YEARBOOK OF THE
UNITED NATIONS
1988

Volume 42

Yearbook of the United Nations, 1988

Volume 42   Sales No. E.93.I.100

Prepared by the Yearbook Section of the Department of Public Information, United Nations, New York. Although the *Yearbook* is based on official sources, it is not an official record.

Chief Editor: Yobert K. Shamapande.

Senior Editors: Kathryn Gordon, Christine B. Koerner.

Editors/Writers: Matthias Gueldner, Lynn Homa, Peter Jackson, Tamara Lee, Jens S. Nielsen, Donald Paneth, Melody C. Pfeiffer.

Contributing Editors/Writers: Choolwe Beyani, Vanessa J. Brooks, Helen Fogarassy, Eugene Forson, Monika Gutestam, James A. Beresford Lubin, Dmitri Marchenkov, Nina Nagy, Vasant V. Nevrekar, Hugi Olafsson, Richard O. Omotoye, Janet E. Root, Ian Steele, Narelle Townsend, Elena Voloshina.

Copy Editor: Alison M. Koppelman.

Editorial Assistants: Georgina Kettles, Nidia H. Morisset, Melinda Robertson, Joyce B. Rosenblum, Leonard M. Simon.

Typesetter: Sunita Chabra.

Indexer: Elaine P. Adam.

YEARBOOK
OF THE
UNITED
NATIONS
1988

Volume 42

Department of Public Information
United Nations, New York

Martinus Nijhoff Publishers
DORDRECHT / BOSTON / LONDON

Published by Martinus Nijhoff Publishers

P.O. Box 163, 3300 AD Dordrecht, The Netherlands

Kluwer Academic Publishers incorporates the
publishing programmes of Martinus Nijhoff Publishers

Sold and distributed in the U.S.A. and Canada
by Kluwer Academic Publishers,
101 Philip Drive, Norwell, MA 02061, U.S.A.

In all other countries, sold and distributed
by Kluwer Academic Publishers Group,
P.O. Box 322, 3300 AH Dordrecht, The Netherlands

Coventry University

Yearbook of the United Nations, 1988
Vol. 42
ISBN: 0-7923-2716-0
ISSN: 0082-8521

UNITED NATIONS PUBLICATION
SALES NO. E.93.I.100

S/0 2531

Printed in the United States of America

Foreword

THE EVENTS OF 1988 REPRESENTED VIVID EVIDENCE that multilateralism was far more capable of inspiring confidence and achieving results than any of its alternatives. Millions around the world witnessed a gratifying demonstration of the potential of the United Nations and the validity of the hopes they placed in it.

Major strides were made to secure peaceful solutions to long-standing regional questions, including the situations in Afghanistan and the Middle East, the Iran-Iraq war, the question of Cyprus, the independence of Namibia and the prospects for peace in South-East Asia and elsewhere. Those efforts were coupled with the joint expression of the two super-Powers of the time that nuclear war could not be won and must never be fought and the initiation of a constructive dialogue between their Governments to reduce and eventually eliminate the incalculable dangers of modern weapons.

In the economic sphere, the Organization remained engaged in fulfilling its responsibility to humanity to tackle critical humanitarian needs as well as to promote social and economic development on a global scale.

But this volume of the *Yearbook of the United Nations* is more than a random collection of dry facts of these pressing human concerns—it is one more chapter in a vital and dynamic record of the Organization. And it is a tribute to the work of my distinguished predecessor, Secretary-General Javier Pérez de Cuéllar. Readers of all persuasions should find something captivating in the crowded happenings and complex issues chronicled in these pages.

Boutros BOUTROS-GHALI
Secretary-General
New York
March 1993

Contents

Part One: *Political and security questions*

Part Two: *Regional questions*

Part Three: *Economic and social questions*

I. DEVELOPMENT POLICY AND INTERNATIONAL
ECONOMIC CO-OPERATION 317

INTERNATIONAL ECONOMIC RELATIONS, 317: Development and economic co-operation, 317. ECONOMIC SURVEYS AND TRENDS, 325. DEVELOPMENT PLANNING AND PUBLIC ADMINISTRATION, 326. RURAL DEVELOPMENT, 327. SPECIAL ECONOMIC AREAS, 328: Developing countries, 328.

II. OPERATIONAL ACTIVITIES FOR DEVELOPMENT 332

GENERAL ASPECTS, 332: Financing of operational activities, 336; Inter-agency co-operation, 337. TECHNICAL CO-OPERATION THROUGH UNDP, 337: UNDP Governing Council, 339; UNDP operational activities, 339; Programme planning and management, 344; Financing, 347; Administrative questions, 353. OTHER TECHNICAL CO-OPERATION, 354: UN programmes, 354; United Nations Volunteers, 357; Technical co-operation among developing countries, 359. UN CAPITAL DEVELOPMENT FUND, 360.

III. ECONOMIC ASSISTANCE, DISASTERS AND EMERGENCY RELIEF 361

ECONOMIC ASSISTANCE, 361: Critical economic situation in Africa, 361; Countries and areas in other regions, 377; Front-line and other bordering States, 380. DISASTERS, 381: Review of disaster and emergency assistance, 381; Office of the UN Disaster Relief Co-ordinator, 383; Disaster relief efforts, 385; Disaster preparedness and prevention, 394. EMERGENCY RELIEF AND ASSISTANCE, 395.

IV. INTERNATIONAL TRADE, FINANCE AND TRANSPORT 403

UNCTAD VII FOLLOW-UP, 403. INTERNATIONAL TRADE, 403: Trade policy, 404; Trade promotion and facilitation, 408; Commodities, 410; Services, 412; Consumer protection, 412. FINANCE, 413: Financial policy, 413. TRANSPORT, 419: Maritime transport, 419. PROGRAMME AND FINANCES OF UNCTAD, 423: Organizational questions, 425.

V. TRANSNATIONAL CORPORATIONS 427

DRAFT CODE OF CONDUCT, 427. STANDARDS OF ACCOUNTING AND REPORTING, 428. COMMISSION ON TNCs, 428. CENTRE ON TNCs, 431.

VI. NATURAL RESOURCES, ENERGY AND CARTOGRAPHY 436

NATURAL RESOURCES, 436: Exploration, 436; Mineral resources, 437; Water resources, 437. ENERGY, 438: Energy resources development, 438; New and renewable energy sources, 440; Nuclear energy, 442. CARTOGRAPHY, 444.

VII. SCIENCE AND TECHNOLOGY 445

FINANCIAL RESOURCES FOR SCIENCE AND TECHNOLOGY, 445: Resource mobilization, 445; UN Fund for Science and Technology for Development, 445. INSTITUTIONAL ARRANGEMENTS, 447: Advisory Committee, 447; Centre for Science and Technology, 447; Co-ordination in the UN system, 448. TECHNOLOGY TRANSFER, 448: Draft code of conduct, 449. BRAIN DRAIN, 450. RELATED QUESTIONS, 451.

VIII. ENVIRONMENT 452

GENERAL ASPECTS, 452: International co-operation, 452; UNEP programme, 452; Environmental education and training, 454; UNEP Fund, 455. ENVIRONMENTAL ACTIVITIES, 456: Environment and development, 456; Environmental monitoring and assessment, 458; Protection against harmful products and pollutants, 459; Global climate, 462; Ecosystems, 464; Technical co-operation, 470.

Part Four: *Trusteeship and decolonization*

Part Five: *Legal questions*

Part Six: *Administrative and budgetary questions*

Part Seven: *Intergovernmental organizations related to the United Nations*

Appendices

Indexes

About the 1988 edition of the *Yearbook*

The 1988 *YEARBOOK OF THE UNITED NATIONS* marks the beginning of the process to eliminate the remaining backlog editions (1988, 1989 and 1990). Its scope, content and breadth of coverage have been restructured and redefined to enhance its focus on the main issues and activities during 1988. As in previous volumes, this volume has been designed to serve as the most comprehensive reference tool for use by the research community and those interested in the activities of the United Nations and its related organizations. The Department of Public Information of the United Nations is committed to clear the backlog and maintain the publication of the current volumes of the *Yearbook* on a timely annual schedule.

Structure and scope of articles

The book is subject-oriented, divided into seven major parts: political and security questions, regional questions, economic and social questions, trusteeship and decolonization, legal questions, administrative and budgetary questions, and intergovernmental organizations related to the United Nations.

The first six parts of the *Yearbook* are devoted to summarizing pertinent United Nations activities, including those of intergovernmental and expert bodies, major reports, Secretariat activities and, in selected cases, the views of States in written communications. Part Seven briefly describes the activities of each specialized agency, the International Atomic Energy Agency and the General Agreement on Tariffs and Trade, based on information prepared by them.

Activities of United Nations bodies. All resolutions, decisions and other major activities of the principal organs and, where applicable, those of subsidiary bodies are either reproduced or summarized in the respective articles. The texts of all resolutions and decisions of substantive nature adopted in 1988 by the General Assembly, the Security Council and the Economic and Social Council are reproduced or summarized under the relevant topic. These texts are followed by the procedural details giving date of adoption, meeting number and vote totals (in favour-against-abstaining); information on their approval by a sessional or subsidiary body prior to final adoption, with document symbols of drafts, approved amendments and committee reports; and a list of sponsors. Also given are the document symbols of any financial implications and relevant meeting numbers. Details of any recorded or roll-call vote on the resolution/decision as a whole also follow the text. The texts of resolutions and decisions of a purely procedural nature are not reproduced, but are summarized and their numbers highlighted in bold type.

Major reports. Most 1988 reports of the Secretary-General, along with selected reports from other United Nations sources, such as seminars and working groups, are summarized briefly with their document symbols appearing in the REFERENCES.

Secretariat activities. The operational activities of the United Nations for development and humanitarian assistance are described under the relevant topics. For major activities financed outside the United Nations regular budget, information is given, wherever available, on contributions and expenditures. Financial data are generally obtained from the audited accounts prepared for each fund and cover the 1988 calendar year unless otherwise specified.

Views of States. Written communications sent to the United Nations by Member States and circulated as documents of the principal organs have been summarized in selected cases, under the relevant topic. Substantive actions by the Security Council have been analysed and brief reviews of the Council's deliberations given, particularly in cases where an issue was taken up but no resolution was adopted.

Terminology

Formal titles of bodies, organizational units, conventions, declarations and officials are given in full on first mention in an article or sequence of articles. They are also used in resolution/decision texts, and in the SUBJECT INDEX under the key word of the title. Short titles may be used in subsequent references.

How to find information in the *Yearbook*

As in previous volumes, information in the 1988 edition may be located in a number of ways: by the table of contents, which highlights the broad subjects and subheadings; by the SUBJECT INDEX, which may be used to locate individual topics and specific references to the bodies dealing with each topic; and by the INDEX OF RESOLUTIONS AND DECISIONS, which provides a numerical list of all resolutions and substantive decisions adopted in 1988 by the principal organs, with page numbers for their text. The *Yearbook* also contains five appendices. APPENDIX I comprises a list of Member States with dates of their admission to the United Nations; APPENDIX II reproduces the Charter of the United Nations, including the Statute of the International Court of Justice; APPENDIX III gives the structure of the principal organs of the United Nations, including the members, officers and date and place of sessions of each body; APPENDIX IV provides the agenda for each session of the principal organs in 1988; and APPENDIX V gives the location and addresses of the United Nations Information Centres and Services worldwide.

ABBREVIATIONS COMMONLY USED IN THE *YEARBOOK*

ACABQ	Advisory Committee on Administrative and Budgetary Questions
ACC	Administrative Committee on Co-ordination
ANC	African National Congress of South Africa
ASEAN	Association of South-East Asian Nations
CCAQ	Consultative Committee on Administrative Questions
CCISUA	Co-ordinating Committee for Independent Staff Unions and Associations of the United Nations System
CCSQ	Consultative Committee on Substantive Questions
CDP	Committee for Development Planning
CEDAW	Committee on the Elimination of Discrimination against Women
CERD	Committee on the Elimination of Racial Discrimination
CFA	Committee on Food Aid Policies and Programmes (WFP)
CILSS	Permanent Inter-State Committee on Drought Control in the Sahel
CMEA	Council for Mutual Economic Assistance
COPUOS	Committee on the Peaceful Uses of Outer Space
CPC	Committee for Programme and Co-ordination
CSDHA	Centre for Social Development and Humanitarian Affairs
DIEC	Development and International Economic Co-operation
DIESA	Department of International Economic and Social Affairs
DPI	Department of Public Information
DTCD	Department of Technical Co-operation for Development
EC	European Community
ECA	Economic Commission for Africa
ECDC	economic co-operation among developing countries
ECE	Economic Commission for Europe
ECLAC	Economic Commission for Latin America and the Caribbean
ECOWAS	Economic Community of West African States
EEC	European Economic Community
ESC	Economic and Social Council
ESCAP	Economic and Social Commission for Asia and the Pacific
ESCWA	Economic and Social Commission for Western Asia
FAO	Food and Agriculture Organization of the United Nations
FICSA	Federation of International Civil Servants' Associations
GA	General Assembly
GATT	General Agreement on Tariffs and Trade
GDP	gross domestic product
GEMS	Global Environmental Monitoring System
GNP	gross national product
IAEA	International Atomic Energy Agency
ICAO	International Civil Aviation Organization
ICITO	Interim Commission for the International Trade Organization
ICJ	International Court of Justice
ICRC	International Committee of the Red Cross
ICSC	International Civil Service Commission
IDA	International Development Association
IDB	Industrial Development Board (UNIDO)
IDDA	Industrial Development Decade for Africa
IEFR	International Emergency Food Reserve
IFAD	International Fund for Agricultural Development
IFC	International Finance Corporation
ILC	International Law Commission
ILO	International Labour Organisation
IMF	International Monetary Fund
IMO	International Maritime Organization
INCB	International Narcotics Control Board
INSTRAW	International Research and Training Institute for the Advancement of Women
IPF	indicative planning figure (UNDP)
ITC	International Trade Centre (UNCTAD/GATT)
ITO	International Trade Organization
ITU	International Telecommunication Union
IUCN	International Union for Conservation of Nature and Natural Resources
IYY	International Youth Year
JAG	Joint Advisory Group on the International Trade Centre
JIU	Joint Inspection Unit
JUNIC	Joint United Nations Information Committee
LDC	least developed country
NATO	North Atlantic Treaty Organization
NGO	non-governmental organization
NPT	Treaty on the Non-Proliferation of Nuclear Weapons
NRSE	new and renewable sources of energy
NSGT	Non-Self-Governing Territory
OAS	Organization of American States
OAU	Organization of African Unity
ODA	official development assistance
OECD	Organisation for Economic Co-operation and Development
OPEC	Organization of Petroleum Exporting Countries
PAC	Pan Africanist Congress of Azania
PLO	Palestine Liberation Organization
SC	Security Council
SDR	special drawing right
S-G	Secretary-General
SNPA	Substantial New Programme of Action for the 1980s for the Least Development Countries
SPC	Special Political Committee
SWAPO	South West Africa People's Organization (Namibia)
TC	Trusteeship Council
TCDC	technical co-operation among developing countries
TDB	Trade and Development Board (UNCTAD)
TNC	transnational corporation
UN	United Nations
UNCDF	United Nations Capital Development Fund
UNCHS	United Nations Centre for Human Settlements (Habitat)
UNCITRAL	United Nations Commission on International Trade Law
UNCTAD	United Nations Conference on Trade and Development
UNDOF	United Nations Disengagement Observer Force (Golan Heights)
UNDP	United Nations Development Programme
UNDRO	Office of the United Nations Disaster Relief Co-ordinator
UNEF	United Nations Emergency Force
UNEP	United Nations Environment Programme
UNESCO	United Nations Educational, Scientific and Cultural Organization
UNFDAC	United Nations Fund for Drug Abuse Control
UNFICYP	United Nations Peace-keeping Force in Cyprus
UNFPA	United Nations Population Fund
UNFSTD	United Nations Fund for Science and Technolgy for Development
UNHCR	Office of the United Nations High Commissioner for Refugees
UNIC	United Nations Information Centre
UNICEF	United Nations Children's Fund
UNIDF	United Nations Industrial Development Fund (UNIDO)
UNIDIR	United Nations Institute for Disarmament Research
UNIDO	United Nations Industrial Development Organization
UNIFIL	United Nations Interim Force in Lebanon
UNIIMOG	United Nations Iran-Iraq Military Observer Group
UNITAR	United Nations Institute for Training and Research
UNPAAERD	United Nations Programme of Action for African Economic Recovery and Development 1986-1990
UNRFNRE	United Nations Revolving Fund for Natural Resources Exploration
UNRISD	United Nations Research Institute for Social Development
UNRWA	United Nations Relief and Works Agency for Palestine Refugees in the Near East
UNSCEAR	United Nations Scientific Committee on the Effects of Atomic Radiation
UNSDRI	United Nations Social Defence Research Institute
UNSO	United Nations Sudano-Sahelian Office
UNTAG	United Nations Transition Assistance Group (Namibia)
UNTSO	United Nations Truce Supervision Organization (Israel and neighbouring States)
UNU	United Nations University
UNV	United Nations Volunteers
UPU	Universal Postal Union
WFC	World Food Council
WFP	World Food Programme
WHO	World Health Organization
WIPO	World Intellectual Property Organization
WMO	World Meteorological Organization
WTO	World Tourism Organization
YUN	*Yearbook of the United Nations*

EXPLANATORY NOTE ON DOCUMENTS

References at the end of each article in Parts One to Six of this volume give the symbols of the main documents issued in 1988 on the topic, arranged in the order in which they are referred to in the text. The following is a guide to the principal document symbols:

A/- refers to documents of the General Assembly, numbered in separate series by session. Thus, A/43/- refers to documents issued for consideration at the forty-third session, beginning with A/43/1. Documents of special and emergency special sessions are identified as A/S- and A/ES-, followed by the session number.

A/C.- refers to documents of six of the Assembly's Main Committees, e.g. A/C.1/- is a document of the First Committee, A/C.6/-, a document of the Sixth Committee. The symbol for documents of the seventh Main Committee, the Special Political Committee, is A/SPC/-. A/BUR/- refers to documents of the General Committee. A/AC.- documents are those of the Assembly's *ad hoc* bodies and A/CN.-, of its commissions; e.g. A/AC.105/- identifies documents of the Assembly's Committee on the Peaceful Uses of Outer Space, A/CN.4/-, of its International Law Commission. Assembly resolutions and decisions since the thirty-first (1976) session have been identified by two arabic numerals: the first indicates the session of adoption; the second, the sequential number in the series. Resolutions are numbered consecutively from 1 at each session. Decisions of regular sessions are numbered consecutively, from 301 for those concerned with elections and appointments, and from 401 for all other decisions. Decisions of special and emergency special sessions are numbered consecutively, from 11 for those concerned with elections and appointments, and from 21 for all other decisions.

E/- refers to documents of the Economic and Social Council, numbered in separate series by year. Thus, E/1988/- refers to documents issued for consideration by the Council at its 1988 sessions, beginning with E/1988/1. E/AC.-, E/C.- and E/CN.-, followed by identifying numbers, refer to documents of the Council's subsidiary *ad hoc* bodies, committees and commissions. For example, E/C.1/-, E/C.2/- and E/C.3/- refer to documents of the Council's sessional committees, namely, the First (Economic), Second (Social) and Third (Programme and Co-ordination) Committees, respectively; E/CN.5/- refers to documents of the Council's Commission for Social Development, E/CN.7/-, to documents of its Committee on Natural Resources. E/ICEF/- documents are those of the United Nations Children's Fund. Symbols for the Council's resolutions and decisions, since 1978, consist of two arabic numerals: the first indicates the year of adoption and the second, the sequential number in the series. There are two series: one for resolutions, beginning with 1 (resolution 1988/1); and one for decisions, beginning, since 1983, with 101 (decision 1988/101).

S/- refers to documents of the Security Council. Its resolutions are identified by consecutive numbers followed by the year of adoption in parentheses, beginning with resolution 1(1946).

T/- refers to documents of the Trusteeship Council. No resolutions were adopted by the Council at its fifty-fifth session. The Council's decisions are not numbered.

ST/-, followed by symbols representing the issuing department or office, refers to documents of the United Nations Secretariat.

Documents of certain bodies bear special symbols, including the following:

ACC/-	Administrative Committee on Co-ordination
CD/-	Conference on Disarmament
CERD/-	Committee on the Elimination of Racial Discrimination
DC/-	Disarmament Commission
DP/-	United Nations Development Programme
HS/-	Commission on Human Settlements
ITC/-	International Trade Centre
LOS/PCN/-	Preparatory Commission for the International Sea-Bed Authority and for the International Tribunal for the Law of the Sea
TD/-	United Nations Conference on Trade and Development
UNEP/-	United Nations Environment Programme
UNITAR/-	United Nations Institute for Training and Research

Many documents of the regional commissions bear special symbols. These are sometimes preceded by the following:

E/ECA/-	Economic Commission for Africa
E/ECE/-	Economic Commission for Europe
E/ESCAP/-	Economic and Social Commission for Asia and the Pacific
E/ESCWA/-	Economic and Social Commission for Western Asia
LC/G.-	Economic Commission for Latin America and the Caribbean

"L" in a symbol refers to documents of limited distribution, such as draft resolutions; "CONF." to documents of a conference; "INF." to those of general information. Summary records are designated by "SR.", verbatim records by "PV.", each followed by the meeting number.

United Nations sales publications each carry a sales number with the following components separated by periods: a capital letter indicating the language(s) of the publication; two arabic numerals indicating the year; a Roman numeral indicating the subject category; a capital letter indicating a subdivision of the category, if any; and an arabic numeral indicating the number of the publication within the category. Examples: E.88.V.4; E/F.R.88.II.E.8; E.88.IX.3.

Report of the Secretary-General

Report of the Secretary-General on the work of the Organization

Following is the Secretary-General's report on the work of the Organization, submitted to the General Assembly and dated 14 September 1988. The Assembly took note of it on 17 October (**decision 43/404.**)

I

Last year, in my report on the work of the Organization, I said that the sails of the small boat in which all the people of the Earth were gathered seemed to have caught a light but favourable wind. At the time, with the clouds of controversy still dark, a less cautious metaphor would have appeared unwarranted. A succession of developments has, however, justified my reasoned hope. With careful and patient navigation, the vessel has come within sight of large sections of the shore.

The developments of the past months have not been fortuitous. They are the result of diplomatic activity sustained over the years by the United Nations and intensified recently. On matters of international peace and security, the principal organs of the United Nations have increasingly functioned in the manner envisaged in the Charter. The working relationship of the Security Council and the Secretary-General has rarely if ever been closer. I am thankful for this as also for the recent improvement in international relations at the global level that has opened new possibilities for successful action by the world body. Multilateralism has proved itself far more capable of inspiring confidence and achieving results than any of its alternatives. Millions around the world have had a gratifying demonstration of the potential of the Organization and the validity of the hopes they place in it.

The international situation is still, of course, marked by points of strain and danger, visible or lurking. Complacency about the resolution of complex problems that still face us is impermissible. However, the possibilities of bringing peace to troubled regions through the efforts of the United Nations have plainly come into view.

II

The conclusion of the Geneva Accords in April represented a major stride in the effort to secure a peaceful solution of the situation relating to Afghanistan and provides a basis for the exercise by all Afghans of their right to self-determination. It is the first instance of the world's two most powerful States becoming co-guarantors of an agreement negotiated under the auspices of the Secretary-General. The full implementation of the Accords in good faith by all the signatories will significantly serve the goal of peace in the region and the world. Immediately after the Accords came into effect, the United Nations Good Offices Mission for Afghanistan and Pakistan (UNGOMAP) began monitoring their implementation, including the withdrawal of foreign troops from Afghanistan. Moreover, within weeks thereafter, the United Nations initiated a humanitarian and economic assistance programme, with a Co-ordinator specially appointed by me, to help the people of Afghanistan in meeting their serious economic and humanitarian needs at this critical moment in their history.

On 20 August, a cease-fire was secured in the eight-year-long Iran-Iraq war in the context of the full implementation of Security Council resolution 598(1987). A United Nations Iran-Iraq Military Observer Group (UNIIMOG) was deployed as at the time and date of the cease-fire. Simultaneously, invitations were extended to the two Governments to send their representatives for direct talks at a high level under my auspices. The talks started on schedule on 25 August. The entire process has exemplified the efficacy of a mandate entrusted to the Secretary-General when actively supported by the Security Council and backed by the complementary efforts of other Member States. For success in the complex task of implementing Security Council resolution 598(1987), it is essential that both Iran and Iraq continue to act on the conviction that genuine peace will provide to each of them opportunities for reconstruction and progress that a fragile situation cannot. On my part, I will do my utmost to help achieve the just and lasting solution envisaged by the Security Council.

There has been an improvement in prospects for the independence of Namibia. Recent diplomatic activity has made a significant contribution to the peace process in southern Africa, which should facilitate a settlement in Namibia without further delay. The date of 1 November 1988 has been recommended for beginning the implementation of Security Council resolution 435(1978). In the light of these developments, the Secretariat has undertaken a review of its contingency plans in order to hold itself in readiness for the timely emplacement of the United Nations Transition Assistance Group in Namibia. It is my hope that current efforts will finally succeed in bringing independence to the people of Namibia.

For many years, the question of Cyprus has involved the continuous exercise of the good offices of the Secretary-General on the basis of a mandate entrusted to him by the Security Council. My latest initiative has evoked greater receptivity from both sides. At the discussion the leaders of the two sides had in my presence on 24 August, they expressed their willingness to meet without any preconditions and to attempt to achieve by 1 June 1989 a negotiated settlement of all aspects of the Cyprus problem. Confirming their desire to cooperate with me in my mission, they agreed to start talks on 15 September and to review with me the progress achieved at the initial stage.

During the past year, the prospects for peace in South-East Asia have also improved, through the initiation of a dialogue between the Kampuchean parties and other concerned countries. This is an encouraging trend as it confirms the interest on all sides in achieving a political solution to the problem. I sincerely hope that concrete progress will soon be achieved on the main substantive issues. I have presented to the parties a number of specific ideas intended to facilitate the elaboration of a framework for a comprehensive political settlement. I remain at their disposal to help bring this process to fruition.

After long effort, an appropriate climate has been established for a just and durable solution of the problem of Western Sahara. Along with the head of the Organization of African Unity, I submitted a peace plan to which the parties concerned conveyed their acceptance with some remarks and comments on 30 August. This will entail a significant operation in the area for the United Nations, with both civilian and military components. I hope that, with the necessary goodwill on all sides, we will soon witness a final settlement of the problem, which will undoubtedly help consolidate the present favourable trend in the region.

All these problems, in their different contexts, have been moved towards solutions in consonance with the principles of the Charter of the United Nations, with diplomatic activity at multilateral and other levels proceeding in convergent directions. For itself, the United Nations does not seek, and was never meant to seek, any kind of diplomatic autarky; what it requires is that diplomacy among Governments, especially those which are concerned with a particular issue, situation or region, should help realize the aims that it has defined. With the United Nations indicating the principles and the direction for efforts to settle a dispute, all relevant points of diplomatic contact and influence in the network of multilateral rela-

tionships can be coherently drawn upon to achieve the objectives of peace. Recently, we have had encouraging evidence of the practicality of this process.

There are other regional problems that continue to cause international concern. The situation in the Middle East, a critically important region of the globe, has repercussions on relationships in a far wider sphere. The members of the Security Council have recently expressed their grave concern over the continued deterioration of the situation in the Palestinian territories occupied by Israel since 1967, including Jerusalem. The uprising since December 1987 has vividly demonstrated the dangers of stalemate resulting from inability to agree on a negotiating process. Even the urgently required measures to enhance the safety and protection of the Palestinian people of the territories, through the application of the Fourth Geneva Convention relative to the Protection of Civilian Persons in Time of War of 12 August 1949, will neither remove the causes of the events that prompted Security Council resolution 605(1987) nor bring peace to the region. As the underlying problems can only be resolved through a comprehensive, just and lasting settlement based on Security Council resolutions 242(1967) and 338(1973), and taking fully into account the legitimate rights of the Palestinian people, including self-determination, what is needed is an urgent effort by the international community, led by the Security Council, to promote an effective negotiating process towards a solution that will secure the interests of both the Israeli and the Palestinian peoples and enable them to live in peace with each other. The next few months may provide opportunities to accelerate this endeavour.

The situation in Central America is the result of convulsions within societies originating in underdevelopment and unjust socio-economic structures. The signing of the Guatemala Procedure in August 1987 signalled the determination of the five Central American Presidents to find solutions to the region's problems free from outside interference and the pressure of geopolitical conflicts. I agreed to participate in the impartial international verification of the process of pacification. Furthermore, at the request of the General Assembly, I formulated a special plan for economic cooperation for Central America, which was considered by the Assembly in May. However, a year after the signing of the Guatemala Procedure, the momentum for peace appears to be faltering and the considerable progress made to date seems to be seriously threatened. The principal merit of the Agreement lay in its requirement for simultaneous progress on two broad fronts: democratization and the cessation of armed hostilities. Its success depends on full compliance and a concerted effort by the signatories as well as the co-operation of all the Governments and parties involved.

The situation in Korea is a legacy of the Second World War and its aftermath. Sustained dialogue between North and South Korea could lead to real progress towards resolving the outstanding issues. It is necessary for all those who are in a position to do so to help foster an atmosphere conducive to an amicable solution of differences between the two sides. Both Governments are aware of my readiness to assist them whenever and in whatever manner they desire.

The region of southern Africa is suffering from a conflict with three dimensions: the question of Namibia, the acts of destabilization against the neighbouring States of South Africa and the system of *apartheid* in South Africa itself. I have already referred to the progress made on the question of Namibia. Acts of destabilization have threatened peace in the whole region. Developments in, or relating to, the continuance of a situation of racial discrimination, which is so repugnant to the spirit of our age, lend further force to the repeated—and hitherto unheeded—urgings of the international community that *apartheid* be dismantled. These urgings provide a renewed opportunity to the Government of South Africa to signal an acceptance of what is just as well as inevitable—the end of *apartheid*. I would appeal to that Government to respond to them in that spirit. Postponing or evading this change of course is fraught with dangers which all the people of the country and its neighbours would certainly wish to avoid.

III

The present juncture of efforts and potentialities opens fresh perspectives for our common political endeavour. This seems to have prompted the observation increasingly heard in recent months that we may be entering a new phase of world affairs. I take the observation as neither a politician's promise nor a scientist's conclusion. A vast range of actions and policies is required to prove it right. If opportunities for breakthroughs on a variety of issues are to be seized, it seems to be important that we keep in mind the implications of our experience, whether of success or of stalemate, in the efforts to resolve the major political questions on our agenda. In this report, I shall deal with these implications and the emerging outlook for the United Nations. As the resurgence in public interest in the Organization has been rather sudden, it is appropriate to recall the long background of efforts, accomplishments and set-backs behind our current experience.

We are all aware of the reasons why, during the first four decades of its existence, the United Nations has been unable to put in place the reliable system of collective security that its Charter envisaged. This system was based on the assumption that the grand alliance of the victors of the Second World War would continue and develop into their joint custodianship of world peace. Furthermore, in the words of one of the principal architects of the world organization, the late President Roosevelt, the system implied "the end of the system of unilateral actions, exclusive alliances and spheres of influence and balances of power and all the other expedients which have been tried for centuries and have always failed". The chastening experience of the most extensive war fought on this planet was expected to transform the older patterns of power relations.

However, developments during the early years of the Organization went contrary to expectations. The assumed radical change was hindered by a variety of factors as far as relationships at the highest plane of global power were concerned. A whole set of circumstances created a continuing climate of mutual suspicion and fear. In such a climate, the great Powers often looked at the United Nations from different angles, with the result that issues that could have been resolved through their joint endeavour became instead added subjects of controversy between them. An almost insuperable obstacle was thus placed in the way of the United Nations to give world peace a durable foundation.

In the difficult phase that naturally ensued— and that has lasted for decades—many who believed in the essentiality of the United Nations were thrown on the defensive. They were driven to enumerate the political achievements of the United Nations in specific cases, but these appeared slim in comparison with the great unresolved issues of our time. I believe that the accomplishments of the world Organization, at any stage of its career, were far larger than what appeared from the case usually made in its defence. Along with the undeniable central fact that the United Nations was often brought to an impasse, in the field of maintaining international peace and security, by the inability of the permanent members of the Security Council to develop a common approach, there was also the fact, equally central, that the United Nations did not allow this factor to block its endeavours; with ingenuity and realism, it found other ways of at least defusing conflicts. If, in one vital respect, it fell short of the Charter, in other respects it kept pace with, and often served as a catalyst of, the process of rapid and peaceful change.

The United Nations played a decisive role in the process of decolonization, which has changed the political complexion of the globe and given vast populations control over their destiny. It gave authoritative definition to human rights and devised monitoring and other mechanisms for encouraging greater respect for them. It codified international law. In partnership with its specialized agencies, it established guidelines to deal with new problems and emerging concerns ranging from the environment, population, the law of the sea, the safeguarding of the rights of the hitherto disadvantaged segments of society like women, children, the aging and the handicapped to terrorism, drug abuse and the incidence of AIDS. It has responded to situations of disaster and dire human need; it has provided protection to refugees. It has had notable successes in the campaign for conquest of avoidable disease in the poorer parts of the world; it has taken measures towards food security and child survival. It has raised consciousness of global economic imperatives; through its development programmes and the specialized agencies, it has represented a vital source of economic and technical assistance to developing countries.

In the political field, even when disabled by differences among the permanent members of the Security Council, the United Nations has displayed a capacity for innovation and played a role that on no reckoning can be considered peripheral. It has repeatedly acted to limit and control armed conflicts; without the peace-keeping operations launched by it, the theatres of conflict would have undoubtedly represented far greater danger to the wider peace. On major international disputes, it has suggested terms of just settlement. The formulation of such terms is the first requirement for bringing a dispute within a manageable scope and weeding out its implacable elements: this requirement the United Nations has repeatedly sought to fulfil. Above all, the Organization has maintained emphasis on the great objectives of arms limitation and disarmament, the self-determination of peoples and the promotion of human rights, which are essential for the strengthening of universal peace.

These achievements have been made against the backdrop of the most massive transition in the history of the human race. The emergence of new States has taken place at the same time that there has been a proliferation of global concerns, stemming partly from the emerging problems I mentioned above, partly from the impact of advancing technologies and partly from a new mass consciousness of rights leading to the non-acceptance of old inequities within or between societies. The United Nations has not only given shape and expression to the sense of world community but established a basis for nations to develop a concerted response to their common problems.

IV

Our experience has thus shown that co-operative management of a variety of global problems, reflect-ing a community of interest among Member States, is an entirely workable idea. We have now come to, or are nearing, a stage where the extension of this approach to resolving some of the major political issues on our agenda is within our reach.

Changes in perceptions and attitudes, of which we have had pronounced signs since the last session of the General Assembly, suggest that we may be witnessing a transition, however slow or occasionally uncertain, towards a new pattern of relationships at the global level. The transition has the logic of necessity behind it. It is certainly justified by the insupportable cost and the incalculable dangers of a self-perpetuating arms race. It could derive support from the realization that security cannot be viewed in military terms alone nor does the application of military power resolve situations in traditionally expected ways. It is, or can be, propelled by the need for greater attention to the problems of economic modernization or to the social problems that economic growth has left untouched. It is evidenced by trends towards horizontal co-operation between States adhering to different social systems without prejudice to their political alignments. It would seem to respond to the multi-polarity of the world's economic power. All these factors, combined with the technological revolution and the sense of global interdependence, seem to call for radical adjustments of outlook on the part of the world's leadership. There is, of course, no guarantee against temporary reverses or set-backs in the process, nor can ambivalence in the relationships of power blocs be excluded. However, the direction appears to be better set and helped by weightier factors now than at any time in recent years. How this transition will affect the United Nations and how it has been affected by the United Nations are questions of practical import that merit the most serious reflection on our part.

The world community has rightly acclaimed the statesmanship displayed by the leaders of the Union of Soviet Socialist Republics and the United States of America in jointly expressing their shared perception that a nuclear war cannot be won and must never be fought, in initiating a constructive dialogue between their Governments and in concluding the Treaty on the Elimination of Their Intermediate-Range and Shorter-Range Missiles, in December 1987. I believe that the international community, articulating its political consciousness through the United Nations, is more than a witness to agreements that narrow the division between the world's most powerful States. It is deeply affected by, and concerned with, the issues at stake. The sustained emphasis by the United Nations on the goals of arms limitation and disarmament, especially in the nuclear field, and the declared nonalignment of the majority of its Member States, with its implied negation of the concept of expanding spheres of rival influence, have helped to provide the political and mental environment for the ongoing process of mutual accommodation between the great Powers. Not only the mathematics of the arms equation and its economic cost but also the attitudes of the world beyond have been factors behind this process.

V

There is a school of thought that holds that the great Powers do not need the world organization except as a symbol of the world community and that its meetings merely provide a convenient opportunity for periodic bilateral exchanges. The view seems to derive support from the dissatisfaction with the working of the United Nations expressed by one or another of these Powers at different times. However, it fails to recognize their interest in maintaining their positions of respect and influence in a changing world situation. There can hardly be a better place than the United Nations for any Power, large or small, to enhance its influence in the best sense of the term. The United Nations offers every country a forum where, with its resources of knowledge and experience, it can take a lead in framing the universal agenda, draw attention to new concerns and new ways of solving problems and contribute to the process of peaceful change. For a country, large or small, to turn its back, to whatever extent, on the United Nations would be to surrender a good part of its actual or potential influence. To follow a two-track policy—at one level, to owe allegiance to the Charter, and, at the other, to seek to marginalize the United Nations—would be to act contrary to the goal of harmonizing the actions of nations in the attainment of their common ends.

Moreover, while, in the normal course, the great Powers, like others, resolve or reduce their differences through negotiations outside the United Nations, they need the United Nations to come to grips with issues that concern other nations and that, in one way or another, impinge on their own relationships as well. In this respect, the great Powers need to show a sensitivity to the expressed wishes of the majority of Member States. I have not the slightest doubt that these wishes are based on genuine concerns and not on any primordial opposition, far less hostility, to the policies of one or another major Power. All this argues for greater, not less, support of the United Nations, for engagement and not grudging participation in its work.

I welcome the efforts being made to control rhetorical inflation in the debates of the General Assembly, to promote civility in dialogue and indeed to develop, even if gradually, a balance between debate and negotiation, the parliamentary and the diplomatic approaches, which are equally part and parcel of the United Nations. Continuing public debate is meant to exert pressure towards negotiations; when it can no longer do so, it defeats the aims of its own sponsors. Resolutions are meant to keep alive the goals to be achieved and to ensure that these goals are not lost sight of in a multitude of other concerns. In that perspective, they can become an indispensable factor for the successful outcome of negotiations and can be perceived as resolutions in the full sense of the term, not as incantations or mere formulations of theory. But they become ineffective when they look like stock resolutions. There needs to be an adjustment of political attitudes on all sides to the double requirement of making resolutions more purposeful and of paying respect to them as genuine expressions or reminders of widely shared concerns.

VI

A primary fact of the present world situation is that, while the power to destroy the Earth is concentrated in a few hands, the power to make and strengthen peace is widely dispersed.

This makes the engagement of the United Nations—the only instrumentality that can ensure the full representation of all concerned parties and relevant viewpoints—central to the great task of resolving regional conflicts. The Organization's long experience of handling these conflicts has certain implications that, I feel, need to be taken into account for sound and workable policies in future.

Some of these implications flow so directly from the Charter that to restate them can look like emphasizing the obvious. Yet, at the hopeful stage we have reached now, they have gained fresh pertinence from a practical point of view. The Charter obligation of settling international disputes by peaceful means and in conformity with the principles of justice and international law, for instance, would imply that these disputes should be kept under constant review by the Security Council. This, in turn, would preclude an attitude of passivity towards a conflict when it is in a phase of relative quiescence. It would certainly not justify tacit acceptance of an inherently brittle *status quo* in the context of any conflict.

Another implication of our current and recent experience is that when an armed conflict erupts and as long as it persists the utmost care needs to be taken by other Powers, global or regional, not to add to its size or intensity. This does not exclude sympathy with the side perceived to be the victim. As I said in my annual report five years ago, regional conflicts have been viewed as wars by proxy among more powerful nations. The improved bilateral relations between the major Powers could arrest this dangerous trend. But not only they are involved. When the tensions or differences between the major or middle-sized Powers are grafted onto a conflict that could otherwise be confined to those immediately involved, the conflict is not only widened: it becomes intractable as one or the other party feels encouraged in its obduracy and neither feels any incentive to explore the possibilities of compromise. Moreover, the Charter obligation of activating or supporting the United Nations in resolving a conflict is inconsistent with what may be called permissive neutrality.

The whole Charter system of collective security rests on the permanent members of the Security Council applying a sense of common purpose to addressing a conflict as soon as it erupts. As long as they view regional problems in the framework of their own rivalries, solutions will be blocked. Once this dark shadow is removed from the diplomatic landscape these problems can be addressed in the right perspective. This would result in a more judicious and principled use of the veto. A principle underlying the Charter is that membership of the Security Council, both permanent and non-permanent, is to be regarded as service to the cause of peace rather than as a function of unilateral positions or interests. With the adoption of resolution 598(1987) by the Security Council, there has been a reassuring and unanimous interest in restoring the Council's peace-making capacity. I believe that fresh avenues have been opened for a consideration again of some of the ideas I submitted in my annual reports in 1982 and 1983 about making the Security Council more effective.

The effectiveness of the Security Council, however, requires that once it has made a determination on a dispute all Member States give it full support in the sense not only of accepting an agreed text but of providing strong diplomatic backing for it. The Charter certainly calls for the application of the collective influence of Member States to lending irresistible weight to a just solution. Furthermore, in carrying out its duties under the responsibility of maintaining international peace and security, the Security Council acts on behalf of all Member States.

Peace-keeping operations have proved to be an inescapable necessity in the context of many conflicts. Their success, however, depends not only on the consent of the parties but also on the consistent support of the Security Council, on a clear and practicable mandate, on the readiness of Member States to volunteer troops and on adequate financial arrangements. These considerations become more important in view of the evolving world situation, which could well assign a broader role to the peace-keeping operations of the United Nations. They might possibly have to be extended to the maritime environment and adapted to new types of situations that have international implications. I believe that attention should be paid to the need for the United Nations to be better prepared for launching peace-keeping operations, sometimes at short notice. In the broad context of these operations, it is gratifying that all permanent members of the Security Council are now in favour of the peace-keeping aspect of the Organization's work. The valour, heroism and sacrifice of the soldiers of peace who man these operations evoke the most heartfelt tribute from all of us.

Peace-keeping, of course, can only be a palliative if it is not made to serve as a prelude to, or to accompany, negotiations towards a comprehensive settlement. A situation of stalemate or worse about the resolution of the dispute underlying a conflict can cause frustration and despair, which, in the long run, may jeopardize the usefulness of the peace-keeping operation itself, regardless of how well it has managed to moderate or control the conflict.

Moreover, I feel that better possibilities for peacemaking can be realized by the employment of a more forthright kind of diplomacy. Let us not forget that peace is secured by agreements, not by the illusion of agreements. When negotiations are envisaged, the adoption of a resolution by the Security Council lays the ground for—but does not necessarily conclude—the diplomatic process required. Negotiations on the basis of the resolution are rendered more difficult if different interpretations are put on its provisions by its framers. The adoption of an agreed text on a controversial issue has certainly the merit of defining the terms of its settlement; in this sense, a vague definition (providing a certain latitude for negotiations) is preferable to no definition at all. However, what is required for solutions to emerge is not merely the endorsement of an agreed text by the members of the Council but also their shared understanding of that text and co-ordinated policy on its basis. A cohesive approach in the spirit of the Charter, regardless of differences of perception, interest or ideology, is indispensable for resolving conflicts.

VII

Strengthening the prospects of peace can entail concrete operations for the United Nations in addition to those of peace-keeping. As peace initiatives addressed to specific situations make headway, the tasks, essential from both the political and the humanitarian points of view, of providing relief to the affected populations and arranging the rehabilitation of those displaced fall primarily on the United Nations. The special programme of humanitarian and economic assistance for Afghanistan is a particularly significant example as is the increased co-operation programme in support of efforts for peace in Central America. In addition, emergency relief efforts organized, for instance, for Ethiopia, Lebanon and Mozambique demonstrate the continuing engagement of the United Nations in the alleviation of the massive suffering caused by conflicts or other adverse circumstances. The work in the past years of the United Nations High Commissioner for Refugees, the United Nations Relief and Works Agency for Palestine Refugees in the Near East, the World Food Programme, the United Nations Children's Fund and others in meeting the basic needs of destitute refugees and displaced or suffering populations has established a sound basis for this kind of effort. I am grateful for the generous response of Governments to the calls made for material support.

VIII

Resolving conflicts is a prime responsibility of the United Nations, but avoiding them is equally necessary for the maintenance of peace.

The continents of Asia, Africa and Latin America have been the scene of a large number of armed conflicts during the existence of the United Nations. It is one of the most disquieting features of our age that inter-State conflicts should occur when Governments could easily avail themselves of the machinery of the United Nations or of other multilateral organizations to help resolve their disputes. The number of those killed in hostilities between Iran and Iraq provides a massive—and, I hope, conclusive—testimony to the human cost of war.

Fortunately, there are also glimmerings of hope in diverse areas of Asia, Africa and Latin America. Some signs of developing common regional perspectives are visible at several points of the globe. Moreover, encouraging examples have been set of States resorting to judicial settlement of their disputes. I would appeal to Governments to make it a practice, as far as possible, to refer justiciable cases to the International Court of Justice. A tradition will thus be established of having recourse to law, which can avert many possible conflicts, with their incalculable waste. Moreover, the hopes we derive from a change of perception and attitude at the global level will be considerably fortified if similar changes dispel fears and suspicions at the regional level.

In the late twentieth century, violent civil strife and social turmoil are not confined to any one region of the globe. In its current state of flux, human society contains smouldering elements, which often flare in explosive violence. The inter-nationalization of crime, with traffic in drugs and terrorism its most appalling signs, can subvert friendly relations among nations unless Member States strengthen their multilateral co-operation in saving the present and future generations from a new kind of scourge. The United Nations has taken an unequivocal stand on ways and means of fighting these new dangers to human society. These means can be used only if Member States maintain and strengthen a sense of social solidarity.

Global society has been lately much afflicted by disregard for international law. It is obvious that international confidence would rest on quicksand if the domestic necessities felt by Governments were allowed to override the international obligations they have solemnly undertaken. Without international law respected by all States there can be no stable framework for multilateral co-operation in our highly complex world of sovereign States and conflicting interests. It sounds axiomatic yet it needs to be stressed that States or other international persons are bound by treaties that have been properly concluded and that have entered into force. The principle that treaties must be complied with and carried out in good faith, commonly expressed in the maxim *pacta sunt servanda*, is basic to the Charter. Respect for international agreements is not only one of the fundamental principles of international law; it is the foundation of the organized international community. If this principle were abandoned, the whole superstructure of contemporary international law and organization, including the functioning of the United Nations, the effectiveness of the decisions of its competent organs and resort to international arbitration or judicial settlement of justiciable disputes, would collapse. It is in the equal interest of all States, large or small, to work towards a world where nations will operate within a complete, coherent and viable system of law. Any movement away from this goal holds equal danger for all.

IX

Disarmament and the regulation of armaments, with the least diversion for armaments of the world's human and economic resources, to use the language of the Charter, will remain a decisive test of the improvement of international relations and the strengthening of peace. The Charter envisaged a system for regulating armaments when the arms race had nowhere reached its present scale and when it did not threaten to be, as it is now, both a cause and an effect of tensions between States at the regional as well as the global levels.

Over the years, considerable work has been done in formulating the principles that should govern disarmament and defining the issues involved in it. However, the translation of these principles into actual plans has remained an elusive goal. In a global climate of distrust, at times exaggerated, the arms race acquired an air of inevitability and discussions about halting and reversing it appeared futile. However, the refreshing change signified by the signing of the Treaty on the Elimination of Their Intermediate-Range and Shorter-Range Missiles by the USSR and the United States as well as the prospect of a reduction in strategic nuclear weapons seemed to furnish a propitious background to the special session of the General Assembly devoted to disarmament, which was held from 31 May to 25 June this year. The impressive number of national leaders that attended the session was an indication of the level of concern—and hope—felt all over the world on this issue. The proceedings had a largely non-polemical tone and the bulk of the text proposed for adoption was generally agreed upon.

It was no doubt disappointing that these favourable circumstances did not lead to the adoption of a concluding document with consensus on its entirety. At least two of the questions that blocked this adoption related to controversial issues regarding situations in the Middle East and southern Africa. This showed how regional concerns cast a shadow over the consideration of issues of global war and peace. Nevertheless, the emergence of a better-focused outlook on disarmament was confirmed by a shared acceptance of some important propositions, which provide a basis for productive discussions and action in the General Assembly:

Disarmament is not the exclusive responsibility of the two most powerful States, but a joint undertaking of all States;

While nuclear disarmament must continue to be the primary concern, conventional disarmament has acquired a new importance and urgency;

The qualitative aspect of the arms race needs to be addressed along with its quantitative aspect;

National security needs to be viewed in the broader context of global issues and international concerns;

The goals of disarmament and arms limitation need to be pursued in conjunction with efforts to resolve conflicts, build confidence and promote economic and social development;

The existing machinery for disarmament can and should be utilized better.

Other promising elements in the proceedings of the special session were the common standpoints on the need to conclude a chemical weapons convention at the earliest, to consider the phenomenon of arms transfers, with their impact on situations of actual or potential conflict, to mobilize

modern technology in the cause of disarmament and to encourage States with major space capabilities to contribute actively to the objective of the exclusively peaceful use of outer space. It was also agreed that the potentially important role of the United Nations in the verification of multilateral disarmament and arms control agreements needed to be studied in depth.

I believe that, the absence of an agreed final text at the recent special session notwithstanding, all these elements can serve to lend further breadth and substance and a pragmatic tone to the international agenda for disarmament. Immediate attention needs to be directed to the negotiation of those measures in which agreement is possible in the foreseeable future. These include a further reduction of nuclear weapons of the two greatest military Powers and the conclusion of a convention on the prohibition of the development, production, stockpiling, acquisition, transfer and use of chemical weapons and on their destruction. The latter has become a compelling need in view of the shocking evidence, which has been documented in the case of the Iran-Iraq war, of the use of chemical weapons. The vast growth in the arsenals of conventional weapons, particularly in the regional context, intertwined as it is with arms transfers, also requires urgent consideration.

The Treaty on the Non-Proliferation of Nuclear Weapons, designed to serve as a barrier against the acquisition of nuclear weapons, is the multilateral agreement in the field of arms limitation which has been signed by the largest number of States. Nevertheless, there is a growing concern that intensified efforts are needed to remove the very real danger of the proliferation of these weapons, both vertical and horizontal, which exists today. An important step towards mitigating this danger would be universal adherence to the Treaty. The Fourth Review Conference of the Parties to the Treaty to be held in 1990 will furnish an opportunity to find new ways and means to strengthen the non-proliferation régime. The success of this Conference would provide a strong impetus to efforts aimed at achieving a complete cessation of nuclear-weapons tests and halting the continuous refinement and spread of these weapons.

Agreements or mechanisms with limited participation, fundamentally important though they are, cannot by themselves transform the political environment caused by the present arms situation or secure the commitment of all required for disarmament measures. Nor can the verification of multilateral arms limitation and disarmament agreements and the relationship between disarmament and development be dealt with successfully except in the multilateral framework. To a great extent, a durable improvement in international relations depends on the success of the United Nations in discharging its mandate in this field.

X

The fortieth anniversary of the proclamation of the Universal Declaration of Human Rights comes at a time when the evolving world situation lends fresh point and urgency to the notions of human dignity and larger freedom expressed in the Charter.

A most deplorable feature of the present international scene is the frequency and magnitude of violations of fundamental human rights in different countries and regions. Summary arrests and executions, disappearances of individuals, the systematic practice of torture and killings of unarmed demonstrators continue to impose a heavy burden on the world's conscience. There have been reports of the forced exodus and even massacres of large groups of human beings. Timely demonstration of serious concern by Member States is essential if such appalling situations are to be checked now and prevented in future.

The Organization's work in the field of human rights, beginning with the Declaration, joined later by the two International Covenants on Human Rights and the Optional Protocol to the International Covenant on Civil and Political Rights to form the International Bill of Human Rights, has set universally accepted standards for the observance of human rights. The work continues as we approach, for example, the adoption of conventions protecting the rights of two especially vulnerable groups: children and migrant workers. A basis has been laid for constructive dialogue between Governments and the relevant expert committees. This year witnessed the first session of the newest such body, the Committee against Torture. Yet the struggle remains to give living reality to the provisions that have been made for promoting respect for human rights. Unless a consciousness of these rights becomes a vital element in the political ethos of a society, they are likely to be denied or truncated.

The key elements are knowledge by the individual citizens of their basic human rights and how to protect them and the existence of adequate national laws, procedures and practice for safeguarding them. For the United Nations, therefore, the twin goals guiding activities in this field, this year and in the years to come, will be the widest dissemination of information on human rights and the provision of advisory services and technical assistance for their protection. The mechanisms patiently developed for monitoring violations of human rights and drawing the attention of concerned Governments to them, often confidentially by the Secretary-General, and the functioning of the United Nations organs as focal points for the expression of their concerns by Governments and non-governmental organizations are proving to be invaluable in the great campaign of universalizing the enjoyment of human rights.

The existing machinery needs to be continually strengthened. Universal ratification and faithful implementation of human rights instruments are of the utmost importance. It is in all these diverse ways that the world community can develop methods to confront and remedy denials of human rights. A strong human rights programme can make our task in other areas significantly easier.

XI

In the economic sphere, the international community needs to act urgently in three areas: debt, trade and commodities, and human resources development.

For many developing countries, the crushing burden of external debt is crippling the development effort. Some progress has been made in dealing with debt problems of the poorest countries, especially those in Africa. I am happy to note the contribution to that end made by the report of the Advisory Group on Financial Flows for Africa, which I constituted last year. But the problems of the middle-income countries are no less pressing. The co-responsibility of debtor and creditor countries for the debt crisis has been increasingly recognized as has the mutual interest in breaking the current deadlock. There is a need promptly to fulfil the commitments made as well as to intensify the search for innovative solutions. Pursuant to a resolution of the General Assembly at the forty-second session, I have personally met with a group of eminent personalities to explore ways and means of finding durable, equitable and mutually agreed solutions to the debt problems of developing countries. I shall make a report to the Assembly separately on this subject.

Debt relief is only one aspect of the problem. Complementary action is needed in increasing financial flows, in particular concessional flows, to support development efforts. An improved international environment is also a prerequisite to restoring and accelerating the pace of economic development. Central to this is progress towards the resumption of more vigorous and healthy growth in international trade. It is imperative that Governments make every effort to achieve concrete results by the time of the mid-term review of the Uruguay Round of trade negotiations to be held in Montreal in December. I have also stressed on many occasions the urgency of taking a fresh look at the commodities problem, to see what more can be done in a practical way to alleviate the plight of commodity-dependent countries.

Ultimately, development means improving the human condition. I am gratified by the efforts made by the United Nations and the specialized agencies to draw attention to the importance of human resources development and to spur action to alleviate critical poverty. I hope that these initiatives will gather further momentum in all of the affected parts of the developing world.

The United Nations Programme of Action for African Economic Recovery and Development gives me the special responsibility of monitoring developments in Africa. We are currently engaged in a review of progress made so far under the Programme of Action. Despite earnest efforts to carry out adjustments in their national economic policies, most African countries have found little reprieve from the harsh impact of climatic conditions and an unfavourable external economic environment. It seems to me that, while a promising start has been made, a faster implementation of the commitments made by the developed countries is needed to avert a serious set-back to the overall process.

The international community responds generously to emergency requirements and to calls for immediate alleviation of dire needs. Unfortunately, international assistance programmes do not attract the same measure of support when long-term development is at stake. As is demonstrated in Africa, such programmes are necessary if the affected groups are to resume productive lives. Failing this, millions continue to languish in poverty, depending on external assistance for their survival. Remedial action needs to be taken so that they can again become self-reliant and contribute to national development.

Considering the interrelatedness of issues and the interdependence of national economies and bearing in mind the dramatic changes that have occurred in the world economy during the past 40 years, it seems to be imperative that the United Nations system strive to achieve greater harmony and coherence in our collective response to the challenges facing us today and those that lie ahead. However, even as the crucial role of the Organization in the political sphere is being widely supported, the question of how best to utilize its capacity to find integrated solutions to economic and social issues in all their aspects still remains subject to debate.

In my report last year, I had made some suggestions on how to strengthen the Economic and Social Council for fulfilling its responsibilities under the Charter. The Special Commission, established by the Council, has carried out a thorough and useful review of the intergovernmental machinery of the United Nations in the economic and social sectors. It was unfortunate that the Commission could not agree on a set of recommendations about the many activities in the economic and social fields which it discussed. Nevertheless, its discussions reveal substantial areas of agreement on important general principles, which could provide a basis for future action.

I welcome the Council's resolution on revitalization which, when implemented, can greatly enhance its ability to give policy guidelines as well as to monitor and co-ordinate the economic and social activities of the United Nations system. The Council's resolution and the report of the Special Commission will be extremely helpful for further deliberations in the context of the ongoing reform process. I should like to touch upon two elements relevant to this process.

First, the Council's effectiveness depends upon its ability to provide authoritative guidance towards a clear definition of priorities. I continue to believe that this ability will be strengthened if the Council meets at a sufficiently high political level, preferably ministerial, to consider issues of major importance for the international community. Such meetings would enhance the Council's status, credibility and effectiveness.

Second, and closely related to the above, Member States need to consider practical steps to identify those issues which are relatively more important and timely for intergovernmental consideration. In doing so, full consideration needs to be given to the fact that financial, monetary, trade and development issues are interrelated and have profound political and social implications. The concept of sustainable development in its broadest sense has relevance in this context.

When global problems call for global solutions, the value of the United Nations to Member States is apparent to all. Successful global initiatives, whether in the political field (which I mentioned earlier) or in the economic, social or humanitarian sphere, mean operational activities at country or subregional level. Two examples may suffice here:

The global AIDS initiative launched under the leadership of the World Health Organization is already being reflected in country-level activities supported by the United Nations Development Programme, which has been designated the operational arm in this important venture, together with the United Nations Population Fund and the United Nations Children's Fund for which maternal and child health are primary concerns.

The International Conference on Drug Abuse and Illicit Trafficking, held at Vienna in 1987, assigned a greatly increased role and responsibility to the United Nations, which it is fully committed to meet. Here again, at the country level, the United Nations Fund for Drug Abuse Control and the United Nations Development Programme have joined forces to assist in the development and implementation of specific actions.

It is most encouraging that specific focus has been placed by Member States on operational activities for development in the course of the past 12 months. Conditions may now be ripe for the introduction of significant improvements in the nature and organization of these activities to ensure that they are fully responsive to a rapidly changing and diversified context and able to match rising expectations.

The links between specific global goals and provision of support for related national and subregional efforts can surely be built on to ensure that, in the preparation of a fourth international development strategy for the 1990s, we will be able to count on direct support from some of the operational activities of the system in the achievement of specific objectives. This would add both strength and coherence to our overall efforts in the economic and social fields.

XII

The state of the Earth's environment is preeminently a problem that should evoke a solidarity of response from all nations. It has, however, reached a stage where, without a global ethic and the necessary law, it can give rise to divisive issues with political implications.

The problem is linked with those of poverty, the growth in the world's population to 5 billion and the prospects for sustainable development. It also involves issues of international responsibility. As such, it has too many aspects for any single country or even a group of countries to be able to deal with effectively. A coherent and well–co-ordinated approach can be developed only at the multilateral level.

This year, with the apprehension that the greenhouse effect has begun to affect our planet, public anxiety around the world has increased about the deterioration of the environment. The United Nations Environment Programme has proceeded, together with the World Meteorological Organization and the International Council of Scientific Unions, to develop internationally accepted assessments of the reality as well as the causes and impact of climatic change. The aim is to co-ordinate government policies to prevent, limit, delay or adapt to this change. With the help of a dialogue between scientists and policy makers, an international agreement needs to be evolved and, if necessary, one or more legal instruments adopted in order to address the effects of this ominous phenomenon in planetary experience.

A constructive precedent has been established in this context with the adoption of the Montreal Protocol on Substances that Deplete the Ozone Layer at a conference convened by UNEP in September 1987. This as well as the 1985 Vienna Convention for the Protection of the Ozone Layer constitute a major step in the development of international environmental law and set an example of managing a world problem before it leads to irreversible damage to human health and the environment.

These reassuring signs of progress notwithstanding, the crisis deepens as a growing population finds itself driven to use irreplaceable natural resources. Desertification, soil erosion, deforestation, swollen cities becoming gigantic sources of pollution, on the one side, and the emission of pollutants into the air by industry, on the other, can have a cumulative and well-nigh unmanageable effect. The unprecedented drought in certain agricultural areas, the acid rain and the more recent phenomenon of trafficking in, and dumping of, toxic wastes are examples of the vexatious issues that need to be forestalled by timely action. Here again, guidelines have been formulated preparatory to a global convention governing the environmentally sound management of hazardous wastes and their movement across frontiers. The issue will require exchange of information, technical assistance in monitoring and control and emergency response in case of accident.

As the Conference on Sustainable Development convened by the Prime Minister of Norway at Oslo in June so lucidly brought out, all issues in the field of environment call for a genuine working partnership among nations in the interest of keeping their common home in good condition.

XIII

Considering the vast sweep and scope of the possibilities now opening for constructive multilateral action through the United Nations, the financial health of the Organization needs to be immediately restored. The United Nations cannot function without money. It is still seriously short of funds. This situation includes both an immediate shortage of cash, which threatens insolvency in the next few months, and the virtual depletion of reserves. Lack of reserves means that the Organization will not be able to mount new operations.

The impact of the crisis is heightened by the increasing responsibilities of peacemaking and peace-keeping which the Organization has had to assume. Taking into account the new operations which the United Nations is likely to undertake in the next 12 months, its total annual expenses will rise very significantly.

I must ask the General Assembly to consider urgently both the cash and reserves aspects of this crisis and to find ways to ensure that it does not persist. These ways may have to include both new methods of raising money such as voluntary contributions or interest-free loans and also such fundamental measures as changes in the scale of assessments.

I welcome the recent decision of the United States to move towards full compliance with its international legal obligation to pay its assessed contributions to the United Nations. This is a most positive development. Partial payment of arrears will not, however, resolve the financial crisis of the Organization. Until and unless the outstanding contributions of all Member States are paid, the Organization will continue to operate with inadequate current income and virtually without reserves. Meanwhile, if the Organization is to sustain its present and foreseeable peacemaking and peace-keeping operations, its reserves must be replenished by the other means that I have mentioned above.

XIV

Reform and renewal in the United Nations has been one of my main preoccupations. As Secretary-General, I have shared the feeling that the accretions of four decades and a certain inflation of activity had encouraged a bureaucratic resistance to self-review and that we needed a leaner and more effective apparatus. As I have submitted two progress reports on this subject to the General Assembly, the second in April this year, it is not necessary to go into the details of the implementation of Assembly resolution 41/213. I may summarize some of the main points here:

Reform is the joint responsibility of both Member States and the Secretariat. As far as the Secretariat is concerned, a good part of the process pertaining to administration and finance has been completed ahead of the three-year schedule. The appropriations for the programme budget of the current biennium assume an overall vacancy rate of 15 per cent in the Professional and 10 per cent in other categories of staff.

Extensive restructuring has been undertaken in the political and administrative areas of the Secretariat and is under way in the area of public information.

A number of steps have been taken to improve co-ordination among the organizations of the United Nations system and a close look has been taken at field offices so as to avoid duplication and share resources, wherever possible.

A thorough assessment of our management information systems, in the light of current technology, has been initiated with a view to their eventual integration and the better provision of information required by Member States and the Secretariat.

Restructuring in the economic and social fields is related to the intergovernmental review. I have elsewhere in this report dwelt on this in the context of the work of the Economic and Social Council.

There are limits to the economies that can be effected in the Secretariat. An example is the provision of conference and documentation services essential to the conduct of discussions on issues on the international agenda. Without a decrease in meetings included in future calendars of conferences, post reductions of the size that were recommended in this area would gravely disrupt these services. But a decrease in meetings would mean some curtailing of the activities of the intergovernmental machinery and this would require a decision not by the Secretariat, but by Member States.

This brings us face to face with the fact that the Secretariat has grown not through a self-propelled process, but in response to the demands of the more extended intergovernmental machinery it must service. A rationalization of the structures of the Organization at the intergovernmental level would require decisions by Governments based on a re-examination of priorities among programmes and procedures for a better use of available resources. Such decisions, if acceptable to the generality of membership, would lend further substance to the process of reform.

I must add here that the staff of the Organization has faced conditions of severe strain in the most remarkable spirit. It is the undiminished loyalty of the staff to the Organization that has enabled it to perform its most vital functions, despite a very high vacancy rate. Responding to recent positive developments in the political situation, they have shown readiness and enthusiasm for a higher level of activity in the cause of peace. However, there is a limit to the additional effort that can be reasonably required from the staff. I feel that if Member States wish the Organization to maintain, as it must, the highest standards of competence and integrity, they need to ensure that conditions of employment of the staff remain competitive.

Reform is not an end in itself but a means of improving the services the Organization renders to Member States. The emerging world situation, with major conflicts on the way to solution, is bound to impose additional responsibilities on the Organization—political, economic and humanitarian. It would be paradoxical and discordant if the Organization should face financial difficulties precisely when it has to meet the demands of a more constructive phase of international affairs.

XV

The advent of a new year, decade or century, or even a new millennium, does not necessarily open a new page in the calendar of human experience. There seems to be a growing consciousness, however, that, while humanity has made phenomenal progress in the twentieth century, it has also reaped a harvest of wars and upheavals which, with better wisdom, could have been avoided. The current and preceding decades have witnessed much dangerous confusion. It is not a fanciful supposition that Governments will adjust better to a qualitatively changed and changing world environment. If the expectation is right, the United Nations will be used more purposefully than it has been before. I have in mind the use made of it by all Powers—the great, the medium and the small.

The Charter and the working of the world Organization do not promise a problem-free world. What they promise is a rational and peaceful way of solving problems. Perfect justice in relations between nations may be unattainable but inequities can be reduced. To the great dangers of the proliferation of nuclear and conventional weapons, political disputes, violations of human rights, the prevalence of poverty and threats to the environment have been added new sources of conflict. There is a need for the world's wealth of political intelligence and imagination—and compassion—to be employed in coping with these dangers. It can be done through constant and systematic effort only within the United Nations. Non-governmental organizations play an invaluable role in this respect, especially in campaigns for disarmament and human rights; the future is bound to call for even greater dedication from them. Failure to comprehend and come to terms with the demands of emerging situations will mean suffering and privation for the weak and erosion of prestige for the strong. Greater support for the Organization is, therefore, called for not as an exercise in piety nor in a sudden and passing burst of idealism, but in sober and enlightened recognition of necessity in handling the complexities of international affairs.

Javier PÉREZ DE CUÉLLAR
Secretary-General

PART ONE

Political and security questions

Chapter I

International peace and security

The Organization's activities in the maintenance of international peace and security were recognized by the award of the 1988 Nobel Peace Prize to the United Nations peace-keeping forces. At the time of the award, in September, the United Nations had nearly 10,000 peace-keeping forces and observers on duty in seven regions of the world.

The Secretary-General characterized the award as a tribute to the idealism of all who had served the Organization, in particular to the valour and sacrifices of those who had contributed and continued to contribute to peace-keeping operations.

The President of the General Assembly, in his statement on the occasion, noted that United Nations peace-keeping operations had helped prevent conflicts and had promoted the purposes and principles of the Charter of the United Nations in general. He observed that the new international atmosphere provided a concrete opportunity for the United Nations to play an even broader role in the system of collective security, of which peace-keeping operations were a fundamental instrument.

The General Assembly welcomed the award with deep appreciation, expressing the conviction that United Nations peace-keeping operations were an integral component of enhancing the effectiveness of the Organization in the maintenance of international peace and security (resolution 43/59 A).

The principal organs of the United Nations on matters of international peace and security continued to function in the manner envisaged in the Charter. International relations at the global level improved markedly, opening up new possibilities for United Nations peacemaking efforts.

The Assembly adopted a number of resolutions relating to issues of peace and security at both the regional and international levels. It recognized the strong resolve of peoples to strengthen international peace and security and promote economic and social development. It reaffirmed the lasting importance and validity of the 1984 Declaration on the Right of Peoples to Peace (43/22) as well as the fact that peace and security and development were interrelated and inseparable (43/23).

The Assembly, noting the tenth anniversary of the 1978 Declaration on the Preparation of Societies for Life in Peace, underscored the important role that the Declaration played in promoting world peace and international security, common understanding and mutually beneficial co-operation (43/87). It expressed the firm conviction that ensuring international peace and security required concerted efforts and close co-operation among States (43/89).

With regard to regional security questions, the Assembly reaffirmed that the security of the Mediterranean was closely linked with European security and with international peace and security and that efforts were necessary to reduce tension and armaments and to promote peace, security and co-operation in the region (43/84). It affirmed that the implementation of confidence- and security-building measures would contribute to strengthening regional as well as international peace and security (43/85). It called for the continuation and intensification of result-oriented political dialogue and co-operation, in accordance with the United Nations Charter (43/86).

Strengthening of international security

Implementation of the 1970 Declaration

In December 1988, the General Assembly, reaffirmed the validity of its 1970 Declaration on the Strengthening of International Security[1] and again urged all States to seek, through the effective use of the United Nations Charter, the peaceful settlement of disputes and the elimination of the focal points of crisis and tension.

The Assembly included the question of the strengthening of international security in its agenda for the first time in 1969, at the request of the USSR,[2] and has since then discussed it annually.

The Secretary-General, in a September 1988 report and subsequent addendum,[3] transmitted replies from Member States to a 1987 Assembly invitation[4] to submit their views on the implementation of the Declaration. Six States had sent substantive replies as at 23 November 1988.

GENERAL ASSEMBLY ACTION

On 7 December, the General Assembly, on the recommendation of the First Committee, adopted **resolution 43/88** by recorded vote.

Review of the implementation of the Declaration on the Strengthening of International Security

The General Assembly,

Having considered the item entitled "Review of the implementation of the Declaration on the Strengthening of International Security",

Aware of the increasing interdependence among nations and of the fact that in the present-day world there is no alternative to a policy of peaceful coexistence, détente and co-operation among States on the basis of equality, irrespective of their economic or military power, political and social systems or size or geographic location,

Convinced that a comprehensive and just solution to pressing international problems, such as achieving peace and security, disarmament and development, can be assured only through negotiations, based on the principles of the Charter of the United Nations, in which all countries participate on an equal footing,

Reiterating its conviction that, in the continuing search by the international community for lasting security, multilateral action has an increasingly important role,

Reaffirming the role of the United Nations as an indispensable forum for negotiations and reaching agreements on measures to promote and strengthen international peace and security,

Stressing the need for the main organs of the United Nations responsible for the maintenance of peace and security, particularly the Security Council, to contribute more effectively to the promotion of international peace and security by seeking solutions to unresolved problems and crises in the world,

Recalling the Declaration on Principles of International Law concerning Friendly Relations and Co-operation among States in accordance with the Charter of the United Nations, the Declaration on the Inadmissibility of Intervention and Interference in the Internal Affairs of States and the Manila Declaration on the Peaceful Settlement of International Disputes,

Welcoming the fact that a favourable climate has recently developed within the international community and progress has been recorded in some important fields of arms limitation and disarmament, as well as in the resolution of certain focal points of crisis in the world,

Encouraged by the Treaty between the United States of America and the Union of Soviet Socialist Republics on the Elimination of Their Intermediate-Range and Shorter-Range Missiles, which represents a valuable initial step in the reduction of nuclear weapons,

Noting that the progress in the resolution of certain regional conflicts and the easing of tensions present the international community of nations with the opportunity to take a significant step towards the realization of international peace and security,

Welcoming also the continuation of the process within the framework of the Conference on Security and Co-operation in Europe,

Noting with concern that despite the positive processes and developments, the provisions of the Declaration on the Strengthening of International Security have not been fully implemented and that international relations are still characterized by the policy of competition for spheres of influence, domination and exploitation in many parts of the world by the continuation of the arms race, particularly in nuclear weapons, and the danger of its extension into outer space, by the recourse to the use or threat of use of force, military intervention and interference and foreign occupation and by the infringement of the independence, sovereignty and territorial integrity of countries,

Concerned particularly by the lack of solutions to the world economic problems, in which the deeper underlying problems of a structural nature have been compounded by cyclical factors and which has further aggravated the inequalities and injustices in international economic relations, all of which pose a grave threat to global peace and security,

1. *Reaffirms* the validity of the Declaration on the Strengthening of International Security, and calls upon all States to contribute effectively to its implementation;

2. *Urges once again* all States to abide strictly, in their international relations, by their commitment to the Charter of the United Nations and, to this end:

(a) To refrain from the use or threat of use of force, intervention, interference, aggression, foreign occupation and colonial domination or measures of political and economic coercion, which violate the sovereignty, territorial integrity, independence and security of other States, as well as the permanent sovereignty of peoples over their natural resources;

(b) To refrain from supporting or encouraging any such act for any reason whatsoever and to reject and refuse recognition of situations brought about by any such act;

(c) To seek, through more effective utilization of the means provided for in the Charter, the peaceful settlement of disputes and the elimination of the focal points of crisis and tension, which constitute a threat to international peace and security;

3. *Calls upon* all States, in particular the nuclear-weapon States and other militarily significant States, to take immediate steps aimed at:

(a) Promoting and using effectively the system of collective security as envisaged in the Charter;

(b) Halting effectively the arms race and achieving general and complete disarmament under effective international control and, to this end, to conduct serious, meaningful and effective negotiations with a view to implementing the recommendations and decisions contained in the Final Document of the Tenth Special Session of the General Assembly and to fulfilling the priority tasks listed in the Programme of Action set forth in section III of the Final Document;

4. *Invites* all States, in particular the major military Powers and States members of military alliances, to refrain, especially in critical situations and in crisis areas, from actions, including military activities and manoeuvres, conceived within the context of East-West confrontation and used as a means of pressure or threat to and destabilization of other States and regions;

5. *Expresses its conviction* that the gradual military disengagement of the great Powers and their military alliances from various parts of the world should be promoted;

6. *Emphasizes* the role that the United Nations has in the maintenance of international peace and security and in economic and social development and progress for the benefit of all mankind;

7. *Stresses* that there is a need further to enhance the effectiveness of the Security Council in discharging its principal role of maintaining international peace and security and to enhance the authority and enforcement capacity of the Council in accordance with the Charter;

8. *Reiterates* the need for the Security Council, in particular its permanent members, to ensure the effective implementation of its decisions in compliance with the relevant provisions of the Charter;

9. *Emphasizes* that there can be no lasting peace and security in the world without the solution of the international economic problems, particularly those of the developing countries, and the ensuring of the sustained growth and development of the world economy;

10. *Considers* that respect for and promotion of human rights and fundamental freedoms in their civil, political, economic, social and cultural aspects, on the one hand, and the strengthening of international peace and security, on the other, mutually reinforce each other;

11. *Reaffirms* the legitimacy of the struggle of peoples under colonial domination, foreign occupation or racist régimes and their inalienable right to self-determination and independence, and urges Member States to increase their support for and solidarity with them and their national liberation movements and to take urgent and effective measures for the speedy completion of the implementation of the Declaration on the Granting of Independence to Colonial Countries and Peoples and for the final elimination of colonialism, racism and *apartheid;*

12. *Calls upon* all States, particularly the members of the Security Council, to take appropriate and effective measures to promote the fulfilment of the objective of the denuclearization of Africa in order to avert the serious danger that the nuclear capability of South Africa constitutes to the African States, in particular the frontline States, as well as to international peace and security;

13. *Reaffirms* that the democratization of international relations is an imperative necessity enabling, under the conditions of interdependence, the full development and independence of all States, as well as the attainment of genuine security, peace and co-operation in the world, and stresses its firm belief that the United Nations offers the best framework for the promotion of these goals;

14. *Invites* Member States to submit their views on the question of the implementation of the Declaration on the Strengthening of International Security, and requests the Secretary-General to submit a report to the General Assembly at its forty-fourth session on the basis of the replies received;

15. *Decides* to include in the provisional agenda of its forty-fourth session the item entitled "Review of the implementation of the Declaration on the Strengthening of International Security".

General Assembly resolution 43/88

7 December 1988   Meeting 73   128-1-22 (recorded vote)

Approved by First Committee (A/43/913) by recorded vote (102-1-25), 30 November (meeting 54); 14-nation draft (A/C.1/43/L.88); agenda item 72.
Sponsors: Algeria, Bangladesh, Egypt, India, Indonesia, Madagascar, Malaysia, Pakistan, Romania, Sri Lanka, Sudan, Tunisia, Uganda, Yugoslavia.
Meeting numbers. GA 43rd session: 1st Committee 47-54; plenary 73.

Recorded vote in Assembly as follows:

In favour: Afghanistan, Algeria, Angola, Antigua and Barbuda, Argentina, Bahamas, Bahrain, Bangladesh, Barbados, Benin, Bhutan, Bolivia, Botswana, Brazil, Brunei Darussalam, Bulgaria, Burkina Faso, Burma, Burundi, Byelorussian SSR, Cameroon, Canada,[a] Cape Verde, Central African Republic, Chad, Chile, China, Colombia, Comoros, Congo, Costa Rica, Côte d'Ivoire, Cuba, Cyprus, Czechoslovakia, Democratic Kampuchea, Democratic Yemen, Djibouti, Dominican Republic, Ecuador, Egypt, El Salvador, Ethiopia, Fiji, Gabon, Gambia, German Democratic Republic, Ghana, Guatemala, Guinea, Guyana, Haiti, Honduras, Hungary, India, Indonesia, Iran, Iraq, Jamaica, Jordan, Kenya, Kuwait, Lao People's Democratic Republic, Lebanon, Lesotho, Liberia, Libyan Arab Jamahiriya, Madagas-

car, Malawi, Malaysia, Maldives, Mali, Malta, Mauritania, Mauritius, Mexico, Mongolia, Morocco, Mozambique, Nepal, Nicaragua, Niger, Nigeria, Oman, Pakistan, Panama, Papua New Guinea, Paraguay, Peru, Philippines, Poland, Qatar, Romania, Rwanda, Saint Lucia, Saint Vincent and the Grenadines, Samoa, Sao Tome and Principe, Saudi Arabia, Senegal, Seychelles, Sierra Leone, Singapore, Solomon Islands, Somalia, Sri Lanka, Sudan, Suriname, Swaziland, Syrian Arab Republic, Thailand, Togo, Trinidad and Tobago, Tunisia, Uganda, Ukrainian SSR, USSR, United Arab Emirates, United Republic of Tanzania, Uruguay, Vanuatu, Venezuela, Viet Nam, Yemen, Yugoslavia, Zaire, Zambia, Zimbabwe.
Against: United States.
Abstaining: Australia, Austria, Belgium, Denmark, Finland, France, Germany, Federal Republic of, Greece, Iceland, Ireland, Israel, Italy, Japan, Luxembourg, Netherlands, New Zealand, Norway, Portugal, Spain, Sweden, Turkey, United Kingdom.

[a]Later advised the Secretariat it had intended to abstain.

Implementation of the 1978 Declaration on societies and peace

On the tenth anniversary of the adoption of the 1978 Declaration on the Preparation of Societies for Life in Peace,[5] the General Assembly reaffirmed its validity and called on all States to spare no efforts towards its full implementation and to adhere strictly to the principles enshrined in it.

The Declaration invited all States to establish, maintain and strengthen a just and durable peace for present and future generations and, in particular, to observe certain principles, including those which stated that every nation and human being, regardless of race, conscience, language or sex, had the inherent right to life in peace; a war of aggression is a crime against peace; and every State had the duty to refrain from propaganda for wars of aggression, to promote equitable political, economic, social and cultural co-operation, to respect the right of all peoples to self-determination, independence, equality, sovereignty, the territorial integrity of States and the inviolability of their frontiers, and to discourage colonialism and racism and advocacy of hatred and prejudice.

GENERAL ASSEMBLY ACTION

On the recommendation of the First Committee, the General Assembly, on 7 December 1988, adopted **resolution 43/87** by recorded vote.

Tenth anniversary of the adoption of the Declaration on the Preparation of Societies for Life in Peace

The General Assembly,

Considering that the year 1988 marks the tenth anniversary of the adoption of the Declaration on the Preparation of Societies for Life in Peace,

Reiterating that the promotion of peace is one of the primary purposes of the United Nations and that its attainment is the most cherished ideal of the peoples of the world,

Welcoming the active promotion of the idea of the preparation of societies for life in peace by Governments, the United Nations and international and national organizations, as reflected in the reports of the Secretary-General prepared in accordance with General Assembly resolutions 33/73 of 15 December 1978, 36/104 of 9 December 1981 and 39/157 of 17 December 1984,

Welcoming also the growing involvement of major political, social and religious movements in the promotion of peace,

Recalling its resolution 42/91 of 7 December 1987 on the implementation of the Declaration,

Noting with satisfaction that the issue of the preparation of societies for life in peace was given a prominent place in the observances of the International Year of Peace,

Recognizing the determination of States to undertake efforts towards a more peaceful and secure world through tangible disarmament,

Aware of the timeliness of the Declaration as well as the valuable experience gained in the course of the implementation of its principles and objectives,

1. *Solemnly reaffirms* the lasting validity of the purposes and principles enshrined in the Declaration on the Preparation of Societies for Life in Peace, based on the Charter of the United Nations;

2. *Noting with appreciation* the important role that the Declaration has played in promoting world peace and international security, common understanding and mutually beneficial co-operation;

3. *Calls upon* all States to spare no efforts towards the fullest implementation of the Declaration at the national and international levels and towards increasing its national and international role by strictly adhering to the principles enshrined in that document.

General Assembly resolution 43/87

7 December 1988　　　Meeting 73　　　128-0-24 (recorded vote)

Approved by First Committee (A/43/913) by recorded vote (103-0-26), 30 November (meeting 54); 18-nation draft (A/C.1/43/L.87); agenda item 72.

Sponsors: Afghanistan, Algeria, Bulgaria, Cameroon, Costa Rica, German Democratic Republic, Hungary, Indonesia, Madagascar, Mongolia, Panama, Peru, Philippines, Poland, Syrian Arab Republic, Tunisia, Viet Nam, Yugoslavia.

Meeting numbers. GA 43rd session: 1st Committee 47-54; plenary 73.

Recorded vote in Assembly as follows:

In favour: Afghanistan, Algeria, Angola, Antigua and Barbuda, Argentina, Bahamas, Bahrain, Bangladesh, Barbados, Benin, Bhutan, Bolivia, Botswana, Brazil, Brunei Darussalam, Bulgaria, Burkina Faso, Burma, Burundi, Byelorussian SSR, Cameroon, Cape Verde, Central African Republic, Chad, Chile, China, Colombia, Comoros, Congo, Costa Rica, Côte d'Ivoire, Cuba, Cyprus, Czechoslovakia, Democratic Kampuchea, Democratic Yemen, Djibouti, Dominican Republic, Ecuador, Egypt, El Salvador, Ethiopia, Fiji, Gabon, Gambia, German Democratic Republic, Ghana, Guatemala, Guinea, Guyana, Haiti, Honduras, Hungary, India, Indonesia, Iran, Iraq, Jamaica, Jordan, Kenya, Kuwait, Lao People's Democratic Republic, Lebanon, Lesotho, Liberia, Libyan Arab Jamahiriya, Madagascar, Malawi, Malaysia, Maldives, Mali, Malta, Mauritania, Mauritius, Mexico, Mongolia, Morocco, Mozambique, Nepal, Nicaragua, Niger, Nigeria, Oman, Pakistan, Panama, Papua New Guinea, Paraguay, Peru, Philippines, Poland, Qatar, Romania, Rwanda, Saint Kitts and Nevis, Saint Lucia, Saint Vincent and the Grenadines, Samoa, Sao Tome and Principe, Saudi Arabia, Senegal, Seychelles, Sierra Leone, Singapore, Solomon Islands, Somalia, Sri Lanka, Sudan, Suriname, Swaziland, Syrian Arab Republic, Thailand, Togo, Trinidad and Tobago, Tunisia, Uganda, Ukrainian SSR, USSR, United Arab Emirates, United Republic of Tanzania, Uruguay, Vanuatu, Venezuela, Viet Nam, Yemen, Yugoslavia, Zaire, Zambia, Zimbabwe.

Against: None.

Abstaining: Australia, Austria, Belgium, Canada, Denmark, Finland, France, Germany, Federal Republic of, Greece, Iceland, Ireland, Israel, Italy, Japan, Luxembourg, Netherlands, New Zealand, Norway, Portugal, Spain, Sweden, Turkey, United Kingdom, United States.

Comprehensive system of international peace and security

Pursuant to the request of the General Assembly in 1987,[6] the Secretary-General, in a report of October 1988,[7] presented the views of Member States and non-governmental organizations

(NGOs) on how to contribute to the development of a dialogue on ways and means of promoting comprehensive security based on the United Nations Charter and within the United Nations framework. The Secretariat also studied statements and deliberations at the 1986 and 1987 regular and special sessions of the Assembly, as well as statements made in the First Committee and other subsidiary bodies and organs of the Assembly, and in the Security Council. In addition, informal consultations were undertaken with the Chairmen of the regional groups and individual delegations with a view to exploring ways and means of organizing an exchange of views on the matter.

The report noted that in the course of its consideration of ways to promote an exchange of views on the subject, the Organization had made use of a variety of methods, ranging from the appointment of formal committees to informal groups such as *ad hoc* committees, contact groups, friends of the chairman or rapporteurs. Among the examples cited were the Special Committee on the Charter of the United Nations and on the Strengthening of the Role of the Organization, the Special Committee on Peace-keeping Operations, the Special Committee on Principles of International Law Concerning Friendly Relations and Co-operation among States, and the Special Committee on Enhancing the Effectiveness of the Principle of the Non-Use of Force in International Relations.

Various opinions were expressed during the Assembly's 1987 session on ways to approach the subject. Suggestions included discussions on means to reinforce the effectiveness of the Charter through supplementary measures and norms; a concerted analysis of the implementation of Charter provisions in order to determine those which had not been utilized to their fullest potential; and a clear definition of the areas where new concepts and approaches had emerged so as to ensure that international efforts in that regard were not to the detriment or at the expense of existing norms and practices. It was proposed that thought be given to convening a special Assembly session with broad participation as the forum most competent to examine the issue of a comprehensive system of international peace and security.

Summarizing the views of those regional groups and individual delegations which were consulted informally, the report stated that one group of Member States suggested consideration of the question by the Assembly's First Committee or its other Committees during and outside the regular sessions, as well as by the Special Committee on the Charter, the Security Council, and regional and intergovernmental organizations. It was also suggested that the United Nations take initiatives in that field and participate actively in introducing dialogue on the question in various forums. At the same time, the view was expressed that there was no need to introduce any new agenda item on the subject in the United Nations bodies and specialized agencies and that the existing agenda items should be examined in such a manner as to promote the concept of strengthening international peace and security.

It was also stated that the existing United Nations bodies were competent and possessed the expertise to discuss questions relating to international peace and security. Consequently, any concrete proposals should be considered in the appropriate United Nations forums. The same group of Member States also maintained that the Charter contained the necessary ideas concerning international peace and security and anything that could lead to a redefinition of international security should be avoided.

Certain delegations had expressed preference for an approach which sought to examine concrete proposals relating to the system of international peace and security. The Secretary-General believed that, although they had suggested varying approaches, Member States were clearly in agreement on the desirability of strengthening the United Nations and increasing its effectiveness. It also appeared that further deliberations and consultations would be needed to bring about greater understanding and a wider consensus. For his part, the Secretary-General said he stood ready to assist the Assembly in discussing the subject—formally or informally—and to study general or specific aspects of it as the Assembly would judge to be of assistance to Member States.

A number of international and national NGOs and political and public figures suggested that scholars whose research was relevant to the study of a "new definition" of global security should be consulted both by their respective Governments and by the Organization. They also underlined the need for growing co-operation between the academic community, politicians and diplomats to broaden the scope of activities conducive to global security.

The five permanent members of the Security Council, in a statement issued after a meeting of their Foreign Ministers with the Secretary-General on 28 September during which they had exchanged views on a wide range of major international issues,[8] placed particular emphasis on efforts to resolve regional conflicts. They noted with satisfaction the marked improvement in international relations at the global level and the general trend towards dialogue and peaceful settlement of disputes since their previous meeting with the Secretary-General in September 1987. They welcomed the active involvement of the United Na-

tions in the process and stressed their continuing confidence in the Organization, which they believed had an increasingly significant role to play in the achievement of international peace and security.

At its February/March 1988 meeting, the Special Committee on the Charter of the United Nations and on the Strengthening of the Role of the Organization completed a draft Declaration on the Prevention and Removal of Disputes and Situations Which May Threaten International Peace and Security and on the Role of the United Nations in this Field, which the General Assembly approved in **resolution 43/51**. In **resolution 43/164**, the Assembly invited the International Law Commission to continue elaborating a draft Code of Crimes against the Peace and Security of Mankind.

GENERAL ASSEMBLY ACTION

On 7 December, the General Assembly, on the recommendation of the First Committee, adopted **resolution 43/89** by recorded vote.

Comprehensive approach to strengthening international peace and security in accordance with the Charter of the United Nations

The General Assembly,

Convinced of the need to strengthen further the role and effectiveness of the United Nations on the basis of full and universal implementation of its Charter, in order to ensure international peace and security on a comprehensive basis covering all States and all aspects of their interrelationship,

Expressing the firm conviction that ensuring international peace and security requires concerted efforts and close co-operation among all States on the basis of the Charter of the United Nations in order to resolve issues of crucial importance in the following spheres: disarmament, peaceful settlement of disputes and conflicts, international economic co-operation and development, protection of the environment, and human rights and fundamental freedoms,

Affirming that the system of security embodied in the Charter is the fundamental and irreplaceable mechanism for the preservation or restoration of international peace and security,

Reaffirming that in the interest of ensuring international peace and security on a comprehensive basis all States should adhere strictly to the fundamental principles of international law, especially respect for the sovereignty, equality, political independence and territorial integrity of States, non-intervention and non-interference in internal affairs, refraining from the threat or use of force, peaceful settlement of disputes, self-determination of peoples, respect for human rights and fundamental freedoms, co-operation among States and compliance in good faith with their obligations assumed in accordance with the Charter,

Bearing in mind the report of the Secretary-General on the ways and means of organizing an exchange of views on the subject among the States Members of the United Nations,

Taking note of the suggestions, ideas and views expressed in the deliberations on this matter,

1. *Encourages* Member States to contribute to an international dialogue, primarily within the framework of the United Nations, its Security Council and General Assembly and their subsidiary bodies, in order to find universally acceptable ways and means and to co-ordinate practical measures to strengthen on a comprehensive basis the system of security laid down in the Charter of the United Nations and to enhance the role and effectiveness of the United Nations in the maintenance of international peace and security in all aspects;

2. *Calls upon* all States to intensify their practical efforts towards ensuring international security in all its aspects through peaceful means, in accordance with the purposes and principles of the Charter;

3. *Decides* to include in the agenda of its forty-fourth session an item entitled ''Comprehensive approach to strengthening international peace and security in accordance with the Charter of the United Nations''.

General Assembly resolution 43/89

7 December 1988   Meeting 73   97-3-45 (recorded vote)

Approved by First Committee (A/43/914) by recorded vote (83-2-39), 30 November (meeting 54); 13-nation draft (A/C.1/43/L.74/Rev.1 & Corr.1); agenda item 73.
Sponsors: Bulgaria, Byelorussian SSR, Czechoslovakia, German Democratic Republic, Hungary, Lao People's Democratic Republic, Madagascar, Mongolia, Poland, Romania, Ukrainian SSR, USSR, Viet Nam.
Meeting numbers. GA 43rd session: 1st Committee 47-54; plenary 73.

Recorded vote in Assembly as follows:

In favour: Afghanistan, Algeria, Angola, Antigua and Barbuda, Argentina, Australia, Austria, Bahamas, Bahrain, Bangladesh, Barbados, Bhutan, Botswana, Brazil, Bulgaria, Burkina Faso, Burma, Burundi, Byelorussian SSR, Canada, Cape Verde, Colombia, Congo, Costa Rica, Cuba, Cyprus, Czechoslovakia, Democratic Yemen, Ecuador, Egypt, Ethiopia, Finland, German Democratic Republic, Ghana, Guinea, Guyana, Hungary, India, Indonesia, Iran, Iraq, Jamaica, Jordan, Kuwait, Lao People's Democratic Republic, Lebanon, Lesotho, Liberia, Libyan Arab Jamahiriya, Madagascar, Malaysia, Maldives, Mali, Mauritius, Mexico, Mongolia, Mozambique, Nepal, New Zealand, Nicaragua, Nigeria, Norway, Oman, Panama, Papua New Guinea, Peru, Poland, Qatar, Romania, Saint Lucia, Saint Vincent and the Grenadines, Sao Tome and Principe, Saudi Arabia, Seychelles, Singapore, Solomon Islands, Somalia, Sri Lanka, Sudan, Sweden, Syrian Arab Republic, Togo, Trinidad and Tobago, Tunisia, Uganda, Ukrainian SSR, USSR, United Arab Emirates, United Republic of Tanzania, Vanuatu, Venezuela, Viet Nam, Yemen, Yugoslavia, Zaire, Zambia, Zimbabwe.

Against: Israel, Japan, United States.

Abstaining: Belgium, Brunei Darussalam, Central African Republic, Chad, Chile, China, Comoros, Côte d'Ivoire, Denmark, Djibouti, Dominican Republic, El Salvador, Fiji, France, Gabon, Gambia, Germany, Federal Republic of, Greece, Guatemala, Haiti, Honduras, Iceland, Ireland, Italy, Kenya, Luxembourg, Malawi, Morocco, Netherlands, Niger, Pakistan, Paraguay, Philippines, Portugal, Rwanda, Saint Kitts and Nevis, Samoa, Senegal, Sierra Leone, Spain, Suriname, Swaziland, Turkey, United Kingdom, Uruguay.

The Chairman of the First Committee, in introducing the item, noted that the relaxation in international relations had created a more favourable background for the consideration of items relating to international security. In that connection, he said the United Nations was the proper instrument to which the international community must turn to find acceptable answers to issues relating to peace and security.

Dialogue to improve the international situation

In 1988, the General Assembly again underlined the need for a result-oriented political dialogue to improve the international situation. The item had been included in its agenda for the first time in 1986, when the Assembly adopted a resolution on the subject.[9]

GENERAL ASSEMBLY ACTION

In accordance with the recommendation of the First Committee, the General Assembly, on 7 December, adopted **resolution 43/86** by recorded vote.

Need for a result-oriented political dialogue to improve the international situation

The General Assembly,

Having considered the item entitled ''Need for a result-oriented political dialogue to improve the international situation'',

Welcoming the favourable trends in the current international environment, in particular the first, though limited, step in the field of nuclear disarmament and the progress reached in solving regional conflicts,

Noting with satisfaction the growing awareness that dialogue and co-operation are imperative in order further to improve international relations, generate a climate of trust and resolve global problems facing humanity,

Conscious of the urgent need for progress in reducing the levels of armament, both nuclear and conventional, and in solving global problems such as the development of equitable international economic relations, measures to alleviate the external indebtedness of the developing countries, protection of the environment and the elimination of racism and *apartheid*, as well as the removal of hunger and poverty,

Considering that durable peace and security cannot be achieved through confrontation, but only through policies of dialogue and co-operation as well as by measures aimed at strengthening the United Nations in accordance with its Charter, particularly in the nuclear and space age,

1. *Reaffirms* the obligation of States to abide strictly by the purposes and principles of the Charter of the United Nations;

2. *Calls* for the continuation and intensification of result-oriented political dialogue and co-operation at the multilateral, regional and bilateral levels, in accordance with the relevant principles of the Charter;

3. *Reaffirms its appeal* to all Member States to enhance the role of the United Nations as a forum for political dialogue and negotiation in order to preserve peace, strengthen international security, promote arms limitation and disarmament, develop equitable international economic relations, implement the right to self-determination of peoples under colonial domination and foreign occupation, eradicate racism and *apartheid*, promote and protect human rights and fundamental freedoms and settle other urgent international issues;

4. *Appeals* to Member States to consider ways and means of strengthening the role and efficiency of the General Assembly as the most representative international forum for dialogue and co-operation, as well as of increasing the political authority of its resolutions;

5. *Welcomes* the recent encouraging co-operation among the members of the Security Council enabling the Council to carry out more effectively its primary

responsibility for the maintenance of international peace and security in accordance with the Charter;

6. *Encourages* the Secretary-General to continue his efforts, in accordance with the Charter, to facilitate dialogue and co-operation as a means to reduce tensions, to promote the peaceful settlement of regional and international conflicts and to enhance international peace and security;

7. *Stresses* the importance of a more adequate consideration of the report of the Secretary-General on the work of the Organization.

General Assembly resolution 43/86

7 December 1988   Meeting 73   127-1-24 (recorded vote)

Approved by First Committee (A/43/913) by recorded vote (100-1-25), 30 November (meeting 54); draft by German Democratic Republic (A/C.1/43/L.85/Rev.1); agenda item 72.

Meeting numbers. GA 43rd session: 1st Committee 47-54; plenary 73.

Recorded vote in Assembly as follows:

In favour: Afghanistan, Algeria, Angola, Antigua and Barbuda, Argentina, Bahamas, Bahrain, Bangladesh, Barbados, Benin, Bhutan, Bolivia, Botswana, Brazil, Brunei Darussalam, Bulgaria, Burkina Faso, Burma, Burundi, Byelorussian SSR, Cameroon, Cape Verde, Central African Republic, Chad, China, Colombia, Comoros, Congo, Costa Rica, Côte d'Ivoire, Cuba, Cyprus, Czechoslovakia, Democratic Kampuchea, Democratic Yemen, Djibouti, Dominican Republic, Ecuador, Egypt, El Salvador, Ethiopia, Fiji, Gabon, Gambia, German Democratic Republic, Ghana, Guatemala, Guinea, Guyana, Haiti, Honduras, Hungary, India, Indonesia, Iran, Iraq, Jamaica, Jordan, Kenya, Kuwait, Lao People's Democratic Republic, Lebanon, Lesotho, Liberia, Libyan Arab Jamahiriya, Madagascar, Malawi, Malaysia, Maldives, Mali, Malta, Mauritania, Mauritius, Mexico, Mongolia, Morocco, Mozambique, Nepal, Nicaragua, Niger, Nigeria, Oman, Pakistan, Panama, Papua New Guinea, Paraguay, Peru, Philippines, Poland, Qatar, Romania, Rwanda, Saint Kitts and Nevis, Saint Lucia, Saint Vincent and the Grenadines, Samoa, Sao Tome and Principe, Saudi Arabia, Senegal, Seychelles, Sierra Leone, Singapore, Solomon Islands, Somalia, Sri Lanka, Sudan, Suriname, Swaziland, Syrian Arab Republic, Thailand, Togo, Trinidad and Tobago, Tunisia, Uganda, Ukrainian SSR, USSR, United Arab Emirates, United Republic of Tanzania, Uruguay, Vanuatu, Venezuela, Viet Nam, Yemen, Yugoslavia, Zaire, Zambia, Zimbabwe.

Against: United States.

Abstaining: Australia, Austria, Belgium, Canada, Chile, Denmark, Finland, France, Germany, Federal Republic of, Greece, Iceland, Ireland, Israel, Italy, Japan, Luxembourg, Netherlands, New Zealand, Norway, Portugal, Spain, Sweden, Turkey, United Kingdom.

Introducing the draft in the Committee, the German Democratic Republic said its initiative stemmed from the fact that all the major political forces of the world had expressed their commitment to a policy of dialogue and co-operation. In addition, there had been an expression of readiness by States to strengthen the United Nations.

In an earlier statement, the German Democratic Republic said that international dialogue on fundamental issues facing mankind was becoming more result-oriented and that all the major political currents favoured a policy of dialogue and co-operation. The United Nations was becoming a centre for harmonizing the activities of States, as envisaged in the Charter.

Regional and international peace and security

Improvements in international relations during 1988 made possible the settlement of regional conflicts under United Nations auspices and with the co-operation of the two super-Powers—the USSR and the United States. The new international cli-

mate coincided with a resurgence of public interest in the Organization, making possible regional approaches to resolving regional conflicts. The Assembly, in December, affirmed that all regional and subregional peace and security endeavours should take into account the characteristics of each region. It further affirmed that the implementation of confidence- and security-building measures, taking into account the United Nations Charter and the specificity of each particular region, would contribute to the strengthening of regional as well as international peace and security.

GENERAL ASSEMBLY ACTION

On 7 December, the General Assembly, on the recommendation of the First Committee, adopted **resolution 43/85** without vote.

Strengthening of regional and international peace and security

The General Assembly,

Bearing in mind that the fundamental responsibility of the United Nations under the Charter is to maintain international peace and security,

Recognizing the need to remove the risk of armed conflicts between States by promoting a change in the international climate from confrontation to peaceful relations and co-operation and by taking appropriate measures to strengthen international peace and security,

Noting with satisfaction the continuing efforts of the Secretary-General to bring about the peaceful resolution of regional conflicts in order to achieve international peace and security,

Noting also with satisfaction that the United Nations peace-keeping forces were awarded the Nobel Peace Prize on 29 September 1988 for effective contribution to the maintenance of international peace and security,

Affirming that all regional and subregional peace and security endeavours should take into account the characteristics of each region, as well as measures adopted therein to strengthen mutual confidence to assure the security of all States involved,

Noting with appreciation the voluntary contributions made by States towards regional and subregional peace-keeping arrangements,

Desiring to facilitate the efforts of the Secretary-General towards the resolution of such conflicts,

Welcoming the positive trends towards the peaceful settlement of various regional and subregional conflicts and the important role played in that regard by the Secretary-General,

1. *Urges* all States, in the implementation of agreements reached with the United Nations regarding peace-keeping arrangements, further to strengthen co-operation with the Secretary-General in the discharge of his functions deriving from the Charter of the United Nations as well as from the mandates and decisions of the Security Council and the General Assembly;

2. *Affirms* that the adoption and implementation of confidence- and security-building measures, taking into account the Charter and the specificity of each particular region, would contribute to the strengthening of regional as well as international peace and security.

General Assembly resolution 43/85

7 December 1988   Meeting 73   Adopted without vote

Approved by First Committee (A/43/913) without vote, 30 November (meeting 54); draft by Cameroon (A/C.1/43/L.84/Rev.2); agenda item 72.
Meeting numbers. GA 43rd session: 1st Committee 47-54; plenary 73.

The original draft by Cameroon had contained a provision recommending the strengthening of the Secretary-General's role in the implementation of agreements reached with the United Nations regarding peace-keeping arrangements which would further enhance the attainment of international peace and security.

Introducing the draft in the Committee, Cameroon said its premise was that the process of peace-keeping arrangements and their implementation involved broad areas of conflict resolution, crisis management and confidence-building measures. In its recent successes, the United Nations had reinforced its fundamental responsibility to maintain international peace and security through various peace-keeping arrangements. While it was undisputed that the Security Council had a central role in maintaining international peace and security, that role must not be divorced from those of other organs of the Organization. The Assembly and its Main Committees, especially the First Committee, bore an equally important responsibility for initiating dialogue, addressing the progressive development of ideas and norms of peace and reviewing major issues of universal concern in the field of disarmament and security, thus facilitating more productive endeavours globally. The veto system in the Council tended to hide consensus opinion among the vast majority of States, all of which had a right to security and shared concerns for peaceful development and progress. The Assembly, on the other hand, presented the world at large with the opportunity to monitor the true collective opinion of States.

South Atlantic zone of peace

Brazil first brought up the question of a zone of peace and co-operation in the South Atlantic at the 1986 General Assembly session, when the Assembly declared the Atlantic Ocean, in the region situated between Africa and South America, a zone of peace and co-operation.[10]

In 1987, the Assembly commended the efforts of the States of the zone to promote peace and regional co-operation and urged them to continue their actions aimed at fulfilling the goals of the declaration through the adoption of concrete programmes; it called on all States to co-operate in promoting the objectives of the zone.[11]

The first meeting of the States of the Zone of Peace and Co-operation of the South Atlantic took place at Rio de Janeiro, Brazil, from 25 to 29 July 1988. The participants were Angola, Argentina, Benin, Brazil, Cape Verde, the Congo, Côte d'Ivoire, Equatorial Guinea, Gabon, the Gambia, Ghana, Guinea, Guinea-Bissau, Liberia, Nigeria, Sao Tome and Principe, Senegal, Sierra Leone, Togo, Uruguay and Zaire.

The participants, in a 33-point final document,[12] reiterated their determination to develop their relations under conditions of peace and freedom, in an environment free from tensions, and in conformity with the principles and rules of international law and with the United Nations Charter. They expressed their purpose to reinforce constructive relations based on dialogue, understanding, mutual interest and respect for the sovereign equality of all States, to the benefit of the peoples of the region as well as the international community as a whole. They emphasized the importance of the 1982 United Nations Convention on the Law of the Sea[13] as an essential pillar in the process of strengthening co-operation and peace in the South Atlantic region and expressed their willingness to consult and exchange information on matters related to the development and implementation of the Convention, including mutual knowledge of national legislation and the promotion of studies in that regard. Agreement was also expressed on the necessity of further consultations in conformity with the aims of the declaration establishing the zone of peace.[10] In that connection, the participants decided to meet periodically to pursue common objectives and to take steps to create the post of a co-ordinator who would facilitate the achievement of the objectives of the declaration.

In a September 1988 report,[14] the Secretary-General transmitted the views of 11 Governments on the declaration.

GENERAL ASSEMBLY ACTION

On 14 November, the General Assembly adopted **resolution 43/23** by recorded vote.

Zone of peace and co-operation of the South Atlantic
The General Assembly,

Recalling its resolution 41/11 of 27 October 1986, in which it solemnly declared the Atlantic Ocean, in the region situated between Africa and South America, the ''Zone of peace and co-operation of the South Atlantic'',

Affirming that the questions of peace and security and those of development are interrelated and inseparable, and considering that co-operation among all States, in particular those of the region, for peace and development is essential to promote the objectives of the zone of peace and co-operation of the South Atlantic,

Recalling also its resolution 42/16 of 10 November 1987, in which it urged States of the region to continue their actions aiming at fulfilling the goals of the declaration, specially through the adoption and implementation of specific programmes for this purpose,

Noting with appreciation the efforts of States of the zone towards fulfilling the goals of the declaration,

1. *Takes note* of the report submitted by the Secretary-General in accordance with resolution 42/16;

2. *Welcomes* the holding of the first meeting of States of the Zone of Peace and Co-operation of the South Atlantic at Rio de Janeiro, from 25 to 29 July 1988, and takes note of the Final Document of the meeting;

3. *Commends* initiatives by States of the zone to promote peace and regional co-operation in the South Atlantic;

4. *Calls upon* all States to co-operate in the promotion of the objectives of peace and co-operation established in the declaration of the zone of peace and co-operation of the South Atlantic and to refrain from any action inconsistent with those objectives, particularly actions which aggravate or may create situations of tension and potential conflict in the region;

5. *Requests* the relevant organizations, organs and bodies of the United Nations system to render all necessary assistance that States of the zone may seek in their joint efforts to implement the declaration of the zone of peace and co-operation of the South Atlantic;

6. *Requests* the Secretary-General to keep the implementation of resolution 41/11 under review and to submit a report to the General Assembly at its forty-fourth session, taking into account, *inter alia*, the views expressed by Member States;

7. *Decides* to include in the provisional agenda of its forty-fourth session the item entitled "Zone of peace and co-operation of the South Atlantic".

General Assembly resolution 43/23

14 November 1988   Meeting 47   144-1-7 (recorded vote)

24-nation draft (A/43/L.25 & Add.1); agenda item 31.

Sponsors: Angola, Argentina, Benin, Brazil, Cameroon, Cape Verde, Congo, Côte d'Ivoire, Equatorial Guinea, Gabon, Gambia, Ghana, Guinea, Guinea-Bissau, Liberia, Nepal, Nigeria, Sao Tome and Principe, Senegal, Sierra Leone, Togo, Uruguay, Venezuela, Zaire.

Recorded vote in Assembly as follows:

In favour: Afghanistan, Albania, Algeria, Angola, Antigua and Barbuda, Argentina, Australia, Austria, Bahamas, Bahrain, Bangladesh, Barbados, Benin, Bhutan, Bolivia, Botswana, Brazil, Brunei Darussalam, Bulgaria, Burkina Faso, Burma, Burundi, Byelorussian SSR, Cameroon, Canada, Cape Verde, Central African Republic, Chad, Chile, China, Colombia, Comoros, Congo, Côte d'Ivoire, Cuba, Cyprus, Czechoslovakia, Democratic Kampuchea, Democratic Yemen, Denmark, Djibouti, Dominican Republic, Ecuador, Egypt, El Salvador, Equatorial Guinea, Ethiopia, Fiji, Finland, Gabon, Gambia, German Democratic Republic, Ghana, Greece, Guatemala, Guinea, Guinea-Bissau, Guyana, Haiti, Honduras, Hungary, Iceland, India, Indonesia, Iran, Iraq, Ireland, Israel, Jamaica, Jordan, Kenya, Kuwait, Lao People's Democratic Republic, Lebanon, Lesotho, Liberia, Libyan Arab Jamahiriya, Madagascar, Malaysia, Maldives, Mali, Malta, Mauritania, Mauritius, Mexico, Mongolia, Morocco, Mozambique, Nepal, New Zealand, Nicaragua, Niger, Nigeria, Norway, Oman, Pakistan, Panama, Papua New Guinea, Paraguay, Peru, Philippines, Poland, Portugal, Qatar, Romania, Rwanda, Saint Kitts and Nevis, Saint Lucia, Saint Vincent and the Grenadines, Samoa, Sao Tome and Principe, Saudi Arabia, Senegal, Seychelles, Sierra Leone, Singapore, Solomon Islands, Somalia, Spain, Sri Lanka, Sudan, Suriname, Swaziland, Sweden, Syrian Arab Republic, Thailand, Togo, Trinidad and Tobago, Tunisia, Turkey, Uganda, Ukrainian SSR, USSR, United Arab Emirates, United Kingdom, United Republic of Tanzania, Uruguay, Venezuela, Viet Nam, Yemen, Yugoslavia, Zaire, Zambia, Zimbabwe.

Against: United States.

Abstaining: Belgium, France, Germany, Federal Republic of, Italy, Japan, Luxembourg, Netherlands.

Security and co-operation in the Mediterranean

The Secretary-General forwarded the views of nine States on strengthening security and co-operation in the Mediterranean to the General Assembly in September 1988,[15] in reply to its 1987 invitation[16] for States' ideas and suggestions regarding their potential contribution to strengthening peace in the region.

As summarized in the Secretary-General's report, the majority of States that addressed the subject expressed their concern at the persistent tension in the region. They pointed out that the continuing presence of non-regional Powers and the stockpiling in the area of weapons, including nuclear weapons, had created a dangerous situation. The policies of aggression, intimidation, intervention and interference in the internal affairs of the countries in the region were blamed by several States for the persistent tension and were seen as a considerable threat to its peace and security.

Several States emphasized the intimate link between strengthening security and co-operation in the Mediterranean and similar action in Europe and in other regions. Towards that end, a number of States called for extended dialogue between countries participating in the Conference on Security and Co-operation in Europe and the non-participating Mediterranean countries.

Among suggestions for strengthening security and co-operation in the region was the establishment of a Mediterranean forum—to include government representatives, scientific, educational, cultural, artistic and other institutions, and eminent individuals specializing in Mediterranean studies—as a multidisciplinary framework for promoting co-operation. Another State reiterated its proposal for the application to the region of agreed confidence-building measures; the reduction of armed forces; the withdrawal of ships carrying nuclear-weapons; the rejection of nuclear weapons deployment on the territory of non-nuclear Mediterranean countries; an undertaking by nuclear Powers not to use such weapons against any country in the Mediterranean which did not permit their deployment on its soil; and the establishment of a chemical-weapon-free zone.

GENERAL ASSEMBLY ACTION

On 7 December 1988, in accordance with the recommendation of the First Committee, the General Assembly adopted **resolution 43/84** without vote.

Strengthening of security and co-operation in the Mediterranean region

The General Assembly,

Recalling its resolutions 36/102 of 9 December 1981, 37/118 of 16 December 1982, 38/189 of 20 December 1983, 39/153 of 17 December 1984, 40/157 of 16 December 1985, 41/89 of 4 December 1986 and 42/90 of 7 December 1987,

Recognizing the importance of promoting peace, security and co-operation in the Mediterranean region and of strengthening further the economic, commercial and cultural links in the region,

Expressing concern at the persistent tension in parts of the Mediterranean region and the consequent threat to peace,

Deeply concerned at the continuing military operations in the Mediterranean and the grave dangers that they create for peace, security and general equilibrium in the region,

Considering, in this regard, the urgency of all States to conform in their actions to the purposes and principles of the Charter of the United Nations, as well as to the provisions of the Declaration on Principles of International Law concerning Friendly Relations and Co-operation among States in accordance with the Charter of the United Nations,

Reaffirming the need to intensify and promote peace and security and to strengthen co-operation in the region, as provided for in the Mediterranean chapter of the Final Act of the Conference on Security and Co-operation in Europe, signed at Helsinki on 1 August 1975,

Recalling the declarations of successive meetings of non-aligned countries concerning the Mediterranean, as well as official declarations on, and contributions to, peace and security in the Mediterranean region made by individual countries,

Reaffirming also the primary role of Mediterranean countries in the promotion of security and co-operation in the Mediterranean region,

Recalling also, in this connection, the Final Declaration adopted at Valletta on 11 September 1984 by the Mediterranean members of the Movement of Non-Aligned Countries, and the commitments assumed by the participants that opened the process of joint efforts with the objective of contributing to peace, security and co-operation in the region,

Taking note of the important meeting of Ministers for Foreign Affairs of the Mediterranean members of the Movement of Non-Aligned Countries held at Brioni, Yugoslavia, on 3 and 4 June 1987,

Welcoming the efforts realized by the Mediterranean members of the Movement of Non-Aligned Countries to strengthen regional co-operation in various fields among themselves and between them and the European countries,

Noting the adoption by the Stockholm Conference on Confidence- and Security-Building Measures and Disarmament in Europe of the Document of the Stockholm Conference on concrete, militarily significant, politically binding and verifiable confidence- and security-building measures,

Noting also the new developments evolving in the ongoing negotiations on nuclear and conventional disarmament in Europe, which have a direct relevance and importance for peace and security in the Mediterranean,

Recognizing the strong desire of the non-aligned Mediterranean countries to intensify the process of dialogue and consultations with the European-Mediterranean and other European countries aimed at strengthening efforts towards the promotion of peace, security and co-operation in the region, and thus contributing to the stabilization of the situation in the Mediterranean,

Taking note of the debate on this item during its various sessions and, in particular, of the report of the Secretary-General on this item,

1.   *Reaffirms:*

(a)   That the security of the Mediterranean is closely linked with European security and with international peace and security;

(b)   That further efforts are necessary for the reduction of tension and of armaments and for the creation of conditions of security and fruitful co-operation in all fields for all countries and peoples of the Mediterranean, on the basis of the principles of sovereignty, independence, territorial integrity, security, non-intervention and non-interference, non-violation of international borders, non-use of force or threat of use of force, the inadmissibility of the acquisition of territory by force, peaceful settlement of disputes and respect for permanent sovereignty over natural resources;

(c)   That just and viable solutions are needed for existing problems and crises in the region on the basis of the provisions of the Charter and of relevant resolutions of the United Nations, the withdrawal of foreign forces of occupation and the right of peoples under colonial or foreign domination to self-determination and independence;

2.   *Takes note* of paragraph 24 of the Document of the Stockholm Conference on Confidence- and Security-Building Measures and Disarmament in Europe, which, *inter alia*, confirms the intention of the participants in the Conference on Security and Co-operation in Europe to develop good-neighbourly relations with all States of the region, with due regard to reciprocity and in the spirit of the principles contained in the Declaration on Principles Guiding Relations between Participating States, so as to promote confidence and security and make peace prevail in the region in accordance with the provisions contained in the Mediterranean chapter of the Final Act of the Conference on Security and Co-operation in Europe;

3.   *Calls upon* all States participating in the Vienna meeting of the Conference on Security and Co-operation in Europe to take all possible measures and to exert every effort in order to ensure substantial and balanced results of this meeting in the implementation of the principles and goals of the Final Act, including those provisions relating to the Mediterranean, as well as the continuity of the multilateral process initiated by the Conference, which also has great significance for the strengthening of peace, security and co-operation;

4.   *Urges* all States to co-operate with the Mediterranean States in the further efforts required to reduce tension and promote peace, security and co-operation in the region in accordance with the purposes and principles of the Charter of the United Nations and with the provisions of the Declaration on Principles of International Law concerning Friendly Relations and Co-operation among States in accordance with the Charter of the United Nations;

5.   *Encourages once again* efforts to intensify existing forms and to promote new forms of co-operation in various fields, particularly those aimed at reducing tension and strengthening confidence and security in the region;

6.   *Reaffirms also* the importance of intensifying and constantly promoting contacts in all fields where common interests exist in order to eliminate gradually, through co-operation, the causes preventing the faster social and economic development of the Mediterranean States, particularly the developing States of the region;

7.   *Takes note*, in this regard, of the idea of the establishment of a Mediterranean forum as a multidiscipli-

nary framework for the promotion of co-operation in the region, which would bring together not only the representatives of Governments but also of scientific, educational, cultural and other institutions, as well as prominent individuals specializing in Mediterranean studies;

8. *Welcomes* any further communication to the Secretary-General from all States of proposals, declarations and recommendations on strengthening peace, security and co-operation in the Mediterranean region;

9. *Renews its invitation* to the Secretary-General to give due attention to the question of peace, security and co-operation in the Mediterranean region and, if requested to do so, to render advice and assistance to Mediterranean countries in their concerted efforts to promote peace, security and co-operation in the region;

10. *Invites* the States members of the relevant regional organizations to lend support and to submit to the Secretary-General concrete ideas and suggestions on their potential contribution to the strengthening of peace and co-operation in the Mediterranean region;

11. *Requests* the Secretary-General to submit to the General Assembly at its forty-fourth session, on the basis of all replies received and notifications submitted in the implementation of the present resolution and taking into account the debate on this question during its forty-third session, an updated report on the strengthening of security and co-operation in the Mediterranean region;

12. *Decides* to include in the provisional agenda of its forty-fourth session the item entitled ''Strengthening of security and co-operation in the Mediterranean region''.

General Assembly resolution 43/84

7 December 1988   Meeting 73   Adopted without vote

Approved by First Committee (A/43/912) without vote, 30 November (meeting 54); 8-nation draft (A/C.1/43/L.86); agenda item 71.
Sponsors: Algeria, Cyprus, Libyan Arab Jamahiriya, Malta, Morocco, Romania, Tunisia, Yugoslavia.
Meeting numbers. GA 43rd session: 1st Committee 47-54; plenary 73.

REFERENCES

(1)YUN 1970, p. 105, GA res. 2734(XXV), 16 Dec. 1970. (2)YUN 1969, p. 70. (3)A/43/603 & Add.1. (4)YUN 1987, p. 114, GA res. 42/92, 7 Dec. 1987. (5)YUN 1978, p. 165, GA res. 33/73, 15 Dec. 1978. (6)YUN 1987, p. 118, GA res. 42/93, 7 Dec. 1987. (7)A/43/732. (8)S/20224. (9)YUN 1986, p. 111, GA res. 41/91, 4 Dec. 1986. (10)*Ibid.*, p. 369, GA res. 41/11, 27 Oct. 1986. (11)YUN 1987, p. 355, GA res. 42/16, 10 Nov. 1987. (12)A/43/512. (13)YUN 1982, p. 181. (14)A/43/576 & Add.1. (15)A/43/579. (16)YUN 1987, p. 250, GA res. 42/90, 7 Dec. 1987.

Review of peace-keeping operations

The Special Committee on Peace-keeping Operations held two meetings in 1988, on 10 February and 25 August.[1] In addition, it held six sessions of informal consultations between 30 March and 22 August.

The Committee recommended that the General Assembly consider the renewal of its mandate, namely, to carry out a comprehensive review of the whole question of peace-keeping operations in all its aspects with a view to strengthening the role of the United Nations in that field.

Various proposals and suggestions on its mandate were put forward after extensive deliberations and exchanges of views. Some delegations submitted ideas regarding agenda items for the Committee, including the financial aspect of peace-keeping operations. Issues discussed included United Nations publications on peace-keeping operations, compilation of a registry containing information on the availability of troops and provisions of logistical assistance for peace-keeping operations.

In a statement on 17 October before the Special Political Committee, Nigeria, the Chairman of the Special Committee, said the year had witnessed positive developments in peace-keeping operations whose importance was underscored by the award of the Nobel Peace Prize. Their prominence had been brought about by the significant shift in international relations, with dialogue and co-operation replacing strident rhetoric and conflict. Nevertheless, they were confronted by numerous problems, particularly financial difficulties. In view of the near certainty of further peace-keeping activities in the future, Nigeria urged the Secretariat to expedite ongoing consultations on the establishment of a special fund for peace-keeping operations. Calling for attention also to the practical aspects of such operations, it proposed a register of countries willing to contribute troops, with countries designating the units to be held in reserve on a stand-by basis. It also suggested the preparation by the Secretariat of a manual on peace-keeping operations.

On 14 April, a spokeswoman for the Secretary-General announced that Japan had made a special contribution of $20 million to be used for peace-keeping and peace-making activities, in connection with the Iran-Iraq conflict and the situations relating to Afghanistan and Lebanon. According to the statement, the Secretary-General regarded the Japanese contribution as a source of encouragement to the United Nations and expressed the hope that it would be emulated by many others.

To mark United Nations Day on 24 October, a videotaped message by the Secretary-General was beamed to United Nations peace-keeping forces around the world. The Secretary-General stated that among the many functions the United Nations had been requested to carry out, none was more vital than the maintenance of peace as personified by its peace-keeping operations. The dedication and sacrifice of the men and women in such operations over the past 40 years deserved the gratitude of the international community as a whole and it was, therefore, particularly satisfying that the 1988 Nobel Peace Prize was awarded to the peace-keeping forces.

In June 1988, the Secretariat's Department of Public Information published a full-colour brochure entitled *United Nations Peace-Keeping*.

In response to the increasing demand for his good offices in the maintenance of international peace and security and for United Nations peace-keeping operations, the Secretary-General announced structural changes in his Executive Office and the Office of Special Political Affairs. The latter, to be headed by only one Under-Secretary-General, was to be responsible for the conduct of all existing peace-keeping operations, with the exception of the United Nations Good Offices Mission in Afghanistan and Pakistan, as well as for the planning and conduct of future peace-keeping operations. The services of the Secretary-General's Military Adviser would continue to be available to the Office.

GENERAL ASSEMBLY ACTION

On 6 December, the General Assembly, on the recommendation of the Special Political Committee, adopted **resolution 43/59 A** without vote.

The General Assembly,

Recalling its resolutions 1874(S-IV) of 27 June 1963, 2006(XIX) of 18 February 1965, 2053 A (XX) of 15 December 1965, 2249(S-V) of 23 May 1967, 2308(XXII) of 13 December 1967, 2451(XXIII) of 19 December 1968, 2670(XXV) of 8 December 1970, 2835(XXVI) of 17 December 1971, 2965(XXVII) of 13 December 1972, 3091(XXVIII) of 7 December 1973, 3239(XXIX) of 29 November 1974, 3457(XXX) of 10 December 1975, 31/105 of 15 December 1976, 32/106 of 15 December 1977, 33/114 of 18 December 1978, 34/53 of 23 November 1979, 35/121 of 11 December 1980, 36/37 of 18 November 1981, 37/93 of 10 December 1982, 38/81 of 15 December 1983, 39/97 of 14 December 1984, 40/163 of 16 December 1985, 41/67 of 3 December 1986 and 42/161 of 8 December 1987,

Welcoming with deep appreciation the award of the 1988 Nobel Peace Prize to the United Nations peace-keeping forces,

Noting with satisfaction the resumption of the work of the Special Committee on Peace-keeping Operations,

Convinced that the United Nations peace-keeping operations are an integral component of enhancing the effectiveness of the United Nations in the maintenance of international peace and security,

Taking into account that increasing activities in the field of United Nations peace-keeping require increasing human, financial and material resources for the Organization,

Aware of the extremely difficult financial situation of the United Nations peace-keeping forces in the light of the heavy burden on the troop contributors, especially those from developing countries,

Emphasizing that the current political atmosphere is propitious for achieving progress in the work of the Special Committee,

Bearing in mind the fact that constructive exchanges of views on various practical aspects of peace-keeping operations can contribute favourably to the smooth and effective functioning of these operations,

Having examined the report of the Special Committee,

1. *Takes note* of the report of the Special Committee on Peace-keeping Operations;

2. *Urges* the Special Committee, in accordance with its mandate, to continue its efforts for a comprehensive review of the whole question of peace-keeping operations in all their aspects with a view to strengthening the role of the United Nations in this field, taking into account the difficult financial situation of peace-keeping operations and the need for maximum cost efficiency;

3. *Invites* Member States to submit observations and suggestions to the Secretary-General by 1 March 1989 on peace-keeping operations in all their aspects, with particular emphasis on practical proposals to make these operations more effective;

4. *Requests* the Secretary-General to prepare, within existing resources, a compilation of the above-mentioned observations and suggestions and to submit it to the Special Committee during its session in 1989;

5. *Requests* the Special Committee to submit a report on its work to the General Assembly at its forty-fourth session;

6. *Decides* to include in the provisional agenda of its forty-fourth session the item entitled "Comprehensive review of the whole question of peace-keeping operations in all their aspects".

General Assembly resolution 43/59 A

6 December 1988   Meeting 71   Adopted without vote

Approved by Special Political Committee (A/43/795) without vote, 2 November (meeting 16); 6-nation draft (A/SPC/43/L.6); agenda item 78.
Sponsors: Argentina, Canada, Egypt, German Democratic Republic, Japan, Nigeria.
Meeting numbers. GA 43rd session: SPC 5, 11-13, 16; plenary 71.

By **decision 43/455** of 21 December, the Assembly, on the recommendation of the Fifth (Administrative and Budgetary) Committee, decided to include in the provisional agenda of its forty-fourth (1989) session an item on the administrative and budgetary aspects of the financing of United Nations peace-keeping operations.

Special Committee membership

In 1988, the General Assembly approved China's request to become a member of the Special Committee on Peace-keeping Operations and increased the Committee's membership to 34 (for a list of members, see APPENDIX III).

GENERAL ASSEMBLY ACTION

On 6 December, on the recommendation of the Special Political Committee, the General Assembly adopted **resolution 43/59 B** without vote.

The General Assembly,

Recalling its resolution 2006(XIX) of 18 February 1965, by which the Special Committee on Peace-keeping Operations was established,

Recognizing the importance of peace-keeping operations,

Convinced that the participation of the People's Republic of China will benefit the work of the Special Committee,

1. *Decides* to increase the membership of the Special Committee on Peace-keeping Operations to thirty-four;

2. *Approves* the request of the People's Republic of China to become a member of the Special Committee.

General Assembly resolution 43/59 B

6 December 1988   Meeting 71   Adopted without vote

Approved by Special Political Committee (A/43/795) without vote, 2 November (meeting 16); 6-nation draft (A/SPC/43/L.7); agenda item 78.
Sponsors: Argentina, Canada, Egypt, German Democratic Republic, Japan, Nigeria.
Meeting numbers. GA 43rd session: SPC 5, 11-13, 16; plenary 71.

Introducing the text in the Special Political Committee, Nigeria recalled that China's application for membership enjoyed the support of all delegations. Expressing its gratitude, China said it would work with all other Member States in fulfilling its obligations.

REFERENCE

(1)A/43/566.

Other aspects

Right of peoples to peace

In response to a 1986 General Assembly resolution,[1] the Secretary-General submitted in September 1988 a report, with later addendum,[2] reviewing measures taken by 14 Member States to implement the 1984 Declaration on the Right of Peoples to Peace.[3] In the Declaration, the Assembly declared that preservation of that right was a fundamental obligation of each State and appealed for appropriate measures to implement it.

GENERAL ASSEMBLY ACTION

On 11 November 1988, the General Assembly adopted **resolution 43/22** by recorded vote.

Right of peoples to peace

The General Assembly,

Recalling its Declaration on the Right of Peoples to Peace, approved on 12 November 1984,

Referring to its resolutions 40/11 of 11 November 1985 and 41/10 of 24 October 1986,

Having in mind the Universal Declaration of Human Rights which emphasizes that recognition of the inherent dignity and of the equal and inalienable rights of all members of the human family is the foundation of freedom, justice and peace in the world,

Recognizing the strong resolve of peoples to strengthen international peace and security and promote economic and social development,

Noting with satisfaction the positive events and trends in the field of disarmament, the resolution of crisis situations and the strengthening of international peace and security,

Reaffirming that the implementation of the right of peoples to peace constitutes a fundamental concern of each State,

Having considered the report of the Secretary-General on the implementation of the Declaration on the Right of Peoples to Peace,

1. *Takes note with appreciation* of the report of the Secretary-General;

2. *Reaffirms* the lasting importance and validity of the Declaration on the Right of Peoples to Peace;

3. *Considers* that the efforts of non-governmental organizations and world public opinion play an important role in the implementation of the Declaration;

4. *Invites* all States and international organizations to continue their efforts towards the implementation of the Declaration at the national and international levels;

5. *Calls upon* all States and relevant organizations of the United Nations system, as well as non-governmental organizations, to inform the Secretary-General about the measures taken to implement the Declaration;

6. *Requests* the Secretary-General to submit a report to the General Assembly at its forty-fifth session on the basis of replies received;

7. *Decides* to include in the provisional agenda of its forty-fifth session an item entitled ''Implementation of the Declaration on the Right of Peoples to Peace''.

General Assembly resolution 43/22

11 November 1988   Meeting 46   118-0-29 (recorded vote)

15-nation draft (A/43/L.22 & Add.1); agenda item 21.
Sponsors: Bulgaria, Byelorussian SSR, Cuba, Czechoslovakia, German Democratic Republic, Lao People's Democratic Republic, Libyan Arab Jamahiriya, Madagascar, Mauritania, Mauritius, Mongolia, Nicaragua, Romania, Syrian Arab Republic, Viet Nam.

Recorded vote in Assembly as follows:

In favour: Afghanistan, Algeria, Angola, Antigua and Barbuda, Argentina, Bahamas, Bahrain, Bangladesh, Barbados, Benin, Bhutan, Bolivia, Botswana, Brunei Darussalam, Bulgaria, Burkina Faso, Burma, Burundi, Byelorussian SSR, Cameroon, Cape Verde, Central African Republic, Chad, Chile, China, Colombia, Comoros, Congo, Côte d'Ivoire, Cuba, Cyprus, Czechoslovakia, Democratic Yemen, Dominican Republic, Ecuador, Egypt, El Salvador, Equatorial Guinea, Ethiopia, Gabon, Gambia, German Democratic Republic, Ghana, Grenada, Guinea, Guinea-Bissau, Guyana, Haiti, Honduras, Hungary, India, Indonesia, Iran, Iraq, Jamaica, Jordan, Kenya, Kuwait, Lao People's Democratic Republic, Lebanon, Lesotho, Liberia, Libyan Arab Jamahiriya, Madagascar, Malawi, Malaysia, Maldives, Mali, Mauritania, Mauritius, Mexico, Mongolia, Morocco, Mozambique, Nepal, Nicaragua, Nigeria, Oman, Pakistan, Panama, Papua New Guinea, Paraguay, Peru, Philippines, Poland, Qatar, Romania, Rwanda, Saint Kitts and Nevis, Saint Lucia, Sao Tome and Principe, Saudi Arabia, Seychelles, Sierra Leone, Somalia, Sri Lanka, Sudan, Suriname, Swaziland, Syrian Arab Republic, Thailand, Togo, Trinidad and Tobago, Tunisia, Uganda, Ukrainian SSR, USSR, United Arab Emirates, United Republic of Tanzania, Uruguay, Vanuatu, Venezuela, Viet Nam, Yemen, Yugoslavia, Zaire, Zambia, Zimbabwe.

Against: None.

Abstaining: Australia, Austria, Belgium, Brazil, Canada, Denmark, Djibouti,[a] Fiji, Finland, France, Germany, Federal Republic of, Greece, Iceland, Ireland, Israel, Italy, Japan, Luxembourg, Netherlands, New Zealand, Norway, Portugal, Samoa, Senegal, Spain, Sweden, Turkey, United Kingdom, United States.

[a]Later advised the Secretariat it had intended to vote in favour.

Science and peace

By a letter of 9 March 1988,[4] Costa Rica requested that an item on science and peace be included in the agenda of the 1988 session of the General Assembly. In an accompanying explanatory memorandum, Costa Rica said it was necessary to promote among all scientists a steadfast attitude in favour of using science for peaceful purposes, in order to promote the social and economic development of mankind. It also proposed that every year the week of 11 November be devoted to ''science and peace''.

Explaining before the Special Political Committee why it had requested inclusion of the item, Costa Rica recalled that in 1986, within the framework of the International Year of Peace, an international association of scientists had proposed holding an International Week of Scientists for Peace to encourage the use of scientific progress for peace and the well-being of mankind. The observance of the Week had met with increasing success during its first two years, Costa Rica added.

GENERAL ASSEMBLY ACTION

The General Assembly, on 6 December 1988, on the recommendation of the Special Political Committee, adopted **resolution 43/61** without vote.

Science and peace

The General Assembly,

Considering that progress in science and technology profoundly affects international peace and security, economic and social development, respect for human rights and many other aspects of civilization and culture,

Considering also that political and economic decisions have a decisive effect on the direction of scientific research and the use of the results obtained thereby,

Recalling that scientific and technological achievements must be used to advance socio-economic progress and the effective enjoyment of human rights throughout the world,

Considering further that the arms race absorbs a substantial proportion of the scientific talent and financial resources used in related research and development, which, in a more peaceful and secure world, could be used to solve other pressing problems facing mankind,

Recalling that in its resolution 40/3 of 24 October 1985, by which it proclaimed the International Year of Peace, it recognized the role of science for peace,

Recalling also its resolution 42/13 of 28 October 1987 on the achievements of the International Year of Peace, in which it urged Member States, intergovernmental and non-governmental organizations and the world community to persevere in their efforts, developing initiatives conducive to the objectives of the Year, and expressed the hope that the ideals and objectives contained in the Proclamation of the International Year of Peace would continue to be an inspiration for concerted action,

Affirming that it is necessary to promote greater awareness among scientists world wide of the usefulness of science to increase international peace, security and cooperation, the social and economic development of mankind, the promotion of human rights and the protection of the environment,

Affirming, in particular, the need for scientists to establish a free and open dialogue between one another, and with political leaders and the public in general, with regard to scientific developments and their present and potential implications for our civilization,

Considering the importance of encouraging scientists to work towards constructive objectives, to improve the climate for arms control and disarmament, and to promote a dialogue on important topics in connection with the positive contributions that scientific knowledge can make to peace, security and ecological balance,

Noting with appreciation the joint efforts made by scientists and members of other professional groups to promote the achievement of those aims through the holding of the First International Week of Scientists for Peace from 10 to 16 November 1986 and the Second International Week of Scientists for Peace from 9 to 15 November 1987,

Considering that the celebration each year of a special week of action devoted to the topic ''Science and peace'' is an important means of generating and increasing public interest in this topic and of stimulating activities and initiatives leading to the study and dissemination of information on the links between progress in science and technology and the maintenance of peace and security,

1. *Decides* to proclaim the ''International Week of Science and Peace'', which will take place each year during the week in which 11 November falls;

2. *Urges* Member States and intergovernmental and non-governmental organizations to encourage universities and other institutions of advanced studies, scientific academies and institutes, and professional associations and individuals in the scientific community to hold, during that Week, lectures, seminars, special debates and other activities conducive to the study and dissemination of information on the links between progress in science and technology and the maintenance of peace and security;

3. *Urges* Member States to promote international cooperation among scientists by facilitating exchanges of experts and information;

4. *Requests* the Secretary-General to draw the attention of Member States and interested organizations to the importance of the International Week of Science and Peace and invite them to report to him on their activities and initiatives in connection with this event, and to report thereon to the General Assembly at its forty-fifth session.

General Assembly resolution 43/61

6 December 1988   Meeting 71   Adopted without vote

Approved by Special Political Committee (A/43/822) without vote, 8 November (meeting 21); 45-nation draft (A/SPC/43/L.9); agenda item 140.
Sponsors: Antigua and Barbuda, Argentina, Bangladesh, Bolivia, Brunei Darussalam, Cameroon, Colombia, Comoros, Congo, Costa Rica, Cyprus, Dominican Republic, Ecuador, El Salvador, Fiji, Grenada, Guatemala, Haiti, Honduras, India, Jamaica, Malaysia, Mauritius, Morocco, Nepal, Pakistan, Panama, Papua New Guinea, Paraguay, Peru, Philippines, Poland, Romania, Saint Lucia, Samoa, Senegal, Sierra Leone, Singapore, Sri Lanka, Togo, Trinidad and Tobago, Uruguay, Vanuatu, Yugoslavia, Zaire.

REFERENCES

[1]YUN 1986, p. 119, GA res. 41/10, 24 Oct. 1986. [2]A/43/602 & Add.1. [3]YUN 1984, p. 119, GA res. 39/11, annex, 12 Nov. 1984. [4]A/43/141.

Chapter II

Disarmament

During 1988, the momentum was sustained towards the general improvement in international relations, particularly between the USSR and the United States and between the two major military alliances. The 1987 Treaty between the United States of America and the Union of Soviet Socialist Republics on the Elimination of Their Intermediate-Range and Shorter-Range Missiles (INF Treaty) went into effect on 1 June 1988. Progress was also made in the deliberations at the Vienna Conference on Security and Co-operation in Europe in the field of confidence- and security-building measures as well as new negotiations on conventional armaments in Europe. In the United Nations and in other forums, both the USSR and the United States indicated their intention to move towards a gradual reduction of their armed forces.

The focus of United Nations disarmament activities in 1988 was the fifteenth special session of the General Assembly, or third special session devoted to disarmament, which was held from 31 May to 25 June. The special session produced a more focused outlook on disarmament and provided a basis for productive discussion and action at the forty-third regular session of the Assembly, which adopted resolutions on a range of arms limitation and disarmament matters.

At Geneva, the 40-nation Conference on Disarmament, the multilateral negotiating body, continued to make progress in the negotiations on a convention banning the production, stockpiling and use of chemical weapons, although the problem of verification remained unsolved. The Conference continued to experience differences in positions and approaches on such long-standing agenda items as a nuclear-weapons test ban, the nuclear-arms race and nuclear disarmament, prevention of nuclear war, nuclear-weapon-free zones, zones of peace and the relationship between disarmament and development. In view of the need to intensify current multilateral negotiations, the General Assembly welcomed the offer of France to host a conference on chemical weapons in 1989.

The Disarmament Commission, a deliberative body composed of United Nations Member States, submitted to the Assembly at its special session a special report containing specific recommendations on the items included in its agenda.

General aspects

In 1988, a number of communications were received, from countries individually or in groups, concerning arms control and disarmament.

On 3 June, the USSR and the United States transmitted to the Secretary-General a joint statement by their leaders following a summit meeting at Moscow from 29 May to 1 June.[1] They reaffirmed their solemn conviction that a nuclear war could not be won and must never be fought, their determination to prevent any war between their States and their disavowal of any intention to achieve military superiority. On 25 July,[2] the two countries transmitted to the President of the Conference on Disarmament the text of the Agreement between the United States of America and the Union of Soviet Socialist Republics on Notifications of Launches of Intercontinental Ballistic Missiles and Submarine-Launched Ballistic Missiles, signed on 31 May. On 8 March,[3] the United States transmitted the text of the Agreement between the United States of America and the Union of Soviet Socialist Republics on the Establishment of Nuclear Risk Reduction Centers, together with its two Protocols, signed in September 1987.

Third special session on disarmament

Work of the Preparatory Committee

In accordance with a recommendation at its 1987 session,[4] as endorsed by the General Assembly,[5] the open-ended Preparatory Committee for the Third Special Session of the General Assembly Devoted to Disarmament held its third session in New York (25 January–5 February 1988) to consider substantive issues related to the special session.

The Preparatory Committee, in its report to the special session,[6] recommended a number of organizational procedures, including the provisional agenda for the session. It annexed an informal paper prepared by the Chairman, containing suggested elements for consideration under substantive items of the provisional agenda. These suggestions related to an assessment and review of the state of affairs in arms limitation and disarmament negotiations, an examination of developments and trends with a view to the elaboration of appropriate concrete and practical measures, and consideration of the role of the United Nations in the field of disarmament and the effectiveness of the disarmament machinery, as well as United Nations information and education activities in disarmament.

By **decision S-15/22** of 31 May, the General Assembly endorsed the report of the Preparatory Committee and its recommendations.

Work of the special session

The General Assembly convened its fifteenth special session, the third special session devoted to disarmament (New York, 31 May–25 June 1988) in accordance with a 1986 resolution.[7] The first two special sessions on disarmament were held in 1978[8] and 1982.[9]

Addressing the special session, the President said its task was to point the way to a more secure world, ultimately free of weapons of mass destruction and the threat or use of force. The Secretary-General stated that all major questions of security and disarmament had bilateral, regional and global dimensions and suggested that the international community should encourage the two major military Powers to sustain and develop the momentum of their mutual relationship, to broaden their understanding and to make progress on issues that had global implications.

On 31 May, by **decision S-15/23**, the Assembly adopted the agenda for the special session (for list of agenda items, see APPENDIX IV). It decided that items 1 to 9 and 16 would be considered in plenary meeting and allocated items 10 to 15 to the Committee of the Whole (see below).

On 14 and 25 June, by **resolutions S-15/1 A and B**, the Assembly approved the first[10] and second[11] reports of the Credentials Committee.

The Assembly had before it special reports of the Conference on Disarmament[12] and the Disarmament Commission;[13] reports of the *Ad Hoc* Committee on the World Disarmament Conference[14] and the *Ad Hoc* Committee on the Indian Ocean;[15] and reports of the Secretary-General on the World Disarmament Campaign,[16] on developments in the field of arms limitation and disarmament since 1982, including the status of negotiations in bilateral and multilateral forums,[17] on objective information on military matters[18] and on programmes and activities undertaken by the United Nations in the area of women and peace.[19]

The Assembly also received many proposals from delegations both during the general debate and in the Committee of the Whole, covering all agenda items. Some were of a comprehensive nature outlining general approaches to disarmament, while others dealt with specific proposals.

On the question of nuclear disarmament, India submitted working papers outlining an action plan for ushering in a nuclear-weapon-free and non-violent world order and on issues surrounding new technologies and the arms race.[20] The German Democratic Republic submitted papers calling on the Assembly to make specific recommendations to promote the process of nuclear disarmament leading to the ultimate goal of total elimination of nuclear weapons[21] and for the creation of a nuclear-weapon-free corridor in Central Europe.[22]

New Zealand submitted a proposal calling for the early conclusion of a comprehensive-test-ban treaty through multilateral negotiations in the Conference on Disarmament.[23]

The five Nordic States—Denmark, Finland, Iceland, Norway and Sweden—submitted a memorandum[24] advocating progress in a number of areas relating to non-proliferation and nuclear disarmament to ensure the prolongation and continued effectiveness of the non-proliferation régime after 1995.

Proposals on nuclear-weapon-free zones were submitted by Egypt, recommending that all States in the Middle East declare their intention not to introduce nuclear weapons in the region and suggesting ways to promote that objective,[25] while a paper by the German Democratic Republic[26] focused on ways of freeing the planet from nuclear weapons and suggested that the time was appropriate for consideration of the whole question of nuclear-weapon-free zones. New Zealand called for express support of the 1967 Treaty for the Prohibition of Nuclear Weapons in Latin America (Treaty of Tlatelolco) and the 1985 South Pacific Nuclear-Free-Zone Treaty (Treaty of Rarotonga), in particular by those States which had been invited to observe restrictions within the zones created by the Treaties.[23]

Denmark proposed that appropriate action be taken by the Assembly, reflecting the increased recognition of the importance of conventional disarmament.[27] The USSR proposed the elimination of foreign military presence and military bases abroad by the year 2000.[28] The United Kingdom proposed language for inclusion in a final document of the session on the transfer of conventional weapons,[29] while Trinidad and Tobago proposed language on the use or transfer of prohibited weapons and weapons which cause unnecessary human suffering.[30]

Argentina outlined criteria for the early conclusion of a convention prohibiting all chemical weapons and installations for their production, and for ensuring universal accession to such a convention,[31] and the United Kingdom proposed a text dealing with chemical weapons, for inclusion in a final document.[32] On the question of radiological weapons, the Netherlands and Sweden proposed that adequate attention be given to the urgent need for the elaboration of a globally agreed prohibition against attacks on nuclear facilities.[33] Proposals were also submitted on naval armaments and disarmament[34] and on the prevention of an arms race in outer space.[35]

As to verification of disarmament agreements, several proposals were submitted. Canada and the Netherlands focused on the role of the United Nations in this regard and proposed an in-depth study on the subject by a group of experts.[36] France focused on the role of the United Nations in contractual verification, investigation procedures and collection of space data.[37] Argentina, Greece, India, Mexico, Sweden and the United Republic of Tanzania proposed an integrated multilateral verification system within the United Nations.[38] A similar proposal was submitted by Bulgaria, Czechoslovakia and the USSR,[39] and Norway submitted a memorandum on procedures for verification of alleged use of chemical weapons.[40]

Several papers were also submitted on the overall role of the United Nations in the field of disarmament,[41] as well as on the conduct of a comprenhensive United Nations study on nuclear weapons.[42]

Other proposals were made on the relationship between disarmament and development[43] and on the danger of radiation arising from the clandestine dumping of nuclear wastes.[44]

A general debate on disarmament took place from 1 to 14 June. In the course of 20 meetings, the Assembly heard 135 speakers, including 23 heads of State or Government, 1 Vice-President, 6 Deputy Prime Ministers and 61 Ministers for Foreign Affairs and other heads of delegation. In addition, representatives of the non-member States of the Democratic People's Republic of Korea, the Holy See, the Republic of Korea and Switzerland, as well as the Director General of the International Atomic Energy Agency (IAEA), made statements. The Assembly was also addressed by representatives of the League of Arab States, the Organization of the Islamic Conference, the Palestine Liberation Organization and the South West Africa People's Organization.

On the recommendation of the Preparatory Committee,[6] the Assembly, by **decision S-15/21** of 31 May, established a Committee of the Whole to consider the substantive items on the agenda. The Committee established three working groups: Working Group I dealt with the assessment of the implementation of the decisions and recommendations of the first and second special sessions on disarmament; Working Group II dealt with the assessment of developments and trends relevant to the disarmament process and the relationship between disarmament and development; and Working Group III dealt with the role of the United Nations in the field of disarmament, the effectiveness of the disarmament machinery, and educa-

tional and information activities. The Committee heard statements by 87 non-governmental organizations and 20 peace and disarmament research institutes.

The Committee's report to the Assembly[45] contained, in an annex, a list of the proposals submitted by Member States.

After three weeks of deliberations, the Assembly did not take action on any of the proposals submitted and was unable to reach full agreement on a concluding document. Specifically, no compromise was reached on issues such as nuclear-weapon-free zones and zones of peace, the nuclear-weapon capabilities of South Africa and Israel, the investigatory role of the Secretary-General with regard to the use of chemical weapons and the relationship between disarmament and development.

Consequently, on 25 June, by **decision S-15/24**, the Assembly took note of the report of the Committee of the Whole as the concluding document of the fifteenth special session of the Assembly.

Review of the third special session

The General Assembly, in accordance with a 1987 decision,[5] considered at its regular session in 1988 the agenda item "Review of the implementation of the recommendations and decisions adopted by the General Assembly at its fifteenth special session".

On 7 December, on the recommendation of the First Committee, the Assembly adopted **resolution 43/77 B** by recorded vote.

Third special session of the General Assembly devoted to disarmament

The General Assembly,

Convinced that, in the international community's continuing search for lasting security, multilateral action has an increasingly important role,

Welcoming the fact that during recent years a favourable climate has developed within the international community and progress has been recorded in some important fields of disarmament,

Encouraged by the Treaty between the United States of America and the Union of Soviet Socialist Republics on the Elimination of Their Intermediate-Range and Shorter-Range Missiles, which represents a valuable initial step in the reduction of nuclear weapons,

Taking into account that, despite the positive processes and developments, the general situation with regard to armament is far from satisfactory,

Stressing the necessity of mutually complementary bilateral, regional and global approaches for success in disarmament negotiations and the attainment of peace and security,

Expressing its regret that the fifteenth special session of the General Assembly, the third special session devoted to disarmament, ended without agreement on a concluding document,

Reaffirming the validity of the Final Document of the Tenth Special Session of the General Assembly, the first special session devoted to disarmament, which reflected a historic consensus on the part of the international community that the halting and reversing of the arms race, in particular the nuclear-arms race, and the achievement of genuine disarmament are tasks of primary importance and urgency,

1. *Considers* that the fifteenth special session of the General Assembly served the purpose of increasing awareness of the areas where future efforts should be concentrated and underscored the urgency that States should work resolutely for the common cause of curbing the arms race, particularly in the nuclear field, and achieving disarmament;

2. *Takes note with appreciation* of the numerous constructive proposals submitted by Member States to the General Assembly at its fifteenth special session aimed at advancing disarmament and increasing security;

3. *Calls upon* all Member States to contribute to the strengthening of the role of the United Nations in the field of disarmament, as it provides the most appropriate forum for all Member States to contribute actively and collectively to the consideration and resolution of disarmament issues that have a bearing on their security;

4. *Considers* that the contribution of the special sessions of the General Assembly devoted to disarmament has been useful in reviewing and assessing the results of the efforts of Member States in moving forward deliberations and negotiations on all disarmament and related issues, and that they can provide a new direction and impetus for these efforts;

5. *Decides* to include in the provisional agenda of its forty-fifth session an item entitled ''Special sessions on disarmament''.

General Assembly resolution 43/77 B

7 December 1988   Meeting 73   152-0-2 (recorded vote)

Approved by First Committee (A/43/858) by recorded vote (132-0-2), 17 November (meeting 41); 22-nation draft (A/C.1/43/L.65); agenda item 66.
Sponsors: Algeria, Bangladesh, Colombia, Cuba, Djibouti, Ecuador, Egypt, Ethiopia, German Democratic Republic, Ghana, India, Indonesia, Madagascar, Malaysia, Morocco, Pakistan, Romania, Sri Lanka, Sweden, Tunisia, Viet Nam, Yugoslavia.
Meeting numbers. GA 42nd session: 1st Committee 3-25, 32, 41; plenary 73.

Recorded vote in Assembly as follows:

In favour: Afghanistan, Albania, Algeria, Angola, Antigua and Barbuda, Argentina, Australia, Austria, Bahamas, Bahrain, Bangladesh, Barbados, Belgium, Belize, Benin, Bhutan, Bolivia, Botswana, Brazil, Brunei Darussalam, Bulgaria, Burkina Faso, Burma, Burundi, Byelorussian SSR, Cameroon, Canada, Cape Verde, Central African Republic, Chad, Chile, China, Colombia, Comoros, Congo, Costa Rica, Côte d'Ivoire, Cuba, Cyprus, Czechoslovakia, Democratic Kampuchea, Democratic Yemen, Denmark, Djibouti, Dominican Republic, Ecuador, Egypt, El Salvador, Ethiopia, Fiji, Finland, France, Gabon, Gambia, German Democratic Republic, Germany, Federal Republic of, Ghana, Greece, Guatemala, Guinea, Guyana, Haiti, Honduras, Hungary, Iceland, India, Indonesia, Iran, Iraq, Ireland, Israel, Italy, Jamaica, Japan, Jordan, Kenya, Kuwait, Lao People's Democratic Republic, Lebanon, Lesotho, Liberia, Libyan Arab Jamahiriya, Luxembourg, Madagascar, Malawi, Malaysia, Maldives, Mali, Malta, Mauritania, Mauritius, Mexico, Mongolia, Morocco, Mozambique, Nepal, Netherlands, New Zealand, Nicaragua, Niger, Nigeria, Norway, Oman, Pakistan, Panama, Papua New Guinea, Paraguay, Peru, Philippines, Poland, Portugal, Qatar, Romania, Rwanda, Saint Kitts and Nevis, Saint Lucia, Saint Vincent and the Grenadines, Samoa, Sao Tome and Principe, Saudi Arabia, Senegal, Seychelles, Sierra Leone, Singapore, Solomon Islands, Somalia, Spain, Sri Lanka, Sudan, Suriname, Swaziland, Sweden, Syrian Arab Republic, Thailand, Togo, Trinidad and Tobago, Tunisia, Turkey, Uganda, Ukrainian SSR, USSR, United Arab Emirates, United Republic of Tanzania, Uruguay, Vanuatu, Venezuela, Viet Nam, Yemen, Yugoslavia, Zaire, Zambia, Zimbabwe.
Against: None.
Abstaining: United Kingdom, United States.

REFERENCES

[1]A/S-15/28. [2]CD/845, CD/847. [3]CD/815. [4]YUN 1987, p. 29. [5]*Ibid.,* GA res. 42/40, 30 Nov. 1987. [6]A/S-15/1.

[7]YUN 1986, p. 21, GA res. 41/60 G, 3 Dec. 1986. [8]YUN 1978, p. 17. [9]YUN 1982, p. 11. [10]A/S-15/36. [11]A/S-15/36/Add.1. [12]A/S-15/2. [13]A/S-15/3. [14]A/S-15/4. [15]A/S-15/5. [16]A/S-15/9. [17]A/S-15/8 & Corr.1. [18]A/S-15/7. [19]A/S-15/40. [20]A/S-15/12. [21]A/S-15/23. [22]A/S-15/48. [23]A/S-15/16. [24]A/S-15/14. [25]A/S-15/AC.1/25. [26]A/S-15/32. [27]A/S-15/AC.1/3. [28]A/S-15/AC.1/12. [29]A/S-15/AC.1/23. [30]A/S-15/AC.1/26, A/S-15/AC.1/27. [31]A/S-15/AC.1/9. [32]A/S-15/AC.1/22. [33]A/S-15/AC.1/4. [34]A/S-15/AC.1/13, A/S-15/AC.1/16. [35]A/S-15/AC.1/8. [36]A/S-15/25. [37]A/S-15/34. [38]A/S-15/AC.1/1. [39]A/S-15/AC.1/15. [40]A/S-15/13. [41]A/S-15/43, A/S-15/AC.1/2, A/S-15/AC.1/7, A/S-15/AC.1/11, A/S-15/AC.1/14, A/S-15/AC.1/24. [42]A/S-15/AC.1/5. [43]A/S-15/42. [44]A/S-15/AC.1/17. [45]A/S-15/50.

Comprehensive approaches to disarmament

In 1988, all the principal intergovernmental disarmament bodies again discussed enhancing the United Nations role in disarmament and increasing the efficiency of the existing machinery for deliberations and negotiations on the topic. (In addition to the activities of those bodies, this section deals with the measures taken to follow up on the decisions adopted at the 1978 and 1982 special sessions, along with developments relating to a proposed world disarmament conference.)

UN disarmament bodies and their activities in 1988

The United Nations continued its disarmament efforts in 1988, mainly through the General Assembly and its First Committee, the Disarmament Commission (a subsidiary organ of the Assembly) and the Conference on Disarmament (a multilateral negotiating forum at Geneva).

Disarmament Commission

The Disarmament Commission, composed of all United Nations Member States, met in New York from 2 to 20 May 1988.[1] It also met on 1 December to elect its officers and consider the provisional agenda for its 1989 session.

The Commission's agenda in 1988 included items on aspects of the arms race, particularly a general approach to negotiations on nuclear and conventional disarmament; reduction of military budgets; South Africa's nuclear capability; review of the United Nations role in disarmament; naval armaments and disarmament; issues related to conventional disarmament; verification in all its aspects; and guidelines for confidence-building measures.

The Commission established a committee of the whole, which in turn set up a contact group to consider aspects of the arms race and elaboration of a general approach to disarmament negotiations.

The group met between 4 and 17 May. In the course of its work, the group updated some of the texts under consideration and made some progress towards narrowing areas of disagreement, but it was unable to reach a consensus on a complete set of recommendations. The Commission also established two consultation groups to deal with the reduction of military budgets and confidence-building measures, respectively. Substantive and open-ended consultations were held on naval armaments and disarmament, and a working group was established for each of the other agenda items.

The Commission prepared a special report to the General Assembly at its third special session on disarmament, summarizing the work of the Commission and its subsidiary bodies from 1983 to 1988 inclusive.[2]

GENERAL ASSEMBLY ACTION

On 7 December 1988, on the recommendation of the First Committee, the General Assembly adopted **resolution 43/78 A** without vote.

Report of the Disarmament Commission

The General Assembly,

Having considered the special and annual reports of the Disarmament Commission,

Emphasizing again the importance of an effective follow-up to the relevant recommendations and decisions contained in the Final Document of the Tenth Special Session of the General Assembly, the first special session devoted to disarmament,

Taking into account the relevant sections of the Concluding Document of the Twelfth Special Session of the General Assembly, the second special session devoted to disarmament,

Also taking into account widespread views expressed during the fifteenth special session of the General Assembly, the third special session devoted to disarmament,

Considering the role that the Disarmament Commission has been called upon to play and the contribution that it should make in examining and submitting recommendations on various problems in the field of disarmament and in the promotion of the implementation of the relevant decisions of the tenth special session,

Recalling its resolutions 33/71 H of 14 December 1978, 34/83 H of 11 December 1979, 35/152 F of 12 December 1980, 36/92 B of 9 December 1981, 37/78 H of 9 December 1982, 38/183 E of 20 December 1983, 39/148 R of 17 December 1984, 40/152 F of 16 December 1985, 41/86 E of 4 December 1986 and 42/42 G of 30 November 1987,

1. *Takes note* of the special and annual reports of the Disarmament Commission;

2. *Commends* the Disarmament Commission for its adoption by consensus of a set of principles of verification on disarmament issues as well as a set of guidelines for appropriate types of confidence-building measures and for the implementation of such measures on a global or regional level, which were recommended to the General Assembly for consideration;

3. *Notes* that the Disarmament Commission has yet to conclude its consideration of some items on its agenda, but notes also with appreciation the progress achieved on some of these;

4. *Recalls* the role of the Disarmament Commission as the specialized, deliberative body within the United Nations multilateral disarmament machinery that allows for in-depth deliberations on specific disarmament issues, leading to the submission of concrete recommendations on those issues;

5. *Stresses* the importance for the Disarmament Commission to work on the basis of a relevant agenda of disarmament topics, thereby enabling the Commission to concentrate its efforts and thus optimize its progress on specific subjects in accordance with resolution 37/78 H;

6. *Requests* the Disarmament Commission to continue its work in accordance with its mandate, as set forth in paragraph 118 of the Final Document of the Tenth Special Session of the General Assembly, and with paragraph 3 of resolution 37/78 H, and to that end to make every effort to achieve specific recommendations, at its 1989 substantive session, on the outstanding items on its agenda, taking into account the relevant resolutions of the General Assembly as well as the results of its 1988 substantive session;

7. *Also requests* the Disarmament Commission to meet for a period not exceeding four weeks during 1989 and to submit a substantive report, containing specific recommendations on the items included in its agenda, to the General Assembly at its forty-fourth session;

8. *Requests* the Secretary-General to transmit to the Disarmament Commission the special and annual reports of the Conference on Disarmament, together with all the official records of the fifteenth special session and the forty-third session of the General Assembly relating to disarmament matters, and to render all assistance that the Commission may require for implementing the present resolution;

9. *Also requests* the Secretary-General to ensure full provision to the Commission and its subsidiary bodies of interpretation and translation facilities in the official languages and to assign, as a matter of priority, all the necessary resources and services to this end;

10. *Decides* to include in the provisional agenda of its forty-fourth session the item entitled "Report of the Disarmament Commission".

General Assembly resolution 43/78 A

7 December 1988   Meeting 73   Adopted without vote

Approved by First Committee (A/43/859) without vote, 10 November (meeting 33); 18-nation draft (A/C.1/43/L.3), orally revised; agenda item 67 *(a)*.

Sponsors: Australia, Austria, Bahamas, Byelorussian SSR, Cameroon, Canada, China, Czechoslovakia, Denmark, Ecuador, Germany, Federal Republic of, Hungary, Jordan, Romania, Sri Lanka, Sweden, Togo, Uruguay.

Meeting numbers. GA 43rd session: 1st Committee 3-25, 32, 33; plenary 73.

Conference on Disarmament

The Conference on Disarmament, the 40-member multilateral negotiating body, met twice in 1988 at Geneva (2 February–29 April and 7 July–20 September).[3] Holding 48 plenary meetings and 18 informal meetings, it considered a nuclear-test ban, cessation of the nuclear-arms race and nuclear disarmament, prevention of nuclear war, chemical weapons, prevention of an arms race in outer space, security assurances to non-nuclear-weapon States,

radiological weapons and a comprehensive programme of disarmament. The Conference re-
established *ad hoc* committees on chemical
weapons, assurances to non-nuclear-weapon
States, radiological weapons, the prevention of an
arms race in outer space and the comprehensive
programme of disarmament (details of these questions are discussed elsewhere in this chapter). It
continued to consider, but did not take action on,
the possibility of increasing its membership by not
more than four States. It also held informal consultations on the improved and effective functioning of the Conference.

Report of the Secretary-General. In October,[4] the Secretary-General, pursuant to a
1987 General Assembly resolution,[5] drew the attention of Member States to the participation in
the work of the Conference on Disarmament of
States not Conference members.

GENERAL ASSEMBLY ACTION

On 7 December, on the recommendation of the
First Committee, the General Assembly adopted
two resolutions on the work of the Conference on
Disarmament (43/78 M and I).

The Assembly adopted **resolution 43/78 M** by
recorded vote.

Report of the Conference on Disarmament
The General Assembly,

Recalling its resolutions 34/83 B of 11 December 1979,
35/152 J of 12 December 1980, 36/92 F of 9 December
1981, 37/78 G of 9 December 1982, 38/183 I of 20 December 1983, 39/148 N of 17 December 1984, 40/152 M
of 16 December 1985, 41/86 M of 4 December 1986 and
42/42 L of 30 November 1987,

Having considered the report of the Conference on Disarmament,

Convinced that the Conference on Disarmament, as the
single multilateral negotiating body on disarmament,
should play the central role in substantive negotiations
on priority questions of disarmament,

Expressing its regret that the Conference on Disarmament
was not able in 1988 either to establish *ad hoc* committees or to commence negotiations on nuclear issues on
its agenda,

Expressing its expectation that the Conference on Disarmament, in view of the positive current processes in some
important fields of disarmament, would be in a position to reach concrete agreements on disarmament issues to which the United Nations has assigned greatest
priority and urgency and which have been under consideration for a number of years,

Considering that it is more than ever imperative in the
present circumstances to give an additional impetus to
negotiations on disarmament at all levels and to achieve
genuine progress in the immediate future,

1. *Reaffirms* the role of the Conference on Disarmament as the single multilateral disarmament negotiating forum of the international community;

2. *Notes with satisfaction* that further progress has been
made in the negotiations on the elaboration of a draft
convention on the complete and effective prohibition of

the development, production and stockpiling of all chemical weapons and on their destruction, and urges the
Conference on Disarmament to intensify further its work
with a view to completing negotiations on such a draft
convention as soon as possible;

3. *Calls upon* the Conference on Disarmament to intensify its work, to further its mandate more earnestly
through substantive negotiations, within the framework
of *ad hoc* committees as the most appropriate mechanism,
and to adopt concrete measures on the specific priority
issues of disarmament on its agenda, in accordance with
the Programme of Action set forth in section III of the
Final Document of the Tenth Special Session of the
General Assembly;

4. *Urges* the Conference on Disarmament to provide
negotiating mandates to *ad hoc* committees on all agenda
items, in keeping with the fundamental role of the Conference as identified in the Final Document of the Tenth
Special Session;

5. *Requests* the Conference on Disarmament to submit a report on its work to the General Assembly at its
forty-fourth session;

6. *Decides* to include in the provisional agenda of its
forty-fourth session the item entitled ''Report of the
Conference on Disarmament''.

General Assembly resolution 43/78 M

7 December 1988   Meeting 73   136-3-14 (recorded vote)

Approved by First Committee (A/43/859) by recorded vote (117-3-14), 17
November (meeting 41); 30-nation draft (A/C.1/43/L.66); agenda item 67
(b).

Sponsors: Algeria, Bangladesh, Brazil, Burma, Cuba, Djibouti, Ecuador, Egypt,
Ethiopia, Ghana, India, Indonesia, Iran, Kenya, Madagascar, Malaysia, Mex-
ico, Morocco, Nigeria, Pakistan, Peru, Romania, Sri Lanka, Sudan, Sweden,
Tunisia, Venezuela, Viet Nam, Yugoslavia, Zaire.

Meeting numbers. GA 43rd session: 1st Committee 3-25, 31, 41; plenary 73.

Recorded vote in Assembly as follows:

In favour: Afghanistan, Albania, Algeria, Angola, Antigua and Barbuda,
Argentina, Australia, Austria, Bahamas, Bahrain, Bangladesh, Barbados,
Belize, Benin, Bhutan, Bolivia, Botswana, Brazil, Brunei Darussalam, Bul-
garia, Burkina Faso, Burma, Burundi, Byelorussian SSR, Cameroon, Cape
Verde, Central African Republic, Chad, Chile, China, Colombia, Comoros,
Congo, Costa Rica, Côte d'Ivoire, Cuba, Cyprus, Czechoslovakia,
Democratic Kampuchea, Democratic Yemen, Djibouti, Dominican Republic,
Ecuador, Egypt, El Salvador, Ethiopia, Fiji, Finland, Gabon, Gambia, Ger-
man Democratic Republic, Ghana, Greece, Guatemala, Guinea, Guyana,
Haiti, Honduras, Hungary, India, Indonesia, Iran, Iraq, Ireland, Jordan,
Kenya, Kuwait, Lao People's Democratic Republic, Lebanon, Lesotho, Li-
beria, Libyan Arab Jamahiriya, Madagascar, Malawi, Malaysia, Maldives,
Mali, Malta, Mauritania, Mauritius, Mexico, Mongolia, Morocco, Mozam-
bique, Nepal, New Zealand, Nicaragua, Niger, Nigeria, Oman, Pakistan,
Panama, Papua New Guinea, Paraguay, Peru, Philippines, Poland, Qatar,
Romania, Rwanda, Saint Kitts and Nevis, Saint Lucia, Saint Vincent and
the Grenadines, Samoa, Sao Tome and Principe, Saudi Arabia, Senegal,
Seychelles, Sierra Leone, Singapore, Solomon Islands, Somalia, Sri Lanka,
Sudan, Suriname, Swaziland, Sweden, Syrian Arab Republic, Thailand,
Togo, Trinidad and Tobago, Tunisia, Uganda, Ukrainian SSR, USSR, United
Arab Emirates, United Republic of Tanzania, Uruguay, Vanuatu, Venezuela,
Viet Nam, Yemen, Yugoslavia, Zaire, Zambia, Zimbabwe.

Against: France, United Kingdom, United States.

Abstaining: Belgium, Canada, Denmark, Germany, Federal Republic of,
Iceland, Israel, Italy, Japan, Luxembourg, Netherlands, Norway, Portugal,
Spain, Turkey.

The Assembly also adopted **resolution 43/78 I**
by recorded vote.

Report of the Conference on Disarmament
The General Assembly,

Recalling the relevant portions of the Final Document
of the Tenth Special Session of the General Assembly,
in particular paragraph 120,

Bearing in mind that considerable and urgent work remains to be accomplished in the field of disarmament,

Convinced that the Conference on Disarmament, as the single multilateral negotiating forum for global disarmament questions, should fully take into account the Programme of Action set forth in section III of the Final Document of the Tenth Special Session,

Having considered the report of the Conference on Disarmament, which the Conference adopted by consensus,

1. *Takes note* of the report of the Conference on Disarmament on its 1988 session;

2. *Reaffirms* that the Conference on Disarmament plays a vital role in the field of disarmament for the world community;

3. *Reaffirms also* its support for the efforts of the Conference on Disarmament in fulfilling its tasks, and calls upon all Conference members and observer States to contribute as effectively as possible to this end;

4. *Requests* the Conference on Disarmament to continue and to intensify its work on the various substantive items on its agenda;

5. *Also requests* the Conference on Disarmament to submit a report on its work to the General Assembly at its forty-fourth session;

6. *Decides* to include in the provisional agenda of its forty-fourth session the item entitled ''Report of the Conference on Disarmament''.

General Assembly resolution 43/78 I

7 December 1988   Meeting 73   96-0-53 (recorded vote)

Approved by First Committee (A/43/859) by recorded vote (73-0-53), 17 November (meeting 41); 12-nation draft (A/C.1/43/L.50); agenda item 67 (b).

Sponsors: Australia, Belgium, Canada, Denmark, France, Germany, Federal Republic of, Iceland, Italy, Japan, Netherlands, Norway, Spain.

Meeting numbers. GA 43rd session: 1st Committee 3-25, 32, 41; plenary 73.

Recorded vote in Assembly as follows:

In favour: Antigua and Barbuda, Australia, Austria, Bahamas, Bahrain, Belgium, Belize, Benin, Bhutan, Botswana, Brunei Darussalam, Bulgaria, Burkina Faso, Byelorussian SSR, Canada, Cape Verde, Central African Republic, Chad, Chile, China, Colombia, Comoros, Costa Rica, Côte d'Ivoire, Czechoslovakia, Democratic Kampuchea, Denmark, Djibouti, El Salvador, Fiji, Finland, France, Gabon, Gambia, German Democratic Republic, Germany, Federal Republic of, Ghana, Greece, Guatemala, Guinea, Haiti, Honduras, Hungary, Iceland, Ireland, Israel, Italy, Japan, Lao People's Democratic Republic, Lebanon, Lesotho, Liberia, Luxembourg, Malawi, Malaysia, Mali, Malta, Mauritius, Mongolia, Morocco, Nepal, Netherlands, New Zealand, Niger, Nigeria, Norway, Papua New Guinea, Paraguay, Philippines, Poland, Portugal, Qatar, Romania, Saint Kitts and Nevis, Saint Lucia, Saint Vincent and the Grenadines, Samoa, Saudi Arabia, Senegal, Seychelles, Singapore, Solomon Islands, Spain, Swaziland, Sweden, Thailand, Togo, Trinidad and Tobago, Turkey, Ukrainian SSR, USSR, United Kingdom, Uruguay, Vanuatu, Yemen, Zaire.

Against: None.

Abstaining: Afghanistan, Algeria, Angola, Argentina, Bangladesh, Barbados, Bolivia, Brazil, Burma, Burundi, Cameroon, Congo, Cuba, Cyprus, Democratic Yemen, Dominican Republic, Ecuador, Egypt, Ethiopia, Guyana, India, Indonesia, Iran, Iraq, Jordan, Kenya, Kuwait, Libyan Arab Jamahiriya, Madagascar, Maldives, Mauritania, Mexico, Nicaragua, Oman, Pakistan, Panama, Peru, Rwanda, Sierra Leone, Somalia, Sudan, Suriname, Syrian Arab Republic, Tunisia, Uganda, United Arab Emirates, United Republic of Tanzania, United States, Venezuela, Viet Nam, Yugoslavia, Zambia, Zimbabwe.

UN role in disarmament

Disarmament Commission consideration. In accordance with a General Assembly request of 1987,[6] the Disarmament Commission[1] in 1988 continued its consideration of the role of the United Nations in disarmament. Working Group II, established on 2 May to deal with the topic, held five meetings and a number of informal con-

sultations between 4 and 19 May. The Working Group, which had 31 working papers before it, set up an open-ended contact group, which held seven meetings between 4 and 16 May.

In carrying out its work, the contact group agreed to use an annex to the 1987 report of the Commission[7] as the basis for its discussion, on the understanding that all the other documents, views and proposals put forward would be considered on an equal footing. The group discussed machinery aspects of the United Nations role and submitted to the Working Group a working paper that had formed the basis for its deliberations. The paper dealt with the General Assembly and its organs, the Security Council, the Secretary-General, the Conference on Disarmament and other organs. It pointed out that other proposals on the same elements were also before the Commission and that, in addition, proposals had been submitted regarding the *Ad Hoc* Committee on the Indian Ocean, the World Disarmament Campaign, the specialized agencies, review conferences, Disarmament Week and regional arrangements. The paper outlined areas in which some progress had been made and those on which substantial divergencies remained.

On 19 May, the Working Group agreed to incorporate part of the 1987 annex and the working paper into an annex to its own report[2] and recommended that the new annex, which had not been agreed upon, be transmitted to the General Assembly at its special session (see above).

On 7 December, on the recommendation of the First Committee, the General Assembly adopted **resolution 43/75 R** without vote.

Review of the role of the United Nations in the field of disarmament

The General Assembly,

Recalling its resolutions 39/151 G of 17 December 1984, 40/94 O of 12 December 1985, 41/59 O of 3 December 1986 and 42/38 O of 30 November 1987,

Bearing in mind that the primary purpose of the United Nations is to maintain international peace and security,

Reaffirming its conviction that genuine and lasting peace can be created only through the effective implementation of the security system provided for in the Charter of the United Nations and the speedy and substantial reduction of arms and armed forces, by international agreement and mutual example, leading ultimately to general and complete disarmament under effective international control,

Reaffirming that the United Nations, in accordance with its Charter, has a central role and primary responsibility in the sphere of disarmament,

Recognizing the need for the United Nations, in discharging its central role and primary responsibility in the sphere of disarmament, to play a more active role in the field of disarmament in accordance with its primary purpose under the Charter to maintain international peace and security,

Taking into account the part of the report of the Disarmament Commission relating to this question, and noting the progress made in the consideration of the question at the fifteenth special session of the General Assembly, the third special session devoted to disarmament,

Bearing in mind the common desire expressed at its third special session devoted to disarmament on the necessity to strengthen the role of the United Nations in the field of disarmament and the increased reaffirmation of faith in the United Nations as an indispensable instrument for international peace and security,

1. *Requests* the Disarmament Commission to continue its consideration of the role of the United Nations in the field of disarmament as a matter of priority at its next substantive session, in 1989, with a view to the elaboration of concrete recommendations and proposals, as appropriate, taking into account, *inter alia*, the views and suggestions of Member States as well as the aforementioned documents on the subject;

2. *Also requests* the Disarmament Commission to submit its report on the subject, including findings, recommendations and proposals, as appropriate, to the General Assembly at its forty-fourth session;

3. *Decides* to include in the provisional agenda of its forty-fourth session the item entitled "Review of the role of the United Nations in the field of disarmament: report of the Disarmament Commission".

General Assembly resolution 43/75 R

7 December 1988　　　Meeting 73　　　Adopted without vote

Approved by First Committee (A/43/856) without vote, 10 November (meeting 33); 33-nation draft (A/C.1/43/L.69/Rev.1); agenda item 64 *(j)*.
Sponsors: Australia, Bahamas, Burkina Faso, Burundi, Cameroon, Canada, Central African Republic, Chad, Congo, Côte d'Ivoire, Ethiopia, France, Gabon, Germany, Federal Republic of, Guinea, Guinea-Bissau, Hungary, Italy, Japan, Liberia, Madagascar, Mali, Morocco, New Zealand, Papua New Guinea, Philippines, Samoa, Senegal, Singapore, Thailand, Togo, Ukrainian SSR, Zaire.
Meeting numbers. GA 43rd session: 1st Committee 3-25, 32, 33; plenary 73.

Role of the Security Council

In response to a 1987 General Assembly request,[8] the Secretary-General submitted in November 1988[9] a note on action taken regarding the role of the Security Council in the area of disarmament. The Assembly had called on the Council to take the necessary steps for the effective implementation of Article 26 of the Charter of the United Nations with a view to enhancing the central role of the United Nations in facilitating solutions to the issues of arms limitation, disarmament and the strengthening of international peace and security. The President of the Council informed the Secretary-General that the Assembly request, as well as the views of the Ukrainian SSR and the USSR on the role of the Council in disarmament, had been circulated to the members of the Council.

UN resolutions on disarmament

In response to a 1987 General Assembly request,[10] the Secretary-General submitted a report in August 1988, with later addenda,[11] containing information from nine Member States regarding developments in arms limitation and disarmament, including the implementation of relevant Assembly resolutions.

GENERAL ASSEMBLY ACTION

On the recommendation of the First Committee, the General Assembly on 7 December adopted **resolution 43/75 H** by recorded vote.

Implementation of General Assembly resolutions in the field of disarmament

The General Assembly,

Recalling its resolution 42/38 J of 30 November 1987,

Taking note of the report of the Secretary-General,

Recalling paragraph 115 of the Final Document of the Tenth Special Session of the General Assembly, in which it is stated, *inter alia*, that the Assembly has been and should remain the main deliberative organ of the United Nations in the field of disarmament and should make every effort to facilitate the implementation of disarmament measures,

Mindful of the fact that the role of the United Nations in the field of disarmament could be strengthened substantially through an increased effort by Member States to implement faithfully General Assembly resolutions in the field of disarmament,

Convinced of the importance of treating recommendations of the General Assembly in the field of disarmament with due respect in accordance with the obligations assumed by Member States under the Charter of the United Nations,

1. *Deems it important* that all Member States make every effort to facilitate the consistent implementation of General Assembly resolutions in the field of disarmament, and thus show their resolve to arrive at mutually acceptable, comprehensively verifiable and effective disarmament measures;

2. *Invites* all Member States that have not yet done so to make available to the Secretary-General their views and suggestions on ways and means to improve the situation with regard to the implementation of General Assembly resolutions in the field of disarmament;

3. *Requests* the Secretary-General to submit to the General Assembly at its forty-fourth session, in accordance with resolution 42/38 J, a report that includes information provided by Member States concerning the implementation of General Assembly resolutions in the field of disarmament, as well as their views on possible avenues to improve the situation in this respect;

4. *Calls upon* all Member States to render every assistance to the Secretary-General so that he may fulfil the request contained in paragraph 3 above;

5. *Decides* to continue its consideration of the issue of the implementation of General Assembly resolutions in the field of disarmament at its forty-fourth session.

General Assembly resolution 43/75 H

7 December 1988　　　Meeting 73　　　131-2-20 (recorded vote)

Approved by First Committee (A/43/856) by recorded vote (106-2-23), 16 November (meeting 39); 3-nation draft (A/C.1/43/L.20/Rev.1); agenda item 64 *(g)*.
Sponsors: Cameroon, Czechoslovakia, Ukrainian SSR.
Meeting numbers. GA 43rd session: 1st Committee 3-25, 32, 39; plenary 73.

Recorded vote in Assembly as follows:

In favour: Afghanistan, Algeria, Angola, Antigua and Barbuda, Argentina, Bahamas, Bahrain, Bangladesh, Barbados, Belize, Benin, Bhutan, Bolivia, Botswana, Brazil, Brunei Darussalam, Bulgaria, Burkina Faso, Burma, Burundi, Byelorussian SSR, Cameroon, Cape Verde, Central African Republic, Chad, Chile, China, Colombia, Comoros, Congo, Costa Rica, Côte d'Ivoire, Cuba, Cyprus, Czechoslovakia, Democratic Kampuchea, Democratic Yemen, Djibouti, Dominican Republic, Ecuador, Egypt, El Salvador, Ethiopia, Fiji, Gabon, Gambia, German Democratic Republic, Ghana, Guatemala, Guinea, Guyana, Haiti, Honduras, Hungary, Indonesia, Iran, Iraq, Jamaica, Jordan, Kenya, Kuwait, Lao People's Democratic Republic, Lebanon, Lesotho, Liberia, Libyan Arab Jamahiriya, Luxembourg, Madagascar, Malawi, Malaysia, Maldives, Mali, Malta, Mauritania, Mauritius, Mexico, Mongolia, Morocco, Mozambique, Nepal, Nicaragua, Niger, Nigeria, Norway, Oman, Pakistan, Panama, Papua New Guinea, Paraguay, Peru, Philippines, Poland, Portugal, Qatar, Romania, Rwanda, Saint Kitts and Nevis, Saint Lucia, Saint Vincent and the Grenadines, Samoa, Sao Tome and Principe, Saudi Arabia, Senegal, Seychelles, Sierra Leone, Singapore, Solomon Islands, Somalia, Sri Lanka, Sudan, Suriname, Swaziland, Syrian Arab Republic, Thailand, Togo, Trinidad and Tobago, Tunisia, Uganda, Ukrainian SSR, USSR, United Arab Emirates, United Republic of Tanzania, Uruguay, Vanuatu, Venezuela, Viet Nam, Yemen, Yugoslavia, Zaire, Zambia, Zimbabwe.

Against: Israel, United States.

Abstaining: Australia, Austria, Belgium, Canada, Denmark, Finland, France, Germany, Federal Republic of, Greece, Iceland, India, Ireland, Italy, Japan, Netherlands, New Zealand, Spain, Sweden, Turkey, United Kingdom.

Role of UN organizations and programmes

In accordance with a 1986 General Assembly request,[12] the Secretary-General submitted in October 1988 a report on the contribution of the specialized agencies and other organizations and programmes of the United Nations system to the cause of arms limitation and disarmament,[13] outlining the continued efforts in that regard of IAEA, four specialized agencies and five organizations and programmes.

By **decision 43/422** of 7 December, the Assembly, taking note of the Secretary-General's report, deferred consideration of the item.

Follow-up to the General Assembly's special sessions on disarmament

At its regular session in 1988, the General Assembly adopted 23 resolutions relating to the implementation of recommendations adopted at its special sessions devoted to disarmament—the first held in 1978 as the tenth special session,[14] the second held in 1982 as the twelfth special session[15] and the third held in 1988 as the fifteenth special session (see above, under "General aspects"). In 1978, the Assembly had adopted a Final Document,[16] and in 1982, a Concluding Document.[17] The Assembly was unable to reach agreement on a document in 1988.

This section deals with resolutions on disarmament and international security, international arms tranfers, scientific and technological developments, the United Nations advisory services programme, international co-operation for disarmament, guidelines for confidence-building measures and the 1990s as the third disarmament decade.

Other resolutions relating to these agenda items and dealing with various specific issues are discussed elsewhere in the chapter.

Disarmament and international security

In the Final Document of the tenth special session, the General Assembly had acknowledged that genuine and lasting peace could be created only through the effective implementation of the security system provided for in the Charter and the speedy and substantial reduction of arms and armed forces, by international agreement and mutual example, leading ultimately to general and complete disarmament under effective international control.

In 1985, the Assembly had noted that the Security Council, which is vested with the responsibility of maintaining international peace and security under Article 26 of the Charter, had not given consideration to the escalating arms race and had called on it to initiate due procedures.[18]

In 1988, the Assembly was again seized of the question of international peace and security.

On 7 December, the General Assembly, on the recommendation of the First Committee, adopted **resolution 43/76 A** by recorded vote.

Disarmament and international security

The General Assembly,

Recalling its resolutions 34/83 A of 11 December 1979, 35/156 J of 12 December 1980, 36/97 K of 9 December 1981, 37/100 E of 13 December 1982, 38/73 H of 15 December 1983, 39/63 K of 12 December 1984 and 40/151 A of 16 December 1985,

Expressing the growing alarm of the world community over the dangers of the arms race, in particular the nuclear-arms race, and its adverse social and economic consequences,

Noting that the present state of the international situation requires that the disarmament principles embodied in the Charter of the United Nations become part and parcel of any collective efforts aimed at ensuring a truly safe world, including those undertaken by the Security Council,

Reaffirming that the United Nations under its Charter plays a central role and bears main responsibility in the area of disarmament and the strengthening of international security,

Recalling paragraph 13 of the Final Document of the Tenth Special Session of the General Assembly, in which the Assembly acknowledged that genuine and lasting peace can only be created through the effective implementation of the security system provided for in the Charter and the speedy and substantial reduction of arms and armed forces, by international agreement and mutual example,

Recalling that, under Article 26 of the Charter, the Security Council is responsible for formulating, with the assistance of the Military Staff Committee, plans for establishing an arms regulation system,

Noting the fact that the Security Council, which is vested under the Charter with the principal responsibility for maintaining international peace and security, has not yet conducted any examination of the question of the adverse effects of the arms race, especially in the nuclear field, on international peace and security, as provided for in the relevant General Assembly resolutions,

Welcoming the entry into force of the Treaty between the United States of America and the Union of Soviet Socialist Republics on the Elimination of Their Intermediate-Range and Shorter-Range Missiles, which opens the process of genuine disarmament,

Mindful of the need to use all avenues for further progress through effective measures in the field of disarmament,

1. *Calls upon* the Security Council, in particular its permanent members, within the framework of its main task, to contribute to establishing and maintaining international peace and security with the least possible diversion of world human and economic resources to armament, and to take the necessary steps for the effective implementation of Article 26 of the Charter of the United Nations with a view to enhancing the central role of the United Nations in facilitating solutions to the issues of arms limitation, primarily in the nuclear field, and disarmament, as well as the strengthening of international peace and security;

2. *Recommends* that the nuclear-weapon States, which at the same time are the five permanent members of the Security Council, hold joint meetings and provide regular information to the General Assembly, as well as to the Conference on Disarmament, about the state of affairs as regards the range of issues related to disarmament, especially in the nuclear field, the prevention of a nuclear war and the status of the current agreements in the field of arms limitation and disarmament, and about progress at those negotiations which include the participation of the nuclear-weapon States;

3. *Recommends* that the Security Council consider the question of establishing, under Article 29 of the Charter, such subsidiary bodies as it deems necessary for the performance of its functions to facilitate a solution to disarmament issues;

4. *Requests* the Secretary-General to submit to the General Assembly at its forty-fourth session a report on the implementation of the present resolution within the framework of the agenda item entitled "Review and implementation of the Concluding Document of the Twelfth Special Session of the General Assembly".

General Assembly resolution 43/76 A

7 December 1988   Meeting 73   129-1-21 (recorded vote)

Approved by First Committee (A/43/857) by recorded vote (109-1-21), 17 November (meeting 41); draft by Cyprus (A/C.1/43/L.24); agenda item 65.
Meeting numbers. GA 43rd session: 1st Committee 3-26, 41; plenary 73.

Recorded vote in Assembly as follows:

In favour: Afghanistan, Algeria, Angola, Antigua and Barbuda, Argentina, Bahamas, Bahrain, Bangladesh, Barbados, Belize, Benin, Bhutan, Bolivia, Botswana, Brazil, Brunei Darussalam, Bulgaria, Burkina Faso, Burma, Burundi, Byelorussian SSR, Cameroon, Cape Verde, Central African Republic, Chad, Chile, China, Colombia, Comoros, Congo, Costa Rica, Côte d'Ivoire, Cuba, Cyprus, Czechoslovakia, Democratic Kampuchea, Democratic Yemen, Djibouti, Dominican Republic, Ecuador, Egypt, El Salvador, Ethiopia, Fiji, Gabon, Gambia, German Democratic Republic, Ghana, Greece, Guatemala, Guinea, Guyana, Honduras, Hungary, India, Indonesia, Iran, Iraq, Jamaica, Jordan, Kenya, Kuwait, Lao People's Democratic Republic, Lebanon, Lesotho, Liberia, Libyan Arab Jamahiriya, Madagascar, Malawi, Malaysia, Maldives, Mali, Malta, Mauritania, Mauritius, Mexico, Mongolia, Morocco, Mozambique, Nepal, Nicaragua, Niger, Nigeria, Oman, Pakistan, Panama, Papua New Guinea, Paraguay, Peru, Philippines, Poland, Qatar, Romania, Rwanda, Saint Kitts and Nevis, Saint Lucia, Saint Vincent and the Grenadines, Samoa, Sao Tome and Principe, Saudi Arabia, Senegal, Seychelles, Sierra Leone, Singapore, Solomon Islands, Somalia, Sri Lanka, Sudan, Suriname, Swaziland, Syrian Arab Republic, Thai-

land, Togo, Trinidad and Tobago, Tunisia, Uganda, Ukrainian SSR, USSR, United Arab Emirates, United Republic of Tanzania, Uruguay, Vanuatu, Venezuela, Viet Nam, Yemen, Yugoslavia, Zaire, Zambia, Zimbabwe.
Against: United States.
Abstaining: Australia, Austria, Belgium, Canada, Denmark, Finland, France, Germany, Federal Republic of, Iceland, Ireland, Israel, Italy, Japan, Luxembourg, Netherlands, New Zealand, Norway, Portugal, Spain, Sweden, United Kingdom.

International arms transfers

In 1988, the General Assembly, in the context of the strengthening of international peace and security, considered the question of international arms transfers. In its 1978 Final Document,[16] the Assembly had advocated that negotiations should be carried out on the balanced reduction of armed forces and conventional armaments, as well as on the limitation of international transfer of conventional weapons, based on the principle of undiminished security.

GENERAL ASSEMBLY ACTION

On 7 December, on the recommendation of the First Committee, the General Assembly adopted by recorded vote **resolution 43/75 I**.

International arms transfers

The General Assembly,

Reaffirming the central role of the United Nations in strengthening international peace and security and promoting disarmament,

Bearing in mind that, in accordance with the Charter of the United Nations, Member States have undertaken to promote the establishment and maintenance of international peace and security with the least diversion for armaments of the world's human and economic resources,

Also bearing in mind the inherent right to self-defence embodied in Article 51 of the Charter,

Taking into account the general principles outlined in paragraph 22 of the Final Document of the Tenth Special Session of the General Assembly,

Also taking into account the conclusions and recommendations of the United Nations studies entitled *Study on Conventional Disarmament, Study on all the Aspects of Regional Disarmament, Study on the Economic and Social Consequences of the Arms Race and Military Expenditures, The Relationship between Disarmament and Development, Reduction of Military Budgets, Relationship between Disarmament and International Security,* and *Comprehensive Study on Confidence-building Measures,*

Further taking into account the action programme set forth in the Final Document of the International Conference on the Relationship between Disarmament and Development,

1. *Expresses its conviction* that arms transfers in all their aspects deserve serious consideration by the international community, *inter alia,* because of:

(*a*) Their potential effects in areas where tension and regional conflict threaten international peace and security and national security;

(*b*) Their known and potential negative effects on the process of the peaceful social and economic development of all peoples;

(*c*) Increasing illicit and covert arms trafficking;

2. *Requests* Member States to consider, *inter alia,* the following measures relating to these concerns:

(a) Reinforcement of their national systems of control and vigilance concerning production and transport of arms;

(b) Examination of ways and means of refraining from acquiring arms additional to those needed for legitimate national security requirements, taking into account the specific characteristics of each region;

(c) Examination of the ways and means of providing for more openness and transparency with regard to world-wide arms transfers;

3. *Requests* the Disarmament Commission to take into account the above-mentioned matters in its deliberations on the issue of conventional disarmament;

4. *Requests* the Secretary-General to seek the views and proposals of Member States on the matters contained in paragraphs 1 and 2 above and to collect all other relevant information for submission to the General Assembly at its forty-fourth session;

5. *Also requests* the Secretary-General to carry out thereafter, with the assistance of governmental experts, a study on ways and means of promoting transparency in international transfers of conventional arms on a universal and non-discriminatory basis, also taking into consideration the views of Member States as well as other relevant information, including that on the problem of illicit arms trade, for submission to the General Assembly at its forty-sixth session;

6. *Further requests* the Secretary-General to make available, within the framework of the World Disarmament Campaign, information concerning the question of arms transfers and their consequences for international peace and security;

7. *Decides* to include in the provisional agenda of its forty-fourth session an item entitled "International arms transfers".

General Assembly resolution 43/75 I

7 December 1988   Meeting 73   110-1-38 (recorded vote)

Approved by First Committee (A/43/856) by recorded vote (93-0-36), 18 November (meeting 42); 20-nation draft (A/C.1/43/L.22/Rev.2); agenda item 64.

Sponsors: Australia, Bolivia, Cameroon, Canada, Colombia, Costa Rica, El Salvador, Germany, Federal Republic of, Guatemala, Honduras, Italy, Luxembourg, Netherlands, Norway, Paraguay, Peru, Philippines, Samoa, Sweden, United Kingdom.

Financial implications. ACABQ, A/43/7/Add.9; 5th Committee, A/43/938; S-G, A/C.1/43/L.80 & Corr.1, A/C.5/43/49.

Meeting numbers. GA 43rd session: 1st Committee 3-25, 29, 42; 5th Committee 41; plenary 73.

Recorded vote in Assembly as follows:

In favour: Albania, Antigua and Barbuda, Argentina, Australia, Austria, Bahamas, Bangladesh, Barbados, Belgium, Belize, Benin, Bhutan, Bolivia, Botswana, Brunei Darussalam, Bulgaria, Burkina Faso, Burma, Burundi, Byelorussian SSR, Cameroon, Canada, Cape Verde, Central African Republic, Chad, Colombia, Comoros, Congo, Costa Rica, Côte d'Ivoire, Czechoslovakia, Denmark, Dominican Republic, Ecuador, El Salvador, Finland, France, Gabon, Gambia, German Democratic Republic, Germany, Federal Republic of, Ghana, Greece, Guatemala, Guinea, Guyana, Haiti, Honduras, Hungary, Iceland, Indonesia, Ireland, Israel, Italy, Jamaica, Japan, Jordan,* Kenya, Lao People's Democratic Republic, Lesotho, Liberia, Luxembourg, Malaysia, Mali, Malta, Mauritius, Mexico, Mongolia, Nepal, Netherlands, New Zealand, Nicaragua, Niger, Nigeria, Norway, Panama, Paraguay, Peru, Philippines, Poland, Portugal, Romania, Rwanda, Saint Kitts and Nevis, Saint Lucia, Saint Vincent and the Grenadines, Samoa, Senegal, Seychelles, Sierra Leone, Singapore, Somalia, Spain, Sri Lanka, Suriname, Swaziland, Sweden, Thailand, Togo, Trinidad and Tobago, Turkey, Uganda, Ukrainian SSR, USSR, United Kingdom, Uruguay, Vanuatu, Venezuela, Yugoslavia, Zaire.

Against: Djibouti.*

Abstaining: Afghanistan, Algeria, Angola, Bahrain, Brazil, Chile,† China, Cuba, Cyprus, Democratic Yemen, Egypt, Ethiopia, Fiji, India, Iraq, Kuwait, Libyan Arab Jamahiriya, Madagascar, Malawi, Maldives, Mauritania, Morocco, Mozambique, Oman, Pakistan, Papua New Guinea, Saudi Ara-

bia, Solomon Islands, Sudan, Syrian Arab Republic, Tunisia, United Arab Emirates, United Republic of Tanzania, United States, Viet Nam, Yemen, Zambia, Zimbabwe.

*Later advised the Secretariat it had intended to abstain.

†Later advised the Secretariat it had intended to vote in favour.

Scientific and technological developments

In the 1978 Final Document, the General Assembly had stressed the importance of both qualitative and quantitative measures for halting the arms race, including negotiations on the limitation and cessation of qualitative improvement of armaments, especially weapons of mass destruction and the development of new means of warfare, so that scientific and technological achievements might be used solely for peaceful purposes.

GENERAL ASSEMBLY ACTION

On 7 December, on the recommendation of the First Committee, the Assembly adopted **resolution 43/77 A** by recorded vote.

Scientific and technological developments and their impact on international security

The General Assembly,

Recalling that, at its tenth special session, the first special session devoted to disarmament, it unanimously stressed the importance of both qualitative and quantitative measures in the process of disarmament,

Observing that at no stage since the first special session devoted to disarmament has the qualitative aspect of the arms race been seriously addressed by the international community,

Noting with concern the existing potential in technological advances for application to military purposes, thus escalating the level and sophistication of armaments,

Recognizing that such a development will have a negative impact on the security environment while causing a major setback to disarmament efforts,

Stressing, in this context, the importance of effectively addressing this problem and ensuring that scientific and technological developments are not exploited for military purposes but harnessed for the common benefit of mankind,

Emphasizing that the proposal contained in the present resolution is without prejudice to research and development efforts being undertaken for peaceful purposes,

Recognizing the interests of the international community in the subject and the need to follow closely such developments,

1. *Requests* the Secretary-General to follow future scientific and technological developments, especially those which have potential military applications, and to evaluate their impact on international security, with the assistance of qualified consultant experts, as appropriate, and to submit a report to the General Assembly at its forty-fifth session;

2. *Invites* Member States to establish panels at the national level to monitor and evaluate such developments and disseminate the assessments provided by the Secretary-General;

3. *Also invites* all Member States to communicate to the Secretary-General their views and proposals as well as the evaluations of the national panels;

4. *Requests* the Secretary-General to submit to the General Assembly at its forty-fourth session a report on the implementation of the present resolution;

5. *Decides* to include in the provisional agenda of its forty-fourth session an item entitled "Scientific and technological developments and their impact on international security".

General Assembly resolution 43/77 A

7 December 1988   Meeting 73   129-7-14 (recorded vote)

Approved by First Committee (A/43/858) by recorded vote (109-7-14), 17 November (meeting 41); 8-nation draft (A/C.1/43/L.54/Rev.1); agenda item 66.

Sponsors: Byelorussian SSR, Hungary, India, Indonesia, Poland, Romania, Sri Lanka, Venezuela.

Financial implications. ACABQ, A/43/7/Add.9; 5th Committee, A/43/938; S-G, A/C.1/43/L.77, A/C.5/43/47.

Meeting numbers. GA 43rd session: 1st Committee 3-25, 30, 41; 5th Committee 41; plenary 73.

Recorded vote in Assembly as follows:

In favour: Afghanistan, Algeria, Angola, Antigua and Barbuda, Argentina, Australia, Austria, Bahamas, Bahrain, Bangladesh, Barbados, Belize, Benin, Bhutan, Bolivia, Botswana, Brazil, Bulgaria, Burkina Faso, Burma, Burundi, Byelorussian SSR, Cameroon, Cape Verde, Central African Republic, Chad, Chile, China, Colombia, Comoros, Congo, Costa Rica, Côte d'Ivoire, Cuba, Cyprus, Czechoslovakia, Democratic Kampuchea, Democratic Yemen, Djibouti, Dominican Republic, Ecuador, Egypt, El Salvador, Ethiopia, Fiji, Finland, Gabon, Gambia, German Democratic Republic, Ghana, Guatemala, Guinea, Guyana, Haiti, Honduras, Hungary, India, Indonesia, Iran, Iraq, Ireland, Jamaica, Jordan, Kenya, Kuwait, Lao People's Democratic Republic, Lebanon, Lesotho, Liberia, Libyan Arab Jamahiriya, Madagascar, Malawi, Maldives, Mali, Malta, Mauritania, Mauritius, Mexico, Mongolia, Morocco, Mozambique, Nepal, Nicaragua, Niger, Nigeria, Oman, Pakistan, Panama, Papua New Guinea, Paraguay, Peru, Poland, Qatar, Romania, Rwanda, Saint Kitts and Nevis, Saint Lucia, Saint Vincent and the Grenadines, Samoa, Sao Tome and Principe, Saudi Arabia, Senegal, Seychelles, Sierra Leone, Solomon Islands, Somalia, Sri Lanka, Sudan, Suriname, Swaziland, Sweden, Syrian Arab Republic, Togo, Trinidad and Tobago, Tunisia, Uganda, Ukrainian SSR, USSR, United Arab Emirates, United Republic of Tanzania, Uruguay, Vanuatu, Venezuela, Viet Nam, Yemen, Yugoslavia, Zaire, Zambia, Zimbabwe.

Against: France, Germany, Federal Republic of, Israel, Italy, Spain, United Kingdom, United States.

Abstaining: Belgium, Canada, Denmark, Greece, Iceland, Japan, Luxembourg, Malaysia, Netherlands, New Zealand, Norway, Portugal, Singapore, Turkey.

Fellowship, training and advisory services programme

In October 1988,[19] the Secretary-General submitted to the General Assembly a report on the United Nations disarmament fellowship, training and advisory services programme, stating that 25 fellows had been selected to participate in 1988. The programme, comprising lectures, seminars and research projects on disarmament and security matters, began on 15 July at Geneva and ended in New York on 23 November. In the course of their work, the fellows visited IAEA headquarters at Vienna and, at the invitation of the States concerned, offices and institutions in the Federal Republic of Germany, Hungary, Japan, Sweden, the USSR and the United States.

The report described the implementation in 1988 of the regional disarmament programme, which was intended to assist Governments through the organization of training courses at the regional and subregional levels, and the implementation of disarmament advisory services, which aimed to further international co-operation, especially among developing countries, to contribute to disarmament efforts.

GENERAL ASSEMBLY ACTION

On 7 December, on the recommendation of First Committee, the General Assembly, adopted **resolution 43/76 F** without vote.

United Nations disarmament fellowship, training and advisory services programme

The General Assembly,

Recalling its decision, contained in paragraph 108 of the Final Document of the Tenth Special Session of the General Assembly, the first special session devoted to disarmament, to establish a programme of fellowships on disarmament, as well as its decisions contained in annex IV to the Concluding Document of the Twelfth Special Session of the General Assembly, the second special session devoted to disarmament, in which it decided, *inter alia*, to continue the programme and to increase the number of fellowships from twenty to twenty-five as from 1983,

Noting with satisfaction that the programme has already trained an appreciable number of public officials selected from geographical regions represented in the United Nations system, most of whom are now in positions of responsibility in the field of disarmament affairs in their respective countries or Governments,

Recalling its resolutions 37/100 G of 13 December 1982, 38/73 C of 15 December 1983, 39/63 B of 12 December 1984, 40/151 H of 16 December 1985, 41/60 H of 3 December 1986 and 42/39 I of 30 November 1987,

Noting with satisfaction that the programme, as designed, has enabled an increased number of public officials, particularly from the developing countries, to acquire more expertise in the sphere of disarmament,

Believing that the forms of assistance available to Member States, particularly to developing countries, under the programme will enhance the capabilities of their officials to follow ongoing deliberations and negotiations on disarmament, both bilateral and multilateral,

1. *Reaffirms* its decisions contained in annex IV to the Concluding Document of the Twelfth Special Session of the General Assembly and the report of the Secretary-General approved by resolution 33/71 E of 14 December 1978;

2. *Expresses its appreciation* to the Governments of the Federal Republic of Germany, Hungary, Japan, Sweden, the Union of Soviet Socialist Republics and the United States of America for inviting the 1988 fellows to study selected activities in the field of disarmament, thereby contributing to the fulfilment of the overall objectives of the programme;

3. *Commends* the Secretary-General for the diligence with which the programme has continued to be carried out;

4. *Requests* the Secretary-General to continue the implementation of the programme within existing resources;

5. *Also requests* the Secretary-General to report to the General Assembly at its forty-fourth session on the implementation of the programme.

General Assembly resolution 43/76 F

7 December 1988   Meeting 73   Adopted without vote

Approved by First Committee (A/43/857) without vote, 14 November (meeting 35); 21-nation draft (A/C.1/43/L.64); agenda item 65 (g).

Sponsors: Algeria, Argentina, Djibouti, Ethiopia, German Democratic Republic, Ghana, Greece, Hungary, Indonesia, Kenya, Liberia, Mauritania, Morocco,

New Zealand, Nigeria, Philippines, Sierra Leone, Sri Lanka, Venezuela, Viet Nam, Zaire.
Meeting numbers. GA 43rd session: 1st Committee 3-25, 31, 35; plenary 73.

International co-operation for disarmament

On 7 December, on the recommendation of the First Committee, the General Assembly adopted **resolution 43/78 C** by recorded vote.

International co-operation for disarmament

The General Assembly,

Reaffirming the importance of achieving international co-operation in the field of arms limitation and disarmament,

Taking into account that since its forty-second session there have been important and encouraging developments in the areas of arms limitation and disarmament,

Stressing that disarmament can only be achieved through active and sustained joint efforts of all States,

Stressing also the vital importance of proceeding to balanced, mutually acceptable, fully verifiable and effective measures of arms limitation and disarmament, in accordance with established priorities, for the preservation of peace and the strengthening of international security,

Stressing further that the necessary balance between bilateral and multilateral approaches to arms limitation and disarmament should be secured through a significantly enhanced role of the United Nations and its respective bodies in this field,

1. *Invites* all States further to increase co-operation for achieving effective arms limitation and disarmament agreements on the basis of reciprocity, equality, undiminished security, non-use of force and the rule of law in international relations;

2. *Calls upon* all States to aim at strengthening the effectiveness of the United Nations in fulfilling its central role and primary responsibility in the sphere of disarmament and to contribute actively to the consideration and resolution of all disarmament issues that have a bearing on their security and other fundamental interests;

3. *Also invites* all States to consider, in a spirit of co-operation, ways and means to facilitate both bilateral and multilateral solutions to disarmament.

General Assembly resolution 43/78 C

7 December 1988　　Meeting 73　　136-1-13 (recorded vote)

Approved by First Committee (A/43/859) by recorded vote (116-1-13), 16 November (meeting 39); draft by Czechoslovakia (A/C.1/43/L.16/Rev.1); agenda item 67.

Meeting numbers. GA 43rd session: 1st Committee 3-25, 35, 39; plenary 73.

Recorded vote in Assembly as follows

In favour: Afghanistan, Algeria, Angola, Antigua and Barbuda, Argentina, Australia, Austria, Bahamas, Bahrain, Bangladesh, Barbados, Belize, Benin, Bhutan, Bolivia, Botswana, Brazil, Brunei Darussalam, Bulgaria, Burkina Faso, Burma, Burundi, Byelorussian SSR, Cameroon, Cape Verde, Central African Republic, Chad, Chile, Colombia, Comoros, Congo, Costa Rica, Côte d'Ivoire, Cuba, Cyprus, Czechoslovakia, Democratic Yemen, Denmark, Djibouti, Dominican Republic, Ecuador, Egypt, El Salvador, Ethiopia, Fiji, Finland, Gabon, Gambia, German Democratic Republic, Ghana, Greece, Guatemala, Guinea, Guyana, Haiti, Honduras, Hungary, Iceland, India, Indonesia, Iran, Iraq, Ireland, Jamaica, Japan, Jordan, Kenya, Kuwait, Lao People's Democratic Republic, Lebanon, Lesotho, Liberia, Libyan Arab Jamahiriya, Madagascar, Malawi, Malaysia, Maldives, Mali, Mauritania, Mauritius, Mexico, Mongolia, Morocco, Mozambique, Nepal, New Zealand, Nicaragua, Niger, Nigeria, Norway, Oman, Pakistan, Panama, Papua New Guinea, Paraguay, Peru, Philippines, Poland, Qatar, Romania, Rwanda, Saint Kitts and Nevis, Saint Lucia, Saint Vincent and the Grenadines, Samoa, Sao Tome and Principe, Saudi Arabia, Senegal, Seychelles, Sierra Leone, Solomon Islands, Somalia, Sri Lanka, Sudan, Suriname, Swaziland,

Sweden, Syrian Arab Republic, Thailand, Togo, Trinidad and Tobago, Tunisia, Uganda, Ukrainian SSR, USSR, United Arab Emirates, United Republic of Tanzania, Uruguay, Vanuatu, Venezuela, Viet Nam, Yemen, Yugoslavia, Zaire, Zambia, Zimbabwe.

Against: United States.

Abstaining: Belgium, Canada, France, Germany, Federal Republic of, Israel, Italy, Luxembourg, Malta, Netherlands, Portugal, Spain, Turkey, United Kingdom.

Confidence-building measures

In 1986,[20] the Disarmament Commission had provisionally approved guidelines for confidence-building measures and for their global or regional implementation.

In response to a 1987 Assembly request,[21] the Commission, on 2 May 1988, established a consultation group to finalize the draft guidelines. The group held six meetings between 5 and 18 May. It considered the three outstanding paragraphs contained in an annex to the 1986 report of the Commission and adopted a compromise text which it recommended to the Commission. On 19 May, the Commission adopted by consensus the report of the consultation group and the recommendations contained therein, which formed part of its own report to the Assembly at its third special session.[2]

GENERAL ASSEMBLY ACTION

On 7 December, on the recommendation of the First Committee, the General Assembly adopted **resolution 43/78 H** without vote.

Guidelines for confidence-building measures

The General Assembly,

Recalling its resolution 42/39 F, adopted without a vote on 30 November 1987,

Taking note of the report of the Disarmament Commission containing the agreed text of the guidelines for appropriate types of confidence-building measures and for the implementation of such measures on a global or regional level,

Appreciative of the work accomplished by the Disarmament Commission in finalizing the text of these guidelines,

Reaffirming its conviction that confidence-building measures, especially when applied in a comprehensive manner, have a potential to contribute significantly to the enhancement of peace and security and to promote and facilitate the attainment of disarmament measures,

Mindful of the fact that confidence-building measures, while neither a substitute nor a pre-condition for arms limitation and disarmament measures, can be conducive to achieving progress in disarmament,

Realizing that effective disarmament and arms limitation measures which directly limit or reduce military potential have particularly high confidence-building value,

Appealing to all States to consider the widest possible use of confidence-building measures in their international relations,

Aware that there are situations peculiar to specific regions which have a bearing on the nature of the confidence-building measures feasible in those regions,

Noting with satisfaction the encouraging results of specific confidence-building measures agreed upon and implemented in some regions,

Pointing to the example of progress in the implementation of confidence- and security-building measures adopted at Stockholm in 1986 that has contributed to more stable relations and increased security, reducing the risk of military confrontation in Europe,

1. *Endorses* the guidelines for appropriate types of confidence-building measures and for the implementation of such measures on a global or regional level, as adopted by consensus by the Disarmament Commission at its 1988 substantive session;

2. *Recommends* these guidelines to all States for implementation, fully taking into account the specific political, military and other conditions prevailing in a region, on the basis of initiatives and with the agreement of the States of the region concerned;

3. *Requests* the Secretary-General to submit a report to the General Assembly at its forty-fifth session on the implementation of these guidelines on the basis of national reports on accumulated relevant experience;

4. *Decides* to include in the provisional agenda of its forty-fifth session an item entitled ''Implementation of the guidelines for appropriate types of confidence-building measures''.

General Assembly resolution 43/78 H

7 December 1988   Meeting 73   Adopted without vote

Approved by First Committee (A/43/859) without vote, 15 November (meeting 38); 23-nation draft (A/C.1/43/L.49), orally revised; agenda item 67.
Sponsors: Australia, Austria, Bahamas, Belgium, Byelorussian SSR, Cameroon, Canada, Costa Rica, Denmark, Finland, German Democratic Republic, Germany, Federal Republic of, Greece, Hungary, Italy, Luxembourg, Netherlands, Norway, Poland, Portugal, Spain, Sweden, United Kingdom.
Meeting numbers. GA 43rd session: 1st Committee 3-25, 32, 38; plenary 73.

Implementation of the Declaration of the 1980s as the Second Disarmament Decade

In 1980, the General Assembly had declared the 1980s as the Second Disarmament Decade.[22] In its review and appraisal of that Declaration in 1985, the Assembly, on the recommendation of the Disarmament Commission, had requested the Secretary-General to report annually on the implementation of the Declaration.[23]

In an August 1988 report and later addendum,[24] the Secretary-General reported that, pursuant to the Assembly's request, he had received information from Bulgaria, the Byelorussian SSR, Cuba, Ghana and the USSR, which reflected their continuing commitment to the objectives of the 1980 Declaration.

Declaration of the 1990s as the Third Disarmament Decade

On 7 December, the General Assembly, on the recommendation of the First Committee, adopted **resolution 43/78 L** without vote.

Consideration of the declaration of the 1990s as the Third Disarmament Decade

The General Assembly,

Recalling its resolution 35/46 of 3 December 1980, in which it declared the 1980s as the Second Disarmament Decade,

Recalling also its resolution 34/75 of 11 December 1979, in which it directed the Disarmament Commission to prepare elements of a draft resolution entitled ''Declaration of the 1980s as the Second Disarmament Decade'' for submission to the General Assembly at its thirty-fifth session for consideration and adoption,

Bearing in mind that the Second Disarmament Decade declared by its resolution 35/46 is coming to an end,

Reaffirming the responsibility of the United Nations in the attainment of disarmament,

Noting the progress in the disarmament talks between the Union of Soviet Socialist Republics and the United States of America and its positive impact on the attainment of global peace and security,

Desirous of maintaining the current momentum in the disarmament process,

Convinced that a third disarmament decade will accelerate the disarmament process,

1. *Decides* to declare the decade of the 1990s as the Third Disarmament Decade;

2. *Directs* the Disarmament Commission, at its 1989 substantive session, to prepare elements of a draft resolution to be entitled ''Declaration of the 1990s as the Third Disarmament Decade'' and to submit them to the General Assembly at its forty-fourth session for consideration and adoption;

3. *Requests* the Secretary-General to seek the views and suggestions of Member States and of relevant specialized agencies and the International Atomic Energy Agency on the possible elements to be included in the Declaration of the 1990s as the Third Disarmament Decade and to make these available to the Disarmament Commission at its 1989 substantive session;

4. *Also requests* the Secretary-General to render all necessary assistance to the Disarmament Commission in implementing the present resolution;

5. *Decides* to include in the provisional agenda of its forty-fourth session an item entitled ''Declaration of the 1990s as the Third Disarmament Decade''.

General Assembly resolution 43/78 L

7 December 1988   Meeting 73   Adopted without vote

Approved by First Committee (A/43/859) without vote, 10 November (meeting 33); 8-nation draft (A/C.1/43/L.63); agenda item 67.
Sponsors: Argentina, Ethiopia, German Democratic Republic, Indonesia, Nigeria, Poland, Thailand, Zaire.
Meeting numbers. GA 43rd session: 1st Committee 3-25, 31, 33; plenary 73.

General and complete disarmament

Under the subject of general and complete disarmament, the General Assembly discussed the issues of information on military matters, disarmament and development, naval armaments and disarmament, and a review conference of the parties to the Treaty on the Prohibition of the Emplacement of Nuclear Weapons and Other Weapons of Mass Destruction on the Sea-Bed and the Ocean Floor and in the Subsoil Thereof.

Information on military matters

In response to a 1987 General Assembly request,[25] the Secretary-General issued a report in May 1988, with subsequent addenda,[26] for consideration at the fifteenth special session of the Assembly, containing the views of the Byelorussian SSR, the German Democratic Republic, the Federal Republic of Germany (on behalf of the member States of the European Community), Hungary, Poland and the United States on ways of ensuring confidence and furthering openness and transparency in military matters.

The report also supplied information on the question of the international system for standardized reporting of military expenditures, implementation of which had been recommended by the Assembly in 1987[25] and which was aimed at achieving a realistic comparison of military budgets. Of the 24 States reporting on their military expenditures in 1987, 22 had used the reporting system.

GENERAL ASSEMBLY ACTION

On 7 December 1988, on the recommendation of the First Committee, the General Assembly adopted **resolution 43/75 G** by recorded vote.

Objective information on military matters

The General Assembly,

Recalling paragraph 105 of the Final Document of the Tenth Special Session of the General Assembly, the first special session devoted to disarmament, in which the Assembly encouraged Member States to ensure a better flow of information with regard to the various aspects of disarmament to avoid dissemination of false and tendentious information concerning armaments and to concentrate on the danger of escalation of the arms race and on the need for general and complete disarmament under effective international control,

Taking into account the attention paid to the questions of openness and of ensuring an exchange of objective information in the military field at its fifteenth special session, the third special session devoted to disarmament,

Noting with satisfaction that recent agreements in the field of arms limitation and disarmament have provided for qualitatively new standards of openness,

Believing that the adoption of confidence-building measures to promote openness and transparency would contribute to the prevention of misperceptions of military capabilities and intentions which would induce States to undertake armaments programmes leading to the acceleration of the arms race, in particular the nuclear-arms race, and to heightened international tensions,

Believing also that balanced and objective information on all military matters, in particular of nuclear-weapon States and other militarily significant States, would contribute to the building of confidence among States and to the conclusion of concrete disarmament agreements, and thereby help to halt and reverse the arms race,

Recognizing that greater openness and transparency would contribute to enhancing security,

Convinced that greater openness on military activities, *inter alia*, through transmittal of relevant information on these activities, including on the levels of military budgets, would contribute to increased confidence among States,

Taking into account the work undertaken in the Disarmament Commission on the reduction of military budgets,

Noting with satisfaction that an increased number of States have provided annual reports on military expenditures in conformity with the international system for the standardized reporting of military expenditures under the auspices of the United Nations,

1. *Takes note* of the report of the Secretary-General on this subject to the third special session of the General Assembly devoted to disarmament;

2. *Reaffirms its firm conviction* that a better flow of objective information on military capabilities would help relieve international tension and contribute to the building of confidence among States on a global, regional or subregional level and to the conclusion of concrete disarmament agreements;

3. *Recommends* that those States and global, regional and subregional organizations which have already expressed support for the principle of practical and concrete confidence-building measures of a military nature on a global, regional or subregional level should intensify their efforts with a view to adopting such measures;

4. *Recommends* that all States, in particular nuclear-weapon States and other militarily significant States, should implement the international system for the standardized reporting of military expenditures, with the aim of achieving a realistic comparison of military budgets, facilitating the availability of objective information on, as well as objective assessment of, military capabilities and contributing to the process of disarmament;

5. *Invites* all Member States to communicate to the Secretary-General before 30 April 1989 measures they have adopted towards these ends, for submission to the General Assembly at its forty-fourth session;

6. *Also invites* all Member States also to communicate to the Secretary-General their views on ways and means of further consolidating the emerging trend towards greater openness in military matters, specifically with regard to the provisions of objective information on military matters, for consideration by the Disarmament Commission at its 1990 session;

7. *Decides* to include in the provisional agenda of its forty-fourth session the item entitled ''Objective information on military matters''.

General Assembly resolution 43/75 G

7 December 1988   Meeting 73   130-0-10 (recorded vote)

Approved by First Committee (A/43/856) by recorded vote (109-0-9), 17 November (meeting 40); 31-nation draft (A/C.1/43/L.19/Rev.2); agenda item 64 *(f)*.

Sponsors: Australia, Belgium, Botswana, Bulgaria, Canada, Czechoslovakia, Denmark, France, German Democratic Republic, Germany, Federal Republic of, Greece, Hungary, Iceland, Italy, Japan, Netherlands, New Zealand, Norway, Philippines, Poland, Portugal, Romania, Samoa, Spain, Swaziland, Sweden, Thailand, Turkey, USSR, United Kingdom, United States.

Meeting numbers. GA 43rd session: 1st Committee 3-25, 31, 40; plenary 73.

Recorded vote in Assembly as follows:

In favour: Afghanistan, Antigua and Barbuda, Argentina, Australia, Austria, Bahamas, Bangladesh, Barbados, Belgium, Belize, Benin, Bhutan, Bolivia, Botswana, Brunei Darussalam, Bulgaria, Burkina Faso, Burma, Burundi, Byelorussian SSR, Cameroon, Canada, Cape Verde, Central African Republic, Chad, Chile, Colombia, Comoros, Congo, Costa Rica, Côte d'Ivoire, Cyprus, Czechoslovakia, Democratic Kampuchea, Denmark, Djibouti, Dominican Republic, Ecuador, El Salvador, Fiji, Finland, France, Gabon, Gambia, German Democratic Republic, Germany, Federal Republic of, Ghana, Greece, Guatemala, Guinea, Guyana, Haiti, Honduras, Hungary, Iceland, India, Indonesia, Iran, Ireland, Israel, Italy, Jamaica, Japan, Kenya, Lao People's Democratic Republic, Lesotho, Liberia, Madagascar, Malawi, Malaysia, Maldives, Mali, Malta, Mauritius, Mexico, Mongolia, Mozambique, Nepal, Netherlands, New Zealand, Nicaragua, Niger, Nigeria, Norway, Pakistan, Panama, Papua New Guinea, Paraguay, Peru, Philippines, Poland, Portugal, Qatar, Romania, Rwanda, Saint Kitts and Nevis, Saint

Lucia, Saint Vincent and the Grenadines, Samoa, Sao Tome and Principe, Senegal, Seychelles, Sierra Leone, Singapore, Solomon Islands, Somalia, Spain, Sri Lanka, Sudan, Suriname, Swaziland, Sweden, Thailand, Togo, Trinidad and Tobago, Turkey, Uganda, Ukrainian SSR, USSR, United Kingdom, United Republic of Tanzania, United States, Uruguay, Vanuatu, Venezuela, Viet Nam, Yugoslavia, Zaire, Zambia, Zimbabwe.

Against: None.

Abstaining: Algeria, Bahrain, Brazil, Cuba, Egypt, Iraq, Jordan, Libyan Arab Jamahiriya, Saudi Arabia, United Arab Emirates.

Naval armaments and disarmament

In 1988, the Disarmament Commission continued consideration of naval armaments and disarmament, on the basis of the 1985 study on the naval arms race,[27] the 1987 Chairman's paper on the topic,[28] and working papers submitted by delegations in 1987 and 1988.

As in 1987, the Chairman of the Commission entrusted a group with substantive open-ended consultations on the topic. Eight meetings were held on various aspects of the question, including the possibility of measures of naval arms limitation and disarmament and the desirability of applying confidence-building measures at sea, resulting in a number of substantive findings and recommendations. These were incorporated into a working paper by the Chairman[29] to form the basis for further discussion of the subject at the third special session devoted to disarmament.

On 19 May, the Commission adopted the report of the Chairman, which was incorporated into its own report to the special session.[2]

GENERAL ASSEMBLY ACTION

On 7 December, the General Assembly, on the recommendation of the First Committee, adopted **resolution 43/75 L** by recorded vote.

Naval armaments and disarmament

The General Assembly,

Recalling its resolution 38/188 G of 20 December 1983, by which it requested the Secretary-General, with the assistance of qualified governmental experts, to carry out a comprehensive study on the naval arms race,

Recalling also its resolution 40/94 F of 12 December 1985, by which it requested the Disarmament Commission to consider the issues contained in the study entitled *The Naval Arms Race*, both its substantive content and its conclusions, taking into account all other relevant present and future proposals, with a view to facilitating the identification of possible measures in the field of naval arms reductions and disarmament, pursued within the framework of progress towards general and complete disarmament, as well as confidence-building measures in this field,

Recalling further its resolution 42/38 K of 30 November 1987, by which it requested the Disarmament Commission to continue, at its 1988 session, the substantive consideration of the question and to report on its deliberations and recommendations to the General Assembly not later than at its forty-third session,

Having examined the report of the Chairman of the Disarmament Commission on the substantive consideration of the question of the naval arms race and disarmament during the 1988 session of the Commission, which met with the approval of all delegations participating

in the substantive consultations and which, in their view, should be discussed at the forty-third session of the General Assembly,

1. *Takes note with satisfaction* of the report on the substantive consideration of the question of the naval arms race and disarmament by the Chairman of the Disarmament Commission;

2. *Requests* the Disarmament Commission to continue, at its forthcoming session in 1989, the substantive consideration of the question and to report on its deliberations and recommendations to the General Assembly at its forty-fourth session;

3. *Also requests* the Disarmament Commission to inscribe on the agenda for its 1989 session the item entitled "Naval armaments and disarmament";

4. *Decides* to include in the provisional agenda of its forty-fourth session the item entitled "Naval armaments and disarmament".

General Assembly resolution 43/75 L

7 December 1988   Meeting 73   152-1-1 (recorded vote)

Approved by First Committee (A/43/856) by recorded vote (134-1), 16 November (meeting 39); 14-nation draft (A/C.1/43/L.37); agenda item 64 *(h)*.

Sponsors: Australia, Austria, Bulgaria, China, Finland, France, German Democratic Republic, Iceland, Indonesia, Malaysia, Mexico, Sri Lanka, Sweden, Yugoslavia.

Meeting numbers. GA 43rd session: 1st Committee 3-25, 29, 39; plenary 73.

Recorded vote in Assembly as follows:

In favour: Afghanistan, Albania, Algeria, Angola, Antigua and Barbuda, Argentina, Australia, Austria, Bahamas, Bahrain, Bangladesh, Barbados, Belgium, Belize, Benin, Bhutan, Bolivia, Botswana, Brazil, Brunei Darussalam, Bulgaria, Burkina Faso, Burma, Burundi, Byelorussian SSR, Cameroon, Canada, Cape Verde, Central African Republic, Chad, Chile, China, Colombia, Comoros, Congo, Costa Rica, Côte d'Ivoire, Cuba, Cyprus, Czechoslovakia, Democratic Kampuchea, Democratic Yemen, Denmark, Djibouti, Dominican Republic, Ecuador, Egypt, El Salvador, Ethiopia, Fiji, Finland, France, Gabon, Gambia, German Democratic Republic, Germany, Federal Republic of, Ghana, Greece, Guatemala, Guinea, Guyana, Haiti, Honduras, Hungary, Iceland, India, Indonesia, Iran, Iraq, Ireland, Italy, Jamaica, Japan, Jordan, Kenya, Kuwait, Lao People's Democratic Republic, Lebanon, Lesotho, Liberia, Libyan Arab Jamahiriya, Luxembourg, Madagascar, Malawi, Malaysia, Maldives, Mali, Malta, Mauritania, Mauritius, Mexico, Mongolia, Morocco, Mozambique, Nepal, Netherlands, New Zealand, Nicaragua, Niger, Nigeria, Norway, Oman, Pakistan, Panama, Papua New Guinea, Paraguay, Peru, Philippines, Poland, Portugal, Qatar, Romania, Rwanda, Saint Kitts and Nevis, Saint Lucia, Saint Vincent and the Grenadines, Samoa, Sao Tome and Principe, Saudi Arabia, Senegal, Seychelles, Sierra Leone, Singapore, Solomon Islands, Somalia, Spain, Sri Lanka, Sudan, Suriname, Swaziland, Sweden, Syrian Arab Republic, Thailand, Togo, Trinidad and Tobago, Tunisia, Turkey, Uganda, Ukrainian SSR, USSR, United Arab Emirates, United Kingdom, United Republic of Tanzania, Uruguay, Vanuatu, Venezuela, Viet Nam, Yemen, Yugoslavia, Zaire, Zambia, Zimbabwe.

Against: United States.

Abstaining: Israel.*

*Later advised the Secretariat it had intended to vote in favour.

Disarmament and development

The 1987 International Conference on the Relationship between Disarmament and Development[30] had adopted a Final Document, which the General Assembly welcomed and decided should be considered by the third special session on disarmament.[31] The Assembly also requested the Secretary-General to take appropriate action to implement the action programme adopted by the Conference.

GENERAL ASSEMBLY ACTION

On 7 December 1988, on the recommendation of the First Committee, the General Assembly adopted **resolution 43/75 B** without vote.

Relationship between disarmament and development

The General Assembly,

Recalling the provisions of the Final Document of the Tenth Special Session of the General Assembly related to the relationship between disarmament and development,

Recalling also the adoption on 11 September 1987 of the Final Document of the International Conference on the Relationship between Disarmament and Development,

1. *Requests* the Secretary-General to take action through the appropriate organs, within available resources, for the implementation of the action programme adopted at the International Conference on the Relationship between Disarmament and Development, and to submit a report to the General Assembly at its forty-fourth session;

2. *Decides* to include in the provisional agenda of its forty-fourth session an item entitled "Relationship between disarmament and development".

General Assembly resolution 43/75 B

7 December 1988   Meeting 73   Adopted without vote

Approved by First Committee (A/43/856) without vote, 10 November (meeting 33); draft by German Democratic Republic, Romania, Zimbabwe, for non-aligned States (A/C.1/43/L.8/Rev.1); agenda item 64.
Meeting numbers. GA 43rd session: 1st Committee 3-25, 32, 33; plenary 73.

Review conference of sea-bed Treaty

The first and second review conferences of the parties to the Treaty on the Prohibition of the Emplacement of Nuclear Weapons and Other Weapons of Mass Destruction on the Sea-Bed and the Ocean Floor in the Subsoil Thereof[32] were held in 1977[33] and 1983.[34] The Second Conference, in its Final Declaration, had decided that a third review conference should be held not earlier than 1988 and not later than 1990.

GENERAL ASSEMBLY ACTION

On 7 December 1988, on the recommendation of the First Committee, the General Assembly adopted **resolution 43/75 M** without vote.

Review Conference of the Parties to the Treaty on the Prohibition of the Emplacement of Nuclear Weapons and Other Weapons of Mass Destruction on the Sea-Bed and the Ocean Floor and in the Subsoil Thereof

The General Assembly,

Recalling its resolution 2660(XXV) of 7 December 1970, in which it commended the Treaty on the Prohibition of the Emplacement of Nuclear Weapons and Other Weapons of Mass Destruction on the Sea-Bed and the Ocean Floor and in the Subsoil Thereof,

Bearing in mind the provisions of article VII of that Treaty concerning the holding of review conferences,

Also bearing in mind that, in its Final Declaration, the Second Review Conference of the Parties to the Treaty on the Prohibition of the Emplacement of Nuclear Weapons and Other Weapons of Mass Destruction on the Sea-Bed and the Ocean Floor and in the Subsoil Thereof, held at Geneva from 12 to 23 September 1983, decided that a third review conference should be held at Geneva at the request of a majority of States parties not earlier than 1988 and not later than 1990,

Recalling also its resolution 38/188 B of 20 December 1983, in which it made an assessment of the outcome of the Second Review Conference,

Bearing in mind also all the relevant paragraphs of the Final Document of the Tenth Special Session of the General Assembly,

1. *Notes* that, following appropriate consultations, a preparatory committee for the Third Review Conference of the Parties to the Treaty on the Prohibition of the Emplacement of Nuclear Weapons and Other Weapons of Mass Destruction on the Sea-Bed and the Ocean Floor and in the Subsoil Thereof is to be established prior to holding a further review conference in 1989;

2. *Requests* the Secretary-General to render the necessary assistance and to provide such services, including summary records, as may be required for the Review Conference and its preparation;

3. *Recalls* its expressed hope for the widest possible adherence to the Treaty.

General Assembly resolution 43/75 M

7 December 1988   Meeting 73   Adopted without vote

Approved by First Committee (A/43/856) without vote, 10 November (meeting 33); 46-nation draft (A/C.1/43/L.39); agenda item 64.
Sponsors: Argentina, Australia, Austria, Belgium, Botswana, Brazil, Bulgaria, Byelorussian SSR, Canada, Czechoslovakia, Denmark, Dominican Republic, Ecuador, Finland, German Democratic Republic, Ghana, Greece, Guinea-Bissau, Hungary, Iceland, India, Iran, Iraq, Ireland, Italy, Japan, Jordan, Malaysia, Malta, Mexico, Mongolia, Nepal, New Zealand, Norway, Poland, Portugal, Romania, Spain, Sweden, Ukrainian SSR, USSR, United Kingdom, United States, Viet Nam, Yugoslavia, Zambia.
Meeting numbers. GA 43rd session: 1st Committee 3-26, 33; plenary 73.

Comprehensive programme of disarmament

A comprehensive programme of disarmament, as envisaged in the Final Document[16] of the General Assembly's first special session on disarmament in 1978, had been considered annually since 1980 by the Assembly. In 1988, the Conference on Disarmament was unable to reconcile all differences and complete the draft programme.

Consideration by the Conference on Disarmament. The Conference on Disarmament continued consideration of a draft comprehensive programme of disarmament between 4 and 8 April and between 29 August and 2 September, in accordance with a 1987 Assembly request[35] that it resolve outstanding issues and conclude negotiations on a programme in time for submission to the third special session on disarmament.

The *Ad Hoc* Committee of the Conference, in April, made some progress, but the report of the Conference to the special session[56] reflected points of difference remaining on a number of issues.

The Committee met again between 28 July and 1 September with a view to submitting the comprehensive programme to the Assembly at its 1988 regular session. It also considered a new proposal by Peru relating to the establishment of a zone of peace and co-operation in the South Pacific.[37] Although further progress was made in harmonizing positions and narrowing areas of disagreement, the Committee was unable to complete elaboration of the programme and agreed to consider it again in 1989.

GENERAL ASSEMBLY ACTION

On 7 December, on the recommendation of the First Committee, the General Assembly adopted **resolution 43/78 K** without vote.

Comprehensive programme of disarmament

The General Assembly,

Recalling its resolution 42/42 I of 30 November 1987, in which it urged the Conference on Disarmament to resume the work on the elaboration of the comprehensive programme of disarmament at the outset of its 1988 session with a view to resolving outstanding issues and concluding negotiations on the programme,

Having examined the report of the *Ad Hoc* Committee on the Comprehensive Programme of Disarmament concerning its work during the 1988 session of the Conference on Disarmament, which is an integral part of the report of the Conference, and noting the agreement of the *Ad Hoc* Committee that it should resume its work at the outset of the 1989 session of the Conference with the firm intention of completing the elaboration of the programme for its submission to the General Assembly, at the latest at its forty-fourth session,

Decides to include in the provisional agenda of its forty-fourth session the item entitled "Comprehensive programme of disarmament".

General Assembly resolution 43/78 K

7 December 1988   Meeting 73   Adopted without vote

Approved by First Committee (A/43/859) without vote, 10 November (meeting 33); draft by Mexico (A/C.1/43/L.60); agenda item 67.

Meeting numbers. GA 43rd session: 1st Committee 3-25, 31, 33; plenary 73.

Verification

The Disarmament Commission, pursuant to a 1987 request of the General Assembly,[38] continued consideration of the item on verification in all its aspects in Working Group IV, which held eight meetings between 5 and 18 May 1988. The Group had before it information from 13 Member States in response to the 1987 Assembly resolution,[39] a working paper by the Chairman[40] and another by Canada.[41] The Group considered a number of suggestions for possible recommendations in three major areas of the subject, namely, principles, provisions and techniques, and the role of the United Nations and its Members in the field of verification. It reached agreement on those areas and adopted a text[2] by consensus, which it recommended that the Commission submit to the Assembly for consideration at the special session.

GENERAL ASSEMBLY ACTION

On 7 December, on the recommendation of the First Committee, the General Assembly adopted two resolutions on verification in all its aspects. **Resolution 43/81 A** was adopted without vote.

Compliance with arms limitation and disarmament agreements

The General Assembly,

Recalling its resolution 42/38 M of 30 November 1987,

Conscious of the abiding concern of all Member States for preserving respect for rights and obligations arising from treaties and other sources of international law,

Convinced that observance of the Charter of the United Nations, relevant treaties and other sources of international law is essential for the strengthening of international security,

Mindful, in particular, of the fundamental importance of full implementation and strict observance of agreements on arms limitation and disarmament if individual nations and the international community are to derive enhanced security from them,

Stressing that any violation of such agreements not only adversely affects the security of States parties but can also create security risks for other States relying on the constraints and commitments stipulated in those agreements,

Stressing also that any weakening of confidence in such agreements diminishes their contribution to global or regional stability and to further disarmament and arms limitation efforts and undermines the credibility and effectiveness of the international legal system,

Recognizing in this context that, *inter alia*, full confidence in compliance with existing agreements can enhance the negotiation of arms limitation and disarmament agreements,

Believing that compliance with arms limitation and disarmament agreements by States parties is, therefore, a matter of interest and concern to all members of the international community, and noting the role that the United Nations could play in that regard,

Convinced that resolution of non-compliance questions that have arisen with regard to agreements on arms limitations and disarmament would contribute to better relations among States and the strengthening of world peace and security,

1.   *Urges* all States parties to arms limitation and disarmament agreements to implement and comply with the entirety of the provisions of such agreements;

2.   *Calls upon* all Member States to give serious consideration to the implications of non-compliance with those obligations for international security and stability, as well as for the prospects for further progress in the field of disarmament;

3.   *Also calls upon* all Member States to support efforts aimed at the resolution of non-compliance questions, with a view to encouraging strict observance by all parties of the provisions of arms limitation and disarmament agreements and maintaining or restoring the integrity of such agreements;

4.   *Requests* the Secretary-General to provide Member States with assistance that may be necessary in this regard;

5.   *Welcomes* efforts by States parties to develop additional co-operative measures, as appropriate, that can increase confidence in compliance with existing arms limitation and disarmament agreements and reduce the possibility of misinterpretation and misunderstanding;

6.   *Decides* to include in the provisional agenda of its forty-fourth session the item entitled "Compliance with arms limitation and disarmament agreements".

General Assembly resolution 43/81 A

7 December 1988   Meeting 73   Adopted without vote

Approved by First Committee (A/43/894) without vote, 18 November (meeting 43); 38-nation draft (A/C.1/43/L.53); agenda item 139.

Sponsors: Australia, Austria, Cameroon, Canada, Colombia, Costa Rica, Côte d'Ivoire, Czechoslovakia, Denmark, Ecuador, El Salvador, Finland, France, German Democratic Republic, Germany, Federal Republic of, Greece, Hungary, Iceland, Italy, Japan, Morocco, Netherlands, New Zealand, Norway, Peru, Philippines, Poland, Portugal, Romania, Samoa, Sierra Leone, Spain, Sweden, Thailand, Turkey, United States, Uruguay, Zaire.

Meeting numbers. GA 43rd session: 1st Committee 3-25, 27, 43; plenary 73.

Resolution 43/81 B was adopted by recorded vote.

Study on the role of the United Nations in the field of verification

The General Assembly,

Recalling its resolutions 40/152 O of 16 December 1985, 41/86 Q of 4 December 1986 and 42/42 F of 30 November 1987,

Underlining the important role that the United Nations, in accordance with its Charter, has to play in the sphere of disarmament,

Recalling that all the peoples of the world have a vital interest in the success of disarmament negotiations and that, consequently, all States have the duty to contribute to efforts in the field of disarmament,

Noting that the critical importance of verification of and compliance with arms limitation and disarmament agreements is universally recognized,

Stressing that the issue of verification of and compliance with arms limitation and disarmament agreements is a matter of concern to all nations,

Reiterating its view that:

(a) Disarmament and arms limitation agreements should provide for adequate and effective measures of verification satisfactory to all parties concerned in order to create the necessary confidence and to ensure that they are being observed by all parties;

(b) The form and modalities of the verification to be provided for in any specific agreement depend upon and should be determined by the purposes, scope and nature of the agreement;

(c) Agreements should provide for the participation of parties directly or through United Nations organs in the verification process;

(d) Where appropriate, a combination of several methods of verification as well as other compliance procedures should be employed,

Recalling that:

(a) In the context of international disarmament negotiations, the problem of verification should be further examined and adequate methods and procedures in this field should be considered;

(b) Every effort should be made to develop appropriate methods and procedures that are non-discriminatory and that do not interfere unduly with the internal affairs of other States or jeopardize their economic and social development,

Conscious of the fact that the United Nations is already playing a useful role in the field of verification,

Taking note of all proposals that have been put forward in the field of verification by Member States, including those by Canada and the Netherlands, France and the countries of the Six-Nation Initiative,

1. *Recognizes* that the United Nations, in accordance with its role and responsibilities established under the Charter, can make a significant contribution in the field of verification, in particular of multilateral agreements;

2. *Notes with satisfaction* the completion by the Disarmament Commission of its work on the subject of verification in all its aspects;

3. *Endorses* the general principles of verification drawn up by the Disarmament Commission and contained in its report;

4. *Requests* the Secretary-General to undertake, with the assistance of a group of qualified governmental experts, an in-depth study of the role of the United Nations in the field of verification that would:

(a) Identify and review existing activities of the United Nations in the field of verification of arms limitation and disarmament;

(b) Assess the need for improvements in existing activities as well as explore and identify possible additional activities, taking into account organizational, technical, operational, legal and financial aspects;

(c) Provide specific recommendations for future action by the United Nations in this context;

5. *Requests* the Secretary-General to submit a comprehensive report on the subject to the General Assembly at its forty-fifth session;

6. *Decides* to include in the provisional agenda of its forty-fifth session the item entitled "Verification in all its aspects".

General Assembly resolution 43/81 B

7 December 1988   Meeting 73   150-1 (recorded vote)

Approved by First Committee (A/43/894) by recorded vote (130-1), 18 November (meeting 43); 35-nation draft (A/C.1/43/L.75); agenda item 139.

Sponsors: Argentina, Australia, Austria, Bahamas, Belgium, Botswana, Bulgaria, Cameroon, Canada, Colombia, Costa Rica, Denmark, Finland, France, Germany, Federal Republic of, Greece, Hungary, Iceland, India, Italy, Japan, Mexico, Netherlands, New Zealand, Norway, Portugal, Romania, Samoa, Singapore, Spain, Sweden, Thailand, United Republic of Tanzania, Uruguay, Zaire.

Financial implications. ACABQ, A/43/7/Add.9; 5th Committee, A/43/938; S-G, A/C.1/43/L.81, A/C.5/43/39.

Meeting numbers. GA 43rd session: 1st Committee 3-25, 41, 43; 5th Committee 41; plenary 73.

Recorded vote in Assembly as follows:

In favour: Afghanistan, Albania, Algeria, Angola, Antigua and Barbuda, Argentina, Australia, Austria, Bahamas, Bahrain, Bangladesh, Barbados, Belgium, Belize, Benin, Bhutan, Bolivia, Botswana, Brazil, Brunei Darussalam, Bulgaria, Burkina Faso, Burma, Burundi, Byelorussian SSR, Cameroon, Canada, Central African Republic, Chad, Chile, China, Colombia, Comoros, Congo, Costa Rica, Côte d'Ivoire, Cuba, Cyprus, Czechoslovakia, Democratic Kampuchea, Democratic Yemen, Denmark, Djibouti, Dominican Republic, Ecuador, Egypt, El Salvador, Ethiopia, Fiji, Finland, France, Gabon, Gambia, German Democratic Republic, Germany, Federal Republic of, Ghana, Greece, Guatemala, Guinea, Guyana, Haiti, Honduras, Hungary, Iceland, India, Indonesia, Iran, Iraq, Ireland, Israel, Italy, Japan, Jordan, Kenya, Kuwait, Lao People's Democratic Republic, Lebanon, Lesotho, Liberia, Libyan Arab Jamahiriya, Luxembourg, Madagascar, Malawi, Malaysia, Maldives, Mali, Malta, Mauritania, Mauritius, Mexico, Mongolia, Morocco, Mozambique, Nepal, Netherlands, New Zealand, Nicaragua, Niger, Nigeria, Norway, Oman, Pakistan, Panama, Papua New Guinea, Paraguay, Peru, Philippines, Poland, Portugal, Qatar, Romania, Rwanda, Saint Kitts and Nevis, Saint Lucia, Saint Vincent and the Grenadines, Samoa, Sao Tome and Principe, Saudi Arabia, Senegal, Seychelles, Sierra Leone, Singapore, Solomon Islands, Somalia, Spain, Sri Lanka, Sudan, Suriname, Swaziland, Sweden, Thailand, Togo, Trinidad and Tobago, Tunisia, Turkey, Uganda, Ukrainian SSR, USSR, United Arab Emirates, United Kingdom, United Republic of Tanzania, Uruguay, Vanuatu, Venezuela, Viet Nam, Yemen, Yugoslavia, Zaire, Zambia, Zimbabwe.

Against: United States.

Proposed world disarmament conference

In 1987, the Secretary-General had submitted to the Assembly[42] the views of 10 Member

States—including the five nuclear-weapon States—on convening a world disarmament conference, first endorsed by the Assembly in 1965.[43] The Assembly had requested the *Ad Hoc* Committee on the World Disarmament Conference,[44] which held no session in 1987, to report to the third special session devoted to disarmament. The Committee met on 14 January and 27 April 1988. Its report[45] summarized its work since 1982, taking note of the important developments which had taken place in the field of disarmament, particularly in the bilateral sphere. However, while recognizing the continuing validity of the initiative for convening a conference, the Committee recommended that, given the divergence of views on the subject, the work of the Committee be suspended until such time as the Assembly deemed it appropriate to reactivate it.

REFERENCES

[1]A/43/42. [2]A/S-15/3. [3]A/43/27. [4]A/43/623. [5]YUN 1987, p. 22, GA res. 42/42 B, 30 Nov. 1987. [6]*Ibid.*, p. 24, GA res. 42/38 O, 30 Nov 1987. [7]*Ibid.*, p. 19. [8]*Ibid.*, p. 24, GA res. 42/39 A, 30 Nov. 1987. [9]A/43/798. [10]YUN 1987, p. 26, GA res. 42/38 J, 30 Nov. 1987. [11]A/43/492 & Add.1-3. [12]YUN 1986, p. 29, GA res. 41/59 D, 3 Dec. 1986. [13]A/43/650. [14]YUN 1978, p. 17. [15]YUN 1982, p. 11. [16]YUN 1978, p. 39, GA res. S-10/2, 30 June 1978. [17]YUN 1982, p. 18, GA dec. S-12/24, 10 July 1982. [18]YUN 1985, p. 27, GA res. 40/151 A, 16 Dec. 1985. [19]A/43/719. [20]YUN 1986, p. 22. [21]YUN 1987, p. 31, GA res. 42/39 F, 30 Nov. 1987. [22]YUN 1980, p. 102, GA res. 35/46, annex, 3 Dec. 1980. [23]YUN 1985, p. 22, GA res. 40/152 L, 16 Dec. 1985. [24]A/43/507 & Add.1. [25]YUN 1987, p. 36, GA res. 42/38 I, 30 Nov. 1987. [26]A/S-15/7 & Add.1,2. [27]YUN 1985, p. 30. [28]YUN 1987, p. 37. [29]A/CN.10/113. [30]YUN 1987, p. 83. [31]*Ibid.*, p. 84, GA res. 42/45, 30 Nov. 1987. [32]YUN 1970, p. 18, GA res. 2660(XXV), annex, 7 Dec. 1970. [33]YUN 1977, p. 44. [34]YUN 1983, p. 47. [35]YUN 1987, p. 39, GA res. 42/42 I, 30 Nov. 1987. [36]CD/834. [37]CD/CPD/WP.91. [38]YUN 1987, p. 34, GA res. 42/42 F, 30 Nov. 1987. [39]A/CN.10/106 & Add.1-3. [40]A/CN.10/107. [41]A/CN.10/111. [42]YUN 1987, p. 39. [43]YUN 1965, p. 62, GA res. 2030(XX), 29 Nov. 1965. [44]YUN 1987, p. 40, GA res. 42/41, 30 Nov. 1987. [45]A/S-15/4.

Nuclear disarmament

Prevention of nuclear war

Consideration by the Conference on Disarmament. The Conference on Disarmament considered the question of the prevention of nuclear war from 7 to 11 March and from 8 to 12 August 1988.[1] In addition to previous documentation, it had before it two new texts submitted by the USSR and the United States: the Agreement between the United States of America and the Union of Soviet Socialist Republics on the Establishment of Nuclear Risk Reduction Centers, along with Protocols I and II, signed at Washington, D.C., on 15 September 1987;[2] and the Agreement between the same two countries on Notifications of Launches of Intercontinental Ballistic Missiles and Submarine-Launched Ballistic Missiles, signed at Moscow on 31 May 1988.[3] As in previous years, no consensus was reached on a mandate proposed by the Group of 21 neutral and non-aligned States (Algeria, Argentina, Brazil, Burma, Cuba, Egypt, Ethiopia, India, Indonesia, Iran, Kenya, Mexico, Morocco, Nigeria, Pakistan, Peru, Sri Lanka, Sweden, Venezuela, Yugoslavia, Zaire) for an *ad hoc* committee to consider all relevant proposals, including appropriate and practical measures for preventing nuclear war.[4]

Disarmament Commission consideration. The Disarmament Commission also considered the question of nuclear disarmament and the prevention of nuclear war. In its report to the third special session of the General Assembly devoted to disarmament,[5] the Commission recommended that all States should co-operate for the adoption of practical and appropriate measures to prevent the outbreak of a nuclear war and to avoid the use of nuclear weapons, and that the Conference on Disarmament should undertake, as a matter of the highest priority, negotiations towards that end. It also recommended that the General Assembly welcome the 1987 Agreement on the Establishment of Nuclear Risk Reduction Centers in the United States and the USSR.[2]

GENERAL ASSEMBLY ACTION

On 7 December 1988, the General Assembly, on the recommendation of the First Committee, adopted **resolution 43/78 B** by recorded vote.

Non-use of nuclear weapons and prevention of nuclear war

The General Assembly,

Recalling that, in accordance with paragraph 20 of the Final Document of the Tenth Special Session of the General Assembly, the first special session devoted to disarmament, effective measures of nuclear disarmament and the prevention of nuclear war have the highest priority and that this commitment was reaffirmed by the Assembly at its twelfth special session, the second special session devoted to disarmament,

Recalling also that, in paragraph 58 of the Final Document, it is stated that all States, in particular nuclear-weapon States, should consider as soon as possible various proposals designed to secure the avoidance of the use of nuclear weapons, the prevention of nuclear war and related objectives, where possible through international agreement, and thereby ensure that the survival of mankind is not endangered,

Recalling further that, at its fifteenth special session, the third special session devoted to disarmament, it was generally recognized that the prevention of nuclear war was of utmost concern and that specific efforts, bilateral, regional or multilateral, should be vigorously pursued and measures should be strengthened to reduce and ultimately eliminate the risk of nuclear war,

Reaffirming that the nuclear-weapon States have the primary responsibility for nuclear disarmament and for undertaking measures aimed at preventing the outbreak of nuclear war,

Welcoming measures taken by the Union of Soviet Socialist Republics and the United States of America to reduce the risk of nuclear war,

Stressing that a nuclear war cannot be won and must never be fought,

Recalling that, in the Political Declaration adopted at the Eighth Conference of Heads of State or Government of Non-Aligned Countries, held at Harare from 1 to 6 September 1986, all nuclear-weapon States were called upon to enter early into an internationally binding commitment not to be the first to use or threaten to use nuclear weapons,

Emphasizing that for the sake of international peace and security, military concepts and doctrines must be of a strictly defensive character,

1. *Considers* that the solemn declarations by two nuclear-weapon States made or reiterated at the twelfth special session of the General Assembly, concerning their respective obligations not to be the first to use nuclear weapons, offer an important avenue to decrease the danger of nuclear war;

2. *Expresses the hope* that those nuclear-weapon States which have not yet done so will consider making similar declarations with respect to not being the first to use nuclear weapons;

3. *Requests* the Conference on Disarmament to commence negotiations on the item in its agenda concerning prevention of nuclear war and to consider, *inter alia*, the elaboration of an international instrument of a legally binding character laying down the obligation not to be the first to use nuclear weapons;

4. *Decides* to include in the provisional agenda of its forty-fourth session the item entitled "Non-use of nuclear weapons and prevention of nuclear war".

General Assembly resolution 43/78 B

7 December 1988   Meeting 73   127-17-6 (recorded vote)

Approved by First Committee (A/43/859) by recorded vote (104-17-7), 11 November (meeting 34); 6-nation draft (A/C.1/43/L.4); agenda item 67 (j).

Sponsors: Bulgaria, Cuba, German Democratic Republic, Hungary, Mongolia, Romania.

Meeting numbers. GA 43rd session: 1st Committee 3-25, 27, 34; plenary 73.

Recorded vote in Assembly as follows:

In favour: Afghanistan, Algeria, Angola, Antigua and Barbuda, Argentina, Austria, Bahamas, Bahrain, Bangladesh, Barbados, Belize, Benin, Bhutan, Bolivia, Botswana, Brazil, Brunei Darussalam, Bulgaria, Burkina Faso, Burma, Burundi, Byelorussian SSR, Cameroon, Cape Verde, Central African Republic, Chad, Comoros, Congo, Costa Rica, Côte d'Ivoire, Cuba, Cyprus, Czechoslovakia, Democratic Yemen, Djibouti, Dominican Republic, Ecuador, Egypt, El Salvador, Ethiopia, Fiji, Finland, Gabon, Gambia, German Democratic Republic, Ghana, Guatemala, Guinea, Guyana, Haiti, Honduras, Hungary, India, Indonesia, Iran, Iraq, Jamaica, Jordan, Kenya, Kuwait, Lao People's Democratic Republic, Lebanon, Lesotho, Liberia, Libyan Arab Jamahiriya, Madagascar, Malawi, Malaysia, Maldives, Mali, Malta, Mauritania, Mauritius, Mexico, Mongolia, Morocco, Mozambique, Nepal, Nicaragua, Niger, Nigeria, Oman, Pakistan, Panama, Papua New Guinea, Paraguay, Peru, Philippines, Poland, Qatar, Romania, Rwanda, Saint Kitts and Nevis, Saint Lucia, Saint Vincent and the Grenadines, Samoa, Sao Tome and Principe, Saudi Arabia, Senegal, Seychelles, Sierra Leone, Solomon Islands, Somalia, Sri Lanka, Sudan, Suriname, Swaziland, Sweden, Syrian Arab Republic, Thailand, Togo, Trinidad and Tobago, Tunisia, Uganda, Ukrainian SSR, USSR, United Arab Emirates, United Republic of Tanzania, Uruguay, Vanuatu, Venezuela, Viet Nam, Yemen, Yugoslavia, Zaire, Zambia, Zimbabwe.

Against: Australia, Belgium, Canada, Denmark, France, Germany, Federal Republic of, Italy, Japan, Luxembourg, Netherlands, New Zealand, Norway, Portugal, Spain, Turkey, United Kingdom, United States.

Abstaining: Chile, Colombia, Greece, Iceland, Ireland, Israel.

The Assembly also adopted **resolution 43/78 F** on 7 December, again on the First Committee's recommendation and by recorded vote.

Prevention of nuclear war

The General Assembly,

Convinced that the prevention of nuclear war and the reduction of the risk of nuclear war are matters of the highest priority and of vital interest to all people of the world,

Recalling the provisions of paragraphs 47 to 50 and 56 to 58 of the Final Document of the Tenth Special Session of the General Assembly, the first special session devoted to disarmament, regarding the procedures designed to secure the avoidance of nuclear war,

Reiterating that it is the shared responsibility of all Member States to save succeeding generations from the scourge of another world war, which would inevitably be a nuclear war,

Noting that at the Conference of Ministers for Foreign Affairs of the Non-Aligned Countries held at Nicosia from 7 to 10 September 1988, the Ministers stated that, being aware that the gravest danger confronting humanity today was the nuclear threat, they welcomed the recent developments in the field of disarmament, which they considered a historic achievement, and emphasized the need to encourage that positive trend through the immediate adoption of measures for the prevention of nuclear war,[a]

Recognizing that the prevention of nuclear war requires disarmament measures, and welcoming the first bilateral nuclear disarmament agreement between the Union of Soviet Socialist Republics and the United States of America on the elimination of all land-based intermediate-range nuclear forces,

Aware of the essential complementarity which links both bilateral and multilateral disarmament negotiations,

Having considered the report of the Conference on Disarmament on its 1988 session,

Taking into account the deliberations on this item at the fifteenth special session of the General Assembly, the third special session devoted to disarmament, and at its forty-third session,

1. *Notes with regret* that, despite the fact that the Conference on Disarmament has discussed the question of the prevention of nuclear war for several years, it has been unable even to establish a subsidiary body to consider appropriate and practical measures to prevent it;

2. *Reiterates its conviction* that, in view of the urgency of the matter and the inadequacy or insufficiency of existing measures, it is necessary to devise suitable steps to expedite effective action for the prevention of nuclear war;

3. *Again requests* the Conference on Disarmament to undertake, as a matter of the highest priority, negotiations with a view to achieving agreement on appropriate and practical measures that could be negotiated and adopted individually for the prevention of nuclear war and to establish for that purpose an *ad hoc* committee on the subject at the beginning of its 1989 session;

4. *Decides* to include in the provisional agenda of its forty-fourth session the item entitled "Prevention of nuclear war".

---

[a]A/43/667-S/20212.

General Assembly resolution 43/78 F

7 December 1988   Meeting 73   136-3-14 (recorded vote)

Approved by First Committee (A/43/859) by recorded vote (116-3-14), 11 November (meeting 34); 27-nation draft (A/C.1/43/L.43); agenda item 67 (I).

Sponsors: Algeria, Argentina, Bangladesh, Brazil, Bulgaria, Cameroon, Colombia, Congo, Costa Rica, Djibouti, Ecuador, Egypt, German Democratic Republic, India, Indonesia, Malaysia, Mexico, Mongolia, Morocco, Nigeria, Pakistan, Peru, Romania, Uruguay, Venezuela, Viet Nam, Yugoslavia.

Meeting numbers. GA 43rd session: 1st Committee 3-25, 31, 34; plenary 73.

Recorded vote in Assembly as follows:

In favour: Afghanistan, Albania, Algeria, Angola, Antigua and Barbuda, Argentina, Australia, Austria, Bahamas, Bahrain, Bangladesh, Barbados, Belize, Benin, Bhutan, Bolivia, Botswana, Brazil, Brunei Darussalam, Bulgaria, Burkina Faso, Burma, Burundi, Byelorussian SSR, Cameroon, Cape Verde, Central African Republic, Chad, Chile, China, Colombia, Comoros, Congo, Costa Rica, Côte d'Ivoire, Cuba, Cyprus, Czechoslovakia, Democratic Kampuchea, Democratic Yemen, Djibouti, Dominican Republic, Ecuador, Egypt, El Salvador, Ethiopia, Fiji, Finland, Gabon, Gambia, German Democratic Republic, Ghana, Greece, Guatemala, Guinea, Guyana, Haiti, Honduras, Hungary, India, Indonesia, Iran, Iraq, Ireland, Jordan, Kenya, Kuwait, Lao People's Democratic Republic, Lebanon, Lesotho, Liberia, Libyan Arab Jamahiriya, Madagascar, Malawi, Malaysia, Maldives, Mali, Malta, Mauritania, Mauritius, Mexico, Mongolia, Morocco, Mozambique, Nepal, New Zealand, Nicaragua, Niger, Nigeria, Oman, Pakistan, Panama, Papua New Guinea, Paraguay, Peru, Philippines, Poland, Qatar, Romania, Rwanda, Saint Kitts and Nevis, Saint Lucia, Saint Vincent and the Grenadines, Samoa, Sao Tome and Principe, Saudi Arabia, Senegal, Seychelles, Sierra Leone, Singapore, Solomon Islands, Somalia, Sri Lanka, Sudan, Suriname, Swaziland, Sweden, Syrian Arab Republic, Thailand, Togo, Trinidad and Tobago, Tunisia, Uganda, Ukrainian SSR, USSR, United Arab Emirates, United Republic of Tanzania, Uruguay, Vanuatu, Venezuela, Viet Nam, Yemen, Yugoslavia, Zaire, Zambia, Zimbabwe.

Against: France, United Kingdom, United States.

Abstaining: Belgium, Canada, Denmark, Germany, Federal Republic of, Iceland, Israel, Italy, Japan, Luxembourg, Netherlands, Norway, Portugal, Spain, Turkey.

On the same date, the Assembly, on the recommendation of the First Committee, adopted **resolution 43/76 E** by recorded vote.

Convention on the Prohibition of the Use of Nuclear Weapons

The General Assembly,

Alarmed by the threat to the survival of mankind and to the life-sustaining system posed by nuclear weapons and by their use, inherent in concepts of deterrence,

Conscious of an increased danger of nuclear war as a result of the intensification of the nuclear-arms race and the serious deterioration of the international situation,

Convinced that nuclear disarmament is essential for the prevention of nuclear war and for the strengthening of international peace and security,

Also convinced that a prohibition of the use or threat of use of nuclear weapons would be a step towards the complete elimination of nuclear weapons leading to general and complete disarmament under strict and effective international control,

Recalling that in paragraph 58 of the Final Document of the Tenth Special Session of the General Assembly, it is stated that all States should actively participate in efforts to bring about conditions in international relations among States in which a code of peaceful conduct of nations in international affairs could be agreed upon and that would preclude the use or threat of use of nuclear weapons,

Reaffirming that the use of nuclear weapons would be a violation of the Charter of the United Nations and a crime against humanity, as declared in its resolutions 1653(XVI) of 24 November 1961, 33/71 B of 14 December 1978, 34/83 G of 11 December 1979, 35/152 D of 12 December 1980 and 36/92 I of 9 December 1981,

Noting with regret that the Conference on Disarmament, during its 1988 session, was not able to undertake negotiations with a view to achieving agreement on an international convention prohibiting the use or threat of use of nuclear weapons under any circumstances, taking as a basis the text annexed to General Assembly resolution 41/60 F of 3 December 1986 and 42/39 C of 30 November 1987,

1.   *Reiterates its request* to the Conference on Disarmament to commence negotiations, as a matter of priority, in order to reach agreement on an international convention prohibiting the use or threat of use of nuclear weapons under any circumstances, taking as a basis the draft Convention on the Prohibition of the Use of Nuclear Weapons annexed to the present resolution;

2.   *Also requests* the Conference on Disarmament to report to the General Assembly at its forty-fourth session on the results of those negotiations.

ANNEX
Draft Convention on the Prohibition of the Use of Nuclear Weapons

The States Parties to this Convention,

Alarmed by the threat to the very survival of mankind posed by the existence of nuclear weapons,

Convinced that any use of nuclear weapons constitutes a violation of the Charter of the United Nations and a crime against humanity,

Convinced that this Convention would be a step towards the complete elimination of nuclear weapons leading to general and complete disarmament under strict and effective international control,

Determined to continue negotiations for the achievement of this goal,

Have agreed as follows:

Article 1

The States Parties to this Convention solemnly undertake not to use or threaten to use nuclear weapons under any circumstances.

Article 2

This Convention shall be of unlimited duration.

Article 3

1.   This Convention shall be open to all States for signature. Any State that does not sign the Convention before its entry into force in accordance with paragraph 3 of this article may accede to it at any time.

2.   This Convention shall be subject to ratification by signatory States. Instruments of ratification or accession shall be deposited with the Secretary-General of the United Nations.

3.   This Convention shall enter into force on the deposit of instruments of ratification by twenty-five Governments, including the Governments of the five nuclear-weapon States, in accordance with paragraph 2 of this article.

4.   For States whose instruments of ratification or accession are deposited after the entry into force of this Convention, it shall enter into force on the date of deposit of their instruments of ratification or accession.

5.   The depositary shall promptly inform all signatory and acceding States of the date of each signature, the date of deposit of each instrument of ratification or accession and the date of the entry into force of this Convention, as well as of the receipt of other notices.

6. This Convention shall be registered by the depositary in accordance with Article 102 of the Charter of the United Nations.

Article 4

This Convention, of which the Arabic, Chinese, English, French, Russian and Spanish texts are equally authentic, shall be deposited with the Secretary-General of the United Nations, who shall send duly certified copies thereof to the Government of the signatory and acceding States.

In witness whereof, the undersigned, being duly authorized thereto by their respective Governments, have signed this Convention, opened for signature at _____ on the _____ day of _____ one thousand nine hundred and _____.

General Assembly resolution 43/76 E

7 December 1988   Meeting 73   133-17-4 (recorded vote)

Approved by First Committee (A/43/857) by recorded vote (112-17-4), 11 November (meeting 34); 14-nation draft (A/C.1/43/L.55); agenda item 65 (c).

Sponsors: Algeria, Argentina, Bangladesh, Bhutan, Ecuador, Egypt, Ethiopia, India, Indonesia, Madagascar, Malaysia, Romania, Viet Nam, Yugoslavia.

Meeting numbers. GA 43rd session: 1st Committee 3-25, 30, 34; plenary 73.

Recorded vote in Assembly as follows:

In favour: Afghanistan, Albania, Algeria, Angola, Antigua and Barbuda, Argentina, Austria, Bahamas, Bahrain, Bangladesh, Barbados, Belize, Benin, Bhutan, Bolivia, Botswana, Brazil, Brunei Darussalam, Bulgaria, Burkina Faso, Burma, Burundi, Byelorussian SSR, Cameroon, Cape Verde, Central African Republic, Chad, Chile, China, Colombia, Comoros, Congo, Costa Rica, Côte d'Ivoire, Cuba, Cyprus, Czechoslovakia, Democratic Kampuchea, Democratic Yemen, Djibouti, Dominican Republic, Ecuador, Egypt, El Salvador, Ethiopia, Fiji, Finland, Gabon, Gambia, German Democratic Republic, Ghana, Guatemala, Guinea, Guyana, Haiti, Honduras, Hungary, India, Indonesia, Iran, Iraq, Jamaica, Jordan, Kenya, Kuwait, Lao People's Democratic Republic, Lebanon, Lesotho, Liberia, Libyan Arab Jamahiriya, Madagascar, Malawi, Malaysia, Maldives, Mali, Malta, Mauritania, Mauritius, Mexico, Mongolia, Morocco, Mozambique, Nepal, Nicaragua, Niger, Nigeria, Oman, Pakistan, Panama, Papua New Guinea, Paraguay, Peru, Philippines, Poland, Qatar, Romania, Rwanda, Saint Kitts and Nevis, Saint Lucia, Saint Vincent and the Grenadines, Samoa, Sao Tome and Principe, Saudi Arabia, Senegal, Seychelles, Sierra Leone, Singapore, Solomon Islands, Somalia, Sri Lanka, Sudan, Suriname, Swaziland, Sweden, Syrian Arab Republic, Thailand, Togo, Trinidad and Tobago, Tunisia, Uganda, Ukrainian SSR, USSR, United Arab Emirates, United Republic of Tanzania, Uruguay, Vanuatu, Venezuela, Viet Nam, Yemen, Yugoslavia, Zaire, Zambia, Zimbabwe.

Against: Australia, Belgium, Canada, Denmark, France, Germany, Federal Republic of, Iceland, Italy, Luxembourg, Netherlands, New Zealand, Norway, Portugal, Spain, Turkey, United Kingdom, United States.

Abstaining: Greece, Ireland, Israel, Japan.

Climatic effects of nuclear war

Pusuant to a 1986 General Assembly request,[6] the Secretary-General submitted in May 1988[7] the report of the group of consultant experts appointed by him to study the climatic and potential physical effects of nuclear war, including nuclear winter, and to examine, *inter alia*, its socio-economic consequences. The group examined the atmospheric and climatic consequences of nuclear war and its effects on natural ecosystems, agriculture, health and socio-economic systems.

The group reported that conclusive scientific evidence indicated that a major nuclear war, especially if targeted areas were large cities and industrial centres in the northern hemisphere in summer, would entail the high risk of global environmental disruption, with significant reduction of temperatures in that hemisphere and a decrease in rainfall of as much as 80 per cent in temperate and tropical latitudes. The resulting agricultural and ecological devastation would be aggravated by chemical pollutants, an increase in ultraviolet radiation and the likely persistence of radioactive "hotspots". The group concluded that the widespread impact of a nuclear exchange would constitute a severe threat to world food production and distribution, with the prospect of starvation, a complete breakdown of health care, an increase in damaging ultraviolet radiation and billions of deaths due to direct and indirect effects.

The socio-economic consequences in a world intimately interconnected economically, socially and environmentally would be grave. In addition, the immediate and direct effects of nuclear explosions and the global environmental consequences would each exacerbate the other.

In the group's view, the co-operative, international scientific effort that had identified the new dimensions of nuclear warfare should be continued so as to refine current findings and explore new possibilities. It further suggested that the scientific advances so far achieved should be pursued internationally and underscored the importance of dialogue between the scientific community and public policy makers.

GENERAL ASSEMBLY ACTION

On 7 December, on the recommendation of the First Committee, the General Assembly adopted **resolution 43/78 D** by recorded vote.

Climatic effects of nuclear war, including nuclear winter

The General Assembly,

Recalling that, in the Final Document of the Tenth Special Session of the General Assembly, the first special session devoted to disarmament, after referring specifically to the threat to the very survival of mankind posed by the existence of nuclear weapons, it declared, in paragraph 18, that removing the threat of world war—a nuclear war—is the most acute and urgent task of the present day,

Recalling also its resolutions 40/152 G of 16 December 1985 and 41/86 H of 4 December 1986, by which it requested the Secretary-General, with the assistance of a group of consultant experts chosen by him, bearing in mind the advisability of wide geographical representation and of their qualifications in a broad range of scientific fields, to carry out a study on the climatic and potential physical effects of nuclear war, including nuclear winter, which would examine, *inter alia*, its socio-economic consequences,

Having examined the report of the Secretary-General entitled *Study on the Climatic and Other Global Effects of Nuclear War,*[a]

---

[a]Sales No. E.89.IX.1.

Gravely concerned by the conclusions of that study,

1. *Takes note* of the *Study on the Climatic and Other Global Effects of Nuclear War;*

2. *Expresses its appreciation* to the Secretary-General and the group of consultant experts that assisted him in the preparation of the study;

3. *Commends* the study and its conclusions to the attention of all Member States;

4. *Invites* all Member States to communicate to the Secretary-General their views on the study before 1 September 1989;

5. *Requests* the Secretary-General to make the necessary arrangements for the reproduction of the study as a United Nations publication and to give it the widest possible distribution.

General Assembly resolution 43/78 D

7 December 1988   Meeting 73   145-0-9 (recorded vote)

Approved by First Committee (A/43/859) by recorded vote (125-0-9), 10 November (meeting 33); 7-nation draft (A/C.1/43/L.34); agenda item 67 *(g)*.
Sponsors: Bangladesh, India, Mexico, Pakistan, Samoa, Sweden, Ukrainian SSR.
Meeting numbers. GA 43rd session: 1st Committee 3-25, 30, 33; plenary 73.

Recorded vote in Assembly as follows:

In favour: Afghanistan, Albania, Algeria, Angola, Antigua and Barbuda, Argentina, Australia, Austria, Bahamas, Bahrain, Bangladesh, Barbados, Belize, Benin, Bhutan, Bolivia, Botswana, Brazil, Brunei Darussalam, Bulgaria, Burkina Faso, Burma, Burundi, Byelorussian SSR, Cameroon, Canada, Cape Verde, Central African Republic, Chad, Chile, China, Colombia, Comoros, Congo, Costa Rica, Côte d'Ivoire, Cuba, Cyprus, Czechoslovakia, Democratic Kampuchea, Democratic Yemen, Denmark, Djibouti, Dominican Republic, Ecuador, Egypt, El Salvador, Ethiopia, Fiji, Finland, Gabon, Gambia, German Democratic Republic, Ghana, Greece, Guatemala, Guinea, Guyana, Haiti, Honduras, Hungary, Iceland, India, Indonesia, Iran, Iraq, Ireland, Israel, Italy, Jamaica, Japan, Jordan, Kenya, Kuwait, Lao People's Democratic Republic, Lebanon, Lesotho, Liberia, Libyan Arab Jamahiriya, Madagascar, Malawi, Malaysia, Maldives, Mali, Malta, Mauritania, Mauritius, Mexico, Mongolia, Morocco, Mozambique, Nepal, New Zealand, Nicaragua, Niger, Nigeria, Norway, Oman, Pakistan, Panama, Papua New Guinea, Paraguay, Peru, Philippines, Poland, Qatar, Romania, Rwanda, Saint Kitts and Nevis, Saint Lucia, Saint Vincent and the Grenadines, Samoa, Sao Tome and Principe, Saudi Arabia, Senegal, Seychelles, Sierra Leone, Singapore, Solomon Islands, Somalia, Spain, Sri Lanka, Sudan, Suriname, Swaziland, Sweden, Syrian Arab Republic, Thailand, Togo, Trinidad and Tobago, Tunisia, Uganda, Ukrainian SSR, USSR, United Arab Emirates, United Republic of Tanzania, Uruguay, Vanuatu, Venezuela, Viet Nam, Yemen, Yugoslavia, Zaire, Zambia, Zimbabwe.

Against: None.

Abstaining: Belgium, France, Germany, Federal Republic of, Luxembourg, Netherlands, Portugal, Turkey, United Kingdom, United States.

Nuclear arms limitation and disarmament

In 1988, the international community remained concerned with the subject of preventing a nuclear war and continued to explore ways of achieving nuclear-arms limitation, banning nuclear-weapon tests, freezing nuclear-weapons production, strengthening the security of non-nuclear-weapon States and creating nuclear-weapon-free zones in many parts of the world.

Following the signing in December 1987 of the INF Treaty between the USSR and the United States,[8] the parties ratified it on 28 and 27 May 1988, respectively. The Treaty came into force on 1 June.

Consideration by the Conference on Disarmament. The Conference on Disarmament considered the question of the cessation of the nuclear-arms race and nuclear disarmament from 15 to 26 February and from 18 to 29 July.[1] In Febru-

ary, the Conference once again considered a proposal[9] on a draft mandate for an *ad hoc* committee to be established to elaborate on paragraph 50 of the Final Document of the Tenth Special Session of the Assembly,[10] dealing with negotiations of agreements to achieve nuclear disarmament, and to identify substantive issues for multilateral negotiations. The Conference, in its report[11] to the third special session of the Assembly devoted to disarmament, summarized its work on this issue since 1982 and indicated its failure to reach a consensus on the draft mandate. The Conference also received documentation from several States and welcomed the documents relating to the INF Treaty[12] by the two major nuclear-weapon States. It expressed the hope for an early conclusion by those States of a treaty on a 50 per cent reduction in their strategic offensive arms.

Despite further informal consultations in July, the Conference was unable to resolve the issue of the *ad hoc* committee.

GENERAL ASSEMBLY ACTION

On 7 December, on the First Committee's recommendation, the Assembly adopted **resolution 43/78 E** by recorded vote.

Cessation of the nuclear-arms race and nuclear disarmament

The General Assembly,

Believing that all nations have a vital interest in negotiations on nuclear disarmament because the existence of nuclear weapons jeopardizes the vital security interests of both nuclear and non-nuclear-weapon States alike,

Recalling that, in paragraphs 11 and 47 of the Final Document of the Tenth Special Session of the General Assembly, the first special session devoted to disarmament, the Assembly stated that the nuclear-arms race, far from contributing to the strengthening of the security of all States, on the contrary weakens it and increases the danger of the outbreak of a nuclear war,

Noting that at the Conference of Ministers for Foreign Affairs of the Non-Aligned Countries held at Nicosia from 7 to 10 September 1988, the Ministers welcomed the recent developments in the field of disarmament, which they considered a historic achievement, expressed the hope that they would result in further substantive progress in the field of current and future bilateral and multilateral negotiations on disarmament, and emphasized as well the need to encourage this positive trend through the immediate adoption of measures for the reversal of the nuclear-arms race, so as to remove the threat of a nuclear holocaust which endangers the very survival of mankind,[a]

Welcoming proposals on the complete elimination of nuclear weapons throughout the world and, especially, the signing of the Treaty between the United States of America and the Union of Soviet Socialist Republics on the Elimination of Their Intermediate-Range and Shorter-Range Missiles,

---

[a]A/43/667-S/20212.

Considering that it is necessary to halt all testing, production and deployment of nuclear weapons of all types and versions and their delivery systems as a first step in the process that should lead to the achievement of substantial reductions in nuclear forces, and welcoming in this context the proposals to that end forwarded by the leaders of Argentina, Greece, India, Mexico, Sweden and the United Republic of Tanzania in their various declarations,

Noting that, at the fifteenth special session of the General Assembly, the third special session devoted to disarmament, and at the 1988 session of the Conference on Disarmament, several proposals on nuclear disarmament were introduced by Member States and that there was general agreement that nuclear disarmament remains a priority objective and represents a central task facing mankind,

Taking into account that all nuclear-weapon States, in particular those with the most important nuclear arsenals, bear a special responsibility for the fulfilment of the task of achieving the goals of nuclear disarmament,

Convinced of the imperative need to take constructive multilateral action towards halting and reversing the nuclear-arms race,

1. *Reaffirms* that both bilateral and multilateral negotiations on the nuclear and space arms race are by nature complementary to one another;

2. *Believes* that efforts should be intensified with a view to initiating, as a matter of the highest priority, multilateral negotiations in accordance with the provisions of paragraph 50 of the Final Document of the Tenth Special Session of the General Assembly;

3. *Again requests* the Conference on Disarmament to establish an *ad hoc* committee at the beginning of its 1989 session to elaborate on paragraph 50 of the Final Document and to submit recommendations to the Conference as to how it could best initiate multilateral negotiations of agreements, with adequate measures of verification, in appropriate stages for:

   (a) Cessation of the qualitative improvement and development of nuclear-weapon systems;

   (b) Cessation of the production of all types of nuclear weapons and their means of delivery and of the production of fissionable material for weapons purposes;

   (c) Substantial reduction in existing nuclear weapons with a view to their ultimate elimination;

4. *Requests* the Conference on Disarmament to report to the General Assembly at its forty-fourth session on its consideration of this subject;

5. *Decides* to include in the provisional agenda of its forty-fourth session the item entitled "Cessation of the nuclear-arms race and nuclear disarmament".

General Assembly resolution 43/78 E

7 December 1988   Meeting 73   135-13-5 (recorded vote)

Approved by First Committee (A/43/859) by recorded vote (114-13-6), 11 November (meeting 34); 15-nation draft (A/C.1/43/L.42); agenda item 67 (k).

Sponsors: Argentina, Bangladesh, Cameroon, Costa Rica, Ecuador, German Democratic Republic, India, Indonesia, Malaysia, Mexico, Mongolia, Romania, Sweden, United Republic of Tanzania, Venezuela.

Meeting numbers. GA 43rd session: 1st Committee 3-25, 31, 34; plenary 73.

Recorded vote in Assembly as follows:

In favour: Afghanistan, Albania, Algeria, Angola, Antigua and Barbuda, Argentina, Austria, Bahamas, Bahrain, Bangladesh, Barbados, Belize, Benin, Bhutan, Bolivia, Botswana, Brazil, Brunei Darussalam, Bulgaria, Burkina Faso, Burma, Burundi, Byelorussian SSR, Cameroon, Cape Verde, Central African Republic, Chad, Chile, China, Colombia, Comoros, Congo, Costa Rica, Côte d'Ivoire, Cuba, Cyprus, Czechoslovakia, Democratic Kampuchea, Democratic Yemen, Djibouti, Dominican Republic, Ecuador, Egypt, El Salvador, Ethiopia, Fiji, Finland, Gabon, Gambia, German Democratic Republic, Ghana, Greece, Guatemala, Guinea, Guyana, Haiti, Honduras, Hungary, India, Indonesia, Iran, Iraq, Ireland, Jordan, Kenya, Kuwait, Lao People's Democratic Republic, Lebanon, Lesotho, Liberia, Libyan Arab Jamahiriya, Madagascar, Malawi, Malaysia, Maldives, Mali, Malta, Mauritania, Mauritius, Mexico, Mongolia, Morocco, Mozambique, Nepal, New Zealand, Nicaragua, Niger, Nigeria, Oman, Pakistan, Panama, Papua New Guinea, Paraguay, Peru, Philippines, Poland, Qatar, Romania, Rwanda, Saint Kitts and Nevis, Saint Lucia, Saint Vincent and the Grenadines, Samoa, Sao Tome and Principe, Saudi Arabia, Senegal, Seychelles, Sierra Leone, Singapore, Solomon Islands, Somalia, Sri Lanka, Sudan, Suriname, Swaziland, Sweden, Syrian Arab Republic, Thailand, Togo, Trinidad and Tobago, Tunisia, Uganda, Ukrainian SSR, USSR, United Arab Emirates, United Republic of Tanzania, Uruguay, Vanuatu, Venezuela, Viet Nam, Yemen, Yugoslavia, Zaire, Zambia, Zimbabwe.

Against: Belgium, Canada, France, Germany, Federal Republic of, Italy, Luxembourg, Netherlands, Norway, Portugal, Spain, Turkey, United Kingdom, United States.

Abstaining: Australia, Denmark, Iceland, Israel, Japan.

Bilateral nuclear-arms negotiations

On 7 December, on the recommendation of the First Committee, the General Assembly adopted **resolution 43/75 E** without vote.

Nuclear disarmament

The General Assembly,

Recalling its resolutions 41/59 F of 3 December 1986 and 42/38 H of 30 November 1987,

Reaffirming the determination to save succeeding generations from the scourge of war as expressed in the Preamble to the Charter of the United Nations,

Convinced that the most acute and urgent task of the present day is to remove the threat of a world war—a nuclear war,

Recalling and reaffirming the statements and provisions on nuclear disarmament set forth in the Final Document of the Tenth Special Session of the General Assembly, and, in particular, provisions that "effective measures of nuclear disarmament and the prevention of nuclear war have the highest priority", contained in paragraph 20, and that "in the task of achieving the goals of nuclear disarmament, all the nuclear-weapon States, in particular those among them which possess the most important nuclear arsenals, bear a special responsibility", contained in paragraph 48,

Bearing in mind that the ultimate goal of nuclear disarmament is the complete elimination of nuclear weapons,

Noting that the leaders of the Union of Soviet Socialist Republics and the United States of America agreed in their joint statement issued at Geneva on 21 November 1985 that "a nuclear war cannot be won and must never be fought" and the common desire they expressed in the same statement calling for early progress in areas where there is common ground, including the principle of a 50 per cent reduction in the nuclear arms of the Soviet Union and the United States appropriately applied,

Noting also that the Union of Soviet Socialist Republics and the United States of America have conducted intensive negotiations on various issues of disarmament,

Noting further that the Conference on Disarmament has not played its due role in the field of nuclear disarmament,

Believing that the qualitative aspect of the arms race needs to be addressed along with its quantitative aspect,

Bearing in mind that the Governments and peoples of various countries expect that the Union of Soviet Socialist Republics and the United States of America will reach agreement on halting the nuclear-arms race and further reducing nuclear weapons,

1. *Welcomes* the signing and ratification of the Treaty between the United States of America and the Union of Soviet Socialist Republics on the Elimination of Their Intermediate-Range and Shorter-Range Missiles, and calls upon the two States strictly to observe and fully to implement the Treaty;

2. *Urges* the Union of Soviet Socialist Republics and the United States of America, which possess the most important nuclear arsenals, further to discharge their special responsibility for nuclear disarmament, to take the lead in halting the nuclear-arms race and to negotiate in earnest with a view to reaching early agreement on the drastic reduction of their nuclear arsenals;

3. *Reiterates its belief* that bilateral and multilateral efforts for nuclear disarmament should complement and facilitate each other;

4. *Decides* to include in the provisional agenda of its forty-fourth session the item entitled ''Nuclear disarmament''.

General Assembly resolution 43/75 E

7 December 1988   Meeting 73   Adopted without vote

Approved by First Committee (A/43/856) without vote, 11 November (meeting 34); draft by China (A/C.1/43/L.14); agenda item 64 *(e)*.
Meeting numbers. GA 43rd session: 1st Committee 3-25, 30, 34; plenary 73.

On the same date, the Assembly, also on the recommendation of the First Committee, adopted **resolution 43/75 A** by recorded vote.

Bilateral nuclear-arms negotiations

The General Assembly,

Recalling its resolutions 40/18 of 18 November 1985, 41/86 N of 4 December 1986 and 42/38 D of 30 November 1987,

Recalling also the Harare Appeal on Disarmament, adopted by the Eighth Conference of Heads of State or Government of Non-Aligned Countries, held at Harare from 1 to 6 September 1986, the Havana Appeal,[a] adopted by the Ministers for Foreign Affairs of Non-Aligned Countries at the special ministerial meeting devoted to disarmament issues held at Havana from 26 to 30 May 1988, and the final documents of the Conference of Ministers for Foreign Affairs of Non-Aligned Countries held at Nicosia from 7 to 10 September 1988,[b]

Gravely concerned about the continuing escalation of the arms race, especially in nuclear weapons and other weapons of mass destruction, despite the fact that this increases the risk of nuclear war and endangers the survival of humanity,

Convinced that the alternative today in the nuclear age is not between war or peace, but between life and death, which makes the prevention of nuclear war the principal task of our times,

Also convinced that international peace and security can be ensured only through general and complete disarmament under effective international control and that one of the most urgent tasks is to halt and reverse the arms race and to undertake concrete measures of disarmament, particularly nuclear disarmament,

Further convinced that, in the interest of mankind as a whole, the Union of Soviet Socialist Republics and the

United States of America, in their bilateral nuclear-arms negotiations, should continue their endeavours with the ultimate objective of achieving general and complete disarmament under effective international control,

Welcoming the ratification and commencement of implementation by the Union of Soviet Socialist Republics and the United States of America of the Treaty on the Elimination of Their Intermediate-Range and Shorter-Range Missiles,

Affirming that bilateral and multilateral negotiations on disarmament should facilitate and complement each other and that progress at the bilateral level should not be used to postpone or prohibit action at the multilateral level,

1. *Calls upon* the Union of Soviet Socialist Republics and the United States of America to exert every effort to achieve the goal they set themselves of a treaty on a 50 per cent reduction in strategic offensive arms as part of the process leading to the complete elimination of nuclear weapons;

2. *Also calls upon* the two Governments to intensify their efforts with the objective of achieving agreements in other areas, in particular the issue of a nuclear-test ban, as a matter of urgency;

3. *Invites* the Governments of the Union of Soviet Socialist Republics and the United States of America to keep the General Assembly and the Conference on Disarmament duly informed of progress made in their negotiations.

---

[a]A/S-15/27 & Corr.1.
[b]A/43/667-S/20212.

General Assembly resolution 43/75 A

7 December 1988   Meeting 73   141-0-12 (recorded vote)

Approved by First Committee (A/43/856) by recorded vote (120-0-13), 14 November (meeting 36); draft by Zimbabwe, for non-aligned States (A/C.1/43/L.7); agenda item 64.
Meeting numbers. GA 43rd session: 1st Committee 3-25, 32, 36; plenary 73.

Recorded vote in Assembly as follows:

In favour: Afghanistan, Algeria, Angola, Antigua and Barbuda, Argentina, Australia, Austria, Bahamas, Bahrain, Bangladesh, Barbados, Belize, Benin, Bhutan, Bolivia, Botswana, Brazil, Brunei Darussalam, Bulgaria, Burkina Faso, Burma, Burundi, Byelorussian SSR, Cameroon, Canada, Cape Verde, Central African Republic, Chad, Chile, China, Colombia, Comoros, Congo, Costa Rica, Côte d'Ivoire, Cuba, Cyprus, Czechoslovakia, Democratic Kampuchea, Democratic Yemen, Denmark, Djibouti, Dominican Republic, Ecuador, Egypt, El Salvador, Ethiopia, Fiji, Finland, Gabon, Gambia, German Democratic Republic, Ghana, Greece,* Guatemala, Guinea, Guyana, Haiti, Honduras, Hungary, Iceland, India, Indonesia, Iran, Iraq, Ireland, Jamaica, Japan, Jordan, Kenya, Kuwait, Lao People's Democratic Republic, Lebanon, Lesotho, Liberia, Libyan Arab Jamahiriya, Madagascar, Malawi, Malaysia, Maldives, Mali, Malta, Mauritania, Mauritius, Mexico, Mongolia, Morocco, Mozambique, Nepal, New Zealand, Nicaragua, Niger, Nigeria, Norway, Oman, Pakistan, Panama, Papua New Guinea, Paraguay, Peru, Philippines, Poland, Qatar, Romania, Rwanda, Saint Kitts and Nevis, Saint Lucia, Saint Vincent and the Grenadines, Samoa, Sao Tome and Principe, Saudi Arabia, Senegal, Seychelles, Sierra Leone, Singapore, Solomon Islands, Somalia, Sri Lanka, Sudan, Suriname, Swaziland, Sweden, Syrian Arab Republic, Thailand, Togo, Trinidad and Tobago, Tunisia, Uganda, Ukrainian SSR, USSR, United Arab Emirates, United Republic of Tanzania, Uruguay, Vanuatu, Venezuela, Viet Nam, Yemen, Yugoslavia, Zaire, Zambia, Zimbabwe.

Against: None.

Abstaining: Belgium, France, Germany, Federal Republic of, Israel, Italy, Luxembourg, Netherlands, Portugal, Spain, Turkey, United Kingdom, United States.

*Later advised the Secretariat it had intended to abstain.

Also on 7 December, the Assembly, again on the First Committee's recommendation, adopted **resolution 43/75 O** by recorded vote.

Bilateral nuclear-arms negotiations

The General Assembly,

Recalling that at their meeting at Geneva in November 1985 the leaders of the Union of Soviet Socialist Republics and the United States of America committed themselves to the objective of working out effective agreements aimed at preventing an arms race in space and terminating it on Earth,

Taking note of the joint statement between the Union of Soviet Socialist Republics and the United States of America issued following meetings held in Moscow from 29 May to 1 June 1988,[a]

Taking note with satisfaction of the report in the joint statement that a joint draft text of a treaty on reduction and limitation of strategic offensive arms had been elaborated, through which process the two sides had recorded extensive and significant areas of agreement and detailed positions on remaining areas of disagreement,

Noting the importance of the verification procedures contained in the Treaty between the United States of America and the Union of Soviet Socialist Republics on the Elimination of Their Intermediate-Range and Shorter-Range Missiles as an example of the high standards of verification that are now achievable in arms control agreements, both bilateral and multilateral,

Believing that, through negotiations pursued in a spirit of flexibility and with full account taken of the security interests of all States, it is possible to achieve far-reaching and effectively verifiable agreements,

Firmly convinced that an early agreement in these negotiations, in accordance with the principle of undiminished security at the lowest possible level of armaments, would be of crucial importance for the strengthening of international peace and security,

Further convinced that the international community should encourage the Government of the Union of Soviet Socialist Republics and the Government of the United States of America in their endeavours, taking into account both the importance and complexity of their negotiations,

1. *Welcomes* the ratification by the Union of Soviet Socialist Republics and the United States of America of the Treaty on the Elimination of Their Intermediate-Range and Shorter-Range Missiles;

2. *Also welcomes* the successful commencement of the implementation of the provisions of that Treaty;

3. *Calls upon* the Government of the Union of Soviet Socialist Republics and the Government of the United States of America to spare no effort in seeking, in accordance with the security interests of all States and the universal desire for progress towards disarmament, the attainment of all the agreed objectives in the negotiations, that is, the resolution of a complex of questions concerning space and strategic nuclear arms with all these questions considered and resolved in their interrelationship;

4. *Invites* the two Governments concerned to keep other States Members of the United Nations duly informed of progress in their negotiations, in accordance with paragraph 114 of the Final Document of the Tenth Special Session of the General Assembly;

5. *Expresses its firmest possible encouragement and support* for the bilateral negotiations and their successful conclusion.

---

[a]A/S-15/28.

General Assembly resolution 43/75 O

7 December 1988   Meeting 73   103-0-46 (recorded vote)

Approved by First Committee (A/43/856) by recorded vote (70-0-58), 14 November (meeting 36); 16-nation draft (A/C.1/43/L.47); agenda item 64.

Sponsors: Australia, Belgium, Canada, Denmark, France, Germany, Federal Republic of, Greece, Italy, Japan, Netherlands, New Zealand, Norway, Portugal, Spain, Turkey, United Kingdom.

Meeting numbers. GA 43rd session: 1st Committee 3-25, 27, 36; plenary 73.

Recorded vote in Assembly as follows:

In favour: Antigua and Barbuda, Australia, Austria, Bahamas, Bahrain, Barbados, Belgium, Belize, Benin, Bhutan,* Brunei Darussalam, Bulgaria, Burkina Faso, Burundi,* Byelorussian SSR, Cameroon, Canada, Cape Verde, Central African Republic,* Chad, Chile, China, Colombia, Comoros, Costa Rica, Côte d'Ivoire, Czechoslovakia, Denmark, Djibouti, Dominican Republic, El Salvador, Fiji, Finland, France, Gabon, Gambia, German Democratic Republic, Germany, Federal Republic of, Greece, Guatemala, Guinea, Haiti, Honduras, Hungary, Iceland, Ireland, Israel, Italy, Jamaica, Japan, Jordan, Kenya, Kuwait, Lao People's Democratic Republic, Lebanon, Liberia, Luxembourg, Malaysia, Mali, Malta, Mauritius, Mongolia, Morocco, Netherlands, New Zealand, Norway, Papua New Guinea, Paraguay, Philippines, Poland, Portugal, Qatar, Romania, Rwanda, Saint Kitts and Nevis, Saint Lucia, Saint Vincent and the Grenadines, Samoa, Saudi Arabia, Senegal, Seychelles, Sierra Leone, Singapore, Solomon Islands, Somalia, Spain, Sri Lanka, Suriname, Swaziland, Sweden, Thailand, Trinidad and Tobago, Tunisia, Turkey, Ukrainian SSR, USSR, United Arab Emirates, United Kingdom, United States, Uruguay, Vanuatu, Viet Nam, Zaire.

Against: None.

Abstaining: Afghanistan, Algeria, Angola, Argentina, Bangladesh, Bolivia, Botswana, Brazil, Burma, Congo, Cuba, Cyprus, Democratic Yemen, Ecuador, Egypt, Ethiopia, Ghana, Guyana, India, Indonesia, Iran, Iraq, Lesotho, Libyan Arab Jamahiriya, Madagascar, Maldives, Mexico, Mozambique, Nepal, Nicaragua, Niger, Nigeria, Oman, Pakistan, Panama, Peru, Sudan, Syrian Arab Republic, Togo, Uganda, United Republic of Tanzania, Venezuela, Yemen, Yugoslavia, Zambia, Zimbabwe.

*Later advised the Secretariat it had intended to abstain.

Prohibition of nuclear weapons

In 1988, the General Assembly again considered the question of adequate verified cessation and prohibition of the production of fissionable material for weapons purposes. To that end, a proposal was made in the Conference on Disarmament that a group of experts be created within the framework of the Conference to study the problem, with the participation of all nuclear Powers at the stage of complete elimination of their nuclear weapons.

GENERAL ASSEMBLY ACTION

On 7 December, the General Assembly, on the recommendation of the First Committee, adopted **resolution 43/75 K** by recorded vote.

Prohibition of the production of fissionable material for weapons purposes

The General Assembly,

Recalling its resolutions 33/91 H of 16 December 1978, 34/87 D of 11 December 1979, 35/156 H of 12 December 1980, 36/97 G of 9 December 1981, 37/99 E of 13 December 1982, 38/188 E of 20 December 1983, 39/151 H of 17 December 1984, 40/94 G of 12 December 1985, 41/59 L of 3 December 1986 and 42/38 L of 30 November 1987, in which it requested the Conference on Disarmament, at an appropriate stage of the implementation of the Programme of Action set forth in section III of the Final Document of the Tenth Special Session of the General Assembly, and of its work on the item entitled "Nuclear weapons in all aspects", to consider urgently the question of adequately verified cessation and prohibition of the production of fissionable material for nuclear weapons and other nuclear explosive devices and to keep the Assembly informed of the progress of that consideration,

Noting that the agenda of the Conference on Disarmament for 1988 included the item entitled "Nuclear weapons in all aspects" and that the programme of work of the Conference for both parts of its 1988 session contained the item entitled "Cessation of the nuclear-arms race and nuclear disarmament",

Recalling the proposals and statements made in the Conference on Disarmament on those items,

Considering that the cessation of production of fissionable material for weapons purposes and the progressive conversion and transfer of stocks to peaceful uses would be a significant step towards halting and reversing the nuclear-arms race,

Considering also that the prohibition of the production of fissionable material for nuclear weapons and other explosive devices would be an important measure in facilitating the prevention of the proliferation of nuclear weapons and explosive devices,

Requests the Conference on Disarmament, at an appropriate stage of its work on the item entitled "Nuclear weapons in all aspects", to pursue its consideration of the question of adequately verified cessation and prohibition of the production of fissionable material for nuclear weapons and other nuclear explosive devices and to keep the General Assembly informed of the progress of that consideration.

General Assembly resolution 43/75 K

7 December 1988　　Meeting 73　　144-1-7 (recorded vote)

Approved by First Committee (A/43/856) by recorded vote (126-1-6), 11 November (meeting 34); 21-nation draft (A/C.1/43/L.32); agenda item 64 (i).

Sponsors: Australia, Austria, Bahamas, Bangladesh, Botswana, Cameroon, Canada, Denmark, Finland, Greece, Indonesia, Ireland, Japan, Netherlands, New Zealand, Norway, Philippines, Romania, Samoa, Sweden, Uruguay.
Meeting numbers. GA 43rd session: 1st Committee 3-25, 32, 34; plenary 73.

Recorded vote in Assembly as follows:

In favour: Afghanistan, Albania, Algeria, Angola, Antigua and Barbuda, Australia, Austria, Bahamas, Bahrain, Bangladesh, Barbados, Belgium, Belize, Benin, Bhutan, Bolivia, Botswana, Brunei Darussalam, Bulgaria, Burkina Faso, Burma, Burundi, Byelorussian SSR, Cameroon, Canada, Cape Verde, Central African Republic, Chad, Chile, Colombia, Comoros, Congo, Costa Rica, Côte d'Ivoire, Cuba, Cyprus, Czechoslovakia, Democratic Yemen, Denmark, Djibouti, Dominican Republic, Ecuador, Egypt, El Salvador, Ethiopia, Fiji, Finland, Gabon, Gambia, German Democratic Republic, Germany, Federal Republic of, Ghana, Greece, Guatemala, Guinea, Guyana, Haiti, Honduras, Hungary, Iceland, Indonesia, Iran, Iraq, Ireland, Israel, Italy, Jamaica, Japan, Jordan, Kenya, Kuwait, Lao People's Democratic Republic, Lebanon, Lesotho, Liberia, Libyan Arab Jamahiriya, Madagascar, Malawi, Malaysia, Maldives, Mali, Malta, Mauritania, Mauritius, Mexico, Mongolia, Morocco, Mozambique, Nepal, Netherlands, New Zealand, Nicaragua, Niger, Nigeria, Norway, Oman, Pakistan, Panama, Papua New Guinea, Paraguay, Peru, Philippines, Poland, Portugal, Qatar, Romania, Rwanda, Saint Lucia, Saint Vincent and the Grenadines, Samoa, Sao Tome and Principe, Saudi Arabia, Senegal, Seychelles, Sierra Leone, Singapore, Solomon Islands, Somalia, Spain, Sri Lanka, Sudan, Suriname, Swaziland, Sweden, Syrian Arab Republic, Thailand, Togo, Trinidad and Tobago, Tunisia, Turkey, Uganda, Ukrainian SSR, USSR, United Arab Emirates, United Republic of Tanzania, Uruguay, Vanuatu, Venezuela, Viet Nam, Yemen, Yugoslavia, Zaire, Zambia, Zimbabwe.

Against: France.

Abstaining: Argentina, Brazil, China, India, Luxembourg, United Kingdom, United States.

Cessation of nuclear-weapon tests

In 1988, efforts continued towards the negotiation of a comprehensive test-ban treaty in the Disarmament Commission, the Conference on Disarmament and the General Assembly. On 21 January, the heads of State of Argentina, Greece, India, Mexico, Sweden and the United Republic of Tanzania declared in the Stockholm Declaration[13] that any agreement which left room for continued testing would not be acceptable and that a comprehensive test ban was long overdue.

Note by the Secretary General. Pursuant to a 1987 General Assembly request,[14] the Secretary General submitted the first annual register[15] of information on nuclear explosions, compiled on the basis of information provided to him between 15 September 1987 and 14 September 1988.[16] The register contained information on nuclear-test explosions reported by the USSR in 1987 and 1988, and on explosions detected in 1987 by New Zealand, a non-nuclear-weapon State.

Disarmament Commission consideration. In 1988, as part of its effort to compile proposals for recommendations on a general approach to various aspects of the arms race and questions relating to both nuclear and conventional disarmament, the Disarmament Commission was again unable to reach agreement on a text for a recommendation covering the negotiation of a comprehensive nuclear-test-ban treaty.[5]

Consideration by the Conference on Disarmament. The Conference on Disarmament considered the question of a nuclear-test ban from 15 to 26 February and from 18 to 29 July.

New proposals on a mandate for an *ad hoc* committee on the issue were made by Czechoslovakia[17] and the Group of 21,[18] but the Conference again could not agree on such a mandate.

By letters dated 5 August[19] and 16 August,[20] Indonesia, Mexico, Peru, Sri Lanka, Venezuela and Yugoslavia informed the Conference that they had formally submitted to the three depositary Governments of the 1963 Treaty Banning Nuclear Weapon Tests in the Atmosphere, in Outer Space and under Water (partial test-ban Treaty)[21] an amendment proposing to convert that Treaty into a comprehensive test ban.

The Conference also considered the reports of the *Ad Hoc* Group of Scientific Experts to Consider International Co-operative Measures to Detect and Identify Seismic Events, which met at Geneva for its twenty-fifth (7-18 March)[22] and twenty-sixth sessions (25 July–5 August).[23] The Group's reports gave an account of its work on developing the overall concept of a modern international seismic-data exchange system based on the expeditious exchange of parameter (level I) and waveform (level II) data and the processing of such data at international data centres. The first phase of activities commenced on an experiment focusing on the exchange and analysis of seismic wave-form segments. The experiment was intended to test methods and procedures to extract, process and transmit the data expeditiously.

A document entitled "Verification of a comprehensive nuclear-test ban: establishing a global seismological network incorporating small-aperture arrays"[24] was submitted by Norway, a non-member of the Conference participating in the Group.

The Conference reported to the third special session on disarmament[11] and to the 1988 regular session[1] of the General Assembly on the issue of a nuclear-test ban.

GENERAL ASSEMBLY ACTION

On 7 December 1988, the General Assembly adopted, on the recommendation of the First Committee, two resolutions (43/63 A and B) on the cessation of all nuclear-test explosions. **Resolution 43/63 A** was adopted by recorded vote.

The General Assembly,

Bearing in mind that the complete cessation of nuclear-weapon tests, which has been examined for more than thirty years and on which the General Assembly has adopted more than fifty resolutions, is a basic objective of the United Nations in the sphere of disarmament, to the attainment of which it has repeatedly assigned the highest priority,

Stressing that on eight different occasions it has condemned such tests in the strongest terms and that, since 1974, it has stated its conviction that the continuance of nuclear-weapon testing will intensify the arms race, thus increasing the danger of nuclear war,

Recalling that the Secretary-General, addressing a plenary meeting of the General Assembly on 12 December 1984, after appealing for a renewed effort towards a comprehensive test-ban treaty, emphasized that no single multilateral agreement could have a greater effect on limiting the further refinement of nuclear weapons and that a comprehensive test-ban treaty is the litmus test of the real willingness to pursue nuclear disarmament,

Taking into account that the three nuclear-weapon States that act as depositaries of the 1963 Treaty Banning Nuclear Weapon Tests in the Atmosphere, in Outer Space and under Water undertook in article I of that Treaty to conclude a treaty resulting in the permanent banning of all nuclear-test explosions, including all those explosions underground, and that such an undertaking was reiterated in 1968 in the preamble to the Treaty on the Non-Proliferation of Nuclear Weapons, article VI of which further embodies their solemn and legally binding commitment to take effective measures relating to cessation of the nuclear-arms race at an early date and to nuclear disarmament,

Noting that the Third Review Conference of the Parties to the Treaty on the Non-Proliferation of Nuclear Weapons, in its Final Declaration adopted on 21 September 1985, called upon the nuclear-weapon States parties to the Treaty to resume trilateral negotiations in 1985 and upon all the nuclear-weapon States to participate in the urgent negotiation and conclusion of a comprehensive nuclear-test-ban treaty, as a matter of the highest priority, in the Conference on Disarmament,

Recalling that the leaders of the six States associated with the five-continent peace and disarmament initiative affirmed in the Stockholm Declaration, adopted on

21 January 1988, that "Any agreement that leaves room for continued testing would not be acceptable",

Taking note with satisfaction of the progress made in the Conference on Disarmament by the *Ad Hoc* Group of Scientific Experts to Consider International Co-operative Measures to Detect and Identify Seismic Events on the seismic verification of a comprehensive test ban,

1. *Reiterates once again its grave concern* that nuclear-weapon testing continues unabated, against the wishes of the overwhelming majority of Member States;

2. *Reaffirms its conviction* that a treaty to achieve the prohibition of all nuclear-test explosions by all States for all time is a matter of the highest priority;

3. *Reaffirms also its conviction* that such a treaty would constitute a contribution of the utmost importance to the cessation of the nuclear-arms race;

4. *Urges once more* all nuclear-weapon States, in particular the three depositary Powers of the Treaty Banning Nuclear Weapon Tests in the Atmosphere, in Outer Space and under Water and of the Treaty on the Non-Proliferation of Nuclear Weapons, to seek to achieve the early discontinuance of all test explosions of nuclear weapons for all time and to expedite negotiations to this end;

5. *Appeals* to all States members of the Conference on Disarmament to promote the establishment by the Conference at the beginning of its 1989 session of an *ad hoc* committee with the objective of carrying out the multilateral negotiation of a treaty on the complete cessation of nuclear-test explosions;

6. *Recommends* to the Conference on Disarmament that such an *ad hoc* committee should comprise two working groups dealing, respectively, with the following interrelated questions: contents and scope of the treaty, and compliance and verification;

7. *Decides* to include in the provisional agenda of its forty-fourth session the item entitled "Cessation of all nuclear-test explosions".

General Assembly resolution 43/63 A

7 December 1988   Meeting 73   136-4-13 (recorded vote)

Approved by First Committee (A/43/831) by recorded vote (118-3-13), 15 November (meeting 37); 11-nation draft (A/C.1/43/L.13); agenda item 52.

Sponsors: Ecuador, Indonesia, Ireland, Mexico, Pakistan, Peru, Romania, Sri Lanka, Sweden, Venezuela, Yugoslavia.

Meeting numbers. GA 43rd session: 1st Committee 3-25, 28, 37; plenary 73.

Recorded vote in Assembly as follows:

In favour: Afghanistan, Albania, Algeria, Angola, Antigua and Barbuda, Argentina, Australia, Austria, Bahamas, Bahrain, Bangladesh, Barbados, Belize, Benin, Bhutan, Bolivia, Botswana, Brazil, Brunei Darussalam, Bulgaria, Burkina Faso, Burma, Burundi, Byelorussian SSR, Cameroon, Cape Verde, Central African Republic, Chad, Chile, Colombia, Comoros, Congo, Costa Rica, Côte d'Ivoire, Cuba, Cyprus, Czechoslovakia, Democratic Yemen, Denmark, Djibouti, Dominican Republic, Ecuador, Egypt, El Salvador, Ethiopia, Fiji, Finland, Gabon, Gambia, German Democratic Republic, Ghana, Greece, Grenada, Guatemala, Guinea, Guyana, Haiti, Honduras, Hungary, India, Indonesia, Iran, Iraq, Ireland, Jamaica, Jordan, Kenya, Kuwait, Lao People's Democratic Republic, Lebanon, Lesotho, Liberia, Libyan Arab Jamahiriya, Madagascar, Malawi, Malaysia, Maldives, Mali, Malta, Mauritania, Mauritius, Mexico, Mongolia, Morocco, Mozambique, Nepal, New Zealand, Nicaragua, Niger, Nigeria, Norway, Oman, Pakistan, Panama, Papua New Guinea, Paraguay, Peru, Philippines, Poland, Qatar, Romania, Rwanda, Saint Kitts and Nevis, Saint Lucia, Samoa, Sao Tome and Principe, Saudi Arabia, Senegal, Seychelles, Sierra Leone, Singapore, Solomon Islands, Somalia, Sri Lanka, Sudan, Suriname, Swaziland, Sweden, Syrian Arab Republic, Thailand, Togo, Trinidad and Tobago, Tunisia, Uganda, Ukrainian SSR, USSR, United Arab Emirates, United Republic of Tanzania, Uruguay, Vanuatu, Venezuela, Viet Nam, Yugoslavia, Zaire, Zambia, Zimbabwe.

Against: France, United Kingdom, United States, Yemen.*

Abstaining: Belgium, Canada, China, Germany, Federal Republic of, Iceland, Israel, Italy, Japan, Luxembourg, Netherlands, Portugal, Spain, Turkey.

*Later advised the Secretariat it had intended to vote in favour.

Resolution 43/63 B was also adopted by recorded vote.

The General Assembly,

Bearing in mind the determination, proclaimed since 1963 in the Treaty Banning Nuclear Weapon Tests in the Atmosphere, in Outer Space and under Water, to seek to achieve the discontinuance of all test explosions of nuclear weapons for all time and to continue negotiations to this end,

Bearing in mind also that in 1968 the Treaty on the Non-Proliferation of Nuclear Weapons recalled such determination and included in its article VI an undertaking by each of its parties to pursue negotiations in good faith on effective measures relating to the cessation of the nuclear-arms race at an early date,

Recalling that in its resolution 2028(XX) of 19 November 1965, adopted unanimously, it had stressed that one of the basic principles on which the treaty to prevent the proliferation of nuclear weapons should be based was that such treaty, which was then to be negotiated, should embody an acceptable balance of mutual responsibilities and obligations of the nuclear and non-nuclear Powers,

Recalling also that the Third Review Conference of the Parties to the Treaty on the Non-Proliferation of Nuclear Weapons, in its Final Declaration adopted by consensus on 21 September 1985, expressed its deep regret that a comprehensive multilateral nuclear-test-ban treaty had not been concluded so far and called for the urgent negotiation and conclusion of such a treaty as a matter of the highest priority,

Noting that article II of the Treaty Banning Nuclear Weapon Tests in the Atmosphere, in Outer Space and under Water provides a procedure for the consideration and eventual adoption of amendments to the Treaty by a conference of its parties,

1. *Welcomes* the submission to the Depositary Governments of the Treaty Banning Nuclear Weapon Tests in the Atmosphere, in Outer Space and under Water of an amendment proposal for consideration at a conference of the parties to the Treaty convened for that purpose in accordance with article II of the Treaty;

2. *Decides* to include in the provisional agenda of its forty-fourth session an item entitled "Amendment of the Treaty Banning Nuclear Weapon Tests in the Atmosphere, in Outer Space and under Water".

General Assembly resolution 43/63 B

7 December 1988   Meeting 73   127-3-21 (recorded vote)

Approved by First Committee (A/43/831) by recorded vote (108-3-21), 15 November (meeting 37); 8-nation draft (A/C.1/43/L.23); agenda item 52.
Sponsors: Ecuador, Indonesia, Mexico, Peru, Romania, Sri Lanka, Venezuela, Yugoslavia.
Meeting numbers. GA 43rd session: 1st Committee 3-25, 29, 37; plenary 73.

Recorded vote in Assembly as follows:

In favour: Afghanistan, Albania, Algeria, Angola, Antigua and Barbuda, Argentina, Bahamas, Bahrain, Bangladesh, Barbados, Belize, Benin, Bhutan, Bolivia, Botswana, Brazil, Brunei Darussalam, Bulgaria, Burkina Faso, Burma, Burundi, Byelorussian SSR, Cameroon, Cape Verde, Central African Republic, Chad, Chile, Colombia, Comoros, Congo, Costa Rica, Côte d'Ivoire, Cuba, Cyprus, Czechoslovakia, Democratic Yemen, Djibouti, Dominican Republic, Ecuador, Egypt, El Salvador, Ethiopia, Fiji, Gabon, Gambia, German Democratic Republic, Ghana, Grenada, Guatemala, Guinea, Guyana, Haiti, Honduras, Hungary, India, Indonesia, Iran, Iraq, Jamaica, Jordan, Kenya, Kuwait, Lao People's Democratic Republic, Lebanon, Lesotho, Liberia, Libyan Arab Jamahiriya, Madagascar, Malawi, Malaysia, Maldives, Mali, Malta, Mauritania, Mauritius, Mexico, Mongolia, Morocco, Mozambique, Nepal, Nicaragua, Niger, Nigeria, Oman, Pakistan, Panama, Papua New Guinea, Paraguay, Peru, Philippines, Poland,

Qatar, Romania, Rwanda, Saint Kitts and Nevis, Saint Lucia, Sao Tome and Principe, Saudi Arabia, Senegal, Seychelles, Sierra Leone, Singapore, Solomon Islands, Somalia, Sri Lanka, Sudan, Suriname, Swaziland, Syrian Arab Republic, Thailand, Togo, Trinidad and Tobago, Tunisia, Uganda, Ukrainian SSR, USSR, United Arab Emirates, United Republic of Tanzania, Uruguay, Vanuatu, Venezuela, Viet Nam, Yemen, Yugoslavia, Zaire, Zambia, Zimbabwe.
Against: France, United Kingdom, United States.
Abstaining: Australia, Austria, Belgium, Canada, Denmark, Finland, Germany, Federal Republic of, Greece, Iceland, Ireland, Israel, Italy, Japan, Luxembourg, Netherlands, New Zealand, Norway, Portugal, Spain, Sweden, Turkey.

On 7 December, as recommended by the First Committee, the Assembly adopted **resolution 43/64** by recorded vote.

Urgent need for a comprehensive nuclear-test-ban treaty

The General Assembly,

Convinced that a nuclear war cannot be won and must never be fought,

Convinced also of the consequent urgent need for an end to the nuclear-arms race and the immediate and verifiable reduction and ultimate elimination of nuclear weapons,

Convinced further that an end to nuclear testing by all States in all environments for all time is an essential step in order to prevent the qualitative improvement and development of nuclear weapons and their further proliferation and to contribute, along with other concurrent efforts to reduce nuclear arms, to the eventual elimination of nuclear weapons,

Welcoming the ongoing negotiations between the Union of Soviet Socialist Republics and the United States of America in accordance with their joint statement of 17 September 1987, and noting the significant developments on improved verification arrangements to facilitate the ratification of the Treaty between the United States of America and the Union of Soviet Socialist Republics on the Limitation of Underground Nuclear Weapon Tests, signed on 3 July 1974, and the Treaty between the United States of America and the Union of Soviet Socialist Republics on Underground Nuclear Explosions for Peaceful Purposes, signed on 28 May 1976,

Welcoming also the conclusion on 8 December 1987 of the historic Treaty between the United States of America and the Union of Soviet Socialist Republics on the Elimination of Their Intermediate-Range and Shorter-Range Missiles and the agreement in principle on and progress made towards an agreement for 50 per cent reductions in the strategic nuclear forces of the Union of Soviet Socialist Republics and the United States of America,

Recalling the proposals by the leaders of the Six-Nation Initiative to promote an end to nuclear testing,

Convinced that the most effective way to achieve the discontinuance of all nuclear tests by all States in all environments for all time is through the conclusion, at an early date, of a verifiable, comprehensive nuclear-test-ban treaty that will attract the adherence of all States,

Reaffirming the particular responsibilities of the Conference on Disarmament in the negotiation of a comprehensive nuclear-test-ban treaty,

1. *Reaffirms its conviction* that a treaty to achieve the prohibition of all nuclear-test explosions by all States in all environments for all time is a matter of fundamental importance;

2. *Urges*, therefore, that the following actions be taken in order that a comprehensive nuclear-test-ban treaty may be concluded at an early date:

(*a*) The Conference on Disarmament should intensify its consideration of item 1 of its agenda entitled "Nuclear-test ban" and initiate substantive work on all aspects of a nuclear-test-ban treaty at the beginning of its 1989 session;

(*b*) States members of the Conference on Disarmament, in particular the nuclear-weapon States, and all other States should co-operate in order to facilitate and promote such work;

(*c*) The nuclear-weapon States, especially those that possess the most important nuclear arsenals, should agree promptly to appropriate verifiable and militarily significant interim measures, with a view to realizing a comprehensive nuclear-test-ban treaty;

(*d*) Those nuclear-weapon States that have not yet done so should adhere to the Treaty Banning Nuclear Weapon Tests in the Atmosphere, in Outer Space and under Water;

3. *Also urges* the Conference on Disarmament:

(*a*) To take immediate steps for the establishment, with the widest possible participation, of an international seismic monitoring network with a view to the further development of its potential to monitor and verify compliance with a comprehensive nuclear-test-ban treaty;

(*b*) In this context, to take into account the progress achieved by the *Ad Hoc* Group of Scientific Experts to Consider International Co-operative Measures to Detect and Identify Seismic Events, including work on the routine exchange and use of wave-form data, and other relevant initiatives or experiments by individual States and groups of States;

(*c*) To initiate detailed investigation of other measures to monitor and verify compliance with such a treaty, including an international network to monitor atmospheric radioactivity;

4. *Calls upon* the Conference on Disarmament to report to the General Assembly at its forty-fourth session on progress made;

5. *Decides* to include in the provisional agenda of its forty-fourth session the item entitled "Urgent need for a comprehensive nuclear-test-ban treaty".

General Assembly resolution 43/64

7 December 1988   Meeting 73   146-2-6 (recorded vote)

Approved by First Committee (A/43/832) by recorded vote (127-2-6), 15 November (meeting 37); 31-nation draft (A/C.1/43/L.51); agenda item 53.
Sponsors: Australia, Austria, Bahamas, Barbados, Brunei Darussalam, Cameroon, Canada, Colombia, Costa Rica, Denmark, Ecuador, Fiji, Finland, Greece, Iceland, Ireland, Jamaica, Japan, Liberia, New Zealand, Nigeria, Norway, Papua New Guinea, Philippines, Samoa, Singapore, Solomon Islands, Sweden, Thailand, Vanuatu, Zaire.
Meeting numbers. GA 43rd session: 1st Committee 3-25, 30, 37; plenary 73.

Recorded vote in Assembly as follows:

In favour: Afghanistan, Albania, Algeria, Angola, Antigua and Barbuda, Australia, Austria, Bahamas, Bahrain, Bangladesh, Barbados, Belgium, Belize, Benin, Bhutan, Bolivia, Botswana, Brunei Darussalam, Bulgaria, Burkina Faso, Burma, Burundi, Byelorussian SSR, Cameroon, Canada, Cape Verde, Central African Republic, Chad, Chile, Colombia, Comoros, Congo, Costa Rica, Côte d'Ivoire, Cuba, Cyprus, Czechoslovakia, Democratic Yemen, Denmark, Djibouti, Dominican Republic, Ecuador, Egypt, El Salvador, Ethiopia, Fiji, Finland, Gabon, Gambia, German Democratic Republic, Germany, Federal Republic of, Ghana, Greece, Grenada, Guatemala, Guinea, Guyana, Haiti, Honduras, Hungary, Iceland, Indonesia, Iran, Iraq, Ireland, Italy, Jamaica, Japan, Jordan, Kenya, Kuwait, Lao People's Democratic Republic, Lebanon, Lesotho, Liberia, Libyan Arab Jamahiriya, Luxembourg, Madagascar, Malawi, Malaysia, Maldives, Mali, Malta, Mauritania, Mauritius, Mexico, Mongolia, Morocco, Mozambique, Nepal, Netherlands, New Zealand, Nicaragua, Niger, Nigeria, Norway, Oman, Pak-

istan, Panama, Papua New Guinea, Paraguay, Peru, Philippines, Poland, Portugal, Qatar, Romania, Rwanda, Saint Kitts and Nevis, Saint Lucia, Saint Vincent and the Grenadines, Samoa, Sao Tome and Principe, Saudi Arabia, Senegal, Seychelles, Sierra Leone, Singapore, Solomon Islands, Somalia, Spain, Sri Lanka, Sudan, Suriname, Swaziland, Sweden, Syrian Arab Republic, Thailand, Togo, Trinidad and Tobago, Tunisia, Turkey, Uganda, Ukrainian SSR, USSR, United Arab Emirates, United Republic of Tanzania, Uruguay, Vanuatu, Venezuela, Viet Nam, Yemen, Yugoslavia, Zaire, Zambia, Zimbabwe.
Against: France, United States.
Abstaining: Argentina, Brazil, China, India, Israel, United Kingdom.

Nuclear-weapons freeze

Since 1982, the General Assembly had annually called for a freeze on nuclear weapons, but no action had been taken by the nuclear-weapon States. In 1988, the Assembly again considered the issue of a nuclear-arms freeze.

GENERAL ASSEMBLY ACTION

On 7 December, the General Assembly, on the recommendation of the First Committee, adopted **resolution 43/76 B** by recorded vote.

Nuclear-arms freeze

The General Assembly,

Recalling that in the Final Document of the Tenth Special Session of the General Assembly, the first special session devoted to disarmament, adopted in 1978 and unanimously and categorically reaffirmed in 1982 during the twelfth special session of the General Assembly, the second special session devoted to disarmament, the Assembly expressed deep concern over the threat to the very survival of mankind posed by the existence of nuclear weapons and the continuing arms race,

Convinced that, in this nuclear age, lasting world peace can be based only on the attainment of the goal of general and complete disarmament under effective international control,

Welcoming the improvement of the relations between the Union of Soviet Socialist Republics and the United States of America and the conclusion of the Treaty on the Elimination of Their Intermediate-Range and Shorter-Range Missiles, as well as their agreement in principle to reduce by 50 per cent their strategic nuclear arsenals,

Convinced of the urgency further to pursue negotiations for the substantial reduction and qualitative limitation of existing nuclear arms,

Considering that a nuclear-arms freeze, while not an end in itself, would constitute an effective step to prevent the continued increase and qualitative improvement of existing nuclear weaponry during the period when the negotiations take place, and that at the same time it would provide a favourable environment for the conduct of negotiations to reduce and eventually eliminate nuclear weapons,

Convinced that the undertakings derived from the freeze can be effectively verified,

Noting with deep concern that nuclear-weapon States have not so far taken any action in response to the call made in the relevant resolutions on the question of a nuclear-arms freeze,

1. *Urges once more* the Union of Soviet Socialist Republics and the United States of America, as the two major nuclear-weapon States, to agree to an immediate nuclear-arms freeze, which would, *inter alia*, provide for

a simultaneous total stoppage of any further production of nuclear weapons and a complete cut-off in the production of fissionable material for weapons purposes;

2. *Calls upon* all nuclear-weapon States to agree, through a joint declaration, to a comprehensive nuclear-arms freeze, whose structure and scope would be the following:

(a) It would embrace:

(i)   A comprehensive test ban on nuclear weapons and on their delivery vehicles;

(ii) The complete cessation of the manufacture of nuclear weapons and of their delivery vehicles;

(iii) A ban on all further deployment of nuclear weapons and of their delivery vehicles;

(iv) The complete cessation of the production of fissionable material for weapons purposes;

(b) It would be subject to appropriate and effective measures and procedures of verification;

3. *Requests* the nuclear-weapon States to submit a joint report, or separate reports, to the General Assembly, prior to the opening of its forty-fourth session, on the implementation of the present resolution;

4. *Decides* to include in the provisional agenda of its forty-fourth session an item entitled ''Nuclear-arms freeze''.

General Assembly resolution 43/76 B

7 December 1988   Meeting 73   135-12-3 (recorded vote)

Approved by First Committee (A/43/857) by recorded vote (116-13-3), 17 November (meeting 40); 7-nation draft (A/C.1/43/L.26/Rev.1); agenda item 65 *(b)*.

Sponsors: India, Indonesia, Mexico, Pakistan, Peru, Romania, Sweden.

Meeting numbers. GA 43rd session: 1st Committee 3-25, 29, 40; plenary 73.

Recorded vote in Assembly as follows:

In favour: Afghanistan, Albania, Algeria, Angola, Antigua and Barbuda, Argentina, Australia, Austria, Bahamas, Bahrain, Bangladesh, Belize, Benin, Bhutan, Bolivia, Botswana, Brazil, Brunei Darussalam, Bulgaria, Burkina Faso, Burma, Burundi, Byelorussian SSR, Cameroon, Cape Verde, Central African Republic, Chad, Chile, Colombia, Comoros, Congo, Costa Rica, Côte d'Ivoire, Cuba, Cyprus, Czechoslovakia, Democratic Yemen, Denmark, Djibouti, Dominican Republic, Ecuador, Egypt, El Salvador, Ethiopia, Fiji, Finland, Gabon, Gambia, German Democratic Republic, Ghana, Greece, Guatemala, Guinea, Guyana, Haiti, Honduras, Hungary, India, Indonesia, Iran, Iraq, Ireland, Jamaica, Jordan, Kenya, Kuwait, Lao People's Democratic Republic, Lebanon, Lesotho, Liberia, Libyan Arab Jamahiriya, Madagascar, Malawi, Malaysia, Maldives, Mali, Malta, Mauritania, Mauritius, Mexico, Morocco, Mozambique, Nepal, New Zealand, Nicaragua, Niger, Nigeria, Norway, Oman, Pakistan, Panama, Papua New Guinea, Paraguay, Peru, Philippines, Poland, Qatar, Romania, Rwanda, Saint Kitts and Nevis, Saint Lucia, Saint Vincent and the Grenadines, Samoa, Sao Tome and Principe, Saudi Arabia, Senegal, Seychelles, Sierra Leone, Singapore, Solomon Islands, Somalia, Sri Lanka, Sudan, Suriname, Swaziland, Sweden, Syrian Arab Republic, Thailand, Togo, Trinidad and Tobago, Tunisia, Uganda, Ukrainian SSR, USSR, United Arab Emirates, United Republic of Tanzania, Uruguay, Vanuatu, Venezuela, Viet Nam, Yemen, Yugoslavia, Zaire, Zambia, Zimbabwe.

Against: Belgium, Canada, France, Germany, Federal Republic of, Israel, Italy, Japan, Luxembourg, Netherlands, Turkey, United Kingdom, United States.

Abstaining: China, Iceland, Spain.

Security of non-nuclear-weapon States

The Conference on Disarmament considered, from 28 March to 1 April and from 22 to 26 August, effective international arrangements to assure non-nuclear-weapon States against the use or threat of use of nuclear weapons (also known as negative security assurances). It had on 2 February re-established an *ad hoc* committee to continue negotiations with a view to reaching agreement on

the subject. The Committee, at both sessions,[25] considered the question of a single ''common formula'' to assure non-nuclear-weapon States against the use or threat of use of nuclear weapons. In that connection, it also discussed an alternative option whereby nuclear-weapon States would set aside their various unilateral declarations to facilitate effective negotiations and the adoption of a convention, and a further proposal for nuclear-weapon States to give negative security assurances to categories of non-nuclear-weapon States. The discussion, however, revealed that difficulties relating to differing perceptions of security interests of nuclear-weapon and non-nuclear-weapon States persisted and the complex nature of the issues involved continued to prevent agreement on a ''common formula'' for inclusion in a convention. The Committee recommended that work continue to overcome the difficulties.

The Conference adopted the reports of the Committee, which were considered by the General Assembly at its third special session on disarmament[11] and its 1988 regular session.[1]

GENERAL ASSEMBLY ACTION

On 7 December, the General Assembly, on the recommendation of the First Committee, adopted by recorded vote **resolution 43/69**.

Conclusion of effective international arrangements to assure non-nuclear-weapon States against the use or threat of use of nuclear weapons

The General Assembly,

Bearing in mind the need to allay the legitimate concern of the States of the world with regard to ensuring lasting security for their peoples,

Convinced that nuclear weapons pose the greatest threat to mankind and to the survival of civilization,

Deeply concerned at the continuing escalation of the arms race, in particular the nuclear-arms race, and the possibility of the use or threat of use of nuclear weapons,

Convinced that nuclear disarmament and the complete elimination of nuclear weapons are essential to remove the danger of nuclear war,

Taking into account the principle of the non-use of force or threat of force enshrined in the Charter of the United Nations,

Deeply concerned about the possibility of the use or threat of use of nuclear weapons,

Recognizing that the independence, territorial integrity and sovereignty of non-nuclear-weapon States need to be safeguarded against the use or threat of use of force, including the use or threat of use of nuclear weapons,

Considering that, until nuclear disarmament is achieved on a universal basis, it is imperative for the international community to develop effective measures to ensure the security of non-nuclear-weapon States against the use or threat of use of nuclear weapons from any quarter,

Recognizing that effective measures to assure the non-nuclear-weapon States against the use or threat of use of nuclear weapons can constitute a positive contribution to the prevention of the spread of nuclear weapons,

Recalling its resolutions 3261 G (XXIX) of 9 December 1974 and 31/189 C of 21 December 1976,

Bearing in mind paragraph 59 of the Final Document of the Tenth Special Session of the General Assembly, in which it urged the nuclear-weapon States to pursue efforts to conclude, as appropriate, effective arrangements to assure non-nuclear-weapon States against the use or threat of use of nuclear weapons,

Desirous of promoting the implementation of the relevant provisions of the Final Document of the Tenth Special Session,

Recalling also its resolutions 33/72 B of 14 December 1978, 34/85 of 11 December 1979, 35/155 of 12 December 1980, 36/95 of 9 December 1981, 37/81 of 9 December 1982, 38/68 of 15 December 1983, 39/58 of 12 December 1984, 40/86 of 12 December 1985, 41/52 of 3 December 1986 and 42/32 of 30 November 1987,

Recalling further paragraph 12 of the Declaration of the 1980s as the Second Disarmament Decade, contained in the annex to its resolution 35/46 of 3 December 1980, which states, *inter alia*, that all efforts should be exerted by the Committee on Disarmament urgently to negotiate with a view to reaching agreement on effective international arrangements to assure non-nuclear-weapon States against the use or threat of use of nuclear weapons,

Noting the in-depth negotiations undertaken in the Conference on Disarmament and its *Ad Hoc* Committee on Effective International Arrangements to Assure Non-Nuclear-Weapon States against the Use or Threat of Use of Nuclear Weapons, with a view to reaching agreement on this item,

Taking note of the proposals submitted under that item in the Conference on Disarmament, including the drafts of an international convention,

Taking note of the decision of the Eighth Conference of Heads of State or Government of Non-Aligned Countries, held at Harare from 1 to 6 September 1986, as well as the relevant recommendations of the Organization of the Islamic Conference reiterated in the Final Communiqué of the Seventeenth Islamic Conference of Foreign Ministers, held at Amman from 21 to 25 March 1988,[a] calling upon the Conference on Disarmament to reach an urgent agreement on an international convention to assure non-nuclear-weapon States against the use or threat of use of nuclear weapons,

Noting the support expressed in the Conference on Disarmament and in the General Assembly for the elaboration of an international convention to assure non-nuclear-weapon States against the use or threat of use of nuclear weapons, as well as the difficulties pointed out in evolving a common approach acceptable to all,

1. *Reaffirms* the urgent need to reach agreement on effective international arrangements to assure non-nuclear-weapon States against the use or threat of use of nuclear weapons;

2. *Notes with satisfaction* that in the Conference on Disarmament there is no objection, in principle, to the idea of an international convention to assure non-nuclear-weapon States against the use or threat of use of nuclear weapons, although the difficulties as regards evolving a common approach acceptable to all have also been pointed out;

3. *Appeals* to all States, especially the nuclear-weapon States, to demonstrate the political will necessary to reach agreement on a common approach and, in particular, on a common formula that could be included in an international instrument of a legally binding character;

4. *Recommends* that further intensive efforts should be devoted to the search for such a common approach or common formula and that the various alternative approaches, including, in particular, those considered in the Conference on Disarmament, should be further explored in order to overcome the difficulties;

5. *Recommends* that the Conference on Disarmament should actively continue negotiations with a view to reaching early agreement and concluding effective international arrangements to assure non-nuclear-weapon States against the use or threat of use of nuclear weapons, taking into account the widespread support for the conclusion of an international convention and giving consideration to any other proposals designed to secure the same objective;

6. *Decides* to include in the provisional agenda of its forty-fourth session the item entitled "Conclusion of effective international arrangements to assure non-nuclear-weapon States against the use or threat of use of nuclear weapons".

---

[a]A/43/393-S/19930.

General Assembly resolution 43/69

7 December 1988   Meeting 73   152-0-3 (recorded vote)

Approved by First Committee (A/43/837) by recorded vote (133-0-4), 10 November (meeting 33); draft by Pakistan (A/C.1/43/L.18); agenda item 58.
Meeting numbers. GA 43rd session: 1st Committee 3-25, 28, 33; plenary 73.

Recorded vote in Assembly as follows:

In favour: Afghanistan, Albania, Algeria, Angola, Antigua and Barbuda, Argentina, Australia, Austria, Bahamas, Bahrain, Bangladesh, Barbados, Belgium, Belize, Benin, Bhutan, Bolivia, Botswana, Brunei Darussalam, Bulgaria, Burkina Faso, Burma, Burundi, Byelorussian SSR, Cameroon, Canada, Cape Verde, Central African Republic, Chad, Chile, China, Colombia, Comoros, Congo, Costa Rica, Côte d'Ivoire, Cuba, Cyprus, Czechoslovakia, Democratic Kampuchea, Democratic Yemen, Denmark, Djibouti, Dominican Republic, Ecuador, Egypt, El Salvador, Ethiopia, Fiji, Finland, France, Gabon, Gambia, German Democratic Republic, Germany, Federal Republic of, Ghana, Greece, Grenada, Guatemala, Guinea, Guyana, Haiti, Honduras, Hungary, Iceland, Indonesia, Iran, Iraq, Ireland, Israel, Italy, Jamaica, Japan, Jordan, Kenya, Kuwait, Lao People's Democratic Republic, Lebanon, Lesotho, Liberia, Libyan Arab Jamahiriya, Luxembourg, Madagascar, Malawi, Malaysia, Maldives, Mali, Malta, Mauritania, Mauritius, Mexico, Mongolia, Morocco, Mozambique, Nepal, Netherlands, New Zealand, Nicaragua, Niger, Nigeria, Norway, Oman, Pakistan, Panama, Papua New Guinea, Paraguay, Peru, Philippines, Poland, Portugal, Qatar, Romania, Rwanda, Saint Kitts and Nevis, Saint Lucia, Saint Vincent and the Grenadines, Samoa, Sao Tome and Principe, Saudi Arabia, Senegal, Seychelles, Sierra Leone, Singapore, Solomon Islands, Somalia, Spain, Sri Lanka, Sudan, Suriname, Swaziland, Sweden, Syrian Arab Republic, Thailand, Togo, Trinidad and Tobago, Tunisia, Turkey, Uganda, Ukrainian SSR, USSR, United Arab Emirates, United Kingdom, United Republic of Tanzania, Uruguay, Vanuatu, Venezuela, Viet Nam, Yemen, Yugoslavia, Zaire, Zambia, Zimbabwe.
Against: None.
Abstaining: Brazil, India, United States.

On the same date, the Assembly, again on the First Committee's recommendation, adopted by recorded vote **resolution 43/68**.

Conclusion of effective international arrangements on the strengthening of the security of non-nuclear-weapon States against the use or threat of use of nuclear weapons

The General Assembly,

Deeply concerned at the continuing escalation of the arms race, in particular the nuclear-arms race, and the possibility of the use or threat of use of nuclear weapons,

Convinced that nuclear disarmament and the complete elimination of nuclear weapons are essential to remove the danger of war,

Considering that, until complete nuclear disarmament is achieved on a universal basis, it is imperative for the international community to develop effective arrangements to ensure the security of non-nuclear-weapon States against the use or threat of use of nuclear weapons,

Noting the general desire to conclude effective international measures to that end at an early date,

Noting also the unilateral declarations on the security of non-nuclear-weapon States against the use or threat of use of nuclear weapons, made by all nuclear-weapon States,

Desirous of promoting the implementation of paragraph 59 of the Final Document of the Tenth Special Session of the General Assembly, the first special session devoted to disarmament,

Recognizing that effective measures of such security assurances to non-nuclear-weapon States would constitute an important contribution to the non-proliferation of nuclear weapons,

Aware of the in-depth negotiations on this subject in the Conference on Disarmament during the past ten years,

Recalling the relevant parts of the special report of the Committee on Disarmament[a] submitted to the General Assembly at its twelfth special session, the second special session devoted to disarmament, and of the special report of the Conference on Disarmament submitted to the Assembly at its fifteenth special session, the third special session devoted to disarmament, as well as of the annual report of the Conference on its 1988 session,

Welcoming the unanimous support in the Conference on Disarmament for continuing the search for a common approach to the substance of negative security assurances and, in particular, to a "common formula", which could be included in a legally binding instrument,

Recognizing the need for a fresh look at the issue, in particular by the nuclear-weapon States, in order to overcome the difficulties encountered at the negotiations in previous years,

Taking note of the proposals on this subject submitted to the Conference on Disarmament,

Considering that the non-nuclear-weapon States having no nuclear weapons on their territories have every right to receive reliable, uniform and unconditional international legal assurances against the use or threat of use of nuclear weapons,

1.   *Reaffirms* the urgent need, pending the achievement of complete nuclear disarmament, to reach an early agreement on effective international arrangements to assure non-nuclear-weapon States against the use or threat of use of nuclear weapons;

2.   *Recommends* that the Conference on Disarmament pursue intensive negotiations in its *Ad Hoc* Committee on Effective International Arrangements to Assure Non-Nuclear-Weapon States against the Use or Threat of Use of Nuclear Weapons at the beginning of its 1989 session, with a view to reaching such an agreement, taking into account the widespread support in the Conference for the conclusion of an international convention;

3.   *Appeals* to all States, in particular the nuclear-weapon States, to demonstrate willingness and to exercise the flexibility necessary to reach agreement on a common approach to, including the possibility of a common formula in, an international instrument or instruments of a le-

gally binding character, to assure non-nuclear-weapon States against the use or threat of use of nuclear weapons;

4.   *Decides* to include in the provisional agenda of its forty-fourth session the item entitled "Conclusion of effective international arrangements on the strengthening of the security of non-nuclear-weapon States against the use or threat of use of nuclear weapons".

---

[a]The Committee on Disarmament was redesignated the Conference on Disarmament as from 7 February 1984.

General Assembly resolution 43/68

7 December 1988   Meeting 73   117-17-16 (recorded vote)

Approved by First Committee (A/43/836) by recorded vote (99-17-16), 10 November (meeting 33); 7-nation draft (A/C.1/43/L.21); agenda item 57.
Sponsors: Angola, Bulgaria, Byelorussian SSR, Czechoslovakia, Lao People's Democratic Republic, Mongolia, USSR.
Meeting numbers. GA 43rd session: 1st Committee 3-25, 31, 33; plenary 73.

Recorded vote in Assembly as follows:

In favour: Afghanistan, Algeria, Angola, Antigua and Barbuda, Bahamas, Bahrain, Bangladesh, Barbados, Belize, Benin, Bhutan, Bolivia, Botswana, Bulgaria, Burkina Faso, Burma, Burundi, Byelorussian SSR, Cameroon, Cape Verde, Central African Republic, Chad, Comoros, Congo, Costa Rica, Côte d'Ivoire, Cuba, Cyprus, Czechoslovakia, Democratic Yemen, Djibouti, Dominican Republic, Ecuador, Egypt, El Salvador, Ethiopia, Fiji, Finland, Gabon, Gambia, German Democratic Republic, Ghana, Grenada, Guatemala, Guinea, Guyana, Haiti, Hungary, India, Indonesia, Iran, Iraq, Jamaica, Jordan, Kenya, Kuwait, Lao People's Democratic Republic, Lebanon, Lesotho, Liberia, Libyan Arab Jamahiriya, Madagascar, Malawi, Malaysia, Maldives, Mali, Mauritania, Mauritius, Mexico, Mongolia, Morocco, Mozambique, Nepal, Nicaragua, Niger, Nigeria, Oman, Pakistan, Panama, Paraguay, Peru, Philippines, Poland, Qatar, Romania, Rwanda, Saint Kitts and Nevis, Saint Lucia, Saint Vincent and the Grenadines, Saudi Arabia, Senegal, Seychelles, Sierra Leone, Solomon Islands, Somalia, Sri Lanka, Sudan, Suriname, Swaziland, Syrian Arab Republic, Thailand, Togo, Trinidad and Tobago, Tunisia, Uganda, Ukrainian SSR, USSR, United Arab Emirates, United Republic of Tanzania, Vanuatu, Venezuela, Viet Nam, Yemen, Yugoslavia, Zaire, Zambia, Zimbabwe.
Against: Australia, Belgium, Canada, Denmark, France, Germany, Federal Republic of, Iceland, Italy, Japan, Luxembourg, Netherlands, Norway, Portugal, Spain, Turkey, United Kingdom, United States.
Abstaining: Argentina, Austria, Brazil, Chile, China, Colombia, Greece, Honduras, Ireland, Israel, Malta, New Zealand, Papua New Guinea, Samoa, Sweden, Uruguay.

Nuclear non-proliferation

Nuclear-weapon-free zones and zones of peace

In 1988, the international community again discussed the establishment of nuclear-weapon-free zones and zones of peace in various regions of the world. Generally, there was continued support for the establishment of such zones in the effort to promote nuclear disarmament and enhance and strengthen the nuclear non-proliferation régime. New proposals were made for the establishment of such zones in the Balkans and in Central and Northern Europe.[26] In June, an International Meeting for Nuclear-Weapon-Free Zones was held at Berlin.[27] On 21 April and 21 October, the USSR and China, respectively, ratified Protocols 2 and 3 of the Treaty of Rarotonga (South Pacific Nuclear-Free-Zone Treaty).

Africa

Since 1964, when the Declaration on the Denuclearizaton of Africa was adopted by the Organization of African Unity (OAU),[28] the General Assembly had annually called for its implementation. In 1988, as in previous years, the Assembly adopted two resolutions—one on the implementation of the Declaration and the other on the nuclear capability of South Africa.

Disarmament Commission consideration. The Disarmament Commission continued consideration in 1988 of South Africa's nuclear capability, in response to a 1987 Assembly request.[29] The Commission established Working Group I, which based its work on the text of conclusions and recommendations contained in the Commission's 1987 report. It also took into consideration, *inter alia*, the 1984 report of the United Nations Institute for Disarmament Research on South Africa's nuclear capability.[30] The Group held nine meetings between 4 and 17 May.

The Commission reported to the third special session of the Assembly on disarmament that, while significant progress had been made in its work on the text of conclusions and recommendations, no consensus had been reached on the text as a whole.[5] It recommended that work continue in 1989 with a view to elaborating concrete recommendations.

Report of the Secretary-General. In an October 1988 report,[31] the Secretary-General informed the Assembly that he had continued to follow relevant developments in South Africa and had been in contact with OAU and IAEA, which had provided him with updated information regarding South Africa's nuclear capability in accordance with a 1987 Assembly request.[29] With regard to the possibility of signing the Treaty on the Non-Proliferation of Nuclear Weapons[32] and the subsequent conclusion of safeguards agreements, discussions were held in August 1988 between the three depositary Governments (USSR, United Kingdom, United States) and South Africa. Those discussions were not conclusive, however, and South Africa continued to hold wide-ranging discussions with many Governments. The depositary Governments indicated that they were resolved to press South Africa further to accede to the Treaty, in the best interest of the countries of the region and of the world.

The Director General of IAEA reported that the General Conference, on 23 September, had resolved to decide in 1989 on a recommendation of the Board of Governors to suspend South Africa from IAEA membership.

GENERAL ASSEMBLY ACTION

On 7 December, the General Assembly, on the recommendation of the First Committee, adopted **resolution 43/71 A** by recorded vote.

Implementation of the Declaration

The General Assembly,

Bearing in mind the Declaration on the Denuclearization of Africa adopted by the Assembly of Heads of State and Government of the Organization of African Unity at its first ordinary session, held at Cairo from 17 to 21 July 1964,

Recalling its resolution 1652(XVI) of 24 November 1961, its earliest on the subject, as well as its resolutions 2033(XX) of 3 December 1965, 31/69 of 10 December 1976, 32/81 of 12 December 1977, 33/63 of 14 December 1978, 34/76 A of 11 December 1979, 35/146 B of 12 December 1980, 36/86 B of 9 December 1981, 37/74 A of 9 December 1982, 38/181 A of 20 December 1983, 39/61 A of 12 December 1984, 40/89 A of 12 December 1985, 41/55 A of 3 December 1986 and 42/34 A of 30 November 1987, in which it called upon all States to consider and respect the continent of Africa and its surrounding areas as a nuclear-weapon-free zone,

Recalling that in its resolution 33/63 it vigorously condemned any overt or covert attempt by South Africa to introduce nuclear weapons into the continent of Africa and demanded that South Africa refrain forthwith from conducting any nuclear explosion in the continent or elsewhere,

Bearing in mind the provisions of resolution CM/Res.1101(XLVI)/Rev.1 on the denuclearization of Africa adopted by the Council of Ministers of the Organization of African Unity at its forty-sixth ordinary session, held at Addis Ababa from 20 to 25 July 1987,

Having taken note of the report of the United Nations Institute for Disarmament Research entitled "South Africa's nuclear capability", undertaken in co-operation with the Department of Disarmament Affairs of the Secretariat and in consultation with the Organization of African Unity, as well as of the report of the Disarmament Commission,

Noting the actions taken by those Governments which have taken measures to restrict co-operation with South Africa in nuclear and other fields,

Expressing regret that, despite the threat that South Africa's nuclear capability constitutes to international peace and security and, in particular, to the realization of the objective of the Declaration on the Denuclearization of Africa, the Disarmament Commission, although it made some progress during its substantive session in 1988, failed once again to reach a consensus on this important item on its agenda,

1. *Strongly renews its call* upon all States to consider and respect the continent of Africa and its surrounding areas as a nuclear-weapon-free zone;

2. *Reaffirms* that the implementation of the Declaration on the Denuclearization of Africa adopted by the Assembly of Heads of State and Government of the Organization of African Unity would be an important measure to prevent the proliferation of nuclear weapons and to promote international peace and security;

3. *Expresses once again its grave alarm* at South Africa's possession and continued development of nuclear-weapon capability;

4. *Condemns* South Africa's continued pursuit of a nuclear capability and all forms of nuclear collaboration by any State, corporation, institution or individual with the racist régime that enable it to frustrate the objective of the Declaration on the Denuclearization of Africa, which seeks to keep Africa free from nuclear weapons;

5. *Calls upon* all States, corporations, institutions and individuals to desist from further collaboration with the racist régime that may enable it to frustrate the objective of the Declaration on the Denuclearization of Africa;

6. *Demands once again* that the racist régime of South Africa refrain from manufacturing, testing, deploying, transporting, storing, using or threatening to use nuclear weapons;

7. *Appeals* to all States that have the means to do so to monitor South Africa's research on and development and production of nuclear weapons and to publicize any information in that regard;

8. *Demands once again* that South Africa submit forthwith all its nuclear installations and facilities to inspection by the International Atomic Energy Agency;

9. *Requests* the Secretary-General to provide all necessary assistance that the Organization of African Unity may seek regarding the modalities and elements for the preparation and implementation of the relevant convention or treaty on the denuclearization of Africa;

10. *Decides* to include in the provisional agenda of its forty-fourth session the item entitled "Implementation of the Declaration on the Denuclearization of Africa".

General Assembly resolution 43/71 A

7 December 1988   Meeting 73   151-0-4 (recorded vote)

Approved by First Committee (A/43/839) by recorded vote (132-0-4), 17 November (meeting 40); draft by United Republic of Tanzania, for African Group (A/C.1/43/L.31, part A); agenda item 60.
Meeting numbers. GA 43rd session: 1st Committee 3-25, 28, 40; plenary 73.

Recorded vote in Assembly as follows:

In favour: Afghanistan, Albania, Algeria, Angola, Antigua and Barbuda, Argentina, Australia, Austria, Bahamas, Bahrain, Bangladesh, Barbados, Belgium, Belize, Benin, Bhutan, Bolivia, Botswana, Brazil, Brunei Darussalam, Bulgaria, Burkina Faso, Burma, Burundi, Byelorussian SSR, Cameroon, Canada, Cape Verde, Central African Republic, Chad, Chile, China, Colombia, Comoros, Congo, Costa Rica, Côte d'Ivoire, Cuba, Cyprus, Czechoslovakia, Democratic Kampuchea, Democratic Yemen, Denmark, Djibouti, Dominican Republic, Ecuador, Egypt, El Salvador, Ethiopia, Fiji, Finland, Gabon, Gambia, German Democratic Republic, Germany, Federal Republic of, Ghana, Greece, Grenada, Guatemala, Guinea, Guyana, Haiti, Honduras, Hungary, Iceland, India, Indonesia, Iran, Iraq, Ireland, Italy, Jamaica, Japan, Jordan, Kenya, Kuwait, Lao People's Democratic Republic, Lebanon, Lesotho, Liberia, Libyan Arab Jamahiriya, Luxembourg, Madagascar, Malawi, Malaysia, Maldives, Mali, Malta, Mauritania, Mauritius, Mexico, Mongolia, Morocco, Mozambique, Nepal, Netherlands, New Zealand, Nicaragua, Niger, Nigeria, Norway, Oman, Pakistan, Panama, Papua New Guinea, Paraguay, Peru, Philippines, Poland, Portugal, Qatar, Romania, Rwanda, Saint Kitts and Nevis, Saint Lucia, Saint Vincent and the Grenadines, Samoa, Sao Tome and Principe, Saudi Arabia, Senegal, Seychelles, Sierra Leone, Singapore, Solomon Islands, Somalia, Spain, Sri Lanka, Sudan, Suriname, Swaziland, Sweden, Syrian Arab Republic, Thailand, Togo, Trinidad and Tobago, Tunisia, Turkey, Uganda, Ukrainian SSR, USSR, United Arab Emirates, United Republic of Tanzania, Uruguay, Vanuatu, Venezuela, Viet Nam, Yemen, Yugoslavia, Zaire, Zambia, Zimbabwe.
Against: None.
Abstaining: France, Israel, United Kingdom, United States.

On the same date, the Assembly adopted **resolution 43/71 B**, also on the First Committee's recommendation and by recorded vote.

Nuclear capability of South Africa

The General Assembly,

Having considered the report of the Secretary-General on South Africa's nuclear capability,

Recalling its resolutions 34/76 B of 11 December 1979, 35/146 A of 12 December 1980, 36/86 A of 9 December 1981, 37/74 B of 9 December 1982, 38/181 B of 20 December 1983, 39/61 B of 12 December 1984, 40/89 B of 12 December 1985, 41/55 B of 3 December 1986 and 42/34 B of 30 November 1987,

Bearing in mind the Declaration on the Denuclearization of Africa adopted by the Assembly of Heads of State and Government of the Organization of African Unity

at its first ordinary session, held at Cairo from 17 to 21 July 1964,

Recalling that, in paragraph 12 of the Final Document of the Tenth Special Session of the General Assembly, it noted that the massive accumulation of armaments and the acquisition of armaments technology by racist régimes, as well as their possible acquisition of nuclear weapons, present a challenging and increasingly dangerous obstacle to a world community faced with the urgent need to disarm,

Recalling also that, in its resolution 33/63 of 14 December 1978, it vigorously condemned any overt or covert attempt by South Africa to introduce nuclear weapons into the continent of Africa and demanded that South Africa refrain forthwith from conducting any nuclear explosion in the continent or elsewhere,

Bearing in mind the provisions of resolution CM/Res.1101(XLVI)/Rev.1 on the denuclearization of Africa adopted by the Council of Ministers of the Organization of African Unity at its forty-sixth ordinary session, held at Addis Ababa from 20 to 25 July 1987,

Noting with regret the non-implementation by *apartheid* South Africa of resolution GC(XXX)/RES/468 adopted on 3 October 1986 by the General Conference of the International Atomic Energy Agency during its thirtieth regular session,

Having taken note of the report of the United Nations Institute for Disarmament Research entitled "South Africa's nuclear capability", undertaken in co-operation with the Department for Disarmament Affairs of the Secretariat and in consultation with the Organization of African Unity,

Expressing regret that despite the threat that South Africa's nuclear-weapon capability constitutes to international peace and security and, in particular, to the realization of the objective of the Declaration on the Denuclearization of Africa, the Disarmament Commission, although it made some progress during its substantive session in 1988, failed once again to reach a consensus on this important item on its agenda,

Alarmed that South Africa's nuclear facilities, particularly those that remain unsafeguarded, enable it to develop and acquire the capability of producing fissionable material for nuclear weapons,

Gravely concerned that South Africa, in flagrant violation of the principles of international law and the relevant provisions of the Charter of the United Nations, has continued its acts of aggression and subversion against the peoples of the independent States of southern Africa,

Deeply indignant at the persistent policy of hostility by the racist régime of South Africa as demonstrated by its constant encroachment into the territory of Angola, which constitutes an act of aggression against the sovereignty and territorial integrity of that country,

Expressing its grave disappointment that, despite repeated appeals by the international community, certain Western States and Israel have continued to collaborate with the racist régime of South Africa in the military and nuclear fields and that some of these States have, by a ready recourse to the use of veto, consistently frustrated every effort in the Security Council to deal decisively with the question of South Africa,

Recalling its decision taken at the tenth special session that the Security Council should take appropriate effective steps to prevent the frustration of the implementation of the decision of the Organization of African Unity for the denuclearization of Africa,

Stressing the need to preserve peace and security in Africa by ensuring that the continent is a nuclear-weapon-free zone,

1. *Takes note* of the report of the Secretary-General on South Africa's nuclear capability;

2. *Condemns* the massive buildup of South Africa's military machine, in particular its frenzied acquisition of nuclear-weapon capability for repressive and aggressive purposes and as an instrument of blackmail;

3. *Also condemns* all forms of nuclear collaboration by any State, corporation, institution or individual with the racist régime of South Africa, in particular the decision by some Member States to grant licences to several corporations in their territories to provide equipment and technical and maintenance services for nuclear installations in South Africa;

4. *Reaffirms* that the acquisition of nuclear-weapon capability by the racist régime constitutes a very grave danger to international peace and security and, in particular, jeopardizes the security of African States and increases the danger of the proliferation of nuclear weapons;

5. *Expresses its full support* for the African States faced with the danger of South Africa's nuclear capability;

6. *Commends* the actions taken by those Governments which have taken measures to restrict co-operation with South Africa in nuclear and other fields;

7. *Demands* that South Africa and all other foreign interests put an immediate end to the exploration for and exploitation of uranium resources in Namibia;

8. *Calls upon* all States, corporations, institutions and individuals to terminate forthwith all forms of military and nuclear collaboration with the racist régime;

9. *Requests* the Disarmament Commission to consider once again as a matter of priority during its substantive session in 1989 South Africa's nuclear capability, taking into account, *inter alia*, the findings of the report of the United Nations Institute for Disarmament Research on South Africa's nuclear capability;

10. *Requests* the Secretary-General to provide all necessary assistance that the Organization of African Unity may seek regarding the modalities and elements for the preparation and implementation of the relevant convention or treaty on the denuclearization of Africa;

11. *Commends* the adoption by the Security Council of resolutions 558(1984) of 13 December 1984 and 591(1986) of 28 November 1986 on the question of South Africa, with a view to blocking the existing loopholes in the arms embargo so as to render it more effective and prohibiting, in particular, all forms of co-operation and collaboration with the racist régime of South Africa in the nuclear field;

12. *Demands once again* that South Africa submit forthwith all its nuclear installations and facilities to inspection by the International Atomic Energy Agency;

13. *Requests* the Secretary-General to follow very closely South Africa's evolution in the nuclear field and to report thereon to the General Assembly at its forty-fourth session.

General Assembly resolution 43/71 B

7 December 1988   Meeting 73   138-4-12 (recorded vote)

Approved by First Committee (A/43/839) by recorded vote (116-4-13), 17 November (meeting 40); draft by United Republic of Tanzania, for African Group (A/C.1/43/L.31, part B), orally revised; agenda item 60.
Meeting numbers. GA 43rd session: 1st Committee 3-25, 28, 40; plenary 73.

Recorded vote in Assembly as follows:

In favour: Afghanistan, Albania, Algeria, Angola, Antigua and Barbuda, Argentina, Austria, Bahamas, Bahrain, Bangladesh, Barbados, Belize, Benin, Bhutan, Bolivia, Botswana, Brazil, Brunei Darussalam, Bulgaria, Burkina Faso, Burma, Burundi, Byelorussian SSR, Cameroon, Cape Verde, Central African Republic, Chad, China, Comoros, Congo, Costa Rica, Côte d'Ivoire, Cuba, Cyprus, Czechoslovakia, Democratic Kampuchea, Democratic Yemen, Denmark, Djibouti, Dominican Republic, Ecuador, Egypt, El Salvador, Ethiopia, Fiji, Finland, Gabon, Gambia, German Democratic Republic, Ghana, Greece, Grenada, Guatemala, Guinea, Guyana, Haiti, Honduras, Hungary, Iceland, India, Indonesia, Iran, Iraq, Ireland, Jamaica, Jordan, Kenya, Kuwait, Lao People's Democratic Republic, Lebanon, Lesotho, Liberia, Libyan Arab Jamahiriya, Madagascar, Malawi, Malaysia, Maldives, Mali, Malta, Mauritania, Mauritius, Mexico, Mongolia, Morocco, Mozambique, Nepal, New Zealand, Nicaragua, Niger, Nigeria, Norway, Oman, Pakistan, Panama, Papua New Guinea, Peru, Philippines, Poland, Qatar, Romania, Rwanda, Saint Kitts and Nevis, Saint Lucia, Saint Vincent and the Grenadines, Samoa, Sao Tome and Principe, Saudi Arabia, Senegal, Seychelles, Sierra Leone, Singapore, Solomon Islands, Somalia, Sri Lanka, Sudan, Suriname, Swaziland, Sweden, Syrian Arab Republic, Thailand, Togo, Trinidad and Tobago, Tunisia, Turkey, Uganda, Ukrainian SSR, USSR, United Arab Emirates, United Republic of Tanzania, Uruguay, Vanuatu, Venezuela, Viet Nam, Yemen, Yugoslavia, Zaire, Zambia, Zimbabwe.

Against: France, Israel, United Kingdom, United States.

Abstaining: Australia, Belgium, Canada, Chile, Colombia, Germany, Federal Republic of, Italy, Japan, Luxembourg, Netherlands, Portugal, Spain.

Latin America

The General Assembly remained seized in 1988 of the item on the signature and ratification of Additional Protocol I of the 1967 Treaty for the Prohibition of Nuclear Weapons in Latin America (Treaty of Tlatelolco), concerning the application of the Treaty to territories in the region for which outside States had *de jure* or *de facto* responsibility. Three of those States—the Netherlands, the United Kingdom and the United States—became parties to the Protocol in 1971, 1969, and 1981, respectively. France signed it in 1979, but had not ratified it.

The Treaty's Additional Protocol II had been ratified by the five nuclear-weapon States by 1979.[33]

GENERAL ASSEMBLY ACTION

On the recommendation of the First Committee, the General Assembly, on 7 December 1988, adopted **resolution 43/62** by vote.

Implementation of General Assembly resolution 42/25 concerning the signature and ratification of Additional Protocol I of the Treaty for the Prohibition of Nuclear Weapons in Latin America (Treaty of Tlatelolco)

The General Assembly,

Recalling its resolutions 2286(XXII) of 5 December 1967, 3262(XXIX) of 9 December 1974, 3473(XXX) of 11 December 1975, 32/76 of 12 December 1977, S-10/2 of 30 June 1978, 33/58 of 14 December 1978, 34/71 of 11 December 1979, 35/143 of 12 December 1980, 36/83 of 9 December 1981, 37/71 of 9 December 1982, 38/61 of 15 December 1983, 39/51 of 12 December 1984, 40/79 of 12 December 1985, 41/45 of 3 December 1986 and 42/25 of 30 November 1987 concerning the signature and ratification of Additional Protocol I of the Treaty for the Prohibition of Nuclear Weapons in Latin America (Treaty of Tlatelolco),

Taking into account that within the zone of application of that Treaty, to which twenty-three sovereign States are already parties, there are some territories which, inspite of not being sovereign political entities, are nevertheless in a position to receive the benefits deriving from the Treaty through its Additional Protocol I, to which the four States that *de jure* or *de facto* are internationally responsible for those territories may become parties,

Considering that it is not fair that the peoples of some of those territories are deprived of such benefits without being given the opportunity to express their opinion in this connection,

Recalling that three of the States to which Additional Protocol I is open—the United Kingdom of Great Britain and Northern Ireland, the Kingdom of the Netherlands and the United States of America—became parties to the Protocol in 1969, 1971 and 1981, respectively,

1. *Deplores* that the signature of Additional Protocol I by France, which took place on 2 March 1979, has not yet been been followed by the corresponding ratification, notwithstanding the time already elapsed and the pressing invitations which the General Assembly has addressed to it;

2. *Once more urges* France not to delay any further such ratification, which has been requested so many times and which appears all the more advisable, since France is the only one of the four States to which the Protocol is open that is not yet party to it;

3. *Decides* to include in the provisional agenda of its forty-fourth session an item entitled ''Implementation of General Assembly resolution 43/62 concerning the signature and ratification of Additional Protocol I of the Treaty for the Prohibition of Nuclear Weapons in Latin America (Treaty of Tlatelolco)''.

General Assembly resolution 43/62

7 December 1988   Meeting 73   149-0-5

Approved by First Committee (A/43/830) by recorded vote (128-0-6), 15 November (meeting 37); 15-nation draft (A/C.1/43/L.40); agenda item 51.
Sponsors: Bahamas, Barbados, Bolivia, Costa Rica, Ecuador, Guatemala, Honduras, Jamaica, Mexico, Nicaragua, Panama, Suriname, Trinidad and Tobago, Uruguay, Venezuela.
Meeting numbers. GA 43rd session: 1st Committee 3-25, 28, 37; plenary 73.

Middle East

In a July 1988 report,[34] submitted in response to a 1987 General Assembly request,[35] the Secretary-General forwarded the views of four Member States—Burkina Faso, Chad, Egypt and Oman—on the establishment of a nuclear-weapon-free zone in the Middle East.

Egypt had also proposed,[36] at the third special session of the Assembly devoted to disarmament, the formulation of a model draft treaty and the preparation of a study on verification and inspection measures relating to the establishment of a nuclear-free zone in the Middle East.

GENERAL ASSEMBLY ACTION

On 7 December, on the recommendation of the First Committee, the General Assembly adopted **resolution 43/65** without vote.

Establishment of a nuclear-weapon-free zone in the region of the Middle East

The General Assembly,

Recalling its resolutions 3263(XXIX) of 9 December 1974, 3474(XXX) of 11 December 1975, 31/71 of 10 December 1976, 32/82 of 12 December 1977, 33/64 of 14 December 1978, 34/77 of 11 December 1979, 35/147 of 12 December 1980, 36/87 of 9 December 1981, 37/75 of 9 December 1982, 38/64 of 15 December 1983, 39/54 of 12 December 1984, 40/82 of 12 December 1985, 41/48 of 3 December 1986 and 42/28 of 30 November 1987 on the establishment of a nuclear-weapon-free zone in the region of the Middle East,

Recalling also the recommendations for the establishment of such a zone in the Middle East consistent with paragraphs 60 to 63, and in particular paragraph 63 *(d)*, of the Final Document of the Tenth Special Session of the General Assembly,

Emphasizing the basic provisions of the above-mentioned resolutions, which call upon all parties directly concerned to consider taking the practical and urgent steps required for the implementation of the proposal to establish a nuclear-weapon-free zone in the region of the Middle East and, pending and during the establishment of such a zone, to declare solemnly that they will refrain, on a reciprocal basis, from producing, acquiring or in any other way possessing nuclear weapons and nuclear explosive devices and from permitting the stationing of nuclear weapons on their territory by any third party, to agree to place all their nuclear facilities under International Atomic Energy Agency safeguards and to declare their support for the establishment of the zone and deposit such declarations with the Security Council for consideration, as appropriate,

Reaffirming the inalienable right of all States to acquire and develop nuclear energy for peaceful purposes,

Emphasizing also the need for appropriate measures on the question of the prohibition of military attacks on nuclear facilities,

Bearing in mind the consensus reached by the General Assembly at its thirty-fifth session that the establishment of a nuclear-weapon-free zone in the region of the Middle East would greatly enhance international peace and security,

Desirous of building on that consensus so that substantial progress can be made towards establishing a nuclear-weapon-free zone in the region of the Middle East,

Emphasizing the essential role of the United Nations in the establishment of a nuclear-weapon-free zone in the region of the Middle East,

Having examined the report of the Secretary-General,

1. *Urges* all parties directly concerned to consider seriously taking the practical and urgent steps required for the implementation of the proposal to establish a nuclear-weapon-free zone in the region of the Middle East in accordance with the relevant resolutions of the General Assembly and, as a means of promoting this objective, invites the countries concerned to adhere to the Treaty on the Non-Proliferation of Nuclear Weapons;

2. *Calls upon* all countries of the region that have not done so, pending the establishment of the zone, to agree to place all their nuclear activities under International Atomic Energy Agency safeguards;

3. *Invites* those countries, pending the establishment of a nuclear-weapon-free zone in the region of the Middle East, to declare their support for establishing such a zone, consistent with paragraph 63 *(d)* of the Final Document of the Tenth Special Session of the General Assembly, and to deposit those declarations with the Security Council;

4. *Also invites* those countries, pending the establishment of the zone, not to develop, produce, test or otherwise acquire nuclear weapons or permit the stationing on their territories, or territories under their control, of nuclear weapons or nuclear explosive devices;

5. *Invites* the nuclear-weapon States and all other States to render their assistance in the establishment of the zone and at the same time to refrain from any action that runs counter to both the letter and the spirit of the present resolution;

6. *Extends its thanks* to the Secretary-General for his report containing the views of parties concerned regarding the establishment of a nuclear-weapon-free zone in the region of the Middle East;

7. *Takes note* of the above-mentioned report;

8. *Requests* the Secretary-General to undertake a study on effective and verifiable measures which would facilitate the establishment of a nuclear-weapon-free zone in the Middle East, taking into account the circumstances and characteristics of the Middle East, as well as the views and the suggestions of the parties of the region, and to submit this study to the General Assembly at its forty-fifth session;

9. *Requests* parties of the region to submit to the Secretary-General their views and suggestions with respect to the measures called for in paragraph 8 above;

10. *Requests* the Secretary-General to submit to the General Assembly at its forty-fourth session a progress report on the implementation of the present resolution;

11. *Decides* to include in the provisional agenda of its forty-fourth session the item entitled ''Establishment of a nuclear-weapon-free zone in the region of the Middle East''.

General Assembly resolution 43/65

7 December 1988   Meeting 73   Adopted without vote

Approved by First Committee (A/43/833) without vote, 15 November (meeting 38); draft by Egypt (A/C.1/43/L.11/Rev.1 & Corr.1); agenda item 54.
Financial implications. ACABQ, A/43/7/Add.9; 5th Committee, A/43/938; S-G, A/C.1/43/L.76, A/C.5/43/38.
Meeting numbers. GA 43rd session: 1st Committee 3-25, 33, 38; 5th Committee 41; plenary 73.

Nuclear weapons and Israel

In an October 1988 report,[37] submitted in response to a 1987 General Assembly request,[38] the Secretary-General indicated that he had continued to follow closely Israeli nuclear activities. He forwarded to the Assembly the text of a resolution adopted by the General Conference of IAEA in September 1988, condemning Israel's refusal to submit its nuclear facilities to IAEA safeguards, in compliance with a 1981 Security Council resolution,[39] and requesting IAEA, pending the acceptance by Israel to place all its nuclear facilities under its safeguards, to prepare a technical study on different modalities of application of IAEA safeguards in the region.

GENERAL ASSEMBLY ACTION

On 7 December 1988, on the recommendation of the First Committee, the General Assembly adopted **resolution 43/80** by recorded vote.

Israeli nuclear armament

The General Assembly,

Bearing in mind its previous resolutions on Israeli nuclear armament, the latest of which is 42/44 of 30 November 1987,

Recalling its resolution 42/28 of 30 November 1987, in which, *inter alia*, it called for placing all nuclear facilities in the region under International Atomic Energy Agency safeguards, pending the establishment of a nuclear-weapon-free zone in the Middle East,

Recalling also Security Council resolution 487(1981) of 19 June 1981, in which, *inter alia*, the Council called upon Israel urgently to place all its nuclear facilities under International Atomic Energy Agency safeguards,

Noting that only Israel has been specifically called upon by the Security Council to place its nuclear facilities under International Atomic Energy Agency safeguards,

Noting with grave concern Israel's persistent refusal to commit itself not to manufacture or acquire nuclear weapons, despite repeated calls by the General Assembly, the Security Council and the International Atomic Energy Agency,

Taking into consideration resolution GC(XXXII)/RES/487 of 23 September 1988 adopted by the General Conference of the International Atomic Energy Agency, in which the General Conference strongly condemned the continued refusal by Israel to renounce the possession of nuclear weapons and to submit all its nuclear facilities to the Agency's safeguards in compliance with Security Council resolution 487(1981),

Deeply alarmed by the information with regard to the continuing production, development and acquisition of nuclear weapons by Israel,

Aware of the grave consequences that endanger international peace and security as a result of Israel's development and acquisition of nuclear weapons and Israel's collaboration with South Africa to develop nuclear weapons and their delivery systems,

Deeply concerned that the declared Israeli policy of attacking and destroying nuclear facilities devoted to peaceful purposes is a part of its nuclear armament policy,

1. *Reiterates its condemnation* of Israel's refusal to renounce any possession of nuclear weapons;

2. *Reiterates also its condemnation* of the co-operation between Israel and South Africa;

3. *Requests once more* the Security Council to take urgent and effective measures to ensure that Israel complies with Council resolution 487(1981);

4. *Demands once more* that Israel place all its nuclear facilities under International Atomic Energy Agency safeguards;

5. *Calls upon* all States and organizations that have not yet done so to discontinue co-operating with and giving assistance to Israel in the nuclear field;

6. *Reiterates its request* to the International Atomic Energy Agency to suspend any scientific co-operation with Israel that could contribute to its nuclear capabilities;

7. *Requests also* the International Atomic Energy Agency to inform the Secretary-General of any steps Israel may take to place its nuclear facilities under Agency safeguards;

8. *Requests* the Secretary-General to follow closely Israeli nuclear activities and to report to the General Assembly at its forty-fourth session;

9. *Decides* to include in the provisional agenda of its forty-fourth session the item entitled "Israeli nuclear armament".

General Assembly resolution 43/80

7 December 1988　　　Meeting 73　　　99-2-51 (recorded vote)

Approved by First Committee (A/43/861) by recorded vote (87-2-45), 15 November (meeting 37); draft by Algeria, Bahrain, Democratic Yemen, Djibouti, Iraq, Jordan (for Arab Group), Kuwait, Lebanon, Libyan Arab Jamahiriya, Mauritania, Morocco, Oman, Qatar, Saudi Arabia, Somalia, Sudan, Syrian Arab Republic, Tunisia, United Arab Emirates, Yemen (A/C.1/43/L.6); agenda item 69.

Meeting numbers. GA 43rd session: 1st Committee 3-25, 29, 37; plenary 73.

Recorded vote in Assembly as follows:

In favour: Afghanistan, Albania, Algeria, Angola, Argentina, Bahrain, Bangladesh, Benin, Bhutan, Botswana, Brazil, Brunei Darussalam, Bulgaria, Burkina Faso, Burundi, Byelorussian SSR, Cameroon, Cape Verde, Central African Republic, Chad, China, Comoros, Congo, Cuba, Cyprus, Czechoslovakia, Democratic Kampuchea, Democratic Yemen, Djibouti, Egypt, Ethiopia, Gabon, Gambia, German Democratic Republic, Ghana, Guatemala, Guinea, Guyana, Haiti, Hungary, India, Indonesia, Iran, Iraq, Jordan, Kenya, Kuwait, Lao People's Democratic Republic, Lebanon, Libyan Arab Jamahiriya, Madagascar, Malaysia, Maldives, Mali, Mauritania, Mauritius, Mexico, Mongolia, Morocco, Mozambique, Nicaragua, Niger, Nigeria, Oman, Pakistan, Peru, Philippines, Poland, Qatar, Romania, Rwanda, Saint Lucia, Sao Tome and Principe, Saudi Arabia, Senegal, Seychelles, Sierra Leone, Somalia, Sri Lanka, Sudan, Suriname, Syrian Arab Republic, Thailand, Togo, Trinidad and Tobago, Tunisia, Turkey, Uganda, Ukrainian SSR, USSR, United Arab Emirates, United Republic of Tanzania, Vanuatu, Venezuela, Viet Nam, Yemen, Yugoslavia, Zambia, Zimbabwe.

Against: Israel, United States.

Abstaining: Antigua and Barbuda, Australia, Austria, Bahamas, Barbados, Belgium, Belize, Bolivia, Canada, Chile, Colombia, Costa Rica, Côte d'Ivoire, Denmark, Dominican Republic, Ecuador, El Salvador, Fiji, Finland, France, Germany, Federal Republic of, Greece, Honduras, Iceland, Ireland, Italy, Japan, Lesotho, Liberia, Luxembourg, Malawi, Malta, Nepal, Netherlands, New Zealand, Norway, Panama, Papua New Guinea, Paraguay, Portugal, Saint Kitts and Nevis, Saint Vincent and the Grenadines, Samoa, Singapore, Solomon Islands, Spain, Swaziland, Sweden, United Kingdom, Uruguay, Zaire.

Before approving the text as a whole, the First Committee approved, by recorded votes, the sixth preambular paragraph (77-19-32), the ninth preambular paragraph (69-21-35), paragraph 2 (79-19-28), paragraph 5 (71-24-31) and paragraph 6 (72-23-32). Separate votes were requested in the Assembly for the same paragraphs which were adopted, respectively, by recorded votes of 90 to 19, with 35 abstentions; 78 to 21, with 43 abstentions; 91 to 19, with 35 abstentions; 82 to 24, with 35 abstentions; and 81 to 23, with 39 abstentions.

South Asia

In 1987, the General Assembly had welcomed a proposal for the conclusion of a bilateral or regional nuclear-test-ban agreement in South Asia and had noted another proposal to convene, under the auspices of the United Nations, a conference on nuclear non-proliferation in South Asia.[40]

The Secretary-General, in an August 1988 report on developments in respect of the establishment of a nuclear-weapon-free zone in South Asia,[41] transmitted the view of Maldives which, while supporting the creation of such a zone, considered as premature any proposal to conclude bilateral or regional agreements or the convening of an international conference, without prior consultation among States of the region.

On 7 December, the General Assembly, on the recommendation of the First Committee, adopted **resolution 43/66** by recorded vote,

Establishment of a nuclear-weapon-free zone in South Asia

The General Assembly,

Recalling its resolutions 3265 B (XXIX) of 9 December 1974, 3476 B (XXX) of 11 December 1975, 31/73 of 10 December 1976, 32/83 of 12 December 1977, 33/65 of 14 December 1978, 34/78 of 11 December 1979, 35/148 of 12 December 1980, 36/88 of 9 December 1981, 37/76 of 9 December 1982, 38/65 of 15 December 1983, 39/55 of 12 December 1984, 40/83 of 12 December 1985, 41/49 of 3 December 1986 and 42/29 of 30 November 1987 concerning the establishment of a nuclear-weapon-free zone in South Asia,

Reiterating its conviction that the establishment of nuclear-weapon-free zones in various regions of the world is one of the measures which can contribute effectively to the objectives of non-proliferation of nuclear weapons and general and complete disarmament,

Believing that the establishment of a nuclear-weapon-free zone in South Asia, as in other regions, will assist in the strengthening of the security of the States of the region against the use or threat of use of nuclear weapons,

Noting with appreciation the declarations issued at the highest level by Governments of South Asian States that are developing their peaceful nuclear programmes reaffirming their undertaking not to acquire or manufacture nuclear weapons and to devote their nuclear programmes exclusively to the economic and social advancement of their peoples,

Welcoming the recent proposal for the conclusion of a bilateral or regional nuclear-test-ban agreement in South Asia,

Taking note of the proposal to convene, under the auspices of the United Nations, a conference on nuclear non-proliferation in South Asia, as soon as possible, with the participation of the regional and other concerned States,

Bearing in mind the provisions of paragraphs 60 to 63 of the Final Document of the Tenth Special Session of the General Assembly, regarding the establishment of nuclear-weapon-free zones, including in the region of South Asia,

Taking note of the report of the Secretary-General,

1. *Reaffirms* its endorsement, in principle, of the concept of a nuclear-weapon-free zone in South Asia;

2. *Urges once again* the States of South Asia to continue to make all possible efforts to establish a nuclear-weapon-free zone in South Asia and to refrain, in the mean time, from any action contrary to this objective;

3. *Calls upon* those nuclear-weapon States that have not done so to respond positively to this proposal and to extend the necessary co-operation in the efforts to establish a nuclear-weapon-free zone in South Asia;

4. *Requests* the Secretary-General to communicate with the States of the region and other concerned States in order to ascertain their views on the issue and to promote consultations among them with a view to exploring the best possibilities of furthering the efforts for the establishment of a nuclear-weapon-free zone in South Asia;

5. *Also requests* the Secretary-General to report on the subject to the General Assembly at its forty-fourth session;

6. *Decides* to include in the provisional agenda of its forty-fourth session the item entitled ''Establishment of a nuclear-weapon-free zone in South Asia''.

General Assembly resolution 43/66

7 December 1988   Meeting 73   116-3-34 (recorded vote)

Approved by First Committee (A/43/834) by recorded vote (99-2-32), 15 November (meeting 37); 2-nation draft (A/C.1/43/L.5); agenda item 55.
Sponsors: Bangladesh, Pakistan.
Meeting numbers. GA 43rd session: 1st Committee 3-25, 28, 37; plenary 73.
Recorded vote in Assembly as follows:

In favour: Albania, Antigua and Barbuda, Australia, Bahamas, Bahrain, Bangladesh, Barbados, Belgium, Belize, Benin, Bolivia, Botswana, Brunei Darussalam, Burkina Faso, Burundi, Cameroon, Canada, Central African Republic, Chad, Chile, China, Colombia, Comoros, Costa Rica, Côte d'Ivoire, Democratic Kampuchea, Djibouti, Dominican Republic, Ecuador, Egypt, El Salvador, Fiji, Finland, Gabon, Gambia, Germany, Federal Republic of, Ghana, Greece, Grenada, Guatemala, Guinea, Guyana, Haiti, Honduras, Iran, Iraq, Ireland, Israel, Italy, Jamaica, Japan, Jordan, Kenya, Kuwait, Lebanon, Lesotho, Liberia, Libyan Arab Jamahiriya, Luxembourg, Malawi, Malaysia, Maldives, Mali, Malta, Mauritania, Mexico, Morocco, Mozambique, Nepal, Netherlands, New Zealand, Niger, Nigeria, Oman, Pakistan, Panama, Papua New Guinea, Paraguay, Peru, Philippines, Portugal, Qatar, Romania, Rwanda, Saint Kitts and Nevis, Saint Lucia, Saint Vincent and the Grenadines, Samoa, Saudi Arabia, Senegal, Sierra Leone, Singapore, Solomon Islands, Somalia, Spain, Sri Lanka, Sudan, Suriname, Swaziland, Thailand, Togo, Trinidad and Tobago, Tunisia, Turkey, Uganda, United Arab Emirates, United Kingdom, United Republic of Tanzania, United States, Uruguay, Vanuatu, Venezuela, Yemen, Zaire, Zambia, Zimbabwe.
Against: Bhutan, India, Mauritius.
Abstaining: Afghanistan, Algeria, Angola, Argentina, Austria, Brazil, Bulgaria, Burma, Byelorussian SSR, Cape Verde, Congo, Cuba, Cyprus, Czechoslovakia, Democratic Yemen, Denmark, Ethiopia, France, German Democratic Republic, Hungary, Iceland, Indonesia, Lao People's Democratic Republic, Madagascar, Mongolia, Nicaragua, Norway, Poland, Seychelles, Sweden, Ukrainian SSR, USSR, Viet Nam, Yugoslavia.

1971 Declaration of the Indian Ocean as a Zone of Peace

Pursuant to a 1987 General Assembly request,[42] the *Ad Hoc* Committee on the Indian Ocean held two sessions in 1988 (New York, 11-15 April, 11-22 July)[43] as it continued to consider practical measures for achieving the implementation of the 1971 Declaration of the Indian Ocean as a Zone of Peace.[44]

The Committee also continued the preparatory work for the convening of the Conference on the Indian Ocean. In April, it was unable to arrive at a decision on Sri Lanka's invitation to hold its second session at Colombo, owing to formal objection by one delegation. The Committee adopted by consensus its report to the third special session of the Assembly on disarmament,[45] in which it urged the Assembly to reaffirm its full support for the implementation of the Declaration and requested the continued assistance of the Secretary-General to enable the completion of its remaining preparatory work for the early convening of the Conference.

In July, the open-ended Working Group of the Committee agreed on 20 substantive issues and principles,[46] which it considered a good basis for further elaboration in the subsequent preparation of a draft final document of the Conference on the Indian Ocean. The Committee agreed to update

a 1983 document[47] containing the views of its members on a zone of peace which were arranged on the basis of an informal list of seven topics: geographical limits; foreign military presence; nuclear weapons; security; peaceful settlement of disputes; use of the Indian Ocean by foreign vessels and aircraft; and other matters.

GENERAL ASSEMBLY ACTION

On 7 December, on the recommendation of the First Committee, the General Assembly adopted **resolution 43/79** without vote.

Implementation of the Declaration of the Indian Ocean as a Zone of Peace

The General Assembly,

Recalling the Declaration of the Indian Ocean as a Zone of Peace, contained in its resolution 2832(XXVI) of 16 December 1971, and recalling also its resolutions 2992(XXVII) of 15 December 1972, 3080(XXVIII) of 6 December 1973, 3259 A (XXIX) of 9 December 1974, 3468(XXX) of 11 December 1975, 31/88 of 14 December 1976, 32/86 of 12 December 1977, S-10/2 of 30 June 1978, 33/68 of 14 December 1978, 34/80 A and B of 11 December 1979, 35/150 of 12 December 1980, 36/90 of 9 December 1981, 37/96 of 13 December 1982, 38/185 of 20 December 1983, 39/149 of 17 December 1984, 40/153 of 16 December 1985, 41/87 of 4 December 1986, 42/43 of 30 November 1987 and other relevant resolutions,

Reaffirming that the establishment of zones of peace in various regions of the world under appropriate conditions, to be clearly defined and determined freely by the States concerned in the zone, taking into account the characteristics of the zone and the principles of the Charter of the United Nations, and in conformity with international law, can contribute to strengthening the security of States within such zones and to international peace and security as a whole,

Recalling also the report of the Meeting of the Littoral and Hinterland States of the Indian Ocean,

Reaffirming its conviction that concrete action for the achievement of the objectives of the Declaration of the Indian Ocean as a Zone of Peace would be a substantial contribution to the strengthening of international peace and security, as well as to the independence, sovereignty, territorial integrity and peaceful development of the States of the region,

Convinced that agreement on such action should be facilitated by encouraging developments in international relations that could have beneficial effects on the region,

Also convinced that the continued military presence of the great Powers in the Indian Ocean area, conceived in the context of their confrontation, gives urgency to the need to take practical steps for the early achievement of the objectives of the Declaration,

Further convinced that the political and security climate in the Indian Ocean area is an important consideration bearing on the question of the urgent convening of the Conference on the Indian Ocean at Colombo and that the further easing of tension in the area would enhance the prospect of success of the Conference,

Considering that the creation of a zone of peace requires co-operation and agreement among the States of the region to ensure conditions of peace and security within the area, as envisaged in the Declaration,

Recalling the decision of the *Ad Hoc* Committee to make every effort, in consideration of the political and security climate in the Indian Ocean area and of progress made in the harmonization of views, to finalize, in accordance with its normal methods of work, all preparations for the Conference, including dates for its convening,

Noting that, in accordance with resolution 42/43, the *Ad Hoc* Committee submitted a report, adopted by consensus, to the Assembly at its fifteenth special session, the third special session devoted to disarmament, and urged it to reaffirm its full support for the implementation of the Declaration,

Noting also that the *Ad Hoc* Committee has requested the Secretary-General to continue to extend to it all necessary assistance in order to facilitate the intensification of the Committee's work towards the implementation of its mandate and to enable the completion of its remaining preparatory work for the early convening of the Conference, as repeatedly called for by the Assembly, in particular in its resolution 42/43,

1. *Takes note* of the report of the *Ad Hoc* Committee on the Indian Ocean;

2. *Reaffirms* full support for the achievement of the objectives of the Declaration of the Indian Ocean as a Zone of Peace;

3. *Reiterates and emphasizes* its decision to convene the Conference on the Indian Ocean at Colombo, as a necessary step for the implementation of the Declaration of the Indian Ocean as a Zone of Peace adopted in 1971;

4. *Renews* the mandate of the *Ad Hoc* Committee as defined in the relevant resolutions, and requests the Committee to intensify its work with regard to the implementation of its mandate;

5. *Notes with satisfaction* that in the implementation of the mandate of the *Ad Hoc* Committee, including the preparatory work for the convening of the Conference, as called for in the relevant resolutions recommended by the Committee and adopted by the General Assembly by consensus, progress has been made by the Working Group of the *Ad Hoc* Committee in its meetings during the sessions of the Committee in 1988;

6. *Urges* the *Ad Hoc* Committee to intensify its discussions of substantive issues and principles, including those identified by the Chairman of the Working Group in his report dated 14 July 1988, with the aim of elaborating elements that might be taken into consideration during the subsequent preparation of a draft final document of the Conference;

7. *Requests* the *Ad Hoc* Committee to hold two preparatory sessions during the first half of 1989, the first with a duration of one week and the second with a duration of two weeks, for completion of the remaining preparatory work relating to the Conference on the Indian Ocean to enable the convening of the Conference at Colombo in 1990 in consultation with the host country;

8. *Notes* that the *Ad Hoc* Committee will, during its preparatory sessions in 1989, continue to keep under review the need to organize its work more effectively in order to enable it to fulfil its mandate;

9. *Decides* that the *Ad Hoc* Committee should commemorate the tenth anniversary of the Meeting of the Littoral and Hinterland States of the Indian Ocean,

which took place in July 1979, during its preparatory sessions in 1989;

10. *Requests* the Chairman of the *Ad Hoc* Committee to continue his consultations on the participation in the work of the Committee by States Members of the United Nations which are not members of the Committee, with the aim of resolving this matter at the earliest possible date;

11. *Also requests* the Chairman of the *Ad Hoc* Committee to consult the Secretary-General at the appropriate time on the establishment of a secretariat for the Conference;

12. *Requests* the *Ad Hoc* Committee to submit to the General Assembly at its forty-fourth session a full report on the implementation of the present resolution;

13. *Requests* the Secretary-General to continue to render all necessary assistance to the *Ad Hoc* Committee, including the provision of summary records, in recognition of its preparatory function.

General Assembly resolution 43/79

7 December 1988   Meeting 73   Adopted without vote

Approved by First Committee (A/43/860) without vote, 10 November (meeting 33); draft by Committee on the Indian Ocean (A/43/29); agenda item 68.

Financial implications. 5th Committee, A/43/939; S-G, A/C.1/43/L.73, A/C.5/43/58.

Meeting numbers. GA 43rd session: 1st Committee 3-26, 33; 5th Committee 41; plenary 73.

Preparation for the 1990 Review Conference of NPT

The 1968 Treaty on the Non-Proliferation of Nuclear Weapons[32] provides for the holding of review conferences at intervals of five years. The first three conferences were held in 1975,[48] 1980[49] and 1985.[50] The 1985 Conference had proposed to the depositary Governments, in its Final Declaration, that a fourth conference be held in 1990.

At the request of 66 States, transmitted by the USSR, the United Kingdom and the United States,[51] the General Assembly included an item on the implementation of the conclusions of the Third Review Conference and establishment of a preparatory committee for the fourth conference in the agenda of its 1988 regular session.

GENERAL ASSEMBLY ACTION

On 7 December, on the recommendation of the First Committee, the General Assembly adopted **resolution 43/82** by recorded vote.

Implementation of the conclusions of the Third Review Conference of the Parties to the Treaty on the Non-Proliferation of Nuclear Weapons and establishment of a Preparatory Committee for the Fourth Review Conference

The General Assembly,

Recalling its resolution 2373(XXII) of 12 June 1968, the annex to which contains the Treaty on the Non-Proliferation of Nuclear Weapons,

Bearing in mind the provisions of article VIII, paragraph 3, of that Treaty concerning the holding of successive review conferences,

Noting that, in the Final Declaration of the Third Review Conference of the Parties to the Treaty on the Non-Proliferation of Nuclear Weapons, held at Geneva from 27 August to 21 September 1985, the Conference proposed to the Depositary Governments that a fourth conference to review the operation of the Treaty be convened in 1990, and also noting that there appears to be a consensus among the parties that the Fourth Review Conference should be held at Geneva in August/September of that year,

1. *Notes* that, following appropriate consultations, an open-ended preparatory committee has been formed of parties to the Treaty on the Non-Proliferation of Nuclear Weapons serving on the Board of Governors of the International Atomic Energy Agency or represented in the Conference on Disarmament, as well as any party to the Treaty that may express its interest in participating in the work of the preparatory committee;

2. *Requests* the Secretary-General to render the necessary assistance and to provide such services, including summary records, as may be required for the Fourth Review Conference of the Parties to the Treaty on the Non-Proliferation of Nuclear Weapons and its preparation.

General Assembly resolution 43/82

7 December 1988   Meeting 73   137-0-11 (recorded vote)

Approved by First Committee (A/43/895) by recorded vote (119-0-9), 15 November (meeting 38); 60-nation draft (A/C.1/43/L.45); agenda item 141.
Sponsors: Afghanistan, Australia, Austria, Bangladesh, Belgium, Bulgaria, Cameroon, Canada, Colombia, Cyprus, Czechoslovakia, Democratic Yemen, Denmark, Ecuador, Egypt, Finland, German Democratic Republic, Germany, Federal Republic of, Ghana, Greece, Guinea, Hungary, Iceland, Iraq, Ireland, Italy, Japan, Kenya, Lao People's Democratic Republic, Liberia, Luxembourg, Malaysia, Mexico, Mongolia, Morocco, Netherlands, New Zealand, Nigeria, Norway, Peru, Philippines, Poland, Portugal, Romania, Samoa, Spain, Sri Lanka, Sweden, Syrian Arab Republic, Thailand, Togo, Tunisia, Turkey, USSR, United Kingdom, United States, Uruguay, Venezuela, Yemen.
Meeting numbers. GA 43rd session: 1st Committee 3-25, 28, 38; plenary 73.

Recorded vote in Assembly as follows:

In favour: Afghanistan, Antigua and Barbuda, Australia, Austria, Bahamas, Bahrain, Bangladesh, Barbados, Belgium, Belize, Benin, Bhutan, Bolivia, Botswana, Brunei Darussalam, Bulgaria, Burkina Faso, Burundi, Byelorussian SSR, Cameroon, Canada, Cape Verde, Central African Republic, Chad, Chile, Colombia, Comoros, Congo, Costa Rica, Côte d'Ivoire, Cyprus, Czechoslovakia, Democratic Kampuchea, Democratic Yemen, Denmark, Djibouti, Dominican Republic, Ecuador, Egypt, El Salvador, Ethiopia, Fiji, Finland, Gabon, Gambia, German Democratic Republic, Germany, Federal Republic of, Ghana, Greece, Guatemala, Guinea, Haiti, Honduras, Hungary, Iceland, Indonesia, Iran, Iraq, Ireland, Italy, Japan, Jordan, Kenya, Kuwait, Lao People's Democratic Republic, Lebanon, Liberia, Libyan Arab Jamahiriya, Luxembourg, Madagascar, Malawi, Malaysia, Maldives, Mali, Malta, Mauritania, Mauritius, Mexico, Mongolia, Morocco, Mozambique, Nepal, Netherlands, New Zealand, Nicaragua, Niger, Nigeria, Norway, Oman, Pakistan, Panama, Papua New Guinea, Paraguay, Peru, Philippines, Poland, Portugal, Qatar, Romania, Rwanda, Saint Kitts and Nevis, Saint Lucia, Saint Vincent and the Grenadines, Samoa, Sao Tome and Principe, Saudi Arabia, Senegal, Seychelles, Sierra Leone, Singapore, Solomon Islands, Somalia, Spain, Sri Lanka, Sudan, Suriname, Swaziland, Sweden, Syrian Arab Republic, Thailand, Togo, Trinidad and Tobago, Tunisia, Turkey, Uganda, Ukrainian SSR, USSR, United Arab Emirates, United Kingdom, United States, Uruguay, Vanuatu, Venezuela, Viet Nam, Yemen, Yugoslavia, Zaire.
Against: None.
Abstaining: Angola, Argentina, Brazil, Cuba, Guyana, India, Israel, Lesotho, United Republic of Tanzania, Zambia, Zimbabwe.

REFERENCES

[1]A/43/27. [2]CD/814 & CD/815. [3]CD/845 & CD/847. [4]CD/515/Rev. 4. [5]A/S-15/3. [6]YUN 1986, p. 37, GA res. 41/86 H, 4 Dec. 1986. [7]A/43/351. [8]YUN 1987, p. 47. [9]CD/819. [10]YUN 1978, p. 39, GA res. S-10/2, 30 June 1978. [11]CD/834. [12]CD/797-800. [13]CD/807 & Add.1,2. [14]YUN 1987, p. 54, GA res. 42/38 C, 30 Nov. 1987. [15]A/43/625.

[16]A/43/152 & Add.1-6. [17]CD/863. [18]CD/829. [19]CD/852. [20]CD/860. [21]YUN 1963, p. 137. [22]CD/818. [23]CD/853. [24]CD/862. [25]CD/825 & CD/868. [26]A/S-15/26 & A/43/485. [27]A/43/741. [28]YUN 1964, p. 69. [29]YUN 1987, p. 61, GA res. 42/34 B, 30 Nov. 1987. [30]YUN 1984, p. 39. [31]A/43/701. [32]YUN 1968, p. 17, GA res. 2373(XXII), annex, 12 June 1968. [33]YUN 1979, p. 46. [34]A/43/484. [35]YUN 1987, p. 64, GA res. 42/28, 30 Nov. 1987. [36]A/S-15/AC.1/25. [37]A/43/693. [38]YUN 1987, p. 66, GA res. 42/44, 30 Nov. 1987. [39]YUN 1981, p. 282, SC res. 487(1981), 19 June 1981. [40]YUN 1987, p. 67, GA res. 42/29, 30 Nov. 1987. [41]A/43/505. [42]YUN 1987, p. 85, GA res. 42/43, 30 Nov. 1987. [43]A/43/29. [44]YUN 1971, p. 34, GA res. 2832(XXVI), 16 Dec. 1971. [45]A/S-15/5. [46]A/AC.159/L.85. [47]A/AC.159/L.55 & Add.1-5. [48]YUN 1975, p. 27. [49]YUN 1980, p. 51. [50]YUN 1985, p. 56. [51]A/43/191/Rev.1.

Prohibition or restriction of other weapons

Progress was made in 1988 by the Conference on Disarmament in elaborating a convention banning the development, production and stockpiling of chemical, biological and radiological weapons. In addition, efforts to prevent an arms race in outer space continued to receive attention both within and outside the United Nations.

Chemical and biological weapons

During 1988, efforts continued in the Conference on Disarmament and in the General Assembly towards the elaboration of a convention on a comprehensive ban of chemical weapons.

During the Assembly's 1988 regular session, the United States proposed the convening of a conference to consider actions to uphold the authority and, in its words, to reverse the serious erosion of the 1925 Geneva Protocol for the Prohibition of the Use in War of Asphyxiating, Poisonous and Other Gases, and of Bacteriological Methods of Warfare. France offered to host the conference, which was later scheduled to take place in Paris from 7 to 11 January 1989.

In May and August 1988, the Security Council, in **resolutions 612(1988) and 620(1988)**, condemned the continued use of chemical weapons, contrary to the obligations under the Geneva Protocol, and called on States to continue to apply, establish or strengthen strict control of the export of chemical products serving for the production of chemical weapons. It also decided to consider appropriate and effective measures should there be any future use of chemical weapons.

Consideration by the Conference on Disarmament. The Conference on Disarmament continued negotiations on a convention banning chemical and biological weapons from 14 to 25 March and from 15 to 19 August.[1]

The *Ad Hoc* Committee on Chemical Weapons, re-established by the Conference on 9 February, held 21 meetings between 12 February and 12 September and its Chairman also held informal consultations. The Committee submitted to the Conference a report on its inter-sessional work in January[2] and a special report,[3] submitted in view of the third special session of the Assembly devoted to disarmament. Both reports contained the rolling text of the draft convention, reflecting the stage of negotiations reached.

New documents were submitted to the Conference on the multilateral exchange and provision of data relevant to the convention by the Federal Republic of Germany[4] and the USSR;[5] on the order, method and technology for the destruction of chemical weapons and their facilities by the Federal Republic of Germany and Italy,[6] the USSR[7] and the United States;[8] and on the use of chemical weapons by Australia,[9] the Federal Republic of Germany[10] and Iran.[11] The United States made proposals for monitoring chemical activities not prohibited by a convention,[12] and the Federal Republic of Germany put forward a case for checks on production facilities in the industry and a list of super-toxic lethal chemicals relevant to the convention.[13] The USSR disclosed the size of its chemical weapons stockpile[14] and the United Kingdom provided information on its past production of chemical warfare agents.[15]

Other ideas and proposals were put forward in working papers submitted to the *Ad Hoc* Committee. New documents on verification problems were submitted by the German Democratic Republic, on the possible composition, size and decision-making process of the executive council of the envisaged verification inspectorate;[16] by Canada, on factors involved in determining the inspectorate's personnel and resource requirements;[17] and by Finland[18] and Norway[19] (both non-members), on verification procedures.

The work of the Committee was conducted in three working groups. It was decided to focus efforts in the first instance on articles III to XVI of the proposed convention and to consider articles I and II—on general provisions and on definitions and criteria—in July. On 29 April, the Conference adopted the report of the *Ad Hoc* Committee,[3] which formed an integral part of its own report to the third special session of the Assembly on disarmament.[20]

In July, the Committee continued the negotiations and further elaboration of the convention and agreed that its three working groups would consider, respectively: permitted activities and economic and technological development; general provisions on scope, definitions and criteria, declarations, elimination of chemical weapons, chemical weapons production facilities and assistance;

and national implementation measures, the organization to achieve the objectives of the convention, consultations, co-operation and fact-finding. The Committee Chairman conducted open-ended consultations to prepare for multilateral trial inspections in the chemical industry.

On 20 September, the Conference adopted the *Ad Hoc* Committee's report,[21] which formed part of its own report to the General Assembly at its 1988 regular session.[1] The *Ad Hoc* Committee recommended to the Conference that further negotiation and drafting of the convention make use of the appendices to its report and other documents reflecting the results of the work of the Committee. It also recommended that it examine further the question of undiminished security during the destruction period and the proper place in the text of the proposed convention for provisions concerning the issue. The Committee further recommended that it be re-established at the outset of the 1989 session.

Report of the Secretary-General. Pursuant to a 1987 request of the General Assembly,[22] the Secretary-General reported in October 1988[23] that the group of experts he had appointed to assist him in the development of further technical guidelines and procedures for the timely and efficient investigation of reports of the possible use of chemical and bacteriological (biological) or toxin weapons had been unable to complete its final consolidated report. Accordingly, he recommended that, given the importance of the task, more time be provided for completing the mandate. In an annex to the report, the Secretary-General provided replies received from 21 Member States in response to his request for names of qualified experts and laboratories that might be in a position to assist him in his mandate.

GENERAL ASSEMBLY ACTION

On 7 December, the General Assembly, on the recommendation of the First Committee, adopted **resolution 43/74 A** without vote.

Measures to uphold the authority of the 1925 Geneva Protocol and to support the conclusion of a chemical weapons convention

The General Assembly,

Recalling its resolution 42/37 C of 30 November 1987,

Recalling also the rules and principles of international humanitarian law applicable in armed conflict,

Reaffirming its dedication to protecting humanity from chemical and biological warfare,

Expressing deep dismay at the use of chemical weapons in violation of the Protocol for the Prohibition of the Use in War of Asphyxiating, Poisonous or Other Gases, and of Bacteriological Methods of Warfare, signed at Geneva on 17 June 1925, and of other rules of customary international law, at indications of their emergence in an increasing number of national arsenals and at the growing risk that they may be used again,

Recalling the provisions of the 1925 Geneva Protocol and other relevant rules of customary international law,

Recalling also the necessity for adherence by all States to the Convention on the Prohibition of the Development, Production and Stockpiling of Bacteriological (Biological) and Toxin Weapons and on Their Destruction, signed in London, Moscow and Washington on 10 April 1972,

Bearing in mind the resolutions of the Security Council on chemical weapons adopted during 1988,

Noting that prompt and impartial investigation of reports of possible use of chemical and bacteriological weapons would further enhance the authority of the Geneva Protocol,

Taking note of the report of the Secretary-General on the meeting of the group of qualified experts established in pursuance of General Assembly resolution 42/37 C to develop further the technical guidelines and procedures available to the Secretary-General for the timely and efficient investigation of reports of the possible use of chemical and bacteriological (biological) or toxin weapons,

Recalling that, in its resolution 620(1988) of 26 August 1988, the Security Council decided to consider immediately, taking into account the investigations of the Secretary-General, appropriate and effective measures in accordance with the Charter of the United Nations,

Expressing its appreciation for the work of the Secretary-General, and noting the procedures available to him in support of the principles and objectives of the Geneva Protocol,

1. *Renews its call* to all States to observe strictly the principles and objectives of the Protocol for the Prohibition of the Use in War of Asphyxiating, Poisonous or Other Gases, and of Bacteriological Methods of Warfare, and condemns vigorously all actions that violate this obligation;

2. *Calls upon* all States that have not yet done so to accede to the 1925 Geneva Protocol;

3. *Urges* the Conference on Disarmament to pursue as a matter of continuing urgency its negotiations on a convention on the prohibition of the development, production, stockpiling and use of all chemical weapons and on their destruction;

4. *Calls upon* all States to be guided in their national policies by the need to curb the spread of chemical weapons pending the conclusion of such a convention;

5. *Requests* the Secretary-General to carry out promptly investigations in response to reports that may be brought to his attention by any Member State concerning the possible use of chemical and bacteriological (biological) or toxin weapons that may constitute a violation of the Geneva Protocol or other rules of customary international law in order to ascertain the facts of the matter, and to report promptly the results of any such investigation to all Member States, in accordance with the procedures established by the General Assembly in its resolution 42/37 C;

6. *Also requests* the Secretary-General, pursuant to resolution 42/37 C, with the assistance of the group of qualified experts provided by interested Member States, to continue his efforts to develop further technical guidelines and procedures available to him for the timely and efficient investigation of such reports of the possible use of chemical and bacteriological (biological) or toxin weapons, and to report to Member States as soon as possible;

7. *Requests* Member States and the relevant international organizations to co-operate fully with the Secretary-General in the above-mentioned work;

8. *Decides* to include in the provisional agenda of its forty-fourth session the item entitled "Chemical and bacteriological (biological) weapons".

General Assembly resolution 43/74 A

7 December 1988   Meeting 73   Adopted without vote

Approved by First Committee (A/43/855) without vote, 16 November (meeting 39); 31-nation draft (A/C.1/43/L.52/Rev.1); agenda item 63.

Sponsors: Australia, Austria, Belgium, Bulgaria, Cameroon, Canada, Colombia, Côte d'Ivoire, Denmark, Ecuador, France, German Democratic Republic, Germany, Federal Republic of, Greece, Iceland, Italy, Japan, Liberia, Netherlands, New Zealand, Norway, Poland, Portugal, Spain, Sweden, Thailand, Turkey, USSR, United States, Uruguay, Zaire.

Financial implications. ACABQ, A/43/7/Add.9; 5th Committee, A/43/938; S-G, A/C.1/43/L.79 & Corr.1, A/C.5/43/46 & Add.1.

Meeting numbers. GA 43rd session: 1st Committee 3-25, 36, 39; 5th Committee 41; plenary 73.

On the same date and on the recommendation of the First Committee, the Assembly adopted **resolution 43/74 C** without vote.

Chemical and bacteriological (biological) weapons

The General Assembly,

Recalling its previous resolutions relating to the complete and effective prohibition of the development, production and stockpiling of all chemical weapons and to their destruction,

Reaffirming the urgent necessity, particularly following recent United Nations reports, of strict observance by all States of the principles and objectives of the Protocol for the Prohibition of the Use in War of Asphyxiating, Poisonous or Other Gases, and of Bacteriological Methods of Warfare, signed at Geneva on 17 June 1925, and taking note with satisfaction of the proposal to convene a conference to that effect,

Reaffirming also the urgent necessity of the adherence by all States to the Convention of the Prohibition of the Development, Production and Stockpiling of Bacteriological (Biological) and Toxin Weapons and on Their Destruction, signed in London, Moscow and Washington on 10 April 1972,

Taking note of the Final Document of the Second Review Conference of the Parties to the Convention on the Prohibition of the Development, Production and Stockpiling of Bacteriological (Biological) and Toxin Weapons and on Their Destruction, adopted by consensus on 26 September 1986, and, in particular, of article IX of the Final Declaration of the Conference,

Having considered the report of the Conference on Disarmament, which incorporates, *inter alia*, the report of its *Ad Hoc* Committee on Chemical Weapons, and noting that following the precedents set over the past four years, consultations are continuing during the intersessional period, thus increasing the time devoted to negotiations,

Convinced of the necessity that all efforts be exerted for the continuation and successful conclusion of negotiations on the prohibition of the development, production, stockpiling and use of all chemical weapons and on their destruction,

Expressing the hope that the conference referred to above will also give a strong impetus to that end,

Conscious of the need to share data relevant to the negotiations on a future convention banning all chemical weapons on a global basis and of the fact that the provision of such data would be an important confidence-building measure,

Noting the bilateral and other discussions, including the ongoing exchange of views between the Union of the Soviet Socialist Republics and the United States of America in the framework of the multilateral negotiations, on issues related to the prohibition of chemical weapons,

Noting with appreciation the efforts made at all levels by States to facilitate the earliest conclusion of a convention and, in particular, the concrete steps designed to promote confidence and to contribute directly to that goal,

1. *Takes note with satisfaction* of the work of the Conference on Disarmament during its 1988 session regarding the prohibition of chemical weapons, and in particular appreciates the progress in the work of its *Ad Hoc* Committee on Chemical Weapons on that question and the tangible results recorded in its report;

2. *Expresses again none the less its regret and concern* that, notwithstanding the progress made in 1988, a convention on the complete and effective prohibition of the development, production, stockpiling and use of all chemical weapons and on their destruction has not yet been elaborated;

3. *Urges again* the Conference on Disarmament, as a matter of high priority, to intensify, during its 1989 session, the negotiations on such a convention and to reinforce further its efforts by, *inter alia*, increasing the time during the year that it devotes to such negotiations, taking into account all existing proposals and future initiatives, with a view to the final elaboration of a convention at the earliest possible date, and to re-establish its *Ad Hoc* Committee on Chemical Weapons for this purpose with the mandate to be agreed upon by the Conference at the beginning of its 1989 session;

4. *Requests* the Conference on Disarmament to report to the General Assembly at its forty-fourth session on the results of its negotiations;

5. *Encourages* Member States to take further initiatives to promote confidence and openness in the negotiations and to provide further information to facilitate prompt resolution of outstanding issues, thus contributing to an early agreement on, and universal adherence to, a convention on the prohibition of the development, production, stockpiling and use of all chemical weapons and on their destruction;

6. *Recognizes* the importance of declarations made by States on whether or not they possess chemical weapons and of further international exchanges of data in connection with the negotiations on a multilateral convention on the complete and effective prohibition of the development, production, stockpiling and use of chemical weapons and on their destruction;

7. *Welcomes* the offer by the French Government to convene in Paris from 7 to 11 January 1989 a conference of the States parties to the Protocol for the Prohibition of the Use in War of Asphyxiating, Poisonous and Other Gases, and of Bacteriological Methods of Warfare, and of other interested States;

8. *Expresses* the hope that all States will contribute actively to the objectives of the conference.

General Assembly resolution 43/74 C

7 December 1988   Meeting 73   Adopted without vote

Approved by First Committee (A/43/855) without vote, 16 November (meeting 39); 33-nation draft (A/C.1/43/L.67); agenda item 63.

Sponsors: Argentina, Australia, Austria, Belgium, Bulgaria, Canada, Denmark, Finland, France, German Democratic Republic, Germany, Federal Republic of, Greece, Hungary, Iceland, Ireland, Italy, Japan, Malaysia, Mexico, Mongolia, Netherlands, Norway, Philippines, Poland, Portugal, Samoa, Spain, Sweden, Turkey, Ukrainian SSR, United Kingdom, Uruguay, Viet Nam.

Meeting numbers. GA 43rd session: 1st Committee 3-25, 36, 39; plenary 73.

Follow-up to the 1986 Review Conference

At the 1987 *Ad Hoc* Meeting of Scientific and Technical Experts[24] of the parties to the 1971 Convention on the Prohibition of the Development, Production and Stockpiling of Bacteriological (Biological) and Toxin Weapons and on Their Destruction,[25] the modalities for a standard procedure for the exchange of information and data on bacteriological and toxin weapons were finalized and adopted. The modalities provided for the first exchange of such information to take place by 15 October 1987 and thereafter by 15 April on an annual basis. In 1988, the second exchange of data and information took place in accordance with that procedure.

GENERAL ASSEMBLY ACTION

On 7 December 1988, on the recommendation of the First Committee, the General Assembly adopted **resolution 43/74 B** without vote.

Second Review Conference of the Parties to the Convention on the Prohibition of the Development, Production and Stockpiling of Bacteriological (Biological) and Toxin Weapons and on Their Destruction

The General Assembly,

Recalling its resolution 2826(XXVI) of 16 December 1971, in which it commended the Convention on the Prohibition of the Development, Production and Stockpiling of Bacteriological (Biological) and Toxin Weapons and on Their Destruction and expressed the hope for the widest possible adherence to the Convention,

Recalling its resolution 39/65 D of 12 December 1984, in which it noted that, at the request of a majority of States parties to the Convention, a second Review Conference of the Parties to the Convention would be held in 1986,

Recalling that the States parties to the Convention met at Geneva from 8 to 26 September 1986 to review the operation of the Convention with a view to assuring that the purposes of the preamble to and the provisions of the Convention, including the provisions concerning negotiations on chemical weapons, were being realized,

Recalling also its resolution 41/58 A of 3 December 1986, in which it, *inter alia*, noted with appreciation that on 26 September 1986, the Second Review Conference of the Parties to the Convention on the Prohibition of the Development, Production and Stockpiling of Bacteriological (Biological) and Toxin Weapons and on Their Destruction adopted by consensus a Final Declaration,

Pursuing its resolution 42/37 B, and noting with satisfaction that at the time of the Second Review Conference of the Parties to the Convention there were more than a hundred States parties to the Convention, including all the permanent members of the Security Council,

1. *Notes with appreciation* that, in accordance with the Final Declaration of the Second Review Conference of the Parties to the Convention on the Prohibition of the Development, Production and Stockpiling of Bacteriological (Biological) and Toxin Weapons and on Their Destruction, an *Ad Hoc* Meeting of Scientific and Technical Experts from States parties to the Convention was held at Geneva from 31 March to 15 April 1987, which adopted by consensus a report finalizing the modalities for the exchange of information and data agreed to in the Final Declaration, thus enabling States parties to follow a standardized procedure;

2. *Notes* that the *Ad Hoc* Meeting of Scientific and Technical Experts from States parties to the Convention agreed in its report that the first exchange of information and data should take place not later than 15 October 1987 and that thereafter information to be given on an annual basis should be provided through the Department for Disarmament Affairs of the Secretariat not later than 15 April;

3. *Notes with satisfaction* that the second such exchange of information and data has commenced, and calls upon States that have not yet exchanged information and data to do so;

4. *Requests* the Secretary-General to render the necessary assistance and to provide such services as may be required for the implementation of the relevant parts of the Final Declaration;

5. *Calls upon* all States that have not ratified or acceded to the Convention to do so without delay, thus contributing to the achievement of universal adherence to the Convention and to international confidence.

General Assembly resolution 43/74 B

7 December 1988   Meeting 73   Adopted without vote

Approved by First Committee (A/43/855) without vote, 16 November (meeting 39); 38-nation draft (A/C.1/43/L.59); agenda item 63.
Sponsors: Australia, Austria, Belgium, Bolivia, Bulgaria, Byelorussian SSR, Canada, Chile, China, Czechoslovakia, Denmark, Finland, France, German Democratic Republic, Germany, Federal Republic of, Greece, Guyana, Hungary, Iran, Ireland, Italy, Japan, Liberia, Mongolia, Netherlands, New Zealand, Norway, Pakistan, Poland, Romania, Spain, Sweden, Ukrainian SSR, USSR, United Kingdom, United States, Zaire.
Meeting numbers. GA 43rd session: 1st Committee 3-25, 27, 39; plenary 73.

New weapons of mass destruction, including radiological weapons

In 1988, the Conference on Disarmament continued consideration of the general question of new types and systems of weapons of mass destruction, including radiological weapons. However, the positions of Member States remained divided, in particular with regard to the need to initiate negotiations on specific types of new weapons, once such weapons had been identified.

At its 1988 regular session, the General Assembly requested the Conference on Disarmament to continue its negotiations on the prohibition of radiological weapons with a view to a prompt conclusion of its work (resolution 43/75 C) and to intensify further its efforts to reach an agreement prohibiting armed attacks against nuclear facilities (43/75 J).

Consideration by the Conference on Disarmament. The Conference on Disarmament considered the item "New types of weapons of mass destruction and new systems of such weapons; radiological weapons" from 28 March to 1 April and from 22 to 26 August.[1]

The *Ad Hoc* Committee on Radiological Weapons, re-established on 2 February, held six meetings from 29 February to 26 August, with a view to reaching agreement on a convention prohibiting the development, production, stockpiling and use of such weapons. It also held a number of informal consultations and re-established two contact groups. Contact group A discussed possible elements for a convention, such as the definition of radiological weapons, the peaceful uses of such weapons, the cessation of the use or threat of use of these weapons, and measures of verification and compliance. Contact group B considered issues relevant to the prohibition of attacks against nuclear facilities, in particular those pertaining to verification and compliance, as well as other main elements.

The *Ad Hoc* Committee took note of IAEA's readiness to provide technical assistance to the Conference in its work relating to the prohibition of armed attacks against nuclear installations.

On 26 April, the Conference adopted the Committee's report as part of its own report to the Assembly's third special session on disarmament.[20] That report reflected the current state of issues before the Committee.[26]

On 6 September, the Conference adopted the report of the Committee on the second part of its session as part of its own report to the 1988 regular Assembly session.[1] That report[27] indicated that the work of the Committee had contributed to the clarification of the different approaches to the issues under consideration. The Committee recommended that it be re-established at the beginning of the 1989 session of the Conference and that it draw on the annexes of its report as a basis for future work.

Report of the Secretary-General. In an October 1988 report on the prohibition of attacks on nuclear facilities,[28] prepared in response to a 1987 Assembly request,[29] the Secretary-General referred to the relevant parts of the report of the Conference on Disarmament to the Assembly,[1] which dealt with the report of the *Ad Hoc* Committee on Radiological Weapons.

GENERAL ASSEMBLY ACTION

On 7 December, on the recommendation of the First Committee, the General Assembly adopted **resolution 43/75 C** without vote.

Prohibition of the development, production, stockpiling and use of radiological weapons
The General Assembly,
Recalling its resolution 42/38 B of 30 November 1987,
1. *Takes note* of the part of the report of the Conference on Disarmament on its 1988 session and that of

the special report of the Conference on Disarmament that deal with the question of radiological weapons, in particular the reports of the *Ad Hoc* Committee on Radiological Weapons;

2. *Recognizes* that the *Ad Hoc* Committee in 1988 made a further contribution to the clarification and better understanding of different approaches that continue to exist with regard to both of the important subjects under consideration;

3. *Takes note* of the recommendation of the Conference on Disarmament that the *Ad Hoc* Committee on Radiological Weapons should be re-established at the beginning of its 1989 session;

4. *Requests* the Conference on Disarmament to continue its negotiations on the subject with a view to a prompt conclusion of its work, taking into account all proposals presented to the Conference to this end and drawing upon the annexes to its report as a basis of its future work, the result of which should be submitted to the General Assembly at its forty-fourth session;

5. *Requests* the Secretary-General to transmit to the Conference on Disarmament all relevant documents relating to the discussion of all aspects of the issue by the General Assembly at its forty-third session;

6. *Decides* to include in the provisional agenda of its forty-fourth session the item entitled "Prohibition of the development, production, stockpiling and use of radiological weapons".

General Assembly resolution 43/75 C

7 December 1988   Meeting 73   Adopted without vote

Approved by First Committee (A/43/856) without vote, 14 November (meeting 35); 4-nation draft (A/C.1/43/L.9); agenda item 64 *(b)*.
Sponsors: Hungary, Indonesia, Sweden, United Kingdom.
Meeting numbers. GA 43rd session: 1st Committee 3-25, 27, 35; plenary 73.

On the same date, again on the First Committee's recommendation, the Assembly adopted **resolution 43/75 J** by recorded vote.

Prohibition of the development, production, stockpiling and use of radiological weapons
The General Assembly,

Recalling its resolutions 37/99 C of 13 December 1982, 38/188 D of 20 December 1983, 39/151 J of 17 December 1984, 40/94 D of 12 December 1985, 41/59 A and I of 3 December 1986 and 42/38 F of 30 November 1987 on, *inter alia*, the conclusion of an agreement prohibiting military attacks against nuclear facilities,

Taking note of the report of the Secretary-General on this subject submitted pursuant to resolution 42/38 F,

Gravely concerned that armed attacks against nuclear facilities, though carried out with conventional weapons, could be tantamount to the use of radiological weapons,

Recalling also that Additional Protocol I of 1977 to the Geneva Conventions of 12 August 1949 prohibits attacks on nuclear electricity-generating stations,

Deeply concerned that the destruction of nuclear facilities by conventional weapons causes the release into the environment of huge amounts of dangerous radioactive material, which results in serious radioactive contamination,

Firmly convinced that the Israeli attack against the safeguarded nuclear facilities in Iraq constitutes an unprecedented danger to international peace and security,

Recalling further resolutions GC(XXVII)/RES/407 and GC(XXVII)/RES/409, adopted on 14 October 1983, in

which the General Conference of the International Atomic Energy Agency urged all member States to support actions in international forums to reach an international agreement that prohibits armed attacks against nuclear installations devoted to peaceful purposes,

1. *Reaffirms* that armed attacks of any kind against nuclear facilities are tantamount to the use of radiological weapons, owing to the dangerous radioactive forces that such attacks cause to be released;

2. *Requests once again* the Conference on Disarmament to intensify further its efforts to reach, as early as possible, an agreement prohibiting armed attacks against nuclear facilities;

3. *Requests again* the International Atomic Energy Agency to provide the Conference on Disarmament with the technical studies that could facilitate the conclusion of such an agreement;

4. *Requests* the Secretary-General to report to the General Assembly at its forty-fourth session on the progress made in the implementation of the present resolution.

General Assembly resolution 43/75 J

7 December 1988   Meeting 73   116-2-29 (recorded vote)

Approved by First Committee (A/43/856) by recorded vote (99-2-30), 14 November (meeting 35); 2-nation draft (A/C.1/43/L.25); agenda item 64 *(b)*.
Sponsors: Iraq, Jordan.
Meeting numbers. GA 43rd session: 1st Committee 3-25, 27, 35; plenary 73.

Recorded vote in Assembly as follows:

In favour: Afghanistan, Albania, Algeria, Angola, Antigua and Barbuda, Argentina, Bahrain, Bangladesh, Barbados, Belize, Benin, Bhutan, Bolivia, Botswana, Brazil, Brunei Darussalam, Bulgaria, Burkina Faso, Burundi, Byelorussian SSR, Cameroon, Cape Verde, Central African Republic, Chad, Chile, China, Comoros, Congo, Costa Rica, Côte d'Ivoire, Cuba, Cyprus, Czechoslovakia, Democratic Kampuchea, Democratic Yemen, Djibouti, Dominican Republic, Ecuador, Egypt, El Salvador, Gabon, Gambia, German Democratic Republic, Ghana, Guatemala, Guinea, Guyana, Haiti, Honduras, Hungary, India, Indonesia, Iran, Iraq, Jamaica, Jordan, Kenya, Kuwait, Lao People's Democratic Republic, Lebanon, Lesotho, Libyan Arab Jamahiriya, Luxembourg,* Madagascar, Malawi, Malaysia, Maldives, Mauritania, Mauritius, Mexico, Mongolia, Morocco, Mozambique, Nepal, Nicaragua, Niger, Nigeria, Oman, Pakistan, Panama, Papua New Guinea, Paraguay, Peru, Philippines, Poland, Romania, Rwanda, Saint Kitts and Nevis, Saint Lucia, Saint Vincent and the Grenadines, Sao Tome and Principe, Saudi Arabia, Senegal, Seychelles, Sierra Leone, Solomon Islands, Sri Lanka, Sudan, Suriname, Swaziland, Syrian Arab Republic, Togo, Trinidad and Tobago, Tunisia, Turkey, Uganda, Ukrainian SSR, USSR, United Arab Emirates, Vanuatu, Viet Nam, Yemen, Yugoslavia, Zaire, Zambia, Zimbabwe.

Against: Israel, United States.

Abstaining: Australia, Austria, Bahamas, Belgium, Canada, Colombia, Denmark, Fiji, Finland, France, Germany, Federal Republic of, Greece, Iceland, Ireland, Italy, Japan, Liberia, Malta, Netherlands, New Zealand, Norway, Portugal, Samoa, Somalia, Spain, Sweden, United Kingdom, Uruguay, Venezuela.

*Later advised the Secretariat it had intended to abstain.

Also on 7 December, the Assembly adopted **resolution 43/72**, on the recommendation of the First Committee and by recorded vote.

Prohibition of the development and manufacture of new types of weapons of mass destruction and new systems of such weapons
The General Assembly,

Recalling its previous resolutions on the prohibition of the development and manufacture of new types of weapons of mass destruction and new systems of such weapons,

Bearing in mind paragraph 77 of the Final Document of the Tenth Special Session of the General Assembly,

Determined to prevent the emergence of new types of weapons of mass destruction that have characteristics comparable in destructive effect to those of weapons of mass destruction identified in the definition of weapons of mass destruction adopted by the United Nations in 1948,

Noting that in the course of its 1988 session the Conference on Disarmament considered the item entitled "New types of weapons of mass destruction and new systems of such weapons; radiological weapons",

Taking into account the section of the report of the Conference on Disarmament relating to this question,

1. *Reaffirms* that effective measures should be undertaken to prevent the emergence of new types of weapons of mass destruction;

2. *Requests* the Conference on Disarmament, in the light of its existing priorities, to keep under review, with expert assistance, as appropriate, the questions of the prohibition of the development and manufacture of new types of weapons of mass destruction and new systems of such weapons with a view to making, when necessary, recommendations on undertaking specific negotiations on the identified types of such weapons;

3. *Calls upon* all States, immediately following the recommendation of the Conference on Disarmament, to give favourable consideration to these recommendations;

4. *Requests* the Secretary-General to transmit to the Conference on Disarmament all documents relating to the consideration of this item by the General Assembly at its forty-third session;

5. *Requests* the Conference on Disarmament to submit a report on results achieved to the General Assembly for consideration at its forty-fourth session;

6. *Decides* to include in the provisional agenda of its forty-fifth session the item entitled "Prohibition of the development and manufacture of new types of weapons of mass destruction and new systems of such weapons: report of the Conference on Disarmament".

General Assembly resolution 43/72

7 December 1988   Meeting 73   152-0-2 (recorded vote)

Approved by First Committee (A/43/840) by recorded vote (134-0-2), 18 November (meeting 42); 21-nation draft (A/C.1/43/L.38/Rev.1), orally revised; agenda item 61.

Sponsors: Afghanistan, Angola, Benin, Bulgaria, Burkina Faso, Byelorussian SSR, Cuba, Czechoslovakia, Democratic Yemen, Ethiopia, German Democratic Republic, Hungary, Lao People's Democratic Republic, Mongolia, Mozambique, Poland, Romania, Syrian Arab Republic, Ukrainian SSR, USSR, Viet Nam.

Meeting numbers. GA 43rd session: 1st Committee 3-25, 31, 39, 42; plenary 73.

Recorded vote in Assembly as follows:

In favour: Afghanistan, Albania, Algeria, Angola, Antigua and Barbuda, Argentina, Australia, Austria, Bahamas, Bahrain, Bangladesh, Barbados, Belgium, Belize, Benin, Bhutan, Bolivia, Botswana, Brazil, Brunei Darussalam, Bulgaria, Burkina Faso, Burma, Burundi, Byelorussian SSR, Cameroon, Canada, Cape Verde, Central African Republic, Chad, Chile, China, Colombia, Comoros, Congo, Costa Rica, Côte d'Ivoire, Cuba, Cyprus, Czechoslovakia, Democratic Yemen, Denmark, Djibouti, Dominican Republic, Ecuador, Egypt, El Salvador, Ethiopia, Fiji, Finland, France, Gabon, Gambia, German Democratic Republic, Germany, Federal Republic of, Ghana, Greece, Grenada, Guatemala, Guinea, Guyana, Haiti, Honduras, Hungary, Iceland, India, Indonesia, Iran, Iraq, Ireland, Italy, Jamaica, Japan, Jordan, Kenya, Kuwait, Lao People's Democratic Republic, Lebanon, Lesotho, Liberia, Libyan Arab Jamahiriya, Luxembourg, Madagascar, Malawi, Malaysia, Maldives, Mali, Malta, Mauritania, Mauritius, Mexico, Mongolia, Morocco, Mozambique, Nepal, Netherlands, New Zealand, Nicaragua, Niger, Nigeria, Norway, Oman, Pakistan, Panama, Papua New Guinea, Paraguay, Peru, Philippines, Poland, Portugal, Qatar, Romania, Rwanda, Saint Kitts and Nevis, Saint Lucia, Saint Vincent and the Grenadines, Samoa, Sao Tome and Principe, Saudi Arabia, Senegal, Seychelles, Sierra Leone, Singapore, Solomon Islands, Somalia, Spain, Sri Lanka, Sudan, Suriname, Swaziland, Sweden, Syrian Arab Republic, Thailand, Togo, Trinidad and Tobago, Tunisia, Turkey, Uganda, Ukrainian SSR, USSR, United Arab Emirates, United Kingdom, United Republic of Tanzania, Uruguay, Vanuatu, Venezuela, Viet Nam, Yemen, Yugoslavia, Zaire, Zambia, Zimbabwe.

Against: None.

Abstaining: Israel, United States.

In related action, the Assembly, by **decision 43/423** of 7 December, included in the provisional agenda of its forty-fourth (1989) session the item entitled "Liability for the illegal transfer and/or use of prohibited weapons and weapons or substances which cause unnecessary human suffering".

Dumping of radioactive wastes

In 1988, the question of the dumping of industrial waste was a major concern of the international community. The Council of Ministers of OAU, in May, adopted a resolution,[30] declaring such dumping in Africa by transnational corporations and enterprises to be a crime against Africa and calling on African countries to put an end to agreements or arrangements either concluded or in the process of being concluded for the dumping of nuclear and industrial wastes. It also requested international organizations and agencies to assist African countries to establish mechanisms for monitoring and controlling the movement and disposal of such wastes and that the issue be placed on the agenda of the General Assembly. The Group of African States subsequently requested the inclusion of the item.[31] The matter was also discussed, on the basis of a working paper by Nigeria,[32] at the third special session of the Assembly on disarmament. The paper proposed that the Assembly reflect the growing awareness of the dangers posed to mankind by the clandestine disposal of nuclear and industrial wastes and condemn those activities. It also proposed that the Assembly call on States to take steps, including domestic legislation, barring transnationals and other enterprises within their jurisdiction from such activities.

In September, the General Conference of IAEA adopted a resolution, calling on IAEA to ensure that it in no way allowed nuclear-waste dumping practices, and to give priority to requests by developing countries for assistance in nuclear-waste management. IAEA was also requested to establish a working group of experts to elaborate an internationally agreed code of practice for international transactions involving nuclear wastes. The United Nations Environment Programme was also working towards the drafting of a convention on the control of the transboundary movement of hazardous wastes.

The Conference on Disarmament, in its ongoing negotiations for a convention on the prohibition of radiological weapons, also addressed the issue of the dumping of radioactive wastes for hostile purposes or in armed conflict, or the deliberate use of any radioactive material to cause destruction, damage or injury through the decay of such material.

GENERAL ASSEMBLY ACTION

On 7 December, on the recommendation of the First Committee, the Assembly adopted **resolution 43/75 Q** by recorded vote.

Prohibition of the dumping of radioactive wastes for hostile purposes

The General Assembly,

Bearing in mind resolution CM/RES.1153(XLVIII) concerning the dumping of nuclear and industrial wastes in Africa, adopted on 25 May 1988 by the Council of Ministers of the Organization of African Unity at its forty-eighth ordinary session, held at Addis Ababa from 19 to 23 May 1988,

Recalling resolution GC(XXXII)/RES/490 on the dumping of nuclear wastes, adopted on 23 September 1988 by the General Conference of the International Atomic Energy Agency at its thirty-second regular session,

Considering its resolution 2602 C (XXIV) of 16 December 1969, in which it requested the Conference of the Committee on Disarmament, *inter alia*, to consider effective methods of control against the use of radiological methods of warfare,

Determined to prevent all nuclear-waste dumping practices that would infringe upon the sovereignty of States,

Desirous of promoting the implementation of paragraph 76 of the Final Document of the Tenth Special Session of the General Assembly,

Aware of the in-depth consideration of the question of the dumping of radioactive wastes for hostile purposes in the Conference on Disarmament during its 1988 session,

1. *Calls upon* all States to ensure that no nuclear-waste dumping practices occur that would infringe upon the sovereignty of States;

2. *Welcomes* the decision of the International Atomic Energy Agency to establish a representative technical working group of experts with the objective of establishing an internationally agreed code of practice for international transactions involving nuclear wastes;

3. *Requests* the Conference on Disarmament to take into account, in the ongoing negotiation for a convention on the prohibition of radiological weapons, the deliberate employment of nuclear wastes to cause destruction, damage or injury by means of radiation produced by the decay of such material;

4. *Requests* the Secretary-General to transmit to the Conference on Disarmament all documents relating to the consideration of this item by the General Assembly at its forty-third session;

5. *Also requests* the Conference on Disarmament to include in its report to the General Assembly at its forty-fourth session the developments on the ongoing negotiations on this subject.

General Assembly resolution 43/75 Q

7 December 1988   Meeting 73   129-1-10 (recorded vote)

Approved by First Committee (A/43/856) by recorded vote (103-3-11), 18 November (meeting 42); 9-nation draft (A/C.1/43/L.62/Rev.2); agenda item 64.
Sponsors: Argentina, Brazil, Indonesia, Nigeria, Pakistan, Romania, Sri Lanka, Syrian Arab Republic, Thailand.
Meeting numbers. GA 43rd session: 1st Committee 3-25, 32, 42; plenary 73.

Recorded vote in Assembly as follows:

In favour: Afghanistan, Albania, Algeria, Antigua and Barbuda, Argentina, Australia, Austria, Bahrain, Bangladesh, Belgium, Belize, Bolivia, Botswana, Brazil, Brunei Darussalam, Bulgaria, Burma, Burundi,* Byelorussian SSR, Canada, Cape Verde, Central African Republic,* Chile, China, Colombia, Comoros, Costa Rica, Cuba, Cyprus, Czechoslovakia, Democratic Yemen, Denmark, Djibouti, Dominican Republic, Ecuador, El Salvador, Ethiopia, Fiji, Finland, France, Gambia, German Democratic Republic, Germany, Federal Republic of, Ghana, Greece, Guatemala, Guinea, Guyana, Haiti, Honduras, Hungary, Iceland, India, Indonesia, Iran, Iraq, Ireland, Israel, Italy, Jamaica, Japan, Jordan, Kenya,† Kuwait, Lao People's Democratic Republic, Lebanon, Lesotho, Liberia, Libyan Arab Jamahiriya, Luxembourg, Madagascar, Malawi, Malaysia, Maldives, Malta, Mauritania, Mauritius, Mexico, Mongolia, Nepal, Netherlands, New Zealand, Nicaragua, Nigeria, Norway, Oman, Pakistan, Panama, Papua New Guinea, Paraguay, Peru, Philippines, Poland, Portugal, Qatar, Romania, Rwanda, Saint Kitts and Nevis, Saint Lucia, Saint Vincent and the Grenadines, Samoa, Sao Tome and Principe, Saudi Arabia, Seychelles, Sierra Leone, Singapore, Solomon Islands, Somalia, Spain, Sri Lanka, Suriname, Swaziland, Sweden, Syrian Arab Republic, Thailand, Trinidad and Tobago, Turkey, Ukrainian SSR, USSR, United Arab Emirates, United Kingdom, United States, Uruguay, Vanuatu, Venezuela, Viet Nam, Yemen, Yugoslavia, Zimbabwe.

Against: Togo.

Abstaining: Angola, Bahamas, Barbados, Burkina Faso, Congo, Mali, Niger, United Republic of Tanzania, Zaire, Zambia.

*Later advised the Secretariat it had intended to abstain.

†Later advised the Secretariat it had intended not to participate in the vote.

On the same date, also on the First Committee's recommendation, the Assembly adopted **resolution 43/75 T** by recorded vote.

Dumping of radioactive wastes

The General Assembly,

Bearing in mind resolution CM/RES.1153(XLVIII), concerning the dumping of nuclear and industrial wastes in Africa, adopted on 25 May 1988 by the Council of Ministers of the Organization of African Unity at its forty-eighth ordinary session, held at Addis Ababa from 19 to 23 May 1988,

Mindful of the serious concerns raised by the Council of Ministers of the Organization of African Unity at its forty-eighth session concerning the grave implications that the dumping of nuclear and industrial wastes could have on the national security of African countries,

Recalling resolution GC(XXXII)/RES/490 on the dumping of nuclear wastes, adopted on 23 September 1988 by the General Conference of the International Atomic Energy Agency at its thirty-second regular session,

Considering its resolution 2602 C (XXIV) of 16 December 1969, in which it requested the Conference of the Committee on Disarmament, *inter alia*, to consider effective methods of control against the use of radiological methods of warfare,

Aware of the potential hazards underlying the dumping of nuclear wastes and also the transboundary radiological consequences, which could have adverse implications on regional and international security and in particular on the security of the developing countries,

Desirous of promoting the implementation of paragraph 76 of the Final Document of the Tenth Special Session of the General Assembly,

Aware also of the consideration by the Conference on Disarmament during its 1988 session of the question of the dumping of radioactive wastes, which cause destruction, damage or injury by means of radiation produced by decay of such material,

1. *Condemns* all nuclear-waste dumping practices that would infringe upon the sovereignty of States;

2. *Expresses profound concern* regarding practices of dumping nuclear and industrial wastes in Africa, which have grave implications on the national security of African countries;

3. *Calls upon* all States to ensure that no radioactive waste is dumped in the territory of other States in infringement of their sovereignty;

4. *Requests* the Conference on Disarmament to take into account, in the ongoing negotiations for a convention on the prohibition of radiological weapons, the dumping of radioactive wastes in the territory of other States;

5. *Requests* the Secretary-General to transmit to the Conference on Disarmament all documents relating to the consideration of the present item by the General Assembly at its forty-third session;

6. *Requests* the Conference on Disarmament to include in its report to the General Assembly at its forty-fourth session the developments on the ongoing negotiations on this subject;

7. *Requests* the Secretary-General to prepare a report, in consultation with relevant international organizations, on the dumping of radioactive wastes in all its aspects in Africa, including all steps taken or envisaged to monitor, control and put a halt to such activities, and to submit his report to the General Assembly at its forty-fourth session;

8. *Decides* to include in the provisional agenda of its forty-fourth session an item entitled "Dumping of radioactive wastes".

General Assembly resolution 43/75 T

7 December 1988   Meeting 73   141-0-13 (recorded vote)

Approved by First Committee (A/43/856) by recorded vote (125-0-13), 18 November (meeting 42); draft by Romania, and Zaire, for African Group (A/C.1/43/L.72/Rev.1); agenda item 64 *(k)*.
Meeting numbers. GA 43rd session: 1st Committee 3-25, 28, 42; plenary 73.

Recorded vote in Assembly as follows:

In favour: Afghanistan, Albania, Algeria, Angola, Antigua and Barbuda, Argentina, Australia, Austria, Bahamas, Bahrain, Bangladesh, Barbados, Belize, Benin, Bhutan, Bolivia, Botswana, Brazil, Brunei Darussalam, Bulgaria, Burkina Faso, Burma, Burundi, Byelorussian SSR, Cameroon, Cape Verde, Central African Republic, Chad, Chile, China, Colombia, Comoros, Congo, Costa Rica, Côte d'Ivoire, Cuba, Cyprus, Czechoslovakia, Democratic Kampuchea, Democratic Yemen, Denmark, Djibouti, Dominican Republic, Ecuador, Egypt, El Salvador, Ethiopia, Fiji, Finland, Gabon, Gambia, German Democratic Republic, Ghana, Greece, Guatemala, Guinea, Guyana, Haiti, Honduras, Hungary, Iceland, India, Indonesia, Iran, Iraq, Ireland, Jamaica, Jordan, Kenya, Kuwait, Lao People's Democratic Republic, Lebanon, Lesotho, Liberia, Libyan Arab Jamahiriya, Madagascar, Malawi, Malaysia, Maldives, Mali, Malta, Mauritania, Mauritius, Mexico, Mongolia, Morocco, Mozambique, Nepal, New Zealand, Nicaragua, Niger, Nigeria, Norway, Oman, Pakistan, Panama, Papua New Guinea, Paraguay, Peru, Philippines, Poland, Qatar, Romania, Rwanda, Saint Kitts and Nevis, Saint Lucia, Saint Vincent and the Grenadines, Samoa, Sao Tome and Principe, Saudi Arabia, Senegal, Seychelles, Sierra Leone, Singapore, Solomon Islands, Somalia, Sri Lanka, Sudan, Suriname, Swaziland, Sweden, Syrian Arab Republic, Thailand, Togo, Trinidad and Tobago, Tunisia, Turkey, Uganda, Ukrainian SSR, USSR, United Arab Emirates, United Republic of Tanzania, Uruguay, Vanuatu, Venezuela, Viet Nam, Yemen, Yugoslavia, Zaire, Zambia, Zimbabwe.
Against: None.
Abstaining: Belgium, Canada, France, Germany, Federal Republic of, Israel, Italy, Japan, Luxembourg, Netherlands, Portugal, Spain, United Kingdom, United States.

Conventional weapons

Conventional disarmament

Some noteworthy developments took place in the conventional disarmament field in 1988. The two major military alliances undertook substan-

tive preparatory work towards new negotiations on conventional armed forces in Europe that would supersede the Vienna Talks on Mutual Reduction of Forces and Armaments and Associated Measures in Central Europe. The "Group of 23" (the 16 North Atlantic Treaty Organization (NATO) parties and the 7 Warsaw Treaty parties) discussed the mandate for the new negotiations, to take place in the context of the Conference on Security and Co-operation in Europe (CSCE), and agreed that the new forum would be known as "Negotiations on Conventional Armed Forces in Europe". The United States and the USSR also indicated their intention to reduce their armed forces significantly and to ensure that those forces would be largely of a defensive character.

Disarmament Commission consideration. In response to two 1987 General Assembly resolutions,[33] the Disarmament Commission continued consideration of the question of conventional disarmament, with a view to facilitating the identification of possible measures in the fields of conventional arms reduction and disarmament. The Commission established Working Group III, which had before it the *Study on Conventional Disarmament*,[34] the views of Member States on the *Study*,[35] and working papers presented by China,[36] Denmark,[37] Hungary,[38] India[39] and the United Kingdom.[40] The Group held seven meetings and a number of informal consultations between 4 and 17 May. It was unable to reach agreement on a set of recommendations and therefore recommended that the work of the Commission on conventional disarmament continue in 1989.

On 19 May, the Commission adopted the Group's report, which was incorporated into its own report to the General Assembly at its third special session on disarmament.[41]

GENERAL ASSEMBLY ACTION

On 7 December, on the recommendation of the First Committee, the General Assembly adopted **resolution 43/75 D** without vote.

Conventional disarmament

The General Assembly,

Recalling its resolution 42/38 E of 30 November 1987,

Welcoming the wide support expressed by Member States for greater attention to be given to conventional disarmament,

Also welcoming the increased awareness of the implications of many aspects of the conventional arms buildup, both in its qualitative and its quantitative aspect,

Taking into account that conventional disarmament is a necessary part of the disarmament process,

Recalling the central role of the United Nations in the field of disarmament,

Having examined the reports of the Disarmament Commission to the General Assembly at its fifteenth special session and at its forty-third session,

1. *Maintains* that the United Nations should continue to encourage and facilitate disarmament efforts in all fields;

2. *Requests* the Disarmament Commission to continue at its 1989 session the substantive consideration of issues related to conventional disarmament and to report to the General Assembly at its forty-fourth session with a view to facilitating possible measures in the fields of conventional arms reduction and disarmament;

3. *Also requests* the Disarmament Commission for this purpose to include in the agenda for its 1989 session an item entitled "Substantive consideration of issues related to conventional disarmament";

4. *Decides* to include in the provisional agenda of its forty-fourth session the item entitled "Conventional disarmament".

General Assembly resolution 43/75 D

7 December 1988   Meeting 73   Adopted without vote

Approved by First Committee (A/43/856) without vote, 15 November (meeting 38); draft by Denmark (A/C.1/43/L.10/Rev.1), orally revised; agenda item 64 *(d)*.
Meeting numbers. GA 43rd session: 1st Committee 3-25, 38; plenary 73.

On the same date, the Assembly, also on the recommendation of the First Committee, adopted **resolution 43/75 F** without vote.

Conventional disarmament

The General Assembly,

Reaffirming the determination to save succeeding generations from the scourge of war as expressed in the Preamble to the Charter of the United Nations,

Recalling the Final Document of the Tenth Special Session of the General Assembly, and particularly its paragraph 81, which provides that together with negotiations on nuclear disarmament measures, the limitation and gradual reduction of armed forces and conventional weapons should be resolutely pursued within the framework of progress towards general and complete disarmament, and which stresses that States with the largest military arsenals have a special responsibility in pursuing the process of conventional armaments reductions,

Also recalling that in the same document it is stated, *inter alia*, that priorities in disarmament negotiations shall be: nuclear weapons; other weapons of mass destruction, including chemical weapons; conventional weapons, including any which may be deemed to be excessively injurious or to have indiscriminate effects; and reduction of armed forces, and that it stresses that nothing should preclude States from conducting negotiations on all priority items concurrently,

Further recalling that in the same document it is stated that effective measures of nuclear disarmament and the prevention of nuclear war have the highest priority, and that real progress in the field of nuclear disarmament could create an atmosphere conducive to progress in conventional disarmament on a world-wide basis,

Aware of the dangers to world peace and security originating from, and the loss in human life and property caused by, wars and conflicts fought with conventional weapons, as well as of their possible escalation into a nuclear war in regions with a high concentration of conventional and nuclear weapons,

Also aware that with the advance in science and technology, conventional weapons tend to become increasingly lethal and destructive and that conventional armaments consume large amounts of resources,

Believing that resources released through disarmament, including conventional disarmament, can be used for the social and economic development of people of all countries, particularly the developing countries,

Noting that the ongoing conventional disarmament negotiations in Europe have gained increasing importance,

Bearing in mind its resolution 36/97 A of 9 December 1981 and the *Study on Conventional Disarmament* conducted in accordance with that resolution, as well as its resolutions 41/59 C and 41/59 G of 3 December 1986, and 42/38 E and 42/38 G of 30 November 1987, and the consideration by the Disarmament Commission at its 1988 session of the question of conventional disarmament,

Bearing in mind also the efforts made to promote conventional disarmament and the related proposals and suggestions, as well as the initiatives taken by various countries in this regard,

1. *Reaffirms* the importance of the efforts aimed at resolutely pursuing the limitation and gradual reduction of armed forces and conventional weapons within the framework of progress towards general and complete disarmament;

2. *Believes* that the military forces of all countries should not be used other than for the purpose of self-defence;

3. *Urges* the countries with the largest military arsenals, which bear a special responsibility in pursuing the process of conventional armaments reductions, and the member States of the two major military alliances to conduct negotiations on conventional disarmament in earnest through appropriate forums, with a view to reaching early agreement on the limitation and gradual and balanced reduction of armed forces and conventional weapons under effective international control in their respective regions, particularly in Europe, which has the largest concentration of arms and forces in the world;

4. *Encourages* all States, while taking into account the need to protect security and maintain necessary defensive capabilities, to intensify their efforts and take, either on their own or in a regional context, appropriate steps to promote progress in conventional disarmament and enhance peace and security;

5. *Requests* the Disarmament Commission to consider further, at its 1989 substantive session, issues related to conventional disarmament;

6. *Decides* to include in the provisional agenda of its forty-fourth session the item entitled "Conventional disarmament".

General Assembly resolution 43/75 F

7 December 1988   Meeting 73   Adopted without vote

Approved by First Committee (A/43/856) without vote, 15 November (meeting 38); draft by China (A/C.1/43/L.15); agenda item 64 *(d)*.
Meeting numbers. GA 43rd session: 1st Committee 3-25, 30, 38; plenary 73.

Regional approach to conventional disarmament

In 1988, the Assembly continued consideration of the question of conventional disarmament on a regional scale, including confidence- and security-building measures and conventional disarmament in Europe.

The Conference of Ministers for Foreign Affairs of Non-Aligned Countries (Nicosia, Cyprus, 7-10 September)[42] recommended that States should consider and adopt measures at the regional level to strengthen peace and security through the limitation and reduction of armed forces and conventional weapons. It also noted the negotiations on conventional disarmament in Europe between the Warsaw Pact and NATO in the context of CSCE.

GENERAL ASSEMBLY ACTION

On 7 December, the General Assembly, on the recommendation of the First Committee, adopted **resolution 43/75 S** by recorded vote.

Conventional disarmament on a regional scale

The General Assembly,

Recalling its resolutions 40/94 A of 12 December 1985, 41/59 M of 3 December 1986 and 42/38 N of 30 November 1987,

Taking note of the final documents of the Conference of Ministers for Foreign Affairs of Non-Aligned Countries held at Nicosia from 7 to 10 September 1988,

Reiterating the primary responsibility of the militarily significant States, especially nuclear-weapon States, for halting and reversing the arms race, and the priority assigned to nuclear disarmament in the context of the advances towards general and complete disarmament,

Drawing attention to the fact that together with negotiations on nuclear disarmament measures, conventional disarmament measures should be resolutely pursued, in the context of which conventional disarmament on a regional scale acquires urgency and renewed importance,

Affirming that regional or subregional arms limitation and disarmament processes complement and enhance global disarmament efforts,

Expressing its firm support for all regional and subregional peace and disarmament endeavours that take into account the characteristics of each region, as well as for unilateral measures to strengthen mutual confidence and assure the security of all States involved, making possible regional agreements on arms limitation in the future,

Emphasizing that the adoption of such disarmament measures should take place in an equitable and balanced manner in order to ensure the right of each State to security and that no individual State or group of States may obtain advantages over others at any stage of this process,

Noting with satisfaction the positive trend towards the peaceful settlement of various regional and subregional conflicts and the important role played in that regard by the United Nations,

1. *Expresses its satisfaction* at the initiatives towards arms limitation and disarmament adopted jointly or unilaterally by some countries at the regional and subregional levels, as well as at the systematic implementation of confidence-building measures, limitation of the acquisition of conventional weapons and the reduction of military spending, with a view to allocating the resources thus released to the socio-economic development of their peoples;

2. *Expresses its keen satisfaction* at efforts to bring about the peaceful solution of conflict situations and regional and subregional crises, which would facilitate setting in motion specific measures for conventional disarmament on a regional scale through negotiated agreements under strict and effective international control;

3. *Again expresses firm support* for the United Nations system, and for the Secretary-General in particular, in the efforts to find solutions to conflict situations, thereby reaffirming the primary role of the United Nations in promoting peace and disarmament, and for the strict observance of the principles and norms embodied in the Charter of the United Nations;

4. *Encourages* the Secretary-General to persevere in his current peace efforts in various areas of tension in the world;

5. *Requests* the United Nations to provide assistance to States and regional institutions that might request it with a view to establishing disarmament measures on a regional scale;

6. *Appeals* to all States to facilitate the progress of regional disarmament, refraining from any action, including the threat or use of force, that might impede the achievement of this objective;

7. *Decides* to include in the provisional agenda of its forty-fourth session the item entitled ''Conventional disarmament on a regional scale''.

General Assembly resolution 43/75 S

7 December 1988   Meeting 73   125-0-23 (recorded vote)

Approved by First Committee (A/43/856) by recorded vote (110-0-18), 17 November (meeting 40); 18-nation draft (A/C.1/43/L.70/Rev.1), orally revised; agenda item 64.

Sponsors: Bangladesh, Bolivia, Cameroon, Colombia, Costa Rica, Dominican Republic, Ecuador, El Salvador, Guatemala, Honduras, Pakistan, Panama, Paraguay, Peru, Philippines, Romania, Sri Lanka, Uruguay.

Meeting numbers. GA 43rd session: 1st Committee 3-25, 30, 40; plenary 73.

Recorded vote in Assembly as follows:

In favour: Algeria, Antigua and Barbuda, Argentina, Australia, Austria, Bahamas, Bangladesh, Barbados, Belgium, Belize, Benin, Bhutan, Bolivia, Botswana, Brazil, Brunei Darussalam, Bulgaria, Burkina Faso, Burma, Burundi, Byelorussian SSR, Cameroon, Canada, Cape Verde, Central African Republic, Chad, Chile, China, Colombia, Comoros, Congo, Costa Rica, Côte d'Ivoire, Czechoslovakia, Democratic Kampuchea, Denmark, Dominican Republic, Ecuador, Egypt, El Salvador, Fiji, Finland, France, Gabon, Gambia, German Democratic Republic, Germany, Federal Republic of, Ghana, Greece, Guatemala, Guinea, Guyana, Haiti, Honduras, Hungary, Iceland, Indonesia, Iran, Ireland, Italy, Jamaica, Japan, Kenya, Lao People's Democratic Republic, Lebanon, Lesotho, Liberia, Luxembourg, Madagascar, Malawi, Malaysia, Maldives, Mali, Malta, Mauritania, Mauritius, Mexico, Mongolia, Morocco, Nepal, Netherlands, New Zealand, Nicaragua, Niger, Nigeria, Norway, Pakistan, Panama, Papua New Guinea, Paraguay, Peru, Philippines, Poland, Portugal, Qatar,* Romania, Rwanda, Saint Lucia, Saint Vincent and the Grenadines, Samoa, Saudi Arabia, Senegal, Seychelles, Sierra Leone, Singapore, Solomon Islands, Spain, Sri Lanka, Suriname, Swaziland, Sweden, Thailand, Togo, Trinidad and Tobago, Tunisia, Turkey, Uganda, Ukrainian SSR, USSR, United Kingdom, Uruguay, Vanuatu, Venezuela, Yugoslavia, Zaire.

Against: None.

Abstaining: Afghanistan, Angola, Bahrain, Cuba, Cyprus, Democratic Yemen, Djibouti, Ethiopia, India, Iraq, Israel, Jordan, Libyan Arab Jamahiriya, Mozambique, Somalia, Sudan, Syrian Arab Republic, United Arab Emirates, United Republic of Tanzania, United States, Viet Nam, Zambia, Zimbabwe.

*Later advised the Secretariat it had intended to abstain.

Europe

The General Assembly in 1986[43] had welcomed the measures adopted at the Stockholm Conference on Confidence- and Security-building Measures and Disarmament in Europe, covering the whole of Europe and designed to reduce the dangers of armed conflict and of misunderstanding or miscalculation of military activities.

Significant progress towards that end had since been achieved and agreement reached on a new regulating forum in the CSCE context. In 1988, it was agreed that the new forum would be known as ''Negotiations on Conventional Armed Forces in Europe''.

On 7 December, on the First Committee's recommendation, the Assembly adopted **resolution 43/75 P** without vote.

Confidence- and security-building measures and conventional disarmament in Europe

The General Assembly,

Determined to achieve progress in disarmament,

Reaffirming the need for continued efforts to build confidence, to lessen the risk of military confrontation and to enhance mutual security,

Reaffirming also the great importance of increasing security and stability in Europe through the establishment of a stable, secure and verifiable balance of conventional armed forces at lower levels, as well as through increased openness and predictability of military activities,

Considering that further negotiations in the field of confidence- and security-building measures, as well as a new negotiation on conventional armaments and forces, both within the framework of the process of the Conference on Security and Co-operation in Europe, should promote the process of strengthening confidence, improving security and developing co-operation in Europe, thereby contributing to international peace and security,

1. *Welcomes* the progress achieved so far in the deliberations at Vienna on issues concerning the above-mentioned negotiations;

2. *Urges* Member States that will participate in the above-mentioned negotiations to contribute actively to the attainment of their objectives as agreed;

3. *Invites* all States to consider the possibility of taking appropriate measures with a view to reducing the risk of confrontation and strengthening security, taking due account of their specific regional conditions.

General Assembly resolution 43/75 P

7 December 1988   Meeting 73   Adopted without vote

Approved by First Committee (A/43/856) without vote, 18 November (meeting 43); 10-nation draft (A/C.1/43/L.61/Rev.2); agenda item 64.

Sponsors: Austria, Belgium, Canada, France, Germany, Federal Republic of, Greece, Hungary, Italy, Poland, Spain.

Meeting numbers. GA 43rd session: 1st Committee 3-25, 43; plenary 73.

Convention on excessively injurious conventional weapons and its Protocols

As at 31 December 1988,[44] the number of States parties to the 1980 Convention on Prohibitions or Restrictions on the Use of Certain Conventional Weapons Which May Be Deemed to Be Excessively Injurious or to Have Indiscriminate Effects and its three Protocols (dealing with non-detectable fragments; mines, booby traps and other devices; and incendiary weapons)[45] was 30, following accession by Cyprus and ratification

by France during the year. The Convention and Protocols had entered into force in 1983.[46]

The Secretary-General submitted, in response to a 1987 Assembly request,[47] a report[48] containing information on action taken with respect to the Convention and Protocols between 1 September 1987 and 31 August 1988.

On 7 December 1988, the General Assembly, on the recommendation of the First Committee, adopted **resolution 43/67** without vote.

Convention on Prohibitions or Restrictions on the Use of Certain Conventional Weapons Which May Be Deemed to Be Excessively Injurious or to Have Indiscriminate Effects

The General Assembly,

Recalling its resolutions 32/152 of 19 December 1977, 35/153 of 12 December 1980, 36/93 of 9 December 1981, 37/79 of 9 December 1982, 38/66 of 15 December 1983, 39/56 of 12 December 1984, 40/84 of 12 December 1985, 41/50 of 3 December 1986 and 42/30 of 30 November 1987,

Recalling with satisfaction the adoption, on 10 October 1980, of the Convention on Prohibitions or Restrictions on the Use of Certain Conventional Weapons Which May Be Deemed to Be Excessively Injurious or to Have Indiscriminate Effects, together with the Protocol on Non-Detectable Fragments (Protocol I), the Protocol on Prohibitions or Restrictions on the Use of Mines, Booby Traps and Other Devices (Protocol II) and the Protocol on Prohibitions or Restrictions on the Use of Incendiary Weapons (Protocol III),

Reaffirming its conviction that general agreement on the prohibition or restriction of use of specific conventional weapons would significantly reduce the suffering of civilian populations and of combatants,

Taking note with satisfaction of the report of the Secretary-General,

1. *Notes with satisfaction* that an increasing number of States have either signed, ratified, accepted or acceded to the Convention on Prohibitions or Restrictions on the Use of Certain Conventional Weapons Which May Be Deemed to Be Excessively Injurious or to Have Indiscriminate Effects, which was opened for signature in New York on 10 April 1981;

2. *Also notes with satisfaction* that, consequent upon the fulfilment of the conditions set out in article 5 of the Convention, the Convention and the three Protocols annexed thereto entered into force on 2 December 1983;

3. *Urges* all States that have not yet done so to exert their best endeavours to become parties to the Convention and the Protocols annexed thereto as early as possible, so as ultimately to obtain universality of adherence;

4. *Notes* that, under article 8 of the Convention, conferences may be convened to consider amendments to the Convention or any of the annexed Protocols, to consider additional protocols relating to other categories of conventional weapons not covered by the existing annexed Protocols, or to review the scope and operation of the Convention and the Protocols annexed thereto and to consider any proposal for amendments to the Convention or to the existing Protocols and any pro-

posals for additional protocols relating to other categories of conventional weapons not covered by the existing Protocols;

5. *Requests* the Secretary-General as depositary of the Convention and its three annexed Protocols to inform the General Assembly from time to time of the state of adherence to the Convention and its Protocols;

6. *Decides* to include in the provisional agenda of its forty-fourth session the item entitled "Convention on Prohibitions or Restrictions on the Use of Certain Conventional Weapons Which May Be Deemed to Be Excessively Injurious or to Have Indiscriminate Effects".

General Assembly resolution 43/67

7 December 1988   Meeting 73   Adopted without vote

Approved by First Committee (A/43/835) without vote, 10 November (meeting 33); 22-nation draft (A/C.1/43/L.44); agenda item 56.
Sponsors: Australia, Austria, Belgium, Byelorussian SSR, Cuba, Denmark, Ecuador, Finland, France, German Democratic Republic, Greece, Ireland, Italy, Netherlands, New Zealand, Nigeria, Norway, Samoa, Sweden, USSR, Viet Nam, Yugoslavia.
Meeting numbers. GA 43rd session: 1st Committee 3-25, 30, 33; plenary 73.

Prevention of an arms race in outer space

Consideration by the Conference on Disarmament. The Conference on Disarmament considered the prevention of an arms race in outer space from 29 February to 4 March and from 1 to 5 August.[1]

The *Ad Hoc* Committee, re-established by the Conference, held 17 meetings between 8 March and 7 September to examine and identify issues pertaining to the item, existing agreements and proposals and future initiatives.

New documents submitted under the item included the Stockholm Declaration of the Six-Nation Initiative, adopted on 21 January 1988 by the heads of State or Government of Argentina, Greece, India, Mexico, Sweden and the United Republic of Tanzania, on the complete banning of anti-satellite weapons,[49] a USSR document on establishing an international system of verification of the non-deployment of weapons of any kind in outer space,[50] and a Venezuela proposal[51] to amend article IV of the Treaty on Principles Governing the Activities of States in the Exploration and Use of Outer Space, including the Moon and Other Celestial Bodies (outer space Treaty).[52] The Committee also received a number of working papers.

The *Ad Hoc* Committee, in its reports to the Conference,[53] concluded that its work had advanced and developed further the examination and identification of issues relevant to the prevention of an arms race in outer space. It considered that the legal régime applicable to outer space did not by itself guarantee the prevention of an arms race and recognized the need to enhance the effectiveness of the régime and for strict compliance with existing bilateral and multilateral agreements. The Committee acknowledged the importance of paragraph 80 of the Final Document of the first special session devoted to disarmament,[54] which called for further measures and international negotiations to be held in accordance with the spirit of the outer space Treaty. It also gave preliminary consideration to a number of proposals and initiatives to prevent an arms race in outer space and to ensure exploration for peaceful purposes.

The Committee recommended that it be re-established at the beginning of the Conference's 1989 session with an adequate mandate, taking into account all relevant factors, including the work of the Committee since 1985.

Report of the Secretary-General. Pursuant to a 1987 Assembly request,[55] the Secretary-General, in an August 1988 report and later addenda,[56] informed the Assembly that he had received the views on all aspects of the question of the prevention of an arms race in outer space from 11 Member States.

GENERAL ASSEMBLY ACTION

On 7 December, on the recommendation of the First Committee, the General Assembly adopted **resolution 43/70** by recorded vote.

Prevention of an arms race in outer space
The General Assembly,
Inspired by the great prospects opening up before mankind as a result of man's entry into outer space,
Recognizing the common interest of all mankind in the exploration and use of outer space for peaceful purposes,
Reaffirming that the exploration and use of outer space, including the Moon and other celestial bodies, shall be carried out for the benefit and in the interest of all countries, irrespective of their degree of economic or scientific development, and shall be the province of all mankind,
Reaffirming also the will of all States that the exploration and use of outer space, including the Moon and other celestial bodies, shall be for peaceful purposes,
Recalling the obligation of all States, in accordance with the Charter of the United Nations, to refrain from the threat or use of force, including in their space activities,
Recalling that the States parties to the Treaty on Principles Governing the Activities of States in the Exploration and Use of Outer Space, including the Moon and Other Celestial Bodies, have undertaken, in article III, to carry on activities in the exploration and use of outer space, including the Moon and other celestial bodies, in accordance with international law and the Charter of the United Nations, in the interest of maintaining international peace and security and promoting international co-operation and understanding,
Reaffirming, in particular, article IV of the above-mentioned Treaty, which stipulates that States parties to the Treaty undertake not to place in orbit around the Earth any objects carrying nuclear weapons or any other kinds of weapons of mass destruction, install such weapons on celestial bodies or station such weapons in outer space in any other manner,
Reaffirming also paragraph 80 of the Final Document of the Tenth Special Session of the General Assembly,

in which it is stated that in order to prevent an arms race in outer space further measures should be taken and appropriate international negotiations held in accordance with the spirit of the Treaty,

Bearing in mind its resolutions 36/97 C and 36/99 of 9 December 1981, as well as resolutions 37/83 of 9 December 1982, 37/99 D of 13 December 1982, 38/70 of 15 December 1983, 39/59 of 12 December 1984, 40/87 of 12 December 1985, 41/53 of 3 December 1986 and 42/33 of 30 November 1987 and the relevant paragraphs of the Political Declaration adopted by the Eighth Conference of Heads of State or Government of Non-Aligned Countries, held at Harare from 1 to 6 September 1986,

Recognizing the importance and urgency of preventing an arms race in outer space and the readiness of all States to contribute to that common objective,

Gravely concerned at the danger posed to all mankind by an arms race in outer space and, in particular, by the impending threat of the exacerbation of the current state of insecurity by developments that could further undermine international peace and security and retard the pursuit of general and complete disarmament,

Encouraged by the widespread interest expressed by Member States in the course of negotiations on and following the adoption of the above-mentioned Treaty in ensuring that the exploration and use of outer space should be for peaceful purposes, and taking note of proposals submitted to the General Assembly at its tenth special session and at its regular sessions and to the Conference on Disarmament,

Noting the grave concern expressed by the Second United Nations Conference on the Exploration and Peaceful Uses of Outer Space at the extension of an arms race into outer space and the recommendations made to the competent organs of the United Nations, in particular the General Assembly, and also to the Committee on Disarmament,

Noting also that in 1988 the *Ad Hoc* Committee on the Prevention of an Arms Race in Outer Space, taking into account its previous efforts since its establishment, undertook the examination and identification of various issues, existing agreements and existing proposals, as well as future initiatives relevant to the prevention of an arms race in outer space, and that this contributed to a better understanding of a number of problems and to a clearer perception of the various positions,

Convinced that additional measures should be examined in the search for effective and verifiable bilateral and multilateral agreements in order to prevent an arms race in outer space,

Emphasizing the paramount importance of strict compliance with existing arms limitation and disarmament agreements relevant to outer space, and with the existing legal régime concerning the use of outer space,

Emphasizing also the necessity of maintaining the effectiveness of relevant existing treaties, and in this context reaffirming the vital importance of strict compliance with the Treaty on the Limitation of Anti-Ballistic Missile Systems,

Recognizing that bilateral negotiations between the Union of Soviet Socialist Republics and the United States of America could facilitate the multilateral negotiations for the prevention of an arms race in outer space in accordance with paragraph 27 of the Final Document of the Tenth Special Session,

Noting the importance in this context of bilateral negotiations between the Union of Soviet Socialist Republics and the United States of America that have continued since 1985, including at their summit meetings in Washington and Moscow on a complex of questions concerning space and nuclear arms,

Hopeful that concrete results would emerge from these negotiations as soon as possible,

Emphasizing the mutually complementary nature of bilateral and multilateral efforts in the field of preventing an arms race in outer space,

Taking note of that part of the report of the Conference on Disarmament relating to this question,

Welcoming the re-establishment of an *Ad Hoc* Committee on the Prevention of an Arms Race in Outer Space during the 1988 session of the Conference on Disarmament, in the exercise of the negotiating responsibilities of this sole multilateral negotiating body on disarmament, to continue to examine and to identify, through substantive and general consideration, issues relevant to the prevention of an arms race in outer space,

1. *Reaffirms* that general and complete disarmament under effective international control warrants that outer space shall be used exclusively for peaceful purposes and that it shall not become an arena for an arms race;

2. *Recognizes*, as stated in the report of the *Ad Hoc* Committee of the Conference on Disarmament, that the legal régime applicable to outer space by itself does not guarantee the prevention of an arms race in outer space, that this legal régime plays a significant role in the prevention of an arms race in that environment, the need to consolidate and reinforce that régime and enhance its effectiveness, and the importance of strict compliance with existing agreements, both bilateral and multilateral;

3. *Emphasizes* that further measures with appropriate and effective provisions for verification to prevent an arms race in outer space should be adopted by the international community;

4. *Calls upon* all States, in particular those with major space capabilities, to contribute actively to the objective of the peaceful use of outer space and to take immediate measures to prevent an arms race in outer space in the interest of maintaining international peace and security and promoting international co-operation and understanding;

5. *Reiterates* that the Conference on Disarmament, as the single multilateral disarmament negotiating forum, has the primary role in the negotiation of a multilateral agreement or agreements, as appropriate, on the prevention of an arms race in outer space in all its aspects;

6. *Requests* the Conference on Disarmament to consider as a matter of priority the question of preventing an arms race in outer space;

7. *Also requests* the Conference on Disarmament to intensify its consideration of the question of the prevention of an arms race in outer space in all its aspects, taking into account all relevant proposals and initiatives, including those presented in the *Ad Hoc* Committee at the 1988 session of the Conference and at the forty-third session of the General Assembly;

8. *Further requests* the Conference on Disarmament to re-establish an *ad hoc* committee with an adequate mandate at the beginning of its 1989 session, with a view to undertaking negotiations for the conclusion of an agreement or agreements, as appropriate, to prevent an arms race in outer space in all its aspects;

9. *Urges* the Union of Soviet Socialist Republics and the United States of America to pursue intensively their bilateral negotiations in a constructive spirit aimed at reaching early agreement for preventing an arms race in outer space, and to advise the Conference on Disarmament periodically of the progress of their bilateral sessions so as to facilitate its work;

10. *Calls upon* all States, especially those with major space capabilities, to refrain, in their activities relating to outer space, from actions contrary to the observance of the relevant existing treaties or to the objective of preventing an arms race in outer space;

11. *Takes note* of the report of the Secretary-General on the question of the prevention of an arms race in outer space, submitted in accordance with resolution 42/33 of 30 November 1987;

12. *Requests* the Conference on Disarmament to report on its consideration of this subject to the General Assembly at its forty-fourth session;

13. *Requests* the Secretary-General to transmit to the Conference on Disarmament all documents relating to the consideration of this subject by the General Assembly at its forty-third session;

14. *Decides* to include in the provisional agenda of its forty-fourth session the item entitled ''Prevention of an arms race in outer space''.

General Assembly resolution 43/70

7 December 1988   Meeting 73   154-1 (recorded vote)

Approved by First Committee (A/43/838) by recorded vote (137-1), 18 November (meeting 42); 29-nation draft (A/C.1/43/L.12/Rev.1); agenda item 59.
Sponsors: Argentina, Bangladesh, Brazil, Cameroon, Djibouti, Egypt, Ethiopia, Ghana, India, Indonesia, Iran, Ireland, Jordan, Malaysia, Mexico, Morocco, Nigeria, Pakistan, Peru, Romania, Sri Lanka, Sudan, Suriname, Sweden, Uruguay, Venezuela, Viet Nam, Yugoslavia, Zimbabwe.
Meeting numbers. GA 43rd session: 1st Committee 3-25, 30, 42; plenary 73.

Recorded vote in Assembly as follows:

In favour: Afghanistan, Albania, Algeria, Angola, Antigua and Barbuda, Argentina, Australia, Austria, Bahamas, Bahrain, Bangladesh, Barbados, Belgium, Belize, Benin, Bhutan, Bolivia, Botswana, Brazil, Brunei Darussalam, Bulgaria, Burkina Faso, Burma, Burundi, Byelorussian SSR, Cameroon, Canada, Cape Verde, Central African Republic, Chad, Chile, China, Colombia, Comoros, Congo, Costa Rica, Côte d'Ivoire, Cuba, Cyprus, Czechoslovakia, Democratic Kampuchea, Democratic Yemen, Denmark, Djibouti, Dominican Republic, Ecuador, Egypt, El Salvador, Ethiopia, Fiji, Finland, France, Gabon, Gambia, German Democratic Republic, Germany, Federal Republic of, Ghana, Greece, Grenada, Guatemala, Guinea, Guyana, Haiti, Honduras, Hungary, Iceland, India, Indonesia, Iran, Iraq, Ireland, Israel, Italy, Jamaica, Japan, Jordan, Kenya, Kuwait, Lao People's Democratic Republic, Lebanon, Lesotho, Liberia, Libyan Arab Jamahiriya, Luxembourg, Madagascar, Malawi, Malaysia, Maldives, Mali, Malta, Mauritania, Mauritius, Mexico, Mongolia, Morocco, Mozambique, Nepal, Netherlands, New Zealand, Nicaragua, Niger, Nigeria, Norway, Oman, Pakistan, Panama, Papua New Guinea, Paraguay, Peru, Philippines, Poland, Portugal, Qatar, Romania, Rwanda, Saint Kitts and Nevis, Saint Lucia, Saint Vincent and the Grenadines, Samoa, Sao Tome and Principe, Saudi Arabia, Senegal, Seychelles, Sierra Leone, Singapore, Solomon Islands, Somalia, Spain, Sri Lanka, Sudan, Suriname, Swaziland, Sweden, Syrian Arab Republic, Thailand, Togo, Trinidad and Tobago, Tunisia, Turkey, Uganda, Ukrainian SSR, USSR, United Arab Emirates, United Kingdom, United Republic of Tanzania, Uruguay, Vanuatu, Venezuela, Viet Nam, Yemen, Yugoslavia, Zaire, Zambia, Zimbabwe.
Against: United States.

Before approving the draft as a whole, the First Committee approved, by recorded votes, the eleventh and eighteenth preambular paragraphs by 121 to 1, with 13 abstentions, and by 121 to 1, with 11 abstentions, respectively, and paragraph 8 by 123 to 1, with 13 abstentions. The Assembly adopted the same paragraphs by recorded votes of 138 to 1, with 13 abstentions; 139 to 1, with 11

abstentions; and 139 to 1, with 13 abstentions, respectively.

REFERENCES

[1]A/43/27. [2]CD/795. [3]CD/831 & Corr.1. [4]CD/828. [5]CD/808. [6]CD/822. [7]CD/789. [8]CD/830. [9]CD/854 & CD/872. [10]CD/826. [11]CD/827. [12]CD/802. [13]CD/791, CD/792, CD/869. [14]CD/790. [15]CD/856. [16]CD/812. [17]CD/823. [18]CD/843 & CD/873. [19]CD/857 & CD/861. [20]A/S-15/2. [21]CD/874. [22]YUN 1987, p. 70, GA res. 42/37 C, 30 Nov. 1987. [23]A/43/690 & Add.1. [24]YUN 1987, p. 71. [25]YUN 1971, p. 19, GA res. 2826(XXVI), annex, 16 Dec. 1971. [26]CD/820. [27]CD/864. [28]A/43/622. [29]YUN 1987, p. 74, GA res. 42/38 F, 30 Nov. 1987. [30]A/43/398. [31]A/43/142. [32]A/S-15/AC.1/17. [33]YUN 1987, pp. 75 & 76, GA res. 42/38 E & G, 30 Nov. 1987. [34]YUN 1984, p. 65. [35]A/CN.10/86 & Add.1. [36]A/CN.10/95. [37]A/CN.10/88. [38]A/CN.10/98. [39]A/CN.10/100. [40]A/CN.10/103. [41]A/S-15/3. [42]A/43/667-S/20212. [43]YUN 1986, p. 71, GA res. 41/59 E, 3 Dec. 1986. [44]*Multilateral Treaties Deposited with the Secretary-General: Status as at 31 December 1988* (ST/LEG/SER.E/7), Sales No. E.89.V.3. [45]YUN 1980, p. 76. [46]YUN 1983, p. 66. [47]YUN 1987, p. 77, GA res. 42/30, 30 Nov. 1987. [48]A/43/589. [49]CD/807. [50]CD/817. [51]CD/851. [52]YUN 1966, p. 41, GA res. 2222(XXI), annex, 19 Dec. 1966. [53]CD/834 & CD/870. [54]YUN 1978, p. 39, GA res. S-10/2, 30 June 1978. [55]YUN 1987, p. 79, GA res. 42/33, 30 Nov. 1987. [56]A/43/506 & Corr.1 & Add.1,2.

Other disarmament issues

The question of military budgets continued to occupy the attention of various disarmament bodies, notably the Disarmament Commission, where work continued on a text of principles to govern further actions of States in that regard. The Secretary-General presented an updated report on the economic and social consequences of the arms race.

Reduction of military budgets

Although agreement by the Disarmament Commission on the last paragraph of the proposed principles that should govern the action of States in freezing and reducing military budgets was not reached in 1988, some progress was achieved with respect to the question of transparency and comparability of military data.

Disarmament Commission consideration. The Disarmament Commission, pursuant to a 1987 General Assembly request,[1] continued consideration of the text of paragraph 7, the last outstanding paragraph, of the set of principles to govern further actions of States in freezing and reducing military expenditures, as elaborated in 1986[2] and 1987.[3] That paragraph dealt with the principles of transparency, comparability and availability of data, through the use of the standardized international reporting instrument.

A consultation group, established by the Commission on 2 May, held seven meetings and a number of informal consultations between 4 and 18 May. It considered a formulation proposed by the Chairman, as well as other proposals for paragraph 7 which had been submitted in 1986 and 1987. While a general agreement was reached on most of the elements of paragraph 7, the group was unable to achieve a consensus formulation. It recommended to the Commission a draft text of the principles, which was subsequently submitted to the Assembly's third special session on disarmament.[4]

Report of the Secretary-General. In September, with later addenda,[5] the Secretary-General, pursuant to a 1985 Assembly request,[6] submitted a report on military expenditures, as disclosed by 31 States. As in previous years, a majority of the reporting States used the standard reporting instrument, consisting of a matrix designed to show how much each force group (such as land, naval and air forces) spent in each resource category (such as personnel, procurement and operations).

GENERAL ASSEMBLY ACTION

On 7 December, on the recommendation of the First Committee, the General Assembly adopted **resolution 43/73** without vote.

Reduction of military budgets

The General Assembly,

Deeply concerned about the ever-spiralling arms race and growing military expenditures, which constitute a heavy burden for the economies of all nations and have extremely harmful effects on world peace and security,

Reaffirming once again the provisions of paragraph 89 of the Final Document of the Tenth Special Session of the General Assembly, the first special session devoted to disarmament, according to which the gradual reduction of military budgets on a mutually agreed basis, for example, in absolute figures or in terms of percentage, particularly by nuclear-weapon States and other militarily significant States, would contribute to curbing the arms race and would increase the possibilities for the reallocation of resources now being used for military purposes to economic and social development, particularly for the benefit of the developing countries,

Convinced that the freezing and reduction of military budgets would have favourable consequences on the world economic and financial situation and might facilitate efforts made to increase international assistance for the developing countries,

Recalling that at its twelfth special session, the second special session devoted to disarmament, all Member States unanimously and categorically reaffirmed the validity of the Final Document of the Tenth Special Session, as well as their solemn commitment to it,

Recalling also that in the Declaration of the 1980s as the Second Disarmament Decade, it is provided that during this period renewed efforts should be made to reach agreement on the reduction of military expenditures and the reallocation of resources thus saved to economic and social development, especially for the benefit of developing countries,

Recalling further the provisions of its relevant resolutions, in which it considered that a new impetus should be given to the endeavours to achieve agreements to freeze, reduce or otherwise restrain, in a balanced manner, military expenditures, including adequate measures of verification satisfactory to all parties concerned,

Aware of the various proposals submitted by Member States and of the activities carried out so far within the framework of the United Nations in the field of the reduction of military budgets,

Considering that the identification and elaboration of the principles that should govern further actions of States in freezing and reducing military budgets and the other current activities within the framework of the United Nations related to the question of the reduction of military budgets should be regarded as having the fundamental objective of reaching international agreements on the reduction of military expenditures,

Noting that the Disarmament Commission, at its 1986 substantive session, agreed upon the above-mentioned principles with the exception of one outstanding paragraph on which it was generally felt that further consideration was needed,

1. *Declares again its conviction* that it is possible to achieve international agreements on the reduction of military budgets without prejudice to the right of all States to undiminished security, self-defence and sovereignty;

2. *Appeals* to all States, in particular to the most heavily armed States, pending the conclusion of agreements on the reduction of military expenditures, to exercise self-restraint in their military expenditures with a view to reallocating the funds thus saved to economic and social development, particularly for the benefit of developing countries;

3. *Reaffirms* that the human and material resources released through the reduction of military expenditures could be reallocated for economic and social development, particularly for the benefit of the developing countries;

4. *Requests* the Disarmament Commission to continue consideration of the item entitled "Reduction of military budgets" and, in this context, to conclude, at its 1989 substantive session, its work on the last outstanding paragraph of the principles that should govern further actions of States in the field of freezing and reduction of military budgets, and to submit its report and recommendations to the General Assembly not later than at its forty-fourth session;

5. *Draws anew the attention* of Member States to the fact that the identification and elaboration of the principles that should govern further actions of States in freezing and reducing military budgets could contribute to harmonizing the views of States and creating confidence among them conducive to achieving international agreements on the reduction of military budgets;

6. *Urges* all Member States, in particular the most heavily armed States, to reinforce their readiness to cooperate in a constructive manner with a view to reaching agreements to freeze, reduce or otherwise restrain military expenditures;

7. *Decides* to include in the provisional agenda of its forty-fourth session the item entitled "Reduction of military budgets".

General Assembly resolution 43/73

7 December 1988　　　Meeting 73　　　Adopted without vote

Approved by First Committee (A/43/841) without vote, 14 November (meeting 36); 9-nation draft (A/C.1/43/L.58/Rev.1); agenda item 62.

Sponsors: Bangladesh, Indonesia, Ireland, Nigeria, Peru, Romania, Senegal, Sweden, USSR.
Meeting numbers. GA 43rd session: 1st Committee 3-25, 29, 36; plenary 73.

Economic and social consequences of the arms race

In May 1988, the Secretary-General, pursuant to 1985[7] and 1986[8] General Assembly requests, submitted a report[9] which updated, with the assistance of a group of consultant experts, a 1982 report on the economic and social consequences of the arms race and of military expenditures.[10]

The 1988 report sought to highlight the harmful effects of the arms race on world peace and security, the economy and the social welfare of States. Specifically, it dealt with the economic and technological implications of the various categories of armaments and forces; the natural, economic and human resources devoted to the arms race and the implications of policy decisions; the economic development and social welfare implications of military outlays; and the international consequences of the arms race. It also made recommendations to reduce and reverse the negative consequences of the arms race, while avoiding consequent counter-productive effects.

The group of experts concluded that military expenditures had extensive social and economic consequences, particularly among the leading high-technology military spenders, and contributed to economic stagnation and structural dislocation. In some developing countries, economic development and military spending were competing priorities.

In the experts' view, there was a close correlation between disarmament and the reallocation of national resources for development, while, at the international level, the progress made in arms limitation and conflict settlement should allow the attention of the international community to be shifted to problems of underdevelopment, insecurity and ecological deterioration. Furthermore, industrialized countries should assume a greater responsibility for fostering development co-operation in the context of official development assistance. The experts emphasized the promotion of international action, for both disarmament and development, and in that regard suggested a more effective role for the United Nations system.

The experts proposed that national studies be conducted on the macro-economic dimensions and social consequences of converting resources from military to civilian use. In addition, they supported the call for a periodic assessment of the impact of world-wide military spending on global economic prospects, and suggested that the United Nations support studies on the effects of military expenditures on international trade and finance and the impact of arms reduction on the national and international economy.

The group endorsed the idea of an improved and comprehensive data base on military budgets and expenditures to facilitate the above studies and suggested the encouragement of national policies of self-restraint in military expenditures until appropriate international agreements were negotiated.

GENERAL ASSEMBLY ACTION

On 7 December, on the recommendation of the First Committee, the General Assembly adopted **resolution 43/78 J** by recorded vote.

Economic and social consequences of the armaments race and its extremely harmful effects on world peace and security

The General Assembly,

Having considered the item entitled ''Economic and social consequences of the armaments race and its extremely harmful effects on world peace and security'',

Recalling its resolutions 2667(XXV) of 7 December 1970, 2831(XXVI) of 16 December 1971, 3075(XXVIII) of 6 December 1973, 32/75 of 12 December 1977, 35/141 of 12 December 1980, 40/150 of 16 December 1985 and 41/86 I of 4 December 1986,

Deeply concerned that the arms race, particularly in nuclear armaments and military expenditures, continues to increase at an alarming speed, representing a heavy burden for the economies of all States and constituting a grave danger for world peace and security,

Recalling also the numerous statements made by the representatives of Governments during the disarmament negotiations and particularly at the fifteenth special session of the General Assembly, the third special session devoted to disarmament, to the effect that the vastly increased military budgets have also contributed to current economic problems in certain States and that existing and planned military programmes constitute a huge waste of precious resources which might otherwise be used to elevate living standards of all peoples and solve the problems confronting developing countries in achieving economic and social development,

Reaffirming the need for all Governments and peoples to be informed about and to understand the situation prevailing in the field of the arms race and disarmament,

Bearing in mind the objectives of the World Disarmament Campaign, solemnly launched at the twelfth special session, which is intended to promote public interest in and support for the reaching of agreements on measures of arms limitation and disarmament,

Recalling further paragraph 93 (c) of the Final Document of the Tenth Special Session of the General Assembly, the first special session devoted to disarmament, in which it is provided that the Secretary-General shall periodically submit reports to the Assembly on the economic and social consequences of the armaments race and its extremely harmful effects on world peace and security,

Considering that the elaboration of such reports should be viewed as a measure aimed at building confidence among States,

1. *Welcomes with satisfaction* the updated report of the Secretary-General on the economic and social consequences of the arms race and military expenditures;

2. *Expresses its thanks* to the Secretary-General and the consultant experts as well as to the Governments and international organizations that have rendered assistance in the updating of the report;

3. *Recommends* that the report be brought to the attention of public opinion and also taken into account in future actions by the United Nations in the field of disarmament;

4. *Requests* the Secretary-General to make the necessary arrangements for the reproduction of the report as a United Nations publication and to give it broad publicity in the framework of the World Disarmament Campaign;

5. *Recommends* that all Governments ensure the widest possible distribution of the report, including its translation into the respective national languages;

6. *Invites* the specialized agencies as well as intergovernmental, national and non-governmental organizations to use their facilities to make the report widely known;

7. *Reaffirms* its decision to keep the item entitled ''Economic and social consequences of the armaments race and its extremely harmful effects on world peace and security'' under constant review, and decides to include it in the provisional agenda of its forty-sixth session.

General Assembly resolution 43/78 J

7 December 1988   Meeting 73   143-1-9 (recorded vote)

Approved by First Committee (A/43/859) by recorded vote (125-1-9), 14 November (meeting 36); 15-nation draft (A/C.1/43/L.57); agenda item 67 *(h)*.

Sponsors: Bangladesh, Czechoslovakia, Ecuador, Indonesia, Malaysia, Mali, Mexico, Nigeria, Romania, Sweden, Tunisia, USSR, Uruguay, Yugoslavia, Zaire.

Meeting numbers. GA 43rd session: 1st Committee 3-25, 32, 36; plenary 73.

Recorded vote in Assembly as follows:

In favour: Afghanistan, Albania, Algeria, Angola, Antigua and Barbuda, Argentina, Australia, Austria, Bahamas, Bahrain, Bangladesh, Barbados, Belize, Benin, Bhutan, Bolivia, Botswana, Brazil, Brunei Darussalam, Bulgaria, Burkina Faso, Burma, Burundi, Byelorussian SSR, Cameroon, Canada, Cape Verde, Central African Republic, Chad, Chile, China, Colombia, Comoros, Congo, Costa Rica, Côte d'Ivoire, Cuba, Cyprus, Czechoslovakia, Democratic Kampuchea, Democratic Yemen, Denmark, Djibouti, Dominican Republic, Ecuador, Egypt, El Salvador, Ethiopia, Fiji, Finland, Gabon, Gambia, German Democratic Republic, Ghana, Greece, Guatemala, Guinea, Guyana, Haiti, Honduras, Hungary, Iceland, India, Indonesia, Iran, Iraq, Ireland, Japan, Jordan, Kenya, Kuwait, Lao People's Democratic Republic, Lebanon, Lesotho, Liberia, Libyan Arab Jamahiriya, Madagascar, Malawi, Malaysia, Maldives, Mali, Malta, Mauritania, Mauritius, Mexico, Mongolia, Morocco, Mozambique, Nepal, New Zealand, Nicaragua, Niger, Nigeria, Norway, Oman, Pakistan, Panama, Papua New Guinea, Paraguay, Peru, Philippines, Poland, Qatar, Romania, Rwanda, Saint Kitts and Nevis, Saint Lucia, Saint Vincent and the Grenadines, Samoa, Sao Tome and Principe, Saudi Arabia, Senegal, Seychelles, Sierra Leone, Singapore, Solomon Islands, Somalia, Spain, Sri Lanka, Sudan, Suriname, Swaziland, Sweden, Syrian Arab Republic, Thailand, Togo, Trinidad and Tobago, Tunisia, Turkey, Uganda, Ukrainian SSR, USSR, United Arab Emirates, United Republic of Tanzania, Uruguay, Vanuatu, Venezuela, Viet Nam, Yemen, Yugoslavia, Zaire, Zambia, Zimbabwe.

Against: United States.

Abstaining: Belgium, France, Germany, Federal Republic of, Israel, Italy, Luxembourg, Netherlands, Portugal, United Kingdom.

REFERENCES

[1]YUN 1987, p. 82, GA res. 42/36, 30 Nov. 1987. [2]YUN 1986, p. 76. [3]YUN 1987, p. 81. [4]A/S-15/3. [5]YUN 1985, p. 84, GA res. 40/91 B, 12 Dec. 1985. [6]YUN 1985, p. 84, GA res. 40/91 B, 12 Dec. 1985. [7]*Ibid.*, p. 88, GA res. 40/150, 16 Dec. 1985. [8]YUN 1986, p. 79, GA res. 41/86 I, 4 Dec. 1986. [9]A/43/368. [10]YUN 1982, p. 145.

PUBLICATION
Study on the Economic and Social Consequences of the Arms Race and Military Expenditures, Sales No. E.89.IX.2.

Information and studies

World Disarmament Campaign

As in previous years, the World Disarmament Campaign—launched by the General Assembly in 1982 at the start of its second special session devoted to disarmament[1]—continued to inform, educate and generate public understanding and support for the disarmament objectives of the United Nations.

The Sixth United Nations Pledging Conference for the World Disarmament Campaign was held on 27 October 1988, during Disarmament Week.

Reports of the Secretary-General. In May 1988,[2] in response to a request of the Preparatory Committee for the Third Special Session of the General Assembly Devoted to Disarmament, the Secretary-General submitted an evaluation of the World Disarmament Campaign's activities and financial situation from 1982 to 1988. He observed that the Campaign had firmly established its place on the international disarmament scene and had become the focal point for contact between organizations, research/educational institutes, individuals and the United Nations Department for Disarmament Affairs (DDA). Support from non-governmental organizations (NGOs) and Member States had been crucial to the Campaign's effective functioning. Despite its financial constraints, the Campaign had translated the objectives given to it by the Assembly and implemented activities to further its goals. It had offered a structured framework for fostering public understanding of the efforts of the United Nations in disarmament.

In an October report,[3] the Secretary-General informed the Assembly of activities carried out by the United Nations system, including publishing and dissemination of information material, particularly in connection with the third special session on disarmament, and the holding of special events and publicity programmes. Within the Campaign framework, DDA, in co-operation with the Soviet Peace Committee, convened a United Nations meeting of experts (Dagomys, USSR, 12-16 April) to discuss the conceptual issues and technical aspects of verification.

The Department of Public Information (DPI) continued to inform the public about United Nations activities concerning disarmament through radio, television, press releases, films and photographs, and by organizing events at Headquarters and United Nations information centres around the world. For the third special session on disarmament, DPI, in co-operation with DDA, organized a number of activities for NGOs.

Financing

The Sixth United Nations Pledging Conference for the World Disarmament Campaign was held in New York on 27 October, with 66 delegations participating.

Either during the Conference or at other times during the year, the following pledges were earmarked for the Campaign: Australia ($A 30,000), Austria ($10,000), Canada ($Can 25,000), Cyprus ($1,000), Finland (50,000 markka), German Democratic Republic (100,000 mark), Greece ($5,000), Indonesia ($5,000), Mexico ($5,000), New Zealand ($5,000), Norway ($15,000), Philippines (10,000 pesos), Sri Lanka ($5,000), Sweden (150,000 kronor), Zaire ($1,000); for the United Nations Institute for Disarmament Research: Australia ($A 20,000), Canada ($Can 25,000), China ($10,000), German Democratic Republic (50,000 mark), USSR (200,000 roubles and $20,000); for the regional centre in Asia: Nepal ($7,000), New Zealand ($5,000), Norway ($10,000); for the regional centre in Latin America and the Caribbean: Colombia ($1,000), Peru ($15,000), Uruguay ($1,000).

GENERAL ASSEMBLY ACTION

On 7 December, on the recommendation of the First Committee, the General Assembly adopted **resolution 43/76 C** by recorded vote.

World Disarmament Campaign

The General Assembly,

Recalling that in paragraph 15 of the Final Document of the Tenth Special Session of the General Assembly, the first special session devoted to disarmament, it declared that it was essential that not only Governments but also the peoples of the world recognize and understand the dangers in the present situation and stressed the importance of mobilizing world public opinion on behalf of disarmament,

Recalling also its resolution 42/39 G of 30 November 1987,

Having examined the reports of the Secretary-General of 19 May 1988 and 4 October 1988 on the implementation of the programme of activities of the World Disarmament Campaign by the United Nations system,

Having also examined the part of the report of the Secretary-General of 10 October 1988 dealing with the activities of the Advisory Board on Disarmament Studies relating to the implementation of the World Disarmament Campaign, as well as the Final Act of the Sixth United Nations Pledging Conference for the Campaign, held on 27 October 1988,

1. *Reiterates its commendation* of the manner in which, as described in the above-mentioned reports, the World Disarmament Campaign has been geared by the Secretary-General in order to guarantee "the widest possible dissemination of information and unimpeded ac-

cess for all sectors of the public to a broad range of information and opinions on questions of arms limitation and disarmament and the dangers relating to all aspects of the arms race and war, in particular nuclear war";

2. *Recalls* that, as was also agreed by consensus in the Concluding Document of the Twelfth Special Session of the General Assembly, the second special session devoted to disarmament, it is likewise an essential requisite for the universality of the Campaign that it receive "the co-operation and participation of all States";

3. *Endorses once more* the statement made by the Secretary-General on the occasion of the Third United Nations Pledging Conference for the World Disarmament Campaign to the effect that such co-operation implies that adequate funds be made available and that consequently the criterion of universality also applies to pledges, since a campaign without world-wide participation and funding will have difficulty in reflecting this principle in its implementation;

4. *Reiterates its regret* that most of the States that have the largest military expenditures have not so far made any financial contribution to the Campaign;

5. *Decides* that at its forty-fourth session there should be a seventh United Nations Pledging Conference for the World Disarmament Campaign, and expresses the hope that on that occasion all those Member States that have not yet announced any voluntary contribution may do so;

6. *Reiterates its recommendation* that the voluntary contributions made by Member States to the World Disarmament Campaign Voluntary Trust Fund should not be earmarked for specific activities inasmuch as it is most desirable that the Secretary-General enjoy full freedom to take the decisions he deems fit within the framework of the Campaign previously approved by the General Assembly and in exercise of the powers vested in him in connection with the Campaign;

7. *Notes with appreciation* that the Secretary-General has given permanent character to his instructions to the United Nations information centres and regional commissions to give wide publicity to the Campaign and, whenever necessary, to adapt, as far as possible, United Nations information materials to local languages;

8. *Requests* the Secretary-General to submit to the General Assembly at its forty-fourth session a report covering both the implementation of the programme of activities of the Campaign by the United Nations system during 1989 and the programme of activities contemplated by the system for 1990;

9. *Decides* to include in the provisional agenda of its forty-fourth session the item entitled "World Disarmament Campaign".

General Assembly resolution 43/76 C

7 December 1988   Meeting 73   144-0-10 (recorded vote)

Approved by First Committee (A/43/857) by recorded vote (128-0-10), 14 November (meeting 35); 15-nation draft (A/C.1/43/L.33); agenda item 65 (e).

Sponsors: Bangladesh, Bulgaria, Byelorussian SSR, Egypt, German Democratic Republic, Indonesia, Mexico, Pakistan, Peru, Philippines, Romania, Sri Lanka, Sweden, Venezuela, Yugoslavia.

Meeting numbers. GA 43rd session: 1st Committee 3-25, 29, 35; plenary 73.

Recorded vote in Assembly as follows:

In favour: Afghanistan, Albania, Algeria, Angola, Antigua and Barbuda, Argentina, Australia, Austria, Bahamas, Bahrain, Bangladesh, Barbados, Belize, Benin, Bhutan, Bolivia, Botswana, Brazil, Brunei Darussalam, Bulgaria, Burkina Faso, Burma, Burundi, Byelorussian SSR, Cameroon, Cape

Verde, Central African Republic, Chad, Chile, China, Colombia, Comoros, Congo, Costa Rica, Côte d'Ivoire, Cuba, Cyprus, Czechoslovakia, Democratic Kampuchea, Democratic Yemen, Denmark, Djibouti, Dominican Republic, Ecuador, Egypt, El Salvador, Ethiopia, Fiji, Finland, Gabon, Gambia, German Democratic Republic, Ghana, Greece, Guatemala, Guinea, Guyana, Haiti, Honduras, Hungary, Iceland, India, Indonesia, Iran, Iraq, Ireland, Israel, Jamaica, Japan, Jordan, Kenya, Kuwait, Lao People's Democratic Republic, Lebanon, Lesotho, Liberia, Libyan Arab Jamahiriya, Madagascar, Malawi, Malaysia, Maldives, Mali, Malta, Mauritania, Mauritius, Mexico, Mongolia, Morocco, Mozambique, Nepal, New Zealand, Nicaragua, Niger, Nigeria, Norway, Oman, Pakistan, Panama, Papua New Guinea, Paraguay, Peru, Philippines, Poland, Qatar, Romania, Rwanda, Saint Kitts and Nevis, Saint Lucia, Saint Vincent and the Grenadines, Samoa, Sao Tome and Principe, Saudi Arabia, Senegal, Seychelles, Sierra Leone, Singapore, Solomon Islands, Somalia, Spain, Sri Lanka, Sudan, Suriname, Swaziland, Sweden, Syrian Arab Republic, Thailand, Togo, Trinidad and Tobago, Tunisia, Turkey, Uganda, Ukrainian SSR, USSR, United Arab Emirates, United Republic of Tanzania, Uruguay, Vanuatu, Venezuela, Viet Nam, Yemen, Yugoslavia, Zaire, Zambia, Zimbabwe.

Against: None.

Abstaining: Belgium, Canada, France, Germany, Federal Republic of, Italy, Luxembourg, Netherlands, Portugal, United Kingdom, United States.

Regional centres for peace and disarmament

On 7 December 1988, the General Assembly adopted three resolutions on regional centres for peace and disarmament—expressing satisfaction that the centre in Africa had become operational (43/76 D), welcoming the inauguration of a centre in Latin America (43/76 H) and welcoming the signing of an agreement on the establishment of a centre in Asia (43/76 G).

Africa

In October 1988,[4] the Secretary-General reported to the General Assembly on the activities of the United Nations Regional Centre for Peace and Disarmament in Africa, which was established in 1986, at Lomé, Togo,[5] and which during the initial phase functioned under the auspices of DDA. The Centre's activities included the organization of training programmes on the peaceful settlement of disputes, the prevention and management of crises and confidence-building among African States, the organization of seminars and conferences, research and study, advisory services to Member States and the dissemination of information and documentation. The Secretary-General reaffirmed the continuing need for voluntary contributions to ensure the viability and effective functioning of the Centre.

GENERAL ASSEMBLY ACTION

On 7 December, on the recommendation of the First Committee, the General Assembly adopted **resolution 43/76 D** without vote.

United Nations Regional Centre for Peace and Disarmament in Africa

The General Assembly,

Recalling its resolutions 40/151 G of 16 December 1985, 41/60 D of 3 December 1986 and 42/39 J of 30 November 1987,

Taking note of the Political Declaration adopted by the Eighth Conference of Heads of State or Government

of the Non-Aligned Countries, held at Harare from 1 to 6 September 1986, in which the heads of State or Government, *inter alia,* reaffirmed the need to strengthen the role of the regional bodies in mobilizing support for the World Disarmament Campaign and, in this regard, welcomed the establishment of the United Nations Regional Centre for Peace and Disarmament in Africa at Lomé,

Bearing in mind resolution AHG/Res.164(XXIII), adopted by the Assembly of Heads of State and Government of the Organization of African Unity at its twenty-third ordinary session, held at Addis Ababa from 27 to 29 July 1987, by which it, *inter alia,* endorsed the Lomé Declaration on Security, Disarmament and Development in Africa and the Programme of Action for Peace, Security and Co-operation in Africa,

Taking into account the report of the Secretary-General,

1. *Expresses its satisfaction* that the United Nations Regional Centre for Peace and Disarmament in Africa, inaugurated on 24 October 1986, has become operational;

2. *Commends* the Secretary-General for his efforts in taking the necessary measures to ensure the effective functioning of the Centre, and requests him to continue to lend all the necessary support to the Centre;

3. *Expresses its gratitude* to the Member States and the international, governmental and non-governmental organizations that have already made contributions to ensure the functioning of the Centre;

4. *Appeals once again* to Member States, as well as to international, governmental and non-governmental organizations, to make voluntary contributions in order to strengthen the effective functioning of the Centre;

5. *Requests* the Secretary-General to submit a report to the General Assembly at its forty-fourth session on the implementation of the present resolution.

General Assembly resolution 43/76 D

7 December 1988　　　　Meeting 73　　　　Adopted without vote

Approved by First Committee (A/43/857) without vote, 14 November (meeting 35); draft by United Republic of Tanzania, for African Group (A/C.1/43/L.41); agenda item 65 *(h).*

Meeting numbers. GA 43rd session: 1st Committee 3-25, 28, 35; plenary 73.

Latin America

As agreed by the General Assembly in 1986,[6] the United Nations Regional Centre for Peace, Disarmament and Development in Latin America was established on 1 January 1987 and inaugurated at Lima, Peru, on 9 October of that year.

In an October 1988 report,[7] the Secretary-General stated that the Centre's initial activities had focused on disseminating information and on establishing contacts with relevant institutions and organizations, as well as responding to queries from the public, with a view to promoting better understanding of and generating wider support for the objectives of the United Nations in the field of arms limitation and disarmament. Efforts were being made to set up a resource centre that could be used by organizations and individuals concerned with issues of peace, security, disarmament and development.

In response to a 1987 Assembly request,[8] a conference of experts on the strengthening of political co-operation in Latin America in the areas of peace, disarmament, development and security was held (Lima, 6-9 December), preceded by a preparatory meeting from 4 to 6 May. The Centre also hosted a conference on conflict zones, peace and development during Disarmament Week.

GENERAL ASSEMBLY ACTION

On 7 December, on the recommendation of the First Committee, the General Assembly adopted **resolution 43/76 H** without vote.

United Nations Regional Centre for Peace, Disarmament and Development in Latin America

The General Assembly,

Recalling its resolutions 41/60 J of 3 December 1986 and 42/39 K of 30 November 1987,

Welcoming the inauguration of the United Nations Regional Centre for Peace, Disarmament and Development in Latin America on 9 October 1987,

Recalling also the Acapulco Commitment to Peace, Development and Democracy signed by the heads of State of States members of the Permanent Mechanism for Consultation and Concerted Political Action on 29 November 1987, as well as the meeting of Ministers for Foreign Affairs of the Permanent Mechanism held at Cartagena, Colombia, in February 1988,

Taking into account that the scope of action of the Centre includes Latin America and the Caribbean,

Also welcoming the holding by the Centre of the Workshop-Seminar of Experts on Disarmament from 4 to 6 May 1988,

Taking note of the final documents of the Conference of Ministers for Foreign Affairs of the Movement of Non-Aligned Countries, held at Nicosia from 7 to 10 September 1988,

Expressing its gratitude to the Member States that have made valuable contributions to the functioning of the Centre,

Convinced that in carrying out its activities the Centre will seek to promote relationships based upon mutual confidence and security among countries of the region in a spirit of harmony, solidarity and co-operation aimed at the implementation of measures that foster peace, disarmament and social and economic development in Latin America and the Caribbean,

1. *Reaffirms* that the United Nations Regional Centre for Peace, Disarmament and Development in Latin America, in conformity with its mandate contained in resolution 41/60 J, is called upon to explore new avenues for concerted political action among the countries of the region and to strengthen further the intra–Latin American and Caribbean links in a framework of harmony, solidarity and co-operation that will enable the region to become an effective area of peace;

2. *Takes note with satisfaction* of the holding of the Conference of Experts on the Strengthening of Political Co-operation in Latin America and the Caribbean in the fields of peace, disarmament, development and security, within the framework of the World Disarmament Campaign, at Lima from 6 to 9 December 1988, which will also examine various conceptual and organizational aspects of the Centre to enable it to fulfil its objectives;

3. *Recommends* that the Centre hold two meetings during 1989 with a view to reaffirming its role as a centre for documentary collection, diffusion and dissemination, as a forum for the promotion of peace, disarmament and development measures in the context of the World Disarmament Campaign and as an organ for the co-ordination of studies, research and programmes in the fields of its competence;

4. *Invites once again* Member States and international, governmental and non-governmental organizations to make voluntary contributions to the Centre;

5. *Decides* to rename the Centre "United Nations Regional Centre for Peace, Disarmament and Development in Latin America and the Caribbean";

6. *Requests* the Secretary-General to transmit that appeal to all Member States in order to ensure the effective functioning of the Centre;

7. *Also requests* the Secretary-General to report to the General Assembly at its forty-fourth session on the implementation of the present resolution.

General Assembly resolution 43/76 H

7 December 1988   Meeting 73   Adopted without vote

Approved by First Committee (A/43/857) without vote, 14 November (meeting 35); 18-nation draft (A/C.1/43/L.71), orally revised; agenda item 65 *(i)*.
Sponsors: Argentina, Bolivia, Brazil, Colombia, Costa Rica, Dominican Republic, Ecuador, El Salvador, Guatemala, Honduras, Mexico, Nepal, Panama, Paraguay, Peru, Togo, Uruguay, Venezuela.
Meeting numbers. GA 43rd session: 1st Committee 3-25, 30, 35; plenary 73.

Asia

The Secretary-General, in an October 1988 report,[9] informed the General Assembly that, pursuant to its 1987 decision,[10] the United Nations Regional Centre for Peace and Disarmament in Asia was established at Kathmandu, Nepal, on 8 June 1988. The Centre was to provide substantive support for initiatives and other activities mutually agreed on by Member States of the Asian region for the implementation of measures for peace and disarmament.

Action was taken to establish a trust fund for the Centre, and the Secretary-General appealed for voluntary contributions to meet its administrative needs and substantive activities.

GENERAL ASSEMBLY ACTION

On 7 December, the General Assembly, on the recommendation of the First Committee, adopted **resolution 43/76 G** without vote.

United Nations Regional Centre for Peace and Disarmament in Asia

The General Assembly,

Recalling its resolution 42/39 D of 30 November 1987, by which it decided to establish the United Nations Regional Centre for Peace and Disarmament in Asia with headquarters at Kathmandu,

Taking into account its decision that the Centre should provide, on request, substantive support for the initiatives and other activities mutually agreed upon by Member States of the Asian region for the implementation of measures for peace and disarmament through appropriate utilization of available resources, and should co-ordinate the implementation of regional activities in Asia under the World Disarmament Campaign,

1. *Takes note with satisfaction* of the report of the Secretary-General of 19 October 1988;

2. *Welcomes* the signing of an agreement and a memorandum of understanding between the Government of Nepal and the United Nations regarding the establishing of the United Nations Regional Centre for Peace and Disarmament in Asia;

3. *Commends* the administrative measures taken by the Secretary-General to ensure the establishment and functioning of the Centre, and requests him to continue lending all possible support;

4. *Invites* Member States and interested organizations to make voluntary contributions for the effective functioning of the Centre;

5. *Requests* the Secretary-General to report to the General Assembly at its forty-fourth session on the implementation of the present resolution.

General Assembly resolution 43/76 G

7 December 1988   Meeting 73   Adopted without vote

Approved by First Committee (A/43/857) without vote, 14 November (meeting 35); draft by Nepal (A/C.1/43/L.68); agenda item 65 *(d)*.
Meeting numbers. GA 43rd session: 1st Committee 3-25, 30, 35; plenary 73.

Disarmament Week

Disarmament Week, an annual event starting on United Nations Day, 24 October, and aimed at fostering the objectives of disarmament, was observed on 28 October 1988 at United Nations Headquarters at a special meeting of the General Assembly's First Committee. Statements to mark the occasion were made by the First Committee Chairman, a Vice-President of the Assembly, the Secretary-General and representatives of the five regional groups.

In an August report and later addendum,[11] the Secretary-General submitted information received from nine Member States, as well as from the United Nations system and international NGOs, on their activities to promote the Week's objectives.

GENERAL ASSEMBLY ACTION

On 7 December, on the recommendation of the First Committee, the General Assembly adopted **resolution 43/78 G** without vote.

Disarmament Week

The General Assembly,

Noting that there have been important developments of late in the areas of arms limitation and disarmament efforts which provide a sense of strong encouragement and hope for a more secure world,

Noting at the same time that, despite the positive developments, the arms race still poses a grave threat to world peace and security,

Stressing the vital importance of eliminating the threat of a nuclear and conventional war, ending the nuclear and conventional arms race and bringing about disarmament,

Emphasizing anew the need for and the importance of world public opinion in support of halting and reversing the global arms race in all its aspects,

Taking into account the aspirations of the world public to prevent an arms race in space and to terminate it on Earth,

Noting with satisfaction the broad and active support by Governments and international and national organizations of the decision taken by the General Assembly at its tenth special session, the first special session devoted to disarmament, regarding the proclamation of the week starting 24 October, the day of the foundation of the United Nations, as a week devoted to fostering the objectives of disarmament,

Recalling the recommendations concerning the World Disarmament Campaign contained in annex V to the Concluding Document of the twelfth special session of the General Assembly, the second special session devoted to disarmament, in particular the recommendation that Disarmament Week should continue to be widely observed,

Noting the support for the further observance of Disarmament Week expressed by Member States at the fifteenth special session of the General Assembly, the third special session devoted to disarmament,

1. *Takes note with satisfaction* of the report of the Secretary-General on the follow-up measures undertaken by States and governmental and non-governmental organizations in holding Disarmament Week;

2. *Commends* all States and international and national governmental and non-governmental organizations for their energetic support of and active participation in Disarmament Week since its first observance ten years ago;

3. *Invites* all States that so desire, in carrying out appropriate measures at the local level on the occasion of Disarmament Week, to take into account the elements of the model programme for Disarmament Week prepared by the Secretary-General;

4. *Invites* Governments to continue, in accordance with General Assembly resolution 33/71 D of 14 December 1978, to inform the Secretary-General of activities undertaken to promote the objectives of Disarmament Week;

5. *Invites* international and national non-governmental organizations to take an active part in Disarmament Week and to inform the Secretary-General of the activities undertaken;

6. *Invites* the Secretary-General to use the United Nations information organs as widely as possible to promote better understanding among the world public of disarmament problems and the objectives of Disarmament Week;

7. *Requests* the Secretary-General, in accordance with paragraph 4 of resolution 33/71 D, to submit to the General Assembly at its forty-fourth session a report on the implementation of the present resolution.

General Assembly resolution 43/78 G

7 December 1988   Meeting 73   Adopted without vote

Approved by First Committee (A/43/859) without vote, 14 November (meeting 35); 17-nation draft (A/C.1/43/L.48); agenda item 67 *(m)*.
Sponsors: Afghanistan, Angola, Bulgaria, Byelorussian SSR, Cuba, Czechoslovakia, German Democratic Republic, Japan, Lao People's Democratic Republic, Mongolia, Mozambique, New Zealand, Papua New Guinea, Philippines, Samoa, Ukrainian SSR, Viet Nam.
Meeting numbers. GA 43rd session: 1st Committee 3-25, 30, 35; plenary 73.

Disarmament studies and research

UN Institute for Disarmament Research

In a report outlining the activities of the United Nations Institute for Disarmament Research (UNIDIR) for the period September 1987 to September 1988,[12] the Secretary-General said it organized a conference on disarmament research, with the assistance of the Institute for World Economics and International Relations of the USSR (Sochi, USSR, 22-24 March). Representatives of 46 institutes and organizations from different regions participated. Preparations continued for the convening of a conference on conventional disarmament in Europe, rescheduled for January 1989.

As part of its lecture programme, UNIDIR, with the co-operation of the United Nations Information Service and in association with the Geneva International Peace Research Institute, organized a symposium on United States–USSR negotiations on nuclear and space arms (Geneva, 18 April). UNIDIR issued seven publications and, in March, commenced publication of a quarterly newsletter. Work continued to expand, update and maintain the sample files of the computerized data base.

The UNIDIR fellowship programme, enabling scholars from developing countries to undertake research on disarmament, continued. A survey was conducted of medium-term perspectives in the field of disarmament and arms limitation, with a view to defining the future research agenda. Three research projects were initiated: on national concepts of verification, on verification by airborne systems, and a second project on problems related to outer space.

Advisory Board on Disarmament Studies

The Advisory Board on Disarmament Studies held two sessions in New York in 1988, its eighteenth (26-29 April) and nineteenth (26-30 September).[13] The Board reviewed the situation in the area of disarmament, including studies and implementation of the World Disarmament Campaign, and discussed its own role. In addition, it continued to act as the Board of Trustees of UNIDIR.

The Board approved the report of the Director on the activities of UNIDIR (see above) and its own work programme for 1989. It also directed the secretariat to investigate the matter of the scheduling of its second annual sessions, which since 1986 had taken place in late September, in contravention of a 1979 General Assembly decision according to which no subsidiary organ was permitted to meet at Headquarters during a regular Assembly session, unless explicitly authorized.[14]

In considering the proposed annual budget of UNIDIR for 1989, the Board noted that there had been a significant increase in the number of donors, with 17 new donors either having made or pledged voluntary contributions during the period under review, in response to the Director's fund-raising efforts. Contributions for 1989 totalled $958,000, including $392,600 in nonconvertible currencies.

The Board adopted the proposed 1989 budget estimates and recommended a subvention of $221,100 from the United Nations regular budget towards meeting the costs of the Director and staff, raising UNIDIR's net income to $1,179,100. In October,[15] the Secretary-General reported to the General Assembly's Fifth (Administrative and Budgetary) Committee accordingly. The Advisory Committee on Administrative and Budgetary Questions recommended that the Assembly approve the subvention for 1989, which the Assembly did by **resolution 43/218 A** on the revised budget appropriations for 1988-1989, under the section on disarmament affairs activities.

UN disarmament studies programme

The Advisory Board, which advised the Secretary-General on various aspects of United Nations studies on disarmament and arms limitation, reported that two studies, on the climatic and other global effects of nuclear war and on the economic and social consequences of the arms race and military expenditures, had been completed. The Board discussed the question of verification, emphasizing its significance as well as the difficulties involved, and was informed of a number of proposals, submitted to the third special session of the Assembly on disarmament, which might lead to subjects for United Nations studies: multilateral verification, developments in nuclear weapons and certain aspects of conventional arms transfers.

GENERAL ASSEMBLY ACTION

On 7 December, the General Assembly, on the recommendation of the First Committee, adopted **resolution 43/75 N** by recorded vote.

Comprehensive United Nations study on nuclear weapons

The General Assembly,

Conscious of the central role and primary responsibility of the United Nations in the sphere of disarmament, in accordance with the Charter,

Recognizing that nuclear disarmament and arms limitation remain a priority objective and represent a central task of the international community,

Recalling the report of the Secretary-General entitled *Comprehensive Study on Nuclear Weapons*, which was submitted to the General Assembly in 1980,

Recognizing also that since then many important developments have taken place in the area of nuclear arms, including the continued qualitative improvement and development of nuclear-weapon systems,

Noting the importance attached by the international community to the complete cessation of nuclear testing within the framework of an effective disarmament process,

Noting also the full-scale stage-by-stage talks on nuclear testing between the Union of Soviet Socialist Republics and the United States of America,

Bearing in mind the critical importance of an early and significant reduction of nuclear arms and recent progress in this field,

Taking note of the reports of the Secretary-General entitled *Study on the Climatic and Other Global Effects of Nuclear War, Concepts of Security* and *Study on Deterrence,*

Convinced that a comprehensive United Nations study on new developments concerning different aspects of nuclear weapons would make a valuable contribution to the dissemination of factual information and to international understanding of the issues involved,

1. *Requests* the Secretary-General to carry out, with the assistance of qualified governmental experts and taking into account recent relevant studies, a comprehensive update of the *Comprehensive Study on Nuclear Weapons* that provides factual and up-to-date information on and pays regard to the political, legal and security aspects of:

(a)   Nuclear arsenals and pertinent technological developments;

(b)   Doctrines concerning nuclear weapons;

(c)   Efforts to reduce nuclear weapons;

(d)   Physical, environmental, medical and other effects of use of nuclear weapons and of nuclear testing;

(e)   Efforts to achieve a comprehensive nuclear-test ban;

(f)   Efforts to prevent the use of nuclear weapons and their horizontal and vertical proliferation;

(g)   The question of verification of compliance with nuclear-arms limitation agreements;

2. *Recommends* that the study, while aiming at being as comprehensive as possible, should be based on open material and such further information as Member States may wish to make available for the purpose of the study;

3. *Invites* all Governments to co-operate with the Secretary-General so that the objectives of the study may be achieved;

4. *Requests* the Secretary-General to submit the final report to the General Assembly well in advance of its forty-fifth session.

General Assembly resolution 43/75 N

7 December 1988   Meeting 73   141-1-9 (recorded vote)

Approved by First Committee (A/43/856) by recorded vote (122-1-9), 17 November (meeting 41); 18-nation draft (A/C.1/43/L.46); agenda item 64.

Sponsors: Argentina, Australia, Austria, German Democratic Republic, Hungary, India, Indonesia, Ireland, Mexico, New Zealand, Pakistan, Peru, Romania, Samoa, Sri Lanka, Sweden, Venezuela, Yugoslavia.

Financial implications. ACABQ, A/43/7/Add.9; 5th Committee, A/43/938; S-G, A/C.1/43/L.78, A/C.5/43/48.

Meeting numbers. GA 43rd session: 1st Committee 3-26, 41; 5th Committee 41; plenary 73.

Recorded vote in Assembly as follows:

In favour: Afghanistan, Albania, Algeria, Angola, Antigua and Barbuda, Argentina, Australia, Austria, Bahamas, Bahrain, Bangladesh, Barbados, Belize, Benin, Bhutan, Bolivia, Botswana, Brazil, Brunei Darussalam, Bulgaria, Burkina Faso, Burma, Burundi, Byelorussian SSR, Cameroon, Canada, Cape Verde, Central African Republic, Chad, Chile, Colombia, Comoros, Congo, Costa Rica, Côte d'Ivoire, Cuba, Cyprus, Czechoslovakia, Democratic Yemen, Denmark, Djibouti, Dominican Republic, Ecuador, Egypt, El Salvador, Ethiopia, Fiji, Finland, Gabon, Gambia, German Democratic Republic, Ghana, Greece, Guatemala, Guinea, Guyana, Haiti, Honduras, Hungary, Iceland, India, Indonesia, Iran, Iraq, Ireland, Jamaica, Japan, Jordan, Kenya, Kuwait, Lao People's Democratic Republic, Leba-

non, Lesotho, Liberia, Libyan Arab Jamahiriya, Madagascar, Malawi, Malaysia, Maldives, Mali, Malta, Mauritania, Mauritius, Mexico, Mongolia, Morocco, Mozambique, Nepal, New Zealand, Nicaragua, Niger, Nigeria, Norway, Oman, Pakistan, Panama, Papua New Guinea, Paraguay, Peru, Philippines, Poland, Qatar, Romania, Rwanda, Saint Kitts and Nevis, Saint Lucia, Saint Vincent and the Grenadines, Samoa, Sao Tome and Principe, Saudi Arabia, Senegal, Seychelles, Sierra Leone, Singapore, Solomon Islands, Somalia, Spain, Sri Lanka, Sudan, Suriname, Swaziland, Sweden, Syrian Arab Republic, Thailand, Togo, Trinidad and Tobago, Tunisia, Turkey, Uganda, Ukrainian SSR, USSR, United Arab Emirates, United Republic of Tanzania, Uruguay, Vanuatu, Venezuela, Viet Nam, Yemen, Yugoslavia, Zambia, Zimbabwe.

Against: United States.

Abstaining: Belgium, France, Germany, Federal Republic of, Israel, Italy, Luxembourg, Netherlands, Portugal, United Kingdom.

By **resolution 43/81 B**, the Assembly requested the Secretary-General to undertake a study on the role of the United Nations in the field of verification.

Parties and signatories to disarmament agreements

In October 1988, the Secretary-General submitted to the General Assembly his annual report on the status of multilateral disarmament agreements,[16] based on information received from the States depositaries of those instruments. Listing the parties to and signatories as at 31 July 1988, the report also contained similar information on the Convention on the Prohibition of Military or Any Other Hostile Use of Environmental Modification Techniques, the Agreement Governing the Activities of States on the Moon and Other Celestial Bodies, and the Convention on Prohibitions or Restrictions on the Use of Certain Conventional Weapons Which May Be Deemed to Be Excessively Injurious or to Have Indiscriminate Effects, of which the Secretary-General is the depositary, as well as on the South Pacific Nuclear-Free-Zone Treaty, of which the Director of the South Pacific Bureau for Economic Co-operation is the depositary.

As at 31 December 1988, the following numbers of States had become parties to the multilateral agreements covered in the Secretary-General's report (listed in chronological order, with the years in which they were initially signed or opened for signature).[17]

(Geneva) Protocol for the Prohibition of the Use in War of Asphyxiating, Poisonous or Other Gases, and of Bacteriological Methods of Warfare (1925): 112 parties

The Antarctic Treaty (1959): 38 parties

Treaty Banning Nuclear Weapon Tests in the Atmosphere, in Outer Space and under Water (1963): 117 parties

Treaty on Principles Governing the Activities of States in the Exploration and Use of Outer Space, including the Moon and Other Celestial Bodies (1967): 89 parties

Treaty for the Prohibition of Nuclear Weapons in Latin America (1967): 31 parties

Treaty on the Non-Proliferation of Nuclear Weapons (1968): 139 parties

Treaty on the Prohibition of the Emplacement of Nuclear Weapons and Other Weapons of Mass Destruction on the Sea-Bed and the Ocean Floor and in the Subsoil Thereof (1971): 81 parties

Convention on the Prohibition of the Development, Production and Stockpiling of Bacteriological (Biological) and Toxin Weapons and on Their Destruction (1972): 110 parties

Convention on the Prohibition of Military or Any Other Hostile Use of Environmental Modification Techniques (1977): 55 parties

Agreement Governing the Activities of States on the Moon and Other Celestial Bodies (1979): 7 parties

Convention on Prohibitions or Restrictions on the Use of Certain Conventional Weapons Which May Be Deemed to Be Excessively Injurious or to Have Indiscriminate Effects (1981): 30 parties

South Pacific Nuclear-Free-Zone Treaty (1985): 11 parties

REFERENCES

[1]YUN 1982, p. 31. [2]A/S-15/9. [3]A/43/642. [4]A/43/689. [5]YUN 1986, p. 85. [6]YUN 1986, p. 86, GA res. 41/60 J, 3 Dec. 1986. [7]A/43/614. [8]YUN 1987, p. 88, GA res. 42/39 K, 30 Nov. 1987. [9]A/43/568. [10]YUN 1987, p. 89, GA res. 42/39 D, 30 Nov. 1987. [11]A/43/508 & Add.1. [12]A/43/687. [13]A/43/685. [14]YUN 1979, p. 440, GA dec. 34/401. [15]A/C.5/43/20. [16]A/43/686. [17]*The United Nations Disarmament Yearbook*, vol. 13: *1988*, Sales No. E.89.IX.5.

Chapter III

Peaceful uses of outer space

During 1988, the United Nations continued to promote international co-operation in the use of outer space for peaceful purposes through the Committee on the Peaceful Uses of Outer Space (Committee on outer space) and its Scientific and Technical and Legal Sub-Committees. In December, the General Assembly endorsed the Committee's recommendations on a variety of issues (resolution 43/56).

Science, technology and law

General aspects

The Committee on outer space,[1] in accordance with a 1987 General Assembly resolution,[2] continued its consideration, as a matter of priority, of ways and means of maintaining outer space for peaceful purposes. The Committee, at its thirty-first session (New York, 13-23 June), agreed that an effective way to maintain outer space for peaceful purposes was to strengthen international co-operation in the exploration and peaceful uses of outer space, through multilateral, regional and bilateral co-operative activities and the promotion of specific projects to assist all countries, especially developing countries.

The Committee decided to consider at its next session the advisability of the Assembly's declaring 1992 as international space year, and recommended that the Scientific and Technical Sub-Committee at its next session, scheduled for February/March 1989, consider possible activities during such a year. It also recommended that a new item, on a review of the current status of spin-off benefits of space technology, be included in the agenda of its next session.

Implementation of the recommendations of the 1982 Conference on outer space

The Secretary-General in August[3] reported on the progress made in implementing the recommendations of the Second (1982) United Nations Conference on the Exploration and Peaceful Uses of Outer Space (UNISPACE-82).[4] The report covered the Working Group of the Whole to Evaluate the Implementation of the Recommendations of UNISPACE-82, inter-agency and regional co-operation, various studies, the United Nations Programme on Space Applications, technical advisory services, the International Space Information Service and voluntary contributions.

The Working Group was re-established in 1988 by the Scientific and Technical Sub-Committee with a view to improving the execution of international co-operation activities, particularly those included in the United Nations Programme on Space Applications (see below), and to increase such co-operation and make it more efficient.[5]

The Working Group, meeting in New York between 18 and 26 February, proposed that the emphasis of the Programme on Space Applications remain on long-term, project-oriented, on-the-job training in specific areas of space technology, and recommended that the activities proposed for 1988 and 1989 by the Expert on Space Applications be fully implemented (see below). Other recommendations dealt with promoting better access to and experiences of space-related subjects in higher education, intensive participation of international and regional financial and development institutions, extensive regional co-operation on space-related projects, greater interaction among application specialists and experimental and theoretical scientists and greater co-operation with non-governmental organizations. The Working Group encouraged countries with relevant capabilities to provide financial and technical assistance to developing countries for the development of low-cost community receivers for communication satellites and low-cost power sources to operate the system in unelectrified areas.

In addition, the Working Group renewed its 1987 recommendation[6] that the Committee on outer space request all Member States and international organizations with space-related activities to inform the Secretary-General of activities that could be the subject of greater international co-operation. Nine Member States (Austria, Bulgaria, Czechoslovakia, Denmark, Netherlands, Pakistan, Sweden, United States, USSR) responded to the Secretary-General's request for such information.[7]

The Working Group's report was adopted by the Sub-Committee and annexed to its report,[5] and its recommendations were endorsed by the Committee on outer space.[1] The Committee recommended that the Working Group be reconvened in 1989 to continue its work.

One of the recommendations of UNISPACE-82 was that an international space information service be established within the Outer Space Affairs Division of the United Nations, consisting initially of a directory of sources of information and data services. Accordingly, the Division in 1988 issued *Information Systems on Space Science and Technology: A Directory,*[8] which summarized the principal functions of institutions that operated space science and technology information systems. It also highlighted the areas of specialization of each of the centres, the type of system in operation there, the geographical areas covered by their collections, the languages of the systems, the users for whom service was provided and the class of services provided, the availability of training opportunities and the possibilities of collaborative arrangements with other institutions world-wide.

UN Programme on Space Applications

In 1988, the United Nations Programme on Space Applications continued to focus on providing long-range fellowships for in-depth training and technical advisory services to Member States and regional institutions; acquiring and disseminating space-related information; organizing a series of regional and international training courses, seminars, workshops and technical expert meetings; and promoting greater co-operation between developed and developing countries as well as among developing countries. Programme activities were described in a December report of the United Nations Expert on Space Applications to the Scientific and Technical Sub-Committee.[9]

The Programme received the following fellowship offers in 1988: Austria renewed its annual offer of two fellowships for training in microwave technology; Brazil renewed its offer of 10 fellowships for training and research in remote-sensing technology; the German Democratic Republic offered three fellowships in basic space sciences, satellite geodesy and remote sensing; and the USSR renewed its annual offer of 10 fellowships in geodesy, cartography and aerial photography and established six additional fellowships in the areas of scientific instrument manufacturing, theoretical and experimental astrophysics, systems and methods of space-information processing and studies of Earth rotation and lithosphere-plate movement using space technology. The European Space Agency (ESA) renewed its annual offer of four fellowships in communications engineering, telecommunications, remote-sensing information systems and satellite meteorology.

In 1988, the Programme conducted one seminar, two training courses and two workshops: the United Nations/ESA Training Course on Applications of Remote-Sensing and Agro-Meteorological Data to Drought Assessment and Vegetation Monitoring (Nairobi, Kenya, 6-22 April),[10] the United Nations International Seminar on the Development and Applications of Satellite Communication Systems (Beijing, China, 19-23 September),[11] the United Nations/ESA Workshop on Microwave Remote-Sensing Technology (Bangkok, Thailand, 26-30 September),[12] the thirteenth United Nations/Food and Agriculture Organization of the United Nations (FAO)/United Nations Educational, Scientific and Cultural Organization International Training Course on the Applications of Remote Sensing to Water Resources (Rome, Italy, 12-30 September; Sardinia, Italy, 2-7 October)[13] and the United Nations Workshop on Regional Space Information Systems (Lima, Peru, 24-28 October).[14]

The Committee on outer space[1] noted with satisfaction that a guidebook, *Fellowship and Training Opportunities Offered Within the Framework of the United Nations Space Applications Programme*, had been issued, along with corresponding booklets, for the use of applicants to fellowship programmes and training courses.

As part of its mandated technical advisory services, the Programme provided assistance to the Economic Commission for Africa (ECA) in revising a project document on the establishment of a remote-sensing information programme for Africa, an ECA remote-sensing training centre at Ile Ife, Nigeria, in developing a training curriculum for a postgraduate diploma course, a project in China aimed at establishing a national telecommunications development centre, the Economic and Social Commission for Western Asia in preparing a draft proposal on improving indigenous capabilities in remote-sensing technology by providing education to educators and Member States in the Indian Ocean region and on the Atlantic coast of Africa in preparing proposals on using space technology and information in evaluating, managing and assessing marine and coastal resources.

In 1988, Australia, Austria, Brazil, Canada, China, France, the German Democratic Republic, the Federal Republic of Germany, Italy, Nigeria, Norway, Pakistan, Peru, Thailand, the USSR and the United States provided support to Programme activities.

The United Nations Expert on Space Applications, in a report[15] considered by the Scientific and Technical Sub-Committee in 1988, proposed that the Programme in 1989 continue to focus on implementing UNISPACE-82 recommendations. Activities proposed for 1989 included: long-range fellowship programmes for in-depth education, research and training of space technologists and application specialists in order to stimulate the growth of indigenous capability and an autonomous technological base; provision of technical advisory services on space technology to Member States on request; six additional workshops and training courses; collaboration with the University of Tennessee's Space Institute (United States) and the American Institute for Aeronautics and Astronautics in organizing an international symposium on the roles of developing countries in space commercialization; and updating the directories *Education, Training, Research and Fellowship Opportunities in Space Science and Technology and its Applications* and *Information Systems on Space Science and Technology.* The Committee on outer space[1] recommended that the General Assembly approve the activities proposed for 1989.

Co-ordination in the UN system

The Scientific and Technical Sub-Committee[5] continued to stress the necessity of ensuring continuous and effective consultations and co-ordination in the field of outer space activities among United Nations organizations and of avoiding duplication of activities. The Committee on outer space[1] noted with appreciation the participation in its work and that of its Sub-Committees by United Nations bodies and specialized agencies, and requested that concerned organizations continue to keep it informed of their activities relating to the peaceful uses of outer space. The Committee endorsed the view of the Sub-Committee that the United Nations should continue to seek the support of the United Nations Development Programme (UNDP) and other international funding institutions and that the Secretariat should take note of, and operate within, UNDP funding procedures.

The *Ad Hoc* Inter-Agency Meeting on Outer Space Activities (Geneva, 3-5 October),[16] convened by the Administrative Committee on Co-ordination, found that the existing inter-agency machinery for consultation and co-ordination in applying space technology had worked satisfactorily.

The co-ordination of outer space activities within the United Nations system in 1989, 1990 and future years was discussed in a November report of the Secretary-General,[17] prepared at the request of the Scientific and Technical Sub-Committee. The report covered remote sensing, communications, meteorology, use of space technology for land, maritime and aeronautical mobile services and other activities.

Science and technology aspects

At its twenty-fifth session (New York, 16-26 February),[5] the Scientific and Technical Sub-Committee continued to examine remote sensing of the earth by satellites, including its applications for developing countries, the use of nuclear power sources in outer space and the geostationary orbit, among other issues. In accordance with a 1987 General Assembly request,[2] the Sub-Committee paid special attention to the theme "microgravity experiments in space and their applications".

Remote sensing of the Earth by satellites

The Scientific and Technical Sub-Committee[5] reiterated the view that remote sensing from outer space should be carried out, taking into account the urgent need to assist the developing countries. The Sub-Committee noted the remote-sensing activities of the United Nations Department of Technical Co-operation for Development carried out for the benefit of developing countries, as well as those of FAO, which were applied to agriculture, forestry, rangelands and fisheries. It emphasized the importance of making remote-sensing data available at a reasonable cost and in a timely manner, and noted the continuing programmes of France, the USSR and the United States for remote-sensing satellites and the planned remote-sensing satellite systems of Brazil, Canada, China, India, Japan and ESA.

The Committee on outer space[1] recognized the importance of continuing international efforts to ensure the continuity, compatibility and complementarity of remote-sensing systems. It also recognized the example of international co-operation evidenced by the free distribution of meteorological information, and encouraged all countries and agencies to continue that practice. The Committee endorsed the decision of the Sub-Committee to retain the topic as a priority item on the agenda for the next session.

Nuclear power sources and safety in spacecraft

The Scientific and Technical Sub-Committee reconvened the Working Group on the Use of Nuclear Power Sources in Outer Space, which met in New York from 22 to 25 February.[5] The Group considered the complete dispersal (burn-up) of the fuel of a nuclear reactor versus its intact re-entry. It was noted that complete dispersal might not be possible with certain types of nuclear reactor fuel. The Group also took note of the concept of a nuclear-fuel containment system which would withstand the heat of re-entry, aerodynamic forces and impact with the ground, guaranteeing that no radioactive material would be released to the environment. It stated that the feasibility and safety aspects of the two concepts required further investigation.

The Group considered the possibility that a space object carrying a nuclear power source could collide with a particle of space debris. It noted that the probability of such a collision could become considerable in view of the long orbital lifetime of nuclear power sources and encouraged national studies of the issue. It was of the opinion that, if the core of a nuclear reactor returning to the Earth became flooded, it should be designed in such a way that it would remain sub-critical in all credible scenarios.

The Sub-Committee adopted the Group's report, and the Committee on outer space[1] endorsed the Sub-Committee's recommendations that the topic be retained as a priority item on the 1989 agenda of the Working Group. The Committee also agreed that the Sub-Committee should have more time in 1989 to consider the safe use of nuclear power sources and recommended that the Secretariat take that into account in preparing the provisional agenda.

Technical aspects of the geostationary orbit

In January, the Secretariat issued a study on the physical nature and technical attributes of the geostationary orbit.[18] A geostationary satellite is one that remains above a fixed point on the Earth's surface by maintaining a rotation along the equatorial plane, at an altitude of about 36,000 kilometres, that is synchronous with the Earth's orbit. The study covered scientific aspects of the geostationary orbit, the current occupation of the orbit, space objects crossing the orbit and determination of the position of objects in the orbit. At the end of 1987, there were nearly 300 space objects in or close to the geostationary orbit, the majority of which were inactive. The Sub-Committee took note of the various current and planned satellite communications programmes of Member States and international organizations. The Committee on outer space[1] endorsed the recommendation of the Sub-Committee that it continue consideration of the item at its next session.

Other questions

The Scientific and Technical Sub-Committee[5] heard special technical presentations by China on microgravity science/space experiments, as well as on remote sensing; by the USSR on the Mir space station and life sciences, including space medicine; and by the United States on microgravity experiments in space, manned space flight, remote sensing, the ecosphere-biosphere, planetary exploration, life sciences and astronomy.

On the subject of space transportation programmes, the Sub-Committee noted developments in China, France, India, Japan, the USSR, the United Kingdom, the United States and ESA, and stressed the importance of international co-operation in providing all countries with access to the benefits of space science and technology.

In its consideration of matters relating to life sciences, including space medicine, the Sub-Committee noted that studies of human physiology during manned space flights had led to important advances in medical knowledge, particularly studies of biological rhythms in space in the absence of normal terrestrial environmental rhythms, which had implications for such phenomena as jet-lag. The microgravity conditions of space flight had also been used to study techniques for processing pharmaceutical products and for growing single crystals of protein in order to study their molecular structure, as well as for investigating the effects of microgravity on plants, animals and humans. Studies were also continuing on the use of controlled ecological life-support systems to maintain a habitable environment during long space flights. The Sub-Committee noted that such studies had important potential benefits for all and that efforts should be made to promote international co-operation to enable all countries to benefit from them.

The Committee on Space Research (COSPAR) and the International Astronautical Federation (IAF) presented to the Sub-Committee a progress report on the international geosphere-biosphere (global change) programme. The Sub-Committee noted the importance of assessing global changes in the climate and their impact on life and the important role of space science and technology in that effort. It took particular note of the recent observations of the ozone hole over Antarctica and the need for further studies of it.

On the subject of planetary exploration, the Sub-Committee noted the ongoing work directed towards investigating planets, asteroids and comets and the plans to conduct a detailed mapping of Venus, to probe Jupiter's atmosphere, to observe the polar region of the Sun, to probe the surface of a comet nucleus and ultimately to return samples of the Martian surface to Earth.

In its consideration of matters relating to astronomy, the Sub-Committee noted that the use of astronomical spacecraft for making observations from above the atmosphere had greatly advanced knowledge of the universe by permitting observations to be made in all regions of the electromagnetic spectrum. Studies at infrared, visible, ultraviolet, X-ray and gamma-ray wavelengths had provided new information concerning the evolution of stars, galaxies and the universe as a whole. Satellites were being developed to gather additional information.

The Committee on outer space[1] endorsed the decision of the Sub-Committee to continue consideration of those issues at its next session.

COSPAR and IAF on 16 and 17 February conducted a symposium on microgravity experiments in space and their applications, which had been designated for the special attention of the Sub-Committee in 1988. The Committee on outer space[1] endorsed the Sub-Committee's recommendation that it focus on the theme "Space technology as an instrument for combating environmental problems, particularly those of developing countries" at its 1989 session. The theme would relate to problems such as desertification, deforestation, floods, erosion and pest infestation.

Bulgaria, the German Democratic Republic, Hungary, Sweden and the United States submitted reviews of national and international space activities in 1988[19] to the Committee on outer space. COSPAR submitted a report[20] on the progress of space research in 1987-1988 and IAF[21] reported on highlights in space technology and applications in 1988. They jointly submitted to the Committee a report on environmental effects of space activities.[22]

Legal aspects

The Legal Sub-Committee of the Committee on outer space held its twenty-seventh session at Geneva from 14 to 31 March 1988.[23] It continued to consider the elaboration of draft principles relevant to the use of nuclear power sources in outer space, matters relating to the definition and delimitation of outer space, and ways to ensure the rational and equitable use of the geostationary orbit. It also adopted a new agenda item.

Nuclear power sources in outer space

On 14 March 1988, the Legal Sub-Committee re-established its Working Group on the elaboration of draft principles relevant to the use of nuclear power sources in outer space. The Group had before it a working paper submitted by Canada and two submitted by China.

The Canadian paper proposed seven revised draft principles concerning: (1) the applicability of international law; (2) safety assessment and notification; (3) guidelines and criteria for safe use; (4) notification of re-entry; (5) assistance to States; (6) the responsibility of States; and (7) compensation. The Chinese papers proposed two draft principles concerning the relation with other international treaties and the settlement of disputes.

The Working Group reached a consensus on principle 1, stating that activities involving the use of nuclear power sources in outer space should be carried out in accordance with international law, and added an eighth draft principle, based on China's proposal, on dispute settlement procedures.

The Committee on outer space[1] recommended that the Legal Sub-Committee continue consideration of the item in 1989. It also agreed that the Sub-Committee should be allocated more time to consider the safe use of nuclear power sources, and recommended that the Secretariat

take that into account in preparing the provisional agenda of the Sub-Committee.

Geostationary orbit and definition of outer space

On 14 March, the Legal Sub-Committee re-established its Working Group on matters relating to the definition and delimitation of outer space and to the character and utilization of the geostationary orbit.

The Working Group continued consideration of issues raised in previous years.[24] In order to facilitate further discussion of issues on which converging opinions had emerged, the Chairman convened an open-ended working party of States' representatives ("Friends of the Chairman") for informal consultations. After the conclusion of those consultations, the Chairman presented to the Group a text declaring that all States should be guaranteed equitable access to the geostationary orbit. The text was generally accepted by the "Friends of the Chairman" to be a valid basis for further negotiations in the context of developing a legal régime for the geostationary orbit.

The Committee on outer space[1] recommended that the Legal Sub-Committee continue to consider the item in 1989.

New agenda item

On 29 March, the Legal Sub-Committee adopted by consensus a new agenda item entitled "Consideration of the legal aspects related to the application of the principle that the exploration and utilization of outer space should be carried out for the benefit and in the interests of all States, taking into particular account the needs of developing countries".

The Committee on outer space[1] recommended that the Sub-Committee consider the item in 1989.

GENERAL ASSEMBLY ACTION

On 6 December 1988, on the recommendation of the Special Political Committee, the General Assembly adopted **resolution 43/56** without vote.

International co-operation in the peaceful uses of outer space

The General Assembly,

Recalling its resolution 42/68 of 2 December 1987,

Deeply convinced of the common interest of mankind in promoting the exploration and use of outer space for peaceful purposes and in continuing efforts to extend to all States the benefits derived therefrom, and of the importance of international co-operation in this field, for which the United Nations should continue to provide a focal point,

Reaffirming the importance of international co-operation in developing the rule of law, including the relevant norms of space law and their important role in international co-operation for the exploration and use of outer space for peaceful purposes,

Gravely concerned at the extension of an arms race into outer space,

Recognizing that all States, in particular those with major space capabilities, should contribute actively to the goal of preventing an arms race in outer space as an essential condition for the promotion of international co-operation in the exploration and use of outer space for peaceful purposes,

Aware of the need to increase the benefits of space technology and its applications and to contribute to an orderly growth of space activities favourable to the socio-economic advancement of mankind, in particular the peoples of developing countries,

Taking note of the progress achieved in the further development of peaceful space exploration and application as well as in various national and co-operative space projects, which contribute to international co-operation in this field,

Taking note also of the report of the Secretary-General on the implementation of the recommendations of the Second United Nations Conference on the Exploration and Peaceful Uses of Outer Space,

Having considered the report of the Committee on the Peaceful Uses of Outer Space on the work of its thirty-first session,

1. *Endorses* the report of the Committee on the Peaceful Uses of Outer Space;

2. *Invites* States that have not yet become parties to the international treaties governing the uses of outer space to give consideration to ratifying or acceding to those treaties;

3. *Notes* that the Legal Sub-Committee of the Committee on the Peaceful Uses of Outer Space at its twenty-seventh session, in its working groups, continued its work as mandated by the General Assembly in its resolution 42/68;

4. *Endorses* the recommendations of the Committee on the Peaceful Uses of Outer Space that the Legal Sub-Committee at its twenty-eighth session, taking into account the concerns of all countries, particularly those of developing countries, should:

(*a*) Continue the elaboration of draft principles relevant to the use of nuclear power sources in outer space through its working group;

(*b*) Continue, through its working group, its consideration of matters relating to the definition and delimitation of outer space and to the character and utilization of the geostationary orbit, including consideration of ways and means to ensure the rational and equitable use of the geostationary orbit without prejudice to the role of the International Telecommunication Union;

(*c*) Consider the legal aspects related to the application of the principle that the exploration and utilization of outer space should be carried out for the benefit and in the interests of all States, taking into particular account the needs of developing countries;

5. *Urges* the Legal Sub-Committee at its twenty-eighth session, in the context of paragraph 4 (*c*) above, to pursue, with a view to finalizing, its consideration of the question of the establishment of a working group under this agenda item in order to ensure a satisfactory outcome of the substantive deliberations under this item;

6. *Notes* that the Scientific and Technical Sub-Committee of the Committee on the Peaceful Uses of Outer Space at its twenty-fifth session continued its work as mandated by the General Assembly in its resolution 42/68;

7. *Endorses* the recommendations of the Committee on the Peaceful Uses of Outer Space that the Scientific and Technical Sub-Committee at its twenty-sixth session, taking into account the concerns of all countries, particularly those of developing countries, should:

(*a*) Consider the following items on a priority basis:

(i) United Nations Programme on Space Applications and the co-ordination of space activities within the United Nations system;

(ii) Implementation of the recommendations of the Second United Nations Conference on the Exploration and Peaceful Uses of Outer Space;

(iii) Matters relating to remote sensing of the Earth by satellites including, *inter alia*, applications for developing countries;

(iv) Use of nuclear power sources in outer space;

(*b*) Consider the following items:

(i) Questions relating to space transportation systems and their implications for future activities in space;

(ii) Examination of the physical nature and technical attributes of the geostationary orbit; examination of its utilization and applications, including, *inter alia*, in the field of space communications, as well as other questions relating to space communications developments, taking particular account of the needs and interests of developing countries;

(iii) Matters relating to life sciences, including space medicine;

(iv) Progress in the geosphere-biosphere (global change) programme; the Committee on Space Research and the International Astronautical Federation should be invited to present reports and arrange a special presentation on this subject;

(v) Matters relating to planetary exploration;

(vi) Matters relating to astronomy;

(vii) The theme fixed for the special attention of the 1989 session of the Scientific and Technical Sub-Committee: "Space technology as an instrument for combating environmental problems, particularly those of developing countries" (the theme relates to problems such as desertification, deforestation, floods, erosion and pest infestation that are of particular interest to developing countries); the Committee on Space Research and the International Astronautical Federation should be invited to arrange a symposium, with as wide a participation as possible, to be held during the first week of the Sub-Committee's session, after the adjournment of its meetings, to complement discussions within the Sub-Committee;

8. *Considers*, in the context of paragraph 7 (*a*) (ii) above, that it is particularly urgent to implement the following recommendations:

(*a*) All countries should have the opportunity to use the techniques resulting from medical studies in space;

(*b*) Data banks at the national and regional levels should be strengthened and expanded and an international space information service should be established to function as a centre of co-ordination;

(c) The United Nations should support the creation of adequate training centres at the regional level, linked, whenever possible, to institutions implementing space programmes; necessary funding for the development of such centres should be made available through financial institutions;

(d) The United Nations should organize a fellowship programme through which selected graduates or post-graduates from developing countries should get in-depth, long-term exposure to space technology or applications; it is also desirable to encourage the availability of opportunities for such exposures on other bilateral and multilateral bases outside the United Nations system;

9. *Endorses* the recommendation of the Committee on the Peaceful Uses of Outer Space that the Scientific and Technical Sub-Committee should reconvene, at its twenty-sixth session, the Working Group of the Whole to Evaluate the Implementation of the Recommendations of the Second United Nations Conference on the Exploration and Peaceful Uses of Outer Space, with a view to improving the execution of activities relating to international co-operation, particularly those included within the United Nations Programme on Space Applications, and to proposing concrete steps to increase such co-operation as well as to make it more efficient;

10. *Endorses* the recommendations of the Working Group of the Whole, as endorsed by the Committee on the Peaceful Uses of Outer Space and as contained in paragraphs 4 and 5 of the report of the Working Group of the Whole;

11. *Endorses* the decision of the Committee on the Peaceful Uses of Outer Space to consider at its thirty-second session the advisability of the General Assembly declaring 1992 as international space year, as well as its request that the Scientific and Technical Sub-Committee consider recommendations regarding possible activities that might be undertaken during an international space year, including those of interest for developing countries, taking note of the major contributions of the relevant international organizations planning an international space year;

12. *Decides* that, during the twenty-sixth session of the Scientific and Technical Sub-Committee, the Working Group on the Use of Nuclear Power Sources in Outer Space shall be reconvened to conduct additional work on the basis of its previous reports and of subsequent reports of the Scientific and Technical Sub-Committee;

13. *Endorses* the United Nations Programme on Space Applications for 1989, as proposed to the Committee on the Peaceful Uses of Outer Space by the Expert on Space Applications;

14. *Emphasizes* the urgency and importance of implementing fully the recommendations of the Second United Nations Conference on the Exploration and Peaceful Uses of Outer Space as early as possible;

15. *Reaffirms* its approval of the recommendation of the Conference regarding the establishment and strengthening of regional mechanisms of co-operation and their promotion and creation through the United Nations system;

16. *Expresses its appreciation* to all Governments that have made or expressed their intention to make contributions towards carrying out the recommendations of the Conference;

17. *Invites* all Governments to take effective action for the implementation of the recommendations of the Conference;

18. *Urges* all States, in particular those with major space capabilities, to contribute actively to the goal of preventing an arms race in outer space as an essential condition for the promotion of international co-operation in the exploration and use of outer space for peaceful purposes;

19. *Takes note* of the views expressed and documents circulated during the thirty-first session of the Committee on the Peaceful Uses of Outer Space and during the forty-third session of the General Assembly concerning ways and means of maintaining outer space for peaceful purposes;

20. *Requests* the Committee on the Peaceful Uses of Outer Space to continue to consider, as a matter of priority, ways and means of maintaining outer space for peaceful purposes and to report thereon to the General Assembly at its forty-fourth session;

21. *Requests* the Committee on the Peaceful Uses of Outer Space to consider at its thirty-second session a new agenda item entitled "Spin-off benefits of space technology: review of current status";

22. *Affirms* that the interference that satellite systems to be newly established may cause to systems already registered with the International Telecommunication Union shall not exceed the limits specified in the relevant provision of the Radio Regulations of the Union applicable to space services;

23. *Requests* all organs, organizations and bodies of the United Nations system and other intergovernmental organizations working in the field of outer space or on space-related matters to co-operate in the implementation of the recommendations of the Conference;

24. *Requests* the Secretary-General to report to the General Assembly at its forty-fourth session on the implementation of the recommendations of the Conference;

25. *Requests* the specialized agencies and other international organizations to continue and, where appropriate, enhance their co-operation with the Committee on the Peaceful Uses of Outer Space and to provide it with progress reports on their work relating to the peaceful uses of outer space;

26. *Requests* the Committee on the Peaceful Uses of Outer Space to continue its work, in accordance with the present resolution, to consider, as appropriate, new projects in outer space activities and to submit a report to the General Assembly at its forty-fourth session, including its views on which subjects should be studied in the future.

General Assembly resolution 43/56

6 December 1988   Meeting 71   Adopted without vote

Approved by Special Political Committee (A/43/767) without vote, 24 October (meeting 10); draft by Austria, for Working Group (A/SPC/43/L.5); agenda item 75.
Meeting numbers. GA 43rd session: SPC 6-10; plenary 71.

In **resolution 43/70**, the Assembly called on all States, in particular those with major space capabilities, to contribute to the objective of the peaceful use of outer space and to take immediate measures to prevent an arms race in outer space. It requested the Conference on Disarmament to consider as a priority matter the question of preventing an arms race in outer space.

REFERENCES

[1]A/43/20. [2]YUN 1987, p. 102, GA res. 42/68, 2 Dec. 1987. [3]A/43/562. [4]YUN 1982, p. 162. [5]A/AC.105/409 & Corr.1. [6]YUN 1987, p. 96. [7]A/AC.105/401 & Corr.1 & Add.1-4. [8]A/AC.105/397/Rev.1. [9]A/AC.105/421. [10]A/AC.105/413. [11]A/AC.105/416. [12]A/AC.105/417. [13]A/AC.105/414. [14]A/AC.105/422. [15]A/AC.105/396 & Corr.1. [16]ACC/1988/PG/13 & Corr.1. [17]A/AC.105/415. [18]A/AC.105/404 & Add.1. [19]A/AC.105/428 & Add.1. [20]A/AC.105/425. [21]A/AC.105/426. [22]A/AC.105/420. [23]A/AC.105/411. [24]YUN 1987, p. 101.

Spacecraft launchings

In 1988, seven countries (France, Federal Republic of Germany, India, Japan, Mexico, United States, USSR) and ESA[1] provided information to the United Nations on the launching of objects into orbit or beyond, in accordance with a 1961 General Assembly resolution[2] and article IV of the Convention on Registration of Objects Launched into Outer Space,[3] which had entered into force in 1976.

Convention on registration of launchings

In 1988, Antigua and Barbuda succeeded to and China acceded to the Convention on Registration of Objects Launched into Outer Space,[4] bringing the number of States parties to the Convention to 37.

REFERENCES

[1]ST/SG/SER.E/175, 176 & Add.1-6, 177-195. [2]YUN 1961, p. 35, GA res. 1721 B (XVI), 20 Dec. 1961. [3]YUN 1974, p. 63, GA res. 3235(XXIX), annex, 12 Nov. 1974. [4]*Multilateral Treaties Deposited with the Secretary-General: Status as at 31 December 1988* (ST/LEG/SER.E/7), Sales No. E.89.V.3.

Chapter IV

Other political questions

In 1988, questions related to information, effects of atomic radiation and Antarctica were again on the General Assembly's agenda.

The Assembly requested that the 1988 recommendations of the Committee on Information be implemented within existing resources (resolution 43/60 A) and called on Member States, United Nations organizations and other groups to contribute to the International Programme for the Development of Communication of the United Nations Educational, Scientific and Cultural Organization (43/60 B).

As to atomic radiation, the Assembly requested the United Nations Scientific Committee on the Effects of Atomic Radiation to continue to work to increase knowledge of the levels, effects and risks of ionizing radiation (43/55).

On the issue of Antarctica, the Assembly expressed its conviction that for any minerals régime on Antarctica to be beneficial to all mankind, it should be negotiated with the full participation of all members of the international community; it regretted that, notwithstanding its previous resolutions calling for a moratorium on negotiations without such full participation, the Antarctic Treaty Consultative Parties had proceeded with negotiations and adopted a convention on the regulation of Antarctic mineral resources activities (43/83 A). The Assembly also appealed to those Parties to exclude South Africa from their meetings (43/83 B).

In the ongoing efforts towards finding a solution to the Cyprus question, the Security Council expressed its strong support for the Secretary-General's good offices mission and, on his recommendation, twice extended the mandate of the United Nations Peace-keeping Force in Cyprus.

During 1988, the Security Council held a total of 55 meetings and adopted 20 resolutions. The Assembly resumed and concluded its forty-second session and held the major part of its forty-third session, with 152 items on its agenda. It also held its fifteenth special session, devoted to disarmament.

The Assembly requested continued co-operation between the United Nations and the Organization of the Islamic Conference (43/2) and the League of Arab States (43/3). It also invited the Agency for the Prohibition of Nuclear Weapons in Latin America and the Caribbean to participate in its work in the capacity of observer (43/6).

As there were no new admissions to the United Nations during 1988, its membership remained at 159.

Information

The public information activities of the United Nations continued to focus on two broad objectives: publicizing the Organization's goals and work, and enhancing the information capabilities of developing countries. Those activities were carried out by the Department of Public Information (DPI) of the Secretariat, the United Nations Educational, Scientific and Cultural Organization (UNESCO) and the Joint United Nations Information Committee (JUNIC). Information policies and activities were considered by the General Assembly's Committee on Information at its tenth session (New York, 27 June–13 July, 8 and 9 September). In its report to the Assembly,[1] the Committee submitted 20 draft recommendations, with proposed amendments, most of which related to the operations of DPI. The Assembly acted on those recommendations in **resolution 43/60 A**.

Mass communication

At its 1988 session, the Committee on Information focused on the establishment of a new, more just and more effective world information and communication order, examined the public information policies and activities of the United Nations in the light of the evolution of international relations, and evaluated the efforts made and progress achieved by the United Nations system in the field of information and communication.

The Committee recommended, *inter alia*, that the United Nations system and developed countries be urged to co-operate with the developing countries to strengthen their information and communication infrastructures and promote their access to advanced communication technology. It also recommended that DPI strengthen its co-operation with the Broadcasting Organization of Non-Aligned Countries, the News Agencies Pool of Non-Aligned Countries and its economic information project (Eco-Pool), and the news agencies of developing countries.

Proposed new world
information and communication order

The Committee on Information recommended that all countries and the United Nations system co-operate in establishing a new world information and communication order, based on the free circulation and wider and better balanced dissemination of information, guaranteeing diversity of sources and access to information and, in particular, recognizing the need to change the dependent status of developing countries in the area of information.

The Committee also recommended that the mass media be encouraged to give wider coverage to the efforts of the international community towards global development and the efforts of developing countries to achieve economic, social and cultural progress.

International Programme for the
Development of Communication

Pursuant to a 1987 General Assembly resolution,[2] the Director-General of UNESCO reported on two issues:[3] implementation of the International Programme for the Development of Communication (IPDC)—a project aimed at helping developing countries to build their communication infrastructure—and the social, economic and cultural effects of the accelerated development of communication technologies.

At its ninth session (Paris, 2-8 February 1988), the IPDC Intergovernmental Council approved contributions from the IPDC Special Account for 55 projects, including 24 current ones that required additional funding. Three of the projects were interregional, 16 regional and 36 national.

Africa received allocations of $570,000; Asia and the Pacific, $475,000; Latin America and the Caribbean, $450,000; the Arab States, $350,000; and interregional projects, $110,000.

Among the projects in Africa were editorial training at the Pan African News Agency, computerization of Cameroon News and the launching of a rural radio network in Guinea. Projects in Latin America and the Caribbean included the modernization of television training facilities at the Caribbean Institute of Mass Communication, the promotion of exchanges and improvement of audio-visual production in the region, and the consolidation and development of the Latin American and Caribbean Broadcasting Union. Asia and the Pacific received allocations for, among other things, a community broadcasting development project in Tonga, press development and the training of women in communication for nutrition and health. The Arab States received allocations for

the Khalifa Broadcasting Training Institute in Yemen, the higher institute of journalism in Morocco and the acquisition of mobile units for the production of films and video materials in Egypt, among others.

Interregional activities included skills acquisition in engineering, planning and management for the development of broadcasting and the creation of an interregional network of women journalists.

During the year, UNESCO continued its collaborative research into the impact of new communication technologies. Thirty interdisciplinary studies of such technologies and their impact were in progress in all regions of the world. The studies, which were co-ordinated by research institutes or non-governmental organizations, included an assessment of the impact of direct broadcasting satellites in the Maghreb region of Africa and in various Asian countries, popular media and the new technologies in the Caribbean and the impact of new technologies on the endogenous cultures of Africa.

GENERAL ASSEMBLY ACTION

On 6 December, acting on the recommendation of the Special Political Committee, the General Assembly adopted **resolution 43/60 B** by recorded vote.

The General Assembly,

Recalling its resolutions 34/181 and 34/182 of 18 December 1979, 35/201 of 16 December 1980, 36/149 A of 16 December 1981, 37/94 A and B of 10 December 1982, 38/82 A of 15 December 1983, 39/98 A and B of 14 December 1984, 40/164 A and B of 16 December 1985, 41/68 A and B of 3 December 1986 and 42/162 A and B of 8 December 1987,

Recalling the relevant provisions of the final documents of the first Conference of the Ministers of Information of Non-Aligned Countries, held at Jakarta from 26 to 30 January 1984, and of the Second Conference, held at Harare from 10 to 12 June 1987, the Declarations of the Seventh and Eighth Conferences of Heads of State or Government of Non-Aligned Countries held at New Delhi from 7 to 12 March 1983, and at Harare from 1 to 6 September 1986, and the Final Political Declarations adopted by the Conferences of Ministers for Foreign Affairs of Non-Aligned Countries, held at Luanda from 4 to 7 September 1985 and at Nicosia from 7 to 10 September 1988,

Recalling the relevant resolutions adopted by the Assembly of Heads of State and Government of the Organization of African Unity at its eighteenth ordinary session, held at Nairobi from 24 to 27 June 1981, and the Conference of Ministers of Information of States members of the Organization of African Unity at its third ordinary session, held at Addis Ababa from 27 to 30 March 1985, and at its first extraordinary session, held at Cairo from 20 to 25 November 1985, especially those encouraging regional co-operation in the field of information,

Recalling the relevant provisions of the Final Act of the Conference on Security and Co-operation in Europe, signed at Helsinki on 1 August 1975, and those of the Concluding Document of the meeting of representatives of the participating States of the Conference on Security and Co-operation in Europe, held at Madrid from 11 November 1980 to 9 September 1983,

Recalling article 19 of the Universal Declaration of Human Rights, which provides that everyone has the right to freedom of opinion and expression and that this right includes freedom to hold opinions without interference and to seek, receive and impart information and ideas through any media and regardless of frontiers, and article 29, which stipulates that these rights and freedoms may in no case be exercised contrary to the purposes and principles of the United Nations,

Recalling also the relevant provisions of the Declaration on the Preparation of Societies for Life in Peace,

Conscious that, in order progressively to remedy existing imbalances, it is essential to strengthen and intensify the development of infrastructure, networks and resources in the communications field and thus encourage a free flow and a wider and better balanced dissemination of information,

Emphasizing its full support for the International Programme for the Development of Communication of the United Nations Educational, Scientific and Cultural Organization, which constitutes an essential instrument for the development of human and material resources and communication infrastructures in the developing countries,

Recognizing the central role of the United Nations Educational, Scientific and Cultural Organization in the field of information and communications within its mandate, as well as the progress accomplished by that organization in that field,

1. *Takes note* of the report of the Director-General of the United Nations Educational, Scientific and Cultural Organization;

2. *Recalls* the Declaration on Fundamental Principles concerning the Contribution of the Mass Media to Strengthening Peace and International Understanding, to the Promotion of Human Rights and to Countering Racialism, *Apartheid* and Incitement to War, adopted on 28 November 1978 by the General Conference of the United Nations Educational, Scientific and Cultural Organization;

3. *Considers* that the International Programme for the Development of Communication of the United Nations Educational, Scientific and Cultural Organization represents a significant step towards the gradual elimination of existing imbalances in the field of information and communications, and welcomes the decisions adopted by the Intergovernmental Council of the Programme at its ninth session, held in Paris from 2 to 8 February 1988;

4. *Expresses its appreciation* to all Member States that have made or pledged a contribution towards the implementation of the International Programme for the Development of Communication;

5. *Again calls upon* Member States and organizations and bodies of the United Nations system as well as other international governmental and non-governmental organizations and concerned public and private enterprises to respond to the appeals of the Director-General of the United Nations Educational, Scientific and Cultural Organization to contribute to the International Programme for the Development of Communication by making

financial resources available as well as staff, equipment, technologies and training resources;

6. *Recalls* resolution 4/22 of 27 October 1980 concerning the reduction of telecommunication tariffs for news exchanges, adopted by the General Conference of the United Nations Educational, Scientific and Cultural Organization, and takes note of the efforts made by Member States in this respect;

7. *Reaffirms* its support for the United Nations Educational, Scientific and Cultural Organization, its Constitution and the ideals reflected in it;

8. *Invites* the Director-General of the United Nations Educational, Scientific and Cultural Organization to continue his efforts in the information and communication field and to submit to the General Assembly, at its forty-fourth session, a detailed report on the application of the International Programme for the Development of Communication as well as on the social, economic and cultural effects of the accelerated development of communication technologies;

9. *Reaffirms* the ongoing efforts of the United Nations Educational, Scientific and Cultural Organization, which retains the central role in the field of information, gradually to eliminate existing imbalances, particularly with respect to the development of infrastructures and production capacities, and to encourage a free flow and wider and better balanced dissemination of information with a view to the establishment of a new world information and communication order, seen as an evolving and continuous process, in accordance with the relevant consensus resolutions of the United Nations Educational, Scientific and Cultural Organization.

General Assembly resolution 43/60 B

6 December 1988   Meeting 71   141-1-11 (recorded vote)

Approved by Special Political Committee (A/43/902) by recorded vote (111-1-11), 23 November (meeting 33); draft by Tunisia, for Group of 77 (A/SPC/43/L.13); agenda item 79.

Meeting numbers. GA 43rd session: SPC 14-20, 24, 33; plenary 71.

Recorded vote in Assembly as follows:

In favour: Afghanistan, Algeria, Angola, Antigua and Barbuda, Argentina, Austria, Bahamas, Bahrain, Bangladesh, Barbados, Belize, Benin, Bhutan, Bolivia, Botswana, Brazil, Brunei Darussalam, Bulgaria, Burkina Faso, Burma, Burundi, Byelorussian SSR, Cameroon, Cape Verde, Central African Republic, Chad, Chile, China, Colombia, Comoros, Costa Rica, Côte d'Ivoire, Cuba, Cyprus, Czechoslovakia, Democratic Kampuchea, Democratic Yemen, Djibouti, Dominican Republic, Ecuador, Egypt, El Salvador, Ethiopia, Fiji, Finland, France, Gabon, Gambia, German Democratic Republic, Ghana, Greece, Grenada, Guatemala, Guinea, Guinea-Bissau, Guyana, Haiti, Honduras, Hungary, India, Indonesia, Iran, Iraq, Ireland, Italy, Jamaica, Jordan, Kenya, Kuwait, Lao People's Democratic Republic, Lebanon, Lesotho, Liberia, Libyan Arab Jamahiriya, Luxembourg, Madagascar, Malawi, Malaysia, Maldives, Mali, Malta, Mauritania, Mauritius, Mexico, Mongolia, Morocco, Mozambique, Nepal, New Zealand, Nicaragua, Niger, Nigeria, Oman, Pakistan, Panama, Papua New Guinea, Paraguay, Peru, Philippines, Poland, Portugal, Qatar, Romania, Rwanda, Saint Kitts and Nevis, Saint Lucia, Saint Vincent and the Grenadines, Samoa, Sao Tome and Principe, Saudi Arabia, Senegal, Seychelles, Sierra Leone, Singapore, Solomon Islands, Somalia, Spain, Sri Lanka, Sudan, Swaziland, Sweden, Syrian Arab Republic, Thailand, Togo, Trinidad and Tobago, Tunisia, Turkey, Uganda, Ukrainian SSR, USSR, United Arab Emirates, United Republic of Tanzania, Uruguay, Vanuatu, Venezuela, Viet Nam, Yemen, Yugoslavia, Zaire, Zambia, Zimbabwe.

Against: United States.

Abstaining: Australia, Belgium, Canada, Denmark, Germany, Federal Republic of, Iceland, Israel, Japan, Netherlands, Norway, United Kingdom.

UN public information

The Committee on Information recommended that the United Nations system, through its information services, co-operate in promoting a more comprehensive and realistic image of the activities and potential of the United Nations. Other recom- mendations dealt with co-operation by DPI with the News Agencies Pool of Non-Aligned Countries and with UNESCO, the dissemination by DPI of infor- mation concerning United Nations activities regard- ing human rights, the right to freedom of opinion and expression under the 1948 Universal Decla- ration of Human Rights,[4] the serious economic situation in Africa and other global economic prob- lems, the World Disarmament Campaign, the Mid- dle East situation, *apartheid*, the illegal occupation of Namibia and peace-keeping operations. The Com- mittee made a number of other recommendations concerning the organization and operation of DPI.

DPI activities

During 1988, DPI, through its radio, visual and publications services and information centres (see below under respective headings for details), con- tinued to implement United Nations information activities.

In September 1988,[5] the Secretary-General re- ported on questions relating to information, including implementation, mainly by DPI, of the 1987 recom- mendations of the Committee on Information, as endorsed by the General Assembly.[6]

In accordance with requests by the Assembly, DPI developed a multi-media public information programme, in co-operation with the United Na- tions Centre for Human Rights, focusing on the fortieth anniversary of the 1948 Universal Decla- ration. A feasibility study was completed on the con- solidation and co-ordination of all United Nations public information activities, with DPI as the focal point.

In line with the major priority assigned to Africa's economic crisis, DPI's bimonthly publication *African Recovery* continued to report on major developments and key issues. DPI worked closely with the Non- Governmental Liaison Service of the United Na- tions Office at Geneva in its major "Africa Four Years On" conference (April 1988). It also supported the Non-Governmental Liaison Service at Head- quarters in its outreach activities, including the "Africa Focus" project in 10 United States and Cana- dian cities.

Information material on the external debt of de- veloping countries was being prepared in 1988 and several television series on development issues were initiated.

The ninth annual training programme for broad- casters and journalists from developing countries was held (20 September–28 October 1988) to pro- vide training and briefings on major issues before the United Nations to 16 young journalists.

DPI also continued promoting United Nations activities for disarmament—most of them focused

on the fifteenth special session of the General As- sembly, the third special session devoted to disarm- ament (see PART ONE, Chapter II)—through press releases, lectures, briefings, film screenings and ex- hibits.

Activities were also undertaken in connection with the campaign against *apartheid* and the strug- gle for the independence of Namibia.

Systematic monitoring and evaluation of activi- ties continued to be emphasized. Those functions were to be carried out by the Programme Evalua- tion and Communications Research Unit of the Division for Committee Liaison and Administra- tive Services in the reorganized DPI. In addition, a modest function seeking to generate data on pub- lic opinion trends about the United Nations was to be added for the purpose of providing a relia- ble information base.

DPI provided coverage of all United Nations in- tergovernmental meetings in both English and French and issued daily summaries of meetings.

With regard to the 1987 recommendation that the Secretary-General continue to intensify his ef- forts to secure adequate resources for continuing the *World Newspaper Supplement*, the Secretary- General said that the principle held by the agen- cies supporting the project was that it should be self-supporting and the participating major newspapers were continuing to find ways towards that end.

The policies and activities of DPI during 1988 were reviewed by the Committee on Information. It had before it, among others, reports on: the en- hancement of co-operation with Member States in DPI's short-wave broadcasts;[7] improvement in the distribution of taped radio programmes and curtailment of certain DPI radio programmes (see below);[8] the reassessment of the effectiveness of the *UN Chronicle;*[9] and DPI's progress in recruit- ing nationals from developing countries to achieve a more balanced geographical distribution of its staff.[10]

In April,[11] the Secretary-General reported on action taken by DPI on 1986 recommendations of the Committee for Programme and Co-ordination (CPC).[12] The restructuring of DPI, he said, should provide a good opportunity to implement those recommendations. The recent decision on the clarification of the terms "redisseminator" and "target audience" would no doubt facilitate the solving of a number of other problems associated with the implementation of activities, monitoring, evaluation, feedback mechanisms, dissemination etc. In June 1988,[13] CPC took note of the report.

Radio and Visual Services Division

The Committee on Information in 1988 recom- mended that the Secretary-General be requested to strengthen and expand the Middle East/Arabic Unit of the DPI Radio and Visual Services Division as the producer of Arabic television and radio programmes, and to ensure full programming by the Caribbean Unit, including implementation of the provisions of a 1983 Assembly resolution,[14] by which the Assembly had requested the introduction of full programming in French/Creole and limited programming in Dutch/Papiamento.

The Secretariat reported on the results of steps taken by DPI to improve the distribution of taped radio programmes and resume the ones that had been curtailed. As at June 1988, DPI produced 31 different regular taped programmes in 16 languages: Arabic, Bengali, Chinese, English, French, Hindi, Indonesean, Portuguese, Russian, Sesotho, Spanish, Swahili, Tswana, Turkish, Xhosa and Zulu. An average of approximately 2,500 tapes/cassettes were distributed each week.

Taped radio programmes were distributed by airmail and pouch by the newly created Dissemination Division of DPI to more than 1,460 recipients and users in some 161 countries and Territories. Feedback concerning the utilization of those programmes was provided through contacts with broadcasting organizations, listeners' mail, reports from United Nations information centres (UNICs) and information provided by delegations and staff members.

Among measures taken by DPI to resume curtailed radio programmes in some non-official languages was collaboration with a number of national and local broadcasting organizations in adapting United Nations programmes.

UN information centres and services

In his September 1988 report on information questions,[5] the Secretary-General also dealt with the strengthening of the United Nations information centres and services. He stated that, with the establishment of regional desks in the Information Centres Division at Headquarters, it would be possible for DPI to evaluate and manage more accurately and effectively the activities of its 67 operational UNICs and services. Further, as a result of the introduction of office automation for the UNICs by modernizing communications equipment, 25 UNICs were being linked with Headquarters through electronic mail. In addition, DPI had introduced a new system of rotation of UNIC directors and Headquarters officials, with clear procedures and guidelines for the appointment of the former, including the designation of qualified female candidates to those posts. Media profiles were being developed for all countries in which UNICs were operating, to help identify the countries that could benefit from DPI's training programmes in broadcasting.

In June,[13] CPC took note of an April report of JUNIC on the policies for distributing material through UNICs.[15]

Co-ordination in the UN system

The Joint United Nations Information Committee, the inter-agency co-ordinating body for information activities in the United Nations system, held its fifteenth session at Geneva (29-31 March 1988).[16] It considered the current public image of the United Nations system and recognized the need for agreed projects that would positively enhance that image. It further discussed inter-agency projects, such as the publications *Development Forum* and *Africa Recovery Report;* the work of the Non-Governmental Liaison Services at Geneva and in New York, which played a particularly important role in development education; audio-visual information dissemination; and international expositions, years, decades and other special events.

JUNIC stressed the need for information departments to avoid overlapping and duplication of work. Also, system-wide priority issues, such as the theme of Africa economic recovery and development and the full and equal participation of women in development, called for mutually supporting activities and co-operation in the field of information.

GENERAL ASSEMBLY ACTION

On 6 December, on the recommendation of the Special Political Committee, the General Assembly adopted **resolution 43/60 A** by recorded vote.

The General Assembly,

Recalling its previous resolutions on questions relating to information,

Reaffirming the mandate given to the Committee on Information by the General Assembly in its resolution 34/182 of 18 December 1979,

Taking note of the report of the Secretary-General on questions relating to information,

Encouraging the Secretary-General to continue necessary action in order to increase the efficiency and effectiveness of the Department of Public Information of the Secretariat, with particular emphasis on securing a co-ordinated approach to priority issues before the Organization,

Taking note of the comprehensive report of the Committee on Information, which served as an important basis and stimulated further deliberations,

1. *Urges* the full implementation of the following recommendations:

(1) All countries, the United Nations system as a whole and all others concerned should co-operate in the establishment of a new world information and communication order, seen as an evolving and continuous process, and based, *inter alia*, on the free circulation and wider and better balanced dissemination of information, guaranteeing diversity of sources of information and free access to information and, in particular, the urgent need to change the dependent status of the developing countries in the field of information and communication, as the principle of sovereign equality among nations extends also to this field, and intended also to strengthen peace and international understanding, enabling all persons to participate effectively

in political, economic, social and cultural life and promoting human rights, understanding and friendship among all nations. The ongoing efforts of the United Nations Educational, Scientific and Cultural Organization, which retains the central role in this field, to eliminate gradually the existing imbalances in the field of information and communication and to encourage a free flow and a wider and better balanced dissemination of information in accordance with the relevant resolutions of that organization, adopted by consensus, should be reaffirmed;

(2) Considering the important role that the media worldwide can freely play, particularly under the present situation, it is recommended that:

(a) The mass media should be encouraged to give wider coverage to the efforts of the international community towards global development and, in particular, the efforts of the developing countries to achieve economic, social and cultural progress;

(b) The United Nations system as a whole should co-operate in a concerted manner, through its information services, in promoting a more comprehensive and realistic image of the activities and potential of the United Nations system in all its endeavours, in accordance with the principles and purposes of the Charter of the United Nations and General Assembly resolutions, with particular emphasis on the right to self-determination and the elimination of all forms of racism, aggression, foreign domination and occupation, in order to create a climate of confidence, the strengthening of multilateralism and the promotion of the development activities in the United Nations system;

(c) All countries should be urged to extend assistance to journalists for the free and effective performance of their professional tasks and to ensure respect for their physical integrity;

(3) Considering the existing imbalances in the international distribution of news, particularly that affecting the developing countries, it is recommended that urgent attention should be given to the elimination of existing imbalances by, *inter alia*, diversifying the sources of information and respecting the interests, aspirations and socio-cultural values of all peoples;

(4) The United Nations system as a whole, particularly the United Nations Educational, Scientific and Cultural Organization, and the developed countries should be urged to co-operate in a concerted manner with the developing countries towards strengthening the information and communication infrastructures in the latter countries and promoting their access to advanced communications technology, in accordance with the priorities attached to such areas by the developing countries, with a view to enabling them to develop their own information and communications policies freely and independently and in the light of their social and cultural values, taking into account the principle of freedom of the press and information. In this regard, support should be provided for the continuation and strengthening of practical training programmes for broadcasters and journalists from developing countries;

(5) Note should be taken with appreciation of regional efforts, especially among the developing countries, as well as co-operation between developed and developing countries to develop further the media infrastructure in the developing countries, especially in the areas of training and dissemination of information, with a view to encouraging a free flow and a wider and better balanced dissemination of information;

(6) Article 19 of the Universal Declaration of Human Rights, which provides that everyone has the right to freedom of opinion and expression and that this right includes freedom to hold opinions without interference and to seek, receive and impart information and ideas through any media and regardless of frontiers, and article 29, which stipulates that these rights and freedoms may in no case be exercised contrary to the purposes and principles of the United Nations, should be recalled;

(7) The relevant paragraphs of General Assembly resolution 59(I) of 14 December 1946, in which the Assembly stated, *inter alia*, that freedom of information is a fundamental human right, must be reiterated;

(8) The primary role that the General Assembly is to play in elaborating, co-ordinating and harmonizing United Nations policies and activities in the field of information having been reaffirmed, the Secretary-General is requested to ensure that the activities of the Department of Public Information, as the focal point of the public information tasks of the United Nations, are strengthened and improved, keeping in view the purposes and principles of the Charter of the United Nations and the priority areas such as those stated in section III, paragraph 1, of General Assembly resolution 35/201 of 16 December 1980 and other pertinent resolutions of the Assembly and the recommendations of the Committee on Information, so as to ensure an objective and more coherent coverage of, as well as better knowledge about, the United Nations and its work. The Secretary-General is further requested to ensure that the Department of Public Information:

(a) Co-operate more regularly with the United Nations Educational, Scientific and Cultural Organization, especially at the working level, with a view to maximizing the contributions of the Department to the efforts of that organization in further promoting the attainment of a free flow and a wider and better balanced dissemination of information;

(b) Strengthen its co-operation with the Movement of Non-Aligned Countries, with the News Agencies Pool of Non-Aligned Countries, with the Eco-Pool of the News Agencies of Non-Aligned Countries and with the Broadcasting Organization of Non-Aligned Countries, as well as with intergovernmental and regional organizations and with the news agencies of the developing countries. In this regard, the Department of Public Information should monitor, as appropriate, important meetings of the Movement, in particular its summit meetings, as well as those of intergovernmental and regional organizations, as this constitutes a concrete step towards the promotion of a wider and better balanced dissemination of information;

(c) Continue to disseminate information about the United Nations activities in the field of human rights, decolonization and the elimination of all forms of racial discrimination and foreign occupation;

(d) Give the widest possible dissemination of information pertaining to acute world economic prob-

lems in general and, in particular, to the severe economic difficulties of the least developed countries and
the need for strengthening the international economic
co-operation aimed at resolving the external debt
problems of developing countries;

(e) Do its utmost to disseminate widely and to
publicize the United Nations Programme of Action
for African Economic Recovery and Development
1986-1990 and the tremendous efforts of the African
countries towards recovery and development, as well
as the positive response by the international community to alleviate the serious economic situation prevailing in Africa;

(f) Continue adequate coverage of the World Disarmament Campaign;

(g) Disseminate adequately and accurately, in
conformity with relevant United Nations resolutions
on the question of Palestine and the situation in the
Middle East, information relating to the struggle of
the Palestinian people, particularly its current uprising, and of the Arab population in the Palestinian and
other Arab territories occupied by Israel since 1967,
including Jerusalem, for the attainment and exercise
of their inalienable national rights, and report thereon
to the Committee on Information at its substantive
session in 1989;

(h) Strengthen its activities and the dissemination
of information on the policies and practices of *apartheid*, giving due attention to the unilateral measures
and official censorship imposed on the local and international media with regard to all aspects of this
issue, and report to the Committee on Information
at its substantive session in 1989;

(i) Further intensify its efforts in order to alert
world public opinion to the illegal occupation of Namibia and continue to disseminate adequately and accurately, with the full assistance of the United Nations
Council for Namibia and the United Nations system
as a whole, information relating to the struggle of the
oppressed people of Namibia for self-determination,
national independence and freedom as well as to the
need for the full and speedy implementation of the
United Nations plan for the independence of Namibia;

(j) Continue adequate coverage of the United Nations activities pertaining to the situation in the Non-
Self-Governing Territories;

(k) Further cover adequately and with impartiality the activities of all United Nations peace-keeping
operations, in view of the paramount importance of
such operations for the maintenance of international
peace and security;

(l) Continue to disseminate information concerning United Nations resolutions on terrorism in all its
forms, including General Assembly resolutions 40/61
of 9 December 1985 and 42/159 of 7 December 1987;

(m) Strengthen its information programmes relating to women and their role in society;

(n) Strengthen its coverage of the efforts made by
the United Nations system and Member States in their
campaign against illicit trafficking of narcotics and
drug abuse;

(9) In the light of the present international situation, the Department of Public Information should
continue its efforts to promote an informed understanding of the work and purposes of the United Nations system among the peoples of the world and to

strengthen the image of the United Nations system
as a whole. In this connection, the Secretary-General
is requested to ensure that the Department of Public
Information:

(a) Continue to maintain consistent editorial independence and accuracy in reporting for all material it produces, taking necessary measures to ensure
that its output contains objective and equitable information about issues before the Organization, reflecting divergent opinions where they occur;

(b) In the context of the review of its role, performance and method of work, continue to explore
the feasibility of applying modern technologies for the
collection, production, storage, dissemination and distribution of information materials, including the use
of satellite facilities, and report to the Committee on
Information at its substantive session in 1989 with regard to the effects of the application of such technologies on prevailing arrangements;

(c) Consider expanding the programme of telephone news bulletins that are paid for by its users;

(d) Continue its co-operation with those countries
which have expressed readiness to assist the United
Nations in resuming the short-wave broadcasts
through their respective national networks free of
charge and encourage expansion of this type of co-
operation with those developed and developing countries with recognized capabilities in this field;

(e) Take adequate measures to resume the taped
radio programmes, which it temporarily curtailed,
bearing in mind the objective of their effective utilization and maximum audience impact and report on
this matter to the General Assembly at its forty-fourth
session;

(f) Continue its annual training programme for
broadcasters and journalists from developing
countries;

(g) Extend all assistance to educational institutions of Member States and continue to organize seminars for educators and education policy makers;

(h) Guarantee daily coverage of all United Nations meetings through issuance of daily press releases
in the working languages, reflecting the views of all
delegations with accuracy and objectivity. It should
also continue to co-operate closely with and provide
assistance to members of the United Nations Correspondents Association, taking into account their
needs and requirements, especially in the area of press
releases, which provide them with the necessary raw
material for adequate reporting, and through press
conferences and briefings;

(i) Use the official languages of the United Nations adequately in its documents and audio-visual
documentation and make balanced use of the two
working languages of the Secretariat;

(j) Ensure timely distribution of its material to
subscribers and to United Nations information
centres;

(10) In view of the proposals of the Department
of Public Information to eliminate certain programmes, the Secretary-General is requested to stop
any action on the proposed elimination and to submit a comprehensive report on the matter to the
General Assembly at its forty-fourth session;

(11) The Secretary-General is urged to continue
his efforts to secure a sound and stable financial basis

for the Department of Public Information to produce its publications on time, particularly *Development Forum, The United Nations Yearbook*, the *UN Chronicle*, the *Africa Recovery Report* and the *World Newspaper Supplement*, and to ensure that they retain their editorial policy of intellectual independence and reflect adequately the United Nations activities, and to submit a report thereon to the Committee on Information at its 1989 substantive session;

(12) The unique function of the United Nations information centres, recognized as one of the most important means of disseminating information about the United Nations among the peoples of the world, should be enhanced. In this regard, United Nations information centres should intensify direct and systematic communication exchange with local media information and educational institutions and nongovernmental organizations recognized by the Economic and Social Council in a mutually beneficial way and arrange for constant evaluation of their activities in this regard. Every effort should be made to establish close co-ordination with other field offices of the United Nations system, particularly those of the United Nations Development Programme, in order to avoid duplication of work, taking into account the functional autonomy of the United Nations information centres. The Department of Public Information should ensure open and unhindered access by all people to all United Nations information centres and to all materials distributed through the centres. It is also urged to accelerate the process of linking the remaining United Nations information centres that have not been linked with electronic mail;

(13) In recognition of the need for co-ordinating information activities of the United Nations system and of the important role that the Joint United Nations Information Committee plays in this regard, the Department of Public Information is encouraged to continue its active participation in the work of that Committee;

(14) It is recognized that the free distribution of materials is necessary in the public information activities of the United Nations. However, as demands increase and whenever it is desirable and possible, the Department of Public Information should actively encourage the sale of its materials;

(15) The Secretary-General is requested to ensure that the reorganization and restructuring of the Department of Public Information strengthen and improve the output of the mandated programmes and activities of the Department, taking into account the need for equitable geographical distribution of posts in the Department;

(16) The Secretary-General is requested to take effective steps to increase in the Department of Public Information the representation of underrepresented developing countries and of other underrepresented groups of countries, especially at the senior levels, in conformity with the relevant provisions of the Charter of the United Nations, and to submit a report to the Committee on Information at its substantive session in 1989;

(17) The Secretary-General is requested to ensure full programme delivery by the Caribbean Unit, including implementation of the provisions of General Assembly resolution 38/82 B of 15 December 1983,

and to submit a report to the Committee on Information at its substantive session in 1989 on the measures taken in the implementation of the present recommendation;

(18) The Secretary-General is requested to maintain the functions of the Middle East/Arabic Unit as the producer of Arabic television and radio programmes, to strengthen and expand this Unit to enable it to function in an effective manner and to report to the Committee on Information at its substantive session in 1989 on the implementation of the present recommendation;

(19) The United Nations system, particularly the United Nations Educational, Scientific and Cultural Organization, should aim at providing all possible support and assistance to the developing countries with due regard to their interests and needs in the field of information and to action already taken within the United Nations system, including, in particular:

(a) Development of human resources as indispensable for the improvement of information and communication systems in developing countries and support for the continuation and strengthening of practical training programmes, such as those already operating under both public and private auspices throughout the developing world;

(b) Creation of conditions that will gradually enable the developing countries to produce, by using their own resources, the communications technology suited to their national needs, as well as the necessary programme material, specifically for radio and television broadcasting;

(c) Assistance in establishing and promoting telecommunication links at subregional, regional and interregional levels, especially among developing countries;

(20) In this regard, full support for the International Programme for the Development of Communication of the United Nations Educational, Scientific and Cultural Organization, which constitutes an important step in the development of these infrastructures, should always be provided;

2. *Requests* that the provisions of the present resolution relating to the activities of the Department of Public Information be implemented within existing resources, taking into account the priorities set by the General Assembly;

3. *Requests* the Secretary-General to report to the Committee on Information at its substantive session in 1989 on the implementation of the present resolution;

4. *Also requests* the Secretary-General to report to the General Assembly at its forty-fourth session on the implementation of the present resolution;

5. *Takes note with appreciation* of the conclusions and recommendations of the Committee for Programme and Co-ordination and requests the Secretary-General to submit a detailed report to the Committee on Information at its eleventh session on the implementation of General Assembly resolution 41/213 of 19 December 1986, bearing in mind resolution 42/211 of 21 December 1987;

6. *Requests* the Committee on Information to report to the General Assembly at its forty-fourth session;

7. *Decides* to include in the provisional agenda of its forty-fourth session the item entitled "Questions relating to information".

General Assembly resolution 43/60 A

6 December 1988   Meeting 71   128-8-16 (recorded vote)

Approved by Special Political Committee (A/43/902) by recorded vote (100-8-15), 23 November (meeting 33); draft by Tunisia, for Group of 77 (A/SPC/43/L.12); agenda item 79.
Financial implications. S-G, A/SPC/43/L.25.
Meeting numbers. GA 43rd session: SPC 14-20, 24, 33; plenary 71.

Recorded vote in Assembly as follows:

In favour: Afghanistan, Algeria, Angola, Antigua and Barbuda, Argentina, Bahamas, Bahrain, Bangladesh, Barbados, Belize, Benin, Bhutan, Bolivia, Botswana, Brazil, Brunei Darussalam, Bulgaria, Burkina Faso, Burma, Burundi, Byelorussian SSR, Cameroon, Cape Verde, Central African Republic, Chad, Chile, China, Colombia, Comoros, Costa Rica, Côte d'Ivoire, Cuba, Cyprus, Czechoslovakia, Democratic Kampuchea, Democratic Yemen, Djibouti, Dominican Republic, Ecuador, Egypt, El Salvador, Ethiopia, Fiji, Gabon, Gambia, German Democratic Republic, Ghana, Grenada, Guatemala, Guinea, Guinea-Bissau, Guyana, Honduras, Hungary, India, Indonesia, Iran, Iraq, Ireland, Jamaica, Jordan, Kenya, Kuwait, Lao People's Democratic Republic, Lebanon, Lesotho, Liberia, Libyan Arab Jamahiriya, Madagascar, Malawi, Malaysia, Maldives, Mali, Mauritania, Mauritius, Mexico, Mongolia, Morocco, Mozambique, Nepal, Nicaragua, Niger, Nigeria, Oman, Pakistan, Panama, Papua New Guinea, Paraguay, Peru, Philippines, Poland, Qatar, Romania, Rwanda, Saint Kitts and Nevis, Saint Lucia, Saint Vincent and the Grenadines, Samoa, Sao Tome and Principe, Saudi Arabia, Senegal, Seychelles, Sierra Leone, Singapore, Solomon Islands, Somalia, Sri Lanka, Sudan, Swaziland, Syrian Arab Republic, Thailand, Togo, Trinidad and Tobago, Tunisia, Uganda, Ukrainian SSR, USSR, United Arab Emirates, United Republic of Tanzania, Uruguay, Vanuatu, Venezuela, Viet Nam, Yemen, Yugoslavia, Zaire, Zambia, Zimbabwe.

Against: Belgium, Canada, Germany, Federal Republic of, Israel, Japan, Netherlands, United Kingdom, United States.

Abstaining: Australia, Austria, Denmark, Finland, France, Greece, Iceland, Italy, Luxembourg, Malta, New Zealand, Norway, Portugal, Spain, Sweden, Turkey.

The Assembly adopted a number of other resolutions and a decision relating to information issues.

In **resolution 43/26 D**, it requested the Secretary-General to direct DPI to assist the United Nations Council for Namibia in implementing its information dissemination programme. In **resolution 43/46**, it requested him to continue to give widespread publicity to the work of the United Nations in decolonization.

In **resolution 43/50 F**, the Assembly appealed to Governments, intergovernmental and non-governmental organizations, information media and individuals to co-operate with the Centre against *Apartheid* and DPI in disseminating information on the deteriorating situation in South Africa. It requested, in **resolution 43/175 B**, that the Secretary-General ensure the continued co-operation of DPI in covering the question of Palestine and, in **resolution 43/175 C**, requested DPI to continue its special information programme on the Palestine question in 1989, with emphasis on public opinion in Europe and North America.

The Assembly, in **resolution 43/76 C**, noted that the Secretary-General had instructed UNICs to give wide publicity to the World Disarmament Campaign, adapting as far as possible United Nations information materials to local languages.

In **decision 43/410**, the Assembly requested the Secretary-General, through DPI, to continue an intensified campaign to publicize the facts concerning military activities and arrangements in colonial Territories impeding the implementation of the 1960 Declaration on the Granting of Independence to Colonial Countries and Peoples.[17]

REFERENCES

[1]A/43/21. [2]YUN 1987, p. 344, GA res. 42/162 B, 8 Dec. 1987. [3]A/43/670. [4]YUN 1948-49, p. 535, GA res. 217 A (III), 10 Dec. 1948. [5]A/43/639. [6]YUN 1987, p. 346, GA res. 42/162 A, 8 Dec. 1987. [7]A/AC.198/1988/3. [8]A/AC.198/1988/6. [9]A/AC.198/1988/7. [10]A/AC.198/1988/5. [11]E/AC.51/1988/11. [12]YUN 1986, p. 367. [13]A/43/16. [14]YUN 1983, p. 366, GA res. 38/82 B, 15 Dec. 1983. [15]E/AC.51/1988/12. [16]ACC/1988/8. [17]YUN 1960, p. 49, GA res. 1514(XV), 14 Dec. 1960.

Radiation effects

The United Nations Scientific Committee on the Effects of Atomic Radiation held its thirty-seventh session in 1988 (Vienna, 6-17 June), continuing its work on the levels, effects and risks of ionizing radiation from all sources, as requested by the General Assembly in 1987.[1] The report, including scientific annexes, presented to the Assembly in 1988,[2] was the tenth substantive report prepared by the Committee since its establishment in 1955;[3] its preparation took place from the thirty-first (1982) to thirty-seventh sessions.

The report contained a summary of the main conclusions reached by the Committee regarding radiation levels and doses received by the world's population, and expected to be received in the future, from various natural and man-made sources of radiation, and an assessment of the risks of induction of various types of harm by radiation, both in the short and the long term. The report also dealt with methods of comparing exposures, regarding which the Committee concluded that it preferred to follow its practice of comparing collective dose commitments from the main radiation sources rather than estimated detriments.

GENERAL ASSEMBLY ACTION

On 6 December, on the recommendation of the Special Political Committee, the General Assembly adopted **resolution 43/55** without vote.

Effects of atomic radiation
The General Assembly,

Recalling its resolution 913(X) of 3 December 1955, by which it established the United Nations Scientific Committee on the Effects of Atomic Radiation, and its subsequent resolutions on the subject, including resolution 42/67 of 2 December 1987, in which, *inter alia*, it requested the Scientific Committee to continue its work,

Taking note with appreciation of the report of the United Nations Scientific Committee on the Effects of Atomic Radiation,

Reaffirming the desirability of the Scientific Committee continuing its work,

Concerned about the potentially harmful effects on present and future generations, resulting from the levels of radiation to which man is exposed,

Conscious of the continued need to examine and compile information about atomic and ionizing radiation and to analyse its effects on man and his environment,

Bearing in mind the decision of the Scientific Committee to submit, as soon as the relevant studies are completed, shorter reports with supporting scientific documents on the specialized topics mentioned by the Committee,

1. *Commends* the United Nations Scientific Committee on the Effects of Atomic Radiation for the valuable contribution it has been making in the course of the past thirty-three years, since its inception, to wider knowledge and understanding of the levels, effects and risks of atomic radiation and for fulfilling its original mandate with scientific authority and independence of judgement;

2. *Notes with satisfaction* the continued and growing scientific co-operation between the Scientific Committee and the United Nations Environment Programme;

3. *Requests* the Scientific Committee to continue its work, including its important co-ordinating activities, to increase knowledge of the levels, effects and risks of ionizing radiation from all sources;

4. *Endorses* the Scientific Committee's intentions and plans for its future activities of scientific review and assessment on behalf of the General Assembly;

5. *Requests* the Scientific Committee to continue at its next session the review of the important problems in the field of radiation and to report thereon to the General Assembly at its forty-fourth session;

6. *Requests* the United Nations Environment Programme to continue providing support for the effective conduct of the Scientific Committee's work and for the dissemination of its findings to the General Assembly, the scientific community and the public;

7. *Expresses its appreciation* for the assistance rendered to the Scientific Committee by Member States, the specialized agencies, the International Atomic Energy Agency and non-governmental organizations, and invites them to increase their co-operation in this field;

8. *Invites* Member States, the organizations of the United Nations system and non-governmental organizations concerned to provide further relevant data about doses, effects and risks from various sources of radiation, which would greatly help in the preparation of the Scientific Committee's future reports to the General Assembly.

General Assembly resolution 43/55

6 December 1988   Meeting 71   Adopted without vote

Approved by Special Political Committee (A/43/754) without vote, 13 October (meeting 4); 25-nation draft (A/SPC/43/L.2); agenda item 74.

Sponsors: Argentina, Australia, Austria, Bangladesh, Canada, China, Costa Rica, Czechoslovakia, Denmark, Egypt, France, Germany, Federal Republic of, India, Indonesia, Japan, Netherlands, New Zealand, Nigeria, Poland, Swaziland, Sweden, USSR, United Kingdom, United States, Uruguay.

Meeting numbers. GA 43rd session: SPC 3, 4; plenary 71.

REFERENCES

[1]YUN 1987, p. 356, GA res. 42/67, 2 Dec. 1987. [2]A/43/45. [3]YUN 1955, p. 21, GA res. 913(X), 3 Dec. 1955.

Antarctica

Minerals régime

Pursuant to a 1987 General Assembly resolution,[1] the Secretary-General submitted in August 1988 a report on an eventual minerals régime on Antarctica.[2] In 1987, the Assembly had reaffirmed that any such régime should take fully into account the interests of the international community and had called on the Antarctic Treaty Consultative Parties—Argentina, Australia, Belgium, Brazil, Chile, China, France, German Democratic Republic, Germany, Federal Republic of, India, Italy, Japan, New Zealand, Norway, Poland, South Africa, USSR, United Kingdom, United States, Uruguay[a]—to impose a moratorium on the negotiations to establish a minerals régime until all members of the international community could participate fully in such negotiations.

The Secretary-General said he had received a letter from Australia[3] conveying a statement by the Chairman of the Antarctic Treaty Special Consultative Meeting on Antarctic Mineral Resources (Wellington, New Zealand, 2 May–2 June), regarding the adoption on 2 June of a convention to regulate mineral resources activities in Antarctica. According to the Chairman, the aim of the convention was to fill a significant gap in the 1959 Antarctic Treaty system. The convention prohibited exploration for and extraction of mineral resources unless a rigorous procedure for permission to do so was followed. It provided for an advisory committee of scientific and technical experts to undertake comprehensive environmental evaluations at all stages of the decision-making process, and for a system of protected areas so that parts of Antarctica of special sensitivity could be placed off limits for minerals activity.

The Secretary-General further reported that, on 18 August, New Zealand had transmitted an authenticated copy of the Final Act of the Fourth Antarctic Treaty Consultative Meeting on Antarctic Mineral Resources.

On 8 June, he had received a statement[4] by Antigua and Barbuda, Bangladesh, Brunei Darussalam, Cameroon, the Congo, Ghana, Indonesia, Kenya, Malaysia, Nepal, Nigeria, Oman, Pakistan, Rwanda, Sri Lanka, the Sudan, Uganda, Zambia and Zimbabwe, expressing the utmost regret and deep concern about the adoption of the convention.

Concluding, the Secretary-General said he was not in a position to provide any evaluation of the negotiations of the Antarctic Treaty Consultative

[a]Spain and Sweden became Consultative Parties in September 1988.

Parties as he was not in receipt of an invitation to their meetings.

GENERAL ASSEMBLY ACTION

On 7 December, on the recommendation of the First Committee, the General Assembly adopted **resolution 43/83 A** by roll-call vote.

The General Assembly,

Having considered the item entitled "Question of Antarctica",

Recalling its resolutions 38/77 of 15 December 1983, 39/152 of 17 December 1984, 40/156 A and B of 16 December 1985, 41/88 A and B of 4 December 1986 and 42/46 A and B of 30 November 1987,

Recalling also the relevant paragraphs of the Political Declaration adopted by the Eighth Conference of Heads of State or Government of Non-Aligned Countries, held at Harare from 1 to 6 September 1986, and the resolution on Antarctica adopted by the Council of Ministers of the Organization of African Unity at its forty-second ordinary session, held at Addis Ababa from 10 to 17 July 1985, as well as the decision of the Council of Ministers of the League of Arab States meeting at Tunis on 17 and 18 September 1986 and resolution 25/5-P(IS) adopted by the Fifth Islamic Summit Conference of the Organization of the Islamic Conference, held at Kuwait from 26 to 29 January 1987,

Taking into account the debates on this item held since its thirty-eighth session,

Welcoming the increasing awareness of and interest in Antarctica shown by the international community,

Convinced of the advantages to the whole of mankind of a better knowledge of Antarctica,

Affirming its conviction that, in the interest of all mankind, Antarctica should continue forever to be used exclusively for peaceful purposes and that it should not become the scene or object of international discord,

Reaffirming the principle that the international community is entitled to information covering all aspects of Antarctica and that the United Nations should be made the repository for all such information in accordance with General Assembly resolutions 41/88 A and 42/46 B,

Conscious of the particular significance of Antarctica to the international community in terms, *inter alia*, of international peace and security, environment, its effects on global climatic conditions, economy and scientific research,

Taking into account all aspects pertaining to all areas covered by the Antarctic Treaty system,

Taking note with appreciation of the reports of the Secretary-General on the question of Antarctica,

Reaffirming that the management, exploration, exploitation and use of Antarctica should be conducted in accordance with the purposes and principles of the Charter of the United Nations and in the interest of maintaining international peace and security and of promoting international co-operation for the benefit of mankind as a whole,

1. *Expresses its conviction* that any minerals régime on Antarctica, in order to be of benefit to all mankind, should be negotiated with the full participation of all members of the international community;

2. *Further expresses its deep regret* that the Antarctic Treaty Consultative Parties have proceeded with negotiations and adopted on 2 June 1988 a convention on the regulation of Antarctic mineral resource activities, notwithstanding General Assembly resolutions 41/88 B and 42/46 B, calling for the imposition of a moratorium on negotiations to establish a minerals régime until such time as all members of the international community can fully participate in such negotiations;

3. *Reiterates its call* upon the Antarctic Treaty Consultative Parties to invite the Secretary-General or his representative to all meetings of the Treaty parties, including their consultative meetings;

4. *Requests* the Secretary-General to submit a report on his evaluations thereon to the General Assembly at its forty-fourth session;

5. *Urges* all States Members of the United Nations to co-operate with the Secretary-General and to continue consultations on all aspects relating to Antarctica;

6. *Decides* to include in the provisional agenda of its forty-fourth session the item entitled "Question of Antarctica".

General Assembly resolution 43/83 A

7 December 1988   Meeting 73   100-0-6 (roll-call vote)

Approved by First Committee (A/43/911 & Corr.1) by roll-call vote (77-0-7), 22 November (meeting 46); 21-nation draft (A/C.1/43/L.82); agenda item 70.
Sponsors: Antigua and Barbuda, Bangladesh, Brunei Darussalam, Cameroon, Congo, Ghana, Indonesia, Kenya, Malaysia, Mali, Nepal, Nigeria, Oman, Pakistan, Rwanda, Sri Lanka, Sudan, Uganda, Zaire, Zambia, Zimbabwe.
Meeting numbers. GA 43rd session: 1st Committee 44-46; plenary 73.

Roll-call vote in Assembly as follows:

In favour: Albania, Algeria, Angola, Antigua and Barbuda, Bahamas, Bahrain, Bangladesh, Barbados, Belize, Benin, Bhutan, Bolivia, Botswana, Brunei Darussalam, Burkina Faso, Burma, Burundi, Cameroon, Cape Verde, Central African Republic, Chad, Comoros, Congo, Costa Rica, Côte d'Ivoire, Cyprus, Democratic Kampuchea, Dominican Republic, Egypt, Ethiopia, Gabon, Gambia, Ghana, Guatemala, Guinea, Guyana, Haiti, Honduras, Indonesia, Iran, Iraq, Jamaica, Jordan, Kenya, Kuwait, Lebanon, Liberia, Libyan Arab Jamahiriya, Madagascar, Malawi, Malaysia, Maldives, Mali, Malta, Mauritania, Mauritius, Mexico, Morocco, Mozambique, Nepal, Niger, Nigeria, Oman, Pakistan, Panama, Paraguay, Philippines, Qatar, Romania, Rwanda, Saint Kitts and Nevis, Saint Lucia, Saint Vincent and the Grenadines, Sao Tome and Principe, Saudi Arabia, Senegal, Seychelles, Sierra Leone, Singapore, Solomon Islands, Somalia, Sri Lanka, Sudan, Suriname, Swaziland, Syrian Arab Republic, Thailand, Togo, Trinidad and Tobago, Tunisia, Uganda, United Arab Emirates, United Republic of Tanzania, Vanuatu, Yemen, Yugoslavia, Zaire, Zambia, Zimbabwe.

Against: None.

Abstaining: China, Fiji, Ireland, Portugal, Turkey, Venezuela.

During the roll-call vote in plenary, the following 46 States announced that they were not participating: Afghanistan, Argentina, Australia, Austria, Belgium, Brazil, Bulgaria, Byelorussian SSR, Canada, Chile, Colombia, Cuba, Czechoslovakia, Denmark, Ecuador, El Salvador, Finland, France, German Democratic Republic, Germany, Federal Republic of, Greece, Hungary, Iceland, India, Israel, Italy, Japan, Lao People's Democratic Republic, Lesotho, Luxembourg, Mongolia, Netherlands, New Zealand, Nicaragua, Norway, Papua New Guinea, Peru, Poland, Spain, Sweden, Ukrainian SSR, USSR, United Kingdom, United States, Uruguay, Viet Nam.

In the Committee, 40 States made such an announcement.

Participation of South Africa

Also in August 1988,[5] the Secretary-General submitted a report in response to a 1987 resolution,[6] by which the Assembly had viewed with concern the continuing participation of South Africa in the meetings of the Antarctic Treaty Consultative Parties and appealed to the Parties to take urgent measures to exclude South Africa from such meetings. In a May 1988 reply to a note verbale of the Secretary-General, Australia, on behalf of the Parties, recalled an earlier note on the subject reproduced in a 1987 report of the Secretary-General.[7] That note, Australia stated, continued fully to reflect the Parties' position.

GENERAL ASSEMBLY ACTION

On 7 December, on the recommendation of the First Committee, the General Assembly adopted **resolution 43/83 B** by roll-call vote.

The General Assembly,

Recalling its resolution 42/46 A of 30 November 1987,

Having considered the item entitled "Question of Antarctica",

Noting with regret that the racist *apartheid* régime of South Africa, which has been suspended from participation in the General Assembly of the United Nations, has continued to participate in the meetings of the Antarctic Treaty Consultative Parties,

Recalling the resolution on Antarctica adopted by the Council of Ministers of the Organization of African Unity at its forty-second ordinary session, held at Addis Ababa from 10 to 17 July 1985,

Recalling also the relevant paragraphs of the Political Declaration adopted by the Eighth Conference of Heads of State or Government of Non-Aligned Countries, held at Harare from 1 to 6 September 1986,

Recalling further that the Antarctic Treaty is, by its terms, intended to further the purposes and principles embodied in the Charter of the United Nations,

Noting that the policy of *apartheid* practised by the racist minority régime of South Africa, which has been universally condemned, constitutes a threat to regional and international peace and security,

1. *Views with concern* the continuing participation of the *apartheid* régime of South Africa in the meetings of the Antarctic Treaty Consultative Parties;

2. *Appeals once again* to the Antarctic Treaty Consultative Parties to take urgent measures to exclude the racist *apartheid* régime of South Africa from participation in the meetings of the Consultative Parties at the earliest possible date;

3. *Invites* the States parties to the Antarctic Treaty to inform the Secretary-General on the actions taken regarding the provisions of the present resolution;

4. *Requests* the Secretary-General to submit a report in this regard to the General Assembly at its forty-fourth session;

5. *Decides* to include in the provisional agenda of its forty-fourth session the item entitled "Question of Antarctica".

General Assembly resolution 43/83 B

7 December 1988   Meeting 73   111-0-10 (roll-call vote)

Approved by First Committee (A/43/911 & Corr.1) by roll-call vote (89-0-5), 22 November (meeting 46); draft by Zaire, for African Group (A/C.1/43/L.83); agenda item 70.

Meeting numbers. GA 43rd session: 1st Committee 44-46; plenary 73.

Roll-call vote in Assembly as follows:

In favour: Afghanistan, Albania, Algeria, Angola, Antigua and Barbuda, Argentina, Bahamas, Bahrain, Bangladesh, Barbados, Belize, Benin, Bhutan, Bolivia, Brazil, Brunei Darussalam, Burkina Faso, Burma, Burundi, Cameroon, Cape Verde, Central African Republic, Chad, China, Colombia, Comoros, Congo, Costa Rica, Cuba, Cyprus, Democratic Kampuchea, Democratic Yemen, Djibouti, Dominican Republic, Ecuador, Egypt, El Salvador, Ethiopia, Fiji, Gabon, Gambia, German Democratic Republic, Ghana, Guatemala, Guinea, Guyana, Haiti, Honduras, India, Indonesia, Iran, Iraq, Jamaica, Jordan, Kenya, Kuwait, Lao People's Democratic Republic, Lebanon, Liberia, Libyan Arab Jamahiriya, Madagascar, Malaysia, Maldives, Mali, Mauritania, Mexico, Mongolia, Morocco, Mozambique, Nepal, Nicaragua, Niger, Nigeria, Oman, Pakistan, Panama, Peru, Philippines, Qatar, Romania, Rwanda, Saint Kitts and Nevis, Saint Lucia, Saint Vincent and the Grenadines, Sao Tome and Principe, Saudi Arabia, Senegal, Seychelles, Sierra Leone, Singapore, Solomon Islands, Somalia, Sri Lanka, Sudan, Suriname, Syrian Arab Republic, Thailand, Togo, Trinidad and Tobago, Tunisia, Uganda, United Arab Emirates, United Republic of Tanzania, Vanuatu, Venezuela, Viet Nam, Yemen, Yugoslavia, Zaire, Zambia, Zimbabwe.

Against: None.

Abstaining: Botswana, Côte d'Ivoire, Ireland, Lesotho, Malawi, Malta, Mauritius, Paraguay, Portugal, Swaziland.

During the roll-call vote in plenary, the following 33 States announced that they were not participating: Australia, Austria, Belgium, Bulgaria, Byelorussian SSR, Canada, Chile, Czechoslovakia, Denmark, Equatorial Guinea, Finland, France, Germany, Federal Republic of, Greece, Hungary, Iceland, Israel, Italy, Japan, Luxembourg, Netherlands, New Zealand, Norway, Papua New Guinea, Poland, Spain, Sweden, Turkey, Ukrainian SSR, USSR, United Kingdom, United States, Uruguay.

In the Committee, 31 States made such an announcement.

REFERENCES

[1]YUN 1987, p. 358, GA res. 42/46 B, 30 Nov. 1987. [2]A/43/564. [3]A/43/434. [4]A/43/396. [5]A/43/565 & Add.1. [6]YUN 1987, p. 358, GA res. 42/46 A, 30 Nov. 1987. [7]*Ibid.*, p. 357.

Cyprus question

Throughout 1988, the Secretary-General continued his mission of good offices concerning Cyprus, entrusted to him by the Security Council. In February, Oscar Camilión assumed his functions as the Secretary-General's Special Representative in Cyprus. The Secretary-General appealed to all concerned to take stock of the situation afresh and to make positive gestures that would create favourable conditions for the resumption of negotiations. In bringing the leaders of the two sides together for talks, he conveyed to them through his Special Representative certain specific suggestions regarding an early meeting at which they would agree to hold urgent non-binding discussions with a view to achieving, by an agreed date, an overall settlement on the basis of 1977[1] and 1979[2] high-level agreements. Negotiations between the two sides took place on various occasions during the year.

The Security Council twice extended the mandate of the United Nations Peace-keeping Force in Cyprus (UNFICYP)—on 15 June (resolution 614(1988)) and 15 December (resolution 625(1988))—which continued its peace-keeping and humanitarian tasks.

Although the question of Cyprus was included in the agenda of the forty-third (1988) General Assembly session (**decisions 42/465** of 19 September and **43/402** of 23 September), it was not discussed. However, in suspending the session on 22 December, the Assembly retained the question on its agenda (**decision 43/459**).

Cyprus and Turkey addressed communications to the Secretary-General on various aspects of the situation throughout the year. Those from Turkey forwarded letters from the Turkish Cypriot community signed by Rauf R. Denktas as ''President of the Turkish Republic of Northern Cyprus'', or by Ozer Koray as the ''representative'' of that ''Republic''.

In February, George Vassiliou was elected President of Cyprus. In a pre-election statement,[3] Cyprus brought to the Secretary-General's attention what it called ominous developments, saying that it had requested United Nations assistance to help facilitate the temporary transfer of Greek Cypriots from the occupied areas so as to allow them to vote. However, the pseudo Minister for Foreign Affairs of the illegal entity in the Turkish-occupied area had stated that the Greek Cypriots there were considered citizens of the Turkish Republic of Northern Cyprus and would not be authorized to vote. In reply,[4] Mr. Koray said that no applicant was refused permission to cross to the South; in fact, the 70 Greek Cypriots and Maronites who had applied did cross during the two weeks of the elections.

In a statement of 13 February,[5] Mr. Denktas stressed that the elections were for the head of the Greek Cypriot Administration in southern Cyprus only and not the ''President of Cyprus'' as a whole. He expressed the hope that the new leader would adopt a constructive and realistic posture towards a negotiated solution on the basis of a binational, bizonal federation, as previously agreed and as also envisaged by the Secretary-General's 1986 draft framework agreement.[6] On 22 February,[7] Mr. Denktas, reiterating that Mr. Vassiliou had been elected solely by Greek Cypriots and was their leader only, invited him for informal talks. Repeating his invitation on 26 February for a meeting on equal terms,[8] Mr. Denktas underlined that the stumbling-block to a settlement in Cyprus was the false title of ''the

Republic'' or ''Government of Cyprus'', which, he said, had been usurped for 24 years.

Report of the Secretary-General (May/June). In his report to the Security Council on the United Nations operation in Cyprus from 1 December 1987 to 31 May 1988,[9] the Secretary-General summarized UNFICYP activities and his good offices mission and reported on the situation regarding the maintenance of the *status quo*.

He noted that during the period under review, UNFICYP continued to monitor the military forces of both sides and there was no significant change in its estimate of the number of Turkish soldiers in Cyprus. Although the Turkish force's tank replacement programme was complete, most of the tanks that were to have been withdrawn were still on the island. In addition, while there was no apparent increase in the manpower of the Cyprus National Guard, its modernization programme had continued with the acquisition of some new armoured vehicles, a few anti-tank helicopters and a limited air-defence capability. During the reporting period, there was no change in the situation in Varosha (a community near the port of Famagusta, just inside the Turkish and Turkish Cypriot forces' cease-fire line), where students continued to be accommodated in hotels inside the fenced area and no date for their departure had been obtained. The presence of settlers from Turkey in the northern part of the island continued to be a matter of great concern to the Cyprus Government. The Turkish Government and the Turkish Cypriot side had not changed their position in that regard, and the Secretary-General urged that, in view of the sensitivity of the issue and its possible bearing on future negotiations, nothing should be done to change the demographic composition of the island.

The Secretary-General stated that a serious threat to the *status quo* resulted from a decision in mid-April by the Turkish Cypriot side to change existing practice for the control of persons passing between the northern and southern parts of the island. The new practice required that certain categories of Cypriots and foreign nationals using the Ledra Palace crossing point should present passports for stamping. The Secretary-General shared the assessment of the Cyprus Government, which had protested that the new practice purported to establish procedures at the crossing point appropriate to that of an international frontier and was in violation of a 1983 Security Council resolution,[10] and urged Mr. Denktas to restore the *status quo* without delay.

Cyprus again complained about the desecration of churches in the north and provided photographs of two specific sites. The Secretary-General considered it the responsibility of those concerned to ensure that no desecration or destruction took place.

Cyprus also protested the changing of place-names in the northern part, which the Turkish Cypriot side said had resulted from the need to bring place-names into conformity with modern Turkish usage.

It further protested the decision of the Turkish Cypriot side to expropriate Greek Cypriot–owned immovable property in the island's northern part and to transfer it to Turkish Cypriot individuals and organizations. Responding to specific complaints regarding property in the Kyrenia and Famagusta districts, the Turkish Cypriot side restated its earlier position that, in accordance with existing procedures, no actual transfer of ownership had taken place. The Turkish Cypriot authorities also refuted as not correct allegations about distribution to individuals of property listed as archaeological sites in the Famagusta area.

The United Nations High Commissioner for Refugees (UNHCR) continued to help the displaced and the needy on the island. The Secretary-General noted that, during the period under review, the Committee on Missing Persons in Cyprus held four sessions, including 16 meetings, and focused its attention on interviewing Greek Cypriot and Turkish Cypriot witnesses concerning those cases before it. The Committee decided to undertake in future a general review of the investigations and reports concerning cases presented to it so far.

The Secretary-General reported that, in view of both tension and hope prevailing on the island, the need for UNFICYP to continue to fulfil its indispensable role was even more important, and recommended that the Security Council extend the Force's mandate for a further six months. Referring to that recommendation, he indicated that Cyprus, Greece and the United Kingdom had agreed, while Turkey, supporting the position of the Turkish Cypriot side, had indicated that the draft resolution (see below) was unacceptable as a basis for UNFICYP's extension and that its position on the issue would be explained before the Council.[11]

SECURITY COUNCIL ACTION (June)

The Security Council met on 15 June to consider the Secretary-General's report and recommendation to extend UNFICYP's mandate. Cyprus, Greece and Turkey were invited, at their request, to participate in the discussion without the right to vote. The Council also extended an invitation under rule 39 of its provisional rules of procedure[b] to Ozer Koray.

On that day, the Council unanimously adopted **resolution 614(1988)**.

The Security Council,

Taking note of the report of the Secretary-General on the United Nations operation in Cyprus of 31 May 1988,

Noting the recommendation by the Secretary-General that the Security Council extend the stationing of the United Nations Peace-keeping Force in Cyprus for a further period of six months,

Noting also that the Government of Cyprus has agreed that in view of the prevailing conditions in the island it is necessary to keep the Force in Cyprus beyond 15 June 1988,

Reaffirming the provisions of resolution 186(1964) of 4 March 1964 and other relevant resolutions,

1. *Extends once more* the stationing in Cyprus of the United Nations Peace-keeping Force established under resolution 186(1964) for a further period ending on 15 December 1988;

2. *Requests* the Secretary-General to continue his mission of good offices, to keep the Security Council informed of the progress made and to submit a report on the implementation of the present resolution by 30 November 1988;

3. *Calls upon* all the parties concerned to continue to co-operate with the Force on the basis of the present mandate.

Security Council resolution 614(1988)

15 June 1988   Meeting 2816   Adopted unanimously

Draft prepared in consultations among Council members (S/19936).

Mr. Koray said the Turkish Cypriot side rejected *in toto* the resolution as a basis for extending UNFICYP's mandate; it could not accept any resolution which purported to endorse the Greek Cypriot side as the so-called "Government of the Republic of Cyprus". The position of the Turkish Cypriot side continued to be that the principle, scope, modalities and procedures of co-operation of the Turkish Republic of Northern Cyprus and UNFICYP should be based only on decisions to be taken solely by the Government of that Republic.

Supporting that position, Turkey said the resolution contained a number of controversial elements to which it had fundamental objections and it could not consent to a renewal of UNFICYP's mandate on that basis.

Report of the Secretary-General (November/December). Reporting to the Security Council on the United Nations operation in Cyprus from 1 June to 30 November 1988,[12] the Secretary-General updated information on UNFICYP activities, his good offices mission and the question of the maintenance of the *status quo.*

At his invitation, the leaders of the two sides met the Secretary-General in Geneva on 24 August and expressed their readiness to seek a negotiated solution, acknowledging that that would require a determined and sustained effort by both sides, as well as the creation of an atmosphere of mutual confidence. They agreed to meet without any pre-

[b]Rule 39 of the Council's provisional rules of procedure states: "The Security Council may invite members of the Secretariat or other persons, whom it considers competent for the purpose, to supply it with information or to give other assistance in examining matters within its competence."

conditions and to attempt to achieve by 1 June 1989 a negotiated settlement of all aspects of the Cyprus question. They met in private in Cyprus, together with the Secretary-General's Special Representative, between 16 September and 7 November. Those talks enabled them to explain to each other their views and concerns about a wide range of key issues.

The Secretary-General met with the two leaders again on 22 and 23 November in New York to review the outcome of the first round of talks, which had proved helpful in building a good working relationship and in clarifying many of the issues and difficulties facing the two sides, and to decide on how to proceed. Both sides agreed with his suggestion that the next round of talks, to begin at Nicosia on 19 December 1988, be devoted to developing, on a non-committal basis, a wide range of options for resolving the issues, taking into account the interests and concerns of both sides. They also accepted his invitation for a meeting with him again in March 1989 to launch the next phase of talks.

The Secretary-General noted, however, that while it was the first time in the past quarter of a century that the leaders of both sides had committed themselves to a personal and sustained effort to reach an overall settlement and to try to achieve that by a specific date, their positions on the main issues remained far apart. The positive rapport created between the two leaders and their personal commitment to the negotiating process was an auspicious beginning, which could be sustained only if both sides found a way to tackle the difficult issues confronting them. It was vital that during the coming months the parties manifested the necessary will to break free from their long-held positions and seek solutions that would reconcile the interests of each community. It was important that all Cypriots should feel that the talks represented a joint effort towards a common goal.

The Secretary-General said that both sides had expressed concern on several occasions about the strength of military forces on the island. UNFICYP, for its part, remained concerned about the level of forces in Cyprus and continued to monitor them. During the period under review, Greek Cypriots held numerous demonstrations close to the United Nations buffer zone, forcing their way inside the zone on several occasions. Those events were marked by violence against UNFICYP personnel, leading to dangerous situations in two areas of the buffer zone in Nicosia. Cyprus had since assured the Force Commander that it would in future take whatever steps were necessary to ensure respect for the *status quo* in the buffer zone.

The Secretary-General noted that in Varosha the situation regarding the students had not changed and efforts were still being made to secure a date for their departure. With regard to the question relating to procedures at the Ledra Palace crossing point, the situation prevailing before his May/June report had been restored.

As in his previous report, the Secretary-General, referring to his recommendation that the Council extend UNFICYP's mandate for a further six months, indicated that Cyprus, Greece and the United Kingdom had agreed, while Turkey, supporting the position of the Turkish Cypriot side, indicated that the draft resolution (see below) was unacceptable as a basis for UNFICYP's extension and that its position on the issue would be explained before the Council.[(13)]

The Committee on Missing Persons in Cyprus continued its interviews of witnesses and pursued its activities with a view to reaching conclusions on the cases before it as soon as possible.

SECURITY COUNCIL ACTION (December)

The Security Council met on 15 December to consider the Secretary-General's report and recommendation to extend the UNFICYP mandate. Cyprus, Greece and Turkey were invited, at their request, to participate without the right to vote. Ozer Koray was also invited to participate under rule 39 of the provisional rules of procedure.[b]

The Council unanimously adopted **resolution 625(1988)**.

The Security Council,

Taking note of the report of the Secretary-General on the United Nations operation in Cyprus of 30 November 1988,

Noting the recommendation by the Secretary-General that the Security Council extend the stationing of the United Nations Peace-keeping Force in Cyprus for a further period of six months,

Noting also that the Government of Cyprus has agreed that in view of the prevailing conditions in the island it is necessary to keep the Force in Cyprus beyond 15 December 1988,

Reaffirming the provisions of resolution 186(1964) of 4 March 1964 and other relevant resolutions,

1. *Extends once more* the stationing in Cyprus of the United Nations Peace-keeping Force established under resolution 186(1964) for a further period ending on 15 June 1989;

2. *Requests* the Secretary-General to continue his mission of good offices, to keep the Security Council informed of the progress made and to submit a report on the implementation of the present resolution by 31 May 1989;

3. *Calls upon* all the parties concerned to continue to co-operate with the Force on the basis of the present mandate.

Security Council resolution 625(1988)

15 December 1988   Meeting 2833   Adopted unanimously

Draft prepared in consultations among Council members (S/20324).

Mr. Koray, for the Turkish Cypriot side, voiced reservations on the resolution similar to those expressed in June (see above). Turkey also objected to the text for reasons similar to those stated previously. Following consultations in the Council, the President concluded the meeting with the following statement:[14]

"The members of the Security Council expressed their support for the effort launched on 24 August 1988 by the Secretary-General in the context of the mission of good offices in Cyprus. They welcomed the readiness of the two parties to seek negotiated settlement of all aspects of the Cyprus problem by 1 June 1989.

"They called upon all parties for full co-operation with the Secretary-General in ensuring the success of the process currently under way."

Peace-keeping and humanitarian assistance

The United Nations Peace-keeping Force in Cyprus, established by the Security Council in 1964,[15] continued throughout 1988 to supervise the cease-fire lines of the Cyprus National Guard and of the Turkish and Turkish Cypriot forces. It also provided security for civilians in the area between the lines; discharged its functions with regard to the security, welfare and well-being of the Greek Cypriots living in northern Cyprus; regularly visited Turkish Cypriots residing in the south; and supported United Nations relief operations.

The area between the cease-fire lines—the buffer zone—was kept under constant surveillance by UNFICYP through a system of 142 observation posts, 50 of which were permanently manned as at 30 November. The number of cease-fire violations remained at a low level, but the number of shooting incidents increased slightly. UNFICYP continued to be successful in restoring the *status quo ante*. In Nicosia, the Force continued its efforts to reduce tension at certain points where troops of both sides continued to be in dangerous proximity to each other and where a significant number of cease-fire violations and other related incidents had occurred. The UNFICYP civilian police continued to work in close co-operation with both the Cyprus and the Turkish Cypriot police, contributing to the protection and movement of civilians between the cease-fire lines. UNFICYP also continued to monitor new civilian construction projects close to the lines in Nicosia to ensure their civilian nature and alleviate concerns on both sides.

Overflights of the buffer zone continued, with nine such flights by Turkish forces or civilian aircraft and eight from the south; all overflights were protested.

Temporary visits to the south by Greek Cypriots living in the north continued through the good offices of UNFICYP. Thirty Greek Cypriots trans- ferred permanently to the south, leaving 639 residing in the north. UNFICYP continued visiting Turkish Cypriots living in the south and assisting them in maintaining contact with their relatives in the north; 30 reunions involving 180 persons were arranged. Frequent contacts between members of the Maronite community residing on opposite sides of the lines continued.

Emergency medical services, including medical evacuation and the delivery of medicines, were provided for both civilian communities, and the anti-mosquito programme arranged by UNFICYP continued. UNFICYP distributed 454 tons of food and other related items provided by Cyprus and the Cyprus Red Cross to Greek Cypriots in the north. Food continued to be provided by the World Food Programme to some 22,000 children and persons in social welfare institutions.

As co-ordinator of humanitarian assistance to Cyprus, UNHCR continued to assist the displaced and the needy and to promote bicommunal projects regarding sewerage, conservation work and rehabilitation of the handicapped. Two major multisectoral projects provided $10 million to assist in communal and bicommunal activities. The 1988 programme was co-ordinated by the Cyprus Red Cross Society and involved constructing medical and educational facilities and overseas procurement of equipment and supplies for health, education, agriculture, veterinary services and water resources management.

Joint activities were maintained between the Greek Cypriot and the Turkish Cypriot communities in the framework of ongoing projects, assisted by the United Nations Development Programme (UNDP). Regular joint meetings took place under the Nicosia Master Plan, whose main focus was to ensure the best utilization of funds made available by UNHCR and the Federal Republic of Germany for projects in the old walled city of Nicosia. The European Economic Community agreed to provide 4 million European currency units to fund projects on both sides in the walled city. With UNDP funding, emergency assistance and expertise were provided to halt damage to the Selimiye-St. Sophia national monument in the Turkish Cypriot quarter of Nicosia.

Commanded by Major-General Günther G. Greindl of Austria, UNFICYP, as at 30 November 1988, had a strength of 2,124, including 35 civilian police. Its military contingents came from Austria (410), Canada (575), Denmark (341), Finland (7), Ireland (8), Sweden (7) and the United Kingdom (741). Civilian police were from Australia (20) and Sweden (15).

UNFICYP financing

In 1988, contributions to UNFICYP, which continued to be financed by voluntary contributions and by troop-contributing Governments, totalled $20,412,776 from 23 countries. Estimated six-month costs totalled some $46 million, of which troop-contributing Governments absorbed in the order of $33 million for such items as regular pay and allowances and normal *matériel* expenses, while United Nations expenditures amounted to $13 million.

The accumulated deficit for UNFICYP since its inception in 1964 was in the order of $164.2 million as at 30 November 1988.

Expressing concern over the precarious financial situation which continued to place an unfair burden on the troop-contributing countries, the Secretary-General, on 26 February[16] and 14 September 1988,[17] renewed his appeal to States for voluntary contributions to finance UNFICYP, again stressing its indispensable contribution to international peace by maintaining calm in Cyprus, a condition crucial to his mission of good offices. Annexed to his appeals were details of the Force's financing.

REFERENCES

[1]YUN 1977, p. 344. [2]YUN 1979, p. 421. [3]A/42/916-S/19506. [4]A/42/940-S/19672. [5]A/42/920-S/19519. [6]YUN 1986, p. 239. [7]A/42/923-S/19524. [8]A/42/926-S/19555. [9]S/19927. [10]YUN 1983, p. 254, SC res. 541(1983), 18 Nov. 1983. [11]S/19927/Add.1. [12]S/20310. [13]S/20310/Add.1. [14]S/20330. [15]YUN 1964, p. 165, SC res. 186(1964), 4 Mar. 1964. [16]S/19577. [17]S/20213.

Institutional machinery

Security Council

In 1988, the Security Council held 55 meetings and adopted 20 resolutions. Twenty-one meetings were devoted to the situation in the Middle East and related questions; nine each to the situation in South Africa and related questions, and to the situation between Iran and Iraq, including four to Iran's complaint against the United States regarding the shooting down of its passenger airliner; four to Tunisia's complaint against Israel following the assassination in Tunis of four persons, among them a member of the Executive Committee of the Palestine Liberation Organization; two each to the extension of the mandate of UNFICYP, a complaint by the Republic of Korea regarding the blowing up in mid-air, on 29 November 1987, of its passenger airliner, the question of the Falkland Islands (Malvinas) and the situation in Nicaragua; one each to the situation in Afghanistan, Angola and Western Sahara; and one (private) to consideration and adoption of the Council's report to the General Assembly.

Agenda

The Security Council considered 14 agenda items during 1988—its forty-third year. It continued the practice of adopting at each meeting the agenda for that meeting (for list of agenda items, see APPENDIX IV). Seven items were included in the Council's agenda for the first time. They concerned: the destruction on 29 November 1987 of a Korean Air Lines passenger aircraft (see PART TWO, Chapter III); the United Kingdom's decision to conduct military manœuvres in the Falkland (Malvinas) Islands from 7 to 31 March 1988 (see PART FOUR, Chapter I); the United States' decision of 16 March to send American troops to Honduran territory (see PART TWO, Chapter II); a complaint by Tunisia of violation of its sovereignty and territorial integrity by Israel on 16 April, which resulted in the loss of human life (see PART TWO, Chapter IV); the destruction of a civil aircraft of Iran Air by a United States missile (see PART TWO, Chapter III); the situation relating to Afghanistan (see PART TWO, Chapter III); and the situation in Angola (see PART TWO, Chapter I). The Council President issued a statement in connection with an attack by South Africa on the territory of Botswana (see PART TWO, Chapter I).

On 15 September,[1] the Secretary-General notified the General Assembly, in accordance with Article 12, paragraph 2, of the Charter of the United Nations, of 12 matters relative to the maintenance of international peace and security which the Council had discussed since his previous annual notification.[2] He listed 126 other matters not discussed by the Council during the period, but of which it remained seized. By **decision 43/415** of 29 November, the Assembly took note of those matters.

Membership

In 1988, the question of equitable representation on the Security Council and increase in its membership again was not considered. By **decision 43/458** of 22 December, the General Assembly decided to include the item in the provisional agenda of its forty-fourth (1989) session.

Pursuant to rule 15 of the provisional rules of procedure of the Security Council, the Secretary General, in December,[3] reported to the Council the credentials of Canada, Colombia, Ethiopia, Finland and Malaysia, which had been elected by the General Assembly on 26 October as non-permanent Council members for a two-year term beginning 1 January 1989. In his opinion, those credentials were in order.

Report for 1987/88

At a private meeting on 8 November 1988, the Security Council unanimously adopted its report covering the period from 16 June 1987 to 15 June

1988.[4] The General Assembly took note of the report by **decision 43/416** of 29 November.

General Assembly

The General Assembly met in two regular sessions during 1988, to resume and conclude its forty-second (1987) session and to hold the major part of its forty-third.

The first part of the forty-second session had been held from 15 September to 21 December 1987[5] and resumed in 1988 from 29 February to 2 March, from 18 to 23 March, from 11 to 13 May, on 16 and 17 August and on 19 September, when it was declared closed after concluding consideration of the remaining agenda items. The Assembly also held its fifteenth special session, devoted to disarmament (see PART ONE, Chapter II), from 31 May to 25 June 1988.

The forty-third regular session opened on 20 September and continued until its suspension on 22 December. During the general debate, from 26 September to 13 October, the Assembly heard 153 statements by heads of State or Government and heads or members of delegations.

Agenda

As decided by the General Assembly in 1987,[6] six items remained on its agenda for its resumed forty-second session in 1988. On 16 August 1988, the Assembly, by **decision 42/402 B**, included in the agenda of its forty-second session an additional item on the financing of the United Nations Iran-Iraq Military Observer Group.

On 19 September, the Assembly included items in the draft agenda of its forty-third session on: armed Israeli aggression against Iraqi nuclear installations and its grave consequences for the established international system concerning the peaceful uses of nuclear energy, the non-proliferation of nuclear weapons and international peace and security (**decision 42/463**); the current financial crisis of the United Nations (**decision 42/464**); the question of Cyprus (**decision 42/465**); and consequences of the prolongation of the armed conflict between Iran and Iraq (**decision 42/466**).

The forty-third session initially had 149 items on the agenda, which was adopted by the Assembly on 23 September; three additional items were later included.[7] (For list and allocation of agenda items, see APPENDIX IV.) The agenda was adopted by **decision 43/402**. Under the same decision, the Assembly allocated the items to the appropriate Main Committees and decided to hold one plenary meeting on item 77, on the report of the Special Committee to Investigate Israeli Practices Affecting the Human Rights of the Population of the Occupied Territories, on the understanding that the Special Political Committee would remain seized of the item for its customary consideration. The request for a special meeting on the uprising in the Israeli-occupied territories under agenda item 77 had been made by Democratic Yemen for the Arab Group of Member States at the United Nations.[8]

Inclusion of the items and their allocation to the Assembly's Main Committees or plenary meetings[9] had been recommended by the General Committee[10] on the basis of the preliminary[11] and annotated preliminary[12] list of items, a 141-item provisional agenda[13] and a seven-item supplementary list.[14]

Following a statement by its President that, with the exception of seven items, consideration of the 1988 agenda had been concluded, the Assembly, by **decision 43/459** of 22 December, retained those seven items. They were 15 (c), 37, 46, 47, 48, 82 and 137 (for the titles of the items, see APPENDIX IV).

Organization of the 1988 session

On 23 September 1988, by **decision 43/401**, the General Assembly, on the recommendation of the General Committee,[15] adopted a number of provisions concerning the organization of the forty-third (1988) session.

The Committee's recommendations concerned rationalization of the Assembly's work; the schedule of meetings; meeting records; the general debate; explanations of vote, right of reply and length of statements; concluding statements; election of the Chairmen of the Main Committees; questions related to the programme budget; documentation; resolutions; special conferences; meetings of subsidiary organs; and the closing date of the 1988 session.

Subsidiary organs

By **decision 43/403 A** of 20 September, adopted on the recommendation of the Committee on Conferences,[16] the General Assembly authorized the *Ad Hoc* Committee of the Whole of the General Assembly on the Review and Appraisal of the United Nations Programme of Action for African Economic Recovery and Development 1986-1990 to hold meetings during the 1988 session.

By **decision 43/403 B**, adopted on 23 September and 14 November, on the recommendations of the Committee on Conferences[17] and the General Committee,[15] the Assembly authorized the following subsidiary organs to hold meetings during the 1988 session: Advisory Board on Disarmament Studies; Advisory Committee on the

United Nations Educational and Training Programme for Southern Africa; Committee of Trustees of the United Nations Fund for South Africa; Committee on Relations with the Host Country; Committee on the Exercise of the Inalienable Rights of the Palestinian People; Intergovernmental Group to Monitor the Supply and Shipping of Oil and Petroleum Products to South Africa; Selection Panel for Human Rights Prizes; Special Committee against *Apartheid;* United Nations Council for Namibia; Working Group on the Financing of the United Nations Relief and Works Agency for Palestine Refugees in the Near East; and World Food Council.

Representatives' credentials

At its first meeting on 11 October 1988, the Credentials Committee examined a memorandum of the previous day from the Secretary-General indicating that credentials of representatives to the General Assembly's forty-third session had been submitted by 123 Member States. The Legal Counsel explained that the memorandum related solely to Member States that had submitted formal credentials.

On 5 December, at its second meeting, the Committee examined a 2 December memorandum from the Secretary-General, which was orally updated by the Legal Counsel, reporting that formal credentials from 24 other Member States had been received. In addition, information concerning the appointment of their representatives to the forty-third session had been communicated to the Secretary-General by six Member States, by means of a cable, letter or note verbale. The Committee Chairman proposed that the Committee accept the credentials of all those Member States, including those that had communicated by cable, letter or note verbale, on the understanding that the latter would submit formal credentials as soon as possible.

At each meeting, the Committee, acting without vote on an oral proposal by its Chairman, adopted a draft resolution by which it accepted the credentials received. The Committee also recommended two draft resolutions to the Assembly. On 18 October and 9 December, the Assembly, by **resolutions 43/10 A and B**, respectively, approved the first[18] and second [19] reports of the Credentials Committee.

REFERENCES

[1]A/43/611. [2]YUN 1987, p. 362. [3]S/20358. [4]A/43/2. [5]YUN 1987, p. 363. [6]*Ibid.*, GA dec. 42/460, 21 Dec. 1987. [7]A/43/251 & Add.1-2. [8]A/43/751. [9]A/43/252 & Add.1,2. [10]A/43/250 & Corr.1 & Add.1,2. [11]A/43/50. [12]A/43/100 & Add.1. [13]A/43/150. [14]A/43/200. [15]A/43/250. [16]A/43/599. [17]A/43/600 & Add.1. [18]A/43/715. [19]A/43/715/Add.1.

PUBLICATIONS
Index to Proceedings of the General Assembly, Forty-third session—1988/1989, Part I—Subject Index; Conclusion of the Forty-second session—1987/1988 (ST/LIB/SER.B/A.44 (Part I)), Sales No. E.89.I.10 (Part I); Part II—Index to Speeches (ST/LIB/SER.B/A.44 (Part II)), Sales No.E.89.I.10 (Part II). *Index to Proceedings of the Security Council, Forty-third year—1988* (ST/LIB/SER.B/S.25), Sales No. E.89.I.11.

Co-operation with other intergovernmental organizations

League of Arab States

In accordance with a 1987 General Assembly resolution,[1] the Secretary-General reported in August 1988 on the co-operation between the United Nations and the League of Arab States (LAS).[2]

The report described consultations and exchanges of information that had taken place between the two organizations and summarized follow-up action on proposals for co-operation agreed on in 1983,[3] as well as progress made on proposals adopted at a 1985 joint United Nations/LAS meeting on social development.[4]

The report of the second joint meeting of representatives of the United Nations and of LAS and its specialized organizations (Geneva, 29 June–1 July 1988) was issued as an addendum[5] to the Secretary-General's report. Taking note with satisfaction of the progress achieved, the meeting stressed the need further to strengthen and enhance co-operation and agreed to develop an effective programme of co-operative activities based on the multi- and bilateral proposals adopted in 1983. The meeting agreed on specific conclusions and recommendations in the following areas: international peace and security; economic, financial and technical co-operation; food and agriculture; industrial development; maritime transport; proposed co-operation between the Arab Maritime Transport Academy, UNDP and the International Maritime Organization; telecommunications; standardization and metrology; co-operation between LAS and the United Nations regional commissions; and co-operation between the LAS General Department for Economic Affairs and United Nations agencies and organizations.

The meeting also identified priorities for co-operation in the fields of social development, labour matters, human resources, cultural affairs, refugees, humanitarian activities and emergencies.

In carrying out projects in the Arab region, the meeting recommended that the United Nations and the specialized agencies give priority to co-operation with Arab organizations and utilize Arab expertise.

Statements in the Security Council. In 1988, the Secretary-General of LAS and its Permanent Observer to the United Nations made statements at a total of six Security Council meetings, in which they had been invited to participate in accordance with rule 39 of the Council's provisional rules of procedure.[b] Those meetings dealt with the Middle East situation, including the occupied Arab territories, and Tunisia'a complaint about violation by Israel of its territorial integrity and sovereignty on 16 April which resulted in the loss of human life.

GENERAL ASSEMBLY ACTION

On 17 October, the General Assembly adopted **resolution 43/3** by recorded vote.

Co-operation between the United Nations and the League of Arab States

The General Assembly,

Recalling its previous resolutions on the promotion of co-operation between the United Nations and the League of Arab States, in particular resolution 42/5 of 15 October 1987,

Having considered the report of the Secretary-General on co-operation between the United Nations and the League of Arab States,

Recalling the Articles of the Charter of the United Nations which encourage activities through regional arrangements for the promotion of the purposes and principles of the United Nations,

Noting with appreciation the desire of the League of Arab States to consolidate and develop the existing ties with the United Nations in all areas relating to the maintenance of international peace and security, and to co-operate in every possible way with the United Nations in the implementation of United Nations resolutions relating to the question of Palestine and the situation in the Middle East,

Aware of the vital importance for the countries members of the League of Arab States of achieving a just, comprehensive and durable solution to the Middle East conflict and the question of Palestine, the core of the conflict,

Realizing that the strengthening of international peace and security is directly related, *inter alia*, to disarmament, decolonization, self-determination and the eradication of all forms of racism and racial discrimination,

Taking note with satisfaction of the second joint meeting of the representatives of the United Nations and other organizations of the United Nations system and the representatives of the League of Arab States and its specialized organizations, held at Geneva from 29 June to 1 July 1988, as called for in General Assembly resolution 42/5, to evaluate the progress achieved in their co-operation during the past five years,

Convinced that the maintenance and further strengthening of co-operation between the United Nations and other organizations of the United Nations system and the League of Arab States contribute to the work of the United Nations system and to the promotion of the purposes and principles of the United Nations,

Recognizing the need for closer co-operation between the United Nations system and the League of Arab States and its specialized organizations in realizing the goals and objectives set forth in the Strategy for Joint Arab Economic Development adopted by the Eleventh Arab Summit Conference, held at Amman from 25 to 27 November 1980,

Taking note with appreciation that consultations have been initiated for the purpose of drafting an agreement of co-operation between the United Nations and the League of Arab States,

Having heard the statement of the Permanent Observer of the League of Arab States of 17 October 1988 on co-operation between the United Nations and the League of Arab States, and having noted the emphasis placed therein on follow-up actions and procedures on the recommendations in the political, social and cultural fields adopted at the meetings between the representatives of the General Secretariat of the League of Arab States and its specialized organizations and the secretariats of the United Nations and other organizations of the United Nations system, held at Tunis from 28 June to 1 July 1983 and at Geneva from 29 June to 1 July 1988, as well as on the recommendations relating to political matters contained in the relevant resolutions of the General Assembly,

1. *Takes note with satisfaction* of the report of the Secretary-General;

2. *Expresses its appreciation* to the Secretary-General for the follow-up action taken by him on the proposals adopted at the meeting between representatives of the General Secretariat of the League of Arab States and its specialized organizations and the secretariats of the United Nations and other organizations of the United Nations system held at Tunis and the sectoral meeting on social development in the Arab region, held at Amman from 19 to 21 August 1985, as well as to the specialized agencies and other organizations of the United Nations system for their efforts to facilitate the implementation of the Tunis and Amman proposals;

3. *Requests* the Secretary-General to continue to strengthen co-operation with the General Secretariat of the League of Arab States for the purpose of implementing United Nations resolutions relating to the question of Palestine and the situation in the Middle East in order to achieve a just, comprehensive and durable solution to the Middle East conflict and the question of Palestine, the core of the conflict;

4. *Requests* the Secretariat of the United Nations and the General Secretariat of the League of Arab States, within their respective fields of competence, further to intensify their co-operation towards the realization of the purposes and principles of the Charter of the United Nations, the strengthening of international peace and security, disarmament, decolonization, self-determination and the eradication of all forms of racism and racial discrimination;

5. *Also requests* the Secretary-General to continue his efforts to strengthen co-operation and co-ordination between the United Nations and other organizations of the United Nations system and the League of Arab States and its specialized organizations in order to enhance their capacity to serve the mutual interests of the two organizations in the political, economic, social and cultural fields;

6. *Further requests* the Secretary-General to continue to co-ordinate the follow-up action to facilitate the implementation of the proposals of a multilateral nature

adopted at the Tunis meeting in 1983, and to take appropriate action regarding the multilateral proposals adopted at the Amman meeting in 1985, and at the Geneva meeting in 1988, including the following measures:

(a) Promotion of contacts and consultations between the counterpart programmes, organizations and agencies concerned;

(b) Setting up of joint sectoral inter-agency working groups;

7. *Calls upon* the specialized agencies and other organizations and programmes of the United Nations system:

(a) To continue to co-operate with the Secretary-General and the programmes, organizations and agencies concerned within the United Nations system and the League of Arab States and its specialized organizations in the follow-up of multilateral proposals aimed at strengthening and expanding co-operation in all fields between the United Nations system and the League of Arab States and its specialized organizations;

(b) To maintain and increase contacts and consultations with the counterpart programmes, organizations and agencies concerned regarding projects of a bilateral nature, in order to facilitate their implementation;

(c) To associate whenever possible with organizations and institutions of the League of Arab States in the execution and implementation of development projects in the Arab region;

(d) To inform the Secretary-General, not later than 15 May 1989, of the progress of their co-operation with the League of Arab States and its specialized organizations, in particular the follow-up action taken on the multilateral and bilateral proposals adopted at the Tunis, Amman and Geneva meetings;

8. *Takes note with appreciation* of the regional workshop on human resources development in the Arab region convened in Kuwait on 28 and 29 November 1987, in implementation of paragraph 6 *(c)* of resolution 41/4;

9. *Decides* that, in order to intensify co-operation and for the purpose of review and appraisal of progress as well as to prepare comprehensive periodic reports, a general meeting between the United Nations system and the League of Arab States should take place once every three years and inter-agency sectoral meetings should be organized annually on areas of priority and wide importance in the development of the Arab States, the time and place to be determined by consultations between the United Nations and the League of Arab States;

10. *Recommends* that, in order to make the already existing co-operation comprehensive and meaningful, as well as to give it a legal and formal status, the Secretary-General of the United Nations and the Secretary-General of the League of Arab States should take necessary steps to conclude an agreement of co-operation between the United Nations and the League of Arab States when the text of such an agreement is finalized by the two organizations, as called for in paragraph 10 of General Assembly resolution 42/5;

11. *Invites* the Secretary-General of the United Nations and the Secretary-General of the League of Arab States to initiate consultations for the purpose of holding a preparatory meeting in 1989 between the Department of Disarmament Affairs of the United Nations Secretariat and the League of Arab States with a view to considering the possibility of holding a seminar on disarmament matters in the Arab region in 1990;

12. *Recommends* that the United Nations and the other organizations of the United Nations system should utilize Arab expertise to the extent possible in projects undertaken in the Arab region;

13. *Requests* the Secretary-General of the United Nations, in close co-operation with the Secretary-General of the League of Arab States, to hold periodic consultations, as and when appropriate, between representatives of the Secretariat of the United Nations and of the General Secretariat of the League of Arab States on follow-up policies, projects, actions and procedures;

14. *Also requests* the Secretary-General to submit to the General Assembly at its forty-fourth session a progress report on the implementation of the present resolution;

15. *Decides* to include in the provisional agenda of its forty-fourth session the item entitled ''Co-operation between the United Nations and the League of Arab States''.

General Assembly resolution 43/3

17 October 1988   Meeting 32   146-2 (recorded vote)

20-nation draft (A/43/L.7); agenda item 25.

Sponsors: Algeria, Bahrain, Democratic Yemen, Djibouti, Iraq, Jordan, Kuwait, Lebanon, Libyan Arab Jamahiriya, Mauritania, Morocco, Oman, Qatar, Saudi Arabia, Somalia, Sudan, Syrian Arab Republic, Tunisia, United Arab Emirates, Yemen.

Recorded vote in Assembly as follows:

In favour: Afghanistan, Albania, Algeria, Angola, Antigua and Barbuda, Argentina, Australia, Austria, Bahamas, Bahrain, Bangladesh, Barbados, Belgium, Belize, Benin, Bhutan, Bolivia, Botswana, Brazil, Brunei Darussalam, Bulgaria, Burkina Faso, Burma, Burundi, Byelorussian SSR, Cameroon, Canada, Cape Verde, Central African Republic, Chad, Chile, China, Colombia, Congo, Costa Rica, Côte d'Ivoire, Cuba, Cyprus, Czechoslovakia, Democratic Kampuchea, Democratic Yemen, Denmark, Djibouti, Dominican Republic, Ecuador, Egypt, El Salvador, Ethiopia, Fiji, Finland, France, Gabon, Gambia, German Democratic Republic, Germany, Federal Republic of, Ghana, Greece, Grenada, Guinea, Guinea-Bissau, Guyana, Haiti, Honduras, Hungary, Iceland, India, Indonesia, Iran, Iraq, Ireland, Italy, Jamaica, Japan, Jordan, Kenya, Kuwait, Lao People's Democratic Republic, Lebanon, Lesotho, Liberia, Libyan Arab Jamahiriya, Luxembourg, Madagascar, Malawi, Malaysia, Maldives, Mali, Malta, Mauritania, Mauritius, Mexico, Mongolia, Morocco, Mozambique, Nepal, Netherlands, New Zealand, Nicaragua, Nigeria, Norway, Oman, Pakistan, Panama, Papua New Guinea, Paraguay, Peru, Philippines, Poland, Portugal, Qatar, Romania, Rwanda, Saint Kitts and Nevis, Samoa, Sao Tome and Principe, Saudi Arabia, Senegal, Seychelles, Sierra Leone, Singapore, Somalia, Spain, Sri Lanka, Sudan, Suriname, Sweden, Syrian Arab Republic, Thailand, Togo, Trinidad and Tobago, Tunisia, Turkey, Ukrainian SSR, USSR, United Arab Emirates, United Kingdom, United Republic of Tanzania, Uruguay, Vanuatu, Venezuela, Viet Nam, Yemen, Yugoslavia, Zaire, Zambia, Zimbabwe.

Against: Israel, United States.

Organization of the Islamic Conference

In response to a 1987 General Assembly resolution,[6] the Secretary-General submitted in August 1988 a report on co-operation between the United Nations and the Organization of the Islamic Conference.[7]

The report described consultations which had taken place between representatives of the two organizations since the Secretary-General's 1987 report;[8] it also outlined co-operation in political and security matters and in the areas of economic, social and cultural development. The third general meeting between representatives of the two organizations (Geneva, 4-6 July 1988) noted with satisfaction the progress achieved in the seven designated priority areas of co-operation—food security and agriculture; science and technology development; investment mechanisms and joint ventures; education and eradication of illiteracy; refugee assistance; technical co-operation; development of trade—despite resource constraints, and made specific recommendations for those and other areas of co-operation.

Statements in the Security Council. During 1988, the Permanent Observer of the Conference, under rule 39 of the Security Council's provisional rules of procedure,[b] participated in two Council meetings, which dealt with the situation in the occupied Arab territories.

GENERAL ASSEMBLY ACTION

On 17 October, the General Assembly adopted without vote **resolution 43/2**.

Co-operation between the United Nations and the Organization of the Islamic Conference

The General Assembly,

Having considered the report of the Secretary-General on co-operation between the United Nations and the Organization of the Islamic Conference,

Taking into account the desire of both organizations to co-operate more closely in their common search for solutions to global problems, such as questions relating to international peace and security, disarmament, self-determination, decolonization, fundamental human rights and the establishment of a new international economic order,

Recalling the Articles of the Charter of the United Nations which encourage activities through regional co-operation for the promotion of the purposes and principles of the United Nations,

Noting the strengthening of co-operation between the specialized agencies and other organizations of the United Nations system and the Organization of the Islamic Conference,

Taking note of the third general meeting between representatives of the secretariats of the United Nations and other organizations of the United Nations system and the secretariat of the Organization of the Islamic Conference, held at Geneva from 4 to 6 July 1988, in compliance with General Assembly resolution 42/4 of 15 October 1987,

Noting the encouraging progress made in the seven priority areas of co-operation as well as in the identification of other areas of co-operation,

Convinced that the strengthening of co-operation between the United Nations and other organizations of the United Nations system and the Organization of the Islamic Conference contributes to the promotion of the purposes and principles of the United Nations,

Recalling its resolutions 37/4 of 22 October 1982, 38/4 of 28 October 1983, 39/7 of 8 November 1984, 40/4 of 25 October 1985, 41/3 of 16 October 1986 and 42/4 of 15 October 1987,

1. *Takes note with satisfaction* of the report of the Secretary-General;

2. *Approves* the conclusions and recommendations of the third general meeting between representatives of the secretariats of the United Nations and other organiza-

tions of the United Nations system and the secretariat of the Organization of the Islamic Conference;

3. *Notes with satisfaction* the active participation of the Organization of the Islamic Conference in the work of the United Nations towards the realization of the purposes and principles of the Charter of the United Nations;

4. *Requests* the United Nations and the Organization of the Islamic Conference to continue co-operation in their common search for solutions to global problems, such as questions relating to international peace and security, disarmament, self-determination, decolonization, fundamental human rights and the establishment of a new international economic order;

5. *Encourages* the specialized agencies and other organizations of the United Nations system to continue to expand their co-operation with the Organization of the Islamic Conference, particularly by negotiating co-operation agreements, and invites them to multiply the contacts and meetings of focal points for co-operation in priority areas of interest to the United Nations and the Organization of the Islamic Conference;

6. *Requests* the Secretary-General to strengthen co-operation and co-ordination between the United Nations and other organizations of the United Nations system and the Organization of the Islamic Conference to serve the mutual interests of the two organizations in the political, economic, social and cultural fields;

7. *Recommends* that a co-ordination meeting of the focal points of the lead agencies of the United Nations and the Organization of the Islamic Conference should be organized during 1989 at a time and place to be determined through consultations with the organizations concerned;

8. *Expresses its appreciation* for the efforts of the Secretary-General in the promotion of co-operation between the United Nations and the Organization of the Islamic Conference, and expresses the hope that he will continue to strengthen the mechanisms of co-operation between the two organizations;

9. *Also requests* the Secretary-General to report to the General Assembly at its forty-fourth session on the state of co-operation between the United Nations and the Organization of the Islamic Conference;

10. *Decides* to include in the provisional agenda of its forty-fourth session the item entitled "Co-operation between the United Nations and the Organization of the Islamic Conference".

General Assembly resolution 43/2

17 October 1988   Meeting 32   Adopted without vote

Draft by Jordan (A/43/L.2); agenda item 24.

Observer status for OPANAL

In a letter of 15 August 1988,[9] Mexico requested the General Assembly, under rule 14 of its rules of procedure, that an item regarding observer status for the Agency for the Prohibition of Nuclear Weapons in Latin America and the Caribbean (OPANAL) in the General Assembly be included in the agenda of its forty-third session. In an explanatory memorandum, Mexico recalled that the Agency was established by the Treaty for the Prohibition of Nuclear Weapons in Latin

America (Treaty of Tlatelolco) as an independent organization to ensure compliance with the obligations assumed by States parties under the Treaty. It noted that as the Assembly had included in its agenda items on the prohibition of nuclear weapons in Latin America and had adopted many resolutions on the question, participation by OPANAL in those items that were of concern to it would facilitate the Organization's work.

GENERAL ASSEMBLY ACTION

On 17 October, the General Assembly adopted without vote **resolution 43/6**.

Observer status for the Agency for the Prohibition of Nuclear Weapons in Latin America and the Caribbean in the General Assembly

The General Assembly,

Noting the desire of the Agency for the Prohibition of Nuclear Weapons in Latin America and the Caribbean for co-operation between the United Nations and the Agency,

1. *Decides* to invite the Agency for the Prohibition of Nuclear Weapons in Latin America and the Caribbean to participate in the sessions and the work of the General Assembly in the capacity of observer;

2. *Requests* the Secretary-General to take the necessary action to implement the present resolution.

General Assembly resolution 43/6

17 October 1988   Meeting 32   Adopted without vote

23-nation draft (A/43/L.3); agenda item 142.

Sponsors: Antigua and Barbuda, Bahamas, Barbados, Bolivia, Colombia, Costa Rica, Dominican Republic, Ecuador, El Salvador, Grenada, Guatemala, Haiti, Honduras, Jamaica, Mexico, Nicaragua, Panama, Paraguay, Peru, Suriname, Trinidad and Tobago, Uruguay, Venezuela.

REFERENCES

[1]YUN 1987, p. 368, GA res. 42/5, 15 Oct. 1987. [2]A/43/509. [3]YUN 1983, p. 394. [4]YUN 1985, p. 731. [5]A/43/509/Add.1. [6]YUN 1987, p. 370, GA res. 42/4, 15 Oct. 1987. [7]A/43/498 & Add.1. [8]YUN 1987, p. 370. [9]A/43/192.

Other institutional questions

National liberation movements

By **resolution 43/160 A**, the General Assembly decided that the Palestine Liberation Organization and the South West Africa People's Organi-zation were entitled to have their communications relating to the sessions and work of the Assembly issued and circulated directly, and without intermediary, as official Assembly documents. It also decided that they were entitled to have their communications relating to the sessions and work of all international conferences convened under the Assembly's auspices issued and circulated directly, and without intermediary, as official conference documents.

By **resolution 43/160 B**, the Assembly once again called on the States concerned to accord to the delegations of the national liberation movements recognized by the Organization of African Unity and/or by the League of Arab States and accorded observer status by international organizations, the facilities, privileges and immunities necessary for the performance of their functions, in accordance with the relevant provisions of the 1975 Vienna Convention on the Representation of States in Their Relations with International Organizations of a Universal Character.[1] (For details, see PART FIVE, Chapter V.)

Composition of UN organs

In 1988, as in every year since 1979, consideration of the question of the composition of the relevant organs of the United Nations was deferred, based on a recommendation of the Special Political Committee, which reported that none of its members had requested to speak on the substance of the item.[2] Acting on that recommendation, the General Assembly on 6 December adopted **decision 43/420**, by which it included the item in the provisional agenda of its forty-fourth (1989) session.

Implementation of UN resolutions

On 7 December, by **decision 43/421**, the General Assembly, at the request of Cyprus, deferred consideration of the item on implementation of the resolutions of the United Nations and decided to include it in the provisional agenda of its forty-fourth (1989) session.

REFERENCES

[1]YUN 1975, p. 880. [2]A/43/774.

PART TWO

Regional questions

Chapter I

Africa

In 1988, the United Nations continued to consider and act on a number of political issues in Africa, in particular South Africa's *apartheid* policy and its aggression against neighbouring States. It was also kept informed about other conflicts among African States.

The question of *apartheid* was debated by the General Assembly, the Security Council and the Special Committee against *Apartheid*, among others. The Assembly adopted a series of resolutions dealing with South Africa's *apartheid* policies, which showed continuing agreement among the majority of Member States on *apartheid* and on the Organization's role in the struggle to abolish it.

The Security Council, in June, strongly condemned South Africa for its latest attacks on Botswana. Allegations of aggressive acts by South Africa were made to the Council by Mozambique, Namibia and Zambia. In September, the Council called on South Africa to cease its continued illegal occupation of Namibia.

Following requests by Angola and Cuba concerning the redeployment and withdrawal of Cuban troops from Angola, the Security Council in December decided to establish under its authority a United Nations Angola Verification Mission and requested the Secretary-General to take the necessary steps to implement that decision.

In March, June and November, the Council called on South Africa to stay the execution and commute the death sentences of anti-*apartheid* activists. In the case of the Sharpeville Six, it urged all States and organizations to use their influence to save their lives.

The Assembly reaffirmed the sovereignty of the Comoros over the Indian Ocean island of Mayotte. It also appealed for contributions to the United Nations Educational and Training Programme for Southern Africa, which provided scholarships for students from the region, and called for continued co-operation with the Organization of African Unity.

South Africa and *apartheid*

South Africa's system of enforced racial separation—the policy of *apartheid*—continued to be of major concern to the international community throughout 1988. The General Assembly, the Security Council and various other United Nations

bodies continued their activities aimed at pressuring the *apartheid* régime into dismantling its system of racial discrimination, which had been condemned as a crime against humanity. In the Assembly's view, comprehensive mandatory sanctions under Chapter VII of the Charter of the United Nations remained the most peaceful and effective means through which the international community could exert pressure on South Africa.

As in previous years, the world community was particularly concerned with the escalation of repression and State-induced terror against opponents of *apartheid*; the continued intransigence of South Africa demonstrated through the extension of the state of emergency, the large number of arbitrary arrests, the increased use of vigilante groups and the muzzling of the press; its acts of aggression and destabilization against neighbouring States; and the continuing illegal occupation of Namibia (see PART FOUR, Chapter III).

It was against this political background that the General Assembly in December adopted eleven resolutions aimed at sustaining and strengthening international pressure against the *apartheid* policies of South Africa.

General aspects

Activities of the Committee against *Apartheid*. The Special Committee against *Apartheid*, in its annual report to the General Assembly and the Security Council,[1] reviewed the situation in South Africa and the Committee's activities aimed at intensifying the international campaign against it. The report, which included recommendations for further action, covered the period until August 1988; developments later in the year were described in the Committee's 1989 report.[2]

The Committee followed with grave concern the rapidly deteriorating situation in and around South Africa and the régime's mounting reign of terror in the face of unprecedented nation-wide resistance to *apartheid*.

It reported that despite the intensification of South Africa's repression and annihilation of opponents, resistance to *apartheid* persisted and was now taking different forms. An alliance between organized black workers and youth was developing into a significant component of the strategic resistance, as was the role of church leaders and religious institutions. There was also growing opposition by democratic whites, as prominent Afrikaners raised their voices in opposition to *apartheid*. The End Conscription Campaign, the biggest organization of whites affiliated with the United Democratic Front (UDF), carried out effective campaigns against induction into the South African Defence Force, as a result of which the organization was virtually banned in August.

During 1988, the Committee repeatedly drew the international community's attention to South Africa's repressive policies by issuing statements, especially in connection with arrests and detentions of anti-*apartheid* activists. It also drew attention to the fact that the *apartheid* régime continued arbitrarily to impose death sentences and carry out executions as part of an ongoing campaign aimed at crushing and suppressing the struggle for liberation. The Committee condemned those executions and urged the Governments and peoples of the world to intervene to prevent further executions.

The Committee continued to promote an international campaign against South Africa's racial policies. It organized, assisted and participated in a number of meetings, conferences and seminars to mobilize public opinion against the *apartheid* régime and for comprehensive and mandatory sanctions as well as sports and cultural boycotts against South Africa. The Committee also campaigned for the release of all political prisoners and the improvement of the situation of women and children under *apartheid*.

In the conclusions to its 1988 report, the Committee stated that the Pretoria régime had escalated its repression, trying to crush every opposition in the country; at the same time, the Government had recently pursued diplomatic efforts aimed at settling the conflict in southern Africa.

The renewal of the state of emergency and the series of repressive measures against anti-*apartheid* organizations and domestic and foreign media suggested that the régime could advance its objectives only through the indiscriminate use of force and State-sponsored terrorism; the enactment of those measures was designed to stifle opposition to its so-called reforms and to the nationwide municipal elections scheduled for October 1988.

According to the Committee, Pretoria's constitutional scheme excluded blacks from participation in Parliament and restricted them to "homelands" and township councils. The so-called reforms gave an appearance of power-sharing without substance. As the centre-piece of the reformist scheme, the National Council, soon to be called the Great Indaba, was intended to be an advisory body. In the Committee's view, the

scheme preserved the fragmentation of the population, maintaining the most critical national issues as the domain for decision-making by whites. As long as the state of emergency remained in effect, political prisoners and detainees remained imprisoned, anti-*apartheid* and political organizations continued to be banned, a peaceful solution remained elusive and the country continued its downward spiral into violence.

Thus, *apartheid* was not only being aggressively maintained, but was camouflaged through "reforms". Therefore, the challenge to the international community remained as high as ever, and the imposition of sanctions continued to be of crucial significance.

Recent developments proved once more, in the Committee's opinion, that the régime could not solve the conflict in the country through violence; despite relentless attacks on all fronts, the opposition was regrouping; its activities ranged from armed resistance to strikes and boycotts. It was imperative that the international community exercise further economic and political pressure in order to induce the régime to introduce fundamental changes towards the eradication of *apartheid*.

The Committee recommended that the Assembly: condemn the *apartheid* system and the régime's acts of repression, aggression, destabilization and terrorism; reaffirm the legitimacy of the struggle, including armed resistance, for the elimination of *apartheid*; call for assistance to the national liberation movements as well as to the front-line States subjected to aggression and destabilization by South Africa; demand that the *apartheid* régime lift the state of emergency and end its repressive policies and violent practices, release all political prisoners and detainees, rescind the bans on political organizations and individuals and repeal restrictions on the freedom of the press; emphasize that only negotiations with the genuine representatives of the resisting majority could bring about a peaceful, just and lasting settlement of the racial conflict; request the Security Council to adopt comprehensive and mandatory sanctions; and, pending their adoption, call on States to terminate military, nuclear, financial, technological and other relations with South Africa, strengthen and coordinate measures and strictly enforce their implementation.

The Committee further recommended that the Assembly urge the international community to intensify its efforts to implement fully United Nations resolutions on cultural, sports, consumer and other boycotts and to facilitate implementation of the policy of cultural isolation of South Africa; urge ratification or accession to the international conventions against *apartheid*, including the International Convention against *Apartheid* in Sports, which had entered into force on 3 April; convene a special session in 1989 on *apartheid* and its destructive consequences; and authorize the Committee to continue mobilizing international action against *apartheid* through publicity, meetings, seminars, conferences, hearings, consultations, missions and other related activities.

In **resolution 43/50 F**, the Assembly endorsed the Committee's work programme.

International action to eliminate *apartheid*

In accordance with a 1987 Assembly resolution,[3] the Secretary-General in October 1988[4] submitted replies from 28 Governments to his request for information regarding the Assembly's appeal to consider, pending mandatory sanctions by the Security Council, national legislative or other measures to increase the pressure on the South African régime. Such measures included the cessation of further investment in and financial loans to South Africa; an end to all promotion of and support for trade with South Africa; prohibition of the sale of krugerrand and all other coins minted in South Africa; cessation of all military, police or intelligence co-operation with South Africa, in particular the sale of computer equipment; an end to nuclear collaboration with South Africa; and cessation of the export and sale of oil to South Africa.

Some of the Governments that sent replies emphasized that they did not maintain any relations with South Africa, in conformity with resolutions and decisions of the United Nations and/or regional organizations. Others reaffirmed previous policies concerning cessation of links with South Africa and newly adopted measures. All replies affirmed commitment to those policies and adherence to the 1987 as well as other Assembly resolutions.

Special Committee's conclusions and recommendations. The Special Committee against *Apartheid* concluded that although the international community had taken a number of positive steps to isolate South Africa and put pressure on the authorities to dismantle *apartheid*, there were still loopholes in the economic measures. While some States were gradually reducing their economic links with South Africa, others were filling the gap in defiance of United Nations resolutions calling for the complete isolation of the régime. The techniques adopted by some corporations to disinvest while maintaining links with South Africa through licensing and other arrangements had attracted attention and criticism.

The Committee considered the total isolation of South Africa to be an urgent task of the international community, as it would force the Government to accept the inevitable course of events and to undertake negotiations with the leaders recognized by the overwhelming majority of the people of South Africa.

Action by the Council for Namibia. The Council for Namibia, in a November report[5] on contacts between Member States and South Africa since the adoption of a November 1987 General Assembly resolution on the situation in Namibia resulting from its occupation by South Africa,[6] observed that, while the majority of States had taken measures to comply with the numerous United Nations resolutions calling for total eradication of *apartheid*, some Member States, as well as their multinational corporations, continued to do business as usual with the racist régime. In the Council's view, the continued opposition to comprehensive and mandatory sanctions by those same trade and political partners of South Africa constituted the single most significant impediment to genuine international efforts to end *apartheid*, thus encouraging South Africa to resist the will of the international community.

GENERAL ASSEMBLY ACTION

On 5 December 1988, the General Assembly adopted **resolution 43/50 K** by recorded vote.

Concerted international action for the elimination of *apartheid*

The General Assembly,

Alarmed by the continuous aggravation of the situation in South Africa caused by the policy of *apartheid*, and in particular by the extension and further tightening of the nation-wide state of emergency,

Convinced that the root-cause of the crisis in southern Africa is the policy of *apartheid*,

Noting with grave concern that in order to perpetuate *apartheid* in South Africa the authorities there have committed acts of aggression and breaches of the peace,

Convinced that only the total eradication of *apartheid* and the establishment of majority rule on the basis of the free and fair exercise of universal adult suffrage can lead to a peaceful and lasting solution in South Africa,

Noting that the so-called reforms in South Africa have the effect of further entrenching the *apartheid* system and further dividing the people of South Africa,

Recognizing that the policy of bantustanization deprives the majority of the people of their citizenship and makes them foreigners in their own country,

Recognizing the responsibility of the United Nations and the international community to take all necessary action for the eradication of *apartheid*, and, in particular, the need for increased and effective pressure on the South African authorities as a peaceful means of achieving the abolition of *apartheid*,

Encouraged, in this context, by the growing international consensus, as demonstrated by the adoption of Security Council resolution 569(1985) of 26 July 1985, and the increase in and expansion of national, regional and intergovernmental measures to this end,

Considering sanctions to be the most effective peaceful means available to the international community to increase pressure on the South African authorities,

Convinced of the vital importance of the strict observance of Security Council resolution 418(1977) of 4 November 1977, by which the Council instituted a mandatory arms embargo against South Africa, and Council resolution 558(1984) of 13 December 1984 concerning the import of arms, ammunition and military vehicles produced in South Africa, and of the need to make these embargoes fully effective in conformity with Council resolution 591(1986) of 28 November 1986,

Commending the national policies not to sell and export oil to South Africa,

Considering that measures to ensure effective and scrupulous implementation of such embargoes through international co-operation are essential and urgent,

Noting, in this respect, the efforts undertaken by the Intergovernmental Group to Monitor the Supply and Shipping of Oil and Petroleum Products to South Africa,

Noting with deep concern that, through a combination of military and economic pressures, in violation of international law, the authorities of South Africa have resorted to economic reprisals and aggression against, and destabilization of, neighbouring States,

Alarmed by the seriously deteriorating situation of millions of refugees, returnees and displaced persons in southern Africa caused by these policies and actions,

Considering that contacts between *apartheid* South Africa and the front-line and other neighbouring States, necessitated by geography, colonial legacy and other reasons, should not be used by other States as a pretext for legitimizing the *apartheid* system or justifying attempts to break the international isolation of that system,

Convinced that the existence of *apartheid* will continue to lead to ever-increasing resistance by the oppressed people, by all possible means, and increased tension and conflict that will have far-reaching consequences for southern Africa and the world,

Convinced that policies of collaboration with the *apartheid* régime, instead of respect for the legitimate aspirations of the genuine representatives of the great majority of the people, will encourage its repression and aggression against neighbouring States and its defiance of the United Nations,

Expressing its full support for the legitimate aspiration of African States and peoples, and of the Organization of African Unity, for the total liberation of the continent of Africa from colonialism and racism,

1. *Strongly condemns* the policy of *apartheid* that deprives the majority of the South African population of their dignity, fundamental freedoms and human rights;

2. *Strongly condemns* the South African authorities for the killings, arbitrary mass arrests and detention of members of mass organizations as well as other individuals who are opposing the *apartheid* system and the state of emergency, and for the detention of and use of violence against children;

3. *Further condemns* the overt and the covert aggressive actions, which South Africa has carried out for the destabilization of neighbouring States, as well as those aimed against refugees from South Africa and Namibia;

4. *Demands* that the authorities of South Africa:

(a) Release immediately and unconditionally Nelson Mandela and all other political prisoners, detainees and restrictees;

(b) Immediately lift the state of emergency;

(c) Abrogate discriminatory laws and lift bans on all organizations and individuals, as well as end restrictions on and censorship of news media;

(d) Grant freedom of association and full trade union rights to all workers of South Africa;

(e) Initiate without pre-conditions a political dialogue with genuine leaders of the majority population with a view to eradicating *apartheid* without delay and establishing a representative government;

(f) Eradicate the bantustan structures;

(g) Immediately end the destabilization of front-line and other States;

5. *Urges* the Security Council to consider without delay the adoption of effective mandatory sanctions against South Africa;

6. *Also urges* the Security Council to take steps for the strict implementation of the mandatory arms embargo instituted by it in resolution 418(1977) and of the arms embargo requested in its resolution 558(1984) and, within the context of the relevant resolutions, to secure an end to military and nuclear co-operation with South Africa and the import of military equipment or supplies from South Africa;

7. *Appeals* to all States that have not yet done so, pending mandatory sanctions by the Security Council, to consider national legislative or other appropriate measures to increase the pressure on the *apartheid* régime of South Africa, such as:

(a) Cessation of further investment in, and financial loans to, South Africa;

(b) An end to all promotion of and support for trade with South Africa;

(c) Prohibition of the sale of krugerrand and all other coins minted in South Africa;

(d) Cessation of all forms of military, police or intelligence co-operation with the authorities of South Africa, in particular the sale of computer equipment;

(e) An end to nuclear collaboration with South Africa;

(f) Cessation of export and sale of oil to South Africa;

(g) Other measures within the economic and commercial fields;

8. *Recognizes* the pressing need, existing and potential, of South Africa's neighbouring States for economic assistance, as a complement and not as an alternative to sanctions against South Africa, and appeals to all States, organizations and institutions:

(a) To increase assistance to the front-line States and the Southern African Development Co-ordination Conference in order to increase their economic strength and independence from South Africa;

(b) To increase humanitarian, legal, educational and other such assistance and support to the victims of *apartheid*, to the liberation movements recognized by the Organization of African Unity and to all those struggling against *apartheid* and for a non-racial, democratic society in South Africa;

9. *Welcomes* the Oslo Declaration and Plan of Action adopted by the International Conference on the Plight of Refugees, Returnees and Displaced Persons in Southern Africa, which was held at Oslo from 22 to 24 August 1988;

10. *Appeals* to all Governments and organizations to take appropriate action for the cessation of all academic, cultural, scientific and sports relations that would support the *apartheid* régime of South Africa, as well as relations with individuals, institutions and other bodies endorsing or based on *apartheid*;

11. *Commends* the States that have already adopted voluntary measures against the *apartheid* régime of South

Africa in accordance with General Assembly resolution 42/23 G of 20 November 1987 and invites those which have not yet done so to follow their example;

12. *Reaffirms* the legitimacy of the struggle of the oppressed people of South Africa for the total eradication of *apartheid* and for the establishment of a non-racial, democratic society in which all the people, irrespective of race, colour or creed, enjoy fundamental freedoms and human rights;

13. *Pays tribute to and expresses solidarity with* organizations and individuals struggling against *apartheid* and for a non-racial, democratic society in accordance with the principles of the Universal Declaration of Human Rights;

14. *Requests* the Secretary-General to report to the General Assembly at its forty-fourth session on the implementation of the present resolution.

General Assembly resolution 43/50 K

5 December 1988   Meeting 68   142-2-2 (recorded vote)

25-nation draft (A/43/L.42 & Add.1); agenda item 36.

Sponsors: Angola, Australia, Austria, Cuba, Denmark, Egypt, Finland, Ghana, Greece, Iceland, India, Ireland, Libyan Arab Jamahiriya, Madagascar, New Zealand, Nigeria, Norway, Philippines, Senegal, Somalia, Sweden, Trinidad and Tobago, United Republic of Tanzania, Zambia, Zimbabwe.

Meeting numbers. GA 43rd session: plenary 60-66, 68.

Recorded vote in Assembly as follows:

In favour: Afghanistan, Albania, Algeria, Angola, Antigua and Barbuda, Argentina, Australia, Austria, Bahamas, Bahrain, Bangladesh, Barbados, Belgium, Belize, Benin, Bhutan, Bolivia, Botswana, Brazil, Brunei Darussalam, Bulgaria, Burkina Faso, Burma, Burundi, Byelorussian SSR, Cameroon, Canada, Cape Verde, Central African Republic, Chad, China, Colombia, Comoros, Congo, Costa Rica, Côte d'Ivoire, Cuba, Cyprus, Czechoslovakia, Democratic Kampuchea, Democratic Yemen, Denmark, Djibouti, Dominican Republic, Ecuador, Egypt, El Salvador, Equatorial Guinea, Ethiopia, Fiji, Finland, France, Gabon, Gambia, German Democratic Republic, Ghana, Greece, Grenada, Guatemala, Guinea, Guinea-Bissau, Guyana, Haiti, Honduras, Hungary, Iceland, India, Indonesia, Iran, Iraq, Ireland, Israel, Italy, Jamaica, Japan, Jordan, Kenya, Kuwait, Lao People's Democratic Republic, Lebanon, Liberia, Libyan Arab Jamahiriya, Luxembourg, Madagascar, Malawi, Malaysia, Maldives, Mali, Malta, Mauritania, Mauritius, Mexico, Mongolia, Morocco, Mozambique, Nepal, Netherlands, New Zealand, Nicaragua, Niger, Nigeria, Norway, Oman, Pakistan, Panama, Papua New Guinea, Peru, Philippines, Poland, Qatar, Romania, Rwanda, Saint Kitts and Nevis, Saint Lucia, Saint Vincent and the Grenadines, Samoa, Sao Tome and Principe, Saudi Arabia, Senegal, Seychelles, Sierra Leone, Singapore, Solomon Islands, Somalia, Spain, Sri Lanka, Sudan, Suriname, Swaziland, Sweden, Syrian Arab Republic, Thailand, Togo, Trinidad and Tobago, Tunisia, Turkey, Uganda, Ukrainian SSR, USSR, United Arab Emirates, United Republic of Tanzania, Uruguay, Venezuela, Viet Nam, Yemen, Yugoslavia, Zaire, Zambia, Zimbabwe.

Against: United Kingdom, United States.

Abstaining: Germany, Federal Republic of, Portugal.

Sanctions and boycotts

The Special Committee reported in 1988 that the international campaign to isolate and put pressure on South Africa had intensified and was marked by significant new developments.

In an initiative to promote gold sanctions against South Africa, the World Gold Commission, a London-based anti-*apartheid* organization, was launched in June. Convinced that non–South African gold suppliers could mine enough gold to satisfy the world's jewellery industry, the Commission had formulated specific proposals with respect to the imposition of gold sanctions against South Africa, notably a ban on gold imports, the release of gold from national reserves and the establishment of a fund for the training of students in the techniques of mining and marketing gold.

The Commission had reported that the Italian jewellery industry, the largest buyer of South African gold, could feasibly switch from South African to non–South African gold. Those findings prompted all three Italian trade union federations to launch a campaign focusing on the jewellery manufacturing centres of northern Italy. The work of both the Commission and the trade unions led a significant number of Italian manufacturers to take steps to obtain their gold supplies from countries other than South Africa.

People's sanctions were also a major force behind the initiatives to tighten, expand and increase the scope of sanctions against South Africa. Examples included the refusal of consumers to purchase South African products, the refusal of workers to handle goods from South Africa and the demands of shareholders to have stocks divested from companies operating in or having links to South Africa. Trade unions and anti-*apartheid* movements were instrumental in organizing people's sanctions.

In its conclusions, the Committee said that sanctions continued to be of crucial significance. The sanctions imposed by a number of countries had significantly contributed to common efforts of the international community and had had a considerable impact even if their implementation had been at times hesitant and on the whole unco-ordinated. Partly as a result of sanctions, South Africa's economy was experiencing slow rates of growth, and the compound effects of disinvestment, the denial of long-term credit and the lack of new capital investment were beginning to be felt. The Committee welcomed in that context the new measures adopted or being considered by the Commonwealth and the United States Congress. It noted that as a result of measures undertaken in recent years, South Africa's trade with the Nordic countries had virtually ceased and that with the United States had decreased.

The Committee regretted, however, that while some countries were gradually reducing their economic links with South Africa, others were filling that gap, notable among them the Federal Republic of Germany, which had become the largest exporter to South Africa, followed by Japan and the United Kingdom. Equally disturbing in the Committee's view was the fact that some newly industrialized countries, particularly in the Far East, were filling the economic gap created by sanctions.

The Committee considered that sanctions should be targeted at key areas of the economy, such as banning imports of coal and agricultural products, the supply of loans and credit, the transfer of technology and direct air flights to and from South Africa. The Committee also called for the strengthening of sanctions as well as improved co-ordination, standardization and implementation and a more effective centralized monitoring and reporting system. States deciding to introduce sanctions should adopt national legislative measures to penalize violators.

Action by the Council for Namibia. In a November report on contacts between Member States and South Africa,[5] the Council for Namibia expressed the view that opposition to comprehensive and mandatory sanctions by some countries constituted the single most significant impediment to genuine international efforts to end *apartheid*. It therefore was of utmost importance for the Security Council to reconsider the imposition of mandatory sanctions against the Pretoria régime under Chapter VII of the Charter.

The call for sanctions was repeated in the Council's annual report to the General Assembly.[7]

Action by the Committee on colonial countries. The Special Committee on the Situation with regard to the Implementation of the Declaration on the Granting of Independence to Colonial Countries and Peoples (Committee on colonial countries), in August,[8] reiterated its request to all States, pending the imposition of comprehensive mandatory sanctions, to act individually or collectively to effectively isolate South Africa politically, economically, militarily and culturally and encouraged those Governments that had unilaterally taken certain measures against it to take additional ones.

On 5 December, the General Assembly adopted **resolution 43/50 C** by recorded vote.

Comprehensive and mandatory sanctions against the racist régime of South Africa

The General Assembly,

Recalling its resolution 42/23 C of 20 November 1987,

Recalling also its earlier resolutions and those of the Security Council calling for concerted international action to force the racist régime of South Africa to eradicate *apartheid*,

Having considered the report of the Special Committee against *Apartheid*, in particular paragraphs 188 to 194,

Noting with satisfaction the entering into force on 3 April 1988 of the International Convention against *Apartheid* in Sports,

Gravely concerned at the continuing defiance by the *apartheid* régime of the will of the international community, the régime's provocative non-compliance with resolutions of the Security Council and the General Assembly, its escalating terror against the people of South Africa, its continuing illegal occupation of Namibia, and its acts of military aggression and political and economic destabilization against independent African States,

Expressing serious concern at the continuing violation of the arms embargo against South Africa,

Noting with grave concern that some Member States and transnational corporations have continued economic relations with South Africa, while some others have begun

to exploit opportunities created by sanctions imposed by other States thus substantially increasing their trade with South Africa,

1. *Reaffirms* that *apartheid* is a crime against humanity and a threat to international peace and security, and that it is a primary responsibility of the United Nations to assist in efforts to eliminate *apartheid* without further delay;

2. *Encourages* States that have not yet done so to accede to the International Convention against *Apartheid* in Sports, and calls upon all States to support the work of the Commission against *Apartheid* in Sports;

3. *Calls upon* those States which have increased their trade with South Africa and, particularly, Japan, which recently emerged as the most important trading partner of South Africa, to sever trade relations with South Africa;

4. *Decides once again* that the imposition of comprehensive and mandatory sanctions by the Security Council under Chapter VII of the Charter of the United Nations would be the most appropriate, effective and peaceful means to bring *apartheid* to an end and to discharge the responsibilities of the United Nations for the maintenance of international peace and security, which are threatened and violated by the *apartheid* régime;

5. *Urgently requests* the Security Council, therefore, to consider immediate action under Chapter VII of the Charter with a view to applying comprehensive and mandatory sanctions against the racist régime of South Africa and calls upon those Governments which are opposed to the application of comprehensive and mandatory sanctions to reassess their policies and cease their opposition to the application of such sanctions by the Security Council;

6. *Appeals* to the Governments of the United Kingdom of Great Britain and Northern Ireland and the United States of America to co-operate in the imposition of comprehensive, mandatory sanctions by the international community against racist South Africa as a means for achieving peaceful change in that country;

7. *Urges* the Security Council to strengthen the mandatory arms embargo imposed by its resolutions 418(1977) of 4 November 1977 and 558(1984) of 13 December 1984 in order to bring to an end the continued violations of the arms embargo.

General Assembly resolution 43/50 C

5 December 1988   Meeting 68   123-12-19 (recorded vote)

38-nation draft (A/43/L.32 & Corr.1 & Add.1); agenda item 36.
Sponsors: Algeria, Angola, Antigua and Barbuda, Benin, Burkina Faso, Burundi, Byelorussian SSR, Congo, Cuba, Ethiopia, German Democratic Republic, Ghana, Hungary, India, Indonesia, Iran, Kenya, Liberia, Libyan Arab Jamahiriya, Madagascar, Malaysia, Mali, Mongolia, Mozambique, Nepal, Niger, Nigeria, Senegal, Somalia, Sudan, Syrian Arab Republic, Tunisia, Uganda, Ukrainian SSR, USSR, United Republic of Tanzania, Zambia, Zimbabwe.
Financial implications. 5th Committee, A/43/901 & Corr.1; S-G, A/C.5/43/50 & Add.1.
Meeting numbers. GA 43rd session: 5th Committee 39, 40, 42; plenary 60-66, 68.

Recorded vote in Assembly as follows:

In favour: Afghanistan, Albania, Algeria, Angola, Antigua and Barbuda, Argentina, Bahamas, Bahrain, Bangladesh, Barbados, Belize, Benin, Bolivia, Brazil, Brunei Darussalam, Bulgaria, Burkina Faso, Burma, Burundi, Byelorussian SSR, Cameroon, Cape Verde, Central African Republic, Chad, China, Colombia, Comoros, Congo, Costa Rica, Côte d'Ivoire, Cuba, Cyprus, Czechoslovakia, Democratic Kampuchea, Democratic Yemen, Djibouti, Dominican Republic, Ecuador, Egypt, El Salvador, Ethiopia, Fiji, Gabon, Gambia, German Democratic Republic, Ghana, Grenada, Guatemala, Guinea, Guinea-Bissau, Guyana, Haiti, Hungary, India, Indonesia, Iran, Iraq, Jamaica, Jordan, Kenya, Kuwait, Lao People's Democratic Republic, Lebanon, Liberia, Libyan Arab Jamahiriya, Madagascar, Malaysia, Maldives, Mali, Mauritania, Mauritius, Mexico, Mongolia, Morocco, Mozambique, Nepal, Nicaragua, Niger, Nigeria, Oman, Pakistan, Panama, Papua New Guinea, Peru, Philippines, Poland, Qatar, Romania, Rwanda, Saint Kitts and Nevis, Saint Lucia, Saint Vincent and the Grenadines, Samoa, Sao Tome and Principe, Saudi Arabia, Senegal, Seychelles, Sierra Leone, Singapore, Solomon Islands, Somalia, Sri Lanka, Sudan, Suriname, Syrian Arab Republic, Thailand, Togo, Trinidad and Tobago, Tunisia, Turkey, Uganda, Ukrainian SSR, USSR, United Arab Emirates, United Republic of Tanzania, Uruguay, Venezuela, Viet Nam, Yemen, Yugoslavia, Zaire, Zambia, Zimbabwe.

Against: Belgium, Canada, France, Germany, Federal Republic of, Israel, Italy, Japan, Luxembourg, Netherlands, Portugal, United Kingdom, United States.

Abstaining: Australia, Austria, Bhutan, Botswana, Denmark, Equatorial Guinea, Finland, Greece, Honduras, Iceland, Ireland, Lesotho, Malawi, Malta, New Zealand, Norway, Spain, Swaziland, Sweden.

SECURITY COUNCIL CONSIDERATION

The Security Council met in March to consider the situation in South Africa. On 8 March, the Council voted on a draft resolution[9] by Algeria, Argentina, Nepal, Senegal, Yugoslavia and Zambia, which would have had the Council impose sanctions under Chapter VII of the United Nations Charter. The proposed sanctions, in accordance with Article 41, were to include the prohibition of the import of South African iron, steel, krugerrand and all other coins minted in South Africa. Also prohibited would have been computer exports to South Africa; investment in and loans to South Africa; the promotion of and support for trade with it; the export and sale of oil to it; and all forms of military, police or intelligence co-operation. The vote was 10 to 2, with 3 abstentions, as follows:

In favour: Algeria, Argentina, Brazil, China, Italy, Nepal, Senegal, USSR, Yugoslavia and Zambia.

Against: United Kingdom, United States.

Abstaining: France, Federal Republic of Germany, Japan.

The draft was not adopted owing to the negative vote of permanent members. (For further details on the Council's consideration and action on the question of South Africa, see below.)

National measures against South Africa

In accordance with a 1987 General Assembly request,[10] the Secretary-General in November submitted a report on implementation of national measures adopted against South Africa.[11] The report dealt with the nature and scope of measures taken against South Africa, the degree of their applicability and the machinery for monitoring and reporting. It further discussed problems relating to their implementation, in particular the existence or absence of co-ordination and the degree of enforcement.

Annexed to the report was a description of measures regarding trade in commodities, financial flows and investment, transfer of technology, and transport and services, prepared by a consultant to the Centre against *Apartheid*.

GENERAL ASSEMBLY ACTION

On 5 December 1988, the General Assembly adopted **resolution 43/50 D** by recorded vote.

Imposition, co-ordination and strict monitoring of measures against racist South Africa

The General Assembly,

Recalling its resolutions on sanctions against South Africa,

Taking note of the report of the Special Committee against *Apartheid*, in particular paragraphs 191 to 194, and of the Secretary-General's report on implementation of national measures adopted against South Africa,

Considering that measures taken by States individually and some collectively, while commendable, vary in coverage and degree of enforcement, which allows for the exploitation of existing gaps and loopholes,

Concerned at the increasing number of States that exploit the trade gaps created by the imposition of these measures,

Commending the action taken by labour unions, women's organizations, student groups and other anti-*apartheid* organizations for the isolation of the *apartheid* régime,

1. *Urges* all States that have not yet done so, pending the imposition of comprehensive and mandatory sanctions, to adopt legislative and/or comparable measures to impose effective sanctions against South Africa and, in particular:

   (a) To impose embargoes on the supply of all products, technologies, skills and services that can be used for the military and nuclear industry of South Africa, including military intelligence;

   (b) To impose embargoes on the supply of oil and petroleum products;

   (c) To prohibit the import of coal, gold, other minerals and agricultural products from South Africa and Namibia;

   (d) To induce transnational corporations, banks and financial institutions to withdraw effectively from South Africa by ceasing equity and non-equity investment, transfer of technology and know-how, and provision of credit and loans;

   (e) To sever all air, sea and other transport links with South Africa;

   (f) To prevent, through appropriate measures, their citizens from serving in South Africa's armed forces and other sensitive sectors;

   (g) To take appropriate measures to ensure the effectiveness of the sports and cultural boycott of the racist régime of South Africa;

2. *Also urges* all States to monitor strictly the implementation of the above measures and adopt when necessary legislation providing for penalties on individuals and enterprises violating those measures;

3. *Requests* the Secretary-General to report to the General Assembly at its forty-fourth session on new legislative and/or comparable measures adopted and implemented by States against South Africa, especially in areas in which the South African economy depends on the outside world.

General Assembly resolution 43/50 D

5 December 1988   Meeting 68   136-4-14 (recorded vote)

44-nation draft (A/43/L.33 & Corr.1 & Add.1); agenda item 36.

Sponsors: Albania, Algeria, Angola, Antigua and Barbuda, Benin, Burkina Faso, Burundi, Byelorussian SSR, Cameroon, Congo, Cuba, Ethiopia, German Democratic Republic, Ghana, Hungary, India, Indonesia, Kenya, Liberia, Libyan Arab Jamahiriya, Madagascar, Malaysia, Mali, Mongolia, Mozambique, Nepal, Niger, Nigeria, Philippines, Senegal, Somalia, Sudan, Syrian Arab Repub-

lic, Togo, Trinidad and Tobago, Tunisia, Uganda, Ukrainian SSR, USSR, United Republic of Tanzania, Viet Nam, Yugoslavia, Zambia, Zimbabwe.
Financial implications. 5th Committee, A/43/901 & Corr.1; S-G, A/C.5/43/50 & Add.1.
Meeting numbers. GA 43rd session: 5th Committee 39, 40, 42; plenary 60-66, 68.

Recorded vote in Assembly as follows:

In favour: Afghanistan, Albania, Algeria, Angola, Antigua and Barbuda, Argentina, Australia, Bahamas, Bahrain, Bangladesh, Barbados, Belize, Benin, Bhutan, Bolivia, Botswana, Brazil, Brunei Darussalam, Bulgaria, Burkina Faso, Burma, Burundi, Byelorussian SSR, Cameroon, Canada, Cape Verde, Central African Republic, Chad, China, Colombia, Comoros, Congo, Costa Rica, Côte d'Ivoire, Cuba, Cyprus, Czechoslovakia, Democratic Kampuchea, Democratic Yemen, Denmark, Djibouti, Dominican Republic, Ecuador, Egypt, El Salvador, Ethiopia, Fiji, Finland, Gabon, Gambia, German Democratic Republic, Ghana, Grenada, Guatemala, Guinea, Guinea-Bissau, Guyana, Haiti, Honduras, Hungary, Iceland, India, Indonesia, Iran, Iraq, Jamaica, Jordan, Kenya, Kuwait, Lao People's Democratic Republic, Lebanon, Liberia, Libyan Arab Jamahiriya, Madagascar, Malaysia, Maldives, Mali, Malta, Mauritania, Mauritius, Mexico, Mongolia, Morocco, Mozambique, Nepal, New Zealand, Nicaragua, Niger, Nigeria, Norway, Oman, Pakistan, Panama, Papua New Guinea, Peru, Philippines, Poland, Qatar, Romania, Rwanda, Saint Kitts and Nevis, Saint Lucia, Saint Vincent and the Grenadines, Samoa, Sao Tome and Principe, Saudi Arabia, Senegal, Seychelles, Sierra Leone, Singapore, Solomon Islands, Somalia, Sri Lanka, Sudan, Suriname, Swaziland, Sweden, Syrian Arab Republic, Thailand, Togo, Trinidad and Tobago, Tunisia, Turkey, Uganda, Ukrainian SSR, USSR, United Arab Emirates, United Republic of Tanzania, Uruguay, Venezuela, Viet Nam, Yemen, Yugoslavia, Zaire, Zambia, Zimbabwe.

Against: Germany, Federal Republic of, Portugal, United Kingdom, United States.

Abstaining: Austria, Belgium, Equatorial Guinea, France, Greece, Ireland, Israel, Italy, Japan, Lesotho, Luxembourg, Malawi, Netherlands, Spain.

Oil embargo

The 11-member Intergovernmental Group to Monitor the Supply and Shipping of Oil and Petroleum Products to South Africa, established by the General Assembly in 1986,[12] reported to the Assembly in October.[13] The Group focused its attention on the flow of oil and petroleum products to the country and on ways and means to assist Member States in implementing embargoes or comparable policies. It also concerned itself with the role of companies that owned oil refineries in South Africa and with transnational corporations (TNCs) that had assisted South Africa in converting coal to oil and in its hydrocarbon exploration projects. It collected and evaluated its own information on oil deliveries to South Africa, but also considered information on violations of the oil embargo from other sides. On 10 June, the Group and the Special Committee against *Apartheid* had established a task force on the hearings on the oil embargo against South Africa, to be held during the first half of 1989.

The Group had noted that large foreign oil companies and corporations controlled a significant portion of the oil refining and distribution infrastructure in South Africa. The international community attached special importance to an oil embargo because of Pretoria's dependence on outside sources of petroleum and on outside aid in procuring and transporting the petroleum it needed. South Africa had attempted to lessen its dependence on external petroleum supplies by resorting to the conversion of coal to motor fuels and by stockpiling crude oil and petroleum products.

However, oil-from-coal conversion satisfied only one fourth of the country's motor fuel demand and, combined with stockpile drawdowns, could maintain motor fuel supplies at normal levels for only six to seven months. Offshore oil exploration had not resulted in significant discoveries.

Efforts to make an oil embargo mandatory had failed. Owing to its voluntary nature, the oil embargo had neither been strictly applied nor closely monitored, and had therefore not been fully effective.

The Group recirculated a questionnaire sent in 1987 to Member States concerning measures they had taken to prevent the supply and shipping of oil and petroleum products to South Africa. In 1988, it received 36 replies; in 1987, 50 Governments had responded, 29 of which again sent replies in 1988. Many Governments either annexed their legislation or comparable measures with respect to the oil embargo, referred to legislation and policies concerning the prohibition of any form of trade or transaction with South Africa or announced that they did not have any oil trade with that country. Some States had not introduced specific legislative or other measures, but instead had incorporated the embargo as a general policy of sanctions.

In its conclusions, the Group stated that a mandatory oil embargo was urgently needed; despite an almost universally declared policy that no oil or petroleum products should be supplied to South Africa, that policy was not being implemented unanimously.

In order to tighten all loopholes in the embargo, the Group suggested that the administrative measures enforced by States that export, ship and handle oil include "end user" and other destination restriction clauses to prevent companies and traders from attempting to circumvent the embargo by falsifying discharge certificates and other documentation.

The Group recommended that the Assembly request the Security Council to consider invoking Chapter VII of the Charter to impose a mandatory embargo on the supply and shipment of oil and petroleum products to South Africa. Pending such a decision, the Assembly should request Member States to adopt legislative or comparable measures to that effect.

Action by the Committee on colonial countries. At its August session,[8] the Committee on colonial countries called on those oil-producing and oil-exporting countries that had not done so to take effective measures to terminate the supply of crude oil and petroleum products to South Africa.

GENERAL ASSEMBLY ACTION

On 5 December, the General Assembly adopted by recorded vote **resolution 43/50 J.**

Oil embargo against South Africa

The General Assembly,

Having considered the report of the Intergovernmental Group to Monitor the Supply and Shipping of Oil and Petroleum Products to South Africa,

Recalling its resolutions on an oil embargo against South Africa, in particular resolution 42/23 F of 20 November 1987,

Noting that, while oil-exporting States have committed themselves to an oil embargo against South Africa, very few major shipping States have done so,

Concerned that the racist régime of South Africa has been able to circumvent the oil embargoes and comparable measures adopted by States,

Commending action taken by labour unions, student groups and anti-*apartheid* organizations against companies involved in the violation of the oil embargo against South Africa, and for the enforcement of the embargo,

Convinced that an effective oil embargo against South Africa would complement the arms embargo against the *apartheid* régime, and serve to curtail both its acts of aggression against the front-line States and its repression of the people of South Africa and Namibia,

1. *Takes note* of the report of the Intergovernmental Group to Monitor the Supply and Shipping of Oil and Petroleum Products to South Africa;

2. *Urges* the Security Council to take action without further delay to impose a mandatory embargo on the supply and shipping of oil and petroleum products to South Africa as well as the supply of equipment and technology to, financing of and investment in its oil industry and coal liquefaction projects;

3. *Requests* all States concerned, pending a decision by the Security Council, to adopt effective measures and/or legislation to broaden the scope of the oil embargo in order to ensure the complete cessation of the supply and shipping of oil and petroleum products to South Africa and Namibia, whether directly or indirectly, and in particular:

   (*a*) To apply strictly the "end users" clause and other conditions concerning restriction on destination to ensure compliance with the embargo;

   (*b*) To compel the companies originally selling or purchasing oil or petroleum products, as appropriate to each nation, to desist from selling, reselling or otherwise transferring oil and petroleum products to South Africa and Namibia, whether directly or indirectly;

   (*c*) To establish strict control over the supply of oil and petroleum products to South Africa and Namibia by intermediaries, oil companies and traders by placing responsibility for the fulfilment of the contract on the first buyer or seller of oil and petroleum products who would, therefore, be liable for the actions of these parties;

   (*d*) To prevent access by South Africa to other sources of energy, including the supply of raw materials, technical know-how, financial assistance and transport;

   (*e*) To prohibit all assistance to *apartheid* South Africa, including the provision of finance, technology, equipment or personnel for the prospecting, development or production of hydrocarbon resources, the construction or operation of oil-from-coal or oil-from-gas plants or the development and operation of plants producing fuel substitutes and additives such as ethanol and methanol;

   (*f*) To prevent South African corporations from maintaining or expanding their holdings in oil companies or properties outside South Africa;

   (*g*) To terminate the transport of oil to South Africa by ships flying their flags, or by ships that are ultimately owned, managed or chartered by their nationals or by companies within their jurisdiction;

   (*h*) To develop a system for registration of ships, registered or owned by their nationals, that have unloaded oil in South Africa in contravention of embargoes imposed;

   (*i*) To impose penal action against companies and individuals that have been involved in violating the oil embargo, and to publicize cases of successful prosecutions in conformity with their national laws;

   (*j*) To gather, exchange and disseminate information regarding violations of the oil embargo, including ways and means to prevent such violations, and to take concerted measures against violators;

4. *Decides* to hold hearings in April 1989 on the strengthening of the oil embargo against South Africa, to be organized by the Intergovernmental Group in co-operation with the Special Committee against *Apartheid*;

5. *Requests* the Intergovernmental Group to submit to the General Assembly at its forty-fourth session a report on the implementation of the present resolution, including proposals for strengthening the mechanism to monitor the supply and shipment of oil and petroleum products to South Africa;

6. *Requests* all States to extend their co-operation to the Intergovernmental Group in the implementation of the present resolution;

7. *Requests* the Secretary-General to provide the Intergovernmental Group with all necessary assistance for the implementation of the present resolution.

General Assembly resolution 43/50 J

5 December 1988   Meeting 68   138-2-14 (recorded vote)

23-nation draft (A/43/L.41 & Add.1); agenda item 36.

Sponsors: Albania, Algeria, Angola, Antigua and Barbuda, Cuba, German Democratic Republic, Indonesia, Iran, Kuwait, Libyan Arab Jamahiriya, Mongolia, New Zealand, Nicaragua, Nigeria, Norway, Senegal, Somalia, Syrian Arab Republic, Trinidad and Tobago, Ukrainian SSR, United Republic of Tanzania, Venezuela, Viet Nam.

Financial implications. 5th Committee, A/43/901 & Corr.1; S-G, A/C.5/43/50 & Add.1.

Meeting numbers. GA 43rd session: 5th Committee 39, 40, 42; plenary 60-66, 68.

Recorded vote in Assembly as follows:

In favour: Afghanistan, Albania, Algeria, Angola, Antigua and Barbuda, Argentina, Australia, Austria, Bahamas, Bahrain, Bangladesh, Barbados, Belize, Benin, Bhutan, Bolivia, Brazil, Brunei Darussalam, Bulgaria, Burkina Faso, Burma, Burundi, Byelorussian SSR, Cameroon, Cape Verde, Central African Republic, Chad, China, Colombia, Comoros, Congo, Costa Rica, Côte d'Ivoire, Cuba, Cyprus, Czechoslovakia, Democratic Kampuchea, Democratic Yemen, Denmark, Djibouti, Dominican Republic, Ecuador, Egypt, El Salvador, Equatorial Guinea, Ethiopia, Fiji, Finland, Gabon, Gambia, German Democratic Republic, Ghana, Grenada, Guatemala, Guinea, Guinea-Bissau, Guyana, Haiti, Honduras, Hungary, Iceland, India, Indonesia, Iran, Iraq, Ireland, Italy, Jamaica, Jordan, Kenya, Kuwait, Lao People's Democratic Republic, Lebanon, Liberia, Libyan Arab Jamahiriya, Madagascar, Malaysia, Maldives, Mali, Malta, Mauritania, Mauritius, Mexico, Mongolia, Morocco, Mozambique, Nepal, New Zealand, Nicaragua, Niger, Nigeria, Norway, Oman, Pakistan, Panama, Papua New Guinea, Peru, Philippines, Poland, Qatar, Romania, Rwanda, Saint Kitts and Nevis, Saint Lucia, Saint Vincent and the Grenadines, Samoa, Sao Tome and Principe, Saudi Arabia, Senegal, Seychelles, Sierra Leone, Singapore, Solomon Islands, Somalia, Spain, Sri Lanka, Sudan, Suriname, Sweden, Syrian Arab Republic, Thailand, Togo, Trinidad and Tobago, Tunisia, Turkey, Uganda, Ukrainian SSR, USSR, United Arab Emirates, United Republic of Tanzania, Uruguay, Venezuela, Viet Nam, Yemen, Yugoslavia, Zaire, Zambia, Zimbabwe.

Sports and cultural boycott

The Special Committee continued its activities aimed at strengthening international efforts to curtail cultural and sporting contacts with South Africa, mainly through its regular publication of registers of entertainers, actors and sportspersons who had performed in South Africa and by supporting activities of non-governmental organizations (NGOs) in that regard.

A major development designed to strengthen the existing boycott of *apartheid* in sports was the entry into force on 3 April of the International Convention against *Apartheid* in Sports which the General Assembly adopted in 1985.[14] As of 31 December 1988, 75 States had signed the Convention, 36 of which had ratified or approved it. In addition, 1 had acceded to the Convention.[15] In a statement of 18 March, the Chairman of the Special Committee urged States that had signed the Convention to expedite their processes of becoming parties.

On 14 April, a register of sports contacts for 1987 was released. Like previous registers, it included a cumulative list, by country, of sportspersons who had participated in sports events in South Africa. An increasing number of requests for deletion from the register were received.

On 25 January, the President of the International Tennis Federation announced that players would no longer be required to play in South Africa. In June, the International Olympic Committee (IOC) convened a special meeting and issued a declaration denouncing *apartheid* and urging all international sports organizations to cut their remaining ties with South Africa. IOC also announced that it would establish a co-ordination commission to study and follow all matters concerning *apartheid* in sports.

International boxing organizations also expressed their opposition to *apartheid* and cooperated with the Special Committee in efforts to isolate *apartheid* sports. The World Boxing Council undertook firm measures against boxers competing in South Africa. In September, the International Amateur Boxing Federation decided to expel Israel for five years following the participation of Israeli boxers in competitions in South Africa.

In August, the Special Committee adopted policy guidelines for implementation of a cultural boycott of South Africa. The policy sought to persuade artists, entertainers and others not to perform in South Africa or to engage in any cultural contacts with it. The guidelines were endorsed by the participants in the Symposium on Culture against *Apartheid*, organized jointly by the Special Committee, the Ministry of Culture of Greece and the Hellenic Association for the United Nations (Athens, 2-4 September).

A register of entertainers, actors and others who had performed in South Africa between January 1981 and June 1988 was published by the Special Committee in August. The register also contained a list of persons whose names had been deleted since the publication of the 1987 register. Several of the few remaining internationally known entertainers and artists pledged they would not again undertake cultural activities in *apartheid* South Africa and their names were therefore deleted from the register.

GENERAL ASSEMBLY ACTION

In **resolution 43/50 D**, the General Assembly urged States, pending the imposition of comprehensive and mandatory sanctions against South Africa, to adopt comparable measures, including action to ensure the effectiveness of the sports and cultural boycott of the racist régime of South Africa. **Resolution 43/50 K** contained an appeal to Governments and organizations to cease academic, cultural, scientific and sports relations that would support the *apartheid* régime, as well as relations with individuals, institutions and other bodies endorsing or based on *apartheid*. In **resolution 43/50 C**, the Assembly encouraged States that had not yet done so to accede to the International Convention against *Apartheid* in Sports, and called on all States to support the work of the Commission against *Apartheid* in Sports, which was to be established under the Convention. In **resolution 43/26 A**, the Assembly condemned the continuing collaboration between South Africa and certain Western and other countries, including cultural contacts, stating that such collaboration helped prolong South Africa's control over Namibia.

Relations with South Africa

Military and nuclear relations

Despite a mandatory arms embargo, South Africa continued to build up its military strength and to trade in armaments. It also increased its security and defence budget, which for 1988/89 was 22 per cent over the previous year's budget. As in the past, actual defence spending for the period was expected to exceed the allocated amount significantly.

In addition to increasing its military and security expenditures, the régime expanded its armaments industry, as well as the export of military equipment. According to the South African Minister for Defence, the Armaments Corporation of

South Africa had over the previous 13 years exported weapons to 39 countries, with sales totalling $800 million annually.

In the Special Committee's view, the régime appeared to have acquired the military technology to upgrade its existing armaments. Loopholes allowed South Africa to circumvent the arms embargo, as did the absence or non-enforcement of laws and regulations banning all forms of military collaboration with South Africa, the thriving international market of weapons and military technology and the lack of firm international action against embargo violations.

In January 1988, the Federal Republic of Germany informed the Committee that it had completed its investigations into the alleged sale of blueprints of naval submarines to South Africa by a German company. A fiscal review was dropped after the authorities concluded that the plans were not detailed enough to enable the construction of a U-boat. The Committee noted, however, that no public prosecutor had been assigned to the case and that the fiscal authorities seemed to have focused on possible violations of the country's export laws. A parliamentary committee was investigating the case.

In February, it was reported that Austrian spotter planes were among the military items recently acquired by South Africa. Also in February, the Special Committee requested an investigation of reported arms exports from South Africa to Sri Lanka.

In March, South Africa participated in an arms exhibition at Santiago, Chile. The Committee had urged Chile to cancel its invitation and expressed astonishment that two South African naval vessels had been invited to pay an official call to Chilean ports.

In June, the Special Committee requested the Federal Republic of Germany and the United Kingdom to investigate alleged deliveries of high-tech dual-purpose, multi-sensor platforms to South Africa involving British Aerospace and Messerschmit-Bölkow-Blohm. The equipment, produced in accordance with the requirements of the South African Defence Force, was capable of being used for locating tanks, missiles, grenades and other ammunition, as well as for preparing military operations. The two Governments reportedly had issued export licences on the basis of South Africa's assurance that the system would be used for satellites. By the time the matter had been brought to the attention of the Federal Republic of Germany, one platform had already been delivered.

On 2 November, the Committee encouraged Finland not to proceed with the purchase of Crotale missiles from the French company Thomson-CSF, which was linked to South Africa. In a reply received on 21 November, the Finnish Government indicated that the purchase did not contradict the spirit of the United Nations sanctions against South Africa.

In August, South Africa indicated to the International Atomic Energy Agency its intention to adhere to the 1968 Treaty on the Non-Proliferation of Nuclear Weapons[16] and to open its nuclear facilities to international inspection, but only on condition that it be allowed to trade in nuclear fuels and technology. In exchange, it would undertake not to produce nuclear weapons.

The Committee called again on all States to terminate relations with South Africa, including those in the military and nuclear fields.

The Committee also considered South Africa's relations with Israel, including its military relations, which were covered in a separate report (see below).

Activities of the Council for Namibia. The Council for Namibia, in its 1988 annual report,[7] noted that in addition to its vast military-industrial complex and the most formidable army in Africa, South Africa possessed a nuclear-weapon capability. Its nuclear programme had been developed with the assistance and collaboration of certain Western and other countries, including Israel. South Africa's role as a major uranium producer, which to a considerable extent came from illegally occupied Namibia, had given it a formidable advantage in securing support from Western countries for its own nuclear programme. The Council called on States to terminate all military and nuclear collaboration with South Africa.

Action by the Committee on colonial countries. In August,[8] the Committee on colonial countries, condemning the military and nuclear intelligence collaboration with South Africa, urged the Security Council to adopt further measures to widen the scope of its 1977 resolution[17] on a mandatory arms embargo to make it more effective and comprehensive. The Committee also called for scrupulous observance of the Council's 1984 resolution[18] enjoining Member States to refrain from importing South African armaments.

GENERAL ASSEMBLY ACTION

On 5 December, the Assembly adopted **resolution 43/50 B** by recorded vote.

Military collaboration with South Africa

The General Assembly,

Recalling its resolutions and those of the Security Council on the arms embargo, as well as other resolutions on collaboration with South Africa,

Taking note of the report of the Special Committee against *Apartheid*, including annex I thereof,

Considering that the full implementation of an arms embargo against South Africa is an essential element of international action against *apartheid*,

Taking note of the statement adopted on 18 December 1987 by the Security Council Committee established by resolution 421(1977) of 9 December 1977 concerning the question of South Africa, which "noted with alarm and great concern that large quantities of arms and military equipment, including highly sophisticated *matériel*, were still reaching South Africa directly or via clandestine routes",

Regretting that some countries surreptitiously continue to deal in arms with South Africa and allow South Africa to participate in international arms exhibitions,

1. *Strongly urges* those States which directly or indirectly infringe the arms embargo and continue to collaborate with South Africa in the military, nuclear, and military intelligence and technology fields, in particular certain Western States and Israel, to terminate forthwith such acts;

2. *Urges* the Security Council to consider immediate steps to ensure the scrupulous and full implementation of the arms embargo imposed by the Council in resolution 418(1977) of 4 November 1977 and its effective monitoring;

3. *Requests* the Special Committee against *Apartheid* to keep the matter under constant review and to report thereon to the General Assembly and the Security Council as appropriate.

General Assembly resolution 43/50 B

5 December 1988   Meeting 68   123-2-29 (recorded vote)

40-nation draft (A/43/L.31 & Corr.1 & Add.1); agenda item 36.

Sponsors: Albania, Algeria, Angola, Benin, Botswana, Burkina Faso, Burundi, Byelorussian SSR, Congo, Cuba, Ethiopia, German Democratic Republic, Ghana, India, Indonesia, Kenya, Liberia, Libyan Arab Jamahiriya, Madagascar, Malaysia, Mali, Mongolia, Mozambique, Nepal, Niger, Nigeria, Philippines, Senegal, Somalia, Sudan, Trinidad and Tobago, Tunisia, Uganda, Ukrainian SSR, USSR, United Republic of Tanzania, Viet Nam, Yugoslavia, Zambia, Zimbabwe.

Meeting numbers. GA 43rd session: plenary 60-66, 68.

Recorded vote in Assembly as follows:

In favour: Afghanistan, Albania, Algeria, Angola, Argentina, Bahrain, Bangladesh, Barbados, Belize, Benin, Bhutan, Bolivia, Botswana, Brazil, Brunei Darussalam, Bulgaria, Burkina Faso, Burma, Burundi, Byelorussian SSR, Cameroon, Cape Verde, Central African Republic, Chad, China, Colombia, Comoros, Congo, Costa Rica, Côte d'Ivoire, Cuba, Cyprus, Czechoslovakia, Democratic Kampuchea, Democratic Yemen, Djibouti, Dominican Republic, Ecuador, Egypt, El Salvador, Equatorial Guinea, Ethiopia, Fiji, Gabon, Gambia, German Democratic Republic, Ghana, Guatemala, Guinea, Guinea-Bissau, Guyana, Haiti, Hungary, India, Indonesia, Iran, Iraq, Jamaica, Jordan, Kenya, Kuwait, Lao People's Democratic Republic, Lebanon, Liberia, Libyan Arab Jamahiriya, Madagascar, Malaysia, Maldives, Mali, Mauritania, Mauritius, Mexico, Mongolia, Morocco, Mozambique, Nepal, Nicaragua, Niger, Nigeria, Oman, Pakistan, Panama, Papua New Guinea, Peru, Philippines, Poland, Qatar, Romania, Rwanda, Saint Kitts and Nevis, Saint Lucia, Saint Vincent and the Grenadines, Sao Tome and Principe, Saudi Arabia, Senegal, Seychelles, Sierra Leone, Singapore, Solomon Islands, Somalia, Sri Lanka, Sudan, Suriname, Swaziland, Syrian Arab Republic, Thailand, Togo, Trinidad and Tobago, Tunisia, Turkey, Uganda, Ukrainian SSR, USSR, United Arab Emirates, United Republic of Tanzania, Uruguay, Venezuela, Viet Nam, Yemen, Yugoslavia, Zaire, Zambia, Zimbabwe.

Against: Israel, United States.

Abstaining: Antigua and Barbuda, Australia, Austria, Bahamas, Belgium, Canada, Chile, Denmark, Finland, France, Germany, Federal Republic of, Greece, Honduras, Iceland, Ireland, Italy, Japan, Lesotho, Luxembourg, Malawi, Malta, Netherlands, New Zealand, Norway, Portugal, Samoa, Spain, Sweden, United Kingdom.

Aspects of military and nuclear collaboration with South Africa were taken up in a number of other Assembly resolutions. In **resolution 43/50 D**, the Assembly urged States to impose embargoes on the supply of all products, technologies, skills and services that could be used for South Africa's nuclear and military industry, including military intelligence. In **resolution 43/50 K**, it urged the Security Council to take steps for strict implementation of the arms embargo and to secure an end to military and nuclear co-operation with South Africa and the import of military equipment or supplies from it.

In **resolutions 43/71 A and B**, the Assembly condemned South Africa's continued pursuit of a nuclear capability and all forms of nuclear collaboration with it, and called on all concerned to desist from further collaboration. In **resolution 43/88**, the Assembly called on States, particularly Security Council members, to promote the denuclearization of Africa in order to avert the serious danger that the nuclear capability of South Africa constituted to African States, in particular the front-line States, as well as to international peace and security.

In **decision 43/410**, the Assembly considered that the acquisition of nuclear-weapon capability by South Africa constituted a further effort on its part to terrorize and intimidate independent States in the region into submission, while posing a threat to all mankind. The Assembly condemned the continuing support to South Africa in the military and nuclear fields and expressed concern at the grave consequences for international peace and security of the collaboration between South Africa and certain Western Powers, Israel and other countries in the military and nuclear fields. It called on States to end such collaboration, in particular to halt the supply of equipment, technology, nuclear materials and related training, which increased South Africa's nuclear capability.

Foreign investments and credits

According to the Special Committee, South Africa relied heavily on trade credits, but its relations with international finance remained tenuous. However, while long-term credits to South Africa had virtually ceased, short-term credits—whose main sources were the Federal Republic of Germany and the United Kingdom—were increasing. Japan, the United States and the Commonwealth (except for the United Kingdom) had banned new loans to South Africa, and some countries had also stopped export credit guarantees. South Africa had been able to attract limited amounts of capital from Far Eastern countries with large capital surpluses. Otherwise, there was little prospect of South Africa's having access to external capital lending. In 1988, studies by the United States Congress and the Commonwealth Secretariat showed that international financial confidence in South Africa had eroded.

In the area of investments, a reported 500 TNCs had sold their holdings in South Africa since corporations started withdrawing from there in the

1970s. Of United States–based TNCs with subsidiaries in South Africa, 60 per cent had disinvested since 1985. Of United Kingdom–based corporations, about 20 per cent had withdrawn; this represented a significant volume of disinvestment, since an estimated 40 per cent of all foreign investment in South Africa was United Kingdom-based. Companies based in the Federal Republic of Germany had disinvested about 6 per cent of their operations. Disinvestment by companies based in Australia, Canada, Denmark, the Netherlands and other Western European States had also taken place.

According to the Special Committee, two trends had emerged: the number of companies ending their direct investment in South Africa had dropped in 1988 from their peak 1987 levels, and a number of firms had retained non-equity links with South Africa under agreements affecting such matters as licences, technology transfers, management, assembly, distribution and franchise. Such arrangements, while allowing withdrawing companies to avoid public criticism, afforded them continued profit-making opportunities and provided South Africa with a continued flow of technology.

GENERAL ASSEMBLY ACTION

Foreign investments and credits were addressed by the General Assembly in **resolution 43/50 D**, urging States to adopt a number of unilateral measures, including inducing banks and financial institutions effectively to withdraw from South Africa by ceasing to provide loans and credits. In **resolution 43/50 K**, the Assembly made a similar call, appealing at the same time for national legislative and other appropriate measures to increase the pressure on South Africa.

Related action was also taken in **resolution 43/29**.

Transnational corporations

Activities of the Commission on TNCs. Among the documents considered at the April 1988 session of the Commission on TNCs[19] were three reports of the Secretary-General, dealing respectively with the activities of TNCs in South Africa and Namibia,[20] the responsibilities of home countries of such corporations,[21] and the follow-up to the public hearings on their activities.[22] (For details see PART THREE, Chapter V.) Following their consideration, the Commission recommended a draft resolution for adoption by the Economic and Social Council. The Council acted on it by adopting **resolution 1988/56**.

The role of TNCs in South Africa was addressed by the General Assembly in several 1988 resolutions. In **resolution 43/50 D**, the Assembly called on States to induce TNCs effectively to withdraw from South Africa by ceasing equity and non-equity investment and the transfer of technology and know-how. In **resolution 43/97**, the Assembly called on all States whose TNCs continued to do business with South Africa to terminate those dealings.

IMF and World Bank
relations with South Africa

In 1988, as in previous years, United Nations bodies called on the International Monetary Fund (IMF) and the International Bank for Reconstruction and Development (World Bank) to terminate their relations with South Africa. The Economic and Social Council, in **resolution 1988/53**, deplored the financial and other links of IMF with South Africa in disregard of repeated General Assembly resolutions, and urgently called on it to end such collaboration.

The Assembly, in **resolution 43/30**, regretted that the World Bank and IMF continued to maintain links with the racist Pretoria régime, expressed the view that all links should be discontinued and, pending such action, called on those organizations not to extend any support or loans to South Africa.

Israel–South Africa relations

In response to a 1987 General Assembly request to keep relations between South Africa and Israel under review,[23] the Special Committee, in an annex to its 1988 report,[1] covered recent developments concerning relations between the two countries.

Figures in the Special Committee's report covering the second half of 1988[2] indicated a decline in trade between the two countries. However, information emanating from South Africa indicated the contrary. According to the South African press, total trade between Israel and South Africa rose to $341 million in 1988, up from $247 million in 1987. Imports of goods from South Africa to Israel in 1988—major among them mineral products, petrol, coal and base metal—exceeded exports by some $80 million. Exports from Israel totalled $131 million, mainly chemical products, precious stones, metals and machinery, but also medical and optical products, rubber, plastics and textiles.

The Special Committee found that despite having taken limited measures against South Africa, Israel continued to have dealings with that country, particularly in the military field, a fact of particular concern to the Committee. Israel's military collaboration with South Africa extended not only to arms trade and upgrading of South Africa's weaponry systems, but also to training and advising its forces. In view of the veil of secrecy surrounding the nature and length of the military agreements between the two countries, the Committee felt that Israel's affirmation that it would refrain from new undertakings with South Africa in the realm of defence did not adequately contribute to the international community's efforts towards isolating South Africa and eliminating *apartheid* as soon as possible.

By a July letter to the Centre against *Apartheid*, Israel said it would continue its endeavour to curtail its relations with South Africa and would refrain from new undertakings in the realm of defence. It added that no new investments in South Africa had been approved and that cultural ties had been completely severed with those institutes connected in any way with the *apartheid* régime. It said that Israeli civil servants were forbidden to visit South Africa and that Israeli authorities, including its Customs Services, had taken all necessary steps to prevent Israel from being used as a transit point for the transfer of goods and services to and from South Africa. Israel also mentioned its training programmes for black South Africans and invitations to some prominent black leaders to visit Israel.

The Committee said that however useful such programmes and visits might be, they could not substitute for restrictive measures against South Africa.

Although data were limited because of the secretive nature of the relations between the two countries, information suggesting continuing collaboration between them, particularly in the military field, did exist. According to the Committee, Israel's arms sales to South Africa amounted to about 10 per cent of its total annual arms exports. A joint missile programme was believed to have started in 1987. In August 1988, South Africa unveiled a modernized and integrated navigation and weapon system, which Israeli experts were believed to have helped develop. In the vein of trade for military use, Israel's State television claimed that Israel imported steel from South Africa for its arms industry.

Concluding, the Special Committee recommended that the General Assembly authorize it to keep the relations between the two countries under review, that it condemn the continuing collaboration between them and that it call on Israel to cease such collaboration.

GENERAL ASSEMBLY ACTION

On December 5, the General Assembly adopted **resolution 43/50 E** by recorded vote.

Relations between South Africa and Israel

The General Assembly,

Recalling its resolution 42/23 D of 20 November 1987,

Having considered the report of the Special Committee against *Apartheid*, particularly annex I on recent developments concerning relations between South Africa and Israel,

1. *Calls upon* Israel to abide by the relevant resolutions of the General Assembly and the Security Coun-

cil by terminating forthwith all forms of military, nuclear, intelligence, economic and other collaboration, particularly its long-term contracts for military supplies, with South Africa;

2. *Requests* the Special Committee against *Apartheid* to continue to monitor the relations between South Africa and Israel and keep them under constant review, including the implementation of the measures adopted by Israel, and report to the General Assembly and the Security Council as appropriate.

General Assembly resolution 43/50 E

5 December 1988   Meeting 68   106-23-26 (recorded vote)

36-nation draft (A/43/L.34 & Corr.1 & Add.1); agenda item 36.
Sponsors: Albania, Algeria, Angola, Benin, Botswana, Burkina Faso, Burundi, Byelorussian SSR, Congo, Cuba, Ethiopia, German Democratic Republic, Ghana, India, Indonesia, Iran, Kenya, Liberia, Libyan Arab Jamahiriya, Madagascar, Malaysia, Mali, Mongolia, Mozambique, Niger, Nigeria, Somalia, Sudan, Tunisia, Uganda, Ukrainian SSR, USSR, United Republic of Tanzania, Viet Nam, Zambia, Zimbabwe.
Financial implications. 5th Committee, A/43/901 & Corr.1; S-G, A/C.5/43/50 & Add.1.
Meeting numbers. GA 43rd session: 5th Committee 39, 40, 42; plenary 60-66, 68.

Recorded vote in Assembly as follows:

> *In favour:* Afghanistan, Albania, Algeria, Angola, Argentina, Bahrain, Bangladesh, Barbados, Benin, Bhutan, Bolivia, Botswana, Brazil, Brunei Darussalam, Bulgaria, Burkina Faso, Burma, Burundi, Byelorussian SSR, Cape Verde, Chad, China, Comoros, Congo, Cuba, Cyprus, Czechoslovakia, Democratic Kampuchea, Democratic Yemen, Djibouti, Ecuador, Egypt, Ethiopia, Gabon, Gambia, German Democratic Republic, Ghana, Guatemala, Guinea, Guinea-Bissau, Guyana, Haiti, Hungary, India, Indonesia, Iran, Iraq, Jamaica, Jordan, Kenya, Kuwait, Lao People's Democratic Republic, Lebanon, Liberia, Libyan Arab Jamahiriya, Madagascar, Malaysia, Maldives, Mali, Mauritania, Mauritius, Mexico, Mongolia, Morocco, Mozambique, Nepal, Nicaragua, Niger, Nigeria, Oman, Pakistan, Panama, Papua New Guinea, Peru, Philippines, Poland, Qatar, Romania, Rwanda, Sao Tome and Principe, Saudi Arabia, Senegal, Seychelles, Sierra Leone, Somalia, Sri Lanka, Sudan, Suriname, Swaziland, Syrian Arab Republic, Thailand, Togo, Trinidad and Tobago, Tunisia, Turkey, Uganda, Ukrainian SSR, USSR, United Arab Emirates, United Republic of Tanzania, Venezuela, Viet Nam, Yemen, Yugoslavia, Zambia, Zimbabwe.
>
> *Against:* Australia, Austria, Belgium, Canada, Denmark, Dominican Republic, Finland, France, Germany, Federal Republic of, Greece, Iceland, Ireland, Israel, Italy, Luxembourg, Netherlands, New Zealand, Norway, Portugal, Spain, Sweden, United Kingdom, United States.
>
> *Abstaining:* Antigua and Barbuda, Bahamas, Belize, Cameroon, Central African Republic, Chile, Colombia, Costa Rica, Côte d'Ivoire, El Salvador, Equatorial Guinea, Fiji, Grenada, Honduras, Japan, Lesotho, Malawi, Malta, Saint Kitts and Nevis, Saint Lucia, Saint Vincent and the Grenadines, Samoa, Singapore, Solomon Islands, Uruguay, Zaire.

In **resolution 43/106**, the Assembly denounced the collusion between Israel and South Africa and expressed support for the 1983 Declaration of the International Conference on the Alliance between South Africa and Israel.[24] Israel was among the countries condemned for maintaining ties with South Africa, which, according to the Assembly, encouraged the latter to persist in suppressing the aspirations of the people to self-determination and independence. In **resolution 43/92**, Israel, together with other countries, was again condemned for collaborating with South Africa in many areas, including the military and nuclear fields, thus encouraging it to persist in its brutal oppression of the peoples of southern Africa and the denial of their human rights. In **resolution 43/80**, the Assembly reiterated its condemnation of the cooperation between the two countries in the field of nuclear armament.

Situation in South Africa

General political situation. In its 1988[1] and 1989 reports,[2] the Special Committee against *Apartheid* provided information on the general political situation in South Africa during 1988. According to those reports, the Government had shown no genuine inclination towards finding a solution for the political crisis in the country. Instead, it had tried to crush opposition by extending the state of emergency, thereby creating an atmosphere of terror in which the police, the army and vigilante groups acted with virtual impunity. Parallel to the internal suppression, the Government had stepped up its terrorist activities abroad against members of national liberation movements with the aim of weakening them and undermining their standing within the international community.

On 24 February, Pretoria imposed severe restrictions on the activities of 17 leading anti-*apartheid* organizations and 18 individuals committed to peaceful forms of struggle, as well as on the Congress of South African Trade Unions (COSATU). In imposing those restrictions, the régime appeared, in the words of the Committee, to be trying to woo back white voters and to avert a popular boycott of the nation-wide municipal elections scheduled for 26 October (see below), which, in the Committee's opinion, were an attempt by Pretoria to reassert its authority and give a semblance of legitimacy to its régime and its new proposed constitutional plan of power-sharing based on ethnicity.

The régime had developed ways to deal with the economic crisis of the country in parallel with its political strategy. A recently announced economic package emphasized privatization, deregulation, drastic cuts in official expenditures and a wage freeze in the public sector. Aimed at boosting private investment and production as well as reducing public sector deficits, the economic restructuring would, in the Committee's view, lead to deterioration of the living standards of low income groups, particularly black workers.

Repression of the population. Under the prolonged state of emergency, which was extended once more in June, police violence increased, as did attacks by vigilante groups and death squads against *apartheid* opponents, resulting in the creation of a new category of people in South Africa: internal refugees from repression.

Detention without charge or trial, even of children, and attacks and murders by vigilante groups were used to intimidate the opposition. In that climate of State-induced terror, foreign and domestic media were severely restricted.

Under the cover of the state of emergency, the basic *apartheid* laws continued to be enforced. Human rights monitors estimated that since the state of emergency was imposed in 1986, more than 30,000 persons had been detained for varying periods of time.

The 1988 Amnesty International report pointed to an unprecedented increase in the application of death sentences for political offences. The case of the so-called Sharpeville Six focused the attention of the international community on death sentences in political cases (see below).

Resistance to apartheid. As government pressure increased, so did resistance against *apartheid*. As mounting repression hindered the activities of political organizations, the black labour movement and religious organizations became leading opposition forces. Anti-*apartheid* resistance was adopting different political forms, switching from high-profile, mass-recruitment rallies to a system of block and street committees. In that process of political regrouping, the alliance between organized black workers and youth continued to grow in significance.

The National Anti-*Apartheid* Conference, convened by COSATU in September 1988 with the participation of more than 70 organizations, attempted to discuss unity and organization against repression and one person one vote in a democratic South Africa. Although the Conference was banned, it generated a debate on the content of political alliances, and some of the scheduled participants met in secret at Cape Town to discuss ways of continuing the process of creating a broader coalition. The nation-wide boycott of the municipal elections on 26 October indicated both the depth of the popular rejection of the structures created by the régime and the ability of community groups to organize themselves in spite of the state of emergency.

The black labour movement continued to play an important role in the opposition to *apartheid*, fighting not only for economic but also for political objectives, in actions often co-ordinated with other grass-roots organizations. An important development was the growing efforts of the trade union federations—COSATU and the National Council of Trade Unions—to take united action in opposition to the 1988 Labour Relations Amendment Act, which was designed to undermine the activities of the non-racial labour movement. In June, both federations called for three days of national protest against the Labour Bill, the state of emergency and the restrictions on anti-*apartheid* organizations. In spite of threats by management and authorities, more than 2 million blacks participated in the stay-away.

The Committee noted that despite gains made by the non-racial trade unions at collective bargaining, black South Africans still earned the lowest average monthly income. By far the most important demands precipitating strikes were, therefore, for improved wages and working conditions.

There were 1,025 strikes in 1988, resulting in the loss of 914,388 work-days; an estimated 161,534 black workers, as opposed to 145 white workers, participated in the strikes.

Despite a sustained attack on youth organizations since 1984, actions by youth and students demonstrated that their organizations had partly survived the effects of the state of emergency. In line with the general political trend, the anti-*apartheid* youth and student organizations were engaged in efforts to strengthen their political constituency by reaching out to youths in churches, sports organizations, township clubs and other such bodies. Finding common ground for political action seemed to be the major purpose of those efforts.

The Committee also reported that church leaders and religious institutions were opposing *apartheid* more forcefully than ever. The South African Council of Churches (SACC) continued to lead the churches in opposing the régime and also in providing humanitarian aid to the victims of *apartheid*. In June, religious leaders attended an SACC convocation to discuss the situation in South Africa and to formulate non-violent strategies for fighting *apartheid*. In September, SACC decided to defy any laws entrenching residential segregation and to condemn the Labour Relations Amendment Act as an instrument of racism. SACC also endorsed the decision to boycott the October municipal elections and resolved to oppose the media restrictions imposed under the state of emergency.

The Special Committee further reported wider opposition by democratic whites, individuals and organizations such as the End Conscription Campaign, which was eventually banned in August, the Five Freedoms Forum and the Johannesburg Democratic Action Committee. The Institute for a Democratic Alternative for South Africa sponsored several meetings between whites, in particular Afrikaners, and African National Congress (ANC) representatives, in an attempt to widen the range of forces opposed to *apartheid*.

ECONOMIC AND SOCIAL COUNCIL ACTION

In **resolution 1988/41**, the Economic and Social Council dealt with the infringement of trade union rights in South Africa. It condemned the increased repression of the independent black trade union movement; demanded that it cease; demanded the unconditional release of trade unionists; and requested immediate recognition of the population's right to form and join trade unions.

GENERAL ASSEMBLY ACTION

On 5 December, the General Assembly adopted **resolution 43/50 A** by recorded vote.

International solidarity with the liberation struggle in South Africa

The General Assembly,

Recalling its resolution 42/23 A of 20 November 1987,

Having considered the report of the Special Committee against *Apartheid*, in particular paragraphs 183 to 194,

Gravely concerned at the escalating repression of and State terror against opponents of *apartheid* and the increasing intransigence of the racist régime of South Africa, exemplified by the continuous extension of the state of emergency, the imposition of severe restrictions on peaceful anti-*apartheid* organizations and individuals, the increasing number of arbitrary detentions, trials, torture and killings, including those of women and children, the increased use of vigilante groups and the stifling of the press,

Noting with serious concern the racist régime's continuing acts of aggression and destabilization against neighbouring independent African States, including assassinations and abductions of freedom fighters in those States and elsewhere, and the continuing illegal occupation of Namibia,

1. *Reaffirms* its full support to the majority of the South African people in their struggle, under the leadership of their national liberation movements, the African National Congress of South Africa and the Pan Africanist Congress of Azania, to eradicate *apartheid* totally, so that all the people of South Africa as a whole, irrespective of race, colour or creed, may enjoy equal and full political and other rights, and participate freely in the determination of their destiny;

2. *Reaffirms also* the legitimacy of the struggle of the people of South Africa and their right to choose the necessary means, including armed struggle, to attain the eradication of *apartheid*, and the establishment of a free, democratic, unfragmented and non-racial South Africa;

3. *Condemns* the racist régime and its policies and practices of *apartheid* and, in particular, the execution of patriots and captured freedom fighters in South Africa and demands that the racist régime:

(a) Stop the execution of political prisoners at present on death row;

(b) Recognize prisoner-of-war status of captured freedom fighters in accordance with the Geneva Conventions of 12 August 1949 and Additional Protocol I of 1977 thereto;

4. *Demands again*:

(a) The lifting of the state of emergency;

(b) The immediate and unconditional release of Nelson Mandela and all other political prisoners and detainees;

(c) The lifting of the ban on all political organizations and opponents of *apartheid*;

(d) The safe return of all political exiles;

(e) The withdrawal of the régime's troops from black townships;

(f) The repeal of restrictions on the freedom of the press;

(g) The end of the policy of bantustanization and forced population removals;

(h) The end of military and paramilitary activities aimed at the neighbouring countries;

5. *Demands in particular* that all detained children be unconditionally released and that the abhorrent practice of applying repressive measures to children and minors cease immediately;

6. *Considers* that the implementation of the above demands would create the appropriate conditions for free consultations among all the people of South Africa with a view to negotiating a just and lasting solution to the conflict in that country;

7. *Appeals* to all States, intergovernmental and non-governmental organizations, mass media, and city and other local authorities as well as individuals to increase urgently political, economic, educational, legal, humanitarian and all other forms of necessary assistance to the people of South Africa and their national liberation movements;

8. *Also appeals* to all States, intergovernmental and non-governmental organizations to step up material, financial and other forms of support to the front-line and other neighbouring independent States;

9. *Urges* all countries to contribute generously to the Action for Resisting Invasion, Colonialism and *Apartheid* Fund set up by the Eighth Conference of Heads of State or Government of Non-Aligned Countries with the aim of increasing support to the national liberation movements fighting the *apartheid* régime and to the front-line and other neighbouring independent States;

10. *Decides* to continue the authorization of adequate financial provision in the regular budget of the United Nations to enable the South African liberation movements recognized by the Organization of African Unity—namely, the African National Congress of South Africa and the Pan Africanist Congress of Azania—to maintain offices in New York in order to participate effectively in the deliberations of the Special Committee against *Apartheid* and other appropriate bodies;

11. *Requests* Governments and intergovernmental and non-governmental organizations to exert their influence towards the implementation of the present resolution.

General Assembly resolution 43/50 A

5 December 1988   Meeting 68   131-3-21 (recorded vote)

46-nation draft (A/43/L.30/Rev.1 & Add.1); agenda item 36.
Sponsors: Albania, Algeria, Angola, Antigua and Barbuda, Bangladesh, Benin, Botswana, Burkina Faso, Burundi, Byelorussian SSR, Cameroon, Congo, Cuba, Ethiopia, German Democratic Republic, Ghana, Hungary, India, Indonesia, Iran, Kenya, Liberia, Libyan Arab Jamahiriya, Madagascar, Malaysia, Mali, Mongolia, Mozambique, Nepal, Niger, Nigeria, Philippines, Senegal, Somalia, Sudan, Syrian Arab Republic, Togo, Trinidad and Tobago, Tunisia, Uganda, Ukrainian SSR, USSR, United Republic of Tanzania, Yugoslavia, Zambia, Zimbabwe.
Financial implications. 5th Committee, A/43/901 & Corr.1; S-G, A/C.5/43/50 & Add.1.
Meeting numbers. GA 43rd session: 5th Committee 39, 40, 42; plenary 60-66, 68.

Recorded vote in Assembly as follows:

In favour: Afghanistan, Albania, Algeria, Angola, Antigua and Barbuda, Argentina, Bahamas, Bahrain, Bangladesh, Barbados, Belize, Benin, Bhutan, Bolivia, Botswana, Brazil, Brunei Darussalam, Bulgaria, Burkina Faso, Burma, Burundi, Byelorussian SSR, Cameroon, Cape Verde, Central African Republic, Chad, Chile, China, Colombia, Comoros, Congo, Costa Rica, Côte d'Ivoire, Cuba, Cyprus, Czechoslovakia, Democratic Kampuchea, Democratic Yemen, Djibouti, Dominican Republic, Ecuador, Egypt, El Salvador, Equatorial Guinea, Ethiopia, Fiji, Gabon, Gambia, German Democratic Republic, Ghana, Grenada, Guatemala, Guinea, Guinea-Bissau, Guyana, Haiti, Honduras, Hungary, India, Indonesia, Iran, Iraq, Jamaica, Jordan, Kenya, Kuwait, Lao People's Democratic Republic, Lebanon, Lesotho, Liberia, Libyan Arab Jamahiriya, Madagascar, Malawi, Malaysia, Maldives, Mali, Mauritania, Mauritius, Mexico, Mongolia, Morocco, Mozambique, Nepal, Nicaragua, Niger, Nigeria, Oman, Pakistan, Panama, Papua New Guinea, Peru, Philippines, Poland, Qatar, Romania, Rwanda, Saint Kitts and Nevis, Saint Lucia, Saint Vincent and the Grenadines, Samoa, Sao Tome and Principe, Saudi Arabia, Senegal, Seychelles, Sierra Leone, Singapore, Solomon Islands, Somalia, Sri Lanka, Sudan, Suriname, Swaziland, Syrian Arab Republic, Thailand, Togo, Trinidad and Tobago, Tunisia, Turkey, Uganda, Ukrainian SSR, USSR, United Arab Emirates, United

Republic of Tanzania, Uruguay, Venezuela, Viet Nam, Yemen, Yugoslavia, Zaire, Zambia, Zimbabwe.
Against: Portugal, United Kingdom, United States.
Abstaining: Australia, Austria, Belgium, Canada, Denmark, Finland, France, Germany, Federal Republic of, Greece, Iceland, Ireland, Israel, Italy, Japan, Luxembourg, Malta, Netherlands, New Zealand, Norway, Spain, Sweden.

On 28 November, by **decision 43/414**, the Assembly took note of the Special Political Committee's report on hearings of organizations and individuals in connection with South Africa's *apartheid* policies.[25] Altogether, the Committee heard statements by 14 persons.

Municipal elections

Nation-wide municipal elections of black representatives to officially sanctioned "community councils" were scheduled for 26 October 1988. Organizations such as the banned UDF and the Azanian People's Organization rejected the elections, which were widely boycotted. The constitutional plan envisaged that the municipal council representatives elected would become political representatives to the regional and national councils and the building blocks of the National Council, which, through an intricate consultative process, would devise a "new constitution" providing Africans with limited political representation at the national level.

The Special Committee Chairman, in a statement of 12 October, denounced South Africa's plans to conduct municipal elections, saying that, far from answering the black majority's demands for full political rights, the régime was trying to impose an official body for blacks that would function solely in an advisory capacity. That scheme, he said, would further entrench the current constitution, which had been overwhelmingly rejected by the black majority in 1984 and declared null and void by both the Security Council[26] and the General Assembly.[27] The Committee considered that the scheduled elections were devoid of any legitimacy since they were to take place amid a state of emergency, severe restrictions on popular organizations and their leaders and a general climate of harassment, intimidation and violence against the anti-*apartheid* opposition. The municipal officials chosen in the so-called elections would have no more legitimacy than the current councillors, who continued to be rejected by the black majority.

On the average, only 5 per cent of the eligible voters in the African townships voted.

GENERAL ASSEMBLY ACTION

On 26 October 1988, the General Assembly adopted **resolution 43/13** by recorded vote.

Pretoria's racial "municipal elections"
The General Assembly,

Recalling its resolution 38/11 of 15 November 1983, in which it stated its conviction that the "constitutional proposals" were aimed at depriving the indigenous African majority of all fundamental rights and further entrenching *apartheid* and accordingly rejected them,

Reaffirming that *apartheid* is a crime against humanity and a threat to international peace and security,

Gravely concerned that the so-called nation-wide municipal elections of 26 October 1988 are an extension of the "constitutional proposals" of 1983,

Welcoming the united resistance of the oppressed people of South Africa against these "municipal elections",

Alarmed that the Pretoria racist régime has declared illegal all advocacy against these "municipal elections" and further intensified repressive State violence, including the bombing of buildings that house the offices of anti-*apartheid* organizations as well as the mass arrest and detention of its opponents, in a bid to crush all resistance to these "municipal elections",

Reaffirming the legitimacy of the struggle of the oppressed people of South Africa for the elimination of *apartheid* and for the establishment of a society in which all the people of South Africa as a whole, irrespective of race, colour or creed, will enjoy equal and full political and other rights and participate freely in the determination of their destiny,

Firmly convinced that the holding of these "municipal elections" will further aggravate the already explosive situation inside *apartheid* South Africa,

1. *Declares* that the "municipal elections" are contrary to the principles of the Charter of the United Nations and that the enforcement of the "municipal elections" and their results will inevitably aggravate tension and conflict in South Africa and in southern Africa as a whole;

2. *Rejects* these "municipal elections" and all insidious manoeuvres by the racist minority régime of South Africa further to entrench white minority rule and *apartheid*;

3. *Also rejects* any so-called "negotiated settlement" based on the outcome of the "municipal elections" and other extensions of the "constitutional proposals" of 1983;

4. *Solemnly declares* that only the total eradication of *apartheid* and the establishment of a non-racial democratic society based on majority rule, through the full and free exercise of adult suffrage by all the people in a united and non-fragmented South Africa, can lead to a just and lasting solution of the explosive situation in South Africa;

5. *Requests* the Security Council, as a matter of urgency, to consider the serious implications of the so-called "municipal elections" and to take all necessary measures, in accordance with the Charter, to avert the further aggravation of tension and conflict in South Africa and in southern Africa as a whole.

General Assembly resolution 43/13

26 October 1988   Meeting 37   146-0-2 (recorded vote)

Draft by United Republic of Tanzania (A/43/L.16); agenda item 36.

Recorded vote in Assembly as follows:

In favour: Afghanistan, Albania, Algeria, Angola, Antigua and Barbuda, Argentina, Australia, Austria, Bahamas, Bahrain, Bangladesh, Belgium, Belize, Benin, Bhutan, Bolivia, Botswana, Brazil, Brunei Darussalam, Bulgaria, Burkina Faso, Burma, Burundi, Byelorussian SSR, Cameroon, Canada, Cape Verde, Central African Republic, Chad, China, Colombia, Comoros, Congo, Costa Rica, Côte d'Ivoire, Cuba, Cyprus, Czechoslovakia, Democratic Kampuchea, Democratic Yemen, Denmark, Djibouti, Dominica, Dominican Republic, Ecuador, Egypt, El Salvador, Equatorial Guinea, Ethiopia, Fiji, Finland, France, Gabon, Gambia, German Democratic Republic, Germany, Federal Republic of, Ghana, Greece, Guatemala, Guinea-Bissau, Guyana, Haiti, Honduras, Hungary, Iceland, India, Indonesia, Iran, Iraq, Ireland, Italy,

Jamaica, Japan, Jordan, Kenya, Kuwait, Lao People's Democratic Republic, Lebanon, Lesotho, Liberia, Libyan Arab Jamahiriya, Luxembourg, Madagascar, Malaysia, Maldives, Mali, Malta, Mauritania, Mauritius, Mexico, Mongolia, Morocco, Mozambique, Nepal, Netherlands, New Zealand, Nicaragua, Niger, Nigeria, Norway, Oman, Pakistan, Panama, Papua New Guinea, Peru, Philippines, Poland, Portugal, Qatar, Romania, Rwanda, Saint Kitts and Nevis, Saint Lucia, Saint Vincent and the Grenadines, Sao Tome and Principe, Saudi Arabia, Senegal, Seychelles, Sierra Leone, Singapore, Somalia, Spain, Sri Lanka, Sudan, Swaziland, Sweden, Syrian Arab Republic, Thailand, Togo, Trinidad and Tobago, Tunisia, Turkey, Uganda, Ukrainian SSR, USSR, United Arab Emirates, United Republic of Tanzania, Uruguay, Vanuatu, Venezuela, Viet Nam, Yemen, Yugoslavia, Zaire, Zambia, Zimbabwe.

Against: None.

Abstaining: United Kingdom, United States.

The General Assembly, in **resolution 43/106**, commended the efforts of the democratic forces within various sections of the South African society striving for the abolition of *apartheid* and the creation of a united non-racial democratic society. It condemned the holding of municipal elections, the restrictions imposed on democratic movements, the extension of the state of emergency, the wanton killing of peaceful demonstrators and the increased attacks on religious community leaders.

In **resolution 43/157**, the Assembly reaffirmed that *apartheid* should be abolished and that the systematic denial or abridgement of the right to vote on the grounds of race or colour was a gross violation of human rights and that the right to participate in a political system based on common and equal citizenship and universal franchise was essential for the exercise of periodic and genuine elections.

Opponents of *apartheid*

There was a substantial escalation in the number of political trials in 1988, which continued to be used as a weapon to silence opposition and deprive anti-*apartheid* organizations of their leadership. According to South Africa's Centre for Applied Legal Studies, 37 political trials involving 112 accused were completed between December 1987 and March 1988 alone. In the middle of 1988, 62 trials were taking place involving 691 accused, including five treason trials with 50 accused, and at least 70 political prisoners were on death row, the most prominent of whom were the so-called Sharpeville Six.

The six prisoners, accused in the murder of a black deputy mayor of the Sharpeville township by a crowd protesting a rent increase in September 1984, had been sentenced in 1985 on the basis of the doctrine of "common purpose", according to which a group could share in the aim of committing a murder, even if it did not actually take part in the crime. Upholding their convictions and sentences, the Appeal Court acknowledged that it had not been proved that their conduct had contributed causally to the mayor's death. Domestic and international pressure persuaded the authorities to commute their death sentences on 23 November to terms of imprisonment ranging from 18 to 25 years.

International action was also called for in the case of another death-row prisoner, 24-year-old Paul Tefo Setlaba, scheduled to be executed on 24 November. He was sentenced to death in 1986 on charges of murder relating to the death of a police informer, also on the basis of common purpose.

In a statement of 29 November, the Special Committee Chairman welcomed the release from prison of Pan Africanist Congress of Azania (PAC) President Zephania Mothopeng. At the same time, he expressed hope that this humanitarian gesture was also a political one and would be followed by the release of Nelson Mandela and the other political prisoners, which had to be the first step in the negotiations for a peaceful resolution of the conflict in South Africa. The Special Committee considered that Member States, intergovernmental organizations and NGOs should redouble their efforts to that effect.

On 9 December, the Acting Chairman of the Special Committee called for international efforts to secure the release of three UDF leaders convicted of high treason and of eight other opponents of *apartheid* convicted of terrorism. The Special Committee considered the sentences of Patrick Lekota (12 years), Popo Molefe (10 years), Moses Chikane (10 years) and Thomas Manthata (6 years) to be flagrant examples of using the judiciary as an instrument to suppress any political opposition to the *apartheid* rule. The harsh judgement rendered after a three-year trial, was widely condemned both within and outside South Africa.

On 29 March, the Chairman issued a statement condemning the assassination of the head of the ANC mission in Paris, Dulcie September. On 8 April, the Chairman condemned the attempted assassination at Maputo, Mozambique, of ANC activist Albie Sachs, who was seriously injured by a car bomb.

SECURITY COUNCIL ACTION

On 2 March,[28] Sierra Leone, on behalf of the Group of African States, requested an urgent meeting of the Security Council to consider the situation in South Africa. Zambia made several similar requests, on 2 March,[29] 15 March,[30] 16 June[31] and 23 November.[32] On the basis of those requests, the Council held seven meetings between 3 March and 23 November.

Meeting numbers. SC 2793-2797, 2799, 2817, 2830.

The Council invited the following countries, at their request, to participate in the discussion without the right to vote: Botswana, Bulgaria, Czechoslovakia, Guyana, India, Kuwait, Malaysia, Nigeria, Pakistan, Sierra Leone, Somalia, South Africa, Tunisia, Zimbabwe. Under rule 39[a] of the Council's provisional rules of procedure, the Council also invited the Chairman of the Special Committee against *Apartheid*, the Acting Chairman of the Committee on colonial countries and the President of the United Nations Council for Namibia. Under the same rule, at the request of Algeria, Senegal and Zambia, it invited Neo Mnumzana, representative of ANC,[33] Lesaoana Makhanda, representative of PAC,[34] and Helmut Angula, representative of the South West Africa People's Organization (SWAPO).[35]

On 16 March, the Council adopted **resolution 610(1988)** unanimously.

The Security Council,

Recalling its resolutions 503(1982) of 9 April 1982, 525(1982) of 7 December 1982, 533(1983) of 7 June 1983 and 547(1984) of 13 January 1984 in which, *inter alia*, it expressed its grave concern that the Pretoria régime's practice of sentencing to death and executing its opponents has adverse consequences on the search for a peaceful resolution of the South African situation,

Gravely concerned at the deteriorating situation in South Africa, the worsening human suffering resulting from the *apartheid* system and, *inter alia*, the South African régime's renewed state of emergency, its imposition on 24 February 1988 of severe restrictions on eighteen anti-*apartheid* and labour organizations and eighteen individuals committed to peaceful forms of struggle and the harassment and detention of church leaders on 29 February, all of which further undermine the possibilities of a peaceful resolution of the South African situation,

Having considered the question of the death sentences passed on 12 December 1985 in South Africa on Mojalefa Reginald Sefatsa, Reid Malebo Mokoena, Oupa Moses Diniso, Theresa Ramashamola, Duma Joseph Khumalo and Francis Don Mokhesi, known as the Sharpeville Six, as well as the decision to execute them on Friday, 18 March 1988,

Conscious that the Court proceedings of the Sharpeville Six show that none of the six young South Africans convicted of murder was found by the Court to have caused the actual death of the Councillor and that they were convicted of murder and sentenced to death only because the Court found that they had a "common purpose" with the actual perpetrators,

Deeply concerned at the Pretoria régime's decision to execute the Sharpeville Six on Friday, 18 March 1988, in defiance of world-wide appeals,

Convinced that these executions, if carried out, will further inflame an already grave situation in South Africa,

1. *Calls upon* the South African authorities to stay execution and commute the death sentences imposed on the Sharpeville Six;

2. *Urges* all States and organizations to use their influence and take urgent measures, in conformity with

---

[a]Rule 39 of the Council's provisional rules of procedure states: "The Security Council may invite members of the Secretariat or other persons, whom it considers competent for the purpose, to supply it with information or to give other assistance in examining matters within its competence."

the Charter of the United Nations, the resolutions of
the Security Council and relevant international instruments, to save the lives of the Sharpeville Six.

Security Council resolution 610(1988)

16 March 1988   Meeting 2799   Adopted unanimously

6-nation draft (S/19627).
Sponsors: Algeria, Argentina, Nepal, Senegal, Yugoslavia, Zambia.

Earlier, on 8 March, the Council had voted on
a draft resolution which would have had the Council impose sanctions under Chapter VII of the
Charter. The draft was not adopted owing to the
negative vote of permanent Council members. (For
further details see above.)

On 17 June, following South Africa's rejection
of an appeal to reopen the case to ensure a fair
trial, the Security Council adopted **resolution
615(1988)** unanimously.

The Security Council,

Recalling its resolutions 503(1982) of 9 April 1982,
525(1982) of 7 December 1982, 533(1983) of 7 June 1983,
547(1984) of 13 January 1984 and 610(1988) of 16 March
1988 in which, *inter alia*, it expressed its grave concern
that the Pretoria régime's practice of sentencing to death
and executing its opponents has adverse consequences
on the search for a peaceful resolution of the South African situation,

Gravely concerned at the deteriorating situation in South
Africa, the worsening human suffering resulting from
the *apartheid* system and, *inter alia*, the South African régime's renewed state of emergency on 9 June 1988, its
imposition on 24 February 1988 of severe restrictions
on eighteen anti-*apartheid* and labour organizations and
eighteen individuals committed to peaceful forms of
struggle and the harassment and detention of church
leaders on 29 February, all of which further undermine
the possibilities of a peaceful resolution of the South African situation,

Having considered the question of the death sentences
passed on 12 December 1985 in South Africa on Mojalefa Reginald Sefatsa, Reid Malebo Mokoena, Oupa
Moses Diniso, Theresa Ramashamola, Duma Joseph
Khumalo and Francis Don Mokhesi, known as the Sharpeville Six, as well as the decision to execute them,

Conscious that the Court proceedings of the Sharpeville
Six show that none of the six young South Africans convicted of murder was found by the Court to have caused
the actual death of the Councillor and that they were
convicted of murder and sentenced to death only because the Court found that they had a "common purpose" with the actual perpetrators,

Deeply concerned at the decision on 13 June 1988 of the
Pretoria Supreme Court to reject an appeal to reopen
the case to ensure a fair trial,

Deeply concerned also at the Pretoria régime's decision
to execute the Sharpeville Six in defiance of world-wide
appeals,

Convinced that these executions, if carried out, will further inflame an already grave situation in South Africa,

1. *Calls once again upon* the South African authorities
to stay execution and commute the death sentences imposed on the Sharpeville Six;

2. *Urges* all States and organizations to use their influence and take urgent measures, in conformity with

the Charter of the United Nations, the resolutions of
the Security Council and relevant international instruments, to save the lives of the Sharpeville Six.

Security Council resolution 615(1988)

17 June 1988   Meeting 2817   Adopted unanimously

6-nation draft (S/19940).
Sponsors: Algeria, Argentina, Nepal, Senegal, Yugoslavia, Zambia.

Following South Africa's decision to implement
the death sentence against Mr. Setlaba, the Council, on 23 November, adopted **resolution
623(1988)**.

The Security Council,

Having learned with grave concern of the intention of the
South African authorities to implement the death sentence imposed on Mr. Paul Tefo Setlaba, an anti-*apartheid*
activist, on the basis of so-called "common purpose",

Strongly urges the Government of South Africa to stay
execution and commute the death sentence imposed on
Mr. Paul Tefo Setlaba in order to avoid further aggravat-
ing the situation in South Africa.

Security Council resolution 623(1988)

23 November 1988   Meeting 2830   13-0-2

6-nation draft (S/20290).
Sponsors: Algeria, Argentina, Nepal, Senegal, Yugoslavia, Zambia.

Vote in Council as follows:

In favour: Algeria, Argentina, Brazil, China, France, Germany, Federal
Republic of, Italy, Japan, Nepal, Senegal, USSR, Yugoslavia, Zambia.
Against: None.
Abstaining: United Kingdom, United States.

South Africa informed the Secretary-General
that it rejected the Council resolutions: in a 16
March letter,[36] it expressed strong objection to
resolution 610(1988), which it regarded as interference in an internal South African matter. On
17 June,[37] it expressed its regret that the Security Council had found it appropriate to express
its views on the case of the Sharpeville Six by
adopting resolution 615(1988).

Women and children under *apartheid*

Report of the Secretary-General. Pursuant to
a 1986 resolution[38] and a 1987 decision[39] of the
Economic and Social Council, the Secretary-
General transmitted to the 1988 session of the
Commission on the Status of Women (see PART
THREE, Chapter XIII) a report on new developments from 1 September 1985 to 30 September
1987 concerning the situation of women under
apartheid in South Africa and Namibia and on assistance to women who had become refugees as
a result of *apartheid*.[40]

In his report, the Secretary-General stated that
black women in particular continued to suffer from
the inhuman practice of *apartheid*. As they had not
been able to change conditions affecting their daily
lives, such as free movement, access to education,
employment and basic services, their situation
deserved increased attention and international assistance. Although considerable effort had been

made so far to provide assistance, it was not sufficient to meet the growing needs. Because of intensified repressive action, attention and assistance were not only essential for meeting pressing needs, but also for enabling the population to develop their potential to take an active part in constructing a new society.

ECONOMIC AND SOCIAL COUNCIL

On 26 May, on the recommendation of its Second (Social) Committee, the Economic and Social Council adopted **resolution 1988/23** by recorded vote.

Women and children under *apartheid*

The Economic and Social Council,

Recalling its resolution 1986/22 of 23 May 1986 on women and children under *apartheid*,

Noting the concern of women throughout the world about the continuing degradation and abuse to which African women and children are subjected daily by the white minority régime of South Africa,

Recalling that that concern was expressed in the Nairobi Forward-looking Strategies for the Advancement of Women, which also contain proposals for various forms of assistance to be rendered to women and children inside South Africa and to those who have become refugees,

Recognizing that the inhuman exploitation and dispossession of the African people by the white minority régime are directly responsible for the appalling conditions in which African women and children live,

Also recognizing that the equality of women cannot be achieved without the success of the struggle for national liberation and self-determination of the people of South Africa against the racist régime of Pretoria,

Referring to the report of the Secretary-General on new developments concerning the situation of women under *apartheid* in South Africa and Namibia and measures of assistance to women from South Africa and Namibia who have become refugees as a result of the practice of *apartheid*,

1. *Condemns unequivocally* the South African régime for the imposition of the state of emergency, the forcible separation of black families, the detention and imprisonment of women and children and the banning of seventeen non-violent anti-*apartheid* democratic organizations, as well as individuals;

2. *Urges* the South African régime to accord the Sharpeville Six, one of whom is a woman, a fair trial based on international legal standards and to stop the execution of political prisoners;

3. *Demands* the immediate and unconditional release of all political prisoners, among whom are included an increasing number of women and children;

4. *Commends* the tenacity and bravery of those women inside and outside South Africa who have resisted oppression, who have been detained, tortured or killed, or whose husbands, children or other relatives have been detained, tortured or killed and who, despite this, have remained steadfast in their opposition to the racist régime;

5. *Acknowledges* the efforts of those Governments, nongovernmental organizations and individuals that have campaigned for and applied sanctions against the racist régime;

6. *Appeals* to all countries to support educational, health and social welfare programmes for women and children under *apartheid*;

7. *Also appeals* to the international community for increased assistance to women and children refugees in southern Africa;

8. *Calls upon* Governments, in view of the deterioration of the situation in South Africa, to impose, as a matter of urgency, comprehensive sanctions in accordance with the resolutions of the Security Council and the Nairobi Forward-looking Strategies for the Advancement of Women;

9. *Urges* Member States and organizations of the United Nations system to give effect forthwith, in consultation with the national liberation movements, to the Nairobi Forward-looking Strategies that deal with women and children under *apartheid*, giving particular attention to education, health, vocational training, employment opportunities and the strengthening of the women's sections of the liberation movement;

10. *Requests* the Secretary-General to submit a comprehensive report on monitoring the implementation of the Nairobi Forward-looking Strategies regarding women and children under *apartheid* to the Commission on the Status of Women at its thirty-third session.

Economic and Social Council resolution 1988/23

26 May 1988   Meeting 15   44-2-8 (recorded vote)

Approved by Second Committee (E/1988/90) by recorded vote (34-2-8), 13 May (meeting 9); draft by Commission on women (E/1988/15); agenda item 11.

Recorded vote in Council as follows:

In favour: Australia, Belize, Bolivia, Bulgaria, Byelorussian SSR, China, Colombia, Cuba, Denmark, Djibouti, Egypt, Gabon, German Democratic Republic, Ghana, Greece, Guinea, India, Iran, Iraq, Jamaica, Lesotho, Liberia, Libyan Arab Jamahiriya, Mozambique, Norway, Oman, Pakistan, Panama, Peru, Philippines, Poland, Rwanda, Saudi Arabia, Sierra Leone, Somalia, Sri Lanka, Sudan, Syrian Arab Republic, Trinidad and Tobago, USSR, Uruguay, Venezuela, Yugoslavia, Zaire.

Against: United Kingdom, United States.

Abstaining: Belgium, Canada, France, Germany, Federal Republic of, Ireland, Italy, Japan, Portugal.

GENERAL ASSEMBLY ACTION

In **resolution 43/134**, the General Assembly dealt with torture and inhuman treatment of children in detention in South Africa and Namibia. The Assembly expressed grave concern about reports of the increasing number of repressive measures against children there and demanded the immediate release of children held in detention. It also demanded that the so-called rehabilitation camps and re-education centres in South Africa be immediately dismantled, as they served only to abuse black children physically and mentally.

Aid programmes and inter-agency co-operation

United Nations aid to victims of *apartheid* was provided through national liberation movements and directly to individuals for education and training. Legal assistance, relief and education grants were given by the United Nations Trust Fund for South

Africa to persons persecuted under repressive and discriminatory South African legislation. The United Nations Educational and Training Programme for Southern Africa offered additional educational assistance (see below).

Assistance to national liberation movements

In 1988, several United Nations organizations, notably the United Nations Development Programme (UNDP), continued to provide assistance to national liberation movements recognized by the Organization of African Unity (OAU), namely, ANC and PAC of South Africa and SWAPO of Namibia.

By a July decision,[41] the UNDP Governing Council requested the Administrator to continue to assist the national liberation movements with maximum efficiency and flexibility, in accordance with the first programme of assistance for 1987-1991.

The Administrator reported[42] that the programme continued to emphasize activities intended to: promote professional expertise and human resources development through formal education and other types of training aimed at assisting individuals sponsored by national liberation movements in preparing themselves for eventual technical, managerial and administrative responsibilities in their countries; and foster among followers of national liberation movements self-reliance in countries of asylum.

During the year, 18 projects were being implemented: ANC and PAC had 3 ongoing projects each, SWAPO benefited from 8 projects and 4 projects covered all three national liberation movements. Total UNDP commitments under the national liberation movement indicative planning figure (IPF) amounted to $11 million. Of the 18 projects, 8 were in the education sector ($4.7 million), 4 dealt with planning, programming and aid co-ordination ($1.8 million), 3 were in food production ($1.8 million), 2 were geared to training and supporting health personnel ($3.1 million) and 1 preparatory assistance project was being used to formulate projects in the maintenance and repair of mechanical equipment ($15,000).

All three ongoing ANC projects, with an IPF of $1.6 million, were executed by the United Nations Educational, Scientific and Cultural Organization; they supported ANC's education sector. The PAC programme consisted of two projects in the education sector, being executed by UNDP, and one in food production, being exectued by the Food and Agriculture Organization of the United Nations. UNDP's contribution was $1.2 million.

In addition, 10 projects, focusing on maintenance and repair activities, health services, educational support, development aid co-ordination and food production, were in various

phases of formulation and approval: 6 with ANC, 2 with SWAPO and 2 with PAC. Pipeline project costs were estimated at $3.5 million.

ECONOMIC AND SOCIAL COUNCIL ACTION

In **resolution 1988/53**, the Economic and Social Council requested United Nations organizations to increase their assistance to the liberation movements in South Africa. It noted with satisfaction the arrangements made by several of those bodies that enabled representatives of national liberation movements recognized by OAU to participate as observers in their proceedings and called on those that had not done so to make such arrangements, including defraying costs of the participation of those representatives.

GENERAL ASSEMBLY ACTION

The General Assembly on a number of occasions took action on assistance to national liberation movements recognized by OAU. In **resolution 43/50 A**, it decided to continue the funding of the New York offices of ANC and PAC to enable them to participate effectively in the work of the Special Committee against *Apartheid* and other bodies. It made an urgent appeal for increases of assistance to the people of South Africa and their national liberation movements. A similar appeal was contained in **resolution 43/50 K**. In **resolution 43/106**, the Assembly again called for a substantial increase in all forms of assistance to the victims of racism and *apartheid* through the movements recognized by OAU. In **resolution 43/30**, it reiterated its recommendation that the United Nations system broaden its co-operation with colonial peoples and their movements and be flexible in formulating and preparing assistance programmes. It also recommended that a separate item on assistance to national liberation movements be put on the agenda of future high-level meetings between OAU and the United Nations. It echoed the call of the Economic and Social Council regarding the participation of representatives of the liberation movements as observers in meetings of international institutions on matters concerning their countries.

UN Trust Fund for South Africa

In October,[43] the Secretary-General reported that the United Nations Trust Fund for South Africa, established in 1965[44] to provide assistance to persons persecuted under discriminatory legislation in South Africa and Namibia, had made 11 grants totalling $3.5 million since the previous report.[44] During that period, the Fund received $3.1 million in voluntary contributions from 30 Governments, and a further $918,117 was outstanding. Total income of the Fund since its inception was $32.4 million, and the total amount of grants was $30.4 million. The available balance was $1.9 million as at 31 August 1988.

GENERAL ASSEMBLY ACTION

On 5 December, the General Assembly adopted **resolution 43/50 I** without vote.

United Nations Trust Fund for South Africa

The General Assembly,

Recalling its earlier resolutions on the United Nations Trust Fund for South Africa, in particular resolution 42/23 H of 20 November 1987,

Having considered the report of the Secretary-General on the United Nations Trust Fund for South Africa, to which is annexed the report of the Committee of Trustees of the Trust Fund,

Gravely concerned at the continued nation-wide state of emergency and security regulations which criminalize and stifle political dissent and protest,

Increasingly alarmed by the continued detentions without trials, forced removals, bannings, restriction orders, political trials, death sentences imposed on opponents of *apartheid*, harassment of trade unions, church and other organizations and individuals involved in peaceful protest and dissent,

Reaffirming that increased humanitarian and legal assistance by the international community to those persecuted under repressive and discriminatory legislation in South Africa and Namibia is more than ever necessary to alleviate their plight and sustain their efforts,

Strongly convinced that increased contributions to the Trust Fund and to the voluntary agencies concerned are necessary to enable them to meet the extensive needs for humanitarian and legal assistance,

1. *Endorses* the report of the Secretary-General on the United Nations Trust Fund for South Africa;

2. *Expresses its appreciation* to the Governments, organizations and individuals that have contributed to the Trust Fund and to the voluntary agencies engaged in rendering humanitarian and legal assistance to the victims of *apartheid* and racial discrimination;

3. *Appeals* for generous and increased contributions to the Trust Fund;

4. *Also appeals* for direct contributions to the voluntary agencies engaged in rendering assistance to the victims of *apartheid* and racial discrimination in South Africa and Namibia;

5. *Commends* the Secretary-General and the Committee of Trustees of the Trust Fund for their persistent efforts to promote humanitarian and legal assistance to persons persecuted under repressive and discriminatory legislation in South Africa and Namibia, as well as assistance to their families and to refugees from South Africa.

General Assembly resolution 43/50 I

5 December 1988   Meeting 68   Adopted without vote

41-nation draft (A/43/L.38 & Add.1); agenda item 36.

Sponsors: Antigua and Barbuda, Argentina, Australia, Austria, Bangladesh, Brazil, Canada, China, Denmark, Egypt, Finland, France, Germany, Federal Republic of, Greece, Guyana, Iceland, India, Indonesia, Ireland, Italy, Japan, Madagascar, Malaysia, Malta, Morocco, Netherlands, Nicaragua, Nigeria, Norway, Pakistan, Philippines, Senegal, Somalia, Sudan, Sweden, Syrian Arab Republic, Trinidad and Tobago, Tunisia, Turkey, Venezuela, Yugoslavia.

Meeting numbers. GA 43rd session: plenary 60-66, 68.

Other aspects

Public information

In accordance with a 1987 resolution,[46] the Department of Public Information (DPI) in 1988 continued its activities against the policy and practice of *apartheid*, including dissemination of information.

In a September report on information questions,[47] the Secretary-General stated that in addition to the regular audio and visual materials regularly produced by DPI, new campaign programmes had been formulated with the Centre against *Apartheid*. Access was gained to prestigious television shows where the United Nations story was seen by hundreds of millions of viewers. Projects undertaken included preparation of an exhibit of art against *apartheid*, participation of the cast of the musical *Sarafina* in commemoration of the International Day for the Elimination of Racial Discrimination, preparation of a film vignette for the twenty-fifth anniversary meeting of the Special Committee against *Apartheid*, the observance of the seventieth birthday of Nelson Mandela, a ceremony to honour the president of the World Boxing Council and boxers for individual and collective action against *apartheid* in sports and the organization of a travelling exhibit against *apartheid*, as well as coverage of numerous events at Headquarters and in the field.

GENERAL ASSEMBLY ACTION

On 5 December, the General Assembly adopted **resolution 43/50 H** by recorded vote.

Dissemination of information against the policies of *apartheid* of the régime of racist South Africa

The General Assembly,

Recalling and reaffirming the legislative mandate of its resolutions 32/105 H of 14 December 1977, paragraph 4, and 33/183 I of 24 January 1979, in which it requested the Secretary-General to undertake, in co-operation with Member States, a regular programme of radio broadcasts directed at South Africa,

Recalling also its resolutions 13(I) of 13 February 1946, 595(VI) of 4 February 1952, 1335(XIII) of 13 December 1958, 1405(XIV) of 1 December 1959, 3535(XXX) of 17 December 1975, 32/105 B of 14 December 1977, 33/115 of 18 December 1978, 34/181 and 34/182 of 18 December 1979, 35/201 of 16 December 1980, 36/149 of 16 December 1981 and 40/64 D of 10 December 1985, in which it requested the Secretary-General to intensify and expand radio programmes for broadcast to southern Africa,

Strongly convinced of the need to intensify and expand activities aimed at mobilizing world public opinion against the evil system of *apartheid* in South Africa,

Mindful of the important role of the United Nations and its specialized agencies in the dissemination of information against *apartheid*, as enshrined in the relevant General Assembly resolutions,

Bearing in mind the malicious propaganda activities of the racist régime of South Africa, which continues to commit numerous acts of military aggression and destabilization against the front-line States and other neighbouring States in the region, and the imperative need to effectively counter these activities,

Alarmed at the planned reduction in the establishment of the Anti-*Apartheid* Programmes Section of the Department of Public Information of the Secretariat,

Concerned at the continuous reduction in programme output over the years, and distressed at the prospect of the Department of Public Information's proposal to further reduce radio programmes directed at the people of South Africa and Namibia at this crucial period when the racist régime has escalated its disinformation campaign and mass media black-out,

Bearing in mind resolution 41/213 of 19 December 1986 regarding the restructuring of the administrative and financial functioning of the United Nations and, in particular, the need to ensure that reforms are implemented with flexibility and not have a negative impact on mandated and priority programmes,

Noting with appreciation that the Secretary-General has initiated radio programmes in co-operation with Member States whose broadcasts can be heard in southern Africa in the main languages spoken in South Africa, which are English, Afrikaans, Sesotho, Setswana, Xhosa and Zulu,

Taking into consideration that radio is the commonly and widely used as well as easily accessible medium of communication in the region,

1. *Urges* the Secretary-General to:

(*a*) Intensify, increase and expand these radio broadcasts as well as the production of audio-visual material and to maintain, without interference, the unique linguistic features and characteristics of these programmes;

(*b*) Provide all appropriate technical and financial assistance to radio stations of those Member States which are broadcasting or willing to broadcast to South Africa, in order to enable their radio transmitters to be heard inside South Africa;

(*c*) Ensure regular monitoring and evaluation of the impact of these programmes;

(*d*) Retain and commensurately increase the personnel in these programmes in accordance with the relevant resolutions of the General Assembly, in particular, resolution 42/220 of 21 December 1987;

(*e*) Further strengthen and enhance these radio programmes by engaging, at the upper echelons of the Secretariat and senior policy-making and supervisory levels, personnel from the region who will readily understand, interpret and be responsive to developments in the region;

(*f*) Maintain these radio programmes as an exclusively separate entity for purposes of enhancing their effectiveness;

2. *Appeals* to all Governments, non-governmental organizations and the specialized agencies to co-operate with the Secretary-General in order to ensure the widest possible dissemination of information against *apartheid*, in particular, these radio programmes;

3. *Expresses its appreciation* to those Member States and international organizations which have provided the Department of Public Information of the Secretariat with their broadcasting facilities, as well as their contribution to the Trust Fund for Publicity against *Apart-*

heid, and request those which have not done so to do the same;

4. *Requests* the Secretary-General to report to the General Assembly at its forty-fourth session on the implementation of the present resolution.

General Assembly resolution 43/50 H

5 December 1988   Meeting 68   132-1-21 (recorded vote)

36-nation draft (A/43/L.37 & Corr.1 & Add.1); agenda item 36.

Sponsors: Algeria, Angola, Antigua and Barbuda, Benin, Botswana, Burkina Faso, Burundi, Cameroon, Congo, Cuba, Ethiopia, Ghana, Hungary, Indonesia, Kenya, Liberia, Libyan Arab Jamahiriya, Madagascar, Malaysia, Mali, Mongolia, Mozambique, Nepal, Niger, Nigeria, Philippines, Senegal, Sudan, Syrian Arab Republic, Trinidad and Tobago, Tunisia, Uganda, United Republic of Tanzania, Zaire, Zambia, Zimbabwe.

Financial implications. 5th Committee, A/43/901 & Corr.1; S-G, A/C.5/43/50 & Add.1.

Meeting numbers. GA 43rd session: 5th Committee 39, 40, 42; plenary 60-66, 68.

Recorded vote in Assembly as follows:

In favour: Afghanistan, Albania, Algeria, Angola, Antigua and Barbuda, Argentina, Bahamas, Bahrain, Bangladesh, Barbados, Belize, Benin, Bhutan, Bolivia, Botswana, Brazil, Brunei Darussalam, Bulgaria, Burkina Faso, Burma, Burundi, Byelorussian SSR, Cameroon, Cape Verde, Central African Republic, Chad, China, Colombia, Comoros, Congo, Costa Rica, Côte d'Ivoire, Cuba, Cyprus, Czechoslovakia, Democratic Kampuchea, Democratic Yemen, Djibouti, Dominican Republic, Ecuador, Egypt, El Salvador, Equatorial Guinea, Ethiopia, Fiji, Gabon, Gambia, German Democratic Republic, Ghana, Grenada, Guatemala, Guinea, Guinea-Bissau, Guyana, Haiti, Honduras, Hungary, India, Indonesia, Iran, Iraq, Jamaica, Jordan, Kenya, Kuwait, Lao People's Democratic Republic, Lebanon, Lesotho, Liberia, Libyan Arab Jamahiriya, Madagascar, Malawi, Malaysia, Maldives, Mali, Malta, Mauritania, Mauritius, Mexico, Mongolia, Morocco, Mozambique, Nepal, New Zealand,[a] Nicaragua, Niger, Nigeria, Oman, Pakistan, Panama, Papua New Guinea, Peru, Philippines, Poland, Qatar, Romania, Rwanda, Saint Kitts and Nevis, Saint Lucia, Saint Vincent and the Grenadines, Samoa, Sao Tome and Principe, Saudi Arabia, Senegal, Seychelles, Sierra Leone, Singapore, Solomon Islands, Somalia, Sri Lanka, Sudan, Suriname, Swaziland, Syrian Arab Republic, Thailand, Togo, Trinidad and Tobago, Tunisia, Turkey, Uganda, Ukrainian SSR, USSR, United Arab Emirates, United Republic of Tanzania, Uruguay, Venezuela, Viet Nam, Yemen, Yugoslavia, Zaire, Zambia, Zimbabwe.

Against: United States.

Abstaining: Australia, Austria, Belgium, Canada, Denmark, Finland, France, Germany, Federal Republic of, Greece, Iceland, Ireland, Israel, Italy, Japan, Luxembourg, Netherlands, Norway, Portugal, Spain, Sweden, United Kingdom.

[a]Later advised the Secretariat it had intended to abstain.

Meetings, missions and observances

As part of its work to promote the international campaign against *apartheid*, the Special Committee against *Apartheid* organized or co-sponsored a number of meetings, missions and observances in 1988.

Meetings. Among the meetings supported or sponsored by the Special Committee were a seminar on the role of the Latin American and Caribbean media in the international campaign against *apartheid* (Lima, Peru, 7-9 March); a conference organized by the Association of West European Parliamentarians for Action against *Apartheid* on southern Africa's future and Europe's role (Lusaka, Zambia, 23-30 March); the Anti-*Apartheid* Asia and Oceania Workshop, organized by the Japan Anti-*Apartheid* Committee (Tokyo, 27-29 August); a symposium on culture against *apartheid* (Athens, Greece, 2-4 September); the International NGO Conference for Action to Combat Racism and Racial Discrimination in the Second United Nations Decade (Geneva, 11-14 October); a seminar for teachers on South Africa and *apartheid* (New

York, 28 and 29 October); an international conference on *apartheid* (Lagos, Nigeria, 7-9 November); and a conference of the European Campaign against South African Aggression on Mozambique and Angola (Bonn, Federal Republic of Germany, 8-10 December).

Missions. In his efforts to promote the anti-*apartheid* struggle, the Committee Chairman visited Botswana, Lesotho and Zimbabwe in May and held consultations with the authorities there. He also visited the German Democratic Republic, Hungary, the Ukrainian SSR and the USSR in August, meeting with governmental and non-governmental officials. At the invitation of the President of France, the Chairman attended ceremonies marking the fortieth anniversary of the Universal Declaration of Human Rights (Paris, 10 December).

Observances. As in previous years, the Special Committee held commemorative meetings on the International Day for the Elimination of Racial Discrimination (21 March), the International Day of Solidarity with the Struggling People of South Africa (16 June), the International Day of Solidarity with the Struggle of Women in South Africa and Namibia (9 August), and the Day of Solidarity with South African Political Prisoners (11 October).

Proposed special session

The Special Committee against *Apartheid* participated in the Conference of Foreign Ministers of the Non-Aligned Countries (Nicosia, Cyprus, 7-10 September). The final declaration of the Conference[48] called for the convening in 1989 of a special session of the General Assembly on *apartheid* and its destructive consequences in southern Africa. That call was endorsed by the eightieth Inter-Parliamentary Conference (Sofia, Bulgaria, 19-24 September),[49] in which the Special Committee Chairman also participated. The convening of a special session was among the recommendations the Special Committee made in its report to the General Assembly.[1]

GENERAL ASSEMBY ACTION

On 5 December, the General Assembly adopted **resolution 43/50 G** without vote.

Special session of the General Assembly on *apartheid* and its destructive consequences in southern Africa

The General Assembly,

Gravely concerned at the escalating repression mounted against the opponents of *apartheid* in South Africa,

Further concerned about the racist régime's continued aggression against the front-line States and its destructive consequences,

Taking note of the Declaration of the Conference of Foreign Ministers of Non-Aligned Countries held at Nicosia from 7 to 10 September 1988,

Indignant at the continued non-implementation of the General Assembly and Security Council resolutions by South Africa,

1. *Decides* to hold a special session of the General Assembly on *apartheid* and its destructive consequences in southern Africa before its forty-fourth session, on a date to be determined by the Secretary-General in consultation with the Special Committee against *Apartheid*;

2. *Requests* the Secretary-General to make the necessary administrative arrangements towards the convening of the special session.

General Assembly resolution 43/50 G

5 December 1988   Meeting 68   Adopted without vote

40-nation draft (A/43/L.36 & Corr.1 & Add.1); agenda item 36.

Sponsors: Albania, Algeria, Angola, Antigua and Barbuda, Benin, Botswana, Burkina Faso, Burundi, Cameroon, Congo, Cuba, Ethiopia, German Democratic Republic, Ghana, Hungary, India, Indonesia, Kenya, Liberia, Libyan Arab Jamahiriya, Malaysia, Mali, Mauritius, Mongolia, Mozambique, Nepal, Niger, Nigeria, Philippines, Senegal, Somalia, Sudan, Syrian Arab Republic, Trinidad and Tobago, Tunisia, Uganda, Ukrainian SSR, Viet Nam, Yugoslavia, Zambia.

Financial implications. 5th Committee, A/43/901 & Corr.1; S-G, A/C.5/43/50 & Add.1.

Meeting numbers. GA 43rd session: 5th Committee 39, 40, 42; plenary 60-66, 68.

Work Programme of the Special Committee against *Apartheid*

In its 1988 report,[1] the Special Committee against *Apartheid* recommended that the General Assembly authorize it to continue in its new approach to mobilizing international action against *apartheid* through publicity, meetings, seminars, conferences, hearings, consultations, missions and other relevant activities.

GENERAL ASSEMBLY ACTION

On 5 December, the General Assembly adopted **resolution 43/50 F** by recorded vote.

Programme of work of the Special Committee against *Apartheid*

The General Assembly,

Having considered the report of the Special Committee against *Apartheid*,

1. *Commends* the Special Committee against *Apartheid* for its work in the discharge of its responsibilities in promoting international action against *apartheid*;

2. *Takes note* of the report of the Special Committee and endorses the recommendations contained in paragraph 194 of the report relating to its programme of work;

3. *Decides* to make a special allocation of 400,000 dollars to the Special Committee for 1989 from the regular budget of the United Nations to cover the cost of special projects to be decided upon by the Committee;

4. *Requests* Governments and organizations to provide financial and other assistance for the special projects of the Special Committee and to make generous contributions to the Trust Fund for Publicity against *Apartheid*;

5. *Appeals* to all Governments, intergovernmental and non-governmental organizations, information media and individuals to co-operate with the Centre against *Apartheid* and the Department of Public Information of the Secretariat in their activities against *apartheid*, and in particular in disseminating information on the de-

teriorating situation in South Africa in order to mitigate the effects of the restraints on the press in South Africa and to effectively counteract South African propaganda.

General Assembly resolution 43/50 F

5 December 1988   Meeting 68   144-1-9 (recorded vote)

42-nation draft (A/43/L.35 & Corr.1 & Add.1); agenda item 36.

Sponsors: Algeria, Angola, Antigua and Barbuda, Benin, Botswana, Burkina Faso, Burundi, Cameroon, Congo, Cuba, Ethiopia, German Democratic Republic, Ghana, Hungary, India, Indonesia, Iran, Kenya, Liberia, Libyan Arab Jamahiriya, Madagascar, Malaysia, Mali, Mauritius, Mozambique, Nepal, Niger, Nigeria, Philippines, Senegal, Somalia, Sudan, Syrian Arab Republic, Trinidad and Tobago, Tunisia, Uganda, Ukrainian SSR, USSR, United Republic of Tanzania, Viet Nam, Yugoslavia, Zambia.

Financial implications. 5th Committee, A/43/901 & Corr.1; S-G, A/C.5/43/50 & Add.1.

Meeting numbers. GA 43rd session: 5th Committee 39, 40, 42; plenary 60-66, 68.

Recorded in Assembly as follows:

In favour: Afghanistan, Albania, Algeria, Angola, Antigua and Barbuda, Argentina, Australia, Austria, Bahamas, Bahrain, Bangladesh, Barbados, Belize, Benin, Bhutan, Bolivia, Botswana, Brazil, Brunei Darussalam, Bulgaria, Burkina Faso, Burma, Burundi, Byelorussian SSR, Cameroon, Canada, Cape Verde, Central African Republic, Chad, Chile, China, Colombia, Comoros, Congo, Costa Rica, Côte d'Ivoire, Cuba, Cyprus, Czechoslovakia, Democratic Kampuchea, Democratic Yemen, Denmark, Djibouti, Dominican Republic, Ecuador, Egypt, El Salvador, Equatorial Guinea, Ethiopia, Fiji, Finland, Gabon, Gambia, German Democratic Republic, Ghana, Greece, Grenada, Guatemala, Guinea, Guinea-Bissau, Guyana, Haiti, Honduras, Hungary, Iceland, India, Indonesia, Iran, Iraq, Ireland, Jamaica, Japan, Jordan, Kenya, Kuwait, Lao People's Democratic Republic, Lebanon, Lesotho, Liberia, Libyan Arab Jamahiriya, Madagascar, Malawi, Malaysia, Maldives, Mali, Malta, Mauritania, Mauritius, Mexico, Mongolia, Morocco, Mozambique, Nepal, New Zealand, Nicaragua, Niger, Nigeria, Norway, Oman, Pakistan, Panama, Papua New Guinea, Peru, Poland, Qatar, Romania, Rwanda, Saint Kitts and Nevis, Saint Lucia, Saint Vincent and the Grenadines, Samoa, Sao Tome and Principe, Saudi Arabia, Senegal, Seychelles, Sierra Leone, Singapore, Solomon Islands, Somalia, Spain, Sri Lanka, Sudan, Suriname, Swaziland, Sweden, Syrian Arab Republic, Thailand, Togo, Trinidad and Tobago, Tunisia, Turkey, Uganda, Ukrainian SSR, USSR, United Arab Emirates, United Republic of Tanzania, Uruguay, Venezuela, Viet Nam, Yemen, Yugoslavia, Zaire, Zambia, Zimbabwe.

Against: United States.

Abstaining: Belgium, France, Germany, Federal Republic of, Israel, Italy, Luxembourg, Netherlands, Portugal, United Kingdom.

REFERENCES

[1]A/43/22-S/20248. [2]A/44/22-S/20901 & Corr.2. [3]YUN 1987, p. 128, GA res. 42/23 G, 20 Nov. 1987. [4]A/43/699. [5]A/AC.131/297. [6]YUN 1987, p. 997, GA res. 42/14 A, 6 Nov. 1987. [7]A/43/24. [8]A/43/23. [9]S/19585. [10]YUN 1987, p. 138, GA res. 42/23 B, 20 Nov. 1987. [11]A/43/786. [12]YUN 1986, p. 137, GA res. 41/35 F, 10 Nov. 1986. [13]A/43/44 & Corr.1. [14]YUN 1985, p. 166, GA res. 40/64 G, annex, 10 Dec. 1985. [15]*Multilateral Treaties Deposited with the Secretary-General: Status as at 31 December 1988* (ST/LEG/SER.E/7), Sales No. E.89.V.3. [16]YUN 1968, p. 17, GA res. 2373(XXII), annex, 12 June 1968. [17]YUN 1977, p. 161, SC res. 418(1977), 4 Nov. 1977. [18]YUN 1984, p. 143, SC res. 558(1984), 13 Dec. 1984. [19]E/1988/17. [20]E/C.10/1988/7. [21]E/C.10/1988/8. [22]E/1988/23 & Corr.1,2. [23]YUN 1987, p. 152, GA res. 42/23 D, 20 Nov. 1987. [24]YUN 1983, p. 147. [25]A/43/802. [26]YUN 1984, p. 160, SC res. 554(1984), 17 Aug. 1984. [27]*Ibid.*, p. 161, GA res. 39/2, 28 Sep. 1984. [28]S/19567. [29]S/19568. [30]S/19624. [31]S/19939. [32]S/20289. [33]S/19569. [34]S/19570. [35]S/19571. [36]S/19632. [37]S/19944. [38]YUN 1986, p. 801, ESC res. 1986/25, 23 May 1986. [39]YUN 1987, p. 845, ESC dec. 1987/121, 26 May 1987. [40]E/CN.6/1988/2. [41]E/1988/19 (dec. 88/23). [42]DP/1989/21. [43]A/43/682. [44]YUN 1987, p. 160. [45]YUN 1965, p. 115, GA res. 2054 B (XX), 15 Dec. 1965. [46]YUN 1987, p. 346, GA res. 42/162 A, 8 Dec. 1987. [47]A/43/639. [48]A/43/610-S/20188. [49]A/43/675-S/20215.

South Africa and the front-line States

Prospects for peace in southern Africa received impetus following negotiations sponsored by the United States and supported by the USSR, which resulted in an agreement between Angola, Cuba and South Africa that allowed the inception of the United Nations plan for the independence of Namibia (see PART FOUR, Chapter III) and included a series of practical steps designed to create conditions necessary to settle the conflict.[1] The Security Council, acting on a report of the Secretary-General, decided to establish under its authority the United Nations Angola Verification Mission (UNAVEM) and requested the Secretary-General to take the necessary steps to implement it.

While such peaceful solutions were emerging, the destructive effects of *apartheid*, aggression and destabilization were evident in the region. Recognizing that reality, the General Assembly in December called for a special session focusing on *apartheid* and its destructive consequences in southern Africa to be convened in the latter part of 1989 (see above). Destabilization, carried out directly by South Africa or through Resistência Nacional de Moçambique (RENAMO), had had a profoundly destructive effect on Mozambique.

According to the Special Committee against *Apartheid*, at least 400,000 persons had died because of acts of destabilization, and millions of others had been displaced. In addition, the disruption of its economy had made Mozambique dependent on foreign donors, who supplied it with $800 million plus 500,000 tons of grain each year.

Several violations of Botswana territory and attacks on Botswana nationals, allegedly carried out by South Africa, were reported during the year.

The Special Committee estimated that the nine countries of the Southern African Development Co-ordination Conference—Angola, Botswana, Lesotho, Malawi, Mozambique, Swaziland, the United Republic of Tanzania, Zambia and Zimbabwe—lost $60 billion (at 1988 prices) in gross domestic product between 1980 and 1988 as a result of South Africa's acts of aggression and destabilization. Those sums related to war damage, particularly in Angola and Mozambique, higher spending on defence, loss of economic production, boycotts and embargoes imposed by Pretoria and caring for the growing number of refugees and internally displaced people.

In March, the Chairman of the Special Committee made a statement at a conference on South Africa's future and Europe's role (Lusaka, Zambia, 23-30 March) in which he proposed that an emergency programme be set up for concerted bilateral and multilateral assistance to the front-line States to counter South Africa's economic destabilization, as well as to reduce their dependence on South Africa.[2] In that connection, he emphasized the importance of the Action for Resisting Invasion, Colonialism and *Apartheid* (AFRICA) Fund of the Movement of Non-Aligned Countries in providing support to the national liberation movements and the front-line States.

Action by the Committee on colonial countries. The Committee on colonial countries, in August,[3] urged the United Nations system to extend, as a matter of priority, substantial material assistance to the front-line States to enable them to support more effectively the struggle of the people of Namibia for freedom and independence and to resist the violation of their territorial integrity. It welcomed the establishment of the AFRICA Fund and invited United Nations organizations and agencies to co-operate with the Fund in providing emergency assistance to the front-line States and national liberation movements.

GENERAL ASSEMBLY ACTION

The General Assembly dealt with South Africa's relations with the front-line States in several 1988 resolutions. In **resolution 43/50 A**, it urged countries to contribute generously to the AFRICA Fund and appealed to all States, intergovernmental organizations and NGOs to step up material, financial and other forms of support to the front-line and other neighbouring independent States. Similar calls were made in **resolution 43/26 A**, when the Assembly condemned South Africa for using Namibia as a springboard for armed invasions, subversion, destabilization and aggression against neighbouring African States, particularly Angola. The Assembly, in **resolution 43/116**, reiterated its appreciation to the Secretary-General for his efforts on behalf of the international community to organize and mobilize special programmes of economic assistance to the front-line and other neighbouring States to help them withstand the effects of South Africa's aggression and destabilization. It called on the international community to provide increased assistance to southern African countries to help them strengthen their capacity to provide for the care of refugees, returnees and displaced persons in their countries.

In **resolution 43/209**, the Assembly, reaffirming the importance of close co-operation between the United Nations and the front-line States, strongly urged the international community to provide the assistance necessary to enhance the capacity of those States to withstand the effects of economic measures taken by South Africa, or by the international community against South Africa.

It also appealed for the support of national and collective emergency programmes prepared by the front-line States and other bordering States.

Situation in Angola

UN verification mission

By letters of 17 December, Angola[4] and Cuba[5] informed the Secretary-General that, considering the fact that South Africa had formally undertaken to accept the implementation the 1978 Security Council resolution on Namibia[6] with effect from 1 April 1989, it was their intention to sign, on 22 December, an agreement providing for the redeployment to the north and the withdrawal of Cuban troops from Angola, in accordance with a timetable arrived at by the two countries. As the agreement also provided for verification by the United Nations, Angola and Cuba accordingly asked the Secretary-General to take the necessary steps to recommend to the Security Council that a group of United Nations military observers be set up to carry out that mandate, in conformity with the agreements the two countries had already reached with the Secretariat.

In order to help the Security Council in its consideration of the request, the Secretary-General, on 17 December, submitted a report[7] concerning the proposed arrangements for the operation of such an observer mission. According to the report, the bilateral agreement provided that the withdrawal of Cuban troops would begin on 1 April 1989 (''D-Day'') and would be completed within 27 months. Angola and Cuba had informed the Secretary-General that 3,000 troops would be withdrawn before 1 April. The duration of the observer mission would be approximately 31 months, starting seven days before the beginning of the Cuban troop withdrawal and ending one month after its completion.

The observer group, UNAVEM, would be under the command of a Chief Military Observer who would be responsible to the Secretary-General, who in turn would report to the Security Council. As for the strength of the mission, the Secretary-General estimated that 70 military observers and about 20 civilian support personnel would be needed. An advance party of approximately 30 observers would be deployed on or about 3 January 1989, while the remaining 40 would be deployed on or about 20 March. The Secretary-General estimated that the cost of the full 31-month period of UNAVEM would total approximately $20.4 million, of which $9.8 million would be required during 1989.

Following approval by the Council of the proposed arrangements for an observer mission, the Secretary-General, by a letter of 22 December,[8] reported that on the same date a tripartite agreement had been signed by Angola, Cuba and South Africa, as had the bilateral agreement between Angola and Cuba, as result of which the arrangements for the establishment of UNAVEM had entered into force. The Secretary-General proposed that UNAVEM be composed of contingents from the following Member States: Algeria, Argentina, Brazil, Congo, Czechoslovakia, India, Jordan, Norway, Spain and Yugoslavia. He also informed the President of the Council of his intention to appoint Brigadier-General Péricles Ferreira Gomes (Brazil) as Chief Military Observer.

By a letter of 23 December,[9] the President transmitted to the Secretary-General the Council's approval of his proposals.

SECURITY COUNCIL ACTION

The Security Council met on 20 December 1988, in accordance with an understanding reached in prior consultations. On that date, the Council unanimously adopted **resolution 626(1988)**.

The Security Council,

Noting the decision of Angola and Cuba to conclude a bilateral agreement on 22 December 1988 for the redeployment to the north and the staged and total withdrawal of Cuban troops from Angola, according to the agreed timetable,

Considering the request submitted to the Secretary-General by Angola and Cuba in letters dated 17 December 1988,

Having considered the report of the Secretary-General dated 17 December 1988,

1. *Approves* the report of the Secretary-General and the recommendations therein;

2. *Decides* to establish under its authority a United Nations Angola Verification Mission and requests the Secretary-General to take the necessary steps to this effect in accordance with his aforementioned report;

3. *Also decides* that the Mission shall be established for a period of thirty-one months;

4. *Further decides* that the arrangements for the establishment of the Mission shall enter into force as soon as the tripartite agreement between Angola, Cuba and South Africa on the one hand, and the bilateral agreement between Angola and Cuba on the other, are signed;

5. *Requests* the Secretary-General to report to the Security Council immediately after the signature of the agreements referred to in paragraph 4 and to keep the Council fully informed of further developments.

Security Council resolution 626(1988)

20 December 1988   Meeting 2834   Adopted unanimously

Draft prepared in consultations among Council members (S/20339).

Botswana–South Africa armed incidents

According to a press release issued on 21 June by Botswana[10] and transmitted the following

day, South Africa had violated its territory and carried out two attacks on Botswana nationals in or near the capital city of Gaborone. During the first incident, three unarmed policemen were injured, and in the second, a bomb destroyed a vehicle and damaged a house. Two members of the South African commando unit charged in the attacks were said to have been arrested on the night of 20 June and brought to trial on 22 June, according to a 23 June letter from Botswana.[11]

A similar incident, during which four persons were killed, had been reported in March.[12] In previous years, such as in June 1985,[13] the Security Council condemned a South African attack on Botswana's capital, and in May 1986,[14] the Council considered, but did not act on, charges of further attacks on a village near Gaborone. More allegations against South Africa were brought forward in 1987.[15]

Following consultations, the President of the Security Council on 24 June issued the following statement on behalf of the Council members:[16]

''Members of the Security Council have learnt with a profound sense of shock and indignation of South Africa's latest attacks on the territory of Botswana in flagrant violation of the sovereignty, independence and territorial integrity of that country carried out by the commandos of that régime on the night of 20 June 1988 which resulted in the injury of three unarmed Botswana policemen who were going about their normal duties near the capital city of Gaborone.

''Members of the Security Council further express their grave concern at South Africa's total disregard of the resolutions of the Security Council, in particular Security Council resolution 568(1985) by which the Security Council, *inter alia*, strongly condemned South Africa's attack on Botswana as an act of aggression against that country and a gross violation of its territorial integrity and national sovereignty.

''Members of the Council are also deeply disturbed by the explosion of a bomb in Gaborone West which destroyed a vehicle and damaged a house belonging to a Botswana national on the morning of 21 June 1988. They noted that the Government of Botswana, after a thorough investigation, had reached the conclusion that the two incidents were related.

''They strongly condemn these aggressive acts, provocation and harassment perpetrated by South Africa against the defenceless and peace-loving nation of Botswana in violation of international law.

''They reiterate their call to the South African Government to refrain from any further such aggressive acts and destabilization against Botswana and other front-line and neighbouring States as such acts can only aggravate tensions in southern Africa.

''They further reiterate the fact that peaceful change in southern Africa can only be brought about by the total eradication of *apartheid* which is the root cause of tension and conflict in both South Africa and the region as a whole.''

By a letter of 24 June,[17] South Africa stated that despite its repeated requests that Botswana curtail the activities of terrorists operating from inside its territory, terrorist infiltrations into South Africa continued, and that it was clear that the bulk of terrorists infiltrating South Africa, as well as their armaments, equipment and logistic support, did so through Botswana. South Africa wished to live in peace with all its neighbours, but was compelled to take action when neighbouring States ignored its legitimate concerns regarding terrorist attacks.

Annexed to the letter was a press release of 21 June issued by the South African Defence Force (SADF), according to which a patrol, while gathering information in Botswana near the South African border, was involved in the shooting incident with the Botswana police. The latter fired on the patrol, which was forced to return their fire, wounding members of the Botswana police. This action, the press release said, was not aimed against the Government or the people of Botswana, and the accusation that South Africa was guilty of State terrorism was preposterous. The two persons held in Botswana in connection with the incident had not been involved. Regarding their alleged connections with SADF, no comment would be made unless Botswana provided more details. Further, the action had to be seen against the background that 23 ANC terrorists were being held in connection with 16 acts of terror that had occurred during the previous three months.

Also annexed was a message of 22 June from South Africa to Botswana reiterating that the action had been directed against ANC. South Africa unequivocally denied any complicity in explosions that reportedly had occurred in or near Gaborone on 21 June. Against the background of the incidents, as well as recent bomb explosions in several major South African cities, South Africa considered it imperative that a ministerial meeting between the two countries be convened at the earliest possible date.

By a 28 June letter,[18] South Africa stated that neither Botswana's communication of 2 June nor the Security Council statement correctly reflected the situation, but that the facts were as follows: over the past two years, South Africa had met regularly with the Botswana Government in an attempt to obtain its cooperation in ensuring the security of the common borders against terrorist incursions. Botswana was well aware that its territory continued to be used by terrorist elements infiltrating South Africa, and the frequency of those incursions had increased over the past few weeks. On 8 May, four white terrorists had been apprehended at Broederstroom, near Johannesburg.

They had an arsenal of weapons and ammunition, including a ground-to-air missile, radio equipment, ANC documents and various explosive devices and mines. The action of the SADF unit on 21 June had been aimed at transit facilities and logistic support bases used by terrorists. Arrangements were being made for further discussions with Botswana, South Africa added.

Mozambique–South Africa relations

By a 23 November note,[19] Mozambique reported to the Secretary-General that during an attack on its forces by South African soldiers in Maputo province on 28 July, one South African was killed and some *matériel* was captured. South Africa had since requested the return of the body of the dead soldier and the captured *matériel*. South Africa, by a 13 December letter,[20] refuted the accuracy of Mozambique's report of the incident, stating that the confrontation was between Frente de Libertação de Moçambique (FRELIMO) and RENAMO contingents. Although SADF, which had been patrolling the border on the South African side, had decided to vacate the area, one of its soldiers was killed in the crossfire. Subsequently, the FRELIMO patrol had mistakenly seized some abandoned SADF equipment on South African territory, but had since apologized to South Africa for the incident and had undertaken to return the equipment.

South Africa expressed dismay that the matter had been publicized by Mozambique in a manner not provided for in the 1984 Nkomati accord,[21] while the Joint South Africa/Mozambique Security Commission (JSC), the primary forum for addressing such incidents, was carrying out its investigations.

South Africa annexed to its letter a joint press communiqué issued on 15 November by JSC expressing the determination of the two Governments to work together to counteract forces that were trying to undermine peace and stability.

Mozambique, in a note of 28 December,[22] maintained that the unprovoked attack on its forces by South African soldiers, supposedly searching for ANC personnel, had taken place well within its territory. No Mozambican forces had at any time crossed the border into South Africa, and no ordnance had fallen into South Africa.

REFERENCES

[1]A/44/22. [2]A/43/22. [3]A/43/23. [4]S/20336. [5]S/20337. [6]YUN 1978, p. 915, SC res. 435(1978), 29 Sep. 1978. [7]S/20338. [8]S/20351. [9]S/20352. [10]A/43/418-S/19952. [11]A/43/422-S/19958. [12]A/43/260-S/19697, A/43/271-S/19718, A/43/298-S/19765. [13]YUN 1985, p. 191, SC res. 568(1985), 21 June 1985. [14]YUN 1986, p. 165. [15]YUN 1987, p. 174. [16]S/19959. [17]S/19960. [18]S/19968. [19]A/43/862-S/20293. [20]A/43/965-S/20326. [21]YUN 1984, p. 185. [22]A/44/60-S/20357.

Other States

Comorian island of Mayotte

The question of Mayotte—one of a group of four islands in the Indian Ocean Comoro Archipelago—remained on the General Assembly agenda in 1988. The Islamic Federal Republic of the Comoros acceded to independence on 6 July 1975, following a referendum in 1974. France, the former colonial Power, had continued to administer the island of Mayotte, whose inhabitants had voted to remain associated with it.

In a September report to the General Assembly,[1] the Secretary-General said he had addressed a note verbale to the Comoros and France, drawing their attention to a 1987 Assembly resolution on the question of the island of Mayotte[2] and inviting them to provide him with any pertinent information for inclusion in his report. A similar communication had been sent to OAU. In the 1987 resolution, the Assembly had reaffirmed the sovereignty of the Comoros over Mayotte; invited France to honour the commitments entered into prior to the 1974 referendum on self-determination of the Comoro Archipelago concerning respect for the unity and territorial integrity of the Comoros; called for the translation into practice of the wish expressed by the French President to seek a just solution to the question of Mayotte; and urged France to accelerate the process of negotiations with the Comoros with a view to ensuring Mayotte's effective and prompt return to the latter.

France responded in August that under a December 1976 act adopted by the French Parliament, Mayotte had acquired the status of territorial collectivity of France; the act gave the island a special status that did not close the door to any change. Conscious of its responsibilities and as a demonstration of open-mindedness, France had undertaken to seek a solution to the problem of Mayotte that was in keeping with national as well as international law. France remained prepared to work towards a just and lasting solution that was consistent with the French Constitution and that respected the wishes of the people concerned; it continued to maintain a constructive dialogue with the Comoros at the highest level.

In September, Comoros stated that it had continued to seek ways of promoting progress on the question of Mayotte. In June, following the re-election of François Mitterrand as President of France, the President of the Comoros, on a private visit to France, had expressed to the French President the desire to speak with him before the end of the year to seek a solution to the question

of Mayotte, in accordance with resolutions adopted by international organizations.

Among them, OAU, at the summit meeting of heads of State (Addis Ababa, Ethiopia, May) had again reviewed the situation and reaffirmed the validity of the claim of the Comoros to the island. The Final Declaration adopted by the Conference of Non-Aligned Countries (Cyprus, September) reaffirmed the position of the Non-Aligned Movement in support of returning the island to the Comoros.

The Comoros said it remained confident that the international community, in particular the United Nations, would be able to bring pressure to bear on France so that a satisfactory solution could be found that was consistent with law and justice and conducive to the climate of peace and calm that must prevail in the region.

Concluding, the Secretary-General stated that he had maintained close contact with all parties and had informed them of his readiness to make available his good offices in the search for a peaceful solution to the problem in accordance with the 1987 resolution.

GENERAL ASSEMBLY ACTION

On 26 October 1988, the General Assembly adopted **resolution 43/14** by recorded vote.

Question of the Comorian island of Mayotte
The General Assembly,

Recalling its resolutions 1514(XV) of 14 December 1960, containing the Declaration on the Granting of Independence to Colonial Countries and Peoples, and 2621(XXV) of 12 October 1970, containing the programme of action for the full implementation of the Declaration,

Recalling also its previous resolutions, in particular resolutions 3161(XXVIII) of 14 December 1973, 3291(XXIX) of 13 December 1974, 31/4 of 21 October 1976, 32/7 of 1 November 1977, 34/69 of 6 December 1979, 35/43 of 28 November 1980, 36/105 of 10 December 1981, 37/65 of 3 December 1982, 38/13 of 21 November 1983, 39/48 of 11 December 1984, 40/62 of 9 December 1985, 41/30 of 3 November 1986 and 42/17 of 11 November 1987, in which, *inter alia*, it affirmed the unity and territorial integrity of the Comoros,

Recalling, in particular, its resolution 3385(XXX) of 12 November 1975 on the admission of the Comoros to membership in the United Nations, in which it reaffirmed the necessity of respecting the unity and territorial integrity of the Comoro Archipelago, composed of the islands of Anjouan, Grande-Comore, Mayotte and Mohéli,

Recalling further that, in accordance with the agreements between the Comoros and France, signed on 15 June 1973, concerning the accession of the Comoros to independence, the results of the referendum of 22 December 1974 were to be considered on a global basis and not island by island,

Convinced that a just and lasting solution to the question of Mayotte is to be found in respect for the sovereignty, unity and territorial integrity of the Comoro Archipelago,

Convinced also that a speedy solution of the problem is essential for the preservation of the peace and security which prevail in the region,

Bearing in mind the wish expressed by the President of the French Republic to seek actively a just solution to that problem,

Taking note of the repeated wish of the Government of the Comoros to initiate as soon as possible a frank and serious dialogue with the French Government with a view to accelerating the return of the Comorian island of Mayotte to the Islamic Federal Republic of the Comoros,

Taking note of the report of the Secretary-General,

Bearing in mind the decisions of the Organization of African Unity, the Movement of Non-Aligned Countries and the Organization of the Islamic Conference on this question,

1. *Reaffirms* the sovereignty of the Islamic Federal Republic of the Comoros over the island of Mayotte;

2. *Invites* the Government of France to honour the commitments entered into prior to the referendum on the self-determination of the Comoro Archipelago of 22 December 1974 concerning respect for the unity and territorial integrity of the Comoros;

3. *Calls* for the translation into practice of the wish expressed by the President of the French Republic to seek actively a just solution to the question of Mayotte;

4. *Urges* the Government of France to accelerate the process of negotiations with the Government of the Comoros with a view to ensuring the effective and prompt return of the island of Mayotte to the Comoros;

5. *Requests* the Secretary-General of the United Nations to maintain continuous contact with the Secretary-General of the Organization of African Unity with regard to this problem and to make available his good offices in the search for a peaceful negotiated solution to the problem;

6. *Also requests* the Secretary-General to report on this matter to the General Assembly at its forty-fourth session;

7. *Decides* to include in the provisional agenda of its forty-fourth session the item entitled "Question of the Comorian island of Mayotte".

General Assembly resolution 43/14

26 October 1988   Meeting 37   127-1-25 (recorded vote)

34-nation draft (A/43/L.15); agenda item 32.

Sponsors: Algeria, Bahrain, Benin, Botswana, Burkina Faso, Burundi, Comoros, Cuba, Democratic Yemen, Equatorial Guinea, Gambia, Guinea-Bissau, Guyana, Kenya, Lesotho, Liberia, Libyan Arab Jamahiriya, Madagascar, Mali, Mauritius, Morocco, Oman, Qatar, Sao Tome and Principe, Senegal, Somalia, Sudan, Swaziland, Uganda, United Arab Emirates, United Republic of Tanzania, Yemen, Zambia, Zimbabwe.

Recorded vote in Assembly as follows:

In favour: Afghanistan, Albania, Algeria, Angola, Antigua and Barbuda, Argentina, Bahamas, Bahrain, Bangladesh, Barbados, Belize, Benin, Bhutan, Bolivia, Botswana, Brazil, Brunei Darussalam, Bulgaria, Burkina Faso, Burma, Burundi, Byelorussian SSR, Cameroon, Cape Verde, Central African Republic, Chad, Chile, China, Colombia, Comoros, Congo, Côte d'Ivoire, Cuba, Czechoslovakia, Democratic Kampuchea, Democratic Yemen, Djibouti, Ecuador, Egypt, El Salvador, Equatorial Guinea, Ethiopia, Fiji, Finland, Gabon, Gambia, German Democratic Republic, Grenada, Guatemala, Guinea, Guinea-Bissau, Guyana, Haiti, Honduras, Hungary, Iceland, India, Indonesia, Iran, Iraq, Jamaica, Jordan, Kenya, Kuwait, Lao People's Democratic Republic, Lesotho, Liberia, Libyan Arab Jamahiriya, Madagascar, Malawi, Malaysia, Maldives, Mali, Mauritania, Mauritius, Mexico, Mongolia, Morocco, Mozambique, Nepal, New Zealand, Nicaragua, Nigeria, Oman, Pakistan, Panama, Papua New Guinea, Paraguay, Peru, Philippines, Poland, Qatar, Romania, Rwanda, Saint Kitts and Nevis, Saint Lucia, Sao Tome and Principe, Saudi Arabia, Senegal, Sierra Leone, Singapore, Somalia, Sri Lanka, Sudan, Suriname, Swaziland, Sweden, Syrian Arab Republic, Thailand, Togo, Trinidad and Tobago, Tunisia, Turkey, Uganda, Ukrainian SSR, USSR, United Arab

Emirates, United Republic of Tanzania, Uruguay, Vanuatu, Venezuela, Viet Nam, Yemen, Yugoslavia, Zaire, Zambia, Zimbabwe.

Against: France.

Abstaining: Australia, Austria, Belgium, Canada, Cyprus, Denmark, Dominica, Dominican Republic, Germany, Federal Republic of, Greece, Ireland, Israel, Italy, Japan, Luxembourg, Malta, Netherlands, Niger,[a] Norway, Portugal, Saint Vincent and the Grenadines, Solomon Islands, Spain, United Kingdom, United States.

[a]Later advised the Secretariat it had intended to vote in favour.

Libyan Arab Jamahiriya

On 30 November 1988, the General Assembly, by **decision 43/417**, included in the provisional agenda of its forty-fourth (1989) session an item on the 1986 Declaration of the Assembly of Heads of State and Government of the Organization of African Unity on the aerial and naval military attack against the Socialist People's Libyan Arab Jamahiriya by the United States in April of that year.[3] Although it was included in the agenda of the Assembly's 1988 session, the item was not discussed at that time.

Malagasy islands of Glorieuses, Juan de Nova, Europa and Bassas da India

The item on the question of the Malagasy islands of Glorieuses, Juan de Nova, Europa and Bassas da India was included in the provisional agenda of the General Assembly's 1988 regular session, in accordance with a 1987 Assembly decision.[4] On 23 September, by **decision 43/402**, the Assembly, on the recommendation of the General Committee, included the item in its agenda and allocated it to the Special Political Committee.

On 31 October, the Chairman informed the Committee that he had held consultations with the delegations concerned, in particular France and Madagascar.[5] In view of the ongoing periodic contacts between the authorities of those two countries, it was requested that the Committee postpone consideration of the item to the 1989 regular Assembly session.

By **decision 43/419** of 6 December, the Assembly, acting on the Committee's recommendation, included the item in the provisional agenda of its 1989 session.

REFERENCES

[1]A/43/648. [2]YUN 1987, p. 180, GA res. 42/17, 11 Nov. 1987. [3]YUN 1986, p. 257. [4]YUN 1987, p. 364, GA dec. 42/415, 2 Dec. 1987. [5]A/43/773.

UN Educational and Training Programme for Southern Africa

The United Nations Educational and Training Programme for Southern Africa, financed by a trust fund made up of voluntary contributions, granted or extended 1,358 scholarships in 1987/88. Of those,

879 were awarded to students from South Africa and 479 went to Namibians. The Programme's activities were described in a report of the Secretary-General covering 1 October 1987 to 31 August 1988.[1]

For Namibians, 201 new scholarships were awarded and 278 were extended, while 35 awards were completed. For South Africans, the figures were 406 new awards, 473 extensions and 250 completions. Students studying in Africa numbered 750, while 455 were in North America, 89 in Europe, 61 in Asia and 3 in Latin America and the Caribbean.

The Programme, in accordance with the recommendations of its Advisory Committee, strengthened its co-operation with scholarship agencies, educational institutions and foundations, such as the Commonwealth Fund for Technical Assistance, the World University Service, the International Institute of Education, the Bishop Tutu Southern African Refugee Scholarship Fund and the African-American Institute.

The Advisory Committee noted that the Programme was able to develop its co-operative activities with intergovernmental and non-governmental agencies involved in educational and technical assistance for southern Africa and welcomed the ongoing computerization of its activities.

In his concluding remarks, the Secretary-General again appealed for generous financial and other support for the Programme to meet the increasing demands being made on it.

During the period under review, the Programme received $4,035,132 in voluntary cash contributions from 27 States.

GENERAL ASSEMBLY ACTION

On 22 November, the General Assembly adopted **resolution 43/31** without vote.

United Nations Educational and Training Programme for Southern Africa

The General Assembly,

Recalling its earlier resolutions on the United Nations Educational and Training Programme for Southern Africa, in particular resolution 42/76 of 4 December 1987,

Having considered the report of the Secretary-General containing an account of the work of the Advisory Committee on the United Nations Educational and Training Programme for Southern Africa and the administration of the Programme for the period from 1 October 1987 to 31 August 1988,

Recognizing the valuable assistance rendered by the Programme to the peoples of South Africa and Namibia,

Noting with satisfaction that educational and technical assistance for southern Africa has become a growing concern of the international community,

Fully recognizing the need to provide continuing educational opportunities and counselling to a greater number of student refugees from South Africa and Namibia in a wide variety of professional, cultural and linguistic disciplines, as well as opportunities for vocational and technical training and for advanced studies at graduate and post-graduate levels in the priority fields of study,

Strongly convinced that the continuation and expansion of the Programme is essential in order to meet the ever-increasing demand for educational and training assistance to students from South Africa and Namibia,

1. *Endorses* the report of the Secretary-General on the United Nations Educational and Training Programme for Southern Africa;

2. *Commends* the Secretary-General and the Advisory Committee on the United Nations Educational and Training Programme for Southern Africa for their continuing efforts further to promote generous contributions to the Programme and to enhance co-operation with governmental, intergovernmental and non-governmental agencies involved in educational and technical assistance to southern Africa;

3. *Expresses its appreciation* to all those that have supported the Programme by providing contributions, scholarships or places in their educational institutions;

4. *Appeals* to all States, institutions, organizations and individuals to offer greater financial and other support to the Programme in order to secure its continuation and steady expansion.

General Assembly resolution 43/31

22 November 1988   Meeting 59   Adopted without vote

Approved by Fourth Committee (A/43/789) without vote, 25 October (meeting 13); 59-nation draft (A/C.4/43/L.3); agenda item 111.

Sponsors: Algeria, Argentina, Australia, Austria, Barbados, Belgium, Brazil, Burundi, Byelorussian SSR, Cameroon, Canada, Chile, Colombia, Congo, Costa Rica, Denmark, Djibouti, Egypt, Finland, France, Germany, Federal Republic of, Greece, Iceland, India, Indonesia, Ireland, Italy, Japan, Jordan, Lesotho, Liberia, Luxembourg, Madagascar, Malaysia, Mali, Morocco, Netherlands, New Zealand, Nicaragua, Nigeria, Norway, Panama, Papua New Guinea, Peru, Philippines, Portugal, Spain, Sudan, Swaziland, Sweden, Trinidad and Tobago, Tunisia, Turkey, Ukrainian SSR, United Kingdom, United States, Venezuela, Zambia, Zimbabwe.

Meeting numbers. GA 43rd session: 4th Committee 7-13; plenary 59.

REFERENCE

[1]A/43/681 & Corr.1.

Co-operation between OAU and the UN system

Co-operation between the United Nations and OAU was outlined by the Secretary-General, pursuant to a 1987 General Assembly resolution,[1] in an August 1988 report and a later addendum.[2] Their co-operation encompassed consultations and exchange of information, the situation in southern Africa, economic and social development and information and publicity.

In accordance with a request contained in the 1987 Assembly resolution, the Secretary-General, in consultation with the Secretary-

General of OAU, convened a meeting between representatives of the United Nations system and OAU (New York, 31 August–2 September). The meeting reviewed the current state of co-operation between the two organizations and measures taken or planned to alleviate the adverse socio-economic impact of emergency situations in Africa, including ways of co-operating to bring about a more effective response to such situations.

The meeting stressed the need for an integrated approach, covering preparedness, prevention, response and rehabilitation aspects. Joint efforts should focus on the following: moving from emergency food relief to household food security; rehabilitating and strengthening basic services, especially primary health care and shelter; providing special assistance to vulnerable groups; and enhancing the capacities of key institutions and programmes to address the emergency situation.

Noting that rehabilitation needs were not receiving adequate support, the meeting stated that long-term support of rehabilitation programmes should go hand-in-hand with emergency assistance; both the United Nations system and OAU had an important role to play in mobilizing assistance from the international community for self-sustained recovery and long-term self-reliant development. The meeting recommended that donors establish a capacity within their aid structures to deal specifically with rehabilitation programmes. The United Nations was seen as having an important role to play in supporting the implementation of rehabilitation efforts and the establishment and maintenance of permanent national emergency mechanisms.

The meeting called for intensified efforts to address the root causes of emergency situations and agreed on the need to give priority to environmental aspects of such situations. It also called for co-ordination with regard to programmes for refugees and displaced persons, with new approaches to allow them to become self-reliant and to channel their energies into genuine development.

The meeting emphasized the need for the United Nations to intensify its co-ordination efforts in order to provide timely and effective support to Governments in the field of disaster prevention and preparedness and related areas. Emphasis was further placed on specific responsibilities and capabilities within the United Nations in assisting OAU and African countries in early warning systems, needs assessment, resource mobilization, pipeline management, disaster preparedness, training and support and socio-economic research.

GENERAL ASSEMBLY ACTION

On 25 October, the General Assembly adopted **resolution 43/12** by recorded vote.

Co-operation between the United Nations and the Organization of African Unity

The General Assembly,

Having considered the report of the Secretary-General on co-operation between the United Nations and the Organization of African Unity,

Recalling its previous resolutions on the enhanc : e ent of co-operation between the United Nations and the Organization of African Unity and the practical measures taken for their implementation,

Recalling also its resolutions S-13/2 of 1 June 1986, the annex to which contains the United Nations Programme of Action for African Economic Recovery and Development 1986-1990, and 42/163 of 8 December 1987 on the Programme,

Taking note of the relevant resolutions, decisions and declarations adopted by the Council of Ministers of the Organization of African Unity at its forty-eighth ordinary session, held at Addis Ababa from 19 to 23 May 1988, and by the Assembly of Heads of State and Government of that organization at its twenty-fourth ordinary session, held at Addis Ababa from 25 to 28 May 1988,

Considering the important statement made by the current Chairman of the Assembly of Heads of State and Government of the Organization of African Unity before the General Assembly on 4 October 1988,

Mindful of the need for continued and closer co-operation between the United Nations and the specialized agencies and the Organization of African Unity,

Gravely concerned at the deteriorating situation in southern Africa arising from the continued domination and oppression of the peoples of South Africa and Namibia by the minority racist régime of South Africa and conscious of the need to provide increased assistance to the peoples of the region and to their liberation movements in their struggle against colonialism, racial discrimination and the policies of *apartheid,*

Conscious of its responsibilities to provide economic, material and humanitarian assistance to independent States in southern Africa to help them cope with the situation resulting from the acts of aggression and destabilization committed by the *apartheid* régime of South Africa,

Deeply concerned at the gravity of the situation of the refugees in Africa and the urgent need for increased international assistance to help African countries of asylum,

Recognizing the important role that the United Nations information system could play in disseminating information to bring about a greater awareness of the grave situation prevailing in southern Africa as well as the social and economic problems and the needs of African States and their regional and subregional institutions,

1. *Takes note* of the report of the Secretary-General on co-operation between the United Nations and the Organization of African Unity and of his efforts to strengthen such co-operation;

2. *Notes with appreciation* the increasing and continued participation of the Organization of African Unity in the work of the United Nations and the specialized agencies and its constructive contribution to that work;

3. *Commends* the continued efforts of the Organization of African Unity to promote multilateral co-operation among African States and to find solutions to African problems of vital importance to the international community;

4. *Reaffirms* that the implementation of the United Nations Programme of Action for African Economic Recovery and Development 1986-1990 is the responsibility of the international community as a whole and commends the efforts undertaken by African countries in spite of the effects of the adverse international economic environment;

5. *Calls upon* the Secretary-General of the United Nations to continue to ensure closer co-operation and coordination with the Secretary-General of the Organization of African Unity in the implementation and monitoring of the United Nations Programme of Action for African Economic Recovery and Development 1986-1990, as well as in the search for solutions to Africa's debt and debt-servicing burden, taking into account Africa's common position on its external debt, adopted by the Assembly of Heads of State and Government of the Organization of African Unity at its third extraordinary session, held at Addis Ababa on 30 November and 1 December 1987, and within the terms of the Medium-term Review of the Programme of Action, to consult the Organization of African Unity with a view to establishing a group of experts to undertake an in-depth assessment of the question of commodities of interest to Africa and the scope for export diversification;

6. *Reaffirms* that all Member States and regional and international organizations, in particular those of the United Nations system, should continue to give their maximum support to Africa's Priority Programme for Economic Recovery 1986-1990;

7. *Requests* all Member States, United Nations bodies, the specialized agencies and all other relevant organs of the United Nations, as well as non-governmental organizations, to activate and increase their programme of assistance to African subregional organizations for drought and desertification control such as the Permanent Inter-State Committee on Drought Control in the Sahel and the Intergovernmental Authority for Drought and Development;

8. *Reiterates its appreciation* to the Secretary-General for his efforts, on behalf of the international community, to organize and mobilize special programmes of economic assistance for those African States facing grave economic difficulties, the front-line States and other independent States of southern Africa to help them to withstand the effects of the acts of aggression and destabilization committed by the *apartheid* régime of South Africa;

9. *Requests* the Secretary-General to continue to keep the Organization of African Unity informed periodically of the response of the international community to those special programmes of economic assistance and to continue to co-ordinate efforts with all similar programmes initiated by that organization;

10. *Expresses its appreciation* to the United Nations Development Programme, the Office of the United Nations Disaster Relief Co-ordinator, the World Food Programme, the Food and Agriculture Organization of the United Nations, the World Health Organization, the United Nations Children's Fund, the Office of the United Nations High Commissioner for Refugees and the United Nations Institute for Training and Research for the assistance so far rendered to the African States in dealing with the emergency situation as well as with the critical economic problems that exist on the African continent;

11. *Reiterates* the determination of the United Nations, in co-operation with the Organization of African Unity, to intensify its efforts to eliminate colonialism, racial discrimination and *apartheid* in southern Africa;

12. *Requests* the Secretary-General to take the necessary measures to strengthen co-operation at the political, economic, cultural and administrative levels between the United Nations and the Organization of African Unity in accordance with the relevant resolutions of the General Assembly, particularly with regard to the provision of assistance to the victims of colonialism and *apartheid* in southern Africa;

13. *Urges* the international community to contribute generously to the Assistance Fund for the Struggle against Colonialism and *Apartheid* established by the Organization of African Unity and to the Action for Resisting Invasion, Colonialism and *Apartheid* Fund, established by the Movement of Non-Aligned Countries;

14. *Calls upon* the competent organs of the United Nations and the specialized agencies to continue to ensure the just and equitable representation of Africa at all levels at their respective headquarters and in their regional and field operations;

15. *Urges* all Member States and regional and international organizations, in particular those of the United Nations system, as well as non-governmental organizations to provide material and economic assistance to African countries of asylum to enable them to withstand the heavy burden imposed on their limited resources and weak infrastructure by the presence in their countries of large numbers of refugees;

16. *Calls upon* the United Nations organs—in particular the Security Council, the Economic and Social Council, the Special Committee on the Situation with regard to the Implementation of the Declaration on the Granting of Independence to Colonial Countries and Peoples, the Special Committee against *Apartheid* and the United Nations Council for Namibia—to continue to associate closely the Organization of African Unity with all their activities concerning Africa;

17. *Congratulates* the Secretary-General of the United Nations and the Secretary-General of the Organization of African Unity for reactivating the machinery for co-operation of the two organizations and encourages them to further strengthen the said machinery;

18. *Requests* the Secretary-General of the United Nations to invite the representative of the Secretary-General of the Organization of African Unity to participate in the meetings of the United Nations Steering Committee and its Inter-Agency Task Force and working groups on the implementation of the United Nations Programme of Action for African Economic Recovery and Development 1986-1990;

19. *Also requests* the Secretary-General to ensure that adequate facilities continue to be made available to facilitate continued liaison and consultations on matters of common interest as well as the provision of technical assistance to the General Secretariat of the Organization of African Unity, as required;

20. *Further requests* the Secretary-General to report to the General Assembly at its forty-fourth session on the implementation of the present resolution and on the development of co-operation between the Organization of African Unity and the organizations within the United Nations system.

General Assembly resolution 43/12

25 October 1988 Meeting 36 140-1 (recorded vote)

Draft by United Republic of Tanzania (A/43/L.1 & Corr.1,2); agenda item 26.

Recorded vote in Assembly as follows:

In favour: Afghanistan, Albania, Algeria, Antigua and Barbuda, Argentina, Australia, Austria, Bahamas, Bahrain, Barbados, Belgium, Belize, Benin, Bhutan, Bolivia, Botswana, Brazil, Brunei Darussalam, Bulgaria, Burkina Faso, Burma, Burundi, Byelorussian SSR, Cameroon, Canada, Cape Verde, Central African Republic, Chad, Chile, China, Colombia, Congo, Costa Rica, Côte d'Ivoire, Cuba, Czechoslovakia, Democratic Kampuchea, Democratic Yemen, Denmark, Djibouti, Dominica, Dominican Republic, Ecuador, Egypt, Equatorial Guinea, Ethiopia, Finland, France, Gabon, German Democratic Republic, Germany, Federal Republic of, Ghana, Greece, Grenada, Guinea-Bissau, Guyana, Haiti, Honduras, Hungary, Iceland, India, Indonesia, Iran, Iraq, Ireland, Italy, Jamaica, Japan, Jordan, Kenya, Kuwait, Lao People's Democratic Republic, Lebanon, Lesotho, Liberia, Libyan Arab Jamahiriya, Luxembourg, Madagascar, Malawi, Malaysia, Maldives, Mali, Malta, Mauritania, Mauritius, Mexico, Mongolia, Mozambique, Nepal, Netherlands, New Zealand, Nicaragua, Niger, Nigeria, Norway, Oman, Pakistan, Panama, Peru, Philippines, Poland, Portugal, Qatar, Romania, Rwanda, Saint Kitts and Nevis, Saint Vincent and the Grenadines, Samoa, Sao Tome and Principe, Saudi Arabia, Senegal, Seychelles, Sierra Leone, Singapore, Somalia, Spain, Sri Lanka, Sudan, Swaziland, Sweden, Syrian Arab Republic, Thailand, Togo, Trinidad and Tobago, Tunisia, Turkey, Uganda, Ukrainian SSR, USSR, United Arab Emirates, United Kingdom, United Republic of Tanzania, Uruguay, Venezuela, Viet Nam, Yemen, Yugoslavia, Zaire, Zambia, Zimbabwe.

Against: United States.

The Assembly called for United Nations/OAU co-operation in a number of other resolutions. Among them was **resolution 43/46**, requesting the Secretary-General to continue to disseminate information on decolonization and to maintain a close relationship with OAU by holding periodic consultations and exchanging information. In **resolutions 43/71 A** and **B**, the Assembly asked the Secretary-General to assist OAU in preparing and implementing a convention or treaty on the denuclearization of Africa.

REFERENCES

[1]YUN 1987, p. 183, GA res. 42/9, 28 Oct. 1987. [2]A/43/497 & Add.1.

Chapter II

Americas

Some progress was made in 1988 towards achieving peaceful solutions to the conflicts in Central America. However, outbreaks of violence continued on both sides of the Nicaragua/Honduras border. The civil war in El Salvador continued, with the Government accusing the insurgents of the Frente Farabundo Martí para la Liberación Nacional of engaging in terrorist activities aimed at seizing power. Panama accused the United States of, among other things, mobilizing unauthorized military forces on its territory and withholding payments related to use of the Panama Canal, in violation of treaties signed between the two countries.

The Security Council considered the Nicaragua situation without taking action on it. The General Assembly adopted resolutions exhorting the Central American States to continue their efforts to achieve peace in the region and appealing to countries outside the region to facilitate those efforts (resolution 43/24), and calling for an end to the trade embargo against Nicaragua (43/185). The Assembly also called for greater co-operation between the United Nations and the Organization of American States (43/4).

Central America situation

In his report on the work of the Organization (see p. 3), the Secretary-General said that the procedure for establishing a firm and lasting peace in Central America, signed at the Esquipulas II summit meeting (Guatemala City, August 1987),[1] had signalled the determination of the Presidents of Costa Rica, El Salvador, Guatemala, Honduras and Nicaragua to find solutions to the region's problems free from outside interference and the pressure of geopolitical conflicts. However, a year later, the momentum for peace appeared to be faltering and the considerable progress made so far seemed to be seriously threatened. Noting that the principal merit of the so-called Guatemala Procedure lay in its requirement for simultaneous progress on two broad fronts—democratization and the cessation of armed hostilities—he said its success depended on full compliance and a concerted effort by the signatories, as well as on the

co-operation of all the Governments and parties involved.

That assessment was also reflected in the Uruguay Declaration,[2] adopted by the member States of the Permanent Mechanism for Consultation and Concerted Political Action (Argentina, Brazil, Colombia, Mexico, Peru, Uruguay, Venezuela) at their second meeting (Punta del Este, Uruguay, 27-29 October). Among other things, the Declaration called on the international community, especially those countries with the most resources, to intensify its support for the political, economic and social reconstruction of the countries of the region in order to revitalize the peace process.

Report of the Secretary-General. In response to a 1987 General Assembly request,[3] the Secretary-General in October 1988 submitted a report[4] on the situation in Central America: threats to international peace and security and peace initiatives. He stated that in the months immediately following the signing of the Guatemala Procedure, significant progress had been made towards fulfilling the commitments set forth in it: national reconciliation commissions were established in each country; amnesty decrees were issued, although not all of them fostered open political activity; states of siege or emergency were lifted; relatively firm measures were taken to expand or strengthen political pluralism; and specific action was taken to arrange a cessation of hostilities. In addition, a treaty establishing a Central American Parliament was signed and ratified by four of the five legislative organs. On the other hand, progress had apparently not been made towards fulfilling the commitments on non-use of territory to attack other States and on terminating aid for irregular forces and insurrectionist movements. The Secretary-General appealed to countries outside the region to refrain from action likely to undermine the peace process and instead to facilitate it, emphasizing in that connection the interest and willingness to help of the Contadora Group (Colombia, Mexico, Panama, Venezuela), the Contadora Support Group (Argentina, Brazil, Peru, Uruguay) and the European Community. He appealed to countries in the region and elsewhere to renew their collective commitment to peace, and pledged his support in fulfilment of that objective.

Joint Declaration of the Central American Presidents. On 16 January, the Central American Presidents issued at San José, Costa Rica, a Joint Declaration,[5] reaffirming their determination to comply with the Esquipulas II agreements. Acknowledging that their commitments had not been entirely fulfilled, they promised to comply immediately with their obligations under the agreements, including dialogue, talks leading to a cease-fire agreement, general amnesty and democratization, including the lifting of states of emergency, freedom of the press, political pluralism and an end to the functioning of special courts. They also announced a new mechanism for verifying compliance with the agreements (see below).

Verification process. The Secretary-General, in his report of October, said that the International Verification and Follow-up Commission (established under the Esquipulas II agreements to verify and monitor their fulfilment and composed of the Secretaries-General of the United Nations and the Organization of American States (OAS) or their representatives and the Foreign Ministers of the Central American countries and the Contadora and Support Groups) had stressed the importance of on-site inspection, particularly with regard to the security commitments set forth in the agreements, for objective, independent and effective verification. A joint United Nations/OAS mission sent to evaluate the need for on-site inspection concluded that in view of the lack of unanimity among the five Central American Governments, conditions did not permit on-site verification of commitments regarding a cease-fire, non-use of territory to attack other States and termination of aid for irregular forces and insurrectionist movements (see below).

The Central American Presidents, in their Joint Declaration (see above), emphasized the necessity of verifying the compliance of Governments with the Esquipulas II agreements, particularly the termination of aid for irregular groups, the non-use of territory to support them and freedom of electoral processes. Accordingly, they decided that the primary function of the Executive Commission established under Esquipulas II, consisting of the Central American Foreign Ministers, would thenceforth be to verify, monitor and follow up all the commitments set forth in the agreements and the Joint Declaration. The Commission was also to secure the co-operation of States and impartial bodies that had indicated a desire to co-operate in the Central American peace process.

At its fifth meeting (Guatemala City, 23 and 24 March and 7 April),[6] the Executive Commission agreed that the national reconciliation commissions would verify the fulfilment of those commitments by means of on-site inspections or any other procedures they deemed necessary. The Commis-

sion said it would request the assistance of an auxiliary technical group composed of specialized personnel from Canada, the Federal Republic of Germany and Spain, which had indicated a desire to co-operate. The Commission urged members of irregular armed forces and insurrectionist movements to make serious efforts to reach a cease-fire agreement, and reiterated its vigorous demand to Governments of the region and outside the region to terminate aid to such groups.

GENERAL ASSEMBLY ACTION

On 15 November 1988, the General Assembly adopted **resolution 43/24** without vote.

The situation in Central America: threats to international peace and security and peace initiatives

The General Assembly,

Recalling Security Council resolutions 530(1983) of 19 May 1983 and 562(1985) of 10 May 1985 and its resolutions 38/10 of 11 November 1983, 39/4 of 26 October 1984, 41/37 of 18 November 1986 and 42/1 of 7 October 1987, as well as the initiative of the Secretaries-General of the United Nations and of the Organization of American States of 18 November 1986,

Taking note of the report of the Secretary-General submitted in pursuance of General Assembly resolution 42/1,

Recognizing the far-sighted and unfailing determination, as well as the decisive contribution, of the Contadora Group and its Support Group in favour of peace in Central America,

Convinced that the peoples of Central America wish to achieve peace, reconciliation, development and justice, without outside interference, in accordance with their own decision and their own historical experience, and without sacrificing the principles of self-determination and non-intervention,

Aware that the agreement on "Procedures for the establishment of a firm and lasting peace in Central America" signed at Guatemala City on 7 August 1987 by the Presidents of the Republics of Costa Rica, El Salvador, Guatemala, Honduras and Nicaragua, at the Esquipulas II summit meeting, is the outcome of the decision by Central Americans to take up fully the historical challenge of forging a peaceful destiny for Central America,

Aware also of the political will which inspires them to settle their differences by means of dialogue, negotiation and respect for the legitimate interests of all States, establishing commitments to be fulfilled in good faith, through the verifiable performance of actions aimed at achieving peace, democracy, security, co-operation and respect for human rights,

Recognizing the importance of the Joint Declaration of the Central American Presidents issued at San José on 16 January 1988, whereby they undertook to fulfil immediately, unconditionally and unilaterally the obligations contained in the agreement concluded at the Esquipulas II summit meeting, which must necessarily be "subject to special verification",

Welcoming the recognition given by the Central American Presidents to the tremendous efforts made by the

International Verification and Follow-up Commission in helping to implement the agreement concluded at the Esquipulas II summit meeting,

Bearing in mind the particular importance which the implementation of its resolution 42/231 of 12 May 1988 has for the improvement of the living standards of the Central American people,

1. *Commends* the desire for peace expressed by the Central American Presidents in signing on 7 August 1987 at Guatemala City the agreement on ''Procedures for the establishment of a firm and lasting peace in Central America'' and in issuing on 16 January 1988 at San José their Joint Declaration;

2. *Expresses* its strongest support for the agreement;

3. *Exhorts* the Governments to continue their efforts to achieve a firm and lasting peace in Central America and fervently hopes that the Central American Presidents at their next meeting will evaluate and give a new impetus to the process of fulfilling the undertakings assumed in the agreement concluded at the Esquipulas II summit meeting;

4. *Urges* the five Central American countries to adopt immediately formulae that will enable them to overcome the obstacles impeding the advancement of the regional peace process;

5. *Exhorts* the five Central American countries, with the utmost urgency, to promote and supplement the agreed verification machinery, with the co-operation of regional or extra-regional States and bodies of recognized impartiality and technical capacity, which have shown a desire to collaborate in the Central American peace process;

6. *Requests* the Secretary-General to afford the fullest possible support to the Central American Governments in their efforts to achieve peace, especially by taking the measures necessary for the development and effective functioning of the essential verification machinery;

7. *Appeals* to the countries which are outside the region but which have links with it and interests in it to facilitate the implementation of the agreement concluded at the Esquipulas II summit meeting and to abstain from any action which may impede such implementation;

8. *Urges* the international community and international organizations to increase their technical, economic and financial co-operation with the Central American countries for the implementation of the activities supporting the goals and objectives of the Special Plan of Economic Co-operation for Central America, as stipulated in General Assembly resolution 42/231, and as a way of assisting the efforts being made by the countries of the region to achieve peace and development;

9. *Also requests* the Secretary-General to submit a report to the General Assembly at its forty-fourth session on the implementation of the present resolution;

10. *Decides* to include in the provisional agenda of its forty-fourth session the item entitled ''The situation in Central America: threats to international peace and security and peace initiatives''.

General Assembly resolution 43/24

15 November 1988   Meeting 50   Adopted without vote

13-nation draft (A/43/L.26); agenda item 22.
Sponsors: Argentina, Brazil, Colombia, Costa Rica, El Salvador, Guatemala, Honduras, Mexico, Nicaragua, Panama, Peru, Uruguay, Venezuela.

In related action, the Assembly, by **resolution 43/118**, welcomed the decisions of OAS and the United Nations High Commissioner for Refugees (UNHCR) in support of an international conference on Central American refugees, to be held in Guatemala in May 1989. (For details concerning Central American refugees, see PART THREE, Chapter XV.)

ECONOMIC AND SOCIAL COUNCIL ACTION

The Economic and Social Council, by **resolution 1988/20**, called on the Central American countries and the Contadora Group and its Support Group to encourage and guarantee the full participation of women at all levels in the search for peace, pluralism, democracy and comprehensive development in the region.

Nicaragua situation

By a note of 8 February to the Secretary of State of the United States,[7] Nicaragua protested what it called terrorist and criminal acts committed against its people by United States–supported mercenaries. It said that 18 civilians, including four children, were killed and 18 were injured in an incident on 4 February in which a bus was mined, and that nine people were killed and 31 injured on 6 February when a fragmentation grenade was thrown into a group of civilians protesting the earlier attack.

In a press release issued on 16 March,[8] Honduras alleged that several hundred Nicaraguan troops had entered Honduran territory on 15 March and that bombs had been dropped from aircraft. Honduras had subsequently requested immediate assistance from the United States.

Nicaragua addressed three notes to the Honduran Foreign Minister protesting further attacks. One, of 18 March, described rocket attacks in the Amaka sector, on 17 March, by jets coming from Honduras.[9] Another, of 19 March, alleged that Nicaragua had been infiltrated by approximately 30 mercenaries who had clashed with a unit of the Sandinista army on 18 March.[10] That note also stated that the incursion had been openly supported by the Honduran army, which had fired rifle shots at a Sandinista army border post. Nicaragua charged that aircraft coming from Honduras had violated Nicaraguan airspace on 26 occasions between 15 and 18 March, and that a number of those incursions had been accompanied by attacks on Nicaraguan territory. The third note, also of 19 March, described two attacks by F-5 aircraft in which several bombs were dropped on Nicaragua on 19 March.[11] On 23 March,[12] Honduras, by a note to the Nicaraguan Foreign Minister, charged that approximately 350 Nicaraguan soldiers had entered Honduras the previous day. Nicaragua categorically rejected the accusation.[13]

SECURITY COUNCIL CONSIDERATION

At the urgent request of Nicaragua,[14] the Security Council met on 18 and 22 March to consider what Nicaragua called the serious situation created by the escalation of threats and aggression against it and by the decision of the United States to send troops to Honduras.

Meeting numbers. SC 2802, 2803.

The President, with the consent of the Council, invited Colombia, Costa Rica, Honduras, Nicaragua, Peru, Viet Nam and Zimbabwe, at their request, to participate in the discussion without the right to vote, in accordance with the relevant provisions of the Charter of the United Nations and rule 37[a] of the Council's provisional rules of procedure.

Addressing the Council, Nicaragua, referring to the decision by the United States to send 3,200 troops to Honduras, accused the United States of attempting to abort the Esquipulas II accords (see above) and efforts to achieve a cease-fire in the region. According to Nicaragua, the first grave provocation had occurred on 17 March, when two United States jets coming from Honduras had bombed the Amaka sector, an area bordering Honduras, and two missiles had been launched against Nicaraguan troops in San Andrés de Bocay. Nicaragua stated that it had requested the Secretaries-General of the United Nations and OAS to send a technical mission to investigate the Bocay incident and to make specific recommendations for the disarmament and withdrawal of what it called the mercenary troops located in Honduras. Nicaragua asked Honduras to abide by the accords by dismantling contra bases and by disarming and expelling the mercenaries. It also urged the United States to put an end to what it called its illegal assistance to the contras and to comply with the 1986 ruling of the International Court of Justice (ICJ) concerning military and paramilitary activities in and against Nicaragua[15] (see below).

Honduras replied that Nicaragua had carried out a broad-ranging offensive in the northern part of the country against its own insurgents, and some 1,500 Nicaraguan troops had entered the Bocay sector of Honduras, using artillery and the air force. Honduras reaffirmed its right of self-defence, saying that it had faced repeated acts of aggression by the Sandinista People's Army. Given the excessive military buildup in Nicaragua, Honduras had requested United States assistance in strengthening its security position. The troops dispatched in response to that request would be carrying out readiness exercises and would remain until the Sandinistas withdrew their troops from Honduras. Honduras stated that the 17 March attacks had been carried out against a Sandinista

military post in Bocay, in Honduran territory, which had been providing logistical support for the aggressive activities of the Nicaraguan troops operating in Honduras. The action was intended to cut off the supply of *matériel* and logistical support to those troops. Honduras called on Nicaragua to withdraw its troops from Honduran territory and border areas immediately.

According to the United States, the deployment of troops was designed to show its staunch support for Honduras at a time when that country's territorial integrity was being violated by the Sandinista army. Because the troops had been deployed to an air base rather than to an area of ongoing hostilities, the United States did not believe that its action constituted either a threat or the use of force against Nicaragua. The United States disputed Nicaragua's claim that its troops had been in hot pursuit of insurgents. Rather, it alleged that the invasion had been a planned offensive in clear violation of international law, and was part of a plan to destroy the Nicaraguan resistance as an effective fighting force in order to stifle internal dialogue and demoralize the democratic opposition groups within the country.

Colombia read out a communiqué issued on 18 March by the Contadora and Support Groups, expressing their profound concern at the escalation of the foreign military presence in Honduras; reiterating the need for strict compliance with the principles of non-intervention, prohibition of the threat or use of force and peaceful settlement of disputes; appealing to Honduras and Nicaragua to reduce the tension in their border area immediately; appealing for an end to the foreign military presence in the area; and urging the Secretary-General to dispatch an observer mission immediately. Colombia further stated that it was pleased that the Secretary-General had already proceeded to send the requested observer mission. The communiqué was transmitted to the Secretary-General on 21 March.[16]

Honduras took exception to the communiqué, saying that it could not be accused of failing to abide by its international obligations as a result of exercising its right of self-defence, and said that the only military escalation it was concerned about was that of the Sandinista People's Army, which it said had invaded Honduras. Honduras reiterated its opposition to an observer mission, since a mechanism—the Executive Commission (see above)—had already been set up by the Central

---

[a]Rule 37 of the Council's provisional rules of procedure states: "Any Member of the United Nations which is not a member of the Security Council may be invited, as the result of a decision of the Security Council, to participate, without vote, in the discussion of any question brought before the Security Council when the Security Council considers that the interests of that Member are specially affected, or when a Member brings a matter to the attention of the Council in accordance with Article 35 (1) of the Charter."

American Presidents for the purpose of implementing the peace process. To accede to Nicaragua's request would go against the political will of the Presidents expressed in their Joint Declaration of January (see above). On 23 March, Honduras transmitted to the Secretary-General its reply to the communiqué,[17] stating that it was ironic that increasing concern should be expressed about the presence of United States troops in Honduras when they were sent at the Government's request, and that there should be such an interest in denouncing the presence of foreign troops in Honduras while nothing was said about the 6,000 military advisers from the Soviet bloc which Nicaragua had on its territory.

Nicaragua thanked the Secretary-General for his prompt response to its request to send a technical mission to investigate the recent border incidents. Nicaragua alleged that contrary to the United States declaration that its troops would be stationed 120 miles from the Nicaraguan border, they were currently within 15 miles of the border.

The United States said that Nicaragua's attack on Honduras had been premeditated and that Nicaragua had repeatedly attempted to delay and obstruct cease-fire talks.

The Council adjourned without taking action.

In a letter of 5 April to the President of the Security Council,[18] Honduras requested a meeting of the Council on 11 April to discuss the collateral effects which the restoration of peace in Nicaragua had on the situation in Central America, in the light of recent developments. It withdrew the request on 8 April[19] in view of the results of the Esquipulas II Executive Commission meeting concluded the previous day (see above).

Sapoá agreement

The Government of Nicaragua and the Nicaraguan resistance, meeting at Sapoá, Nicaragua (21-23 March),[20] with the aim of contributing to reconciliation within the framework of the Esquipulas II agreements, agreed to end offensive military operations for 60 days beginning on 1 April 1988, during which a definitive cease-fire would be negotiated. During the first 15 days, the resistance forces were to move to mutually agreed areas. Nicaragua agreed to a general amnesty, to be implemented gradually under the direction of the Secretary-General of OAS. The contras agreed to arrange for and accept humanitarian assistance only, which was to be provided by neutral organizations. Nicaragua guaranteed unrestricted freedom of expression, agreed to allow all persons who had left the country for political or other motives to return without being punished for any political or military activities, and confirmed the right of all persons who had been "reintegrated into a peaceful life" to participate in national, municipal and Central American Parliament elections.

A commission, composed of the President of the Episcopal Conference of Nicaragua and the Secretary-General of OAS, was established to verify compliance with the agreement.

Nicaragua, in a note to the United States Secretary of State on 20 April,[21] accused that country of providing humanitarian aid, through its Agency for International Development (AID), to armed members of the resistance who had remained in Honduras. In a similar note, it accused Honduras of permitting such aid to be provided. Nicaragua charged that this action violated both the Sapoá agreement, requiring that humanitarian aid be provided by neutral organizations, as well as the Esquipulas II agreements, which prohibited aid to irregular forces except that intended for repatriation and relocation assistance. On 21 April,[22] Honduras replied that Nicaragua's protest was unfounded. It stated that the aid had been approved, with the concurrence of Nicaragua, once a provisional cease-fire had been agreed upon, precisely to facilitate the agreements. It was the intention of Honduras that aid reach groups of Nicaraguans who did not enjoy the protection of UNHCR. Nicaragua, in a note of 10 May to the United States Secretary of State,[23] protested a plan by AID, reported in _The New York Times_, to provide cash to the contras, and, in a note of 12 August to the Secretary-General,[24] denounced the approval by the United States Senate of $27 million in so-called humanitarian aid for the contras.

1986 ICJ Judgment

Responding to a 1987 General Assembly request,[25] the Secretary-General in October 1988[26] reported that there had been no new developments regarding compliance with ICJ's 1986 Judgment concerning military and paramilitary activities in and against Nicaragua.[15] (See PART FIVE, Chapter I, for ICJ action on this matter.)

The Assembly, in **resolution 43/11**, urgently called for full and immediate compliance with the Judgment in conformity with the United Nations Charter.

Trade embargo against Nicaragua

In response to a 1987 General Assembly request,[27] the Secretary-General in September 1988 submitted a report[28] summarizing action taken by States to reduce the negative effects of the trade embargo imposed by the United States against Nicaragua in 1985.[29] Czechoslovakia, Denmark, the German Democratic Republic, Malawi, Nicaragua, Norway, the Ukrainian SSR and the USSR had provided information in response to a request of the Secretary-General.

Nicaragua reported that the embargo had had serious, far-reaching consequences, as its economy had relied largely on foreign trade, particularly with North America. In 1980, sales to the United States had represented 36 per cent of its total exports, but by 1986, the percentage had fallen to zero. Nicaragua had also traditionally depended heavily on imports from the United States, especially for intermediate goods for industry, agriculture and construction, capital goods and consumer goods. The embargo had resulted in a loss of $65 million between May 1985 and December 1987 because of higher import prices, mainly on inputs for the production of basic foodstuffs for domestic consumption and for the manufacture of chemicals for export. The most serious effects of the embargo in the medium and long term would be a reduction of public services, including water and power, and a deterioration of the health system. Nicaragua estimated that the damage caused by the embargo between May 1985 and the end of 1987 amounted to $254 million.

With the exception of Denmark and Norway, the above-mentioned States indicated their opposition to the embargo. Denmark, the German Democratic Republic, Norway, the Ukrainian SSR and the USSR described various levels of financial, technical and/or in-kind assistance they had been providing to Nicaragua. These took the form of, among other things, development aid, vocational training, hospital facilities and medical supplies, food and loan deferments.

GENERAL ASSEMBLY ACTION

On 20 December 1988, the Assembly, on the recommendation of the Second (Economic and Financial) Committee, adopted **resolution 43/185** by recorded vote.

Trade embargo against Nicaragua

The General Assembly,

Recalling its resolutions 40/188 of 17 December 1985, 41/164 of 5 December 1986 and 42/176 of 11 December 1987, as well as its resolutions 42/204 of 11 December 1987 and 42/231 of 12 May 1988,

Taking note of the report of the Secretary-General on the trade embargo against Nicaragua,

1. *Deplores* the continuation of the trade embargo contrary to its resolutions 40/188, 41/164 and 42/176 and to the Judgment of the International Court of Justice of 27 June 1986, and once again requests that those measures be immediately revoked;

2. *Requests* the Secretary-General to report to the General Assembly at its forty-fourth session on the implementation of the present resolution.

General Assembly resolution 43/185

20 December 1988   Meeting 83   89-2-50 (recorded vote)

Approved by Second Committee (A/43/915/Add.2) by recorded vote (85-2-38), 23 November (meeting 44); 9-nation draft (A/C.2/43/L.52); agenda item 82 (b).

Sponsors: Algeria, Congo, Democratic Yemen, Libyan Arab Jamahiriya, Mexico, Nicaragua, Panama, Peru, Zimbabwe.

Meeting numbers. GA 43rd session: 2nd Committee 21-26, 30, 42-44; plenary 83.

Recorded vote in Assembly as follows:

In favour: Afghanistan, Albania, Algeria, Angola, Argentina, Australia, Austria, Barbados, Bolivia, Botswana, Brazil, Bulgaria, Burkina Faso, Burma, Burundi, Byelorussian SSR, Cameroon, Cape Verde, China, Colombia, Congo, Cuba, Cyprus, Czechoslovakia, Democratic Yemen, Denmark, Dominican Republic, Ecuador, Ethiopia, Fiji, Finland, German Democratic Republic, Ghana, Greece, Guinea, Guyana, Haiti, Hungary, Iceland, India, Indonesia, Iran, Iraq, Ireland, Kenya, Kuwait, Lao People's Democratic Republic, Lesotho, Liberia, Libyan Arab Jamahiriya, Madagascar, Malawi, Malaysia, Mali, Mexico, Mongolia, Mozambique, New Zealand, Nicaragua, Nigeria, Norway, Pakistan, Panama, Papua New Guinea, Peru, Philippines, Poland, Romania, Sao Tome and Principe, Seychelles, Solomon Islands, Spain, Sudan, Suriname, Swaziland, Sweden, Syrian Arab Republic, Uganda, Ukrainian SSR, USSR, United Arab Emirates, United Republic of Tanzania, Uruguay, Vanuatu, Venezuela, Viet Nam, Yugoslavia, Zambia, Zimbabwe.

Against: Israel, United States.

Abstaining: Antigua and Barbuda, Bahrain, Belgium, Brunei Darussalam, Canada, Central African Republic, Chad, Chile, Costa Rica, Côte d'Ivoire, Djibouti, Egypt, El Salvador, Equatorial Guinea, France, Gabon, Gambia, Germany, Federal Republic of, Grenada, Honduras, Italy, Jamaica, Japan, Jordan, Lebanon, Luxembourg, Malta, Mauritius, Nepal, Netherlands, Niger, Oman, Paraguay, Portugal, Rwanda, Saint Vincent and the Grenadines, Samoa, Saudi Arabia, Senegal, Sierra Leone, Singapore, Somalia, Sri Lanka, Togo, Trinidad and Tobago, Tunisia, Turkey, United Kingdom, Yemen, Zaire.

El Salvador situation

In 1988, El Salvador continued to accuse the Frente Farabundo Martí para la Liberación Nacional–Frente Democrático Revolucionario (FMLN-FDR)—the Salvadorian opposition movement—of terrorist activities that it said were part of a guerrilla war designed to achieve a violent take-over of power. By a communiqué of 6 September,[30] El Salvador denounced an attack on 1 September in which private dwellings were destroyed and two persons were injured in machine-gun fire. On 14 September,[31] it condemned street unrest that had occurred during a demonstration the previous day in which one soldier was killed and several police officers were shot. The Government accused armed opposition groups of using the demonstration to incite disorder. El Salvador also said that FMLN had attacked an army brigade and conducted a transport stoppage, blocking the delivery of humanitarian assistance to victims of hurricane Gilbert. On 26 September,[32] El Salvador charged that the transport stoppage, imposed from 19 to 21 September, had been accompanied by acts of sabotage against the national electricity grid. In addition, it said, a Red Cross ambulance was machine-gunned, offices of the National Telecommunications Administration were destroyed and various military posts were attacked. On 20 December,[33] the Government denounced the abduction by FMLN-FDR of two relief workers and requested humanitarian agencies to intercede to secure their speedy and safe release. El Salvador accused FMLN-FDR of detonating four car bombs on a busy street in the capital on 23 December,[34] resulting in at least three civilian deaths, dozens of casualties and extensive material damage, and of threatening freely elected municipal mayors in three departments. El Salvador asked the special representative of the United Nations Commission on Human Rights, organizations monitoring the human rights situation in El Salvador and Governments to condemn those actions. (See PART THREE, Chapter X, for details on the human rights situation in El Salvador.)

REFERENCES

[1]YUN 1987, p. 188. [2]A/43/791-S/20265. [3]YUN 1987, p. 189, GA res. 42/1, 7 Oct. 1987. [4]A/43/729-S/20234. [5]A/42/911-S/19447. [6]A/42/948-S/19764. [7]A/42/917-S/19508. [8]A/42/931-S/19643. [9]A/42/935-S/19661. [10]A/42/937-S/19666. [11]A/42/934-S/19660. [12]A/42/943-S/19678. [13]A/42/946-S/19698. [14]S/19638. [15]YUN 1986, p. 981. [16]A/42/936-S/19663. [17]A/42/942-S/19677. [18]S/19738. [19]S/19753. [20]A/43/676. [21]S/19831. [22]A/42/951-S/19838. [23]S/19883. [24]A/42/962-S/20127. [25]YUN 1987, p. 191, GA res. 42/18, 12 Nov. 1987. [26]A/43/728. [27]YUN 1987, p. 193, GA res. 42/176, 11 Dec. 1987. [28]A/43/612. [29]YUN 1985, p. 212. [30]A/43/617. [31]A/C.3/43/3. [32]A/C.3/43/4. [33]A/44/67. [34]A/44/68.

Other questions relating to the Americas

Co-operation with OAS

In response to a 1987 General Assembly request,[1] the Secretary-General in September 1988 submitted a report on co-operation between the United Nations and the Organization of American States.[2] He reported that he and the Secretary-General of OAS had collaborated as members of the International Verification and Follow-up Commission provided for under the Esquipulas II agreements (see above). Regarding co-operation in the area of economic, social and cultural development, the Secretary-General reported that the United Nations Development Programme, the Economic Commission for Latin America and the Caribbean, the International Research and Training Institute for the Advancement of Women, the International Labour Organisation, the Food and Agriculture Organization of the United Nations, the United Nations Educational, Scientific and Cultural Organization, the International Civil Aviation Organization, the World Health Organization, the International Maritime Organization, the General Agreement on Tariffs and Trade, the United Nations Centre for Human Settlements and UNHCR had various types of co-operative arrangements with OAS, including technical co-operation, joint workshops and training programmes, and preparation of publications.

GENERAL ASSEMBLY ACTION

On 17 October 1988, the General Assembly adopted **resolution 43/4** without vote.

Co-operation between the United Nations and the Organization of American States

The General Assembly,

Recalling its resolution 42/11 of 28 October 1987, relating to the promotion of co-operation between the United Nations and the Organization of American States,

Having examined the report of the Secretary-General on co-operation between the United Nations and the Organization of American States,

Recalling that the purposes of the United Nations are, *inter alia*, to achieve international co-operation in solving international problems of an economic, social, cultural or humanitarian character, and in promoting and encouraging respect for human rights and fundamental freedoms and to be a centre for harmonizing the actions of nations in the attainment of these common ends,

Bearing in mind that the Charter of the United Nations provides for the existence of regional arrangements or agencies for dealing with such matters relating to the maintenance of international peace and security as are appropriate for regional action, and whose activities are consistent with the purposes and principles of the United Nations,

Recalling also that the Charter of the Organization of American States reaffirms these purposes and principles, and provides that that organization is a regional agency under the terms of the Charter of the United Nations,

Bearing in mind resolution AG/RES.880(XVII-0/87) adopted on 14 November 1987 by the General Assembly of the Organization of American States on co-operation between the two organizations,

Underscoring the need to continue strengthening the co-operation that already exists between the United Nations and the Organization of American States, especially in respect of economic and social development, as well as the initiative by their Secretaries-General regarding co-operation in the peace process in Central America,

Convinced of the need for more efficient and co-ordinated utilization of available economic and financial resources to promote the common objectives of the two organizations,

1. *Takes note* of the report of the Secretary-General on co-operation between the United Nations and the Organization of American States, as well as his efforts to strengthen that co-operation;

2. *Invites* the Secretary-General to continue taking the necessary measures for promoting and expanding co-operation and co-ordination between the United Nations and the Organization of American States in order to increase the capacity of the two organizations for the attainment of their common objectives;

3. *Recommends* that a general meeting should be held between representatives of the Organization of American States and of the United Nations and other organizations of the United Nations system, on a date and at a place to be determined, for the purpose of holding consultations on projects, measures and procedures which will facilitate and broaden co-operation between those organizations;

4. *Recommends* that in 1989 local meetings should be promoted between resident representatives of the two organizations, in each country which is a member of both organizations, in consultation with the national authorities of those countries;

5. *Requests* the Secretary-General to submit to the General Assembly at its forty-fifth session a report on the implementation of the present resolution;

6. *Decides* to include in the provisional agenda of its forty-fifth session the item entitled "Co-operation between the United Nations and the Organization of American States".

General Assembly resolution 43/4

17 October 1988   Meeting 32   Adopted without vote

26-nation draft (A/43/L.8/Rev.1 & Add.1); agenda item 27.
Sponsors: Antigua and Barbuda, Argentina, Barbados, Bolivia, Brazil, Chile, Colombia, Costa Rica, Dominican Republic, Ecuador, El Salvador, Equatorial Guinea, Grenada, Guatemala, Haiti, Honduras, Mexico, Nicaragua, Panama, Paraguay, Peru, Saint Lucia, Trinidad and Tobago, United States, Uruguay, Venezuela.

In related action, the Assembly, in **resolution 43/76 H** on the United Nations Regional Centre for Peace, Disarmament and Development in Latin America, made recommendations regarding the work of the Centre and changed its name to "United Nations Regional Centre for Peace, Disarmament and Development in Latin America and the Caribbean".

Bolivia-Chile

In a continuing dispute over its lack of access to the Pacific Ocean, Bolivia, in a 14 April press release from its Foreign Ministry,[3] reiterated its condemnation of Chile's diversion of the Lauca River in 1962, saying that it demonstrated Chile's total disregard of international law. The diversion of the river had done serious harm to the country and was a major factor in the impoverishment of the rural zone, Bolivia said. In addition, Bolivia condemned what it called a new affront—Chile's recent action changing the name of the Arica–La Paz international railway to "Regional Railway of Arica", which Bolivia said was a prelude to new action designed to reinforce its isolation from the sea. It urged the United Nations and other international institutions to express their solidarity with Bolivia.

Political conditions in Haiti

By a letter of 7 January to the Secretary-General,[4] the United States disputed allegations by Cuba[5] that it had disrupted elections in Haiti. The United States said it had provided $6.6 million to the Haitian Provisional Electoral Commission and had made continued aid dependent on the holding of free and fair elections and respect for their results. The tragic events of 29 November 1987 had resulted in the suspension of the electoral process and the suspension by the United States of all military aid to Haiti, except funds for anti-narcotics co-operation, as well as all economic aid routed through the Government of Haiti. The United States said that its action in cutting off that assistance was a clear signal of its disapproval of the disruption of elections. It reaffirmed its support for the efforts of the Haitian people to secure a democratic political system.

Panama–United States

Panama transmitted several communications to the Secretary-General in 1988 protesting what it called warlike actions taken by the United States in Panama, which it said violated international law as well as the Panama Canal Treaty and the Treaty concerning the Permanent Neutrality and Operation of the Panama Canal, signed by the two Governments in 1977.

By a letter of 9 March,[6] Panama said that its Foreign Minister had announced that certain military exercises being conducted by the United States constituted a prelude to an armed invasion of Panama. He said that United States troops had been mobilized in Panama unilaterally and without authorization, in violation of the 1977 treaties as well as the sovereignty and territorial integrity of Panama.

On 22 March,[7] Panama transmitted excerpts from a message to the nation by its Minister in Charge of the Presidency, issued the previous day, denouncing what he called the United States aggression against Panama. He listed several measures which he said had been arbitrarily imposed by that country on Panama, including obstruction of negotiations on the external debt service, withholding payments for use of the Panama Canal, withholding Panamanian funds deposited in United States bank accounts, banning exports to Panama and barring Panamanian planes and ships from entering the United States. Those actions, he said, were clear manifestations of an undeclared war against Panama.

By a communiqué of 24 March[8] from its Foreign Ministry, Panama said that it had received information that five days earlier, at a briefing at the Southern Command headquarters, an expert in psychological warfare in the United States army had instructed some 40 American journalists on how to misrepresent events in Panama in order to help in ousting the Commander-in-Chief of the Panamanian defence forces. The communiqué stated that article I of the agreement on the implementation of article IV of the Panama Canal Treaty prohibited members of the United States armed forces from engaging in political activity or interfering in the internal affairs of Panama. Panama reaffirmed the illegality of the presence of the Southern Command in its territory and its overt use for destabilizing purposes, and protested the way in which the United States armed forces were endangering the security of Panama and undermining the credibility of the United States press. It accused the United States of manipulating information as part of a plan to subjugate Panama in order to maintain its military bases there beyond 1999.

Panama on 5 April[9] transmitted the text of a decision adopted by the Latin American Council of the Latin American Economic System (Caracas, Venezuela, 28 and 29 March), calling on the United States to revoke immediately the economic enforcement measures taken against Panama, and exhorting it to abide by the provisions of the Panama Canal treaties.

By a letter of 14 April,[10] Panama accused the United States of numerous acts it said were in violation of the United Nations Charter and international law, and said the warlike mobilization of United States armed forces constituted the first and only threat to the Panama Canal since the end of the Second World War. In addition to the increase in troops, those acts included violations of Panamanian airspace and waters, various provocative acts and economic measures, such as the withholding of payments, which had brought about a severe money supply crisis and paralysed banking and a number of production activities.

By a communiqué of 5 July,[11] Panama accused the United States of using the administrative régime of the Panama Canal as a weapon of aggression and economic coercion, in violation of the Panama Canal treaties. It said that the United States had withheld payments amounting to over $100 million which were due to Panama under the treaties, as well as proceeds of income-tax and education-insurance deductions from the salaries of Panamanians employed by the Panama Canal Commission and the United States armed forces. The communiqué said that since October 1979, when the treaties had entered into force, Panama had scrupulously fulfilled its obligations under the treaties and it was determined to ensure the Canal's efficient and safe operation not only while the treaties remained in force but also after it assumed full control and administration of the Canal in 2000.

REFERENCES

[1]YUN 1987, p. 194, GA res. 42/11, 28 Oct. 1987. [2]A/43/552 & Add.1. [3]A/43/332. [4]S/19410. [5]YUN 1987, p. 195. [6]A/43/209-S/19597. [7]A/43/235-S/19674. [8]A/43/254. [9]A/43/287-S/19740. [10]A/43/316-S/19799. [11]A/43/446.

Chapter III

Asia and the Pacific

During 1988, intensified diplomatic activity resulted in major breakthroughs in the conflicts between Iran and Iraq, in Afghanistan and in Kampuchea.

In April, Agreements on the Settlement of the Situation Relating to Afghanistan were signed at Geneva and United Nations military observers were sent to monitor the situation. Describing the Agreements as a major step towards a peaceful solution to the situation in Afghanistan, the Secretary-General said that their full implementation in good faith by all the signatories would serve the goal of regional and world peace.

In August, a United Nations–sponsored cease-fire went into effect in the eight-year Iran-Iraq war, followed by direct talks between the parties under the Secretary-General's auspices. United Nations military observers began overseeing the cease-fire and the withdrawal of forces to internationally recognized boundaries. During the year, the Security Council again condemned the use of chemical weapons in the war, and decided to consider appropriate action should there be any such future use. It again stressed rapid implementation of its resolution 598(1987) as the only basis for a settlement of the conflict. It made that statement after considering the downing in the Persian Gulf of an Iranian passenger plane by the United States navy.

After the Secretary-General had presented specific proposals for a comprehensive political settlement of the Kampuchean problem, all parties and countries concerned agreed to work towards a solution and to examine key substantive issues. The Secretary-General reported that prospects for peace in the region had improved through initiation of the dialogue.

East Asia

Korean question

The annual report of the United Nations Command (UNC) on the maintenance of the 1953 Korean Armistice Agreement[1] was received by the Security Council in June 1988. The report was submitted by the United States[2] on behalf of the Unified Command established pursuant to a 1950 Council resolution.[3] It provided information on the activities of UNC and major incidents and issues discussed during 1987 by the Military Armistice Commission (MAC), established to supervise the Armistice Agreement's implementation and settle violations of it through negotiation.[1]

The report stated that the capability of the Democratic People's Republic of Korea to initiate a major attack against UNC and the Republic of Korea remained a threat to international peace. MAC, which served as the only official channel of communication between the opposing military commanders in Korea and provided a mechanism for defusing serious and accidental incidents to prevent further escalation of tension, held four meetings during 1987. Among the issues it considered, UNC detailed an offensively oriented build-up by the Democratic People's Republic of more than 3,500 tanks, over 2,000 self-propelled artillery pieces, as well as MIG-23 aircraft and SA-3 missiles. Those modern and reinforced forces, deployed close to the demilitarized zone (DMZ), reduced warning time for UNC and the defence forces of the Republic of Korea and posed a serious threat to the south. UNC therefore considered maintenance of defence preparedness and joint UNC/Republic of Korea defence training exercises such as "Team Spirit" essential.

A major incident occurred on 7 October 1987, when a Democratic People's Republic warship, or warships, attacked an unarmed fishing boat of the Republic of Korea and sank it in international waters west of the Republic of Korea island of Paegnyong-Do, killing 11 fishermen. UNC pointed out that the attack violated international law regarding minimum force and insisted that the Democratic People's Republic apologize for the sinking and punish those responsible.

The report stated that in spite of the hostility of the Democratic People's Republic and its use of MAC for propaganda purposes, UNC continued to approach meetings of MAC and its subordinate agencies in the positive manner intended by the Armistice Agreement. It presented numerous proposals to help reduce military tensions, which were, however, rejected by that Republic.

On 22 January 1987, UNC conveyed the Republic of Korea's invitation to the military authorities of both the Democratic People's Republic of Korea and the People's Republic of China to observe the annual "Team Spirit" military training exercises (February/March). The former, however, responded with propaganda against the exercises.

At a 30 July 1987 meeting of MAC, UNC requested that the Korean People's Army/Chinese People's Volunteers (KPA/CPV) return the remains of UNC military personnel killed during the Korean War, as this was both an Armistice and humanitarian issue. It noted that, in the past, remains had been returned through MAC, as required by the Armistice Agreement. KPA/CPV, however, reiterated its position that searching for and disinterring remains did not fall within the purview of MAC, but it agreed to return them whenever they were discovered. Emphasizing its humanitarian actions over the years in returning military and civilian personnel, both alive and deceased, UNC proposed a multinational team composed of representatives of several UNC nations, accompanied by the Neutral Nations Supervisory Commission (NNSC) members of MAC, to assist the Democratic People's Republic's search for UNC military remains.

Earlier, at a 26 May meeting of MAC secretaries, UNC passed to KPA maps of three temporary prisoner-of-war camps and associated burial sites located along the Yalu River in the Democratic People's Republic, which, it felt, should prove helpful in recovering the remains of 374 UNC military and civilian personnel. KPA, however, maintained that the remains would be returned through MAC if and when discovered, and denied any obligation to search for and disinter them based on UNC information.

Concluding, the report stated that, at a 22 September 1987 MAC meeting, UNC expressed concern that the Democratic People's Republic was setting the stage for a serious incident designed to discourage nations from participating in the 1988 Seoul Olympics, and warned that the Republic alone would be held responsible if hostile acts arose from its attempts to create false impressions of high tension in the Korean peninsula.

Throughout 1988, the President of the Security Council received a number of communications from the two Koreas.

On 7 January,[4] the Democratic People's Republic of Korea transmitted its President's New Year address, in which he proposed high-level North-South talks to study the question of reunification. He also proposed that both sides adopt a non-aggression declaration whose implementation could be guaranteed by increasing NNSC authority and organizing a neutral nations' inspection force. By a 21 March communiqué[5] from the KPA Supreme Command and a Foreign Ministry statement[6] two days later, it protested against the 1988 "Team Spirit" military exercises. On 10 May,[7] the Democratic People's Republic denounced a 19 April UNC spe-

cial report[8] which refuted that Republic's July 1987 allegations[9] of UNC violations of the Armistice Agreement, adding that violations committed by United States forces and the Republic of Korea army during January-March 1988 totalled 36,100. A 27 July KPA/CPV report[10] to MAC charged that the latest joint military exercises were the most provocative ever.

The Republic of Korea, on 8 July,[11] transmitted a special declaration by its President enunciating policies that he hoped would open a new chapter of inter-Korean relations and lead to unification. It was followed by a 16 July[12] statement of foreign policy measures in pursuance of that declaration. On 12 July,[13] the Democratic People's Republic denounced the special declaration as a divisionist proposal. On 22 July,[14] it transmitted a letter from its Supreme People's Assembly to the Republic of Korea National Assembly proposing parliamentary talks between the two sides and a draft joint declaration on non-aggression between them. It further conveyed a 20 July[15] letter addressed to the United States Congress from the Supreme People's Assembly proposing talks between the two bodies.

During August and September, the Secretary-General received a request by 10 Western and other States[16] for inclusion of a supplementary item entitled "Fortieth anniversary of the establishment of the Government of the Republic of Korea" in the agenda of the 1988 regular session of the General Assembly. Objections to discussing the anniversary of an individual country, especially a divided nation, were made by China on 16 September[17] and by Afghanistan, Angola, Burundi, Cuba, Madagascar, Mali, Nicaragua, Zambia and Zimbabwe on 19 September.[18] The Democratic People's Republic, on 6[19] and 16 September,[20] denounced the move to include the item as a provocative act designed to wreck North-South dialogue and legalize the division of Korea.

On 15 September,[21] 13 Eastern European and other socialist States requested inclusion in the agenda of the same Assembly session of an additional item on the situation on the Korean peninsula and implementation of the resolution on the question of Korea adopted by the General Assembly in 1975.[22]

On 10 October 1988,[23] the Democratic People's Republic forwarded excerpts from a report by its President, in connection with the fortieth anniversary of the founding of that Republic. A 7 November communiqué[24] described a joint meeting of the Central People's Committee, the Standing Committee of the Supreme People's Assembly and the Administration Council, during which new comprehensive peace proposals to the United States and South Korean authorities were made.

Destruction of Korean airliner

In mid-February 1988, the Security Council considered an allegation by the Republic of Korea that "agents of North Korea" had planted a time-bomb on a Korean Air Lines (KAL) commercial passenger plane, causing it to explode in mid-air off the coast of Burma on 29 November 1987. The Democratic People's Republic of Korea charged Japan, the Republic of Korea and the United States with collusion to fake the incident. It also accused Bahrain of involvement.

The Republic of Korea, on 10 February 1988,[25] presented the findings of its investigation into the destruction of KAL flight 858, maintaining that two agents of the Democratic People's Republic were responsible. On the same day,[26] the Democratic People's Republic forwarded statements of 15, 25 and 26 January from the Korean Central News Agency, its Foreign Ministry and the Central Committee of the National Democratic Front of South Korea, refuting the findings and alleging that the incident had been fabricated to divert attention from civil and political unrest in the South.

Communications condemning the attack on the airliner were received from the Federal Republic of Germany on behalf of the 12 States Members of the European Community (EC),[27] and from Bolivia[28] and Paraguay.[29] Bahrain[30] rejected allegations by the Democratic People's Republic[26] that as a result of bribery it had extradited to the Republic of Korea a woman and the body of a man who, it said, were responsible for the explosion. It said that it had done so out of its commitment to international norms following a request from that Republic.

Japan and the Republic of Korea, on 10 February,[31] requested the Security Council to consider the matter urgently. On 16 February,[32] the Democratic People's Republic objected, stating that Japan, the Republic of Korea and the United States were exploiting the incident for political purposes.

SECURITY COUNCIL CONSIDERATION

The Security Council held meetings on 16 and 17 February to consider the matter. The Democratic People's Republic of Korea and the Republic of Korea were invited, at their request, to participate in the discussion without the right to vote. The Council also invited Bahrain to participate in accordance with rule 37 of the Council's provisional rules of procedure.[a]

Meeting numbers. SC 2791, 2792.

The USSR objected to the Council's consideration of what it said were groundless assertions by the Republic of Korea. Discussion of the matter, it said, would have negative consequences for the situation on the Korean peninsula.

According to the Republic of Korea, a man and a woman—both North Koreans carrying Japanese passports—had boarded a KAL flight from Baghdad, Iraq, to Seoul, placed explosives in an overhead luggage compartment and disembarked at the first stop, Abu Dhabi, United Arab Emirates. Nine hours later, the plane exploded over the sea off the coast of Burma. After the two people had been stopped in Bahrain for questioning, they took poison, resulting in the man's death. The woman, who survived, was extradited to the Republic of Korea and confessed on 23 December. The Republic charged that the terrorist act was intended to disrupt the upcoming Olympic games in Seoul.

The Democratic People's Republic of Korea said the KAL incident was a fake drama put together by authorities in the South, aided by Japan and the United States, because of an insecure political situation in the South.

Bahrain, Japan and the United States rejected the charges of collusion in the affair as groundless, and Japan added that it, too, was a victim because the two accused had pretended to be Japanese.

At the conclusion of the debate, the Council President said it was a tragedy that 115 lives had been lost needlessly.

REFERENCES

[1]YUN 1953, p. 136, GA res. 725(VIII), annex, 7 Dec. 1953. [2]S/19950. [3]YUN 1950, p. 230, SC res. 84(1950), 7 July 1950. [4]S/19413 & Corr.1. [5]S/19658. [6]S/19675. [7]S/19873. [8]S/19800. [9]YUN 1987, p. 199. [10]S/20100. [11]S/19999. [12]S/20028. [13]S/20008. [14]S/20054. [15]S/20088. [16]A/43/196/Rev.1 & Rev.1/Corr.1 & Rev.1/Add.1,2. [17]A/43/616. [18]A/43/619. [19]S/20177. [20]A/43/615. [21]A/43/242. [22]YUN 1975, p.204, GA res. 3390 B (XXX), 18 Nov. 1975. [23]S/20222. [24]S/20268. [25]S/19488. [26]S/19492. [27]S/19507. [28]A/43/111-S/19458. [29]A/43/133-S/19493. [30]S/19515. [31]S/19489. [32]S/19514.

South-East Asia

Kampuchea situation

After nine years of conflict in Kampuchea, the heads of both the Coalition of Democratic Kampuchea and the People's Republic of Kampuchea met for the first time in late 1987 and early 1988 and announced agreement on the need for a peaceful political solution to the problem of Kampuchea.

[a]Rule 37 of the Council's provisional rules of procedure states: "Any Member of the United Nations which is not a member of the Security Council may be invited, as the result of a decision of the Security Council, to participate, without vote, in the discussion of any question brought before the Security Council when the Security Council considers that the interests of that Member are specially affected, or when a Member brings a matter to the attention of the Council in accordance with Article 35 (1) of the Charter."

During the first half of 1988, the Secretary-General and his Special Representative presented to all the parties concerned specific ideas for a comprehensive settlement of the Kampuchea problem.

In November, by resolution 43/19, the General Assembly reiterated that the principal elements of a settlement should be: withdrawal of all foreign forces from Kampuchea; restoration of its independence, sovereignty and territorial integrity; the right of Kampucheans to determine their own destiny; and a commitment by all States to non-interference.

In other action, the Assembly, in December, by **resolution 43/119**, welcomed the call of the Association of South-East Asian Nations (ASEAN) for an international conference on Indo-Chinese refugees, hoped that the conference would be held at the ministerial level early in 1989, and appealed for the necessary support and resources needed by the Office of the United Nations High Commissioner for Refugees (UNHCR) (see PART THREE, Chapter XV).

The four Kampuchean parties—the National United Front for an Independent Neutral Peaceful and Co-operative Cambodia, headed by Prince Norodom Sihanouk; the Khmer People's National Liberation Front (KPNLF), led by Son Sann; the Party of Democratic Kampuchea, led by Khieu Samphan; and the authorities in Phnom Penh, headed by Hun Sen—as well as the Lao People's Democratic Republic, Viet Nam and the six members of ASEAN (Brunei Darussalam, Indonesia, Malaysia, Philippines, Singapore, Thailand) held the Jakarta Informal Meeting (JIM) (Bogor, Indonesia, 25-28 July).[1] Participants agreed to work towards setting up an independent, sovereign neutral and non-aligned Kampuchea based on self-determination and national reconciliation. All shared the view that the two key interlinked issues were the withdrawal of Vietnamese forces, to be carried out in the context of an overall political solution, and the prevention of a recurrence of genocidal practices and cessation of all foreign interference and external arming of opposing Kampuchean forces. They also saw the need to set definite timetables and to provide effective international supervision of those processes. Key issues to be resolved were specified and a working group was set up to make recommendations to a second JIM at ministerial level.

A ministerial meeting of the Movement of Non-Aligned Countries (Nicosia, Cyprus, 5-10 September)[2] established a Committee on Kampuchea, complementary to the JIM process. Some parties called for an international peace-keeping force to oversee a future settlement, while others preferred an international control commission.

Throughout 1988, the Secretary-General received numerous communications relating to the situation in Kampuchea. Among them were letters from China, Democratic Kampuchea, Indonesia, the Lao People's Democratic Republic, Thailand and Viet Nam.

On 6 January,[3] the Lao People's Democratic Republic transmitted, as requested by the People's Republic of Kampuchea, a message from Hun Sen, President of the latter's Council of Ministers, informing of a four-point agreement reached between him and Prince Norodom Sihanouk following their meeting in France from 2 to 4 December 1987. He said the meeting was a prelude to a solution to end the war in Kampuchea and to the restoration of peace there and in South-East Asia. A second round of talks was held on 20 and 21 January 1988.

Democratic Kampuchea, on 31 May,[4] conveyed a message from its President to heads of State or Government of the donor countries to the Kampuchean Humanitarian Assistance Programme, and a statement from its Foreign Ministry, calling on those and other countries to make the granting of humanitarian assistance and other aid to Viet Nam conditional on the total withdrawal of its forces from Kampuchea.

Viet Nam, on 7 July,[5] criticized ASEAN for continuing to slander it and the People's Republic of Kampuchea. Jointly with the Lao People's Democratic Republic, on 8 July,[6] it denounced ASEAN's attempt to turn the upcoming informal Jakarta "cocktail party" into negotiations between Viet Nam and the four Kampuchean parties.

Activities of the Committee of the Conference on Kampuchea. During 1988, the 10-member *Ad Hoc* Committee of the International Conference on Kampuchea met on 12 January, 11 February, 16 June and 1 and 25 August.[7] It undertook one consultation mission in accordance with its mandate to assist in seeking a comprehensive political settlement. The mission visited Beijing, Bangkok and Vienna from 27 June to 8 July.

The mission consulted extensively with the Governments concerned on the prospects for a settlement, in an effort to encourage negotiations leading to the implementation of the Declaration on Kampuchea, adopted in 1981 by the International Conference.[8] They expressed the view that a settlement must be based on the withdrawal of all foreign forces, national reconciliation, the right of Kampucheans to determine their own destiny and the establishment of a non-aligned and neutral Kampuchea.

In Beijing, the Foreign Minister and two Deputy Foreign Ministers informed the mission that China would support all efforts aimed at achieving a fair and reasonable political settlement.

Prince Norodom Sihanouk briefed the mission in Bangkok on the deliberations that had led the three partners of the Coalition Government of Democratic Kampuchea (CGDK) to adopt their declaration of 25 June for the upcoming JIM in July.[9] The Prince said he considered three points in that declaration to be necessary conditions for any settlement. They were the formation of a provisional quadripartite government following the second phase of Vietnamese withdrawal; the simultaneous dismantling of the Phnom Penh régime and CGDK; and the introduction of an international peace-keeping force.

The mission then briefed the ASEAN Foreign Ministers and focused on the upcoming JIM. They also met the CGDK Vice-President in charge of foreign affairs, who supported the June declaration and emphasized that total withdrawal of Vietnamese forces was the key to a solution. While in Bangkok, the mission also met with KPNLF, which stressed that any solution should provide for the disarming of all factions and a United Nations peace-keeping force.

Report of the Secretary-General. The Secretary-General, in response to a 1987 General Assembly request,[10] reported in October 1988[11] that during the year he and his Special Representative, Rafeeuddin Ahmed, had maintained close contact with the States most concerned and other interested parties. Early in 1988, Mr. Ahmed met with Prince Sihanouk in Paris, and, in June in New York, the problem was discussed in detail with the Foreign Ministers of China, Indonesia and Viet Nam.

In the light of those discussions, the Secretary-General felt it was time to formulate specific ideas towards a framework for a comprehensive political settlement. He asked Mr. Ahmed to travel to South-East Asia to present those ideas to the four Kampuchean parties, and to Viet Nam, the Lao People's Democratic Republic and the ASEAN countries. Accordingly, the Special Representative visited Bangkok, Phnom Penh and Vientiane, where he met with the interested parties, before returning to Bangkok for a meeting with ASEAN Foreign Ministers on 4 July.

In September, Mr. Ahmed again travelled to the region to take stock of the situation because of developments in the intervening period, especially the initiative of the Movement of Non-Aligned Countries and JIM.

The Secretary-General held further discussions in New York with Prince Sihanouk, the leaders of the countries of the region and the President of the International Conference on Kampuchea. He stated that the process of dialogue, which the Kampuchean parties and other concerned countries had initiated and seemed determined to pursue until a framework for a comprehensive political settlement was agreed, was encouraging. It confirmed the interest of all sides to abandon confrontation and to seek a political solution through genuine negotiations and mutual accommodation. He was convinced that with good will and co-operation it should be possible to bring peace to Kampuchea.

Meanwhile, the Secretary-General continued to co-ordinate humanitarian relief assistance to the Kampuchean people along the Thai-Kampuchean border. His Special Representative for co-ordination of the programmes, Shah A. M. S. Kibria, had been in close touch with interested Member States.

Some 292,000 Kampucheans were under the care of the United Nations Border Relief Operation (UNBRO). In addition, there were some 14,000 Kampuchean refugees, mainly in the Khao-I-Dang holding centre, assisted by UNHCR. Both groups were totally dependent on international relief. The future of Khao-I-Dang was the subject of particular attention, and the United Nations remained in contact with UNHCR and the Thai Government on that question.

Providing humanitarian assistance to the population within Kampuchea were the United Nations Children's Fund, the World Food Programme, UNHCR, the Food and Agriculture Organization of the United Nations (FAO), five national Red Cross Societies and 16 other voluntary agencies. However, creation of a secure environment for the border camps remained difficult. To combat violent crime at the evacuation sites, the Thai Government replaced Task Force 80 with a Displaced Persons Protection Unit to work closely with UNBRO and the International Committee of the Red Cross (ICRC).

To improve primary education facilities at the evacuation sites, efforts were under way to train 2,000 teachers and teacher trainers, to expand and upgrade the curriculum and to provide the necessary supplies for primary education for all school-age children. Prospects for extending skills-training and educational facilities to secondary level students were being explored with the authorities.

The Secretary-General reported progress on the question of voluntary repatriation of Kampucheans, with the parties concerned indicating willingness to co-operate with UNHCR to speed up the processing of individual applications.

Although Kampuchea was expected to have a better harvest in 1988, its food situation remained fragile following the 1987 drought, although international assistance helped mitigate the effects. Mr. Kibria appealed for funding for a number of projects proposed by FAO to help the population become self-sufficient in basic foods.

At a September 1988 meeting in New York, donors responded to the Secretary-General's appeal for help, providing some $14 million for the Kampuchean Humanitarian Assistance Programme.

In **decision 1988/143** of 27 May, the Economic and Social Council expressed concern at the continued violation of human rights by the foreign occupying force in Kampuchea of Kampuchean nationals, as well as of innocent displaced Kampucheans seeking temporary shelter along the Thai-Kampuchean border; and at the unresolved dilemma of the approximately 292,000 Kampuchean civilians stranded in Thailand as a result of attacks by the foreign forces on the Kampuchean civilian border encampments since 1984.

GENERAL ASSEMBLY ACTION

On 3 November 1988, the General Assembly adopted by recorded vote **resolution 43/19**.

The situation in Kampuchea

The General Assembly,

Recalling its resolutions 34/22 of 14 November 1979, 35/6 of 22 October 1980, 36/5 of 21 October 1981, 37/6 of 28 October 1982, 38/3 of 27 October 1983, 39/5 of 30 October 1984, 40/7 of 5 November 1985, 41/6 of 21 October 1986 and 42/3 of 14 October 1987,

Recalling also the Declaration on Kampuchea and resolution 1(I) adopted by the International Conference on Kampuchea,

Taking note of the report of the Secretary-General on the implementation of General Assembly resolution 42/3,

Deploring that foreign armed intervention and occupation continue and that foreign forces still remain in Kampuchea, thus causing continuing hostilities in that country and seriously threatening international peace and security,

Noting the continued and effective struggle waged against foreign occupation by the Kampuchean forces under the leadership of Samdech Norodom Sihanouk,

Taking note of Economic and Social Council decision 1988/143 of 27 May 1988 on the right of peoples to self-determination and its application to peoples under colonial or alien domination or foreign occupation,

Greatly disturbed that the continued fighting and instability in Kampuchea have forced an additional large number of Kampucheans to flee to the Thai-Kampuchean border in search of food and safety,

Recognizing that the assistance extended by the international community has continued to reduce the food shortages and health problems of the Kampuchean people,

Emphasizing that it is the inalienable right of the Kampuchean people who have sought refuge in neighbouring countries to return safely to their homeland,

Emphasizing also that no effective solution to the humanitarian problems can be achieved without a comprehensive political settlement of the Kampuchean conflict,

Seriously concerned about reported demographic changes being imposed in Kampuchea by foreign occupation forces,

Convinced that, to bring about lasting peace in South-East Asia and reduce the threat to international peace and security, there is an urgent need for the international community to find a comprehensive political solution to the Kampuchean problem, with effective guarantees, that will provide for the withdrawal of all foreign forces from Kampuchea under effective international supervision and control, the creation of an interim administering authority, the promotion of national reconciliation among all Kampucheans under the leadership of Samdech Norodom Sihanouk, the non-return to the universally condemned policies and practices of a recent past and ensure respect for the sovereignty, independence, territorial integrity and neutral and non-aligned status of Kampuchea, as well as the right of the Kampuchean people to self-determination free from outside interference,

Recognizing that the Jakarta Informal Meeting held at Bogor, Indonesia, from 25 to 28 July 1988 was a significant development, which marked for the first time the participation of the parties directly involved and other concerned countries,

Reiterating its conviction that, after the comprehensive political settlement of the Kampuchean question through peaceful means, the countries of the South-East Asian region can pursue efforts to establish a zone of peace, freedom and neutrality in South-East Asia so as to lessen international tensions and to achieve lasting peace in the region,

Reaffirming the need for all States to adhere strictly to the principles of the Charter of the United Nations, which call for respect for the national independence, sovereignty and territorial integrity of all States, non-intervention and non-interference in the internal affairs of States, non-recourse to the threat or use of force and peaceful settlement of disputes,

1. *Reaffirms* its resolutions 34/22, 35/6, 36/5, 37/6, 38/3, 39/5, 40/7, 41/6 and 42/3 and calls for their full implementation;

2. *Reiterates its conviction* that the withdrawal of all foreign forces from Kampuchea under effective international supervision and control, the creation of an interim administering authority, the promotion of national reconciliation among all Kampucheans under the leadership of Samdech Norodom Sihanouk, the non-return to the universally condemned policies and practices of a recent past, the restoration and preservation of the independence, sovereignty, territorial integrity and neutral and non-aligned status of Kampuchea, the reaffirmation of the right of the Kampuchean people to determine their own destiny and the commitment by all States to non-interference and non-intervention in the internal affairs of Kampuchea, with effective guarantees, are the principal components of any just and lasting resolution of the Kampuchean problem;

3. *Takes note with appreciation* the report of the *Ad Hoc* Committee of the International Conference on Kampuchea on its activities during 1987-1988 and requests that the Committee continue its work, pending the reconvening of the Conference;

4. *Authorizes* the *Ad Hoc* Committee to convene when necessary and to carry out the tasks entrusted to it in its mandate;

5. *Reaffirms* its commitment to reconvene the Conference at an appropriate time, in accordance with Conference resolution 1(I), and its readiness to support any other conference of an international nature under the auspices of the Secretary-General;

6. *Requests* the Secretary-General to continue to consult with and assist the Conference and the *Ad Hoc* Committee and to provide them on a regular basis with the necessary facilities to carry out their functions;

7. *Expresses its appreciation once again* to the Secretary-General for taking appropriate steps in following the situation closely and requests him to continue to do so and to exercise his good offices in order to contribute to a comprehensive political settlement;

8. *Expresses its deep appreciation once again* to donor countries, the United Nations and its agencies and other humanitarian organizations, national and international, that have rendered relief assistance to the Kampuchean people, and appeals to them to continue to provide emergency assistance to those Kampucheans who are still in need, especially along the Thai-Kampuchean border and in the various encampments in Thailand;

9. *Reiterates its deep appreciation* to the Secretary-General for his efforts in co-ordinating humanitarian relief assistance and in monitoring its distribution, and requests him to intensify such efforts as necessary;

10. *Urges* the States of South-East Asia, once a comprehensive political solution to the Kampuchean conflict is achieved, to exert renewed efforts to establish a zone of peace, freedom and neutrality in South-East Asia;

11. *Reiterates the hope* that, following a comprehensive political solution, an intergovernmental committee will be established to consider a programme of assistance to Kampuchea for the reconstruction of its economy and for the economic and social development of all States in the region;

12. *Requests* the Secretary-General to report to the General Assembly at its forty-fourth session on the implementation of the present resolution;

13. *Decides* to include in the provisional agenda of its forty-fourth session the item entitled ''The situation in Kampuchea''.

General Assembly resolution 43/19

3 November 1988   Meeting 44   122-19-13 (recorded vote)

64-nation draft (A/43/L.12 & Add.1); agenda item 23.
Sponsors: Antigua and Barbuda, Australia, Barbados, Belgium, Brunei Darussalam, Cameroon, Canada, Chad, Chile, Colombia, Comoros, Costa Rica, Denmark, Djibouti, Dominica, Dominican Republic, Ecuador, Equatorial Guinea, Fiji, France, Gambia, Germany, Federal Republic of, Greece, Grenada, Guatemala, Haiti, Honduras, Iceland, Indonesia, Ireland, Italy, Japan, Lesotho, Liberia, Luxembourg, Malaysia, Maldives, Mauritius, Morocco, Nauru, Nepal, Netherlands, New Zealand, Nigeria, Norway, Oman, Papua New Guinea, Paraguay, Philippines, Saint Kitts and Nevis, Saint Lucia, Saint Vincent and the Grenadines, Samoa, Senegal, Sierra Leone, Singapore, Solomon Islands, Somalia, Spain, Swaziland, Sweden, Thailand, Turkey, United Kingdom, Uruguay, Zambia.
Financial implications. 5th Committee, A/43/766; S-G, A/C.5/43/23.
Meeting numbers. GA 43rd session: 5th Committee 23; plenary 42-44.

Recorded vote in Assembly as follows:

In favour: Antigua and Barbuda, Argentina, Australia, Austria, Bahamas, Bahrain, Bangladesh, Barbados, Belgium, Belize, Bhutan, Bolivia, Botswana, Brazil, Brunei Darussalam, Burkina Faso, Burma, Burundi, Cameroon, Canada, Cape Verde, Central African Republic, Chad, Chile, China, Colombia, Comoros, Costa Rica, Côte d'Ivoire, Cyprus, Democratic Kampuchea, Denmark, Djibouti, Dominica, Dominican Republic, Ecuador, Egypt, El Salvador, Equatorial Guinea, Fiji, Finland, France, Gabon, Gambia, Germany, Federal Republic of, Ghana, Greece, Grenada, Guatemala, Guinea, Guinea-Bissau, Haiti, Honduras, Iceland, Indonesia, Iran, Ireland, Israel, Italy, Jamaica, Japan, Jordan, Kenya, Kuwait, Lesotho, Liberia, Luxembourg, Malawi, Malaysia, Maldives, Mali, Malta, Mauritania, Mauritius, Mexico, Morocco, Nepal, Netherlands, New Zealand, Niger, Nigeria, Norway, Oman, Pakistan, Panama, Papua New Guinea, Paraguay, Peru, Philippines, Portugal, Qatar, Rwanda, Saint Kitts and Nevis, Saint Lucia, Saint Vincent and the Grenadines, Samoa, Sao Tome and Principe, Saudi Arabia, Senegal, Sierra Leone, Singapore, Solomon Islands, Somalia, Spain,

Sri Lanka, Sudan, Suriname, Swaziland, Sweden, Thailand, Togo, Trinidad and Tobago, Tunisia, Turkey, United Arab Emirates, United Kingdom, United States, Uruguay, Venezuela, Yugoslavia, Zaire, Zambia.
Against: Afghanistan, Albania, Angola, Bulgaria, Byelorussian SSR, Cuba, Czechoslovakia, Democratic Yemen, Ethiopia, German Democratic Republic, Hungary, Lao People's Democratic Republic, Mongolia, Nicaragua, Poland, Syrian Arab Republic, Ukrainian SSR, USSR, Viet Nam.
Abstaining: Algeria, Congo, Guyana, India, Iraq, Lebanon, Libyan Arab Jamahiriya, Madagascar, Uganda, United Republic of Tanzania, Vanuatu, Yemen, Zimbabwe.

Participation and representation of Democratic Kampuchea in UN bodies

The question of Democratic Kampuchea's credentials was again raised in the Credentials Committee on 11 October 1988 with respect to the General Assembly's forty-third (1988) regular session. Several States expressed opinions on those credentials, which were accepted when the General Assembly on 18 October adopted **resolution 43/10 A**, approving the Committee's first report.[12]

International security in South-East Asia

Several communications were received by the Secretary-General in 1988 dealing with general aspects of relations among countries in South-East Asia.

By a joint letter, the Federal Republic of Germany and Thailand, on 11 May,[13] transmitted a declaration of the seventh meeting of the European Community and ASEAN Foreign Ministers (Düsseldorf, 2 and 3 May), calling on Viet Nam to withdraw its troops from Kampuchea. A similar call was made by the Toronto Economic Summit (19-21 June), whose final documents were forwarded by Canada on 30 June.[14]

Thailand, on 5 July,[15] conveyed a statement of the ASEAN Foreign Ministers, expressing support for JIM (see above) and welcoming the willingness of Viet Nam and all the Kampuchean factions to participate in it.

Similarly, on 28 July,[16] Greece forwarded a declaration by the 12 EC member States, welcoming JIM, which they hoped would be a starting-point for a peace process.

Brunei Darussalam, on 4 August,[17] transmitted excerpts from the joint communiqué of the twenty-first ASEAN Ministerial Meeting (Bangkok, 4 and 5 July), calling for a durable and comprehensive political settlement and the achievement of national reconciliation in Kampuchea.

China, on 19 December,[18] accused Taiwan of attempts to create what it called ''two Chinas'' or ''one China, one Taiwan'', and hoped that it would stop activities detrimental to China's reunification.

Incidents along the border between the Lao People's Democratic Republic and Thailand were the subject of a number of communications from those States between January and March.[19]

On 11 November, by **decision 43/407**, the General Assembly deferred consideration of the item on peace, stability and co-operation in South-East Asia and included it in the provisional agenda of its forty-fourth (1989) session.

In other related action, the Assembly, in **resolution 43/76 G** of 7 December, welcomed the signing of an agreement and a memorandum of understanding between Nepal and the United Nations concerning the establishment of the United Nations Regional Centre for Peace and Disarmament in Asia, with headquarters in Kathmandu.

China–Viet Nam dispute

Sovereignty over an archipelago in the South China Sea continued to be disputed by China and Viet Nam in 1988. The archipelago was called Nansha by China and Truong Sa by Viet Nam and was also known as Spratly. In 1979,[20] China and Viet Nam had each transmitted documents to the Secretary-General in support of its claim to the islands. Both States had continued to maintain their claims periodically since that time.

From February to May 1988,[21] both forwarded further communications, each charging the other with naval incursions or armed provocations, together with documentation supporting their respective claims to sovereignty over the disputed territory.

REFERENCES
[1]A/43/493-S/20071. [2]A/43/667-S/20212. [3]A/43/80-S/19407. [4]A/43/382-S/19913. [5]A/43/454-S/19994. [6]A/43/455-S/19997. [7]A/CONF.109/13. [8]YUN 1981, p. 242. [9]A/43/429-S/19966. [10]YUN 1987, p. 206, GA res. 42/3, 14 Oct.1987. [11]A/43/730. [12]A/43/715. [13]A/43/373. [14]A/43/435-S/19974. [15]A/43/444-S/19988. [16]A/43/496. [17]A/43/510-S/20091. [18]S/20355. [19]A/43/76-S/19439, A/43/83-S/19414, A/43/87-S/19426, A/43/93-S/19438, A/43/110-S/19457, A/43/113-S/19463, A/43/117-S/19472, A/43/128-S/19481, A/43/137-S/19498, A/43/139-S/19501, A/43/140-S/19504, A/43/151-S/19505, A/43/154-S/19511, A/43/155-S/19512, A/43/158-S/19520, A/43/159-S/19521, A/43/167-S/19539, A/43/174-S/19545, A/43/180-S/19556, A/43/205-S/19586, A/43/225-S/19645, A/43/234-S/19667, A/43/256-S/19688, A/43/306-S/19777, A/43/343-S/19851. [20]YUN 1979, p. 288. [21]A/42/229-S/19662, A/43/168-S/19540, A/43/218-S/19625, A/43/221-S/19634, A/43/240-S/19683, A/43/255-S/19685. [22]A/43/259-S/19694, A/43/266-S/19712, A/43/285-S/19739, A/43/292-S/19746, A/43/307-S/19778, A/43/346-S/19856, A/43/363-S/19887, A/43/365-S/19891.

Western and south-western Asia

Afghanistan situation

Following eight years of conflict and more than six years of negotiations and shuttle diplomacy by the Secretary-General and his Personal Represen-tative, Agreements on the Settlement of the Situation Relating to Afghanistan[1] were signed at Geneva on 14 April 1988. In the four-part Agreements, Afghanistan and Pakistan committed themselves to principles of mutual relations, particularly to non-interference and non-intervention, and to the voluntary return of refugees. By a declaration on international guarantees, the United States and the USSR also undertook to refrain from any form of interference in Afghanistan's or Pakistan's internal affairs. All four States signed an instrument on interrelationships for the settlement of the situation, providing for a phased withdrawal of foreign troops from Afghanistan.

To assist in monitoring implementation of the Agreements, the Secretary-General immediately dispatched 50 United Nations military observers to the region.

In October, the Secretary-General reported that Afghanistan and Pakistan had each charged the other with serious violations of the Agreements, and expressed his deep concern that fighting continued in Afghanistan and that the economic and social problems posed to neighbouring countries by the presence of millions of refugees had not ended.

In November, the General Assembly called on all parties to respect scrupulously and to implement faithfully the April peace settlement (resolution 43/20).

At the end of the year, the Secretary-General again expressed concern over the suffering of the Afghan people and at the slow pace of developments leading to a settlement.

Among the numerous communications addressed to the Secretary-General in 1988 concerning the situation were many from Afghanistan and Pakistan, alleging violations of airspace and territory in the form of reconnaissance flights, bombings, shellings and other acts of aggression and provocation by one against the other. Each continued to lodge protests with the other against such acts and demanded their cessation, while rejecting each other's allegations.[2]

Agreements on the Settlement of the Situation Relating to Afghanistan

Responding to a 1987 General Assembly request,[3] the Secretary-General reported in October 1988[4] on the Afghanistan situation. He said that as part of intensive consultations, his Personal Representative, Diego Cordovez, had visited Washington, D.C., and Moscow in December 1987 for meetings with senior United States and USSR officials. In Moscow, Foreign Minister Eduard Shevardnadze assured him of his Government's determination to conclude the negotiations and requested that a new round of talks be convened at Geneva at an early date. The Secretary-General felt that before this could be done further consultations were necessary, and he subsequently sent Mr. Cordovez to Islamabad and Kabul from 20 January to 9 February 1988.

At Islamabad, Mr. Cordovez met with the Pakistani President, the Prime Minister and the Foreign Minister, and at Kabul with the President and Foreign Minister of Afghanistan. For technical reasons, he was unable to visit Teheran during that trip, but Iran was briefed on the contents of the discussions. Based on those discussions, it was agreed that a round of talks would be held. All Governments concerned had conveyed to the Secretary-General, through Mr. Cordovez, their determination to bring the negotiating process to an early conclusion. A statement by Mikhail Gorbachev that the withdrawal of Soviet troops would begin on 15 May if agreement was reached at Geneva by 15 March provided an important impetus.

Thus, talks in which the Foreign Ministers of Afghanistan and Pakistan participated began at Geneva on 1 March. While there was progress on the question of the time-frame and modalities for the withdrawal of foreign troops, final agreement proved elusive because of a number of other issues to which each side gave varying degrees of relevance and significance, the Secretary-General said.

Following consultations held over a six-week period, it was announced on 8 April that the instruments comprising the settlement were finalized and open for signature. On 14 April, at a ceremony at Geneva presided over by the Secretary-General, the Agreements on the Settlement of the Situation Relating to Afghanistan were signed. They consisted of: a bilateral agreement between Afghanistan and Pakistan on the principles of mutual relations, in particular on non-interference and non-intervention; a declaration on international guarantees; a bilateral agreement between Afghanistan and Pakistan on the voluntary return of refugees; and an agreement on the interrelationships for the settlement of the Afghanistan situation, including a memorandum of understanding on the monitoring arrangements to be provided by the United Nations. On behalf of their respective Governments, the Foreign Ministers of Afghanistan and Pakistan signed the instruments as parties to the settlement. The USSR and United States counterparts signed as State guarantors.

The Agreements came into force on 15 May and, as part of the arrangements, Afghanistan and Pakistan requested the Secretary-General to appoint his Representative and provide assistance for investigating any possible violations of the instruments. Accordingly, he appointed Mr. Cordovez to that post. Major-General Rauli Helminen (Finland) was appointed as his deputy and Benon Sevan (Turkey) as Alternate Representative. Following consultations with the parties, troop-contributing countries and the force commanders of existing United Nations peace-keeping operations, 50 military officers were temporarily detached from those operations to constitute the United Nations Good Offices Mission in Afghanistan and Pakistan (UNGOMAP).

The first review of the Mission's operations was conducted by Mr. Cordovez at Geneva from 24 to 26 May, followed by a broader review when he travelled to the area from 29 June to 10 July. On the latter occasion, he met at Islamabad with the President and the Foreign Minister and, at Kabul, he had meetings with the President, the Prime Minister and the Foreign Minister. He held extensive consultations with the two Governments on compliance with the obligations of the Agreements, as well as with UNGOMAP. He also met with USSR military authorities in the Afghan capital who briefed him on the status of the troop withdrawal, and he visited Teheran, where he kept the Foreign Minister of Iran informed of developments.

According to the report, complaints of alleged violations were filed by both parties with UN-GOMAP. Those from Afghanistan included allegations of border crossings of men and material from Pakistan, cross-border firings, the continued presence in Pakistan of training camps and arms depots for Afghan opposition groups, restrictions placed on refugees who wished to return, political activities hostile to Afghanistan and violations of its airspace by Pakistani aircraft. Those from Pakistan included allegations of violation of its airspace, bombing incidents, acts of sabotage and hostile political activities by Afghanistan. The complaints were investigated and the results were conveyed to both parties in accordance with the procedure laid down in the Agreements.

With a view to enhancing the capacity of the United Nations to meet the needs of humanitarian and economic assistance programmes and to ensure a co-ordinated approach in that regard, the Secretary-General appointed Sadruddin Aga Khan as Co-ordinator for Humanitarian and Economic Assistance Programmes relating to Afghanistan (for details, see PART THREE, Chapter III).

In the Secretary-General's view, the signing of the Geneva Agreements was a major step in the efforts to bring peace to Afghanistan. They laid the basis for the exercise by all Afghans of their right to self-determination and their implementation was essential to the achievement of those objectives. The Secretary-General regretted that the signatories were preoccupied with violations by the other side and considered it imperative that they abide fully by the Agreements' provisions. He also expressed concern that continued fighting in Afghanistan was resulting in heavy casualties and that the suffering of the Afghan people, as well as the economic and social problems of neighbouring countries related to the presence of refugees, had not been brought to an end. A full political settlement was, therefore, urgent.

Concluding, he stated that the United Nations remained committed to promoting conditions under which the Afghans could realize their goals of peace in their country and stability in the region, and urged all Governments to support those endeavours.

In a 14 April letter to the Security Council President,[5] the Secretary-General informed the Council of the conclusion of the Geneva Agreements and the appointments he had made as required under them. He informed Council members that he intended to detach up to 50 military officers from existing United Nations operations and deploy them as inspection teams in Afghanistan and Pakistan. He requested the President to bring the matter to the Council members' attention for their concurrence with those measures. On 25 April,[6] the President conveyed the members' provisional agreement to the proposals pending formal consideration and a decision by the Council.

Iran, on 13 April,[7] stated that the exclusion of the Mujahedin (freedom fighters), refugees and Muslim people of Afghanistan from a process of determination of the destiny of Afghanistan was unacceptable. It called for unconditional withdrawal of what it termed occupation troops from Afghanistan and the establishment of a truly representative Government.

The USSR, on 27 April,[8] said that it considered compliance with the Geneva Agreements the most important condition for restoring peace in Afghanistan and its consolidation as an independent, non-aligned and neutral State. Afghanistan and the USSR transmitted on 15 May[9] a joint statement that, in conformity with the Agreements, the withdrawal of the Soviet troops, which had begun that same day, would be carried out within nine months and that one half of the contingent would be withdrawn by 15 August. On 15 June,[10] the USSR forwarded a letter from its Foreign Minister accusing Pakistan of violating its obligations under the Geneva Agreements. He cited what he called irrefutable facts, including the transfer of weapons from Pakistan to Afghanistan and military training of insurgents by foreign instructors who had entered Afghanistan from that country. He said if Pakistan's actions were not brought into line with its obligations under the Agreements, a situation could develop which might undermine efforts that had led to their conclusion.

Pakistan, on 23 June,[11] stated that investigations had revealed that the Soviet charges were unfounded. It accused Afghanistan of violations of its territory in contravention of the Agreements. On 1 July,[12] the USSR stated that, in spite of Pakistan's assertions to the contrary, armaments and armed opposition groups continued to enter Afghanistan from that country. It charged Pakistan with encouraging Afghan opposition activities aimed at disrupting the return of the Afghan refugees to their homeland.

On 28 June,[13] Afghanistan accused Pakistan of having increased the shipment of arms into Afghanistan and of equipping and inciting the extremists against the Afghan Government, in violation of the Geneva Agreements.

On 6 July,[14] Afghanistan forwarded a statement from its Foreign Ministry criticizing what it called hostile pronouncements made by Pakistan's President at an international conference in Islamabad. It said that by making such assertions, he was further complicating the situation in Afghanistan. On the following day,[15] it conveyed a 27 June statement to the Afghan Parliament by its Foreign Minister accusing Pakistan of continuing to violate the Geneva Agreements.

Refuting the allegations, Pakistan, on 14 July,[16] stated that it was committed to abide by the provisions of the Agreements and that it rejected Afghanistan's efforts to implicate it in its internal affairs. Afghanistan, on 8 August,[17] described Pakistan's response as an attempt to mislead the United Nations and world public opinion. On 21 July,[18] Afghanistan drew attention to the activities of elements linked with the Peshawar-based alliance of seven (liberation movements), which, it said, had resulted in tragedies among the inhabitants of Kabul and other cities.

Afghanistan, on 14 November,[19] accused Pakistan of interfering in its internal affairs and of hindering the repatriation of Afghan refugees. On 23 November,[20] Afghanistan proposed the convening of an international conference on its neutrality and demilitarization, under the aegis of the United Nations. It also forwarded a 29 October statement[21] by its President to the Afghan Parliament, on comprehensive initiatives for peace.

Pakistan, on 18 November,[22] while reaffirming its commitment to the Agreements, called the Afghan allegations unfounded. Further, on 19 December,[23] it opposed Afghanistan's proposal for an international conference. Support for the convening of such a conference was expressed by the USSR in a statement of 2 December.[24]

SECURITY COUNCIL ACTION (October)

In accordance with the agreement reached in prior consultations, the Security Council considered the situation relating to Afghanistan at a meeting on 31 October.

It unanimously adopted **resolution 622(1988)**.

The Security Council,

Recalling the letters dated 14 April and 22 April 1988 from the Secretary-General to the President of the Security Council concerning the agreements on the settlement of the situation relating to Afghanistan, signed at Geneva on 14 April 1988,

Recalling also the letter dated 25 April 1988 from the President of the Security Council to the Secretary-General,

1. *Confirms* its agreement to the measures envisaged in the Secretary-General's letters of 14 and 22 April 1988, in particular the arrangement for the temporary dispatch to Afghanistan and Pakistan of military officers from existing United Nations operations to assist in the mission of good offices;

2. *Requests* the Secretary-General to keep the Security Council informed of further developments, in accordance with the Geneva agreements.

Security Council resolution 622(1988)

31 October 1988   Meeting 2828   Adopted unanimously

Draft prepared in consultations among Council members (S/20250).

GENERAL ASSEMBLY ACTION (November)

The General Assembly, on 3 November, adopted **resolution 43/20** without vote.

The situation in Afghanistan and its implications for international peace and security

The General Assembly,

Having considered the item entitled "The situation in Afghanistan and its implications for international peace and security",

Reaffirming the purposes and principles of the Charter of the United Nations and the obligation of all States to refrain in their international relations from the threat or use of force against the sovereignty, territorial integrity and political independence of any State,

Reaffirming also the inalienable right of all peoples to determine their own form of government and to choose their own economic, political and social system free from outside intervention, subversion, coercion or constraint of any kind whatsoever,

Gravely concerned at the situation in Afghanistan, which resulted from the violation of principles of the Charter of the United Nations and of the recognized norms of inter-State conduct,

Noting the conclusion at Geneva, on 14 April 1988, of the Agreements on the Settlement of the Situation Relating to Afghanistan and the partial withdrawal of foreign troops in accordance with the agreed time-frame,

Aware of the continuing concern of the international community at the sufferings of the Afghan people and the magnitude of the social and economic problems posed to Pakistan and Iran by the presence on their soil of millions of Afghan refugees,

Deeply conscious of the urgent need for a comprehensive political solution of the situation in respect of Afghanistan,

Conscious that a successful final political settlement of the Afghanistan problem would have a favourable impact on the international situation and provide an impetus for the resolution of other acute regional conflicts,

Expressing its appreciation to the Secretary-General and his Personal Representative for their efforts to bring about peace and security,

Taking note of the report of the Secretary-General and the status of the process of political settlement,

1. *Welcomes* the conclusion at Geneva, on 14 April 1988, under United Nations auspices, of the Agreements on the Settlement of the Situation Relating to Afghanistan, which constitute an important step towards a comprehensive political solution of the Afghanistan problem;

2. *Expresses its deep appreciation* to the Secretary-General and his Personal Representative for their constant efforts to achieve a political solution of the Afghanistan problem;

3. *Calls* for the scrupulous respect for and faithful implementation of the Agreements by all parties concerned who should fully abide by their letter and spirit;

4. *Notes* the continuing process of withdrawal of foreign troops from Afghanistan and expresses its expectation that the withdrawal will be completed in accordance with the relevant provisions of the Agreements;

5. *Reiterates* that the preservation of the sovereignty, territorial integrity, political independence and non-aligned character of Afghanistan is essential for a peaceful solution of the Afghanistan problem;

6. *Reaffirms* the right of the Afghan people to determine their own form of government and to choose their economic, political and social system free from outside intervention, subversion, coercion or constraint of any kind whatsoever;

7. *Calls upon* all parties concerned to work for the urgent achievement of a comprehensive political solution and the creation of the necessary conditions of peace and normalcy that would enable the Afghan refugees to return voluntarily to their homeland in safety and honour;

8. *Emphasizes* the need for an intra-Afghan dialogue for the establishment of a broad-based government to ensure the broadest support and immediate participation of all segments of the Afghan people;

9. *Requests* the Secretary-General and his Representative to encourage and facilitate the early realization of a comprehensive political settlement in Afghanistan in accordance with the provisions of the Agreements and of the present resolution;

10. *Renews its appeal* to all States and national and international organizations to continue to extend humanitarian relief assistance with a view to alleviating the hardship of the Afghan refugees, in co-ordination with the United Nations High Commissioner for Refugees;

11. *Welcomes* the appointment of a special co-ordinator for channelling economic and humanitarian assistance to the people of Afghanistan;

12. *Calls upon* all States to provide adequate financial and material resources to the Co-ordinator for Humanitarian and Economic Assistance Programmes Relating to Afghanistan for the purposes of achieving the speedy repatriation and rehabilitation of the Afghan refugees, as well as for the economic and social reconstruction of the country;

13. *Requests* the Secretary-General to keep Member States and the Security Council informed of progress towards the implementation of the present resolution and to submit to the General Assembly at its forty-fourth session a report on the situation in Afghanistan, on progress achieved in the implementation of the Agreements and the political settlement relating to Afghanistan;

14. *Decides* to include in the provisional agenda of its forty-fourth session the item entitled "The situation in

Afghanistan and its implications for international peace and security''.

General Assembly resolution 43/20
3 November 1988   Meeting 45   Adopted without vote
Draft by President (A/43/L.20); agenda item 30.

In pursuance of the mandate given to him by the Assembly, the Secretary-General met in New York with Afghanistan's Prime Minister on 7 November and with the Chairman of the Alliance of Afghan Mujahedin on 10 November, assuring them of his determination to encourage and facilitate the early realization of a comprehensive political settlement as called for by the Assembly.

UN assistance programmes

Afghanistan, on 29 April,[25] requested the inclusion of an additional item on economic and social assistance to Afghanistan in the provisional agenda of the 1988 first regular session of the Economic and Social Council, and asked for an urgent discussion of the item by the Council. On 5 May,[26] Pakistan opposed that proposal, calling it premature, and said it complicated the negotiating process for an interim arrangement acceptable to all the Afghan parties. Afghanistan, on 11 May,[27] called Pakistan's objection politically motivated.

The Economic and Social Council, by **resolution 1988/52** of 26 July, urged Member States to contribute to the United Nations effort to assist the people of Afghanistan. Welcoming the Secretary-General's initiative in that regard, it supported the efforts of the Co-ordinator for United Nations Humanitarian and Economic Assistance Programmes relating to Afghanistan and requested all specialized agencies and United Nations bodies to participate actively.

Iran-Iraq armed conflict

On 20 August 1988, a cease-fire was secured by the United Nations in the eight-year Iran-Iraq war, followed five days later by a first round of direct negotiations between the two nations. Second and third rounds were held in October and November.

Earlier, on 17 July, Iran accepted Security Council resolution 598(1987)[28] by which the Council had outlined a peace plan for the region. On 9 August 1988, by resolution 619(1988), the Council established the United Nations Iran-Iraq Military Observer Group to verify, confirm and supervise the cease-fire and troop withdrawal.

In October, the Secretary-General reported that, although the cease-fire was holding well, there was a pressing need for its consolidation and the earliest possible withdrawal of troops to internationally recognized boundaries.

The Security Council addressed various aspects of the conflict throughout 1988. In March, deploring the escalating hostilities, it urged the two sides to send special emissaries to New York for urgent consultations. In May and August, after considering a total of four expert reports on chemical weapons use in the conflict, the Council condemned their use and decided that any future use would prompt effective measures by the Council in accordance with the United Nations Charter (resolutions 612(1988) and 620(1988)).

Charges of psychological and other abuses of prisoners of war prompted the Secretary-General to send a specialist mission to Iran and Iraq in late July to evaluate the situation.

The General Assembly, at its resumed forty-second session on 19 September, by **decision 42/466**, included in the draft agenda of its forty-third (1988) session an item on the consequences of the prolongation of the armed conflict between Iran and Iraq, but did not discuss the matter. In suspending the forty-third session on 22 December, the Assembly decided to retain the item on its agenda for consideration when it resumed that session in 1989 (**decision 43/459**).

Communications received by the United Nations from the two sides in the first quarter of the year showed no reduction in hostilities. Attacks were reported along the battle fronts, on civilian population centres and on commercial shipping in the Persian Gulf.

Iran complained of violations of international law and its territorial sea and airspace by United States ships and aircraft in the Gulf. Similar charges were made against an Italian ship, while Kuwait protested that Iran had violated its territorial waters in an attack on its fishing boats.

On 18 March, the Secretary-General called on Iran and Iraq to exercise utmost restraint and to end incidents causing loss of innocent lives. He invited the Presidents of both countries to send special emissaries to New York for intensive consultations. On 22 March, he said he was appalled at the sharp escalation of the conflict.

SECURITY COUNCIL ACTION

On 16 March, Security Council members held consultations on the intensified hostilities and the Council President made the following statement on their behalf:[29]

Meeting number. SC 2798.

"The members of the Security Council express grave concern over the fact that the tragic conflict between the Islamic Republic of Iran and Iraq continues and has entered its eighth year.

"They strongly deplore the escalation of the hostilities between these two countries, particularly the attacks against civilian targets and cities that have taken a heavy toll in human lives and caused vast material destruction, in spite of the declared readiness of the belligerent parties to cease such attacks.

"The members of the Council insist that the Islamic Republic of Iran and Iraq immediately cease all such attacks and desist forthwith from all acts that lead to the escalation of the conflict and which thereby create further obstacles in the way of implementation of resolution 598(1987) of 20 July 1987 and undermine the efforts of the Security Council to put an early end to this conflict in accordance with the resolution.

"They are convinced that the recent escalation has demonstrated the need for full and rapid implementation of resolution 598(1987).

"Determined to bring the conflict between the Islamic Republic of Iran and Iraq to an early end, the members of the Council reaffirm their strong commitment to the implementation of resolution 598(1987) as an integrated whole, which is the only basis for a comprehensive, just, honourable and lasting settlement of the conflict.

"They express grave concern that resolution 598(1987), which has a mandatory character, has not yet been implemented.

"The members of the Council take note of the statement made by the Secretary-General to them on 14 March 1988. They encourage him to continue his efforts as endorsed by the Council to secure implementation of resolution 598(1987) and, in this connection, support his intention to invite the Governments of the Islamic Republic of Iran and Iraq to send, at the earliest possible date, their foreign ministers, or another senior official, as a special emissary to New York to enter into urgent and intensive consultations with the Secretary-General. They request the Secretary-General to submit to the Security Council, within three weeks, the report on his consultations with the two sides.

"The members of the Council reaffirm their determination, in accordance with paragraph 10 of resolution 598(1987), to consider promptly, in the light of the Secretary-General's renewed efforts to secure implementation of that resolution, further effective steps to ensure compliance with it."

Communications received during April-August continued to contain allegations of attacks by Iran and Iraq against the other's civilian targets, including the use of chemical weapons (see below).

Iran also charged Kuwait with co-operation with Iraq by allowing its airspace to be used by the latter. The United States accused Iran of attacking its ships in international waters, while Iraq complained of United States attacks on its oil platforms and violations of its sea and air space. Iran also charged France, Italy and the United Kingdom with various violations of international law by their ships in the Gulf, while Iran was accused of attacking Kuwaiti fishermen.

Use of chemical weapons

From January to June, numerous communications continued to be received by the Secretary-General concerning allegations of chemical warfare in the Iran-Iraq conflict. Iran accused Iraq of using chemical weapons against its military, civilian and refugee populations, while Iraq charged that Iran had carried out chemical weapons attacks against its military personnel. In response to requests from both sides for an investigation into the situation,[30] the Secretary-General dispatched expert missions to the two countries in late March/early April and again in July and August. Following consideration of their reports, the Security Council vigorously condemned the continued use of chemical weapons.

Specialist's report (April). On 25 April, the Secretary-General transmitted to the Security Council the report[31] of a medical specialist who had investigated the allegations during visits to Iran from 28 to 31 March and Iraq from 7 to 11 April 1988. The investigation was a continuation of those conducted in 1984,[32] 1985,[33] 1986[34] and 1987.[35] The Secretary-General said the specialist had concluded that chemical weapons continued to be used in the conflict, adding urgency to the concern that such use could escalate and undermine the 1925 Geneva Protocol prohibiting the use of such weapons.

The report covered the mission's terms of reference, review of documentation, methodology, investigations, summary of findings, conclusions and appendices, and was subsequently augmented by an addendum on civilian and military patients examined at hospitals in Iran and Iraq.[36]

The specialist reported that in Iran he found several casualties resulting from mustard-gas attacks and that, compared with previous years, there had been an increase in both the number of victims and the severity of the injuries sustained. There also appeared to be a higher proportion of civilians among those affected. He also stated that all the casualties of chemical attacks he found in Iraq were military personnel.

A total of 66 patients were examined at Teheran, while 39 were seen at the Al Rasheed Military Hospital at Baghdad. A cursory medical observation was also made of the injuries suffered by 72 additional patients in the same Iraqi hospital. The symptoms and signs indicating the use of mustard gas (yperite) included conjunctivitis, skin lesions, respiratory insufficiency, chemical tracheobronchitis and leukopenia.

The specialist concluded that the patients he had examined had been affected by chemical weapons whose main aggressive chemical was mustard gas. While in some cases in Iran an acetylcholine esterase-inhibiting substance had also been used, there was no conclusive evidence that it had been used in Iraq.

In a 27 April letter,[37] Iran expressed disappointment that the report failed to address the task for which the dispatch of the mission was requested. It said that despite repeated requests, the team did not visit Halabja where, it alleged, the most extensive use of chemical weapons against civilians had taken place.

SECURITY COUNCIL ACTION (May)

The Security Council met on 9 May pursuant to an agreement reached during prior consultations. It unanimously adopted **resolution 612(1988)**.

The Security Council,

Having considered the report of 25 April 1988 of the mission dispatched by the Secretary-General to investigate allegations of the use of chemical weapons in the conflict between the Islamic Republic of Iran and Iraq,

Dismayed by the mission's conclusions that chemical weapons continue to be used in the conflict and that their use has been on an even more intensive scale than before,

1. *Affirms* the urgent necessity of strict observance of the Protocol for the Prohibition of the Use in War of Asphyxiating, Poisonous or Other Gases, and of Bacteriological Methods of Warfare, signed at Geneva on 17 June 1925;

2. *Condemns vigorously* the continued use of chemical weapons in the conflict between the Islamic Republic of Iran and Iraq contrary to the obligations under the Geneva Protocol;

3. *Expects* both sides to refrain from the future use of chemical weapons in accordance with their obligations under the Geneva Protocol;

4. *Calls upon* all States to continue to apply or to establish strict control of the export to the parties to the conflict of chemical products serving for the production of chemical weapons;

5. *Decides* to remain seized of the matter and expresses its determination to review the implementation of the present resolution.

Security Council resolution 612(1988)

9 May 1988   Meeting 2812   Adopted unanimously

3-nation draft (S/19869).
Sponsors: Germany, Federal Republic of, Italy, Japan.

On 16 May,[38] Iran expressed displeasure at the failure of the Council to acknowledge that Iraq was responsible for the use of chemical weapons, since such use had been documented in several United Nations expert reports and Council statements. Accusing the United Nations of delaying the specialist mission's dispatch, Iran claimed it was sent after the effects on the people and the environment had worn off and a large number of the wounded had by then died or been discharged from the hospitals.

From mid-May to early July, further charges of chemical warfare were made by both Iran and Iraq. While Iran again complained of attacks on its military and civilian populations, Iraq accused Iran of chemical attacks on its military forces.

On 28 June, the Secretary-General announced that he was sending, at the Security Council's request, another mission, composed of three mem-

bers, to investigate further allegations of chemical weapons use against Iran. Iran had also made such requests on 19[39] and 25 May[40] and 27 June.[41] After Iraq made a similar request on 3 July[42] for the mission to investigate Iran's use of chemical weapons against it, he requested the same mission to visit Iraq.

Specialists' reports (July and August). Two reports on the further use of chemical weapons were submitted to the Security Council in July. On 20 July,[43] the Secretary-General transmitted a report by two specialists who had investigated further allegations from Iran during a mission to the country from 1 to 5 July. The specialists concluded that chemical weapons continued to be used against Iranian forces and that their use had been intensifying and had become more frequent.

The report covered the mission's terms of reference, review of documentation, methodology, investigations, summary of findings, conclusions and appendices, and was subsequently augmented by an addendum on the 44 patients examined by the specialists. Symptoms and signs indicating the use of mustard gas included lesions of erythema, darkening of the skin, blisters and respiratory lesions. In the Hamid area south-west of Ahvaz, chemical analysis of soil samples and weapon fragments had shown evidence of mustard gas. The experts also concluded that bombs similar to those used in 1984, 1986 and 1987 had again been directed against Iranian forces.

On 25 July,[44] the Secretary-General transmitted a second report by the same two specialists who had investigated further allegations from Iraq during a mission to the country on 10 and 11 July. They concluded that chemical weapons were used against Iraqi forces.

The specialists were able to determine conclusively that the nine Iraqi soldiers they examined at the hospitals in As Sulaymaniyah and Baghdad were affected by mustard gas. Further, fragments of mortar grenades discovered after an alleged Iranian attack at As Sulaymaniyah were found to contain mustard gas. An examination of mortar ammunition claimed to have been captured from the Iranian forces confirmed that they were designed to be filled with solid or liquid material which could include chemical agents. On the basis of their current investigation, the specialists said that the number of casualties and the extent of their injuries seemed less extensive than previously found.

On 3 August,[45] Iran requested the Secretary-General to send another expert team to investigate an alleged chemical bombardment the preceding day on the Sheikh Othman District in Oshnaviyeh. On 5 August, the President of the Security Council informed the Secretary-General that the Council members considered that, in the light of resolution 612(1988), any new allegation ought to be investigated. Consequently, the Secretary-General dispatched three specialists who investigated the allegations during a mission to Iran from 12 to 14 August. Their report[46] was forwarded to the Council on 19 August. Based on the evidence obtained, the specialists concluded that mustard gas had been used in the air attack, affecting Iranian civilians. An analysis of air and soil samples from Oshnaviyeh had confirmed the presence of that gas.

SECURITY COUNCIL ACTION (August)

Pursuant to an agreement reached in prior consultations, the Security Council met on 26 August to consider the mission reports. It unanimously adopted **resolution 620(1988)**.

The Security Council,

Recalling its resolution 612(1988) of 9 May 1988,

Having considered the reports of 20 and 25 July and of 2 and 19 August 1988 of the missions dispatched by the Secretary-General to investigate allegations of the use of chemical weapons in the conflict between the Islamic Republic of Iran and Iraq,

Deeply dismayed by the missions' conclusions that there had been continued use of chemical weapons in the conflict between the Islamic Republic of Iran and Iraq and that such use against Iranians had become more intense and frequent,

Profoundly concerned by the danger of possible use of chemical weapons in the future,

Bearing in mind the current negotiations in the Conference on Disarmament on the complete and effective prohibition of the development, production and stockpiling of chemical weapons and on their destruction,

Determined to intensify its efforts to end all use of chemical weapons in violation of international obligations now and in the future,

1. *Condemns resolutely* the use of chemical weapons in the conflict between the Islamic Republic of Iran and Iraq, in violation of obligations under the Protocol for the Prohibition of the Use in War of Asphyxiating, Poisonous or Other Gases, and of Bacteriological Methods of Warfare, signed at Geneva on 17 June 1925, and in defiance of its resolution 612(1988);

2. *Encourages* the Secretary-General to carry out promptly investigations in response to allegations brought to his attention by any Member State concerning the possible use of chemical and bacteriological (biological) or toxic weapons that may constitute a violation of the 1925 Geneva Protocol or other relevant rules of customary international law, in order to ascertain the facts of the matter, and to report the results;

3. *Calls upon* all States to continue to apply, to establish or to strengthen strict control of the export of chemical products serving for the production of chemical weapons, in particular to parties to a conflict, when it is established or when there is substantial reason to believe that they have used chemical weapons in violation of international obligations;

4. *Decides* to consider immediately, taking into account the investigations of the Secretary-General, appropriate and effective measures in accordance with the Charter of the United Nations, should there be any fu-

ture use of chemical weapons in violation of international law, wherever and by whomever committed.

Security Council resolution 620(1988)

26 August 1988   Meeting 2825   Adopted unanimously

4-nation draft (S/20151).

Sponsors: Germany, Federal Republic of, Italy, Japan, United Kingdom.

Treatment of prisoners of war

The treatment of prisoners of war (POWs) was taken up in a number of letters to the Secretary-General.

Iraq informed the Secretary-General on 10 March 1988[47] that, on 16 December 1987, the Iranian news agency had reported that Iran had released 450 Iraqi POWs who had sought political asylum in Iran. Iraq charged Iran with using mental and physical pressure, in violation of the 1949 Geneva Convention relative to the Treatment of Prisoners of War (third Geneva Convention), to force the POWs to abandon their faith and fight against Iraq. On 28 March,[48] Iraq accused Iran of hindering ICRC from discharging its functions under the same Convention. Iraq said that tens of thousands of Iraqi POWs were in need of protection under that Convention and called on the Secretary-General to dispatch a mission to investigate the fate of Iraqi POWs.

On 2 July,[49] Iraq transmitted a note verbale from ICRC informing Iraq that during its visits to 15 Iranian camps and 6 hospitals in 1987, it was not given access to 7,327 previously registered POWs or to thousands of others whom it knew were being held in Iran. Such violations, Iraq said, required the Security Council's attention. Iraq also repeated its call for the dispatch of an investigative mission to examine the conditions of Iraqi POWs in Iran. On 7 July,[50] Iraq forwarded a film showing that the remains of a considerable number of its POWs had been found in the Mawat region, making it clear that Iran had killed, mutilated and burned them after tying up some of them.

Iran accused Iraq on 11 July[51] of violating the third Geneva Convention in respect of Iranian civilians interned in Iraq as POWs and of Iranian POWs in that country. It listed 10 instances of their ill-treatment by Iraq and requested the United Nations to investigate.

On 17 October,[52] Iraq transmitted a memorandum to ICRC at Baghdad concerning the exchange of POWs. It informed ICRC of its agreement that the exchange of POWs should begin on condition that Iran reciprocated, adding that since the exchange was a humanitarian matter and in response to an ICRC request, Iraq's agreement was unrelated to the other issues referred to in resolution 598(1987).[28]

Iran, on 21 October,[53] informed ICRC that it was prepared to repatriate POWs in accordance with resolution 598(1987) and the Secretary-General's implementation plan and to continue the repatriation of disabled, wounded and sick POWs on humanitarian grounds, should Iraq reciprocate.

On 8 November,[54] Iraq told ICRC that it was prepared to begin immediately repatriation of all sick and wounded POWs on humanitarian grounds and that it would begin to return POWs who were already registered. It emphasized the need to commence registration of non-registered POWs in accordance with the arrangements proposed by ICRC. On 24 November,[55] Iraq announced the conclusion of an agreement between Iran, Iraq and ICRC on the exchange of 1,158 Iraqi and 411 Iranian sick or wounded POWs.

Iran, on 29 November,[56] complained to ICRC that Iraq had violated the Memorandum of Understanding by refusing to repatriate 22 sick and wounded POWs on the first day of exchange and that it had not repatriated a total of 67 such POWs. Iran said it was ready to repatriate all sick and wounded Iraqi POWs.

On 28 November,[57] Iraq informed ICRC of a report by the Iranian news agency that Iran had suspended the transfer of sick and disabled Iraqi POWs the preceding day and that those transfers would not be resumed until after the release of Iranian POWs whom Iraq had not freed during the initial phase of the prisoner-exchange operation. Iraq said that its agreement with Iran stipulated that the transfer of POWs would be made daily on a reciprocal basis and that the operation would be completed within 10 days beginning on 22 November. Iraq accused Iran of delaying the start of the operation by two days and of trying to reduce the number of POWs agreed on for each transfer; it said Iran had suspended the exchange of POWs after what it called its fraudulent moves became apparent.

On 7 December,[58] Iraq transmitted a letter to ICRC in reply to Iran's allegation of Iraqi violation of the agreement, accusing Iran of duplicity and of misleading Iranian and world public opinion.

On 10 December,[59] Iran said while it had presented to ICRC a list of unregistered Iraqi sick and wounded POWs at the stipulated time, Iraq had not done so in respect of Iranian POWs and had thus violated the Memorandum of Understanding for the second time.

Report of the mission on POWs. On 24 August,[60] the Secretary-General transmitted to the Security Council a report by three specialists who had enquired into the situation of POWs being held in the two countries. Both Iran[61] and Iraq[49],[50] had requested him to send such a mission.

The Secretary-General said he had dispatched the mission to those countries as an extraordinary measure and in accordance with his responsibility under the United Nations Charter. Its task was to ascertain the facts and inquire into concerns expressed by both countries regarding the condition of their POWs, with a view to ensuring the observance of international law. The Secretary-General pointed out, however, that important developments had taken place since the mission's dispatch, including a cease-fire (see below), and that the negotiations that would follow were expected to lead to lasting peace between the two countries. He said he was encouraged by the mission's conclusion that on the issue of repatriation the views of the parties were convergent and, in substance, consistent with the third Geneva Convention.

The specialists visited Iran from 24 to 30 July and Iraq from 31 July to 5 August. In Iran, they visited five POW camps and found the prisoners' material conditions, on the whole, acceptable, although on some points their further improvement was desirable. They were, however, concerned at the prisoners' psychological condition and said they had faced emotional stress which required further observation. An important factor affecting the POWs' state of mind was the general atmosphere in the camps, resulting from the religious and political influence of the Cultural Committee, and they recommended that the latter's role and activities be reconsidered.

Referring to Iraq's concerns about the 7,327 POWs who were registered by ICRC prior to 1984 but not seen by it since then, and the 20,000 to 30,000 missing who had not been registered by ICRC as POWs, the specialists said they had established that, apart from POWs who had died and could be accounted for, Iran knew the whereabouts and current status of those other prisoners and was able to make the information available. They believed that the existing state of affairs would change after the cease-fire, but said that further diplomatic efforts in that regard were needed.

In Iraq, the specialists found the material conditions of POWs they visited generally acceptable, although improvements were necessary in some instances. While psychological pressure on Iranian POWs was said to have increased, there was no evidence of systematic indoctrination. The specialists noted that the POW camps were visited regularly by ICRC whose recommendations were generally complied with, and said that the problem of non-registration of POWs was a legacy of the past which Iraq was now ready to solve. They credited Iraq for allowing ICRC to register every prisoner in its camps and were disappointed that considerations of reciprocity had again brought that process to a halt. The mission reported that the main problem with regard to the civilian internees resulted from the uncertainty of their future in Iraq, Iran or wherever they would be allowed to live. A number of them had not been interned in civilian camps but were being treated as POWs. Any reproach to Iraq for keeping them in captivity had met with the argument that they had been fighting against Iraq. As they were being treated like POWs, they were expected to be repatriated as such.

Both Iran and Iraq informed the mission that they agreed to a key role for ICRC; that repatriation would be carried out as quickly as possible; that no one should be forcibly repatriated; and that it would be necessary for some prisoners to find third countries of asylum.

Declaration of a cease-fire

By a 17 July letter from its President,[62] Iran conveyed its acceptance of Security Council resolution 598(1987),[28] which had outlined a peace plan for the region, including a cease-fire, an end to all military actions, withdrawal of forces to internationally recognized boundaries, United Nations observers to supervise those actions and an impartial body to inquire into the responsibility for the conflict. President Seyed Ali Khamenei stated that his country was accepting the 1987 resolution because of the importance Iran attached to saving human lives and to establishing justice and regional and international peace and security. Also, the war, which had been started by Iraq on 22 September 1980, had reached unprecedented dimensions, drawing other countries into it and engulfing innocent civilians—a manifestation of which was the shooting down of Iran Air flight 655 (see below).

Despite a 19 July call from the Secretary-General and the Security Council urging both sides to exercise maximum restraint and refrain from any act that might endanger the Secretary-General's effort, further incidents of fighting continued to be reported.

On 19 July,[63] Iran charged that on that day Iraq had bombarded its industrial installations at Bushehr, Mahshahr and Imam Khomeini, killing and wounding workers; it also accused Iraq of violating its airspace. The following day,[64] it reported that Iraq had carried out ground and air attacks against Iranian targets. On 21 July,[65] Iran complained that Iraq on 19 July had also attacked the Piranshahr and Mehran areas.

On 25 July,[66] Iran informed the Secretary-General of Iraqi artillery attacks against Sardasht on 23 July, killing five and wounding 15, and its bombardment of the Kazand-e-Gharb city on 24 July, killing seven and wounding 50. The following day,[67] it charged Iraq with initiating attacks in its north-western region at a time when the Iranian Foreign Minister was visiting New York to announce his country's willingness to co-operate

with the Secretary-General to facilitate immediate implementation of resolution 598(1987). On 27 July 1988,[68] Iran complained of Iraqi aerial attacks during the preceding three days against civilian targets, wounding students and villagers and damaging crops and fields.

Iraq, on 18 July,[69] transmitted a statement issued by the General Command of the Iranian Armed Forces concerning resolution 598(1987). Through a statement of its Deputy Prime Minister and Foreign Minister, on 19 July 1988,[70] it pointed out that the General Command statement affirmed Iran's resolve to mobilize its military capabilities for the purpose of continuing its aggression against Iraq. It pointed out that while Iraq had accepted resolution 598(1987) upon its adoption, Iran had done so after rejecting it for a whole year. On 20 July,[71] Iraq forwarded a letter from its Deputy Prime Minister and Foreign Minister proposing practical steps for achieving a comprehensive and durable peace in the shortest possible time, in the light of developments following Iran's acceptance of the 1987 resolution.

On 6 August 1988,[72] Iraq transmitted a message from its President, declaring readiness for a cease-fire on the condition that Iran declared unequivocally and officially its agreement to enter into direct negotiations with Iraq, leading to the implementation of all the provisions of resolution 598(1987). If Iran refused to agree to such negotiations, it alone would be responsible for rejecting the path of peace.

On 7 August,[73] Iran conveyed its acceptance of direct talks to take place after the cease-fire and said that, having accepted resolution 598(1987) unconditionally, it considered any insistence on holding talks before the cease-fire as a pre-condition for the implementation of that resolution; the subsequent Iraqi position had signalled its reconsideration of that pre-condition.

SECURITY COUNCIL ACTION

The Security Council again took up the Iran-Iraq situation on 8 August, inviting both States to participate in the discussions without the right to vote.

Meeting number. SC 2823.

The Secretary-General informed the Council[74] that as a result of his diplomatic efforts towards achieving implementation of its 1987 resolution,[28] and in exercise of his mandate, he was calling on Iran and Iraq to observe a cease-fire and to discontinue all military action on land, at sea and in the air as of 0300 hours GMT on 20 August 1988. Both parties assured him that they would observe the cease-fire and agreed to the deployment of United Nations observers at that time. He was inviting Iran and Iraq to direct talks under his auspices at Geneva on 25 August.

Noting that military activity had decreased in the preceding few days, the Secretary-General appealed to all concerned to exercise the utmost restraint and to refrain from any hostile activity before the cease-fire came into effect.

On the same day, the Council President made the following statement:[75]

"The Security Council welcomes the statement just made by the Secretary-General concerning the implementation of its resolution 598(1987) of 20 July 1987 on the Iran/Iraq conflict.

"The Council endorses the Secretary-General's announcement that the cease-fire demanded in the resolution shall come into effect at 0300 (GMT) on 20 August 1988, and that direct talks under his auspices between the two parties shall begin on 25 August.

"The Council further endorses the appeal of the Secretary-General to both parties to exercise the utmost restraint and expects them to refrain from all hostile activities in the period before the entry into effect of the cease-fire.

"The Council reiterates its determination that its resolution 598(1987) be fully implemented as an integral whole and reaffirms its full support for the continuing efforts of the Secretary-General to this end."

Iran, on 8 August,[76] stated that it was prepared to refrain from all military actions beginning that same day.

Appointment of a Personal Representative

On 1 September, the Secretary-General appointed Jan K. Eliasson (Sweden) as his Personal Representative on issues pertaining to the implementation of resolution 598(1987). From 1980 to 1986, Mr. Eliasson had accompanied Olof Palme (Sweden), who was during that period the Secretary-General's Special Representative dealing with the Iran-Iraq conflict, on missions to both countries.

UN Iran-Iraq Military Observer Group

In August 1988, the Security Council established a team of unarmed United Nations observers to supervise the cease-fire between Iran and Iraq and the withdrawal of forces to internationally recognized boundaries, as called for in resolution 598(1987).

Report of the Secretary-General (August). In a 7 August 1988 report,[77] the Secretary-General recommended that, as soon as the cease-fire date had been set, the Council establish an observer team, to be known as the United Nations Iran-Iraq Military Observer Group (UNIIMOG), which would also assist the parties as might be mutually agreed.

As set out in resolution 598(1987), UNIIMOG's terms of reference would be: to establish with the parties agreed cease-fire lines; to monitor compliance with the cease-fire; to investigate alleged violations and restore the situation if a violation had taken place; to prevent, through negotiation, any other change in the *status quo*; to supervise, verify and confirm the withdrawal of all forces to the internationally recognized boundaries; and to obtain the agreement of the parties to other arrangements which, pending negotiation of a comprehensive settlement, could help reduce tension and build confidence between them, such as the establishment of areas of separation of forces, limitations on the number and calibre of weapons, and patrolling of certain sensitive areas in or near Shatt al-Arab.

The Secretary-General reported that on 20 July he had announced the sending of a technical team to Iran and Iraq to work out the modalities for the dispatch of United Nations observers. The team was led by Lieutenant-General Martin Vadset, Chief of Staff of the United Nations Truce Supervision Organization (UNTSO), and included a senior political adviser, a civilian logistics expert and four military observers of UNTSO. It was assisted by small teams which had been stationed at Baghdad and Teheran since 1984. During its visit to both capitals, the team held detailed discussions relevant to the establishment and deployment of UNIIMOG.

On the basis of General Vadset's report, the Secretary-General estimated that UNIIMOG would need up to 350 military observers, in addition to military support staff and civilian administrative and logistics personnel. The Group would consist of a headquarters and two detachments, one in each country.

Outlining his plan of action for deploying UNIIMOG, the Secretary-General said the duration of its deployment would depend on progress made in implementing other aspects of resolution 598(1987); subject to this, he suggested that UNIIMOG be stationed initially in the area for six months. He estimated the cost of UNIIMOG for that period at approximately $74 million, to be borne by Member States in accordance with Article 17, paragraph 2, of the Charter.

SECURITY COUNCIL ACTION (August)

On 9 August 1988, the Security Council met, in accordance with an understanding reached during prior consultations, to consider the Secretary-General's report. Iran and Iraq were invited to participate in the debate without the right to vote.

The Council unanimously adopted **resolution 619(1988)**.

The Security Council,
Recalling its resolution 598(1987) of 20 July 1987,

1. *Approves* the report of the Secretary-General contained in document S/20093 on the implementation of paragraph 2 of resolution 598(1987) of the Security Council;

2. *Decides* to set up immediately, under its authority, a United Nations Iran-Iraq Military Observer Group and requests the Secretary-General to take the necessary steps to this effect, in accordance with his above-mentioned report;

3. *Also decides* that the United Nations Iran-Iraq Military Observer Group shall be established for a period of six months, unless the Council decides otherwise;

4. *Requests* the Secretary-General to keep the Security Council fully informed of further developments.

Security Council resolution 619(1988)

9 August 1988   Meeting 2824   Adopted unanimously

Draft prepared in consultations among Council members (S/20097).

Report of the Secretary-General (October). Responding to resolution 619(1988), the Secretary-General submitted on 25 October an interim report[78] on UNIIMOG during its first two months of operation.

He reported that the cease-fire came into effect at 0300 hours GMT on 20 August. By that time, 307 United Nations military observers and the main elements of the Canadian signals unit were in Iran and Iraq and 51 patrols were deployed on the first day. Those patrols had the double task of verifying the forward-defended localities (FDLs) occupied by the two sides when the cease-fire came into effect and of defusing confrontations resulting from actual or alleged breaches of the cease-fire. Because of the length of the cease-fire line (some 1,400 kilometres) and the nature of the terrain, ranging from rugged mountains in the north to desert and marshy swamps in the south, it took UNIIMOG some time to verify some limited areas along the whole length of the line. In some areas there was disagreement between the two sides about where the FDLs were on 20 August. However, in general, UNIIMOG succeeded quickly in establishing the necessary data-base to carry out its task of monitoring compliance with the cease-fire.

Before the cease-fire came into effect, the Secretary-General had proposed to the two sides that a number of activities be considered as violations. As of 24 October, UNIIMOG had received 1,072 complaints of alleged violations, only 235 of which had been confirmed as such.

The Secretary-General concluded that although there had been some serious breaches, the cease-fire was holding well and there had been no fighting for over two months. However, he conveyed to the Council his concern that the current state of affairs was inherently unstable. There were points on the cease-fire line where the two sides remained in dangerous proximity; as long as that situation continued, there was danger that fighting could resume. There was, therefore, a pressing need for the current cease-fire to be consolidated and for the earliest possible withdrawal to the internationally recognized boundaries.

From August to mid-December, both Iran and Iraq alleged violations of the cease-fire in numerous communications to the Secretary-General.

Composition

On 9 August,[79] the Secretary-General proposed to the Council that UNIIMOG be composed of contingents from the following Member States: Argentina, Australia, Austria, Bangladesh, Canada, Denmark, Finland, Ghana, Hungary, India, Indonesia, Ireland, Italy, Kenya, Malaysia, New Zealand, Nigeria, Norway, Poland, Senegal, Sweden, Turkey, Yugoslavia, Zambia. On 10 August,[80] the President informed the Secretary-General of the Council's agreement.

Also, on 10 August,[81] the Secretary-General informed the Council of his intention, with its consent, to appoint Major-General Slavco Jovic of Yugoslavia as Chief Military Observer (CMO) of UNIIMOG. On 11 August,[82] the President conveyed the Council's agreement to that proposal.

On 23 August,[83] the Secretary-General informed the Council President of his intention to add Peru and Uruguay to the list of contingents included in UNIIMOG. The President informed him on 26 August[84] that the Council agreed with his proposal.

As of 24 October, UNIIMOG's military strength was 828, made up of contingents from 26 Member States. In addition, 37 military police provided by Ireland and 4 medical orderlies from Austria were to join before the end of October. One hundred and two civilian staff members had been assigned to UNIIMOG.

UNIIMOG headquarters were at Baghdad and Teheran, with the CMO and his senior staff spending alternate weeks at each capital.

Financing

On 10 August,[85] the Secretary-General requested the General Assembly to include in the agenda of its resumed forty-second session an additional urgent item on the financing of UNIIMOG. By **decision 42/402 B** of 16 August, the Assembly added the item to the list of those allocated to the Fifth (Administrative and Budgetary) Committee.

On 11 August,[86] the Secretary-General submitted to the Assembly a report on the financing of UNIIMOG. He estimated the costs for the six-month period from 9 August 1988 to 8 February 1989 at $75.6 million gross ($73.8 million net). In order to act immediately on the Security Council's decision establishing UNIIMOG, he had sought the concurrence of the Advisory Committee on Administrative and Budgetary Questions (ACABQ) to enter into commitments not to exceed $3.7 million until the Assembly decided on UNIIMOG financing at its resumed session.

On 16 August, the Chairman of ACABQ recommended that the Assembly approve an appropriation large enough to allow UNIIMOG to initiate and carry on its operations until ACABQ and the Assembly had completed an in-depth review of the Group's financing.

GENERAL ASSEMBLY ACTION

On 17 August, the General Assembly adopted without vote **resolution 42/233**.

Financing of the United Nations Iran-Iraq Military Observer Group

The General Assembly,

Having considered the report of the Secretary-General on the financing of the United Nations Iran-Iraq Military Observer Group, established pursuant to Security Council resolution 619(1988) of 9 August 1988 for the period from 9 August 1988 to 8 February 1989 inclusive, and the related statement of the Chairman of the Advisory Committee on Administrative and Budgetary Questions,

Reaffirming its previous decisions regarding the fact that, in order to meet the expenditures caused by such operations, a different procedure from the one applied to meet expenditures of the regular budget of the United Nations is required,

Taking into account the fact that the economically more developed countries are in a position to make relatively larger contributions and that the economically less developed countries have a relatively limited capacity to contribute towards peace-keeping operations involving heavy expenditures,

Bearing in mind the special responsibilities of the States permanent members of the Security Council in the financing of such operations, as indicated in General Assembly resolution 1874(S-IV) of 27 June 1963 and other resolutions of the Assembly,

Urging all concerned to implement strictly Security Council resolution 598(1987) of 20 July 1987 in all its parts,

1. *Decides* to appropriate an amount of $35.7 million, inclusive of the amount of $3.7 million authorized with the concurrence of the Advisory Committee on Administrative and Budgetary Questions, under the terms of General Assembly resolution 42/227 of 21 December 1987, for the operation of the United Nations Iran-Iraq Military Observer Group for an initial period of approximately three months of the six-month period authorized by the Security Council beginning 9 August 1988 and requests the Secretary-General to establish a special account for the Group;

2. *Decides,* as an *ad hoc* arrangement, to apportion:

(a) An amount of $20,664,945 for the above-mentioned initial period among the States permanent members of the Security Council in the proportions determined by the scale of assessments for the years 1986, 1987 and 1988;

(b) An amount of $14,105,070 for the above-mentioned initial period among the economically de-

veloped Member States which are not permanent members of the Security Council in the proportions determined by the scale of assessments for the years 1986, 1987 and 1988;

(c) An amount of $912,492 for the above-mentioned initial period among the economically less developed Member States in the proportions determined by the scale of assessments for the years 1986, 1987 and 1988;

(d) An amount of $17,493 for the above-mentioned initial period to the following of the economically less developed Member States in the proportions determined by the scale of assessments for the years 1986, 1987 and 1988: Afghanistan, Angola, Antigua and Barbuda, Bangladesh, Belize, Benin, Bhutan, Botswana, Burkina Faso, Burundi, Cape Verde, Chad, Comoros, Democratic Yemen, Djibouti, Dominica, Ethiopia, Grenada, Guinea, Guinea-Bissau, Haiti, Lao People's Democratic Republic, Lesotho, Malawi, Maldives, Mali, Mozambique, Nepal, Niger, Papua New Guinea, Rwanda, Saint Kitts and Nevis, Saint Lucia, Saint Vincent and the Grenadines, Samoa, Sao Tome and Principe, Senegal, Seychelles, Solomon Islands, Somalia, Sudan, Suriname, Uganda, United Republic of Tanzania, Vanuatu, Yemen and Zimbabwe;

3. *Decides* that, for the purpose of the present resolution, the term "economically less developed Member States" in paragraph 2 (c) above shall mean all Member States except Australia, Austria, Belgium, the Byelorussian Soviet Socialist Republic, Canada, Czechoslovakia, Denmark, Finland, the German Democratic Republic, Germany, Federal Republic of, Iceland, Ireland, Italy, Japan, Luxembourg, the Netherlands, New Zealand, Norway, Poland, South Africa, Sweden, the Ukrainian Soviet Socialist Republic and the Member States referred to in paragraphs 2 (a) and (d) above;

4. *Decides* that, in accordance with the provisions of its resolution 973(X) of 15 December 1955, there shall be set off against the apportionment among Member States, as provided for in paragraph 2 above, their respective share in the Tax Equalization Fund of the estimated staff assessment income of $700,000 approved for the above-mentioned initial period;

5. *Invites* voluntary contributions to the United Nations Iran-Iraq Military Observer Group both in cash and in the form of services and supplies acceptable to the Secretary-General, to be administered in accordance with the procedure established under the terms of paragraph 2 of General Assembly resolution 34/9 D of 17 December 1979;

6. *Decides* to include in the draft agenda of its forty-third session the item entitled "Financing of the United Nations Iran-Iraq Military Observer Group";

7. *Requests* the Secretary-General to submit to the General Assembly by 1 October 1988, through the Advisory Committee on Administrative and Budgetary Questions, an updated report on the financing of the United Nations Iran-Iraq Military Observer Group, including the status of voluntary contributions;

8. *Also requests* the Secretary-General to take all necessary action to ensure that the United Nations Iran-Iraq Military Observer Group is administered with a maximum of efficiency and economy.

General Assembly resolution 42/233
17 August 1988   Meeting 115   Adopted without vote

Approved by Fifth Committee (A/42/963) without vote, 16 August (meeting 71); draft by Chairman (A/C.5/42/L.26), orally revised, and orally amended by Canada and by Japan; agenda item 145.
Meeting numbers. GA 42nd session: 5th Committee 70, 71; plenary 114, 115.

Report of the Secretary-General (October). In an October report,[87] the Secretary-General submitted revised cost estimates for UNIIMOG financing. Based on experience gained since UNIIMOG's commencement, he estimated the cost for establishing the mission and for maintaining it from 9 August 1988 to 8 February 1989 at some $58.7 million gross ($58.1 million net). There were other possible costs of about $20 million relating to the military signals unit assigned to UNIIMOG during its initial phase, for which no agreement had been reached with the Member States concerned.

For the 12 months beyond 8 February 1989, the Secretary-General submitted an estimate of $99.7 million gross ($98.4 million net), on the basis of which the Assembly might authorize him to enter into commitments for UNIIMOG.

The Secretary-General also reported that, in response to the Assembly's invitation, voluntary contributions to UNIIMOG in cash and kind had been received from Iran, Iraq, Italy, Japan, Morocco, New Zealand, Switzerland and the USSR.

ACABQ, in November 1988,[88] recommended that the Secretary-General be authorized to enter into commitments for the 12-month period beginning 8 February 1989 at a monthly rate not to exceed $7,986,000 ($7,889,000 net). His authority would be subject to obtaining ACABQ's prior concurrence for the actual level of commitments to be entered into for each mandate period that might be approved subsequent to 8 February.

GENERAL ASSEMBLY ACTION

On 21 December, on the recommendation of the Fifth Committee, the General Assembly adopted without vote **resolution 43/230**.

Financing of the United Nations Iran-Iraq Military Observer Group

The General Assembly,

Having considered with appreciation the report of the Secretary-General on the financing of the United Nations Iran-Iraq Military Observer Group, the related report of the Advisory Committee on Administrative and Budgetary Questions and the statements of the representative of the Secretary-General and the Chairman of the Advisory Committee thereon,

Bearing in mind Security Council resolution 619(1988) of 9 August 1988, by which the Council established the United Nations Iran-Iraq Military Observer Group,

Recalling its resolution 42/233 of 17 August 1988 on the financing of the United Nations Iran-Iraq Military Observer Group,

Recognizing that the costs of the United Nations Iran-Iraq Military Observer Group are expenses of the Or-

ganization to be borne by Member States in accordance with Article 17, paragraph 2, of the Charter of the United Nations,

Mindful of the fact that it is essential to provide the United Nations Iran-Iraq Military Observer Group with the necessary financial resources to enable it to fulfil its responsibilities under the relevant resolutions of the Security Council,

Urging all Member States to make every possible effort to ensure payment of their assessed contributions to the United Nations Iran-Iraq Military Observer Group in full and on time,

Reaffirming its previous decisions regarding the fact that, in order to meet the expenditures caused by such operations, a different procedure is required from the one applied to meet expenditures of the regular budget of the United Nations,

Taking into account the fact that the economically more developed countries are in a position to make relatively larger contributions and that the economically less developed countries have a relatively limited capacity to contribute towards peace-keeping operations involving heavy expenditures,

Bearing in mind the special responsibilities of the States permanent members of the Security Council in the financing of such operations, as indicated in General Assembly resolution 1874(S-IV) of 27 June 1963 and other resolutions of the Assembly,

Noting with appreciation that voluntary contributions in cash and in kind have been made to the United Nations Iran-Iraq Military Observer Group by certain Governments,

I

1. *Decides* to appropriate to the Special Account referred to in paragraph 1 of General Assembly resolution 42/233 an amount of 18.3 million United States dollars gross, in addition to the 35.7 million dollars gross previously appropriated, for the operation of the United Nations Iran-Iraq Military Observer Group for the six-month period as authorized by the Security Council, from 9 August 1988 to 8 February 1989, inclusive;

2. *Decides also,* as an *ad hoc* arrangement, and without prejudice to the positions of principle that may be taken by Member States in any consideration by the General Assembly of arrangements for the financing of peace-keeping operations, to apportion the amount of 18.3 million dollars among Member States in accordance with the scheme set out in Assembly resolution 42/233; the scale of assessments for the year 1988 shall be applied against a portion thereof, that is 6,854,300 dollars being the amount pertaining on a *pro rata* basis to the period ending 31 December 1988, and the scale of assessments for the year 1989 shall be applied against the balance, that is 11,445,700 dollars, for the period thereafter;

3. *Decides further* that, in accordance with the provisions of its resolution 973(X) of 15 December 1955, the apportionment among Member States, as provided for in paragraph 2 above, shall take into consideration the decrease in their respective share in the Tax Equalization Fund of the estimated staff assessment income of 200,000 dollars of the amount approved for the period from 9 August 1988 to 8 February 1989, inclusive;

4. *Authorizes* the Secretary-General to enter into commitments for the United Nations Iran-Iraq Military Ob-

server Group at a rate not to exceed 7,986,000 dollars gross (7,889,000 dollars net) per month, with prior concurrence of the Advisory Committee on Administrative and Budgetary Questions, for the twelve-month period from 9 February 1989, should the Security Council decide to continue the Military Observer Group beyond the period of six months authorized under its resolution 619(1988), the said amount to be apportioned among Member States in accordance with the scheme set out in the present resolution and the action to be taken in accordance with paragraph 5 below;

5. *Decides* that the voluntary contributions received in cash in the amount of 11 million dollars shall be credited as income to the Special Account for the United Nations Iran-Iraq Military Observer Group and that this amount shall be taken into account in calculating the total amount to be assessed on Member States for future mandate periods, including the next mandate period, on the basis of proposals by the Secretary-General and the related recommendations of the Advisory Committee on Administrative and Budgetary Questions consistent with the status of collection of assessed contributions and legal obligations of the Military Observer Group, and requests that a report thereon be submitted to the General Assembly at its forty-fourth session;

6. *Requests* the Secretary-General to take all necessary measures to ensure that the United Nations Iran-Iraq Military Observer Group shall be administered with a maximum of efficiency and economy, bearing in mind the flexibility suggested in paragraph 24 of the report of the Advisory Committee on Administrative and Budgetary Questions;

7. *Emphasizes*, in this regard, the important role the Advisory Committee on Administrative and Budgetary Questions has to play within its terms of reference;

II

1. *Invites* voluntary contributions to the United Nations Iran-Iraq Military Observer Group, acceptable to the Secretary-General, in cash, in convertible or readily usable currencies, and in the form of supplies and services;

2. *Decides* that voluntary contributions in cash made as outright grants shall be considered income to be credited to the Special Account for the United Nations Iran-Iraq Military Observer Group and shall be taken into account in calculating the total amount to be assessed on Member States; to this end, the Secretary-General shall inform the General Assembly in each of his reports on the Military Observer Group of the amount of assessed contributions collected and of such voluntary contributions received; and the Secretary-General shall propose to the Assembly, through the Advisory Committee on Administrative and Budgetary Questions, when and to what extent the voluntary contributions in cash as outright grants can be deducted from the total amount to be assessed on Member States, taking into consideration the status of collection of assessed contributions and the legal obligations of the Military Observer Group, including reimbursement to troop contributors;

3. *Decides also* that contributions in cash made available to the Secretary-General on a voluntary basis as advances shall not be considered as income in determining the total amount to be assessed on Member States;

unless otherwise specified by the donor, such contributions shall be deposited in the Suspense Account for the United Nations Iran-Iraq Military Observer Group established under resolution 42/233;

4. *Requests* the Secretary-General to submit to the General Assembly, through the Advisory Committee on Administrative and Budgetary Questions, at the earliest possible stage a report containing technical guidelines relating to the treatment and valuation of voluntary contributions in the form of supplies and services to the United Nations Iran-Iraq Military Observer Group;

5. *Agrees*, pending the submission of the report called for in paragraph 4 above, that voluntary contributions in the form of supplies and services to the United Nations Iran-Iraq Military Observer Group may be accepted as outright grants; the cash value of such contributions in respect of budgeted requirements may eventually reduce the total amount to be assessed on Member States; in this regard, the Secretary-General should make adequate and timely information available as to what supplies and services will be required in order to facilitate offers of such contributions;

6. *Decides* that, on receipt of the report requested in paragraph 4 above, the General Assembly will consider appropriate procedures and guidelines for the treatment of voluntary contributions in the form of supplies and services other than as outright grants;

III

1. *Requests* the Secretary-General to undertake and submit to the General Assembly at its forty-fourth session, through the Advisory Committee on Administrative and Budgetary Questions, the following studies, taking into account the related proposals of the Advisory Committee, as well as the views expressed by Member States at the forty-third session of the Assembly:

(a) A comprehensive study on how economies of scale could be achieved through administrative co-ordination of the various United Nations peace-keeping operations;

(b) A study proposing procedures and criteria by which Governments may offer the services of civilian personnel for peace-keeping operations, corresponding to those by which military personnel are made available;

(c) An analysis of the problems involved in starting up peace-keeping and related operations and of possible solutions, including the establishment of a fund and the use of the existing Working Capital Fund;

(d) A study on the feasibility and cost-effectiveness of creating a reserve stock of communications and other equipment;

(e) A review, in the context of the report on standard rates of reimbursement, of the background and development of reimbursement to Member States contributing troops to peace-keeping operations;

2. *Also requests* the Secretary-General to make the studies called for in paragraph 1 above available to the Special Committee on Peace-keeping Operations for its information and use;

3. *Welcomes* the assurances offered, on behalf of the Secretary-General, that careful consideration will be given to the present format and to the amount of information that should be included in future reports of the Secretary-General on the financing of the United Na-

tions Iran-Iraq Military Observer Group and other peace-keeping operations;

4. *Requests* the Secretary-General to provide the General Assembly at its forty-fourth session with relevant information in order to enable it to identify any possible anomalies in the composition of the existing groups of Member States on the basis of the criteria set out in Assembly resolution 3101(XXVIII) of 11 December 1973 and taking into account the views expressed at its forty-second and forty-third sessions.

General Assembly resolution 43/230

21 December 1988   Meeting 84   Adopted without vote

Approved by Fifth Committee (A/43/978) without vote, 18 December (meeting 50); draft by Finland (A/C.5/43/L.16); agenda item 147.
Meeting numbers. GA 43rd session: 5th Committee 25, 29, 33, 35-37, 50; plenary 84.

Shooting down of Iran Air flight 655

In July 1988, after an Iranian civil airliner was shot down by the United States navy in the Persian Gulf, the Security Council expressed deep distress over the tragic loss of life and stressed the need for full implementation of its resolution 598(1987)[28] as the only basis for a settlement of the conflict between Iran and Iraq.

On 3 July,[89] Iran stated that, earlier that day, United States naval forces in the Persian Gulf had shot down an Iranian passenger airliner on a scheduled flight from Bandar-e Abbas, Iran, to Dubai, United Arab Emirates, killing all 290 passengers on board, including 66 children and the crew. Calling the attack an act of aggression and a violation of international law, which threatened civil aviation in the region, Iran expected the United Nations to condemn what it called a massacre of innocent passengers and to prevent future such occurrences.

By a letter of 6 July,[90] the United States replied that its forces, which had operated in international waters of the Persian Gulf, had exercised their inherent right to self-defence under international law by responding to an attack by Iran. According to its version of the incident, the *USS Vincennes*, operating on 3 July in international waters, sent a helicopter on a patrol following indications that some dozen Iranian small boats were congregating to attack neutral merchant shipping. A group of Iranian patrol aircraft fired at the helicopter, which turned back to the ship without returning fire. Shortly afterwards, when the *USS Vincennes* and another United States vessel were approaching the Iranian boats, at least four of them turned towards them and began closing in on them. Both warships then opened fire on the boats, sinking two and damaging a third. In the course of exercising its right to self-defence, the *USS Vincennes* fired at what it believed to be hostile Iranian military aircraft, after sending repeated warnings to which the aircraft did not respond.

The United States said it regretted the loss of life and was conducting a full investigation. It would also co-operate with any International Civil Aviation Organization (ICAO) investigation into the incident. On 11 July,[91] the United States announced that its President had decided to offer compensation, on an *ex gratia* basis, to the families of the victims of the airline incident. The offer, a humanitarian effort consistent with international practice, was made on a voluntary basis and not as a legal liability or obligation. The United States, however, held Iran responsible for the incident, as it had refused for almost a year to accept and implement Security Council resolution 598(1987) while it continued attacks on neutral shipping in the international waters of the Persian Gulf.

The USSR, on 5 July,[92] transmitted a statement from the TASS news agency holding the United States command responsible for the airline tragedy, which, it said, demonstrated that it was necessary for the United States naval fleet to leave the Persian Gulf, where peace and security could be ensured by a United Nations naval force. The incident was also deplored in communications from several other countries.

SECURITY COUNCIL ACTION

Responding to a 5 July request from Iran,[93] the Security Council held four meetings between 14 and 20 July to consider the shooting down of the Iranian airliner. The Council invited the following, at their request, to participate in the discussion without the right to vote: Cuba, Gabon, India, Iran, Libyan Arab Jamahiriya, Nicaragua, Pakistan, Romania, Syrian Arab Republic, United Arab Emirates.

At its meeting on 20 July, the Council unanimously adopted **resolution 616(1988)**.

The Security Council,

Having considered the letter dated 5 July 1988 from the Acting Permanent Representative of the Islamic Republic of Iran addressed to the President of the Security Council,

Having heard the statement of the representative of the Islamic Republic of Iran, Minister for Foreign Affairs, Ali Akbar Velayati and the statement of the representative of the United States of America, Vice-President George Bush,

Deeply distressed that a civil aircraft of Iran Air—scheduled international flight 655—was destroyed in flight over the Strait of Hormuz by a missile fired from the United States warship *USS Vincennes*,

Stressing the need for a full explanation of the facts of the incident based upon impartial investigation,

Gravely disturbed at the increasing exacerbation of tension in the Gulf region,

1. *Expresses its deep distress* at the downing of an Iranian civil aircraft by a missile fired from a United States warship and profound regret over the tragic loss of innocent lives;

2. *Expresses its sincere condolences* to the families of the victims of the tragic incident and to the peoples and Governments of their countries of origin;

3. *Welcomes* the decision of the International Civil Aviation Organization, in response to the request of the Islamic Republic of Iran, ''to institute an immediate fact-finding investigation to determine all relevant facts and technical aspects of the chain of events relating to the flight and destruction of the aircraft'' and welcomes the announcements by the United States of America and by the Islamic Republic of Iran of their decisions to co-operate with the International Civil Aviation Organization investigation;

4. *Urges* all parties to the Convention on International Civial Aviation, signed at Chicago in 1944, to observe to the fullest extent, in all circumstances, the international rules and practices concerning the safety of civil aviation, in particular those of the annexes to that Convention, in order to prevent the recurrence of incidents of the same nature;

5. *Stresses* the need for a full and rapid implementation of its resolution 598(1987) of 20 July 1987, as the only basis for a comprehensive, just, honourable and durable settlement of the conflict between the Islamic Republic of Iran and Iraq, and reaffirms its support to the efforts of the Secretary-General to implement that resolution, committing itself to work with him in the development of his implementation plan.

Security Council resolution 616(1988)

20 July 1988   Meeting 2821   Adopted unanimously

Draft prepared in consultations among Council members (S/20038).
Meeting numbers. SC 2818-2821.

In a statement after the vote, the United States called the shooting down of the airliner a tragic accident. Having initiated its own investigation, the United States endorsed the actions by the ICAO Council to commence its own investigation and looked forward to co-operating with ICAO in that regard and in its efforts to improve civil avia-

tion safety in the Persian Gulf in order to prevent a recurrence of similar incidents.

REFERENCES
[1]S/19835. [2]A/43/81-S/19411, A/43/82-S/19412, A/43/84-S/19422, A/43/136-S/19497, A/43/156-S/19517, A/43/204-S/19582, A/43/211-S/19606, A/43/212-S/19607, A/43/269-S/19716, A/43/299-S/19766, A/43/300-S/19767, A/43/301-S/19768, A/43/335-S/19843, A/43/342-S/19850, A/43/349-S/19859, A/43/359-S/19879, A/43/364-S/19890, A/43/378-S/19905, A/43/391-S/19925, A/43/400-S/19932, A/43/409-S/19941 & Corr.1, A/43/412-S/19945, A/43/428-S/19964, A/43/440-S/19984, A/43/503-S/20087, A/43/515-S/20101, A/43/577-S/20160, A/43/585-S/20167, A/43/598-S/20180 & Corr.1, A/43/641-S/20201, A/43/649-S/20204, A/43/783-S/20260, A/43/848-S/20282, A/43/849-20283, A/43/908-S/20309. [3]YUN 1987, p. 215, GA res. 42/15, 10 Nov. 1987. [4]A/43/720-S/20230. [5]S/19834. [6]S/19836. [7]S/19763. [8]A/43/344. [9]A/43/374. [10]A/43/406. [11]A/43/424. [12]A/43/439-S/19978. [13]A/43/431-S/19969. [14]A/43/447-S/19990. [15]A/43/451-S/19996. [16]A/43/465-S/20019. [17]A/43/511-S/20098. [18]A/43/474-S/20044. [19]S/20269. [20]A/43/906-S/20305. [21]A/43/804-S/20270. [22]S/20277. [23]A/43/983. [24]A/43/934. [25]E/1988/66. [26]E/1988/84. [27]E/1988/86. [28]YUN 1987, p. 223, SC res. 598(1987), 20 July 1987. [29]S/19626. [30]S/19650, S/19665, S/19730, S/19822. [31]S/19823 & Corr.1. [32]YUN 1984, p. 232. [33]YUN 1985, p. 247. [34]YUN 1986, p. 233. [35]YUN 1987, p. 232. [36]S/19823/Add.1. [37]A/43/338-S/19844. [38]S/19886. [39]S/19892. [40]S/19902. [41]S/19967. [42]S/19982. [43]S/20060 & Add.1. [44]S/20063/Add.1. [45]S/20084. [46]S/20134. [47]S/19609. [48]S/19695. [49]S/19980 & Corr.1. [50]S/19993. [51]S/20012. [52]S/20232. [53]S/20237. [54]S/20267. [55]S/20296. [56]S/20304. [57]S/20298. [58]S/20313. [59]S/20335. [60]S/20147. [61]S/20020. [62]S/20027. [63]S/20035. [64]S/20041. [65]S/20048. [66]S/20059. [67]S/20064. [68]S/20065. [69]S/20022. [70]S/20031. [71]S/20039. [72]S/20092. [73]S/20094. [74]S/20095. [75]S/20096. [76]S/20099. [77]S/20097. [78]S/20242. [79]S/20104. [80]S/20105. [81]S/20111. [82]S/20112. [83]S/20154. [84]S/20155. [85]A/42/244. [86]A/42/244/Add.1 & Corr.1. [87]A/43/696. [88]A/43/768. [89]S/19979. [90]S/19989. [91]S/20005. [92]S/19987. [93]S/19981.

Chapter IV

Middle East

Throughout 1988, the United Nations continued its efforts for a peaceful settlement of the Middle East situation. The year was a decisive one for the Palestinian freedom struggle, as the popular uprising by Palestinians in the West Bank and Gaza Strip—known as *intifadah*—which began in December 1987 against Israeli occupation, gathered momentum.

The United Nations Special Committee to Investigate Israeli Practices Affecting the Human Rights of the Population of the Occupied Territories (Committee on Israeli practices) and the Committee on the Exercise of the Inalienable Rights of the Palestinian People (Committee on Palestinian rights) reported on the deteriorating conditions in the territories. The latter Committee continued to press for the implementation of its original (1976) recommendations—on the rights of the Palestinians to return to their homes and property and to achieve self-determination, national independence and sovereignty in Palestine—and for the convening of an international peace conference on the Middle East under United Nations auspices. Although by the end of the year sufficient agreement on the terms for a conference did not exist, there was growing international recognition that such a step was essential for a political solution of the Arab-Israeli conflict. Accordingly, the General Assembly called again for the convening of such a conference and the participation of all parties to the conflict on an equal footing, including the Palestine Liberation Organization (PLO) (resolution 43/176). Meanwhile, the Palestine National Council declared a State of Palestine, a move which the General Assembly acknowledged in December (43/177).

The epicentre of the Middle East crisis, the question of Palestine, continued to depend on solving such complex questions as the status of Jerusalem, the applicability of the 1949 Geneva Conventions to the territories occupied by Israel since 1967, and the relationship between Israel and its Arab neighbours. The Assembly reaffirmed that the question of Palestine was the core of the Middle East conflict and that no comprehensive, just and lasting peace would be achieved without the full exercise by the Palestinian people of their inalienable national rights— including the right to return to their homes and property and to achieve self-determination, national independence and sovereignty.

By two January resolutions, the Security Council demanded that Israel desist from deporting Palestinians from the occupied territories (resolutions 607(1988) and 608(1988)). Human rights conditions in the territories were addressed by the Commission on Human Rights.

The cycle of violence in Lebanon continued, with that country repeatedly requesting the convening of the Security Council in response to armed Israeli incursions into its territory. The Council was, however, unable to take effective action due to the repeated negative vote of a permanent member. The Council twice extended the mandate of the United Nations Interim Force in Lebanon, as well as the mandate of the United Nations Disengagement Observer Force, deployed since 1974 to secure the Israeli-Syrian border. In July, the Council condemned the abduction on 17 February in southern Lebanon of Lieutenant-Colonel William Higgins, a military observer of the United Nations Truce Supervision Organization, and demanded his immediate release (618(1988)).

The Council also convened in April after the assassination in Tunis of Khalil al-Wazir, a member of the PLO Executive Committee, and condemned the aggression against the sovereignty of Tunisia, urging Member States to prevent such acts (611(1988)).

In response to the emergency situation in the West Bank and Gaza, the United Nations increased its assistance to the Palestinians. The United Nations Development Programme earmarked an additional $4 million from its Special Programme Resources, and appeals for funds from the international donor community received substantial response. In consultation with PLO, the Commissioner-General of the United Nations Relief and Works Agency for Palestine Refugees in the Near East (UNRWA) prepared urgent proposals for improving the infrastructure of the refugee camps and for seeking funds of approximately $65 million. UNRWA maintained its assistance to over 2.2 million refugees in Jordan, Lebanon, the Syrian Arab Republic, the West Bank and the Gaza Strip.

In February and March 1988, the Assembly considered a move by the United States to close the PLO Observer Mission to the United Nations in New York and urged it to desist from taking action inconsistent with its international legal obligations. In May, the Assembly called on the United States to submit the dispute to arbitration, thereby endorsing an advisory opinion of the International Court of Justice.

Middle East situation

The Palestinian uprising, or *intifadah*, against Israel's occupation of the West Bank, Gaza and East Jerusalem overshadowed the situation in the Middle East and underlined the urgency to find an effective negotiating process towards a solution. However, negotiations remained at a standstill and no consensus was found on the modalities of setting in motion an international peace conference under United Nations auspices.

In December, the General Assembly adopted two resolutions dealing with the situation, again declaring that peace in the region must be based on a comprehensive, just and lasting solution negotiated under United Nations auspices, and reaffirming its call for the convening of an international conference (resolution 43/54 A). It requested the Security Council to consider measures needed to convene a conference, including establishment of a preparatory committee, and asked the Secretary-General to continue his efforts with the parties concerned to facilitate its convening (43/176).

Reports of the Secretary-General. Pursuant to a 1987 request by the General Assembly,[1] the Secretary-General submitted in November 1988 a report[2] on developments in the Middle East situation, stating that the *intifadah* had been a dominating political factor in the region. It was the focus of the Arab Summit Conference at Algiers, Algeria, in June 1988[3] and the inspiration behind the November session of the Palestine National Council (PNC) at Algiers.[4] Born of the frustration and despair of a population that had lived under occupation for more than 20 years, the *intifadah* was a direct result of the stalemate in the search for a peaceful settlement of the Arab-Israeli conflict, and was evidence of the Palestinian people's commitment to exercise their legitimate rights, including self-determination.

The *intifadah* had also generated an intense debate in Israel about the peace process and Israel's role in the occupied territories. Although sufficient agreement did not exist to convene an international peace conference (see below), the Secretary-General said he was encouraged that all members of the Security Council believed that it was desirable to convene such a conference. However, the loss of life and injuries on both sides during the *intifadah* compelled consideration of fundamental questions beyond procedural matters.

The time was right for the Council to commit itself to a thorough review of the situation in order to adopt a pragmatic approach, taking into account the concerns and security interests of all parties. The Secretary-General stressed that, with the full support of the Council and the co-operation of the major Powers, progress could be made towards a just and lasting peace. The protracted and explosive nature of the Arab-Israeli conflict made urgent concentrated efforts necessary. The growth of extremism and the alarming proliferation of weapons in the area constituted trends that had to be reversed if disaster was to be averted.

The Secretary-General believed that the recent session of PNC had generated a new momentum in the diplomatic process and offered fresh opportunities for progress. Every gesture towards peace should be nurtured to overcome the deep mistrust felt on all sides. Concluding, he reiterated the fundamental importance of devising a negotiating process that could secure the interests of both Israelis and Arabs and enable them to live in peace with each other.

In an October 1988 report with a later addendum,[5] the Secretary-General submitted replies from nine Member States to his request for information on steps taken to implement three 1987 Assembly resolutions on the Middle East situation. By two of those resolutions,[6] the Assembly had called on States to adopt a number of measures concerning relations with Israel and had called on States concerned to abide by the relevant Assembly resolutions. By the third,[7] it had requested the Secretary-General to continue his efforts for the convening of a peace conference and to apprise the Assembly of his consultations (see below).

GENERAL ASSEMBLY ACTION

On 6 December 1988, the General Assembly adopted **resolution 43/54 A** by recorded vote.

The General Assembly,

Having discussed the item entitled "The situation in the Middle East",

Reaffirming its resolutions 36/226 A and B of 17 December 1981, ES-9/1 of 5 February 1982, 37/123 F of 20 December 1982, 38/58 A to E of 13 December 1983, 38/180 A to D of 19 December 1983, 39/146 A to C of 14 December 1984, 40/168 A to C of 16 December 1985, 41/162 A to C of 4 December 1986 and 42/209 A to D of 11 December 1987,

Recalling Security Council resolutions 425(1978) of 19 March 1978, 497(1981) of 17 December 1981, 508(1982) of 5 June 1982, 509(1982) of 6 June 1982, 511(1982) of 18 June 1982, 512(1982) of 19 June 1982, 513(1982) of 4 July 1982, 515(1982) of 29 July 1982, 516(1982) of 1 August 1982, 517(1982) of 4 August 1982, 518(1982) of 12 August 1982, 519(1982) of 17 August 1982, 520(1982) of 17 September 1982, 521(1982) of 19 September 1982 and 555(1984) of 12 October 1984 and other relevant resolutions,

Taking note of the reports of the Secretary-General of 31 March 1988, 30 September 1988, 11 October 1988, and 28 November 1988,

Reaffirming the need for continued collective support for the decisions adopted by the Twelfth Arab Summit Conference, held at Fez, Morocco, on 25 November 1981 and from 6 to 9 September 1982, which were confirmed by subsequent Arab summit conferences, including the Arab Summit Conference held at Algiers from 7 to 9 June 1988, reiterating its previous resolutions on the question of Palestine and its support for the Palestine Liberation Organization as the sole legitimate representative of the Palestinian people, and considering that the convening of the International Peace Conference on the Middle East, under the auspices of the United Nations, in accordance with General Assembly resolution 38/58 C and other relevant resolutions related to the question of Palestine, would contribute to the promotion of peace in the region,

Welcoming all efforts contributing towards the realization of the inalienable rights of the Palestinian people through the achievement of a comprehensive, just and lasting peace in the Middle East, in accordance with the United Nations resolutions relating to the question of Palestine and to the situation in the Middle East,

Welcoming the world-wide support extended to the just cause of the Palestinian people and the other Arab countries in their struggle against Israeli aggression and occupation in order to achieve a comprehensive, just and lasting peace in the Middle East and the full exercise by the Palestinian people of its inalienable national rights, as affirmed by previous resolutions of the General Assembly on the question of Palestine and on the situation in the Middle East,

Gravely concerned that the Palestinian territory occupied since 1967, including Jerusalem, and the other occupied Arab territories still remain under Israeli occupation, that the relevant resolutions of the United Nations have not been implemented and that the Palestinian people is still denied the restoration of its land and the exercise of its inalienable national rights in conformity with international law, as reaffirmed by resolutions of the United Nations,

Reaffirming the applicability of the Geneva Convention relative to the Protection of Civilian Persons in Time of War, of 12 August 1949, to the Palestinian territory occupied since 1967, including Jerusalem, and the other occupied Arab territories,

Reaffirming also all relevant United Nations resolutions which stipulate that the acquisition of territory by force is inadmissible under the Charter of the United Nations and the principles of international law and that Israel must withdraw unconditionally from the Palestinian territory occupied since 1967, including Jerusalem, and the other occupied Arab territories,

Reaffirming further the imperative necessity of establishing a comprehensive, just and lasting peace in the region, based on full respect for the Charter and the principles of international law,

Gravely concerned also at the continuing Israeli policies involving the escalation and expansion of the conflict in the region, which further violate the principles of international law and endanger international peace and security,

Stressing once again the great importance of the time factor in the endeavours to achieve an early comprehensive, just and lasting peace in the Middle East,

1. *Reaffirms its conviction* that the question of Palestine is the core of the conflict in the Middle East and that no comprehensive, just and lasting peace in the region will be achieved without the full exercise by the Palestinian people of its inalienable national rights and the immediate, unconditional and total withdrawal of Israel from the Palestinian territory occupied since 1967, including Jerusalem, and the other occupied Arab territories;

2. *Reaffirms further* that a just and comprehensive settlement of the situation in the Middle East cannot be achieved without the participation on an equal footing of all the parties to the conflict, including the Palestine Liberation Organization, the representative of the Palestinian people;

3. *Declares once more* that peace in the Middle East is indivisible and must be based on a comprehensive, just and lasting solution of the Middle East problem, under the auspices of the United Nations and on the basis of its relevant resolutions, which ensures the complete and unconditional withdrawal of Israel from the Palestinian territory occupied since 1967, including Jerusalem, and the other occupied Arab territories, and which enables the Palestinian people, under the leadership of the Palestine Liberation Organization, to exercise its inalienable rights, including the right to return and the right to self-determination, national independence and the establishment of its independent sovereign State in Palestine, in accordance with the resolutions of the United Nations relating to the question of Palestine, in particular General Assembly resolutions ES-7/2 of 29 July 1980, 36/120 A to F of 10 December 1981, 37/86 A to D of 10 December 1982, 37/86 E of 20 December 1982, 38/58 A to E of 13 December 1983, 39/49 A to D of 11 December 1984, 40/96 A to D of 12 December 1985, 41/43 A to D of 2 December 1986 and 42/66 A to D of 2 December 1987;

4. *Considers* the Arab Peace Plan adopted unanimously at the Twelfth Arab Summit Conference, held at Fez, Morocco, on 25 November 1981 and from 6 to 9 September 1982, and reiterated by the Extraordinary Summit Conference of the Arab States, held at Casablanca, Morocco, from 7 to 9 August 1985, as well as relevant efforts and action to implement the Fez plan, as an important contribution towards the realization of the inalienable rights of the Palestinian people through the achievement of a comprehensive, just and lasting peace in the Middle East;

5. *Condemns* Israel's continued occupation of the Palestinian territory occupied since 1967, including Jerusalem, and the other occupied Arab territories, in violation of the Charter of the United Nations, the principles of international law and the relevant resolutions of the United Nations, and demands the immediate, unconditional and total withdrawal of Israel from all the territories occupied since 1967;

6. *Rejects* all agreements and arrangements which violate the inalienable rights of the Palestinian people and contradict the principles of a just and comprehensive solution to the Middle East problem to ensure the establishment of a just peace in the area;

7. *Deplores* Israel's failure to comply with Security Council resolutions 476(1980) of 30 June 1980 and 478(1980) of 20 August 1980 and General Assembly resolutions 35/207 of 16 December 1980 and 36/226 A and B of 17 December 1981; determines that Israel's decision to annex Jerusalem and to declare it as its "capital" as well as the measures to alter its physical character,

demographic composition, institutional structure and status are null and void and demands that they be rescinded immediately; and calls upon all Member States, the specialized agencies and all other international organizations to abide by the present resolution and all other relevant resolutions and decisions;

8. *Condemns* Israel's aggression, policies and practices against the Palestinian people in the occupied Palestinian territory and outside this territory including expropriation, establishment of settlements, annexation and other terrorist, aggressive and repressive measures, which are in violation of the Charter and the principles of international law and the relevant international conventions;

9. *Strongly condemns* the imposition by Israel of its laws, jurisdiction and administration on the occupied Syrian Arab Golan, its annexationist policies and practices, the establishment of settlements, the confiscation of lands, the diversion of water resources and the imposition of Israeli citizenship on Syrian nationals, and declares that all these measures are null and void and constitute a violation of the rules and principles of international law relative to belligerent occupation, in particular the Geneva Convention relative to the Protection of Civilian Persons in Time of War, of 12 August 1949;

10. *Considers* that the agreements on strategic co-operation between the United States of America and Israel, signed on 30 November 1981, and the continued supply of modern arms and *matériel* to Israel, augmented by substantial economic aid, including the Agreement on the Establishment of a Free Trade Area between the two Governments, have encouraged Israel to pursue its aggressive and expansionist policies and practices in the Palestinian territory occupied since 1967, including Jerusalem, and the other occupied Arab territories, and have had adverse effects on efforts for the establishment of a comprehensive, just and lasting peace in the Middle East and pose a threat to the security of the region;

11. *Calls once more upon* all States to put an end to the flow to Israel of any military, economic, financial and technological aid, as well as of human resources, aimed at encouraging it to pursue its aggressive policies against the Arab countries and the Palestinian people;

12. *Strongly condemns* the continuing and increasing collaboration between Israel and the racist régime of South Africa, especially in the economic, military and nuclear fields, which constitutes a hostile act against the African and Arab States and enables Israel to enhance its nuclear capabilities, thus subjecting the States of the region to nuclear blackmail;

13. *Reaffirms its call* for convening the International Peace Conference on the Middle East, under the auspices of the United Nations, with the participation of the five permanent members of the Security Council and all parties to the conflict, including the Palestine Liberation Organization, the sole legitimate representative of the Palestinian people, on an equal footing, and that the Conference should be effective with full authority, in order to achieve a comprehensive and just solution based on the withdrawal of Israel from the occupied Palestinian territory, including Jerusalem, and the other occupied Arab territories, and the attainment of the inalienable rights of the Palestinian people in accordance with United Nations resolutions relevant to the question of Palestine and the situation in the Middle East;

14. *Endorses the call* for setting up a preparatory committee, within the framework of the Security Council, with the participation of the permanent members of the Council, to take the necessary action to convene the Conference;

15. *Requests* the Secretary-General to report to the Security Council periodically on the development of the situation and to submit to the General Assembly at its forty-fourth session a comprehensive report covering the developments in the Middle East in all their aspects.

General Assembly resolution 43/54 A

6 December 1988   Meeting 71   103-18-30 (recorded vote)

20-nation draft (A/43/L.44 & Add.1); agenda item 40.
Sponsors: Bahrain, Bangladesh, Cuba, Djibouti, Indonesia, Iraq, Kuwait, Malaysia, Mauritania, Morocco, Oman, Pakistan, Qatar, Saudi Arabia, Sudan, Tunisia, United Arab Emirates, Yemen, Yugoslavia, Zimbabwe.
Meeting numbers. GA 43rd session: plenary 68-71.

Recorded vote in Assembly as follows:

In favour: Afghanistan, Albania, Algeria, Angola, Argentina, Bahrain, Bangladesh, Benin, Bhutan, Bolivia, Botswana, Brazil, Brunei Darussalam, Bulgaria, Burkina Faso, Burundi, Byelorussian SSR, Cape Verde, Central African Republic, Chad, China, Colombia, Comoros, Cuba, Cyprus, Czechoslovakia, Democratic Kampuchea, Democratic Yemen, Djibouti, Ecuador, Egypt, Ethiopia, Gabon, German Democratic Republic, Ghana, Greece, Guatemala, Guinea, Guinea-Bissau, Guyana, Hungary, India, Indonesia, Iran, Iraq, Jordan, Kenya, Kuwait, Lao People's Democratic Republic, Lebanon, Lesotho, Libyan Arab Jamahiriya, Madagascar, Malaysia, Maldives, Mali, Mauritania, Mauritius, Mexico, Mongolia, Morocco, Mozambique, Nepal, Nicaragua, Niger, Nigeria, Oman, Pakistan, Peru, Philippines, Poland, Qatar, Romania, Rwanda, Saint Lucia, Sao Tome and Principe, Saudi Arabia, Senegal, Seychelles, Sierra Leone, Singapore, Somalia, Sri Lanka, Sudan, Swaziland, Syrian Arab Republic, Thailand, Togo, Trinidad and Tobago, Tunisia, Turkey, Uganda, Ukrainian SSR, USSR, United Arab Emirates, United Republic of Tanzania, Vanuatu, Venezuela, Viet Nam, Yemen, Yugoslavia, Zambia, Zimbabwe.

Against: Australia, Belgium, Canada, Denmark, El Salvador, France, Germany, Federal Republic of, Iceland, Ireland, Israel, Italy, Luxembourg, Netherlands, New Zealand, Norway, Portugal, United Kingdom, United States.

Abstaining: Antigua and Barbuda, Austria, Bahamas, Barbados, Belize, Burma, Cameroon, Chile, Côte d'Ivoire, Fiji, Finland, Grenada, Haiti, Honduras, Jamaica, Japan, Liberia, Malawi, Malta, Panama, Papua New Guinea, Paraguay, Saint Kitts and Nevis, Saint Vincent and the Grenadines, Samoa, Solomon Islands, Spain, Sweden, Uruguay, Zaire.

Proposed peace conference under UN auspices

Throughout 1988, the evolving *intifadah* and its blood toll on both the Arab and the Israeli sides underscored the urgency of resolving the political impasse through the convening of an international peace conference on the Middle East.

Reports of the Secretary-General. Pursuant to a 1987 request by the Security Council,[8] the Secretary-General, in a January 1988 report[9] to the Council on the situation in the occupied territories (see below, under "Territories occupied by Israel"), stated that the underlying problem in the Middle East could be resolved only through a political settlement responsive both to the Palestinian population's refusal to accept a future under Israeli occupation and to Israel's determination to ensure its security and the well-being of its people. Such a settlement should be based on Council resolutions of 1967[10] and 1973[11] and should take fully into account the legitimate rights of the Palestinian people, including self-determination. It should be negotiated by means of an international conference under United Nations auspices, with the participation of all the parties concerned.

Each side must put aside resentment and understand better the legitimate interests of the other. The Secretary-General believed that an urgent effort was required by the international community, led by the Council, to promote an effective negotiating process, as required by the Charter of the United Nations.

In response to its 1987 request,[12] the Secretary-General reported in March 1988[13] to the Assembly on the outcome of his contacts with the Council President regarding the status of consultations on an international peace conference. The President stated that the Council members were deeply concerned at the lack of substantive progress in solving the Middle East crisis, one of the most serious sources of instability in the world. They were convinced that the latest developments, particularly in the occupied territories, called for urgent action, and all members agreed that it was desirable to convene an international conference. Almost all declared support for an early convening of a substantive conference under United Nations auspices, with the participation of all parties concerned and of the five permanent Council members. They expressed readiness to help overcome remaining obstacles, and most members reiterated support for the 1983 Assembly resolution outlining the basis for the conference,[14] stressing that PLO should have the status of a full-fledged participant. One Council member, however, was of the opinion that no progress was possible on the basis of the 1983 resolution. A peace initiative currently under way would involve an international conference convened by the Secretary-General and would include permanent Council members, as well as Israel and interested Arab neighbours. Such a conference should bring about prompt and direct negotiations between those neighbours and Israel and should not have the right to veto the results of direct negotiations or to impose solutions.

In statements of concerned parties, submitted in response to a note verbale of the Secretary-General of 9 March and contained in the report, Egypt and Jordan supported the conference's convening, while Israel continued to object, favouring instead direct negotiations with its neighbours. Lebanon approved in principle but did not consider that the situation of its own case should be linked to the solution of the Middle East question; Israel's occupation should be dealt with from the angle of implementing the will of the international community, including Israel's withdrawal from Lebanese territory. The Syrian Arab Republic supported an international conference provided that Israel withdrew from all occupied Arab territories and that the inalienable rights of the Palestinian people were guaranteed. PLO reaffirmed its support of such a conference with its participation as the sole legitimate representative of the

Palestinian people, and with a view to realizing their national rights.

In accordance with another Assembly request of 1987,[7] the Secretary-General, in September 1988,[15] again reported on his contacts with the Council President regarding the proposed conference. The President indicated that, due to the situation in the occupied territories and a lack of true progress towards a solution, the Council members were more convinced than ever of the need for urgent action with a view to a comprehensive settlement of the Palestinian problem. Again, all members believed it was desirable to hold a conference and invited the Secretary-General to pursue efforts in that regard. Almost all favoured an early convening of a substantive conference under United Nations auspices, and most of them reaffirmed their support for conducting the conference based on the 1983 Assembly resolution,[14] stressing PLO's full-fledged participation. In addition, pending a settlement based on those objectives, some members requested interim measures for the occupied territories, such as establishing a provisional United Nations administration. One member, in contrast, considered the 1983 resolution[14] as one-sided, unbalanced and not conducive to a negotiated settlement.

Updating earlier stated positions of concerned parties, the Secretary-General said Israel continued to advocate direct negotiations with its neighbours rather than an international conference, adding that the parties directly involved in the Arab-Israeli dispute bore primary responsibility for structuring the negotiating forum and for determining its agenda and procedure. PLO maintained that it was incumbent on the United Nations to assume administrative responsibility for the occupied territories concurrently with cessation of Israeli occupation and withdrawal of its troops and, thereafter, for a transitional period pending establishment of a sovereign and independent Palestinian State. Such a step would contribute towards the convening of a conference and the achievement of peace.

In both his March[13] and September[15] reports, the Secretary-General concluded that the necessary agreement did not exist for the convening of an international conference. Though all Security Council members believed it desirable to do so and the replies of States indicated agreement on an international framework for the negotiation of a settlement, deep differences remained about the nature of the framework, its powers, the basis on which it would be convened and about who should participate.

According to the Secretary-General, the violence and suffering in the territories underlined the need for progress on the diplomatic front. The continuing occupation was not acceptable to the inhabitants and would not become so. It was necessary therefore to find a political solution that satisfied both the legitimate political rights of the Palestinian people and the right of Israel to live in peace within secure recognized boundaries. There was urgent need to establish a process acceptable to all for negotiating a just, lasting and comprehensive settlement.

In February 1988, the Secretary-General circulated in the Security Council[16] relevant paragraphs of an Assembly resolution of 2 December 1987[17] and another of 11 December 1987,[1] reaffirming the call for convening the conference and for setting up a preparatory committee, and requesting the Secretary-General to continue his efforts in that regard, in consultation with the Council.

Action by the Committee on Palestinian rights. In its annual report to the General Assembly,[18] the Committee on Palestinian rights stated its decision to exert all efforts to promote the early convening of an international peace conference on the Middle East, while urging understanding and further co-operation of all concerned for the resolution of a problem fundamentally important to international peace and security. Citing the grave situation in the occupied territories, the Committee decided to give priority to ensuring the safety and protection of Palestinians under Israeli occupation, in accordance with the 1949 Geneva Conventions. It was strengthened in its resolve by the overwhelming consensus of the international community in favour of a negotiated settlement through a conference.

The Committee, however, noted with regret the Secretary-General's conclusion that sufficient agreement did not exist to permit convening the conference. It was of the view that the uprising in the occupied territories and the repressive policies and practices of Israel there, as well as its violations of the sovereignty and territorial integrity of countries in the area, had created a critical situation making it imperative to advance towards a comprehensive, just and lasting settlement of the Palestinian question.

At the same time, events during the year had brought about greatly increased support for the proposed conference. The Committee accordingly stressed the need for members of the Security Council, and others who had not shown willingness to co-operate, to reconsider their positions.

GENERAL ASSEMBLY ACTION

On 15 December 1988, the General Assembly adopted **resolution 43/176** by roll-call vote.

Question of Palestine

The General Assembly,

Having considered the reports of the Secretary-General of 31 March 1988 and 30 September 1988,

Having noted with appreciation the statement made on 13 December 1988 by the Chairman of the Palestine Liberation Organization,

Stressing that achieving peace in the Middle East would constitute a significant contribution to international peace and security,

Aware of the overwhelming support for the convening of the International Peace Conference on the Middle East,

Noting with appreciation the endeavours of the Secretary-General to achieve the convening of the Conference,

Welcoming the outcome of the nineteenth Extraordinary Session of the Palestine National Council as a positive contribution towards a peaceful settlement of the conflict in the region,

Aware of the ongoing uprising *(intifadah)* of the Palestinian people since 9 December 1987, aimed at ending Israeli occupation of Palestinian territory occupied since 1967,

1. *Affirms* the urgent need to achieve a just and comprehensive settlement of the Arab-Israeli conflict, the core of which is the question of Palestine;

2. *Calls for* the convening of the International Peace Conference on the Middle East, under the auspices of the United Nations, with the participation of all parties to the conflict, including the Palestine Liberation Organization, on an equal footing, and the five permanent members of the Security Council, based on Security Council resolutions 242(1967) of 22 November 1967 and 338(1973) of 22 October 1973 and the legitimate national rights of the Palestinian people, primarily the right to self-determination;

3. *Affirms* the following principles for the achievement of comprehensive peace:

(*a*) The withdrawal of Israel from the Palestinian territory occupied since 1967, including Jerusalem, and from the other occupied Arab territories;

(*b*) Guaranteeing arrangements for security of all States in the region, including those named in resolution 181(II) of 29 November 1947, within secure and internationally recognized boundaries;

(*c*) Resolving the problem of the Palestine refugees in conformity with General Assembly resolution 194(III) of 11 December 1948, and subsequent relevant resolutions;

(*d*) Dismantling the Israeli settlements in the territories occupied since 1967;

(*e*) Guaranteeing freedom of access to Holy Places, religious buildings and sites;

4. *Notes* the expressed desire and endeavours to place the Palestinian territory occupied since 1967, including Jerusalem, under the supervision of the United Nations for a limited period, as part of the peace process;

5. *Requests* the Security Council to consider measures needed to convene the International Peace Conference on the Middle East, including the establishment of a preparatory committee, and to consider guarantees for security measures agreed upon by the Conference for all States in the region;

6. *Requests* the Secretary-General to continue his efforts with the parties concerned, and in consultation with the Security Council, to facilitate the convening of the Conference, and to submit progress reports on developments in this matter.

General Assembly resolution 43/176

15 December 1988   Meeting 82   138-2-2 (roll-call vote)

30-nation draft (A/43/L.53 & Add.1); agenda item 37.

Sponsors: Afghanistan, Angola, Bangladesh, Bulgaria, Burkina Faso, Cuba, Cyprus, Djibouti, Egypt, German Democratic Republic, Hungary, India, Indonesia, Jordan, Lao People's Democratic Republic, Madagascar, Malaysia, Mali, Malta, Morocco, Pakistan, Senegal, Sri Lanka, Sudan, Ukrainian SSR, Vanuatu, Viet Nam, Yemen, Yugoslavia, Zambia.
Meeting numbers. GA 43rd session: plenary 71, 77-82.

Roll-call vote in Assembly as follows:

In favour: Afghanistan, Albania, Algeria, Angola, Antigua and Barbuda, Argentina, Australia, Austria, Bahamas, Bahrain, Bangladesh, Barbados, Belgium, Benin, Bhutan, Bolivia, Botswana, Brazil, Brunei Darussalam, Bulgaria, Burkina Faso, Burma, Burundi, Byelorussian SSR, Cape Verde, Central African Republic, Chad, China, Colombia, Comoros, Côte d'Ivoire, Cuba, Cyprus, Czechoslovakia, Democratic Kampuchea, Democratic Yemen, Denmark, Djibouti, Ecuador, Egypt, Equatorial Guinea, Ethiopia, Finland, France, Gabon, Gambia, German Democratic Republic, Germany, Federal Republic of, Ghana, Greece, Guinea, Guinea-Bissau, Guyana, Haiti, Hungary, Iceland, India, Indonesia, Iraq, Ireland, Italy, Japan, Jordan, Kenya, Kuwait, Lao People's Democratic Republic, Lebanon, Lesotho, Liberia, Libyan Arab Jamahiriya, Luxembourg, Madagascar, Malawi, Malaysia, Maldives, Mali, Malta, Mauritania, Mauritius, Mexico, Mongolia, Morocco, Mozambique, Nepal, Netherlands, New Zealand, Nicaragua, Niger, Nigeria, Norway, Oman, Pakistan, Panama, Papua New Guinea, Peru, Philippines, Poland, Portugal, Qatar, Romania, Rwanda, Saint Lucia, Saint Vincent and the Grenadines, Samoa, Sao Tome and Principe, Saudi Arabia, Senegal, Seychelles, Sierra Leone, Singapore, Somalia, Spain, Sri Lanka, Sudan, Suriname, Swaziland, Sweden, Syrian Arab Republic, Thailand, Togo, Trinidad and Tobago, Tunisia, Turkey, Uganda, Ukrainian SSR, USSR, United Arab Emirates, United Kingdom, United Republic of Tanzania, Uruguay, Vanuatu, Venezuela, Viet Nam, Yemen, Yugoslavia, Zaire, Zambia, Zimbabwe.
Against: Israel, United States.
Abstaining: Canada, Costa Rica.

UN Truce Supervision Organization

In November 1988,[2] the Secretary-General provided an overview of the activities of the three peace-keeping operations in the Middle East: two peace-keeping forces—the United Nations Disengagement Observer Force (UNDOF) (see below, under "Israel and the Syrian Arab Republic") and the United Nations Interim Force in Lebanon (UNIFIL) (see below, under "Lebanon")—and one observer mission, the United Nations Truce Supervision Organization (UNTSO). Apart from assisting UNDOF and UNIFIL, UNTSO maintained observer groups of its own—the Observer Group in Beirut, which was established by the Security Council in August 1982 following the occupation of West Beirut by Israeli troops, with a reduced strength by 1988 of 14 observers following the withdrawal of Israeli forces from the Beirut area in September 1983; and the Observer Group in Egypt, where with the Government's agreement some 50 observers had remained since 1979 when the second United Nations Emergency Force was withdrawn. In addition to liaison offices at Cairo and Ismailia, the Observer Group in Egypt maintained six observation posts in the Sinai. A major incident during 1988 was the abduction in February of Lieutenant-Colonel William Higgins, the Chief of the Observer Group Lebanon, an unarmed military group of UNTSO assigned to assist UNIFIL (see also below, under "Lebanon").

REFERENCES
[1]YUN 1987, p. 255, GA res. 42/209 B, 11 Dec. 1987. [2]A/43/867-S/20294. [3]A/43/407-S/19938. [4]A/43/827-S/20278. [5]A/43/683 & Add.1. [6]YUN 1987, pp. 319 & 269, GA res. 42/209 C & D, 11 Dec. 1987. [7]*Ibid.*, p. 261, GA

res. 42/209 A, 11 Dec. 1987. [8]*Ibid.*, p. 305, SC res. 605(1987), 22 Dec. 1987. [9]S/19443. [10]YUN 1967, p. 257, SC res. 242(1967), 22 Nov. 1967. [11]YUN 1973, p. 213, SC res. 338(1973), 22 Oct. 1973. [12]YUN 1987, p. 260, GA res. 42/66 D, 2 Dec. 1987. [13]A/43/272-S/19719. [14]YUN 1983, p. 278, GA res. 38/58 C, 13 Dec. 1983. [15]A/43/691-S/20219. [16]S/19532, S/19536. [17]YUN 1987, p. 265, GA res. 42/66 A, 2 Dec. 1987. [18]A/43/35.

Palestine question

The question of Palestine remained at the core of an intensifying Arab-Israeli conflict which brought with it an escalating uprising of the Palestinian people against Israeli occupation in the West Bank, Gaza Strip and East Jerusalem. The uprising, which had begun on 9 December 1987[1] and was known in Arabic as *intifadah*, served tragically to focus international attention on the area and the underlying political context as a whole, while greatly increasing awareness of the need to resolve the Palestine question. The *intifadah* was supported by the Seventeenth Islamic Conference of Foreign Ministers at its Session of Islamic Solidarity with the Uprising of the Palestinian People (Amman, Jordan, 21-25 March),[2] and the Arab Summit Conference (Algiers, 7-9 June).[3]

A large number of States, human rights agencies and United Nations bodies, including the Committee on Palestinian rights,[4] reported instances of Palestinian armed struggle and Israeli counteractions throughout 1988. Measures by Israel against Palestinians included military force—in addition to administrative and judicial policies authorizing the use of force against civilians—detentions and expulsions.

The nineteenth extraordinary session of PNC (Algiers, 12-15 November)[5] culminated in the proclamation of an independent State of Palestine in the land of Palestine, with Jerusalem as its capital. PNC decided to provide all means and possibilities for the intensification of the uprising, with a view to ensuring its continuation and escalation. It invited the United Nations to place the occupied Palestinian territories under international supervision to protect their population and terminate Israeli occupation. It affirmed the determination of PLO to reach a comprehensive political settlement of the question of Palestine within the framework of the Charter and the rules of international law. PNC insisted on: the need to convene an effective international conference that should guarantee the Palestinians' right to self-determination; Israel's withdrawal from all Palestinian and Arab territories; cancellation of all measures of attachment and annexation; and removal of Israeli settlements. It renewed its commitment to United Nations resolutions and once again rejected terrorism in all forms, including State terrorism.

Numerous States endorsed PNC's proclamation and recognized the new State in communications to the Secretary-General, which were transmitted to the Assembly.

Israel commented on 21 November[6] that no unilateral step could substitute for a negotiated settlement. Hence, any recognition or legitimation of the PNC declaration would only reinforce an illusion that the outcome of desired negotiations could be prejudged by unilateral acts or declarations. PLO had not changed its basic character, policy or adherence to terrorism; peace between Israel and its neighbours would be reached solely by negotiation and those assisting PLO only helped prevent regional peace.

Although invited to participate in deliberations on the Palestine question when it came before the General Assembly on 1 December, PLO Chairman Yasser Arafat was denied an entry visa by the United States, the host country of United Nations Headquarters in New York. The Assembly, deploring the failure of the host country to approve the requested visa, urged the United States by **resolution 43/48** to reverse that decision. In the light of the United States failure to respond favourably, the Assembly, by **resolution 43/49**, decided to consider the question of Palestine in plenary at Geneva, from 13 to 15 December (see PART FIVE, Chapter V).

The Assembly acknowledged the proclamation by PNC of the State of Palestine and decided that the designation "Palestine" would forthwith be used in place of "Palestine Liberation Organization" in the United Nations system (resolution 43/177). After considering the 1988 recommendations of the Committee on Palestinian rights,[4] the Assembly again drew the Security Council's attention to the fact that action was still awaited on the Committee's original 1976 recommendations[7] for resolving the Palestinian problem (43/175 A); requested resources and co-operation to enable the Division for Palestinian Rights of the Secretariat to perform its tasks (43/175 B); and asked that the Department of Public Information (DPI) continue its special information programme on Palestine (43/175 C). The Assembly again determined that Israel's 1980 decision[8] to impose jurisdiction over Jerusalem was illegal (43/54 C).

Both the Economic and Social Council (1988/54) and the Assembly (43/178) regretted that the Organization's 1988-1990 programme of economic and social assistance to the Palestinian people had not been developed as requested by the Assembly in 1987.[9] Therefore, both organs requested that the United Nations Centre for Human Settlements (Habitat) be charged with future development of the programme, in co-operation with PLO, and decided to extend to occupied Palestine the same preferential treatment accorded to the least devel-oped countries (LDCs), calling for the granting of trade concessions for Palestinian exports based on certificates of origin issued by Palestinian bodies designated by PLO.

GENERAL ASSEMBLY ACTION

On 15 December 1988, the General Assembly adopted **resolution 43/177** by roll-call vote.

Question of Palestine

The General Assembly,

Having considered the item entitled "Question of Palestine",

Recalling its resolution 181(II) of 29 November 1947, in which, *inter alia*, it called for the establishment of an Arab State and a Jewish State in Palestine,

Mindful of the special responsibility of the United Nations to achieve a just solution to the question of Palestine,

Aware of the proclamation of the State of Palestine by the Palestine National Council in line with General Assembly resolution 181(II) and in exercise of the inalienable rights of the Palestinian people,

Affirming the urgent need to achieve a just and comprehensive settlement in the Middle East which, *inter alia*, provides for peaceful coexistence for all States in the region,

Recalling its resolution 3237(XXIX) of 22 November 1974 on the observer status for the Palestine Liberation Organization and subsequent relevant resolutions,

1. *Acknowledges* the proclamation of the State of Palestine by the Palestine National Council on 15 November 1988;

2. *Affirms* the need to enable the Palestinian people to exercise their sovereignty over their territory occupied since 1967;

3. *Decides* that, effective as of 15 December 1988, the designation "Palestine" should be used in place of the designation "Palestine Liberation Organization" in the United Nations system, without prejudice to the observer status and functions of the Palestine Liberation Organization within the United Nations system, in conformity with relevant United Nations resolutions and practice;

4. *Requests* the Secretary-General to take the necessary action to implement the present resolution.

General Assembly resolution 43/177

15 December 1988   Meeting 82   104-2-36 (roll-call vote)

29-nation draft (A/43/L.54 & Add.1); agenda item 37.

Sponsors: Afghanistan, Angola, Bangladesh, Bulgaria, Cuba, Cyprus, Djibouti, Egypt, German Democratic Republic, India, Indonesia, Jordan, Lao People's Democratic Republic, Madagascar, Malaysia, Mali, Malta, Mongolia, Morocco, Pakistan, Senegal, Sri Lanka, Sudan, Ukrainian SSR, Vanuatu, Viet Nam, Yemen, Yugoslavia, Zambia.

Meeting numbers. GA 43rd session: plenary 71, 77-82.

Roll-call vote in Assembly as follows:

In favour: Afghanistan, Albania, Algeria, Angola, Argentina, Bahrain, Bangladesh, Benin, Bolivia, Botswana, Brazil, Brunei Darussalam, Bulgaria, Burkina Faso, Burma, Burundi, Byelorussian SSR, Cape Verde, Chad, China, Colombia, Comoros, Cuba, Cyprus, Czechoslovakia, Democratic Kampuchea, Democratic Yemen, Djibouti, Ecuador, Egypt, Equatorial Guinea, Ethiopia, Gabon, Gambia, German Democratic Republic, Ghana, Guinea, Guinea-Bissau, Guyana, Haiti, Hungary, India, Indonesia, Iraq, Jordan, Kenya, Kuwait, Lao People's Democratic Republic, Lebanon, Libyan Arab Jamahiriya, Madagascar, Malaysia, Maldives, Mali, Malta, Mauritania, Mauritius, Mexico, Mongolia, Morocco, Mozambique, Nicaragua, Niger, Nigeria, Oman, Pakistan, Panama, Papua New Guinea, Peru, Philippines, Poland, Qatar, Romania, Rwanda, Saint Lucia, Saint Vincent and the Grenadines, Samoa, Sao Tome and Principe, Saudi Arabia, Senegal, Seychelles, Sierra Leone, Singapore, Somalia, Sri Lanka, Sudan, Suriname, Swaziland, Syrian Arab Republic, Thailand, Togo, Tunisia, Turkey, Uganda, Ukrainian SSR, USSR, United Arab Emirates, United Republic of Tanzania, Vanuatu, Viet Nam, Yemen, Yugoslavia, Zambia, Zimbabwe.

Against: Israel, United States.

Abstaining: Antigua and Barbuda, Australia, Austria, Bahamas, Barbados, Belgium, Bhutan, Canada, Central African Republic, Costa Rica, Côte d'Ivoire, Denmark, Finland, France, Germany, Federal Republic of, Greece, Iceland, Ireland, Italy, Japan, Lesotho, Liberia, Luxembourg, Malawi, Nepal, Netherlands, New Zealand, Norway, Portugal, Spain, Sweden, Trinidad and Tobago, United Kingdom, Uruguay, Venezuela, Zaire.

Activities of the Committee on Palestinian rights. In its October 1988 report to the General Assembly,[4] the Committee on Palestinian rights—established in 1975[10]—stressed that, since its first report in 1976,[7] it had made a number of annual recommendations, which the Assembly had as a basis for the resolution of the Palestinian question. However, despite the increasing urgency of its appeals, the Security Council had not acted on or implemented those recommendations. The Committee remained convinced that positive Council action would advance prospects for attaining a comprehensive, just and lasting solution.

The Committee's efforts to promote such a solution acquired particular urgency in the light of the grave deterioration of the situation in the territories. Despite the international outcry over repeated violations of human rights there and the adoption of several Council resolutions requesting the occupying Power to abide by relevant international instruments and United Nations resolutions, Israel continued to resort to military force against the Palestinians resisting occupation, and to engage in armed attacks against the integrity and sovereignty of countries in the region. The Committee expressed greatest concern at the mounting casualties and suffering inflicted on Palestinian civilians and warned that Israel's intransigence would further exacerbate the situation, jeopardize international efforts towards a just and lasting settlement, and further endanger international peace and security. It reasserted that no solution could be achieved as long as the Palestinian people was denied its inalienable rights, including those to self-determination, national independence and sovereignty, to return to homes and property, and to establish an independent and sovereign State.

Accordingly, the Committee repeatedly appealed to the Security Council to take appropriate action to secure United Nations objectives, and again accorded priority to the convening of the proposed international peace conference on the Middle East in conformity with the 1983 Assembly resolution.[11] In that respect, it stressed the urgent need for additional concrete and constructive efforts by all Governments.

The Committee continued monitoring developments relating to Palestine and exerted efforts to promote implementation of its recommendations. On an ongoing basis, it gathered information from the media, Governments and reports of missions, individuals, experts and eyewitnesses, which indicated a serious deterioration of the situation.

Among its 1988 recommendations, the Committee reaffirmed the need for positive action by the Security Council on its original recommendations[7] and those adopted by the 1983 International Conference on the Question of Palestine.[12] It reasserted that Israeli evacuation of the territories occupied by force and in violation of the Charter and United Nations resolutions was a *conditio sine qua non* for the exercise by the Palestinian people of its inalienable rights and the establishment of an independent Arab State in Palestine as envisaged in a 1947 resolution,[13] which had been implemented only in part. The Committee was further convinced that the United Nations and the international community as a whole must urgently intensify their efforts to bring this about. It considered it imperative for the Security Council to act towards convening an international peace conference in accordance with 1983[11] and 1986[14] resolutions, and appealed to the Secretary-General to ensure that active consultations were undertaken within the Council's framework for that purpose.

The Committee called on the international community, in particular on the parties to the Geneva Convention relative to the Protection of Civilian Persons in Time of War of 12 August 1949 (fourth Geneva Convention), to do all in their power to ensure respect for the Convention by Israel. It called on the Security Council to appeal to those parties that had diplomatic relations with Israel to ensure respect for the instrument under all circumstances and to urge Israel to abide by its provisions.

Annexed to the Committee's report were the conclusions and recommendations of symposia and seminars held in 1988 on the question of Palestine, organized by the Division for Palestinian Rights: the nineteenth and twentieth United Nations seminars (European regional seminar, Berlin, 25-29 April; and North American regional seminar, New York, 27 and 28 June); followed by the United Nations North American regional NGO symposium (New York, 29 June–1 July), the United Nations European regional NGO symposium (Geneva, 29 and 30 August) and the international NGO meeting (Geneva, 31 August–2 September).

GENERAL ASSEMBLY ACTION

Following consideration of the report of the Committee on Palestinian rights, the General Assembly adopted, on 15 December 1988, three resolutions on the question of Palestine (resolutions 43/175 A-C).

Resolution 43/175 A was adopted by roll-call vote.

The General Assembly,
Recalling its resolutions 181(II) of 29 November 1947, 194(III) of 11 December 1948, 3236(XXIX) of 22 November 1974, 3375(XXX) and 3376(XXX) of 10 November 1975, 31/20 of 24 November 1976, 32/40 of 2 December 1977, 33/28 of 7 December 1978, 34/65 A

and B of 29 November 1979 and 34/65 C and D of 12 December 1979, ES-7/2 of 29 July 1980, 35/169 of 15 December 1980, 36/120 of 10 December 1981, ES-7/4 of 28 April 1982, ES-7/5 of 26 June 1982, ES-7/9 of 24 September 1982, 37/86 A of 10 December 1982, 38/58 A of 13 December 1983, 39/49 A of 11 December 1984, 40/96 A of 12 December 1985, 41/43 A of 2 December 1986 and 42/66 A of 2 December 1987,

Having considered the report of the Committee on the Exercise of the Inalienable Rights of the Palestinian People,

1. *Expresses its appreciation* to the Committee on the Exercise of the Inalienable Rights of the Palestinian People for its efforts in performing the tasks assigned to it by the General Assembly;

2. *Endorses* the recommendations of the Committee contained in paragraphs 141 to 148 of its report and draws the attention of the Security Council to the fact that action on the Committee's recommendations, as repeatedly endorsed by the General Assembly at its thirty-first session and subsequently, is still awaited;

3. *Requests* the Committee to continue to keep under review the situation relating to the question of Palestine as well as the implementation of the Programme of Action for the Achievement of Palestinian Rights and to report and make suggestions to the General Assembly or the Security Council, as appropriate;

4. *Authorizes* the Committee to continue to exert all efforts to promote the implementation of its recommendations, including representation at conferences and meetings and the sending of delegations, to make such adjustments in its approved programme of seminars and symposia and meetings for non-governmental organizations as it may consider necessary, and to report thereon to the General Assembly at its forty-fourth session and thereafter;

5. *Requests* the Committee to continue to extend its co-operation to non-governmental organizations in their contribution towards heightening international awareness of the facts relating to the question of Palestine and creating a more favourable atmosphere for the full implementation of the Committee's recommendations, and to take the necessary steps to expand its contacts with those organizations;

6. *Requests* the United Nations Conciliation Commission for Palestine, established under General Assembly resolution 194(III), as well as other United Nations bodies associated with the question of Palestine, to co-operate fully with the Committee and to make available to it, at its request, the relevant information and documentation which they have at their disposal;

7. *Decides* to circulate the report of the Committee to all the competent bodies of the United Nations and urges them to take the necessary action, as appropriate, in accordance with the Committee's programme of implementation;

8. *Requests* the Secretary-General to continue to provide the Committee with all the necessary facilities for the performance of its tasks.

General Assembly resolution 43/175 A

15 December 1988   Meeting 82   123-2-20 (roll-call vote)

16-nation draft (A/43/L.50 & Corr.1 & Add.1); agenda item 37.

Sponsors: Afghanistan, Cuba, Cyprus, German Democratic Republic, India, Indonesia, Jordan, Madagascar, Malaysia, Mali, Pakistan, Senegal, Ukrainian SSR, Vanuatu, Yugoslavia, Zambia.

Meeting numbers. GA 43rd session: plenary 71, 77-82.

Roll-call vote in Assembly as follows:

In favour: Afghanistan, Albania, Algeria, Angola, Antigua and Barbuda, Argentina, Bahamas, Bahrain, Bangladesh, Barbados, Benin, Bhutan, Bolivia, Botswana, Brazil, Brunei Darussalam, Bulgaria, Burkina Faso, Burma, Burundi, Byelorussian SSR, Cape Verde, Central African Republic, Chad, Chile, China, Colombia, Comoros, Côte d'Ivoire, Cuba, Cyprus, Czechoslovakia, Democratic Kampuchea, Democratic Yemen, Djibouti, Ecuador, Egypt, Equatorial Guinea, Ethiopia, Gabon, Gambia, German Democratic Republic, Ghana, Greece, Guatemala, Guinea, Guinea-Bissau, Guyana, Haiti, Hungary, India, Indonesia, Iran, Iraq, Jordan, Kenya, Kuwait, Lao People's Democratic Republic, Lebanon, Lesotho, Liberia, Libyan Arab Jamahiriya, Madagascar, Malawi, Malaysia, Maldives, Mali, Malta, Mauritania, Mauritius, Mexico, Mongolia, Morocco, Mozambique, Nepal, Nicaragua, Niger, Nigeria, Oman, Pakistan, Papua New Guinea, Paraguay, Peru, Philippines, Poland, Qatar, Romania, Rwanda, Saint Lucia, Saint Vincent and the Grenadines, Samoa, Sao Tome and Principe, Saudi Arabia, Senegal, Seychelles, Sierra Leone, Singapore, Somalia, Spain, Sri Lanka, Sudan, Suriname, Swaziland, Syrian Arab Republic, Thailand, Togo, Trinidad and Tobago, Tunisia, Turkey, Uganda, Ukrainian SSR, USSR, United Arab Emirates, United Republic of Tanzania, Uruguay, Vanuatu, Venezuela, Viet Nam, Yemen, Yugoslavia, Zaire, Zambia, Zimbabwe.

Against: Israel, United States.

Abstaining: Australia, Austria, Belgium, Canada, Costa Rica, Denmark, Finland, France, Germany, Federal Republic of, Iceland, Ireland, Italy, Japan, Luxembourg, Netherlands, New Zealand, Norway, Portugal, Sweden, United Kingdom.

The Assembly also adopted **resolution 43/175 B** by roll-call vote.

The General Assembly,

Having considered the report of the Committee on the Exercise of the Inalienable Rights of the Palestinian People,

Taking note, in particular, of the relevant information contained in paragraphs 96 to 128 of that report,

Recalling its resolutions 32/40 B of 2 December 1977, 33/28 C of 7 December 1978, 34/65 D of 12 December 1979, 35/169 D of 15 December 1980, 36/120 B of 10 December 1981, 37/86 B of 10 December 1982, 38/58 B of 13 December 1983, 39/49 B of 11 December 1984, 40/96 B of 12 December 1985, 41/43 B of 2 December 1986 and 42/66 B of 2 December 1987,

Recalling that 1989 is the thirtieth anniversary of the Declaration of the Rights of the Child and the tenth anniversary of the International Year of the Child,

1. *Takes note with appreciation* of the action taken by the Secretary-General in compliance with General Assembly resolution 42/66 B;

2. *Requests* the Secretary-General to provide the Division for Palestinian Rights of the Secretariat with the necessary resources and to ensure that it continues to discharge the tasks detailed in paragraph 1 of General Assembly resolution 32/40 B, paragraph 2 *(b)* of resolution 34/65 D, paragraph 3 of resolution 36/120 B, paragraph 3 of resolution 38/58 B, paragraph 3 of resolution 40/96 B and paragraph 2 of resolution 42/66 B, in consultation with the Committee on the Exercise of the Inalienable Rights of the Palestinian People and under its guidance;

3. *Also requests* the Secretary-General to direct the Division for Palestinian Rights to pay particular attention to the plight of Palestinian children in the occupied Palestinian territories in its programme of work for 1989;

4. *Further requests* the Secretary-General to ensure the continued co-operation of the Department of Public Information and other units of the Secretariat in enabling the Division for Palestinian Rights to perform its tasks and in covering adequately the various aspects of the question of Palestine;

5. *Invites* all Governments and organizations to lend their co-operation to the Committee on the Exercise of

the Inalienable Rights of the Palestinian People and the Division for Palestinian Rights in the performance of their tasks;

6. *Takes note with appreciation* of the action taken by Member States to observe annually on 29 November the International Day of Solidarity with the Palestinian People, and of the issuance by them of special postage stamps for the occasion.

General Assembly resolution 43/175 B

15 December 1988   Meeting 82   123-2-20 (roll-call vote)

16-nation draft (A/43/L.51 & Corr.1 & Add.1); agenda item 37.
Sponsors: Afghanistan, Cuba, Cyprus, German Democratic Republic, India, Indonesia, Jordan, Madagascar, Malaysia, Mali, Pakistan, Senegal, Ukrainian SSR, Vanuatu, Yugoslavia, Zambia.
Meeting numbers. GA 43rd session: plenary 71, 77-82.

Roll-call vote in Assembly as follows:

In favour: Afghanistan, Albania, Algeria, Angola, Antigua and Barbuda, Argentina, Bahamas, Bahrain, Bangladesh, Barbados, Benin, Bhutan, Bolivia, Botswana, Brazil, Brunei Darussalam, Bulgaria, Burkina Faso, Burma, Burundi, Byelorussian SSR, Cape Verde, Central African Republic, Chad, Chile, China, Colombia, Comoros, Côte d'Ivoire, Cuba, Cyprus, Czechoslovakia, Democratic Kampuchea, Democratic Yemen, Djibouti, Ecuador, Egypt, Equatorial Guinea, Ethiopia, Gabon, Gambia, German Democratic Republic, Ghana, Greece, Guatemala, Guinea, Guinea-Bissau, Guyana, Haiti, Hungary, India, Indonesia, Iran, Iraq, Jordan, Kenya, Kuwait, Lao People's Democratic Republic, Lebanon, Lesotho, Liberia, Libyan Arab Jamahiriya, Madagascar, Malawi, Malaysia, Maldives, Mali, Malta, Mauritania, Mauritius, Mexico, Mongolia, Morocco, Mozambique, Nepal, Nicaragua, Niger, Nigeria, Oman, Pakistan, Papua New Guinea, Paraguay, Peru, Philippines, Poland, Qatar, Romania, Rwanda, Saint Lucia, Saint Vincent and the Grenadines, Samoa, Sao Tome and Principe, Saudi Arabia, Senegal, Seychelles, Sierra Leone, Singapore, Somalia, Spain, Sri Lanka, Sudan, Suriname, Swaziland, Syrian Arab Republic, Thailand, Togo, Trinidad and Tobago, Tunisia, Turkey, Uganda, Ukrainian SSR, USSR, United Arab Emirates, United Republic of Tanzania, Uruguay, Vanuatu, Venezuela, Viet Nam, Yemen, Yugoslavia, Zaire, Zambia, Zimbabwe.
Against: Israel, United States.
Abstaining: Australia, Austria, Belgium, Canada, Costa Rica, Denmark, Finland, France, Germany, Federal Republic of, Iceland, Ireland, Italy, Japan, Luxembourg, Netherlands, New Zealand, Norway, Portugal, Sweden, United Kingdom.

In related action, the Assembly, reaffirming the importance of implementing the 1960 Declaration on the Granting of Independence to Colonial Countries and Peoples,[15] urged States, the United Nations system and international organizations to support the Palestinian people through PLO in its struggle for self-determination and independence in accordance with the Charter (**resolution 43/106**).

Public information activities

The Committee on Palestinian rights[4] followed up on the implementation of a 1987 General Assembly request[16] that DPI continue in 1988-1989 its special information programme on the question of Palestine, with particular emphasis on public opinion in Europe and North America.

DPI accordingly disseminated press releases, publications and audio-visual material, in addition to organizing fact-finding missions and regional and national encounters for journalists. Its coverage of the Palestine question focused increasingly on news items and information concerning the situation in the occupied territories in relation to the uprising, and on efforts to convene an international peace conference under United

Nations auspices. United Nations information centres (UNICs) throughout the world organized information activities and made available to the public United Nations information materials on the question of Palestine.

The *UN Chronicle* reported extensively on consideration given to the Palestine question by the Assembly and the Security Council, particularly since the beginning of the uprising. DPI continued to distribute in Arabic, English, French, German and Spanish a brochure on the Committee on Israeli practices as well as the booklet *The United Nations and the Question of Palestine*. The Arabic and Middle East Radio Unit provided broad coverage of the *intifadah* in its weekly programmes and telephone feeds to radio stations of the region. United Nations activities and events, including observance of 30 November 1988 as the International Day of Solidarity with the Palestinian People, received broad coverage. Two feature programmes in the *Perspective* series dealt with new initiatives to convene the proposed peace conference. A 22-minute film, *Palestinian Portraits*, was produced in English and widely screened and loaned out by 34 UNICs and film libraries of the United Nations Development Programme (UNDP). DPI prepared 241 television news packages for worldwide dissemination and provided delegations with video-cassette dubs and excerpts on subjects related to the question.

DPI once again organized activities to acquaint the media with facts and developments pertaining to the Palestine question. A team of 10 high-level journalists participated in a news mission to the Middle East, visiting Egypt, Jordan, the Syrian Arab Republic and Tunisia between 13 March and 2 April. It organized two regional encounters for journalists: the first (Nairobi, Kenya, 2-5 February) was attended by 18 journalists from Africa and the second (Vienna, 17-20 May) by 20 journalists from Europe. In addition, African national journalists' encounters were held at Kinshasa (Zaire), Dar-es-Salaam (United Republic of Tanzania) and Addis Ababa (Ethiopia) between 29 January and 8 February. National encounters for Europe were held between 16 and 25 May at Madrid (Spain), Brussels (Belgium) and Stockholm (Sweden).

GENERAL ASSEMBLY ACTION

On 15 December, the General Assembly adopted **resolution 43/175 C** by roll-call vote.

The General Assembly,

Having considered the report of the Committee on the Exercise of the Inalienable Rights of the Palestinian People,

Taking note, in particular, of the information contained in paragraphs 129 to 140 of that report,

Recalling its resolution 42/66 C of 2 December 1987,

Convinced that the world-wide dissemination of accurate and comprehensive information and the role of non-governmental organizations and institutions remain of vital importance in heightening awareness of and support for the inalienable rights of the Palestinian people to self-determination and to the establishment of an independent sovereign Palestinian State,

1. *Takes note with appreciation* of the action taken by the Department of Public Information of the Secretariat in compliance with General Assembly resolution 42/66 C;

2. *Requests* the Department of Public Information, in full co-operation and co-ordination with the Committee on the Exercise of the Inalienable Rights of the Palestinian People, to continue its special information programme on the question of Palestine in 1989, with particular emphasis on public opinion in Europe and North America and, in particular:

(a) To disseminate information on all the activities of the United Nations system relating to the question of Palestine, including reports of the work carried out by the relevant United Nations organs;

(b) To continue to issue and update publications on the various aspects of the question of Palestine, including Israeli violations of the human rights of the Arab inhabitants of the occupied territories as reported by the relevant United Nations organs;

(c) To expand its audio-visual material on the question of Palestine, including the production of special series of radio programmes and television broadcasts;

(d) To organize fact-finding news missions to the area for journalists;

(e) To organize regional and national encounters for journalists.

General Assembly resolution 43/175 C

15 December 1988   Meeting 82   127-2-17 (roll-call vote)

16-nation draft (A/43/L.52 & Corr.1 & Add.1); agenda item 37.
Sponsors: Afghanistan, Cuba, Cyprus, German Democratic Republic, India, Indonesia, Jordan, Madagascar, Malaysia, Mali, Pakistan, Senegal, Ukrainian SSR, Vanuatu, Yugoslavia, Zambia.
Meeting numbers. GA 43rd session: plenary 71, 77-82.

Roll-call vote in Assembly as follows:

In favour: Afghanistan, Albania, Algeria, Angola, Antigua and Barbuda, Argentina, Austria, Bahamas, Bahrain, Bangladesh, Barbados, Benin, Bhutan, Bolivia, Botswana, Brazil, Brunei Darussalam, Bulgaria, Burkina Faso, Burma, Burundi, Byelorussian SSR, Cape Verde, Central African Republic, Chad, Chile, China, Colombia, Comoros, Côte d'Ivoire, Cuba, Cyprus, Czechoslovakia, Democratic Kampuchea, Democratic Yemen, Djibouti, Ecuador, Egypt, Equatorial Guinea, Ethiopia, Finland, Gabon, Gambia, German Democratic Republic, Ghana, Greece, Guatemala, Guinea, Guinea-Bissau, Guyana, Haiti, Hungary, India, Indonesia, Iran, Iraq, Jordan, Kenya, Kuwait, Lao People's Democratic Republic, Lebanon, Lesotho, Liberia, Libyan Arab Jamahiriya, Madagascar, Malawi, Malaysia, Maldives, Mali, Malta, Mauritania, Mauritius, Mexico, Mongolia, Morocco, Mozambique, Nepal, Nicaragua, Niger, Nigeria, Oman, Pakistan, Panama, Papua New Guinea, Paraguay, Peru, Philippines, Poland, Qatar, Romania, Rwanda, Saint Lucia, Saint Vincent and the Grenadines, Samoa, Sao Tome and Principe, Saudi Arabia, Senegal, Seychelles, Sierra Leone, Singapore, Somalia, Spain, Sri Lanka, Sudan, Suriname, Swaziland, Sweden, Syrian Arab Republic, Thailand, Togo, Trinidad and Tobago, Tunisia, Turkey, Uganda, Ukrainian SSR, USSR, United Arab Emirates, United Republic of Tanzania, Uruguay, Vanuatu, Venezuela, Viet Nam, Yemen, Yugoslavia, Zaire, Zambia, Zimbabwe.

Against: Israel, United States.

Abstaining: Australia, Belgium, Canada, Costa Rica, Denmark, France, Germany, Federal Republic of, Iceland, Ireland, Italy, Japan, Luxembourg, Netherlands, New Zealand, Norway, Portugal, United Kingdom.

Jerusalem

The Secretary-General forwarded in October 1988[17] replies received from nine States to his notes verbales of 17 February on the implementation of a General Assembly resolution of 1987[18] concerning the transfer by some States of their

diplomatic missions to Jerusalem in violation of a Security Council resolution of 1980.[19] Since Israel's occupation in 1967 of Arab territories, including Jerusalem,[20] the Assembly had repeatedly determined that Israel's decision to annex Jerusalem and declare it the capital of Israel was null and void, as were its actions to alter the physical character, demographic composition, institutional structure and status of the city, and demanded that those measures be rescinded.

GENERAL ASSEMBLY ACTION

On 6 December 1988, the General Assembly adopted **resolution 43/54 C** by recorded vote.

The General Assembly,

Recalling its resolutions 36/120 E of 10 December 1981, 37/123 C of 16 December 1982, 38/180 C of 19 December 1983, 39/146 C of 14 December 1984, 40/168 C of 16 December 1985, 41/162 C of 4 December 1986 and 42/209 D of 11 December 1987, in which it determined that all legislative and administrative measures and actions taken by Israel, the occupying Power, which had altered or purported to alter the character and status of the Holy City of Jerusalem, in particular the so-called "Basic Law" on Jerusalem and the proclamation of Jerusalem as the capital of Israel, were null and void and must be rescinded forthwith,

Recalling Security Council resolution 478(1980) of 20 August 1980, in which the Council, *inter alia*, decided not to recognize the "Basic Law" and called upon those States that had established diplomatic missions at Jerusalem to withdraw such missions from the Holy City,

Having considered the report of the Secretary-General of 28 November 1988,

1. *Determines* that Israel's decision to impose its laws, jurisdiction and administration on the Holy City of Jerusalem is illegal and therefore null and void and has no validity whatsoever;

2. *Deplores* the transfer by some States of their diplomatic missions to Jerusalem in violation of Security Council resolution 478(1980), and their refusal to comply with the provisions of that resolution;

3. *Calls once more upon* those States to abide by the provisions of the relevant United Nations resolutions, in conformity with the Charter of the United Nations;

4. *Requests* the Secretary-General to report to the General Assembly at its forty-fourth session on the implementation of the present resolution.

General Assembly resolution 43/54 C

6 December 1988   Meeting 71   143-2-7 (recorded vote)

25-nation draft (A/43/L.46 & Add.1); agenda item 40.
Sponsors: Algeria, Bahrain, Bangladesh, Cuba, Democratic Yemen, Djibouti, Egypt, Indonesia, Iraq, Kuwait, Libyan Arab Jamahiriya, Malaysia, Mauritania, Morocco, Oman, Pakistan, Qatar, Saudi Arabia, Sudan, Syrian Arab Republic, United Arab Emirates, Tunisia, Yemen, Yugoslavia, Zimbabwe.
Meeting numbers. GA 43rd session: plenary 68-71.

Recorded vote in Assembly as follows:

In favour: Afghanistan, Albania, Algeria, Angola, Argentina, Australia, Austria, Bahamas, Bahrain, Bangladesh, Barbados, Belgium, Belize, Benin, Bhutan, Bolivia, Botswana, Brazil, Brunei Darussalam, Bulgaria, Burkina Faso, Burma, Burundi, Byelorussian SSR, Canada, Cape Verde, Central African Republic, Chad, Chile, China, Colombia, Comoros, Côte d'Ivoire, Cuba, Cyprus, Czechoslovakia, Democratic Kampuchea, Democratic Yemen, Denmark, Djibouti, Ecuador, Egypt, Ethiopia, Fiji, Finland, France, Gabon,

Gambia, German Democratic Republic, Germany, Federal Republic of, Ghana, Greece, Grenada, Guatemala, Guinea, Guinea-Bissau, Guyana, Haiti, Hungary, Iceland, India, Indonesia, Iran, Iraq, Ireland, Italy, Jamaica, Japan, Jordan, Kenya, Kuwait, Lao People's Democratic Republic, Lebanon, Lesotho, Libyan Arab Jamahiriya, Luxembourg, Madagascar, Malaysia, Maldives, Mali, Malta, Mauritania, Mauritius, Mexico, Mongolia, Morocco, Mozambique, Nepal, Netherlands, New Zealand, Nicaragua, Niger, Nigeria, Norway, Oman, Pakistan, Panama, Papua New Guinea, Paraguay, Peru, Philippines, Poland, Portugal, Qatar, Romania, Rwanda, Saint Lucia, Saint Vincent and the Grenadines, Samoa, Sao Tome and Principe, Saudi Arabia, Senegal, Seychelles, Sierra Leone, Singapore, Solomon Islands, Somalia, Spain, Sri Lanka, Sudan, Swaziland, Sweden, Syrian Arab Republic, Thailand, Togo, Trinidad and Tobago, Tunisia, Turkey, Uganda, Ukrainian SSR, USSR, United Arab Emirates, United Kingdom, United Republic of Tanzania, Uruguay, Vanuatu, Venezuela, Viet Nam, Yemen, Yugoslavia, Zaire, Zambia, Zimbabwe.

Against: El Salvador, Israel.

Abstaining: Antigua and Barbuda, Cameroon, Honduras, Liberia, Malawi, Saint Kitts and Nevis, United States.

Assistance to Palestinians

Under their respective mandates, various organizations of the United Nations system continued to provide assistance in 1988 to the Palestinian people. They responded in particular to the emergency conditions in the occupied territories due to the *intifadah* and repressive Israeli reactions. Notable among them were the United Nations Relief and Works Agency for Palestine Refugees in the Near East, which maintained an extensive programme of education, health and relief services as well as humanitarian assistance to Palestine refugees (see below, under ''Palestine refugees''), and UNDP, whose economic and social assistance programme was primarily for the non-refugee population.

As requested by the General Assembly in 1987,[9] the Secretary-General, in June 1988,[21] reported on progress in implementing the programme of economic and social assistance to the Palestinian people in: research, analysis and organization of data; infrastructure; agriculture; industry; employment; education and vocational training; health; social welfare; and human settlements. He also gave an overview of the United Nations response to the *intifadah*-related emergency situation in the territories. In addition to UNDP and UNRWA, the following reported on their implementation and development of the programme: ESCWA, FAO, ILO, ITC, UNCHS, UNCTAD, UNESCO, UNFPA, UNICEF, UNU, UPU, WHO and WIPO.

The Secretary-General recalled that in a January 1988 report to the Security Council,[22] he had asked the UNRWA Commissioner-General to prepare urgently proposals for improving the infrastructure of the refugee camps and to seek the necessary funds. In the past, refugees had sometimes expressed reservations about improving the infrastructure for fear that it would make the camps more permanent; the recent disturbances, however, had attracted world attention to the squalid living conditions in many camps, especially in the Gaza Strip.

In February/March, UNRWA prepared a package of projects, which were estimated at $65 mil-

lion. The package was presented to an informal meeting of major donors and host Governments, immediately followed by a meeting of the UNRWA Advisory Commission. Proposed activities included improvement of sewerage, shelters, road maintenance, upgrading of health and education facilities, a new hospital block and water supply in Gaza, and expansion of vocational training and university scholarship programmes, as well as strengthening income-generating and small development projects. By June, some $25 million was pledged in cash and kind.

UNRWA also expanded its educational, health and relief programmes to deal with the emergency situation. Additional budget provisions were made to meet hospitalization costs resulting from it. Emergency aid in the form of food, supplies and cash was provided to refugees and to a small number of non-refugees.

Many Palestinians expressed the hope that a concerted international effort would be undertaken to revive the territories' economy. In that context, the Secretary-General requested the UNDP Administrator to study the possibility of expanding the UNDP programme. Pursuant to that request, the Administrator in turn requested the UNDP Governing Council, at its special session in February, urgently to reinforce the programme through an additional allocation of $4 million from Special Programme Resources, over and above the $8 million previously allocated for 1987-1991.[23] The Council, on 19 February,[24] acceded to that request and appealed to Governments and intergovernmental institutions to respond immediately through further voluntary contributions.

At the special session, Japan announced a special contribution of $1 million, subject to parliamentary approval. Italy indicated that it intended to select certain projects for official consideration for co-funding. The Administrator informed the Council that those and other indications made it appear that substantially increased resources would be available. In consultation with PLO, UNDP sought to attract additional financial support.

In May, UNDP sent a five-day programming and operational review mission to the West Bank and Gaza to discuss the implementation of its programme. The mission concluded that the unrest and demonstrations that characterized the situation there had an inevitable effect on programme delivery. Nevertheless, the programme continued to operate at full strength under the supervision of the UNDP office at Jerusalem, and UNDP continued to plan its activities in consultation with all parties directly concerned, in particular the Palestinian inhabitants. The mission found renewed interest by donor Governments in assistance to the

Palestinians, and agreement was reached on new projects proposed by UNDP.

In an April report,[25] the Administrator provided additional financial and programming information on UNDP's assistance to the Palestinians. He stated that, notwithstanding the recent tragic events in the territories, project planning and implementation continued at a satisfactory rate. A revised programme was designed in March to serve as a framework for full utilization of the $8 million approved for the fourth programming cycle (1987-1991), plus the $4 million approved in February 1988. Projects under the accrued $12 million programme were formulated with an eye to the growing possibilities of attracting funds from Governments and non-governmental institutions. A list of 23 projects planned for implementation during the remainder of 1987-1991 was annexed to the report. UNDP reinforced its invitation to other United Nations organizations to utilize the management facilities and programming capacity of its Jerusalem office for projects sponsored by them. WHO, ILO and UNFPA had already launched projects with UNDP assistance, while consultations on possible co-operation were under way with the United Nations Industrial Development Organization (UNIDO).

UNDP's new role would provide a much larger range of project activities, greater emphasis on basic development projects, a structure for easy incorporation of external inputs and greater reliance on local assessment of basic needs. In addition to infrastructure projects already under implementation, UNDP proposed four new projects: a water-purification project in the Gaza Strip ($400,000); a sewage system for the Nablus area ($300,000); construction of commercial centres to establish income-generating small businesses ($750,000); and assistance to municipalities ($1 million). In agriculture, three UNDP projects were completed by March 1988, covering training, development and a hydrology laboratory at the cost of some $619,000. FAO continued to provide two fellowships in agricultural economics and one in animal production, with a total budget of $68,500. It also assisted Al-Quds University at Jerusalem to develop its curriculum in agriculture. In education, UNDP-assisted projects dealing with pre-primary education and promotion of vocational training were completed by March at a cost of $1.8 million, to which UNDP contributed $632,700.

On 29 April, pursuant to a decision of the Administrative Committee on Co-ordination,[26] the Director-General for Development and International Economic Co-operation convened a meeting of United Nations bodies to discuss assistance to the Palestinian people of the occupied territories. All participants expressed willingness to expand their activities there, provided additional funding was available.

UNCTAD, through its Special Economic Unit (Palestinian people), continued to prepare reports and technical publications on developments in the economic conditions of the occupied territories. ESCWA collaborated with UNCTAD in preparing a study on the Palestinian financial sector under Israeli occupation. An August report by the UNCTAD secretariat[27] updated major economic developments in the territories and analysed their external trade (see below, under "Economic and social conditions of Palestinians").

UNICEF worked on reducing water-related diseases in 25 villages in the West Bank, Gaza and the Jordan Valley for the benefit of 140,000 people, in addition to health education campaigns, with estimated expenditures amounting to $160,000 in 1988. A pilot project was initiated to introduce communities, on a self-help basis, to early childhood stimulation and development for, eventually, 10,000 children at a total cost of $230,000. UNICEF also provided an expanded immunization programme and diarrhoeal disease control. UNFPA approved $88,000 to support three WHO collaborating centres for primary health care research in the West Bank and Gaza.

UNCHS was preparing an in-depth study on future needs for infrastructure in the Palestinian territories. Pursuant to two 1987 resolutions of the Commission on Human Settlements,[28] UNCHS prepared reports on housing requirements of a future independent Palestinian State and on the reconstruction needed in Palestinian camps in Lebanon. By a resolution of 12 April 1988,[29] the Commission requested the UNCHS Executive Director to assist Palestinians in rebuilding their houses destroyed by the occupying authorities and to report on progress made.

UNDP completed in March 1988 a project on training in industrial management and had two others—on industrial olive-oil development and on glass and ceramics—under way with a funding of $690,000, while UPU provided two training fellowships to the Arab Faculty of Posts (Damascus, Syrian Arab Republic) for two Palestinian nationals.

In conclusion,[21] the Secretary-General stated that the programme of assistance had inevitably been affected by the uprising in the territories. Nevertheless, in spite of serious disruptions due to strikes, curfews and violent actions during recent months, measurable progress had been achieved by all United Nations agencies involved. Additional projects had become operational or had been identified, even though the pace of project delivery slowed down from time to time.

Developments in the territories had the effect of attracting far greater international attention, and additional funds for development assistance, as well as relief services, had been forthcoming. However, additional funding was urgently needed. As more resources became available, the Secretary-General would continue to implement and develop the programme further.

ECONOMIC AND SOCIAL COUNCIL ACTION

On 26 July 1988, on the recommendation of its Third (Programme and Co-ordination) Committee, the Economic and Social Council adopted **resolution 1988/54** by roll-call vote.

Assistance to the Palestinian people

The Economic and Social Council,

Recalling General Assembly resolution 42/166 of 11 December 1987,

Recalling also Economic and Social Council resolution 1987/77 of 8 July 1987,

Bearing in mind the Declaration on the Granting of Independence to Colonial Countries and Peoples,

Recalling the Programme of Action for the Achievement of Palestinian Rights, adopted by the International Conference on the Question of Palestine,

Taking into account the uprising of the Palestinian people in the occupied Palestinian territories against the Israeli occupation, including its economic and social policies and practices,

Affirming that the Palestinian people cannot develop their national economy as long as the Israeli occupation persists,

Aware of the increasing need to provide economic and social assistance to the Palestinian people,

1. *Takes note* of the report of the Secretary-General on assistance to the Palestinian people;

2. *Regrets* that the programme of economic and social assistance to the Palestinian people has not been developed as requested by the General Assembly in its resolution 42/166;

3. *Requests* the Secretary-General to charge the United Nations Centre for Human Settlements (Habitat) with supervising the development of the programme and to provide it with the funds needed to engage twenty experts to prepare an adequate programme, in close co-operation with the Palestine Liberation Organization, taking into account the uprising of the Palestinian people in the occupied Palestinian territories and its implications;

4. *Expresses its appreciation* to those States, United Nations bodies and intergovernmental and non-governmental organizations that have provided assistance to the Palestinian people;

5. *Urges* the international community, the organizations of the United Nations system, other intergovernmental organizations and non-governmental organizations to disburse their aid or any other forms of assistance to the occupied Palestinian territories solely for the benefit of the Palestinian people and in a manner that will not serve to prolong the Israeli occupation;

6. *Calls* for the provision of emergency assistance to the Palestinian people in the occupied Palestinian territories, including the dispatch of teams of orthopaedic surgeons;

7. *Requests* the international community, the organizations of the United Nations system, other intergovernmental organizations and non-governmental organizations to sustain and increase their assistance to the

Palestinian people in close co-operation with the Palestine Liberation Organization;

8. *Decides* to extend to the occupied Palestinian territories the same preferential treatment accorded to the least developed countries, pending the elimination of the Israeli occupation and the assumption of full control by the Palestinian people over their national economy without external interference;

9. *Calls* for the treatment on a transit basis of Palestinian exports and imports passing through neighbouring ports and points of exit and entry;

10. *Also calls* for the granting of trade concessions and concrete preferential measures for Palestinian exports;

11. *Further calls* for the implementation of development projects in the occupied Palestinian territories, including the cement plant referred to in General Assembly resolution 39/223 of 18 December 1984;

12. *Condemns* the occupying Power, Israel, for its brutal economic and social policies and practices against the Palestinian people in the occupied Palestinian territories;

13. *Requests* United Nations bodies not to extend any form of assistance to the occupying Power, Israel;

14. *Stresses* that aid is not and cannot be a substitute for a genuine and just solution to the question of Palestine;

15. *Requests* the Secretary-General to issue immediately a corrigendum to his report on assistance to the Palestinian people, bringing the language strictly into line with General Assembly resolution 42/166 and the present resolution;

16. *Requests* the Secretary-General to report to the General Assembly at its forty-fourth session, through the Economic and Social Council, on the progress made in the implementation of the present resolution.

Economic and Social Council resolution 1988/54

26 July 1988   Meeting 38   33-1-17 (roll-call vote)

Approved by Third Committee (E/1988/107) by vote (29-1-15), 15 July (meeting 8); 18-nation draft (E/1988/C.3/L.5); amended in Council by 12 nations (E/1988/L.48); agenda item 19.

Sponsors of draft: Afghanistan, Algeria, Bangladesh, Democratic Yemen, Egypt, German Democratic Republic, Iraq, Kuwait, Libyan Arab Jamahiriya, Morocco, Pakistan, Saudi Arabia, Somalia, Sudan, Syrian Arab Republic, Tunisia, Yemen, Zimbabwe.

Sponsors of amendment: Egypt, German Democratic Republic, Iraq, Libyan Arab Jamahiriya, Morocco, Pakistan, Saudi Arabia, Somalia, Sudan, Syrian Arab Republic, Tunisia, Zimbabwe.

Financial implications: S-G, E/1988/C.3/L.13.

Roll-call vote in Council as follows:

In favour: Bolivia, Bulgaria, Byelorussian SSR, China, Cuba, Egypt, German Democratic Republic, Ghana, Guinea, India, Iran, Iraq, Lesotho, Liberia, Libyan Arab Jamahiriya, Mozambique, Oman, Pakistan, Panama, Peru, Philippines, Poland, Rwanda, Saudi Arabia, Sierra Leone, Somalia, Sri Lanka, Sudan, Syrian Arab Republic, USSR, Venezuela, Yugoslavia, Zaire.

Against: United States.

Abstaining: Australia, Belgium, Canada, Colombia, Denmark, France, Germany, Federal Republic of, Greece, Ireland, Italy, Jamaica, Japan, Norway, Portugal, Trinidad and Tobago, United Kingdom, Uruguay.

An amendment in the Council calling for the insertion of paragraph 15, requesting the Secretary-General to issue a corrigendum to his report,[21] was adopted by a roll-call vote of 34 to 1, with 16 abstentions. The Sudan, introducing the amendment on behalf of its sponsors, said they had first acquiesced in the ruling by the President that the matter should be dealt with by the Secretariat, but had become convinced that the Secretariat found itself constrained. The language of the Secretary-General's report was not consistent with the corresponding 1987 Assembly resolution,[9] as had been pointed out in the Third Committee on several occasions. By adopting the amendment, the Council could dispose of the issue.

GENERAL ASSEMBLY ACTION

On 20 December, on the recommendation of the Second (Economic and Financial) Committee, the General Assembly adopted **resolution 43/178** by recorded vote.

Assistance to the Palestinian people

The General Assembly,

Recalling its resolution 42/166 of 11 December 1987,

Taking note of Economic and Social Council resolution 1988/54 of 26 July 1988,

Bearing in mind the Declaration on the Granting of Independence to Colonial Countries and Peoples,

Recalling the Programme of Action for the Achievement of Palestinian Rights, adopted by the International Conference on the Question of Palestine,

Taking into account the *intifadah* of the Palestinian people in the occupied Palestinian territory, including Jerusalem, against the Israeli occupation including its economic and social policies and practices,

Affirming that the Palestinian people cannot develop their national economy as long as the Israeli occupation persists,

Taking into consideration the recent steps taken by Jordan concerning the occupied Palestinian West Bank,

Aware of the increasing need to provide economic and social assistance to the Palestinian people,

1. *Takes note* of the report of the Secretary-General on assistance to the Palestinian people;

2. *Regrets* that the programme of economic and social assistance to the Palestinian people has not been developed as requested by the General Assembly in its resolution 42/166;

3. *Requests* the Secretary-General to charge the United Nations Centre for Human Settlements (Habitat) with supervising the development of the programme and to provide it with the funds needed to engage twenty experts to prepare an adequate programme, in close co-operation with the Palestine Liberation Organization, taking into account the *intifadah* of the Palestinian people in the occupied Palestinian territory, including Jerusalem, and its implications;

4. *Expresses its appreciation* to those States, United Nations bodies and intergovernmental and non-governmental organizations that have provided assistance to the Palestinian people;

5. *Urges* Member States, organizations of the United Nations system and intergovernmental and non-governmental organizations to disburse their aid or any other forms of assistance to the occupied Palestinian territory solely for the benefit of the Palestinian people and in a manner that will not serve to prolong the Israeli occupation;

6. *Calls* for the provision of emergency assistance to the Palestinian people in the occupied Palestinian territory, including the dispatch of teams of orthopaedic surgeons;

7. *Requests* Member States, organizations of the United Nations system and intergovernmental and non-governmental organizations to sustain and increase their assistance to the Palestinian people, in close co-operation with the Palestine Liberation Organization;

8. *Requests* all Member States and donors that provide any form of assistance to the occupied Palestinian West Bank to sustain and increase that assistance and to channel it to the Palestinian people through their representative, the Palestine Liberation Organization;

9. *Decides* to extend to the occupied Palestinian territory the same preferential treatment accorded the least developed countries, pending the elimination of the Israeli occupation and the assumption of full control by the Palestinian people over their national economy without external interference;

10. *Calls* for treatment on a transit basis of Palestinian exports and imports passing through neighbouring ports and points of exit and entry;

11. *Also calls* for the granting of trade concessions and concrete preferential measures for Palestinian exports on the basis of certificates of origin issued by Palestinian bodies designated by the Palestine Liberation Organization;

12. *Further calls* for the implementation of development projects in the occupied Palestinian territory, including the projects mentioned in its resolution 39/223 of 18 December 1984;

13. *Condemns* the occupying Power, Israel, for its brutal economic and social policies and practices against the Palestinian people in the occupied Palestinian territory;

14. *Requests* United Nations bodies not to extend any form of assistance to the occupying Power, Israel;

15. *Stresses* that aid is not and cannot be a substitute for a genuine and just solution to the question of Palestine;

16. *Requests* the Secretary-General to report to the General Assembly at its forty-fourth session, through the Economic and Social Council, on the progress made in the implementation of the present resolution.

General Assembly resolution 43/178

20 December 1988   Meeting 83   118-14-13 (recorded vote)

Approved by Second Committee (A/43/750/Add.2) by recorded vote (90-14-14), 4 November (meeting 32); 10-nation draft (A/C.2/43/L.13/Rev.2); agenda item 12.

Sponsors: Algeria, Bahrain, Cuba, Democratic Yemen, Egypt, Iraq, Mauritania, Pakistan, Saudi Arabia, Tunisia.

Meeting numbers. GA 43rd session: 2nd Committee 24, 32; plenary 83.

Recorded vote in Assembly as follows:

In favour: Afghanistan, Albania, Algeria, Angola, Antigua and Barbuda, Argentina, Bahrain, Bangladesh, Barbados, Benin, Bhutan, Bolivia, Botswana, Brazil, Brunei Darussalam, Bulgaria, Burkina Faso, Burma, Burundi, Byelorussian SSR, Cameroon, Cape Verde, Central African Republic, Chad, China, Congo, Cote d'Ivoire, Cuba, Cyprus, Czechoslovakia, Democratic Kampuchea, Democratic Yemen, Djibouti, Dominican Republic, Ecuador, Egypt, Equatorial Guinea, Ethiopia, Gabon, Gambia, German Democratic Republic, Ghana, Grenada, Guinea, Guinea-Bissau, Guyana, Hungary, India, Indonesia, Iran, Iraq, Jamaica, Jordan, Kenya, Kuwait, Lao People's Democratic Republic, Lesotho, Liberia, Libyan Arab Jamahiriya, Madagascar, Malawi, Malaysia, Maldives, Mali, Malta, Mauritania, Mauritius, Mexico, Mongolia, Morocco, Mozambique, Nepal, Nicaragua, Niger, Nigeria, Oman, Pakistan, Panama, Papua New Guinea, Paraguay, Peru, Philippines, Poland, Qatar, Romania, Rwanda, Saint Vincent and the Grenadines, Samoa, Sao Tome and Principe, Saudi Arabia, Senegal, Seychelles, Singapore, Solomon Islands, Somalia, Sri Lanka, Sudan, Suriname, Swaziland, Syrian Arab Republic, Thailand, Togo, Trinidad and Tobago, Tunisia, Turkey, Uganda, Ukrainian SSR, USSR, United Arab Emirates, United Republic of Tanzania, Uruguay, Vanuatu, Venezuela, Viet Nam, Yemen, Yugoslavia, Zaire, Zambia.

Against: Australia, Belgium, Canada, Denmark, France, Germany, Federal Republic of, Iceland, Israel, Luxembourg, Netherlands, Norway, Portugal, United Kingdom, United States.

Abstaining: Austria, Chile, Colombia, Costa Rica, Fiji, Finland, Greece, Ireland, Italy, Japan, New Zealand, Spain, Sweden.

Speaking before the vote in the Second Committee, Israel supported the idea of assistance to the Palestinians through UNDP, but said it would not receive the experts mentioned in paragraph 3 or any mission of inquiry. Channelling assistance to the territories through PLO was preposterous, and the suggestion of granting the occupied territories the preferential treatment accorded to LDCs had nothing to do with assistance in the conventional sense. The suggestion that Palestinian exports be granted trade concessions and preferential measures on the basis of certificates of origin issued by Palestinian bodies designated by PLO was indicative of the text's true intentions: producers or exporters not paying ransom to PLO would not get such concessions or preferential treatment. Instead of assistance, the text called for international approval of a PLO boycott, discrimination, economic warfare and extortion; it was an attempt to politicize the Second Committee's work and its real intention was to call for sanctions against Israel.

REFERENCES

(1)YUN 1987, p. 296. (2)A/43/273-S/19720. (3)A/43/407-S/19938. (4)A/43/35. (5)A/43/827-S/20278. (6)A/43/842. (7)YUN 1976, p. 235. (8)YUN 1980, p. 399. (9)YUN 1987, p. 272, GA res. 42/166, 11 Dec. 1987. (10)YUN 1975, p. 248, GA res. 3376(XXX), 10 Nov. 1975. (11)YUN 1983, p. 278, GA res. 38/58 C, 13 Dec. 1983. (12)*Ibid.*, p. 274. (13)YUN 1947-48, p. 247, GA res. 181 A (II), 29 Nov. 1947. (14)YUN 1986, p. 267, GA res. 41/43 D, 2 Dec. 1986. (15)YUN 1960, p. 49, GA res. 1514(XV), 14 Dec. 1960. (16)YUN 1987, p. 267, GA res. 42/66 C, 2 Dec. 1987. (17)A/43/683 & Add.1. (18)YUN 1987, p. 269, GA res. 42/209 D, 11 Dec. 1987. (19)YUN 1980, p. 426, SC res. 478(1980), 20 Aug. 1980. (20)YUN 1967, p. 209. (21)A/43/367-E/1988/82 & Corr.1,2. (22)S/19443. (23)DP/1988/13. (24)E/1988/19 (dec. 88/10). (25)DP/1988/23 & Corr.1. (26)ACC/1988/DEC/1-18 (dec. 1988/5). (27)TD/B/1183 & Corr.1. (28)YUN 1987, pp. 720 & 721. (29)A/43/8 (res. 11/10).

Incidents and disputes involving Arab countries and Israel

Israel and Iraq

At the close of its forty-second session on 19 September 1988, the General Assembly, by **decision 42/463**, included in the draft agenda of its forty-third session, beginning the following day, the item on armed Israeli aggression against Iraqi nuclear installations, which had been on its agenda since 1981[1] following the bombing that year by Israel of a nuclear research centre near Baghdad. However, the Assembly took no action on the item and, in suspending its forty-third session on 22 December, retained the item on the agenda of that session by **decision 43/459**.

Lebanon

Hostilities and violence continued to characterize the situation in Lebanon during 1988. Although the camps war in West Beirut between rival militias abated somewhat in July, new casualties continued to occur and hundreds of families were displaced by outbreaks of fighting. In central Lebanon, heavy shelling forced the closure of all schools in mid-March.

The fate of Alex Collett, a British journalist kidnapped in March 1985 while on assignment for UNWRA, remained unresolved, no word having been received from his kidnappers since 1986.

In February 1988, Lieutenant-Colonel William Higgins, a United States military observer of UNTSO serving with UNIFIL, was abducted in southern Lebanon, an action condemned by the Security Council (resolution 618(1988)).

Israel and Lebanon

The situation between Israel and Lebanon remained tense during 1988. Israel Defence Forces continued to occupy parts of southern Lebanon, which Israel had declared as its "security zone". Throughout the year, Lebanon addressed numerous communications to the Secretary-General and the Presidents of the Security Council and the General Assembly accusing Israel of ongoing military attacks against its territory, causing death and injury to many innocent civilians and widespread destruction and property damage. The Security Council convened throughout the year to consider aspects of the Middle East situation related to Lebanon. The Council met on three occasions (January, May and December) at Lebanon's request to consider specific charges of armed Israeli incursions, but was unable to take action due to the repeated negative vote of a permanent member (United States). By those resolutions, the Council would have called for urgent implementation of its previous resolutions demanding that Israel withdraw all its military forces from Lebanon. Israel maintained that it was forced to protect its territory and population from terrorist attacks launched from Lebanon.

In January and July, the Council unanimously extended UNIFIL's mandate for six months and, in July, demanded the immediate release of Lieutenant-Colonel William Higgins, who had been abducted while on duty on 17 February.

At the request of Lebanon for a Council meeting after bombing and rocket attacks by Israel, the Council convened on 15 and 18 January. Further hostile incidents were reported by Lebanon during March and April, as contained in the report of the Security Council for the period 16 June 1987 to 15 June 1988.[2] The incidents ranged from destruction of property to unlawful deportations, detentions and deliberate bombings of houses, resulting in civilian deaths. On 3 May, Lebanon reported that Israel had again invaded its southern territory, and requested another Council meeting. The Council subsequently convened on 6, 9 and 10 May.

Lebanon continued to inform of deportations, air attacks, detentions, arrests and destruction by Israel, including deportations of Palestinians into Lebanon,[3] the bombings of refugee camps and clinics,[4] attacks on Lebanese villages with air-to-ground missiles[5] and the arrest of Lebanese citizens on Lebanese territory, with subsequent sentencing by Israeli courts under Israeli law,[6] in violation of the fourth Geneva Convention. On 9 December, Lebanon reported a further massive attack against its territory by Israeli air, land and sea forces and again requested a Council meeting; the Council met on 14 December.

SECURITY COUNCIL CONSIDERATION (January)

Following two incidents on 2 January—the bombing by Israel of blocks of flats near Sidon and rocket attacks against two villages 80 kilometres from the Israeli border,[7] which resulted in 26 deaths, dozens of wounded and substantial material damage—Lebanon requested on 7 January[8] an urgent meeting of the Security Council. Acceding to the request, the Council held one meeting on 15 January and two on 18 January.

Meeting numbers. SC 2782-2784.

At their request, Israel, Jordan, Kuwait, Lebanon, Mauritania, Morocco, Saudi Arabia and the Syrian Arab Republic were invited to participate without the right to vote. At the request of Algeria,[9] the Acting Permanent Observer of the League of Arab States (LAS) was invited under rule 39[a] of the Council's provisional rules of procedure. Also at Algeria's request,[10] the Council decided, by 10 votes to 1 (United States), with 4 abstentions (France, Germany, Federal Republic of, Italy, United Kingdom), that an invitation to participate also be accorded to the PLO Permanent Observer. The invitation, though not made pursuant to rules 37[b] or 39, conferred on PLO the same rights as those conferred on a Member State when invited pursuant to rule 37.

Before the vote, the United States, which had requested it, said the only legal basis on which the Council might grant a hearing to persons speaking on behalf of non-governmental entities was rule 39. The United States opposed extending to PLO the same rights to participate as if it represented a Member State and did not agree with recent practice in the Council which appeared selectively to try to enhance the prestige of those who wished to speak through a departure from the Council's rules.

On 18 January, the Council voted on a draft resolution[11] submitted by Algeria, Argentina, Nepal, Senegal, Yugoslavia and Zambia. By that text, the Council would have strongly deplored Israel's repeated attacks against Lebanese territory and all other measures against the civilian population; strongly requested that Israel cease all acts of encroachment of land, construction of roads and setting up of fences that violated the border, and any attempts to occupy or change the status of Lebanese territory or impede the return of the effective authority of the Government of Lebanon in its sovereign territory; and reaffirmed its calls for strict respect for Lebanon's sovereignty, independence, unity and territorial integrity within its internationally recognized boundaries. It would also have reaffirmed Council resolutions of 1978[12] and 1982,[13] which demanded that Israel withdraw all its military forces unconditionally, and the Secretary-General would have been requested to continue consultations with Lebanon and other parties directly concerned with regard to implementing those resolutions.

The vote was 13 to 1, with 1 abstention, as follows:

In favour: Algeria, Argentina, Brazil, China, France, Germany, Federal Republic of, Italy, Japan, Nepal, Senegal, USSR, Yugoslavia, Zambia.

Against: United States.

Abstaining: United Kingdom.

The draft was not adopted owing to the negative vote of a permanent member.

Speaking before the vote, Lebanon charged Israel with violating its sovereignty. Any attempt by Israel to deny that violation and to justify it citing reasons of security was unacceptable. Israel's stepped-up inhuman policies and acts of oppression had claimed increasing numbers of civilian victims and caused widespread destruction of cities, villages and farmlands; the Council had a responsibility to impose security and peace in an extremely explosive area that might erupt at any moment.

Israel said that if Lebanon's sovereignty was in question, it was violated by Iran, the Syrian Arab Republic and PLO, which were using Lebanon for terrorist attacks against Israel. Israel itself was taking ongoing self-defence measures that were restrained,

[a]Rule 39 of the Council's provisional rules of procedure states: "The Security Council may invite members of the Secretariat or other persons, whom it considers competent for the purpose, to supply it with information or to give other assistance in examining matters within its competence."

[b]Rule 37 of the Council's provisional rules of procedure states: "Any Member of the United Nations which is not a member of the Security Council may be invited, as the result of a decision of the Security Council, to participate, without vote, in the discussion of any question brought before the Security Council when the Security Council considers that the interests of that Member are specially affected, or when a Member brings a matter to the attention of the Council in accordance with Article 35(1) of the Charter."

temporary but necessary for its security in the absence of a Lebanese Government capable of assuming its responsibilities. Israel had no territorial claim against Lebanon but wanted restoration of Lebanese sovereignty by a strong central Government over all of Lebanon and security arrangements until such a Government emerged.

The PLO Observer averred that the exercise of State terrorism by Israel against Palestinian refugee camps and civilians in south Lebanon were acts of aggression and manifestations of genocide. Israel's total, unconditional and immediate withdrawal from Lebanon was a *conditio sine qua non* for achieving a comprehensive, just and lasting peace.

Speaking after the vote, the United States—stressing its support for Lebanon's independence, sovereignty and territorial integrity within its internationally recognized boundaries—said that continuing a review of the situation in southern Lebanon, without an attendant concern for the security of northern Israel, would have no consequence; peace and stability could not come to south Lebanon until the border between the two countries was secure.

SECURITY COUNCIL CONSIDERATION (May)

By a letter of 3 May,[14] Lebanon informed the Secretary-General that the day before large contingents of the Israeli army had again invaded southern Lebanon. An estimated 2,000 soldiers, supported by tanks, artillery and military helicopters, had crossed the southern Lebanese border, passed through the so-called security zone, an area Israel continued to occupy, and penetrated some 15 kilometres north to the town of Lebbaya. Lebanon charged Israel with heavy shelling of villages, raiding and destroying houses, ruining crops, terrorizing the population and arresting many. The invasion was accompanied by the deployment of Israeli navy vessels along the Lebanese coast between Sidon and Tyre, as well as overflights by the Israeli air force, which dropped flare canisters on those and other towns.

At the request of Lebanon,[15] the Council met on 6, 9 and 10 May to consider the situation in southern Lebanon.

Meeting numbers. SC 2811, 2813, 2814.

At their request, Bahrain, Israel, Jordan, Kuwait, Lebanon, the Libyan Arab Jamahiriya, Qatar, Saudi Arabia, Somalia, the Syrian Arab Republic and Tunisia were invited to participate without the right to vote. At Algeria's request,[16] an invitation was also extended to the Permanent Observer of LAS under rule 39[a] of the Council's provisional rules of procedure.

Algeria further requested[17] that an invitation be extended to the Permanent Observer of PLO to participate in the debate, in accordance with the

Council's past practice. The President stated that the proposal was not made pursuant to rule 37[b] or 39 but that, if approved, the invitation would confer on PLO the same rights of participation as those conferred on a Member State under rule 37.

The request was approved by 10 votes to 1 (United States), with 4 abstentions (France, Germany, Federal Republic of, Italy, United Kingdom). The United States, which had requested the vote, reiterated its previously stated position (see above).

On 10 May, the Council voted on a draft resolution[18] sponsored by Algeria, Argentina, Nepal, Senegal, Yugoslavia and Zambia, by which the Council would have condemned Israel's recent invasion of southern Lebanon; repeated the call for immediate Israeli withdrawal and for the cessation of all acts violating Lebanon's sovereignty and its population's security; reaffirmed its call for strict respect for Lebanon's sovereignty, independence, unity and territorial integrity within its internationally recognized boundaries; reaffirmed the urgent need to restore international peace and security by implementing Council resolutions of 1978[12] and 1982;[13] and requested the Secretary-General to continue consultations with Lebanon and other parties directly concerned.

The vote was 14 to 1, as follows:

> *In favour:* Algeria, Argentina, Brazil, China, France, Germany, Federal Republic of, Italy, Japan, Nepal, Senegal, USSR, United Kingdom, Yugoslavia, Zambia.
> *Against:* United States.

The draft was not adopted owing to the negative vote of a permanent member.

Repeating its charges before the Council, Lebanon called the invasion an unjustified flagrant violation of its sovereignty, territorial waters and national airspace, flouting the Charter, international law and Council resolutions. The Council was duty-bound to act to pre-empt Israel from continuously perpetrating a policy of violence and expansion.

Israel reiterated that it had no territorial claims to any Lebanese territory. The current arrangements on Israel's northern border resulted from security constraints and were designed solely to protect its northern population centres against repeated attacks emanating from Lebanese territory. Those security arrangements would be essential only as long as there was no central Lebanese authority capable of preventing such attacks. Israel wished to see Lebanese sovereignty restored in all areas of the country by a central Government that would effectively unify the State and be responsible for security within its territory and borders.

During its two-day operation in southern Lebanon, carried out to prevent terrorist groups from re-establishing an infrastructure from which they launched attacks on Israel, Israel had made every effort to avoid civilian casualties. It respected the universal principles of sovereignty and territorial integrity, but could not allow its own sovereignty and territorial integrity to be compromised. It believed that the only feasible solution to the problems on both sides of the border could be found in mutually agreed, adequate security arrangements, which were essential as long as there was no central Lebanese authority.

Speaking after the vote, the United States said the Council should not address the problems of southern Lebanon in resolutions that failed to recognize the attacks and reprisals originating on both sides of the Israeli-Lebanese border. The United States had called publicly and repeatedly for the withdrawal of all foreign troops from Lebanon and the extension of central-government authority through the Council.

SECURITY COUNCIL CONSIDERATION (December)

On 9 December, Israeli air and naval forces heavily bombarded the Lebanese town of Na'imah and the surrounding hills, as well as the Shuwayfat-Sa'diyat-Bi'wirta triangle 20 kilometres south of Beirut. Helicopters then carried out an airborne landing of Israeli troops, which was followed by severe clashes. According to Lebanon,[19] the attack and resistance to it resulted in large-scale human and material losses.

At Lebanon's request,[20] the Council met on 14 December to consider the situation. Israel and Lebanon were invited at their request to participate without the right to vote under rule 37[b] of the Council's provisional rules of procedure.

Meeting number. SC 2832.

The Council voted on a draft resolution by Algeria, Argentina, Nepal, Senegal, Yugoslavia and Zambia.[21] By wording almost identical to the texts put forward in January and May, the Council would have strongly deplored the most recent attack, requested that Israel cease immediately all such attacks and reaffirmed the urgent need to implement the Council's resolutions on Lebanon.

The draft received 14 votes to 1, as follows:

In favour: Algeria, Argentina, Brazil, China, France, Germany, Federal Republic of, Italy, Japan, Nepal, Senegal, USSR, United Kingdom, Yugoslavia, Zambia.

Against: United States.

The text was not adopted owing to the negative vote of a permanent member.

Lebanon stated that the attack was further proof that Israel considered as fair game Lebanon's sovereignty and territorial integrity, its soil and territorial waters. The operation, timed to mark the first anniversary of the *intifadah*, was aimed at restoring the confidence of the Israeli army, which had failed to quell the Palestinian uprising. Lebanon appealed to the Council—which, it said, was responsible for protecting the sovereignty of Member States, as well as for maintaining international peace and security—to protect its sovereignty, redress the injustice inflicted on its people and stop the bloodshed, by deterring Israel through a firm and courageous stance.

Israel repeated its position that it had no territorial claims with regard to Lebanon; its mere desire was to ensure the security of its population from attacks emanating from there. On 9 December it had targeted in a limited operation the headquarters of the General Command of the Popular Front for the Liberation of Palestine—a PLO faction led by Ahmed Jibril—and its terrorist training camps in the hills north of Dammur.

After the vote, the United States explained that it opposed the draft resolution because it criticized action by one party while ignoring attacks originating from the other side of the border. Requesting Israel to cease all attacks against Lebanese territory regardless of provocation would deny its right to self-defence.

UNIFIL

During 1988, at the request of Lebanon and on the recommendation of the Secretary-General, the Security Council twice extended the mandate of the United Nations Interim Force in Lebanon, in January and July, each time for a six-month period. Established by the Council in 1978[22] following Israel's invasion of Lebanon in March of that year,[23] UNIFIL was entrusted with restoring international peace and security; confirming the withdrawal of Israeli forces from Lebanese territory; and re-establishing the Lebanese Government's effective authority in the area.

After a second Israeli invasion in 1982,[24] the Council authorized[25] the Force additionally to provide protection and humanitarian assistance to the local population.

Composition

As of July 1988,[26] UNIFIL had a strength of 5,844 troops. It was composed of contingents from nine countries: Fiji, 701; Finland, 543; France, 502; Ghana, 901; Ireland, 744; Italy, 52; Nepal, 856; Norway, 906; Sweden, 639. The Force was assisted by 64 unarmed military observers of UNTSO organized as Observer Group Lebanon (OGL). The Lebanese army unit serving with UNIFIL maintained a strength of 128.

On 30 March,[27] the Secretary-General informed the President of the Security Council that the current Commander of UNIFIL, Lieutenant-General Gustav Hägglund of Finland, in office since 1 June 1986, was being recalled by his Government to assume a new command. Therefore, the Secretary-General intended, subject to Council approval, to appoint Lieutenant-General

Lars-Eric Wahlgren of Sweden as the new Commander from 1 July 1988. The Council agreed to that appointment on 20 April.[28]

Report of the Secretary-General (January). The Secretary-General reported to the Security Council on developments in the UNIFIL area of operation from 25 July 1987 to 22 January 1988.[29]

During that period, seven members of the Force lost their lives, including two Nepalese soldiers killed by hostile firing and two French, one Irish, one Nepalese and one Swedish soldier who died from accidents or other causes. In addition, an Australian military observer from UNTSO assigned to OGL was killed by a mine and a Canadian observer was severely injured in the same incident; 11 soldiers were wounded by hostile action. Since the establishment of UNIFIL, 151 members of the Force had died, 60 of them as a result of firing and mine or bomb explosions, 63 in accidents and 28 from other causes. More than 200 had been wounded by firing and mine or bomb explosions.

The situation in UNIFIL's area of operation remained essentially unchanged. Israel continued to maintain in southern Lebanon its "security zone", manned by Israel Defence Forces (IDF) and the so-called South Lebanon Army (SLA). Within the UNIFIL area, IDF and SLA maintained 57 positions, 15 of which were located within the battalion sectors. Of these, 14 were manned permanently. During the reporting period, three IDF/SLA positions were closed in the Nepalese battalion sector and one was closed in the Finnish sector.

Armed resistance groups continued to launch frequent operations against IDF and SLA using small arms, rocket-propelled grenades, rockets and mortars, as well as mines and roadside bombs. UNIFIL recorded 60 such operations from August to December 1987, and nine in the first half of January 1988. In two cases, attacks were carried out by armed elements estimated to number up to 200 men.

Until the middle of October 1987, most of the resistance operations in the UNIFIL area were directed against two adjacent SLA positions on Tallet Huqban, overlooking the villages of Kafra and Yatar in the Nepalese battalion sector. In numerous instances, the personnel in those positions fired at civilian as well as UNIFIL targets within their range. During August 1987, 13 women and children were injured by unprovoked firing from those positions. In some instances, local armed elements retaliated, notably on 29 August when some 200 armed elements infiltrated the area and attacked the positions on Tallet Huqban with mortars, rocket-propelled grenades and machine-guns. On 14 October, IDF/SLA evacuated the two positions on Tallet Huqban and UNIFIL occupied one of them. The other position, heavily mined by IDF, was left vacant.

IDF/SLA continued firing frequently from their positions or when on patrol. When attacked, they generally responded with heavy artillery and tank and mortar shelling, also employing helicopter gunships. Such firing at or near UNIFIL positions increased, particularly in the Irish battalion sector. Frequently the firing was unprovoked and apparently deliberate, causing UNIFIL to protest some 300 such incidents to the Israeli military authorities.

While the Norwegian battalion sector had previously been relatively quiet, the situation changed in early August when IDF asserted its intention to operate in the area and SLA personnel increasingly objected to UNIFIL check-point controls. This resulted in harassment of and attacks on UNIFIL positions, including the shelling of a Norwegian patrol by an IDF tank and several instances of forced entry into UNIFIL positions by SLA personnel.

On 32 occasions, unidentified armed elements fired at or near UNIFIL positions, and, on 25 August 1987, a Nepalese soldier was killed and three others were wounded west of Kafra. On 12 January 1988, an Australian captain was killed and a Canadian major was seriously injured when their OGL patrol vehicle hit a land-mine west of the village of Shama in the "security zone".

The Force continued to co-operate with the Lebanese authorities and humanitarian assistance agencies in extending aid to the local population. Some 3,000 Lebanese civilians were treated at the UNIFIL hospital at Naqoura, including more than 250 in-patients.

In conclusion, the Secretary-General noted that UNIFIL had been prevented from making further progress to implement in full the objectives of Council resolution 425(1978).[22] Ten years later, the conditions still did not exist for UNIFIL to perform its functions fully or fulfil its mandate completely. Although the circumstances under which UNIFIL was established had changed, the objectives set by resolution 425(1978) remained valid. The Lebanese authorities maintained that Israel should withdraw completely and allow UNIFIL's deployment to the international border. Israel, however, with its own forces and those of SLA, continued to maintain a "security zone" in southern Lebanon, saying that it could not allow the deployment of UNIFIL to the border as there was no central Government in Beirut able to exercise authority throughout the area. In its view, UNIFIL as a peace-keeping force was not able, under its current terms of reference, to assume such responsibility.

The Secretary-General stressed that the Force could not implement its mandate successfully without the full co-operation of the Israeli authorities, whose position was an essential factor. He believed that the somewhat limited level of violence in southern Lebanon during the period under review was particularly due to the presence of UNIFIL, which maintained calm in the area after IDF/SLA's withdrawal from Tallet Huqban and the subsequent return of thousands of inhabitants to Yatar and Kafra.

On 20 January 1988,[30] the Secretary-General received a request from Lebanon for UNIFIL's extension for a further six-month period. He observed that, although the state of affairs in which the Force found itself after 10 years of deployment was contrary to the expectations of the Council, UNIFIL remained an important mechanism for conflict control in a very volatile situation which, without UNIFIL, could quickly escalate into a wider conflict.

SECURITY COUNCIL ACTION (January)

The Security Council met on 29 January to consider the Secretary-General's report and, without debate, unanimously adopted **resolution 609(1988)**.

The Security Council,

Recalling its resolutions 425(1978) and 426(1978) of 19 March 1978, 501(1982) of 25 February 1982, 508(1982) of 5 June 1982, 509(1982) of 6 June 1982 and 520(1982) of 17 September 1982, as well as all its resolutions on the situation in Lebanon,

Having studied the report of the Secretary-General on the United Nations Interim Force in Lebanon of 22 January 1988, and taking note of observations expressed therein,

Taking note of the letter dated 20 January 1988 from the Permanent Representative of Lebanon to the United Nations addressed to the Secretary-General,

Responding to the request of the Government of Lebanon,

1. *Decides* to extend the present mandate of the United Nations Interim Force in Lebanon for a further interim period of six months, that is, until 31 July 1988;

2. *Reiterates* its strong support for the territorial integrity, sovereignty and independence of Lebanon within its internationally recognized boundaries;

3. *Re-emphasizes* the terms of reference and general guidelines of the Force as stated in the report of the Secretary-General of 19 March 1978, approved by resolution 426(1978), and calls upon all parties concerned to co-operate fully with the Force for the full implementation of its mandate;

4. *Reiterates* that the Force should fully implement its mandate as defined in resolutions 425(1978), 426(1978) and all other relevant resolutions;

5. *Requests* the Secretary-General to continue consultations with the Government of Lebanon and other parties directly concerned on the implementation of the present resolution and to report to the Security Council thereon.

Security Council resolution 609(1988)

29 January 1988　　　Meeting 2788　　　Adopted unanimously

Draft prepared in consultations among Council members (S/19461).

Report of the Secretary-General (July). In his report on UNIFIL covering the period from 23 January to 25 July 1988,[26] the Secretary-General stated that the situation in the UNIFIL area re-

mained essentially unchanged, with Israel continuing to control the so-called security zone in southern Lebanon, through IDF/SLA. Within the UNIFIL area, IDF and SLA maintained a total of 54 positions, with IDF personnel being observed in SLA positions on many occasions, especially at night.

Resistance groups continued to launch frequent attacks against IDF and SLA, using small arms, rocket-propelled grenades, rockets and mortars, as well as mines and roadside bombs. From January to June, UNIFIL recorded an average of 19 such operations each month, with many more in the "security zone" where UNIFIL was not deployed. On 28 January, some 150 men attacked SLA positions at Rshaf and Brashit. IDF/SLA continued to respond with heavy artillery, tank and mortar shelling, at times employing Israeli helicopter gunships and shelling villages in retaliation.

During the period under review, two Force members, an Irish and a French soldier, lost their lives in accidents; 15 soldiers suffered injuries, 1 as a result of hostile fire and 5 from mine explosions. This brought to 153 the number of killed and 220 wounded members of the Force since its establishment.

In addition to co-operating in rendering humanitarian assistance in the area, UNIFIL provided its Naqoura hospital to treat some 5,000 Lebanese civilians, 250 of them as in-patients.

The Secretary-General regretted to inform the Council that no further progress was made towards attaining the objectives of Council resolution 425(1978),[22] namely the withdrawal of Israeli forces from Lebanese territory, restoration of international peace and security, and re-establishment of the Lebanese Government's authority in the area.

The Secretary-General reported that the Lebanese authorities viewed with increasing frustration and apprehension the apparent permanence of the Israeli military presence on Lebanese territory, rejecting it as a matter of principle. They were convinced that Israel's early withdrawal and the deployment of UNIFIL to the internationally recognized boundary would improve considerably the prospects for solving the very serious problems facing Lebanon. Israel restated its position regarding the Lebanese Government's inability to exercise effective authority in preventing its territory from being used to launch attacks against Israel. The Secretary-General averred that, however much Israel had a legitimate interest in protecting itself, that interest was not legitimately served by maintaining Israeli military forces in Lebanon and thus infringing on Lebanon's sovereignty and territorial integrity.

He referred to a message received from the President of Lebanon on 11 July, urging a renewal of efforts aimed at exploring practical steps towards implementing the Council's requests, particularly resolution 425(1978), and asking the United Nations to start a new momentum. Concerning Lebanon's request of 13 July for a renewal of UNIFIL's mandate,[31] the Secretary-General restated that the Force played an important role in controlling the level of violence in a very volatile situation prone to even wider conflict. Furthermore, the Force provided humanitarian support to the inhabitants of the area, a role which would be enhanced through co-operation with his newly appointed Special Representative for the Reconstruction and Development of Lebanon (see PART THREE, Chapter III). In recommending renewal of the UNIFIL mandate, the Secretary-General urged again that efforts be made to bring about Israel's withdrawal from Lebanon.

SECURITY COUNCIL ACTION (July)

On 29 July 1988, without debate, the Security Council, having considered the Secretary-General's report, unanimously adopted **resolution 617(1988)**.

The Security Council,

Recalling its resolutions 425(1978) and 426(1978) of 19 March 1978, 501(1982) of 25 February 1982, 508(1982) of 5 June 1982, 509(1982) of 6 June 1982 and 520(1982) of 17 September 1982, as well as all its resolutions on the situation in Lebanon,

Having studied the report of the Secretary-General on the United Nations Interim Force in Lebanon of 25 July 1988, and taking note of observations expressed therein,

Taking note of the letter dated 13 July 1988 from the Permanent Representative of Lebanon to the United Nations addressed to the Secretary-General,

Responding to the request of the Government of Lebanon,

1. *Decides* to extend the present mandate of the United Nations Interim Force in Lebanon for a further interim period of six months, that is, until 31 January 1989;

2. *Reiterates* its strong support for the territorial integrity, sovereignty and independence of Lebanon within its internationally recognized boundaries;

3. *Re-emphasizes* the terms of reference and general guidelines of the Force as stated in the report of the Secretary-General of 19 March 1978, approved by resolution 426(1978), and calls upon all parties concerned to co-operate fully with the Force for the full implementation of its mandate;

4. *Reiterates* that the Force should fully implement its mandate as defined in resolutions 425(1978), 426(1978) and all other relevant resolutions;

5. *Requests* the Secretary-General to continue consultations with the Government of Lebanon and other parties directly concerned on the implementation of the present resolution and to report to the Security Council thereon.

Security Council resolution 617(1988)

29 July 1988   Meeting 2822   Adopted unanimously

Draft prepared in consultations among Council members (S/20069).

Financing

The Secretary-General reported in November 1988[32] that, as at 30 September, contributions totalling $1,208.5 million had been received for the operation of UNIFIL out of $1,538.8 million apportioned among Member States since the inception of the Force on 19 March 1978. Of the unpaid balance of $330.3 million, only $105.1 million could be considered collectible, leaving a shortfall of $225.2 million, including $19.6 million due from China transferred to a special account in accordance with a 1981 General Assembly resolution.[33] As a consequence, UNIFIL was unable to meet its obligations on a current basis, particularly to troop-contributing countries, which had never been paid on a current and full basis in accordance with established rates. The UNIFIL Suspense Account, set up in 1979[34] to facilitate reimbursement to them for equipment and supplies, had thus far not achieved that purpose. Troop-contributing countries had expressed serious concern about the heavy burden placed on their Governments.

As at 30 September 1988, voluntary contributions totalling $1.3 million had been received from Governments, in addition to $3 million to defray expenses for the prospective acquisition of logistic equipment and supplies. Use of the latter voluntary contribution was subject to consultation with the donor Government based on proposals from the Secretariat.

For the mandate periods from 1 February 1988 to 31 January 1989, $141,180,000 gross ($139,416,000 net) was authorized for UNIFIL.[35] The costs of UNIFIL for the 12-month period beginning 1 February 1989 were estimated at $143,340,000 gross ($141,072,000 net), based on an average Force strength of 5,850 troops. On a net basis, that was $1,656,000 (1.2 per cent) more than the estimate for the previous period. In the event that future decisions of the Security Council required additional commitments, authorization was to be sought from the General Assembly if in session at the time, or by recourse to the 1987 Assembly resolution on unforeseen and extraordinary expenses for the biennium 1988-1989,[36] with the prior concurrence of the Advisory Committee on Administrative and Budgetary Questions (ACABQ). In the latter case, if the amounts exceeded the financial limit stipulated in the resolution, a special Assembly session would have to be convened.

In December 1988,[37] ACABQ reported that the audited accounts for the UNIFIL Special Account indicated a ''surplus'' balance of $6,313,362 as at 31 December 1987 for the 1986-1987 biennium, representing an excess of income over expenditure due to interest and miscellaneous credits accrued to the account, ''income'' referring to assessed contributions irrespective of collectibility. However, due to the withholding of contributions by Member States, the surplus balance had been drawn upon to the full extent. ACABQ was of the view that savings could be achieved in the maintenance of transport equipment and supplies and services. It therefore recommended that the UNIFIL budget for the 12 months beginning 1 February 1989 not exceed $142,842,000 gross ($140,574,000 net) and that the Assembly approve accordingly commitment authority up to $11,903,500 gross ($11,714,500 net) per month.

GENERAL ASSEMBLY ACTION

On 21 December 1988, on the recommendation of the Fifth (Administrative and Budgetary) Committee, the General Assembly adopted **resolution 43/229** by recorded vote.

Financing of the United Nations Interim Force in Lebanon

The General Assembly,

Having considered the report of the Secretary-General on the financing of the United Nations Interim Force in Lebanon and the related report of the Advisory Committee on Administrative and Budgetary Questions,

Bearing in mind Security Council resolution 425(1978) of 19 March 1978, by which the Council established the United Nations Interim Force in Lebanon, and the subsequent resolutions by which the Council extended the mandate of the Force, the latest of which was resolution 617(1988) of 29 July 1988,

Recalling its resolution S-8/2 of 21 April 1978 on the financing of the United Nations Interim Force in Lebanon and its subsequent resolutions thereon, the latest of which was resolution 42/223 of 21 December 1987,

Reaffirming its previous decisions regarding the fact that, in order to meet the expenditures caused by such operations, a different procedure from the one applied to meet expenditures of the regular budget of the United Nations is required,

Taking into account the fact that the economically more developed countries are in a position to make relatively larger contributions and that the economically less developed countries have a relatively limited capacity to contribute towards peace-keeping operations involving heavy expenditures,

Bearing in mind the special responsibilities of the States permanent members of the Security Council in the financing of such operations, as indicated in General Assembly resolution 1874(S-IV) of 27 June 1963 and other resolutions of the Assembly,

Having regard to the financial position of the Special Account for the United Nations Interim Force in Lebanon, as set forth in the report of the Secretary-General, and referring to paragraph 18 of the report of the Advisory Committee on Administrative and Budgetary Questions,

Recalling its resolution 34/9 E of 17 December 1979 and the subsequent resolutions in which it decided that the provisions of regulations 5.2 (_b_), 5.2 (_d_), 4.3 and 4.4 of the Financial Regulations of the United Nations should be suspended, the latest of which was resolution 42/223,

Mindful of the fact that it is essential to provide the United Nations Interim Force in Lebanon with the necessary financial resources to enable it to fulfil its responsibilities under the relevant resolutions of the Security Council,

Noting with appreciation that voluntary contributions have been made to the United Nations Interim Force in Lebanon by certain Governments,

Concerned that the Secretary-General is continuing to face increasing difficulties in meeting the obligations of the United Nations Interim Force in Lebanon on a current basis, including reimbursement to current and former troop-contributing States, resulting from the withholding of contributions by certain Member States,

Concerned also that the surplus balances in the Special Account for the United Nations Interim Force in Lebanon have, in effect, been drawn upon to the full extent to supplement the income received from contributions for meeting expenses of the Force,

Concerned further that the application of the provisions of regulations 5.2 (_b_), 5.2 (_d_), 4.3 and 4.4 of the Financial Regulations of the United Nations would aggravate the already difficult financial situation of the United Nations Interim Force in Lebanon,

1. _Decides_ to appropriate to the Special Account referred to in section I, paragraph 1, of General Assembly resolution S-8/2 an amount of 141,180,000 United States dollars authorized by the Assembly in paragraph 3 of its resolution 42/223 for the operation of the United Nations Interim Force in Lebanon from 1 February 1988 to 31 January 1989, inclusive;

2. _Decides,_ as an _ad hoc_ arrangement, without prejudice to the positions of principle that may be taken by Member States in any consideration by the General Assembly of arrangements for the financing of peace-keeping operations, to apportion the amount of 141,180,000 dollars among Member States in accordance with the scheme set out in Assembly resolution 33/14 of 3 November 1978 and the provisions of section V, paragraph 1, of resolution 34/9 B of 17 December 1979, section VI, paragraph 1, of resolution 35/115 A of 10 December 1980, section VI, paragraph 1, of resolution 36/138 A of 16 December 1981, section IX, paragraph 1, of resolution 37/127 A of 17 December 1982, and section VII, paragraphs 1 and 2, of resolution 39/71 A of 13 December 1984; the scale of assessments for the year 1988 shall be applied against a portion thereof, that is, 129,415,000 dollars being the amount pertaining on a _pro rata_ basis to the period from 1 February to 31 December 1988 inclusive, and the scale of assessments for the year 1989 shall be applied against the balance, that is, 11,765,000 dollars for the period thereafter;

3. _Decides_ that there shall be set off against the apportionment among Member States, as provided for in paragraph 2 above, their respective share in the estimated income of 20,000 dollars other than staff assessment income approved for the period from 1 February 1988 to 31 January 1989, inclusive;

4. _Decides_ that, in accordance with the provisions of its resolution 973(X) of 15 December 1955, there shall be set off against the apportionment among Member States, as provided for in paragraph 2 above, their respective share in the Tax Equalization Fund of the estimated staff assessment income of 1,744,000 dollars approved for the period from 1 February 1988 to 31 January 1989, inclusive;

5. _Authorizes_ the Secretary-General to enter into commitments for the United Nations Interim Force in Lebanon at a rate not to exceed 11,903,500 dollars gross (11,714,500 dollars net) per month for the twelve-month period beginning 1 February 1989, should the Security Council decide to continue the Force beyond the period of six months authorized under its resolution 617(1988), the said amount to be apportioned among Member

States in accordance with the scheme set out in the present resolution and the scale of assessments for the years 1989 and 1990;

6. *Decides* that the provisions of regulations 5.2 *(b)*, 5.2 *(d)*, 4.3 and 4.4 of the Financial Regulations of the United Nations shall be suspended in respect of the amount of 6,313,362 dollars, which otherwise would have to be surrendered pursuant to those provisions, this amount to be entered in the account referred to in the operative part of General Assembly resolution 34/9 E and held in suspense until a further decision is taken by the Assembly;

7. *Requests* the Secretary-General to take all necessary measures to ensure that the United Nations Interim Force in Lebanon shall be administered with a maximum of efficiency and economy;

8. *Renews its invitation* to Member States and other interested parties to make voluntary contributions to the United Nations Interim Force in Lebanon both in cash and in the form of services and supplies acceptable to the Secretary-General, and also to make voluntary contributions in cash to the Suspense Account established in accordance with resolution 34/9 D of 17 December 1979.

General Assembly resolution 43/229

21 December 1988   Meeting 84   134-1-8 (recorded vote)

Approved by Fifth Committee (A/43/957) by recorded vote (103-1-7), 12 December (meeting 45); 18-nation draft (A/C.5/43/L.7), orally revised; agenda item 124 *(b)*.

Sponsors: Austria, Canada, Denmark, Fiji, Finland, France, Germany, Federal Republic of, Ghana, Iceland, Ireland, Italy, Lebanon, Nepal, Netherlands, New Zealand, Norway, Samoa, Sweden.

Meeting numbers. GA 43rd session: 5th Committee 44, 45; plenary 84.

Recorded vote in Assembly as follows:

In favour: Antigua and Barbuda, Argentina, Australia, Austria, Bahamas, Bahrain, Bangladesh, Barbados, Belgium, Belize, Benin, Bhutan, Bolivia, Botswana, Brazil, Brunei Darussalam, Bulgaria, Burkina Faso, Burma, Burundi, Byelorussian SSR, Cameroon, Canada, Central African Republic, Chad, Chile, China, Colombia, Comoros, Congo, Costa Rica, Côte d'Ivoire, Cyprus, Czechoslovakia, Denmark, Djibouti, Dominican Republic, Ecuador, Egypt, Ethiopia, Fiji, Finland, France, Gabon, Gambia, German Democratic Republic, Germany, Federal Republic of, Ghana, Greece, Grenada, Guatemala, Guinea, Guinea-Bissau, Guyana, Haiti, Honduras, Hungary, Iceland, India, Indonesia, Ireland, Israel, Italy, Jamaica, Japan, Jordan, Kenya, Kuwait, Lao People's Democratic Republic, Lebanon, Lesotho, Liberia, Luxembourg, Madagascar, Malawi, Malaysia, Malta, Mauritania, Mauritius, Mexico, Mongolia, Morocco, Nepal, Netherlands, New Zealand, Nicaragua, Niger, Nigeria, Norway, Oman, Pakistan, Panama, Papua New Guinea, Paraguay, Peru, Philippines, Portugal, Qatar, Romania, Rwanda, Saint Lucia, Saint Vincent and the Grenadines, Samoa, Sao Tome and Principe, Saudi Arabia, Senegal, Sierra Leone, Singapore, Solomon Islands, Somalia, Spain, Sri Lanka, Sudan, Swaziland, Sweden, Thailand, Togo, Trinidad and Tobago, Tunisia, Turkey, Uganda, Ukrainian SSR, USSR, United Arab Emirates, United Kingdom, United Republic of Tanzania, United States, Uruguay, Vanuatu, Venezuela, Yugoslavia, Zaire, Zambia, Zimbabwe.

Against: Syrian Arab Republic.

Abstaining: Cuba, Iran, Iraq, Libyan Arab Jamahiriya, Maldives, Poland, Viet Nam, Yemen.

Abduction of OGL Chief William Higgins

Special report of the Secretary-General (March). In March 1988, the Secretary-General reported[38] to the Security Council on developments relating to the kidnapping, on 17 February, of Lieutenant-Colonel William Richard Higgins, a United States officer serving since January as Chief of Observer Group Lebanon of UNTSO. According to the testimony of Lebanese eyewitnesses, Colonel Higgins was abducted from his car by armed men in the Tyre Pocket outside the UNIFIL area on his way to UNIFIL headquarters at Naqoura after having met with a local leader of the Amal movement. UNIFIL headquarters was alerted by radio and numerous additional checkpoints were established and patrols increased, but subsequent search measures were to no avail.

On 18 February, the Under-Secretary-General for Special Political Affairs, Marrack Goulding, met at Beirut with Lebanon's President Amin Gemayel and Acting Prime Minister Salim Hoss, who both pledged their full support for efforts to free the Colonel, as well as with the Minister of State for Southern Affairs, Nabih Berri, who promised that the Amal movement he headed would do what it could to find him.

On 19 February, the kidnappers sent to a news agency in Beirut copies of Colonel Higgins' identity card and on 23 February a video tape showing him reading their conditions for his release. Continuing searches by UNIFIL and the Amal movement were not successful; however, UNIFIL received a number of reports suggesting that he might be held north of the Litani River.

The Secretary-General affirmed that UNIFIL would maintain all possible efforts to locate the Colonel and secure his release.

Report of the Secretary-General (July). In his July report on UNIFIL,[26] the Secretary-General expressed distress that, despite continuing efforts to obtain his release, Colonel Higgins remained in captivity. He underlined that at the time of his abduction the Colonel was serving the United Nations under the authority of the Security Council. The Secretary-General appealed to Member States having influence in the matter to do everything in their power to help secure the officer's release.

SECURITY COUNCIL ACTION

On 29 July, after extending UNIFIL's mandate (see above), the Security Council unanimously adopted **resolution 618(1988)**.

The Security Council,

Taking note of paragraph 23 of the Secretary-General's report on the United Nations Interim Force in Lebanon concerning the abduction of Lieutenant-Colonel William Richard Higgins, a military observer of the United Nations Truce Supervision Organization serving with the Force,

Recalling the Secretary-General's special report on the United Nations Interim Force in Lebanon,

Recalling also its resolution 579(1985) of 18 December 1985, which, *inter alia*, condemned unequivocally all acts of hostage-taking and abduction and called for the immediate release of all hostages and abducted persons wherever and by whomever they are being held,

1. *Condemns* the abduction of Lieutenant-Colonel Higgins;

2. *Demands* his immediate release;

3. *Calls upon* Member States to use their influence in any way possible to promote the implementation of the present resolution.

Security Council resolution 618(1988)
29 July 1988   Meeting 2822   Adopted unanimously
6-nation draft (S/20070).
Sponsors: Argentina, France, Italy, Nepal, USSR, United States.

Israel and the Syrian Arab Republic

UNDOF

The United Nations Disengagement Observer Force, established by the Security Council in 1974[39] and headquartered at Damascus, continued to supervise the observance of the cease-fire in the Golan Heights, as called for by the Agreement on Disengagement of Forces between Israel and the Syrian Arab Republic.[40] Its mandate was renewed by the Council, in May and November 1988, each time for six months. The General Assembly and the Commission on Human Rights also dealt with the situation in the Golan Heights in the light of Israel's 1981 decision[41] to impose its laws, jurisdiction and administration on the area (see also PART THREE, Chapter X).

Composition

As of November 1988,[42] UNDOF had a strength of 1,350 troops, up from 1,339 in May. It had contingents from four countries—Austria, 536; Canada, 227; Finland, 419; and Poland, 161, including four officers deployed to the United Nations Good Offices Mission in Afghanistan and Pakistan in accordance with Security Council **resolution 622(1988)** (see PART TWO, Chapter III)— and seven United Nations military observers assigned from UNTSO. In addition, UNTSO observers of the Israel-Syria Mixed Armistice Commission assisted UNDOF as needed.

On 23 June,[43] the Secretary-General informed the President of the Security Council that Major-General Gustaf Welin (Sweden), the Commander of UNDOF since 1 July 1986, was being recalled by his Government to assume a new command. Therefore, the Secretary-General intended, subject to Council approval, to appoint Major-General Adolf Radauer (Austria) as the new Commander with effect from 10 September 1988. The Council agreed to the appointment on 29 June.[44]

Activities

Reports of the Secretary-General. Before the expiration of the mandate of UNDOF on 31 May and 30 November 1988, the Secretary-General reported to the Security Council on UNDOF activities for two six-month periods, from 14 November 1987 to 20 May 1988[45] and from 21 May to 17 November 1988.[42]

The functions and guidelines of UNDOF remained as mandated in 1974[39] and the Force continued to fulfil its tasks effectively with the co-operation of the parties, facilitated by close contact of the Force Commander and his staff with the military liaison staff of Israel and the Syrian Arab Republic. Restrictions on freedom of movement still existed and the Secretary-General engaged in efforts to correct the problem. The cease-fire was maintained and no serious incidents occurred.

UNDOF supervised the area of separation by means of static positions and observation posts, manned 24 hours a day, and by foot and mobile patrols operating at irregular intervals on predetermined routes by day and night, in addition to temporary outposts and patrols. It also conducted fortnightly inspections of armament and forces in the area of limitation. The safety of Syrian shepherds grazing their flocks close to and west of the separation area continued to be of concern to UNDOF and intensified patrolling of new mine-cleared paths helped prevent incidents. Mines continued to pose a threat to the Force; during the two reporting periods, mine-clearing teams cleared 39,159 and 44,820 square metres, respectively, destroying a considerable number of mines and quantities of other military explosives, including ammunition. The Force also continued to assist the International Committee of the Red Cross in its humanitarian activities.

Despite the current quiet in the Israel-Syria sector, the Secretary-General cautioned that the situation in the Middle East as a whole continued to be potentially dangerous and was likely to remain so, unless a comprehensive settlement of all aspects of the problem was reached. Stating in each report that he considered UNDOF's continued presence in the area to be essential, the Secretary-General, with the agreement of the Syrian Arab Republic and Israel, recommended that its mandate be extended for a further six months.

SECURITY COUNCIL ACTION (May and November)

On 31 May 1988, without debate, the Security Council adopted **resolution 613(1988)** unanimously.

The Security Council,

Having considered the report of the Secretary-General on the United Nations Disengagement Observer Force,

Decides:

(*a*) To call upon the parties concerned to implement immediately Security Council resolution 338(1973) of 22 October 1973;

(*b*) To renew the mandate of the United Nations Disengagement Observer Force for another period of six months, that is, until 30 November 1988;

(*c*) To request the Secretary-General to submit, at the end of this period, a report on the developments in the situation and the measures taken to implement resolution 338(1973).

Security Council resolution 613(1988)
31 May 1988   Meeting 2815   Adopted unanimously
Draft prepared in consultations among Council members (S/19911).

On 30 November, again without debate, the Council adopted **resolution 624(1988)** unanimously.

The Security Council,

Having considered the report of the Secretary-General on the United Nations Disengagement Observer Force,

Decides:

(a) To call upon the parties concerned to implement immediately Security Council resolution 338(1973) of 22 October 1973;

(b) To renew the mandate of the United Nations Disengagement Observer Force for another period of six months, that is, until 31 May 1989;

(c) To request the Secretary-General to submit, at the end of this period, a report on the developments in the situation and the measures taken to implement resolution 338(1973).

Security Council resolution 624(1988)

30 November 1988   Meeting 2831   Adopted unanimously

Draft prepared in consultations among Council members (S/20300).

Following the adoption of each resolution, the President of the Council made the following statement:[46]

"As is known, the report of the Secretary-General on the United Nations Disengagement Observer Force states, in paragraph 24: 'Despite the present quiet in the Israel-Syria sector, the situation in the Middle East as a whole continues to be potentially dangerous and is likely to remain so, unless and until a comprehensive settlement covering all aspects of the Middle East problem can be reached.' That statement of the Secretary-General reflects the view of the Security Council."

Financing

The Secretary-General reported[47] that, as at 30 September 1988, assessments totalling $843.4 million had been apportioned among Member States for UNDOF since its inception on 31 May 1974[39] to 30 November 1988 and for the second United Nations Emergency Force (UNEF-II), established in 1973[48] and liquidated in 1980.[49] Contributions received from 1973 to 1988 amounted to $768.4 million. Of the unpaid assessed balance due of $75 million, only $6.4 million was considered collectible, leaving a shortfall of $68.6 million. That amount represented $32.6 million in payments withheld by Member States and $36 million transferred to a special account in accordance with a 1981 General Assembly resolution.[33] Therefore, troop contributors had not been reimbursed in full or on time.

In 1987,[50] the Assembly had appropriated $17,664,000 for UNDOF for the period from 1 December 1987 to 31 May 1988 and authorized the commitment of a rate not to exceed $2,944,000 gross ($2,893,000 net) per month for the period from 1 June to 30 November 1988 should the Security Council decide to continue UNDOF beyond 31 May, which it did (see above). For the 12-month period starting 1 December 1988, the estimated

costs were $3,019,000 gross ($2,963,000 net) per month. Those estimates assumed an average force strength of 1,327 troops, all ranks, as well as the continuance of existing responsibilities. On a net basis, that was $840,000 (2.4 per cent) more than the estimate for the previous period.

In December 1988,[37] ACABQ reported that the audited accounts of UNEF/UNDOF for the 1986-1987 biennium showed a "surplus" balance of $2,413,235 as at 31 December 1987, representing excess of income over expenditures due to interest and miscellaneous credits accrued to the account, with "income" referring to "assessed contributions" irrespective of collectibility. As a consequence of contributions withheld by Member States, the surplus had in effect been drawn upon in full. ACABQ recommended that the Secretary-General's cost estimate for UNDOF in 1988/89 be approved and that its requirements for the 12-month period begining 1 December 1988 not exceed $36,228,000 gross ($35,556,000 net).

GENERAL ASSEMBLY ACTION

On 21 December 1988, the General Assembly, on the recommendation of the Fifth Committee, adopted **resolution 43/228** by recorded vote.

Financing of the United Nations Disengagement Observer Force

The General Assembly,

Having considered the report of the Secretary-General on the financing of the United Nations Disengagement Observer Force, as well as the related report of the Advisory Committee on Administrative and Budgetary Questions,

Bearing in mind Security Council resolution 350(1974) of 31 May 1974, by which the Council established the United Nations Disengagement Observer Force, and the subsequent resolutions by which the Council extended the mandate of the Force, the latest of which was resolution 624(1988) of 30 November 1988,

Recalling its resolution 3211 B (XXIX) of 29 November 1974 on the financing of the United Nations Emergency Force and the United Nations Disengagement Observer Force and its subsequent resolutions thereon, the latest of which was resolution 42/70 A of 3 December 1987,

Reaffirming its previous decisions regarding the fact that, in order to meet the expenditures caused by such operations, a different procedure from the one applied to meet expenditures of the regular budget of the United Nations is required,

Taking into account the fact that the economically more developed countries are in a position to make relatively larger contributions and that the economically less developed countries have a relatively limited capacity to contribute towards peace-keeping operations involving heavy expenditures,

Bearing in mind the special responsibilities of the States permanent members of the Security Council in the financing of such operations, as indicated in General Assembly resolution 1874(S-IV) of 27 June 1963 and other resolutions of the Assembly,

Having regard to the financial position of the Special Account for the United Nations Emergency Force and the United Nations Disengagement Observer Force, as set forth in the report of the Secretary-General, and referring to paragraph 6 of the report of the Advisory Committee on Administrative and Budgetary Questions,

Recalling its resolution 33/13 E of 14 December 1978 and the subsequent resolutions in which it decided that the provisions of regulations 5.2 *(b)*, 5.2 *(d)*, 4.3 and 4.4 of the Financial Regulations of the United Nations should be suspended, the latest of which was resolution 42/70 B of 3 December 1987,

Mindful of the fact that it is essential to provide the United Nations Disengagement Observer Force with the necessary financial resources to enable it to fulfil its responsibilities under the relevant resolutions of the Security Council,

Concerned that the Secretary-General continues to face difficulties in meeting the obligations of the Forces on a current basis, particularly those due to the Governments of troop-contributing States,

Recognizing that, in consequence of the withholding of contributions by certain Member States, the surplus balances in the Special Account for the United Nations Emergency Force and the United Nations Disengagement Observer Force have, in effect, been drawn upon to the full extent to supplement the income received from contributions for meeting expenses of the Forces,

Concerned that the application of the provisions of regulations 5.2 *(b)*, 5.2 *(d)*, 4.3 and 4.4 of the Financial Regulations of the United Nations would aggravate the already difficult financial situation of the Forces,

1. *Decides* to appropriate to the Special Account referred to in section II, paragraph 1, of General Assembly resolution 3211 B (XXIX) the amount of 17,664,000 United States dollars gross (17,358,000 dollars net) authorized and apportioned by section III of Assembly resolution 42/70 A for the operation of the United Nations Disengagement Observer Force for the period from 1 June to 30 November 1988, inclusive;

2. *Decides also* to appropriate to the Special Account an amount of 18,114,000 dollars for the operation of the United Nations Disengagement Observer Force for the period from 1 December 1988 to 31 May 1989, inclusive;

3. *Decides further,* as an *ad hoc* arrangement, without prejudice to the positions of principle that may be taken by Member States in any consideration by the General Assembly of arrangements for the financing of peacekeeping operations, to apportion the amount of 18,114,000 dollars among Member States in accordance with the scheme set out in Assembly resolution 3101(XXVIII) of 11 December 1973 and the provisions of section II, paragraph 2 *(b)* and *(c)*, and section V, paragraph 1, of resolution 3374 C (XXX) of 2 December 1975, section V, paragraph 1, of resolution 31/5 D of 22 December 1976, section V, paragraph 1, of resolution 32/4 C of 2 December 1977, section V, paragraph 1, of resolution 33/13 D of 8 December 1978, section V, paragraph 1, of resolution 34/7 C of 3 December 1979, section V, paragraph 1, of resolution 35/45 A of 1 December 1980, section V, paragraph 1, of resolution 36/66 A of 30 November 1981, section V, paragraph 1, of resolution 37/38 A of 30 November 1982 and section V, paragraphs 1 and 2, of resolution 39/28 A of 30 November 1984; the scale of assessments for the year 1988 shall be applied against a portion thereof, that is,

3,019,000 dollars, being the amount pertaining on a *pro rata* basis to the period ending 31 December 1988, and the scale of assessments for the year 1989 shall be applied against the balance, that is, 15,095,000 dollars, for the period thereafter;

4. *Decides* that there shall be set off against the apportionment among Member States, as provided for in paragraph 3 above, their respective share in the estimated income of 6,000 dollars other than staff assessment income approved for the period from 1 December 1988 to 31 May 1989, inclusive;

5. *Decides* that, in accordance with the provisions of its resolution 973(X) of 15 December 1955, there shall be set off against the apportionment among Member States, as provided for in paragraph 3 above, their respective share in the Tax Equalization Fund of the estimated staff assessment income of 330,000 dollars approved for the period from 1 December 1988 to 31 May 1989, inclusive;

6. *Authorizes* the Secretary-General to enter into commitments for the United Nations Disengagement Observer Force at a rate not to exceed 3,019,000 dollars gross (2,963,000 dollars net) per month for the period from 1 June to 30 November 1989, inclusive, should the Security Council decide to continue the Force beyond the period of six months authorized under its resolution 624(1988), the said amount to be apportioned among Member States in accordance with the scheme set out in the present resolution;

7. *Decides* that the provisions of regulations 5.2 *(b)*, 5.2 *(d)*, 4.3 and 4.4 of the Financial Regulations of the United Nations shall be suspended in respect of the amount of 2,413,235 dollars, which otherwise would have to be surrendered pursuant to those provisions, this amount to be entered into the account referred to in the operative part of General Assembly resolution 33/13 E and held in suspense until a further decision is taken by the Assembly;

8. *Stresses* the need for voluntary contributions to the United Nations Disengagement Observer Force, both in cash and in the form of services and supplies acceptable to the Secretary-General;

9. *Requests* the Secretary-General to take all necessary action to ensure that the United Nations Disengagement Observer Force is administered with a maximum of efficiency and economy.

General Assembly resolution 43/228

21 December 1988   Meeting 84   133-2-8 (recorded vote)

Approved by Fifth Committee (A/43/956) without vote, 12 December (meeting 45); 13-nation draft (A/C.5/43/L.6); agenda item 124 *(a)*.

Sponsors: Australia, Austria, Canada, Denmark, Fiji, Finland, Germany, Federal Republic of, Ghana, Ireland, Nepal, New Zealand, Norway, Sweden.

Meeting numbers. GA 43rd session: 5th Committee 44, 45; plenary 84.

Recorded vote in Assembly as follows:

In favour: Antigua and Barbuda, Argentina, Australia, Austria, Bahamas, Bahrain, Bangladesh, Barbados, Belgium, Belize, Benin, Bhutan, Bolivia, Botswana, Brazil, Brunei Darussalam, Bulgaria, Burkina Faso, Burma, Burundi, Byelorussian SSR, Cameroon, Canada, Central African Republic, Chad, Chile, China, Colombia, Comoros, Congo, Costa Rica, Côte d'Ivoire, Cyprus, Czechoslovakia, Denmark, Djibouti, Dominican Republic, Ecuador, Egypt, Ethiopia, Fiji, Finland, France, Gabon, Gambia, German Democratic Republic, Germany, Federal Republic of, Ghana, Greece, Grenada, Guatemala, Guinea, Guinea-Bissau, Guyana, Haiti, Honduras, Hungary, Iceland, India, Indonesia, Ireland, Israel, Italy, Jamaica, Japan, Jordan, Kenya, Kuwait, Lao People's Democratic Republic, Lebanon, Lesotho, Liberia, Luxembourg, Madagascar, Malawi, Malaysia, Malta, Mauritania, Mauritius, Mexico, Mongolia, Morocco, Nepal, Netherlands, New Zealand, Nicaragua, Niger, Nigeria, Norway, Oman, Pakistan, Panama, Papua New Guinea, Paraguay, Peru, Philippines, Portugal, Qatar, Romania,

Rwanda, Saint Lucia, Saint Vincent and the Grenadines, Samoa, Sao Tome and Principe, Saudi Arabia, Senegal, Sierra Leone, Singapore, Solomon Islands, Somalia, Spain, Sri Lanka, Swaziland, Sweden, Thailand, Togo, Trinidad and Tobago, Tunisia, Turkey, Uganda, Ukrainian SSR, USSR, United Arab Emirates, United Kingdom, United Republic of Tanzania, United States, Uruguay, Vanuatu, Venezuela, Yugoslavia, Zaire, Zambia, Zimbabwe.

Against: Libyan Arab Jamahiriya, Syrian Arab Republic.

Abstaining: Algeria, Cuba, Iran, Iraq, Maldives, Sudan, Viet Nam, Yemen.

Israel and Tunisia

Assassination of PLO
Executive Committee member in Tunis

By a letter of 19 April 1988,[51] Tunisia informed the President of the Security Council that, on 16 April, a terrorist commando unit had killed a Tunisian citizen and three Palestinians, one of whom was Khalil al-Wazir, also known as Abu Jihad, a member of the PLO Executive Committee and deputy commander-in-chief of its forces, in his residence in the northern suburbs of Tunis. The preliminary investigation indicated that the commando unit had sophisticated naval and aerial military support, the latter through an Israeli Boeing 707, which was in fact a military aircraft whose electronic equipment jammed the local telecommunications network. Statements by Israeli officials confirmed that direct responsibility for the action lay with the Israeli Government, which had financed and ordered Mr. al-Wazir's execution.

Tunisia requested an urgent meeting of the Council to consider what it called a new deliberate attack on its territorial integrity and sovereignty, in violation of an October 1985 Council resolution,[52] adopted after an Israeli air raid on a Tunis suburb. It invited the Council to take appropriate steps to prevent the repetition of such acts.

In response to Tunisia's request, the Council held four meetings between 21 and 25 April. At their request, the following States were invited to participate without the right to vote: Bahrain, Bangladesh, Congo, Cuba, Djibouti, Egypt, Gabon, Greece, Jordan, Kuwait, Lao People's Democratic Republic, Lebanon, Libyan Arab Jamahiriya, Mauritania, Morocco, Mozambique, Pakistan, Qatar, Saudi Arabia, Somalia, Sudan, Syrian Arab Republic, Tunisia, Turkey, Ukrainian SSR, United Arab Emirates, Yemen, Zimbabwe.

At Algeria's request,[53] an invitation under rule 39[a] of the Council's provisional rules of procedure was extended to the Permanent Observer of LAS. Also at Algeria's request,[54] the Council decided, by 10 votes to 1 (United States), with 4 abstentions (France, Germany, Federal Republic of, Italy, United Kingdom), that an invitation be accorded to the Observer of PLO. The invitation, though not made pursuant to rules 37[b] or 39, conferred on PLO the same rights as those conferred on a Member State when invited under rule 37. The United States, which had requested the vote, reiterated its previously stated position, objecting

to giving PLO the same rights as a Member State (see above, under "Israel and Lebanon").

Tunisia charged that the attack was premeditated, as evidenced clearly by the preliminary findings of a committee of inquiry set up by the Government, namely: at the very time when the assassination took place, an Israeli military aircraft, disguised as a civilian airliner, was flying not far from the Tunisian coast, providing logistic support to a group of terrorists, and the plane was equipped with ultra-sophisticated electronic equipment which was able to jam the telecommunications network in the area. The terrorists fled in rented vehicles, which were left on the beach 15 kilometres from the scene of the crime; footprints showed that they entered and left Tunisia by sea. Statements by Israeli leaders also established the Israeli Government's responsibility for the operation.

Recalling that this was not the first Israeli terrorist attack on its territory, Tunisia said the Council was duty-bound to condemn the political assassination and State terrorism practised by Israel, whose involvement in the assassination was a violation of the sovereignty and territorial integrity of an independent State, showing the terrorist nature of its practices and its defiance of international law.

Israel, which did not participate in the Council's proceedings, said in a 21 April statement that the request for Council action was based on unsubstantiated allegations and that it was saddening, in view of the need for action against international terrorism, that the Council was discussing the fate of a terrorist who had openly accepted responsibility for the murder of many innocent men, women and children.

Before the vote, the United States explained that it would abstain because the draft resolution disproportionately placed all blame for the latest round in the rising spiral of violence in the Middle East on one event, while failing to mention other actions that preceded it. It also included language that was suggestive of sanctions under Chapter VII of the Charter.

The Council adopted **resolution 611(1988)** on 25 April.

The Security Council,

Having considered the letter dated 19 April 1988, in which Tunisia made a complaint against Israel following the new act of aggression committed by the latter against the sovereignty and territorial integrity of Tunisia,

Having heard the statement by the Minister for Foreign Affairs of Tunisia,

Having noted with concern that the aggression perpetrated on 16 April 1988 in the locality of Sidi Bou Said has caused loss of human life, particularly the assassination of Mr. Khalil al-Wazir,

Recalling that in accordance with Article 2, paragraph 4, of the Charter of the United Nations, all Member States shall refrain in their international relations from the threat or use of force against the territorial integrity or political independence of any State, or acting in any other manner inconsistent with the purposes of the United Nations,

Considering that in its resolution 573(1985) of 4 October 1985, adopted following the act of aggression committed on 1 October 1985 by Israel against the sovereignty and territorial integrity of Tunisia, it has condemned Israel and has demanded that Israel refrain from perpetrating such acts of aggression or from threatening to do so,

Gravely concerned by the act of aggression which constitutes a serious and renewed threat to peace, security and stability in the Mediterranean region,

1. *Condemns* vigorously the aggression, perpetrated on 16 April 1988 against the sovereignty and territorial integrity of Tunisia in flagrant violation of the Charter of the United Nations, international law and norms of conduct;

2. *Urges* Member States of the United Nations to take measures to prevent such acts against the sovereignty and territorial integrity of all States;

3. *Expresses its determination* to take the appropriate steps to ensure the implementation of the present resolution;

4. *Requests* the Secretary-General to report urgently to the Security Council any new elements available to him and relating to this aggression;

5. *Decides* to remain seized of the matter.

Security Council resolution 611(1988)

25 April 1988   Meeting 2810   14-0-1

6-nation draft (S/19819).
Sponsors: Algeria, Argentina, Nepal, Senegal, Yugoslavia, Zambia.
Meeting numbers. SC 2807-2810.

Vote in Council as follows:

In favour: Algeria, Argentina, Brazil, China, France, Germany, Federal Republic of, Italy, Japan, Nepal, Senegal, USSR, United Kingdom, Yugoslavia, Zambia.
Against: None.
Abstaining: United States.

REFERENCES

[1]YUN 1981, p. 275. [2]A/43/2. [3]A/43/541-S/20132. [4]A/43/737-S/20235. [5]A/43/746-S/20240. [6]A/43/661-S/20207. [7]A/43/79-S/19406. [8]S/19415. [9]S/19432. [10]S/19433. [11]S/19434. [12]YUN 1978, p. 312, SC res. 425(1978) & 426(1978), 19 Mar. 1978. [13]YUN 1982, p. 450, SC res. 509(1982), 6 June 1982. [14]A/43/350-S/19860. [15]S/19861. [16]S/19867. [17]S/19870. [18]S/19868. [19]A/43/927-S/20317. [20]S/20318. [21]S/20322. [22]YUN 1978, p. 312, SC res. 425(1978), 19 Mar. 1978. [23]*Ibid.*, p. 296. [24]YUN 1982, p. 428. [25]*Ibid.*, p. 450, SC res. 511(1982), 18 June 1982. [26]S/20053 & Corr.1. [27]S/19808. [28]S/19809. [29]S/19445. [30]S/19440. [31]A/43/461-S/20014. [32]A/43/826 & Corr.1. [33]YUN 1981, p. 1299, GA res. 36/116 A, 10 Dec. 1981. [34]YUN 1979, p. 352, GA res. 34/9 D, 17 Dec. 1979. [35]YUN 1987, p. 293, GA res. 42/223, 21 Dec. 1987. [36]*Ibid.*, p. 1110, GA res. 42/227, 21 Dec. 1987. [37]A/43/941. [38]S/19617. [39]YUN 1974, p. 205, SC res. 350(1974), 31 May 1974. [40]*Ibid.*, p. 198. [41]YUN 1981, p. 309. [42]S/20276. [43]S/19972. [44]S/19973. [45]S/19895. [46]S/19912, S/20306. [47]A/43/769. [48]YUN 1973, p. 213, SC res. 340(1973), 25 Oct. 1973. [49]YUN 1980, p. 361. [50]YUN 1987, p. 291, GA res. 42/70 A, 3 Dec. 1987. [51]S/19798. [52]YUN 1985, p. 287, SC res. 573(1985), 4 Oct. 1985. [53]S/19815. [54]S/19814.

Territories occupied by Israel

The territories occupied by Israel as a result of previous armed conflicts in the Middle East com-prised the Gaza Strip, the West Bank of the Jordan River, including East Jerusalem, and the Golan Heights in the Syrian Arab Republic. The political and security situation in the West Bank and Gaza Strip deteriorated progressively during 1988, following the beginning in late 1987 of the uprising, or *intifadah*, and with tensions remaining high in the Golan Heights. The Security Council and the General Assembly took action on various aspects of that situation.

The uprising also brought a noticeable increase in deportations of Palestinians from the occupied territories. The Security Council, by resolution 607(1988) in January, called on Israel to refrain from such deportations and requested it to abide by the 1949 Geneva Convention relative to the Protection of Civilian Persons in Time of War (fourth Geneva Convention). The Council called again in January on Israel to rescind the order to deport Palestinian civilians and to ensure their safe and immediate return, requesting that it desist from deporting any others (608(1988)).

In November, the Assembly, addressing the uprising, condemned Israel's persistent policies and practices violating the human rights of Palestinians in the occupied territories, in particular the opening of fire by the Israeli army and settlers that resulted in the killing and wounding of defenceless Palestinians; beatings and breaking of bones; deportation and detention of Palestinian civilians; restrictive economic measures; demolition of houses; collective punishment; and denial of access to the media. The Assembly reaffirmed that Israel's occupation in no way changed the territories' status and demanded that Israel abide by the fourth Geneva Convention (resolution 43/21).

In seven resolutions adopted in December, dealing with aspects of the situation considered by the Committee on Israeli practices, the Assembly reaffirmed that occupation itself was a grave violation of the human rights of the civilian population in those Arab territories, and condemned Israeli policies and practices affecting a variety of aspects of Palestinian life (43/58 A); condemned Israel's failure to acknowledge the applicability of the fourth Geneva Convention to the territories (43/58 B); demanded that Israel rescind the illegal measures of deporting Palestinians and facilitate their immediate return (43/58 E); called on Israel to release all Palestinians and other Arabs arbitrarily detained or imprisoned (43/58 D) and to rescind all measures taken against Palestinian educational institutions (43/58 G); condemned Israel's persistence in changing the physical character, demographic composition, institutional structure and legal status of the occupied Golan Heights (43/58 F); and demanded that Israel desist from such action in all of the occupied territories (43/58 C).

The Economic and Social Council condemned the application of an iron-fist policy by Israel against Palestinian women and their families in the occupied territories (1988/25).

Report of the Committee on Palestinian rights. Repressive Israeli measures to quell the Palestinian uprising led to a grave deterioration of the situation, the Committee on Palestinian rights reported in October 1988.[1] Despite the international outcry over repeated violations of human rights in the occupied territories and requests by the Security Council to abide by the relevant international instruments and United Nations resolutions, Israel continued to resort to military force against the Palestinians resisting the occupation and to engage in armed attacks against the integrity and sovereignty of countries in the region.

The Committee expressed great concern at the mounting casualties and suffering inflicted on the Palestinians and warned that Israel's intransigence would further exacerbate the situation and jeopardize international efforts towards a just and lasting settlement. The urgency of taking measures to protect Palestinians under occupation, to guarantee the safety and security and the legal and human rights of Palestinian refugees in the territories and to alleviate their suffering were paramount concerns in the Committee's programme of work during the year under review.

The Committee estimated that, by 27 September, 248 Palestinians had been shot to death by Israeli armed forces since the beginning of the uprising; another 126 had died from beatings, teargas inhalation and other causes related to actions by those forces and Israeli settlers. Thousands of Palestinians had been wounded or had suffered crushed bones in random beatings by Israeli soldiers implementing a policy of might to suppress the uprising, announced by the Israeli Defence Minister in January.

A high proportion of the victims were youths and children, the Committee noted with alarm, adding that the casualty toll was probably higher than reported since many feared arrest if they sought hospital treatment. Furthermore, repeated sealing off of areas, measures restricting activities of the press, and detention and harassment of journalists and human rights workers made it difficult to collect systematic information. At the same time, the growing involvement of armed Israeli settlers in attacks against the Palestinians seemed to be endorsed through an announced policy by the authorities allowing settlers to shoot demonstrators carrying what appeared to be fire-bombs. Humanitarian assistance organizations reported that medical personnel were refused access to camps and villages closed by the military, that hospitals had been attacked, and that patients and medical personnel had been beaten and arrested. In view of the high number of casualties, the Committee noted that the health situation—particularly in Gaza—had reached catastrophic proportions and that hospitals were facing severe shortages because the authorities were restricting access to medical supplies.

Israeli authorities had resorted to a policy of mass arrests, administrative detention without charge or trial, and deportations, in attempts to eradicate the leadership of the uprising. Human rights organizations estimated that, by the end of September, about 5,500 Palestinians were in detention, of whom 2,500 were under administrative detention without charge or trial, and that 33 had been deported, with deportation orders on another 25, in defiance of Security Council resolutions and the fourth Geneva Convention (see below). Collective punishment against the entire Palestinian population also escalated, including the closing off of areas as military zones; prevention of the delivery of foodstuffs, fuel and medicines; disruption of electricity and telephone services; and mass destruction of trees, crops and homes. Some 236 homes were reported destroyed as at 23 September, displacing thousands of Palestinians, while hundreds more were reportedly scheduled for demolition.

Other measures to suppress the uprising included restrictions on freedom of movement or travel and the intensification of measures against Palestinian economic, social and cultural institutions. West Bank universities were repeatedly closed, as were most schools in the Gaza Strip. A large number of schools were sequestered by the Israeli army for its own use, and school property was destroyed. The Palestinian Press Service was closed for six months, and other publications were harassed through closings, disruption of distribution and arrest of journalists. Trade unions and community groups were also harassed, and stringent administrative and economic measures were directed at strengthening Israel's hold on the territories at the same time that it intensified its *de facto* annexation.

By May 1988, the area of land confiscated by Israel since 1967 was almost 2.8 million dunums (1 dunum = 1,000 square metres), which was more than half the land area of the occupied Palestinian territories. The number of settlements had reached 170 in the West Bank and 20 in the Gaza Strip, with plans for new settlements and expansion of existing ones. Concurrently, stringent restrictions continued to be imposed on water use, new construction, the granting of credit and other activities necessary to develop the territories.

The Committee considered that every effort should be made to ensure the safety and protection of Palestinians in the occupied territories.

Report of the Committee on Israeli practices. In its report covering the period from 4 September 1987 to 26 August 1988,[2] the Committee on Israeli practices reflected on the overall situation in the territories, the uprising and specific incidents as they occurred. It described changes instituted by the Israeli Government in the administration of justice as a consequence of the uprising and followed up on practices by Israeli settlers and underground activists. The report included examples of harassment and physical mistreatment, collective punishment, expulsions and deportations, economic and social maltreatment, and unduly harsh treatment of detainees.

While Israel had continued to withhold its cooperation, the Committee benefited from the cooperation of Egypt, Jordan, the Syrian Arab Republic and PLO. The report was based on oral and written evidence presented to the Committee by Governments, organizations and individuals, as well as media sources.

The accumulation of frustrations suffered by the civilian population over the years as a result of Israel's persistent policy of annexation and colonization in the territories occupied in June 1967, and the humiliation and suffering brought about by that policy, were bound to provoke a violent reaction, the Committee stated. The restrictions imposed in the framework of the ''iron-fist policy'' since 1985 and the increasing determination of the young generation of Palestinians to oppose the arbitrary rules set by the occupants had prepared the ground for such confrontation. Thus, the explosion of violence sparked off by an incident in the Gaza Strip in December 1987 had quickly spread to the entire occupied territories.

The uprising was marked by heavy casualties, with hundreds of civilians killed by security forces or settlers, or under other circumstances. The death toll included casualties caused by shooting, beating, gas inhalation or electrocution. While several thousands of civilians were physically injured, the entire Palestinian population suffered as a result of Israel's policy of ''force, power and blows''.

Day-to-day life in the territories since the start of the uprising was characterized by constant unrest and violent clashes, sparing almost no single village or locality. The pattern of disturbances included demonstrations, stone-throwing and commercial strikes on the one hand, and the use of teargas, clubs, rubber and live bullets, curfews and various economic sanctions by the occupation authorities on the other. Acts of aggression by Israeli settlers against Palestinians contributed to a further deterioration in the climate of tension and terror. Information and evidence collected by the Committee also revealed the arbitrary deportation of Palestinians; the illegal demolition of houses as a form of collective punishment; severe limitations on the freedom of expression, which tended in particular to limit or prevent adequate media coverage of events related to the uprising; and the general closure of all educational institutions for several months.

The new situation in the territories engendered a considerable amount of administrative and other forms of detention. Several thousand Palestinians, including minors, had been or continued to be detained in various prisons and detention centres, sometimes even inside Israel itself, illustrating that legal guarantees such as the right to fair trial were often denied to Palestinians. Furthermore, the unprecedented increase in the prison population aggravated already critical detention conditions and the plight of detainees.

The Committee stressed that a year earlier it had warned of an explosive situation that seemed bound to provoke yet more dramatic events. The tragic developments stemmed from the basic reality that occupation itself constituted a violation of human rights, a fact consistently denied by Israel, which asserted that the territories it had occupied in 1967 constituted part of the State of Israel and that therefore measures such as the establishment of colonies and the transfer of Israeli citizens thereto did not constitute annexation. That attitude, the Committee said, was a violation by Israel of its international obligations as a party to the fourth Geneva Convention.

In view of the grave developments, the Committee stressed the responsibility of the international community to prevent a further deterioration of the situation and to protect the civilian population, whose basic rights could be ensured in the long run only through negotiation of a comprehensive, just and lasting settlement of the Arab-Israeli conflict. In the mean time, the Committee made specific recommendations to restore the basic rights of the civilians in the territories. It recommended full application by Israel of the relevant provisions of the fourth Geneva Convention, that Israel give the International Committee of the Red Cross (ICRC) access to detained persons, and that Israel and other Member States fully support the activities of ICRC and UNRWA.

GENERAL ASSEMBLY ACTION

On 6 December 1988, acting on the recommendation of the Special Political Committee and following consideration of the report of the Committee on Israeli practices, the General Assembly adopted **resolution 43/58 A** by recorded vote.

The General Assembly,

Guided by the purposes and principles of the Charter of the United Nations and by the principles and provisions of the Universal Declaration of Human Rights,

Aware of the uprising *(intifadah)* of the Palestinian people since 9 December 1987 against Israeli occupation, which has received significant attention and sympathy from world public opinion,

Deeply concerned at the alarming situation in the Palestinian territory occupied since 1967, including Jerusalem, as well as in the other occupied Arab territories, as a result of the continued occupation by Israel, the occupying Power, and of its persistent policies and practices against the Palestinian people,

Bearing in mind the provisions of the Geneva Convention relative to the Protection of Civilian Persons in Time of War, of 12 August 1949, as well as of other relevant conventions and regulations,

Taking into account the need to consider measures for the impartial protection of the Palestinian people under the Israeli occupation,

Recalling all its resolutions on the subject, in particular resolutions 32/91 B and C of 13 December 1977, 33/113 C of 18 December 1978, 34/90 A of 12 December 1979, 35/122 C of 11 December 1980, 36/147 C of 16 December 1981, ES-9/1 of 5 February 1982, 37/88 C of 10 December 1982, 38/79 D of 15 December 1983, 39/95 D of 14 December 1984, 40/161 D of 16 December 1985, 41/63 D of 3 December 1986, 42/160 D of 8 December 1987 and 43/21 of 3 November 1988,

Recalling also the relevant Security Council resolutions, in particular resolutions 605(1987) of 22 December 1987, 607(1988) of 5 January 1988 and 608(1988) of 14 January 1988,

Recalling further the relevant resolutions adopted by the Commission on Human Rights, in particular its resolutions 1983/1 of 15 February 1983, 1984/1 of 20 February 1984, 1985/1 A and B and 1985/2 of 19 February 1985, 1986/1 A and B and 1986/2 of 20 February 1986, 1987/1, 1987/2 A and B and 1987/4 of 19 February 1987, 1988/1 A and B and 1988/2 of 15 February 1988 and 1988/3 of 22 February 1988, and by other United Nations organs concerned and the specialized agencies,

Having considered the report of the Special Committee to Investigate Israeli Practices Affecting the Human Rights of the Population of the Occupied Territories, which contains, *inter alia*, self-incriminating public statements made by officials of Israel, the occupying Power,

Having also considered the reports of the Secretary-General of 21 January 1988, 29 September 1988 and 21 November 1988,

1. *Commends* the Special Committee to Investigate Israeli Practices Affecting the Human Rights of the Population of the Occupied Territories for its efforts in performing the tasks assigned to it by the General Assembly and for its thoroughness and impartiality;

2. *Deplores* the continued refusal by Israel to allow the Special Committee access to the occupied territories;

3. *Demands* that Israel allow the Special Committee access to the occupied territories;

4. *Reaffirms* the fact that occupation itself constitutes a grave violation of the human rights of the civilian population of the occupied Arab territories;

5. *Condemns* the continued and persistent violation by Israel of the Geneva Convention relative to the Protection of Civilian Persons in Time of War, of 12 August 1949, and other applicable international instruments, and condemns in particular those violations which the Convention designates as "grave breaches" thereof;

6. *Declares once more* that Israel's grave breaches of that Convention are war crimes and an affront to humanity;

7. *Reaffirms*, in accordance with the Convention, that the Israeli military occupation of the Palestinian and other Arab territories is of a temporary nature, thus giving no right whatsoever to the occupying Power over the territorial integrity of the occupied territories;

8. *Strongly condemns* the following Israeli policies and practices:

(a) Annexation of parts of the occupied territories, including Jerusalem;

(b) Imposition of Israeli laws, jurisdiction and administration on the Syrian Arab Golan, which has resulted in the effective annexation of that territory;

(c) Illegal imposition and levy of heavy and disproportionate taxes and dues;

(d) Establishment of new Israeli settlements and expansion of the existing settlements on private and public Arab lands, and transfer of an alien population thereto;

(e) Eviction, deportation, expulsion, displacement and transfer of Arab inhabitants of the occupied territories and denial of their right to return;

(f) Confiscation and expropriation of private and public Arab property in the occupied territories and all other transactions for the acquisition of land involving the Israeli authorities, institutions or nationals on the one hand and the inhabitants or institutions of the occupied territories on the other;

(g) Excavation and transformation of the landscape and the historical, cultural and religious sites, especially at Jerusalem;

(h) Pillaging of archaeological and cultural property;

(i) Destruction and demolition of Arab houses;

(j) Collective punishment, mass arrests, administrative detention and ill-treatment of the Arab population;

(k) Ill-treatment and torture of persons under detention;

(l) Interference with religious freedoms and practices as well as family rights and customs;

(m) Interference with the system of education and with the social and economic and health development of the population in the Palestinian and other occupied Arab territories;

(n) Interference with the freedom of movement of individuals within the Palestinian and other occupied Arab territories;

(o) Illegal exploitation of the natural wealth, resources and population of the occupied territories;

9. *Strongly condemns*, in particular, the following Israeli policies and practices:

(a) Implementation of an "iron-fist" policy against the Palestinian people in the occupied Palestinian territory since 4 August 1985;

(b) Escalation of Israeli brutality since the beginning of the uprising (*intifadah*) on 9 December 1987;

(c) Ill-treatment and torture of children and minors under detention and/or imprisonment;

(d) Closure of headquarters and offices of trade unions and social organizations and harassment of their leaders, as well as attacks on hospitals and their personnel;

(e) Interference with the freedom of the press, including censorship, detention or expulsion of journalists, closure and suspension of newspapers and magazines, as well as denial of access to international media;

(f) Killing and wounding of defenceless demonstrators;

(g) Breaking of bones and limbs of thousands of civilians;

(h) House and/or town arrests;

(i) Usage of toxic gas, which resulted, *inter alia*, in the killing of many Palestinians;

10. *Condemns also* the Israeli repression against and closing of the educational institutions in the occupied Syrian Arab Golan, particularly the prohibition of

Syrian textbooks and the Syrian educational system, the deprivation of Syrian students from pursuing their higher education in Syrian universities, the denial of the right to return to Syrian students receiving their higher education in the Syrian Arab Republic, the forcing of Hebrew on Syrian students, the imposition of courses that promote hatred, prejudice and religious intolerance, and the dismissal of teachers, all in clear violation of the Geneva Convention;

11.   *Strongly condemns* the arming of Israeli settlers in the occupied territories to commit acts of violence against Palestinian and Arab civilians and the perpetration of acts of violence by these armed settlers against individuals, causing death and injury and wide-scale damage to Arab property;

12.   *Requests* the Security Council to ensure Israel's respect for and compliance with all the provisions of the Geneva Convention relative to the Protection of Civilian Persons in Time of War, of 12 August 1949, in the Palestinian and other Arab territories occupied since 1967, including Jerusalem, and to initiate measures to halt Israeli policies and practices in those territories;

13.   *Urges* the Security Council to consider the current situation in the Palestinian territory occupied by Israel since 1967, taking into account the recommendations contained in the reports of the Secretary-General of 21 January 1988 and 21 November 1988, and with a view to securing international protection for the defenceless Palestinian people until the withdrawal of Israel, the occupying Power, from the occupied Palestinian territory;

14.   *Reaffirms* that all measures taken by Israel to change the physical character, demographic composition, institutional structure or legal status of the occupied territories, or any part thereof, including Jerusalem, are null and void, and that Israel's policy of settling parts of its population and new immigrants in the occupied territories constitutes a flagrant violation of the Geneva Convention and of the relevant resolutions of the United Nations;

15.   *Demands* that Israel desist forthwith from the policies and practices referred to in paragraphs 8, 9, 10 and 11 above;

16.   *Calls upon* Israel, the occupying Power, to take immediate steps for the return of all displaced Arab and Palestinian inhabitants to their homes or former places of residence in the territories occupied by Israel since 1967, in implementation of Security Council resolution 237(1967) of 14 June 1967;

17.   *Urges* international organizations, including the specialized agencies, in particular the International Labour Organisation, the United Nations Educational, Scientific and Cultural Organization and the World Health Organization, to continue to examine the educational and health conditions of Palestinian and Arab workers in the occupied Palestinian and other Arab territories, including Jerusalem;

18.   *Reiterates its call* upon all States, in particular those States parties to the Geneva Convention, in accordance with article 1 of that Convention, and upon international organizations, including the specialized agencies, not to recognize any changes carried out by Israel in the occupied territories and to avoid actions, including those in the field of aid, which might be used by Israel in its pursuit of the policies of annexation and colonization

or any of the other policies and practices referred to in the present resolution;

19.   *Requests* the Special Committee, pending early termination of Israeli occupation, to continue to investigate Israeli policies and practices in the Arab territories occupied by Israel since 1967, to consult, as appropriate, with the International Committee of the Red Cross in order to ensure the safeguarding of the welfare and human rights of the population of the occupied territories and to report to the Secretary-General as soon as possible and whenever the need arises thereafter;

20.   *Also requests* the Special Committee to submit regularly periodic reports to the Secretary-General on the present situation in the occupied Palestinian territory;

21.   *Further requests* the Special Committee to continue to investigate the treatment of civilians in detention in Arab Palestinian and other Arab territories occupied by Israel since 1967;

22.   *Condemns* Israel's refusal to permit persons from the occupied territories to appear as witnesses before the Special Committee and to participate in conferences and meetings held outside the occupied Palestinian territory;

23.   *Requests* the Secretary-General:

(*a*)   To provide all necessary facilities to the Special Committee, including those required for its visits to the occupied territories, so that it may investigate the Israeli policies and practices referred to in the present resolution;

(*b*)   To continue to make available additional staff as may be necessary to assist the Special Committee in the performance of its tasks;

(*c*)   To circulate regularly and periodically the reports mentioned in paragraph 20 above to the States Members of the United Nations;

(*d*)   To ensure the widest circulation of the reports of the Special Committee and of information regarding its activities and findings, by all means available, through the Department of Public Information of the Secretariat and, where necessary, to reprint those reports of the Special Committee that are no longer available;

(*e*)   To report to the General Assembly at its forty-fourth session on the tasks entrusted to him in the present resolution;

24.   *Calls upon* Israel, the occupying Power, to allow the reopening of the Roman Catholic Medical Facility Hospice at Jerusalem in order to continue to provide needed health and medical services to the Arab population in the city;

25.   *Decides* to include in the provisional agenda of its forty-fourth session the item entitled "Report of the Special Committee to Investigate Israeli Practices Affecting the Human Rights of the Population of the Occupied Territories".

General Assembly resolution 43/58 A

6 December 1988   Meeting 71   106-2-43 (recorded vote)

Approved by Special Political Committee (A/43/904) by recorded vote (89-2-32), 28 November (meeting 34); draft by Afghanistan, Bangladesh, Brunei Darussalam, Burkina Faso, Comoros, Cuba, India, Indonesia, Jordan (for Arab Group), Madagascar, Malaysia, Nicaragua, Pakistan, Zambia (A/SPC/43/L.26); agenda item 77.

Financial implications. 5th Committee, A/43/931; S-G, A/SPC/43/L.33, A/C.5/43/51.

Meeting numbers. GA 43rd session: SPC 28-32, 34; 5th Committee 41; plenary 71.

Recorded vote in Assembly as follows:

In favour: Afghanistan, Albania, Algeria, Angola, Argentina, Bahamas, Bahrain, Bangladesh, Benin, Bhutan, Bolivia, Botswana, Brazil, Brunei Darussalam, Bulgaria, Burkina Faso, Burma, Burundi, Byelorussian SSR,

Cape Verde, China, Comoros, Cuba, Cyprus, Czechoslovakia, Democratic Kampuchea, Democratic Yemen, Djibouti, Ecuador, Egypt, El Salvador, Ethiopia, Gabon, Gambia, German Democratic Republic, Ghana, Guatemala, Guinea, Guinea-Bissau, Guyana, Honduras, Hungary, India, Indonesia, Iran, Iraq, Jamaica, Jordan, Kenya, Kuwait, Lao People's Democratic Republic, Lebanon, Lesotho, Libyan Arab Jamahiriya, Madagascar, Malaysia, Maldives, Mali, Mauritania, Mauritius, Mexico, Mongolia, Morocco, Mozambique, Nepal, Nicaragua, Niger, Nigeria, Oman, Pakistan, Panama, Papua New Guinea, Paraguay, Peru, Philippines, Poland, Qatar, Romania, Rwanda, Sao Tome and Principe, Saudi Arabia, Senegal, Seychelles, Sierra Leone, Singapore, Somalia, Sri Lanka, Sudan, Swaziland, Syrian Arab Republic, Thailand, Togo, Trinidad and Tobago, Tunisia, Turkey, Uganda, Ukrainian SSR, United Arab Emirates, United Republic of Tanzania, Vanuatu, Venezuela, Viet Nam, Yemen, Yugoslavia, Zambia, Zimbabwe.

Against: Israel, United States.

Abstaining: Antigua and Barbuda, Australia, Austria, Barbados, Belgium, Belize, Cameroon, Canada, Central African Republic, Colombia, Costa Rica, Côte d'Ivoire, Denmark, Dominican Republic, Fiji, Finland, France, Germany, Federal Republic of, Greece, Grenada, Haiti, Iceland, Ireland, Italy, Japan, Liberia, Luxembourg, Malawi, Malta, Netherlands, New Zealand, Norway, Portugal, Saint Kitts and Nevis, Saint Lucia, Saint Vincent and the Grenadines, Samoa, Solomon Islands, Spain, Sweden, United Kingdom, Uruguay, Zaire.

Before adopting the text as a whole, the Assembly adopted paragraph 6 by a recorded vote of 80 to 23, with 45 abstentions. The paragraph was approved by the Committee by a recorded vote of 71 to 20, with 29 abstentions.

The Palestinian uprising

Gravely concerned at the situation created by the widespread uprising of Palestinians in the occupied territories and the resulting massive Israeli repression, the Security Council had, in December 1987,[3] deplored Israel's practices, particularly the Israeli army's firing at defenceless civilians, and called on Israel to abide immediately by the fourth Geneva Convention and to desist from such practices. The Secretary-General was requested to examine the situation by all available means and to recommend ways to ensure the safety of Palestinians under Israeli occupation.

During 1988, the uprising gained momentum, with its escalation exponentially increasing international attention to the inhuman conditions in the territories occupied by Israel. Avenues open to negotiation were blocked by deep mutual distrust on both the Arab and Israeli sides and by diametrically opposed political and legal positions. The Security Council did not adopt an operational resolution on the conflict due to the repeated negative vote of a permanent member.

Report of the Secretary-General. On 21 January 1988,[4] in response to the December 1987 Security Council resolution,[3] the Secretary-General reported on the results of a visit to Israel and the occupied territories by the Under-Secretary-General for Special Political Affairs, Marrack Goulding, from 8 to 17 January, which was undertaken to examine the situation on the spot and make recommendations to the Council on ways to ensure the safety and protection of the Palestinian population. At meetings with Mr. Goulding, the Israeli Minister for Foreign Affairs,

the Defence Minister and the Co-ordinator of Government Operations in the territories stated that, since Israel did not accept the applicability of the fourth Geneva Convention, the Council had no role to play in the security of the territories, for which Israel itself was exclusively responsible.

The Ministers agreed that the situation was serious, with the Israel Defence Forces (IDF) being surprised by the extent of the disturbances. As a largely conscript army trained to defend against external attack, IDF lacked expertise in riot control and, although Israel regretted the civilian casualties, the current disorder in the refugee camps could not be tolerated and firm measures would, if necessary, be taken to suppress it. A political solution had to be found to the underlying problem, and Israel remained committed to the search for a negotiated settlement. Meanwhile, law and order had to be restored.

Throughout Mr. Goulding's visit, nearly all camps in the Gaza Strip were under curfew or had been declared closed military areas, as were many of the West Bank camps. However, during visits to Rafah (Gaza Strip), Dheisheh (Bethlehem) and Balata (Nablus) camps and in other meetings, about 200 Palestinian men and women indicated that they rejected Israeli occupation and insisted that the Palestinian problem was not one of refugees but a political problem requiring a political solution. They complained bitterly about Israeli practices, especially the behaviour of the security forces, and about the Israeli settlements and the obstruction of Palestinian economic development. It was widely maintained that the practices had to be made known to a world which, after 20 years of occupation, seemed to have forgotten the territories. There was criticism of the failure of Member States to secure implementation of the dozens of United Nations resolutions, both on the situation in the territories and on the wider political issue of a just and lasting settlement.

Overall, the atmosphere in the territories, especially in the refugee camps, was marked by tension and unrest, with commercial strikes in almost all towns and most educational institutions closed. More than 2,000 Palestinians, many under the age of 16 and some as young as 11 or 12, had been detained in the month since the beginning of the uprising, while deportations continued. Most acutely affected were residents of the refugee camps, particularly in the Gaza Strip, where normal life had been totally disrupted by curfews and the closing off of camps to non-residents, including relief workers. While at first the Israeli Ministers had believed the rebellion leading to such a situation had been orchestrated by PLO and fundamentalist Islamic groups, they had since concluded that the situation was a spontaneous outburst. It was a reaction supported by Palestinians of all ages and walks of life to 20 years of occupation and to a lack of hope for its early end.

The behaviour of the Israeli security forces was described by the Palestinians consulted, without exception, as not only harsh but random and capricious, in such incidents as the beating of bystanders, the deliberate humiliation of Palestinians who refused to co-operate with Israeli forces, the use of physical and psychological pressure at detention centres and during interrogations, and the prevention of medical assistance to the wounded and injured. Other complaints concerned the lack of outlets for political activity; the taking of land, especially for Israeli settlements; deportations and other human rights violations; interruption of education; shortcomings in the judicial system; and heavy taxation and economic discrimination.

The Co-ordinator of Government Operations said that the security forces had very strict orders against mistreatment of the civilian population; there were isolated cases in which those orders were not properly observed but such cases were severely dealt with by the Israeli authorities. He offered to investigate any individual case that was brought to his attention and to take up any specific case of alleged obstruction of UNRWA activities by the security forces. On the economic questions, he asserted that Israel spent more in the territories than it received in tax revenue and that health and education services there were better than the Palestinians would admit. Israel wanted foreign countries to contribute to the territories' development and would give them a free hand, subject only to security requirements and observance of Israeli procedures.

While the report emphasized that assistance and protection could not be a substitute for a political settlement, it considered forms of protection available to the international community to help the population in the territories. The Secretary-General noted that, unless there was a change in Israel's position, the deployment of United Nations forces in the territories was not currently practicable, but should not be lost sight of. Such forces could be a valuable ingredient in implementing a negotiated settlement or in transitional arrangements that might be agreed on. A measure of legal protection to the population was nevertheless provided by ICRC, whose activities the Secretary-General commended. He recommended a concerted international effort to induce Israel to comply with relevant United Nations resolutions and the fourth Geneva Convention, and the working towards a peaceful, just settlement through an international conference under United Nations auspices.

The negotiation of a settlement would be exceptionally difficult, requiring all concerned to move from positions to which they were strongly attached. The Secretary-General's fundamental recommendation focused on an urgent effort by the international community, led by the Security Council, to promote an effective negotiating process as required by the Charter, thereby unblocking the current impasse.

SECURITY COUNCIL CONSIDERATION (January/February)

The Security Council considered the Secretary-General's report at five meetings held between 27 January and 1 February.

Meeting numbers. SC 2785-2787, 2789, 2790.

With the consent of the Council, the President invited Czechoslovakia, Egypt, India, Indonesia, Israel, Jordan, Kuwait, the Libyan Arab Jamahiriya, Malaysia, Morocco, Qatar, the Sudan, the Syrian Arab Republic and Zimbabwe, at their request, to participate without the right to vote. PLO's participation, requested by Algeria,[5] was approved by 10 votes to 1 (United States), with 4 abstentions (France, Germany, Federal Republic of, Italy, United Kingdom). The United States, which had requested the vote, took the position that, under the Council's provisional rules of procedure, rule 39[a] was the only legal basis on which the Council might grant a hearing to non-governmental entities. It had for decades supported a generous interpretation of that rule and would not object had the matter been raised under it. However, the United States opposed special *ad hoc* departures from orderly procedure and consequently opposed extending to PLO the same rights of participation as a Member State. It believed in listening to all points of view, but not if that required violating the rules; in particular, it did not agree with recent Council practice that appeared to try to enhance selectively the prestige of those wishing to speak through a departure from the rules of procedure.

At Algeria's request,[6] LAS was invited to participate under rule 39, as was the Organization of the Islamic Conference (OIC), at Kuwait's request.[7]

After discussing the Secretary-General's report and the issues raised in it, the Council voted on 1 February on a draft resolution[8] submitted by Algeria, Argentina, Nepal, Senegal, Yugoslavia and Zambia. By the text, the Council would have called again on Israel to desist from its policies and practices violating the human rights of the Palestinian people and accept the applicability of the fourth Geneva Convention; requested that it facilitate the tasks of ICRC and UNRWA and that all Member States give them their full support; and affirmed the urgent need to achieve a comprehensive settlement under United Nations auspices.

The vote was 14 to 1, as follows:

In favour: Algeria, Argentina, Brazil, China, France, Germany, Federal Republic of, Italy, Japan, Nepal, Senegal, USSR, United Kingdom, Yugoslavia, Zambia.

Against: United States.

The draft was not adopted owing to the negative vote of a permanent Council member.

Israel told the Council that it was not dealing with peaceful, non-violent demonstrations, but with violent disturbances deliberately geared to undermine normal life, employing means to kill and maim. Having failed in war, terrorism and all other violent means at their disposal, the Arab rejectionists now sought the strategy of anarchy. Israel maintained that it had decided to act *de facto* in accordance with the humanitarian provisions of the fourth Geneva Convention and to co-operate with ICRC, but not to accept its *de jure* applicability to the territories.

The PLO Observer stressed that the issue was not the restoration of law and order, but a confrontation by the occupying Power with the Palestinians and their rising up to demand the right to life in peace and freedom, untarnished by the presence of Israeli occupation, military or otherwise; all iron-fist measures would not bend that determination. Ending Israeli occupation of Palestinian and other Arab territories, including Jerusalem, would definitely contribute to the endeavours of a comprehensive settlement and to peace. Meanwhile, in addressing immediate ways to protect the civilian population in the territories, the mere presence of the United Nations there as a symbol of protection and admission of responsibility was important. The Council should respond to the tragic situation and address the root cause, in keeping with the remedy prescribed in the relevant Assembly resolutions.

Explaining its negative vote, the United States said the text could detract from ongoing diplomatic efforts with the parties directly concerned on ways to resolve the Palestinian conflict; agreement on a negotiating process and the appropriate auspices for negotiations could not be imposed on those parties even by implication, which the draft resolution attempted to do.

SECURITY COUNCIL CONSIDERATION (March and April)

At the request of Tunisia,[9] as Chairman of the Group of Arab States, the Security Council held further meetings on the situation in the occupied territories, on 30 March and 14 and 15 April.

Meeting numbers. SC 2804-2806.

At their request, Bangladesh, India, Israel, Jordan, Kuwait, the Libyan Arab Jamahiriya, Pakistan, Saudi Arabia, the Syrian Arab Republic and Tunisia were invited to participate without voting rights. The Acting Chairman of the Committee on Palestinian rights was invited, at his own request, under rule 39[a] of the provisional rules of procedure.

Algeria requested[10] PLO's participation, which was approved by the same vote as in January, after the United States restated its negative position on such participation (see above). LAS was invited to participate at Algeria's request,[11] as was OIC, as requested by Jordan.[12]

On 15 April, the Council voted on a draft resolution[13] put forward by the same six States that had proposed the February text (see above). By wording similar to that text, the Council would have condemned Israel for violating the Palestinians' human rights, particularly the killing and wounding of defenceless civilians; urged it to abide immediately and scrupulously by the fourth Geneva Convention, to rescind its deportation orders on Palestinian civilians and ensure the safe and immediate return of those already deported, and to desist from such deportations; and affirmed the need to achieve a comprehensive, just and lasting settlement of the Arab-Israeli conflict under United Nations auspices.

The vote was 14 to 1 (United States), following the same voting pattern as on 1 February, and the draft was thus rejected owing to the negative vote of a permanent member.

Although opposing the deportations, the United States felt the Council should desist from rhetoric and unproductive texts which would cut across the objective of finding a way to peace in the Middle East. The draft neither contributed to easing tension nor promoted the cause of peace.

Israel said that, during the disturbances, its soldiers had found themselves in extremely trying conditions but had exercised utmost restraint. It regretted any loss of life but, when confronted with unbridled mob violence, it had to quell it to restore order. Those who readily relied on the fourth Geneva Convention could not deny that that remained any administration's foremost responsibility. Also, political negotiations could not proceed under the threat of any violence.

The PLO Observer stressed that the Council was called upon to adopt all measures ensuring the effective protection of Palestinians and to require the occupying forces to cease immediately arbitrary measures violating human rights and international law. The Council must follow closely the situation through measures available to the United Nations, entrust the Secretary-General with the task of pursuing constructive efforts along those lines, and support the Secretary-General's endeavours to convene an international peace conference under United Nations auspices.

The Acting Chairman of the Committee on Palestinian rights appealed to the Secretary-General to implement his recommendations[4] calling for the provision of necessary humanitarian assistance to suffering Palestinians.

SECURITY COUNCIL ACTION (August)

After consultations, the President of the Security Council, on 26 August, issued a statement on behalf of its members:[14]

"The members of the Security Council are gravely concerned by the continued deterioration of the situation in the Palestinian territories occupied by Israel since 1967, including Jerusalem, and especially by the current grave and serious situation resulting from the closing-off of areas, the imposition of curfews and the consequent increase in the numbers of injuries and deaths that have occurred.

"The members of the Council are profoundly concerned by the persistence of Israel, the occupying Power, in continuing its policy of deporting Palestinian civilians in contravention of Security Council resolutions and the Geneva Convention relative to the Protection of Civilian Persons in Time of War, of 12 August 1949, as demonstrated on 17 August 1988 by its expulsion of four Palestinian civilians to Lebanon and its decision to expel 40 more. The members of the Council request Israel immediately to desist from deporting any Palestinian civilians and immediately to ensure the safe return of those already deported.

"The members of the Council consider that the current situation in the occupied territories, described in the first paragraph above, has grave consequences for endeavours to achieve a comprehensive, just and lasting peace in the Middle East.

"They reaffirm that the above-mentioned Geneva Convention is applicable to the Palestinian and other Arab territories occupied by Israel since 1967, including Jerusalem, and request the high contracting parties to ensure respect for the Convention.

"Recalling Security Council resolutions, the members of the Council will keep the situation in the occupied Palestinian territories, including Jerusalem, under review."

GENERAL ASSEMBLY ACTION (November)

On 3 November, the General Assembly adopted **resolution 43/21** by recorded vote.

The uprising _(intifadah)_ of the Palestinian people

The General Assembly,

Aware of the uprising _(intifadah)_ of the Palestinian people since 9 December 1987 against Israeli occupation, which has received significant attention and sympathy from world public opinion,

Deeply concerned at the alarming situation in the Palestinian territories occupied since 1967, including Jerusalem, as well as in the other occupied Arab territories, as a result of the continued occupation by Israel, the occupying Power, and of its persistent policies and practices against the Palestinian people,

Reaffirming that the Geneva Convention relative to the Protection of Civilian Persons in Time of War, of 12 August 1949, is applicable to all the Palestinian and other Arab territories occupied by Israel since 1967, including Jerusalem,

Recalling its relevant resolutions as well as Security Council resolutions 605(1987) of 22 December 1987, 607(1988) of 5 January 1988 and 608(1988) of 14 January 1988,

Recognizing the need for increased support and aid for, and solidarity with, the Palestinian people under Israeli occupation,

Conscious of the urgent need to resolve the underlying problem through a comprehensive, just and lasting settlement, including a solution to the Palestinian problem in all its aspects,

1. _Condemns_ Israel's persistent policies and practices violating the human rights of the Palestinian people in the occupied Palestinian territories, including Jerusalem, and, in particular, such acts as the opening of fire by the Israeli army and settlers that result in the killing and wounding of defenceless Palestinian civilians, the beating and breaking of bones, the deportation of Palestinian civilians, the imposition of restrictive economic measures, the demolition of houses, collective punishment and detentions, as well as denial of access to the media;

2. _Strongly deplores_ the continuing disregard by Israel, the occupying Power, of the relevant decisions of the Security Council;

3. _Reaffirms_ that the occupation by Israel of the Palestinian territories since 1967, including Jerusalem, in no way changes the legal status of those territories;

4. _Demands_ that Israel, the occupying Power, abide immediately and scrupulously by the Geneva Convention relative to the Protection of Civilian Persons in Time of War, of 12 August 1949, and desist forthwith from its policies and practices that are in violation of the provisions of the Convention;

5. _Calls upon_ all the High Contracting Parties to the Convention to take appropriate measures to ensure respect by Israel, the occupying Power, for the Convention in all circumstances, in conformity with their obligation under article 1 thereof;

6. _Invites_ Member States, the organizations of the United Nations system, governmental, intergovernmental and non-governmental organizations, and the mass communications media to continue and enhance their support for the Palestinian people;

7. _Urges_ the Security Council to consider the current situation in the occupied Palestinian territories, taking into account the recommendations contained in the report of the Secretary-General;

8. _Requests_ the Secretary-General to examine the present situation in the occupied Palestinian territories by all means available to him and to submit periodic reports thereon, the first such report no later than 17 November 1988.

General Assembly resolution 43/21

3 November 1988   Meeting 45   130-2-16 (recorded vote)

54-nation draft (A/43/L.21 & Add.1); agenda item 77.

Sponsors: Afghanistan, Algeria, Bahrain, Bangladesh, Brunei Darussalam, Bulgaria, Burkina Faso, Byelorussian SSR, Comoros, Cuba, Cyprus, Czechoslovakia, Democratic Yemen, Djibouti, Egypt, Gambia, German Democratic Republic, Ghana, India, Indonesia, Iraq, Jordan, Kuwait, Lao People's Democratic Republic, Lebanon, Libyan Arab Jamahiriya, Madagascar, Malaysia, Mali, Malta, Mauritania, Mongolia, Morocco, Nicaragua, Niger, Oman, Pakistan, Poland, Qatar, Saudi Arabia, Senegal, Sierra Leone, Somalia, Sudan, Syrian Arab Republic, Tunisia, Ukrainian SSR, USSR, United Arab Emirates, Viet Nam, Yemen, Yugoslavia, Zambia, Zimbabwe.

Recorded vote in Assembly as follows:

In favour: Afghanistan, Albania, Algeria, Angola, Argentina, Australia, Austria, Bahamas, Bahrain, Bangladesh, Barbados, Belgium, Benin, Bhutan, Bolivia, Botswana, Brazil, Brunei Darussalam, Bulgaria, Burkina Faso, Burma, Burundi, Byelorussian SSR, Cameroon, Cape Verde, Central African Republic, Chile, China, Colombia, Comoros, Congo, Cuba, Cyprus, Czechoslovakia, Democratic Yemen, Democratic Kampuchea, Denmark, Djibouti, Ecuador, Egypt, Ethiopia, Fiji, Finland, France, Gabon, Gambia, German Democratic Republic, Germany, Federal Republic of, Ghana, Greece, Guatemala, Guinea, Guinea-Bissau, Guyana, Hungary, India,

Indonesia, Iran, Iraq, Ireland, Italy, Japan, Jordan, Kenya, Kuwait, Lao People's Democratic Republic, Lebanon, Lesotho, Libyan Arab Jamahiriya, Luxembourg, Madagascar, Malawi, Malaysia, Mali, Malta, Mauritania, Mauritius, Mexico, Mongolia, Morocco, Mozambique, Nepal, Netherlands, New Zealand, Nicaragua, Niger, Nigeria, Norway, Oman, Pakistan, Panama, Papua New Guinea, Paraguay, Peru, Philippines, Poland, Portugal, Qatar, Romania, Rwanda, Sao Tome and Principe, Saudi Arabia, Senegal, Seychelles, Sierra Leone, Singapore, Somalia, Spain, Sri Lanka, Sudan, Swaziland, Sweden, Syrian Arab Republic, Thailand, Trinidad and Tobago, Tunisia, Turkey, Uganda, Ukrainian SSR, USSR, United Arab Emirates, United Republic of Tanzania, Uruguay, Vanuatu, Venezuela, Viet Nam, Yemen, Yugoslavia, Zambia, Zimbabwe.

Against: Israel, United States.

Abstaining: Antigua and Barbuda, Belize, Canada, Costa Rica, Dominica, Dominican Republic, El Salvador, Equatorial Guinea, Grenada, Iceland, Saint Kitts and Nevis, Saint Lucia, Saint Vincent and the Grenadines, Samoa, United Kingdom, Zaire.

In Israel's view, the text encouraged intransigence, incited hostility and promoted even more violence. It did not call on the residents of the territories to exercise restraint and ignored completely the violent nature of the activities directed against both Jews and Arabs, which had obliged Israel to take measures in order to restore calm. Furthermore, the text did not even allude to a political solution on the basis of Security Council resolutions 242(1967) and 338(1973).

Report of the Secretary-General (November). In response to the Assembly's request, the Secretary-General noted in a follow-up report of 21 November[15] that the Secretariat's Centre for Human Rights had on 10 November contacted Israel regarding the dispatch of a senior official to the occupied territories to examine the situation on the spot. On 14 November, Israel replied that the request was being considered by the Government, but, having received no further word, the Secretary-General requested an update of the information in the October report[2] of the Committee on Israeli practices (see above).

The update, annexed to the Secretary-General's report, summarized Israeli press reports from 1 September to 1 November, as well as information from UNRWA and ICRC, concluding that the situation in the occupied territories had worsened, with civilian deaths and injuries continuing to be widespread, along with other serious violations of human rights. The Secretary-General was deeply distressed by the high number of casualties, stating that the Israeli countermeasures of deportations, administrative detentions and collective punishments such as the imposition of curfews, the blowing up of houses and the closure of schools could only aggravate the tension already prevailing in the area. He reaffirmed that, under the fourth Geneva Convention, the civilian population of the territories was entitled to safety and protection. However, those measures, urgent as they were, would not resolve the conflict's underlying problem. The Secretary-General, therefore, remained fully committed to the search for a comprehensive, just and lasting settlement.

Fourth Geneva Convention

In 1988, the General Assembly and the Commission on Human Rights (see PART THREE, Chapter X) again reaffirmed that the fourth Geneva Convention of 12 August 1949 applied to the Israeli-occupied territories. Continuing disregard of the Convention—the main international instrument in humanitarian law that applied to the occupied territories—was reported throughout the year by the Committee on Israeli practices, which cited Israel's policy of annexation, settlements, deportations and ill-treatment of detainees in flagrant violation of the Convention.

Report of the Committee on Israeli practices. In its October 1988 report,[2] the Committee on Israeli practices stressed that Israel's general policy towards the occupied territories was based on the principle that they were part of the State of Israel and that therefore measures such as the establishment of colonies in the occupied territories and the transfer of Israeli citizens thereto did not constitute a process of annexation. That represented a flagrant violation of Israel's international obligations as a State party to the fourth Geneva Convention, which stipulated that military occupation was to be considered as a temporary, *de facto* situation, giving no right to the occupying Power over the territorial integrity of occupied territories. Israel's attitude was reflected in Prime Minister Shamir's statement (reported in *Ha'aretz* on 19 October 1987) that Jerusalem, Samaria, the Sharon, the Galilee and the Golan Heights were one entity and that it was a dangerous illusion to say that the people of Israel would ever cut itself from those areas.

Reports of the Secretary-General. In his January report to the Security Council,[4] the Secretary-General stated that Palestinians had requested the deployment of United Nations forces in the occupied territories, either to protect the inhabitants against Israeli security forces or to replace those forces in the populated areas. The Secretary-General stated that he had considered both possibilities, but, under the fourth Geneva Convention, the occupying Power was responsible for maintaining law and order and for protecting the civilian population. Since the prior consent of the parties to a conflict was a principle of United Nations peace-keeping operations, Israel's non-agreement was a serious deterrent.

With regard to the civilian population's entitlement to safety under the Convention, the Secretary-General reported that ICRC, the guardian of the 1949 Geneva Conventions, had frequently alluded to Israeli violations, which had also been the subject of numerous Security Council resolutions. Those violations included attempts to alter the status of Jerusalem, the establishment of Israeli settlements in the territories, deportations of Palestinian civilians, collective punishments such as curfews applied to whole districts, and the destruction of houses. There was also evidence that IDF used disproportionate force in dealing with demonstrations, leading to fatalities.

Pending a political settlement, the most effective way to ensure the safety and protection of the civilian population of the territories would be for Israel to apply in full the Convention's provisions. To that end, the Secretary-General recommended that the Security Council appeal to all the High Contracting Parties having diplomatic relations with Israel to use all means at their disposal to persuade Israel to change its position. Meanwhile, he urged Israel to introduce temporary measures, including: training IDF personnel in the rules of international humanitarian law (an obligation under the Convention); issuing orders for IDF personnel to assist, in all circumstances, in the provision of medical care to wounded persons; and ordering IDF not to obstruct delivery of essential food and medical supplies.

The Secretary-General, in November,[15] again stressed that it was essential that the occupying Power scrupulously apply the Convention's provisions.

In September,[16] the Secretary-General reported, in accordance with a 1987 General Assembly resolution[17] on the application of the fourth Geneva Convention, that, in a letter of 7 July 1988, Israel had maintained that, in view of the *sui generis* status of Judaea, Samaria and the Gaza District, the *de jure* applicability of the Convention to those areas was doubtful. Israel preferred to leave aside the legal question of the status of those areas and had decided, since 1967, to act in *de facto* accordance with the Convention's humanitarian provisions.

GENERAL ASSEMBLY ACTION

On 6 December, on the recommendation of the Special Political Committee, the General Assembly adopted **resolution 43/58 B** by recorded vote.

The General Assembly,

Recalling Security Council resolution 465(1980) of 1 March 1980, in which, *inter alia*, the Council affirmed that the Geneva Convention relative to the Protection of Civilian Persons in Time of War, of 12 August 1949, is applicable to the Arab territories occupied by Israel since 1967, including Jerusalem,

Recalling also its resolutions 3092 A (XXVIII) of 7 December 1973, 3240 B (XXIX) of 29 November 1974, 3525 B (XXX) of 15 December 1975, 31/106 B of 16 December 1976, 32/91 A of 13 December 1977, 33/113 A of 18 December 1978, 34/90 B of 12 December 1979, 35/122 A of 11 December 1980, 36/147 A of 16 December 1981, 37/88 A of 10 December 1982, 38/79 B of 15 December 1983, 39/95 B of 14 December 1984, 40/161 B of 16 December 1985, 41/63 B of 3 December 1986 and 42/160 B of 8 December 1987,

Taking note of the reports of the Secretary-General of 21 January 1988, 15 September 1988 and 21 November 1988,

Considering that the promotion of respect for the obligations arising from the Charter of the United Nations and other instruments and rules of international law is among the basic purposes and principles of the United Nations,

Bearing in mind the provisions of the Geneva Convention,

Noting that Israel and the concerned Arab States whose territories have been occupied by Israel since June 1967 are parties to the Convention,

Taking into account that States parties to the Convention undertake, in accordance with article 1 thereof, not only to respect but also to ensure respect for the Convention in all circumstances,

1. *Reaffirms* that the Geneva Convention relative to the Protection of Civilian Persons in Time of War, of 12 August 1949, is applicable to the Palestinian and other Arab territories occupied by Israel since 1967, including Jerusalem;

2. *Condemns once again* the failure of Israel, the occupying Power, to acknowledge the applicability of the Convention to the territories it has occupied since 1967, including Jerusalem;

3. *Strongly demands* that Israel acknowledge and comply with the provisions of the Convention in the Palestinian and other Arab territories it has occupied since 1967, including Jerusalem;

4. *Urgently calls upon* all States parties to the Convention to exert all efforts in order to ensure respect for and compliance with its provisions in the Palestinian and other Arab territories occupied by Israel since 1967, including Jerusalem;

5. *Requests* the Secretary-General to report to the General Assembly at its forty-fourth session on the implementation of the present resolution.

General Assembly resolution 43/58 B

6 December 1988   Meeting 71   148-1-4 (recorded vote)

Approved by Special Political Committee (A/43/904) by recorded vote (121-1-4), 28 November (meeting 34); draft by Afghanistan, Bangladesh, Brunei Darussalam, Burkina Faso, Comoros, Cuba, Egypt, India, Indonesia, Jordan (for Arab Group), Madagascar, Malaysia, Nicaragua, Pakistan, Zambia (A/SPC/43/L.27); agenda item 77.

Meeting numbers. GA 43rd session: SPC 28-32, 34; plenary 71.

Recorded vote in Assembly as follows:

In favour: Afghanistan, Albania, Algeria, Angola, Antigua and Barbuda, Argentina, Australia, Austria, Bahamas, Bahrain, Bangladesh, Barbados, Belgium, Belize, Benin, Bhutan, Bolivia, Botswana, Brazil, Brunei Darussalam, Bulgaria, Burkina Faso, Burma, Burundi, Byelorussian SSR, Cameroon, Canada, Cape Verde, Central African Republic, Chad, Chile, China, Colombia, Comoros, Costa Rica, Cuba, Cyprus, Czechoslovakia, Democratic Kampuchea, Democratic Yemen, Denmark, Djibouti, Dominican Republic, Ecuador, Egypt, El Salvador, Ethiopia, Fiji, Finland, France, Gabon, Gambia, German Democratic Republic, Germany, Federal Republic of, Ghana, Greece, Grenada, Guatemala, Guinea, Guinea-Bissau, Guyana, Haiti, Honduras, Hungary, Iceland, India, Indonesia, Iran, Iraq, Ireland, Italy, Jamaica, Japan, Jordan, Kenya, Kuwait, Lao People's Democratic Republic, Lebanon, Lesotho, Libyan Arab Jamahiriya, Luxembourg, Madagascar, Malaysia, Maldives, Mali, Malta, Mauritania, Mauritius, Mexico, Mongolia, Morocco, Mozambique, Nepal, Netherlands, New Zealand, Nicaragua, Niger, Nigeria, Norway, Oman, Pakistan, Panama, Papua New Guinea, Paraguay, Peru, Philippines, Poland, Portugal, Qatar, Romania, Rwanda, Saint Kitts and Nevis, Saint Lucia, Saint Vincent and the Grenadines, Samoa, Sao Tome and Principe, Saudi Arabia, Senegal, Seychelles, Sierra Leone, Singapore, Solomon Islands, Somalia, Spain, Sri Lanka, Sudan, Swaziland, Sweden, Syrian Arab Republic, Thailand, Togo, Trinidad and Tobago, Tunisia, Turkey, Uganda, Ukrainian SSR, USSR, United Arab Emirates, United Kingdom, United Republic of Tanzania, Uruguay, Vanuatu, Venezuela, Viet Nam, Yemen, Yugoslavia, Zambia, Zimbabwe.

Against: Israel.

Abstaining: Côte d'Ivoire, Liberia, United States, Zaire.

Before adopting the text as a whole, the Assembly adopted paragraph 1 by a recorded vote of 150 to 1. The Special Political Committee had approved the same provision by a recorded vote of 122 to 1. The vote had been requested by Israel, which stated that it supported paragraph 1, but not the text as a whole, as it did nothing to resolve the problems it sought to address.

Deportation of Palestinians

According to the Committee on Israeli practices,[2] the period since the beginning of the uprising was characterized by a noticeable increase in expulsions and deportations from the occupied territories, carried out in spite of international protest against such illegal practices.

On 5 January,[18] the Chairman of the Committee on Palestinian rights reported that Israeli authorities had decided to expel nine Palestinians, five from the West Bank and four from the Gaza Strip, accusing them of being instigators of the *intifadah*. The nine had been on a protest hunger strike in their respective prisons, where they were to remain until a decision was taken on their appeal against the expulsion orders.

By a letter of 12 January,[19] the Committee Chairman drew the urgent attention of the Security Council to the continuing deterioration of the situation in the territories owing to Israel's policies and practices, including use of live ammunition against demonstrators, mass arrests, detentions and deportations.

Reports of further expulsions continued to be received during 1988. On 12 April,[20] Lebanon protested that the previous day Israel had transported eight Palestinians by helicopter into the so-called security zone, then forcing them out of there, so that later that day they arrived at Rachaya in southern Lebanon. Lebanon condemned the deportations and Israel's exploitation of its territory for that purpose, in violation of Lebanese sovereignty. In reporting the same incident on 13 April,[21] the Acting Chairman of the Committee on Palestinian rights added that Israel had decided to deport another 12 Palestinians, according to *The New York Times*. Seventeen citizens from the village of Chabaa inside the so-called "security zone" who had committed no crime were deported by Israeli forces on 24 May, according to a communication by Lebanon of the following day.[22]

On 4 August, the Committee's Acting Chairman stated that on 1 August, as also communicated by Mauritania,[23] eight Palestinians from the West Bank and Gaza were deported to southern Lebanon on charges of inciting the uprising, and Israel declared its intention to deport six more. An additional four Palestinians from Gaza were deported to southern Lebanon on 17 August, an action protested by Lebanon the following day.[24]

The Committee on Palestinian rights, in October,[1] stated that a total of 33 Palestinians had been deported and there were deportation orders for another 25.

SECURITY COUNCIL ACTION (January and August)

At the request of Jordan on behalf of the Arab Group,[25] the Security Council convened on 5 January to consider the question of deportations of Palestinians from the occupied territories.

Israel, at its own request, was invited to participate without the right to vote under rule 37[b] of the Council's provisional rules of procedure. At Algeria's request,[26] the Council decided by 10 votes to 1 (United States), with 4 abstentions (France, Germany, Federal Republic of, Italy, United Kingdom), that PLO also be invited to participate. Though not made pursuant to rules 37 or 39,[a] the invitation gave PLO the same rights as those of a Member State invited under rule 37.

In requesting the vote, the United States reiterated its position that PLO should not be given the same rights as a Member State; it believed in hearing all points of view but not if that required violating the Council's rules.

Speaking before the Council, Israel maintained that the recent violence was not spontaneous and that a network of subversive organizers had been apprehended. In a few hard-core cases, Israel had decided on deportation—a right it had under international law; it would not countenance attempts to interfere with its legitimate responsibility of maintaining orderly government in all areas under its control.

The United States found that harsh deportation measures were unnecessary to maintain order; they increased tension rather than creating a political atmosphere conducive to reconciliation.

On 5 January, the Council unanimously adopted **resolution 607(1988)**.

The Security Council,
Recalling its resolution 605(1987) of 22 December 1987,
Expressing grave concern over the situation in the occupied Palestinian territories,
Having been apprised of the decision of Israel, the occupying Power, to "continue the deportation" of Palestinian civilians in the occupied territories,
Recalling the Geneva Convention relative to the Protection of Civilian Persons in Time of War, of 12 August 1949, and in particular articles 47 and 49 of same,
1. *Reaffirms once again* that the Geneva Convention relative to the Protection of Civilian Persons in Time of War, of 12 August 1949, is applicable to Palestinian and other Arab territories occupied by Israel since 1967, including Jerusalem;
2. *Calls upon* Israel to refrain from deporting any Palestinian civilians from the occupied territories;

3. *Strongly requests* Israel, the occupying Power, to abide by its obligations arising from the Convention;

4. *Decides* to keep the situation in the Palestinian and other Arab territories occupied by Israel since 1967, including Jerusalem, under review.

Security Council resolution 607(1988)

5 January 1988   Meeting 2780   Adopted unanimously

6-nation draft (S/19403).
Sponsors: Algeria, Argentina, Nepal, Senegal, Yugoslavia, Zambia.

On 13 January, four Palestinians were deported to Lebanon, while five others received deportation notices which were under appeal.

The following day, the Council again took up the question of deportations, inviting Israel and Lebanon to participate without voting rights. As it had done in January, the Council also invited PLO to participate, at Algeria's request.[27] It did so after voting on the matter at the request of the United States. The pattern of the voting was identical to that at the previous meeting, with the United States maintaining its position on PLO's eligibility to participate (see above).

Lebanon said the four Palestinians were currently in the Israeli-occupied "security zone" of southern Lebanon, without shelter or home; ICRC should be allowed to meet those individuals and bring them to Palestinian territory. The Council had the responsibility to adopt prompt measures required by international humanitarian law.

Israel rejected as false the depiction of its actions to remove a handful of leading terrorists of the Habash and Fatah groups in words appropriate to mass expulsion and uprooting of entire populations. In its recent meetings and resolutions, the Council had condoned all Palestinian violence and condemned all Israeli countermeasures, thus pushing the peace process farther away.

PLO refuted Israel's argument that it had to deport the Palestinians in question because they rejected due process of justice, and reasserted that in any case under article 49 of the fourth Geneva Convention the occupying Power was prohibited from deporting persons. The deportations also violated the Universal Declaration of Human Rights, article 9 of which stated that no one should be subjected to arbitrary arrest, detention or exile.[28]

On 14 January, the Council adopted **resolution 608(1988)**.

The Security Council,

Reaffirming its resolution 607(1988) of 5 January 1988,

Expressing its deep regret that Israel, the occupying Power, has, in defiance of that resolution, deported Palestinian civilians,

1. *Calls upon* Israel to rescind the order to deport Palestinian civilians and to ensure the safe and immediate return to the occupied Palestinian territories of those already deported;

2. *Requests* that Israel desist forthwith from deporting any other Palestinian civilians from the occupied territories;

3. *Decides* to keep the situation in the Palestinian and other Arab territories occupied by Israel since 1967, including Jerusalem, under review.

Security Council resolution 608(1988)

14 January 1988   Meeting 2781   14-0-1

6-nation draft (S/19429).
Sponsors: Algeria, Argentina, Nepal, Senegal, Yugoslavia, Zambia.
Vote in Council as follows:

In favour: Algeria, Argentina, Brazil, China, France, Germany, Federal Republic of, Italy, Japan, Nepal, Senegal, USSR, United Kingdom, Yugoslavia, Zambia.

Against: None.

Abstaining: United States.

The United States said that, while not minimizing the seriousness of deportations and urging Israel to avoid further deportations, it did not believe that selective attention to that issue in the Council was justified or served a useful purpose. It also noted that the four deported individuals declined to appeal to the Israeli Supreme Court, thus not allowing the judicial process to run its course.

In a 26 August statement on behalf of the Council members[14] (see above, under "The Palestinian uprising"), the Council President expressed profound concern over Israel's policy of deporting Palestinians, as demonstrated by the four expelled on 17 August and its decision to expel 40 more. He requested Israel to desist from those policies and to ensure immediately the safe return of those already deported.

Report of the Secretary-General (August). Israel's position on the deportation question, as reported by the Secretary-General in August 1988,[29] in response to a 1987 request of the General Assembly,[30] was that the continuing threat posed by terrorist activity to Israel's security accounted for its measures to ensure the maintenance of public order as contemplated by international law. Expulsion orders against individuals had been issued in the most extreme cases and were subject first to the review of an advisory committee and then to Israel's High Court of Justice. That Court had upheld the legality of such expulsion orders on appeal. An addendum to the report contained responses by the Byelorussian SSR and the Ukrainian SSR, condemning Israel's actions and supporting United Nations resolutions concerning protection of the population of the occupied territories.

GENERAL ASSEMBLY ACTION (December)

On 6 December 1988, on the recommendation of the Special Political Committee, the General Assembly adopted **resolution 43/58 E** by recorded vote.

The General Assembly,

Recalling Security Council resolutions 605(1987) of 22 December 1987, 607(1988) of 5 January 1988 and 608(1988) of 14 January 1988,

Taking note of the reports of the Secretary-General of 21 January 1988, 25 August 1988 and 21 November 1988,

Alarmed by the deportation of Palestinians from the occupied Palestinian territory by the Israeli authorities, especially in 1988,

Recalling the Geneva Convention relative to the Protection of Civilian Persons in Time of War, of 12 August 1949, in particular article 1 and the first paragraph of article 49, which read as follows:

"*Article 1*

"The High Contracting Parties undertake to respect and to ensure respect for the present Convention in all circumstances."

"*Article 49*

"Individual or mass forcible transfers, as well as deportations of protected persons from occupied territory to the territory of the occupying Power or to that of any other country, occupied or not, are prohibited, regardless of their motive. . .",

Reaffirming the applicability of the Geneva Convention to the Palestinian and other Arab territories occupied by Israel since 1967, including Jerusalem,

1. *Strongly deplores* the continuing disregard by Israel, the occupying Power, of the relevant decisions of the Security Council and resolutions of the General Assembly;

2. *Demands* that the Government of Israel, the occupying Power, rescind the illegal measures taken by the Israeli authorities in deporting Palestinians, especially in 1988, and that it facilitate their immediate return;

3. *Calls upon* Israel, the occupying Power, to cease forthwith the deportation of Palestinians and to abide scrupulously by the provisions of the Geneva Convention relative to the Protection of Civilian Persons in Time of War, of 12 August 1949;

4. *Requests* the Secretary-General to report to the General Assembly as soon as possible but not later than the beginning of its forty-fourth session on the implementation of the present resolution.

General Assembly resolution 43/58 E

6 December 1988   Meeting 71   152-1-1 (recorded vote)

Approved by Special Political Committee (A/43/904) by recorded vote (121-1-3), 28 November (meeting 34); draft by Afghanistan, Bangladesh, Brunei Darussalam, Burkina Faso, Comoros, Cuba, Egypt, India, Indonesia, Jordan (for Arab Group), Madagascar, Malaysia, Nicaragua, Pakistan, Zambia (A/SPC/43/L.30/Rev.1); agenda item 77.

Meeting numbers. GA 43rd session: SPC 28-32, 34; plenary 71.

Recorded vote in Assembly as follows:

In favour: Afghanistan, Albania, Algeria, Angola, Antigua and Barbuda, Argentina, Australia, Austria, Bahamas, Bahrain, Bangladesh, Barbados, Belgium, Belize, Benin, Bhutan, Bolivia, Botswana, Brazil, Brunei Darussalam, Bulgaria, Burkina Faso, Burma, Burundi, Byelorussian SSR, Cameroon, Canada, Cape Verde, Central African Republic, Chad, Chile, China, Colombia, Comoros, Costa Rica, Côte d'Ivoire, Cuba, Cyprus, Czechoslovakia, Democratic Kampuchea, Democratic Yemen, Denmark, Djibouti, Dominican Republic, Ecuador, Egypt, El Salvador, Ethiopia, Fiji, Finland, France, Gabon, Gambia, German Democratic Republic, Germany, Federal Republic of, Ghana, Greece, Grenada, Guatemala, Guinea, Guinea-Bissau, Guyana, Haiti, Honduras, Hungary, Iceland, India, Indonesia, Iran, Iraq, Ireland, Italy, Jamaica, Japan, Jordan, Kenya, Kuwait, Lao People's Democratic Republic, Lebanon, Lesotho, Liberia, Libyan Arab Jamahiriya, Luxembourg, Madagascar, Malawi, Malaysia, Maldives, Mali, Malta, Mauritania, Mauritius, Mexico, Mongolia, Morocco, Mozambique, Nepal, Netherlands, New Zealand, Nicaragua, Niger, Nigeria, Norway, Oman, Pakistan, Panama, Papua New Guinea, Paraguay, Peru, Philippines, Poland, Portugal, Qatar, Romania, Rwanda, Saint Kitts and Nevis, Saint Lucia, Saint Vincent and the Grenadines, Samoa, Sao Tome and Principe, Saudi Arabia, Senegal, Seychelles, Sierra Leone, Singapore, Solomon Islands, Somalia, Spain, Sri Lanka, Sudan, Swaziland, Sweden, Syrian Arab Republic, Thailand, Togo, Trinidad and Tobago, Tunisia, Turkey, Uganda, Ukrainian SSR, USSR, United Arab Emirates, United Kingdom, United Republic of Tanzania, Uruguay, Vanuatu, Venezuela, Viet Nam, Yemen, Yugoslavia, Zaire, Zambia, Zimbabwe.

Against: Israel.

Abstaining: United States.

Palestinian detainees

Report of the Committee on Israeli practices. In its October 1988 report,[2] the Committee on Israeli practices cited extensive evidence of detainees being treated under harsh conditions in the occupied territories. The exceptional situation created by the uprising had resulted in an unprecedented increase in the number of detainees, which had led to the opening of new detention centres and to a worsening of already critical conditions. By mid-May, an estimated 1,900 Palestinians were held in administrative detention. In addition to existing prisons, army detention centres had increased in number, and Israeli military government buildings and police stations were often used temporarily for detention purposes. Detainees were also held in centres inside Israel itself, in violation of the fourth Geneva Convention. Inmates were faced with overcrowding, physical and psychological ill-treatment, and lack of adequate health services, nutrition and clothing. Some of those detained were no older than 11 or 12 years. Testimonies also referred to the practice of repeatedly detaining the same persons, turning them into so-called special cases who spent most of their lives in prison, or to the arbitrary detention of several members of the same family.

Written information submitted to the Committee referred to incidents where individuals had died during interrogation, where prison staff were replaced by harsher military police, and where prisoners had been tortured, beaten and kept in wretched conditions without adequate sanitation, water, food and medical care. When brought to light through the Israeli judicial system, punishments for serious, routine ill-treatment of prisoners took the form of demotions in rank or imprisonment for several months.

Reports of the Secretary-General. In January,[4] the Secretary-General reported to the Security Council allegations of routine violence in detention centres, as well as in the whole system of administrative detention, with the purpose of interrogation being normally to extract a confession for use in proceedings in the military courts. Heavy physical and psychological pressure was used for that purpose by the General Security Services, which applied techniques such as hooding to prevent permanent physical disfigurement.

Annexed to the Secretary-General's 21 November 1988 report on the *intifadah*[15] were summaries of events in the occupied territories reported in the Israeli press from 1 September to 1 November, including details on Arab detainees. ICRC delegates were visiting approximately 6,200 persons in eight military detention centres, more than 2,100 of whom were administrative detainees.

In August,[31] the Secretary-General reported that, in response to his 5 February note verbale to Israel regarding steps it had taken to implement the 1987 General Assembly resolution on arbitrary detentions,[32] Israel stated on 7 July that that resolution bore unconcealed bias; detention and imprisonment in Judaea, Samaria and Gaza were legal measures taken against terrorism and violence. Israel was responsible under international law for maintaining public order and security, a duty it carried out in conformity with the utmost regard to preserving the rule of law and protecting human rights. Due process was guaranteed by allowing detainees and prisoners to petition Israel's High Court of Justice, and ICRC delegates were allowed regular visits to prisons and detention centres.

GENERAL ASSEMBLY ACTION

On 6 December, on the recommendation of the Special Political Committee, the General Assembly adopted **resolution 43/58 D** by recorded vote.

The General Assembly,

Recalling Security Council resolution 605(1987) of 22 December 1987,

Recalling also its resolutions 38/79 A of 15 December 1983, 39/95 A of 14 December 1984, 40/161 A of 16 December 1985, 41/63 A of 3 December 1986, 42/160 A of 8 December 1987 and 43/21 of 3 November 1988,

Taking note of the report of the Special Committee to Investigate Israeli Practices Affecting the Human Rights of the Population of the Occupied Territories,

Taking note also of the reports of the Secretary-General of 21 January 1988, 25 August 1988 and 21 November 1988,

1. *Deplores* the Israeli arbitrary detention or imprisonment of thousands of Palestinians;

2. *Calls upon* Israel, the occupying Power, to release all Palestinians and Arabs arbitrarily detained and imprisoned as a result of their resistance against occupation in order to attain self-determination;

3. *Requests* the Secretary-General to report to the General Assembly as soon as possible but not later than the beginning of its forty-fourth session on the implementation of the present resolution.

General Assembly resolution 43/58 D

6 December 1988   Meeting 71   150-2 (recorded vote)

Approved by Special Political Committee (A/43/904) by recorded vote (118-2-2), 28 November (meeting 34); draft by Afghanistan, Bangladesh, Brunei Darussalam, Burkina Faso, Comoros, Cuba, Egypt, India, Indonesia, Jordan (for Arab Group), Madagascar, Malaysia, Nicaragua, Pakistan, Zambia (A/SPC/43/L.29/Rev.1); agenda item 77.

Meeting numbers. GA 43rd session: SPC 28-32, 34; plenary 71.

Recorded vote in Assembly as follows:

In favour: Afghanistan, Albania, Algeria, Angola, Antigua and Barbuda, Argentina, Australia, Austria, Bahamas, Bahrain, Bangladesh, Barbados, Belgium, Belize, Benin, Bhutan, Bolivia, Botswana, Brazil, Brunei Darussalam, Bulgaria, Burkina Faso, Burma, Burundi, Byelorussian SSR, Cameroon, Canada, Cape Verde, Central African Republic, Chad, China, Colombia, Comoros, Costa Rica, Côte d'Ivoire, Cuba, Cyprus, Czechoslovakia, Democratic Kampuchea, Democratic Yemen, Denmark, Djibouti, Dominican Republic, Ecuador, Egypt, El Salvador, Ethiopia, Fiji, Finland, France, Gabon, Gambia, German Democratic Republic, Germany, Federal Republic of, Ghana, Greece, Grenada, Guatemala, Guinea, Guinea-Bissau, Guyana, Haiti, Honduras, Hungary, Iceland, India, Indonesia, Iran, Iraq, Ireland, Italy, Jamaica, Japan, Jordan, Kenya, Kuwait, Lao People's Democratic Republic, Lebanon, Lesotho, Liberia, Libyan Arab Jamahiriya, Luxembourg, Madagascar, Malawi, Malaysia, Maldives, Mali, Malta, Mauritania, Mauritius, Mexico, Mongolia, Morocco, Mozambique, Nepal, Netherlands, New Zealand, Nicaragua, Niger, Nigeria, Norway, Oman, Pakistan, Panama, Papua New Guinea, Paraguay, Peru, Philippines, Poland, Portugal, Qatar, Romania, Rwanda, Saint Kitts and Nevis, Saint Lucia, Saint Vincent and the Grenadines, Samoa, Sao Tome and Principe, Saudi Arabia, Senegal, Seychelles, Sierra Leone, Singapore, Solomon Islands, Somalia, Spain, Sri Lanka, Sudan, Swaziland, Sweden, Syrian Arab Republic, Togo, Trinidad and Tobago, Tunisia, Turkey, Uganda, Ukrainian SSR, USSR, United Arab Emirates, United Kingdom, United Republic of Tanzania, Uruguay, Vanuatu, Venezuela, Viet Nam, Yemen, Yugoslavia, Zaire, Zambia, Zimbabwe.

Against: Israel, United States.

Israeli settlements

Report of the Committee on Palestinian rights. In its October 1988 report,[1] the Committee on Palestinian rights drew attention to the increasing demolition of houses by Israel in the occupied territories and the growing involvement of Israeli settlers in attacks against the Palestinian population, which seemed to be endorsed by the authorities' announced policy of allowing settlers to shoot demonstrators carrying what appeared to be fire-bombs. The number of settlements had reached 170 in the West Bank and 20 in Gaza, with new construction and expansion announced. On the other hand, stringent restrictions were imposed for Arabs on water use, new construction, credit-granting and other activities necessary to develop the territories.

Report of the Committee on Israeli practices. Similarly, the Committee on Israeli practices, also in October,[2] reported that Israel continued to annex Palestinian territory and establish or plan settlements. In April, following a drastic drop in the sale of flats in the territories, owing to unrest, Israel decided on measures to boost construction there and, in June, it was announced that 10 provisional settlements were to be converted into permanent ones. According to the *Jerusalem Post* of 4 March, the Israeli Finance Minister had agreed to add $6.5 million to funds available for Jewish settlements in the territories.

Reports of the Secretary-General. The Secretary-General reported in January[4] to the Security Council on complaints by Palestinians that land was being taken for Israeli settlements and that those settlements were given privileged access to water supplies. Israeli Ministers rejected those and other complaints, describing them as politically motivated exaggerations or distortions.

In September,[33] the Secretary-General reported that, in response to his query of 5 February on the implementation of a 1987 General Assembly resolution[34] demanding that Israel desist from changing the legal status or demographic composition of the territories, Israel had stated on 7 July that, in view of the *sui generis* status of Judaea, Samaria and the Gaza District, the *de jure* applicability of the fourth Geneva Convention to those areas was doubtful and it preferred to leave aside the legal question of status, having decided since 1967 to act in *de facto* accordance with the humanitarian provisions of that Convention.

GENERAL ASSEMBLY ACTION

On 6 December 1988, on the recommendation of the Special Political Committee, the General Assembly adopted **resolution 43/58 C** by recorded vote.

The General Assembly,

Recalling Security Council resolution 465(1980) of 1 March 1980,

Recalling also its resolutions 32/5 of 28 October 1977, 33/113 B of 18 December 1978, 34/90 C of 12 December 1979, 35/122 B of 11 December 1980, 36/147 B of 16 December 1981, 37/88 B of 10 December 1982, 38/79 C of 15 December 1983, 39/95 C of 14 December 1984, 40/161 C of 16 December 1985, 41/63 C of 3 December 1986 and 42/160 C of 8 December 1987,

Expressing grave anxiety and concern at the present serious situation in the Palestinian and other occupied Arab territories, including Jerusalem, as a result of the continued Israeli occupation and the measures and actions taken by Israel, the occupying Power, designed to change the legal status, geographical nature and demographic composition of those territories,

Taking note of the reports of the Secretary-General of 21 January 1988, 15 September 1988 and 21 November 1988,

Confirming that the Geneva Convention relative to the Protection of Civilian Persons in Time of War, of 12 August 1949, is applicable to all Palestinian and other Arab territories occupied by Israel since June 1967, including Jerusalem,

1. *Determines* that all such measures and actions taken by Israel in the Palestinian and other Arab territories occupied since 1967, including Jerusalem, are in violation of the relevant provisions of the Geneva Convention relative to the Protection of Civilian Persons in Time of War, of 12 August 1949, and constitute a serious obstacle to the efforts to achieve a comprehensive, just and lasting peace in the Middle East and therefore have no legal validity;

2. *Strongly deplores* the persistence of Israel in carrying out such measures, in particular the establishment of settlements in the Palestinian and other occupied Arab territories, including Jerusalem;

3. *Demands* that Israel comply strictly with its international obligations in accordance with the principles of international law and the provisions of the Geneva Convention;

4. *Demands once more* that Israel, the occupying Power, desist forthwith from taking any action which would result in changing the legal status, geographical nature or demographic composition of the Palestinian and other Arab territories occupied since 1967, including Jerusalem;

5. *Urgently calls upon* all States parties to the Geneva Convention to respect and to exert all efforts in order to ensure respect for and compliance with its provisions in all Palestinian and other Arab territories occupied by Israel since 1967, including Jerusalem;

6. *Requests* the Secretary-General to report to the General Assembly at its forty-fourth session on the implementation of the present resolution.

General Assembly resolution 43/58 C

6 December 1988　　Meeting 71　　149-1-2 (recorded vote)

Approved by Special Political Committee (A/43/904) by recorded vote (119-1-4), 28 November (meeting 34); draft by Afghanistan, Bangladesh, Brunei Darussalam, Burkina Faso, Comoros, Cuba, Egypt, India, Indonesia, Jordan (for Arab Group), Madagascar, Malaysia, Nicaragua, Pakistan, Zambia (A/SPC/43/L.28); agenda item 77.

Meeting numbers. GA 43rd session: SPC 28-32, 34; plenary 71.

Recorded vote in Assembly as follows:

In favour: Afghanistan, Albania, Algeria, Angola, Antigua and Barbuda, Argentina, Australia, Austria, Bahamas, Bahrain, Bangladesh, Barbados, Belgium, Belize, Benin, Bhutan, Bolivia, Botswana, Brazil, Brunei Darussalam, Bulgaria, Burkina Faso, Burma, Burundi, Byelorussian SSR, Cameroon, Canada, Cape Verde, Central African Republic, Chad, Chile, China, Colombia, Comoros, Costa Rica, Côte d'Ivoire, Cuba, Cyprus, Czechoslovakia, Democratic Kampuchea, Democratic Yemen, Denmark, Djibouti, Dominican Republic, Ecuador, Egypt, El Salvador, Ethiopia, Fiji, Finland, France, Gabon, Gambia, German Democratic Republic, Germany, Federal Republic of, Ghana, Greece, Grenada, Guatemala, Guinea, Guinea-Bissau, Guyana, Haiti, Honduras, Hungary, India, Indonesia, Iran, Iraq, Ireland, Italy, Jamaica, Japan, Jordan, Kenya, Kuwait, Lao People's Democratic Republic, Lebanon, Lesotho, Libyan Arab Jamahiriya, Luxembourg, Madagascar, Malawi, Malaysia, Maldives, Mali, Malta, Mauritania, Mauritius, Mexico, Mongolia, Morocco, Mozambique, Nepal, Netherlands, New Zealand, Nicaragua, Niger, Nigeria, Norway, Oman, Pakistan, Papua New Guinea, Paraguay, Peru, Philippines, Poland, Portugal, Qatar, Romania, Rwanda, Saint Kitts and Nevis, Saint Lucia, Saint Vincent and the Grenadines, Samoa, Sao Tome and Principe, Saudi Arabia, Senegal, Seychelles, Sierra Leone, Singapore, Solomon Islands, Somalia, Spain, Sri Lanka, Sudan, Swaziland, Sweden, Syrian Arab Republic, Thailand, Togo, Trinidad and Tobago, Tunisia, Turkey, Uganda, Ukrainian SSR, USSR, United Arab Emirates, United Kingdom, United Republic of Tanzania, Uruguay, Vanuatu, Venezuela, Viet Nam, Yemen, Yugoslavia, Zaire, Zambia, Zimbabwe.

Against: Israel.

Abstaining: Liberia, United States.

Golan Heights

Report of the Committee on Israeli practices. In its October 1988 report,[2] the Committee on Israeli practices indicated that tension prevailed in the Syrian territory under Israeli occupation, with reported disturbances and arrests of residents of Majdal Shams in the northern Golan Heights. The Syrian Arab Republic reported to the Committee in May that Israeli human rights violations in the Golan Heights had intensified. Annexation, introduction of settlers, Judaization and expropriation of water continued, as confirmed by official Israeli statements. In addition, detention and imprisonment, oppression, house arrest and raids, imposition of curfews and repression of freedom of expression escalated.

Meanwhile, the economic position of the population was increasingly deteriorating as a result of Israeli policies, which treated the occupied areas as dependent on the Israeli economy and as a major consumer market for Israeli products. Israel had blocked the marketing of agricultural produce, the mainstay of the population there. Furthermore, the occupation authorities insisted on eliminating any national character from the population and cutting the people off from their national historic and cultural roots with the Syrian Arab Republic. The level of education and health care provided in the schools also deteriorated.

Report of the Secretary-General. In response to a 1987 resolution of the General Assembly[35] calling on Member States not to recognize Israel's imposition of its laws, jurisdiction and administration on the occupied Syrian Arab Golan, the Secretary-General reported on 26 August 1988[36] that seven States had expressed support for the provisions of that resolution. Israel's position remained as first expressed in 1981,[37] namely, that it could not be expected to maintain indefinitely a military administration merely to accommodate the Syrian Arab Republic's interest in persistent conflict and that its legislation applied to the Golan Heights did not diminish the local population's rights.

GENERAL ASSEMBLY ACTION

On 6 December 1988, the General Assembly adopted **resolution 43/54 B** by recorded vote.

The General Assembly,

Having discussed the item entitled "The situation in the Middle East",

Taking note of the report of the Secretary-General of 28 November 1988,

Recalling Security Council resolution 497(1981) of 17 December 1981,

Reaffirming its resolutions 36/226 B of 17 December 1981, ES-9/1 of 5 February 1982, 37/123 A of 16 December 1982, 38/180 A of 19 December 1983, 39/146 B of 14 December 1984, 40/168 B of 16 December 1985, 41/162 B of 4 December 1986 and 42/209 C of 11 December 1987,

Recalling its resolution 3314(XXIX) of 14 December 1974, in which it defined an act of aggression, *inter alia*, as "the invasion or attack by the armed forces of a State of the territory of another State, or any military occupation, however temporary, resulting from such invasion or attack, or any annexation by the use of force of the territory of another State or part thereof" and provided that "no consideration of whatever nature, whether political, economic, military or otherwise, may serve as a justification for aggression",

Reaffirming the fundamental principle of the inadmissibility of the acquisition of territory by force,

Reaffirming once more the applicability of the Geneva Convention relative to the Protection of Civilian Persons in Time of War, of 12 August 1949, to the Palestinian territory occupied since 1967, including Jerusalem, and the other occupied Arab territories,

Noting that Israel's record, policies and actions establish conclusively that it is not a peace-loving Member State and that it has not carried out its obligations under the Charter of the United Nations,

Noting also that Israel has refused, in violation of Article 25 of the Charter, to accept and carry out the numerous relevant decisions of the Security Council, in particular resolution 497(1981), thus failing to carry out its obligations under the Charter,

1. *Strongly condemns* Israel for its failure to comply with Security Council resolution 497(1981) and General

Assembly resolutions 36/226 B, ES-9/1, 37/123 A, 38/180 A, 39/146 B, 40/168 B, 41/162 B and 42/209 C;

2. *Declares once more* that Israel's continued occupation of the Syrian Arab Golan and its decision of 14 December 1981 to impose its laws, jurisdiction and administration on the occupied Syrian Arab Golan constitute an act of aggression under the provisions of Article 39 of the Charter of the United Nations and General Assembly resolution 3314(XXIX);

3. *Declares once more* that Israel's decision to impose its laws, jurisdiction and administration on the occupied Syrian Arab Golan is illegal and therefore null and void and has no validity whatsoever;

4. *Declares* all Israeli policies and practices of, or aimed at, annexation of the Palestinian territory occupied since 1967, including Jerusalem, and of the other occupied Arab territories, to be illegal and in violation of international law and of the relevant United Nations resolutions;

5. *Determines once more* that all actions taken by Israel to give effect to its decision relating to the occupied Syrian Arab Golan are illegal and invalid and shall not be recognized;

6. *Reaffirms its determination* that all relevant provisions of the Regulations annexed to the Hague Convention IV of 1907, and the Geneva Convention relative to the Protection of Civilian Persons in Time of War, of 12 August 1949, continue to apply to the Syrian territory occupied by Israel since 1967, and calls upon the parties thereto to respect and ensure respect for their obligations under these instruments in all circumstances;

7. *Determines once more* that the continued occupation of the Syrian Arab Golan since 1967 and its annexation by Israel on 14 December 1981, following Israel's decision to impose its laws, jurisdiction and administration on that territory, constitute a continuing threat to international peace and security;

8. *Strongly deplores* the negative vote by a permanent member of the Security Council which prevented the Council from adopting against Israel, under Chapter VII of the Charter, the "appropriate measures" referred to in resolution 497(1981) unanimously adopted by the Council;

9. *Further deplores* any political, economic, financial, military and technological support to Israel that encourages it to commit acts of aggression and to consolidate and perpetuate its occupation and annexation of the Palestinian territory occupied since 1967, including Jerusalem, and the other occupied Arab territories;

10. *Firmly emphasizes once more* its demand that Israel, the occupying Power, rescind forthwith its illegal decision of 14 December 1981 to impose its laws, jurisdiction and administration on the Syrian Arab Golan, which resulted in the effective annexation of that territory;

11. *Reaffirms once more* the overriding necessity of the total and unconditional withdrawal by Israel from the Palestinian territory occupied since 1967, including Jerusalem, and the other occupied Arab territories, which is an essential prerequisite for the establishment of a comprehensive and just peace in the Middle East;

12. *Determines once more* that Israel's record, policies and actions confirm that it is not a peace-loving Member State, that it has persistently violated the principles contained in the Charter and that it has carried out neither its obligations under the Charter nor its commitment under General Assembly resolution 273(III) of 11 May 1949;

13. *Calls once more upon* all Member States to apply the following measures:

(a) To refrain from supplying Israel with any weapons and related equipment and to suspend any military assistance that Israel receives from them;

(b) To refrain from acquiring any weapons or military equipment from Israel;

(c) To suspend economic, financial and technological assistance to and co-operation with Israel;

(d) To sever diplomatic, trade and cultural relations with Israel;

14. *Reiterates its call* to all Member States to cease forthwith, individually and collectively, all dealings with Israel in order totally to isolate it in all fields;

15. *Urges* non-member States to act in accordance with the provisions of the present resolution;

16. *Calls upon* the specialized agencies and other international organizations to conform their relations with Israel to the terms of the present resolution;

17. *Requests* the Secretary-General to report to the General Assembly at its forty-fourth session on the implementation of the present resolution.

General Assembly resolution 43/54 B

6 December 1988   Meeting 71   83-21-45 (recorded vote)

22-nation draft (A/43/L.45 & Add.1); agenda item 40.
Sponsors: Algeria, Bahrain, Bangladesh, Cuba, Democratic Yemen, Djibouti, Indonesia, Iraq, Kuwait, Libyan Arab Jamahiriya, Malaysia, Mauritania, Morocco, Oman, Pakistan, Qatar, Saudi Arabia, Sudan, Syrian Arab Republic, United Arab Emirates, Yemen, Zimbabwe.
Meeting numbers. GA 43rd session: plenary 68-71.

Recorded vote in Assembly as follows:

In favour: Afghanistan, Albania, Algeria, Angola, Bahrain, Bangladesh, Benin, Bhutan, Botswana, Brunei Darussalam, Bulgaria, Burkina Faso, Burundi, Byelorussian SSR, Cape Verde, China, Comoros, Cuba, Cyprus, Czechoslovakia, Democratic Kampuchea, Democratic Yemen, Djibouti, Ethiopia, Gabon, German Democratic Republic, Ghana, Greece, Guinea, Guinea-Bissau, Guyana, Hungary, India, Indonesia, Iran, Iraq, Jordan, Kenya, Kuwait, Lao People's Democratic Republic, Lebanon, Lesotho, Libyan Arab Jamahiriya, Madagascar, Malaysia, Maldives, Mali, Mauritania, Mauritius, Mexico, Mongolia, Morocco, Mozambique, Nicaragua, Niger, Nigeria, Oman, Pakistan, Poland, Qatar, Rwanda, Sao Tome and Principe, Saudi Arabia, Senegal, Seychelles, Sierra Leone, Somalia, Sri Lanka, Sudan, Syrian Arab Republic, Tunisia, Turkey, Uganda, Ukrainian SSR, USSR, United Arab Emirates, United Republic of Tanzania, Vanuatu, Viet Nam, Yemen, Yugoslavia, Zambia, Zimbabwe.
Against: Australia, Belgium, Belize, Canada, Denmark, Finland, France, Germany, Federal Republic of, Iceland, Ireland, Israel, Italy, Japan, Luxembourg, Netherlands, New Zealand, Norway, Portugal, Sweden, United Kingdom, United States.
Abstaining: Antigua and Barbuda, Argentina, Austria, Bahamas, Barbados, Bolivia, Brazil, Burma, Cameroon, Central African Republic, Chad, Colombia, Côte d'Ivoire, Ecuador, Egypt, El Salvador, Fiji, Grenada, Guatemala, Haiti, Honduras, Jamaica, Liberia, Malawi, Malta, Nepal, Panama, Papua New Guinea, Paraguay, Peru, Philippines, Saint Kitts and Nevis, Saint Lucia, Saint Vincent and the Grenadines, Samoa, Singapore, Solomon Islands, Spain, Swaziland, Thailand, Togo, Trinidad and Tobago, Uruguay, Venezuela, Zaire.

On the same date, the Assembly, on the recommendation of the Special Political Committee, adopted **resolution 43/58 F** by recorded vote.

The General Assembly,

Deeply concerned that the Arab territories occupied since 1967 have been under continued Israeli military occupation,

Recalling Security Council resolution 497(1981) of 17 December 1981,

Recalling also its resolutions 36/226 B of 17 December 1981, ES-9/1 of 5 February 1982, 37/88 E of 10 December 1982, 38/79 F of 15 December 1983, 39/95 F of 14 December 1984, 40/161 F of 16 December 1985, 41/63 F

of 3 December 1986, 42/160 F of 8 December 1987 and 43/21 of 3 November 1988,

Having considered the report of the Secretary-General of 26 August 1988,

Recalling its previous resolutions, in particular resolutions 3414(XXX) of 5 December 1975, 31/61 of 9 December 1976, 32/20 of 25 November 1977, 33/28 and 33/29 of 7 December 1978, 34/70 of 6 December 1979 and 35/122 E of 11 December 1980, in which, *inter alia,* it called upon Israel to put an end to its occupation of the Arab territories and to withdraw from all those territories,

Reaffirming once more the illegality of Israel's decision of 14 December 1981 to impose its laws, jurisdiction and administration on the Syrian Arab Golan, which has resulted in the effective annexation of that territory,

Reaffirming that the acquisition of territory by force is inadmissible under the Charter of the United Nations and that all territories thus occupied by Israel must be returned,

Recalling the Geneva Convention relative to the Protection of Civilian Persons in Time of War, of 12 August 1949,

1. *Strongly condemns* Israel, the occupying Power, for its refusal to comply with the relevant resolutions of the General Assembly and the Security Council, particularly Council resolution 497(1981), in which the Council, *inter alia,* decided that the Israeli decision to impose its laws, jurisdiction and administration on the occupied Syrian Arab Golan was null and void and without international legal effect and demanded that Israel, the occupying Power, should rescind forthwith its decision;

2. *Condemns* the persistence of Israel in changing the physical character, demographic composition, institutional structure and legal status of the occupied Syrian Arab Golan;

3. *Determines* that all legislative and administrative measures and actions taken or to be taken by Israel, the occupying Power, that purport to alter the character and legal status of the Syrian Arab Golan are null and void and constitute a flagrant violation of international law and of the Geneva Convention relative to the Protection of Civilian Persons in Time of War, of 12 August 1949, and have no legal effect;

4. *Strongly condemns* Israel for its attempts to impose forcibly Israeli citizenship and Israeli identity cards on the Syrian citizens in the occupied Syrian Arab Golan, and calls upon it to desist from its repressive measures against the population of the Syrian Arab Golan;

5. *Calls once again upon* Member States not to recognize any of the legislative or administrative measures and actions referred to above;

6. *Requests* the Secretary-General to report to the General Assembly at its forty-fourth session on the implementation of the present resolution.

General Assembly resolution 43/58 F

6 December 1988   Meeting 71   149-1-3 (recorded vote)

Approved by Special Political Committee (A/43/904) by recorded vote (118-1-5), 28 November (meeting 34); draft by Afghanistan, Bangladesh, Brunei Darussalam, Burkina Faso, Comoros, Cuba, Egypt, India, Indonesia, Jordan (for Arab Group), Madagascar, Malaysia, Nicaragua, Pakistan, Zambia (A/SPC/43/L.31); agenda item 77.
Meeting numbers. GA 43rd session: SPC 28-32, 34; plenary 71.

Recorded vote in Assembly as follows:

In favour: Afghanistan, Albania, Algeria, Angola, Antigua and Barbuda, Argentina, Australia, Austria, Bahamas, Bahrain, Bangladesh, Barbados, Belgium, Belize, Benin, Bhutan, Bolivia, Botswana, Brazil, Brunei Darussalam, Bulgaria, Burkina Faso, Burma, Burundi, Byelorussian SSR, Cameroon, Canada, Cape Verde, Central African Republic, Chad, Chile, China, Colombia, Comoros, Côte d'Ivoire,* Cuba, Cyprus, Czechoslovakia, Democratic Kampuchea, Democratic Yemen, Denmark, Djibouti, Dominican Republic, Ecuador, Egypt, El Salvador, Ethiopia, Fiji, Finland, France, Gabon, Gambia, German Democratic Republic, Germany, Federal Republic of, Ghana, Greece, Grenada, Guatemala, Guinea, Guinea-Bissau, Guyana, Haiti, Honduras, Hungary, Iceland, India, Indonesia, Iran, Iraq, Ireland, Italy, Jamaica, Japan, Jordan, Kenya, Kuwait, Lao People's Democratic Republic, Lebanon, Lesotho, Libyan Arab Jamahiriya, Luxembourg, Madagascar, Malawi, Malaysia, Maldives, Mali, Malta, Mauritania, Mauritius, Mexico, Mongolia, Morocco, Mozambique, Nepal, Netherlands, New Zealand, Nicaragua, Niger, Nigeria, Norway, Oman, Pakistan, Panama, Papua New Guinea, Paraguay, Peru, Philippines, Poland, Portugal, Qatar, Romania, Rwanda, Saint Kitts and Nevis, Saint Lucia, Saint Vincent and the Grenadines, Samoa, Sao Tome and Principe, Saudi Arabia, Senegal, Seychelles, Sierra Leone, Singapore, Solomon Islands, Somalia, Spain, Sri Lanka, Sudan, Swaziland, Sweden, Syrian Arab Republic, Thailand, Togo, Trinidad and Tobago, Tunisia, Turkey, Uganda, Ukrainian SSR, USSR, United Arab Emirates, United Kingdom, United Republic of Tanzania, Uruguay, Vanuatu, Venezuela, Viet Nam, Yemen, Yugoslavia, Zambia, Zimbabwe.

Against: Israel.

Abstaining: Liberia, United States, Zaire.

*Later advised the Secretariat it had intended to abstain.

Israeli measures against educational institutions

Report of the Committee on Palestinian rights. The Committee on Palestinian rights reported in October 1988[1] that universities and other educational institutions in the West Bank, which had suffered frequent closings and disruptions prior to the uprising, were closed from December 1987 to May 1988, and then again for varying periods. Most schools in the Gaza Strip were also repeatedly closed. A large number of schools were sequestered by the army for its own use and school property was destroyed. All teachers newly appointed for the 1987/88 academic year were dismissed.

Report of the Committee on Israeli practices. The Committee on Israeli practices[2] detailed information it had received regarding freedom of education for Palestinians in the territories during the current academic year. That included the killing and physical mistreatment of students, detention of some 1,000 students as well as teachers, and the fining of students. Israel was charged with trying to change the entire structure of universities by interfering in their internal affairs and by preventing the appointment of professors and the admission of students. It was also accused of imposing financial constraints and taxes on the educational institutions and of trying to modify their curriculum to suit its views.

Reports of the Secretary-General. The Secretary-General reported to the Security Council in January 1988[4] that education in the territories had been interrupted through the closing of schools and universities, especially through the denial of laissez-passers for an adequate period to Palestinian students pursuing higher education in other countries. In November,[15] the Secretary-General summarized reports

in the Israeli press from 1 September to 1 November on instances of Israeli military forces interfering with Palestinian educational facilities. In September, it was reported, several vocational training centres at Tulkarm were raided and 14 educational centres were shut down, on the grounds that they had violated an order closing down all educational institutions in the West Bank until 1 October.

The Secretary-General informed the General Assembly[38] that no reply had been received by 25 August from Israel to his February request for information on steps it had taken or envisaged to implement a 1987 Assembly demand[39] that it rescind all actions and measures against universities and educational institutions, ensure their freedom and refrain from hindering their effective operation.

GENERAL ASSEMBLY ACTION

On 6 December 1988, on the recommendation of the Special Political Committee, the General Assembly adopted **resolution 43/58 G** by recorded vote.

The General Assembly,

Bearing in mind the Geneva Convention relative to the Protection of Civilian Persons in Time of War, of 12 August 1949,

Deeply concerned at the continued and intensified harassment by Israel, the occupying Power, against educational institutions in the occupied Palestinian territories,

Recalling Security Council resolution 605(1987) of 22 December 1987,

Recalling also its resolutions 38/79 G of 15 December 1983, 39/95 G of 14 December 1984, 40/161 G of 16 December 1985, 41/63 G of 3 December 1986, 42/160 G of 8 December 1987 and 43/21 of 3 November 1988,

Taking note of the reports of the Secretary-General of 21 January 1988, 25 August 1988 and 21 November 1988,

Taking note of the relevant decisions adopted by the Executive Board of the United Nations Educational, Scientific and Cultural Organization concerning the educational and cultural situation in the occupied territories,

1. *Reaffirms* the applicability of the Geneva Convention relative to the Protection of Civilian Persons in Time of War, of 12 August 1949, to the Palestinian and other Arab territories occupied by Israel since 1967, including Jerusalem;

2. *Condemns* Israeli policies and practices against Palestinian students and faculties in schools, universities and other educational institutions in the occupied Palestinian territories, especially the opening of fire on defenceless students, causing many casualties;

3. *Condemns* the systematic Israeli campaign of repression against and closing of universities, schools and other educational and vocational institutions in the occupied Palestinian territory, restricting and impeding the academic activities of Palestinian universities by subjecting the selection of courses, textbooks and education programmes, the admission of students and the appointment of faculty members to the control and supervision of the military occupation authorities, in clear contravention of the Geneva Convention;

4. *Demands* that Israel, the occupying Power, comply with the provisions of that Convention, rescind all actions and measures against all educational institutions, ensure the freedom of those institutions and refrain forthwith from hindering the effective operation of the universities, schools and other educational institutions;

5. *Requests* the Secretary-General to report to the General Assembly as soon as possible but not later than the beginning of its forty-fourth session on the implementation of the present resolution.

General Assembly resolution 43/58 G

6 December 1988   Meeting 71   147-2-3 (recorded vote)

Approved by Special Political Committee (A/43/904) by recorded vote (116-2-5), 28 November (meeting 34); draft by Afghanistan, Bangladesh, Brunei Darussalam, Burkina Faso, Comoros, Cuba, Egypt, India, Indonesia, Jordan (for Arab Group), Madagascar, Malaysia, Nicaragua, Pakistan, Zambia (A/SPC/43/L.32); agenda item 77.

Meeting numbers. GA 43rd session: SPC 28-32, 34; plenary 71.

Recorded vote in Assembly as follows:

In favour: Afghanistan, Albania, Algeria, Angola, Antigua and Barbuda, Argentina, Australia, Austria, Bahamas, Bahrain, Bangladesh, Barbados, Belgium, Belize, Benin, Bhutan, Bolivia, Botswana, Brazil, Brunei Darussalam, Bulgaria, Burkina Faso, Burundi, Byelorussian SSR, Cameroon, Canada, Cape Verde, Central African Republic, Chad, China, Colombia, Comoros, Costa Rica, Côte d'Ivoire,* Cuba, Cyprus, Czechoslovakia, Democratic Kampuchea, Democratic Yemen, Denmark, Djibouti, Dominican Republic, Ecuador, Egypt, El Salvador, Ethiopia, Fiji, Finland, France, Gabon, Gambia, German Democratic Republic, Germany, Federal Republic of, Ghana, Greece, Guatemala, Guinea, Guinea-Bissau, Guyana, Haiti, Honduras, Hungary, Iceland, India, Indonesia, Iran, Iraq, Ireland, Italy, Jamaica, Japan, Jordan, Kenya, Kuwait, Lao People's Democratic Republic, Lebanon, Lesotho, Libyan Arab Jamahiriya, Luxembourg, Madagascar, Malawi, Malaysia, Maldives, Mali, Malta, Mauritania, Mauritius, Mexico, Mongolia, Morocco, Mozambique, Nepal, Netherlands, New Zealand, Nicaragua, Niger, Nigeria, Norway, Oman, Pakistan, Panama, Papua New Guinea, Paraguay, Peru, Philippines, Poland, Portugal, Qatar, Romania, Rwanda, Saint Kitts and Nevis, Saint Lucia, Saint Vincent and the Grenadines, Samoa, Sao Tome and Principe, Saudi Arabia, Senegal, Seychelles, Sierra Leone, Singapore, Solomon Islands, Somalia, Spain, Sri Lanka, Sudan, Swaziland, Sweden, Syrian Arab Republic, Thailand, Togo, Trinidad and Tobago, Tunisia, Turkey, Uganda, Ukrainian SSR, USSR, United Arab Emirates, United Kingdom, United Republic of Tanzania, Uruguay, Vanuatu, Venezuela, Viet Nam, Yemen, Yugoslavia, Zambia, Zimbabwe.

Against: Israel, United States.

Abstaining: Chile, Liberia, Zaire.

*Later advised the Secretariat it had intended to abstain.

Economic and social conditions of Palestinians

Report of the Secretary-General. In his January report to the Security Council on the situation in the occupied territories,[(4)] the Secretary-General stated that the recent disturbances had attracted world attention to the squalid living conditions in many of the refugee camps in the territories, especially in the Gaza Strip, resulting from the lack of such basic amenities as paved roads, sewerage, water, lighting and minimum-standard housing. The Commissioner-General of UNRWA had expressed an urgent need to rehabilitate many UNRWA installations, such as schools, health centres and food distribution centres. Therefore, the Secretary-General had asked the Commissioner-General to prepare urgently proposals for improving the camps' infrastructure.

The Secretary-General also stated that Palestinians felt it was a deliberate Israeli policy to obstruct the territories' economic development. Israeli authorities maintained that the accusation was un-

founded and that they would welcome foreign assistance for the development of the territories, provided that each project complied with Israel's overriding security requirements and with Israeli procedures. Many Palestinians consulted said they hoped for a concerted international effort to revive the territories' economy, perhaps initially through an expansion of UNDP's programme. The Secretary-General asked the UNDP Administrator to study that possibility (see above, under "Assistance to Palestinians").

Heavy taxation was a frequent complaint, many of the proceeds benefiting Israel rather than the territories, for which the budget was not published. Economic discrimination was also frequently cited, with the purpose of hindering agricultural and industrial development and keeping the Palestinians as both a captive market and a source of cheap labour for Israel.

Israeli Ministers meeting with Under-Secretary-General Goulding said, to the contrary, that there had been great improvements in the economic and social situation since 1967, especially regarding consumption and social services. They drew a favourable comparison between Israel's record and that of Egypt and Jordan during 1948-1967. They agreed that more needed to be done to enhance the economic and social conditions, but were disappointed by the poor response of the international community to Israel's invitation to provide funds for developing the territories.

Report of the Committee on Palestinian rights. In its October report,[(1)] the Committee on Palestinian rights noted that the Israeli authorities had adopted a number of stringent administrative and economic measures directed at further strengthening their control over key aspects of life in the territories and at stifling Palestinian resistance. Back taxes were collected aggressively and the direct export of agricultural produce from the territories was prohibited. In addition, the amount of money Palestinians were permitted to bring into the territories was reduced to one fifth of the amount previously allowed, thus almost eliminating the possibility of indirect export and severely reducing remittances from Palestinians working abroad, on which many families depended. Shops of an essential nature, such as bakeries and pharmacies, were repeatedly closed by the authorities, while others were forcibly opened to break protest strikes.

Finance and trade

In response to a 1987 Economic and Social Council resolution,[(40)] the Secretary-General submitted in June 1988 a note[(41)] on a number of studies under way on finance and trade in the occupied territories. In addition to compiling information on Israeli financial practices in the occupied Golan Heights to complete an in-depth study on the financial sector in the territories, submitted in part in 1987,[42] a second study on recent economic developments in the territories with special reference to the external trade sector was being conducted by UNCTAD in co-operation with the Economic and Social Commission for Western Asia as part of its 1988/89 work programme.

That report[43] was before the Trade and Development Board when it met in September/October 1988. The report showed that most of the key economic indicators analysed by UNCTAD's Special Economic Unit (Palestinian people) reflected basic structural deficiencies owing to a lack of indigenous institutions to steer the economy and the predominance of Israeli economic interests.

The potential for sustained development of the Palestinian economy was constrained by a process of transformation in the traditional sector, unaccompanied by policies and measures to absorb and regulate the pressures of readjustment. Israeli occupation brought a host of pressures on the Palestinian economy, which aggravated its development performance and resulted in a steady decline in traditional branches without parallel encouragement of growth in modern sectors. The effects of occupation reduced agricultural employment opportunities; encouraged the flight of labour from the traditional sector into labour-intensive sectors of the Israeli economy; neglected the needs of Palestinian productive sectors or reoriented them to serving Israeli production and consumption interests; and imposed control over trade channels, ensuring Israeli domination of Palestinian trade. Those effects were profoundly felt by the small and unsophisticated Palestinian economy, confronted with the challenge of competing on unequal and unprotected terms with the articulated, highly capitalized and technologically advanced Israeli economy.

The mechanisms for better planning and supporting the Palestinian economy had been eroded through 21 years of occupation. While power over economic management had been assumed by the Israeli authorities, they failed to fulfil the concomitant responsibilities; moreover, the concentration of that power within the jurisdiction of the Israeli military authorities continued to inhibit economic performance and potential. In those circumstances, stable and rational development and concomitant policies and measures could not emerge spontaneously.

The problems plaguing the Palestinian economy had acquired fresh urgency and significance after the beginning of the *intifadah*, which had many economic implications and repercussions and posed new development challenges for both the Palestinians and the Israeli occupation authorities.

By July 1988, there were few indications that the Israeli authorities intended to rescind restric-

tions affecting Palestinian development, including those instituted since the beginning of the year. Their main concern regarding the economic effects of the uprising was the damage to the Israeli economy as a result of Palestinian labour absenteeism, particularly in agriculture, construction, services and industry, and the reduced market for certain Israeli exports such as textiles, foodstuffs and other consumer goods, which featured prominently in Palestinian markets. The economic costs to Israel during the first five months of unrest were estimated at $800 million and included increased security costs and declines of 15-20 per cent in tourism revenues, 20 per cent in construction activities and more than 3 per cent in agricultural and industrial output, as well as indirect costs caused by manpower shortages arising from extra duty in the Israeli armed forces.

Palestinian economic resistance measures included: proposals for a boycott of Israeli products and promotion of Palestinian self-sufficiency; calls for supporting indigenous Palestinian production facilities; a return to agriculture; creation of alternative employment opportunities for Palestinians who ceased to work as migrant labourers in Israel or resigned their posts in the Israeli administration; and a ''tax revolt''.

The trade sector was increasingly being linked to the economy of Israel, with a growing deficit in merchandise trade, resulting in unfavourable patterns and terms of trade for the territories. Whereas there was no trade with Israel until 1967, the growth of imports from Israel over the occupation period was more than nine-and-a-half-fold between 1970 and 1986, bringing Israel's share of Palestinian imports to 90 per cent. A number of recommendations contained in the report for policy action were aimed at relaxing the severe constraints on external trade and therefore on the growth and development of the Palestinian economy.

Despite numerous measures aimed at constraining Palestinian economic activities during the uprising, the Palestinian people had demonstrated initiatives aimed at promoting self-reliance, which deserved to be supported by international development assistance.

The Board, on 5 October,[44] took note of the report.

ECONOMIC AND SOCIAL COUNCIL ACTION

On 28 July 1988, the Economic and Social Council adopted **resolution 1988/65** by roll-call vote.

Israeli economic practices in the occupied Palestinian and other Arab territories

The Economic and Social Council,

Recalling General Assembly decision 40/432 of 17 December 1985, in which the Assembly requested the

Secretary-General to prepare a report on the financial and trade practices of the Israeli occupation authorities in the occupied Palestinian and other Arab territories,

Recalling also Economic and Social Council resolution 1987/87 of 8 July 1987 and General Assembly decision 42/449 of 17 December 1987,

1. *Takes note* of the note by the Secretary-General concerning progress in the implementation of General Assembly decision 40/432 and Economic and Social Council resolution 1987/87;

2. *Requests* the Secretary-General to speed up the preparation of the required report on the trade practices of the Israeli occupation authorities in the occupied Palestinian territories and on the financial and trade practices of the Israeli occupation authorities in the occupied Syrian Arab Golan and to report to the General Assembly at its forty-fourth session, through the Economic and Social Council, on the implementation of the present resolution;

3. *Also requests* the Secretary-General to use the terminology decided upon in the relevant General Assembly resolutions.

Economic and Social Council resolution 1988/65

28 July 1988   Meeting 40   49-1 (roll-call vote)

11-nation draft (E/1988/L.44); agenda item 6.

Sponsors: Bulgaria, German Democratic Republic, Iran, Iraq, Libyan Arab Jamahiriya, Oman, Pakistan, Saudi Arabia, Somalia, Sudan, Syrian Arab Republic.

Meeting numbers. ESC 32, 33, 37, 40.

Roll-call vote in Council as follows:

In favour: Australia, Belgium, Bolivia, Bulgaria, Byelorussian SSR, Canada, China, Colombia, Cuba, Denmark, Egypt, France, German Democratic Republic, Germany, Federal Republic of, Ghana, Greece, Guinea, India, Iran, Iraq, Ireland, Italy, Jamaica, Japan, Lesotho, Liberia, Libyan Arab Jamahiriya, Mozambique, Norway, Oman, Pakistan, Panama, Peru, Philippines, Poland, Portugal, Rwanda, Saudi Arabia, Sierra Leone, Somalia, Sri Lanka, Sudan, Syrian Arab Republic, USSR, United Kingdom, Uruguay, Venezuela, Yugoslavia, Zaire.

Against: United States.

Palestinian women

Following consideration of a report by the Secretary-General on the situation of Palestinian women living within and outside the occupied territories[45] (see PART THREE, Chapter XIII), the Economic and Social Council, by **resolution 1988/25** of 26 May 1988, condemned the application of an "iron-fist" policy by Israel against Palestinian women and their families and requested the Commission on the Status of Women to monitor the implementation of the 1985 Nairobi Forward-looking Strategies for the Advancement of Women[46] concerning assistance to Palestinian women. The Council reaffirmed that Palestinian women could not participate in attaining the objectives of equality, development and peace without realizing their inalienable rights to return to their homes, to exercise self-determination and to establish an independent State. The Secretary-General was urgently requested to send an expert mission to investigate the situation of Palestinian women and children, in the light of the recent tragic developments in the territories.

REFERENCES

[1]A/43/35. [2]A/43/694. [3]YUN 1987, p. 305, SC res. 605(1987), 22 Dec. 1987. [4]S/19443. [5]S/19455. [6]S/19456. [7]S/19453. [8]S/19466. [9]S/19700. [10]S/19706. [11]S/19705, S/19776. [12]S/19773. [13]S/19780. [14]S/20156. [15]A/43/806. [16]A/43/608. [17]YUN 1987, p. 308, GA res. 42/160 B, 8 Dec. 1987. [18]A/43/77-S/19405. [19]A/43/86-S/19424. [20]A/43/296-S/19758. [21] A/43/302-S/19769. [22]A/43/377. [23]A/43/504-S/20090. [24]A/43/541-S/20132. [25]S/19402. [26]S/19404. [27]S/19430. [28]YUN 1948-49, p. 535, GA res. 217 A (III), 10 Dec. 1948. [29]A/43/558 & Add.1. [30]YUN 1987, p. 314, GA res. 42/160 E, 8 Dec. 1987. [31]A/43/557. [32]YUN 1987, p. 311, GA res. 42/160 A, 8 Dec. 1987. [33]A/43/609. [34]YUN 1987, p. 312, GA res. 42/160 C, 8 Dec. 1987. [35]*Ibid.*, p. 318, GA res. 42/160 F, 8 Dec. 1987. [36]A/43/559. [37]YUN 1981, p. 312. [38]A/43/560. [39]YUN 1987, p. 316, GA res. 42/160 G, 8 Dec. 1987. [40]*Ibid.*, p. 324, ESC res. 1987/87, 8 July 1987. [41]A/43/432-E/1988/68. [42]YUN 1987, p. 323. [43]TD/B/1183 & Corr.1. [44]A/43/15, vol. II. [45]E/CN.6/1988/8 & Corr.1. [46]YUN 1985, p. 937.

Palestine refugees

More than 2 million refugees were registered with the United Nations Relief and Works Agency for Palestine Refugees in the Near East as at 30 June 1988[1] in five areas of the Middle East: in and outside camps in the Israeli-occupied West Bank (385,634) and Gaza Strip (459,074); Jordan (870,490); Lebanon (288,176); and the Syrian Arab Republic (265,221).

The General Assembly addressed the Palestinian refugee problem and UNRWA's relief activities in 10 resolutions adopted in December 1988. The resolutions dealt with: assistance to Palestine refugees (43/57 A) and to displaced persons (43/57 C); the Working Group on the Financing of UNRWA (43/57 B); scholarships for higher education and vocational training (43/57 D); a proposed University of Jerusalem "Al-Quds" for Palestine refugees (43/57 J); Palestine refugees in Palestinian territory occupied by Israel since 1967 (43/57 E); resumption of the ration distribution to Palestine refugees (43/57 F); refugee protection (43/57 I); revenues from refugee properties (43/57 H); and the return of population and refugees displaced since 1967 (43/57 G).

UN Agency for Palestine refugees

As at 30 June 1988,[1] Palestine refugees registered with UNRWA in its five areas of operation numbered 2,268,595, to whom the Agency rendered educational, health and relief services, in addition to emergency measures in response to the Palestinian uprising. Emergency situations, such as the civil war in Lebanon ongoing since 1978,[2] seriously challenged the Agency in carrying out its mandate, while the evolving *intifadah* required

UNRWA throughout 1988 to work under emergency measures in the West Bank and Gaza Strip.

The UNRWA Commissioner-General's reports on the Agency's work during the periods 1 July 1987–30 June 1988[1] and 1 July 1988–30 June 1989[3] indicated that, since the beginning of the uprising, various developments had affected the Agency's operations and its ability to discharge its functions effectively. UNRWA repeatedly called on Israeli authorities to respect its privileges and immunities, as well as its premises. Nevertheless, camps were barricaded, access roads were blocked and the telephone connection between UNRWA's Vienna headquarters and its field office in the Gaza Strip was inoperative after 16 March 1988. The number of refugee shelters sealed or demolished for punitive reasons increased, as did the number of staff arrested and detained without charge or trial. Interference with the movement of staff increased due to obstructions in obtaining clearances and to frequent curfews. Many staff members also complained of maltreatment. With UNRWA becoming increasingly involved in emergency operations, a Programme Planning and Evaluation Office was established at headquarters to examine the longer-term implications of that trend.

UNRWA's education programme provided nine grades of general education, vocational and technical training, in-service teacher training and some higher education for Palestine refugees. The curricula followed those prescribed in the respective host countries. Despite adversarial circumstances, 349,321 Palestine refugee children served by 10,101 teachers enrolled in 1988 in 633 UNRWA elementary and preparatory schools. An additional 58,941 pupils attended government and private schools. Vocational, technical and pre-service teacher training was provided in eight training centres with a total enrolment of 4,668 teachers and 468 instructors. The UNRWA Institute of Education provided in-service training courses for 572 teachers and, at the university level, 297 scholars benefited from the Agency's scholarship programme. Some 27 new classrooms were completed or under construction during the year. Total 1988 expenditure on the education programme was $112.6 million.

The UNRWA health programme provided sanitation services and curative and preventive medical services through 100 health clinics and 35 subsidized hospitals, which counted 228,785 bed-days utilized by refugees during 1988. Some 35,500 schoolchildren received full mid-day meals in 92 supplementary feeding centres six days a week. Fifteen new dental units were provided through the UNRWA budget or donations, with six of them—including a mobile unit—in Jordan, five in the West Bank and two each in Gaza and Lebanon. Dental teams to service those units and new posts of dental hygienists were established to assist in the preventive oral health programme. Four new clinical laboratories were established, two in the West Bank and one each in Lebanon and the Syrian Arab Republic, while other health facilities were upgraded. Expenditures on the health programme amounted to $38.3 million during 1988.

Under the relief service programme, 32,560 families, representing 7.6 per cent of the registered refugee population, received, as special hardship cases, assistance consisting of food, clothing, blankets, cash aid, cash grants for income-generating projects, assistance in the repair or reconstruction of shelters and preferential access to vocational and teacher training. The general welfare programme comprised casework, women's activities, adult training courses, education and training of the disabled, self-support projects and assistance to refugees in emergency situations. The cost in 1988 of the relief services programme amounted to $19.7 million.

Lebanon. UNRWA operations were profoundly affected by the conditions of emergency prevailing throughout much of Lebanon due to recurrent waves of intense armed conflict, which also impeded compliance with a 1987 Assembly request that UNRWA headquarters be relocated to its former Beirut site.[4]

Nearly all schools stayed open most of the time; basic health services, bolstered by mobile medical teams in heavily damaged areas, continued to operate with only limited interruptions related to security conditions; and the relief programme was expanded to include four general distributions of emergency rations to all registered and non-registered Palestine refugees in Lebanon.

UNRWA again sought access to the three besieged refugee camps—Shatila and Burj el-Barajneh in the southern outskirts of Beirut and Rashidieh near Tyre—which had not been possible since 1985. Several hundred families from camps in southern Lebanon fled north seeking alternative shelter, with nearly 100 of them occupying UNRWA schools in the Saida region. The Agency made representations to government officials, leaders of militias and popular committees to stem the new flow of refugees and obtain assurances for their safe return to Rashidieh and other camps in the vicinity of Tyre. Despite continuing high tension in the region, those displaced eventually returned or found alternative accommodations.

In the wake of the wholesale damage inflicted on Shatila and Burj el-Barajneh, UNRWA continued emergency operations and began repairing roads, water supplies and piping, as well as removing heavy rubble. In September, UNRWA started payments to selected families to help them repair their shelters. In October, it began clearance and repair operations in both camps and, after infrastructural restoration, distributed cash grants to families whose shelters were destroyed or damaged.

Damage to UNRWA installations and refugee shelters was estimated to be 85 per cent in Shatila (1,530 shelters) and 60 per cent in Burj el-Barajneh (2,390 shelters), with repair costs of $3.2 million. A further $1.2 million was required to repair some 2,100 damaged shelters in three camps south of the Litani River: El-Buss, Burj el-Shemali and Rashidieh.

Following the abduction of two Agency staff—a Norwegian and a Swede—on 5 February, who were released unharmed on 1 March, UNRWA reduced the number of international staff in Lebanon to the minimum required to maintain essential services at levels permitted by the security conditions.

Renewed fighting in May and June between rival Palestinian factions in the Beirut camps resulted in an estimated 100 killed, 500 wounded and many newly displaced refugee families, and had an adverse effect on UNRWA programmes. By the end of June, heavy shelling by artillery, mortars, rockets and machine-guns had all but destroyed the Shatila camp, where only about 40 families remained.

West Bank and Gaza Strip. In the West Bank and Gaza, the *intifadah* and Israel's response affected virtually all Agency activities, stretching its health services to the limit due to the increased case-load. Individuals, including UNRWA personnel, were arrested or detained without charge or trial in substantial numbers. There were indiscriminate beatings and deliberate damage to property, including Agency premises, which were used as observation posts and interrogation or detention centres. Houses were demolished or sealed and entrances to refugee camps were blocked, while economic pressures by Israel multiplied.

The freedom of movement of staff was increasingly interfered with, particularly after the requirement of passes, in late 1988, following imposition of curfews. Few such passes were allotted to UNRWA staff, seriously affecting essential services, including delivery of emergency health care.

To aid the West Bank and Gaza, UNRWA, at an informal meeting (Vienna, 29 February and 1 March) with representatives of major donor and host Governments, presented a plan of action estimated at some $65 million and requiring three years (1988-1990) for implementation. It related to the expansion of relief activities, improvement of camp infrastructure and creation of new employment opportunities through economic development schemes. As at 30 June, some $32.2 million had been pledged or paid in cash and commodities, more than half of which was specified for food, medical supplies and equipment, hospitalization and related costs. More than $10 million was also pledged towards special projects to improve the living conditions of refugees in the occupied territories.

Health services, with emphasis on preventive rather than curative care, were provided through a network of 41 health centres, 6 maternal and child health sub-centres, 15 dental clinics, 8 maternity wards, 13 laboratories and 46 supplementary feeding centres. The Agency subsidized more than 400 beds in private hospitals for use by Palestine refugees, which was, however, insufficient for all cases requiring in-patient care.

Starting in September, 15 additional emergency medical teams were established to reinforce the available infrastructure of the 33 health centres or points throughout the West Bank. Duty hours were extended to provide afternoon shifts in the camps where confrontations between the inhabitants and Israeli security forces occurred most frequently. Six additional health buses were acquired to improve the transportation of injured persons, and equipment was procured to upgrade services and capacities in casualty care. Nutritional support was expanded and additional funds were earmarked to cover emergency medical supplies and extra hospital expenses. In February, after establishing eight additional medical teams to operate clinics in Gaza, UNRWA opened an emergency clinic in Beach camp and two night-duty clinics. In September, the first physiotherapy clinic was established in the Balata health centre near Nablus.

Education was seriously affected by a loss of instruction time in schools and training centres. As a result of the enforced closure of all educational institutions in the West Bank from 4 February until late May, pupils in elementary and preparatory schools missed approximately 40 per cent of scheduled class time. The authorities allowed elementary schools to reopen on 23 May and preparatory schools on 29 May but directed them to close on 21 July, despite an earlier declaration to extend the school year to 18 August. The 1987/88 school year in the Gaza Strip, which was seriously affected by curfews, strikes and violent incidents, was not completed until late October, following the implementation of a crash programme after the summer recess to make up for time lost during the first half of 1988.

In its medium-term plan for 1988-1990, UNRWA identified priority school-construction requirements, including the construction of additional classrooms, replacement of unsuitable premises and improvements to existing facilities. The impact on training centres was more devastating, with three of them in the West Bank closed, along with other educational institutions, by a February order of the Israeli Government, causing the loss of all but 44 days of the scheduled instruction time. The centre in Gaza had been closed since the beginning of January, completing only about 50 days. Thus, would-be 1988 graduates had to enrol for the 1988/89 academic year.

Addressing the need for small-scale income-generating enterprises, 51 projects were given loans in the West Bank for industrial workshops, food production and essential services under a joint programme established in January by UNRWA and other aid agencies.

Jordan and the Syrian Arab Republic. Due to the weakening economies of Jordan and the Syrian Arab Republic, Palestine refugees faced difficulties there. The economy also slackened in the Persian Gulf States, which had traditionally absorbed an important share of the Palestinian skilled and semi-skilled labour force. UNRWA schools in Jordan and the Syrian Arab Republic operated satisfactorily throughout the year. The Amman and Wadi Seer training centres in Jordan provided 28 courses in vocational and technical fields for 1,170 students; the centre in Amman also provided 300 places for trainee teachers.

Under the Agency's health programme, two new health centres in the Jordanian Baqa'a and Marka refugee camps, funded by Canada, were completed in August 1987 and April 1988, respectively. A survey of the Qabr Essit camp near Damascus, Syrian Arab Republic, found that the water used in refugee shelters was often contaminated and that 60 per cent of the children suffered from intestinal parasites. That led to the launching of a health education campaign and the subsequent upgrading of the water system and sewer lines with UNICEF funds.

Report of the Secretary-General. The Secretary-General reported in January to the Security Council[5] that UNRWA played the leading role in providing registered refugees in the Gaza Strip with a wide variety of assistance and protection, as well as support for their day-to-day efforts to cope with life under occupation. ICRC assisted especially the families of detainees, and many Palestinian and international voluntary agencies played their part.

The Secretary-General concluded that in the case of registered refugees in the West Bank and Gaza, who numbered 818,983 (373,586 in the West Bank and 445,397 in Gaza) or about 55 per cent of the Palestinian population there, UNRWA was clearly best placed to provide general assistance. However, the number of UNRWA international staff had declined over the years, to nine in the West Bank (where there were 19 refugee camps) and six in Gaza (where there were eight camps) as at the uprising's initiation. The Secretary-General believed that international staff currently played an especially valuable role, as they could gain easier access to Israeli authorities in emergency situations. Their mere presence at points of confrontation had a significant impact on the way the civilian population was treated by the security forces. He therefore asked the UNRWA Commissioner-General to examine the addition of extra international staff in the territories

to enhance general refugee assistance and urged Member States to respond generously to the appeal for their financing.

The Secretary-General deemed it essential that Israel honour UNRWA privileges and immunities in full, especially the right of its personnel to freedom of movement in all circumstances and the inviolability of its premises and installations. In view of the current disturbances, it also seemed desirable that the Commissioner-General be permitted to provide humanitarian assistance, on an emergency basis and as a temporary measure, to non-refugees in serious need of assistance.

GENERAL ASSEMBLY ACTION

On 6 December 1988, on the recommendation of the Special Political Committee, the General Assembly adopted **resolution 43/57 A** by recorded vote.

Assistance to Palestine refugees

The General Assembly,

Recalling its resolution 42/69 A of 2 December 1987 and all its previous resolutions on the question, including resolution 194(III) of 11 December 1948,

Taking note of the report of the Commissioner-General of the United Nations Relief and Works Agency for Palestine Refugees in the Near East, covering the period from 1 July 1987 to 30 June 1988,

1. *Notes with deep regret* that repatriation or compensation of the refugees as provided for in paragraph 11 of General Assembly resolution 194(III) has not been effected, that no substantial progress has been made in the programme endorsed by the Assembly in paragraph 2 of its resolution 513(VI) of 26 January 1952 for the reintegration of refugees either by repatriation or resettlement and that, therefore, the situation of the refugees continues to be a matter of serious concern;

2. *Expresses its thanks* to the Commissioner-General and to all the staff of the United Nations Relief and Works Agency for Palestine Refugees in the Near East, recognizing that the Agency is doing all it can within the limits of available resources, and also expresses its thanks to the specialized agencies and private organizations for their valuable work in assisting the refugees;

3. *Reiterates its request* that the headquarters of the Agency should be relocated to its former site within its area of operations as soon as practicable;

4. *Notes with regret* that the United Nations Conciliation Commission for Palestine has been unable to find a means of achieving progress in the implementation of paragraph 11 of General Assembly resolution 194(III), and requests the Commission to exert continued efforts towards the implementation of that paragraph and to report to the Assembly as appropriate, but no later than 1 September 1989;

5. *Directs attention* to the continuing seriousness of the financial position of the Agency, as outlined in the report of the Commissioner-General;

6. *Notes with profound concern* that, despite the commendable and successful efforts of the Commissioner-General to collect additional contributions, this increased level of income to the Agency is still insufficient to cover essential budget requirements in the present year and

that, at currently foreseen levels of giving, deficits will recur each year;

7. *Calls upon* all Governments, as a matter of urgency, to make the most generous efforts possible to meet the anticipated needs of the Agency, particularly in the light of the budgetary deficit projected in the report of the Commissioner-General, and therefore urges non-contributing Governments to contribute regularly and contributing Governments to consider increasing their regular contributions.

General Assembly resolution 43/57 A

6 December 1988   Meeting 71   152-0-1 (recorded vote)

Approved by Special Political Committee (A/43/903) by recorded vote (121-0-1), 28 November (meeting 34); draft by United States (A/SPC/43/L.14); agenda item 76.

Meeting numbers. GA 43rd session: SPC 22, 24, 26, 27, 34; plenary 71.

Recorded vote in Assembly as follows:

In favour: Afghanistan, Algeria, Angola, Antigua and Barbuda, Argentina, Australia, Austria, Bahamas, Bahrain, Bangladesh, Barbados, Belgium, Belize, Benin, Bhutan, Bolivia, Botswana, Brazil, Brunei Darussalam, Bulgaria, Burkina Faso, Burma, Burundi, Byelorussian SSR, Cameroon, Canada, Cape Verde, Central African Republic, Chad, Chile, China, Colombia, Comoros, Costa Rica, Côte d'Ivoire, Cuba, Cyprus, Czechoslovakia, Democratic Kampuchea, Democratic Yemen, Denmark, Djibouti, Dominican Republic, Ecuador, Egypt, El Salvador, Ethiopia, Fiji, Finland, France, Gabon, Gambia, German Democratic Republic, Germany, Federal Republic of, Ghana, Greece, Grenada, Guatemala, Guinea, Guinea-Bissau, Guyana, Haiti, Honduras, Hungary, Iceland, India, Indonesia, Iran, Iraq, Ireland, Italy, Jamaica, Japan, Jordan, Kenya, Kuwait, Lao People's Democratic Republic, Lebanon, Lesotho, Liberia, Libyan Arab Jamahiriya, Luxembourg, Madagascar, Malawi, Malaysia, Maldives, Mali, Malta, Mauritania, Mauritius, Mexico, Mongolia, Morocco, Mozambique, Nepal, Netherlands, New Zealand, Nicaragua, Niger, Nigeria, Norway, Oman, Pakistan, Panama, Papua New Guinea, Paraguay, Peru, Philippines, Poland, Portugal, Qatar, Romania, Rwanda, Saint Kitts and Nevis, Saint Lucia, Saint Vincent and the Grenadines, Samoa, Sao Tome and Principe, Saudi Arabia, Senegal, Seychelles, Sierra Leone, Singapore, Solomon Islands, Somalia, Spain, Sri Lanka, Sudan, Swaziland, Sweden, Syrian Arab Republic, Thailand, Togo, Trinidad and Tobago, Tunisia, Turkey, Uganda, Ukrainian SSR, USSR, United Arab Emirates, United Kingdom, United Republic of Tanzania, United States, Uruguay, Vanuatu, Venezuela, Viet Nam, Yemen, Yugoslavia, Zaire, Zambia, Zimbabwe.

Against: None.

Abstaining: Israel.

UNRWA financing

The Agency's income to its General Fund and ongoing activities amounted to $206.1 million in 1988.[3] To maintain the regular programmes at their planned levels, UNRWA spent $204.3 million; the balance enabled it to replenish its much-depleted working capital reserve, which amounted to $29.3 million—considered inadequate when measured against UNRWA's size of operation and manner of funding. Thus, the Commissioner-General stressed that the financial position still needed strengthening to achieve a measure of fiscal security. Expenditure on capital and special projects was planned at $14.9 million for 1988, of which $6.8 million was funded by special donations and $2.3 million from the General Fund.

According to the financial report and audited financial statements of UNRWA for the year ended 31 December 1988,[6] the 1988 budget of UNRWA amounted to $247 million, of which $190.2 million was for the General Fund. Project funds were $18.6 million for ongoing activities and $14.9 million for capital and special projects, giving $223.7 million for the regular budget.

Extraordinary emergency budgets included the Lebanon Emergency Fund of $8 million, representing the unspent balance of funds donated in 1987, and two new funds established during 1988 in response to the emergency situation created by the uprising in the occupied territories. The Extraordinary Measures in the Occupied Territories Fund had a budget of $15.1 million in response to increasing needs. It was intended for extra-regular activities in the territories to alleviate the hardship of the Palestine refugees owing to the civil unrest. A second fund—the Expanded Programme of Assistance—was established to improve the infrastructure in terms of better housing and new or expanded sewerage systems, and to provide UNRWA with better facilities to run its education, health and relief programmes in the territories. For 1988, $200,000 was budgeted under that programme, representing first allotments set up for the initial preparation and administration of funds received in response to the Commissioner-General's presentation to major donors in February 1988, the aim of which was to solicit about $65 million for various projects to improve the environmental conditions of the refugee population in the West Bank and Gaza.

The Agency ended 1988 with an excess of income over expenditure under the General Fund amounting to $3.5 million, largely owing to the unexpected depreciation of the Jordanian dinar during the second half of 1988. However, the large deficits of earlier years had left a much depleted working capital.

Reallocations from the General Fund to projects totalled $2.3 million for such urgent construction projects as class-rooms in Jordan, the Syrian Arab Republic, the West Bank and Gaza to avoid triple shifts; a new field office in the Syrian Arab Republic; moving an education development centre at Amman; the Baqa'a school in Jordan; and warehouses in Gaza. In 1988, 70 UNWRA projects funded by special contributions were under implementation, and a loan scheme, running in its fourth year to assist housing and education projects, had outstanding loans of $3.8 million as at 31 December 1988, as compared with $5.8 million a year earlier.

The Commissioner-General noted that, in response to his February 1987 appeal[7] for $20.6 million to cover UNRWA emergency operations in Lebanon, $15.5 million had been received or pledged, of which some $9.8 million was obligated or expended. Major items funded through 30 June 1988 included $4.9 million for food and other emergency supplies, $1.6 million for hospitalization and other health services, $1 million for additional staff and $650,000 for replacement of school supplies and furniture. The remaining $5.7 million was to be used for additional emergency

relief expenditures, the repair of Agency installations and cash grants under the accommodation
assistance programme to refugee families whose
homes in the camps were damaged or destroyed.
Although that programme was not under way in
Lebanon as at 30 June, the balance of the $20.6
million requested would be needed once UNRWA
was allowed to proceed with those activities.

On 21 December, the General Assembly, by **resolution 43/216**, accepted the financial report and
audited financial statements of UNRWA for the year
ended 31 December 1987,[8] together with the
report of the Board of Auditors, and requested the
Commissioner-General to report in 1989 on steps
taken to implement the Board's recommendations.

Working Group on UNRWA financing

In a report covering its meetings of 14 September and 11 October 1988,[9] the Working Group on
the Financing of UNWRA expressed concern that
income in 1988 might be insufficient to cover the
cost of maintaining services. The Agency's financial situation promised to be less healthy than in
1987. Projections indicated that cash contributions
to the General Fund would fall short by $2 million
of the budgeted requirements of $176.6 million.
Under the two special emergency programmes
funded by special contributions, the $7 million bal-
ance remaining at the start of 1988 in the Lebanon Emergency Fund, earmarked to repair shelters,
was expected to be exhausted by the end of the year,
and the expanded programme in the occupied territories, operative since February 1988, had funding assured only to the end of the year.

The budget for 1989 was estimated to increase
by $11 million (or 5 per cent), to about $218 million, which would meet growing requirements for
UNRWA services brought about by increases in the
school population, expanded use of Agency health
services and unavoidable staff salary increases. A
corresponding increase in contributions would
have to be sought. Moreover, construction costs
were expected to be about $15 million, a substan-
tial increase over 1988, as many projects had been
delayed due to insufficient contributions. Should
the Lebanon Emergency Fund be continued, additional funds would have to be sought, and although funds specially pledged for projects in the
occupied territories were available through 1989,
only a limited amount of funding for the emergency measures would extend beyond 1988.

The Working Group took note that the
Commissioner-General envisaged an annual
growth of 5 per cent in expenditure over the next
few years simply to maintain UNRWA's regular
programmes at current levels. That would require
a corresponding increase in contributions and continued strict control over expenditure if deficits and
eventual cuts in services were to be avoided.

To circumvent the projected deficit, the Working Group urged that Governments start contributing or make more generous contributions,
make additional contributions for construction
projects and pay their contributions as early as
possible in the calendar year.

GENERAL ASSEMBLY ACTION

On 6 December 1988, on the recommendation
of the Special Political Committee, the General Assembly adopted **resolution 43/57 B** without vote.

Working Group on the Financing of the United Nations Relief and Works Agency for Palestine Refugees in the Near East

The General Assembly,

Recalling its resolutions 2656(XXV) of 7 December
1970, 2728(XXV) of 15 December 1970, 2791(XXVI)
of 6 December 1971, 2964(XXVII) of 13 December
1972, 3090(XXVIII) of 7 December 1973, 3330(XXIX)
of 17 December 1974, 3419 D (XXX) of 8 December
1975, 31/15 C of 23 November 1976, 32/90 D of 13 December 1977, 33/112 D of 18 December 1978, 34/52 D
of 23 November 1979, 35/13 D of 3 November 1980,
36/146 E of 16 December 1981, 37/120 A of 16 December 1982, 38/83 B of 15 December 1983, 39/99 B of 14
December 1984, 40/165 B of 16 December 1985, 41/69 B
of 3 December 1986 and 42/69 B of 2 December 1987,

Recalling also its decision 36/462 of 16 March 1982,
whereby it took note of the special report of the Working Group on the Financing of the United Nations Relief and Works Agency for Palestine Refugees in the Near
East and adopted the recommendations contained therein,

Having considered the report of the Working Group,

Taking into account the report of the Commissioner-
General of the United Nations Relief and Works Agency
for Palestine Refugees in the Near East, covering the
period from 1 July 1987 to 30 June 1988,

Deeply concerned at the critical financial situation of the
Agency, which permits the provision of only minimum
services to the Palestine refugees,

Emphasizing the continuing need for extraordinary efforts in order to maintain, at least at their present minimum level, the activities of the Agency, as well as to enable the Agency to carry out essential construction,

1. *Commends* the Working Group on the Financing
of the United Nations Relief and Works Agency for
Palestine Refugees in the Near East for its efforts to assist in ensuring the Agency's financial security;

2. *Takes note with approval* of the report of the Working Group;

3. *Requests* the Working Group to continue its efforts,
in co-operation with the Secretary-General and the
Commissioner-General, for the financing of the Agency
for a further period of one year;

4. *Requests* the Secretary-General to provide the
necessary services and assistance to the Working Group
for the conduct of its work.

General Assembly resolution 43/57 B

6 December 1988   Meeting 71   Adopted without vote

Approved by Special Political Committee (A/43/903) without vote, 28 November (meeting 34); 16-nation draft (A/SPC/43/L.15); agenda item 76.

Sponsors: Austria, Bangladesh, Canada, Denmark, Germany, Federal Republic of, India, Indonesia, Liberia, Malaysia, Netherlands, New Zealand, Pakistan, Philippines, Spain, Sweden, Yugoslavia.
Meeting numbers. GA 43rd session: SPC 22, 24, 26, 27, 34; plenary 71.

Legal matters

UNRWA staff and premises

During the 1987/88 reporting period, the number of UNRWA staff arrested and detained without charge continued to increase.[1] Israeli authorities also deported one staff member from the Gaza Strip. However, the number of staff kidnapped or detained in Lebanon decreased.

As UNRWA remained unable to obtain adequate, timely information on reasons for the arrests and detentions, it was unable to ascertain whether the staff members' official functions were involved or whether their rights and duties flowing from the Charter, the 1946 Convention on the Privileges and Immunities of the United Nations[10] and UNRWA Staff Regulations and Rules were duly respected.

Staff movements in and out of the occupied territories continued to be restricted; sometimes entry permits were refused. From late 1988 on, the authorities insisted that local staff in the Gaza Strip could move during curfew only if they possessed permits; however, very few staff were issued curfew permits, which were often of limited duration, with time-consuming renewal procedures. Israeli authorities continuously summoned Agency staff for interrogation during official hours without adequate notice.

UNRWA also stated increasing concern over forcible entries of its premises by Israeli military personnel, sometimes accompanied by injuries to staff and damage to property. UNRWA protested such actions as a violation of its privileges and immunities.

Compensation claims

In 1988, UNRWA reported that no progress had been made with regard to its claims against the Governments of: Israel (for loss of and damage to UNRWA property during the 1967 hostilities, Israel's invasion of Lebanon in 1982 and its military action before then); Jordan (arising from the 1967 hostilities and the disturbances in 1970 and 1971); and the Syrian Arab Republic (relating mainly to the levy of certain taxes from which UNRWA believed it was exempt under existing agreements). Those claims had been reported in 1986.[11] The Secretary-General, in September 1988,[12] also stated that there had been no progress with regard to UNRWA claims against Israel resulting from its 1982 invasion of Lebanon.

In **resolution 43/57 I**, the General Assembly called anew on Israel to compensate UNRWA for damage to its property and facilities resulting from Israel's invasion of Lebanon, without prejudice to Israel's responsibility for all damages resulting from that invasion.

In July, Israel informed UNRWA that, because of temporary budgetary constraints, it had to withhold payment of clearance, warehousing and transport charges payable to the Agency under the 1967 Comay-Michelmore provisional agreement concerning assistance to Palestine refugees. To prevent delayed clearance of goods and to minimize costs, UNRWA temporarily advanced the sums needed, on the understanding that the amount would be reimbursed, and requested Israel to revert as at 1 January 1989 to the *status quo ante* and the procedures envisaged under the agreement. As a result of Israel's failure to do so due to its alleged financial situation, the Agency had to spend an additional $800,000 to carry out its programmes in the occupied territories.

Other aspects

Humanitarian assistance to displaced and other persons

During 1988, in addition to providing relief in the form of basic food commodities, blankets, clothing, shelter repair and cash grants, UNRWA continued to provide a small measure of humanitarian assistance to persons who had been displaced as a result of the June 1967 and subsequent hostilities but who were not registered with UNRWA as refugees.

GENERAL ASSEMBLY ACTION

On 6 December 1988, the General Assembly, on the recommendation of the Special Political Committee, adopted **resolution 43/57 C** without vote.

Assistance to persons displaced as a result of the June 1967 and subsequent hostilities
The General Assembly,

Recalling its resolution 42/69 C of 2 December 1987 and all its previous resolutions on the question,

Taking note of the report of the Commissioner-General of the United Nations Relief and Works Agency for Palestine Refugees in the Near East, covering the period from 1 July 1987 to 30 June 1988,

Concerned about the continued human suffering resulting from the hostilities in the Middle East,

1. *Reaffirms* its resolution 42/69 C and all its previous resolutions on the question;

2. *Endorses,* bearing in mind the objectives of those resolutions, the efforts of the Commissioner-General of the United Nations Relief and Works Agency for Palestine Refugees in the Near East to continue to provide humanitarian assistance as far as practicable, on an emergency basis and as a temporary measure, to other persons in the area who are at present displaced and in serious need of continued assistance as a result of the June 1967 and subsequent hostilities;

3. *Strongly appeals* to all Governments and to organizations and individuals to contribute generously for the above purposes to the United Nations Relief and Works Agency for Palestine Refugees in the Near East and to

the other intergovernmental and non-governmental organizations concerned.

General Assembly resolution 43/57 C

6 December 1988   Meeting 71   Adopted without vote

Approved by Special Political Committee (A/43/903) without vote, 28 November (meeting 34); 20-nation draft (A/SPC/43/L.16); agenda item 76.
Sponsors: Austria, Belgium, Canada, Denmark, Finland, Germany, Federal Republic of, Greece, India, Indonesia, Ireland, Italy, Japan, Malaysia, Mali, Netherlands, Norway, Pakistan, Philippines, Sri Lanka, Sweden.
Meeting numbers. GA 43rd session: SPC 22, 24, 26, 27, 34; plenary 71.

Repatriation of refugees

In September 1988,[13] the Secretary-General reported on compliance with the General Assembly's 1987 call[14] on Israel to take immediate steps for the return of all displaced inhabitants and to desist from measures obstructing their return. By a note verbale of 7 July, Israel had stated that its position had been fully set out in successive annual replies to the Secretary-General, most recently in 1987.[15] It continued to make every effort to review individual cases of resettlement based on their merits and, as a result, the total number of persons returned to the administered territories was approximately 75,000.

The Commissioner-General pointed out to the Secretary-General that UNRWA was not involved in arrangements for the return of either refugees or displaced persons who were not registered with it. Its information was based on requests made by returning registered refugees who wanted a transfer of their benefit entitlements and a correction of their records; thus, it would not necessarily be aware of registered refugees not requesting services. As far as was known to UNRWA, 181 registered refugees had returned to the West Bank between 1 July 1987 and 30 June 1988, and 27 had returned to the Gaza Strip. The number of displaced registered refugees who were known by UNRWA to have returned to the occupied territories since June 1967 was about 11,300. Those records, however, might be incomplete.

GENERAL ASSEMBLY ACTION

On 6 December 1988, on the recommendation of the Special Political Committee, the General Assembly adopted **resolution 43/57 G** by recorded vote.

The return of population and refugees displaced since 1967

The General Assembly,

Recalling Security Council resolution 237(1967) of 14 June 1967,

Recalling also its resolutions 2252(ES-V) of 4 July 1967, 2452 A (XXIII) of 19 December 1968, 2535 B (XXIV) of 10 December 1969, 2672 D (XXV) of 8 December 1970, 2792 E (XXVI) of 6 December 1971, 2963 C and D (XXVII) of 13 December 1972, 3089 C (XXVIII) of 7 December 1973, 3331 D (XXIX) of 17 December 1974, 3419 C (XXX) of 8 December 1975, 31/15 D of 23 November 1976, 32/90 E of 13 December 1977,

33/112 F of 18 December 1978, 34/52 E of 23 November 1979, ES-7/2 of 29 July 1980, 35/13 E of 3 November 1980, 36/146 B of 16 December 1981, 37/120 G of 16 December 1982, 38/83 G of 15 December 1983, 39/99 G of 14 December 1984, 40/165 G of 16 December 1985, 41/69 G of 3 December 1986 and 42/69 G of 2 December 1987,

Having considered the report of the Commissioner-General of the United Nations Relief and Works Agency for Palestine Refugees in the Near East, covering the period from 1 July 1987 to 30 June 1988, and the report of the Secretary-General,

1. *Reaffirms* the inalienable right of all displaced inhabitants to return to their homes or former places of residence in the territories occupied by Israel since 1967, and declares once more that any attempt to restrict, or to attach conditions to, the free exercise of the right to return by any displaced person is inconsistent with that inalienable right and inadmissible;

2. *Considers* any and all agreements embodying any restriction on, or condition for, the return of the displaced inhabitants as null and void;

3. *Strongly deplores* the continued refusal of the Israeli authorities to take steps for the return of the displaced inhabitants;

4. *Calls once more upon* Israel:

   (a) To take immediate steps for the return of all displaced inhabitants;

   (b) To desist from all measures that obstruct the return of the displaced inhabitants, including measures affecting the physical and demographic structure of the occupied territories;

5. *Requests* the Secretary-General, after consulting with the Commissioner-General of the United Nations Relief and Works Agency for Palestine Refugees in the Near East, to report to the General Assembly, before the opening of its forty-fourth session, on Israel's compliance with paragraph 4 above.

General Assembly resolution 43/57 G

6 December 1988   Meeting 71   129-2-23 (recorded vote)

Approved by Special Political Committee (A/43/903) by recorded vote (99-2-23), 28 November (meeting 34); 17-nation draft (A/SPC/43/L.20); agenda item 76.
Sponsors: Afghanistan, Bangladesh, Brunei Darussalam, Burkina Faso, Comoros, Cuba, Egypt, India, Indonesia, Madagascar, Malaysia, Mali, Nicaragua, Pakistan, Yugoslavia, Zambia, Zimbabwe.
Meeting numbers. GA 43rd session: SPC 22, 24, 26, 27, 34; plenary 71.

Recorded vote in Assembly as follows:

In favour: Afghanistan, Albania, Algeria, Angola, Antigua and Barbuda, Argentina, Bahamas, Bahrain, Bangladesh, Barbados, Belize, Benin, Bhutan, Bolivia, Botswana, Brazil, Brunei Darussalam, Bulgaria, Burkina Faso, Burma, Burundi, Byelorussian SSR, Cameroon, Cape Verde, Central African Republic, Chad, Chile, China, Colombia, Comoros, Cuba, Cyprus, Czechoslovakia, Democratic Kampuchea, Democratic Yemen, Djibouti, Dominican Republic, Ecuador, Egypt, El Salvador, Ethiopia, Fiji, Gabon, Gambia, German Democratic Republic, Ghana, Greece, Grenada, Guatemala, Guinea, Guinea-Bissau, Guyana, Haiti, Honduras, Hungary, India, Indonesia, Iran, Iraq, Jamaica, Japan, Jordan, Kenya, Kuwait, Lao People's Democratic Republic, Lebanon, Lesotho, Libyan Arab Jamahiriya, Madagascar, Malawi, Malaysia, Maldives, Mali, Malta, Mauritania, Mauritius, Mexico, Mongolia, Morocco, Mozambique, Nepal, Nicaragua, Niger, Nigeria, Oman, Pakistan, Panama, Papua New Guinea, Paraguay, Peru, Philippines, Poland, Qatar, Romania, Rwanda, Saint Kitts and Nevis, Saint Lucia, Saint Vincent and the Grenadines, Samoa, Sao Tome and Principe, Saudi Arabia, Senegal, Seychelles, Sierra Leone, Singapore, Solomon Islands, Somalia, Spain, Sri Lanka, Sudan, Syrian Arab Republic, Thailand, Togo, Trinidad and Tobago, Tunisia, Turkey, Uganda, Ukrainian SSR, USSR, United Arab Emirates, United Republic of Tanzania, Uruguay, Vanuatu, Venezuela, Viet Nam, Yemen, Yugoslavia, Zambia, Zimbabwe.

Against: Israel, United States.

Food aid

The Secretary-General reported in September 1988[16] that UNRWA had continued distributing rations to the most needy sector of the refugee population, known as special hardship cases, who numbered 119,512 in December 1987. The Agency provided emergency food assistance in Lebanon, the West Bank and Gaza. Two distributions of food were made to all registered refugees in Lebanon and *ad hoc* distributions were made to camp inhabitants and others affected by the fighting. In the West Bank, food supplies had been distributed in camps and other areas of refugee concentration, as well as to some 87,000 schoolchildren in the Gaza Strip. However, due to continued financial constraints, a general ration distribution to all refugees, as requested by the General Assembly in 1987,[17] was not possible.

The Commissioner-General noted[1] that, whenever possible, normal relief programmes were carried out and additional measures were adopted. In the Gaza Strip, dry food commodities sufficient for one person for one month, pre-packed in plastic bags, were distributed through schools, and *ad hoc* arrangements were made to reach families without school-age children. Approximately 2,750 tons of supplies, either purchased by or donated to UNRWA, were distributed to registered refugees in the Gaza Strip, with about 87,000 schoolchildren and 6,166 families benefiting monthly from the distributions. In the West Bank, some 1,840 tons of commodities were distributed to registered refugees and non-refugees, with an average of 62,770 refugees, 4,700 non-refugees and 14,500 schoolchildren benefiting monthly.

GENERAL ASSEMBLY ACTION

On 6 December, on the recommendation of the Special Political Committee, the General Assembly adopted **resolution 43/57 F** by recorded vote.

Resumption of the ration distribution to Palestine refugees

The General Assembly,

Recalling its resolutions 36/146 F of 16 December 1981, 37/120 F of 16 December 1982, 38/83 F of 15 December 1983, 39/99 F of 14 December 1984, 40/165 F of 16 December 1985, 41/69 F of 3 December 1986, 42/69 F of 2 December 1987 and all its previous resolutions on the question, including resolution 302(IV) of 8 December 1949,

Having considered the report of the Commissioner-General of the United Nations Relief and Works Agency for Palestine Refugees in the Near East, covering the period from 1 July 1987 to 30 June 1988, and the report of the Secretary-General,

Deeply concerned at the interruption by the Agency, owing to financial difficulties, of the general ration distribution to Palestine refugees in all fields,

1. *Regrets* that its resolutions 37/120 F, 38/83 F, 39/99 F, 40/165 F, 41/69 F and 42/69 F have not been implemented;

2. *Calls once again upon* all Governments, as a matter of urgency, to make the most generous efforts possible and to offer the necessary resources to meet the needs of the United Nations Relief and Works Agency for Palestine Refugees in the Near East, particularly in the light of the interruption by the Agency of the general ration distribution to Palestine refugees in all fields, and therefore urges non-contributing Governments to contribute regularly and contributing Governments to consider increasing their regular contributions;

3. *Requests* the Commissioner-General of the United Nations Relief and Works Agency for Palestine Refugees in the Near East to resume on a continuing basis the interrupted general ration distribution to Palestine refugees in all fields;

4. *Requests* the Secretary-General, in consultation with the Commissioner-General, to report to the General Assembly at its forty-fourth session on the implementation of the present resolution.

General Assembly resolution 43/57 F

6 December 1988   Meeting 71   130-20-3 (recorded vote)

Approved by Special Political Committee (A/43/903) by recorded vote (100-20-4), 28 November (meeting 34); 16-nation draft (A/SPC/43/L.19); agenda item 76.
Sponsors: Afghanistan, Bangladesh, Brunei Darussalam, Burkina Faso, Comoros, Cuba, Egypt, Indonesia, Madagascar, Malaysia, Mali, Nicaragua, Pakistan, Yugoslavia, Zambia, Zimbabwe.
Meeting numbers. GA 43rd session: SPC 22, 24, 26, 27, 34; plenary 71.

Recorded vote in Assembly as follows:

In favour: Afghanistan, Albania, Algeria, Angola, Antigua and Barbuda, Argentina, Bahamas, Bahrain, Bangladesh, Barbados, Belize, Benin, Bhutan, Bolivia, Botswana, Brazil, Brunei Darussalam, Bulgaria, Burkina Faso, Burma, Burundi, Byelorussian SSR, Cameroon, Cape Verde, Central African Republic, Chad, Chile, China, Colombia, Comoros, Costa Rica, Côte d'Ivoire, Cuba, Cyprus, Czechoslovakia, Democratic Kampuchea, Democratic Yemen, Djibouti, Dominican Republic, Ecuador, Egypt, El Salvador, Ethiopia, Fiji, Gabon, Gambia, German Democratic Republic, Ghana, Guatemala, Guinea, Guinea-Bissau, Guyana, Haiti, Honduras, Hungary, India, Indonesia, Iran, Iraq, Jamaica, Jordan, Kenya, Kuwait, Lao People's Democratic Republic, Lebanon, Lesotho, Liberia, Libyan Arab Jamahiriya, Madagascar, Malawi, Malaysia, Maldives, Mali, Malta, Mauritania, Mauritius, Mexico, Mongolia, Morocco, Mozambique, Nepal, Nicaragua, Niger, Nigeria, Oman, Pakistan, Panama, Papua New Guinea, Paraguay, Peru, Philippines, Poland, Qatar, Romania, Rwanda, Saint Kitts and Nevis, Saint Lucia, Saint Vincent and the Grenadines, Samoa, Sao Tome and Principe, Saudi Arabia, Senegal, Seychelles, Sierra Leone, Singapore, Solomon Islands, Somalia, Sri Lanka, Sudan, Swaziland, Syrian Arab Republic, Thailand, Togo, Trinidad and Tobago, Tunisia, Turkey, Uganda, Ukrainian SSR, USSR, United Arab Emirates, United Republic of Tanzania, Uruguay, Vanuatu, Venezuela, Viet Nam, Yemen, Yugoslavia, Zaire, Zambia, Zimbabwe.
Against: Australia, Belgium, Canada, Denmark, Finland, France, Germany, Federal Republic of, Iceland, Ireland, Israel, Italy, Japan, Luxembourg, Netherlands, New Zealand, Norway, Portugal, Sweden, United Kingdom, United States.
Abstaining: Austria, Greece, Spain.

Education and training services

Schools and teacher training

UNWRA's education programmes continued to provide nine grades of general education, vocational and technical training, pre-service teacher training and scholarships for higher education for Palestine refugees. The programme operated with technical assistance from UNESCO.

In 1988, expenditures on the education programme amounted to $112.4 million: $43.3 million in Jordan; $30.9 million in the Gaza Strip; $18.1 million in the West Bank; $11.7 million in the Syrian Arab Republic; $5.5 million in Lebanon; and $2.8 million at headquarters (Vienna).

As at 15 October, 351,136 pupils were enrolled in UNRWA schools, some 1,750 more than the previous year, as follows: 134,435 in Jordan; 91,222 in the Gaza Strip; 53,378 in the Syrian Arab Republic; 39,275 in the West Bank; and 32,826 in Lebanon. In addition, 110,339 refugee pupils attended government and private schools.

In the West Bank, 90 of 98 schools remained closed by the Israeli authorities for a large part of 1988. In the Gaza Strip, there was considerable disruption due to frequent curfews, strikes and widespread unrest. In Jordan and the Syrian Arab Republic, schools operated satisfactorily. In Lebanon, despite the generally disturbed situation, the majority of schools functioned with only local and short-lived interruptions.

During the 1987/88 academic year, UNRWA provided places for 3,904 vocational trainees and 850 teacher trainees in its eight training centres.

Proposed University of Jerusalem "Al-Quds"

In keeping with a General Assembly request of 1987,[18] the Secretary-General reported in June 1988[19] on the establishment of a university for Palestine refugees at Jerusalem. The proposed "Al-Quds" University, first considered by the Assembly in 1980,[20] had since been the subject of annual reports by the Secretary-General with regard to measures taken towards its establishment, including a functional feasibility study. To assist in the preparation of the study and at the Secretary-General's request, the United Nations University made available the services of an expert who was to visit the area and meet with Israeli officials. By a note verbale of 3 May, the Secretary-General requested Israel to facilitate the expert's visit at a mutually convenient date.

Israel replied on 24 May that its position remained unchanged;[21] it had consistently voted against the resolution calling for the establishment of the University, whose sponsors sought to exploit higher education in order to politicize issues totally extraneous to genuine academic pursuits. Therefore, Israel was unable to assist in taking the matter further.

In view of Israel's position, the feasibility study could not be completed as planned.

GENERAL ASSEMBLY ACTION

On 6 December 1988, on the recommendation of the Special Political Committee, the General Assembly adopted **resolution 43/57 J** by recorded vote.

University of Jerusalem "Al-Quds" for Palestine refugees

The General Assembly,

Recalling its resolutions 36/146 G of 16 December 1981, 37/120 C of 16 December 1982, 38/83 K of 15 December 1983, 39/99 K of 14 December 1984, 40/165 D and K of 16 December 1985, 41/69 K of 3 December 1986 and 42/69 K of 2 December 1987,

Having considered the report of the Secretary-General,

Having also considered the report of the Commissioner-General of the United Nations Relief and Works Agency for Palestine Refugees in the Near East, covering the period from 1 July 1987 to 30 June 1988,

1. *Emphasizes* the need for strengthening the educational system in the Arab territories occupied since 5 June 1967, including Jerusalem, and specifically the need for the establishment of the proposed university;

2. *Requests* the Secretary-General to continue to take all necessary measures for establishing the University of Jerusalem "Al-Quds", in accordance with General Assembly resolution 35/13 B of 3 November 1980, giving due consideration to the recommendations consistent with the provisions of that resolution;

3. *Calls once more upon* Israel, the occupying Power, to co-operate in the implementation of the present resolution and to remove the hindrances that it has put in the way of establishing the University of Jerusalem "Al-Quds";

4. *Requests* the Secretary-General to report to the General Assembly at its forty-fourth session on the progress made in the implementation of the present resolution.

General Assembly resolution 43/57 J

6 December 1988   Meeting 71   152-2 (recorded vote)

Approved by Special Political Committee (A/43/903) by recorded vote (122-2-1), 28 November (meeting 34); 18-nation draft (A/SPC/43/L.23); agenda item 76.

Sponsors: Afghanistan, Bangladesh, Brunei Darussalam, Burkina Faso, Comoros, Cuba, Egypt, India, Indonesia, Jordan, Madagascar, Malaysia, Mali, Nicaragua, Pakistan, Yugoslavia, Zambia, Zimbabwe.

Meeting numbers. GA 43rd session: SPC 22, 24, 26, 27, 34; plenary 71.

Recorded vote in Assembly as follows:

In favour: Afghanistan, Albania, Algeria, Angola, Antigua and Barbuda, Argentina, Australia, Austria, Bahamas, Bahrain, Bangladesh, Barbados, Belgium, Belize, Benin, Bhutan, Bolivia, Botswana, Brazil, Brunei Darussalam, Bulgaria, Burkina Faso, Burma, Burundi, Byelorussian SSR, Cameroon, Canada, Cape Verde, Central African Republic, Chad, Chile, China, Colombia, Comoros, Costa Rica, Côte d'Ivoire, Cuba, Cyprus, Czechoslovakia, Democratic Kampuchea, Democratic Yemen, Denmark, Djibouti, Dominican Republic, Ecuador, Egypt, El Salvador, Ethiopia, Fiji, Finland, France, Gabon, Gambia, German Democratic Republic, Germany, Federal Republic of, Ghana, Greece, Grenada, Guatemala, Guinea, Guinea-Bissau, Guyana, Haiti, Honduras, Hungary, Iceland, India, Indonesia, Iran, Iraq, Ireland, Italy, Jamaica, Japan, Jordan, Kenya, Kuwait, Lao People's Democratic Republic, Lebanon, Lesotho, Liberia, Libyan Arab Jamahiriya, Luxembourg, Madagascar, Malawi, Malaysia, Maldives, Mali, Malta, Mauritania, Mauritius, Mexico, Mongolia, Morocco, Mozambique, Nepal, Netherlands, New Zealand, Nicaragua, Niger, Nigeria, Norway, Oman, Pakistan, Panama, Papua New Guinea, Paraguay, Peru, Philippines, Poland, Portugal, Qatar, Romania, Rwanda, Saint Kitts and Nevis, Saint Lucia, Saint Vincent and the Grenadines, Samoa, Sao Tome and Principe, Saudi Arabia, Senegal, Seychelles, Sierra Leone, Singapore, Solomon Islands, Somalia, Spain, Sri Lanka, Sudan, Swaziland, Sweden, Syrian Arab Republic, Thailand, Togo, Trinidad and Tobago, Tunisia, Turkey, Uganda, Ukrainian SSR, USSR, United Arab Emirates, United Kingdom, United Republic of Tanzania, Uruguay, Vanuatu, Venezuela, Viet Nam, Yemen, Yugoslavia, Zaire, Zambia, Zimbabwe.

Against: Israel, United States.

Scholarships

The Secretary-General reported in September 1988[22] on responses to the General Assembly's 1987 appeal[23] to augment special allocations for scholarships and grants to Palestine refugees, for which UNRWA acted as recipient and trustee.

The 1988 activities of responding States and institutions included the provision by Japan of 15 fellowships to UNRWA vocational training instructors. The Federal Republic of Germany offered 25 scholarships in 1988 to Palestine refugee graduates of UNRWA vocational training centres, to be awarded in 1989. UNESCO granted six fellowships in 1988 and WIPO and UPU also followed up in offering additional fellowships. WHO sponsored nine regional and international fellowships to Palestine refugee health staff in its post-graduate training programme aimed at developing the technical and managerial skills of UNRWA's department of health staff and at meeting future replacement needs. Three Palestinians continued their studies in agricultural economics and animal production through the FAO project on specialized training in agricultural development, which also provided expertise to the Al-Quds Open University.

GENERAL ASSEMBLY ACTION

On 6 December 1988, on the recommendation of the Special Political Committee, the General Assembly adopted **resolution 43/57 D** by recorded vote.

Offers by Member States of grants and scholarships for higher education, including vocational training, for Palestine refugees

The General Assembly,

Recalling its resolution 212(III) of 19 November 1948 on assistance to Palestine refugees,

Recalling also its resolutions 35/13 B of 3 November 1980, 36/146 H of 16 December 1981, 37/120 D of 16 December 1982, 38/83 D of 15 December 1983, 39/99 D of 14 December 1984, 40/165 D of 16 December 1985, 41/69 D of 3 December 1986 and 42/69 D of 2 December 1987,

Cognizant of the fact that the Palestine refugees have, for the last four decades, lost their homes, lands and means of livelihood,

Having considered the report of the Secretary-General,

Having also considered the report of the Commissioner-General of the United Nations Relief and Works Agency for Palestine Refugees in the Near East, covering the period from 1 July 1987 to 30 June 1988,

1. *Urges* all States to respond to the appeal contained in General Assembly resolution 32/90 F of 13 December 1977 and reiterated in subsequent relevant resolutions in a manner commensurate with the needs of Palestine refugees for higher education, including vocational training;

2. *Strongly appeals* to all States, specialized agencies and non-governmental organizations to augment the special allocations for grants and scholarships to Palestine refugees in addition to their contributions to the regular budget of the United Nations Relief and Works Agency for Palestine Refugees in the Near East;

3. *Expresses its appreciation* to all Governments, specialized agencies and non-governmental organizations that responded favourably to General Assembly resolutions 41/69 D and 42/69 D;

4. *Invites* the relevant specialized agencies and other organizations of the United Nations system to continue, within their respective spheres of competence, to extend assistance for higher education to Palestine refugee students;

5. *Appeals* to all States, specialized agencies and the United Nations University to contribute generously to the Palestinian universities in the Palestinian territory occupied by Israel since 1967, including, in due course, the proposed University of Jerusalem "Al-Quds" for Palestine refugees;

6. *Also appeals* to all States, specialized agencies and other international bodies to contribute towards the establishment of vocational training centres for Palestine refugees;

7. *Requests* the United Nations Relief and Works Agency for Palestine Refugees in the Near East to act as the recipient and trustee for the special allocations for grants and scholarships and to award them to qualified Palestine refugee candidates;

8. *Requests* the Secretary-General to report to the General Assembly at its forty-fourth session on the implementation of the present resolution.

General Assembly resolution 43/57 D

6 December 1988   Meeting 71   153-0-1 (recorded vote)

Approved by Special Political Committee (A/43/903) by recorded vote (123-0-1), 28 November (meeting 34); 17-nation draft (A/SPC/43/L.17); agenda item 76.

Sponsors: Afghanistan, Bangladesh, Brunei Darussalam, Burkina Faso, Comoros, Cuba, Egypt, Indonesia, Jordan, Madagascar, Malaysia, Mali, Nicaragua, Pakistan, Yugoslavia, Zambia, Zimbabwe.

Meeting numbers. GA 43rd session: SPC 22, 24, 26, 27, 34; plenary 71.

Recorded vote in Assembly as follows:

In favour: Afghanistan, Albania, Algeria, Angola, Antigua and Barbuda, Argentina, Australia, Austria, Bahamas, Bahrain, Bangladesh, Barbados, Belgium, Belize, Benin, Bhutan, Bolivia, Botswana, Brazil, Brunei Darussalam, Bulgaria, Burkina Faso, Burma, Burundi, Byelorussian SSR, Cameroon, Canada, Cape Verde, Central African Republic, Chad, Chile, China, Colombia, Comoros, Costa Rica, Côte d'Ivoire, Cuba, Cyprus, Czechoslovakia, Democratic Kampuchea, Democratic Yemen, Denmark, Djibouti, Dominican Republic, Ecuador, Egypt, El Salvador, Ethiopia, Fiji, Finland, France, Gabon, Gambia, German Democratic Republic, Germany, Federal Republic of, Ghana, Greece, Grenada, Guatemala, Guinea, Guinea-Bissau, Guyana, Haiti, Honduras, Hungary, Iceland, India, Indonesia, Iran, Iraq, Ireland, Italy, Jamaica, Japan, Jordan, Kenya, Kuwait, Lao People's Democratic Republic, Lebanon, Lesotho, Liberia, Libyan Arab Jamahiriya, Luxembourg, Madagascar, Malawi, Malaysia, Maldives, Mali, Malta, Mauritania, Mauritius, Mexico, Mongolia, Morocco, Mozambique, Nepal, Netherlands, New Zealand, Nicaragua, Niger, Nigeria, Norway, Oman, Pakistan, Panama, Papua New Guinea, Paraguay, Peru, Philippines, Poland, Portugal, Qatar, Romania, Rwanda, Saint Kitts and Nevis, Saint Lucia, Saint Vincent and the Grenadines, Samoa, Sao Tome and Principe, Saudi Arabia, Senegal, Seychelles, Sierra Leone, Singapore, Solomon Islands, Somalia, Spain, Sri Lanka, Sudan, Swaziland, Sweden, Syrian Arab Republic, Thailand, Togo, Trinidad and Tobago, Tunisia, Turkey, Uganda, Ukrainian SSR, USSR, United Arab Emirates, United Kingdom, United Republic of Tanzania, United States, Uruguay, Vanuatu, Venezuela, Viet Nam, Yemen, Yugoslavia, Zaire, Zambia, Zimbabwe.

Against: None.

Abstaining: Israel.

Property rights

Report of the Secretary-General. In September 1988,[24] the Secretary-General reported on responses to his request for information on steps taken to implement the General Assembly's 1987 resolution[25] on revenues derived from Palestinian refugee properties.

In its reply of 7 July 1988, Israel reiterated its position as set out in statements to the Special Political Committee, most recently in 1987,[26] that

there was no legal basis for taking the steps proposed, as property rights within the borders of a
sovereign State were subject exclusively to the
domestic laws of that State. The right of States to
regulate and dispose of property within their territory and the income derived from that property
was a generally accepted principle. Significantly,
the resolution's sponsors made no suggestion regarding confiscated property in Arab countries of
some 800,000 Jewish refugees as a result of the
1948 war, estimated to be worth billions of dollars.
Israel stressed that there could be no difference
in law, justice or equity between the claims of Arab
and Jewish property owners.

No reply had been received from any other Member State regarding implementation of the resolution.

Report of the Conciliation Commission. The
United Nations Conciliation Commission for Palestine, in its report covering the period from 1 September 1987 to 31 August 1988,[27] stated that
events that had occurred in the area since the preceding reporting period had further complicated an
already very complex situation. As far as the Commission was concerned, the circumstances that had
limited its possibilities of action remained essentially unchanged. Nevertheless, it continued to hope
that the situation would improve towards the achievement of a comprehensive, just and lasting peace
in the Middle East, thus enabling it to carry forward its work in accordance with its mandate as
defined by the Assembly in 1948.[28]

GENERAL ASSEMBLY ACTION

On 6 December 1988, on the recommendation
of the Special Political Committee, the General
Assembly adopted **resolution 43/57 H** by recorded vote.

Revenues derived from Palestine refugee properties

The General Assembly,

Recalling its resolutions 35/13 A to F of 3 November
1980, 36/146 C of 16 December 1981, 37/120 H of 16 December 1982, 38/83 H of 15 December 1983, 39/99 H
of 14 December 1984, 40/165 H of 16 December 1985,
41/69 H of 3 December 1986, 42/69 H of 2 December
1987 and all its previous resolutions on the question,
including resolution 194(III) of 11 December 1948,

Taking note of the report of the Secretary-General,

Taking note also of the report of the United Nations Conciliation Commission for Palestine, covering the period
from 1 September 1987 to 31 August 1988,

Recalling that the Universal Declaration of Human
Rights and the principles of international law uphold
the principle that no one shall be arbitrarily deprived
of his or her private property,

Considering that the Palestine Arab refugees are entitled to their property and to the income derived therefrom, in conformity with the principles of justice and equity,

Recalling in particular its resolution 394(V) of 14 December 1950, in which it directed the United Nations Conciliation Commission for Palestine, in consultation with
the parties concerned, to prescribe measures for the pro-

tection of the rights, property and interests of the Palestine Arab refugees,

Taking note of the completion of the programme of identification and evaluation of Arab property, as announced
by the United Nations Conciliation Commission for
Palestine in its twenty-second progress report, and of
the fact that the Land Office had a schedule of Arab
owners and file of documents defining the location, area
and other particulars of Arab property,

1. *Requests* the Secretary-General to take all appropriate steps, in consultation with the United Nations Conciliation Commission for Palestine, for the protection
and administration of Arab property, assets and property rights in Israel and to establish a fund for the receipt of income derived therefrom, on behalf of the right-
ful owners;

2. *Calls once more upon* Israel to render all facilities and
assistance to the Secretary-General in the implementation of the present resolution;

3. *Calls upon* the Governments of all the other Member States concerned to provide the Secretary-General
with any pertinent information in their possession concerning Arab property, assets and property rights in Israel, which would assist the Secretary-General in the
implementation of the present resolution;

4. *Deplores* Israel's refusal to co-operate with the
Secretary-General in the implementation of the resolutions on the question;

5. *Requests* the Secretary-General to report to the
General Assembly at its forty-fourth session on the implementation of the present resolution.

General Assembly resolution 43/57 H

6 December 1988   Meeting 71   124-2-25 (recorded vote)

Approved by Special Political Committee (A/43/903) by recorded vote (97-
2-24), 28 November (meeting 34); 17-nation draft (A/SPC/43/L.21);
agenda item 76.

Sponsors: Afghanistan, Bangladesh, Brunei Darussalam, Burkina Faso,
Comoros, Cuba, Egypt, India, Indonesia, Madagascar, Malaysia, Mali, Nicaragua, Pakistan, Yugoslavia, Zambia, Zimbabwe.

Meeting numbers. GA 43rd session: SPC 22, 24, 26, 27, 34; plenary 71.

Recorded vote in Assembly as follows:

In favour: Afghanistan, Albania, Algeria, Angola, Antigua and Barbuda,
Argentina, Bahamas, Bahrain, Bangladesh, Barbados, Belize, Benin, Bhu-
tan, Bolivia, Botswana, Brazil, Brunei Darussalam, Bulgaria, Burkina Faso,
Burma, Burundi, Byelorussian SSR, Cape Verde, Central African Repub-
lic, Chad, Chile, China, Colombia, Comoros, Cuba, Cyprus, Czechoslovakia,
Democratic Kampuchea, Democratic Yemen, Djibouti, Dominican Republic,
Ecuador, Egypt, El Salvador, Ethiopia, Fiji, Gabon, Gambia, German
Democratic Republic, Ghana, Greece, Guatemala, Guinea, Guinea-Bissau,
Guyana, Honduras, Hungary, India, Indonesia, Iran, Iraq, Jamaica, Jordan,
Kenya, Kuwait, Lao People's Democratic Republic, Lebanon, Lesotho,
Libyan Arab Jamahiriya, Madagascar, Malaysia, Maldives, Mali, Malta,
Mauritania, Mauritius, Mexico, Mongolia, Morocco, Mozambique, Nepal,
Nicaragua, Niger, Nigeria, Oman, Pakistan, Panama, Papua New Guinea,
Paraguay, Peru, Philippines, Poland, Qatar, Romania, Rwanda, Saint Kitts
and Nevis, Saint Lucia, Saint Vincent and the Grenadines, Samoa, Saudi
Arabia, Senegal, Seychelles, Sierra Leone, Singapore, Solomon Islands,
Somalia, Spain, Sri Lanka, Sudan, Swaziland, Syrian Arab Republic, Thai-
land, Togo, Trinidad and Tobago, Tunisia, Turkey, Uganda, Ukrainian SSR,
USSR, United Arab Emirates, United Republic of Tanzania, Uruguay, Vanu-
atu, Venezuela, Viet Nam, Yemen, Yugoslavia, Zambia, Zimbabwe.

Against: Israel, United States.

Abstaining: Australia, Austria, Belgium, Cameroon, Canada, Costa Rica,
Côte d'Ivoire, Denmark, Finland, France, Germany, Federal Republic of,
Iceland, Ireland, Italy, Japan, Liberia, Luxembourg, Malawi, Netherlands,
New Zealand, Norway, Portugal, Sweden, United Kingdom, Zaire.

Refugee protection

Reports of the Secretary-General. In his January
1988 report to the Security Council on the situation in the occupied territories,[5] the Secretary-

General explored four possible ways of protecting the civilian population in the territories, some 55 per cent of which were refugees registered with UNRWA. One such way was physical protection by United Nations peace-keeping forces. Another was legal protection, meaning intervention with the security or judicial authorities on behalf of those threatened. Protection could also take the form of general assistance, with an outside agency intervening to help individuals or groups to resist violations of rights and cope with life under occupation. Finally, protection by publicity was afforded through the presence of the international media, ready to publish events.

On the basis of those definitions, the Secretary-General explored ways for the international community to help ensure the civilian population's protection. With regard to physical protection, he said the introduction of United Nations forces into the territories could detract from the occupying Power's responsibilities under the fourth Geneva Convention. Also, their deployment would require the consent of Israel, which had voiced its disagreement. The idea, however, should not be lost sight of, as Israel had accepted international forces in other contexts of the Arab-Israeli conflict and United Nations forces could again be a valuable ingredient in implementing a negotiated settlement or in transitional arrangements for the territories.

A measure of legal protection was provided by ICRC, and general assistance was provided by agencies, most prominently UNRWA. In order to improve general assistance, the Secretary-General had requested the UNRWA Commissioner-General to examine the possibility of extra international staff, stressing at the same time that Israel should honour UNRWA privileges and immunities in full. The Commissioner-General should be permitted to extend humanitarian assistance on an emergency basis and as a temporary measure to non-refugees in serious need because of the recent disturbances.

The need to publicize the situation in the territories was stressed by the Palestinians, as was the importance of unhindered access by the international media. It was argued that world attention had a potentially beneficial influence, both on Israel's practices in the territories and on its willingness to negotiate. It was suggested that the Secretary-General appoint a United Nations ombudsman to reside in the territories. The Secretary-General concluded that the practicability of all the aforementioned ideas depended on Israel's full consent and co-operation.

The Secretary-General reported in September 1988[12] on implementation of a 1987 Assembly resolution[29] holding Israel responsible for the security of the Palestine refugees in the occupied territories and calling on it to compensate UNRWA for the damage to its property and facilities resulting from Israel's 1982 invasion of Lebanon.

The report reproduced Israel's reply of 7 July 1988 to the Secretary-General's request for information on steps taken or envisaged to comply with the resolution. Israel said it had fully set forth its position on the subject in statements to the Special Political Committee and in a 1987 report of the Secretary-General.[30] The adoption of the resolution was hypocritical, anachronistic and out of place. Despite its withdrawal from Lebanon in 1985, Israel was still being blamed for the "suffering" of Palestinians there and, not surprisingly, for Arab persecution of Palestinian refugees. In recent years, thousands of Palestinians had been killed and wounded in Lebanese refugee camps in vicious fighting totally unconnected with Israel; likewise, Palestinian refugee camps in Jordan and the Syrian Arab Republic were the scenes of considerable human misery. The selective and distorted presentation of the Palestinian refugees' situation in Arab countries clearly illustrated the resolution's double standards and its disregard for the refugees' general welfare.

The Secretary-General cited the UNRWA Commissioner-General's report for the period 1 July 1987 to 30 June 1988[1] to the effect that the Commissioner-General had continued his efforts to do everything feasible to contribute to the refugees' safety and security.

GENERAL ASSEMBLY ACTION

On 6 December 1988, on the recommendation of the Special Political Committee, the General Assembly adopted **resolution 43/57 I** by recorded vote.

Protection of Palestine refugees

The General Assembly,

Recalling Security Council resolutions 508(1982) of 5 June 1982, 509(1982) of 6 June 1982, 511(1982) of 18 June 1982, 512(1982) of 19 June 1982, 513(1982) of 4 July 1982, 515(1982) of 29 July 1982, 517(1982) of 4 August 1982, 518(1982) of 12 August 1982, 519(1982) of 17 August 1982, 520(1982) of 17 September 1982 and 523(1982) of 18 October 1982,

Recalling in particular recent Security Council resolutions 605(1987) of 22 December 1987, 607(1988) of 5 January 1988 and 608(1988) of 14 January 1988,

Recalling its resolutions ES-7/5 of 26 June 1982, ES-7/6 and ES-7/8 of 19 August 1982, ES-7/9 of 24 September 1982, 37/120 J of 16 December 1982, 38/83 I of 15 December 1983, 39/99 I of 14 December 1984, 40/165 I of 16 December 1985, 41/69 I of 3 December 1986, 42/69 I of 2 December 1987 and 43/21 of 3 November 1988,

Taking note of the report of the Secretary-General dated 21 January 1988, submitted in accordance with Security Council resolution 605(1987),

Having considered the report of the Secretary-General,

Having also considered the report of the Commissioner-General of the United Nations Relief and Works Agency for Palestine Refugees in the Near East, covering the period from 1 July 1987 to 30 June 1988,

Gravely concerned and alarmed by the deteriorating situation in the Palestinian territory occupied by Israel since 1967, including Jerusalem,

Taking into account the need to consider measures for the impartial protection of the Palestinian civilian population under Israeli occupation,

Referring to the humanitarian principles of the Geneva Convention relative to the Protection of Civilian Persons in Time of War, of 12 August 1949, and to the obligations arising from the regulations annexed to the Hague Convention IV of 1907,

Deeply concerned at the marked deterioration in the security situation experienced by the Palestine refugees as stated by the Commissioner-General in his report,

Deeply distressed at the suffering of the Palestinian and Lebanese population which resulted from continuing Israeli acts of aggression against Lebanon and other hostile acts,

Deeply distressed at the tragic situation of the civilian population in and around the Palestinian refugee camps in Lebanon which resulted from the fighting,

Noting with appreciation the efforts of the Secretary-General and the support of the Commissioner-General for organizing a co-ordinated and comprehensive programme of assistance for Lebanon by the United Nations inter-agency group, as reflected in paragraph 17 of the Commissioner-General's report,

Reaffirming its support for the sovereignty, unity and territorial integrity of Lebanon, within its internationally recognized boundaries,

1. *Holds* Israel responsible for the security of the Palestine refugees in the Palestinian and other Arab territories occupied since 1967, including Jerusalem, and calls upon it to fulfil its obligations as the occupying Power in this regard, in accordance with the pertinent provisions of the Geneva Convention relative to the Protection of Civilian Persons in Time of War, of 12 August 1949;

2. *Calls upon* all the High Contracting Parties to the Convention to take appropriate measures to ensure respect by Israel, the occupying Power, for the Convention in all circumstances in conformity with their obligation under article I thereof;

3. *Urges* the Security Council to consider the current situation in the occupied Palestinian territory, taking into account the recommendations contained in the report of the Secretary-General;

4. *Urges* the Secretary-General, in consultation with the Commissioner-General of the United Nations Relief and Works Agency for Palestine Refugees in the Near East, to continue their efforts in support of the upholding of the safety and security and the legal and human rights of the Palestine refugees in all the territories under Israeli occupation in 1967 and thereafter;

5. *Calls once again upon* Israel, the occupying Power, to release forthwith all arbitrarily detained Palestine refugees, including the employees of the United Nations Relief and Works Agency for Palestine Refugees in the Near East;

6. *Welcomes* the provision by the Commissioner-General, in consultation with the Government of Leb-

anon, to provide housing to the Palestine refugees whose houses were demolished or razed;

7. *Welcomes also* the provision by the Commissioner-General, in consultation with the Government of Lebanon, to provide emergency housing repairs for the shelters and Agency installations that have been partly damaged or destroyed in the fighting;

8. *Calls once again upon* Israel to compensate the Agency for the damage to its property and facilities resulting from the Israeli invasion of Lebanon, without prejudice to Israel's responsibility for all damages resulting from that invasion;

9. *Requests* the Secretary-General, in consultation with the Commissioner-General, to report to the General Assembly, before the opening of its forty-fourth session, on the implementation of the present resolution.

General Assembly resolution 43/57 I

6 December 1988   Meeting 71   151-2-1 (recorded vote)

Approved by Special Political Committee (A/43/903) by recorded vote (121-2), 28 November (meeting 34); 16-nation draft (A/SPC/43/L.22/Rev.1); agenda item 76.

Sponsors: Afghanistan, Bangladesh, Brunei Darussalam, Burkina Faso, Comoros, Cuba, Egypt, Indonesia, Madagascar, Malaysia, Mali, Nicaragua, Pakistan, Yugoslavia, Zambia, Zimbabwe.

Meeting numbers. GA 43rd session: SPC 22, 24, 26, 27, 34; plenary 71.

Recorded vote in Assembly as follows:

In favour: Afghanistan, Albania, Algeria, Angola, Antigua and Barbuda, Argentina, Australia, Austria, Bahamas, Bahrain, Bangladesh, Barbados, Belgium, Belize, Benin, Bhutan, Bolivia, Botswana, Brazil, Brunei Darussalam, Bulgaria, Burkina Faso, Burma, Burundi, Byelorussian SSR, Cameroon, Canada, Cape Verde, Central African Republic, Chad, Chile, China, Colombia, Comoros, Costa Rica, Côte d'Ivoire, Cuba, Cyprus, Czechoslovakia, Democratic Kampuchea, Democratic Yemen, Denmark, Djibouti, Dominican Republic, Ecuador, Egypt, El Salvador, Ethiopia, Fiji, Finland, France, Gabon, Gambia, German Democratic Republic, Germany, Federal Republic of, Ghana, Greece, Grenada, Guatemala, Guinea, Guinea-Bissau, Guyana, Haiti, Honduras, Hungary, Iceland, India, Indonesia, Iran, Iraq, Ireland, Italy, Jamaica, Japan, Jordan, Kenya, Kuwait, Lao People's Democratic Republic, Lebanon, Lesotho, Liberia, Libyan Arab Jamahiriya, Luxembourg, Madagascar, Malawi, Malaysia, Maldives, Mali, Malta, Mauritania, Mauritius, Mexico, Mongolia, Morocco, Mozambique, Nepal, Netherlands, New Zealand, Nicaragua, Niger, Nigeria, Norway, Oman, Pakistan, Panama, Papua New Guinea, Paraguay, Peru, Philippines, Poland, Portugal, Qatar, Romania, Rwanda, Saint Kitts and Nevis, Saint Lucia, Saint Vincent and the Grenadines, Samoa, Sao Tome and Principe, Saudi Arabia, Senegal, Seychelles, Sierra Leone, Singapore, Solomon Islands, Somalia, Spain, Sri Lanka, Sudan, Swaziland, Sweden, Syrian Arab Republic, Thailand, Togo, Trinidad and Tobago, Tunisia, Turkey, Uganda, Ukrainian SSR, USSR, United Arab Emirates, United Kingdom, United Republic of Tanzania, Uruguay, Vanuatu, Venezuela, Viet Nam, Yemen, Yugoslavia, Zambia, Zimbabwe.

Against: Israel, United States.

Abstaining: Zaire.

Removal and resettlement of refugees

Reports of the Secretary-General. The Secretary-General reported in September 1988[31] that, in response to his request for information on steps taken to implement a 1987 General Assembly resolution[32] calling on Israel to refrain from resettling Palestine refugees in the West Bank and from destroying their camps, Israel replied on 7 July that its position had been fully set out in annual statements to the Special Political Committee and in a 1987 report of the Secretary-General.[33]

The Secretary-General noted that the UNRWA Commissioner-General would not object if refugees in the camps voluntarily sought better housing, whether by improving existing housing or by moving into new housing. He would, however, strongly object if any pressure or coercion were used to make refugees move or comply with any scheme. Refugees would not lose eligibility for UNRWA services on relocation outside the camps.

In another September report, the Secretary-General reproduced[34] Israel's response of 7 July to a 1987 Assembly resolution[35] demanding that it desist from removing and resettling Palestine refugees in the Gaza Strip and from destroying their shelters. Israel said its position had been set out in successive annual replies to the Secretary-General, most recently in 1987.[36] It considered the resolution distorted, unbalanced and inaccurate, in that it intentionally ignored the improved living conditions in the Gaza District since 1967, the considerable increase of pupils attending school, the significant drop in illiteracy, the development of medical care, the improvement in environmental services such as water supply and sewage and waste disposal, and the community development projects initiated by Israel that had enabled 10,000 families to leave refugee camps and relocate to new residential areas. Notwithstanding the omission of those facts, Israel continued to undertake and encourage assistance and rehabilitation projects for refugees.

The Secretary-General stated that, according to UNRWA, house demolitions as punitive actions continued during 1988, as did the practice of requiring refugee families to demolish their shelters as a pre-condition for new housing. Also, refugee shelters were demolished on the grounds that they had been built without proper authority on State land outside camp boundaries. Families affected by demolitions from as far back as 1971, including those categorized as living in hardship conditions, continued to live in unsatisfactory circumstances despite Israel's assurances that they would be housed.

According to information available to the Commissioner-General, Israeli authorities had to date allocated 3,914 plots of land in the Gaza Strip for housing projects. A total of 2,583 plots had been built on by 3,673 refugee families comprising 22,732 persons, buildings on 257 plots were under construction, 937 plots were vacant and 137 had been built on by non-refugees. In addition, 3,034 refugee families, consisting of 18,823 persons, had moved into 2,666 completed housing units, comprising 5,893 rooms. Refugee families were continuing to purchase plots of land at subsidized rates for construction of houses in projects developed by the Israeli authorities.

GENERAL ASSEMBLY ACTION

On 6 December 1988, on the recommendation of the Special Political Committee, the General Assembly adopted **resolution 43/57 E** by recorded vote.

Palestine refugees in the Palestinian territory occupied by Israel since 1967

The General Assembly,

Recalling Security Council resolution 237(1967) of 14 June 1967,

Recalling also its resolutions 2792 C (XXVI) of 6 December 1971, 2963 C (XXVII) of 13 December 1972, 3089 C (XXVIII) of 7 December 1973, 3331 D (XXIX) of 17 December 1974, 3419 C (XXX) of 8 December 1975, 31/15 E of 23 November 1976, 32/90 C of 13 December 1977, 33/112 E of 18 December 1978, 34/52 F of 23 November 1979, 35/13 F of 3 November 1980, 36/146 A of 16 December 1981, 37/120 E and I of 16 December 1982, 38/83 E and J of 15 December 1983, 39/99 E and J of 14 December 1984, 40/165 E and J of 16 December 1985, 41/69 E and J of 3 December 1986 and 42/69 E and J of 2 December 1987,

Having considered the report of the Commissioner-General of the United Nations Relief and Works Agency for Palestine Refugees in the Near East, covering the period from 1 July 1987 to 30 June 1988, and the two reports of the Secretary-General,

Recalling the provisions of paragraph 11 of its resolution 194(III) of 11 December 1948, and considering that measures to resettle Palestine refugees in the Palestinian territory occupied by Israel since 1967 away from their homes and property from which they were displaced constitute a violation of their inalienable right of return,

Alarmed by the reports received from the Commissioner-General that the Israeli occupying authorities, in contravention of Israel's obligation under international law, persist in their policy of demolishing shelters occupied by refugee families,

1. *Reiterates strongly its demand* that Israel desist from the removal and resettlement of Palestine refugees in the Palestinian territory occupied by Israel since 1967 and from the destruction of their shelters;

2. *Requests* the Commissioner-General of the United Nations Relief and Works Agency for Palestine Refugees in the Near East to address the acute situation of the Palestine refugees in the Palestinian territory occupied by Israel since 1967 and accordingly to extend all the services of the Agency to those refugees;

3. *Requests* the Secretary-General, in co-operation with the Commissioner-General, to resume issuing identification cards to all Palestine refugees and their descendants in the occupied Palestinian territory, irrespective of whether or not they are recipients of rations and services of the Agency;

4. *Requests* the Secretary-General, after consulting with the Commissioner-General, to report to the General Assembly, before the opening of its forty-fourth session, on the implementation of the present resolution and in particular on Israel's compliance with paragraph 1 above.

General Assembly resolution 43/57 E

6 December 1988   Meeting 71   152-2 (recorded vote)

Approved by Special Political Committee (A/43/903) by recorded vote (121-2), 28 November (meeting 34); 18-nation draft (A/SPC/43/L.18/Rev.1); agenda item 76.

Sponsors: Afghanistan, Bangladesh, Brunei Darussalam, Burkina Faso, Comoros, Cuba, Egypt, India, Indonesia, Madagascar, Malaysia, Mali, Nicaragua, Pakistan, Sierra Leone, Yugoslavia, Zambia, Zimbabwe.

Meeting numbers. GA 43rd session: SPC 22, 24, 26, 27, 34; plenary 71.

Recorded vote in Assembly as follows:

In favour: Afghanistan, Albania, Algeria, Angola, Antigua and Barbuda, Argentina, Australia, Austria, Bahamas, Bahrain, Bangladesh, Barbados, Belgium, Belize, Benin, Bhutan, Bolivia, Botswana, Brazil, Brunei Darussalam, Bulgaria, Burkina Faso, Burma, Burundi, Byelorussian SSR, Cameroon, Canada, Cape Verde, Central African Republic, Chad, Chile, China, Colombia, Comoros, Costa Rica, Côte d'Ivoire, Cuba, Cyprus, Czechoslovakia, Democratic Kampuchea, Democratic Yemen, Denmark, Djibouti, Dominican Republic, Ecuador, Egypt, El Salvador, Ethiopia, Fiji, Finland, France, Gabon, Gambia, German Democratic Republic, Germany, Federal Republic of, Ghana, Greece, Grenada, Guatemala, Guinea, Guinea-Bissau, Guyana, Haiti, Honduras, Hungary, Iceland, India, Indonesia, Iran, Iraq, Ireland, Italy, Jamaica, Japan, Jordan, Kenya, Kuwait, Lao People's Democratic Republic, Lebanon, Lesotho, Liberia, Libyan Arab Jamahiriya, Luxembourg, Madagascar, Malawi, Malaysia, Maldives, Mali, Malta, Mauritania, Mauritius, Mexico, Mongolia, Morocco, Mozambique, Nepal, Netherlands, New Zealand, Nicaragua, Niger, Nigeria, Norway, Oman, Pakistan, Panama, Papua New Guinea, Paraguay, Peru, Philippines, Poland, Portugal, Qatar, Romania, Rwanda, Saint Kitts and Nevis, Saint Lucia, Saint Vincent and the Grenadines, Samoa, Sao Tome and Principe, Saudi Arabia, Senegal, Seychelles, Sierra Leone, Singapore, Solomon Islands, Somalia, Spain, Sri Lanka, Sudan, Swaziland, Sweden, Syrian Arab Republic, Thailand, Togo, Trinidad and Tobago, Tunisia, Turkey, Uganda, Ukrainian SSR, USSR, United Arab Emirates, United Kingdom, United Republic of Tanzania, Uruguay, Vanuatu, Venezuela, Viet Nam, Yemen, Yugoslavia, Zaire, Zambia, Zimbabwe.

Against: Israel, United States.

REFERENCES

[1]A/43/13 & Add.1. [2]YUN 1978, p. 358. [3]A/44/13 & Corr.1 & Add.1. [4]YUN 1987, p. 327, GA res. 42/69 A, 2 Dec. 1987. [5]S/19443. [6]A/44/5/Add.3. [7]YUN 1987, p. 285. [8]A/43/5/Add.3. [9]A/43/702. [10]YUN 1946-47, p. 100, GA res. 22 A (I), annex, 13 Feb. 1946. [11]YUN 1986, p. 342. [12]A/43/656. [13]A/43/655. [14]YUN 1987, p. 331, GA res. 42/69 G, 2 Dec. 1987. [15]*Ibid.*, p. 331. [16]A/43/654. [17]YUN 1987, p. 332, GA res. 42/69 F, 2 Dec. 1987. [18]*Ibid.*, p. 334, GA res. 42/69 K, 2 Dec. 1987. [19]A/43/408. [20]YUN 1980, p. 443, GA res. 35/13 B, 3 Nov. 1980. [21]YUN 1987, p. 333. [22]A/43/652. [23]YUN 1987, p. 335, GA res. 42/69 D, 2 Dec. 1987. [24]A/43/581. [25]YUN 1987, p. 336, GA res. 42/69 H, 2 Dec. 1987. [26]*Ibid.*, p. 337. [27]A/43/582. [28]YUN 1948-49, p. 174, GA res. 194(III), 11 Dec. 1948. [29]YUN 1987, p. 337, GA res. 42/69 I, 2 Dec. 1987. [30]*Ibid.*, p. 337. [31]A/43/657. [32]YUN 1987, p. 341, GA res. 42/69 J, 2 Dec. 1987. [33]*Ibid.*, p. 341. [34]A/43/653. [35]YUN 1987, p. 340, GA res. 42/69 E, 2 Dec. 1987. [36]*Ibid.*, p. 339.

Chapter V

Regional economic and social activities

The five United Nations regional commissions continued their efforts to promote economic and social development in their respective regions during 1988.

Four of the commissions held their regular sessions in April—the Economic and Social Commission for Asia and the Pacific (ESCAP), the Economic Commission for Europe (ECE), the Economic Commission for Africa (ECA) and the Economic Commission for Latin America and the Caribbean (ECLAC). The Economic and Social Commission for Western Asia (ESCWA) did not meet in a regular session but held a special session on 8 June.

Several resolutions were adopted by the General Assembly in 1988 concerning the commissions. The resolutions covered a special plan of economic co-operation for Central America (42/231); co-operation between the United Nations and the Latin American Economic System (43/5); and the Second Transport and Communications Decade in Africa (43/179). Among resolutions adopted by the Economic and Social Council pertaining to the commissions were: the co-ordination of drug control activities in Africa (1988/11); and the Khartoum Declaration: Towards a Human-focused Approach to Socio-economic Recovery and Development in Africa (1988/66). The question of Israel's membership in ECE was again deferred (decision 1988/172).

Regional co-operation

The executive secretaries of the five regional commissions, under the chairmanship of the Director-General for Development and International Economic Co-operation, met twice in 1988 (New York, 12 and 13 May, and Geneva, 14 July). At the May meeting, they reviewed the economic and social developments in each region, highlighting important issues that had emerged from the four commission sessions held in 1988. It was noted that a general picture of conciliation seemed to have emerged due to the improvement in East-West relations. Human resources development was emphasized at the sessions of ECA, ECE and ESCAP, while the debt problem was of central concern at the ECLAC session. The meeting also dis-

cussed preparation of an international development strategy for the fourth United Nations development decade (1991-2000) (see also PART THREE, Chapter I), restructuring the economic and social sectors of the United Nations, strengthening collaboration and co-operation between and among the regional commissions and official travel to and representation at conferences and meetings.

At the July meeting, the executive secretaries reviewed progress made in improving the interface between the commissions and the Economic and Social Council.

In a June 1988 report to the Council on regional co-operation,[1] the Secretary-General drew attention to issues and decisions of the commissions calling for Council action or attention, highlighted the work of the commissions, reported on progress achieved by the commissions in promoting interregional economic and technical co-operation among developing countries, and reviewed their co-operative activities and problems in the transport field. He also gave an account of the May meeting of the executive secretaries.

In **decision 1988/173** of 28 July, the Council took note of the Secretary-General's report on regional co-operation. In **decision 1988/181** of 29 July, it took note of a number of reports considered by it in its general discussion of international economic and social policy, including summaries of: the economic survey of Europe in 1987-1988;[2] the economic and social survey of Asia and the Pacific, 1987;[3] the survey of economic and social developments in the ESCWA region, 1987;[4] the survey of economic and social conditions in Africa, 1986-1987;[5] and the economic survey of Latin America and the Caribbean, 1987.[6]

In other action, the Council, in **resolution 1988/15** of 25 May, requested the Secretary-General to convene annually meetings of heads of national drug law enforcement agencies of States of the Asian and Pacific, African, and Latin American and Caribbean regions. The meetings would be held at the capitals of States in the regions that might wish to act as host or at the headquarters of the regional commission concerned.

Human rights

Following consideration of a report of the Secretary-General on regional arrangements for the promotion and protection of human rights (see

PART THREE, Chapter X), the General Assembly, in **resolution 43/152** of 8 December, noted that contacts between regional bodies and commissions and the United Nations were continuing to be pursued and strengthened through advisory services and technical assistance, particularly those relating to organizing regional and subregional training courses in human rights, and asked the Secretary-General to encourage those developments. States in areas where regional arrangements in human rights did not exist were invited to consider concluding agreements to establish suitable regional machinery for promoting and protecting human rights.

REFERENCES

[1]E/1988/69. [2]E/1988/52. [3]E/1988/57. [4]E/1988/59. [5]E/1988/60. [6]E/1988/61.

Africa

The Economic Commission for Africa held its twenty-third session/fourteenth meeting of the Conference of Ministers at Niamey, Niger, from 14 to 17 April 1988.[1] Among the issues discussed were the mid-term review and appraisal of the United Nations Programme of Action for African Economic Recovery and Development 1986-1990 (UNPAAERD) (see PART THREE, Chapter III) and Africa's Priority Programme for Economic Recovery, 1986-1990 (APPER), and the food and agriculture situation in Africa. The Ministers also considered the report of the Technical Preparatory Committee of the Whole,[2] which met at Niamey from 6 to 13 April. Subjects covered in the report included natural resources and energy, industrial development, transport and communications, social development, trade and development, recommendations of ECA subsidiary organs and sectoral bodies, economic co-operation and integration, the proposed United Nations Development Programme (UNDP)–sponsored management facility, ECA and African development, statutory issues, and the report of the eighth meeting of the Conference of Ministers of African Least Developed Countries (LDCs).

The Conference of Ministers adopted 34 resolutions covering such issues as the campaign against locusts and grasshoppers, drought and desertification, women's integration in the development process, the brain drain from Africa, development of industry in North Africa, promotion of tourism, experiments in grass-roots development, and support to countries of the southwestern Indian Ocean affected by tropical cyclones and natural disasters.

Five resolutions were submitted to the Economic and Social Council for action. They dealt with the Khartoum Declaration: Towards a Human-focused Approach to Socio-economic Recovery and Development in Africa; the United Nations Transport and Communications Decade in Africa (1978-1988); the biennial report of the Executive Secretary; proposals for extension of the 1984-1989 medium-term plan to 1990-1991; and updating the 1988-1989 programme budget.

Several subsidiary bodies of ECA met during the year. The Conference of Ministers Responsible for Human Resources Planning, Development and Utilization (Khartoum, Sudan, 12 and 13 March) reviewed the status of human resources development in Africa and endorsed the Khartoum Declaration. It also discussed the brain drain from Africa and the United Nations Special Action Programme for Administration and Management. The Conference of African Ministers of Transport, Communications and Planning (Kinshasa, Zaire, 23 and 24 March) reviewed progress made during the United Nations Transport and Communications Decade in Africa. The Ministers adopted seven resolutions, one of which was on the proclamation of a second transport and communications decade.

The Conference of Ministers of African LDCs (Niamey, 13 and 14 April) examined a report by the Intergovernmental Committee of Experts of African LDCs (Niamey, 1-4 April) on the economic and social conditions of those countries.

The Committee of Officials and the Council of Plenipotentiaries of the Tangier Multinational Programming and Operational Centre (MULPOC) met at Tangier, Morocco, from 14 to 16 and on 17 and 18 March, respectively. The two bodies discussed the MULPOC's activities, considered a progress report on the establishment of a Preferential Trade Area for North Africa and reviewed problems of drought and desertification. No other MULPOC met during the year.

Meetings of the Joint Conference of African Planners, Statisticians and Demographers (Addis Ababa, Ethiopia, 21-28 March) and the Africa Regional Co-ordinating Committee for the Integration of Women in Development (Niamey, 3-5 April) also took place in 1988.

These and other developments were reflected in the biennial report of the Executive Secretary for 1988-1989.[3]

Economic and social trends

In its survey of economic and social conditions in Africa, 1987-1988,[4] ECA reported that the African economy improved somewhat during 1988, but not enough to spur a growth in per capita income. Gross domestic product (GDP) grew by 2.3 per cent, 1.6 per cent higher than in 1987. However, with a population growth rate of about 3 per cent, per capita GDP growth was negative

(−0.7 per cent), continuing the declining trend that began in the early 1980s.

At the subregional level, performance was mixed. North African output grew by 2.4 per cent compared to only 0.4 per cent in 1987. Overall GDP in West Africa rose by 2 per cent, with the Sahel countries doing particularly well due to improved agricultural production following above-average rains. In Central Africa, economic performance remained weak with GDP growing by less than 2 per cent; however, there was some improvement over 1987. East and southern Africa was the only subregion that turned in a lower growth rate in 1988 than 1987, with output rising by 2.5 per cent in 1988 against 3.8 per cent in 1987.

The impetus for GDP growth was attributable to agriculture, which benefited from a combination of above-average rains and policy reforms conceived along the lines advocated in UNPAAERD[5] and APPER. According to the Food and Agriculture Organization of the United Nations (FAO), agricultural output rose by 3.8 per cent in 1988 compared to a fall of 1.2 per cent in 1987. FAO reported a 20.7 per cent increase in cereal production during the year, reaching 78.8 million tons. Industrial crop production also rose in 1988. However, that generally coincided with lower commodity prices worldwide. In the non-food sector, including forestry, it was noted that rapid deforestation was occurring in wide areas of the Sahel and East Africa. The tropical forests of Africa were being depleted at an average rate of 1.3 million hectares per year.

Manufacturing value added rose by 5 per cent in 1988, adding to the 3.1 per cent rise in 1987. The gain largely reflected the improved supply of agricultural raw material and a higher level of capacity utilization. However, declining investments in the industrial sector resulted in lower capital stock and capacity. The regional employment growth rate in the manufacturing sector had slowed from 5.7 per cent in 1975-1980 to only 1.9 per cent in 1980-1986.

The mining sector as a whole recovered in 1988, its value added growth estimated at 4.7 per cent compared to a fall of 3.1 per cent in 1987. However, the inability of several countries to capitalize on increased global demand for metals and a rise in oil production that was only marginal led to an uneven performance in the mineral sector.

External constraints on Africa's recovery tightened in 1988, with external debt rising from $220.3 billion in 1987 to $230 billion in 1988. As a result, the scheduled debt ratio amounted to about 40 per cent of exports of goods and services. Also, total export commodity prices fell 12.9 per cent in 1988, while imports became more expensive. Domestic demand grew by only 1.5 per cent for the whole of Africa, with private consumption rising by 2 per cent, further evidence of a continuing deterioration in living standards.

Public spending was reduced in 1988, contributing to a drop in fiscal deficit as a proportion of GDP that began in 1986 (9.2 per cent of GDP) and 1987 (8.6 per cent) and continued into 1988 (6.7 per cent). That came at the expense of such important sectors as health, education, agriculture and development expenditure in general. The rise in total nominal expenditures grew mostly as a result of the debt-service burden, which rose to 36 per cent of current expenditure in 1988 as compared to 26.7 per cent in 1986.

Activities in 1988

Development policy and regional economic co-operation

In his biennial report for 1988-1989,[3] the Executive Secretary said that, in the area of regional development strategies, ECA continued to review national development planning practices in Africa in the light of the objectives and priorities of the 1980 Lagos Plan of Action for the Implementation of the Monrovia Strategy for the Economic Development of Africa and the Final Act of Lagos,[6] APPER and UNPAAERD. Those activities aimed to initiate actions at the national, subregional, regional and international levels to implement a process of sustained socio-economic growth and development in African countries.

Regarding economic co-operation and integration, ECA's research programme emphasized sectoral planning with a view to co-ordinating and harmonizing national development plans at the subregional level. The problems and potentials of co-ordinating national projects with subregional dimensions in agriculture, industry, trade and transport and communications were extensively analysed.

In policy formulation, ECA promoted the search for an alternative to existing policy frameworks, particularly those associated with conventional structural adjustment programmes, in order to make them more coherent and consistent with Africa's real development priorities and objectives as stipulated in regionally agreed development strategies.

By a 15 April resolution on multisectoral planning,[7] the Conference of Ministers asked the ECA secretariat to organize a workshop on the integration of the informal sector in the development planning process and regional planning in Africa. Donors and United Nations agencies were invited to provide support and financial assistance for the workshop.

In another resolution of the same date,[8] the Ministers appealed to member States to undertake national efforts to widen the scope of national income accounting data, training of manpower, acquisition of technical know-how and material, such as computing hardware and software, to strengthen or initiate modelling capability. The ECA secretariat was asked to continue to assist countries to initiate or strengthen model-building capabilities and to seek technical and financial assistance from donor countries and organizations to support its efforts and those of collaborating institutions in the area of modelling. It was also asked to organize a meeting of experts on global modelling to draw up a plan of action for Africa and the global modelling systems.

African Institute for Economic Development and Planning

In a 15 April resolution on ECA's African Institute for Economic Development and Planning (IDEP) (Dakar, Senegal),[9] the Conference of Ministers requested IDEP to continue and strengthen its training programmes and start its planned expanded research and new advisory/consultancy services. It urged member States to pay their annual contributions regularly and called on those with arrears to pay them at the rate of at least 10 per cent per year. The Ministers invited UNDP to continue its support to IDEP, while shifting emphasis to research and creation of capacity for IDEP's new advisory and consultancy services. They invited the African Development Bank also to assist IDEP in developing its advisory and consultancy services and to use IDEP as a consultant. The Executive Director was asked to support IDEP's implementation of its five-year plan, especially by funding posts, and to request the General Assembly for regular posts for IDEP in the context of the 1990-1991 programme budget.

Least developed countries

The ECA secretariat continued to focus on the implementation of the Substantial New Programme of Action (SNPA) for the 1980s for LDCs (see PART THREE, Chapter I). As the 1980s drew to a close, the primary objective of SNPA of introducing major structural changes in LDCs was far from being achieved, partly because of the neglect of transformational investment in favour of short-term stabilization measures to redress persistent balance-of-payments disequilibria. All indications were that the social and economic conditions in African LDCs had deteriorated sharply during the 1980s. In addition to structural limitations, there had been the impact of the protracted drought, deteriorating terms of trade, inadequate official development assistance and other resource flows and mounting external debt.

The eighth meeting of the Conference of Ministers of African LDCs (Niamey, 13 and 14 April)[10] decided to devote its 1989 meeting to

preparing for the second (1990) United Nations conference on LDCs. It also discussed economic and social conditions in African LDCs in 1986-1987; progress made towards implementing SNPA; and the development and utilization of human resources in African LDCs. It also reviewed ECA activities with regard to African LDCs in 1986-1987 and the work programme for 1988-1989.

On 15 April,[11] the ECA Conference of Ministers approved the devotion of the 1989 meeting of the Conference of Ministers of African LDCs to preparations for the 1990 conference. It called on African LDCs to evaluate progress made in implementing SNPA and to participate actively in the preparatory meetings for the conference. African and international organizations, especially ECA, the United Nations Conference on Trade and Development (UNCTAD) and the Organization of African Unity (OAU), were asked to provide technical assistance to the African LDCs in evaluating progress made in implementing SNPA and in formulating the new strategy to be presented to the conference.

Food and agriculture

During 1988, ECA, in collaboration with FAO, continued to build up national capabilities in agricultural development policy, planning and programming, with field missions being undertaken to selected countries in the eastern, southern and West African subregions. Reports were submitted to member countries suggesting measures for harmonizing national food plans and policies. Problems highlighted in the reports included institutional inadequacies, limited participation in planning and policy-making at the grass-roots level, absence of realism in planning and policy objectives due to lack of data, and scarcity of funds. Recognizing the importance of agricultural data to development, ECA improved the agricultural data base for women and fielded a mission to conduct a survey of ongoing efforts in ECA countries. It also assisted member countries in developing systems for collection, synthesis, analysis, processing and storage of agricultural data.

ECA carried out activities to strengthen co-operation and trade in food and agricultural products, improve institutions and increase the food crop and livestock production. Several reports and publications were produced on topics such as the production of cereals and tubers with special emphasis on the role of women, non-conventional food sources, increased production of strategic food commodities, improving women's land rights, and multinational co-operation in fishery development. At the subregional level, ECA assisted member States of the Lusaka-based MULPOC to establish a maize research network. It also initiated a feasibility study on increased maize production and marketing for the Gisenyi-based MULPOC countries.

In the area of agricultural marketing, two advisory service missions were fielded to a number of countries. They focused on establishing agricultural marketing policies and institutions and improving the structure and management of agricultural co-operatives. A workshop was organized in September, in co-operation with FAO, on policy changes and their implications for grain-marketing agencies. At a seminar in Yaoundé, Cameroon, in June, the problems of food security and reducing food losses were discussed. Financed under a bilateral German project, it was attended by pest-control and storage specialists together with marketing officials. ECA continued to assist member countries in formulating policies for efficient organization and distribution of agricultural inputs to small farmers, and in harmonizing their pricing policies on staple food crops in order to stimulate interregional trade.

Population

Population policies and development planning, demographic analysis in the context of economic and social development planning, and regional training and research continued to be the focus of ECA's population programme in 1988. As in the past, the provision of advisory services to member States was emphasized.

ECA carried out several studies: one reviewed and analysed legislative instruments for formulating and implementing population policies in member States and suggested a framework for use in formulating legislation to achieve a specific population-policy objective; in another, social, cultural and legislative factors affecting family formation and fertility in selected African countries were examined; a third made a comparative analysis of mortality levels, patterns, trends and differentials and their life tables in middle Africa.

Under the Population Information Network in Africa (POPIN–Africa), a meeting was held for African press and media personnel on the dissemination of population information in the region (Dakar, Senegal, November). The meeting was organized jointly with the Pan-African News Agency and the Union of National Radio and Television Organizations in Africa. The POPIN–Africa Technical Working Group held its first meeting at Addis Ababa in December.

On 15 April,[12] the Conference of Ministers expressed concern about the financial problems facing the Institut de formation et de recherche démographiques (IFORD) and about the non-payment of contributions by the majority of member countries of the Regional Institute for Population Studies. The Ministers urged African Governments to pay their current arrears and to pay contributions regularly in the future. Member countries of IFORD were urged to respond urgently to the financial crisis facing that institution by paying their 1987 and 1988 contributions. The Ministers appealed to the Executive Director of the United Nations Population Fund to continue funding the institutes at current levels to ensure their service to member States.

Natural resources and energy

In 1988, ECA organized the third Regional Conference on the Development and Utilization of Mineral Resources in Africa (Kampala, Uganda, 6-15 June). The Conference, in the Kampala Programme of Action, recommended the development of capital and technological capabilities; restructuring of existing national mineral policies to sustain co-operation among member States; the growth of small-scale mining of precious and semi-precious stones; an in-depth study of copper and aluminium processing facilities and prospects for intra-African trade in copper- and aluminium-based products; and the establishment of mechanisms to finance new mineral resources development projects.

During the year, ECA provided technical support to the Central African Mineral Resources Development Centre (Brazzaville, Congo) and the Eastern and Southern African Mineral Resources Development Centre (Dodoma, United Republic of Tanzania). Advisory missions were undertaken to Chad and Guinea to survey the exploitation of soda ash and small-scale gold mining.

ECA continued to provide advisory assistance to member States and river basin organizations on a broad range of activities in the area of water resources development and management. The Organization for the Development of the Senegal River was aided in formulating a project involving a study of river basin development. To assist the Lake Chad Basin Commission in its efforts to save Lake Chad, which had shrunk to one tenth of its size due to drought conditions, ECA and UNDP helped prepare a water resources development project that was submitted for UNDP financing. In October, an interregional meeting on river and lake basin development was held at Addis Ababa.

In the energy sector, ECA emphasized the major issues of exploration, evaluation and development of resources; integrating energy policies into overall socio-economic planning; research, training and information; and institution-building. Missions were mounted to Burundi, the Niger, Rwanda, the Sudan, Uganda, Zaire, Zambia and Zimbabwe and the main findings were presented in reports outlining measures to improve energy planning, policies and management in African States. A seminar and study tour in the USSR were organized by ECA on the planning of integrated energy resources development, which aimed to sensitize member States to the importance of energy planning. ECA also provided substantive servicing to a meeting of the Council of the African Regional Centre for Solar Energy (Bujumbura, Burundi, June).

On 15 April,[13] the Conference of Ministers welcomed the establishment of the African Organization for Cartography and Remote Sensing after the merging of the African Association of Cartography and the African Remote Sensing Council and expressed appreciation to Algeria for providing headquarters facilities in Algiers. They appealed to the former members of those organizations in arrears with their contributions to pay them as quickly as possible and to the member States to pay their contributions to the budget of the new organization. The Executive Secretary was requested, in collaboration with the executive heads of the relevant United Nations bodies and the Secretary-General of OAU, to provide technical and financial assistance to cartography and remote sensing projects and to African member States for training in those fields.

Science and technology

Under its programme in science and technology, ECA developed policies, machinery, capabilities and manpower for science and technology, and promoted regional and interregional co-operation.

During the year, advisory services were provided to: Benin on developing local capacity for producing school science equipment; Mauritius on defining a technology policy and mechanisms for accelerated technological development; and the Ghana Technology Transfer Centre on elaborating modalities for executing aspects of a UNDP project and on selecting foreign consultants to lead local teams. An advisory mission was also undertaken to the African Regional Centre for Technology (Dakar) to assist in a tripartite review meeting for a UNDP project and in the recruitment of project staff.

Regarding the development of manpower for science and technology, ECA organized a subregional workshop on developing indigenous capacity for the local production of school science equipment in the Economic Community of the Great Lakes Countries (CEPGL) region. The workshop recommended that Burundi, Rwanda and Zaire should co-operate in establishing common facilities to produce school science equipment and called on ECA and CEPGL to assist in mobilizing financing.

ECA collaborated with the United Nations Centre for Science and Technology for Development and the German Development Foundation in organizing a regional meeting at Brazzaville in December to review the implementation of the 1979 Vienna Programme of Action on Science and Technology for Development.[14] The meeting noted the institutional, financial and other constraints inhibiting the implementation of the Programme of Action and urged the adoption of innovative approaches to incorporate science and technology in the development process and bring about closer understanding between the science and technology system and potential users in the production and service sectors.

By a 15 April resolution,[15] the Conference of Ministers approved the recommendations of a 1987 meeting of the Intergovernmental Committee of Experts for Science and Technology Development. Member States were called on to give active support to the ECA secretariat and its co-operating agencies in implementing those recommendations. The Ministers decided that each MULPOC should co-ordinate the activities of the respective working group of the Intergovernmental Committee. The MULPOCs were requested to keep their member States and economic groupings in the subregion fully informed of the tasks of the working groups, and the ECA Executive Secretary was asked to ensure the implementation of the resolution with the co-operation of the OAU secretariat.

On the same date,[16] the Ministers recommended that the ECA secretariat, in collaboration with OAU and the United Nations Educational, Scientific and Cultural Organization (UNESCO), should work out modalities to ensure a complementary relationship between the activities of the Intergovernmental Committee and of the Standing Conference of Heads of National Science and Technology Policy-making Bodies of African member States of UNESCO.

Environment

ECA environmental activities focused on developing environmental capabilities, including the conservation of resources and pollution control. Combating drought and desertification control were priority areas and were among the key factors accounting for the social and economic crisis in Africa.

Advisory services on combating desertification and managing drought were undertaken in four countries. In Ethiopia, work focused on establishing a central authority to co-ordinate desertification control activities. In Zimbabwe, activities promoted public participation in environmental conservation, self-sufficiency in food production, establishment of wood-lots and afforestation. For Somalia, the mission recommended sand-dune fixation, management of range and salinized lands, and public participation in resource management to combat desertification. For Djibouti, the mission concentrated on the establishment of a ministry or department of environment rather than a forestry department to address the diverse environmental issues facing the country. In order to exchange experiences on drought and desertification control, two study tours for member States were conducted to China and the USSR in June and October 1988. The tours focused mainly on desert sylviculture and methods of sand-dune stabilization.

On 15 April,[17] the Conference of Ministers urged member States to establish appropriate national mechanisms for implementing the 1977 United Nations Plan of Action to Combat Desertification[18] and the 1984 Regional Plan of Action to Combat the Impact of Drought in Africa.[19] The ECA Executive Secretary was urged to explore the feasibility of starting a co-operation process between all African countries as envisaged in the Regional Plan. ECA was requested to support the established subregional organizations to combat more effectively the problems of drought and desertification. The Executive Secretary was asked to report in 1989 on implementation of the resolution.

In 1988, the African Centre of Meteorological Applications for Development (ACMAD) was established in Niamey. A joint venture between ECA and the World Meteorological Organization, the Centre would collect, process and analyse meteorological data and provide information to users for application to agricultural production, water resources management and other human activities that depended on the weather.

On 15 April,[20] the Conference of Ministers urged member States that had not done so to approve ACMAD's constitution and decided that they should contribute $1 million, representing a 50 per cent contribution annually to ACMAD's recurrent annual budget. A formula was adopted for the contribution by member States to the annual budget and annexed to the resolution. The Executive Secretary was asked to consult with donors with a view to obtaining contributions towards making the Centre operational and the Chairman of ACMAD's Board of Governors was asked to report in 1989 on progress made in implementing the resolution.

Transport, communications and tourism

During 1988, ECA continued to provide advisory services, undertake studies, issue technical publications and organize professional meetings on transport and tourism. In the field of general and multimodal transport, advisory services were rendered to Burundi, Rwanda and Zaire to determine the extent to which they could containerize exports or imports through the ports of Dar es Salaam, United Republic of Tanzania, and Mombasa, Kenya. Recommendations were made which could help in the opening up of land-locked countries.

Guidelines for the evaluation of international road-transport practices were prepared, including the facilitation of international road traffic. Also,

attention was given to promoting an African industry to manufacture transport equipment and spare parts in order to reduce imports.

In the field of shipping, ECA activities included an assessment of Africa's capabilities to promote a shipbuilding and repair industry, identification of the main bottle-necks hampering the smooth flow of African maritime trade and proposed solutions, and an attempt to establish a ministerial conference on maritime transport for eastern and southern Africa. Several port-based activities were also undertaken. With regard to inland water transport, the main activities were identification of transport facilitation problems and ways to ease Africa's international traffic flow and a study of activities to ensure the safety of navigation on lakes Kivu and Tanganyika.

The main activity in air transport was the preparation of an African policy to meet changes in the air transport environment, i.e., deregulation in the United States, liberalization in Europe, noise restrictions and the introduction of a computerized reservation system. ECA organized a Special Conference of African Ministers of Civil Aviation to discuss those issues (Yamoussoukro, Côte d'Ivoire, November).

In communications, activities included studies, the organization of seminars, technical assistance to member States, technical publications and participation in professional conferences. In July 1988, a regional seminar on satellite communications technology was held in Moscow in collaboration with UNDP and the International Telecommunication Union. Also, a seminar on planning of rural telecommunications for French- and Portuguese-speaking African countries was held at Yaoundé in October/November. Technical assistance missions were undertaken at the request of telecommunications organizations in Chad, Sao Tome and Principe, Uganda and the United Republic of Tanzania.

On 15 April,[21] the Conference of Ministers reaffirmed that intra-African tourism was a component of the African policy on the economic, social, cultural and political integration of the continent and was a determining factor of development. The Executive Secretary was asked to intensify co-operation within international organizations to help African countries develop tourism programmes, conduct a study on tourism activities of subregional intergovernmental organizations in Africa, establish subregional programmes for joint promotion of inter-State tourism, establish an African association of tourism and draw up model management contracts for various types of hotel infrastructure to be submitted to member States for appraisal. He was further requested to establish subregional and regional tourism and hotel institutes, develop training programmes to upgrade tourism and hotel services at various levels, publish an African directory for educational and training facilities, and organize African tourism events alongside existing continental, subregional and national trade fairs.

Transport and Communications Decade

In response to a 1986 request of the Conference of African Ministers of Transport, Communications and Planning,[22] ECA, in January 1988, prepared an in-depth evaluation of the United Nations Transport and Communications Decade in Africa (1978-1988),[23] proclaimed by the General Assembly in 1977.[24] The report gave the context and background to the Decade's proclamation, analysed the concept of its programme and outlined the institutional mechanisms for its implementation. It also described the Decade programme, analysed its results and discussed its impact.

The report concluded that the Decade had enabled Africa to equip itself with a global strategy suited to its needs. However, the strategy had major shortcomings in its conceptual relevance.

With regard to quantitative results, in the programme's first phase (1980-1983), a total of $7 billion, or 47 per cent, was secured out of the $15 billion estimated cost. In terms of project implementation, 300 of 1,091 projects in the first phase, or 27 per cent, were reported completed by the end of 1983. Many projects from the first phase were transferred to the second (1984-1988). At the end of 1987, 164 of the 1,048 projects in phase II were completed. It was projected that the implementation rate of that phase would be about 45 per cent.

Three main objectives were well covered during the Decade's implementation: integration, opening up of land-locked regions and mobilization of resources. The least covered objectives were harmonization, restructuring and industrial promotion. Although it was difficult to show the full impact the Decade might have had on improving transport conditions and communications efficiency, the Decade did generate considerable momentum with regard to creating political awareness through the Conference of Ministers of Transport, Communications and Planning. Also, it gave a major boost to the future development of transport and communications by equipping Africa with a strategy and policy as well as institutions and mechanisms for their implementation. The report recommended that a second transport and communications decade in Africa be declared, that the expertise and experience acquired during the first Decade be maintained by retaining and/or reappointing the statutory and executing agencies and that there should be a two-year preparatory period between the end of the first and the launching of the second decade. The report also recommended activities to be undertaken by ECA during the two-year preparatory period and stated that African States should devote more financial resources to the second decade than they had to the first.

In a March report on progress in implementing the Decade's second phase,[25] ECA stated that there was very little improvement reported in 1987 over 1986. With 236 projects, roads and road transport was the largest subsector in the programme. Information was obtained on 192 of those projects, of which 62 were reported completed and a further 70 in progress, for a 32 per cent completion rate. A further 20 projects would be completed by the end of 1988, implying that 82 (35 per cent) of the projects would be completed during phase II of the Decade. Of the 70 rail transport projects on which information was received, 14 were completed, which represented no change from the previous year, and 40 projects were under implementation compared with 31 the previous year. Thus, there was no significant improvement in project implementation. Of the 38 projects in the maritime transport subsector, 7 were reported completed and 2 in progress, compared with 2 reported completed the previous year. Information was available on 55 of the 70 projects in the ports subsector, 9 of which were reported completed and 30 were under implementation.

Of the 94 projects in air transport, information was obtained on 69, showing that 11 were completed and 31 in progress, for a completion rate of 16 per cent; 33 had not been started and no information was given on 19 others. Thus, even if all 31 projects under implementation were to be completed during the year, only 42 (45 per cent) of the projects would be completed by the end of the Decade.

Of the 45 projects in the inland water transport sector, information was available for only 19. Of those, 2 were reported completed and 5 in progress. Even if all 5 projects under implementation were to be completed during the year, still only 7 (16 per cent) of the total would be completed during the Decade. In multimodal transport, information was available on 7 projects of the 11 in the subsector; 4 were completed and 3 were under implementation.

In the telecommunications subsector, 149 projects were monitored out of 215, representing a significant improvement in terms of monitoring. Projects reported as completed rose to 34, or 23 per cent of those monitored. A further 60 projects were under implementation.

In broadcasting, projects monitored increased from 64 to 100 in 1988, representing 83 per cent of the 120 projects in the subsector. Only 15 projects were completed and 33 were in progress. By the end of the Decade, less than one third of the projects would be completed. As to postal services, information was available on 115 of the 135 projects, with 6 projects reported completed and 30 under implementation.

The stagnation in implementation rate in 1987 had been matched by a lack of growth in assistance from major financing institutions. Although World Bank assistance in 1987 was 90 per cent higher than in 1986, it was 3.8 per cent less than in 1985. During 1985-1986, African Development Bank assistance declined 47.7 per cent.

The evaluation of the Decade was discussed by the Conference of African Ministers of Transport, Communications and Planning (Kinshasa, 23 and 24 March),[26] which recommended that member States should adopt the principle of launching a second decade.

On 15 April,[27] the ECA Conference of Ministers endorsed the recommendation of the Conference that a second decade be declared for the period 1991-2000 and recommended to the General Assembly, through the Economic and Social Council, that it declare a second decade. The Ministers endorsed a number of other decisions of the Conference: to convene a meeting of African Ministers responsible for civil aviation to consider an African aeronautic policy; to convene a meeting of experts on facilitation of inland water transport in Africa; to establish, within the Tangier MULPOC, a committee for the development of transport, including harmonization of transport infrastructure and facilitation of administrative and customs procedures in the North African subregion; to promote the use of African intergovernmental organizations as executing agencies for transport and communications projects; to reactivate the Trans-African Highways Bureau in ECA and urge African countries to allocate resources to maintain and rehabilitate roads; to urge African member States to give high priority to completing Pan-African Telecommunications Network links and making greater use of existing links for intra-African communications traffic; and to establish ministerial conferences on maritime transport in African subregions. The Ministers reiterated their 1987 appeal[28] to UNDP to provide ECA with financial assistance to reactivate and operate the Trans-African Highways Bureau and appealed to other financial institutions and donor countries also to lend financial support.

ECONOMIC AND SOCIAL COUNCIL ACTION

On 28 July 1988, the Economic and Social Council, on the recommendation of its First (Economic) Committee, adopted **resolution 1988/67** without vote.

Transport and Communications Decade in Africa

The Economic and Social Council,

Recalling resolution 291(XIII) of 26 February 1977 of the Conference of Ministers of the Economic Commission for Africa, Economic and Social Council resolution 2097(LXIII) of 29 July 1977 and General Assembly resolution 32/160 of 19 December 1977,

Noting the financial support provided by the General Assembly, the United Nations Development Programme and donor countries for the implementation of the programme of the Transport and Communications Decade in Africa,

Taking into account the report on the in-depth evaluation of the Transport and Communications Decade in Africa, which concluded that the Decade gave a major boost to the future development of transport and communications by equipping Africa with a policy and strategy, as well as institutions and mechanisms for their implementation,

Considering resolution 84/44 of the fourth meeting of the Conference of African Ministers of Transport, Communications and Planning, in which the Conference recommended that Governments of States members of the Economic Commission for Africa decide, in principle, to approve the launching of a second United Nations transport and communications decade in Africa,

Noting the report on progress in the implementation of the second phase of the programme of the Decade and the report on the sixth meeting of the Conference of African Ministers of Transport, Communications and Planning,

Conscious that air transport is one of the key factors in economic development and integration in Africa,

Noting the concern expressed by the Conference of African Ministers of Transport, Communications and Planning about the adverse consequences for African air transport of the new civil aeronautic policies emanating from outside the continent,

Bearing in mind resolution 86/55 of the fifth meeting of the Conference of African Ministers of Transport, Communications and Planning, in which the Conference, *inter alia,* called upon the Economic Commission for Africa to provide support to the various African subregional organizations and to assist them in co-ordinating their transport and communications programmes,

Mindful of the heavy investments made by States members of the Economic Commission for Africa in the Pan-African Telecommunications Network and the substantial achievement made in establishing it,

Noting that the in-depth evaluation of the Decade has revealed great deficiencies in the inland water transport systems in Africa,

1. *Takes note* of resolution 88/73 of 24 March 1988 of the Conference of African Ministers of Transport, Communications and Planning, in which the Conference recommended that:

(*a*) A second United Nations transport and communications decade in Africa should be declared for the period 1991-2000 in order to sustain the momentum of the activities begun during the first Decade;

(*b*) The expertise and experience acquired during the first Decade should be retained by continuing the institutional arrangements for the first Decade, namely, the Conference of African Ministers of Transport, Communications and Planning as the permanent policy-making body, the Economic Commission for Africa as the lead agency responsible, in collaboration with other organizations of the United Nations system, for preparing the programme for the Decade and for harmonizing, co-ordinating and monitoring activities, and the Inter-Agency Co-ordinating Committee as the technical body accountable to the Conference of Ministers;

(c) There should be a two-year preparatory period between the end of the first Decade and the launching of the second;

2. *Recommends* that the General Assembly, in the light of the outcome of the preparations referred to in paragraph 1 *(c)* of the present resolution, consider declaring the period 1991-2000 the Second Transport and Communications Decade in Africa;

3. *Expresses its appreciation* for the generous support of the Administrator of the United Nations Development Programme and those members of the international community that were able to provide financial and technical assistance for carrying out the activities of the first Decade;

4. *Appeals* to the Administrator of the United Nations Development Programme to continue to provide support for activities related to the two-year preparatory period, 1989-1990;

5. *Requests* donor countries and international financial institutions to intensify their support for the accelerated development of transport and communications in Africa.

Economic and Social Council resolution 1988/67

28 July 1988   Meeting 40   Adopted without vote

Approved by First Committee (E/1988/117) without vote, 20 July (meeting 18); draft by ECA (E/1988/69), orally amended by Vice-Chairman following informal consultations; agenda item 7.

By **decision 1988/173** of 28 July, the Council took note of the Secretary-General's report on the Transport and Communications Decade in Africa.[29]

GENERAL ASSEMBLY ACTION

On 20 December 1988, the General Assembly, on the recommendation of the Second (Economic and Financial) Committee, adopted **resolution 43/179** without vote.

Second Transport and Communications Decade in Africa

The General Assembly,

Recalling its resolution 32/160 of 19 December 1977,

Recalling also Economic and Social Council resolution 2097(LXIII) of 29 July 1977,

Emphasizing the need for full implementation of the goals and objectives of the Transport and Communications Decade in Africa, especially in the light of continuing inadequacies in the field of transport and communications in Africa,

1. *Endorses* Economic and Social Council resolution 1988/67 of 28 July 1988;

2. *Declares* the period 1991-2000 the Second Transport and Communications Decade in Africa;

3. *Requests* the Secretary-General, in consultation with the Organization of African Unity and existing African regional and subregional economic groups, as well as relevant United Nations agencies, to undertake the necessary preparatory arrangements for the Second Transport and Communications Decade in Africa, and

to submit to the General Assembly, through the Economic and Social Council, a progress report at its forty-fourth session and a final report at its forty-fifth session.

General Assembly resolution 43/179

20 December 1988   Meeting 83   Adopted without vote

Approved by Second Committee (A/43/750/Add.2) without vote, 23 November (meeting 44); draft by United Republic of Tanzania, for African Group (A/C.2/43/L.18), orally revised following informal consultations; agenda item 12.

Meeting numbers. GA 43rd session: 2nd Committee 28, 44; plenary 83.

Trade and finance

During 1988, ECA carried out activities under subprogrammes for domestic, intra-African and non-African trade; international financial and monetary policies; and activities of transnational corporations.

As part of ECA assistance to the member countries of the North African MULPOC, a mission went to Egypt, the Libyan Arab Jamahiriya, Morocco and Tunisia to brief those countries on the technical issues involved in establishing the Preferential Trade Area for North Africa and to advise them on national action required to promote it.

ECA participated in the fifth All-Africa Trade Fair (Kinshasa, 16-31 July), organizing workshops and seminars on intra-African trade and the Industrial Development Decade for Africa (the 1980s), proclaimed by the General Assembly in 1980.[30] The following were presented: a paper on the development and expansion of intra-African trade; a statistical analysis of intra-African trade; a compendium of decisions, recommendations and resolutions on intra-African trade; and issues of the *African Trade Bulletin*. ECA also participated in a workshop on the United Nations Electronic Data Interchange for Administration, Commerce and Transport (EDIFACT) (Baghdad, Iraq, 14 and 15 December). Organized by ESCWA and ECE, it discussed the possibilities of developing interregional co-operation in the development and application of EDIFACT in trade transactions.

Regarding international monetary and financial relations, ECA participated in the fourteenth General Assembly of the Association of African Development Finance Institutions (Abidjan, Côte d'Ivoire, 25-29 May) and serviced an extraordinary meeting of Governors of African Central Banks on the establishment of an African Monetary Fund (Abidjan, 4 June).

A regional workshop on the integration of women in trade and commerce (Niamey, 31 March–2 April) had before it an ECA report on the role and contribution of African women in domestic trade. On 15 April,[31] the Conference of Ministers called on African Governments and public and local authorities to recognize the important role played by women in trade and commerce and their significant contribution to the economic development process in Africa. They appealed to the authorities to improve conditions in African traditional markets in rural and urban areas and to African Governments to encourage the granting of loans to African women to improve their trade and commercial activities. The Ministers requested development financing institutions, especially UNDP, the African Development Bank Group, the World Bank Group, the Arab Bank for Economic Development in Africa, the Islamic Development Bank and the International Fund for Agricultural Development, to encourage greater participation of African women in trade and commerce. They also requested the ECA Executive Secretary, the OAU Secretary-General, the UNCTAD Secretary-General, the Executive Director of the International Trade Centre and the Director of the International Research and Training Institute for the Advancement of Women to draw up a joint programme for training African business women and traders in rural and urban areas.

Public administration and finance

During 1988, ECA assisted member States in developing and implementing programmes in public administration, management and finance. In February, assistance was provided to the Ministry of Local Government in Uganda in assessing, evaluating and streamlining its newly reformed structures. In September, technical advisory services were rendered to Cameroon, in co-operation with the Ministry of Public Service and the State General Inspectorate for Administrative Reform, in formulating an administrative reform strategy and in proposing measures to enhance the efficiency of the public service. With the African Association for Public Administration and Management, ECA organized a subregional seminar on critical skills for public policy management (Serrekunda, Gambia, 30 May–3 June). In June, ECA assisted the Institute of Development Management (Gaborone, Botswana) to conduct a regional seminar on management training and development (Mbabane, Swaziland).

By a 15 April resolution[32] on support for the United Nations Special Action Programme in Public Administration and Management for Africa (SAPAM) (see below), the Conference of Ministers commended the initiative of the United Nations system, particularly ECA, UNDP and the United Nations Department of Technical Co-operation for Development (DTCD), with the support of African countries in formulating SAPAM. Donor countries and funding agencies, particularly UNDP, were urged to make contributions for SAPAM's timely implementation.

In response to a 1987 request,[33] the Secretary-General submitted a report on SAPAM[34] to the Economic and Social Council. SAPAM, established on the recommendation of the Seventh (1984) Meeting of Experts on the United Nations Programme in Public Administration and Finance,[35] was based on the concept that inadequate public administration and management in Africa had adversely contributed to the manner in which African Governments had responded to problems, and that an integrated approach, supported by the international community, would improve management capabilities and help to ameliorate the economic and social situation.

SAPAM's mandate was to: inject technical and managerial expertise within international technical assistance frameworks; carry out training programmes to fill vacancies in critical functional areas; organize programmes to revitalize key institutions responsible for national capacity-building, policy formulation and central guidance; design special programmes to improve the management performance of public enterprises; and identify mechanisms at the national level to spearhead sustained implementation of proposed measures.

The report outlined SAPAM's role in meeting the technical co-operation needs of African countries and described its implementation, which would imply the mobilization over a 10-year period of some $400 million. Contributions were envisaged from three main sources: UNDP; special grants from donor Governments and agencies; and the African Development Bank and the World Bank.

With regard to future action, SAPAM would be presented to a meeting of donor Governments and agencies for their consideration and support and would be reviewed by the Ninth Meeting of Experts on the United Nations Programme in Public Administration and Finance in 1989.

ECONOMIC AND SOCIAL COUNCIL ACTION

On 25 May 1988, the Economic and Social Council, on the recommendation of its First Committee, adopted **resolution 1988/7** without vote.

Public administration and finance for development

The Economic and Social Council,

Recalling General Assembly resolutions 35/56 of 5 December 1980, the annex to which contains the International Development Strategy for the Third United Nations Development Decade, 36/194 of 17 December 1981 on the United Nations Conference on the Least Developed Countries, particularly paragraph 3 thereof, 34/137 of 14 December 1979 on the role of the public sector in promoting the economic development of developing countries, and 35/80 of 5 December 1980, 39/219 of 18 December 1984 and 40/213 of 17 December 1985 on the role of qualified national personnel in the social and economic development of developing countries,

Reiterating the importance of the effective and speedy implementation of General Assembly resolution S-13/2 of 1 June 1986 on the United Nations Programme of Action for African Economic Recovery and Development 1986-1990,

Recalling also all relevant Council resolutions concerning public administration and finance for development,

Stressing the importance of public administration systems for economic and social development in developing countries and of accelerating the development of the low-income countries, in particular the least developed countries,

1. *Takes note* of the report of the Secretary-General on the Special Action Programme in Public Administration and Management for Africa;

2. *Notes* the process of reviewing the public administration and managerial needs of African countries and the progress made so far in identifying the project proposals, the utilization of the trust fund established by the Administrator of the United Nations Development Programme, the interest expressed in the Special Action Programme by donor countries, and the support provided by the United Nations Development Programme in collaboration with other organizations of the United Nations system;

3. *Requests* the United Nations Development Programme to intensify its efforts to mobilize additional financial resources for the implementation of the Special Action Programme, and urges donor countries and institutions, as well as regional development banks, to the extent possible, to make available additional resources for the Programme;

4. *Urges* all organs and organizations of the United Nations system and the international community to provide full and effective support in order to accelerate the implementation of projects identified under the Special Action Programme, to initiate, at the request of interested countries, projects at the subregional and regional levels, and to take early action to identify further projects at the country level;

5. *Invites* the Secretary-General to submit to the Council at its first regular session of 1989 a progress report on activities undertaken under the Special Action Programme;

6. *Requests* the Secretary-General to include updated information on the Special Action Programme in Public Administration and Management for Africa in his report to the *Ad Hoc* Committee of the Whole of the General Assembly on the Review and Appraisal of the United Nations Programme of Action for African Economic Recovery and Development 1986-1990.

Economic and Social Council resolution 1988/7

25 May 1988   Meeting 13   Adopted without vote

Approved by First Committee (E/1988/94) without vote, 18 May (meeting 2); draft by Lesotho, for African States (E/1988/C.1/L.1), orally revised; agenda item 8.

Social development

Human resources development

In 1988, ECA activities in the area of human resources development focused on problems such as the absence of institutional machineries and policies for human resources development; the inappropriateness of education and training to the needs for African socio-economic development activities; declining standards of instruction in education and training; and increasing underutilization and wastage of human resources.

In the area of manpower planning, advisory missions went to Uganda and Somalia where workshops were organized to propose measures on national manpower policy formulation and on improving the structure and functional delineation of manpower planning machineries in those countries. Other workshops were organized in Ethiopia, Kenya, the United Republic of Tanzania and Zimbabwe on various topics, including the techniques of curriculum planning and development, improving technical capabilities through higher learning, and defining ways to create employment.

The International Conference on the Human Dimension of Africa's Economic Recovery and Development (Khartoum, 5-8 March) culminated in the adoption of the Khartoum Declaration: Towards a Human-focused Approach to Socioeconomic Recovery and Development in Africa.

The Declaration gave an overall assessment of the human condition in Africa and discussed the human dimension of structural adjustment programmes. It also contained a series of recommendations for action at the national, regional, subregional and international levels on incorporating the human factor in the recovery and structural adjustment process, special measures for the social sector and vulnerable groups, manpower development and utilization for the long term, and the role of regional, international and non-governmental organizations (NGOs).

In its conclusions, the Declaration affirmed that the human dimension was the *sine qua non* of economic recovery and stated that there could be no real structural adjustment or economic recovery in the absence of the human imperative. That imperative meant that the vulnerable and the impoverished, the uprooted and the ravaged, women, children, youth, disabled, aged, the rural and urban poor, every group and individual in society who was in some way disadvantaged had to be given paramount consideration in the socioeconomic development process. In the service of that principle, health, education, welfare and all related sectors became indispensable components of national policies, programmes, plans and regional or subregional collaboration.

The centre-piece of UNPAAERD,[5] of which the Declaration was an organic part of the follow-up, enshrined a shared partnership between Africa and the rest of the international community whereby Africa would act and the international community would respond through donor reforms and increased assistance. Noting that the international community had not fulfilled its part of the bargain and that African economic recovery continued to be threatened, the Declaration stated that, if adjustment with a human face did not succeed, then the failure would be laid at the feet of the international community.

The Conference recommended that the Declaration be endorsed by the third ECA Conference of African Ministers Responsible for Human Resources Planning, Development and Utilization and hoped that the Ministers would transmit it to the ECA Conference of Ministers. The Declaration could then be transmitted to the General Assembly.

The third meeting of the Conference of African Ministers Responsible for Human Resources Planning, Development and Utilization (Khartoum, 12 and 13 March)[36] endorsed the Khartoum Declaration.

On 15 April,[37] the ECA Conference of Ministers endorsed the Declaration and annexed it to its resolution. Member States were urged to implement its recommendations by making the human dimension an essential focus of their recovery and long-term development programmes. The Ministers urged international financial institutions, bilateral and multilateral donors, the United Nations system and NGOs to implement its recommendations, ensuring that its concerns were reflected in their assistance programmes to African countries. They asked the Secretary-General to transmit the Declaration to the *Ad Hoc* Committee of the Whole on the implementation of UNPAAERD (see PART THREE, Chapter III) and to institute actions to mobilize the support of the United Nations system and the international community in implementing the Declaration's recommendations. The United Nations Inter-Agency Task Force on the Follow-up of the Implementation of UNPAAERD was called on to intensify efforts to strengthen co-operation between United Nations agencies in search for solutions to Africa's problems of human development within the context of recovery and long-term development. The Ministers asked the ECA Executive Secretary to disseminate the Declaration and, with the Chairman of the Inter-Agency Task Force, to report in 1989 on its implementation.

ECONOMIC AND SOCIAL COUNCIL ACTION

On 27 June,[38] the Sudan transmitted the Khartoum Declaration to the Secretary-General. On 28 July, the Economic and Social Council, on the recommendation of its First Committee, adopted **resolution 1988/66** without vote.

Khartoum Declaration: Towards a Human-focused Approach to Socio-economic Recovery and Development in Africa

The Economic and Social Council,

Convinced of the need for urgent and concerted measures at the national, subregional, regional and international levels to improve the human condition and sustain human resources development and utilization through the period of recovery and beyond in Africa,

1. *Welcomes* the thrust of the Khartoum Declaration: Towards a Human-focused Approach to Socio-

economic Recovery and Development in Africa, adopted by the International Conference on the Human Dimension of Africa's Economic Recovery and Development in March 1988;

2. *Commends* the Inter-Agency Task Force on the Follow-up of the Implementation of the United Nations Programme of Action for African Economic Recovery and Development 1986-1990 at the Regional Level for having successfully convened the Conference;

3. *Expresses its gratitude* to the Government of the Sudan for hosting the Conference and, in particular, to the Prime Minister of the Sudan for his patronage of the Conference;

4. *Welcomes* the commitment of the States members of the Economic Commission for Africa to implement the recommendations of the Khartoum Declaration by making the human dimension an essential focus of their recovery and long-term development programmes;

5. *Urges* international financial institutions, bilateral and multilateral donors, organizations of the United Nations system and non-governmental organizations to contribute actively to the implementation of the recommendations contained in the Khartoum Declaration, with a view to ensuring that concern for the human dimension is adequately taken into account in their programmes of assistance to African countries;

6. *Requests* the Secretary-General to transmit the Khartoum Declaration to the *Ad Hoc* Committee of the Whole of the General Assembly on the Review and Appraisal of the United Nations Programme of Action for African Economic Recovery and Development 1986-1990 and to the General Assembly at its forty-third session;

7. *Urges* the Secretary-General to institute the action necessary to mobilize the United Nations system and the international community in support of the implementation of the recommendations contained in the Khartoum Declaration;

8. *Calls upon* the Inter-Agency Task Force to intensify its efforts to strengthen further the co-operation among the organizations of the United Nations system in the search for solutions to Africa's problems of human development within the context of recovery and long-term development.

Economic and Social Council resolution 1988/66

28 July 1988   Meeting 40   Adopted without vote

Approved by First Committee (E/1988/117) without vote, 19 July (meeting 17); draft by ECA (E/1988/69), orally amended by Vice-Chairman following informal consultations; agenda item 7.

In **resolution 43/27** of 18 November, the General Assembly adopted the conclusions of the mid-term review of UNPAAERD, which contained a number of recommendations on human resources.

Crime prevention and criminal justice

ECA participated in the preparations for the Eighth (1990) United Nations Congress on the Prevention of Crime and the Treatment of Offenders. In that connection, it contributed to the International Meeting of Experts on the Development of United Nations Standards for the Prevention of Juvenile Delinquency (Riyadh, Saudi Arabia, 28 and 29 February), the Interregional

Meeting on the Prevention of Delinquency, Juvenile Justice and the Protection of the Young: Policy Approaches and Direction (Vienna, 18-22 April), the Committee on Crime Prevention and Control (Vienna, 22-31 August) and the Inter-Agency Meeting on Follow-up to the Seventh (1985) United Nations Congress on the Prevention of Crime and the Treatment of Offenders (Vienna, 1 and 2 September).

On 15 April,[39] the Conference of Ministers adopted the statute of the African Institute for the Prevention of Crime and the Treatment of Offenders, to be headquartered at Kampala. For the first four years following adoption of the statute, the following member States, in addition to the host country, would serve on the Institute's Governing Board: Rwanda and Zaire (representing the Gisenyi MULPOC subregion); Botswana and the United Republic of Tanzania (Lusaka MULPOC); Ghana and Guinea (Niamey MULPOC); Egypt and Morocco (Tangier MULPOC); and the Central African Republic and Equatorial Guinea (Yaoundé MULPOC). Half of that group would retire after two years, to be replaced by the same number of member States elected in accordance with the provisions in the statute. The Governing Board was requested to establish a work programme and budget for the Institute, the gross financial contribution from the host country, and a formula for annual contributions of member States. The Ministers urged member States to sign the statute as soon as possible, and invited governmental, non-governmental and international organizations, as well as the United Nations, to support the Institute technically and financially. The text of the statute was annexed to the resolution.

Drug abuse

In **resolution 1988/11** of 25 May on the co-ordination of drug control activities in the African region, the Economic and Social Council expressed concern at the increasing incidence of drug abuse and illicit trafficking in the region. It requested that the Secretary-General establish within ECA a focal point to co-ordinate and promote measures to combat drug abuse and illicit traffic throughout Africa. States of the region were called on to accede to existing international conventions on narcotic drugs and psychotropic substances and urged to establish national agencies to combat drug abuse and illicit traffic.

Youth

Youth and social welfare activities focused primarily on issues of youth employment and juvenile delinquency. The ECA secretariat compiled a _Directory of Youth Organizations in African Countries_, which provided information on the various youth organizations and their structures, activities and achievements. A study on the impact of rural youth employment programmes on rural development was completed and circulated to planners, policy makers and practitioners in member States. It assessed the impact of youth programmes on the rural sector, such as increase in productivity and contribution to the overall transformation of rural life. A report on juvenile delinquency, crime and justice in the light of socio-economic conditions was prepared on the basis of case-studies. ECA participated in a seminar on street children, organized by Ethiopia (Addis Ababa, 29 November–2 December).

Women and development

Efforts to include women's issues in development planning were continued during the year. An _ad hoc_ expert group meeting on guidelines for the incorporation of women's concerns in national development plans was held (Addis Ababa, 24-28 November). Training programmes were implemented to ensure that women's needs were adequately formulated and reflected in development programmes, with emphasis on women from Portuguese-speaking countries. A seminar on project formulation and implementation was held (Sao Tome and Principe, 16-27 May) for women from Angola, Cape Verde, Guinea-Bissau, Mozambique and Sao Tome and Principe.

Special attention was given to enhancing women's skills and employment opportunities by means of three major operational projects: improving the role of women in the informal sector; improving women's access to credit through training in management and credit techniques; and training in optimal nutritional use of food donated for relief and food-for-work activities. A subregional seminar on measures to improve women's management skills (Douala, Cameroon, 28 November–2 December) examined existing management training programmes and the economic, cultural and social environments in which women managers worked. Its purpose was also to promote exchanges between trainers and extension workers involved in women's activities. Case-studies were undertaken on the role of women in agro-industries in Botswana, Lesotho, the United Republic of Tanzania and Zimbabwe and on women managers in the informal sector in Kenya, Mauritius, Swaziland and Zambia.

On 15 April,[40] the Conference of Ministers appealed to the relevant bodies, especially the two UNDP bureaux for Africa and ECA, to ensure that the programme for the integration of women in development within the five MULPOCs was maintained. The ECA Executive Secretary was requested to take steps to reinstate the posts for the co-ordinators within the MULPOCs. The Ministers recommended that the United Nations take action to ensure that professional women at ECA and especially at the African Training and Research Centre for Women were given permanent posts and asked member Governments to encourage direct working relations between NGOs and national machineries for the integration of women in development.

PADIS

During 1988, the Pan-African Documentation and Information System (PADIS) focused on establishing a network for the exchange of development information and improving the information infrastructure of ECA member States. A total of 1,300 new records were added to the PADIS bibliographic data base on socio-economic development literature. Two new data bases were opened: one on ongoing research projects in the eastern and southern African countries and the other on African development institutions. Eleven member States designated national participating centres, bringing the total number of countries participating in PADIS to 27.

Among advisory missions carried out during 1988 were two to assess the needs and capacities of national participating centres in Cape Verde and Swaziland. A mission to Ethiopia concluded a preliminary investigation for the establishment of an industrial and technological information network. The Association of African Universities benefited from an advisory mission to reorganize its documentation centre.

In April, the Information and Documentation Committee of the Joint Conference of African Planners, Statisticians and Demographers reviewed the implementation of PADIS during 1986-1988 and examined its work programme for 1988-1990. A meeting of the Standing Committee on the Harmonization and Standardization of Information Systems at ECA-sponsored Regional and Subregional Institutions was held at Addis Ababa in March. A major technical consultative seminar on national information and informatics policies was held at Addis Ababa from 28 November to 1 December.

Programme, organizational and administrative questions

ECA work programme, financing and staffing

Activities carried out by ECA and its secretariat during 1988 were financed mainly from the regular budget of the United Nations and extra-budgetary funds. For substantive activities, resources came from direct regular budget allocation by the General Assembly, through other United Nations units and from specialized agencies. Resources for the implementation of substan-

tive activities were increased greatly for the 1988-1989 biennium from the low level of 1986-1987 when the Organization, because of its financial crisis, took a series of measures to reduce expenditure. In **resolution 43/218 A** of 21 December on the programme budget for the biennium 1988-1989, the Assembly revised the budget for ECA from the $44.2 million appropriated in 1987[41] to $51.2 million.

In a biennial report on staff and administrative questions,[25] the ECA Executive Secretary said that, as at 31 December 1988, Africans held 162 of 187 Professional posts subject to geographical distribution in the ECA secretariat, compared to 158 at the end of 1986. Efforts were being made to ensure that all member States were represented in the secretariat, and the number not represented dropped from 11 to 10 between 1986 and 1988. The proportion of women employed in ECA rose from 7.5 per cent in 1980 to 11.5 per cent. That, however, was still short of the 30 per cent established by the Assembly in 1985.[42]

With regard to progress made in implementing the 1986 recommendations of Group of High-level Intergovernmental Experts to Review the Efficiency of the Administrative and Financial Functioning of the United Nations,[43] posts in the ECA secretariat had been reduced by only 6.7 per cent against the 15 per cent recommended for the United Nations as a whole. The relatively low rate of reduction at ECA was due largely to the efforts of the Conference of Ministers and of the African Group in New York. With regard to the status of the construction of new conference facilities, a timetable for completion by 1993 had been established (see PART SIX, Chapter III).

In its audited financial statements for the biennium ended 31 December 1987,[44] the Board of Auditors stated that budgetary control of the ECA MULPOCs was ineffective and that their operational activities *vis-à-vis* expenditures was very low. It cited several weaknesses in the financial and operational functions of PADIS, including non-identification of implementation costs in the 1986-1987 and 1988-1989 ECA programme budgets, and project goals that were very ambitious and unrealistic, with achievement falling far short of the goals. Also at ECA, the accounting for contributions to a trust fund had not followed the practice provided in the United Nations financial rules. In October,[45] the Advisory Committee on Administrative and Budgetary Questions (ACABQ) agreed with the views of the Board regarding the MULPOCs and PADIS.

In **resolution 43/216** of 21 December, the General Assembly endorsed the concurring observations and recommendations of the Board of Auditors and ACABQ, duly taking into account the divergent views expressed in the Fifth (Administrative and

Budgetary) Committee on the question of the MULPOCs and PADIS.

REFERENCES

(1)E/1988/37. (2)E/ECA/CM.14/39. (3)E/ECA/CM.16/2. (4)E/1989/68. (5)YUN 1986, p. 446, GA res. S-13/2, annex, 1 June 1986. (6)YUN 1980, p. 548. (7)E/1988/37 (res. 624(XXIII)). (8)*Ibid.* (res. 623(XXIII)). (9)*Ibid.* (res. 622(XXIII)). (10)E/ECA/CM.14/40. (11)E/1988/37 (res. 643(XXIII)). (12)*Ibid.* (res. 625(XXIII)). (13)*Ibid.* (res. 628(XXIII)). (14)YUN 1979, p. 636. (15)E/1988/37 (res. 629(XXIII)). (16)*Ibid.* (res. 630(XXIII)). (17)*Ibid.* (res. 635(XXIII)). (18)YUN 1977, p. 509. (19)YUN 1984, p. 617. (20)E/1988/37 (res. 651(XXIII)). (21)*Ibid.* (res. 640(XXIII)). (22)YUN 1986, p. 536. (23)E/ECA/TCD/55. (24)YUN 1977, p. 603, GA res. 32/160, 19 Dec. 1977. (25)E/ECA/CM.14/15. (26)E/ECA/CM.14/24. (27)E/1988/37 (res. 639(XXIII)). (28)YUN 1987, p. 519. (29)A/43/325-E/1988/54. (30)YUN 1980, p. 662, GA res. 35/66 B, 5 Dec. 1980. (31)E/1988/37 (res. 627(XXIII)). (32)*Ibid.* (res. 632(XXIII)). (33)YUN 1987, p. 386, ESC res. 1987/55, 28 May 1987. (34)E/1988/21. (35)YUN 1984, p. 409. (36)E/ECA/CM.14/20. (37)E/1988/37 (res. 631(XXIII)). (38)A/43/430. (39)E/1988/37 (res. 642(XXIII)). (40)*Ibid.* (res. 626(XXIII)). (41)YUN 1987, p. 1106, GA res. 42/226 A, 21 Dec. 1987. (42)YUN 1985, p. 1239, GA res. 40/258 B, 18 Dec. 1985. (43)YUN 1986, p. 1050. (44)A/43/5, vol. I. (45)A/43/674 & Corr.1.

Asia and the Pacific

The Economic and Social Commission for Asia and the Pacific, at its forty-fourth session (Jakarta, Indonesia, 11-20 April 1988), adopted 11 resolutions on a variety of urgent economic and social issues.[1]

With the region's population fast approaching 3 billion, the Commission adopted a Plan of Action to develop those vast human resources.[2] Known as the Jakarta Plan of Action on Human Resources Development in the ESCAP Region, the Plan focused on employment and manpower development, science and technology and the quality of life. In two resolutions related to the Plan, the Commission called on the Executive Secretary to conduct a survey on the quality of life in the ESCAP region as a major initial activity of the Plan[3] and a study on the implications of changes in demographic situations for the various aspects of human resources development.[4]

To achieve environmentally sound and sustainable development, the very basic needs of all people had to be met, the Commission stated.[5] Despite some progress, the region still battled with such environmental problems as depletion of natural resources, desertification and environmental degradation. Recalling that the General Assembly had included "A long-term strategy for sustainable and environmentally sound development" in its 1988 agenda, the Commission invited ESCAP members to integrate environmental considerations into their development policies and programmes. The Commis-

sion also decided to convene a ministerial conference on the environment in 1990. (See also PART THREE, Chapter VIII.)

The continuing deterioration in the economic and social conditions in LDCs, in spite of national and international efforts, was a cause of deep concern, the Commission said.[6] Recalling the Substantial New Programme of Action (SNPA) for the 1980s for LDCs, endorsed by the General Assembly in 1981,[7] it urged donor countries whose official development assistance (ODA) to LDCs had not reached 0.15 per cent of their gross national product (GNP), or which had not doubled their ODA, to attain those targets.

By another resolution, the Commission invited its members to participate actively in the formulation of a regional social development strategy to the year 2000 and beyond, with special reference to the social aspects of rural development.[8]

Concerned that millions in the region were living either completely without shelter or in shelter unfit for human habitation, the Commission[9] urged all members to commit themselves to the objectives of the Global Strategy for Shelter to the Year 2000, adopted by the Assembly in 1987.[10]

Recognizing the importance of technical and economic co-operation among developing countries, the Commission recommended that regional intergovernmental programming exercises to promote such co-operation continue to be held, and asked the ESCAP Executive Secretary to give them greater emphasis.[11]

The Asia and Pacific Telecommunications Development Conference (New Delhi, India, February) recommended that ESCAP take action on recommendations made in a report known as "The missing link" that related to telecommunication sector priority. Following up, the Commission adopted a resolution in which it called on the Executive Secretary to consult with interested members on the matter.[12]

As the Pacific island countries, especially the small, remote and least developed ones, had not been fully represented at Commission sessions, ESCAP requested the Executive Secretary to increase and diversify Pacific subregional representation on the secretariat Professional staff.[13]

In 1987, the Assembly had proclaimed 1990 as International Literacy Year.[14] In response, the Commission, inviting its members to participate in the preparation of the Year at both the national and regional levels, recommended that special attention be paid to implementing the Regional Programme for the Universalization and Renewal of Primary Education and the Eradication of Illiteracy in Asia and the Pacific.[15]

In his message to ESCAP at its forty-fourth session, the Secretary-General said the region had recently shown remarkable vitality, despite depressed commodity prices, rising debt burdens and protectionist measures worldwide. However, the least developed and Pacific island countries had been unable to achieve any significant economic growth and still needed special support. On an encouraging note, many developing countries in the region were giving special attention to modernizing their infrastructures and upgrading human resources.

The Executive Secretary reported that the developing Asian and Pacific countries had achieved a 6 per cent average growth in 1987 despite various difficulties, an improvement of almost 2 per cent over 1986 and nearly double the growth rate of the rest of the developing world. However, that was an average figure which would have been reduced to 3 per cent had it not been for the strong growth of China and the three newly industrializing economies of East Asia.

Among the region's unresolved problems, the inability of its social progress to keep pace with economic development was arguably at the forefront. Many overdue social changes, reforms and improvements were needed if the continued success of growth itself was not to be undermined. The outgrowth of that imbalance was mounting social tension and such urgent new concerns as unemployed youth, rising crime and drug abuse, as well as excessive rural-urban migration, inadequate welfare for the aged and a lack of academic and institutional readiness for the current technological revolution. Massive illiteracy also continued to be a widespread problem.

With the admission of American Samoa as an associate member of ESCAP, membership stood at 38 member States and 10 associate members in 1988 (see APPENDIX III).

Economic and social trends

The diverse economies of the developing ESCAP region turned in more vigorous and geographically balanced performances during 1988 than in the previous year, according to the annual *Economic and Social Survey of Asia and the Pacific 1988*,[16] a summary of which was issued in April 1989.[17] The continued robustness of economic activity in the industrial countries contributed strongly to that vigour.

The underlying strength of growth capacity in many countries was illustrated by the economies of Malaysia, the Philippines and Singapore, which continued a strong recovery from the difficult situations they had encountered in 1985-1986. Malaysia was expected to post a growth rate of 7.4 per cent in 1988, compared with 5.2 per cent in 1987. The Philippines, which had experienced over 10 per cent contraction in 1984-1985, showed a marked recovery, with 5.9 per cent growth in 1987 and 6.7 per cent in 1988. Singapore's economic growth picked up from 1.8 per cent in 1986 to 8.8

per cent in 1987 and was expected to exceed 11 per cent in 1988. A similar rate of growth was estimated for Thailand in 1988, compared with 8.4 and 4.7 per cent in 1987 and 1986. The strong performance of those economies was supported both by export demand for their manufactures and their primary commodities and by strong domestic demand from consumer and investment spending. The latter was partly stimulated by an upsurge in foreign direct investment flows from Japan and the East Asian newly industrializing economies.

Indonesia continued to expect constrained economic growth of a projected 4 per cent for the year, due mainly to slackening oil prices. China and East Asia showed some signs of weakened growth in 1988, although their current rates remained high. China found itself threatened with inflation due to a high demand pressure that had come after rapid income growth, along with shortages of energy and raw material supplies. It was projected that the real growth rate of China's overall economy might moderate from 1987's level of 9.4 per cent, even though an 11 per cent nominal growth of GNP was estimated for 1988.

In Hong Kong, growth was expected to be just more than half of the 13.6 per cent achieved in 1987, while the rate for the Republic of Korea was projected to be slightly less than the 11.1 per cent recorded in 1987. Increasing constraints faced in export markets, rising domestic costs and inflation tended to put a brake on the growth performance of those economies.

With the exception of India, the performance of the major South Asian economies remained rather subdued during 1988. India, however, was expected to accelerate the pace of economic growth in 1988, overcoming the effects of the adverse weather situation in 1987, when the rate slumped to 2 per cent. The growth rates of Pakistan in 1987 and 1988, although lower than the two previous years, were still relatively high and more stable than other South Asian countries. In Sri Lanka, GDP growth rate, estimated at 3.4 per cent, was more than double the 1.4 per cent of 1987, when the country was drought-stricken. Growth rates of LDCs remained depressed during the year, with the exception of Bhutan, Maldives and Nepal. Bhutan's economic growth showed a sudden spurt, reaching 15 per cent in 1987. Bangladesh showed a 2-3 per cent loss of agricultural income in 1988 due to devastating floods and cyclones in 1987-1988. However, exports of light manufactures showed a possible growth of almost 30 per cent for Bangladesh, while Nepal's were forecast to reach a 45 per cent increase.

International trade provided a strong stimulus to the economic growth of the region in 1988. Markets generally were buoyant for both primary commodities and manufactures in most parts of the world. Strong economic growth rates in industrialized countries meant sustained demand for exports from the ESCAP region. Demand also remained high within the region itself. Of special significance for Asian exports since 1985 was the dynamic growth of the Japanese market, which benefited many economies, particularly those in East and South-East Asia.

Oil prices declined in 1988, affecting mostly the economies of Brunei Darussalam and Indonesia. Prices for some other commodities rose and recoveries were relatively strong in the cases of copper, copra and other coconut products, palm oil, rice, rubber, sugar and timber. Prices of cotton, coffee, cocoa, jute, tin and tea, however, remained stagnant.

The current balance of payments (on goods, services and private transfers) of economies in the region benefited in 1987-1988 from the generally strong upsurge in exports. The countries in East and South-East Asia, because of the stronger performance of their manufactures exports and favourable commodity prices, benefited more than the countries in South Asia, which, in general, made slower progress in their attempt to achieve long-term viability in the balance of payments.

Foreign direct investment flows to the developing ESCAP countries had grown in importance in recent years. Several favourable characteristics of developing economies of the region, as well as a record of high and stable economic growth, in contrast to that of other developing regions, had made the Asian and Pacific region a large potential destination of foreign investment flows. Within the region itself, the inward foreign direct investment stock and flows remained heavily concentrated in the East and South-East Asian economies. For example, those economies received above 90 per cent of the inflows averaging $4.82 billion in 1981-1985. But although the share of foreign direct investment stock in the developing countries of the region was relatively high, the region's share in the stock of foreign direct investment worldwide stood at only 8 per cent in 1985.

During the 1980s, with their currencies pegged to the United States dollar or to baskets of currencies in which the dollar had a major weight, the developing countries of the region had to adjust to the large realignments among the currencies of the main industrial countries. For most of the decade, the exchange rate issue centred on how to cope with the sharp appreciation of the dollar and then its similar depreciation against all other major international currencies.

In **decision 1988/181** of 29 July, the Economic and Social Council took note of the summary of the economic and social survey of Asia and the Pacific 1987.[18]

Least developed and island economies

Many of the region's least developed and island countries received severe set-backs in their socio-economic development efforts owing to natural calamities during 1987 and 1988, which ranged from severe floods, cyclones, tidal waves, earthquakes and heavy rains to drought in some countries. While generally failing to achieve either long-term structural diversification or the 7.2 per cent per annum growth target envisaged in SNPA,[19] some countries showed signs of improvement in 1988.

Agriculture, the largest sector of most LDC's, remained vulnerable to the vagaries of nature; in many, growth rates of food-grains output remained below population growth rates, requiring continued dependence on food imports, thus draining scarce foreign exchange resources. Despite various efforts, growth in the industrial sector continued to be weak as compared with other developing countries in the region.

The trade opportunities of LDCs suffered from a lack of diversification in both commodity composition and market orientation. However, some countries marked a good growth rate in exports, led by light manufactures, especially garments.

Social development

Traditionally the formal education system had received great attention in developing economies throughout the region as a means of equalizing opportunities in the society. But although vocational and technical training had been stressed, along with emphasis on universal primary education (especially in countries with growing industrial sectors), in several economies facilities had not expanded fast enough to satisfy demands.

There was concern that educational expansion in developing economies had resulted in unemployment of the educated, because there was evidence that unemployment in urban areas was concentrated among workers in their teens and early twenties. While the system had increased the supply of workers with educational credentials in the labour force, suitable job opportunities to match the earnings expectation of those workers could not keep pace.

Women

The role of women in the development process had received increasing attention in recent years. It appeared (though no statistical data were available) that throughout the region women's participation in productive activity remained generally lower than that of men. Women's jobs also tended to be concentrated in agriculture, especially at the relatively low stage of economic development of countries, and in the services at a higher stage. In all sectors, women tended to hold jobs requiring relatively low levels of skill and responsibility.

Although education of women was of crucial significance in terms of a number of family-oriented development and welfare activities, such as family planning and health, child care and welfare, women in the region had generally tended to lag behind men in educational achievements. Over the years, women's access to and position in the educational system had improved only slightly in most countries. Regarding secondary and tertiary schooling, however, the disparity between men and women tended to be less in some countries, judging from enrolment ratios. This was probably due to the fact that secondary education remained limited to the elite and upper classes in most developing countries.

Activities in 1988

During the year, ESCAP continued to monitor closely the socio-economic situations and issues at the national, regional and international levels that might have impact on the region's development prospects. Activities were undertaken in a wide variety of areas, including population, food and agriculture, international trade, energy and natural resources.

Agriculture and rural development

The sector covering food, agriculture and rural development continued to be beset with many problems in 1988 that hindered national progress. They included limited technical knowledge among farmers, lack of required inputs, absence of integrated rural planning, unfavorable prices of primary commodities, declining soil fertility and heavy dependence on weather. Included in the activities was a planning workshop on socio-economic constraints on the use of new and renewable sources of energy (Bangkok, Thailand, September), a regional symposium on farm broadcasting (Bangkok, November/December) and a planning workshop on country studies to assess the impact of low agricultural export prices at the farm level (Bangkok, December).

The Commission endorsed the technical recommendations of the ESCAP and World Bank/UNDP Resource Recovery (Waste Recycling) International Seminar on Waste-water Reclamation and Reuse for Aquaculture (Calcutta, India, December) and suggested that public health aspects of sewage-fed aquaculture be further studied. It expressed support of the ESCAP/FAO/UNIDO Fertilizer Advisory, Development and Information Network for Asia and the Pacific in its continued work to promote the balanced and judicious use of fertilizer through the development of human resources by means of training, workshops, seminars and study tours; advisory services and research; and dissemination of timely and reliable fertilizer-related information.

The first phase of an inter-agency project on the action plan for multiplication of participatory rural development experience on a socially significant scale was implemented at the Regional Review Meeting on Participatory Rural Development (Dhaka, Bangladesh, July). Also, eight grass-roots cadres participated in training programmes in Bangladesh, India and Nepal during November and December.

Concerning the environment, progress was made on the Regional Network of Research and Training Centres on Desertification Control in Asia and the Pacific, including the production of a film on the extent of the problem within the region. Several meetings were held in Bangkok, including an expert group meeting on environmental impact assessment of development projects (August), a consultative meeting on integrated environmental impact assessment for the eastern seaboard development programme (November) and roving seminars on promotion of environmental awareness in accordance with findings and recommendations of the World Commission on Environment and Development (December) (the last also in Dhaka and Kuala Lumpur, Malaysia).

Human settlements

Progress was made towards implementing the Commission's April 1988 resolution[9] in which it urged members to commit themselves to the Global Strategy for Shelter to the Year 2000.[10] With France's support, two projects were under implementation: developing building-component industries through the application of updated modular coordination rules, and guidelines for innovative community-based housing finance and credit systems for low-income households. Among meetings held was a national training seminar for trainers in community participation in human settlements programmes (Manila, Philippines, September) and a seminar-cum-study tour on urban transport (Yokohama/Osaka, Japan, October/November).

International trade

In 1988, the mid-term review of the Uruguay Round of multilateral trade negotiations of the General Agreement on Tariffs and Trade (GATT) (see PART SEVEN, Chapter XVIII) had revealed that, while progress had been achieved in some sectors, much was required in others. The Commission decided to continue to provide appropriate technical and advisory support to developing countries in the region and to conduct relevant studies and seminars so as to equip them to participate effectively in the negotiations and adopt appropriate trade policy measures. In secretariat activities covering raw materials and commodities, particular attention was paid to the usefulness of co-operative commodity arrangements among producing countries of jute, silk and tropical timber.

Activities were also undertaken regarding trade facilitation, organizing the next Asia-Pacific International Trade Fair to be held in 1990-1991 and conducting studies on foreign investment incentive schemes relating to Bangladesh, Malaysia, the Philippines, the Republic of Korea and Sri Lanka.

The Committee on Trade held its twenty-sixth session at Bangkok from 28 November to 2 December 1988. Also, a workshop for the development and strengthening of trade information services in the South Pacific was organized at Suva, Fiji (October) and an expert group meeting on sericulture took place at Khon Kaen, Thailand (December).

Least developed countries

The wide disparity between the rapid economic progress and development in several of the region's developing countries and the continued unfavourable economic situation in LDCs became a cause for concern during 1988. Some progress had been made in implementing SNPA[19] during the year, with most LDCs launching extensive development programmes. However, lack of resources hindered them from achieving their goals, and it was urgent that an appropriate action programme for the 1990s be formulated. ESCAP had taken action, pursuant to its April resolution,[6] in helping to prepare for the Second United Nations Conference on LDCs in 1990.

Support for LDCs was reiterated by UNDP and DTCD, with the former rendering special support to countries with special needs. In particular, it was committed to participating in a rehabilitation programme for countries stricken by war and had extended emergency assistance to two LDCs hit by natural disasters in 1988. UNDP co-ordinated assistance to five LDCs of the region.

Technology for development

During 1988, the region witnessed a heightened awareness among policy planners and decision makers of development based on science and technology. That was attributable in part to the efforts of the ESCAP secretariat, which took action pursuant to the Tokyo Programme on Technology for Development in Asia and the Pacific. ESCAP initiated co-operative projects in five areas: research, development and demonstration projects in selected areas of technology; identification of technological needs, capabilities and levels of technological development; finding practical ways of sharing information; promotion of regional co-operative activities; and initiating measures for the technological development of the least developed, land-locked and island developing countries.

The Asian and Pacific Centre for Transfer of Technology (with the financial support of UNDP) contributed to implementing the Tokyo Programme, especially in the areas of science and technology information-sharing and management and the promotion of technology utilization.

Transnational corporations

In 1988, the Commission noted that transnational corporations (TNCs) accounted for a significant part of total investment in only a few developing countries, with such investments tending to be concentrated in the higher-income, larger and better-endowed developing countries. Therefore, the Commission agreed that it might be desirable for developing countries to improve their investment climate to maintain their share of foreign investment.

In China, Hong Kong, India, Indonesia, Malaysia, the Philippines, the Republic of Korea and Singapore, advisory services were undertaken during 1988 to assist them with projects relating to TNCs. Research activities were undertaken in data collection under a project on TNCs in the international trade of primary commodities and studies were made under the second phase of a project on TNCs and the environment. Several publications were completed, including the *Asian-Pacific TNC Review 1988*, *The Socio-economic Impact of Transnational Corporations in the Fast Food Industry*, *Transnational Corporations and Environment Management in Selected Asian and Pacific Developing Countries* and *Transnational Corporations from Developing Asian Economies: Host Country Perspectives*.

In June, the ESCAP/United Nations Centre on Transnational Corporations Joint Unit on TNCs held a seminar at Bangkok on the role of foreign direct investment and trade in services and development. The Joint Unit also continued to collect, analyse and disseminate information relating to TNC activities in the region, including information and research publications on: laws, regulations and general policies pertaining to them; foreign direct investment flows and non-equity arrangements; and data sources, research activities and information services pertaining to or carried out in the region. Activities to further the development of national information systems on TNCs and the establishment of a regional information network continued with the formulation of a pilot project proposal for the Association of South-East Asian Nations.

Shipping, transport and communications

The Committee on Shipping, Transport and Communications, at its twelfth session (Bangkok, 12-16 December 1988), noted that in recent years multimodal transport had become increasingly important, owing to demand for fast, efficient shipment of goods and rapid changes in technology. There was also a tremendous need in the developing countries for assistance in the introduction of multimodalism.

In the area of road transport, UNDP financed a project to develop rural road infrastructure, which was designed to strengthen the training as well as research and development capacities of several regional institutions in order to organize training courses for ESCAP member countries.

In railway transport, the secretariat carried out activities relating to modernization, transfer of technology, development of railways, computerized railway operation and electrification, and organized seminars, study tours, symposia and workshops. Regarding air transport, a project was carried out on air cargo management systems applicable to developing countries of the region. In telecommunications and postal services, a programme was being undertaken by the secretariat relating to the development of postal services in rural areas.

Advisory services were provided to Bangladesh, Nepal and the Philippines on information and data collection for ESCAP railway statistics; to India for a site survey of rail/wheel wear and derailment and in connection with the implementation of the UNDP project on developing rural road infrastructure; and to China and Indonesia in connection with the implementation of the same UNDP project.

Transport and Communications Decade for Asia and the Pacific

At its 1988 session, the Commission endorsed a proposal to convene a senior-level meeting of ESCAP to consider the findings of an intercountry mission which was to take place within the framework of the 1989 mid-term review of the Transport and Communications Decade for Asia and the Pacific (1985-1994). The Commission felt that long-term projects such as the Asian Highway, the Trans-Asian Railway, the Asian Railway master plan and rail-cum-sea transport development under the programme for the Decade should be continued during the Decade's second half. It also felt that human resources development, technology transfer, strengthening of interregional and intraregional transport and communication linkages, promotion of regional co-operation and integrated transport planning should be accorded priority and be included in the Decade's regional programme of action.

In an April report to the Economic and Social Council,[20] the Secretary-General reviewed the implementation of the Decade's programmes, which the Commission in 1987 had recommended be accorded priority.[21] He reported that of 54 projects under the regional programme of action, 15 had been completed, 15 were under implementation, 9 had been submitted to UNDP for funding and 15 were to be submitted for financial assistance from donor countries.

The Secretary-General stated that an effective way of raising the public's awareness of the Decade would be for each member and associate member of ESCAP to issue a set of commemorative stamps. The ESCAP secretariat had received a positive response from some countries to its suggestion in that regard.

By **decision 1988/173** of 28 July, the Economic and Social Council took note of the Secretary-General's report.

Population

The Committee on Population and Social Development held its first session in 1988 (Bangkok, 21-25 November). A regional study on emerging issues of population aging was organized to develop policies and programmes concerning the elderly. Training programmes were organized on the use of microcomputers for analysis of mortality data. A study on the implications of demographic changes for the development of human resources was initiated. Technical assistance activities involved strengthening the formulation of population policies and programmes through the provision of advisory services on population and development. Also, efforts were made to improve the Commission's dissemination and exchange of population information and to develop population information centres and networks in countries of the region.

The final meeting of the Study Directors on Emerging Issues of the Aging of Population was held in Bangkok in May. A regional seminar on frameworks for population and development planning was also held (Bangkok, June), as was an *ad hoc* expert group meeting on integration of population and development policies (Bangkok, August/September). The Asia-Pacific population information consultative workshop was conducted (Bangkok, October/November). In addition, 18 candidates from the region were awarded 1988-1989 fellowships for training at the International Institute for Population Sciences in Bombay, India.

Women in development

Legal literacy among women was regarded by the Commission as having particular importance and it noted the secretariat's efforts towards that end during 1988. Such literacy was especially pertinent in the developing countries, where the majority of women were, in many cases, not aware of their legal rights. National workshops to promote legal literacy among women were held (Colombo, Sri Lanka, June; Manila, July; Jakarta, Indonesia, September; Dhaka, Bangladesh, December).

The secretariat also continued to implement the multi-year project on the development of the

Women's Information Network for Asia and the Pacific, with a workshop on management of women's information centres being held (Bangkok, December). Advisory services were provided to Australia, Brunei Darussalam, Burma, China, Fiji, Indonesia, Japan, the Republic of Korea, Samoa, Thailand and Tonga to assist the strengthening of national structures and mechanisms, including national policies and programmes, for the integration of women in development.

Statistics

The Commission noted with concern that demands for data were placing a strain on national statistical offices, whose resources were static or declining. It felt that it was particularly important to develop existing statistical methodology, especially in the quality control of data, so as to enhance the accuracy and reliability of the information supplied. In 1988, many countries had benefited greatly from the regional advisory services provided by the secretariat in such areas as population censuses and surveys, data processing and household surveys.

Several meetings covering statistics issues were held in 1988: an expert group meeting on computerized information systems for Governments (Bangkok, June); an advanced course on statistics related to poverty, inequality and basic needs (Bangkok, July); and an advanced course on planning, implementing and evaluating agricultural census (Bangkok, July/August). A number of advisory services were also rendered in 1988. A technical review of the National Household Survey Capability Programme was conducted in Bangladesh, while another appraised household survey activities in two provinces of China. Advisory services assisted in the review and improvement of national accounts in Bangladesh, Brunei Darussalam and Thailand; others assisted in the planning, organization, conducting of pre-tests, processing and analysis of population and housing censuses and demographic surveys in Bangladesh, Hong Kong, the Lao People's Democratic Republic, Malaysia, Maldives, Nepal, Pakistan, Papua New Guinea, the Philippines, Samoa, Sri Lanka, Tonga, Vanuatu and Viet Nam.

Organizational questions

Admission of American Samoa

In 1987, the United States, as the ESCAP member responsible for the international relations of American Samoa, had presented the Territory's application for admission as an associate member of ESCAP.[22] The application was considered and unanimously endorsed by the Commission at its April 1988 session. On 28 July, the Economic and Social Council, by adopting **decision 1988/170**, amended the Commission's terms of reference to include American Samoa as an associate member.

REFERENCES

[1]E/1988/35. [2]*Ibid.* (res. 274(XLIV)). [3]*Ibid.* (res. 273(XLIV)). [4]*Ibid.* (res. 272(XLIV)). [5]*Ibid.* (res. 267(XLIV)). [6]*Ibid.* (res. 271 (XLIV)). [7]YUN 1981, p. 410, GA res. 36/194, 17 Dec. 1981. [8]E/1988/35 (res. 265(XLIV)). [9]*Ibid.* (res. 268(XLIV)). [10]YUN 1987, p. 718, GA res. 42/191, 11 Dec. 1987. [11]E/1988/35 (res. 264(XLIV)). [12]*Ibid.* (res. 270(XLIV)). [13]*Ibid.* (res. 269(XLIV)). [14]YUN 1987, p. 654, GA res. 42/104, 7 Dec. 1987. [15]E/1988/35 (res. 266(XLIV)). [16]*Economic and Social Survey of Asia and the Pacific 1988*, Sales No. E.89.II.F.3. [17]E/1989/55. [18]YUN 1987, p. 533. [19]YUN 1981, p. 406. [20]E/1988/55. [21]YUN 1987, p. 537. [22]*Ibid.*, p. 545.

Europe

The forty-third session of the Economic Commission for Europe (Geneva, 12-21 April 1988)[1] took place in an improved political climate in East-West relations, which had opened up new prospects for enhanced co-operation. Such co-operation included the 1987 signing of the Treaty between the United States and the USSR on the elimination of intermediate-range and shorter-range nuclear missiles (see PART ONE, Chapter II), the resumed negotiations on disarmament issues and many other peaceful initiatives. Particular reference was made to the entry into force in 1987 of the Single European Act and the European Community's objective to establish a common internal market in 1992. Several delegations, however, focused on the deceleration in output growth and the unfavourable short-term prospects for a number of countries of the region. They also highlighted the need for more growth-oriented national economic policies and for international co-operation.

At its April session, the Commission adopted a resolution on its work as a whole and its future activities, in which it again called on member Governments to take full advantage of its potential for dialogue and for strengthening economic relations and multilateral co-operation in the region.[2] Sixteen decisions were also adopted on various aspects of the Commission's work. The Commission approved an Overall Economic Perspective to the Year 2000,[3] and adopted a Regional Strategy for Environmental Protection and Rational Use of Natural Resources in ECE Member Countries Covering the Period up to the Year 2000 and Beyond, and a Declaration on Conservation of Flora, Fauna and Their Habitats.[4] Other decisions related to the work of the World Commission on Environment and Development;[5] ECE's contribution to the follow-up of the World Conference to Review and Appraise the

Achievements of the United Nations Decade for Women;[6] agriculture;[7] a new international codification system for medium- and high-rank coals;[8] rail and combined transport;[9] the possible introduction of summertime throughout all European ECE countries;[10] policy implications of a study on European timber trends and prospects to the year 2000 and beyond;[11] the adoption of rules for Electronic Data Interchange for Administration, Commerce and Transport and related data elements, segments and messages (EDIFACT);[12] the work programme of the Committee on the Development of Trade;[13] co-operation in the development of transport;[14] building regulations;[15] economic co-operation in the Mediterranean;[16] standardization and related activities;[17] and engineering industries and automation.[18]

During the first eight months of 1988, some 120 East-West joint venture contracts were signed compared with only a handful during the early 1980s. Noting that those joint ventures were being established at an accelerating pace as an innovative form for developing trade and industrial co-operation between Eastern and Western partners, ECE issued a guide on the legal aspects of such ventures.[19]

In February, six Balkan countries agreed to mutual co-operation in a wide range of economic activities. Noting ECE's previous help in fostering co-operation among those countries, some delegations indicated that the Commission's future assistance in that area would be welcomed. Delegations emphasized, however, that care had to be taken that internal integration processes among groupings of countries did not produce external disintegration among other countries in the region.

Economic trends

According to the summary of the economic survey of Europe, 1988-1989,[20] the region experienced growth in 1988. This occurred despite forecasts to the contrary, as a slow-down had been expected in the market economies following turbulent activity in world-wide financial markets in 1987. Instead, outputs in those economies rose by just over 4 per cent, which was attributed to a number of factors, including the impact of lower inflation, reductions in fiscal imbalances, major improvements in corporate profitability and, in general, widespread progress in raising supply-side efficiency.

GDP of the market economies of Western Europe rose from 2.5 to 3.6 per cent in 1988—the largest increase since 1976. Consequently, employment in Western Europe rose by some 1 per cent and unemployment fell from a 1987 average of 9.3 per cent to 8.8 per cent.

Although the centrally planned economies of Europe shared in the general acceleration of world-wide output growth in 1988, goals for the year were not reached. Imbalances in domestic markets increased in most countries. Declining import demand in the USSR and low competitiveness in Western markets affected growth in Eastern Europe.

The volume of Soviet exports to the West increased by some 13 per cent in the first three quarters of the year, with higher oil exports playing an important part. Soviet imports grew by 11 per cent in volume after falling sharply in the previous two years. But despite this, 1988 was another difficult year for Soviet trade with the West. Export prices of fuels fell by 15 per cent, while import prices rose rapidly, led by higher prices for cereals. This caused the annual trade balance with the West to swing from a surplus of $1 billion to a deficit of $2.5 billion. Adjusted for valuation effects, Soviet net indebtedness was estimated to have increased by over $1 billion.

After several years of stagnation, the volume of Eastern European exports to the West increased by 7 per cent in the first three quarters of 1988. But although Eastern Europe's trade surplus in convertible currencies increased, the increase of the invisibles deficit led to a small decline in the current account surplus to about $1 billion. The area's net indebtedness declined from almost $76 billion in 1987 to $73 billion at the end of 1988.

Among the centrally planned economies of Eastern Europe and the USSR, individual performances varied. In Hungary, adjustments in the external sector, combined with far-reaching economic reforms, had had priority over the pace of economic expansion and GDP stagnated. Romania had continued to give priority to external adjustment: in 1988 that affected not only the standard of living but also investment and output growth. The German Democratic Republic had tried to combine external adjustment with economic growth, but in 1988 output decelerated for the third consecutive year and fell below the Eastern European average.

There had been signs in recent years of increasing imbalances in the domestic markets of centrally planned economies. In the USSR, the inadequate supplies of consumer goods became the principal economic problem in 1988. Open inflation in Hungary and Poland, which had been reported for several years, reached 17 and 60 per cent, respectively, in 1988. Inflationary pressures seemed to be increasing in other countries, although it manifested in other ways. Domestic imbalances had also worsened in Poland and Romania, where extensive rationing had been in force for some years.

Activities in 1988

Regional economic co-operation

When the Senior Economic Advisers to ECE Governments (twenty-fourth session, Geneva,

15-19 February) met in 1988,[21] they were joined by representatives of UNCTAD, the Council for Mutual Economic Assistance (CMEA), the European Economic Community and the European Free Trade Association (EFTA). Discussions covered the situations in countries of both market and centrally planned economies. The Advisers finalized the full version of the Overall Economic Perspective to the Year 2000,[22] which was intended as an aid to policy makers who sought solutions through co-operation among ECE member countries. The document showed that a continuation of past trends was untenable owing to imbalances and that new approaches to solving economic and social problems were needed, namely in the form of enhanced international co-operation. The Perspective was divided into two parts. Part one contained chapters covering the overall economic perspective and scenarios exploring long-term economic growth conditions. Part two's chapters dealt with human resources development; energy prospects; environment problems and economic development; and science and technology in long-term economic development. In April, ECE approved the Perspective.[3]

During the year, the Senior Economic Advisory held an *ad hoc* meeting on personal and collective services sectors development (Geneva, 24 and 25 October) and a symposium on the national and international aspects of long-term prospects in ECE countries (Budapest, Hungary, 4-7 October).

International trade

The Committee on the Development of Trade (thirty-seventh session, Geneva, 5-9 December)[23] considered recent and prospective trends in intraregional and interregional trade; matters arising from the April session of ECE; compensation trade in the region; practical measures to examine obstacles to intraregional trade and to promote and diversify trade; promoting trade through industrial co-operation; improved business contacts; trade problems of the economically developing member States; and improvement of international trade procedures and international contract practices in industry.

The Committee adopted its work programme for 1988-1993, which included a number of continuing activities, such as an analysis of recent and prospective trade trends, policies and problems; promotion and diversification of East-West trade; and consideration of means for creating favourable conditions for industrial co-operation.

A number of meetings were held by various bodies of the Committee during 1988: the Working Party on Facilitation of International Trade Procedures met from 13 to 16 September; a meeting of experts on data elements and automatic data interchange was held on 14 and 15 September; and the Working Party on International Contract Prac-

tices in Industry held its thirty-second (27-29 June) and thirty-third (28-30 November) sessions.

In April,[12] ECE noted that the Working Party on the Facilitation of International Trade Procedures had adopted the rules for EDIFACT and recommended that they be named the United Nations Rules for Electronic Data Interchange for Administration, Commerce and Transport.

Transport

At its forty-ninth session (Geneva, 1-5 February),[24] the Inland Transport Committee discussed the application of international transport agreements of interest to ECE Governments, an analysis of the transport situation in member countries and emerging development trends, and specific issues related to road, rail and inland water transport.

Working parties or expert groups of the Committee also convened during 1988. They conducted meetings on the transport of dangerous goods, road traffic safety, construction of vehicles, noise, combined transport, customs questions affecting transport, transport trends and economics, transport statistics, transport of perishable foodstuffs, road transport, lighting and light-signalling, pollution and energy, brakes and running gear, general safety provisions, passive safety, rail transport, developing a European railway network, inland water transport, standardizing technical requirements for vessels and ships' papers, and standardizing rules of the road and signs and signals in inland navigation.

In April, ECE requested the Inland Transport Committee to analyse the conditions for closer international co-operation between national railways, appropriate commercial autonomy for international traffic management, and international railway services according to prevailing market conditions.[9]

The Commission again asked the Committee to co-operate with the Mediterranean transport centres and recommended to the Economic and Social Council that it grant United Nations status to the Transport Study Centre for the Eastern Mediterranean (Volos, Greece), the Transport Study Centre for the Western Mediterranean (Barcelona, Spain) and the Transport Training Centre (Istanbul, Turkey), on the understanding that there would be no financial implications for the regular United Nations budget.[16] On 28 July, the Council agreed to ECE's recommendation when it adopted **decision 1988/169**, adding that such status would take effect after agreements had been concluded between the United Nations and the respective Governments concerning the conditions of such status.

Industry

The Chemical Industry Committee (twenty-first session, Geneva, 5-7 October)[25] discussed major issues confronting the industry, such as restructuring of the industry changes in fiscal policy, enterprises, technology policies, manpower problems, the problem of the image of the industry, environmental considerations and safety. The Committee reviewed chemical market data on aromatic hydrocarbons and olefins, and agreed that a new group of rapporteurs, on chlor-alkaline products, should be created. It also endorsed a report on the use and disposal of wastes from phosphoric acid and titanium dioxide production and reviewed the report of the first *ad hoc* meeting for the study on membrane technology in the chemical industry. The second such meeting was held at Geneva in December. The Group of Experts on the Periodic Survey of the Chemical Industry held its fourteenth session (3 and 4 October). A seminar on the use of electronic energy in the chemical industry was held at Lyons, France (7-10 November), and preparations for a seminar on the role of the chemical industry in environmental protection took place on 26 and 27 May.

The Working Party on Engineering Industries and Automation (eighth session, Geneva, 22-24 February)[26] examined the medium- and long-term assessment of engineering industries within national, regional and global economies and took note of the Commission's decision to delete from its work programme the project on the medium- and long-term impact of automation on the economy and its individual sectors. It also discussed the 1985 and 1986 annual reviews of engineering industries and automation and the preparation of the 1987 review. Several current and proposed studies were discussed, including the preparation of a feasibility study on ECE work on robotics and flexible manufacturing systems and trends towards computer-integrated manufacturing, and a study on food-processing machinery, including packaging techniques. A project on a consulting system for industrial technologies was also proposed. Other topics brought under discussion included environmental and resource-saving problems, statistics of engineering industries and automation, and activities of United Nations and other international bodies.

Meetings held included one on questions of statistics concerning engineering industries and automation (17-19 October), an *ad hoc* meeting for the study on food-processing machinery and a seminar entitled "Shipbuilding 2000 Maritime Conference—BALTEXPO '88" (Gdansk, Poland, 5-9 September).

In April, the Commission approved the 1988-1992 work programme and the calendar of meetings of the Working Party.[18]

The Steel Committee (fifty-sixth session, Geneva, 26-28 October)[27] reviewed short- and medium-term trends in the steel market and recent statistics on the industry. It examined projects in progress, including one on the importance of the iron and steel industry in the economic activity of ECE members and another on the recuperation and economic utilization of by-products of the iron and steel industry.

During the year, activities included an expert meeting on the steel market, a seminar on new applications for steel in view of the challenge from substitute materials and a preparatory meeting for a seminar on the economic and technical aspects of the modernization of the steel industry.

Energy resources

The Senior Advisers to ECE Governments on Energy (sixth session, Geneva, 24-27 May),[28] pursuant to a 1987 Commission decision,[29] reviewed, among other things, ECE activities regarding general energy and the energy situation in the region, as well as the general energy work programme for 1988-1992.

The Coal Committee (eighty-fourth session, Geneva, 26-29 September)[30] focused on general energy problems in the region, with particular attention paid to the compilation of energy balances of ECE countries for past and future years. Current developments, international trade and medium- and long-term perspectives of the coal industry were discussed, as was scientific and technical co-operation in preparation and utilization of coal. The Committee also adopted its 1988-1992 work programme. Meetings held in 1988 included an *ad hoc* meeting on the elaboration of a new international scientific classification of medium- and high-rank coals (13 and 14 June). Expert meetings were held on productivity and management problems in the coal industry (20-22 June), on the utilization and preparation of solid fuels (14-16 June) and on opencast mines (Karlovy Vary, Czechoslovakia, 16-20 May). The Working Party on Coal Trade and Coal Statistics held its second session (Donetsk, Ukrainian SSR, 30 May–2 June).

The Committee on Electric Power (forty-sixth session, Geneva 25-28 January)[31] examined, among other things, selected technical and economic problems, including the rational use and distribution of electricity outside major urban areas; electric power stations; new developments in geothermal energy; the interconnection of electric power transmission systems of the Balkan countries; and the relationship between electricity and the environment. Expert groups met on problems of planning and operating large power systems (8-10 June); electric power stations (12-14 December); and the relationship between electricity and the environment (14-16 December). A seminar was held on the impact of atmospheric protection measures on thermal power stations (Essen, Federal Republic of Germany, 19-21 September).

The Committee on Gas (thirty-fourth session, Geneva, 18-21 January)[32] examined several issues, including general energy problems in the region. Medium- and long-term prospects and current developments were discussed, with topics covering natural gas and liquefied petroleum gas markets in 1986 and future prospects; the transport and storage of gas; natural gas resources; investments in the gas industry; and development of international co-operation. Two expert groups on gas met during the year: one on its use and distribution (12-14 September) and the other on its transport and storage (14-16 September).

In April,[8] ECE endorsed the Coal Committee's 1987 decision to approve a new International Codification System for Medium- and High-rank Coals and recommended that the Economic and Social Council consider appropriate measures for the System's world-wide application.

ECONOMIC AND SOCIAL COUNCIL ACTION

On 28 July, the Economic and Social Council, on the recommendation of its First Committee, adopted **resolution 1988/68** without vote.

International trade and co-operation in the field of coal

The Economic and Social Council,

Aware of the need to facilitate international trade and co-operation in the field of coal,

Recalling the adoption by the Economic Commission for Europe in 1956 of the International Classification of Hard Coals by Type,

1. *Welcomes* the adoption by the Economic Commission for Europe of the International Codification System for Medium- and High-rank Coals, which was elaborated in close collaboration with States not members of the Commission and with international organizations;

2. *Invites* States Members of the United Nations, international organizations and the regional commissions to consider the possibility of taking appropriate measures for ensuring the world-wide application of the International Codification System.

Economic and Social Council resolution 1988/68

28 July 1988   Meeting 40   Adopted without vote

Approved by First Committee (E/1988/117) without vote, 21 July (meeting 19); 3-nation draft (E/1988/C.1/L.6), orally amended by Vice-Chairman; agenda item 7.

Sponsors: Bulgaria, Poland, Portugal.

Water

In April, ECE adopted a decision on co-operation in the field of environmental protection and water resources,[4] which also included the adoption of the Regional Strategy for Environmental Protection and Rational Use of Natural Resources in ECE Member Countries Covering the Period up to the Year 2000 and Beyond (see below, under "Environment"). It also endorsed the recommendations of the 1987 seminar on protection of soil and aquifers against non-point source pollution as well as ECE recommendations on waste-water treatment.[33]

The Regional Strategy and the Declaration had been drafted by the Senior Advisers to ECE Governments on Environmental and Water Problems (first session, Geneva, 29 February–4 March).[34] The Advisers also formulated recommendations on waste-water treatment, liability in case of accidental pollution and an ecosystems approach to water management. They analysed the existing situation and future prospect with regard to the utilization of water resources and pollution control in the region and reviewed a draft charter on groundwater management. The Advisers' work programme was approved, taking into consideration, among other things, preparations for a symposium on rational use of water through on-farm operations of irrigation, scheduled for 1989. Meetings included the Working Party on Water Problems (8-11 November) and a seminar on dam safety (Rovaniemi, Finland, 29 August–3 September).

Agriculture and timber

The Committee on Agricultural Problems (thirty-ninth session, Geneva, 7-10 March)[35] reviewed reports on trade and commodities; activities of other international organizations; European trade in agricultural products; the report on the twenty-fourth (1987) Conference of FAO[36] and its activities in Europe; and the market situation of selected commodities, such as grains, livestock and meat, and milk and dairy products. It also adopted its 1988-1992 work programme. Groups of experts on standardization met during the year to discuss poultry meat, eggs and egg products, fruit juices, and fresh fruit and vegetables.

Working parties also met on the standardization of perishable produce (7-11 November) and on agrarian structure and farm rationalization (26-30 September). A joint FAO/ECE Working Party on Mechanization of Agriculture also met (24-27 October) and an *ad hoc* meeting to consider the standardization of porcine and bovine meat was held (1 and 2 June). Symposia were held on agriculture and fish farming (Warsaw, Poland, 10-13 May) and on development of biotechnology in food and feed production (Budapest, 13-17 June).

The ECE Timber Committee (forty-sixth session, Geneva, 11-14 October)[37] discussed activities carried out by other ECE bodies, international organizations and FAO. The Committee considered a report of meetings held by the Joint FAO/ECE/ILO Committee on Forest Working Techniques and Training of Forest Workers (29-31 August), which included a proposal that its name be changed to the Joint FAO/ECE/ILO Committee on Forestry Technology, Management and Training to reflect better the scope of its activities. The Timber Committee postponed its decision until the

FAO European Forestry Commission had considered the proposal at its June 1989 session. It also considered a report by the Joint FAO/ECE Working Party on Forest Economics and Statistics (24-26 February) and examined a draft study on the trade in and markets for tropical hardwoods.

A team of specialists on wood and energy met in February and several seminars were held during the year covering: reforestation methods after harvesting, in particular artificial regeneration (Eberswalde-Finow, German Democratic Republic, 9-13 May); products from the Mediterranean forest (Florence, Italy, 20-24 September); and employment of contractors in forest work (Loubières, France, 26-30 September).

In April,[11] ECE welcomed the Declaration on the policy implications of a study on European timber trends and prospects to the year 2000 and beyond, which had been unanimously adopted by the 1987 joint session of the Timber Committee and the European Forestry Commission[33] and recommended that ECE member Governments take the Declaration into account when reviewing their forestry policies.

Science and technology

Meeting in 1988, the Senior Advisers to ECE Governments on Science and Technology (sixteenth session, Geneva, 19-23 September)[38] discussed safety aspects of biotechnology, current developments in science and technology policies, transfer of technology and social and economic development in biotechnology.

It was stressed that since neither *in vitro* DNA-modified nor -unmodified organisms, released deliberately or accidentally, would respect national boundaries, an international safety approach was needed for biotechnology. It was suggested that those possible adverse effects should be made known to the public at large through the mass media, Governments, scientists and industry. However, the positive effects of the technology should also be made clear via similar means.

The ways and means of facilitating technology transfer needed to be considered in areas relating to environmental protection; elaboration of measures aimed at drawing up legal, administrative and organizational arrangements; analysis of relevant national legislation; and the development on a cooperative basis of new technologies.

During the year, a seminar was held on the prediction of earthquakes (Lisbon, Portugal, 14-18 November).

Environment

The Senior Advisers to ECE Governments on Environmental and Water Problems[34] (see above, under "Water") considered two draft instruments: the Declaration on Conservation of Flora, Fauna and Their Habitats, which had been finalized in 1987;[33] and the Regional Strategy for Environmental Protection and Rational Use of Natural Resources in ECE Member Countries Covering the Period up to the Year 2000 and Beyond, which was first proposed in 1986.[39] After further revising the draft Regional Strategy, the Advisers decided that both instruments would be submitted to the Commission for consideration. Low-waste technology and waste management were also discussed, as was work done by a task force on the relationship between economic activities and protection of flora, fauna and their habitats. Other subjects considered included water management (see above, under "Water") and air pollution problems.

At an *ad hoc* meeting of experts on the report of the World Commission on Environment and Development (Geneva, 10-12 October), it was stressed that sustainable development was to be used as the guiding principle in the interrelated objectives of economic growth, environmental protection and sound development within the ECE region. It was agreed that progress towards sustainable development implied changes and adequate measures in economic policies in three directions: acceptance of higher costs, not as set against more goods and services but against less degradation of the environment; important financial requirements; and an increased effort in basic research to solve environment-related problems. Activities in the area of sustainable development could include: optimal use of chemicals in European agriculture; international standards for environmental protection; and long-term prospects for energy-efficiency in the region.

Other 1988 meetings of the Senior Advisers included an *ad hoc* meeting on hazardous waste management (5-7 September).

In April,[4] ECE adopted the Declaration and the Regional Strategy.

Transboundary air pollution

The Executive Body for the Convention on Long-range Transboundary Air Pollution (sixth session, Sofia, Bulgaria, 31 October–4 November) adopted a protocol to the Convention concerning the control of emissions of nitrogen oxides or their transboundary fluxes.[40] Other topics discussed were strategies and policies of parties and signatories to the 1979 Convention[41] for the abatement of air pollution; critical loads for forests, crops and materials, and for sulphur and nitrogen; and volatile organic compounds. Progress reports were considered on the effects of major air pollutants on human health and the environment, and on the technologies for and economic aspects of emission control.

Meetings of other groups held during the year included the Group of Economic Experts on Air Pollution (13-15 June), the Working Group on Effects (29-31 August) and the Steering Body to the Co-operative Programme for Monitoring and Evaluation of the Long-range Transmission of Air Pollutants in Europe (31 August–2 September). Also, an *ad hoc* meeting to elaborate a draft framework agreement on environmental impact assessment in a transboundary context was held (18-21 October).

Human settlements

The Committee on Housing, Building and Planning (forty-ninth session, Geneva, 13-16 September)[42] discussed current trends and policies in the human settlements situation and reviewed its work. In the areas of urban renewal and modernization policies, it was reported that public participation had become standard practice and that techniques to incorporate public opinions and views had been further developed with positive results. Regarding housing, it was noted that rent levels and housing expenditure, in general, were increasing in most market-economy countries. Declines in new construction and scarcity of land for housing were significant reasons causing tight vacancy rates in some market-economy countries. The Committee also studied human settlements problems in southern Europe, urban and regional planning, housing policies, building and settlements statistics. Recommendations that had emerged from a seminar on policies for energy conservation in buildings (Espoo, Finland, 6-10 June) were reviewed and its report endorsed.

Also held were a seminar on the evaluation of housing quality (Copenhagen, Denmark, 3-7 October) and the Sixth Conference on Urban and Regional Research (Leipzig, German Democratic Republic, 17-21 October).

Statistics

The Conference of European Statisticians (thirty-sixth plenary session, Geneva, 13-17 June)[43] discussed annual and multi-annual statistical programmes throughout the region and the marketing of services. In reviewing its work on environment statistics, the Conference acknowledged the need to co-ordinate international efforts. Requests for environment statistics were growing noticeably in a large number of countries, particularly among the general public. As to the direction of future work, the Conference noted that, along with its own conclusions, ECE had requested it to place environment statistics among its four priority areas. The Conference also discussed the organization and operation of statistical services, including the use of computers and the development of statistical information systems,

and methodologies in collecting, processing, disseminating, and analysing statistical data.

Meetings that dealt with statistics in 1988 included: Working Parties on National Accounts and Balances (2-5 May) and on Transport Statistics (5-8 December); a seminar on integrated statistical information systems and related matters (Bratislava, Czechoslovakia, 16-20 May); and a meeting on statistics concerning engineering industries and automation (17-19 October).

Standardization

The Tenth Meeting of Government Officials Responsible for Standardization Policies (Geneva, 30 May–3 June)[44] noted that developments in standardization had been very rapid both within and between the European Communities, EFTA and CMEA, and that the GATT Agreement on Technical Barriers to Trade was under renegotiation as part of the Uruguay Round of multilateral trade negotiations. Standardization took on even more importance in the perspective of the planned establishment of the so-called single European market in 1992. ECE provided the only forum in which information about standardization developments could be exchanged and policies co-ordinated between all parties concerned.

At the international level, considerable progress was reported by the International Electrotechnical Commission (IEC) in a number of areas, such as that of increasing the speed at which international standards were produced, and that of increasing the co-operation between IEC and the International Organization for Standardization.

In April,[17] ECE endorsed a recommendation made by the Group of Experts on Standardization Policies that a one-day seminar on metrology be held during the Tenth Meeting and authorized the Meeting to convene a three-day meeting of experts in the first half of 1989 to prepare for the Eleventh Meeting.

Also in April,[10] ECE reiterated its invitation to all European ECE members to introduce summertime and invited Governments to consider making provisions to ensure that a medium-term period of summertime would be applied for the same years in all European ECE countries.

Other activities

ECE/UNDP joint projects

Several meetings were held in 1988 regarding ECE/UNDP operational projects. The Steering Committee of the Trans-European North-South Motorway Project met at Istanbul (8-10 June). The Executive Technical Experts Committee also met (Belgrade, Yugoslavia, 12 October), as did the Steering Committee of the Statistical Computing Project, Phase 2 (Geneva, 9-11 November).

An *ad hoc* meeting on the inter-country project on international co-operative research on low-calorie solid fuel technology also took place (Belgrade, 10-12 October).

Women

In April,[6] ECE requested the Executive Secretary to continue assessing developments with respect to the economic role of women in the region, in conjunction with the work of the principal subsidiary bodies and with other research activities of the secretariat.

Programme questions

In April,[2] ECE approved its 1988-1989 work programme and endorsed, in principle, a work programme for 1988-1992.

Membership

In 1987,[45] the Economic and Social Council, after considering the Executive Secretary's report on his consultations with member States on the question of admitting Israel to the Commission, had decided to defer consideration of a draft decision on the matter to its July 1988 session. On 28 July 1988, the Council, by **decision 1988/172**, deferred consideration of the draft decision to its second regular session of 1989.

REFERENCES

[1]E/1988/36. [2]*Ibid.* (res. 1(43)). [3]*Ibid.* (dec. P(43)). [4]*Ibid.* (dec. E(43)). [5]*Ibid.*(dec. A(43)). [6]*Ibid.* (dec. B(43)). [7]*Ibid.* (dec. C(43)). [8]*Ibid.* (dec. D(43)). [9]*Ibid.* (dec. F(43)). [10]*Ibid.* (dec. G(43)). [11]*Ibid.* (dec. H(43)). [12]*Ibid.* (dec. I(43)). [13]*Ibid.* (dec. J(43)). [14]*Ibid.* (dec. K(43)). [15]*Ibid.* (dec. L(43)). [16]*Ibid.* (dec. M(43)). [17]*Ibid.* (dec. N(43)). [18]*Ibid.* (dec. O(43)). [19]*East-West Joint Ventures: Economic, Business, Financial and Legal Aspects*, Sales No. E.88.II.E.18. [20]E/1989/61. [21]ECE/EC.AD./31. [22]*Overall Economic Perspective to the Year 2000*, Sales No. E.88.II.E.4. [23]ECE/TRADE/164. [24]ECE/TRANS/72. [25]ECE/CHEM/70. [26]ECE/ENG.AUT/34. [27]ECE/STEEL/63. [28]ECE/ENERGY/13. [29]YUN 1987, p. 548. [30]ECE/COAL/117. [31]ECE/EP/76. [32]ECE/GAS/92. [33]YUN 1987, p. 549. [34]ECE/ENVWA/3 & Add.1,2. [35]ECE/AGRI/96. [36]YUN 1987, p. 1204. [37]ECE/TIM/42. [38]ECE/SC.TECH./35. [39]YUN 1986, p. 559. [40]ECE/EB.AIR/18. [41]YUN 1979, p. 710. [42]ECE/HBP/74. [43]ECE/CES/32. [44]ECE/STAND/30. [45]YUN 1987, p. 550, ESC dec. 1987/164, 8 July 1987.

Latin America and the Caribbean

Celebrating its fortieth anniversary in 1988, the Economic Commission for Latin America and the Caribbean, which held its twenty-second session at Rio de Janeiro, Brazil, from 20 to 27 April,[1] focused on open trade, structural adjustment and economic growth as three of the region's top priorities.

The Commission adopted 11 resolutions at its 1988 session. In connection with preparations for a new international development strategy for the fourth United Nations development decade (the 1990s), ECLAC was requested to prepare a report for analysis by the Committee of High-level Government Experts in 1989.[2] The Commission also resolved that the Committee would analyse ways of intensifying economic co-operation among developing countries of the region[3] and urged ECLAC member countries to intensify their support for ECLAC activities aimed at strengthening technical co-operation among developing countries.[4]

After considering a report by the World Commission on Environment and Development, ECLAC ordered a review of its programmes aimed at contributing to sustainable development.[5] It emphasized the need for alternative solutions for strengthening the region's role in the international economic system and resuming the process of sustained development that had been affected by the economic crisis and external debt.[6]

The Commission expressed support for the Latin American and Caribbean Institute for Economic and Social Planning (ILPES) on its twenty-fifth anniversary[7] and called for adequate financing for the Latin American Demographic Centre.[8] It further adopted the calendar of conferences for 1988-1990[9] and the 1990-1991 work programme,[10] and admitted Aruba as an associate member of the Commission.[11]

It also recommended to the Economic and Social Council that the twenty-third session of ECLAC be held at Caracas, Venezuela, in 1990;[12] the recommendation was approved by the Council on 28 July (**decision 1988/171**).

The Caribbean Development and Co-operation Committee held its eleventh session in St. Croix, United States Virgin Islands (18-22 November).[13] It adopted resolutions regarding support for Haiti and the Dominican Republic, policies on harmful wastes in the environment, a programme of assistance to small island developing countries and its own role. The Committee also admitted Aruba as an associate member.

Taking up the question of co-operation between the United Nations and the Latin American Economic System, the General Assembly requested the Secretary-General to promote a 1989 meeting between the respective secretariats to identify areas for broader co-operation (resolution 43/5).

After reviewing the Secretary-General's Special Plan of Economic Co-operation for Central America, the Assembly urged the international community to support the Plan (42/231) and recommended a meeting early in 1989 between the Central American Governments, the co-operating community, the United Nations system, international financial institutions and intergovernmental organizations to review support for the Plan's goals and objectives (43/210).

Economic trends

During 1988, the economic crisis in Latin America and the Caribbean reached dramatic proportions, according to a summary of the *Economic Survey of Latin America and the Caribbean, 1988*.[14] Per capita output fell for the first time since the recession of 1981-1983, to an amount barely equal to that obtained in 1978. Inflation more than doubled, averaging an unprecedented 530 per cent and real wages and salaries decreased in most countries.

The region's economy had performed badly for eight consecutive years and gave evidence that imbalances associated with debt servicing, the fiscal crisis and the scarcity of foreign exchange had acquired a momentum of their own, reflected in growing inflationary pressures, weakening investment and reduced leeway for implementing economic policy.

Export earnings grew during 1988 due to a rise in the prices of non-energy commodities. However, in most countries the rise did not boost economic growth, as earnings were not used to increase imports but to finance the increased outward transfer of resources, which rose by nearly 75 per cent to $28.9 billion—one of the highest levels since the debt crisis began in 1982.

During the year, the region's GDP rose by only 0.7 per cent, which was lower than that of 1987 and also lower than the growth rate of the population. Consequently, per capita product fell by 1.5 per cent to a level 6.5 per cent lower than in 1980.

The poor economic growth rate of the region was particularly influenced by conditions in three countries that accounted for nearly three quarters of the regional product: the Brazilian economy remained virtually stagnant, while very slight growth was recorded in Argentina and Mexico. It was also affected by sharp drops in economic activity in Panama (−20 per cent), Nicaragua (−9 per cent) and Peru (−8.5 per cent), as well as slower growth in most other economies of the region.

The most notable rise in inflation took place for the third consecutive year in Nicaragua where, between September 1987 and September 1988, consumer prices rose by close to 7,800 per cent. Inflation in Peru rose from 115 per cent in 1987 to 1,720 per cent in 1988, while Brazil recorded a 930 per cent rise. Argentina's inflation rose from 175 to nearly 390 per cent, Ecuador's by 86 per cent and the Dominican Republic's by 57 per cent. Inflation intensified in Bolivia, Colombia and Costa Rica but remained under 30 per cent. In Uruguay, inflation flared up again after slackening for the two preceding years. Venezuela showed a rate of 35 per cent and Chile 13 per cent. Barbados, Jamaica, Haiti, Honduras, Panama and Trinidad and Tobago recorded rises in inflation of under 10 per cent. Mexico's rate dropped from 160 per cent in 1987 to 52 per cent in 1988.

The growth in foreign trade during 1988 made it possible to finance nearly 80 per cent of the net payments of interest and profits. This growth, combined with the greater trade surplus, resulted in only a slight rise in the deficit on current account from $9.8 billion in 1987 to nearly $10 billion. However, external financing shrank considerably, so that overall balance of payments moved from a surplus of $4.1 billion in 1987 to a deficit of $5.1 billion in 1988.

The net transfer of resources abroad rose dramatically. Those transfers, which in the preceding two years had followed a downward pattern, rose from $16.6 billion in 1987 to $28.7 billion in 1988—equal to nearly a quarter of the value of the region's exports of goods and services and about 4 per cent of GDP.

Because of the low influx of new loans and the rise in debt conversion transactions in a number of countries, the external debt of Latin America and the Caribbean fell in 1988 for the first time in absolute terms. Estimates showed that the amount fell from $410 billion to $401 billion, mostly due to reductions of some 7 per cent in the debts of Bolivia and Chile and of close to 5.5 per cent in those of Brazil and Mexico.

The year marked the prolongation of the ongoing economic crisis of the region in the 1980s. However, 1988 differed from previous years in one important aspect: the rise in the international prices of many of the region's primary exports, excluding petroleum. Although that increase in the purchasing power of exports should have facilitated greater rates of economic expansion, that scenario did not occur, partly because higher interest rates spurred the transfer of resources abroad and, especially, because of the extremely limited access to new financing. Also, the weight of the accumulated effect of the crisis worked against whatever adjustment policies were in place to handle it.

The management of economic policy had become increasingly difficult since the beginning of the decade. Public finances had been affected by downward trends in income and upward pressures on spending. Also, the drop in real wages associated with rising inflation not only had aggravated domestic problems but had also caused considerable social and political tension. It had become increasingly difficult to overcome long-standing structural obstacles to development, such as antiquated educational systems, inefficient agrarian structures, the scanty application of technical progress to production and out-of-date financial and tax systems. The recession had also served to accentuate the acutely unequal distribution of wealth, long present in many Latin American societies.

For their part, the Governments of the main highly indebted Latin American countries had tried various ways to reduce their debts. In December, the Ministers of Finance of seven countries of the region met in Rio de Janeiro to examine available options. Three points were recognized as crucial to resolving the crisis. First, a consensus was emerging that some multilateral organizations should be established to collaborate with the countries in their efforts to repurchase part of their old debt or to convert it into new, long-term securities. Secondly, although creditors had continuously insisted that any solution be kept within the rules of the market and be voluntary, that principle should be kept within certain limits; at very least it should be accepted that maximum interest rates might be fixed on the accumulated debt. Thirdly, a larger amount of new financing was required from multinational organizations such as the Inter-American Development Bank (IDB), the World Bank and the International Monetary Fund.

In **decision 1988/181** of 29 July, the Economic and Social Council took note of the summary of the economic survey of Latin America and the Caribbean, 1987.[15]

Activities in 1988

Development policy and regional economic co-operation

In 1988, ECLAC's Economic Development Division continued to examine the short-term economic evolution of all the countries of the region and considered and recommended economic policies and strategies to promote strong, sustained, equitable and autonomous development. Activities in the area of information and documentation for economic and social development were carried out by the Latin America Centre for Economic and Social Documentation.

Operational activities for technical co-operation in fiscal review and policy were also undertaken. Seven technical reports were published on such topics as an accounting framework for evaluating fiscal policy in Latin America, fiscal policy in the 1980s, the measurement and breakdown of the public deficit in Latin America and the results of four national case-studies. National seminars were held to discuss the results of the case-studies, and a regional meeting on methodologies for measuring the public deficit and evaluating fiscal policy also took place.

With regard to stabilization, adjustment and the external debt, progress was made at the ECLAC subregional headquarters in Mexico in modernizing the recording of debt in the Central American countries. Computerized data-processing systems were installed, and the recording systems used by agencies in some countries were converted to centralized systems covering the entire national debt.

ECLAC provided technical assistance to the ministers responsible for following up the Special Plan of Economic Co-operation for Central America (see below). In co-ordination with the secretariat of the General Treaty on Central American Economic Integration, the Central American Research Institute for Industry and UNDP, work continued on drafting a document on the assessment of industrial reconversion needs in Central America.

The Commission continued in 1988 to monitor international economic trends, especially changes in the economies of the industrialized countries, in order to ascertain their effects on the region's development. A number of studies by international and national bodies were analysed, including some conducted by countries of the Organisation for Economic Co-operation and Development (OECD). To help establish tentative guidelines for a medium- and long-term industrialization strategy for the countries of the region, a study was also made of changes in production patterns. Activities in the area of economic projections were ongoing, providing the quantitative framework for prospective studies.

In 1988, ECLAC participated in meetings, seminars and conferences under its programme on development issues and policies. These included: courses/seminars on the Planning Information System for Latin America and the Caribbean (INFOPLAN) (Caracas, 4-8 April; Managua, Nicaragua, 18-22 April; La Paz, Bolivia, 25-29 April); a subregional course on strategic planning in information (San José, Costa Rica, 5-9 April); the twenty-fourth session of the Committee for Development Planning (New York, 12-14 April); an INFOPLAN course on management of information systems (San José, 25-29 April); a meeting on the progress of debt negotiations in Mexico, organized by the World Institute for Development Economics Research of the United Nations University (Mexico City, 2 May); a seminar on underutilization of manpower—situation and policies, organized by the International Labour Organisation (Buenos Aires, Argentina, 7 June); a working group on economic issues (Washington, D.C., 9 September); a seminar on debt and structural adjustment (Managua, 18-22 September); a seminar on industrial policy in developing countries, organized by the Economic System Reform Institute of China and the Friedrich Ebert Foundation (Beijing, 20 September–4 October); an international colloquium on strategies of development in Latin American countries, organized by Fundación Raúl Prebisch, El Colegio de México and Instituto Tecnológico Autónomo de México (Mexico City, 17-22 October); a seminar on international energy prospects: case-study of Latin America (Rio de Janeiro, 24-27 October); a seminar on economic reporting, organized by the International Press Service (Buenos Aires, 3-5 November); and a meeting of officials of integration bodies responsible for the Special Plan of Economic Co-operation for Central America (Guatemala City, 7-8 November), to make arrangements for the preparatory meeting of the Support Committee of the Central American Development Co-operation Group (New York, 28 and 29 November).

Industrial, scientific and technological development

In the area of industrial development, the main activities of ECLAC focused in 1988 on industrial restructuring at the international level and in Latin America, support for small- and medium-scale industry and the capital goods industry. Closer contacts were systematically sought with the Latin American entrepreneurial sector, academic circles and international bodies working in related fields, including the World Bank, OECD and IDB.

Training courses were given on industrial and technological policies and problems within the framework of ILPES. The year also marked the inception of a multidivisional project on changes in production patterns and international competitiveness, in which the following divisions, in addition to the Industry and Technology Division, participated: the Joint ECLAC/FAO Agriculture Division, the Transport and Communications Division, the Natural Resources and Energy Division and the International Trade and Development Division.

In addition, a regional preparatory assistance project financed by UNDP on technological innovation and international competitiveness was formulated, and several publications on research project results were published.

Regarding science and technology, ECLAC activities focused on technological development and the region's challenges as related to the current worldwide revolution in the field. Also, case-studies were carried out on technological innovation and international competitiveness in a number of countries, including Argentina, Brazil, Colombia, Costa Rica and Mexico. A methodological approach was also developed for studying the links between international trade and the transfer of technology.

In 1988, a seminar on industrial restructuring and international competitiveness was organized (Santiago, Chile, 5-7 December). ECLAC participated in a United States social scientists working group on Latin America (New Orleans, 17-19 March); a meeting on the regional co-operation programme in the field of pharmaceuticals, organized by the Latin American Economic System (SELA) (Caracas, 11-13 May); a seminar on joint investment in co-operation with developing countries, organized by the Government of Italy (Bergamo and Modena, 12-16 June); a World Bank seminar on technological change (Washington, D.C., 6 and 7 July); a seminar on trends in Brazil at the beginning of the twenty-first century (São Paulo, 1-5 August); a meeting on evaluation of UNDP regional programmes on technology exchange, organized by OECD (Paris, 14 and 15 September); and a forum on the capital goods industry as a tool in the development of Peru (Lima, 24-27 November).

International trade and development finance

The International Trade and Development Division focused on three main areas in 1988: Latin America and the proposed new international economic order; economic relations between Latin America and other regions; and economic integration and co-operation.

Under the first topic, in a follow-up of the current multilateral trade negotiations within GATT, known as the Uruguay Round, reports which sought to identify the strategic interest pursued by the Latin American countries were prepared and analysed in collaboration with UNCTAD.

Concerning commodities, three main lines of activity were developed. The first dealt with the growing role of commodity exchanges, especially futures markets, in the pricing of commodities. This was done on the basis of special studies made of the London Metal Exchange, the Chicago grain market and the New York tropical commodities market. The second dealt with the impact of the latest forms of technological progress on market prospects for some commodities. The third line involved a global examination of the current status of Latin America's export commodities and the various factors that affected market prospects.

Various activities were carried out with respect to services, with a report being published on Latin American co-operation and work being carried out on producer services on the one hand and on service-sector statistics on the other.

In 1988, the Division organized a seminar on main issues and prospects for the participation of the Latin American and Caribbean countries in the Uruguay Round (Santiago, 26-28 October); the first subregional seminar on informatics (Lima, 21 and 22 November); a Latin American seminar on the improvement of statistics on services (Lima, 23 and 24 November); a regional seminar on producer services (Lima, 25 and 26 November); and a seminar on co-operation in science and technology (Montevideo, Uruguay, 5-7 December).

The Division also participated in a number of meetings and seminars during the year, including a meeting of ministers responsible for Central American integration (Guatemala City, 7 and 8

January); a meeting of Central American vice-presidents (Guatemala City, 21-23 January); a seminar on direct foreign investment and trade in services (Lima, 29 January–5 February); a meeting on development strategies and alternatives in times of crisis (Quito, Ecuador, 29 February–2 March); a national seminar on services (Havana, Cuba, 29 February–4 March); a second meeting of agencies responsible for services (Caracas, 12 March); a second meeting of regional economic bodies, convened by SELA (Caracas, 22 March); a seminar on external debt, macro-economic policies and growth (Mendoza, Argentina, 29-31 March); a seminar of European parliamentarians on peace and development in Central America (Oxford, England, 7-11 April); a meeting on the 1988-1990 work programme of the Association of Latin American and Caribbean Economists (Havana, 16-29 April); a round table on trade policies and food security (Santiago, 7-10 May); the eighteenth general meeting of the Latin American Association of Development Financing Institutions (Buenos Aires, 16-19 May); a meeting on trade strategy and negotiations in Latin America (Caracas, 6 and 7 June); a meeting of experts to analyse the relations between debt and trade (Caracas, 16 and 17 June); a meeting of ministers responsible for economic integration (Guatemala City, 17 and 18 June); the eighth meeting of Latin American and Caribbean agencies responsible for economic integration and co-operation (Lima, 21 and 22 July); a meeting of vice-ministers responsible for economic integration (Guatemala City, 26-30 July); a seminar on trade negotiations and the Uruguay Round (San José, 27-30 July); a colloquium on the international economy (La Paz, 10-12 August); a seminar on the impact of United States policies on Central America (San José, 10-13 August); the first meeting of the programme on co-operation with respect to regional integration (San José, 12-16 October); a seminar on industrial prospects in Nicaragua (Managua, 16-20 October); a seminar on the Andean Group and the Uruguay Round (Santa Cruz, Bolivia, 29 October–2 November); the forty-fourth session of the Contracting Parties to GATT (Geneva, 7-9 November); a seminar on adjustment programmes and the external debt, organized jointly by the Centre for Latin American Monetary Studies and the Central Bank of Costa Rica (San José, 25 and 26 November); a regional seminar on producer services (Lima, 25 and 26 November); and a seminar on co-operation and regional integration of Central America and Europe (Maastricht, Netherlands, 4-16 December).

Natural resources and energy

Promotion and support of co-operation between countries of the region in the management of water resources, development and conservation of high-altitude river basins, co-operation in the exploitation of minerals and assistance in the elaboration of national policies concerning the oceans all came under the focus of the Natural Resources and Energy Division during 1988. The Division also carried out its mandates to follow up on the implementation of the 1977 Mar del Plata Action Plan[16] and the International Drinking Water Supply and Sanitation Decade (1981-1990), proclaimed by the General Assembly in 1980,[17] and undertook studies on natural disasters, the quality of water in the region and water supply and sanitation for the most disadvantaged sectors of society.

In the area of maritime resources, support continued to be provided for the activities of Governments under the 1982 United Nations Convention on the Law of the Sea,[18] and particularly activities arising from the Preparatory Commission for the International Sea-Bed Authority and for the International Tribunal for the Law of the Sea. Concerning mineral resources, support continued to be provided for the work programme of the Latin American Mining Organization (OLAMI), particularly in setting up the second phase of the Latin American Regional Mining Information and Documentation System. A technical *ad hoc* working group was set up to assist the mining/metallurgical sector of the region in promoting intraregional trade in products, inputs and mining-related capital goods. The group was set up in conjunction with a number of groups and institutions throughout the region, including OLAMI and LATINEQUIP, a consortium comprising the Banco de la Provincia de Buenos Aires, the Banco del Estado de São Paulo and the Nacional Financiera S.A. of Mexico.

The Division organized two events in 1988: a consultative meeting of the project on training in the management of water resource projects and systems (Mendoza, 21-23 March) and a meeting of the group of experts advising the Latin American Group in the Preparatory Commission for the International Sea-Bed Authority and for the International Tribunal for the Law of the Sea (Santiago, 9-11 November).

In the specific area of energy, the Division concentrated on the themes of energy forecasting, energy prices and their impact on world energy markets and the updating of ECLAC's energy data bank. A study was undertaken on short-term energy forecasting using time-series techniques, with particular emphasis on the use of the Auto-regressive Integrated Moving Average method. Work also progressed on the study of the use of vector autoregression as an energy forecast method.

Studies on energy pricing were also undertaken, including one to examine the patterns of change in retail prices of refined oil products in selected

Latin American countries during the 1970s and 1980s, and another to examine the dependence of various oil-deficit Latin American countries since the 1960s. At ECLAC subregional headquarters in Mexico, studies were carried out on the development of new and renewable sources of energy in Central America.

Technical assistance was provided to the six national electricity corporations in connection with the initiation of work on the draft programme of regional activities in the electricity subsector of Central America and the updating, jointly with the World Bank, of the catalogue of priority projects in the electricity subsector.

In 1988, ECLAC participated in meetings, seminars and conferences under its programmes on energy and natural resources. These included: a round-table meeting on international participation in the forestry development of Honduras (Tegucigalpa, 24-27 January); the eleventh meeting of the Central American Regional Electrical Interconnection Group (San Salvador, El Salvador, 25 and 26 February); a seminar on the operation of interconnected systems (Managua, 17-24 March); the fourth session of the Committee on the Development and Utilization of New and Renewable Sources of Energy and the seventh session of the Inter-Agency Group on New and Renewable Sources of Energy (New York, 28 March–8 April); a regional seminar on schemes for low-frequency load shedding (Mexico City, 20-22 April); a seminar on water and electricity tariffs (Washington, D.C., 6-8 June); a meeting on the development of new and renewable sources of energy in Central America and Panama (Mexico City, 25-27 July); the second international course on the development and management of river basins (Trento, Italy, 29 August–21 October); a seminar on the management of ecosystems (Turrialba, Costa Rica, 19-30 September); a regional seminar on water supply and sanitation (Recife, Brazil, 29 September–5 October); a seminar on water supply and sanitation for low-income populations in rural and periurban areas (Olinda, Pernambuco, Brazil, 29 September–5 October); a meeting on a systematic approach to rural development (Lima, 2-4 November); an international workshop on the management of the Panama Canal basin (Panama, 9-16 November); a seminar on energy saving (Culiacán, Mexico, 23-28 November); the first meeting of the Support Committee of the Central American Development Co-operation Group (New York, 27-30 November); and a meeting on intraregional trade in products, inputs, machinery and mining equipment (Montevideo, 5-9 December).

Transport

Some of the most important activities of the transport programme were carried out under the project on interior cargo terminals, funded by the Netherlands. The programme also collaborated with the Meeting of Ministers for Public Works and Transport of the Southern Cone Countries in formulating an annex on international transport by railroads to the Agreement on International Land Transport among the Southern Cone Countries. Support was provided to the Latin American Maritime Transport Commission of SELA in building a regional consensus in preparation for the October/November Review Conference on the Convention on a Code of Conduct for Liner Conferences (see PART THREE, Chapter IV). Also, ECE and UNCTAD were aided in establishing standards for the electronic transfer of administrative, trade and transport data.

National seminars on structural changes in the international transport chain and their impact on the policies of Latin American countries were held during 1988 in Argentina, Bolivia, Brazil, Chile, Colombia, Costa Rica, Ecuador, Paraguay, Peru and Uruguay. The programme organized a meeting on international rail transport (Buenos Aires, 6-8 April), a seminar on the future of container transport on the west coast of South America (Santiago, 19-22 April) and a national seminar on the uniform system of maritime transport statistics (Buenos Aires, 21 October).

The Commission participated in international, regional and national meetings, seminars and conferences under its transport programme. These included: a meeting of the *ad hoc* transport group of the Government on strengthening Mexico's transport relations with other Latin American countries (Mexico City, 25 and 26 January); a symposium on aeronautical development in the twenty-first century (Santiago, 15 and 16 March); the first meeting of the Permanent Tripartite Commission on the Los Libertadores–Buenos Aires–La Paz–Matarani Interoceanic Corridor (Jujuy, Argentina, 28 and 29 March); a meeting of Ministers for Public Works and Transport and the Physical Integration Council of the Board of the Cartagena Agreement (Quito, 16-20 May); a semi-annual meeting of the Caribbean Shipping Association (Basseterre, Saint Kitts and Nevis, 30 and 31 May); a national seminar on multimodal transport and the Hamburg Rules (Mexico City, 8 and 9 June); a meeting of experts on public works and transport of the Southern Cone countries (La Paz, 17-19 August); the sixth meeting of national customs directors of the Latin American Integration Association (Mar del Plata, Argentina, 17 and 18 October); the ninth meeting of national customs directors of Latin America, Spain and Portugal (Mar del Plata, 19-21 October); the third Latin American Congress on Public Transport/third Latin American meeting on urban transport (Lima, 7-10 November); a workshop on road maintenance planning (Santiago, 7-25 November); and the third Latin American and Caribbean seminar on experiences in road maintenance (Piriá-polis, Uruguay, 28 November–2 December).

Social development

The Social Development Division carried out a wide range of activities in 1988 relating to the social aspects of the current economic crisis. Studies were conducted on changes in various social actors, such as the trade union movement, urban dwellers and youth. A study was prepared on occupational changes and social mobility up until the period just prior to the outbreak of the crisis. Consideration was also given to the question of how to adapt broad social policies, through a study on the role of the State in development and on the different proposals to achieve greater economic equity. Studies were also undertaken on the challenges posed by the crisis to planning in the areas of health, education and housing, as well as on proposals aimed at securing the full incorporation of the poorest sectors, both rural and urban, into development.

Of particular importance was a seminar on social development options in the 1990s (San José, 15-18 November), where the national experiences of Argentina, Brazil, Colombia, Costa Rica, Guatemala, Mexico and Peru in economic and social development and social policies were presented. The main subjects discussed were related to diagnostic study of the social and economic situation of the region and of the countries under review, the challenges of the near future and the necessary interconnection between economic policy and social policy in the perspective of development aimed at achieving greater equity and democracy.

Also during the year, ECLAC participated in: an interregional preparatory meeting for the Eighth United Nations Congress on the Prevention of Crime and the Treatment of Offenders (Vienna, 14-18 March); a conference on social security, organized by the Mexican Social Security Institute and the Inter-American Center for Social Security Studies (Mexico, 17-19 March); a training workshop in planning (Madrid, Spain, 11-22 April); a seminar on youth, expectations and the future (Santiago, 8-10 June); a meeting on changes in the social structure of Latin America, organized by the Latin American Council for the Social Sciences (Porto Alegre, Brazil, 22-25 August); the tenth session of the Committee on Crime Prevention and Control (Vienna, 23-31 August); the XIV World Congress of the International Political Science Association (Washington, D.C., 28-31 August); the Conference on Social Conflict in Latin America (Cartagena, Colombia, 29 August–1 September); an inter-agency meeting on crime prevention and criminal justice (Vienna, 1 and 2 September); the annual meeting of the American Political Science Association (Washing-ton, D.C., 1-4 September); the XVII Latin American Congress on Sociology (Montevideo, 2-6 December); and a conference on the prospects for social development in Latin America, organized by the Italy/FAO Training Programme in the Planning of Agricultural Development Policies and Projects (Buenos Aires, 8-14 December).

Population

The work of the Latin American Demographic Centre (CELADE) was aimed at furthering the economic and social development of the countries in the region through a programme of work addressing problems relating specifically to population and development. The Centre established close ties with national institutions concerned with economic and social development in the region, paying particular attention to sectoral policy needs and to the needs of the less privileged groups in the population. Those groups were the subject of studies on such topics as the incorporation of women into development and the socio-economic situation of the aged.

Within the framework of the 1987 agreement concluded at the Esquipulas II Summit,[19] a project was formulated with the Intergovernmental Committee for Migration with the aim of helping to solve the problems of displaced populations in Central America. Consultations were held with international institutions associated with this problem, including, in particular, the Office of the United Nations High Commissioner for Refugees. A feasibility study was carried out on the installation of national systems for the provision of information on displaced populations, and a draft request for assistance from the United Nations Population Fund (UNFPA) was prepared.

CELADE began helping countries to utilize systems for obtaining disaggregated data on population and housing, for making projections of small areas by microcomputer and for facilitating the inclusion of population variables in development planning. Such systems included REDATAM (retrieval of data for small areas by microcomputer) and PANDEM (package for demographic analysis by microcomputer). Work was also begun on the creation of a Latin American and Caribbean population information network (POPIN), as part of a strategy designed to increase the use of research findings and of numerical data by the public and private sectors.

In 1988, CELADE inaugurated an annual postgraduate course at its headquarters in Santiago. The 10-month course covered population dynamics and development programmes and policies in an action-oriented structure, the aim being to increase the number of professionals in the individual countries who were capable of helping to incorporate demographic factors in development programmes. The teaching programme also included short-term training activities such as regional and national courses, seminars and workshops.

The population programme organized the Latin American seminar on collection and processing of demographic data (Santiago, 23-27 May) and a workshop on the incorporation of women in development projects (Buenos Aires, 24 July–6 August).

It also participated in an UNFPA inter-agency consultative meeting (New York, 28 and 29 January); a meeting on fertility and family planning organized by the International Union for the Scientific Study of Population (Bangkok, 22 March–2 April); the UNFPA Global Conference (New York, 7 and 8 April); an expert group meeting on international transmission of population-policy experiences (New York, 27-30 June); a POPIN working group meeting on microcomputer and other training strategy for 1988-1991 (New York, 5-8 July); a workshop on the demographic consequences of economic development: implications for agrarian and rural development, organized by the Cuban Centre for Demographic Studies and the University of Havana (Havana, 5-15 July); the fourth meeting of the health sector of Central America and Panama and the eighth Latin American meeting of the Econometric Society (San José, August); the first meeting of the Regional Census Co-ordinating Committee, organized by the secretariat of the Caribbean Community (Georgetown, Guyana, 4-6 October); a conference on dissemination and use of census data, sponsored by UNFPA, the United States Agency for International Development, the International Statistical Programmes Centre and the Egyptian Central Agency for Public Mobilization and Statistics (Cairo, 9-13 October); a seminar on evaluation of information networks in Latin America, organized by the Cuban Centre for Demographic Studies (Havana, 20-22 October); a consultative workshop of the United Nations Asia-Pacific POPIN (Bangkok, 26 October–3 November); a seminar on household, employment and unemployment surveys, organized by the Ministry of the Economy, Industry and Commerce and the Department of Statistics and Censuses (San José, November); a scientific workshop on population aging, organized by the Cuban Centre for Demographic Studies (Havana, November); a workshop on population in the Dominican Republic in the year 2000, organized by UNDP to collect background data for the formulation of a global population programme (Santo Domingo, November); the sixth regional conference of officials responsible for employment planning in Latin America and the Caribbean (Guatemala City, December); a subregional seminar on municipal information for Central America, Mexico and the Caribbean (San José, December); and a Central American subregional workshop for producers and users of statistics and indicators relating to women in development, organized by the International Research and Training Institute for the Advancement of Women, the United Nations Statistical Office and the National Centre for Women and the Family of Costa Rica (San José, December).

Integration of women

The fourth Regional Conference on the Integration of Women into the Economic and Social Development of Latin America and the Caribbean was held in 1988 (Guatemala City, 27-30 September). Its purpose was to evaluate what had been done to meet the requirements of the Regional Plan of Action for the Integration of Women into Latin American Economic and Social Development, in the light of the 1985 Nairobi Forward-looking Strategies for the Advancement of Women,[20] and taking into consideration the impact of the economic crisis on the situation of women. The Conference made a number of recommendations for action at the national level, as well as at the international and regional levels. It also concluded that, in 1988, there was a consensus that the advancement of women was a matter not only for women but for the entire society.

The Presiding Officers of the Regional Conference on the Integration of Women into the Economic and Social Development of Latin America and the Caribbean held their eighth meeting in 1988 (Guatemala City, 26 September).

Meetings and seminars participated in by ECLAC included: the thirty-second session of the Commission on the Status of Women (Vienna, 14-23 March); a seminar on policies on young women in Latin America (Montevideo, 22-24 March); an *ad hoc* inter-agency meeting on women (Vienna, 24 and 25 March); a training workshop on the evaluation of income-generating projects of peasant women (Santiago, 12-15 April); an inter-regional consultative meeting on women in co-operatives: implications for development (Bulgaria, 20-24 June); a seminar on the world of women, continuity and change (Santiago, 26 July); a United Nations interregional seminar on women and the economic crisis: impact, policies and prospects (Vienna, 3-7 October); an expert group meeting on social support measures for advancement of women (Vienna, 14-18 November); a regional seminar on women in human settlements and development management (Lima, 21-25 November); and the first national encounter of the Centre for the Prevention of Domestic Violence and Assistance to Battered Women (Chapadmalal, Argentina, 24-26 November).

Environment

The activities of the environment programme, carried out by the Joint ECLAC/UNEP Development and Environment Unit, were aimed first at strengthening the incorporation of the environmental dimension into the work performed by the ECLAC system and then at promoting action in the countries of the region regarding strategies and policies for bringing about environmentally sustainable development.

ECLAC/UNEP began work on the second phase of a project on technical co-operation for the integration of environmental considerations into development planning in Latin America and the Caribbean. Under the project, preparation began for studies for Argentina, Ecuador, Honduras and Peru concerning relations between the environment and macro-economic variables within the context of those countries' recent development pattern. Work also began on preliminary technical reports for use in considering methods for evaluating environmental impact, and studies were reviewed concerning the relationship between external debt and the processes of environmental deterioration in the region. Another project was begun on natural and cultural environments within national accounts and inventories.

The first seminar on the rehabilitation of terraces and other traditional technologies was organized by ECLAC in 1988 (Lima, 4-6 May). It also participated in a meeting on environmental management (Caracas, 25-28 April); a conference on structural adjustment in the third world (Burlington, United States, 28-30 April); and a meeting to establish the Latin American headquarters of the International Institute for Environment and Development (Buenos Aires, 6 and 7 May); an international conference on the regulation theory (Barcelona, Spain, 15-19 June); a conference on prospects for the future, including environmental sustainability (Campinhas, Brazil, 3-8 July); a conference on enviromental management of development and national heritage accounts (San Juan, Argentina, 16 August); the first and second series of Ibero-American technical meetings, on environmental engineering and development and on mining (Bogotá, Colombia, 9-13 October and 20-26 November); and a seminar/workshop on economic policy, organized by the International Press Service (Buenos Aires, 3-5 November).

Human settlements

The human settlements programme, carried out through a joint unit of ECLAC and the United Nations Centre for Human Settlements (UNCHS),

strengthened its research and development activities, especially in relation to the functioning of metropolitan centres, the strengthening of local government capacity to manage human settlements and the formulation of housing policies in the context of national development strategies. The unit also did preliminary work on the role of non-governmental and community organizations in managing the habitat.

Concerning training, an agreement was reached on the establishment of a regional training system of policy-making and financial administration for urban development projects in Latin America. Also, the joint unit increased significantly its technical support activities and exchanges of experience with countries in the region, as part of a policy aimed at establishing closer contact with national agencies operating in the housing and human settlements sector. The unit contributed to the Commission's efforts to assess the economic and social effects of natural disasters.

The unit participated in several meetings during 1988: a seminar on rural local governments and social participation, organized jointly with Chilean Agrarian Research Group (Santiago, 28 and 29 July); a meeting of experts on formulating an international plan for low-cost housing in the third world, organized by ECLAC, the International Union of Architects and UNCHS (Santiago, 22-26 August); a regional seminar on natural disasters and the planning of human settlements, organized by Ecuador, ECLAC, UNCHS and the Office of the United Nations Disaster Relief Co-ordinator (Quito, 3-8 October); a meeting of experts on the establishment of a regional training programme in municipal administration and finance, organized by ECLAC, the World Bank, IDB, the International Union of Local Authorities and UNCHS; an international seminar on technologies for human settlements, organized by the Instituto Eduardo Torroja, Spain (Madrid, 1-9 May); a seminar on the quality of life, organized by the Municipality of Lanús, Argentina (Buenos Aires, 15-20 May); a meeting on Latin American experiences in urban renewal and participation, organized by the Dominican Centre for Legal Advisory Assistance and Research of the Dominican Republic (Santo Domingo, 21-27 September); a seminar on metropolitan alternatives (Mexico City, 19-21 October); the second meeting on the programme for a regional training system in urban management and planning (Quito, 21-23 November); the second Latin American Congress on Metropolitan Areas, organized by the National Commission for the Buenos Aires Metropolitan Area (Buenos Aires, 21-25 November); and an international seminar on financing the development of large cities, organized by the

Union of Ibero-American Capitals (Buenos Aires, 13-16 December).

Food and agriculture

As a result of work completed in 1987, significant collaboration was made possible with FAO in preparing a study on potentials for agricultural and rural development in Latin America and the Caribbean. FAO subsequently submitted the study to its October 1988 Regional Conference at Recife, Brazil.

Further analysis was undertaken both of the dynamic links between agriculture and industry and of the resulting transformations in agriculture. The main objective of the research—which included several case-studies—was to generate clear perceptions of the determinants of technological change in agriculture. The study of the region's agricultural entrepreneurs focused on the conditions under which that class developed, the position it adopted *vis-à-vis* government policies and its links to other productive agents, such as the industrial sector.

Progress was made in improving the criteria and methods of agricultural planning. A review was undertaken of the quantitative instruments used in the various phases of the sectoral planning process, in order to determine the effects on agriculture of the economic crisis and the resulting adjustment policies. ECLAC also collaborated in the training activities in policies and plans for agricultural development organized by ILPES and FAO.

Organized by the food and agriculture programme were a meeting on the role of agricultural entrepreneurs in Latin America (Santiago, 26-29 July) and a later workshop on the same subject (Santiago, 12-15 December); and an expert meeting on the production of citrus products in Central America (Mexico City, 24 and 25 November).

Meetings, seminars and conferences participated in by ECLAC included a seminar on biotechnology and food security (Mexico City, 24-30 March); the first seminar/workshop on rural development (Valdivia, Chile, 29-31 July); an international conference of agrarian economists (Buenos Aires, 24-31 August); a seminar on development and promotion of associations of agricultural producers (Rio de Janeiro, 17 September–6 October); a seminar on the role of the peasant economy in the agricultural recovery and development strategy (San José, 26-28 September); a meeting of the Inter-institutional Group for the Agricultural Sector (GISA) (Tegucigalpa, 27 September–1 October); an inter-American course on agricultural censuses (Santiago, 28 November–16 December); a seminar on the evolution of the peasant class in Chile and the need for integrated rural development (Los Angeles, Chile, 1 and 2 December); a meeting in support of the evaluation programme groups of the Institute of Nutrition of Central America and Panama (San José, 7-11 December); and the third meeting of GISA, convened by the permanent secretariat of the General Treaty on Central American Economic Integration (Panama, 13-17 December).

Statistics and economic projections

The development of the ECLAC statistics programme focused in 1988 on three major activities: expansion of data banks; technical co-operation; and dissemination of information, technological innovations and international standards.

In the context of enlarging data banks, priority was given to organizing data bases to be incorporated into on-line data banks, while at the same time expanding the coverage of subject-matter and countries included and providing a more timely distribution of information. The fastest-growing data banks were those of national accounts, foreign trade, balance of payments and statistics on social development. Work was also carried out towards the creation of an on-line data bank for analysing foreign trade data for the countries of the region, obtained via trade data from the developed countries and other non-customs sources, thereby offering the possibility of obtaining provisional but more up-to-date information.

Seminars organized by the programme were on: co-ordination of national statistics (Buenos Aires, 28 June–1 July); census administration and strategy (Lima, 24-28 October); national accounts (Buenos Aires, 14-18 November); telematics, statistics and producer services (Lima, 21-27 November); and census cartography (San José, 28 November–1 December). A round table on household surveys focusing on advances and prospects was also held (Tegucigalpa, 16-19 November).

ECLAC also participated in the sixth meeting of the Permanent Executive Committee of the Inter-American Statistical Conference (Aguascalientes, Mexico, 21-24 February); a co-ordination meeting on the inter-agency project on critical poverty in Latin America (Bogotá, 6-12 March); a technical seminar on measuring poverty in Argentina, Brazil and Uruguay (Montevideo, 10-15 April); the twenty-fourth session of the Committee for Development Planning (New York, 12-15 April); technical meetings on defining methodologies for national accounts in Brazil (Brasília, 1-6 May); a tripartite meeting on the project on information systems for public management in Guatemala (Guatemala City, 6-14 May); a meeting of the Committee on Programming and Co-ordination of the Household Surveys Programme in Honduras (Tegucigalpa, 8-14 May); a tripartite meeting of the project on change of the base year of Venezuela's national accounts (Caracas, 22-28 May); an interregional workshop on statistical data processing and data bases in developing countries (Geneva, 24 May–3 June); the twenty-second session of the Sub-Committee on Statistical

Activities of the Administrative Committee on Co-ordination (Geneva, 6-10 June); a seminar on widely used techniques for statistical data processing (Santiago, 20 June-1 July); a regional seminar on co-ordination of national statistics (Buenos Aires, 26 June-2 July); a tripartite meeting on the project on support for the development of the National Statistical System of Guatemala (Guatemala City, 27 September-1 October); a seminar on producer services (Lima, 25 and 26 November); and a round table on household survey advances and prospects under the Honduras/ECLAC/IDB project (San José, 27 November-2 December).

Transnational corporations

The joint ECLAC/Centre on Transnational Corporations unit continued work towards implementing the resolutions and mandates of the member States of both ECLAC and the Commission on Transnational Corporations. The unit focused on two areas: identifying the contribution and impact of TNCs on development in the region and its studies of particular issues in individual countries and sectors. Particular emphasis was placed on the manufacturing industry and services in research on the role of TNCs in international competitiveness.

The question of the transformation of the productive structures became a focus of the activities of the joint unit in 1988, and was linked to other research programmes such as that related to experiences and alternative policies on direct foreign investment in the countries of the region. Within that same area, emphasis was placed on the elaboration of a regional directory of foreign investment. The overall aim was to increase the data available on the activities of TNCs operating in the region and the impact of such activities, and systematically to elaborate homogeneous and comparable statistical series that would reinforce the position of the countries of the region in their negotiations with TNCs.

In 1988, the joint unit participated in the April session of the Commission on TNCs and in a workshop on debt-equity swaps (Caracas, 27-29 April).

Co-operation between the United Nations and the Latin American Economic System

Since the establishment of the Latin American Economic System in 1975, the ECLAC secretariat had frequently supplied its Permanent Secretariat with direct support and collaboration, the Secretary-General stated in a June 1988 report to the General Assembly.[21] The report was submitted pursuant to a 1987 Assembly resolution,[22] in which the Assembly had emphasized the need to reinforce collaboration between the United Nations and SELA.

Co-operation between ECLAC and SELA had been highly varied and fruitful over the years, involving frequent participation in meetings convened by SELA and the preparation of numerous specialized documents. Notably, an important document on regional economic security was published in 1982, while work on a document outlining Latin America's response to the international economic crisis became the starting-point for the 1984 Quito Declaration and Plan of Action,[23] adopted by the Latin American Economic Conference.

Several ongoing working links existed between ECLAC and SELA, including a project jointly implemented with UNDP and UNCTAD involving services, commodities and multilateral international negotiations, for which a number of meetings were held at government level. In 1987, ECLAC was the venue of the annual meeting of integration and co-operation organizations convened by SELA. In addition, in recent months the ECLAC secretariat had participated in SELA meetings, held to prepare a regional co-operation strategy to establish the Latin American and Caribbean Trade Information and External Sector Support Programme and to analyse a proposal for creating a Latin American reserve fund. Additional areas in which ECLAC and other United Nations bodies worked together with SELA included projects on science and technology, industrial development and technology, transportation and TNCs.

In January 1988, a meeting promoted by SELA was held at Caracas with bodies that had close links to it. Areas of co-ordinated activities between SELA and ECLAC were identified, including those relating to the industrialization of Latin America and the use to which its purchasing power was put. The two bodies agreed to intensify co-operation.

ECLAC had always attached great importance to the co-ordination of its activities with the Organization of American States and SELA.

GENERAL ASSEMBLY ACTION

On 17 October 1988, the General Assembly adopted **resolution 43/5** without vote.

Co-operation between the United Nations and the Latin American Economic System
The General Assembly,

Recalling its resolution 42/12 of 28 October 1987 on co-operation between the United Nations and the Latin American Economic System,

Having considered the report of the Secretary-General on co-operation between the United Nations and the Latin American Economic System,

Taking into account decision 282 of 20 September 1988 on co-operation between the United Nations and the Latin American Economic System, adopted at the fourteenth regular session of the Latin American Council, in which the conviction was expressed that General Assembly resolution 42/12 represents an important step towards further development of co-operation between the Latin American Economic System and the United Nations system,

Considering that the Economic Commission for Latin America and the Caribbean has developed close ties of co-operation with the Latin American Economic System and that, in the course of the last year, efforts have been successfully made at co-ordinating and mutually strengthening their activities,

Considering also that since 1976 the Permanent Secretariat of the Latin American Economic System has carried out various programmes with the support of the United Nations Development Programme in areas that are considered of priority for the economic development of the region,

Considering further that the Latin American Economic System is developing joint activities with specialized agencies and other bodies and programmes of the United Nations system, such as the United Nations Conference on Trade and Development, the United Nations Educational, Scientific and Cultural Organization, the United Nations Industrial Development Organization, the World Meteorological Organization, the World Health Organization, the World Intellectual Property Organization, the United Nations Environment Programme, the United Nations Centre on Transnational Corporations, the Office of the United Nations Disaster Relief Co-ordinator and the United Nations Institute for Training and Research,

1. _Takes note with satisfaction_ of the report of the Secretary-General;

2. _Expresses satisfaction_ with decision 282 of the Latin American Council of the Latin American Economic System;

3. _Expresses its gratitude_ for the constant efforts made by the Latin American Economic System in promoting co-operation among the countries of Latin America and the Caribbean, and consultation and co-ordination of their positions on subjects of vital importance to the region, as well as in enhancing their economic and social development;

4. _Welcomes with satisfaction_ the dialogue which the Ministers for Foreign Affairs of Latin American and Caribbean countries are holding on the occasion of the ordinary sessions of the Latin American Council of the Latin American Economic System;

5. _Urges_ the Economic Commission for Latin America and the Caribbean to broaden and deepen its co-ordination and mutual support activities with the Latin American Economic System, as well as its participation in common efforts to harmonize action among the various regional and subregional entities in the economic field;

6. _Urges_ the United Nations Development Programme to strengthen and broaden its support to the programme that the Permanent Secretariat of the Latin American Economic System is carrying out within the framework of the 1989-1991 work programme approved by the Latin American Council;

7. _Urges_ the specialized agencies and other organizations and programmes of the United Nations system to continue to intensify their co-operation with the activities of the Latin American Economic System;

8. _Requests_ the Secretary-General of the United Nations to promote, in close collaboration with the Permanent Secretary of the Latin American Economic System, the holding of a meeting in 1989 between their respective secretariats, with the aim of identifying those areas in which it will be possible to broaden co-operation between the United Nations system and the Latin American Economic System;

9. _Also requests_ the Secretary-General to continue to take the necessary measures to strengthen and intensify co-operation between the United Nations system and the Latin American Economic System, and to inform the General Assembly at its forty-fourth session of the implementation of the present resolution.

General Assembly resolution 43/5

17 October 1988   Meeting 32   Adopted without vote

26-nation draft (A/43/L.6); agenda item 28.
Sponsors: Argentina, Barbados, Bolivia, Brazil, Chile, Colombia, Costa Rica, Cuba, Dominican Republic, Ecuador, El Salvador, Grenada, Guatemala, Guyana, Haiti, Honduras, Jamaica, Mexico, Nicaragua, Panama, Paraguay, Peru, Suriname, Trinidad and Tobago, Uruguay, Venezuela.

Special plan of economic co-operation for Central America

A proposed special plan of economic co-operation for Central America was submitted by the Secretary-General to the General Assembly in April 1988,[24] pursuant to a 1987 resolution.[25] The Secretary-General requested funding of $4,370,690 for the special programme.

The proposal gave a brief history of the economies of Central America and the main characteristics of the current crisis. The countries involved had witnessed a deterioration in their levels of economic activity, and the international recession had gradually helped to exacerbate the most conspicuous areas of strangulation in both everyday life and the financial sphere. Significant manifestations of the crisis had emerged in the form of contraction of the subregional common market; capital flight and brain drain from the region; shrinking investment; political and military conflicts; displaced persons and refugees; and increased dependence on and vulnerability to the influence of foreign countries.

The plan was designed to concentrate on those economic and social aspects that were directly linked to the preservation and consolidation of peace, and to coincide with the priorities of the Governments of the region and supplement their national development efforts. Specifically, the Secretary-General pointed to problems requiring immediate action under the plan, caused by the damaging effects of war on the population and infrastructure and by the 1987 drought.

Strategies for emergency assistance were outlined in several areas under the plan, including assistance to refugees and repatriated persons; food aid; and urgent needs for fuel and thermal, hydro-electric and electrical energy.

In order to help reactivate the economy, financial constraints on the region needed to be eased. Several measures were proposed to help reduce the heavy burden of foreign debt carried by the Central American countries, including debt outstanding to private agents, bilateral public debt and multilateral debt. The Secretary-General proposed a method of financing to reactivate the Central American Common Market and reduce temporary imbalances in countries' balance of payments. That suggestion included a proposal for facilitating liquidity in the region's payments system and for strengthening the Central American Monetary Stabilization Fund.

In the area of economic revitalization, programmes were proposed for industrial rehabilitation; agricultural development; trade concessions; reconstruction of the infrastructure; and investments in the energy sector. Social development programmes included investments in the social, health, education and housing sectors; strengthening the productive capacity of marginal groups; food security; reinforcement of co-operatives; and strengthening the Central American Bank for Economic Integration. The report also outlined the role of the United Nations system in the special plan, internal and international responsibilities, and institutional mechanisms for implementing the plan.

In his October report on the situation in Central America,[26] the Secretary-General stressed that the root of the Central American crisis was to be found in the unjust economic and social structures that had traditionally characterized the region, and which were exacerbated by the current economic recession.

UNDP action. On 1 July,[27] the UNDP Governing Council allocated $20 million for the Special Plan of Economic Co-operation for Central America.

GENERAL ASSEMBLY ACTION

At its resumed forty-second session, the General Assembly, on 12 May 1988, adopted **resolution 42/231** without vote.

Special plan of economic co-operation for Central America

The General Assembly,

Recalling its resolution 42/1 of 7 October 1987, in which it expressed its firmest support for the agreement on "Procedures for the establishment of a firm and lasting peace in Central America", signed by Central American Presidents at Guatemala City on 7 August 1987, at the Esquipulas II summit meeting, and its resolution 42/204 of 11 December 1987, in which it requested the Secretary-General to formulate, in consultation with the Governments of the region and the appropriate organs and organizations of the United Nations system, a special plan of co-operation for Central America to be submitted for consideration by the General Assembly at its current session,

Bearing in mind the Joint Declaration of Central American Presidents, issued at San José on 16 January 1988,[a] and the agreement adopted at Guatemala City on 7

April 1988[b] by the Executive Commission, composed of the Central American Ministers for Foreign Affairs in accordance with the agreement concluded at the Esquipulas II summit meeting,

Reiterating its appreciation to the Contadora Group and the Support Group for their contribution to the peace process in Central America,

Noting with satisfaction the Joint Political Declaration and the Joint Economic Communiqué[c] adopted by the European Community and the States parties to the General Treaty on Central American Economic Integration and Panama at the Ministerial Conference on Political Dialogue and Economic Co-operation between the European Community and its member States, and the States of Central America and of the Contadora Group, held at Hamburg, Federal Republic of Germany, on 29 February and 1 March 1988,

Considering that fulfilment of the agreement concluded at the Esquipulas II summit meeting and the implementation of a special plan of economic co-operation for Central America require political will and determination so that peace and development can be consolidated in the region,

Reaffirming its conviction that peace and development are inseparable,

Deeply concerned about the emergency situation in Central America and alarmed by the seriousness of the economic and social crisis it is facing,

Aware of the complexity and seriousness of the situation of the refugees and displaced persons in the Central American region, and of its effect on the social and economic development of the area,

Convinced of the urgent need for concerted action by the international community in support of the commitments made by the Central American countries to improve the living conditions of their peoples and to achieve social justice as a foundation for a stable and lasting peace,

1. *Expresses its appreciation* to the Secretary-General for formulating and submitting the Special Plan of Economic Co-operation for Central America, prepared in accordance with General Assembly resolutions 42/1 and 42/204;

2. *Also expresses its appreciation* for the important support provided by the United Nations Development Programme, the Economic Commission for Latin America and the Caribbean and the various regional integration and co-operation bodies in the preparation of the Special Plan;

3. *Requests* the Secretary-General, with the assistance of the United Nations Development Programme and in close co-ordination with the Governments of Central America and in consultation with donors, to use his best efforts in the promotion, co-ordination, monitoring and follow-up of the Special Plan and to make, as soon as possible, institutional arrangements in order to facilitate the fulfilment of the commitments of the international community;

4. *Emphasizes* the urgent need to provide the Central American countries with financial resources on concessional and favourable terms, in addition to those they are already receiving from the international community;

5. *Requests* all bodies, organs and organizations of the United Nations system, taking into account the

---

[a]A/42/911-S/19447.
[b]A/42/948-S/19764.
[c]A/42/258.

emergency situation faced by the Central American countries, to take immediate steps to mobilize additional financial resources and to participate actively in the implementation of the activities supporting the goals and objectives of the Special Plan;

6. *Urges* the organs and specialized agencies of the United Nations system, in particular the United Nations Development Programme, the Food and Agriculture Organization of the United Nations, the Office of the United Nations High Commissioner for Refugees, the United Nations Children's Fund, the International Fund for Agricultural Development, the United Nations Population Fund, the United Nations Industrial Development Organization, the World Bank and the International Monetary Fund, to continue and expand, to the extent possible, their assistance programmes on a priority basis, and to co-operate with the Secretary-General in the implementation of the activities supporting the goals and objectives of the Special Plan;

7. *Urges* the international community and international organizations to increase their technical, economic and financial co-operation with the Central American countries for the implementation of the activities supporting the goals and objectives of the Special Plan, as a way of contributing to the efforts being made under the agreement concluded at the Esquipulas II summit meeting to attain peace and development;

8. *Recognizes* the vital importance of the Central American economic integration process as a fundamental element for the economic and social development of the region and urges all Governments and international organizations to contribute to the strengthening of this process;

9. *Decides* to review and evaluate the progress in the implementation of the Special Plan of Economic Co-operation for Central America at its forty-fourth session and requests the Secretary-General to submit a report on the implementation of the present resolution with whatever recommendations are deemed appropriate.

General Assembly resolution 42/231

12 May 1988   Meeting 112   Adopted without vote

51-nation draft (A/42/L.49 & Add.1); agenda items 34 & 86.

Sponsors: Algeria, Argentina, Austria, Bahrain, Barbados, Belgium, Belize, Bolivia, Brazil, Canada, Cape Verde, Colombia, Congo, Costa Rica, Cuba, Denmark, Ecuador, El Salvador, Ethiopia, Finland, France, Germany, Federal Republic of, Greece, Guatemala, Honduras, Iceland, India, Ireland, Italy, Luxembourg, Mauritania, Mexico, Morocco, Netherlands, Nicaragua, Norway, Pakistan, Panama, Peru, Philippines, Portugal, Rwanda, Spain, Sweden, Tunisia, Uganda, United Republic of Tanzania, Uruguay, Venezuela, Yugoslavia, Zambia.

Meeting numbers. GA 42nd session: plenary 28, 110-112.

The Assembly again took up the matter at its forty-third session and, on 20 December 1988, on the recommendation of the Second Committee, adopted **resolution 43/210** without vote.

Special Plan of Economic Co-operation for Central America

The General Assembly,

Recalling its resolutions 42/1 of 7 October 1987, 42/110 of 7 December 1987 and 42/204 of 11 December 1987 and, in particular, its resolution 42/231 of 12 May 1988, in which it urged the international community and international organizations to increase their technical, economic and financial co-operation with the Central American countries for the implementation of the activities

supporting the goals and objectives of the Special Plan of Economic Co-operation for Central America,

Reiterating the importance of the commitment made in the agreement signed by Central American Presidents at Guatemala City on 7 August 1987, at the Esquipulas II summit meeting, to promote and strengthen democracy in the Central American countries through the creation of a system of economic and social well-being and justice, and jointly to seek special economic assistance from the international community,

Having considered the report of the Secretary-General on the situation in Central America,

Noting with satisfaction the agreement reached by the Governments of Central America with regard to the mechanisms for implementing the Special Plan, and recognizing the need to continue consultations on those mechanisms with the co-operating countries and international organizations, in accordance with its resolution 42/231,

Deeply concerned about the emergency situation in Central America and alarmed at the seriousness of the economic and social crisis that it faces, which has been accentuated by the catastrophic effects of recent climatic phenomena in the region,

Reaffirming its conviction that peace and development are inseparable,

1. *Expresses its appreciation* to the Secretary-General for his report on the situation in Central America and for the efforts that he has made to promote the Special Plan of Economic Co-operation for Central America;

2. *Welcomes* decision 88/31 of 1 July 1988, adopted by the Governing Council of the United Nations Development Programme, in particular paragraph 9 *(b)* thereof, in which funds were allocated for the promotion, co-ordination, implementation and follow-up of the Special Plan;

3. *Welcomes with satisfaction* the elaboration by the Central American Governments, in co-ordination with the United Nations Development Programme and in consultation with the co-operating community, of mechanisms for the implementation of its resolution 42/231 and the ongoing consultations on those mechanisms;

4. *Recommends* the convening of a meeting, early in 1989, in close co-ordination with the United Nations Development Programme, between the Governments of Central America, the bilateral and multilateral co-operating community, the organs and organizations of the United Nations system, multilateral, regional and subregional international financial institutions and intergovernmental organizations, for the purpose of reviewing the evolution of the development process, including assistance requirements, and of discussing the programmes and projects that could be implemented as soon as possible in support of the goals and objectives of the Special Plan;

5. *Urges* Member States and observers, intergovernmental organizations, international financial institutions, the organs, organizations and specialized agencies of the United Nations system and regional and subregional organs and agencies, taking into account the emergency situation faced by the Central American countries, to participate actively and to adopt immediate measures for the implementation of the activities in support of the goals and objectives of the Special Plan;

6. *Emphasizes* the urgent need to provide the Central American countries with financial resources on

concessional and favourable terms, in addition to those which they are already receiving from the international community;

7. *Welcomes* the convening of the International Conference on Central American Refugees, to be held in Guatemala in May 1989;

8. *Decides* to review and evaluate the progress in the implementation of the Special Plan of Economic Co-operation for Central America at its forty-fourth session, in the light of the report requested of the Secretary-General in its resolution 42/231.

General Assembly resolution 43/210

20 December 1988   Meeting 83   Adopted without vote

Approved by Second Committee (A/43/918/Add.2) without vote, 30 November (meeting 45); 41-nation draft (A/C.2/43/L.46), orally revised following informal consultations; agenda item 86.

Sponsors: Algeria, Argentina, Austria, Bangladesh, Belgium, Bolivia, Brazil, Canada, Colombia, Congo, Costa Rica, Cuba, Denmark, Ecuador, El Salvador, Finland, France, Germany, Federal Republic of, Greece, Guatemala, Honduras, India, Ireland, Italy, Japan, Luxembourg, Mauritania, Mexico, Morocco, Netherlands, Nicaragua, Norway, Panama, Peru, Portugal, Spain, Sweden, Tunisia, Uruguay, Venezuela, Yugoslavia.

Meeting numbers. GA 43rd session: 2nd Committee 26, 28-30, 36-38, 42, 45; plenary 83.

REFERENCES

[1]E/1988/38. [2]*Ibid.* (res. 498(XXII)). [3]*Ibid.* (res. 492(XXII)). [4]*Ibid.* (res. 491(XXII)). [5]*Ibid.* (res. 496(XXII)). [6]*Ibid.* (res. 499(XXII)). [7]*Ibid.* (res. 493(XXII)). [8]*Ibid.* (res. 494(XXII)). [9]*Ibid.* (res. 495(XXII)). [10]*Ibid.* (res. 497(XXII)). [11]*Ibid.* (res. 490(XXII)). [12]*Ibid.* (res. 500(XXII)). [13]E/1990/43. [14]*Economic Survey of Latin America and the Caribbean, 1988*, Sales No. E.89.II.G.2 (summary, E/1989/59). [15]YUN 1987, p. 551. [16]YUN 1977, p. 555. [17]YUN 1980, p. 712, GA res. 35/18, 10 Nov. 1980. [18]YUN 1982, p. 181. [19]YUN 1987, p. 188. [20]YUN 1985, p. 937. [21]A/43/433. [22]YUN 1987 p. 554, GA res. 42/12, 28 Oct. 1987. [23]YUN 1984, p. 635. [24]A/42/949. [25]YUN 1987, p. 189, GA res. 42/1, 7 Oct. 1987, & p. 447, GA res. 42/204, 11 Dec. 1987. [26]A/43/729-S/20234. [27]E/1988/19 (dec. 88/31 A).

Western Asia

The many sources of tension in the region covered by the Economic and Social Commission for Western Asia had far-reaching and disruptive repercussions on the Commission's activities and, in particular, on the individual countries of the region, the ESCWA Executive Secretary stated in an April 1988 report.[1] The Iraq-Iran war, which ended in mid-1988, resulted in widespread negative consequences that were devastating for the region's development. The destruction resulting from the civil war in Lebanon had led that country to making reconstruction, rather than development, its priority. Also, an outbreak of protest by Palestinians in the territories occupied by Israel in December 1987 escalated during 1988 into the *intifadah*, or uprising, and was cause for further social and economic disruption (see PART TWO, Chapter IV).

Pursuant to its 1987 decision that future sessions of ESCWA would be held biennially,[2] no regular session of the Commission was held in 1988. However, in June, ESCWA held its third special session[3] to consider a proposal by the Secretary-General for the temporary relocation outside Iraq of ESCWA's staff and its secretariat. The Commission decided not to agree to the Secretary-General's proposal[4] (see "Programme, organizational and administrative questions", below).

Economic and social trends

During the 1980s, the performance of the region's economy was hampered by a number of unfavourable developments,[5] according to a summary of the survey of economic and social developments in the ESCWA region during the Third United Nations Development Decade (the 1980s). Those developments included a sharp deterioration in the terms of trade of primary commodities and oil, coupled with wars, military conflicts and political instability.

In contrast to the growth target of 7 per cent average annual gross domestic product (GDP) for the developing countries set by the International Development Strategy for the Decade,[6] an average annual GDP growth rate of −1.4 per cent was experienced during the 1980-1987 period. Hence, the region recorded an average annual per capita GDP growth rate of −4.7 per cent. The average annual growth rates in the manufacturing and agricultural sectors from 1980 to 1986 were 5.9 and 2.9 per cent, respectively. The region witnessed a negative 13.5 per cent average annual growth rate in exports and a negative 2.6 per cent rate with respect to imports during the period. The share of gross investment in total GDP in the ESCWA region rose marginally from 23 per cent in 1980 to 24 per cent in 1987.

GDP growth rates varied considerably among the various subgroups in the region, and from one country to another. The average annual GDP growth rate for Gulf Co-operation Council (GCC) countries (Bahrain, Kuwait, Oman, Qatar, Saudi Arabia and the United Arab Emirates) generated the greatest share of total GDP for the region as a whole, amounting to 82.2 and 70 per cent in 1980 and 1987, respectively. The average annual GDP growth rate for those countries was negative (−3.7 per cent). Countries with diversified economies (Egypt, Iraq, Jordan, Lebanon and the Syrian Arab Republic) achieved a 6.1 per cent growth over the period, while the two least developed countries in the region—Democratic Yemen and Yemen—showed a 4.8 per cent growth rate.

On 29 July, by **decision 1988/181**, the Economic and Social Council took note of, among other documents, a summary of the survey of economic and social developments in the ESCWA region, 1987.[7]

As the end of the Development Decade approached, the region's oil-exporting countries witnessed a decline in oil revenues to less than 30 per cent of their level at the start of the Decade in nominal terms, and below 20 per cent in real terms. The sharp decrease strongly impacted the region's economy, as oil exports accounted for 60 per cent or more of total exports in 10 of the 14 ESCWA countries. For most GCC members, oil still accounted for over 90 per cent of total exports, over 35 per cent of GDP and about two thirds of government revenues. Hence declining oil revenues during the Decade had severe ramifications on the balance of payments, national budgets and economic activities in most countries in Western Asia.

The countries of the Organization of Petroleum Exporting Countries (OPEC), which earlier had led the international oil market, had to readjust and respond to the continued "glut" in the market as non-OPEC oil producers more than compensated for the cutbacks made by OPEC countries, while world demand for oil decreased. The world economic recession of 1980-1982 was a leading factor in this, prompting OPEC members to reduce the official price of benchmark crude in March 1983 by about 15 per cent—from $34 to $29 per barrel—and to cut the cartel's production quota to 17.5 million barrels per day.

But world oil demand grew in 1988 by an unexpected 3 per cent, mainly due to higher consumption in the United States (up 9 per cent) and Japan (up 4.9 per cent). Much of United States imports came from three ESCWA countries: Iraq, Kuwait and Saudi Arabia. Total United States imports from those countries rose almost 70 per cent. This increase in ESCWA sales to the United States could be attributed in part to formula pricing which reduced the cost disadvantage of transportation.

The downturn in oil revenues, met by contractional government fiscal policies, led to recessions in those countries during most of the Decade. Also, employment opportunities for workers from other countries in the region and many other developing countries outside the region were reduced. This particularly affected the ESCWA labour-sending countries of Democratic Yemen, Egypt, Jordan, Lebanon and Yemen, which had become increasingly dependent on partially financing their external trade deficits from the transfer of remittances by their nationals working in the GCC countries.

In the light of current and projected trends, readjustment policies pursued in most countries of the region since 1986 were expected to continue. Rises in taxes and import tariffs were likely, as Governments sought to increase revenues. New sources of income and employment opportunities also needed to be established and/or developed.

The balance of payments of the ESCWA region came under increasing pressure as the Development Decade progressed. Factors in evidence included virtual erosion of the substantial trade surplus existing at the outset of the period, sharp reduction in net imports of services, inability of aid-giving countries to maintain their disbursements (thereby adversely affecting developing countries) and steep depreciation or devaluation of the currencies of several countries (notably Egypt, Jordan, Lebanon and the Syrian Arab Republic). Such unfavourable developments resulted in a $3 billion draw on reserves in the period 1982-1987. The highly unfavourable situation prevailing in the international oil market throughout most of the period under review, the rising tide of protectionism in world trade, and the prevailing political situation in the region all contributed to the decline. Cessation of hostilities between Iraq and Iran in August 1988 and establishment of the Arab Co-operation Council greatly improved prospects.

Agricultural development and growth in the region as a whole were below expectations during the Decade. Production grew at an annual rate of 2.9 per cent, 1.1 per cent short of the 4 per cent target set by the Decade Strategy to meet minimum nutritional and industrial needs.

Towards the end of the 1980s, the Governments of many ESCWA countries had taken measures conducive to higher agricultural output, with pricing policies expected to contribute to higher production and slower growth in demand.

The region overall saw its manufacturing value added (MVA) grow 5.9 per cent per year during the 1980-1986 period, well below the 9 per cent United Nations target. The top performance of 13.4 per cent was achieved by the least developed countries—Democratic Yemen and Yemen—due mainly to the low level of industrial development in the base year. By 1987 and 1988, most countries in the region showed significant improvement in manufacturing, particularly Bahrain, Egypt, Saudi Arabia and the United Arab Emirates. Although impeded by declining oil revenues, manufacturing activities during the 1980-1988 period were given higher priority and directed generally towards the promotion of large-scale, capital-intensive heavy industries such as petrochemicals, oil refining, fertilizers, cement, steel rods and bars and aluminium.

Social conditions in Western Asia varied widely among countries during the Decade. Whereas GCC countries had a relatively high level of social welfare, States with lower per capita incomes provided very little in social welfare to the deprived. Nevertheless, in the region as a whole, social programmes expanded. Concrete progress was made in implementing the Strategy of the Decade towards education.

The region's illiteracy rate was estimated to have fallen to about 50 per cent. The gross enrolment ratio in primary education rose above 85 per cent, and was nearly 100 per cent in 10 of the 14 ESCWA countries. Health conditions also continued to improve. In several countries, particularly those of GCC, inhabitants enjoyed free health services. However, the rural population, well over half the region's population, was generally left outside the mainstream development and there was a wide and growing gap between rural and urban per capita income in most countries.

Approximately 20 per cent of the region's total population were between the ages of 15 and 24. While they benefited from greater education and health services, this generation faced rapidly rising living costs and new forms of crime and delinquency. Youth programmes were neither numerous nor adequate. Meanwhile, the problem of aging received slightly more attention. The increasing prominence of the nuclear family, along with greater mobility for the young, would mean that more assistance to that group would be needed in the future.

The plight of disabled persons, numbering as many as 10 million, posed a serious socio-economic problem to the region in the wake of war, compounded by social and environmental factors and cultural and health-related factors.

During the Decade, progress was made in building the basic science and technology infrastructure and producing qualified manpower and skilled workers in the region, but there remained a marked imbalance between the demand and supply of qualified manpower in most countries.

Imports of technical services included notably: telecommunications; medical equipment and services; petrochemical industries; commercial airline support systems; water supply and sewage treatment plants; and nuclear power plants. About 80 per cent of non-military technology in the region was supplied by France, the Federal Republic of Germany, Italy, Japan, the United Kingdom and the United States.

Most ESCWA countries experienced two sets of environmental problems during the Decade: air, water and soil pollution of large urban and rural centres, and rapid population growth, with depletion of resources and deficiencies in basic services. Few controls were exercised over industrial development to eliminate the hazards of dangerous emissions and the disposal of untreated solid and liquid wastes from factories. Despite expressed concern, many environmental problems such as desertification, soil degradation and depletion, urbanization of cultivated and grazing lands, water and air pollution worsened in Western Asia. The desired ecological balance would be difficult to achieve without an integrated approach to development at the national and regional levels.

Activities in 1988

Despite a high vacancy rate of approximately 34 per cent, the ESCWA secretariat in 1988 implemented a substantial amount of the 1988-1989 work programme,[8] completing 29 of 68 outputs planned for 1988—an implementation rate of 43 per cent (not including 55 outputs which were at various stages of progress at the end of the year).

Transport and communications

The ESCWA transport and communications programme in 1988 succeeded in initiating work on an ESCWA manual for transport project appraisal; keeping ESCWA member countries abreast of the latest developments in multimodal transport; formulating regional maritime development policies; surveying and recommending appropriate road construction techniques to the authorities concerned in ESCWA countries; studying container traffic; and promoting regional co-operation in transportation.

Another major aim of the programme was to implement in Western Asia the objectives of the Transport and Communications Decade for Asia and the Pacific (1985-1994).[9] To carry out the mandates of the General Assembly,[10] Economic and Social Council[11] and ESCWA[12] resolutions, the programme fully implemented the preparatory assistance project for the Decade, whose final report was discussed in an intergovernmental/interagency meeting (Baghdad, 13-15 December).

Energy

Under the ESCWA energy programme, several reports and surveys were published in 1988. Two technical publications of energy data were prepared and distributed to all bodies concerned as a step towards establishing an energy data bank. Further, two surveys of energy-related activities and developments undertaken in the ESCWA region in 1987 and 1988 were completed. They covered recent developments in the energy sector in petroleum exploration and prospecting, production, processing, transportation, distribution, local consumption and exportation, as well as a comprehensive review of progress made in the electricity sector towards expanding and improving national grids and regional co-operation for the interconnection of electricity grids.

A report to the Commission was prepared on progress towards regional and international co-operation in the peaceful uses of nuclear energy. Also, as the whole region still depended heavily on oil, whether as the major source of energy or of material wealth, a technical publication was undertaken on the impact of changing conditions in the oil market on energy policies. Projects for promoting renewable and non-conventional sources of energy in the region, such as solar, wind and biomass, were formulated as well.

Oil

Oil was the major focus of a report on 1988 energy-related activities in ESCWA countries by the Natural Resources, Science and Technology Committee.[13] Oil prices fell globally during most of 1988, as members of OPEC, including those in the ESCWA region, substantially increased production levels, in many cases beyond their own quotas, while the cessation of hostilities between Iraq and Iran also brought more oil to the international market.

Restructuring in the international oil market continued the trend of recent years towards vertical concentration, with major sales of oil and gas reserves as well as downstream operations in 1988. In the United States, more refineries were sold in 1988 than any year since 1982, while in Europe ownership of 3.5 per cent of the refinery capacity of the European Economic Community had passed to oil-exporting countries, including Kuwait. Kuwait also owned over 4,500 outlets worldwide, through which it sold oil products directly to consumers in major oil-consuming countries. Kuwait intended to purchase more retail facilities, and was exploring possibilities in the Far East, France, the Federal Republic of Germany and the United States. Saudi Arabia also made a major investment in 1988 in downstream facilities, purchasing a half interest in refineries and retail outlets in the United States. The United Arab Emirates took steps in that direction, acquiring a 10 per cent interest in a Spanish refining group and increasing its interest in Total-CFP (France).

The region also benefited from the fact that relatively new or recently updated refineries built in the region for export purposes enjoyed a technological advantage over older installations and generally performed better than refineries in other parts of the world.

Plans were under way throughout the region to increase pipeline capacities. Iraq's programme to expand its pipeline system in the region would result in a pipeline-system export capacity surpassing that of Saudi Arabia by 1990. Iraq relied increasingly on overland transport during the earlier 1980s when hostilities made shipping difficult, but planned to make less use of trucks as its pipelines became operational. Oman and Yemen were expanding their existing oil pipelines and were expected to increase their export capacities by 70,000 and 200,000 barrels per day, respectively.

Shipping, historically the most important oil export route, benefited from the cessation of hostilities between Iraq and Iran in the latter part of 1988, such that the tanker industry performed better than at any time since the early 1970s. Plans were laid to widen shipping lanes and the Suez Canal.

Gas

The ESCWA region participated to some extent in the international gas market through sales of liquefied natural gas (LNG) and liquefied petroleum gas (LPG), mainly to Japan. However, its share of international gas reserves—18 per cent—were much smaller than its share of oil reserves. The largest reserves were found in Iraq, Qatar, Saudi Arabia and the United Arab Emirates. The international trade of gas was rising, along with gas consumption in general. One forecast predicted that natural gas consumption would reach 22 per cent of total world energy consumption by the year 2000. Gas reserves in the ESCWA region grew by 15.6 per cent during 1988, following the discovery of new fields and the positive reassessment of existing reserves.

Most gas was consumed within the producing country and transport networks were geared towards local markets. In fact, the high cost of transporting gas was a major factor inhibiting the rate of growth of exports. The system relied heavily on pipelines and, as gas use rose, pipeline construction was expected to increase.

Exploration activities in the field of oil and gas suffered worldwide during 1988 owing to fluctuating oil prices and the high costs involved, but did continue in countries such as Democratic Yemen, Egypt, the Syrian Arab Republic and Yemen where there was some geological evidence of the possibility of increasing oil reserves.

Electricity

Rural electrification was a priority in many ESCWA countries, and progress was made during 1988. The region continued to interconnect national electricity grids. The co-operative efforts of the 1980s were rewarded: a project was under way to connect the Jordanian and Egyptian electricity grids, Jordan and Iraq were studying the feasibility of interconnecting their grids, and a completed interconnection between Iraq and Turkey allowed Iraq to export electricity to Turkey in 1988. Work began on interconnecting the electricity grids of several other countries, the first phase involving Bahrain, Kuwait, Qatar and Saudi Arabia. Plans to interconnect Democratic Yemen and Yemen were also discussed in 1988 and financing was secured.

Iraq's post-war reconstruction placed an important emphasis on electricity, and hydroelectrical power in particular. Several major projects were expected to be completed by 1993 both to meet increasing local demand and to provide additional surpluses for export. Other countries' projects included: Bahrain's plans for a $770 million power and desalination plant; an agreement between Egypt and the

USSR to construct three power stations; three new substations in Jordan's industrial area and a dam for both irrigation and export of power; two new gas turbines and reassessment of plans in Qatar, where power demands were growing 10 per cent per year; Kuwait's Subiya power station, which would include a water desalination facility; and Saudi Arabia's combined power and water desalination plant at Shuqaiq, completed in 1988.

Renewable energy sources

New and renewable sources of energy were promoted by Governments and organizations in the ESCWA region. While the private sector had invested in such projects in some countries, its involvement had probably been held back by the low price of conventional energy that continued into 1988, but some activity was under way. Projects included plans for a factory in Saudi Arabia to produce solar lighting systems, medical refrigerators and pumping systems, telecommunications and warning lights. A Jordanian firm issued a licence to a firm in Gibraltar to produce solar heating equipment for sale in Gibraltar, Spain and the United States. Solar water heaters were also used in Jordan, totalling 100,000 units by the end of 1987. Several energy-generating projects began operating in Egypt in 1988, and were making ice, desalinating water and pumping water. One wind farm generating 400 kilowatts contributed to the local power grid. A wind farm in Jordan also began operating in 1988.

Food and agriculture

A main achievement concerning food and agriculture in 1988 was the ESCWA secretariat's publication of the recurrent *Agriculture and Development in Western Asia*, which presented an assessment of the year's agricultural development, analysed some emerging trends and tackled critical national and regional agricultural problems. A plan of action was formulated to combat desertification in Iraq, and a desertification-control project was also set up for Democratic Yemen. Many training workshops were held on varied subjects, from resource conservation to credit management to computerized planning. Evaluations of rural development projects and programmes were carried out for two countries, and an assessment of agricultural policies at farm level in two countries of the region was published.

Population

ESCWA's population programme in 1988 produced substantial demographic and related socio-economic data necessary for development planning and policy-making. Work on the upcoming publication of *Demographic and Related Socio-economic Data Sheets of the Economic and Social Commission for Western Asia* (issue no. 6) went forward. A study of patterns and trends of infant mortality in Bahrain, Egypt, Jordan, Kuwait, the Syrian Arab Republic and the United Arab Emirates was published, along with another on socio-economic differentials of child mortality in Jordan. The *Population Bulletin of ESCWA* and the *Trilingual Demographic Dictionary* were published. An advanced training workshop for member States on organizing and administrating population and housing censuses was organized, and a fully computerized labour data base established (to be updated continuously). Four technical studies relating to working women in Western Asia and to international migration were launched. Attention was given to manpower planning and to agricultural, technical and vocational education.

Development issues

The ESCWA region's two least developed countries, Democratic Yemen and Yemen, were the object of special measures in their favour. The programme's main contribution was to assess the economic and social conditions prevailing there and analyse obstacles impeding their efforts to promote development and economic transformation. A more comprehensive review and analysis of the region's national, regional and subregional performance was published, entitled *Survey of Economic and Social Developments in the ESCWA Region*.

Social development

A Conference on the Capabilities and Needs of Disabled Persons in the ESCWA region, to take place in November 1989 at Amman, Jordan, was prepared starting in 1988. Social aspects of rural development, including the role of the co-operative movement, were studied. Other areas receiving attention were the aged and social security. The Commission drew a regional profile on aging as input for the second review and appraisal of the International Plan of Action on Aging endorsed by the General Assembly in 1982[14] (see PART THREE, Chapter XIV). A review of social security systems in the region was also made.

Under a subprogramme on women and development, work progressed on a technical publication on the employment of women in the informal sector and on the recurrent publication of a directory of Arab professional women active in technical co-operation among developing countries. Reports to the Commission dealt with improving women's participation in both rural and urban economies through skills training, and with identification of women's needs through case-studies or project assessments such as women trainers for maintenance skills of electrical appliances and participation of women in food and textile industries. Other activities provided information to women, Governments, non-governmental organizations and other bodies dealing with women's issues.

Programme, organizational and administrative questions

At its headquarters in Baghdad, Iraq,[3] on 8 June, ESCWA held a third special session to consider a request by the Secretary-General of the United Nations to relocate the staff of its secretariat temporarily outside Iraq.

ESCWA's Executive Secretary summarized the Secretary-General's reasons for his proposal under three main headings. First: the safety and security of the staff. The Executive Secretary recalled how, after ESCWA's establishment in 1973, it had been decided in 1976 to relocate temporarily from Beirut, Lebanon, to Amman, Jordan, because of civil strife and conflict in Lebanon. It had re-established its headquarters in Beirut in 1977, but by 1979 had moved on to Baghdad.

Second: repeated relocation and instability had meant that ESCWA had been unable to perform its functions or had encountered difficulty in carrying them out in an optimum manner in keeping with its capacities and its mission. Because of the Iran-Iraq war, the Commission had found difficulty in pursuing its activities, since the host country had been obliged to impose restrictions on external contacts in contravention of the ESCWA Headquarters Agreement.

Third: the Commission had continued to suffer from its inability to attract qualified staff to work in the secretariat, which had affected its capacity to implement programmes. Despite the excellent facilities provided by Iraq, security reasons had forced ESCWA to evacuate staff members' dependants from Baghdad.

The Commission decided by consensus not to agree to relocate temporarily its staff from its current headquarters to a site outside Iraq and reaffirmed its determination to maintain its permanent headquarters at Baghdad.[4]

REFERENCES

[1]E/ESCWA/88/1/Rev.1. [2]YUN 1987, p. 562. [3]E/1988/98. [4]*Ibid.* (res. 163(S-3)). [5]E/1989/67. [6]YUN 1980, p. 503, GA res. 35/56, annex, 5 Dec. 1980. [7]YUN 1987, p. 559. [8]E/ESCWA/C.1/15/4(Part I)/Rev.1. [9]YUN 1985, p. 623. [10]YUN 1984, p. 624, GA res. 39/227, 18 Dec. 1984. [11]*Ibid.* p. 623, ESC res. 1984/78, 27 July 1984. [12]YUN 1985, p. 666. [13]E/ESCWA/NR/89/12/Rev.1. [14]YUN 1982, p. 1184, GA res. 37/51, 3 Dec. 1984.

PART THREE

Economic and social questions

Chapter I

Development policy and international economic co-operation

Continuing instability in the world economy, particularly in exchange and interest rates, following the sudden decline in equity prices in October 1987 was a major subject of discussion in several United Nations bodies during 1988. An overall slow-down in growth of the global economy was predicted at the beginning of the year; modest prosperity was achieved instead, but it was highly uneven and major imbalances persisted, which most affected the debt-distressed developing countries where long-term improvements had already been interrupted by the severity of their economic problems.

In December, the General Assembly established an *Ad Hoc* Committee of the Whole for the Preparation of the International Development Strategy for the Fourth United Nations Development Decade (1991-2000), with a view to finalizing the strategy for adoption in 1990 (resolution 43/182). Various organizations of the United Nations system were asked to contribute to the preparatory process. Having considered the Secretary-General's report on the overall socio-economic perspective of the world economy to the year 2000, the Assembly requested him to update the report so as to enhance its utility as a background document for the strategy's preparation (43/194).

Also in December, the Assembly urged the international community to create, as a priority, a supportive international economic environment for growth and development that would reinforce the efforts of developing countries to revitalize their development process and eradicate poverty (43/195). It also reaffirmed the validity of the official development assistance target, established at 0.7 per cent of the gross national product of developed countries, and appealed to donor countries to achieve the target (43/197).

The *World Economic Survey 1988* reviewed main international economic developments and included a comprehensive analysis of the global effects of the indebtedness and fiscal imbalances of developed countries, particularly as they affected the development of developing countries. The process of economic reform in the centrally planned economies and China was also analysed. The *Trade and Development Report, 1988* also discussed debt, payment imbalances and economic growth and addressed the role of services in the world economy.

In April, the Committee for Development Planning found that prospects for the world economy

were clouded by market volatility and the uncertainty surrounding unsustainable trends. There were also uncertainties about how to reduce fiscal imbalances among developed market-economy countries, whether international trade would become more or less protectionist and what would be the future of net capital flows to developing countries.

The special development problems of both the least developed countries (LDCs) and island developing countries were highlighted as preparations began for the Second United Nations Conference on LDCs, to be held in 1990. Technical co-operation and public administration issues also received attention, with human resources development being increasingly linked to economic growth.

International economic relations

Development and economic co-operation

During 1988, several United Nations bodies, including the General Assembly and the Economic and Social Council, discussed various aspects of development and economic co-operation. During its general discussion of international economic and social policy in July, the Council focused on economic trends and the need to achieve more widespread and sustained development.

CDP activities. At its April 1988 session,[1] the Committee for Development Planning (CDP) stated that, in the face of major structural imbalances in the world economy, inadequacies of both national policies and international co-operation threatened the sustainability of growth in many countries and regions. The international system needed strengthening; as a new régime was established, development strategies would come to the fore. Prompt action to reduce the international debts of debt-distressed developing countries was an essential prerequisite of any successful strategy to deal with the long-term issues of the 1990s. In CDP's view, such action would include moratoriums for African countries on payments on public and publicly guaranteed debts, with concessional interest rates on rescheduled amounts for low-income severely debt-distressed countries and reduced interest rates on Paris Club reschedulings for others. As to private debt, particularly that of the middle-income countries in Latin America and elsewhere, action was needed to facilitate debt reduction by commercial banks.

During the 1980s, debt-distressed countries had cut investment, reduced public expenditure and imposed deflationary contraction on their economies. In low-income countries, the share of public expenditure on education and health fell, while that on defence and general public administration rose. For reasons of both efficiency and equity, Governments should adjust to short-term economic and fiscal constraints by making the objectives of policy the safeguarding of human development programmes through restructuring to reduce inefficiency and improve delivery and targeting by such means as low-cost technologies and emphasis on basic services. The ultimate objective of economic development should be human development, whereby growth occurred as a consequence of local resource mobilization.

Economic and Social Council general discussion. During its general discussion of international economic and social policy in July 1988,[2] the Economic and Social Council focused on economic trends, particularly the considerable regional disparities in economic performance during the second half of the 1980s and the economic measures required to achieve more widespread and sustained development during the rest of the decade and the 1990s. In addition, the Council discussed the global and regional economic outlook and efforts to increase stability in the world economy. It also addressed the questions of resource transfers, international trade and primary commodities, human resources development, the participation of women in the economy, the environment and sustainable development, global policies, domestic measures, the international development strategy for the 1990s and the role of the Council itself.

The Council had before it the *World Economic Survey 1988*,[3] prepared by the United Nations Department of International Economic and Social Affairs (DIESA). The *Survey* examined the world economy in the late 1980s, the main features of and prospects for world economic development, trends in international trade, international finance, debt and instability, and the international oil market. It also discussed economic reforms in the centrally planned economies and China, the causes and effects of the external fiscal imbalances of developed countries, and growth and adjustment in small and medium-sized developing countries during the 1980s.

Also before the Council was a report of the Secretary-General containing the first biennial summary of the main research findings on major global economic and social trends, policies and emerging issues.[4] Prepared in response to a 1986 Council request,[5] the report was based on information supplied by organizations of the United Nations system and/or recent reports and studies published by them. It included information on major trends in the world economy in the areas of global output, agricultural production, industrial production and structural change, world trade and balance of payments, commodity prices, capital flows, population, employment and education. The report also addressed salient policy issues (structural adjustment and trade policy), sectoral issues (science and technology, energy, transnational corporations (TNCs) and food supplies, food aid and food security) and emerging issues (the impact of economic growth on the environment, urbanization and human settlements, women in development, poverty, hunger and malnutrition, and the development of human resources).

The report stated that the broadest conclusion to which the research findings of the system pointed was that of growing interdependence and interlinkages in the world system. That had always been an important theme in studies of international economy, and it had been powerfully underlined by research on issues that had emerged in recent decades. TNCs had profoundly affected international economic integration, and environmental issues had vast implications for international co-operation that derived from the physical unity of the planet. The research of the international organizations thus had a strong policy orientation; it sought to furnish information on the nature and magnitude of major problems, documented policy experience and proposed national and co-operative approaches.

On 29 July, by **decision 1988/181**, the Council took note of the *The World Economic Survey 1988* and the Secretary-General's report on the main research findings of the system on major global economic and social trends, policies and emerging issues.

GENERAL ASSEMBLY ACTION

The Second (Economic and Financial) Committee devoted a major portion of its work during the General Assembly's 1988 session to development and economic co-operation, making recommendations on a number of topics (see APPENDIX IV, agenda item 82). A list of pertinent documents was included in part I of the Committee's report on that item,[6] which the Assembly took note of on 20 December 1988 by **decision 43/436**. In related action, the Assembly, in **resolution 43/162**, called on the Secretary-General to continue to seek Member States' proposals on procedures to be adopted with regard to the codification and progressive development of principles and norms of international law relating to the new international economic order, and recommended that the Sixth (Legal) Committee consider making a final decision at the Assembly's 1989 session on an appropriate forum in which to complete the elaboration of the codification and development process. In **resolution 43/196**, the Assembly decided to consider in 1989 the question of convening a United Nations conference on environment and development no later than 1992.

The Assembly deferred consideration of the launching of global negotiations on international economic co-operation for development and, on 22 December 1988, by **decision 43/457**, decided to include it in the provisional agenda of its 1989 session.

Preparations for a strategy for the fourth UN development decade

In accordance with a 1987 General Assembly request,[7] the Secretary-General submitted in June 1988 a report[8] on preparation of a new international development strategy for the 1990s. The report, based on consultations held with senior officials of the United Nations system, noted that although the Strategy for the Third United Nations Development Decade (the 1980s), adopted by the Assembly in 1980,[9] was quickly outdated by the unanticipated worsening of the international economic situation, it was generally recognized that the short-term adjustment problems of the world economy should not obscure the importance of longer-term perspectives. The report concluded that in spite of some hesitation, a new strategy was an opportunity to study the prospects ahead and their implications, to strengthen commitments for international economic co-operation in general and international development in particular, and to examine major issues in the international economic system. To rally international support, a new strategy would have to focus on a limited set of essential, realistic objectives and the policies needed to meet them. Indicators of strategic developments in the world economy should be monitored to trigger action when there were deviations from the predicted track.

Annexed to the Secretary-General's report was a decision[10] of the Administrative Committee on Co-ordination (ACC) (Geneva, 20 and 21 April), by which it agreed that adoption of a new strategy was desirable in view of increasing interdependence and the changing circumstances and priorities of the 1990s. The new strategy should deal with development problems in an integrated manner and not exclusively in economic terms, be global in scope, flexible to allow for changing conditions, and give due attention to the development of infrastructure, particularly transport and communications. The ACC Task Force on Long-term

Development Objectives should be asked to review ongoing work in various parts of the system on trends and problems relating to the 1990s and to identify any additional studies that were needed.

The Task Force (sixteenth session, Geneva, 13-16 September)[11] considered the ongoing work in the United Nations system on trends and issues relating to the 1990s, as well as the need for additional studies in the light of concerns likely to be relevant to the new strategy. It also discussed the identification of suitable indicators to be agreed on in the new strategy and the need to arrange for research co-operation at the working level in the system.

ECONOMIC AND SOCIAL COUNCIL ACTION

On 29 July 1988, the Economic and Social Council adopted **resolution 1988/76** without vote.

International development strategy for the fourth United Nations development decade

The Economic and Social Council,

Recalling General Assembly resolution 42/193 of 11 December 1987,

Having considered the report of the Secretary-General on the preparation of a new international development strategy,

Taking note of the statements made at the second regular session of 1988 of the Economic and Social Council,

Aware of the potential contribution of an international development strategy towards enhanced public support for international economic and social co-operation for development,

1. *Recommends* that the General Assembly initiate a comprehensive process for the preparation of an international development strategy for the fourth United Nations development decade for the period 1991-2000;

2. *Requests* all States to contribute actively to the formulation of the strategy;

3. *Stresses* the important supportive role envisaged for the Secretary-General in the preparation of the international development strategy;

4. *Invites* the Committee for Development Planning to continue its activities related to the preparation of the strategy with a view to providing concrete inputs to the strategy.

Economic and Social Council resolution 1988/76

29 July 1988   Meeting 41   Adopted without vote

Draft by Vice-President (E/1988/L.53), based on informal consultations on draft by Tunisia, for Group of 77 (E/1988/L.47); agenda item 5.
Meeting numbers. ESC 34-36, 38, 41.

GENERAL ASSEMBLY ACTION

On 20 December 1988, on the recommendation of the Second Committee, the General Assembly adopted **resolution 43/182** by recorded vote.

Preparation of an international development strategy for the fourth United Nations development decade

The General Assembly,

Recalling its resolution 42/193 of 11 December 1987 and Economic and Social Council resolution 1988/76 of 29

July 1988 on an international development strategy for the fourth United Nations development decade,

1. *Decides* to establish an *Ad Hoc* Committee of the Whole for the Preparation of the International Development Strategy for the Fourth United Nations Development Decade, and requests the *Ad Hoc* Committee to submit a progress report to the General Assembly for consideration at its forty-fourth session, with a view to finalizing the strategy in time for its adoption in 1990;

2. *Invites* the Committee for Development Planning to continue its activities related to the preparation of the strategy in support of the work and consideration of the *Ad Hoc* Committee;

3. *Invites* the United Nations Conference on Trade and Development, the regional commissions and other organizations and specialized agencies of the United Nations system to include in their agendas, during 1989, items regarding their contributions to the preparation of the strategy;

4. *Requests* the Secretary-General of the United Nations Conference on Trade and Development and the executive heads of the other organs, organizations and bodies of the United Nations system to contribute effectively to the preparatory process for the strategy by providing all appropriate input, including relevant documentation, using comprehensive analytical studies;

5. *Requests* the Secretary-General, in this context, to entrust the Director-General for Development and International Economic Co-operation with the responsibility for overall co-ordination of the contributions of relevant secretariats of the United Nations system to the formulation of the strategy.

General Assembly resolution 43/182

20 December 1988   Meeting 83   151-0-1 (recorded vote)

Approved by Second Committee (A/43/915/Add.1) by recorded vote (114-0-1), 9 December (meeting 48); draft by Tunisia, for Group of 77 (A/C.2/43/L.40/Rev.1), orally revised; agenda item 82 *(a)*.
Financial implications. 5th Committee, A/43/982; S-G, A/C.2/43/L.81, A/C.5/43/62.
Meeting numbers. GA 43rd session: 2nd Committee 21-26, 30, 31, 41, 48, 49; 5th Committee 50; plenary 83.

Recorded vote in Assembly as follows:

In favour: Afghanistan, Albania, Algeria, Angola, Antigua and Barbuda, Argentina, Australia, Austria, Bahrain, Bangladesh, Barbados, Belgium, Benin, Bhutan, Bolivia, Botswana, Brazil, Brunei Darussalam, Bulgaria, Burkina Faso, Burma, Burundi, Byelorussian SSR, Cameroon, Canada, Cape Verde, Central African Republic, Chad, Chile, China, Colombia, Comoros, Congo, Costa Rica, Côte d'Ivoire, Cuba, Cyprus, Czechoslovakia, Democratic Kampuchea, Democratic Yemen, Denmark, Djibouti, Dominican Republic, Ecuador, Egypt, El Salvador, Equatorial Guinea, Ethiopia, Fiji, Finland, France, Gabon, Gambia, German Democratic Republic, Germany, Federal Republic of, Ghana, Greece, Grenada, Guinea, Guinea-Bissau, Guyana, Haiti, Honduras, Hungary, Iceland, India, Indonesia, Iran, Iraq, Ireland, Israel, Italy, Jamaica, Japan, Jordan, Kenya, Kuwait, Lao People's Democratic Republic, Lebanon, Lesotho, Liberia, Libyan Arab Jamahiriya, Luxembourg, Madagascar, Malawi, Malaysia, Maldives, Mali, Malta, Mauritania, Mauritius, Mexico, Mongolia, Morocco, Mozambique, Nepal, Netherlands, New Zealand, Nicaragua, Niger, Nigeria, Norway, Oman, Pakistan, Panama, Papua New Guinea, Paraguay, Peru, Philippines, Poland, Portugal, Qatar, Romania, Rwanda, Saint Vincent and the Grenadines, Samoa, Sao Tome and Principe, Saudi Arabia, Senegal, Seychelles, Sierra Leone, Singapore, Solomon Islands, Somalia, Spain, Sri Lanka, Sudan, Suriname, Swaziland, Sweden, Syrian Arab Republic, Thailand, Togo, Trinidad and Tobago, Tunisia, Turkey, Uganda, Ukrainian SSR, USSR, United Arab Emirates, United Kingdom, United Republic of Tanzania, Uruguay, Vanuatu, Venezuela, Viet Nam, Yemen, Yugoslavia, Zaire, Zambia, Zimbabwe.
Against: None.
Abstaining: United States.

Also on 20 December, by **decision 43/437**, the Assembly took note of the Secretary-General's report on the preparation of a new international development strategy.

Fulfilment of the ODA target

On 20 December 1988, on the recommendation of the Second Committee, the General Assembly adopted **resolution 43/197** by recorded vote.

Fulfilment of the target for official development assistance

The General Assembly,

Noting that the problem of increasing poverty in developing countries can only be solved effectively through policies aimed at sustained economic growth and development and that transfers of financial resources to developing countries are important for achieving those objectives,

Stressing, in this context, that official development assistance plays an important role for developing countries, particularly for the poorest among them,

Referring to the target of 0.7 per cent of the gross national product of developed countries for official development assistance, adopted by the General Assembly in resolution 2626(XXV) of 24 October 1970 on the International Development Strategy for the Second United Nations Development Decade and reaffirmed in its resolution 35/56 of 5 December 1980 on the International Development Strategy for the Third United Nations Development Decade,

Concerned that total official development assistance, as a percentage of the gross national product of developed countries, has stagnated at a level significantly below the target of 0.7 per cent,

Stressing the need to continue to improve the quality of official development assistance,

Recalling the increased demands on multilateral development institutions to play a major role in addressing the development problems of developing countries,

1. *Reaffirms* the agreed target of 0.7 per cent of the gross national product of developed countries for official development assistance contained in the International Development Strategy for the Third United Nations Development Decade, as adopted;

2. *Expresses its appreciation* to those donor countries that have already achieved the target of 0.7 per cent, or have increased their official development assistance with a view to achieving that target, and urges them to continue their efforts;

3. *Appeals* to donor countries that have not yet reached the target of 0.7 per cent to make their best efforts to reach it as quickly as possible by pursuing specific measures that will make their efforts more effective, taking into account the necessity of improving the quality of official development assistance;

4. *Stresses* the importance of achieving the target of 0.15 per cent of the gross national product of donor countries for official development assistance for the least developed countries, or doubling official development assistance to those countries, in compliance with the Substantial New Programme of Action for the 1980s for the Least Developed Countries and the conclusions of the mid-term global review of progress towards the implementation of the Substantial New Programme of Action;

5. *Requests* the Director-General for Development and International Economic Co-operation to include in-

formation on compliance with the present resolution in his report for the triennial policy review of operational activities for development.

General Assembly resolution 43/197

20 December 1988   Meeting 83   148-0-1 (recorded vote)

Approved by Second Committee (A/43/915/Add.8) by recorded vote (121-0-1), 6 December (meeting 47); 8-nation draft (A/C.2/43/L.31/Rev.1), orally revised; agenda item 82.

Sponsors: Belgium, Canada, Denmark, Finland, France, Netherlands, Norway, Sweden.

Meeting numbers. GA 43rd session: 2nd Committee 21-26, 38, 46, 47; plenary 83.

Recorded vote in Assembly as follows:

In favour: Afghanistan, Albania, Algeria, Angola, Antigua and Barbuda, Argentina, Australia, Austria, Bahrain, Bangladesh, Barbados, Belgium, Benin, Bhutan, Bolivia, Botswana, Brazil, Brunei Darussalam, Bulgaria, Burkina Faso, Burma, Burundi, Byelorussian SSR, Cameroon, Canada, Cape Verde, Central African Republic, Chad, Chile, China, Colombia, Comoros, Congo, Costa Rica, Côte d'Ivoire, Cuba, Cyprus, Czechoslovakia, Democratic Kampuchea, Democratic Yemen, Denmark, Djibouti, Dominican Republic, Ecuador, Egypt, El Salvador, Equatorial Guinea, Ethiopia, Fiji, Finland, France, Gabon, Gambia, German Democratic Republic, Germany, Federal Republic of, Ghana, Greece, Grenada, Guinea, Guinea-Bissau, Guyana, Haiti, Honduras, Iceland, India, Indonesia, Iran, Iraq, Ireland, Italy, Jamaica, Japan, Jordan, Kenya, Kuwait, Lao People's Democratic Republic, Lebanon, Lesotho, Liberia, Libyan Arab Jamahiriya, Luxembourg, Madagascar, Malawi, Malaysia, Maldives, Mali, Malta, Mauritania, Mauritius, Mexico, Mongolia, Morocco, Mozambique, Nepal, Netherlands, New Zealand, Nicaragua, Niger, Nigeria, Norway, Oman, Pakistan, Panama, Papua New Guinea, Paraguay, Peru, Philippines, Portugal, Qatar, Romania, Rwanda, Saint Vincent and the Grenadines, Samoa, Sao Tome and Principe, Saudi Arabia, Senegal, Seychelles, Sierra Leone, Singapore, Solomon Islands, Somalia, Spain, Sri Lanka, Sudan, Suriname, Swaziland, Sweden, Syrian Arab Republic, Thailand, Togo, Trinidad and Tobago, Tunisia, Turkey, Uganda, Ukrainian SSR, USSR, United Arab Emirates, United Kingdom, United Republic of Tanzania, Uruguay, Vanuatu, Venezuela, Viet Nam, Yemen, Yugoslavia, Zaire, Zambia, Zimbabwe.

Against: None.

Abstaining: United States.

Entrepreneurship

In accordance with a 1986 General Assembly request,[(12)] the Secretary-General submitted, through the Economic and Social Council, a report on indigenous entrepreneurs in economic development.[(13)]

The report introduced the issues by defining the terms entrepreneur and entrepreneurship and noting that entrepreneurship was an essential dimension of economic and social development. With regard to indigenous entrepreneurs, the report stated that developing countries in which indigenous entrepreneurship was weak tended to become dependent on transnational companies and foreign entrepreneurs. Thus, Governments attached high priority to promoting high-level indigenous entrepreneurship and management, capable of holding its own in international competition.

Commenting on general national policies relevant to the emergence of indigenous entrepreneurs, the report specifically drew attention to the need for a legal and regulatory framework which should not be overly complex, the question of widening and protecting markets, the need to improve credit and capital markets and the importance of education. The report also discussed recent national and international efforts to train and support entrepreneurs. It noted that most

models of programmes to promote entrepreneurship included four components: access to finance, technical assistance, training and social promotion of the poorest social groups. Experience suggested that imported models of entrepreneurship were adaptable to local conditions and could be useful complements to national programmes. Non-governmental organizations, with the support of official aid programmes, were often best suited to assist entrepreneurs in the informal sector.

The Assembly, by **decision 43/435** of 20 December, took note of the Secretary-General's report.

ECONOMIC AND SOCIAL COUNCIL ACTION

On 29 July 1988, the Economic and Social Council adopted **resolution 1988/74** without vote.

National entrepreneurship in economic development

The Economic and Social Council,

Reaffirming General Assembly resolution 41/182 of 8 December 1986 on indigenous entrepreneurs in economic development,

Recognizing the responsibility of the international community, in particular that of the developed countries, to promote and endeavour to provide an equitable international economic environment supportive of the development of developing countries,

Bearing in mind that the promotion and development of national entrepreneurship require a dynamic process of capital formation in developing countries, which is related to the availability to those countries of financial and technical resources and broader market opportunities for them,

Convinced that entrepreneurship is an important dimension of economic and social development and that entrepreneurs in the public and private sectors can play an important role in mobilizing resources and promoting economic growth and socio-economic development,

Aware that many countries are actively seeking to encourage, strengthen and improve the effectiveness of national entrepreneurs in expanding and modernizing productive capacities, particularly by increasing productivity and technological capabilities, and in contributing generally to the development process,

Bearing in mind that the development of national entrepreneurship and its positive contribution to the development process should be pursued within the framework of the overall economic and social development strategy of each country in accordance with its economic and social system and specific objectives, needs and conditions,

Recognizing the important role that national entrepreneurs in all countries can play in economic development and technological progress, in the creation of new sources of employment, in the more efficient utilization of human resources and in the acquisition of new technologies,

Recognizing also the important role of Governments in promoting the development of national entrepreneurial activity,

Recognizing further that organs and organizations of the United Nations system are currently undertaking work in this field,

Noting the work of non-governmental organizations that are active in fostering positive entrepreneurial activity in interested developing countries,

1. *Takes note* of the report of the Secretary-General;

2. *Requests* the Secretary-General to undertake a study of measures to promote the contribution of national entrepreneurs to the economic development of developing countries, taking into account the need for a positive international economic environment and focusing on the following:

(a) The experience of developed and developing countries in establishing legal, technical and financial frameworks conducive to the positive contribution of national entrepreneurs to development;

(b) Programmes to help entrepreneurs achieve increased access to domestic and international finance, in order to enhance capital formation in developing countries;

(c) Technical assistance and financial support provided by interested donor countries for activities to promote entrepreneurial skills in interested developing countries;

(d) The acquisition, diffusion, creation and development of technologies, including new technologies, in national entrepreneurial activities;

3. *Requests* the Secretary-General to include in the report requested in paragraph 4 of the present resolution a section on international factors affecting the growth and competitiveness of enterprises of developing countries, including the need for broader market opportunities;

4. *Further requests* the Secretary-General, avoiding duplication and within existing resources, to prepare a report on the issues dealt with in the present resolution and to submit it to the General Assembly at its forty-fifth session, through the Economic and Social Council.

Economic and Social Council resolution 1988/74

29 July 1988   Meeting 41   Adopted without vote

5-nation draft (E/1988/L.40/Rev.2), orally revised; agenda item 2.
Sponsors: Canada, Germany, Federal Republic of, Japan, United Kingdom, United States.
Meeting numbers. ESC 34, 41.

Eradication of poverty

Following the adoption of **resolution 1988/47** on extreme poverty by the Economic and Social Council on 27 May 1988 (see PART THREE, Chapter XII), the General Assembly's Second Committee considered the question of international co-operation for the eradication of poverty in developing countries.

GENERAL ASSEMBLY ACTION

On 20 December, the General Assembly, on the recommendation of the Second Committee, adopted **resolution 43/195** by recorded vote.

International co-operation for the eradication of poverty in developing countries

The General Assembly,

Recalling its resolutions 3201(S-VI) and 3202(S-VI) of 1 May 1974, containing the Declaration and the Programme of Action on the Establishment of a New International Economic Order, 3281(XXIX) of 12 De-

cember 1974, containing the Charter of Economic Rights and Duties of States, and 3362(S-VII) of 16 September 1975 on development and international economic co-operation,

Taking note of Economic and Social Council resolution 1988/47 of 27 May 1988 on extreme poverty,

Aware that the adverse economic situation of developing countries, exacerbated by large structural imbalances in the world economy, has hindered the development process in those countries and their capacity to undertake social and economic programmes for, *inter alia*, the eradication of poverty,

Deeply concerned that a significant percentage of the world's population lives in conditions of absolute poverty and that, in developing countries, poverty can be a threat to social and political stability,

Stressing that the eradication of poverty is one of the most important development objectives requiring action by the international community at all levels,

Noting the importance of achieving effective international co-operation designed to support national efforts aimed at the eradication of poverty,

Aware that the eradication of poverty is made more difficult by a range of factors in the international economic environment that impede growth and development in the developing countries, such as the worsening in the terms of trade, intensified protectionism, high real interest rates, depressed commodity prices and the heavy burden of external debt,

Deeply concerned that negative effects of structural adjustment programmes in developing countries have exacerbated poverty, particularly among vulnerable groups in those countries, and have limited the ability of those countries to attain their socio-economic objectives,

Emphasizing the need for new and imaginative approaches to the eradication of poverty in developing countries as an integral part of the promotion of growth and development in those countries,

1. *Urges* the international community to create, as a priority, a supportive international economic environment for growth and development that will reinforce the efforts of developing countries to revitalize their development process and eradicate poverty;

2. *Requests* the regional commissions, in accordance with their mandates, to contribute more effectively to the strengthening of regional and subregional co-operation and to study options, including new approaches oriented towards the revitalization of growth and development in developing countries, in order to enable those countries to address effectively the eradication of poverty;

3. *Requests* the Secretary-General to submit to the General Assembly at its forty-fourth session a report analysing the impact of the economic crisis in developing countries on the intensity of poverty in those countries and containing recommendations for effective international policy measures for the urgent and permanent eradication of poverty in accordance with the present resolution.

General Assembly resolution 43/195

20 December 1988   Meeting 83   128-1-21 (recorded vote)

Approved by Second Committee (A/43/915/Add.6) by recorded vote (97-1-19), 9 December (meeting 48); draft by Tunisia, for Group of 77 (A/C.2/43/L.56/Rev.1), orally revised; agenda item 82 *(f)*.
Meeting numbers. GA 43rd session: 2nd Committee 21-26, 43, 48, 49; plenary 83.

In favour: Afghanistan, Albania, Algeria, Angola, Antigua and Barbuda, Argentina, Bahrain, Bangladesh, Barbados, Benin, Bhutan, Bolivia, Botswana, Brazil, Brunei Darussalam, Bulgaria, Burkina Faso, Burma, Burundi, Byelorussian SSR, Cameroon, Cape Verde, Central African Republic, Chad, Chile, China, Colombia, Comoros, Congo, Costa Rica, Côte d'Ivoire, Cuba, Cyprus, Czechoslovakia, Democratic Kampuchea, Democratic Yemen, Djibouti, Dominican Republic, Ecuador, Egypt, El Salvador, Equatorial Guinea, Ethiopia, Fiji, Gabon, Gambia, German Democratic Republic, Ghana, Grenada, Guinea, Guinea-Bissau, Guyana, Haiti, Honduras, Hungary, India, Indonesia, Iran, Iraq, Jamaica, Jordan, Kenya, Kuwait, Lao People's Democratic Republic, Lebanon, Lesotho, Liberia, Libyan Arab Jamahiriya, Madagascar, Malawi, Malaysia, Maldives, Mali, Malta, Mauritania, Mauritius, Mexico, Mongolia, Mozambique, Nepal, Nicaragua, Niger, Nigeria, Oman, Pakistan, Panama, Papua New Guinea, Paraguay, Peru, Philippines, Poland, Qatar, Romania, Rwanda, Saint Vincent and the Grenadines, Samoa, Sao Tome and Principe, Saudi Arabia, Senegal, Seychelles, Sierra Leone, Singapore, Solomon Islands, Somalia, Sri Lanka, Sudan, Suriname, Swaziland, Syrian Arab Republic, Thailand, Togo, Trinidad and Tobago, Tunisia, Turkey, Uganda, Ukrainian SSR, USSR, United Arab Emirates, United Republic of Tanzania, Uruguay, Vanuatu, Venezuela, Viet Nam, Yemen, Yugoslavia, Zaire, Zambia, Zimbabwe.

Against: United States.

Abstaining: Australia, Austria, Belgium, Canada, Denmark, Finland, France, Germany, Federal Republic of, Greece, Iceland, Ireland, Italy, Japan, Luxembourg, Netherlands, New Zealand, Norway, Portugal, Spain, Sweden, United Kingdom.

Long-term trends in economic and social development

In accordance with a 1985 request of the General Assembly,[14] the Secretary-General submitted in September 1988 a report[15] on the overall socio-economic perspective of the world economy to the year 2000. A summary of the report[16] was considered by the Economic and Social Council in July.

The report, prepared by DIESA with contributions from various parts of the United Nations system, attempted to place the economic events of the 1980s in historical perspective by reviewing a number of trends. A baseline scenario to the year 2000, prepared on the assumption of essentially unchanged policies, was presented. It was noted, however, that past attempts to forecast and project long-term trends had not been very successful—the expectations at the beginning of the 1970s were overthrown by the turbulence of the world economy, and those for the 1980s proved even more mistaken—and that the projections for the 1990s should be seen in that light.

Following a brief overview of world economic performance and policy in the 1980s, the report presented the baseline and alternative scenarios. It then considered: demographic and labour force trends and issues (population trends and structure, urbanization, international migration); trends and problems in the physical state of the world (energy, environment, human settlements); human resource development and social policy (education, health, social policy); and structural and technological change (structural trends in world production and trade, new and emerging technologies, the diffusion process of new technologies, structural changes in world manufacturing, world trade in non-fuel primary commodities). The report concluded that the outlook for the 1990s depended on progress made in national policy-making and in international co-operation. It was impossible to look forward to the 1990s without the impression that the forces seeking an internationalization of the world economy and those seeking to retain a measure of national and local autonomy would have to find new solutions and compromises. At one extreme of the perspective was the spectre of stagnation and environmental disaster; at the other there were opportunities to relieve poverty, improve the quality of life, safeguard the environment for future generations, stabilize the world economy and move towards a global community. The world's actual course would be decided by how Governments met the challenges facing them.

In October,[17] ACC decided that a small group of high-level officials should be convened to review the work of the United Nations system on long-term issues and to relate it to the preparation and future monitoring of an international development strategy for the fourth United Nations development decade.

On 29 July, by **decision 1988/179**, the Economic and Social Council took note of the summary of the Secretary-General's report and invited the Assembly, when considering the full report, to examine the feasibility of continuing the assessment of long-term trends in economic and social development.

GENERAL ASSEMBLY ACTION

On 20 December, on the recommendation of the Second Committee, the General Assembly adopted **resolution 43/194** without vote.

Examination of long-term trends in economic and social development

The General Assembly,

Recalling its resolutions 3508(XXX) of 15 December 1975, 32/57 of 8 December 1977, 34/57 of 29 November 1979, 37/249 of 21 December 1982 and 40/207 of 17 December 1985,

Recognizing that restoration of the economic and social development process of the developing countries is indispensable for the sustained growth of the international economy and world-wide well-being,

Considering that an examination of long-term social and economic trends, and their forecasted interaction, would be useful in the elaboration of the international development strategy for the fourth United Nations development decade, called for in its resolution 42/193 of 11 December 1987,

Conscious of the expediency of continuing to identify potential problem areas and critical issues in the world economy in order further to strengthen the capability for anticipating and responding to them by means of mutually supportive, co-ordinated policies,

Aware of the role that the United Nations is mandated to play and capable of playing in the formulation of future-oriented common approaches to key international economic and social issues,

1. *Takes note with interest* of the report of the Secretary-General on the overall socio-economic perspective of the world economy to the year 2000;

2. *Requests* the Secretary-General to update, as appropriate, the report on the overall socio-economic perspective of the world economy to the year 2000, in co-operation with the Secretary-General of the United Nations Conference on Trade and Development, taking into account the debate in the General Assembly at its forty-third session and the earlier discussion in the Economic and Social Council at its second regular session of 1988 as well as the views expressed by the Committee for Development Planning, so as to enhance its utility as one of the background documents for the preparation of the international development strategy for the fourth United Nations development decade;

3. *Also requests* the Secretary-General to prepare a comprehensive report, in time for the middle of the decade, on the basis of the updated overall socio-economic perspective of the world economy to the year 2000, and to consider the preparation of a subsequent report towards the end of the decade, selecting for topic-oriented studies the areas of common concern which warrant the special attention of the international community.

General Assembly resolution 43/194

20 December 1988   Meeting 83   Adopted without vote

Approved by Second Committee (A/43/915/Add.6) without vote, 6 December (meeting 47); draft by Vice-Chairman (A/C.2/43/L.73), based on informal consultations on draft by Poland (A/C.2/43/L.51); agenda item 82 *(f)*.
Meeting numbers. GA 43rd session: 2nd Committee 21-26, 43, 47; plenary 83.

Reactivation of economic growth and development

On 29 July 1988, by **decision 1988/178**, the Economic and Social Council decided to transmit a draft decision[18] on reactivation of economic growth and development in developing countries to the General Assembly's 1988 session for consideration and action. By that text, the Council would have decided to reaffirm the urgency of reactivating economic growth and development in developing countries and to recommend that the Assembly convene a special session in 1990 to be devoted to ways of achieving sustained growth in the world economy. On 10 October,[19] the Secretary-General submitted the draft decision to the Assembly.

GENERAL ASSEMBLY ACTION

On 20 December, by **decision 43/443**, the General Assembly decided to convene a resumed forty-third session, not later than the end of February 1989, for the Second Committee to consider further and take a final decision on convening a special session of the Assembly in 1990 devoted to international economic co-operation, in particular to the revitalization of economic growth and development in the developing countries. It also decided to transmit to the resumed session a draft decision[20] by which the Assembly would decide to convene such a special session and to initiate the preparatory process for it in January 1989.

Confidence-building

On 29 July 1988, the Economic and Social Council, by **decision 1988/180**, decided to defer to its July 1989 session consideration of a draft resolution submitted by Poland on confidence-building in international economic relations.[21] By that text, the Council would have called on Member States to pursue policies to strengthen confidence and partnership in international economic relations, address jointly issues facing the world economy, promote new ideas and develop a common sense of purpose, particularly regarding development issues. It would also have invited all States and United Nations bodies, particularly the United Nations Conference on Trade and Development (UNCTAD), the regional commissions and the specialized agencies, to exchange views on confidence-building and on ways to enhance it through concrete, co-operative measures. The Secretary-General would have been asked to keep the matter under review, take action to identify and promote confidence-building measures, establish a repertory of such measures and submit it to the General Assembly in 1990, through the Council.

In November 1988, the General Assembly's Second Committee had before it a draft resolution on international co-operation for development: towards confidence and common approaches,[22] submitted by Poland. By that text, which was subsequently withdrawn, the Assembly would have invited all States and bodies of the United Nations system to undertake measures to contribute to fostering confidence, predictability and reliability in international economic relations, and to promote common approaches to international economic issues, especially those confronting the developing countries. It would have asked the Secretary-General to keep the matter under review and assemble information on the relevant ongoing and planned activities of the system, and to report thereon in 1990, through the Economic and Social Council. It would have appealed to Governments to continue to use the potential of the United Nations to promote constructive, concerted and mutually supportive economic policies of Member States.

REFERENCES

[1]E/1988/16. [2]A/43/3/Rev.1. [3]*World Economic Survey 1988: Current Trends and Policies in the World Economy* (E/1988/50), Sales No. E.88.II.C.1. [4]E/1988/65. [5]YUN 1986, p. 884, ESC res. 1986/51, 22 July 1986. [6]A/43/915. [7]YUN 1987, p. 378, GA res. 42/193, 11 Dec. 1987. [8]A/43/376-E/1988/67 & Corr.1. [9]YUN 1980, p. 503, GA res. 35/56, annex, 5 Dec. 1980. [10]ACC/1988/DEC/1-18 (dec. 1988/1). [11]ACC/1988/17. [12]YUN 1986, p. 399, GA res. 41/182, 8 Dec. 1986. [13]A/43/360-E/1988/63. [14]YUN 1985, p. 416, GA res. 40/207, 17 Dec. 1985. [15]A/43/554. [16]E/1988/62. [17]ACC/1988/DEC/19-31 (dec. 1988/21). [18]E/1988/L.42.

(19)A/C.2/43/L.3.   (20)A/C.2/43/L.39.   (21)E/1988/L.34.
(22)A/C.2/43/L.50.

OTHER PUBLICATIONS

Joint Venture as a Form of International Economic Co-operation (ST/CTC/93), Sales. No. E.88.II.A.12. *Entrepreneurship and Economic Development* (ST/ESA/206), Sales No. E.88.II.A.13.

Economic surveys and trends

The *World Economic Survey 1988*[1] stated that the growth of gross world product in 1987 was slightly above 3 per cent, somewhat higher than in 1986. Short-term trends indicated that the world economy would continue to expand during 1988 and 1989, but at a lower rate.

The *Survey* reviewed the main international economic developments, analysed their implications and presented short- and medium-term forecasts for the different regions of the world. The first global stock exchange crisis in October 1987 gave evidence of the internationalization of financial relations, and fears of similar turbulence to come contributed to the instability of key parameters in the international economy—exchange rates and interest rates.

Per capita incomes in virtually all industrial countries grew steadily during the 1980s. Moderate increases in gross domestic product (GDP), some improvement in the terms of trade—particularly for oil importers—and slow population growth raised per capita incomes at an annual rate of 1 to 3 per cent in most countries since 1982, a trend likely to continue in the medium term.

Most countries in South and East Asia, including the most populous, achieved consistent increases in per capita income during the decade. Underlying economic trends and current policy stances indicated a consolidation of those gains in the short to medium term. In West Asia, armed conflicts and a large drop in oil prices at mid-decade adversely affected incomes and output. While the drop in per capita incomes halted in 1987 and incomes were still above those of most developing countries, prospects for a decisive improvement in the short term were uncertain.

In most countries of Africa, per capita incomes fell without respite during the 1980s. A legacy of policy failures in agriculture, ineffective industrialization strategies and extremely low primary commodity prices largely explained the disappointing performance in sub-Saharan Africa. Since 1986, output growth had also slowed markedly in the economies of North Africa. In the short term, prospects for the continent remained highly uncertain; room for manoeuvre on the domestic front appeared limited, structural policies would take time to bear fruit, and export earnings and prices of primary commodities would probably remain weak.

For the majority of countries in Latin America and the Caribbean, per capita incomes had fallen since 1981; for almost half of them, they fell again in 1987. Inflation accelerated considerably in 1987, reaching three digits in the large countries by early 1988. The need to confront domestic disequilibria and a heavy debt burden made it unlikely that investment ratios would soon recover. Unprecedented adjustment took place in the trade balance of the region, which shifted from deficit into surplus to the tune of $30 billion. Largely as a result of that shift, which absorbed savings and cut into investments, sustainable growth was not expected in the foreseeable future if present policies continued.

The UNCTAD *Trade and Development Report, 1988*[2] noted that the world economy was characterized by considerable diversity. The output of developing countries in Africa, Latin America and West Asia was advancing only weakly following declines in the rhythm of activity in 1987. The debt crisis, bad harvests in some countries and the behaviour of export prices and volumes all contributed to that outcome.

In Western Europe also, growth appeared to be lagging somewhat behind the already slow pace recorded in 1987, so that no significant improvement in unemployment levels was to be expected in most countries. For the developing countries of East Asia, the extraordinarily rapid expansion of exports experienced in 1987 continued to be the primary engine of growth. In China, a rapid expansion of domestic demand continued to drive the economy forward, and government policy aimed at moderating the expansion. In Japan, a buoyant rise in domestic demand was offsetting the relatively modest rise in net imports triggered by the appreciation of the yen; and for the United States, increased domestic demand and a revival of export growth, following the depreciation of the dollar, continued to provide a stimulus.

For the socialist countries of Eastern Europe and the developing countries of South Asia, growth in 1987 fell far short of earlier years, largely because of poor harvests. In South Asia, that was primarily the result of drought, and the decline in agricultural output was expected to be rapidly reversed. In Eastern Europe, weather was also a factor, but certain managerial and organizational deficiencies were also evident. The process of economic reform accelerated markedly in the region, particularly in the USSR.

ECONOMIC AND SOCIAL COUNCIL ACTION

On 29 July 1988, the Economic and Social Council adopted **resolution 1988/75** without vote.

Early identification of world economic developments
The Economic and Social Council,

Emphasizing the common interest in a more balanced and sustained growth and development of the world economy,

Recognizing the importance of short-term and medium-term analysis of the most acute problems in the world economy,

Convinced that the United Nations provides an appropriate framework for the early identification and analysis of emerging problems in the world economy and international economic relations,

Recalling General Assembly resolution 32/197 of 20 December 1977, by which the United Nations Secretariat was requested to concentrate, *inter alia*, on identifying and bringing to the attention of Governments emerging economic and social issues of international concern,

1. *Acknowledges* that the economic research and analysis activities of the United Nations should continue to be carried out within existing resources and on a co-ordinated basis and should include:

(*a*) The continuous gathering, updating and analysis of the necessary data from a wide range of sources, including national and international sources;

(*b*) The provision of timely and reliable information to Governments;

(*c*) Applied research;

2. *Requests* the Secretary-General to prepare a survey of the mechanisms and means currently available within the United Nations system for the early identification, analysis and monitoring of world economic developments and to include it in the *World Economic Survey 1989* as an annex.

Economic and Social Council resolution 1988/75

29 July 1988   Meeting 41   Adopted without vote

Draft by Vice-President (E/1988/L.50), based on informal consultations on draft by Bulgaria, Byelorussian SSR, German Democratic Republic, Mongolia, Poland and USSR (E/1988/L.38/Rev.1); agenda item 2.
Meeting numbers. ESC 33, 41.

REFERENCES

[1]*World Economic Survey 1988: Current Trends and Policies in the World Economy* (E/1988/50), Sales No. E.88.II.C.1. [2]*Trade and Development Report, 1988* (UNCTAD/TDR/8), Sales No. E.88.II.D.8.

OTHER PUBLICATION

Modelling of World Economic Development (ST/ESA/195), Sales No. E.88.II.C.2.

Development planning and public administration

In 1988, the human resources element of development was discussed by CDP. The United Nations Department of Technical Co-operation for Development (DTCD) continued its programme of technical co-operation in public administration and finance with a budget of $24.9 million.

Development planning

The Committee for Development Planning held its twenty-fourth session in New York from 12 to 15 April 1988.[1] It discussed aspects of the world economy, including policy issues for the 1990s (see above). It also considered human resources development (see PART THREE, Chapter XII), iden-

tification of the least developed among the developing countries (see below) and arrangements for its future work.

In the face of major structural imbalances in the world economy, inadequacies of both national policies and international co-operation threatened the sustainability of growth in many countries and regions. Technological change, shifting comparative advantage, and population and environmental changes complicated the formulation of effective national policies and increased the need for international co-operation. In addition to reducing absolute poverty, diversifying exports and integrating environmental concerns into economic decision-making, other domestic issues varied from country to country. As policy makers digested the results of differing experiences of other countries, they had started to pursue greater autonomy and market discipline for State enterprises, encourage entrepreneurship in the private sector and reform pricing policies and fiscal systems.

A critical social issue in all countries was unemployment and marginalization. In developing countries, underemployment, or disguised unemployment, was more important than open unemployment; a very large informal sector absorbed workers who would otherwise be unemployed.

The mobilization of resources for development was a central task in developing countries. In all countries there was scope for improving financial intermediation and the functioning of domestic capital markets to utilize private savings better. There was also need for fiscal reform to increase revenues and for reducing military expenditures and subsidies to urban consumers and inefficient State enterprises.

Developing countries needed counter-cyclical policies to face external and domestic economic shocks. They could include guaranteed commodity prices for domestic producers, sinking funds to retire debt accumulated during slack export demand or to sustain income levels during a drought or other disturbance to domestic supply, and special measures to protect vulnerable groups. Other approaches to facilitate a more flexible response to shocks included decentralized decision-making in the State enterprise sector. CDP noted that a number of countries were experimenting with performance contracts to strengthen manager incentives and minimize costs. In some cases, privatization could offer possibilities for increasing efficiency.

ECONOMIC AND SOCIAL COUNCIL ACTION

By **decision 1988/181** of 29 July 1988, the Economic and Social Council took note of the report of CDP on its 1988 session. On 17 October, by **decision 1988/185**, the Council decided that the 1989 session of CDP should be held from 9 to 12 May.

Technical co-operation

During 1988,[2] DTCD executed 153 projects in development issues and policies with delivery of $33.2 million against budgets of $42.2 million. Of total project expenditures, 41.8 per cent was for Africa, 25.2 per cent for Asia and the Pacific, 23.6 per cent for the Mediterranean, Middle East, Europe and interregional programme, and 9.4 per cent for the Americas.

During the year, requests for technical assistance in development planning were strongly influenced by international economic instability and onerous foreign debt and balance-of-payments problems. DTCD's assistance therefore focused on activities related to national economic structural adjustment and recovery programmes, particularly in the case of Africa. A main thrust was on applied, immediately useful assistance in such areas as short-term and operational planning, project planning and monitoring and the co-ordination of external assistance; the development of innovative methodologies and modalities to enhance the effectiveness and efficiency of technical co-operation was intensified. Training and other means of developing national technical capacities in development were stressed.

Public administration

On 25 May 1988, the Economic and Social Council, by **decision 1988/115**, requested the Secretary-General to convene the Ninth Meeting of Experts on the United Nations Programme in Public Administration and Finance in early 1989 to review the United Nations regular programme of work in public administration and finance as well as the progress made in the Special Action Programme in Public Administration and Management for Africa and United Nations technical co-operation activities, giving particular attention to identifying new ways to strengthen technical co-operation among developing countries. The Council also decided that the Meeting should accord special attention to enhancing the role of public administration in developing countries in the promotion and management of development alternatives so as to facilitate a balanced and accelerated process of development.

Technical co-operation

In 1988,[2] DTCD implemented 120 projects in public administration and finance with delivery of $18.6 million against budgets of $24.9 million. Both budgets and delivery increased more than 30 per cent over 1987. Of 1988 expenditures, 52.7 per cent was in Africa, 27.7 per cent in Asia and the Pacific, 11.8 per cent in the Mediterranean, Middle East, Europe and interregional programme, 7.8 per cent in the Americas. Interregional advisers undertook 22 missions (compared to 37 in 1987) in the areas of tax administration and resource mobilization, management development and training, government budgeting and financial management, including accounting and auditing, public enterprise and administrative reform.

While a number of projects had multi-sectoral dimensions, most fell broadly into the fields of organization and management improvement, training and management development, personnel administration and labour power planning, public administration policy analysis and development, information management and data processing, and regional and local administration. Improved productivity and performance in public services was a priority objective of programmes, as was human resource development.

In public financial management, tax policies and administration were strengthened in a number of countries as a means of improving resource mobilization. The focus in public financial management projects varied from streamlining budgetary systems to improving legislative accountability. The establishment of financial information systems to strengthen public financial management was also used in a number of projects. Concern continued in many developing countries about the financial difficulties of public enterprises, especially with regard to large deficits and subsidies.

Three public administration and finance meetings were organized: an interregional seminar on management training for scientific and technical personnel (Manila, Philippines); an interregional seminar on the application of audit standards in the public sector (Vienna); and an interregional training programme on improving government accounting and financial reporting (Malawi).

REFERENCES
[1]E/1988/16. [2]DP/1989/46/Add.1.

Rural development

The ACC Task Force on Rural Development (sixteenth meeting, New York, 11-13 May 1988)[1] reviewed work accomplished since its 1987 meeting[2] in three areas: joint action at the country and regional levels, people's participation in rural development, and monitoring and evaluation. It also discussed the definition of rural development projects oriented towards alleviating rural poverty, an issue currently under discussion by the World Bank, and progress attained regarding implementation of the Nairobi Forward-looking Strategies for the Advancement of Women[3] as pertaining to rural women. Reports of panels on people's participation in rural development and on monitoring and evaluation were annexed to the Task Force's report.

In response to a 1981 Economic and Social Council decision,[4] the Secretary-General transmitted the second review and analysis of agrarian reform and rural development,[5] prepared by the Food and Agriculture Organization of the United Nations in collaboration with other concerned United Nations organizations and bodies, as a follow-up to the 1979 World Conference on Agrarian Reform and Rural Development (WCARRD).[6] The first such report had been submitted in 1984.[7]

The report delineated the dimensions and trends of rural poverty, described international developments and policies during the period 1983-1986 and discussed the policies and progress of national Governments in various fields in ameliorating rural poverty and improving the conditions of rural people.

Concluding, the report stated that there had been little advance in rural poverty alleviation during 1983-1986, except in Asia. The major causes behind the seemingly incongruous simultaneous increase in food availability and hunger could be laid to policy choices by both developed and developing countries, population dynamics and the general economic environment. With regard to population increase, an important aspect was the problem facing rural youth. A review of agrarian reforms indicated the absence of new programmes by countries. While many countries continued their land settlement programmes, none had succeeded in keeping pace with even the annual increase in agricultural population. Inequalities in land holdings continued to be large in all regions, especially in Latin America and the Near East. Population pressure had resulted in an increase in landlessness and near-landlessness in many Asian countries.

A bright spot was the continuing progress towards people's participation in development. Also, the critical role of women in rural development was beginning to be reflected in almost all programmes and projects, though more work needed to be done in that regard. A determined political commitment followed by energetic action was imperative from countries on the commemoration of the tenth anniversary of WCARRD.

REFERENCES

[1]ACC/1988/PG/7. [2]YUN 1987, p. 388. [3]YUN 1985. p. 937. [4]YUN 1981, p. 400, ESC dec. 1981/185, 23 July 1981. [5]E/1988/56. [6]YUN 1979, p. 500. [7]YUN 1984, p. 411.

Special economic areas

The development problems of the least developed and island developing countries were considered by various United Nations bodies during 1988.

Preparations began for the Second United Nations Conference on the Least Developed Countries, planned for September 1990. In December, on the recommendation of CDP and the Economic and Social Council, the General Assembly added Mozambique to the list of LDCs.

Developing countries

Least developed countries

The special problems of the officially designated LDCs were considered in several United Nations forums during 1988. With the inclusion of Mozambique in the United Nations list of LDCs, the number rose to 42. The others were Afghanistan, Bangladesh, Benin, Bhutan, Botswana, Burkina Faso, Burma, Burundi, Cape Verde, Central African Republic, Chad, Comoros, Democratic Yemen, Djibouti, Equatorial Guinea, Ethiopia, Gambia, Guinea, Guinea-Bissau, Haiti, Kiribati, Lao People's Democratic Republic, Lesotho, Malawi, Maldives, Mali, Mauritania, Nepal, Niger, Rwanda, Samoa, Sao Tome and Principe, Sierra Leone, Somalia, Sudan, Togo, Tuvalu, Uganda, United Republic of Tanzania, Vanuatu, Yemen.

Identification of LDCs

By **decision 1988/105** of 5 February 1988, the Economic and Social Council requested CDP to consider including Mozambique in the list of LDCs and to submit its recommendation to the Council in July.

In April,[1] CDP considered the eligibility of Mozambique and Zambia for inclusion in the list, examining data pertaining to three formal criteria—per capita GDP, share of manufacturing output in GDP, and adult literacy rate. CDP concluded that Mozambique met the existing criteria for inclusion in the list.

With regard to the case of Zambia, which had been carried over from its 1987 session,[2] while concerned about the deteriorating state of Zambia's economy, CDP concluded that the existing criteria and the procedures for their application did not warrant its inclusion in the list.

CDP reiterated its reluctance to apply the existing criteria, which it had deemed inadequate for some time. In view of its concern, it included an item on the criteria in the programme of work for its 1989 session.

ECONOMIC AND SOCIAL COUNCIL ACTION

On 13 July, the Economic and Social Council, by **decision 1988/153**, endorsed the CDP conclusion and recommended that the General Assembly approve Mozambique's inclusion in the list of LDCs.

By **decision 43/431** of 20 December, the General Assembly decided to include Mozambique in the list of LDCs.

Programme of Action for the 1980s

ACC held the eighth interagency consultation on the follow-up of the Substantial New Programme of Action (SNPA) for the 1980s for LDCs at Geneva on 16 and 17 May 1988.[3] SNPA had been adopted in 1981 by a United Nations Conference[4] and endorsed later that year by the General Assembly.[5] The consultation discussed support to adjustment programmes in LDCs and co-ordination arrangements. It also considered preparatory arrangements for the Second United Nations Conference on LDCs.

Preparations for the Second UN Conference on LDCs

In accordance with a 1987 General Assembly request,[6] the Secretary-General submitted a report in October 1988 on the state of preparations for the Second United Nations Conference on LDCs.[7] The Secretary-General noted that preparatory meetings were planned for 1989 and 1990 and that it was proposed to hold the Conference in Paris from 3 to 14 September 1990.

Within the United Nations system, preparations for the Conference had been discussed at the eighth inter-agency consultation on the follow-up of SNPA; preparations had also been initiated at the regional level.

The Secretary-General of UNCTAD, in collaboration with the Netherlands, convened a meeting of eminent persons at The Hague on 15 and 16 September, bringing together 24 high-level experts on development problems. The meeting focused on identifying constraints and bottle-necks that had hindered the development efforts of LDCs during the 1980s and on national and international measures required to accelerate their development process in the 1990s. UNCTAD planned further high-level meetings in 1989.

The eighth inter-agency consultation on the follow-up of SNPA (see above) reviewed the preparatory process and noted the need for co-ordination between the different programmes of relevance to LDCs, particularly the United Nations Programme of Action for African Economic Recovery and Development 1986-1990.[8] The consultation conducted an exchange of views on issues related to the development of LDCs and discussed contributions of United Nations organizations and agencies to the 1990 Conference.

UNDP action. On 1 July,[9] the Governing Council of the United Nations Development Programme (UNDP) requested the Administrator

to assist LDCs to ensure their full participation in the preparations for the 1990 Conference and in the Conference itself, deciding that such assistance should be funded from the Special Measures Fund for LDCs. He was also asked to report to the Council's February 1989 special session on UNDP participation in Conference preparations.

On 20 December, on the recommendation of the Second Committee, the General Assembly adopted **resolution 43/186** without vote.

Second United Nations Conference on the Least Developed Countries

The General Assembly,

Recalling its resolution 42/177 of 11 December 1987, in which it decided to convene the Second United Nations Conference on the Least Developed Countries at a high level in Paris in September 1990,

Recalling also its decision to convene one session of the Meeting of Governmental Experts of Donor Countries and Multilateral and Bilateral Financial and Technical Assistance Institutions with Representatives of the Least Developed Countries early in 1989 followed by one session of the Intergovernmental Group on the Least Developed Countries, as Preparatory Committee for the Second United Nations Conference on the Least Developed Countries, early in 1990 in order to prepare for the Conference,

Reiterating its request to the Secretary-General to obtain, as has been the past practice, extrabudgetary resources to ensure the effective participation of the representatives of the least developed countries through provision of the resources necessary to finance the travel expenses of at least two representatives from each least developed country to attend the two preparatory meetings,

Taking note of the report of the Secretary-General on the Second United Nations Conference on the Least Developed Countries,

Expressing deep concern at the continuing deterioration in the overall socio-economic situation of the least developed countries,

1. *Emphasizes* the crucial importance of adequate preparation for the Second United Nations Conference on the Least Developed Countries, taking into account the priorities to be put forward by the least developed countries themselves;

2. *Calls upon* all Governments, intergovernmental and multilateral institutions and others concerned to take appropriate steps to ensure that adequate preparations are made for the Conference and to participate effectively in the two above-mentioned preparatory meetings, as well as in the Conference itself;

3. *Requests* all concerned organs, organizations and bodies of the United Nations system to submit, before the first preparatory meeting, reports containing a review of the implementation of the Substantial New Programme of Action for the 1980s for the Least Developed Countries within their fields of competence and proposals for further action as input to the preparations for the Conference;

4.   *Notes* the steps being taken by the Secretary-General of the United Nations, with the assistance of the Director-General for Development and International Economic Co-operation and the Secretary-General of the United Nations Conference on Trade and Development, and urges them to ensure full mobilization and co-ordination of all organs, organizations and bodies of the United Nations system in the preparations for the Conference;

5.   *Takes note with appreciation* of decision 88/30 on the Second United Nations Conference on the Least Developed Countries, adopted by the Governing Council of the United Nations Development Programme on 1 July 1988, in which the Administrator of the United Nations Development Programme was requested, in close consultation with the Secretary-General of the United Nations Conference on Trade and Development, to assist the least developed countries to ensure that they are able to participate fully in the preparations, including preparatory meetings, for the Conference and in the Conference itself;

6.   *Requests* the Secretary-General to submit a report to the General Assembly at its forty-fourth session on the state of preparations for the Conference.

General Assembly resolution 43/186

20 December 1988   Meeting 83   Adopted without vote

Approved by Second Committee (A/43/915/Add.2) without vote, 23 November (meeting 44); draft by Vice-Chairman (A/C.2/43/L.66), based on informal consultations on draft by Tunisia, for Group of 77 (A/C.2/43/L.54); agenda item 82 *(b)*.
Meeting numbers. GA 43rd session: 2nd Committee 21-26, 30, 36, 37, 43, 44; plenary 83.

Technical co-operation

In March 1988,[10] the Secretary-General transmitted to the General Assembly a Joint Inspection Unit (JIU) report on technical co-operation between organizations of the United Nations system and LDCs. The report outlined financing, programming, implementation and co-ordination aspects of the technical co-operation activities of the United Nations system. Conclusions and recommendations focused on improving the effectiveness of technical co-operation through co-ordination of agencies, along with closer analysis of efforts to assess effectiveness from the viewpoint of the beneficiary countries.

In May,[11] the Secretary-General transmitted ACC's comments on the JIU report. ACC members agreed that there was a need to streamline and strengthen modalities, mechanisms and co-ordination for technical co-operation with LDCs. It noted, however, that fuller discussion of existing specific intersecretariat mechanisms needed to occur before certain recommendations, such as one to eliminate some planning meetings, could be implemented.

Island developing countries

In accordance with a 1986 General Assembly request,[12] the Secretary-General submitted in August 1988 a report[13] on the specific problems and special needs of island developing countries. Taking into account the views of United Nations bodies and agencies, as well as the findings of a Group of Experts on Island Developing Countries (Malta, 24 and 25 May 1988), the report stated that many problems of those countries were those of development in general, but were more pronounced in their impact on island developing countries, particularly the small ones.

The report discussed the problems and prospects of island developing countries, giving special attention to those that were small in terms of population, land area and gross national product. With regard to domestic resources, the report considered natural and geographical factors (lack of natural resources, depletion of non-renewable resources, environmental problems, fresh water supplies, vulnerability to natural disasters, transport and communications), economic activities (diseconomies of scale, agriculture, trade policy issues, the role of tourism and services, marine and submarine resources) and human and institutional problems (shortages and gaps in manpower, other institutional constraints, migration, cultural problems). As to the transfer of external resources, the report considered aid, external debt and remittances.

In its conclusions and recommendations, the report outlined possible measures at the national level (development strategies, institution building, human resource development, entrepreneurship and foreign investment, technological development, food and agriculture, fisheries, services, infrastructural development, environment, disaster preparedness, participation in international forums), regional co-operation and international support measures (external financial and technical assistance, trade, migration).

GENERAL ASSEMBLY ACTION

On 20 December 1988, on the recommendation of the Second Committee, the General Assembly adopted **resolution 43/189** without vote.

Specific measures in favour of island developing countries

The General Assembly,

Recalling the Declaration and the Programme of Action on the Establishment of a New International Economic Order, contained in its resolutions 3201(S-VI) and 3202(S-VI) of 1 May 1974, the Charter of Economic Rights and Duties of States, contained in its resolution 3281(XXIX) of 12 December 1974, resolution 3362(S-VII) of 16 September 1975 on development and international economic co-operation, and the International Development Strategy for the Third United Nations Development Decade, contained in the annex to its resolution 35/56 of 5 December 1980,

Reiterating the call for specific action in favour of island developing countries contained in its resolution 41/163 of 5 December 1986, and in resolutions 98(IV) of 31 May 1976, 111(V) of 3 June 1979 and 138(VI) of 2 July 1983 of the United Nations Conference on Trade and Development, as well as decision 86/33 of 27 June 1986 of the Governing Council of the United Nations Development

Programme on the special needs of island developing countries,

Recognizing that, in addition to the general problems facing developing countries, island developing countries also suffer handicaps arising from the interplay of such factors as their smallness, remoteness, geographical dispersion, vulnerability to natural disasters, the fragility of their ecosystems, constraints in transport and communications, great distances from market centres, a highly limited internal market, lack of natural resources, weak indigenous technological capacity, the acute problem of obtaining fresh water supplies, heavy dependence on imports and a small number of commodities, depletion of non-renewable resources, migration, particularly of personnel with high-level skills, shortage of administrative personnel and heavy financial burdens,

Recognizing also that many of the above factors occur concurrently in island developing countries, resulting in economic and social vulnerability and dependence, particularly in those countries which are small and/or geographically dispersed,

1. *Reaffirms* its resolution 41/163 and other relevant resolutions of the General Assembly and of the United Nations Conference on Trade and Development, and calls for their immediate and effective implementation;

2. *Expresses its appreciation* to States and to organizations and bodies within and outside the United Nations system that have responded to the special needs of island developing countries;

3. *Welcomes* the initiative of the Secretary-General of the United Nations Conference on Trade and Development in convening a meeting of the Group of Experts on Island Developing Countries at Valletta on 24 and 25 May 1988, and expresses its appreciation to the Government of Malta for acting as host to the meeting;

4. *Takes note* of the report of the Valletta meeting and of the report of the Secretary-General on specific problems and special needs of island developing countries;

5. *Welcomes* the efforts made by island developing countries to adopt policies that address their specific problems, including efforts at regional co-operation and integration, and calls upon those countries to continue to pursue, in accordance with their national objectives, policies and priorities, further measures to render their economies less vulnerable to the adverse consequences of their specific situations;

6. *Appeals* to the international community:

(a) To maintain and, if possible, increase the level of concessional financial and technical assistance provided to island developing countries;

(b) To maximize access of island developing countries to concessional financial and technical assistance by taking into account the specific development needs and problems facing those countries;

(c) To consider reviewing the mechanisms of existing procedures used in providing concessional resources to island developing countries;

(d) To ensure that assistance conforms to the national and, as appropriate, regional priorities of island developing countries;

(e) To provide support to island developing countries over a mutually agreed and, where appropriate, longer time-frame to enable them to achieve economic growth and development;

(f) To consider improving existing arrangements for the compensation of island developing countries for adverse effects on their export earnings and to consider wider adoption of such arrangements;

(g) To continue to ensure that a concerted effort is made to assist island developing countries, at their request, in improving their administrative capacities and in satisfying their overall needs with regard to the development of human resources;

7. *Calls upon* the international community to consider improving measures, within existing trade arrangements, in favour of island developing countries according to their special circumstances, taking into account particularly the special needs and problems of small island developing countries;

8. *Urges once again* relevant organizations of the United Nations system to take adequate measures to respond positively to the particular needs of island developing countries and to report on such measures, as appropriate;

9. *Urges* the United Nations Conference on Trade and Development to strengthen its role as the focal point for specific action at the global level in favour of island developing countries and to act as a catalyst in this regard, *inter alia*, by organizing and facilitating the cross-regional interchange of information and experience in full co-operation with regional and subregional organizations, both within and outside the United Nations system, as appropriate;

10. *Calls upon* the Secretary-General, taking into account work already done on this issue, including that envisaged in paragraph 9 above, to identify within the appropriate inter-agency framework the problems of island developing countries, in particular those of small island developing countries, in order to elaborate specific measures that the international community might take to address those problems;

11. *Requests* the Secretary-General to convene a meeting of governmental experts of island developing countries and donor countries and organizations to review the problems of island developing countries and propose appropriate concrete action with respect to those countries;

12. *Also requests* the Secretary-General to submit a report to the General Assembly at its forty-fifth session on the implementation of the present resolution.

General Assembly resolution 43/189

20 December 1988   Meeting 83   Adopted without vote

Approved by Second Committee (A/43/915/Add.2) without vote, 9 December (meeting 48); draft by Vice-Chairman (A/C.2/43/L.79), orally revised, based on informal consultations on draft by Tunisia, for Group of 77 (A/C.2/43/L.57); agenda item 82 (b).

Financial implications. 5th Committee, A/43/967; S-G, A/C.2/43/L.83, A/C.5/43/60.

Meeting numbers. GA 43rd session: 2nd Committee 21-26, 30, 36, 37, 43, 48; 5th Committee 47; plenary 83.

REFERENCES

(1)E/1988/16. (2)YUN 1987, p. 389. (3)ACC/1988/11. (4)YUN 1981, p. 406. (5)*Ibid.*, p. 410, GA res. 36/194, 17 Dec. 1981. (6)YUN 1987, p. 392, GA res. 42/177, 11 Dec. 1987. (7)A/43/698. (8)YUN 1986, p. 446, GA res. S-13/2, annex, 1 June 1986. (9)E/1988/19 (dec. 88/30). (10)A/43/228. (11)A/43/228/Add.1. (12)YUN 1986, p. 408, GA res. 41/163, 5 Dec. 1986. (13)A/43/513 & Corr.1.

PUBLICATION

The Least Developed Countries—1988 Report (TD/B/1202), Sales No. E.89.II.D.3.

Chapter II

Operational activities for development

In 1988, some $7 billion in concessional loans and grants was made available to developing countries through the United Nations system, representing 14 per cent of total official development assistance to those countries from all sources during the year. Following its consideration of the annual report of the Director-General for Development and International Economic Co-operation on United Nations operational activities, the General Assembly, in December, invited members of the organs and organizations of the system to address operational activities for development in their governing bodies, with a view to arriving at a co-ordinated and system-wide approach to the issue.

The United Nations Development Programme (UNDP) registered a record year in 1988 with total income of $1.2 billion. Expenditures during the year from UNDP central resources totalled $1.1 billion, of which $832 million was spent on field programme activities. Following a mid-term review of resources for the fourth programming cycle (1987-1991), the UNDP Governing Council made additional programme allocations of $490 million to country and intercountry indicative planning figures and $110 million to Special Programme Resources.

The United Nations Department of Technical Co-operation for Development (DTCD) had 953 projects under execution in 1988 with total delivery of $149.4 million. In line with its emphasis on human resources development, there was a significant rise in expenditures for training and more stress on management development and technical training. A considerable increase in the United Nations Population Fund's share of DTCD's programme enabled DTCD to resume active involvement in statistics and population-related activities.

The United Nations Volunteers programme expanded in 1988 with an estimated 1,534 volunteers in service at the end of the year, supported by the Special Voluntary Fund.

In 1988, project expenditures by the United Nations Capital Development Fund totalled $34 million, and $74.9 million was approved in new commitments.

General aspects

In his report providing statistical data on United Nations operational activities for development covering 1988,[1] the Director-General for Development and International Economic Co-operation (DIEC) stated that preliminary figures indicated that some $7 billion in concessional resources (grants and loans) was made available to developing countries through the United Nations system, an increase of 11 per cent over 1987. That amount represented 14 per cent of the total official development assistance (ODA) to developing countries in 1988 ($51 billion). Although the system's concessional resources increased by $0.8 billion over 1987, their overall proportion in total ODA remained the same.

Total expenditures on operational activities overall by the system, including humanitarian assistance, amounted to $7.8 billion in 1988 as against $6.9 billion in 1987. That total comprised: development grants, $3.3 billion; concessional loans, $3.7 billion; and grant-financed refugee, humanitarian, special economic and disaster relief activities, $0.8 billion.

Grant assistance through UNDP and UNDP-administered funds totalled $917.5 million in 1988; through the World Food Programme (WFP), $878 million; through the United Nations Children's Fund (UNICEF), $399.5 million; and through the United Nations Population Fund (UNFPA), $129.9 million. Grant assistance through specialized agencies during the year totalled $825.9 million.

Net transfers from the International Development Association (IDA) grew by 7 per cent to $3.5 billion in 1988, representing a less vigorous increase than the 16 per cent recorded in 1987. As for net transfers of non-concessional (not ODA) loans from the World Bank, they went from an already sizeable negative balance of $2.2 billion in 1987 to some $4.6 billion in 1988.

Policy review. In response to a series of requests by the General Assembly in a 1987 resolution,[2] the DIEC Director-General, in his annual report to the Economic and Social Council and the Assembly in 1988,[3] addressed selected policy and management issues. The issues mainly corresponded to those identified in the course of a review of case-studies on the functioning of operational activities of the system undertaken in 1987.[4]

In addition to mobilization of financial resources, the report discussed issues that would need to be addressed by various entities of the system, noting that implementation of the 1987 Assembly resolution on operational activities for development[2] would require a major effort by all the organizations of the United Nations development system. With respect to specific items, the report reviewed the work of the Consultative Committee on Substantive Questions (Operational Activities) (CCSQ(OPS)) of the Administrative Committee on Co-ordination (ACC), described the nature and scope of the activities of the Joint Consultative Group on Policy (JCGP) (UNDP, UNFPA, UNICEF, WFP and the International Fund for Agricultural Development (IFAD)) and discussed integrating women in development programmes, rationalization of field office structures and procurement of equipment.

The Director-General concluded that two actions were particularly important: the scope for linkages between global objectives and targets set for the 1990s and the potential contribution of the operational activities of the United Nations to their achievement in some fields could be explored more systematically; and a forward-looking approach should be taken to adapt the activities and structures of United Nations organizations to match a rapidly changing and increasingly complex and diversified environment.

The Director-General said it was his intention to launch a broader study of emerging trends in operational activities. Such a study would provide a basis for developing responses to the problems that the United Nations system would be expected to address in the 1990s and would involve far-reaching modifications in the content and organization of development co-operation. It was his opinion that issues related to the role and functions of the resident co-ordinator and the rationalization of field office structures would also benefit from examination in the course of such a long-term review.

The Director-General also submitted consolidated information on responses from governing bodies of the organs and organizations of the United Nations system on the findings of the case-studies on the functioning of operational activities of the system undertaken in 1987.[4] Information on programming, simplification, decentralization and harmonization of rules and procedures, the role of UNDP as a central funding agency, country-level co-ordination, structure and technical advice and other issues was received from the governing bodies of UNICEF, UNDP, UNFPA and the United Nations Centre for Human Settlements (Habitat), as well as from WFP, ILO, FAO, UNESCO, WHO, UPU and IFAD.

The Director-General noted that the extent and depth of responses by governing bodies varied considerably and suggested that they might wish to review the consolidated responses to identify both common positions and differences in emphasis or approach. While the case-studies covered only a small sample of the issues relating to operational activities in selected developing countries, the most important findings related to problems frequently cited in other studies and evaluations and confirmed the statements of the General Assembly on the need for improvements. The responses of governing bodies revealed some difficulties likely to be encountered in formulating long- and medium-term goals and improved policies and procedures, as well as in adjusting the country-level structures of the system.

Member States would find in the responses further evidence of the need for greater coherence and co-ordination of their policies on operational activities. While the intentions of Member States to ensure optimum service and support to the developing countries had been clearly expressed in the Assembly, differences in interpretation or emphasis underlined the complexity of the process of achieving reforms and improvement of operational activities to which the system was firmly committed.

UNDP Council action. In response to the General Assembly's 1987 request[2] for governing bodies of the United Nations development system to discuss the 1987 report on case-studies on the functioning of the operational activities for development of the United Nations system,[4] the UNDP Administrator submitted a report to the Governing Council on UNDP's response to that report.[5]

The Administrator grouped the recommendations of the report on case-studies under the following headings and commented on them: the importance of the United Nations system of technical co-operation; programming and co-ordination; the functions of the resident co-ordinator; concentration of UNDP assistance in more needy countries; reinforcing the role of UNDP; decentralization of UNDP; closer co-operation between multilateral financial assistance sources and United Nations agencies; substantive support to Governments in meeting their development planning needs; nongovernmental organizations (NGOs); and field representation and common premises.

On 1 July,[6] the Governing Council decided to submit a series of conclusions on the subject to the Economic and Social Council. It concurred with the views expressed in the 1987 report regarding the importance of assistance from the United Nations system for technical co-operation and acknowledged the important role of UNDP as the central funding and co-ordinating mechanism.

The Council also concurred with a number of the report's recommendations, including those regarding the need for coherent co-ordination at the country level; the importance of the relationship between recipient Governments and resident co-ordinators; the need for decentralization of the management of operational activities and the pursuit of increased harmonization of procedures; self-reliance in programming approaches; the need for operational activities to respond to the varied and changing requirements of developing countries; the need for more attention to be paid to reinforcing the central funding role of UNDP; increasing the flow of development information to the field; the provision by the United Nations system of maximum assistance to recipient Governments to strengthen their capacity to co-ordinate external assistance; and the important role of NGOs in some areas of operational activities.

The Council welcomed the Administrator's decision[5] to raise the project approval limit of resident representatives to $700,000 and encouraged steps towards further decentralization. It recognized that UNDP was not serving the wider role envisaged by the Assembly in 1977[7] and 1986[8] and expressed interest in a study being carried out by the DIEC Director-General to assess constraints on the use of the UNDP country programme as a frame of reference of operational activities and in further reflections on the concept of joint programming. It was particularly interested in which organizations of the system and which resources could be covered by such processes.

The Council considered that collaboration with the international financial institutions should take into account the special character, mandates and policies of the institutions involved and respect their differences. It also considered that the system's capacity for analytical work at the country level could be enhanced by ensuring that representatives of specialized agencies had technical functions and capacities in their sectoral areas, and by strengthening resident co-ordinators' capacity to draw on that expertise in support of government programmes.

ACC consideration. In response to a 1987 General Assembly request,[2] CCSQ(OPS) (Geneva, 6-8 April 1988)[9] reviewed its work. It considered its current arrangements to be working satisfactorily, particularly considering the limited budgetary provisions for its substantive secretariat.

At its first regular session of 1988 (Geneva, 20 and 21 April), ACC decided[10] to approve the extension of the budget estimates for continuing operation of the substantive secretariat of CCSQ(OPS) at its current level of expenditure, for a futher period of one year ending on 30 April 1989.

ECONOMIC AND SOCIAL COUNCIL ACTION

In July, on the recommendation of its Third (Programme and Co-ordination) Committee, the Economic and Social Council adopted **decision 1988/165** without vote.

Operational activities for development

At its 39th plenary meeting, on 27 July 1988, the Economic and Social Council decided to recommend that the General Assembly at its forty-third session consider and take appropriate action on the draft decision contained in document E/1988/C.3/L.14, the text of which is annexed to the present decision.

ANNEX
Operational activities for development

The Economic and Social Council:

(a) Takes note of the report of the Director-General for Development and International Economic Co-operation on operational activities for development;

(b) Takes note also of the extract from the report of the Governing Council of the United Nations Development Programme, the report of the Executive Board of the United Nations Children's Fund[a] and the thirteenth annual report of the Committee on Food Aid Policies and Programmes;[b]

(c) Takes note further of the statements of the Director-General for Development and International Economic Co-operation and of the representatives of the organizations of the United Nations system made before the Third (Programme and Co-ordination) Committee of the Council;

(d) Stresses the importance of the views expressed by Governments on those statements and on the report of the Director-General;

(e) Notes the measures taken by the Director-General to implement General Assembly resolution 42/196 of 11 December 1987 and also notes the additional measures proposed, bearing in mind that priority should be given to the completion of the tasks specifically mentioned in that resolution and that the reports requested should be submitted in time to facilitate their proper consideration by the Economic and Social Council during the triennial review of operational activities for development in 1989;

(f) Requests the Governing Council of the United Nations Development Programme at its thirty-sixth session, when reviewing the functioning of the Working Group of the Committee of the Whole of the Governing Council, to take duly into account the comments made by Governments, as reflected in the report of the Governing Council to the Special Commission of the Economic and Social Council on the In-depth Study of the United Nations Intergovernmental Structure and Functions in the Economic and Social Fields.

---

[a]E/1988/18.
[b]E/1988/77.

Economic and Social Council decision 1988/165

Adopted without vote

Approved by Third Committee (E/1988/116) without vote, 22 July (meeting 14); oral proposal by Chairman; agenda item 16.

In other action on 27 July, the Council, by **decision 1988/166**, asked the Secretary-General to make available to the General Assembly in 1988 his note[11] transmitting the reports of the governing bodies of the United Nations system on the

1987 report on the functioning of the operational activities of the system, co-operation with the World Bank, and the review and rationalization of field office structures (see above).

On 20 December, on the recommendation of the Second (Economic and Financial) Committee, the General Assembly adopted **resolution 43/199** without vote.

Operational activities for development
The General Assembly,

Recalling its resolution 2688(XXV) of 11 December 1970, 32/197 of 20 December 1977, 41/171 of 5 December 1986 and 42/196 of 11 December 1987,

Stressing that the primary objective of the operational activities of the United Nations system is to promote the self-reliance of developing countries through multilateral co-operation and, in this context, emphasizing the need to maintain this multilateral character,

Reaffirming the exclusive responsibility of the Government of the recipient country for formulating national development plans, priorities and objectives, as set out in the consensus of 1970 contained in the annex to its resolution 2688(XXV), and emphasizing that the integration of the operational activities of the United Nations system with national programmes would enhance the impact and relevance of those activities,

Emphasizing the central role of the General Assembly and the Economic and Social Council as forums for overall policy guidance and co-ordination of operational activities for development of the United Nations system,

Reaffirming the central funding and co-ordinating role of the United Nations Development Programme in technical co-operation within the United Nations system, in conformity with the consensus of 1970 and General Assembly resolution 32/197,

Reaffirming also that the operational activities for development of the United Nations system are carried out for the benefit of all developing countries, at their request and in accordance with their own policies and priorities for development,

Bearing in mind the urgent and specific needs of the least developed countries,

Aware of the acute problems of island and land-locked developing countries and their particular needs for development to overcome their economic difficulties,

Recalling the United Nations Programme of Action for African Economic Recovery and Development 1986-1990,

Recalling also its resolution 42/231 of 12 May 1988 on the Special Plan of Economic Co-operation for Central America,

Reaffirming the importance attached to the integration of women in United Nations development programmes, both as agents and as beneficiaries of development, calling on the funding and executing agencies to intensify efforts to increase the participation of women, especially those from developing countries, and reiterating its request to the Director-General for Development and International Economic Co-operation, taking into account the requirements of Economic and Social Council resolution 1987/86 of 8 July 1987 in this regard, to report on such efforts and on the establishment of mechanisms

for generating baseline information and measuring results,

1. *Takes note* of the report of the Economic and Social Council;

2. *Takes note also* of the report of the Director-General for Development and International Economic Co-operation on the operational activities for development of the United Nations system;

3. *Notes* the encouraging result of the 1988 United Nations Pledging Conference for Development Activities and stresses the continuing need for a real and significant increase in resources for operational activities for development on a continuous, predictable and assured basis;

4. *Urges* all countries to increase their voluntary contributions for operational activities for development, in particular those countries whose overall involvement is not commensurate with their capacity;

5. *Requests* the Director-General, in the triennial policy review of operational activities for development, to report fully on the implementation thus far of Assembly resolutions 41/171 and 42/196, and to prepare his reports in a comprehensive manner, setting out the interrelationship among problems and factors where appropriate, identifying options available and putting forward his specific recommendations, including possible scenarios for their implementation;

6. *Reaffirms* the primary responsibility of recipient Governments for co-ordinating development assistance at the country level, stresses the need for improved functioning of co-ordination of the United Nations system at the country level, and requests the Director-General:

(a) To report on the action taken by governing bodies of the organizations of the United Nations system, in response to paragraph 24 of General Assembly resolution 42/196, to review and rationalize their field office structures in order to enhance co-operation, coherence and efficiency, and to make comments on possible improvements in the field structure from those standpoints;

(b) In this context, to make specific proposals for enhancing the functioning of the resident co-ordinator system, including proposals on the inter-agency arrangements concerned, within the framework of the role of the resident co-ordinators described in Assembly resolutions 32/197, 41/171 and 42/196;

(c) In the context of subparagraphs *(a)* and *(b)* above, to make specific proposals on ways and means of achieving the objective of the provision to recipient Governments by the United Nations system at the field level of technical advice in a multisectoral and integrated manner, including the deployment of substantive and technical personnel, as envisaged in resolution 32/197 and stressed in paragraph 24 of resolution 42/196;

(d) To provide information on the roles of the United Nations Development Programme resident representative and the United Nations resident co-ordinator with respect to the field representation of the organizations of the United Nations system;

7. *Emphasizes* the importance of flexibility, simplification and harmonization of procedures for operational activities of the United Nations system, so as to increase the responsiveness of those operational activities to the needs and priorities of recipient countries, to reduce the administrative burden on those countries and to allow them to better manage and co-ordinate external assistance; requests the Director-General to make specific

proposals on those subjects in his report, as requested by the Assembly in resolution 42/196; reiterates the view that decentralization of the operational activities of the United Nations system to the field level should, within established principles of accountability, foster appropriate flexibility and responsiveness to the needs of developing countries; and renews its request for information on measures taken by organizations of the system in this regard;

8. *Requests* the Director-General to submit his recommendations on innovative, practical and effective measures to increase substantially procurement from developing countries for consideration during the triennial policy review to be undertaken in 1989, taking into account the need for the full implementation of the preferential arrangements for developing countries and making maximum use of national institutions and firms of those countries, as well as giving due regard to regional comparative advantage consistent with the principle of international competitive bidding and bearing in mind the need to take concrete measures to achieve equitable geographical distribution of procurement through the increased utilization of supply sources from developing and underutilized donor countries;

9. *Stresses* that technical co-operation among developing countries should become a widely used modality for development co-operation within the United Nations development system and in this connection draws the attention of the Director-General to the need for formulating specific proposals for consideration during the triennial review;

10. *Urges* all relevant organizations and bodies of the United Nations system to co-operate fully with the Director-General in the implementation of General Assembly resolutions 41/171 and 42/196 and to provide all the information requested in those resolutions;

11. *Urges* the governing bodies of the organizations of the United Nations system in the field of operational activities, in co-operation with the Economic Commission for Africa, the Organization of African Unity and the existing subregional economic groupings, as appropriate, to provide increased support, as a matter of priority, to African countries in the implementation, follow-up and monitoring of the priority themes of the United Nations Programme of Action for African Economic Recovery and Development 1986-1990;

12. *Emphasizes* the crucial importance of adequate preparations for the Second United Nations Conference on the Least Developed Countries, taking into account the priorities put forward by those countries themselves, and notes with appreciation decision 88/30 of 1 July 1988 of the Governing Council of the United Nations Development Programme, in which the Administrator of the United Nations Development Programme was requested, in close consultation with the Secretary-General of the United Nations Conference on Trade and Development, to assist the least developed countries to ensure that they are able to participate fully in the preparations, including preparatory meetings, for the Conference and in the Conference itself;

13. *Welcomes* Governing Council decision 88/50 of 1 July 1988, adopted in response to paragraph 34 of Assembly resolution 42/196, to initiate consideration by a group of experts of the successor arrangements for support costs from the standpoint of the best ways of meeting the requirements of developing countries;

14. *Invites* the Governing Council, when considering the successor arrangements for support costs, to take into consideration the possibilities of the new arrangements promoting coherence, efficiency and effectiveness of action by the relevant organizations of the United Nations system;

15. *Also invites* the Governing Council to examine the current practices in the designation of executing agencies for projects under regional, interregional and global programmes, taking into account the desirability of utilizing the services of relevant and competent United Nations organs and programmes;

16. *Further invites* the Governing Council to consider the following at its thirty-sixth session, in 1989, and to report thereon to the Assembly at its forty-fourth session, through the Economic and Social Council:

(*a*) The question of holding its future sessions and the future sessions of its subsidiary bodies at United Nations Headquarters;

(*b*) The possibility of changing its name to "Governing Council of the United Nations Development Programme and the United Nations Population Fund";

17. *Welcomes* the review and assessment being conducted by the United Nations Population Fund of its experience in the field of population and requests that an appropriate summary of the main findings, conclusions and recommendations be submitted to the Assembly at its forty-fourth session;

18. *Invites* States members of the relevant organs and organizations of the United Nations system to address the issue of operational activities for development in the governing bodies of those organs and organizations, with a view to arriving at a co-ordinated and system-wide approach to this issue.

General Assembly resolution 43/199

20 December 1988   Meeting 83   Adopted without vote

Approved by Second Committee (A/43/917) without vote, 6 December (meeting 47); draft by Vice-Chairman (A/C.2/43/L.78), orally amended by Netherlands, based on informal consultations on drafts by Canada, Denmark, Italy, Japan, Netherlands, New Zealand, Norway, Sweden, United Kingdom (A/C.2/43/L.42) and by Tunisia, for Group of 77 (A/C.2/43/L.44); agenda item 84.

Meeting numbers. GA 43rd session: 2nd Committee 31-36, 42, 44, 47, 49; plenary 83.

Financing of operational activities

Expenditures

In his report on 1988 operational activities,[1] the DIEC Director-General stated that net transfers made available to developing countries through the United Nations system amounted to $7 billion, an increase of 11 per cent over 1987. Total expenditures on operational activities overall, including humanitarian assistance by the United Nations system, totalled $7.8 billion in 1988. Of that amount, development grants accounted for $3.3 billion compared with $2.8 billion in 1987, concessional loans for $3.7 billion, an increase of $0.2 billion over 1987, and grants for refugee, humanitarian, special economic and disaster relief activities, $0.8 billion ($0.6 billion in 1987).

Expenditures on United Nations operational activities, including technical assistance expenditures on training and consultants included in World Bank loans and IDA credits, but excluding WFP budgetary and extrabudgetary expenditures, totalled $3.4 billion in 1988 compared with $3.2 billion in 1987.

Total expenditure of the member organizations of JCGP in 1988 was $2.78 billion compared to $1.98 billion in 1987.

Contributions

Contributions from Governments and other sources for operational activities for development of the United Nations system increased by some 12 per cent in dollar terms, from $7.1 billion in 1987 to $8.3 billion in 1988. The increase was affected by exchange rate movements, particularly those of the United States dollar against other major donor currencies.

Contributions to UNDP, UNDP-administered funds and trust funds, UNFPA, UNICEF, WFP and other United Nations funds and programmes totalled $3 billion compared with $2.7 billion in 1987. Continued increases in contributions to core funds of UNICEF, UNDP and UNFPA were reported; increases for UNICEF in dollar terms were 24 and 15 per cent for 1987 and 1988, respectively, for UNDP, 12 and 7 per cent, respectively, and for UNFPA, 12 per cent for each year. Contributions to the specialized agencies for operational activities also rose in 1988, reaching $3.8 billion compared with the 1987 total of $3.4 billion.

Contributions to IDA and IFAD and capital subscription payments to the World Bank and the International Finance Corporation (IFC) rose to $4.4 billion from $3.6 billion in 1987.

Contributions to United Nations bodies for refugee, humanitarian, special economic and disaster relief activities totalled $614.9 million in 1988 compared with $611.2 million the previous year.

UN Pledging Conference for Development Activities

The 1988 United Nations Pledging Conference for Development Activities was held in New York on 1 and 2 November to receive government pledges for 1989 to United Nations funds and programmes concerned with development and related assistance.

As at 30 June 1989, pledges from 138 countries for 22 participating funds and programmes amounted to over $1,442 million, with $862.2 million designated for UNDP.

Inter-agency co-operation

Inter-agency co-operation on matters concerning operational activities for development was discussed at two meetings of ACC's CCSQ(OPS) in 1988. The first session was held at Geneva (6-8 April)[9] (see above) and the second in New York (21-23 September).[12]

REFERENCES

[1]A/44/324/Add.4-E/1989/106/Add.4. [2]YUN 1987, p. 401, GA res. 42/196, 11 Dec. 1987. [3]A/43/426-E/1988/74 & Add.1 & Add.1/Corr.1 & Add.2,3. [4]YUN 1987, p. 399. [5]DP/1988/64. [6]E/1988/19 (dec. 88/56). [7]YUN 1977, p. 438, GA res. 32/197, 20 Dec. 1977. [8]YUN 1986, p. 414, GA res. 41/171, 5 Dec. 1986. [9]ACC/1988/7. [10]ACC/1988/DEC/1-18 (dec. 1988/10). [11]E/1988/76. [12]ACC/1988/14.

Technical co-operation through UNDP

In his annual report for 1988,[1] the UNDP Administrator stated that UNDP had another record year for income received, with total income of $1,209 million. The value and volume of new projects approved during the year, however, decreased compared to the 1987 levels. Pledges to UNDP for 1989 were a record $1.2 billion, an increase of 7 per cent in real terms over pledges for 1988.

Five major donors (Finland, France, Italy, Spain, Switzerland) raised their contributions by 8 per cent or more in United States dollar terms. Among recipient contributors, nine countries (Brazil, China, Colombia, Cuba, India, Indonesia, Pakistan, Saudi Arabia, Thailand) each pledged more than $1 million.

Expenditures from UNDP central resources in 1988 totalled $1,109.4 million, of which $832 million was spent on field programme activities, $99.8 million on agency support costs, $172.3 million on UNDP administrative and programme support costs, and $5.6 million on sectoral support and other field-level costs. Of the $832 million in field programme expenditure, $676.5 million was delivered under indicative planning figure (IPF) resources.

Project expenditures rose from $702.1 million in 1987 to an estimated $832.5 million in 1988. Expenditures for international experts and fellowships increased by 18.6 per cent and 22.1 per cent, respectively, while for sub-contracts and equipment they increased by 10.9 per cent and 22.8 per cent, respectively.

The value of new projects approved in 1988 was $708.5 million compared to $714.6 million in 1987, while the number decreased from 1,977 in 1987 to 1,794. During the year, the three leading sectors by their numerical share were: a general category including trade and finance, health, employment, culture and science and technology; development strategies, policies and planning; and agriculture.

The majority of UNDP programmes continued to emphasize more efficient economic management while addressing issues of critical poverty. Other programmes were directed to promoting productivity increases in agriculture and industry, public sector efficiency, economic reactivation through the diversification of industry and exports, greater incentives for the private sector and the application of technology in development. UNDP also continued to emphasize the incorporation of women in development, co-operation with NGOs as partners in development, and the increased use of United Nations Volunteers, Transfer of Knowledge through Expatriate Nationals and short-term advisory services as means of providing highly skilled, low-cost services to development efforts world-wide.

In Africa, overall economic performance remained unsatisfactory in 1988, as the debt burden, unfavourable terms of trade and a net outflow of resources severely restricted growth. Country and intercountry programmes in the fourth cycle (1987-1991) supported the African countries in their implementation of the United Nations Programme of Action for African Economic Recovery and Development 1986-1990 (UNPAAERD), adopted by the General Assembly in 1986.[2] Programmes also reflected UNDP efforts to help African Governments to implement structural adjustment measures and address social issues emanating from economic reform.

Economic growth in the developing Asian-Pacific countries was a robust 8 per cent in 1988. Major factors in the region's performance were the agricultural recovery in South and South-East Asia after adverse weather in 1987, strong industrial and export growth combined with increased consumer spending, and fast growing investments. The composition of UNDP-supported projects in the region reflected a changing pattern of development. Industry and science and technology expanded, while agriculture, forestry and fisheries, although declining modestly, remained the largest sector, with 21 per cent of allocated funds in 1988. Within many projects, training grew in importance relative to equipment.

The economies of Latin America and the Caribbean continued to evolve unfavourably in 1988 with a low growth rate, capital flight and an external debt of some $400 billion at year's end. The UNDP programme in the region emphasized economic management, agriculture, transport, natural resources and environmental management.

While economic conditions in the Arab States benefited from a relatively high average per capita income of $2,000, a number of factors underscored the development challenge faced by the region in 1988. Population growth rates averaged 3.1 per cent in the first half of the 1980s. The region produced only about 75 per cent of its food needs during the same period. While some countries and some groups enjoyed high standards of living, the basic needs of many remained unmet. In 1988, UNDP emphasized the role of women in develop-

ment, the private sector as a facilitator for development, NGOs and the environment.

Social and political changes in Europe led to an increase in projects that addressed debt-restructuring, the environment and development of the private sector. During 1988, several missions were carried out by Arab countries in biotechnology, computer software, water resources management and agricultural technologies in European countries in order to establish co-operative links.

UNDP administered six funds during 1988: the United Nations Capital Development Fund (UNCDF) (see below), the United Nations Trust Fund for Sudano-Sahelian Activities (see PART THREE, Chapter VIII), the United Nations Revolving Fund for Natural Resources Exploration (UNRFNRE) (see PART THREE, Chapter VI), the United Nations Development Fund for Women (UNIFEM) (see PART THREE, Chapter XIII), the United Nations Fund for Science and Technology for Development (UNFSTD) (see PART THREE, Chapter VII) and the United Nations Volunteers programme (UNV) (see below).

In the area of emergency and disaster relief, UNDP collaborated with the Office of the United Nations Disaster Relief Co-ordinator and other international agencies. It approved 43 relief projects in 1988 while providing follow-up assistance to countries struck by disasters in previous years. Disasters to which UNDP responded included desert locust infestations in the Sudan, a hurricane in Jamaica, a typhoon in the Philippines and flooding in Bangladesh (see PART THREE, Chapter III).

On 1 July,[3] the UNDP Governing Council took note of the Administrator's report for 1987[4] and encouraged him to pursue the measures that had led to an increase and improvement in the implementation of programmes and to an improvement of the quality of UNDP-supported projects. It reaffirmed the continued applicability of the basic principles governing UNDP activities and stressed that UNDP should be enabled to fulfil its mandate as the central funding and co-ordinating agent for technical co-operation provided by the United Nations system. It welcomed the information provided by the Administrator on the increasing involvement and role of UNDP in diverse areas of development co-operation and the evolving co-operation between UNDP and the World Bank, which was based on the full recognition of the respective mandates and policies of both institutions. It called on UNDP and the executing agencies to collaborate more closely in order to respond effectively and efficiently to the priority needs of developing countries and took note of UNDP's support to the private sector at the express request of Governments. The Council decided to devote the high-level segment of its 1989 session to the role of UNDP in the 1990s and requested the Administrator to submit a comprehensive report to it at that time.

UNDP Governing Council

In 1988 in New York, the UNDP Governing Council held organizational meetings on 16 and 19 February and a special session to consider pending issues from 17 to 19 February; it held its thirty-fifth regular session at Geneva from 6 June to 1 July.[5] At the organizational meetings, the Council adopted decisions on its schedule of meetings in 1988 and other organizational matters,[6] and on the election of the members of the Working Group of the Committee of the Whole.[7]

At its special session, the Council adopted eleven decisions on: country, intercountry, interregional and global programmes and projects (see below); the report of the Chairman of the Working Group of the Committee of the Whole;[8] co-operation with WHO and other agencies against AIDS (see PART THREE, Chapter XI); UNIFEM (see PART THREE, Chapter XIII); the mid-term review of resources for the fourth programming cycle (see below); IPFs for the fourth programming cycle (see below); UNDP response to emergency, medium-term and long-term development requirements in Africa (see PART THREE, Chapter III); the role of UNDP in the West Bank and the Gaza Strip (see PART TWO, Chapter IV); change of name of the Office for Projects Execution (see below); delegation of authority for project approval (see below); and financing of technical co-operation among developing countries (see below).

The Budgetary and Finance Committee met between 6 June and 1 July to consider financial, budgetary and administrative matters, the Committee of the Whole met between 7 June and 1 July to consider evaluation matters, country and intercountry programmes and projects, UNFPA country and intercountry programmes and projects, and the report of the Chairman of the Working Group of the Committee of the Whole, and the drafting group met between 13 and 30 June to consider proposals for draft decisions.

Forty-seven decisions were adopted at the June/July session; those not covered in this chapter dealt with: women in development and UNIFEM (see PART THREE, Chapter XIII); human resources development (see PART THREE, Chapter XII); assistance to national liberation movements recognized in its area by the Organization of African Unity (see PART TWO, Chapter I); the role of UNDP in implementing UNPAAERD (see PART THREE, Chapter III); UNFPA (see PART THREE, Chapter IX); UNRFNRE (see PART THREE, Chapter VI); UNFSTD and the Energy Account (see PART THREE, Chapters VI and VII);

activities in the field of drug abuse control (see PART THREE, Chapter XVI); the Second United Nations Conference on the Least Developed Countries (see PART THREE, Chapter I); the fight against locust and grasshopper infestation in Africa (see PART THREE, Chapter III); the report of the World Commission on Environment and Development and the Environmental Perspective to the Year 2000 and Beyond (see PART THREE, Chapter VIII); and the activities of the United Nations Sudano-Sahelian Office and assistance to other drought-stricken countries in Africa (see PART THREE, Chapters III and VIII).

On 1 July,[9] the Council approved the agenda and organization of work at its thirty-fifth session. Decisions were taken on future Council sessions[10] and the provisional agenda for 1989.[11] The Council also took note of several reports and other documents.[12]

GENERAL ASSEMBLY ACTION

By **decision 43/445** of 20 December, the General Assembly decided to refer a paragraph on operational activities for development to the Economic and Social Council for consideration and action in 1989. By that paragraph, the value of the Governing Council's Committee of the Whole and its Working Group would be recognized or the Council would be called on to terminate the Working Group.

UNDP operational activities

Country and intercountry programmes

In a report to the Governing Council's 1988 special session,[13] the Administrator analysed eight country programmes, which he submitted for approval. Three of the programmes were in Africa, three in the Arab States and two in Europe. The small number of country programmes reflected the approach of the end of programming for the fourth IPF cycle.

The largest IPF in the programmes submitted was $27.8 million (from previous and current programmes) for Yemen, which also topped the list of total resources programmed, with $42.2 million, including large sums of non-IPF resources. The smallest IPF in the programmes submitted was $2 million for the Libyan Arab Jamahiriya, although the programme was much larger ($14 million) due to the inclusion of substantial resources from other donors. The report included information on the timing, preparations, financing, major development objectives and orientation of the submitted programmes, distribution of resources by sector and attention to global priorities.

On 17 February,[14] the Council approved the eight new programmes.

On 1 July,[15] the Council approved a further 13 country programmes for the duration of their programme period and within the limits of their IPFs for the period 1987-1991. Of those programmes, nine were from Africa, two were from the Arab States, one was from Asia and one from Latin America and the Caribbean. The Council also took note of the extension of a country programme for Iran and of the proposed regional programme for the Arab States, and approved emergency assistance to meet short and intermediate needs for desert locust control.

By the same decision, the Council took note of a report by the Administrator on the analysis of country programme trends during the third (1982-1986) and fourth (1987-1991) IPF cycles.[16] The Administrator analysed 131 country programmes which were common to both cycles in order to investigate what longer-term trends could be observed.

In a section of his annual report for 1988[1] on project results of global and interregional programmes, the Administrator stated that UNDP supported international co-operation in basic and applied research and its dissemination, particularly in the areas of food crops and health. The global programme in agriculture emphasized improving varieties of food crops such as maize, rice, sorghum and millet by combining higher yields with resistance to insects, disease and environmental stress. It had created successful networks in several developing countries to test and adapt new varieties of those crops. Nearly 800 rice scientists from developing countries were linked to the International Rice Testing Programme at the International Rice Research Institute (IRRI) in the Philippines. In 1988, 1,215 sets of 25 types of rice strains were distributed to 46 countries, where 33 improved varieties performed well under varying conditions. A total of 130 trainees from 17 countries were trained at IRRI. Co-operation continued with the International Fertilizer Development Centre in Mussel Shoals, Alabama, United States, to increase crop output through efficient use of fertilizers. Over 400 people from 63 countries participated in training courses. The $11 million UNDP contribution to agricultural research centres was combined with nearly $250 million provided by other donors.

With regard to clean water and adequate sanitation, UNDP and partner United Nations agencies applied innovative strategies to provide such facilities to the developing world through the International Drinking Water Supply and Sanitation Decade (1981-1990) (see also PART THREE, Chapter VI). Five new intercountry projects for low-income communities were allocated $10.8 million in 1988, bringing total UNDP support for the sector to $370 million since the Decade was launched.

Almost 700 communities in 13 countries had participated in the UNDP programme on the promotion of the role of women in water and environmental sanitation services. Preparations were being made to extend the programme to seven more countries and an office was opened in Abidjan, Côte d'Ivoire, to encourage closer co-operation with other African organizations. Additional funding for the programme in 1988 was granted by the Canadian International Development Agency.

In the health sector, UNDP and WHO in March 1988 formed an "Alliance to Combat AIDS", under which UNDP resident representatives were charged with seeing that assistance for AIDS from all United Nations organizations was co-ordinated within the framework of national AIDS plans. UNDP also helped to mobilize external funds. UNDP and WHO also played leading roles in the launching of the "Global Blood Safety Initiative", which was designed to ensure safe blood supplies throughout the world in order to stem the spread of AIDS and other diseases.

Development programmes involving fisheries, energy, trade, environment, education and urban management were also supported by UNDP in 1988.

Country programmes by region

Africa

In a report on implementation of selected country programmes in the Africa region during 1988,[17] the Administrator stated that the remaining 11 of the 45 fourth cycle (1987-1991) programmes of UNDP assistance in the 42 countries of the region were approved in 1988 (see above).

At the start of the fourth cycle, $1.4 billion of programmable resources were estimated as being available to the region through UNDP core resources and associated funds. At the end of the second year of the cycle, the estimates were revised to $1.8 billion, some $368 million of that increase resulting from supplementary allocations to the 1987-1991 IPFs made by the Governing Council in 1988 (see below).

The rate of delivery of IPF resources, which sank to a low point in the middle of the third cycle (1982-1986), rebounded sharply to the full level of available resources; in 1988, it was estimated to be almost double the total for 1984. Although the strong showing in 1988 was predictable for the second year of a cycle, intensive financial management and monitoring practices and the increased ceiling for project approvals by resident representatives (from $400,000 to $700,000) were also contributing factors. Government cost-sharing increased rapidly, from $9.3 million in 1982 to $28 million in 1988, as did the proportion of government-executed projects.

In 1988, a total of 1,968 projects had current budgets funded from UNDP core resources. As in previous years, most of the available resources (69.1 per cent) were allocated to large-scale projects. A comparison of the four UNDP budget components (personnel plus sub-contracts, training, equipment and miscellaneous) showed a declining trend in expenditure on project personnel and an upward one in expenditure on training, especially in the fourth cycle. The decline in project personnel and sub-contractor expenditure, despite the rising costs of expertise, was attributable to a tendency towards shorter assignments and more use of national experts and consultants.

The distribution of resources by sector for the region for 1987-1991 was as follows: agriculture, forestry and fisheries, 28.9 per cent; general development, policy and planning, 23.5 per cent; natural resources, 10.7 per cent; transport and communications, 11.1 per cent; industry, 8.4 per cent; employment, 7.2 per cent; education, 5.5 per cent; science and technology, 3.9 per cent; and other sectors, 0.8 per cent.

The report assessed 23 country programmes of the region. Reviews of a number of them— Botswana, Burkina Faso, Cameroon, Ethiopia, Gambia, Ghana, Guinea-Bissau, Lesotho, Liberia, Malawi, Mali, Nigeria, Togo, Zaire—were carried out during the year.

At the regional level, human resources development programmes for the building of regional and subregional centres of excellence in technical, scientific, administration and management training accounted for the majority of the $90 million of projects approved in 1988. A $5.7 million programme with 16 training centres for strengthening management institutions in Africa became fully operational in 1988; the focus was on management organization, curriculum development and consultancy capabilities.

The African Project Development Facility, sponsored by UNDP, IFC, the African Development Bank and 14 donor countries, became fully operational. Field operations conducted from regional offices in Abidjan and Nairobi reviewed nearly 1,000 proposals for funding, UNDP budgets for which ranged from $300,000 to $4.8 million, with an average of $1.4 million per project.

A substantial number of projects in the area of food production, which ranked as one of the foremost priorities of the regional programme, were approved during 1988. Significant efforts were initiated in marine and inland fisheries, the livestock sector and crop protection. Also, in support of NGO activities, a $2.4 million project was approved to provide organizational and management support to indigenous NGO associations and to iden-

tify and develop opportunities for grass-roots participation in UNDP country programmes. Within the women in development programme, three projects were started, three others were formulated and one continued to receive preparatory assistance. The three being implemented were on raising the agricultural productivity of women in Africa, improving the role of African women in informal-sector production and management, and African women water users.

Infrastructure development centred on the transport and communications sectors with a $4.8 million programme being approved in 1988, including $1.3 million in cost-sharing.

Arab States and Europe

In his report on the implementation of selected country programmes in the Arab States and Europe during 1988,[18] the Administrator said that by the end of the year, all country programmes for the fourth cycle had been approved with the exception of Lebanon. In view of the slightly improved operational conditions in certain areas of Lebanon, UNDP decided in mid-1988 to proceed with a revitalization of the country programme, albeit at a measured pace, beginning with the appointment of the Resident Representative in July 1988.

In terms of the overall level of approvals of IPFs, there was a 90 per cent increase in 1988 with $240.7 million approved, compared with $126.9 million in 1987. The sectoral distribution of the ongoing projects was as follows: agriculture, forestry and fisheries, 19 per cent; development planning, 15 per cent; industry, 15 per cent; transport and communications, 13 per cent; natural resources, 12 per cent; science and technology, 7 per cent; education, 5 per cent; employment, 5 per cent; health, 3 per cent; trade, 2 per cent; and other areas, 4 per cent.

The report reviewed the country programmes for Bahrain, Jordan, Libyan Arab Jamahiriya, Poland, Portugal, Qatar, Romania, Saudi Arabia, the Sudan and Yemen. With regard to the fourth regional programme for the Arab States, 1988-1992, approved by the Governing Council in July[15] in the amount of $46.4 million, the report stated that it was based on assessment of the previous regional programme (1983-1988). The report outlined important lessons which were applied in preparing the new programme: the need to concentrate efforts on a few priority areas; the need to incorporate considerations of human resources development into every project, with the role of women emerging as specially important; the need to recognize the critical importance of networking arrangements to improve the efficiency of technical co-operation; the need to identify projects according to the priorities of the various subregional groups; and the need to increase Arab/European co-operation particularly throughout the Mediterranean basin.

Under the new programme, two main priority themes, increased food security through the expansion of food production and the acquisition of technology, were to receive almost half of IPF resources. Underscoring both those themes was a strong emphasis on human resources development, which would also be an important component in water development, environment, energy, trade and transport and communications.

The regional programme for Europe, approved by the Council in 1987,[19] was in full implementation in 1988, with 37 ongoing projects. Of particular note was the promotion of the linkage between participating Arab and European countries, particularly in terms of developing an outreach programme that would share with the Arab countries the successful experience of Europe's regional programme in such areas as energy planning. A mid-term review was scheduled for the end of the first quarter of 1989.

The report reviewed two country projects— remote-sensing application to agriculture in Egypt and improvement of the quality of drinking-water in Morocco—and one regional project on Bayoud (a date-palm disease) control. It also noted that UNDP emphasized a number of special themes in its technical co-operation programme (the role of women in development, the private sector in development, environment and support to NGOs) and described the incorporation of those themes into the country and regional programmes.

The report also discussed co-ordination of assistance with regard to Lebanon, Somalia and the Sudan and in connection with the locust invasion of countries in North and West Africa (see PART THREE, Chapter III). It was also noted that, at the headquarters level, contacts were made with specialized executing agencies with a view to improving the rate and quality of assistance delivered.

Asia and the Pacific

In a report on implementation of selected country programmes in Asia and the Pacific during 1988,[20] the Administrator stated that, with the Governing Council's approval of the country programme for Maldives in July,[15] only the country programme for Iran remained to be approved.

Total IPF resources available to the region for the fourth cycle were $1.5 billion, which included carry-over from the previous cycle and reflected the significant increase in IPF levels approved by the Council in July (see below). Eighty-five per cent of the resources for the region were allocated for country-specific projects and 15 per cent for intercountry projects. For 1988, it was estimated that cost-sharing contributions by the recipient and third parties amounted to almost 8 per cent of total funds disbursed.

In 1988, country and regional projects delivered assistance from IPF resources valued at an estimated $240 million, representing a marginal increase over the 1987 level of $234 million. Sectoral allocation of IPF resources confirmed past trends, with an increased share going to industry and science and technology. The three largest sectors were: agriculture, forestry and fisheries (21 per cent); industry (19 per cent); and natural resources (12 per cent).

During the year, mid-term reviews of country programmes were held for China, the Lao People's Democratic Republic and Nepal. The review of China's programme included sectoral reviews covering industry, agriculture, forestry, energy and economic planning. It concluded that the country programme remained valid and effective in meeting China's technical assistance requirements.

Nepal's review was introduced through a series of sectoral meetings in August 1988, covering agriculture, forestry, energy, industry, finance and economic planning. Emphasis was placed on identifying issues of a cross-sectoral nature and particular attention was paid to private sector development, NGO involvement and participation of women in development. The Lao People's Democratic Republic's review focused on implementing the country programme and the evolving role of UNDP in the context of bilateral and other multilateral agency activities.

The second year of the fourth intercountry programming cycle was marked by an increase in UNDP assistance disbursed to over $35 million. The total amount of new IPF resources allocated to the programme was $211 million. However, those figures did not give the complete delivery picture, as the intercountry programme continued to generate an ever-growing amount of cost-sharing and co-financing from participating and donor countries, with each UNDP dollar helping to mobilize the equivalent of $1.60 in additional spending. In terms of ongoing projects, transport and communications continued to receive the largest allocation, with 24 per cent of all programmed resources, followed by natural resources (19 per cent) and agriculture, forestry and fisheries (16 per cent).

At the subregional level, total programmed resources for the South Pacific amounted to approximately $35 million and would actually exceed the allocations from IPFs to those countries. The members of the Association of South-East Asian Nations would receive nearly $11 million and the nine least developed countries (LDCs) of the region a similar amount.

The Administrator's report also discussed special themes that were assuming importance in the region—management of the environment, women in development, NGOs, private sector development and technical co-operation among developing countries (TCDC)—and aid co-ordination.

Latin America and the Caribbean

In a report on implementation of selected country programmes in Latin America and the Caribbean during 1988,[21] the Administrator stated that, in addition to the actual expenditure of $59 million in 1987 and the estimated delivery of $67 million in 1988, the region had committed an IPF of $100 million by December 1988, leaving a balance of $85 million to be committed for the remaining years of the fourth cycle (1987-1991). The overall UNDP programme in the region was considerably larger than was suggested by IPF resources because cost-sharing, management services agreements and Special Programme Resources (SPRs) made it possible to carry out additional activities for a total of $552 million. IPF resources during the fourth cycle amounted to 37.6 per cent ($333 million) of total resources available.

By sector, general development issues received the largest percentage (30.6) of resources, followed by agriculture (14.3 per cent), transport (12.7 per cent) and natural resources (9.2 per cent). Those sectors were closely associated with the aim of improving the capacity to import since they were related to exports of primary goods.

An important characteristic of the programme in 1988 was the increased importance of government execution, which was by far the preferred method of project execution in the region. Execution by Governments accounted for 27 per cent of total delivery, followed by DTCD, which accounted for 12.1 per cent of executions.

The report provided information on reviews which took place during 1988 on the country programmes for Chile, Ecuador and Panama; a review of the programme for Haiti was also carried out but would be reported on separately. Also reviewed were a number of individual projects under implementation in 1988 in the areas of economic management, equity and growth, and science and technology.

Special themes receiving attention in 1988 were improving the environment for private sector development and regional co-operation and mobilization of resources for environmental action. A meeting was held in New York in June, attended by nine NGOs and consortia, where recommendations were made to strengthen co-operation among those organizations and UNDP, as well as to improve the treatment of gender issues and the role of women in development. The report also contained information on the co-ordination of the Special Plan of Economic Co-operation for Central America (see PART TWO, Chapter V).

Indicative planning figures

In a report to the special session of the Governing Council,[22] the Administrator provided details on the revision of certain country IPFs resulting from changes in the basic data used to calculate them (per capita gross national product (GNP)) and from action taken by the General Assembly with respect to the list of LDCs.[23] Under the revised data, 21 countries would receive an IPF increase, including Burma as a new LDC. No reductions were calculated for countries whose revised per capita GNP had increased. The Administrator also proposed a new methodology for effecting changes in IPFs when basic data were modified.

Also, in response to a 1987 Governing Council request,[24] the Administrator had initiated consultations with recipient Governments on the net contributor provisions established by the Council in 1985.[25] He reported that the position of several Governments with respect to achieving net contributor status had not formally been communicated, but it seemed likely that some countries would not achieve it. Given the Council's 1987 confirmation of the net contributor provision,[24] he stated that he intended to reduce programme activity to a level commensurate with anticipated voluntary contributions in those instances where net contributor status would clearly not be achieved.

On 19 February,[26] the Council confirmed its agreement that, in instances where the official revision of basic data of GNP used in calculating IPFs was detrimental to country IPFs, no downward revision should be made to IPFs of the current programming cycle (1987-1991). Also, where revision would change the status of the country to that of a net contributor, no action would be taken during the current cycle. The Council approved the recalculation of country IPFs for the fourth cycle and confirmed the proposed methodology by which future revision to IPFs resulting from changes in per capita GNP would be considered. It took note of the likely outcome of the Administrator's intention to reduce programme activity to a level commensurate with anticipated voluntary contributions in instances where it was clear that net contributor status would not be achieved and noted a statement by the Associate Administrator that proposals on the basis of the round of consultations with Governments expected to achieve net contributor status would be submitted to the Council at its 1988 regular session.

On 1 July,[27] the Council decided that net contributor obligations would be waived for any year in respect of which the per capita GNP of net contributor countries fell below the thresholds established in 1985, and to defer consideration of the issue of net contributor status to 1989 on the understanding that the Administrator could postpone taking action until March of that year.

In May,[28] the Administrator recommended, based on an increase in voluntary contributions in non–United States dollar currencies, and due to the decline in the United States dollar, that the Council base a revised resource allocation decision on additional resources of $676 million available at the end of the fourth cycle. From that amount, $76 million would have to be set aside for agency support costs.

On 1 July,[29] the Council decided that $490 million would be distributed between country and intercountry IPFs in accordance with the criteria established in 1985,[25] and agreed that distribution of country IPFs should take into consideration the loss of purchasing power of IPFs due to exchange rate fluctuations. It decided that the additional country IPFs would be calculated as follows: 50 per cent would be distributed proportionally to the existing IPFs for the fourth cycle and 50 per cent in accordance with the Council's 1985 decision; and the resultant IPFs were to constitute floors and ceilings in substitution for those established in 1985. The Council further decided that the national liberation movement IPF, the Namibia IPF and the multi-island IPFs should be increased by a percentage equal to the average increase for countries belonging to the group with a per capita GNP between $750 and $1,500; it also increased the multi-island IPF by $2.5 million for the cycle.

Programme planning and management

In accordance with a 1987 Governing Council request,[30] the Administrator submitted a review of programme and project activities.[31] With regard to improving programme and project quality, the Administrator described the procedural framework established for mid-term reviews of country and intercountry programmes, noting that for all programmes over $10 million, at least one review was required, ideally taking place at the mid-point in the programme. As to programme management information, revised procedures for monitoring, reporting and evaluation included formats for project performance evaluation reports for project managers and the resident representative to report on project tripartite reviews. A computerized system would be introduced to link planned management actions with receipt of reports to enable headquarters to monitor compliance with project reporting requirements. In the context of the Country Programme Management Plan mechanism, a computerized system was

being developed to capture information/data on fourth cycle programmes to facilitate monitoring of programme implementation.

A new Programme and Projects Manual was issued in February 1988 containing revised guidelines on project formulation, which emphasized the importance of undertaking basic preliminary investigations before embarking on project formulation and included a clearer and more logical project document format.

On 1 July,[32] the Governing Council commended the Administrator for making available the new Programme and Projects Manual and welcomed the formulation and issuance of more rigorous and comprehensive guidelines on project formulation and management, including a new project document format. The Council asked the Administrator to carry out jointly with the recipient Government a mid-term review for each country programme approved for the fourth programming cycle and took note of the format envisaged for the mid-term review reports to be prepared at the field level. The Administrator was invited to undertake an evaluation of the country programme mid-term review process and to include in his report both aggregated data on all mid-term reviews and an analysis of the main findings and results of different reviews. He was also invited to report to the Council in 1989 on the timetable envisaged for the different mid-term reviews and measures taken to carry out reviews of regional, interregional and global programmes, as well as on how and when he intended to report to the Council on those reviews.

Standard modalities of technical co-operation

In response to a 1987 Governing Council request,[30] the Administrator included in his review of programme and project activities[31] proposals for standard modalities of technical co-operation. He noted that he was in the process of gathering information from all major donors on the terms, procedures and modalities under which technical co-operation was provided by them. That information would be used to draft an inventory of practices and undertake a comparative analysis. Although the response to requests for information had been disappointing, analyses were being undertaken on material already published on technical co-operation procedures. In a second phase, detailed consultations would take place with donor and recipient Governments to identify areas of common concern and interest, with a view to overcoming the main difficulties that recipient Governments faced in co-ordinating and programming technical co-operation inputs from different sources.

On 1 July,[32] the Council noted the Administrator's request to major donor countries for information. It asked him to make use of existing sources of information and invited the major donors to provide any other supplementary information specified by the Administrator for the purpose of harmonizing both bilateral and multilateral technical co-operation. The Administrator was urged to intensify efforts towards harmonization in carrying out technical co-operation in the United Nations system through harmonization of programming cycles, document formats and procedures.

Project Development Facility

In his review of programme and project activities,[31] the Administrator included a progress report on the operations of the Project Development Facility, which had been established on an experimental basis until the end of the third programming cycle (1982-1986) and subsequently extended. The Facility was financed from Special Programme Resources (SPR) and was reimbursed for the costs of missions when they led to a project financed from the IPF. If a project did not result from the use of the Facility, then the costs remained chargeable against SPR. The Administrator stated that the Facility had been widely used by many countries in all regions. It had been used intensively to identify and appraise complex projects, particularly in Asia, where some countries had used the mechanism for a relatively large number of missions. The Administrator noted that the Facility needed no further replenishment, as its experimental operation until the end of the cycle could be expected to continue on the basis of reimbursements, permitting the fielding of some 15 missions per quarter.

On 1 July,[32] the Governing Council asked the Administrator to include in the next review of the operations of the Facility detailed data on the selection and recruitment of consultants for field missions and statistics related to consultants.

Government execution

In response to a 1987 Governing Council request,[33] the Administrator submitted in March 1988 a report[34] summarizing the principal observations and findings of an evaluation report on government execution, which assessed the impact and cost-effectiveness of government-executed projects. With regard to programming responsibilities, the evaluation report recommended that UNDP should ensure that when programmes were formulated and reviewed, the usefulness of the modalities to be used to execute the programme were assessed; UNDP endorsed that recommendation. As to operational issues, greater focus was needed on the contribution of the modality to effectiveness and more evaluations and attention to the reasons for project success would promote that; UNDP concurred. In connection with accounting proce-

dures, it was recommended that: UNDP payments by the field office that were not advanced to Governments should be recorded as expenditures on a component and/or budget line-item basis from monthly inter-office vouchers; direct payments by headquarters should be recorded as expenditures instead of as an advance; co-operating agency payments should be recorded as expenditures from their semi-annual reports; executing Governments should report only on funds actually advanced to them; and add-on funds should be credited to government-executed projects based on recorded expenditures and programmed accordingly. UNDP fully accepted those recommendations. The report also made recommendations regarding auditing of government-executed projects, which would require administration of the audit process by UNDP staff; the Administrator concurred.

On 1 July,[35] the Council encouraged Governments to continue to expand government execution and urged the Administrator to renew his efforts to involve the executing agencies in the use of that modality. It took note of the recommendations on programming responsibilities and operational issues and approved those on accounting, auditing and reporting procedures. The Administrator was asked to implement those procedures so that Governments could assume entire responsibility for the custody, use and reporting of financial outcomes of government-executed projects. He was also asked to ensure greater commitment to the allocation of add-on funds, including for accounting, reporting and auditing.

The Council invited the Administrator to present in 1990 specific proposals and recommendations for the implementation of a 1987 General Assembly resolution,[36] which called for further support and flexibility to facilitate government execution, and to report on the impact of the revised accounting, reporting and auditing procedures both on UNDP's work-load and on Governments' commitment and capacity to assume responsibility for those procedures or to contribute to costs incurred by UNDP for that purpose, out of the add-on funds. The Council authorized the Administrator to continue, in 1989 and 1990, to charge additional staff resources approved in 1987[33] at the level of up to $400,000 per year to the support-costs line of UNDP, and to establish a small unit with two Professional staff plus supporting services, to administer and monitor audit requirements at a cost not exceeding $300,000 per year to the support-costs line in 1988, 1989 and 1990. The Administrator was asked to examine the use of add-on funds.

Agency accountability

In response to a 1987 Governing Council request,[30] the Administrator submitted in April

1988 a report on agency accountability,[37] which described management measures being undertaken by UNDP to improve project performance and accountability, reviewed the legal position regarding the application of penalty schemes and discussed options to be explored to ensure effective implementation of projects.

On 1 July,[38] the Council stated that it looked forward to receiving in 1989 a further report from the Administrator on his efforts and urged UNDP and its executing agencies to participate fully and collaborate in the exploration of the options put forward in his April report. It asked the Administrator to include in his 1989 report an explanation of his efforts to reach agreement on a standard basic agreement between UNDP and those executing agencies which had yet to sign one. The Council stressed the importance of the role of executing agencies in providing sectoral and subsectoral expertise as well as their role in project formulation and execution. It also stressed the importance of that expertise to the resident coordinator as a support to his function of ensuring coherence of the United Nations system's operational activities for development at the field level.

Evaluation

In March 1988,[39] the UNDP Administrator described steps taken by him to improve evaluation policies and procedures introduced by UNDP. He reviewed evaluation activities undertaken in 1987 and proposed a work programme for 1988-1989. He also discussed integration of evaluation results into UNDP activities, system strengthening, strengthening Government evaluation capacity and external relations.

On 1 July,[40] the Governing Council stressed that particular attention should be paid to enhancing the evaluation capacity of developing countries and asked the Administrator to review the staffing arrangements of the Central Evaluation Office and make proposals in 1989 within the framework of the 1990-1991 budget.

Procurement

In response to two 1987 Governing Council decisions,[41] the Administrator submitted a report on procurement of equipment and services from developing countries.[42] The first part of the report dealt with procurement statistics and steps to increase procurement from developing and underutilized major donor countries, while the second part dealt with the mandate, work programme, staffing and budget of the Inter-Agency Procurement Services Unit (IAPSU) and its place in the structure of UNDP and the United Nations. The Administrator said that the future role of IAPSU should continue to be to serve as a focal point and co-ordinating centre for procurement matters, providing advice and direct support to United Nations agencies, lending institutions and, as appropriate, NGOs and bilateral aid organizations.

On 1 July,[43] the Council noted with concern the continuing difficulty experienced in obtaining adequate statistical information on procurement activities within the United Nations development system. It called on agencies to continue to provide to IAPSU full statistical information on their procurement activities and to co-operate fully with IAPSU with a view to enhancing the utility of that information. It reaffirmed that the overall objective and overriding concern of IAPSU should be the procurement of equipment at the lowest possible cost consistent with the maintenance of adequate standards. It also reaffirmed the need to achieve equitable geographical distribution of procurement through the increased use of supply sources from developing and underutilized donor countries. The Administrator was requested to urge the participating and executing agencies to observe and implement the preferential arrangements for developing countries. He was invited, in association with IAPSU, DTCD and other executing agencies of the United Nations system, to consider means by which information on procurement opportunities could be made more readily available to the headquarters of agencies, UNDP headquarters in New York and IAPSU at Geneva. The Administrator was also requested to report to the Council in 1989 on developments in the area of procurement by the United Nations development system, with particular emphasis on the need for greater access to information and transparency of activity.

Also on 1 July,[44] the Council noted the increase in 1987 of procurement of goods and equipment from developing countries and recognized the efforts of IAPSU to promote such procurement, including the production of country-specific binders providing information on goods and equipment available to the United Nations development system. It called on IAPSU to continue to intensify assistance to developing countries wishing to increase their involvement in United Nations procurement activities and recognized that increased procurement from developing countries depended on action by all parties, including UNDP, United Nations funding and executing agencies and Governments. The Council authorized continuation of two temporary posts in IAPSU and decided to review the Unit's staffing in 1989 in the context of the 1990-1991 budget. It invited the Inter-Agency Procurement Working Group to respond positively to invitations from developing countries when determining the venue of its annual meeting, thereby ensuring that those countries benefited from contact with agency procurement personnel.

Pre-investment activities

As requested by the Governing Council in 1982,[45] the Administrator submitted his third biennial report on pre-investment activities.[46] The report described progress achieved by the Administrator in strengthening the pre-investment role of UNDP, with emphasis on the 1986-1987 biennium. During UNDP's third programming cycle (1982-1986), reported investment commitments from all sources of finance—domestic, multilateral, bilateral, whether public or private—resulting from UNDP-assisted pre-investment projects and investment-oriented projects increased from $6.6 billion in 1982 to $9.4 billion in 1986. Developing countries continued to lead the way as the major source of finance, with multilateral organizations coming second, followed by various bilateral sources. The principal source of reported investment commitments continued to be the public sector, but the share of private sources, from both developed and developing countries, was rising and grew from $350 million in 1982 to about $1.4 billion in 1986. Also during the third cycle, the number of development finance institutions with which UNDP had established special interest or co-operative arrangements rose from 7 to 10. The total of those investment commitments increased from $2.4 billion in 1982 to some $3.8 billion in 1986, with the World Bank consistently being the largest single source of follow-up finance, followed by the regional development banks.

The report described measures taken to stimulate UNDP's pre-investment function, special relationships with development finance institutions, co-operative arrangements with agencies, reimbursable aid arrangements, project development facilities and training in investment development. It concluded that to accomplish its goals of increasing pre-investment and improving linkages between UNDP-assisted pre-investment activities and follow-up investment from sources of finance, UNDP would have to focus on a more intensive application of its co-operative arrangements with development finance institutions and agencies of the United Nations system. UNDP would intensify its efforts to finance pre-investment studies, from both IPFs and resources available through the various facilities established for that purpose, and to link those studies with sources of finance. Emphasis would be placed on continuing UNDP training programmes in investment development, particularly those seminars held in collaboration with development finance institutions.

On 1 July,[47] the Council noted its appreciation of the increase in the number of development finance institutions with which UNDP had established arrangements and the rise in investment commitment made by most of them. It encouraged the Administrator to seek an improvement in in-vestment commitment from those institutions where there had been a decline. The Council commended the Administrator for initiating reimbursable aid mechanisms to finance pre-investment activities and for strengthening UNDP's links with the Caribbean and African Project Development Facilities. It encouraged him to continue to collaborate with international development and finance institutions in providing training in pre-investment studies and investment development techniques to the staff of UNDP and Governments of developing countries. The Administrator was asked to report whenever necessary on UNDP activities in the area.

NGO collaboration and grass-roots activities

In a March report,[48] the Administrator described UNDP action in 1987 to involve grass-roots organizations and NGOs in UNDP-supported activities and its efforts to strengthen co-operation with NGOs through small-scale development activities.

On 1 July,[49] the Council noted the initiative taken in establishing the Partners in Development Programme as part of plans to strengthen co-operation through support to small-scale grass-roots development activities undertaken by indigenous NGOs in recipient countries, and to strengthen the technical and managerial capabilities of those organizations, and requested the Administrator to report on the work of the Programme in 1989. It endorsed activities under way leading to the establishment of an Africa 2000 Network of African NGOs working to support communities in natural resources management, community forestry, food production and environmental protection activities; it also endorsed the setting up of a UNDP-administered trust fund for that purpose, to which Governments and organizations were invited to contribute. The Administrator was asked to take steps to strengthen the capacity of recipient Governments to work with NGOs by helping with data collection, facilitating dialogue, providing appropriate institutional support and involving NGOs in programme and project design. He was also asked to examine ways of simplifying procedures and practices to facilitate collaboration with grass-roots groups and NGOs. The Council urged the Administrator to continue measures, including training, to strengthen UNDP staff capabilities to support co-operation with NGOs and grass-roots organizations. It requested him to report in 1989 on measures taken.

Financing

In his review of the financial situation in 1988,[50] the Administrator stated that, as a result of the surplus of main programme income over expenditure, the balance of UNDP general resources increased from $532.2 million at 31 December 1987 to $581.6 million at 31 December 1988. Income from voluntary contributions totalled $936.1 million. After applying the accounting linkage for local office costs, income amounted to $931 million ($18 million lower than forecast). That resulted primarily from one Government not paying its pledge in 1988. Most Member States paid in full, with over 97 per cent of pledges for 1988 paid during the year. Fluctuations in exchange rates in 1988 impacted on UNDP resources in two ways: the value of pledges made in national currencies, in dollar terms, decreased by $23.5 million between 31 December 1987 and the date paid; and the value of assets held by UNDP in various currencies, including transactional gains or losses on exchange, decreased, in dollar terms, by $10.5 million. The Administrator reported that, for the third year in a row, there was a substantial increase in the dollar value of pledges made to UNDP. Even with the reduced level of pledges in 1988 resulting from exchange rate fluctuations, pledges for 1988 were 9.8 per cent higher than for 1987.

Field programme expenditures in 1988 totalled $832.5 million, of which $678 million represented expenditures against IPFs (including $1 million in respect of add-on funds), $109.2 million against cost-sharing and $45.3 million against supplementary programmes in the UNDP account. IPF expenditure of $678 million represented an increase of almost 15 per cent over 1987.

In his annual report,[1] the Administrator noted that 1988 was another record year for income received, with total income of $1,209 million. The amount comprised contributions to UNDP's main programme, all cost-sharing arrangements and UNDP-administered funds.

Total expenditures from UNDP central resources amounted to $1,109.4 million, of which $832.5 million was spent on field programme activities, $99.8 million on agency support costs, $172.3 million on UNDP administrative and programme support costs and $5.6 million on sectoral support and other field-level costs.

Through its 112 field offices serving in 152 countries and territories, UNDP offered Governments and their other development partners numerous services extending beyond its central responsibilities. Field offices continued to play a central role in catalysing linkages to obtain parallel financing; figures reported by 42 UNDP field offices indicated that at least $249 million in parallel financing could be attributed directly to UNDP-assisted activities during 1988. Field offices also continued to support non-UNDP-financed projects through UNDP's field infrastructure. In 1988, 80 offices reported assistance in implementing 1,364 non-UNDP-financed projects with total expenditures of

$364 million. UNDP also assisted recipients of World Bank loans by placing at their disposal its field-based delivery system to support implementation of Bank-financed technical co-operation projects. Those management services were also available to recipients of bilateral assistance. The value of management services agreements signed in 1988, excluding IFAD, amounted to $45.6 million.

Investment commitments related to UNDP-assisted projects amounted to an estimated $9.2 billion in 1988, a decline of 12 per cent from 1987. The World Bank Group provided $3.8 billion or 41 per cent of those investment commitments in 1988 compared with 23 per cent in 1987. Developing countries provided $2.9 billion, a substantial drop from the $5.2 billion reported in 1987. Investment commitments from bilateral sources totalled $1.7 billion, a 30 per cent increase over 1987. As in previous years, the public sector was the principal source of reported investment commitments in 1988, with $8 billion contributed—87 per cent of those funds. The private sector commitment was $1.2 billion, $1 billion greater than in 1987.

In 1988, project expenditures by the Office for Project Services (OPS) reached over $200 million, a 29 per cent increase over 1987. Levels of expenditures increased for all sources of funds, with the largest amount, $79.5 million, disbursed under projects financed from UNDP core funds, an increase of 25 per cent over 1987. Management services constituted 31 per cent of the OPS projects budget, with disbursements of $67.5 million in 1988, a 32 per cent increase over the previous year.

The audited financial statements of UNDP for 1988[51] showed that the total of unexpended UNDP resources increased from $723 million in 1987 to $776.7 million as at 31 December 1988.

Contributions. The audited financial statements for 1988[52] showed that total income from contributions to the UNDP account was $1,070.8 million. That included contributions from Governments and other sources as follows: voluntary contributions, $931 million ($936.1 million, less transfers to government local office costs of $5.1 million); voluntary contributions to the Special Measures Fund for the Least Developed Countries (SMF/LDC), $15.9 million; cost-sharing contributions, $115.1 million; and cash counterpart contributions for projects, $12.7 million. Exchange adjustments on the collection of contributions of $3.8 million were deducted to derive the total.

As at 31 December 1988, pledges made in 1988 to the UNDP account for use in 1989 amounted to $578.5 million; pledges for 1989 for SMF/LDC amounted to $6.7 million. The financial statements gave a breakdown of contributions by Governments in 1988 and of pledges for 1989.

In his annual report,[1] the UNDP Administrator stated that during 1988 five major donor countries raised their contributions by 8 per cent or more in United States dollar terms. Among recipient donors, nine countries (Brazil, China, Colombia, Cuba, India, Indonesia, Pakistan, Saudi Arabia, Thailand) each pledged more than $1 million. Pledges made by the Federal Republic of Germany, the Netherlands, Norway and the United States maintained their positions among the top donors.

On 1 July,[29] the Governing Council reaffirmed its 1985 decision[25] whereby it had decided that for the purposes of forward planning an assumed average annual growth of total voluntary contributions of at least 8 per cent on a basis of the target of $700 million anticipated for 1986 should apply, and appealed to all contributors to increase their contributions in order to achieve that goal.

Mid-term review of resources

In accordance with a 1985 decision,[25] which provided for a mid-term review of resources for the fourth programming cycle (1987-1991), the Governing Council decided on 19 February 1988[52] to consider resources available and the outlook for the remainder of the cycle at its regular session later in the year. The Administrator was asked to report on programme delivery, implementation rates for the various parts of the programme and utilization of resources. He was also asked to provide an estimate of the resource outlook for the remainder of the cycle and make recommendations for using resources available, taking into account views expressed by Council members.

In a May report,[28] the Administrator gave an overview of the existing UNDP resource situation and an analysis of the variances with the resource scenario underlying fourth cycle programme allocations established in 1985.[25] The net effect of those variances (an increase in voluntary contributions and depreciation of the United States dollar versus many other currencies) was that UNDP was likely to hold at the end of 1988 resources available for programming of $549 million, assuming the value of the dollar *vis-à-vis* other currencies remained more or less constant. That projected balance compared with an originally foreseen amount of some $10 million for the end of 1988. The amount available at the end of 1987 was some $455 million.

The Administrator presented a revised resource scenario for the fourth programming cycle as a whole, which indicated that $600 million would be available for new programme allocations. He proposed that part of the additional resources be set aside for an increase of SPR (see below) and that the remainder, and major part, be used for an increase in IPFs (see above). The Administra-

tor recommended that an increase in the operational reserve should be deferred.

On 1 July,[29] the Governing Council agreed to maintain the operational reserve at its current level of $200 million and decided to review the need to increase the reserve on an annual basis. Considering that the forecasts of likely additional resources contained in the Administrator's report were based on assumptions which might or might not be realized, the Council asked the Administrator to restrict commitments against categories for both additional IPFs and SPR and to review the resource situation each year in the light of voluntary contributions, exchange rates and other related factors; he was to report annually. The Council also decided that if the increase in resources did not materialize, equal proportional amounts would be deducted from SPR and IPF allocations. If, on the other hand, the resources should increase over and above the amounts foreseen, any additional resources would be distributed in accordance with the 1985 decision on fourth programming cycle resources.[25]

Special Programme Resources

In his May report on the mid-term review of resources,[28] the Administrator provided details on additional funding needs with respect to activities financed from SPR. In response to a 1987 request of the Governing Council,[53] he provided information on categorization of SPR activities and criteria for contingencies in order for the Council to review the criteria. He proposed that the categorization of SPR activities should comprise: disaster relief; programme development; TCDC and related activities; other activities; and contingencies and unearmarked funds. He stated that the total amount needed during the balance of the fourth programming cycle to finance SPR activities was estimated to exceed $120 million.

On 1 July,[29] the Governing Council decided that of the $600 million in extra resources available for programming, SPR would receive $8.38 million, which would be augmented by $101.62 million, making a total of $110 million. That amount would be allocated as follows: $30 million for activities already agreed by the Council and included under the categories of SPR activities proposed by the Administrator (see above); $20 million for the Special Plan of Economic Co-operation for Central America (see PART TWO, Chapter V); and $60 million for a Special Programme for Management Development and Related Institution-building, to be known as the Management Development Programme, as proposed by the Administrator.[54] The Council specified that: the Programme would be available to all countries wishing to participate, with no more than 50 per cent of resources being allocated to programmes in one region; it would operate only in response to requests from developing countries to assist them to design and/or implement long-term, sectoral or multisectoral programmes of management development and related institution-building; no conditionality would be applied in the use of those funds or in the Programme's activities other than normal UNDP requirements; the use of the facility would not be related to the implementation of any policy other than that of the Governments concerned; and UNDP activities in that area should not be conditional upon those of any other organization. The Administrator was asked to provide in 1989 details of guidelines for the use of the Programme and a report on its operation.

GENERAL ASSEMBLY ACTION

In **decision 43/445** of 20 December, the General Assembly referred a paragraph on operational activities for development to the Economic and Social Council for consideration and action in 1989. By that paragraph, the establishment of a management development programme as an instrument for focused support of national efforts to improve public administration in developing countries would be welcomed.

Budgets

Revised 1988-1989 budget

Revised budget estimates of UNDP as a whole for the biennium 1988-1989[55] amounted to $397.3 million (gross) and $333 million (net). The 0.8 per cent increase in gross estimates over estimates approved in 1987[56] was attributable to a volume increase in respect of the Office for Project Services, amounting to $3.7 million, which was partially offset by an overall cost decrease of $0.5 million. The revised estimates took account of the change in currency parities between 1 February 1987, the basis of the Administrator's original budget estimates, and 1 February 1988. The result was an overall currency release of $3.4 million. As regards inflation, an increase in headquarters costs as a result of an increase in projected inflation was more than offset by a decrease in projected inflation in certain developing countries. The net effect was a reduction of $1.4 million. The revised estimates embodied an overall inflation rate of 6 per cent, comprising 4 per cent at headquarters and 7 per cent at the field offices.

The report containing the revised budget estimates[55] also contained a presentation on the funding mechanisms used by UNDP to meet the costs of its programme support and administrative services. It also included proposals regarding the presentation of the 1990-1991 biennial budget.

On 1 July,[57] the Governing Council approved revised appropriations of $416,183,100 (gross) to finance the 1988-1989 biennial budget, and resolved that income estimates of $66,197,300 should be used to offset the gross appropriations, resulting in net appropriations of $349,985,800. It requested the Administrator to prepare an overall review of the most appropriate senior management structure for UNDP as a whole, to be presented to the Council in 1989, in the context of the 1990-1991 biennial budget estimates. He was also asked to undertake a detailed review of the role and functions of the Office for Project Services, taking into account the work-load, structure and staffing of the Office, and to report in 1989. The Council took note of the funding mechanisms used by UNDP and decided to keep the issue under review in the context of the biennial budget presentation. It approved changes for the presentation of the 1990-1991 budget estimates and took note of the carry-forward of $2.6 million of the 1986-1987 support-cost earnings of the Office for Project Services for use in 1988-1989.

Review of 1987 financial situation

In an April report,[58] the Administrator provided a comprehensive financial review of activities financed from the UNDP account during 1987 and of the financial position as at the end of that year. He included estimates of anticipated resources and expenditures for 1988 and 1989, as well as information on cost-sharing activities, the status of SMF/LDC and SPR, the placement of UNDP funds, the status of the operational reserve, the utilization of accumulated non-convertible currencies, agency support-cost arrangements, the status of the Reserve for Construction Loans to Governments, management and other support services and the Senior Industrial Development Field Adviser programme (see below, under "Sectoral support").

On 1 July,[59] the Governing Council urged the Administrator, in co-operation with recipient Governments and executing agencies, to continue to improve programme delivery so that it was better aligned with the available balance of resources, without compromising the quality of the programme. It requested him to continue to report on problems related to the utilization of non-convertible currencies, decided that the level of the operational reserve should be $200 million, fully funded, and approved the Administrator's proposals in respect of the Reserve for Construction Loans to Governments, renaming it Reserve for Field Accommodation.

UNDP-administered funds

During 1988, twelve new trust funds were established by the Administrator on behalf of UNDP.[60] They were to finance: a demographic and economic census of population and housing in Senegal; an African training and management services project; the Steering Committee and secretariat for UNPAAERD; the Africa 2000 Network (addressing problems of environmental degradation); the rehabilitation and reconstruction of Afghanistan; the administration of the residual funds of the United Nations Special Relief Office in Bangladesh; emergency assistance to Bangladesh in the wake of severe flooding; technical and capital assistance to Palestinians in the West Bank and Gaza Strip; the participation of parliamentarians, spiritual leaders and the media in development activities; preparation of an international research programme on tropical forestry; the development of policies and plans to make motherhood safer; and the co-ordination of international agricultural research. Contributions to those funds received during the year amounted to $16,819,885 out of a total trust fund income of $28.5 million. A trust fund arrangement was also established on behalf of UNCDF and another on behalf of UNIFEM. The value of those arrangements was approximately $671,000.

In March 1988,[61] the Administrator informed the Governing Council of the full utilization of the Trust Fund for Assistance to Colonial Countries and Peoples. Since no additional contributions had been received, the Fund had become inoperative and the Administrator recommended that it be closed and the residual amount of approximately $900 be transferred to general resources of UNDP.

On 1 July,[62] the Governing Council took note of the Administrator's report on trust funds established by him in 1987.[53] It requested him to provide, in future reports, summary information, at the aggregate level, on all trust funds established by him since 1981. It agreed that the Trust Fund for Assistance to Colonial Countries and Peoples be closed and that its unspent balance be transferred to the general resources of UNDP, and requested the Administrator to take appropriate action to submit the proposal to the General Assembly in 1988.

GENERAL ASSEMBLY ACTION

By **decision 43/446** of 20 December 1988, the General Assembly took note of the decision of the UNDP Governing Council to close the Trust Fund for Assistance to Colonial Countries and Peoples and to transfer the balance of $900 to UNDP general resources.

Emergency Operation Trust Fund

In March 1988,[63] the Administrator informed the Governing Council of action taken to implement a 1983 General Assembly resolution[64] on liquidation of the United Nations Emergency Operation Trust Fund and allocation of its remaining balance. With regard to the sum allocated to

the UNDP Trust Fund for Countries Afflicted by Famine and Malnutrition, of total available funds as at 31 December 1987 of some $42.9 million, 144 projects with total budgets of $42.3 million had been approved or accepted in principle. As to the amount allocated to the Pérez-Guerrero Trust Fund for Economic and Technical Co-operation among Developing Countries, the balance as at 31 December 1987 was $7 million, of which $5 million was in the form of preserved capital and $2 million in disposable resources.

In a decision of 27 June and 1 July,[65] the Council took note of the Administrator's report.

Agency support costs

ACC action. In April 1988, ACC adopted a decision[66] by which it submitted to the Governing Council a statement on the effect of changes in the exchange rate of the United States dollar on support-cost reimbursements by UNDP. ACC noted that the existing support-cost arrangements, established in 1981,[67] were due to expire in 1991. The substantial decline in the value of the dollar which had taken place since 1985 could not have been foreseen in 1981; that decline had rendered the increase in support-cost reimbursement to executing agencies very inadequate in comparison with the shortfalls sustained. ACC requested special *ad hoc* arrangements for the reimbursement of support costs for 1987 to compensate European-based executing agencies for the severe difficulties encountered owing to the depreciation of the dollar against the currencies of the headquarters' countries concerned. In an annex to its decision, ACC listed 14 executing agencies and proposed additional support-cost reimbursements for 1987.

In May,[68] the Administrator transmitted the ACC statement to the Governing Council.

Also in May,[69] the Administrator submitted requests from seven executing agencies (ILO, FAO, UNESCO, ITU, UNIDO, the United Nations Conference on Trade and Development and the International Trade Centre) for the additional reimbursement of support costs for 1987 as a result of currency fluctuations. The Council was requested to review the requests in conjunction with the ACC statement.

On 1 July,[70] the Council authorized the Administrator to make a special *ad hoc* additional support-cost reimbursement for 1987 to the executing agencies listed by ACC in the amounts proposed, less any amounts reimbursed under existing arrangements. It emphasized that the authorization was exceptional and that it would not consider further requests for support-cost reimbursements in excess of the amounts authorized through 1991. The Administrator was asked to bring the decision to the attention of ACC and to inform the governing bodies of the executing agencies, through ACC, that: the Council considered that the approval of the request should enhance the capacity of executing agencies to support UNDP projects entrusted to them and improve the quality of project execution by agencies; and that the Council intended to examine the relationship between the agencies and UNDP—including the best way for UNDP to provide technical assistance to developing countries, accountability and appropriate compensation arrangements to those agencies, Governments and other providers of services for UNDP-funded projects—with a view to devising successor arrangements for agency support costs to operate from January 1992. The Administrator was asked to inform the Council of ACC's reponse.

Also on 1 July,[71] the Council, having considered the requests by seven executing agencies for additional reimbursement of support costs and noting that two other agencies had subsequently submitted such requests, authorized the Administrator to reimburse the nine agencies with headquarters in Europe in accordance with the provisions of the 1981 arrangements.

Ex post facto *report*

In accordance with a 1984 Governing Council decision,[72] the Administrator submitted his third *ex post facto* report on agency support costs,[73] covering 1986 and 1987. The report examined information received from agencies and analysed trends in agency support-cost income and expenditure, as well as agency technical co-operation project expenditure.

On 1 July,[74] the Council expressed its concern at the increase in the ratio between agency support-cost expenditure and total technical co-operation project expenditure. It asked the Administrator to continue to submit, on a biennial basis, an *ex post facto* report.

Successor arrangements

On 1 July,[75] the Governing Council considered that the successor arrangements for agency support costs dealt with in a 1987 General Assembly resolution[36] should be examined in the wider context of the evolving relationship of UNDP, Governments and the executing agencies of the United Nations system. It decided to establish a small group of experts in international development to study the issues and to make recommendations no later than 28 February 1990. The Administrator was asked to circulate the group's report and recommendations immediately, together with the comments of the specialized agencies, to all members of the Council. The Council also asked the Administrator, after consultations with the Council and United Nations agencies, to make proposals in February 1989 on the composition of the group, its working methods, terms of reference, timetable and work programme, and an estimate of all costs and financing.

Sectoral support

On 1 July 1988,[76] the Governing Council recalled its 1986[77] and 1987[78] decisions on sectoral support and reiterated its wish to continue to co-operate with UNIDO in providing the services of Senior Industrial Development Field Advisers (SIDFAs) to developing countries. It expressed the hope that the open-ended intersessional working group established by the Industrial Development Board would complete its work on the review of SIDFAs so that the Board could decide on the matter in October 1988. The UNIDO Director-General and the UNDP Administrator could then conclude a memorandum of understanding. The Council recalled that the UNDP contribution to the SIDFA programme was linked to the integration of SIDFAs into UNDP field offices. It agreed to review in 1989 the part of its 1987 decision[78] dealing with classification of SIDFAs and asked the Administrator to provide, in his report on the annual review of the financial situation, information for that purpose.

Management services

In response to a 1987 Governing Council request,[53] the Administrator reviewed the experience gained in providing management services to developing countries.[79] The report recapitulated the legislative background to and described the status and growth of management services operations. The process of determining management fees was also explained.

The report indicated that the use of management services had grown dramatically. As at March 1988, 63 agreements were in effect with total budgets of $241.4 million. Expenditures from all funding sources—development banks, bilateral donors and IFAD—totalled $87.4 million in 1987.

The Administrator concluded that management services afforded Governments an existing and flexible mechanism that could be used to mobilize project inputs more rapidly. There was no indication that the multilateral character of the UNDP programme or its role as a central funding agency for technical assistance had in any way been affected by the use of the management services modality. He believed that management services tended to be supportive of UNDP's overall efforts to improve coordination at the field level. Given that the experience, albeit of limited duration, had proved positive, the Administrator recommended that UNDP continue to provide such services, reporting to the Governing Council every two years on the status of management services agreements, with an analysis of any emerging trends.

On 1 July,[80] the Council noted with satisfaction that the activities undertaken under management services agreements had been carried out in accordance with the principles and guidelines of a 1983 decision.[81] It authorized the Administrator to continue to provide such services in accordance with those principles and guidelines. He was also requested to report to the Council every two years, beginning in 1990, on the status of management services, with an analysis of any trends that might appear over the longer term and including information, by individual donor, on the level of voluntary contributions to UNDP general resources compared with amounts provided under management services agreements.

Accounts and auditing

Accounts for 1987

The financial statements of UNDP for the year ended 31 December 1987, together with the report of the Board of Auditors, were submitted to the General Assembly in August 1988.[82] The statements also covered UNDP-administered trust funds.

The Advisory Committee on Administrative and Budgetary Questions, in October,[83] commented on the Board's findings.

By **resolution 43/216**, the Assembly accepted the financial report and audited financial statements and the audit opinions and report of the Board of Auditors and requested the Governing Council of UNDP to require the Administrator to take immediate steps to correct the situations or conditions that gave rise to the qualification of audit opinions of the Board. The Assembly urged the panel of external auditors, administrations, governing bodies of the executing agencies and other parties to solve the problem regarding certification of programme expenditures executed and reported by United Nations executing agencies in co-operation with UNDP and UNFPA.

Audit reports for 1986

In April 1988, the Administrator submitted to the Governing Council the audited accounts and audit reports of participating and executing agencies relating to the funds allocated to them by UNDP as at 31 December 1986.[84] He included comments on substantive observations of the auditors, UNDP follow-up with agencies on such observations and a summary of action taken by UNDP in response to a 1987 Council decision[85] on the preparation of audit reports.

On 1 July,[86] the Council noted with concern that the Board of Auditors' opinion on the 1986 accounts was qualified on several counts and noted with satisfaction that the Administrator was taking steps to correct the situations that gave rise to

those qualifications. It recognized that the audit opinion on UNDP accounts would remain qualified as long as audited accounts of executing agencies had not been received by the Board when it issued its opinion on UNDP accounts. The Administrator was asked to bring that problem to the attention of the Panel of External Auditors. The Council suggested that the Economic and Social Council invite the executing agencies to consider providing UNDP with annual audited accounts. It welcomed the Administrator's proposals concerning the management and administration of the audit process in connection with Government-executed projects and considered that existing UNDP procedures for recording unliquidated obligations should continue to be applied pending the Panel of External Auditors' examination of those procedures. It welcomed the measures taken by the Administrator to provide fuller disclosure in UNDP financial statements of overexpenditure on projects funded from cost-sharing and Government cash-counterpart contributions, accepting that the existing basis of recording income and expenditure for those contributions, and for trust funds, should continue pending consideration by the Panel. Noting that a comparison of actual expenditure against appropriation estimates would, for 1987, be provided in a schedule contained in the annual audited UNDP financial statements, the Council decided to retain for the time being a single appropriation line for UNDP core activities. The Administrator was asked to consider having the budget decision presented in more appropriation lines and to report on the matter in 1989.

Financial regulations

On 1 July,[87] the Governing Council decided that its Budgetary and Finance Committee would consider in 1990 a proposed financial regulation (mainly dealing with currencies of contributions and their utilization) and other matters on which consensus was not achieved at the Council's current session, as specified in the annex to a 1986 note on the matter.[88]

Administrative questions

Project personnel

In pursuance of a 1987 Governing Council decision,[85] the Administrator reported on his efforts to update and refine data on project personnel.[89] The report also addressed the Council's request for case-studies of a representative number of projects with varying component mixes of personnel to determine to what extent the objectives of projects had been achieved and whether the right mix of experts in terms of quality and cost had been used. The Administrator made recommendations covering project design, an agreement on conditions of service for national Professional project personnel, the status of such personnel and monitoring and reporting.

On 1 July,[32] the Council endorsed the Administrator's proposal that a comprehensive data base on the participation in the programme of national Professional project personnel be established. It recommended that UNDP and the executing agencies provide training in United Nations system practices and procedures to such personnel and that efforts be made to regularize their legal status in consultation with their Governments.

In-house technical expertise

On 1 July,[90] the Governing Council requested the Administrator to report to it on the role of and need for in-house technical expertise in UNDP, including the appropriate role of the Technical Advisory Division, in the programme and project cycle.

Change of name of the Office for Projects Execution

In February 1988,[91] the Administrator informed the Governing Council of his decision to rename the Office for Projects Execution as the Office for Project Services, indicating that the designation of what was in effect UNDP's operational arm better reflected the essence of its activities in the service of both Governments and UNDP's funding partners.

On 18 February,[92] the Council took note of the Administrator's decision.

Delegation of project approval authority

In February,[93] the Administrator informed the Council that, effective 1 March 1988, the level at which resident representatives would have the authority to approve projects would be raised from $400,000 to $700,000, subject to certain conditions.

On 18 February,[94] the Council took note of the Administrator's action.

Action by other organs of the UN system

On 1 July,[95] the Governing Council requested the Administrator to submit to it in February 1989 a report indicating action which UNDP had taken or intended to take in response to decisions of other organs of the United Nations system in 1988.

REFERENCES

[1]DP/1989/13 & Add.1-5. [2]YUN 1986, p. 446, GA res. S-13/2, annex, 1 June 1986. [3]E/1988/19 (dec. 88/15). [4]YUN 1987, p. 406. [5]E/1988/19. [6]*Ibid.* (dec. 88/1). [7]*Ibid.* (dec. 88/2). [8]*Ibid.* (dec. 88/4). [9]*Ibid.* (dec. 88/14). [10]*Ibid.* (dec. 88/59). [11]*Ibid.* (dec. 88/60). [12]*Ibid.* (dec. 88/58). [13]DP/1988/3. [14]E/1988/19 (dec. 88/3). [15]*Ibid.* (dec. 88/33). [16]DP/1988/31. [17]DP/1989/28. [18]DP/1989/29. [19]YUN 1987, p. 410. [20]DP/1989/30. [21]DP/1989/31. [22]DP/1988/9. [23]YUN 1987, p. 390, GA dec. 42/428, 11 Dec. 1987. [24]*Ibid.*, p. 417. [25]YUN 1985, p. 471. [26]E/1988/19 (dec. 88/8). [27]*Ibid.* (dec. 88/31 C). [28]DP/1988/26. [29]E/1988/19 (dec. 88/31 A). [30]YUN 1987, p. 414. [31]DP/1988/19 & Add.1-4. [32]E/1988/19 (dec. 88/17). [33]YUN 1987, p. 415. [34]DP/1988/19/Add.2. [35]E/1988/19 (dec. 88/18). [36]YUN 1987, p. 401, GA res. 42/196, 11 Dec. 1987. [37]DP/1988/19/Add.4. [38]E/1988/19 (dec. 88/19). [39]DP/1988/14. [40]E/1988/19 (dec. 88/25). [41]YUN 1987, p. 416. [42]DP/1988/20. [43]E/1988/19 (dec. 88/20). [44]*Ibid.* (dec. 88/21). [45]YUN 1982, p. 642. [46]DP/1988/25. [47]E/1988/19 (dec. 88/26). [48]DP/1988/15. [49]E/1988/19 (dec. 88/27). [50]DP/1989/54 & Add.1. [51]A/44/5/Add.1. [52]E/1988/19 (dec. 88/7). [53]YUN 1987, p. 419. [54]DP/1988/76. [55]DP/1988/52 & Add.1,2. [56]YUN 1987, p. 418. [57]E/1988/19 (dec. 88/46). [58]DP/1988/51 & Add.1,2. [59]E/1988/19 (dec. 88/45 A). [60]DP/1989/57 & Add.1. [61]DP/1988/57. [62]E/1988/19 (dec. 88/47). [63]DP/1988/22. [64]YUN 1983, p. 537, GA res. 38/201, 20 Dec. 1983. [65]E/1988/19 (dec. 88/58). [66]ACC/1988/DEC/1-18 (dec. 1988/8). [67]YUN 1981, p. 449. [68]DP/1988/66. [69]DP/1988/67. [70]E/1988/19 (dec. 88/52). [71]*Ibid.* (dec. 88/53). [72]YUN 1984, p. 448. [73]DP/1988/54 & Corr.1. [74]E/1988/19 (dec. 88/51). [75]*Ibid.* (dec. 88/50). [76]*Ibid.* (dec. 88/45 B). [77]YUN 1986, p. 431. [78]YUN 1987, p. 421. [79]DP/1988/59. [80]E/1988/19 (dec. 88/54). [81]YUN 1983, p. 460. [82]A/43/5/Add.1. [83]A/43/674 & Corr.1. [84]DP/1988/5 & Add.1 & Add.1/Corr.1. [85]YUN 1987, p. 422. [86]E/1988/19 (dec. 88/49). [87]*Ibid.* (dec. 88/48). [88]DP/1986/63. [89]DP/1988/19/Add.1. [90]E/1988/19 (dec. 88/16). [91]DP/1988/INF/1. [92]E/1988/19 (dec. 88/11). [93]DP/1988/INF/2. [94]E/1988/19 (dec. 88/12). [95]*Ibid.* (dec. 88/55).

Other technical co-operation

UN programmes

In 1988, the United Nations, mainly through DTCD, continued to provide technical assistance to developing countries. In a report[1] to the UNDP Governing Council, the Secretary-General addressed various policy issues and described DTCD's technical co-operation programme and those of other United Nations entities.

In 1988, the United Nations delivered a technical co-operation programme of $269 million, compared with $229 million in 1987, an increase of 17 per cent in project expenditures. Of that amount, DTCD executed a programme of $149.4 million. UNDP-financed projects represented $97.2 million; projects financed by UNFPA accounted for $20.3 million; $25.1 million was financed by trust funds; and $6.8 million was expended under the United Nations regular programme for technical co-operation. In comparison with 1987, budgets increased by $19.8 million (12 per cent) in 1988 to $182.8 million, and the delivery of $149.4 million was up 10 per cent. The implementation rate was 82 per cent.

DTCD activities

In his report on technical co-operation activities,[1] the Secretary-General stated that in 1988 DTCD had under execution 953 projects with total delivery of $149.4 million against budgets of $182.8 million. The volume of expenditures for UNDP-financed projects increased by $9 million and accounted for 65 per cent of total expenditures, as in 1987. There was a marked increase in the UNFPA-funded share of project expenditures, which partly offset the sharp drop in UNDP trust funds, which fell by 72 per cent or over $8 million.

By sector, natural resources and energy represented 38.1 per cent of total expenditures, or $56.9 million. Development planning was the second largest sector, representing 19.3 per cent or $28.8 million. Statistics had expenditures of $21.3 million (14.3 per cent); public administration and finance, $18.6 million (12.4 per cent); population, $9.4 million (6.3 per cent); the United Nations Educational and Training Programme for Southern Africa, $6.7 million (4.5 per cent); social development, $5.6 million (3.8 per cent); and others, $2.1 million.

By geographic area, the DTCD-executed programme included expenditures of $66.5 million for Africa, $38.8 million for Asia and the Pacific, $30 million for the Middle East, Mediterranean, Europe and interregional projects, and $14.1 million for the Americas. The largest growth was in Asia, where the programme increased by $6.8 million. Project delivery in Africa remained the largest, but its share of the total delivery decreased from 47 per cent to 45 per cent.

DTCD executed 153 projects in development issues and policies during 1988, with delivery of $33.2 million against budgets of $42.2 million: 41.8 per cent for Africa; 9.4 per cent for the Americas; 25.2 per cent for Asia and the Pacific; and 23.6 per cent for the Mediterranean, Middle East, Europe and interregional programme.

Requests from developing countries for technical assistance in development planning were strongly influenced by international economic instability and onerous foreign debt and balance-of-payment problems. DTCD's assistance therefore focused on activities related to national economic structural adjustment and recovery programmes, particularly in the case of Africa. A main thrust was on applied, immediately useful assistance in such areas as short-term and operational planning, project planning and monitoring and the co-ordination of external assistance. DTCD intensified the development of innovative methodologies and modalities to enhance the effectiveness and efficiency of its technical co-operation. Training and other means of developing national technical capacities in development planning were stressed. It provided assistance in computerized investment project banks and in co-ordinating international financial and technical co-operation, particularly in Latin America and Africa. In Burkina Faso, for example, an integrated project bank was developed

to enable the Government to monitor its entire public investment programme and select investment projects on the basis of economic and financial criteria and priorities.

Innovative methodologies and modalities developed by DTCD included the first planning model designed especially for island developing countries of the Pacific, which filled an important vacuum. In relation to that, training in sub-national planning was provided to national professionals associated with DTCD's planning projects in eight Pacific island countries at a workshop held at the United Nations Centre for Regional Development at Nagoya, Japan. In addition, interregional projects were formulated under the regular programme to develop applied econometric and data-bank models specifically for LDCs.

In rural development, a multisectoral project in the Lao People's Democratic Republic assisted in establishing an agricultural promotion centre, which developed pragmatic approaches for agricultural production and exceeded its objectives in road-building, rice cultivation and forestry. In Swaziland, a project combining income generation, training and social infrastructure expanded from one to several regions of the country. Also in grass-roots development, support continued for the Trickle-Up programme of very small loans for productive sectors of the population. In 1988, a manual translated into all the United Nations official languages was produced to help replicate the system world-wide. With regard to inter-agency co-operation, DTCD expanded its technical scrutiny of WFP projects.

DTCD delivery in the energy sector during 1988 was $15.8 million, compared to $21.3 million in 1987, and was allocated as follows: Asia and the Pacific, $9.1 million or 57.5 per cent; the Middle East, Mediterranean, Europe and interregional programme, $2.5 million or 16 per cent; Africa, $2.1 million or 13.5 per cent; and the Americas, $2.1 million or 13 per cent. The decreased 1988 expenditures reflected the lower priority assigned in 1985-1987 to the energy sector by developing countries in response to lower prices in the world oil market. A total of 78 advisory missions to 49 countries were undertaken by headquarters staff to provide advice on energy policy, resource evaluation and exploration, design of projects and feasibility studies in the broad range of energy fields covered by DTCD: petroleum, coal, natural gas, electric power, energy planning and conservation, geothermal, solar and wind energy, multisource renewable energy packages, computerized data banks and microcomputer-based energy analysis.

In cartography, remote sensing and public works, there were 69 projects under execution during 1988 with delivery of $9.5 million against budgets of about $10 million, a significant increase over the 64 projects with delivery of $6.9 million in 1987. Projects in cartography, surveying, mapping and hydrography included institution-building, transfer of technical expertise to national cartographic and hydrographic institutions and provision of training and equipment. Substantive assistance was provided to five countries in the design and evaluation of remote-sensing proposals related to outer space, including advice on the feasibility of particular remote-sensing projects and assistance to resource managers in gathering data for locating, managing and monitoring natural resources.

Total 1988 delivery for mineral resources was $12.5 million against budgets of $17 million, up from $11.1 million and budgets of $12 million in 1987. Advisory missions increased sharply to 120 in 1988 from 59 in 1987. As in 1987, most new requests were in mineral sector planning and programming, investment promotion, rehabilitation of production facilities and fields requiring highly specialized expertise. Thirty new projects were initiated in 1988. Almost all were concerned with institution-strengthening and training, investment promotion and mineral-sector planning and strategies, and about half of them were in Africa.

While the number of DTCD water projects decreased from 126 in 1987 to 113 in 1988, the budget for the sector increased from $24 million to $24.3 million. The regional distribution was as follows: Africa, 54.4 per cent; Asia and the Pacific, 21.6 per cent; the Americas, 9.8 per cent; and the Middle East, Mediterranean, Europe and inter-regional programme, 14.1 per cent. Rural water supply continued to comprise a significant part of the technical assistance programme, with some 18 per cent of all projects. While nearly a quarter of those were concerned with institutional support and training, there was an increase in projects to improve management and planning of water resources. In addition to UNDP-financed projects, 42 interregional advisory missions, sponsored by the United Nations regular programme of technical co-operation, covered such fields as water legislation, well drilling, computerized data management and hydrogeology.

During 1988, DTCD implemented 120 projects in public administration and finance with delivery of $18.6 million against a budget of $24.9 million, an increase of more than 30 per cent compared to 1987. Interregional advisers in development administration and finance undertook 22 missions in the following areas: tax administration and resource mobilization; management development and training; and government budgeting and financial management, including accounting and auditing, public enterprise and administrative reform. Improved productivity and performance in public services continued to be a priority objec-

tive of technical assistance programmes. Along with reforming public services, many developing countries continued to make progress in supporting human resource development, training managers and technical personnel in the public sector and upgrading national training institutions. In an environment of declining official capital flows and increasing external debt burdens, many developing countries were able to achieve considerable fiscal adjustment by cutting spending and generating additional revenues. Governments were helped through projects aimed at closing tax loopholes, expanding tax bases and introducing tax reforms.

In statistics, DTCD provided support for the execution of 180 projects with a total delivery of $21.3 million in 1988, compared with $16.1 million in 1987. Headquarters staff undertook 121 project-related or direct advisory missions to 60 countries; of those, 11 were carried out by interregional advisers. Technical co-operation continued to be aimed at strengthening national services and capabilities for collecting, processing and disseminating a broad range of development-related statistics, from general economic statistics and national accounts to social and demographic statistics, and statistics on women and special population groups, such as disabled persons. Over 40 countries were assisted in the use of microcomputer systems to support population data processing and general statistical work.

In the population sector, DTCD had 112 projects under execution with total delivery of $9.4 million, compared to 98 projects with delivery of $7.9 million in 1987. Its activities heightened awareness of the implications of demographic levels and trends. In Africa, for example, a number of countries had adopted or were in the process of adopting population policies aimed at fertility reduction, and training had increased at both national and interregional levels, particularly using new microcomputer technologies. In response to the continuing need for human resources with population skills and background, projects in population and development training and research continued at the country level, with particular emphasis on the Africa region, and at the interregional level, through renewed support to the Cairo Demographic Centre and the United Nations/USSR Interregional Training and Research Programme in Population and Development.

In the area of population dynamics, increased use was made of computers in completing the analysis of the 1980 round of censuses and in the preparation of population projections. The dissemination of census results was made an integral part of the census analysis programme. In several African countries—Benin, Burkina Faso, Liberia, the Sudan and Togo—the results of demographic analyses and population projects were produced speedily through the use of computers, with follow-up seminars generating interest in all government sectors. Computer packages assembled and distributed by DTCD were used extensively to evaluate data, estimate fertility and mortality levels, construct life tables and compute population projects. In population policy and development, DTCD continued to assist 30 countries to strengthen population units for research and studies, formulate population policies and integrate population variables into national development planning.

The United Nations Centre for Social Development and Humanitarian Affairs (CSDHA) continued, in co-operation with DTCD, to carry out technical co-operation activities in social development. With financing provided by DTCD, CSDHA fielded several *ad hoc* advisory missions: to Guatemala to assist the Government in strengthening voluntary social welfare organizations; to Hungary to launch a UNDP-financed project on strengthening social welfare and health programmes; to the United Republic of Tanzania to participate in a joint UNDP/World Bank project on the social aspects of adjustment; and to Yugoslavia to help establish an institute on aging. DTCD and CSDHA also co-operated in formulating World Bank proposals for technical assistance loans for social sector management in Argentina and Brazil.

In 1988, delivery for project personnel was $74.6 million, of which 44.9 per cent was for Africa, 25.1 per cent for the Mediterranean, Middle East, Europe and interregional programme, 17.7 per cent for Asia and the Pacific, and 12.3 per cent for the Americas. The expenditures reflected an increase of $9.4 million over 1987. Expenditures for equipment for technical co-operation projects executed by DTCD totalled $31.8 million and for contracts $6.8 million. Also during 1988, 42 per cent or $13.2 million of all equipment purchases and 29 per cent or $2 million of all contracts awarded were for projects in Africa, in line with the priority being accorded to providing assistance to African countries.

The training component accounted for $29.7 million in 1988, a significant increase over the $22.6 million in 1987. Africa had the largest share, with 45.3 per cent, Asia and the Pacific had 32.7 per cent, the Americas, 4.9 per cent, and the Mediterranean, Middle East, Europe and interregional programme, 17.1 per cent.

A total of 4,141 training awards were implemented in 1988, including fellowships, study tours, seminars and workshops, compared with 3,773 in 1987. Fellows and participants from 143 countries were trained in 83 host countries. Over 2,200 United Nations fellows/participants were trained in developing countries.

UNDP Council action. On 1 July 1988,[2] the Governing Council took note of the Secretary-General's report on United Nations technical co-operation activities during 1987.[3]. It welcomed the high rate of project implementation by DTCD, its efforts to hold down support costs and the steps taken by it to promote greater use of project evaluation as a tool to augment the quality and effectiveness of technical co-operation. DTCD was urged to take measures to ensure feedback of the results of evaluation into project formulation, and to co-ordinate its evaluation procedures with those of UNDP and UNFPA. The Council reiterated the continuing importance of greater co-operation between UNDP and DTCD, *inter alia*, in the preparation of round-table meetings and national technical co-operation assessments and programmes in keeping with the needs of developing countries. DTCD was requested to extend all necessary support to assist African countries in improving their managerial capacities through training and institution-building, and funding agencies were called on to make maximum use of DTCD's expertise in economic management. The Council encouraged DTCD to continue to co-operate closely with UNDP and to contribute to the Special Action Programme in Public Administration and Management for Africa. It urged DTCD to promote TCDC and requested it to intensify its efforts to promote the full integration of women in development, taking into account their concerns in all aspects of its programmes. The Secretary-General was to report to the Council on specific measures taken in that respect, including information on the participation of women in its training programmes and seminars and as experts in its programme. He was also to report on the major conclusions of DTCD's study, on behalf of ACC, on improving the quality of experts for development projects.

United Nations Volunteers

In his annual report,[4] the UNDP Administrator stated that at the end of 1988 there were 1,534 serving volunteers. That number was expected to increase to 2,000 by the end of 1989.

Of the $8 million available in the Special Voluntary Fund (SVF) in 1988, $2.9 million was carried forward from 1987, $1.3 million was received in voluntary contributions, $3.6 million came from the partial offset of external costs, and $160,000 was earned in interest. Of the total, $2.8 million was paid for travel costs of volunteers assigned in 1988 and for the repatriation of volunteers who completed their assignments. The remaining $5.2 million was carried forward to 1989.

A breakdown of contributions by Governments to UNV in 1988 and of pledges for 1989 was set out in the audited financial statements for 1988.[5]

In response to a 1987 Governing Council request,[6] the Administrator submitted a report on the review of the UNV programme.[7] The review had been conducted by consultants using information collected from user agencies, donor and recipient Governments, bilateral volunteer organizations and UNDP field staff in seven developing countries. Resident representatives had also supplied written responses to a questionnaire. The report presented the Administrator's views on 67 recommendations generated by the review as well as his recommendations concerning the future funding of UNV. The review's recommendations fell within six broad categories: the UNV concept and mandate, general management and administration issues, programme finance, programming, recruitment and training.

The Administrator concluded that the management of UNV should be financed through a core budget, which would be part of UNDP's administrative budget, and that the volunteer recruitment and back-stopping should be financed through a per capita charge. He believed that his proposals would provide strengthening and stability of the UNV management and flexibility in staffing its operations side in line with the changing level of volunteers. He noted that he had accepted and implemented many useful recommendations. Others were being studied for possible implementation. Some had serious implications for work-loads and budgets and could not be implemented currently. Still others touched fundamental issues not only of volunteerism, but also of the nature of multilateral co-operation programmes. The Administrator assured the Council that future review exercises would be conducted, which would assist UNDP and UNV in serving the developing countries.

UNDP Council action. On 1 July,[8] the Council noted with satisfaction the Administrator's intention to prepare and circulate a programme advisory note on the appropriate use of volunteers and to draw its contents to the attention of United Nations organizations. It invited volunteer-sending organizations to continue to assist in the work of the United Nations system, either by participating in the UNV programme by providing volunteers or by supporting the government or other local counterpart contribution to a United Nations project. The Council noted the Administrator's intention to undertake periodic evaluations of the UNV programme and invited him to report on them. He was asked also to inform the Council of the results of consultation meetings with other volunteer-sending organizations. The Council invited him to report in 1990 on the desirability of continuing separate UNV programme youth activities and agreed that the Domestic Development Services should be known as the Participating Development Programme

(PDP) and should retain a separate identity. It recognized the need to streamline recruitment procedures and improve co-operation with volunteer-sending societies so that the universal character of the UNV programme could be reflected in the diversity of the volunteers' countries of origin, and asked the Administrator to report in 1990 on steps taken. The Council recommended that the Administrator make efforts towards increasing the representation of women and older volunteers. It stressed the need for adequate and improved pre-assignment preparation for all volunteers, cross-cultural orientation, language training, precise job descriptions and increased attention to matching the volunteer's skills with the assignment.

Also on 1 July,[9] the Council decided that, with effect from 1988, project budgets should be charged on a *pro forma* basis $2,500 per year per serving volunteer to cover the balance of external costs that could not be met from SVF. It also decided that 85 per cent annually of income accruing to SVF, from voluntary general contributions and interest income, be utilized to meet the balance of external costs which were not covered by the $2,500 charge to project budgets. It further decided that annually the remaining 15 per cent of the income of SVF could be utilized in support of activities such as pilot and experimental projects of UNV and PDP/Youth Programmes, the cost of PDP specialists in the field, the orientation and briefing of volunteers, PDP specialists and government officials, and special recruitment campaigns. The Council invited member States to increase their contributions to SVF to enable the UNV programme to meet its commitment with the least possible augmentation of project costs, bearing in mind that 75 per cent of volunteers served in least developed, land-locked developing or island developing countries. It noted that the Administrator was empowered to receive Fund contributions for specific as well as general purposes and asked him to report to it, beginning in 1990, on the financial status of SVF and activities funded by it, as part of his biennial report on UNV.

In a 1 July decision on revised budget estimates for 1988-1989,[10] the Council decided that, for the time being, provision would be made for up to 40 UNV Programme Officers to be financed from the UNV programme budget at an average annual cost of $25,000 per post, including an adequate level of support services. The Administrator was asked to present proposals on the criteria to be applied in establishing UNV Programme Officer posts in the context of his 1990-1991 biennial budget estimates. The Council approved a revised core budget for the UNV programme amounting to $16 million for 1988-1989, chargeable to the biennial budget of UNDP, a level intended to provide headquarters and field-level support to 1,000 serving volunteers. It authorized the Administrator to supplement the core budget by an additional annual charge to UNDP general resources of $3,500 per serving volunteer over the established base of 1,000, as of 31 December of the previous year, which could be used for additional staffing units at a rate of one unit per 70 additional serving volunteers. He was to report on the exercise of those authorities in the context of the biennial budget.

Technical co-operation among developing countries

In his annual report for 1988,[4] the Administrator said that there had been a rapid expansion of TCDC activities. Estimated expenditures for such activities from IPF funds for 1987 and 1988 were $104.9 million compared to $55.7 million for 1985-1986. That amounted to 7.3 per cent of total IPFs available to all developing countries and territories in 1987-1988 as opposed to 5.3 per cent in 1985-1986. Expenditures for regional and interregional and global IPFs were $83 million and $15.4 million or 37 and 25 per cent, respectively, of IPF funds available for those programmes. Country programme IPF expenditures for 1987-1988 of $6.5 million represented 1.4 per cent of IPF spending.

The Information Referral System (INRES)–South data base continued to improve, with 700 new institutions registered during the year, bringing their number to almost 4,000. The number of enquiries responded to by INRES-South during 1988 exceeded 100 per month. The addition of a microcomputer-based data entry and retrieval system made it possible for the data base to be distributed to users equipped with similar microcomputers.

The Special Unit for TCDC, which facilitated the exchange of qualified experts between developing countries, assisted TCDC programming in Egypt and Pakistan and with the Latin American Economic System during 1988. Over 500 new TCDC projects emerged from those exercises.

TCDC financing

In response to a Governing Council decision of 19 February,[11] the Administrator submitted in April a report on strengthening the capacity of UNDP to promote and support TCDC, including its financing.[12]. The report outlined the status of TCDC in UNDP's programme policies and procedures, as well as the role of TCDC in programmes and projects being assisted from country, regional, interregional and global IPFs. The status and functions of the Special Unit for TCDC were reviewed, together with the use of SPR for promoting TCDC, especially through TCDC programming. Con-

straints to the fuller utilization of TCDC modalities were highlighted and some remedial measures proposed.

In response to a 1987 request of the High-level Committee on the Review of TCDC,[13] the Administrator submitted a report[14] summarizing the views of the United Nations development system on a 1985 report by the Joint Inspection Unit (JIU)[15] on the implementation of the 1978 Buenos Aires Plan of Action on TCDC[16] and the comments of ACC[15]. The Administrator's report highlighted the progress made and difficulties encountered in implementing the JIU recommendations. It was noted that further information on the implementation of those recommendations would be obtained in preparation for the 1989 session of the High-level Committee. That information would be presented to the Council along with the decisions of the Committee.

On 1 July,[17] the Council asked the Administrator to intensify measures to comply with the General Assembly's 1987 request[18] that steps be taken to enable each developing country to have the choice of executing each technical co-operation project, totally or in part, within the framework of TCDC or according to the traditional method of technical assistance. The Council took note of the Administrator's efforts to assist the Special Unit for TCDC in its staffing constraints, and urged him to present proposals and recommendations to strengthen the Unit in the light of its growing responsibilities in the context of his review of the overall staffing needs of UNDP for the 1990-1991 biennium.

GENERAL ASSEMBLY ACTION

In **resolution 43/190**, the General Assembly reaffirmed the role of TCDC in the socio-economic development of developing countries and in agricultural development in particular. It called on developing countries, in the context of their primary responsibility for promoting technical co-operation among themselves, to place greater emphasis on technical co-operation in food and agriculture and to strengthen and improve the mechanisms for such co-operation at the national, subregional and regional levels, especially their national focal points, so as to facilitate policy co-ordination and exchange of experience. Developed countries and organizations of the United Nations system were urged to provide financial and technical assistance for TCDC in food and agriculture, including through participation in tripartite co-operative agreements and other arrangements. The Assembly recommended that United Nations organizations and other international development and financing institutions, within their respective spheres of competence, give priority in their programmes of work to TCDC in food and agriculture.

REFERENCES

[1]DP/1989/46 & Add.1, 2 & Add.2/Corr.1 & Add.3. [2]E/1988/19 (dec. 88/37). [3]YUN 1987, p. 423. [4]DP/1989/13/Add.1. [5]A/44/5/Add.1. [6]YUN 1987, p. 427. [7]DP/1988/46/Add.1. [8]E/1988/19 (dec. 88/38 A). [9]*Ibid.* (dec. 88/38 B). [10]*Ibid.* (dec. 88/46). [11]*Ibid.* (dec. 88/13). [12]DP/1988/71. [13]YUN 1987, p. 429. [14]DP/1988/72. [15]YUN 1985, p. 490. [16]YUN 1978, p. 467. [17]E/1988/19 (dec. 88/43). [18]YUN 1987, p. 432, GA res. 42/180, 11 Dec. 1987.

UN Capital Development Fund

In his annual report for 1988,[1] the Administrator said that the United Nations Capital Development Fund, which provides capital assistance for small-scale investment projects, primarily in LDCs, received pledges for 1988 of $36 million. New project commitments approved by the Fund from its general resources grew to about $74 million. The Administrator noted, however, that the increased level of project activities could not be maintained without an increase in contributions. Of the 245 UNCDF-financed projects in progress at the end of 1988, 114 benefited from technical assistance financed by UNDP, an indication of the complementarity which continued to characterize UNCDF relations with other sources of financing.

On 1 July,[2] the UNDP Governing Council requested the Administrator to review the staffing arrangements of UNCDF in relation to its current and future work-load and to make proposals in 1989 within the framework of the 1990-1991 budget proposal.

REFERENCES

[1]DP/1989/13 & Add.1-5. [2]E/1988/19 (dec. 88/44).

Chapter III

Economic assistance, disasters and emergency relief

Countries facing severe economic difficulties and those requiring aid for reconstruction, rehabilitation and development continued to receive special assistance from the United Nations system during 1988. Several countries required assistance in the aftermath of natural or man-made disasters.

During the year, the mid-term review and appraisal of the implementation of the United Nations Programme of Action for African Economic Recovery and Development 1986-1990 was carried out. In November, the General Assembly adopted the conclusions of the mid-term review and appraisal and decided to conduct a final review and appraisal in 1991 (resolution 43/27).

In December, the Assembly urgently appealed to all international organizations to increase assistance in response to the reconstruction, economic recovery and development needs of Benin, the Central African Republic, Democratic Yemen, Djibouti, Ecuador, Madagascar and Vanuatu (43/211), all of which were facing special economic and financial difficulties. The Assembly also requested continued assistance for Chad (43/205) and Somalia (43/206).

The United Nations system, particularly the Office of the United Nations Disaster Relief Coordinator, continued to assist countries stricken by disasters. The Assembly, in October, requested the United Nations system and other multilateral organizations to assist Bangladesh to strengthen its capacity to assess, predict, prevent and mitigate natural disasters (43/9). Also in October, States were called on to assist Jamaica following hurricane Gilbert in September (43/7) and to respond urgently to the Sudan's needs following torrential rain and floods in August (43/8). The Assembly also urged States to contribute generously to relief, rehabilitation and reconstruction efforts in Costa Rica, Nicaragua, Panama and other countries affected by hurricane Joan which struck in October (43/17).

In February (resolution 1988/2) and May (1988/3), the Economic and Social Council called on the international community to support locust and grasshopper control activities undertaken by African countries; that request was echoed by the Assembly in December (resolution 43/203).

Both the Assembly and the Council (resolutions 43/207 and 1988/50, respectively) requested continued assistance for Lebanon in its reconstruction and development efforts. In July, the Council also urged Member States to contribute to the United Nations effort to assist the people of Afghanistan (1988/52), while the Assembly, in December, called for assistance to Mozambique (43/208).

Economic assistance

In 1988, the United Nations continued to provide special economic assistance to countries with severe economic problems affecting their development efforts. Some programmes were designed to support national reconstruction efforts after natural or man-made disasters, while others aimed to help overcome obstacles to national development posed by weak infrastructure. Some countries were land-locked or were small, island developing countries; a number of countries had been classified by the General Assembly as least developed.

The mid-term review and appraisal of the United Nations Programme of Action for African Economic Recovery and Development 1986-1990 (UNPAAERD) was carried out in 1988.

Critical economic situation in Africa

In accordance with a 1986 request of the General Assembly,[1] the Secretary-General submitted a report in August 1988,[2] prepared in the context of the mid-term review and appraisal of UNPAAERD, adopted by the Assembly in 1986.[3]

The report, which built on the Secretary-General's report on the critical economic situation in Africa presented to the Assembly in 1987,[4] noted that the mid-term review and appraisal was taking place against a backdrop of a continuing deterioration in Africa's economic situation. Economic performance during 1986-1988 was generally disappointing. The gross domestic product (GDP) of the region rose by 1 per cent in 1986 and 0.8 per cent in 1987; however, per capita income fell by 2 and 2.2 per cent in those years. The report, following the major themes of UNPAAERD, reviewed actions taken by African Governments, the international community and the United Nations system. It assessed the economic situation in Africa and made recommendations for further national, subregional, regional and international actions to accelerate UNPAAERD's implementation.

With regard to policy reforms, the report stated that African countries should continue to pursue policies aimed at accelerating recovery and improving their economic performance. Particular attention needed to be given to domestic economic management, effective mobilization and utilization of domestic resources, rationalization of public investment policies, development and utilization of human resources, development and implementation of population policies, protection of the environment, improvement of international competitiveness and diversification of production. Attention should also be given to developing the food and agricultural sector and agro-related industries, to the fight against pests, drought and desertification, and to other sectoral priorities identified in UNPAAERD. Efforts were needed to mitigate the adverse socio-economic effects of adjustment measures and to ensure that short-term actions were compatible with medium- and long-term structural transformation. While primarily the responsibility of African Governments, bilateral partners, multilateral financial institutions and the United Nations system had an indispensable role to play in supporting a framework of policy reforms and development objectives consistent with long-term development strategies. Africa's bilateral and multilateral partners needed to co-ordinate their efforts and co-operate with Africa within an agreed framework; consultative groups and round-table meetings were suitable mechanisms for that. People's participation in the recovery and development process needed to be broadened and made more effective, particularly through promoting increased access to development resources and benefits, creating favourable conditions for decentralized decision-making and encouraging greater entrepreneurship at all levels.

The report noted that Africa's efforts at economic restructuring and policy reforms were severely limited by the external constraints posed by the problems of debt, commodities and capital resource flows. Financial flows to Africa, especially concessional flows, had to be increased and their quality improved. A number of possible actions were considered to be particularly relevant: donor countries should substantially increase their official development assistance (ODA) to Africa; co-financing funds pledged under the World Bank's Special Programme of Assistance for low-income, debt-distressed countries should be made available as soon as possible; agreed commitments to replenishments of the African Development Fund, the International Fund for Agricultural Development (IFAD) and the International Development Association (IDA) should be fulfilled as soon as possible; measures should be implemented to enhance the co-ordination of external assistance; terms of existing multilateral loans should be adjusted to provide increased concessionality and more favourable grace and maturity periods; and efforts should be made to stimulate the flow of non-concessional resources. Integral to increased resource flows were continuing efforts by African countries to sustain policy reform measures, improve public expenditure programmes, ensure that scarce resources were put to effective use and improve the management of aid. Measures were also needed to improve the investment climate to encourage local and foreign private investment.

Possible measures to increase export earnings included: accelerating ongoing initiatives to make the Common Fund for Commodities operational; reducing domestic agriculture subsidies by industrialized countries on products competing with those of Africa; removing barriers to African exports; increasing the resources of the International Monetary Fund (IMF) compensatory financing facility; and establishing a generalized programme to stabilize export earnings of African countries. Also, efforts had to be made by African countries to diversify exports and initiate measures to bring the production and supply of their commodities into line with medium- and long-term demand.

With regard to the debt problem, the report recommended that consultations should be intensified with regard to official bilateral debt (broadening the conversion of bilateral ODA loans into grants embracing all ODA debts of African countries, consolidating non-concessional, officially guaranteed debt and debt-service payments into long-term loans at interest rates comparable to those on IDA credits, and allowing African countries to repay part of their bilateral official debts in local currencies to be used to finance development projects and programmes); multilateral debt (refinancing IMF purchases on concessional terms and implementing a concessional facility to repay outstanding World Bank debt by low-income African countries that were pursuing reform measures); and commercial bank loans (special debt relief measures in favour of African countries, including more flexible conditions, lower interest rates, longer maturity and grace periods, disposal of claims at discounts and debt-equity swaps). Both the public and private sectors in African countries would need to improve the management of their foreign debt, negotiate more effectively with foreign creditors, co-ordinate new borrowing and exercise more effective control over external borrowing.

The report also made recommendations with regard to economic co-operation and integration, South-South co-operation, mitigating the impact of destabilization, and peace and stability.

One addendum to the report[5] comprised a statistical annex, while the other,[6] prepared in response to Economic and Social Council **decision 1988/161** of 27 July 1988, discussed investment of transnational corporations in Africa. The latter addendum addressed trends in foreign direct investment, opportunities for increased investment and impediments and policy measures, and suggested possible international actions.

CPC/ACC Joint Meetings. The 1988 Joint Meetings of the Committee for Programme and Co-ordination (CPC) and the Administrative Committee on Co-ordination (ACC) (Geneva, 4 and 5 July)[7] discussed the implementation of UNPAAERD. They had before them a background paper summarizing the actions of several organizations of the United Nations system in response to UNPAAERD and outlining policy issues relevant to its implementation. The Committees suggested initiatives for further action, including the need to strengthen subregional groupings in Africa, in view of their contributions to recovery and development in the region.

UNDP activities. In response to a 1987 Governing Council decision,[8] the Administrator of the United Nations Development Programme (UNDP) submitted a report on the role of UNDP in implementing UNPAAERD.[9] It updated his 1987 report on the subject[10] and incorporated the views and observations of the Working Group of the Committee of the Whole during the Governing Council's special session in February 1988.[11]

The report described a number of consultative processes in which UNDP was involved and which were strengthening co-ordination for a more effective implementation of UNPAAERD. It also highlighted the most significant of UNDP's special initiatives to address areas of major concern to African countries in their implementation of UNPAAERD, particularly at the regional level. UNDP's contribution to the implementation of UNPAAERD's priorities had been largely through the machinery of its country programmes and the intercountry programme for Africa for the fourth programming cycle (1987-1991). During the fourth cycle, indicative planning figure (IPF) resources totalling $1.21 billion had been allocated, under country and intercountry programmes, to projects and programmes in sub-Saharan Africa, representing an increase of $240 million or 24.7 per cent over the third (1982-1986) cycle. Of the total IPF resources allocated, over $1 billion was for the implementation of 42 country programmes. Cost-sharing budgets for Africa had also increased and the trend was expected to continue.

The report also described UNDP's leading role and activities in aid co-ordination and resource mobilization for African countries, particularly through the round-table process, and reviewed developments with respect to national technical co-operation assessments and programmes. It concluded by summarizing action taken by UNDP, in the context of UNPAAERD, in four specific areas: the private sector; economic and technical co-operation among developing countries; the promotion of women; and co-operation with non-governmental organizations (NGOs).

On 19 February,[12] the Governing Council requested the Administrator to submit proposals for supplementary staffing and related costs in response to emergency and medium- and long-term development requirements in Africa. In response to that request, the Administrator submitted a report[13] in which he proposed expanding UNDP's capacity to cope with emergency operations in Africa, the annual cost of which would be $7.8 million. That represented a 5 per cent increase in UNDP's core budget and a 16 per cent increase in its Africa operations budget.

On 1 July,[14] the Governing Council welcomed the approval of all the fourth-cycle country programmes and the intercountry programmes which reflected the priorities contained in UNPAAERD and called on the Administrator, in concert with the recipient countries, to intensify efforts to speed up programme delivery in Africa. It requested the Administrator, in consultation with relevant United Nations organs and bodies, recipient countries and intergovernmental organizations, to do his utmost to speed up the approval process for projects submitted by those organizations so as to support subregional economic integration efforts in Africa. He was also requested to continue his efforts to mobilize additional resources and urged to identify more concrete and innovative approaches and actions in support of UNPAAERD and to consult with African Governments in formulating them. The Council also urged UNDP to continue to strengthen its ties with NGOs and ensure their greater involvement in the implementation of UNDP-sponsored programmes. The Administrator was urged to support the implementation of the United Nations Plan of Action to Combat Desertification[15] and to support emergency activities against locusts. He was also requested to ensure continued support for actions of the United Nations Steering Committee for the implementation of UNPAAERD, to ensure the involvement of women in UNDP programmes and projects related to UNPAAERD's priority areas and to report to the Council in 1989.

UNCTAD action. In an August 1988 progress report[16] to the Trade and Development Board of the United Nations Conference on Trade and Development (UNCTAD) on UNPAAERD's implementation, the UNCTAD secretariat stated that the UNCTAD contribution involved three main strands:

ongoing programmes having elements of particular relevance to African countries and to UNPAAERD priorities, relating particularly to programmes on trade in commodities, structural adjustment, debt and resource flows, intra-African trade, South-South co-operation and trade with socialist countries, technology transfer, transportation, and the Special Programme for Least Developed, Land-locked and Island Developing Countries; technical co-operation activities; and organization of and participation in inter-agency meetings, regional/subregional or country seminars and other forums implementing UNPAAERD or having similar goals.

Also in August,[17] the secretariat reported on the interaction between the international economic environment and the efforts of African countries in implementing UNPAAERD. It noted that the external economic environment since the adoption of UNPAAERD had not been conducive to African development efforts and suggested a number of actions and initiatives that could be expanded and acted on in order to support African countries' efforts towards economic recovery and development. It noted that the international community could contribute to UNPAAERD's implementation by strengthening its co-operation with African countries in ways that would support economic growth and recovery.

On 5 October,[18] the Trade and Development Board adopted a set of agreed conclusions regarding UNCTAD's contribution to UNPAAERD and asked the UNCTAD Secretary-General to take them fully into account in implementing UNPAAERD; it supported his efforts to mobilize resources to enable UNCTAD to play its role in implementing UNPAAERD in the remaining two years. The Board called on States, intergovernmental organizations and NGOs to contribute resources to support the UNCTAD secretariat's activities in implementing UNPAAERD.

Ad Hoc Committee of the Whole. In accordance with a 1987 General Assembly resolution,[19] the *Ad Hoc* Committee of the Whole of the General Assembly on the Review and Appraisal of UNPAAERD met in New York from 15 to 23 September 1988.[20] Arrangements for the *Ad Hoc* Committee's meetings were outlined in a resolution and two decisions of the Economic and Social Council (see below). The Council had had before it a note by the Secretary-General,[21] outlining some considerations with regard to possible documentation for the *Ad Hoc* Committee. The Committee established two working groups which held informal meetings, one on the critical economic situation in Africa and the problems and constraints facing Africa's development efforts, and the other on the response of the international community, including the United Nations system, and its commitment to support and complement Africa's efforts. The Committee recommended a draft resolution on

the mid-term review and appraisal to the General Assembly for adoption (see below).

ECONOMIC AND SOCIAL COUNCIL ACTION

On 5 February 1988, the Economic and Social Council adopted **resolution 1988/1** without vote.

Arrangements for the meeting of the *Ad Hoc* Committee of the Whole of the General Assembly on the Review and Appraisal of the United Nations Programme of Action for African Economic Recovery and Development 1986-1990

The Economic and Social Council,

Recalling General Assembly resolution 42/163 of 8 December 1987 on the United Nations Programme of Action for African Economic Recovery and Development 1986-1990,

Having considered the note by the Secretary-General on the review and appraisal of the United Nations Programme of Action for African Economic Recovery and Development 1986-1990,

1. *Takes note with appreciation* of the arrangements proposed by the Secretary-General in his note on the review and appraisal of the United Nations Programme of Action for African Economic Recovery and Development 1986-1990;

2. *Requests* the governing bodies of all relevant organizations of the United Nations system to include an item on the review and appraisal of the United Nations Programme of Action for African Economic Recovery and Development 1986-1990 in the agendas of their forthcoming meetings and to report as soon as possible, at the latest by 31 July 1988, on both the outcome of their deliberations on the matter and their contributions in support of the implementation of the Programme of Action since its adoption, to the *Ad Hoc* Committee of the Whole of the General Assembly on the Review and Appraisal of the United Nations Programme of Action for African Economic Recovery and Development 1986-1990;

3. *Invites* all Governments to communicate in writing to the Secretary-General as soon as possible, at the latest by 31 July 1988, their contributions and information on their efforts in support of the implementation of the Programme of Action since its adoption;

4. *Invites* intergovernmental and non-governmental organizations to report on their contributions, particular perspectives and efforts related to the implementation of the Programme of Action and to make specific recommendations on further measures that need to be taken, for submission to the *Ad Hoc* Committee.

Economic and Social Council resolution 1988/1

5 February 1988   Meeting 4   Adopted without vote

Draft by Somalia, for African States (E/1988/L.14), orally revised; agenda item 3.

Meeting numbers. ESC 3, 4.

The Council, in May, adopted **decision 1988/148** without vote.

Arrangements for the meeting of the *Ad Hoc* Committee of the Whole of the General Assembly on the Review and Appraisal of the United Nations Programme of Action for African Economic Recovery and Development 1986-1990

At its 17th plenary meeting, on 27 May 1988, the Economic and Social Council decided on the following arrangements for the meeting of the *Ad Hoc* Committee of the Whole of the General Assembly on the Review and Appraisal of the United Nations Programme of Action for African Economic Recovery and Development 1986-1990:

(*a*) The Bureau should be constituted at the highest possible level and be composed of a Chairman, three Vice-Chairmen and a Rapporteur;

(*b*) The provisional agenda for the *Ad Hoc* Committee of the Whole should be as follows:

(i) Opening of the session;

(ii) Election of officers;

(iii) Adoption of the agenda;

(iv) Organization of work;

(v) Mid-term review and appraisal of the United Nations Programme of Action for African Economic Recovery and Development 1986-1990;

(vi) Adoption of the report of the *Ad Hoc* Committee of the Whole to the General Assembly at its forty-third session;

(*c*) The *Ad Hoc* Committee of the Whole, in carrying out its mandate, should submit its findings to the General Assembly and propose concrete measures and recommendations for the full implementation of the United Nations Programme of Action for African Economic Recovery and Development 1986-1990 within the agreed time-frame;

(*d*) Invitations to attend the meeting should be sent to the relevant organs, organizations and bodies of the United Nations system and concerned non-governmental organizations in consultative status with the Economic and Social Council, as well as interested intergovernmental organizations and other non-governmental organizations concerned;

(*e*) Member States should be represented at the highest possible level;

(*f*) The proceedings of the *Ad Hoc* Committee of the Whole should be governed by the rules of procedure of the General Assembly.

Economic and Social Council decision 1988/148

Adopted without vote

Draft by Vice-President (E/1988/L.30), based on informal consultations; agenda item 5.
Meeting numbers. ESC 11, 17.

In further action, the Council, in July, adopted **decision 1988/154** without vote.

Arrangements for the mid-term review and appraisal of the United Nations Programme of Action for African Economic Recovery and Development 1986-1990

At its 37th plenary meeting, on 25 July 1988, the Economic and Social Council, pursuant to its decision 1988/148 of 27 May 1988, decided:

(*a*) That the *Ad Hoc* Committee of the Whole of the General Assembly on the Review and Appraisal of the United Nations Programme of Action for African Economic Recovery and Development 1986-1990 should establish the following two working groups:

(i) Working Group on the Critical Economic Situation in Africa and the Problems and Constraints facing Africa's Development Efforts;

(ii) Working Group on the Response of the International Community, including the United Nations

System, and its Commitment to Support and Complement Africa's Efforts;

(*b*) That the *Ad Hoc* Committee, scheduled to meet from 6 to 19 September 1988, should be rescheduled to meet from 12 to 23 September 1988;

(*c*) That the general discussion in the *Ad Hoc* Committee should not exceed two working days and that Governments should bear that in mind in preparing for the review and appraisal;

(*d*) That the final outcome of the review and appraisal should preferably consist of a single document.

Economic and Social Council decision 1988/154

Adopted without vote

Draft by Vice-President (E/1988/L.36/Rev.1), based on informal consultations; agenda item 4.
Financial implications. S-G, E/1988/L.37.
Meeting numbers. ESC 31, 33, 37.

GENERAL ASSEMBLY ACTION

On 18 November, the General Assembly adopted **resolution 43/27** without vote.

Mid-term review and appraisal of the implementation of the United Nations Programme of Action for African Economic Recovery and Development 1986-1990

The General Assembly,

Recalling its resolution S-13/2 of 1 June 1986, the annex to which contains the United Nations Programme of Action for African Economic Recovery and Development 1986-1990,

Recalling also its resolution 42/163 of 8 December 1987,

Emphasizing that the African economic crisis is one that concerns the international community as a whole and that the accelerated implementation of the Programme of Action requires further effective action by all parties concerned,

Taking note of the report of the Secretary-General on the mid-term review of the implementation of the Programme of Action,

Taking note of the mid-term assessment of the implementation of the Programme of Action, prepared by the Permanent Steering Committee of the Organization of African Unity at its fourteenth ordinary session,[a]

Taking note also of the contribution made by individual Governments, intergovernmental organizations and non-governmental organizations to the work of the *Ad Hoc* Committee of the Whole of the General Assembly on the Review and Appraisal of the United Nations Programme of Action for African Economic Recovery and Development 1986-1990,

Taking note further of the report of the *Ad Hoc* Committee of the Whole,

1. *Adopts* the conclusions of the mid-term review and appraisal of the implementation of the United Nations Programme of Action for African Economic Recovery and Development 1986-1990, consisting of an assessment of the responses and measures to accelerate the implementation of the Programme of Action, as set forth in the annex to the present resolution;

2. *Decides* to conduct a final review and appraisal of the implementation of the Programme of Action at its forty-sixth session.

---

[a]A/43/596.

ANNEX
Mid-term review and appraisal of the United Nations
Programme of Action for African Economic Recovery
and Development 1986-1990 and recommendations
for the acceleration of its implementation

I. Introduction

1. The United Nations Programme of Action for African Economic Recovery and Development 1986-1990, which was adopted by the General Assembly in response to the critical economic situation in Africa, is based on mutual commitment and co-operation between Africa and the international community.

2. In the Programme of Action, Africa committed itself to launch long-term programmes for self-sustaining socio-economic development and growth. The international community committed itself to assisting Africa in achieving this objective.

3. The African countries committed themselves to giving priority attention to necessary economic reform as mentioned in Africa's Priority Programme for Economic Recovery 1986-1990 adopted by the Assembly of Heads of State and Government of the Organization of African Unity at its twenty-first ordinary session, held at Addis Ababa from 18 to 20 July 1985, as a basis for broad-based, sustained economic development; the rehabilitation and development of agriculture; other sectors supportive of agriculture; measures to combat drought and desertification; and the efficient development and utilization of human resources.

4. The international community recognized that the economic recovery and development efforts of African countries must be supplemented by complementary action on its part through intensified co-operation and substantially increased support. It also realized that lasting solutions to the serious exogenous constraints, over which Africa has no control, will have to be found, since their persistence will impede the efforts of the African countries. It therefore committed itself to making every effort to provide sufficient resources to support and supplement the African development effort. The international community further appreciated that Africa's efforts would be greatly facilitated if flows of external resources were predictable and assured and if the quality and modality of external assistance and co-operation were improved. It also recognized that, to bring about an improvement in the external economic environment, the international community should address and examine the external factors that aggravate the African situation, especially in terms of trade and the need to deal urgently with commodity issues and alleviate Africa's debt burden. The Programme of Action equally emphasizes the importance for the international community to increase official development assistance to African countries and to improve its quality and effectiveness.

5. The Programme of Action provides an important framework for co-operation between Africa and the international community, and all parties wish to reaffirm their commitment to the Programme of Action. The continuing gravity of the economic situation in Africa requires that all partners take urgent and decisive actions to accelerate and ensure the effective implementation of the Programme of Action during its remaining period.

6. In the Programme of Action, the international community recognized the importance to African economic development of genuine peace and security, as well as of the strengthening of international co-operation.

7. The review of measures taken to implement the Programme of Action demonstrates that most African countries have adopted significant policy reforms to improve the overall management of their economies. The determination with which African countries are pursuing and strengthening these reforms is courageous and commendable, particularly since in many countries such measures involve severe social costs and political risks. Many countries have also faced continuing climatic problems and natural calamities. The political will demonstrated by African countries and the commendable reform and policy reorientation measures that have been put in place should be sustained. Appropriate reforms should be embarked upon by those countries that have not yet initiated the process. The Governments of African countries should also play a key role in the process of co-ordination of external assistance.

8. For its part, the international community has taken important initiatives in support of the African efforts, through the Special Programme of Assistance of the World Bank, the Enhanced Structural Adjustment Facility of the International Monetary Fund and new bilateral aid commitments. Resource commitments to Africa for the years 1988-1990 will increase and disbursements will assist countries implementing reforms. Furthermore, the international community has declared its intention to continue to support the efforts of African Governments to implement the Programme of Action.

9. The reform and restructuring that are being undertaken by African countries and the ongoing initiatives taken by the international community thus constitute an important beginning. However, the overall performance of the African economies remains unsatisfactory. Despite earnest efforts to carry out adjustments in their national economic policies, most African countries have found little reprieve from the harsh impact of climatic conditions and an unfavourable external economic environment. Internal constraints, and the adverse impact of exogenous factors to which African economies are highly susceptible, are impeding the reform process and are severely hampering African development.

10. Dealing with the African crisis is a priority concern for the international community and the United Nations. It is therefore a matter of urgency that the promising actions that have been taken by all parties concerned to implement the Programme of Action should be strengthened and accelerated. Sustained and unfaltering efforts made by African countries must be matched by substantial and urgent efforts by the international community to provide support to them at the required levels and to create an international environment favourable to the process of reform and restructuring.

II. Assessment of the implementation of the United Nations Programme of Action for African Economic Recovery and Development 1986-1990

A. *Response of African countries*

11. The Programme of Action was designed and adopted to provide an important framework for co-operation between Africa and the international community in fostering economic recovery and development

on the African continent. The continuing gravity of the economic situation in Africa requires that all partners take urgent and decisive actions to accelerate and ensure the effective implementation of the Programme of Action during its remaining term.

1. *Agricultural development*

12. Agriculture, on which more than 75 per cent of Africa's people depend for their livelihood, has been a major area of sectoral reform. More countries have given higher priority to channelling resources to agriculture, with the particular aim of making progress towards food security and achieving increased agricultural production. As regards export crops, almost all countries have implemented price incentive measures, and some have adopted measures to liberalize marketing policies, to increase the share of the export value retained by farmers and to bring prices into line with world market levels. A large number of African countries have instituted a wide range of measures to mitigate food emergencies. Approximately half the countries in the region now have various types of national emergency preparedness mechanisms, about eighteen countries have early warning systems and many have set up national food security arrangements.

13. The efforts of African countries to ensure food self-sufficiency and to increase their exports have been hindered, among other things, by the following factors:

(*a*) The recurrence and persistence of such phenomena as drought, locust infestation and floods;

(*b*) The decline of international commodity prices at a time when African Governments raised prices for producers;

(*c*) Competition from food exports that benefit from all kinds of direct or indirect support measures;

(*d*) The inflow of lower-priced agricultural products concurrently with the adoption by many African Governments of import liberalization policies.

2. *Other sectors in support of agriculture*

14. To enhance agricultural development, attention has been given to the rehabilitation and maintenance of infrastructure that supports agriculture. In particular, emphasis has been placed on the production of agricultural tools, small-scale irrigation equipment, fertilizer, pesticides and other chemicals. Within the general constraint of scarce foreign exchange, efforts have been made to modernize, rehabilitate and expand food-processing and other agro-based industries. Inadequate transportation facilities also remain a critical bottle-neck in many countries. Similarly, the agro-based manufacturing sector has stagnated or grown only marginally.

3. *Drought and desertification*

15. African countries are determined to reduce the effects of drought and desertification. The measures taken to that effect include the development of water sources, the building of small dams and the development of renewable sources of energy to replace fuelwood. Despite cyclones, floods and other calamities, the countries affected are resolutely determined to pursue activities to combat drought and desertification. Overall, the African countries are determined to fight against every new threat to their environment, including the dumping of industrial or toxic waste in the continent.

4. *Human resources*

16. African Governments have always considered that human resources development and planning are key

to the economic recovery and development of the continent and that the efficient utilization of these resources should become a major objective of their national policies. Since the adoption of the Programme of Action, the majority of African countries have put particular emphasis on formulating national literacy and vocational training programmes, elaborating information systems, setting up project appraisal machinery and, in certain cases, improving educational systems. Adapting training and educational systems to the development objectives of the Programme of Action is difficult, among other reasons, because of budgetary constraints.

17. African countries have also adopted measures to promote the effective participation of the population in the development process. In so doing, they have put particular emphasis on the role of African women, not only as beneficiaries but also as agents of development. However, as underlined in the Khartoum Declaration, adopted on 8 March 1988 by the International Conference on the Human Dimension of Africa's Economic Recovery and Development,[b] internal and external constraints may counter the efforts undertaken by Africa to fully develop its human resources, especially in the high-priority fields of health and education.

18. Particular attention has been paid by some African countries to their population policies on the basis of the Kilimanjaro Programme of Action for African Population and Self-Reliant Development, adopted by the Second African Population Conference and endorsed by the Economic Commission for Africa in 1984. A growing number of countries are putting in place national policies designed to harmonize population growth with economic and environmental capacities, and formulating specific policies and action plans to address population issues in a long-run development perspective. Effective implementation of these policies, however, still faces immense problems, which include a lack of resources, in particular trained personnel, and a low level of public support. Future efforts must focus on overcoming these problems.

5. *Policy reforms*

19. Since the adoption of the Programme of Action, most African countries have adopted significant policy reforms to improve the overall management of their economies. About thirty countries are undertaking stabilization or structural adjustment programmes in conjunction with the World Bank and the International Monetary Fund. These efforts are intended to improve economic performance, bring about accelerated recovery within the context of the Programme of Action and lay the foundation for self-sustaining growth and development.

20. The determination with which most African countries are pursuing and strengthening economic policy reforms is courageous and commendable, particularly since in many countries such measures involve social costs and political risks. However, reforms have not been adopted by all Governments; nor are they being pursued with equal vigour in all countries. Policy reform takes time to have a demonstrable impact on economic performance. Available data on the achievement of structural adjustment programmes, while incomplete, suggest that economic reform is beginning to make a

---

[b]A/43/430.

positive impact in a number of countries. Nevertheless, in some other countries the impact remains to be fully felt, and the overall economic situation in Africa remains critical. However, there is no doubt that improvement of the economic situation requires that appropriate reform policies and programmes be vigorously implemented and sustained, taking into account the need to improve them continuously.

21. Most African Governments have instituted policy reforms aimed at economic structural transformation and improvement of the overall management of their economies, especially in the following areas: *(a)* public investment management systems, institutions and practices; *(b)* public enterprises; *(c)* reform of public services to make them more oriented towards achieving national development goals; *(d)* lowering of budget deficits and reduction and redirection of public expenditure; *(e)* mobilization of domestic saving and increase in investment; *(f)* financial and debt management; *(g)* reduction and reversal, where possible, of foreign exchange leakage; *(h)* encouragement of the role of the productive private sector and market forces in the efficient allocation of resources; and *(i)* promotion of foreign trade in general and intra-African trade in particular.

22. Experience in the implementation of stabilization or structural adjustment programmes currently instituted has revealed substantial concerns to African Governments, bilateral donors, multilateral financial institutions and non-governmental organizations, notably:

(a) African Governments need to play the central role in the design and formulation of structural adjustment programmes, including the development of "policy framework papers";

(b) Projections of financial flows, including export earnings, have often been overly optimistic;

(c) The short-term adjustment or stabilization targets of structural adjustment programmes should be integrated with long-term development objectives;

(d) The importance attached to macro-economic indicators should not obscure the need to pay adequate attention to institutional, social and sectoral factors that are critical to the structural transformation of African economies. Supply responses are only partly tied to relative price levels. Market liberalization involves more than just the removal of controls. Strategies of sequencing, timing and complex institutional restructuring are critical to the success of market reform in Africa;

(e) To avoid straining the social, cultural and political framework and to be credible and sustainable, structural adjustment programmes must be designed so as to be sensitive to the internal conditions of the countries concerned. In implementing expenditure reductions as part of adjustment efforts, care should be taken to ensure that such reductions, especially those in basic health, nutrition, education and other social services are not made in areas where they would worsen the situation of the poorest and most vulnerable groups;

(f) Realignment of exchange rates and rises in producers' prices have not always generated the full expected benefits because of structural rigidities that continue to characterize the current stage of development of most African countries. In part this has occurred because African countries have not had the human and financial resources fully to address these rigidities.

23. In spite of all the measures taken, the overall performance of the economies of African countries re-

mains unsatisfactory. Domestic structural problems and adverse exogenous developments, to which the African countries are highly susceptible, have complicated the reform process by restraining overall economic growth. In certain cases, weaknesses in the management and coordination of external assistance at the level of recipient countries and of bilateral and multilateral assistance agencies had led to delays in the disbursement and utilization of external resources already available.

24. Domestic impediments include the effects of recurrent drought and other natural calamities such as cyclones, floods and locust and grasshopper infestation in some areas, infrastructural and institutional deficiencies, marketing problems, low capacity for domestic resource mobilization, strong dependency of export income on a limited number of commodities, excessive dependence on imports of consumer goods and production inputs, human resources and population factors, refugee flows, shortage of skilled labour and armed conflicts. The external constraints include weak demand for African exports, low commodity prices, inadequate and stagnating foreign real resource flows, and a high debt and debt-servicing burden. Indeed, these constraints, coupled with natural calamities, continue to be major obstacles to economic recovery and development in the region.

25. In southern Africa, the situation continues to be adversely affected by the policies of political and economic destabilization and acts of aggression pursued by the South African régime against the front-line and neighbouring States. The violence inherent in the system of *apartheid* has resulted in loss of human lives, the destruction of social and economic infrastructures, the diversion of substantial resources and efforts away from economic development to defence spending, the disruption of economic development and an increase in refugees and displaced persons throughout the region. The United Nations has estimated that losses for the member countries of the Southern African Development Coordination Conference for the period 1980-1986 amounted to 25 billion to 30 billion United States dollars. These factors have been the main reasons for the sharp decline of economic growth and have consequently undermined development efforts in the region, including the implementation of the Programme of Action.

6. *Implementation at the regional and subregional levels*

26. At the regional and subregional levels, a number of concrete actions have been taken to promote recovery and development, in particular, as related to the formulation and implementation of joint programmes in the key economic sectors and the strengthening of mechanisms for these efforts. The search for agreements between neighbouring countries on food supplies aimed at ensuring a better complementarity between surplus and deficit zones has progressed. Other important actions have included the establishment of regional networks for crop protection and of mechanisms for co-operation among national early warning systems. In 1987 and 1988, a number of key intra-African conferences were convened to review and promote the implementation of the Programme of Action. The major constraints on subregional and regional co-operation have been associated with infrastructural bottle-necks and scarce external financial support to date.

B. *Response of the international community*

1. *Response of other countries*

(a) *Resource flows*

27. In support of the goals of the Programme of Action, the international community has made commitments to provide an increased level of financial assistance to African countries, both bilaterally and multilaterally. Net resource flows to Africa increased from 17.9 billion dollars in 1985 to 19.9 billion dollars in 1986 and 22.9 billion dollars in 1987 in nominal terms. However, measured in real terms, resource flows were lower in 1986 and 1987 than in 1985.

28. Official development assistance has been a steady and vital source of funding for Africa, accounting for over 73 per cent of net resource flows to the region. Total bilateral disbursements of development assistance to African countries remained relatively constant in real terms in 1986 and 1987. Many donors made substantial increases in their bilateral assistance to African countries. Official development assistance reported by the member countries of the Development Assistance Committee of the Organisation for Economic Co-operation and Development, the Organization of Petroleum Exporting Countries and the multilateral institutions increased in current dollars. In sub-Saharan Africa, it rose from 11.7 billion dollars in 1986 to 13.3 billion dollars in 1987, but that reflects no increase when measured at 1986 prices and exchange rates. According to the Organisation for Economic Co-operation and Development, export credits to sub-Saharan Africa are estimated to have fallen from 0.8 million dollars in 1985 to 0.4 million dollars in 1986 and to 0 in 1987. The limited data available suggest that other private commercial flows remained unchanged. Member countries of the Council for Mutual Economic Assistance continued their economic assistance to Africa.

29. The multilateral institutions, with the support of bilateral donors, are playing an important role in international efforts to increase financial flows to Africa. Disbursement from the International Development Association rose from 0.9 billion dollars in fiscal year 1985 to 1.2 billion dollars in 1986 and 1.6 billion dollars in 1987. The World Bank initiated a Special Programme of Assistance for the low-income heavily indebted African countries that combines additional disbursement from the International Development Association with additional co-financing by bilateral donors. It is estimated that the programme will increase resource flows to sub-Saharan Africa by about 3 billion dollars over the period 1988-1990. In 1986 and 1987, there was a substantial net transfer of resources from Africa to the International Monetary Fund. In response to the economic situation in African countries, the Fund undertook several initiatives. In particular, its members reached agreement on an Enhanced Structural Adjustment Facility that will increase the concessional resources available to low-income countries by 6 billion special drawing rights over the period 1988-1990. The African Development Bank reached agreement on a trebling of its authorized capital and on a 50-per-cent increase in the African Development Fund. That has enabled it to increase commitments from 2 billion dollars in 1984-1985 to 3.8 billion dollars in 1986-1987. Net disbursements by the International Fund for Agricultural Development increased from 50 million dollars in 1983 to

85 million dollars in 1986. Those new multilateral flows, supported by bilateral donors, constitute a major new commitment of resources to Africa in support of the continent's efforts to achieve sustainable and growth-oriented development. Many parties, in particular the African countries, have expressed dissatisfaction with the methods by which conditionality for adjustment are developed. Efforts are under way to increase the participation of all parties to resolve those differences and such efforts should be reinforced.

30. The contribution of resources has been largely undermined by the growth in debt-service obligations and the decrease in export earnings, resulting in a marked deterioration of the external financial position of many African countries. Various estimates have been made of Africa's external resource requirements. The Advisory Group on Financial Flows to Africa, which, contrary to its mandate, considered the needs of only sub-Saharan Africa excluding Nigeria, estimated the requirements to be at least 5 billion dollars per annum above their level in 1986-1987. Other estimates differ from that, depending on the country coverage, assumptions and methodology used, but in general suggest that assistance flows should be increased in support of the Programme of Action. Increased flows should be forthcoming within the period of the Programme of Action when disbursements from new multilateral initiatives and bilateral commitments are fully implemented.

(b) *Trade and commodities*

31. In many parts of the developing world and in Africa in particular, the recent growth of the global economy has not yet resulted in a gathering of momentum in the development process. Most African countries have found it difficult to increase their export earnings, although those earnings are a critical factor in their economic recovery and development. Protectionism remains a constraint to efforts by African countries to expand their trade. Non-tariff measures against exports from African countries, some of which are applied progressively to processed commodities, are an impediment to the expansion of the region's exports. There remains scope for dismantling the non-tariff barriers that impede access by African countries to the markets of industrialized countries. The Uruguay Round of multilateral trade negotiations, agreed upon since the adoption of the Programme of Action, will provide an opportunity to address some of the difficulties that Africa faces in the area of international trade.

32. In spite of the recent improvement in some commodity prices, Africa's financial problems have been aggravated by the continuing decline of many commodity prices. Moreover, those prices continue to be at historically very low levels. This has been induced by a complex array of market forces, often beyond the control of African countries. A majority of these countries depend on no more than three export commodities for the bulk of their foreign exchange earnings, which serve as the principal source of external resources for development. Africa's total commodity earnings fell by 18 billion dollars in 1986 and 1987 remained below their 1985 level. It was agreed in the Programme of Action to deal urgently with commodity issues in the framework of an overall approach taking into account the special interests of the African countries. The matter was discussed at the seventh session of the United Nations Conference on Trade and Development. Changing

global conditions have contributed to Africa's significant losses in foreign exchange from falling export earnings; this problem can be addressed only through a long-term and overall approach, including efforts to increase the capacity of African countries to process, market, distribute and transport non-traditional exports. Moreover, there has been an overall deterioration in the terms of trade of sub-Saharan African countries. Over the short and medium terms, a major sustained improvement in commodity prices is not expected. However, aid, debt-relief and direct foreign investment can only supplement trade in that respect.

33.   Existing arrangements to provide compensatory financing for shortfalls in commodity earnings, such as the Stabex and Sysmin arrangements of the European Economic Community and the Compensatory Financing Facility of the International Monetary Fund, have been important but insufficient in themselves to deal with the magnitude and nature of the difficulties that Africa faces in commodity export markets. The speedy activation of the Common Fund for Commodities, in particular, its Second Account, may help to overcome these difficulties. The new Compensatory and Contingency Financing Facility of the International Monetary Fund will also be available to help to offset fluctuations in export earnings for those countries that are able to meet the conditions for its use.

(c)   *Debt*

34.   The external indebtedness of African countries has become one of the important factors constraining recovery and development in the continent, since debt servicing draws substantially on scarce financial resources that otherwise could be used for development purposes in the region. Debt service obligations were equivalent to 29 per cent of export earnings in 1985, 43 per cent in 1986 and 39 per cent in 1987. Debt service payments in these years were equivalent to 29 per cent, 29 per cent and 25 per cent of export earnings respectively.

35.   The economic situation of many of the countries of the region and their low levels of income make the debt burden particularly heavy. Most outstanding debt is to official bilateral and multilateral agencies. These agencies have responded with a number of initiatives to lighten the debt burden, particularly of the low-income African countries. Efforts have also been initiated to address the debt problems of African middle-income countries. The economic recovery and development of Africa calls for continued efforts in this area.

36.   A number of bilateral donors have converted official development assistance loans to some African countries into grants—a process that began in 1978. Conversions to date affect only one sixth of Africa's official development assistance debt but cover more than half of that of the least developed countries of the region. Commitments have been made by a number of donors to make further conversions, and proposals have been made to further reduce the stock of debt. Progress has been made in providing lengthened grace and maturity periods in rescheduling in the Paris Club. Rescheduling does not reduce the stock of debt. Proposals are under discussion to provide additional relief. African countries have expressed three concerns regarding the process of rescheduling: the lack of a medium-term and long-term perspective; rescheduling terms that are not adapted to debtors' capacity to pay;

and the excessive duration of the rescheduling process itself.

37.   Africa's continuing search for solutions to the problems of its external indebtedness prompted African Governments to hold an extraordinary summit meeting at Addis Ababa from 30 November to 1 December 1987 devoted to Africa's external debt. This meeting resulted in the adoption of Africa's common position on external indebtedness. The economic summit meeting of the seven largest industrialized countries, held at Toronto from 19 to 21 June 1988,[c] addressed Africa's debt and development problems. The summit achieved consensus on rescheduling official debt of the poorest developing countries that are undertaking internationally approved adjustment programmes, allowing official creditors to choose among several options. The likely overall impact of these measures is difficult to quantify because it is not clear yet what the total amount of relief would be. It is the shared responsibility of all parties concerned to develop lasting and durable solutions to the problems of Africa's external indebtedness.

(d)   *Quality and modalities of external assistance*

38.   Some progress has been made in improving the quality and modalities of external assistance, notably by improving the quality of bilateral flows; increasing the pace of disbursement; increasing the concessionality of assistance; and strengthening the co-ordination of donor programmes, notably through the expansion and improvement of consultative groups and United Nations Development Programme round-table meetings and through the introduction of "policy framework papers". Nevertheless, considerable scope remains for future improvement, particularly in relation to quick disbursement, wherever appropriate.

(e)   *Structural adjustment programmes*

39.   An important consideration relates to the developmental framework within which external assistance is provided. The implementation of structural adjustment programmes has given rise to general concerns, such as human, social and political consequences, as well as long-term financing needs for Africa's economic recovery and development efforts. These concerns have resulted in a dialogue on the nature and content of adjustment programmes. This has led to greater understanding and increased awareness of the need to ensure that such programmes form an integral part of a longer-term strategy for economic growth, incorporate a human dimension and do not have an adverse impact on vulnerable groups and would take due account of the specific economic situation and national development priorities of each country. This is now being reflected in actions by African Governments and donor agencies.

40.   The efforts of the African countries to achieve sustained growth and development through structural reform are seriously constrained by the adverse external environment as it relates to the situation in Africa, in particular, with respect to export earnings, the debt service burden and concessional finance.

2.   *Response of the United Nations system*

41.   The organizations of the United Nations system were invited to attach high priority to Africa in their global operations, taking into account the priorities of the Programme of Action. These organizations are now

---

[c]A/43/435-S/19974.

devoting more than 35 per cent of their resources to Africa, with expenditures amounting to more than 1 billion dollars annually.

42. The Secretary-General has taken important actions to sensitize the international community to the serious economic situation in Africa, to ensure a co-ordinated response by the United Nations system to the implementation of the Programme of Action and to monitor and report on the implementation of the Programme of Action. Although the contributions of the organizations of the United Nations system were diversified and useful, they were, however, insufficient. In view of the deterioration in Africa's financial situation after the Programme of Action was adopted, the Secretary-General appointed a high-level Advisory Group on Financial Flows to Africa; its report was issued in February 1988. The Secretary-General also established a United Nations Steering Committee with the participation of all relevant bodies of the United Nations to co-ordinate and monitor their response to the Programme of Action. In addition, an inter-agency task force, which acts as the operational arm of the Steering Committee, has been established under the chairmanship of the Executive Secretary of the Economic Commission for Africa.

3. South-South co-operation

43. Progress in co-operation between African countries and other developing countries has been registered in a number of areas, such as trade, finance, technology and technical assistance. Some countries have contributed through bilateral assistance and programmes of technical co-operation among developing countries. In the field of trade, the first round of negotiations of the global system of trade preferences among developing countries was completed at the ministerial meeting on the Global System of Trade Preferences among Developing Countries of the Group of Seventy-seven held at Belgrade from 11 to 13 April 1988. The participants in the global system signed a contractual document that seeks to facilitate their trade relations. The potential for South-South co-operation is considerable, and every effort should be made by the international community to support the expansion and intensification of such co-operation.

4. Non-governmental organizations

44. Most non-governmental organizations, both African and non-African, are contributing to Africa's economic recovery and development through effective programmes at the grass-roots level. Significant resources are mobilized by non-governmental organizations, from both the general public and official aid institutions, for economic and social projects and programmes as well as for humanitarian activities. These efforts support the goals of the Programme of Action and deserve to be commended. One development has been the emergence and growing presence of the community of indigenous African non-governmental organizations as important actors in Africa's development effort. They are engaging in closer dialogue with African Governments, official development agencies and non-African non-governmental organizations in order further to clarify and define their own role in Africa's recovery and development. They are contributing their own experience to the implementation of development policies, especially those oriented towards the poorest groups.

III. Measures for accelerating the implementation of the United Nations Programme of Action for African Economic Recovery and Development 1986-1990

A. Role of the African countries

1. Agricultural development

45. In the course of implementing the Programme of Action, African countries should continue to concentrate their efforts on agriculture and its supporting sectors, the rehabilitation and development of agro-industries, the fight against drought, desertification and pests, and on the other sectoral priorities identified in the Programme.

46. It is important that development programmes give due recognition to the factors critical to increased agricultural production. These factors include investment in appropriate technology, research and development and agricultural inputs. African countries should intensify their efforts to establish early warning systems and national food security arrangements, diversify exports, improve export performance and maintain the incomes of farmers at appropriate levels.

47. The traditional role of women as producers of a significant proportion of food should be protected and strengthened when new agricultural production methods are introduced. More attention must be given to ensure that women have access to agricultural extension services, credit, land titles and, not least, new technologies.

2. Other sectors in support of agriculture

48. Increased attention and financial resources should be directed to the rehabilitation and maintenance of productive infrastructures in the sectors that support agriculture, including transport and communications. Emphasis should continue to be placed on the production of agricultural tools, small-scale irrigation equipment, spare parts, fertilizers, pesticides and other chemicals. Greater attention should be given to rehabilitating, modernizing and expanding food-processing and other agro-based industries, by mobilizing the resources needed as well as providing training and credit in rural areas and promoting entrepreneurial development programmes.

3. Drought and desertification

49. The environment and natural resources should become important considerations in development co-operation. Environmental activities must go hand in hand with efforts to enhance economic growth and combat poverty, as there is a clear link between economic well-being and the quality of the environment. Better management of the natural resource base is a major factor in moving towards sustainable development. Action should be intensified to improve the economic situation and combat more effectively environmental degradation arising, in particular, from drought, desertification, deforestation, floods, locust and grasshopper infestation and the dumping of toxic and industrial wastes.

4. Human resources

50. Since many internal constraints are linked to weaknesses in education, training and management systems and since human resources play a key role in the long-term development prospects of the continent, the effective development and utilization of human resources of the region must be made a major objective of national policy. In consequence, the African countries should place greater emphasis on population policies and programmes, including the Kilimanjaro Programme of Action.

51. The participation of people in the recovery and development process should continue to be broadened and made more effective, particularly through promoting increased access to development resources and benefits, creating favourable conditions for decentralized decision-making, encouraging greater entrepreneurship at all levels and promoting individual initiative and private enterprise.

52. African countries and their development partners should give particular importance to human resources development, especially by integrating the human dimension in the design and implementation of structural adjustment programmes. As stated in the Programme of Action, the role and contribution of women in the development process are of crucial importance. However, women often remain at the periphery of economic systems and decision-making processes. There is thus an urgent need to strengthen the participation of women in all areas of the economy and at all levels of development planning and implementation. Moreover, African countries should allocate substantial resources to make it possible for women to participate more fully as active economic agents in development programmes, especially in rural areas.

5. *Policy reforms*

53. African countries should continue to pursue the balanced development of all sectors of their economy. Particular attention should be given to domestic economic management, the effective mobilization and utilization of domestic resources, in particular through the encouragement of savings, and action to contain or reverse capital flight with the support of the international community and to provide an environment conducive to direct investment. Special attention should be given to the rationalization of public investment policies, the development and effective implementation of appropriate human resources and population policies, industrial development, the improvement of international competitiveness and the diversification of production.

54. Structural adjustment programmes should be designed in such a way as to mitigate their adverse socio-economic effects, ensure that the human dimension is integrated in them, further improve the well-being of the poor and disadvantaged in African societies, notably through redirecting social and developmental expenditures, and make short-term stabilization and adjustment measures compatible with and built into long-term structural transformation.

55. Bearing in mind that they have the central role to play in the design and implementation of their adjustment programmes, African Governments, with the support of their development partners, should give particular attention to the following so that adjustment programmes are based on a realistic and pragmatic approach of the problems of each country:

(a) In designing economic structural adjustment programmes, the following should be taken into account:

(i) The need for adjustment programmes to be realistic and consistent with projected financial resources and the external and internal environment;

(ii) Harmonization of the programme with long-term objectives and strategies, with particular, continued emphasis on self-sustaining economic development and growth;

(iii) Provision of compensatory programmes to minimize the adverse effects of redeployment of labour and the social costs of adjustment to the poor;

(iv) Social infrastructure and human resource development, including environmental, cultural and political concerns;

(v) A pragmatic approach to the respective roles of the public and private sectors;

(b) Social indicators need to be developed to monitor the impact of these programmes on the population;

(c) African countries should increase their efforts in the search for a viable conceptual and practical framework for economic structural adjustment programmes in keeping with the long-term development objectives and strategies at the national, subregional and regional levels;

(d) It is essential that the process of reform be implemented as soon as possible by those countries that have not yet done so and sustained and supported by those that have already started it.

6. *Trade*

56. African countries need to make special efforts in order to make African products more competitive in international markets, and to adopt appropriate policies and reinforce mechanisms to expand and diversify their exports.

57. Decisions on diversification are primarily the responsibility of African countries. These decisions should take into account the agricultural, industrial and other development objectives. Horizontal and vertical diversification of their economies, as well as increased participation in the processing, marketing and distribution of their commodities are long-term development objectives towards which African countries need to make further efforts in the context of intensified international co-operation between producers and consumers.

58. Adequate structures should be established or improved in order to promote the transfer, adoption, adaptation and the application of appropriate technologies, the development of communication infrastructure and the improvement of marketing networks and thus form a solid base for reinforcing the efficiency of exports.

59. African Governments should enhance their participation in all major international trade negotiations, notably the Uruguay Round of multilateral trade negotiations, so as to better achieve a reduction in tariff and non-tariff barriers that have a negative impact on their ability to export.

7. *Economic co-operation and integration*

60. For the effective implementation of the Programme of Action, African countries should intensify their efforts towards economic co-operation and integration in accordance with the objectives of the Lagos Plan of Action for the Implementation of the Monrovia Strategy for the Economic Development of Africa, adopted by the Assembly of Heads of State and Government of the Organization of African Unity at its second extraordinary session, held at Lagos on 28 and 29 April 1980. Among the measures that should be taken are the following:

(a) Strengthening and rationalization of existing subregional groupings, the creation, as appropriate, of new ones and their effective utilization for co-ordinated planning and development at the subregional level;

(b) Implementation of measures for the co-ordination of economic and social policies subregionally, as well as for joint planning and development of multicountry projects in key economic sectors;

(c) Promotion of intra-African trade in primary and processed commodities;

(d) Promotion of domestic policies that encourage the movement of goods, skills and capital among the African countries.

8. *Peace and stability*

61. Every effort must be made to achieve political settlements of international and regional conflicts so that scarce resources can be directed towards economic recovery and development. In this context, African countries should, with the support of the international community, intensify their efforts to end the acts of aggression and destabilization of the *apartheid* régime in South Africa, which is the single most destructive form of conflict in the region.

B. *Role of the international community*

1. *Role of other countries*

(a) *Resource flows*

62. Financial flows to Africa, in particular concessional flows, should be increased substantially, especially to sub-Saharan African countries, and provided on a continuous, predictable, assured and fast-disbursing basis, as appropriate. Such an increase in resources for Africa would be facilitated if all developed countries allocated 0.7 per cent of their gross domestic product to official development assistance.

63. Most resource flows to Africa will continue to be provided through official bilateral assistance and by multilateral institutions, but flows of private capital should also be encouraged. The following actions are particularly relevant:

(a) Donor countries, particularly those whose assistance to Africa has decreased in the past two years or is at a low level, should aim to increase their official development assistance to Africa in real terms. These resources should be provided on a sustained and fast-disbursing basis and directed to the priorities of recovery and development;

(b) Bilateral co-financing funds pledged under the World Bank's Special Programme of Assistance for low-income, debt-distressed countries should be made available as soon as possible, and donors should expedite the disbursement of the resources that they have agreed to provide for this purpose;

(c) The agreed commitments to an increase in the capital of the World Bank, to the fifth replenishment of the African Development Fund and to the eighth replenishment of the International Development Association should be fulfilled without delay. In addition, negotiations on the third replenishment of the International Fund for Agricultural Development should be concluded promptly, and those on a ninth replenishment of the International Development Association should be undertaken as soon as possible;

(d) Efforts should be continued to improve the quality of bilateral flows, particularly through more rapid disbursement of assistance already pledged and increased concessionality, meeting the recurrent local costs of programmes and projects, using local equipment, indigenous competence and expertise and improving procedures, guidelines and formats for the procurement of equipment;

(e) The co-ordination of donor programmes, undertaken in close co-operation with the recipient countries, should be improved further. The important role of the consultative groups and round-table meetings in this regard should be enhanced.

(b) *Trade and commodities*

64. An increase in Africa's export earnings and a reduction in the adverse impact on African economies of year-to-year fluctuations in those earnings would both contribute to the attainment of sustained non-inflationary growth and assist African countries in their efforts to implement the Programme of Action. These improvements in export earnings would be facilitated by an international environment more favourable to African exports and by continued efforts to diversify exports.

65. Particular attention should be given to the following:

(a) The mid-term review of the Uruguay Round of multilateral trade negotiations scheduled for December 1988 should give a new impulse to the negotiations in the General Agreement on Tariffs and Trade, in which the concerns of African countries should be given particular attention. All countries involved in the Uruguay Round should endeavour to improve the international trading environment, particularly as it concerns African exports. This applies especially to measures affecting processed and non-traditional exports because these offer the greatest hope for Africa to increase and diversify its export base in the longer run. There is need for greater liberalization of trade in agricultural products, and special attention should be given to the provisions of existing régimes concerning trade in tropical products of interest to African countries. In this connection, the Uruguay Round should be used to develop improved discipline and rules, addressing the problems of market access, subsidies that directly or indirectly affect trade and the harmonization of health and sanitary standards;

(b) Ongoing initiatives to make the Common Fund for Commodities fully operational should be completed in the shortest possible time, bearing in mind that a number of developmental programmes have already been approved or considered by producers and consumers, for possible financing under its Second Account;

(c) Programmes for the stabilization of export earnings of African countries, along the lines of the Stabex and Sysmin, should be considered by other countries;

(d) The Compensatory and Contingency Financing Facility of the International Monetary Fund should have an enhanced role in responding to Africa's short-term external contingency needs;

(e) Within the context of the Programme of Action, the Secretary-General of the United Nations should consult with the United Nations Conference on Trade and Development, other relevant organizations and interested Governments with a view to establishing a group of experts to undertake an in-depth assessment of the question of African commodities and the scope for export diversification.

(c) *External debt*

66. Many countries have taken measures to reduce the burden of Africa's external debt, and such action should be continued, in order to limit the burden that debt imposes on recovery, reform and development of

the African countries. Debt rescheduling should be supplemented by other multilateral and bilateral measures. Every effort should be made by the international community to find lasting, durable and growth-oriented solutions that cover various categories of debt, various creditors and various debtor countries and that respond to Africa's development needs. Recognizing the major contribution that progress in this area would make to the success of the Programme of Action, ongoing initiatives, including those agreed upon at the economic summit meeting held at Toronto from 19 to 21 June 1988, should be pursued urgently, with the following being taken into account:

(a) Official bilateral debt
(i) Non-concessional officially guaranteed debt and debt-service payments of low-income African countries should be rescheduled on more generous terms;
(ii) Creditor countries' efforts to write off or otherwise remove the burden of official development assistance loans, *inter alia*, by repayment in local currencies, of low-income countries pursuing structural adjustment programmes, should be continued;
(iii) In addition, donor countries should increase the grant element in their future assistance to poorer African countries.

(b) Multilateral debt
(i) Every effort should be made to ensure the speedy and full implementation of the initiatives of international financial institutions, especially the Enhanced Structural Adjustment Facility of the International Monetary Fund, in order to ensure that necessary concessional resource flows are available to low-income countries in Africa that are undertaking structural adjustment;
(ii) The proposal to establish a mechanism, financed by voluntary contributions, to alleviate, on a concessional basis, the outstanding World Bank debt of low-income countries that are pursuing reform measures should also be considered urgently.

(c) Commercial loans and credits
Various new methods of reducing the commercial debt of developing countries have been developed. The application of these methods to ease the commercial debt of African countries should be promoted.

67. The common position of Africa on addressing the problem of the continent on external debt adopted by the Assembly of Heads of State and Government of the Organization of African Unity at its third extraordinary session, held at Addis Ababa on 30 November and 1 December 1987, should be taken account of and seriously considered by the international community.

(d) *Supporting reform within a broad development framework*
68. African countries have the responsibility for formulating and implementing the economic reforms that form part of the process of recovery and longer-term development. In supporting these reforms, Africa's international partners should keep in mind this imperative for longer-term economic and social development. In this context, the human dimension should be a central concern. Intensified efforts should be made by all parties to develop and use appropriate indicators to measure and monitor closely the improvement of conditions of human well-being as reforms proceed. Instruments should also be developed to provide early warning of deteriorating human conditions.

2. *Economic co-operation and integration*
69. Special efforts should be made by the international community to support ongoing efforts of African countries to strengthen co-operation and the rapid achievement of economic integration in the region. International assistance to national projects should be complemented by greater support for regional and subregional projects, particularly in the priority sectors.

3. *Impact of destabilization policies of South Africa*
70. Recovery and development efforts in the countries of the southern African subregion continue to be frustrated by acts of aggression and destabilization by the South African régime. The international community as a whole should exert greater pressure on the *apartheid* régime to abolish its abhorrent policies and immediately stop its acts of destabilization and aggression in the region. In the absence of an end to these acts of destabilization, increased assistance should be given to the member countries of the Southern African Development Co-ordination Conference in order to compensate for the costs of destabilization, to allow these countries to implement their recovery and development programmes effectively and to strengthen co-operation among them so that they can reduce their dependence on South Africa. Furthermore, provisions of relief assistance should be expanded to include the rehabilitation of populations affected by emergency situations in order to restore, *inter alia*, their productive capacities. In particular, contributions to the Action for Resisting Invasion, Colonialism and *Apartheid* Fund and United Nations funds and other means to support the victims of *apartheid* and the front-line States should be continued and be increased, where possible.

4. *Human resources*
71. Responsibility for the development, planning and utilization of their human resources falls first and foremost on the African countries. The international community should support their efforts by providing the necessary financial and technical assistance to promote their human resources development.

5. *South-South co-operation*
72. South-South co-operation in supporting the implementation of the Programme of Action should be enhanced. Action already initiated in the agricultural sector should be intensified, and additional projects should be identified to assist African countries, either individually or collectively, in improving the production of staple food items. Particular emphasis should be placed on technological co-operation, especially in agro-related and consumer-goods industries, to enable Africa to benefit from the expertise and experience of other, more advanced developing countries. The same obtains for the exchange of experience and skills in the development of human resources. To achieve these objectives, individual countries and subregional and regional groupings in Africa and other developing regions should agree on specific plans of action, with time-bound and sectoral targets.

6. *Support by the United Nations system*
73. Co-operation and co-ordination among the various organizations of the United Nations system in the

implementation and monitoring of the Programme of Action should be further strengthened. In order to ensure the capacity of the Secretary-General to carry out his responsibilities with regard to the Programme of Action, the secretariats of the United Nations Steering Committee and of the Inter-Agency Task Force should be given appropriate support for the duration of the Programme. Adequate funding, both budgetary and extra-budgetary, should be provided for this purpose.

74. At the national level, further efforts to improve co-ordination within the United Nations system should be taken in the context of the country-programming framework of the United Nations and the role of the resident co-ordinator. In the programmes of the United Nations system, particular emphasis should be placed on the priority sectors for the recovery and development of Africa.

75. In view of the important role of non-governmental organizations in mobilizing and making the public more aware as regards development, the United Nations system should increase its co-operation with non-governmental organizations for the implementation of the Programme of Action.

General Assembly resolution 43/27

18 November 1988   Meeting 56   Adopted without vote

Draft by *Ad Hoc* Committee of the Whole (A/43/664 & Corr.1); agenda item 39.
Meeting numbers. GA 43rd session: plenary 55, 56.

In **resolution 43/217, section VII**, the Assembly approved the conclusions and recommendations of CPC[22] regarding UNPAAERD. CPC recommended that regular budget resources for the Economic Commission for Africa and other relevant entities for the 1990-1991 biennium be made commensurate with the priority accorded to Africa and UNPAAERD by the Assembly. Noting that a large portion of resources allocated to UN-PAAERD was to come from extrabudgetary resources, CPC expressed concern that they might not materialize and recommended that the Secretary-General redouble his efforts to ensure adequate resources for UNPAAERD's implementation. It also recommended that information on factors affecting UNPAAERD's implementation be provided to the *Ad Hoc* Committee of the Whole and that the Secretary-General take into consideration all relevant views in pursuing the matter of financial flows for Africa.

Benin

In response to a 1987 General Assembly request,[23] the Secretary-General submitted in August 1988 a report[24] containing information on the special programme of economic assistance for Benin, whose economic performance continued to decline in 1988. In April, the first stage of formulating a financial stabilization and structural adjustment programme was completed, following consultations between the Government and a joint IMF/World Bank mission. A timetable was drawn up for the implementation of a series of measures

during the year. It was estimated that donor support, which took account of the economic and social impact of the measures undertaken by Benin in implementing a financial stabilization and structural adjustment programme, would be of key importance to achieving the desired goals.

In the area of external assistance and aid co-ordination, a round-table conference was tentatively scheduled for late 1988 or early 1989. It was expected that this forum would provide an opportunity for dialogue between the Government and bilateral and multilateral donors concerning programmes to stimulate economic recovery and the country's needs for external assistance to support those programmes.

In a later report,[25] the Secretary-General noted that external development assistance to Benin in 1988 totalled $209.8 million, of which $178.6 million was for capital expenses and technical assistance. Donor contributions to the latter amount comprised: bilateral, $88.1 million; multilateral, $67.6 million; United Nations system, $14.2 million; NGOs, $8.6 million.

Following several years of drought, several Benin provinces suffered flood rains in August/September 1988, which resulted in 70,000 flood victims and loss of crops and stocks, and left thousands homeless.

For General Assembly action on economic assistance to Benin, see **resolution 43/211**.

Central African Republic

In his August 1988[24] report on special programmes of economic assistance, the Secretary-General said that, according to World Bank estimates, the financing requirement of the Central African Republic to meet its investment programme for 1987-1992, after taking account of expected external financing, had a shortfall of $20 million in 1988. The shortfall was expected to decline to $5 million by 1992. The investment programme aimed, in particular, to revitalize the commercial exploitation of the country's forestry resources, strengthen receipts from the diamond industry and stimulate the private sector, especially at the level of small and medium-sized enterprises. Social investment would focus on developing the country's human resources and improving health conditions. In accordance with recommendations made at a round-table conference held at Geneva in June 1987,[26] follow-up consultations were scheduled for programmes in rural development, education, training and employment, and for small and medium-sized enterprises.

In a later report,[25] the Secretary-General stated that in the Central African Republic between 1987 and 1988, GDP declined in real terms. The external current account went further into deficit in 1988, despite a contraction of imports;

the deficit for the year represented 18 per cent of GDP. The fall in prices of the Central African Republic's exports (coffee, tobacco) contributed to those results. Export revenues also suffered from declines in the quantities of cotton, coffee and wood exported. Exacerbating the current account shortfall was the country's land-locked situation, which added to transport and insurance costs. The situation with regard to public finances also deteriorated in 1988. Recurrent costs were in excess of revenues, and capital expenditures were markedly curtailed. At year's end, the country's public debt totalled $598 million, with debt servicing consuming 16 per cent of export revenues.

For General Assembly action on economic assistance to the Central African Republic, see **resolution 43/211**.

Chad

In response to a 1987 request of the General Assembly,[27] the Secretary-General, in his August 1988 report on special programmes of economic assistance,[24] provided information on Chad. In January, Chad appealed for food donations and financial assistance to help meet an estimated food deficit of 141,000 tonnes. In March, the Government appealed for financial assistance to transport 7,500 tonnes of food to deficit areas.

In a later report on the situation in Chad,[28] the Secretary-General stated that a favourable pattern of rainfall in 1987/88 resulted in a striking recovery in agricultural output. GDP in 1988 was estimated to have risen by 21 per cent over 1987. An agreement was signed by Chad and the World Bank in 1988 that would provide Chad with a financial rehabilitation credit of $45 million, which was to cover the years 1988 to 1990 and aimed to improve performance in a number of sectors, specifically the public, cotton and banking sectors and public enterprises. However, Chad continued to confront serious financial constraints. In the balance of payments, the deficit on current transactions was expected to rise to as much as 25 per cent of GDP if unilateral flows of assistance to the public sector were excluded. According to World Bank data, Chad's external debt totalled $269.6 million at the end of 1987.

A new development plan for 1989-1992 was under preparation, with World Bank assistance and UNDP funding, succeeding the interim plan of 1986-1988. Under the round-table process, two sets of consultations between the Government and donors were held in 1988. The first, in February, was on rehabilitation of the transport and communications sector, where projects costing $98 million were presented. Donors made commitments for 75 per cent of that amount. In December, consultations were held on rehabilitating the prefecture of Borkou-Ennedi-Tibesti in northern Chad.

A programme costing $43 million was presented covering rural and urban development and including environmental protection measures. Pledges by donors totalled $27 million.

In 1988, technical assistance valued at $71.7 million was provided to Chad, of which 55 per cent was bilateral assistance, 36 per cent was provided by multilateral organizations, including the United Nations, and 9 per cent was provided by 12 NGOs. Countries providing technical assistance were (in order of volume of assistance) France, the United States, Switzerland, Egypt, the Federal Republic of Germany, the Netherlands and China.

GENERAL ASSEMBLY ACTION

On 20 December, on the recommendation of the Second (Economic and Financial) Committee, the General Assembly adopted **resolution 43/205** without vote.

Special economic assistance to Chad

The General Assembly,

Recalling its resolution 42/200 of 11 December 1987 and its previous resolutions on assistance in the reconstruction, rehabilitation and development of Chad, on emergency humanitarian assistance to Chad and on special economic assistance to that country,

Having considered the report of the Secretary-General on special economic assistance to Chad, dealing with, *inter alia*, the economic and financial situation of Chad, the status of assistance provided for the rehabilitation and reconstruction of the country and the progress made in organizing and executing the programme of assistance for that country,

Considering that the effects of war, natural calamities and disasters are compromising all the reconstruction and development efforts of the Government of Chad,

Noting the numerous appeals launched by the Government of Chad and governmental and non-governmental organizations regarding the seriousness of the food and health situation in Chad,

Noting also that the donor round table on assistance in the rehabilitation and reconstruction of northern Chad will be convened by the Government of Chad, in collaboration with the United Nations Development Programme, on 14, 15 and 16 December 1988,

Recognizing the need for emergency economic assistance to Chad,

Noting with satisfaction that the implementation of the interim plan for 1986-1988 is now drawing to an end and that a development plan for 1989-1992 is being prepared,

Recalling the round table on assistance to Chad, convened by the United Nations Development Programme at Geneva on 4 and 5 December 1985, in accordance with the arrangements agreed upon at the International Conference on Assistance to Chad, held in November 1982,

1. *Expresses its gratitude* to the States and governmental and non-governmental organizations that responded and are continuing to respond generously to the appeals of the Government of Chad and of the Secretary-General by furnishing assistance to Chad;

2. *Expresses its appreciation* to the Secretary-General for his efforts to make the international community aware of the difficulties of Chad and to mobilize assistance for that country;

3. *Renews the request* made to States, competent United Nations organizations and programmes and international economic and financial institutions to continue:

(a) To provide the necessary humanitarian assistance to the people of Chad, who have suffered from the combined effects of the war, drought, flooding and the invasion of predators;

(b) To contribute to the rehabilitation and development of Chad;

4. *Notes with satisfaction* that the sectoral follow-up meetings envisaged by the round table on assistance to Chad, held at Geneva in December 1985, took place in December 1986 and February 1988 at Ndjamena;

5. *Requests* the Secretary-General:

(a) To contribute, in co-operation with the United Nations Development Programme, to the preparation of a development plan for Chad for 1989-1992;

(b) To continue to assess, in close collaboration with the humanitarian agencies concerned, the humanitarian needs, particularly in the areas of food and health, of the displaced populations;

(c) To mobilize special humanitarian assistance for persons who have suffered as a result of the war, natural calamities and disasters, and for the resettlement of displaced persons;

6. *Invites* States and competent United Nations organizations and programmes to participate actively in the donor round table on assistance in the rehabilitation and reconstruction of northern Chad, to be held on 14, 15 and 16 December 1988;

7. *Calls upon* the Secretary-General to keep the situation in Chad under review and to report thereon to the General Assembly at its forty-fourth session.

General Assembly resolution 43/205

20 December 1988   Meeting 83   Adopted without vote

Approved by Second Committee (A/43/918/Add.2) without vote, 15 November (meeting 42); 28-nation draft (A/C.2/43/L.33); agenda item 86.
Sponsors: Algeria, Argentina, Burkina Faso, Burundi, Cameroon, Cape Verde, Central African Republic, Chad, China, Colombia, Comoros, Congo, Côte d'Ivoire, Egypt, France, Gabon, Guinea, Guinea-Bissau, Japan, Mali, Mauritania, Morocco, Niger, Senegal, Togo, Tunisia, United Kingdom, Zaire.
Meeting numbers. GA 43rd session: 2nd Committee 26, 28-30, 36-38, 40, 42; plenary 83.

Djibouti

In response to a 1987 General Assembly request,[23] the Secretary-General, in his August 1988 report,[24] provided information on the situation in Djibouti, which had instituted a number of measures to improve its budgetary and financial situation. The 1988 budget aimed to increase revenues by further improving the collection of indirect taxes, raising certain taxes and imposing profit taxes on public enterprises. Government expenditures were to be kept to a necessary minimum and the civil service would continue to be subject to financial constraints. However, as in previous years, it was expected that external assistance would be required to balance the budget.

In February, Djibouti appealed to the international community for assistance in coping with the consequences of the 1987 drought and requested UNDP to co-ordinate efforts to mobilize resources. To that end, UNDP approved an emergency grant of $50,000 for the purchase of various items and for the services of a consultant to assist the Government in project preparation.

In a later report,[25] the Secretary-General stated that external assistance to Djibouti in 1988 totalled $102 million, of which $78 million was provided by bilateral donors and $24 million by multilateral institutions. Among sectors, education led in its share of total assistance, followed by transport and communications, housing, agriculture, water and natural resources.

For General Assembly action on economic assistance to Djibouti, see **resolution 43/211**.

Madagascar

In 1988, Madagascar entered its fifth consecutive year of implementing serious structural adjustment measures, formulated in co-operation with the World Bank and IMF, said the Secretary-General in an August 1988 report.[24] Those efforts continued within the structural policy framework for the period 1987-1990, the main objective of which was to increase the growth rate of GDP and exports. In the 1987-1990 phase of adjustment, particular attention was being given to increasing the efficiency of allocation and use of public resources.

At the fifth meeting of the Consultative Group for Madagascar (Paris, 28 and 29 January), held under the auspices of the World Bank, Madagascar presented its strategy for continued structural adjustment in the immediate future and donors pledged a total of $700 million for 1988 and 1989.

In a later report,[25] the Secretary General noted that, after almost a decade of efforts aimed at financial stabilization and structural adjustment of the economy, Madagascar began in 1988 to experience the beginnings of economic growth.

Total aid disbursements to Madagascar in 1988 totalled $382.5 million, with the World Bank, the European Development Fund, the African Development Bank, IMF and UNDP accounting for 39 per cent of contributions.

For General Assembly action regarding economic assistance to Madagascar, see **resolution 43/211**.

Countries and areas in other regions

Central America

In response to a 1987 General Assembly request,[29] the Secretary-General submitted in April 1988 a Special Plan of Economic Co-operation for Central America.[30] The report gave the background and main characteristics of the crisis in the Central American countries and outlined an emergency programme (assistance to refugees, food aid, urgent energy needs), programmes of immediate action (foreign debt, financing to reactivate the Central American Common Market and reduce temporary imbalances in countries' balance of payments) and economic reactivation and social development. The report also discussed institutional and management capacity aspects, the role of the United Nations system, internal and international responsibility, and institutional mechanisms for implementing the Special Plan.

In **resolution 42/231** of 12 May 1988, the Assembly urged the international community and international organizations to increase their technical, economic and financial co-operation with the Central American countries to implement the activities supporting the Special Plan.

In an October report on the situation in Central America,[31] the Secretary-General stated that not only had economic development been adversely affected by the political turmoil in the region, but the economic crisis was perpetuating unjust socio-economic structures and prolonging internal conflicts, thus frustrating efforts to arrive at a consensus concerning the socio-political model for Central American societies.

In **resolution 43/210** of 20 December, the Assembly recommended the convening of a meeting early in 1989 to review the evolution of the development process, including assistance requirements, and to discuss the programmes and projects that could be implemented as soon as possible in support of the Special Plan's goals and objectives. It urged Member States and observers, intergovernmental organizations, international financial institutions and the United Nations system to adopt immediate measures to implement activities in support of the Special Plan.

Democratic Yemen

In his August 1988 report on special programmes of economic assistance,[24] the Secretary-General provided information on Democratic Yemen's economic situation and its rehabilitation and reconstruction efforts following devastating floods in 1982. Most of the aid-assisted programmes under the reconstruction and rehabilitation programme had been completed or were close to completion. Two UNDP-funded projects were due to be completed in 1988: the reconstruction of the Abyan Delta and flood control at Wadi Bana and Wadi Hassan.

For General Assembly action regarding economic assistance to Democratic Yemen, see **resolution 43/211**.

Ecuador

In his August 1988 report to the General Assembly,[24] the Secretary-General described international assistance programmes and donor support to Ecuador following the March 1987 earthquakes. Total emergency assistance by United Nations programmes and agencies amounted to $158,450. In addition, bilateral donors channelled $313,385 in emergency assistance through the Office of the United Nations Disaster Relief Co-ordinator (UNDRO).

Bilateral donors and the European Community provided direct emergency assistance in cash and kind valued at $7.5 million. Emergency assistance from NGOs and private institutions approximated $700,000, while bilateral donations channelled through the Red Cross amounted to $730,000.

For General Assembly action regarding economic assistance to Ecuador, see **resolution 43/211**.

Vanuatu

In his August 1988 report on special programmes of economic assistance,[24] the Secretary-General described external assistance to Vanuatu, an island developing country, which was struck by a cyclone in 1987.[32] In a later report,[25] he stated that in January and February 1988, Vanuatu had again been struck by cyclones, following each of which UNDP had provided $50,000 in emergency relief assistance. UNDP also initiated a $300,000 reconstruction project covering longer-term rehabilitation.

As to the economy, copra exports had been declining but that had been offset by increases in the export of meat and hides, trochus shells and cocoa. Vanuatu's tourist industry contributed significantly to foreign exchange earnings. A significant development in the industry had been the national airline's acquisition of its first aircraft, which came into service in the second half of 1988.

A round-table meeting of donors to Vanuatu was held at Geneva in October 1988, providing an opportunity for dialogue between the Government and potential donors on the country's economic situation in order to secure and integrate additional assistance into the overall plan. Two new donors offered new aid funds and one traditional donor offered additional technical assistance.

GENERAL ASSEMBLY ACTION

On 20 December, on the recommendation of the Second Committee, the General Assembly adopted **resolution 43/211** without vote.

Assistance to Benin, the Central African Republic, Democratic Yemen, Djibouti, Ecuador, Madagascar and Vanuatu

The General Assembly,

Recalling its resolution 42/205 of 11 December 1987 on assistance to Benin, the Central African Republic,

Democratic Yemen, Djibouti, Ecuador, the Gambia, Madagascar, Nicaragua and Vanuatu and its previous resolutions on assistance to the countries concerned,

Having considered the relevant report of the Secretary-General,

Noting with satisfaction the financial, economic and technical support that Member States, the specialized agencies and other organizations of the United Nations system and regional, interregional and intergovernmental organizations have been providing to those countries,

Deeply concerned that those countries continue to face special economic and financial difficulties owing to a variety of factors,

Noting that Benin continues to experience grave economic and financial difficulties, characterized by a marked balance-of-payments disequilibrium, the heavy burden of its external debt and a lack of resources necessary for the implementation of its planned economic and social development programme, and that its situation is even more precarious following the disastrous floods that caused substantial material damage and loss of human lives during the months of August, September and October 1988,

Noting the persistence of the grave difficulties that the Government of the Central African Republic continues to face in the efforts that it has been making since 1982 to re-establish the economic stability of the country, as well as the importance of mobilizing more supplementary resources in order to enable it to achieve its objectives in its development programme,

Noting that severe and harsh climatic conditions coupled with chronic aridity preclude the possibility of any meaningful agricultural activities, and that the lingering effects of recurrent drought and the presence of large numbers of refugees and displaced persons are having a devastating impact on the already precarious economic and social development of Djibouti,

Noting the efforts made by the Government of Democratic Yemen in its rehabilitation and reconstruction programmes in response to the devastating consequences of the floods in 1982,

Bearing in mind the economic and financial consequences of the earthquakes of March 1987 in Ecuador and their negative impact on its balance of payments, the current account deficit amounting to 776 million United States dollars and the public sector deficit amounting to more than 305 million dollars in the months following March 1987, and taking into account the fact that all the efforts made by the Government of Ecuador to improve that adverse situation have not produced the desired results owing to the domestic economic recession and the effects of the international economic crisis, which seriously impede the entire economic and social development process,

Noting that Madagascar's economic and social development efforts are being thwarted by the adverse effects of the cyclones and floods that afflict that country periodically, particularly those of December 1983, January and April 1984 and March 1986, and that the execution of reconstruction and rehabilitation programmes requires the mobilization of sizeable resources exceeding the country's real possibilities,

Noting that Vanuatu, an island developing country, continues to experience severe constraints in its economic and social development as a consequence, *inter alia*, of declining export prices leading to a deterioration in its terms of trade and of a high population growth rate coupled with a shortage of skilled manpower,

Noting the particularly difficult problems faced by island developing countries in responding to negative and special economic circumstances, as referred to in the report of the Secretary-General called for in its resolution 41/163 of 5 December 1986 and in its resolution 43/189 of 20 December 1988,

Noting that Benin, the Central African Republic, Democratic Yemen, Djibouti and Vanuatu are among the countries classified as least developed countries,

Having heard the statements of Member States at the forty-third session of the General Assembly on the situations currently prevailing in those countries,

1. *Expresses its appreciation* to the Secretary-General for the steps he has taken to mobilize resources for carrying out the special programmes of economic assistance to those countries;

2. *Expresses its appreciation* for the efforts undertaken by the Governments of those countries to overcome their economic and financial difficulties;

3. *Also expresses its appreciation* for the assistance provided or pledged to those countries by Member States, specialized agencies and other organizations of the United Nations system and regional, interregional and intergovernmental organizations;

4. *Further expresses its appreciation* for the action taken by the United Nations and the specialized agencies, in particular the United Nations Development Programme and the Office of the United Nations Disaster Relief Coordinator, and for the contributions of the international community with regard to the immediate assistance provided to the population and areas affected by the earthquakes in Ecuador in March 1987;

5. *Welcomes* the successful conclusion of the round-table meeting for Vanuatu, conducted by the United Nations Development Programme on 28 October 1988;

6. *Notes with concern* that the assistance made available to those countries has not been adequate to meet their urgent requirements and that additional assistance is needed;

7. *Reaffirms* the need for all Governments and international organizations to fulfil the commitments undertaken within the framework of the Substantial New Programme of Action for the 1980s for the Least Developed Countries;

8. *Appeals* to Member States, international financial institutions, the specialized agencies and organizations and programmes of the United Nations system to respond generously and urgently to the needs of those countries as identified in the report of the Secretary-General;

9. *Appeals* to the specialized agencies, organizations and programmes of the United Nations system and to the international community to provide the necessary assistance to the rehabilitation and reconstruction programmes in Ecuador, which are essential to the most affected areas and populations and whose implementation is impeded by the national budgetary constraints resulting from the economic crisis, and requests the Secretary-General to use his good offices to promote greater participation by the international community and the United Nations system in the implementation of those programmes;

10. *Invites* the international community to contribute to the special accounts established at United Na-

tions Headquarters by the Secretary-General for the purpose of facilitating the channelling of contributions to the countries facing special difficulties;

11. *Urgently appeals* to all international organizations, in particular the specialized agencies and other organizations of the United Nations system, regional organizations, humanitarian organizations and voluntary agencies, to continue and increase, to the extent possible, their assistance in response to the reconstruction, economic recovery and development needs of those countries;

12. *Requests* the Secretary-General to take the necessary steps, in collaboration with the organs, agencies and programmes of the United Nations system, in accordance with General Assembly resolution 41/192 of 8 December 1986 on special programmes of economic assistance, to provide assistance for all disasters, natural or otherwise, striking those countries and to mobilize the necessary resources to enable them to meet their short-, medium- and long-term needs;

13. *Also requests* the Secretary-General to keep the question of assistance to those countries and their economic situation under review and to report to the General Assembly at its forty-fifth session on the implementation of the present resolution.

General Assembly resolution 43/211

20 December 1988   Meeting 83   Adopted without vote

Approved by Second Committee (A/43/918/Add.2) without vote, 6 December (meeting 47); draft by Vice-Chairman (A/C.2/43/L.67), orally amended by Democratic Yemen; agenda item 86.
Meeting numbers. GA 43rd session: 2nd Committee 26, 28-30, 36-38, 45, 47; plenary 83.

Front-line and other bordering States

In response to a 1987 request of the General Assembly,[33] the Secretary-General submitted a report in July 1988, with later addenda,[34] on action taken by the international community to assist the front-line States (Angola, Botswana, Mozambique, United Republic of Tanzania, Zambia, Zimbabwe) and other bordering States to withstand the effects of economic measures taken by South Africa, or by the international community against South Africa.

The report first described urgent humanitarian, economic and technical assistance being provided by the United Nations to Angola, Malawi and Mozambique, where complex emergency situations prevailed. Following an inter-agency mission to Angola in 1987, the Secretary-General launched an appeal to the international donor community during his February 1988 visit there. That was followed by a donor meeting at Geneva in May, when over $75 million was pledged towards Angola's overall emergency requirements. An inter-agency mission also visited Malawi in 1987 and estimated that some $90.8 million would be required in 1988 to meet the needs of some 360,000 displaced persons from neighbouring Mozambique. The Secretary-General launched an appeal in March 1988 for generous contributions to the projects and programmes recommended by the mission (see

also PART THREE, Chapter XV). In 1988, Mozambique again requested the Secretary-General's assistance to mobilize international humanitarian support to cope with the grave consequences of externally-supported acts of destabilization and the impact of a limited drought. An inter-agency mission visited the country in February, an international appeal was launched by the Secretary-General in March and an international donor meeting was held in April at Maputo.

In response to a request by the Secretary-General for information on specific measures taken to assist front-line and other States bordering on South Africa, replies were received from 24 Member States and 14 organizations of the United Nations system. Information was also received from the Southern African Development Co-ordination Conference (SADCC). In addition, it was noted that efforts were being made by the United Nations system and SADCC to expand and strengthen their co-operation.

GENERAL ASSEMBLY ACTION

On 20 December, on the recommendation of the Second Committee, the General Assembly adopted **resolution 43/209** by recorded vote.

Special assistance to front-line States
The General Assembly,

Recalling its resolutions 41/199 of 8 December 1986 and 42/201 of 11 December 1987,

Having considered the report of the Secretary-General,

Deeply concerned at the continuing deteriorating situation in southern Africa, which has aggravated the economic problems confronting the front-line States and other bordering States, arising from the *apartheid* policies of the Pretoria régime,

Conscious of the responsibility of the international community to address the problems of the region,

Commending the concerted and determined efforts of the countries of the region to cope with the prevailing adverse conditions by strengthening their economic co-operation and lessening their dependence on South Africa, particularly in the areas of transportation, communications and related sectors,

Reaffirming the importance of close co-operation between the United Nations and the front-line States,

Mindful of Security Council resolutions 568(1985) of 21 June 1985, 571(1985) of 20 September 1985 and 581(1986) of 13 February 1986, in which the Council, *inter alia*, requested the international community to render assistance to the front-line States,

1. *Expresses its appreciation* to the Secretary-General for his efforts regarding assistance to the front-line States;

2. *Strongly urges* the international community to continue to provide in a timely and effective manner the financial, material and technical assistance necessary to enhance the individual and collective capacity of the front-line States and other bordering States to withstand the effects of economic measures taken by South Africa, or by the international community against South Africa, in accordance with their national and regional plans and strategies;

3.   *Requests* the Secretary-General to continue mobilizing organs, organizations and bodies of the United Nations system so that they may respond to such requests for assistance as might be forthcoming from individual States or the appropriate subregional organization, and further urges all States to respond favourably to such requests;

4.   *Appeals* to all States and appropriate intergovernmental and non-governmental organizations to support the national and collective emergency programmes prepared by the front-line States and other bordering States to overcome the critical problems arising from the situation in South Africa;

5.   *Notes with appreciation* the assistance being rendered to the front-line States by donor countries and intergovernmental organizations;

6.   *Requests* the Secretary-General to report to the General Assembly at its forty-fourth session on the progress made in the implementation of the present resolution.

General Assembly resolution 43/209

20 December 1988   Meeting 83   152-0-1 (recorded vote)

Approved by Second Committee (A/43/918/Add.2) by recorded vote (139-0-1), 23 November (meeting 44); 38-nation draft (A/C.2/43/L.49); agenda item 86.

Sponsors: Afghanistan, Algeria, Angola, Argentina, Austria, Barbados, Benin, Botswana, Burundi, Canada, Cape Verde, Congo, Cuba, Denmark, Ethiopia, Finland, German Democratic Republic, Ghana, Iceland, Liberia, Libyan Arab Jamahiriya, Madagascar, Mali, Mauritania, Mexico, Morocco, Mozambique, New Zealand, Norway, Sierra Leone, Somalia, Sweden, Tunisia, Uganda, United Republic of Tanzania, Zaire, Zambia, Zimbabwe.

Meeting numbers. GA 43rd session: 2nd Committee 26, 28-30, 36-38, 43, 44; plenary 83.

Recorded vote in Assembly as follows:

In favour: Afghanistan, Albania, Algeria, Angola, Antigua and Barbuda, Argentina, Australia, Austria, Bahrain, Bangladesh, Barbados, Belgium, Benin, Bhutan, Bolivia, Botswana, Brazil, Brunei Darussalam, Bulgaria, Burkina Faso, Burma, Burundi, Byelorussian SSR, Cameroon, Canada, Cape Verde, Central African Republic, Chad, Chile, China, Colombia, Comoros, Congo, Costa Rica, Côte d'Ivoire, Cuba, Cyprus, Czechoslovakia, Democratic Kampuchea, Democratic Yemen, Denmark, Djibouti, Dominican Republic, Ecuador, Egypt, El Salvador, Equatorial Guinea, Ethiopia, Fiji, Finland, France, Gabon, Gambia, German Democratic Republic, Germany, Federal Republic of, Ghana, Greece, Grenada, Guatemala, Guinea, Guinea-Bissau, Guyana, Haiti, Honduras, Hungary, Iceland, India, Indonesia, Iran, Iraq, Ireland, Italy, Jamaica, Japan, Jordan, Kenya, Kuwait, Lao People's Democratic Republic, Lebanon, Lesotho, Liberia, Libyan Arab Jamahiriya, Luxembourg, Madagascar, Malawi, Malaysia, Maldives, Mali, Malta, Mauritania, Mauritius, Mexico, Mongolia, Morocco, Mozambique, Nepal, Netherlands, New Zealand, Nicaragua, Niger, Nigeria, Norway, Oman, Pakistan, Panama, Papua New Guinea, Paraguay, Peru, Philippines, Poland, Portugal, Qatar, Romania, Rwanda, Saint Lucia, Saint Vincent and the Grenadines, Samoa, Sao Tome and Principe, Saudi Arabia, Senegal, Seychelles, Sierra Leone, Singapore, Solomon Islands, Somalia, Spain, Sri Lanka, Sudan, Suriname, Swaziland, Sweden, Syrian Arab Republic, Thailand, Togo, Trinidad and Tobago, Tunisia, Turkey, Uganda, Ukrainian SSR, USSR, United Arab Emirates, United Kingdom, United Republic of Tanzania, Uruguay, Vanuatu, Venezuela, Viet Nam, Yemen, Yugoslavia, Zaire, Zambia, Zimbabwe.

Against: None.

Abstaining: United States.

The Assembly, in **resolution 43/50 A**, appealed to all States and intergovernmental and non-governmental organizations to increase material, financial and other support to the front-line and other neighbouring independent States. In **resolution 43/116**, the Assembly reiterated its appreciation to the Secretary-General for his efforts to organize and mobilize special programmes of economic assistance for the front-line and other neighbouring States to help them withstand the

effects of South Africa's aggression and destabilization, and called on the international community to increase assistance to southern African countries to enable them to strengthen their capacity to provide for the care of refugees, returnees and displaced persons in their countries.

REFERENCES

[1]YUN 1986, p. 446, GA res. S-13/2, 1 June 1986. [2]A/43/500 & Corr.1. [3]YUN 1986, p. 446, GA res. S-13/2, annex, 1 June 1986. [4]YUN 1987, p. 437. [5]A/43/500/Add.1. [6]A/43/500/Add.2. [7]E/1988/79. [8]YUN 1987, p. 439. [9]DP/1988/24. [10]YUN 1987, p. 438. [11]DP/1988/10. [12]E/1988/19 (dec. 88/9). [13]DP/1988/65. [14]E/1988/19 (dec. 88/24). [15]YUN 1977, p. 509. [16]TD/B/1181. [17]TD/B/1182. [18]A/43/15, vol. II (dec. 363(XXXV)). [19]YUN 1987, p. 440, GA res. 42/163, 8 Dec. 1987. [20]A/43/664 & Corr.1. [21]E/1988/40. [22]A/43/16. [23]YUN 1987, p. 449, GA res. 42/205, 11 Dec. 1987. [24]A/43/483. [25]A/45/358. [26]YUN 1987, p. 442. [27]*Ibid.*, p. 443, GA res. 42/200, 11 Dec. 1987. [28]A/44/418. [29]YUN 1987, p. 447, GA res. 42/204, 11 Dec. 1987. [30]A/42/949. [31]A/43/729-S/20234. [32]YUN 1987, p. 456. [33]*Ibid.*, p. 166, GA res. 42/201, 11 Dec. 1987. [34]A/43/449 & Add.1,2.

Disasters

In 1988, UNDRO continued to be the focal point in the United Nations system for disaster management; its mandate covered all aspects of disaster relief and mitigation (prevention and preparedness). UNDRO also provided Governments with assistance in pre-disaster planning.

Review of disaster and emergency assistance

In accordance with a 1987 General Assembly decision,[1] the Secretary-General submitted a progress report[2] on the status of the implementation of that decision, by which he had been asked to proceed with the implementation of the conclusions and recommendations contained in his 1987 report on the capacity of the United Nations system in the area of disaster relief, preparedness and prevention.[3]

With regard to recommendations concerning UNDRO, the Secretary-General stated that a study was under way by the Advisory Management Service to adjust UNDRO's work programme and organization in order to focus attention on sudden natural disasters and on preparation and prevention measures. The report of a joint UNDRO/UNDP task force, established to work out improved modalities for co-operation, was annexed to the Secretary-General's report. The task force made several specific recommendations to strengthen co-operation between UNDP and UNDRO and its report also dealt with co-operative arrangements between all organizations in the field, including the strengthening of government mechanisms to deal with disasters. The Secretary-General noted that steps were being taken to strengthen UNDRO's capacity to manage disaster-related information.

In connection with operations at the field level, the UNDRO/UNDP task force addressed issues related to the responsibilities of United Nations resident co-ordinators and their colleagues in the field, particularly to the need for a standing United Nations disaster response team in disaster-prone countries.

As to United Nations Headquarters arrangements, the Secretary-General had entrusted the Director-General for Development and International Economic Co-operation with the responsibility of ensuring that he was kept fully informed on potential and existing disaster situations so as to be in a position to take appropriate action. In that regard, a close working relationship had been established with UNDRO, a major concern being to ensure a timely, adequate and co-ordinated response by the United Nations system.

The suggestion that a technical panel be convened to advise the Secretary-General on ways to take advantage of technological advances in dealing with disaster and emergency situations was being considered in connection with the International Decade for Natural Disaster Reduction (see below).

GENERAL ASSEMBLY ACTION

On 20 December, on the recommendation of the Second Committee, the General Assembly adopted **resolution 43/204** without vote.

Special economic and disaster relief assistance
The General Assembly,
Recalling its resolution 2816(XXVI) of 14 December 1971, by which it established the Office of the United Nations Disaster Relief Co-ordinator,
Recalling also its resolution 42/169 of 11 December 1987 and taking note of Economic and Social Council resolution 1988/51 of 26 July 1988,
Taking note with interest of the reports of the Secretary-General on the activities of the Office of the Co-ordinator and on special economic and disaster relief assistance,
Recognizing that activities related to disaster preparedness and prevention were significantly greater than in 1986-1987, and appreciating, in this regard, the contribution of bilateral donors and intergovernmental and non-governmental organizations, as well as the good performance of the Office of the Co-ordinator in strengthening the national emergency services of affected developing countries by providing, *inter alia*, advice and expertise on the utilization of early warning systems and on the elaboration and implementation of disaster contingency plans for pre-disaster planning and post-disaster periods,
1. *Encourages* the Office of the United Nations Disaster Relief Co-ordinator to expand further its informa-

tion base and its capacity to disseminate timely and reliable disaster-related information and to continue to update its profiles of disaster-prone countries, as well as to develop its International Disaster Management Information Network, bearing in mind the report to be prepared by the Secretary-General in response to the request made by the General Assembly in paragraph 5 of its resolution 42/169;
2. *Notes with interest* the close co-operation between the Office of the Co-ordinator and the United Nations Development Programme, as described in the final report of the joint United Nations Development Programme/Office of the United Nations Disaster Relief Co-ordinator task force;
3. *Requests* the Office of the Co-ordinator to strengthen its relationship with Member States, in particular with national focal points in disaster-prone countries, and, in this connection, recognizes the need to hold meetings at the regional and/or international level, at appropriate intervals, with the participation of heads of national emergency relief services of donor and recipient countries.

General Assembly resolution 43/204

20 December 1988   Meeting 83   Adopted without vote

Approved by Second Committee (A/43/918/Add.2) without vote, 30 November (meeting 45); draft by Vice-Chairman (A/C.2/43/L.70), based on informal consultations on draft by Tunisia, for Group of 77 (A/C.2/43/L.59); agenda item 86.
Meeting numbers. GA 43rd session: 2nd Committee 26, 28-30, 36-38, 43, 45; plenary 83.

Humanitarian assistance

On the recommendation of the Third (Social, Humanitarian and Cultural) Committee, the General Assembly, on 8 December, adopted **resolution 43/131** without vote.

Humanitarian assistance to victims of natural disasters and similar emergency situations
The General Assembly,
Recalling that one of the purposes of the United Nations is to achieve international co-operation in solving international problems of an economic, social, cultural or humanitarian character, and in promoting and encouraging respect for human rights and fundamental freedoms for all without distinction as to race, sex, language, or religion,
Reaffirming the sovereignty, territorial integrity and national unity of States, and recognizing that it is up to each State first and foremost to take care of the victims of natural disasters and similar emergency situations occurring on its territory,
Deeply concerned about the suffering of the victims of natural disasters and similar emergency situations, the loss in human lives, the destruction of property and the mass displacement of populations that result from them,
Bearing in mind that natural disasters and similar emergency situations have grave consequences for the economic and social plans of all countries concerned,
Desiring that the international community should respond speedily and effectively to appeals for emergency humanitarian assistance made in particular through the Secretary-General,
Mindful of the importance of humanitarian assistance for the victims of natural disasters and similar emergency situations,

Recognizing that the international community makes an important contribution to the sustenance and protection of such victims, whose health and life may be seriously endangered,

Considering that the abandonment of the victims of natural disasters and similar emergency situations without humanitarian assistance constitutes a threat to human life and an offence to human dignity,

Concerned about the difficulties that victims of natural disasters and similar emergency situations may experience in receiving humanitarian assistance,

Convinced that, in providing humanitarian assistance, in particular the supply of food, medicines or health care, for which access to victims is essential, rapid relief will avoid a tragic increase in their number,

Aware that alongside the action of Governments and intergovernmental organizations, the speed and efficiency of this assistance often depends on the help and aid of local and non-governmental organizations working with strictly humanitarian motives,

Recalling that, in the event of natural disasters and similar emergency situations, the principles of humanity, neutrality and impartiality must be given utmost consideration by all those involved in providing humanitarian assistance,

1. *Reaffirms* the importance of humanitarian assistance for the victims of natural disasters and similar emergency situations;

2. *Reaffirms also* the sovereignty of affected States and their primary role in the initiation, organization, coordination and implementation of humanitarian assistance within their respective territories;

3. *Stresses* the important contribution made in providing humanitarian assistance by intergovernmental and non-governmental organizations working with strictly humanitarian motives;

4. *Invites* all States in need of such assistance to facilitate the work of these organizations in implementing humanitarian assistance, in particular the supply of food, medicines and health care, for which access to victims is essential;

5. *Appeals*, therefore, to all States to give their support to these organizations working to provide humanitarian assistance, where needed, to the victims of natural disasters and similar emergency situations;

6. *Urges* States in proximity to areas of natural disasters and similar emergency situations, particularly in the case of regions that are difficult to reach, to participate closely with the affected countries in international efforts with a view to facilitating, to the extent possible, the transit of humanitarian assistance;

7. *Calls upon* all the intergovernmental, governmental and non-governmental organizations dealing with humanitarian assistance to co-operate as closely as possible with the Office of the United Nations Disaster Relief Co-ordinator or any other *ad hoc* mechanism set up by the Secretary-General in the co-ordination of aid;

8. *Requests* the Secretary-General to seek the views of Governments, intergovernmental, governmental and non-governmental organizations with regard to the possibility of enhancing the effectiveness of international mechanisms and increasing the speed of assistance in the best possible conditions for the victims of natural disasters and similar emergency situations, where needed, and to report his findings to the General Assembly at its forty-fifth session;

9. *Decides* to consider this question at its forty-fifth session.

General Assembly resolution 43/131

8 December 1988   Meeting 75   Adopted without vote

Approved by Third Committee (A/43/877) without vote, 22 November (meeting 49); 35-nation draft (A/C.3/43/L.38/Rev.1), orally revised; agenda item 105.

Sponsors: Bahrain, Bangladesh, Belgium, Benin, Burkina Faso, Burundi, Cameroon, Central African Republic, Chad, Costa Rica, Côte d'Ivoire, Denmark, France, Gabon, Guatemala, Italy, Jamaica, Japan, Jordan, Luxembourg, Malta, Mauritania, Morocco, Nepal, Niger, Philippines, Portugal, Samoa, Senegal, Sierra Leone, Thailand, Togo, United Kingdom, United States, Zaire.

Meeting numbers. GA 43rd session: 3rd Committee 36-38, 42, 46, 49, 50; plenary 75.

Office of the UN Disaster Relief Co-ordinator

During 1988, UNDRO—the specialized office of the United Nations Secretary-General for all disaster-related matters—continued to cover all aspects of disaster relief and mitigation (prevention and preparedness). It was also heavily involved in the preparatory work for the International Decade for Natural Disaster Reduction (see below) and in strengthening its collaborative relationship with UNDP (see above). UNDRO's organizational structure was adjusted to reflect new requirements.

In a report[4] on UNDRO activities in 1988-1989, the Secretary-General discussed major developments concerning the Office as a whole, disaster relief co-ordination, disaster mitigation (prevention and preparedness), disaster information and administration and finance. He noted that UNDRO's limited resources for disaster relief co-ordination were under great strain. Owing to the increased vulnerability of communities to natural hazards and other emergencies, the number of disasters grew, as well as the magnitude of their human, economic and social impact. Disaster situations in which UNDRO was involved ranged from those of short duration to those requiring sustained attention over a longer period of time and covered man-made as well as natural disasters.

Donor meetings were valuable forums for presenting emergency appeals of countries in need of assistance to the international donor community. In 1988, UNDRO organized or participated in such meetings for Mozambique (Maputo, April), Angola (Geneva, May) and Bangladesh (New York, November). In addition, UNDRO used regular information meetings to offer government representatives and intergovernmental and non-governmental organizations providing emergency assistance the opportunity to gather and exchange information on specific disaster situations and on their financing.

Contributions in 1988 from multilateral and bilateral sources and from NGOs and Red Cross and Red Crescent Societies totalled $1,037 million for disasters in 25 countries affecting some 85 million people. Some $626 million of the contributions in 1988 were donated for disasters that occurred in Ethiopia, Lebanon, Mozambique and the Sudan prior to that year.

Major disasters requiring the involvement of UNDRO in 1988 included: earthquakes in Armenia (USSR), China, India and Nepal; floods in Bangladesh, Benin, Brazil, Burkina Faso, Chad, China, Cuba, Rwanda, the Sudan and Thailand; a cyclone in Bangladesh; fires in Burma; hurricanes in Costa Rica, Haiti, Jamaica, Nicaragua and Panama; drought in Djibouti; a typhoon in the Philippines; and displaced persons in the Sudan and Uganda.

A report of the Secretary-General on UNDRO activities in 1986 and 1987[5] was submitted to the Economic and Social Council and the General Assembly in June 1988.

UNDRO financing

UNDRO activities continued to be financed mainly from the United Nations regular budget and voluntary contributions to a number of trust funds administered by the United Nations Disaster Relief Co-ordinator.

In 1987,[6] the General Assembly had appropriated $7,289,400 in UNDRO activities in the 1988-1989 biennium. By **resolution 43/218 A** of 21 December 1988, the Assembly revised that appropriation to $6,944,800.

ECONOMIC AND SOCIAL COUNCIL ACTION

On 26 July, the Economic and Social Council, on the recommendation of its Third (Programme and Co-ordination) Committee, adopted **resolution 1988/51** without vote.

Assistance in cases of natural disaster and other disaster situations: Office of the United Nations Disaster Relief Co-ordinator

The Economic and Social Council,

Recalling General Assembly resolution 2816(XXVI) of 14 December 1971, by which the Assembly established the Office of the United Nations Disaster Relief Co-ordinator and, *inter alia,* recognized the need to ensure prompt, effective and efficient responses, in times of natural disaster and other disaster situations, that would bring to bear the resources of the United Nations system, prospective donor countries and voluntary agencies,

Recalling also other pertinent resolutions, in particular General Assembly resolution 41/201 of 8 December 1986,

Bearing in mind General Assembly resolution 42/169 of 11 December 1987, in which the Assembly decided to designate the 1990s as a decade in which the international community, under the auspices of the United Nations, would pay special attention to fostering international co-operation in the field of natural disaster reduction,

Reaffirming that the primary responsibility for the administration of disaster relief operations and for disaster preparedness lies with the Governments of the affected countries and recognizing that available resources and efforts are being devoted by the Governments of those countries towards the alleviation of disaster-related problems,

Noting the increased number of requests to the Office of the United Nations Disaster Relief Co-ordinator for assistance in disaster relief and mitigation and for related information,

Reaffirming also that shortage of resources has been one of the major constraints on an effective response of the United Nations to disaster situations and continues to hamper the full achievement of a rapid and effective response to the needs of countries affected by disasters and that, if the shortage is to be overcome, efforts will be required by the international community to provide both funds and assistance in kind,

Reaffirming that, within the United Nations system, the Office of the United Nations Disaster Relief Co-ordinator is the focal point for disaster relief matters and therefore should be provided by the donor community, the United Nations and the other organizations of the United Nations system with the support necessary for it to discharge its responsibilities for disaster relief and mitigation,

Affirming the necessity of implementing the conclusions of the report of the Secretary-General on the implementation of General Assembly resolution 41/201,

1. *Takes note with satisfaction* of the report of the Secretary-General on the activities of the Office of the United Nations Disaster Relief Co-ordinator and of the statement made by the Co-ordinator before the Third (Programme and Co-ordination) Committee of the Economic and Social Council on 7 July 1988;

2. *Emphasizes* that it is essential for the Office of the United Nations Disaster Relief Co-ordinator to be placed, and kept, on a sound financial basis, and calls upon the international community to respond positively and expeditiously to the appeals of the Secretary-General for contributions to the United Nations Trust Fund for Disaster Relief Assistance in order to meet relief needs resulting from natural disasters and other disaster situations;

3. *Recognizes* that activities related to disaster preparedness and prevention were significantly greater in 1986-1987 than in the previous biennium, and appreciates the good performance of the Office of the United Nations Disaster Relief Co-ordinator in participating in strengthening the national emergency services of affected developing countries by providing, *inter alia,* advice and expertise on the utilization of early warning systems and on the elaboration and implementation of disaster contingency plans for pre-disaster planning and the post-disaster period, and in giving assistance to regional, interregional and global activities on the medium-term and longer-term aspects of disaster mitigation;

4. *Invites* the Secretary-General to request the United Nations Development Programme, in co-operation with the Office of the United Nations Disaster Relief Co-ordinator, to facilitate further the integration of disaster prevention projects in the planning of national programmes;

5. *Recognizes* that at the country level, particularly in disaster-prone countries, it is important that the organizations of the United Nations system concerned be

organized, under the resident co-ordinator, in an emergency operations group, in accordance with General Assembly resolution 36/225 of 17 December 1981, and welcomes the practical steps taken by the United Nations Development Programme and the Office of the United Nations Disaster Relief Co-ordinator to improve further their co-operation with Governments and voluntary agencies;

6. *Invites* the Secretary-General to provide the Office of the United Nations Disaster Relief Co-ordinator with the support necessary for it to continue to provide high-quality service to recipient countries, and to encourage the organizations of the United Nations system to contribute to this endeavour;

7. *Requests* the Secretary-General to include information on the implementation of the present resolution in his next biennial report on the Office, to be submitted to the General Assembly at its forty-fifth session, through the Economic and Social Council at its second regular session of 1990;

8. *Invites* the Secretary-General to continue to implement, by concrete measures, the conclusions of his report on the implementation of General Assembly resolution 41/201.

Economic and Social Council resolution 1988/51

26 July 1988   Meeting 38   Adopted without vote

Approved by Third Committee (E/1988/111) without vote, 21 July (meeting 13); draft by Tunisia, for Group of 77 (E/1988/C.3/L.4/Rev.1); agenda item 15.

GENERAL ASSEMBLY ACTION

On 20 December, by **decision 43/447**, the General Assembly endorsed Council resolution 1988/51.

Disaster relief efforts

Drought-stricken areas

Sudano-Sahelian region

The United Nations Sudano-Sahelian Office (UNSO) continued in 1988, under UNDP supervision, to assist countries in drought preparedness, recovery and rehabilitation, and medium- to long-term development, and in implementing the 1977 Plan of Action to Combat Desertification (see also PART THREE, Chapter VIII).

In a report to the UNDP Governing Council on UNSO activities during 1988,[7] the UNDP Administrator stated that climatic and related developments in the Sudano-Sahelian countries in 1988 generally improved. Many countries benefited from higher rainfall, although in some cases, particularly the Sudan, the rains had extremely damaging consequences. While agriculture was expected to fare better in terms of higher yields, medium- and long-term prospects regarding protection of productive resources had not improved. For example, flooding in the Sudan was aggravated by the poor soil and water-retention capacity in the catchment areas of the Blue Nile.

With some exceptions, the region was not stricken by any major, climate-induced famines. However, there was a resurgence, after years of dormancy, of the desert locust, which caused extensive damage in the drylands of the region.

The report covered the main functional areas of UNSO in support of the 22 countries of the Sudano-Sahelian region: co-operation with Governments in planning, co-ordination and monitoring at the country level; projects and programmes; resource mobilization; facilitating international co-ordination; serving as the focal point of the United Nations for regional organizations, particularly the Permanent Inter-State Committee on Drought Control in the Sahel (CILSS) and the Intergovernmental Authority for Drought and Development (IGADD); and information and public awareness. The report also covered activities related to drought and desertification control carried out by other entities within UNDP and summarized arrangements to strengthen UNSO's operating capacity.

In his annual report covering 1988 UNDP activities,[8] the Administrator stated that new projects and extensions of projects sponsored by UNSO increased by $25 million in 1988, bringing their total value to over $100 million at the end of the year. Programmes ranged from large-scale integrated land management projects in the Niger and the Sudan to afforestation and fuelwood plantation projects in Ethiopia and the Sudan, and sand-dune fixation and alternative energy projects in Cape Verde and Somalia. UNSO also assisted CILSS with an environmental education project and IGADD with study tours.

Funds mobilized by UNSO for desertification control through the end of 1988 reached $103.6 million.

UNDP Council action. On 1 July,[9] the UNDP Governing Council, having considered the Administrator's report on UNSO's 1987 activities,[10] encouraged the Administrator to capitalize on UNSO's experience and potential regarding environmental issues in the context of the follow-up by UNDP of the 1987 General Assembly resolution[11] on the report of the World Commission on Environment and Development. It renewed its appeal to Governments, organizations and individuals to contribute to UNSO's general resources and earmarked projects, and to make use of its services.

UNCTAD action. The UNCTAD secretariat submitted a report in July 1988 to the Trade and Development Board on the drought and the external trade of the countries members of IGADD.[12] IGADD comprised six countries—Djibouti, Ethiopia, Kenya, Somalia, the Sudan and Uganda—all of which, except Kenya, were least developed countries (LDCs). The report described IGADD's institutional background, the drought and environmental conditions, the external trade of IGADD members, action taken by them, and international support and related measures.

As to bases for future action, the report highlighted some domestic policy measures and international support that would help to streamline the effectiveness of the external sector of IGADD countries.

On 5 October,[13] the Trade and Development Board asked the UNCTAD Secretary-General to transmit the report, together with views of delegations, to the IGADD secretariat and to international organizations and agencies, including UNDP. The IGADD secretariat was asked to keep UNCTAD informed of developments in the external trade of its members and the UNCTAD secretariat was asked to continue to assist IGADD members.

ECONOMIC AND SOCIAL COUNCIL ACTION

On 7 July, a UNDP representative reported orally to the Economic and Social Council's Third Committee on assistance to the drought-stricken areas of Djibouti, Ethiopia, Kenya, Somalia, the Sudan and Uganda. On 26 July, by **decision 1988/158**, the Council took note of the report.

Storms and floods

Treacherous weather took a serious toll in many parts of the world during 1988. In August and September, flood waters in Bangladesh affected 45 million people out of a total population of 110 million. The official death toll was 1,664 persons. The Sudan was also devastated by torrential rains and widespread floods.

In Jamaica, a severe hurricane devastated the island in September, causing extensive damage and destruction to property, agriculture and infrastructure. In Nicaragua, a severe hurricane in October caused widespread damage to property and disrupted its economic activities.

UNCTAD action. On 5 October,[14] the Trade and Development Board requested the UNCTAD secretariat to study the impact of floods and cyclones on the medium- and long-term economic growth and development of the affected developing countries, particularly LDCs, and to identify requirements for the resumption and maintenance of a modest pace of sustained growth and development of their economies.

Hurricane in Jamaica

In his report on UNDRO activities,[4] the Secretary-General stated that a major hurricane— hurricane Gilbert—struck Jamaica on 12 Septem-

ber 1988, with winds of up to 125 miles per hour. The hurricane moved across Jamaica from east to west, tearing off roofs and destroying crops, vegetation and infrastructure. At least 500,000 people were left homeless and damage was estimated at over $800 million. Other Caribbean islands, notably Guadeloupe, Martinique, Puerto Rico and Saint Lucia, also suffered damage to infrastructure and plantations.

An alert was issued to the international community on 12 September and was followed on the same day by a report containing a preliminary assessment of damage. UNDRO dispatched the Manager of the Pan-Caribbean Disaster Preparedness and Prevention Project from Antigua to Jamaica to assist the authorities and the UNDP/UNDRO Resident Representative in co-ordinating relief efforts.

In a 19 September letter,[15] Jamaica appealed to the international community for support and assistance in view of the magnitude of the disaster.

In his annual report covering 1988,[16] the UNDP Administrator stated that multilateral and bilateral donor response to Jamaica's appeal for assistance resulted in the shipment of building materials, medicines, fertilizers and other materials for emergency relief and longer-term rehabilitation. Following Jamaica's request for UNDP assistance in the financial management and tracking of goods and services delivered, a computerized emergency information and management system was installed to provide the Government with a monitoring and follow-up capacity.

GENERAL ASSEMBLY ACTION

On 18 October, the General Assembly adopted **resolution 43/7** without vote.

Emergency assistance to Jamaica

The General Assembly,

Recalling its resolution 42/169 of 11 December 1987 on an international decade for natural disaster reduction,

Deeply distressed by the number of afflicted persons and the destruction wrought by hurricane Gilbert which, on 12 September 1988, struck the island of Jamaica,

Conscious of the efforts of the Government and people of Jamaica to save lives and alleviate the sufferings of the victims of the hurricane,

Noting the enormous effort that will be required to alleviate the grave situation caused by this natural disaster,

Conscious also of the prompt response being made by Governments, international agencies, non-governmental organizations and private individuals to provide emergency relief,

Recognizing that the magnitude of the disaster and its long-term effects will require, as a complement to the effort being made by the people and Government of Jamaica, a demonstration of international solidarity and humanitarian concern to ensure broad multilateral co-operation in order to meet the immediate emergency situation in the affected areas, as well as to undertake the process of reconstruction,

1. *Expresses its solidarity and support* to the Government and people of Jamaica;

2. *Expresses its appreciation* to the States, international agencies and non-governmental organizations that are providing emergency relief to that country;

3. *Calls upon* all States to contribute generously to the relief and reconstruction efforts in the affected areas;

4. *Requests* the Secretary-General, in collaboration with the international financial institutions and the bodies and agencies of the United Nations system, to assist the Government of Jamaica in identifying the emergency, medium-term and long-term needs and in mobilizing resources, as well as to help with the task of reconstruction of the country undertaken by the Government.

General Assembly resolution 43/7

18 October 1988   Meeting 33   Adopted without vote

57-nation draft (A/43/L.5 & Add.1); agenda item 149.

Sponsors: Algeria, Antigua and Barbuda, Argentina, Bahamas, Bangladesh, Barbados, Belize, Bolivia, Brazil, Cameroon, Canada, Chile, Colombia, Costa Rica, Cuba, Democratic Yemen, Dominica, Dominican Republic, Ecuador, El Salvador, Ethiopia, Gambia, Ghana, Grenada, Guatemala, Guyana, Haiti, Honduras, Italy, Jamaica, Japan, Lesotho, Liberia, Madagascar, Malaysia, Mexico, Morocco, Mozambique, Netherlands, Nigeria, Panama, Peru, Philippines, Saint Kitts and Nevis, Saint Lucia, Saint Vincent and the Grenadines, Sao Tome and Principe, Senegal, Sudan, Suriname, Trinidad and Tobago, Tunisia, United Kingdom, United States, Uruguay, Venezuela, Zimbabwe.

Floods in Bangladesh

In his report on UNDRO activities,[4] the Secretary-General stated that unusually heavy rainfall between 20 and 28 August led to peak flood levels of the Brahmaputra, Ganges and Meghna rivers in Bangladesh in early September. By mid-September, flood waters covered 53 districts of a total of 64; 45 million people out of a population of 110 million were directly affected and enormous damage was done to crops, and transport and communications systems. An inter-agency mission visited Bangladesh from 13 to 18 September to assess the damage and identify priority relief needs. In a 10 October note verbale to the Secretary-General,[17] Bangladesh appealed for international assistance. A Special Meeting on Assistance to Bangladesh (New York, 16 November) had before it the report of the Joint Task Force of the Government of Bangladesh and the United Nations on the 1988 floods.[18] It estimated the extent of damage caused by the floods, its macro-economic and social impact and immediate supply requirements. The report also assessed damage following the recession of flood waters and outlined the Government's reconstruction and rehabilitation plans. Disaster preparedness and flood control strategies were also discussed.

The Secretary-General stated that the value of Bangladesh's reconstruction needs was assessed by the Joint Task Force at over $1 billion. Before the 16 November meeting, $200 million of international assistance had been made available or

pledged; after the meeting some $500 million became available.

GENERAL ASSEMBLY ACTION

On 18 October, the General Assembly adopted **resolution 43/9** without vote.

Short-term, medium-term and long-term solutions to the problems of natural disasters in Bangladesh

The General Assembly,

Recalling its resolution 40/231 of 17 December 1985 following the disastrous cyclone that struck Bangladesh in 1985,

Recalling also its resolution 42/169 of 11 December 1987 on an international decade for natural disaster reduction,

Noting with concern the devastating consequences of the recent floods in Bangladesh, the worst in living memory, that have caused significant loss of life, unprecedented human suffering to tens of millions of stranded and homeless people subjected to hunger and water-borne disease and incalculable damage to crops, livestock, communications and infrastructure,

Taking note of the statement made on 10 October 1988 by the representative of Bangladesh, in which he elaborated the details of these concerns,

Deeply conscious of the macro-economic impact of such calamities, which constitutes an insurmountable burden on the economy and development plans of a least developed country like Bangladesh, causing irrecoverable set-back in growth and necessitating extremely difficult adjustment, and that the cost of damage inflicted by such catastrophes often exceeds the net inflow of development assistance,

Recognizing the strenuous efforts of the Government and people of Bangladesh to save lives, to alleviate the suffering and hardship suffered by the victims of the floods and to initiate urgent recovery measures, including immediate relief and rehabilitation measures,

Recognizing also that the magnitude of the damage and devastation is beyond the ability of Bangladesh alone to rectify or to meet, requiring national efforts to be supplemented by sustained international financial and technical assistance over the long term,

Emphasizing in this connection the importance of measures noted in the report of the Secretary-General on special economic and disaster relief assistance to Bangladesh, submitted to the General Assembly at its forty-first session,

Aware that Bangladesh is particularly vulnerable to recurrent disasters that have the potential of becoming annual visitations of destruction far beyond its capacity either to control or to effectively mitigate,

Conscious of the fact that international assistance and investment over time are required to mitigate and prevent the consequences of such disasters,

Noting with appreciation the support and solidarity displayed by the countries of South Asia in assisting Bangladesh in the immediate aftermath of the floods,

Welcoming the efforts of the Government of Bangladesh, initiated at the highest level, to strengthen bilateral co-operation with concerned countries of the region through the establishment of task forces of experts to study and make recommendations for flood management and water flows and to find durable solutions to the problems in these areas,

Expressing the hope that these multiple bilateral approaches will strengthen co-operation, co-ordination and convergence of mutual interests leading to practical arrangements to promote solutions for the assessment, prediction, prevention and mitigation of natural disasters and to joint approaches for a permanent solution,

Recognizing the responsibility of the United Nations system to facilitate studies at the request of concerned Governments, including those of natural disasters of a geophysical origin, to improve capacities of countries to mitigate the effects of natural disasters, to foster scientific and engineering endeavours to close critical gaps in knowledge, to disseminate existing and new information and to develop measures for prediction, prevention and mitigation of natural disasters through programmes of technical assistance and technology transfer,

Aware that considerable expertise and technical capabilities are available within the organizations of the United Nations system to strengthen preparedness and prevention capabilities of disaster-prone countries through the promotion of a long-term and effective solution of the problems caused by natural disasters,

1. *Expresses its gratitude* to Member States, international organizations within and outside the United Nations system, non-governmental organizations and individuals and groups that have so generously assisted the Government of Bangladesh in its immediate relief and rehabilitation efforts;

2. *Expresses its deep appreciation* to the Secretary-General for the urgent steps he has taken to mobilize humanitarian assistance and, through the appointment of the United Nations Disaster Relief Co-ordinator as his Special Representative, to co-ordinate activities of the United Nations agencies in the field for purposeful and unified assistance by the international community;

3. *Appeals* to all Member States, specialized agencies in the field and other organs and bodies of the United Nations system, as well as international economic and financial institutions, to respond urgently and generously in sustaining development assistance to Bangladesh, particularly in its plans and programmes for longer-term rehabilitation and reconstruction;

4. *Requests* relevant organizations and bodies of the United Nations system and other multilateral organizations to take appropriate measures to provide assistance to Bangladesh to strengthen its capacity to assess, predict, prevent and mitigate natural disasters, particularly assistance for disaster preparedness and prevention programmes and to implement its plans and programmes for seeking a long-term and effective solution of the problems caused by floods and other natural disasters;

5. *Requests* the Secretary-General, through the Office of the United Nations Disaster Relief Co-ordinator and in co-operation with other relevant agencies of the United Nations system, to assist the Government of Bangladesh in preparing its own feasibility plan to meet such exigencies;

6. *Requests* the Secretary-General to report to the General Assembly at its forty-fourth session on the implementation of the present resolution.

General Assembly resolution 43/9

18 October 1988   Meeting 33   Adopted without vote

56-nation draft (A/43/L.10/Rev.1 & Add.1); agenda item 151.
Sponsors: Algeria, Antigua and Barbuda, Bahamas, Bahrain, Bangladesh, Barbados, Belize, Burkina Faso, Burundi, Cameroon, Canada, Cape Verde, Chad, China, Colombia, Costa Rica, Cuba, Democratic Yemen, Djibouti,

Ethiopia, Gambia, Gabon, Grenada, Guinea, Iraq, Italy, Jamaica, Japan, Lesotho, Libyan Arab Jamahiriya, Madagascar, Maldives, Mauritania, Mauritius, Mexico, Morocco, Mozambique, Nepal, Niger, Pakistan, Panama, Paraguay, Peru, Philippines, Rwanda, Saint Vincent and the Grenadines, Senegal, Somalia, Sri Lanka, Sudan, Swaziland, Tunisia, Turkey, United Arab Emirates, United Kingdom, United Republic of Tanzania.
Meeting numbers. GA 43rd session: plenary 25, 33.

Emergencies in China

Floods, hailstorms, a typhoon and an earthquake ravaged several provinces of China during 1988. In his report on UNDRO activities,[4] the Secretary-General stated that there had been floods in Fujiang province in May, hailstorms and rainstorms in Heilongjiang province, floods and a typhoon in Zhejiang province and floods in Shanxi province, all in August, and earthquakes in Yunnan province in November. The UNDP/UNDRO Resident Representative, in co-operation with government authorities, transmitted detailed reports. UNDRO issued 17 information reports during the year and promptly provided $30,000 in cash grants to bridge the gap until the arrival of other assistance. Australia, Canada and the Netherlands channelled their contributions through UNDRO and UNDP. Contributions reported to UNDRO in 1988 amounted to $3.2 million.

Hurricane in Nicaragua, Costa Rica, Panama and other countries

Between 22 and 25 October 1988, hurricane Joan struck Nicaragua, Costa Rica, Panama and other countries of the region. The Secretary-General reported[4] that, in Nicaragua, early warnings led to the evacuation of some 300,000 people. UNDRO launched an appeal and issued 13 reports between October and December 1988 on the emergency. The value of relief contributions reported to UNDRO totalled some $32 million. In response to the UNDRO appeal, Canada and the United Kingdom transferred cash contributions, which were used to buy zinc sheets and motor saws locally. An UNDRO emergency grant of $25,000 was used on a cost-sharing basis with UNDP to provide household utensils and medical equipment.

GENERAL ASSEMBLY ACTION

On 28 October, the General Assembly adopted **resolution 43/17** without vote.

Emergency assistance to Nicaragua, Costa Rica, Panama and other countries affected by hurricane Joan

The General Assembly,

Recalling its resolutions 42/169 of 11 December 1987 on an international decade for natural disaster reduction and 35/56 of 5 December 1980, the annex to which contains the International Development Strategy for the Third United Nations Development Decade,

Deeply concerned by the large number of afflicted persons and also by the destruction caused by hurricane

Joan, which between 22 and 25 October 1988 struck Nicaragua, Costa Rica, Panama and other countries of the region,

Aware of the efforts of the Governments and peoples of the region to save lives and alleviate the suffering of the victims of hurricane Joan,

Aware also of the enormous effort that will be required to alleviate the grave situation caused by this natural disaster,

Welcoming the prompt response of the Governments, the organs, organizations and specialized agencies of the United Nations system and also of the international and regional agencies, the non-governmental organizations and the private individuals that are providing emergency relief,

Recognizing that the magnitude of the disaster and its medium- and long-term effects will require, as a complement to the efforts being made by the peoples and Governments of Nicaragua, Costa Rica, Panama and other countries of the region, a demonstration of international solidarity and humanitarian concern to trigger broad multilateral co-operation in order to meet the immediate emergency situation in the affected areas and initiate the process of reconstruction,

1. *Expresses its solidarity and support* to Nicaragua, Costa Rica, Panama and other countries of the region affected by the natural disaster;

2. *Expresses its gratitude* to all the States of the international community, the international agencies and the non-governmental organizations that are providing emergency relief to the affected countries;

3. *Urges* all the States of the international community, as a matter of urgency, to contribute generously to the relief, rehabilitation and reconstruction efforts in the affected areas;

4. *Expresses its appreciation* to the Secretary-General for the steps taken to co-ordinate and mobilize the relief, rehabilitation and reconstruction efforts;

5. *Requests* the Secretary-General, in close collaboration with the Governments of Nicaragua, Costa Rica, Panama and the affected countries of the region, and the international financial institutions, organs, organizations and specialized agencies of the United Nations system to assist those countries in mobilizing the additional financial resources necessary for the implementation of the medium- and long-term plans and programmes of rehabilitation and reconstruction.

General Assembly resolution 43/17

28 October 1988   Meeting 40   Adopted without vote

26-nation draft (A/43/L.19 & Corr.1); agenda item 152.
Sponsors: Argentina, Bahamas, Barbados, Belize, Bolivia, Brazil, Chile, Colombia, Costa Rica, Cuba, Dominican Republic, Ecuador, Grenada, Guatemala, Guyana, Honduras, Jamaica, Mexico, Nicaragua, Panama, Paraguay, Peru, Suriname, Trinidad and Tobago, Uruguay, Venezuela.

Floods in the Sudan

The Secretary-General reported[4] that, on 6 August 1988, UNDRO issued an appeal on behalf of 2 million people in and around Khartoum, Sudan, made homeless by floods. UNDRO dispatched two relief co-ordination officers to Khartoum to assess needs, monitor contributions and assist the UNDP resident co-ordinator. By 30 August, contributions in cash and kind reported directly to UNDRO amounted to over $18.5 million, excluding supplies for which no monetary value was indicated.

GENERAL ASSEMBLY ACTION

On 18 October, the General Assembly adopted **resolution 43/8** without vote.

Emergency assistance to the Sudan

The General Assembly,

Recalling its resolutions 35/56 of 5 December 1980, the annex to which contains the International Development Strategy for the Third United Nations Development Decade, and 42/169 of 11 December 1987 on an international decade for natural disaster reduction,

Recalling also the Substantial New Programme of Action for the 1980s for the Least Developed Countries, in particular the section concerning disaster assistance for least developed countries,

Deeply concerned by the extensive and unprecedented damage and devastation in the Sudan caused by torrential rain and floods in August 1988,

Extremely concerned about the destruction of hundreds of thousands of buildings and dwellings and by the fact that large sectors of the nation's infrastructure have been completely disrupted, in particular, roads, railway lines, water supplies, electricity supplies, hospitals and health centres, schools and other public utilities and communication systems,

Considering that over 120,000 hectares of cultivated land and over 7,000 small farmers' schemes were inundated, and about 600 villages and islands have completely disappeared and thereby over 1.5 million persons were left without shelter or food,

Fully cognizant of the economic difficulties already faced by the Sudan, particularly resulting from its high level of indebtedness and compounded further by a massive influx of refugees and 2 million displaced persons,

Recognizing that the Sudan has shouldered the major part of the burden in dealing with the disasters, but that the magnitude of devastation and damage is far beyond the means and abilities of the Sudan alone to rectify,

Reaffirming the need for the international community to respond fully to requests for emergency humanitarian assistance as well as rehabilitation and reconstruction of a least developed country, facing grave and compounded disaster situations,

Noting with appreciation the response to date of various countries and intergovernmental and non-governmental organizations in emergency relief operations,

Noting that the Secretary-General has sent an interagency mission to the Sudan to assess emergency conditions and that a United Nations Development Programme/World Bank multi-donor flood recovery programme mission is currently in the Sudan, at the request of its Government, to assess the impact of floods and to prepare a two-year reconstruction programme,

1. *Expresses its solidarity* with the Government and people of the Sudan in facing the complex disaster situations;

2. *Expresses its gratitude* to the States and intergovernmental and non-governmental organizations that rendered support and assistance to the Government of the Sudan in its relief and rehabilitation efforts;

3. *Expresses its appreciation* to the Secretary-General for the steps he has taken to co-ordinate and mobilize relief and rehabilitation efforts;

4. *Calls upon* all States to contribute generously and respond urgently and effectively to the needs of relief operations, rehabilitation and reconstruction;

5. *Requests* the Secretary-General, in close co-operation with the Government of the Sudan, to co-ordinate efforts of the United Nations system to help the Sudan in its emergency, rehabilitation and reconstruction efforts, to mobilize resources for the implementation of those programmes and to keep the international community informed of those needs;

6. *Also requests* the Secretary-General to apprise the Economic and Social Council at its first regular session of 1989 of his efforts and to report to the General Assembly at its forty-fourth session on the implementation of the present resolution.

General Assembly resolution 43/8

18 October 1988   Meeting 33   Adopted without vote

40-nation draft (A/43/L.9 & Add.1); agenda item 150.
Sponsors: Algeria, Bangladesh, Cameroon, Chile, Colombia, Comoros, Congo, Cuba, Democratic Yemen, Djibouti, Ecuador, Egypt, Ethiopia, Gambia, Guinea-Bissau, Jamaica, Jordan, Kenya, Kuwait, Libyan Arab Jamahiriya, Madagascar, Malaysia, Mauritania, Mexico, Mozambique, Pakistan, Peru, Philippines, Qatar, Romania, Rwanda, Sao Tome and Principe, Somalia, Sri Lanka, Sudan, Tunisia, Uganda, United Arab Emirates, United Republic of Tanzania, Yemen.

Other disasters

Earthquake in Nepal

The UNDP Administrator reported[19] that, on the morning of 21 August 1988, an earthquake measuring 6.7 on the Richter scale shook remote mountainous regions of central and eastern Nepal. The earthquake killed more than 700 people and caused widespread damage to homes, roads, bridges, and drinking-water and irrigation systems.

Through the efforts of UNDRO and the UNDP Resident Representative, who was asked by the Government to co-ordinate the external relief efforts, $3.6 million was mobilized for emergency relief and an assessment was made of needs for longer-term rehabilitation.

Earthquake in the USSR

The Secretary-General reported[4] that, on 7 December 1988, an earthquake of 6.9 on the Richter scale hit the northern part of the Soviet Socialist Republic of Armenia. Some 24,593 lives were lost and more than 8,000 people were partially or fully disabled. The Government estimated that about half a million people were left homeless. Economic damage was estimated at between $21 billion and $33 billion. Total foreign relief aid from 74 countries was the highest reported to UNDRO for a single natural disaster.

Locust and grasshopper infestation in Africa

At each of its three sessions in 1988, the Economic and Social Council discussed the continuing locust and grasshopper infestation in Africa, which had been the subject of a 1986 General As-

sembly resolution[20] and a 1987 report of the Director-General of the Food and Agriculture Organization of the United Nations (FAO).[21]

ECONOMIC AND SOCIAL COUNCIL ACTION

On 5 February, the Council adopted **resolution 1988/2** without vote.

Fight against the locust and grasshopper infestation in Africa

The Economic and Social Council,

Recalling General Assembly resolution 41/185 of 8 December 1986 on the fight against locust and grasshopper infestation in Africa,

Concerned about the unrelentingly destructive effects of the current locust and grasshopper infestation in many regions of Africa,

1. *Calls upon* the international community to give high priority to the fight against the locust and grasshopper infestation in Africa, in particular the new infestation of several regions in Mauritania;

2. *Invites* the Director-General of the Food and Agriculture Organization of the United Nations to report to the Economic and Social Council at its second regular session of 1988 on the situation of the locust and grasshopper infestation in Africa.

Economic and Social Council resolution 1988/2

5 February 1988   Meeting 4   Adopted without vote

2-nation draft (E/1988/L.15), orally revised; agenda item 3.
Sponsors: Iraq, Mauritania.

On 24 May, the Council adopted **resolution 1988/3** without vote.

Fight against the locust and grasshopper infestation in Africa

The Economic and Social Council,

Recalling General Assembly resolution 41/185 of 8 December 1986 and Council resolution 1988/2 of 5 February 1988,

Deeply concerned at the magnitude and gravity of the present locust and grasshopper infestation in Africa,

Alarmed by the unrelentingly destructive effects of the locust and grasshopper infestation on many African countries,

Fully aware of the urgent need to spare no effort to counter and eradicate the infestation, as well as the need to take adequate preventive measures against future outbreaks,

Noting that the resources of Africa are insufficient to control the infestation, which will need to be countered by concerted efforts at the national, regional and international levels,

1. *Expresses its deep concern* at the worsening desert locust and grasshopper infestation in Africa, which may adversely affect food production and cause renewed famine, and reaffirms the need to accord the highest priority to locust and grasshopper control and eradication;

2. *Notes with appreciation* the efforts of affected countries, donors and regional and international organizations, in particular the Food and Agriculture Organization of the United Nations, acting individually and jointly, to contain the infestation;

3. *Urges* donors to increase financial and technical assistance for current and future programmes of locust

and grasshopper control, in keeping with the increased requirements of the evolving situation;

4. *Calls upon* the international community to support fully the locust and grasshopper control activities undertaken by African countries, including the gathering and dissemination of information and prevention, co-ordination and funding activities, as well as the strengthening and establishment of national, regional and international early warning systems for the monitoring of locust and grasshopper infestations;

5. *Supports* the efforts of the Maghreb countries within the framework of their joint programme of co-ordination to fight against locust and grasshopper infestation, and invites those countries willing to participate in the eradication of that scourge to contribute resources to the common fund established for that purpose by the Governments of Algeria, the Libyan Arab Jamahiriya, Mauritania, Morocco and Tunisia;

6. *Invites* the Director-General of the Food and Agriculture Organization of the United Nations, in close co-operation with the relevant organizations of the United Nations system, to undertake an assessment of the prevailing techniques used in the fight against locust and grasshopper infestation, with a view to identifying and applying more effective and environmentally sound methods;

7. *Invites* the appropriate bodies, organizations and programmes of the United Nations system to give the necessary priority, in their regular activities, to the fight against the locust and grasshopper infestation in Africa;

8. *Requests* the Secretary-General, in consultation with the Director-General of the Food and Agriculture Organization of the United Nations, to take the necessary measures in this regard;

9. *Invites* the Director-General of the Food and Agriculture Organization of the United Nations to keep the situation under constant review and to strengthen that organization's capabilities with regard to the overall co-ordination of the Emergency Centre for Locust Operations;

10. *Requests* the Secretary-General to transmit to the General Assembly at its forty-third session the text of the report of the Director-General of the Food and Agriculture Organization of the United Nations to be made to the Council at its second regular session of 1988.

Economic and Social Council resolution 1988/3

24 May 1988　　　　Meeting 12　　　　Adopted without vote

Draft by Denmark, France, Germany, Federal Republic of, Italy, Norway, Portugal, Somalia (for African States), Spain, United Kingdom (E/1988/L.25), orally revised; agenda item 1.
Meeting numbers. ESC 6, 11, 12.

On 18 July, a representative of FAO made an oral report to the Council's First (Economic) Committee on the locust and grasshopper situation in Africa. By **decision 1988/177** of 29 July, the Council took note of FAO's oral report.

UNDP action. On 1 July,[22] the UNDP Governing Council endorsed an interregional project on locust and grasshopper control.[23] The two-year project, to be executed by FAO with UNDP financing of $3.3 million, would provide emergency assistance to meet short and intermediate needs for desert locust control. The Council urged

UNDP, and appealed to other sources of financing, to provide countries affected with resources to cope with the outbreaks of desert locusts and grasshoppers and to contain expected infestations. UNDP and other sources of financing were invited to provide those countries with resources to enable them to devise and implement a regional strategy to control the locust scourge with a view to its eventual eradication. The Council requested UNDP regional offices involved in the fight against locust and grasshopper infestation to co-ordinate their activities closely with the affected countries and/or the appropriate international, regional and subregional organizations, with a view to obtaining effective control of the infestations while safeguarding the environment. It invited donor countries to continue to provide the affected countries with the necessary products, equipment and aircraft.

FAO report. In response to the 24 May request by the Economic and Social Council (see above), the Secretary-General, in October,[24] transmitted to the General Assembly a report by the Director-General of FAO on the desert locust plague in Africa. The report stated that, during 1988, the desert locust situation had further deteriorated despite large-scale campaigns in many countries. In March, there was a major swarm invasion of north-west Africa, followed by a southward movement of swarms from spring breeding there into the Sahelian zone in March—much earlier than foreseen. Also, notwithstanding the spraying of over 5 million hectares in north-west Africa, further swarms reached the Sahelian countries between May and July, many of which moved east, reaching Chad and the Sudan in May and northern Ethiopia in late July. In addition, widespread and abundant monsoon rainfall provided favourable breeding conditions. The total invasion area thus extended from Senegal and Mauritania to the Sudan, Ethiopia, Djibouti and Yemen, covering an area of some 8 million square kilometres.

Aerial and ground campaigns had been conducted against all major infestations south of the Sahara with two objectives in mind—limitation of damage to agricultural crops and the destruction of as many infestations as possible to reduce a further spread. Through its Emergency Centre for Locust Operations, FAO continued to co-ordinate the control campaign and, together with the affected countries, analysed the development of the situation, evaluated the needs and worked closely with donors to ensure support. Although those activities were focused on emergency operations, it was recognized that further research was necessary to improve methods of locust survey and control, to find alternative control methods and to accelerate longer-term predictions. Unless the weather became less suitable for locusts, the plague would continue to threaten the livelihood of hundreds of millions of people in over 50 countries. (See also PART SEVEN, Chapter III.)

GENERAL ASSEMBLY ACTION

On 20 December, on the recommendation of the Second Committee, the General Assembly adopted **resolution 43/203** without vote.

International strategy for the fight against locust and grasshopper infestation, particularly in Africa

The General Assembly,

Recalling its resolution 41/185 of 8 December 1986 and taking note of Economic and Social Council resolution 1988/3 of 24 May 1988 concerning the fight against locust and grasshopper infestation in Africa,

Taking note also of Economic and Social Council resolution 1988/2 of 5 February 1988, in which the Council drew particular attention to the critical situation in one of the regions where the locust and grasshopper infestation had originated,

Recalling its resolutions S-13/2 of 1 June 1986 on the United Nations Programme of Action for African Economic Recovery and Development 1986-1990 and 41/29 of 31 October 1986 on the emergency situation in Africa, in which it recognized that food production on that continent must be increased to meet the needs of its populations,

Aware that, in its resolution 42/169 of 11 December 1987 on an international decade for natural disaster reduction, it had included grasshopper and locust infestations among the types of natural disasters to be covered by the decade,

Taking note of resolution CM/Res.1173(XLVIII) on locust control in Africa, adopted by the Council of Ministers of the Organization of African Unity at its forty-eighth ordinary session, held at Addis Ababa from 19 to 23 May 1988,[a]

Deeply concerned at the exceptional seriousness and the potential and real dangers of the current locust and grasshopper infestation, particularly in Africa, despite the laudable efforts of the affected countries, with the assistance of the international community, as recognized in the report of the Director-General of the Food and Agriculture Organization of the United Nations on the desert locust plague in Africa,

Aware that, in the course of the current infestation, swarms of locusts and grasshoppers have affected or may invade the great majority of African countries and other countries in Asia, Latin America, the Caribbean and Europe, and concerned at the disastrous consequences that may result for food production and agriculture in the world,

Taking into account, in that context, the potential problem created by billions of insects capable of devouring as much as 80,000 tons of vegetation and cereal crops per swarm daily, of migrating great distances from their original habitat and of obliterating the livelihood of hundreds of millions of people in some sixty countries, as stated in the status reports of the Food and Agriculture Organization of the United Nations,

Alarmed by the unrelentingly destructive effects of the current invasion of locusts and grasshoppers in many countries of Africa and other geographical regions, and concerned at the economic and social consequences, including the reduction in agricultural output, which could continue for several years, the consequent displacement of affected populations and, in particular, the impact on the ecological environment and on medium- and long-term economic and social development,

Convinced that since, of the total area to be treated, only a small portion of the infested areas in Africa have benefited from locust and grasshopper control campaigns, it can be expected, given the extreme seriousness of the current situation, that the cycle of invasion will last beyond 1989 for a minimum period of five years, during which it can be predicted that the plague will intensify and extend to areas that were previously spared,

Aware that current campaigns for locust and grasshopper control have so far been unable to put an end to the infestation, in particular because of the limited financial resources of the affected countries, and convinced that the fight against the plague, which, by virtue of its recurrent nature and geographical extent, is international in scope, requires increased and co-ordinated mobilization of appropriate human, scientific, technical, material and financial resources,

Noting with satisfaction the readiness of donor countries resolutely to support action to fight locust and grasshopper infestation, in the knowledge that the resources of the affected countries and the emergency operations are not in themselves adequate to halt the plague on a lasting basis,

Conscious of the urgent need to define an effective strategy for fighting the locust and grasshopper peril while protecting the health of the populations concerned and the natural ecosystems,

Bearing in mind the recommendations of the International Conference on the Locust Plague, held at Fez, Morocco, on 28 and 29 October 1988,[b]

1. *Takes note with interest* of the report of the Director-General of the Food and Agriculture Organization of the United Nations on the desert locust plague in Africa;

2. *Expresses its deep concern* at the worsening locust and grasshopper infestations, especially in Africa, which may adversely affect food production and result in renewed famine, and reaffirms the need to accord the highest priority to locust and grasshopper control and eradication;

3. *Notes with appreciation* the efforts of the affected countries and expresses its gratitude to donor countries, organizations of the United Nations system and other competent institutions in their efforts to contain the infestation, in particular the Emergency Centre for Locust Operations of the Food and Agriculture Organization of the United Nations, the Joint Anti-Locust and Anti-Avarian Organization, the Desert Locust Control Organization for East Africa and the Joint Committee of Mahgreb Experts on Locust and Grasshopper Control;

4. *Invites* all countries recently threatened by the invasion of desert locusts to take all appropriate measures to develop their own national means of protection against locusts and grasshoppers and to contribute to the implementation of regional infestation control programmes, and encourages the affected countries to continue their efforts in that area;

---

[a]A/43/398.
[b]A/C.2/43/9.

5. *Calls upon* the donor countries and organizations to continue to assist the affected countries to strengthen their control capacities by making available to them, particularly at the current critical stage, *inter alia*, reconnaissance and spraying aircraft, means of transport and liaison, degradable insecticides, spraying equipment, and, where necessary, specialized technicians, and to continue this assistance as long as the infestation lasts;

6. *Calls upon* the international community, particularly the developed countries, to support fully the locust and grasshopper control activities undertaken at the national and regional levels by the affected countries, particularly in Africa, specifically in the areas of data collection and dissemination of information, prevention, co-ordination and funding, the establishment of national and regional early warning systems, and the strengthening of existing national systems for the protection of plant life;

7. *Invites* the international community, particularly the developed countries, to help the affected countries to improve to a considerable extent the present methods of monitoring and control and, specifically, to use remote-sensing techniques as a means of improving the quality of meteorological observations and forecasting in the affected countries, particularly in the regions where locust and grasshopper infestations originate;

8. *Also invites* the international community, including the organizations of the United Nations system and specifically the United Nations Development Programme, to continue to contribute to the funding for the establishment of programmes agreed on by the affected countries for the training of specialized personnel in the modern techniques of locust and grasshopper control;

9. *Calls upon* the international scientific community to develop co-ordinated research programmes to identify new and more effective methods of control, with a view to establishing a reliable forecasting system that would permit a better understanding of the relationship between climatic phenomena and the bio-ecology of the desert locust;

10. *Requests* the Director-General of the Food and Agriculture Organization of the United Nations, in close co-operation with the relevant organizations of the United Nations system, including the United Nations Environment Programme, the World Health Organization and the United Nations Development Programme, to undertake an assessment of the pesticides and techniques currently used in the fight against locust and grasshopper infestation, in particular the biological fight against the reproduction of larvae, and to test the efficacy of those pesticides and techniques, bearing in mind their effects on the natural environment and the health of the people living in the affected zones;

11. *Urges* the multilateral financial and development institutions, including the United Nations Development Programme, to give high priority, within the framework of their activities, to the fight against locust and grasshopper infestation and to grant financial and technical assistance to the affected countries, particularly those which have issued appeals for international assistance or have declared a state of emergency;

12. *Requests* the Secretary-General to seek the views of the international *ad hoc* group of experts established as part of the preparations for the International Decade for Natural Disaster Reduction on the fight against locust and grasshopper infestation, with particular reference to the scope of research programmes on its biological, bio-climatic and chemical aspects and on the risks of mutation that might make locusts more resistant to insecticides or to the effects of climate;

13. *Also requests* the Secretary-General, in co-operation with the Director-General of the Food and Agriculture Organization of the United Nations, to consult with Member States and competent organizations concerning the establishment, under the auspices of the United Nations and the technical and organizational responsibility of the Food and Agriculture Organization of the United Nations, of an international operational entity operating at the regional or subregional levels to provide direct support to the countries affected and to undertake co-ordinated actions to control locusts and grasshoppers, particularly in regions that are seriously infested and/or to which access is difficult;

14. *Requests* the Director-General of the Food and Agriculture Organization of the United Nations to establish, to that end, a focused and action-oriented working group of representatives of the affected countries, the donor countries and relevant organizations to prepare a detailed plan to fight locust and grasshopper infestation, including the necessary modalities and means for the establishment of such an operational entity;

15. *Agrees* that the actions proposed above will be financed through extrabudgetary resources and requests the Secretary-General, in co-operation with the Director-General of the Food and Agriculture Organization of the United Nations, to mobilize voluntary contributions, if appropriate through a pledging conference, for the fight against locust and grasshopper infestation;

16. *Encourages* the Secretary-General to keep under review the question of the locust and grasshopper infestation, particularly in Africa, and to undertake, in consultation with the Director-General of the Food and Agriculture Organization of the United Nations, the necessary action to make the world community more aware of the disastrous cumulative consequences of locust and grasshopper infestation, specifically with respect to food security;

17. *Decides* to include in the provisional agenda of its forty-fourth session the question of locust and grasshopper infestation, particularly in Africa, and requests the Secretary-General to submit to the General Assembly at that session, through the Economic and Social Council at its second regular session of 1989, a detailed report on the implementation of the provisions of the present resolution, including a report of the Director-General of the Food and Agriculture Organization of the United Nations on developments in the fight against locust and grasshopper infestation.

General Assembly resolution 43/203

20 December 1988   Meeting 83   Adopted without vote

Approved by Second Committee (A/43/918) without vote, 23 November (meeting 44); draft by Albania, Argentina, Bahamas, Bahrain, Bangladesh, Barbados, Belgium, Bolivia, Brazil, Canada, Chile, China, Colombia, Costa Rica, Cuba, Democratic Yemen, Denmark, Dominican Republic, Ecuador, El Salvador, Fiji, France, German Democratic Republic, Germany, Federal Republic of, Greece, Grenada, Guatemala, Guyana, Haiti, Honduras, Indonesia, Iran, Iraq, Ireland, Italy, Jamaica, Japan, Lao People's Democratic Republic, Luxembourg, Malta, Nepal, Netherlands, Nicaragua, Pakistan, Panama, Papua New Guinea, Paraguay, Peru, Philippines, Poland, Portugal, Qatar, Romania, Saint Kitts and Nevis, Saint Lucia, Saint Vincent and the Grenadines, Samoa, Saudi Arabia, Singapore, Spain, Sri Lanka, Sweden, Thailand, Trinidad and Tobago, Turkey, United Kingdom, United

States, Uruguay, Vanuatu, Venezuela, Yemen, Yugoslavia, Zaire (for African Group) (A/C.2/43/L.41/Rev.1); agenda item 86.
Meeting numbers. GA 43rd session: 2nd Committee 26, 28-30, 36-38, 41, 44; plenary 83.

Disaster preparedness and prevention

In his report on UNDRO activities during 1988 and 1989,[4] the Secretary-General stated that disaster mitigation (prevention and preparedness) activities fell into two broad categories: those of a technical and preventive nature involving the scientific and engineering aspects of disaster reduction and related legislation, including estimating the frequency and magnitude of future hazards, delineation of high-risk areas, identifying restrictions to be placed on land use and urban development in such areas and reinforcing structures to resist the largest hazards that could reasonably be expected; and logistical planning or preparedness activities involving preparation of plans for alert and evacuation in the face of imminent danger, as well as for post-disaster rescue and provision of food and shelter for victims. Related aspects included establishing criteria for decision-making to implement the elements of the plan, training local officials and educating the population in high-risk areas. Comprehensive disaster mitigation programmes recommended by UNDRO and implemented with UNDRO assistance in a number of countries involved a five-step sequence of activities covering those categories.

Since 1988 coincided with the preparation phase for the International Decade for Natural Disaster Reduction (see below), the period was one of increased world-wide awareness of the benefits of disaster preparedness and prevention, and the number of requests to UNDRO for assistance increased accordingly. The report described regional and national projects carried out during the year. In addition to regional workshops and seminars, an international training seminar on engineering aspects of earthquake mitigation was held at Dushanbe, USSR, in October.

International Decade for Natural Disaster Reduction

In response to a 1987 resolution,[25] in which the General Assembly designated the 1990s as a decade in which the international community, under the auspices of the United Nations, would pay special attention to fostering international co-operation in the field of natural disaster reduction, the Secretary-General submitted in October 1988 a progress report on preparations for the decade.[26]

The report noted that it was not possible to estimate the loss of human lives and damage caused by natural disasters, especially since many went unreported. However, major disasters in 1988 alone, which included extensive floods in Bangladesh and the Sudan, a hurricane in the Caribbean, a typhoon in China, an earthquake in the border region of India and Nepal, a landslide in Venezuela and locust infestations in northern Africa, accounted for at least 18,000 deaths and a minimum of $3 billion in material damage.

The report gave examples of the potential of disaster-mitigation measures for reducing human and material losses and outlined preparations for the International Decade for Natural Disaster Reduction. It noted that the Secretary-General, in February 1988, established a steering committee on the Decade to assist him in developing a framework to attain its objectives and goals. In addition, he appointed a panel of 25 eminent scientists and experts which held two meetings in 1988 (Geneva, 5-8 July; New York, 3-6 October). Two additional metings were tentatively scheduled for 1989. In March 1988, in Washington D.C., the United Nations, in co-operation with the United States National Academy of Sciences, convened an informal meeting of scientists, engineers and representatives of the United Nations system to review the possible orientation of and preparatory arrangements for the Decade. Also, on 29 July, the Director-General for Development and International Economic Co-operation drew the attention of Member States to the provision of the 1987 Assembly resolution[25] regarding the establishment of national committees. Governments were asked to provide information on action taken towards establishing such committees or other official bodies for the Decade. The report also commented on co-operation with non-governmental and intergovernmental organizations and on funding and secretariat support.

The report stated that the United Nations system had a critical catalytic and facilitating role in inspiring and supporting the activities of local communities, national authorities, regional organizations and the international community as a whole. It was also called on to become an international centre for exchanging information, storing documentation and co-ordinating international efforts. Several United Nations entities had a long tradition in promoting the study of natural disaster phenomena and the application of counter-disaster measures. Many activities of those entities lent themselves to achieving the Decade's goals and objectives and that experience was being mobilized in the preparations.

GENERAL ASSEMBLY ACTION

On 20 December, on the recommendation of the Second Committee, the General Assembly adopted **resolution 43/202** without vote.

International Decade for Natural Disaster Reduction

The General Assembly,

Considering that natural disasters, particularly in the past two decades, have adversely affected the lives of at least 800 million people and caused considerable damage to infrastructure and property worldwide, especially in developing countries,

Recalling that in 1988 many countries suffered severe natural disasters, such as the extensive floods in the Sudan and Bangladesh, typhoons in the Philippines, hurricanes in countries of Latin America and the Caribbean, locust infestations, mainly in Africa, and other natural disasters in several regions of the developing world, and recognizing the pressing need for reducing the impact of natural disasters for all people, in particular those in developing countries,

Recognizing the important responsibility of the United Nations system as a whole for promoting international co-operation in the study of natural disasters and in the development of techniques to mitigate risks arising therefrom, as well as for providing assistance and co-ordinating disaster relief, preparedness and prevention,

Recalling its resolution 42/169 of 11 December 1987, in which it decided to designate the 1990s as a decade in which the international community, under the auspices of the United Nations, would pay special attention to fostering international co-operation in the field of natural disaster reduction,

Taking note of Economic and Social Council resolution 1988/51 of 26 July 1988 on assistance in cases of natural disaster and other disaster situations,

Noting with appreciation the progress that has been made in the preparations for the International Decade for Natural Disaster Reduction, within the United Nations system as well as by Member States, since the adoption of resolution 42/169,

Welcoming the establishment by the Secretary-General of the international *ad hoc* group of experts on the Decade,

Convinced that concerted international action for the reduction of natural disasters over the course of the 1990s would give genuine impetus to a series of concrete measures at the national, regional and international levels,

Welcoming the fact that national committees on natural disaster reduction have been established in some countries and that preparations for establishing such committees are under way in other countries,

1. *Takes note with interest* of the progress report of the Secretary-General on the preparations for the International Decade for Natural Disaster Reduction;

2. *Notes with satisfaction* the progress made by the international *ad hoc* group of experts on the Decade in the preparations for the Decade;

3. *Reiterates its request* to the Secretary-General, made in paragraph 5 of resolution 42/169, to develop an appropriate framework of action at all levels for attaining the objective and goals referred to in paragraphs 3 and 4 of that resolution;

4. *Requests* the Secretary-General further to strengthen co-ordination within the United Nations system in order to ensure better preparation of the Decade;

5. *Calls upon* all Governments further to prepare for participation during the Decade in concerted international action for the reduction of natural disasters by, as appropriate, establishing national committees in co-operation with the relevant scientific and technological communities;

6. *Also calls upon* Governments to keep the Secretary-General informed of their countries' plans and of assistance that can be provided so that the United Nations may become an international centre for the exchange of information and the co-ordination of international efforts concerning activities in support of the objective and goals of the Decade, thus enabling each Member State to benefit from the experience of other countries;

7. *Emphasizes* the importance of technical co-operation among developing countries and mutual assistance in the transfer of technology, and encourages the international community to play a prominent role as promoter and catalyst of technical and scientific co-operation among developing countries in the field of natural disaster reduction;

8. *Expresses its appreciation* to those countries which have provided or pledged voluntary contributions for the preparation of the report to be submitted to the General Assembly at its forty-fourth session pursuant to paragraph 5 of resolution 42/169, and calls upon other countries, international organizations and other organizations to provide voluntary contributions for that purpose;

9. *Requests* the Secretary-General to bring to the attention of the international *ad hoc* group of experts on the Decade in its future work the increasingly serious problems of locust infestation and floods;

10. *Requests* the Secretary-General to incorporate in the report to be submitted pursuant to paragraph 5 of resolution 42/169 a definition of the catalytic and facilitating role of the United Nations system, including that described in paragraph 6 above, and to submit that report to the General Assembly at its forty-fourth session through the Economic and Social Council, as requested in resolution 42/169.

General Assembly resolution 43/202

20 December 1988   Meeting 83   Adopted without vote

Approved by Second Committee (A/43/918) without vote, 23 November (meeting 44); draft by Austria, Burundi, China, Czechoslovakia, France, Germany, Federal Republic of, Greece, Hungary, Iceland, Ireland, Italy, Japan, Mongolia, Poland, Tunisia (for Group of 77), Turkey (A/C.2/43/L.37/Rev.1); agenda item 86.

Meeting numbers. GA 43rd session: 2nd Committee 26, 28-30, 36-38, 40, 44; plenary 83.

REFERENCES

[1]YUN 1987, p. 452, GA dec. 42/433, 11 Dec. 1987. [2]A/43/731. [3]YUN 1987, p. 451. [4]A/45/271-E/1990/78 & Corr.1. [5]A/43/375-E/1988/73 & Corr.1. [6]YUN 1987, p. 1106, GA res. 42/226 A, 21 Dec. 1987. [7]DP/1989/50. [8]DP/1989/13/Add.2 (Part II). [9]E/1988/19 (dec. 88/41). [10]YUN 1987, p. 453. [11]*Ibid.*, p. 679, GA res. 42/187, 11 Dec. 1987. [12]TD/B/1180. [13]A/43/15, vol. II (dec. 361(XXXV)). [14]*Ibid.* (dec. 362(XXXV)). [15]A/43/243. [16]DP/1989/13/Add.1. [17]A/43/245. [18]SG/CONF.4/1. [19]DP/1989/13/Add.2 (Part I). [20]YUN 1986, p. 483, GA res. 41/185, 8 Dec. 1986. [21]YUN 1987, p. 458. [22]E/1988/19 (dec. 88/32). [23]DP/PROJECTS/REC/29 & Corr.1. [24]A/43/688. [25]YUN 1987, p. 459, GA res. 42/169, 11 Dec. 1987. [26]A/43/723.

Emergency relief and assistance

Afghanistan

Following the signing on 14 April 1988 of the Geneva Accords between Afghanistan and Pakistan on the one hand and by the USSR and the United States as guarantors on the other, which began the peace process in Afghanistan after nine years of war (see PART TWO, Chapter III), the Secretary-General, on 11 May, appointed Sadruddin Aga Khan as Co-ordinator for United Nations Humanitarian and Economic Assistance Programmes relating to Afghanistan.

Since 1979, more than 5.5 million people had had to abandon their homes, lands and country to seek asylum in other countries, particularly Iran and Pakistan, and more than 2 million had also fled their homes to the apparent safety of urban centres and remote rural areas. The return of those displaced persons to their home areas would be one of the world's largest operations, as it amounted to the resettlement of some 45 per cent of Afghanistan's total population. The war not only had caused the reported deaths of almost a million people but had resulted in the permanent disablement of tens of thousands. As a consequence, there were hundreds of thousands of widows, orphans and disabled people who would need care and assistance for years to come. In addition, Afghanistan had suffered extensive damage to all sectors of its economy.

On 10 June, the Secretary-General launched an appeal for humanitarian relief and economic assistance to Afghanistan comprising two phases. The first related to immediate relief and rehabilitation and was allocated an 18-month time frame with a total cost of some $1.2 billion. The second consisted of longer-term rehabilitation of the country's infrastructure covering three years with a cost of some $839.6 million.

On 14 June 1988, a Conference on United Nations Humanitarian and Economic Assistance Programmes relating to Afghanistan was held in New York. The Conference had before it a report by the Co-ordinator,[1] in which he stated that the co-ordinated programme was a collaborative undertaking involving many agencies and programmes of the United Nations system. Inter-agency meetings were held in New York on 28 and 29 April and at Geneva on 23 May. The Co-ordinator visited the executive heads of FAO, IFAD, UNDP, the United Nations Children's Fund (UNICEF), the Office of the United Nations High Commissioner for Refugees (UNHCR), the World Food Programme (WFP) and the World Health Organization (WHO) and had consultations with the International Committee of the Red Cross and the League of Red Cross and Red Crescent Societies. At the end of May, he led a mission to the region and had discussions with the Governments of Afghanistan, Iran and Pakistan. The Co-ordinator outlined the programme and his own role, described arrangements required to assist voluntary repatriation, and discussed other components of the programme—food aid and related logistical support; agriculture, irrigation and rural development; health programmes and water supply; human resources and culture; and communications, industry and natural resources.

On 24 June, the Afghanistan Emergency Trust Fund, administered by the Co-ordinator, was established to receive cash donations. Inputs of food and other contributions in kind would be routed directly to the agency or programme concerned, with the Co-ordinator being informed of such contributions.

In his first consolidated report,[2] the Co-ordinator stated that a number of countries pledged or deposited initial contributions at the 14 June Conference and further pledges and contributions were received following visits by him to a number of donor countries. Those initiatives brought the total donor response to some $97 million by 31 August.

A Pledging Conference on United Nations Humanitarian and Economic Assistance Programmes relating to Afghanistan was held in New York on 12 October, to which the Co-ordinator submitted a report containing background information on programmes and projects.[3] He noted that the prolific deployment of mines was one of the most damaging aspects of the Afghanistan conflict and that his Office was developing training programmes in mine-clearance and mass public information and education in mine-recognition and avoidance. In response to the need for treatment and rehabilitation of the large number of disabled persons, particularly those suffering from war-related injuries, the Co-ordinator established a Committee on Actions for Disabled Afghans, the first meeting of which took place at Geneva on 1 September. The continuing conflict and fluid political situation within the country obstructed an early return of refugees from Iran and Pakistan. The Co-ordinator therefore initiated a series of missions to assess conditions and needs within Afghanistan, the first of which took place in late August and early September. He identified a number of projects to be carried out during the first 18 months of the relief and rehabilitation programme and gave estimates of their cost.

At the Pledging Conference, the Secretary-General and the Co-ordinator launched "Operation Salam", following which donors announced their pledges. The most important pledge was that of the USSR, the equivalent of $660 million, mostly in kind. Other generous pledges were made by a number of donors, both at the Conference and in the following weeks. The United States advised the Co-ordinator of its planned contribution in 1989: $33.1 million in food aid to WFP, $20 million to UNHCR and $2 million for the de-mining programme.

As at 31 December 1988, the total donor response to the Secretary-General's appeal amounted to some $890 million both in cash and in kind.

ECONOMIC AND SOCIAL COUNCIL ACTION

On 26 July, the Economic and Social Council, on the recommendation of its Third Committee, adopted **resolution 1988/52** without vote.

United Nations assistance programmes relating to Afghanistan

The Economic and Social Council,

Having considered the report of the Co-ordinator for United Nations Humanitarian and Economic Assistance Programmes relating to Afghanistan made before the Third (Programme and Co-ordination) Committee of the Council on 21 July 1988,

Convinced that a co-ordinated programme of assistance and relief efforts will entail collaborative undertakings by many different agencies and programmes within the United Nations system,

1. *Welcomes* the initiative of the Secretary-General, and supports the efforts of the Co-ordinator for United Nations Humanitarian and Economic Assistance Programmes relating to Afghanistan;

2. *Urges* all Member States to contribute to the fullest extent possible to the United Nations effort to assist the people of Afghanistan;

3. *Requests* all specialized agencies and United Nations bodies to participate actively in the fulfilment of the United Nations humanitarian and economic assistance programmes relating to Afghanistan.

Economic and Social Council resolution 1988/52

26 July 1988   Meeting 38   Adopted without vote

Approved by Third Committee (E/1988/111) without vote, 21 July (meeting 13); 21-nation draft (E/1988/C.3/L.10); agenda item 15.

Sponsors: Afghanistan, Australia, Belgium, Canada, Denmark, Finland, France, German Democratic Republic, Greece, India, Iran, Ireland, Japan, Norway, Pakistan, Portugal, Spain, Sweden, USSR, United Kingdom, United States.

Lebanon

In response to a 1987 General Assembly request,[4] the Secretary-General submitted a report on assistance for the reconstruction and development of Lebanon between August 1987 and July 1988.[5] He summarized the general situation affecting assistance efforts, including the overall performance of the Lebanese economy. With regard to the role of the United Nations, although the system had significantly upgraded its activities and presence in Lebanon, lack of political stability and security problems made it difficult for it to carry out its reconstruction and development programmes.

On receiving the findings of a high-level interagency mission which visited Lebanon in October 1987 to reassess emergency relief needs, the Secretary-General, in December, launched an appeal to the international community for approximately $85 million on behalf of the 250,000 most affected Lebanese families. As at 31 July 1988, over $70 million had been pledged by donor nations to United Nations agencies, the Lebanese Government and NGOs.

In order to ensure a co-ordinated and responsible distribution of donations received, the Secretary-General appointed Ragnar Gudmundsson as Special Representative for the Reconstruction and Development of Lebanon. He was also appointed the UNDP Resident Representative/Resident Co-ordinator for operational activities; he assumed his functions at Beirut in July 1988.

Because of the prevailing circumstances in Lebanon, United Nations activities continued to focus on providing emergency relief aid and the maintenance of essential services, such as health care and water supply. The report summarized the activities of the following United Nations programmes and specialized agencies: UNICEF, UNDP, UNDRO, UNHCR, WFP, ILO, FAO, UNESCO and WHO. The United Nations Interim Force in Lebanon provided humanitarian assistance in its area of operation in order to alleviate emergency needs and the United Nations Relief and Works Agency for Palestine Refugees in the Near East assisted Palestine refugees there (see PART TWO, Chapter IV).

The Secretary-General concluded that relief assistance from the international community in response to his appeal, either through United Nations channels or on a bilateral basis, significantly alleviated the suffering of the Lebanese people. Although there were signs of a slight improvement in the economic situation in the first half of 1988, the United Nations would continue its efforts to mobilize support in terms of emergency relief aid and assistance for Lebanon's reconstruction and development.

The future economic development of Lebanon and the well-being of its people depended on the restoration of peace, stability and mutual trust among the various parties. Circumstances permitting, the Secretary-General intended to send a high-level interagency mission to evaluate emergency needs and might again have to appeal for additional emergency relief assistance. He called on the parties concerned to promote the restoration of peace and stability in Lebanon.

UNDP action. On 1 July,[6] the UNDP Governing Council asked the Administrator to take urgent steps, in collaboration with the Government and the World Bank, to obtain the statistical data needed to adjust Lebanon's interim illustrative indicative planning figure (IPF) for the fourth planning cycle (1987-1991). He was also asked to continue to approve projects submitted by the Government to be financed by the IPF for the fourth cycle and by remaining funds brought forward from the third cycle. In addition, he was asked, in co-operation with the Government, to accelerate programme activities in Lebanon. In that regard, the Council authorized expenditures in the next year up to 60 per cent of the current provisional IPF for the fourth cycle and the carry-over from the third cycle. The Council decided to consider the situation in Lebanon as a matter of priority in 1989.

ECONOMIC AND SOCIAL COUNCIL ACTION

On 26 July, the Economic and Social Council, on the recommendation of its Third Committee, adopted **resolution 1988/50** without vote.

Assistance for the reconstruction and development of Lebanon

The Economic and Social Council,

Referring to General Assembly resolution 42/199 of 11 December 1987 and previous resolutions in which the Assembly requested the specialized agencies and other organizations and bodies of the United Nations system to expand and intensify their programmes of assistance in response to the needs of Lebanon,

Aware of the deteriorating socio-economic conditions of the Lebanese people and the magnitude of their unmet needs,

Noting with great concern the unprecedented inflation in Lebanon during the last four years and the catastrophic erosion of the value of the Lebanese currency, which is now worth only one hundredth of its value in October 1984,

Appeals to all Member States and all organizations of the United Nations system to continue and intensify their efforts to mobilize all possible assistance for the Government of Lebanon in its reconstruction and development efforts, in accordance with the relevant resolutions and decisions of the General Assembly and the Economic and Social Council.

Economic and Social Council resolution 1988/50

26 July 1988   Meeting 38   Adopted without vote

Approved by Third Committee (E/1988/111) without vote, 15 July (meeting 8); 21-nation draft (E/1988/C.3/L.3); agenda item 15.
Sponsors: Algeria, Bahrain, Bangladesh, Canada, France, Greece, Iraq, Italy, Japan, Jordan, Kuwait, Lebanon, Libyan Arab Jamahiriya, Morocco, Oman, Qatar, Somalia, Sudan, Syrian Arab Republic, Tunisia, Yugoslavia.

GENERAL ASSEMBLY ACTION

On 20 December, on the recommendation of the Second Committee, the General Assembly adopted **resolution 43/207** without vote.

Assistance for the reconstruction and development of Lebanon

The General Assembly,

Recalling its resolution 42/199 of 11 December 1987 and its previous resolutions on assistance for the reconstruction and development of Lebanon,

Taking note of Economic and Social Council resolution 1988/50 of 26 July 1988 and recalling the previous relevant resolutions and decisions of the Council,

Noting with deep concern the grave deterioration of the economic situation in Lebanon,

Reaffirming the urgent need for further international action to assist the Government of Lebanon in its continuing efforts for reconstruction and development,

Welcoming the determined efforts of the Government of Lebanon in undertaking its reconstruction and rehabilitation programme,

Noting with appreciation the appointment by the Secretary-General of the Special Representative for the Reconstruc-

tion and Development of Lebanon and Resident Co-ordinator of the operational activities for development of the United Nations system in Lebanon,

Taking note of the report of the Secretary-General and of the statements made on 8 November 1988 by the Under-Secretary-General for Political and General Assembly Affairs and Secretariat Services and by the Special Representative of the Secretary-General,

Noting with satisfaction that the United Nations Development Programme is resuming its programme in Lebanon,

1. *Expresses its appreciation* to the Secretary-General for his report and for the steps he has taken to mobilize assistance to Lebanon;

2. *Commends* the Under-Secretary-General for Political and General Assembly Affairs and Secretariat Services for his co-ordination of system-wide assistance to Lebanon;

3. *Requests* the Secretary-General to continue and intensify his efforts to mobilize all possible assistance within the United Nations system to help the Government of Lebanon in its reconstruction and development efforts;

4. *Expresses its appreciation* for the appointment by the Secretary-General of the Special Representative for the Reconstruction and Development of Lebanon and Resident Co-ordinator of the operational activities for development of the United Nations system in Lebanon;

5. *Calls upon* the organs, organizations and bodies of the United Nations system to intensify their programmes of assistance and to expand them in response to the pressing needs of Lebanon, and to take the necessary steps to ensure that their offices at Beirut are adequately staffed at the senior level;

6. *Requests* the Secretary-General to report to the General Assembly at its forty-fourth session on the progress made in the implementation of the present resolution.

General Assembly resolution 43/207

20 December 1988   Meeting 83   Adopted without vote

Approved by Second Committee (A/43/918/Add.2) without vote, 21 November (meeting 43); 10-nation draft (A/C.2/43/L.45); agenda item 86.
Sponsors: Bahrain, France, Italy, Jordan, Lebanon, Madagascar, Mauritania, Saudi Arabia, Tunisia, Spain.
Meeting numbers. GA 43rd session: 2nd Committee 26, 28-30, 36-38, 42, 43; plenary 83.

Mozambique

In accordance with a 1986 General Assembly request,[7] an oral report was made on 7 July 1988 to the Economic and Social Council's Third Committee on assistance to Mozambique. By **decision 1988/158** of 26 July, the Council took note of that report.

In an August report to the Assembly,[8] the Secretary-General stated that he had consulted with the Government of Mozambique on the implementation of the 1986 resolution on assistance to it.[7] He had been informed that, while Mozambique was endeavouring to maintain its regular development programmes, much of its energy and resources were taken up in pursuing its emergency and rehabilitation programme (1987-1990), which combined short-term emergency relief with rehabilitation and development activities, with the support of the international community. Since a comprehensive report, prepared by Mozambique in collaboration with the United Nations for a donors' conference in April 1988 (see below), covered emergency and rehabilitation needs, the Government decided that there was no need for another full report to be submitted to the Assembly until its emergency and rehabilitation programme was fully launched and funded. The Secretary-General therefore submitted an interim report on assistance to Mozambique.

The interim report stated that social and economic conditions in Mozambique had been deteriorating since the early 1980s, when the country began to experience sabotage, terrorism and a major disruption of its social life as a result of externally supported acts of destabilization. Together with adverse climatic conditions in a number of regions, the situation brought about a decline in agricultural production of over 50 per cent between 1981 and 1986. The internal conflict continued unabated, resulting in over 2.2 million Mozambicans being affected by severe food shortages and an additional 1.1 million displaced from their homes. In 1987, the Government launched its emergency and rehabilitation programme with substantial support from the World Bank, IMF and the United Nations system. Since the programme's introduction, real GDP was estimated to have risen by 4 per cent in 1987 and rural and industrial production had grown by 10 per cent.

On 26 and 27 April 1988, under the aegis of the United Nations, the Conference on Emergency Assistance to Mozambique was held at Maputo, attended by delegations from 37 countries and many intergovernmental and non-governmental organizations. The Conference raised some $270 million against a target of $330 million, with the bulk of contributions directed towards food aid and logistical requirements.

The report discussed the deterioration in Mozambique's economy since the early 1980s and described the evolution of the emergency situation, including recent developments such as floods, a tropical depression, late and insufficient rainfall and infestations of pests. Violence continued to disrupt relief efforts in many areas and lack of security hampered relief distribution to outlying districts. Since government forces had retaken several zones from bandits, a massive return of Mozambicans in Malawi to those zones was foreseen, adding to the country's food shortage.

The report concluded by outlining new economic policies instituted by the Government and action undertaken within the context of the emergency and rehabilitation programme.

GENERAL ASSEMBLY ACTION

On 20 December, on the recommendation of the Second Committee, the General Assembly adopted **resolution 43/208** without vote.

Assistance to Mozambique

The General Assembly,

Recalling Security Council resolution 386(1976) of 17 March 1976,

Recalling also its relevant resolutions, in particular resolution 41/197 of 8 December 1986, in which it urged the international community to respond effectively and generously to the call for assistance to Mozambique,

Having considered the report of the Secretary-General on assistance to Mozambique, including the annex thereto,

Considering that Mozambique continues to face a complex emergency situation of extreme proportions, as illustrated in the report of the Secretary-General,

Noting with deep concern that Mozambique has continued to suffer from the cumulative and negative impact of externally supported acts of destabilization, as well as persistent natural disasters, resulting in, *inter alia*, enormous losses of human life, widespread destruction of infrastructure and large numbers of displaced persons, which, combined with an adverse international economic situation, have led to an overall retrogression of the country's development,

Recognizing that substantial international assistance is still required for the implementation of emergency, reconstruction and development projects,

Stressing that a proper response to the emergency situation in Mozambique requires the reinforcement of relief aid with additional rehabilitation and development assistance,

1. *Takes note* of the report of the Secretary-General on assistance to Mozambique, including the annex thereto;

2. *Welcomes* the efforts undertaken by the Government of Mozambique, as reflected in its emergency and economic recovery programmes, and, in this context, stresses the imperative need for substantial international assistance in support of these efforts;

3. *Expresses its appreciation* to, and commends, the Secretary-General and the relevant organizations of the United Nations system for the measures taken to organize international assistance programmes for Mozambique;

4. *Expresses its gratitude* to all States and regional, intergovernmental and non-governmental organizations that have rendered assistance to Mozambique;

5. *Notes,* however, that the total assistance provided to date to Mozambique continues to fall short of the country's urgent requirements;

6. *Reiterates its appeal* to the international community to continue to provide relief aid, including food aid and logistics support, so as to improve distribution capability and prevent further widespread starvation;

7. *Draws the attention* of the international community to the non-food sectors, as described in the documents of the Conference on Emergency Assistance to Mozambique, held at Maputo on 26 and 27 April 1988, the funding of which continues to lag, particularly the agriculture, health and education sectors;

8. *Calls upon* Member States, regional and interregional organizations and other intergovernmental and non-governmental organizations to provide and expand technical, financial and other material assistance to Mozambique wherever possible, especially in the form of grants, and urges them to give priority to the inclusion of Mozambique in their development assistance programmes;

9. *Invites* the appropriate organizations and programmes of the United Nations system, in particular the United Nations Development Programme, the Food and Agriculture Organization of the United Nations, the International Fund for Agricultural Development, the World Food Programme, the World Health Organization, the United Nations Children's Fund, the United Nations Population Fund and the United Nations Industrial Development Organization, to maintain and increase their current and future programmes of assistance to Mozambique;

10. *Requests* the Secretary-General:

(a) To continue his efforts to mobilize the financial, technical and material assistance required by Mozambique;

(b) To continue to co-ordinate the work of the United Nations system, in close co-operation with the Government of Mozambique, in the implementation of the country's emergency and rehabilitation programmes;

(c) To keep the situation in Mozambique under constant review, to maintain close contact with Member States, organs and organizations of the United Nations system, and to apprise the Economic and Social Council, at its second regular session of 1989, of the status of the programmes of assistance to Mozambique;

(d) To prepare, on the basis of consultations with the Government of Mozambique, a report on the implementation of the emergency and rehabilitation programmes for that country and to submit the report to the General Assembly at its forty-fifth session.

General Assembly resolution 43/208

20 December 1988   Meeting 83   Adopted without vote

Approved by Second Committee (A/43/918/Add.2) without vote, 21 November (meeting 43); 44-nation draft (A/C.2/43/L.48); agenda item 86.

Sponsors: Afghanistan, Algeria, Angola, Argentina, Austria, Bangladesh, Barbados, Brazil, Bulgaria, Burkina Faso, Burundi, Canada, Cape Verde, Chad, China, Congo, Cuba, Egypt, Ethiopia, German Democratic Republic, Ghana, Italy, Madagascar, Mali, Mauritania, Mongolia, Morocco, Mozambique, Nepal, Nicaragua, Nigeria, Pakistan, Portugal, Romania, Sao Tome and Principe, Spain, Sudan, Tunisia, Uganda, United Republic of Tanzania, Yugoslavia, Zaire, Zambia, Zimbabwe.

Meeting numbers. GA 43rd session: 2nd Committee 26, 28-30, 36-38, 42, 43; plenary 83.

Somalia

On 31 October 1988, the President of Somalia drew the attention of the Secretary-General to the grave humanitarian situation that had developed in the northern provinces of Somalia as a result of attacks by armed bandits on towns and villages and on public installations, and to the urgent need for emergency assistance to help cope with the large numbers of displaced persons and the repair, rehabilitation and reconstruction of vital public facilities and installations. The President stated that more than 600,000 people were estimated to be in camps and another 400,000 were scattered about the countryside. In one town alone (Hargeysa), 70 per cent of permanent dwellings had been destroyed or badly damaged. Schools, hospitals, public markets and power and water installations had been destroyed.

GENERAL ASSEMBLY ACTION

On 20 December, on the recommendation of the Second Committee, the General Assembly adopted **resolution 43/206** without vote.

Emergency assistance to Somalia

The General Assembly,

Taking note of the message addressed to the Secretary-General by the head of State of Somalia, in which he drew attention to the grave humanitarian situation that has developed in the northern provinces of Somalia as a result of attacks by armed bandits on towns and villages and on public installations, and appealed for emergency assistance to help the Government cope with the large numbers of displaced persons and the repair, rehabilitation and reconstruction of vital public facilities and installations,

Conscious of the critical economic problems already confronting Somalia, as well as the great burden that has been imposed on its economy by the massive presence of over 700,000 refugees,

Bearing in mind that Somalia has been included in the list of least developed countries of the world and that its social and economic infrastructure is barely sufficient to meet the needs of its own inhabitants,

Recognizing that the widespread destruction that has taken place in the northern provinces of Somalia requires the immediate response of the international community for an emergency assistance programme that would provide food, water and shelter for the inhabitants made homeless as a result of these events, and for a programme of emergency assistance and rehabilitation to enable the affected population to return to their homes and become self-reliant,

1. *Expresses* its solidarity with the Government and people of Somalia in facing the complex disaster situation in the northern provinces;

2. *Welcomes* the current efforts of the Secretary-General and the appropriate organizations of the United Nations system and the assistance so far provided to the people and Government of Somalia in coping with the emergency;

3. *Requests* the Secretary-General to continue his efforts to mobilize international assistance and to co-ordinate the efforts of the appropriate organizations of the United Nations system in order to respond in a concerted and effective manner to the request of the Government of Somalia for humanitarian assistance, and to carry out an assessment of priority humanitarian needs, in close co-operation with the government authorities and with the organizations of the United Nations system, and bring the findings to the attention of the international community without delay;

4. *Calls upon* all States and the competent intergovernmental and non-governmental organizations to provide financial, material and technical assistance to ensure an effective response to the needs identified by the Secretary-General for relief operations, rehabilitation and reconstruction;

5. *Requests* the Secretary-General to apprise the Economic and Social Council at its first regular session of 1989 of his efforts and to report to the General Assembly at its forty-fourth session on the implementation of the present resolution.

General Assembly resolution 43/206

20 December 1988   Meeting 83   Adopted without vote

Approved by Second Committee (A/43/918/Add.2) without vote, 15 November (meeting 42); draft by Zaire, for African Group (A/C.2/43/L.38); agenda item 86.
Meeting numbers. GA 43rd session: 2nd Committee 26, 28-30, 36-38, 40, 42; plenary 83.

Sudan

In June 1988, the Prime Minister of the Sudan requested the Secretary-General to alert the international community to the grave situation in his country and to appeal for emergency assistance to respond to the urgent requirements of the affected people. In an October report to the General Assembly on emergency assistance to the Sudan,[9] the Secretary-General stated that over the preceding few years the Sudan had found it increasingly difficult to cope with the cumulative impact of ongoing or recurrent emergencies such as internal strife, floods, drought, widespread famine, locust depredations and influxes of refugees from neighbouring countries. Those emergencies had created additional social and economic burdens for the Sudanese people who were already adversely affected by the depressed state of the country's economy.

In response to the Government's request for support in order to undertake a review of the situation, to update data on the number, condition and background of the affected population and to develop a strategy for early implementation of a programme of immediate emergency assistance, the Secretary-General sent a high-level mission to the Sudan in July. However, torrential rains and devastating floods in early August effectively paralysed Khartoum until mid-September, wrought additional destruction in several parts of the country and delayed implementation of the agreed programme by two months.

In late September, a follow-up inter-agency mission travelled to all accessible parts of the country where large numbers of displaced people were reported. The mission discussed its findings and recommendations with the Prime Minister before leaving the country on 11 October. The Secretary-General noted that the Assembly had adopted **resolution 43/8** on 18 October dealing with the floods in the Sudan. His report responded to the Assembly's request that he keep the international community informed of the Sudan's emergency, rehabilitation and reconstruction needs.

Following a description of the background to the crisis in the Sudan, the report outlined the response of the United Nations to the emergency and summarized a policy statement of the Government. It then described an overall emergency strategy for assistance to displaced persons, to be based on a three-pronged approach focused on the

geographic areas where the needs of the people were the most acute.

With regard to emergency humanitarian requirements, it was estimated that the total cost would amount to some $69.7 million.

GENERAL ASSEMBLY ACTION

On 6 December, on the recommendation of the Second Committee, the General Assembly adopted **resolution 43/52** without vote.

Special programme of assistance to the Sudan
The General Assembly,

Recalling its resolution 43/8 of 18 October 1988 on emergency assistance to the Sudan, in which it recognized the disastrous impact of torrential rains and unprecedented floods that devastated Khartoum and the north of the country in August 1988, causing the destruction of over 300,000 dwellings and widespread damage to the country's social and economic infrastructure,

Recalling the Substantial New Programme of Action for the 1980s for the Least Developed Countries,

Deeply concerned about the serious plight of over two million Sudanese nationals who have been displaced or seriously affected by civil strife, famine and drought,

Noting that these grave problems are in addition to those already created in the country by the presence of over one million refugees,

Deeply conscious of the urgent need to take emergency action to alleviate the suffering of these victims and improve the conditions of life of the displaced population,

Conscious of the great efforts of the Government and the people of the Sudan in responding to the urgent humanitarian needs of the displaced population,

Noting with satisfaction the prompt response made by a number of Governments, international agencies and non-governmental organizations in providing emergency relief,

Recognizing that the magnitude of these disasters and their long-term consequences will require, in addition to the ongoing efforts of the Government and the people of the Sudan, a demonstration of international solidarity and humanitarian concern to ensure broad support in order to meet immediate emergency as well as longer-term rehabilitation needs,

Taking note of the report of the Secretary-General concerning the findings and recommendations of a high-level mission, which assessed the conditions of the displaced population and assisted in the formulation of an interim assistance programme focusing on the urgent humanitarian and rehabilitation requirements of the displaced,

1. *Expresses its solidarity* with the Government and the people of the Sudan in facing a grave and complex humanitarian and economic situation;

2. *Expresses its gratitude and appreciation* to Governments and international and non-governmental organizations that provided support and assistance to the Government of the Sudan in its relief and rehabilitation efforts;

3. *Recognizes* the valuable efforts of the Government of the Sudan to provide assistance to the people affected;

4. *Recognizes also* the importance of intense and wide co-operation with international relief organizations, as well as non-governmental organizations, to ensure the

provision of humanitarian assistance where needed in all areas affected;

5. *Takes note* of the interim assistance programme contained in the report of the Secretary-General;

6. *Calls upon* all States to contribute generously to programmes for the relief and rehabilitation of displaced persons;

7. *Expresses its appreciation* to the Secretary-General for his efforts to make the international community more aware of the enormous difficulties facing the displaced population and to mobilize assistance to the Sudan;

8. *Welcomes* the decision of the Secretary-General to organize, as requested by the Government of the Sudan and in close co-operation with the United Nations Development Programme and the World Bank, a meeting of bilateral donors and pertinent international institutions and non-governmental organizations in order to mobilize resources needed to implement a follow-up

emergency assistance programme covering the rehabilitation and resettlement needs of displaced persons;

9. *Requests* the Secretary-General to apprise the Economic and Social Council at its first regular session of 1989 of his efforts and to report thereon to the General Assembly at its forty-fourth session.

General Assembly resolution 43/52

6 December 1988   Meeting 70   Adopted without vote

Approved by Second Committee (A/43/918/Add.1) without vote, 10 November (meeting 40); draft by Vice-Chairman (A/C.2/43/L.34), based on informal consultations on 29-nation draft (A/C.2/43/L.20); agenda item 86 *(b)*.
Meeting numbers. GA 43rd session: 2nd Committee 26, 28-30, 36-38, 40; plenary 70.

REFERENCES

[1]SG/CONF.3/1. [2]UNOCA/1988/1 & Add.1. [3]SG/CONF.3/2. [4]YUN 1987, p. 463, GA res. 42/199, 11 Dec. 1987. [5]A/43/727. [6]E/1988/19 (dec. 88/31 B). [7]YUN 1986, p. 465, GA res. 41/197, 8 Dec. 1986. [8]A/43/514. [9]A/43/755.

Chapter IV

International trade, finance and transport

Although global trade expanded rapidly in 1988, growth was largely concentrated in the developed market-economy countries. Some areas of the world, particularly countries of Africa and Latin America, continued to perform unsatisfactorily, due mainly to their debt burden and the economic disorder caused by it. Prices of primary commodities showed some improvement, enhancing the import capacity of some commodity producers, but that was more than offset by a large increase in the price of manufactures.

Two landmarks in international trade during the year gave cause for renewed optimism. First, negotiations under the Global System of Trade Preferences were successfully concluded, which, it was hoped, would be a catalyst for creating a potentially dynamic preferential market among developing countries, stimulating global trade and making developing countries more important trading partners for industrialized countries. Secondly, the final obstacle towards implementing the Common Fund for Commodities was overcome and the Agreement was expected to come into force in 1989.

The gravity of the debt problem, which dominated the relationship between the developed and the developing countries, was discussed by the Trade and Development Board of the United Nations Conference on Trade and Development (UNCTAD) and by the General Assembly. In December, the Assembly noted that it was essential to reaffirm the shared responsibility of all parties involved and requested the Secretary-General to continue his efforts towards a common understanding on a solution (resolution 43/198). Following consideration of a report of the Secretary-General on international monetary issues, the Assembly requested him to monitor the international monetary situation and provide information on proposals for convening a conference on the topic (43/187).

In the area of international transport, seaborne trade and maritime transport improved in 1988 as the world economy showed signs of recovery and the price of oil fell. However, the disequilibrium between demand and supply of tonnage remained a serious problem for the industry. Developing countries were also plagued by the high proportion of freight costs to cost, insurance and freight import values as compared to that for developed market-economy countries.

UNCTAD VII follow-up

In September/October 1988,[1] the UNCTAD Trade and Development Board (TDB) evaluated progress made in implementing the Final Act of the seventh (1987) session of the Conference (UNCTAD VII).[2]

Following a debate on the issue, the TDB President summed up the views expressed. There was general agreement on the importance of carrying forward the implementation of the Final Act in order to revitalize development, growth and international trade. Representatives noted that some progress had been achieved and certain advances made since UNCTAD VII, particularly in relation to official resource flows to certain groups of developing countries. However, there was a general sense among members of the Group of 77 developing countries that overall progress in the implementation process had been slow and fell short of expectations based on the commitment embodied in the Final Act. They cited the inadequacy of responses to the debt problem of developing countries, their overall need for external resources for development on appropriate conditions, the unavailability of liquidity, exchange instability, the need to strengthen the role of the commodity sector, commitments on standstill and roll-back, structural adjustment, progress in the Uruguay Round of multilateral trade negotiations in areas of interest to developing countries, maintenance of the generalized, non-discriminatory and non-reciprocal character of the generalized system of preferences and support for the development efforts of the least developed countries (LDCs).

The importance of follow-up work by the UNCTAD intergovernmental machinery, including the Board, and by the UNCTAD secretariat was stressed.

REFERENCES
[1]A/43/15, vol. II. [2]YUN 1987, p. 465.

International trade

International trade grew faster than expected in 1987, according to the *World Economic Survey 1988*,[1] with the volume of world trade increasing by just over 4 per cent. The growth was mostly accounted for by a noticeable improvement in non-oil trade. The value of world trade rose by around 15 per cent in United States dollar terms, partly reflecting the fall of the dollar in 1987. Exports increased to approximately $2.4 trillion; agricultural exports increased by about 4 per cent and exports of manufactures attained a growth rate of 5 per cent after a 3.5 per cent increase in 1986. There were indications that the rate of increase of exports was likely to be sustained in 1988.

The improved performance of world trade was due mainly to an increase in the imports of the developed market economies and to the vigorous performance in the non-fuel exports of the developing countries. Total imports of the developed market economies grew by over 5 per cent. This growth reflected not only buoyant trade among those economies, but also an increase in their imports from developing countries. Developing countries as a whole increased their imports by 2.5 per cent, although imports of the energy-exporting developing countries declined. There was an increase of almost 23 per cent in current dollar terms of the export of manufactures from the newly industrializing economies to the developed market economies.

Trade policy

The UNCTAD *Trade and Development Report, 1988*[2] stated that, despite repeated commitments by the major trading nations towards the liberalization of international trade, the extent to which trade flows were managed was on the increase. The gradual abandonment of multilateralism in favour of the bilateral approach to resolving international trade conflicts translated itself into increasing protectionism through the application of a wide range of non-tariff measures (NTMs), which had serious consequences for the exports of the developing countries in particular. The resurgence of protectionist trade policies was a response to wide fluctuations in exchange rates, to demand-management policies to control inflation and the attendant slow economic growth of the developed market economies, and to the increasing competitiveness of the exports of the newly industrializing countries.

The *World Economic Survey 1988*[1] observed that the signing of a bilateral trade agreement between Canada and the United States in December 1987 and the imminent conclusion of a similar agreement between Mexico and the United States, although indicative of the trend towards bilateralism in international trade relations, should significantly expand the area of freer trade.

An encouraging sign was the continuing belief of countries in the multilateral system, as demonstrated through the growing use of the General Agreement on Tariffs and Trade (GATT) dispute settlement procedures and the number of countries wishing to join GATT. The progress made in the Uruguay Round of multilateral trade negotiations and the intense interest generated by the mid-term review of those negotiations were also testimony to the desire of countries to strengthen the multilateral trading system.

Uruguay Round of multilateral trade negotiations

The end of 1988 marked the mid-term of the Uruguay Round of multilateral trade negotiations, which were launched in September 1986 at Punta del Este, Uruguay.[3] The mid-term review was intended to address the difficulties that had emerged and to provide a timely impetus to the negotiating process (see PART SEVEN, Chapter XVIII).

TDB, as mandated by UNCTAD VII,[4] considered developments and issues in the Uruguay Round of particular concern to developing countries. The UNCTAD secretariat submitted a document by the Group of 77 setting forth its views.[5] On 30 September, TDB decided to annex the document to its report.[6]

According to the Group of 77, the progress achieved so far in the Round was clearly uneven. The developing countries were disconcerted by the unsatisfactory progress recorded in such areas as the implementation of standstill and roll-back commitments, tropical products, textiles and agriculture. In general, the positions and interests of the developing countries were not being given favourable consideration in keeping with the spirit of the Punta del Este meeting in 1986. In particular, the developing countries called on the developed countries to fulfil their commitments on standstill and roll-back of NTMs and to provide restriction-free entry for tropical products into their markets. They were also of the view that there should be a clear demonstration of political will to return the textiles trade to the GATT rules and that concrete progress should be achieved towards removing distortions and liberalizing trade in agriculture. The Group of 77 stressed that the principle of differential and more favourable treatment for developing countries, as provided for in the Punta del Este Declaration,[3] should also be assessed at the mid-term review in December 1988. The Group also pointed to other developments which risked jeopardizing the outcome of the negotiations, including the tendency on the part of some developed countries to link trade in goods with matters such as developing countries' policies on foreign direct investment, protection of intellectual property, services and fair labour standards, and the continuing monetary and financial instability in the world economy and its effect on the developing countries.

Technical assistance

On 10 May,[7] TDB requested the secretariats of UNCTAD and the United Nations Development Programme (UNDP) to finalize expeditiously consultations on project proposals for technical assistance to developing countries in connection with the Uruguay Round. It invited UNDP to consider favourably and expedite its decision on the project proposals and called on the UNCTAD Secretary-General to take steps to make fully operational the programme of technical assistance, keep interested member States informed of the programmes under implementation and continue to consult with other organizations in order to enhance co-ordination and complementarity of technical assistance activities.

GENERAL ASSEMBLY ACTION

The General Assembly, on 20 December 1988, on the recommendation of the Second (Economic and Financial) Committee, adopted **resolution 43/188** without vote.

Report of the Trade and Development Board
The General Assembly,

Recalling its resolution 1995(XIX) of 30 December 1964, as amended, on the establishment of the United Nations Conference on Trade and Development and the Final Act adopted by the Conference at its seventh session, held at Geneva from 9 July to 3 August 1987,

Recalling also its resolution 42/175 of 11 December 1987 on the seventh session of the Conference,

Noting that the *Trade and Development Report, 1988* has made a constructive contribution to the consideration by the Trade and Development Board, at the first part of its thirty-fifth session, of the interdependence of problems of trade, development finance and the international monetary system, as well as to the Board's consideration of the debt and development problems of the developing countries,

1. *Takes note* of the report of the Trade and Development Board on the second part of its thirty-fourth session, and the first part of its thirty-fifth session;

2. *Welcomes* the review of the implementation of the guidelines contained in the annex to Board resolution 222(XXI) of 27 September 1980 undertaken by the Board at its thirty-fifth session and urges the Governments concerned to implement fully the relevant provisions contained in Board resolution 358(XXXV) of 5 October 1988;

3. *Urges* all Governments, bearing in mind their particular contributions, commensurate with their economic weight, and their commitments as embodied in the Final Act, to give full and prompt effect to the policies and measures agreed to therein through continuing action, individually and collectively and in competent international organizations, in pursuit of the objective of revitalizing development, growth and international trade;

4. *Requests* the Board, in accordance with its mandate, to keep under review the implementation of the relevant provisions of the Final Act;

5. *Welcomes* the contribution of the Board to intergovernmental discussions on the interdependence of economic issues and policies, particularly in the interrelated areas of trade, money, finance, debt, commodities and development, and notes the efforts under way to enhance the outcome of the Board's debates on interdependence, as well as the substantive linkages with other discussions on related questions in the United Nations Conference on Trade and Development and other organizations;

6. *Stresses* that it is important that the Uruguay Round of multilateral trade negotiations respond positively to the interests and concerns of all parties thereto, in accordance with its objectives, and that it promote growth and development, particularly in developing countries;

7. *Invites* the Board to continue to follow closely developments and issues in the Uruguay Round that are of particular concern to the developing countries;

8. *Notes* that the Board has been requested to review and study, in depth, developments in the international trading system; in doing so it could, respecting the principles of most-favoured-nation treatment and non-discrimination, make recommendations on principles and policies related to international trade and make proposals as to the strengthening and improvement of the trading system, with a view to giving it a more universal and dynamic character, as well as to making it more responsive to the needs of developing countries and supportive of accelerated economic growth and development, particularly of developing countries;

9. *Notes also* the imminent entry into force of the Agreement Establishing the Common Fund for Commodities and invites the ratifying States, with the active support of the secretariat of the United Nations Conference on Trade and Development, to take the necessary action to bring the Common Fund into operation at an early date as an important and useful instrument of international co-operation on commodities;

10. *Takes note* of Board decision 356(XXXIV) of 10 May 1988 containing agreed conclusions regarding trade relations among countries having different economic and social systems, urges the Board to elaborate further a programme for the promotion of trade and economic co-operation among countries having different economic and social systems, in particular East-South trade, and requests the Secretary-General of the United Nations Conference on Trade and Development, in his consultations referred to in paragraph 105 (27) of the Final Act, to seek ways and means of broadening and strengthening inter-system trade relations, in particular East-South trade;

11. *Invites* the Board to contribute effectively to the preparations for the international development strategy for the fourth United Nations development decade, in close co-operation with the *Ad Hoc* Committee of the Whole for the Preparation of the International Development Strategy for the Fourth United Nations Development Decade.

General Assembly resolution 43/188

20 December 1988   Meeting 83   Adopted without vote

Approved by Second Committee (A/43/915/Add.2) without vote, 6 December (meeting 47); draft by Vice-Chairman (A/C.2/43/L.77 & Corr.1), based on informal consultations on draft by Tunisia, for Group of 77 (A/C.2/43/L.55); agenda item 82 *(b)*.

Meeting numbers. GA 43rd session: 2nd Committee 21-26, 30, 42-44, 46, 47; plenary 83.

Data base on trade measures

On 10 May,[8] TDB, recognizing that the UNCTAD data base on trade measures was a valuable source of information on general and product-specific trade measures, decided that the UNCTAD secretariat should provide the information contained in the data base and noted that any dissemination would be the secretariat's responsibility. It also decided that the Intergovernmental Group of Experts on Definitions and Methodology Employed in the UNCTAD Data Base on Trade Measures should examine the methodology employed in the data base to improve its utility for analytical purposes and make provision for the comments of member States to be reflected in it. The UNCTAD secretariat was asked to take action on the recommendations of the Group of Experts.

The Group, at its second session (Geneva, 16-20 May 1988),[9] examined questions of definitions and methodology employed in the data base and adopted recommendations for submission to TDB. The recommendations covered measures for the inclusion of comments of member States, expansion of country coverage and scope of trade measures, the updating of the data base, questions relating to nomenclature and verification, use of data base material, analysis, technical assistance and co-operation with other organizations. The Group urged the secretariat to continue to refine the methodology, to examine the comparability of data to improve its assessment of NTMs, and to give priority to the needs of developing countries in this area.

On 5 October,[6] TDB took note of the Group's report.

Protectionism and structural adjustment

In April/May 1988, TDB conducted its annual review of protectionism and structural adjustment. UNCTAD VII[4] had agreed that the review should have wider coverage by taking into account the specific interests of developing countries.

The Board had before it a two-part UNCTAD secretariat report,[10] part I of which covered developments in trade action and trade legislation in 1987, assessed official trade intervention and discussed selected issues such as tropical products, trade measures in high technology sectors and national mechanisms for fighting protectionism. It also gave a profile of tariffs in developed market-economy countries and addressed the prospects for trade expansion for developing countries that could result from tariff liberalization. Part II examined trends in production and trade in all sectors and their underlying factors. It also discussed economic policies and structural adjustment in pursuit of international competitiveness. An addendum to the report[11] contained statistical information.

The Board also had before it information provided by member States[12] on action taken by them relevant to agreements and commitments in an UNCTAD VI (1983) resolution that dealt with the subject.[13]

The Administrative Committee on Co-ordination (ACC), in April, adopted a decision[14] in which it agreed that achieving a stronger social consensus was a particularly important condition for effective stabilization and structural adjustment programmes. It called for action among organizations of the United Nations system to develop a system-wide approach to structural adjustment and related issues.

In October,[15] ACC considered that increased collaboration and concerted action within the United Nations system should continue to promote structural adjustment policies that would lead to a more efficient allocation of resources and provide an adequate basis for renewed growth and development. It also considered that the United Nations system should pool its information and experience so as to assist developing countries in formulating their medium- and long-term development policies and, in particular, in devising the best way to address social priorities, including the needs of the most disadvantaged, during the adjustment process.

GENERAL ASSEMBLY ACTION

In October 1988, the Second Committee had before it a draft resolution[16] on protectionism and structural adjustment, consideration of which had been postponed annually by the Assembly since 1980. By the draft, the Assembly would urge developed countries to refrain from introducing new tariff and non-tariff barriers affecting the exports of developing countries, eliminate existing barriers, and provide market access for the products of those countries.

On 20 December, by **decision 43/438**, the Assembly, on the recommendation of the Second Committee, deferred consideration of the draft until its 1989 session.

In **resolution 43/198** on the external debt crisis, the Assembly stressed that a supportive international economic environment, together with a growth-oriented development approach, was needed by debtor countries to alleviate the political and social costs of structural adjustment programmes and adjustment fatigue in order to restore their economic growth, development and credit-worthiness.

Trade preferences

Generalized system of preferences

TDB's Special Committee on Preferences (fifteenth session, Geneva, 24 May-1 June)[17] considered the secretariat's eleventh general report[18] on the implementation of the generalized system of preferences (GSP), which described changes and improvements in GSP and provided information on its trade effects.

In 1988, the European Economic Community (EEC), under its scheme, started to define product coverage in terms of a combined goods nomenclature. It also introduced a new method to calculate the setting of preferential limits in textiles and suspended the Republic of Korea from preferences. The United States decided to graduate Hong Kong, the Republic of Korea, Singapore and Taiwan from its scheme.

In analysing the trade effects of GSP from available information, the report stated that, although in 1986 more than $40 billion of imports from developing countries received preferential access to developed countries, less than one fourth of dutiable imports from beneficiaries had actually received preferential treatment.

The Special Committee on Preferences also considered the report of its Working Group on Rules of Origin on its 1987 session,[19] and a report on technical co-operation in 1986 and 1987 in connection with GSP.[19]

Sri Lanka, on behalf of the Group of 77 developing countries, submitted a draft decision,[20] by which the Special Committee would have agreed that preference-giving countries should try to improve significantly their GSP schemes by expanding product coverage and deepening the preferential margins to duty-free levels. It would have requested preference-giving countries to refrain from excluding products already in their schemes, declared that they should ensure the maintenance and improvement of preferential margins sufficient to enable beneficiary countries to penetrate the market and maintain a position in it, urged Governments, particularly those of preference-giving countries, to make financial and other contributions to the UNCTAD Trust Fund for technical assistance programmes on GSP and requested the UNCTAD secretariat to produce a consolidated digest of all schemes. The draft was considered by a Contact Group of the Chairman, but agreement could not be reached on a consolidated text. The Special Committee decided to annex the draft to its report to TDB and agreed on the need for further work on rules of origin and on the importance of technical assistance for better utilization of GSP.

Global system of trade preferences among developing countries

The Ministerial Meeting on the Global System of Trade Preferences among Developing Countries (GSTP) was held at Belgrade, Yugoslavia, from 11 to 13 April 1988,[21] and culminated in the adoption of the Agreement on the Global System of Trade Preferences among Developing Countries.[22] The Agreement, by which the Meeting's participants established GSTP to promote and sustain mutual trade and develop economic co-operation among developing countries through exchange of concessions, comprised 34 articles covering establishment and aims, principles, components and schedules of concessions of GSTP, negotiations, a committee of participants, ground rules, consultations and settlement of disputes and final provisions. Annexes to the Agreement listed the 48 participants in the Agreement and dealt with rules of origin, additional measures in favour of LDCs and schedules of concessions.

The Agreement stipulated that GSTP would be reserved for the exclusive participation of members of the Group of 77, would be based on the principle of mutuality of advantages in such a way as to benefit equitably all participants, would be negotiated step by step, improved and extended in successive stages, with periodic reviews, and would reinforce subregional, regional and interregional groupings. The Agreement would enter into force 30 days after 15 of the participating States had deposited their instruments of ratification. The Agreement's operation would be the responsibility of a Committee of Participants, which would, on the Agreement's entry into force, carry forward the task of launching the next round of negotiations.

The Meeting decided the Chairman of the Group of 77 should continue negotiations in order to find an appropriate and acceptable arrangement for China's participation in GSTP.

By the Belgrade Declaration, the Meeting announced the opening of the Agreement for signature and called on signatories to conclude expeditiously the ratification procedures. It called on signatories and other members of the Group of 77 to undertake preparatory work for the next round of negotiations, which would facilitate the process of accession and carry forward the exchange of trade concessions. Participants were urged to implement fully all commitments regarding special treatment for and additional measures in favour of LDCs. The Ministers also adopted resolutions on special measures of assistance for the Palestinian people, by which they called for granting trade concessions and concrete preferential measures to Palestinian exports, and on Panama, by which they expressed their rejection of the coercive economic measures being applied against Panama which affected the autonomy and threatened the economic security of a Group of 77 member country and called for their immediate revocation.

The Ministerial Meeting was preceded by a Meeting of Senior Officials (6-9 April) which recommended the draft Belgrade Declaration for adoption.

Trade among countries having different economic and social systems

At its April/May session, TDB had before it a report by the UNCTAD secretariat on trends and policies in trade and economic co-operation among countries having different economic and social systems.[23] The report described major trends in the economic performance of the socialist countries of Eastern Europe and innovations in their foreign trade management systems, and inter-systems trade and economic co-operation. It then discussed action arising from the relevant provisions of the Final Act of UNCTAD VII.[24] On the question of elaborating a programme for further promoting inter-systems trade and economic co-operation, the report suggested that the Board's session might provide an opportunity to exchange opinions, to be further examined at a later stage by a group of experts with a view to finalizing the issue at TDB's spring 1989 session. Regarding the UNCTAD Secretary-General's consultations with Governments for further strengthening of inter-systems trade, as called for by UNCTAD VII, the report proposed an approach that would identify modalities appropriate for trade expansion. The results of those consultations could also be reported to the Board's spring 1989 session. As to technical assistance to promote trade between developing countries and the socialist countries of Eastern Europe, UNCTAD was revising a programme for the remaining years of the fourth programming cycle of UNDP (1987-1991).

On 10 May,[25] TDB agreed on the feasibility of elaborating a programme for the further promotion of trade and economic co-operation among countries having different systems, particularly East-South trade. It also agreed that a number of additional inputs to the programme, an outline of which it annexed to its decision, should be transmitted to the Board at its spring 1989 session. Those inputs would be supplemented by a report by the UNCTAD Secretary-General on his consultations with Governments. In his consultations, the Secretary-General would also discuss the composition and terms of reference of an intergovernmental group of experts that might contribute to elaborating the programme.

TDB agreed that it was necessary to improve further the secretariat's analytical work and asked the UNCTAD Secretary-General to highlight the following topics in his 1989 report: influences and policy implications of the principal factors in inter-systems trade, including the impact of structural adjustment and economic reform processes; financing of inter-systems trade and economic co-operation, including the relative role of different payment arrangements; and GSP schemes of the socialist countries of Eastern Europe.

The UNCTAD Secretary-General was asked to develop further, in co-operation with UNDP, technical assistance to developing countries, particularly LDCs, in their trade and economic co-operation with the socialist countries of Eastern Europe. UNDP was invited to expedite its decision on technical assistance projects submitted by UNCTAD.

Trade promotion and facilitation

During 1988, United Nations bodies continued to assist developing countries to promote their exports and to facilitate the movement of goods in international commerce. The International Trade Centre (ITC) continued to play a leading role in the delivery of technical co-operation projects.

International Trade Centre

During 1988, ITC, under the joint sponsorship of UNCTAD and GATT, continued to serve as a focal point for United Nations assistance to developing countries in formulating and implementing trade promotion programmes.[26]

In 1988, ITC's expenditures on technical co-operation activities rose by 24.6 per cent to some $26.3 million, after two consecutive years at about $21 million. The increase was largely attributable to expenditure on UNDP projects, particularly the interregional, regional and national projects that became fully operational in 1988. Those projects contributed to a rise of 34 per cent in the annual expenditures under UNDP-financed projects, bringing the total to $13 million. In addition, increased trust fund contributions from a number of traditional donor countries were paralleled by a 16.7 per cent increase in expenditures, which reached $13.3 million in 1988.

ITC assistance to developing countries in institutional infrastructure for trade promotion at the national level sought increasingly to improve the overall institutional framework for foreign trade by strengthening existing institutions, encouraging the reallocation of functions according to clearer and better co-ordinated strategies, and improving co-ordination mechanisms between Governments and business organizations active in foreign trade. Some 30 ITC technical co-operation projects were operational under the subprogramme in all developing regions.

In export market development, over 100 projects were operational in 1988 in trade information, product and market development and export development of commodities.

Under the specialized national trade promotion services subprogramme, ITC continued to provide assistance to improve administrative and technical skills in export packaging, export finance, costing and pricing, trade fairs and commercial publicity, export quality control, national commercial representation, legal aspects of foreign trade, export co-operation schemes for small and medium-sized enterprises, export-oriented joint ventures and the international physical distribution of goods.

The total value of ITC assistance to LDCs in 1988 constituted over 30 per cent of its total programme resources. The subprogramme focused attention on urgent export development problems affecting products from a number of LDCs, namely coffee, tea, cotton yarns and grey cloth. ITC also gave priority in its training events to participants from LDCs and a number of those events were oriented towards the export development requirements of those countries.

Other ITC technical assistance subprogrammes dealt with commodity promotion, which concentrated mainly on jute products; human resource development for trade promotion, which continued to emphasize the strengthening of training institutions, training of trainers and developing training materials; import operations and techniques; and technical co-operation with national chambers of commerce. The Centre also carried out work on trade between developing countries and the socialist countries of Eastern Europe, technical and economic co-operation among developing countries, and the participation of women in trade promotion activities.

During the year, 11 projects were evaluated, 5 in Africa, 2 in Asia and the Pacific, 1 in Latin America and 3 interregional projects; 5 were financed by UNDP and 6 from trust funds. It was observed that some projects were unrealistically designed, in that resources were insufficient to meet objectives. It was also noticeable that some project objectives were not specific enough or were equated with the implementation of activities, which did not facilitate the evaluation of end-results.

JAG action. The Joint Advisory Group (JAG) on ITC (twenty-first session, Geneva, 11-15 April)[27] had before it the annual report on ITC activities during 1987,[24] a report on an evaluation of supply-demand surveys as an area of activity[28] and a report of a meeting on that subject (Geneva, 12-14 January 1988).[29]

In its general recommendations, JAG proposed that future annual reports should be improved to include suggestions for future action; expanded extrabudgetary resources should be made available to ITC in order to improve the ability of developing countries to secure export revenues; ITC should strengthen its co-operation with international development assistance bodies, regional development banks and bilateral assistance agencies; more intensive use should be made of expertise available in developing countries in connection with ITC's enterprise approach, which in turn should be fostered—because of its emphasis on

exports—to enable developing countries to improve their export capabilities in the short and medium term; ITC should seek to expand and diversify its technical co-operation work in commodities and intensify its actions in favour of LDCs; and technical co-operation in support of technical consultancy enterprises in developing countries should be expanded.

In reviewing ITC activities by subprogrammes, JAG recommended that ITC should continue its efforts to assist national trade promotion organizations in implementing strategies and programmes, including the exchange of information among them; it should continue to assist in developing and consolidating trade information services, especially the Latin American service (PLACIEX); the Executive Director should report on studies concerning charging for trade information services and make recommendations; ITC should continue marketing assistance to developing countries in the area of non-traditional exports and foster production development for export through the promotion of joint ventures; it should expand enterprise-oriented technical co-operation and promote wider dissemination among developing countries of its reports on technical co-operation; it should study the possibility of providing assistance in organizing export services fairs, the upgrading of the commercial representation of developing countries and the international physical distribution of goods; special attention should be given to the training of trainers and personnel of national trade promotion organizations, and timely information on training events and expanded participation in those events should be pursued, with closer co-operation with UNCTAD and GATT in training activities; and the participation of women in training programmes should also be fostered. JAG also recommended that high priority should be given to assisting LDCs and an increased flow of resources should be sought towards that end, as well as contingency funds to respond to urgent requests for technical assistance. ITC should be encouraged to utilize to the fullest extent possible available expertise in the socialist countries of Eastern Europe, and efforts should be increased to enhance the participation of women in trade promotion activities.

Financial report

On 21 December 1988, in **resolution 43/216**, the General Assembly accepted the financial report and audited financial statements and report of the Board of Auditors on ITC for the biennium ending 31 December 1987.[30]

Restrictive business practices

The UNCTAD Intergovernmental Group of Experts on Restrictive Business Practices postponed its seventh session (originally scheduled to be held from 3 to 7 October) to 1989.

Commodities

The UNCTAD Committee on Commodities held its thirteenth session at Geneva from 5 to 13 December 1988.[31] The Committee had before it a report on recent developments in the world commodity situation,[32] which reviewed the commodity export earnings of developing countries during 1985 and 1986, commodity prices in 1987 and 1988 and the outlook for prices, and the operation of international commodity agreements. Information on the disposal of non-commercial stocks was provided in an annex to the report.

The report noted that there had been a general upward but fluctuating trend in commodity prices in 1987 and the first half of 1988. Despite the price index for the principal commodity exports of developing countries having reached, in June 1988, its highest level in more than six years, it was still considerably below its 1979-1981 average in both nominal and real terms. Particular commodity groups and individual commodities were also subject to divergent movements and considerable fluctuations. Although prices of agricultural raw materials, vegetable oilseeds and oils and some minerals had improved, there had been little change in the market situation of tropical beverages.

In 1985 and 1986, the developing countries saw a steady general decline in their commodity export earnings, thus exacerbating their debt-servicing obligations. Nevertheless, very few developing countries had resorted to International Monetary Fund compensatory financing to make up for the shortfall. Supply and demand of commodities were also affected by agricultural support policies, particularly those of the United States, EEC and Japan, concern for which resulted in inclusion of a comprehensive negotiating mandate on agriculture in the Uruguay Round of multilateral trade negotiations.

Also before the Committee was a report on results of comprehensive consultations with producers and consumers on individual commodities not covered by international commodity agreements/arrangements (bananas, bauxite, cotton and cotton yarns, hard fibres and products, manganese, meat, phosphates, tea and vegetable oils and oilseeds, excluding olive oil),[33] and a review of the Committee's work programme, the implementation of decisions relating to it and proposals for further work.[34]

On 13 December,[35] the Committee adopted an agreed conclusion, stating that it would continue to undertake a comprehensive review of the commodity situation and outlook. Several topics would be included in the review, in particular the results of the in-depth assessment of African commodities and the scope for export diversification, to be undertaken within the framework of the United Nations Programme of Action for African Economic Recovery and Development (see preceding chapter).

With respect to individual commodities, the Committee would consider the results of intergovernmental consultations, negotiations and follow-up action on commodities not covered by existing international agreements. The Committee endorsed the programme of its Working Party on Diversification, Processing, Marketing and Distribution, including Transportation, and requested that a study on those issues be prepared for the United Nations Conference on LDCs scheduled for September 1990, identifying their particular needs and problems. In a broader framework, the Committee would consider developments relating to market access for commodities and ways of improving the competitiveness of natural products with respect to synthetics and substitutes. It would also analyse factors affecting the expansion of commodity trade, particularly the identification of further possibilities for strengthening co-operation on individual commodity markets, aimed at stimulating the consumption of those commodities and expansion of trade.

GENERAL ASSEMBLY ACTION

In accordance with a 1987 General Assembly decision,[36] the Assembly's Second Committee had before it in 1988 a draft resolution on commodities[37] submitted by the Group of 77 in 1985.[38]

By **decision 43/438** of 20 December, the Assembly deferred consideration of the draft until 1989.

Common Fund for Commodities

With the ratification by Maldives on 11 July 1988 of the Agreement Establishing the Common Fund for Commodities, the main outstanding condition for the Agreement's entry into force (that ratifying countries should represent two thirds of the Fund's directly contributed capital) was fulfilled. The Agreement would be brought into force at a meeting of ratifying countries to be convened by the UNCTAD Secretary-General. At the December 1988 meeting of the Committee on Commodities (see above), the UNCTAD Secretary-General suggested 30 June 1989 as a possible date for the entry into force.

Signatures and ratifications

As at 31 December 1988,[39] the 1980 Agreement Establishing the Common Fund for Commodities[40] had been signed by 120 States and EEC, and 103 States had formally adhered by ratifying, accepting, approving or acceding to it. Of those, Maldives and Mauritania signed the Agreement during 1988, and Cuba, Honduras, Maldives and Swaziland ratified it.

Individual commodities

In accordance with an UNCTAD VII request,[41] the UNCTAD Secretary-General in 1988 convened a number of consultations with producers and consumers on several commodities not covered by international commodity agreements or arrangements. A report by the UNCTAD secretariat to the December 1988 meeting of the Committee on Commodities[33] described antecedents and possible options for future producer-consumer co-operation in respect of the individual commodities concerned. In an oral update to the Committee on the consultations, an UNCTAD secretariat representative stated that there had been four consultations on bananas, five on bauxite, six on cotton, five on hard fibres, four on manganese, two on meat, four on phosphates, six on tea and four on vegetable oils. The results had been modest, although the principal exporters of bananas had indicated the desire to revise and update the draft programme on research and development and to explore the possibilities for negotiating an international agreement on bananas, without economic clauses.

Agricultural commodities

Cocoa. Buffer stock purchases of cocoa beans, under the 1986 International Cocoa Agreement,[42] resumed in January 1988, having been suspended in June 1987. At a March meeting of the International Cocoa Council, the time-limit for depositing instruments of ratification, acceptance or approval of the Agreement by signatory Governments was extended until 30 September 1988. At a September meeting, the time-limit was again extended until 30 September 1989. During 1988,[39] France accepted the Agreement, Italy ratified it and Trinidad and Tobago and Yugoslavia acceded to it.

Rubber. The International Rubber Agreement, 1987,[43] entered into force provisionally on 29 December 1988, when Governments representing at least 75 per cent of net exports and imports had deposited their instruments of ratification, accession, acceptance or approval or had indicated that they would apply the Agreement provisionally.

During 1988,[39] six countries ratified or accepted the Agreement, bringing the total to eight; 14 countries agreed to apply the Agreement provisionally.

Sugar. The International Sugar Agreement, 1987,[43] came into force provisionally on 24 March 1988. The International Sugar Council, on 18 May, decided to extend for an indefinite period the validity of the conditions for accession for the countries listed in Annexes A and B of the Agreement.

During 1988,[39] 16 countries ratified, acceded to or accepted the Agreement, bringing the total to 22 countries and EEC; 24 countries agreed to apply the Agreement provisionally, bringing the total to 33.

Minerals and metals

Copper. In accordance with a recommendation of the 1987 Preparatory Meeting on Copper,[44] the United Nations Conference on Copper, 1988, met at Geneva from 13 to 24 June 1988 to negotiate the establishment of an autonomous producer-consumer forum or group for copper. During the Conference, the Intergovernmental Group of Experts on Market Development for Copper met on 13, 14 and 16 June.[45] The Group discussed the structure of market development activities, their funding and the policies and strategies of various organizations in their approach to market development.

On 24 June,[46] the Conference requested the UNCTAD Secretary-General to make arrangements to reconvene the Conference as early as possible for a period of two weeks in order to conclude negotiations on an autonomous producer-consumer forum or group for copper. He was also requested to prepare revised, annotated, draft terms of reference reflecting the outcome of the negotiations and to submit them to the Conference's next session. Statements of position on the resolution were reproduced in a separate document.[47]

Iron ore. The Intergovernmental Group of Experts on Iron Ore[48] held its second session from 7 to 11 March 1988 at Geneva, the first having been held in 1986.[49]

The Group considered statistical issues and the impact and effect of energy costs on the consumption of metallics, such as scrap, pig iron and directly reduced iron (sponge iron), and reviewed the current market situation and outlook for iron ore. The Group recommended that TDB convene a third session in 1989, with a view to continuing the review of statistics and market developments relating to iron ore and reporting thereon to the Fifth Preparatory Meeting on Iron Ore.

Tin. On the recommendation of the Preparatory Meeting on Tin (Geneva, 11-15 April 1988),[50] the United Nations Tin Conference, 1988, met at Geneva from 21 November to 2 December[51] to discuss the negotiation of the establishment of an intergovernmental producer-consumer forum or group for tin.

On 2 December, the Conference adopted a resolution[52] by which it decided that it should be reconvened in order to complete the negotiation of the draft terms of reference for an international tin study group, which were contained in an annex to the resolution. The UNCTAD Secretary-General was requested to make arrangements for the reconvening of the Conference in March/April 1989.

Tungsten. At its twentieth session (Geneva, 7-11 November),[53] the Committee on Tungsten reviewed the question of stabilizing the tungsten market with a view to enabling producing and consuming countries to agree on market stabilization measures and the convening of a negotiating conference. The Committee had before it reports by the UNCTAD secretariat on recent developments and short-term outlook in the tungsten market[54] and major aspects of structural change in consumption.[55]

With regard to its future work, it was the general view of participants that the Committee should consider studies relating to structural change and its effect on consumption and supply; competition from substitutes, the recycling of tungsten scrap and developments in the tool sectors; consumption trends for intermediate products; price elasticities for tungsten in individual consuming industries; and a survey of mine and plant closures and idle capacities.

The Committee agreed that the UNCTAD secretariat would undertake, for the twenty-first (1989) session, an in-depth analysis of substitution prospects with emphasis on ceramics and cermets. It would also review existing research and development programmes to promote new applications for tungsten and a survey of industry and government views on the need for additional programmes. The Committee decided to retain the 1988 agenda for its 1989 session.

Services

A section of the *Trade and Development Report, 1988*[2] was devoted to the role of services in the world economy.

The *Report* examined the growing role of the service sector in the developed market economies, particularly in generating new employment. It also reviewed international trade in services and observed the position of services with respect to other components of the current account in different countries; explained the broader strategic role of services; and examined policy issues arising from transnationalization of services, including discussions in the Uruguay Round of what constituted

appropriate regulation. The *Report* also addressed the role of services in the economies of the socialist countries of Eastern Europe. In its summary of findings, it outlined a series of policy conclusions aimed at identifying appropriate action at the national, regional and international levels to maximize the contribution of services to the development process.

One of the basic issues raised in the study was that of an acceptable definition of trade in services, a subject that became a major issue in the Uruguay Round, where negotiations were being conducted to establish a multilateral framework of rules and principles for trade in services, with a view to expanding such trade under conditions of transparency and progressive liberalization.

The role of services in the process of structural adjustment was also discussed in a report on protectionism and structural adjustment,[10] presented by the UNCTAD secretariat to TDB in April. The report reiterated earlier findings on the reasons for the growth of this sector in the developed market economies, but indicated that those economies had recently been exploring possible policy options for stimulating the producer service sector in support of the manufacturing, agricultural and other service sectors. In many developing countries, however, the producer service sector was not well developed, and that weakness was one of the major factors hindering the shift from low value-added agricultural and industrial sectors to higher value-added production.

In another report[56] submitted to TDB in April, the UNCTAD secretariat outlined its latest findings on international trade in goods and services and concluded that there was a need to ensure that developing countries shared the experiences of the advanced countries and that they participated in multilateral efforts to establish an improved system of internationally comparable data on services. In view of the priority need for developing countries to develop a services infrastructure and the producer services sector, their international competitiveness in both goods and services would have to be pursued through multilateral cooperation and negotiation. The report also stated that the UNCTAD secretariat and some developed countries had been responding to requests for technical assistance from developing countries to assess the role of the service sector in their economies.

Consumer protection

As a follow-up to the adoption by the General Assembly in 1985[57] of a set of guidelines for consumer protection, the Economic and Social

Council, in 1988, discussed the implementation of these guidelines.

On 27 July 1988, on the recommendation of its Third (Programme and Co-ordination) Committee, the Economic and Social Council adopted **resolution 1988/61** without vote.

Consumer protection

The Economic and Social Council,

Recalling General Assembly resolution 39/248 of 9 April 1985, in which the Assembly adopted guidelines for consumer protection,

1. *Urges* all Governments to implement the guidelines for consumer protection and encourages them to develop further, as appropriate, national legislation and policies in this field;

2. *Requests* the Secretary-General to continue to promote, subject to the availability of extrabudgetary resources, the implementation of the guidelines and to ensure system-wide co-ordination in this regard;

3. *Also requests* the Secretary-General, in co-operation with the development funds and programmes of the United Nations, the regional commissions and other relevant bodies and agencies of the United Nations system, to continue to provide assistance to Governments, in particular those of developing countries, in implementing the guidelines;

4. *Further requests* the Secretary-General to report to the Economic and Social Council at its second regular session of 1990 on the implementation of the present resolution.

Economic and Social Council resolution 1988/61

27 July 1988   Meeting 39   Adopted without vote

Approved by Third Committee (E/1988/114) without vote, 15 July (meeting 8); 15-nation draft (E/1988/C.3/L.6), orally revised; agenda item 17.
Sponsors: Australia, Canada, Egypt, Germany, Federal Republic of, Greece, India, Japan, Netherlands, Norway, Pakistan, Somalia, Spain, United Kingdom, Uruguay, Venezuela.
Financial implications. S-G, E/1988/C.3/L.8.

REFERENCES

[1]*World Economic Survey 1988: Current Trends and Policies in the World Economy* (E/1988/50), Sales No. E.88.II.C.1. [2]*Trade and Development Report, 1988* (UNCTAD/TDR/8), Sales No. E.88.II.D.8. [3]YUN 1986, p. 1210. [4]YUN 1987, p. 472. [5]TD/B/1186. [6]A/43/15, vol. II. [7]*Ibid.*, vol. I (dec. 355(XXXIV)). [8]*Ibid.* (dec. 354(XXXIV)). [9]TD/B/1176. [10]TD/B/1160. [11]TD/B/1160/Add.1. [12]TD/B/1161 & Add.1-3. [13]YUN 1983, p. 544. [14]ACC/1988/DEC/1-18 (dec. 1988/3). [15]ACC/1988/DEC/19-31 (dec. 1988/19). [16]A/C.2/43/L.7. [17]TD/B/1177. [18]TD/B/C.5/111 & Add.1. [19]YUN 1987, p. 473. [20]TD/B/C.5/L.63. [21]GSTP/MM/BELGRADE/12 (vol. II). [22]GSTP/MM/BELGRADE/12 (vol. I). [23]TD/B/1164 & Add.1. [24]YUN 1987, p. 475. [25]A/43/15, vol. I (dec. 356(XXXIV)). [26]ITC/AG(XXI)/114 & Add.1. [27]ITC/AG(XXI)/112. [28]ITC/AG(XXI)/109. [29]ITC/AG(XXI)/109/Add.1. [30]A/43/5, vol. II. [31]TD/B/1201. [32]TD/B/C.1/299. [33]TD/B/C.1/300. [34]TD/B/C.1/301 & Corr.1. [35]TD/B/1201 (25(XIII)). [36]YUN 1987, p. 481. [37]A/C.2/43/L.7. [38]YUN 1985, p. 567. [39]*Multilateral Treaties Deposited with the Secretary-General: Status as at 31 December 1988* (ST/LEG/SER.E/7), Sales No. E.89.V.3. [40]YUN 1980, p. 621. [41]YUN 1987, p. 480. [42]YUN 1986, pp. 502-503. [43]YUN 1987, p. 482. [44]*Ibid.*, p. 483. [45]TD/B/C.1/297. [46]TD/COPPER/10. [47]TD/COPPER/11 & Add.1. [48]TD/B/C.1/296. [49]YUN 1986, p. 504. [50]TD/TIN/PM/3. [51]TD/TIN.7/11. [52]TD/TIN.7/10. [53]TD/B/C.1/302. [54]TD/B/C.1/TUNGSTEN/77. [55]TD/B/C.1/TUNGSTEN/76 & Corr.1. [56]TD/B/1162. [57]YUN 1985, p. 571, GA res. 39/248, annex, 9 Apr. 1985.

Finance

Financial policy

The Committee for Development Planning (CDP), in the report on its April session,[1] noted that reform of the international monetary system was necessary to ensure adequate levels and an appropriate distribution of international liquidity, more symmetrical balance-of-payment adjustment processes, and less volatile exchange rates. Particular responsibilities rested with the major industrialized countries to achieve greater co-operation in the pursuit of their national and fiscal policies in the interest of global economic growth and stability. Even more urgent, said CDP, was the problem of finding an enduring and comprehensive solution to the external debt problem of the developing countries (see below).

At the national level, policy stances in many developing countries had changed as policy makers pursued greater autonomy and market discipline for state enterprises and placed more emphasis on encouraging entrepreneurship in the private sector and reforms of pricing policies and fiscal systems.

The *World Economic Survey 1988*[2] observed that three sets of financial events had captured the attention of policy makers in 1987: severe strains in the international strategy for managing developing country debt, the need for central banks to finance increased amounts of the current-account deficit of the United States, and the October crash in all the major stock markets of the world. Those developments highlighted the instability of international financial relations in the late 1980s, although none of the events erupted into a full-blown international crisis. However, the potential for crisis remained.

The *Survey* stated that domestic efforts to restore growth and stability were in many cases frustrated by the international financial situation, notably the net outflow of resources from several large debtor countries. If the United States was to reverse its deficit and run a trade surplus sufficient to meet the interest payments on its debt, that shift would have to be of the order of 5 per cent of its GNP. In the case of developing countries, where a revival of investment was necessary, the required shift was in the opposite direction; a renewed flow of capital was needed, not decades of merely paying off past debts. In both cases much time would be required and the correction of those situations would continue into the 1990s.

The prevailing uncertainty in the world economy would be reduced if a co-operative framework were established, embodying at least three elements: redirecting capital and trade flows in a manner consonant with the needs of stability and widespread growth; a timetable for achieving that objective; and recognition of the need to sustain adequate financial flows throughout the adjustment process in order to avert the disruptive effect of sudden financial contraction.

International monetary situation

In accordance with a 1987 General Assembly decision,[3] the Secretary-General submitted in October 1988 a report on current international monetary issues.[4] The report discussed recent developments in the international monetary system, issues in the management of the international monetary system, balance-of-payments adjustment in developing countries, and issues likely to challenge the functioning of the system in the future. The report noted that the international monetary system continued to be pressured by the large external imbalances of major OECD countries and the debt and adjustment problems of the developing countries.

Balance-of-payments adjustment in the developed countries, although showing some modest improvement, remained critical. The developing countries displayed a marked change in their current-account situation, but this was achieved mainly through sharp import cuts and substantial currency depreciations. This all contributed to imbalances in world trade, which added further to the deflationary process. Despite massive adjustment efforts, the over-indebtedness of the developing countries persisted. The international monetary system failed to provide a working mechanism to correct trade imbalances among the industrialized countries and this impeded the ability of the developing countries to achieve economic recovery.

The report pointed to the need for more effective macro-economic policy co-ordination among industrialized countries and proposed a much broader use of the IMF surveillance framework as a means of achieving this, as it would allow for the inclusion of developing countries in the process. It also considered that, in terms of growth-oriented adjustment, IMF-supported programmes should be tailored to the specific characteristics of the economic structure of individual borrowing countries and confined to external variables such as balance on current account and the level of international reserves. IMF facilities were also strengthened in support of macro-economic adjustment and structural reform, concessional lending, contingency financing and stand-by or extended arrangement.

The report also identified issues that would require attention in the future to achieve the efficient functioning of the international monetary system. They included: the symmetry of the balance-of-payments adjustment process between deficit and surplus countries and the appropriate roles of monetary and fiscal policies in that process; debt relief and reductions of protection against developing countries' exports; the amount and distribution of international liquidity; and relations among international capital mobility, the functioning of financial markets and exchange rates. Also identified was the integration of socialist countries into a universal monetary system.

Recent proposals for convening an international conference on monetary and financial issues were summarized in an annex to the Secretary-General's report.

GENERAL ASSEMBLY ACTION

On 20 December, on the recommendation of the Second Committee, the General Assembly adopted **resolution 43/187** by recorded vote.

International conference on money and finance
The General Assembly,

Taking note with appreciation of the report of the Secretary-General on current international monetary issues,

Requests the Secretary-General to continue to monitor the international monetary situation and to prepare an updated version of his report thereon for submission to the General Assembly at its forty-fourth session and to provide updated information on the proposals for convening an international conference on monetary issues made in recent years by Governments, prominent persons and organizations.

General Assembly resolution 43/187

20 December 1988   Meeting 83   127-19-5 (recorded vote)

Approved by Second Committee (A/43/915/Add.2) by recorded vote (112-19-5), 5 December (meeting 46); draft by Tunisia, for Group of 77 (A/C.2/43/L.53); agenda item 82 (b).

Meeting numbers. GA 43rd session: 2nd Committee 21-26, 30, 36, 37, 43, 46; plenary 83.

Recorded vote in Assembly as follows:

In favour: Afghanistan, Albania, Algeria, Angola, Antigua and Barbuda, Argentina, Bahrain, Bangladesh, Barbados, Benin, Bhutan, Bolivia, Botswana, Brazil, Brunei Darussalam, Bulgaria, Burkina Faso, Burma, Burundi, Byelorussian SSR, Cameroon, Cape Verde, Central African Republic, Chad, Chile, China, Colombia, Comoros, Congo, Costa Rica, Côte d'Ivoire, Cuba, Cyprus, Czechoslovakia, Democratic Kampuchea, Democratic Yemen, Djibouti, Dominican Republic, Ecuador, Egypt, El Salvador, Equatorial Guinea, Ethiopia, Fiji, Gabon, Gambia, German Democratic Republic, Ghana, Grenada, Guinea, Guinea-Bissau, Guyana, Haiti, Honduras, India, Indonesia, Iran, Iraq, Jamaica, Jordan, Kenya, Kuwait, Lao People's Democratic Republic, Lebanon, Lesotho, Liberia, Libyan Arab Jamahiriya, Madagascar, Malawi, Malaysia, Maldives, Mali, Malta, Mauritania, Mauritius, Mexico, Mongolia, Morocco, Mozambique, Nepal, Nicaragua, Niger, Nigeria, Oman, Pakistan, Panama, Papua New Guinea, Paraguay, Peru, Philippines, Poland, Qatar, Romania, Rwanda, Saint Vincent and the Grenadines, Samoa, Sao Tome and Principe, Saudi Arabia, Senegal, Seychelles, Sierra Leone, Singapore, Solomon Islands, Somalia, Sri Lanka, Sudan, Suriname, Swaziland, Syrian Arab Republic, Thailand, Togo, Trinidad and Tobago, Tunisia, Uganda, Ukrainian SSR, USSR, United Arab Emirates, United Republic of Tanzania, Uruguay, Vanuatu, Venezuela, Viet Nam, Yemen, Yugoslavia, Zaire, Zambia, Zimbabwe.

Against: Australia, Austria, Belgium, Canada, Denmark, France, Germany, Federal Republic of, Greece, Iceland, Ireland, Israel, Italy, Japan, Luxembourg, Netherlands, Portugal, Spain, United Kingdom, United States.

Abstaining: Finland, New Zealand, Norway, Sweden, Turkey.

By **decision 43/442** of 20 December 1988, the General Assembly, on the recommendation of the Second Committee, decided to defer until its forty-fourth session consideration of a draft resolution[5] entitled "International conference on money and finance for development". The draft, by which the Assembly would have called on the Secretary-General to carry out consultations on convening a conference on money and finance for development, had been considered by the Assembly in 1987[6] and deferred to the 1988 session.

Net transfer of resources from developing to developed countries

In accordance with a 1987 request,[7] the Secretary-General submitted to the Economic and Social Council in June a report on the net transfer of resources from developing to developed countries.[8] The report examined the interactions between changes in the terms of trade and changes in the pattern of financial flows to and from developing countries and how negative net transfers affected the level of real expenditure, particularly domestic investment because of its implications for long-term economic growth. In response to a 1987 General Assembly request,[9] the report included a section on the links between the level of a net overall transfer of real resources from developing to developed countries and the attainment of the growth target for developing countries set in the International Development Strategy for the Third United Nations Development Decade (the 1980s).

The report noted that, during the 1980s, the terms of trade for most groups of developing countries deteriorated, causing their ratio of debt service to export revenue to rise, even without further borrowing, and the ratios of outstanding debt to exports also worsened. Those developments led to a drop in the inflow of new commercial lending as banks' perception of risk rose. There was also a slow-down in the growth of bilateral and multilateral official flows. As a result of that pattern, 1987 was the fifth consecutive year of negative net transfers to developing countries.

The report observed that a sudden negative net transfer was one dimension of a debt problem and had to be seen in the context of a country's overall debt situation, adding that it should not be assumed that all negative transfers must be reversed. The international community had before it a number of proposals for debt relief for heavily indebted countries of Africa and Latin America. In the case of low-income countries, particularly in Africa, proposals emphasized the need to reduce interest payments on past debts *vis-à-vis* official creditors. For the middle-income highly indebted countries, an effective response to the transfer problem had to take the form of reducing outflows. One option that was increasingly being considered by debtor countries was to reduce their outstanding stock of debt by capturing the discount on it that applied in the secondary market. Another option was to exchange present debt for new debt instruments with an interest rate that was both fixed and below market rates.

Along those lines, proposals had been made to establish a multilateral debt conversion facility that would enable creditor banks to convert their developing countries' debt at a discount into long-term bonds with fixed interest rates. The report stated that it was in the interest of the international community to consider such proposals against the need to ensure that the balance between finance and adjustment was not struck at the expense of the long-term requirements for growth and development.

By **decision 1988/160** of 27 July, the Economic and Social Council requested the Secretary-General to continue to monitor the evolution of the phenomenon of the net transfer of resources from developing to developed countries and to devote a separate chapter of the *World Economic Survey 1989* to analysing the phenomenon.

External debt problems

At its April session,[1] CDP stated that prompt action to reduce the international debts of debt-distressed developing countries, particularly in Africa and Latin America, was an essential prerequisite of any successful strategy to deal with the critical long-term issues of the 1990s. In the Committee's view, such action would include a multi-year moratorium for African countries on interest and principal payments on public and publicly guaranteed debts, with highly concessional interest rates on the rescheduled amounts for low-income, severely debt-distressed countries; and reduced interest rates on Paris Club (a creditor group) reschedulings for others. As to private debt—particularly that of the middle-income countries in Latin America and elsewhere—official action was needed to facilitate an orderly process of debt reduction on the part of commercial banks.

The year 1987 was characterized by frustration among debtor countries and disillusionment among creditor institutions, according to the *World Economic Survey 1988*.[2] In 1988, however, there was an improvement in the debtor/creditor relationship. Negotiations replaced unilateral action and several debtor countries renewed adjustment programmes with IMF and the World Bank as those two institutions tried to improve their ability to address the adjustment needs of the developing countries. Although no comprehensive strategy evolved to manage the debt problem, several new features were added to the menu of options from which debtors and creditors could design their debt-restructuring packages.

The *Survey* also addressed the issue of the United States foreign debt, noting that, as the supplier of the major currency for international transactions, it had been able to borrow almost entirely in its own currency and was not susceptible to a foreign exchange crisis of the sort afflicting developing countries. The major concerns about the growing external indebtedness of the United States were related to the risks it posed for the stability of the world financial system, the rate of growth of the debt, its absolute magnitude and the question of whether the world's wealthiest country should appropriate such a large portion of the surplus savings of the rest of the world as a way of sustaining levels of domestic expenditures that substantially exceeded domestic output.

The *Trade and Development Report, 1988*,[10] having considered a possible debt relief scenario, concluded that, if debtor countries were given relief equivalent to about one half of the discount at which their debt was being traded on secondary markets, they could break out of the vicious circle of over-indebtedness and stagnation, and grow out of their debt problem.

Trade and Development Board consideration. At its April/May session, TDB had before it an UNCTAD secretariat report[11] providing information for a review of the implementation of a 1980 Board resolution[12] containing guidelines on dealing with the debt problems of developing countries.

The report's introduction highlighted the considerable deterioration of the economic and financial situation of developing countries and identified the debt overhang as an obstacle to restoring financial viability and development. The report reviewed trends in the rescheduling practices of official creditors in the Paris Club, the main changes being the granting of a greater degree of debt relief through measures such as rescheduling a higher proportion of debt service and of previously rescheduled debt; an improvement in cover policies of export credit agencies; a lengthening of maturities for poorer countries and the acceptance of an IMF Structural Adjustment Facility programme rather than an upper credit tranche arrangement; and the introduction of multi-year rescheduling agreements.

While acknowledging the positive developments in Paris Club practices, the report noted that the adequacy of existing arrangements had to be assessed in the light of both the gravity of the debt problems of developing countries and the criteria adopted by the international community. The report observed that traditional rescheduling techniques needed to be supplemented with measures to reduce the effective stock of debt. It proposed a selective relaxation of the principle whereby debt-service obligations arising from all bilateral

non-concessional debt had eventually to be met in full and referred to various options, some of which had been proposed by some creditor Governments and multilateral institutions, including: debt cancellation, reduction of interest rates, temporary waivers of interest payments and debt conversions. The report also called for the introduction of improved and more flexible multi-year rescheduling agreements and for extending eligibility to countries with structural debt difficulties. It further stated that conditionality should be supportive of medium-term development programmes and consistent with growth targets. It also saw scope for expanding creditor participation in the Paris Club to all official creditors and to multilateral institutions.

TDB decided to take up the matter again in September, when it had before it a note by the UNCTAD secretariat updating developments in official debt rescheduling.[13] With regard to creditor policies towards poorer debtors, the report noted that, at the Toronto Economic Summit of the seven largest developed market-economy countries (Toronto, Canada, 19-21 June),[14] agreement was reached on modalities concerning concessional relief on official bilateral debt owed by poorer countries and rescheduled in the Paris Club. The agreement provided for a menu of options for official creditors, including concessional interest rates on shorter maturities, longer repayment periods at commercial rates, partial write-offs of debt-service obligations during the consolidation period, or a combination of those options.

As to official debt reschedulings in 1988, the report stated that there had been a considerable slow-down in the number of agreements during the first eight months of the year, when official creditors concluded seven agreements with developing countries compared with 13 agreements during the first eight months of 1987. Only 10 countries went to the Paris Club between September 1987 and August 1988, against 21 in the preceding 12 months. That development reflected considerable delays in negotiating new adjustment programmes supported by IMF, which were a prerequisite for commencing Paris Club rescheduling exercises.

The TDB President summed up the debate on the issue, noting that there had been convergence on a number of points but that there remained considerable differences of view and/or of emphasis.

On 5 October,[15] TDB urged Governments to implement fully and further improve implementation of the agreed features contained in the Board's 1980 resolution,[12] by: enhancing the medium- and long-term perspective of the rescheduling process by ensuring that it took fully into account the development policies and programmes of each country concerned, giving consideration to rescheduling agreements on a multi-year basis; improving co-ordination between the Paris Club and multilateral financial forums designed to co-ordinate new financial flows to debtor countries; implementing expeditiously the decisions on concessional debt relief agreed on at the Toronto Economic Summit[14] in such a way that resources were additional to aid allocations and to donors' existing aid programmes; noting the important role of concessional terms and conditions and extended maturity periods in rescheduling operations; accelerating and simplifying the negotiation in the context of the Paris Club of bilateral agreements between creditor and debtor Governments; and improving the co-ordination of the contributions of the parties involved for solving external debt problems of a developing debtor country in the context of its medium- and long-term development policies.

TDB noted that calls had been made by developing countries and other countries to extend the benefits of the menu of options endorsed by the Toronto Economic Summit.[14] It invited the Chairman of the Paris Club to continue to invite the UNCTAD Secretary-General to participate in its meetings, agreed to undertake in 1992 a further review of the implementation of the guidelines contained in its 1980 resolution[12] and asked the UNCTAD Secretary-General to include in his reports an analysis of problems that developing debtor countries had encountered in debt-rescheduling procedures.

A draft resolution on the need for debt reduction was submitted by Egypt on behalf of the Group of 77 and the Board decided to annex it to its report.[16] By that resolution, the Board would have urged that a debt strategy be developed, agreed on and implemented to swiftly yield durable and equitable solutions for all developing countries having debt-servicing difficulties. The strategy should provide for reduction of the volume of debt and/or interest charges to align debt-servicing obligations with the capacity to pay, while meeting the needs of the population and attaining the high levels of investment required to sustain growth. To that end the following measures would be taken by creditor Governments, commercial banks and multilateral financial institutions: reduction of outstanding commercial bank debt of developing countries with the active encouragement of creditor Governments directly and/or through mechanisms such as an international debt facility; provision of concessional financing to reduce debts of developing countries to multilateral institutions; substantial write-off and other concessional relief on debt owed to official bilateral creditors and a significant increase in the total volume of official development assistance; and devising suitable mechanisms to lower the real rates of interest on all debt owed to commercial banks,

multilateral institutions and bilateral creditors. The UNCTAD Secretary-General would have been asked to monitor the implementation of the resolution and to report to the Board in 1989.

ACC consideration. The Administrative Committee on Co-ordination (ACC) (Geneva, 20 and 21 April 1988) discussed the question of debt and development and adopted a decision[17] endorsing the Secretary-General's suggestion for greater co-operation among the relevant agencies and entities of the system in analytical work in debt and development. It agreed that the Director-General for Development and International Economic Co-operation should follow the matter up with the organizations concerned.

Report of the Secretary-General. In response to a 1987 General Assembly request,[18] the Secretary-General submitted a September report on the debt problem.[19] In preparing the report, a broad process of consultations had been undertaken by the Secretary-General; written submissions were solicited from authorities in different countries and an international group of experts was convened informally at Geneva on 14 and 15 July. Views were obtained from multilateral institutions and from the United Nations system, including CDP and ACC (see above). On 10 and 11 September, the Secretary-General held informal consultations in New York with a number of eminent personalities. The results of those consultations were summarized in an annex to the report.

After discussing questions of debt, growth and adjustment and the recent development of the debt strategy, the report outlined elements of a possible approach to international debt policy. It concluded that a durable solution of the debt problem was one that would explicitly address the imbalances between debt-servicing obligations and capacities. Eliminating those imbalances would entail relieving the external financial constraints on adjustment and growth in debtor countries, ensuring that the improvement in their net transfer of financial resources was used in the most socially and developmentally appropriate way and improving the global economic environment.

The report suggested debt-reduction measures for different groups of countries: low-income debtor countries; countries heavily indebted to official creditors; and highly indebted middle-income countries. The report also discussed the need for higher financial flows, the adjustment efforts of debtor countries, and the adjustment efforts of industrialized countries.

GENERAL ASSEMBLY ACTION

On 20 December, on the recommendation of the Second Committee, the General Assembly adopted **resolution 43/198** by recorded vote.

External debt crisis and development: towards a durable solution of the debt problems

The General Assembly,

Recalling its resolutions 41/202 of 8 December 1986 on strengthened international economic co-operation aimed at resolving the external debt problems of developing countries and 42/198 of 11 December 1987 on furthering international co-operation regarding the external debt problems,

Recalling Trade and Development Board resolutions 165(S-IX) of 11 March 1978, 222(XXI) of 27 September 1980 and 358(XXXV) of 5 October 1988 and the relevant recommendations of the mid-term global review of progress towards the implementation of the Substantial New Programme of Action for the 1980s for the Least Developed Countries,

Recalling the Final Act adopted by the United Nations Conference on Trade and Development at its seventh session,

Recognizing that the deteriorating economic situation faced by those developing countries with a heavy debt burden, which constitutes a major obstacle to their economic growth and sustained development, can be a threat to their economic, social and political stability,

Emphasizing that the world-wide impact and the wide range of implications of indebtedness of developing countries on today's increasingly interdependent world economy can be a threat to the political stability of those countries,

Recognizing that, in the present circumstances, adjustment efforts are needed on the part of all countries, collectively and individually, each country contributing to the common objective in accordance with its capacities and weight in the world economy, while concern remains about the political and social implications associated with the structural adjustment programme in indebted developing countries,

Welcoming the increasing acceptance of further diversifying the range of options that, *inter alia*, reduce the stock and service of debt and contribute to the achievement of a durable solution to the external indebtedness of developing countries,

Acknowledging the continuing need for strengthening effective international co-operation in order to resolve the problem of external indebtedness of developing countries on a durable, equitable and mutually agreed basis, in particular through improvement in the international economic environment,

Noting that, although efforts have been made by the international community to deal with the debt problem, it is essential, owing to the gravity of the problem, to reaffirm the shared responsibility of all parties involved,

Deeply concerned that debt-service obligations remain high, that the factors determining the capacity to pay have not moved in consonance with the debt-service obligations of the majority of developing countries, and that prospects for reducing the adverse effects of the debt burden on the development process in developing countries continue to be uncertain,

Noting with concern that the net outflow of financial resources from developing countries as a whole, exacerbated by the debt crisis and the deterioration in the terms of trade, deprives those countries of resources needed for financing their growth and development,

1. *Expresses its appreciation* to the Secretary-General for his involvement in the debt issue and for his report entitled "Towards a durable solution of the debt problem";

2. *Stresses* that the debt crisis in an increasingly interdependent world economy has a wide impact, often with political implications, having a bearing not only on relations between creditors and debtors but also on prospects for the world community as a whole, thereby requiring a broad approach with political impetus and continued close co-operation;

3. *Expresses deep concern* that the overall indebtedness of debtor developing countries has persisted and often increased, that their growth and development are severely limited, and that their economic and social prospects continue to be a cause of serious concern;

4. *Stresses* that a supportive international economic environment, together with a growth-oriented development approach, is needed for supporting the efforts of debtor developing countries in dealing with their external indebtedness and alleviating the political and social costs of structural adjustment programmes and adjustment fatigue, thus contributing to the restoration of their economic growth, development and credit-worthiness;

5. *Urges* the international community to continue to search, through dialogue and shared responsibility, for a durable, equitable and mutually agreed growth-oriented and development-oriented solution to the external indebtedness of developing countries;

6. *Invites* the multilateral financial institutions to continue to review conditionality criteria, taking into account, *inter alia*, social objectives, growth and development priorities of developing countries and changing conditions of the world economy, and stresses further the need for increased co-operation between the International Monetary Fund, the World Bank and other multilateral financial institutions, which should not lead to cross-conditionality;

7. *Reaffirms* that a major objective of any debt strategy should be that debtor developing countries achieve an adequate level of growth sufficient to enable them to satisfy their social, economic and development needs, which will in turn enhance their ability to service debt, and urges all concerned parties to develop new ways and means to sustain effectively policies aimed at attaining such a level of growth;

8. *Recognizes* that efforts to resolve the debt problem should include policies in creditor countries and debtor countries that are supportive of export growth and diversification in the latter;

9. *Recognizes* that there is need to broaden further the range of approaches that, *inter alia*, reduce the stock and service of debt, including expansion of the scope and implementation of currently utilized financial techniques;

10. *Recognizes* that the external indebtedness of some other countries with serious debt-servicing problems gives rise to considerable concern, and invites all those involved to take into account, as appropriate, the above provisions in addressing those problems;

11. *Requests* the Secretary-General to continue his efforts, through a process of high-level consultations, as appropriate, with heads of State or Government and other parties concerned, to contribute to a common understanding on a solution to the external indebtedness of developing countries in the context of their growth and development;

12. *Also requests* the Secretary-General to take any other appropriate measures for the implementation of the present resolution and to report thereon to the General Assembly at its forty-fourth session.

General Assembly resolution 43/198

20 December 1988   Meeting 83   150-1-1 (recorded vote)

Approved by Second Committee (A/43/916) by recorded vote (115-1-1), 9 December (meeting 48); draft by Tunisia, for Group of 77 (A/C.2/43/L.15/Rev.2), orally revised; agenda item 83.

Meeting numbers. GA 43rd session: 2nd Committee 16-21, 24, 28, 48; plenary 83.

Recorded vote in Assembly as follows:

In favour: Afghanistan, Albania, Algeria, Angola, Antigua and Barbuda, Argentina, Australia, Austria, Bahrain, Bangladesh, Barbados, Belgium, Benin, Bhutan, Bolivia, Botswana, Brazil, Brunei Darussalam, Bulgaria, Burkina Faso, Burma, Burundi, Byelorussian SSR, Cameroon, Canada, Cape Verde, Central African Republic, Chad, Chile, China, Colombia, Comoros, Congo, Costa Rica, Côte d'Ivoire, Cuba, Cyprus, Czechoslovakia, Democratic Kampuchea, Democratic Yemen, Denmark, Djibouti, Dominican Republic, Ecuador, Egypt, El Salvador, Equatorial Guinea, Ethiopia, Fiji, Finland, France, Gabon, Gambia, German Democratic Republic, Germany, Federal Republic of, Ghana, Greece, Grenada, Guatemala, Guinea, Guinea-Bissau, Guyana, Haiti, Honduras, Hungary, Iceland, India, Indonesia, Iran, Iraq, Ireland, Italy, Jamaica, Jordan, Kenya, Kuwait, Lao People's Democratic Republic, Lebanon, Lesotho, Liberia, Libyan Arab Jamahiriya, Luxembourg, Madagascar, Malawi, Malaysia, Maldives, Mali, Malta, Mauritania, Mauritius, Mexico, Mongolia, Morocco, Mozambique, Nepal, Netherlands, New Zealand, Nicaragua, Niger, Nigeria, Norway, Oman, Pakistan, Panama, Papua New Guinea, Paraguay, Peru, Philippines, Poland, Portugal, Qatar, Romania, Rwanda, Saint Vincent and the Grenadines, Samoa, Sao Tome and Principe, Saudi Arabia, Senegal, Seychelles, Sierra Leone, Singapore, Solomon Islands, Somalia, Spain, Sri Lanka, Sudan, Suriname, Swaziland, Sweden, Syrian Arab Republic, Thailand, Togo, Trinidad and Tobago, Tunisia, Turkey, Uganda, Ukrainian SSR, USSR, United Arab Emirates, United Kingdom, United Republic of Tanzania, Uruguay, Vanuatu, Venezuela, Viet Nam, Yemen, Yugoslavia, Zaire, Zambia, Zimbabwe.

Against: United States.

Abstaining: Japan.

By **decision 43/444** of 20 December, the Assembly, on the Second Committee's recommendation, deferred to its 1989 session consideration of a draft decision on the establishment of an Advisory Commission on Debt and Development. By that draft,[20] submitted by Tunisia on behalf of the Group of 77, the Assembly would have established an Advisory Commission on Debt and Development to develop innovative approaches and evolve proposals on all types of debt. The Commission would have been established for at least three years and would have submitted annual reports to the Assembly. The Secretary-General would have been requested to appoint the Commission's members, organize its support staff and report to the Assembly in 1989.

Taxation

The Economic and Social Council in May considered the report of the 1987 meeting of the *Ad Hoc* Group of Experts on International Co-operation in Tax Matters.[21]

ECONOMIC AND SOCIAL COUNCIL ACTION

On 25 May, the Economic and Social Council, on the recommendation of its First (Economic) Committee, adopted **decision 1988/114** without vote.

***Ad Hoc* Group of Experts on International Co-operation in Tax Matters**

At its 13th plenary meeting, on 25 May 1988, the Economic and Social Council decided:

(a) To take note of the report of the Secretary-General on the work of the *Ad Hoc* Group of Experts on International Co-operation in Tax Matters;

(b) To endorse the proposals of the *Ad Hoc* Group, contained in paragraphs 28 and 29 of that report, for changing the frequency, duration and organization of its meetings, on the understanding that the new arrangements would not require any additional financial resources.

Economic and Social Council decision 1988/114

Adopted without vote

Approved by First Committee (E/1988/93) without vote, 18 May (meeting 2); draft agreed upon during informal consultations; agenda item 7.

REFERENCES

[1]E/1988/16. [2]*World Economic Survey 1988* (E/1988/50), Sales No. E.88.II.C.1. [3]YUN 1987, p. 486, GA dec. 42/440, 11 Dec. 1987. [4]A/43/749 & Corr.1. [5]A/C.2/43/L.6. [6]YUN 1987, p. 493. [7]*Ibid.*, p. 469, ESC. res. 1987/93, 9 July 1987. [8]E/1988/64. [9]YUN 1987, p. 470, GA dec. 42/429, 11 Dec. 1987. [10]*Trade and Development Report 1988* (UNCTAD/TDR/8), Sales No. E.88.II.D.8. [11]TD/B/1167. [12]YUN 1980, p. 616. [13]TD/B/1167/Add.1. [14]A/43/435-S/19974. [15]A/43/15, vol. II (dec. 358(XXXV)). [16]A/43/15, vol. II. [17]ACC/1988/DEC/1-18 (dec. 1988/2). [18]YUN 1987, p. 489, GA res. 42/198, 11 Dec. 1987. [19]A/43/647. [20]A/C.2/43/L.19. [21]YUN 1987, p. 496.

Transport

Maritime transport

In 1988, the total volume of international seaborne trade amounted to an estimated 3.7 billion tons, an increase of 4.1 per cent over 1987. The *Review of Maritime Transport, 1988,*[1] stated that the growth in the international economy and the fall in oil prices contributed in large part to the increase, which restored seaborne trade to approximately the 1980 level. Developing countries generated 46.5 per cent of all goods loaded and 24.9 per cent of goods unloaded, while the developed market economies accounted for 45 per cent and 68 per cent respectively. The socialist countries' shares were 8.5 per cent of goods loaded and 7.1 per cent of goods unloaded.

The size of the world merchant fleet continued its declining trend. At mid-1988, the total deadweight of the world merchant fleet had declined by 0.7 per cent from the previous year to 627.9 million tons. Ownership remained concentrated in the developed market-economy and open-registry countries, while the developing countries owned 20.9 per cent and the socialist countries of Eastern Europe and Asia owned 10.2 per cent. Developing countries, especially in Africa and Oceania, continued to be subject to a rate more than double that paid by developed market-economy countries for freight costs in relation to the total cost, insurance, freight (c.i.f.) value of imports. World shipping continued to be faced with the problem of tonnage oversupply.

Shipping

At its thirteenth session (Geneva, 14-22 March 1988),[2] the UNCTAD Committee on Shipping, as requested at its 1986 session,[3] considered the major issue of the imbalance between supply and demand in ocean shipping. It had before it an UNCTAD secretariat report on the issue,[4] supplementing a 1986 report,[5] which concluded that the large and continuing imbalance between supply and demand in world shipping had not greatly diminished. Surplus tonnage as at mid-1986 remained at over 130 deadweight tons (dwt) or about 20 per cent of the world merchant fleet. Excess shipbuilding capacity was at 4.5 million compensated gross tons (cgt) or 30 per cent on a world-wide basis. Excess capacity was thus likely to continue well into the 1990s unless further substantial capacity reductions were undertaken. This confirmed previous findings[5] that the major cause of the shipping crisis lay in the high level and scale of government financial subsidies as well as indirect support measures to the acquisition, operation and building of new ships over the past decade. To address the fundamental structural crisis of the shipbuilding industry would require consideration of national, regional and international shipping policy measures along with simultaneous consideration of the world shipbuilding situation. The report suggested that the Committee consider adopting a ''Common Measure of Understanding on Shipping and Shipbuilding Questions'' containing principles to be followed by the international community that would promote the orderly development of their merchant marines and promote their effective participation in world shipping. Such an instrument would provide guidelines for the shipping and shipbuilding industries to adapt to rapidly changing fluctuations in world-wide demand for shipping services.

By a 22 March resolution,[6] the Committee urged all UNCTAD member States to consider adopting and implementing shipping policies which would promote a more balanced situation in world shipping. It requested the UNCTAD secretariat to continue to monitor developments in world shipping and shipbuilding, with particular reference to the imbalance between supply and demand; and to prepare, for consideration by the Committee at its 1990 session, a report containing proposals for the international community to consider with a view to avoiding imbalance situations and promoting a more balanced development of world shipping, taking into account the special interest of developing countries and the recognized need to assist them in developing their merchant marines.

Ocean freight rates

With regard to the issue of ocean freight rates and their effects on exports of developing countries, the Committee on Shipping had before it an UNCTAD secretariat study[7] undertaken in response to a 1983 UNCTAD VI request.[8] The study noted that, for many primary commodities exported by developing countries, the bulk of ocean transport charges or increases appeared to be borne largely by exporters and that, since ocean freight costs represented a large proportion of commodity prices, those costs absorbed a large part of export earnings. The report contained a number of recommendations for action to be taken by exporting developing countries and in the context of UNCTAD consultations to deal with the problem of ocean freight costs.

On 22 March,[9] the Committee on Shipping requested the UNCTAD secretariat to update existing studies on the maritime transportation of selected commodities and prepare studies analysing the impact of conditions of ocean transport services, particularly ocean freight rates, on exports of manufactured goods from developing countries, in order to provide them with information required for making appropriate decisions in that area.

Ports

On 22 March,[9] the Committee on Shipping invited the UNCTAD Secretary-General to convene in 1989 an *ad hoc* intergovernmental group of port experts to review practical problems in respect of the development, improvement and operation of ports. He was asked to examine the secretariat's work on problems arising in setting up transshipment facilities in developing countries, data processing in port operation and documentation, and maintenance of port equipment; to study possibilities for regional co-operation in developing countries regarding ports; and to propose follow-up action for local, national and intergovernmental consideration. The Committee also asked the UNCTAD Secretary-General to review and monitor UNCTAD's work in port management training and advisory services and to prepare a report for the Committee's 1990 session with recommendations for future work.

Multimodal transport

The *Review of Maritime Transport, 1988*,[1] stated that, although there was virtually no increase in the number of multimodal transport operators in 1988, scattered indications showed that some existing services had expanded: parcel service operations; unit-train operations, particularly double-stack train operations in the United States; the Trans-Siberian container service; and container train services in India, Kenya and Malaysia. Sea-air services from Japan also grew significantly, as did traffic through the main interface points for sea-air multimodal services in the developing countries, notably at Dubai and Singapore. The international physical distribution system was undergoing great changes, including a tendency to shift production bases from one country to another. In addition, new and various combinations of sea-air, truck and rail multimodal transportation were being offered. To facilitate the movement of goods through this form of transport, and in response to a 1986 resolution of the Committee on Shipping,[10] an informal meeting was held in October 1988 on elaboration of a standard multimodal transport document.

The Committee on Shipping considered the results of the work carried out since 1986 by the Group of Experts to Develop and Recommend Model Rules for Multimodal Container Tariffs.[11] On 22 March,[6] the Committee endorsed the standard sequence and model container tariff rules contained in the final report of the Group of Experts[10] and recommended their use in existing and/or new container tariff rules as appropriate. It requested the UNCTAD secretariat to commence operation of a reference library for multimodal container tariff rules and to explore the possibilities of electronic storage and retrieval of data. Concerning the standardization of containers, and especially the adverse implications for the port facilities of developing countries of introducing higher and heavier containers, the Committee instructed the secretariat to monitor closely developments in that area at International Organization for Standardization meetings and to report at regular intervals to UNCTAD member States and to the Committee on Shipping.

The Committee requested the secretariat to produce in the UNCTAD working languages reports on rights and duties of container terminal operators and users, and on the commercial risk factor in container terminal management. The secretariat was also to prepare a detailed inventory of, and report on, studies carried out on multimodal transport and containerization, to complete outstanding studies, and to present the results to the Committee's 1990 session.

International maritime legislation and conventions

Maritime fraud

The Committee on Shipping considered a progress report by the UNCTAD secretariat on the establishment of a Maritime Fraud Prevention Exchange (MFPE).[11] Details concerning the structure and operation of MFPE had been agreed on and the organization, renamed Maritime Advisory Exchange, started operation on 1 December 1988. On 22 March,[9] the Committee recommended that Governments of UNCTAD States members urge the relevant commercial parties to utilize the services to be provided by MFPE, once established, as a means to combat maritime fraud, and invited States members and interested commercial parties to inform the secretariat of MFPE's effectiveness and positive contribution. The secretariat was also requested to promote MFPE and to monitor its activities.

The Committee also requested the secretariat to continue monitoring work on formulating Uniform Rules for incorporation in sea waybills and other similar documents as a means to reduce the incidence of maritime fraud and facilitate trade.

Maritime liens and mortgages

The Joint Intergovernmental Group of Experts on Maritime Liens and Mortgages and Related Subjects, established by UNCTAD and the International Maritime Organization, held its fourth (London, 16-20 May)[12] and fifth (Geneva, 12-20 December)[13] sessions in 1988.

In May, the Group considered the text of revised draft articles on maritime liens and mortgages and a report on the current practices of bareboat charter registration.[14] The main issues to be considered included the determination of the number of claims to be given maritime lien status and their priority, the right of the States to grant other liens or rights of retention to secure claims other than those specified in the convention, and whether or not the convention should include provisions dealing with the question of bareboat charter registration.

The Group also considered two new draft articles. One sought to clarify terms used in the draft convention in consideration of the practice, adopted by several States, of permitting a vessel to temporarily fly the flag of a State other than that of the vessel's registration. The other aimed to protect the holders of mortgages, ''hypothèques'' or charges in such cases. It was agreed that the Group's December session should be wholly devoted to completing the work on preparing the draft provisions on maritime liens and mortgages. In March,[9] the Committee on Shipping had urged the Group to complete its work during 1989 and to submit its final report to the Committee in 1990.

In December, the Group further considered the revised draft articles[15] and submissions from Greece, Liberia, the United Kingdom and Hong Kong. It also examined relevant provisions of the international conventions to which reference had been made in drafting article 12 (scope of application), regarding the possible application of the draft convention to ships registered in non-contracting States.

Convention on a Code of Conduct for Liner Conferences

The United Nations Convention on a Code of Conduct for Liner Conferences, which entered into force in 1983,[16] had 72 States parties as at 31 December 1988.[17] Mauritania, Somalia and Zambia became parties during 1988.

In accordance with article 52 of the Convention, a Review Conference was convened at Geneva from 31 October to 18 November 1988.[18] The Conference carried out a general review of the Convention's implementation and working and considered a number of specific issues relating to the Convention and its implementation: technological and structural changes in world liner shipping, the scope of the Convention's application, reservations to the Convention, modalities of its implementation, and the subject of non-conference lines.

With regard to the rules of procedure, there was a difference of views between certain groups as to the manner and extent to which non-contracting parties should participate in the Conference. The Conference adopted a resolution by which it decided that there was a need for a resumed session to complete its tasks and called on all participating States to assist the Conference to conclude its work at the resumed session. It asked the United Nations Secretary-General to make arrangements to convene a resumed session at Geneva for three weeks in 1989 and asked the Conference President and the UNCTAD Secretary-General to consult with all States entitled to attend the Review Conference on outstanding questions pertaining to rules of procedure. Following agreement on the rules, a two-day meeting should be convened when the rules would be presented to all States entitled to attend the Review Conference for their approval and recommendation of the rules to the resumed session for adoption.

United Nations Convention on the Carriage of Goods by Sea

The United Nations Convention on the Carriage of Goods by Sea, 1978, was to enter into force 12 months after 20 States had become contracting parties. By 31 December 1988, 14 countries had acceded to or ratified the Convention while 27 had signed it. In 1988, Botswana, Nigeria and Sierra Leone ratified or acceded to the Convention.[17]

Convention on Conditions for Registration of Ships

The United Nations Convention on Conditions for Registration of Ships, adopted in 1986,[3] was to enter into force 12 months after the date on which no fewer than 40 States, the combined tonnage of which amounted to at least 25 per cent of world tonnage, had become contracting parties. As at 31 December 1988, 13 States had signed the Convention and two States (Côte d'Ivoire and Mexico) had ratified it.[17] Mexico ratified the Convention in 1988.

Transport centres for the Mediterranean region

On 28 July, by **decision 1988/169**, the Economic and Social Council decided to confer United Nations status on the Transport Study Centre for the Eastern Mediterranean (Volos, Greece), the Transport Study Centre for the Western Mediterranean (Barcelona, Spain), and the Transport Training Centre (Istanbul, Turkey), upon the conclusion of agreements between the United Nations and the respective Governments concerning the conditions of such status. This was subject to the understanding that there would be no financial implications for the regular budget of the United Nations.

Transport of dangerous goods

In response to a 1987 Economic and Social Council request,[19] the Council, in May 1988, received an oral report from the United Nations Secretariat on the work of the Committee of Experts on the Transport of Dangerous Goods and on its staffing arrangements.[20] By **decision 1988/109** of 24 May, the Council took note of the oral report.

Committee of Experts. The Committee of Experts on the Transport of Dangerous Goods (fifteenth session, Geneva, 5-14 December)[21] paid special attention to co-ordinating its own activities with those of other international organizations whose activities impinged on the transport of dangerous goods. Liaison was established with the secretariats responsible for the draft global convention on the control of transboundary movements of hazardous wastes (United Nations Environment Programme) and the International Programme on Chemical Safety (World Health Organization) to ensure that their work did not duplicate existing agreements and instruments on the safe transport of dangerous goods. During its first two decades, the Committee had elaborated technical recommendations and persuaded regulatory authorities to take cognizance of them. In its third decade, the Committee's role was twofold: to adapt the recommendations to technical progress; and to respond to suggestions to amend the recommendations to facilitate total harmonization. The Committee was structured to make recommendations embodying a balance between undue risks on the one hand and unwarranted restrictions on trade on the other.

During the 1987-1988 biennium, the Committee completed its work on a new régime of testing and classification of very insensitive explosives and a radically new scheme for classifying organic peroxides. It also amended extensively its recommendations on intermediate bulk containers and aerosols and took a major decision concerning the way it listed dangerous goods in order to facilitate harmonization of the provisions for road and rail transport in the Economic Commission for Europe region.

In accordance with Economic and Social Council **decision 1988/149** of 26 May 1988, endorsing the Secretary-General's decision to appoint an expert designated by China as a full member of the Committee,[22] the Government of China participated in the Committee's work as a full member. Portugal was represented by an observer for the first time and India formally requested to become a full member. The Committee welcomed those developments as further steps towards widening the geographical scope of its decision-making base.

The Committee's Group of Rapporteurs met at Geneva from 7 to 11 March[23] and from 8 to 12 August;[24] its Group of Experts on Explosives met at Geneva from 1 to 5 August.[25]

Technical assistance and training

During 1988, UNCTAD's technical co-operation and training programme in shipping, ports and multimodal transport totalled 39 projects at both the regional and national levels, involving a total expenditure of $3.25 million (as against $3.55 million in 1987).

The TRAINMAR programme, which had as its objective the reinforcement of local training activities, continued to expand; new centres in Africa, Latin America and the Middle East commenced regular association with TRAINMAR in addition to the existing 22 port and shipping training centres. A TRAINMAR general meeting was held in September at Bremen, Federal Republic of Germany, at which the basis for a permanent system of co-operation was discussed. A new regional programme was established in the Caribbean with funds from France. New courses were funded by Norway and the United States, while the secretariat provided course material on multimodal transport.

UNCTAD continued to promote and assist in organizing international workshops on various aspects of international shipping, primarily for the benefit of developing countries. A new programme—JOBMAR—was designed to improve the practical management skills of middle/senior managers from developing countries by providing "on-the-job" experience in countries with a more advanced maritime sector. It was ready for a 1 January 1989 launching, and some 20 to 25 participants would be trained initially. Progress was also made in developing two new training packages, one for equipment manage-

ment and one for equipment procurement, under the Improving Port Performance project. A regional project financed by UNDP to assist the land-locked African countries in improving access to shipping became operational in 1988.

REFERENCES

[1]*Review of Maritime Transport, 1988* (TD/B/C.4/320), Sales No. E.89.II.D.16. [2]TD/B/1158. [3]YUN 1986, p. 519. [4]TD/B/C.4/312 & Corr.1 & Add.1. [5]YUN 1986, p. 518. [6]TD/B/1158 (res. 62(XIII)). [7]TD/B/C.4/313. [8]YUN 1983, p. 571. [9]TD/B/1158 (res. 61(XIII)). [10]YUN 1986, p. 523. [11]TD/B/C.4/314 & Corr.1. [12]TD/B/C.4/AC.8/15. [13]TD/B/C.4/AC.8/19. [14]TD/B/C.4/AC.8/12. [15]TD/B/C.4/AC.8/17 & Add.1-4. [16]YUN 1983, p. 572. [17]*Multilateral Treaties Deposited with the Secretary-General: Status as at 31 December 1988* (ST/LEG/SER.E/7), Sales No. E.89.V.3. [18]TD/CODE.2/7. [19]YUN 1987, p. 503, ESC res. 1987/54, 28 May 1987. [20]E/1988/SR.6,7. [21]ST/SG/AC.10/15 & Add.1-3. [22]E/1988/97. [23]ST/SG/AC.10/C.2/29. [24]ST/SG/AC.10/C.2/31. [25]ST/SG/AC.10/C.1/20.

Programme and finances of UNCTAD

UNCTAD programme

The Trade and Development Board—the executive body of UNCTAD—held two sessions in 1988 at Geneva. The second part of its thirty-fourth session was held from 25 April to 6 May and on 10 May;[1] the first part of its thirty-fifth session was held from 19 to 30 September and on 5 October.[2]

The Board adopted one resolution and 11 decisions during 1988. At its April/May session, it adopted decisions on the reverse transfer of technology (see PART THREE, Chapter VII), the continued updating of the UNCTAD data base on trade measures (see above), technical assistance activities provided in connection with the Uruguay Round of multilateral trade negotiations (see above), and trade relations among countries having different economic and social systems and all trade flows resulting therefrom (see above). At its September/October session, the Board adopted a resolution on its review of the implementation of guidelines on the debt-service obligations of developing countries (see above). Decisions adopted at that session related to the review of measures agreed upon by the *Ad Hoc* Intergovernmental Working Group on the In-depth Study of the United Nations Intergovernmental Structure and Functions in the Economic and Social Fields, a review of arrangements for rationalizing the Board's regular sessions and UNCTAD's calendar of meetings (see below). Other decisions dealt with drought and the external sector of the countries members of the Intergovernmental Authority on Drought and Development, the effects of floods and cyclones on the development and growth of developing countries, and UNCTAD's contribution to the implementation of the United Nations Programme of Action for African Economic Recovery and Development 1986-1990 (see preceding chapter).

On 26 July, by **decision 1988/155**, the Economic and Social Council took note of TDB's report on the second part of its thirty-fourth session.[1]

Aspects of the UNCTAD programme were dealt with in a number of General Assembly resolutions not covered in this chapter, including those on the preparation of an international development strategy for the fourth United Nations development decade (**resolution 43/182**); the reverse transfer of technology (**43/184**); the Second United Nations Conference on the Least Developed Countries (**43/186**); specific measures in favour of island developing countries (**43/189**); and examination of long-term trends in economic and social development (**43/194**).

Programme policy

Medium-term plan (1984-1989)

The Working Party on the Medium-term Plan and the Programme Budget held its fourteenth (2-9 February),[3] fifteenth (23-30 March)[4] and sixteenth (21-25 November)[5] sessions in 1988.

At its March session,[4] the Working Party had before it a report by the UNCTAD Secretary-General on the third revision of the UNCTAD sections of the United Nations medium-term plan for 1984-1989.[6] The proposed revisions updated mandates emanating from the Final Act of UNCTAD VII[7] and from TDB and its committees. On 5 May,[1] TDB took note of the revisions, and, bearing in mind a statement of the Chairman of the Working Party, in which he summarized considerations that had arisen in informal consultations on the revisions, transmitted them to the appropriate United Nations bodies for consideration.

In May/June,[8] the Committee for Programme and Co-ordination recommended approval of the proposed revisions subject to a number of modifications.

Programme budget, 1988-1989

By **resolution 43/218 A** of 21 December 1988, the General Assembly, on the recommendation of the Fifth (Administrative and Budgetary) Committee, approved a revised appropriation for UNCTAD of $76,958,200 for the 1988-1989 biennium.

Programme evaluation

At its February session,[3] the Working Party on the Medium-term Plan and the Programme Budget had before it a report by the UNCTAD Secretary-General on programme evaluation in UNCTAD.[9]

The report provided information on the consolidation of programme evaluation in UNCTAD and summarized five self-evaluation studies that had been planned for 1987.

In a series of agreed conclusions, the Working Party welcomed progress made in implementing the programme evaluation system and the initial practical results obtained. It noted the gradual strengthening of the internal independent component and invited the Secretary-General to keep it informed on future developments.

In a July report on programme evaluation in UNCTAD,[10] the UNCTAD Secretary-General discussed the further development of the evaluation process, with particular reference to methodological developments, the evolution of programme evaluation in the United Nations system, the importance of feedback for evaluation purposes, evaluation findings and their application and a better integration of evaluations of substantive programmes and of technical co-operation activities. It also discussed implementation of the evaluation plan for 1988 and summarized the results of six self-evaluations conducted during the year.

At its November session,[5] the Working Party on the Medium-term Plan and the Programme Budget adopted a series of agreed conclusions in which it again welcomed progress made in implementing programme evaluation and asked the UNCTAD Secretary-General to keep it informed of future developments. It also welcomed the secretariat's intention to pay increased attention to evaluating its contribution to technical co-operation projects in order to improve their overall quality.

Technical co-operation

Total UNCTAD project expenditures in 1988 for technical co-operation activities grew to $12.2 million from $11.8 million in 1987.[11] Allocations from UNDP, totalling $10.1 million, were the main source of funds. Activities were also funded from funds-in-trust ($1.5 million) and the United Nations regular programme of technical co-operation ($0.6 million). In 1988 there were 145 approved projects under implementation. Activities remained predominantly inter-country, in the light of the international nature of trade and economic co-operation. Activities in Africa continued to constitute the largest share of project expenditures, with a delivery of $3.9 million in 1988 (44 per cent). The next largest programme was the Americas with $1.8 million (21 per cent), followed by Asia and the Pacific with $1.4 million (16 per cent), the Arab States with $1 million (13 per cent) and Europe with $0.5 million (6 per cent).

The main sectors in which UNCTAD provided assistance were: international trade, resources for development, commodities, economic co-operation among developing countries, maritime and multimodal transport, data management and cross-sectoral and other activities.

At its February session,[3] the Working Party on the Medium-term Plan and the Programme Budget considered UNCTAD's 1987 technical co-operation activities.[12] In a series of agreed conclusions, it invited the UNCTAD Secretary-General to take into account the need for: adequate transparency in project formulation and implementation; clear criteria for assessing and reporting on the state of implementation of projects and their interrelationships with other projects; projects to be based on the requirements of participating developing countries; better use of proper channels for selecting projects at the regional level; and efforts to improve procedures relating to updating the roster and selection of experts. The Working Party hoped that the recovery in the level of resources for UNCTAD technical co-operation activities would be further strengthened and expressed its appreciation to bilateral donors and multilateral aid agencies for their support to those activities. It invited UNDP to continue to expand its support.

The Working Party also considered technical co-operation at its November session[5] and, in its agreed conclusions, requested the secretariat to report on progress in implementing its February conclusions, taking into account views expressed at the November session with reference to: project presentation and design; mobilization of resources; arrangements for financing substantive and administrative back-stopping of projects; procedures for recruiting experts; and project evaluation. The Working Party recommended that efforts be made to secure more regular contacts between the secretariat and bilateral donors and beneficiaries, called on the secretariat to explore new patterns for funding technical co-operation projects, invited UNDP and other funding sources to take into account UNCTAD's specialized expertise and its mandate when selecting executing agencies for projects in trade and development, and requested the UNCTAD Secretary-General to include in future technical assistance reports, on a triennial basis, an analysis of trends in volume of resources allocated to UNCTAD.

Organizational questions

Calendar of UNCTAD meetings

By a 10 May decision,[13] TDB approved a calendar of meetings for the remainder of 1988.

On 5 October,[14] it approved the calendar of meetings for the remainder of 1988 and for 1989.

UNCTAD intergovernmental machinery.

On 5 October,[15] TDB reaffirmed its 1987 decision[16] that measures contained in the 1987 report of the *Ad Hoc* Intergovernmental Working Group on the In-Depth Study of the United Nations Intergovernmental Structure and Functions in the Economic and Social Fields[17] should be implemented within the UNCTAD machinery and its request to the UNCTAD Secretary-General to ensure full implementation of measures falling within his competence. It decided to review in 1990 measures relating to methods of work in UNCTAD.

UNCTAD publications. In accordance with a recommendation contained in the report of the *Ad Hoc* Intergovernmental Working Group on the In-Depth Study of the United Nations Intergovernmental Structure and Functions in the Economic and Social Fields, which was endorsed by TDB in 1987,[16] an *Ad Hoc* Working Group on Publications met between 26 May and 7 July 1988.[18] It reviewed UNCTAD's publications and made a number of recommendations regarding reproduction and printing, cost evaluation, sales and dissemination policy and follow-up.

In October,[2] TDB took note of the Group's report and endorsed its recommendations.

Rationalization of TDB's sessions. On 5 October,[19] TDB, having reviewed its 1986 decision on rationalization of its regular sessions,[20] decided to reaffirm that decision.

Twenty-fifth anniversary of UNCTAD

On 20 December, on the recommendation of the Second Committee, the General Assembly adopted **resolution 43/183** without vote.

Twenty-fifth anniversary of the establishment of the United Nations Conference on Trade and Development

The General Assembly,

Recalling its resolution 1995(XIX) of 30 December 1964,

Noting that the United Nations Conference on Trade and Development intends to celebrate its twenty-fifth anniversary in 1989,

Noting also that the United Nations Conference on Trade and Development will use the occasion of its twenty-fifth anniversary as an important opportunity to inform and mobilize all concerned, with a view to achieving its goals and objectives as contained in its mandate,

Expressing its appreciation of the important achievements of the United Nations Conference on Trade and Development in fulfilling its mandate,

1. *Decides* to observe, at its forty-fourth session, the twenty-fifth anniversary of the United Nations Confer-

ence on Trade and Development in a manner befitting the role and achievements of that organ;

2. *Invites* the Trade and Development Board to contribute, as appropriate, to the celebration of that anniversary.

General Assembly resolution 43/183

20 December 1988   Meeting 83   Adopted without vote

Approved by Second Committee (A/43/915/Add.2) without vote, 15 November (meeting 42); draft by Tunisia, for Group of 77 (A/C.2/43/L.22); agenda item 82 *(b)*.

Meeting numbers. GA 43rd session: 2nd Committee 21-26, 30, 42; plenary 83.

REFERENCES

[1]A/43/15, vol. I. [2]A/43/15, vol. II. [3]TD/B/1157. [4]TD/B/1159. [5]TD/B/1198. [6]TD/B/WP/55 & Corr.1. [7]YUN 1987, p. 465. [8]A/43/16. [9]TD/B/1145. [10]TD/B/1184. [11]TD/B/WP/68. [12]YUN 1987, p. 498. [13]A/43/15, vol. I (dec. 357(XXXIV)). [14]A/43/15, vol. II (dec. 364(XXXV)). [15]*Ibid.* (dec. 359 (XXXV)). [16]YUN 1987, p. 499. [17]*Ibid.*, p. 498. [18]TD/B/1185. [19]A/43/15, vol. II (dec. 360(XXXV)). [20]YUN 1986, p. 517.

Chapter V

Transnational corporations

Transnational corporations (TNCs) continued to be major players in the world economy. World-wide flows of foreign direct investment continued to expand in 1988, but most were directed towards the developed economies, particularly the United States and Western Europe. A significant development was the emergence of the countries of Central and Eastern Europe as prospective hosts for foreign direct investment.

The Commission on TNCs in April discussed, among other issues, the activities of TNCs in South Africa and Namibia, TNCs and issues relating to the environment, transnational banks in developing countries and the activities of the Centre on TNCs and its joint units established with the regional commissions. The Commission's Intergovernmental Working Group of Experts in March discussed international accounting issues.

Draft code of conduct

Work on formulating a code of conduct on TNCs, first considered in 1975,[1] continued in 1988. In accordance with a 1987 Economic and Social Council request,[2] the Secretary-General, in January 1988,[3] transmitted the report of the Chairman presiding at the Commission's special session, who had held consultations with the Bureau of that session with the aim of preparing a draft code of conduct for the reconvened special session.

Annexed to the report was a proposed text of the draft code,[4] which covered, in the conduct of TNC activities, observance of national laws and regulations, adherence to economic goals and development objectives, renegotiation of contracts, adherence to socio-cultural objectives, respect for human rights, non-collaboration by TNCs with South Africa, non-interference in internal affairs and intergovernmental relations, abstention from corrupt practices, ownership and control, employment conditions, balance of payments and financing, transfer pricing, taxation, competition, transfer of technology, consumer protection, environmental protection and disclosure of information. Also covered were the treatment of TNCs (nationalization and compensation, jurisdiction and dispute settlement), intergovernmental co-

operation and implementation of the code at the national and international levels.

Pursuant to Economic and Social Council **decision 1988/104** of 5 February 1988, the enlarged Bureau of the special session met on 8 April to consider the draft text. It reached agreement on a set of recommendations to serve as guiding principles in future consultations and negotiations on the code of conduct.

Also in April,[5] the Commission considered the Chairman's report[3] and the draft code.[4] In presenting the topic, the Executive Director of the Centre on TNCs expressed concern that, after 12 years, the code had still not been finalized and called on delegations to be flexible and to make a real effort to reach a compromise on the remaining unsettled questions in order to complete the code.

The Commission took note of the Chairman's report and requested the Centre to prepare another report on the subject for its 1989 session.

The Economic and Social Council, in **resolution 1988/58**, reiterated the importance of the expeditious completion of the code of conduct.

International arrangements related to TNCs

In 1988, the Centre on TNCs continued to collect, monitor and analyse developments in international, regional and bilateral arrangements related to TNCs.

In a February 1988 report on international arrangements and agreements related to TNCs,[6] the Secretary-General analysed general principles of conduct by TNCs and their treatment by Governments, regional and multilateral agreements referring to entry, ownership and financing of TNCs, employment and labour, transfer of technology, protection of consumers and of the environment, jurisdiction, conflicting requirements, and settlement of investment disputes and investment insurance. He concluded that developments in the late 1980s showed important changes as regards some of the activities at the multilateral level. Certain multilateral instruments dealing with TNCs' conduct relating to specific products or issues had been adopted and major new efforts to limit national protectionist and regulatory measures, directed at trade and services, were under way. The Secretary-General noted the shift of emphasis in international negotiations to formulating standards of treatment of TNCs rather than their standards of conduct, but a body of principles concerning their conduct and treatment was beginning to emerge. There was a need for a comprehensive statement of agreed standards, such as that found in the draft code of conduct.

In April,[5] the Commission took note of the report and requested the Centre to update it for its 1989 session.

REFERENCES

[1]YUN 1975, p. 484. [2]YUN 1987, p. 508, ESC res. 1987/57, 28 May 1987. [3]E/1988/39. [4]E/1988/39/Add.1. [5]E/1988/17. [6]E/C.10/1988/5.

Standards of accounting and reporting

The sixth session of the Intergovernmental Working Group of Experts on International Standards of Accounting and Reporting was held in New York from 7 to 17 March 1988.[1] The Group had before it reports of the Secretary-General on current developments in accounting and reporting by TNCs,[2] an international survey of financial reporting practices of TNCs,[3] consolidation procedures and segmentation of aggregated data,[4] objectives and concepts underlying financial reporting,[5] numerical data on the largest service TNCs[6] and appropriate measures to give effect to the work of the Group.[7]

The Group noted the usefulness of the annual review of important current developments in accounting and reporting and observed that such a report would gain in utility if it contained an analysis of global as well as national trends and covered as wide a range of countries as practicable.

With regard to the international survey of the financial statements of 200 TNCs, the Group suggested that more TNCs from African and Asian countries should be included, as well as TNCs whose shares were not publicly traded. The Group determined the time of circulation of the list of TNCs to be surveyed and decided that the final results should be presented to the Group in 1989.

Regarding consolidation procedures, the Group agreed that consolidated financial statements should be prepared in accordance with legal requirements and/or accounting standards and that, where the enterprise was considered to have met the conditions for inclusion in the consolidation, it should be excluded only in exceptional circumstances. The Group stated that segmentation of aggregated data should not be required beyond the level at which amounts could be allocated to segments on a reliable basis. As regards the objec-

tives and concepts underlying financial reporting, the Group noted that agreement had been reached on several items, including the objective of financial statements.

In discussing further steps to be taken in relation to the development of a comprehensive information system of TNCs, the Group requested the Centre to continue to review the development of such a system and to report in 1989.

The Group recommended to the Commission on TNCs for adoption a draft resolution on the renewal of its mandate. It also adopted a document containing all the agreed conclusions of the Group and its *ad hoc* predecessor. The document was seen as a significant contribution to the process of standard-setting and particularly useful for developing countries in training and understanding current international trends. The Group agreed that a number of complex issues remained to be tackled, including information disclosure requirements regarding the economic and social responsibilities of TNCs and disclosure by banks.

In April,[8] the Commission recommended the continuation of the Group's mandate. It agreed that the results of the Group's work should be brought to the attention of Governments, standard-setting bodies, the accountancy profession, TNCs and other interested parties through United Nations publications, advisory services and technical assistance.

The Commission approved the report of the Group and the provisional agenda for its seventh (1989) session,[9] and determined the measures to be taken in order to give effect to the Group's work.[10]

By **decision 1988/164** of 27 July, the Economic and Social Council decided that the seventh session of the Group should be held from 7 to 17 March 1989 instead of from 27 February to 10 March.

REFERENCES

[1]E/C.10/1988/6. [2]E/C.10/AC.3/1988/2. [3]E/C.10/AC.3/1988/3. [4]E/C.10/AC.3/1988/4. [5]E/C.10/AC.3/1988/5. [6]E/C.10/AC.3/1988/6. [7]E/C.10/AC.3/1988/7. [8]E/1988/17 (res. 1988/1). [9]*Ibid.* (dec. 1988/1). [10]*Ibid.* (dec. 1988/2).

PUBLICATION

Conclusions on Accounting and Reporting by Transnational Corporations (ST/CTC/92), Sales No. E.88.II.A.18.

Commission on TNCs

The Commission on TNCs held its fourteenth session in New York from 6 to 15 April 1988.[1] Among subjects it discussed were recent developments related to TNCs and international economic relations, activities of the Centre on TNCs during the biennium 1986-1987, the draft code of conduct on TNCs, international standards of accounting and reporting, TNCs in South Africa and Namibia, TNCs and the environment, TNCs in services, the role of transnational banks, the question of expert advisers, the role of the Commission and its agenda for 1989.

On 27 July 1988, the Economic and Social Council took note of the report of the Commission on its fourteenth session (**decision 1988/163**) and approved the provisional agenda and documentation for its fifteenth (1989) session (**decision 1988/162**).

TNCs in South Africa and Namibia

The Commission considered the role of TNCs in South Africa and Namibia, having before it three reports of the Secretary-General, prepared in response to a 1987 request of the Economic and Social Council.[2]

The first, on the activities of TNCs in the region and the collaboration of such corporations with the racist minority régime there,[3] presented information on recent changes in foreign direct investment and in bank lending to South Africa and focused on the shift towards non-equity forms of participation by TNCs in the economy of the region. The second report dealt with the responsibilities of home countries with respect to TNCs operating in the region in violation of United Nations decisions.[4] A report on the follow-up to the recommendations of the 1985 Panel of Eminent Persons,[5] established to conduct public hearings on the activities of TNCs in South Africa and Namibia,[6] reviewed the Panel's recommendations for adoption by TNCs and their home Governments. In order to induce TNCs to follow the recommendations, the Panel had added a number of suggested measures to international organizations, home country Governments, financial institutions and the general public. The report contained lists of TNCs which had disposed of their equity interests, those maintaining interests in the region, those in the process of disposing of their equity interests, and those which had reduced them.

The reports found that an increasing number of TNCs had terminated their operations in South Africa and Namibia. However, recent disinvestments had had an ambiguous effect, since TNCs continued to maintain their links with South Africa through licensing agreements and other non-equity arrangements.

ECONOMIC AND SOCIAL COUNCIL ACTION

On 27 July 1988, by **decision 1988/163**, the Economic and Social Council took note of the report on the follow-up to the recommendations of the Panel of Eminent Persons.

On the same date, on the recommendation of its First (Economic) Committee, the Council adopted **resolution 1988/56** by roll-call vote.

Activities of transnational corporations in South Africa and Namibia

The Economic and Social Council,

Recalling its resolutions concerning the activities of transnational corporations in South Africa and Namibia, in particular resolution 1981/86 of 2 November 1981, in which it requested the Secretary-General to make arrangements for the organization of public hearings on the activities of transnational corporations in South Africa and Namibia,

Noting with grave concern the continued deterioration of the situation in South Africa and Namibia, as evidenced by the escalating brutality, indiscrimate killing and mass arrest of innocent persons, including women and children, by the authorities of the racist minority régime,

Noting with concern that the deadline of 1 January 1987, proposed by the Panel of Eminent Persons established to conduct the public hearings on the activities of transnational corporations in South Africa and Namibia, for effecting significant changes in the operations of transnational corporations in South Africa and Namibia has not been met,

1. *Reiterates* its condemnation of the racist minority régime in South Africa and its brutal perpetuation of the inhuman system of *apartheid* and the illegal occupation of Namibia;

2. *Condemns* those transnational corporations that, through covert and overt activities in South Africa and Namibia, continue their systematic and clandestine circumventing of laws and measures imposed by the Governments of their home countries, as well as the disinvestment programmes of some transnational corporations that are aimed at retaining profitable economic links with South Africa;

3. *Welcomes* as an initial step the measures taken by some Governments of home countries of transnational corporations to impose restrictions on further investments in South Africa and on bank loans to the racist oppressive régime, and, in the light of new investments and contractual arrangements by which South Africa continues to have access to investment, technologies and resources, calls upon home countries to ensure full and effective compliance with the measures adopted, such as those prescribing disinvestment;

4. *Appeals* to Governments of home countries of transnational corporations to impose similar and additional measures on transnational corporations operating in Namibia;

5. *Reiterates* that continued collaboration, especially of transnational corporations, with the racist régime in South Africa, through trade and various traditional and innovative investments and contractual arrangements, helps perpetuate and strengthen the *apartheid* régime in its war of aggression and acts of destabilization against front-line States and other neighbouring countries and in its illegal occupation of Namibia, and urges all countries to desist from such collaboration;

6. *Urges* the Governments of home countries of transnational corporations that have not yet done so to adopt measures aimed at ensuring that transnational corporations cease to contribute to maintaining the policies

of *apartheid* of South Africa and its illegal occupation of Namibia;

7. *Urges* all transnational corporations, in accordance with the provisions of General Assembly resolutions, to stop immediately all forms of collaboration with the racist régime in South Africa as a measure to force the racist régime to abandon *apartheid*, which constitutes a crime against humanity and an affront to human dignity, and to terminate its illegal occupation of Namibia;

8. *Reaffirms* that the elimination of *apartheid* and the termination of the illegal occupation of Namibia by the racist régime will require an effective, concerted programme of international action, endorsed and supervised in a systematic manner by the United Nations, Governments and other relevant bodies and supported by monitoring and follow-up activities;

9. *Requests* the Secretary-General to take all necessary steps to establish by 1989 a panel of eminent persons to conduct public hearings in Europe on the activities of transnational corporations in South Africa and Namibia, with a view to further mobilizing public opinion to induce home Governments and transnational corporations to cease any kind of collaboration with the South African régime;

10. *Further requests* the Secretary-General:

(a) To continue the useful work carried out by the Secretariat in collecting and disseminating information on the activities of transnational corporations in South Africa and Namibia;

(b) To take all necessary measures to publicize the list contained in the report of the Secretary-General on the follow-up to the recommendations of the Panel of Eminent Persons established to conduct the public hearings on the activities of transnational corporations in South Africa and Namibia, with a view to mobilizing public opinion in home countries of transnational corporations still operating in South Africa and Namibia;

(c) To report annually to the Commission on Transnational Corporations, the Economic and Social Council, the General Assembly and the Security Council on the implementation of the present resolution, until the abolition of *apartheid* and the termination of South Africa's illegal occupation of Namibia have been achieved;

(d) To prepare an updated study on the activities of transnational corporations in South Africa and Namibia, dealing in particular with the impact of their disinvestment programmes and the replacement of investment by non-equity links, and on the responsibilities of home countries with respect to transnational corporations operating in South Africa and Namibia in violation of the relevant United Nations resolutions and decisions, bearing in mind the recommendations made by the Panel of Eminent Persons;

(e) To include in this updated study an examination of which countries have become the main home countries of transnational corporations operating in South Africa and Namibia;

(f) To take all necessary steps to ensure the immediate implementation of the recommendations of the Panel of Eminent Persons.

Economic and Social Council resolution 1988/56

27 July 1988   Meeting 39   41-2-7 (roll-call vote)

Approved by First Committee (E/1988/113) by roll-call vote (38-2-8), 19 July (meeting 17); draft by Commission on TNCs (E/1988/17), orally amended by Vice-Chairman following informal consultations; agenda item 8.

Roll-call vote in Council as follows:

In favour: Australia, Bolivia, Bulgaria, Byelorussian SSR, Canada, China, Colombia, Cuba, Denmark, Egypt, German Democratic Republic, Ghana, Greece, Guinea, India, Iran, Iraq, Italy, Jamaica, Liberia, Libyan Arab Jamahiriya, Mozambique, Norway, Oman, Pakistan, Panama, Peru, Philippines, Poland, Rwanda, Saudi Arabia, Sierra Leone, Somalia, Sri Lanka, Sudan, Trinidad and Tobago, USSR, Uruguay, Venezuela, Yugoslavia, Zaire.

Against: United Kingdom, United States.

Abstaining: Belgium, France, Germany, Federal Republic of, Ireland, Japan, Lesotho, Portugal.

Before adopting the text as a whole, the Council adopted paragraphs 5, 7 and 9 by separate roll-call votes. Paragraphs 5 and 7 were each adopted by 40 votes to 2, with 8 abstentions, while paragraph 9 received 39 votes to 2, with 9 abstentions. The Committee had approved paragraphs 5 and 7 by separate roll-call votes of 34 to 2, with 9 abstentions, and 37 to 2, with 9 abstentions, respectively.

Expert advisers

In February,[7] the Secretariat informed the Commission on TNCs that in 1988 it was to elect new expert advisers to serve until the end of the sixteenth (1990) session. The Commission thanked the retiring expert advisers for their valuable contribution and selected four new advisers with a business background, five with a trade union background and six with an academic or other background. It was agreed that one additional expert with a business background would be selected at a later date in consultation between the Commission's Chairman and the Executive Director of the Centre.

On 27 July, by **decision 1988/163**, the Economic and Social Council took note of a letter dated 3 June 1988 from the Chairman to the President of the Council informing him of the selection of the additional expert.[8]

Transborder data flows

Role of transnational banks

The Secretary-General submitted to the Commission on TNCs a report on the role of transnational banks in developing countries.[9] It described the changes in the composition of the global network of transnational banks characterized by limited expansion during the 1980s and how developing countries had been affected thereby. It noted the decline of transnational banks as the main suppliers of international finance and the shift in the nationality of such banks—while French and Japanese banks had increased the number of their foreign offices, banks from the Federal Republic of Germany, the United Kingdom and the United States had reduced theirs—and stressed that the role of transnational banks in developing countries was affected by host country regulations. The report also mentioned as a special case the widespread establishment by transnational banks of entities in offshore financial centres, which provided favourable taxation treatment, secrecy, lack of exchange controls and the near absence of regulations on international banking business. The report concluded that the activity of transnational banks in developing countries was increasingly taking securitized forms and remained largely confined to assisting foreign trade finance and participating in local markets.

In April, the Commission took note of the Secretary-General's report and asked him to continue further studies on the role of transnational banks in developing countries and to report in 1989.

By **resolution 1988/58**, the Economic and Social Council requested the Centre on TNCs to study new forms of debt, such as supplier loans and export credits, and make proposals on ways of making the terms of repayment comport with the developing countries' capacity to pay.

TNCs in services other than banking

The Secretary-General submitted a report to the Commission on TNCs on the role of TNCs in services other than banking.[10] It focused on service TNCs and their characteristics, such as propensity to transnationalize, diversification, home country and industry distribution and geographical spread of their affiliates. It briefly assessed the organizational forms of the service TNCs abroad—particularly non-equity ventures and co-operative arrangements—and concluded that the growing role of services in foreign direct investment had resulted from both the expansion of service TNCs and investment in services by industrial TNCs.

The Commission took note of the report and asked the Secretary-General to continue research on TNCs in services other than banking and to report to the Commission in 1989.

By **resolution 1988/58**, the Economic and Social Council requested the Centre on TNCs to prepare a report on the relationship between developing countries and TNCs in services from the perspective of developing countries.

Role of the Commission on TNCs in promoting international economic co-operation

On 27 July, on the recommendation of its First Committee, the Economic and Social Council adopted **resolution 1988/57** without vote.

Role of the Commission on Transnational Corporations in promoting alternative and new forms of international economic co-operation

The Economic and Social Council,

Reaffirming its resolutions 1908(LVII) of 2 August 1974 and 1913(LVII) of 5 December 1974,

Reiterating the important role of the United Nations in promoting equitable and mutually beneficial international economic co-operation as a major factor in economic development and well-being, world wide, particularly in developing countries,

Noting with appreciation the important role of the Commission on Transnational Corporations and the United Nations Centre on Transnational Corporations in strengthening the capacity of developing countries in their dealings with transnational corporations by promoting technical co-operation, research and information activities in accordance with their mandates,

Recognizing that alternative and new forms of international investment, scientific and technological exchange and equity and non-equity co-operation, including joint ventures, should contribute to sustained growth and development world wide, particularly in developing countries,

1. *Calls* for the further strengthening of the role of the Commission on Transnational Corporations and the United Nations Centre on Transnational Corporations, as the focal points within the United Nations system for issues related specifically to transnational corporations and for co-ordination with other intergovernmental bodies and secretariats on all matters in that regard;

2. *Emphasizes* the need to enhance the work of the Centre in providing consultative, advisory and other types of technical assistance to developing countries, in conducting analytical research and studies and in gathering and disseminating information related to the development of alternative and new forms of international investment, scientific and technological exchange and other co-operative arrangements, including joint ventures, pertaining to the operations of transnational corporations, particularly in view of the development needs of the developing countries;

3. *Requests* the Secretary-General to report to the Commission at its fifteenth session on the implementation of the present resolution, including the improvement of co-operation and co-ordination within the United Nations system in accordance with the mandate of the Centre.

Economic and Social Council resolution 1988/57

27 July 1988   Meeting 39   Adopted without vote

Approved by First Committee (E/1988/113) without vote, 19 July (meeting 17); draft by Commission on TNCs (E/1988/17); agenda item 8.

REFERENCES

[1]E/1988/17. [2]YUN 1987, p. 148, ESC res. 1987/56, 28 May 1987. [3]E/C.10/1988/7. [4]E/C.10/1988/8. [5]YUN 1985, p. 149. [6]E/1988/23 & Corr.1-3. [7]E/C.10/1988/15 & Add.1. [8]E/1988/99. [9]E/C.10/1988/12. [10]E/C.10/1988/13.

PUBLICATIONS

Joint Venture as a Form of International Economic Co-operation (ST/CTC/93), Sales No. E.88.II.A.12. *Data Goods and Data Services in the Socialist Countries of Eastern Europe* (ST/CTC/80), Sales No. E.88.II.A.20.

Centre on TNCs

In 1988, the United Nations Centre on TNCs continued to develop an information system, to conduct research and to carry out technical co-operation activities. It also acted as the substantive secretariat to the Commission on TNCs and the Intergovernmental Working Group of Experts on International Standards of Accounting and Reporting.

In response to a 1987 request by the Commission,[1] the Secretary-General submitted a report on the Centre's activities.[2] It summarized the Centre's work on securing an effective code of conduct and other international arrangements and agreements related to TNCs. It also contained information on the Centre's activities aimed at minimizing the negative effects of TNCs and enhancing their contribution to development, and strengthening the capabilities of developing countries in dealing with TNCs.

Information system

In 1988, the Centre's information system continued to record and supply statistical data on foreign direct investment and related flows, having access to governmental sources and International Monetary Fund balance-of-payment and international financial statistics tapes, as well as data from other intergovernmental organizations.

The Centre increased to 30 the number of countries or territories on which it gathered data by official national source on the total inward and outward stocks and/or flows of foreign direct investment. The developing countries or territories for which data were collected were Bangladesh, Brazil, Chile, China, Colombia, Hong Kong, Indonesia, Malaysia, Panama, Peru, the Philippines, the Republic of Korea, Singapore, Thailand and Venezuela; the developed countries were Australia, Canada, Denmark, Finland, France, the Federal Republic of Germany, Japan, the Netherlands, New Zealand, Norway, Portugal, Sweden, Switzerland, the United Kingdom and the United States.

The Centre also collected and computerized basic numerical data on the world's largest TNCs in the manufacturing and extractive sectors. It expanded its collection of foreign investment laws and contracts and agreements, particularly in the areas of petroleum and mining.

A data base of bibliographic citations was created by the Centre, in co-operation with the United Nations Electronic Services Division and the Dag Hammarskjöld Library. The data base contained references to books, periodicals, serials, articles, and documents by governmental and intergovernmental organizations dealing with TNCs, foreign direct investment and the institutional and regulatory frameworks pertaining to them. The first product of the data base was *Transnational Corporations: A Selective Bibliography, 1983-1987.*

The Centre continued to respond to requests from government institutions for assistance in developing and refining national information systems on TNCs, with a view to increasing the effectiveness of those systems.

During 1988, requests from Governments, trade unions, business organizations, academic institutions and the media increased. The information system received 1,940 requests for which the responses required research; in addition, 2,100 short-answer requests were received.

A report of the Secretary-General to the Commission[3] described experience gained in the use of the information system on TNCs. It concluded with some observations on the information needs of developing countries and an exploration of further steps that might be taken to improve the system.

Joint units with regional commissions

Joint units established between the Centre on TNCs and the United Nations regional commissions continued to operate in 1988 in Africa, Asia and the Pacific, Europe, Latin America and the Caribbean, and Western Asia.[4] Each unit's work programme, tailored to the region's specific needs, included research on the economic, social and institutional issues of TNCs, information dissemination, training and advisory services.

The joint unit with the Economic Commission for Africa (ECA) undertook research within the context of the United Nations Programme of Action for African Economic Recovery and Development 1986-1990.[5] Particular attention was given to the following projects: the role of TNCs in the food-processing industry in selected African countries; the role of TNCs in regional co-operation, based on national experiences of the region covered by the Customs and Economic Union of Central Africa; the integration of women in development; and the role of TNCs in the development of informatics. The provision of information on foreign direct investment gained prominence in the activities of the joint unit. In collaboration with ECA's Pan-African Documentation and Information System, the unit started to collect all available macro- and micro-data relating to the main TNCs operating in the region.

The joint unit with the Economic Commission for Europe focused its research activities on the contribution to *Transnational Corporations in World Development: Trends and Prospects.* Research was carried out on Japanese foreign direct investment in Europe. In the area of technical assistance, the unit directed a workshop on negotiating and implementing agreements with TNCs (Port Moresby, Papua New Guinea). The unit assisted the Centre in preparing, organizing and implementing a workshop on frameworks for international services. Work continued on setting up and organizing at Geneva the Centre's Regional European Documentation Centre on TNCs.

The joint unit established with the Economic and Social Commission for Asia and the Pacific (ESCAP) completed its research project on TNCs based in Asian developing economies. In collaboration with the United Nations Environment Programme, it undertook a research project on the environmental aspects of TNC activities in the region. It undertook a re-examination of the role of TNCs in the tourism industry in Thailand and conducted a research project on TNCs in the international trade of primary commodities. In order to enhance the dissemination of information, the unit published in 1988 an edition of the *Asia-Pacific TNC Review*. During the year, it provided administrative and technical support to training workshops and advisory missions conducted by the Centre, including seminars on legal aspects of transnational investments in developing countries (Singapore, 2-13 May) and on the role of foreign direct investment and trade in services and development (Bangkok, Thailand, 6-9 June). The unit also continued activities leading to the development of national information systems and the establishment of an information network among ESCAP member countries.

The joint unit established with the Economic Commission for Latin America and the Caribbean focused its research on analysing the behaviour of TNCs and their impact on the development process in Latin America. Studies were conducted on policy alternatives and experiences with regard to foreign direct investment; the impact of TNCs on the industrial structure of developing countries; debt equity conversion; and the behaviour of transnational banks and the international debt crisis. In the field of technical co-operation, the joint unit identified potential investors in selected industrial sectors in connection with the programme of industrial restructuring in Peru.

The joint unit with the Economic and Social Commission for Western Asia completed studies on the impact of the operations of TNCs on the development of Oman and on the experience of Egypt in external financing during the period of 1974-1986. It initiated the preparation of studies on Arab petrochemicals and rising protectionism in the developed market economies and on institutional arrangements and procedures for screening and monitoring the activities of TNCs in Western Asia. Information was gathered on TNCs operating in the region as an input to the Centre's directory on foreign direct investment.

TNCs and developing countries

On 27 July 1988, on the recommendation of its First Committee, the Economic and Social Council adopted **resolution 1988/58** by roll-call vote.

Strengthening the role of the Commission on Transnational Corporations and the activities of the United Nations Centre on Transnational Corporations in support of developing countries

The Economic and Social Council,

Reaffirming its resolutions 1908(LVII) of 2 August 1974 and 1913(LVII) of 5 December 1974 on the impact of transnational corporations on the development process and on international relations,

Noting the reports of the Secretary-General submitted to the Commission on Transnational Corporations at its fourteenth session,

Noting also the important contribution made by the Commission and the United Nations Centre on Transnational Corporations to furthering the understanding of the operations of transnational corporations and the effects of their activities on developing host countries and on the international economic situation,

1. *Reaffirms* the validity of the mandates of the Commission on Transnational Corporations and the United Nations Centre on Transnational Corporations;

2. *Emphasizes* the need for the Centre to reinforce its role in strengthening the capacity of developing host countries in their dealings with transnational corporations by providing, through its technical co-operation programme, advisory services to those countries at their request, and urges all funding agencies of the United Nations, in particular the United Nations Development Programme, to co-operate actively in that task;

3. *Requests* the Centre to continue its studies on political, economic and social issues and on the global trends and determinants of the flow of foreign direct investment and the impact of those trends and the expansion of transnational corporations on developing countries;

4. *Requests* the Centre, in continuing its work in the area of transnational corporations in services, to prepare, in co-operation with the appropriate organs, organizations and bodies of the United Nations system, a comprehensive report on the relationship between developing countries and transnational corporations in services from the perspective of developing countries;

5. *Reaffirms* the importance of continuing consideration of the issues related to the activities of transnational banks and their corporate strategies and the different mechanisms currently envisaged to alleviate the debt problem and their potential impact on the capital accounts of developing countries; in that context, consideration should also be given to the effective repayment capacity of debtor developing countries, allowing for the maintenance of satisfactory growth in their economies;

6. *Recognizes* that debt other than bank lending, such as supplier loans and export credits handled by transnational corporations, is of concern to developing countries, and requests the Centre to study such forms of debt comprehensively, with a view to making concrete proposals on ways and means of making the modalities and terms of payment comport with the capacity of developing countries to pay and with their growth and development process;

7. *Expresses concern* that some transnational corporations have relocated environmentally dangerous operations and processes in developing countries, and requests the Centre to intensify its study of the environmental impact of the operations of transnational corporations in developing countries and to provide technical assistance to developing host countries, at their request, for the development of adequate environmental protection policies relating to the operations of transnational corporations;

8. *Requests* the Centre to assist in the preparation of the report of the Secretary-General on illegal traffic in toxic and dangerous products and wastes in accordance with General Assembly resolution 42/183 of 11 December 1987 and in the expeditious publication of the fourth issue of the *Consolidated List of Products Whose Consumption*

and/or Sale Have Been Banned, Withdrawn, Severely Restricted or Not Approved by Governments;

9. *Also requests* the Centre to study the role of transnational corporations in the least developed countries in a comprehensive manner, and requests the Secretary-General to submit a report thereon to the Commission on Transnational Corporations at its fifteenth session;

10. *Reiterates* the need for the Centre to intensify its technical co-operation with host developing countries, at their request, in dealing with transnational corporations in services;

11. *Reiterates also* the importance of the expeditious completion of the code of conduct on transnational corporations, and requests the Secretary-General to continue to assist the Chairman presiding at the special session of the Commission in implementing the tasks assigned to him by the Economic and Social Council in resolution 1987/57 of 28 May 1987;

12. *Requests* the Secretary-General to report on the implementation of the present resolution to the Commission on Transnational Corporations at its fifteenth session under the appropriate agenda items.

Economic and Social Council resolution 1988/58

| 27 July 1988 | Meeting 39 | 36-5-9 (roll-call vote) |

Approved by First Committee (E/1988/113) by roll-call vote (34-5-9), 19 July (meeting 17); draft by Commission on TNCs (E/1988/17); agenda item 8.

Roll-call vote in Council as follows:

In favour: Bolivia, Bulgaria, Byelorussian SSR, China, Colombia, Cuba, Egypt, German Democratic Republic, Ghana, Guinea, India, Iran, Iraq, Jamaica, Lesotho, Liberia, Libyan Arab Jamahiriya, Mozambique, Oman, Pakistan, Panama, Peru, Philippines, Poland, Rwanda, Saudi Arabia, Sierra Leone, Somalia, Sri Lanka, Sudan, Trinidad and Tobago, USSR, Uruguay, Venezuela, Yugoslavia, Zaire.

Against: Australia, France, Germany, Federal Republic of, United Kingdom, United States.

Abstaining: Belgium, Canada, Denmark, Greece, Ireland, Italy, Japan, Norway, Portugal.

By **decision 1988/161** of 27 July, the Council requested the Secretary-General to include in the report to the *Ad Hoc* Committee of the Whole of the General Assembly on the Review and Appraisal of the United Nations Programme of Action for African Economic Recovery and Development 1986-1990[5] the contribution made by the Centre from June 1986 to July 1988 in support of the Programme's implementation. It also requested the Secretary-General to submit a report to the *Ad Hoc* Committee proposing ways for TNCs to increase foreign direct investment in Africa, with a view to stimulating the region's economic recovery and development.

Research

The Centre continued to examine, monitor and analyse multilateral, regional and bilateral agreements relating to TNCs. A report of the Secretary-General on the negotiation, adoption, implementation and follow-up of the regional and multilateral agreements relating to foreign direct investment and TNCs, and their impact on the elaboration of standards of conduct and treatment for TNCs was submitted to the Commission.[6]

In 1988, the Centre completed work on the fourth survey of TNCs in world development. A report of the Secretary-General to the Commission[7] said the survey described the main behaviour of TNCs in the 1980s and analysed their impact on the world economy. Most of what was observed could be traced to one main theme, the continuation of the process of transnationalization. The recent growth of TNCs was different in important respects from previous periods of expansion. Small and medium-sized companies, including some from developing countries, were expanding more rapidly than larger firms. TNCs from Japan and Western Europe were rapidly expanding their transnational activities, while firms from the United States were expanding more slowly and, in some instances, contracting. Corporations were transnationalizing more rapidly in service activities than in manufacturing. At the same time, forms of transnationalization were changing, with various non-equity arrangements either replacing or supplementing foreign direct investment. Research findings indicated that the activities of TNCs were becoming increasingly concentrated in the developed market economies.

In April,[8] the Commission took note of the report and requested the Centre to prepare another study in 1989 on recent developments related to TNCs and international economic relations and to prepare the fifth survey on TNCs in 1993.

The Centre's research programme during 1988 developed a number of the themes that were raised in the fourth survey. They were summarized in a report of the Secretary-General.[9] Of particular importance were the impact of new and emerging technologies on strategies of TNCs and the distribution of world-wide flows of foreign direct investment.

During 1988, the Centre published two issues of the *CTC Reporter*, its semi-annual magazine, and four issues of *Transnationals*, a quarterly newsletter.

The Centre carried out research on the role of TNCs in the process of sustainable development and was represented at various intergovernmental and professional conferences. It assisted host developing countries on issues related to hazardous waste. In a report on TNCs and their impact on the environment,[10] the Secretary-General provided an update on the activities of international organizations, individual Governments, non-governmental organizations and industry in ensuring industrial process safety. The report focused on the responses of TNCs to industrial accidents. In April,[8] the Commission took note of the report and encouraged the Centre to assist host Governments in integrating the activities of TNCs in a policy of sustainable development. It requested the Centre to report in 1989.

Technical co-operation

In 1988,[11] developing countries continued to reappraise their policies towards foreign investment and technology transfer. In order to attract greater inflows, many developing countries sought the

Centre's assistance in reformulating their foreign investment and technology policies.

The Centre completed or initiated 100 advisory and information projects in 41 developing countries. Of those, 50 were in 18 African countries, 29 were in 14 countries in Asia and the Pacific, and 21 were in 10 countries in Latin America and the Caribbean.

The majority of advisory and information services were related to the formulation of foreign investment policies, laws and regulations relating to foreign investment and technology transfer, the formulation of model contracts and agreements, and the streamlining of institutional mechanisms and administrative procedures for approving, monitoring and promoting foreign investment. The rest pertained to specific sectors and to issues such as export-processing zones and transfer pricing. Thirty-two projects were completed or initiated in the forestry, manufacturing, mining, petroleum, telecommunication and tourism sectors. The Centre implemented 32 training projects consisting of 23 workshops, round-table meetings or seminars and 9 study tours and fellowships. It continued its sponsorship of the study tour programme for several developing countries.

After finalization and distribution of the curricula relating to TNCs for advanced courses in transnational law, economics and business, three seminars were held for representatives of higher educational institutions in Asia.

Activities to support harmonization efforts within regional institutions continued during 1988. The secretariat of the Preferential Trade Area for Eastern and Southern African States (PTA), with the Centre's assistance, entered the second phase of its programme of rationalization and harmonization of PTA investment codes. The Centre also assisted the Organization of Eastern Caribbean States in its efforts to harmonize its foreign investment and technology transfer policies, laws and regulations. A major study was prepared, which provided an analytical background to the foreign investment policies, laws and regulations in the subregion and made suggestions on common approaches to promote intraregional benefits. In the area of services, the Centre began a joint project with the Junta del Acuerdo de Cartagena, Colombia, to examine technology transfer through TNCs in services to the Andean Pact subregion. In order to influence the tailoring of debt-equity swaps to particular domestic situations of developing countries within the general framework of debt management solutions, the Centre, together with the Latin American Economic System, organized an international seminar on debt-equity swaps (Caracas, Venezuela, April).

The Centre developed an extensive technical assistance programme that utilized TNC linkages for the development of entrepreneurship and technology-based small and medium-sized enterprises in developing countries. During 1988, the programme was launched in Argentina.

A report of the Secretary-General to the Commission on TNCs focused on the Centre's role in meeting the technical assistance requirements of developing countries.[12] In April,[8] the Commission took note of the report and requested the Secretary-General to submit to it in 1989 a further report on the subject. It reaffirmed the importance it attached to the Centre's technical co-operation programme.

Financing

The Centre's technical co-operation programme continued to be financed mainly by extra-budgetary resources from the Centre's Trust Fund and from allocations from the United Nations Development Programme (UNDP).[4] Total extra-budgetary resources in 1988 amounted to $5,568,280. Contributions to the Trust Fund reached $2,934,587; the significant increase was attributed to continuing support by several donor countries and the input made by new donors. The Fund's opening balance was $1,050,548 and interest income amounted to $300,000. Resources made available by UNDP totalled $1,283,145. Total disbursements in 1988 amounted to $3,115,137; advisory projects accounted for $988,552 and workshops and other training activities for $1,523,573.

REFERENCES

[1]YUN 1987, p. 513. [2]E/C.10/1988/3. [3]E/C.10/1988/14. [4]E/C.10/1989/3. [5]YUN 1986, p. 446, GA res. S-13/2, annex, 1 June 1986. [6]E/C.10/1988/5. [7]E/C.10/1988/2. [8]E/1988/17. [9]E/C.10/1988/10 and Corr.1. [10]E/C.10/1988/11. [11]DP/1989/46/Add.2. [12]E/C.10/1988/9.

PUBLICATIONS

Bilateral Investment Treaties (ST/CTC/65), Sales No. E.88.II.A.1. *Foreign Direct Investment in the People's Republic of China* (ST/CTC/73), Sales No. E.88.II.A.3. *Transnational Corporations in Biotechnology* (ST/CTC/61), Sales No. E.88.II.A.4. *International Income Taxation and Developing Countries* (ST/CTC/56), Sales No. E.88.II.A.6. *Transnational Corporations in World Development: Trends and Prospects* (ST/CTC/89), Sales No. E.88.II.A.7. *Transnational Corporations: A Selective Bibliography 1983-1987*, vol. I (ST/CTC/76, vol. I), Sales No. E.88.II.A.9; vol. II (ST/CTC/76, vol. II), Sales No. E.88.II.A.10.

Chapter VI

Natural resources, energy and cartography

During 1988, the United Nations Revolving Fund for Natural Resources Exploration continued to assist developing countries in natural resources exploration and development. It became operational in the Asia region with projects in China and the Philippines.

In December, the General Assembly requested the Secretary-General to outline a programme of action to accelerate the exploration and development of the energy resources of developing countries and to undertake appropriate studies and analyses (resolution 43/193). It endorsed the report of the Committee on the Development and Utilization of New and Renewable Sources of Energy and urged members of the Committee to consider further measures to strengthen United Nations activities in that area (43/192).

In October, the Assembly urged all States to strive for international co-operation in carrying out the work of the International Atomic Energy Agency and in applying measures to strengthen the safety of nuclear installations (43/16).

In May, the Economic and Social Council requested the Secretary-General to implement the recommendations adopted at the Fifth (1987) United Nations Conference on the Standardization of Geographical Names (decision 1988/116).

Natural resources

Exploration

UN Revolving Fund for
Natural Resources Exploration

The United Nations Revolving Fund for Natural Resources Exploration assists developing countries in natural resources exploration and development. During 1988,[1] it pursued two goals—more equitable distribution of projects and greater variety in the type of minerals being sought. The Fund became active in the Asia region with new mineral targets: pyrophyllite in China and chromite in the Philippines. In addition, the Fund expanded its geothermal activities with a project in Mexico and the evaluation of other potential projects in Latin America and the Caribbean, Asia and the Pacific and Africa.

The Fund had 12 projects operating during 1988, including nine mineral exploration projects (Argentina, China, Côte d'Ivoire, Ghana, Haiti, Honduras, Peru, Philippines, Rwanda), one feasibility study (Congo) and two geothermal projects (Mexico, Saint Lucia).

Peru requested the Fund to extend its exploration activities into two new areas, resulting in the identification of more than 230 million cubic metres of gold-bearing gravels containing about 1.5 million ounces of recoverable gold. The Government was seeking financing to bring the deposit into production.

Exploration for gold in Ghana began early in the year with financial support from Sweden. By the end of 1988, geophysical and geochemical investigations had been completed and a zone of gold mineralization about 1 kilometre long identified.

The Fund's project in Haiti was completed in 1988 and its report listed gold in the area known as Faille B. The project involved the drilling of 3,200 metres, consisting of 31 boreholes, 97 line kilometres of geophysical surveys and analysis of more than 8,300 samples. The reserves discovered amounted to approximately 520,000 tonnes with a grade of 14 grams of gold per tonne. The Fund was assisting the Government in attracting investment to bring the discovery into production.

Projects in Rwanda and Côte d'Ivoire were concluded without significant mineral discoveries. However, in Rwanda, results would assist co-operatives in the exploration of modest quantities of gold.

In the Congo, the Fund's offshore phosphate feasibility study entered an advanced stage with the signing of a contract with the Bureau de recherches géologiques et minières of France. Activities would include bulk sampling and environmental, marketing, infrastructure and economic studies.

In a March 1988 report,[2] the Administrator of the United Nations Development Programme (UNDP) presented a review of the terms and conditions of Fund assistance with a view to seeing whether they could be made more attractive to recipient countries without sacrificing the intention to build up the revolving Fund from successful projects. The Administrator concluded that the terms and conditions should not be changed.

On 1 July,[3] the UNDP Governing Council took note of the Administrator's report and approved his recommendations; noted his approval of supplementary short-term financing for the offshore phosphate feasibility study in the Congo; approved exploration for precious and base metals in Ghana; noted the success of the Fund in obtaining joint financing of its projects; and renewed its appeal to Member States to contribute to the Fund.

Financing

In 1988, project expenditures totalled $6.9 million compared to $4.6 million in 1987. Total income was $2.9 million, which included voluntary contributions of $2.3 million from eight Governments. By year's end, the Fund's balance stood at $3.4 million.

Mineral resources

Technical co-operation

The 1988 activities of the United Nations Department of Technical Co-operation for Development (DTCD) were described in a report of the Secretary-General.[4]

During the year, there was increased interest in investment programmes, human resources development, efforts to attract the private sector to mining, and the transfer of technology. Total assistance delivered by DTCD for mineral resources was $12.5 million, up from $11.1 million in 1987. The distribution of expenditures was $7.5 million in Africa, $1.8 million each in Asia and the Pacific and in the Americas, and $1.4 million in the Mediterranean, Middle East, Europe and interregional programme. Advisory missions increased to 120, up from 59 in 1987.

DTCD provided legal, technical, economic and negotiating expertise to the Dominican Republic in negotiations related to the FALCONDO nickel project, nickel being the country's major foreign exchange earner. As part of a gold investment promotion project in Guyana, a compendium of information for prospective investors was prepared and advertised through a commercially printed prospectus. In Burkina Faso, a geochemical survey, follow-up field checking and assistance in connection with the recovery of gold were completed.

With the World Bank, DTCD initiated a review of investment conditions in African countries aimed at reversing the decline of mining production. Support to negotiations for a titanium oxide mining operation between Senegal and the Du Pont company of the United States led to an investment agreement. DTCD advisers reviewed mineral investment contracts in Bolivia, Brazil, Ethiopia, Guinea, Haiti, Indonesia, Kenya, Malaysia, Malta, Pakistan, Peru and the Philippines.

An interregional seminar on small-scale mining in developing countries was held at Ankara, Turkey, from 19 to 25 September 1988, organized by DTCD with the support of UNDP.

Water resources

The traditional approach to water resources management dealt with water almost exclusively as a natural resource. The other uses of fresh water as a major component of ecosystems and a carrier of matter in natural cycles and its role in socio-economic development were taken into account by the United Nations Environment Programme (UNEP) in its programme for the environmentally sound management of inland water. During 1988,[5] attention under the programme focused on the Lake Chad basin, which had deteriorated as a result of a prolonged dry period.

UNEP assisted the Lake Chad Basin Commission by outlining the necessary steps for the preparation of a water master plan and an action programme for the environmentally sound management of the basin through: lake inflow and water balance control; reinforcing the recharge of underground waters; development of sound water use; water and soil conservation projects; improvement of rain-fed and irrigated agriculture; and restoration of vegetation.

While the implementation of the action plan for the Zambezi River system was primarily a matter for the Southern African Development Co-ordination Conference, UNEP's concern with the development of large international basins focused on an advanced decision support system for basin management. In 1988, in co-operation with the International Institute for Applied Systems Analysis, UNEP continued to develop and test an interactive programme for the decision support system. A case-study of the Zambezi basin was prepared to demonstrate the methodology to the institutions involved in the implementation of the Zambezi plan.

In the Mekong Delta, one way to increase food production lay in more intensive agriculture and improvement of water and land management through restoration of the agricultural productivity of the acid sulphate soils, though the method of improvement of acid soils was not feasible over large areas. In co-operation with the USSR Commission for UNEP, a survey mission was dispatched to the Delta to establish two pilot farms covering at least 5,000 hectares each. Some 12 Vietnamese specialists underwent training in the USSR in rational agricultural land use and water resources development, and another 16 were trained in the technology of intensive rice growing in the Delta.

Projects were also developed for the protection and development of the Lake Xolotlán basin in Nicaragua and the Orinoco-Apure river system in Venezuela.

UNEP was equally concerned with the environmentally sound management of ground-water resources. An expert group meeting was held

(Bahrain, March) to discuss the preparation of an action plan for the management of the Damman aquifer. Experts from Bahrain, Kuwait, Oman, Qatar, Saudi Arabia, the United Arab Emirates, the Arab Centre for the Study of Arid Zones and Dry Lands and the Economic and Social Commission for Western Asia attended. They agreed on the need to prevent the pollution of recharge water by industrial and domestic waste and to co-operate in conserving ground-water resources.

Inter-agency co-ordination

The Intersecretariat Group for Water Resources of the Administrative Committee on Co-ordination (ninth session, Geneva, 17, 18 and 21 October 1988)[6] discussed the preparation of a strategy for the implementation in the 1990s of the Mar del Plata Action Plan for the development of water resources, adopted in 1977 by the United Nations Water Conference.[7] It also considered the water situation in Africa, operation and maintenance for water resources, data collection and dissemination, water demand management, and the implications of the 1987 report of the World Commission on Environment and Development[8] in regard to water resources development and utilization.

Technical co-operation

During 1988,[4] better use and fuller development of water resources continued to be of major interest to Member States, as DTCD shifted its focus to longer-term water resources planning and assessment of resource availability. The number of projects decreased from 126 in 1987 to 113 in 1988, while the total budget for the sector increased from $24 million in 1987 to $24.3 million in 1988. The regional distribution of funds was as follows: Africa, $10.5 million or 54.5 per cent; Asia and the Pacific, $4.1 million or 21.6 per cent; the Middle East, Mediterranean, Europe and inter-regional programme, $2.7 million or 14.1 per cent; and the Americas, $1.9 million or 9.8 per cent.

Rural water supply continued to comprise a significant part of the technical assistance programme, with about 18 per cent of all projects. While a quarter of those projects were concerned with institutional support and training for technicans and professionals, there was an increase in the number of projects to improve the management and planning of water resources.

The most significant rural water supply project in 1988 was carried out in the Abeche-Mongo area of Chad. The project undertook to sink about 500 boreholes to provide potable water to a population of 35,000.

Assistance related to dams and other hydraulic structures also increased. Project support was provided to hydraulic research centres in Bangladesh, India, Iran and Viet Nam. A project on dam safety and monitoring was begun in India and a similar project formulated for China.

In Bangladesh, which had been plagued by floods, the physical models previously used for hydraulic studies were being replaced by mathematical models.

In water management and planning, two projects stood out: water resources management in three river basins of Tamil Nadu, India, financed by a World Bank loan to the state Government, aimed to demonstrate that improved management and more efficient use could make more water available; in Yemen, a project was helping to establish a technical secretariat to support the High Water Council in setting up a water resource data base and preparing a national master plan.

In addition to UNDP-financed projects, 42 interregional advisory missions were sponsored under the United Nations Regular Programme of Technical Co-operation, covering such areas as water legislation, water well drilling, computerized data management and hydrogeology. Activities under the Programme included the convening of an interregional seminar on river and lake basin development, emphasizing the African region (Addis Ababa, Ethiopia, October), and an international seminar on women's role in the water resources sector (Bamako, Mali, November).

REFERENCES

[1]DP/1989/49 & Corr.1. [2]DP/1988/48 & Corr.1. [3]E/1988/19 (dec. 88/40). [4]DP/1989/46/Add.1. [5]UNEP/GC.15/4. [6]ACC/1988/PG/14. [7]YUN 1977, p. 555. [8]YUN 1987, p. 679.

PUBLICATIONS

Ground Water in Eastern, Central and Southern Africa (ST/TCD/6 & Corr.1), Sales No. E.88.II.A.5. *Water Resources Planning to Meet Long-term Demand: Guidelines for Developing Countries* (ST/TCD/8), Sales No. E.88.II.A.17. *Acquisition of Marine Surveying Technologies—Addis Ababa* (ST/ESA/202), Sales No. E.88.II.A.19. *Legal and Institutional Factors Affecting the Implementation of the International Drinking Water Supply and Sanitation Decade* (ST/TCD/7), Sales No. E.88.II.A.21.

Energy

Energy resources development

In an August 1988 report[1] to the General Assembly, the Secretary-General focused on energy exploration and development trends in developing countries. Since his previous report,[2] the dimensions of the oil price collapse in 1986 and its subsequent stabilization in 1987 at about half the level that had prevailed had become clearer. Investments by national oil companies in the developing world had suffered in oil-exporting countries because of massive production over-capacities and great reduction in foreign exchange revenues from oil sales.

The expectation in oil-importing countries that savings on oil imports could be channelled to the development of indigenous energy resources had hardly materialized. Corporate cash flows had also been reduced, with consequent cut-backs in investments, because of the oil glut and fears of another oil price collapse to the low levels of $6 to $9 a barrel reached in mid-1986. Such investments had been further reduced by the failure of hundreds of independent oil corporations that had prospered during the 1970s and the first half of the 1980s in North America, the North Sea and elsewhere because of high oil prices.

The report analysed energy consumption trends, provided data on energy exploration, development and production, discussed investments and changes in petroleum industry structures, and described new methods of energy financing. It concluded that the energy-deficient developing countries had not been able to adjust to changes in the global energy situation because of their lack of financial resources and technologies. Their energy import bill still weighed heavily on their total foreign exchange. With a resumption of economic growth, the import dependence of oil-importing developing countries would become even more pronounced.

During the next decade, it was expected that the world energy demand, particularly for oil, would again increase pressures for higher prices. There was a need for international co-operation to ensure stability in energy investments, production and consumption patterns, and, in that connection, the role of the United Nations merited consideration. A country-by-country survey of available energy projections and plans to the year 2000 might be initiated. The results of such a survey and their implications for energy self-reliance could then be submitted to the Assembly in 1990.

UNDP action. The UNDP Energy Office/Energy Account promoted activities in the energy sector of developing countries and provided technical advice to UNDP on energy-related projects. On 1 July,[3] the UNDP Governing Council, having considered the report of the Administrator on new arrangements in UNDP in the areas of science, technology and energy,[4] recommended that the name of the United Nations Fund for Science and Technology for Development be changed to the United Nations Fund for Science, Technology and Energy. It also decided to close the Energy Office; the Energy Account would remain as a sub-account of the Fund. (See PART THREE, Chapter VII.)

Technical co-operation

The Secretary-General, in a report to the UNDP Governing Council on United Nations technical co-operation activities,[5] stated that the budget of DTCD in the energy sector during 1988 was $15.8 million, compared to $21.3 million in 1987. Expenditures were as follows: $9.1 million for Asia and the Pacific; $2.5 million for the Middle East, Europe, the Mediterranean and interregional programme; and $2.1 million each for Africa and the Americas. The decrease in expenditures reflected the lower priority given to the energy sector by developing countries in response to lower world oil prices. A total of 78 advisory missions were carried out in 49 countries during the year in the areas of petroleum, coal, natural gas, electric power, energy planning and conservation, geothermal, solar and wind energy, multi-source renewable energy packages, computerized data banks and microcomputer-based energy analysis.

GENERAL ASSEMBLY ACTION

On 20 December 1988, on the recommendation of the Second Committee, the General Assembly adopted without vote **resolution 43/193**.

Development of the energy resources of developing countries

The General Assembly,

Recalling the Declaration and the Programme of Action on the Establishment of a New International Economic Order, contained in its resolutions 3201(S-VI) and 3202(S-VI) of 1 May 1974, the Charter of Economic Rights and Duties of States, contained in its resolution 3281(XXIX) of 12 December 1974, its resolution 3362(S-VII) of 16 September 1975 on development and international economic co-operation, and the International Development Strategy for the Third United Nations Development Decade, contained in the annex to its resolution 35/56 of 5 December 1980,

Recalling also its resolution 40/208 of 17 December 1985 on the development of the energy resources of developing countries,

Reaffirming the importance of the development of the energy resources of developing countries and the need for measures by the international community to assist and support the efforts of the developing countries, in particular the energy-deficient among them, to develop their energy resources, in order to meet their needs through co-operation, assistance and investment in the field of conventional and of new and renewable sources of energy, consistent with their national plans and priorities,

1. *Reaffirms* its resolution 40/208 and calls for the effective implementation of all its provisions;

2. *Welcomes* the report of the Secretary-General on energy exploration and development trends in developing countries;

3. *Notes with concern* that these trends have been on the decline in recent years, and therefore requests the Secretary-General to outline a programme of action aimed at the acceleration of the exploration and development of the energy resources of developing countries;

4. *Welcomes* the convening of symposia and other similar undertakings called for in resolution 40/208 and calls upon interested Member States, in co-operation

with the appropriate organs, organizations and bodies of the United Nations system, to continue to explore ways and means to support the efforts of developing countries in the exploration and development of their energy resources;

5. *Requests* the Secretary-General to continue to undertake appropriate studies and analyses of trends in energy exploration and development of energy resources of developing countries, taking into account the activities of relevant organizations of the United Nations system in this field, and to report to the General Assembly at its forty-fifth session, through the Economic and Social Council at its second regular session of 1990.

General Assembly resolution 43/193

20 December 1988   Meeting 83   Adopted without vote

Approved by Second Committee (A/43/915/Add.5) without vote, 15 November (meeting 42); draft by Tunisia, for Group of 77 (A/C.2/43/L.27), orally revised; agenda item 82 *(e)*.

Meeting numbers. GA 43rd session: 2nd Committee 21-26, 30, 42; plenary 83.

New and renewable energy sources

Implementation of the Nairobi Programme

The Secretary-General, in response to a 1986 request,[6] submitted a report in January 1988[7] to the Committee on the Development and Utilization of New and Renewable Sources of Energy, concerning trends and policy considerations as well as technological developments, as identified in the 1981 Nairobi Programme of Action for the Development and Utilization of New and Renewable Sources of Energy.[8]

The report stated that a slow-down in global economic growth had been accompanied by slack energy markets and decreasing prices. The supply of petroleum continued to be abundant. Supplies of coal and natural gas showed small increases, while nuclear electricity capacities grew markedly. The report stressed that current abundant energy supplies pertained only to the commercial sector of the global energy economy. The rural sector in developing countries was largely disconnected from international energy markets and therefore did not benefit. It relied for energy on traditional sources, including fuelwood, charcoal, draught animal power and agricultural and animal residues.

More than 2 billion rural inhabitants depended on fuelwood, the majority living in areas where fuelwood scarcity was acute. The fuelwood crisis was affecting their nutrition, health and living standards; it was imperative to address that situation. A considerable increase in woodlot planting, widespread use of improved forest management techniques and utilization of fast-growing and appropriate species were essential. Further, the demand for fuelwood could be reduced through conversion to efficient stoves and kilns and to alternative sources of energy such as biogas, gasifiers, small-scale hydropower and wind and solar energy.

Recent technological developments in the use of energy sources had generally been of an incremental nature without major breakthroughs, according to the report. Development efforts had been set back by the unfavourable economic climate and the lack of competitiveness resulting from lower hydrocarbon prices. The report pointed out that the overview presented referred only to already accomplished technology; it did not consider prospects opened up by research progress in such areas as the advanced turbines derived from aircraft technology for the utilization of biomass, the renewed interest in the production of hydrogen and developments in superconductivity deemed to be promising for energy applications.

In another report submitted to the Committee in February,[9] the Secretary-General discussed the mobilization of financial resources as well as inter-agency co-ordination for implementing the Nairobi Programme of Action. Reviewing the background and trends in and mechanisms for resource mobilization, he concluded that there was a whole range of multilateral, bilateral, domestic, public and private mechanisms for funding activities. Consultative meetings, convened at the national, regional and global levels, were flexible mechanisms for co-ordinating resources. The Inter-Agency Group on New and Renewable Sources of Energy, established in 1983,[10] served as a focal point for co-ordination of activities, for the avoidance of duplication and overlapping and for monitoring the implementation of the Nairobi Programme.

Technical co-operation

In response to a 1986 request of the Committee on the Development and Utilization of New and Renewable Sources of Energy,[6] the Secretary-General, in February,[11] submitted a report by the UNDP Administrator on UNDP's activities in the area of new and renewable energy sources. The report reviewed the energy situation; areas of concentration and activities of the UNDP Energy Account; UNDP activities; collaborative arrangements, including those with the United Nations Institute for Training and Research in the Centre for Small Energy Resources and the Information Centre for Heavy Crude and Tar Sands; and the financial situation. An appendix showed that UNDP funding of activities in the area of new and renewable sources of energy, energy conservation and planning in developing countries during the 1980s totalled $319.5 million.

DTCD, reporting on its technical co-operation activities,[5] stated that in the area of new and renewable energy resources, solar and wind energy development programmes had progressed significantly. In China, small but technically advanced experimental wind power stations had been set up in Zhejiang and Fukien provinces; project data had been computerized and were playing a key role in developing larger, commercial-size wind turbine generators. In Mongolia, a new project would expand rural power supply through local wind pumps, solar water and air heaters and biogas digesters for cattle farms. Another project in Mongolia would identify the potential national market for photovoltaic system applications. In Romania, a solar energy project developed photovoltaic solar cell and module fabrication technologies and established a module fabrication facility; it also tested a solar photovoltaic water pumping system for agriculture applications. In India, a project was testing solar thermal equipment. In Cuba, a project would establish a facility for the production of crystalline silicon using national quartz. A project in Cape Verde had determined the wind régime for sizing of units at potential wind power sites and formulated the procedure for measuring solar radiation.

Three geothermal projects were completed in 1988. In the Philippines, four sites for the direct use of geothermal energy for agro-industrial purposes were found to be economically feasible, 18 engineers were trained and equipment was installed. In Honduras, a pre-feasibility study on the geothermal potential in the central region was concluded, leading to a government decision to develop geothermal resources for low- to medium-scale power generation. In China, a project evaluated the use of geothermal energy to meet district heating requirements in the Beijing and Tianjin areas.

Research and development

The Secretary-General, in response to a 1986 request[6] from the Committee on the Development and Utilization of New and Renewable Sources of Energy, submitted in January 1988 a report on United Nations activities in research, development and demonstration and in information systems related to new and renewable sources of energy.[12] He said the activities carried out in research, development and demonstration had been largely concerned with applying existing knowledge and with supporting activities in developing countries that promoted institution-building and policy formulation, the launching of research and pilot projects, and the development of research methods. In view of the limited resources available for those activities, the importance of co-ordination and co-operative arrangements could not be overemphasized.

A substantial number of activities had been carried out with regard to information systems. Some of them involved the establishment or extension of information systems, while others concerned technical and financial co-operation with developing countries promoting institution-building and technical know-how. Coverage of the information systems within the United Nations system was uneven and incomplete. For example, only one activity was reported on a data base on draught animal power, and no activity was reported on a system of information dealing with geothermal energy, peat and large-scale hydropower, apart from statistical activities on those sources. It was apparent that while there might be an abundance of information in some areas, potential users were not aware of its availability and location. There was a need for an effective referral service to improve the access to information.

Committee on new and renewable sources of energy

The Committee on the Development and Utilization of New and Renewable Sources of Energy held its fourth session in New York from 28 March to 8 April 1988.[13] The Committee, which was established in 1982[14] by the General Assembly as an intergovernmental group to promote the Nairobi Programme of Action,[8] adopted two resolutions and a decision.

The first resolution[15] concerned enhancing the activities of the United Nations system to implement the Programme of Action. The Committee decided to include in the provisional agenda for its fifth (1990) session the contribution of new and renewable sources of energy to integrated rural development and the specific issues of direct solar-to-electrical energy conversion and utilization of agricultural residues and urban wastes for energy production. The Committee invited States to inform it of their activities and evaluations with regard to those themes and invited States and organizations to convene meetings to examine them. It requested the Secretary-General to prepare reports on the current stage of achievements in relation to those themes and on the more effective exchange of information and experience regarding new and renewable sources of energy.

By the second resolution,[16] on follow-up action regarding research, development and demonstration, and information systems, the Committee noted the report of the 1987 Colloquium of High-level Experts on New and Renewable Sources of Energy.[17] It called for the implementation of the Colloquium's short-term proposals regarding efficient utilization of energy, identification of success stories and innovations, and promotion of joint ventures in developing countries, and of a longer-term proposal on the feasibility of a network of international centres in the area of new and renewable sources of energy. The Committee requested the Secretary-General to convene an *ad hoc* panel of experts to prepare recommendations regarding information systems on such sources of energy.

The decision[18] set forth the provisional agenda and documentation for the Committee's fifth session.

Following informal consultations, the First (Economic) Committee of the Economic and Social Council agreed on 20 July to take no action on a draft decision introduced by Tunisia, on behalf of the Group of 77,[19] requesting the Secretary-General to submit a report in 1989 containing proposals on the composition, terms of reference and institutional, legal and financial implications of an expert group on the development and utilization of new and renewable sources of energy, to complement the work of the Committee.

On 26 July, by **decision 1988/157**, the Council took note of the Committee's report on its fourth session.[13]

GENERAL ASSEMBLY ACTION

On 20 December, on the recommendation of the Second Committee, the General Assembly adopted without vote **resolution 43/192.**

Report of the Committee on the Development and Utilization of New and Renewable Sources of Energy

The General Assembly,

Recalling its resolutions concerning new and renewable sources of energy, in particular resolution 41/170 of 5 December 1986,

Stressing that trends in the energy sector do not diminish the importance of the continued development of new and renewable sources of energy,

Considering that new and renewable sources of energy could constitute a significant share of total world energy supplies, particularly in developing countries,

Noting the continuing need to strengthen the activities of the United Nations in the field of development and utilization of new and renewable sources of energy,

1. *Takes note* of the report of the Committee on the Development and Utilization of New and Renewable Sources of Energy on its fourth session and endorses the resolutions and decision contained therein;

2. *Reaffirms* the importance of the Nairobi Programme of Action for the Development and Utilization of New and Renewable Sources of Energy as the basic framework for action in that field and calls for its speedy and full implementation;

3. *Urges* the States members of the Committee, at its fifth session, to consider further measures to strengthen the activities of the United Nations in this field, particularly to enable the Committee to assure full and more effective implementation of the Nairobi Programme of Action;

4. *Invites* interested States to inform the Committee, at its fifth session, of their ongoing technical and scientific activities and/or evaluations with regard to selected substantive themes, and invites interested States, organizations of the United Nations system and other interested organizations to convene technical and scientific meetings, related to the substantive themes, that would contribute to the examination of such themes in depth, and to inform the Committee, also at its fifth session, of the results of those meetings;

5. *Calls upon* the international community to implement effectively the proposals contained in the conclusions and recommendations of the Colloquium of High-level Experts on New and Renewable Sources of Energy, held at Castelgandolfo, Italy, in 1987, as contained in paragraph 2 of resolution 2(IV) of 8 April 1988 of the Committee, which are aimed at giving new impetus to the implementation of the Nairobi Programme of Action, and requests the Secretary-General to convene an *ad hoc* panel of experts to prepare specific recommendations regarding information systems on new and renewable sources of energy;

6. *Reiterates* the need to pursue actively ways and means of mobilizing adequate additional financial resources commensurate with the needs of developing countries in the field of new and renewable sources of energy and emphasizes the need to utilize existing channels fully, including the United Nations Trust Fund for New and Renewable Sources of Energy, and urges donor countries to continue voluntary contributions to that Fund;

7. *Reaffirms* the importance of increasing inter-agency co-operation within the United Nations system, as well as co-ordination of development activities for new and renewable sources of energy at all levels.

General Assembly resolution 43/192

20 December 1988   Meeting 83   Adopted without vote

Approved by Second Committee (A/43/915/Add.4) without vote, 30 November (meeting 45); draft by Vice-Chairman (A/C.2/43/L.69), orally revised, based on informal consultations on draft by Tunisia, for Group of 77 (A/C.2/43/L.24); agenda item 82 (d).

Meeting numbers. GA 43rd session: 2nd Committee 21-26, 30, 45; plenary 83.

Nuclear energy

IAEA report

Total installed nuclear power generating capacity in the world increased by about 4.3 per cent during 1988, reaching 311 gigawatts by the end of the year. Nuclear power plants accounted for about 17 per cent of the world's electricity generation; 14 nuclear power plants came on line during the year, in France, the Federal Republic of Germany, Japan, the Republic of Korea, Spain, the USSR, the United Kingdom and the United States, bringing the world total to 429. Two reactors, with a total capacity of 335 megawatts, were permanently shut down in the USSR and the United Kingdom. Construction began on six plants in China, France, Japan, the USSR and the United Kingdom. (See PART SEVEN, Chapter I, for further information on activities of the International Atomic Energy Agency.)

In July 1988, the Secretary-General transmitted the 1987 report of IAEA to the General Assembly.[20] The Agency's Director General presented and updated the report in a statement to the Assembly on 27 October. He pointed out that developing countries would have an increasing need for electricity for irrigation, industrialization and transport, as would industrialized countries with relatively low levels of energy consumption. He said there was little reliance by Governments on renewable energy sources, but rather an increasing reliance on coal and gas, along with a considerable increase in carbon dioxide emissions. He was not suggesting that nuclear power would be a panacea against the greenhouse effect, acid rain or dying forests and lakes, but that nuclear power was one large-scale source of energy that did not give rise to acid rain or greenhouse gases.

He suggested that a thorough examination of environmentally responsible and practical energy policies be conducted under United Nations auspices. Among the issues to be considered would be: how much energy would be needed in the coming decades for industrial and social development in both industrialized and developing countries; to what extent efficiency gains in energy production and use offset increased needs; to what extent sulphur dioxide and nitrogen oxide could be eliminated from fossil fuel emissions and at what cost; to what extent the problems caused by those gases and carbon dioxide could be alleviated by greater use of natural gas and nuclear power; the possible contribution of renewable energy sources; the possibility of nuclear fusion; and the problems associated with nuclear power.

He said that more education was needed on the subject of radiation. While each person received an average annual dose of 2.4 millisieverts from natural sources, activities related to nuclear power gave 0.0002 millisieverts annually.

While IAEA had no mandate regarding toxic waste, the question of nuclear dumping had been the subject of a Board of Governors resolution in 1988. The Director General also discussed concerns that increased reliance on nuclear power might lead to a proliferation of nuclear weapons. He stressed that most countries had renounced nuclear weapons and adhered to IAEA safeguards—95 per cent of the nuclear installations and fissile material in non-nuclear-weapon States were covered by those safeguards, and all five nuclear-weapon States experienced some safeguards inspection. In addition, he suggested that if a nuclear-weapon-free zone were established in the Middle East, as had been proposed (see PART ONE, Chapter II), verification responsibilities could be entrusted to IAEA.

GENERAL ASSEMBLY ACTION

On 28 October, the General Assembly adopted without vote **resolution 43/16**.

Report of the International Atomic Energy Agency

The General Assembly,

Having received the report of the International Atomic Energy Agency to the General Assembly for the year 1987,

Taking note of the statement of the Director General of the International Atomic Energy Agency of 27 October 1988, which provides additional information on the main developments in the Agency's activities during 1988,

Recognizing the importance of the work of the Agency to promote further the application of atomic energy for peaceful purposes, as envisaged in its statute,

Also recognizing the special needs of the developing countries for technical assistance by the Agency in order to benefit effectively from the application of nuclear technology for peaceful purposes as well as from the contribution of nuclear energy to their economic development,

Conscious of the importance of the work of the Agency in the implementation of safeguards provisions of the Treaty on the Non-Proliferation of Nuclear Weapons and other international treaties, conventions and agreements designed to achieve similar objectives, as well as in ensuring, as far as it is able, that the assistance provided by the Agency or at its request or under its supervision or control is not used in such a way as to further any military purpose, as stated in article II of its statute,

Recognizing the importance of the work of the Agency on nuclear power, nuclear safety, radiological protection and radioactive waste management, including its work directed towards assisting developing countries in planning for the introduction of nuclear power in accordance with their needs,

Again stressing the need for the highest standards of safety in the design and operation of nuclear plants so as to minimize risks to life, health and the environment,

Welcoming the initiation of a project under the auspices of the Agency by the world's four major fusion partners for a conceptual design of an international thermonuclear experimental reactor,

Noting with appreciation the adoption of a joint protocol relating to the application of the Vienna Convention on Civil Liability for Nuclear Damage and the Paris Convention on Third Party Liability in the Field of Nuclear Energy, which would have the effect of extending the existing civil liability régime and avoiding possible conflicts of the applicable law,

Bearing in mind resolutions GC(XXXII)/RES/487 on Israeli nuclear capabilities and threat, GC(XXXII)/RES/489 on measures to strengthen international co-operation in nuclear safety and radiological protection, GC(XXXII)/RES/490 on dumping of nuclear wastes, GC(XXXII)/RES/491 on liability for nuclear damage, GC(XXXII)/RES/492 on the Convention on the Physical Protection of Nuclear Material, GC(XXXII)/RES/493 on the Convention on Early Notification of a Nuclear Accident and the Convention on Assistance in the case of a Nuclear Accident or Radiological Emergency, GC(XXXII)/RES/494 on the Agency's contribution to sustainable development and GC(XXXII)/RES/503 on South Africa's nuclear capabilities, adopted on 23 September 1988 by the General Conference of the Agency at its thirty-second regular session,

1.   *Takes note* of the report of the International Atomic Energy Agency;

2.   *Affirms* its confidence in the role of the Agency in the application of nuclear energy for peaceful purposes;

3.   *Urges* all States to strive for effective and harmonious international co-operation in carrying out the work

of the Agency, pursuant to its statute; in promoting the use of nuclear energy and the application of the necessary measures to strengthen further the safety of nuclear installations and to minimize risks to life, health and the environment; in strengthening technical assistance and co-operation for developing countries; and in ensuring the effectiveness and efficiency of the Agency's safeguards system;

4. *Requests* the Secretary-General to transmit to the Director General of the International Atomic Energy Agency the records of the forty-third session of the General Assembly relating to the Agency's activities.

General Assembly resolution 43/16

28 October 1988   Meeting 40   Adopted without vote

3-nation draft (A/43/L.17); agenda item 14.
Sponsors: Algeria, Canada, German Democratic Republic.
Meeting numbers. GA 43rd session: plenary 38-40.

Conventions

In accordance with a 1987 decision of the General Assembly,[21] the Secretary-General submitted a report in October 1988[22] on accession by the United Nations to the Convention on Early Notification of a Nuclear Accident and to the Convention on Assistance in the Case of a Nuclear Accident or Radiological Emergency. The Conventions had been adopted in 1986;[23] the Notification Convention entered into force in 1986 and the Assistance Convention in 1987.

As at 21 July 1988, 29 States were parties to the Notification Convention and 23 States to the Assistance Convention. The Conventions also were open for accession by international organizations having competence in respect to matters covered by the Conventions. As at 21 July 1988, no international organization had acceded to either of them. Annexed to the Secretary-General's report were declarations indicating the extent of the competence of the United Nations in matters covered by each of the Conventions.

On 20 December, the Assembly, by **decision 43/441**, transmitted the Secretary-General's report to its 1989 session for further consideration.

REFERENCES
[1]A/43/476 & Corr.1. [2]YUN 1986, p. 577. [3]E/1988/19 (dec. 88/39). [4]DP/1988/47. [5]DP/1989/46/Add.1. [6]YUN 1986, p. 581. [7]A/AC.218/15. [8]YUN 1981, p. 689. [9]A/AC.218/16. [10]YUN 1983, p. 681. [11]A/AC.218/17. [12]A/AC.218/13. [13]A/43/36. [14]YUN 1982, p. 896, GA res 37/250, 21 Dec. 1982. [15]A/43/36 (res. 1(IV)). [16]*Ibid.* [17]YUN 1987, p. 579. [18]A/43/36 (dec. 1(IV)). [19]E/1988/C.1/L.7. [20]A/43/488. [21]YUN 1987, p. 581, GA dec. 42/443, 11 Dec. 1987. [22]A/43/714. [23]YUN 1986, p. 1101.

PUBLICATIONS
Coastal Areas Resource Development: Energy in Small Islands (ST/ESA/198), Sales No. E.88.II.A.2. *New and Renewable Sources of Energy for Development* (ST/ESCAP/580), Sales No. E.88.II.F.7. *Energy Balances and Electricity Profiles 1988* (ST/ESA/STAT/SER.W/5), Sales No. E/F.90.XVII.15.

Cartography

DTCD projects in cartography (surveying, mapping and hydrography) continued during 1988.[1] They included institution-building, transfer of technical expertise to national cartographic and hydrographic institutions and provision of training and equipment. Fellowships and grants for study tours were awarded to candidates from all over the world for studies in photogrammetry, cadastral systems, cartographic and photographic procedures, cartography, digital mapping, computer communications and networking, cadastral surveying and land information, geodetic science and hydrography.

In March 1988,[2] the Secretary-General submitted to the Economic and Social Council a report on the Fifth United Nations Conference on the Standardization of Geographical Names, held in 1987.[3]

By **decision 1988/116** of 25 May, the Council took note of the report; endorsed the Conference's recommendation to convene the Sixth Conference in 1992; requested the Secretary-General to implement the Fifth Conference's recommendations, especially with regard to the work of the United Nations Group of Experts on Geographical Names; and approved the statute and rules of procedure of the Group. On 24 May, by **decision 1988/111**, the Council decided to hold the fourteenth session of the Group at Geneva from 17 to 26 May 1989 instead of in September 1989.

REFERENCES
[1]DP/1989/46/Add.1. [2]E/1988/22 & Add.1. [3]YUN 1987, p. 575.

Chapter VII

Science and technology

The United Nations continued in 1988 to strengthen the scientific and technological capacities of developing countries by mobilizing financial resources, encouraging the flow of technology to those countries and upgrading institutional arrangements. The framework of these efforts was, as in previous years, the 1979 Vienna Programme of Action on Science and Technology for Development. Preparations for the Programme's end-of-decade review were carried out by the United Nations Centre for Science and Technology for Development, the Advisory Committee on Science and Technology for Development and other United Nations bodies.

The Centre and the Task Force on Science and Technology for Development of the Administrative Committee on Co-ordination proposed policy guidelines for harmonizing activities in science and technology within the United Nations system. The Advisory Committee met in September 1988 and warned that the debt crisis could affect investment in science and technology in developing countries.

The United Nations Fund for Science and Technology for Development finished its second year of operation, providing technical advisory services to the United Nations Development Programme, in addition to being a multilateral funding mechanism for science and technology activities.

Consultations on an international code of conduct on the transfer of technology continued, but differences on some outstanding issues remained. Transfer of technology continued to be a focus of various activities by the United Nations Conference on Trade and Development (UNCTAD).

The problem of the reverse transfer of technology, or brain drain, was the subject of a meeting of government experts in March. The General Assembly, in resolution 43/184, requested the UNCTAD Secretary-General to take into account the experts' recommendations in the future work of the UNCTAD Committee on Transfer of Technology.

Financial resources for science and technology

Resource mobilization

At its September 1988 session (see below),[1] the Advisory Committee on Science and Technology

for Development recommended that developing countries set targets for investment in science and technology in the key sectors of their development plans. Such targets would encourage political commitment to a course of action and would serve as yardsticks for measuring progress. The Committee also recommended that donor countries channel a growing share of investment to education and to science and technology, as those fields were likely to be hard hit in the current era of great debt burdens and declining living standards. The external debt crisis could have ruinous effects on many countries' scientific and technological capabilities, the Committee warned. Resources for the growth of science and technology would in the main part be internal, with foreign financing playing a relatively small role, although external financing could play a significant role for the least developed countries. The Committee noted that the development of endogenous capacities in science and technology was not a major issue on the policy agenda of donor agencies.

UN Fund for Science and Technology for Development

The United Nations Fund for Science and Technology for Development (UNFSTD) was established as a trust fund within the United Nations Development Programme (UNDP) in 1987,[2] taking over the responsibilities of the former United Nations Financing System for Science and Technology for Development. Its responsibilities were to help finance, design and implement activities to strengthen the endogenous scientific and technological capacities of developing countries; collaborate with multilateral and bilateral programmes and non-governmental entities for that purpose; and serve as a focal point for science and technology within UNDP.

UNFSTD expenditures for 1987-1988 under core and co-financing arrangements were over $17 million.[3] Voluntary contributions for 1988, pledged by 26 countries in November 1987, totalled $0.7 million, and the Fund received an additional $0.25 million in early 1988. Thirty-two countries pledged $1.4 million in November 1988. About 40 per cent of the limited core resources came from developing countries. The Fund made vigorous efforts to reduce its administrative expenses, which were about 11 per cent of its overall expenditure. Under the

Fund's predecessor, the Financing System, a threshold level of $10 million had been stipulated, in roughly equal amounts from core and non-core resources. That overall threshold level had approximately been met, while the share of core funding had been much less than that of non-core funding.

In a March 1988 report to the UNDP Governing Council,[4] the UNDP Administrator stated that UNFSTD was an essential element in the overall machinery of the United Nations dealing with science and technology, which included the Intergovernmental Committee on Science and Technology for Development, the Advisory Committee on Science and Technology for Development and the United Nations Centre for Science and Technology for Development, which served as the secretariat for both committees. The Administrator proposed that the Energy Office and Energy Account be closed and that their responsibilities and resources be transferred to UNFSTD.

Also under the management of UNFSTD were two technical consultancy services to developing countries: the Transfer of Knowledge through Expatriate Nationals (TOKTEN) and short-term advisory services (STAS). The Administrator noted that the joint management of those services and the Energy Office under UNFSTD, as well as the strengthening of the relationship of the Centre with UNFSTD and UNDP, had led to administrative cost savings and the enhancement of UNDP's effectiveness in science, technology and energy-related matters.

The new institutional arrangements had led to a broad strategy for science and technology activities within UNDP. The Administrator identified five areas of concentration, in line with the mandate laid down by the Intergovernmental Committee in 1987:[5] the formulation of national science and technology strategies and master plans, including forecasting of technology and assessment of impact; introducing new appropriate technologies and upgrading traditional technologies; providing access to expertise needed to acquire and adapt advanced technologies for countries with the required technical infrastructure; improving commercial utilization and management of research, including the proper use of technology business incubation centres; and strengthening the establishment and use of relevant scientific and technological information systems. An effective way for UNFSTD to enhance UNDP's work in science and technology was to promote technological change through new initiatives and pilot activities, often of an experimental nature.

UNDP action. On 1 July,[6] the UNDP Governing Council took note of the new arrangements for the work of UNDP in science, technology and energy and recommended to the General Assembly that it consider that issue and the possible change of UNFSTD to the United Nations Fund for Science, Technology and Energy. The Council affirmed the importance of UNFSTD as a focal point in UNDP for assistance in strengthening the national, subregional and regional capacities of developing countries to manage technological change and for stimulating international technological co-operation. The Council decided to close the Energy Office, but to retain the Energy Account as a sub-account of UNFSTD. It invited all Governments to increase their pledges to the core resources of the Fund as well as to the projected activities through individual co-financing arrangements and other co-operative modalities.

Technical co-operation activities

In the field of devising national science and technology strategies, UNFSTD undertook five projects in 1987 and 1988: in Burundi, Cyprus, Ethiopia and Jordan, as well as with the countries of the Gulf Co-operation Council. Their purpose was to assist countries with critically scarce human and financial resources to make appropriate choices of technology and to allocate technical resources to priority needs.[3]

Among activities to initiate new technologies assisted by the Fund were: an assessment of how biotechnology could be used to utilize Zambia's abundant raw materials and agricultural waste products; the establishment of a Computer Science Division at the Asian Institute of Technology (Bangkok, Thailand); training at the National Remote Sensing Centre in China; and the introduction of new advances in drip irrigation techniques in semi-arid environments in China. The Fund supported several projects in non-conventional energy: geothermal energy in Costa Rica and Djibouti, biogas in Cape Verde and photovoltaic technology in Maldives, Mauritius and Seychelles. The Fund also supported efforts to upgrade traditional technologies, like the woodstove development programme in West Africa and use of the soapberry plant in East Africa to treat schistosomiasis.

The Fund developed systems to serve as data bases and dissemination instruments, among them the Technological Information Pilot System, used in 10 countries in Africa, Asia, the Arab States and Latin America, and the Technology Expert Knowledge System, a proposed computer-based system using the existing network of UNDP offices around the world. In order to promote the commercial use of scientific research, UNFSTD launched a major programme on technological innovation and entrepreneurship in collaboration with the National Business Incubator Association of the United States and the European Business Incubator Network. Among other developments in that area, the first of 50 planned innovation centres was opened in Wuhan, China, and a conference on the matter was organized in Gabon following missions to Côte d'Ivoire, Gabon, Nigeria and Zimbabwe. In the area of quality control and maintenance, a UNFSTD-supported National Food Technology and Quality Control Research Centre was inaugurated in China in September 1988. The Fund supported the maintenance of scientific instruments in Africa and the training of technicians in Latin America.

Apart from being a multilateral funding mechanism for science and technology activities, UNFSTD also provided technical advisory services to UNDP in those fields. It responded to 132 requests for advice from UNDP bureaux and field offices in the 1987-1988 period. These included preparation of technical memoranda for projects, participation in various project appraisal committees and in the UNDP Action Committee, and assistance in monitoring and evaluation.

UNFSTD drew upon experts from professional societies and the international scientific community for project appraisal and evaluation, often at minimal cost. The two services working with the Fund, STAS and TOKTEN, provided additional sources of advice, fielding over 910 missions in 1987 and 1988. The fourth international TOKTEN workshop (New Delhi, India, February 1988) discussed ideas to widen the scheme. The year marked the tenth anniversary of TOKTEN and was the best in its history, with 449 consultancies completed, bringing the total to 2,270. About 26 countries had UNDP-supported TOKTEN programmes, to which they had allocated over $12 million of indicative planning figure (IPF) resources. STAS completed 70 assignments in 1988, bringing the total to 131 from the beginning of its operation in 1985. STAS services were voluntary, with only travel and per diem being provided either by the beneficiary organization or through IPF resources.

REFERENCES

[1]A/CN.11/91. [2]YUN 1987, p. 599. [3]DP/1989/48. [4]DP/1988/47. [5]YUN 1987, p. 600. [6]E/1988/19 (dec. 88/39).

Institutional arrangements

Advisory Committee

The Advisory Committee on Science and Technology for Development, established to provide policy and planning advice to the Intergovernmental Committee (which did not meet in 1988), held its eighth session at Goa, India, from 26 to 30 September 1988.[1] It focused on the implementation of the 1979 Vienna Programme of Action on Science and Technology for Development[2] in the light of the technological and economic changes of the 1980s; endogenous capacity-building; the development of human resources; the development of strategies to foster linkages between research and development institutions and the productive sectors; the need for information systems for developing countries to improve their access to available science and technology or industrial information; national strategies for international co-operation; and financial resources for science and technology for development (see above).

The Advisory Committee called on member Governments to renew their commitments to applying science and technology to the development of all countries through national efforts supported by vigorous international co-operation. The Vienna Programme of Action had crystallized and given international support to a wide range of efforts, even though progress in science and technology had proceeded quite independently from the agreement reached at Vienna. But with a new—and usually more difficult—situation facing developing countries, it was essential for the community of nations to reaffirm the political will and commitment to build endogenous science and technology capacities in developing countries, to restructure international scientific and technological relations and to strengthen the role of the United Nations system in those areas. The Committee recommended that individual countries set mid- to long-term targets for investments in science and technology in key sectors of their development plans. It stressed three guiding principles for mobilizing science and technology in the service of development: the need for an endogenous scientific and technological capability; the need for greater social equity; and the need for a wider understanding of the implications of unchecked resource development and for the formulation of a strategy for sustainable development. The spirit of international co-operation achieved in the Vienna Programme of Action had to be revived, reaffirmed and extended; only in that way would it be possible to make effective the potential contribution of science and technology to development.

Centre for Science and Technology

Serving as the secretariat of the Intergovernmental Committee, the Advisory Committee and the Task Force on Science and Technology for Development of the Administrative Committee on Co-ordination (ACC), the Centre for Science and Technology for Development worked in 1988 on many activities with the common goal of serving as a basis for the end-of-decade (1989) review of the Vienna Programme of Action.[2]

A report by the Secretary-General to the Intergovernmental Committee[3] stated that the Centre's expanded activities, implemented with reduced resources, were designed to make its work more relevant and responsive to Member States' needs, to alert Member States to the implications of the increased market penetration of new and emerging areas of science and technology, and to promote inter-agency co-operation at the secretariat and country levels.

Pursuant to a 1987 resolution of the Intergovernmental Committee on the end-of-decade review,[4] the Centre addressed a questionnaire to all national focal points, requesting Member States to report on their experiences and constraints encountered in the implementation of the Vienna Programme. A total of 37 replies were received, with developing countries indicating that limited financial resources for science and technology were an obstacle to the implementation of the Programme. In addition, many United Nations entities reported on their experiences with the Programme, with some stating that they had encountered conceptual difficulties with it, in addition to financial ones.

The Centre also carried out analytical studies on trends in science and technology in the 1980s in all regions of the developing world, as well as in the developed world. The latter study recommended that the donor community and the United Nations system increase their effectiveness in bilateral and multilateral co-operation programmes in science and technology. Based on these studies, the Centre organized four regional meetings and one interregional meeting of experts, which came to the following conclusions: the results of the Vienna Programme of Action lagged considerably behind the expectations of developing Member States, in particular in regard to the mobilization of additional resources for the promotion of science and technology; the main thrust of the Programme had not always been clearly perceived; the gap between developed and developing countries in science and technology remained and was widening; special efforts would be required to improve the access of developing countries to new and emerging technologies; and there was a need for new approaches in the implementation of the Programme.

Other activities of the Centre included: launching pilot studies on endogenous capacity-building in selected developing countries; organizing meetings of experts on drought and desertification and on energy technologies; publishing Advance Technology Alert System *Bulletins* and a renewed *Update* newsletter; co-sponsoring with the United Nations Environment Programme and the World Meteorological Organization the first World Congress on Climate and Development (Hamburg, Federal Republic of Germany, 7-10 November 1988); formulating policy guidelines for harmonizing science and technology activities in the United Nations system; conducting inter-agency missions to developing countries; providing basic scientific and technical literature to Portuguese-speaking African countries; assisting interested Member States to develop their science and technology information infrastructure; and bringing out a directory of national and regional sources of science and technology information of the United Nations system.

Co-ordination in the UN system

The ninth session of the Task Force on Science and Technology for Development, established by ACC as a mechanism of inter-agency co-operation in implementing tasks assigned to the Intergovernmental Committee, was held in New York from 7 to 10 March 1988.[5] Subjects considered by the Task Force included: co-ordination at the country level; policy guidelines for the harmonization of policies in science and technology in the United Nations system; follow-up to the 1987 cross-organizational programme analysis and the cross-organizational review of the medium-term plans in science and technology for development;[4] and preparations for the end-of-decade review of the implementation of the Vienna Programme of Action.

The Task Force agreed that its future work should be issue-oriented and, while necessarily focused on science and technology, be better integrated with other bodies dealing with broader aspects such as operational activities and long-term development strategies. It agreed to devote a substantial portion of its time at future sessions to a comprehensive discussion of specific substantive topics of inter-agency importance, like science and technology policy and planning and south-south co-operation. The Task Force requested the Centre for Science and Technology for Development to prepare a compendium of the various activities being undertaken by the organizations of the United Nations system in new and emerging areas of science and technology. Four developing countries (Colombia, Jordan, Kenya and Thailand) were to be assisted in assessing the impact of United Nations activities in science and technology.

REFERENCES

[1]A/CN.11/91. [2]YUN 1979, p. 636. [3]A/CN.11/88. [4]YUN 1987, p. 596. [5]ACC/1988/PG/4.

Technology transfer

UNCTAD activities. In a report to the UNCTAD Trade and Development Board,[1] the UNCTAD secretariat outlined its technical assistance activities, including its programmes in the area of technology transfer, which were mainly channelled through the Advisory Service on Transfer of Technology (ASTT).

In response to an expansion of UNCTAD's technical co-operation programme, the secretariat listed measures under way to improve project design and delivery, including: focusing activities around the main programme areas, channelling requests for which UNCTAD had neither expertise nor capacity to other organizations; ensuring the adequacy of substantive and technical backstopping and of administrative and support services; having UNDP headquarters appraise all major UNDP-financed projects; and updating the roster of experts and consultants for selection for assignment under the UNCTAD co-operation programme.

The activities of ASTT focused in 1988 on human resources development and on the interrelated aspects of technology policies, sectoral issues and institution-building in the area of technology transfer and development.

An interregional seminar on technology selection and negotiation (Kuala Lumpur, Malaysia, 12-16 December) was organized in co-operation with the Islamic Development Bank. Another interregional seminar on technology transfer through joint ventures (Moscow, 21-25 November) was held in co-operation with the USSR Ministry of External Economic Relations and the Chamber of Commerce and Industry and was financed by UNDP. A regional seminar for Africa (Arusha, United Republic of Tanzania, 9-29 March) on technology transfer and development perspectives of the food-processing sector was held in co-operation with the Southern African Development Co-ordination Conference, the Programme of Development Co-operation (Helsinki, Finland) and the Eastern and Southern African Management Institute. A seminar on technology transfer for Asian developing countries (Beijing, China, 31 October–16 November) was organized in co-operation with the Ministry of Foreign Economic Relations and Trade and with the Programme of Development Co-operation. A workshop and on-the-job training were organized at Maseru, Lesotho, in March.

UNCTAD assisted the African, Caribbean and Pacific Group of States' secretariat in preparing a draft programme of action in the field of technology. A regional project on transfer and utilization of technology in least developed and island developing countries of Asia and the Pacific was further evolved with UNDP. ASTT participated in advisory and programme review missions to Burundi, Kenya, Nepal, Thailand and Tunisia.

The second UNCTAD Enterprise Symposium (Geneva, 13 and 14 October),[2] with the theme of ''Transfer of technology for efficiency and growth—the entrepreneur's perspective'', was a forum for a variety of views on technology flows and their impact on development. In summing up the Symposium, its Chairman stated that the 1980s had seen a general decline in cross-border flows of technology to the developing world and a widening of the technology gap with the industrialized nations. That was attributable to the debt crisis of the third world and a consequent fall in foreign investment; the slump in commodity prices; and shortening innovation cycles in the developed world, which forced many industries to focus on staying competitive in advanced markets. Some actions that could help revive technology flows to developing nations were: the easing of the debt crisis through global action; putting increased emphasis on carrying out the adaptation of technology in recipient countries rather that the countries of supply; reducing barriers that inhibited the effective transfer of technology; and improving education and training in developing countries. It was also vital for developing countries to focus on improving the utilization of their most plentiful resource—manpower—and to encourage them to liberalize further their regulations concerning technology inflows.

Draft code of conduct

In a response to a 1987 General Assembly request,[3] the Secretary-General of UNCTAD submitted in October 1988 a report on progress made in the negotiations on an international code of conduct on the transfer of technology.[4] He and the President of the United Nations Conference on an International Code of Conduct on the Transfer of Technology continued in 1988 their consultations with regional groups and Governments with a view to identifying appropriate solutions to outstanding issues.

The draft code consisted of a preamble and the following chapters: (1) definitions and scope of application; (2) objectives and principles; (3) national regulation of transfer-of-technology transactions; (4) restrictive practices; (5) responsibilities and obligations of parties to transfer-of-technology transactions; (6) special treatment for developing countries; (7) international collaboration; (8) international institutional machinery; and (9) applicable law and settlement of disputes. Most of the outstanding issues concerned chapters 4 and 9.

During the 1988 consultations, the developing countries put forward a set of elements relating to the outstanding issues, which in their view could serve as a basis for reconvening the Conference. Those proposals were communicated to all other regional groups and China for consideration. China and the socialist countries of Eastern Europe said they could accept the proposals as the basis for reconvening the Conference, but the developed market-economy countries thought the proposals were not a basis for a successful resolution of the outstanding issues and, accordingly, they could not accede to the suggestion that the Conference be reconvened. However, the groups agreed that the consultations on the draft code should continue with a view to exploring further avenues of action for the future.

On 20 December, the General Assembly, by **decision 43/439**, took note of the UNCTAD Secretary-General's report.

REFERENCES
[1]TD/B/WP/68. [2]UNCTAD/EDM/1. [3]YUN 1987, p. 603, GA res. 42/172, 11 Dec. 1987. [4]A/43/763.

Brain drain

In 1988, UNCTAD and UNDP continued to search for solutions to the problem of the outflow of skilled personnel from developing countries, known as the reverse transfer of technology or brain drain.

UNCTAD activities. Pursuant to a 1985 General Assembly request,[1] the UNCTAD Secretary-General convened the Fourth Meeting of Governmental Experts on the Reverse Transfer of Technology (Geneva, 14-18 March 1988).[2] The Meeting considered the current situation with respect to all aspects of the international migration of skilled personnel from developing countries, focusing on the nature, scale and effect of such flows, taking into account the concerns of all parties, with a view to proposing to UNCTAD and other concerned organizations what further work might be carried out on the subject.

In their agreed conclusions and recommendations, the experts stated that, as the continuing outflow of skilled personnel from developing countries seriously hampered their development, there was a need for appropriate policies to avoid the brain drain; that it was necessary to improve the quantity, quality and coverage of information on international migration of skilled personnel from developing countries; and that developed countries should consider favourably the adoption of policies that encouraged greater participation by developing country emigrants in the development of their home countries. The work done by the Inter-Agency Group on Reverse Transfer of Technology was said to be of major significance for a comprehensive and complementary response from the United Nations system.

On 3 May,[3] the UNCTAD Trade and Development Board recommended to the General Assembly for adoption a draft resolution (see below).

UNDP activities. In 1988, nearly 450 expert voluntary consultancies were completed by TOK-TEN,[4] which enabled developing countries to recapture some of of the skills and experience lost through the brain drain by sending expatriate experts on short-term voluntary assignments. UNDP covered only air fares and subsistence allowances, so a TOKTEN consultancy cost between $3,000 and $4,000 per work-month. Since its inception in 1977, TOKTEN had funded over 2,200 consultancies, to which $10 million had been committed in UNDP/IPF resources. In 1988, TOKTEN was operating in 26 countries.

GENERAL ASSEMBLY ACTION

On 20 December, the General Assembly, on the recommendation of the Second (Economic and Financial) Committee, having considered a note by the Secretary-General containing the report of the Fourth Meeting of Governmental Experts on the Reverse Transfer of Technology,[5] adopted **resolution 43/184** without vote.

Reverse transfer of technology

The General Assembly,

Recalling its resolutions 3201(S-VI) and 3202(S-VI) of 1 May 1974, 3281(XXIX) of 12 December 1974, 3362(S-VII) of 16 September 1975, 35/56 of 5 December 1980 and 40/191 of 17 December 1985,

Conscious that the development process of the developing countries is crucially dependent on the availability of highly trained personnel and that the acquisition of skills and their efficient utilization are a crucial component of the social, economic and technological transformation of those countries,

Convinced that the continuing outflow of skilled personnel from developing countries seriously hampers their development and has implications of global concern,

Recognizing the urgent need to formulate appropriate policies to avoid the "brain drain" and to obviate its adverse effects,

1. *Takes note* of the outcome of the Fourth Meeting of Governmental Experts on the Reverse Transfer of Technology, held at Geneva from 14 to 18 March 1988;

2. *Requests* the Secretary-General of the United Nations Conference on Trade and Development to make the necessary arrangements so that future work on the reverse transfer of technology can be considered by the Committee on Transfer of Technology in the context of the elaboration of its work programme, taking into account the conclusions and recommendations of the Fourth Meeting of Governmental Experts and of the work accomplished by previous meetings of governmental experts on the subject;

3. *Invites* other relevant organs and bodies of the United Nations system and other relevant international organizations to take into consideration in their work, as appropriate, individually and in the context of the work of the Inter-Agency Group on Reverse Transfer of Technology, the economic, social and developmental aspects of the reverse transfer of technology and international policy initiatives in this area at the multilateral level.

General Assembly resolution 43/184

20 December 1988   Meeting 83   Adopted without vote

Approved by Second Committee (A/43/915/Add.2) without vote, 23 November (meeting 44); draft by TDB (A/C.2/43/L.47); agenda item 82 *(b)*.
Meeting numbers. GA 43rd session: 2nd Committee 21-26, 30, 42-44; plenary 83.

REFERENCES

[1]YUN 1985, p. 720, GA res. 40/191, 17 Dec. 1985. [2]TD/B/1169. [3]A/43/15, vol. I (dec. 353(XXXIV)). [4]DP/1989/13/Add.1. [5]A/43/369.

Related questions

In **resolution 43/61**, the General Assembly decided to proclaim the "International Week of Science and Peace", which would take place each year during the week in which 11 November fell, and requested the Secretary-General to draw the attention of Member States and interested organizations to the importance of the Week.

In **resolution 43/77 A**, the Assembly requested the Secretary-General to follow future scientific and technological developments, especially those with potential military applications, and to evaluate their impact on international security.

Assembly **resolutions 43/109, 43/110 and 43/111** addressed topics in the field of human rights and scientific and technological developments. The subject was also on the agenda of the 1988 session of the Commission on Human Rights (see PART THREE, Chapter X).

Chapter VIII

Environment

Environmental problems, including global warming and depletion of the ozone layer, became increasingly prominent in the international public debate and political agenda in 1988. The United Nations Environment Programme (UNEP) continued its efforts to monitor and assess those problems and to protect the Earth's environment. An international conference held in Canada addressed the growing evidence that industrial gases might be responsible for global warming. The General Assembly, by resolution 43/212, urged States to prohibit all transboundary movement of toxic and dangerous wastes carried out without the prior consent of the importing country's authorities. The Economic and Social Council, by resolution 1988/71, stressed the importance of the active participation of all Governments in preparing for the the the global convention on transboundary movements of hazardous wastes.

The UNEP Governing Council held its first special session in March, at Nairobi, Kenya, focusing on the system-wide medium-term environment programme for 1990-1995. UNEP continued its various activities in conserving biodiversity and protected areas, controlling soil erosion and forest loss, protecting the marine environment and collecting information on such topics as air and water quality, food contamination and ozone depletion.

General aspects

International co-operation

As a result of the 1972 United Nations Conference on the Human Environment, the General Assembly established that year the institutional and financial arrangements for international co-operation on the environment.[1] It also established the Governing Council of UNEP and set out its role of environmental policy guidance.

ECONOMIC AND SOCIAL COUNCIL ACTION

On 28 July 1988, on the recommendation of its First (Economic) Committee, the Economic and Social Council adopted **resolution 1988/69** without vote.

International co-operation on the environment
The Economic and Social Council,
Recalling General Assembly resolution 2997(XXVII) of 15 December 1972 on institutional and financial arrangements for international environmental co-operation, in particular, section III, paragraph 4, thereof,

Reiterating the need to keep under review the problem of additional costs that may be incurred by developing countries in the implementation of environmental programmes and projects,

Reaffirming the need for additional financial resources to be provided by donor countries and organizations to assist developing countries in identifying, analysing, monitoring, preventing and managing environmental problems in accordance with their national development plans, priorities and objectives,

1. *Requests* the Executive Director of the United Nations Environment Programme, in co-operation with the competent organizations, to carry out an up-to-date review of the problem referred to in General Assembly resolution 2997(XXVII), section III, paragraph 4, and to report thereon to the General Assembly at its forty-fourth session, through the Economic and Social Council;

2. *Calls upon* all Governments to request their central economic and sectoral agencies to ensure that their policies, programmes and budgets encourage sustainable development and to strengthen the role of their environmental and natural resource agencies in advising and assisting the central and other sectoral agencies in that task;

3. *Requests* the organizations of the United Nations system concerned to include in their reports to the General Assembly at its forty-fourth session an account of the measures they have taken to give effect to the provisions of General Assembly resolutions 42/184 and 42/187 of 11 December 1987 calling on them to provide additional resources to developing countries.

Economic and Social Council resolution 1988/69

28 July 1988   Meeting 40   Adopted without vote

Approved by First Committee (E/1988/118) without vote, 21 July (meeting 19); draft by Tunisia, for Group of 77 (E/1988/C.1/L.2), orally revised following informal consultations; agenda item 11.

UNEP programme

Programme policy

Pursuant to a 1987 General Assembly resolution,[2] the UNEP Governing Council in 1988 held its first special session (Nairobi, 14-18 March)[3] to consider and approve the United Nations system-wide medium-term environment programme for 1990-1995 and to consider the global environmental programme of the proposed United Nations medium-term plan, which had been extended to cover 1990-1991.[4] The medium-term plan of UNEP for 1990-1995 was also before the Council.

In an introductory report,[5] the UNEP Executive Director outlined the goals and organization of the system-wide medium-term environment programme covering 1990-1995. The programme had been submitted by the Administrative Committee on Co-ordination (ACC), which stated, in its annual report to the Council,[6] that the programme constituted an overall strategy and planning framework for United Nations action on the environment. The ACC report discussed general co-ordination policy issues on environmental matters and the integration of environmental considerations into development planning and projects.

The system-wide medium-term environment programme was an expression of the catalytic and co-ordinating role of UNEP in respect of the efforts of the United Nations system to address environmental issues as a dimension of its overall activities, the Executive Director noted. The programme corresponded closely in its philosophy and approach to UNEP's 1987 report, "Environmental Perspective to the Year 2000 and Beyond", adopted by the Assembly as a broad framework to guide action and co-operation on policies and programmes aimed at achieving environmentally sound development.[7] That report, in turn, drew on the 1987 report of the World Commission on Environment and Development titled "Our common future", which emphasized the need for environmentally sustainable development and which was welcomed by the Assembly.[8]

In his introductory statement to the Council,[9] the Executive Director described the basis of the Council's mandate to orchestrate a sustained and multisectoral response by the United Nations system. What was expected from member Governments of the Council was, first and foremost, firm guidance on the long-term strategy for achieving a system-wide application of sustainable development.

On 18 March,[10] the Governing Council resolved to exercise fully the role expected of it with respect to the follow-up of the Environmental Perspective to the Year 2000 and Beyond, the report of the World Commission on Environment and Development and the system-wide medium-term environment programme for 1990-1995; it also decided to follow up on the relevant Assembly resolutions at its fifteenth (1989) session. The Council emphasized that sustainable and environmentally sound development should be one of the main objectives of the proposed international development strategy for the fourth United Nations development decade (1991-2000) (see PART THREE, Chapter I).

System-wide medium-term environment programme, 1990-1995

The system-wide medium-term environment programme for 1990-1995 was developed by UNEP in collaboration with other United Nations organizations and submitted to the UNEP Governing Council in a report by ACC.[11] Its structure was derived from that of the first such programme, covering 1984-1989, which in turn flowed from the evolving structures decided upon by the Council since its establishment.

The report stated that problems related to the misuse of natural resources and pollution would dominate the concerns of both developing and developed countries well into the twenty-first century. Many of them would be eased by the wide application of better environmental management techniques, while others would require changes in social and economic structures. A prerequisite for environmentally sound development was the achievement of an equitable system of international economic relations. Another fundamental goal was the elimination of poverty on the one hand and excessive consumption on the other. The issues addressed by the programme were the human environment, including atmosphere, water, terrestrial ecosystems, coastal and island systems, oceans, lithosphere, human settlements and the environment, human health and welfare, energy, industry and transportation, and peace, security and the environment; and environmental assessment, management and awareness.

While describing the strategies for achieving progress in each of these areas, the report stressed that the programme was not a rigid prescription for action, but rather reflected fundamental policies and priorities which were to be translated into action programmes by UNEP and other United Nations bodies.

On 18 March,[12] the Council approved the programme and decided that, at its 1991 session, ACC should present a revised programme for 1990-1995 incorporating policy guidelines that the Council would provide at its 1989 session. The Council brought the programme to the attention of the General Assembly and urged the organizations and programmes of the United Nations system to co-operate closely in its implementation.

UNEP medium-term plan, 1990-1995

UNEP's medium-term plan for 1990-1995, described in a report by the Executive Director,[13] proposed 13 programmes which were to constitute UNEP's contribution towards the objectives of the system-wide programme.

On 18 March,[14] the Governing Council approved the plan and requested the Executive Director to use it as a guide for formulating UNEP's next three programme budgets.

UN medium-term plan, 1984-1989

The General Assembly in 1987 had extended the United Nations medium-term plan for 1984-

1989 to cover 1990-1991,[4] requiring revision of the environment chapter to take into account the new system-wide programme. The proposed revisions were submitted to the Secretary-General by the Executive Director.[15]

On 18 March,[16] the Governing Council took note of the proposed revisions and recommended to the Assembly that the global programme on the environment of the United Nations medium-term plan beginning in 1992 be structured along the lines of the system-wide medium-term environment programme to ensure uniformity of content and to facilitate co-ordination of the environmental activities being undertaken by the United Nations system.

Regional and subregional programmes

Cairo Programme for African Co-operation

The UNEP Governing Council, on 18 March 1988,[17] urged the governing bodies of the organizations of the United Nations system to give priority to the provision of financial and technical assistance for the effective implementation of each of the programme areas of the Cairo Programme for African Co-operation, adopted in 1985.[18] It noted with appreciation UNEP's involvement in and support for the Programme and urged the Executive Director to continue to give priority to its implementation in UNEP's next three programme budgets.

Latin America and the Caribbean

On 18 March,[19] the Governing Council expressed its appreciation to UNEP for its support for the Action Plan for the Protection of the Marine Environment and Coastal Areas of the South-East Pacific and the Action Plan for the Caribbean Environment Programme. The Council decided that, in developing the medium-term plan of UNEP for 1990-1995, priority should continue to be given to those two plans, and requested the Executive Director to continue providing technical and financial support for activities under them.

1990 state-of-the-environment report

On 18 March,[20] the Governing Council decided that the topic of the state-of-the-environment report for 1990 should be children and the environment, and requested the Executive Director to prepare the report in co-operation with the United Nations Children's Fund.

Environmental education and training

UNEP in 1988 published the "International Strategy for Action in the Field of Environmental Education and Training for the 1990s", replacing the Tbilisi Declaration of 1977, which had provided guiding principles for environmental education for 10 years.[21] The Strategy defined nine major areas of action: access to environmental information; research and experimentation; development of programmes and teaching materials; training of personnel; incorporation of an environmental dimension into technical and vocational education; its incorporation into general university education; educating and informing the public; provision of specialist environmental training; and development of international and regional co-operation. Those principles were or would be reflected in phase VI of the UNEP/United Nations Educational, Scientific and Cultural Organization (UNESCO) International Environmental Education Programme, which remained the major international vehicle for the promotion of environmental education.

A joint UNESCO/UNEP steering committee, set up to provide overall guidance for the Education Programme, met at Bangkok, Thailand, in November 1988 to review environmental education in Asia and the Pacific. National workshops and seminars on environmental education were held in Sri Lanka in February, Egypt and Bolivia in March, Jamaica and Ecuador in May, Uganda in June/July and Jordan in October. A proposal for a primary environmental science curriculum for 16 Pacific island States was discussed at a workshop in Fiji in July. A regional seminar on the integration of environmental issues into education was held in Senegal in May, and subregional seminars on that issue were held in Argentina in September and in Costa Rica in December. An Afro-Arab training course on the incorporation of environmental education into industrial education was held in Egypt in October/November, and the advisory committee on the environmental training network for Latin America and the Caribbean met in Venezuela in April.

UNEP continued to provide training designed to promote acceptance of sustainable development. Those activities took two forms: general attempts to build awareness of the environment, directed at such groups as policy makers, engineers, industrialists and trade unionists; and specialized training to perfect the problem-solving skills of professionals whose work affected the environment.

In 1988, UNEP supported the establishment of environmental training networks in Africa, Asia and the Pacific and western Asia similar to the one established in 1983 in Latin America and the Caribbean, which had trained more than 800 professionals in different environmental fields. A second awareness-building workshop for 40 key personnel from ministries of planning, environment and education in French-speaking African countries was held at Rabat, Morocco, in November. UNESCO, UNEP and the USSR organized a two-week international training course on geological aspects of environmental protection for 15 participants from seven developing countries. The annual postgraduate course on the ecological aspects of resource development, land management and impact assessment was held at the Technical University of Dresden in the German Democratic Republic.

Public information

To secure coverage of its priority issues, UNEP continued to make use of the editorially independent Television Trust for the Environment (TVE), established in 1984. In 1988, the Trust distributed more than 200 programmes free of charge to television stations in 22 developing countries and started a quarterly bulletin in English and French with news on the latest productions coming out world-wide. Using computer equipment donated by International Business Machines (IBM), TVE established the world's first environment and development television programme data base, accessible through the ''Green-net'' computer link-up. Since 1984, TVE had arranged nearly 60 international television co-productions seen by millions in more than 80 countries, and had mobilized close to $15 million for its projects. About 5,000 television stations, development agencies and nongovernmental organizations (NGOs) subscribed to the service.

UNEP stepped up its media relations in 1988. It held a training course in Mauritius, in co-operation with UNESCO, for journalists from five African countries. Efforts were concentrated on joint publications, such as the three-volume directory *Coral Reefs of the World*, written with the International Union for Conservation of Nature and Natural Resources.

UNEP supported the Environment Liaison Centre in publishing its *Ecoforum* magazine, and also supported the magazine *African Journalist*, issued by the Union of African Journalists, which continued to stimulate more and better environmental media coverage in 30 African countries. A similar project for the Arab region was managed by the Arab Office for Youth and Environment. A network of 12 UNEP regional youth focal points was established and a framework for their activities was defined at a January meeting at Nairobi. The principal ceremonies for World Environment Day on 5 June, held at Bangkok, emphasized the role of women in environmental protection and sustainable development.

UNEP Fund

Contributions to the Environment Fund in 1988 exceeded those of 1980, hitherto the year in which contributions had been the highest.[21] At the end of the year, $34.47 million had been either paid or pledged to the Fund. In real terms, however, contributions had declined steadily since 1979. The number of contributors also continued to fall: from 90 in 1985 to 65 in 1988.

Commitments for programme and reserve activities totalled $27.53 million in 1988, including: support measures, $5.24 million; desertification control, $3.58 million; monitoring and assessment, $3.54 million; oceans, $3.11 million; information exchange, $2.58 million; terrestrial ecosystems management, $2.42 million; technical and regional co-operation, $1.93 million; technology and environment, $1.69 million; water, $1.39 million; environmental health, $0.71 million; peace, arms race and environment, $0.18 million; and reserve, $1.15 million. Geographical distribution of Fund commitments was as follows: global projects, $17.98 million (65.3 per cent of total commitments); interregional projects, $1.54 million (5.6 per cent); Africa, $3.46 million (12.6 per cent); Asia, $2.35 million (8.5 per cent); Latin America, $1.93 million (7 per cent); Europe, $0.24 million (0.9 per cent); and North America, $0.03 million (0.1 per cent).

Commitments accounted for only 84 per cent of allocations in 1988, due to difficulty in committing funds provided in non-convertible currencies and a perceived need to hold back some resources to provide for essential commitments in 1989. The largest share of Fund project commitments was implemented by UNEP directly and amounted to 53 per cent of the total. The Executive Director expressed a desire to reduce that share so that co-operating agencies, supporting organizations and UNEP would each account for approximately one third of total commitments during the 1990-1991 biennium.

ECONOMIC AND SOCIAL COUNCIL ACTION

On 28 July, on the recommendation of its First Committee, the Economic and Social Council adopted **resolution 1988/72** without vote.

International co-operation on the environment: the Environment Fund

The Economic and Social Council,

Having considered the report of the Governing Council of the United Nations Environment Programme on the work of its first special session,

Expressing its concern at the almost complete stagnation in nominal terms of the resources available to the Environment Fund, at a time when the challenges facing the international community in the field of the environment and in the achievement of sustained, environmentally sound and socially just development by the developing countries continue to multiply and assume critical importance,

Considering that a 50 per cent increase in real terms in the resources of the Environment Fund is desirable,

1. *Takes note* of the report of the Governing Council of the United Nations Environment Programme on the work of its first special session;

2. *Recognizes* the resolve of the Governing Council to exercise fully the role expected of it in accordance with its mandate;

3. *Welcomes* the request of the Governing Council to the governing bodies of the organizations of the United Nations system to give priority to the provision of financial and technical assistance for the effective implementation of the Cairo Programme for African Co-operation in each of its programme areas;

4. *Expresses its appreciation* to those Governments that have substantially increased their contributions to the Environment Fund;

5. *Considers* it essential to increase the resources of the Environment Fund substantially;

6. *Calls upon* Governments of developed countries that have not contributed in the past to the Environment Fund to do so at a level commensurate with that of other developed countries, in order to give the Fund a much wider base, and encourages those Governments that are contributing to the Fund to continue to do so and, if possible, to increase their contributions in accordance with their capacity to do so.

Economic and Social Council resolution 1988/72

28 July 1988   Meeting 40   Adopted without vote

Approved by First Committee (E/1988/118) without vote, 22 July (meeting 20); draft by Tunisia, for Group of 77 (E/1988/C.1/L.11), orally revised following informal consultations; agenda item 11.

REFERENCES
[1]YUN 1972, p. 331, GA res. 2997(XXVII), 15 Dec. 1972. [2]YUN 1987, p. 692, GA res. 42/185, 11 Dec. 1987. [3]A/43/25. [4]YUN 1987, p. 1118, GA res. 42/215, 21 Dec. 1987. [5]UNEP/GCSS.I/6 & Corr.1 & Add.2. [6]UNEP/GCSS.I/5. [7]YUN 1987, p. 661, GA res. 42/186, 11 Dec. 1987. [8]*Ibid.*, p. 679, GA res. 42/187, 11 Dec. 1987. [9]UNEP/GCSS.I/6/Add.3. [10]A/43/25 (dec. SS.I/1). [11]UNEP/GCSS.I/2 & Corr.1,2. [12]A/43/25 (dec. SS.I/3). [13]UNEP/GCSS.I/3 & Corr.1. [14]A/43/25 (dec. SS.I/6). [15]UNEP/GCSS.I/4. [16]A/43/25 (dec. SS.I/7). [17]*Ibid.* (dec. SS.I/5). [18]YUN 1985, p. 793. [19]A/43/25 (dec. SS.I/4). [20]*Ibid.* (dec. SS.I/2). [21]UNEP/GC.15/4.

Environmental activities

Environment and development

The Secretary-General in May 1988 submitted to the General Assembly, through the Economic and Social Council, a progress report[1] on the implementation of a 1987 resolution[2] that endorsed the principle of sustainable development.

The Secretary-General stated that a number of Governments had notified the UNEP Executive Director that the resolution and the report of the World Commission on Environment and Development were under consideration. The Secretariat intended to request Governments to provide relevant information by 31 December 1988. The governing bodies of eight United Nations organs, organizations and programmes reported that they had reviewed the resolution and/or the World Commission's report with a view to taking the recommendations into account in their programmes. Eight other organizations reported that they expected to consider the resolution and report when their governing bodies next met. Further information was provided at the secretariat level of 13 United Nations bodies.

On 28 July, by **decision 1988/175**, the Economic and Social Council took note of the report. On 1 July,[3] the Governing Council of the United Nations Development Programme (UNDP) stressed the need for additional financial resources and strengthened technical co-operation to assist developing countries in dealing with environmental problems. It requested the UNDP Administrator to assist recipient countries in enhancing their capacity to integrate environmental concerns into their development strategies and programmes, and to report on the manner in which agencies that designed, implemented and evaluated UNDP-funded projects took environmental aspects into account.

In October, ACC agreed that co-operation among the organizations of the United Nations system should be strengthened in order to enable them effectively to assist Member States in selected priority areas, and decided to consider the question of sustainable and environmentally sound development at its first regular session of 1989.[4]

At the Oslo Conference on Sustainable Development (Oslo, Norway, 9 and 10 July),[5] the Secretary-General, the executive heads of 22 United Nations organizations and members of the World Commission on Environment and Development identified priority issues for United Nations action on sustainable development towards the year 2000 and beyond. They also agreed to include in their programmes and budgets for 1990-1991, as well as in their medium-term plans, measures responding to the World Commission's recommendations regarding the promotion of sustainable development by enhancing global economic growth and social development.

GENERAL ASSEMBLY ACTION

On 20 December, on the recommendation of the Second (Economic and Financial) Committee, the Assembly adopted **resolution 43/196** without vote.

United Nations conference on environment and development

The General Assembly,

Recalling its resolution 42/186 of 11 December 1987, by which it adopted the Environmental Perspective to the Year 2000 and Beyond as a broad framework to guide national action and international co-operation on policies and programmes aimed at achieving environmentally sound development,

Recalling also its resolution 42/187 of 11 December 1987, in which it welcomed the report of the World Commission on Environment and Development,

Bearing in mind that the United Nations Conference on the Human Environment, convened in 1972 in accordance with Assembly resolution 2398(XXIII) of 3 December 1968, recommended that the Assembly convene a second United Nations conference on the subject,

Believing it highly desirable that a United Nations conference on environment and development be convened no later than 1992,

Aware that serious environmental problems are arising in all countries and that these problems must be progressively addressed through preventive measures at their source,

Emphasizing the common goal of all countries to strengthen international co-operation for the promotion of growth and development worldwide and recognizing that, in view of the global character of major environmental problems, all countries have a common interest in pursuing policies aimed at achieving sustainable and environmentally sound development within a sound ecological balance,

Noting that the critical objectives for environment and development policies that follow from the need for sustainable and environmentally sound development must include creating a healthy, clean and safe environment, reviving growth and improving its quality, remedying the problems of poverty and the satisfaction of human needs through raising the standard of living and the quality of life, addressing the issues of population and of conserving and enhancing the resource base, reorienting technology and managing risk and merging environment and economics in decision-making,

Aware that a supportive international economic environment that would result in sustained economic growth and development in all countries, particularly in developing countries, is of major importance for sound management of the environment,

Stressing that it is important for all countries to take effective measures for the protection, restoration and enhancement of the environment in accordance, *inter alia*, with their respective capabilities, and, at the same time, acknowledging the efforts being made in all countries in this regard, including international co-operation between developed and developing countries,

Noting the fact that the largest part of the current emission of pollutants into the environment, including toxic and hazardous wastes, originates in developed countries, and therefore recognizing that those countries have the main responsibility for combating such pollution,

Reaffirming the need for additional financial resources from the international community effectively to support developing countries in identifying, analysing, monitoring, managing or preventing environmental problems in accordance with their national development plans, priorities and objectives,

Reaffirming also the need for developed countries and the appropriate organs and organizations of the United Nations system to strengthen technical co-operation with the developing countries to enable them to develop and strengthen their capacity for identifying, analysing, monitoring, managing or preventing environmental problems in accordance with their national development plans, priorities and objectives,

Recognizing the importance of international co-operation in the research and development of environmentally sound technology and recognizing the need for an international exchange of experience and knowledge as well as the promotion of the transfer of technology for the protection and enhancement of the environment, especially in developing countries, in accordance with national laws, regulations and policies,

Reaffirming the need for the international community to play a catalytic role in technical co-operation among developing countries in the field of the environment, and inviting the appropriate organs and organizations of the United Nations system to co-operate, at the request of the parties concerned, in the promotion and strengthening of such co-operation,

Aware that threats to the environment often have a transboundary impact and that their urgent nature requires strengthened international co-operative action, *inter alia*, by assessing and providing early warning to the world community on serious environmental threats within the framework of Earthwatch,

Taking note with appreciation of the progress report of the Secretary-General on the implementation of resolution 42/187,

Recalling that, in its resolution 42/187, the General Assembly invited Governments, in co-operation with the regional commissions and the United Nations Environment Programme and, as appropriate, intergovernmental organizations, to support and engage in follow-up activities, such as conferences, at the national, regional and global levels,

Noting the importance of exploring the best ways and means to promote sustainable and environmentally sound development in all countries, taking into account General Assembly resolutions 42/186 and 42/187,

Considering in this context that the conference could, *inter alia:*

(a) Review trends in policies and action taken by all countries and international organizations to protect and enhance the environment and to examine how environmental concerns have been incorporated in economic and social policies and planning since the United Nations Conference on the Human Environment in 1972,

(b) Assess major environmental problems, risks and opportunities associated with economic activities in all countries,

(c) Make recommendations for further strengthened international co-operative action within a set of priorities to be established by the conference, define the research and development effort required to implement such recommendations, and indicate financial requirements for their implementation, together with a definition of possible sources for such financing,

1. *Decides* to consider at its forty-fourth session the question of the convening of a United Nations conference on the subject of the present resolution no later than 1992, with a view to taking an appropriate decision at that session on the exact scope, title, venue and date of such a conference and on the modalities and financial implications of holding the conference;

2. *Requests* the Secretary-General, with the assistance of the Executive Director of the United Nations Environment Programme, urgently to obtain the views of Governments on:

(a) The objectives, content, title and scope of the conference;

(b) Appropriate ways of preparing for the conference;

(c) A suitable time and place and other modalities for the conference;
and to submit those views to the General Assembly at its forty-fourth session, through the Economic and Social Council, and to make them available to the Governing Council of the United Nations Environment Programme at its fifteenth session;

3. *Also requests* the Secretary-General, with the assistance of the Executive Director, to obtain the views of appropriate organs, organizations and programmes of the United Nations system and relevant intergovernmental and non-governmental organizations on the objectives, content and scope of the conference, and to submit those views to the General Assembly at its forty-fourth session, through the Economic and Social Council, and to make them available to the Governing Council at its fifteenth session;

4. *Further requests* the Secretary-General, with the assistance of the Executive Director, to prepare a statement of the financial implications of preparing and convening the conference, and to submit that statement to the General Assembly at its forty-fourth session, through the Economic and Social Council, and to make it available to the Governing Council at its fifteenth session;

5. *Invites* the Governing Council to consider the documents referred to in paragraphs 2 to 4 above and, on the basis of that consideration, to submit to the General Assembly at its forty-fourth session, through the Economic and Social Council, its views on the matters referred to in the present resolution, in particular its views on the objectives, content and scope of the conference.

General Assembly resolution 43/196

20 December 1988   Meeting 83   Adopted without vote

Approved by Second Committee (A/43/915/Add.7) without vote, 6 December (meeting 47); 43-nation draft (A/C.2/43/L.36/Rev.2), orally revised following informal consultations; agenda item 82 *(g)*.

Sponsors: Argentina, Austria, Bangladesh, Barbados, Belize, Bolivia, Brazil, Canada, China, Colombia, Costa Rica, Czechoslovakia, Denmark, Ecuador, Egypt, Finland, Guatemala, Guyana, Honduras, Iceland, India, Indonesia, Jamaica, Kenya, Lesotho, Maldives, Malta, Mexico, Netherlands, New Zealand, Nicaragua, Norway, Peru, Poland, Romania, Samoa, Sweden, Tunisia, Ukrainian SSR, Uruguay, Venezuela, Yugoslavia, Zimbabwe.

Meeting numbers. GA 43rd session: 2nd Committee 21-26, 38, 47; plenary 83.

Environmental monitoring and assessment

Earthwatch, the environmental assessment arm of UNEP, continued in 1988 to collect and disseminate information on changes in the global environment, such as ozone depletion, climate change, soil loss and deforestation.[6]

UNEP continued to hold training seminars and expert group meetings on environmental monitoring and data collection. Among these were the second Economic Commission for Europe (ECE) workshop on integrated monitoring, a meeting on remote-sensing technologies for biosphere studies and a workshop on the evaluation of air pollution pressure through pine-needle analysis and mapping.

In October 1988, the Secretary-General submitted to the Second Committee the text of a draft resolution[7] on international ecological security. The Assembly in 1987 had deferred consideration of the draft until 1988.[8] On 29 November, the sponsors of that draft, Czechoslovakia and the Ukrainian SSR, introduced a revised draft resolution[9] on international co-operation in the monitoring, assessment and anticipation of environmental threats. On the recommendation of the Second Committee, the Assembly, by **decision 43/440** of 20 December, deferred consideration of the draft until 1989.

Global Environmental Monitoring System

The Global Environmental Monitoring System (GEMS), through its Programme Activity Centre, continued to co-ordinate the collection of environmental data at the global, regional and national levels and to make them available to managers and planners of natural resources and the environment. These activities encompassed monitoring, data management and environmental assessment.

In March, GEMS was instructed by the Bureau of the African Ministerial Conference on the Environment to co-ordinate environmental monitoring activities in Africa. In 1988, UNEP collected detailed information on eight African countries' needs for resource monitoring and assessment capabilities.

Together with other agencies and organizations, UNEP was developing a satellite-based methodology to map and monitor tropical forests. It continued to co-operate with the World Meteorological Organization (WMO) in monitoring climate systems and with UNESCO and the Swiss Federal Institute of Technology in a world glacier-monitoring service. That project also encompassed the publication in 1988 of the fifth volume in a series on the fluctuation of glaciers covering 1980-1985, and an inventory of the world's glaciers, scheduled for publication in 1989. Attention was given to the development of methods of studying the effects of pollution on forest ecosystems. The newly constituted World Conservation Monitoring Centre gathered data on the status of endangered species, parks and protected areas and trade in animal products. The Monitoring and Assessment Research Centre (MARC) continued to collect and analyse data for the next edition of the environmental data report, to be published in 1989. UNEP also collaborated with the World Resources Institute in the preparation of *World Resources 1988-1989*, issued in November 1988. An interactive environmental data base was being established at MARC in order to offer instant access to the best environmental data.

Three major global assessments were undertaken by UNEP and the World Health Organization (WHO) in air quality, freshwater quality and food contamination. Regarding urban air quality, studies had found that in many industrialized countries, while the levels of sulphur dioxide, particulate matter and lead were improving as a result of various control and prevention strategies, there was still cause for concern in many cities. Data on urban air quality in developing countries, while scanty, indicated deteriorating conditions. While water pollution in cities in developing countries could be severe, water resources did not in general suffer greatly from pollution. Severe pathogen pollution could be found in many rivers in South America, the Indian subcontinent, South-East Asia and probably Africa. Eutrophication, often linked to organic waste, was a problem in many small lakes in Europe, the United States and Asia. Increased levels of nitrate in ground water were found in many western European countries and the United States. Salinization of ground water was found to be extremely widespread in Sahelian Africa and in the arid belt from the Middle East to India. Levels of contaminants in food, particularly in industrialized countries, were generally well within established limits, with the exception, in several countries, of organochlorine pesticides in human milk, mercury and polychlorinated biphenyls in fish, lead in canned foods and aflatoxins in nuts and cereals. In developing countries, however, while the situation was less clear, there were indications that the levels of contaminants, particularly for organochlorine pesticides and aflatoxins, were in excess of health guidelines.

Global Resource Information Database

The Global Resource Information Database (GRID), the principal data management programme within GEMS, continued its efforts to make environmental data available to environmental managers and decision makers with the help of its computer-based Geographic Information System. In December, IBM donated some $6 million worth of computer hardware to UNEP for use in the GRID programme, including two mainframe computers and 15 micro-based systems.

By year's end, the GRID training course for third world professionals, sponsored by the Swiss Directorate for Development Co-operation, had trained 20 persons from as many countries. A GRID scientific and technical advisory group meeting was held at Nairobi (18-21 January), and an expert meeting on hardware and software was held in Washington, D.C. (15-17 November).

INFOTERRA

UNEP's International Environmental Information System, INFOTERRA, continued to assist developing countries in gathering scientific and technological information on environment and resource management issues. The INFOTERRA network continued to grow, with 700 new information sources registered during the reporting period. The number of national focal points (NFPs) increased to 134 with the addition of Lesotho. During 1988, more than 14,000 people from some 90 countries made use of INFOTERRA's information services. Several new publications were issued, and a training course for new staff from 10 English- and French-speaking NFPs was held (Nairobi, 14-18 November). Several INFOTERRA NFPs organized events for World Environment Day, using the promotional kits distributed to them on behalf of the UNEP information service.

1988 state of the world environment

UNEP's 1988 state-of-the-environment report[10] focused on the public and the environment, with special emphasis on the role of women. The report covered the environmental movement, perceptions and attitudes towards environmental issues, public participation in environmental activities, the special role of women and the role of the media.

Protection against harmful products and pollutants

Registration of harmful products

The International Register of Potentially Toxic Chemicals (IRPTC), UNEP's chemical information exchange network, continued in 1988 to expand its computerized files, which included some 600 chemicals of international concern. Scientific and technical information was given to Governments, research institutions, international organizations, NGOs and industry for hazard assessment, risk evaluation and disposal or control.

IRPTC files were made available for use on minicomputers to Canadian users in June, and ways of making that system available outside Canada were explored. An updated version of the Registry of Chemicals Currently Being Tested for Toxic Effects was published in October. An international workshop on the use of classification systems for chemicals based on their toxicity and hazards was organized in Leningrad, and an expert consultation on a regional information exchange network for chemicals was organized in Moscow. IRPTC participated in a meeting of an *ad hoc* working group of experts on prior informed consent and other modalities to supplement the London Guidelines for the Exchange of Information on Chemicals in International Trade[11] (Dakar, Senegal, 19-23 September), organized in response to a 1987 decision by the UNEP Governing Council on the exchange of information on chemicals in international trade. Also in response to that decision, IRPTC continued to implement the London Guidelines by maintaining and distributing a list of designated national authorities; processing and disseminating notifications of control action to those authorities and other appropriate bodies; maintaining regular contacts with the authorities on national implementation of the Guidelines; and developing and maintaining a computerized data base of notifications of control action received in IRPTC. IRPTC continued to participate in the updating of the United Nations consolidated list of products whose consumption and/or sale had been banned, withdrawn, severely restricted or not approved by Governments. An expert consultation meeting (Geneva, 21-24 November), held in response to a 1987 decision of the Governing Council,[12] examined the short- and long-term financial position of IRPTC.[13]

Health-related monitoring

The Food and Agriculture Organization of the United Nations (FAO)/UNEP/WHO Panel of Experts on Environmental Management for Vector Control held its eighth session (Nairobi, September), focusing on education and training in environmental management of water resource development projects.

A symposium on genetic monitoring for the protection of human health and environment was held to promote and encourage research in environmental mutagenesis in Latin America (San José, Costa Rica, 6-11 March). UNEP co-operated with the International Labour Organisation (ILO) and WHO in the International Programme on Chemical Safety (IPCS), providing an effort to assess the risks of chemicals to human health and the environment and to strengthen national capabilities in chemical safety. IPCS held an expert group meeting (Rome, Italy, 20-29 September) on categories of information useful for the identification of hazards during the manufacture, storage and transport of chemicals. It subsequently produced an annotated check-list of that information. It also published a survey on facilities dealing with poisonings, covering 200 institutions in 40 countries, which showed that only 11 developing countries had a full range of facilities to respond to poisonings. In 1988, IPCS published 15 documents on potentially toxic chemicals in the Environmental Health Criteria series, bringing the number of chemicals evaluated to 75. The preparation of 75 international chemical safety cards, giving health and safety information on chemicals for use by factory, agricultural and other workers and employers, was in the pilot phase. A consultation on the pilot phase (Brussels, Belgium, 11-15 April) and a meeting for the peer review of the cards (Rome, 7-11 November) were held.

Other meetings sponsored or co-sponsored by IPCS during the year dealt with chemicals and the aging process, an environmental health review of vinylidene chloride, revision of WHO guidelines for drinking-water quality, the effects of vehicle exhaust, environmental reduction of asbestos, development of a poison information package for developing countries, food additives, pesticide residues, chemical hazards and methods for assessing adverse effects of pesticides.

Several projects were initiated in the area of agricultural chemicals in 1988. In April/May, an independent consultant evaluated a joint UNEP/International Centre of Insect Physiology and Ecology (ICIPE) project on training for self-reliance in ecological pest management in Africa, concluding that the overall impact of the training courses had been positive. From August to October, a working group appointed by ICIPE identified five areas of research which could be addressed in a longer-term programme for locust control. Scientists and donor agencies, including UNEP, met at Cairo, Egypt, in December to discuss such a programme, agreeing that the pursuit of alternative control strategies would be promoted through an international research network. In September/October, a consultant reviewed current activities in Botswana, Malawi, Zambia and Zimbabwe for the control of the tsetse fly and the reduction of animal trypanosomiasis in Africa under the Zambezi Action Plan. A joint FAO/UNEP meeting was held at Rome in November to review the guidelines on biological control in developing countries, which had just been completed. Two Soviet scientists undertook a mission to conduct a feasibility study for a project on training in zoonosis epidemiology, control and prevention in Mongolia. Between May and October, training aids on the safe use and handling of pesticides were prepared for 150 women's group leaders in Thailand. Under the FAO/UNEP Co-operative Global Programme for the Implementation and Development of Integrated Pest Control in Agriculture, a Latin American intercountry programme for the development and application of integrated pest control in cotton growing was developed and implemented, and it was expected that its guidelines would be used in all the cotton-growing countries of Central and South America.

Traffic in toxic and dangerous products and wastes

In response to a 1987 General Assembly resolution,[14] the Secretary-General in May 1988 submitted a report on illegal traffic in toxic and dangerous products and wastes.[15] The report was based on information which Governments and international organizations had submitted to the UNEP Executive Director on instances of illegal traffic in toxic products and wastes that had occurred in the past five years. Information came from 16 countries—seven of which cited concrete examples of illegal traffic—and 27 organizations.

The Secretary-General concluded that the number of responses would seem to indicate increased international traffic in toxic and dangerous products and wastes. The movement of hazardous wastes tended to go from developed to developing countries or to countries whose standards of environmental protection were more permissive. Movements of toxic products—mostly pesticides—followed a similar trend. It was likely that environmentally hazardous substances would be increasingly transferred to developing countries as a result of improved environmental standards and decreasing waste-disposal capacities in developed countries. Part of such international movements might not be deemed illegal in the recipient countries themselves, even though they could pose risks to human health and to the environment. Several developing countries were enacting legislation to prevent them from being used as "dumping places" for environmentally hazardous substances. The prospect of an increased flow of hazardous products and wastes underscored the importance of adherence to the London Guidelines, which apparently had not been complied with in many of the reported cases. A global convention on the control of the transboundary movements of hazardous wastes, which was being negotiated under the aegis of UNEP, was urgently needed (see below).

ECONOMIC AND SOCIAL COUNCIL ACTION

On 28 July, on the recommendation of its First Committee, the Economic and Social Council adopted **resolution 1988/70** without vote.

Traffic in toxic and dangerous products and wastes

The Economic and Social Council,

Taking into account General Assembly resolution 42/183 of 11 December 1987,

Noting that the preliminary report of the Secretary-General on illegal traffic in toxic and dangerous products and wastes indicates a trend of increased international traffic in toxic and dangerous products and wastes, which in most cases has tended to flow from developed to developing countries,

Concerned that part of this traffic is carried out in contravention of existing national legislation and relevant international instruments,

Emphasizing the urgent need for all States to transmit pertinent information requested by the Executive Director of the United Nations Environment Programme in response to General Assembly resolution 42/183,

Taking into account the increase in this traffic as reported by various organizations of the United Nations system, non-governmental organizations and the international media,

Deeply concerned at the rising incidence of dumping of toxic wastes in many countries, particularly in the developing countries,

Considering the potential danger to the health of the population and to the environment of all States posed by toxic and dangerous products and wastes,

1. *Requests* the Secretary-General, in preparing his report to the General Assembly at its forty-fourth session, to draw on information provided by the United Nations Environment Programme and other organizations of the United Nations system, in line with internationally accepted guidelines and principles, and to focus on the following:

(*a*) A quantitative and geographical assessment, by region of origin and of destination, of the illegal traffic in toxic and dangerous products and wastes;

(*b*) A classification of types of toxic and dangerous products and wastes according to their nature, their potential toxicity and the probability of their being traded or dumped;

2. *Also requests* the Secretary-General to submit conclusions and recommendations on different mechanisms that can be devised to monitor and control the illegal traffic in toxic and dangerous products and wastes;

3. *Further requests* the Secretary-General to increase his efforts to obtain information on illegal traffic in toxic and dangerous wastes and on steps taken to eliminate or reduce this type of traffic.

Economic and Social Council resolution 1988/70

28 July 1988   Meeting 40   Adopted without vote

Approved by First Committee (E/1988/118) without vote, 22 July (meeting 20); draft by Tunisia, for Group of 77 (E/1988/C.1/L.3), orally revised following informal consultations; agenda item 11.

GENERAL ASSEMBLY ACTION

On 20 December, on the recommendation of the Second Committee, the Assembly adopted **resolution 43/212** without vote.

Responsibility of States for the protection of the environment: prevention of the illegal international traffic in, and the dumping and resulting accumulation of, toxic and dangerous products and wastes affecting the developing countries in particular

The General Assembly,

Recalling its resolution 42/183 of 11 December 1987 on traffic in toxic and dangerous products and wastes,

Taking note of Economic and Social Council resolutions 1988/70 and 1988/71 of 28 July 1988,

Concerned about the increase in the illegal international traffic in, and the dumping and resulting accumulation of, toxic and dangerous products and wastes, in contravention of existing national legislation and relevant international legal instruments, adversely affecting many countries, particularly developing countries, as well as international waters,

Stressing the obligation of all States, in accordance with their responsibilities, to protect the environment and, in this overall context, stressing also the need for all States to prevent the illegal international traffic in, and the dumping and resulting accumulation of, toxic and dangerous products and wastes adversely affecting many countries, in particular developing countries,

1. *Urges* all States, bearing in mind their respective responsibilities, to take the necessary legal and technical measures in order to halt and prevent the illegal international traffic in, and the dumping and resulting accumulation of, toxic and dangerous products and wastes;

2. *Also urges* all States to prohibit all transboundary movement of toxic and dangerous wastes carried out without the prior consent of the competent authorities of the importing country or without full recognition of the sovereign rights of transit countries;

3. *Further urges* all States in this connection to prohibit such movement without prior notification in writing of the competent authorities of all countries concerned, including transit countries, and to provide all information required to ensure the proper management of the wastes and full disclosure of the nature of the substances to be received or transported;

4. *Urges* all States generating toxic and dangerous wastes to make every effort to treat and dispose of them in the country of origin to the maximum extent possible consistent with environmentally sound disposal;

5. *Requests* the *Ad Hoc* Working Group of Legal and Technical Experts with a Mandate to Prepare a Global Convention on the Control of the Transboundary Movements of Hazardous Wastes, established by the United Nations Environment Programme, to give due consideration to the present resolution and to take into account the various views expressed during the forty-third session of the General Assembly on the respective responsibilities for the prevention of the illegal international traffic in, and the dumping and resulting accumulation of, toxic and dangerous products and wastes;

6. *Calls upon* the international community, in particular the developed countries, to strengthen its scientific and technical co-operation with the developing countries and to provide appropriate assistance to them in their efforts to eliminate the adverse consequences of toxic and dangerous products and wastes for human health and the environment.

General Assembly resolution 43/212

20 December 1988   Meeting 83   Adopted without vote

Approved by Second Committee (A/43/919) without vote, 6 December (meeting 47); draft by Vice-Chairman (A/C.2/43/L.74), orally revised, based on draft by Tunisia, for Group of 77 (A/C.2/43/L.23); agenda item 143.
Meeting numbers. GA 43rd session: 2nd Committee 21-26, 30, 47; plenary 83.

Transboundary movements of hazardous wastes

The Executive Director of UNEP, as authorized by a 1987 decision of the Governing Council,[16] convened the third session of the *Ad Hoc* Working Group of Legal and Technical Experts with a Mandate to Prepare a Global Convention on the Control of Transboundary Movements of Hazardous Wastes (Geneva, 7-16 November 1988). The draft convention was to be submitted to a diplomatic conference for adoption early in 1989.

ECONOMIC AND SOCIAL COUNCIL ACTION

On 28 July, on the recommendation of its First Committee, the Economic and Social Council adopted **resolution 1988/71** without vote.

Global convention on the control of transboundary movements of hazardous wastes

The Economic and Social Council,

Noting the work of the *Ad Hoc* Working Group of Legal and Technical Experts with a Mandate to Prepare a Global Convention on the Control of Transboundary Movements of Hazardous Wastes, convened by the Executive Director of the United Nations Environment Programme pursuant to Governing Council decision 14/30 of 17 June 1987, and that the draft of the convention will be submitted to a diplomatic conference for adoption by Governments in Basel, Switzerland, in early 1989,

1. *Stresses* the importance of the active participation of all Governments in the preparatory work for the global convention on the control of transboundary movements of hazardous wastes, with a view to its speedy and successful completion;

2. *Requests* the Secretary-General to report to the General Assembly at its forty-fourth session on developments in regard to the convention.

Economic and Social Council resolution 1988/71

28 July 1988   Meeting 40   Adopted without vote

Approved by First Committee (E/1988/118) without vote, 22 July (meeting 20); draft by Chairman (E/1988/C.1/L.10), based on informal consultations; agenda item 11.

Atomic radiation and nuclear dumping

In August, the United Nations Scientific Committee on the Effects of Atomic Radiation issued a report on the sources, effects and risks of ionizing radiation.[17] The report gave a historical review of the Committee's work and outlined the levels and effects of radiation from such sources as nuclear explosions, nuclear power production and medical exposures. It summarized the developments and trends in the field and presented the highlights and conclusions to be drawn from the most recent studies in radiation physics and biology.

On 6 December, the Assembly adopted **resolution 43/55**, requesting the Committee to continue its work and noting with satisfaction the continued and growing scientific co-operation between the Committee and UNEP.

On 28 July, the Economic and Social Council, by **decision 1988/174**, requested the Secretary-General—through UNEP's Governing Council and in co-operation with the Director General of the International Atomic Energy Agency—to submit a report to the Assembly at its 1989 session on the effects of the dumping of nuclear wastes on the environment.

Global climate

In January 1988, UNEP organized an internal seminar to identify environmental sectors that might be sensitive to climate change. The Intergovernmental Panel on Climate Change, a forum in which Governments were examining greenhouse warming and global climate change, held its first session at Geneva in November, with representatives from 30 Governments and 19 international organizations. One of the main objectives of the UNEP climate change programme was to improve understanding of the probable effect of greenhouse gas warming on socio-economic systems in various regions. To that end, several regional studies on the effect of climate change on society were planned. In response to a 1987 decision of the Governing Council,[18] UNEP commissioned the Beijer Institute to prepare a report on possible responses by Governments and international agencies to anticipated climate change.

UNEP sponsored numerous meetings dealing with climate change during the year, including a seminar on climate and agriculture, world conferences on climate and development and on the changing atmosphere, and a workshop on drought early-warning systems. Seminars on climate impact assessment techniques were held at Kathmandu, Nepal, and New Delhi, India, in March. The UNEP *Ad Hoc* Working Group on El Niño and the Southern Oscillation (Bangkok, 11-15 January) concluded that the recent El Niño events had been associated with world-wide climatic anomalies, such as droughts in Australia, Brazil, Ethiopia and India and widespread temperature anomalies in the northern hemisphere. The Group adopted objectives and a work plan for the next two years.

In October,[19] ACC decided to consider in 1989 the question of world climate change and requested UNEP, in co-operation with WMO and other concerned organizations, to prepare an issues paper as the basis for its discussion.

On 9 September, in a letter to the Secretary-General,[20] Malta requested that an item entitled "Declaration proclaiming climate as part of the common heritage of mankind" be added to the agenda of the 1988 session of the Assembly.

GENERAL ASSEMBLY ACTION

On 6 December, on the recommendation of the Second Committee, the Assembly adopted **resolution 43/53** without vote.

Protection of global climate for present and future generations of mankind

The General Assembly,

Welcoming with appreciation the initiative taken by the Government of Malta in proposing for consideration by the Assembly the item entitled "Conservation of climate as part of the common heritage of mankind",

Concerned that certain human activities could change global climate patterns, threatening present and future generations with potentially severe economic and social consequences,

Noting with concern that the emerging evidence indicates that continued growth in atmospheric concentrations of "greenhouse" gases could produce global warming with an eventual rise in sea levels, the effects of which could be disastrous for mankind if timely steps are not taken at all levels,

Recognizing the need for additional research and scientific studies into all sources and causes of climate change,

Concerned also that emissions of certain substances are depleting the ozone layer and thereby exposing the earth's surface to increased ultra-violet radiation, which may pose a threat to, *inter alia*, human health, agricultural productivity and animal and marine life, and re-affirming in this context the appeal, contained in its resolution 42/182 of 11 December 1987, to all States that have not yet done so to consider becoming parties to the Vienna Convention for the Protection of the Ozone Layer, adopted on 22 March 1985, and the Montreal Protocol on Substances that Deplete the Ozone Layer, adopted on 16 September 1987, as soon as possible,

Recalling its resolutions 42/186 and 42/187 of 11 December 1987 on the Environmental Perspective to the Year 2000 and Beyond and on the report of the World Commission on Environment and Development, respectively,

Convinced that changes in climate have an impact on development,

Aware that a considerable amount of valuable work, particularly at the scientific level and in the legal field, has already been initiated on climate change, in particular by the United Nations Environment Programme, the World Meteorological Organization and the International Council of Scientific Unions and under the auspices of individual States,

Welcoming the convening in 1990 of a second World Climate Conference,

Recalling also the conclusions of the meeting held at Villach, Austria, in 1985, which, *inter alia*, recommended a programme on climate change to be promoted by Governments and the scientific community with the collaboration of the World Meteorological Organization, the United Nations Environment Programme and the International Council of Scientific Unions,

Convinced that climate change affects humanity as a whole and should be confronted within a global framework so as to take into account the vital interests of all mankind,

1. *Recognizes* that climate change is a common concern of mankind, since climate is an essential condition which sustains life on earth;

2. *Determines* that necessary and timely action should be taken to deal with climate change within a global framework;

3. *Reaffirms* its resolution 42/184 of 11 December 1987, in which, *inter alia*, it agreed with the Governing Council of the United Nations Environment Programme that the Programme should attach importance to the problem of global climate change and that the Executive Director of the United Nations Environment Programme should ensure that the Programme co-operates closely with the World Meteorological Organization and the International Council of Scientific Unions and maintains an active, influential role in the World Climate Programme;

4. *Considers* that activities in support of the World Climate Programme, approved by the Congress and Executive Council of the World Meteorological Organization and elaborated in the system-wide medium-term environment programme for the period 1990-1995, which was approved by the Governing Council of the

United Nations Environment Programme, should be accorded high priority by the relevant organs and programmes of the United Nations system;

5. *Endorses* the action of the World Meteorological Organization and the United Nations Environment Programme in jointly establishing an Intergovernmental Panel on Climate Change to provide internationally coordinated scientific assessments of the magnitude, timing and potential environmental and socio-economic impact of climate change and realistic response strategies, and expresses appreciation for the work already initiated by the Panel;

6. *Urges* Governments, intergovernmental and non-governmental organizations and scientific institutions to treat climate change as a priority issue, to undertake and promote specific, co-operative action-oriented programmes and research so as to increase understanding on all sources and causes of climate change, including its regional aspects and specific time-frames as well as the cause and effect relationship of human activities and climate, and to contribute, as appropriate, with human and financial resources to efforts to protect the global climate;

7. *Calls upon* all relevant organizations and programmes of the United Nations system to support the work of the Intergovernmental Panel on Climate Change;

8. *Encourages* the convening of conferences on climate change, particularly on global warming, at the national, regional and global levels in order to make the international community better aware of the importance of dealing effectively and in a timely manner with all aspects of climate change resulting from certain human activities;

9. *Calls upon* Governments and intergovernmental organizations to collaborate in making every effort to prevent detrimental effects on climate and activities which affect the ecological balance, and also calls upon non-governmental organizations, industry and other productive sectors to play their due role;

10. *Requests* the Secretary-General of the World Meteorological Organization and the Executive Director of the United Nations Environment Programme, utilizing the Intergovernmental Panel on Climate Change, immediately to initiate action leading, as soon as possible, to a comprehensive review and recommendations with respect to:

(a) The state of knowledge of the science of climate and climatic change;

(b) Programmes and studies on the social and economic impact of climate change, including global warming;

(c) Possible response strategies to delay, limit or mitigate the impact of adverse climate change;

(d) The identification and possible strengthening of relevant existing international legal instruments having a bearing on climate;

(e) Elements for inclusion in a possible future international convention on climate;

11. *Also requests* the Secretary-General to bring the present resolution to the attention of all Governments, as well as intergovernmental organizations, non-governmental organizations in consultative status with the Economic and Social Council and well-established scientific institutions with expertise in matters concerning climate;

12. *Further requests* the Secretary-General to report to the General Assembly at its forty-fourth session on the implementation of the present resolution;

13. *Decides* to include this question in the provisional agenda of its forty-fourth session, without prejudice to the application of the principle of biennialization.

General Assembly resolution 43/53

6 December 1988   Meeting 70   Adopted without vote

Approved by Second Committee (A/43/905) without vote, 23 November (meeting 44); 21-nation draft (A/C.2/43/L.17/Rev.1); agenda item 148.

Sponsors: Australia, Canada, Colombia, El Salvador, Fiji, Finland, India, Jamaica, Malta, Morocco, New Zealand, Norway, Papua New Guinea, Poland, Samoa, Solomon Islands, Sweden, Togo, United Kingdom, Vanuatu, Venezuela.

Meeting numbers. GA 43nd session: 2nd Committee 21-26, 30, 44; plenary 70.

Ecosystems

Atmosphere

Protection of the ozone layer

Activities addressing the depletion of the ozone layer continued to build on the 1985 Vienna Convention for the Protection of the Ozone Layer[21] and the 1987 Montreal Protocol on Substances that Deplete the Ozone Layer.[22]

The Ozone Trends Panel—set up by UNEP, WMO and three United States agencies in 1986—published a report in 1988 which found that the atmospheric concentrations of trace gases important in controlling stratospheric ozone had continued to increase globally because of human activities and that ozone losses in general were greater than had been predicted, primarily as a result of chlorofluorocarbons. The report confirmed the repeated sudden decreases in the amount of Antarctic ozone in the spring, and stated that evidence strongly indicated that man-made chlorine species were primarily responsible for the ozone hole over Antarctica.

UNEP organized a series of expert group meetings (The Hague, Netherlands, October) to review measures for controlling ozone-depleting gases and their effectiveness, as called for in the Montreal Protocol. Scientists attending the meeting confirmed that while implementation of the Montreal Protocol would do much to stabilize the ozone layer, it would be insufficient to repair the Antarctica hole.

UNEP and WMO co-sponsored the World Conference on the Changing Atmosphere: Implications for Global Security (Toronto, Canada, 27-30 June), which urged immediate action to counter the ongoing degradation of the atmosphere, including the development of a plan to protect the atmosphere, speedy ratification of the Montreal Protocol, the reduction of carbon dioxide emissions to approximately 80 per cent of the 1988 level by 2005 and establishment of a World Atmosphere Fund. The Advisory Group on Greenhouse Gases (Toronto, 1 and 2 July), continuing its role of advising the executive heads of UNEP, the International Council of Scientific Unions and WMO, approved the establishment of three working groups to review analyses of limitation strategies, indicators for management of climatic change and costs of adaptation and limitation strategies.

The WMO/UNEP Background Air Pollution Monitoring Network continued to publish data regularly and held a training course at Budapest, Hungary, for observers at its stations.

Terrestrial ecosystems

Soil management

Soil erosion had become so severe in many areas of the developing world that controlling it was a matter of life and death to many low-income farmers. The rate of soil loss had reached 26 billion tons annually, which was equivalent to 20 million tons of grain. The United States reported that it had reversed the rate of soil erosion through legislation and increased public awareness of the serious environmental threat. A project to assess global soil degradation, initiated in 1987, was implemented by the International Soil Reference and Information Centre in the Netherlands in association with FAO and other agencies. In April, the project published a set of guidelines for general assessment of the status of human-induced soil degradation, which was adopted at a regional workshop for Latin American soil scientists in Montevideo, Uruguay, in March. A procedure manual for small-scale map and data base compilation was completed in December.

In the context of implementing the 1985 Cairo Programme for African Co-operation,[23] the Soil Research Institute of the Council for Scientific and Industrial Research at Kumasi, Ghana, agreed to assume responsibility for the co-ordination of the African Soils and Fertilizers Network. Initial activities included a training workshop with the University of Zimbabwe (Harare, 24 May–9 June), the second meeting of the Network's management and planning group (Kampala, Uganda, 4 and 5 December) and the All-Africa Soil Science Society Conference (Kampala, 5-10 December). UNEP supported the International Conference on Soil Classification (Alma-Ata, USSR, 12-16 September) and an international workshop on classification, management and use potential of swell-shrink soils (Nagpur, India, 24-28 October).

Forest and mountain ecosystems

Amid growing concern over the continuing destruction of forest ecosystems in general and tropical forests in particular, UNEP played an active role in the implementation of the FAO-co-ordinated Tropical Forestry Action Plan[24] by strengthening its conservation component. More than 10 national forestry sector reviews had been completed and 33 were being developed under the Plan. Six African countries expressed interest in reafforestation plans recommended by the African Ministerial Conference on the Environment. UNEP provided resources to enable participants from developing countries to attend workshops on forest research, conservation and nature management.

An expert meeting on compensation mechanisms for conserving tropical forest ecosystems was held at Nairobi in March, addressing issues such as debt swaps and the development of methodologies to assess the real value of forest ecosystems. A training seminar on agroforestry applications for arid and semi-arid French-speaking African countries was organized at Samarkand, USSR, in May. Missions visited Costa Rica and Peru, resulting in proposals to train local experts. Two expert missions produced proposals for a plan to improve forestry conservation and management in the United Republic of Tanzania. A UNEP-supported forestry sector overview in Uganda was published.

An international seminar on the ecology and management of natural resources in high mountain areas (Cajamarca, Peru, 20-27 August) was organized as part of a pilot project that had been active in encouraging farmers' participation in training, rescuing traditional technologies and improving living conditions.

Protection of endangered species

The non-sustainable and exploitative use of natural resources was expected to result in the loss of perhaps a quarter of the Earth's species during the next 20-30 years. Among the measures demonstrated to be effective in preserving biological diversity were establishing protected areas, incorporating the maximum amount of biological diversity in those areas and providing secure scientific management for them, promoting regional and national conservation strategies, encouraging the application of international conservation conventions, protecting particular species from destructive exploitation and encouraging Governments to apply to non-protected lands the conservation principles outlined in the World Charter for Nature[25] and the World Conservation Strategy,[26] which in 1988 was being updated and expanded.

In response to a 1987 decision of the Governing Council on the establishment of a biological diversity convention,[27] UNEP surveyed Governments—58 of which had replied—on their activities related to the conservation of biological diversity. A meeting of experts (Nairobi, 29-31 August) concluded that a global convention should proceed only if it were truly comprehensive with a sound basis in science, practical in defining obligations and goals, adequately funded by Governments, capable of co-ordinating efforts under other conventions on the subject, and provided for a transfer of resources to allow for its implementation in poorer countries, which were the custodians of much of the Earth's biological heritage. An *ad hoc* working group of experts (Geneva, 16-18 November), building on the work of the Nairobi meeting, determined that an umbrella convention to rationalize existing international instruments was neither desirable nor possible, given political and logistical difficulties, and that other ways to achieve that goal should be sought. The Group endorsed the view that a new global legal instrument and other measures were required for the conservation of biological diversity and proposed that the Governing Council should decide on how to resolve several important issues critical to such a convention.

UNEP continued in 1988 to provide the secretariat for the Convention on International Trade in Endangered Species of Wild Fauna and Flora (CITES) at Lausanne, Switzerland. Six technical assistance missions took place during the year to assist developing countries in implementing the Convention. The Ivory Co-ordination Unit continued its work on an ivory quota system and a survey of ivory trade and stocks. The CITES African Elephant Working Group agreed at its first meeting (Nairobi, October/November) to submit a comprehensive elephant conservation strategy to Governments for consideration. UNEP also provided the secretariat for the Convention on the Conservation of Migratory Species of Wild Animals; the first meeting of its Scientific Council and the second meeting of the Conference of the Parties to the Convention were held at Geneva in October. The Conference discussed the development of agreements among States on conservation of species and populations and directed that priority should be given to a global review of the conservation status of small cetaceans, including freshwater species.

The Ecosystem Conservation Group, comprising the four major global conservation organizations—UNEP, FAO, UNESCO and the International Union for Conservation of Nature and Natural Resources (IUCN)—at its fifteenth general meeting, reviewed activities for implementing the Action Plan for Biosphere Reserves. UNEP had drawn up a project on training of biosphere reserve managers in Africa in co-operation with UNESCO.

Among the activities intended to help preserve the genetic diversity of the world's crop plants was a project sponsored by UNEP and the International Board for Plant Genetic Resources, in which samples of the germ plasm of 11 genera of plants were collected in Zaire for deposit in the Board's gene bank network. An international consultation on the conservation of medicinal plants was held in March, and a pan-African workshop on plant genetic resources (Nairobi, 26-30 September) called for greater African co-operation through networking on germ-plasm research and the development of projects to conserve important plant species.

An agreement was reached between FAO and the European Association of Animal Production to expand the newly established data bank for Europe to hold a summary of genetic characteristics of breeds from developing countries, thus making the data bank a global one. FAO, with support from UNEP, continued to provide technical inputs for the establishment of regional gene banks for animal genetic resources. Studies began as a step towards the creation of such gene banks in Africa, Asia and Latin America for the cryogenic storage of semen and embryos of endangered breeds. UNEP continued its support to the regional Microbiological Resources Centres in Brazil, Egypt, Guatemala, Kenya, Senegal and Thailand, which enabled them to carry out training activities and pilot projects for the application of microbial resources in environmental management. UNEP also supported the International Microbial Strain Data Network as a means of collating knowledge about and ensuring access to data on the location and availability of strains with desired properties. The Network held two training courses—in Guatemala and the United States—for potential users and operators. In the area of biotechnology, the joint United Nations Industrial Development Organization/WHO/UNEP Working Group on Biotechnology Safety continued its work, and an international conference (Cardiff, United Kingdom, 5-8 April) discussed the need to proceed with caution and to raise the level of understanding and confidence among the general public about the release of genetically engineered organisms into the environment.

Lithosphere

Addressing the environmental aspects of the lithosphere, the UNEP/UNESCO/USSR project on geology and environment continued, and the proceedings of a 1985 workshop (Tashkent, USSR) on the impact of water management projects on the hydrogeological and engineering geological conditions of the lithosphere were published. In September 1988, a joint workshop of the Scientific Council on Problems of the Environment/UNEP Carbon and Sulphur Units was held on the shores of Lake Baikal in the USSR, which holds nearly 20 per cent of the world's freshwater reserves. The workshop was the first to appraise all major biogeochemical elements with respect to their integrated feedbacks in a biogeochemical supercycle. The proceedings of the workshop were to form part of a publication series on the transport of carbon and minerals in major world rivers, lakes and estuaries.

Desertification control

Desertification continued to be a major environmental problem, worsened by the persistent droughts reported in the northern hemisphere during 1988. Heavy rains broke the drought of previous years in Africa, but also caused catastrophic floods and an unprecedented desert locust plague in the Maghreb countries, the western Sahel, eastern Africa and the Arabian peninsula. Efforts to combat desertification were in most countries limited to isolated sectoral anti-desertification projects whose impact was hampered by the lack of a clearly defined framework for desertification control within national development plans as well as inadequate human and financial resources.

In response to those problems, UNEP during the year made a major effort to assist the 16 Governments that had fully or partly developed national desertification control plans. UNEP and the United Nations Sudano-Sahelian Office (UNSO) consulted with various Governments to agree on steps to formulate concrete project proposals on priority areas identified under those national action plans. In compliance with a 1987 decision of the Governing Council,[28] the Executive Director consulted with representatives of Governments and United Nations agencies on enhancing the efficiency of the Consultative Group for Desertification Control, a new approach to the special account for financing desertification control programmes and means of financing implementation of the United Nations Plan of Action to Combat Desertification.[29] A meeting of officials and experts at Geneva in July made various recommendations in those areas, which were discussed in detail in a report to the Governing Council on implementation of the Plan of Action.[30]

The Inter-Agency Working Group on Desertification continued to co-ordinate a programme for the establishment of regional networks on desertification. The programme culminated in 1988 in the creation of a major operational sand-dune mapping, stabilization and afforestation network for the Middle East and North Africa, an arid lands forestry network for the Sahelian and north Sudanian zones of Africa and five Caribbean and Latin American technical co-operation networks on watershed management, all established by FAO. The network of research and training centres for desertification control in Asia and the Pacific and the Latin American and Caribbean environmental training network also continued to consolidate their programmes. UNEP was funding a three-year project to establish an NGO network of research

and information on the development of sustainable livelihoods in arid and semi-arid lands in Africa.

In 1988, UNEP continued its efforts to implement the Plan of Action to Combat Desertification, providing technical assistance to Governments in integrating desertification control plans into national development plans and programmes. In addition, the UNEP Desertification Control Programme Activity Centre assisted 15 African countries in formulating pilot projects for the rehabilitation of villages and the sustainable development of stock-raising zones in semi-arid areas, with the aim of fostering grass-roots participation. UNEP initiated a study in the Sudan and Uganda to identify local sources of minerals and assess their usability as low-cost soil ameliorants and fertilizers. At the request of Uganda, UNEP undertook a study on the production of stabilized soil/lime bricks and roofing tiles, a technology that can considerably reduce the amount of deforestation resulting from the traditional production of fire-baked clay bricks. Other activities included co-ordination and support of various sand-dune stabilization and afforestation programmes, training programmes, the assessment and mapping of desertification and preparation of an arid lands bibliography data base and a wind erosion bibliographic referral system.

Implementation in the Sudano-Sahelian region

In 1988, many areas of the Sudano-Sahelian region received torrential downpours that resulted in serious flooding and massive soil erosion, particularly in Burkina Faso, Mali and the Sudan.

The Plan of Action to Combat Desertification was implemented in the Sudano-Sahelian region by UNSO, which supported a desertification control programme in 22 countries, consisting, as at September 1988, of 64 ongoing projects with total funding of some $71 million. An in-house study conducted in late 1987 and early 1988 on the role of UNSO refined its role to include, *inter alia:* co-ordination and harmonization of a wide spectrum of drought-related and desertification control activities; assistance in the mobilization of external financial resources needed for implementation of such activities; management of the United Nations Trust Fund for Sudano-Sahelian Activities; intensification of public interest in the plight of the region; co-operation with Governments of the region in carrying out their activities; identification, development, financing and monitoring of programmes; and mobilization of resources. It was decided to establish a regional office of UNSO at Nairobi to serve as a link between UNEP and UNSO, to function as an extended arm of UNEP in East Africa in implementing the Plan of Action, and to act as a United Nations liaison with the

Intergovernmental Authority for Drought and Development and its member States in developing and implementing their drought-related programmes and desertification control activities.

In 1988, projects were carried out in the areas of afforestation and reforestation, alternative energy sources aimed at conserving fuelwood, rangeland management, water resources, soil protection and dune stabilization and integrated land management.

Freshwater ecosystems

UNEP's programme for the environmentally sound management of inland water (EMINWA) focused in 1988 on the Lake Chad basin, which had deteriorated because of drought. UNEP outlined steps for the preparation of a water master plan and an action programme for the environmentally sound management of the basin. A survey mission was dispatched to the Mekong Delta to establish two pilot farms with a view to increasing food production. Projects were developed for the development of the Lake Xolotlán basin in Nicaragua and the Orinoco-Apure river system in Venezuela.

On the subject of environmentally sound development of ground-water resources, an expert group met in Bahrain in March to discuss the preparation of an action plan for the Damman aquifer. The fourth planning meeting on the freshwater part of the World Climate Programme, organized by UNESCO and WMO (Paris, 12-16 September), agreed that in climate and water resource development projects attention had to be focused on studies of hydrological data in the context of climate variability and change, modelling of the hydrological cycle and a methodology for the application of climatological data to water resources projects. In the context of the International Drinking Water Supply and Sanitation Decade (1981-1990), UNEP and WHO established water quality surveillance systems in villages in Indonesia, Peru and Zambia, with plans for similar projects in the United Republic of Tanzania and Vanuatu.

A first draft code of conduct on accidental pollution of transboundary inland waters was prepared by representatives of 13 European countries under the auspices of ECE. The code of conduct was to be used as guidance for solving similar problems throughout the world. A series of guidelines on environmental impact assessment methods was prepared, aimed at helping Governments, institutions and individuals to highlight environmental components in the design of water resources projects. Training seminars and workshops were held on environmentally sound lake management (Japan), environmentally sound water management (Egypt, the Niger and Thailand) and the management of water resource development

projects (USSR). During the year, UNEP published recommended syllabuses on the integration of environmental aspects into water resources engineering education, following a world-wide survey conducted with UNESCO.

The Advisory Group on Water Resources, focusing on the preparation of guidelines for sustainable water management and on the implementation of the EMINWA programme, held two sessions in 1988. Expert group meetings were held on the organization of ecological investigations dealing with water and soil resources development and on international river basin development.

Marine ecosystems

UNEP's activities with regard to oceans and coastal areas included global and regional programme elements that concentrated on issues that could benefit from UNEP's co-ordinating role and from the Environment Fund.

UNEP continued to support the Joint Group of Experts on the Scientific Aspects of Marine Pollution (GESAMP) and co-sponsored six GESAMP working groups dealing with specific environmental problems: evaluation of the hazards of harmful substances carried by ship; review of potentially harmful substances; interchange of pollutants between the atmosphere and the oceans; coastal modelling; state of the marine environment; and long-term ecological consequences of low-level contamination of the marine environment. The reports produced by these working groups provided the scientific basis for the formulation of proposals for government action in pursuance of regional seas conventions. Assessments of the state of the marine environment, co-ordinated by UNEP with the assistance of several other organizations, were completed during the year in 14 regions, covering practically all the world's coastal waters. These reports were intended to be used by GESAMP to finalize a global report on health of the oceans and by States in assessing their marine pollution control priorities. Six regional overviews on the potential impact of expected climatic changes on coastal and marine ecosystems were prepared. Eight new reference methods for studying marine pollution were prepared, two were revised and four were translated into French and Spanish.

Regional seas programme

Mediterranean region. In the Mediterranean region in 1988, the number of countries that had ratified the Protocol for the Protection of the Mediterranean Sea against Pollution from Land-Based Sources and the Protocol concerning Mediterranean Specially Protected Areas rose to 12 and 13, respectively. Pledges to the Trust Fund totalled $3,988,035 for 1988. During their fifth ordinary meeting, the contracting parties approved joint measures to prevent mercury pollution; approved environmental quality criteria for shellfish waters; agreed to amend the Protocol on land-based sources; and decided to allow the Regional Oil Combating Centre to deal with dangerous substances other than oil. Numerous technical meetings and training programmes were organized, on issues such as oil pollution control, microbiological methods for determining the quality of beaches and management of liquid waste treatment plants. Pilot coastal zone development projects continued, and the Regional Centre for the Reduction of Seismic Risk in Mediterranean Coastal Areas was inaugurated at Genoa, Italy. Documents published included six volumes of the Mediterranean Action Plan technical report series and *Futures of the Mediterranean Basin 2000-2025*.

Kuwait region. The Council of the Regional Organization for the Protection of the Marine Environment (ROPME) held its sixth meeting in Kuwait in April and approved UNEP proposals for future co-operation on coastal zone management, strengthening national and regional capabilities for monitoring the marine environment and public awareness. The Council also agreed to a UNEP initiative for an in-depth evaluation of the Kuwait Action Plan. An extraordinary meeting of the ROPME Council (Kuwait, 31 October and 1 November) endorsed the reorientation of the Action Plan towards concrete achievable targets and approved the actions proposed for cleaning up the sea area after the eight-year conflict in the region.

West and Central African region. In May, the steering committee for the marine environment of the region agreed to a rescheduling of unpaid pledges to the Trust Fund, but the continuing failure of most Governments to contribute had seriously retarded implementation of the Action Plan. Despite these financial problems, the network of institutions and laboratories participating in marine-pollution monitoring grew to 23 in 10 countries during the year. A manual on methods for evaluating and controlling coastal erosion in the region was also completed.

Wider Caribbean region. In 1988, the UNEP Regional Co-ordinating Unit for the Wider Caribbean reached full staffing and its information network became operational. Fifteen Governments had ratified or acceded to the Convention for the Protection and Development of the Marine Environment of the Wider Caribbean Region and its Protocol concerning Co-operation in Combating Oil Spills. Four umbrella projects—co-ordination and common costs; environmental management of coastal areas; assessment and control of marine pollution; and environmental training, education and public awareness—were being implemented.

East Asian seas region. Four projects were completed within the framework of the East Asian Seas Action Plan, leaving four ongoing and two being formulated. The seventh meeting of the East Asian seas co-ordinating body (Yogyakarta, Indonesia, 17-19 July) reviewed the progress of the Action Plan and requested UNEP to prepare for a meeting of experts in 1989 to look into the feasibility of preparing a draft convention as a possible legal framework for

the Action Plan. The regional report on the state of the marine environment was completed and a regional study on the socio-economic implications of expected climate changes was initiated.

South-East Pacific region. Protocols on environmental impact assessment and specially protected areas were being prepared, following the entry into force of the Convention on the Protection of the Marine Environment and Coastal Area of the South-East Pacific. About 200 experts benefited from seminars, workshops and other activities carried out under the Action Plan. The regional institutional network comprised 50 institutions conducting research in 29 areas of interest.

Red Sea and Gulf of Aden region. Following a proposal from the secretariat of the Red Sea and Gulf of Aden Environment Programme concerning marine conservation surveys in Democratic Yemen, Somalia and the Sudan, UNEP was drafting a project on strengthening research and monitoring capabilities in Democratic Yemen for assessment of pollution in the marine environment.

South Pacific region. A wide range of activities continued within the framework of the South Pacific Regional Environment Programme (SPREP). An intergovernmental review meeting on the SPREP Action Plan (Noumea, New Caledonia, 27 June–1 July) approved a concentration on six major programme elements: monitoring, research and control of pollution; management of specially protected areas, historic sites and exotic organisms; inland water quality, pesticides and pollution control; natural resource management, environmental planning and administration; environmental education, training and information; and impact of climatic changes and sea-level rise. A training course on the basic techniques for assessing environmental impacts on the marine environment and coastal areas of the South Pacific was also held (Cali, Colombia, 8-12 February).

Eastern African region. Somalia in 1988 ratified the Convention for the Protection, Management and Development of the Marine and Coastal Environment of the Eastern African Region. Somalia was assisted in assessing pollution in Mogadishu harbour, where the M.V. *Ariadne* had spilled hazardous chemicals when it went aground in 1985. A national oil spill contingency plan for Mauritius was developed by the International Maritime Organization (IMO) and UNEP, and a national action plan for the protection, management and development of the marine and coastal environment of the United Republic of Tanzania was prepared.

South Asian seas region. UNEP, with the assistance of IUCN and IMO, had initiated two projects in the South Asian seas region and was in the process of formulating a third. The regional report on the state of the marine environment was completed and the regional report on the socio-economic implications of expected climatic changes was being finalized.

UNEP served as the secretariat for the Committee on Seas of the African Ministerial Conference on the Environment. At its second meeting in December, the Committee finalized its organization and established a mechanism for the exchange of information and expertise between the African subregions on protection and development of the marine and coastal environment. The Committee declared an African Decade for the Protection of the Marine and Coastal Environment, 1991-2000.

UNEP continued its efforts to promote the implementation of the Global Plan of Action for the Conservation, Management and Utilization of Marine Mammals. A regional action plan for the protection of the Mediterranean monk seal was prepared by experts participating in the Mediterranean Action Plan. An extensive evaluation of the development of the Global Plan of Action and its achievements to the end of 1988 was undertaken. The Planning and Co-ordinating Committee reviewed progress in the implementation of the Plan and made recommendations regarding its future orientation and co-ordination.

Some other relevant meetings concerning the marine environment that were sponsored by UNEP were: a western South American marine geology symposium (Santiago, Chile); an international symposium on living resources and fisheries (Valparaiso, Chile); and a training course on the assessment of pollution from land-based sources (Singapore).

Environment and technology

In response to the growing concern that greenhouse gases were inducing climate change, UNEP took steps to become a source of comprehensive information on the environmental impacts of energy systems and management options. During the year, UNEP developed a mailing list of close to 1,500 addresses of institutions and individuals with an interest in energy and environment, which was used in distributing publications from the Energy Report Series. Preparatory work was done on a project that would enhance the computerized energy planning system popularly known as LEAP (Less Developed Country Energy Alternatives Planning System) by allowing for the tracking of environmental impacts of different energy policies generated in the planning system. Preparations were also made for a project to apply the results of impact studies to assess and manage the health and environmental risks of energy and other complex industrial systems. Preparatory work for the African Ministerial Conference on the Environment energy network was carried out, and the first meeting of the network was held at Dakar in February.

UNEP continued to contribute to the achievement of environmentally sustainable industrial development by providing technical guidelines and reviews, information transfer, technical co-operation and training.

UNEP sponsored several diagnostic missions of experts on industry and environment issues in Africa and Asia, arranged training programmes for industrial managers and organized study tours for government and industry specialists to upgrade their skills in pollution prevention and control. Workshops on hazardous waste management were held in Malaysia and Mexico, and a workshop on clean technologies was held at Cairo. ILO and UNEP continued training activities for employers; seminars were held in Barbados, Jamaica and Trinidad and Tobago. In addition, UNEP worked closely with industry associations to stimulate and support environmental initiatives. A handbook on community awareness and preparedness for industrial accidents at the local level was released, and a special issue of *Industry and Environment* dealt with the working environment. Four expert group meetings on industrial accidents were held in Paris during the year.

Human settlements

UNEP and the United Nations Centre for Human Settlements (Habitat) completed in 1988 a demonstration project in Democratic Yemen, initiated in 1985 to provide a model for the planning and building of human settlements taking the environment specially into account. In addition to the demonstration housing units and other infrastructure, the project also produced a technical report and a video film to be used as training tools and guidance material for similar projects expected to be initiated under the Government's sponsorship.

Technical co-operation

The technical co-operation activities of UNEP were described in an addendum to the report of the Secretary-General to the UNDP Governing Council on United Nations technical co-operation.[31] Technical assistance to developing countries, including the provision of experts, equipment, training, grants and fellowships, was central to the work of UNEP. Its technical co-operation programme allocation amounted to $2.6 million in 1988.

In October,[32] ACC decided that, following a consultant's review, a joint meeting of its Consultative Committee on Substantive Questions (Operational Activities) and the designated officials on environmental matters should be convened on the approaches to be followed by United Nations organizations regarding environmental guidelines and their application to the operational activities of the United Nations system.

REFERENCES

[1]A/43/353-E/1988/71. [2]YUN 1987, p. 679, GA res. 42/187, 11 Dec. 1987. [3]E/1988/19 (dec. 88/57). [4]ACC/1988/DEC/19-31 (dec. 1988/20). [5]A/43/462. [6]UNEP/GC.15/4. [7]A/C.2/43/L.5. [8]YUN 1987, p. 712, GA dec. 42/442, 11 Dec. 1987. [9]A/C.2/43/L.25/Rev.2. [10]UNEP/GC.15/7/Add.1. [11]YUN 1987, p. 697. [12]*Ibid.*, p. 698. [13]UNEP/GC.15/4, Supp.1. [14]YUN 1987, p. 699, GA res. 42/183, 11 Dec. 1987. [15]E/1988/72. [16]YUN 1987, p. 699. [17]A/43/45. [18]YUN 1987, p. 701. [19]ACC/1988/DEC/19-31 (dec. 1988/22). [20]A/43/241. [21]YUN 1985, p. 804. [22]YUN 1987, p. 700. [23]YUN 1985, p. 793. [24]YUN 1986, p. 666. [25]YUN 1982, p. 1024, GA res. 37/7, annex, 28 Oct. 1982. [26]YUN 1980, p. 717. [27]YUN 1987, p. 686. [28]*Ibid.*, p. 704. [29]YUN 1977, p. 509. [30]UNEP/GC.15/9/Add.4. [31]DP/1989/46/Add.2. [32]ACC/1988/DEC/19-31 (dec. 1988/24).

Chapter IX

Population and human settlements

In 1988, the world population reached 5.2 billion; the United Nations estimated that it would grow by more than 90 million each year during the 1990s, with more than 90 per cent of the growth taking place in the developing countries, where about one third of the population was homeless. The United Nations Population Fund had programmes and projects in 127 developing countries and continued to focus on the needs of 56 priority countries. At the end of 1988, the United Nations Centre for Human Settlements was carrying out 219 projects in 94 countries.

The General Assembly adopted resolutions in December on the 1987 International Year of Shelter for the Homeless (43/180) and on a Global Strategy for Shelter to the Year 2000 (43/181).

Follow-up to the 1984 Conference on Population

UNFPA activities. The Executive Director of the United Nations Population Fund (UNFPA), in a December 1988 report[1] to the Population Commission, reviewed the Fund's mandate, re-examined its recent realignment and decentralization of authority and responsibility, surveyed the financial scope of its activities and considered its programme of work, as part of the follow-up to the 1984 International Conference on Population.[2] The report reviewed the strategy for UNFPA assistance in sub-Saharan Africa, the Fund's intercountry programme, which consisted of an interregional and four regional programmes, the modification of criteria for priority countries, evaluation activities, and women, population and development. It examined the following aspects of the UNFPA work programme: family planning; population information, education and communication; basic data collection; utilization of population data and research for policy formulation and development planning; and special programmes for women, youth and the aging.

The Executive Director concluded that UNFPA would concentrate on enhanced programme delivery by strengthening its field offices, improving monitoring, supervision and feedback, and making more use of evaluation and research. It would also continue to improve the outreach of its pro-

grammes by adapting them to conditions in each country, by providing adequate means of family planning, by involving the community and by extending services to scattered and poorly served populations.

Reports of the Secretary-General. Two reports were presented by the Secretary-General on follow-up to the recommendations of the Conference.

In one report,[3] he provided an overview of the main activities in the area of population carried out by the various organs, organizations and bodies of the United Nations system. The overview was accompanied by an account of changes in the institutional and legislative framework and in the organizational structure of programmes. It also included a description of the resources devoted to population activities and the co-ordination mechanisms of the units and organizations engaged in them. The activities covered were: socio-economic development, the environment and population; the role and status of women; development of population policies; population goals and policies, including population growth, morbidity and mortality, reproduction and the family, population distribution and internal migration, international migration and population structure; and the promotion of knowledge and policy through data collection and analysis, research, and management, training, information, education and communication.

In the other report,[4] the Secretary-General gave an overview of population activities undertaken by nine intergovernmental and 81 non-governmental organizations (NGOs), with the principal characteristics of those organizations and their relationships with the United Nations system.

REFERENCES
[1]E/CN.9/1989/6. [2]YUN 1984, p. 714. [3]E/1989/11. [4]E/CN.9/1989/7.

UN Population Fund

UNFPA activities

During 1988, the United Nations Population Fund continued to focus on the priority areas designated by the Governing Council of the United Nations Development Programme (UNDP) in

1981.[1] They included: family planning; information, education and communication; basic data collection; and the utilization of population data and research for policy formulation and development planning. Work also went forward on such special programmes as: women, population and development; youth; the question of aging; and acquired immunodeficiency syndrome (AIDS). The UNFPA Executive Director reported on those activities in her annual report to the UNDP Governing Council.[2]

Total UNFPA income in 1988 was $178.9 million, compared to $156.1 million in 1987. Project allocations totalled $169.1 million, including a $24.1 million carry-over from 1987, compared to $133.7 million in project allocations in 1987. Expenditures were $167.3 million, compared to $140.5 million in 1987, and included $91.4 million for country programmes, $38.5 million for intercountry programmes, $26.7 million for administrative services and $10.7 million for agency support costs.

At year's end, UNFPA was assisting 3,266 projects—2,403 country and 863 regional and intercountry projects. In 1988, 95 projects were completed, bringing the cumulative total to 2,944.

Assistance to family planning amounted to $87 million, or 51.5 per cent of total allocations. UNFPA supported almost 500 country and intercountry family-planning projects, concentrating on integrating planning services with maternal and child health programmes (MCH/FP). It made special efforts to strengthen services in sub-Saharan Africa, where maternal and infant mortality remained very high. The Regional Training Centre for Family Health in Mauritius conducted 9 eight-week courses in 1988 for a total of 93 trainees. The curriculum included a clinical orientation on fertility management. The University of Brussels (Belgium) conducted 2 three-month MCH/FP training courses. UNFPA assessed the training needs in the Africa region, with the assistance of the Margaret Sanger Center of Planned Parenthood of New York. As a participant in the Global Programme on AIDS of the World Health Organization (WHO), UNFPA took part in various forums to gain a better understanding of the interaction between human immunodeficiency virus infection and contraceptive practice and to explore the role MCH/FP could play in AIDS control programmes.

In the area of information, education and communication, UNFPA provided assistance totalling $26.1 million, or 15.5 per cent of expenditures. It added Colombia, Democratic Yemen and the Niger to the countries undertaking in-school and out-of-school population education activities. In addition, family-life education components were integrated into literacy programmes in Bangladesh, Malawi and the Syrian Arab Republic. UNFPA continued to receive requests from

Governments of developing countries for support in establishing sex education projects, for example, to address adolescent fertility and AIDS. Among the countries assisted were Burundi, Cape Verde and Nicaragua.

Several projects were approved that aimed at improving the coverage of population and related issues in the mass media; they included support to mass communication institutes in Ghana, Kenya, Zambia and Zimbabwe, as well as continued assistance to the Asian Institute for Broadcasting Development.

With regard to programmes on population dynamics and the formulation and evaluation of population policies, UNFPA provided $31.3 million, or 18.7 per cent of total allocations. It undertook to develop the most suitable methodological approaches, to strengthen national technical capacity, to support research and to set up required institutional arrangements. Principal activities included studies of the social and economic consequences of population trends; the interrelationship between population, environment, resources and development; the formulation and evaluation of population policies; and the integration of population factors into national development plans. Training courses were held dealing with various aspects of demography and of population and development. UNFPA provided assistance to 23 projects to support United Nations international personnel, to 38 projects to support training activities and to 40 projects to purchase equipment.

Assistance for basic data collection totalled $15 million, or 8.9 per cent of total allocations. UNFPA continued to provide assistance to strengthen developing countries' self-reliance in population data collection and analysis and to increase their capacity to plan, design and implement basic data collection and analysis using integrated statistical systems that included population censuses and intercensal demographic surveys. It emphasized the quality of data, its gender specificity, international comparability and effective utilization. It also stressed tabulating, analysing and disseminating data on particular groups—youth, elderly, female-headed households and, to the extent possible, refugees. UNFPA funded a conference (Cairo, Egypt, October 1988) to discuss utilization of census data; it was attended by 292 data producers and users, academics and technical specialists from 73 countries.

Programmes directed to women, population and development, youth, the question of aging and AIDS totalled $5.9 million of total allocations, or 3.5 per cent. UNFPA gave priority to the training of its staff in the area of women in development. It conducted a number of training workshops on aspects of incorporating women's concerns into population programmes. Most UNFPA-supported youth projects dealt with population and family-life education, communication and, to some extent, family planning. It provided assistance for research into adolescent and youth problems; approved support for a training research programme on reproductive health in adolescence, to be carried out by WHO; and commissioned a global review of factors affecting adolescent birth rates. Projects dealing with the question of aging cut across functional, regional and programme lines. For example, aging-related projects might be included in the sector on population policy formulation, as in the interregional project on population aging, old-age security and social and economic policies, or they might focus on the consequences of population changes, as in the regional project on analysis of the consequences of the changing population structure in Europe.

UNFPA continued to work within the scope of the strategies set by WHO's Global Programme on AIDS. It co-ordinated its activities with those of the other members of the Programme's Management Committee. It integrated MCH/FP activities with those specifically designed to combat AIDS—structurally, by promoting the incorporation of MCH/FP units of Ministries of Health into national AIDS commissions and, operationally, by placing those units in the service of AIDS-related activities. Through arrangements with the Programme, during the year UNFPA participated in 12 meetings of donors, held in selected countries, to review medium-term national AIDS plans and propose levels of funding. Discussions indicated, for example, that Sierra Leone needed increased supplies of condoms and that Zaire needed surgical gloves and sterile syringes.

On 1 July 1988,[3] the UNDP Governing Council took note of the reports of the Executive Director on UNFPA's 1987 activities[4] and noted the proportions of assistance allocated to the highest priority programme areas, particularly the increase in resources for family planning. The Council endorsed modified criteria and their threshold levels to be used in designating priority countries (per capita gross national product of $750 or under, gross reproduction rate of 2 or more, infant mortality rate of 120 or more, annual population increment of 100,000 or more, agricultural population density of 2 or more persons per hectare and female literacy rate of 40 per cent or under). It welcomed the Fund's increased emphasis on monitoring and evaluation as part of its programming process and the continued increase in assistance to sub-Saharan Africa; it urged steps to augment the resource base so that support for programmes in other regions was maintained at current levels. Further, the Council noted UNFPA's efforts to fight the AIDS pandemic and to incorporate women's concerns in population programmes.

Country and intercountry programmes

In 1988, UNFPA focused on the needs of 56 priority countries. Of the $123.5 million allocated to country programmes in 1988, $94.8 million was allocated to the priority countries.

Intercountry (regional, interregional and global) allocations totalled $45.5 million.

On 1 July,[5] the UNDP Governing Council approved country programmes for Benin, Bhutan, Cape Verde, Colombia, Costa Rica, Gabon, Guatemala, Lesotho, Nepal, Paraguay, Peru, Swaziland, Turkey, Uganda, Viet Nam and Zambia, and regional programmes for 1988-1991 in sub-Saharan Africa, the Arab States and Europe, Asia and the Pacific, and Latin America and the Caribbean.

Strategy for sub-Saharan Africa

Responding to a 1987 decision by the UNDP Governing Council,[6] the UNFPA Executive Director submitted in April 1988[7] an overview of UNFPA assistance to the sub-Saharan Africa area in recent years as well as its proposed regional programme for 1988-1991.

In the preceding four years, UNFPA assistance to the region totalled $94.8 million, of which $21.6 million was for regional programmes. UNFPA had endeavoured to strengthen African countries' capacity to plan, develop and implement national population programmes. Its regional strategy aimed at reinforcing technical advisory services and their deployment at subregional levels and instituting training programmes to remedy the shortage of qualified personnel within country programmes.

UNFPA-supported regional activities included basic data collection, the study of population dynamics and policy formulation, family planning, and information, education and communication. Its regional and national efforts continued to require strengthening, guidance, monitoring and evaluation. The experience of recent years indicated that weaknesses in the technical backstopping structure had placed constraints on effective implementation of some activities at the country level. Training activities were still inadequate. Research had been virtually non-existent due to financial and manpower contraints.

For 1988-1991, UNFPA proposed to provide assistance to the region totalling $36.4 million. Of that amount, $17.1 million would be for training activities, $14.9 million for support advisory services, $2.3 million for information dissemination, $1.5 million for research, and $0.6 million would be reserved for urgent, innovative and emerging needs.

On 1 July,[5] the UNDP Governing Council approved the regional programme for the sub-Saharan Africa area, 1988-1991.

Work programmes

The UNFPA Executive Director, in a report on the work plan for 1989-1992,[8] took the 1989 estimated income of $190 million as the base and assumed a constant annual increase of 8 per cent for 1990-1992. On the basis of those assumptions, a total income of $856.1 million was expected, including $205.2 million for 1990, $221.6 million for 1991 and $239.3 million for 1992. After deductions for operational costs and additions to the operational reserve, programmable resources were expected to total $664.6 million for the four years— $146.1 million for 1989, $158.9 million for 1990, $172.8 million for 1991 and $186.8 million for 1992. The income estimates did not include a contribution from the United States, which had withdrawn support from UNFPA starting in 1986.

The Executive Director, in another report,[9] gave the status of financial implementation of UNDP Governing Council–approved UNFPA country programmes and projects, with details on expenditures and allocations by year, region and country.

On 1 July,[10] the Governing Council approved the work plan for 1989-1992. It also authorized the net additional approval authority in accordance with the work plan in the amounts of $63.7 million for 1989, to bring the total for 1989 to 100 per cent of the 1989 level, or $179 million; $42.3 million for 1990, to bring the total for 1990 to 75 per cent of the new programmable resources for 1990, or $119.2 million; $48 million for 1991, to bring the total for 1991 to 50 per cent of the new programmable resources for 1991, or $86.4 million; and $46.7 million for 1992, to bring the total for 1992 to 25 per cent of the new programmable resources for 1992.

Women, population and development

The Executive Director, in response to a 1987 UNDP Governing Council decision,[11] submitted a report on the implementation strategy to strengthen the capacity of UNFPA to deal with issues concerning women, population and development.[12] In 1987-1988, activities focused on training of staff on the conceptual and operational aspects of involving women in population policies, programme procedures and guidelines; undertaking project reviews to identify facilitating and constraining factors from a gender perspective; and strengthening the capacities of and collaboration with governmental organizations and NGOs.

In May 1988, UNFPA updated its guidelines on women, population and development, based on the recommendations of the 1984 International Conference on Population[13] and the 1985 Nairobi Forward-Looking Strategies for the Advancement of Women.[14] The updated guidelines took into account inquiries from field staff regarding the definition of programmes and projects designed to benefit women. They identified in detail specific activities that UNFPA considered critical for the integration of women into population and development endeavours. Such activities included education and training, skill development, entrepreneurial undertakings, awareness creation for both the public and planners, exchange of information, data collection and research. The guidelines also stressed the importance of strengthening national technical capabilities at the governmental and non-governmental levels.

During 1988, UNFPA conducted a number of training workshops on incorporating women's concerns into population programmes. It also carried out in-depth project reviews in Guinea-Bissau, Honduras, Indonesia, Jordan, Paraguay, Zaire and Zambia to assess the impact of various activities on women and the extent of women's participation.

On 1 July,[3] the UNDP Governing Council noted the efforts of UNFPA to extend training on the incorporation of women's concerns in population programmes and welcomed the adoption of measures to ensure that programming reflected attention to gender-specific issues. The Council encouraged UNFPA to increase support for activities to improve the status of women.

Financial and administrative questions

Financial situation

On 1 January 1988, UNFPA's balance was $24,062,609. During the year, the Fund received income of $177,996,371 and had expenditures of $167,212,569, which resulted in an excess of income over expenditures of $10,783,802. As at 31 December, the Fund's balance was $31,846,411; unspent 1988 allocations amounted to $39,235,456.

Budget for 1988-1989

In May 1988,[15] the UNFPA Executive Director submitted to the UNDP Governing Council revised budget estimates for administrative and programme support services (APSS) for the 1988-1989 biennium. The total supplementary proposals in the revised budget amounted to $3 million. On a gross basis, which included $4.2 million of estimated earned credits, appropriations would increase from $59.5 million approved by the Council in 1987[16] to $62.5 million.

On 1 July,[17] the Governing Council approved a supplementary appropriation of $3,709,700 to bring the total appropriation of the revised 1988-1989 budget for APSS from $59,523,700 to

$63,233,400 gross, resulting in total appropriations of $59,033,400 net by applying overhead credits available to UNFPA in the estimated amount of $3,800,000 and the miscellaneous income from trust funds for support services in the amount of $400,000.

Contributions

During 1988, 88 countries and Territories paid a total of $168 million in voluntary contributions to UNFPA, compared with $149.3 million from 77 countries and Territories in 1987. Total income in 1988 amounted to $178 million, which included additions and adjustments to pledges for prior years, exchange-rate and currency re-evaluation adjustments, interest, donations and other miscellaneous income. Pledges for 1989 and future years totalled $120.4 million from 81 countries and Territories.

Accounts for 1987

The Board of Auditors made a number of observations and recommendations following its audit of the UNFPA financial statements for the year ended 31 December 1987.[18]

On 21 December, the General Assembly, by **resolution 43/216**, accepted the UNFPA financial report and requested the Fund to take immediate steps to correct the situations that gave rise to the opinion of the Board of Auditors.

Staffing

In May 1988,[19] the Executive Director submitted a report to the UNDP Governing Council reviewing UNFPA's overall staffing requirements in the field and at headquarters. Bearing in mind the priority of UNFPA's field programmes, particularly the strategy of assistance to sub-Saharan Africa, he proposed an increase of 61 posts, from 342 posts to 403 posts in the field establishment. Of the new posts, 52 would be established in sub-Saharan Africa, 3 in UNFPA field offices in the Arab States and Europe and 8 in Latin America and the Caribbean, while 2 posts would be abolished in Asia and the Pacific.

On 1 July,[17] the Govering Council took note of the report and considered, in view of the complexity of the population field and programmes undertaken by the Fund, that the second Assistant Secretary-General post should be staffed at its designated level, without prejudice to the overall application of the relevant provisions of a 1987 General Assembly resolution.[20] It also approved the establishment in the APSS budget of four new international Professional field posts and of 57 new local posts as temporary posts. It decided to establish 289 existing temporary local posts as regular posts in the APSS budget, and confirmed the

classification of six international Professional posts in the field at the D-1 level, effective from 1 January 1988.

UN Population Award

The Secretary-General transmitted to the General Assembly a report by the UNFPA Executive Director on the 1988 United Nations Population Award.[21] A total of 12 nominations were received by the Committee for the Award. The Committee selected Shidzue Kato, who founded the Family Planning Federation of Japan, and the Asociación Pro-Bienestar de la Familia Colombiana of Colombia as recipients.

On 20 December, by **decision 43/435**, the Assembly took note of the transmittal by the Secretary-General.

The Trust Fund for the United Nations Population Award stood at $456,139 as at 1 January 1988. Interest income amounted to $33,426, while expenditures totalled $37,490. After a contribution of $150,000 from Japan, the closing balance as at 31 December 1988 totalled $602,502.

REFERENCES

[1]YUN 1981, p. 782. [2]DP/1989/32 (Parts I-III). [3]E/1988/19 (dec. 88/34 A). [4]YUN 1987, p. 632. [5]E/1988/19 (dec. 88/34 C). [6]YUN 1987, p. 634. [7]DP/1988/37/Add.2. [8]DP/1988/34. [9]DP/1988/35. [10]E/1988/19 (dec. 88/34 B). [11]YUN 1987, p. 635. [12]DP/1989/36. [13]YUN 1984, p. 714. [14]YUN 1985, p. 937. [15]DP/1988/39. [16]YUN 1987, p. 636. [17]E/1988/19 (dec. 88/36). [18]A/43/5/Add.7. [19]DP/1988/42. [20]YUN 1987, p. 1101, GA res. 42/213 A, 21 Dec. 1987. [21]A/43/336.

PUBLICATIONS

Guide to Sources of International Population Assistance, 1988, Sales No. E.87.III.H.1. *Mortpak-Lite, The United Nations Software Package for Mortality Measurements* (ST/ESA/SER.A/104), Sales No. E.88.XIII.2. *Mortality of Children under Age 5—World Estimates and Projections 1950-2025* (ST/ESA/SER.A/105), Sales No. E.88.XIII.4. *Adolescent Reproductive Behaviour: Evidence from Developed Countries*, vol. I (ST/ESA/SER.A/109), Sales No. E.88.XIII.8. *Demographic Yearbook, 1988* (ST/ESA/STAT/SER.R/18), Sales No. E/F.89.XIII.1. *Levels and Trends of Contraceptive Use as Assessed in 1988* (ST/ESA/SER.A/110), Sales No. E.89.XIII.4. *Population Bulletin of the United Nations*, No. 27—1988 (ST/ESA/SER.N/27), Sales No. E.89.XIII.7

Human settlements

At its eleventh session (New Delhi, India, 6-12 April 1988),[1] the Commission on Human Settlements recommended that the General Assembly request Governments to sustain the momentum generated during the 1987 International Year of Shelter for the Homeless and to implement concrete and innovative programmes to improve the shelter and neighbourhoods of the poor and disadvantaged. The Commission further recommended that the Assembly adopt a Global

Strategy for Shelter to the Year 2000 and urge Governments to develop appropriate national and sub-national strategies for shelter.

The Commission also considered the use of the term "settlements" in relation to Israeli colonies in occupied territories, the reconstruction of Palestinian homes, and assistance to victims of *apartheid* and colonialism in southern Africa.

In addition, the Commission urged States to respect international obligations regarding the protection of the civilian population and human settlements in armed conflicts; recommended the mobilization of new and greater international financial resources for shelter; and examined themes for its twelfth (1989) session, deciding to include "Maintenance of buildings and infrastructure and its financing and cost-recovery".

On 26 July 1988, the Economic and Social Council, by **decision 1988/156**, took note of the report of the Commission on the work of its eleventh session.[1]

Human settlements activities

International Year of Shelter for the Homeless

The International Year of Shelter for the Homeless (IYSH) was observed in 1987.[2] It had been proclaimed by the General Assembly in 1982[3] to improve the shelter and neighbourhoods of some of the global poor and disadvantaged by the end of 1987 and to demonstrate ways of improving the situation by the year 2000. The United Nations Centre for Human Settlements (UNCHS), also known as Habitat, performed the role of lead agency in the United Nations system for coordinating IYSH activities.

In February 1988,[4] the UNCHS Executive Director reported to the Commission on Human Settlements on IYSH activities and achievements. As at 31 December 1987, 130 Governments had reported the adoption of new or revised national shelter strategies and specific measures to improve shelter, dealing with such issues as land, finance, infrastructure, institutions, building materials production and employment generation. The report also discussed IYSH activities carried out by organizations of the United Nations system, intergovernmental organizations, NGOs, multilateral financial institutions and bilateral financial aid agencies.

Assessing the accomplishments of IYSH, the report stated that emphasis had been placed on action-oriented methods, that progress had been promising, that more than 600 demonstration projects had been carried out in more than 100 countries, and that a body of practical knowledge had been accumulated. IYSH subregional meetings, in which more than 100 Member States par-

ticipated, had served to identify the most appropriate approaches for providing shelter to the poor. UNCHS had published two books, more than 10 special topic publications, 15 monographs and 12 *IYSH Bulletins* aimed at disseminating information on experience of various countries in shelter improvement.

On 11 April,[5] the Commission on Human Settlements welcomed the success achieved by IYSH, requested the UNCHS Executive Director to transmit his report to the General Assembly and recommended to the Assembly the adoption of a draft resolution.

GENERAL ASSEMBLY ACTION

On 20 December 1988, on the recommendation of the Second (Economic and Financial) Committee, the General Assembly adopted **resolution 43/180** without vote.

International Year of Shelter for the Homeless
The General Assembly,

Recalling its resolution 37/221 of 20 December 1982, by which it proclaimed the year 1987 International Year of Shelter for the Homeless,

Recalling also, in particular, the objectives of the Year as contained in resolution 37/221,

Having considered the report of the Executive Director of the United Nations Centre for Human Settlements (Habitat) entitled "International Year of Shelter for the Homeless: activities and achievements", and the comments of the Commission on Human Settlements and of the Economic and Social Council on that report,

1. *Welcomes* the success achieved in attaining the objectives of the International Year of Shelter for the Homeless;

2. *Takes note with appreciation* of the numerous and encouraging reports, which had been received from a total of one hundred and thirty countries as at 31 December 1987, on activities, policies, programmes and projects undertaken by those countries within the context of the Year and towards the successful attainment of its objectives;

3. *Commends* Governments, organizations and bodies of the United Nations system and intergovernmental and non-governmental organizations for the efforts and resources that were effectively mobilized for the programme of activities for the Year;

4. *Requests* Governments to sustain the momentum generated by the programme for the Year and to continue implementing concrete and innovative programmes aimed at improving the shelter and neighbourhoods of the poor and the disadvantaged;

5. *Requests* the Executive Director of the United Nations Centre for Human Settlements (Habitat) to continue to assist Governments in their efforts towards that goal, within the framework of the Global Strategy for Shelter to the Year 2000;

6. *Recommends* that Governments indicate, if possible on World Habitat Day, the concrete actions to be taken and the specific targets to be achieved during each successive year;

7. *Also recommends* that Governments maintain, where appropriate, the national focal points and national com-

mittees for the International Year of Shelter for the Homeless for the purpose of monitoring and assessing the progress achieved in improving the shelter and neighbourhoods of the poor and the disadvantaged;

8. *Requests* the Secretary-General to inform the General Assembly periodically, through the Economic and Social Council, on progress achieved in improving the shelter and neighbourhoods of the poor and the disadvantaged.

General Assembly resolution 43/180

20 December 1988   Meeting 83   Adopted without vote

Approved by Second Committee (A/43/750/Add.3) without vote, 10 November (meeting 40); draft by Vice-Chairman (A/C.2/43/L.30), based on informal consultations on draft by Commission on Human Settlements (A/43/8); agenda item 12.

Global Strategy for Shelter to the Year 2000

In response to a 1987 General Assembly resolution,[6] the UNCHS Executive Director submitted in February 1988 to the Commission on Human Settlements a report on a Global Strategy for Shelter to the Year 2000.[7] The report had four parts: the first discussed the objectives, rationale and general principles of the Strategy; the second, the reorganization of the shelter sector, mobilization and allocation of financial resources, and shelter production and improvement; the third, guidelines for international action; and the fourth, a plan of action and a timetable for the first phase. The report concluded that the global shelter situation was worsening and that anxiety about it was being expressed not only with regard to its current effects on people but in relation to the future implications for society of the unfavourable supply trend.

To achieve the Strategy's objectives, emphasis would have to be placed on action in the areas of macro-economic policy, institutional co-ordination, legislation and regulation, data collection and analysis, financial resources and mechanisms for shelter and infrastructure, land, infrastructural development, and building materials and technology.

Implementing the Strategy, Member States would review their shelter policies in the light of the Strategy; formulate national strategies for shelter for all; decide on specific targets; develop plans of action to implement their strategies; and report to the Commission on progress. The plan of action also set forth activities to be carried out by the Commission, the General Assembly, UNCHS, and international and intergovernmental agencies and NGOs.

On 12 April,[8] the Commission adopted the report of the UNCHS Executive Director as an addendum[9] to the report on its eleventh session, and recommended to the General Assembly the adoption of a draft resolution.

GENERAL ASSEMBLY ACTION

On 20 December, on the recommendation of the Second Committee, the General Assembly adopted **resolution 43/181** without vote.

Global Strategy for Shelter to the Year 2000

The General Assembly,

Bearing in mind the Vancouver Declaration on Human Settlements, 1976, and the recommendations for national action adopted at Habitat: United Nations Conference on Human Settlements,

Recalling its resolution 35/56 of 5 December 1980, the annex to which contains the International Development Strategy for the Third United Nations Development Decade, in which, *inter alia*, the importance of the provision of basic shelter and infrastructure was stressed,

Recalling also its resolution 37/221 of 20 December 1982, by which it proclaimed the year 1987 International Year of Shelter for the Homeless,

Recalling further its resolution 42/191 of 11 December 1987, in which it decided that there should be a Global Strategy for Shelter to the Year 2000,

Recalling the Nairobi Forward-looking Strategies for the Advancement of Women,

Recalling Commission on Human Settlements resolutions 9/9 of 16 May 1986 and 10/17 of 16 April 1987 on the participation of women in the solution of human settlements problems,

Recalling also Commission on Human Settlements resolution 10/16 of 16 April 1987 on the effect of the external debt of the developing countries and their ability to raise the funds needed to solve the housing problems of the homeless up to the year 2000,

Taking note of Commission on Human Settlements resolution 11/7 of 11 April 1988 entitled "Co-ordination and co-operation with agencies and organizations within the United Nations system",

Convinced that the continuous, co-ordinated and widely based efforts of Governments, organizations of the United Nations system, other intergovernmental and non-governmental organizations and individuals, when guided by an appropriate strategy, will reverse the alarming trends in the field of human settlements and produce clear and visible improvements in the shelter and neighbourhoods of the poor and disadvantaged by the year 2000, and that this should be a global responsibility,

Encouraged by action already taken or being taken in many countries to prepare national shelter strategies and to adopt other measures that will promote achievement of the goal of shelter for all,

Recognizing that, despite such efforts, more than one billion people have shelter unfit for human habitation, that this number will increase dramatically, partly as a result of population and urbanization trends, and that determined measures must be taken aimed at profiting from these trends, rather than being penalized by them,

Also recognizing that the International Year of Shelter for the Homeless has confirmed the need to intensify national and international efforts to produce, deliver and improve shelter for all, with specific emphasis on the poor and disadvantaged,

Convinced that shelter problems are universal, that no country has yet completely met its shelter needs and that every country can profit from the experience of others,

Also convinced that shelter problems are a global concern requiring solutions that relate to other global problems and also requiring the efforts of all countries to reach such solutions, that the demand for shelter in each country can be met by applying a set of common principles, but that goals can only be met by the individual efforts of each Government acting in its own political, economic, social and cultural context,

Recognizing that the core of the Global Strategy for Shelter to the Year 2000 consists of integrated national shelter strategies that need to be based on a full understanding of the scale and nature of the problem and the national resource base available to address the problem,

Recognizing also that national shelter strategies need to contain four complementary parts: clear and measurable objectives; national mobilization and distribution of financial resources; promotion of shelter production and improvement with special reference to the management of land, the provision of infrastructure and encouragement of the use of appropriate building materials and technology; and the gradual reorganization of the shelter sector,

1. *Adopts* the Global Strategy for Shelter to the Year 2000;

2. *Decides* that the main objective of the Strategy is to facilitate adequate shelter for all by the year 2000, that the main focus should therefore be on improving the situation of the disadvantaged and the poor and that the following fundamental objectives and principles should form the basis of the Strategy:

(*a*) Enabling policies, whereby the full potential and resources of all governmental and non-governmental actors in the field of human settlements are utilized, must be at the heart of national and international efforts;

(*b*) Women, as income-earners, home-makers and heads of households, and women's organizations fulfil a crucial role as contributors to the solution of human settlements problems, which should be fully recognized and reflected in equal participation of women in the elaboration of housing policies, programmes and projects, and the specific interests and capabilities of women should be adequately represented in human settlements policy formulation and in government mechanisms employed at all levels for the implementation of housing policies, programmes and projects;

(*c*) Shelter and development are mutually supportive and interdependent, and policies must be developed in full recognition of the important links between shelter and economic development;

(*d*) The concept of sustainable development implies that the provision of shelter and urban development must be reconcilable with a sustainable management of the environment;

3. *Designates* the Commission on Human Settlements as the United Nations intergovernmental body responsible for co-ordinating, evaluating and monitoring the Strategy and the United Nations Centre for Human Settlements (Habitat) as the secretariat for the Strategy and the lead agency for co-ordinating and monitoring the relevant programmes and activities of other United Nations organizations and agencies concerned;

4. *Urges* Governments to develop appropriate national and sub-national strategies for shelter in the light of the guidelines provided in the report of the Executive Director of the United Nations Centre for Human Settlements (Habitat) entitled "Global Strategy for Shelter to the Year 2000" and to report regularly to the Commission on Human Settlements, beginning at its twelfth session, on their relevant experience and on progress achieved in implementing those strategies;

5. *Requests* the Executive Director to monitor the relevant global experience and progress of all countries in implementing the Strategy and to report thereon to the Commission, beginning at its thirteenth session;

6. *Decides* to review and clarify the Strategy on a biennial basis, within regular budgetary resources, with the assistance of experts selected on the basis of equitable geographic representation, and to revise the Strategy in the light of global and national experience from all regions and subregions;

7. *Requests* the Commission on Human Settlements, as the body designated to co-ordinate implementation of the Strategy, to report biennially to the General Assembly on progress made in its implementation;

8. *Also requests* the Commission to strengthen, within existing resources, its role in regard to the promotion of innovative measures by which bilateral and multilateral financial institutions may support the shelter strategies of developing countries, for example, by way of suitably devised loan agreements that would lead to the building up of national revolving funds for shelter;

9. *Requests* financial institutions and creditor countries to consider, as one of the conditions for the success of the Strategy, immediate measures to reduce the external debts by their conversion into long-term loans;

10. *Adopts* the guidelines for steps to be taken at the national and international levels, as set out in the annex to the present resolution, in support of the guidelines for national and international action contained in the Global Strategy for Shelter to the Year 2000, prepared pursuant to its resolution 42/191;

11. *Calls upon* all States and others in a position to do so to make generous contributions to the United Nations Habitat and Human Settlements Foundation to facilitate implementation of the Strategy.

ANNEX

I. Guidelines for steps to be taken at the national level

A. *Considerations for Governments when formulating a national shelter strategy*

1. A national shelter strategy must spell out clear operational objectives for the development of shelter conditions both in terms of the construction of new housing and the upgrading and maintenance of existing housing stock and infrastructure and services.

2. In the definition of those objectives, development of shelter should be seen as a process whereby conditions are gradually improved for both men and women. The objectives need to address the scale of the problem, while the "adequate" standard aimed at should be identified on the basis of an analysis of the standards and options affordable to the target population and society at large. The objectives should be based on a comprehensive view of the magnitude and nature of the problem and of the available resource base, including the potential contribution of men and women. In addition to finance, land, manpower and institutions, building materials and technology also have to be considered irrespective of whether they are held by the public or private, formal or informal sector.

3. The objectives of the shelter sector need to be linked to the goals of overall economic policy, social policy, settlement policy and environmental policy.

4. The strategy needs to outline the action through which the objectives can be met. In an enabling strategy, actions such as the provision of infrastructure may mean the direct involvement of the public sector in shelter con-

struction. The objective of "facilitating adequate shelter for all" also implies that direct government support should mainly be allocated to the most needy population groups.

5. The public sector is responsible for developing and implementing measures for national shelter policies and for the adoption of measures to stimulate the desired action by other sectors. This can be done through measures in areas such as the locally based small-scale building-materials industry, appropriate financial schemes or training programmes.

6. Another important component is the development of administrative, institutional and legislative tasks that are the direct responsibility of the Government, for example, land registration and regulation of construction.

7. An analysis of affordability will provide the criteria for defining the right priorities and appropriate approaches and standards for public sector involvement. Likewise, such an analysis gives the criteria for planning the indirect involvement of the public sector, that is, the type of activities to be promoted and the appropriate way of going about it.

8. The appropriate institutional framework for the implementation of a strategy must be identified, which may require much institutional reorganization. Each agency involved must have a clear understanding of its role within the overall organizational framework and of the tasks expected of it. Mechanisms for the co-ordination of inter- and intra-agency activities need to be developed. Mechanisms such as shelter coalitions are recommended and may be developed in partnership with the private and non-governmental sectors. Finally, arrangements for the continuous monitoring, review and revision of the strategy must be developed.

B. *Steps to be taken by Governments when implementing a national strategy*

9. Work for the preparation of the strategy must be organized. For instance, a task force may be appointed for the actual work and a steering committee ensuring high-level political commitment set up to guide its work. Alternatively it may be possible to use existing mechanisms. Equal participation of women should be ensured at all levels.

10. Needs and resources must be assessed. Estimates are required of the needs in housing construction and in upgrading and maintenance, including housing-related infrastructure, as well as of the resources that can be mobilized during the period to the year 2000 to cover those needs.

11. Shelter options and standards that are affordable by the target groups and society at large must be analysed, taking into account both the scale of need and all the resources available—finance, land, manpower and institutions, building materials and technology.

12. Objectives must be set for the construction of new housing and for the upgrading and maintenance of the existing housing stock in terms both of the scale of the activities and of the housing standards to be met.

13. Action must be identified through which those objectives can be realistically met. The estimated required resources for this action must not exceed those that can be made available by society. The action in-

cludes both direct government involvement and measures needed to encourage, facilitate and integrate active participation of other sectors in shelter delivery.

14. A plan of action must be prepared in consultation and partnership with non-governmental organizations, people and their representatives, which:

(*a*) Lists the activities that are the direct responsibility of the public sector;

(*b*) Lists the activities to be taken to facilitate and encourage the other actors to carry out their part of the task;

(*c*) Outlines resource allocation to the aforementioned activities;

(*d*) Outlines the institutional arrangements for the implementation, co-ordination, monitoring and review of the strategy;

(*e*) Outlines a schedule for the activities of the various agencies.

II. Guidelines for steps to be taken at the international level

15. International action will be necessary to support the activities of countries in their endeavour to improve the housing situation of their poor and disadvantaged inhabitants. Such assistance should support national programmes and use know-how available locally and within the international community.

16. The goal of external assistance should be to enhance and support national capabilities to develop and implement national action components of the Global Strategy for Shelter to the Year 2000.

17. Mutual co-operation and exchange of information and expertise between developing countries in human settlement work stimulate and enrich national human settlement work.

18. The United Nations Centre for Human Settlements (Habitat) will act as the co-ordinating agency in the implementation of the Global Strategy for Shelter to the Year 2000, on the basis of biennial plans to be drawn up with the involvement of experts working with Governments and the Centre at the regional and subregional levels.

19. As the co-ordinating agency for the Strategy, the United Nations Centre for Human Settlements (Habitat) will stimulate international and national action by incorporating the Strategy in its future medium-term plans and biennial work programmes.

20. An inter-agency-level working arrangement will be made within the existing budget to provide continuous co-ordination of the Strategy.

21. The United Nations Centre for Human Settlements (Habitat) will prepare a reporting format to facilitate monitoring by the Commission on Human Settlements of progress achieved in the implementation of the Global Strategy.

General Assembly resolution 43/181

20 December 1988   Meeting 83   Adopted without vote

Approved by Second Committee (A/43/750/Add.3) without vote, 9 December (meeting 48); draft by Vice-Chairman (A/C.2/43/L.29), based on informal consultations on draft by Commission on Human Settlements (A/43/8); agenda item 12.

Meeting numbers. GA 43rd session: 2nd Committee 48, 49; plenary 83.

Human settlements and development

In response to a 1985 General Assembly resolution,[10] the Secretary-General reported in

June 1988[11] on an overall socio-economic perspective of the world economy to the year 2000, which included a section on human settlements. The report stated that increased investment in shelter, infrastructure and related services could be a major source of economic growth. Using inputs that were primarily domestic, it could provide a degree of insulation from external economic shocks and could be used to counter a recession.

The limited available evidence suggested a decline in average shelter conditions in the past decade, especially in the developing countries. In many cities, 40-50 per cent of the people lived in slums or squatter settlements. Approximately 1 billion people had housing of very poor quality, and that number might double by the year 2000. In recent years, rented housing had accounted for one quarter to two thirds of the housing market of large cities in the developing countries. It had increased in response to increases in land values that prevented squatting and inexpensive owner-occupancy. Local authorities were partly responsible for overcrowded conditions, particularly where they prohibited informal construction yet enforced rent controls that discouraged new, authorized construction.

On 11 April,[12] the Commission on Human Settlements requested the UNCHS Executive Director to prepare a report for the Commission's 1989 session on the Centre's contribution to international efforts towards sustainable development within the area of human settlements. The Commission invited Governments to provide the Executive Director with their views on how UNCHS might contribute to international efforts towards sustainable development. It further decided to consider in 1989 the issue of sustainable development as a follow-up to the report of the World Commission on Environment and Development within UNCHS.[13] It decided also to consider the formulation of priority items to be added to the Global Strategy for Shelter to the Year 2000 and to the medium-term plan for the period beginning 1992 resulting from the mandate of the Commission and UNCHS to contribute towards sustainable ecological, economic and social development.

Human settlements and political, economic and social issues

Use of the term "settlements"

The Commission on Human Settlements adopted on 12 April[14] a resolution on the use of the term "settlements" in relation to Israeli colonies in occupied territories. It recommended to the General Assembly the adoption of a draft resolution proposing that the term "Israeli colonies in occupied territories" be used instead of "Israeli settlements" in United Nations documentation.

Following informal consultations, the Assembly's Second Committee decided not to take action on the draft resolution.

Reconstruction of Palestinian homes

On 12 April,[15] the Commission called on the Israeli authorities in the occupied territories to cease the blowing up and destruction of Palestinians' houses, reiterated the right of Palestinians whose houses had been destroyed to rebuild and live in them again, and requested the UNCHS Executive Director, with other concerned United Nations bodies, to assist in their rebuilding.

Safeguarding human settlements against acts of war

The Commission, on 12 April,[16] adopted a resolution on safeguarding human settlements against acts of war and chemical warfare, urging Member States to respect international obligations regarding the protection of the civilian population and civilian objects, including human settlements, condemning the use of chemical weapons and urging that their use be stopped.

Situation between Iraq and Iran

On 12 April,[17] the Commission condemned aggression and the use of force to settle disputes, called on Iraq and Iran to respond to a 1987 Security Council resolution[18] and to end their conflict in accordance with international law, and confirmed that humanitarian co-operation between the peoples of the world required an atmosphere of peace.

Assistance to victims of apartheid

On 12 April,[19] the Commission condemned the *apartheid* régime in South Africa for its inhuman repression, forced removal of the African population from their homes, illegal occupation of Namibia and aggression against the front-line and other neighbouring States. It commended the UNCHS Executive Director for efforts to implement its 1987 resolution on *apartheid*,[20] and also commended States members of the Organization of African Unity and other supporting members of the international community for their efforts against *apartheid*. It called on the international community to extend political and material support to the front-line States and material assistance to the displaced and homeless victims in the region.

UN programmes

Habitat Centre

The UNCHS work programme for 1988-1989 was based on eight subprogrammes:[21] policies and strategies, settlement planning, shelter and community services, indigenous construction sector, low-cost infrastructure, land, mobilization of financial resources, and institutions and management.

Under the first subprogramme, a publication entitled *A New Agenda for Human Settlements* was distributed. The UNCHS Executive Director established a task force and a steering committee to facilitate the Centre's work in connection with the Global Strategy for Shelter to the Year 2000.

Under the second subprogramme, a paper on the relationship between urbanization and sustainable development was presented at the International Conference on Environment and Development (Milan, Italy, March). The second version of the UNCHS human settlements data base software was completed; it was reviewed at an international workshop on statistical data processing and data bases in developing countries (Geneva, 30 May–3 June). Research on rural settlements development continued with the Centre's participation in an international symposium on involuntary resettlement processes (Zagreb, Yugoslavia, 25-31 July).

The development of methodologies under the third subprogramme for community-based shelter and services improvements in urban low-income settlements generated practical experience for evolving shelter strategies, which in turn were incorporated in the Global Strategy for Shelter. UNCHS, supported by the Danish International Development Agency, offered support services to national and local authorities in strengthening their capacity to work with low-income communities on improving shelter and environment. Thirty-one participants from eight Asian countries took part in a workshop on housing in development, organized by UNCHS and the Katholieke Universiteit Leuven (Bangkok, Thailand, 21 January–5 February).

Under the fourth subprogramme, a number of technical publications were prepared, including data sheets on soil construction technology, a compendium on selected local building materials, a bibliography on earth construction technology and a report on development of the construction industry for delivery of low-income shelter and infrastructure. The Centre collaborated with the Economic Commission for Africa in formulating a project document for the establishment of pilot plants for building materials in 23 African countries. Several missions were undertaken: with the Agency for Technical Co-

operation of the Federal Republic of Germany, to the Caribbean on the training of women in construction skills; to the National Housing Authority in Zambia on promoting local building materials; and to Chile, Poland, Singapore, Switzerland, the United Kingdom and the United States to finalize a paper on the maintenance of buildings and infrastructure, financing and cost recovery.

A number of reports and publications were prepared under the fifth subprogramme, on new and renewable sources of energy, energy auditing in human settlement development, water supply and waste disposal.

Work continued under the sixth subprogramme on assessing the organizational and technical requirements for setting up and operating low-technology land-registration systems through local governments.

Research on human settlements financed under the seventh subprogramme focused on mobilizing public and private resources and efficiently channelling them. A trainers' manual on urban finance and management, containing a municipal finance and expenditure control software simulation model, was published by UNCHS and the World Bank's Economic Development Institute. The manual and software were tested during a trainers' workshop (Dakar, Senegal, May/June). A workshop on urban local government finance training for Latin American countries was held (Quito, Ecuador, November), as were two senior policy workshops on urban finance and management training in the African region during June, at Nairobi, Kenya, and Dakar.

Under the eighth subprogramme, case-studies were prepared on urban management practice in both intermediate cities and metropolitan areas in developing countries. A summary of training capabilities of selected training institutions in North Africa was distributed.

On 11 April,[22] the Commission on Human Settlements reconfirmed the role of UNDP's country programming as a framework for operational activities for development.

Financing

The UNCHS work programme was financed from the United Nations regular budget and from extrabudgetary resources. Extrabudgetary resources during 1988-1989[23] were expected from programme support income from the execution of projects financed by UNDP and trust funds ($4,994,000), a subvention from the World Food Programme ($248,000), programme support from the Fund of the United Nations Environment Programme ($99,000) and the United Nations Habitat and Human Settlements Foundation. Estimated income for the Foundation was $14.5 million.[24]

The UNCHS Executive Director estimated that expenditures and commitments of the Foundation in 1990-1991 would total $11.2 million.[25] He also estimated carry-over income from 1988-1989 (including the reserve fund) of $4.4 million, as well as investment and miscellaneous income and savings from liquidation of prior years' obligations of $370,000.

On 21 December, by **resolution 43/216**, the General Assembly accepted the financial report and audited financial statements and the audit opinions and report of the Board of Auditors regarding the Foundation for the biennium ended 31 December 1987.[26]

REFERENCES

[1]A/43/8. [2]YUN 1987, p. 715. [3]YUN 1982, p. 1043, GA res. 37/221, 20 Dec. 1982. [4]HS/C/11/2. [5]A/43/8 (res. 11/1). [6]YUN 1987, p. 718, GA res. 42/191, 11 Dec. 1987. [7]HS/C/11/3. [8]A/43/8 (res. 11/2). [9]A/43/8/Add.1. [10]YUN 1985, p. 416, GA res. 40/207, 17 Dec. 1985. [11]E/1988/62. [12]A/43/8 (res. 11/4). [13]YUN 1987, p. 679. [14]A/43/8 (res. 11/3). [15]*Ibid.* (res. 11/10). [16]*Ibid.* (res. 11/8). [17]*Ibid.* (res. 11/9). [18]YUN 1987, p. 223, SC res. 598(1987), 20 July 1987. [19]A/43/8 (res. 11/11). [20]YUN 1987, p. 720. [21]HS/C/12/2. [22]A/43/8 (dec. 11/13). [23]HS/C/12/9/Add.2. [24]HS/C/12/9. [25]HS/C/12/9/Add.1. [26]A/43/5/Add.8.

Chapter X

Human rights

During 1988, the United Nations continued to promote human rights and fundamental freedoms world-wide and to curtail their violations.

Protection of detained persons was a substantial part of the United Nations work in human rights. In December, the General Assembly adopted the Body of Principles for the Protection of All Persons under Any Form of Detention or Imprisonment (resolution 43/173). The Working Group on Enforced or Involuntary Disappearances continued to investigate cases of such violations, while the Working Group on Slavery, renamed the Working Group on Contemporary Forms of Slavery, continued to examine issues related to slavery-like practices.

Work progressed on draft declarations concerning the unacknowledged detention of persons; freedom and non-discrimination in respect of the right of everyone to leave any country, including his own; independence and impartiality of the judiciary, jurors and assessors; the right and responsibility of individuals, groups and organs of society to promote and protect universally recognized human rights and fundamental freedoms; the rights of indigenous peoples; and the rights of persons belonging to national, ethnic, religious and linguistic minorities.

There was also progress on the elaboration of a convention on the protection of the rights of migrant workers and their families, as well as on a draft body of principles and guarantees for the protection of mentally ill persons and for the improvement of mental health care. Meanwhile, a draft convention on the rights of the child was adopted in first reading. Work also began on the elaboration of a second optional protocol to the International Covenant on Civil and Political Rights, aimed at abolishing the death penalty.

The Economic and Social Council decided in May that mandates of special rapporteurs on thematic issues should be for two years and that they should continue to report annually (decision 1988/129). The Council also recommended that the General Assembly proclaim an international year of the world's indigenous populations (resolution 1988/37).

In December, the Assembly launched a World Public Information Campaign on Human Rights (43/128) and adopted a resolution in commemoration of the fortieth anniversary of the adoption of the Universal Declaration of Human Rights

(43/90). Activities continued under the United Nations programme of advisory services in the field of human rights, and the United Nations Voluntary Fund for Advisory Services and Technical Assistance in the Field of Human Rights became operational in 1988.

The Commission on Human Rights at its forty-fourth session, held in February/March, examined situations involving alleged violations of human rights on a large scale in several countries, as well as cases involving mercenaries and mass exoduses, and the implications of scientific and technological developments for human rights. Its deliberations resulted in the adoption of 78 resolutions and 7 decisions. Its Sub-Commission on Prevention of Discrimination and Protection of Minorities at its fortieth session, held in August/September, adopted 40 resolutions and 13 decisions.

Discrimination

Racial discrimination

Second Decade to Combat Racism and Racial Discrimination (1983-1993)

Implementation of the Programme for the Decade

During 1988, United Nations efforts to implement the Programme of Action for the Second Decade to Combat Racism and Racial Discrimination were carried out in accordance with the plan of activities for 1985-1989 put forward in 1984.[1] In 1987,[2] the General Assembly approved a plan of activities for the remainder of the Decade, 1990-1993.

Reports of the Secretary-General. Pursuant to an Economic and Social Council request of 1987,[3] the Secretary-General submitted, in April 1988, his annual report with later addenda,[4] summarizing activities undertaken or planned by Governments, United Nations bodies, specialized agencies and non-governmental organizations (NGOs) to achieve the Decade's objectives. In response to an Assembly request of 1984,[5] he submitted to the Council a report containing information received, as at 28 January, from 12 Governments on legislative, administrative and other measures they had taken to implement the Programme.[6]

As requested by the Assembly in 1987,[2] the Secretary-General submitted, in September 1988,[7] a report containing information on action taken by United Nations bodies, national legislation to combat racism and racial discrimination, seminars and training courses, the Trust Fund for the Programme of the Decade, and the plan of activities for the Second Decade. He noted that a training course on preparing national legislation prohibiting racism and racial discrimination had taken place in 1987[8] and drew attention to his April 1988 report to the Council on the subject.[9] On 24 May, by **decision 1988/108**, the Council took note of the Secretary-General's report on the training course.

The Secretary-General submitted to the Assembly in September a report[10] containing the views of three Governments, one specialized agency and one intergovernmental organization on his 1986 report on the role of private group action to combat racism and racial discrimination.[11]

Also in September,[12] the Secretary-General gave an overview of texts submitted by 44 States for the global compilation of national legislation against racism and racial discrimination which the Assembly, in 1985, had requested him to compile and publish.[13]

Human Rights Commission action. On 29 February,[14] the Commission expressed concern that, despite the efforts of the international community, the principal objectives of the first Decade for Action to Combat Racism and Racial Discrimination (1973-1983) had not been attained. It commended all States that had ratified or acceded to the international instruments relevant to the Decade and appealed to others to do the same. It urged co-operation from States and international organizations in implementing the plan of activities for 1985-1989 and appealed for generous contributions to the Trust Fund for the Programme for the Decade. Within the plan of activities for 1985-1989, the Commission selected as its topic for 1990 the human rights of individuals belonging to ethnic groups in countries of immigration. The Secretary-General was requested to prepare a handbook of recourse procedures for victims of racism and racial discrimination.

Also on 29 February,[15] the Commission recommended for adoption by the Economic and Social Council a resolution authorizing Special Rapporteur Asbjorn Eide (Norway) to complete his 1987 study on assessing the achievements made and obstacles encountered during the first Decade,[8] which the Council did by **resolution 1988/32** (see below).

Sub-Commission action. On 25 August,[16] the Sub-Commission on Prevention of Discrimination and Protection of Minorities endorsed the decision of its Special Rapporteur, Mr. Eide, to make a renewed call for additional information to complete the study and called on him to include in his final report, to be presented in 1989, recommendations on steps that could be taken by the Sub-Commission to prevent discrimination. It recommended that the Secretary-General convene a seminar on current manifestations of racism and their causes.

In September,[17] the Special Rapporteur reported on the progress he had made on the study.

Other action. At its thirty-sixth session (Geneva, 1-12 August),[18] the Committee on the Elimination of Racial Discrimination (CERD) decided to revise and update its study on progress made towards achieving the objectives of the International Convention on the Elimination of All Forms of Racial Discrimination,[19] which it had prepared in 1978 for the World Conference to Combat Racism and Racial Discrimination.[20] The Convention was adopted by the General Assembly in 1965[21] and had been in force since 1969.[22]

A global consultation (Geneva, 3-6 October 1988) considered the international challenge of racism; the origins of racism and racial discrimination; contemporary forms of racism; vulnerable groups and racism; and co-ordination and strengthening of international action against racism and racial discrimination.

ECONOMIC AND SOCIAL COUNCIL ACTION

On 24 May 1988, the Economic and Social Council adopted **resolution 1988/6** without vote.

Implementation of the Programme of Action for the Second Decade to Combat Racism and Racial Discrimination

The Economic and Social Council,

Reaffirming the purpose set forth in the Charter of the United Nations of achieving international co-operation in solving international problems of an economic, social, cultural or humanitarian character, and in promoting and encouraging respect for human rights and fundamental freedoms for all without distinction as to race, sex, language or religion,

Recalling the proclamation by the General Assembly, in its resolution 38/14 of 22 November 1983, of the Second Decade to Combat Racism and Racial Discrimination,

Recalling also the Programme of Action for the Second Decade to Combat Racism and Racial Discrimination, approved by the General Assembly in its resolution 38/14 to achieve the objectives of the Second Decade,

Reaffirming the plan of activities for the period 1985-1989, to be implemented by the Secretary-General in accordance with General Assembly resolution 39/16 of 23 November 1984,

Recalling the plan of activities for the period 1990-1993, approved by the General Assembly in its resolution 42/47 of 30 November 1987,

Conscious of the responsibility conferred upon it by the General Assembly for co-ordinating and, in particular, evaluating the activities undertaken in the implementation of the Programme of Action for the Second Decade,

Bearing in mind, in particular, its mandate under General Assembly resolution 41/94 of 4 December 1986 to submit an annual report containing, *inter alia*:

(a) An enumeration of the activities undertaken or contemplated to achieve the objectives of the Second Decade, including the activities of Governments, United Nations bodies, the specialized agencies and other international and regional organizations, as well as non-governmental organizations,

(b) A review and appraisal of those activities,

(c) Its suggestions and recommendations,

Having examined the reports of the Secretary-General on the implementation of the Programme of Action for the Second Decade,

Emphasizing the need to ensure the co-ordination of activities undertaken by various United Nations bodies and specialized agencies for the purpose of implementing the Programme of Action for the Second Decade,

Noting that, despite the efforts of the international community, the principal objectives of the first Decade for Action to Combat Racism and Racial Discrimination and the first years of the Second Decade have not been attained, and that millions of human beings continue to be victims of varied forms of racism, racial discrimination and *apartheid*,

Aware of the efforts of the international community to improve the protection of the human rights of migrant workers, including those from the developing countries,

1. *Reaffirms* the importance of achieving the objectives of the Second Decade to Combat Racism and Racial Discrimination;

2. *Requests* the Secretary-General, when reporting on the activities undertaken to implement the Programme of Action for the Second Decade to Combat Racism and Racial Discrimination, to assess the impact of the actions and decisions taken on the elimination of racism and racial discrimination;

3. *Also requests* the Secretary-General to continue to ensure that the Centre for Human Rights of the Secretariat abides by the letter and spirit of the resolutions on the implementation of the Programme of Action for the Second Decade;

4. *Reaffirms* the necessity of co-ordinating the full range of programmes being implemented by the United Nations system as they relate to the objectives of the Second Decade;

5. *Invites* all Governments, United Nations bodies, the specialized agencies and other intergovernmental organizations, as well as interested non-governmental organizations in consultative status with the Economic and Social Council, to participate fully in the implementation of the plan of activities for the period 1985-1989;

6. *Urgently requests* the Secretary-General to ensure the effective and immediate implementation of those activities proposed for the first half of the Decade that have not yet been undertaken;

7. *Invites* the Secretary-General to proceed with the implementation of the activities for the period 1990-1993 listed in the annex to General Assembly resolution 42/47, and requests him, in this context, to accord the highest priority to measures to combat *apartheid;*

8. *Commends* those Governments, United Nations bodies, specialized agencies and other intergovernmental

and non-governmental organizations that have intensified and expanded their efforts to ensure the rapid elimination of *apartheid* and all forms of racism and racial discrimination, and urges them to redouble such efforts;

9. *Invites* all Governments to take or continue to take all necessary measures to combat all forms of racism and racial discrimination and to support the work of the Second Decade by making contributions to the Trust Fund for the Programme for the Decade for Action to Combat Racism and Racial Discrimination, in order to ensure further implementation of activities for the Second Decade;

10. *Decides*, as a matter of priority, to give particular attention to the specific activities of the Programme of Action for the Second Decade that are directed towards the elimination of *apartheid*, in view of the present explosive situation in southern Africa;

11. *Requests* the Secretary-General, in his reports, to continue to pay special attention to the situation of migrant workers and their families;

12. *Also requests* the Secretary-General to organize in 1989 a seminar on cultural dialogue between the countries of origin and the host countries of migrant workers;

13. *Emphasizes* the importance of public information activities in combating racism and racial discrimination and in mobilizing public support for the objectives of the Second Decade, and, in this context, commends the efforts of the Co-ordinator for the Second Decade to Combat Racism and Racial Discrimination;

14. *Further requests* the Secretary-General to present, in his future annual reports to the Council on the implementation of the Programme of Action for the Second Decade, more detailed information on the relevant activities of all Governments, United Nations bodies, the specialized agencies, intergovernmental organizations, and non-governmental organizations in consultative status with the Economic and Social Council.

Economic and Social Council resolution 1988/6

24 May 1988   Meeting 12   Adopted without vote

Draft by Sudan, for African States (E/1988/L.24); agenda item 2.
Financial implications. S-G, E/1988/L.26.
Meeting numbers. ESC 7-12.

On 27 May, the Council, on the recommendation of its Second (Social) Committee, adopted **resolution 1988/32** without vote.

Measures to combat racism and racial discrimination and the role of the Sub-Commission on Prevention of Discrimination and Protection of Minorities

The Economic and Social Council,

Mindful of its resolution 1984/24 of 24 May 1984, in which it authorized the Sub-Commission on Prevention of Discrimination and Protection of Minorities to entrust Mr. Asbjorn Eide, Special Rapporteur, with carrying out a study on the achievements of, and obstacles encountered during, the first Decade for Action to Combat Racism and Racial Discrimination,

Having considered Sub-Commission resolution 1987/6 of 31 August 1987 and Commission on Human Rights resolution 1988/15 of 29 February 1988,

1. *Authorizes* the Special Rapporteur to proceed with the collection of the information he needs to complete the study, as specified in his progress report;

2. *Requests* the Secretary-General to provide all necessary assistance to the Special Rapporteur in his efforts to collect the information he needs.

Economic and Social Council resolution 1988/32

27 May 1988   Meeting 16   Adopted without vote

Approved by Second Committee (E/1988/89/Add.1) without vote, 23 May (meeting 20); draft by Commission on Human Rights (E/1988/12 & Corr.1); agenda item 10.

GENERAL ASSEMBLY ACTION

On 8 December 1988, on the recommendation of the Third (Social, Humanitarian and Cultural) Committee, the General Assembly adopted **resolution 43/91** without vote.

Second Decade to Combat Racism and Racial Discrimination

The General Assembly,

Reaffirming its objective set forth in the Charter of the United Nations to achieve international co-operation in solving international problems of an economic, social, cultural or humanitarian character, and in promoting and encouraging respect for human rights and fundamental freedoms for all without distinction as to race, sex, language or religion,

Reaffirming its firm determination and its commitment to eradicate totally and unconditionally racism in all its forms, racial discrimination and *apartheid,*

Recalling the Universal Declaration of Human Rights, the International Convention on the Elimination of All Forms of Racial Discrimination, the International Convention on the Suppression and Punishment of the Crime of *Apartheid,* the International Convention against *Apartheid* in Sports, and the Convention against Discrimination in Education adopted by the United Nations Educational, Scientific and Cultural Organization on 14 December 1960,

Recalling also its resolution 3057(XXVIII) of 2 November 1973, on the first Decade for Action to Combat Racism and Racial Discrimination, and its resolution 38/14 of 22 November 1983, on the Second Decade to Combat Racism and Racial Discrimination,

Recalling further the two World Conferences to Combat Racism and Racial Discrimination, held at Geneva in 1978 and 1983, respectively,

Bearing in mind the *Report of the Second World Conference to Combat Racism and Racial Discrimination,*

Convinced that the Second World Conference represented a positive contribution by the international community towards attaining the objectives of the Decade, through its adoption of a Declaration and an operational Programme of Action for the Second Decade to Combat Racism and Racial Discrimination,

Noting with concern that, despite the efforts of the international community, the principal objectives of the first Decade for Action to Combat Racism and Racial Discrimination were not attained and that millions of human beings continue to this day to be the victims of varied forms of racism, racial discrimination and *apartheid,*

Recalling its resolutions 39/16 of 23 November 1984 and 42/47 of 30 November 1987,

Emphasizing once again the necessity of attaining the objectives of the Second Decade to Combat Racism and Racial Discrimination,

Having considered the reports of the Secretary-General submitted within the framework of the implementation of the Programme of Action for the Second Decade,

Convinced of the need to take more effective and sustained international measures for the elimination of all forms of racism and racial discrimination and the total eradication of *apartheid* in South Africa,

Aware of the importance and the magnitude of the phenomenon of migrant workers, as well as the efforts undertaken by the international community to improve the protection of the human rights of migrant workers and their families,

1. *Declares once again* that all forms of racism and racial discrimination, particularly in their institutionalized form, such as *apartheid,* or resulting from official doctrines of racial superiority or exclusivity, are among the most serious violations of human rights in the contemporary world and must be combated by all available means;

2. *Decides* that the international community, in general, and the United Nations, in particular, should continue to give the highest priority to programmes for combating racism, racial discrimination and *apartheid,* and to intensify their efforts, during the Second Decade to Combat Racism and Racial Discrimination, to provide assistance and relief to the victims of racism and all forms of racial discrimination and *apartheid,* especially in South Africa and Namibia and in occupied territories and territories under alien domination;

3. *Appeals* to all Governments and to international and non-governmental organizations to increase and intensify their activities to combat racism, racial discrimination and *apartheid* and to provide relief and assistance to the victims of these evils;

4. *Takes note* of the reports submitted by the Secretary-General containing information on the activities of Governments, specialized agencies, regional intergovernmental organizations and non-governmental organizations, as well as United Nations organs, to give effect to the Programme of Action for the Second Decade to Combat Racism and Racial Discrimination;

5. *Notes* the efforts made to co-ordinate all the programmes currently under implementation by the United Nations system that relate to the objectives of the Decade and encourages the Co-ordinator for the Second Decade to Combat Racism and Racial Discrimination to continue his efforts;

6. *Requests* the Secretary-General to continue the study on the effects of racial discrimination on the children of minorities, in particular those of migrant workers, in the field of education, training and employment, and to submit, *inter alia,* specific recommendations for the implementation of measures to combat the effects of that discrimination;

7. *Again requests* the Secretary-General to transmit his study on the role of private group action to combat racism and racial discrimination to Governments, specialized agencies, regional intergovernmental organizations and non-governmental organizations in consultative status with the Economic and Social Council in order to obtain their views and an indication from them of further relevant materials, and to submit to the General Assembly at its forty-fourth session a final report on this topic;

8. *Requests* the Secretary-General to prepare and issue as soon as possible a collection of model legisla-

tion for the guidance of Governments in the enactment of further legislation against racial discrimination;

9. *Renews its invitation* to the United Nations Educational, Scientific and Cultural Organization to expedite the preparation of teaching materials and teaching aids to promote teaching, training and educational activities on human rights and against racism and racial discrimination, with particular emphasis on activities at the primary and secondary levels of education;

10. *Requests* the Sub-Commission on Prevention of Discrimination and Protection of Minorities of the Commission on Human Rights to update the study on racial discrimination;

11. *Also requests* the Sub-Commission to complete as soon as possible the study of the results achieved and the obstacles encountered during the first Decade for Action to Combat Racism and Racial Discrimination and the first half of the Second Decade;

12. *Notes* the holding at Geneva, from 3 to 6 October 1988, of a meeting on the global consultations on racial discrimination and requests the Secretary-General to transmit the recommendations of the global consultations to the organs of the United Nations and to the specialized agencies concerned with the view to their implementation;

13. *Welcomes* the decision of the Economic and Social Council contained in resolution 1988/6 of 24 May 1988 to organize in 1989 a seminar on cultural dialogue between the countries of origin and the host countries of migrant workers;

14. *Emphasizes* the importance of adequate recourse procedures for victims of racism and racial discrimination and therefore requests the Secretary-General, in the light of the results of the seminars held on this topic, to prepare and finalize, with the appropriate assistance of qualified experts if possible, a handbook of recourse procedures;

15. *Considers* that all the parts of the Programme of Action for the Second Decade to Combat Racism and Racial Discrimination should receive equal attention in order to attain the objectives of the Second Decade;

16. *Affirms once again* the need for the implementation of the plan of activities proposed for the period 1990-1993 contained in the annex to General Assembly resolution 42/47;

17. *Invites* the Secretary-General to proceed without delay with the preparations for the activities scheduled for the biennium 1990-1991;

18. *Requests* the Secretary-General to accord the highest priority, in executing the plan of activities, to measures for combating *apartheid;*

19. *Also requests* the Secretary-General to continue to accord, in his reports, special attention to the situation of migrant workers and their families;

20. *Invites* all Governments, United Nations bodies, the specialized agencies and other intergovernmental organizations, as well as interested non-governmental organizations in consultative status with the Economic and Social Council, to participate fully in the implementation of the plans of activities for the periods 1985-1989 and 1990-1993 by intensifying and broadening their efforts to bring about the speedy elimination of *apartheid* and all forms of racism and racial discrimination;

21. *Considers* that voluntary contributions to the Trust Fund for the Programme for the Decade for Action to Combat Racism and Racial Discrimination are in-

dispensable for the implementation of the above-mentioned programmes;

22. *Notes with regret* that the present situation of the Trust Fund is not encouraging;

23. *Strongly appeals,* therefore, to all Governments, organizations and individuals in a position to do so to contribute generously to the Trust Fund and, to this end, requests the Secretary-General to undertake appropriate contacts and initiatives to encourage contributions;

24. *Reiterates its request* to the Economic and Social Council, throughout the Second Decade, to submit annually to the General Assembly a report containing, *inter alia:*

(*a*) An enumeration of the activities undertaken or contemplated to achieve the objectives of the Second Decade, including the activities of Governments, United Nations bodies, the specialized agencies and other international and regional organizations, as well as non-governmental organizations;

(*b*) A review and appraisal of those activities;

(*c*) Its suggestions and recommendations;

25. *Requests* the Secretary-General to report to the General Assembly at its forty-fourth session on the implementation of the present resolution;

26. *Decides* to keep the item entitled "Implementation of the Programme of Action for the Second Decade to Combat Racism and Racial Discrimination" on its agenda throughout the Second Decade and to consider it as a matter of the highest priority at its forty-fourth session.

General Assembly resolution 43/91

8 December 1988   Meeting 75   Adopted without vote

Approved by Third Committee (A/43/775) without vote, 27 October (meeting 23); draft by United Republic of Tanzania, for African Group (A/C.3/43/L.7); agenda item 87.
Financial implications. 5th Committee, A/43/845; S-G, A/C.3/43/L.18, A/C.5/43/28.
Meeting numbers. GA 43rd session: 3rd Committee 4-14, 16, 23; 5th Committee 36; plenary 75.

Convention on the Elimination of Racial Discrimination

Accessions and ratifications

As at 31 December 1988,[23] 127 States were parties to the International Convention on the Elimination of All Forms of Racial Discrimination, adopted by the General Assembly in 1965[21] and in force since 1969.[22] Antigua and Barbuda, the Congo and Mauritania became parties during 1988.

In August, the Secretary-General reported to the Assembly on the status of the Convention as at 1 August.[24]

GENERAL ASSEMBLY ACTION

On 8 December 1988, the General Assembly, on the recommendation of the Third Committee, adopted **resolution 43/95** without vote.

Status of the International Convention on the Elimination of All Forms of Racial Discrimination
The General Assembly,

Recalling its relevant resolutions adopted since 1973, the most recent of which is resolution 41/104 of 4 December 1986,

Noting with satisfaction the entry into force, on 3 December 1982, of the competence of the Committee on the Elimination of Racial Discimination to receive and consider communications from individuals or groups of individuals under article 14 of the International Convention on the Elimination of All Forms of Racial Discrimination,

1. *Takes note* of the report of the Secretary-General on the status of the International Convention on the Elimination of All Forms of Racial Discrimination;

2. *Expresses its satisfaction* at the number of States that have ratified the Convention or acceded thereto;

3. *Reaffirms once again its conviction* that ratification of or accession to the Convention on a universal basis and implementation of its provisions are necessary for the realization of the objectives of the Second Decade to Combat Racism and Racial Discrimination;

4. *Requests* those States which have not yet become parties to the Convention to ratify it or accede thereto;

5. *Calls upon* the States parties to the Convention to consider the possibility of making the declaration provided for in article 14 of the Convention;

6. *Requests* the Secretary-General to submit to the General Assembly at its forty-fifth session a report concerning the status of the Convention, in accordance with Assembly resolution 2106 A (XX) of 21 December 1965.

General Assembly resolution 43/95

8 December 1988   Meeting 75   Adopted without vote

Approved by Third Committee (A/43/777) without vote, 27 October (meeting 23); 23-nation draft (A/C.3/43/L.8), amended by 12 nations (A/C.3/43/L.14); agenda item 91.
Sponsors of draft: Argentina, Australia, Bahamas, Barbados, Belgium, Brazil, Bulgaria, Canada, Cuba, Cyprus, Djibouti, Egypt, Germany, Federal Republic of, Hungary, India, Italy, Luxembourg, Morocco, New Zealand, Portugal, Rwanda, Spain, Yugoslavia.
Sponsors of amendments: Costa Rica, Denmark, Ecuador, France, Iceland, Italy, Netherlands, Norway, Peru, Senegal, Sweden, Uruguay.
Meeting numbers. GA 43rd session: 3rd Committee 4-14, 16, 23; plenary 75.

The Third Committee adopted amendments to the resolution[25] by a recorded vote of 80 to none, with 59 abstentions.

Implementation of the Convention

CERD activities. The Committee on the Elimination of Racial Discrimination, set up under article 8 of the Convention, held only one curtailed session in 1988, its thirty-sixth (Geneva, 1-12 August),[18] owing to the non-payment of assessed contributions by a number of States parties over several years. Normally the Committee annually held two 3-week sessions.

Most of the Committee's work was devoted to examining reports submitted by States parties on measures taken to implement the Convention's provisions. After considering reports by 13 States under article 9 of the Convention, the Committee provided a summary of its members' views on each country report and of statements made by the States parties concerned.

In conformity with article 15 of the Convention, CERD considered documents related to Trust and Non-Self-Governing Territories transmitted to it by the Trusteeship Council (see PART FOUR, Chapter II) and by the Special Committee on the Situation with regard to the Implementation of the Declaration on the Granting of Independence to Colonial Countries and Peoples. The Committee appointed the members of its three working groups—Atlantic Ocean and Caribbean Territories, including Gibraltar; Pacific and Indian Ocean Territories; and African Territories—to examine the documents submitted under article 15 and to report on their findings. Due to its curtailed session, the Committee took note of the documents and postponed their consideration until its next session.

The Committee continued to consider, in conformity with article 14 of the Convention, communications from individuals or groups of individuals claiming violation of their rights under the Convention by a State party recognizing CERD competence to receive and consider such communications. Twelve of the States parties had declared such recognition—Costa Rica, Denmark, Ecuador, France, Iceland, Italy, Netherlands, Norway, Peru, Senegal, Sweden, Uruguay. The text of the Committee's opinion on its sole communication was annexed to its report.

CERD also considered activities to implement the Programme of Action for the Second Decade to Combat Racism and Racial Discrimination (see above).

Concerning its critical financial situation, the Committee recommended a draft resolution by which the Assembly would have authorized the Secretary-General to ensure, on a temporary basis, the financing of the expenses of the members of the Committee from the United Nations regular budget until a more permanent solution was found. The twelfth meeting of States parties (New York, 15 January 1988) had recommended that, as an exceptional measure pending resolution of the current financial difficulties, the Committee hold one session in 1988, extended if possible, and, if the situation remained unchanged, one similar session in 1989. The Secretary-General reported that, as at 1 September 1988, the total of outstanding assessments and arrears amounted to $149,328.[26]

GENERAL ASSEMBLY ACTION

On 8 December 1988, on the recommendation of the Third Committee, the General Assembly adopted **resolution 43/96** without vote.

Report of the Committee on the Elimination of Racial Discrimination

The General Assembly,

Recalling its previous resolutions concerning the reports of the Committee on the Elimination of Racial Discrimination and resolution 41/104 of 4 December 1986 on the status of the International Convention on the Elimination of All Forms of Racial Discrimination, as well as its other relevant resolutions on the implementation of the Programme of Action for the Second Decade to Combat Racism and Racial Discrimination,

Reiterating the importance of the International Convention on the Elimination of All Forms of Racial Discrimination, which is the most widely accepted human rights instrument adopted under the auspices of the United Nations,

Aware of the importance of the contributions of the Committee to the efforts of the United Nations to combat racism and all other forms of discrimination based on race, colour, descent or national or ethnic origin,

Welcoming the report of the Committee on the work of its thirty-sixth session,

Reiterating once again the need to intensify the struggle for the elimination of racism and racial discrimination throughout the world, especially the elimination of the system of *apartheid* in South Africa and Namibia,

Emphasizing the obligation of all States parties to the Convention to take legislative, judicial and other measures in order to secure full implementation of the provisions of the Convention,

Recalling the urgent appeals made by the Secretary-General, the General Assembly, the eleventh and twelfth meetings of States parties to the Convention and the Committee itself to the States parties to honour their financial obligation under the Convention,

Expressing its appreciation for the efforts of the members of the Committee to explore ways and means to overcome the Committee's current financial crisis,

Gravely concerned that, despite those appeals and other efforts, the meeting schedule of the Committee has been interrupted and the proper functioning of the Committee continues to deteriorate,

Having considered the report of the Secretary-General on the question of financing the expenses of the members of the Committee,

1. *Expresses its profound concern* at the fact that a number of States parties to the International Convention on the Elimination of All Forms of Racial Discrimination have still not fulfilled their financial obligations, which led to the cancellation of the February/March 1988 session and the curtailment by one week of the August 1988 session of the Committee on the Elimination of Racial Discrimination;

2. *Expresses once again its concern* that such a situation led to further delay in discharging the substantive obligations of the Committee under the Convention;

3. *Commends* the Committee for its work with regard to the implementation of the Convention and the Programme of Action for the Second Decade to Combat Racism and Racial Discrimination;

4. *Takes note with appreciation* of the report of the Committee on the work of its thirty-sixth session;

5. *Calls upon* States parties to fulfil their obligations under article 9, paragraph 1, of the Convention and to submit in due time their periodic reports on measures taken to implement the Convention;

6. *Notes with appreciation* the measures taken by the Committee with a view to improving the reporting procedure and streamlining its own method of examination of reports submitted by States parties;

7. *Strongly appeals* to all States parties to fulfil their financial obligations under article 8, paragraph 6, of the Convention and to pay their outstanding contributions and, if possible, their contributions for 1989 before

1 February 1989 so as to enable the Committee to meet regularly;

8. *Endorses* the decision taken at the twelfth meeting of States parties to the Convention that, as an exceptional measure, pending resolution of its current financial difficulties, the Committee should hold one extended session if possible in 1989;

9. *Invites* the Secretary-General to ensure, if possible, that the Committee holds its regular session in 1989 for at least three weeks;

10. *Requests* the Secretary-General to report to the General Assembly at its forty-fourth session on the financial situation of the Committee and possible administrative and legal measures for improving the situation facing the Committee;

11. *Decides* to consider the report at its forty-fourth session under the item entitled ''Elimination of all forms of racial discrimination''.

General Assembly resolution 43/96

8 December 1988   Meeting 75   Adopted without vote

Approved by Third Committee (A/43/777) without vote, 27 October (meeting 23); 32-nation draft (A/C.3/43/L.9); agenda item 91.
Sponsors: Algeria, Australia, Bulgaria, Colombia, Cuba, Cyprus, Djibouti, Egypt, Ethiopia, Finland, France, Germany, Federal Republic of, Hungary, India, Iraq, Italy, Libyan Arab Jamahiriya, Luxembourg, Mexico, Nicaragua, Nigeria, Norway, Pakistan, Poland, Rwanda, Senegal, Sweden, USSR, United Kingdom, United Republic of Tanzania, Venezuela, Yugoslavia.
Meeting numbers. GA 43rd session: 3rd Committee 4-14, 16, 23; plenary 75.

Measures against nazism

Human Rights Commission action. On 8 March,[27] the Commission urged all States to ensure full international co-operation for the prosecution and just punishment of those who had committed war crimes and crimes against humanity, preferably in the place where they committed their deeds.

On 10 March,[28] the Commission resolutely condemned all totalitarian or other ideologies, including Nazi, Fascist and neo-Fascist, based on racial or ethnic exclusiveness, intolerance, hatred or terror, and called on Governments, specialized agencies, intergovernmental and international non-governmental organizations to intensify measures against all such ideologies and practices. It further called on Governments to educate youth against those ideologies and practices. States were asked to ensure the thorough investigation, detection, arrest, extradition and punishment of all war criminals and persons guilty of crimes against humanity who had not been brought before a court and appropriately punished.

Reports of the Secretary-General. In response to a General Assembly request of 1986,[29] the Secretary-General, in April 1988, summarized comments of 15 Governments and two specialized agencies on measures to be taken against Nazi, Fascist and neo-Fascist activities and all other forms of totalitarian ideology and practices based on racial intolerance, hatred and terror.[30] By **decision 1988/145** of 27 May, the Economic and Social Council took note of the Secretary-General's report.

In an earlier report,[31] the Secretary-General summarized action he had taken on the subject, as well as action by the General Assembly and the Commission on Human Rights, since 1985.

On 8 December 1988, on the recommendation of the Third Committee, the General Assembly adopted **resolution 43/150** without vote.

Measures to be taken against Nazi, Fascist and neo-Fascist activities and all other forms of totalitarian ideologies and practices based on apartheid, racial discrimination and racism, and the systematic denial of human rights and fundamental freedoms

The General Assembly,

Recalling that the United Nations emerged from the struggle against nazism, fascism, totalitarian ideologies and régimes, aggression and foreign occupation, and that the peoples expressed their resolve in the Charter of the United Nations to save succeeding generations from the scourge of war,

Aware of the determination proclaimed by the peoples of the world in the Charter to reaffirm faith in fundamental human rights, in the dignity and worth of the human person, in the equal rights of men and women and of nations large and small and to promote social progress and better standards of life in larger freedom,

Noting with regret that in the contemporary world there continue to exist various forms of totalitarian ideologies and practices which entail contempt for the individual or a denial of the intrinsic dignity and equality of all human beings and of equality of opportunity in the civil, political, economic, social and cultural spheres, including the practices of *apartheid,* racial discrimination and racism,

Emphasizing that the doctrines of political, racial or ethnic superiority on which the totalitarian entities and régimes are based contradict the spirit and principles of the United Nations and that the application of such doctrines in practice leads to wars, mass and flagrant violations of human rights and crimes against humanity, such as genocide, and creates serious obstacles to friendly relations among nations and the development of all countries,

Acknowledging with satisfaction the fact that many States have established legal provisions designed to prevent the revival of Nazi, Fascist and neo-Fascist groups and organizations and are extraditing war criminals and persons having committed crimes against mankind,

Mindful of the principles of international co-operation in the detection, arrest, extradition and punishment of persons guilty of war crimes and crimes against humanity, set forth in its resolution 3074(XXVIII) of 3 December 1973,

Reaffirming that the prosecution and punishment of war crimes and crimes against peace and humanity, as laid down in its resolutions 3(I) of 13 February 1946 and 95(I) of 11 December 1946, constitute a universal commitment for all States,

Recalling its resolutions 2331(XXII) of 18 December 1967, 2438(XXIII) of 19 December 1968, 2545(XXIV) of 11 December 1969, 2713(XXV) of 15 December 1970, 2839(XXVI) of 18 December 1971, 34/24 of 15 Novem-

ber 1979, 35/200 of 15 December 1980, 36/162 of 16 December 1981, 37/179 of 17 December 1982, 38/99 of 16 December 1983, 39/114 of 14 December 1984, 40/148 of 13 December 1985 and 41/160 of 4 December 1986,

1. *Again resolutely condemns* all totalitarian or other ideologies and practices, including Nazi, Fascist and neo-Fascist, that are based on *apartheid,* racial discrimination and racism, and the systematic denial of human rights and fundamental freedoms, or which have such consequences;

2. *Expresses its determination* to resist all totalitarian ideologies, and especially their practices, which deprive people of basic human rights and fundamental freedoms and of equality of opportunity;

3. *Calls upon* all States to take the necessary measures to ensure the thorough investigation, detection, arrest, extradition and punishment of all war criminals and persons guilty of crimes against humanity who have not yet been brought before a court and appropriately punished;

4. *Also calls upon* all Governments to pay constant attention to educating the young in the spirit of respect for international law and fundamental human rights and freedoms and against Fascist, neo-Fascist and other totalitarian ideologies and practices based on terror, hatred and violence;

5. *Further calls upon* all States, in accordance with the basic principles of international law, to refrain from practices aimed at the violation of basic human rights, particularly the right to self-determination;

6. *Appeals* to States that have not yet done so to consider becoming parties to the International Covenants on Human Rights, the Convention on the Prevention and Punishment of the Crime of Genocide, the International Convention on the Elimination of All Forms of Racial Discrimination, the Convention on the Non-Applicability of Statutory Limitations to War Crimes and Crimes against Humanity and the International Convention on the Suppression and Punishment of the Crime of *Apartheid;*

7. *Invites* all States and international organizations to submit to the Secretary-General their comments and information on the implementation of the present resolution;

8. *Requests* the Secretary-General to submit a report, through the Economic and Social Council, to the General Assembly at its forty-fifth session in the light of the discussion that will take place in the Commission on Human Rights and on the basis of comments provided by States and international organizations.

General Assembly resolution 43/150

8 December 1988   Meeting 75   Adopted without vote

Approved by Third Committee (A/43/868) without vote, 30 November (meeting 57); 15-nation draft (A/C.3/43/L.73/Rev.1), orally revised, and orally amended by India; agenda item 12.

Sponsors: Afghanistan, Angola, Bulgaria, Byelorussian SSR, Cuba, Czechoslovakia, German Democratic Republic, Hungary, Lao People's Democratic Republic, Mongolia, Nicaragua, Poland, Ukrainian SSR, USSR, Viet Nam.

Meeting numbers. GA 43rd session: 3rd Committee 49-57; plenary 75.

Other aspects of discrimination

Religious freedom

Reports of the Secretary-General. As requested by the Commission on Human Rights in

1987,[32] the Secretary-General submitted in 1988 an addendum[33] to the 1986 compendium of national legislation and regulations on freedom of religion or belief, highlighting measures taken to combat intolerance or discrimination.[34] The addendum contained the legislative and regulatory texts of 22 countries.

Also in response to the Commission's request,[32] the Secretary-General summarized the views of 14 States on the contribution that might be made by an international instrument to eliminate all forms of intolerance and discrimination based on religion or belief.[35]

Report of the Special Rapporteur. In January,[36] Special Rapporteur Angelo Vidal D'Ameida Ribeiro (Portugal), appointed in 1986,[37] submitted to the Commission on Human Rights a report containing a summary of replies from Governments regarding alleged infringements of the provisions of the 1981 Declaration on the Elimination of All Forms of Intolerance and Discrimination Based on Religion or Belief,[38] received from various sources. An analysis of information collected by the Special Rapporteur pointed to the persistence of incidents and measures inconsistent with the provisions of the Declaration.

He recommended drawing up an international convention on the elimination of all forms of intolerance and discrimination based on religion or belief and establishing, within the Commission, an open-ended working group to consider a draft convention on freedom of religion and belief. States were urged to facilitate the formulation of international standards and to adapt their legislation to that of existing international norms, calling on United Nations bodies for technical assistance in drafting new legislative provisions. The Special Rapporteur outlined a series of measures for States to prevent and eliminate discrimination based on religion or belief, including bilateral and multilateral action. He noted that NGOs concerned with human rights and religious communities could play an important role in promoting and protecting religious tolerance and in giving widespread publicity to the relevant existing international standards.

Human Rights Commission action. As requested by the General Assembly in 1987,[39] the Commission continued in 1988 to consider measures to implement the 1981 Declaration. On 8 March,[40] it extended its Special Rapporteur's mandate for two years and asked the Secretary-General to provide him with the assistance required. It called on Governments which had not done so to co-operate with him. The Commission urged States, in accordance with their own constitutional system and relevant international instruments, to provide adequate constitutional and legal guarantees of freedom of thought, conscience,

religion and belief and to take measures to combat intolerance and encourage understanding, tolerance and respect in matters relating to freedom of religion or belief. It considered it desirable to enhance United Nations promotional activities relating to freedom of religion or belief and asked the Secretary-General to accord high priority to disseminating the text of the 1981 Declaration and to publish and widely distribute the 1987 study on the dimensions of the problems of intolerance and of discrimination on the grounds of religion or belief[32] prepared by the Sub-Commission's Special Rapporteur, Elizabeth Odio Benito (Costa Rica). The United Nations University (UNU) and other academic and research institutions were invited to undertake studies on how to achieve such understanding. The Sub-Commission was asked to compile provisions relating to the elimination of intolerance based on religion contained in the 1981 Declaration and other international instruments, and to examine the issues that should be considered prior to drafting a further international instrument on the issue. The Commission asked the Secretary-General to report on the implementation of its resolution in 1989.

The Commission's decision to extend the Special Rapporteur's mandate for two years and its request to the Secretary-General to provide him with all the assistance he required was approved on 27 May by Economic and Social Council **decision 1988/142**.

Sub-Commission action. On 1 September,[41] the Sub-Commission recommended that the Commission consider establishing a pre-sessional, open-ended working group to draft an international instrument on freedom of religion or belief immediately after the mandate of the working group to draft a convention on the rights of the child had ended.

On the same date,[42] the Sub-Commission, noting the Commission's requests of 8 March (see above),[40] requested Theo van Boven (Netherlands) to prepare a working paper to assist the Sub-Commission in carrying out its task.

GENERAL ASSEMBLY ACTION

On 8 December 1988, on the recommendation of the Third Committee, the General Assembly adopted **resolution 43/108** without vote.

Elimination of all forms of religious intolerance

The General Assembly,

Conscious of the need to promote universal respect for, and observance of, human rights and fundamental freedoms for all without distinction as to race, sex, language or religion,

Reaffirming its resolution 36/55 of 25 November 1981, by which it proclaimed the Declaration on the Elimination of All Forms of Intolerance and of Discrimination Based on Religion or Belief,

Recalling its resolution 42/97 of 7 December 1987, in which it requested the Commission on Human Rights to continue its consideration of measures to implement the Declaration,

Encouraged by the efforts being made by the Commission on Human Rights and by the Sub-Commission on Prevention of Discrimination and Protection of Minorities to study relevant developments affecting the implementation of the Declaration,

Taking note of Commission on Human Rights resolution 1988/55 of 8 March 1988 and Economic and Social Council decision 1988/142 of 27 May 1988, whereby the mandate of the Special Rapporteur appointed to examine incidents and governmental actions in all parts of the world that are incompatible with the provisions of the Declaration and to recommend remedial measures as appropriate was extended for two years,

Noting with satisfaction that the Commission on Human Rights decided, by that resolution, that the study of the current dimensions of the problems of intolerance and discrimination based on religion or belief by the Special Rapporteur of the Sub-Commission on Prevention of Discrimination and Protection of Minorities should be published in all official languages of the United Nations and should be widely distributed, and that the Sub-Commission has been invited to continue its in-depth consideration of the issue and to report to the Commission at its forty-fifth session,

Emphasizing that non-governmental organizations and religious bodies and groups at every level have an important role to play in the promotion of tolerance and the protection of freedom of religion or belief,

Seriously concerned that intolerance and discrimination on the grounds of religion or belief continue to exist in many parts of the world,

Believing that further efforts are therefore required to promote and protect the right to freedom of thought, conscience, religion and belief and to eliminate all forms of intolerance and discrimination based on religion or belief,

1. *Reaffirms* that freedom of thought, conscience, religion and belief is a right guaranteed to all without discrimination;

2. *Urges* States, therefore, in accordance with their respective constitutional systems and with such internationally accepted instruments as the Universal Declaration of Human Rights, the International Covenant on Civil and Political Rights and the Declaration on the Elimination of All Forms of Intolerance and of Discrimination Based on Religion or Belief to provide, where they have not already done so, adequate constitutional and legal guarantees of freedom of thought, conscience, religion and belief, including the provision of effective remedies where there is intolerance or discrimination based on religion or belief;

3. *Urges* all States to take all appropriate measures to combat intolerance and to encourage understanding, tolerance and respect in matters relating to freedom of religion or belief and, in this context, to examine where necessary the supervision and training of their civil servants, educators and other public officials to ensure that, in the course of their official duties, they respect different religions and beliefs and do not discriminate against persons professing other religions or beliefs;

4. *Invites* the United Nations University and other academic and research institutions to undertake programmes and studies on the encouragement of understanding, tolerance and respect in matters relating to freedom of religion or belief;

5. *Considers* it desirable to enhance the promotional and public information activities of the United Nations in matters relating to freedom of religion or belief;

6. *Invites* the Secretary-General to continue to give high priority to the dissemination of the text of the Declaration on the Elimination of All Forms of Intolerance and of Discrimination Based on Religion or Belief, in all the official languages of the United Nations, and to take all appropriate measures to make the text available for use by United Nations information centres, as well as by other interested bodies;

7. *Requests* the Secretary-General in this context to invite interested non-governmental organizations to consider what further role they could envisage playing in the implementation of the Declaration and in its dissemination in national and local languages;

8. *Urges* all States to consider disseminating the text of the Declaration in their respective national languages and to facilitate its dissemination in national and local languages;

9. *Welcomes* the renewal for two years of the mandate of the Special Rapporteur appointed to examine incidents and governmental actions in all parts of the world that are incompatible with the provisions of the Declaration and to recommend remedial measures as appropriate;

10. *Notes* that the Commission on Human Rights also intends to consider at its forty-fifth session the question of a binding international instrument in this field and emphasizes, in this connection, the relevance of General Assembly resolution 41/120 of 4 December 1986 entitled ''Setting international standards in the field of human rights'';

11. *Requests* the Commission on Human Rights to continue its consideration of measures to implement the Declaration and to report, through the Economic and Social Council, to the General Assembly at its forty-fourth session;

12. *Decides* to include in the provisional agenda of its forty-fourth session the item entitled ''Elimination of all forms of religious intolerance'' and to consider the report of the Commission on Human Rights under that item.

General Assembly resolution 43/108

8 December 1988   Meeting 75   Adopted without vote

Approved by Third Committee (A/43/869) without vote, 23 November (meeting 51); 23-nation draft (A/C.3/43/L.53); agenda item 97.
Sponsors: Austria, Belgium, Canada, Colombia, Costa Rica, Côte d'Ivoire, Fiji, Finland, France, Germany, Federal Republic of, Ireland, Luxembourg, Netherlands, New Zealand, Norway, Philippines, Portugal, Samoa, Senegal, Sweden, United States, Uruguay, Venezuela.
Meeting numbers. GA 43rd session: 3rd Committee 39-43, 46, 51; plenary 75.

Indigenous populations

Human Rights Commission action. On 8 March,[43] the Commission urged the Sub-Commission's Working Group on Indigenous Populations to intensify its efforts to elaborate international standards to promote and protect the human rights of such populations. It appealed to

Governments, organizations and individuals to contribute to the United Nations Voluntary Fund for Indigenous Populations (see below).

Also on 8 March,[44] the Commission recommended for adoption by the Economic and Social Council a resolution on the promotion of indigenous peoples' rights, which the Council adopted as **resolution 1988/35** (see below).

On 9 March,[45] the Commission recommended that the Council authorize the appointment of Miguel Alfonso Martínez (Cuba) as the Sub-Commission's Special Rapporteur to prepare an outline on the possible purposes, scope and sources of a study on the potential utility of treaties, agreements and other constructive arrangements between indigenous populations and Governments to ensure the promotion and protection of the human rights and fundamental freedoms of indigenous populations, which the Council did by **decision 1988/134** of 27 May. The Commission asked the Special Rapporteur to pay particular attention to the ongoing development of universally relevant standards and the need to develop innovative, forward-looking approaches to relationships between indigenous populations and Governments and to submit the outline to the Sub-Commission for consideration by the Working Group on Indigenous Populations in 1988 (see below), together with views expressed by Governments and other parties interested in the study. The Commission asked the Secretary-General to bring its resolution, the outline and the deliberations of the Sub-Commission thereon to the attention of Governments, specialized agencies and NGOs, with a view to obtaining comments before the Commission's 1989 session.

Working Group activities. At its sixth session (Geneva, 1-5 August 1988), the Working Group on Indigenous Populations[46] reviewed developments on the protection of the rights of indigenous populations and discussed the evolution of standards concerning indigenous rights. Special Rapporteur Martínez presented an outline of his study on treaties, agreements and other constructive arrangements between States and indigenous populations,[47] which the Group endorsed. The Group recommended to the Sub-Commission that it recommend full authorization from the Economic and Social Council in 1989 for the Special Rapporteur to proceed with the study, which the Sub-Commission did on 1 September.[48] Documents and other written statements submitted to the Group were contained in an addendum to the Group's report.[49]

Sub-Commission action. On 1 September,[50] the Sub-Commission asked the Secretary-General to ensure that participation in the seminar on social and economic relations between indigenous peoples and States, and any future seminars or meetings of experts on indigenous rights, included representation of indigenous peoples' organizations. It recommended for adoption by the Economic and Social Council a resolution recommending that the Secretary-General consider including courses and seminars for indigenous peoples and other vulnerable groups in the programme of advisory services in the field of human rights.

On the same date,[51] the Sub-Commission suggested that the Secretary-General organize during the first half of 1991 a meeting of experts to review national experience in the operation of schemes of local, internal self-government for indigenous populations as part of the plan of activities to be implemented during the second half of the Second Decade to Combat Racism and Racial Discrimination, approved by the General Assembly in 1987.[2] It also decided to invite the Working Group on Indigenous Populations to discuss in 1989 the possible programme and agenda of such a meeting.

Also on 1 September,[52] the Sub-Commission delegated two of its members to prepare a summary of information on the relocation of Hopi and Navajo families, for submission in 1989.

ECONOMIC AND SOCIAL COUNCIL ACTION

On 27 May, on the recommendation of its Second Committee, the Economic and Social Council adopted **resolution 1988/35** without vote.

Study of the problem of discrimination against indigenous populations

The Economic and Social Council,

Taking note of Commission on Human Rights resolution 1988/48 of 8 March 1988,

Recalling the final report of Mr. J. R. Martínez Cobo, Special Rapporteur on the problem of discrimination against indigenous populations, in which he recommended the organization of international seminars under the programme of advisory services in the field of human rights,

Recalling also the recommendations of the Second World Conference to Combat Racism and Racial Discrimination, in particular those relating to the protection of indigenous rights and to the use of education and the mass media to combat racial discrimination,

1. *Requests* the Secretary-General to include the recognition and promotion of the rights of indigenous peoples in future United Nations activities under the Programme of Action for the Second Decade to Combat Racism and Racial Discrimination and to invite representatives of indigenous nations, peoples and communities, including non-governmental organizations, to participate in the planning and implementation of these activities;

2. *Requests* the Secretary-General to organize in 1988, as part of the programme of advisory services in the field of human rights, a seminar on the effects of racism and racial discrimination on the social and economic relations between indigenous peoples and States;

3. *Encourages* all States to ensure that educational and informational activities, including national celebrations, give an accurate interpretation of history and do not perpetuate or justify theories of racial superiority or the subjugation of indigenous or other peoples.

Economic and Social Council resolution 1988/35

27 May 1988   Meeting 16   Adopted without vote

Approved by Second Committee (E/1988/89/Add.1) without vote, 23 May (meeting 20); draft by Commission on Human Rights (E/1988/12 & Corr.1); agenda item 10.

Other action. The seminar on the effects of racism and racial discrimination on social and economic relations between indigenous peoples and States, scheduled for 1988, did not take place until 1989.

Draft declaration

Human Rights Commission action. On 8 March,[43] the Commission encouraged Governments and indigenous organizations and communities to review the preliminary draft principles on rights of indigenous populations presented by the Working Group on Indigenous Populations in 1987.[53]

Also on 8 March,[54] the Commission recommended for adoption by the Economic and Social Council a resolution, the text of which the Council adopted as **resolution 1988/36** (see below).

ECONOMIC AND SOCIAL COUNCIL ACTION

On 27 May 1988, the Economic and Social Council, on the recommendation of its Second Committee, adopted **resolution 1988/36** without vote.

Draft declaration of principles on the rights of indigenous populations

The Economic and Social Council

1. *Requests* the Chairman/Rapporteur of the Working Group on Indigenous Populations of the Sub-Commission on Prevention of Discrimination and Protection of Minorities, Mrs. Erica-Irene Daes, to prepare a working paper containing a set of principles and preambular paragraphs for inclusion in a draft declaration of principles on the rights of indigenous populations, for consideration by the Working Group at its sixth session, in 1988;

2. *Requests* the Secretary-General to give all necessary assistance to the Chairman/Rapporteur in the completion of this task.

Economic and Social Council resolution 1988/36

27 May 1988   Meeting 16   Adopted without vote

Approved by Second Committee (E/1988/89/Add.1) without vote, 23 May (meeting 20); draft by Commission on Human Rights (E/1988/12 & Corr.1); agenda item 10.

Working Group activities. In August,[46] the Working Group on Indigenous Populations had before it a working paper prepared by its Chairman/Rapporteur, Erica-Irene A. Daes (Greece), containing a set of draft preambular paragraphs

and principles for insertion into a universal declaration on indigenous rights.[55] The 14 draft principles in preliminary wording already adopted by the Working Group in 1987[53] were maintained, with a few minor changes and additions and in a different order. The Working Group recommended that the Sub-Commission ask Governments, indigenous peoples, intergovernmental and non-governmental organizations to submit written observations and suggestions for the draft prior to 31 January 1989 and that the Chairman/Rapporteur prepare a first revised text of the draft based on those observations and suggestions and on comments made by the Group.

Sub-Commission action. On 1 September,[56] the Sub-Commission adopted the recommendations of the Working Group and asked the Secretary-General to give it all necessary assistance.

International Year of Indigenous Populations

Human Rights Commission action. On 9 March,[57] the Commission recommended a resolution for adoption by the Economic and Social Council, which adopted it as **resolution 1988/37** (see below).

ECONOMIC AND SOCIAL COUNCIL ACTION

On 27 May 1988, the Economic and Social Council, on the recommendation of its Second Committee, adopted **resolution 1988/37 without vote.**

Proposal to proclaim an international year of the world's indigenous populations

The Economic and Social Council,

Recalling its resolution 1982/34 of 7 May 1982, by which it authorized the establishment of a working group on indigenous populations with the mandate to review developments pertaining to the promotion and protection of the human rights and fundamental freedoms of indigenous populations, giving special attention to the evolution of standards,

Recalling also its resolution 1986/34 of 23 May 1986,

Noting that the Sub-Commission on Prevention of Discrimination and Protection of Minorities, in its resolution 1987/16 of 2 September 1987, endorsed the recommendation that the Working Group on Indigenous Populations should make every effort to complete a draft declaration on indigenous rights as soon as possible,

Conscious of the continuing struggle of indigenous populations throughout the world to enjoy their inalienable human rights and fundamental freedoms,

Recommends that the General Assembly should, at an appropriate time, proclaim an international year of the world's indigenous populations.

Economic and Social Council resolution 1988/37

27 May 1988   Meeting 16   Adopted without vote

Approved by Second Committee (E/1988/89/Add.1) without vote, 23 May (meeting 20); draft by Commission on Human Rights (E/1988/12 & Corr.1); agenda item 10.

Working Group activities. The Working Group on Indigenous Populations, in August,[46] recommended to the Sub-Commission that an international year of the world's indigenous populations, originally scheduled by the Working Group and the Sub-Commission for 1992,[53] be held in 1993 to coincide with the end of the Second Decade to Combat Racism and Racial Discrimination.

Sub-Commission action. On 1 September,[58] the Sub-Commission adopted the Working Group's recommendation and asked the Secretary-General to bring the matter to the attention of the General Assembly.

UN Voluntary Fund for Indigenous Populations

In an October report,[59] the Secretary-General stated that a total of $124,568 in contributions to the United Nations Voluntary Fund for Indigenous Populations had been received from seven Governments as at 1 October 1988. In addition, two NGOs, one based in Canada and the other in Japan, had contributed $814.81 and $755, respectively. The Fund's Board of Trustees held its first session (Geneva, April), at which it examined requests for financial assistance for 86 indigenous representatives. Of those requests, 27 travel and subsistence grants were awarded to beneficiaries from 19 countries to participate in the 1988 session of the Working Group on Indigenous Populations.

The General Assembly, by **decision 43/427** of 8 December, took note of the Secretary-General's report and called on Governments, NGOs and representatives of indigenous groups to consider contributing to the Fund and to disseminate information about its activities. It asked the Secretary-General to report on the Fund's status in 1990.

Migrant workers

Draft convention

Human Rights Commission action. The Commission, on 10 March,[60] welcomed the progress made by the Working Group on the Drafting of an International Convention on the Protection of the Rights of All Migrant Workers and Their Families, established by the General Assembly in 1979,[61] on the second reading of the draft convention. It invited Member States to continue co-operating with the Working Group, reiterated its hope for a completion of the convention as soon as possible and asked the Secretary-General to report on further progress in 1989.

Working Group activities. The Working Group on the Drafting of an International Convention on the Protection of the Rights of All Migrant Workers and Their Families held its seventh inter-sessional meeting from 31 May to 10 June[62] and its ninth session from 27 September to 7 October,[63] both in New York.

At those meetings, the Group adopted in second reading articles 51-55 of part IV, on other rights of migrant workers and members of their families in a regular situation; articles 57-62 of part V, on provisions applicable to particular categories of migrant workers and their families; one unnumbered article under part VIII, dealing with general provisions; articles 63-69 *bis* of part VI, on the promotion of sound, equitable and humane conditions in connection with lawful international migration of workers and their families; and articles 70-72 of part VII, on the application of the convention.

GENERAL ASSEMBLY ACTION

On 8 December 1988, on the recommendation of the Third Committee, the General Assembly adopted **resolution 43/146** by recorded vote.

**Measures to improve the situation and
ensure the human rights
and dignity of all migrant workers**

The General Assembly,

Reaffirming once more the permanent validity of the principles and standards set forth in the basic instruments regarding the international protection of human rights, in particular in the Universal Declaration of Human Rights, the International Covenants on Human Rights, the International Convention on the Elimination of All Forms of Racial Discrimination and the Convention on the Elimination of All Forms of Discrimination against Women,

Bearing in mind the principles and standards established within the framework of the International Labour Organisation and the United Nations Educational, Scientific and Cultural Organization, and the importance of the task carried out in connection with migrant workers and their families in other specialized agencies and in various organs of the United Nations,

Reiterating that, in spite of the existence of an already established body of principles and standards, there is a need to make further efforts to improve the situation and ensure the human rights and dignity of all migrant workers and their families,

Recalling its resolution 34/172 of 17 December 1979, in which it decided to establish a working group open to all Member States to elaborate an international convention on the protection of the rights of all migrant workers and their families,

Recalling also its resolutions 35/198 of 15 December 1980, 36/160 of 16 December 1981, 37/170 of 17 December 1982, 38/86 of 16 December 1983, 39/102 of 14 December 1984, 40/130 of 13 December 1985, 41/151 of 4 December 1986 and 42/140 of 7 December 1987, in which it renewed the mandate of the Working Group on the Drafting of an International Convention on the Protection of the Rights of All Migrant Workers and Their Families and requested it to continue its work,

Having examined the progress made by the Working Group at its seventh inter-sessional meeting, held from

31 May to 10 June 1988, and at the current session of the General Assembly, from 27 September to 7 October 1988, during which the Working Group continued with the second reading of the draft convention,

1. *Takes note with satisfaction* of the two most recent reports of the Working Group on the Drafting of an International Convention on the Protection of the Rights of All Migrant Workers and Their Families and, in particular, of the progress made by the Working Group on the drafting, in second reading, of the draft convention;

2. *Decides* that, in order to enable it to complete its task as soon as possible, the Working Group shall again hold an inter-sessional meeting of two weeks' duration in New York, immediately after the first regular session of 1989 of the Economic and Social Council;

3. *Invites* the Secretary-General to transmit to Governments the two most recent reports of the Working Group so as to enable the members of the Working Group to continue the drafting, in second reading, of the draft convention during the inter-sessional meeting to be held in the spring of 1989, as well as to transmit the results obtained at that meeting to the General Assembly for consideration during its forty-fourth session;

4. *Also invites* the Secretary-General to transmit the above-mentioned documents to the competent organs of the United Nations and to the international organizations concerned, for their information, so as to enable them to continue their co-operation with the Working Group;

5. *Decides* that the Working Group shall meet during the forty-fourth session of the General Assembly, preferably at the beginning of the session, to conclude, if possible, the second reading of the draft international convention on the protection of the rights of all migrant workers and their families;

6. *Requests* the Secretary-General to do everything possible to ensure adequate Secretariat services for the Working Group for the timely fulfilment of its mandate, both at its inter-sessional meeting to be held after the first regular session of 1989 of the Economic and Social Council and during the forty-fourth session of the General Assembly.

General Assembly resolution 43/146

8 December 1988   Meeting 75   154-1-2 (recorded vote)

Approved by Third Committee (A/43/868) by vote (136-1-2), 29 November (meeting 56); 25-nation draft (A/C.3/43/L.69), orally revised; agenda item 12.
Sponsors: Algeria, Argentina, Bangladesh, Bolivia, Botswana, China, Colombia, Ecuador, Greece, India, Italy, Mali, Mauritania, Mexico, Morocco, Nicaragua, Pakistan, Peru, Philippines, Portugal, Rwanda, Senegal, Tunisia, Turkey, Yugoslavia.
Financial implications. 5th Committee, A/43/936; S-G, A/C.3/43/L.83, A/C.5/43/56 & Add.1.
Meeting numbers. GA 43rd session: 3rd Committee 49-56; 5th Committee 43; plenary 75.

Recorded vote in Assembly as follows:

In favour: Afghanistan, Albania, Algeria, Angola, Antigua and Barbuda, Argentina, Australia, Austria, Bahamas, Bahrain, Bangladesh, Barbados, Belgium, Belize, Benin, Bolivia, Botswana, Brazil, Brunei Darussalam, Bulgaria, Burkina Faso, Burma, Burundi, Byelorussian SSR, Cameroon, Canada, Cape Verde, Central African Republic, Chad, Chile, China, Colombia, Comoros, Congo, Costa Rica, Côte d'Ivoire, Cuba, Cyprus, Czechoslovakia, Democratic Kampuchea, Democratic Yemen, Denmark, Djibouti, Dominica, Dominican Republic, Ecuador, Egypt, El Salvador, Equatorial Guinea, Ethiopia, Fiji, Finland, France, Gabon, Gambia, German Democratic Republic, Ghana, Greece, Grenada, Guatemala, Guinea, Guinea-Bissau, Guyana, Haiti, Honduras, Hungary, Iceland, India, Indonesia, Iran, Iraq, Ireland, Israel, Italy, Jamaica, Japan, Jordan, Kenya, Kuwait, Lao People's Democratic Republic, Lebanon, Lesotho, Liberia, Libyan Arab Jamahiriya, Luxembourg, Madagascar, Malawi, Malaysia, Maldives, Mali, Malta,

Mauritania, Mauritius, Mexico, Mongolia, Morocco, Mozambique, Nepal, Netherlands, New Zealand, Nicaragua, Niger, Nigeria, Norway, Oman, Pakistan, Panama, Papua New Guinea, Paraguay, Peru, Philippines, Poland, Portugal, Qatar, Romania, Rwanda, Saint Kitts and Nevis, Saint Lucia, Saint Vincent and the Grenadines, Samoa, Sao Tome and Principe, Saudi Arabia, Senegal, Seychelles, Sierra Leone, Singapore, Solomon Islands, Somalia, Spain, Sri Lanka, Sudan, Suriname, Swaziland, Sweden, Syrian Arab Republic, Thailand, Togo, Trinidad and Tobago, Tunisia, Turkey, Uganda, Ukrainian SSR, USSR, United Arab Emirates, United Republic of Tanzania, Uruguay, Vanuatu, Venezuela, Viet Nam, Yemen, Yugoslavia, Zaire, Zambia, Zimbabwe.
Against: United States.
Abstaining: Germany, Federal Republic of, United Kingdom.

Protection of minorities

As in previous years, the Commission on Human Rights set up an informal open-ended working group to elaborate a draft declaration on the rights of persons belonging to national, ethnic, religious and linguistic minorities. The group, which held five meetings on 10, 11, 16 and 18 February and 8 March, adopted provisionally in first reading draft article 3 and considered draft articles 4 and 5. Annexed to the group's report[64] were the texts of articles 1-3, on which preliminary agreement had been reached, proposals relating to articles 4-6 for consideration by the group and written proposals submitted by Bulgaria and the USSR on preambular paragraphs 4 and 5 and article 4.

On 9 March,[65] the Commission decided to set up another working group in 1989 to continue consideration of the draft declaration and asked the Secretary-General to provide the group with the assistance it needed.

On 1 September,[66] the Sub-Commission invited one of its members to prepare a working paper on possible ways and means to facilitate the peaceful and constructive resolution of situations involving racial, national, religious and linguistic minorities and asked the Secretary-General to provide the assistance needed to complete the task.

HIV- and AIDS-related discrimination

On 1 September,[67] the Sub-Commission decided that one of its members should be asked to prepare, and submit in 1989, a concise note setting forth methods by which a study could be made on the problem of discrimination against persons infected with the human immunodeficiency virus or suffering from the acquired immunodeficiency syndrome.

REFERENCES

[1]YUN 1984, p. 785. [2]YUN 1987, p. 730, GA res. 42/47, annex, 30 Nov. 1987. [3]*Ibid.*, p. 729, ESC res. 1987/2, 26 May 1987. [4]E/1988/9 & Add.1,2. [5]YUN 1984, p. 787, GA res. 39/16, 23 Nov. 1984. [6]E/1988/8. [7]A/43/644. [8]YUN 1987, p. 729. [9]E/1988/10. [10]A/43/631. [11]YUN 1986, p. 682. [12]A/43/637. [13]YUN 1985, p. 837, GA res. 40/22, 29 Nov. 1985. [14]E/1988/12 (res. 1988/16). [15]*Ibid.* (res. 1988/15). [16]E/CN.4/1989/3 (dec. 1988/101). [17]E/CN.4/Sub.2/1988/5. [18]A/43/18. [19]Sales No. E.79.XIV.4. [20]YUN 1978, p. 661. [21]YUN 1965, p. 440, GA res. 2106 A (XX), annex, 21 Dec. 1965. [22]YUN 1969, p. 488. [23]*Multilateral Treaties*

Deposited with the Secretary-General: Status as at 31 December 1988
(ST/LEG/SER.E/7), Sales No. E.89.V.3. (24)A/43/517.
(25)A/C.3/43/L.14. (26)A/43/607. (27)E/1988/12 (res. 1988/47).
(28)*Ibid.* (res. 1988/63). (29)YUN 1986, p. 687, GA res. 41/160,
4 Dec. 1986. (30)A/43/305-E/1988/26. (31)E/CN.4/1988/49.
(32)YUN 1987, p. 735. (33)E/CN.4/1988/43 & Add.1-7. (34)YUN
1986, p. 688. (35)E/CN.4/1988/44 & Add.1-7. (36)E/CN.4/1988/45
& Add.1 & Add.1/Corr.1. (37)YUN 1986, p. 689, ESC dec.
1986/134, 23 May 1986. (38)YUN 1981, p. 881, GA res. 36/55,
25 Nov. 1981. (39)YUN 1987, p. 736, GA res. 42/97, 7 Dec.
1987. (40)E/1988/12 (res. 1988/55). (41)E/CN.4/1989/3 (res.
1988/32). (42)*Ibid.* (dec. 1988/112). (43)E/1988/12 (res. 1988/44).
(44)*Ibid.* (res. 1988/48). (45)*Ibid.* (res. 1988/56). (46)E/CN.4/
Sub.2/1988/24. (47)E/CN.4/Sub.2/1988/24/Add.1. (48)E/CN.4/
1989/3 (res. 1988/20). (49)E/CN.4/Sub.2/1988/24/Add.2.
(50)E/CN.4/1989/3 (res. 1988/21). (51)*Ibid.* (dec. 1988/106). (52)*Ibid.*
(dec. 1988/105). (53)YUN 1987, p. 737. (54)E/1988/12 (res.
1988/49). (55)E/CN.4/Sub.2/1988/25. (56)E/CN.4/1989/3 (res.
1988/18). (57)E/1988/12 (res. 1988/58). (58)E/CN.4/1989/3 (res.
1988/19). (59)A/43/706. (60)E/1988/12 (res. 1988/77). (61)YUN
1979, p. 875, GA res. 34/172, 17 Dec. 1979. (62)A/C.3/43/1.
(63)A/C.3/43/7. (64)E/CN.4/1988/36. (65)E/1988/12 (res.
1988/64). (66)E/CN.4/1989/3 (res. 1988/36). (67)*Ibid.* (dec.
1988/111).

Civil and political rights

Covenant on Civil and Political Rights and Optional Protocol

Accessions and ratifications

As at 31 December 1988,[1] the International
Covenant on Civil and Political Rights and the
Optional Protocol thereto, adopted by the General
Assembly in 1966[2] and in force since 1976,[3]
had been ratified or acceded to by 87 and 43
States, respectively. No States became parties to
the Covenant during 1988, but the Gambia, Hungary and Togo acceded to the Optional Protocol,
and the Gambia made the declaration under article 41 of the Covenant recognizing the competence
of the Human Rights Committee to consider
claims that a State party was not fulfilling its obligations under the Covenant.

In his report to the Assembly on the International
Covenants on Human Rights,[4] the Secretary-
General provided information on the status of the
Covenant and the Protocol as at 31 July 1988 (see
below, under "Advancement of human rights").

Human Rights Commission action. On 7
March,[5] the Commission appealed to States that
had not done so to become parties to the Covenant and Optional Protocol and to consider making the declaration provided for in article 41. A
similar appeal was made by the Assembly later in
the year, by **resolution 43/114**. The Commission
asked the Secretary-General to provide technical
assistance to States not parties to the Covenant
with a view to assisting them to ratify or accede
to it and to report in 1989 on the status of the Covenant and its Protocol.

Also on 7 March,[6] the Commission decided to
consider in 1989 the elaboration of a second optional protocol to the Covenant aimed at abolishing the death penalty, and asked the Secretary-
General to inform the Assembly of its decision.

Sub-Commission action. On 1 September,[7]
the Sub-Commission transmitted to the Commission an analysis concerning the elaboration of a
second optional protocol, presented by its Special
Rapporteur in 1987.[8]

Implementation

The Human Rights Committee, established
under article 28 of the Covenant, held three sessions in 1988: the thirty-second in New York from
21 March to 8 April; and the thirty-third from 11
to 29 July[9] and the thirty-fourth from 24 October to 11 November, both at Geneva.[10]

At those sessions, the Committee considered
reports from 13 States (Australia, Barbados, Belgium, Central African Republic, Colombia, Ecuador, France, Guinea, Japan, Mexico, Netherlands, Norway, United Kingdom) under article 40
of the Covenant. It adopted views on six communications from individuals claiming that their
rights under the Covenant had been violated.
Those cases concerned the Netherlands, Peru (2),
Sweden (2) and Uruguay. The Committee decided
that 11 other such cases were inadmissible.

On 23 March, the Committee adopted its
general comment on article 17 of the Covenant,
which provided for the right of every person to be
protected against arbitrary or unlawful interference with his privacy, family, home or correspondence, as well as against unlawful attacks on his
honour and reputation. General comments were
intended to assist States parties to fulfil their reporting obligations and to promote implementation of the Covenant. In accordance with a 1985
Economic and Social Council decision,[11] the
Secretary-General, by a 12 April note,[12] transmitted the Committee's general comments to the
Council.

Taking note of the Committee's report, the Assembly, in **resolution 43/114**, urged those parties
that had not submitted their reports under article
40 to do so.

States of emergency

Human Rights Commission action. On 8
March,[13] the Commission requested its Sub-
Commission to continue to give attention to states
of siege or emergency.

The Commission,[5] as did the Assembly by
resolution 43/114, underlined the importance of
strict observation of the agreed condition and
procedure for derogation under article 4 of the
Convenant, bearing in mind the need for States
parties to provide the fullest possible information

during states of emergency in order to assess the justification and appropriateness of measures taken.

Report of the Special Rapporteur and Sub-Commission action. As requested by the Economic and Social Council in 1985,[14] Special Rapporteur Leandro Despouy (Argentina) submitted in July 1988 the second annual report containing information on four States, which, since 1 January 1985, had proclaimed, extended or terminated a state of emergency.[15] The first annual report was issued in 1987.[16] The Special Rapporteur made recommendations on: model legal provisions applicable in emergency situations; the effect of states of emergency on human rights; the protection of persons likely to be most affected by a state of emergency; undeclared states of emergency; government co-operation with human rights organizations; limits to the imposition of states of emergency; and training for officials responsible for declaring, promulgating, disseminating and communicating relevant orders. Annexed to his report were the texts of norms of international law applicable to states of emergency communicated to the Special Rapporteur and a dated list of replies received from Governments, United Nations bodies, intergovernmental organizations and NGOs. In a later report,[17] the Special Rapporteur provided updated information, as requested by the Sub-Commission on 1 September.[18]

Self-determination of peoples

Human Rights Commission action. By five resolutions adopted in 1988, the Commission on Human Rights reaffirmed the right to self-determination for the people of Afghanistan,[19] Kampuchea,[20] Palestine,[21] South Africa and Namibia[22] and Western Sahara.[23] A sixth resolution adopted under the agenda item pertained to the use of mercenaries to impede the right of peoples to self-determination.[24]

Report of the Secretary-General. Pursuant to General Assembly requests of 1987,[25] the Secretary-General submitted a September 1988 report with later addendum[26] summarizing action taken in 1988 on the right of peoples to self-determination and on the speedy granting of independence to colonial countries by the Commission on Human Rights and the Economic and Social Council. The report presented the views of nine Governments, five United Nations bodies, three specialized agencies and five NGOs.

GENERAL ASSEMBLY ACTION

As in previous years, the General Assembly adopted in 1988 two resolutions on the right to self-determination, a right it repeatedly reaffirmed for individual Non-Self-Governing Territories (see PART FOUR, Chapter I). On 8 December, on the recommendation of the Third Committee, it adopted **resolution 43/105** without vote.

Universal realization of the right of peoples to self-determination

The General Assembly,

Reaffirming the importance, for the effective guarantee and observance of human rights, of the universal realization of the right of peoples to self-determination enshrined in the Charter of the United Nations and embodied in the International Covenants on Human Rights, as well as in the Declaration on the Granting of Independence to Colonial Countries and Peoples contained in General Assembly resolution 1514(XV) of 14 December 1960,

Welcoming the progressive exercise of the right to self-determination by peoples under colonial, foreign or alien occupation and their emergence into sovereign statehood and independence,

Deeply concerned about the continuation of acts or threats of foreign military intervention and occupation that are threatening to suppress, or have already suppressed, the right to self-determination of an increasing number of sovereign peoples and nations,

Expressing grave concern that, as a consequence of the persistence of such actions, millions of people have been and are being uprooted from their homes as refugees and displaced persons, and emphasizing the urgent need for concerted international action to alleviate their condition,

Recalling the relevant resolutions regarding the violation of the right of peoples to self-determination and other human rights as a result of foreign military intervention, aggression and occupation, adopted by the Commission on Human Rights at its thirty-sixth, thirty-seventh, thirty-eighth, thirty-ninth, fortieth, forty-first, forty-second, forty-third and forty-fourth sessions,

Reiterating its resolutions 35/35 B of 14 November 1980, 36/10 of 28 October 1981, 37/42 of 3 December 1982, 38/16 of 22 November 1983, 39/18 of 23 November 1984, 40/24 of 29 November 1985, 41/100 of 4 December 1986 and 42/94 of 7 December 1987,

Taking note of the report of the Secretary-General,

1. *Reaffirms* that the universal realization of the right of all peoples, including those under colonial, foreign and alien domination, to self-determination is a fundamental condition for the effective guarantee and observance of human rights and for the preservation and promotion of such rights;

2. *Declares its firm opposition* to acts of foreign military intervention, aggression and occupation, since these have resulted in the suppression of the right of peoples to self-determination and other human rights in certain parts of the world;

3. *Calls upon* those States responsible to cease immediately their military intervention and occupation of foreign countries and territories and all acts of repression, discrimination, exploitation and maltreatment, particularly the brutal and inhuman methods reportedly employed for the execution of these acts against the peoples concerned;

4. *Deplores* the plight of the millions of refugees and displaced persons who have been uprooted as a result

of the aforementioned acts and reaffirms their right to return to their homes voluntarily in safety and honour;

5. *Requests* the Commission on Human Rights to continue to give special attention to the violation of human rights, especially the right to self-determination, resulting from foreign military intervention, aggression or occupation;

6. *Requests* the Secretary-General to report on this issue to the General Assembly at its forty-fourth session under the item entitled "Importance of the universal realization of the right of peoples to self-determination and of the speedy granting of independence to colonial countries and peoples for the effective guarantee and observance of human rights".

General Assembly resolution 43/105

8 December 1988   Meeting 75   Adopted without vote

Approved by Third Committee (A/43/778) without vote, 27 October (meeting 23); 23-nation draft (A/C.3/43/L.5); agenda item 96.
Sponsors: Brunei Darussalam, Chile, Colombia, Comoros, Costa Rica, Djibouti, Ecuador, Jordan, Kuwait, Malaysia, Mauritania, Morocco, Nepal, Oman, Pakistan, Papua New Guinea, Philippines, Qatar, Samoa, Saudi Arabia, Somalia, Sudan, Thailand.
Meeting numbers. GA 43rd session: 3rd Committee 4-16, 23; plenary 75.

Also on 8 December, on the Third Committee's recommendation, the Assembly adopted **resolution 43/106** by recorded vote.

Importance of the universal realization of the right of peoples to self-determination and of the speedy granting of independence to colonial countries and peoples for the effective guarantee and observance of human rights

The General Assembly,

Reaffirming its faith in the importance of the implementation of the Declaration on the Granting of Independence to Colonial Countries and Peoples contained in its resolution 1514(XV) of 14 December 1960,

Reaffirming the importance of the universal realization of the right of peoples to self-determination, national sovereignty and territorial integrity and of the speedy granting of independence to colonial countries and peoples as imperatives for the full enjoyment of all human rights,

Reaffirming the obligation of all Member States to comply with the principles of the Charter of the United Nations and the resolutions of the United Nations regarding the exercise of the right to self-determination by peoples under colonial and foreign domination,

Recalling its resolution 1514(XV) and all relevant resolutions concerning the implementation of the Declaration on the Granting of Independence to Colonial Countries and Peoples,

Recalling also its resolutions on the question of Namibia, in particular resolutions 2145(XXI) of 27 October 1966 and S-14/1 of 20 September 1986, as well as the relevant Security Council resolutions, in particular resolutions 385(1976) of 30 January 1976, 435(1978) of 29 September 1978 and 601(1987) of 30 October 1987,

Recalling further the Declaration adopted by the World Conference on Sanctions against Racist South Africa and the Declaration of the International Conference for the Immediate Independence of Namibia and the Programme of Action on Namibia,

Recalling the Luanda Declaration and Programme of Action adopted by the United Nations Council for Na-

mibia at its extraordinary plenary meetings, held at Luanda from 18 to 22 May 1987,

Recalling also the final communiqué adopted by the United Nations Council for Namibia at its ministerial meeting held at United Nations Headquarters on 2 October 1987,

Bearing in mind the outcome of the International Conference on the Alliance between South Africa and Israel, held at Vienna from 11 to 13 July 1983,

Recalling with satisfaction the holding at Tunis from 7 to 9 August 1984 of the Conference of Arab Solidarity with the Struggle for Liberation in Southern Africa,

Taking note of resolutions CM/Res.1147(XLVIII) on Namibia and CM/Res.1148(XLVIII) on South Africa adopted by the Council of Ministers of the Organization of African Unity at its forty-eighth ordinary session, held at Addis Ababa from 19 to 23 May 1988,

Taking note also of the statement issued on 29 September 1988 by the President of the Security Council, on behalf of the members of the Council, in which he expressed their concern that so long after the adoption of Council resolution 435(1978) the Namibian people had not yet attained their self-determination and independence and strongly urged South Africa to comply forthwith with the resolutions and decisions of the Council, in particular resolution 435(1978), and to co-operate with the Secretary-General in its immediate, full and definitive implementation,

Gravely concerned about the continuation of the illegal occupation of Namibia by South Africa and the continued violations of the human rights of the people in the Territory and of the other peoples still under colonial domination and alien subjugation,

Gravely concerned about the continuation of the news blackout in Namibia by the racist régime of Pretoria,

Expressing support and solidarity with students, workers and parents in Namibia in their demand for the removal of the racist South African military bases from the vicinity of the schools,

Reaffirming that the system of *apartheid* imposed on the South African people constitutes a violation of the fundamental rights of that people, a crime against humanity and a constant threat to international peace and security,

Reaffirming its resolution 39/2 of 28 September 1984, and recalling Security Council resolution 554(1984) of 17 August 1984, in which the Council rejected the so-called "new constitution" as null and void, Council resolution 569(1985) of 26 July 1985 and the statement made by the President of the Council on 13 June 1986 on the nation-wide state of emergency in South Africa,

Deeply concerned about the continued terrorist acts of aggression committed by the Pretoria régime against independent African States in the region, in particular the unprovoked attacks against Botswana, Mozambique, Zambia and Zimbabwe,

Recalling its resolution 42/95 of 7 December 1987 condemning the holding of an all-white election by the racist régime in May 1987, in the midst of the state of emergency, accompanied by the muzzling of the press and the increased brutal repression of the majority, which once again clearly manifested the *apartheid* régime's arrogant defiance and intransigence,

Alarmed by the latest manoeuvre the racist régime has employed to gain credibility, namely, the staging of fraudulent municipal elections on 26 October 1988, which were designed to entrench further white supremacy,

Deeply concerned about the banning of nineteen mass democratic organizations and eighteen individuals, including the restrictions imposed on Govan Mbeki, as well as the outright banning of the End Conscription Campaign, which is committed to peaceful means of struggle against *apartheid*,

Alarmed by the increasing number of assassinations and abductions of members and leaders of the national liberation movements in Africa and elsewhere by hit squads deployed and paid by the racist régime,

Deeply concerned about the racist régime's increased attacks on the religious community and its individual leaders and the recent bombings of the offices of the mass democratic organizations, including those of the Southern Africa Catholic Bishop's Conference at Pretoria, by agents of the régime,

Deeply indignant at the persistent policy of hostility by the racist régime of South Africa against Angola, which constitutes an act of aggression against the sovereignty and territorial integrity of that country,

Recalling Security Council resolutions 527(1982) of 15 December 1982 and 535(1983) of 29 June 1983 on Lesotho, and Council resolutions 568(1985) of 21 June 1985 and 572(1985) of 30 September 1985 on Botswana,

Reaffirming the national unity and territorial integrity of the Comoros,

Recalling the Political Declaration adopted by the First Conference of Heads of State and Government of the Organization of African Unity and the League of Arab States, held at Cairo from 7 to 9 March 1977,

Recalling also the Geneva Declaration on Palestine and the Programme of Action for the Achievement of Palestinian Rights, adopted by the International Conference on the Question of Palestine,

Considering that the denial of the inalienable rights of the Palestinian people to self-determination, sovereignty, independence and return to Palestine and the brutal suppression by the Israeli forces of the heroic uprising, the *intifadah*, of the Palestinian population in the occupied territories, as well as the repeated Israeli aggression against the population of the region, constitute a serious threat to international peace and security,

Recalling Security Council resolutions 605(1987) of 22 December 1987, 607(1988) of 5 January 1988 and 608(1988) of 14 January 1988 on the deterioration of the situation of the Palestinian people in the occupied territories,

Deeply concerned and alarmed at the deplorable consequences of Israel's continuing acts of aggression against Lebanon and recalling all the relevant resolutions of the Security Council, in particular resolutions 425(1978) of 19 March 1978, 508(1982) of 5 June 1982, 509(1982) of 6 June 1982, 520(1982) of 17 September 1982 and 521(1982) of 19 September 1982,

1. *Calls upon* all States to implement fully and faithfully all the resolutions of the United Nations regarding the exercise of the right to self-determination and independence by peoples under colonial and foreign domination;

2. *Reaffirms* the legitimacy of the struggle of peoples for their independence, territorial integrity, national unity and liberation from colonial domination, *apartheid* and foreign occupation by all available means, including armed struggle;

3. *Reaffirms* the inalienable right of the Namibian people, the Palestinian people and all peoples under foreign and colonial domination to self-determination, national independence, territorial integrity, national unity and sovereignty without foreign interference;

4. *Strongly condemns* those Governments that do not recognize the right to self-determination and independence of all peoples still under colonial domination and alien subjugation, notably the peoples of Africa and the Palestinian people;

5. *Calls once again* for the full and immediate implementation of the declarations and programmes of action on Namibia and on Palestine adopted by the international conferences on those questions;

6. *Reaffirms once again* its vigorous condemnation of the continued illegal occupation of Namibia by racist South Africa;

7. *Condemns once again* the racist régime of South Africa for its installation of a so-called "interim administration" at Windhoek and declares that action to be illegal, null and void;

8. *Strongly condemns* the illegal, occupationist and racist régime of South Africa for its increased brutal repression of the Namibian people, as manifested by the continued arrest and detention without trial of leaders of the South West Africa People's Organization, trade unionists and church leaders, the cold-blooded murder and torture of children, women and the elderly, and the bombing and destruction of social and educational institutions by the racist army, police and murder squads, and demands the immediate and unconditional release of all Namibians imprisoned and detained by the Pretoria régime;

9. *Vehemently condemns* the racist régime of Pretoria for the news blackout in Namibia, the repeated destruction of editorial offices of independent papers such as *The Namibian* and the arrest of their staff members with a view to preventing them from exposing the atrocities committed by the racist troops and murder squads against the innocent civilian population;

10. *Strongly condemns* the racist régime for the brutal attack by its occupation troops against peaceful demonstrators gathered at Windhoek on 29 September 1988 to mark the tenth anniversary of the adoption of Security Council resolution 435(1978);

11. *Further condemns* the policy of "bantustanization" and reiterates its support for the oppressed people of South Africa in its just and legitimate struggle against the racist minority régime of Pretoria;

12. *Reaffirms* its rejection of the so-called "new constitution" as null and void and reiterates that peace in South Africa can be guaranteed only by the establishment of majority rule through the full and free exercise of adult suffrage by all the people in a united and undivided South Africa;

13. *Commends* the efforts of the democratic forces within the various sections of South African society that are striving towards the abolition of *apartheid* and the creation of a united non-racial democratic society in South Africa and, in this connection, recalls with satisfaction the Dakar Declaration, adopted at the meeting organized by the Institute for a Democratic Alternative for South Africa at Dakar from 9 to 12 July 1987;

14. *Strongly condemns* the holding of municipal elections on 26 October 1988, which will further entrench white supremacy, and demands the calling of free and

fair elections based on universal adult suffrage in a united and democratic South Africa;

15. *Vehemently condemns* the banning and restrictions imposed on the mass democratic movements and individuals using peaceful means of struggle against *apartheid*, as well as the restrictions imposed on Govan Mbeki, leader of the African National Congress of South Africa, who was recently released from Robben Island, and demands that these restrictions and bannings be immediately lifted;

16. *Strongly condemns* the wanton killing of peaceful and defenceless demonstrators and workers on strike, as well as the arbitrary arrests of leaders and activists of the mass democratic movement, including women and young children, and demands their immediate and unconditional release, in particular that of Nelson Mandela and Zephania Mothopeng;

17. *Strongly condemns* South Africa for the imposition, renewal and extension of the state of emergency under its repugnant Internal Security Act and calls for the immediate lifting of the state of emergency, as well as the repeal of the Internal Security Act;

18. *Strongly condemns* the increased attacks on the religious community and its leaders, and demands that the racist Pretoria régime bring to justice those responsible for the bombing of the mass democratic organizations, including the Southern Africa Catholic Bishop's Conference;

19. *Condemns* South Africa for its increasing oppression of the Namibian people, for the massive militarization of Namibia and for its armed attacks launched against the States in the region in order to destabilize them politically and to sabotage and destroy their economies;

20. *Strongly condemns* the establishment and use of armed terrorist groups by South Africa with a view to pitting them against the national liberation movements and destabilizing the legitimate Governments of southern Africa;

21. *Calls once again* for the full implementation of the provisions of the Declaration adopted by the World Conference on Sanctions against Racist South Africa and of the Declaration of the International Conference for the Immediate Independence of Namibia and the Programme of Action on Namibia;

22. *Demands once again* the immediate implementation of General Assembly resolutions ES-8/2 of 14 September 1981 and S-14/1 of 20 September 1986;

23. *Urges* all States, the specialized agencies, organizations of the United Nations system and other international organizations to extend their support to the Namibian people through their sole and legitimate representative, the South West Africa People's Organization, in its struggle to gain its right to self-determination and national independence in accordance with the Charter of the United Nations;

24. *Strongly condemns* the racist régime for its wanton arrests and detention of women and children in South Africa and Namibia and demands their immediate and unconditional release;

25. *Strongly condemns* the persistent policy of hostility and the repeated armed attacks by the racist régime of South Africa against Angola, which constitute acts of aggression against the sovereignty and the territorial integrity of that country;

26. *Demands* that the Pretoria régime respect the sovereignty and territorial integrity of Angola and the principle of non-interference in the internal affairs of other States, and demands the immediate payment of compensation to Angola for damages caused, in accordance with the relevant decisions and resolutions of the Security Council;

27. *Commends* the Government of Angola for its political will, diplomatic flexibility and constructive spirit in the search for a negotiated solution to the problems of southern Africa and welcomes the ongoing negotiations among Angola, Cuba and South Africa, mediated by the United States of America, aimed at seeking a peaceful solution to the conflict in south-western Africa;

28. *Strongly reaffirms* its solidarity with the independent African countries and national liberation movements that are victims of murderous acts of aggression and destabilization by the racist régime of Pretoria, and calls upon the international community to render increased assistance and support to these countries in order to enable them to strengthen their defence capacity, defend their sovereignty and territorial integrity and peacefully rebuild and develop;

29. *Reaffirms* that the practice of using mercenaries against sovereign States and national liberation movements constitutes a criminal act, and calls upon the Governments of all countries to enact legislation declaring the recruitment, financing and training of mercenaries in their territories and the transit of mercenaries through their territories to be punishable offences, and prohibiting their nationals from serving as mercenaries, and to report on such legislation to the Secretary-General;

30. *Strongly condemns* the continued violation of the human rights of the peoples still under colonial domination and alien subjugation, the continuation of the illegal occupation by the racist minority régime in southern Africa and the denial to the Palestinian people of their inalienable rights;

31. *Strongly condemns* the racist régime of Pretoria for its acts of destabilization against Lesotho, and strongly urges the international community to continue to extend maximum assistance to Lesotho to enable it to fulfil its international humanitarian obligations towards refugees and to use its influence on the racist régime so that it desists from such acts against Lesotho;

32. *Strongly condemns* the unprovoked and unwarranted military attacks of 14 June 1985, 19 May 1986 and 20 June 1988 on the capital of Botswana and demands that the racist régime pay full and adequate compensation to Botswana for the loss of life and damage to property;

33. *Strongly condemns* the escalation of massacres of defenceless people and the continuing destruction of economic and social infrastructures perpetrated against Mozambique by armed terrorists, who are an extension of the South African army of aggression;

34. *Denounces* the collusion between Israel and South Africa and expresses support for the Declaration of the International Conference on the Alliance between South Africa and Israel;

35. *Strongly condemns* the policy of those Western States, Israel and other States whose political, economic, military, nuclear, strategic, cultural and sports relations with the racist minority régime of South Africa encourage that régime to persist in its suppression of the aspirations of the peoples to self-determination and independence;

36. *Again demands* the immediate application of the mandatory arms embargo against South Africa, imposed

under Security Council resolution 418(1977) of 4 November 1977, by all countries and more particularly by those countries that maintain military and nuclear co-operation with the racist Pretoria régime and continue to supply it with related *matériel;*

37. *Reaffirms* all relevant resolutions adopted by the Organization of African Unity and the United Nations on the question of Western Sahara, including General Assembly resolution 42/78 of 4 December 1987, and calls upon the current Chairman of the Assembly of Heads of State and Government of the Organization of African Unity and the Secretary-General of the United Nations to continue their efforts to find a just and lasting solution to this question;

38. *Notes* the contacts between the Government of the Comoros and the Government of France in the search for a just solution to the problem of the integration of the Comorian island of Mayotte into the Comoros, in accordance with the resolutions of the Organization of African Unity and the United Nations on this question;

39. *Calls* for a substantial increase in all forms of assistance given by all States, United Nations organs, the specialized agencies and non-governmental organizations to the victims of racism, racial discrimination and *apartheid* through national liberation movements recognized by the Organization of African Unity;

40. *Demands* the immediate and unconditional release of all persons detained or imprisoned as a result of their struggle for self-determination and independence, full respect for their fundamental individual rights and compliance with article 5 of the Universal Declaration of Human Rights, under which no one shall be subjected to torture or to cruel, inhuman or degrading treatment;

41. *Strongly condemns* the constant and deliberate violations of the fundamental rights of the Palestinian people, as well as the expansionist activities of Israel in the Middle East, which constitute an obstacle to the achievement of self-determination and independence by the Palestinian people and a threat to peace and stability in the region;

42. *Urges* all States, the specialized agencies, organizations of the United Nations system and other international organizations to extend their support to the Palestinian people through its sole and legitimate representative, the Palestine Liberation Organization, in its struggle to regain its right to self-determination and independence in accordance with the Charter;

43. *Expresses its appreciation* for the material and other forms of assistance that peoples under colonial rule continue to receive from Governments, organizations of the United Nations system and intergovernmental organizations, and calls for a substantial increase in that assistance;

44. *Urges* all States, the specialized agencies and other competent organizations of the United Nations system to do their utmost to ensure the full implementation of the Declaration on the Granting of Independence to Colonial Countries and Peoples and to intensify their efforts to support peoples under colonial, foreign and racist domination in their just struggle for self-determination and independence;

45. *Requests* the Secretary-General to give maximum publicity to the Declaration on the Granting of Independence to Colonial Countries and Peoples and to give the widest possible publicity to the struggle of oppressed peoples for the achievement of their self-determination and national independence and to report periodically to the General Assembly on his activities in this regard;

46. *Decides* to consider this item at its forty-fourth session on the basis of the reports on the strengthening of assistance to colonial territories and peoples that Governments, organizations of the United Nations system and intergovernmental and non-governmental organizations have been requested to submit.

General Assembly resolution 43/106

8 December 1988   Meeting 75   124-15-15 (recorded vote)

Approved by Third Committee (A/43/778) by recorded vote (116-16-13), 27 October (meeting 23); draft by United Republic of Tanzania, for African Group (A/C.3/43/L.6), orally revised; agenda item 96.

Meeting numbers. GA 43rd session: 3rd Committee 4-16, 23; plenary 75.

Recorded vote in Assembly as follows:

In favour: Afghanistan, Albania, Algeria, Angola, Antigua and Barbuda, Argentina, Bahamas, Bahrain, Bangladesh, Barbados, Belize, Benin, Bhutan, Bolivia, Botswana, Brazil, Brunei Darussalam, Bulgaria, Burkina Faso, Burma, Burundi, Byelorussian SSR, Cameroon, Cape Verde, Central African Republic, Chad, China, Colombia, Comoros, Congo, Côte d'Ivoire, Cuba, Cyprus, Czechoslovakia, Democratic Kampuchea, Democratic Yemen, Djibouti, Dominica, Dominican Republic, Ecuador, Egypt, Ethiopia, Gabon, Gambia, German Democratic Republic, Ghana, Grenada, Guatemala, Guinea, Guinea-Bissau, Guyana, Haiti, Hungary, India, Indonesia, Iran, Iraq, Jamaica, Jordan, Kenya, Kuwait, Lao People's Democratic Republic, Lebanon, Lesotho, Liberia, Libyan Arab Jamahiriya, Madagascar, Malaysia, Maldives, Mali, Mauritania, Mauritius, Mexico, Mongolia, Morocco, Mozambique, Nepal, Nicaragua, Niger, Nigeria, Oman, Pakistan, Panama, Papua New Guinea, Peru, Philippines, Poland, Qatar, Romania, Rwanda, Saint Kitts and Nevis, Saint Lucia, Saint Vincent and the Grenadines, Sao Tome and Principe, Saudi Arabia, Senegal, Seychelles, Sierra Leone, Singapore, Solomon Islands, Somalia, Sri Lanka, Sudan, Suriname, Swaziland, Syrian Arab Republic, Thailand, Togo, Trinidad and Tobago, Tunisia, Turkey, Uganda, Ukrainian SSR, USSR, United Arab Emirates, United Republic of Tanzania, Uruguay, Vanuatu, Venezuela, Viet Nam, Yemen, Yugoslavia, Zambia, Zimbabwe.

Against: Belgium, Canada, Denmark, Finland, France, Germany, Federal Republic of, Iceland, Israel, Italy, Luxembourg, Netherlands, Norway, Sweden, United Kingdom, United States.

Abstaining: Australia, Austria, El Salvador, Equatorial Guinea, Fiji, Greece, Ireland, Japan, Malawi, Malta, New Zealand, Portugal, Samoa, Spain, Zaire.

Afghanistan

On 22 February,[19] the Commission, by a roll-call vote of 31 to 5, with 6 abstentions, reaffirmed its profound concern that the people of Afghanistan continued to be denied their right to self-determination, to determine their own form of government and to choose their economic, political and social system free from outside intervention, subversion, coercion or constraint. It called for a political settlement based on the withdrawal of foreign troops, full respect for Afghanistan's independence, sovereignty, territorial integrity and non-aligned status, and strict observance of the principle of non-interference. The Commission requested the Secretary-General to continue searching for a political solution, urged all concerned to continue co-operating with him and appealed for humanitarian relief assistance, in co-ordination with the United Nations High Commissioner for Refugees (UNHCR), to alleviate the hardship of Afghan refugees.

Kampuchea

Human Rights Commission action. By a roll-call vote of 31 to 7, with 3 abstentions, the Commission, on 22 February,[20] reiterated its condemnation of persistent gross violations of human rights in Kampuchea and reaffirmed that the continued illegal occupation of Kampuchea by foreign forces deprived Kampucheans of their right to self-determination and constituted the primary human rights violation in that country. It emphasized that the withdrawal of all foreign forces, restoration of Kampuchea's independence, sovereignty and territorial integrity, recognition of the Kampucheans' right to self-determination and the commitment by all States to non-interference in its internal affairs were essential for a solution to the Kampuchean problem. The Commission reaffirmed its call for an end to hostilities and an immediate withdrawal of foreign forces, to enable Kampucheans to exercise their fundamental rights free from foreign interference, to determine their future through free and fair elections under United Nations supervision, to make possible the return of all refugees and to allow for efforts towards a political solution within the framework of the 1981 Declaration on Kampuchea.[27] The Secretary-General was asked urgently to intensify efforts towards a political settlement and restoration of human rights in Kampuchea. The Commission noted the 1987 report of the *Ad Hoc* Committee of the International Conference on Kampuchea[28] and asked it to continue its work. It recommended that the Economic and Social Council continue to consider measures to implement recommendations to achieve the full enjoyment of fundamental human rights and freedoms of the Kampuchean people.

ECONOMIC AND SOCIAL COUNCIL ACTION

In May 1988, on the recommendation of its Second Committee, the Economic and Social Council adopted **decision 1988/143** by recorded vote.

Right of peoples to self-determination and its application to peoples under colonial or alien domination or foreign occupation

At its 16th plenary meeting, on 27 May 1988, the Economic and Social Council fully endorsed Commission on Human Rights resolution 1988/6 of 22 February 1988, by which the Commission, *inter alia*, reaffirmed that the continuing occupation of Kampuchea by foreign forces deprived the people of Kampuchea of the exercise of their right to self-determination and constituted the primary violation of human rights in that country at the current time. The Council reaffirmed its decisions 1981/154 of 8 May 1981, 1982/143 of 7 May 1982, 1983/155 of 27 May 1983, 1984/148 of 24 May 1984, 1985/155 of 30 May 1985, 1986/146 of 23 May 1986 and 1987/155 of 29 May 1987 and reiterated its call for the withdrawal of all foreign forces from Kampuchea in order to allow the people of Kampuchea to exercise their fundamental freedoms and human rights, including the right to self-determination as contained in the Declaration on Kampuchea adopted by the International Conference on Kampuchea on 17 July 1981 and in General

Assembly resolutions 34/22 of 14 November 1979, 35/6 of 22 October 1980, 36/5 of 21 October 1981, 37/6 of 28 October 1982, 38/3 of 27 October 1983, 39/5 of 30 October 1984, 40/7 of 5 November 1985, 41/6 of 21 October 1986 and 42/3 of 14 October 1987.

The Council expressed its grave concern at the unresolved dilemma of the approximately 292,000 Kampuchean civilians still stranded in Thailand as a result of the armed attacks by the foreign forces in Kampuchea on the Kampuchean civilian encampments along the Thai-Kampuchean border since 1984. In that connection, the Council recalled the statements made by the Secretary-General on 27 December 1984 and 13 March 1985, in which, *inter alia*, he appealed to all concerned to avoid endangering the lives of those Kampuchean civilians and adding to the misery and deprivation that already afflicted those most unfortunate people.

The Council also expressed its grave concern at the continued violation of human rights by the foreign occupying force in Kampuchea of Kampuchean nationals in their homeland, as well as of innocent Kampuchean displaced persons seeking temporary shelter in encampments along the border.

The Council requested the Secretary-General to report to the Council any further violations of humanitarian principles perpetrated against Kampuchean civilian refugees by the foreign occupying troops along the border, and also requested him to continue to monitor closely the developments in Kampuchea and to intensify efforts, including the use of his good offices, to bring about a comprehensive political settlement of the Kampuchean problem and the restoration of fundamental human rights there.

The Council recalled the communiqués issued by the *Ad Hoc* Committee of the International Conference on Kampuchea on 17 January and 15 February 1985. The Council noted the visits undertaken by the Chairman and members of the Committee to a number of countries in 1987 in an effort to find a comprehensive political solution to the Kampuchean problem. The Council also noted with appreciation the ongoing efforts of the Committee and requested that the Committee continue its work, pending the reconvening of the Conference.

Economic and Social Council decision 1988/143

40-9-2 (recorded vote)

Approved by Second Committee (E/1988/89/Add.1) by vote (37-8), 23 May (meeting 21); 44-nation draft (E/1988/C.2/L.6); agenda item 10.

Sponsors: Bangladesh, Belgium, Belize, Brunei Darussalam, Cameroon, Canada, Colombia, Costa Rica, Denmark, Fiji, Gambia, Germany, Federal Republic of, Greece, Haiti, Honduras, Iceland, Italy, Japan, Liberia, Luxembourg, Malaysia, Morocco, Nepal, Netherlands, Norway, Oman, Pakistan, Papua New Guinea, Philippines, Rwanda, Saint Lucia, Samoa, Senegal, Sierra Leone, Singapore, Somalia, Spain, Sudan, Thailand, Togo, Turkey, United Kingdom, Uruguay, Zaire.

Recorded vote in Council as follows:

In favour: Australia, Belgium, Belize, Canada, China, Colombia, Denmark, Djibouti, Egypt, France, Gabon, Germany, Federal Republic of, Ghana, Greece, Guinea, Ireland, Italy, Jamaica, Japan, Lesotho, Liberia, Norway, Oman, Pakistan, Panama, Peru, Philippines, Portugal, Rwanda, Saudi Arabia, Sierra Leone, Somalia, Sri Lanka, Sudan, United Kingdom, United States, Uruguay, Venezuela, Yugoslavia, Zaire.

Against: Bulgaria, Byelorussian SSR, Cuba, German Democratic Republic, India, Libyan Arab Jamahiriya, Poland, Syrian Arab Republic, USSR.

Abstaining: Iraq, Trinidad and Tobago.

Palestinians

By a resolution of 22 February,[21] adopted by a roll-call vote of 30 to 4, with 8 abstentions, the

Commission condemned Israel for its continued occupation of the Palestinian and other Arab territories and called on it to withdraw, in compliance with its obligations under the Charter of the United Nations. It reaffirmed the right of the Palestinians to self-determination, to regain their rights in accordance with the Charter and United Nations resolutions, and to return to their homes and property. The Commission reaffirmed the right of the Palestine Liberation Organization (PLO), as the sole legitimate representative of the Palestinian people, to participate fully in all efforts concerning the question of Palestine. Reaffirming its support for an international peace conference on the Middle East, the Commission expressed deep regret at the negative attitude of some States towards the conference. States, United Nations bodies and other international organizations were urged to support the Palestinians, through PLO, in the struggle to restore their rights. The Secretary-General was requested to make available to the Commission, prior to its 1989 session, all information pertaining to the implementation of its resolution and to transmit the resolution to Israel.

South Africa and Namibia

Human Rights Commission action. The Commission, by a 29 February resolution adopted by a roll-call vote of 33 to 3, with 7 abstentions,[22] called on States to take steps to enable the people of South Africa and Namibia to exercise fully and without further delay their right to self-determination and independence. It reaffirmed the right of Namibians to self-determination, freedom and independence in a united Namibia, as well as the legitimacy of their struggle and that of the oppressed people of South Africa by all means, including armed struggle. It urged all States to assist them and called for the full implementation of the 1986 Paris[29] and Vienna Declarations[30] and the Programme of Action adopted in the same year by the International Conference for the Immediate Independence of Namibia.[30] The Commission rejected the so-called "constitutional initiative", including the "statutory council". Condemning South Africa's acts of aggression and destabilization against front-line and other neighbouring States, it demanded the imposition of mandatory sanctions against South Africa. The Commission also condemned: the policy of bantustanization; the illegal occupation of Namibia and South Africa's attempts to dismember its territory; and censorship and other restrictions imposed on the media. It demanded the immediate release of all people detained or imprisoned as a result of their struggle for self-determination and that South Africa end its acts of aggression and withdraw its occupation forces from Angola.

In a related resolution,[31] the Commission reaffirmed the inalienable right of the oppressed people of Namibia to self-determination and independence and reiterated that that right could be exercised by the Namibians only in accordance with conditions determined by the Security Council in 1978.[32]

Sub-Commission action. On 25 August,[33] the Sub-Commission asked the Secretary-General to make available, through the Centre for Human Rights, to the authorities of the new Constituent Assembly of Namibia, when it was duly constituted, such human rights advisory services as they might require and expressed its willingness to assist them. On the same date,[34] the Sub-Commission appealed to the international community to assist concerned parties in their efforts to bring about the independence of Namibia, in accordance with a 1978 Security Council resolution.[35]

(For human rights violations in South Africa and Namibia, see below, under "Human rights violations". For details on the situation in Namibia, see PART FOUR, Chapter III.)

Western Sahara

On 22 February,[23] by a roll-call vote of 27 to none, with 15 abstentions, the Commission reaffirmed that the question of Western Sahara was one of decolonization to be completed through the exercise of the people's right to self-determination and independence. It also reaffirmed that a political solution lay in the implementation of a 1983 OAU resolution quoted in a General Assembly resolution.[36] It joined in the Assembly's appeal to the parties to the conflict to display the political will to implement that resolution, as well as others adopted in 1985,[37] 1986[38] and 1987.[39] The Commission took note of a joint decision of the OAU Chairman and the United Nations Secretary-General to send a mission to Western Sahara to collect relevant technical information to assist them in discharging the mandate entrusted to them by the Assembly in those resolutions. It again requested the parties to the conflict, the Kingdom of Morocco and the Frente Popular para la Liberación de Saguia el-Hamra y de Río de Oro, to negotiate directly with a view to bringing about a cease-fire and creating conditions for a referendum for self-determination.

Mercenaries

Human Rights Commission action. On 22 February,[24] the Commission, by a roll-call vote of 30 to 11, with 1 abstention, condemned the increased recruitment, financing, training, assembly, transit and use of mercenaries and urged all States to prohibit such activities. It denounced any State that persisted in recruiting mercenaries and providing facilities for launching armed aggression against other States, and called on all States to ensure, by administrative and legislative measures, that States, territories under their control and their nationals were not used for mercenarism. Taking note of the Special Rapporteur's report (see below), the Commission decided to continue his mandate for another year so that he might submit further conclusions and recommendations. It asked him to: develop further the position that mercenarism violated human rights and thwarted the self-determination of peoples; strengthen his co-operation and co-ordination with concerned bodies of the United Nations system; study credible and reliable reports of mercenary activity in African and other developing countries; and to submit in 1989 a report to the Commission and a preliminary report to the General Assembly. All Governments were urged to facilitate the Special Rapporteur's task and to invite him to conduct on-site visits where appropriate. The Secretary-General was asked to provide all necessary assistance to the Special Rapporteur and to appeal to Governments to assist him in the performance of his duties. The Commission recommended that the Economic and Social Council ensure the necessary financial resources and staff to implement its resolution.

ECONOMIC AND SOCIAL COUNCIL ACTION

In May, on the recommendation of its Second Committee, the Economic and Social Council adopted **decision 1988/126** by recorded vote.

Use of mercenaries as a means of impeding the exercise of the right of peoples to self-determination

At its 16th plenary meeting, on 27 May 1988, the Economic and Social Council, taking note of Commission on Human Rights resolution 1988/7 of 22 February 1988, approved the decision of the Commission to continue for another year the mandate of the Special Rapporteur to examine the question of the use of mercenaries as a means of impeding the exercise of the right of peoples to self-determination in order to enable him to submit further conclusions and recommendations to the Commission, and also approved the Commission's request to the Secretary-General to continue to provide all necessary assistance to the Special Rapporteur, including the necessary financial resources and sufficient staff.

Economic and Social Council decision 1988/126

39-13-2 (recorded vote)

Approved by Second Committee (E/1988/89/Add.1) by recorded vote (38-13-2), 23 May (meeting 20); draft by Commission on Human Rights (E/1988/12 & Corr.1); agenda item 10.

Recorded vote in Council as follows:

In favour: Belize, Bolivia, Bulgaria, Byelorussian SSR, China, Colombia, Cuba, Djibouti, Egypt, Gabon, German Democratic Republic, Ghana, Guinea, India, Iran, Iraq, Jamaica, Lesotho, Liberia, Libyan Arab Jamahiriya, Mozambique, Pakistan, Panama, Peru, Philippines, Poland, Rwanda, Saudi Arabia, Sierra Leone, Somalia, Sri Lanka, Sudan, Syrian Arab Republic, Trinidad and Tobago, USSR, Uruguay, Venezuela, Yugoslavia, Zaire.

Against: Belgium, Canada, Denmark, France, Germany, Federal Republic of, Greece, Ireland, Italy, Japan, Norway, Portugal, United Kingdom, United States.

Abstaining: Australia, Oman.

Reports of the Special Rapporteur. Pursuant to a 1987 General Assembly request,[40] the Secretary-General, on 3 October 1988,[41] transmitted a report prepared by Special Rapporteur Enrique Bernales Ballesteros (Peru). The report reviewed the history of mercenarism, drawing attention to mercenary practices affecting the right of peoples to self-determination. It presented information on the international handling of complaints, the current state of international law on the subject, the instruments in force concerning mercenarism and the work of the United Nations *Ad Hoc* Committee on the Drafting of an International Convention against the Recruitment, Use, Financing and Training of Mercenaries (see PART FIVE, Chapter II). The report discussed complaints received relating to mercenary activities and the legislative provisions enacted by some States to combat and punish mercenary practices. The report contained a typology of mercenary activities and analysed the definition of "mercenary". It concluded, among other things, that mercenary practices had increased, had spread from Africa to other continents and had become a complex phenomenon. It further concluded that the main areas of mercenary activity were in southern Africa and Central America and recommended further investigation of complaints received concerning those areas.

The Secretary-General, on 21 October, transmitted the Special Rapporteur's preliminary report to the General Assembly.[42] The Special Rapporteur described his visit to Angola in August at the invitation of the Government, where he met with government officials, members of the South West Africa People's Organization and the African National Congress of South Africa regarding the alleged presence of mercenaries in Angola, supported by the Government of South Africa. He recommended the adoption of policies to penalize mercenary activities, support for the *Ad Hoc* Committee, reiteration by the Assembly of its condemnation of the practice, and the thorough investigation of complaints of mercenary practices in southern and south-west Africa.

GENERAL ASSEMBLY ACTION

On 8 December 1988, on the recommendation of the Third Committee, the General Assembly adopted **resolution 43/107** by recorded vote.

Use of mercenaries as a means to violate human rights and to impede the exercise of the right of peoples to self-determination

The General Assembly,

Bearing in mind the need for strict observance of the principles of sovereign equality, political independence, territorial integrity of States and self-determination of peoples, as well as scrupulous respect for the principle of the non-use or threat of the use of force in international relations, enshrined in the Charter of the United Nations and developed in the Declaration on Principles of International Law concerning Friendly Relations and Co-operation among States in accordance with the Charter of the United Nations,

Reaffirming the legitimacy of the struggle of peoples and their liberation movements for their independence, territorial integrity, national unity and liberation from colonial domination, *apartheid* and foreign intervention and occupation, and that their legitimate struggle can in no way be considered as or equated to mercenary activity,

Deeply concerned about the increasing menace that the activities of mercenaries represent for all States, particularly African, Central American and other developing States,

Recognizing that the use of mercenaries is a threat to international peace and security,

Recognizing also that the activities of mercenaries are contrary to fundamental principles of international law, such as non-interference in the internal affairs of States, territorial integrity and independence, and seriously impede the process of self-determination of peoples struggling against colonialism, racism and *apartheid* and all forms of foreign domination,

Recalling all of its relevant resolutions, particularly resolution 42/96 of 7 December 1987, in which it denounced the practice of using mercenaries, in particular against developing countries and national liberation movements,

Recalling also Security Council resolutions 239(1967) of 10 July 1967, 405(1977) of 14 April 1977, 419(1977) of 24 November 1977, 496(1981) of 15 December 1981 and 507(1982) of 28 May 1982, in which the Council, *inter alia*, condemned any State that persisted in permitting or tolerating the recruitment of mercenaries, and the provision of facilities to them, with the objective of overthrowing the Governments of States Members of the United Nations,

Welcoming Commission on Human Rights resolution 1988/7 of 22 February 1988, in which the Commission condemned the increased recruitment, financing, training, assembly, transit and use of mercenaries,

Reaffirming its decision, in its resolution 32/130 of 16 December 1977, to accord priority to the search for solutions to the mass and flagrant violations of human rights of peoples and persons affected by situations such as those resulting, *inter alia*, from aggression and threats against national sovereignty, national unity and territorial integrity,

Recalling the relevant resolutions of the Organization of African Unity and the convention adopted by the Assembly of Heads of State and Government of the Organization of African Unity at its fourteenth ordinary session, held at Libreville from 2 to 5 July 1977, condemning and outlawing the use of mercenaries and its adverse effects on the independence and territorial integrity of African States,

Deeply concerned about the loss of life, the substantial damage to property and the short-term and long-term negative effects on the economy of southern African countries resulting from mercenary aggression,

Taking note with appreciation of the reports of the Special Rapporteur of the Commission on Human Rights on the question of the use of mercenaries as a means of impeding the exercise of the right of peoples to self-determination,

1. *Condemns* the increased recruitment, financing, training, assembly, transit and use of mercenaries, as well as all other forms of support to mercenaries for the purpose of destabilizing and overthrowing the Governments of southern Africa and Central America and of other developing States and fighting against the national liberation movements of peoples struggling for the exercise of their right to self-determination;

2. *Strongly condemns* the racist régime of South Africa for its increasing use of groups of armed mercenaries against national liberation movements and for the destabilization of the Governments of southern African States;

3. *Denounces* any State that persists in the recruitment, or permits or tolerates the recruitment, of mercenaries and provides facilities to them for launching armed aggression against other States;

4. *Calls upon* all States to exercise the utmost vigilance against the menace posed by the activities of mercenaries and to ensure, by both administrative and legislative measures, that the territory of those States and other territories under their control, as well as their nationals, are not used for the recruitment, assembly, financing, training and transit of mercenaries, or the planning of such activities designed to destabilize or overthrow the Government of any State and to fight the national liberation movements struggling against racism, *apartheid*, colonial domination and foreign intervention and occupation for their independence, territorial integrity and national unity;

5. *Urges* all States to take the necessary measures under their respective domestic laws to prohibit the recruitment, financing, training and transit of mercenaries on their territory;

6. *Calls upon* all States to extend humanitarian assistance to victims of situations resulting from the use of mercenaries, as well as from colonial or alien domination or foreign occupation;

7. *Considers* it inadmissible to use channels of humanitarian and other assistance to finance, train and arm mercenaries;

8. *Welcomes* the provisions of Commission on Human Rights resolution 1988/7 aimed at giving the Special Rapporteur on the question of the use of mercenaries the full opportunity to carry out his mandate most effectively;

9. *Expresses its appreciation* to the Special Rapporteur for his reports and especially for his preliminary conclusions and recommendations;

10. *Decides* to examine at its forty-fourth session the question of the use of mercenaries as a means to violate human rights and to impede the exercise of the right of peoples to self-determination under the item entitled "Importance of the universal realization of the right of peoples to self-determination and of the speedy granting of independence to colonial countries and peoples for the effective guarantee and observance of human rights";

11. *Emphasizes* the importance of having the Special Rapporteur present his report during the consideration of the item entitled "Importance of the universal realization of the right of peoples to self-determination and of the speedy granting of independence to colonial countries and peoples for the effective guarantee and observance of human rights", and requests the Secretary-General to make the same report available to the *Ad Hoc* Committee on the Drafting of an International Convention against the Recruitment, Use, Financing and Training of Mercenaries, for its information.

General Assembly resolution 43/107

8 December 1988   Meeting 75   125-10-21 (recorded vote)

Approved by Third Committee (A/43/778/Add.1) by recorded vote (107-10-22), 29 November (meeting 56); 37-nation draft (A/C.3/43/L.12), orally revised, and orally amended by Morocco; agenda item 96.

Sponsors: Algeria, Angola, Benin, Botswana, Bulgaria, Burkina Faso, Cameroon, Congo, Cuba, Ethiopia, German Democratic Republic, Ghana, Guinea, India, Kenya, Lesotho, Libyan Arab Jamahiriya, Madagascar, Malawi, Mongolia, Nicaragua, Nigeria, Panama, Peru, Rwanda, Sierra Leone, Somalia, Sudan, Swaziland, Syrian Arab Republic, Togo, Uganda, Ukrainian SSR, United Republic of Tanzania, Viet Nam, Zambia, Zimbabwe.

Meeting numbers. GA 43rd session: 3rd Committee 4-16, 56; plenary 75.

Recorded vote in Assembly as follows:

In favour: Afghanistan, Albania, Algeria, Angola, Antigua and Barbuda, Argentina, Bahamas, Bahrain, Bangladesh, Barbados, Belize, Benin, Bhutan, Bolivia, Botswana, Brazil, Brunei Darussalam, Bulgaria, Burkina Faso, Burma, Burundi, Byelorussian SSR, Cameroon, Cape Verde, Central African Republic, Chad, China, Colombia, Comoros, Congo, Côte d'Ivoire, Cuba, Cyprus, Czechoslovakia, Democratic Kampuchea, Democratic Yemen, Djibouti, Dominica, Dominican Republic, Ecuador, Egypt, Ethiopia, Fiji, Gabon, Gambia, German Democratic Republic, Ghana, Grenada, Guatemala, Guinea, Guinea-Bissau, Guyana, Haiti, Hungary, India, Indonesia, Iran, Iraq, Jamaica, Jordan, Kenya, Kuwait, Lao People's Democratic Republic, Lebanon, Lesotho, Liberia, Libyan Arab Jamahiriya, Madagascar, Malawi, Malaysia, Maldives, Mali, Malta, Mauritania, Mexico, Mongolia, Morocco, Mozambique, Nepal, Nicaragua, Niger, Nigeria, Pakistan, Panama, Papua New Guinea, Peru, Philippines, Poland, Qatar, Romania, Rwanda, Saint Kitts and Nevis, Saint Lucia, Saint Vincent and the Grenadines, Sao Tome and Principe, Saudi Arabia, Senegal, Seychelles, Sierra Leone, Singapore, Solomon Islands, Somalia, Sri Lanka, Sudan, Suriname, Swaziland, Syrian Arab Republic, Thailand, Togo, Trinidad and Tobago, Tunisia, Uganda, Ukrainian SSR, USSR, United Arab Emirates, United Republic of Tanzania, Uruguay, Vanuatu, Venezuela, Viet Nam, Yemen, Yugoslavia, Zaire, Zambia, Zimbabwe.

Against: Belgium, France, Germany, Federal Republic of, Italy, Japan, Luxembourg, Netherlands, Portugal, United Kingdom, United States.

Abstaining: Australia, Austria, Canada, Costa Rica, Denmark, El Salvador, Equatorial Guinea, Finland, Greece, Honduras, Iceland, Ireland, Israel, Mauritius, New Zealand, Norway, Paraguay, Samoa, Spain, Sweden, Turkey.

Before the vote in the Assembly, Nigeria introduced an amendment to paragraph 11,[43] which was adopted by a recorded vote of 123 to 6, with 21 abstentions.

Rights of detained persons

Administration of justice

Human Rights Commission action. On 8 March,[13] the Commission urged its Sub-Commission to pursue consideration of the issue of independence and impartiality of the judiciary, jurors and assessors and the independence of lawyers, based on a 1985 report of the Sub-Commission's Special Rapporteur.[44] It requested the Sub-Commission to continue to give attention to the question of a declaration against the unacknowledged detention of persons. The Commission also called on its special rapporteurs and working groups to give attention to the effective protection of human rights in the administration of justice, particularly the unacknowledged detention of persons, and asked the Secretary-General to provide the necessary resources to ensure close co-operation between the Centre for Human Rights and the Centre for Social Development and Humanitarian Affairs. It also asked him to continue to assist States, at their request, in implementing existing international human rights standards in the administration of justice.

Report of the Secretary-General. The Secretary-General presented to the Sub-Commission in June succinct information on the work of the Human Rights Committee and CERD, developments elsewhere in the human rights programme, and activities within the United Nations programme on crime prevention and control related to the rights of persons detained or imprisoned. The Secretary-General covered extra-legal, arbitrary and summary executions; safeguards guaranteeing protection of the rights of those facing the death penalty; the report of the Working Group on Enforced or Involuntary Disappearances (see below); torture and other cruel, inhuman or degrading treatment or punishment; the draft body of principles for the protection of persons under any form of detention; preparation for the Eighth (1990) United Nations Congress on the Prevention of Crime and the Treatment of Offenders (see PART THREE, Chapter XII); juvenile justice; victims of crime and abuse of power; the independence of the judiciary; and draft basic principles on the use of force and firearms by law enforcement officials.

Sub-Commission action. On 17 August,[45] the Sub-Commission asked the Secretary-General to communicate to the Committee on Crime Prevention and Control, in time for consideration at its August 1988 session (see PART THREE, Chapter XII), suggestions relating to the draft principles on the effective prevention and investigation of extra-legal, arbitrary and summary executions and the draft basic principles on the use of force and firearms by law enforcement officials.

GENERAL ASSEMBLY ACTION

On 8 December 1988, on the recommendation of the Third Committee, the General Assembly adopted **resolution 43/153** without vote.

Human rights in the administration of justice

The General Assembly,

Guided by the principles embodied in articles 3, 5, 9, 10 and 11 of the Universal Declaration of Human Rights, as well as the relevant provisions of the International Covenant on Civil and Political Rights, in particular article 6, which explicitly states that no one shall be arbitrarily deprived of his life and prohibits the imposition of the death penalty for crimes committed by persons below eighteen years of age,

Guided also by the relevant principles embodied in the Convention against Torture and Other Cruel, Inhuman or Degrading Treatment or Punishment and in the International Convention on the Elimination of All Forms of Racial Discrimination,

Calling attention to the Declaration of Basic Principles of Justice for Victims of Crime and Abuse of Power and the safeguards guaranteeing protection of the rights of those facing the death penalty, as well as to the Basic Principles on the Independence of the Judiciary, the Code of Conduct for Law Enforcement Officials and the Standard Minimum Rules for the Treatment of Prisoners,

Convinced of the importance of the finalization and adoption of the draft Body of Principles for the Protection of All Persons under Any Form of Detention or Imprisonment,

Reaffirming the importance of the principles contained in its resolution 41/120 of 4 December 1986 on setting international standards in the field of human rights,

Recalling its resolutions 40/146 of 13 December 1985, 41/149 of 4 December 1986 and 42/143 of 7 December 1987 on human rights in the administration of justice,

Recognizing the important contribution of the Commission on Human Rights in the field of human rights in the administration of justice, as reflected in its resolutions 1988/33 of 8 March 1988 on human rights in the administration of justice, 1988/40 of 8 March 1988 on the independence and impartiality of the judiciary, jurors and assessors and the independence of lawyers, 1988/45 of 8 March 1988 on administrative detention without charge or trial and 1988/68 of 10 March 1988 on summary or arbitrary executions,

Acknowledging the important work accomplished in this field by the United Nations within the framework of its programme of work in crime prevention and criminal justice, as reaffirmed, *inter alia*, by the Economic and Social Council in its resolution 1988/44 of 27 May 1988 and the results of the Committee on Crime Prevention and Control at its tenth session,

Convinced of the need for further co-ordinated and concerted action in promoting respect for human rights in the administration of justice,

1. *Reaffirms* the importance of the full implementation of United Nations norms and standards on human rights in the administration of justice;

2. *Urges* Member States to develop strategies for the practical implementation of these standards, in particular:

(*a*) To adopt in national legislation and practice existing international standards relating to human rights in the administration of justice, and to make them available to all persons concerned;

(*b*) To design realistic and effective mechanisms for the full implementation of these standards and to provide the necessary administrative and judicial structures for their continuous monitoring;

(*c*) To devise measures to promote the observance of these standards, as well as public awareness about their important role, in particular through their widespread dissemination and through educational and promotional activities;

(*d*) To include, where appropriate, references to the implementation of these standards in their reports under the various international human rights instruments;

(*e*) To increase, as far as possible, their support to technical co-operation and advisory services at all levels for the more effective implementation of these standards, either directly or through international funding agencies such as the United Nations Development Programme, when developing countries include specific projects in their country programmes;

3. *Notes with appreciation* that the United Nations system continues to give special attention to the elaboration of standards in this field, as mandated by the Economic and Social Council in its resolution 1986/10 of 21 May 1986, including on the use of force and firearms by law enforcement officials as well as with regard to unacknowledged detention of persons and on the independence and impartiality of the judiciary, jurors and assessors and independence of lawyers;

4. *Encourages* the relevant bodies within the United Nations pursuing the setting of new standards in this field to continue their efforts with regard to subjects such as extra-legal, summary or arbitrary executions, or the question of states of emergency;

5. *Urges* all bodies working on these issues to take fully into account the provisions of its resolution 41/120;

6. *Emphasizes* the importance of education and public information programmes in this field for law students, the legal profession and all those responsible for the administration of justice;

7. *Stresses* the significant role of the regional commissions concerned, the specialized agencies, the United Nations institutes in the area of human rights and crime prevention and criminal justice and other organizations of the United Nations system, as well as intergovernmental and non-governmental organizations, including national professional associations concerned with promoting United Nations standards in this field;

8. *Welcomes* the steps initiated by the Centre for Human Rights and the Crime Prevention and Criminal Justice Branch of the Centre for Social Development and Humanitarian Affairs of the Secretariat to ensure closer co-operation, with regard to the prevention of crime and the treatment of offenders, on all matters of human rights in the administration of justice, especially with respect to criminal violations of human rights and mass victimization;

9. *Requests* the Secretary-General:

(*a*) To continue to provide all necessary support to United Nations bodies working on the setting of standards in this field;

(*b*) To continue to assist Member States, at their request, in implementing existing international human rights standards in the administration of justice, in particular under the programme of advisory services;

(*c*) To develop further the recently created focal points within the Centre for Human Rights and the Centre for Social Development and Humanitarian Affairs to monitor the human rights aspects of the administration of justice within the various elements of United Nations programmes in this field, as well as the work of specialized agencies, regional organizations and non-governmental organizations in consultative status, and to provide, as appropriate, advice on co-ordination and other relevant issues in this field;

(*d*) To co-ordinate the various technical advisory services carried out by the Centre for Human Rights and the Crime Prevention and Criminal Justice Branch with a view to undertaking joint programmes and strengthening existing mechanisms for the protection of human rights in the administration of justice;

(*e*) To draw the attention of special rapporteurs and working groups in the field of human rights to the importance of questions relating to the effective protection of human rights in the administration of justice, in particular with regard to states of emergency;

10. *Encourages* the development of diversified funding strategies, including recourse to voluntary and mixed multilateral and bilateral contributions for specific projects on human rights in the administration of justice, and the increasing involvement of United Nations

development agencies, in particular the United Nations Development Programme;

11. *Draws the attention* of the Commission on Human Rights and its Sub-Commission on Prevention of Discrimination and Protection of Minorities, as well as of the regional preparatory meetings for the Eighth United Nations Congress on the Prevention of Crime and the Treatment of Offenders, to the issues raised in the present resolution;

12. *Decides* to consider at its forty-fourth session the question of human rights in the administration of justice.

General Assembly resolution 43/153

8 December 1988   Meeting 75   Adopted without vote

Approved by Third Committee (A/43/868) without vote, 30 November (meeting 57); 19-nation draft (A/C.3/43/L.76), orally revised; agenda item 12.
Sponsors: Argentina, Australia, Austria, Belgium, Canada, Colombia, Costa Rica, Cyprus, Denmark, Finland, Germany, Federal Republic of, Iceland, Italy, Netherlands, New Zealand, Norway, Samoa, Sweden, United Kingdom.
Meeting numbers. GA 43rd session: 3rd Committee 49-57; plenary 75.

Treatment of prisoners and detainees

In connection with the Sub-Commission's review of developments in the administration of justice and the human rights of detainees, the Secretary-General submitted in June 1988 a report[46] summarizing information received from 14 Governments. Also in June,[47] he summarized information from two specialized agencies, one United Nations body and two intergovernmental organizations. In July,[48] he presented a synopsis of material from NGOs.

Draft principles
for the protection of detainees

Sub-Commission action. A five-member sessional Working Group on Detention, set up by the Sub-Commission, met from 10 to 17 and on 22 and 26 August to consider, among other things, a draft Body of Principles for the Protection of All Persons under Any Form of Detention or Imprisonment.[49] The Working Group decided to recommend to the Sub-Commission that it bring to the attention of the General Assembly's Sixth (Legal) Committee Working Group charged with drafting the text certain questions concerning the text which were annexed to the body of principles provisionally approved by the Group in 1987.[50] On 1 September,[51] the Sub-Commission thus requested the Secretary-General to do so. The draft text and questions were also annexed to the report of the Working Group on Detention. Also on 1 September,[52] the Sub-Commission asked the Secretary-General to transmit the annex to Governments, the Centre for Social Development and Humanitarian Affairs, the Working Group on Enforced and Involuntary Disappearances, intergovernmental organizations and NGOs for comments and suggestions and to transmit a summary of that information to the Working Group on Detention prior to its 1989 session.

Sixth Committee Working Group. In accordance with a 1987 General Assembly decision,[53]

a Working Group of the Sixth Committee met from 4 October to 16 November 1988 to complete the elaboration of the draft Body of Principles.[54] The Working Group considered questions left pending at the Assembly's 1987 session and examined suggestions by delegations to the text, as provisionally adopted. The Group reviewed the draft for accuracy and consistency, thus completing its elaboration. The text, as contained in the Working Group's report, was submitted to the Sixth Committee for consideration and adoption.

GENERAL ASSEMBLY ACTION

On 9 December 1988, on the recommendation of the Sixth Committee, the General Assembly adopted **resolution 43/173** without vote.

Body of Principles for the Protection of All Persons under Any Form of Detention or Imprisonment
The General Assembly,

Recalling its resolution 35/177 of 15 December 1980, in which it referred the task of elaborating the draft Body of Principles for the Protection of All Persons under Any Form of Detention or Imprisonment to the Sixth Committee and decided to establish an open-ended working group for that purpose,

Taking note of the report of the Working Group on the Draft Body of Principles for the Protection of All Persons under Any Form of Detention or Imprisonment, which met during the forty-third session of the General Assembly and completed the elaboration of the draft Body of Principles,

Considering that the Working Group decided to submit the text of the draft Body of Principles to the Sixth Committee for its consideration and adoption,

Convinced that the adoption of the draft Body of Principles would make an important contribution to the protection of human rights,

Considering the need to ensure the wide dissemination of the text of the Body of Principles,

1. *Approves* the Body of Principles for the Protection of All Persons under Any Form of Detention or Imprisonment, the text of which is annexed to the present resolution;

2. *Expresses its appreciation* to the Working Group on the Draft Body of Principles for the Protection of All Persons under Any Form of Detention or Imprisonment for its important contribution to the elaboration of the Body of Principles;

3. *Requests* the Secretary-General to inform the States Members of the United Nations or members of specialized agencies of the adoption of the Body of Principles;

4. *Urges* that every effort be made so that the Body of Principles becomes generally known and respected.

ANNEX
Body of Principles for the Protection of All Persons under Any Form of Detention or Imprisonment

Scope of the Body of Principles

These principles apply for the protection of all persons under any form of detention or imprisonment.

Use of terms

For the purposes of the Body of Principles:

(a) "Arrest" means the act of apprehending a person for the alleged commission of an offence or by the action of an authority;

(b) "Detained person" means any person deprived of personal liberty except as a result of conviction for an offence;

(c) "Imprisoned person" means any person deprived of personal liberty as a result of conviction for an offence;

(d) "Detention" means the condition of detained persons as defined above;

(e) "Imprisonment" means the condition of imprisoned persons as defined above;

(f) The words "a judicial or other authority" mean a judicial or other authority under the law whose status and tenure should afford the strongest possible guarantees of competence, impartiality and independence.

Principle 1

All persons under any form of detention or imprisonment shall be treated in a humane manner and with respect for the inherent dignity of the human person.

Principle 2

Arrest, detention or imprisonment shall only be carried out strictly in accordance with the provisions of the law and by competent officials or persons authorized for that purpose.

Principle 3

There shall be no restriction upon or derogation from any of the human rights of persons under any form of detention or imprisonment recognized or existing in any State pursuant to law, conventions, regulations or custom on the pretext that this Body of Principles does not recognize such rights or that it recognizes them to a lesser extent.

Principle 4

Any form of detention or imprisonment and all measures affecting the human rights of a person under any form of detention or imprisonment shall be ordered by, or be subject to the effective control of, a judicial or other authority.

Principle 5

1. These principles shall be applied to all persons within the territory of any given State, without distinction of any kind, such as race, colour, sex, language, religion or religious belief, political or other opinion, national, ethnic or social origin, property, birth or other status.

2. Measures applied under the law and designed solely to protect the rights and special status of women, especially pregnant women and nursing mothers, children and juveniles, aged, sick or handicapped persons shall not be deemed to be discriminatory. The need for, and the application of, such measures shall always be subject to review by a judicial or other authority.

Principle 6

No person under any form of detention or imprisonment shall be subjected to torture or to cruel, inhuman or degrading treatment or punishment.[a] No circumstance whatever may be invoked as a justification for torture or other cruel, inhuman or degrading treatment or punishment.

Principle 7

1. States should prohibit by law any act contrary to the rights and duties contained in these principles, make any such act subject to appropriate sanctions and conduct impartial investigations upon complaints.

2. Officials who have reason to believe that a violation of this Body of Principles has occurred or is about to occur shall report the matter to their superior authorities and, where necessary, to other appropriate authorities or organs vested with reviewing or remedial powers.

3. Any other person who has ground to believe that a violation of this Body of Principles has occurred or is about to occur shall have the right to report the matter to the superiors of the officials involved as well as to other appropriate authorities or organs vested with reviewing or remedial powers.

Principle 8

Persons in detention shall be subject to treatment appropriate to their unconvicted status. Accordingly, they shall, whenever possible, be kept separate from imprisoned persons.

Principle 9

The authorities which arrest a person, keep him under detention or investigate the case shall exercise only the powers granted to them under the law and the exercise of these powers shall be subject to recourse to a judicial or other authority.

Principle 10

Anyone who is arrested shall be informed at the time of his arrest of the reason for his arrest and shall be promptly informed of any charges against him.

Principle 11

1. A person shall not be kept in detention without being given an effective opportunity to be heard promptly by a judicial or other authority. A detained person shall have the right to defend himself or to be assisted by counsel as prescribed by law.

2. A detained person and his counsel, if any, shall receive prompt and full communication of any order of detention, together with the reasons therefor.

3. A judicial or other authority shall be empowered to review as appropriate the continuance of detention.

Principle 12

1. There shall be duly recorded:

(a) The reasons for the arrest;

(b) The time of the arrest and the taking of the arrested person to a place of custody as well as that of his first appearance before a judicial or other authority;

(c) The identity of the law enforcement officials concerned;

(d) Precise information concerning the place of custody.

2. Such records shall be communicated to the detained person, or his counsel, if any, in the form prescribed by law.

Principle 13

Any person shall, at the moment of arrest and at the commencement of detention or imprisonment, or promptly thereafter, be provided by the authority responsible for his arrest, detention or imprisonment, respectively,

---

[a]The term "cruel, inhuman or degrading treatment or punishment" should be interpreted so as to extend the widest possible protection against abuses, whether physical or mental, including the holding of a detained or imprisoned person in conditions which deprive him, temporarily or permanently, of the use of any of his natural senses, such as sight or hearing, or of his awareness of place and the passing of time.

with information on and an explanation of his rights and how to avail himself of such rights.

Principle 14

A person who does not adequately understand or speak the language used by the authorities responsible for his arrest, detention or imprisonment is entitled to receive promptly in a language which he understands the information referred to in principle 10, principle 11, paragraph 2, principle 12, paragraph 1, and principle 13 and to have the assistance, free of charge, if necessary, of an interpreter in connection with legal proceedings subsequent to his arrest.

Principle 15

Notwithstanding the exceptions contained in principle 16, paragraph 4, and principle 18, paragraph 3, communication of the detained or imprisoned person with the outside world, and in particular his family or counsel, shall not be denied for more than a matter of days.

Principle 16

1. Promptly after arrest and after each transfer from one place of detention or imprisonment to another, a detained or imprisoned person shall be entitled to notify or to require the competent authority to notify members of his family or other appropriate persons of his choice of his arrest, detention or imprisonment or of the transfer and of the place where he is kept in custody.

2. If a detained or imprisoned person is a foreigner, he shall also be promptly informed of his right to communicate by appropriate means with a consular post or the diplomatic mission of the State of which he is a national or which is otherwise entitled to receive such communication in accordance with international law or with the representative of the competent international organization, if he is a refugee or is otherwise under the protection of an intergovernmental organization.

3. If a detained or imprisoned person is a juvenile or is incapable of understanding his entitlement, the competent authority shall on its own initiative undertake the notification referred to in the present principle. Special attention shall be given to notifying parents or guardians.

4. Any notification referred to in the present principle shall be made or permitted to be made without delay. The competent authority may however delay a notification for a reasonable period where exceptional needs of the investigation so require.

Principle 17

1. A detained person shall be entitled to have the assistance of a legal counsel. He shall be informed of his right by the competent authority promptly after arrest and shall be provided with reasonable facilities for exercising it.

2. If a detained person does not have a legal counsel of his own choice, he shall be entitled to have a legal counsel assigned to him by a judicial or other authority in all cases where the interests of justice so require and without payment by him if he does not have sufficient means to pay.

Principle 18

1. A detained or imprisoned person shall be entitled to communicate and consult with his legal counsel.

2. A detained or imprisoned person shall be allowed adequate time and facilities for consultations with his legal counsel.

3. The right of a detained or imprisoned person to be visited by and to consult and communicate, without delay or censorship and in full confidentiality, with his legal counsel may not be suspended or restricted save in exceptional circumstances, to be specified by law or lawful regulations, when it is considered indispensable by a judicial or other authority in order to maintain security and good order.

4. Interviews between a detained or imprisoned person and his legal counsel may be within sight, but not within the hearing, of a law enforcement official.

5. Communications between a detained or imprisoned person and his legal counsel mentioned in the present principle shall be inadmissible as evidence against the detained or imprisoned person unless they are connected with a continuing or contemplated crime.

Principle 19

A detained or imprisoned person shall have the right to be visited by and to correspond with, in particular, members of his family and shall be given adequate opportunity to communicate with the outside world, subject to reasonable conditions and restrictions as specified by law or lawful regulations.

Principle 20

If a detained or imprisoned person so requests, he shall if possible be kept in a place of detention or imprisonment reasonably near his usual place of residence.

Principle 21

1. It shall be prohibited to take undue advantage of the situation of a detained or imprisoned person for the purpose of compelling him to confess, to incriminate himself otherwise or to testify against any other person.

2. No detained person while being interrogated shall be subject to violence, threats or methods of interrogation which impair his capacity of decision or his judgement.

Principle 22

No detained or imprisoned person shall, even with his consent, be subjected to any medical or scientific experimentation which may be detrimental to his health.

Principle 23

1. The duration of any interrogation of a detained or imprisoned person and of the intervals between interrogations as well as the identity of the officials who conducted the interrogations and other persons present shall be recorded and certified in such form as may be prescribed by law.

2. A detained or imprisoned person, or his counsel when provided by law, shall have access to the information described in paragraph 1 of the present principle.

Principle 24

A proper medical examination shall be offered to a detained or imprisoned person as promptly as possible after his admission to the place of detention or imprisonment, and thereafter medical care and treatment shall be provided whenever necessary. This care and treatment shall be provided free of charge.

Principle 25

A detained or imprisoned person or his counsel shall, subject only to reasonable conditions to ensure security and good order in the place of detention or imprisonment, have the right to request or petition a judicial or other authority for a second medical examination or opinion.

Principle 26

The fact that a detained or imprisoned person underwent a medical examination, the name of the physician and the results of such an examination shall be duly recorded. Access to such records shall be ensured. Modalities therefore shall be in accordance with relevant rules of domestic law.

Principle 27

Non-compliance with these principles in obtaining evidence shall be taken into account in determining the admissibility of such evidence against a detained or imprisoned person.

Principle 28

A detained or imprisoned person shall have the right to obtain within the limits of available resources, if from public sources, reasonable quantities of educational, cultural and informational material, subject to reasonable conditions to ensure security and good order in the place of detention or imprisonment.

Principle 29

1. In order to supervise the strict observance of relevant laws and regulations, places of detention shall be visited regularly by qualified and experienced persons appointed by, and responsible to, a competent authority distinct from the authority directly in charge of the administration of the place of detention or imprisonment.

2. A detained or imprisoned person shall have the right to communicate freely and in full confidentiality with the persons who visit the places of detention or imprisonment in accordance with paragraph 1 of the present principle, subject to reasonable conditions to ensure security and good order in such places.

Principle 30

1. The types of conduct of the detained or imprisoned person that constitute disciplinary offences during detention or imprisonment, the description and duration of disciplinary punishment that may be inflicted and the authorities competent to impose such punishment shall be specified by law or lawful regulations and duly published.

2. A detained or imprisoned person shall have the right to be heard before disciplinary action is taken. He shall have the right to bring such action to higher authorities for review.

Principle 31

The appropriate authorities shall endeavour to ensure, according to domestic law, assistance when needed to dependent and, in particular, minor members of the families of detained or imprisoned persons and shall devote a particular measure of care to the appropriate custody of children left without supervision.

Principle 32

1. A detained person or his counsel shall be entitled at any time to take proceedings according to domestic law before a judicial or other authority to challenge the lawfulness of his detention in order to obtain his release without delay, if it is unlawful.

2. The proceedings referred to in paragraph 1 of the present principle shall be simple and expeditious and at no cost for detained persons without adequate means.

The detaining authority shall produce without unreasonable delay the detained person before the reviewing authority.

Principle 33

1. A detained or imprisoned person or his counsel shall have the right to make a request or complaint regarding his treatment, in particular in case of torture or other cruel, inhuman or degrading treatment, to the authorities responsible for the administration of the place of detention and to higher authorities and, when necessary, to appropriate authorities vested with reviewing or remedial powers.

2. In those cases where neither the detained or imprisoned person nor his counsel has the possibility to exercise his rights under paragraph 1 of the present principle, a member of the family of the detained or imprisoned person or any other person who has knowledge of the case may exercise such rights.

3. Confidentiality concerning the request or complaint shall be maintained if so requested by the complainant.

4. Every request or complaint shall be promptly dealt with and replied to without undue delay. If the request or complaint is rejected, or in case of inordinate delay, the complainant shall be entitled to bring it before a judicial or other authority. Neither the detained or imprisoned person nor any complainant under paragraph 1 of the present principle shall suffer prejudice for making a request or complaint.

Principle 34

Whenever the death or disappearance of a detained or imprisoned person occurs during his detention or imprisonment, an inquiry into the cause of death or disappearance shall be held by a judicial or other authority, either on its own motion or at the instance of a member of the family of such a person or any person who has knowledge of the case. When circumstances so warrant, such an inquiry shall be held on the same procedural basis whenever the death or disappearance occurs shortly after the termination of the detention or imprisonment. The findings of such inquiry or a report thereon shall be made available upon request, unless doing so would jeopardize an ongoing criminal investigation.

Principle 35

1. Damage incurred because of acts or omissions by a public official contrary to the rights contained in these principles shall be compensated according to the applicable rules on liability provided by domestic law.

2. Information required to be recorded under these principles shall be available in accordance with procedures provided by domestic law for use in claiming compensation under the present principle.

Principle 36

1. A detained person suspected of or charged with a criminal offence shall be presumed innocent and shall be treated as such until proved guilty according to law in a public trial at which he has had all the guarantees necessary for his defence.

2. The arrest or detention of such a person pending investigation and trial shall be carried out only for the purposes of the administration of justice on grounds and under conditions and procedures specified by law. The imposition of restrictions upon such a person which are not strictly required for the purpose of the deten-

tion or to prevent hindrance to the process of investigation or the administration of justice, or for the maintenance of security and good order in the place of detention shall be forbidden.

Principle 37

A person detained on a criminal charge shall be brought before a judicial or other authority provided by law promptly after his arrest. Such authority shall decide without delay upon the lawfulness and necessity of detention. No person may be kept under detention pending investigation or trial except upon the written order of such an authority. A detained person shall, when brought before such an authority, have the right to make a statement on the treatment received by him while in custody.

Principle 38

A person detained on a criminal charge shall be entitled to trial within a reasonable time or to release pending trial.

Principle 39

Except in special cases provided for by law, a person detained on a criminal charge shall be entitled, unless a judicial or other authority decides otherwise in the interest of the administration of justice, to release pending trial subject to the conditions that may be imposed in accordance with the law. Such authority shall keep the necessity of detention under review.

General clause

Nothing in this Body of Principles shall be construed as restricting or derogating from any right defined in the International Covenant on Civil and Political Rights.

General Assembly resolution 43/173

9 December 1988   Meeting 76   Adopted without vote

Approved by Sixth Committee (A/43/889) without vote, 25 November (meeting 48); 10-nation draft (A/C.6/43/L.17), orally revised; agenda item 138.
Sponsors: Austria, Brazil, Canada, Italy, Jamaica, Netherlands, Portugal, Samoa, Spain, Uruguay.
Meeting numbers. GA 43rd session: 6th Committee 45-48; plenary 76.

Torture and cruel treatment

Report of the Special Rapporteur. In January, Special Rapporteur Peter H. Kooijmans (Netherlands), in his third report to the Commission,[55] said he continued to receive requests for urgent action concerning people who were allegedly being tortured or who it was feared might be. He brought 14 of those requests to the immediate attention of the respective Governments, appealing to them to ensure that the physical and mental integrity of the individual was protected. In addition, the Special Rapporteur decided to retransmit allegations sent previously to 17 Governments. He discussed his 1987 visit to Argentina, Colombia and Uruguay.

The Special Rapporteur presented a number of conclusions and recommendations, some of which were taken up by the Commission.

Human Rights Commission action. Commending the Special Rapporteur for his report, the Commission, on 8 March,[56] endorsed his recommendations concerning strict measures against members of the medical profession who

had, in that capacity, practised torture. The Commission encouraged all States to sign and ratify the 1984 Convention against Torture and Other Cruel, Inhuman or Degrading Treatment or Punishment.[57] It underlined the Special Rapporteur's recommendation to declare incommunicado detention illegal and to institute a system of periodic visits by independent experts to places of detention. The Commission also emphasized the importance of training programmes for law and security personnel.

It decided to extend the Special Rapporteur's mandate for two years and asked the Secretary-General to provide all the assistance he might need and to report to the Commission in 1989. On 27 May, the Economic and Social Council, by **decision 1988/130**, approved those requests. The Commission also asked the Secretary-General to appeal to Governments to co-operate with the Special Rapporteur.

Convention against torture

As at 31 December 1988, 39 States had ratified or acceded to the Convention against Torture and Other Cruel, Inhuman or Degrading Treatment or Punishment, 11 of them in 1988.[1] The Convention was adopted by the General Assembly in 1984[57] and opened for signature in 1985.[58] It entered into force during 1987.[59] The optional provisions of articles 21 and 22 (under which a party recognizes the competence of the Committee against Torture, set up under the Convention, to receive and consider communications from or on behalf of individuals claiming to be victims of a violation of the Convention by a State party) also entered into force in 1987.[59] Twelve parties had made the required declarations. The Secretary-General reported on the status of the Convention as at 1 August 1988.[60]

Human Rights Commission action. On 8 March,[61] the Commission reiterated its request to all States to become parties to the Convention as a matter of priority and invited all ratifying or acceding States to consider making the declarations provided for in articles 21 and 22. It requested the Secretary-General to continue submitting annual reports on the Convention's status and to ensure that there were appropriate staff and facilities for the effective functioning of the Committee against Torture.

Also on 8 March,[62] the Commission noted that the financial cost of the implementation machinery under the Convention was onerous and might delay its universal acceptance. Bearing in mind that the Economic and Social Council considered annual reports on the activities of the relevant monitoring bodies and could make recommendations to the General Assembly, the Commission recommended that the Council give the matter due attention and asked the Secretary-General to prepare for the Council an overview of the various methods applied under different human rights instruments regarding their financial implications (see below, under "Advancement of human rights").

Draft optional protocol

As requested by the Commission in 1986,[63] the Secretary-General in January 1988[64] submitted a progress report on conventions containing ideas similar to those contained in a draft optional protocol to the 1984 Convention on torture, submitted by Costa Rica in 1980, providing for a system of periodic visits by a committee of experts to places of detention or imprisonment within the jurisdiction of States parties to the Convention. The Secretary-General stated that he had received information from the Council of Europe concerning the 1987 European Convention for the prevention of torture and inhuman or degrading treatment or punishment[65] and that the Organization of American States had provided information on the 1985 Inter-American Convention to Prevent and Punish Torture.[66]

Committee against Torture

The Committee against Torture, established as a monitoring body under the Convention, at its first session (Geneva, 18-22 April 1988),[67] elected its officers and adopted its agenda and rules of procedure. Annexed to the Committee's report were a list of States parties to the Convention as at 22 April 1988; a list of Committee members; rules of procedure and provisional guidelines on the form and content of initial reports to be submitted under article 19; and a list of initial reports to be submitted by States parties and their due dates.

GENERAL ASSEMBLY ACTION

On 8 December 1988, on the recommendation of the Third Committee, the General Assembly adopted **resolution 43/132** without vote.

Status of the Convention against Torture and Other Cruel, Inhuman or Degrading Treatment or Punishment

The General Assembly,

Recalling article 5 of the Universal Declaration of Human Rights and article 7 of the International Covenant on Civil and Political Rights, both of which provide that no one shall be subjected to torture or to cruel, inhuman or degrading treatment or punishment,

Recalling also the Declaration on the Protection of All Persons from Being Subjected to Torture and Other Cruel, Inhuman or Degrading Treatment or Punishment, adopted by the General Assembly in its resolution 3452(XXX) of 9 December 1975,

Recalling further its resolution 39/46 of 10 December 1984, by which it adopted and opened for signature,

ratification and accession the Convention against Torture and Other Cruel, Inhuman or Degrading Treatment or Punishment and called upon all Governments to consider signing and ratifying the Convention as a matter of priority, and its resolutions 40/128 of 13 December 1985, 41/134 of 4 December 1986 and 42/123 of 7 December 1987, as well as Commission on Human Rights resolutions 1987/30 of 10 March 1987, 1988/31 and 1988/36 of 8 March 1988,

Mindful of the relevance, for the eradication of torture and other cruel, inhuman or degrading treatment or punishment, of the Code of Conduct for Law Enforcement Officials and of the Principles of Medical Ethics relevant to the role of health personnel, particularly physicians, in the protection of prisoners and detainees against torture and other cruel, inhuman or degrading treatment or punishment,

Convinced of the importance of the finalization of the draft Body of Principles for the Protection of All Persons under Any Form of Detention or Imprisonment,

Seriously concerned about the alarming number of reported cases of torture and other cruel, inhuman or degrading treatment or punishment taking place in various parts of the world,

Determined to promote the full implementation of the prohibition, under international and national law, of the practice of torture and other cruel, inhuman or degrading treatment or punishment,

Welcoming the decision of the Commission on Human Rights, in its resolution 1988/32 of 8 March 1988, to extend for two years the mandate of the Special Rapporteur to examine questions relevant to torture,

1. *Welcomes* the first report of the Committee against Torture;

2. *Takes note with appreciation* of the report of the Secretary-General on the status of the Convention against Torture and Other Cruel, Inhuman or Degrading Treatment or Punishment;

3. *Recognizes* the importance of making appropriate administrative and financial arrangements to enable the Committee to carry out in an effective and efficient manner the functions entrusted to it under the Convention, and to ensure the long-term viability of the Committee as an essential mechanism for overseeing the effective implementation of the provisions of the Convention;

4. *Appreciates* the fact that the Committee has given early attention to the development of an effective reporting system on implementation by States parties to the Convention;

5. *Requests* the Secretary-General to ensure the provision of appropriate staff and facilities for the effective performance of the functions of the Committee;

6. *Again requests* all States to become parties to the Convention as a matter of priority;

7. *Once again invites* all States, upon ratification of or accession to the Convention, or subsequently, to consider the possibility of making the declarations provided for in articles 21 and 22 thereof;

8. *Requests* the Secretary-General to submit to the Commission on Human Rights at its forty-fifth session and to the General Assembly at its forty-fourth session a report on the status of the Convention against Torture and Other Cruel, Inhuman or Degrading Treatment or Punishment;

9. *Decides* to consider the report of the Secretary-General at its forty-fourth session under the item enti-

tled "Torture and other cruel, inhuman or degrading treatment or punishment".

General Assembly resolution 43/132

8 December 1988   Meeting 75   Adopted without vote

Approved by Third Committee (A/43/878) without vote, 23 November (meeting 51); 30-nation draft (A/C.3/43/L.49); agenda item 106.

Sponsors: Argentina, Australia, Austria, Belgium, Brazil, Bulgaria, Canada, Colombia, Costa Rica, Cyprus, Denmark, Ecuador, Finland, France, Germany, Federal Republic of, Greece, Guinea, Italy, Luxembourg, Mexico, Netherlands, New Zealand, Norway, Peru, Portugal, Samoa, Spain, Sweden, Uruguay, Venezuela.

Meeting numbers. GA 43rd session: 3rd Committee 39-43, 46, 51; plenary 75.

Fund for victims of torture

On 8 March,[68] the Commission on Human Rights appealed to Governments, organizations and individuals to contribute to the Voluntary Fund for Victims of Torture, established in 1981.[69] It asked the Secretary-General to transmit its appeal to all Governments, to help make the Fund's humanitarian work better known and to inform it annually of the Fund's operations.

In his annual report to the Assembly on the status of the Fund,[70] the Secretary-General said that, at its seventh session (Geneva, 22-26 February 1988), the Fund's Board of Trustees had recommended grants of some $900,000, which corresponded closely to available resources. The grants focused on therapy and rehabilitation projects and were extended to some 32 countries in Africa, the Americas, Asia and Europe.

During the period 16 October 1987 to 15 October 1988, the Fund received $903,427 from 22 States. Contributions were also received from a number of individuals. In addition, pledges totalling $140,000 were made by two States.

GENERAL ASSEMBLY ACTION

On 8 December 1988, on the recommendation of the Third Committee, the General Assembly adopted **resolution 43/133** without vote.

United Nations Voluntary Fund for Victims of Torture

The General Assembly,

Recalling article 5 of the Universal Declaration of Human Rights, which states that no one shall be subjected to torture or to cruel, inhuman or degrading treatment or punishment,

Recalling also the Declaration on the Protection of All Persons from Being Subjected to Torture and Other Cruel, Inhuman or Degrading Treatment or Punishment,

Recalling with satisfaction the entry into force on 26 June 1987 of the Convention against Torture and Other Cruel, Inhuman or Degrading Treatment or Punishment,

Recalling its resolution 36/151 of 16 December 1981, in which it noted with deep concern that acts of torture took place in various countries, recognized the need to provide assistance to the victims of torture in a purely humanitarian spirit and established the United Nations Voluntary Fund for Victims of Torture,

Convinced that the struggle to eliminate torture includes the provision of assistance in a humanitarian spirit to the victims and members of their families,

Taking note of the report of the Secretary-General,

1.   *Expresses its gratitude and appreciation* to the Governments, organizations and individuals that have already contributed to the United Nations Voluntary Fund for Victims of Torture;

2.   *Calls upon* all Governments, organizations and individuals in a position to do so to respond favourably to requests for initial as well as further contributions to the Fund;

3.   *Invites* Governments to make contributions to the Fund, if possible on a regular basis, in order to enable the Fund to provide continuous support to projects that depend on recurrent grants;

4.   *Expresses its appreciation* to the Board of Trustees of the Fund for the work it has carried out;

5.   *Expresses its appreciation* to the Secretary-General for the support given to the Board of Trustees of the Fund;

6.   *Requests* the Secretary-General to make use of all existing possibilities, including the preparation, production and dissemination of information materials, to assist the Board of Trustees of the Fund in its efforts to make the Fund and its humanitarian work better known and in its appeal for contributions.

General Assembly resolution 43/133

8 December 1988   Meeting 75   Adopted without vote

Approved by Third Committee (A/43/878) without vote, 23 November (meeting 51); 26-nation draft (A/C.3/43/L.51); agenda item 106.

Sponsors: Australia, Austria, Belgium, Brazil, Canada, Cyprus, Denmark, Finland, France, Germany, Federal Republic of, Greece, Iceland, Ireland, Italy, Japan, Kenya, Libyan Arab Jamahiriya, Luxembourg, Netherlands, New Zealand, Norway, Senegal, Spain, Sweden, United Kingdom, United States.

Meeting numbers. GA 43rd session: 3rd Committee 39-43, 46, 51; plenary 75.

Torture and inhuman treatment of detained children in South Africa

On 29 February,[71] the Commission on Human Rights, vigorously condemning the detention, torture and inhuman treatment of children in South Africa, demanded their immediate and unconditional release and asked the Secretary-General to intervene with South Africa to end those practices in South Africa and Namibia and to report in 1989. It demanded the immediate dismantling of so-called "rehabilitation camps" or "re-education centres", which only served the racist régime's strategy of mentally and physically abusing black South African children, and the total abolition of the *apartheid* system. The Commission requested relevant United Nations bodies, specialized agencies and NGOs to launch a world-wide campaign to draw attention to the need to monitor and expose the inhuman practices associated with *apartheid* targeted at children. It appealed to the international community to adopt measures to bring pressure against South Africa until it dismantled *apartheid*. It asked the *Ad Hoc* Working Group of Experts on southern Africa to pay special attention to the question and to report in 1989. The Secretary-General was asked to assist the Working Group in discharging its responsibilities.

The *Ad Hoc* Working Group, in January 1988,[72] recounted testimony from witnesses and press reports concerning arrests, torture and other ill-treatment and harassment of black children and adolescents in South Africa. (For details of the Group's activities, see below, under "Human rights violations".)

GENERAL ASSEMBLY ACTION

On 8 December 1988, on the recommendation of the Third Committee, the General Assembly adopted **resolution 43/134** without vote.

Torture and inhuman treatment of children in detention in South Africa and Namibia

The General Assembly,

Recalling its resolution 42/124 of 7 December 1987 and taking note of Commission on Human Rights resolution 1988/11 of 29 February 1988,

Recalling also the relevant provisions of the Declaration on the Protection of All Persons from Being Subjected to Torture and Other Cruel, Inhuman or Degrading Treatment or Punishment, the Convention against Torture and Other Cruel, Inhuman or Degrading Treatment or Punishment and the Declaration on the Rights of the Child,

Recalling with satisfaction the holding of the International Conference on Children, Repression and the Law in *Apartheid* South Africa at Harare, from 24 to 27 September 1987,

Appalled at evidence that children in South Africa and Namibia continue to be subjected to detention, torture and inhuman treatment,

Gravely concerned about reports of the increasing number of repressive measures targeted against children in South Africa and Namibia,

1. *Expresses its profound outrage* at evidence of detention, torture and inhuman treatment of children in South Africa and Namibia;

2. *Vigorously condemns* the *apartheid* racist régime for increasing detention, torture and inhuman treatment of children in South Africa and Namibia;

3. *Demands* the immediate and unconditional release of children held in detention in those countries;

4. *Demands also* the immediate dismantlement of the so-called "rehabilitation camps" and "re-education centres" in South Africa, since they only serve the racist régime's strategy of physically and mentally abusing black South African children;

5. *Strongly condemns* the racist régime of South Africa for its forced recruitment, torture and inhuman treatment of Namibian children with the objective of turning them into their agents against the Namibian people;

6. *Requests* all relevant United Nations bodies, specialized agencies and non-governmental organizations to intensify the world-wide campaign aimed at drawing attention to, monitoring and exposing these inhuman practices;

7. *Requests* the Commission on Human Rights to continue to pay special attention to the question of detention, torture and other inhuman treatment of children in South Africa and Namibia;

8. *Requests* the Secretary-General to submit a report to the General Assembly at its forty-fourth session on the implementation of the present resolution;

9. *Decides* to consider this question at its forty-fourth session under the item entitled "Torture and other cruel, inhuman or degrading treatment or punishment".

General Assembly resolution 43/134

8 December 1988   Meeting 75   Adopted without vote

Approved by Third Committee (A/43/878) without vote, 23 November (meeting 51); 33-nation draft (A/C.3/43/L.52); agenda item 106.

Sponsors: Algeria, Angola, Austria, Botswana, Bulgaria, Burkina Faso, Congo, Costa Rica, Côte d'Ivoire, Cuba, Denmark, Egypt, Ethiopia, Greece, Guinea, Ireland, Kenya, Libyan Arab Jamahiriya, Mongolia, Morocco, Nigeria, Norway, Philippines, Rwanda, Senegal, Sudan, Swaziland, Sweden, Tunisia, United Republic of Tanzania, Zaire, Zambia, Zimbabwe.

Meeting numbers. GA 43rd session: 3rd Committee 39-43, 46, 51; plenary 75.

Detention on grounds of mental illness

The World Health Organization (WHO) provided the Commission with information on consultations it had held on persons detained on the grounds of mental illness. The consultations stressed the need for agreement on a set of principles for protecting the mentally ill, including protection from neglect as well as abuse, and the treatment of mental illness in the same way as other illnesses, recognizing the divergent legal, cultural and economic situations of those in need of assistance.

Human Rights Commission action. On 9 March,[73] the Commission requested the Sub-Commission's sessional working group, set up in 1984,[74] to complete work on the draft body of guidelines, principles and guarantees of the rights of persons detained on the grounds of mental ill-health or mental disorders, taking into account information provided in February by WHO.[75] It asked the Secretary-General to assist the working group to complete its work.

Sub-Commission action. On 1 September,[76] the Sub-Commission adopted the draft body of principles and guarantees for the protection of mentally-ill persons and for the improvement of mental health care, approved by its sessional working group in August,[77] and submitted it to the Commission for further consideration.

GENERAL ASSEMBLY ACTION

On 8 December, on the recommendation of the Third Committee, the General Assembly adopted **resolution 43/109** without vote.

Implications of scientific and technological developments for human rights

The General Assembly,

Recalling its resolution 33/53 of 14 December 1978, in which it requested the Commission on Human Rights to urge the Sub-Commission on Prevention of Discrimination and Protection of Minorities to undertake, as a matter of priority, a study of the question of the protection of those detained on the grounds of mental ill-health, with a view to formulating guidelines,

Mindful of the Principles of Medical Ethics relevant to the role of health personnel, particularly physicians, in the protection of prisoners and detainees against torture and other cruel, inhuman or degrading treatment or punishment,

Recalling also its resolution 42/98 of 7 December 1987, in which it again urged the Commission and the Sub-

Commission to expedite their consideration of this question, so that the Commission could submit its views and recommendations, including a draft body of guidelines, principles and guarantees, to the General Assembly at its forty-fourth session, through the Economic and Social Council,

Endorsing Commission resolution 1988/62 of 9 March 1988,

Taking note of Sub-Commission resolution 1988/28 of 1 September 1988,

Expressing deep concern at the repeated evidence of the misuse of psychiatry to detain persons on non-medical grounds, as reflected in the report of the Special Rapporteur of the Sub-Commission,

Reaffirming its conviction that detention of persons in mental institutions on account of their political views or on other non-medical grounds is a violation of their human rights,

1. _Welcomes_ the progress made by the Working Group of the Sub-Commission on Prevention of Discrimination and Protection of Minorities, which enabled the Sub-Commission, at its fortieth session, to adopt the draft body of principles and guarantees for the protection of mentally-ill persons and for the improvement of mental health care;

2. _Invites_ the Commission on Human Rights to consider the subject at its forty-fifth session in the light of the Sub-Commission's recommendations.

General Assembly resolution 43/109

8 December 1988   Meeting 75   Adopted without vote

Approved by Third Committee (A/43/870) without vote, 23 November (meeting 51); 14-nation draft (A/C.3/43/L.45); agenda item 98.

Sponsors: Belgium, Bolivia, Colombia, Costa Rica, Côte d'Ivoire, Germany, Federal Republic of, Italy, Luxembourg, Morocco, Norway, Samoa, Singapore, Sweden, United Kingdom.

Meeting numbers. GA 43rd session: 3rd Committee 39-43, 46, 51; plenary 75.

Unacknowledged detention

On 8 March,[13] the Commission on Human Rights requested its Sub-Commission to continue to give attention to a draft declaration against the unacknowledged detention of persons.

In August, the Working Group on Detention, having made a preliminary review of the text of the draft declaration which was annexed to its report,[49] recommended to the Sub-Commission that it circulate the draft to Governments, the United Nations Centre for Social Development and Humanitarian Affairs, and intergovernmental and nongovernmental organizations for comments.

Detention without charge or trial

Human Rights Commission action. On 8 March,[78] the Commission, taking note of a 1987 explanatory paper by Special Rapporteur Louis Joinet (France) on administrative detention without charge or trial,[79] invited all Governments, specialized agencies, regional intergovernmental organizations and NGOs to assist by forwarding answers to a questionnaire sent to them on the subject. It requested the Sub-Commission to consider the Special Rapporteur's analysis and make any proposals deemed necessary on the questionnaire.

Sub-Commission action. On 1 September,[80] the Sub-Commission approved a recommendation of the Working Group on Detention[49] that the Sub-Commission consider the Special Rapporteur's study as a matter of priority (see above). It asked the Special Rapporteur to report in 1989 and the Secretary-General to assist him.

Report of the Special Rapporteur. In November,[81] the Special Rapporteur presented an analysis of the issues dealt with in his 1987 paper on administrative detention without charge or trial[79] based on replies to questionnaires from 22 Governments, 3 specialized agencies, 3 intergovernmental organizations and 12 NGOs. He stated that due to problems of co-ordination, classification of the purposes of detention had been reduced from six to four categories: prevention of serious disturbances of public order; measures relating to the status of foreigners; disciplinary measures; and situations of poverty or social maladjustment. The Special Rapporteur discussed possible proposals to the Commission, which comprised suggestions made by NGOs concerning flagrant abuses of administrative detention.

Hostage-taking

Human Rights Commission action. On 8 March,[82] the Commission strongly condemned those responsible for hostage-taking in all circumstances and demanded the immediate release of those being held. It called on States to take preventive and punitive steps to put an immediate end to cases of abduction and unlawful restraint. It asked the Secretary-General, whenever a State so requested, to use all available means to secure the release of persons held hostage.

Sub-Commission action. On 1 September,[83] the Sub-Commission called on all parties involved in the war in Lebanon to release immediately and unconditionally all their detainees and hostages and to use their influence on those who might have control of those being held.

Detained UN staff members

Human Rights Commission action. On 8 March,[84] the Commission appealed to Member States to respect the rights of staff members and others acting under the authority of the United Nations and their families. It asked the Secretary-General to continue his efforts to ensure that the human rights and privileges and immunities of United Nations staff members and their families were fully respected and to submit an updated report on the situation of international civil servants and their families detained, imprisoned, missing or held in a country against their will, including those cases that had been successfully settled five years prior to the Commission's 1989 session.

Report of the Secretary-General. In response to the Commission's request, the Secretary-General, on 19 August 1988,[85] submitted a report updating developments pertaining to the detention of international civil servants and their families.

Sub-Commission action. On 31 August,[86] by a vote of 18 to 1, with 3 abstentions, the Sub-Commission decided that one of its members should examine the human rights violations of staff members of the United Nations system, their families and experts, as well as the repercussions of those violations on the operation of United Nations organs and agencies. The Secretary-General, heads of the specialized agencies and the various United Nations staff representative organs were asked to assist the designated member.

Extra-legal executions

In January 1988, Special Rapporteur S. Amos Wako (Kenya) submitted to the Commission on Human Rights his sixth report with later addenda[87] on summary or arbitrary executions. The report was based on information received from Governments, NGOs, groups and individuals and described allegations of imminent or actual executions, which had been communicated to the Governments concerned. It summarized replies from those Governments and presented developments regarding international standards for the proper investigation of all deaths under suspicious circumstances. The Special Rapporteur reviewed the current situation in countries where summary or arbitrary executions had been widely reported and situations in restored or new democracies.

The Special Rapporteur recommended: human rights training programmes for law enforcement officers; ratification by Governments of international human rights instruments and the Optional Protocol to the International Covenant on Civil and Political Rights[2] and a review of national laws and regulations; government machinery to check and control law enforcement organs, including military forces; and support by Governments and international organizations for United Nations efforts to adopt an international instrument incorporating international standards for the proper investigation of all deaths under suspicious circumstances. Annexed to the report was an account of the Special Rapporteur's visit to Suriname (16-24 August 1987) to investigate alleged killings by members of the military.

Human Rights Commission action. On 10 March,[88] the Commission recommended a resolution on summary or arbitrary executions for adoption by the Economic and Social Council (see below).

Sub-Commission action. On 1 September,[89] the Sub-Commission asked the Secretary-General to provide a document describing action by other international forums towards international standards for the investigation of suspicious deaths in detention, including autopsies.

ECONOMIC AND SOCIAL COUNCIL ACTION

On 27 May 1988, the Economic and Social Council, on the recommendation of its Second Committee, adopted **resolution 1988/38** without vote.

Summary or arbitrary executions

Economic and Social Council,

Recalling the Universal Declaration of Human Rights, which proclaims the right to life, liberty and security of person,

Having regard to the provisions of the International Covenant on Civil and Political Rights, in which it is stated that every human being has the inherent right to life, that this right shall be protected by law, and that no one shall be arbitrarily deprived of his life,

Recalling General Assembly resolution 34/175 of 17 December 1979, in which the Assembly reaffirmed that mass and flagrant violations of human rights were of special concern to the United Nations and urged the Commission on Human Rights to take timely and effective action in existing and future cases of mass and flagrant violations of human rights,

Mindful of General Assembly resolutions 36/22 of 9 November 1981, 37/182 of 17 December 1982, 38/96 of 16 December 1983, 39/110 of 14 December 1984, 40/143 of 13 December 1985, 41/144 of 4 December 1986 and 42/141 of 7 December 1987,

Recalling resolution 1982/13 of 7 September 1982 of the Sub-Commission on Prevention of Discrimination and Protection of Minorities, in which the Sub-Commission recommended that effective measures should be adopted to prevent summary or arbitrary executions,

Reaffirming its resolution 1984/50 of 25 May 1984 and the safeguards guaranteeing protection of the rights of those facing the death penalty annexed thereto, which were endorsed by the Seventh United Nations Congress on the Prevention of Crime and the Treatment of Offenders in its resolution 15, and welcoming the on-going work of the Committee on Crime Prevention and Control on summary and arbitrary executions,

Welcoming the close co-operation established between the Centre for Human Rights, the Crime Prevention and Criminal Justice Branch of the Centre for Social Development and Humanitarian Affairs of the Secretariat and the Committee on Crime Prevention and Control with regard to the elaboration of the principles on the effective prevention and investigation of arbitrary and summary executions, including extra-legal executions,

Deeply alarmed at the occurrence on a large scale of summary or arbitrary executions, including extra-legal executions,

Convinced of the need for appropriate action to combat and eventually eliminate the abhorrent practice of summary or arbitrary executions, which are a flagrant violation of the most fundamental right, the right to life,

1. *Strongly condemns,* once again, the large number of summary or arbitrary executions, including extra-legal executions, which continue to take place in various parts of the world;

2. *Appeals urgently* to Governments, United Nations bodies, the specialized agencies, regional intergovernmental organizations and non-governmental organizations to take effective action to combat and eliminate summary or arbitrary executions, including extra-legal executions;

3. *Takes note with appreciation* of the report of the Special Rapporteur, Mr. S. Amos Wako, and welcomes his recommendations for eliminating summary or arbitrary executions;

4. *Decides* to renew the mandate of the Special Rapporteur for two years and decides that he should continue to report annually and submit further conclusions and recommendations to the Commission at its forty-fifth and forty-sixth sessions;

5. *Requests* the Special Rapporteur in carrying out his mandate to continue to examine situations of summary or arbitrary executions;

6. *Also requests* the Special Rapporteur in carrying out his mandate to respond effectively to information that comes before him, in particular when a summary or arbitrary execution is imminent or threatened or when such an execution has occurred;

7. *Encourages* Governments, international organizations and non-governmental organizations to organize training programmes and to support projects with a view to providing training or education for law enforcement officials on human rights issues connected with their work, and appeals to the international community to support endeavours to that end;

8. *Invites* Governments, international organizations and non-governmental organizations to support the efforts made in United Nations forums towards the adoption of an international instrument that would incorporate international standards for the proper investigation of all cases of death in suspicious circumstances, including provision for adequate autopsy;

9. *Endorses* the proposals of the Special Rapporteur concerning the elements to be included in such international standards;

10. *Requests* the Secretary-General to continue to provide all necessary assistance to the Special Rapporteur;

11. *Also requests* the Secretary-General to consider ways of publicizing the work of the Special Rapporteur, as well as his recommendations, particularly within the framework of the information activities of the Centre for Human Rights;

12. *Urges* all Governments, in particular those that have consistently not responded to communications transmitted to them by the Special Rapporteur, and all others concerned, to co-operate with and assist the Special Rapporteur so that he may carry out his mandate effectively;

13. *Again requests* the Secretary-General to continue to make the utmost effort in cases where the minimum standard of legal safeguards provided for in articles 6, 14 and 15 of the International Covenant on Civil and Political Rights appears not to have been respected;

14. *Requests* the Commission on Human Rights to consider the question of summary or arbitrary executions as a matter of high priority at its forty-fifth session under the agenda item entitled ''Question of the violation of human rights and fundamental freedoms in any part of the world, with particular reference to colonial and other dependent countries and territories''.

Economic and Social Council resolution 1988/38

27 May 1988   Meeting 16   Adopted without vote

Approved by Second Committee (E/1988/89/Add.1) without vote, 23 May (meeting 20); draft by Commission on Human Rights (E/1988/12 & Corr.1); agenda item 10.

GENERAL ASSEMBLY ACTION

On 8 December 1988, on the recommendation of the Third Committee, the General Assembly adopted **resolution 43/151** without vote.

Summary or arbitrary executions

The General Assembly,

Recalling the provisions of the Universal Declaration of Human Rights, in which it is stated that every human being has the right to life, liberty and security of person,

Having regard to the provisions of the International Covenant on Civil and Political Rights, in which it is stated that every human being has the inherent right to life, that this right shall be protected by law and that no one shall be arbitrarily deprived of his life,

Recalling also its resolution 34/175 of 17 December 1979, in which it reaffirmed that mass and flagrant violations of human rights are of special concern to the United Nations and urged the Commission on Human Rights to take timely and effective action in existing and future cases of mass and flagrant violations of human rights,

Recalling further its resolution 36/22 of 9 November 1981, in which it condemned the practice of summary or arbitrary executions, and its resolutions 37/182 of 17 December 1982, 38/96 of 16 December 1983, 39/110 of 14 December 1984, 40/143 of 13 December 1985, 41/144 of 4 December 1986 and 42/141 of 7 December 1987,

Deeply alarmed at the continued occurrence on a large scale of summary or arbitrary executions, including extra-legal executions,

Recalling resolution 1982/13 of 7 September 1982 of the Sub-Commission on Prevention of Discrimination and Protection of Minorities, in which the Sub-Commission recommended that effective measures should be adopted to prevent the occurrence of summary or arbitrary executions,

Recalling also Economic and Social Council resolution 1984/50 of 25 May 1984 and the safeguards guaranteeing protection of the rights of those facing the death penalty annexed thereto, which resolution was endorsed by the Seventh United Nations Congress on the Prevention of Crime and the Treatment of Offenders in its resolution 15,

Welcoming the close co-operation established between the Centre for Human Rights, the Crime Prevention and Criminal Justice Branch of the Centre for Social Development and Humanitarian Affairs of the Secretariat and the Committee on Crime Prevention and Control with regard to the elaboration of the principles on the effective prevention and investigation of arbitrary and summary executions, including extra-legal executions,

Taking note of the recommendation by the Committee on Crime Prevention and Control concerning ''Draft principles on the effective prevention and investigation of extra-legal, arbitrary and summary executions'' for consideration and adoption by the Economic and Social Council,

Convinced of the need for appropriate action to combat and eventually eliminate the abhorrent practice of summary or arbitrary executions, which represents a flagrant violation of the most fundamental human right, the right to life,

1. *Once again strongly condemns* the large number of summary or arbitrary executions, including extra-legal executions, that continue to take place in various parts of the world;

2. *Demands* that the practice of summary or arbitrary executions be brought to an end;

3. *Appeals urgently* to Governments, United Nations bodies, the specialized agencies, regional intergovernmental organizations and non-governmental organizations to take effective action to combat and eliminate summary or arbitrary executions, including extra-legal executions;

4. *Recalls* Economic and Social Council resolution 1982/35 of 7 May 1982, in which the Council decided to appoint a special rapporteur to consider the questions related to summary or arbitrary executions;

5. *Welcomes* Economic and Social Council resolution 1988/38 of 7 May 1988, in which the Council decided to renew the mandate of the Special Rapporteur, Mr. S. A. Wako, for two years, while keeping the annual reporting cycle, and requested the Commission on Human Rights to consider the question of summary or arbitrary executions as a matter of high priority at its forty-fifth session;

6. *Urges* all Governments, in particular those which have consistently not responded to communications transmitted to them by the Special Rapporteur, and all others concerned, to co-operate with and assist the Special Rapporteur so that he may carry out his mandate effectively;

7. *Requests* the Special Rapporteur, in carrying out his mandate, to respond effectively to information that comes before him, in particular when a summary or arbitrary execution is imminent or threatened, or when such an execution has recently occurred; and, furthermore, to promote exchanges of views between Governments and those who provide reliable information to the Special Rapporteur, where the Special Rapporteur considers that such exchanges of information might be useful;

8. *Welcomes* the recommendations made by the Special Rapporteur in his reports to the Commission on Human Rights at its forty-third and forty-fourth sessions with a view to eliminating summary or arbitrary executions;

9. *Encourages* Governments, international organizations and non-governmental organizations to organize training programmes and to support projects with a view to training or educating law enforcement officials in human rights issues connected with their work, and appeals to the international community to support endeavours to that end;

10. *Invites* Governments, international organizations and non-governmental organizations to support the efforts made in United Nations forums towards the adoption of an international instrument that would incorporate international standards for proper investigation of all cases of death in suspicious circumstances, including provision for adequate autopsy;

11. *Endorses* the proposals of the Special Rapporteur concerning the elements to be included in such international standards;

12. *Considers* that the Special Rapporteur, in carrying out his mandate, should continue to seek and receive information from Governments, United Nations bodies, specialized agencies, regional intergovernmental organizations, non-governmental organizations in consultative status with the Economic and Social Council, as well as medical and forensic experts;

13. *Requests* the Secretary-General to continue to provide all necessary assistance to the Special Rapporteur so that he may effectively carry out his mandate;

14. *Again requests* the Secretary-General to continue to use his best endeavours in cases where the minimum standard of legal safeguards provided for in articles 6, 14 and 15 of the International Covenant on Civil and Political Rights appear not to have been respected;

15. *Requests* the Commission on Human Rights at its forty-fifth session, on the basis of the report of the Special Rapporteur to be prepared in conformity with Economic and Social Council resolutions 1982/35, 1983/36, 1984/35, 1985/40, 1986/36, 1987/60 and 1988/38, to make recommendations concerning appropriate action to combat and eventually eliminate the abhorrent practice of summary or arbitrary executions.

General Assembly resolution 43/151

8 December 1988   Meeting 75   Adopted without vote

Approved by Third Committee (A/43/868) without vote, 30 November (meeting 57); 25-nation draft (A/C.3/43/L.74), orally revised; agenda item 12.
Sponsors: Austria, Belgium, Canada, Colombia, Costa Rica, Cyprus, Denmark, Finland, France, Germany, Federal Republic of, Greece, Iceland, Italy, Kenya, Luxembourg, Morocco, Netherlands, Norway, Portugal, Samoa, Senegal, Spain, Sweden, United Kingdom, Zambia.
Meeting numbers. GA 43rd session: 3rd Committee 54, 57; plenary 75.

Disappearance of persons

Human Rights Commission action. On 8 March,[90] the Commission requested the Working Group on Enforced or Involuntary Disappearances to report on its work in 1989 and 1990 and to present recommendations to help eliminate the practice of enforced or involuntary disappearances. The Commission decided to extend the Group's mandate for two years and encouraged Governments to consider inviting it to their countries. It asked the Secretary-General to ensure that the Group received all necessary assistance, particularly staff and resources.

ECONOMIC AND SOCIAL COUNCIL ACTION

In May, the Economic and Social Council, on the recommendation of its Second Committee, adopted **decision 1988/107** without vote.

Question of enforced or involuntary disappearances

At its 10th plenary meeting, on 13 May 1988, the Economic and Social Council, taking note of Commission on Human Rights resolution 1988/34 of 8 March 1988, approved the decision of the Commission to extend for two years the mandate of the Working Group on Enforced or Involuntary Disappearances. The Council also approved the request of the Commission to the Secretary-General to ensure that the Working Group received all necessary assistance, in particular the staff and resources it required to perform its functions, especially in carrying out missions or holding sessions in countries that would be prepared to receive them.

Economic and Social Council decision 1988/107
									Adopted without vote

Approved by Second Committee (E/1988/89) without vote, 11 May (meeting 6); draft by Commission on Human Rights (E/1988/12 & Corr.1); agenda item 10.

Working Group activities. The five-member Working Group on Enforced or Involuntary Disappearances, established in 1980,[91] held three sessions in 1988: its twenty-fourth (New York, 23-27 May) and twenty-fifth and twenty-sixth (Geneva, 12-16 September and 30 November–9 December).[92]

During those sessions, the Group held 14 meetings with government representatives and 28 meetings with representatives of human rights organizations, associations of relatives of missing persons and families or witnesses directly concerned with reports on enforced or involuntary disappearances. Two members of the Group visited Colombia from 24 October to 2 November and provided the Commission with a report on the problem of disappearances there.[93]

In 1988, the Group received reports of some 4,200 cases of enforced or involuntary disappearances and transmitted 3,440 newly reported cases to the Governments concerned. Among the cases which occurred in 1988, 60 were clarified, 50 of them under the urgent-action procedure.

The Group recommended that the Commission: again urge Governments to take steps to protect the families of disappeared persons against intimidation or ill-treatment; call on Governments to co-operate with the Group and to ensure that in states of emergency the necessary human rights guarantees were maintained; and ask Governments to invite the Group to visit their countries and to make use of the advisory services of the United Nations, particularly human rights training of security forces and the judiciary by qualified experts. Annexed to the Group's report were graphs showing the development of disappearances for the period 1974 to 1988 in countries with more than 50 transmitted cases.

GENERAL ASSEMBLY ACTION

On 8 December 1988, on the recommendation of the Third Committee, the General Assembly adopted **resolution 43/159** without vote.

Question of enforced or involuntary disappearances
The General Assembly,

Recalling its resolution 33/173 of 20 December 1978 concerning disappeared persons, and its resolution 42/142 of 7 December 1987 on the question of enforced or involuntary disappearances,

Deeply concerned about the persistence, in certain cases, of the practice of enforced or involuntary disappearances, and about the fact that, in certain cases, the families of disappeared persons have been the target of intimidation and ill-treatment,

Expressing its profound emotion at the anguish and sorrow of the families concerned, who are unsure of the fate of their relatives,

Convinced of the need to continue implementing the provisions of its resolution 33/173 and of the other United Nations resolutions on the question of enforced or involuntary disappearances, with a view to finding solutions for cases of disappearances and helping to eliminate such practices,

Bearing in mind Commission on Human Rights resolution 1988/34 of 8 March 1988,

1. *Expresses its appreciation* to the Working Group on Enforced or Involuntary Disappearances for its humanitarian work and to those Governments that have co-operated with it;

2. *Welcomes* the decision of the Commission on Human Rights to extend for two years the term of the mandate of the Working Group, as defined in Commission resolution 20(XXXVI) of 29 February 1980, while maintaining the principle of annual reporting by the Working Group;

3. *Also welcomes* the provisions made by the Commission on Human Rights in its resolution 1986/55 of 13 March 1986 to enable the Working Group to fulfil its mandate with greater efficiency;

4. *Further welcomes* the progress made in the preparation of the draft declaration on enforced or involuntary disappearances;

5. *Appeals* to the Governments concerned, particularly those which have not yet replied to the communications addressed to them by the Working Group, to co-operate fully with the Working Group so as to enable it, with respect for its working methods based on discretion, to perform its strictly humanitarian role, and in particular to reply more quickly to the requests for information addressed to them by the Working Group;

6. *Encourages* the Governments concerned to consider the wish of the Working Group, when such a wish is expressed, to visit their countries, thus enabling the Working Group to fulfil its mandate even more effectively;

7. *Extends its warm thanks* to the Governments that have invited the Working Group;

8. *Appeals* to the Governments concerned to take steps to protect the families of disappeared persons against any intimidation or any ill-treatment of which they may be the target;

9. *Calls upon* the Commission on Human Rights to continue to study this question as a matter of priority and to take any step it may deem necessary to the pursuit of the task of the Working Group when it considers the report to be submitted by the Working Group to the Commission at its forty-fifth session;

10. *Renews its request* to the Secretary-General to continue to provide the Working Group with all necessary facilities.

General Assembly resolution 43/159

8 December 1988			Meeting 75			Adopted without vote

Approved by Third Committee (A/43/868) without vote, 30 November (meeting 57); 22-nation draft (A/C.3/43/L.82); agenda item 12.

Sponsors: Austria, Belgium, Canada, Colombia, Costa Rica, Cyprus, Denmark, France, Germany, Federal Republic of, Greece, Italy, Luxembourg, Netherlands, Norway, Portugal, Rwanda, Samoa, Senegal, Spain, United Kingdom, United States, Yugoslavia.

Meeting numbers. GA 43rd session: 3rd Committee 49-57; plenary 75.

Disappearance of children

On 10 March,[94] the Commission approved a 1987 Sub-Commission request[95] to appoint one or more members to establish and maintain contact with the authorities and institutions responsible for reporting on the situation of disappeared children in Argentina who had been located in Paraguay. It authorized the Secretary-General to provide all the assistance necessary to implement its resolution.

On 27 May, the Economic and Social Council, by **decision 1988/138**, endorsed the Commission's approval of the Sub-Commission's request and authorized the Secretary-General to provide assistance.

In August,[96] Sub-Commission member Theo van Boven (Netherlands) presented a report on disappeared children in Argentina who had been located in Paraguay. He had visited Argentina from 12 to 15 July where he met with government officials, NGOs, judges, lawyers, psychologists and health professionals. He recommended urging Paraguay to return the children to their country of origin, firm international co-operation and international mechanisms to help find disappeared children and reintegrate them into their legitimate families.

Other aspects of civil and political rights

Slavery

Human Rights Commission action. The Commission, on 8 March,[97] endorsed the Sub-Commission's 1987 recommendation to change the name of the Working Group on Slavery to the Working Group on Contemporary Forms of Slavery,[98] and asked the Sub-Commission and the Group to draw up a plan of action on its future work for submission in 1989. The Commission decided to transmit to Member States the Sub-Commission's 1987 recommendation that any step taken to interfere with the freedom of attendance and speech before the Group be strongly condemned. It recommended that the Sub-Commission consider appointing a special rapporteur to review the implementation by Member States, United Nations organs and other appropriate bodies of the recommendations made and the measures taken by United Nations organs and executing agencies, international organizations and Member States to prevent and suppress contemporary forms of slavery and to submit recommendations in 1989. The Secretary-General was asked to report to the Economic and Social Council on the implementation of a 1983 decision.[99] The Commission recommended a draft, which the Council adopted (see below).

On 27 May 1988, the Economic and Social Council, on the recommendation of its Second Committee, adopted **resolution 1988/34** without vote.

Working Group on Contemporary Forms of Slavery of the Sub-Commission on Prevention of Discrimination and Protection of Minorities

The Economic and Social Council,

Taking note of Commission on Human Rights resolution 1988/42 of 8 March 1988,

Recalling its resolutions 1982/20 of 4 May 1982 and 1983/30 of 26 May 1983 on the suppression of the traffic in persons and of the exploitation of the prostitution of others,

Recalling also General Assembly resolutions 38/107 of 16 December 1983 and 40/103 of 13 December 1985 on the prevention of prostitution,

Desiring to give further follow-up to the excellent report of its Special Rapporteur, Mr. J. Fernand-Laurent, on the suppression of the traffic in persons and the exploitation of the prostitution of others,

Commending the Sub-Commission on Prevention of Discrimination and Protection of Minorities and, in particular, its Working Group on Contemporary Forms of Slavery for their work on contemporary forms of slavery,

Aware of the complexity of the issue of the suppression of the traffic in persons and of the exploitation of the prostitution of others and of the need for further co-ordination and co-operation to implement the recommendations made by the Special Rapporteur and by various United Nations bodies,

1. *Invites* all Member States to draw up a special programme for the prevention of child prostitution, the suppression of its exploitation and the social rehabilitation of its victims;

2. *Recommends* that the United Nations Children's Fund allocate technical and financial support to Member States that are developing countries to set up experimental programmes for the prevention of child prostitution and the social rehabilitation of its victims;

3. *Encourages* the United Nations Educational, Scientific and Cultural Organization to carry out the study on the legal and effective protection of minors from pornography that was recommended by the international meeting of experts held in Madrid from 18 to 21 March 1986;

4. *Invites* Member States that belong to the International Criminal Police Organization to request that organization to make the fight against the international traffic in children one of its priorities;

5. *Decides* to apply the provisions of the present resolution, where appropriate, to young women and recommends that the Secretary-General and Member States do likewise;

6. *Requests* the Secretary-General to urge the following bodies to send representatives to the sessions of the Working Group on Contemporary Forms of Slavery: Commission on the Status of Women, Centre for Social Development and Humanitarian Affairs of the Secretariat, United Nations Children's Fund, United Nations Development Programme, United Nations University, International Labour Organisation, Food and Agriculture Organization of the United Nations,

United Nations Educational, Scientific and Cultural Organization, World Health Organization, World Bank, International Monetary Fund and International Criminal Police Organization;

7. *Also requests* the Secretary-General to prepare a survey of the recommendations made by the Working Group since its inception;

8. *Endorses* the recommendation made by the Commission on Human Rights in its resolution 1988/42 that the Sub-Commission on Prevention of Discrimination and Protection of Minorities consider appointing a special rapporteur to review the implementation of the recommendations made and the appropriate measures taken by United Nations organs and specialized agencies, other international organizations and Member States and to submit recommendations with a view to achieving further progress in the prevention and suppression of slavery-like practices, the traffic in persons and the exploitation of the prostitution of others, as well as other contemporary forms of slavery;

9. *Decides*, in the light of the recommendations made in its resolution 1983/30 and in General Assembly resolutions 38/107 and 40/103, to consider the question of the suppression of the traffic in persons and of the exploitation of the prostitution of others at its first regular session of 1989 under the agenda item entitled "Human rights".

Economic and Social Council resolution 1988/34

27 May 1988   Meeting 16   Adopted without vote

Approved by Second Committee (E/1988/89/Add.1) without vote, 23 May (meeting 20); draft by Commission on Human Rights (E/1988/12 & Corr.1); agenda item 10.

Report of the Secretary-General. In June,[100] the Secretary-General presented a survey of recommendations made by the Working Group since its inception in 1975.[101]

Working Group activities. The Sub-Commission's five-member Working Group on Contemporary Forms of Slavery, at its thirteenth session (Geneva, 1-5 and 12 August),[102] reviewed and made a number of recommendations on developments in slavery and the slave trade, including the sale of children and child labour (see below, under "Other human rights questions"), debt bondage, traffic in persons and exploitation of the prostitution of others, and slavery-like practices of *apartheid* and colonialism.

As requested by the Commission (see above), the Group drew up its plan of action for the period 1989 to 1991.

Sub-Commission action. On 1 September,[103] the Sub-Commission approved the Group's plan of action. It asked the Secretary-General to seek means to facilitate the participation of indigenous peoples in the Group and to prepare an annotated agenda of the work of the Group for each of its sessions.

Right to leave a country

Human Rights Commission action. On 8 March,[104] the Commission thanked the Sub-

Commission's Special Rapporteur for the first part of his final report and for the preliminary draft declaration on the right of everyone to leave any country, including his own, and to return to his country,[105] and asked that the Sub-Commission be provided with the entire report. It requested the Secretary-General to continue to assist the Special Rapporteur.

Report of the Special Rapporteur. In June,[106] Special Rapporteur Chama L. C. Mubanga-Chipoya (Zambia) submitted his final report on current trends and developments regarding the right to leave any country including one's own, and to return to one's own country, and the evolution of related international legal provisions.

The Special Rapporteur concluded that freedom of movement within a country had progressed substantially and noted some progress in the right of a national to leave his own country. National security and public order were among the most common permissible restrictions on the right to leave one's country. He recommended that national laws include provisions on the right of nationals and aliens to leave the country and the right of nationals and permanent residents to return, and effective measures for developed and developing countries to eliminate the problem of the "brain drain". The Special Rapporteur also made suggestions to Governments regarding travel documents. He called for due attention to the conditions of refugees and the reunification of families and discussed the adoption of a draft declaration on freedom and non-discrimination relating to the right of everyone to leave any country, including his own.

Annexes to the Special Rapporteur's report were contained in an addendum[107] and included the draft declaration, a questionnaire on recent practice and legislation of States and the development of international law and a list of related communications, draft principles on freedom and non-discrimination formulated by the Sub-Commission in 1963, and the 1986 Strasbourg Declaration on the Right to Leave and Return.

Sub-Commission action. On 1 September,[108] the Sub-Commission decided to examine further in 1989 the Special Rapporteur's recommendations, as well as the draft declaration on freedom and non-discrimination in respect of the right of everyone to leave any country, including his own, and to return to his country. It also asked the Secretary-General to transmit the draft declaration to Member States, specialized agencies and other intergovernmental and non-governmental organizations for comments.

Human rights and fundamental freedoms

Human Rights Commission action. On 8 March,[109] the Commission expressed concern that persons were detained for seeking to exercise peacefully their human rights and fundamental freedoms, particularly the rights to freedom of expression, assembly and association. It asked Governments to release all persons deprived of their liberty for seeking peacefully to exercise those rights and freedoms or to promote and defend them and called on Governments, pending such release, to take effective measures to safeguard the human rights and fundamental freedoms of such persons.

Sub-Commission action. On 1 September,[110] the Sub-Commission called for the release of all persons detained, in violation of their rights to freedom of speech, association and assembly, for defending the human rights of others and for publicizing alleged violations of such human rights. It urged the Commission to finalize the drafting of a declaration on the right and responsibility of individuals, groups and organs of society to promote and protect universally recognized human rights and fundamental freedoms (see below, under "Advancement of human rights").

Freedom of speech

Human Rights Commission action. On 8 March,[111] the Commission, expressing concern at the extensive detention of persons who exercised their right to freedom of opinion and expression, appealed to States to ensure respect and support for those who exercised it and to release those detained solely for doing so. It requested the Sub-Commission to continue considering the right to freedom of opinion and expression and to recommend to the Commission in 1989 further measures to promote and safeguard that right.

Sub-Commission action. On 1 September,[80] the Sub-Commission requested Danilo Türk (Yugoslavia) to prepare a proposal for a study called for by the Commission concerning the right to freedom of expression and opinion, to serve as a basis for future decisions of the Sub-Commission.

Independence of the judicial system

Human Rights Commission action. On 8 March,[112] the Commission requested the Sub-Commission to review and finalize the draft declaration on the independence of justice, as proposed by Special Rapporteur L. M. Singhvi (India) in 1985,[44] with a view to its submission in 1989. The Sub-Commission was asked to take into account the comments of Governments, the Centre for Social Development and Humanitarian Affairs and other relevant parties.

Report of the Special Rapporteur. In July, Special Rapporteur L. M. Singhvi presented comments received, as at 7 June, on the draft declaration on the independence and impartiality of the judiciary, jurors and assessors and the independence of lawyers from 19 Governments and the Centre for Social Development and Humanitarian Affairs.[113] He also submitted a revised version of the draft declaration.[114]

Sub-Commission action. On 1 September,[115] the Sub-Commission referred the draft declaration to the Commission for further consideration.

REFERENCES

[1]*Multilateral Treaties Deposited with the Secretary-General: Status as at 31 December 1988* (ST/LEG/SER.E/7), Sales No. E.89.V.3. [2]YUN 1966, p. 423, GA res. 2200 A (XXI), annex, 16 Dec. 1966. [3]YUN 1976, p. 609. [4]A/43/518. [5]E/1988/12 (res. 1988/27). [6]*Ibid.* (dec. 1988/104). [7]E/CN.4/1989/3 (res. 1988/22). [8]YUN 1987, p. 760. [9]A/43/40. [10]A/44/40. [11]YUN 1985, p. 853, ESC dec. 1985/105, 8 Feb. 1985. [12]E/1988/49. [13]E/1988/12 (res. 1988/33). [14]YUN 1985, p. 854, ESC res. 1985/37, 30 May 1985. [15]E/CN.4/Sub.2/1988/18. [16]YUN 1987, p. 741. [17]E/CN.4/Sub.2/1988/18 & Add.1. [18]E/CN.4/1989/3 (res. 1988/24). [19]E/1988/12 (res. 1988/4). [20]*Ibid.* (res. 1988/6). [21]*Ibid.* (res. 1988/3). [22]*Ibid.* (res. 1988/8). [23]*Ibid.* (res. 1988/5). [24]*Ibid.* (res. 1988/7). [25]YUN 1987, pp. 741 & 742, GA res. 42/94 & 42/95, 7 Dec. 1987. [26]A/43/633 & Add.1. [27]YUN 1981, p. 242. [28]YUN 1987, p. 204. [29]YUN 1986, p. 123. [30]*Ibid.*, p. 925. [31]E/1988/12 (res. 1988/10). [32]YUN 1978, pp. 915 & 916, SC res. 435(1978) & 439(1978), 28 Sep. & 13 Nov. 1978. [33]E/CN.4/1989/3 (res. 1988/5). [34]*Ibid.* (res. 1988/7). [35]YUN 1978, p. 915, SC res. 435(1978), 28 Sep. 1978. [36]YUN 1983, p. 1087, GA res. 38/40, 7 Dec. 1983. [37]YUN 1985, p. 1138, GA res. 40/50, 2 Dec. 1985. [38]YUN 1986, p. 965, GA res. 41/16, 31 Oct. 1986. [39]YUN 1987, p. 1032, GA res. 42/78, 4 Dec. 1987. [40]*Ibid.*, p. 750, GA res. 42/96, 7 Dec. 1987. [41]A/43/632. [42]A/43/735. [43]A/43/L.49 & Corr.1. [44]YUN 1985, p. 873. [45]E/CN.4/1989/3 (dec. 1988/103). [46]E/CN.4/Sub.2/1988/13. [47]E/CN.4/Sub.2/1988/14. [48]E/CN.4/Sub.2/1988/15. [49]E/CN.4/Sub.2/1988/28. [50]YUN 1987, p. 754. [51]E/CN.4/1989/3 (dec. 1988/107). [52]*Ibid.* (res. 1988/17). [53]YUN 1987, p. 754, GA dec. 42/426, 7 Dec. 1987. [54]A/C.6/43/L.9. [55]E/CN.4/1988/17 & Add.1. [56]E/1988/12 (res. 1988/32). [57]YUN 1984, p. 813, GA res. 39/46, annex, 10 Dec. 1984. [58]YUN 1985, p. 863. [59]YUN 1987, p. 755. [60]A/43/519. [61]E/1988/12 (res. 1988/36). [62]*Ibid.* (res. 1988/31). [63]YUN 1986, p. 706. [64]E/CN.4/1988/16. [65]E/CN.4/Sub.2/1987/12/Add.3. [66]E/CN.4/Sub.2/1987/12/Add.1. [67]A/43/46. [68]E/1988/12 (res. 1988/35). [69]YUN 1981, p. 906, GA res. 36/151, 16 Dec. 1981. [70]A/43/779. [71]E/1988/12 (res. 1988/11). [72]E/CN.4/1988/8. [73]E/1988/12 (res. 1988/62). [74]YUN 1984, p. 820. [75]E/CN.4/1988/66. [76]E/CN.4/1989/3 (res. 1988/28). [77]E/CN.4/Sub.2/1988/23. [78]E/1988/12 (res. 1988/45). [79]YUN 1987, p. 758. [80]E/CN.4/1989/3 (dec. 1988/110). [81]E/CN.4/Sub.2/1988/12. [82]E/1988/12 (res. 1988/38). [83]E/CN.4/1989/3 (res. 1988/23). [84]E/1988/12 (res. 1988/41). [85]E/CN.4/Sub.2/1988/17. [86]E/CN.4/1989/3 (res. 1988/9). [87]E/CN.4/1988/22 & Add.1,2. [88]E/1988/12 (res. 1988/68). [89]E/CN.4/1989/3 (dec. 1988/109). [90]E/1988/12 (res. 1988/34). [91]YUN 1980, p. 843. [92]E/CN.4/1989/18. [93]E/CN.4/1989/18/Add.1. [94]E/1988/12 (res. 1988/76). [95]YUN 1987, p. 764. [96]E/CN.4/Sub.2/1988/19. [97]E/1988/12 (res. 1988/42). [98]YUN 1987, p. 765. [99]YUN 1983, p. 849, ESC dec. 1983/143, 4 Mar. 1983. [100]E/CN.4/Sub.2/1988/29. [101]YUN 1975, p. 639. [102]E/CN.4/Sub.2/1988/32. [103]E/CN.4/1989/3 (res. 1988/31). [104]E/1988/12 (res. 1988/46). [105]YUN 1987, p. 766. [106]E/CN.4/Sub.2/1988/35. [107]E/CN.4/Sub.2/1988/35/Add.1 & Corr.1. [108]E/CN.4/1989/3 (res. 1988/39). [109]E/1988/12 (res. 1988/39). [110]E/CN.4/1989/3 (res. 1988/38). [111]E/1988/12 (res. 1988/37).

(112)*Ibid.* (res. 1988/40). (113)E/CN.4/Sub.2/1988/20 & Corr.1. (114)E/CN.4/Sub.2/1988/20/Add.1 & Corr.1. (115)E/CN.4/1989/3 (res. 1988/25).

Economic, social and cultural rights

Report of the Secretary-General. In accordance with a 1987 request of the Commission on Human Rights,[1] the Secretary-General submitted in 1988 a report[2] containing replies from 10 Governments, 6 specialized agencies and 17 NGOs on their policies regarding the implementation, promotion and protection of economic, social and cultural rights.

Human Rights Commission action. On 7 March,[3] by a roll-call vote of 30 to 9, with 3 abstentions, the Commission appealed to States to pursue policies for the implementation of economic, social, cultural, civil and political rights, and called on them to co-operate in promoting social progress and better standards of life in larger freedom. The Commission again asked the Secretary-General to invite Governments, United Nations organs, specialized agencies and NGOs to comment on their policies for the implementation, promotion and protection of economic, social and cultural rights and to report to the Commission in 1989. The Commission asked its Sub-Commission to appoint a special rapporteur to study problems, policies and progressive measures relating to a more effective realization of those rights.

Sub-Commission action. In response to the Commission's request, the Sub-Commission, on 1 September,[4] decided to appoint Danilo Türk (Yugoslavia) as its Special Rapporteur to prepare a study of problems, policies and progressive measures relating to the more effective realization of economic, social and cultural rights. It recommended that he take account of its guidelines, which were outlined in a 1987 resolution.[1] The Special Rapporteur was asked to submit a preliminary report in 1989. The Sub-Commission recommended that the Commission and the Economic and Social Council request the Secretary-General to provide the Special Rapporteur with all the assistance he needed.

Covenant on Economic, Social and Cultural Rights

As at 31 December 1988, the International Covenant on Economic, Social and Cultural Rights, adopted by the General Assembly in 1966[5] and in force since 1976,[6] had been ratified or acceded to by 92 States.[7] In 1988, Guatemala became a party to it.

In his report to the General Assembly on the International Covenants on Human Rights,[8] the Secretary-General provided information on the status of ratifications, accessions and signatures to the Covenant as at 1 August, as well as on other questions related to its implementation (see also below, under "Advancement of human rights").

Implementation of the Covenant

Human Rights Commission action. The Commission, on 7 March,[9] encouraged States parties to the Covenant to support and co-operate with the Committee on Economic, Social and Cultural Rights, established in 1985[10] to oversee implementation of the Covenant from 1987 on. It welcomed the Committee's establishment of a sessional working group to consider its methods of work (see below) and asked it to develop general guidelines for preparing reports under the Covenant, taking into account the Secretary-General's guidelines for preparing reports. It encouraged the Committee to consider ways of strengthening dialogue and an information flow with other treaty bodies and invited States parties to identify benchmarks to measure the progressive realization of rights under the Covenant. It requested the Economic and Social Council to identify ways in which international co-operation and technical assistance would contribute to implementation of the Covenant and asked the Secretary-General to intensify co-ordination between United Nations human rights activities and programmes of the development agencies. The Sub-Commission was asked to identify practical strategies for promoting the Covenant, particularly for the most vulnerable and disadvantaged.

Committee on Economic, Social and Cultural Rights. The Committee on Economic, Social and Cultural Rights held its second session at Geneva from 8 to 25 February.[11] It established a sessional five-member working group to consider its methods of work and to develop general guidelines for preparing reports. On 23 February, the Committee discussed recommendations drawn up by the group.

Concerning the rights covered by articles 6 to 9 of the Covenant (the right to work and to favourable conditions of work, trade union rights and the right to social security), the Committee examined reports from Austria[12] and Zaire;[13] by articles 10 to 12 (protection of the family, mothers and children, and the right to an adequate living standard and to physical and mental health), reports from Bulgaria,[14] the Byelorussian SSR,[15] Chile,[16] Denmark,[17] Mongolia,[18] Norway,[19] Poland,[20] Romania[21] and Sweden;[22] and by articles 13 to 15 (the rights to education, including compulsory education, and cultural participation), from Austria,[23] Chile,[24] Yugoslavia[25] and Zaire.[26]

Annexed to the Committee's report was a list of States parties and the status of report submissions, a list of Committee members, and the Secretary-General's statement on the budget implications of the Committee's recommendations.

Other action. The Secretary-General transmitted to the Economic and Social Council the tenth report of the International Labour Organisation (ILO) Committee of Experts on the Application of Conventions and Recommendations[27] on progress towards observance of the Covenant's provisions, within ILO's scope of activities. The report detailed progress in the observance of articles 6 to 10 in 12 States.

In January,[28] the Secretary-General transmitted to the Council the second report of the United Nations Educational, Scientific and Cultural Organization (UNESCO) describing progress made in the observance of articles 13 to 15.

ECONOMIC AND SOCIAL COUNCIL ACTION

On 24 May 1988, the Economic and Social Council adopted **resolution 1988/4** without vote.

International Covenant on Economic, Social and Cultural Rights

The Economic and Social Council,

Mindful of its central responsibilities under the International Covenant on Economic, Social and Cultural Rights,

Recalling its resolution 1985/17 of 28 May 1985, by which it established the Committee on Economic, Social and Cultural Rights, to be entrusted, as from 1987, with the important task of overseeing the implementation of the Covenant,

Recalling also its resolutions and decisions relating to its Sessional Working Group of Governmental Experts on the Implementation of the International Covenant on Economic, Social and Cultural Rights, including resolution 1979/43 of 11 May 1979, which remain in force in so far as they are not superseded or modified by the provisions of resolution 1985/17,

Reaffirming the importance of increasing public awareness of the Committee on Economic, Social and Cultural Rights and the role that non-governmental organizations can play in that regard,

Recalling General Assembly resolutions 41/121 of 4 December 1986 and 42/105 of 7 December 1987 on reporting obligations under United Nations instruments on human rights, which are of relevance to the Committee on Economic, Social and Cultural Rights, and in which the Assembly reaffirmed the importance of maintaining summary records of the proceedings of the bodies supervising the implementation of United Nations instruments on human rights, and bearing in mind the relevance to the work of the Committee of the activities and experience of other United Nations treaty bodies,

Recalling also the request of the General Assembly, in its resolution 42/105, that the Council consider changing the periodicity of reporting under the International Covenant on Economic, Social and Cultural Rights, and the endorsement by the Assembly, in its resolution 42/102 of 7 December 1987, of the invitation extended by the Economic and Social Council to the Committee to consider recommendations relating to its future work,

1. *Takes note with appreciation* of the report of the Committee on Economic, Social and Cultural Rights on its second session, including the conclusions and recommendations adopted by the Committee with respect to its future methods of work;

2. *Urges* all States that have not yet done so to become parties to the International Covenant on Economic, Social and Cultural Rights;

3. *Invites* States parties to the Covenant to follow the recommendations made by the Committee to address the problems of non-submission and extended delays in the submission of periodic reports, in particular regarding the need to submit and present the reports in a timely manner and to complete the entire cycle of initial reports before submitting second reports, and requests the Secretary-General to send appropriate reminders to those States parties whose reports are overdue;

4. *Welcomes* the decisions taken by the Committee on the action it should take to seek supplementary information in cases where reports are incomplete;

5. *Invites* States parties to the Covenant to review the processes followed in the preparation of their periodic reports on the implementation of the Covenant, including consultation and co-ordination with appropriate governmental departments and agencies, compilation of data and training of staff, and to hold, as appropriate, consultations with interested non-governmental organizations, with a view to ensuring full compliance with relevant guidelines, improving the quality of description and analysis in such reports and limiting reports to a reasonable length;

6. *Endorses* the recommendation of the Committee that States parties be requested to submit a single report within two years of the entry into force of the Covenant for the State party concerned and thereafter at five-year intervals, and requests the Secretary-General to inform States parties to the Covenant of this decision;

7. *Welcomes* the decision of the Committee to revise and simplify the guidelines for reports of States parties and to place limits on the time devoted to the consideration of the report of each State party;

8. *Endorses* the request of the Committee that the Secretary-General prepare a report showing clearly the extent and nature of any overlapping of issues dealt with in the principal human rights treaties, with a view to reducing, as appropriate, duplication in the different supervisory bodies of issues raised with respect to any given State party;

9. *Takes note* of the recommendation of the Committee on its future sessions, but considers that, in view of the various recommendations made by the Committee to expedite its consideration of periodic reports, the current provision for one annual session of three weeks' duration should be maintained for the time being;

10. *Authorizes* the Committee to establish, within available resources, a pre-sessional working group to meet for a period of up to one week prior to each session;

11. *Agrees* that an effort should be made to avoid overlapping future sessions of the Committee with sessions of the Commission on Human Rights;

12. *Takes note* of the decision of the Committee to devote one day during each session to a general discussion of one specific right or a particular article of the Covenant in order to develop in greater depth its understanding of the relevant issues;

13. *Welcomes* the decision of the Committee to prepare general comments, based on the various articles and provisions of the Covenant, with a view to assisting States parties in fulfilling their reporting obligations, paying particular attention to relevant practices followed by other treaty bodies, and takes note of the methods of work to be followed at future sessions of the Committee;

14. *Urges* the Committee to encourage States parties, in conformity with article 2, paragraph 1, of the Covenant, to consider identifying bench-marks for measuring achievements in the progressive realization of the rights recognized in the Covenant and, in this context, to pay particular regard to the most vulnerable and disadvantaged persons;

15. *Urges* the specialized agencies, the regional commissions and other appropriate United Nations bodies, in particular the United Nations Development Programme, to extend their full co-operation and support to the Committee on Economic, Social and Cultural Rights by, *inter alia*, enabling their representatives to attend meetings of the Committee and submitting relevant information to the Committee;

16. *Invites* non-governmental organizations in consultative status with the Council to submit to the Committee written statements that might contribute to full and universal recognition and realization of the rights set forth in the Covenant, requests the Secretary-General to make those statements available to the Committee in a timely manner and thanks those organizations that submitted written statements to the Committee for consideration at its second session;

17. *Requests* the Secretary-General to bring the report of the Committee to the attention of the Commission on Human Rights, its Sub-Commission on Prevention of Discrimination and Protection of Minorities, the Human Rights Committee, the Committee on the Elimination of Discrimination against Women, other United Nations organs and their subsidiaries, specialized agencies concerned with providing technical assistance and the regional commissions;

18. *Requests* the Secretary-General to continue his efforts under the programme of advisory services in the field of human rights to assist States parties in discharging their reporting obligations under the Covenant, including the holding of training courses on the preparation of reports on the implementation of the Covenant, and to advise States parties of the availability of such assistance;

19. *Takes note with appreciation* of the conclusions of the Committee on the importance of greater publicity for its work, and encourages the Secretary-General to give publicity to the proceedings of the Committee and to ensure that it receives full administrative support so as to enable it to discharge its functions as effectively as possible;

20. *Requests* the Secretary-General to continue to provide the Committee, upon its request, with relevant data from official United Nations sources, including information from the specialized agencies and the regional commissions;

21. *Decides* to transmit the report of the Committee to the General Assembly at its forty-third session for consideration under the agenda item entitled "International Covenants on Human Rights".

Economic and Social Council resolution 1988/4

24 May 1988   Meeting 12   Adopted without vote

14-nation draft (E/1988/L.22/Rev.1), orally revised; agenda item 3.
Sponsors: Australia, Canada, Costa Rica, Denmark, Ecuador, France, Germany, Federal Republic of, Italy, Mexico, Netherlands, Norway, Peru, Senegal, United Kingdom.
Meeting numbers. ESC 7, 8, 10-12.

Interdependence of economic, social, cultural, civil and political rights

On 8 December 1988, on the recommendation of the Third Committee, the General Assembly adopted **resolution 43/113** by recorded vote.

Indivisibility and interdependence of economic, social, cultural, civil and political rights

The General Assembly,

Mindful of the obligations of States under the Charter of the United Nations to promote social progress and better standards of life in larger freedom and universal respect for, and observance of, human rights and fundamental freedoms for all without distinction as to race, sex, language or religion,

Reaffirming the Universal Declaration of Human Rights, the International Covenant on Civil and Political Rights, the International Covenant on Economic, Social and Cultural Rights and the Declaration on Social Progress and Development,

Recalling that in the preambles to the International Covenants on Human Rights it is recognized that the ideal of free human beings enjoying freedom from fear and want can only be achieved if conditions are created whereby persons may enjoy their economic, social and cultural rights as well as their civil and political rights,

Recalling its resolutions 40/114 of 13 December 1985, 41/117 of 4 December 1986 and 42/102 of 7 December 1987,

Reaffirming the provisions of its resolution 32/130 of 16 December 1977 that all human rights and fundamental freedoms are indivisible and interdependent and that the promotion and protection of one category of rights can never exempt or excuse States from the promotion and protection of the other rights,

Convinced that equal attention and urgent consideration should be given to the implementation, promotion and protection of economic, social, cultural, civil and political rights,

Desirous of removing all obstacles to the full realization of human rights, in particular colonialism, neo-colonialism, racism, racial discrimination in all its forms, *apartheid*, foreign intervention, occupation, aggression and domination,

Recognizing the fundamental rights of every people to exercise full sovereignty over its natural wealth and resources,

Reaffirming that there is a close and multidimensional relationship between disarmament and development, that progress in disarmament would considerably promote progress in development and that resources released through disarmament measures could contribute to the economic and social development and well-being of all peoples, in particular those of the developing countries,

Recognizing that the realization of the right to development may help to promote the enjoyment of all human rights and fundamental freedoms,

Recalling Commission on Human Rights resolutions 1985/42 of 14 March 1985, 1986/15 of 10 March 1986, 1987/19 and 1987/20 of 10 March 1987 and 1988/22 and 1988/23 of 7 March 1988, in which the Commission stated that the implementation, promotion and protection of economic, social and cultural rights have not received sufficient attention within the framework of the United Nations system,

Requesting the Secretary-General to enhance his efforts under the programme of advisory services to States in the implementation, promotion and protection of the human rights and fundamental freedoms set forth in the International Covenants on Human Rights and other United Nations instruments in the field of human rights,

1. *Notes* the essential importance of national efforts and international co-operation to achieve the full and effective realization of all human rights recognized in the International Covenants on Human Rights and other international instruments;

2. *Appeals* to all States to pursue policies directed towards the implementation, promotion and protection of economic, social, cultural, civil and political rights recognized in the International Covenants on Human Rights and other international instruments;

3. *Requests* the Commission on Human Rights to give more attention to the realization of economic, social and cultural rights under the relevant agenda items;

4. *Urges* the Secretary-General to take determined steps, within existing resources, to give publicity to the Human Rights Committee and to the Committee on Economic, Social and Cultural Rights and to ensure that they receive full administrative support in order to enable them to discharge their functions effectively;

5. *Affirms* the importance and relevance, to programmes and activities being undertaken throughout the United Nations system in the field of human rights, of reports submitted by States parties to the International Covenants on Human Rights to the Human Rights Committee and the Committee on Economic, Social and Cultural Rights;

6. *Decides* to consider the question of the indivisibility and interdependence of economic, social, cultural, civil and political rights at its forty-fourth session under the item entitled "International Covenants on Human Rights".

General Assembly resolution 43/113

8 December 1988   Meeting 75   132-1-23 (recorded vote)

Approved by Third Committee (A/43/872) by recorded vote (111-1-23), 23 November (meeting 51); 7-nation draft (A/C.3/43/L.44); agenda item 100.
Sponsors: Bulgaria, Byelorussian SSR, German Democratic Republic, Hungary, Mongolia, Nicaragua, Syrian Arab Republic.
Meeting numbers. GA 43rd session: 3rd Committee 39-43, 46, 51; plenary 75.

Recorded vote in Assembly as follows:

In favour: Afghanistan, Algeria, Angola, Antigua and Barbuda, Argentina, Australia, Bahamas, Bahrain, Bangladesh, Barbados, Belize, Benin, Bhutan, Bolivia, Botswana, Brazil, Brunei Darussalam, Bulgaria, Burkina Faso, Burma, Burundi, Byelorussian SSR, Cameroon, Cape Verde, Central African Republic, Chad, China, Colombia, Comoros, Congo, Costa Rica, Côte d'Ivoire, Cuba, Cyprus, Czechoslovakia, Democratic Yemen, Djibouti, Dominica, Dominican Republic, Ecuador, Egypt, El Salvador, Equatorial Guinea, Ethiopia, Fiji, Gabon, Gambia, German Democratic Republic, Ghana, Grenada, Guatemala, Guinea, Guinea-Bissau, Guyana, Haiti, Honduras, Hungary, India, Indonesia, Iran, Iraq, Jamaica, Jordan, Kenya, Kuwait, Lao People's Democratic Republic, Lebanon, Lesotho, Liberia, Libyan Arab Jamahiriya, Madagascar, Malawi, Malaysia, Maldives, Mali, Malta, Mauritania, Mauritius, Mexico, Mongolia, Morocco, Mozambique, Nepal, New Zealand, Nicaragua, Niger, Nigeria, Oman, Pakistan, Panama, Papua New Guinea, Paraguay, Peru, Philippines, Poland, Qatar, Romania,

Rwanda, Saint Kitts and Nevis, Saint Lucia, Saint Vincent and the Grenadines, Samoa, Sao Tome and Principe, Saudi Arabia, Senegal, Seychelles, Sierra Leone, Singapore, Solomon Islands, Somalia, Sri Lanka, Sudan, Suriname, Syrian Arab Republic, Thailand, Togo, Trinidad and Tobago, Tunisia, Uganda, Ukrainian SSR, USSR, United Arab Emirates, United Republic of Tanzania, Uruguay, Vanuatu, Venezuela, Viet Nam, Yemen, Yugoslavia, Zaire, Zambia, Zimbabwe.
Against: United States.
Abstaining: Austria, Belgium, Canada, Chile, Denmark, Finland, France, Germany, Federal Republic of, Greece, Iceland, Ireland, Israel, Italy, Japan, Luxembourg, Netherlands, Norway, Portugal, Spain, Swaziland, Sweden, Turkey, United Kingdom.

In the Committee, the eighth preambular paragraph was adopted by a recorded vote of 109 to 7, with 17 abstentions. The Assembly retained the paragraph by a recorded vote of 133 to 7, with 16 abstentions.

Right to development

Working Group activities. In 1988, the 15-member Working Group of Governmental Experts on the Right to Development, established by the Economic and Social Council in 1981,[29] held its eleventh session at Geneva from 11 to 22 January.[30]

As requested by the General Assembly in 1987,[31] the Group considered an analytical compilation of comments on implementation of the Declaration on the Right to Development,[32] prepared by the Secretary-General and received from Governments, United Nations bodies, specialized agencies and other governmental and non-governmental organizations. The Group recommended that the Commission on Human Rights remind those who had not replied to expedite their responses and compile statements which might be made by Governments, United Nations bodies, specialized agencies and intergovernmental and non-governmental organizations on the subject. The Group reiterated that urgent action should be taken to implement its 1987 proposals aimed at deepening and widening the concept of the right to development.[33] It felt that there was a need for a mechanism within the United Nations to monitor, review and co-ordinate the actions taken by United Nations bodies and specialized agencies to implement the Declaration within their work programmes. To enhance the right of development, the Group recommended, among other things: a meeting of eminent persons under the aegis of the Commission, to help further implement the Declaration; strengthening of the cultural and educational base of the development process; an extension of United Nations University programmes emphasizing technology and development; that emphasis be placed on the impact of heavy debt on developing countries' right to development; and further studies on obstacles to development. It also recommended measures towards co-ordinated and early implementation of the Declaration.

Human Rights Commission action. On 7 March,[34] the Commission requested the Secretary-General to transmit the Working Group's report to the General Assembly in 1988 and to circulate it among Governments, United Nations bodies, specialized agencies and other governmental and non-governmental organizations, asking them once more to offer their comments and views on implementing and further enhancing the Declaration as a matter of urgency. The Commission decided to convene the Working Group during the last week of January 1989 and directed it to study the analytical compilation and to submit final recommendations in 1989. It also decided that in 1989, based on consideration of the Group's report and the views expressed by Commission members, a decision would be taken on further action on the subject. It asked the Secretary-General to assist the Group.

By **decision 1988/128** of 27 May, the Economic and Social Council transmitted the Group's report to the General Assembly and approved its convening in January 1989 and the Commission's request to the Secretary-General to assist the Group.

GENERAL ASSEMBLY ACTION

On 8 December 1988, on the recommendation of the Third Committee, the General Assembly adopted **resolution 43/127** without vote.

Right to development

The General Assembly,

Recalling the proclamation by the General Assembly at its forty-first session of the Declaration on the Right to Development,

Recalling also its resolutions and those of the Commission on Human Rights relating to the right to development, and taking note of Commission resolution 1988/26 of 7 March 1988, approved by the Economic and Social Council,

Reiterating the importance of the right to development for all countries, in particular the developing countries,

Mindful that, pursuant to the proclamation of the Declaration on the Right to Development, the Commission has entered a new phase of its deliberation on this matter, which is directed towards the implementation and further enhancement of the Declaration,

Having considered the report of the Working Group of Governmental Experts on the Right to Development and all other relevant documents submitted to the General Assembly at its forty-third session,

Aware of the interest shown by several Member States, specialized agencies and non-governmental organizations in the work of the Working Group,

1. *Expresses the hope* that the replies of Governments, United Nations bodies and specialized agencies and governmental and non-governmental organizations, submitted at the request of the Secretary-General based on Commission on Human Rights resolution 1988/26 to offer their comments and views on the implementation of the Declaration on the Right to Development, will contain practical proposals for further enhancement of the Declaration;

2. *Endorses* the agreement reached by the Commission that future work on the question of the right to development should proceed step by step and in stages;

3. *Calls upon* the Working Group of Governmental Experts on the Right to Development, at its twelfth session, to study the analytical compilation to be prepared by the Secretary-General of all replies received in response to Commission resolution 1988/26, if necessary together with the individual replies themselves, and to submit to the Commission at its forty-fifth session its final recommendations on those proposals which would best contribute to the further enhancement and implementation of the Declaration at the individual, national and international levels, and especially on the views of the Secretary-General and of Governments on the means of establishing an evaluation system on the implementation and further enhancement of the Declaration;

4. *Calls upon* the Commission to decide at its forty-fifth session, on the basis of its consideration of the report of the Working Group and the views expressed by the members of the Commission during the session, on the future course of action on the question, in particular on practical measures for the implementation and enhancement of the Declaration;

5. *Invites* the Commission to report on the question to the General Assembly at its forty-fourth session, through the Economic and Social Council;

6. *Decides* to consider this question at its forty-fourth session under the item entitled ''Alternative approaches and ways and means within the United Nations system for improving the effective enjoyment of human rights and fundamental freedoms''.

General Assembly resolution 43/127

8 December 1988   Meeting 75   Adopted without vote

Approved by Third Committee (A/43/876) without vote, 17 November (meeting 46); 29-nation draft (A/C.3/43/L.35); agenda item 104.
Sponsors: Algeria, Argentina, Bolivia, Brazil, China, Colombia, Costa Rica, Cuba, Cyprus, Dominican Republic, Ecuador, Egypt, Ethiopia, Guatemala, India, Iraq, Jamaica, Mexico, Morocco, Nicaragua, Peru, Philippines, Rwanda, Sudan, Tunisia, United Republic of Tanzania, Venezuela, Yugoslavia, Zimbabwe.
Meeting numbers. GA 43rd session: 3rd Committee 36-38, 42, 46; plenary 75.

Right to food

Human Rights Commission action. On 7 March,[35] the Commission recommended that Governments which had not done so draw up national food security plans as suggested in 1987 by the Sub-Commission's Special Rapporteur.[33] It urged them to recognize and comply with their obligations, particularly those related to international co-operation based on free consent, and the principles enshrined in the Charter and other instruments. The Commission called on NGOs to support the right to food world-wide and to base their efforts on that right rather than policy statements. The Commission recommended a draft text, which the Economic and Social Council adopted (see below).

ECONOMIC AND SOCIAL COUNCIL ACTION

On 27 May 1988, the Economic and Social Council, on the recommendation of its Second

Committee, adopted **resolution 1988/33** without vote.

The right to food

The Economic and Social Council,

Recalling its decision 1983/140 of 27 May 1983, in which it authorized the Sub-Commission on Prevention of Discrimination and Protection of Minorities to entrust Mr. Asbjorn Eide, Special Rapporteur, with the preparation of a study on the right to adequate food as a human right and recommended that he give special attention to the normative content of the right to food and its significance in relation to the establishment of the new international economic order,

Noting with satisfaction that a comprehensive final study on this subject was presented by the Special Rapporteur to the Sub-Commission at its thirty-ninth session,

Recalling Sub-Commission resolution 1987/27 of 3 September 1987 and Commission on Human Rights resolution 1988/29 of 7 March 1988,

1. *Decides* that the study should be published by the United Nations and given the widest possible circulation;

2. *Decides* to take steps to ensure better co-ordination between specialized agencies and bodies dealing with food-related matters and human rights bodies of the United Nations, if possible through inter-agency cooperative arrangements;

3. *Draws the attention* of the Committee on Economic, Social and Cultural Rights to the study prepared by the Special Rapporteur, and invites the Committee to submit its observations thereon to the Economic and Social Council at an appropriate time.

Economic and Social Council resolution 1988/33

27 May 1988   Meeting 16   Adopted without vote

Approved by Second Committee (E/1988/89/Add.1) without vote, 23 May (meeting 20); draft by Commission on Human Rights (E/1988/12 & Corr.1); agenda item 10.

Right to own property

On 7 March,[36] the Commission on Human Rights appealed to Member States, specialized agencies and other United Nations bodies to communicate their views on the right to own property to the Secretary-General for submission to the General Assembly in 1988, as called for in 1986.[37]

By **decision 1988/145** of 27 May, the Economic and Social Council took note of an April note[38] of the Secretary-General informing the Council of progress made in preparing the report to the Assembly.

Also on 7 March,[39] by a roll-call vote of 31 to 11, the Commission called on States to ensure that their national legislation regarding all forms of property did not impair the enjoyment of human rights and fundamental freedoms, or prejudice the right freely to choose and develop political, social, economic and cultural systems.

Report of the Secretary General. In October,[40] the Secretary-General presented the views of 22 Member States, 2 United Nations bodies, 3 specialized agencies and 6 NGOs on the right

of everyone to own property alone and in association with others and the relationship between that right and other human rights and its impact on the economic and social development of States. He discussed United Nations and regional instruments relating to the right to property.

GENERAL ASSEMBLY ACTION

On 8 December 1988, on the recommendation of the Third Committee, the General Assembly adopted **resolution 43/123** without vote.

Respect for the right of everyone to own property alone as well as in association with others and its contribution to the economic and social development of Member States

The General Assembly,

Recalling its resolution 41/132 of 4 December 1986, in which it expressed the conviction that the full enjoyment by everyone of the right to own property alone as well as in association with others, as set forth in article 17 of the Universal Declaration of Human Rights, is of particular significance in fostering widespread enjoyment of other basic human rights and contributes to securing the goals of economic and social development enshrined in the Charter of the United Nations,

Recalling also Commission on Human Rights resolution 1987/17 of 10 March 1987, in which the Commission urged States, in accordance with their respective constitutional systems and in accordance with the Universal Declaration of Human Rights, to provide, where they have not done so, adequate constitutional and legal provisions to protect the right of everyone to own property alone as well as in association with others and the right not to be arbitrarily deprived of one's property,

Reaffirming the right of States and their peoples freely to choose and develop their political, social, economic and cultural systems and to determine their laws and regulations,

Recognizing the value of constructive dialogue in the national context on the ways and means by which States can promote the full enjoyment of the right of everyone to own property alone as well as in association with others,

Recognizing also in this context the importance of enabling everyone to acquire property, alone or in association with others, by taking practical actions that assist the economic development of developing countries,

Convinced that the right of everyone to own property alone as well as in association with others, as set forth in article 17 of the Universal Declaration of Human Rights, and as reaffirmed in paragraph 11 of the Declaration on the Rights of Disabled Persons and in article 16, paragraph 1 *(h)*, of the Convention on the Elimination of All Forms of Discrimination against Women, is of particular significance in fostering widespread enjoyment of other basic human rights,

Reaffirming, in accordance with article 29 of the Universal Declaration of Human Rights, that, in the exercise of his or her rights and freedoms, everyone shall be subject only to such limitations as are determined by law solely for the purpose of securing due recognition and respect for the rights and freedoms of others and of meeting the just requirements of morality, public order and the general welfare in a democratic society,

Taking note of the report of the Secretary-General on respect for the right of everyone to own property alone as well as in association with others and its contribution to the economic and social development of Member States,

Noting that the comments of Member States and of specialized agencies and other competent bodies of the United Nations system, as outlined in that report, consisted mainly of summaries of legal principles associated with the right to own property and that relatively little attention was given to the role of the right of everyone to own property, alone as well as in association with others, in ensuring the full and free participation of individuals in the economic and social systems of States,

1. *Recognizes* that there exist in Member States many forms of legal property ownership, including private, communal, social and state forms, each of which should contribute to ensuring effective development and utilization of human resources through the establishment of sound bases for political, economic and social justice;

2. *Affirms*, in accordance with article 30 of the Universal Declaration of Human Rights, that nothing in the Declaration, including the right of everyone to own property alone as well as in association with others, may be interpreted as implying for any State, group or person any right to engage in any activity or to perform any act aimed at the destruction of any of the rights and freedoms set forth therein;

3. *Considers* that further measures may be appropriate at the national level to ensure respect for the right of everyone to own property alone as well as in association with others and the right not to be arbitrarily deprived of one's property, as set forth in article 17 of the Universal Declaration of Human Rights;

4. *Urges* States, therefore, in accordance with their respective constitutional systems and with the Universal Declaration of Human Rights, to provide, where they have not done so, adequate constitutional and legal provisions to protect the right of everyone to own property alone as well as in association with others and the right not to be arbitrarily deprived of one's property;

5. *Requests* the Secretary-General to seek the views of Member States and of the specialized agencies and other competent bodies of the United Nations system on the means whereby and the degree to which the right to own property alone as well as in association with others contributes to the development of individual liberty and initiative, which serve to foster, strengthen and enhance the exercise of other human rights and fundamental freedoms;

6. *Suggests* that Member States and the specialized agencies and other competent bodies of the United Nations system, in the context of their remarks on the impact of the right to own property alone as well as in association with others, may wish to address, in particular, the right to own the following types of property:

(*a*) Personal property, including the residence of one's self and family;

(*b*) Economically productive property, including property associated with agriculture, commerce and industry;

7. *Requests* the Secretary-General, within existing resources, to report his findings to the General Assembly at its forty-fifth session;

8. *Decides* to consider this question at its forty-fifth session under the item entitled "Alternative approaches and ways and means within the United Nations system for improving the effective enjoyment of human rights and fundamental freedoms".

General Assembly resolution 43/123

8 December 1988   Meeting 75   Adopted without vote

Approved by Third Committee (A/43/876) without vote, 17 November (meeting 46); draft by United States (A/C.3/43/L.31); agenda item 104.
Meeting numbers. GA 43rd session: 3rd Committee 36-38, 42, 46; plenary 75.

Also on 8 December, on the recommendation of the Third Committee, the Assembly adopted **resolution 43/124** by recorded vote.

The impact of property on the enjoyment of human rights and fundamental freedoms
The General Assembly,

Recalling the Universal Declaration of Human Rights, the Declaration on Social Progress and Development and the Declaration on the Right to Development, which assign property a role in the exercise of human rights and fundamental freedoms,

Recalling also its resolution 42/115 of 7 December 1987 and Commission on Human Rights resolution 1987/18 of 10 March 1987 and taking note of Commission resolution 1988/19 of 7 March 1988 on the impact of property on the enjoyment of human rights and fundamental freedoms,

Taking note of Commission on Human Rights resolution 1988/20 of 7 March 1988 on recovery of nations' assets illegally removed by violators of human rights,

Mindful of the obligations of States under the Charter of the United Nations to promote higher standards of living, full employment, conditions of economic and social progress and development and solutions of international economic, social, health and related problems,

Recognizing the need to promote universal respect for, and observance of, human rights and fundamental freedoms for all without discrimination of any kind as to race, colour, sex, language, religion, political or other opinion, national or social origin, property, birth or other status,

Recognizing also that all peoples have the right to self-determination, by virtue of which they may freely determine their political status and may freely pursue their economic, social and cultural development,

Recognizing further that the right of all peoples to self-determination includes the exercise of their inalienable right to full sovereignty over all their natural wealth and resources,

Convinced that social justice is a prerequisite for lasting peace and that people can achieve complete fulfilment of their aspirations only within a just social order,

Convinced also that social development can be promoted by peaceful coexistence, friendly relations and cooperation among States with different social, economic or political systems,

Reaffirming that, in accordance with article 28 of the Universal Declaration of Human Rights, everyone is entitled to a social and international order in which the rights and freedoms set forth in the Declaration can be fully realized,

Bearing in mind that in no case may human rights and fundamental freedoms be exercised contrary to the purposes and principles of the Charter of the United Nations or to the rights and freedoms of others,

Recalling its resolution 34/137 of 14 December 1979 on the role of the public sector in promoting the economic development of developing countries, in which it emphasized the importance of an efficient public sector in the development process,

Reaffirming that, in accordance with article 6 of the Declaration on Social Progress and Development, social progress and development require the establishment, in conformity with human rights and fundamental freedoms and with the principles of justice and the social function of property, of forms of ownership of land and of the means of production which preclude any kind of exploitation of man, ensure equal rights to property for all and create conditions leading to genuine equality among people,

1. *Takes note* of the report of the Secretary-General;

2. *Reaffirms* the obligation of States to take effective steps with a view to achieving the full realization of civil, political, economic, social and cultural rights;

3. *Recognizes* that there exist in Member States many forms of legal property ownership, including private, communal and State forms, each of which should contribute to ensuring the effective development and utilization of human resources through the establishment of sound bases for political, economic and social justice;

4. *Calls upon* States to ensure that their national legislation with regard to all forms of property shall preclude any impairment of the enjoyment of human rights and fundamental freedoms, without prejudice to their right freely to choose and develop their political, social, economic and cultural systems;

5. *Requests* the Secretary-General, in preparing his report to the General Assembly at its forty-fifth session, in accordance with resolution 43/123 of 8 December 1988, to take into account the present resolution;

6. *Decides* to consider this question at its forty-fifth session under the item entitled ''Alternative approaches and ways and means within the United Nations system for improving the effective enjoyment of human rights and fundamental freedoms''.

General Assembly resolution 43/124

8 December 1988   Meeting 75   129-24-1 (recorded vote)

Approved by Third Committee (A/43/876) by recorded vote (107-24-1), 17 November (meeting 46); draft by German Democratic Republic (A/C.3/43/L.32); agenda item 104.
Meeting numbers. GA 43rd session: 3rd Committee 36-38, 42, 46; plenary 75.

Recorded vote in Assembly as follows:

In favour: Afghanistan, Algeria, Angola, Antigua and Barbuda, Argentina, Bahamas, Bahrain, Bangladesh, Barbados, Belize, Benin, Bhutan, Bolivia, Botswana, Brazil, Brunei Darussalam, Bulgaria, Burkina Faso, Burma, Burundi, Byelorussian SSR, Cameroon, Cape Verde, Central African Republic, Chad, Chile, China, Colombia, Comoros, Congo, Costa Rica, Côte d'Ivoire, Cuba, Cyprus, Czechoslovakia, Democratic Yemen, Dominica, Dominican Republic, Ecuador, Egypt, El Salvador, Equatorial Guinea, Ethiopia, Fiji, Gabon, Gambia, German Democratic Republic, Ghana, Grenada, Guatemala, Guinea, Guinea-Bissau, Guyana, Haiti, Honduras, Hungary, India, Indonesia, Iran, Iraq, Jamaica, Jordan, Kenya, Kuwait, Lao People's Democratic Republic, Lebanon, Lesotho, Liberia, Libyan Arab Jamahiriya, Madagascar, Malawi, Malaysia, Maldives, Mali, Mauritania, Mauritius, Mexico, Mongolia, Morocco, Mozambique, Nepal, Nicaragua, Niger, Nigeria, Pakistan, Panama, Papua New Guinea, Paraguay, Peru, Philippines, Poland, Qatar, Romania, Rwanda, Saint Kitts and Nevis, Saint Lucia, Saint Vincent and the Grenadines, Samoa, Sao Tome and Principe, Saudi Arabia, Senegal, Seychelles, Sierra Leone, Singapore, Solomon Islands, Somalia, Sri Lanka, Sudan, Suriname, Swaziland, Syrian Arab Republic, Thailand, Togo, Trinidad and Tobago, Tunisia, Uganda, Ukrainian SSR, USSR, United Arab Emirates, United Republic of Tanzania, Uruguay,

Vanuatu, Venezuela, Viet Nam, Yemen, Yugoslavia, Zaire, Zambia, Zimbabwe.
Against: Australia, Austria, Belgium, Canada, Denmark, Finland, France, Germany, Federal Republic of, Greece, Iceland, Ireland, Israel, Italy, Japan, Luxembourg, Netherlands, New Zealand, Norway, Portugal, Spain, Sweden, Turkey, United Kingdom, United States.
Abstaining: Malta.

Right to adequate housing

On 7 March,[41] the Commission on Human Rights, by a roll-call vote of 31 to none, with 11 abstentions, expressed deep concern that millions of people did not enjoy the right to adequate housing and reiterated the need for measures to promote the right of all persons to an adequate standard of living for themselves and their families, including adequate housing. It noted the General Assembly's 1987[42] call to States and concerned international organizations to pay special attention to the development of national shelter strategies and settlement improvement programmes within the global strategy for shelter to the year 2000.[43]

ECONOMIC AND SOCIAL COUNCIL ACTION

On 27 May 1988, the Economic and Social Council, on the recommendation of its Second Committee, adopted **resolution 1988/43** without vote.

Realization of the right to adequate housing
The Economic and Social Council,

Recalling its resolutions 1986/41 of 23 May 1986 and 1987/62 of 29 May 1987,

Recalling also General Assembly resolution 41/146 of 4 December 1986,

Taking into account General Assembly resolution 42/146 of 7 December 1987, in which the Assembly requested the Economic and Social Council and its appropriate functional commissions to keep the question of the right to adequate housing under periodic review,

Bearing in mind that the Universal Declaration of Human Rights and the International Covenant on Economic, Social and Cultural Rights provide that all persons have the right to an adequate standard of living for themselves and their families, including adequate housing, and that States should take appropriate steps to ensure the realization of that right,

Recognizing that the provision of housing for the homeless is an integral part of national economic and social development in all countries and an important step towards the realization of the right to development,

Recalling the objectives of the International Year of Shelter for the Homeless,

Noting with appreciation the measures and action taken and the renewed commitments made during the International Year of Shelter for the Homeless by Member States, specialized agencies and intergovernmental and non-governmental organizations to advance the realization of the right to adequate housing,

Recognizing the importance of sustaining the momentum generated by the International Year of Shelter for the Homeless,

1. *Expresses its deep concern* that millions of people do not enjoy the right to adequate housing;

2. *Reaffirms* the provisions of General Assembly resolution 42/146 and the need to take appropriate measures, at the national and international levels, to promote the right of all persons to an adequate standard of living for themselves and their families, including adequate housing;

3. *Calls upon* all States and international organizations concerned to pay special attention to the realization of the right to adequate housing in carrying out measures to develop national shelter strategies and settlement improvement programmes within the framework of the Global Strategy for Shelter to the Year 2000;

4. *Requests* the Secretary-General to submit a report on the social aspects of the situation of homeless people to the General Assembly at its forty-fifth session;

5. *Requests* the General Assembly to consider the question of the realization of the right to adequate housing at its forty-third session under the agenda item entitled ''Report of the Economic and Social Council''.

Economic and Social Council resolution 1988/43

27 May 1988   Meeting 16   Adopted without vote

Approved by Second Committee (E/1988/89/Add.1) without vote, 24 May (meeting 22); 19-nation draft (E/1988/C.2/L.14), orally revised following informal consultations; agenda item 10.

Sponsors: Afghanistan, Bulgaria, Cuba, Czechoslovakia, Ethiopia, German Democratic Republic, Kenya, Lao People's Democratic Republic, Libyan Arab Jamahiriya, Madagascar, Mongolia, Nicaragua, Panama, Sri Lanka, Syrian Arab Republic, Uganda, Ukrainian SSR, USSR, Viet Nam.

Popular participation and human rights

Report of the Secretary-General. As requested by the Commission on Human Rights in 1987,[44] the Secretary-General submitted a report summarizing the views of seven Governments, two United Nations bodies, two specialized agencies and six NGOs on his 1985 study on popular participation as an important factor in the realization of all human rights.[45]

Human Rights Commission action. On 7 March,[46] the Commission invited Governments, United Nations bodies, specialized agencies and NGOs that had not done so to comment on the Secretary-General's 1985 study. It asked the Secretary-General to submit those comments in 1989 and decided to consider at that time a study of laws and practices on the extent to which the right to participation had been established and had evolved at the national level, which the Commission had requested in 1987.[44]

REFERENCES

[1]YUN 1987, p. 767. [2]E/CN.4/1988/9 & Add.1,2. [3]E/1988/12 (res. 1988/22). [4]E/CN.4/1989/3 (res. 1988/33). [5]YUN 1966, p. 419, GA res. 2200 A (XXI), annex, 16 Dec. 1966. [6]YUN 1976, p. 609. [7]*Multilateral Treaties Deposited with the Secretary-General: Status as at 31 December 1988* (ST/LEG/SER.E/7), Sales No. E.89.V.3. [8]A/43/518. [9]E/1988/12 (res. 1988/23). [10]YUN 1985, p. 878, ESC res. 1985/17, 28 May 1985. [11]E/1988/14. [12]E/1984/6/Add.17. [13]E/1984/6/Add.18. [14]E/1986/4/Add.20. [15]E/1986/4/Add.19. [16]E/1986/4/Add.18. [17]E/1986/4/Add.16. [18]E/1986/4/Add.9. [19]E/1986/4/Add.21. [20]E/1986/4/Add.12. [21]E/1986/4/Add.17. [22]E/1986/4/Add.13. [23]E/1982/3/Add.37. [24]E/1982/3/Add.40. [25]E/1982/3/Add.39. [26]E/1982/3/Add.41. [27]E/1988/6. [28]E/1988/7. [29]YUN 1981, p. 924, ESC dec. 1981/149, 8 May 1981. [30]E/CN.4/1988/10. [31]YUN 1987, p. 773, GA res. 42/117, 7 Dec. 1987. [32]YUN 1986, p. 717, GA res. 41/128, annex, 4 Dec. 1986. [33]YUN 1987, p. 773. [34]E/1988/12 (res. 1988/26). [35]*Ibid.* (res. 1988/29). [36]*Ibid.* (res. 1988/18). [37]YUN 1986, p. 721, GA res. 41/132, 4 Dec. 1986. [38]E/1988/24. [39]E/1988/12 (res. 1988/19). [40]A/43/739. [41]E/1988/12 (res. 1988/24). [42]YUN 1987, p. 777, GA res. 42/146, 7 Dec. 1987. [43]*Ibid.*, p. 718, GA res. 42/191, 11 Dec. 1987. [44]*Ibid.*, p. 777. [45]YUN 1985, p. 881. [46]E/1988/12 (res. 1988/21).

Advancement of human rights

On 8 December 1988, on the recommendation of the Third Committee, the General Assembly adopted **resolution 43/125** by recorded vote.

Alternative approaches and ways and means within the United Nations system for improving the effective enjoyment of human rights and fundamental freedoms

The General Assembly,

Recalling that in the Charter of the United Nations the peoples of the United Nations declared their determination to reaffirm faith in fundamental human rights, in the dignity and worth of the human person and in the equal rights of men and women and of nations large and small and to employ international machinery for the promotion of the economic and social advancement of all peoples,

Recalling also the purposes and principles of the Charter to achieve international co-operation in solving international problems of an economic, social, cultural or humanitarian character, and in promoting and encouraging respect for human rights and for fundamental freedoms for all without distinction as to race, sex, language or religion,

Emphasizing the significance and validity of the Universal Declaration of Human Rights and of the International Covenants on Human Rights in promoting respect for and observance of human rights and fundamental freedoms,

Recalling its resolution 32/130 of 16 December 1977, in which it decided that the approach to future work within the United Nations system with respect to human rights questions should take into account the concepts set forth in that resolution,

Recalling also its resolutions 34/46 of 23 November 1979, 35/174 of 15 December 1980, 36/133 of 14 December 1981, 38/124 of 16 December 1983, 39/145 of 14 December 1984, 40/124 of 13 December 1985, 41/131 and 41/133 of 4 December 1986 and 42/119 of 7 December 1987,

Taking into account Commission on Human Rights resolution 1985/43 of 14 March 1985,

Reiterating that the right to development is an inalienable human right and that equality of development opportunities is a prerogative both of nations and of individuals within nations,

Recognizing that the human being is the main subject of development and that everyone has the right to participate in, as well as to benefit from, the development process,

Reiterating once again that the establishment of the new international economic order is an essential element for the effective promotion and full enjoyment of human rights and fundamental freedoms for all,

Reiterating also its profound conviction that all human rights and fundamental freedoms are indivisible and interdependent and that equal attention and urgent consideration should be given to the implementation, promotion and protection of civil and political rights and of economic, social and cultural rights,

Emphasizing the need for the creation, at the national and international levels, of conditions for the promotion and full protection of the human rights of individuals and peoples,

Recognizing that international peace and security are essential elements for the full realization of human rights, including the right to development,

Considering that the resources that would be released by disarmament could contribute significantly to the development of all States, in particular to that of the developing countries,

Reiterating that co-operation among all nations on the basis of respect for the independence, sovereignty and territorial integrity of each State, including the right of every people to choose freely its own socio-economic and political system, is essential for the promotion of peace and development,

Convinced that the primary aim of such international co-operation must be the achievement by all human beings of a life of freedom and dignity and freedom from want,

Concerned, however, about the occurrence of violations of human rights in the world,

Reaffirming that nothing in the Universal Declaration of Human Rights or in the International Covenants on Human Rights may be interpreted as implying for any State, group or person the right to engage in any activity or perform any act aimed at destroying any of the rights and freedoms proclaimed therein,

Affirming that the ultimate aim of development is the steady improvement of the well-being of the entire population, on the basis of its full participation in the process of development and a fair distribution of the benefits therefrom,

Considering that the efforts of the developing countries for their own development should be supported by an increased flow of resources and by the adoption of appropriate and substantive measures for creating an external environment conducive to such development,

Taking into account the Political Declaration adopted by the Eighth Conference of Heads of State or Government of Non-Aligned Countries, held at Harare from 1 to 6 September 1986,

Bearing in mind the stipulations of the final documents of the Conference of Foreign Ministers of the Non-Aligned Countries, held at Nicosia from 7 to 10 September 1988,[a] particularly paragraphs 15 to 18 of the Economic Part,

Emphasizing the special importance of the purposes and principles proclaimed in its Declaration on the Right to Development,

Taking into account Commission on Human Rights resolutions 1988/22 and 1988/26 of 7 March 1988,

Reaffirming the importance of furthering the activities of the organs of the United Nations in the field of human rights in conformity with the principles of the Charter,

Emphasizing that Governments have the duty to ensure respect for all human rights and fundamental freedoms,

1. *Reiterates its request* that the Commission on Human Rights continue its current work on overall analysis with a view to further promoting and strengthening human rights and fundamental freedoms, including the question of the programme and working methods of the Commission, and on the overall analysis of the alternative approaches and ways and means for improving the effective enjoyment of human rights and fundamental freedoms, in accordance with the provisions and concepts of General Assembly resolution 32/130 and other relevant texts;

2. *Affirms* that a primary aim of international co-operation in the field of human rights is a life of freedom, dignity and peace for all peoples and for every human being, that all human rights and fundamental freedoms are indivisible and interrelated and that the promotion and protection of one category of rights should never exempt or excuse States from promoting and protecting the others;

3. *Affirms its profound conviction* that equal attention and urgent consideration should be given to the implementation, promotion and protection of civil and political rights and of economic, social and cultural rights;

4. *Reaffirms* that it is of paramount importance for the promotion of human rights and fundamental freedoms that Member States should assume specific obligations by acceding to or ratifying international instruments in this field and, consequently, that the work within the United Nations system of setting standards in the field of human rights and universal acceptance and implementation of the relevant international instruments should be encouraged;

5. *Reiterates once again* that the international community should accord, or continue to accord, priority to the search for solutions to mass and flagrant violations of human rights of peoples and individuals affected by situations such as those mentioned in paragraph 1 *(e)* of General Assembly resolution 32/130, paying due attention also to other situations of violations of human rights;

6. *Reaffirms* its responsibility for achieving international co-operation in promoting and encouraging respect for human rights and fundamental freedoms for all, and expresses its concern at serious violations of human rights, in particular mass and flagrant violations of these rights, wherever they occur;

7. *Expresses concern* at the present situation as regards the achievement of the objectives and goals for the establishment of the new international economic order, and at its adverse effects on the full realization of human rights, in particular the right to development;

8. *Reaffirms* that the right to development is an inalienable human right;

9. *Reaffirms also* that international peace and security are essential elements for achieving full realization of the right to development;

10. *Recognizes* that all human rights and fundamental freedoms are indivisible and interdependent;

11. *Considers* that all Member States must promote international co-operation on the basis of respect for the independence, sovereignty and territorial integrity of each State, including the right of every people to choose freely its own socio-economic and political system, with

---

[a]A/43/667-S/20212.

a view to solving international economic, social and humanitarian problems;

12. *Expresses concern* at the disparity existing between established norms and principles and the actual situation of all human rights and fundamental freedoms in the world;

13. *Urges* all States to co-operate with the Commission on Human Rights in the promotion and protection of human rights and fundamental freedoms;

14. *Reiterates* the need to create, at the national and international levels, conditions for the full promotion and protection of the human rights of individuals and peoples;

15. *Reaffirms once again* that, in order to facilitate the full enjoyment of all human rights without diminishing personal dignity, it is necessary to promote the rights to education, work, health and proper nourishment through the adoption of measures at the national level, including those that provide for the right of workers to participate in management, as well as the adoption of measures at the international level, including the establishment of the new international economic order;

16. *Decides* that the approach to future work within the United Nations system on human rights matters should also take into account the content of the Declaration on the Right to Development and the need for the implementation thereof;

17. *Decides* to include in the provisional agenda of its forty-fourth session the item entitled "Alternative approaches and ways and means within the United Nations system for improving the effective enjoyment of human rights and fundamental freedoms".

General Assembly resolution 43/125

8 December 1988   Meeting 75   130-1-25 (recorded vote)

Approved by Third Committee (A/43/876) by recorded vote (112-1-25), 17 November (meeting 46); 33-nation draft (A/C.3/43/L.33); agenda item 104.
Sponsors: Algeria, Angola, Argentina, Benin, Bolivia, Burkina Faso, Colombia, Congo, Cuba, Cyprus, Democratic Yemen, Ecuador, Ethiopia, Ghana, India, Iraq, Lao People's Democratic Republic, Madagascar, Mali, Mexico, Mozambique, Nicaragua, Panama, Peru, Romania, Rwanda, Sao Tome and Principe, Syrian Arab Republic, Uganda, United Republic of Tanzania, Viet Nam, Yugoslavia, Zimbabwe.
Meeting numbers. GA 43rd session: 3rd Committee 36-38, 42, 46; plenary 75.

Recorded vote in Assembly as follows:

In favour: Afghanistan, Algeria, Angola, Antigua and Barbuda, Argentina, Bahamas, Bahrain, Bangladesh, Barbados, Belize, Benin, Bhutan, Bolivia, Botswana, Brazil, Brunei Darussalam, Bulgaria, Burkina Faso, Burma, Burundi, Byelorussian SSR, Cameroon, Cape Verde, Central African Republic, Chad, China, Colombia, Comoros, Congo, Costa Rica, Côte d'Ivoire, Cuba, Cyprus, Czechoslovakia, Democratic Kampuchea, Democratic Yemen, Dominica, Dominican Republic, Ecuador, Egypt, El Salvador, Equatorial Guinea, Ethiopia, Fiji, Gabon, Gambia, German Democratic Republic, Ghana, Grenada, Guatemala, Guinea, Guinea-Bissau, Guyana, Haiti, Honduras, Hungary, India, Indonesia, Iran, Iraq, Jamaica, Jordan, Kenya, Kuwait, Lao People's Democratic Republic, Lebanon, Lesotho, Liberia, Libyan Arab Jamahiriya, Madagascar, Malawi, Malaysia, Maldives, Mali, Mauritania, Mauritius, Mexico, Mongolia, Morocco, Mozambique, Nepal, New Zealand, Nicaragua, Niger, Nigeria, Oman, Pakistan, Panama, Papua New Guinea, Paraguay, Peru, Poland, Qatar, Romania, Rwanda, Saint Kitts and Nevis, Saint Lucia, Saint Vincent and the Grenadines, Samoa, Sao Tome and Principe, Saudi Arabia, Senegal, Seychelles, Sierra Leone, Singapore, Solomon Islands, Somalia, Sri Lanka, Sudan, Suriname, Swaziland, Syrian Arab Republic, Thailand, Togo, Trinidad and Tobago, Tunisia, Uganda, Ukrainian SSR, USSR, United Arab Emirates, United Republic of Tanzania, Uruguay, Vanuatu, Venezuela, Viet Nam, Yemen, Yugoslavia, Zaire, Zambia, Zimbabwe.
Against: United States.
Abstaining: Australia, Austria, Belgium, Canada, Chile, Denmark, Finland, France, Germany, Federal Republic of, Greece, Iceland, Ireland, Israel, Italy, Japan, Luxembourg, Malta, Netherlands, Norway, Philippines, Portugal, Spain, Sweden, Turkey, United Kingdom.

Also on 8 December, on the recommendation of the Third Committee, the Assembly adopted **resolution 43/126** by recorded vote.

Alternative approaches and ways and means within the United Nations system for improving the effective enjoyment of human rights and fundamental freedoms

The General Assembly,

Recalling its resolutions relating to the right to development, especially resolution 41/133 of 4 December 1986,

Reiterating the importance of the right to development for all countries, in particular the developing countries,

1. *Stresses* that the achievement of the right to development requires a concerted international and national effort to eliminate economic deprivation, hunger and disease in all parts of the world without discrimination, in accordance with the Declaration and the Programme of Action on the Establishment of a New International Economic Order, the International Development Strategy for the Third United Nations Development Decade and the Charter of Economic Rights and Duties of States;

2. *Emphasizes* that, to this end, international co-operation should aim at the maintenance of stable and sustained economic growth with simultaneous action to increase concessional assistance to developing countries, build world food security, resolve the debt burden, eliminate trade barriers, promote monetary stability and enhance scientific and technological co-operation.

General Assembly resolution 43/126

8 December 1988   Meeting 75   135-8-14 (recorded vote)

Approved by Third Committee (A/43/876) by recorded vote (115-9-13), 17 November (meeting 46); draft by Pakistan (A/C.3/43/L.34), orally revised; agenda item 104.
Meeting numbers. GA 43rd session: 3rd Committee 36-38, 42, 46; plenary 75.

Recorded vote in Assembly as follows:

In favour: Afghanistan, Albania, Algeria, Angola, Antigua and Barbuda, Argentina, Bahamas, Bahrain, Bangladesh, Barbados, Belize, Benin, Bhutan, Bolivia, Botswana, Brazil, Brunei Darussalam, Bulgaria, Burkina Faso, Burma, Burundi, Byelorussian SSR, Cameroon, Cape Verde, Central African Republic, Chad, Chile, China, Colombia, Comoros, Congo, Costa Rica, Côte d'Ivoire, Cuba, Cyprus, Czechoslovakia, Democratic Kampuchea, Democratic Yemen, Djibouti, Dominica, Dominican Republic, Ecuador, Egypt, El Salvador, Equatorial Guinea, Ethiopia, Fiji, Gabon, Gambia, German Democratic Republic, Ghana, Grenada, Guatemala, Guinea, Guinea-Bissau, Guyana, Haiti, Honduras, Hungary, India, Indonesia, Iran, Iraq, Jamaica, Jordan, Kenya, Kuwait, Lao People's Democratic Republic, Lebanon, Lesotho, Liberia, Libyan Arab Jamahiriya, Madagascar, Malawi, Malaysia, Maldives, Mali, Malta, Mauritania, Mauritius, Mexico, Mongolia, Morocco, Mozambique, Nepal, Nicaragua, Niger, Nigeria, Oman, Pakistan, Panama, Papua New Guinea, Paraguay, Peru, Philippines, Poland, Qatar, Romania, Rwanda, Saint Kitts and Nevis, Saint Lucia, Saint Vincent and the Grenadines, Samoa, Sao Tome and Principe, Saudi Arabia, Senegal, Seychelles, Sierra Leone, Singapore, Solomon Islands, Somalia, Sri Lanka, Sudan, Suriname, Swaziland, Syrian Arab Republic, Thailand, Togo, Trinidad and Tobago, Tunisia, Turkey, Uganda, Ukrainian SSR, USSR, United Arab Emirates, United Republic of Tanzania, Uruguay, Vanuatu, Venezuela, Viet Nam, Yemen, Yugoslavia, Zaire, Zambia, Zimbabwe.
Against: Belgium, Canada, France, Germany, Federal Republic of, Japan, Luxembourg, Netherlands, United Kingdom.
Abstaining: Australia, Austria, Denmark, Finland, Greece, Iceland, Ireland, Israel, Italy, New Zealand, Norway, Portugal, Spain, Sweden.

National institutions for human rights protection

Human Rights Commission action. On 10 March,[1] the Commission reaffirmed the importance of developing national institutions for the promotion and protection of human rights and of maintaining their independence and integrity, and encouraged Member States to develop funding and other strategies for the establishment of such institutions. It welcomed the 1987 General Assembly request[2] to update the Secretary-General's report on national institutions[3] and to distribute it at the forty-fourth (1989) session of the Assembly as a United Nations handbook. The Commission further invited the Secretary-General to include in his updated report a list of existing national institutions and all pertinent information provided by Governments, particularly on various models of such institutions and their functioning in implementing international human rights standards.

UN machinery

Commission on Human Rights

The Commission on Human Rights held its forty-fourth session at Geneva from 1 February to 11 March 1988 and adopted 78 resolutions and 7 decisions. In addition, it recommended 9 draft resolutions and 18 draft decisions for adoption by the Economic and Social Council.

On 27 May, by **decision 1988/144**, the Council took note of the Commission's report on its forty-fourth session.[4]

With regard to the organization of its work, the Commission decided[5] to set up informal open-ended working groups on further promotion and encouragement of human rights and fundamental freedoms; on the question of a convention on the rights of the child; on the rights of persons belonging to national, ethnic, religious and linguistic minorities; and for drafting a declaration on the right and responsibility of individuals, groups and organs of society to promote and protect universally recognized human rights and fundamental freedoms.

On 8 March,[6] the Commission recommended a decision for adoption by the Economic and Social Council, stating that the mandates of special rapporteurs should be for two-year periods and that they should continue to report annually. The decision would apply to special rapporteurs on mercenaries, on the implementation of the Declaration on the Elimination of All Forms of Intolerance and of Discrimination Based on Religion or Belief, on the question of torture, on summary and arbitrary executions, and to the Special Rapporteur of the Sub-Commission on Prevention of Discrimination and Protection of Minorities on the adverse consequences for the enjoyment of human rights of political, military, economic and other forms of assistance given to the racist and colonialist régime of South Africa.

On 27 May, by **decision 1988/129**, the Council approved the Commission's recommendation.

Organization of work of the 1989 session

On 2 March,[7] the Commission decided, subject to the approval of the Economic and Social Council, to set up a five-member working group to examine particular human rights violations that might be referred to it at its 1989 session by the Sub-Commission under the confidential procedure governed by a 1970 Council resolution.[8]

On 27 May, by **decision 1988/127**, the Council approved the Commission's decision. On the same date, by **decision 1988/141**, the Council authorized 20 fully serviced additional meetings for the Commission's forty-fifth (1989) session. It noted that the Commission had requested its Chairman to make every effort to organize the session's work within the time normally allotted, with additional meetings only if absolutely necessary.

On 10 March,[9] the Commission had recommended to the Council the above conditions for organizing its 1989 session.

Sub-Commission on Prevention of Discrimination and Protection of Minorities

The Sub-Commission on Prevention of Discrimination and Protection of Minorities held its fortieth session at Geneva from 8 August to 2 September 1988;[10] it adopted 40 resolutions and 13 decisions. It also recommended to the Commission on Human Rights, its parent body, eight draft resolutions and five draft decisions for adoption.

On 25 August,[11] the Sub-Commission decided to continue discussing in 1989 ways of implementing the Commission's resolution on the work of the Sub-Commission, and to review its work biennially thereafter. On 2 September,[12] it approved the composition of its working groups on communications, slavery and indigenous populations, each representing five regions (Africa, Asia, Eastern Europe, Latin America, and Western Europe and other).

Human Rights Commission action. On 8 March,[13] the Commission, noting that steps taken by the Sub-Commission to rationalize and streamline its work had not fully achieved the desired results, set out further guidelines for organizing the Sub-Commission's work. The Chairman of the Sub-Commission was requested to report on their implementation in 1989.

Strengthening the Centre for Human Rights

On 24 August,[14] the Sub-Commission recommended that the Commission adopt a resolution supporting the efforts of the Secretary-General to enhance the role of the Centre for Human Rights as a co-ordinating unit for bodies dealing with the protection of human rights, and inviting him to request Governments, specialized agencies and intergovernmental and non-governmental organizations to express their views on strengthening the Centre's activities.

Public information activities

The Secretary-General presented to the Commission in 1988 a report[15] on the development of public information activities in the human rights field, with special emphasis on preparations for the fortieth anniversary of the Universal Declaration of Human Rights (see below) and activities by the Centre for Human Rights, the United Nations Department of Public Information (DPI) and the United Nations Office at Geneva. They focused on dissemination of human rights information and distribution of teaching materials; organization of symposia, seminars and workshops on human rights issues; production of radio and audio-visual materials; co-ordination within the United Nations system; and special observances. The report noted the establishment of a new section for external relations, publications and documentation within the Centre for Human Rights, aimed at broadening and deepening public understanding of human rights and the Organization's efforts to advance them.

Human Rights Commission action. On 10 March,[16] the Commission encouraged Member States to publicize United Nations human rights activities and give priority to disseminating in their national and local languages the 1948 Universal Declaration of Human Rights,[17] the 1966 International Covenants on Human Rights[18] and other international conventions. It welcomed the Secretary-General's undertaking that DPI would encourage NGOs to carry out activities in support of United Nations work on human rights, and urged DPI to give special attention to the role of the United Nations information centres (UNICs) in the Organization's campaign. The Secretary-General was requested to establish collections of basic reference materials at each UNIC by the end of 1988, to explore the possibility of co-production arrangements for audio-visual programmes on human rights issues, and to finalize the United Nations teaching booklet on human rights. Member States were urged to include in their educational curricula materials relevant to a comprehensive understanding of human rights issues. The Commission encouraged all those responsible for training in the areas of law and its enforcement, the armed forces, medicine, diplomacy and other relevant fields to include appropriate human rights components in their programmes. It also asked the Secretary-General to seek the views of Member States, United Nations organs and NGOs on activities for the proposed world public information campaign on human rights (see below), to ensure proper storage and distribution of United Nations

materials on human rights, to provide adequate funding for public information activities in that field and to report on those activities in 1989.

Sub-Commission action. On 1 September,[19] the Sub-Commission requested the Secretary-General, in co-operation with UNESCO and other organizations, to develop a global programme to prepare teaching materials for all levels of education and for the training of teachers to teach human rights.

World public information campaign

In October 1988, pursuant to a 1987 General Assembly resolution[20] and a 1988 request of the Commission,[16] the Secretary-General submitted to the Assembly a report on the advisability of launching a world public information campaign on human rights.[21] The report outlined the aims and scope of the proposed campaign, its objectives being to increase understanding and awareness of human rights and fundamental freedoms and to educate people as to United Nations efforts and the international machinery to realize them. The campaign, directed to all segments of the world's population, was to be financed from existing United Nations resources supplemented by voluntary contributions.

Activities envisaged under the campaign included workshops and training courses, a yearly programme of at least 30 fellowships and between 20 and 25 internships on human rights, special observances, media coverage and promotion activities, and the preparation and dissemination of printed public information and reference materials. The report also provided background information on dissemination of various human rights instruments; commemorations and anniversaries of the Universal Declaration of Human Rights; advisory services and training programmes (see below); and the development of public information activities in the human rights field.

In another report,[22] the Secretary-General summarized the implementation of a 1987 General Assembly resolution on public information activities.[20] The report noted steps by DPI to establish a collection of basic reference works on human rights at UNICs and to increase promotion of their activities. A teaching booklet was prepared and out-of-stock human rights materials were reprinted and distributed to national focal points. Annexed to the report were replies from Governments to the Assembly's resolution, providing information on their efforts to publicize United Nations activities in the field of human rights.

GENERAL ASSEMBLY ACTION

On 8 December 1988, on the recommendation of the Third Committee, the General Assembly adopted **resolution 43/128** without vote.

Development of public information activities in the field of human rights

The General Assembly,

Reaffirming that activities to improve public knowledge in the field of human rights are essential to the fulfilment of the purposes of the United Nations set out in Article 1, paragraph 3, of the Charter of the United Nations and that carefully designed programmes of teaching, education and information are essential to the achievement of lasting respect for human rights and fundamental freedoms,

Recalling the relevant resolutions on this subject, in particular its resolution 42/118 of 7 December 1987, and taking note of Commission on Human Rights resolution 1988/74 of 10 March 1988,

Recognizing the catalytic effect of United Nations initiatives on national and regional public information activities in the field of human rights,

Recognizing also the valuable role that non-governmental organizations can play in these endeavours,

Emphasizing the importance of adherence by all Governments to the principles contained in the Universal Declaration of Human Rights and believing that the fortieth anniversary of its adoption has provided a focus and renewed impetus to the promotional activities of the United Nations system in the field of human rights,

Believing that a world public information campaign on human rights would be a valuable complement to the activities of the United Nations further to promote and to protect human rights worldwide,

1. *Takes note* of the reports of the Secretary-General on the development of public information activities in the field of human rights and on the advisability of launching, within existing resources, a world public information campaign on human rights;

2. *Reaffirms* the need for information materials on human rights to be carefully designed in clear and accessible form, to be tailored to regional and national requirements and circumstances with specific target audiences in mind and to be effectively disseminated in national and local languages and in sufficient volume to have the desired impact, and for effective use also to be made of the mass media, in particular radio and television and audio-visual technologies, in order to reach wider audiences, with priority being given to children, young people and the disadvantaged, including those in isolated areas;

3. *Appreciates* the measures taken during 1988 by the Secretariat, through the Centre for Human Rights and the Department of Public Information:

(a) To update, increase stocks and extend the language versions of human rights information materials, especially those on the basic United Nations human rights instruments and institutions, and, in this regard, urges the Secretariat to take measures to ensure the further production and effective dissemination of such documents in national and local languages, in cooperation with regional, national and local organizations as well as with Governments, making full and effective use of the United Nations information centres, which have a key promotional role to play in the field of human rights at the regional and national levels;

(b) To establish in the Department of Public Information a new Dissemination Division, which is revising and computerizing the Secretariat's distribution methods so as to target specific audiences better, globally and regionally, and which will assist organizations, schools and non-governmental organizations to identify appropriate material for their use;

(c) To expand audio-visual activities in the field of human rights, and, in this regard, again requests the Secretary-General to explore the possibility of co-production arrangements for future audio-visual programmes so as to achieve maximum public impact at an economical cost;

4. *Encourages* all Member States, in particular in order to follow up the activities of the fortieth anniversary of the adoption of the Universal Declaration of Human Rights, to make special efforts to publicize and to facilitate and encourage publicity for the activities of the United Nations in the field of human rights, and to accord priority to the dissemination, in their respective national and local languages, of the Declaration, the International Covenants on Human Rights and other international conventions and to information and education on the practical ways in which the rights and freedoms enjoyed under these instruments can be exercised;

5. *Urges* all Member States to include in their educational curricula materials relevant to a comprehensive understanding of human rights issues and encourages all those responsible for training in law and its enforcement, the armed forces, medicine, diplomacy and other relevant fields to include appropriate human rights components in their programmes, and, to this end, requests the Secretary-General to draw the attention of Member States to the teaching booklet on human rights, which could serve as a broad and flexible framework adaptable to national circumstances for the structuring and development of human rights teaching;

6. *Notes* the special value, under the advisory services and technical assistance programme, of regional and national training courses and workshops, in co-operation with Governments, regional and national organizations and non-governmental organizations, in promoting practical education and awareness in the field of human rights, and welcomes the priority given to the organization of such activities by the Centre for Human Rights;

7. *Decides* to launch on 10 December 1988, the fortieth anniversary of the Universal Declaration of Human Rights, within existing resources, a World Public Information Campaign on Human Rights, under which the activities of the Organization in this field should be developed and strengthened in a global and practically oriented fashion, engaging the complementary activities of concerned bodies of the United Nations system, Member States and non-governmental organizations;

8. *Requests* the Secretary-General to ensure the fullest effective deployment of the skills and resources of all concerned units of the Secretariat and to make available, within existing resources, and in particular from the budget of the Department of Public Information, adequate funding for developing practical and effective human rights information activities, including those within the programme of the World Public Information Campaign on Human Rights;

9. *Calls upon* the Centre for Human Rights, which has primary responsibility within the United Nations system in the field of human rights, to co-ordinate the substantive activities of the World Campaign pursuant to the direction of the General Assembly and the Com-

mission on Human Rights, and to serve as liaison with Governments, regional and national institutions, non-governmental organizations and concerned individuals in the development and implementation of the World Campaign's activities;

10. *Calls upon* the Department of Public Information, which has primary responsibility for public information activities, to co-ordinate the public information activities of the World Campaign and, in its responsibility as secretariat to the Joint United Nations Information Committee, to promote co-ordinated system-wide information activities in the field of human rights;

11. *Emphasizes* the need for the United Nations to harmonize its activities in the field of human rights with those of other organizations, including the International Committee of the Red Cross, with regard to the dissemination of information on international humanitarian law and, with regard to education for human rights, with the United Nations Educational, Scientific and Cultural Organization, which was requested by the General Assembly in its resolution 38/57 of 9 December 1983 to submit a report to the Assembly at its forty-third session on its human rights teaching and training programmes;

12. *Urges* all Member States that have not yet done so to nominate national focal points that could be supplied with copies of relevant human rights material and that might also serve as points of liaison with the United Nations in the development and implementation of the World Campaign, and requests the Secretary-General to publish the list of such focal points in his report to the General Assembly at its forty-fourth session on the implementation of the present resolution;

13. *Requests* the Secretary-General to submit to the Commission on Human Rights at its forty-fifth session a report on the current and proposed aims and activities of the World Campaign;

14. *Requests* the Commission on Human Rights, at its forty-fifth session, on the basis of the report of the Secretary-General, to give priority consideration to this question with a view to providing appropriate guidance on the aims and activities of the World Campaign;

15. *Also requests* the Secretary-General to submit to the General Assembly at its forty-fourth session a comprehensive report on the implementation of the present resolution for consideration under the item entitled "Alternative approaches and ways and means within the United Nations system for improving the effective enjoyment of human rights and fundamental freedoms".

General Assembly resolution 43/128

8 December 1988   Meeting 75   Adopted without vote

Approved by Third Committee (A/43/876) without vote, 17 November (meeting 46); 18-nation draft (A/C.3/43/L.40), orally revised; agenda item 104.
Sponsors: Australia, Bolivia, Colombia, Cyprus, Ecuador, Germany, Federal Republic of, India, Ireland, Italy, Mexico, Netherlands, Norway, Peru, Philippines, Samoa, Senegal, Sweden, Yugoslavia.
Meeting numbers. GA 43rd session: 3rd Committee 36-38, 42, 46; plenary 75.

Advisory services

In 1988, under the United Nations programme of advisory services in human rights established in 1955,[23] the Centre for Human Rights organized regional workshops on the Universal Declaration of Human Rights (Lomé, Togo, 5-7 April;

Milan, Italy, 7-9 September) and on human rights and the administration of justice (Tunis, Tunisia, 26 September–1 October), and an international seminar on teaching human rights (Geneva, 5-9 December). Training courses were held on the implementation of international human rights standards (Lomé, 8-15 April), reporting obligations under the international human rights instruments (Lisbon, Portugal, 25-29 May; Kigali, Rwanda, 6-17 June) and human rights and the administration of justice (Moscow, 21-25 November). Under the fellowship programme, 31 fellows received training during the year (14 from Africa, 7 from Asia, 6 from Latin America, and 2 each from Eastern and Western Europe). In addition, the Centre awarded some 30 internships to outstanding graduate students. The Commission on Human Rights provided advice to the recently established African Commission on Human Rights and Peoples' Rights of the Organization of African Unity (OAU). In addition, the Centre carried out a number of activities financed by the United Nations Voluntary Fund for Advisory Services and Technical Assistance in the Field of Human Rights (see below).

Reports of the Secretary-General. The Secretary-General presented to the Commission in 1988 a report[24] outlining a medium-term plan of advisory services and technical assistance activities grouped under three main subprogrammes (regional seminars, regional training courses, and expert services and technical assistance), three supportive subprogrammes (fellowships, regional arrangements and national institutions) and *ad hoc* subprogrammes at the national level. An addendum contained a table of requests from Member States for technical assistance to strengthen their legal institutions.

In another report,[25] the Secretary-General communicated to the Sub-Commission replies from three States, two United Nations bodies and three specialized agencies as at 17 August, concerning technical assistance for strengthening legal institutions, as requested by the Sub-Commission in 1987.[26]

Human Rights Commission action. On 8 March,[27] the Commission recommended to the Secretary-General that increased emphasis be placed on expert assistance and activities to develop infrastructures to meet international human rights standards, and requested him to: pursue his efforts for a medium-term plan for advisory services and technical assistance; ensure that the Centre for Human Rights became a focal point for co-ordination of advisory services activities, as well as close co-ordination between activities financed under the regular programme and by the Voluntary Fund; bring the need for further technical legal assistance to the attention of the relevant United Nations bodies and agencies; and report to the Commission in 1989 on progress made in implementing the programme of advisory services. It requested its special rapporteurs and representatives, as well as the Working Group on Enforced or Involuntary Disappearances, to inform Governments of the possibility of availing themselves of services provided under that programme and to include in their recommendations proposals for specific projects. The Commission also appealed to Member States to consider organizing, under the programme of advisory services, national training courses for government personnel on the application of international human rights standards, and encouraged Governments in need of technical assistance to take advantage of relevant expert services.

Voluntary Fund for Advisory Services

The United Nations Voluntary Fund for Advisory Services and Technical Assistance in the Field of Human Rights, established pursuant to a 1987 Commission resolution[28] and endorsed by the Economic and Social Council later that year,[29] became operational in 1988. Activities financed by the Fund included a regional training course for Central American countries on the implementation of international human rights instruments (San Remo, Italy, 12-16 December); a national training course on human rights (Guatemala City, 14-18 November); a national workshop on human rights and the administration of justice (Manila, Philippines, 5-7 December); and publication of a brochure in Portuguese containing the International Bill of Human Rights and of a poster of the Universal Declaration. In addition, the Fund granted seven fellowships and provided assistance, including expert services, under technical cooperation projects in Colombia, Guatemala and Uganda, aimed at developing infrastructures to protect and promote human rights and strengthening relevant national institutions. By the end of 1988, contributions from Governments and NGOs to the Fund totalled some $800,200.

Human Rights Commission action. On 8 March,[30] the Commission called on Governments, intergovernmental and non-governmental organizations and individuals to consider making voluntary contributions to the Fund, and recommended that activities under the Fund be directed towards expert assistance to Governments. It also recommended that the Secretary-General consider financing and implementing through the Fund those projects which could catalyse the realization of international human rights. It requested him to begin operations under the Fund using available resources, to draw the attention of Governments and competent human rights organs to the availability of advisory services and technical assistance under the Fund, and to report to the Commission in 1989 on its operation and administration.

Equatorial Guinea

In a report on the situation in Equatorial Guinea,[31] submitted to the Commission on Human Rights in 1988, the Secretary-General supported the recommendation of Expert Fernando Volio Jiménez (Costa Rica) that the implementation of the plan of action proposed by the United Nations for that country in 1981[32] be entrusted to the National Codification Commission, established by the Government. On 8 March,[33] the Commission recommended that Equatorial Guinea consider becoming a party to the Convention against Torture and Other Cruel, Inhuman or Degrading Treatment or Punishment,[34] and requested it to consider implementing the proposed plan of action, taking into account the Expert's recommendation. The Expert was requested to report in 1989 on progress in implementing the plan.

On 27 May, by **decision 1988/133**, the Economic and Social Council approved the Commission's decision to consider the Expert's report on the manner in which Equatorial Guinea intended to implement the plan of action.

Guatemala

In 1988, the Commission considered a report by Héctor Gros Espiell (Uruguay), appointed in 1987 as the Expert on Guatemala,[35] on advisory services to that country.[36] Following his first visit to Guatemala (20-26 September 1987), the Expert concluded that, despite continued problems, particularly regarding indigenous populations and refugees, the human rights situation there had generally improved, and he recommended a broad programme of assistance to further that process.

Activities during 1988 included three missions by the Expert (20-24 June, 19-21 August, 19-21 November) and the commencement of a technical assistance programme to Guatemala for 1988-1989, financed by the Voluntary Fund for Advisory Services.

Human Rights Commission action. On 8 March,[37] the Commission expressed its appreciation to Guatemala for its collaboration and facilities for the Expert, and requested the Secretary-General to provide Guatemala with advisory services and appropriate assistance to advance democracy and strengthen its human rights institutions. The Commission appealed to Guatemala to give priority to the implementation of measures to prevent any violation of human rights. It asked the Secretary-General to renew the Expert's mandate for one year and requested the Expert to report in 1989.

By **decision 1988/131** of 27 May, the Economic and Social Council approved the extension of the Expert's mandate and the Commission's request to the Secretary-General to provide such advisory services and other forms of assistance in the field of human rights as might be requested by Guatemala.

Sub-Commission action. On 1 September,[38] the Sub-Commission recommended that the Expert on Guatemala, in his forthcoming report, pay particular attention to obstacles resulting from non-co-operation by certain elements of the military, and indicate ways to remedy that situation.

Haiti

In February 1988, André Braunschweig (France), appointed in 1987 as the Expert on Haiti,[39] reported to the Commission on advisory services to that country.[40] Noting that in January 1988 a civilian Government took office in Haiti, the Expert suggested that the country receive assistance to set up an independent judiciary, establish an autonomous police force and reform the prison system. Annexed to the report were extracts from Haiti's 1987 Constitution, relating to human rights.

Human Rights Commission action. On 8 March,[41] the Commission requested Haiti to consider adopting measures to develop full respect for human rights and recommended that it consider becoming a party to existing international human rights instruments. The Secretary-General was asked to provide advisory services and other assistance to encourage Haiti's democratic development. The Commission decided to ask the Secretary-General to extend the Expert's mandate and have him report to the Commission in 1989. It asked the Expert to establish direct contacts with Haiti's Government and the Secretary-General to give him all necessary assistance.

On 27 May, the Economic and Social Council, by **decision 1988/132**, approved the Commission's decision to extend the Expert's mandate for one year and its request to the Secretary-General to give him all necessary assistance.

Further developments. On 20 June, the civilian Government in Haiti was overthrown in a military take-over, which led to a deterioration in the human rights situation. Philippe Texier (France), who replaced Mr. Braunschweig as the Expert on Haiti, continued to follow developments and visited the country from 15 to 22 December. (See also below, under "Human rights violations".)

International human rights instruments

Human rights treaty bodies

In 1988, there were six human rights treaty instruments in force providing for the monitoring of treaty implementation by expert bodies. Those instruments and their respective treaty bodies were the 1965 International Convention on the Elimination of All Forms of Racial Discrimination[42] (Committee on the Elimination of Racial Discrimination); the 1966 International Covenant on Civil and Political Rights[18] (Human Rights Committee); the 1966 International Covenant on Economic, Social and Cultural Rights[18] (Committee on Economic, Social and Cultural Rights); the 1973 International Convention on the Suppression and Punishment of the Crime of _Apartheid_[43] (Group of Three); the 1979 Convention on the Elimination of All Forms of Discrimination against Women[44] (Committee on the Elimination of Discrimination against Women); and the 1984 Convention against Torture and Other Cruel, Inhuman or Degrading Treatment or Punishment[34] (Committee against Torture).

In accordance with a 1987 General Assembly resolution,[45] the Chairmen of the treaty bodies held their second meeting in 1988 (Geneva, 10-14 October).[46]

Note by the Secretary-General. In a May note,[47] submitted to the Economic and Social Council in response to a March 1988 request of the Commission,[48] the Secretary-General provided an overview of methods applied under different human rights instruments as regards their financial implications. The note listed relevant provisions relating to the programme budget implications of United Nations instruments in the field of human rights.

On 27 May, by **decision 1988/145**, the Council took note of the Secretary-General's note.

ECONOMIC AND SOCIAL COUNCIL ACTION

Also on 27 May, on the recommendation of its Second Committee, the Council adopted **resolution 1988/42** without vote.

Effective implementation of international instruments on human rights
The Economic and Social Council,

Affirming that the effective implementation of international instruments on human rights is of major importance to the efforts made by the United Nations, pursuant to the Charter and the Universal Declaration of Human Rights, to promote universal respect for, and observance of, human rights and fundamental freedoms,

Considering that the effective functioning of treaty bodies established in accordance with the relevant provisions of international instruments on human rights plays a fundamental role in this connection and hence represents an important continuing concern of the United Nations,

Recalling the many resolutions adopted by the General Assembly, the Economic and Social Council and the Commission on Human Rights that have affirmed this concern and addressed various aspects of the effective implementation of international instruments on human rights,

Taking note of General Assembly resolution 42/105 of 7 December 1987, concerning reporting obligations of States parties to international instruments on human rights,

1. *Appeals strongly* to all States that have not yet done so to become parties to international instruments on human rights;

2. *Emphasizes* the interest and responsibility of States parties to the various human rights instruments in ensuring that legal, financial and administrative difficulties affecting the functioning of the relevant treaty bodies are appropriately addressed;

3. *Urges* all States parties to the International Convention on the Elimination of All Forms of Racial Discrimination and all States parties to the Convention against Torture and Other Cruel, Inhuman or Degrading Treatment or Punishment to comply fully with their financial obligations under these conventions;

4. *Emphasizes* that the United Nations has an interest in ensuring that difficulties affecting the functioning of the relevant treaty bodies are appropriately addressed;

5. *Affirms* its commitment to relevant provisions of various resolutions of the General Assembly, the Economic and Social Council and the Commission on Human Rights, addressing such issues as:

(a) The importance of effective systems of periodic reporting by States parties to international instruments on human rights for reviewing and assisting efforts to promote and protect the rights and freedoms elaborated in those instruments;

(b) The need for the United Nations to ensure that financial difficulties, which may increasingly impede the functioning of certain human rights treaty bodies and deter universal acceptance of certain international instruments on human rights, are appropriately addressed;

(c) The importance of the application of universally recognized criteria in the implementation of provisions of the international instruments on human rights;

6. *Requests* the Secretary-General fully to inform the General Assembly at its forty-third session, the Economic and Social Council at its first regular session of 1989 and the Commission on Human Rights, as its subsidiary body, at its forty-fifth session, as well as the second meeting of chairmen of human rights treaty bodies, of further developments concerning the effective functioning of treaty bodies established in accordance with the international instruments on human rights.

Economic and Social Council resolution 1988/42

27 May 1988   Meeting 16   Adopted without vote

Approved by Second Committee (E/1988/89/Add.1) without vote, 24 May (meeting 22); 5-nation draft (E/1988/C.2/L.13), orally revised following informal consultations; agenda item 10.

Sponsors: Argentina, Canada, Denmark, Netherlands, Norway.

Sub-Commission action.

In a June note,[49] the Secretary-General transmitted to the Sub-Commission the replies from 10 Governments, as at 1 June, to his invitation, issued in accordance with a 1985 Sub-Commission request,[50] to provide information on circumstances that had prevented them from adhering to human rights instruments.

On 1 September,[51] the Sub-Commission requested the Secretary-General to renew the invitation for submission of information; examine further

the idea of offering legal training to local staff or of providing experts to help draft legislation and regulations, with a view to enabling States to ratify or accede to those instruments; keep under review the idea of designating regional advisers on international human rights standards; continue informal consultations with government representatives on prospects for ratification; and update the table of country-by-country developments in connection with ratification or accession. The Sub-Commission also requested its Chairman to appoint a member to report in 1990 on information received.

Reporting obligations of States parties

In 1988, problems related to the reporting obligations of States parties to international instruments on human rights and to the functioning of bodies established under such instruments were considered at the second meeting of the Chairmen of the treaty bodies.[46] The meeting made recommendations concerning harmonization and consolidation of reporting guidelines, co-ordination of reporting, measures for expediting consideration of reports, and projects for technical assistance and advisory services to help States parties fulfil their reporting obligations.

GENERAL ASSEMBLY ACTION

On 8 December, on the recommendation of the Third Committee, the General Assembly adopted **resolution 43/115** without vote.

Reporting obligations of States parties to international instruments on human rights and effective functioning of bodies established pursuant to such instruments

The General Assembly,

Recalling its resolution 42/105 of 7 December 1987, taking note of Economic and Social Council resolution 1988/42 of 27 May 1988 and Commission on Human Rights resolution 1988/31 of 8 March 1988, and recalling other relevant resolutions,

Affirming that the effective implementation of United Nations instruments on human rights is of major importance to the efforts made by the Organization, pursuant to the Charter of the United Nations and to the Universal Declaration of Human Rights, to promote universal respect for and observance of human rights and fundamental freedoms,

Considering that the effective functioning of treaty bodies established pursuant to international instruments on human rights is indispensable for supervising the implementation of such instruments, including the consideration of periodic reports of States parties,

Aware of its responsibility with respect to the proper functioning of the bodies established to carry out specific functions regarding the implementation of instruments on human rights adopted by the General Assembly,

Reiterating the fundamental importance that it attaches to the fulfilment of reporting obligations under international instruments on human rights,

Recognizing that the effective implementation of instruments on human rights, involving periodic reporting by States parties to the relevant treaty bodies and the efficient functioning of the treaty bodies themselves, not only enhances international accountability in relation to the protection and promotion of human rights but also provides States parties with a valuable opportunity to review policies and programmes affecting the protection and promotion of human rights and to make any appropriate adjustments,

Expressing concern about the increasing backlog of reports on implementation by States parties of United Nations instruments on human rights and about delays in consideration of reports by the treaty bodies,

Recognizing the burden that coexisting reporting systems place upon Member States that are parties to various instruments, as well as upon the respective treaty bodies themselves, and noting that this burden will become more onerous for the United Nations and the States parties as additional instruments come into force,

Conscious that, in establishing additional treaty bodies, long-term problems both in terms of enhanced reporting obligations and of financial implications should be appropriately addressed,

Concerned that the problem of securing sufficient financial resources may increasingly hamper the proper functioning of treaty bodies, as noted with concern in the recent reports of five treaty bodies,

Reaffirming the importance of providing resources for all bodies supervising the implementation of international instruments on human rights, including sufficient financial resources to ensure the effective functioning of the treaty bodies,

Reaffirming the independent, expert character of the treaty bodies,

Taking note of the conclusions and recommendations of the meeting of persons chairing the human rights treaty bodies, held at Geneva from 10 to 14 October 1988,

1. *Once again urges* States parties to international instruments on human rights with reports overdue to make every effort to present their reports as soon as possible and to take advantage of opportunities whereby such reports can be consolidated;

2. *Invites* States parties to international instruments on human rights to review the processes followed in the preparation of their periodic reports with a view to ensuring compliance with relevant guidelines, improving the quality of description and analysis and limiting reports to a reasonable length, taking due consideration of the relevant provisions of those instruments;

3. *Invites* States parties to international instruments on human rights to consider at their meetings further ways of streamlining and otherwise improving reporting procedures, as well as enhancing co-ordination and information flow between the treaty bodies and with relevant United Nations bodies, including the specialized agencies, and requests the Secretary-General to inform the General Assembly of any decisions of the States parties on these issues;

4. *Welcomes* the efforts of the treaty bodies to streamline and rationalize reporting procedures, particularly by extending the periodicity of reporting, improving the efficiency of work methods and harmonizing and simplifying reporting guidelines;

5. *Requests* the Secretary-General to consider, as a matter of priority, the finalization of the detailed reporting manual to assist States parties in the fulfilment of their reporting obligations and to allow each of the treaty bodies the opportunity to comment on the draft manual;

6. *Requests* the Secretary-General to prepare, as requested by the Committee on Economic, Social and Cultural Rights, a report showing the extent and nature of any overlapping of issues dealt with in the international human rights treaties, with a view to reducing, as appropriate, duplication in the supervisory bodies of issues raised with respect to any given State party;

7. *Requests* the Secretary-General to provide from official United Nations sources a compilation of statistics relevant to the consideration by the treaty bodies of the reports of States parties;

8. *Requests* the Secretary-General to strengthen co-ordination between the Centre for Human Rights and the Centre for Social Development and Humanitarian Affairs of the Secretariat with reference to the implementation of human rights treaties and the servicing of treaty bodies;

9. *Requests* the Secretary-General to arrange, within existing resources and taking into account the priorities of the programme of advisory services, further training courses for those countries experiencing the most serious difficulties in meeting reporting obligations under international instruments on human rights;

10. *Invites* the specialized agencies and other United Nations bodies to assist the Secretary-General in the above-mentioned endeavours and to develop complementary training activities in this field;

11. *Calls upon* all States parties to fulfil without delay and in full their financial obligations under the relevant instruments on human rights;

12. *Requests* the Secretary-General to consider ways and means of strengthening collection procedures and making them more effective;

13. *Requests* the Secretary-General to convey to the Commission on Human Rights at its forty-fifth session the conclusions and recommendations of the meeting of persons chairing the human rights treaty bodies together with any views and comments he may have thereon;

14. *Requests* the Commission on Human Rights, in view of its overall responsibilities in the field of human rights, to consider at its forty-fifth session, as a matter of priority, the conclusions and recommendations of that meeting, in particular those identified as matters requiring urgent action, and to report to the General Assembly at its forty-fourth session, through the Economic and Social Council;

15. *Requests* the Secretary-General:

(a) To consider entrusting, within existing resources, an independent expert with the task of preparing a study on possible long-term approaches to the supervision of new instruments on human rights, taking into account the conclusions and recommendations of the meeting of persons chairing the treaty bodies, the deliberations of the Commission on Human Rights and other relevant materials, to be submitted to the General Assembly at its forty-fourth session;

(b) To review the need for adequate staffing resources in regard to the various human rights treaty bodies;

16. *Invites* the persons chairing the human rights treaty bodies to maintain communication and dialogue with each other on common issues and problems and decides to consider at its forty-fourth session the possi-

bility of convening a meeting in 1990 of the persons chairing the treaty bodies;

17. *Decides* to include in the provisional agenda of its forty-fourth session, as a separate item, an item entitled "Effective implementation of international instruments on human rights, including reporting obligations under international instruments on human rights".

General Assembly resolution 43/115

8 December 1988   Meeting 75   Adopted without vote

Approved by Third Committee (A/43/873) without vote, 23 November (meeting 51); 16-nation draft (A/C.3/43/L.50/Rev.1), orally revised; agenda item 101.

Sponsors: Australia, Austria, Belgium, Canada, Colombia, Costa Rica, Denmark, India, Italy, Morocco, Netherlands, Norway, Portugal, Sweden, United Kingdom, Yugoslavia.

Financial implications. 5th Committee, A/43/937; S-G, A/C.3/43/L.62, A/C.5/43/55.

Meeting numbers. GA 43rd session: 3rd Committee 39-43, 50, 51; 5th Committee 42; plenary 75.

International Covenants on Human Rights

Human Rights Commission action. On 7 March 1988,[52] the Commission adopted a resolution on the 1966 International Covenants on Human Rights,[18] which corresponded largely to resolutions adopted by the Economic and Social Council and the General Assembly later in the year (see below). The Commission asked the Secretary-General to consider, within existing resources and possibilities under the programme of advisory services, ways of assisting States parties to the Covenants to prepare their reports, and to report in 1989 on the status of the Covenants and the work of the Committee on Economic, Social and Cultural Rights.

ECONOMIC AND SOCIAL COUNCIL ACTION

On 24 May, the Economic and Social Council adopted **resolution 1988/5** without vote.

International Covenants on Human Rights

The Economic and Social Council,

Mindful that the International Covenants on Human Rights constitute the first all-embracing and legally binding international treaties in the field of human rights and, together with the Universal Declaration on Human Rights, form the core of the International Bill of Human Rights,

Recalling the International Covenant on Economic, Social and Cultural Rights and the International Covenant on Civil and Political Rights, and reaffirming that all human rights and fundamental freedoms are indivisible and interrelated and that the promotion and protection of one category of rights should never exempt or excuse States from the promotion and protection of the other rights,

Bearing in mind the important responsibilities of the Economic and Social Council in the co-ordination of activities to promote the International Covenants on Human Rights,

Considering that the year 1988 marks the fortieth anniversary of the Universal Declaration of Human Rights, which, conceived as a common standard of achievement for all peoples and all nations and having provided the basis for the International Covenants on

Human Rights, has been and rightly continues to be a fundamental source of inspiration for national and international efforts for the promotion and protection of human rights and fundamental freedoms,

Recalling its resolution 1987/4 of 26 May 1987, General Assembly resolutions 41/150 of 4 December 1986, 42/103 and 42/131, both of 7 December 1987, and Commission on Human Rights resolutions 1988/23 and 1988/27, both of 7 March 1988,

Convinced of the continuing need to promote the universal observance and enjoyment of human rights, which contribute to peaceful and friendly relations among nations,

1. *Reaffirms* the importance of the International Covenants on Human Rights in international efforts to promote universal respect for, and observance of, human rights and fundamental freedoms;

2. *Appeals strongly* to all States that have not yet done so to become parties to the International Covenant on Economic, Social and Cultural Rights and the International Covenant on Civil and Political Rights, and to consider acceding to the Optional Protocol to the International Covenant on Civil and Political Rights, so that these instruments acquire genuine universality;

3. *Emphasizes* the importance of the strictest compliance by States parties to the Covenants with their obligations under the International Covenant on Economic, Social and Cultural Rights, the International Covenant on Civil and Political Rights and, where applicable, the Optional Protocol to the International Covenant on Civil and Political Rights;

4. *Invites* the States parties to the International Covenant on Civil and Political Rights to consider making the declaration provided for in article 41 of the Covenant;

5. *Stresses* the importance of avoiding the erosion of human rights by derogation and the necessity for strict observance of the agreed conditions and procedures for derogation under article 4 of the International Covenant on Civil and Political Rights, bearing in mind the need for States parties to provide the fullest possible information during states of emergency, so that the justification and appropriateness of measures taken in those circumstances can be assessed;

6. *Reaffirms* the important role of the Human Rights Committee and the Committee on Economic, Social and Cultural Rights with respect to the implementation by States parties of the International Covenants on Human Rights, and expresses its satisfaction with the serious and constructive manner in which the Committees are exercising their functions;

7. *Invites* the Secretary-General and Member States to implement the measures set out in the annex to General Assembly resolution 41/150 in order to ensure the success of the activities in celebration of the fortieth anniversary of the Universal Declaration of Human Rights;

8. *Decides* to include the question of the International Covenants on Human Rights in the provisional agenda for its first regular session of 1989 and to consider under that question the general comments adopted by the Human Rights Committee and by the Committee on Economic, Social and Cultural Rights.

Economic and Social Council resolution 1988/5

24 May 1988   Meeting 12   Adopted without vote

12-nation draft (E/1988/L.23/Rev.1); agenda item 3.

Sponsors: Bulgaria, Byelorussian SSR, Czechoslovakia, Denmark, German Democratic Republic, Italy, Mongolia, Norway, Poland, Portugal, USSR, United Kingdom.
Meeting numbers. ESC 7, 8, 10-12.

Report of the Secretary-General. In August 1988,[53] the Secretary-General reported to the General Assembly, in response to its 1987 request,[54] on the status of the International Covenants as at 31 July, as well as on questions related to their implementation (see also above, under "Civil and political rights" and "Economic, social and cultural rights").

GENERAL ASSEMBLY ACTION

On 8 December, on the recommendation of the Third Committee, the General Assembly adopted **resolution 43/114** without vote.

International Covenants on Human Rights

The General Assembly,

Recalling its resolutions 33/51 of 14 December 1978, 34/45 of 23 November 1979, 35/132 of 11 December 1980, 36/58 of 25 November 1981, 37/191 of 18 December 1982, 38/116 and 38/117 of 16 December 1983, 39/136 and 39/138 of 14 December 1984, 40/115 and 40/116 of 13 December 1985, 41/32 of 3 November 1986, 41/119 and 41/121 of 4 December 1986 and 42/103 and 42/105 of 7 December 1987,

Taking note of the report of the Secretary-General on the status of the International Covenant on Economic, Social and Cultural Rights, the International Covenant on Civil and Political Rights, and the Optional Protocol to the International Covenant on Civil and Political Rights,

Recalling the International Covenant on Economic, Social and Cultural Rights and the International Covenant on Civil and Political Rights, and reaffirming that all human rights and fundamental freedoms are indivisible and interrelated and that the promotion and protection of one category of rights should never exempt or excuse States from the promotion and protection of the other,

Recognizing the important role of the Human Rights Committee in the implementation of the International Covenant on Civil and Political Rights and the Optional Protocol thereto,

Also recognizing the important role of the Committee on Economic, Social and Cultural Rights in the implementation of the International Covenant on Economic, Social and Cultural Rights,

Bearing in mind the important responsibilities of the Economic and Social Council in relation to the International Covenants on Human Rights,

Welcoming the submission to the General Assembly of the annual report of the Human Rights Committee and the report of the Committee on Economic, Social and Cultural Rights on its second session,

Considering that the effective functioning of treaty bodies established in accordance with the relevant provisions of international instruments on human rights plays a fundamental role and hence represents an important continuing concern of the United Nations,

Noting with concern the critical situation with regard to overdue reports from States parties to the International Covenants on Human Rights,

Taking note with appreciation of the results of the meeting of persons chairing human rights treaty bodies, held at Geneva from 10 to 14 October 1988,

Bearing in mind that 1988 marks the fortieth anniversary of the Universal Declaration of Human Rights,

1. *Takes note with appreciation* of the report of the Human Rights Committee on its thirty-first, thirty-second and thirty-third sessions, including the suggestions and recommendations of a general nature approved by the Committee;

2. *Also takes note with appreciation* of the report of the Committee on Economic, Social and Cultural Rights, including its suggestions and recommendations;

3. *Expresses its satisfaction* with the serious and constructive manner in which both Committees are carrying out their function;

4. *Expresses its appreciation* to the States parties to the International Covenant on Civil and Political Rights that have submitted their reports to the Human Rights Committee under article 40 of the Covenant and urges States parties that have not yet done so to submit their reports as speedily as possible;

5. *Urges* those States parties to the International Covenant on Civil and Political Rights that have been requested by the Human Rights Committee to provide additional information to comply with that request;

6. *Commends* the States parties to the International Covenant on Economic, Social and Cultural Rights that have submitted their reports under article 16 of the Covenant and urges States parties that have not yet done so to submit their reports as soon as possible;

7. *Notes with satisfaction* that the majority of States parties to the International Covenant on Civil and Political Rights and an increasing number of States parties to the International Covenant on Economic, Social and Cultural Rights have been represented by experts in the presentation of their reports, thereby assisting the respective monitoring bodies in their work, and hopes that all States parties to both Covenants will arrange such representation in the future;

8. *Again urges* all States that have not yet done so to become parties to the International Covenant on Economic, Social and Cultural Rights and the International Covenant on Civil and Political Rights, and to consider acceding to the Optional Protocol to the International Covenant on Civil and Political Rights;

9. *Invites* the States parties to the International Covenant on Civil and Political Rights to consider making the declaration provided for in article 41 of the Covenant;

10. *Emphasizes* the importance of the strictest compliance by States parties with their obligations under the International Covenant on Economic, Social and Cultural Rights and the International Covenant on Civil and Political Rights and, where applicable, the Optional Protocol to the International Covenant on Civil and Political Rights;

11. *Calls upon* all States parties to the International Covenant on Economic, Social and Cultural Rights and the International Covenant on Civil and Political Rights to adhere fully to these two Covenants and to all the rights and principles contained therein;

12. *Stresses* the importance of avoiding the erosion of human rights by derogation, and underlines the necessity of strict observance of the agreed conditions and procedures for derogation under article 4 of the International Covenant on Civil and Political Rights, bear-

ing in mind the need for States parties to provide the fullest possible information during states of emergency, so that the justification for and appropriateness of measures taken in these circumstances can be assessed;

13. *Appeals* to States parties to the Covenants that have exercised their sovereign right to make reservations in accordance with relevant rules of international law to consider whether any such reservation should be reviewed;

14. *Urges* States parties to pay active attention to the protection and promotion of civil and political rights, as well as economic, social and cultural rights;

15. *Urges* States parties to the International Covenant on Economic, Social and Cultural Rights, the specialized agencies and other relevant United Nations bodies to extend their full support and co-operation to the Committee on Economic, Social and Cultural Rights;

16. *Requests* the Secretary-General to keep the Human Rights Committee and the Committee on Economic, Social and Cultural Rights informed of the relevant activities of the General Assembly, the Economic and Social Council, the Commission on Human Rights, the Commission on the Status of Women, the Sub-Commission on Prevention of Discrimination and Protection of Minorities, the Committee on the Elimination of Racial Discrimination, the Committee on the Elimination of Discrimination against Women, the Committee against Torture and, where appropriate, other functional commissions of the Economic and Social Council and the specialized agencies, and also to transmit the annual reports of the Human Rights Committee and the Committee on Economic, Social and Cultural Rights to those bodies;

17. *Requests* the Secretary-General to submit to the General Assembly at its forty-fourth session a report on the status of the International Covenant on Economic, Social and Cultural Rights, the International Covenant on Civil and Political Rights and the Optional Protocol to the International Covenant on Civil and Political Rights;

18. *Also requests* the Secretary-General, within existing resources, to ensure that the Human Rights Committee and the Committee on Economic, Social and Cultural Rights are able to hold the necessary sessions and are provided with administrative support and summary records;

19. *Further requests* the Secretary-General to ensure that the Centre for Human Rights of the Secretariat effectively assists the Human Rights Committee and the Committee on Economic, Social and Cultural Rights in the implementation of their respective mandates;

20. *Again urges* the Secretary-General, taking into account the suggestions of the Human Rights Committee, to take determined steps, within existing resources, to give more publicity to the work of that Committee and, similarly, to the work of the Committee on Economic, Social and Cultural Rights;

21. *Encourages* all Governments to publish the texts of the International Covenant on Economic, Social and Cultural Rights, the International Covenant on Civil and Political Rights and the Optional Protocol to the International Covenant on Civil and Political Rights in as many languages as possible and to distribute them and make them known as widely as possible in their territories.

General Assembly resolution 43/114

8 December 1988   Meeting 75   Adopted without vote

Approved by Third Committee (A/43/872) without vote, 30 November (meeting 57); 18-nation draft (A/C.3/43/L.54), orally revised; agenda item 100.
Sponsors: Australia, Bulgaria, Canada, Costa Rica, Cyprus, Denmark, Ecuador, Finland, Hungary, Iceland, Italy, Netherlands, Norway, Peru, Spain, Sweden, USSR, United Kingdom.
Meeting numbers. GA 43rd session: 3rd Committee 39-43, 46, 51, 55, 57; plenary 75.

Fortieth anniversary of the Universal Declaration of Human Rights

Pursuant to 1986[55] and 1987[56] General Assembly resolutions, a range of activities during 1988 commemorated the fortieth anniversary of the Universal Declaration of Human Rights,[17] which was observed on Human Rights Day, 10 December. The Centre for Human Rights held *ad hoc* inter-agency meetings to discuss preparations for the celebration, and a co-ordinating meeting of representatives of the organizations of the United Nations system (Geneva, 15 January) reviewed the work programme for the year. Information about special commemorative activities was received from 38 Governments and the Holy See, as well as from NGOs. The text of the Declaration was available in some 80 languages following its publication in seven new languages in 1988. It was included in a special anniversary edition of the International Bill of Human Rights, together with the texts of the International Covenants. Other activities included workshops, seminars and training courses focusing on the anniversary (see also above, under ''Advisory services'') and the production of reference, information and promotional materials, including the *Human Rights Newsletter* and a new *Bulletin on Human Rights*. Issues related to human rights and the anniversary were also discussed at a global consultation with NGOs (Geneva, 12 December).

Report of the UNESCO Director-General. In November,[57] the Secretary-General transmitted to the Assembly a report of the UNESCO Director-General in connection with the fortieth anniversary of the Declaration, as requested by the Assembly in 1983.[58] The report outlined UNESCO activities in human rights education, information, documentation and the training of specialized groups, as well as activities relating to the International Congress on Human Rights Teaching, Information and Documentation (Malta, 30 August–5 September 1987) and the anniversary.

Sub-Commission action. On 1 September,[59] the Sub-Commission recommended that the Special Committee to Select the Winners of the United Nations Human Rights Prize consider making an award to Nelson Mandela on the occasion of the fortieth anniversary, for his personal life-long struggle against *apartheid* in South Africa.

Other action. On 8 December, at a commemorative meeting held by the Assembly, prizes for outstanding contributions to the promotion and protection of human rights and fundamental freedoms were awarded to M. D. (Baba) Amte (India), John Humphrey (Canada), Adam Lopatka (Poland), Nelson and Winnie Mandela (South Africa) and Monsignor Leonidas Proaño (Ecuador).

GENERAL ASSEMBLY ACTION

On 8 December, the General Assembly adopted **resolution 43/90** without vote.

Fortieth anniversary of the Universal Declaration of Human Rights

The General Assembly,

Reaffirming on the occasion of the fortieth anniversary of the Universal Declaration of Human Rights its significance as a source of inspiration for national and international efforts for the protection and promotion of human rights and fundamental freedoms,

Welcoming the progress made so far in the promotion and protection of human rights and fundamental freedoms since the proclamation of the Declaration,

Recalling that Member States have pledged themselves to achieve, in co-operation with the United Nations, the promotion of universal respect for and observance of human rights and fundamental freedoms,

Recalling also the obligations of Member States under the Charter of the United Nations to respect the principle of equal rights and self-determination of peoples as a basis for the creation of conditions of stability and well-being, which are necessary for peaceful and friendly relations among nations,

Acknowledging that, despite efforts made by the international community to promote and protect human rights, there is a need for constant vigilance by the international community in this field,

Recalling the responsibility of the international community to promote understanding, friendship and peaceful co-operation among peoples, and to ensure that everyone enjoys the inherent right to life, liberty and security of person,

Recalling the International Covenant on Economic, Social and Cultural Rights and the International Covenant on Civil and Political Rights, and reaffirming that all human rights and fundamental freedoms are indivisible and interrelated and that the promotion and protection of one category of rights should never exempt or excuse States from the promotion and protection of the other,

Underlining the importance of the teaching of human rights at all levels,

1. *Stresses* the important role of the Universal Declaration of Human Rights in encouraging Member States to enshrine the principles of the inherent dignity and of the equal and inalienable rights of all members of the human family in national constitutions and laws;

2. *Notes with satisfaction* the progress made so far in the field of human rights, including standard setting and codification, since the proclamation of the Declaration and reaffirms its commitment to further progress in this respect;

3. *Expresses grave concern* at mass and flagrant violations of human rights, including those stemming from racism, all forms of racial discrimination and *apartheid*, and at all violations of human rights that continue to take place in many parts of the world;

4. *Affirms* the responsibility of the United Nations in protecting and promoting human rights and fundamental freedoms and expresses the determination of the United Nations to deal, through appropriate United Nations bodies, with violations of human rights and fundamental freedoms;

5. *Urges* all States to observe the rights and freedoms set forth in the Declaration and appeals to those States which have not yet done so to consider ratifying or acceding to the Convention on the Prevention and Punishment of the Crime of Genocide, the International Convention on the Elimination of All Forms of Racial Discrimination, the International Covenant on Economic, Social and Cultural Rights, the International Covenant on Civil and Political Rights and the Optional Protocol thereto, the International Convention on the Suppression and Punishment of the Crime of *Apartheid*, the Convention on the Elimination of all Forms of Discrimination against Women, and the Convention against Torture and Other Cruel, Inhuman or Degrading Treatment or Punishment;

6. *Reaffirms* the importance of the observance and effective implementation of universally recognized standards in the field of human rights as contained in international human rights instruments;

7. *Invites* the Commission on Human Rights to consider a programme of action in the field of human rights, including:

(*a*) Measures to promote the univeral ratification of or accession to United Nations instruments in the field of human rights and to strengthen United Nations machinery for the promotion and protection of human rights and fundamental freedoms enshrined in the Declaration;

(*b*) Activities to develop human rights institutions and infrastructures, drawing upon the assistance of the United Nations programme of advisory services in the field of human rights, including the Voluntary Fund for Advisory Services and Technical Assistance in the Field of Human Rights, and drawing also upon the relevant capabilities of the specialized agencies in this field, and other available multilateral and bilateral assistance;

(*c*) Activities in the area of public information as may be determined by the Commission in considering the world campaign for human rights;

(*d*) Measures to enhance national and existing regional institutions for the promotion of human rights, through appropriate educational, judicial, legal and other channels, including direct contact among them;

8. *Invites* Member States, the specialized agencies and intergovernmental organizations to draw upon the contributions of non-governmental organizations concerned with the promotion and protection of human rights and fundamental freedoms for the achievement of the above programme of action;

9. *Requests* the Secretary-General to submit to the General Assembly at its forty-eighth session a report on the activities undertaken in pursuance of the present resolution;

10. *Decides* to include in the provisional agenda of its forty-eighth session an item entitled "Forty-fifth anniversary of the Universal Declaration of Human Rights".

General Assembly resolution 43/90

8 December 1988   Meeting 75   Adopted without vote

37-nation draft (A/43/L.47 & Corr.1); agenda item 38.
Sponsors: Afghanistan, Argentina, Australia, Barbados, Bulgaria, Byelorussian SSR, Canada, Central African Republic, Colombia, Costa Rica, Cyprus, Dominican Republic, Ecuador, Egypt, France, Greece, Hungary, India, Iraq, Ireland, Italy, Lebanon, Luxembourg, Mongolia, Morocco, Netherlands, New Zealand, Nigeria, Peru, Philippines, Poland, Samoa, Senegal, Sudan, Ukrainian SSR, USSR, Vanuatu.
Meeting numbers. GA 43rd session: plenary 66, 68, 72, 74, 75.

Also on 8 December, the Assembly was informed that Colombia had withdrawn a draft resolution on human rights based on solidarity.[60] By **decision 43/424** of the same date, the Assembly included the item on preparation of an instrument on human rights based on solidarity in the provisional agenda of its forty-fourth (1989) session.

Electoral processes

On 8 December, on the recommendation of the Third Committee, the General Assembly adopted **resolution 43/157** without vote.

Enhancing the effectiveness of the principle of periodic and genuine elections

The General Assembly,

Aware of its obligations under the Charter of the United Nations to develop friendly relations among nations based on respect for the principle of equal rights and self-determination of peoples and to promote and encourage respect for human rights and fundamental freedoms for all,

Reaffirming the Universal Declaration of Human Rights, which provides that everyone has the right to take part in the government of his or her country, directly or through freely chosen representatives, that everyone has the right of equal access to public service in his or her country, that the will of the people shall be the basis of the authority of government, and that this will shall be expressed in periodic and genuine elections which shall be by universal and equal suffrage and shall be held by secret vote or by equivalent free voting procedures,

Noting that the International Covenant on Civil and Political Rights provides that every citizen shall have the right and the opportunity, without distinction of any kind, such as race, colour, sex, language, religion, political or other opinion, national or social origin, property, birth or other status, to take part in the conduct of public affairs, directly or through freely chosen representatives, to vote and to be elected at genuine periodic elections which shall be by universal and equal suffrage and shall be held by secret ballot, guaranteeing the free expression of the will of the electors, and to have access, on general terms of equality, to public service in his or her country,

Condemning the system of *apartheid* and any other denial or abridgement of the right to vote on the grounds of race, colour, sex, language, religion, political or other opinion, national or social origin, property, birth or other status,

Recalling that all States enjoy sovereign equality and that each State has the right freely to choose and develop its political, social, economic, and cultural systems,

1. *Emphasizes* the significance of the Universal Declaration of Human Rights and the International Cove-

nant on Civil and Political Rights, which establish that the authority to govern shall be based on the will of the people, as expressed in periodic and genuine elections;

2. *Stresses* its conviction that periodic and genuine elections are a necessary and indispensable element of sustained efforts to protect the rights and interests of the governed and that, as a matter of practical experience, the right of everyone to take part in the government of his or her country is a crucial factor in the effective enjoyment by all of a wide range of other human rights and fundamental freedoms, including political, economic, social, and cultural rights;

3. *Declares* that determining the will of the people requires an electoral process which accommodates distinct alternatives, and that this process should provide an equal opportunity for all citizens to become candidates and put forward their political views, individually and in co-operation with others;

4. *Reaffirms* that *apartheid* should be abolished, that the systematic denial or abridgement of the right to vote on the grounds of race or colour is a gross violation of human rights and an affront to the conscience and dignity of mankind, and that the right to participate in a political system based on common and equal citizenship and universal franchise is essential for the exercise of the principle of periodic and genuine elections;

5. *Calls upon* the Commission on Human Rights, at its forty-fifth session, to consider appropriate ways and means of enhancing the effectiveness of the principle of periodic and genuine elections, in the context of full respect for the sovereignty of Member States, and to report to the General Assembly at its forty-fourth session, through the Economic and Social Council;

6. *Decides* to include in the agenda of its forty-fourth session an item entitled "Enhancing the effectiveness of the principle of periodic and genuine elections".

General Assembly resolution 43/157

8 December 1988   Meeting 75   Adopted without vote

Approved by Third Committee (A/43/868) without vote, 30 November (meeting 57); 17-nation draft (A/C.3/43/L.80), orally revised; agenda item 12.
Sponsors: Belgium, Costa Rica, Cyprus, Dominican Republic, France, Germany, Federal Republic of, Honduras, Hungary, India, Italy, Malta, Netherlands, Philippines, Portugal, Spain, United Kingdom, United States.
Meeting numbers. GA 43rd session: 3rd Committee 49-57; plenary 75.

Regional arrangements

In accordance with a 1986 General Assembly resolution,[61] the Secretary-General reported in April 1988 on the state of regional arrangements for the promotion and protection of human rights.[62] The report noted that contacts between regional bodies and commissions and the United Nations continued to be pursued and strengthened through advisory services and technical assistance activities, particularly those relating to training courses on human rights, and summarized action by the Commission on Human Rights in that respect. (See also above, under "Advisory services".)

GENERAL ASSEMBLY ACTION

On 8 December, on the recommendation of the Third Committee, the General Assembly adopted **resolution 43/152** without vote.

Regional arrangements for the promotion and protection of human rights

The General Assembly,

Recalling its resolution 32/127 of 16 December 1977 and all its subsequent resolutions concerning regional arrangements for the promotion and protection of human rights, in particular resolutions 41/153 and 41/154 of 4 December 1986,

Recalling that, in its resolution 41/154, the General Assembly invited the Secretary-General to submit to the Assembly at its forty-third session a report on the state of regional arrangements for the promotion and protection of human rights, and to include therein the results of action taken in pursuance of that resolution,

Recalling Commission on Human Rights resolution 1987/37 of 10 March 1987 and taking note of Commission resolution 1988/54 of 8 March 1988 concerning advisory services in the field of human rights,

Recalling also Commission on Human Rights resolution 1987/41 of 10 March 1987 and taking note of Commission resolution 1988/73 of 10 March 1988 concerning regional arrangements for the promotion and protection of human rights in the Asian-Pacific region,

Having considered the report of the Secretary-General on regional arrangements for the promotion and protection of human rights,

Noting with satisfaction the progress achieved so far in the promotion and protection of human rights at the regional level under the auspices of the United Nations, the specialized agencies and the regional intergovernmental organizations,

Reaffirming that regional arrangements for the promotion and protection of human rights may make a major contribution to the effective enjoyment of human rights and fundamental freedoms and that the exchange of information and experience in this field among the regions, within the United Nations system, may be improved,

1. *Takes note* of the report of the Secretary-General;

2. *Notes with interest* that various contacts between regional bodies and commissions and the United Nations have continued to be pursued and strengthened through advisory services and technical assistance activities, particularly those relating to the organization of regional and subregional training courses in the field of human rights;

3. *Requests* the Secretary-General to continue to consider the possibility of encouraging these developments;

4. *Invites* States in areas where regional arrangements in the field of human rights do not yet exist to consider concluding agreements with a view to the establishment within their respective regions of suitable regional machinery for the promotion and protection of human rights;

5. *Welcomes* the fact that subprogramme 5 of the medium-term plan of activities concerning advisory services and technical assistance activities in the field of human rights, to which the Secretary-General refers in his report, provides for the establishment of regional arrangements where they are still lacking;

6. *Notes* the announcement by the Secretary-General in his report that, for the advancement of the above-mentioned objective, it is useful to hold seminars in the regions concerned which will draw upon the knowledge and experience of the United Nations development agencies in those regions, as well as upon the experience gained through established arrangements in other regions;

7. *Endorses* the appeal made to all Governments, in Commission on Human Rights resolution 1988/54, to consider making use of the possibility offered by the United Nations of organizing, under the programme of advisory services in the field of human rights, information and/or training courses at the national level for appropriate government personnel on the application of international human rights standards and the experience of relevant international bodies;

8. *Requests* the Commission on Human Rights to continue to pay special attention to the most appropriate ways of assisting, at their request, countries of the different regions under the programme of advisory services and to make, where necessary, the relevant recommendations;

9. *Invites* the Secretary-General to submit to the General Assembly at its forty-fifth session a report on the state of regional arrangements for the promotion and protection of human rights and to include therein the results of action taken in pursuance of the present resolution;

10. *Decides* to consider this question further at its forty-fifth session.

General Assembly resolution 43/152

8 December 1988   Meeting 75   Adopted without vote

Approved by Third Committee (A/43/868) without vote, 30 November (meeting 57); 16-nation draft (A/C.3/43/L.75), orally revised; agenda item 12.
Sponsors: Austria, Belgium, Bolivia, Colombia, Costa Rica, Côte d'Ivoire, Ecuador, Gambia, Germany, Federal Republic of, Italy, Netherlands, Norway, Samoa, Senegal, Togo, Uruguay.
Meeting numbers. GA 43rd session: 3rd Committee 49-57; plenary 75.

Asia and the Pacific

In a February report on regional arrangements for the promotion and protection of human rights in Asia and the Pacific,[63] submitted to the Assembly through the Economic and Social Council in response to a 1986 Assembly request,[64] the Secretary-General noted that there had been no substantive change in the mandate of the Economic and Social Commission for Asia and the Pacific (ESCAP) that would enable it to establish a depository centre for United Nations human rights materials at Bangkok, Thailand, but that the ESCAP library continued to receive and disseminate information on human rights.

On 27 May, by **decision 1988/145**, the Economic and Social Council took note of the Secretary-General's report.

Human Rights Commission action. The Commission on Human Rights was apprised of regional arrangements in Asia and the Pacific by a separate report of the Secretary-General,[65] which also summarized the conclusions of a 1987 regional training course on human rights teaching.[66] They included general agreement on the need to advance formal and informal human rights teaching in the region, particularly in rural areas, and on the usefulness of establishing a resource library to collect and disseminate laws, documents and other publications throughout Asia and the Pacific.

On 10 March,[67] the Commission requested the Secretary-General to continue assisting the Executive Secretary of ESCAP in establishing a depository centre, to ensure a continuing flow of human rights materials to the ESCAP library and to report to the Commission in 1989 on the progress achieved. United Nations development agencies in the Asian and Pacific region were encouraged to co-ordinate with ESCAP their efforts to promote the human rights dimension in their activities.

GENERAL ASSEMBLY ACTION

On 8 December, on the recommendation of the Third Committee, the General Assembly adopted **resolution 43/140** without vote.

Regional arrangements for the promotion and protection of human rights in the Asian and Pacific region

The General Assembly,

Recalling its previous resolutions, in particular resolution 41/153 of 4 December 1986, on regional arrangements for the promotion and protection of human rights in the Asian and Pacific region,

Recognizing that regional arrangements make a major contribution to the promotion and protection of human rights and that non-governmental organizations may have a valuable role to play in this process,

Bearing in mind that intergovernmental arrangements for the promotion and protection of human rights have been established in other regions,

Reiterating its appreciation for the report of the Seminar on National, Local and Regional Arrangements for the Promotion and Protection of Human Rights in the Asian Region, held at Colombo from 21 June to 2 July 1982, and the comments on the report of the Seminar received from the Economic and Social Commission for Asia and the Pacific and from States members of the Commission,

Welcoming the designation of the Social Development Division of the Economic and Social Commission for Asia and the Pacific as a regional human rights focal point,

Taking note of Commission on Human Rights resolution 1988/73 of 10 March 1988,

1. *Takes note* of the report of the Secretary-General;

2. *Requests* the Secretary-General to continue to assist and encourage the Executive Secretary of the Economic and Social Commission for Asia and the Pacific to pursue the establishment, within existing resources, of a depository centre for United Nations human rights materials within the Commission at Bangkok, the function of which would include the collection, processing and dissemination of such materials in the Asian and Pacific region;

3. *Renews its invitation* to States members of the Economic and Social Commission for Asia and the Pacific that have not yet done so to communicate to the Secretary-General as soon as possible their comments on the report of the Seminar on National, Local and Regional Arrangements for the Promotion and Protection of Human Rights in the Asian Region and, in par-

ticular, to address themselves to the conclusions and recommendations in the report concerning the development of regional arrangements in Asia and the Pacific;

4. *Requests* the Secretary-General to ensure a continuing flow of human rights material to the library of the Economic and Social Commission for Asia and the Pacific at Bangkok for appropriate dissemination in the region;

5. *Notes* the efforts of United Nations development agencies in the Asian and Pacific region to promote the human rights dimension more actively and systematically in their development activities;

6. *Encourages* United Nations development agencies in the Asian and Pacific region to co-ordinate with the Economic and Social Commission for Asia and the Pacific their efforts to promote the human rights dimension in their activities;

7. *Welcomes* the report of the Secretary-General on the successful training course on human rights teaching held at Bangkok from 12 to 23 October 1987 under the United Nations programme of advisory services in the field of human rights;

8. *Draws attention* to the summary of discussions and conclusions in the report, in particular to the need to advance both formal and informal teaching of human rights in the region, with emphasis on the identification of target groups, particularly in rural areas;

9. *Notes* the general consensus among participants in the training course that it would be useful for the better identification of existing measures and the dissemination of materials to establish a resource library that would collect and disseminate laws, documents and other publications throughout the region;

10. *Requests* the Secretary-General to submit a further report to the General Assembly at its forty-fifth session, through the Economic and Social Council, incorporating information on progress achieved in the implementation of the present resolution;

11. *Decides* to continue its consideration of the question at its forty-fifth session.

General Assembly resolution 43/140

8 December 1988   Meeting 75   Adopted without vote

Approved by Third Committee (A/43/868) without vote, 29 November (meeting 56); 12-nation draft (A/C.3/43/L.63); agenda item 12.

Sponsors: Australia, Bangladesh, China, Cyprus, Fiji, Iran, Jordan, Mongolia, Papua New Guinea, Philippines, Samoa, Sri Lanka.

Meeting numbers. GA 43rd session: 3rd Committee 49-56; plenary 75.

Responsibility to promote and protect human rights

Working group activities. The working group to draft a declaration on the right and responsibility of individuals, groups and organs of society to promote and protect universally recognized human rights and fundamental freedoms met at Geneva from 25 January to 3 February and on 8 March 1988.[68] It provisionally adopted, at first reading, the title and some of the provisions of chapter II of the draft declaration, and accepted in principle a number of paragraphs from the compendium of elements for chapter I. Annexed to the group's report was a compilation of all the texts showing the state of the whole draft declaration.

Human Rights Commission action. On 10 March,[69] the Commission decided to continue at its 1989 session work on elaborating the draft declaration and to make meeting time available to the working group during that session. It recommended a draft resolution for adoption by the Economic and Social Council (see below).

ECONOMIC AND SOCIAL COUNCIL ACTION

On 27 May, on the recommendation of its Second Committee, the Economic and Social Council adopted **resolution 1988/39** without vote.

Question of a draft declaration on the right and responsibility of individuals, groups and organs of society to promote and protect universally recognized human rights and fundamental freedoms

The Economic and Social Council,

Recalling Commission on Human Rights resolution 1988/71 of 10 March 1988,

1. *Authorizes* an open-ended working group of the Commission on Human Rights to meet for a period of one week prior to the forty-fifth session of the Commission, in order to continue to elaborate a draft declaration on the right and responsibility of individuals, groups and organs of society to promote and protect universally recognized human rights and fundamental freedoms;

2. *Requests* the Secretary-General to extend all facilities to the working group for its meetings prior to and during the forty-fifth session of the Commission and in order to enable it to continue its work on the elaboration of the draft declaration to transmit the report of the working group that met prior to and during the forty-fourth session of the Commission, together with the annexes thereto, to all Member States in advance of the next meeting of the working group.

Economic and Social Council resolution 1988/39

27 May 1988   Meeting 16   Adopted without vote

Approved by Second Committee (E/1988/89/Add.1) without vote, 23 May (meeting 20); draft by Commission on Human Rights (E/1988/12 & Corr.1); agenda item 10.

Sub-Commission action. On 1 September,[70] the Sub-Commission called for effective measures of protection for human rights defenders and those threatened with violations of their own human rights, and urged the Commission to finalize a draft declaration as soon as possible.

New international humanitarian order

In an October report with a later addendum,[71] the Secretary-General submitted to the General Assembly replies from seven Governments, five United Nations organs, four specialized agencies, three NGOs and the Independent Commission on International Humanitarian Issues, providing information on humanitarian issues of concern to them, as requested by the Assembly in 1987.[72]

GENERAL ASSEMBLY ACTION

On 8 December, on the recommendation of the Third Committee, the General Assembly adopted **resolution 43/129** without vote.

New international humanitarian order

The General Assembly,

Recalling its resolutions 36/136 of 14 December 1981, 37/201 of 18 December 1982, 38/125 of 16 December 1983, 40/126 of 13 December 1985 and 42/120 and 42/121 of 7 December 1987 relating to the promotion of a new international humanitarian order,

Taking note of the report of the Secretary-General and the comments made by various Governments regarding the humanitarian order and the work done in this regard by the Independent Commission on International Humanitarian Issues,

Noting the actions being taken by the specialized agencies and programmes of the United Nations system with regard to the humanitarian issues, examined by the Independent Commission, that fall within their respective mandates,

Recognizing with concern the continuing need further to strengthen international responses to growing humanitarian challenges and to adjust actions of governmental and non-governmental organizations to new realities in a fast-changing world,

Bearing in mind the importance of creative humanitarian action at the international as well as the regional and national levels to alleviate human suffering and to promote durable solutions to humanitarian problems,

Convinced of the need for an active follow-up to the recommendations and suggestions made by the Independent Commission and of the importance of the role being played in this regard by the Independent Bureau for Humanitarian Issues set up for the purpose,

1. *Expresses its appreciation* to the Secretary-General for his continuing active support for the efforts to promote a new international humanitarian order;

2. *Encourages* Governments as well as governmental and non-governmental organizations that have not yet done so to provide their comments and expertise to the Secretary-General regarding the humanitarian order and the report of the Independent Commission on International Humanitarian Issues;

3. *Invites* the Independent Bureau for Humanitarian Issues to continue and further strengthen its essential role in following up the work of the Independent Commission;

4. *Invites* Governments to make available to the Secretary-General, on a voluntary basis, information and expertise on humanitarian issues of concern to them, in order to identify opportunities for future action;

5. *Requests* the Secretary-General to remain in contact with Governments as well as governmental and non-governmental organizations and the Independent Bureau for Humanitarian Issues and to report to the General Assembly at its forty-fifth session on the progress made by them;

6. *Decides* to review at its forty-fifth session the question of a new international humanitarian order.

General Assembly resolution 43/129

8 December 1988   Meeting 75   Adopted without vote

Approved by Third Committee (A/43/877) without vote, 17 November (meeting 46); 40-nation draft (A/C.3/43/L.36), orally revised; agenda item 105.

Sponsors: Bahrain, Bangladesh, Belgium, Bulgaria, Canada, Chile, Colombia, Costa Rica, Democratic Yemen, Denmark, Djibouti, Egypt, France, German Democratic Republic, Greece, Indonesia, Iraq, Italy, Jamaica, Japan, Jordan, Kuwait, Lebanon, Libyan Arab Jamahiriya, Mauritania, Morocco, Oman, Pakistan, Philippines, Qatar, Romania, Saudi Arabia, Senegal, Somalia, Sri Lanka, Sudan, USSR, United Arab Emirates, Yemen, Yugoslavia.
Meeting numbers. GA 43rd session: 3rd Committee 36-38, 42, 46; plenary 75.

International co-operation in human rights

On 8 December, on the recommendation of the Third Committee, the General Assembly adopted **resolution 43/155** without vote.

International co-operation in solving international problems of a social, cultural or humanitarian character, and in promoting and encouraging universal respect for, and observance of, human rights and fundamental freedoms

The General Assembly,

Recalling its resolution 41/155 of 4 December 1986 and Commission on Human Rights resolution 1987/42 of 10 March 1987,

Conscious that it is a purpose of the United Nations and the task of all Member States to achieve international co-operation in solving international problems of an economic, social, cultural or humanitarian character, and in promoting and encouraging universal respect for, and observance of, human rights and fundamental freedoms for all, without distinction as to race, sex, language or religion,

Desirous of achieving further progress in promoting and encouraging respect for human rights and fundamental freedoms,

Considering that special emphasis should be put on the effective implementation of the principles embodied in the Charter of the United Nations, the Universal Declaration of Human Rights, the International Covenant on Civil and Political Rights, the International Covenant on Economic, Social and Cultural Rights and other relevant international instruments,

Convinced that the effectiveness of United Nations human rights instruments would be enhanced by universal adherence to them as well as by strict compliance of States parties with their voluntarily accepted obligations,

Considering that existing regional arrangements for the promotion and protection of human rights make a major contribution to the effective enjoyment of human rights and fundamental freedoms and that the exchange of information and experience in this field could be further improved,

Emphasizing the necessity for the international community to continue its efforts to take practical measures to prevent mass and flagrant violations and all other violations of human rights, including all forms of discrimination based on distinctions of any kind, such as race, colour, sex, language, religion, political or other opinion, national or social origin, property, birth or other status, which continue to take place in many parts of the world, contrary to the provisions of international instruments in the field of human rights,

Noting the importance that the promotion and protection of human rights has secured on the international agenda and in relations between States,

1. *Calls upon* Member States to implement fully the universally recognized standards for the protection and promotion of human rights enshrined, in particular, in the Charter of the United Nations, the Universal Declaration of Human Rights, the International Covenant on Civil and Political Rights, the International Covenant on Economic, Social and Cultural Rights and other relevant international instruments;

2. *Urges* all States to co-operate fully with the relevant bodies of the United Nations system as well as other intergovernmental forums dealing with the protection and promotion of human rights and fundamental freedoms in any part of the world;

3. *Considers* that such co-operation will make an effective and practical contribution to the implementation of human rights and fundamental freedoms for all;

4. *Expresses its conviction* that the promotion of and respect for human rights and fundamental freedoms, as well as the implementation of universally recognized human rights standards, are particularly important for all countries;

5. *Urges* Member States that have not yet done so to consider ratifying or acceding to the various international instruments in the field of human rights;

6. *Recognizes* the value of common efforts by Governments and intergovernmental and non-governmental organizations at international, regional, bilateral and national levels in the field of human rights;

7. *Considers* that a world public information campaign on human rights would contribute to the promotion and improvement of understanding of human rights;

8. *Emphasizes* that the wide dissemination of information on human rights is an important task and would contribute to the implementation of universally recognized international human rights standards;

9. *Decides* to continue the consideration of this question at its forty-fourth session under the item entitled "Report of the Economic and Social Council".

General Assembly resolution 43/155

8 December 1988   Meeting 75   Adopted without vote

Approved by Third Committee (A/43/868) without vote, 30 November (meeting 57); 4-nation draft (A/C.3/43/L.78), orally revised; agenda item 12.
Sponsors: Austria, Canada, Hungary, Ukrainian SSR.
Meeting numbers. GA 43rd session: 3rd Committee 49-57; plenary 75.

Also on 8 December, on the recommendation of the Third Committee, the General Assembly adopted **resolution 43/130** without vote.

Promotion of international co-operation in the humanitarian field

The General Assembly,

Recalling its resolution 42/121 of 7 December 1987,

Noting that one of the purposes of the United Nations, set forth in its Charter, is to achieve international co-operation in solving international problems of a humanitarian character,

Recalling the Universal Declaration of Human Rights, which proclaims, *inter alia*, that recognition of the inherent dignity and of the equal and inalienable rights of all members of the human family is the foundation of freedom, justice and peace in the world,

Guided by universally accepted human values and common aspiration for a better, more just, safe and humane world,

Noting that international co-operation in the humanitarian field could contribute to attaining the ideals of a new international humanitarian order,

Mindful of the significance of the existing workable system to promote, facilitate and co-ordinate humanitarian activities carried out by Governments, the United Nations system and intergovernmental and non-governmental organizations,

Taking note with satisfaction of the report of the Independent Commission on International Humanitarian Issues and the efforts of the Independent Bureau for Humanitarian Issues to promote public awareness of humanitarian problems and to identify alternative approaches for resolving humanitarian problems,

1. *Calls upon* Governments, the United Nations system and intergovernmental and non-governmental organizations further to develop international co-operation in the humanitarian field;

2. *Reiterates* that international co-operation in the humanitarian field will facilitate better understanding, mutual respect, confidence and tolerance among countries and peoples, thus contributing to a more just and non-violent world;

3. *Invites* Governments to promote, within existing mechanisms, regular exchanges of information and of national experience in addressing humanitarian problems;

4. *Encourages* the international community to contribute substantially and regularly to international humanitarian activities;

5. *Invites* all non-governmental organizations concerned with the humanitarian issues examined by the Independent Commission on International Humanitarian Issues and working with strictly humanitarian motives to bear in mind the recommendations and suggestions made in the report of the Independent Commission in the context of their policies and actions in the field;

6. *Invites* Governments and intergovernmental and non-governmental organizations to forward to the Secretary-General, on a voluntary basis, their comments concerning further development of international co-operation in the humanitarian field;

7. *Requests* the Secretary-General to continue his contacts with Governments, agencies and programmes of the United Nations system and non-governmental organizations concerned, as well as with the Independent Bureau for Humanitarian Issues and, taking into account information received, to submit to the General Assembly at its forty-fifth session a report on possible ways and means of strengthening international co-operation in the humanitarian field.

General Assembly resolution 43/130

8 December 1988   Meeting 75   Adopted without vote

Approved by Third Committee (A/43/877) without vote, 17 November (meeting 46); 8-nation draft (A/C.3/43/L.37), orally revised; agenda item 105.
Sponsors: Bulgaria, German Democratic Republic, Iraq, Jordan, Mongolia, Morocco, USSR, Viet Nam.
Meeting numbers. GA 43rd session: 3rd Committee 36-38, 42, 46; plenary 75.

Displaced persons and humanitarian assistance

On 24 August,[73] the Sub-Commission requested the Secretary-General to offer Burundi all necessary assistance, particularly within the programme of advisory services, to deal with the situation of refugees and displaced persons in that country, and asked him to inform it of the results.

REFERENCES

[1]E/1988/12 (res. 1988/72). [2]YUN 1987, p. 781, GA res. 42/116, 7 Dec. 1987. [3]*Ibid.*, p. 780. [4]E/1988/12 & Corr.1. [5]*Ibid.* (dec. 1988/101). [6]*Ibid.* (res. 1988/30). [7]*Ibid.* (dec. 1988/103). [8]YUN 1970, p. 529, ESC res. 1503(XLVIII), 27 May 1970. [9]E/1988/12 (dec. 1988/107). [10]E/CN.4/1989/3. [11]*Ibid.* (dec. 1988/104). [12]*Ibid.* (dec. 1988/113). [13]E/1988/12 (res. 1988/43). [14]E/CN.4/1989/3 (res. 1988/2). [15]E/CN.4/1988/20 & Add.1. [16]E/1988/12 (res. 1988/74). [17]YUN 1948-49, p. 535, GA res. 217 A (III), 10 Dec. 1948. [18]YUN 1966, pp. 419 & 423, GA res. 2200 A (XXI), annex, 16 Dec. 1966. [19]E/CN.4/1989/3 (res. 1988/35). [20]YUN 1987, p. 782, GA res. 42/118, 7 Dec. 1987. [21]A/43/711. [22]A/43/721. [23]YUN 1955, p. 164, GA res. 926(X), 14 Dec. 1955. [24]E/CN.4/1988/40 & Add.1. [25]E/CN.4/Sub.2/1988/36 & Add.1. [26]YUN 1987, p. 791. [27]E/1988/12 (res. 1988/54). [28]YUN 1987, p. 790. [29]*Ibid.*, ESC dec. 1987/147, 29 May 1987. [30]E/1988/12 (res. 1988/53). [31]E/CN.4/1988/6. [32]YUN 1981, p. 938. [33]E/1988/12 (res. 1988/52). [34]YUN 1984, p. 813, GA res. 39/46, annex, 10 Dec. 1984. [35]YUN 1987, p. 791, ESC dec. 1987/149, 29 May 1987. [36]E/CN.4/1988/42. [37]E/1988/12 (res. 1988/50). [38]E/CN.4/1989/3 (res. 1988/14). [39]YUN 1987, p. 818. [40]E/CN.4/1988/38. [41]E/1988/12 (res. 1988/51). [42]YUN 1965, p. 440, GA res. 2106 A (XX), annex, 21 Dec. 1965. [43]YUN 1973, p. 103, GA res. 3068(XXVIII), annex, 30 Nov. 1973. [44]YUN 1979, p. 895, GA res. 34/180, annex, 18 Dec. 1979. [45]YUN 1987, p. 785, GA res. 42/105, 7 Dec. 1987. [46]A/44/98. [47]E/1988/85. [48]E/1988/12 (res. 1988/31). [49]E/CN.4/Sub.2/1988/27. [50]YUN 1985, p. 889. [51]E/CN.4/1989/3 (res. 1988/30). [52]E/1988/12 (res. 1988/27). [53]A/43/518. [54]YUN 1987, p. 788, GA res. 42/103, 7 Dec. 1987. [55]YUN 1986, p. 736, GA res. 41/150, 4 Dec. 1986. [56]YUN 1987, p. 784, GA res. 42/131, 7 Dec. 1987. [57]A/43/796. [58]YUN 1983, p. 863, GA res. 38/57, 9 Dec. 1983. [59]E/CN.4/1989/3 (res. 1988/108). [60]A/43/L.39/Rev.1. [61]YUN 1986, p. 734, GA res. 41/154, 4 Dec. 1986. [62]A/43/328. [63]A/43/170-E/1988/25. [64]YUN 1986, p. 735, GA res. 41/153, 4 Dec. 1986. [65]E/CN.4/1988/39 & Add.1. [66]YUN 1987, p. 784. [67]E/1988/12 (res. 1988/73). [68]E/CN.4/1988/26. [69]E/1988/12 (res. 1988/71). [70]E/CN.4/1989/3 (res. 1988/38). [71]A/43/734 & Add.1. [72]YUN 1987, p. 792, GA res. 42/120, 7 Dec. 1987. [73]E/CN.4/1989/3 (res. 1988/1).

Human rights violations

Alleged violations of human rights on a large scale in several countries were examined again in 1988 by the General Assembly, the Economic and Social Council and the Commission on Human Rights, as well as by special bodies and appointed officials.

In addition, alleged human rights violations involving the self-determination of peoples (see above, under "Civil and political rights") were discussed with regard to Afghanistan, Kampuchea, South Africa, Western Sahara and the Palestinian people.

Under a procedure established by the Council in 1970[1] to deal with communications alleging denial or violation of human rights, the Working Group on Communications of the Sub-Commission on Prevention of Discrimination and Protection of Minorities met from 25 July to 5 August 1988. After considering the Working Group's confidential report, the Sub-Commission referred to the Commission for consideration situations which appeared to reveal a consistent pattern of gross and reliably attested human rights violations. The Sub-

Commission decided to defer action on certain communications until 1989 and to take no action on certain other communications.

Africa

South Africa and Namibia

Working Group activities. In 1988, the six-member *Ad Hoc* Working Group of Experts on southern Africa, established by the Commission on Human Rights in 1967,[2] submitted to the Commission its interim report,[3] as requested by the Economic and Social Council in 1987.[4] In the report, the Group re-examined its mandate and considered recent developments in South Africa and Namibia. Developments in South Africa dealt with by the Group concerned the right to life, physical integrity and protection from arbitrary arrest and detention; *apartheid*, including bantustanization and forced population removals; the right to education and freedom of expression and of movement; and the right to work, the situation of black workers and trade union rights. Issues relating to Namibia included human rights violations affecting individuals; consequences of the militarization of the Territory; the right to work, to education and to health; and information concerning persons suspected of being guilty of the crime of *apartheid* or of a serious human rights violation.

In July/August, pursuant to Commission and Council resolutions adopted earlier in the year (see below), the Group undertook a fact-finding mission aimed at gathering testimony from witnesses (Geneva, 27 and 28 July; Luanda, Angola, 30 July–2 August; Harare, Zimbabwe, 3-8 August; Lusaka, Zambia, 10-14 August; and Dar-es-Salaam, United Republic of Tanzania, 15-18 August).

Human Rights Commission action. On 26 February,[5] the Commission decided to send an urgent message to South Africa to lift immediately the ban and restrictions imposed from 24 February on a large number of black civic, political and trade union organizations and their leaders, and requested the Secretary-General to intervene urgently with a view to defusing the situation.

On 29 February,[6] by a roll-call vote of 36 to 3, with 4 abstentions, the Commission strongly condemned the escalation of human rights violations in South Africa since the imposition of the state of emergency in June 1986, including widespread detention and incarceration of children, use of torture against political opponents and indiscriminate use of force against unarmed demonstrators, and demanded that South Africa immediately abolish the system of *apartheid* in all its forms. It denounced the policies of "bantustanization" and denationalization, the forced removals of the black population and so-called "voluntary" removals, and rejected South Africa's so-called reforms. Those reforms, it said, fell short of terminating the state of emergency, abolishing *apartheid* laws, dismantling the "bantustans", lifting bans on political organizations and parties and on the return of political exiles and freedom fighters, and ensuring the release of political prisoners.

The Commission demanded that South Africa desist from its brutal repression, torture and harassment of organizations and individuals opposed to *apartheid* and from the abduction and assassination of political refugees and members of liberation movements based in neighbouring States. It also demanded that South Africa repeal its ban on political organizations, release unconditionally all political prisoners and ensure that all South Africans were afforded a unified, free educational system. It condemned the South African régime for military pressures and other destabilization policies towards the front-line States, and called on it to respect international standards on trade union rights.

Urging all States to stop any assistance to South Africa, the Commission called on the Security Council to impose mandatory sanctions against it, and endorsed, pending the adoption of sanctions, other measures adopted by certain countries against South Africa, including prohibition of the transfer of technology; cessation of exports, sales or transport of oil and oil products; cessation of further investments and financial loans and of support for trade; prohibition of the sale of krugerrand and other coins minted in South Africa; prohibition of imports from South Africa; termination of visa-free entry and of the promotion of tourism to South Africa; termination of air and shipping links; cessation of academic, cultural, scientific and sports relations; suspension or abrogation of agreements; termination of double taxation agreements; and a ban on government contracts with majority-owned South African companies.

Taking note of the Working Group's report,[3] the Commission decided that the Group should continue to study human rights violations in South Africa and Namibia, and requested it to continue bringing to the Commission Chairman's attention particularly serious violations. It asked the Group, in co-operation with the Special Committee against *Apartheid*, to continue investigating cases of torture, ill-treatment and deaths of detainees in South Africa, and authorized the Group Chairman to participate in events connected with action against *apartheid* organized under the Committee's auspices. The Commission renewed its request to South Africa to allow on-the-spot investigations by the Group of treatment and living conditions in South African and Namibian prisons, and asked the Group to submit its final report in 1989. The Secretary-General was requested to provide the Group with all possible assistance.

Reaffirming the Namibian people's inalienable right to self-determination and independence under conditions determined by the Security Council in 1978,[7] the Commission, on 29 February,[8] by a roll-call vote of 34 to none, with 9 abstentions, reiterated that South Africa's illegal occupation of Namibia was an act of aggression and condemned South Africa for the militarization of Namibia; the use of mercenaries; the recruitment and training of Namibians for tribal armies; the proclamation of a security zone in Namibia; forcible displacement of Namibians from their homes; torture and brutality against the population and captured freedom fighters; the military conscription of Namibians; the exploitation and depletion of natural resources; and the use of Namibia as a springboard for aggression against the front-line States. The Commission strongly condemned South Africa's attempts to impose a so-called interim government on the Namibian people, declared its laws and proclamations null and void, and called on States to refrain from recognizing or co-operating with any régime imposed by South Africa in Namibia. It also strongly condemned the continued collaboration of certain States and institutions with South Africa and expressed its conviction that such collaboration helped prolong South Africa's domination and control over Namibia. The Commission endorsed the universal rejection of the "linkage" between Namibia's independence and the Cuban military presence in Angola and denounced South Africa's intention to separate parts of the territory from the rest of Namibia. It demanded that South Africa co-operate with the United Nations to bring about Namibia's independence, release immediately all Namibian political prisoners, account for all "disappeared" Namibians and release those who were still alive, and declared South Africa to be liable to compensate the victims and their families and the future lawful Government of an independent Namibia for losses sustained.

The Commission asked Member States to ensure that all corporations and individuals within their jurisdiction fully applied and complied with the provisions of Decree No. 1 for the Protection of the Natural Resources of Namibia,[9] and requested the *Ad Hoc* Working Group of Experts to bring to the Commission Chairman's attention particularly serious human rights violations in Namibia. It further requested South Africa to allow an on-the-spot investigation by the Working Group of treatment and living conditions in Namibian prisons, and asked the Group to report in 1989. The Secretary-General was requested to provide the Group with all necessary assistance.

Sub-Commission action. On 11 August,[10] the Sub-Commission requested the Commission Chairman to address a telegram to South Africa demanding that it immediately release Nelson Mandela and Zephania Mothopeng, President of the Pan African Congress of Azania.

On 25 August,[11] the Sub-Commission reaffirmed that *apartheid* was a crime against humanity and demanded the immediate lifting of the state of emergency, the cessation of all acts of brutality by the South African army and security forces, and the release of all political prisoners. The Sub-Commission, urging South Africa to lift promptly the ban on anti-*apartheid* organizations, strongly condemned it for the recent imposition of capital punishment on 53 opponents of *apartheid*; the continuing acts of international terrorism and destabilization carried out against the front-line and other neighbouring States; and the decision to proceed with local government elections organized along racial lines. It called on States to provide assistance to the people of South Africa and Namibia as well as to the front-line countries and to continue efforts towards South Africa's total economic, cultural and political isolation. It appealed to them to put pressure on South Africa not to proceed with the execution of *apartheid* opponents. Condemning all collaboration with South Africa, the Sub-Commission called on States, particularly Equatorial Guinea and Israel, to cut all military links with that country. It also called for immediate and complete disinvestment from South Africa and urged the foreign companies concerned to ensure that benefits that had accrued to the black labour force were fully respected.

1973 Convention against apartheid

As at 31 December 1988,[12] there were 88 parties to the International Convention on the Suppression and Punishment of the Crime of *Apartheid*, which was adopted by the General Assembly in 1973[13] and entered into force in 1976.[14] In 1988, Colombia and Mauritania acceded to the Convention. In his annual report to the Assembly on the status of the Convention,[15] the Secretary-General provided a list of States that had signed, ratified or acceded to it as at 31 July.

Activities of the Group of Three. The Group of Three (Ethiopia, Nicaragua and Sri Lanka)—established under article IX of the Convention to consider reports by States parties on measures taken to implement the Convention's provisions—held its eleventh session at Geneva from 25 to 28 January.[16]

The Group examined, in the presence of the representatives of the reporting States, initial reports from Argentina, Bangladesh and Sri Lanka; the second periodic report from Algeria; the third periodic report from Mongolia; and the fifth periodic reports from the Byelorussian SSR, Hungary and the Ukrainian SSR.[17]

The Group also continued to consider whether actions of transnational corporations (TNCs) operating in South Africa and Namibia came under the definition of the crime of *apartheid*. It had before it a note by the Secretary-General summarizing the views of seven States parties, a specialized agency and two NGOs.[18] The Group concluded that, by their complicity, such TNCs must be considered, in conformity with article III *(b)* of the Convention, accomplices in the crime of *apartheid* and must be prosecuted for their responsibility in continuing that crime.

Noting with concern that more than 120 reports from States parties were overdue as at 1 February and that 35 States parties had not submitted any report, as listed in a note by the Secretary-General,[19] the Group urged those parties to fulfil their reporting obligations.

The Group made a number of recommendations, some of which were incorporated into a Commission resolution (see below).

Human Rights Commission action. On 29 February,[20] by a roll-call vote of 32 to none, with 11 abstentions, the Commission urged States that had not done so to ratify or accede to the 1973 Convention against *apartheid* without delay and to ratify the 1948 Convention on the Prevention and Punishment of the Crime of Genocide.[21] It called on States parties to the former Convention that had not yet done so to submit their reports as soon as possible, taking into account the general guidelines laid down by the Group of Three in 1978.[22] It reiterated its recommendation that parties be represented during the Group's consideration of their reports. The Commission requested the Secretary-General once again to invite States parties to express their views on the extent and responsibility of TNCs for the continued existence of *apartheid* and asked him to invite States parties, specialized agencies and NGOs to provide it with relevant information concerning the various forms of the crime of *apartheid*, as described in article II. The Group was requested to continue examining the extent and nature of TNCs' responsibility for the *apartheid* system and legal actions that could be taken against TNCs whose operations came under the crime of *apartheid*, and to report to the Commission in 1989. The Secretary-General was asked to assist the Group and to intensify his efforts to disseminate information on the Convention and its implementation.

The Commission called on States parties to terminate their dealings with South Africa and Namibia and to strengthen co-operation in implementing United Nations decisions aimed at preventing, suppressing and punishing the crime of *apartheid*. It appealed to States, United Nations bodies, specialized agencies and NGOs to step up their activities to enhance public awareness by denouncing the crimes committed by South Africa.

GENERAL ASSEMBLY ACTION

On 8 December, on the recommendation of the Third Committee, the General Assembly adopted **resolution 43/97** by recorded vote.

Status of the International Convention on the Suppression and Punishment of the Crime of *Apartheid*

The General Assembly,

Recalling its resolutions 41/103 of 4 December 1986 and 42/56 of 30 November 1987,

Mindful that the International Convention on the Suppression and Punishment of the Crime of *Apartheid* constitutes an important international treaty in the field of human rights and serves to implement the ideals of the Universal Declaration of Human Rights,

Reaffirming its conviction that *apartheid* constitutes a total negation of the purposes and principles of the Charter of the United Nations, a gross violation of human rights and a crime against humanity, seriously threatening international peace and security,

Strongly condemning South Africa's continued policy of *apartheid* and its continued illegal occupation of Namibia, as well as its policy of aggression, State terrorism and destabilization against independent African States,

Alarmed by the aggravation of the situation in South Africa, in particular the further escalation of ruthless repression by the Fascist-like *apartheid* régime,

Mindful of Commission on Human Rights resolution 1988/14 of 29 February 1988, in which the Commission expressed its conviction that the crime of *apartheid* is a form of the crime of genocide,

Stressing that the root cause of the conflict in southern Africa is the policy of *apartheid* and that only the total eradication of *apartheid* can lead to a peaceful and lasting solution of that conflict,

Condemning the continued collaboration of certain States and transnational corporations with the racist régime of South Africa in the political, economic, military and other fields as an encouragement to the intensification of its odious policy of *apartheid*,

Firmly convinced that the legitimate struggle of the oppressed peoples in southern Africa against *apartheid*, racism and colonialism and for the effective exercise of their inalienable right to self-determination and independence demands more than ever all necessary support by the international community and, in particular, further action by the Security Council in accordance with Chapter VII of the Charter of the United Nations,

Underlining that ratification of or accession to the Convention on a universal basis and the implementation of its provisions without any delay are necessary for its effectiveness, and therefore will contribute to the eradication of the crime of *apartheid*,

1. *Takes note* of the report of the Secretary-General on the status of the International Convention on the Suppression and Punishment of the Crime of *Apartheid*;

2. *Commends* those States parties to the Convention which have submitted their reports under article VII thereof;

3. *Appeals once again* to those States which have not yet done so to ratify or to accede to the Convention without further delay, in particular those States which have jurisdiction over transnational corporations operating in South Africa and Namibia and without whose co-operation such operations could not be halted;

4. *Underlines* the importance of the universal ratification of the Convention, which would be an effective contribution to the fulfilment of the ideals of the Universal Declaration of Human Rights, the fortieth anniversary of which is being celebrated in 1988;

5. *Takes note with appreciation* of the report of the Group of Three of the Commission on Human Rights, which was set up under the Convention, and, in particular, of the conclusions and recommendations contained in that report;

6. *Draws the attention* of all States to the opinion expressed by the Group of Three in its report that transnational corporations operating in South Africa and Namibia must be considered accomplices in the crime of *apartheid*, in accordance with article III *(b)* of the Convention;

7. *Calls upon* all States of which the transnational corporations continue to do business with South Africa and Namibia to take appropriate steps to terminate their dealings with South Africa and Namibia;

8. *Requests* the Commission on Human Rights to intensify, in co-operation with the Special Committee against *Apartheid*, its efforts to compile periodically the progressive list of individuals, organizations, institutions and representatives of States deemed responsible for crimes enumerated in article II of the Convention, as well as those against whom or which legal proceedings have been undertaken;

9. *Requests* the Secretary-General to circulate the above-mentioned list among all States parties to the Convention and all Member States and to bring such facts to the attention of the public by all means of mass communication;

10. *Requests* the Secretary-General to invite the States parties to the Convention, the specialized agencies and non-governmental organizations to provide the Commission on Human Rights with relevant information concerning the forms of the crime of *apartheid*, as described in article II of the Convention, committed by transnational corporations operating in South Africa;

11. *Notes* the importance of measures to be taken by States parties in the field of teaching and education for fuller implementation of the Convention;

12. *Appeals* to all States, United Nations organs, the specialized agencies and international and national non-governmental organizations to step up their activities in enhancing public awareness by denouncing the crimes committed by the racist régime of South Africa;

13. *Requests* the Secretary-General to intensify his efforts, through appropriate channels, to disseminate information on the Convention and its implementation with a view to promoting further ratification of or accession to the Convention;

14. *Requests* the Secretary-General to include in his next annual report under General Assembly resolution 3380(XXX) of 10 November 1975 a special section concerning the implementation of the Convention.

General Assembly resolution 43/97

8 December 1988   Meeting 75   128-1-26 (recorded vote)

Approved by Third Committee (A/43/777) by recorded vote (120-2-23), 27 October (meeting 23); 23-nation draft (A/C.3/43/L.10/Rev.1); agenda item 91.
Sponsors: Afghanistan, Algeria, Angola, Bulgaria, Burkina Faso, Cuba, Czechoslovakia, Ethiopia, German Democratic Republic, Ghana, Hungary, India, Lao People's Democratic Republic, Libyan Arab Jamahiriya, Madagascar, Mongolia, Nicaragua, Nigeria, Poland, Syrian Arab Republic, Ukrainian SSR, Viet Nam, Zambia.
Meeting numbers. GA 43rd session: 3rd Committee 4-14, 17, 23; plenary 75.

Recorded vote in Assembly as follows:

In favour: Afghanistan, Albania, Algeria, Angola, Antigua and Barbuda, Argentina, Bahamas, Bahrain, Bangladesh, Barbados, Belize, Benin, Bhutan, Bolivia, Botswana, Brazil, Brunei Darussalam, Bulgaria, Burkina Faso, Burma, Burundi, Byelorussian SSR, Cameroon, Cape Verde, Central African Republic, Chad, China, Colombia, Comoros, Congo, Costa Rica, Côte d'Ivoire, Cuba, Cyprus, Czechoslovakia, Democratic Kampuchea, Democratic Yemen, Djibouti, Dominica, Dominican Republic, Ecuador, Egypt, El Salvador, Ethiopia, Fiji, Gabon, Gambia, German Democratic Republic, Ghana, Grenada, Guatemala, Guinea, Guinea-Bissau, Guyana, Haiti, Honduras, Hungary, India, Indonesia, Iran, Iraq, Jamaica, Jordan, Kenya, Kuwait, Lao People's Democratic Republic, Lebanon, Lesotho, Liberia, Libyan Arab Jamahiriya, Madagascar, Malawi, Malaysia, Maldives, Mali, Mauritania, Mexico, Mongolia, Morocco, Mozambique, Nepal, Nicaragua, Niger, Nigeria, Pakistan, Panama, Papua New Guinea, Peru, Philippines, Poland, Qatar, Romania, Rwanda, Saint Kitts and Nevis, Saint Lucia, Saint Vincent and the Grenadines, Samoa, Sao Tome and Principe, Saudi Arabia, Senegal, Seychelles, Sierra Leone, Singapore, Solomon Islands, Somalia, Sri Lanka, Sudan, Suriname, Swaziland, Syrian Arab Republic, Thailand, Togo, Trinidad and Tobago, Tunisia, Uganda, Ukrainian SSR, USSR, United Arab Emirates, United Republic of Tanzania, Uruguay, Vanuatu, Venezuela, Viet Nam, Yemen, Yugoslavia, Zaire, Zambia, Zimbabwe.
Against: United States.
Abstaining: Australia, Austria, Belgium, Canada, Chile, Denmark, Equatorial Guinea, Finland, France, Germany, Federal Republic of, Greece, Iceland, Ireland, Israel, Italy, Japan, Luxembourg, Malta, Netherlands, New Zealand, Norway, Portugal, Spain, Sweden, Turkey, United Kingdom.

Before adopting the text as a whole, the Assembly adopted paragraphs 6, 7 and 10 by recorded votes of 119 to 17, with 12 abstentions, 123 to 8, with 19 abstentions, and 126 to 15, with 11 abstentions, respectively. The Third Committee had approved the same paragraphs by recorded votes of 113 to 17, with 11 abstentions, 116 to 8, with 16 abstentions, and 117 to 14, with 9 abstentions. The sixth preambular paragraph was adopted by the Assembly by a recorded vote of 122 to 15, with 15 abstentions, having been approved by the Committee by a recorded vote of 114 to 15, with 13 abstentions. By a recorded vote of 118 to 18, with 16 abstentions, the Assembly decided to retain the words "State terrorism" in the fourth preambular paragraph, which had been approved by the Committee by a recorded vote of 110 to 18, with 14 abstentions.

Foreign support of South Africa

Human Rights Commission action. On 29 February,[23] by a roll-call vote of 32 to 7, with 4 abstentions, the Commission expressed satisfaction to the Sub-Commission's Special Rapporteur, Ahmed Khalifa (Egypt), for his 1987 report on the adverse consequences for the enjoyment of human rights of political, military, economic and other forms of assistance to South

Africa.[24] It invited the Rapporteur to continue updating annually the list of banks, TNCs and other organizations assisting South Africa and to report to the Commission through its Sub-Commission; to indicate the volume, nature and adverse human consequences of such assistance; and to intensify co-operation with the Centre on TNCs and the Centre against *Apartheid*. The Commission called on States to co-operate with the Special Rapporteur and disseminate and publicize his report, and asked the Secretary-General to provide the Rapporteur with all necessary assistance, including two economists, and to give the report wide distribution as a United Nations publication.

Also on 29 February,[25] by a roll-call vote of 32 to 7, with 4 abstentions, the Commission vigorously condemned assistance to South Africa by major Western countries and Israel, particularly in the military field, and demanded that that assistance, which it was convinced was a hostile action against the people of South Africa, Namibia and neighbouring States, be immediately terminated. Condemning the continuing nuclear collaboration of some Western States, Israel and others with South Africa, the Commission urged them to stop supplying it with nuclear equipment and technology. It strongly condemned foreign economic activities in Namibia and demanded that TNCs exploiting Namibian resources immediately refrain from new investments or activities, withdraw from the Territory and stop co-operating with South Africa. Noting with appreciation measures taken by some States, parliamentarians, institutions and NGOs to exert pressure on South Africa, the Commission called on them to intensify their efforts to force it to comply with United Nations resolutions and decisions. It also called on Governments that had not done so to take legislative, administrative and other measures to prevent nationals and corporations under their jurisdiction from trading, manufacturing and investing in South Africa and Namibia, to end technological assistance or collaboration in the manufacture of arms and military supplies there, and to cease nuclear collaboration with South Africa.

The Commission rejected all policies that encouraged South Africa to intensify its repression of South Africans and Namibians and to escalate its aggression against neighbouring States, and demanded that South Africa cease all acts of aggression and destabilization against those States. Strongly condemning South Africa for its aggression against Angola and the occupation of a part of its territory, the Commission demanded that South Africa withdraw all its troops from that country. It welcomed the General Assembly's request to the Security Council for complete and mandatory sanctions against South Africa, in particular the prohibition of technological assistance or collaboration in the manufacture of arms and military supplies; cessation of nuclear collaboration; prohibition of loans to and investments in South Africa and the cessation of trade; and an embargo on the supply of petroleum, petroleum products and other strategic goods.

The Commission appealed to States, specialized agencies and NGOs to co-operate with the liberation movements of southern Africa and to intensify, along with regional intergovernmental organizations, their campaign aimed at mobilizing public opinion to enforce economic and other sanctions against South Africa. It urgently requested specialized agencies, particularly the International Monetary Fund (IMF), to refrain from granting loans or financial assistance to South Africa.

Report of the Special Rapporteur. In June, the Special Rapporteur presented to the Sub-Commission an updated report, with a later addendum,[26] listing banks, insurance companies, firms and other enterprises giving direct or indirect military, economic and other assistance to South Africa. The report contained comments on the subject from 12 States, a United Nations body, 2 specialized agencies, 2 regional intergovernmental organizations, 6 NGOs and 3 other organizations.

Sub-Commission action. On 25 August,[27] the Sub-Commission recommended that the Commission recommend to the Economic and Social Council a resolution requesting the Special Rapporteur to continue updating his report and to provide to the Sub-Commission in 1989 a note on the feasibility of consolidating lists of enterprises doing business in South Africa and an analysis of partial disinvestment of foreign enterprises from that country, enumerating techniques employed to avoid total withdrawal from participation in the South African economy.

Note of the Secretary-General. In September,[28] the Secretary-General transmitted the Special Rapporteur's report to the General Assembly.

GENERAL ASSEMBLY ACTION

On 8 December, on the recommendation of the Third Committee, the General Assembly adopted **resolution 43/92** by recorded vote.

Adverse consequences for the enjoyment of human rights of political, military, economic and other forms of assistance given to the racist and colonialist régime of South Africa
The General Assembly,
Recalling its resolutions 3382(XXX) and 3383(XXX) of 10 November 1975, 33/23 of 29 November 1978, 35/32 of 14 November 1980, 37/39 of 3 December 1982, 39/15 of 23 November 1984 and 41/95 of 4 December 1986,
Recalling also its resolutions 3201(S-VI) and 3202(S-VI) of 1 May 1974, containing the Declaration and the Pro-

gramme of Action on the Establishment of a New International Economic Order, and 3281(XXIX) of 12 December 1974, containing the Charter of Economic Rights and Duties of States,

Mindful of its resolution 3171(XXVIII) of 17 December 1973 relating to permanent sovereignty over natural resources of both developing countries and territories under colonial and foreign domination or subjected to the *apartheid* régime,

Recalling its resolutions on military collaboration with South Africa, as well as Security Council resolutions 418(1977) of 4 November 1977, 421(1977) of 9 December 1977, 558(1984) of 13 December 1984 and 569(1985) of 26 July 1985,

Taking into account, in particular, the relevant decisions adopted by the Assembly of Heads of State and Government of the Organization of African Unity at its twenty-fourth ordinary session, held at Addis Ababa from 25 to 28 May 1988, and by the Council of Ministers of that organization at its forty-eighth ordinary session, held at Addis Ababa from 19 to 23 May 1988,[a]

Taking note with satisfaction of the updated report prepared by the Special Rapporteur of the Sub-Commission on Prevention of Discrimination and Protection of Minorities on the adverse consequences for the enjoyment of human rights of political, military, economic and other forms of assistance given to the racist and colonialist régime of South Africa,

Noting with regret that the request contained in its resolution 41/95 with regard to making available to the Special Rapporteur two economists was not implemented,

Reaffirming that any collaboration with the racist régime of South Africa constitutes a hostile act against the oppressed peoples of southern Africa in their struggle for freedom and independence and a contemptuous defiance of the United Nations and of the international community,

Considering that such collaboration enables South Africa to acquire the means necessary to carry out acts of aggression and blackmail against independent African States,

Deeply concerned that the major Western and other trading partners of South Africa continue to collaborate with that racist régime and that their collaboration constitutes the main obstacle to the liquidation of that racist régime and the elimination of the inhuman and criminal system of *apartheid*,

Alarmed at the continued collaboration of certain Western States and Israel with the racist régime of South Africa in the nuclear field,

Regretting that the Security Council has not been in a position to take binding decisions to prevent any collaboration in the nuclear field with South Africa,

Affirming that the highest priority must be accorded to international action to secure the full implementation of the resolutions of the United Nations for the eradication of *apartheid* and the liberation of the peoples of southern Africa,

Conscious of the continuing need to mobilize world public opinion against the political, military, economic and other forms of assistance given to the racist and colonialist régime of South Africa,

1. *Reaffirms* the inalienable right of the oppressed peoples of southern Africa to self-determination, independence and the enjoyment of the natural resources of their territories;

2. *Again reaffirms* the right of those same peoples to dispose of those resources for their greater well-being and to obtain just reparation for the exploitation, depletion, loss or depreciation of those natural resources, including reparation for the exploitation and abuse of their human resources;

3. *Vigorously condemns* the collaboration of certain Western States, Israel and other States, as well as the transnational corporations and other organizations, which maintain or continue to increase their collaboration with the racist and colonialist régime of South Africa, especially in the political, economic, military and nuclear fields, thus encouraging that régime to persist in its inhuman and criminal policy of brutal oppression of the peoples of southern Africa and denial of their human rights;

4. *Reaffirms once again* that States and organizations that give assistance to the racist régime of South Africa become accomplices in the inhuman practices of racial discrimination, colonialism and *apartheid* perpetrated by that régime, as well as in the acts of aggression against the liberation movements and neighbouring States;

5. *Requests* the Security Council once again urgently to consider the imposition of comprehensive and mandatory sanctions under Chapter VII of the Charter of the United Nations against the racist régime of South Africa, in particular:

(a) The prohibition of all technological assistance or collaboration in the manufacture of arms and military supplies in South Africa;

(b) The cessation of all collaboration with South Africa in the nuclear field;

(c) The prohibition of all loans to, and all investments in, South Africa and the cessation of any trade with South Africa;

(d) An embargo on the supply of petroleum, petroleum products and other strategic goods to South Africa;

6. *Appeals* to all States, specialized agencies and non-governmental organizations to extend all possible cooperation to the liberation movements of southern Africa recognized by the United Nations and the Organization of African Unity;

7. *Expresses its appreciation* to the Special Rapporteur of the Sub-Commission on Prevention of Discrimination and Protection of Minorities for his updated report;

8. *Reaffirms* that the updating of the report on the adverse consequences for the enjoyment of human rights of political, military, economic and other forms of assistance given to the racist and colonialist régime of South Africa is of the greatest importance to the cause of fighting *apartheid* and other violations of human rights in South Africa and Namibia;

9. *Invites* the Special Rapporteur:

(a) To continue to update, subject to annual review, the list of banks, transnational corporations and other organizations assisting the racist and colonialist régime of South Africa, giving such details regarding enterprises listed as the Rapporteur may consider necessary and appropriate, including explanations of responses, if any, and to submit the updated report to the General Assembly at its forty-fifth session;

---

[a]A/43/398.

(b) To use all available material from other United Nations organs, Member States, national liberation movements recognized by the Organization of African Unity, specialized agencies and other intergovernmental and non-governmental organizations, as well as other relevant sources, in order to indicate the volume, nature and adverse human consequences of the assistance given to the racist régime of South Africa;

(c) To intensify direct contacts with the United Nations Centre on Transnational Corporations, the Centre against *Apartheid* of the Secretariat and the United Nations Council for Namibia, with a view to consolidating mutual co-operation in updating his report;

10. *Requests* the Secretary-General to give the Special Rapporteur all the assistance, including adequate travel funds, that he may require in the exercise of his mandate, with a view, in particular, to intensifying direct contacts with the United Nations Centre on Transnational Corporations, the Centre against *Apartheid* and the United Nations Council for Namibia, to expanding his work on the annotation of certain selected cases as reflected in the list contained in his report and to continuing the computerization of future updated lists;

11. *Demands* that the Secretary-General, in accordance with Economic and Social Council decision 1986/145 of 23 May 1986, make available to the Special Rapporteur two economists to help him to develop his work of analysis and documentation of some special cases mentioned in his report;

12. *Notes with satisfaction* the disinvestment measures, trade restrictions and other positive measures taken by some countries and transnational corporations, and encourages them to continue in this direction;

13. *Requests* the Special Rapporteur to include in his updated report a list of partial disinvestment of foreign enterprises from South Africa, enumerating various techniques employed to avoid total withdrawal from participation in the South African economy;

14. *Calls upon* the Governments of the countries where the banks, transnational corporations and other organizations named and listed in the updated report are based to take effective action to put a stop to their trading, manufacturing and investing activities in the territory of South Africa as well as in the Territory of Namibia illegally occupied by the racist Pretoria régime;

15. *Urgently requests* all specialized agencies, particularly the International Monetary Fund and the World Bank, to refrain from granting loans or financial assistance of any type to the racist régime of South Africa;

16. *Requests* the Secretary-General to transmit the updated report to the Special Committee against *Apartheid*, the United Nations Council for Namibia, other bodies concerned within the United Nations system and regional international organizations;

17. *Invites* the Secretary-General to give the updated report the widest dissemination, to issue it as a United Nations publication and to make it available to learned societies, research centres, universities, political and humanitarian organizations and other interested groups;

18. *Calls upon* all Governments to co-operate with the Special Rapporteur in making the report even more accurate and informative;

19. *Calls upon* all States, specialized agencies and regional, intergovernmental and other organizations concerned to give wide publicity to the updated report;

20. *Invites* the Commission on Human Rights to give high priority at its forty-fifth session to the consideration of the updated report;

21. *Decides* to consider at its forty-fifth session, as a matter of high priority, the item entitled "Adverse consequences for the enjoyment of human rights of political, military, economic and other forms of assistance given to the racist and colonialist régime of South Africa", in the light of any recommendations which the Sub-Commission on Prevention of Discrimination and Protection of Minorities, the Commission on Human Rights, the Economic and Social Council and the Special Committee against *Apartheid* may wish to submit to it.

General Assembly resolution 43/92

8 December 1988   Meeting 75   129-10-17 (recorded vote)

Approved by Third Committee (A/43/776) by recorded vote (121-10-15), 27 October (meeting 23); draft by United Republic of Tanzania, for African States (A/C.3/43/L.11/Rev.1); agenda item 88.
Financial implications. S-G, A/C.3/43/L.16.
Meeting numbers. GA 43rd session: 3rd Committee 4-14, 16, 23; plenary 75.

Recorded vote in Assembly as follows:

In favour: Afghanistan, Albania, Algeria, Angola, Antigua and Barbuda, Argentina, Bahamas, Bahrain, Bangladesh, Barbados, Belize, Benin, Bhutan, Bolivia, Botswana, Brazil, Brunei Darussalam, Bulgaria, Burkina Faso, Burma, Burundi, Byelorussian SSR, Cameroon, Cape Verde, Central African Republic, Chad, China, Colombia, Comoros, Congo, Costa Rica, Côte d'Ivoire, Cuba, Cyprus, Czechoslovakia, Democratic Kampuchea, Democratic Yemen, Djibouti, Dominica, Dominican Republic, Ecuador, Egypt, El Salvador, Ethiopia, Fiji, Gabon, Gambia, German Democratic Republic, Ghana, Grenada, Guatemala, Guinea, Guinea-Bissau, Guyana, Haiti, Honduras, Hungary, India, Indonesia, Iran, Iraq, Jamaica, Jordan, Kenya, Kuwait, Lao People's Democratic Republic, Lebanon, Lesotho, Liberia, Libyan Arab Jamahiriya, Madagascar, Malaysia, Maldives, Mali, Mauritania, Mauritius, Mexico, Mongolia, Morocco, Mozambique, Nepal, Nicaragua, Niger, Nigeria, Oman, Pakistan, Panama, Papua New Guinea, Peru, Philippines, Poland, Qatar, Romania, Rwanda, Saint Kitts and Nevis, Saint Lucia, Saint Vincent and the Grenadines, Samoa, Sao Tome and Principe, Saudi Arabia, Senegal, Seychelles, Sierra Leone, Singapore, Solomon Islands, Somalia, Sri Lanka, Sudan, Suriname, Swaziland, Syrian Arab Republic, Thailand, Togo, Trinidad and Tobago, Tunisia, Turkey, Uganda, Ukrainian SSR, USSR, United Arab Emirates, United Republic of Tanzania, Uruguay, Vanuatu, Venezuela, Viet Nam, Yemen, Yugoslavia, Zambia, Zimbabwe.

Against: Belgium, France, Germany, Federal Republic of, Israel, Italy, Luxembourg, Netherlands, Portugal, United Kingdom, United States.

Abstaining: Australia, Austria, Canada, Denmark, Equatorial Guinea, Finland, Greece, Iceland, Ireland, Japan, Malawi, Malta, New Zealand, Norway, Spain, Sweden, Zaire.*

*Later advised the Secretariat it had intended to vote against.

Before adopting the resolution as a whole, the Assembly adopted paragraph 3 by a recorded vote of 84 to 32, with 36 abstentions; the Committee had approved the same paragraph by a recorded vote of 80 to 36, with 26 abstentions. The eleventh preambular paragraph was adopted by the Assembly by a recorded vote of 82 to 32, with 37 abstentions, having been approved by the Committee by a recorded vote of 80 to 35, with 27 abstentions.

Trade union rights

In 1988, the *Ad Hoc* Working Group of Experts on southern Africa (see above) continued to study trade union rights and the conditions of black workers. Its findings, included in its interim report[3] to the Commission as requested by the Economic and Social Council in 1987,[4] were submitted to the Council in April by the Secretary-General.[29]

ECONOMIC AND SOCIAL COUNCIL ACTION

On 27 May, on the recommendation of its Second Committee, the Economic and Social Council adopted **resolution 1988/41** without vote.

Infringements of trade union rights in South Africa

The Economic and Social Council,

Recalling its resolution 1987/63 of 29 May 1987,

Having examined the relevant section of the report of the *Ad Hoc* Working Group of Experts on southern Africa of the Commission on Human Rights,

Noting with indignation that dehumanizing conditions imposed on black workers by the Government of South Africa and police intervention in industrial disputes, including mass arrests, banning and even killing of trade unionists, continue,

Aware of the ever-growing importance of the role of the independent black trade union movement in the struggle against *apartheid,*

Gravely concerned at the recent escalation of the repression against the independent black trade union movement, in particular the severe restrictions placed on the Congress of South African Trade Unions, and efforts to impose further restrictions on trade unions through legislative changes,

1. *Takes note* of the relevant section of the report of the *Ad Hoc* Working Group of Experts on southern Africa;

2. *Condemns* the increased repression of the independent black trade union movement by the Government of South Africa;

3. *Demands once again* that the persecution of trade unionists and repression of the independent black trade union movement cease;

4. *Requests once again* immediate recognition of the right of the entire population of South Africa to exercise freedom of association and to form and join trade unions without impediment or discrimination of any kind;

5. *Demands* the immediate unconditional release of all trade unionists imprisoned for exercising their legitimate trade union rights;

6. *Requests* the *Ad Hoc* Working Group of Experts, to continue to study the situation and to report thereon to the Commission on Human Rights and the Economic and Social Council;

7. *Also requests* the *Ad Hoc* Working Group of Experts, in the discharge of its mandate, to consult with the International Labour Organisation and the Special Committee against *Apartheid,* as well as with international and African trade union confederations;

8. *Decides* to consider at its first regular session of l989 the question of allegations regarding infringements of trade union rights in South Africa as a sub-item of the item entitled "Human rights".

Economic and Social Council resolution 1988/41

27 May 1988   Meeting 16   Adopted without vote

Approved by Second Committee (E/1988/89/Add.1) without vote, 23 May (meeting 21); draft by Sudan, for African States (E/1988/C.2/L.11); agenda item 10.

Asia and the Pacific

Afghanistan

Report of the Special Rapporteur. In February, Special Rapporteur Felix Ermacora (Austria) submitted to the Commission a report[30] on the human rights situation in Afghanistan, following visits to that country in 1987 and to Pakistan from 4 to 11 January and from 5 to 11 February 1988.

He noted that in government-controlled areas of Afghanistan, there were certain improvements in the human rights situation, brought about by the policy of reconciliation, including amnesty decrees, changes in the reform process, decrees concerning the return of refugees, the convening of a *Loya Jirgah* (Grand Assembly), the adoption of a new Constitution and the pronouncement of a unilateral cease-fire. However, the Special Rapporteur was of the opinion that the policy had not achieved the desired results, stating that incidents of torture and ill-treatment in prisons and killings of political prisoners continued to be reported. Although the Government claimed to have released more than 7,000 prisoners after proclaiming national reconciliation, the number of political prisoners stood at some 3,000 and 545 others were detained or under investigation. The Special Rapporteur had also received information concerning forced labour of some 3,000 youths.

Noting that some local agreements with the opposition forces had led to the cessation of hostilities in several so-called peace zones, he stated that heavy fighting in combat areas continued and had cost the lives of more than 14,000 civilians in 1987. Acts of brutality in violation of humanitarian law were still being reported, as were acts of terrorism in Afghanistan and Pakistan. There were also cases of detention, conviction and imprisonment of foreign journalists in combat areas. In addition, some 8,000 refugees had recently fled to Pakistan. The total number of refugees remained at about 5 million and official estimates of returnees totalled some 111,000. The Government of Afghanistan continued to take steps to facilitate the return of refugees. The Special Rapporteur had been told that 24 reception centres had been set up in frontier towns and villages.

The Special Rapporteur noted that the new Afghan Constitution adopted in 1987, while proclaiming basic human rights and freedoms, did not provide for the implementation machinery, a system for the protection of those rights or a system to ensure free elections and representation for refugees after their return. Nor did it provide any indication that the existing system would be brought into line with the 1966 International Covenant on Civil and Political Rights.[31] Other deficiencies concerned states of emergency and the reservation system governing many basic rights.

The Special Rapporteur recommended that the amnesty be broadened and that amnestied persons not be put under house arrest or police surveillance. He also recommended that the Government implement the human rights provisions of the new

Constitution; dismantle the system of revolutionary or special tribunals or prosecutors; and investigate the fate of missing persons. He said that the assistance of specialized agencies and NGOs should be extended to areas not under government control, and that the International Committee of the Red Cross (ICRC) should have free access to places requiring humanitarian action. Prisoners held by the opposition should be released and journalists in conflict areas should be protected. The Rapporteur stated that the withdrawal of foreign troops should be accompanied by a universal cease-fire and that adequate precautions should be taken to ensure the protection of civilians during the withdrawal, under the supervision of the international community and humanitarian organizations. Recommendations regarding refugees covered their freedom to return; the creation of conditions conducive to the return of internal refugees; and the holding of elections once foreign troops had withdrawn and the representation of returnees could be ensured.

He further recommended that post-war Afghanistan adopt the status of permanent neutrality and that the United Nations assist it, through the advisory programme, to secure human rights, based on appropriate legislation, monitoring mechanisms and infrastructure to safeguard those rights.

Human Rights Commission action. On 10 March,[32] by a roll-call vote of 29 to 7, with 6 abstentions, the Commission, noting the Special Rapporteur's report, expressed distress at continuing violations of the right to life, liberty and security of individuals as well as freedoms of expression, assembly, movement and association, and concern at the large number of persons detained without due process of law and the conditions of their detention, as well as reports of torture during interrogation and the killing of political prisoners. It noted that widespread human rights violations continued to cause large flows of refugees and displaced persons and expressed concern that the Afghan authorities, with heavy foreign troop support, were acting without respect for international human rights obligations. The intensified armed conflict included indiscriminate bombardments and military operations targeted primarily on villages and agriculture, with severe consequences for civilians. It was also concerned that the education system did not respect the right of parents to ensure their children's religious and moral education.

The Commission urged that all necessary measures be taken to ensure the full enjoyment of human rights in Afghanistan and that the Afghan authorities continue to co-operate with the Commission and its Special Rapporteur. It called again on the parties to the conflict to apply fully the principles and rules of international humanitarian law. It decided to extend the Special Rapporteur's mandate and to have him report to the General Assembly in 1988 and the Commission in 1989. It also asked the Secretary-General to give him all necessary assistance.

On 27 May, the Economic and Social Council, by **decision 1988/136**, approved the Commission's decision to extend for one year the Special Rapporteur's mandate and its request that the Secretary-General give him all necessary assistance.

Interim report of the Special Rapporteur. In October 1988, the Secretary-General transmitted to the Assembly an interim report on the human rights situation in Afghanistan,[33] prepared by the Special Rapporteur in accordance with the Commission's request. The report analysed the human rights aspect of the Geneva Agreements on Afghanistan, signed on 14 April 1988 (see PART TWO, Chapter III), and reviewed recent developments relating, *inter alia*, to the Afghan Constitution and constitutional life; the refugee situation; economic, social and cultural rights; and terrorism.

The Special Rapporteur visited Afghanistan from 11 to 19 September. He noted that, in general, there was greater improvement in the human rights situation in government-controlled areas. The policy of reconciliation had led to elections and the establishment of a National Assembly. The Special Rapporteur listed a number of laws with human rights provisions related to freedom of the press, the right to work, personal liberty, freedom of movement and freedom of assembly, but he also expressed doubts as to whether all of those provisions were being fairly implemented. Although he had been informed that 6,997 prisoners had been freed since January 1988, there were still some 2,100 political prisoners in September and 893 others were detained for common-law crimes. The Special Rapporteur attested to improved detention conditions in at least one prison, but said he had been informed that released prisoners of military age were enrolled directly into the army without any possibility of contacting their families. He said he had also continued to receive allegations of executions, disappearances, torture and other ill-treatment of prisoners. The Government had announced a policy for the creation of demilitarized zones in the region of Panshir and the province of Bamian, where military operations were prohibited, and for peace zones that had been cleared of mines. The Special Rapporteur pointed out that a large number of minefields laid by both sides represented a serious danger to civilians and a major impediment to reconstruction efforts in certain areas.

According to official estimates, the number of refugees had increased by some 100,000 since January, while the number of returnees rose to about

151,000 at the end of August. An estimated 1 million internal refugees had begun to return spontaneously at a rate of some 200 persons a day, following the withdrawal of foreign troops from their regions of origin. That withdrawal was reportedly accompanied by heavy bomb attacks and ''cleaning-up'' operations that included artillery bombardments of residential areas and attacks on civilians that had caused significant losses. The Special Rapporteur had also been informed of the continued use of booby-trap bombs and a sharp increase in the number of victims, including children.

A growing number of terrorist acts was also reported in Afghanistan and Pakistan, causing more than 4,000 civilian deaths. The Special Rapporteur cited three recent terrorist incidents, including rocket attacks on Kabul's airport and residential areas and a bomb blast in a Kabul business centre. He noted that, under the law on terrorism, adopted in Afghanistan in August, all members of the opposition were considered to be terrorists.

The Special Rapporteur estimated the total number of civilian deaths in Afghanistan since 1980 at 1 million. He recommended that the Government: pursue a policy of amnesty; ensure that prisoners and detainees were not tortured or ill-treated and that combatants were treated in conformity with humanitarian law; respect the principles of humanitarian law in combat areas; make every effort to end the growing internal conflict by peaceful means; and oblige the belligerents to apply relevant international instruments, should the international conflict evolve into an internal one. He said opposition movements should: give maps of minefields to the United Nations agencies concerned; respect humanitarian law; refrain from indiscriminate acts; cease their attacks on civilians; and not treat their prisoners as hostages. He also recommended that the troop withdrawal not be accompanied by acts of retaliation or the planting of new mines; that the fate of missing persons be investigated; that ICRC have full access to prisons and detention centres as well as to persons held there; and that consideration be given to advisory services and relief assistance for Afghanistan.

GENERAL ASSEMBLY ACTION

On 8 December, on the recommendation of the Third Committee, the General Assembly adopted **resolution 43/139** without vote.

Situation of human rights in Afghanistan

The General Assembly,

Guided by the principles embodied in the Charter of the United Nations, the Universal Declaration of Human Rights, the International Covenants on Human Rights and the humanitarian rules set out in the Geneva Conventions of 12 August 1949,

Aware of its responsibility to promote and encourage respect for human rights and fundamental freedoms for all and resolved to remain vigilant with regard to violations of human rights wherever they occur,

Emphasizing the obligations of all Governments to respect and protect human rights and to fulfil the responsibilities they have assumed under various international instruments,

Recalling Economic and Social Council resolution 1984/37 of 24 May 1984, in which the Council requested the Chairman of the Commission on Human Rights to appoint a special rapporteur to examine the situation of human rights in Afghanistan, with a view to formulating proposals that could contribute to ensuring full protection of the human rights of all residents of the country before, during and after the withdrawal of all foreign forces,

Recalling all other relevant resolutions, in particular its resolution 42/135 of 7 December 1987,

Taking note of Commission on Human Rights resolution 1988/67 of 10 March 1988 and Economic and Social Council decision 1988/136 of 27 May 1988,

Welcoming the Agreements on the Settlement of the Situation Relating to Afghanistan signed at Geneva on 14 April 1988[a] as a positive development, which, when fully implemented, should contribute to the creation of a situation that will permit the full enjoyment of human rights, including the right to self-determination, by all the people of Afghanistan,

Welcoming the co-operation that the Afghan authorities have extended to international organizations, in particular to the specialized agencies of the United Nations, to the Office of the United Nations High Commissioner for Refugees and to the International Committee of the Red Cross,

Having carefully examined the interim report of the Special Rapporteur on the situation of human rights in Afghanistan, in which, while it is recognized that there have been some improvements in the human rights situation in the area controlled by the Afghan authorities, continuing violations of fundamental human rights within the country are revealed,

Recognizing that a situation of armed conflict continues to exist in Afghanistan, leaving large numbers of victims without protection or assistance and contributing to violations of human rights and humanitarian law throughout the country,

Regretting that the Special Rapporteur was unable to visit areas not under the control of the Afghan authorities,

1. *Commends* the efforts of the Special Rapporteur to fulfil his mandate and takes note of his interim report on the situation of human rights in Afghanistan;

2. *Welcomes* the co-operation that the Afghan authorities extended to the Commission on Human Rights by permitting its Special Rapporteur to visit Afghanistan from 11 to 19 September 1988;

3. *Expresses its serious concern* that, in spite of improvements identified by the Special Rapporteur, acts of war continue and violations of human rights persist with the same frequency as in the past, especially affecting the civilian population and threatening the life and security of innocent men, women and children;

---

[a]S/19835.

4. *Expresses its concern* that, despite the significant reduction in the numbers of political prisoners as a result of various measures, over two thousand persons are still in prison for political reasons, and urges the Afghan authorities to pursue the policy of amnesty and to guarantee that released prisoners are not placed under surveillance or harassed following their release;

5. *Notes with grave concern* the continuing allegations of torture and ill-treatment of prisoners on remand and political prisoners;

6. *Notes with equal concern* the reports of disappearances and urges the Afghan authorities to investigate the fate of all missing persons;

7. *Notes also with concern* indications that the economic, social and cultural situation in Afghanistan has deteriorated over the years of conflict and has now become critical;

8. *Expresses its great concern* that more than five million refugees remain outside the country because they fear the climate of insecurity in Afghanistan, the extensive presence of mines and explosives, and the continued bombardments of the civilian population;

9. *Calls once again upon* all the parties to the conflict, in order to alleviate the suffering of the people of Afghanistan, to apply fully the principles and rules of international humanitarian law and to co-operate fully and effectively with international humanitarian organizations, in particular to facilitate the protection activities of the International Committee of the Red Cross;

10. *Underlines* that in post-war Afghanistan it will be essential to adopt concrete measures aimed at securing the observance of human rights;

11. *Urges* the authorities in Afghanistan to continue to co-operate with the Commission on Human Rights and its Special Rapporteur;

12. *Requests* the Secretary-General to give all necessary assistance to the Special Rapporteur;

13. *Decides* to keep under consideration, during its forty-fourth session, the question of human rights and fundamental freedoms in Afghanistan in order to re-examine this question in the light of additional elements provided by the Commission on Human Rights and the Economic and Social Council.

General Assembly resolution 43/139

8 December 1988   Meeting 75   Adopted without vote

Approved by Third Committee (A/43/868) without vote, 29 November (meeting 56); 19-nation draft (A/C.3/43/L.57); agenda item 12.

Sponsors: Australia, Belgium, Canada, Costa Rica, Denmark, France, Germany, Federal Republic of, Greece, Ireland, Italy, Japan, Luxembourg, Netherlands, Norway, Portugal, Samoa, Spain, Sweden, United Kingdom.

Meeting numbers. GA 43rd session: 3rd Committee 49-56; plenary 75.

Iran

Report of the Special Representative. In January, Special Representative Reynaldo Galindo Pohl (El Salvador) submitted to the Commission a report on the human rights situation in Iran.[34] He summarized information received from 11 victims of alleged human rights violations during informal hearings at Geneva on 12, 14 and 15 January as well as pertinent written information, which was communicated to the Iranian Government and dealt with: summary executions; torture and ill-treatment of prisoners; persecution on religious grounds; violations of the right to liberty and security of person; economic pressure on the followers of the Baha'i faith, such as cancellation of business licences, confiscation of property, dismissal from government positions, loss of pensions and denial of higher education; and the evacuation and resettling of 23 Kurdish villages.

The Special Representative received a list of 14,028 persons allegedly killed by government agents during 1981-1987, including 2,000 names not previously published. Annexed to the report was a list of 60 persons allegedly executed or tortured to death in 1986-1987, which had been submitted to Iran with a request for information or comments. The Special Representative also received lists of 17 Baha'is detained in Iran and believed to be in danger of execution; he was subsequently informed, however, that five of them had been released.

He further examined the views of the Iranian Government, which had stated that international law was only partially compatible with Islamic law and that secularism of international human rights instruments justified Iran's selective adherence thereto. The Special Representative noted that the Iranian Government refused to provide detailed replies to allegations of human rights violations, questioning the terms of his mandate, the method of conveying allegations, the qualifications of witnesses and the use of the term "minority" as applied to the members of the Baha'i faith.

In conclusion, the Special Representative, acknowledging the cultural difficulties of applying fully human rights instruments in Iran, noted that the alleged incompatibility between some provisions of international law and Islamic law was a domestic problem and did not affect international obligations, by which Iran was bound as a United Nations Member and party to the Covenants, and expressed the hope that the Iranian Government would come to the complete recognition of all provisions of those instruments and application of their norms. He stated that the method of conveying allegations of human rights violations was in conformity with international practice. He expressed concern regarding continued allegations of summary executions and detention in danger of execution, ill-treatment and torture in prisons and economic pressure on Baha'is. He believed that acts still occurring in Iran that were inconsistent with human rights instruments justified continuing international concern, study and monitoring.

Human Rights Commission action. On 10 March,[35] by a roll-call vote of 20 to 5, with 14 abstentions, the Commission noted with satisfaction recent releases of prisoners and welcomed the pardoning of prisoners in the hope that it could be the first stage of a process leading to a general amnesty for political prisoners. The Commission expressed concern, however, about allegations of grave human rights violations in Iran, including executions because of political and religious convictions, and of maltreatment and torture in prisons, as well as the existence of summary and informal proceedings, the unawareness of defendants of specific accusations, the lack of legal counsel and other irregularities in respect to fair trial. It shared the Special Representative's opinion that denial by Iran of those allegations as a whole, without providing details, was not sufficient for a sensible assessment of the human rights situation there.

The Commission endorsed the Special Representative's conclusion that acts occurring in Iran were inconsistent with international instruments and justified continuing international concern, study and monitoring, and urged Iran to respect and ensure to all individuals within its territory and under its jurisdiction the rights recognized in the 1966 International Covenant on Civil and Political Rights.[31] Deciding to extend the Special Representative's mandate and have him report to the Assembly in 1988 and to the Commission in 1989, it renewed its urgent appeal to Iran to respond to his request for information and to permit him to visit that country, and requested the Secretary-General to give him all necessary assistance.

ECONOMIC AND SOCIAL COUNCIL ACTION

In May, on the recommendation of its Second Committee, the Economic and Social Council adopted **decision 1988/137** by recorded vote.

Situation of human rights in the Islamic Republic of Iran

At its 16th plenary meeting, on 27 May 1988, the Economic and Social Council, taking note of Commission on Human Rights resolution 1988/69 of 10 March 1988, approved the decision of the Commission to extend the mandate of the Special Representative on the human rights situation in the Islamic Republic of Iran, as contained in Commission resolution 1984/54 of 14 March 1984, for a further year. The Council also approved the Commission's request to the Secretary-General to give all necessary assistance to the Special Representative of the Commission.

Economic and Social Council decision 1988/137

24-8-15 (recorded vote)

Approved by Second Committee (E/1988/89/Add.1) by roll-call vote (24-7-14), 23 May (meeting 20); draft by Commission on Human Rights (E/1988/12 & Corr.1); agenda item 10.

Recorded vote in Council as follows:

In favour: Australia, Belgium, Belize, Canada, Colombia, Denmark, France, Germany, Federal Republic of, Greece, Iraq, Ireland, Italy, Jamaica, Japan, Lesotho, Norway, Panama, Peru, Philippines, Portugal, Rwanda, United Kingdom, United States, Venezuela.
Against: Cuba, Iran, Libyan Arab Jamahiriya, Oman, Pakistan, Somalia, Sri Lanka, Syrian Arab Republic.
Abstaining: China, Djibouti, Egypt, Gabon, German Democratic Republic, Ghana, Guinea, India, Liberia, Saudi Arabia, Sierra Leone, Sudan, Trinidad and Tobago, Yugoslavia, Zaire.

Interim report of the Special Representative. In October, the Secretary-General transmitted to the Assembly an interim report of the Special Representative,[36] prepared in accordance with the Commission's request. The report was again based on oral and written information concerning alleged violations of human rights, and included consideration of views expressed by the Iranian Government. The Special Representative also informed the Assembly of his meeting with a representative of the Government at Geneva on 27 September.

The Special Representative noted Iran's announcement that it was preparing detailed responses to allegations and its promise for increased co-operation, albeit conditional on the non-use of the term "religious minority" applied to Baha'is and on changes in the method of conveying allegations. He further noted a reported increase in the number of executions in July, August and September 1988 and continuing ill-treatment and torture, both physical and psychological, in Iranian prisons, as well as the existence of summary and informal proceedings and other irregularities contravening international standards on fair trial. The number of political prisoners, reportedly affirmed by an Iranian official, stood at 9,000; according to other sources, it was much higher. The Special Representative continued to receive reports on poor conditions in prisons and expressed concern over the suspension of family visits to political prisoners in Evin prison in Teheran. He stated that allegations concerning the Iranian penitentiary system deserved a thorough investigation by the Government and that the elimination of practices inconsistent with human rights instruments had to be considered at the legislative and executive levels.

With regard to alleged violations of the right to freedom of thought, conscience and religion, harassment of the Baha'i community diminished somewhat; no new arrests or executions were reported, and a number of Baha'is were released from prison, including 13 in July alone, while the sentences of others were reduced. However, 140 Baha'is were still said to remain in prison. According to the official Iranian stand, strongly denied by the Baha'i International Community, Baha'is were persecuted not on the grounds of their faith but for engagement in subversive activities. In conclusion, the Special Representative recommended renewal of the urgent appeal to Iran for full co-operation with him and for compliance with its international obligations, and expressed his belief that the persistence of alleged human rights violations justified continuing monitoring of the situation.

GENERAL ASSEMBLY ACTION

On 8 December, on the recommendation of the Third Committee, the General Assembly adopted **resolution 43/137** by recorded vote.

Situation of human rights in the Islamic Republic of Iran

The General Assembly,

Guided by the principles embodied in the Charter of the United Nations, the Universal Declaration of Human Rights and the International Covenants on Human Rights,

Reaffirming that all Member States have an obligation to promote and protect human rights and fundamental freedoms and to fulfil the obligations they have undertaken under the various international instruments in this field,

Recalling its pertinent resolutions, as well as the resolutions of the Commission on Human Rights and the Sub-Commission on Prevention of Discrimination and Protection of Minorities,

Taking note, in particular, of Commission on Human Rights resolution 1988/69 of 10 March 1988, in which the Commission decided to extend the mandate of its Special Representative for one year and requested him to submit an interim report to the General Assembly at its forty-third session on the situation of human rights in the Islamic Republic of Iran, including the situation of minority groups such as the Baha'is, and to submit a final report to the Commission at its forty-fifth session,

Welcoming the recent cease-fire as a positive development that should contribute to a situation in which human rights and fundamental freedoms can be fully enjoyed,

Taking note of the Special Representative's view that the Government of the Islamic Republic of Iran continued, during the period under consideration, to indicate its willingness to increase gradually its co-operation with the competent United Nations organs,

Recognizing as a positive development the undertaking by the Iranian authorities to provide a detailed response to allegations of violations of human rights,

Noting, nevertheless, that a detailed response to individual allegations brought to the attention of the Government of the Islamic Republic of Iran by the Special Representative has yet to be received,

Regretting that, notwithstanding the indication of a greater willingness to co-operate with the Special Representative, a state of full co-operation has yet to be achieved,

Noting the recent contacts between the Special Representative and the Government of the Islamic Republic of Iran, which it is hoped will lead to a state of full co-operation between the Special Representative and that Government, including a visit to the Islamic Republic of Iran, so that he can fulfil his mandate,

Noting that the Baha'is in the Islamic Republic of Iran continue to be subjected to various forms of harassment and discrimination, although there are indications that the intensity of the campaign of persecution against the Baha'is has diminished somewhat in recent months and that a number of them have been released from prison,

1. *Takes note with appreciation* of the interim report of the Special Representative and the considerations and observations contained therein;

2. *Once again urges* the Government of the Islamic Republic of Iran to extend its full co-operation to the Special Representative of the Commission on Human Rights and, in particular, to permit him to visit that country;

3. *Calls upon* the Government of the Islamic Republic of Iran to give immediate effect to its undertaking to provide detailed information concerning the allegations of human rights violations that have been brought to its attention;

4. *Expresses once more its deep concern* about the numerous and detailed allegations of grave human rights violations in the Islamic Republic of Iran to which the Special Representative has referred in his report, namely, those related to the right to life, the right to freedom from torture or cruel, inhuman or degrading treatment or punishment, the right to liberty and security of person, the right to a fair trial and the right to freedom of thought, conscience and religion;

5. *Expresses its grave concern* that, although the Special Representative observes that the number of alleged violations of the right to life continued to decrease during 1987, the information available to him indicates that there was a renewed wave of executions in the period July-September 1988 whereby a large number of persons died because of their political convictions;

6. *Expresses its deep concern* at allegations that ill-treatment and torture, both physical and psychological, continued to be common practice in Iranian prisons, especially during interrogation but also immediately after arrest and before and after the final verdict;

7. *Expresses its deep concern also* at the existence of extremely summary, informal and irregular proceedings, failure to inform defendants of specific accusations against them, lack of legal counsel, absence of an appropriate instance for appeal and other irregularities that contravene international standards on fair trial;

8. *Shares the opinion* of the Special Representative regarding the importance of prompt investigation into all allegations of irregularities in the treatment of political prisoners and other persons in custody, as well as the necessity of adequate redress for those whose human rights have been violated;

9. *Welcomes* the intention of the Special Representative to consider in his report to the Commission on Human Rights at its forty-fifth session several issues pertaining to the legal system applicable in the Islamic Republic of Iran;

10. *Endorses* the conclusion of the Special Representative that acts continue to occur in the Islamic Republic of Iran that are inconsistent with the provisions of international instruments by which that country is bound and that the persistence of alleged violations of human rights continues to justify continuing international concern and continued monitoring by the United Nations of the situation in that country;

11. *Urges* the Government of the Islamic Republic of Iran, as a State party to the International Covenant on Civil and Political Rights, to respect and ensure the rights recognized in that Covenant to all individuals within its territory and subject to its jurisdiction;

12. *Requests* the Secretary-General to give all necessary assistance to the Special Representative;

13. *Decides* to keep under consideration the situation of human rights in the Islamic Republic of Iran, including the situation of minority groups such as the Baha'is, during its forty-fourth session in order to re-examine it in the light of additional elements provided by the Commission on Human Rights and the Economic and Social Council.

General Assembly resolution 43/137
8 December 1988   Meeting 75   61-25-44 (recorded vote)

Approved by Third Committee (A/43/868) by recorded vote (55-23-38), 30
November (meeting 58); 14-nation draft (A/C.3/43/L.41/Rev.1); agenda item
12.
Sponsors: Australia, Austria, Belgium, Canada, Costa Rica, Denmark, Iceland,
Ireland, Luxembourg, Netherlands, Norway, Portugal, Samoa, United Kingdom.
Meeting numbers. GA 43rd session: 3rd Committee 49-58; plenary 75.

Recorded vote in Assembly as follows:

In favour: Antigua and Barbuda, Australia, Austria, Bahamas, Barbados,
Belgium, Belize, Botswana, Canada, Cape Verde, Central African Repub-
lic, Chad, Colombia, Costa Rica, Denmark, Dominica, Ecuador, El Salvador,
Equatorial Guinea, Finland, France, Germany, Federal Republic of, Greece,
Grenada, Guatemala, Honduras, Iceland, Iraq, Ireland, Israel, Italy, Jamaica,
Japan, Jordan, Lesotho, Luxembourg, Malta, Mauritius, Mexico, Nether-
lands, New Zealand, Norway, Panama, Papua New Guinea, Paraguay, Peru,
Philippines, Portugal, Rwanda, Saint Lucia, Saint Vincent and the Grena-
dines, Samoa, Solomon Islands, Spain, Swaziland, Sweden, Togo, Trinidad
and Tobago, United Kingdom, United States, Venezuela.
Against: Albania, Algeria, Angola, Bahrain, Bangladesh, Brunei Darus-
salam, Cuba, Democratic Yemen, Ethiopia, Indonesia, Iran, Kuwait, Lib-
yan Arab Jamahiriya, Malaysia, Nicaragua, Niger, Oman, Pakistan, Qatar,
Romania, Sri Lanka, Sudan, Syrian Arab Republic, United Arab Emirates,
United Republic of Tanzania.
Abstaining: Bhutan, Brazil, Burkina Faso, Burma, Burundi, Cameroon,
Comoros, Côte d'Ivoire, Cyprus, Djibouti, Egypt, Fiji, Gabon, Gambia, Ghana,
Guinea, Guinea-Bissau, Guyana, Haiti, India, Kenya, Lebanon, Liberia, Malawi,
Maldives, Mali, Mauritania, Morocco, Nepal, Nigeria, Saudi Arabia, Sene-
gal, Sierra Leone, Somalia, Suriname, Thailand, Tunisia, Turkey, Uganda,
Yemen, Yugoslavia, Zaire, Zambia, Zimbabwe.

Before the text was approved by the Committee, Pakistan moved to adjourn the debate and requested that no action be taken on the draft resolution. The motion was rejected by a recorded vote
of 40 in favour to 50 against, with 27 abstentions.

Kampuchea

Both the Commission on Human Rights and
the Economic and Social Council reaffirmed that
continued occupation of Kampuchea by foreign
forces constituted the primary violation of human
rights in that country (see above, under "Civil and
political rights").

Europe and the Mediterranean

Albania

Human Rights Commission action. On 2
March,[37] by a roll-call vote of 15 to 11, with 17
abstentions, the Commission decided that con-
sideration of the human rights situation in Alba-
nia should be taken up under its public procedure.
It recommended to the Economic and Social
Council that the confidential material concerning
Albania no longer be restricted.

On 27 May, the Council, by a recorded vote of
11 in favour to 13 against, with 29 abstentions, rejected the Commission's recommendation, which
had been approved by its Second Committee by
a recorded vote of 13 to 10, with 25 abstentions.[38]

Sub-Commission action. On 1 September,[39]
by 12 votes to 4, with 6 abstentions, the Sub-Commission strongly disapproved the inhuman treatment of minorities living in Albania and requested
the Commission to urge Albania to provide adequate constitutional and legal measures consistent

with international human rights instruments with
a view to ensuring freedom of religion or belief
and providing safeguards and remedies against
discrimination on grounds of religion or belief.
The Sub-Commission also asked the Commission
to call on Albania to restore and guarantee all
human rights of ethnic and religious minorities,
particularly the Greek minority, and to free all political prisoners. The Secretary-General was requested to bring to the attention of the Commission and its Special Rapporteur on religious
intolerance allegations of human rights violations
in Albania and to inform the Sub-Commission in
1989 of the Commission's deliberations, as well as
of any consideration of the matter by the General
Assembly or the Economic and Social Council.

Cyprus

Human Rights Commission action. On 10
March,[40] the Commission decided to postpone
consideration of the question of human rights in
Cyprus until its 1989 session, when the Secretary-
General was to report to it.

Report of the Secretary-General. The Secretary-
General reported[41] that the two sides in Cyprus
agreed to achieve a negotiated settlement of the problem by 1 June 1989. The Committee on Missing
Persons in Cyprus held seven sessions during 1988,
and the United Nations Peace-keeping Force in
Cyprus continued, under its mandate, to discharge
humanitarian functions on behalf of the Greek
Cypriots remaining in the northern part of the island, whose number stood at 639 at the end of
November, as well as to make periodic visits to Turkish Cypriots living in the south. (For details, see
PART ONE, Chapter IV.)

Latin America and the Caribbean

Chile

Report of the Special Rapporteur (February).
In a report to the Commission on the human rights
situation in Chile,[42] covering mainly the second
half of 1987, Special Rapporteur Fernando Volio
Jiménez (Costa Rica) said that, during his third
visit to Chile from 8 to 21 December 1987, he was
informed about the detention conditions of 470 persons charged with infringing internal security or
related offences, of whom 367 awaited trial and 65
were convicted. He also received information about
the promulgation of four new secret laws and other
legislation which might place additional obstacles
to judicial investigation of human rights questions
and reports of 52 new cases of alleged torture in
police custody and persons abducted for political
reasons, 136 incidents of unjustified violence, 44

cases of political abductions, 33 arrests not acknowledged by the police and 21 deaths. The Special Rapporteur was told that 644 persons were subject to a ban on entering the country and that 40 exiled Chileans who had lost their Chilean nationality were listed as undesirable aliens. He learned about the lack of progress in judicial investigations of outstanding cases, including those of missing detainees, and about five new disappearances.

The Special Rapporteur examined complaints from legal and other documents regarding violations of the rights to life, physical and moral integrity, liberty, security, proper trial and procedural guarantees, to enter and leave the country freely, and freedom of expression and information, as well as alleged disappearances. He noted the full co-operation of the Chilean Government, except for the Minister of Justice, and stated that a forthcoming plebiscite constituted progress in the sphere of respect for human rights, although more limited than general elections. The Special Rapporteur pointed out that on 14 January 1988 the Government announced its approval of the Constitutional Organizational Act on votes and ballots for the election of the President and parliamentarians and for plebiscites; the Act had to be approved by the Constitutional Court and promulgated. He was informed that a new Act concerning State television was adopted to regulate fairly the time available for each political party taking part in the plebiscite. At the same time, the Special Rapporteur noted that there was no longer a ban on media coverage of terrorist activities, that no new administrative banishment orders were issued in the second half of 1987 and that the Government had decided to end the exile of Chileans forbidden to return to their country. He further referred to an order by the Ministries of the Interior and of Defence, instructing police authorities to avoid maltreatment, including torture, and to the agreements allowing ICRC access to persons detained on the premises of police agencies.

On the other hand, however, the Special Rapporteur noted that two decrees, issued on 1 September, banned media coverage of public activities of individuals or organizations and extended the state of emergency in Chile for three months, permitting authorities to prohibit entry into or departure from the country, restrict freedoms of movement and opinion, suspend the right of assembly and censor correspondence and communications. By another decree of 1 September, the state of a threat to internal law and order had been extended for six months, allowing the detention of persons for up to five days in places other than prison and for a further 15 days if "terrorist acts" occurred, restricting the rights of assembly and expression, prohibiting entry into or ordering the expulsion from Chile of persons propagating doc-

trines contrary to Chile's interests, and banishing individuals to remote parts of the country for renewable periods of up to three months. Yet another decree restricted the freedom of information by subjecting any new publication to prior administrative authorization.

In addition, prolonged periods of incommunicado detention were still frequently ordered, and torture was still practised, although on a smaller scale, as was intimidation, usually carried out by private gangs. Other matters of concern were military courts, characterized by excessively long trials, harshness, wide field of action and their tendency to take over civil cases; the curtailed freedom of the press; and the recurrence of disappearances.

The Special Rapporteur recommended lifting the two states of emergency; ratifying international conventions against torture; speeding up the process of enacting constitutional organization laws; finding urgently the five persons missing since September 1987; clarifying deaths believed to have resulted from illegal executions of opponents of the Chilean political régime; terminating exile without delay; changing the official policy towards the Mapuche population, particularly the legislation on land division; taking measures against acts of intimidation; giving due attention to new and previous allegations of human rights violations; putting an end to unlawful coercion, especially torture; reducing the length of incommunicado detention; and organizing training courses for law-enforcement officials on the proper treatment of persons deprived of their liberty. He also recommended reviewing the system of justice and reforming pertinent legislation, with a view to defining the jurisdictions of the military and civil systems and giving independence to the civil system; revising laws restricting human rights and freedoms, as well as the Code of Penal Procedure, to avert abusive proceedings; and adequately protecting freedom of expression and the activities of the media.

Human Rights Commission action. On 10 March,[43] by a roll-call vote of 34 to none, with 7 abstentions, the Commission expressed again its conviction that the re-establishment of a legal and political order through free elections was fundamental for full respect for human rights in Chile and emphasized the need to re-establish the independence of the Chilean judiciary. It urged the Chilean Government to honour requests from all social and political sectors for the peaceful restoration of democracy and to guarantee full access to all means of communication and control by citizens over the electoral process, as well as the abolition of states of emergency and other restrictions on the freedoms of association and assembly. The Commission expressed its concern at the continuation of such restrictions through the use of repressive methods, particularly military searches and acts of intimidation. It also expressed concern at the persistence of serious human rights violations, such as murder, death in alleged confrontations, abduction, disappearance, torture and ill-treatment, the climate of violence, the maintenance of exile and the denial of fundamental rights during states of emergency, as well as at the failure to conduct full investigations and prosecute those responsible for unresolved cases of such violations.

Expressing dismay at the continued acts of violence from all sources in Chile, the Commission emphasized the need to restore and respect human rights in conformity with various international instruments and, in particular, to: end immediately the application of laws and regulations contrary to the full exercise of those rights; put an immediate end to all forms of torture and desist from intimidation and persecution, abduction, arbitrary arrests and ill-treatment of political prisoners; terminate the activities of gangs and groups violating human rights and punish those responsible, especially their leaders; ensure effective investigations of such violations and judicial remedies against the intimidation of witnesses and defence lawyers, and re-establish the jurisdiction of civilian courts in matters within their competence; guarantee the non-use of anti-terrorist legislation to justify any abuse of authority, torture or inhuman treatment against those who did not commit terrorist acts, as well as due process of law and respect for the rights of persons accused of such acts; end the practice of forced exile and respect the right of Chileans to live in and freely enter or leave their country; restore labour rights and terminate the repression of trade union activities; broaden and guarantee the rights of political parties to campaign peacefully; extend full co-operation to ICRC; and investigate and clarify without delay the fate of disappeared persons who were arrested for political reasons.

The Commission decided to extend the Special Rapporteur's mandate and have him report to the Assembly in 1988 and to the Commission in 1989, and recommended that the Economic and Social Council ensure provision of the necessary resources and staff.

On 27 May, the Council, by **decision 1988/140**, approved the Commission's decision to extend the Special Rapporteur's mandate for one year and its recommendation regarding appropriate financial and staff arrangements.

Sub-Commission action. On 1 September,[44] the Sub-Commission affirmed its conviction that restoring a legal and political system based on the participation of all Chileans and on free expression of the people's will was a prerequisite

for the full and effective enjoyment and exercise of human rights in Chile. It requested the Commission to urge the Chilean authorities to adopt measures to restore democratic institutions and the principle of legality, and specified measures which largely corresponded to those listed in the Commission's March resolution (see above). Urging Chile to respect and promote human rights in accordance with binding international instruments, the Sub-Commission recommended that the Commission continue to study the human rights situation in that country, and requested specialized agencies, intergovernmental organizations and NGOs to provide the Commission and its Special Rapporteur, through the Secretary-General, with any information on that situation. The Secretary-General was asked to report to the Sub-Commission in 1989 on the results of the Special Rapporteur's investigations, as well as on General Assembly and Commission deliberations and resolutions.

Report of the Special Rapporteur (October). In October,[45] the Secretary-General transmitted to the Assembly a report prepared by the Special Rapporteur in accordance with the Commission's request.

The Special Rapporteur noted that Chile had, in May, resumed its co-operation with the Commission, interrupted in March, and had notified him that the number of exiles had been reduced to 518 by 30 August and that the administrative ban on entry to Chile had been lifted on 1 September, ending the exile of all Chileans except the few serving judicial sentences of expulsion. He further noted that the two states of emergency, which had been in force for 15 years, were lifted on 25 August in anticipation of the plebiscite.

Nevertheless, information was received concerning 6 new secret laws promulgated in Chile; 42 cases of violent death, 8 of which were attributed to the Chilean carabineros; 42 new allegations of torture; 64 judicial complaints of unnecessary violence resulting in injury; 1,780 arrests, with proceedings initiated in only 149 cases; and the lack of progress in judicial investigations. Cases of intimidation continued to be reported, as did incidents of prolonged incommunicado detention and an abusive application of restrictions on the freedom of speech. The Special Rapporteur had been informed of police raids in Mapuche communities and of the disadvantage suffered by the 16 opposition political parties, which had access to only 13 per cent of the media space allotted to electoral propaganda in preparing for the plebiscite.

He examined new complaints regarding violations of the rights to life, physical and moral integrity, liberty, security, proper trial and procedural guarantees, freedom of expression and information, and to enter and leave the country, and observed that, while the carabineros were gradually resuming their traditional role of safeguarding public order, terrorist acts continued unabated. Also, the system of justice continued to suffer from major institutional limitations, with the military system undermining and showing a lack of respect for the system of civil justice. The Special Rapporteur expressed concern over some remaining penal laws that were a source of repressive measures, as well as the Code of Military Justice with its excessively wide field of application. Continuing harassment of the media was also of concern; as at 5 August, legal proceedings had been brought against 24 journalists accused of alleged insults to the armed forces, of whom 8 had been indicted and 1 convicted.

The Special Rapporteur recommended the completion without delay of the constitutional act relating to the National Congress; ending the system of enacting so-called ''secret laws''; undertaking urgent reform of several laws containing excessively harsh provisions contrary to liberal and democratic penal law; desisting from harassing the media, dropping proceedings brought against journalists and pardoning those already sentenced; taking measures to combat violence, especially terrorist acts, and to prevent violent deaths; investigating long-standing and recent cases of disappearance; and finding a legal means to apply agreements between Chile and ICRC to persons detained incommunicado.

During his fourth visit to Chile from 2 to 10 October, the Special Rapporteur observed the presidential plebiscite on 5 October, which, he believed, opened the way for completing the transition to a representative democracy. He noted that the current President and his Government, defeated in the plebiscite, respected the popular will.

GENERAL ASSEMBLY ACTION

On 8 December, on the recommendation of the Third Committee, the General Assembly adopted **resolution 43/158** by recorded vote.

Situation of human rights and fundamental freedoms in Chile

The General Assembly,

Guided by the purposes and principles of the Charter of the United Nations and bearing in mind the Universal Declaration of Human Rights, the International Covenant on Economic, Social and Cultural Rights and the International Covenant on Civil and Political Rights,

Aware of its responsibility to promote and encourage respect for human rights and fundamental freedoms, and determined to remain vigilant with regard to violations of human rights wherever they occur,

Noting the obligation of the Government of Chile to respect and protect human rights in accordance with the international instruments to which Chile is a party,

Bearing in mind that the concern of the international community at the situation of human rights in Chile has been expressed by the General Assembly in a number of resolutions, particularly resolution 33/173 of 20 December 1978 on disappeared persons and resolution 42/147 of 7 December 1987, in which the Assembly invited the Commission on Human Rights to take the most appropriate steps for the effective restoration of human rights and fundamental freedoms in that country, including the extension of the mandate of the Special Rapporteur,

Recalling the pertinent resolutions of the Commission on Human Rights, particularly resolution 1988/78 of 10 March 1988, in which the Commission decided, *inter alia*, in view of the persistence of serious violations of human rights in Chile, to extend the mandate of the Special Rapporteur for one year and to consider that subject as a matter of high priority,

Considering the referendum held on 5 October 1988 to be an important step towards the restoration of democracy in Chile,

Noting the formal acceptance of the results of the referendum and the increase in political activity in Chile,

Noting with satisfaction the termination of the two states of emergency and of the prohibition of free movement into and out of the country,

Deploring the fact that, notwithstanding the repeated visits of the Special Rapporteur to Chile and the adoption of positive measures by the Government, the institutional and legal framework that makes violations of human rights possible has remained unchanged,

Noting that, although opposition publications have in some cases been authorized, they are frequently subject to arbitrary restrictions and limitations,

1. *Takes note with interest* of the provisional report of the Special Rapporteur, submitted in accordance with Commission on Human Rights resolution 1988/78;

2. *Welcomes* the positive fact that the Government of Chile has decided to continue to co-operate with the Special Rapporteur and again permitted him to visit the country in October 1988, providing him with free access to the facilities for compiling his report, and expresses its confidence that a further visit will be authorized on the same conditions in the immediate future;

3. *Welcomes* the decision of the Government of Chile to respect the result of the referendum of 5 October 1988 as an expression of the will of the people and an important step towards the rapid restoration of democracy in Chile;

4. *Urges* the Government of Chile to take the necessary measures to facilitate the full re-establishment of a democratic, pluralist and representative system based on the principle of popular sovereignty;

5. *Notes with satisfaction* the decision of the Government of Chile to lift the two states of emergency imposed fifteen years ago, permitting greater political activity in the country;

6. *Expects* that the measures already adopted by the Government of Chile in favour of a transition to democracy will lead to a genuine improvement in the situation of human rights and fundamental freedoms of the Chilean people;

7. *Expresses once again its concern* at the persistence of serious violations of human rights and fundamental freedoms in Chile, as stated in the provisional report of the Special Rapporteur;

8. *Again urges* the Government of Chile to put an end to this situation and to the legislation that makes it possible; to continue adopting measures to permit the restoration of the rule of law in Chile; to ensure the independence of the judiciary and the effectiveness of judicial remedies; to respect human rights in accordance with the principles of the Universal Declaration of Human Rights and to comply with its obligations under various international instruments in order to ensure the enjoyment and effective exercise of human rights and fundamental freedoms;

9. *Urges* the Government of Chile to authorize, in accordance with the recommendations of the Special Rapporteur and in conformity with existing laws, the official publication of the International Covenant on Civil and Political Rights and the International Covenant on Economic, Social and Cultural Rights;

10. *Invites* the Commission on Human Rights to consider at its forty-fifth session, as a matter of high priority, the situation of human rights in Chile, bearing in mind the report of the Special Rapporteur and the pertinent available information, to consider also the measures necessary for the restoration of human rights in Chile, including the extension of the mandate of the Special Rapporteur, and to report to the General Assembly at its forty-fourth session.

General Assembly resolution 43/158

8 December 1988   Meeting 75   97-1-55 (recorded vote)

Approved by Third Committee (A/43/868) by recorded vote (82-1-51), 30 November (meeting 57); 11-nation draft (A/C.3/43/L.81), orally revised, and orally amended by Costa Rica; agenda item 12.
Sponsors: Australia, Austria, Cuba, France, Greece, Italy, Luxembourg, Mexico, Netherlands, Portugal, Spain.
Meeting numbers. GA 43rd session: 3rd Committee 49-57; plenary 75.

Recorded vote in Assembly as follows:

In favour: Afghanistan, Albania, Algeria, Angola, Antigua and Barbuda, Argentina, Australia, Austria, Barbados, Belgium, Benin, Bolivia, Botswana, Bulgaria, Burkina Faso, Burundi, Byelorussian SSR, Canada, Cape Verde, Colombia, Congo, Cuba, Cyprus, Czechoslovakia, Democratic Yemen, Denmark, Dominica, Ecuador, El Salvador, Ethiopia, Finland, France, Gambia, German Democratic Republic, Germany, Federal Republic of, Ghana, Greece, Guatemala, Guinea, Guinea-Bissau, Guyana, Hungary, Iceland, India, Ireland, Italy, Jamaica, Kenya, Kuwait, Lao People's Democratic Republic, Libyan Arab Jamahiriya, Luxembourg, Madagascar, Mali, Malta, Mauritania, Mauritius, Mexico, Mongolia, Mozambique, Netherlands, New Zealand, Nicaragua, Norway, Papua New Guinea, Peru, Philippines, Poland, Portugal, Rwanda, Saint Lucia, Saint Vincent and the Grenadines, Samoa, Sao Tome and Principe, Senegal, Seychelles, Solomon Islands, Spain, Sri Lanka, Swaziland, Sweden, Togo, Trinidad and Tobago, Tunisia, Uganda, Ukrainian SSR, USSR, United Arab Emirates, United Kingdom, United Republic of Tanzania, Uruguay, Vanuatu, Venezuela, Viet Nam, Yugoslavia, Zambia, Zimbabwe.

Against: Chile.

Abstaining: Bahamas, Bahrain, Bangladesh, Bhutan, Brazil, Brunei Darussalam, Burma, Cameroon, Central African Republic, Chad, China, Comoros, Costa Rica, Côte d'Ivoire, Democratic Kampuchea, Djibouti, Egypt, Equatorial Guinea, Fiji, Gabon, Grenada, Haiti, Honduras, Indonesia, Iraq, Israel, Japan, Jordan, Lebanon, Lesotho, Liberia, Malawi, Malaysia, Maldives, Morocco, Nepal, Niger, Nigeria, Oman, Pakistan, Panama, Paraguay, Qatar, Saint Kitts and Nevis, Saudi Arabia, Sierra Leone, Singapore, Somalia, Sudan, Suriname, Thailand, Turkey, United States, Yemen, Zaire.

El Salvador

Report of the Special Representative (January). Special Representative José Antonio Pastor Ridruejo (Spain) submitted to the Commission his final report on the human rights situation in El Salvador,[46] covering mainly the events of 1987.

He noted that the situation of economic, social and cultural rights had deteriorated as a result of a number of factors, including attacks by the

Frente Farabundo Martí para la Liberación Nacional (FMLN) against the national economic infrastructure. He also pointed to a disturbing number of summary executions attributed to the armed forces and Civil Defence, a resurgence of ''death squad'' activities and the persistence by guerrilla organizations in practices incompatible with human rights standards. Cases of disappearance and abduction continued to be reported, as did incidents of maltreatment during interrogation of political prisoners. Activities by the criminal justice system to investigate and punish human rights violations remained unsatisfactory, although the number of political prisoners declined. According to the report, guerrilla organizations were responsible for most casualties among civilians maimed or killed by contact mines, while El Salvador's constitutional authorities remained committed to a policy of respect for human rights, which was reflected in the declining number of attacks on human life. The Special Representative noted that FMLN had also committed itself to respect and promote human rights. At the beginning of 1988, however, the dialogue between the Government and the armed opposition, initiated in 1987, was deadlocked.

The Special Representative recommended to El Salvador's constitutional authorities a speedy repeal of legislation incompatible with international human rights standards and the adoption of laws compatible with those standards, increased monitoring of interrogations of political prisoners, and expanded social reform, particularly of the judicial system. He also recommended that FMLN refrain from planting contact mines in a manner incompatible with international law and from attacking the economic infrastructure. He further recommended that States provide assistance to alleviate and improve the living conditions of Salvadorian citizens who had been displaced or made refugees by the conflict.

Human Rights Commission action. On 10 March,[47] the Commission emphasized the significance of the Special Representative's observation that respect for human rights was an important part of the Government's policy, and took note of the fact that the opposition was associating itself with proposals concerning democratization and respect for human rights. It expressed concern, however, at continuing human rights violations and at the harassment of humanitarian groups by death squads, and trusted that the Salvadorian authorities would continue to investigate those violations and punish the offenders.

Urging the authorities to hasten the adoption of measures to ensure the efficiency of the judicial system, the Commission called on the Government and opposition forces to do their utmost to implement measures to avoid death or harm to the non-combatant population, and urged them to renew the dialogue aimed at achieving a political solution. States were requested to refrain from intervening in El Salvador's internal situation and to encourage the continuation of the dialogue. The Commission recommended the continuation and broadening of reforms in El Salvador to solve socio-economic problems, and requested the Government and opposition forces to continue applying agreements for the evacuation of the war-wounded. It also encouraged the Government to continue to grant refugees and displaced persons facilities to enable their return, and requested United Nations bodies to assist in promoting and protecting human rights in El Salvador. The Commission extended the Special Representative's mandate and decided to consider in 1989 its positive modification in the light of progress made. It requested him to report to the Assembly in 1988 and to the Commission in 1989.

On 27 May, the Economic and Social Council, by **decision 1988/135**, approved the Commission's decision to extend the Special Representative's mandate for one year.

Sub-Commission action. On 1 September,[48] the Sub-Commission expressed its concern at the recent increase in the number of human rights violations in El Salvador and at the persistent inobservance of the fundamental norms of humanitarian law. It recommended that the Special Representative develop in his next report his conclusions that death squads were made up of police and army members acting under the orders of superior officers and that they continued to capture for political reasons. It confirmed that non-combatants must not be subjected to military attacks and encirclements by government forces and requested the Special Rapporteur on human rights and disability to undertake all possible measures for the prompt and regular evacuation of the war-wounded and disabled and to report in 1989.

The Sub-Commission strongly urged the Salvadorian Government to ensure respect for human rights by its military, paramilitary and police forces, expressed the hope that the Government and opposition forces would do everything possible to renew their dialogue, and asked the Secretary-General to report in 1989 on the results of the Special Representative's investigation, as well as on General Assembly and Commission deliberations.

Report of the Special Representative (October). In October, the Secretary-General transmitted to the Assembly a report on the human rights situation in El Salvador,[49] prepared by the Special Representative in accordance with the Commission's request.

The Special Representative, who visited El Salvador from 9 to 15 October, reported that the armed conflict between government and guerrilla forces continued, causing serious human rights violations and a deterioration in the economic situation. He had received information regarding many cases of summary execution attributed to government forces and to guerrilla organizations, most of which were non-combatant civilians. He was also informed of numerous arrests or abductions and disappearances attributed to the State apparatus and to guerrilla forces. The Special Representative noted a decrease in the number of political prisoners from 492 in September 1987 to 45 by 10 October 1988 as a result of the Amnesty Act promulgated in October 1987, and the continuing return of refugees and displaced persons, with 1,200 people repatriated from Honduras in August.

He further noted that the Salvadorian criminal justice system remained unchanged and that of 147 investigations of human rights violations initiated since December 1987 only 24 resulted in arrest warrants for perpetrators. The Special Representative also learned of 14 arrests followed by maltreatment. However, he noted the Government's efforts to strengthen respect for human rights and activities of the governmental Human Rights Commission. The Special Representative reiterated the recommendations made in his January report (see above) and added that El Salvador's constitutional authorities should adopt measures to ensure efficient control of all agencies under their authority and dismiss those responsible for human rights violations; investigate and punish the perpetrators of such violations as soon as possible; and pay urgent attention to the basic needs of peasant populations resettled in combat zones. He further recommended that guerrilla organizations refrain from indiscriminate urban terrorist acts and summary executions, and emphasized the need for both sides to the conflict to create conditions for a dialogue conducive to its early peaceful settlement.

GENERAL ASSEMBLY ACTION

On 8 December, on the recommendation of the Third Committee, the General Assembly adopted **resolution 43/145** without vote.

Situation of human rights and fundamental freedoms in El Salvador

The General Assembly,

Guided by the principles of the Charter of the United Nations, the Universal Declaration of Human Rights, the International Covenant on Civil and Political Rights and the humanitarian rules laid down in the Geneva Conventions of 12 August 1949 and Additional Protocols I and II thereto, of 1977,

Reaffirming that it is the duty of the Governments of all Member States to promote and protect human rights and fundamental freedoms and to fulfil the obligations which they have assumed under the relevant international instruments,

Recalling that, in its resolutions 35/192 of 15 December 1980, 36/155 of 16 December 1981, 37/185 of 17 December 1982, 38/101 of 16 December 1983, 39/119 of 14 December 1984, 40/139 of 13 December 1985, 41/157 of 4 December 1986 and 42/137 of 7 December 1987, it expressed its deep concern at the situation of human rights in El Salvador,

Bearing in mind Commission on Human Rights resolution 32(XXXVII) of 11 March 1981, in which the Commission decided to appoint a special representative on the situation of human rights in El Salvador, and resolutions 1982/28 of 11 March 1982, 1983/29 of 8 March 1983, 1984/52 of 14 March 1984, 1985/35 of 13 March 1985, 1986/39 of 12 March 1986, 1987/51 of 11 March 1987, as well as Commission resolution 1988/65 of 10 March 1988, in which it extended the mandate of the Special Representative for another year and requested him to report to the General Assembly at its forty-third session and the Commission at its forty-fifth session,

Considering that an armed conflict of a non-international character continues to exist in El Salvador in which the parties involved are under an obligation to apply the minimum standards of protection of human rights and humanitarian treatment provided for in article 3 common to the Geneva Conventions of 1949 and in Additional Protocol II thereto, of 1977,

Noting that the Special Representative points out in his report that the question of human rights continues to be an important element of the current policy of the Government of El Salvador,

Concerned, however, because, as the Special Representative has pointed out in his report, there has been an increase in the number of violations of human rights in El Salvador, particularly in the form of threats to human life and integrity, frequent violations of the humanitarian rules of war as well as the systematic destruction of the economic infrastructure as a consequence of the armed conflict,

Concerned also about information reported by the Special Representative regarding the activities of the so-called ''death squads'',

Recalling that on 7 August 1987 at Guatemala City the Central American Governments signed the agreement on the ''Procedures for the establishment of a firm and lasting peace in Central America'', thus manifesting the political will and good faith to fulfil its provisions in order to achieve peace and stability in the region,

Convinced that the strict fulfilment of the commitments assumed by the Government of El Salvador in the agreement signed at Guatemala City will contribute to the promotion, respect and realization of human rights and fundamental freedoms in that country,

Deeply concerned about the interruption of the dialogue between the Government of El Salvador and the Frente Farabundo Martí para la Liberación Nacional-Frente Democrático Revolucionario, the resumption of which in the context of the agreement signed at Guatemala City is one of the best ways of achieving a solution that will help to improve the situation of human rights of the Salvadorian people,

Aware that a negotiated political solution of the Salvadorian conflict can be cut short if external forces do not support the resumption of the dialogue but instead seek in different ways to spur the intensification or prolongation of the war, with ensuing grave effects on the situation of human rights and the possibilities of economic recovery in El Salvador,

1. *Commends* the Special Representative for his report on the situation of human rights in El Salvador;

2. *Notes with interest and emphasizes* that it is important that the Special Representative has indicated in his report that the Government of El Salvador continues to be committed to a policy of respect for human rights, although difficulties are being encountered with regard to the implementation of that policy;

3. *Expresses its concern,* nevertheless, at the fact that there has been an increase in the number of violations of human rights in El Salvador and that non-observance of the humanitarian rules of war continues to be a frequent occurrence;

4. *Recognizes* the efforts made by the Government of El Salvador related to the investigations designed to determine the responsibility of the instigators of serious violations of human rights, and expresses its profound concern at the fact that the capacity of the judicial system in El Salvador continues to be extremely unsatisfactory, despite the efforts of the Government, and consequently urges the competent authorities to accelerate the adoption of the reforms and measures necessary for ensuring its effectiveness;

5. *Notes with satisfaction* the comments of the Special Representative to the effect that new forces have been incorporated into the Salvadorian political process, in a context of pluralistic, representative and participatory democracy;

6. *Notes with satisfaction* that, with the consent of the Government, there have been a number of mass returns of refugees who have decided of their own free will to resettle in rural areas of conflict, and urges the competent authorities to allow and ensure that such persons are assisted in respect of their most basic health and food needs;

7. *Requests,* in accordance with the recommendations of the Special Representative, that the Government of El Salvador and all the authorities, courts and political forces of the country, including the Frente Farabundo Martí para la Liberación Nacional-Frente Democrático Revolucionario, should adopt appropriate measures to eliminate attacks on the lives and integrity of persons, independently of, during and as a result of combat situations, as well as attacks on the economic infrastructure and, in general, all types of action constituting a violation of the fundamental rights and freedoms of the Salvadorian people;

8. *Calls upon* the Government of El Salvador and the Frente Farabundo Martí para la Liberación Nacional-Frente Democrático Revolucionario, within the framework of the agreement signed at Guatemala City, to make every possible effort to create conditions that would make it possible to renew a magnanimous and open dialogue, leading to the achievement of a global political solution that will end the armed conflict and promote the implementation and strengthening of a pluralistic and participatory democratic process that will involve the promotion of social justice, respect for human rights, and the full exercise of the right of the Salvadorian people to determine freely and without external interference of any kind its economic, political and social system, as recognized in the recent ''National Debate'';

9. *Trusts* that the fulfilment of the commitments assumed in the agreement on the "Procedures for the establishment of a firm and lasting peace in Central America" will lead to improving the situation of human rights in El Salvador;

10. *Renews its appeal* to all States to refrain from intervening in the internal situation of El Salvador and, instead of seeking in different ways to spur the prolongation and intensification of the armed conflict, to stimulate dialogue until a just and lasting peace is attained;

11. *Requests* the Government of El Salvador and the Frente Farabundo Martí para la Liberación Nacional-Frente Democrático Revolucionario, with a view to humanizing the conflict, to continue ensuring that the agreements for the evacuation of the war-wounded and war-injured for medical attention will not be made contingent on further prisoner exchanges and negotiations;

12. *Requests* the competent bodies of the United Nations system to provide such advice and assistance as the Government of El Salvador may require in order to enhance the promotion and protection of human rights and fundamental freedoms;

13. *Requests* the Commission on Human Rights at its forty-fifth session to consider the situation of human rights in El Salvador and the mandate of its Special Representative, taking into account the evolution of the situation of human rights in El Salvador and the developments linked to the fulfilment of the agreement signed at Guatemala City;

14. *Decides* to keep under consideration, during its forty-fourth session, the situation of human rights and fundamental freedoms in El Salvador in order to re-examine this situation in the light of the information provided by the Commission on Human Rights and the Economic and Social Council.

General Assembly resolution 43/145

8 December 1988   Meeting 75   Adopted without vote

Approved by Third Committee (A/43/868) without vote, 29 November (meeting 56); 8-nation draft (A/C.3/43/L.68); agenda item 12.
Sponsors: Argentina, Brazil, Colombia, Mexico, Panama, Peru, Uruguay, Venezuela.
Meeting numbers. GA 43rd session: 3rd Committee 49-56; plenary 75.

Haiti

Following military take-overs in June and September, resulting in the suspension of the Constitution and of Parliament, the human rights situation in Haiti continued to deteriorate. In September, 11 people were massacred and 70 seriously injured in an attack on a church during Sunday mass, followed by attacks on two other churches; 23 deaths in prison were reported since April as a result of torture, ill-treatment or summary execution, as well as some 25 cases of non-recognized detention. There were also reports of numerous political assassinations and several cases of disappearance following arrests made by the security forces or unidentified civilians.

Sub-Commission action. On 1 September,[50] the Sub-Commission, noting that the civilian Government which took office in Haiti on 7 February 1988 was overthrown on 20 June, expressed its concern at the continuing deterioration in the human rights situation in that country and urged the Government to observe full respect for the human rights of its citizens. The Sub-Commission expressed the hope that the Expert on Haiti (see above, under "Advancement of human rights") would inform the Commission on the extent to which the evolution of the situation influenced his ability to carry out his mandate and recommended that the Commission consider appointing a special rapporteur to study and report on the human rights situation in Haiti, without prejudice to the need to continue rendering advisory services through the Secretary-General. The Secretary-General was requested to inform the Sub-Commission in 1989 of the Commission's deliberations, as well as of any consideration of the matter by the General Assembly or the Economic and Social Council.

Middle East

Lebanon

Human Rights Commission action. On 10 March,[51] by a roll-call vote of 26 to 1, with 15 abstentions, the Commission strongly condemned Israel's persistence in violating human rights in southern Lebanon, manifested in acts of aggression, bombardments of civilian populations, detention and other arbitrary practices, and called on it to end them immediately and to implement Security Council resolutions requiring its immediate, total and unconditional withdrawal from all Lebanese territory and respect for Lebanon's sovereignty, independence and territorial integrity. It called on Governments assisting Israel to exert pressure to end its aggressive and expansionist policy in southern Lebanon. The Secretary-General was asked to bring the resolution to Israel's attention, to invite Israel to provide information on its implementation, and to report to the General Assembly in 1988 and to the Commission in 1989 on the results of his efforts.

Report of the Secretary-General. In accordance with the Commission's request, the Secretary-General reported to the Assembly in September[52] that he had asked Israel in July for information on the implementation of the Commission's resolution; as at 23 September, he had received no reply.

By **decision 43/428** of 8 December, the Assembly took note of the Secretary-General's report.

Territories occupied by Israel

In 1988, the question of human rights violations in the territories occupied by Israel as a result of the 1967 hostilities in the Middle East was again considered by the Commission. Political and other aspects were considered by the General Assembly, its Special Committee to Investigate Israeli Practices Affecting the Human Rights of the Population of the Occupied Territories and other bodies (see PART TWO, Chapter IV).

Reports of the Secretary-General. As requested in 1987,[53] the Secretary-General reported to the Commission in January 1988[54] that he had brought the Commission's two 1987 resolutions on human rights violations in the Israeli-occupied territories to the attention of Governments and General Assembly and Security Council members, the Committee on Israeli practices, and the Committee on the Exercise of the Inalienable Rights of the Palestinian People; they had also been transmitted to the specialized agencies, the United Nations Relief and Works Agency for Palestine Refugees in the Near East, the Council of Europe, the Organization of African Unity, the Organization of American States and the League of Arab States. Information on human rights in the Israeli-occupied territories, including the resolutions, was disseminated through United Nations press releases, publications, audio-visual programmes, fact-finding missions for media representatives and journalists' encounters on the question of Palestine.

Also in accordance with a 1987 Commission request,[53] the Secretary-General submitted a list of all United Nations reports issued since 13 March 1987 on the situation of the population of the occupied Arab territories.[55]

Human Rights Commission action. On 15 February,[56] by a roll-call vote of 31 to 8, with 4 abstentions, the Commission reaffirmed that occupation itself was a fundamental violation of the human rights of the civilian population of the occupied Arab territories, including Palestine, and that Israel's continuous grave violations of the 1949 Geneva Convention relative to the Protection of Civilian Persons in Time of War (fourth Geneva Convention) and the 1977 Additional Protocols to the Geneva Conventions[57] were war crimes and an affront to humanity. It strongly condemned Israel's policy of physical violence in occupied Palestine and its continued violation of the human rights of the Palestinian people under the "iron fist" policy. The Commission rejected and reiterated its condemnation of Israel's attempts to subject the West Bank and Gaza Strip to Israeli laws and its decision to annex Jerusalem and to change the architecture, demographic and institutional structure or status of the territories, considering those measures null and void.

It condemned again the establishment of Israeli settlements and the arming of settlers in occupied Palestine; aggression against Islamic and Christian holy places and the obstruction of religious freedoms and practices; evacuation, deportation, expulsion, displacement and transfer of Palestinians and the denial of their right to return and the

settlement of alien populations on their land; mass arrests, collective punishment, administrative detention and torture of detainees; and the repression of cultural and educational institutions, the pillaging of archaeological and cultural property and the expropriation of Palestinian resources. The Commission called on the Israeli authorities to implement Security Council resolutions calling for the immediate return of elected mayors to their municipalities and of deported citizens to their homeland, and urged Israel to refrain from policies and practices violating human rights in the occupied territories. It requested the General Assembly to recommend that the Security Council adopt measures against Israel under the United Nations Charter, and asked the Secretary-General to give the resolution wide publicity and to provide the Commission with all United Nations reports on the situation in the occupied territories.

Also on 15 February,[58] by a roll-call vote of 31 to 1, with 11 abstentions, the Commission, reaffirming the applicability of the fourth Geneva Convention to the territories, including Jerusalem, strongly condemned Israel for refusing to apply that Convention and for ill-treating and torturing Palestinian detainees and prisoners, urging it to grant prisoner-of-war status to all captured Palestinian fighters and to treat them accordingly. It also strongly condemned Israel for deporting Palestinians, calling on it to refrain from that policy and to rescind its deportation decisions. The Commission urged Israel to co-operate with and allow ICRC to visit all Palestinian and Arab detainees in Israeli prisons, and also urged States parties to the fourth Geneva Convention to ensure compliance with its provisions in the occupied territories, including Jerusalem. It called on Israel to respect its obligations under the Charter and other international instruments, requested it to release all Arabs detained for fighting for self-determination and liberation and to accord them prisoner-of-war status pending their release, and demanded that it cease all acts of torture and ill-treatment of Palestinian and Arab detainees and prisoners.

By a third resolution,[59] adopted on the same day by a roll-call vote of 31 to 1, with 11 abstentions, the Commission strongly condemned Israel for persistently disregarding and defying United Nations resolutions on the Syrian Golan Heights, and strongly deprecated its failure to end occupation and cease human rights violations. Demanding that Israel allow the Special Committee on Israeli practices access to the occupied Arab territories, the Commission declared once again that Israeli occupation of the Golan Heights and its 1981 decision[60] to impose its laws, jurisdiction and administration on the territory were acts of aggression. It declared that decision null and void and without international legal effect as a violation of international law and the Charter, and called on Israel to rescind it. It condemned Israel's persistence in changing the Golan Heights' physical character, demographic composition, institutional structure and legal status and emphasized that displaced persons must be allowed to return and recover their property. It further emphasized the need for Israel's total and unconditional withdrawal from the occupied Palestinian and Syrian territories, including Jerusalem. The Commission deplored the inhuman treatment, terror and practices applied against Syrian citizens, including the imposition of Israeli citizenship and identity cards on them, which was a flagrant violation of international human rights instruments and humanitarian law, and called on Israel to cease such acts of terrorism. It also condemned Israel for repressing educational institutions in the Golan Heights and imposing courses promoting hatred, prejudice and religious intolerance.

Strongly deploring the negative vote and pro-Israeli position of a Security Council permanent member, which had prevented the Council from adopting measures against Israel under Chapter VII of the Charter, the Commission reaffirmed its request to all Member States not to recognize any jurisdiction, laws or measures established by Israel in the occupied territories, and called on the specialized agencies and other international organizations to conform their relations with Israel to the terms of the Commission's resolution. It asked the Secretary-General to provide the Special Committee on Israeli practices with the resources necessary to visit the occupied territories and investigate Israeli policies and practices, and to give wide publicity to the resolution.

The Secretary-General was requested to report in 1989 on progress in implementing the resolutions and to bring them to the attention of Governments, United Nations organs and agencies, intergovernmental and international humanitarian organizations and NGOs.

Sub-Commission action. On 31 August,[61] by a roll-call vote of 16 to 1, with 7 abstentions, the Sub-Commission affirmed that Israeli occupation constituted a gross violation of human rights in the occupied territories and that acts perpetrated by Israel that caused the death or physical harm to Palestinians, as well as the obstruction of delivery of food and medical supplies to their cities, villages and camps, imposition of curfews and attacks on their houses, mosques and hospitals, were grave violations of international law. It also affirmed the right of Palestinians to resist the occupation by all means, including the uprising, and reaffirmed their inalienable rights to return to their homeland, to self-determination and to establish an independent and sovereign State. Reaffirming that

the fourth Geneva Convention was applicable to the occupied territories and that Israel's violation of its provisions by torturing and ill-treating Palestinian detainees, imposing collective punishment and administrative detention, expelling and deporting Palestinians and destroying their properties were crimes of war, the Sub-Commission condemned Israel for such practices, calling on it to desist from them and withdraw from the occupied territories. It also condemned Israel for occupying and annexing the Golan Heights, its 1981 decision[60] to impose its laws, jurisdiction and administration on that territory, which, the Sub-Commission reaffirmed, was null and void and had no legal validity, and its inhuman treatment and terrorist practices against Syrians for their refusal of Israeli citizenship and identity cards.

The Sub-Commission requested States and international organizations not to recognize Israeli laws or jurisdiction in respect of the Golan Heights, and supported the call to convene an international peace conference on Palestine and the Middle East, in accordance with a 1983 General Assembly resolution.[62] The Secretary-General was asked to provide the Sub-Commission in 1989 with an updated list of reports, studies, statistics, documents and United Nations decisions and resolutions on Palestine and other Arab territories.

Pursuant to a similar request made in 1987,[63] the Secretary-General presented such a list in May 1988.[64]

Other alleged human rights violations

On 10 March,[65] the Commission decided to accept Cuba's invitation to its Chairman and five other members, to be appointed following regional consultations, to visit Cuba to observe the human rights situation, and asked them to report on the results of their mission.

On 27 May, by **decision 1988/139**, the Economic and Social Council approved the Commission's decision.

Mass exoduses

Human Rights Commission action. On 10 March,[66] the Commission invited Governments and international organizations to intensify their co-operation and assistance in efforts to address the problems resulting from mass exoduses of refugees and displaced persons and the causes of such exoduses, and requested States to ensure the implementation of the relevant international instruments to avert new massive flows of refugees and displaced persons. It renewed its request to the Secretary-General to inform the Assembly in 1988 of action taken pursuant to the 1986 report of the

Group of Governmental Experts on International Co-operation to Avert New Flows of Refugees,[67] and asked him to inform the Commission in 1989 of developments concerning efforts to enable the United Nations to anticipate and react more adequately and speedily to cases requiring humanitarian assistance.

Report of the Secretary-General. In response to a 1987 General Assembly request[68] and the Commission's resolution (see above), the Secretary-General submitted in October 1988 a report on human rights and mass exoduses, with a later addendum.[69] He summarized the activities of the United Nations Office for Research and Collection of Information, established in 1987 to provide early warning of situations requiring his attention and to monitor factors related to possible refugee flows and similar emergencies. Those activities focused on identifying existing refugee-related activities and communication channels within the United Nations system; surveying NGOs and services capable of monitoring possible refugee flows; obtaining relevant information on emerging situations; and creating an early-warning system.

The Secretary-General also provided views and information from Brazil, Mexico and the United States on the question of mass exoduses and their related activities.

GENERAL ASSEMBLY ACTION

On 8 December, on the recommendation of the Third Committee, the General Assembly adopted **resolution 43/154** without vote.

Human rights and mass exoduses

The General Assembly,

Mindful of its general humanitarian mandate under the Charter of the United Nations to promote and encourage respect for human rights and fundamental freedoms,

Deeply disturbed by the continuing scale and magnitude of exoduses of refugees and displacements of population in many regions of the world and by the human suffering of millions of refugees and displaced persons,

Conscious of the fact that human rights violations are one of the multiple and complex factors causing mass exoduses of refugees and displaced persons, as indicated in the study of the Special Rapporteur of the Commission on Human Rights on this subject[a] and also in the report of the Group of Governmental Experts on International Co-operation to Avert New Flows of Refugees,

Aware of the recommendations concerning mass exoduses made by the Commission on Human Rights to its Sub-Commission on Prevention of Discrimination and Protection of Minorities and to special rapporteurs to be taken into account when they are studying violations of human rights in any part of the world,

Deeply preoccupied by the increasingly heavy burden being imposed, particularly upon developing countries with limited resources of their own and upon the international community as a whole, by these sudden mass exoduses and displacements of population,

Stressing the need for international co-operation aimed at averting new massive flows of refugees in parallel with the provision of durable solutions to actual refugee situations,

Reaffirming its resolution 41/70 of 3 December 1986, in which it endorsed the conclusions and recommendations contained in the report of the Group of Governmental Experts on International Co-operation to Avert New Flows of Refugees,

Recalling its resolutions 35/196 of 15 December 1980, 37/186 of 17 December 1982, 38/103 of 16 December 1983, 39/117 of 14 December 1984, 40/149 of 13 December 1985, 41/70, 41/148 of 4 December 1986 and 42/144 of 7 December 1987, and Commission on Human Rights resolutions 30(XXXVI) of 11 March 1980, 29(XXXVII) of 11 March 1981, 1982/32 of 11 March 1982, 1983/35 of 8 March 1983, 1984/49 of 14 March 1984, 1985/40 of 13 March 1985, 1986/45 of 12 March 1986, 1987/56 of 11 March 1987 and 1988/70 of 10 March 1988,

Welcoming the steps taken so far by the United Nations to examine the problem of massive outflows of refugees and displaced persons in all its aspects, including its root causes,

1. *Recalls* the recommendation of the Group of Governmental Experts on International Co-operation to Avert New Flows of Refugees that the principal organs of the United Nations should make fuller use of their respective competencies under the Charter of the United Nations for the prevention of new massive flows of refugees and displaced persons;

2. *Invites* all Governments and intergovernmental and humanitarian organizations concerned to intensify their co-operation and assistance in world-wide efforts to address the serious problems resulting from mass exoduses of refugees and displaced persons, and also the causes of such exoduses;

3. *Requests* all Governments to ensure the effective implementation of the relevant international instruments, in particular in the field of human rights, as this would contribute to averting new massive flows of refugees and displaced persons;

4. *Invites* the Commission on Human Rights to keep the question of human rights and mass exoduses under review with a view to making appropriate recommendations concerning further measures to be taken in this matter;

5. *Takes note* of the report of the Secretary-General on human rights and mass exoduses;

6. *Encourages* the Secretary-General to continue to take the necessary steps to discharge the function and responsibilities described in the report of the Group of Governmental Experts on International Co-operation to Avert New Flows of Refugees;

7. *Notes* the establishment by the Secretary-General of the Office for Research and the Collection of Information to co-ordinate information-gathering and analysis with United Nations bodies so as to provide early warning on developing situations requiring the Secretary-General's attention, as well as to provide a focal point within the United Nations system for policy responses;

---

[a]E/CN.4/1503.

8. *Urges* the Secretary-General to use the resources available to consolidate and strengthen the early warning system in the humanitarian area by, *inter alia*, early computerization of the Office for Research and the Collection of Information and strengthened co-ordination among the relevant parts of the United Nations system, especially the Office for Research and the Collection of Information, as well as the Office of the United Nations High Commissioner for Refugees, the Centre for Human Rights of the Secretariat and the relevant specialized agencies;

9. *Requests* the Secretary-General to report to the General Assembly at its forty-fourth session on the strengthened role that the Secretary-General could play in undertaking early warning activities, especially in the humanitarian area, as well as on any further developments relating to the recommendations contained in the report of the Group of Governmental Experts on International Co-operation to Avert New Flows of Refugees;

10. *Decides* to continue consideration of the question of human rights and mass exoduses at its forty-fourth session.

General Assembly resolution 43/154

8 December 1988   Meeting 75   Adopted without vote

Approved by Third Committee (A/43/868) without vote, 30 November (meeting 57); 17-nation draft (A/C.3/43/L.77), orally revised; agenda item 12.
Sponsors: Australia, Canada, Colombia, Costa Rica, Germany, Federal Republic of, Greece, Guatemala, Italy, Luxembourg, Japan, Jordan, Pakistan, Samoa, Senegal, Somalia, Thailand, United States.
Meeting numbers. GA 43rd session: 3rd Committee 49-57; plenary 75.

Genocide

On 7 March,[70] the Commission strongly condemned the crime of genocide and affirmed the necessity for international co-operation towards its elimination. It noted that many States had ratified or acceded to the 1948 Convention on the Prevention and Punishment of the Crime of Genocide[21] and urged those that had not done so to become parties without delay.

Status of the 1948 Convention

As at 31 December 1988,[12] 99 States had ratified, acceded or succeeded to the Convention. Two States—Antigua and Barbuda and the United States—became parties in 1988. In July,[71] the Secretary-General reported to the General Assembly on the status of the Convention as at 1 July 1988.

GENERAL ASSEMBLY ACTION

On 8 December, on the recommendation of the Third Committee, the General Assembly adopted **resolution 43/138** without vote.

Status of the Convention on the Prevention and Punishment of the Crime of Genocide
The General Assembly,
Recalling its resolutions 40/142 of 13 December 1985, 41/147 of 4 December 1986 and 42/133 of 7 December 1987,
Recalling also Commission on Human Rights resolutions 1986/18 of 10 March 1986, 1987/25 of 10 March 1987 and 1988/28 of 7 March 1988,

Recalling its resolution 260 A (III) of 9 December 1948, by which it approved and proposed for signature, ratification or accession the Convention on the Prevention and Punishment of the Crime of Genocide,
Reaffirming once again its conviction that genocide is a crime under international law, contrary to the spirit and aims of the United Nations,
Convinced that international co-operation is necessary in order to liberate mankind from such an odious crime,
Recognizing that crimes of genocide have caused great losses to mankind,
Taking note of the report of the Secretary-General,
1. *Once again strongly condemns* the crime of genocide;
2. *Reaffirms* the necessity of international co-operation in order to liberate mankind from such an odious crime;
3. *Notes with satisfaction* that many States have ratified the Convention on the Prevention and Punishment of the Crime of Genocide or have acceded thereto;
4. *Expresses its conviction* that implementation of the provisions of the Convention by all States is necessary for the prevention and punishment of the crime of genocide;
5. *Urges* those States which have not yet become parties to the Convention to ratify it or accede thereto without further delay;
6. *Invites* the Secretary-General to submit to the General Assembly at its forty-fourth session a report on the status of the Convention.

General Assembly resolution 43/138

8 December 1988   Meeting 75   Adopted without vote

Approved by Third Committee (A/43/868) without vote, 29 November (meeting 56); 5-nation draft (A/C.3/43/L.55); agenda item 12.
Sponsors: Afghanistan, Byelorussian SSR, Pakistan, Poland, USSR.
Meeting numbers. GA 43rd session: 3rd Committee 49-56; plenary 75.

Other aspects of human rights violations

Recovery of assets illegally removed by human rights violators

On 7 March,[72] the Commission, mindful of the need to apply the principle that human rights violators should not be allowed to benefit from their crimes, requested all States concerned to co-operate in the speedy recovery of the assets belonging to the peoples of the Philippines and Haiti illegally removed by the Marcos and Duvalier families, respectively.

Compensation for human rights violations

On 1 September,[73] the Sub-Commission recognized that all victims of gross human rights violations should be entitled to restitution, compensation and the means for rehabilitation, and that in the event of death as a result of such violations the victims' dependants should be entitled to fair and just compensation. It decided to discuss the matter in 1989 with a view to considering the possibility of developing some basic principles and guidelines in that respect.

REFERENCES

[1]YUN 1970, p. 530, ESC res. 1503(XLVIII), 27 May 1970.
[2]YUN 1967, p. 509. [3]E/CN.4/1988/8. [4]YUN 1987, p. 799,
ESC res. 1987/63, 29 May 1987. [5]E/1988/12 (dec. 1988/102).
[6]*Ibid.* (res. 1988/9). [7]YUN 1978, pp. 915 & 916, SC res.
435(1978) & 439(1978), 29 Sep. & 13 Nov. 1978. [8]E/1988/12
(res. 1988/10). [9]YUN 1974, p. 152. [10]E/CN.4/1989/3 (dec.
1988/101). [11]*Ibid.* (res. 1988/4). [12]*Multilateral Treaties Deposited
with the Secretary-General: Status as at 31 December 1988* (ST/LEG/
SER.E/7), Sales No. E.89.V.3. [13]YUN 1973, p. 103, GA res.
3068(XXVIII), annex, 30 Nov. 1973. [14]YUN 1976, p. 575.
[15]A/43/516. [16]E/CN.4/1988/32. [17]E/CN.4/1988/30/Add.1-8.
[18]E/CN.4/1988/31 & Add.1-3. [19]E/CN.4/1988/30. [20]E/1988/12
(res. 1988/14). [21]YUN 1948-49, p. 959, GA res. 260 A (III),
annex, 9 Dec. 1948. [22]YUN 1978, p. 677. [23]E/1988/12 (res.
1988/12). [24]YUN 1987, p. 799. [25]E/1988/12 (res. 1988/13).
[26]E/CN.4/Sub.2/1988/6 & Add.1 & Corr.1. [27]E/CN.4/1989/3
(res. 1988/3). [28]A/43/646. [29]E/1988/27. [30]E/CN.4/1988/25.
[31]YUN 1966, pp. 419 & 423, GA res. 2200 A (XXI), annex,
16 Dec. 1966. [32]E/1988/12 (res. 1988/67). [33]A/43/742.
[34]E/CN.4/1988/24. [35]E/1988/12 (res. 1988/69). [36]A/43/705.
[37]E/1988/12 (res. 1988/17). [38]E/1988/89/Add.1. [39]E/CN.4/
1989/3 (res. 1988/15). [40]E/1988/12 (dec. 1988/105). [41]E/CN.4/
1989/28. [42]E/CN.4/1988/7. [43]E/1988/12 (res. 1988/78).
[44]E/CN.4/1989/3 (res. 1988/16). [45]A/43/624. [46]E/CN.4/
1988/23. [47]E/1988/12 (res. 1988/65). [48]E/CN.4/1989/3 (res.
1988/13). [49]A/43/736. [50]E/CN.4/1989/3 (res. 1988/12).
[51]E/1988/12 (res. 1988/66). [52]A/43/630. [53]YUN 1987, p. 819.
[54]E/CN.4/1988/3. [55]E/CN.4/1988/5. [56]E/1988/12 (res.
1988/1 A). [57]YUN 1977, p. 706. [58]E/1988/12 (res. 1988/1 B).
[59]*Ibid.* (res. 1988/2). [60]YUN 1981, p. 308. [61]E/CN.4/1989/3
(res. 1988/10). [62]YUN 1983, p. 278, GA res. 38/58 C, 13
Dec. 1983. [63]YUN 1987, p. 820. [64]E/CN.4/Sub.2/1988/8.
[65]E/1988/12 (dec. 1988/106). [66]*Ibid.* (res. 1988/70). [67]YUN
1986, p. 851. [68]YUN 1987, p. 821, GA res. 42/133, 7 Dec.
1987. [69]A/43/743 & Add.1. [70]E/1988/12 (res. 1988/28).
[71]A/43/478. [72]E/1988/12 (res. 1988/20). [73]E/CN.4/1989/3
(res. 1988/11).

Other human rights questions

Additional Protocols I and II to the 1949 Geneva Conventions

In response to a 1986 General Assembly request,[1] the Secretary-General reported in August 1988[2] on the status of the two 1977 Protocols Additional to the Geneva Conventions of 12 August 1949 for the protection of war victims.[3] A list of States that had ratified or acceded to the Protocols as at 28 July 1988 was annexed to the report.

As at 31 December 1988, 77 States and the United Nations Council for Namibia had ratified or acceded to Protocol I (on protection of victims of international armed conflicts). Seven States—Democratic People's Republic of Korea, Guyana, Liberia, New Zealand, Nigeria, Qatar and Solomon Islands—did so in 1988. All of these parties—except 11—also adhered to Protocol II (on protection of victims of non-international conflicts). Two States—France and the Philippines—adhered only to Protocol II.

GENERAL ASSEMBLY ACTION

On 9 December, on the recommendation of the Sixth (Legal) Committee, the General Assembly adopted **resolution 43/161** without vote.

Status of the Protocols Additional to the Geneva Conventions of 1949 and relating to the protection of victims of armed conflicts

The General Assembly,

Recalling its resolutions 32/44 of 8 December 1977, 34/51 of 23 November 1979, 37/116 of 16 December 1982, 39/77 of 13 December 1984 and 41/72 of 3 December 1986,

Having considered the report of the Secretary-General on the status of the Protocols Additional to the Geneva Conventions of 1949 and relating to the protection of victims of armed conflicts,

Convinced of the continuing value of established humanitarian rules relating to armed conflicts and the need to respect and ensure respect for these rules in all circumstances within the scope of the relevant international instruments pending the earliest possible termination of such conflicts,

Mindful of the need for consolidating and implementing the existing body of international humanitarian law and for the universal acceptance of such law,

Particularly mindful of the need to protect the civilian population, especially women and children, against the effects of hostilities, and of the role of the International Committee of the Red Cross, the national Red Cross and Red Crescent societies and civil defence organizations in this respect,

Noting with appreciation the continuing efforts of the International Committee of the Red Cross to promote and to disseminate knowledge of the two additional Protocols,

1. *Notes with appreciation* the virtually universal acceptance of the Geneva Conventions of 1949 and the increasingly wide acceptance of the two additional Protocols of 1977;

2. *Notes,* however, the fact that, in comparison with the Geneva Conventions, the number of States parties to the two additional Protocols is still limited;

3. *Appeals* to all States parties to the Geneva Conventions of 1949 that have not yet done so to consider becoming parties also to the additional Protocols at the earliest possible date;

4. *Calls upon* all States becoming parties to Protocol I to consider making the declaration provided for under article 90 of that Protocol;

5. *Requests* the Secretary-General to submit to the General Assembly at its forty-fifth session a report on the status of the additional Protocols based on information received from Member States;

6. *Decides* to include in the provisional agenda of its forty-fifth session the item entitled "Status of the Protocols Additional to the Geneva Conventions of 1949 and relating to the protection of victims of armed conflicts: report of the Secretary-General".

General Assembly resolution 43/161

9 December 1988   Meeting 76   Adopted without vote

Approved by Sixth Committee (A/43/819) without vote, 28 October (meeting 24); 9-nation draft (A/C.6/43/L.5); agenda item 127.
Sponsors: Austria, Denmark, Finland, Iceland, Libyan Arab Jamahiriya, Netherlands, New Zealand, Norway, Sweden.
Meeting numbers. GA 43rd session: 6th Committee 11-13, 21, 24; plenary 76.

Rights of the child

Draft convention

Working group activities. The open-ended working group on a draft convention on the rights of the child met twice in 1988—from 25 January to 5 February and on 7 and 10 March,[4] and from 28 November to 9 December.[5]

At the earlier session, the group completed the first reading of the draft convention and requested that its technical review be completed by 31 August. At the latter session, the group began the second reading of the draft.

Human Rights Commission action. On 10 March,[6] the Commission, noting that the working group had completed the first reading of the draft convention, decided to continue its work on the draft as a matter of highest priority, and requested the Economic and Social Council to authorize a further session of the group in 1988, with a view to completing the second reading. It also requested the Secretary-General to circulate the text of the draft convention to all States to facilitate their participation in its second reading, and to provide the necessary resources for its technical review. The Commission further recommended a draft resolution for adoption by the Council (see below).

ECONOMIC AND SOCIAL COUNCIL ACTION

On 27 May, on the recommendation of its Second Committee, the Economic and Social Council adopted **resolution 1988/40** without vote.

Question of a convention on the rights of the child

The Economic and Social Council,

Taking note of General Assembly resolution 42/101 of 7 December 1987, in which the Assembly requested the Commission on Human Rights to give the highest priority to the elaboration of a draft convention on the rights of the child, to make every effort at its forty-fourth and forty-fifth sessions to complete it, and to submit it, through the Economic and Social Council, to the Assembly at its forty-fourth session, in 1989,

Considering that it was not found possible to complete the work on the draft convention at the forty-fourth session of the Commission,

Taking note of Commission on Human Rights resolution 1988/75 of 10 March 1988,

1. *Authorizes,* within existing resources, the open-ended working group of the Commission on Human Rights to meet for a period of up to two weeks in November-December 1988, with a view to completing the second reading of the draft convention on the rights of the child prior to the forty-fifth session of the Commission so that it may be submitted, through the Economic and Social Council, to the General Assembly at its forty-fourth session;

2. *Requests* the Secretary-General to continue to provide to the working group all the support and facilities necessary for the successful completion of its task, to circulate to all States the report of the working group and

the text of the draft convention as adopted during its first reading, and to provide the resources necessary for the technical review requested by the working group and for the meeting of the working group in November-December 1988.

Economic and Social Council resolution 1988/40

27 May 1988   Meeting 16   Adopted without vote

Approved by Second Committee (E/1988/89/Add.1) without vote, 23 May (meeting 20); draft by Commission on Human Rights (E/1988/12 & Corr.1); agenda item 10.

GENERAL ASSEMBLY ACTION

On 8 December, on the recommendation of the Third Committee, the General Assembly adopted **resolution 43/112** without vote.

Question of a convention on the rights of the child

The General Assembly,

Recalling its previous resolutions, as well as Commission on Human Rights and Economic and Social Council resolutions, on the question of a convention on the rights of the child,

Reaffirming that children's rights require special protection and call for continuous improvement of the situation of children all over the world, as well as their development and education in conditions of peace and security,

Profoundly concerned that the situation of children in many parts of the world remains critical as a result of unsatisfactory social conditions, natural disasters, armed conflicts, exploitation, illiteracy, hunger and disability and convinced that urgent and effective national and international action is called for,

Mindful of the important role of the United Nations Children's Fund and the United Nations in promoting the well-being of children and their development,

Convinced of the positive contribution that an international convention on the rights of the child, as a standard-setting accomplishment of the United Nations in the field of human rights, would make to protecting children's rights and ensuring their well-being,

Noting with appreciation that the first reading of a full text of a draft convention on the rights of the child has been completed by the open-ended working group of the Commission on Human Rights,

Bearing in mind that 1989 marks the thirtieth anniversary of the Declaration on the Rights of the Child and the tenth anniversary of the International Year of the Child,

Considering that these anniversaries could constitute an appropriate target date for completion of the work on a draft convention on the rights of the child and for its adoption by the General Assembly at its forty-fourth session, in 1989,

Bearing in mind the necessity of taking due account of the cultural values and needs of developing countries in the second reading of the draft convention on the rights of the child, in order to achieve the universal recognition of those rights in the future convention,

1. *Welcomes* Economic and Social Council resolution 1988/40 of 27 May 1988, in which the Council authorized a meeting of the open-ended working group of the Commission on Human Rights for a period of up to two weeks in November-December 1988, with a view

to completing the second reading of the draft convention on the rights of the child prior to the forty-fifth session of the Commission;

2. *Requests* the Commission on Human Rights to give the highest priority to the draft convention on the rights of the child and to make every effort at its session in 1989 to complete it and to submit it, through the Economic and Social Council, to the General Assembly at its forty-fourth session;

3. *Invites* all Member States to offer their active support to the completion of the draft convention on the rights of the child in 1989, the year of the thirtieth anniversary of the Declaration on the Rights of the Child and of the tenth anniversary of the International Year of the Child;

4. *Requests* the Secretary-General to provide all the support and facilities necessary for the successful completion and adoption of the draft convention on the rights of the child;

5. *Decides* to include in the provisional agenda of its forty-fourth session an item entitled ''Adoption of the convention on the rights of the child''.

General Assembly resolution 43/112

8 December 1988   Meeting 75   Adopted without vote

Approved by Third Committee (A/43/871) without vote, 28 November (meeting 55); 68-nation draft (A/C.3/43/L.46); agenda item 99.
Sponsors: Algeria, Angola, Argentina, Australia, Austria, Bangladesh, Bolivia, Botswana, Brazil, Bulgaria, Burkina Faso, Byelorussian SSR, Canada, China, Colombia, Congo, Costa Rica, Côte d'Ivoire, Cuba, Cyprus, Czechoslovakia, Democratic Yemen, Denmark, Ecuador, Egypt, Ethiopia, Finland, France, German Democratic Republic, Greece, Hungary, India, Indonesia, Italy, Jordan, Libyan Arab Jamahiriya, Luxembourg, Madagascar, Mexico, Mongolia, Morocco, Netherlands, New Zealand, Nicaragua, Nigeria, Norway, Panama, Peru, Philippines, Poland, Portugal, Romania, Samoa, Senegal, Spain, Sri Lanka, Sweden, Syrian Arab Republic, Tunisia, Ukrainian SSR, USSR, Uruguay, Venezuela, Viet Nam, Yemen, Yugoslavia, Zaire, Zimbabwe.
Meeting numbers. GA 43rd session: 3rd Committee 39-43, 46, 51, 55; plenary 75.

Sale of children and child labour

Reports of the Secretary-General. In a June report[7] submitted to the Sub-Commission in response to its 1987 request,[8] the Secretary-General summarized the recommendations of the Sub-Commission's Working Group on Slavery and Slavery-like Practices (renamed the Working Group on Contemporary Forms of Slavery by the Commission on 8 March 1988) since its first session in 1975,[9] pertaining, *inter alia*, to the sale of children, child prostitution and exploitation of child labour.

A preliminary report on the sale of children,[10] submitted by the Secretary-General to the Sub-Commission in July, provided information relating to organ transplant and the foetus trade received as at 20 June from three States, one United Nations body, three specialized agencies, the Inter-American Commission on Human Rights and nine NGOs. The Secretary-General pointed out, however, that more substantive information was needed to meet the Sub-Commission's 1987 request[8] that those matters be given a deeper and broader accent in the report.

Working Group activities. The Working Group on Contemporary Forms of Slavery, at its thirteenth session (Geneva, 1-5 and 12 August),[11] recommended that the Secretary-General, with the support of interested specialized agencies and NGOs, complete his final report on the sale of children for submission to it in 1989, and that Member States be urged to enact legislation against child pornography and consider establishing national institutions to protect children and to promote their rights. (See also above, under ''Civil and political rights''.)

Sub-Commission action. On 1 September,[12] the Sub-Commission appealed to relevant international institutions to promote the education of children on the dangers of child prostitution and child pornography. It recommended that United Nations agencies dedicated to child welfare study the problem of child labour with a view to assisting in its eradication, and that United Nations and intergovernmental bodies and banks involved in development projects ensure that no child be employed either directly or through local subcontractors. It further recommended for adoption by the Commission a resolution endorsing the recommendations of the Working Group.

Youth and human rights

In 1988, the Sub-Commission considered the question of a report on human rights and youth, entrusted to Special Rapporteur Dumitru Mazilu (Romania) in 1985.[13] On 15 August,[14] by a roll-call vote of 15 to 2, with 4 abstentions, the Sub-Commission requested the Secretary-General to seek assistance from the Government of Romania in establishing contact with the Special Rapporteur to help him complete his report, if he so wished. The Sub-Commission was subsequently informed that Romania had rejected the request to allow a visit to the Special Rapporteur, stating that the Secretariat had no juridical basis to intervene in a matter between a citizen and his Government.

On 1 September,[15] by a roll-call vote of 16 to 4, with 3 abstentions, the Sub-Commission requested the Secretary-General to invoke the applicability of the 1946 Convention on the Privileges and Immunities of the United Nations[16] to ensure the completion of the report and, in case of non-concurrence by Romania with the applicability of that Convention, to bring the matter to the attention of the Commission on Human Rights in 1989. It requested the Commission, in the latter event, to urge the Economic and Social Council to request an advisory opinion from the International Court of Justice on the applicability of the Convention to the case.

Sexual minorities

In June,[17] the Secretary-General transmitted to the Sub-Commission a study on the legal and social problems of sexual minorities (homosexuals, lesbians and transsexuals), including male prostitution, prepared pursuant to a 1983 Economic and Social Council resolution[18] and requested by the Sub-Commission in 1987.[19] The study contained a number of recommendations relating to the protection of the rights of sexual minorities.

Traditional practices affecting the health of women and children

Human Rights Commission action. On 9 March,[20] the Commission requested the Sub-Commission to consider, at its 1988 session, measures to be taken at the national and international levels to eliminate traditional practices affecting the health of women and children, and to report to it in 1990.

Sub-Commission action. On 1 September,[21] the Sub-Commission, concerned about continuing harmful practices violating the rights of women and children and taking into consideration a 1986 study of the special working group on the subject[22] and a pertinent resolution of the Commission,[23] requested one of its members, Halima Embarek Warzazi (Morocco), to study recent developments regarding such practices and to report to it in 1989. It also requested the Secretary-General to provide her with all necessary assistance.

Human rights and science and technology

UNU report. The Secretary-General transmitted to the Commission at its 1988 session a preliminary report on human rights and scientific and technological developments,[24] prepared by the United Nations University (UNU) in response to a 1986 Commission resolution.[25] The report concluded that under prevailing conditions, developments in and transfer of science and technology tended to aggravate inequality of decision-making power and the exercise of autonomy within and among countries as a result of disparities in their institutional competence. The second phase of UNU's work on the subject would focus on assessing various means for minimizing such disparities.

Human Rights Commission action. On 9 March,[26] the Commission invited UNU, in co-operation with other interested academic and research institutions, to continue studying the positive and negative impact of scientific and technological developments on human rights, and expressed the hope that it would be informed of the results in 1990.

Reports of the Secretary-General. The Secretary-General presented to the Commission at its 1988 session a report[27] on the implementation of a 1986 Commission resolution[28] on the use of science and technology exclusively in the interests of international peace and for promoting human rights. The report contained views and comments on that resolution, received as at 27 November 1987 from 10 Governments, one United Nations body and two NGOs.

In June, in response to a 1985 request,[29] the Secretary-General reported to the Sub-Commission on the interrelationship between human rights and international peace.[30] The report concluded that the interrelationship between peace, disarmament and human rights and development was evident in the Charter of the United Nations, its resolutions and decisions and a number of international treaties and declarations, and that measures for strengthening peace and security would promote human rights standards worldwide, contribute to the elimination of all forms of discrimination, and give way to other considerations of a political, economic or social character. Annexed to the report was a list of reports and studies on the subject, published by the United Nations.

Human Rights Commission action. On 9 March,[31] by a roll-call vote of 30 to 9, with 4 abstentions, the Commission stressed once again the urgent need to strengthen peace and halt the arms race, thus contributing to ensuring the right to life, and the importance of implementing disarmament measures that would release substantial resources for socio-economic development, particularly for the benefit of developing countries. It called on States to take measures with a view to prohibiting any war propaganda, and requested the Secretary-General to report to it in 1990, in the light of comments and views from Member States.

GENERAL ASSEMBLY ACTION

On 8 December, on the recommendation of the Third Committee, the General Assembly adopted **resolution 43/111** without vote.

Human rights and scientific and technological developments: the right to life

The General Assembly,

Reaffirming the determination of the peoples of the United Nations to save succeeding generations from the scourge of war, to reaffirm faith in the dignity and worth of the human person, to maintain international peace and security and to develop friendly relations among peoples and international co-operation in promoting and encouraging universal respect for human rights and fundamental freedoms,

Recalling the relevant provisions of the Universal Declaration of Human Rights, the International Covenant on Economic, Social and Cultural Rights and the International Covenant on Civil and Political Rights,

Reaffirming that the inherent dignity and the equal and inalienable rights of all members of the human family are the foundation of freedom, justice and peace in the world,

Recalling the fundamental importance of the right to life,

Conscious that it is only the creative genius of man that makes progress and the development of civilization possible in a peaceful environment, and that human life must be recognized as supreme,

Recalling its resolution 42/99 of 7 December 1987,

Recalling Commission on Human Rights resolution 1988/60 of 9 March 1988,

1. *Reaffirms* that all people have an inherent right to life;

2. *Recalls* the historic responsibility of the Governments of all countries of the world to preserve civilization and to ensure that everyone enjoys his inherent right to life;

3. *Calls upon* all States to do their utmost to assist in implementing the right to life through the adoption of appropriate measures at both the national and international level;

4. *Calls upon* all States, appropriate United Nations bodies, the specialized agencies and intergovernmental and non-governmental organizations concerned to take the necessary measures to ensure that the results of scientific and technological progress, the material and intellectual potential of mankind, are used for the benefit of mankind and for promoting and encouraging universal respect for human rights and fundamental freedoms;

5. *Emphasizes* the importance of promoting international understanding based on tolerance, friendship and peaceful co-operation;

6. *Calls upon* Governments and intergovernmental and non-governmental organizations to intensify their efforts with a view to strengthening mutual understanding and trust in the spirit of peace and respect for human rights;

7. *Decides* to consider this question at its forty-fifth session under the item entitled "Human rights and scientific and technological developments".

General Assembly resolution 43/111

8 December 1988   Meeting 75   Adopted without vote

Approved by Third Committee (A/43/870) without vote, 29 November (meeting 56); 15-nation draft (A/C.3/43/L.48/Rev.1); agenda item 98.

Sponsors: Afghanistan, Bulgaria, Byelorussian SSR, Cuba, Czechoslovakia, German Democratic Republic, Hungary, Lao People's Democratic Republic, Nicaragua, Poland, Romania, Ukrainian SSR, USSR, Viet Nam, Zimbabwe.

Meeting numbers. GA 43rd session: 3rd Committee 39-43, 46, 51, 55, 56; plenary 75.

Implementation of the Declaration on the use of scientific and technological progress

On 9 March,[32] by a roll-call vote of 30 to none, with 13 abstentions, the Commission stressed the importance of the implementation by all States of the 1975 Declaration on the Use of Scientific and Technological Progress in the Interests of Peace and for the Benefit of Mankind,[33] and called on all States to ensure that scientific and technological achievements were placed at the service of mankind. The Commission again requested the Sub-Commission to un-

dertake a study on the use of scientific and technological achievements to ensure the right to work and development and decided to consider that study in 1990.

GENERAL ASSEMBLY ACTION

On 8 December, on the recommendation of the Third Committee, the General Assembly adopted **resolution 43/110** by recorded vote.

Human rights and scientific and technological developments

The General Assembly,

Noting that scientific and technological progress is one of the decisive factors in the development of human society,

Reaffirming once again the great importance of the Declaration on the Use of Scientific and Technological Progress in the Interests of Peace and for the Benefit of Mankind, adopted by the General Assembly in its resolution 3384(XXX) of 10 November 1975,

Considering that implementation of the Declaration will contribute to the strengthening of international peace and the security of peoples and to their economic and social development, as well as to international co-operation in the field of human rights,

Bearing in mind the relevant provisions of the Declaration on Social Progress and Development,

Realizing that the science and technology of our times create possibilities for providing an abundance of material wealth on Earth and establishing conditions for the prosperity of society as well as the all-round development of every person,

Seriously concerned that the results of scientific and technological progress could be used for the arms race and the development of new types of weapons to the detriment of international peace and security and social progress, human rights and fundamental freedoms and the dignity of the human person,

Emphasizing the growing importance of intellectual work, of interaction between science, technology and society, and of the humanistic, moral and ethical orientation of science and of scientific and technological progress,

Convinced that in the era of modern scientific and technological progress the resources of mankind and the activities of scientists should be used for peaceful economic, social and cultural development of countries and for the improvement of the living standards of all people,

Recognizing that the establishment of the new international economic order calls in particular for an important contribution to be made by science and technology to economic and social progress,

Bearing in mind that the exchange and transfer of scientific and technological knowledge is one of the important ways to accelerate the social and economic development of the developing countries,

1. *Stresses* the importance of the implementation by all States of the provisions and principles contained in the Declaration on the Use of Scientific and Technological Progress in the Interests of Peace and for the Benefit of Mankind in order to promote human rights and fundamental freedoms;

2. *Calls upon* all States to make every effort to use the achievements of science and technology in order to promote peaceful social, economic and cultural devel-

opment and progress and to put an end to the use of these achievements for military purposes;

3. *Also calls upon* States to take all necessary measures to place all the achievements of science and technology at the service of mankind and to ensure that they do not lead to the degradation of the natural environment;

4. *Requests* the specialized agencies and other organizations of the United Nations system to take into account in their programmes and activities the provisions of the Declaration;

5. *Requests* the Commission on Human Rights to continue to give special attention, in its consideration of the item entitled "Human rights and scientific and technological developments", to the question of the implementation of the provisions of the Declaration;

6. *Invites* the Commission on Human Rights to take appropriate measures and to assist the Sub-Commission on Prevention of Discrimination and Protection of Minorities in preparing the study requested by the Commission in its resolutions 1982/4 of 19 February 1982, 1984/29 of 12 March 1984, 1986/11 of 10 March 1986 and 1988/61 of 9 March 1988;

7. *Decides* to include in the provisional agenda of its forty-fourth session the item entitled "Human rights and scientific and technological developments".

General Assembly resolution 43/110

8 December 1988   Meeting 75   133-0-24 (recorded vote)

Approved by Third Committee (A/43/870) by recorded vote (106-0-23), 23 November (meeting 51); 38-nation draft (A/C.3/43/L.47); agenda item 98.

Sponsors: Afghanistan, Algeria, Angola, Argentina, Bangladesh, Benin, Bolivia, Bulgaria, Burkina Faso, Burundi, Byelorussian SSR, Colombia, Costa Rica, Côte d'Ivoire, Cuba, Cyprus, Czechoslovakia, Democratic Yemen, German Democratic Republic, Hungary, Lao People's Democratic Republic, Libyan Arab Jamahiriya, Madagascar, Mali, Mongolia, Morocco, Nepal, Nicaragua, Panama, Peru, Poland, Romania, Sierra Leone, Syrian Arab Republic, Ukrainian SSR, USSR, Viet Nam, Zambia.

Meeting numbers. GA 43rd session: 3rd Committee 39-43, 46, 51; plenary 75.

Recorded vote in Assembly as follows:

In favour: Afghanistan, Algeria, Angola, Antigua and Barbuda, Argentina, Bahamas, Bahrain, Bangladesh, Barbados, Belize, Benin, Bhutan, Bolivia, Botswana, Brazil, Brunei Darussalam, Bulgaria, Burkina Faso, Burma, Burundi, Byelorussian SSR, Cameroon, Cape Verde, Central African Republic, Chad, Chile, China, Colombia, Comoros, Congo, Costa Rica, Côte d'Ivoire, Cuba, Cyprus, Czechoslovakia, Democratic Kampuchea, Democratic Yemen, Djibouti, Dominica, Dominican Republic, Ecuador, Egypt, El Salvador, Equatorial Guinea, Ethiopia, Fiji, Gabon, Gambia, German Democratic Republic, Ghana, Grenada, Guatemala, Guinea, Guinea-Bissau, Guyana, Haiti, Honduras, Hungary, India, Indonesia, Iran, Iraq, Jamaica, Jordan, Kenya, Kuwait, Lao People's Democratic Republic, Lebanon, Lesotho, Liberia, Libyan Arab Jamahiriya, Madagascar, Malawi, Malaysia, Maldives, Mali, Malta, Mauritania, Mauritius, Mexico, Mongolia, Morocco, Mozambique, Nepal, Nicaragua, Niger, Nigeria, Oman, Pakistan, Panama, Papua New Guinea, Paraguay, Peru, Philippines, Poland, Qatar, Romania, Rwanda, Saint Kitts and Nevis, Saint Lucia, Saint Vincent and the Grenadines, Samoa, Sao Tome and Principe, Saudi Arabia, Senegal, Seychelles, Sierra Leone, Singapore, Solomon Islands, Somalia, Sri Lanka, Sudan, Suriname, Swaziland, Syrian Arab Republic, Thailand, Togo, Trinidad and Tobago, Tunisia, Uganda, Ukrainian SSR, USSR, United Arab Emirates, United Republic of Tanzania, Uruguay, Vanuatu, Venezuela, Viet Nam, Yemen, Yugoslavia, Zaire, Zambia, Zimbabwe.

Against: None.

Abstaining: Australia, Austria, Belgium, Canada, Denmark, Finland, France, Germany, Federal Republic of, Greece, Iceland, Ireland, Israel, Italy, Japan, Luxembourg, Netherlands, New Zealand, Norway, Portugal, Spain, Sweden, Turkey, United Kingdom, United States.

Computerized personal files

Report of the Special Rapporteur. In July, Special Rapporteur Louis Joinet (France) submitted to the Sub-Commission a final report on guidelines for the regulation of computerized personal data files.[34] The report analysed comments and suggestions on the provisional draft guidelines, proposed by the Rapporteur in 1983,[35] received from Governments and international organizations in response to a 1985 Sub-Commission request.[29] It also commented on proposed amendments with regard to the principles laying a basis for national legislation and to files kept by international organizations and agencies. Annexed to the report were the revised final draft guidelines and a list of bodies that had provided information thereon.

Sub-Commission action. On 1 September,[36] the Sub-Commission recommended a draft resolution to the Commission, by which it would decide to publish the study on the guidelines and recommend them for adoption by the General Assembly.

Hazardous technologies

In a June report with later addenda,[37] the Secretary-General transmitted to the Sub-Commission replies from Argentina and the Philippines, received in response to a 1985 Sub-Commission request,[29] and dealing with transnational corporations and enterprises operating in those countries, whose technologies, processes or products might be hazardous to human lives or health. The report noted that replies were also received from Brunei Darussalam, which stated that it had no comments on the subject, and from Cyprus, stating that there were no such corporations or enterprises operating under its jurisdiction. Annexed to the report was the table of contents of the first volume of the *Anthology of International Policies on Industrial Process Safety*, prepared by the United Nations Centre on Transnational Corporations.

Movement and dumping of toxic and dangerous products and waste

In May, the Secretary-General submitted to the Economic and Social Council a preliminary report on illegal traffic in toxic and dangerous products and wastes[38] (see PART THREE, Chapter VIII).

Sub-Commission action. On 1 September,[39] the Sub-Commission recommended to the Commission a draft resolution, by which it would request States producing toxic and dangerous wastes to ban their exportation to countries technically incapable of their environmentally sound disposal; abrogate existing agreements for the disposal of such wastes and products with those countries; and expedite elaboration of a global convention on the control of transboundary movements of hazardous wastes by the United Nations Environment Programme. The Secretary-General would be requested to report on the convention to the Sub-Commission in 1989.

Chemical weapons and the right to life

On 1 September,[40] the Sub-Commission urged States to curb the spread of chemical weapons and to cut off their supply to countries proven to have used them. It requested the Secretary-General to collect information on the use of chemical weapons and on the danger they represent to life and other human rights, and to report to it in 1989 on the information received.

Human rights of disabled persons

Report of the Special Rapporteur. In June, Special Rapporteur Leandro Despouy (Argentina) submitted to the Sub-Commission a progress report[41] on his study on the relationship between human rights and disability, in response to a 1985 Sub-Commission request.[13] The report analysed information received from Governments and international organizations dealing with the objectives and focus of the study; multilateral activities relating to the disabled; national legislation and practices; and NGO activities. It also provided general observations on the structure and main points of the final report.

Sub-Commission action. On 25 August,[42] the Sub-Commission requested the Special Rapporteur to continue his work and to submit a final report to it in 1990. It also requested the Secretary-General to provide the Rapporteur with all possible assistance.

Human rights of the individual and international law

In response to a 1985 Sub-Commission request,[13] Special Rapporteur Erica-Irene A. Daes (Greece) submitted in July 1988 a study on the status of the individual and contemporary international law,[43] mandated by the Commission on Human Rights in 1981 and authorized by the Economic and Social Council the same year.[44] The study provided an overview of contemporary international law, reviewed institutions and concepts related to the protection of the individual and his responsibilities, discussed the individual as a subject of international duties and as a subject in contemporary international law, and considered the international procedural capacity of the individual

and his position in the European Communities and in the inter-American system.

It concluded that the legal doctrine after the Second World War prevailingly recognized a world community of individuals who were subjects of international law along with States, and that the individual became the bearer of rights under the rules of international law. The study recommended greater popularization of international human rights standards and dissemination of information on the promotion, protection and restoration of those rights; creation or development of mechanisms accessible to individuals for protecting their rights, reviewing violations of such rights and ensuring the redress of those violations, and appealing to international procedures when violations occurred; easier access for individuals to international courts and tribunals; and the accordance of personality under international law with certain rights and responsibilities as a subject of such law. Other recommendations dealt with international instruments and the status of the individual and with proposed studies on related topics.

Sub-Commission action. On 1 September,[45] the Sub-Commission requested the Special Rapporteur to update her study for submission in 1989. It also requested the Secretary-General to provide the Rapporteur with all necessary assistance.

REFERENCES

[1]YUN 1986, p. 776, GA res. 41/72, 3 Dec. 1986. [2]A/43/532. [3]YUN 1977, p. 706. [4]E/CN.4/1988/28 & Corr.1. [5]E/CN.4/1989/48 & Corr.1. [6]E/1988/12 (res. 1988/75). [7]E/CN.4/Sub.2/1988/29. [8]YUN 1987, p. 824. [9]YUN 1975, p. 639. [10]E/CN.4/Sub.2/1988/30. [11]E/CN.4/Sub.2/1988/32. [12]E/CN.4/1989/3 (res. 1988/31). [13]YUN 1985, p. 931. [14]E/CN.4/1989/3 (dec. 1988/102). [15]Ibid. (res. 1988/37). [16]YUN 1946-47, p. 100. [17]E/CN.4/Sub.2/1988/31. [18]YUN 1983, p. 918, ESC res. 1983/30, 26 May 1983. [19]E/CN.4/1988/37 (res. 1987/31). [20]E/1988/12 (res. 1988/57). [21]E/CN.4/1989/3 (res. 1988/34). [22]YUN 1986, p. 778. [23]Ibid., p. 779. [24]E/CN.4/1988/48. [25]YUN 1986, p. 780. [26]E/1988/12 (res. 1988/59). [27]E/CN.4/1988/29. [28]YUN 1986, p. 781. [29]YUN 1985, p. 933. [30]E/CN.4/Sub.2/1988/2. [31]E/1988/12 (res. 1988/60). [32]Ibid., (res. 1988/61). [33]YUN 1975, p. 631, GA res. 3384(XXX), 10 Nov. 1975. [34]E/CN.4/Sub.2/1988/22. [35]YUN 1983, p. 904. [36]E/CN.4/1989/3 (res. 1988/29). [37]E/CN.4/Sub.2/1988/21 & Add.1,2. [38]E/1988/72. [39]E/CN.4/1989/3 (res. 1988/26). [40]Ibid. (res. 1988/27). [41]E/CN.4/Sub.2/1988/11. [42]E/CN.4/1989/3 (res. 1988/8). [43]E/CN.4/Sub.2/1988/33 & Add.1. [44]YUN 1981, p. 976, ESC dec. 1981/142, 5 May 1981. [45]E/CN.4/1989/3 (res. 1988/40).

Chapter XI

Health, food and nutrition

During 1988, the United Nations continued to respond to the international problems relating to health, food and nutrition. The spread of acquired immunodeficiency syndrome (AIDS) posed a greater threat to human health; the World Health Organization reported a 15-fold increase over a four-year period. In October, the General Assembly urged continued support for the world-wide struggle against AIDS (resolution 43/15).

At the mid-point of the United Nations Decade of Disabled Persons (1983-1992), the Economic and Social Council, in May, reiterated the need to launch a special global awareness and fund-raising campaign to give added momentum to the Decade (resolution 1988/45). The Assembly, in December, stressed that, for the second half of the Decade, emphasis should be placed on the equalization of opportunities for disabled persons (43/98).

For the second consecutive year, world food consumption exceeded production, threatening food security and raising prices. In May, the World Food Council adopted the Cyprus Initiative against Hunger in the World, calling for an urgent review of the efforts made to date in reducing hunger. In December, the Assembly called for the strengthening of technical co-operation among developing countries in food and agriculture (43/190). The Assembly also urged the international community to increase aid to developing countries with the aim of increasing food production, thereby stimulating economic growth and social progress (43/191).

Health

Human and environmental health

A wide array of environmental hazards continued to pose a potential threat to human health. Pollutants and hazardous substances became more numerous and more dangerous with increasing industrialization, urbanization and general development.

The World Health Organization (WHO) co-operated with its Member States in building up their ability to deal with environmental hazards. In co-operation with the United Nations Environ-ment Programme (UNEP) and the Food and Agriculture Organization of the United Nations (FAO), WHO continued to monitor and control pollution through the Global Environmental Monitoring System, which provided data on environmental quality throughout the world.

An assessment of global air and water quality based on data collected by WHO and UNEP since the mid-1970s—the most comprehensive assessment of its kind ever made—indicated that more than a billion people lived in areas where the air contained disturbingly high levels of sulphur dioxide and dust. Severe water pollution affected many developing countries. Food contamination, on the other hand, showed a downward trend. (See also PART SEVEN, Chapter V, on the work of WHO.)

AIDS prevention and control

In May, the Secretary-General transmitted to the General Assembly the WHO Director-General's report on a global strategy for the prevention and control of AIDS.[1] The report, requested by the Assembly in 1987,[2] gave an epidemiological overview and described WHO's direction and co-ordination of the global AIDS strategy.

Jointly with the United Kingdom, WHO organized the World Summit of Ministers of Health on Programmes for AIDS Prevention, (London, 26-28 January). By the London Declaration on AIDS Prevention, the ministers undertook to devise national programmes to prevent and contain the spread of human immunodeficiency virus (HIV) infection as part of their countries' health systems.

The World Health Assembly in May endorsed the London Declaration and stressed the need to protect the human rights and dignity of HIV-infected people.

The number of AIDS cases reported to WHO continued to rise rapidly in 1988. As at 1 April, 85,273 cases had been reported by 137 of 173 reporting countries—a 15-fold increase over four years. This included 62,536 cases, or 73 per cent, in the Americas, 90 per cent of which were in the United States. Africa and Europe each reported nearly 13 per cent of the world total, while Asia and the Pacific reported slightly over 1 per cent. The report also described modes of transmission and global epidemiological patterns, and estimated that 5 million to 10 million people were currently infected with HIV world-wide.

In March, WHO and the United Nations Development Programme (UNDP) established an alliance to combat AIDS. The alliance was to support countries in developing, implementing, monitoring and evaluating multisectoral national AIDS plans. In addition, the World Bank was collaborating with WHO in studying the economic impact of AIDS in the developing world and the demographic impact of the disease.

A new WHO AIDS series was launched in January with the publication of *Guidelines for the Development of a National AIDS Prevention and Control Programme.* The second in the series, *Guidelines for Sterilization and High Level Disinfection Methods Effective against HIV,* was published in April. The guidelines were distributed to all ministries of health.

The annual International Conference on AIDS, the major forum of information exchange, was held at Stockholm, Sweden, in June. A major effort was made to support national programmes in evaluating staff needs, defining skills and providing training. The number of training activities under the global programme increased from 20 in 1987 to 61 in 1988.

A range of scientific and technical meetings were held during the year on matters of global importance, such as blood safety, drug and vaccine development, social and behavioural research, HIV-2, health promotion for AIDS prevention and epidemiological surveillance and modelling.

UNDP action. In a report on co-operation against AIDS,[3] the UNDP Administrator recommended that UNDP lend up to $2 million to WHO to finance national AIDS activities between the pledging and the receipt of external funds. He also recommended approval of a $700,000 global blood safety initiative to establish blood transfusion services ensuring adequate and safe blood supplies. The project would be carried out under the WHO global programme on AIDS in co-operation with UNDP, the League of Red Cross and Red Crescent Societies and the International Society of Blood Transfusion. The funds would be used to prepare a meeting of a consortium of international organizations familiar with the technical, economic and structural needs and concerns of government and medical personnel throughout the world and to finance any activities recommended by the consortium.

On 17 February,[4] the UNDP Governing Council noted the Administrator's report and approved the two projects.

UNICEF activities. A February 1988 report of the United Nations Children's Fund (UNICEF) reviewed the impact of AIDS on women and children and the UNICEF response.[5] The report discussed the medical and socio-economic problems created by AIDS for infants, children, adolescents and women in developing countries and outlined a policy framework for the Fund's approach to AIDS. It recommended that UNICEF consider the problem of AIDS as it affected children and women; increase co-operation with Governments, the WHO special programme on AIDS and other multilateral, bilateral and non-governmental organizations (NGOs); continue efforts to ensure the safety of immunization programmes and promote equipment sterilization; train staff in the patterns of the disease; increase support for specific projects on health education; and strengthen maternal and child health and primary health care structures, especially in African countries where such care was inadequate.

In April,[6] the UNICEF Executive Board endorsed the Fund's programme involvement as described in the report.

ECONOMIC AND SOCIAL COUNCIL ACTION

On 27 July, the Economic and Social Council adopted **resolution 1988/55** without vote.

Prevention and control of acquired immunodeficiency syndrome (AIDS)

The Economic and Social Council,

Recalling its resolution 1987/75 of 8 July 1987, General Assembly resolution 42/8 of 26 October 1987, World Health Assembly resolution WHA41.24 of 13 May 1988 and other relevant resolutions,

Recalling also the London Declaration on AIDS Prevention, adopted by the World Summit of Ministers of Health on Programmes for AIDS Prevention on 28 January 1988,

Acknowledging the established leadership and the essential role of the World Health Organization in the global direction and co-ordination of AIDS prevention, control, research and education, and noting with appreciation the efforts of the World Health Organization, other United Nations agencies and funds and national Governments,

1. *Decides* to transmit to the General Assembly for consideration at its forty-third session the report of the Director-General of the World Health Organization on the global strategy for the prevention and control of AIDS;

2. *Notes with satisfaction* the arrangements made by the Secretary-General, in close co-operation with the Director-General of the World Health Organization, to ensure a co-ordinated response by the United Nations system to the AIDS pandemic pursuant to General Assembly resolution 42/8 and Economic and Social Council resolution 1987/75, and welcomes those arrangements within the context of the global strategy;

3. *Invites* the General Assembly to consider the report of the Director-General of the World Health Organization and the present response of the United Nations system to the AIDS pandemic and to take an appropriate decision on further action.

Economic and Social Council resolution 1988/55

27 July 1988   Meeting 39   Adopted without vote

33-nation draft (E/1988/L.43), orally revised following informal consultations; agenda item 17.

Sponsors: Australia, Austria, Belgium, Bulgaria, Canada, Colombia, Cuba, Denmark, Finland, France, German Democratic Republic, Germany, Federal Republic of, Greece, Ireland, Italy, Jamaica, Japan, Netherlands, Norway, Pakistan, Peru, Poland, Portugal, Rwanda, Spain, Sweden, Uganda, USSR, United Kingdom, United States, Uruguay, Venezuela, Zaire.
Meeting numbers. ESC 33, 34, 37, 39.

GENERAL ASSEMBLY ACTION

On 27 October, the General Assembly, on the recommendation of the Second (Economic and Financial) Committee, adopted **resolution 43/15** without vote.

Prevention and control of acquired immunodeficiency syndrome (AIDS)

The General Assembly,

Deeply concerned that acquired immunodeficiency syndrome (AIDS) has assumed pandemic proportions affecting all regions of the world and represents a threat to the attainment of health for all,

Recalling its resolution 42/8 of 26 October 1987, Economic and Social Council resolution 1988/55 of 27 July 1988, World Health Assembly resolution WHA41.24 of 13 May 1988 and other relevant resolutions,

Recalling also the London Declaration on AIDS Prevention, adopted by the World Summit of Ministers of Health on Programmes for AIDS Prevention on 28 January 1988,

Noting with satisfaction the development and implementation of the global strategy for the prevention and control of AIDS prepared by the World Health Organization, including the establishment of appropriate inter-agency mechanisms, and noting with appreciation the efforts of the World Health Organization, other United Nations agencies and funds, and national Governments,

Recognizing the urgent need to pursue multilateral efforts to promote and improve human health, control disease and extend health care in order to accomplish the objective of health for all by the year 2000,

1.   *Reaffirms* the established leadership and the essential role of the World Health Organization in the global direction and co-ordination of AIDS prevention, control, research and education, commends those Governments which have initiated action to establish national programmes for the prevention and control of AIDS in line with the global strategy for the prevention and control of AIDS prepared by the World Health Organization, and urges other Governments to take similar action;

2.   *Takes note* of the World Health Organization Global Programme on AIDS, and stresses the continued need for adequate resources for its implementation and the corresponding need to continue to share the pool of world-wide medical and scientific knowledge and experience in the control and prevention of the disease;

3.   *Notes* that the World Health Organization has declared 1 December 1988 World AIDS Day, and stresses the importance of the appropriate observance of that occasion;

4.   *Affirms* that the struggle against AIDS should be consistent with and not divert attention from other national public health priorities and development goals or divert international efforts and resources needed for overall health priorities;

5.   *Calls upon* all States, in addressing the AIDS problem, to take into account the legitimate concerns of other countries and the interests of inter-State relations;

6.   *Invites* the World Health Organization to continue to facilitate the exchange of information on and promotion of national and international research for the prevention and control of AIDS through the further development of Collaborating Centres of the World Health Organization and similar existing mechanisms;

7.   *Requests* the Secretary-General, in view of all the aspects of the problem, in particular the socio-economic and humanitarian aspects, to continue to ensure, in close co-operation with the Director-General of the World Health Organization and through the appropriate existing mechanisms, a co-ordinated response by the United Nations system to the AIDS pandemic;

8.   *Urges* all appropriate organizations of the United Nations system, including the specialized agencies, bilateral and multilateral agencies and non-governmental and voluntary organizations, in conformity with the global strategy, to continue to support the world-wide struggle against AIDS;

9.   *Invites* the Director-General of the World Health Organization to report to the General Assembly at its forty-fourth session, through the Economic and Social Council, on further developments in the global AIDS pandemic, and requests the Economic and Social Council to consider the report in accordance with its mandate.

General Assembly resolution 43/15

27 October 1988   Meeting 38   Adopted without vote

Approved by Second Committee (A/43/750/Add.1) without vote, 21 October (meeting 20); draft by Vice-Chairman (A/C.2/43/L.12), orally revised, based on informal consultations on 32-nation draft (A/C.2/43/L.10); agenda item 12.
Meeting numbers. GA 43rd session: 2nd Committee 16, 20; plenary 38.

Disabled persons

Implementation of the Programme of Action

Report of the Secretary-General (April). In response to a request by the General Assembly in 1987,[7] the Secretary-General in April 1988 reported[8] to the Economic and Social Council on the implementation of the 1982 World Programme of Action concerning Disabled Persons[9] and the United Nations Decade of Disabled Persons (1983-1992).

Member States and bodies and agencies of the United Nations system had been asked to comment on the Secretary-General's evaluation of the implementation of the Programme of Action during the first half of the Decade as well as on the recommendations of the 1987 global meeting of experts to review the implementation of the Programme.[10] As at 7 April 1988, the Secretary-General had received only 32 replies, 20 from Member States and 12 from United Nations organizations. Because of the small number and late arrival of replies, the Secretary-General said, there were insufficient data on which to establish a priority list for planning global activities and programmes for the remainder of the Decade and beyond. He suggested that the Council might wish to recommend that an additional and more detailed report and analysis be made available to the Assembly, on the understanding that more Governments would respond to the request for comments.

ECONOMIC AND SOCIAL COUNCIL ACTION

On 27 May, the Economic and Social Council, on the recommendation of its Second (Social) Committee, adopted **resolution 1988/45** without vote.

United Nations Decade of Disabled Persons

The Economic and Social Council,

Recalling General Assembly resolution 37/52 of 3 December 1982, by which the Assembly adopted the World Programme of Action concerning Disabled Persons, and resolution 37/53 of 3 December 1982, by which it, *inter alia,* proclaimed the period 1983-1992 the United Nations Decade of Disabled Persons,

Noting that in accordance with General Assembly resolution 39/26 of 23 November 1984, the Global Meeting of Experts to Review the Implementation of the World Programme of Action concerning Disabled Persons at the Mid-Point of the United Nations Decade of Disabled Persons was held at Stockholm from 17 to 22 August 1987,

Reaffirming the validity and value of the World Programme of Action in promoting effective measures for disability prevention, rehabilitation and the full participation and equality of disabled persons in social life and development,

Mindful that Member States bear the ultimate responsibility for the implementation of the World Programme of Action,

Stressing that the Centre for Social Development and Humanitarian Affairs of the Secretariat is the focal point within the United Nations for the implementation and monitoring of the World Programme of Action,

Reiterating the need to give greater publicity to the United Nations Decade of Disabled Persons in order to revitalize it,

Taking note with appreciation of the report of the Secretary-General, submitted in response to General Assembly resolution 42/58 of 30 November 1987 and containing the preliminary conclusions and comments of Member States and relevant organs and bodies of the United Nations system on the recommendations contained in paragraphs 10 to 39 of the report of the Global Meeting of Experts and on the report of the Secretary-General on the evaluation of the implementation of the World Programme of Action,

Noting with regret that owing to the small number of replies to the Secretary-General's request for comments and to the late arrival of those replies, there were not sufficient data on which to base a list of priorities for planning global activities and programmes for the remainder of the Decade and beyond,

1. *Urges* all Member States and relevant organs and bodies of the United Nations system that have not yet done so to submit to the Secretary-General, as soon as possible, their comments in accordance with General Assembly resolution 42/58;

2. *Requests* the Secretary-General to submit to the General Assembly at its forty-third session a more detailed report and analysis, based on the comments received, so that a list of priorities may be established for planning global activities and programmes for the remainder of the United Nations Decade of Disabled Persons and beyond;

3. *Calls upon* Member States, organs and bodies of the United Nations system and other intergovernmental and non-governmental organizations to make all possible efforts in the implementation of the World Programme of Action concerning Disabled Persons and to promote efforts at all levels in the context of the Decade;

4. *Reiterates* the need to launch a special global awareness and fund-raising campaign to give added momentum to the Decade;

5. *Welcomes* the appointment by the Secretary-General of the Special Representative for the Promotion of the United Nations Decade of Disabled Persons, whose activities will be financed from special voluntary contributions;

6. *Expresses its appreciation* to Governments and non-governmental organizations for their voluntary contributions, which have made possible the appointment of the Special Representative;

7. *Requests* the Secretary-General to report to the Commission for Social Development at its thirty-first session on the implementation of the World Programme of Action concerning Disabled Persons during the second half of the Decade, and requests the Commission to give special attention to the implementation of the World Programme of Action.

Economic and Social Council resolution 1988/45

27 May 1988   Meeting 16   Adopted without vote

Approved by Second Committee (E/1988/91) without vote, 20 May (meeting 19); 20-nation draft (E/1988/C.2/L.8); agenda item 12.
Sponsors: Belgium, Canada, China, Colombia, Egypt, Germany, Federal Republic of, Indonesia, Italy, Kenya, Libyan Arab Jamahiriya, Panama, Peru, Philippines, Poland, Rwanda, Senegal, Sierra Leone, Sudan, United States, Yugoslavia.

Report of the Secretary-General (September). In accordance with the Council's request, the Secretary-General in September submitted a new report to the General Assembly on the implementation of the World Programme of Action and the Decade.[11] Eleven more Member States had responded to the request for comments since his April report. Summarizing those comments, the Secretary-General stated that more could and should be done to motivate Governments and organizations to implement the Programme of Action and to undertake activities that would improve the living conditions of persons with disabilities. Experience from the first half of the Decade showed that additional resources had to be mobilized. Priorities for global activities and programmes during the second half of the Decade were suggested, as were national, regional and international activities.

GENERAL ASSEMBLY ACTION

On 8 December 1988, the General Assembly, on the recommendation of the Third (Social, Humanitarian and Cultural) Committee, adopted **resolution 43/98** without vote.

Implementation of the World Programme of Action concerning Disabled Persons and United Nations Decade of Disabled Persons

The General Assembly,

Recalling all its relevant resolutions, including resolution 37/52 of 3 December 1982, by which it adopted the World Programme of Action concerning Disabled Persons, and resolution 37/53 of 3 December 1982, in which it, *inter alia,* proclaimed the period 1983-1992 the United Nations Decade of Disabled Persons,

Recalling its resolution 42/58 of 30 November 1987 and reaffirming all of its relevant provisions,

Noting with appreciation that an interregional meeting of representatives of national committees on disability issues will be held early in 1989 to exchange views and information on enhancing the capabilities of such committees,

Taking note of Economic and Social Council resolution 1988/45 of 27 May 1988, in which the Council, *inter alia,* reiterated the need to launch a special global awareness and fund-raising campaign to give added momentum to the Decade, and in this regard, welcomed the appointment by the Secretary-General of the Special Representative for the Promotion of the United Nations Decade of Disabled Persons,

Noting the important work currently being undertaken by the Sub-Commission on Prevention of Discrimination and Protection of Minorities on human rights and disability, which could serve as a useful basis for the continued efforts to ensure for disabled persons the enjoyment of human rights and fundamental freedoms,

Bearing in mind that the mid-decade review to evaluate the implementation of the World Programme of Action was conducted so that a list of priorities could be established for planning global activities and programmes during the remainder of the Decade and beyond,

Taking into account the concrete measures already carried out by the Governments of Member States, the bodies and organizations of the United Nations system and non-governmental organizations to implement the objectives of the World Programme of Action within the framework of the Decade, and recognizing that much more should be done to improve the living conditions of disabled persons,

Mindful that Member States bear the ultimate responsibility for the implementation of the World Programme of Action,

Recognizing the pivotal role of the United Nations in promoting the exchange of information, experience and expertise and closer regional and interregional co-operation towards more effective strategies and policies to advance the status and welfare of disabled persons,

Stressing that the Centre for Social Development and Humanitarian Affairs of the Secretariat is the focal point within the United Nations for the implementation and monitoring of the World Programme of Action,

Noting with appreciation the steps taken by the United Nations system and by the non-governmental organizations concerned to monitor the implementation of the World Programme of Action,

Concerned that, at the mid-point of the Decade, the resource base of the Voluntary Fund for the United Nations Decade of Disabled Persons is significantly reduced from that prevailing during the first half of the Decade, and that unless this trend is reversed and the resource capacities of the Voluntary Fund are strengthened, many priority requests will not be met and the implementation of the World Programme of Action will be seriously affected,

Mindful that, since developing countries are experiencing difficulties in mobilizing resources, international co-operation should be encouraged to assist in national efforts to implement the World Programme of Action and to achieve the objectives of the Decade,

Having considered the report of the Secretary-General on the implementation of the World Programme of Action concerning Disabled Persons and the United Nations Decade of Disabled Persons,

1. *Reaffirms* the validity of the World Programme of Action concerning Disabled Persons;

2. *Stresses* that, for the second half of the United Nations Decade of Disabled Persons, special emphasis should be placed on the equalization of opportunities for disabled persons;

3. *Urges* Member States, intergovernmental organizations and non-governmental organizations concerned to translate into action at all levels, as appropriate, the priorities for global activities and programmes during the second half of the Decade, such as those set forth in the annex to the present resolution;

4. *Renews its invitation* to all States to give high priority to projects concerning the prevention of disabilities, rehabilitation and the equalization of opportunities for disabled persons within the framework of bilateral assistance, as well as financial support to strengthen organizations of disabled persons;

5. *Invites* Governments to participate actively in the international co-operation with a view to improving the living conditions of disabled persons by encouraging professional experts, in particular disabled persons, in various aspects of rehabilitation and the equalization of opportunity, including those who are in retirement and willing to work with disabled persons;

6. *Requests* the Secretary-General to encourage all organs and bodies of the United Nations system, including regional commissions, international organizations and the specialized agencies, to take into account in their programmes and operational activities the specific needs of disabled persons;

7. *Requests* the Secretary-General to take, *inter alia,* the following measures at the United Nations level:

(*a*) To disseminate widely the text of the World Programme of Action and all manuals and special publications prepared by the United Nations for the International Year of Disabled Persons, in 1981, and the Decade;

(*b*) To examine possible ways in which United Nations meetings, information materials and documents can be made more accessible to disabled persons and to determine the financial implications thereof;

(*c*) To assist Member States in establishing and strengthening national committees on disability issues and similar co-ordinating bodies;

(*d*) To promote and support the establishment of strong national organizations of disabled persons;

8. *Requests* the Secretary-General to conduct a feasibility study on the substantive, financial and administrative implications of alternative ways to mark the end of the Decade in 1992, which would include a review of the global progress achieved and obstacles encountered during the Decade and which would provide a

mechanism for preparing the actions needed until the year 2000 and beyond, and to submit the study to the General Assembly at its forty-fifth session;

9. *Requests* the Secretary-General to strengthen the regional commissions to enable them to promote technical co-operation activities and the sharing of national resources for personnel training, the exchange of information, policy and programme development and research and the participation of disabled persons;

10. *Endorses* the measures proposed by the Secretary-General in his report to strengthen the programmes and activities of the agencies and bodies of the United Nations system and to improve the co-ordination of inter-agency efforts on behalf of disabled persons;

11. *Invites* the Secretary-General and Member States to involve disabled persons to a greater extent in United Nations programmes and activities, *inter alia*, through the provision of employment opportunities;

12. *Requests* the Secretary-General to consider establishing, within existing resources, alternative structures to ensure that the issue of disability is accorded high visibility and to develop the Disabled Persons Unit of the Centre for Social Development and Humanitarian Affairs as a specialized facilitating agent engaging the available resources of the United Nations system and relevant networks outside the United Nations;

13. *Invites* the Centre to expand its close collaboration with intergovernmental and non-governmental organizations active in the field of disability, in particular organizations of disabled persons, and to consult with them on a regular and systematic basis on matters relating to the implementation of the World Programme of Action;

14. *Calls upon* Member States, national committees, the United Nations system and non-governmental organizations to assist in a global information and fund-raising campaign to publicize the Decade through all appropriate means;

15. *Recognizes* the important role of non-governmental organizations, especially those representing disabled persons, in the effective implementation of the World Programme of Action, in raising international awareness of the concerns of disabled persons and in monitoring and evaluating progress achieved during the Decade;

16. *Requests* the Secretary-General to inform the Commission for Social Development at its thirty-first session of the progress of work of the Special Representative for the Promotion of the Decade of Disabled Persons;

17. *Requests* the Secretary-General to continue to administer donated funds, using them for projects under the present structure of the Voluntary Fund for the United Nations Decade of Disabled Persons, and to continue to make new provisions in order to offer a selection of projects to donor countries that may be willing to finance a particular programme under the "Special Purpose Contributions";

18. *Reaffirms* that the resources of the Voluntary Fund should be used to support catalytic and innovative activities in order to implement further the objectives of the World Programme of Action within the framework of the Decade, with priority given, as appropriate, to programmes and projects of the least developed countries;

19. *Invites* Governments and non-governmental organizations to continue their contributions to the Volun-

tary Fund and calls upon Governments and non-governmental organizations that have not yet done so to consider contributing to the Voluntary Fund so as to enable it to respond effectively to the growing demand for assistance;

20. *Requests* the Secretary-General to report to the General Assembly at its forty-fourth session on the implementation of the present resolution;

21. *Decides* to include in the provisional agenda of its forty-fourth session the item entitled "Implementation of the World Programme of Action concerning Disabled Persons and United Nations Decade of Disabled Persons".

ANNEX
Priorities for global activities and programmes during the second half of the United Nations Decade of Disabled Persons

1. Member States, which have the main responsibility for the implementation of the World Programme of Action concerning Disabled Persons, are urged:

(a) To develop and implement national plans of action, using a multisectoral, interdisciplinary approach in consultation with organizations of disabled persons;

(b) To promote the development and functioning of organizations of disabled persons by providing technical and financial support;

(c) To establish and/or strengthen national committees or similar co-ordinating bodies;

(d) To launch a public information and education campaign in which disabled persons are portrayed as equal members of society;

(e) To support cultural activities to promote awareness of the United Nations Decade of Disabled Persons by giving disabled persons the opportunity to participate in musical, artistic and drama activities;

(f) To review, update and, where necessary, improve national legislation to ensure general conformity with international standards;

(g) To consider incorporating in their legislation and planning the rights of the disabled, including those of persons who are:

(i) Hearing-impaired, including the right to have sign language interpretation;

(ii) Visually impaired, including access to Braille material, audio aids and large print information;

(iii) Mentally impaired, including access to easy reading materials;

(iv) Speech-impaired, including access to new technologies;

(h) To formulate and implement disability-related projects for inclusion in technical co-operation programmes financed by the United Nations Development Programme through the country programmes funded by the indicative planning figures;

(i) To review and extend services and benefits available to disabled persons and their families, aimed at ensuring basic level income maintenance and promoting self-directed personal assistance, housing, transport and other facilities needed for independent living;

(j) To train personnel, including disabled persons, to build a national capability to deal with disability;

(k) To establish machinery for appropriate data collection on disabilities, to be used in national planning;

(l) To use indigenous raw materials, scientific expertise and production facilities for the manufacture and

local repair of appropriate technical aids and appliances needed by disabled persons;

(m) To accede to and implement the provisions of the Protocol to the Agreement on the Importation of Educational, Scientific and Cultural Materials, adopted at Nairobi on 26 November 1976 by the General Conference of the United Nations Educational, Scientific and Cultural Organization at its nineteenth session, concerning the duty-free international movement of equipment and material needed to assist the daily living of disabled persons;

(n) To ratify, if they have not yet done so, the Convention concerning Vocational Rehabilitation and Employment (Disabled Persons) adopted in 1983 by the International Labour Conference;

(o) To support research into the special needs of disabled persons and into programmes to benefit them and their families;

(p) To develop services and facilities to promote the rehabilitation and equalization of opportunities of disabled women, elderly disabled persons, mentally ill and other mentally impaired persons, multiple disabled persons, disabled refugees and disabled migrants.

2. Intergovernmental organizations are urged to give priority to issues concerning disabled persons and to take initiatives to implement the World Programme of Action.

3. Non-governmental organizations, which play an important role in the implementation of the World Programme of Action, are urged during the remainder of the Decade:

(a) To establish regular and systematic contacts with the United Nations system and other non-governmental organizations in collecting and disseminating information and research findings, planning activities and sharing innovative experiences and in maximizing the use of available resources;

(b) To mobilize their networks and resources to publicize the aims and objectives of the United Nations Decade of Disabled Persons;

(c) To provide regular information on their activities and meetings to the Disabled Persons Unit of the Centre for Social Development and Humanitarian Affairs of the Secretariat and actively to support its activities.

General Assembly resolution 43/98

8 December 1988   Meeting 75   Adopted without vote

Approved by Third Committee (A/43/810) without vote, 3 November (meeting 31); 31-nation draft (A/C.3/43/L.20), orally revised; agenda item 92.
Sponsors: Bangladesh, Belgium, Cameroon, Canada, China, Colombia, Costa Rica, Denmark, Dominica, Dominican Republic, Egypt, Finland, Germany, Federal Republic of, Greece, Guatemala, Italy, Kenya, Libyan Arab Jamahiriya, Mauritania, Morocco, Norway, Peru, Philippines, Romania, Samoa, Senegal, Sudan, Sweden, United States, Yugoslavia, Zimbabwe.
Meeting numbers. GA 43rd session: 3rd Committee 15-22, 25, 31; plenary 75.

UN trust fund

The Voluntary Fund for the United Nations Decade of Disabled Persons received nearly 70 requests for assistance in the 18-month period ending June 1988.[11] Of those, 24 were approved for funding, involving a resource commitment of $308,213: 4 in Africa, 7 in Asia and the Pacific, 1 in Latin America and the Caribbean, 3 in Western Asia and 9 interregional and global projects.

Projects included promotional activities, support to organizations concerned with disabled persons, data collection and applied research, training, information exchange and technical co-operation. NGOs continued to play a major role as executing agencies. The 1987-1988 biennium saw an increased focus on the integration of disabled persons into society through sports—a priority concern identified in the World Programme of Action.

On 1 April,[12] the Secretary-General appointed a Special Representative for the Promotion of the United Nations Decade of Disabled Persons to strengthen global efforts to implement the Programme of Action. Financed by voluntary contributions, his activities included promoting the objectives of the Decade, raising funds and co-operating with the Disabled Persons Unit of the Centre for Social Development and Humanitarian Affairs. Sweden contributed earmarked funds to the Unit to provide two specialized Professionals and one secretary for an initial period of one year. Other extrabudgetary resources from Sweden were to be used to establish one or two posts for special technical advisers on disability to cover selected Member States in Africa and in Asia and the Pacific. Finland also contributed earmarked funds to the Unit for one Professional and one support-staff post.

The 1988 United Nations Pledging Conference for Development Activities resulted in pledges of only $91,000 from nine Governments—a substantial reduction from the $175,933 pledged in 1987.[13]

The Fund's income in 1988, including special earmarked contributions, totalled $1,030,369; expenditures amounted to $627,792.

REFERENCES

[1]A/43/341-E/1988/80. [2]YUN 1987, p. 645, GA res. 42/8, 26 Oct. 1987. [3]DP/1988/1 & Add.1. [4]E/1988/19 (dec. 88/5). [5]E/ICEF/1988/L.7. [6]E/1988/18 (res. 1988/7). [7]YUN 1987, p. 650, GA res. 42/58, 30 Nov. 1987. [8]E/1988/32. [9]YUN 1982, p. 980. [10]YUN 1987 p. 647. [11]A/43/634 & Add.1. [12]E/CN.5/1989/6. [13]A/44/406/Rev.1.

Food and agriculture

Food problems

World production of staple foods declined by 3 per cent in 1988, falling below aggregate consumption for the second consecutive year. This decline was due to the worst drought in half a century in the United States and Canada, coupled with poor production in many other countries. In a report to the World Food Council (WFC) on the current world food situation,[1] FAO provided an overview of the food supply, food and agricultural trade, official external assistance and food aid, and food availability and nutrition.

While food output, including crops and livestock, decreased by 3.5 per cent in the developed countries in 1988, developing countries increased their overall production by 3.2 per cent (1.2 per cent on a per capita basis).

The decline in cereal supplies and higher international grain prices exacerbated the difficulties for low-income, food-deficit countries facing increased cereal import requirements. World cereal stocks were expected to fall below global food security requirements by the end of the 1988/89 season. FAO estimated that the higher market prices would reduce the volume of food aid in cereals to 3.3 million tons below the level of the previous season.

In April 1988, 23 countries were experiencing exceptional food shortages and required additional and/or emergency food aid. The shortages were particularly severe in Bangladesh, Ethiopia and the Sudan.

In a June report,[2] requested by the Economic and Social Council in 1987,[3] the Secretary-General reviewed trends in international agricultural markets with special reference to the share of developing countries. The Council, in **decision 1988/177** of 29 July, took note of the report.

WFC activities

The 36-member WFC, the highest international body dealing with food problems, held its fourteenth ministerial session at Nicosia, Cyprus, from 23 to 26 May 1988.[4] In its report, WFC stated that the living conditions of the world's poorest people were continuing to deteriorate. Famine and food shortages in developing countries continued to exist despite record food surpluses in other parts of the world. In an attempt to address this problem, WFC adopted the Cyprus Initiative against Hunger in the World, calling for an urgent review and assessment of the efforts made to date in reducing world hunger. It further called for the improvement of current policies and programmes as well as new initiatives to eliminate hunger and malnutrition. It asked its President, with the assistance of an *ad hoc* consultative group, to review the policies and instruments available to combat hunger and malnutrition in developing countries, to identify obstacles that might have hindered their impact and to recommend a course of action to combat hunger more effectively.

WFC called for the pursuit of sustainable global food security through production systems that safeguarded natural resources and protected the environment, emphasized the benefits to all countries of liberalized international trade in agricultural and tropical products, and recommended

that UNDP adopt a proposed project to promote regional and South-South co-operation in the food and agricultural sector. It also reaffirmed the call of its 1987 Beijing Declaration[5] for strengthening South-South co-operation as a means of reinforcing individual and collective self-reliance of the developing countries.

The Economic and Social Council, by **decision 1988/177** of 29 July, took note of the WFC report.

On 20 December 1988, the General Assembly, on the recommendation of the Second Committee, adopted two resolutions on food and agriculture. **Resolution 43/190** was adopted without vote.

Strengthening technical co-operation among developing countries in food and agriculture

The General Assembly,

Recalling its resolution 33/134 of 19 December 1978, in which it endorsed the Buenos Aires Plan of Action for Promoting and Implementing Technical Co-operation among Developing Countries,

Recalling also its other resolutions on technical co-operation among developing countries,

Recalling further resolution 9/85 on economic and technical co-operation among developing countries, adopted on 28 November 1985 by the Conference of the Food and Agriculture Organization of the United Nations,

Noting with appreciation that the World Food Council at its thirteenth and fourteenth sessions called for the further strengthening of technical co-operation among developing countries in food and agriculture, particularly in food production, institution building, training and enhancement of management capability and the development of agro-industries and trade,

Noting with interest the progress already made in technical co-operation among developing countries in food and agriculture, especially in tripartite co-operative agreements and other existing arrangements among international institutions and organizations and developed and developing countries,

Recognizing the expertise and technological capability accumulated by developing countries in the fields of food and agriculture and food production,

Reaffirming that developing countries have the primary responsibility for promoting technical co-operation among themselves in food and agriculture, that developed countries and the United Nations system should assist and support such activities, and that in addition the United Nations system should play a prominent role as promoter and catalyst of technical co-operation among developing countries in food and agriculture, in accordance with the Buenos Aires Plan of Action,

1. *Endorses* the relevant conclusions and recommendations contained in the reports of the World Food Council on the work of its thirteenth and fourteenth sessions;

2. *Reaffirms* the role and importance of technical co-operation among developing countries in their socio-economic development in general and in their agricultural development in particular, and in the reinforcement and final achievement of their individual and collective self-reliance;

3. *Welcomes* the progress made in technical co-operation among developing countries in food and agriculture, and emphasizes that such co-operation should be carried out in accordance with the national development plans, objectives and priorities of the developing countries concerned;

4. *Affirms* that tripartite co-operative agreements and other existing arrangements constitute an effective means of promoting technical co-operation among developing countries in food and agriculture, in particular in food production, and welcomes the progress made so far in this regard;

5. *Calls upon* the developing countries, in the context of their primary responsibility for promoting technical co-operation among themselves, to place greater emphasis on technical co-operation in food and agriculture and to strengthen and improve the mechanisms for such co-operation at the national, subregional and regional levels, especially their national focal points, so as to facilitate policy co-ordination and exchange of experience;

6. *Urges* the developed countries, if so requested by participants in programmes concerning technical co-operation among developing countries, to provide financial and technical assistance to such programmes in food and agriculture, including through participation in tripartite co-operative agreements;

7. *Urges* the organizations of the United Nations system, including the Food and Agriculture Organization of the United Nations, the United Nations Development Programme and the International Fund for Agricultural Development, and other international development and financing institutions, to provide increased financial and technical assistance for technical co-operation among developing countries in food and agriculture, and in particular to encourage and take part in tripartite co-operative agreements and other arrangements;

8. *Recommends* that organizations of the United Nations system and other international development and financing institutions, within their respective spheres of competence, give priority in their programmes of work to technical co-operation among developing countries in food and agriculture;

9. *Requests* the World Food Council to continue its work in identifying effective ways and means of technical co-operation among developing countries in food and agriculture and to make recommendations thereon to the General Assembly through the Economic and Social Council;

10. *Requests* the Secretary-General to include in his report to the General Assembly on technical co-operation among developing countries, to be prepared pursuant to resolution 42/180 of 11 December 1987, information on the implementation of the present resolution, including recommendations for the enhancement of technical co-operation among developing countries in food and agriculture.

General Assembly resolution 43/190

20 December 1987   Meeting 83   Adopted without vote

Approved by Second Committee (A/43/915/Add.3) without vote, 15 November (meeting 42); draft by Bangladesh, Canada, China, Cyprus, Egypt, Germany, Federal Republic of, Mali, Mexico, Pakistan, Sierra Leone, Tunisia for Group of 77, Uruguay and Yugoslavia (A/C.2/43/L.16/Rev.1), orally revised; agenda item 82 (c).

Meeting numbers. GA 43rd session: 2nd Committee 26, 30, 42; plenary 83.

The Assembly also adopted **resolution 43/191** without vote.

Food and agricultural problems

The General Assembly,

Recalling the Declaration and the Programme of Action on the Establishment of a New International Economic Order, contained in its resolutions 3201(S-VI) and 3202(S-VI) of 1 May 1974, the Charter of Economic Rights and Duties of States, contained in its resolution 3281(XXIX) of 12 December 1974, resolution 3362(S-VII) of 16 September 1975 on development and international economic co-operation, and the International Development Strategy for the Third United Nations Development Decade, contained in the annex to its resolution 35/56 of 5 December 1980,

Recalling also its resolutions on food and agricultural problems, in particular resolution 41/191 of 8 December 1986,

Reaffirming the Universal Declaration on the Eradication of Hunger and Malnutrition adopted by the World Food Conference,

Stressing the imperative need to keep food and agricultural issues at the centre of global attention,

Reaffirming that food and agricultural problems in developing countries should be considered in a comprehensive manner in their different dimensions and in their immediate, short-term and long-term perspectives,

Emphasizing that the continuing gravity of the economic situation in Africa, including the persistence of negative trends in the food and agricultural sectors, requires urgent and decisive action by the international community to accelerate and ensure the full implementation of the United Nations Programme of Action for African Economic Recovery and Development 1986-1990, as stressed during the mid-term review of the implementation of the Programme of Action,

Welcoming the support given by the international donor community to agricultural development in developing countries and the efforts of these countries in the development of their food and agricultural sectors,

Noting with concern that the tensions concerning trade in agricultural markets remain very serious, notably owing to the persistence and, in some cases, intensification of all forms of agricultural support, including export subsidies and import restrictions, as pointed out by ministers of Governments of States members of the Organisation for Economic Co-operation and Development at their meeting in Paris on 18 and 19 May 1988,

Reaffirming that the right to food is a universal human right that should be guaranteed to all people and, in that context, believing in the general principle that food should not be used as an instrument of political pressure, either at the national or at the international level,

Deeply concerned about the worsening of the locust infestation and its spread to several regions of the developing world, particularly the recent infestation of large regions of Africa, as described in the status reports of the Food and Agriculture Organization of the United Nations, and about the grave consequences of the infestation for agriculture and food production in the countries of the affected regions,

Welcoming the ongoing work of the Global Information and Early Warning System on Food and Agriculture in monitoring the world food situation and in alerting the international community to impending problems,

Concerned that, despite some slight improvements in 1987, the economies of developing countries continue to suffer from depressed international commodity prices, protectionism and worsening terms of trade, growing debt service burden and net outflow of financial resources from developing countries as a whole, which have had a negative effect on international trade and agriculture, particularly for developing countries,

1. *Notes with concern* that hunger and malnutrition have been increasing since the World Food Conference in 1974, that the number of people suffering from hunger and malnutrition has increased in the 1980s and that the central objective of the Conference remains largely unfulfilled;

2. *Welcomes* the conclusions and recommendations contained in the report of the World Food Council on the work of its fourteenth ministerial session, held at Nicosia from 23 to 26 May 1988, in particular the Cyprus Initiative against Hunger in the World, and calls upon Governments and international and non-governmental organizations to assist the World Food Council fully in implementing the Initiative;

3. *Takes note with appreciation* of the report of the Secretary-General on trends in international agricultural markets with special reference to the share of developing countries;

4. *Stresses* the urgent need for substantial progress in stimulating food production in developing countries and the importance of increasing domestic food production, thereby stimulating national economic growth and social progress in those countries, in particular in Africa and the least developed countries, and helping to resolve the problems of hunger and malnutrition in an effective way;

5. *Urges*, in this context, the members of the international community, in particular the donor countries, to take further determined action in support of the efforts of developing countries by increasing the flow of resources, including concessional flows designated for agricultural development, and to increase their contributions to intergovernmental organizations;

6. *Stresses* the need for donor countries to increase aid commitments to food and agriculture in developing countries and the need to channel assistance through existing organizations and programmes;

7. *Also stresses* that the provision of food aid in the context of emergency situations resulting, *inter alia*, from natural disasters should be reinforced through additional rehabilitation and development assistance in order to help restore food production capacity and self-reliance;

8. *Calls* for a joint effort by all States and relevant international and intergovernmental organizations to improve the food situation and protect the nutritional levels of affected groups, in particular low-income groups, especially during the implementation of structural adjustment programmes;

9. *Affirms* that increasing food production in developing countries will significantly contribute to the eradication of poverty and the elimination of malnutrition, and recommends that a higher priority be given to supporting food production in the national development efforts of those countries in order to ensure adequate food supplies and distribution;

10. *Stresses* that the Uruguay Round of multilateral trade negotiations, launched on the occasion of the Special Session of the Contracting Parties to the General Agreement on Tariffs and Trade, held at Punta del Este, Uruguay, from 15 to 20 September 1986, presents a unique opportunity to develop a more open, viable and durable trading system, to reverse the disquieting rise in protectionism, and to bring agriculture under the strengthened and operationally effective rules and disciplines of the General Agreement on Tariffs and Trade, in accordance with the relevant provisions of the Ministerial Declaration on the Uruguay Round, and urges that concerted efforts to this end should be made at the forthcoming mid-term review of multilateral trade negotiations at Montreal, Canada, taking into account the need to provide special and differential treatment for developing countries, considering their food security objectives and the need to avoid potentially adverse effects on those countries, especially those that import food, bearing in mind the overall benefits of trade liberalization;

11. *Stresses* the need to implement fully the relevant provisions of the Ministerial Declaration concerning tropical products;

12. *Also stresses* the need to improve global economic conditions in order to establish national, subregional and regional food security in developing countries;

13. *Calls upon* the international community to support scientific and technological training and research in developing countries in order to promote agricultural development in those countries, and emphasizes the urgency of strengthening international co-operation in the field of transfer of agricultural technology and of facilitating the free exchange of information on experience and technology relating to food production, processing and storage;

14. *Also calls upon* the international community, through specific and effective measures, to support and complement the efforts made by African Governments to stimulate agriculture and food production and to implement fully the United Nations Programme of Action for African Economic Recovery and Development 1986-1990;

15. *Urges* all States members of the International Fund for Agricultural Development to take decisive action to ensure the timely conclusion of the negotiations on the third replenishment of the resources of the Fund so as to facilitate its adoption by the Governing Council of the Fund in January 1989, thus enabling the Fund to pursue its mandate of assisting developing countries in increasing their food production and in alleviating rural poverty and, to that end, appeals to all parties to make their best efforts to achieve the overall target fixed for the replenishment;

16. *Takes note with satisfaction* of the fact that the target of the Special Programme for Sub-Saharan African Countries Affected by Drought and Desertification of the Fund has been achieved, and appeals for increased contributions to the Fund;

17. *Appeals* to the international community to contribute generously to the World Food Programme so that the pledging target for the period 1989-1990, as set out in General Assembly resolution 42/164 of 11 December 1987, can be attained and the Programme can continue its activity in support of capital investment and in meeting emergency food needs;

18. *Notes with appreciation* the eighth replenishment of the International Development Association for the period 1 July 1987 to 30 June 1990, which provides for a total of 12.4 billion United States dollars, and stresses the need to draw upon those resources for the development of food and agriculture;

19. *Stresses* the need for co-ordinated international action to tackle the long-term problems of migratory pest control, particularly in Africa, and, expressing gratitude for the support of donors and recognizing the efforts made by the affected countries in the fight against the grasshopper and locust infestation, calls upon donors to continue to give high priority to the implementation and continued co-ordination by the Food and Agriculture Organization of the United Nations of emergency control programmes, as well as longer-term measures, against grasshoppers and locusts currently affecting vast areas of Africa, as well as other regions of the developing world, and to remain prepared to provide financial and technical assistance to affected countries at short notice;

20. *Takes note* of the establishment, within the framework of the World Food Council, of the informal *ad hoc* consultative group for the implementation of the Cyprus Initiative against Hunger in the World, and urges all Member States and international organizations to participate actively in the work of the group so as:

(a) To review and assess the policies and instruments currently available to combat chronic hunger and malnutrition in developing countries, particularly in low-income food-deficit countries, and to identify the reasons and obstacles that may have reduced their impact;

(b) To consider concrete and realistic measures that could make existing policies and instruments more effective;

(c) To identify workable initiatives;

(d) To recommend a course of action to combat hunger and malnutrition more effectively;

21. *Requests* the President of the World Food Council to present to the Council at its fifteenth ministerial session an action-oriented report on the Cyprus Initiative against Hunger in the World;

22. *Urges* the World Food Council to continue, within its mandate:

(a) To assess the overall impact of structural adjustment programmes in developing countries on the nutritional levels of their populations, especially among children and low-income groups, and to suggest remedial measures in that area, including ways of stimulating the provision of resources to eliminate the suffering of those groups;

(b) To assess the impact of liberalized international trade in agricultural and tropical products on all countries and especially on the food security and development efforts of developing countries and, in this context, to maintain an active interest in the progress and outcome of the Uruguay Round of multilateral trade negotiations;

(c) To promote activities related to food security and agricultural trade, as well as to regional and South-South co-operation in food and agriculture, within the context of economic growth and the development needs of developing countries;

(d) To stimulate progress in and contribute more actively to the full implementation of the food policy and programme components of the United Nations Programme of Action for African Economic Recovery and Development 1986-1990;

23. *Also urges* the World Food Council to continue to exercise leadership in sensitizing the international community to the nature, extent, causes and consequences of hunger and malnutrition and in recommending appropriate practical policies for remedial action;

24. *Requests* the Secretary-General, in consultation with the World Food Council, the United Nations Conference on Trade and Development and the Food and Agriculture Organization of the United Nations, to submit to the Economic and Social Council, at its second regular session of 1989, an updated comprehensive report on trends in the international market for agricultural and tropical products and on the liberalization of international agricultural trade, together with suggestions on ways and means of increasing the share of developing countries in that trade, while avoiding the potentially adverse short-term effects on developing countries, in particular those that import food.

General Assembly resolution 43/191

20 December 1988   Meeting 83   Adopted without vote

Approved by Second Committee (A/43/915/Add.3) without vote, 9 December (meeting 48); draft by Vice-Chairman (A/C.2/43/L.82), orally revised, based on informal consultations on draft by Tunisia, for Group of 77 (A/C.2/43/L.26); agenda item 82 *(c)*.

Meeting numbers. GA 43rd session: 2nd Committee 26, 30, 42, 48; plenary 83.

Food aid

CFA activities

At its twenty-fifth session (Rome, Italy, 30 May–9 June),[6] the Committee on Food Aid Policies and Programmes (CFA)—the governing body of the World Food Programme (WFP)—conducted its thirteenth annual review of food aid policies and programmes and approved the WFP Executive Director's annual report covering 1987 activities.[7]

Concerned about the continuing increase in emergency food aid necessitated by man-made disasters, CFA recognized the need for additional contributions to the International Emergency Food Reserve (IEFR) (see below). It requested WFP to continue to give attention to environmental deterioration and the need for sustainable development in designing and implementing projects. It also strongly endorsed a $1.8 billion Action Plan for Africa, the main objective of which was to provide a frame of reference for projecting resource flows to Africa in support of the United Nations Programme of Action for African Economic Recovery and Development 1986-1990.[8] The Committee stressed that WFP had a special role to play in Africa, in emergency situations as well as in regard to the environment, human resources development and the maintenance of infrastructure. It urged that triangular transactions and local purchases in African countries be included within the overall framework of the Plan. It also urged all concerned with food aid to co-operate with WFP in implementing the new International Food Aid Information System by providing timely and accurate data.

The Committee approved 24 projects with a combined value of $439.3 million, as well as three budget increases for approved projects, making a combined total of $466.5 million (equivalent to about 1 million tons of food).

At its twenty-sixth session (Rome, 12 December),[9] CFA approved 18 projects with a combined value of $224 million and nine budget increases for approved projects. The combined value amounted to $278.6 million, equivalent to about 437,000 tons of food. The Committee also approved the WFP plan of action for the relief and rehabilitation of Afghanistan.

WFP activities

In 1988, WFP—a joint undertaking of the United Nations and FAO—continued to provide developing countries with food aid for development purposes and emergency relief. The amount of food shipped to developing countries rose sharply in 1988, reaching 3.1 million tons, a 28 per cent increase over the previous record set in 1987.[10]

With the signing of the Geneva Accords in April (see PART TWO, Chapter III), WFP established a special Afghan task force to prepare for the repatriation of some 6 million refugees from Iran and Pakistan to Afghanistan.

For the third consecutive year, WFP spent a record amount on purchases of food—more than $136 million—though slightly less food was bought because of higher commodity prices. Purchases in developing countries reached a record $108.5 million. During the year, WFP was requested to purchase, transport or monitor 972,000 tons of food, worth $240 million, on behalf of bilateral donors. Actual shipments on behalf of bilateral donors rose 71 per cent, to an all-time high of 566,000 tons.[11]

Development assistance

At the end of 1988, WFP had 289 active development projects in its portfolio valued at $3.5 billion. Of those, 157 had components, valued at over $1.4 billion, intended to promote environmentally sustainable development.[11]

WFP in 1988 committed $779 million—representing 1.84 million metric tons of food—for 49 new development projects or project expansions, 25 per cent more than in 1987. It continued to give priority to assisting low-income, food-deficit countries, which received 86 per cent of its commitments in 1988; 3 of every 10 tons of food went to the least developed countries. Commitments for agricultural and rural development, which accounted for 56 per cent of total development commitments, rose from $298 million in 1987 to $433 million in 1988. Human resource de-

velopment accounted for the rest, most of which was allocated to the feeding of vulnerable groups (mothers, infants, pre-school children) and to students at primary schools.

The countries of sub-Saharan Africa continued to receive top priority, but WFP found it increasingly difficult to formulate sound development projects there. In 1988, $266 million was committed for new projects in the region; at 34 per cent of the total, the share was only slightly less than in 1987, although the proportion of commitments had been going down over the last three years, and current indications pointed towards a further decline.

Emergency operations

More than 15 million people in 29 countries—half of whom were refugees and displaced persons—received emergency food assistance through WFP's 65 operations approved in 1988. The year's commitment of 828,000 tons of commodities, valued at $254 million, nearly matched the record set in 1987, continuing the trend of increased need for emergency food aid.[11] Those commitments were drawn mainly from IEFR, which furnished 88 per cent of the commodities.[12]

Man-made disasters continued to require over two thirds of WFP's emergency food aid resources, with long-term assistance needed for large numbers of refugees in Ethiopia, Iran, Malawi, Pakistan and Somalia. Because of the number and severity of hurricanes, typhoons and disastrous floods during the year, 11 per cent of emergency food aid was committed to sudden natural disasters (compared to an average of 3 per cent during the previous three years), its value of $27.5 million unequalled over the previous decade.[10]

Sub-Saharan Africa received 65 per cent of the emergency resources, followed by Asia and the Pacific, 26 per cent, Latin America and the Caribbean, 6 per cent; and North Africa and the Middle East, 3 per cent.

WFP resources

WFP's receipts for 1988 totalled about $1.01 billion, while expenditures amounted to $1.1 billion. Net commitments for development projects and emergency operations totalled $1.03 billion.

Pledges and contributions

For the 1987-1988 biennium, combined total resources contributed or pledged to WFP regular resources, the Food Aid Convention and IEFR reached $1.6 billion, including some 4.5 million tons of food. By the end of 1988, 81 countries had pledged a record $1.24 billion, or 89 per cent of the target—the highest percentage in a decade.[11]

By 31 December 1988, contributions to IEFR for the year amounted to 531,336 tons of food, worth $161.6 million. However, contributions in cereals, at 441,773 tons, fell short of the annual target of 500,000 tons, even though demand substantially exceeded that amount. Twenty-two donors, including two developing countries, contributed to IEFR in 1988.

1986 Food Aid Convention

In 1988, three States (Australia, Federal Republic of Germany, United States) became parties to the Food Aid Convention, 1986, bringing the total number to 14.[13] The Food Aid Convention, together with the Wheat Trade Convention, 1986, constitutes the International Wheat Agreement, 1986.

Agricultural development

In April, the Secretary-General transmitted to the Economic and Social Council a report[14] prepared by FAO reviewing and analysing agrarian reform and rural development. The report, prepared pursuant to a 1981 decision of the Council,[15] concluded that the basic needs of the rural poor were being less well met than they were at the beginning of the decade. If life for the rural poor was to improve by the year 2000, concerted efforts would have to be made by national Governments and the international community.

The President of the International Fund for Agricultural Development, in the IFAD 1988 annual report, said the third replenishment of the Fund, which was nearing completion, should open the path to a high degree of financial autonomy for IFAD by the end of the next decade. He said that a satisfactory and timely outcome of the upcoming third replenishment would enable the Fund to broaden the coverage and further sharpen the impact of its interventions on behalf of the poor.

ECONOMIC AND SOCIAL COUNCIL ACTION

On 29 July, the Economic and Social Council, on the recommendation of its First (Economic) Committee, adopted **resolution 1988/73** without vote.

Third replenishment of the International Fund for Agricultural Development

The Economic and Social Council,

Recalling General Assembly resolution S-13/2 of 1 June 1986, the annex to which contains the United Nations Programme of Action for African Economic Recovery and Development 1986-1990, in which the international community agreed to increase support, whenever possible, to the Special Programme for Sub-Saharan African Countries Affected by Drought and Desertification of the International Fund for Agricultural Development,

Noting with appreciation that the target of $300 million for the Special Programme has been surpassed,

Recalling also its resolution 1987/90 of 9 July 1987 on food and agricultural problems and the Final Act of the seventh session of the United Nations Conference on Trade and Development,

Stressing the imperative need to strengthen international co-operation to intensify the global effort to assist the hundreds of millions of human beings who, as a result of acute poverty, continue to suffer, especially in rural areas, from hunger or chronic undernutrition,

Noting with appreciation the significant role that the International Fund for Agricultural Development has played in addressing, *inter alia*, the needs of the rural poor, including smallholders, the landless, rural women and other marginalized groups,

Noting the appeal made by the Council of Ministers of the Organization of African Unity at its forty-eighth ordinary session to strengthen financing for the fight against poverty and hunger being undertaken by the Fund,

Expressing its appreciation to those recipient developing countries that, by announcing significant increases in their contributions in convertible currency, have ensured that two thirds of their objective of $75 million has already been achieved,

Emphasizing the validity of the unique structure and mandate of the International Fund for Agricultural Development,

Emphasizing also the importance of ensuring the continuity of the lending operations of the Fund,

1. *Calls upon* all countries to demonstrate political will and flexibility so that the replenishment of the International Fund for Agricultural Development can be completed by the end of 1988, before the next session of the Governing Council of the Fund;

2. *Appeals* to all States members of the Fund to ensure that positive action is taken to reach an early agreement on the third replenishment;

3. *Invites* those recipient developing countries that have not yet done so to announce their increased contributions at the earliest possible date.

Economic and Social Council resolution 1988/73

29 July 1988   Meeting 41   Adopted without vote

Approved by First Committee (E/1988/112) without vote, 21 July (meeting 19); draft by Tunisia, for Group of 77 (E/1988/C.1/L.5), orally revised following informal consultations, orally sub-amended by Canada; further orally revised in Council by Committee Chairman, based on informal consultations; agenda item 9.

REFERENCES

(1)WFC/1989/5. (2)E/1988/70. (3)YUN 1987 p. 585, ESC res. 1987/90, 9 July 1987. (4)A/43/19. (5)YUN 1987, p. 586, ESC res. 1987/90, annex, 9 July 1987. (6)WFP/CFA:25/18. (7)YUN 1987, p. 589. (8)YUN 1986, p. 446, GA res. S-13/2, annex, 1 June 1986. (9)WFP/CFA:26/3. (10)WFP/CFA:27/P/4. (11)WFP/CFA:27/12. (12)WFP/CFA:27/SCP:2/14. (13)*Multilateral Treaties Deposited with the Secretary-General: Status as at 31 December 1988* (ST/LEG/SER.E/7), Sales No. E.89.V.3. (14)E/1988/56. (15)YUN 1981, p. 400, ESC dec. 1981/185, 23 July 1981.

Nutrition

The elimination of hunger and malnutrition remained an elusive goal in 1988, despite advances in increasing global food production, the Council of the United Nations University (UNU) stated in its report on 1988 activities.[1] Working towards that goal, UNU continued its research, training and information dissemination activities in the areas of food, nutrition and biotechnology. Research by the UNU-associated Institute of Nutrition on the cognitive effects of iron deficiency on schoolchildren in Bangkok, Thailand, confirmed a clear relationship between test performance and iron status. This research was conducted as part of a project on the social and economic consequences of chronic energy deficiency, which sought to document the behavioural, social and economic effects of chronically low energy intake and to co-ordinate an international effort to apply results of the research to national policies. An International Dietary Energy Consultancy Group was also established in connection with the project.

The International Food Data Systems Project released an updated version of its directory of food composition tables and began publication of a new UNU-sponsored *Journal of Food Composition and Analysis.*

Work began on a joint regional project of the Association of African Universities, and UNU aimed at improving co-ordination of Africa's scientific and technological resources in the areas of food and nutrition. Workshops were held on improving the quality of root and tuber products (Lagos, Nigeria, August-October) and on the development of cereals as weaning foods (Dakar, Senegal, October).

The UNU World Institute for Development Economics Research also focused on the hunger problem. It was studying alternative development strategies and their implications for food entitlements and living standards in five Asian countries. Another study used a simulation model to examine the effects of different economic development scenarios and policy changes on food consumption in sub-Saharan Africa. The investigation focused on why so many African countries, unlike many other developing countries, had been unable to prevent famine and improve nutrition.

In the area of biotechnology, UNU was attempting to strengthen the capacity of scientists in developing countries to employ both traditional and emerging techniques. The former included processes for fermenting foods, and the latter included genetic manipulation of plants and animals as well as new hybrid areas of science, such as bioelectronics. The concluding workshop of the brucellosis research network in Latin America, established to develop vaccines through biotechnology, was held in 1988, and in Africa two small-scale projects on improving food fermentation through biotechnology were initiated.

The FAO/WHO/UNICEF Inter-agency Food and Nutrition Surveillance Programme continued to co-ordinate support for the establishment of national surveillance systems designed to improve the assessment of various nutrition policy options and permit accurate monitoring of changes in nutritional status. Of 10 proposals submitted to the Programme from countries in Africa, Asia and Latin America, 3 were approved in 1988.

Twenty countries participated in an international conference on food and nutrition surveillance in the Americas (Mexico City, September), organized by the Pan American Health Organization (PAHO). Also in the Americas, a regional training course on the methodology of case-study writing in subjects related to food, nutrition and health (Costa Rica, April-June) was given jointly by the Central American Institute of Business Administration, PAHO and UNU.

Malnutrition in South-East Asia was being addressed using a combination of six strategies: development of national nutrition policies, nutrition improvement through primary health care, improved nutrition surveillance capability, national control programmes, information exchange and nutrition research. Vitamin-A and iodine deficiency was vigorously tackled throughout the region.

ACC activities

The fourteenth session of the Sub-Committee on Nutrition and its Advisory Group on Nutrition was held at Geneva from 22 to 26 February.[2] The Sub-Committee drew to the attention of the Administrative Committee on Co-ordination the potentially important interactions between nutrition and AIDS. Two symposia were held during the session, on cash cropping and nutrition and on nutrition and AIDS. The Sub-Committee also examined work in progress in the following areas: nutritional surveillance; women and nutrition; nutrition and infection; and vitamin-A, iron and iodine deficiencies.

REFERENCES

[1]E/1989/37. [2]ACC/1988/PG/1.

Chapter XII

Human resources, social and cultural development

During 1988, United Nations bodies and agencies continued to promote human resources development, social and cultural development, literacy, crime prevention and criminal justice. The year marked the fortieth anniversary of the United Nations programme in the area of crime prevention and criminal justice.

The United Nations Development Programme (UNDP) reviewed its experience in human resources development since 1970, drawing broad conclusions regarding the evolving nature of such development and technical co-operation needs, as well as the longer-term sustainability and impact of institutions after UNDP support had ended.

Under social development, the General Assembly requested the Secretary-General to submit, in 1989, a proposed date and comprehensive outline of a possible programme for an international year of the family (resolution 43/135).

The Committee on Crime Prevention and Control at its tenth session (Vienna, 22-31 August 1988) focused on the implementation of conclusions and recommendations of the Seventh (1985) United Nations Congress on the Prevention of Crime and the Treatment of Offenders and on preparations for the Eighth (1990) Congress.

In January, the World Decade for Cultural Development (1988-1997), proclaimed by the General Assembly in 1986, was launched by the Secretary-General and the Director-General of the United Nations Educational, Scientific and Cultural Organization (UNESCO). As the lead agency, UNESCO continued to make preparations for International Literacy Year (1990).

Human resources

In response to a 1986 request by the UNDP Governing Council,[1] the UNDP Administrator submitted a report in March 1988[2] analysing UNDP experience since 1970 in human resources development (HRD). The analysis was based on a review of over 100 evaluations of projects identifying factors affecting the success of HRD and had involved follow-up visits to several countries.

The Administrator, noting the need for a human resources strategy and planning framework in developing countries, stated that data were lacking on skill availabilities and needs, labour force participation rates, wage rates and incentives needed to correct labour market imbalances and the comparative efficiency of different educational and training systems. Project evaluations pointed to the need for a national focal point where human resources information, not usually found in national accounts and other aggregated data, could be collected and analysed on a continuing basis.

Regarding past experience with project design and linkages, he pointed to a number of factors that compromised project success, including heavy commitments of equipment and tight procurement schedules which were incompatible with more gradualist training requirements; a tendency to stress the development of technical capabilities to the relative neglect of management needs; project formulation without the examination of recurrent cost implications; and unexpected circumstances requiring adjustments and changes in project components. Project experience showed a lack of sensitivity to involving local communities in assessing needs, and designing and implementing projects.

In discussing evolving HRD and technical co-operation needs, the Administrator noted a number of changes that had taken place. There had been a shift away from traditional technical co-operation, characterized by long-term experts and counterpart training overseas, to a need for short-term consultants to upgrade the competence of national staff in very specific fields. In addition, an earlier emphasis on training of counterparts in technical fields was giving way to the training of trainers and the setting up of indigenous training systems. Government policies to stimulate private investment created new demands for technical co-operation, with UNDP being asked to support institutes that taught management and business skills in which private-sector interests were represented. As to high-technology projects, he suggested the formulation of a new type of umbrella consulting project which was highly flexible and from which short-term contracts could be negotiated.

Concerning the sustainability of institutions and measures of project impact, the Administrator stated that project evaluations had concluded that retention of staff trained with UNDP assistance was critical to the process of institution-building and that a key ingredient in project impact was the quality of top management. UNDP resources, he said, were relatively limited and had to be strategically employed. He cautioned against the premature withdrawal of UNDP project support, since evaluations had noted that institutions seldom became self-sustaining as of the official project-termination date.

The Administrator concluded that UNDP's resources were too limited to meet technical needs over an extended period of time and should be used to address critical constraints, for the most part at the national level, by developing systems for policy analysis and more comprehensive human resources planning and by reinforcing training strategies and techniques to respond better to human resources requirements.

Noting with concern the constraints identified in the Administrator's report which limited the impact of UNDP-funded HRD projects, the Governing Council, on 1 July,[3] recommended that they be taken into consideration in designing UNDP-assisted projects. It supported the Administrator's intention to devise a methodology to measure the impact of HRD projects on social and economic development and urged him, in designing HRD projects, to take account of the long-term nature of the institutional process. It asked him to collect and synthesize technical co-operation experience, thus ensuring that future UNDP assistance achieved maximum impact; called on him to support those aspects of the Khartoum Declaration: Towards a Human-focused Approach to Socio-economic Recovery and Development in Africa[4] that were within UNDP's mandate; and urged him to contribute to implementing specific proposals included in the Jakarta Plan of Action on Human Resources Development in the ESCAP (Economic and Social Commission for Asia and the Pacific) Region.[5] The Council requested UNDP to assist those Governments which sought its help to explore the possibility of financing their human resources requirements beyond traditional sources.

The Committee for Development Planning (see PART THREE, Chapter I) in April recommended that greater national and international priority should be given to restructuring human development programmes to reduce inefficiency and improve delivery and targeting.[6]

Education and literacy

International Literacy Year (1990)

In October,[7] the Consultative Committee on Substantive Questions (CCSQ) of the Administrative Committee on Co-ordination was informed of the activities undertaken by UNESCO as the lead agency in preparing and organizing International Literacy Year (1990), proclaimed by the General Assembly in 1987.[8]

Activities included the establishment of a secretariat to co-ordinate the activities of the

United Nations system for the Year, creation of a high-level inter-sectoral task force to deal with its planning and organization, issuance by UNESCO of journals and bulletins and the publication of guides and newsletters. CCSQ noted that all organizations were invited to establish focal points for activities related to the Year.

CCSQ supported UNESCO's initiative to send missions to organizations to discuss joint action that might be taken in relation to the Year.

UN research and training institutes

In June 1988,[9] the Secretary-General submitted his comments on a report prepared by the Joint Inspection Unit (JIU) in 1987[10] on autonomous research institutes of the United Nations. Those institutes were the United Nations Institute for Training and Research (UNITAR), the United Nations Social Defence Research Institute, the United Nations Research Institute for Social Development (see below, under "Social aspects of development"), the United Nations Institute for Disarmament Research (UNIDIR) (see PART ONE, Chapter II), the International Research and Training Institute for the Advancement of Women (see PART THREE, Chapter XIII), the Latin American Demographic Centre and the Latin American and Caribbean Institute for Economic and Social Planning (see PART TWO, Chapter V), and the African Institute for Economic Development and Planning. The JIU report did not cover the research and training institutes of the specialized agencies, nor the United Nations University (UNU) (see below), which had been the subject of an earlier JIU report.[11]

The Secretary-General agreed that the setting up of a reserve fund for each existing institute was a prudent financial measure, but he considered one year's estimated expenditure rather than two and a half to be sufficient; an alternative arrangement could be to encourage donors to create endowment funds (recommendation 1). He stated that assessed contributions would be levied against those countries that participated in the activities of the institutions and would be separate from the assessments under the regular budget of the United Nations (recommendation 2). The income-generating activities suggested by JIU could be a source of support for United Nations research institutes, but the Secretary-General reaffirmed their need to maintain independence and keep within core research mandates (recommendation 3). He stated that, given the specific measures called for in a 1987 General Assembly resolution[12] concerning the finance and administration of UNITAR, it was unnecessary to comment on recommendation 4. He did not currently intend to consider the JIU proposal that UNIDIR cease to exist as an autonomous research institute (recommendation 6).

On 21 December 1988, the Assembly, by **decision 43/453**, took note of the 1987 JIU report and of the Secretary-General's comments.

UN Institute for Training and Research

UNITAR activities

Despite the uncertainty and developments in 1988 concerning the future of UNITAR (see below), the period was marked by intense activities aimed at enhancing the effectiveness of the United Nations. UNITAR's 1988 activities were described by the Executive Director in two reports to the General Assembly, covering the periods 1 July 1986 to 30 June 1988[13] and 1 July 1988 to 30 June 1990.[14] The latter period was characterized by the implementation of a 1987 Assembly resolution,[12] by which the Assembly undertook further restructuring of UNITAR.

The UNITAR training programme focused on international co-operation and multilateral diplomacy, economic and social development, and research on training and training promotion. Training courses and seminars in multilateral diplomacy dealt with orientation to the United Nations, drafting international legal instruments, human rights reporting and techniques of multilateral economic negotiations. Training for economic and social development continued to aim at improving the capacity of developing countries to organize and manage their development programmes and projects.

Under the research programme, financed mainly through special-purpose grants, projects focused on the future of the United Nations and an evaluation of United Nations development decades and strategies. The UNITAR/UNDP Centre for Heavy Crude and Tar Sands organized the Fourth International Conference on Heavy Crude and Tar Sands (Edmonton, Canada, 7-12 August). A workshop organized by the UNITAR/UNDP Centre on Small Energy Resources (Rome, Italy, March) dealt with the overall status of energy for rural development in Africa.

UNITAR financing

In 1988,[15] UNITAR's General Fund income—from government contributions and other sources—totalled $1,330,128, while total expenditure amounted to $1,273,571. Income of the Special-Purpose Grants Fund was $1,967,734, including $1,601,585 in grants, while expenditure totalled $2,287,450.

A summary of principal findings and conclusions for remedial action by the United Nations Board of Auditors, submitted to the General Assembly by the Secretary-General,[16] indicated that 1988 expenditures exceeded allotments, with some projects incurring expenditures even though no allotments had been issued. The Board recommended that expenditures should not be allowed to exceed allotments and that no expenditures should be incurred for any special-purpose projects unless allotments had been issued for the purpose.

The Assembly, by **resolution 43/216**, accepted the financial report and audited financial statements of UNITAR for 1987, as well as the report of the Board of Auditors thereon.[17] The Advisory Committee on Administrative and Budgetary Questions (ACABQ) had no comments on the Board's report.[18]

Restructuring of UNITAR

In response to a General Assembly resolution of 1987,[12] the Secretary-General reported in October 1988 on the restructuring of UNITAR's programme and financing, amendment to the text of its statute and personnel matters.[19] The 1988-1989 core programme, funded largely through the General Fund, was limited to training for international co-operation and multilateral diplomacy. The expanded programme, funded through extrabudgetary resources, included training for economic and social development, and research on the United Nations, energy and natural resources and the future of the main developing regions of the world. A fuller description of the new programme was available in *UNITAR Work Programme 1988-1989*, published by UNITAR.

At the beginning of 1988, UNITAR had a cash deficit of $2,017,030, made up of an accumulated budget deficit from previous years, uncollected pledges from 1987 and earlier years and other receivables. The deficit was financed in large part by borrowing from the United Nations, to which UNITAR was in debt by $2,056,509 at the end of 1987. The debt due to the United Nations at 31 July 1988 amounted to $1,917,888.

The 1988 budget for UNITAR, incorporating programme restructuring measures, was set at the level of $1,069,700 and was approved by the UNITAR Board of Trustees (New York, 11-15 April). The Board encouraged the Executive Director to continue to manage UNITAR with austerity and urged that all the accumulated financial liabilities should be settled, if possible in 1988.

The amendments to the text of UNITAR's statute, approved by the Secretary-General, incorporated the proposals of the Board and focused on the programmatic, financial, administrative and budgetary arrangements of UNITAR affected by its mandated restructuring. The report contained a proposed amendment concerning the status of full-time UNITAR fellows. A large number of amendments dealt with UNITAR's new financial arrangements, notably the operation of a planned new reserve fund (see below) and the principles to govern the financing of its research and training programmes. The text of the new statute as well as the statute previously in force, together with the stated justification for its revisions, were contained in an addendum to the Secretary-General's report.[20]

As to personnel matters, it was decided to abolish, effective 30 June 1988, 14 posts involving 6 in the Professional category and 8 in the General Service category. In accordance with the Assembly's 1987 request,[12] all efforts were made to absorb the released staff within the United Nations system and to ensure that those affected did not suffer loss of rank or benefits. However, that request had to be reconciled with the priorities and provisions of other resolutions requiring staff reduction.

The Secretary-General also discussed the acquisition of the land and subsequent sale of the entire property of the UNITAR building, stating that the objective of the transaction was to establish a reserve fund, the accruing interests of which would be applied to the annual budgetary appropriations of UNITAR. In March 1988, the joint owners of the land confirmed their willingness to sell the property. Subsequently, the Secretary-General sought ACABQ's advice and concurrence on an appropriate means of financing the acquisition of the land. In April, ACABQ informed the Secretary-General that it concurred with his intent to borrow the necessary amount, not to exceed $4.5 million, from funds in his custody, excluding peace-keeping funds. As at the end of 1988, negotiations with the owners of the property were continuing.

GENERAL ASSEMBLY ACTION

On 20 December 1988, on the recommendation of the Second (Economic and Financial) Committee, the General Assembly adopted **resolution 43/201** without vote.

United Nations Institute for Training and Research

The General Assembly,

Recalling its resolutions 41/172 of 5 December 1986 and 42/197 of 11 December 1987,

Having considered the report of the Secretary-General and the report of the Executive Director of the United Nations Institute for Training and Research,

Recognizing the continuing importance and relevance of the mandate of the Institute, particularly in the field of training,

Recognizing also the need for Governments to contribute or increase their voluntary contributions, as appropriate, to the Institute,

Noting with concern the continuing lack of a sufficiently broad base of donor countries supporting the Institute,

Recognizing further the need for the Institute to continue to utilize the services of a small number of senior fellows for its programmes,

Noting with concern that the 1988 United Nations Pledging Conference for Development Activities did not provide the General Fund of the United Nations Institute

for Training and Research with the level of resources required for the Institute to maintain a minimum training programme and institutional structure,

Concerned that the absorption, on an exceptional basis, of several professional staff members of the Institute within the United Nations system, as called for in paragraph 11 of resolution 42/197, has yet to be fully implemented,

1. *Takes note* of the report of the Secretary-General prepared in response to resolution 42/197 and the report of the Executive Director of the United Nations Institute for Training and Research;

2. *Reaffirms* the continuing validity and relevance of the mandate of the Institute, as contained in the amended statute;

3. *Reaffirms also* the continuing validity of resolution 42/197 and calls for the early implementation of all its provisions;

4. *Takes note* of the amendment to the statute of the Institute regarding the designation of alternates to members of the Board of Trustees who are unable to attend any meeting of the Board;

5. *Requests* that the 1989 budgetary proposals of the Institute, as well as those of subsequent years, be submitted to the Advisory Committee on Administrative and Budgetary Questions for review and comment prior to approval by the Board of Trustees of the Institute;

6. *Urges* the Secretary-General to proceed as rapidly as possible with the acquisition of the land and subsequent sale of the entire property of the Institute, as approved in resolution 42/197;

7. *Reiterates* its approval of the recommendation of the Secretary-General that the Institute should, after the sale of the building, repay the amounts currently owed to the United Nations and use the balance to establish a reserve fund for the Institute;

8. *Requests* the Secretary-General to submit to the Board of Trustees at its forthcoming session a complete and current report on his efforts to purchase the land under the Institute building and subsequently to sell the entire property;

9. *Also requests* the Secretary-General, in the event that the necessary financing is not assured, through the sale of the building and/or voluntary contributions, for the administration of the Institute in the first half of 1989, to present to the General Assembly at its forty-fourth session specific recommendations on the future of the Institute, together with detailed financial information;

10. *Authorizes* the Secretary-General, notwithstanding the provisions of article VI, paragraph 1, of the statute of the Institute, to appoint for a one-year period up to nine full-time senior fellows and grant them the status of officials of the United Nations;

11. *Requests* the Secretary-General to consult with the Board of Trustees of the Institute on criteria and qualifications to apply to full-time senior fellows, and to present his recommendations to the General Assembly at its forty-fourth session;

12. *Renews its appeal* to the Secretary-General to give priority consideration to absorbing the remaining four staff members of the Institute who are occupying posts that have been abolished as a result of the restructuring of the Institute;

13. *Encourages* the Secretary-General to explore new modalities for greater interfacing among United Nations research bodies and requests him to report thereon;

14. *Requests* the Secretary-General to report to the General Assembly at its forty-fourth session on the implementation of the present resolution.

General Assembly resolution 43/201

20 December 1988   Meeting 83   Adopted without vote

Approved by Second Committee (A/43/892) without vote, 21 November (meeting 43); draft by Vice-Chairman (A/C.2/43/L.65), based on informal consultations; agenda item 85.
Meeting numbers. GA 43rd session: 2nd Committee 22, 27, 43; plenary 83.

United Nations University

UNU activities

In 1988,[21] UNU, an autonomous academic institution within the United Nations system, carried out its research, training and dissemination projects under eight programme areas: peace, culture and governance; the global economy and development; global life-support systems; alternative rural-urban configurations; science, technology and society; food, nutrition and biotechnology (see PART THREE, Chapter XI); human and social development; and global learning and informatics. Training courses were completed by 39 UNU fellows.

A total of 28 new books were published in various languages by UNU or co-publishers around the world. The University's four journals were published: *ASSET* (three issues); *Journal of Food Composition and Analysis* (four issues); *Food and Nutrition Bulletin* (four issues); and *Mountain Research and Development* (four issues).

UNU continued to make progress in establishing its own research and training centres. In July, the UNU Council approved the establishment of an Institute for New Technologies (Maastricht, Netherlands), which would focus on the implications of new technologies. Discussions continued on the establishment of a research and training centre in Japan that would take the form of an institute of advanced studies. An agreement was signed between UNU and Venezuela concerning biotechnology activities for Latin America and the Caribbean, with a co-ordinating office in Caracas.

UNU Council

The UNU Council met twice during 1988, holding its thirty-first (Brasília, Brazil, 26-30 July) and thirty-second (Tokyo, 6-10 December) sessions.

In July, the Council focused on the effect of continuing financial difficulties, the preparations for the second medium-term perspective for the period 1990-1995 and UNU's institutional structure.

In December, it dealt with a proposed supplementary and revised programme and budget of UNU for 1988-1989 and reports on the development of research and training centres and programmes. It adopted the second medium-term perspective as presented by the Rector of UNU. During 1990-1995, UNU was to conduct its work within five interrelated areas: universal human values and global responsibilities; new directions in the world economy; sustaining global life-support systems; advances in science and technology; and population dynamics and human welfare.

By **decision 1988/113** of 25 May 1988, the Economic and Social Council took note of the report of the UNU Council on the University's work in 1987.[22]

GENERAL ASSEMBLY ACTION

On 20 December 1988, on the recommendation of the Second Committee, the General Assembly adopted **resolution 43/200** without vote.

United Nations University

The General Assembly,

Reaffirming its previous resolutions on the United Nations University,

Having considered the report of the Council of the United Nations University on the work of the University in 1987 and its development in 1988, as presented by the Rector of the University on 25 October 1988,

Noting with appreciation the voluntary contributions made so far from Governments and other sources in support of the University,

Also noting with appreciation the continuing support of the Government of Japan for the overall development of the University, including the construction of a permanent headquarters building at Tokyo,

Expressing its appreciation to the Government of Finland for the continued financial and other support it provides to the first research and training centre established by the University, the World Institute for Development Economics Research,

Taking note of decision 5.2.1 adopted by the Executive Board of the United Nations Educational, Scientific and Cultural Organization at its one hundred and twenty-ninth session, held from 25 May to 10 June 1988,[a]

1. *Welcomes* the achievements of the United Nations University in implementing programmes of research, advanced training and dissemination of knowledge, within the framework of the first medium-term perspective (1982-1987);

2. *Welcomes also* the consolidation of the overall University programme and the restructuring of the University Centre at Tokyo;

3. *Notes with satisfaction* that the World Institute for Development Economics Research has made considerable progress on the three research themes for its initial programme: "Hunger and poverty: the poorest billion"; "Money, finance and trade: reform for world development"; and "Development and technological transformation: the management of change" and that its first substantial research publications will be issued shortly;

4. *Notes with concern* the difficulties encountered by the University in securing the funding for the commencement of the activities of the Institute for Natural Resources in Africa;

5. *Welcomes* the offer made by the Government of the Netherlands relating to the establishment and operation of a research and training centre of the University in the area of new technologies;

[a]129 Ex/Dec.5.2.1.

6. *Requests* the University, when drawing up its report to the General Assembly, to take into account the comments made by Governments in the Assembly on the manner in which the activities of the University are presented, in particular regarding strengthening the analytical content of the report;

7. *Invites* the University to continue and intensify its co-operative activities in areas of common interest with the United Nations and its bodies and specialized agencies, in particular with the United Nations Educational, Scientific and Cultural Organization, on the one hand, and with the international academic and scientific community, including national research centres, on the other, which enhance the responsiveness of the University to global issues and problems and bring its work into closer relation with the concerns of the United Nations system and the world academic community with regard to global issues and problems;

8. *Requests* the University to continue to intensify its fund-raising efforts to build up its Endowment Fund and its Operating Fund in order to increase its core income;

9. *Earnestly appeals* to all States to take cognizance of the progress made by the University and the relevance of its work to the concerns of the United Nations, to contribute urgently and generously to its Endowment Fund and to make operating contributions, including support for its research and training centres and programmes, in order to enable it to fulfil its mandate efficiently, in accordance with its Charter and with the relevant resolutions of the General Assembly.

General Assembly resolution 43/200

20 December 1988   Meeting 83   Adopted without vote

Approved by Second Committee (A/43/892) without vote, 15 November (meeting 42); 21-nation draft (A/C.2/43/L.32), orally revised following informal consultations; agenda item 85.
Sponsors: Argentina, Austria, Bangladesh, Bolivia, Brazil, China, Colombia, Egypt, Finland, Ghana, Guyana, Iceland, Japan, Jordan, Mexico, Morocco, Nepal, Netherlands, Philippines, Poland, Zambia.
Meeting numbers. GA 43rd session: 2nd Committee 22, 27, 38, 42; plenary 83.

REFERENCES

[1]YUN 1986, p. 640. [2]DP/1988/62. [3]E/1988/19 (dec. 88/29). [4]A/43/430. [5]E/1988/35 (res.274 (XLIV)). [6]E/1988/16. [7]ACC/1988/15. [8]YUN 1987, p. 654, GA res. 42/104, 7 Dec. 1987. [9]A/43/397. [10]YUN 1987, p. 654. [11]YUN 1982, p. 992. [12]YUN 1987, p. 656, GA res. 42/197, 11 Dec. 1987. [13]A/43/14. [14]A/45/14. [15]A/44/5/Add.4. [16]A/44/356. [17]A/43/5/Add.4. [18]A/43/674 & Corr. 1. [19]A/43/697. [20]A/43/697/Add.1. [21]E/1989/37. [22]YUN 1987, p. 658.

Social and cultural development

Social aspects of development

Improvement of social life

On 8 December 1988, on the recommendation of the Third (Social, Humanitarian and Cultural) Committee, the General Assembly adopted **resolution 43/156** by recorded vote.

Improvement of social life
The General Assembly,
Bearing in mind that the Members of the United Na-

tions have undertaken in the Charter to promote social progress and better standards of life in larger freedom,

Recalling the principles proclaimed in the Universal Declaration of Human Rights and in the Declaration on Social Progress and Development,

Mindful of the need to establish a harmonious balance between scientific, technological and material progress and the intellectual, spiritual, cultural and moral advancement of mankind,

Considering that the improvement of social life must be based on respect for and the promotion of all human rights and particularly on the elimination of all forms of discrimination,

Recognizing that social progress and development are founded on respect for the dignity and value of the human person,

Considering that healthy recreational, cultural and sports activities contribute to the achievement of a proper level of physical and mental health,

Considering also that the improvement of social life must take place in a continuous and uninterrupted manner,

Mindful that the existing inequalities and imbalances in the international economic system are widening the gap between developed and developing countries and thereby constitute a major obstacle to the development of the developing countries and adversely affect international relations and the promotion of world peace and security,

Conscious that each country has the sovereign right freely to adopt the economic and social system that it deems the most appropriate and that each Government has a primary role in ensuring the social progress and well-being of its people,

Convinced of the urgent necessity rapidly to eradicate colonialism, neo-colonialism, racism and all forms of racial discrimination, *apartheid*, foreign aggression, occupation and domination and all forms of inequality, exploitation and subjugation of peoples, which constitute major obstacles to economic and social progress as well as to the promotion of world peace and security,

Recalling its resolutions 40/100 of 13 December 1985, 41/152 of 4 December 1986 and 42/145 of 7 December 1987,

1. *Acknowledges* that the progress achieved in the world social situation is still inadequate despite the efforts made and that efforts should therefore be redoubled;

2. *Notes with great concern* the slow progress in the implementation of the Declaration on Social Progress and Development;

3. *Reaffirms* that the social aspects and goals of development are an integral part of the overall development process and that it is the sovereign right of each State freely to determine and implement appropriate policies for social development within the framework of its development plans and priorities;

4. *Emphasizes* the importance, for the achievement of social progress, of the establishment of the new international economic order;

5. *Calls upon* Member States to make all efforts to promote the speedy and complete elimination of such fundamental elements hindering economic and social progress and development as colonialism, neo-colonialism, racism and all forms of racial discrimination, *apartheid*, foreign aggression, occupation, and domination and all forms of inequality and exploitation of

peoples, and also to undertake effective measures to lessen international tensions;

6. *Reiterates* that it is the right of everyone to enjoy the greatest possible degree of physical and mental health;

7. *Emphasizes* that participation in cultural, sports and recreational activities and the use of leisure without discrimination of any kind promotes the improvement of social life;

8. *Requests* the Secretary-General to include in his report on the implementation of the Declaration on Social Progress and Development the results attained in the improvement of social life in the world;

9. *Decides* to resume consideration of the question of the improvement of social life at its forty-fifth session.

General Assembly resolution 43/156

8 December 1988   Meeting 75   130-16-9 (recorded vote)

Approved by Third Committee (A/43/868) by recorded vote (110-15-9), 30 November (meeting 57); 6-nation draft (A/C.3/43/L.79), orally revised; agenda item 12.

Sponsors: Bulgaria, Burkina Faso, Cuba, Lao People's Democratic Republic, Nicaragua, Viet Nam.

Meeting numbers. GA 43rd session: 3rd Committee 49-57; plenary 75.

Recorded vote in Assembly as follows:

In favour: Afghanistan, Albania, Algeria, Angola, Antigua and Barbuda, Argentina, Bahamas, Bahrain, Bangladesh, Barbados, Belize, Benin, Bhutan, Bolivia, Botswana, Brazil, Brunei Darussalam, Bulgaria, Burkina Faso, Burma, Burundi, Byelorussian SSR, Cameroon, Cape Verde, Central African Republic, Chad, China, Colombia, Comoros, Congo, Costa Rica, Côte d'Ivoire, Cuba, Cyprus, Czechoslovakia, Democratic Yemen, Djibouti, Dominica, Dominican Republic, Ecuador, Egypt, El Salvador, Equatorial Guinea, Ethiopia, Fiji, Gabon, Gambia, German Democratic Republic, Ghana, Grenada, Guatemala, Guinea, Guinea-Bissau, Guyana, Haiti, Honduras, Hungary, India, Indonesia, Iran, Iraq, Jamaica, Jordan, Kenya, Kuwait, Lao People's Democratic Republic, Lebanon, Lesotho, Liberia, Libyan Arab Jamahiriya, Madagascar, Malaysia, Maldives, Mali, Mauritania, Mauritius, Mexico, Mongolia, Morocco, Mozambique, Nepal, Nicaragua, Niger, Nigeria, Oman, Pakistan, Panama, Papua New Guinea, Paraguay, Peru, Philippines, Poland, Qatar, Romania, Rwanda, Saint Kitts and Nevis, Saint Lucia, Saint Vincent and the Grenadines, Samoa, Sao Tome and Principe, Saudi Arabia, Senegal, Seychelles, Sierra Leone, Singapore, Solomon Islands, Somalia, Sri Lanka, Sudan, Suriname, Swaziland, Syrian Arab Republic, Thailand, Togo, Trinidad and Tobago, Tunisia, Uganda, Ukrainian SSR, USSR, United Arab Emirates, United Republic of Tanzania, Uruguay, Vanuatu, Venezuela, Viet Nam, Yemen, Yugoslavia, Zaire, Zambia, Zimbabwe.

Against: Australia, Austria, Belgium, Canada, Denmark, France, Germany, Federal Republic of, Israel, Luxembourg, Netherlands, New Zealand, Norway, Portugal, Turkey, United Kingdom, United States.

Abstaining: Finland, Greece, Iceland, Ireland, Italy, Japan, Malta, Spain, Sweden.

The family

International year of the family

In response to a General Assembly resolution of 1987,[1] the Secretary-General reported in September 1988[2] on the views and proposals of Governments concerning a United Nations international year of the family. As at 18 August, responses had been received from 45 Governments, of which 39 favoured such a year. Among that group there appeared to be a consensus that the importance of family issues warranted attention and that an international year was an appropriate way of achieving that objective. Governments against an international year considered that it was not appropriate to family issues or that the value of international years, or too many such years, was questionable. Responses indicated that an international year would need to give attention to family issues in an environment fully sensitive to the

goal of advancement of women, as reflected in the 1985 Nairobi Forward-looking Strategies.[3]

GENERAL ASSEMBLY ACTION

On 8 December 1988, on the recommendation of the Third Committee, the General Assembly adopted **resolution 43/135** without vote.

Need to enhance international co-operation in the field of protection and assistance to the family

The General Assembly,

Recalling the resolve of the peoples of the United Nations to promote social progress and better standards of life in larger freedom, with a view to the creation of conditions of stability and well-being, which are necessary for peaceful and friendly relations among nations,

Recalling also its resolution 42/49 of 30 November 1987 and taking note of Economic and Social Council resolution 1988/46 of 27 May 1988 entitled "Achievement of social justice",

Mindful of the importance of the role of the family in society,

Guided by the relevant provisions of the Universal Declaration of Human Rights, the International Covenant on Economic, Social and Cultural Rights and the Declaration on Social Progress and Development, according to which the widest possible protection and assistance should be accorded to the family,

Recalling the Nairobi Forward-looking Strategies for the Advancement of Women and its resolution 42/125 of 7 December 1987 in which it endorsed for action the Guiding Principles for Developmental Social Welfare Policies and Programmes in the Near Future, which call for social welfare policies to give greater attention to the family,

Recognizing the efforts of States at the local, regional and national levels in carrying out specific programmes concerning the family, in which the United Nations may have an important role to play, and in raising awareness, increasing understanding and promoting policies that improve the position and well-being of the family,

Recalling its resolution 42/134 of 7 December 1987 on the need to enhance international co-operation in the field of the protection of and assistance to the family,

Recalling also Economic and Social Council resolutions 1983/23 of 26 May 1983 and 1985/29 of 29 May 1985,

1. *Takes note with appreciation* of the report of the Secretary-General on the possible proclamation of an international year of the family, prepared in pursuance of its resolution 42/134;

2. *Takes note* of the responses to the Secretary-General's inquiry as to the desirability of proclaiming an international year of the family, summarized in his report;

3. *Requests* the Secretary-General to submit to the General Assembly at its forty-fourth session a report containing the proposed date and a comprehensive outline of a possible programme for an international year of the family, in conformity with Assembly decision 35/424 of 5 December 1980 and Economic and Social Council resolution 1980/67 of 25 July 1980 concerning the guidelines for international years and anniversaries;

4. *Invites* Member States that have not yet done so to make their views known to the Secretary-General concerning ways and means of improving the position and

well-being of the family and intensifying efforts as part of an international year of the family;

5. *Requests* the United Nations agencies and organizations, as well as intergovernmental and non-governmental organizations in consultative status with the Economic and Social Council, to submit to the Secretary-General proposals on their participation in an international year of the family, in order to facilitate the preparation of his report;

6. *Decides* to consider the report of the Secretary-General and to take a decision on the final date of an international year of the family at its forty-fourth session, under an item entitled "Families in the development process".

General Assembly resolution 43/135

8 December 1988   Meeting 75   Adopted without vote

Approved by Third Committee (A/43/814) without vote, 11 November (meeting 40); 19-nation draft (A/C.3/43/L.21/Rev.1), orally revised; agenda item 107.
Sponsors: Austria, Colombia, Costa Rica, Cuba, Czechoslovakia, Dominican Republic, Ecuador, German Democratic Republic, Libyan Arab Jamahiriya, Mexico, Mongolia, Panama, Philippines, Poland, Romania, Ukrainian SSR, Uruguay, Venezuela, Viet Nam.
Meeting numbers. GA 43rd session: 3rd Committee 15-22, 27, 31, 40; plenary 75.

Achievement of social justice

On 27 May 1988, on the recommendation of its Second (Social) Committee, the Economic and Social Council adopted **resolution 1988/46** without vote.

Achievement of social justice

The Economic and Social Council,

Mindful of the pledge made by States Members of the United Nations in the Charter to take joint and separate action to promote higher standards of living, full employment and conditions of economic and social progress and development,

Bearing in mind that, in accordance with the Declaration on Social Progress and Development, social progress and development shall be founded on respect for the dignity and value of the human person and shall ensure the promotion of human rights and social justice,

Convinced that more extensive regional and inter-regional co-operation is important in strengthening national efforts to promote social progress,

Mindful of the Guiding Principles for Developmental Social Welfare Policies and Programmes in the Near Future,

Persuaded of the importance of taking measures to ensure co-ordination within the United Nations system in order to develop a comprehensive approach to developmental social welfare, including better integrated and mutually supportive economic and social development policies, aimed at the achievement of social justice,

1. *Considers* that the common purpose of the international community must be to create from varied economic, social and political conditions a global environment conducive to sustained development, the full enjoyment of human rights and fundamental freedoms, social justice and peace;

2. *Recognizes* that social justice is one of the most important goals of social progress;

3. *Reaffirms* the importance of co-operation among countries in promoting a climate conducive to the achievement by individual countries of the goals of development and social justice and progress;

4. *Considers* that such co-operation should continue to be a major focus of the activities of the United Nations and its bodies in accordance with the principles of the Charter;

5. *Recommends* that the Commission for Social Development and other relevant United Nations bodies and specialized agencies take into account the necessity of achieving social justice for all when considering problems of social development.

Economic and Social Council resolution 1988/46

27 May 1988   Meeting 16   Adopted without vote

Approved by Second Committee (E/1988/91) without vote, 20 May (meeting 19); 7-nation draft (E/1988/C.2/L.9); agenda item 12.
Sponsors: Bulgaria, Byelorussian SSR, German Democratic Republic, Poland, Ukrainian SSR, USSR, United States.

GENERAL ASSEMBLY ACTION

On 8 December, the General Assembly adopted **resolution 43/153** on human rights in the administration of justice. The resolution was based in part on a review of United Nations functioning in the field.

Extreme poverty

On 27 May 1988, on the recommendation of its Second Committee, the Economic and Social Council adopted **resolution 1988/47** without vote.

Extreme poverty

The Economic and Social Council,

Concerned that a significant percentage of the world's population lives in conditions of extreme poverty and is forced to live increasingly at the margins of society,

Noting the insufficient attention paid to the phenomenon of extreme poverty, a phenomenon that frequently eludes international and intergovernmental action and current statistical methods,

Recalling its resolution 1987/48 of 28 May 1987, in which it called on non-governmental organizations to participate in follow-up activities to the Interregional Consultation on Developmental Social Welfare Policies and Programmes,

Taking into account the provision of the Declaration on Social Progress and Development to the effect that social progress and development are the common concerns of the international community, which shall supplement, by concerted international action, national efforts to raise the living standards of peoples,

Bearing in mind General Assembly resolution 2543 (XXIV) of 11 December 1969 on the implementation of the Declaration on Social Progress and Development,

Noting the results of the International Conference on the Human Dimension of Africa's Economic Recovery and Development, held at Khartoum from 5 to 8 March 1988, and the Khartoum Declaration adopted by the Conference,[a]

Concerned that a deteriorating international economic situation has adverse social consequences, particularly for developing countries, and contributes to extending

[a]A/43/430.

the boundaries of extreme poverty and increases the number of people living in such conditions,

Bearing in mind the urgent need to take account of the social costs of adjustment policies,

Calling for the strengthening of efforts being made by the international community to alleviate the impact of such policies on those who live in conditions of extreme poverty,

Considering that the Commission for Social Development is the most appropriate United Nations organ for recommending social development policies,

1. *Requests* the Commission for Social Development to study the phenomenon of extreme poverty with a view to examining the interrelationship between social development and the eradication of poverty and report to the Economic and Social Council at its first regular session of 1989;

2. *Invites* all Member States to transmit to the Commission for Social Development any studies or reports that they may have on the problem of extreme poverty or, if they have none, invites them to consider undertaking such studies and to transmit them to the Commission;

3. *Also invites* non-governmental organizations to continue to support follow-up activities to the Interregional Consultation on Developmental Social Welfare Policies and Programmes in accordance with Council resolution 1987/48;

4. *Urges* the Commission for Social Development to suggest, on the basis of an assessment of its studies, strategies that will help put an end to the marginalization of people living in extreme poverty, irrespective of the economic and social system to which they belong, and to submit its views to the Economic and Social Council for consideration at its first regular session of 1991;

5. *Requests* the Secretary-General to include the results of the studies of the Commission for Social Development in his report on the world social situation.

Economic and Social Council resolution 1988/47

27 May 1988   Meeting 16   Adopted without vote

Approved by Second Committee (E/1988/91) without vote, 24 May (meeting 22); 16-nation draft (E/1988/C.2/L.10/Rev.1), orally revised; agenda item 12.

Sponsors: Bolivia, Colombia, Costa Rica, Cuba, Dominican Republic, Ecuador, Haiti, India, Mexico, Pakistan, Peru, Philippines, Poland, Sudan, Uruguay, Venezuela.

Institutional machinery

Centre for Social Development and Humanitarian Affairs

In his annual report on United Nations technical co-operation,[4] the Secretary-General described the activities of the United Nations Office at Vienna/Centre for Social Development and Humanitarian Affairs (UNOV/CSDHA). He stated that, with funds provided by the Department of Technical Co-operation for Development (DTCD), UNOV/CSDHA had fielded several *ad hoc* advisory missions: to Guatemala to assist in strengthening voluntary social welfare organizations; to Hungary to launch a UNDP-financed project on strengthening social welfare and health programmes; and to the United Republic of Tanzania to participate in a joint UNDP/World Bank project on the social

aspects of adjustment. DTCD and CSDHA also had co-operated in formulating World Bank proposals for technical assistance loans for social-sector management in Argentina and Brazil.

In another report on technical co-operation activities,[5] the Secretary-General stated that in 1988 UNOV/CSDHA saw an increased commitment by Governments and international agencies towards tackling the social aspects of development. New initiatives dealt with the social effects of adjustment, HRD, particularly among specific population groups, and the problem of critical poverty. The major thrust of the work of UNOV/CSDHA during the year was in translating social development concepts into programmes and in intensifying co-operation with UNDP. Those efforts aimed to strengthen the social content of development projects and promote a comprehensive approach to programming activities which integrated social objectives and programmes into national development plans and UNDP country programmes.

UN Research Institute for Social Development

In 1988, the United Nations Research Institute for Social Development (UNRISD) focused on carrying out new research programmes, scheduled for completion in 1989, on the social situation of refugees, improvement of development data, the social impact of the sustained economic crisis and adjustment-related food policy. The research phase of the food systems and society project in West Africa was completed, as was the report on the third socio-economic survey of Afghan refugees in Pakistan, which was carried out in collaboration with the Office of the United Nations High Commissioner for Refugees in 1986 and subsequently published as the *Survey of the Social and Economic Conditions of Afghan Refugees in Pakistan*.

In July, the UNRISD Board approved the development of new research efforts in the areas of people's participation in natural resource management, economic reform and social participation in countries with centrally planned economies, and social conflict and development.

The UNRISD research data bank continued to be updated using material from the latest statistical yearbooks and the Economic Time Series data bank. News of UNRISD activities was circulated through a periodic publication, *Research Notes*.

Crime prevention and criminal justice

The United Nations continued in 1988 to focus its activities in crime prevention and criminal justice on the implementation of the conclusions of the Seventh (1985) United Nations Congress on the Prevention of Crime and the Treatment of Offenders[6] and the preparation for the Eighth (1990) Congress.

Report of the Secretary-General. In October 1988,[7] the Secretary-General reported on progress achieved in implementing 1986[8] and 1987[9] General Assembly resolutions. He highlighted the adoption by the Economic and Social Council of **resolution 1988/44** (see below, under "Review of the UN programme") and discussed activities carried out by Member States in implementing the Milan Plan of Action[6] adopted by the Seventh Congress and the norms, guidelines and standards in crime prevention and criminal justice.

Concerning the norms and guidelines, the Secretary-General cited a report[10] he had submitted to the Committee on Crime Prevention and Control (see below) with information from 79 countries indicating that the provisions of the 1979 Code of Conduct for Law Enforcement Officials[11] were considered to be of great importance and that they were generally incorporated into or covered by national legislation or practice. The Secretary-General noted other examples where the norms and guidelines were given serious attention, also by way of reports he had submitted to the Committee: 32 Governments[12] provided information on the application of the 1985 United Nations Standard Minimum Rules for the Administration of Juvenile Justice (Beijing Rules);[13] 74 Governments reported on the implementation of United Nations safeguards guaranteeing protection of the rights of those facing the death penalty;[14] replies of 57 countries demonstrated the vital role of international co-operation to prevent extra-legal, arbitrary and summary executions;[15] and various Governments[16] provided information on measures taken to implement the 1985 Declaration of Basic Principles of Justice for Victims of Crime and Abuse of Power.[17]

Activities within the United Nations system were carried out by ESCAP, UNDP and the Department of Public Information (DPI). ESCAP published *Guidelines on Social Measures for the Prevention of Crime among Youth and on Juvenile Justice: the Role of Youth Organizations in the ESCAP Region*; UNDP continued to support the Latin American Institute for the Prevention of Crime and the Treatment of Offenders (ILANUD) (Costa Rica) and the United Nations African Institute for the Prevention of Crime and the Treatment of Offenders (UNAFRI) (Uganda), as well as projects related to the control of drug abuse; and DPI issued publications of United Nations criminal justice instruments.

The Secretary-General stated that every effort had been made by the Secretariat to implement the recommendations and conclusions of the Seventh Congress. A major report had been submitted to the Committee on Crime Prevention and Control on proposals for concerted international action against the forms of crime identified in the Milan Plan of Action, summarizing initiatives and recommending actions for improved co-operation and mutual assistance.[18]

Preparations for the Eighth (1990) Congress included five interregional preparatory meetings of experts held at Vienna on each of the topics of the provisional agenda of the Congress (see below).

Despite severe resource constraints, every effort had been made by the Secretariat to establish a solid basis for an effective programme of international co-operation in crime prevention and criminal justice. The Secretariat had also initiated activities intended to establish a solid base of regular contacts with Governments and funding agencies, on which a technical assistance programme could be set up. Interregional advisory services continued to be provided to countries, the regional commissions, United Nations interregional and regional institutes and intergovernmental and non-governmental organizations (NGOs). The Secretary-General in 1988 launched an appeal for more voluntary contributions to the United Nations Trust Fund for Social Defence.

GENERAL ASSEMBLY ACTION

On 8 December 1988, on the recommendation of the Third Committee, the General Assembly adopted **resolution 43/99** without vote.

Crime prevention and criminal justice

The General Assembly,

Recalling the responsibility assumed by the United Nations in the field of crime prevention and criminal justice under Economic and Social Council resolution 155 C (VII) of 13 August 1948 and General Assembly resolution 415(V) of 1 December 1950,

Recalling also its resolution 42/59 of 30 November 1987 on crime prevention and criminal justice, in which Member States and the Secretary-General were urged, *inter alia*, to make every effort to translate into action, as appropriate, the respective recommendations, policies and conclusions stemming from the Milan Plan of Action and the relevant resolutions and recommendations adopted unanimously by the Seventh United Nations Congress on the Prevention of Crime and the Treatment of Offenders and to accord priority attention to the forms of crime identified in the Milan Plan of Action by strengthening international co-operation in this field,

Recalling further that in the same resolution the General Assembly endorsed the recommendations related to preparations for the Eighth United Nations Congress on the Prevention of Crime and the Treatment of Offenders, to be held in 1990, contained in Economic and Social Council resolution 1987/49 of 28 May 1987, and requested the Secretary-General to take immediate steps to ensure successful and cost-effective preparations for the Eighth Congress,

Mindful that 1988 marks the fortieth anniversary of the establishment of the United Nations programme of work in crime prevention and criminal justice and that the scope and extent of present-day criminality exceeds what could have been foreseen by Member States when they vested the United Nations with a leading role in this field,

Bearing in mind the objectives of the United Nations in the field of crime prevention and criminal justice, specifically the reduction of criminality, the promotion of more efficient and effective administration of justice, the strengthening of international co-operation and the fight against transnational crime, the observance of human rights and the promotion of the highest standards of fairness, humanity and professional conduct,

Aware that the spread of crime in the contemporary world and its ever-changing patterns and dynamics require a prompt and effective response appropriate to the particular cultural, political, economic and social circumstances and that modern technological advances facilitate crime prevention and control but also make possible the transnational expansion of organized criminality,

Recognizing that issues related to crime have intensified in complexity and gravity and that economic and financial crises in many developing countries have severely affected the functioning of crime prevention and the criminal justice system,

Reaffirming the crucial functions of the Committee on Crime Prevention and Control in developing practical crime prevention and criminal justice policies and strategies as a standing expert body of the Economic and Social Council and as the preparatory body for the quinquennial United Nations congresses on the prevention of crime and the treatment of offenders,

Noting with concern that the severe constraints on the human and financial resources available to the Crime Prevention and Criminal Justice Branch of the Centre for Social Development and Humanitarian Affairs of the Secretariat may jeopardize the success of the Eighth Congress and of the programme as a whole,

1. *Takes note with appreciation* of the report of the Secretary-General on the implementation of its resolution 42/59 and of the relevant recommendations contained therein made by the Committee on Crime Prevention and Control at its tenth session, during which, *inter alia*, it reviewed the results of the interregional preparatory meetings for the Eighth United Nations Congress on the Prevention of Crime and the Treatment of Offenders and endorsed their recommendations;

2. *Invites* the Economic and Social Council, at its first regular session of 1989, to give priority attention to the recommendations of the Committee regarding, in particular, the implementation of the resolutions of the Seventh United Nations Congress on the Prevention of Crime and the Treatment of Offenders, the review of the functioning and programme of work in the field of crime prevention and criminal justice and the preparations for the Eighth Congress;

3. *Welcomes* the efforts made by Member States and the Secretary-General to translate into action the recommendations contained in the Milan Plan of Action, adopted by the Seventh Congress, and urges those Governments which have not yet done so to provide relevant information to the Secretary-General on the implementation of those recommendations;

4. *Stresses* the necessity for Member States to continue to make concerted and systematic efforts to strengthen international co-operation in crime prevention and criminal justice as identified in the Milan Plan of Action and to facilitate the adoption by the Eighth Congress of viable and constructive action-oriented strategies against crime;

5. *Calls upon* all States to become actively involved in the preparations for the Eighth Congress, to partici-

pate in the regional preparatory meetings to be held in 1989 and to be represented in the quinquennial congress at a high level, and encourages the intergovernmental and non-governmental organizations concerned and the professional community, whose substantive contributions to the congresses have always been of great value, to continue to collaborate in the research and other preparatory activities for the Eighth Congress;

6. *Calls upon* the specialized agencies, in particular the International Labour Organisation, the United Nations Educational, Scientific and Cultural Organization, the World Health Organization, the International Civil Aviation Organization and the International Maritime Organization, and other organizations of the United Nations system to give the necessary attention and priority to national, regional and international measures aimed at fighting crime and improving the quality of the administration of justice;

7. *Invites* Member States to contribute to the United Nations Trust Fund for Social Defence as a means of supporting the work of the United Nations in the field of crime prevention and criminal justice and to forward to the Secretary-General proposals for its revitalization;

8. *Encourages* Member States and relevant organizations, in particular the World Bank, the United Nations Development Programme, the Department of Technical Co-operation for Development of the Secretariat and the regional commissions, to support and complement the technical co-operation activities in the field of crime prevention and criminal justice, including the programmes of the United Nations for interregional and regional co-operation for crime prevention, and to provide financial assistance to the regional institutes for the prevention of crime and the treatment of offenders;

9. *Calls upon* the Secretary-General to apply the priorities identified for the United Nations programme of work in crime prevention and criminal justice both to the Eighth Congress and to the work of the United Nations in the field of criminal justice and crime prevention in general;

10. *Requests* the Secretary-General to provide the necessary resources for the preparations for the Eighth Congress, including regional preparatory meetings, and to ensure that the allocation of manpower to the Crime Prevention and Criminal Justice Branch of the Centre for Social Development and Humanitarian Affairs is sufficient to meet its responsibilities and necessary commitments;

11. *Also requests* the Secretary-General to report to the General Assembly at its forty-fourth session on the implementation of the present resolution, providing updated information on the preparations for the Eighth Congress;

12. *Decides* to consider this subject at its forty-fourth session under the item entitled "Crime prevention and criminal justice".

General Assembly resolution 43/99

8 December 1988   Meeting 75   Adopted without vote

Approved by Third Committee (A/43/811) without vote, 3 November (meeting 31); 21-nation draft (A/C.3/43/L.19), orally revised; agenda item 93.
Sponsors: Argentina, Australia, Austria, Bolivia, Canada, Colombia, Costa Rica, Cuba, France, Ghana, Greece, Italy, Norway, Samoa, Senegal, Spain, United Kingdom, United States, Uruguay, Venezuela, Yugoslavia.
Financial implications. 5th Committee, A/43/824; S-G, A/C.3/43/L.22, A/C.5/43/35.
Meeting numbers. GA 43rd session: 3rd Committee 15-22, 25, 31; 5th Committee 33; plenary 75.

Review of the UN programme

In April 1988,[19] the Secretary-General reported on initial steps taken to implement an Economic and Social Council resolution adopted in 1987,[20] covering research and policy development, technical co-operation, and resources and funding.

He discussed action taken by the General Assembly in 1987[9] and outlined activities carried out by the Secretariat, which included research and policy development; preparations for the Eighth Congress; technical co-operation projects on specific crime issues and advisory services; and the encouragement of contributions to the United Nations Trust Fund for Social Defence. He also discussed action taken to foster the optimal functioning of the Committee on Crime Prevention and Control.

The Secretary-General described the activities of the United Nations interregional and regional institutes for the prevention of crime and the treatment of offenders. Those institutes included UNAFRI, ILANUD, the United Nations Social Defence Research Institute (UNSDRI) (Rome), the United Nations Asia and Far East Institute for the Prevention of Crime and the Treatment of Offenders (Fuchu, Japan), the Helsinki Institute for Crime Prevention and Control (Finland) and the Arab Security Studies and Training Centre (Riyadh, Saudi Arabia).

The Secretary-General stated that the involvement of the United Nations system in crime prevention and criminal justice was somewhat limited. There had been close co-operation with NGOs in implementing the recommendations of the Seventh Congress and in preparing for the Eighth.

He concluded that there was a need for vigorous collaboration between States, as an integral part of global co-operation for economic and social development, together with the search for new and effective joint action. He would continue his efforts to reinforce the role of the Secretariat as a central mechanism and catalytic factor in implementing cost-effective activities and programmes in crime prevention and criminal justice.

ECONOMIC AND SOCIAL COUNCIL ACTION

On 27 May 1988, on the recommendation of its Second Committee, the Economic and Social Council adopted **resolution 1988/44** without vote.

Review of the functioning and programme of work of the United Nations in crime prevention and criminal justice

The Economic and Social Council,

Recalling the responsibility assumed by the United Nations in the field of crime prevention and criminal justice under Economic and Social Council resolution 155 C (VII) of 13 August 1948 and General Assembly resolution 415(V) of 1 December 1950,

Bearing in mind its resolutions 1986/11 of 21 May 1986 and 1987/49 and 1987/53, both of 28 May 1987, as

well as General Assembly resolution 42/59 of 30 November 1987,

Noting that 1988 is the fortieth anniversary of the establishment of the programme of the United Nations in the field of crime prevention and criminal justice and that the scope and extent of criminal activity have assumed dimensions that could not have been foreseen by Member States when they entrusted the United Nations with a leading role in this field,

Emphasizing the central role of the Committee on Crime Prevention and Control in assisting the Council in the preparations for the quinquennial United Nations congresses on the prevention of crime and the treatment of offenders and in developing the programme of work of the United Nations in this field, as specified by the General Assembly in its resolution 32/60 of 8 December 1977 and by the Council in its resolution 1979/19 of 9 May 1979,

Conscious that the effective management of the increasing range of United Nations activities in crime prevention and criminal justice, and the efficient preparation of the quinquennial congresses, require professional, technical and specialized work on the part of the Secretariat, as well as close involvement on the part of the Committee,

Noting with concern that the resources available to the Crime Prevention and Criminal Justice Branch of the Centre for Social Development and Humanitarian Affairs of the Secretariat have decreased, while the commitments of the United Nations in this field have increased,

1. *Takes note with appreciation* of the report of the Secretary-General;

2. *Acknowledges* the work accomplished by the Secretariat in implementing its programme of work in this field, including progress in the preparations for the Eighth United Nations Congress on the Prevention of Crime and the Treatment of Offenders, following the directives of the Committee on Crime Prevention and Control and the recommendations of the Economic and Social Council, as specified in its resolutions 1986/11 and 1987/53, while recognizing the major tasks still to be undertaken;

3. *Requests* the Secretary-General to ensure that the United Nations programme of work in crime prevention and criminal justice is supported by adequate resources through such measures as appropriate redeployment of staff and funds, including redeployment from relevant departments at Headquarters, and to ensure that the specialized and technical nature of the programme and the high priority attached by Member States to crime prevention and criminal justice are fully reflected in the management and staffing of the Crime Prevention and Criminal Justice Branch;

4. *Notes with satisfaction* the interest shown in, and the support given to, the Crime Prevention and Criminal Justice Branch by many Governments, as well as by non-governmental organizations and the professional community, which have been involved in the preparations for the Eighth Congress, and invites them to continue to participate actively in such preparations;

5. *Welcomes* the appointment of the Secretary-General of the Eighth United Nations Congress on the Prevention of Crime and the Treatment of Offenders;

6. *Urges* the Secretary-General of the United Nations to pay particular attention to the operational aspects of the programme of work, specifically to assist interested countries in developing self-reliance in the area of crime

prevention through human resources development, the reinforcement of national machinery, the promotion of joint training activities and the development of pilot and demonstration projects, and invites the United Nations Development Programme and the Department of Technical Co-operation for Development of the Secretariat and other agencies that provide funding for technical co-operation to continue to provide effective support and assistance for this endeavour;

7. *Encourages* Governments and intergovernmental and non-governmental organizations, in co-operation with the Secretariat, to play an active role in the formulation and implementation of technical co-operation projects in crime prevention and criminal justice and to allocate adequate resources and expertise for technical assistance activities through, *inter alia*, the United Nations Trust Fund for Social Defence, and urges the Secretary-General to strengthen existing interregional advisory services;

8. *Requests* the Secretary-General to foster further close collaboration between the Secretariat and the United Nations regional and interregional institutes for crime prevention and criminal justice and to co-ordinate the activities of the Crime Prevention and Criminal Justice Branch with those of the institutes, particularly through the reinforcement of existing contacts, the crime information network, substantive support of technical co-operation projects, staff secondment and exchange of expertise and research findings;

9. *Also requests* the Secretary-General to continue to explore ways and means of ensuring the optimal functioning of the Committee on Crime Prevention and Control;

10. *Invites* the Committee on Crime Prevention and Control to give priority attention at its tenth session to reviewing the progress made in the preparations for the Eighth Congress and to make specific recommendations thereon, including recommendations on the staff resources to be provided for the preparation and duration of the Congress, to the Economic and Social Council at its first regular session of 1989;

11. *Requests* the Secretary-General to report to the Economic and Social Council, at its first regular session of 1989, on the implementation of the present resolution, taking into account the conclusions and recommendations of the Committee on Crime Prevention and Control at its tenth session.

Economic and Social Council resolution 1988/44

27 May 1988   Meeting 16   Adopted without vote

Approved by Second Committee (E/1988/91) without vote, 18 May (meeting 14); 14-nation draft (E/1988/C.2/L.4); agenda item 12.
Sponsors: Argentina, Australia, Bolivia, Canada, Colombia, Costa Rica, Cuba, France, Greece, Italy, United Kingdom, Uruguay, Venezuela, Yugoslavia.

Committee on Crime Prevention and Control

The Committee on Crime Prevention and Control held its tenth session at Vienna from 22 to 31 August 1988.

The Committee had before it reports prepared by the Secretary-General relating to the implementation of the conclusions and recommendations of the Seventh Congress, dealing with United Nations activities in crime prevention and control between 1 October 1985 and 31 March 1988;[21] a model

agreement on the transfer of criminal proceedings;[22] a model agreement on the transfer of supervision of foreign offenders conditionally sentenced or conditionally released;[23] alternatives to imprisonment and reduction of the prison population;[24] draft basic principles on the role of lawyers;[25] and the implementation of the Basic Principles on the Independence of the Judiciary,[26] adopted by the Seventh Congress.[27] The implementation of the recommendations of the Seventh Congress was also a subject of discussion at an *ad hoc* inter-agency meeting (Vienna, 1 and 2 September 1988).[28] The Committee also considered reports of the Secretary-General on the review of the functioning and programme of work of the United Nations in crime prevention and criminal justice;[29] on preparations for the Eighth Congress (see below);[30] and on progress achieved on domestic violence,[31] submitted in response to a 1985 General Assembly resolution.[32]

In its report to the Economic and Social Council,[33] the Committee recommended 14 draft resolutions for the Council's adoption: statute of a United Nations interregional crime and justice research institute; implementation of the Declaration of Basic Principles of Justice for Victims of Crime and Abuse of Power;[17] United Nations network of government-appointed national correspondents in the field of crime prevention and control; UNAFRI; procedures for the effective implementation of the Basic Principles on the Independence of the Judiciary;[27] guidelines for the effective implementation of the Code of Conduct for Law Enforcement Officials;[11] concerted international action against the forms of crime identified in the Milan Plan of Action; implementation of United Nations standards and norms in crime prevention and criminal justice; implementation of the safeguards guaranteeing protection of the rights of those facing the death penalty;[34] effective prevention and investigation of extra-legal, arbitrary and summary executions; the Beijing Rules;[13] domestic violence; review of the functioning and programme of the work of the United Nations in crime prevention and criminal justice; and the continuation of preparations for the Eighth Congress. A draft decision concerned the report of the Committee on its tenth session and the provisional agenda and documentation for its eleventh session.

Preparations for the Eighth Congress

Preparations for the Eighth (1990) Congress were entrusted to the Committee on Crime Prevention and Control. In a June report to the Committee,[30] the Secretary-General discussed continuation of the preparations, reported on the provisional agenda, resource allocations and the appointment of the Director-General of

UNOV/CSDHA as the Secretary-General of the Congress, and described the programme of public information activities to be provided by DPI.

Five interregional preparatory meetings of experts were conducted at Vienna on the substantive items of the provisional agenda of the Eighth Congress, as follows: crime prevention and criminal justice in the context of development: realities and perspectives of international co-operation (15-19 February); criminal justice policies in relation to problems of imprisonment, other penal sanctions and alternative measures (30 May-3 June); effective national and international action against organized crime and terrorist criminal activities (14-18 March); prevention of juvenile delinquency, juvenile justice and the protection of the young: policy approaches and directions (18-22 April); and United Nations norms and guidelines in crime prevention and criminal justice: implementation and priorities for further standard-setting (27 June-1 July). Five regional preparatory meetings were planned for 1989. A number of *ad hoc* meetings related to items of the provisional agenda were held in 1988 with the co-operation of Governments and on the initiative and with the support of NGOs and academic institutions.

A planning meeting for the Congress was scheduled to take place from 27 August to 7 September 1990. In April 1988,[35] Cuba extended an invitation to host the Congress at Havana. On 27 May, the Economic and Social Council, by **decision 1988/146**, took note with appreciation of Cuba's offer.

The Secretary-General suggested that the Committee might wish to consider as the theme for the Congress "International criminal justice co-operation for the twenty-first century". He discussed the general preparatory activities for the Congress; categories of participants and observers to be invited; demonstration workshops and information exhibits; and basic documentation.

On 31 August, the Committee approved a draft resolution for adoption by the Economic and Social Council, in which it agreed to the proposed dates and theme of the Congress.

Preparations for the Congress were also discussed at an *ad hoc* inter-agency meeting (Vienna, 1 and 2 September 1988).[28]

UN Trust Fund for Social Defence

The United Nations Trust Fund for Social Defence had a total income in 1988 of $1,617,506, including $1,407,046 in pledged contributions, while expenditures amounted to $1,349,089.

Most of the contributions were earmarked and used to fund UNSDRI activities and to maintain the United Nations–affiliated Helsinki Institute for Crime Prevention and Control.

Cultural development

World Decade for Cultural Development

In January 1988, the Secretary-General and the Director-General of UNESCO launched the World Decade for Cultural Development (1988-1997), proclaimed by the General Assembly in 1986.[36] They were to report biennially on the progress of the Decade to the Assembly, through the Economic and Social Council at its second regular session. In February,[37] the Secretary-General stated that, since the Decade was launched in January, it would be preferable to begin the biennial reporting in 1989 and he would propose, in consultation with the UNESCO Director-General, that the Council postpone consideration of the report to its second regular session of 1989.

On 5 February 1988, the Council, by **decision 1988/101**, decided to consider the report on the progress of the Decade on a biennial basis beginning at its second regular session of 1989 and recommended that the Assembly do the same.

REFERENCES

[1]YUN 1987, p. 618, GA res. 42/134, 7 Dec. 1987. [2]A/43/570. [3]YUN 1985, p. 937. [4]DP/1989/46/Add.1. [5]DP/1989/46/Add.2. [6]YUN 1985, p. 738. [7]A/43/572. [8]YUN 1986, p. 618, GA res. 41/107, 4 Dec. 1986. [9]YUN 1987, p. 623, GA res. 42/59, 30 Nov. 1987. [10]E/AC.57/1988/8 & Corr.1 & Add.1,2. [11]YUN 1979, p. 779, GA res. 34/169, annex, 17 Dec. 1979. [12]E/AC.57/1988/11. [13]YUN 1985, p. 747, GA res. 40/33, annex, 29 Nov. 1985. [14]E/AC.57/1988/9 & Corr.1,2. [15]E/AC.57/1988/5 & Corr.1. [16]A/AC.57/1988/3. [17]YUN 1985, p. 743, GA res. 40/34, annex, 29 Nov. 1985. [18]E/AC.57/1988/16. [19]E/1988/31. [20]YUN 1987, p. 626, ESC res. 1987/53, 28 May 1987. [21]E/AC.57/1988/2. [22]E/AC.57/1988/6 & Corr.1. [23]E/AC.57/1988/7 & Corr.1. [24]E/AC.57/1988/10. [25]E/AC.57/1988/15. [26]E/AC.57/1988/4. [27]YUN 1985, p. 757. [28]ACC/1988/PG/12. [29]E/AC.57/1988/13 & Corr.1. [30]E/AC.57/1988/14. [31]E/AC.57/1988/12. [32]YUN 1985, p. 745, GA res. 40/36, 29 Nov. 1985. [33]E/1988/20. [34]YUN 1984, p. 710, ESC res. 1984/50, annex, 25 May 1984. [35]E/1988/51. [36]YUN 1986, p. 624, GA res. 41/187, 8 Dec. 1986. [37]E/1988/44.

Chapter XIII

Women

In 1988, the United Nations continued the implementation of the Nairobi Forward-looking Strategies for the Advancement of Women, adopted in 1985 to overcome obstacles to the goals and objectives of the United Nations Decade for Women (1976-1985).

At its March session, the Commission on the Status of Women considered several issues concerning women and development, including the economic aspects of women in development and the problems of rural women. It recommended a number of draft resolutions and decisions for adoption by the Economic and Social Council. On the recommendation of the Commission, the Council, in May, endorsed a comprehensive reporting system to monitor, review and appraise the implementation of the Forward-looking Strategies (resolution 1988/22). The system was also endorsed by the General Assembly in December (resolution 43/101) when it emphasized the importance of integrating women into the development process and called on Member States to establish targets to increase women's participation in professional and decision-making positions in their countries.

In July, the Council urged Governments to provide women with adequate education and training facilities and requested United Nations development agencies to pay particular attention to the role of women in rural development, especially in the areas of food, water supply, access to credit facilities and appropriate technologies (1988/29).

The United Nations Development Fund for Women continued to provide resources for plans and projects in developing regions in two priority areas—serving as a catalyst to ensure women's involvement in development activities and supporting innovative and experimental activities benefiting women. In December, the Assembly stressed the importance of strengthening the Fund's technical and financial capacities and invited Governments and others to consider making substantial contributions (43/102).

The Committee on the Elimination of Discrimination against Women considered 11 initial reports and two second periodic reports of States parties to the 1979 Convention on the Elimination of All Forms of Discrimination against Women on their implementation of the Convention. By the end of the year, the Convention had received 95 signatures and 95 accessions.

Advancement of women

Implementation of the Nairobi Strategies

In response to a 1987 request of the General Assembly,[1] the Secretary-General, in September 1988,[2] submitted a report on the implementation of the Nairobi Forward-looking Strategies for the Advancement of Women, adopted in 1985 by the World Conference to Review and Appraise the Achievements of the United Nations Decade for Women.[3] The report discussed action taken by the organizations of the United Nations system to implement the Strategies through monitoring and review and appraisal (see below); the Commission on the Status of Women (see below); separate programmes for the advancement of women; steps to ensure the equalization of opportunities for disabled women; the establishment of new five-year targets at each level for the percentage of women in Professional posts and decision-making positions; and development of a public information strategy on issues relating to women.

The report also reviewed the priority themes for consideration by the Commission on the Status of Women in 1989 dealing with equality (equality in economic and social participation); development (women and education, eradication of illiteracy, employment, health and social services, including population issues and child care); and peace (full participation of women in the construction of their countries and in the creation of just social and political systems).

GENERAL ASSEMBLY ACTION

On 8 December 1988, on the recommendation of the Third (Social, Humanitarian and Cultural) Committee, the General Assembly adopted **resolution 43/101** without vote.

Implementation of the Nairobi Forward-looking Strategies for the Advancement of Women
The General Assembly,
Recalling all its relevant resolutions, in particular resolutions 40/108 of 13 December 1985 and 42/62 of 30 November 1987, in which, *inter alia*, it endorsed the Nairobi Forward-looking Strategies for the Advancement of Women for the period up to the year 2000 and set out measures for their immediate implementation and

for the overall achievement of the goals and objectives of the United Nations Decade for Women: Equality, Development and Peace,

Taking into consideration Economic and Social Council resolutions 1987/18, 1987/19, 1987/20, 1987/21, 1987/22, 1987/23, 1987/24, 1987/25 and 1987/26 of 26 May 1987 and 1988/19, 1988/21, 1988/22 and 1988/29 of 26 May 1988,

Recalling the Guiding Principles for Developmental Social Welfare Policies and Programmes in the Near Future, adopted by the Interregional Consultation on Developmental Social Welfare Policies and Programmes, held at Vienna from 7 to 15 September 1987,

Noting with concern the serious impact of the world economic situation on the programmes and plans for the advancement of women, especially in the global context,

Conscious of the important and constructive contribution to the advancement of the status of women made by the Commission on the Status of Women, the specialized agencies, the regional commissions and other organizations of the United Nations system, Member States and intergovernmental and non-governmental organizations,

Emphasizing once again the priority of the implementation, monitoring, review and appraisal of the Forward-looking Strategies,

Welcoming the significant progress made by the Commission at its special session in 1987 in restructuring its agenda along functional lines, developing the systematic long-term programme of work and strengthening its role and functions, and noting the outcome of the thirty-second session of the Commission, held at Vienna from 14 to 23 March 1988, and, in particular, Economic and Social Council resolutions 1988/19, 1988/21, 1988/22 and 1988/29,

Taking note of Economic and Social Council resolutions on issues relating to women,

Welcoming the designation by the Secretary-General of the advancement of women as one of the priorities of the Organization for the biennium 1988-1989,

Recognizing the need for the Commission to consider at its regular sessions the priority themes for its next five sessions, contained in the annex to Economic and Social Council resolution 1987/24,

1. *Takes note* of the report of the Secretary-General concerning the implementation of the Nairobi Forward-looking Strategies for the Advancement of Women;

2. *Recalls* resolutions 1, 2 and 4 adopted by the Commission on the Status of Women at its special session in 1987, in particular its recommendation that the implementation of the Forward-looking Strategies and the status of women in general should be incorporated as one of the priorities in the introduction of the Organization's medium-term plan for the period 1992-1997;

3. *Reaffirms* the need for the Forward-looking Strategies to be translated immediately into concrete action by Governments, as determined by overall national priorities, as well as by the organizations of the United Nations system, the specialized agencies and intergovernmental and non-governmental organizations;

4. *Reaffirms also* the central role of the Commission in matters related to the advancement of women and calls upon it to promote the implementation of the Forward-looking Strategies to the year 2000 based on the goals of the United Nations Decade for Women: Equality, Development and Peace and the subtheme "Employment, Health and Education", and urges all organizations of

the United Nations system to co-operate with the Commission in this task;

5. *Endorses* Economic and Social Council resolution 1988/19, in which, *inter alia*, the Council decided that the duration of the thirty-fourth session of the Commission, to be held in 1990, should be extended to ten days;

6. *Reaffirms further*, in the implementation of the Forward-looking Strategies, the role of the Centre for Social Development and Humanitarian Affairs of the Secretariat, in particular the Division for the Advancement of Women, as the substantive secretariat of the Commission and as a focal point for matters on women, the catalysing role of the United Nations Development Fund for Women and the role of the International Research and Training Institute for the Advancement of Women in the promotion of the role of women in the context of the participation of women in development;

7. *Requests* the relevant United Nations bodies to continue to provide focused and action-oriented input when reporting to the Commission on the priority themes;

8. *Endorses* the comprehensive reporting system to monitor, review and appraise the implementation of the Forward-looking Strategies, as outlined in the annex to Economic and Social Council resolution 1988/22, which will assist Member States in identifying problems and in developing remedial measures at the national, regional and international levels, and invites Governments and the organizations of the United Nations system, including the regional commissions and the specialized agencies, to report accordingly, through the Commission, to the Economic and Social Council;

9. *Emphasizes*, in the framework of the Forward-looking Strategies, the importance of the total integration of women in the development process, bearing in mind the specific and urgent needs of the developing countries, and calls upon Member States to establish specific targets at each level in order to increase the participation of women in professional and decision-making positions in their countries;

10. *Emphasizes also* the need to give urgent attention to redressing socio-economic inequities at the national and international levels as a necessary step towards the full realization of the goals and objectives of the Forward-looking Strategies;

11. *Urges* that particular attention be given by the United Nations and Governments to the situation of disabled women, and that Governments take steps to ensure the equalization of opportunities and social justice for and political participation of disabled women in each sector of society;

12. *Endorses* Economic and Social Council resolution 1988/29, in which the Council requested the Secretary-General to convene a seminar on women and rural development, using the resources available in the Trust Fund for the Preparatory Activities of the 1985 World Conference to Review and Appraise the Achievements of the United Nations Decade for Women established under Council decision 1983/132;

13. *Endorses also* Economic and Social Council resolution 1988/21, in which the Council recommended that in updating the *World Survey on the Role of Women in Development*, particular emphasis should be given to those factors that contribute to the deteriorating status of women in developing countries, as well as Economic and Social Council resolution 1988/49 of 26 July 1988, in which the Council called upon the Secretary-General to devote a

separate section in the *World Economic Survey* to economic aspects of the situation of women and their contribution to economic development;

14. *Requests* the Commission to explore, at its thirty-third session, the possibility of holding, during the period 1990-1991, an interregional consultation on women in public life;

15. *Once again calls upon* the Secretary-General and the executive heads of the specialized agencies and other United Nations bodies to establish five-year targets at each level for the percentage of women in Professional and decision-making positions, in accordance with the criteria established by the General Assembly, in particular that of equitable geographical distribution, in order that a definite upward trend in the implementation of Assembly resolution 41/206 D of 11 December 1986 be registered in the number of Professional and decision-making positions held by women by 1990, and to set additional targets every five years;

16. *Requests* the Secretary-General to invite Governments, organizations of the United Nations system, including the regional commissions and the specialized agencies, and intergovernmental and non-governmental organizations to report periodically to the Economic and Social Council, through the Commission, on activities undertaken at all levels to implement the Forward-looking Strategies;

17. *Also requests* the Secretary-General to include in his report to the General Assembly at its forty-fourth session on the implementation of the Forward-looking Strategies an assessment of recent developments that are relevant to the priority themes to be considered at the following session of the Commission and to transmit to the Commission a summary of relevant views expressed by delegations during the Assembly's debate;

18. *Further requests* the Secretary-General to report to the General Assembly at its forty-fourth session on measures taken to implement the present resolution;

19. *Requests* the Secretary-General to continue to provide for the existing weekly radio programmes on women in the regular budget of the United Nations, with adequate provisions for broadcasts in different languages, and to develop the focal point for issues relating to women in the Department of Public Information of the Secretariat, which, in concert with the Centre for Social Development and Humanitarian Affairs, should provide a more effective public information programme relating to the advancement of women;

20. *Decides* to consider these questions further at its forty-fourth session under the item entitled ''Forward-looking strategies for the advancement of women to the year 2000''.

General Assembly resolution 43/101

8 December 1988   Meeting 75   Adopted without vote

Approved by Third Committee (A/43/813) without vote, 11 November (meeting 40); draft by Tunisia, for Group of 77 (A/C.3/43/L.23), orally revised; agenda item 95.
Meeting numbers. GA 43rd session: 3rd Committee 15, 23-30, 36, 40; plenary 75.

Monitoring, review and appraisal

In September,[2] the Secretary-General reported on action taken by the organizations of the United Nations system to monitor the review and appraisal of progress in the advancement of women.

The Economic and Social Council, by **resolution 1988/22** (see below), had modified the reporting system proposed by the Secretary-General in January[4] to form part of a two-year cycle of system-wide monitoring of progress in implementing the Strategies, and established a five-year cycle for review and appraisal. The reporting system aimed at simplifying the substantive aspects of monitoring at the global and regional levels and to extend the review and appraisal at the national level to the whole of the Strategies.

For national monitoring purposes, the United Nations Statistical Office completed a women's indicators and statistical data base in co-operation with the Branch for the Advancement of Women of the United Nations Centre for Social Development and Humanitarian Affairs at Vienna and the statistical services of the International Labour Organisation (ILO), the Food and Agriculture Organization of the United Nations, the United Nations Educational, Scientific and Cultural Organization and the World Health Organization. The data contained over 200 statistical series and indicators for monitoring the situation of women in conformity with the Decade's goals and objectives, the implementation of the Strategies and the priority themes. The *Compendium of Statistics and Indicators on the Situation of Women—1986* was prepared using the data base.

On 28 June 1988, the Secretary-General circulated, for the first review and appraisal, a questionnaire to Member States to be returned in early 1989. The first part of the questionnaire consisted of a summary for implementation of the Strategies and the second presented an outline of a national report, including an executive summary.

The Secretary-General noted that systematic monitoring and review and appraisal aspects were being incorporated into the operational activities of the United Nations system and many organizations were elaborating specific procedures.

ECONOMIC AND SOCIAL COUNCIL ACTION

On 26 May 1988, the Economic and Social Council, on the recommendation of its Second (Social) Committee, adopted **resolution 1988/22** without vote.

Establishment of a comprehensive reporting system to monitor, review and appraise the implementation of the Nairobi Forward-looking Strategies for the Advancement of Women

The Economic and Social Council,

Reaffirming the importance attached by the World Conference to Review and Appraise the Achievements of the United Nations Decade for Women: Equality, Development and Peace to monitoring, review and appraisal as outlined in the Nairobi Forward-looking Strategies for the Advancement of Women,

Bearing in mind the guidelines set out in its resolution 1987/18 of 26 May 1987, which the Secretary-General was requested to take into account in further developing and implementing the reporting system to monitor, review and appraise progress in the advancement of women,

Recalling its resolution 1987/22 of 26 May 1987, in which it decided to expand the terms of reference of the Commission on the Status of Women to include the functions of promoting the objectives of equality, development and peace, monitoring the implementation of measures for the advancement of women, and reviewing and appraising progress made at the national, subregional, regional, sectoral and global levels,

Reaffirming the request made by the General Assembly, in its resolution 42/62 of 30 November 1987, that the Secretary-General invite Governments, organizations of the United Nations system, including the regional commissions and the specialized agencies, and intergovernmental and non-governmental organizations to report periodically to the Economic and Social Council, through the Commission, on activities undertaken at all levels to implement the Nairobi Forward-looking Strategies,

Reaffirming the appropriateness of a two-year cycle of system-wide monitoring of progress made in implementing the Nairobi Forward-looking Strategies and a five-year cycle of longer-term review and appraisal to continue the cycle established by the World Conference,

Recognizing that effective monitoring, review and appraisal should be conducted at the national, regional, sectoral and international levels to achieve optimal results,

Mindful of the need to avoid duplication of reporting obligations, in view of the burden that coexisting reporting systems place on Member States, especially those with limited resources, and in view of the financial stringencies facing the United Nations system,

1.   *Endorses* the comprehensive reporting system to monitor, review and appraise the implementation of the Nairobi Forward-looking Strategies for the Advancement of Women, set out in the annex to the present resolution;

2.   *Decides* that its intergovernmental subsidiary bodies, including the regional commissions, should monitor, as necessary, the follow-up to their recommendations relating to the advancement of women;

3.   *Requests* the Secretary-General to include the resolutions of those bodies in the report requested by the General Assembly in resolution 42/178 of 11 December 1987 and the results of their monitoring activities in his biennial report to the Commission on the Status of Women on monitoring the Nairobi Forward-looking Strategies;

4.   *Also requests* the Secretary-General to invite Governments and intergovernmental and non-governmental organizations to report to the Economic and Social Council, through the Commission, on monitoring, review and appraisal of progress at all levels in the implementation of the Nairobi Forward-looking Strategies, in the manner set out in the annex to the present resolution;

5.   *Decides* that the biennial reports of the Secretary-General on monitoring of progress made by the organizations of the United Nations system in the implementation of the Nairobi Forward-looking Strategies should be considered by the Commission in even-numbered years, beginning in 1990;

6.   *Also decides* that, for the purpose of monitoring progress at the national level, the Secretary-General should, within existing resources, make available a summary compilation of available statistical indicators relating to the implementation of the Nairobi Forward-looking Strategies and submit a progress report on national reporting of statistics and indicators on women to the Commission in odd-numbered years, beginning in 1989;

7.   *Urges* the organizations of the United Nations system to incorporate in their regular work programmes, as necessary, monitoring, review and appraisal of the implementation of the Nairobi Forward-looking Strategies and to submit reports thereon to their governing bodies;

8.   *Decides* that the first quinquennial report on review and appraisal of the implementation of the Nairobi Forward-looking Strategies will be considered by the Commission at its thirty-fourth session, in 1990, and that subsequent reports will be considered in 1995 and 2000, so as to continue the five-year cycle of reporting established during the United Nations Decade for Women;

9.   *Encourages* Member States to make use of the reports prepared for the Committee on the Elimination of Discrimination against Women and other relevant international bodies in the preparation of the quinquennial review and appraisal reports, in order to minimize duplication of effort;

10.   *Encourages* the provision of technical assistance to national machinery for the advancement of women and the sharing of support and expertise among such machineries, particularly those in developing countries, to facilitate the preparation of the national reports for the quinquennial review and appraisal;

11.   *Requests* the Commission to make action-oriented recommendations for the further implementation of the Nairobi Forward-looking Strategies following the quinquennial review and appraisal;

12.   *Decides* that, after consideration by the Commission, the monitoring, review and appraisal reports should be made available to the General Assembly so that the Assembly may be kept informed of progress in the implementation of the Nairobi Forward-looking Strategies.

ANNEX
Comprehensive reporting system to monitor, review and appraise the implementation of the Nairobi Forward-looking Strategies for the Advancement of Women

I.   Biennial monitoring of progress made by the organizations of the United Nations system

1.   The Secretary-General should prepare biennial reports on monitoring of the implementation of the Nairobi Forward-looking Strategies for the Advancement of Women by the organizations of the United Nations system, including monitoring at the regional level. The reports should address the three interrelated and mutually reinforcing objectives of the Nairobi Forward-looking Strategies: equality, development and peace. Each objective should be reported on separately, as appropriate.

2.   An introductory commentary should be included covering the basic strategies, relevant institutions, mandates and programmes of action employed to advance each objective.

3.   An account of measures taken for the implementation of the basic strategies for international and regional co-operation set out in chapter V of the Nairobi Forward-looking Strategies should be included under each objective.

4.   The reports should contain specific information on:

(a)   Measures to ensure the integration of the Nairobi Forward-looking Strategies in the programmes of the or-

ganizations of the United Nations system, including measures to strengthen institutional co-ordination and focal points on the status of women;

(b) Progress made by each organization in establishing and meeting five-year targets at each level for the percentage of women in professional and decision-making positions, as called for by the General Assembly.

5. Reports should be prepared according to a standardized format.

6. In order to minimize duplication of effort, the biennial monitoring reports should make use of reports prepared to meet other reporting requirements, *inter alia*, any other reports required under subprogramme 5A of the proposed revisions to the medium-term plan for 1984-1989 to cover the period 1990-1991, the biennial reports requested by the General Assembly in resolution 42/178 of 11 December 1987 and reports on the improvement of the status of women in the United Nations Secretariat, as requested by the General Assembly.

II. Quinquennial review and appraisal

7. The quinquennial review and appraisal will be based on responses from Member States to a questionnaire on the progress achieved in the implementation of the Nairobi Forward-looking Strategies, including an assessment of the effectiveness of methods and programmes introduced and an account of new programmes planned as a result of the national review and appraisal.

8. The national reports should address the three interrelated and mutually reinforcing objectives of the Nairobi Forward-looking Strategies: equality, development and peace. Each objective should be monitored and reported on separately.

9. Each national report should include an introductory commentary covering the basic strategies and programmes of action employed to advance each objective and a review and appraisal of their effectiveness.

10. The national reports should include, under each of the three objectives, an account of measures taken to implement the basic strategies for international and regional co-operation set out in paragraphs 356 to 365 of the Nairobi Forward-looking Strategies.

11. The questionnaires should be simple and direct and structured according to the Nairobi Forward-looking Strategies.

12. The national reports should include an account of the measures taken to meet relevant international standards, such as the Convention on the Elimination of All Forms of Discrimination against Women, the International Convention on the Elimination of All Forms of Racial Discrimination and the conventions of the International Labour Organisation.

13. Non-governmental bodies should be invited to submit reports for the quinquennial review and appraisal.

14. The biennial statistical reports provided by the Secretary-General to the Commission on the Status of Women for monitoring progress at the national level should be consolidated and made available to the Commission for the quinquennial review and appraisal.

15. Every five years, the Commission should review its conclusions on priority themes on the basis of a compilation of relevant resolutions and should select priority themes for the following five-year period.

16. Reports of Member States to relevant international supervisory bodies, such as the Committee on the Elimination of Discrimination against Women, the Com-

mittee on the Elimination of Racial Discrimination, the International Labour Organisation and the United Nations Educational, Scientific and Cultural Organization, and the *World Survey on the Role of Women in Development* should be made available in a consolidated form to the Commission on the Status of Women for consideration in the quinquennial review and appraisal.

17. Reports prepared by the regional commissions on changes in the situation of women within their region, as requested by the General Assembly in resolution 42/178, should be made available to the Commission every five years for the review and appraisal.

Economic and Social Council resolution 1988/22

26 May 1988   Meeting 15   Adopted without vote

Approved by Second Committee (E/1988/90) without vote, 13 May (meeting 9); draft by Commission on women (E/1988/15/Rev.1); agenda item 11.

1990 session of the Commission on the Status of Women

On the recommendation of its Second Committee, the Economic and Social Council, on 26 May 1988, adopted **resolution 1988/19** without vote.

Session of the Commission on the Status of Women in 1990 to review and appraise progress in the implementation of the Nairobi Forward-looking Strategies for the Advancement of Women

The Economic and Social Council,

Recalling its resolution 1987/20 of 26 May 1987, in which it recommended that an extended session of the Commission on the Status of Women be held in 1990, at which Member States would be represented at a high level, in order to review and appraise progress in the implementation of the Nairobi Forward-looking Strategies for the Advancement of Women,

Bearing in mind its resolution 1987/24 of 26 May 1987, in which it endorsed the priority themes to be considered at the next five sessions of the Commission, regardless of any process of review and appraisal that might take place,

Considering the importance of the review and appraisal process to the implementation of the Nairobi Forward-looking Strategies in accordance with General Assembly resolution 40/108 of 13 December 1985, and of the role of non-governmental organizations in that process,

Recalling its resolution 1987/18 of 26 May 1987, in which it established a five-year cycle of review and appraisal of progress in the implementation of the Nairobi Forward-looking Strategies,

Recognizing the role of non-governmental organizations in contributing to the preparations for the session of the Commission in 1990,

Bearing in mind its resolution 1988/22 of 26 May 1988 on the establishment of a comprehensive reporting system to monitor, review and appraise the implementation of the Nairobi Forward-looking Strategies,

Concerned about the limited time and resources available to the Commission and Governments to prepare for the session in 1990,

1. *Decides* that the duration of the thirty-fourth session of the Commission on the Status of Women, to be held in 1990, shall be ten days, in order that the Commission may review and appraise progress made by Governments, international organizations and non-governmental organizations in the implementation of the Nairobi Forward-looking Strategies for the Advancement of Women;

2. *Requests* the Secretary-General to provide additional interpretation facilities, within available resources, so that the Commission may establish a subsidiary body during its thirty-fourth session, in order to make maximum use of the time available;

3. *Decides* that the Commission should review preparations for the 1990 review and appraisal at its thirty-third session, under the agenda item entitled "Monitoring and implementation of the Nairobi Forward-looking Strategies for the Advancement of Women";

4. *Also decides* that the documentation for the 1990 review and appraisal should be prepared according to the requirements of the comprehensive reporting system set out in Council resolution 1988/22 and according to the provisional agenda outlined in the annex to the present resolution;

5. *Encourages* Governments to provide responses of high quality to the questionnaire on which the review and appraisal will be based;

6. *Proposes* that assistance be made available to Governments, on request, for the preparation of their responses to the questionnaire;

7. *Requests* the five regional commissions to hold, within available resources, regional review and appraisal meetings in preparation for the global review and appraisal;

8. *Invites* non-governmental organizations in consultative status with the Economic and Social Council to submit their views, in writing, on their contribution to the 1990 session of the Commission, for presentation in consolidated form to the Commission at its thirty-third session;

9. *Recommends* that in 1990 the Commission make a recommendation to the General Assembly on the convening of a world conference to review and appraise progress in the implementation of the Nairobi Forward-looking Strategies.

ANNEX
Outline of the provisional agenda for the thirty-fourth session of the Commission on the Status of Women
1. Programming and co-ordination matters
2. Priority themes
3. Review and appraisal of the implementation of the Nairobi Forward-looking Strategies for the Advancement of Women:
   (a) Progress at the national level;
   (b) Progress at the regional level;
   (c) Progress at the international level;
   (d) Conclusions and recommendations

Economic and Social Council resolution 1988/19

26 May 1988   Meeting 15   Adopted without vote

Approved by Second Committee (E/1988/90) without vote, 13 May (meeting 9); draft by Commission on women (E/1988/15/Rev.1); agenda item 11.

Programme planning

The Commission on the Status of Women, at its March session, had before it a note by the Secretary-General on programme planning and co-ordination matters.[5] He stated that the first stage for implementing the system-wide medium-term plan for women and development was for each organization of the United Nations system to incorporate that plan, as appropriate, into its own medium-term

proposals. (For details on the system-wide medium-term plan, see below under "Women and development".)

ECONOMIC AND SOCIAL COUNCIL ACTION

On 26 May 1988, on the recommendation of its Second Committee, the Economic and Social Council adopted **resolution 1988/18** without vote.

Programme planning and activities to advance the status of women

The Economic and Social Council,

Reaffirming the high priority that Member States attach to activities to advance the status of women,

Welcoming the priority given by the Secretary-General to the advancement of women in the programme budget for the biennium 1988-1989,

Noting the important roles played by the Commission on the Status of Women and the Committee on the Elimination of Discrimination against Women in achieving the global equality of women,

Concerned that activities to advance the status of women should not suffer disproportionately from the impact of restructuring and retrenchment measures,

Stressing the need to ensure that budgetary resources allocated to activities for the advancement of women are commensurate with the priorities of Governments,

Referring to the reports of the Secretary-General on programme planning matters pertaining to the status of women,

I. Medium-term planning matters

1. *Reiterates* the recommendation made by the Commission on the Status of Women that the Secretary-General should identify the implementation of the Nairobi Forward-looking Strategies for the Advancement of Women and the status of women in general as a global priority for the period 1990-1995 in the introduction to the next medium-term plan;

2. *Requests* the Secretary-General, in preparing his proposals for the next medium-term plan, to formulate a separate major programme on the advancement of women, which should include the four existing or proposed subprogrammes of the global social development issues programme which relate to women and incorporate the intersectoral presentation of activities called for by the General Assembly in resolution 40/108 of 13 December 1985;

II. Programme budget matters

1. *Decides* that the Secretary-General's proposed programme budget for the biennium 1990-1991 and subsequent programme budgets should provide for full funding from the regular budget for the implementation of all aspects of legislative mandates for the advancement of women;

2. *Also decides* that the Trust Fund for the Preparatory Activities for the 1985 World Conference to Review and Appraise the Achievements of the United Nations Decade for Women, established by the Secretary-General pursuant to Economic and Social Council decision 1983/132 of 26 May 1983, should be continued on an interim basis for the biennium 1988-1989 as a special trust fund for the monitoring, review and appraisal of the implementation of the Nairobi Forward-looking Strategies for the Advancement of Women, for the purpose of facilitat-

ing global exchange of information, enhancing the preparation of the work of the Commission on the Status of Women regarding priority themes, and disseminating the results of its discussions of those themes and on monitoring, review and appraisal to a wider audience, in conformity with paragraph 1 of section I above;

3. *Recommends* that the Trust Fund maintain a close and continuous relationship with other United Nations organs, in particular the United Nations Development Fund for Women, with a view to avoiding duplication;

4. *Requests* the Secretary-General to submit a report on the future of the Trust Fund to the Commission on the Status of Women at its thirty-third session;

5. *Reiterates* the recommendation made by the Commission that the Secretary-General should accord the highest priority in the programme budget for the biennium 1988-1989 to the programme elements concerned with policy development in support of the Commission and include activities to that end in the subprogramme on the participation of women in promoting international peace and co-operation;

6. *Reaffirms* the view of the Commission, as expressed in its resolution 32/1 of 16 March 1988, on the level of resources necessary to implement its mandates effectively and efficiently, expressed in its submission to the Special Commission of the Economic and Social Council on the In-depth Study of the United Nations Intergovernmental Structure and Functions in the Economic and Social Fields;

7. *Recommends* that the Branch for the Advancement of Women be renamed the Division for the Advancement of Women, such a change to be carried out without financial implications.

Economic and Social Council resolution 1988/18

| 26 May 1988 | Meeting 15 | Adopted without vote |

Approved by Second Committee (E/1988/90) without vote, 13 May (meeting 9); draft by Commission on women (E/1988/15/Rev.1); agenda item 11.

System-wide co-ordination

The twelfth *ad hoc* inter-agency meeting on women (Vienna, 24-29 March 1988)[6] recommended that the Administrative Committee on Co-ordination (ACC) request its subsidiary bodies dealing with substantive, operational and personnel questions to include regularly in their agendas the implementation of the Nairobi Forward-looking Strategies, together with other measures to advance the status of women. The meeting also adopted recommendations on priority themes of the Commission in 1989 (see above) and 1990, the system-wide medium-term plan for women and development (see below) and the update of the world survey on women in development (see below). The ACC Consultative Committee on Substantive Questions (CCSQ) (Programme Matters) (New York, 3-5 October)[7] took note of the meeting's recommendations.

In January,[8] the Secretary-General submitted a report to the Committee for Programme and Co-ordination (CPC) on the scope and general approach of a 1989 cross-organizational programme analysis on the activities of the United Nations sys-

tem related to the advancement of women (see below).

ECONOMIC AND SOCIAL COUNCIL ACTION

On 26 May 1988, the Economic and Social Council, by **decision 1988/122**, decided to defer until its second regular session consideration of a four-part draft resolution, recommended by the Commission on the Status of Women,[9] concerning system-wide co-ordination of activities to advance the status of women and to integrate women in development.

On 27 July, on the recommendation of its Third (Programme and Co-ordination) Committee, the Council adopted resolutions 1988/60 C and D. **Resolution 1988/60 C** was adopted without vote.

Inter-agency co-ordination in implementing the Nairobi Forward-looking Strategies for the Advancement of Women

The Economic and Social Council,

Recalling its resolutions 1985/46 of 31 May 1985, 1986/71 of 23 July 1986 and 1987/86 of 8 July 1987 concerning the preparation of the system-wide medium-term plan for women and development and the cross-organizational programme analysis of activities related to the advancement of women,

Concerned that many provisions of Commission on the Status of Women resolution 1987/5 of 16 January 1987 relating to the preparation of the final draft of the system-wide medium-term plan for women and development are as yet unimplemented,

1. *Stresses* that the cross-organizational programme analysis to be submitted to the Committee for Programme and Co-ordination in 1989 should present a comprehensive factual picture of the United Nations system's mandates and activities related to the advancement of women, attempt a comprehensive diagnosis of co-ordination problems and suggest remedial action;

2. *Recommends* that the activities analysed should include programme activities at the programme element level, technical co-operation projects and regular programmes of technical assistance, grant-based development assistance, and funding by international development-financing institutions;

3. *Decides* that the legislative mandates to be analysed should include international instruments, intergovernmental resolutions and decisions, other legislative instructions, directives and guidelines, and international strategies, plans and programmes of action relating to the status of women that are still in force;

4. *Further decides* that the directions given by the Commission on the Status of Women, in its resolution 1987/5 and the annex thereto, for the preparation of the final draft of the system-wide medium-term plan for women and development should be fully implemented.

Economic and Social Council resolution 1988/60 C

| 27 July 1988 | Meeting 39 | Adopted without vote |

Approved by Third Committee (E/1988/114) without vote, 15 July (meeting 8); draft by Commission on women (E/1988/C.3/L.1); agenda item 17.

Resolution 1988/60 D was also adopted without vote.

Legislative linkage as a means of co-ordinating the implementation of the Nairobi Forward-looking Strategies for the Advancement of Women

The Economic and Social Council,

Recalling paragraph 320 of the Nairobi Forward-looking Strategies for the Advancement of Women, in which it is stated that specific, appropriate attention should be paid to the advancement of women in the preparation of new instruments and strategies,

Welcoming the decision of the Governing Body of the International Labour Office at its 238th session to place on the agenda of the International Labour Conference in 1989 the question "Night work", as defined in the Night Work (Women) Convention (Revised), 1948 (No. 89) and other relevant conventions,

Requests the Secretary-General to take the necessary measures to ensure that specific action is taken to integrate the concerns of the Nairobi Forward-looking Strategies for the Advancement of Women into the activities mandated by the General Assembly in the following resolutions: resolution 42/104 of 7 December 1987 on the International Literacy Year, resolution 42/106 of 7 December 1987 on the International Conference on the Plight of Refugees, Returnees and Displaced Persons in Southern Africa, resolution 42/163 of 8 December 1987 on the United Nations Programme of Action for African Economic Recovery and Development 1986-1990, resolution 42/177 of 11 December 1987 on the Second United Nations Conference on the Least Developed Countries, resolution 42/186 of 11 December 1987 on the Environmental Perspective to the Year 2000 and Beyond, resolution 42/187 of 11 December 1987 on the report of the World Commission on Environment and Development, and resolution 42/193 of 11 December 1987 on the preparation of the international development strategy for the fourth United Nations development decade.

Economic and Social Council resolution 1988/60 D

27 July 1988   Meeting 39   Adopted without vote

Approved by Third Committee (E/1988/114) without vote, 15 July (meeting 8); draft by Commission on women (E/1988/C.3/L.1); agenda item 17.

National machinery

At its 1988 session, the Commission on the Status of Women considered the issue of national machinery for monitoring and improving the status of women as its priority theme in the area of equality.

A seminar on information systems for the advancement of women for national machinery was held (Vienna, 25-29 January 1988) with support from Japan.

ECONOMIC AND SOCIAL COUNCIL ACTION

On 26 May 1988, on the recommendation of its Second Committee, the Economic and Social Council adopted **resolution 1988/30** without vote.

National machinery for the advancement of women

The Economic and Social Council,

Recalling General Assembly resolution 40/108 of 13 December 1985, in which the Assembly endorsed the Nairobi Forward-looking Strategies for the Advancement of Women,

Bearing in mind its resolution 1986/31 of 23 May 1986, in which it requested the Secretary-General, *inter alia,* to propose guidelines for national machinery to promote the advancement of women and ways to ensure the effective implementation of the Nairobi Forward-looking Strategies,

Recalling its resolution 1987/24 of 26 May 1987, in which it recommended the convening of expert group meetings to assist in the preparation of the work of the Commission on the Status of Women on priority themes and endorsed the topic entitled "National machinery for monitoring and improving the status of women" as one of the three priority themes of the thirty-second session of the Commission,

Recognizing that national machinery or its equivalent is an essential element in the promotion and implementation of the Nairobi Forward-looking Strategies and the Convention on the Elimination of All Forms of Discrimination against Women,

Bearing in mind the recommendations of the Seminar on National Machinery for Monitoring and Improving the Status of Women, held at Vienna from 28 September to 2 October 1987, and the Seminar on Information Systems for the Advancement of Women for National Machinery, held at Vienna from 25 to 29 January 1988,

1. *Urges* countries that have not yet done so to establish national machinery for the advancement of women, or its equivalent, including such machinery at the highest political level;

2. *Urges* Governments that have already established such machinery or its equivalent to recognize its essential importance in the promotion and implementation of national policies for the advancement of women, the Nairobi Forward-looking Strategies for the Advancement of Women and the Convention on the Elimination of All Forms of Discrimination against Women, and therefore requests Governments to provide adequate political, financial and human resources to enable such machinery or its equivalent to function effectively;

3. *Encourages* Governments, in accordance with their own administrative systems, to make every effort in establishing or strengthening national machinery for the advancement of women, or its equivalent, to do so, as appropriate, on the basis of the recommendations of the Seminar on National Machinery for Monitoring and Improving the Status of Women and the Seminar on Information Systems for the Advancement of Women for National Machinery;

4. *Stresses* the importance, for Governments, of establishing and maintaining formal and informal mechanisms for co-operation between national machinery or its equivalent and specialized centres of responsibility in sectoral departments and ministries, including mechanisms to support greater co-ordination of efforts to promote the interests of women in both national and international policies;

5. *Calls upon* Governments to develop information systems that include statistics and indicators on the status of women;

6. *Invites* national machineries or their equivalents to exchange information, bilaterally and multilaterally, on issues of common interest, including information on innovative policies, programmes and research;

7. *Requests* the Secretary-General, in co-operation with the regional commissions, to promote such infor-

mation exchange by supporting regional and subregional meetings of national machineries or their equivalents, using resources from the regular programme of advisory services for the biennium 1988-1989 and from the regular budgets of the five regional commissions thereafter, and by annually updating and distributing the Directory of National Machinery for the Advancement of Women;

8. *Invites* Governments of developing countries to give priority, within the context of their overall requests for development assistance, to proposals for assistance to strengthen national machinery for the advancement of women or its equivalent;

9. *Recommends* that international development agencies respond positively to requests from Governments for assistance in strengthening national machinery for the advancement of women or its equivalent;

10. *Urges* the national machinery for the advancement of women or its equivalent in each Government to participate actively in the preparation of and follow-up to the work of the Commission on the Status of Women by co-ordinating the collection of all forms of information for the comprehensive reporting system to review and appraise the implementation of the Nairobi Forward-looking Strategies and for reports for the Commission's consideration of priority themes;

11. *Endorses* the continuation of the information system on women initiated by the Secretary-General and its further development in official languages of the United Nations, consistent with the priorities determined by Governments and taking advantage of all sources of funding beyond those already mandated, including the contributions of interested Governments;

12. *Recommends* that statistics and other information on women be an integral part of all relevant major statistical and public information programmes of the United Nations system, including those of the United Nations Office at Vienna and the Department of Public Information of the Secretariat;

13. *Recommends* that the services of an interregional adviser be made available, through the regular programme of technical co-operation, to assist, on request, national machineries or their equivalents in carrying out effectively their review and appraisal of the implementation of the Nairobi Forward-looking Strategies and in preparing the reports called for in the Convention on the Elimination of All Forms of Discrimination against Women;

14. *Decides* that the questionnaire to be prepared by the Secretary-General to collect information for the review and appraisal of the implementation of the Nairobi Forward-looking Strategies should contain a specific section on national machinery or its equivalent;

15. *Recommends* that Governments make every effort to support women's non-governmental organizations working to improve the status of women in accordance with the Nairobi Forward-looking Strategies and the Convention on the Elimination of All Forms of Discrimination against Women;

16. *Calls upon* Governments to ensure the effective participation of women and women's non-governmental organizations in decision-making at all levels in order to bring about a lasting improvement in the welfare of societies.

Economic and Social Council resolution 1988/30

26 May 1988   Meeting 15   Adopted without vote

Approved by Second Committee (E/1988/90) without vote, 13 May (meeting 9); draft by Commission on women (E/1988/15/Rev.1); agenda item 11.

Research and Training Institute for the Advancement of Women

The Board of Trustees of the International Research and Training Institute for the Advancement of Women (INSTRAW) held its eighth session at Santo Domingo, Dominican Republic, from 8 to 12 February 1988.[10] The Board reviewed INSTRAW's 1987 activities and considered INSTRAW training strategies on women in development (WID); new communication technologies as applied to WID; the proposed 1988-1989 INSTRAW programme budget; network building through co-operative arrangements with Governments, United Nations bodies and non-governmental, academic and women's organizations; and fund-raising.

In decisions it adopted and brought to the attention of the Economic and Social Council, the Board stated its intention to examine INSTRAW publications in depth for future policy guidelines and action. It recommended that prototype curricula and teaching materials on women and development be developed. It further recommended that INSTRAW communication facilities and linkages with other United Nations information systems be further upgraded and expanded to academic institutions. The regional commissions were requested to assist INSTRAW in establishing new focal points and to co-operate with existing focal points and correspondents. The Board recommended that INSTRAW and the regional commissions jointly co-ordinate their strategies within the system-wide medium-term plan for women and development for the period 1990-1995 and convene consultations prior to the Board's 1989 session.

INSTRAW activities

Reporting on the Institute's work in 1988, the INSTRAW Director stated that the work programme for the year had included 26 programmes in research and training on women and development in five programmatic clusters: statistics, indicators and data on women; issues relevant for policy design; sectoral issues, focusing on inter-agency co-operation in the areas of drinking-water supply and sanitation and new and renewable sources of energy; training methods for WID; and network building. The Director noted that the close interrelationship between the INSTRAW research, training and information programmes had been further strengthened, thus contributing to the expansion of the 1988 work programme.

Within its programme on statistics, indicators and data on women, INSTRAW organized three training workshops: two national workshops (Beijing, China, 2-8 June; Athens, Greece, 10-14 October) and a subregional workshop for Central America (San José, Costa Rica, 5-9 December).

INSTRAW began, in October 1988, implementation of the statistics component of the Economic Commission for Africa (ECA) project, funded by the United Nations Development Programme (UNDP), on improving African women's role in informal-sector production and management. INSTRAW co-operated with ECA and the Economic and Social Commission for Western Asia (ESCWA) in implementing a study on the time-use of women and developing statistics and indicators on the situation of women in the ESCWA region.

Under its programme on alternative approaches to women and development, INSTRAW co-sponsored an international training seminar on women and the economy, focusing on women managers and entrepreneurs (Halifax, Canada, 25-28 July), and co-operated with the Society for International Development in a conference on poverty, development and collective survival: public and private responsibilities (New Delhi, India, March).

INSTRAW, in co-operation with the Bulgarian Academy of Sciences (its focal point in Bulgaria), organized an interregional consultative meeting on women in co-operatives: implications for development (Plovdiv, Bulgaria, 20-24 June).

Under the programme on the role of women and new and renewable sources of energy, INSTRAW prepared, in collaboration with the ILO International Centre for Advanced Technical and Vocational Training (Turin, Italy), a multi-media modular training package on women and new and renewable sources of energy. The package contained a pedagogical scheme, additional reading, a bibliography, a lesson plan, key issue check-lists for group work, a trainer's guide and two evaluation forms; it was supplemented with sound slide packages and transparencies.

The INSTRAW training manual for women entrepreneurs and managers in industry was prepared in collaboration with the United Nations Industrial Development Organization.

The Institute prepared a training package on women and development which was presented during a joint training seminar with UNDP and the United Nations Population Fund (Santo Domingo, 28 November–2 December).

INSTRAW organized an international consultative meeting on communications for women in development (Rome, Italy, 24-28 October) with financial support from Italy and the Friedrich Ebert Stiftung (Federal Republic of Germany).

At the United Nations Pledging Conference for Development Activities held in November 1988, 23 Member States pledged $1,199,364 to INSTRAW

for 1989. As at 31 December 1988, the balance of the Trust Fund for INSTRAW amounted to $1,685,933.

ECONOMIC AND SOCIAL COUNCIL ACTION

On 26 May 1988, the Economic and Social Council, on the recommendation of its Second Committee, adopted **resolution 1988/31** without vote.

International Research and Training Institute for the Advancement of Women

The Economic and Social Council,

Recalling its resolution 1987/25 of 26 May 1987,

Recalling also General Assembly resolution 42/65 of 30 November 1987,

Having considered the report of the Board of Trustees of the International Research and Training Institute for the Advancement of Women on its eighth session,

Convinced that the programme activities of the Institute have helped to promote greater general awareness of the linkages between research, training and information in questions relating to women and development, which is an essential prerequisite for bringing about developmental changes benefiting women and society,

1. *Takes note with satisfaction* of the report of the Board of Trustees of the International Research and Training Institute for the Advancement of Women on its eighth session and the decisions contained therein;

2. *Expresses its satisfaction* with the work done by the Institute in its innovative research on economic activities of women, particularly in the informal sector of the economy, and with its flexible modular approach to training, which strengthens national training capabilities and should be further developed;

3. *Takes note* of the programme budget of the Institute for the biennium 1988-1989, approved by the Board of Trustees at its eighth session, which is consistent with the goals of the Nairobi Forward-looking Strategies for the Advancement of Women;

4. *Recommends* that the Institute, in keeping with its statute, continue to co-operate with the organizations of the United Nations system in the implementation of its programmes and possibly implement research and training projects within its area of competence funded by the United Nations Development Programme;

5. *Renews its appeal* to Governments, intergovernmental and non-governmental organizations and other potential donors to contribute to the United Nations Trust Fund for the International Research and Training Institute for the Advancement of Women.

Economic and Social Council resolution 1988/31

26 May 1988   Meeting 15   Adopted without vote

Approved by Second Committee (E/1988/90) without vote, 13 May (meeting 9); 38-nation draft (E/1988/C.2/L.3); agenda item 11.

Sponsors: Argentina, Bahamas, Bolivia, Bulgaria, Chile, China, Colombia, Costa Rica, Cuba, Cyprus, Dominican Republic, Ecuador, Egypt, El Salvador, France, Greece, Guatemala, Guinea, Haiti, India, Indonesia, Italy, Japan, Kenya, Lesotho, Mexico, Morocco, Panama, Peru, Philippines, Senegal, Spain, Sri Lanka, Sudan, Uruguay, Venezuela, Yugoslavia, Zaire.

REFERENCES

[1]YUN 1987, p. 830, GA res. 42/62, 30 Nov. 1987. [2]A/43/638. [3]YUN 1985, p. 937. [4]E/1988/4 & Corr.1. [5]E/CN.6/1988/10. [6]ACC/1988/PG/2. [7]ACC/1988/15. [8]E/AC.51/1988/2. [9]E/1988/15/Rev.1. [10]E/1988/28.

Women and development

Commission action. The Commission on the Status of Women[1] made a number of recommendations concerning women in development in resolutions it adopted on the system-wide coordination of activities to integrate WID and on rural women and development. Under the priority theme of development, the Commission discussed the problems of rural women, including food, water resources, agricultural technology, rural employment, transportation and environment. It had before it a report of the Secretary-General,[2] prepared in collaboration with United Nations bodies and specialized agencies whose work covered rural women, which outlined the current situation of rural women, indicated the limitations to improving their conditions and suggested policy measures to overcome those limitations.

UNICEF action. At its 1988 session,[3] the Executive Board of the United Nations Children's Fund (UNICEF) discussed a progress report[4] on achievements made in implementing UNICEF's policy on WID, which the Board had adopted in 1987.[5] The report reviewed the follow-up, implementation and field application of the policy and recommendations for action to strengthen UNICEF's commitment towards incorporating women into mainstream development activities. Special orientation and training was required to widen the expertise of programme staff in regional and country offices to assist in monitoring and participate in field-work of selected country programmes. Programme officers specializing in WID issues were needed, as was a personal commitment of senior management, for which an accountability system to monitor programme implementation performance was recommended. The report stressed the importance of organizing training workshops to develop field staff perspectives and skills in areas of operational methodology. The Board endorsed the recommendations for action as proposed in the report.[6]

UNDP action. In a March report with later addendum,[7] the UNDP Administrator discussed the way in which WID perspectives were reflected in the work of UNDP. He also addressed other issues, such as staff training, including the participation of agencies and government representatives; complementarity with the United Nations Development Fund for Women (UNIFEM) (see below); cooperation between the UNDP Division for WID with relevant units of United Nations organizations, agencies, Governments and non-governmental organizations (NGOs); and the 1988 work plan.

On 1 July,[8] the UNDP Governing Council, having considered the report of the Administrator, noted an initiative taken by the Division for WID to examine the feasibility of more gender-responsive programming and asked the Administrator to submit a progress report thereon in 1989. The Council encouraged the expansion and diversification of the staff training programme and requested information on its development in 1989. It further requested the Administrator to report in 1989 on the complementarity between the Division for WID, UNIFEM and INSTRAW and on how WID perspectives were reflected in the work of UNDP.

UNEP activities. The Senior Women's Advisory Group on Sustainable Development of the United Nations Environment Programme contributed to a workshop on women and environment for sustainable development (Bangkok, Thailand), held by the International Council on Social Welfare, Asia and the Pacific.

ECONOMIC AND SOCIAL COUNCIL ACTION

On 26 July 1988, the Economic and Social Council, on the recommendation of its Second Committee, adopted **resolution 1988/29** without vote.

Rural women and development

The Economic and Social Council,

Recalling its resolution 1987/24 and its decision 1987/121, both of 26 May 1987, in which it endorsed the decision of the Commission on the Status of Women to consider problems of rural women as the priority theme under the objective of development at its thirty-second session,

Recognizing that the economic and financial crises that are affecting most of the developing countries have severely affected the socio-economic status of women,

Bearing in mind the enormous burden on women engaged in food production,

Bearing in mind also that the majority of women in developing countries are active in agriculture as farmers in their own right or as wage labourers in commercial agriculture,

Recognizing women's limited access to and control of agricultural resources, such as land, appropriate agricultural technologies, credit and training,

Recognizing that better health and sanitation are among the goals of development,

Bearing in mind that fetching water for domestic use is a major time-consuming task and primarily the responsibility and concern of women,

Recognizing that education is the basis for improving the status of women,

Aware that the lack of education and training for women in developing countries reduces their socio-economic options, particularly employment opportunities,

1. *Urges* Governments:

(a) To undertake projects exclusively designed for rural women;

(b) To involve women in the design, planning and implementation of such projects;

(c) To design projects to improve access to water supplies and sanitation and to promote the development of agricultural technologies and extension services for women;

2. *Urges* Governments to provide women with adequate education and training facilities to ensure their access to equal employment opportunities;

3. *Appeals* to donor countries to increase aid and fellowships to improve the status of women in developing countries;

4. *Requests* the development agencies of the United Nations system to pay particular attention in their programmes to the general role of women in rural development, especially in the areas of food, water supply, access to credit facilities and appropriate technologies;

5. *Requests* the Secretary-General to convene a seminar on women and rural development, using the resources available in the Trust Fund for the Preparatory Activities of the 1985 World Conference to Review and Appraise the Achievements of the United Nations Decade for Women and drawing on the results of the Interregional Seminar on National Experience Relating to the Improvement of the Situation of Women in Rural Areas, held at Vienna from 17 to 28 September 1984 in preparation for the World Conference.

Economic and Social Council resolution 1988/29

26 May 1988   Meeting 15   Adopted without vote

Approved by Second Committee (E/1988/90) without vote, 18 May (meeting 14); draft by Commission on women (E/1988/15/Rev.1); agenda item 11.

Updating the survey on women in development

Pursuant to a 1986 request of the Economic and Social Council,[9] the Secretary-General submitted to the Commission on the Status of Women a report[10] containing the first draft of an update of the 1985 *World Survey on the Role of Women in Development*.[11] The first draft elaborated material contained in a 1987 report of the Secretary-General.[12]

ECONOMIC AND SOCIAL COUNCIL ACTION

On 26 May 1988, on the recommendation of its Second Committee, the Economic and Social Council adopted **resolution 1988/21** without vote.

Updating of the *World Survey on the Role of Women in Development* in the light of the deterioration in the status of women in the developing countries

The Economic and Social Council,

Considering that, in compliance with resolution 1986/64 of 23 July 1986, the Secretary-General submitted to the Commission on the Status of Women, at its thirty-second session, a first draft of the updated *World Survey on the Role of Women in Development,*

Taking into account the fact that the preliminary assessments of that survey and of other studies prepared by specialized agencies and other organizations of the United Nations system point to a deterioration in the status of women in developing countries, which is ap-

parent in worsening working conditions, reduction in income, declining or stagnating health services and reduced access to education,

Considering that this deterioration, which is in marked contrast to expectations for an improvement in the status of women, makes it difficult to achieve the objectives of the United Nations Decade for Women: Equality, Development and Peace and is becoming an obstacle to the effective implementation of the Nairobi Forward-looking Strategies for the Advancement of Women,

Reaffirming the need to examine in depth the role of women in development, in particular the situation of women in developing countries and the problems hindering their advancement,

1. *Recommends* that in updating the *World Survey on the Role of Women in Development* particular emphasis be given to those factors that contribute to the deteriorating status of women in developing countries, namely:

(a) The economic crisis, including the problem of external debt servicing, which has resulted in worsening working conditions, particularly in low-paying employment and in the informal sector of the economy;

(b) The long-term effects of the inability of certain sectors of the economy adequately to absorb female labour;

(c) The decline in women's income, particularly in agricultural regions;

(d) The gap that evidently exists between the income levels of men and women;

(e) The long-term effects of the decline in the levels of education, nutrition and health that is evident in a large number of developing countries as a result of adjustment policies;

2. *Also recommends* that when preparing the updated survey, the Secretary-General make a special effort to adopt approaches that strike a balance between traditional viewpoints on adjustment policies and more innovative approaches that take into account the social cost to women of adjustments arising from, among other things, debt servicing;

3. *Considers* that in the updated survey attention should be devoted to alternative policies for managing the problem of external indebtedness in developing countries, which might in turn help eliminate the current obstacles to the achievement of the objectives of the Nairobi Forward-looking Strategies for the Advancement of Women.

Economic and Social Council resolution 1988/21

26 May 1988   Meeting 15   Adopted without vote

Approved by Second Committee (E/1988/90) without vote, 18 May (meeting 14); draft by Commission on women (E/1988/15/Rev.1); agenda item 11.

Integration of women in economic development programmes

In March, the *ad hoc* inter-agency meeting on women[13] (see above) recommended the organization of a joint activity with interested organizations to consolidate and simplify existing guidelines and check-lists concerning the issue of WID, and that a review be carried out of existing guidelines for projects on the incorporation of WID, in order to prepare a consolidated set of guidelines for use by field staff; UNDP was to initiate the process. In September,[14] CCSQ (Operational Activities) (OPS) agreed to review, in 1989, the consolidated set of guidelines.

ECONOMIC AND SOCIAL COUNCIL ACTION

On 26 July 1988, the Economic and Social Council adopted **resolution 1988/49** without vote.

Economic aspects of women in development

The Economic and Social Council,

Recalling General Assembly resolution 42/178 of 11 December 1987 and the Nairobi Forward-looking Strategies for the Advancement of Women, particularly paragraphs 120, 137, 142, 147, 282 and 312 thereof,

Having reviewed annex I to the *World Economic Survey 1988* on selected indicators of the socio-economic attainment of women and taking into consideration the useful comments made thereon,

Recognizing the essential role of the economic activities of women in both the formal and the informal sectors of the economies of all countries and the positive role of women in promoting growth and development,

Convinced that further analysis of the economic activities of women in developing and developed countries is necessary for the design and implementation of social and economic policies,

Calls upon the Secretary-General to devote a separate section in the *World Economic Survey* to the economic aspects of the situation of women and their contribution to economic development, taking into account, *inter alia*, their participation in the evolution of labour markets.

Economic and Social Council resolution 1988/49

26 July 1988   Meeting 38   Adopted without vote

5-nation draft (E/1988/L.33/Rev.1); agenda item 2.
Sponsors: Bulgaria, Canada, Greece, Nigeria, Poland.
Meeting numbers. ESC 28, 38.

By **decision 1988/122** of 26 May, the Council deferred until its second regular session consideration of a four-part draft resolution (see above, under "System-wide co-ordination").

On 27 July, the Council, on the recommendation of its Third Committee, adopted **resolution 1988/60 B** without vote.

Intergovernmental co-operation to integrate women effectively in economic development programmes and activities

The Economic and Social Council,

Bearing in mind its resolutions 1986/65 of 23 July 1986 and 1987/65 of 8 July 1987,

Recalling General Assembly resolution 42/178 of 11 December 1987,

Emphasizing the central role of the Commission on the Status of Women in promoting co-operation among intergovernmental bodies to integrate women fully in economic development programmes and activities,

1. *Considers* that intergovernmental co-operation in the implementation of the Nairobi Forward-looking Strategies for the Advancement of Women would be considerably strengthened if each of the United Nations intergovernmental bodies concerned were to include in its agenda an item on activities for the implementation of

the Forward-looking Strategies within its field of competence, in particular, activities concerned with monitoring, technical co-operation, institutional co-ordination, research and policy analysis, the participation of women in decision-making, and public information, and transmit its report on that agenda item to the Commission on the Status of Women;

2. *Decides* that the reports requested in Economic and Social Council resolution 1987/65 and decision 1987/182 of 8 July 1987 should first be submitted to the Commission on the Status of Women at its thirty-third session for consideration and then to the Council at its second regular session of 1989;

3. *Requests* the Secretary-General to report on the measures taken in 1986, 1987 and 1988:

(a) To ensure coherent implementation of the Forward-looking Strategies by central, regional and sectoral intergovernmental bodies of the United Nations;

(b) To harmonize the implementation of the Forward-looking Strategies with all relevant United Nations intergovernmental decisions and other international strategies and plans and programmes of action;

4. *Further requests* that the reports referred to in paragraph 2 of the present resolution be consolidated in a single report structured according to the three aspects of co-ordination defined in resolution 1988/60 A;

5. *Recommends* that, in the light of the importance of the overall co-ordination of United Nations activities, particularly between the units of the Secretariat in New York and Vienna, provision continue to be made for the Centre for Social Development and Humanitarian Affairs to maintain liaison in New York.

Economic and Social Council resolution 1988/60 B

27 July 1988   Meeting 39   Adopted without vote

Approved by Third Committee (E/1988/114) without vote, 15 July (meeting 8); draft by Commission on women (E/1988/C.3/L.1); agenda item 17.

Medium-term plan for women and development

ACC action. In March,[13] the *ad hoc* interagency meeting on women (see above) adopted two recommendations on the system-wide medium-term plan for women and development (1990-1995).[15] One recommended that organizations of the United Nations system should continue to incorporate in their planning and policy documents proposals consistent with the plan. The other discussed the preparation by ACC of an initial report on the plan's implementation.

CCSQ(OPS), in April,[16] noted that although most of the activities in the plan would be undertaken by individual organizations, there was considerable scope for joint action, particularly in the area of technical co-operation, training and advisory services.

CPC consideration. In response to a 1987 request of the Economic and Social Council,[17] the Secretary-General submitted to CPC, in January 1988,[18] a report proposing a general framework and approach to preparing a cross-organizational programme analysis (COPA) on the advancement of women, to be reviewed by CPC in 1989. The COPA was to be prepared as a monitoring tool for implementing the system-wide medium-term plan and would also incorporate activities relating to equality and peace.

In May,[19] CPC concluded that the Secretary-General's report provided a useful basis for the COPA, which would cover the main objectives of the Nairobi Forward-looking Strategies of equality, development and peace and encompass the related priority themes of employment, health and education.

ECONOMIC AND SOCIAL COUNCIL ACTION

On 26 May 1988, the Economic and Social Council, by **decision 1988/121**, decided to defer until its second regular session consideration of a draft resolution, recommended by the Commission on the Status of Women,[1] concerning the system-wide medium-term plan for the advancement of women.

On 27 July, on the recommendation of its Third Committee, the Council adopted **resolution 1988/59** without vote.

System-wide medium-term plan for the advancement of women: equality, development and peace

The Economic and Social Council,

Recalling General Assembly resolution 40/108 of 13 December 1985, in which the Assembly endorsed the Nairobi Forward-looking Strategies for the Advancement of Women,

Affirming the interrelationship of the objectives of the United Nations Decade for Women: Equality, Development and Peace as regards the advancement of women and their full integration in political, economic, social and cultural development and that the objectives of the Decade, in conformity with the Nairobi Forward-looking Strategies for the Advancement of Women, should remain in effect in the operational strategies for the advancement of women to the year 2000,

Referring to the Convention on the Elimination of All Forms of Discrimination against Women,

Recalling General Assembly resolution 37/63 of 3 December 1982, in which the Assembly proclaimed the Declaration on the Participation of Women in Promoting International Peace and Co-operation,

Bearing in mind paragraphs 311, 338 and 339 of the Forward-looking Strategies, outlining measures to improve system-wide co-ordination of activities for the advancement of women in the implementation of the Strategies,

Recalling Commission on the Status of Women resolutions 1987/1 of 16 January 1987 on participation of women in promoting international peace and co-operation and preparation of the United Nations medium-term plan for the period 1990-1995 and 1987/2 of 16 January 1987 on women and equality and preparation of the United Nations medium-term plan for the period 1990-1995,

Affirming its determination to give adequate attention to all the goals of the United Nations Decade for Women: Equality, Development and Peace,

1. *Urges* all United Nations bodies, including the regional commissions, and the specialized agencies that have not yet done so to develop and implement comprehensive policies for the advancement of women and to incorporate them in their organization's medium-term plans, statements of objectives, programmes and other major policy statements;

2. *Requests* the Secretary-General, in his capacity as Chairman of the Administrative Committee on Co-ordination and within existing financial resources, to initiate the formulation of a system-wide medium-term plan for the advancement of women, directed towards the objectives of equality, development and peace, for the period 1996-2001, taking into account the priorities recommended by the Economic and Social Council, the provisions of the Nairobi Forward-looking Strategies for the Advancement of Women and the views and decisions of the governing bodies of the organizations of the United Nations system, including the regional commissions, on the content of the plan, as well as experience in developing the system-wide medium-term plan for women and development for the period 1990-1995;

3. *Recommends* all United Nations bodies, including the regional commissions, and the specialized agencies to take Commission on the Status of Women resolutions 1987/1 and 1987/2 into account in the implementation of the system-wide medium-term plan for women and development;

4. *Requests* the Secretary-General to report on the implementation of the present resolution to the Economic and Social Council at its first regular session of 1989, through the Commission on the Status of Women.

Economic and Social Council resolution 1988/59

27 July 1988   Meeting 39   Adopted without vote

Approved by Third Committee (E/1988/114) without vote, 19 July (meeting 10); draft by Commission on women (E/1988/C.3/L.1); agenda item 17.

Technical co-operation

In his annual report on United Nations technical co-operation,[20] the Secretary-General described WID activities, particularly those of the Department of Technical Co-operation for Development (DTCD). Training was emphasized, with another module added to the computer training package demonstrating the impact of changes in the role and status of women on the economy. DTCD maintained close collaboration with IN-STRAW in training, which was also provided through community development projects. DTCD provided seed money to finance a programme on water use and conservation, which included the training of trainers and the purchase of teaching materials and equipment to build a demonstration village sanitary installation. Fellowships awarded to women in the area of population rose from 36 in 1987 to 58 in 1988. Under the United Nations Educational and Training Programme for Southern Africa, the percentage of women from Namibia and South Africa receiving scholarships was 54 per cent and 44 per cent, respectively.

An interregional seminar (Mali) focused on the involvement of women in drawing up and managing water resources programmes. In other projects, special components were designed to improve traditional technologies and acquaint women with ways of benefiting from ongoing development programmes.

The DTCD Task Force on Women focused on the need to involve primary users—community women in rural areas—at the planning stage as well as during other phases of a project cycle.

UN Development Fund for Women

The Consultative Committee on the United Nations Development Fund for Women met twice in 1988, in New York, from 5 to 11 April and from 6 to 12 September.[21] It approved the Fund's 1988-1989 work plan, which featured the implementation of two regional plans—the African Investment Plan, including the development of activities in the northern African States, and the Participatory Action Plan for Latin America and the Caribbean—and the development and implementation of the Asia and Pacific Development Strategy, including preparation of a strategy for programming in Western Asia. The work plan also included the replenishment of two facilities, one for monitoring and evaluation and the other for mainstream programming initiatives.

In April,[22] the UNDP Administrator submitted to the Governing Council (see below) his annual report on the operations, management and budget of the Fund in 1987. The report gave an overview of the management of UNIFEM, highlighting operational activities, and provided information on its financial status.

In a report on the 1988 activities of the Fund,[21] the Administrator stated that activities carried out with organizations of the United Nations included a mission to the Pacific, mounted with the support of the UNDP office in Suva, Fiji. The mission proposed a project for incorporating women in national and project development planning and a strategy for executing it. In Mexico, collaboration between UNDP, UNIFEM and ILO resulted in a proposal aimed at enhancing women's participation in an ongoing UNDP/ILO/government project. In Argentina, a mission resulted in the provision of financial assistance by UNIFEM for activities to enhance women's participation in and benefits from a $20 million credit project of the International Fund for Agricultural Development and the Inter-American Development Bank. In Guatemala, UNIFEM assisted in the formulation of credit programmes to help women producers who were often overlooked in large-scale credit schemes. UNIFEM collaborated with the World Bank in two joint missions.

Activities with intergovernmental organizations included support for a regional conference of the Southern African Development Co-ordination

Conference on women and food technology (Arusha, United Republic of Tanzania, May 1988) and preparation of a plan for co-operation between UNIFEM and the Inter-American Institute for Co-operation on Agriculture (San José, Costa Rica).

The Fund's work with government and national organizations focused on assistance to Zambia in designing a strategy to incorporate the issue of WID into the country's five-year development plan and recommendations to strengthen the Ministry of Community Development, Culture, Youth and Sports in the United Republic of Tanzania. In the Philippines, UNIFEM supported the National Commission on the Role of Filipino Women in preparing a development plan for women. In Guatemala, UNIFEM, in collaboration with national women's organizations, helped to plan a national workshop on women, in preparation for a subregional conference hosted by the Economic Commission for Latin America and the Caribbean (September).

As to project support for developing innovative and experimental activities benefiting women, UNIFEM reviewed some 124 proposals, of which 38 were recommended for funding for a total of $4.9 million. Two specialty areas in which UNIFEM was pioneering approaches dealt with women and food cycle technologies and credit support systems.

At the November 1988 United Nations Pledging Conference for Development Activities, 32 countries pledged $4.7 million to UNIFEM general resources for 1989. Total pledges were expected to reach $7 million, a 23 per cent increase over the previous year.

In October,[23] the Secretary-General transmitted the UNDP Administrator's report on 1987 UNIFEM activities to the General Assembly.

UNDP Council action. On 17 February 1988,[24] the UNDP Governing Council, taking note of a report on UNIFEM[25] containing proposals for changing from full to partial funding, approved that change on the understanding that financial and administrative issues arising from it would be referred to the Council's Budgetary and Finance Committee at its 1988 regular session. At that session (Geneva, 6 June–1 July),[26] the Committee recommended that the Council approve the implementation of the partial funding system, effective 1988; decide that UNIFEM should establish and maintain, on a fully funded basis, an operational reserve of 45 per cent of outstanding recommended project approvals and unspent allocations; and request the Administrator to submit a report on the implementation of the system in 1990.

On 1 July 1988,[27] the Council took note of the Administrator's report on the operations, management and budget of UNIFEM in 1987[22] and its February decision,[24] and adopted the recommendations of the Budgetary and Finance Committee.

GENERAL ASSEMBLY ACTION

On 8 December 1988, the General Assembly, on the recommendation of the Third Committee, adopted **resolution 43/102** without vote.

United Nations Development Fund for Women

The General Assembly,

Reaffirming its decisions set forth in resolution 39/125 of 14 December 1984,

Emphasizing the catalytic role of the United Nations Development Fund for Women in the United Nations development co-operation system, with the goal of ensuring the appropriate involvement of women in mainstream development activities at the pre-investment stages, and supporting activities directly benefiting women in line with national and regional priorities,

Recognizing that the Fund's dynamism lies in its flexibility and the complementarity of its innovative and catalytic priority roles,

Recognizing the initiatives of the Fund to assist national machineries on women, planning and other relevant ministries and intergovernmental organizations to integrate the concerns of women and to ensure their involvement in development programmes at all levels,

Noting the Fund's regional priority frameworks and its increased co-operation with regional and national development banks and larger funds, through which critical resources have been leveraged for women in development activities,

1. *Takes note* of the note by the Secretary-General, containing the report of the Administrator of the United Nations Development Programme on the activities of the United Nations Development Fund for Women;

2. *Notes* the Fund's continued co-operation with units throughout the United Nations system concerned with women and development, and with the planning and sectoral ministries and the national machineries on women in development of developing countries;

3. *Stresses* the importance of the continuous strengthening of the technical and financial capacities of the Fund to enable it to preserve and augment its flexible approaches to supporting activities at the national, regional and global levels, including those of the regional commissions and of the Division for the Advancement of Women of the Centre for Social Development and Humanitarian Affairs of the Secretariat;

4. *Reaffirms* the dual priorities of the Fund to serve as a catalyst in respect of mainstream development activities, as often as possible at pre-investment stages, and to support innovative and experimental activities in line with national and regional priorities, and recognizes the forceful interrelationship between the two approaches;

5. *Expresses its appreciation* to Governments, non-governmental organizations and individuals that have pledged and contributed to the Fund;

6. *Notes with concern* that the Fund's resources have been insufficient to enable it to respond adequately to the increasing number of requests received;

7. *Commends* national committees on the Fund and non-governmental organizations for their initiatives in the development of education and public awareness programmes and resource mobilization on behalf of the Fund;

8. *Invites* Governments, non-governmental organizations and others to consider making substantial contributions to the Fund;

9. *Requests* the Secretary-General to transmit to the Assembly at its forty-fourth session the report of the Administrator of the United Nations Development Programme on the activities of the Fund submitted pursuant to Assembly resolution 39/125.

General Assembly resolution 43/102

8 December 1988	Meeting 75	Adopted without vote

Approved by Third Committee (A/43/813) without vote, 11 November (meeting 40); 5-nation draft (A/C.3/43/L.26), orally revised; agenda item 95.
Sponsors: Colombia, German Democratic Republic, India, Kenya, Norway.
Meeting numbers. GA 43rd session: 3rd Committee 15, 23-30, 36, 40; plenary 75.

REFERENCES

[1]E/1988/15/Rev.1.	[2]E/CN.6/1988/4.	[3]E/1988/18.
[4]E/ICEF/1988/L.1.	[5]YUN 1987, p. 836.	[6]E/1988/18 (res. 1988/6).	[7]DP/1988/15 & Add.1.	[8]E/1988/19 (dec. 88/28).	[9]YUN 1986, p. 791, ESC res. 1986/64, 23 July 1986.	[10]E/CN.6/1988/7.	[11]YUN 1985, p. 944.	[12]YUN 1987, p. 838.	[13]ACC/1988/PG/2.	[14]ACC/1988/14.	[15]YUN 1987, p. 840.	[16]ACC/1988/7.	[17]YUN 1987, p. 840, ESC res. 1987/86, 8 July 1987.	[18]E/AC.51/1988/2.	[19]A/43/16.	[20]DP/1989/46.	[21]DP/1989/51.	[22]DP/1988/50 & Add.1,2.	[23]A/43/643.	[24]E/1988/19 (dec. 88/6).	[25]YUN 1987, p. 842.	[26]DP/1988/78.	[27]E/1988/19 (dec. 88/42).

PUBLICATION

Improving Statistics and Indicators on Women Using Household Surveys (ST/ESA/STAT/SER.F/48), Sales No. E.88.XVII.11.

Status of women

Commission on the Status of Women

The Commission on the Status of Women, at its thirty-second session (Vienna, 14-23 March 1988),[1] recommended 17 draft resolutions and two decisions for adoption by the Economic and Social Council. The resolutions dealt with: women and children under *apartheid;* women and children in Namibia; Palestinian women; women and peace in Central America; discrimination against women; violence against women; international peace and co-operation; rural women and development; the system-wide medium-term plan for the advancement of women; improvement of the status of women in the United Nations system (see PART SIX, Chapter II); programme planning and activities to advance the status of women; system-wide co-ordination of activities to advance the status of women and to integrate WID; the Commission's 1990 session; updating the world survey on women and development; a reporting system to monitor, review and appraise the implementation of the Nairobi Forward-looking Strategies; enlargement of the Commission; and national machinery for the advancement of women. The decisions dealt with the provisional agenda for the Commission's 1989 session and the mandate of the office of the Co-ordinator for the Improvement of the Status of Women in the Secretariat.

ECONOMIC AND SOCIAL COUNCIL ACTION

By **decision 1988/122** of 26 May 1988, the Economic and Social Council deferred until its second regular session consideration of a four-part draft resolution (see above, under "System-wide co-ordination").

On 27 July, on the recommendation of its Third Committee, the Council adopted **resolution 1988/60 A** without vote.

Co-ordinating role of the Commission on the Status of Women

The Economic and Social Council,

Convinced that it must play a more forceful and dynamic role in reviewing and co-ordinating all activities of the United Nations system relevant to women's issues,

Referring to the reports of the Secretary-General and the Administrative Committee on Co-ordination on co-ordination matters pertaining to the status of women,

Considers that the central substantive co-ordinating role of the Commission on the Status of Women in advancing the status of women and integrating women in development has three distinct aspects:

(a) Intergovernmental co-operation, which relates to action taken by the United Nations central, regional and sectoral intergovernmental bodies to achieve a coherent and complementary approach to implementing the Nairobi Forward-looking Strategies for the Advancement of Women within the United Nations;

(b) Inter-agency co-ordination, which relates to measures taken by organizations of the United Nations system to co-ordinate the implementation of the Forward-looking Strategies;

(c) Legislative linkage, which relates to action taken by the Commission on the Status of Women to link the implementation of the Forward-looking Strategies to all relevant United Nations intergovernmental decisions and other international strategies and plans and programmes of action.

Economic and Social Council resolution 1988/60 A

27 July 1988   Meeting 39   Adopted without vote

Approved by Third Committee (E/1988/114) without vote, 15 July (meeting 8); draft by Commission on women (E/1988/C.3/L.1); agenda item 17.

In May 1988, on the recommendation of its Second Committee, the Council adopted **decision 1988/125** without vote.

Enlargement of the Commission on the Status of Women

At its 16th plenary meeting, on 27 May 1988, the Economic and Social Council, recalling its resolution 1987/23 of 26 May 1987, in which it accepted, in principle, the enlargement of the Commission on the Status of Women and decided that the Commission at its thirty-second session should consider proposals to that end and submit them to the Council at its first regular session of 1988, noting that the membership of the

United Nations had increased from 120 Member States in 1966 to 159 Member States and that the Commission had not been enlarged proportionately, bearing in mind the principle of equitable geographical distribution for the allocation of seats, considering that issues related to women had grown in complexity and in number, particularly in the developing world, and recalling its resolution 1988/19 of 26 May 1988, by which it decided that the Commission should hold in 1990 a session of extended duration to review and appraise progress in the implementation of the Nairobi Forward-looking Strategies for the Advancement of Women, decided:

(a) To take action on draft resolution XIII, entitled "Enlargement of the Commission on the Status of Women", contained in the report of the Commission, and the amendments proposed thereto,[a] at its first regular session of 1989;

(b) To invite the Commission to offer its views on the question of its enlargement, in the light of the foregoing considerations and the discussions held during the first regular session of the Council of 1988;

(c) To urge that, in the mean time, consultations should be held with a view to assisting the Council in its consideration of the issue.

---

[a]E/1988/C.2/L.2.

Economic and Social Council decision 1988/125

Adopted without vote

Approved by Second Committee (E/1988/90/Add.1) without vote, 23 May (meeting 21); draft by Vice-Chairman (E/1988/C.2/L.12), based on informal consultations on draft by Commission on women (E/1988/15/Rev.1); agenda item 11.

On 26 May, by **decision 1988/123**, the Council took note of the Commission's report on its 1988 session and approved the provisional agenda and documentation for its 1989 session.

Role of women in society

In December 1988, on the recommendation of the Third Committee, the General Assembly adopted **decision 43/425** without vote.

The role of women in society

At its 75th plenary meeting, on 8 December 1988, the General Assembly, on the recommendation of the Third Committee, having reaffirmed its profound conviction that all Governments, international organizations and intergovernmental and non-governmental organizations should pay due attention in their activities to the importance of the role of women in society in all its interrelated aspects—as mothers, as participants in political, economic, social and cultural development and as participants in public life—and recalling its resolutions 39/123 of 14 December 1984, 40/101 of 13 December 1985, 41/110 of 4 December 1986 and 42/64 of 30 November 1987, decided to recommend that the Commission on the Status of Women, during the consideration at its next sessions of the priority themes under the heading "Equality", including "Equality in economic and social participation" at its thirty-third session, should consider the provisions of the Assembly resolutions on the role of women in society, with a view to formulating recommendations for appropriate action by concerned United Nations organs and bodies, Governments and intergovernmental and non-governmental organizations.

General Assembly decision 43/425

Adopted without vote

Approved by Third Committee (A/43/813) without vote, 11 November (meeting 40); 15-nation draft (A/C.3/43/L.25); agenda item 95.

Sponsors: Argentina, Bolivia, Bulgaria, Burkina Faso, Byelorussian SSR, Cameroon, Cuba, German Democratic Republic, Kenya, Mongolia, Panama, Rwanda, Viet Nam, Zambia, Zimbabwe.

Meeting numbers. GA 43rd session: 3rd Committee 15, 23-30, 36, 40; plenary 75.

Women and peace

The Commission had before it a report of the Secretary-General on access to information and education for peace,[2] one of the areas under the priority theme of peace selected by the Economic and Social Council in 1987.[3] The Secretary-General discussed women's access to information and education for peace and the role of women in education for peace, including family and early childhood development, formal education, society and decision-making processes. He also described the role of the United Nations in promoting the participation of women in education for peace. He concluded that women needed full access to information and education, as well as knowledge of the techniques for the non-violent resolution of conflicts. Special classes, courses and training seminars could encourage women to develop their interests in peace. The Secretary-General suggested a number of issues for further research on the role of women in the education of societies for life in peace and activities to increase women's participation in education for peace.

ECONOMIC AND SOCIAL COUNCIL ACTION

On 26 May 1988, on the recommendation of its Second Committee, the Economic and Social Council adopted **resolution 1988/28** without vote.

Participation of women in promoting international peace and co-operation

The Economic and Social Council,

Reaffirming the interrelationship of the objectives of the United Nations Decade for Women: Equality, Development and Peace,

Expressing the need for equal participation of women in all efforts to strengthen and maintain international peace and security and to promote international co-operation, disarmament, the process of détente and respect for the principles of the Charter of the United Nations,

Referring to General Assembly resolution 37/63 of 3 December 1982, by which the Assembly proclaimed the Declaration on the Participation of Women in Promoting International Peace and Co-operation,

Recalling that the World Conference to Review and Appraise the Achievements of the United Nations Decade for Women: Equality, Development and Peace, in adopting the Nairobi Forward-looking Strategies for the Advancement of Women for the period up to the year 2000,

emphasized that the main principles and directions for women's activities aimed at strengthening peace, formulated in the Declaration, should be put into practice,

Taking note of General Assembly resolution 42/61 of 30 November 1987, in which the Assembly invited the Commission on the Status of Women to give adequate attention to all the priority themes under the headings of equality, development and peace in recognition of the complexity of all the subject areas addressed in the Nairobi Forward-looking Strategies and in other policy documents, including the participation of women in promoting international peace and co-operation,

Stressing that access to information, education for peace and the eradication of violence against women within the family and society are important for the implementation of the Declaration,

Welcoming the Treaty between the United States of America and the Union of Soviet Socialist Republics on the Elimination of Their Intermediate-range and Shorter-range Missiles, signed in Washington, D.C., on 8 December 1987, as an important step in promoting international peace and co-operation and a contribution to the creation of favourable conditions for the attainment of the objectives of the United Nations Decade for Women: Equality, Development and Peace,

Noting that the third special session of the General Assembly devoted to disarmament will provide manifold opportunities to support the participation of women in all activities related to peace, disarmament and security at the national, regional and international levels,

Wishing to encourage the active participation of women in promoting international peace, security and co-operation and the elimination of violence against women within the family and society,

1. *Urges* the Commission on the Status of Women to continue to give adequate attention to the implementation of the Declaration on the Participation of Women in Promoting International Peace and Co-operation and to the elimination of violence against women within the family and society;

2. *Appeals* to all Governments to take practical institutional, educational and organizational measures to facilitate the participation of women on an equal footing with men in activities related to peace, disarmament negotiations and the resolution of conflicts, and to inform the Secretary-General of the activities that they have undertaken at all levels to implement the Declaration;

3. *Invites* Member States to use the third special session of the General Assembly devoted to disarmament as an occasion to support the full participation of women in the establishment of conditions conducive to the maintenance of peace and to the elimination of inequality, poverty and violence against women within the family and society;

4. *Requests* the Secretary-General to report to the General Assembly at its third special session devoted to disarmament on programmes and activities undertaken by the United Nations system relating to women and peace, in particular those activities relating to the implementation of the Declaration on the Participation of Women in Promoting International Peace and Cooperation and the Nairobi Forward-looking Strategies for the Advancement of Women;

5. *Also requests* the Secretary-General to take adequate steps to ensure that publicity is given to the Declaration.

Economic and Social Council resolution 1988/28

26 May 1988   Meeting 15   Adopted without vote

Approved by Second Committee (E/1988/90) without vote, 13 May (meeting 9); draft by Commission on women (E/1988/15/Rev.1); agenda item 11.

GENERAL ASSEMBLY ACTION

On 8 December 1988, on the recommendation of the Third Committee, the General Assembly adopted **resolution 43/104** without vote.

Participation of women in promoting international peace and co-operation

The General Assembly,

Reaffirming the interrelationship of the objectives of the United Nations Decade for Women: Equality, Development and Peace,

Expressing the need for equal opportunity for participation by women in the decision-making process, including that related to peace, disarmament and security at national, regional and international levels, including the United Nations system,

Reaffirming its resolution 37/63 of 3 December 1982, by which it proclaimed the Declaration on the Participation of Women in Promoting International Peace and Co-operation,

Recalling that the World Conference to Review and Appraise the Achievements of the United Nations Decade for Women: Equality, Development and Peace, in adopting the Nairobi Forward-looking Strategies for the Advancement of Women for the period up to the year 2000, emphasized that the main principles and directions formulated in the Declaration for women's activities aimed at strengthening peace should be put into practice,

Convinced that increased efforts are required to eliminate still existing forms of discrimination against women in every field of human endeavour,

Conscious of the need to implement the provisions of the Declaration,

1. *Pledges its determination* to encourage the full participation of women in the economic, social, cultural, civil and political affairs of society and in the endeavour to promote international peace and co-operation;

2. *Appeals* to all Governments to give publicity to the Declaration on the Participation of Women in Promoting International Peace and Co-operation and to take practical institutional, educational and organizational measures to facilitate the participation of women on an equal footing with men in the decision-making process, including that related to peace, disarmament negotiations and the resolution of conflicts;

3. *Invites* all Governments, in accordance with Economic and Social Council resolution 1988/28 of 26 May 1988, to inform the Secretary-General of their activities undertaken at all levels to implement the Declaration;

4. *Requests* the Secretary-General to continue to take adequate steps to ensure that publicity is given to the Declaration;

5. *Invites* the Centre for Social Development and Humanitarian Affairs of the Secretariat, the United Nations University and other bodies within the United Nations system to undertake activities that will further involve women in the process aimed at strengthening international peace and co-operation;

6. *Decides* to consider the further implementation of the Declaration at its forty-fourth session under the item

entitled "Forward-looking strategies for the advancement of women to the year 2000".

General Assembly resolution 43/104

8 December 1988   Meeting 75   Adopted without vote

Approved by Third Committee (A/43/813) without vote, 11 November (meeting 40); 20-nation draft (A/C.3/43/L.29), orally amended by Sweden; agenda item 95.
Sponsors: Angola, Bulgaria, Byelorussian SSR, Cuba, Czechoslovakia, Democratic Yemen, German Democratic Republic, Hungary, Iraq, Lao People's Democratic Republic, Libyan Arab Jamahiriya, Madagascar, Mongolia, Nicaragua, Poland, Romania, Syrian Arab Republic, Ukrainian SSR, USSR, Viet Nam.
Meeting numbers. GA 43rd session: 3rd Committee 15, 23-30, 36, 40; plenary 75.

Women and peace in Central America

On 26 May 1988, the Economic and Social Council, on the recommendation of its Second Committee, adopted **resolution 1988/20** without vote.

Women and peace in Central America

The Economic and Social Council,

Recalling that in adopting the Nairobi Forward-looking Strategies for the Advancement of Women, the World Conference to Review and Appraise the Achievements of the United Nations Decade for Women: Equality, Development and Peace recognized that women must participate fully in all efforts to strengthen and maintain international peace and security and to promote international co-operation,

Recalling also that the World Conference also recognized that the situation of violence and destabilization in Central America hindered the fulfilment of the Nairobi Forward-looking Strategies, which were essential to the advancement of women,

Taking note of the agreement on "Procedures for the establishment of a firm and lasting peace in Central America", signed at the Esquipulas II summit meeting, at Guatemala City, on 7 August 1987, by the Presidents of Costa Rica, El Salvador, Guatemala, Honduras and Nicaragua,

Recognizing the valuable contribution of the Contadora Group and its Support Group to the process of bringing peace to Central America,

Convinced of the exceptional importance to the peoples of Central America, particularly the women, of achieving peace, reconciliation, development and social justice in the region, as well as ensuring their economic, social, cultural, civil and political rights,

Considering that the General Assembly, in its resolution 42/1 of 7 October 1987, requested the Secretary-General to promote a special plan of co-operation for Central America,

Eager to encourage the active participation of women in the promotion of peace and development in Central America,

1. *Expresses its gratification* at the strong desire for peace manifested by the Presidents of the Central American countries in their signing of the agreement on "Procedures for the establishment of a firm and lasting peace in Central America";

2. *Calls upon* the Presidents of the Central American countries to continue their joint efforts to achieve peace in Central America, particularly the efforts aimed at establishing the Central American Parliament, in order to guarantee propitious conditions for the attain-

ment in the region of the objectives of the Nairobi Forward-looking Strategies for the Advancement of Women, and requests the international community to support those efforts;

3. *Urges* all States to support the peace efforts, fully respecting the principles of the self-determination of peoples and non-intervention;

4. *Also urges* the international community to ensure that programmes of technical, economic and financial co-operation for the region take account of the particular needs and interests of Central American women;

5. *Recommends* to the Secretary-General that the special plan of co-operation for Central America should include specific activities in support of the advancement of women in the region;

6. *Exhorts* the Governments of the Central American countries and of the countries of the Contadora Group and its Support Group to encourage and guarantee the full participation of women at all levels in the search for peace, pluralism, democracy and comprehensive development in the Central American region;

7. *Urges* national and international governmental and non-governmental women's organizations to participate in and support actively the process of peace and development in Central America.

Economic and Social Council resolution 1988/20

26 May 1988   Meeting 15   Adopted without vote

Approved by Second Committee (E/1988/90) without vote, 13 May (meeting 9); draft by Commission on women (E/1988/15/Rev.1); agenda item 11.

Palestinian women

Pursuant to a 1986 request of the Economic and Social Council,[4] the Secretary-General submitted to the Commission a report on the situation of Palestinian women living within and outside the occupied Arab territories,[5] based mainly on information received from the United Nations Relief and Works Agency for Palestine Refugees in the Near East. The Secretary-General stated that the difficult living conditions of Palestinian women indicated the need for special attention and assistance. The assistance being provided to the Palestinian people by the United Nations did not focus adequately on women's needs. The Secretary-General suggested that the needs of the Palestinian women should be ascertained through special missions, and programmes of assistance should be designed to go beyond the delivery of services.

ECONOMIC AND SOCIAL COUNCIL ACTION

On 26 May 1988, the Economic and Social Council, on the recommendation of its Second Committee, adopted **resolution 1988/25** by recorded vote.

Situation of Palestinian women

The Economic and Social Council,

Referring to the report of the Secretary-General on the situation of Palestinian women living within and outside the occupied Arab territories,

Mindful of the humanitarian principles and provisions of the Geneva Convention relative to the Protection of Civilian Persons in Time of War of 12 August 1949,

Recalling the Nairobi Forward-looking Strategies for the Advancement of Women, in particular paragraph 260 thereof,

Noting with deep concern the escalating Israeli oppression and ill-treatment of the Palestinian people, including women and children in the occupied Palestinian territories,

1. *Requests* the Secretary-General to submit a comprehensive report on the situation of Palestinian women and children inside and outside the occupied Palestinian territories to the Commission on the Status of Women at its thirty-third session;

2. *Strongly condemns* the application of an "iron-fist" policy by Israel, the occupying Power, against Palestinian women and their families in the occupied Palestinian territories;

3. *Reaffirms* that the Geneva Convention relative to the Protection of Civilian Persons in Time of War is applicable to territories occupied by Israel since 1967, including Jerusalem;

4. *Requests* the Secretary-General, as a matter of urgency, to send a mission composed of experts on the status of women to investigate the situation of Palestinian women and children, in the light of the recent tragic developments in the occupied Palestinian territories;

5. *Requests* the Commission on the Status of Women to monitor the implementation of the provisions of paragraph 260 of the Nairobi Forward-looking Strategies for the Advancement of Women concerning assistance to Palestinian women inside and outside the occupied territories;

6. *Reaffirms* that Palestinian women, as part of a nation whose people are prevented from exercising their basic human and political rights, cannot participate in the attainment of the objectives of the Nairobi Forward-looking Strategies, namely equality, development and peace, without the realization of their inalienable right to return to their homes, their right to self-determination and their right to establish an independent State in accordance with the relevant United Nations resolutions.

Economic and Social Council resolution 1988/25

26 May 1988   Meeting 15   39-1-13 (recorded vote)

Approved by Second Committee (E/1988/90) by recorded vote (33-1-13), 13 May (meeting 9); draft by Commission on women (E/1988/15/Rev.1); agenda item 11.

Recorded vote in Council as follows:

In favour: Bolivia, Bulgaria, Byelorussian SSR, China, Colombia, Cuba, Djibouti, Egypt, Gabon, German Democratic Republic, Ghana, Greece, Guinea, India, Iran, Iraq, Jamaica, Lesotho, Liberia, Libyan Arab Jamahiriya, Mozambique, Oman, Pakistan, Panama, Peru, Philippines, Poland, Rwanda, Saudi Arabia, Sierra Leone, Somalia, Sri Lanka, Sudan, Syrian Arab Republic, Trinidad and Tobago, USSR, Uruguay, Venezuela, Yugoslavia.

Against: United States.

Abstaining: Australia, Belgium, Canada, Denmark, France, Germany, Federal Republic of, Ireland, Italy, Japan, Norway, Portugal, United Kingdom, Zaire.

Women and children under *apartheid*

In accordance with a 1986 request of the Economic and Social Council,[6] the Secretary-General submitted to the Commission a report on political and social developments concerning the situation of women living under *apartheid* in South Africa and in Namibia.[7] He also reviewed assistance to South African and Namibian refugees. The Secretary-General stated that black people, particularly black women, in South Africa and Namibia continued to suffer under *apartheid*, unable to change conditions affecting their daily lives, such as free movement and access to education, employment and other basic services. Their situation deserved full international assistance from Governments and NGOs. Although a considerable effort had been made to provide assistance, it was not sufficient to meet the growing needs.

The Economic and Social Council, by **resolution 1988/23**, urged Member States and United Nations organizations to give effect to the Nairobi Forward-looking Strategies that dealt with women and children under *apartheid*. By **resolution 1988/24**, it called on women to support and assist all bodies struggling to end colonialism in Namibia.

(For details on women and children living under *apartheid*, see PART TWO, Chapter I. For information on the question of Namibia, see PART FOUR, Chapter III.)

Violence against women

The Commission had before it a report of the Secretary-General on efforts to eradicate violence against women within the family and society,[8] one of the areas under the priority theme of peace selected by the Economic and Social Council in 1987.[3] The Secretary-General reviewed international concern on the issue, discussed the nature of violence against women within the family and society and surveyed efforts to eradicate violence against women at the national, regional and international levels. He made a series of recommendations to eradicate violence against women, among them, increasing public awareness; making the issue a priority in relevant United Nations agencies and bodies and other international and regional organizations; reviewing and reformulating educational curricula to emphasize gender equality, partnership, tolerance, mutual respect, self-reliance and self-esteem; and organizing seminars to help women speak out about the problem.

ECONOMIC AND SOCIAL COUNCIL ACTION

On 26 May 1988, on the recommendation of its Second Committee, the Economic and Social Council adopted **resolution 1988/27** without vote.

Efforts to eradicate violence against women within the family and society

The Economic and Social Council,

Recalling the Nairobi Forward-looking Strategies for the Advancement of Women, in which it was stated that violence against women was a major obstacle to the achievement of the objectives of the United Nations Decade for Women: Equality, Development and Peace,

Cognizant of the fact that violence against women exists in various forms in everyday life in all kinds of societies and that concerted and continuous efforts are required for its eradication,

Recalling also the relevant recommendations of the Sixth United Nations Congress on the Prevention of Crime and the Treatment of Offenders, the relevant observations of the Seventh Congress and Economic and Social Council resolution 1984/14 of 24 May 1984 on violence in the family, as well as section IV of Council resolution 1986/10 of 21 May 1986 and General Assembly resolution 40/36 of 29 November 1985 on domestic violence,

Recalling further the relevant provisions of the International Covenant on Economic, Social and Cultural Rights and the Declaration on Social Progress and Development,

Taking note with appreciation of the report of the Secretary-General on efforts to eradicate violence against women within the family and society and the views of the Commission on the Status of Women expressed during its thirty-second session,

Noting and fully appreciating the efforts being undertaken by intergovernmental and non-governmental organizations and researchers throughout the world,

Mindful of the need to continue and accelerate both short-term and long-term efforts already under way to eradicate the problem of violence against women,

1. *Calls upon* Member States to take the necessary steps to give effect to the recommendations contained in the report of the Secretary-General;

2. *Also calls upon* concerned intergovernmental and non-governmental organizations and researchers to continue to consolidate their efforts and establish close collaboration with the relevant units and organizations of the United Nations system in the eradication of violence against women within the family and society;

3. *Invites* organizations and institutions dealing with the various aspects of the problem of violence against women within the family and society in such fields as social welfare, criminal justice, education, health and shelter, as well as research, to establish an international network for co-operation to facilitate complementarity of action;

4. *Requests* the Secretary-General to pursue the implementation of the recommendations contained in his report and, in this regard, to ensure close collaboration between the Branch for the Advancement of Women and the Crime Prevention and Criminal Justice Branch of the Centre for Social Development and Humanitarian Affairs of the Secretariat and with intergovernmental and non-governmental organizations and research institutions concerned;

5. *Also requests* the Secretary-General to bring to the attention of the Committee on Crime Prevention and Control at its tenth session the relevant recommendations of the Expert Group Meeting on Violence in the Family with Special Emphasis on its Effects on Women, held at Vienna from 8 to 12 December 1986, so that the Committee may review them and provide guidance on their implementation;

6. *Further requests* the Secretary-General to ensure that adequate documentation on the issue of violence against women within the family and society is prepared for the Eighth United Nations Congress on the Prevention of Crime and the Treatment of Offenders.

Economic and Social Council resolution 1988/27
26 May 1988   Meeting 15   Adopted without vote

Approved by Second Committee (E/1988/90) without vote, 13 May (meeting 9); draft by Commission on women (E/1988/15/Rev.1); agenda item 11.

Violence against detained women

In accordance with a 1986 request of the Economic and Social Council,[9] the Secretary-General submitted to the Commission a report[10] based on replies from Governments to his request for their views on physical violence against detained women specific to their sex. Replies were received from 41 Governments and dealt with legislative and other measures to prevent such violence.

REFERENCES

[1]E/1988/15/Rev.1. [2]E/CN.6/1988/5. [3]YUN 1987, p. 844, ESC res. 1987/24, 26 May 1987. [4]YUN 1986, p. 802, ESC res. 1986/21, 23 May 1986. [5]E/CN.6/1988/8 & Corr.1. [6]YUN 1986, p. 801, ESC res. 1986/25, 23 May 1986. [7]E/CN.6/1988/2. [8]E/CN.6/1988/6. [9]YUN 1986, p. 805, ESC res. 1986/29, 23 May 1986. [10]E/CN.6/1988/9.

Elimination of discrimination against women

Convention on discrimination against women

The Committee on the Elimination of Discrimination against Women (CEDAW), established under the 1979 Convention on the Elimination of All Forms of Discrimination against Women,[1] held its seventh session in New York from 16 February to 4 March 1988.[2]

The Committee considered 11 initial reports of States parties (Argentina, Australia, Dominican Republic, Indonesia, Jamaica, Japan, Mali, New Zealand, Nigeria, Senegal, Uruguay) and two second periodic reports (Hungary, Sweden) on legislative, juridical, administrative and other measures they had adopted to give effect to the Convention.

CEDAW adopted a general recommendation stating that States parties should make more use of temporary special measures, such as positive action, preferential treatment or quota systems, to advance women's integration into education, the economy, politics and employment. It also recommended that States parties establish or strengthen effective national machinery, institutions and procedures to advise on the impact on women of government policies, monitor the situation of women comprehensively and help formulate new policies and effectively carry out strategies and measures to eliminate discrimination; take steps to ensure the dissemination of the Convention, their reports under article 18 and CEDAW reports

in the language of the States concerned; and include in their reports action taken in respect of the recommendation. On the subject of resources, CEDAW recommended to States parties that they take measures to ensure that adequate resources and services were available to it. A fourth recommendation stated that States parties should take further direct measures in accordance with article 4 of the Convention to ensure the full implementation of article 8 and to ensure to women on equal terms with men and without any discrimination the opportunities to represent their Government at the international level and to participate in the work of international organizations.

CEDAW also suggested that the Economic and Social Council request the General Assembly to approve eight additional meetings of the Committee in 1989 and provide it with the necessary resources (see below).

Meeting of the States Parties. At their fourth meeting (New York, 7 and 8 March 1988),[3] the States parties to the Convention elected 11 members of CEDAW to replace those whose terms were to expire in April 1988 (see APPENDIX III).

The States parties took note of reports submitted in 1986[4] and 1987[5] on reservations to the Convention and of views expressed thereon by the General Assembly and the Economic and Social Council. They endorsed an Assembly request of 1987[6] that the Secretary-General provide a compilation of relevant statistics from official United Nations sources to assist CEDAW in considering periodic reports. They requested the Secretary-General to make available, within existing resources, adequate and appropriate staff to assist CEDAW and to take due account, when preparing the 1990-1991 programme budget, of the Convention's article 17, paragraph 9, by providing the necessary staff and facilities for the effective performance of the Committee.

ECONOMIC AND SOCIAL COUNCIL ACTION

On 27 May 1988, the Economic and Social Council adopted **resolution 1988/48** without vote.

Convention on the Elimination of All Forms of Discrimination against Women

The Economic and Social Council,

Recalling General Assembly resolution 34/180 of 18 December 1979, by which the Assembly adopted the Convention on the Elimination of All Forms of Discrimination against Women,

Taking note of General Assembly resolutions 42/60 of 30 November 1987 and 42/105 of 7 December 1987 and recalling Economic and Social Council resolution 1987/3 of 26 May 1987,

Recalling in particular the decisions of the Fourth Meeting of the States Parties to the Convention on the Elimination of All Forms of Discrimination against Women,

Having considered the report of the Committee on the Elimination of Discrimination against Women on its seventh session, notably general recommendations 5, 6, 7 and 8 and suggestion 1 on ways and means of implementing article 21 of the Convention,

Noting that the Committee agreed, in examining reports, to take due account of the different cultural and socio-economic systems of States parties to the Convention,

1. *Welcomes* the ratification of or accession to the Convention on the Elimination of All Forms of Discrimination against Women by an increasing number of Member States;

2. *Urges* all States that have not yet ratified or acceded to the Convention to consider doing so as soon as possible;

3. *Emphasizes* the importance of the strictest compliance by States parties with their obligations under the Convention;

4. *Takes note* of the report of the Committee on the Elimination of Discrimination against Women on its seventh session;

5. *Reaffirms* the decision of the General Assembly, in paragraph 9 of resolution 42/60, that no action should be taken on decision 4 adopted by the Committee at its sixth session;

6. *Urges* States parties to the Convention to make all possible efforts to submit their initial reports on the implementation of the Convention, as well as their second and subsequent periodic reports, in accordance with article 18 of the Convention and the guidelines of the Committee;

7. *Notes with satisfaction* the efforts made by the Committee to rationalize its procedures and expedite the consideration of periodic reports, and encourages the Committee to continue those efforts;

8. *Notes with deep concern* the problems encountered by the Committee as a result of the lack of resources, including technical and substantive support, and the backlog of reports awaiting examination;

9. *Requests* the Secretary-General, in preparing the proposed programme budget for the biennium 1990-1991, to take due account of article 17, paragraph 9, of the Convention by providing the necessary staff and facilities for the effective performance of the functions of the Committee, in order to enable it to carry out its mandate as efficiently as other human rights treaty bodies;

10. *Recommends* that the General Assembly at its forty-third session consider the request made by the Committee for additional meetings, on an exceptional basis, in order to advance consideration of reports already submitted to the Committee;

11. *Also requests* the Secretary-General, within existing resources and drawing, in particular, on funds available to the Department of Public Information of the Secretariat, to provide for, facilitate and encourage public information activities relating to the Committee and the Convention, giving priority to the dissemination of the Convention in the official languages of the United Nations;

12. *Further requests* the Secretary-General to transmit the report of the Committee to the Commission on the Status of Women for information.

Economic and Social Council resolution 1988/48

27 May 1988   Meeting 16   Adopted without vote

26-nation draft (E/1988/L.28), orally revised, and orally sub-amended by India; agenda item 4.

Sponsors: Australia, Austria, Bulgaria, China, Costa Rica, Cuba, Denmark, Dominican Republic, El Salvador, Ethiopia, Finland, German Democratic Republic, Greece, Ireland, Italy, Mexico, Norway, Poland, Portugal, Rwanda, Spain, Sri Lanka, Sweden, Venezuela, Viet Nam, Yugoslavia.
Meeting numbers. ESC 12, 13, 16.

On 26 May, the Council, on the recommendation of its Second Committee, adopted **resolution 1988/26** without vote.

Elimination of discrimination against women in accordance with the aims of the Convention on the Elimination of All Forms of Discrimination against Women

The Economic and Social Council,

Recalling General Assembly resolutions 42/60 of 30 November 1987 and 42/105 of 7 December 1987 and Economic and Social Council resolution 1987/18 of 26 May 1987,

Taking note of the decisions of the Fourth Meeting of States Parties to the Convention on the Elimination of All Forms of Discrimination against Women,

Taking note of resolution 32/1 of 16 March 1988 adopted by the Commission on the Status of Women in response to the request contained in Economic and Social Council decision 1987/112 of 6 February 1987,

Recalling the emphasis placed by the World Conference to Review and Appraise the Achievements of the United Nations Decade for Women: Equality, Development and Peace, on ratification of or accession to the Convention on the Elimination of All Forms of Discrimination against Women,

1. *Welcomes* the ratification of or accession to the Convention on the Elimination of All Forms of Discrimination against Women by an increasing number of Member States;

2. *Urges* all States that have not yet ratified or acceded to the Convention to do so as soon as possible;

3. *Urges* States parties to the Convention to make all possible efforts to submit their initial reports in accordance with article 18 thereof and the guidelines of the Committee on the Elimination of Discrimination against Women;

4. *Recalls* the articles of the Convention that provide the mandate of the Committee on the Elimination of Discrimination against Women;

5. *Welcomes* the continuing efforts made by the Committee to rationalize its procedures and expedite the consideration of periodic reports submitted in accordance with article 18 of the Convention;

6. *Recalls* the role of the Committee pursuant to article 21, paragraph 1, of the Convention;

7. *Notes with considerable concern* the problems encountered by the Committee as a result of the shortage of resources, including resources for technical and substantive support;

8. *Reaffirms* that resources of the Branch for the Advancement of Women of the Centre for Social Development and Humanitarian Affairs of the Secretariat should be reinforced through various means, including redeployment, in order to enable it to keep pace with its increased work-load and to guarantee proper servicing of all bodies concerned with the advancement of the status of women that are assisted by the Branch;

9. *Recognizes* the special relevance of the periodic reports of States parties to the Convention to the efforts of the Commission on the Status of Women to review

and appraise the implementation of the Nairobi Forward-looking Strategies for the Advancement of Women in those countries;

10. *Recognizes also* that all States Members of the United Nations should take into account all relevant documents when developing strategies to monitor and evaluate progress in the advancement of women and when formulating policies and programmes concerning women at the national, regional and international levels;

11. *Requests* the Secretary-General to disseminate information on the Convention and its implementation, with a view to promoting additional ratifications of or accessions to the Convention;

12. *Recommends* that the Chairman of the Committee on the Elimination of Discrimination against Women and the Chairman of the Commission on the Status of Women each attend meetings of the other body;

13. *Recommends* that the meetings of the Committee on the Elimination of Discrimination against Women be scheduled, whenever possible, to allow for the timely transmission of the results of its work for information to the Commission on the Status of Women during the same year as the Committee's session.

Economic and Social Council resolution 1988/26

26 May 1988   Meeting 15   Adopted without vote

Approved by Second Committee (E/1988/90) without vote, 18 May (meeting 14); draft by Commission on women (E/1988/15/Rev.1), amended by Australia (E/1988/C.2/L.5) and further orally amended; agenda item 11.

GENERAL ASSEMBLY ACTION

On 8 December, the General Assembly, on the recommendation of the Third Committee, adopted **resolution 43/100** without vote.

Convention on the Elimination of All Forms of Discrimination against Women

The General Assembly,

Bearing in mind that one of the purposes of the United Nations, as stated in Articles 1 and 55 of the Charter, is to promote universal respect for human rights and fundamental freedoms for all without distinction of any kind, including distinction as to sex,

Affirming that women and men should participate equally in social, economic and political development, should contribute equally to such development and should share equally in improved conditions of life,

Recalling its resolution 34/180 of 18 December 1979, by which it adopted the Convention on the Elimination of All Forms of Discrimination against Women,

Recalling also its previous resolutions on the Convention, in particular resolution 42/60 of 30 November 1987, as well as Economic and Social Council resolutions 1988/26 of 26 May 1988 and 1988/48 of 27 May 1988,

Taking note of the decisions taken on 7 and 8 March 1988 at the Fourth Meeting of States Parties to the Convention,

Aware of the important contribution that the implementation of the Nairobi Forward-looking Strategies for the Advancement of Women can make to eliminating all forms of discrimination against women and to achieving legal and *de facto* equality between women and men,

Noting the emphasis placed by the World Conference to Review and Appraise the Achievements of the United Nations Decade for Women: Equality, Development and Peace on ratification of and accession to the Convention,

Having considered the report of the Committee on the Elimination of Discrimination against Women on its seventh session,

Noting that the Committee agreed, in examining reports, to take due account of the different cultural and socio-economic systems of States parties to the Convention,

1. *Takes note with concern* of the declining rate of ratification of or accession to the Convention on the Elimination of All Forms of Discrimination against Women by Member States;

2. *Urges* all States that have not yet ratified or acceded to the Convention to do so as soon as possible;

3. *Emphasizes* the importance of the strictest compliance by States parties with their obligations under the Convention;

4. *Takes note* of the report of the Secretary-General on the status of the Convention and requests him to submit annually to the General Assembly a report on the status of the Convention;

5. *Takes note* of the report of the Committee on the Elimination of Discrimination against Women on its seventh session;

6. *Urges* States parties to make all possible efforts to submit their initial reports on the implementation of the Convention in accordance with article 18 thereof and with the guidelines of the Committee;

7. *Takes note* of the general recommendations adopted by the Committee pursuant to its discussion at its seventh session on ways and means of implementing article 21 of the Convention;

8. *Takes note with concern* of the account by the Committee of the present constraints within which it operates and of the problems it has encountered as a result of its lack of resources;

9. *Welcomes* the efforts made by the Committee to rationalize its procedures and expedite the consideration of periodic reports and to develop procedures and guidelines for the consideration of second reports, and strongly encourages the Committee to continue its endeavours to those ends;

10. *Decides* to keep under review the Committee's request for additional meeting time;

11. *Requests* the Secretary-General to make available within existing resources the necessary staff and facilities for the effective performance by the Committee of its functions;

12. *Reaffirms* that, to this end, the resources of the Division for the Advancement of Women of the Centre for Social Development and Humanitarian Affairs of the Secretariat should be reinforced through various means, including redeployment, without prejudice to the current allocation of resources to the United Nations Office at Vienna;

13. *Also requests* the Secretary-General, in preparing the programme budget for the biennium 1990-1991, to take due account of article 17, paragraph 9, of the Convention in providing the necessary staff and facilities for the effective performance by the Committee of its functions in order to enable it to carry out its mandate as efficiently as other human rights treaty bodies;

14. *Requests* the Committee to continue to take into account considerations of cost and effectiveness, as well as other relevant matters, when determining where it will meet;

15. *Requests* the Secretary-General to provide the Committee with an assessment of the costs of holding

meetings at the United Nations Office at Vienna and at United Nations Headquarters in New York based on full servicing of the Committee, including attendance by relevant professional staff from the Division for the Advancement of Women, legal staff expert in human rights treaty implementation and adequate secretarial staff, and to transmit this information to the Economic and Social Council at its first regular session of 1989;

16. *Requests* the Secretary-General, within existing resources and drawing, in particular, on funds available to the Department of Public Information of the Secretariat, to provide, facilitate and encourage public information activities relating to the Committee and the Convention, giving priority to the dissemination of the Convention in the official languages of the United Nations;

17. *Also requests* the Secretary-General to transmit the report of the Committee to the Commission on the Status of Women for information;

18. *Further requests* the Secretary-General to submit to the General Assembly at its forty-fourth session a report on the implementation of the present resolution, and to transmit the report to the Commission on the Status of Women at its thirty-fourth session.

General Assembly resolution 43/100

8 December 1988   Meeting 75   Adopted without vote

Approved by Third Committee (A/43/812) without vote, 11 November (meeting 40); 30-nation draft (A/C.3/43/L.27/Rev.1); agenda item 94.

Sponsors: Australia, Austria, Bulgaria, Canada, China, Costa Rica, Cuba, Denmark, Ecuador, El Salvador, Ethiopia, Finland, German Democratic Republic, Germany, Federal Republic of, Greece, Iceland, Indonesia, Italy, Mexico, Norway, Philippines, Portugal, Rwanda, Spain, Sri Lanka, Sweden, Turkey, USSR, Viet Nam, Yugoslavia.
Meeting numbers. GA 43rd session: 3rd Committee 15, 23-30, 36, 40; plenary 75.

Ratifications, accessions and signatures

As at 31 December 1988, the Convention on the Elimination of All Forms of Discrimination against Women had received 95 signatures and 95 accessions or ratifications. During the year, the Convention was signed and ratified by Sierra Leone.[7]

The Secretary-General submitted to the General Assembly his annual report on the status of the Convention,[8] containing information on signatures, ratifications and accessions as at 31 August 1988 and on reservations made from 1 September 1987 to 31 August 1988.

REFERENCES

[1]YUN 1979, p. 895, GA res. 34/180, annex, 18 Dec. 1979. [2]A/43/38. [3]CEDAW/SP/14. [4]YUN 1986, p. 808. [5]YUN 1987, p. 850. [6]*Ibid.*, p. 785, GA res. 42/105, 7 Dec. 1987. [7]*Multilateral Treaties Deposited with the Secretary-General: Status as at 31 December 1988* (ST/LEG/SER.E/7), Sales No. E.89.V.3. [8]A/43/605.

Chapter XIV

Children, youth and aging persons

During 1988, some 14 million children died in the developing countries, most of them from the effects of frequent infection and prolonged undernutrition. In an effort to reduce infant and child mortality and improve the quality of life for children, the United Nations Children's Fund (UNICEF) continued to pursue its child survival and development strategy, which incorporated immunization and primary health-care programmes; activities to control diarrhoeal diseases through the use of oral rehydration therapy, safe water supply and improved sanitation; support for breast-feeding and growth monitoring, improved nutrition and food security; and efforts to provide basic urban services and meet the needs of children in especially difficult circumstances. Basic education, maternal health care and activities to improve the status of women in development were also among the crucial components of UNICEF's strategy. During the year, UNICEF expended $400 million on programmes in 121 countries and territories, mostly in developing regions. At its 1988 session (18-29 April), the UNICEF Executive Board adopted 25 resolutions covering the full range of the Fund's activities.

The serious education and unemployment problems facing young people were considered by the General Assembly, which, in December, called on all States, United Nations bodies and governmental and non-governmental organizations to give priority to measures supporting education and employment opportunities for young people, and requested the Secretary-General and youth organizations to improve existing channels of communication between youth and the United Nations (resolution 43/94). It also requested that priority be given to the follow-up to International Youth Year (1985) and that the Secretary-General consider including the United Nations Youth Fund among the programmes eligible for funding through the annual United Nations Pledging Conference for Development Activities. Also in December (43/136), the Assembly invited all States to submit their views on measures that should be taken to implement the principles and objectives of the 1965 Declaration on the Promotion among Youth of the Ideals of Peace, Mutual Respect and Understanding between Peoples.

Member States also recognized the needs of an increasing number of elderly people, aged 60 years and over. In December, the Assembly stressed the need to accelerate implementation of the 1982 International Plan of Action on Aging, and called on specialized agencies, regional commissions and other funding organizations to continue their support for activities related to the question of aging (43/93). It also recommended that aging be a priority theme in the medium-term plan starting in 1992 and in the international development strategy for the fourth United Nations development decade (1991-2000). It appealed to Governments, intergovernmental and non-governmental organizations to contribute generously to the United Nations Trust Fund for Aging.

Children

UN Children's Fund

As in previous years, programmes for children were primarily carried out by the United Nations Children's Fund, which provided assistance for child survival and development (CSD), primary health care (PHC), water supply and sanitation, education, social welfare, household food security and emergency relief. Its immunization and oral rehydration therapy (ORT) programmes saved the lives of some 2.5 million children during the year. According to UNICEF, positive changes in international relations, growing support for child-oriented actions, the success of its country programmes and a rapidly developing consensus on the rights of the child gave hope that ambitious goals for children in the 1990s could be achieved. These included: reduced infant and child mortality, universal child immunization (UCI) and PHC, and universal basic education and literacy.

In 1988, UNICEF co-operated in programmes in 121 countries and territories. The majority (42) were in Africa, followed by Asia (34), Latin America and the Caribbean (30), and the Middle East and North Africa (15). UNICEF also provided technical or advisory services in 15 higher-income developing countries.

Programme expenditures totalled $400 million, of which 40 per cent ($158 million) was spent on child health; 17 per cent ($69 million) on water supply and sanitation; 13 per cent ($52 million) on planning and programme support services; 9 per cent ($37 million) on education; 8 per cent ($32 million) on emergency relief; 7 per cent ($29 million) on community and family-based services; and 6 per cent ($23 million) on child nutrition.

In his report on 1988 activities,[1] the UNICEF Executive Director noted that CSD activities continued to gain momentum during the year. Together with the World Health Organization (WHO), the Fund adopted a number of health goals for the year 2000. They included the eradication of polio, the elimination of guinea-worm disease, and a 90 per cent reduction in measles cases, by 1995. UNICEF continued its advocacy for alternative economic-adjustment policies in developing countries, and promoted inter-agency co-operation at all levels. It continued to collaborate also with the United Nations system and non-governmental organizations (NGOs) on key issues related to children and women. The Executive Director noted that issues affecting children were becoming more prominent on national political agendas, and the Fund submitted to its Executive Board a list of goals for the 1990s and strategies to achieve them.

The Executive Board held its 1988 regular session in New York from 18 to 29 April.[2]

Programme policy

Medium-term plan

At its 1988 regular session, the Board reviewed UNICEF's performance in 1987 and endorsed[3] the programme objectives of the medium-term plan for 1987-1991.[4] Their basic goals included: the reduction of maternal, infant and child mortality and the improvement of maternal and child health (MCH); the protection and improvement of children's well-being and their environment; improvements in the well-being of women and their role in development; and appropriate child spacing to protect the health of mothers and children in the overall context of development.

The plan emphasized the need to assess the Fund's goals for the 1990s, to meet the objectives of the child survival and development strategy by the year 2000, and to promote the concept of "adjustment with a human face" (see below).

Global strategy for children

In April, the Board requested[5] the Executive Director to report to its 1989 session on the goals, targets and elements of a global strategy for the well-being of children. The Board considered that this strategy should address basic needs, as well as the main problems and risks facing children, their mothers and families, and strengthen nations' ability to deal with those problems on their own. Special attention would be given to the needs

of the least developed countries and the most effective use of international assistance. The Board recommended the integration of both the global and UNICEF strategies in country programming and the medium-term plan.

Policy reviews

The Executive Board considered, among other matters: an implementation strategy for UNICEF policy on women in development; co-operation in water supply and sanitation; and the impact of acquired immunodeficiency syndrome (AIDS) on women and children and guidelines for the Fund's participation in global events.

The policy review on women in development[6] described activities in Ethiopia, India, Kenya and Togo, and recommended action to incorporate women's needs and priorities into all aspects of UNICEF-supported programmes. The Board endorsed those recommendations in April.[7] (For detailed treatment of UNICEF policy on women in development, see PART THREE, Chapter XIII.)

In response to a 1987 Board request,[8] the report[9] on water, sanitation and health for all by the year 2000 reviewed co-operation in UNICEF-supported programmes since the 1970s, linkages with PHC and guidelines for future action. It recommended that efforts towards the goals of the International Drinking Water Supply and Sanitation Decade be extended to the year 2000 and noted a shift from technology-oriented water and sanitation projects to an emphasis on community mobilization involving women, hygiene education and human resources development.

The Board agreed[10] that the Fund should continue to promote the use of low-cost technologies and advocate their acceptance in national planning and local implementation. It urged that higher priority be given to human resources development and recommended that greater attention be paid to social mobilization.

After consideration of another policy review paper,[11] the Board endorsed[12] the 1988-1989 UNICEF programmes on AIDS, together with the Executive Director's recommendations that the Fund: consider AIDS as it affected children and women in UNICEF country programming exercises; consider education and advocacy in preventive programmes and emphasize the needs of children and mothers affected by the disease; continue efforts to ensure the safety of immunization programmes and promote equipment sterilization in all aspects of MCH care; and strengthen its collaboration with Governments and concerned organizations.

Another report[13] provided guidelines for UNICEF participation in global events for fundraising, advocacy and the development of strategic alliances with other organizations and individuals. In April, the Board approved[14] the guidelines, subject to amendments. It also requested[15] the UNICEF Executive Director to report at its 1989 session on the implementation of 1987 General Assembly resolutions on the Environmental Perspective to the Year 2000 and Beyond[16] and on the report of the World Commission on Environment and Development.[17]

UNICEF Maurice Pate Award

In April 1988, the Executive Director submitted to the Board a proposal[18] to amend the status of the Maurice Pate Memorial Award, established in 1966[19] to commemorate the first UNICEF Executive Director. The proposal broadened the criteria for the award's recipients. The UNICEF Maurice Pate Award may be conferred upon an institution, agency or individual in recognition of an extraordinary contribution to the advancement of the survival, protection and development of children. The Executive Board approved[20] the proposal, subject to amendments, together with an allocation of $25,000 from general resources as the award's stipend.[21] The 1988 Award was presented to Pembinaan Kesejahteraan Keluarga (Family Welfare Movement—PKK) of Indonesia for its role in rallying community participation in CSD activities in that country.

Adjustment with a human face

UNICEF continued its global advocacy for alternative economic-adjustment policies to protect social programmes in the face of budget cuts and ensure that the well-being of children was not sacrificed for the sake of financial stability. Leaders of the seven major industrialized countries attending a Toronto summit meeting made commitments to "offset" official debts, and the International Monetary Fund (IMF) and the World Bank made provisions for the most seriously affected African countries. In July, UNICEF signed an agreement with the African Development Bank at Abidjan, Côte d'Ivoire, for the joint financing of key CSD programmes and the analysis, design and implementation of structural adjustment policies "with a human face". The Amman Declaration of the North-South Round Table meeting, in September, urged that human resources development be a central goal of development.

In April, the Executive Board requested[22] the Fund to continue its assistance to countries interested in initiatives on debt relief for child survival.

Activities related to structural adjustment continued in Brazil, Ghana, Jamaica, Madagascar, Mozambique, the Niger, Sierra Leone and Somalia. The goal of Ghana's Programme of Action to Mitigate the Social Cost of Adjustment was to pro-

tect the poor for two years at a cost of $84 million (about 6 to 8 per cent of the cost of international support for Ghana's structural adjustment programme). In the Philippines, UNICEF continued its advocacy for debt relief for child survival and co-operated in the formulation of alternative adjustment programmes. In Indonesia and Pakistan, advocacy for adjustment with a human face continued to lay the foundation for economic growth to sustain existing social services and protect the poor. In Sri Lanka, a "poverty alleviation" symposium, organized by the Central Bank and based on the Fund's analytical support, provided opportunities for continued UNICEF advocacy. In the Sudan, negotiations were in progress with the Midland Bank of the United Kingdom on debt relief for child survival.

UNICEF programmes by region

Africa

A deteriorating economic situation, armed conflicts, recurrent natural disasters, mass population displacements, growing urbanization, declining food production and increasing malnutrition continued to affect the quality of life and survival prospects of millions of African children in 1988. UNICEF continued to adapt its strategies to the continent's difficult situation, with programme expenditures totalling $146 million, or 36 per cent of its global programme commitment.

In April, the Executive Board endorsed UNICEF programme policies and strategies for Africa[23] and asked the Executive Director to initiate or strengthen, as a priority, programmes aimed at preparing the African child for its role in development.[24] In accordance with Economic and Social Council **resolution 1988/1**, the Board also requested[25] the Executive Director to prepare a report on the Fund's contribution from 1 June 1986 to 31 July 1988 to the implementation of the United Nations Programme of Action for African Economic Recovery and Development 1986-1990.

The Board further approved[26] a five-year policy framework[27] for the Bamako Initiative, adopted at a meeting of African Ministers of Health (Bamako, Mali, September 1987) to revitalize and expand MCH/PHC services in Africa. The Board authorized UNICEF to seek funding from interested donors and approved $2 million from general resources for preparatory work as well as up to $30 million of supplementary-funded resources to initiate action at the country level.

The Executive Director reported significant progress in UNICEF-supported programmes in Africa during the year.[1] Eight countries achieved child immunization coverage levels of 75 per cent or more and another 12 were within striking distance of this goal. The year saw a positive move from ORT, as a means of preventing diarrhoeal dehydration, towards the control of diarrhoeal diseases (CDD) through linkages with water and sanitation projects, breast-feeding and personal hygiene, and their integration with MCH/PHC programmes. With the endorsement of the Bamako Initiative by the Organization of African Unity (OAU) in 1988, many countries began to discuss the realignment of their essential drugs projects with the Initiative's approach.

The Fund provided emergency assistance to many countries, including Angola, Mozambique and the Sudan. The Executive Director released $500,000 from the Emergency Reserve Fund to support NGO activities in southern Sudan, where armed conflict had led to massive population displacements and high death rates caused by malnutrition and disease.

In eastern and southern Africa,[28] programmes to strengthen national and local capacities focused on improvements in health, family food security and nutrition, basic education, and the role of women as producers and mothers. In the area of PHC, several countries had fully integrated their CDD/ORT activities into the expanded programme of immunization (EPI) or MCH/PHC projects, and Kenya, Malawi and Mauritius reported a decline in diarrhoeal cases and deaths. The Fund continued to supply States with oral rehydration salts (ORS) packets and provided training for diarrhoea treatment units. In June, Madagascar became the sixth country in the region to start local ORS production, following the examples of Burundi, the Comoros, Kenya, Mozambique and Zambia. Several countries also made efforts to cope with the spread of malaria and acute respiratory infections (ARI), using staff and equipment from UCI projects.

UNICEF supported national AIDS control plans in several areas, including health education and social mobilization to change sexual behaviour, stronger sterilization procedures in immunization programmes, and the care of AIDS cases and orphans. Steps were taken to reduce maternal and infant mortality by increasing the number of births attended by trained personnel and through support for family planning.

Although there were above-average harvests in the region, many countries, particularly in southern Africa, failed to benefit because of disruptions caused by wars, civil strife and the influx of refugees. UNICEF took steps to estimate the extent of food insecurity and to identify policy options to redress the problem. Direct interventions to improve household food security and nutrition were undertaken in Ethiopia, Mozambique, Somalia and the United Republic of Tanzania, mainly as part of UNICEF/WHO joint nutrition support programmes (JNSP).

As a result of severe economic difficulties and a massive decrease in school enrolments, national education systems continued to suffer. The Fund advocated innovative and cost-effective approaches to basic education that emphasized self-reliant, community-based actions.

In west and central Africa,[29] mid-term programme reviews with UNICEF partners (Ghana, Nigeria and Sierra Leone) and the preparation of new country programme recommendations (Benin, Côte d'Ivoire, Guinea-Bissau, the Niger and Togo) strengthened intersectoral co-ordination and programme development. Although there was a decline in the nutritional status of mothers and children in central and west Africa as a result of economic hardship and rising food prices, some success was achieved in reducing levels of low birth weight and severe and moderate early childhood malnutrition. The Fund supported nutrition surveys, training and health education projects, and helped to equip nutrition rehabilitation centres in most Sahelian countries. With a combination of national immunization days and strengthened routine services, four countries—the Congo, Côte d'Ivoire, Senegal and Togo—raised the coverage rate for all antigens to more than 50 per cent and reported high access to immunization services. Cape Verde and the Gambia achieved better than 75 per cent coverage for six antigens, but in many countries of the region progress towards UCI was impeded by the lack of service infrastructure, especially in rural areas, and by serious financial difficulties. In the difficult economic climate, financial planning and monitoring of national and external inputs became increasingly important to ensure the most efficient use of limited resources.

In January, in conjunction with UNESCO, the Fund organized a regional seminar on development of the young child, which analysed the living conditions of African children and their CSD implications; examined possible interventions for children in difficult circumstances; and reviewed support for CSD programmes through education.

Latin America and the Caribbean

At a regional conference on poverty, held in Colombia in September, it was acknowledged that 170 million people—more than 40 per cent of the region's population—lived in poverty, and that some 61 million of that group lived in extreme poverty. The combination of economic decline, rising inflation, wage reductions and greater unemployment, coupled with heavy external and social debt burdens and environmental deterioration, made it increasingly difficult for Governments to meet the minimum needs of their citizens. Social service budgets stagnated or were cut in many countries, contributing to a high level of child malnutrition and deficient pre-natal and other health care for women. To meet these challenges, the Fund continued its efforts to raise awareness of children's problems and to ensure that activities benefiting poor children and women received the highest priority. UNICEF programme expenditure for the region totalled $37 million, or 9 per cent of total global programme expenditure.

In April,[30] the Executive Board established a special adjustment facility for Latin America and the Caribbean, to be funded from general resources in the amount of $2 million a year for five years, and requested the Executive Director to report in 1990 on its use and allocation criteria. Programme activities in Latin America and the Caribbean in 1988[31] helped to achieve progress in child development; expand primary education and literacy, particularly for women; develop innovative interventions benefiting children in especially difficult circumstances; encourage women's participation in development; and strengthen public awareness of children's needs. Support for immunization increased substantially, but only eight countries, in addition to the English-speaking Caribbean, were expected to attain UCI by 1990.

UNICEF was encouraging the formulation of regional and national CDD/ORT and ARI plans of action and co-sponsored an International Conference on Food and Nutrition Surveillance in September.

Accelerated urbanization, accompanied by unemployment and family disintegration, as well as armed conflict in Central America and violence in Colombia and Peru, resulted in a growing number of children in especially difficult circumstances. The Fund advocated and supported national initiatives to protect children at high risk, and national child boards or committees were established or consolidated in El Salvador, Guatemala and Honduras.

Asia

In 1988, UNICEF programme expenditures in Asia totalled $167 million, some 42 per cent of the Fund's global programme budget. Although a number of countries reported remarkable economic growth,[32] disparities in income distribution, political volatility, external debt burdens and natural disasters significantly affected the situation of women and children and the ability of Governments to deliver services to them. Severe flooding in Bangladesh, drought in Pakistan, and typhoons and hurricanes in the Philippines and Viet Nam meant that an increasing share of the Fund's work reverted to reconstruction, thereby hampering the normal flow of development activities.

Progress was made in many areas, however, most notably in immunization. Rapid increases in coverage were recorded in Indonesia, Pakistan and the Philippines, and the Democratic People's Republic of Korea, Malaysia, the Republic of Korea and Thailand showed signs of achieving UCI before the end of 1990. Diarrhoeal diseases remained among the leading causes of morbidity and mortality in the region, although most countries had established national programmes for CDD. The distribution of ORS and the promotion of ORT were of special importance to the Pacific island countries, where high mortality from diarrhoea underscored the need for integrated CDD programmes.

Nutrition surveillance continued, accompanied by growth monitoring and family food production programmes as an integral part of national agricultural strategies. Increasing attention was paid to the control of iodine deficiency disorders (IDD) through salt iodation and iodized oil supplements. Many countries also pursued vitamin-A deficiency control through surveys, training and capsule distribution, together with iron/folic acid supplementation as part of MCH programmes. A special emergency mission to Bangladesh provided advice on post-flood interventions, and a regional workshop was held in Indonesia (August) to consider the linkage of food and nutrition surveillance with anti-poverty programmes.

In collaboration with NGOs, UNICEF supported skills training and income-generating activities for women and promoted female literacy. In Bangladesh, 26 UNICEF-assisted NGOs developed revolving funds to support income-generating activities and to extend credit to poor women. Training in EPI, health education, nutrition and child development was provided for female leaders in Kampuchea and the Lao People's Democratic Republic. The Fund co-operated in a literacy programme for girls and women in Indonesia, focusing on school drop-outs and illiterate women from the lowest income groups.

In South Central Asia, poverty was aggravated by a higher than usual incidence of drought, floods, earthquakes and human conflict.[33] The reduction of infant mortality remained a priority, and UNICEF tried, with some success, to help Governments introduce broad-based, interrelated services targeted on interventions such as immunization and ORT, combined with improved infant feeding and education for girls. Rates of maternal malnutrition, morbidity and mortality remained high throughout the region, however, as did the proportion of low-weight births.

The summit of the South Asian Association for Regional Co-operation (SAARC) (Islamabad, Pakistan, December) reviewed progress in the situation of children and reiterated the commitment to give the highest priority in national planning and human resources development to the needs of children. The summit declared that 1989 would be the

SAARC Year against Drug Abuse, and 1990, the SAARC Year of the Girl Child.

Middle East and North Africa

In 1988, UNICEF programme expenditures in the Middle East and North Africa amounted to $38 million—10 per cent of the global budget. Despite the continuing economic stagnation and deteriorating circumstances of some countries, child survival efforts in the 17 States where the Fund had active programmes prevented an estimated 72,000 infant deaths during the year,[34] and the number of lives saved was expected to accelerate with a surge in immunization coverage. Immunization rates for important childhood diseases rose to 75 per cent in Iran, Lebanon and Morocco and to 50 per cent outside the war zones in the Sudan. Average coverage levels for children to the age of one year were 73 per cent for diphtheria/pertussis/tetanus (DPT) vaccine and 69 per cent for measles, and the UCI goal of 80 per cent coverage in the region by 1990 seemed well within reach.

In the Sudan, UNICEF relief co-ordination, supply operations and staff dedication were critical factors during the August flood emergency and the meningitis epidemic earlier in the year. In Lebanon, the Fund assisted with water supply and distributed food and drugs through the district-level liaison network used for immunization campaigns. In March, during the first months of the *intifadah* in the West Bank and Gaza, UNICEF deployed an international physiotherapy team to help young people injured in the uprising. During the Iran-Iraq cease-fire in November, the Fund launched rehabilitation initiatives in both countries to help national authorities accelerate the opening or re-opening of rural PHC units in the affected areas.

Social mobilization was used to promote a wide range of activities and issues throughout the region, including immunization in Iran, Morocco and Saudi Arabia; ORT in Iran and Jordan; and the draft Convention on the Rights of the Child (see below) in Algeria, Egypt and Turkey. In March, the Persian Gulf area countries launched a UNICEF-supported communications project to link health educators and media policy makers from Bahrain, Kuwait, Oman, Saudi Arabia and the United Arab Emirates in a sustained effort to support CSD activities. In October, a health education programme jointly sponsored by UNICEF, UNESCO and WHO went public in Bahrain, Egypt, Jordan, Morocco and the Sudan with the aim of turning the region's primary schools into focal points for community self-reliance in PHC.

Other programme developments in the region included an immunization/ORT/breast-feeding campaign in Iran; an expanded pilot project against ARI in Turkey; new emphasis on women's education and development in Democratic Yemen,

Morocco and Oman; training and income-generating activities for women in Egypt and the Sudan; stronger links between water and sanitation projects and CDD in Egypt and the Syrian Arab Republic; and accelerated water drilling in the Sudan. ORT programmes stagnated, except in Iran, Jordan and Syria, and tetanus toxoid coverage, although increasing in the region, remained among the lowest worldwide. An accelerated tetanus toxoid immunization campaign was launched in Egypt in November.

UNICEF programmes by sector

Child survival and development

UNICEF, together with WHO, the World Bank, UNDP and the Rockefeller Foundation, continued to support the Task Force for Child Survival in 1988. In March, a meeting sponsored by the Task Force adopted the "Talloires Declaration" which proposed several CSD goals for the 1990s.

Immunization

With the UCI/1990 goal approaching, coverage accelerated in all regions, led by impressive gains in Asia and eastern and southern Africa. In 1988, more than 60 per cent of children in the developing world received three doses of combined DPT and oral polio vaccine (OPV) before their first birthday, an increase of more than 50 per cent since 1981. The gap between anti-tuberculosis vaccine, the traditional leader in coverage, and the third doses of DPT and OPV was narrowed significantly as a result of reduced drop-out rates, and those achievements, when coupled with increased measles coverage, resulted in an estimated 1.5 million fewer child deaths during the year. Some 240,000 other children were spared the crippling effects of poliomyelitis. Many Middle East and North African countries reached 80 per cent coverage for all antigens during the year, while Latin America and the Caribbean also made progress towards UCI. Rapidly improving coverage rates in China, India, Indonesia, Nigeria, the Philippines and, to some extent, Bangladesh fueled optimism for the attainment of global UCI targets in 1990 and for preventing the deaths of an additional 2 million children a year from immunizable diseases.

Control of diarrhoeal diseases

Public awareness and use of ORT rose significantly between 1980 and 1988 with the result that over 60 per cent of the developing world's population was living within reach of a trained, regularly supplied provider of ORS in 1988. Of the 300 million ORS packets distributed during the year, two thirds were produced in developing countries. UNICEF provided assistance to more than half of the 55 ORS-producer countries, 10 of which were self-sufficient. It was estimated that as many as 1 million child deaths were averted during the year through the use of ORT. In December, the Third International Conference on ORT (Washington, D.C.) addressed the issue of sustainability.

Primary health care

Several trends could be discerned in PHC developments in 1988, including heightened interest in health financing; sustainability; decentralization; management issues and the training of health personnel at the district and community levels; and the integration of vertical programmes. Following the Safe Motherhood Conference (Nairobi, Kenya, 1987), several countries developed programmes or undertook studies and surveys on maternal health care and maternal mortality reduction, and interregional or national seminars on the issue were held in Brazil, Egypt, Indonesia, the Philippines and the Sudan. ARI was increasingly recognized as a major cause of death in children under five years of age in developing countries, and UNICEF began to promote training for health workers in the use of new, simplified diagnostic and management criteria developed by WHO. The two organizations were also developing operational modalities for ARI control in Bolivia, the Gambia and Thailand. The Fund also supported efforts to deal with the prevention and management of malaria by providing drugs in endemic areas.

Acquired immunodeficiency syndrome

During 1988, the direct and indirect impact of AIDS on women and children reached dramatic proportions in many developing countries in Africa and in the Caribbean, where half of all human immunodeficiency virus (HIV)–infected individuals and AIDS cases were women, with a 30 to 50 per cent chance of infecting their newborn children. Data for the year indicated HIV seroprevalence rates of up to 27 per cent for women of reproductive age in urban areas of some African countries, and over 10 per cent in many others. To protect adults and their children from HIV infection, a variety of intensive and creative health education channels were mobilized urgently. In April,[12] the Executive Board approved a policy and programme direction for UNICEF involvement in AIDS-prevention projects that were part of national AIDS plans and consistent with the WHO Global Programme on AIDS. It also approved special prevention projects for supplementary funding in Burundi, Rwanda, Uganda and the United Republic of Tanzania. More than $4 million in supplementary funding was raised from bilateral donors, National Committees and advances from the Infant Mortality Reduction Reserve Fund. UNICEF provided training in AIDS prevention for

its health staff in the field as well as for health workers, and began to add AIDS prevention to other child survival messages. In Uganda, AIDS prevention was included in a UNICEF-assisted school health education project. The Fund also continued to monitor the sterilization of immunization equipment to prevent the transmission of HIV and other infections.

Breast-feeding, nutrition and growth monitoring

UNICEF activities in the area of nutrition concentrated on improving household food security, growth monitoring and promotion, food and nutrition surveillance, promotion of breast-feeding, and the control of micronutrient deficiencies. To bolster household food security, the Fund promoted income-generating activities for women, support for vulnerable households and small farmers, and the production and processing of improved varieties of cassava and soya beans—the staple food for some 40 per cent of the population in sub-Saharan Africa. Growth monitoring and nutrition education were commonly included in community-level PHC and were featured in major programmes, including the Integrated Child Development Service scheme in India, the family nutrition improvement programme in Indonesia, and the Child Pastorate Programme of the National Conference of Bishops in Brazil. Growth-monitoring techniques—weighing, plotting, interpreting and counselling—received greater attention in many countries. Although the gap between awareness of and the practice of breast-feeding remained a major problem among mothers and health professionals, changes in hospital policies led to higher breast-feeding initiation rates and to a reduction of mortality and morbidity in infants.

UNICEF assistance in vitamin-A deficiency control ranged from surveys to support for comprehensive programmes aimed at increasing the production and consumption of dark green leafy vegetables and other dietary sources of the vitamin. The Fund joined with the International Vitamin-A Consultative Group and WHO in preparing and publishing guidelines on the use of vitamin-A supplements to treat and prevent vitamin-A deficiency and xerophthalmia. UNICEF co-operated in IDD control through salt iodation in 24 countries, strengthened monitoring arrangements for salt quality control, and continued its support for the International Council for the Control of IDD.

Childhood disability

During 1988, UNICEF was involved in childhood disability prevention, in the broader context of CSD, including immunization against polio, the control of vitamin-A deficiency and IDD. Activities also included family education on disability prevention. Early detection and community-based rehabilitation activities were reported from 37 countries.

Water supply and sanitation

Sanitation services continued to lag far behind water supply in 1988, and deficits in rural areas were much higher than those in urban areas. The Fund spent $69 million on water supply and sanitation programmes, $4 million more than in the previous year.

Basic education

A global crisis in education, with over 900 million illiterates and 120 million children aged 6 to 11 years out of school, led UNESCO, the World Bank, UNDP and UNICEF to agree to co-sponsor a world conference on basic education for all in 1990. Almost all countries reported the integration of education into CSD activities and the accelerated incorporation of CSD themes in primary school curricula and teacher training. Children's education was threatened by civil strife in several countries. Imaginative responses included rehabilitation training for teachers to cope with war-traumatized children (Mozambique), decentralization to keep schools open (Lebanon), the introduction of child rights into primary school curricula (Thailand), and conflict resolution (Education for Peace) in Central America.

Urban basic services

UNICEF assistance benefiting the urban poor shifted gradually from strategy-oriented goals to impact-oriented targets such as immunization coverage, decrease in infant mortality, access to basic drugs and, ultimately, to PHC and basic services coverage.

In 1988, the coverage and sustainability of EPI in urban areas were addressed by all country offices. Experience indicated that all start-up activities were generally delayed in urban slums and shanty towns by administrative matters and that the countries which achieved the highest immunization coverage in urban areas were those with the greatest experience with large-scale urban basic services (UBS). Immunization campaigns were also found to generate higher demand among the urban poor for PHC. Countries with long traditions in UBS, such as Colombia, India, Indonesia, Peru, the Philippines and Sri Lanka, continued to implement large-scale intersectoral programmes in which the Fund assisted with software and facilities, while channelling other agencies' hardware towards the poor and the poorest.

Women in development

In 1988, the Fund continued its child-specific interventions to strengthen the socio-economic resource base of women. Women-related concerns were fully integrated into situation analyses in Bolivia, the Central African Republic, Egypt, Mexico and Rwanda, and studies on the status of women were completed in Brazil, Burma, Dominica, Indonesia, Oman and the Sudan. Country programme submissions and CSD initiatives reflected heightened awareness of the interrelationship between the socio-economic situation of women and the welfare of the child. Emphasis was placed on non-formal education as a means of reinforcing women's position in both the household and the community. In Bangladesh and Indonesia, national programmes supported women as key disseminators of CSD messages and linked their participation in literacy programmes with economic activities, vocational training and health education. The subregional women's education and child survival programme in Central America expanded, as did functional literacy programmes in Angola, Cape Verde, Chad and Guinea. Brazil, Democratic Yemen and the Lao People's Democratic Republic were developing similar initiatives. Credit programmes geared towards low-income women were consolidated in Bangladesh, Egypt and India, and a subregional programme on income-generating activities was being developed in the Caribbean. In Brazil, an effort was under way to form credit solidarity groups, revolving loan funds and a national institution to extend credit to low-income women. In Africa, emphasis remained on support for co-operatives and credit-sharing groups.

Emergency relief and rehabilitation

During the year, natural disasters were particularly severe and frequent, and they often coincided with the effects of armed conflict. The Fund provided emergency relief totalling $32.2 million to 43 countries to offset the impact of 14 weather-related emergencies (floods, typhoons and hurricanes), 7 epidemics, 12 armed-conflict situations, 3 drought-related conditions and 1 economic emergency. Most assistance went to Africa (25 countries), where Angola, Ethiopia, Mozambique, Somalia and the Sudan remained the most seriously affected countries. The Executive Director's Emergency Reserve Fund made 17 releases totalling $3.5 million to 15 countries during the year.[35]

Children in especially difficult circumstances

UNICEF remained involved in programmes for children in armed conflict and for working and street children. It provided basic services to displaced persons, including children, and was beginning to develop appropriate educational support systems for the psycho-social needs of children in armed conflicts. In 1988, 13 countries in Latin America and 7 countries in other regions submitted projects to the Executive Board for working and street children, and 20 other States were preparing similar projects for supplementary funding. UNICEF signed a letter of agreement for joint activities with project CHILDHOPE and co-operated with the International Labour Organisation (ILO) to publish training materials.

Other activities

During the period October 1987–September 1988, the Fund completed some 218 programme evaluations, 42 per cent of which dealt with immunization and diarrhoeal diseases, 11 per cent with water and environmental sanitation, 10 per cent with education, 8 per cent with nutrition and 5 per cent with women. The supply operations of UNICEF, which accounted for some 50 per cent of programme assistance, amounted to $215 million during 1988.[36]

UNICEF finances

UNICEF income in 1988 totalled $711 million,[37] compared with $572 million in 1987. Income comprised $437 million for general resources and $274 million for supplementary funds, including $39 million in emergency contributions, mostly for Africa. Contributions from Governments and intergovernmental organizations represented 70 per cent of the total ($498 million), and those from private sources 19 per cent ($136 million). Around 1 per cent ($6 million) was received from the United Nations system and 10 per cent ($71 million) from miscellaneous sources, including exchange-rate revaluations of assets and liabilities.

Expenditures in 1988 totalled $516 million, compared with $479 million in 1987. At the United Nations Pledging Conference for Development Activities in November, 75 Governments pledged a total of $263 million for 1989 UNICEF general resources, compared with $213 million in 1987.

New programme commitments of $230,631,000, to be financed from general resources,[38] were approved in April.[21]

Medium-term financial plan

At its 1988 session, the Executive Board approved[39] the medium-term financial plan for the period 1988-1991,[4] including the preparation of up to $200 million in programme expenditures from general resources for 1989, subject to resource availability and the validity of income/expenditure estimates. The plan projected the Fund's total income at $560 million for 1989, $585 million for 1990 and $612 million for 1991, and recommended programme expenditures of $340 million in 1990 and $150 million in 1991.

Financial policy decisions

In April 1988, the Executive Board adopted a set of rules to expand supplementary funding policies and revised the relevant financial regulations.[40] It authorized the temporary allocation of general resources to supplementary-funded projects under certain conditions and decided to discontinue use of the term "noted" projects and refer to them as projects for supplementary funding, or supplementary-funded projects. The Board also acted[41] on problems related to the payment of recurrent costs.[42] It requested UNICEF to help Governments reduce recurrent costs through improved programme management; the use of low-cost technologies and community-based service delivery; and more effective targeting of services towards the needs of vulnerable groups, especially children and women. It also requested the Fund to promote new approaches to local resource generation in recipient countries, to monitor the impact of economic and social-sector policies on vulnerable groups, and to assist in identifying long-term solutions to the financing of recurrent costs. The Board also urged UNICEF to establish operational guidelines for the financing of recurrent costs related to its field activities.

1986 accounts

In response to a 1987 General Assembly request,[43] the Board of Auditors undertook an expanded audit of the 1986 UNICEF accounts. The Board had withheld an audit opinion on the Fund's 1986 financial statement in 1987 because of the timing of income from pledged supplementary resources, the temporary allocation of general resources to supplementary-funded projects, the level of reported expenditures, funding approval for UNICEF fortieth anniversary activities, and technical accounting issues. The audit was completed in March 1988, the accounts were certified, and the Board's conclusions[44] were submitted to the Advisory Committee on Administrative and Budgetary Questions (ACABQ). In October,[45] the Committee considered the Board of Auditors' report and the Secretary-General's note,[46] and forwarded its comments to the UNICEF Executive Director.

Organizational questions

UNICEF structure

In April 1988, the Executive Board reviewed the function and organizational structure of the UNICEF external relations system[47] and requested[48] the Executive Director to address its restructuring in the context of the revised 1988-1989 and 1990-1991 biennial budgets, including a review of regional offices and offices in Geneva, Tokyo and Sydney, as well as the Greeting Card Operation (see below).

UNICEF Board

At its 1988 regular session, the Executive Board adopted 25 resolutions on programme, administrative and budgetary matters. In the light of its increased work-load, it requested the Economic and Social Council to allocate four additional meetings to its two-week regular session.[49]

UNICEF fortieth anniversary (1986)

In 1988, the Executive Director reported to the Board on the Fund's fortieth anniversary in 1986.[50] The report included an overview of fund-raising activities, including the Sport Aid and First Earth Run campaigns. It gave the status of the Special Account for Special Events, and summarized expenditures, income and budget adjustments related to anniversary activities. In April, the Board noted that anniversary events had so far raised a total of $38.9 million against expenditures of $7.7 million, and approved, *post facto*, those expenditures, including $4,696,847 for Sport Aid that was eventually offset by commercial receipts.[51]

Greeting Card Operation

For the third consecutive year, UNICEF's Greeting Card Operation[52] made a record profit ($38.5 million). New sales structures and training programmes were implemented in Asia and Latin America; a programme to test the feasibility of UNICEF retail shops was launched in Europe; and a new product line was tested in the United States. In May, the Fund formally opened the Danny Kaye Visitors Centre at UNICEF House in New York.

The work plan for the 1988 season[53] was endorsed by the Executive Board in April. The Board approved expenditure estimates of $31 million for the financial year 1988/89 and noted that gross revenues were estimated to be $80.2 million.[54]

Draft Convention on the Rights of the Child

At its 1988 session, the Executive Board requested[55] UNICEF to support the United Nations Centre for Human Rights with a technical review of the draft Convention on the Rights of the Child. The aim was to complete the second reading in 1988 and submit it for adoption by the General Assembly in 1989. The Fund was also requested to continue its co-operation with Governments and NGOs to raise awareness of the draft Convention and encourage their participation in the process leading to its adoption.

In May, the Assembly of Heads of State and Government of OAU in Addis Ababa, Ethiopia, adopted a resolution urging completion of the draft Convention and the drafting of an African charter for children. Parliamentarians, religious leaders and media personnel from Africa, Asia and Latin America agreed on specific measures to promote the draft Convention at all levels, and national and regional NGO networks pledged to support regional charters for the protection of child rights.

UNICEF completed a comprehensive examination of the text prior to the second reading, as requested. (For details on the draft Convention, see PART THREE, Chapter X.)

Tenth anniversary (1989) of the International Year of the Child

The Board invited Governments to observe the tenth anniversary of the International Year of the Child (IYC) in 1989 by assessing their achievements in relation to the goals established during IYC. It also requested UNICEF to co-operate with Governments, National Committees and NGOs in attaining the goals through country programmes and advocacy.[56]

International Child Development Centre

In April, the Board took note[57] of the progress report[58] on the organization, planning and initial activities of the International Child Development Centre at Florence, Italy, which began operations in September 1988. The Centre was to provide a forum for international professional exchanges, advocate innovative strategies for the benefit of children, and provide training facilities.

NGO relations

During 1988, UNICEF co-operation with NGOs continued to expand. Rotary International worked with the Fund to combat polio in over 70 countries and was the first institution to receive the International Child Survival Award. The Fund worked closely with NGOs to promote the draft Convention on the Rights of the Child, and, through the NGO Committee on UNICEF, sought to broaden the network of organizations promoting children's rights, breast-feeding and responses to AIDS.

Inter-agency co-operation

In February, the Joint Consultative Group on Policy, comprising UNDP, the United Nations Population Fund (UNFPA), the World Food Programme, UNICEF and the International Fund for Agricultural Development, met with senior representatives of IMF and the World Bank, and agreed to work towards broader adjustment policies that took better account of social implications. In April, the Board welcomed UNICEF's initiative to rationalize the field-office structure of its member organizations, and requested the Executive Director to report on the Fund's operational activities for development.[59]

UNICEF continued to co-operate with the World Bank in such areas as health, nutrition, education, water supply and sanitation, urban development, women in development, and safe motherhood, and it pressed for more attention to nutrition and human issues in the World Bank's consultative groups and UNDP round tables. The long-standing collaboration between the Fund and WHO progressed in 1988 across a broad span of programme fields, and the Third International Conference on ORT (Washington, D.C., December) was co-sponsored by the two organizations together with UNDP, the World Bank and the United States Agency for International Development.

Co-operation with UNESCO emphasized female enrolment in schools, and, as a member of the International Working Group on Education, UNICEF was responsible for female and basic education.

REFERENCES

[1]E/ICEF/1989/2 (Part I) & Corr.1 & (Part II) & Corr.1,2 & Add.1. [2]E/1988/18. [3]*Ibid.* (res. 1988/1). [4]E/ICEF/1988/3. [5]E/1988/18 (res. 1988/17). [6]E/ICEF/1988/L.1. [7]E/1988/18 (res. 1988/6). [8]E/ICEF/1987/11. [9]E/ICEF/1988/L.4. [10]E/1988/18 (res. 1988/2). [11]E/ICEF/1988/L.7 & Add.1. [12]E/1988/18 (res. 1988/7). [13]E/ICEF/1988/L.8/Rev.1. [14]E/1988/18 (res. 1988/8). [15]*Ibid.* (res. 1988/18). [16]YUN 1987, p. 661, GA res. 42/186, 11 December 1987. [17]YUN 1987, p. 679, GA res. 42/187, 11 December 1987. [18]E/ICEF/1988/P/L.37. [19]YUN 1966, p. 385. [20]E/1988/18 (res. 1988/9). [21]*Ibid.* (res. 1988/4). [22]*Ibid.* (res. 1988/20). [23]E/ICEF/1988/L.5. [24]E/1988/18 (res. 1988/23). [25]*Ibid.* (res. 1988/21). [26]*Ibid.* (res. 1988/3). [27]E/ICEF/1988/P/L.40. [28]E/ICEF/1989/5. [29]E/ICEF/1989/6. [30]E/1988/18 (res. 1988/22). [31]E/ICEF/1989/7. [32]E/ICEF/1989/8. [33]E/ICEF/1989/9. [34]E/ICEF/1989/10 & Corr.1. [35]E/ICEF/1989/11. [36]E/ICEF/1989/4. [37]E/ICEF/1989/AB/L.7. [38]E/ICEF/1988/P/L.1. [39]E/1988/18 (res. 1988/10). [40]*Ibid.* (res. 1988/11). [41]*Ibid.* (res. 1988/15). [42]E/ICEF/1988/L.3. [43]YUN 1987, p. 862. [44]A/42/5/Add.2. [45]A/43/674 & Corr.1. [46]A/43/445. [47]E/ICEF/1988/AB/L.1. [48]E/1988/18 (res. 1988/12). [49]*Ibid.* (res. 1988/25). [50]E/ICEF/1988/AB/L.9. [51]E/1988/18 (res. 1988/13). [52]E/ICEF/1989/AB/L.4. [53]E/ICEF/1988/AB/L.6 & Corr.1. [54]E/1988/18 (res. 1988/14). [55]*Ibid.* (res. 1988/16). [56]*Ibid.* (res. 1988/19). [57]*Ibid.* (res. 1988/5). [58]E/ICEF/1988/L.9 & Corr.1 & Add.1. [59]E/1988/18 (res. 1988/24).

Youth

In 1988, United Nations activities on youth—persons aged 15 to 24 years—concentrated on follow-up to guidelines, endorsed by the General Assembly during International Youth Year (IYY) in 1985.[1] Despite serious resource constraints, the United Nations Office at Vienna/Centre for Social Development and Humanitarian Affairs (UNOV/CSDHA), as the focal point on youth matters within the United Nations system, continued to promote the integration of youth in development and to monitor project proposals for funding by the United Nations Youth Fund. Interagency co-operation in the field of youth during the follow-up to IYY resulted in more critical research on youth, intensified technical co-operation

activities and advisory services to Governments, and improved working relations with NGOs and between United Nations bodies at the field level. Additional steps were taken to promote the HOPE '87 initiative aimed at reducing unemployment among young people.

Follow-up to International Youth Year (1985)

In accordance with a 1987 General Assembly resolution,[2] the Secretary-General in a September 1988 report[3] reviewed policies and programmes involving young people, especially in relation to development and peace. He said that efforts to develop long-term planning for youth had expanded youth-related programmes within and outside the United Nations system and increased global awareness of the needs and aspirations of young people. However, planning for youth was hampered by limited financial resources at all levels. He suggested that the United Nations Youth Fund be included among the programmes for which funds were pledged at the United Nations Pledging Conference for Development Activities, and that CSDHA establish a consultative forum of NGOs to discuss their greater involvement in the implementation of youth policies and programmes.

Co-ordination and information

In a March 1988 report on co-ordination and information in the field of youth,[4] submitted in response to a 1987 Economic and Social Council resolution,[5] the Secretary-General described follow-up activities to IYY, reviewed co-ordination efforts in the field of youth, and listed suggestions for further co-ordination and greater resource mobilization.

In co-operation with the Government of China and the All-China Youth Federation, as well as the Department of Technical Co-operation for Development (DTCD) and the Economic and Social Commission for Asia and the Pacific (ESCAP), CSDHA organized an interregional consultative meeting on integrated planning of youth policies, strategies and programmes (Beijing, 17-23 October). The meeting was the first international technical exchange on the implementation of youth guidelines since their endorsement in 1985. The Beijing Statement, adopted by the meeting, emphasized the need for substantive interregional exchanges on youth issues. The Centre also organized a seminar on the prevention and treatment of juvenile delinquency through community participation in co-operation with DTCD (Beijing, 19-25 October). The seminar adopted guidelines and recommendations relating to community-oriented programmes and the strengthening of international co-operation in the field of juvenile justice, including the establishment of a juvenile justice information network.

By **decision 1988/147** of 27 May 1988, the Economic and Social Council took note of the Secretary-General's report.[4]

ACC activity. The informal inter-agency technical working group on youth, at its sixth session (Vienna, 8 and 9 March 1988),[6] reviewed progress after IYY and suggested action to enhance technical assistance in the field of youth. The group underlined the need for Governments to integrate youth policy with their national development planning.

Strengthening communication between youth and the United Nations

In response to a 1987 General Assembly resolution,[7] a September 1988 report[3] of the Secretary-General gave an overview of national, regional and international activities to strengthen communication between the United Nations and youth and with youth organizations.

CSDHA's *Youth Information Bulletin*, published three times a year since January 1988, highlighted major issues and activities. In January, CSDHA and the International Union of Students initiated a quarterly newsletter, *IYY Follow-up*, addressed primarily to national co-ordinating mechanisms and youth NGOs.

Other publications featuring youth issues included the twice-weekly *Newswire* and monthly *Intercom* (UNICEF), the *Bulletin on Narcotics* (Division of Narcotic Drugs), *Momentum* and *The Youth Development Newsletter* (ESCAP), *CEPAL Review* (ECLAC), and *Youth News* (United Nations Volunteers).

The right of youth to education and work

In accordance with a 1987 General Assembly resolution on the right of youth to education and work,[8] and an Assembly request of 1987,[9] the Secretary-General's report described the work of the Institute of HOPE '87 (Hundreds of Original Projects for Employment). The Institute was established in 1987[10] at the initiative of Austria to share nations' expertise with educational and vocational training and to develop programmes that could serve as models. By September 1988, the Institute had negotiated with 17 countries to establish affiliated HOPE '87 offices, prepared a model training manual for HOPE '87 personnel, set up a data bank, and conducted project feasibility studies. In August, Austria approved the establishment and funding of the Institute's Permanent Secretariat, with a 1989 budget of 1.5 million Austrian schillings.

GENERAL ASSEMBLY ACTION

On 8 December, on the recommendation of the Third Committee, the General Assembly adopted **resolution 43/94** without vote.

Question of youth

The General Assembly,

Recalling resolution 40/14 entitled "International Youth Year: Participation, Development, Peace", adopted on 18 November 1985 by the General Assembly acting as United Nations World Conference for the International Youth Year, and its resolution 42/54 of 30 November 1987,

Recalling its resolutions 32/135 of 16 December 1977 and 36/17 of 9 November 1981, by which it adopted guidelines for the improvement of the channels of communication between the United Nations and youth and youth organizations, and its resolution 42/55 of 30 November 1987,

Recalling also its resolutions 40/16 of 18 November 1985 and 42/53 of 30 November 1987, entitled "Opportunities for youth",

Recalling further its resolution 36/29 of 13 November 1981 and its subsequent resolutions in which it, *inter alia*, recognized the need to adopt appropriate measures for securing the implementation and enjoyment by youth of human rights, particularly the right to education and to work,

Having considered the report of the Secretary-General submitted on the basis of its resolutions 42/52, 42/53, 42/54 and 42/55 of 30 November 1987,

Bearing in mind that the preparation for and observance in 1985 of the International Youth Year: Participation, Development, Peace offered a useful and significant opportunity for drawing attention to the situation and the specific needs and aspirations of youth, for increasing co-operation at all levels in dealing with youth issues, for undertaking concerted action programmes in favour of youth and for improving the participation of young people in the study, decision-making processes and resolution of major national, regional and international problems,

Recognizing that the guidelines for further planning and suitable follow-up in the field of youth provide a constructive framework for a long-term strategy in the field of youth,

Expressing its serious interest in systematically consolidating and building further on the results of the International Youth Year in order to contribute to the increasing active participation of young people in the political and socio-economic life of their countries,

Convinced of the importance of the effective and efficient functioning of the channels of communication between the United Nations and youth and youth organizations as a basic prerequisite for the adequate information of young people and their active participation in the work of the United Nations and the specialized agencies at the national, regional and international levels, and also for informing the United Nations of the problems facing youth, with a view to finding solutions to such problems,

Convinced that it is necessary to ensure full enjoyment by youth of the rights stipulated in the Universal Declaration of Human Rights, the International Covenant on Economic, Social and Cultural Rights and the International Covenant on Civil and Political Rights, with special regard to the right to education and to work,

Recognizing that in many countries the majority of young people, under prevailing critical social and economic conditions, are facing serious problems in the exercise of their right to education and to work and that insufficient education and unemployment of young people limit their ability to participate effectively in the development process, and emphasizing the importance of adequate education of young people and access for them to appropriate technical and vocational guidance and training programmes,

1. *Calls upon* all States, all United Nations bodies, in particular the Economic and Social Council through its Commission for Social Development, the specialized agencies and the intergovernmental and non-governmental organizations concerned, in particular youth organizations, to continue to exert all possible efforts for the implementation of the guidelines for further planning and suitable follow-up in the field of youth, in accordance with their experience, conditions and priorities, and to submit to the Secretary-General their views and proposals on the specific ways and means to implement fully the guidelines;

2. *Requests* the Secretary-General to promote and monitor intensively, by using the Centre for Social Development and Humanitarian Affairs of the Secretariat as a focal point, the inclusion of youth-related projects and activities in the programmes of the United Nations bodies and of the specialized agencies, specifically on such themes as communication, health, housing, culture, youth employment and education;

3. *Calls upon* Member States, United Nations bodies, the specialized agencies and other governmental and intergovernmental organizations to implement fully the guidelines relating to the channels of communication adopted by the General Assembly in its resolutions 32/135 and 36/17, not only in general terms but also by concrete measures that take into account the issues of importance to young people;

4. *Requests* the Secretary-General to continue in this respect to make use at the national, regional and international levels of the already existing structures of co-operation between youth and the United Nations system in accordance with the additional guidelines for the improvement of the channels of communication between the United Nations and youth and youth organizations, contained in the annex to resolution 36/17, and to encourage other United Nations bodies and specialized agencies to do the same;

5. *Also requests* the Secretary-General to develop methods that specifically indicate how the channels of communication could efficiently be attuned to youth-related projects and activities of the United Nations organs and of the specialized agencies, and to include in his report thereon to the General Assembly concrete suggestions for co-operation between the United Nations system and the non-governmental youth organizations;

6. *Calls upon* youth mechanisms that have been set up by youth and youth organizations at the national, regional and international levels to continue to act as channels of communication between the United Nations and youth and youth organizations by putting forth their proposals for co-operation with the United Nations system and, where such mechanisms do not exist, recommends that national co-ordinating committees of the International Youth Year should similarly continue to act as channels of communication;

7. *Calls upon* all States, all governmental and non-governmental organizations, interested United Nations bodies, in particular the Economic and Social Council through its Commission for Social Development, and specialized agencies to continue to give priority to the formulation and implementation of effective measures for securing the exercise by youth of the right to education and to work, with a view to resolving the problem of unemployment among youth;

8. *Calls upon* Member States to pay increased attention to the promotion of youth employment in all sectors of the economy in order to enable more young people to obtain appropriate education and vocational training, thereby facilitating their integration into social and professional life;

9. *Invites* national co-ordinating bodies and bodies implementing policies and programmes in the field of youth to give appropriate priority in the activities to be undertaken after the International Youth Year: Participation, Development, Peace to the implementation and the enjoyment by youth of human rights, particularly the right to education and to work;

10. *Stresses* the importance for youth and youth organizations of the freedom of association, in accordance with the relevant national legislation, the Universal Declaration of Human Rights, the International Covenant on Civil and Political Rights and other relevant international human rights instruments, so as to enable their active and direct participation at all stages of implementation of the policies, projects and activities organized at the local, national, regional and international levels in the field of youth, and stresses the need to intensify the efforts for educating youth in accordance with national experience, conditions and priorities and to act effectively as channels of communication;

11. *Emphasizes* that providing education and employment to each young person is a worthy goal for all States and should serve the full development of the human being, which can best be ensured by countries that respect the fundamental rights and freedoms of everyone;

12. *Notes with appreciation* the establishment by the Government of Austria of a permanent secretariat of the Institute of HOPE '87, for the promotion of youth employment;

13. *Recommends* that the Secretary-General continue to explore the possibilities for the Centre for Social Development and Humanitarian Affairs to support, within the framework of its activities, the work of the Institute of HOPE '87 secretariat, including the question of affiliating, on the basis of the relevant regulations of the United Nations and the proposed letter of understanding, as outlined in his report, the Institute of HOPE '87 secretariat to the Centre, on the understanding that the financial resources for the secretariat would be raised exclusively from special voluntary contributions;

14. *Invites* Governments again to include youth representatives in their national delegations to the General Assembly and other relevant United Nations meetings and international conferences dealing with youth-related issues, thus enhancing and strengthening the channels of communication through the discussion of such issues, with a view to finding solutions to the problems confronting youth in the contemporary world;

15. *Requests* the Secretary-General to consider including, on an annual basis, the United Nations Youth Fund among the programmes for which funds are pledged at the United Nations Pledging Conference for Development Activities;

16. *Also requests* the Secretary-General to prepare a report on the implementation of the present resolution,

paying attention to the deliberations and conclusions of the Commission for Social Development in March 1989, and to submit it to the General Assembly at its forty-fourth session under the item entitled "Policies and programmes involving youth";

17. *Decides* to consider the item entitled "Policies and programmes involving youth" at its forty-fourth session on the basis of the report of the Secretary-General.

General Assembly resolution 43/94

8 December 1988   Meeting 75   Adopted without vote

Approved by Third Committee (A/43/809) without vote, 3 November (meeting 31); 17-nation draft (A/C.3/43/L.13/Rev.2), orally revised; agenda item 90.
Sponsors: Austria, Bangladesh, Barbados, Bolivia, Cameroon, Costa Rica, Czechoslovakia, Egypt, Greece, Guatemala, Netherlands, Pakistan, Romania, Samoa, Senegal, Spain, Sudan.
Meeting numbers. GA 43rd session: 3rd Committee 15-22, 25, 31; plenary 75.

Youth declaration on peace

In a letter of 18 August 1988,[11] Romania requested the inclusion in the agenda of the Assembly's forty-third session of a supplementary item dealing with, *inter alia*, evaluating the implementation of the Declaration on the Promotion among Youth of the Ideals of Peace, Mutual Respect and Understanding between Peoples.[12] An explanatory memorandum stated that this inclusion was in line with United Nations declarations aimed at promoting human rights, strengthening peace and countering racism and incitement to war, as well as the follow-up to IYY.

By its **decision 43/402** of 23 September 1988, the General Assembly endorsed Romania's request and allocated the item to the Third Committee.

GENERAL ASSEMBLY ACTION

On 8 December, acting on the recommendation of the Third Committee, the Assembly adopted **resolution 43/136** without vote.

Evaluation of the implementation of the Declaration on the Promotion among Youth of the Ideals of Peace, Mutual Respect and Understanding between Peoples

The General Assembly,

Recalling that one of the fundamental objectives of the United Nations is to save succeeding generations from the scourge of war,

Reaffirming the importance of the strict observance and full implementation of the purposes and principles inscribed in the Charter of the United Nations for the maintenance of international peace and security, the development of friendly relations among nations and understanding and co-operation among States and peoples,

Convinced that young people are interested in their future and wish to live in peace, freedom and friendship among all peoples,

Aware of the important role of youth in society, in all fields of activity, as well as of the fact that youth should also contribute to the further promotion of the common ends of peace and welfare of humankind,

Convinced also that the education of youth in the spirit of the ideals of peace, mutual respect, friendship and

co-operation between peoples should be a priority and permanent task of all States,

Emphasizing the essential role of Governments, governmental and non-governmental organizations, the mass media and educational systems in promoting these ideals among nations and, primarily, among youth,

Reaffirming the lasting validity and importance of the principles and objectives of the Declaration on the Promotion among Youth of the Ideals of Peace, Mutual Respect and Understanding between Peoples, proclaimed by the General Assembly in resolution 2037(XX) of 7 December 1965,

Stressing the necessity of the implementation of the provisions of the Universal Declaration of Human Rights towards the promotion among youth of the ideals of peace, mutual respect and understanding between peoples,

Noting that 1990 will mark the twenty-fifth anniversary of the adoption of the Declaration on the Promotion among Youth of the Ideals of Peace, Mutual Respect and Understanding between Peoples,

1. *Appeals* to all States to adopt effective measures in accordance with their legislation, particularly in the fields of teaching, education, culture and information, in order to strengthen the efforts for the promotion among nations and, primarily, among youth of understanding, mutual respect and friendship among nations, for the creation of an international climate free from mistrust and discord;

2. *Stresses* the role of the mass media in supporting by all means the implementation of these objectives with a view to promoting the ideals and conceptions meant to contribute to the enhancement of friendly relations and co-operation among States;

3. *Invites* all States to submit to the Secretary-General their views and comments on the impact of the Declaration on the Promotion among Youth of the Ideals of Peace, Mutual Respect and Understanding between Peoples since its adoption and on the measures that should be taken, at the national and international levels, for the implementation of the principles and objectives set forth in the Declaration, and requests the Secretary-General to submit a report on the matter to the General Assembly at its forty-fifth session;

4. *Requests* the Commission for Social Development to submit to the General Assembly at its forty-fifth session its views on the present resolution under the item entitled "Policies and programmes involving youth".

General Assembly resolution 43/136

8 December 1988   Meeting 75   Adopted without vote

Approved by Third Committee (A/43/815) without vote, 3 November (meeting 31); draft by Romania (A/C.3/43/L.17/Rev.1), orally revised; agenda item 144.
Meeting numbers. GA 43rd session: 3rd Committee 15-22, 25, 31; plenary 75.

UN Youth Fund

In accordance with its mandate, the United Nations Youth Fund continued to provide technical and material support to catalytic and innovative activities in the field of youth. Special attention was paid to strengthening national capacities, promoting the integration and participation of youth in national development, and expanding the body of knowledge on youth and development. Particular importance was attached to data collection and information exchange activities, as well as applied research on youth.

Since becoming operational in 1984, the Fund had received about 275 requests for assistance, of which 39 were approved for funding as at June 1988, involving a total resource commitment of $300,000. Although the Fund's project grants were modest, $7,500 on average, they had mobilized matching resources, totalling about $1 million since IYY. To give new impetus to resource mobilization for the Fund, the Secretary-General recommended that it be included among activities for which funds were pledged at the annual United Nations Pledging Conference for Development Activities.

REFERENCES

[1]YUN 1985, p. 979, GA res. 40/14, 18 Nov. 1985. [2]YUN 1987, p. 865, GA res. 42/54, 30 Nov. 1987. [3]A/43/601. [4]E/1988/29. [5]YUN 1987, p. 866, ESC res. 1987/51, 28 May 1987. [6]ACC/1988/PG/6. [7]YUN 1987, p. 868, GA res. 42/55, 30 Nov. 1987. [8]*Ibid.*, p. 869, GA res. 42/52, 30 Nov. 1987. [9]*Ibid.*, p. 870, GA res. 42/53, 30 Nov. 1987. [10]*Ibid.*, p. 868. [11]A/43/194 & Rev.1. [12]YUN 1965, p. 480, GA res. 2037(XX), 7 Dec. 1965.

Aging persons

The United Nations continued in 1988 to consider the question of persons aged 60 and over in the context of the Vienna International Plan of Action on Aging, adopted in 1982 by the World Assembly on Aging[1] and endorsed later that year by the General Assembly.[2] The Plan's primary aim was to assist States in strengthening their capacities to deal with aging populations.

The Administrative Committee on Co-ordination (ACC) approved a system-wide approach to implementation of the Plan, formulated in March 1988 at the inter-agency meeting on co-ordination of policies and programmes in the field of aging (see below). The General Assembly welcomed the approach and recommended that the next inter-agency meeting coincide with the second review and appraisal of the Plan in 1989. The Assembly also supported the 1987 recommendation of the Commission for Social Development[3] that the Secretary-General, when preparing the medium-term plan for 1990-1995, give priority to the elaboration of strategies to implement the Plan of Action through co-ordination of United Nations activities on aging and adequate budget allocations.

On 15 April, the Secretary-General officially inaugurated the International Institute on Aging at Valletta, Malta, which was established pursuant to a 1987 resolution of the Economic and Social Council.[4] The Institute, which was to be funded from voluntary contributions by Governments, NGOs and individuals, received seed money and support from DTCD and an initial $300,000 over two years from UNDP. The Secretary-General appointed the UNOV Director-General as Chairperson of the Institute's Board.

In keeping with the same 1987 Economic and Social Council resolution,[4] Yugoslavia requested in 1988 a feasibility study on the establishment of a United Nations–affiliated institute on aging at Belgrade.

A preparatory meeting for the establishment of an African gerontological society was held at Dakar, Senegal (17-22 December), in co-operation with CSDHA. It elaborated the draft statutes, rules of procedure and a work programme that envisaged five main activities: research, training, education, exchange of information, and work on operational projects.

Implementation of the Plan of Action

In February 1988, the Secretary-General circulated to Governments a questionnaire to obtain their views and experiences in implementing the Plan of Action, while UNOV/CSDHA elicited comments from United Nations organizations and NGOs. The results of the inquiry were to be a basis for the second review and appraisal of the Plan in 1989. The 48 responses from Governments as at September 1988 revealed their concern over the escalating cost of social expenditures, the weakening of traditional support systems for the elderly, and the condition of such vulnerable groups as elderly women. Forty-seven States, 28 of which were developing countries, reported having national machineries for action on aging.

To facilitate an exchange of information, CSDHA prepared a *Handbook on Organizations Active in the Field of Aging.* It described the activities of 270 organizations and educational institutions and listed the countries and regions in which they would like to co-operate on aging-related projects. Beginning in 1988, a *Bulletin on Aging* was to be issued three times a year, with one issue devoted to technical and specialized information previously contained in the *Periodical on Aging*, which had been discontinued for want of resources.

The Centre continued its co-operation with NGO committees on aging in New York and Vienna and collaborated with the Committee for the Promotion of Aid to Co-operatives in preparing a *Manual on Co-operatives for Aging.* It also participated in a number of non-governmental conferences, including the Seminar on Elderly Women (Washington, D.C., 30 June) and the Fifth International Conference on Legislation concerning Veterans and War Victims (Bad Ischl, Austria, 21-24 April).

Other activities. The Population Division of the Secretariat's Department of International Economic and Social Affairs was engaged in research to provide planners in developing countries with a better understanding of the socio-economic consequences of aging and available policy options, and the United Nations University continued its research on the impact of aging persons on welfare resources. The Economic and Social Commission for Asia and the Pacific (ESCAP) convened an expert seminar on the promotion of national infrastructure for aging populations in the region (Bangkok, Thailand, 14-17 December 1987), the Economic Commission for Europe (ECE) completed a project on the socio-economic implications of changing age distributions, and the United Nations Educational, Scientific and Cultural Organization (UNESCO) was preparing a survey on the use of the skills and experience of the elderly in the education of young people and adults.

Policy and programme co-ordination

An *ad hoc* inter-agency meeting on system-wide co-ordination of policies and programmes in the field of aging (Vienna, 10 and 11 March)[5] was attended by nine United Nations organizations and the International Institute on Aging. It adopted a system-wide approach to implementation of the Plan of Action to deal with constraints, priority objectives, strategies for implementation, and a framework for co-ordination.

The ACC Consultative Committee on Substantive Questions (Programme Matters), in March,[6] approved the system-wide approach and recommended that a further inter-agency meeting be convened in 1989, in conjunction with the thirty-first session of the Commission for Social Development and the second review and appraisal of the Plan of Action.

Report of the Secretary-General. In September, responding to a 1987 request of the General Assembly,[7] the Secretary-General reported[8] on aging-related activities and preparations for the second review and appraisal of the Plan of Action. He suggested, among other things, that the Assembly endorse a programme of measures to the year 2000; identify aging as a priority theme in the medium-term plan starting in 1992 and in the strategy for the fourth development decade (1991-2000); and urge Governments and concerned bodies to participate in activities marking the tenth anniversary of the World Assembly on Aging in 1992.

GENERAL ASSEMBLY ACTION

On 8 December 1988, on the recommendation of the Third Committee, the General Assembly adopted **resolution 43/93** without vote.

Implementation of the International Plan of Action on Aging and related activities

The General Assembly,

Recalling its resolution 37/51 of 3 December 1982, by which it endorsed the International Plan of Action on

Aging, adopted by consensus by the World Assembly on Aging,

Recalling also its resolution 40/30 of 29 November 1985, in which it expressed its conviction that the elderly must be considered an important and necessary element in the development process at all levels within a given society, and reaffirming that developing countries, in particular, need assistance in order to implement the Plan of Action,

Keeping in mind its resolution 41/96 of 4 December 1986, in which it requested the Secretary-General to review the world aging situation every six years,

Reaffirming its resolution 41/96, in which it urged Governments to intensify their efforts, within the context of their own national priorities, cultures and traditions, to implement the recommendations contained in the Plan of Action,

Reaffirming also its resolution 42/51 of 30 November 1987, in which it considered that the tenth anniversary of the World Assembly on Aging should be marked in 1992 by appropriate follow-up activities in order to maintain awareness on a global level of issues affecting the aging,

Taking into consideration the preliminary findings of the second review and appraisal of the implementation of the Plan of Action, as contained in the report of the Secretary-General on the question of aging, which indicate that co-ordinating mechanisms and national machineries are essential for implementing the Plan of Action,

Noting with concern that the United Nations does not have the necessary resources to deal effectively with requests for assistance and expert advice in the field of aging,

Alarmed by the large reduction in the staff working on the programme on aging at the Centre for Social Development and Humanitarian Affairs of the Secretariat, which makes it difficult for the United Nations Office at Vienna to carry out the mandates given to it in the Plan of Action and reaffirmed repeatedly in General Assembly resolutions,

Taking into consideration that there will be a marked increase in the population over the age of sixty years, and that increasingly women will constitute the majority of these elderly populations,

Acknowledging the request of the Government of Yugoslavia for a feasibility study on the establishment of a United Nations–affiliated institute on aging at Belgrade,

Recalling its requests to the Secretary-General to respond favourably to the request of the African Regional Conference on Aging, held at Dakar in December 1984, for assistance in establishing an African gerontological society,

Acknowledging also the guide for future activities relating to aging in the Asian and Pacific region adopted by the Economic and Social Commission for Asia and the Pacific at the Expert Seminar on the Promotion of National Infrastructures for Aging Populations in Asia and the Pacific, held at Bangkok from 14 to 17 December 1987,

Appreciating the invaluable role played by non-governmental organizations in promoting greater awareness of issues that involve aging and in advocating measures to implement the Plan of Action,

1. *Takes note* of the report of the Secretary-General on the question of aging;

2. *Welcomes* the system-wide approach to issues of aging worked out jointly by the concerned agencies and bodies of the United Nations system at the inter-agency meeting on system-wide co-ordination of policies and pro-

grammes in the field of aging, held at Vienna on 10 and 11 March 1988, and recommends that the next meeting be held to coincide with the second review and appraisal of the International Plan of Action on Aging, in 1989;

3. *Expresses its satisfaction* that the International Institute on Aging has been established in Malta in co-operation with the United Nations and was officially inaugurated by the Secretary-General on 15 April 1988;

4. *Requests* the Secretary-General to report to the General Assembly on the activities of the International Institute on Aging;

5. *Stresses* the imperative need to increase the impetus of the implementation of the Plan of Action at national, regional and international levels, and appeals for resources to be provided commensurate with the requirements;

6. *Urges* the Secretary-General, in compliance with the views of Member States as reflected in his report, to maintain and strengthen the existing programmes on aging and to strengthen the United Nations system-wide co-ordination of policies and programmes on aging, with the Centre for Social Development and Humanitarian Affairs continuing in its role as focal point in the United Nations system for activities relating to aging;

7. *Supports* the recommendation made to the Secretary-General by the Commission for Social Development in its resolution 30/1 of 4 March 1987 that, in preparing the medium-term plan for the period 1990-1995, he should give priority to the careful elaboration of practical strategies to implement the Plan of Action by providing fuller co-ordination of aging activities in the United Nations system and maintaining adequate programme budget allocations;

8. *Recommends* that aging should be considered a priority theme in both the proposed medium-term plan for the period starting in 1992 and in the preparation of an international development strategy for the fourth United Nations development decade (1991-2000);

9. *Urges* that the staff of the Aging Unit of the Centre for Social Development and Humanitarian Affairs be maintained at levels which will permit the Centre to carry out its mandates as the focal point in the United Nations for all matters relating to aging;

10. *Urges* the bodies and organizations of the United Nations system, working in close co-operation with concerned centres and institutes as well as non-governmental organizations, and utilizing the networking mode of operation, to conduct further research and studies in order to assist Member States in developing demographic and socio-economic profiles of their elderly populations, so that ways and means of ensuring the full and effective participation of the elderly in development can be identified;

11. *Requests* the Commission on the Status of Women to pay particular attention to the specific problems faced by elderly women and to the discrimination suffered by these women because of their sex and age;

12. *Decides* to commemorate the tenth anniversary of the World Assembly on Aging in the plenary General Assembly at its forty-seventh session, in 1992, and requests the Commission for Social Development to include in its second review and appraisal of the implementation of the Plan of Action a draft programme of substantive activities to mark this occasion;

13. *Strongly appeals* to Governments and intergovernmental and non-governmental organizations to contribute generously to the United Nations Trust Fund for Aging, bearing in mind that the Fund is particularly well placed to act as a catalyst for resource mobilization;

14. *Welcomes* the Secretary-General's efforts at finding options for the optimal use of the original resources of the Trust Fund for the Promotion of a United Nations Programme for the Aging, which include the formulation of a concerted programme of measures to the year 2000, and the proposal to create a world foundation on aging, which would encourage both the private and the public sector to support the work of the United Nations system in the field of aging;

15. *Calls upon* the specialized agencies, regional commissions and other funding organizations concerned to continue to support activities relating to the question of aging, in particular by providing assistance for projects that fall within their mandate;

16. *Requests* the Secretary-General to report to the General Assembly at its forty-fourth session on the implementation of the present resolution;

17. *Decides* to include in the provisional agenda of its forty-fourth session the item entitled "Question of aging".

General Assembly resolution 43/93

8 December 1988   Meeting 75   Adopted without vote

Approved by Third Committee (A/43/808) without vote, 3 November (meeting 31); 13-nation draft (A/C.3/43/L.15), orally revised; agenda item 89.

Sponsors: Austria, Barbados, Bolivia, Costa Rica, Côte d'Ivoire, Dominica, Dominican Republic, Malta, Samoa, Senegal, Sudan, United States, Yugoslavia.

Meeting numbers. GA 43rd session: 3rd Committee 15-22, 25, 31; plenary 75.

Trust funds

As at June 1988, the United Nations Trust Fund for Aging supported nine projects with a total commitment of $209,700. Three of those projects were interregional and global, and there were two each in Africa, Asia and the Pacific, and Latin America and the Caribbean. Country and regional projects accounted for 72 per cent of all grants by the Fund in 1987-1988, with 42 per cent ($87,811) of resources allocated for information exchange, 36 per cent ($76,600) for support to organizations of the elderly, 12 per cent ($25,000) for research and 10 per cent ($20,300) for training activities.

Among the projects supported in 1988 were a national training course on caretaking for the elderly in China (September); a project on the settlement needs of elderly refugees in Uganda; and a conference on aging demography and well-being in Latin America (Gainesville, United States, 23-25 February), which reviewed the implementation of the Plan of Action in the region and assessed future policy and research priorities. Other projects included, *inter alia*, an international seminar on policies and strategies for the participation of the elderly in development (Rabat, Malta, 2-5 February); an international conference on aging populations in the context of urbanization (Sendai, Japan, 12-16 September); and a meeting of the preparatory group for establishing an African Society of Gerontology.

The Director-General of UNOV continued to manage the Fund. Projects were approved for financing on the recommendation of the Social Development Trust Fund Operations Committee, established in 1987 to appraise funding proposals.

The Fund not only provided direct substantive and financial support to developing countries, but also acted as a catalyst for resource mobilization. In 1987-1988, its grants attracted an estimated $800,000 in additional resources—a ratio of 4:1. Expenditures in 1988 totalled $302,841, leaving a balance of $242,265 as at 31 December 1988. Without an immediate and sustained effort to strengthen the Fund, many constructive projects would fail to materialize, the Secretary-General stated in a September report on the question of aging.[8] He called on Member States to give serious consideration to the Fund's situation and recommended that the Assembly set a goal of mobilizing $2 million by 1992, which could generate an estimated additional $8 million in matching resources.

The Trust Fund for the Promotion of a United Nations Programme for the Aging, established in July 1986[9] on a provisional basis until 31 December 1987, was extended through 1988, on the recommendation of the Secretary-General.[10] Among the options being reviewed for use of the Fund's resources, set at $18,000, was the creation of a world foundation on aging, to encourage private-sector support for United Nations activities in the field.

No action was taken by the Assembly's Third Committee on a proposal to merge the two trust funds into a United Nations International Fund for Aging, administered by UNDP and eligible for funding through the annual United Nations Pledging Conference for Development Activities. The General Assembly had deferred consideration of that proposal in 1986.[11]

REFERENCES

[1]YUN 1982, p. 1184. [2]*Ibid.*, p. 1186, GA res. 37/51, 3 Dec. 1982. [3]YUN 1987, p. 872. [4]*Ibid.*, p. 872, ESC res. 1987/41, 28 May 1987. [5]ACC/1988/PG/5. [6]ACC/1988/15. [7]YUN 1987, p. 873, GA res. 42/51, 30 Nov. 1987. [8]A/43/583. [9]YUN 1986, p. 831. [10]YUN 1987, p. 875. [11]YUN 1986, p. 832, GA dec. 41/124, 4 Dec. 1986.

Chapter XV

Refugees and displaced persons

While the number of refugees swelled to over 12 million in 1988, some events occurred that offered hope for solutions for nearly half the world's refugee population. The signing of an agreement between Afghanistan and Pakistan created an opportunity for millions of Afghans, constituting the world's largest refugee population, to return to their country, and the return of more than 80,000 Ugandans from the Sudan was the largest such movement anywhere in the world. Progress was made towards securing the independence of Namibia, which in turn paved the way for the organized return home of several thousand Namibians. Other large refugee repatriation movements in 1988 included Burundians, Chadians, Ethiopians, Mozambicans and Zimbabweans; Iraqi Kurds; Sri Lankan Tamils; and Central Americans.

The impact of those positive achievements was qualified, however, by an increase in the number of refugees and asylum-seekers world-wide. This was especially true in Africa, where hundreds of thousands of Somalis and Sudanese sought refuge in Ethiopia, and several thousand Ethiopians, Mozambicans and Sudanese fled to neighbouring countries. Those same tendencies also occurred in South-East Asia, where the number of asylum-seekers rose by more than 11 per cent over 1987, and in Europe, where the number increased by almost one third.

While more States acceded to the major international instruments on refugees, bringing the total number of signatories to 106 to the 1951 Convention relating to the Status of Refugees, its 1967 Protocol, or both, there was also an increase in actions by States that deteriorated the plight of asylum-seekers, posing a threat to the humanitarian institution of asylum.

The General Assembly endorsed the Oslo Declaration and Plan of Action, adopted by the International Conference on the Plight of Refugees, Returnees and Displaced Persons in Southern Africa, which called for international action in the fields of protection, assistance, refugee aid and development, emergency preparedness, public information and mobilization of resources to deal with the deteriorating humanitarian situation in southern Africa (resolution 43/116). The Assembly also welcomed decisions to hold conferences on Indo-Chinese (43/119) and Central American (43/118) refugees in 1989.

The Nansen Medal, awarded since 1954 in honour of Fridtjof Nansen, the first League of Nations High Commissioner for Refugees, went in 1988 to Syed Munir Hussain, Secretary of the States and Frontier Regions Ministry of Pakistan from 1982 to 1987. The Medal was awarded for his supervision of the world's largest refugee assistance programme—the Afghan refugee relief operation—for the Pakistani Government.

UNHCR programme and finances

Programme policy

Executive Committee action. At its thirty-ninth session (Geneva, 3-10 October 1988), the Executive Committee of the Programme of the United Nations High Commissioner for Refugees,[1] emphasizing the importance of dealing with the underlying causes of refugee movements, called on the High Commissioner to continue his efforts to provide international protection through voluntary repatriation, local integration in countries of first asylum or resettlement in third countries. The Committee expressed its concern about the lack of adequate international protection for various groups of refugees, including a large number of Palestinians, and hoped that efforts would continue within the United Nations system to address their protection needs. (Palestinian refugees are dealt with in PART TWO, Chapter IV.) States were urged to abide by international prohibitions against expulsion and *refoulement*, or forcible return, of refugees, and were called on, along with the High Commissioner and others, to ensure the protection of refugees from arbitrary detention and violence. The Committee further encouraged all States hosting refugees to consider ways of facilitating their employment, invited States to promote measures favourable to stateless persons and called on the High Commissioner to implement measures intended to address the irregular movement to other countries of refugees who had found protection.

Regarding the promotion and dissemination of refugee law, the Committee called on States that had not done so to accede to the 1951 Convention[2] and the 1967 Protocol relating to the Status of Refugees,[3] and, if applicable, to the 1969 Organization of African Unity (OAU) Convention governing the Specific Aspects of Refugee Problems in Africa,[4] in order to ensure the widest possible application of the basic principles of refugee law. It urged States to initiate or participate in training courses in refugee law and protection, and requested the Office of the High Commissioner (UNHCR) to provide information to the Committee on specific promotional activities world-wide, including their financial implications.

On the subject of international solidarity and refugee protection, the Committee, stressing that the principle of international solidarity was fundamental in encouraging a humanitarian approach to granting asylum and in implementing international protection in general, invited all States to support the protection functions of the High Commissioner, as well as to abide by their own humanitarian responsibilities towards refugees, particularly to safeguard the right to seek and enjoy asylum from persecution and to ensure full respect for the principle of *non-refoulement*.

The Committee recommended that States and UNHCR take into account the following guidelines when dealing with cases of stowaway asylum-seekers: stowaways must be protected against forcible return to their country of origin; they should be allowed to disembark at the first port of call and have their refugee status determined by the authorities without implying a lasting solution in that country; and UNHCR should be requested to assist in finding a durable solution for those found to be refugees.

As to the special needs of refugee women, the Committee called for the reinforcement of measures to enhance their physical security and called on host Governments to strengthen their support of UNHCR's protection activities as they related to women. Relevant Governments were also called on to support the Special Resettlement Programme for Women-at-Risk. The High Commissioner was encouraged to expand his public information activities relating to refugee women and to develop training modules on the special needs of refugee women and the means of addressing them. The Committee requested the High Commissioner to provide at its next session a detailed progress report on the implementation of policies and programmes for refugee women, and called on host countries, the donor community and non-governmental organizations (NGOs) to support the High Commissioner in implementing that programme.

The Committee welcomed plans to organize international conferences on Indo-Chinese and Central American refugees in 1989, and called on the international community to support them (see below). Regarding the Oslo Declaration and Plan of Action, adopted by the International Confer-

ence on the Plight of Refugees, Returnees and Displaced Persons in Southern Africa (see below), the Executive Committee requested the High Commissioner to ensure their implementation and to participate in formulating strategies for rendering humanitarian assistance to internally displaced persons. The High Commissioner was further requested to report to the Committee at its next session on the role of UNHCR in implementing the Declaration and Plan of Action.

Within the framework of strengthening programme planning, implementation and monitoring, the Committee endorsed the High Commissioner's efforts in creating special programmes for refugee women and children, training staff, and providing technical support, evaluation services and the specifications and means of delivering supplies and food aid, and called on him to continue to provide assistance to refugees under the care of national liberation movements recognized by OAU and the United Nations.

The Committee called on the High Commissioner to encourage further study of the issue of durable solutions to the refugee problem, and appealed to Governments to continue to create and promote conditions conducive to attaining such solutions. It supported UNHCR's promotion of voluntary repatriation as the preferred long-term solution, and called for more resources to be devoted to that goal. When voluntary repatriation was not feasible, UNHCR was encouraged to promote local integration and resettlement.

The Committee made a number of recommendations regarding refugee aid and development. Recognizing the need to ensure compatibility between refugee aid and the national development plans of developing refugee-asylum countries, the Committee recommended that low-income asylum countries be provided with assistance to strengthen their social and economic infrastructure to enable them to cope with the burden of dealing with large numbers of refugees and returnees. It called on Governments and the High Commissioner to provide technical support to developing countries in needs assessment, formulation of concrete projects and plans of action in areas hosting large numbers of refugees. The Committee further expressed its desire that the issue of refugee aid and development receive prominent attention by the Sub-Committee on Administrative and Financial Matters in 1989, and requested UNHCR to submit to the Executive Committee at its session that year a report describing in detail the role and mandate of UNHCR and the breakdown of financial resources being allocated to developing asylum countries.

GENERAL ASSEMBLY ACTION

On 8 December 1988, on the recommendation of the Third (Social, Humanitarian and Cultural)

Committee, the General Assembly adopted **resolution 43/117** without vote.

Office of the United Nations High Commissioner for Refugees

The General Assembly,

Having considered the report of the United Nations High Commissioner for Refugees on the activities of his Office, as well as the report of the Executive Committee of the Programme of the High Commissioner on the work of its thirty-ninth session, and having heard the statements made by the High Commissioner on 16 and 18 November 1988,

Recalling its resolution 42/109 of 7 December 1987,

Reaffirming the purely humanitarian and non-political character of the activities of the Office of the High Commissioner, which are undertaken in the common interest of humanity,

Noting with satisfaction that, following recent accessions, more than one hundred States are now parties to the 1951 Convention and the 1967 Protocol relating to the Status of Refugees,

Noting with concern that, despite developments that offer hope for solutions to refugee problems, refugees and displaced persons of concern to the High Commissioner continue to face, in certain situations, distressingly serious problems,

Particularly concerned that in various regions the safety and welfare of refugees and asylum-seekers continue to be seriously jeopardized on account of military or armed attacks and other forms of violence, and noting that further efforts should be made in dealing with the problem of rescuing asylum-seekers in distress at sea and, in this context, also noting the problems relating to stowaway asylum-seekers,

Stressing the fundamental importance of the High Commissioner's function to provide international protection, particularly in the context of the increasing complexity of the contemporary refugee problem, and the need for States to co-operate with the High Commissioner in the exercise of this essential function,

Noting the efforts of the High Commissioner to continue to address the special problems and needs of refugee and displaced women and children, who in many cases are exposed to a variety of difficult situations affecting their physical and legal protection as well as their psychological and material well-being,

Emphasizing the need for States to assist, on as wide a basis as possible, the efforts of the High Commissioner to promote speedy and durable solutions to the problems of refugees,

Realizing in this context that voluntary repatriation or return remains the most desirable solution to the problems facing refugees and displaced persons of concern to the High Commissioner, and welcoming the fact that in various parts of the world it has been possible for significant numbers of them to return voluntarily to their countries of origin,

Recognizing that the enhancement of basic economic and social rights is essential to the achievement of self-sufficiency and family security for refugees, as well as to the process of re-establishing the dignity of the human person and realizing durable solutions to refugee problems,

Recognizing that durable solutions for refugees in developing countries can, in the majority of cases, be achieved through a development-oriented approach and that the heavy burden placed on a host country as a result of growing influxes of refugees requires sufficient resources to redress the negative impact and the strain on its socio-economic infrastructure in rural and urban areas,

Welcoming the conclusions and decisions on refugee aid and development adopted by the Executive Committee of the Programme of the High Commissioner at its thirty-ninth session as a tangible recognition of the need to ensure the compatibility of refugee aid and national development plans of the developing asylum countries,

Commending those States that, despite severe economic and development problems of their own, continue to admit large numbers of refugees and displaced persons of concern to the Office of the High Commissioner into their territories, and emphasizing the need to share the burden of these States to the maximum extent possible through international assistance, in accordance with the conclusions on refugee aid and development adopted by the Executive Committee of the Programme of the High Commissioner at its thirty-ninth session,

Stressing the need for the international community to continue to provide adequate resettlement opportunities for those refugees for whom no other durable solution may be in sight, with particular attention given to refugees who have already spent an inordinately long time in camps,

Welcoming the valuable support extended by Governments to the High Commissioner in carrying out his humanitarian tasks, and recognizing the need for continuing and increasing co-operation between the Office of the High Commissioner and other bodies of the United Nations system and with intergovernmental and non-governmental organizations,

Also welcoming the decision of the Executive Committee of the Programme of the High Commissioner at its thirty-ninth session to open sessions of its two subcommittees and informal meetings to participation as observers by States Members of the United Nations and members of the specialized agencies which are not members of the Executive Committee,

Noting the High Commissioner's continuing efforts to improve the efficiency and effectiveness of the Office, particularly in strengthening field activities and responsibilities,

Commending the High Commissioner and his staff for the dedicated manner in which they discharge their responsibilities, and paying tribute to those staff members who have endangered their lives in the course of their duties,

1. *Strongly reaffirms* the fundamental nature of the function of the United Nations High Commissioner for Refugees to provide international protection and the need for Governments to co-operate fully with his Office in order to facilitate the effective exercise of this function, in particular by acceding to and implementing the relevant international and regional refugee instruments and by scrupulously observing the principles of asylum and *non-refoulement;*

2. *Endorses,* in this regard, the conclusions on international solidarity and refugee protection adopted by the Executive Committee of the Programme of the High Commissioner at its thirty-ninth session;

3. *Notes with particular concern* the continued violation, in certain situations, of the principle of *non-refoulement,*

recalls existing prohibitions as contained in conclusions 4 and 5 adopted by the Executive Committee of the Programme of the High Commissioner at its twenty-eighth session, stresses the need to strengthen measures to protect refugees against such action and appeals to all States to abide by their international obligations, taking fully into account their legitimate security concerns;

4. *Appeals* to all States that have not yet become parties to the 1951 Convention and the 1967 Protocol relating to the Status of Refugees to consider acceding to these instruments in order to enhance their universal character;

5. *Condemns* all violations of the rights and safety of refugees and asylum-seekers, in particular those perpetrated by military or armed attacks against refugee camps and settlements and other forms of violence;

6. *Endorses once again* the conclusions on military and armed attacks on refugee camps and settlements adopted by the Executive Committee of the Programme of the High Commissioner at its thirty-eighth session, and again calls upon all States to observe these principles;

7. *Commends* the High Commissioner for the work undertaken by his Office to identify and meet the special needs of refugee children and, in particular, for the guidelines of the Office on refugee children, and invites the High Commissioner to pursue his efforts on behalf of refugee children, drawing on the valuable contributions that non-governmental organizations continue to make in this area;

8. *Endorses* the conclusions on refugee women adopted by the Executive Committee of the Programme of the High Commissioner at its thirty-ninth session, and urges States to extend their full co-operation to the High Commissioner in his efforts to ensure that the special needs of refugee women in the fields of protection, assistance and durable solutions are met;

9. *Notes* the close connection between the problems of refugees and of stateless persons and invites States actively to explore and promote measures favourable to stateless persons in accordance with international law;

10. *Recognizes* the importance of fair and expeditious procedures for determining refugee status and/or granting asylum in order, *inter alia*, to protect refugees and asylum-seekers from unjustified or unduly prolonged detention or stay in camps, and urges States to establish such procedures;

11. *Recognizes* the importance of achieving durable solutions to refugee problems and, in particular, the need to address in this process the root causes of refugee movements in order to avert new flows of refugees, taking into account the report of the Group of Governmental Experts on International Co-operation to Avert New Flows of Refugees, and to facilitate the solution of existing problems;

12. *Urges* all States to support the High Commissioner in his efforts to achieve durable solutions to the problem of refugees and displaced persons of concern to his Office, primarily through voluntary repatriation or return, including assistance to returnees as appropriate, or, wherever appropriate, through integration into countries of asylum or through resettlement in third countries;

13. *Expresses deep appreciation* for the valuable material and humanitarian response of receiving countries, in particular those developing countries which, despite limited resources, continue to admit, on a permanent or temporary basis, large numbers of refugees and asylum-seekers;

14. *Urges* the international community, in accordance with the principle of international solidarity and burden-sharing, to assist the above-mentioned countries in order to enable them to cope with the additional burden that care for refugees and asylum-seekers represents;

15. *Supports broadly* the purpose of a Project Planning Fund along the lines stipulated in paragraph 32 of the report of the Executive Committee of the Programme of the High Commissioner on the work of its thirty-ninth session and, in particular, the following recommendations:

(*a*) The Office of the High Commissioner should remain a focal point for encouraging refugee-related technical assistance and capital investment in developing asylum countries;

(*b*) Assistance to refugees should be additional to funds earmarked for development programmes in developing asylum countries;

(*c*) The High Commissioner should be requested to prepare a comprehensive report in which the nature and operational aspects of the Project Planning Fund and the mandate of the Office of the High Commissioner, as well as the role of development-oriented agencies and non-governmental organizations, would be clearly defined;

16. *Recognizes with appreciation* the work done by the High Commissioner to put into practice the concept of development-oriented assistance to refugees and returnees, as initiated at the Second International Conference on Assistance to Refugees in Africa and reaffirmed in the Oslo Declaration and Plan of Action adopted by the International Conference on the Plight of Refugees, Returnees and Displaced Persons in Southern Africa, urges the High Commissioner to continue that process, wherever appropriate, in full co-operation with appropriate international agencies, and further urges Governments to support these efforts;

17. *Emphasizes* the essential role of development-oriented organizations and agencies in the implementation of programmes that benefit refugees and returnees, urges the High Commissioner and those organizations and agencies, in accordance with their respective mandates, to strengthen their mutual co-operation towards the attainment of durable solutions, and calls upon the High Commissioner to continue to promote such co-operation;

18. *Welcomes* the various initiatives undertaken by the High Commissioner in regard to the promotion and dissemination of the principles of refugee law and protection and calls upon his Office, in co-operation with Governments, to intensify its activities in this area, bearing in mind the need, in particular, to develop practical applications of refugee law and principles and to continue to organize training courses for governmental and other officials involved in refugee activities;

19. *Calls upon* all Governments to contribute, in a spirit of international solidarity and burden-sharing and in every way feasible, to the High Commissioner's programmes with the aim of ensuring that the needs of refugees, returnees and displaced persons of concern to the High Commissioner are met.

General Assembly resolution 43/117

8 December 1988   Meeting 75   Adopted without vote

Approved by Third Committee (A/43/874) without vote, 23 November (meeting 51); 38-nation draft (A/C.3/43/L.59); agenda item 102.

Sponsors: Austria, Belgium, Canada, Costa Rica, Cyprus, Denmark, El Salvador, Ethiopia, Finland, France, Germany, Federal Republic of, Greece, Guatemala, Honduras, Iceland, Italy, Japan, Netherlands, New Zealand, Nicaragua, Nigeria, Norway, Pakistan, Panama, Philippines, Portugal, Rwanda, Senegal, Somalia, Spain, Sudan, Swaziland, Sweden, Thailand, United Kingdom, Zaire, Zambia, Zimbabwe.
Meeting numbers. GA 43rd session: 3rd Committee 44, 45, 47, 48, 50, 51; plenary 75.

Financial and administrative questions

UNHCR voluntary funds expenditure in 1988 amounted to $545.5 million,[5] compared to $461.4 million in 1987.[6] Of that, $395 million was spent on General Programmes and $150.2 million went to Special Programmes and other trust funds. Total income for 1988 amounted to $529.1 million, compared to $475.6 million in 1987.[7]

Although financial support from the donor community in 1988 was the highest ever received by UNHCR, it was inadequate to cover all programme needs. Against a General Programmes budget of $420 million, $395 million was spent. However, combined contributions and secondary income amounted to only $385 million, forcing the High Commissioner to seek donor approval to advance funds from the 1989 General Programmes reserve to cover the shortfall.

Special appeals were issued in 1988 to meet the needs of new refugee emergency situations, such as Mozambican refugees in southern Africa, Somali and Sudanese refugees in Ethiopia, Burundi refugees in Rwanda and Iraqi Kurds in Iran. Appeals were also made to cover the financial requirements of returnee programmes in Afghanistan, Burundi, Central America, Ethiopia, Sri Lanka, Uganda and Viet Nam, as well as other activities outside the General Programmes.

In October, the UNHCR Executive Committee approved a target of $428.8 million for General Programmes in 1989.

Efforts made in 1988 to expand the donor base and increase contributions to voluntary funds were successful, as the number of donors increased by 19.6 per cent and income increased by 18.2 per cent.

Contributions

Contributions in cash and in kind in 1988 totalled $482.7 million, compared to $427.9 million in 1987. Paid cash contributions amounted to $339.8 million in 1988, and outstanding cash pledges amounted to $86 million. Contributions in kind amounted to $9.6 million, with an additional $47.3 million outstanding. In addition to those contributions, $3,694,608 ($834,948 from Canada and $2,859,660 from the European Economic Community) was transferred to the World Bank for administration and implementation of the Income-Generating Project for Refugee Areas in Pakistan. Intergovernmental organizations provided $47.6 million, while NGOs and private sources provided $6.8 million.

1987 accounts

The audited financial statements on funds administered by UNHCR for the year ended 31 December 1987[7] showed a total expenditure of $461.4 million and a total income of $475.6 million. In October 1988, the Executive Committee took note of the report of the Sub-Committee on Administrative and Financial Matters[8] and the report of the Advisory Committee on Administrative and Budgetary Questions (ACABQ).[9]

On 21 December, in **resolution 43/216**, the General Assembly accepted the financial reports and audited financial statements of UNHCR and endorsed the observations and recommendations of the Board of Auditors and ACABQ.

REFERENCES

[1]A/43/12/Add.1. [2]YUN 1951, p. 520. [3]YUN 1967, p. 769. [4]YUN 1969, p. 470. [5]A/44/5/Add.5. [6]A/44/12. [7]A/43/5/Add.5. [8]A/AC.96/719. [9]A/43/674 & Corr.1.

Refugee assistance and protection

Assistance

During 1988, as in previous years, UNHCR co-operated with concerned Governments and the international community to meet the humanitarian needs of refugees world-wide.[1] Those efforts centred on the promotion of durable solutions, namely, voluntary repatriation, local integration in the country of first asylum or resettlement in another country. In 1988, $239 million was obligated for the promotion of those solutions. Of that amount, $27.8 million was made available under Special Programmes for the rehabilitation of returnees in their country of origin. The largest voluntary repatriation movement of the year was the spontaneous return of more than 80,000 Ugandan refugees. Other major repatriation movements involved a number of African refugee groups, Sri Lankan Tamils from India, Iraqi Kurds and Central Americans. Resettlement in a third country continued to be the only feasible option for a significant number of refugees, including more than 50,000 Indo-Chinese. UNHCR expenditure for promotion of resettlement and transportation of refugees amounted to $18.8 million under General Programmes.

Where political or other factors precluded rapid identification of durable solutions, UNHCR provided intermediate assistance including food, shelter, water, health services and sanitation, clothing, household utensils and basic education. In 1988, the largest care and maintenance programme was that for Afghan refugees in Pakistan, for which $43.3 million was obligated under the

General Programmes. Over $6.2 million of that was devoted to income-generating and self-sufficiency activities, another major UNHCR assistance area during 1988. Care and maintenance programmes were also implemented in Ethiopia, Malawi, Somalia and Thailand. At the same time, refugee operations were recognized as vehicles for economic development. In many cases, UNHCR redirected its operational expenditures to local businesses in order to benefit both host countries and refugees.

UNHCR emergency activities fell into the two broad categories of response and preparedness. Frequently UNHCR was forced to resort to its Emergency Fund, which allowed the High Commissioner to allocate up to $10 million annually. In 1988, $9.9 million from that Fund was used, mainly in response to emergencies in Africa and South-West Asia. UNHCR participated in a co-ordinated effort by the United Nations to promote national emergency preparedness in southern Africa. Other preparedness activities included management training and development of resource materials, an early warning project and a feasibility study on establishing emergency stockpiles.

Social services continued during the year, with an emphasis on promoting the self-sufficiency of refugees. A total of 70 refugee counselling projects were implemented in Africa, Asia, Europe, Latin America and the Middle East, at a cost of $4.3 million. These included provision of information on the availability and use of community resources and establishment of referral links to facilitate access to employment, training and education, health services, housing and social security. Medical facilities and physical, social and mental treatment and rehabilitation support were made available to some 13,000 disabled refugees in several asylum countries at a cost of $1.1 million.

Primary education continued to be provided through multisectoral projects. Post-primary, vocational/technical and academic education was provided by 110 UNHCR programmes. UNHCR promoted co-ordination among the education ministries of Malawi, Mozambique and Zimbabwe in order to improve the quality of the Mozambican curriculum in refugee camps, to develop a refugee teacher-training scheme and to provide Mozambican textbooks to about 70,000 refugee children. Activities had been undertaken for phasing refugee educational schemes into the national system of Somalia, and guidelines on primary education for refugee children were being prepared. The costs of supplies for refugees and for UNHCR operations amounted to $70.9 million in 1988, and some $72.9 million in food aid to refugees was channelled through UNHCR.

In-depth evaluations of UNHCR operations in 1988 concentrated primarily on the extent to which assistance activities were consistent with the durable solutions envisaged in various country programmes. Major evaluations of country and regional programmes were carried out in the Horn of Africa, western and southern Africa and Latin America. During 1988, the UNHCR self-evaluation system underwent the first major change since its introduction in 1980, with self-evaluations being prepared for all major operational activities rather than for individual projects.

To consolidate UNHCR activities aimed at protecting and assisting refugee women, the UNHCR Steering Committee on Refugee Women was established in February 1988 under the chairmanship of the Deputy High Commissioner. The Committee was to assess, review and develop policies, procedures and guidelines; promote public awareness of refugee women's problems; and ensure the availability of adequate human resources for the staffing of activities.

In response to a decision of the Executive Committee (see above), UNHCR formulated a detailed work-plan with a view to integrating the needs of refugee women into the mainstream. Efforts concentrated on institutional changes aimed at ensuring that the needs of women were systematically considered and regularly reported on.

Approximately half the world's refugees were children under 18 years of age. Accordingly, the newly established Working Group on Refugee Children focused on developing guidelines for field offices in their activities concerning refugee children. In August, UNHCR distributed to its officers and relevant organizations *Guidelines on Refugee Children*, which addressed issues such as determination of refugee status for children, the situation of unaccompanied minors and the effects on children of extended residence in refugee camps.

Assistance to refugees in Africa

The overall number of refugees in Africa increased during 1988. Refugees continued to flee from Mozambique into Malawi and from the Sudan into south-western Ethiopia, and two new influxes occurred without advance warning—from north-western Somalia into eastern Ethiopia and from Burundi into Rwanda. The great majority of the Burundi refugees repatriated voluntarily within a few months, and other significant repatriation movements occurred to Chad and Ethiopia (see below). The new and continued refugee influxes required mobilization of substantial emergency assistance. Progress in promoting self-reliance was mixed, with benefits of better harvests in some countries offset by economic difficulties in many asylum countries.

In 1988, the total expenditure in Africa under UNHCR voluntary funds amounted to $250.1 million, of which $175.3 million was obligated under

General Programmes (mainly for care and maintenance operations) and $74.9 million under Special Programmes (mainly for the needs of newly arrived refugees).

ECONOMIC AND SOCIAL COUNCIL ACTION

On 26 July, the Economic and Social Council, by **decision 1988/158**, took note of oral reports made on behalf of the Secretary-General by the High Commissioner on the Second International Conference on Assistance to Refugees in Africa, the International Conference on the Plight of Refugees, Returnees and Displaced Persons in Southern Africa, humanitarian assistance to refugees in Djibouti, assistance to refugees in Somalia, the situation of refugees in the Sudan, assistance to student refugees in southern Africa, and assistance to displaced persons in Ethiopia.

Follow-up to the Second International Conference on Assistance to Refugees in Africa

In response to a 1987 resolution of the General Assembly,[2] the Secretary-General in August 1988 submitted a report[3] on follow-up activities to the Second (1984) International Conference on Assistance to Refugees in Africa.[4]

Nineteen projects aimed at strengthening the social and economic infrastructure of host countries to enable them to deal with large numbers of refugees and returnees had been funded in 15 African countries, four of which had been completed. Planning missions were initiated in Ethiopia, Malawi, Somalia and the Sudan, and eight new projects to benefit refugees and local populations in asylum countries, to be financed through the United Nations Development Programme (UNDP) Trust Fund for Refugee-Related Development Projects in Africa, were being prepared. As at 15 April 1988, total resources under the Trust Fund amounted to $9,069,827, while the commitment for project and programming activities was $6,630,530, leaving a balance of $2,439,297 for financing pipeline projects and additional programming activities.

Refugees in southern Africa

More than 100,000 Mozambicans received assistance under a consolidated emergency programme in the United Republic of Tanzania, Zambia and Zimbabwe. By year's end, 13,000 Mozambicans had been transferred to a new settlement in Zambia.

UNHCR intensified its preparations for the repatriation of Namibian refugees in accordance with a 1978 Security Council resolution,[5] which set out a plan for Namibia's transition to independence. The number of South African refugees reported to have found asylum in other southern African countries remained at about 35,000, over half of whom received UNHCR assistance in 1988.

Malawi

In response to a 1987 Assembly resolution,[6] the Secretary-General in August 1988 submitted a report on assistance to refugees and displaced persons in Malawi.[7] In 1988, some 20,000 Mozambicans per month fled to Malawi, resulting in a total of 552,669 as at 1 June.

An inter-agency mission that visited Malawi in 1987 found that the country's rural subsistence economy was under severe strain owing to the refugee burden. Food production and water resources in the affected areas were insufficient to satisfy the needs of both the Malawi population and the displaced persons. The environment had been severely damaged by wood-cutting and cultivation on fragile hillsides. Health, education and community services were also under heavy strain. The mission concluded that the Malawi economy would not be able to cope with the expanded emergency conditions without major support from the international community and development investment. It was estimated that $90.8 million in emergency assistance would be required in 1988 to finance food, water, health and education, as well as public works programmes designed to increase the amount of cultivable land and expand food production. The proposed action programme of economic development initiatives addressed both emergency needs and long-term development goals.

ECONOMIC AND SOCIAL COUNCIL ACTION

On 24 May, by **decision 1988/110,** the Economic and Social Council took note of an oral report made by the representative of UNHCR on assistance to refugees and displaced persons in Malawi.

GENERAL ASSEMBLY ACTION

On 8 December, on the recommendation of the Third Committee, the Assembly adopted **resolution 43/148** without vote.

Assistance to refugees and displaced persons in Malawi

The General Assembly,

Recalling its resolution 42/132 of 7 December 1987 on assistance to refugees and displaced persons in Malawi,

Having considered the report of the Secretary-General on assistance to refugees and displaced persons in Malawi, as well as on the report of the inter-agency mission on this subject,

Having considered that part of the report of the United Nations High Commissioner for Refugees regarding the situation of refugees and displaced persons in Malawi,

Gravely concerned about the continuing serious social and economic impact of the massive presence of refugees and displaced persons, as well as its far-reaching consequences for the country's long-term development process,

Appreciating the important measures that the Government of Malawi is taking in order to provide shelter, protection, food, education and health and other humanitarian services to thousands of refugees and displaced persons,

Recognizing the heavy burden placed on the people and Government of Malawi and the sacrifices they are making in caring for the refugees and displaced persons, given the country's limited social services and infrastructure, and the need for adequate international assistance to enable them to continue their efforts to provide assistance to the refugees and displaced persons,

Expressing its appreciation for the assistance rendered by Member States, the various organs of the United Nations, the Office of the United Nations High Commissioner for Refugees and international, intergovernmental and non-governmental organizations in support of the refugee programme in Malawi,

Bearing in mind the findings and recommendations of the inter-agency mission to Malawi, particularly on the need to strengthen the country's socio-economic infrastructure in order to enable it to provide for the immediate humanitarian relief requirements of the refugees and displaced persons as well as the long-term national development needs of the country,

Recognizing the need to view refugee-related development projects within local and national development plans,

1. *Takes note* of the report of the Secretary-General on assistance to refugees and displaced persons in Malawi, particularly with regard to the findings and recommendations of the inter-agency mission;

2. *Commends* the measures that the Government of Malawi is taking to provide material and humanitarian assistance to refugees and displaced persons, in spite of the serious economic situation it faces, and stresses the need for additional resources to lessen the impact of the presence of refugees and displaced persons on the country's long-term development process;

3. *Expresses its appreciation* to the Secretary-General, the United Nations High Commissioner for Refugees, donor countries and intergovernmental and non-governmental organizations for their efforts to assist the refugees and displaced persons in Malawi;

4. *Expresses grave concern* at the serious and far-reaching consequences of the massive presence of refugees and displaced persons in the country and its implications for the long-term socio-economic development of the whole country;

5. *Appeals* to Member States, the appropriate organs, organizations and bodies of the United Nations system, intergovernmental and non-governmental organizations and the international financial institutions to continue providing the Government of Malawi with the necessary resources for the implementation of development assistance projects in regions affected by the presence of refugees and displaced persons, as well as the development programmes recommended by the inter-agency mission;

6. *Requests* the Secretary-General to continue his efforts to mobilize the necessary financial and material assistance for the full implementation of ongoing projects in the areas affected by the presence of refugees and displaced persons and programmes recommended in the report of the inter-agency mission;

7. *Requests* the High Commissioner to continue co-ordination with the appropriate specialized agencies in order to consolidate and ensure the continuation of essential services to the refugees and displaced persons in their settlements;

8. *Requests* the Secretary-General to report to the General Assembly at its forty-fourth session, through the Economic and Social Council, on the implementation of the present resolution.

General Assembly resolution 43/148

8 December 1988   Meeting 75   Adopted without vote

Approved by Third Committee (A/43/868) without vote, 29 November (meeting 56); 23-nation draft (A/C.3/43/L.71); agenda item 12.

Sponsors: Algeria, Botswana, Burkina Faso, Chad, Egypt, Ethiopia, Greece, Kenya, Lesotho, Madagascar, Malawi, Mali, Morocco, Nigeria, Philippines, Rwanda, Senegal, Somalia, Sudan, Swaziland, Zaire, Zambia, Zimbabwe.

Meeting numbers. GA 43rd session: 3rd Committee 49-56; plenary 75.

Conference on refugees in southern Africa

The Assembly in 1987[8] had welcomed the OAU decision to hold an International Conference on the Plight of Refugees, Returnees and Displaced Persons in Southern Africa. The Conference (Oslo, Norway, 22-24 August 1988)[9] adopted the Oslo Declaration and Plan of Action, which emphasized the need to link emergency aid to development assistance activities in order to promote self-sufficiency and to minimize the risk of dependency. Accordingly, the Conference urged all States to provide sufficient resources to support both emergency and development programmes on behalf of refugees, returnees and displaced persons. The 90 States participating in the Conference agreed to undertake activities in the areas of emergency preparedness, needs assessment and delivery of assistance, recovery and development, and resource mobilization. In the context of emergency preparedness, the Conference called on the United Nations system, OAU, intergovernmental organizations and NGOs to implement training programmes for relief officials in asylum countries in order to enable better use of resources. On the subject of internally displaced persons, the Conference requested the Secretary-General to conduct studies and consultations aimed at ensuring the timely implementation and co-ordination of relief programmes, and called on the international community to co-operate in ensuring the safe transport of relief and emergency goods.

The Conference recommended voluntary repatriation of refugees wherever possible, while recognizing that local integration or resettlement in a third country was sometimes a necessary alternative, especially in the case of South African and Namibian refugees. The Conference emphasized the need for all members of the international community to share the refugee burden equally, and accordingly urged African States to admit refugees from southern Africa not only into their countries, but also into their national educational and employment systems, enabling them to have access, where feasible, to financial and land resources. As part of the follow-up and evaluation process, the Secretary-General was called on to provide for the regular appraisal of the Declaration and Plan of Action, in co-operation with UNHCR, the World Food Programme (WFP), the United Nations Children's Fund, UNDP, the Food and Agriculture Organization of the United Nations, the World Health Organization and NGOs.

GENERAL ASSEMBLY ACTION

On 8 December, on the recommendation of the Third Committee, the Assembly adopted **resolution 43/116** without vote.

International Conference on the Plight of Refugees, Returnees and Displaced Persons in Southern Africa

The General Assembly,

Recalling its resolution 42/106 of 7 December 1987 on the convening of an International Conference on the Plight of Refugees, Returnees and Displaced Persons in Southern Africa,

Gravely concerned about the constant deterioration of the situation in southern Africa arising from the domination and oppression of the peoples of South Africa and Namibia by the minority racist régime of South Africa,

Having considered the report of the Secretary-General on the International Conference on the Plight of Refugees, Returnees and Displaced Persons in Southern Africa, held at Oslo from 22 to 24 August 1988, and the Oslo Declaration and Plan of Action on the Plight of Refugees, Returnees and Displaced Persons in Southern Africa adopted by the Conference and contained in the annex to that report,

Taking note with appreciation of the active participation of His Excellency General Moussa Traoré, President of the Republic of Mali and current Chairman of the Assembly of Heads of State and Government of the Organization of African Unity, His Excellency Mr. Robert Mugabe, Prime Minister of the Republic of Zimbabwe and Chairman of the Movement of Non-Aligned Countries, and Her Excellency Mrs. Gro Harlem Brundtland, Prime Minister of the Kingdom of Norway, at the Conference,

Aware of the valuable contribution made by the Governments of Norway and the other Nordic countries to the successful convening of the Conference,

Recognizing the importance of the financial and technical assistance provided by the Secretary-General of the United Nations, the United Nations High Commissioner for Refugees and the Administrator of the United Nations Development Programme to the Secretary-General of the Organization of African Unity in the preparation and organization of the Conference,

Noting with satisfaction the successful outcome of the Conference,

Conscious of its responsibility to provide economic, material and humanitarian assistance to independent States in southern Africa in order to assist them in coping with the situation resulting from the acts of aggression and destabilization committed by the *apartheid* régime of South Africa,

Noting the absence of an operational mechanism within the United Nations system dealing specifically with the problems of assistance to internally displaced persons,

Noting with indignation that South Africa's policy of *apartheid*, its illegal occupation of Namibia, and its direct and indirect acts of aggression, intimidation and destabilization through armed terrorists continue to be the main causes of refugee flows and increasing displacement of persons in southern Africa,

Convinced that there is an urgent need for the international community to extend maximum and concerted assistance to southern African countries sheltering refugees, returnees and displaced persons and also to highlight the plight of these persons,

1. *Takes note with satisfaction* of the report of the Secretary-General on the International Conference on the Plight of Refugees, Returnees and Displaced Persons in Southern Africa;

2. *Endorses* the Oslo Declaration and Plan of Action on the Plight of Refugees, Returnees and Displaced Persons in Southern Africa adopted by the Conference;

3. *Calls upon* the international community to provide increased assistance to the countries of southern Africa to enable them to strengthen their capacity to provide the necessary facilities and services for the care and well-being of the refugees, returnees and displaced persons in their countries;

4. *Reiterates its appreciation* to the Secretary-General for his efforts, on behalf of the international community, to organize and mobilize special programmes of economic assistance for the front-line and other neighbouring States to help them to withstand the effects of the acts of aggression and destabilization committed by the *apartheid* régime of South Africa;

5. *Requests* the Secretary-General, the United Nations High Commissioner for Refugees and the Administrator of the United Nations Development Programme to implement those specific tasks and responsibilities assigned to them in the Oslo Declaration and Plan of Action;

6. *Requests* the Secretary-General to undertake studies and consultations in order to consider the need for the establishment, within the United Nations system, of a mechanism or arrangement to ensure the implementation and overall co-ordination of relief programmes to internally displaced persons;

7. *Urges* all Member States, organizations of the United Nations system and governmental and non-governmental organizations to undertake the measures required of them under the Oslo Declaration and Plan of Action;

8. *Expresses its gratitude* to the Government of Norway for acting as host to the Conference, and to all the Nordic countries for their generous assistance towards the convening of the Conference;

9. *Expresses its appreciation* to the Secretary-General of the United Nations, the United Nations High Commissioner for Refugees and the Administrator of the United Nations Development Programme for the valuable assistance that they provided to the Secretary-General of the Organization of African Unity in the organization of the Conference;

10. *Commends* the Organization of African Unity for having convened the Conference and for focusing the attention of the international community on the grave humanitarian problems of the southern African region;

11. *Decides* to consider this question at its forty-fourth session on the basis of a report to be submitted by the Secretary-General.

General Assembly resolution 43/116

8 December 1988   Meeting 75   Adopted without vote

Approved by Third Committee (A/43/874) without vote, 23 November (meeting 51); draft by Zaire, for African Group (A/C.3/43/L.58); agenda item 102.
Meeting numbers. GA 43rd session: 3rd Committee 44, 45, 47, 48, 50, 51; plenary 75.

Student refugees in southern Africa

In response to a 1987 Assembly resolution,[10] the Secretary-General reported on assistance to student refugees in southern Africa from 1 July 1987 to 30 June 1988.[11] Those refugees were South Africans and Namibians who had been granted asylum in Botswana, Lesotho, Swaziland and Zambia. There had been no massive exodus of refugees from either South Africa or Namibia during the period under review, but it was feared that the ongoing school boycott in Namibia, in protest of South Africa's policy of stationing troops close to schools, would intensify and ultimately lead to a substantial increase in the number of Namibian student refugees. In addition, lack of security in countries bordering South Africa necessitated the evacuation of most newly arriving refugees, mostly young males, into other countries in the southern and eastern African regions.

In Botswana, the number of refugees remained stable at about 1,000 South Africans and 200 Namibians. Of these, 180 South Africans and 120 Namibians continued to benefit from educational facilities offered at the Dukwe Settlement. Swaziland was host to 6,500 South Africans, 220 of whom were receiving UNHCR educational assistance. Educational assistance was also provided to South African and/or Namibian students in Cameroon, Ghana, Kenya, Lesotho, Sierra Leone, Zambia and Zimbabwe.

GENERAL ASSEMBLY ACTION

On 8 December, on the recommendation of the Third Committee, the Assembly adopted **resolution 43/149** without vote.

Assistance to student refugees in southern Africa

The General Assembly,

Recalling its resolution 42/138 of 7 December 1987, in which it, *inter alia*, requested the United Nations High Commissioner for Refugees, in co-operation with the Secretary-General, to continue to organize and implement an effective programme of educational and other appropriate assistance for student refugees from South Africa and Namibia who had been granted asylum in Botswana, Lesotho, Swaziland and Zambia,

Having considered the report of the Secretary-General,

Noting with appreciation that some of the projects recommended in the report on assistance to student refugees in southern Africa continue to be successfully implemented,

Noting with concern that the discriminatory and repressive policies that continue to be applied in South Africa and Namibia cause a continued and increasing influx of student refugees into Botswana, Lesotho, Swaziland and Zambia,

Conscious of the burden placed on the limited financial, material and administrative resources of the host countries by the increasing number of student refugees,

Appreciating the efforts of the host countries to deal with their student refugee populations, with the assistance of the international community,

1. *Takes note with satisfaction* of the report of the Secretary-General;

2. *Expresses its appreciation* to the Governments of Botswana, Lesotho, Swaziland and Zambia for granting asylum and making educational and other facilities available to the student refugees, in spite of the pressure that the continuing influx of those refugees exerts on facilities in their countries;

3. *Also expresses its appreciation* to the Governments of Botswana, Lesotho, Swaziland and Zambia for the co-operation that they have extended to the United Nations High Commissioner for Refugees on matters concerning the welfare of the refugees;

4. *Notes with appreciation* the financial and material support provided for the student refugees by Member States, the Office of the United Nations High Commissioner for Refugees, other bodies of the United Nations system and intergovernmental and non-governmental organizations;

5. *Requests* the High Commissioner, in co-operation with the Secretary-General, to continue to organize and implement an effective programme of educational and other appropriate assistance for student refugees from South Africa and Namibia who have been granted asylum in Botswana, Lesotho, Swaziland and Zambia;

6. *Urges* all Member States and intergovernmental and non-governmental organizations to continue contributing generously to the assistance programme for student refugees, through financial support of the regular programmes of the High Commissioner and of the projects and programmes, including unfunded projects, which were submitted to the Second International Conference on Assistance to Refugees in Africa, held at Geneva from 9 to 11 July 1984;

7. *Also urges* all Member States and all intergovernmental and non-governmental organizations to assist the countries of asylum materially and otherwise to enable them to continue to discharge their humanitarian obligations towards refugees;

8. *Appeals* to the Office of the United Nations High Commissioner for Refugees, the United Nations Development Programme and all other competent United Nations bodies, as well as other international and non-governmental organizations, to continue providing humanitarian and development assistance so as to facilitate and expedite the settlement of student refugees from South Africa and Namibia who have been granted asylum in Botswana, Lesotho, Swaziland and Zambia;

9. *Calls upon* agencies and programmes of the United Nations system to continue co-operating with the Secretary-General and the High Commissioner in the implementation of humanitarian programmes of assistance for the student refugees in southern Africa;

10. *Requests* the High Commissioner, in co-operation with the Secretary-General, to continue to keep the mat-

ter under review, to apprise the Economic and Social Council, at its second regular session of 1989, of the current status of the programmes and to report to the General Assembly at its forty-fourth session on the implementation of the present resolution.

General Assembly resolution 43/149

8 December 1988   Meeting 75   Adopted without vote

Approved by Third Committee (A/43/868) without vote, 29 November (meeting 56); 47-nation draft (A/C.3/43/L.72); agenda item 12.

Sponsors: Algeria, Angola, Barbados, Botswana, Brazil, Burkina Faso, Burundi, Central African Republic, China, Côte d'Ivoire, Cuba, Cyprus, Democratic Kampuchea, Djibouti, Egypt, Ethiopia, Guinea, Haiti, India, Indonesia, Jamaica, Kenya, Lebanon, Lesotho, Liberia, Libyan Arab Jamahiriya, Madagascar, Malawi, Malaysia, Mali, Morocco, Niger, Nigeria, Philippines, Rwanda, Senegal, Sierra Leone, Sudan, Swaziland, Togo, Trinidad and Tobago, Uganda, United Republic of Tanzania, Yugoslavia, Zaire, Zambia, Zimbabwe.

Meeting numbers. GA 43rd session: 3rd Committee 49-56; plenary 75.

Refugees in other African countries

Chad

In response to a 1987 Assembly resolution,[12] the Secretary-General in September 1988 submitted a report on emergency assistance to voluntary returnees and displaced persons in Chad.[13] Spontaneous and organized return of Chadians from neighbouring countries, especially Cameroon and Nigeria, continued during 1988. UNHCR continued to provide tools and seeds to returnees, install water supplies and, in collaboration with WFP, distribute food.

GENERAL ASSEMBLY ACTION

On 8 December, on the recommendation of the Third Committee, the Assembly adopted **resolution 43/143** without vote.

Emergency assistance to voluntary returnees and displaced persons in Chad

The General Assembly,

Recalling its resolution 42/128 of 7 December 1987 on emergency assistance to voluntary returnees and displaced persons in Chad, as well as all its previous resolutions on this question,

Taking note of the report of the Secretary-General on emergency assistance to voluntary returnees and displaced persons in Chad,

Deeply concerned about the persistence of the harmful effects of the drought, desertification, floods and infestations of locusts and grasshoppers, which are compounding the already precarious food and health situation in Chad,

Conscious that the large number of voluntary returnees and displaced persons resulting from the war and the drought in Chad poses a serious problem of their integration into society,

Considering that the mass return of returnees to Chad and of displaced persons in the northern region poses serious social and economic problems for the Government of Chad,

Bearing in mind the many appeals made by the Government of Chad for international emergency assistance to the voluntary returnees and displaced persons in Chad,

1. *Endorses* the appeals made by the Government of Chad for emergency assistance to the voluntary returnees and displaced persons in Chad;

2. *Reiterates its appeal* to all States and intergovernmental and non-governmental organizations to support, by generous contributions, the efforts being made by the Government of Chad to assist and resettle the voluntary returnees and displaced persons;

3. *Takes note with satisfaction* of the action undertaken by the various organizations of the United Nations system and the specialized agencies with a view to mobilizing emergency humanitarian assistance to the voluntary returnees and displaced persons in Chad;

4. *Again requests* the United Nations High Commissioner for Refugees and the United Nations Disaster Relief Co-ordinator to mobilize emergency humanitarian assistance to the voluntary returnees and displaced persons in Chad;

5. *Calls upon:*

(*a*) The Secretary-General to continue his efforts to mobilize special humanitarian assistance for the resettlement of displaced persons in the northern region of Chad;

(*b*) The international community to support the efforts made by the Government of Chad to implement the programmes for repatriating and resettling the voluntary returnees and displaced persons in Chad;

6. *Requests* the Secretary-General, in co-operation with the United Nations High Commissioner for Refugees and the United Nations Disaster Relief Co-ordinator, to report to the General Assembly at its forty-fourth session on the implementation of the present resolution.

General Assembly resolution 43/143

8 December 1988   Meeting 75   Adopted without vote

Approved by Third Committee (A/43/868) without vote, 29 November (meeting 56); 37-nation draft (A/C.3/43/L.66); agenda item 12.

Sponsors: Algeria, Burkina Faso, Burundi, Cameroon, Cape Verde, Central African Republic, Chad, Chile, China, Colombia, Comoros, Congo, Costa Rica, Côte d'Ivoire, Democratic Kampuchea, Djibouti, Egypt, France, Gabon, Guinea, Haiti, Indonesia, Japan, Malawi, Mali, Morocco, Niger, Nigeria, Philippines, Rwanda, Senegal, Somalia, Sudan, Thailand, Togo, Tunisia, Zaire.

Meeting numbers. GA 43rd session: 3rd Committee 49-56; plenary 75.

Djibouti

In response to a 1987 Assembly resolution,[14] the Secretary-General in September 1988 submitted a report on humanitarian assistance to refugees in Djibouti.[15] The UNHCR multi-purpose assistance programme for 1988 focused on the improvement of community and preventive health care, nutrition and educational services.

GENERAL ASSEMBLY ACTION

On 8 December, on the recommendation of the Third Committee, the Assembly adopted **resolution 43/142** without vote.

Humanitarian assistance to refugees in Djibouti

The General Assembly,

Recalling its resolutions 41/137 of 4 December 1986 and 42/126 of 7 December 1987 on humanitarian assistance to refugees in Djibouti, as well as all its previous resolutions on this question,

Having considered the report of the Secretary-General on humanitarian assistance to refugees in Djibouti,

Deeply concerned about the plight of the refugees and the constantly increasing inflow of displaced persons which has severely affected the inadequate social services and the infrastructure of the country,

Aware of the heavy economic and social burden placed on the Government of Djibouti and the consequent unfavourable effects on the development of that country, given the delicate nature of its resources,

Appreciating the determined and sustained efforts made by the Government of Djibouti to cope with the growing needs of the refugees and displaced persons, despite its modest economic resources and limited means,

Noting with appreciation the steps taken by the Government of Djibouti, in close co-operation with the United Nations High Commissioner for Refugees, to implement appropriate and lasting solutions with respect to the refugees in Djibouti,

Appreciating the assistance provided by Member States, the specialized agencies, intergovernmental and non-governmental organizations and voluntary agencies to the relief and rehabilitation programmes for the refugees and displaced persons in Djibouti,

1. *Takes note* of the report of the Secretary-General on humanitarian assistance to refugees in Djibouti and appreciates the efforts of the United Nations High Commissioner for Refugees to keep their situation under constant review;

2. *Welcomes* the steps taken by the Government of Djibouti, in close co-operation with the High Commissioner, to implement appropriate and lasting solutions with respect to the refugees in Djibouti;

3. *Expresses its appreciation* to Member States, the specialized agencies, intergovernmental and non-governmental organizations and voluntary agencies for their assistance to the relief and rehabilitation programmes for the refugees and displaced persons in Djibouti;

4. *Urges* the High Commissioner to intensify his efforts to mobilize, on an emergency basis, the necessary resources to implement lasting solutions with respect to the refugees in Djibouti and the constant inflow of displaced persons;

5. *Calls upon* all Member States, the organizations of the United Nations system, the specialized agencies and intergovernmental and non-governmental organizations to continue to support the determined and sustained efforts made by the Government of Djibouti to cope with the urgent needs of the refugees and displaced persons and to implement lasting solutions as regards their situation;

6. *Requests* the Secretary-General to report to the General Assembly at its forty-fourth session, through the Economic and Social Council, on the implementation of the present resolution.

General Assembly resolution 43/142

8 December 1988   Meeting 75   Adopted without vote

Approved by Third Committee (A/43/868) without vote, 29 November (meeting 56); 88-nation draft (A/C.3/43/L.65); agenda item 12.

Sponsors: Angola, Argentina, Bahrain, Bangladesh, Barbados, Benin, Bolivia, Botswana, Brazil, Brunei Darussalam, Burkina Faso, Burundi, Cameroon, Cape Verde, Central African Republic, Chad, China, Colombia, Comoros, Congo, Costa Rica, Cuba, Democratic Yemen, Djibouti, Dominican Republic, Ecuador, Egypt, Equatorial Guinea, Ethiopia, France, Gabon, Gambia, Ghana, Greece, Guinea, Haiti, Honduras, India, Indonesia, Iraq, Italy, Jamaica, Japan, Jordan, Kenya, Kuwait, Lebanon, Lesotho, Liberia, Libyan Arab Jamahiriya, Madagascar, Malawi, Malaysia, Mali, Mauritania, Mauritius, Morocco, Niger, Oman, Pakistan, Panama, Philippines, Qatar, Rwanda, Sao Tome and Principe, Saudi Arabia, Senegal, Sierra Leone, Singapore, Somalia, Sri Lanka, Sudan, Swaziland, Syrian Arab Republic, Thailand, Togo, Trinidad and Tobago, Tunisia, Turkey, Uganda, United Arab Emirates, United Republic of Tanzania, Uruguay, Yemen, Yugoslavia, Zaire, Zambia, Zimbabwe.

Meeting numbers. GA 43rd session: 3rd Committee 49-56; plenary 75.

Ethiopia

In response to a 1987 Assembly resolution,[16] the Secretary-General in September 1988 submitted a report on assistance to displaced persons and returnees in Ethiopia.[17]

Ethiopia reported the largest increase in the number of refugees in 1988, with the number of Sudanese refugees in the south-western region rising from nearly 260,000 to some 350,000, the majority of whom were women and children. The remote location of the camps and the severe malnutrition of some new arrivals continued to demand a high level of support. In May, the High Commissioner appealed for $26.7 million in donations to assist the Sudanese refugees.

In addition, more than 300,000 Somalis entered south-eastern Ethiopia in 1988, a region devoid of natural resources and difficult to reach. Vital supplies were airlifted to those refugees as part of a major relief operation. In July, the High Commissioner appealed for international support for a relief programme valued at $11 million, based on a tentative planning case-load of 120,000, but despite a rapid increase in the number of Somali refugees to some 400,000, only $1.2 million had been contributed in cash by August.

Other assistance in the form of food, agricultural tools, seeds, livestock and home construction materials was provided to Ethiopian refugees returning home from Djibouti, Somalia and the Sudan.

GENERAL ASSEMBLY ACTION

On 8 December, on the recommendation of the Third Committee, the Assembly adopted **resolution 43/144** without vote.

Assistance to refugees and returnees in Ethiopia

The General Assembly,

Recalling all its resolutions, in particular resolution 42/139 of 7 December 1987, as well as all those of the Economic and Social Council, on assistance to displaced persons in Ethiopia,

Taking note of the report of the Secretary-General on assistance to displaced persons in Ethiopia,

Having considered the report of the United Nations High Commissioner for Refugees,

Recognizing the increasing number of refugees and voluntary returnees in Ethiopia,

Deeply concerned about the massive flow of refugees and voluntary returnees into the country and the enormous burden this has placed on the country's infrastructure and meagre resources,

Deeply concerned also about the grave consequences this has entailed for the country's capability to grapple with the effects of the prolonged drought,

Aware of the heavy burden placed on the Government of Ethiopia and of the need for adequate assistance to refugees, voluntary returnees and victims of natural disasters,

1. *Commends* the Office of the United Nations High Commissioner for Refugees and intergovernmental organizations and voluntary agencies for their assistance in mitigating the plight of the large number of refugees and voluntary returnees in Ethiopia;

2. *Appeals* to Member States and to international organizations and voluntary agencies to provide adequate material, financial and technical assistance for relief and rehabilitation programmes for the large number of refugees and voluntary returnees in Ethiopia;

3. *Requests* the United Nations High Commissioner for Refugees to continue his efforts in mobilizing humanitarian assistance for the relief, rehabilitation and resettlement of voluntary returnees and the large number of refugees in Ethiopia;

4. *Requests* the Secretary-General, in co-operation with the High Commissioner, to apprise the Economic and Social Council, at its second regular session of 1989, of the implementation of the present resolution and to report thereon to the General Assembly at its forty-fourth session.

General Assembly resolution 43/144

8 December 1988　　　　Meeting 75　　　　Adopted without vote

Approved by Third Committee (A/43/868) without vote, 29 November (meeting 56); 67-nation draft (A/C.3/43/L.67); agenda item 12.

Sponsors: Afghanistan, Algeria, Angola, Argentina, Bangladesh, Barbados, Benin, Bolivia, Botswana, Burkina Faso, Byelorussian SSR, Cameroon, China, Congo, Côte d'Ivoire, Cuba, Cyprus, Djibouti, Egypt, Ethiopia, German Democratic Republic, Ghana, Greece, Guinea, Guyana, India, Indonesia, Iran, Italy, Jamaica, Japan, Kenya, Lao People's Democratic Republic, Lesotho, Liberia, Madagascar, Malawi, Mali, Mauritania, Mongolia, Morocco, Mozambique, Nicaragua, Niger, Nigeria, Pakistan, Panama, Poland, Romania, Rwanda, Senegal, Sierra Leone, Sri Lanka, Swaziland, Syrian Arab Republic, Togo, Trinidad and Tobago, Uganda, Ukrainian SSR, USSR, United Republic of Tanzania, Viet Nam, Yemen, Yugoslavia, Zaire, Zambia, Zimbabwe.

Meeting numbers. GA 43rd session: 3rd Committee 49-56; plenary 75.

Rwanda

In August, some 55,000 refugees from northern Burundi fled to Rwanda, requiring immediate emergency assistance. A commission, comprising representatives from UNHCR, Burundi, Rwanda and Zaire, with OAU representatives as observers, was established to promote conditions conducive to the early voluntary return of those refugees. Repatriation began spontaneously in October and continued through UNHCR-organized convoys. The great majority of refugees had returned within two months.

Somalia

In response to a 1987 Assembly resolution,[18] the Secretary-General in August 1988 submitted a report on assistance to refugees in Somalia.[19] All of them were Ethiopian, and many were women and children. The second phase of a project to re-enumerate the refugees, consisting of a socio-demographic survey, was begun in 1988.

Concrete steps were taken to promote refugee-related development projects and to identify labour-intensive schemes benefiting both refugees and the local population. The Qorioley Refugee

Settlement Project, approved in May, was to produce a feasibility study and technical plan for the settlement of refugee families who had been living in refugee camps for eight years. The project was intended to serve as a model for other development projects for refugees in Somalia.

UNHCR continued its efforts to promote repatriation and self-sufficiency in Somalia, including road rehabilitation and agricultural development. Food assistance, co-ordinated by WFP, was expected to amount to about 142,000 metric tons in 1988, at an estimated cost of $53 million. On the basis of a nutritional survey conducted in 1988, rations were increased and steps were taken to improve the timing of deliveries.

Prospects for the voluntary repatriation of Ethiopian refugees in Somalia improved during the year as a result of high-level discussions between UNHCR and Somalia, in which the parties agreed on the need to redirect the programme from relief assistance towards repatriation. In Somalia, that included the promotion of area development and rehabilitation projects aimed at creating durable economic assets and helping to redress the ecological and other consequences of the presence of refugees. Another objective was to ensure that refugee services that could contribute to national development were integrated into national structures. In north-western Somalia, however, the UNHCR assistance programme was seriously disrupted by the outbreak of conflict in May.

GENERAL ASSEMBLY ACTION

On the recommendation of the Third Committee, the Assembly, on 8 December, adopted **resolution 43/147** without vote.

Assistance to refugees in Somalia

The General Assembly,

Recalling its resolutions 35/180 of 15 December 1980, 36/153 of 16 December 1981, 37/174 of 17 December 1982, 38/88 of 16 December 1983, 39/104 of 14 November 1984, 40/132 of 13 December 1985, 41/138 of 4 December 1986 and 42/127 of 7 December 1987 on the question of assistance to refugees in Somalia,

Having considered the report of the Secretary-General on assistance to refugees in Somalia,

Deeply concerned about the heavy burden that has been placed on the fragile economy of Somalia by the continuing presence of large numbers of refugees,

Concerned about the need to ensure continuing and adequate supplies of food in refugee camps in Somalia,

Conscious of the pressure that the refugee presence continues to impose on the public services, in particular education, health, transport and communications, and water supplies,

Noting with concern the deleterious effect of the refugee presence on the environment, which has resulted in widespread deforestation, soil erosion and the threat of destruction to an already fragile ecological balance,

1. *Takes note* of the report of the Secretary-General;

2. *Commends* the measures that the Government of Somalia is taking to provide material and humanitarian assistance to refugees, in spite of its own limited resources and fragile economy;

3. *Expresses its appreciation* to the Secretary-General, the United Nations High Commissioner for Refugees, donor countries and intergovernmental and non-governmental organizations for their efforts to assist the refugees in Somalia;

4. *Calls upon* the High Commissioner to ensure, as appropriate, that the care, maintenance and rehabilitation needs of the refugees are adequately covered;

5. *Appeals* to Member States, international organizations and voluntary agencies to render maximum and timely material, financial and technical assistance to enable the Government of Somalia to implement the projects and activities identified in the report of the 1987 interagency mission annexed to the report submitted by the Secretary-General to the General Assembly at its forty-second session as the basis for a comprehensive programme of action combining both refugee-related humanitarian and developmental needs;

6. *Calls upon* the United Nations Development Programme to assume the leading role, as required by the Second International Conference on Assistance to Refugees in Africa, in the conceptualization, implementation and monitoring of refugee-related projects, and to be involved in the mobilization of the financial and technical means required, in close co-operation with the High Commissioner and the World Bank;

7. *Requests* the pertinent organizations of the United Nations system, namely the Food and Agriculture Organization of the United Nations, the International Labour Organisation, the World Health Organization, the United Nations Educational, Scientific and Cultural Organization and the United Nations Children's Fund, as well as the United Nations Environment Programme and the World Food Programme, to prepare, in consultation with the Government of Somalia, detailed project documentation for the implementation of those projects and activities identified in the report of the Secretary-General as priority endeavours for a comprehensive programme of action;

8. *Calls upon* the United Nations Development Programme, the United Nations Environment Programme, the United Nations Sudano-Sahelian Office and the Food and Agriculture Organization of the United Nations to continue and expand their activities in Somalia, in co-operation with the Government of Somalia, to protect and rehabilitate its damaged environment;

9. *Recognizes* the important role that non-governmental organizations are playing with regard to programmes for the care, maintenance and rehabilitation of refugees, particularly in activities related to small-scale development projects, and in the fields of health and agriculture;

10. *Calls upon* the international community to support the activities of non-governmental organizations in Somalia in the planning and implementation of refugee projects and refugee-related development activities;

11. *Requests* the United Nations High Commissioner for Refugees and the Administrator of the United Nations Development Programme to apprise the Economic and Social Council at its second regular session of 1989 of the progress made in their respective fields of responsibility with regard to those provisions of the present resolution which concern them;

12. *Requests* the Secretary-General, in consultation with the High Commissioner and United Nations Development Programme, to submit to the General Assembly at its forty-fourth session a report on the progress achieved in the implementation of the present resolution.

General Assembly resolution 43/147

8 December 1988   Meeting 75   Adopted without vote

Approved by Third Committee (A/43/868) without vote, 29 November (meeting 56); 65-nation draft (A/C.3/43/L.70/Rev.1); agenda item 12.

Sponsors: Bahrain, Bangladesh, Barbados, Botswana, Brunei Darussalam, Burundi, Cameroon, Central African Republic, Chad, China, Colombia, Comoros, Costa Rica, Côte d'Ivoire, Cyprus, Democratic Kampuchea, Djibouti, Dominican Republic, Egypt, Gambia, Guinea, Indonesia, Iran, Iraq, Italy, Jamaica, Japan, Jordan, Kenya, Kuwait, Lebanon, Lesotho, Liberia, Libyan Arab Jamahiriya, Madagascar, Malawi, Malaysia, Mauritania, Morocco, Niger, Nigeria, Oman, Pakistan, Panama, Philippines, Qatar, Samoa, Saudi Arabia, Senegal, Sierra Leone, Singapore, Somalia, Sri Lanka, Sudan, Swaziland, Syrian Arab Republic, Thailand, Togo, Tunisia, Turkey, United Arab Emirates, Yemen, Zaire, Zambia, Zimbabwe.

Meeting numbers. GA 43rd session: 3rd Committee 49-56; plenary 75.

Sudan

In response to a 1987 Assembly resolution,[20] the Secretary-General in August 1988 submitted a report on the situation of refugees in the Sudan.[21] Government sources had indicated that there were approximately 2 million displaced persons and 1 million refugees in that country. The Under-Secretary-General for Special Political Questions, Regional Co-operation, Decolonization and Trusteeship, after discussions with Sudanese authorities, reinstituted the United Nations Emergency Operations Group, composed of the local representatives of the key United Nations agencies, in order to ensure an effective and concerted response to the critical humanitarian situation resulting from drought, civil strife and the presence of refugees. The Group was to co-ordinate emergency and rehabilitation assistance requested by the Government for refugees and displaced persons as well as for the stricken population in drought-affected areas. The Secretary-General in March appealed for assistance in implementing ongoing projects in areas affected by refugees.

UNHCR continued to provide assistance to nearly half of the more than 800,000 refugees estimated to be in the Sudan, the majority of whom were Ethiopian. More than 300,000 Ethiopians were receiving UNHCR assistance; a substantially higher number had spontaneously settled in towns and rural areas and were therefore unassisted.

Some 30,000 Ethiopian refugees, the majority fleeing armed conflict, arrived in eastern Sudan in the second half of 1988. Most were accommodated with relative ease at existing reception centres. As part of the overall effort to link refugee assistance to national development, UNHCR, in co-operation with the World Bank, prepared an agricultural project in southern Kassala province to benefit small farmers, including refugees.

More than 80,000 Ugandan refugees in the Sudan returned to their country of origin in the largest such movement anywhere in the world.

On 8 December, on the recommendation of the Third Committee, the Assembly adopted **resolution 43/141** without vote.

Situation of refugees in the Sudan

The General Assembly,

Recalling its resolution 42/129 of 7 December 1987 and its other previous resolutions on the situation of refugees in the Sudan,

Having considered the report of the Secretary-General on the implementation of resolution 42/129 and the action taken by the concerned organizations, and the report of the United Nations High Commissioner for Refugees,

Expressing its appreciation for the efforts made by the Government of the Sudan for the reception of the refugees and the provision of protection, shelter, food, health, education and other humanitarian services to the ever increasing number of refugees who have been crossing the borders into the Sudan since the early 1960s,

Recognizing the heavy burden shouldered by the people and the Government of the Sudan and the sacrifices they are making in acting as host to more than one million refugees, who constitute approximately 7.5 per cent of the total population of the country,

Concerned that the great majority of the refugees have spontaneously settled in various urban and rural communities throughout the country and are thus sharing the already meagre resources and services allocated to the indigenous population,

Expressing grave concern at the devastating and far-reaching effects of the successive calamities, ranging from the 1984 drought to the heavy rains and floods and the locust infestations, that have afflicted the country, thus exacerbating the already deteriorating situation resulting from the presence of this great number of refugees,

Gravely concerned also that the Government of the Sudan, besides dealing with the difficult prevailing economic and social problems, has the additional task of taking care of more than 1.5 million nationals displaced as a result of the 1984 drought, the civil strife in the southern part of the country and the rains and floods of August 1988,

Recognizing the serious task undertaken by the Government of the Sudan to initiate a wide-ranging rehabilitation programme to redress the impact and damages incurred by the natural disasters,

Considering those serious circumstances, which render the Government of the Sudan less prepared than ever to meet its obligations to its own people, and the more serious consequences, which affect the capacity of the Government of the Sudan to receive and grant asylum to additional numbers of refugees,

Expressing its appreciation for the assistance rendered by Member States and intergovernmental and non-governmental organizations in support of the refugee programme in the Sudan,

1. *Takes note* of the report of the Secretary-General on the situation of refugees in the Sudan and expresses its appreciation for the appeal made by the Secretary-General to Member States and the appropriate organs, organizations and bodies of the United Nations;

2. *Takes note also* of the report submitted by the United Nations High Commissioner for Refugees and in par-

ticular of the new trends identified in the area of refugee aid and development;

3. *Expresses its appreciation* to the Secretary-General, the High Commissioner, donor countries and intergovernmental and non-governmental organizations for their efforts to assist the refugees in the Sudan;

4. *Expresses grave concern* at the serious and far-reaching consequences of the presence of massive numbers of refugees in the country on the security and stability of the country and the overall negative impact on its basic infrastructure, which arrests the socio-economic development of the whole country;

5. *Also expresses grave concern* at the shrinking resources available for refugee programmes in the Sudan and the serious consequences of this situation for the country's ability to continue to act as host and provide assistance to refugees;

6. *Appeals* to Member States, the appropriate organs, organizations and bodies of the United Nations system, intergovernmental and non-governmental organizations and the international financial institutions to provide the Government of the Sudan with the necessary resources for the implementation of development assistance projects in regions affected by the presence of refugees;

7. *Requests* the Secretary-General to mobilize the necessary financial and material assistance for the full implementation of ongoing projects in the areas affected by the presence of refugees;

8. *Requests* the High Commissioner to continue coordination with the appropriate specialized agencies in order to consolidate and ensure the continuation of essential services to the refugees in their settlements;

9. *Requests* the Secretary-General to report to the General Assembly at its forty-fourth session, through the Economic and Social Council, on the implementation of the present resolution.

General Assembly resolution 43/141

8 December 1988   Meeting 75   Adopted without vote

Approved by Third Committee (A/43/868) without vote, 29 November (meeting 56); 59-nation draft (A/C.3/43/L.64); agenda item 12.

Sponsors: Algeria, Argentina, Bahrain, Bangladesh, Botswana, Cameroon, Central African Republic, Chad, China, Colombia, Democratic Kampuchea, Democratic Yemen, Djibouti, Egypt, Guatemala, Guinea, India, Indonesia, Iraq, Italy, Japan, Jordan, Kuwait, Lesotho, Libyan Arab Jamahiriya, Madagascar, Malawi, Malaysia, Mali, Morocco, Nepal, Niger, Nigeria, Oman, Pakistan, Panama, Philippines, Qatar, Romania, Saudi Arabia, Senegal, Sierra Leone, Somalia, Sri Lanka, Sudan, Swaziland, Syrian Arab Republic, Thailand, Togo, Tunisia, Turkey, Uganda, United Arab Emirates, United Republic of Tanzania, Yemen, Yugoslavia, Zaire, Zambia, Zimbabwe.

Meeting numbers. GA 43rd session: 3rd Committee 49-56; plenary 75.

Asia and Oceania

At the request of Sri Lanka, UNHCR in 1988 launched a programme to promote the return of Sri Lankan Tamils from India. Transportation for the returnees was provided by India, and reception, registration and initial assistance were provided by Sri Lanka and UNHCR. Reintegration assistance was also planned for Sri Lankan Tamils returning voluntarily from countries other than India. By year's end, some $8.3 million had been spent towards implementation of the programme.

In India, there were more than 6,000 registered refugees at year's end, mainly from Afghanistan and Iran. UNHCR assistance included primary and secondary education for children, as well as higher education and vocational training for adults. A total of 1,002 refugees in India were resettled in third countries during 1988, and 62 Afghans and 30 Iranians voluntarily repatriated.

During the year, UNHCR expenditure in the region stood at $64.3 million under General Programmes and $18.2 million under Special Programmes.

Indo-China

At the end of 1988, some 156,000 Indo-Chinese asylum-seekers were in UNHCR-assisted camps in Hong Kong, Indonesia, Malaysia, the Philippines, Singapore and Thailand, with Thailand being host to the majority of the case-load. Despite efforts to promote voluntary repatriation, resettlement remained the principal durable solution. The increase in arrivals, particularly "boat people", was not offset by the resettlement of some 50,000 Indo-Chinese in third countries, and the number of registered asylum-seekers in South-East Asian camps, particularly in Hong Kong and Malaysia, rose by 11.5 per cent compared to 1987. Progress was made in Viet Nam, however, with more than 21,000 persons leaving through the reactivated Orderly Departure Programme.

In July, the Foreign Ministers of the Association of South-East Asian Nations called for an international conference on Indo-Chinese refugees to be held in 1989.[22] The UNHCR Executive Committee welcomed the proposal in October 1988.[23]

GENERAL ASSEMBLY ACTION

On 8 December, on the recommendation of the Third Committee, the Assembly adopted **resolution 43/119** without vote.

International Conference on Indo-Chinese Refugees

The General Assembly,

Deeply concerned about the continuing humanitarian and other problems posed by the presence in the South-East Asian region of large numbers of refugees, displaced persons and those seeking refuge,

Recognizing that the problem of refugees, displaced persons and those seeking refuge is of international concern,

Convinced that there is an urgent need for the international community to find a comprehensive and durable solution to the problem which is acceptable to all parties concerned,

Appreciating the continuing efforts of the South-East Asian countries aimed at solving this problem, as well as the endeavours of the international community to provide humanitarian assistance to refugees, displaced persons and those seeking refuge in South-East Asia,

Noting the call in the Joint Statement on Indo-Chinese Refugees, issued at Bangkok on 4 July 1988 by the Ministers for Foreign Affairs of the States members of the Association of South-East Asian Nations at their twenty-first Ministerial Meeting, for the convening of

an International Conference on Indo-Chinese Refugees at the ministerial level, in early 1989, to be preceded by a preparatory conference at the senior official level,

Noting the expressions of support given by all States concerned, including those of the South-East Asian region, to the convening of the Conference,

Taking note of the decision by the Executive Committee of the Programme of the United Nations High Commissioner for Refugees at its thirty-ninth session to endorse the proposal for the convening of the Conference,

Bearing in mind the need for adequate preparation by the parties concerned to ensure the success of the Conference,

1. *Welcomes* the call by the Association of South-East Asian Nations for the convening of an International Conference on Indo-Chinese Refugees and expresses the strong desire that the Conference take place at the ministerial level at the earliest possible date during the first half of 1989;

2. *Also welcomes* the decision by the Executive Committee of the Programme of the United Nations High Commissioner for Refugees on the convening of the Conference;

3. *Requests* the Secretary-General, in close co-operation with the States members of the Association of South-East Asian Nations and other States concerned, to convene the Conference and to extend all possible assistance to the parties concerned for the organization of the Conference;

4. *Appeals* to all States, the specialized agencies and regional, intergovernmental and non-governmental organizations to provide all the necessary support and resources needed by the High Commissioner for the preparation and the holding of the Conference;

5. *Requests* the Secretary-General to apprise the Economic and Social Council at its second regular session of 1989 and to report to the General Assembly at its forty-fourth session on the implementation of the present resolution.

General Assembly resolution 43/119

8 December 1988   Meeting 75   Adopted without vote

Approved by Third Committee (A/43/874) without vote, 23 November (meeting 51); 25-nation draft (A/C.3/43/L.61); agenda item 102.

Sponsors: Australia, Brunei Darussalam, Canada, Chad, China, Denmark, Djibouti, Finland, Guatemala, Honduras, Iceland, Indonesia, Japan, Malaysia, New Zealand, Norway, Philippines, Singapore, Somalia, Sudan, Sweden, Thailand, Turkey, United States, Viet Nam.

Meeting numbers. GA 43rd session: 3rd Committee 44, 45, 47, 48, 50, 51; plenary 75.

Europe and North America

The number of new asylum-seekers in Europe increased to 240,000 during 1988, compared to 188,000 in 1987. Reversing the trend of previous years, most of the new asylum-seekers were of European origin. In addition, Hungary took in some 13,000 Romanian asylum-seekers, on whose behalf it sought UNHCR assistance. Another 50,000 Iraqi nationals were admitted to Turkey and granted temporary sanctuary as well as assistance and protection. UNHCR maintained close contact with Governments and NGOs to ensure preservation of the humanitarian tradition and the principles of the 1951 Convention[24] and the 1967 Protocol[25] relating to the Status of Refugees.

An agreement concluded in August between France, Suriname and UNHCR led to the creation of a tripartite commission to supervise the voluntary repatriation of some 8,000 Surinamese nationals in the French overseas department of Guiana.

In North America, Canada and the United States saw an expansion in their role as countries of first asylum during 1988. In the United States, there was a sharp increase in the number of Central American refugees, and accelerated procedures were introduced to determine the eligibility of their asylum requests.

During the year, UNHCR's operational expenditure in Europe and North America amounted to $19 million under General Programmes and $1.3 million under Special Programmes.

Latin America and the Caribbean

UNHCR had assisted about 124,000 refugees in Central America and Mexico by the end of 1988. The number of returnees increased considerably during the year, especially from Honduras, from where 2,476 Salvadorians and 7,965 Miskito and Sumo Nicaraguans repatriated. More than 37,000 refugees remained in Honduras at year's end, however, including Nicaraguans, Salvadorians and Guatemalans. In addition, 1,921 Guatemalans returned from Mexico, while 41,273 remained. Smaller repatriation movements occurred from the Dominican Republic (to Haiti) and Costa Rica (to El Salvador, Guatemala and Nicaragua), bringing the total number of returnees in the region to 13,684. In southern Latin America, the estimated refugee population stood at 23,900, of whom 7,370 received UNHCR assistance. Though new Chilean asylum-seekers were registered, approximately 900 refugees, mostly Chileans, were assisted in repatriation.

During 1988, UNHCR expenditure in the region totalled $32.8 million under General Programmes and $6.5 million under Special Programmes.

In October,[23] the UNHCR Executive Committee welcomed the September decision of the Governments of Costa Rica, El Salvador, Guatemala, Honduras, Mexico and Nicaragua to hold an international conference on Central American refugees in 1989.[26] The Secretary-General in September had reported[27] that UNHCR was providing support to the Governments of the region to prepare national profiles and programmes of solutions in preparation for the conference.

In October,[28] the Secretary-General reported on threats to international peace and security and peace initiatives in Central America, stating that he was gratified by the concrete measures taken to facilitate the voluntary repatriation of refugees in the region; he emphasized particularly the decision to hold an international conference on the subject.

GENERAL ASSEMBLY ACTION

On 8 December, on the recommendation of the Third Committee, the Assembly adopted **resolution 43/118** without vote.

International Conference on Central American Refugees

The General Assembly,

Recalling its resolutions 42/1 of 7 October 1987 concerning the peace initiatives undertaken in connection with the agreement on "Procedures for the establishment of a firm and lasting peace in Central America", signed by five Central American Presidents at Guatemala City on 7 August 1987 at the Esquipulas II summit meeting, 42/110 of 7 December 1987 on assistance to refugees, returnees and displaced persons of Central America, 42/204 of 11 December 1987 on special economic assistance to Central America and 42/231 of 12 May 1988 on the Special Plan of Economic Cooperation for Central America,

Taking note of the report of the Secretary-General,

Also taking note of the report of the United Nations High Commissioner for Refugees,

Gravely concerned about the present situation in the Central American region, the flows of refugees to neighbouring countries and countries outside the region, and the impact of those flows of refugees on the social and economic development of the area,

Conscious of the need to address the problem of Central American refugees who have found asylum in some Central American countries, including Belize and Mexico, and desirous of contributing to the search for lasting solutions of benefit to the countries and communities of asylum and origin,

Taking into account that, as stated in point 8 of the agreement concluded at the Esquipulas II summit meeting, the Central American countries have undertaken, as a matter of urgency, to address the problem of refugees, including their repatriation and relocation through bilateral and multilateral processes,

Welcoming the establishment of the Preparatory Committee for the International Conference on Central American Refugees, consisting of Costa Rica, El Salvador, Guatemala, Honduras, Mexico and Nicaragua, and emphasizing the importance of the success of their work,

Welcoming with satisfaction the San Salvador communiqué on the Central American refugees, signed on 9 September 1988, whereby it was decided to convene an International Conference on Central American Refugees, to be held at Guatemala City in May 1989,

Emphasizing that the general objective of the Conference is to examine the needs of Central American refugees and concrete proposals for practical solutions to their problems, as a contribution to peace in the region,

Reiterating the paramount importance of humanitarian and apolitical considerations, both in dealing with and in solving the problem of refugees, returnees and displaced persons, and the need to ensure that this approach is strictly observed by the countries of origin and of asylum and other interested participants,

Expressing its appreciation for the work done by the Office of the United Nations High Commissioner for Refugees in support of the preparation for the Conference, and for its co-operation with the Preparatory Committee,

Recognizing the priority given in the Special Plan of Economic Co-operation for Central America to the section of the emergency programme which is designed to promote activities for solving the problem of refugees, displaced persons and repatriated persons,

Recognizing that the task of seeking solutions goes further than emergency activities and is linked with aspects concerning the development of the region and assistance for the displaced populations in the countries of origin and of asylum that are directly affected by the massive presence of refugees,

Emphasizing that, among the possible solutions, voluntary repatriation is the most appropriate solution for solving the problems created by the massive presence of refugees in the countries and communities of asylum,

Recognizing that the tripartite commissions, composed of representatives of the country of asylum, the country of origin and the Office of the High Commissioner, constitute an ongoing mechanism for solving the problem of refugees and that they require support in order to continue the current voluntary repatriation programmes in conditions of personal and material security,

1. *Welcomes* the decision adopted by the countries members of the Preparatory Committee for the International Conference on Central American Refugees to convene the Conference at Guatemala City in May 1989;

2. *Supports* the undertaking made by the countries represented in the Preparatory Committee to continue to deal with the problems relating to the refugees and their voluntary repatriation, as well as with the preparatory work for the Conference and the Conference itself, on a purely humanitarian and apolitical basis;

3. *Welcomes* the decisions in support of the Conference adopted by the General Assembly of the Organization of American States at its eighteenth session and by the Executive Committee of the Programme of the United Nations High Commissioner for Refugees at its thirty-ninth session;

4. *Urges* that, in the context of the Conference, consideration should be given to the problems of displaced persons and to the effects of the massive presence of refugees in countries of asylum, as well as to those solutions which the affected countries deem applicable;

5. *Exhorts* all Member States, organs, specialized agencies and other organizations of the United Nations system, as well as the regional and subregional, intergovernmental and non-governmental organizations engaged in the humanitarian task of helping Central American refugees, to participate in the Conference and to provide all the resources, co-operation and support necessary for preparing and holding it, and for following up the results;

6. *Appeals* to the international community to increase its assistance to the countries of asylum and of origin of Central American refugees in order to strengthen their capacity to provide the means and services necessary for the solution of the problem of refugees, returnees and displaced persons, in accordance with national development programmes;

7. *Requests* the Secretary-General to invite all States to participate in the Conference and to adopt the means necessary for ensuring its success;

8. *Invites* the Secretary-General to establish the necessary co-ordination between the Conference and the implementation of the section of the Special Plan of Economic Co-operation for Central America relating to refugees, displaced persons and repatriated persons;

9. *Requests* the United Nations High Commissioner for Refugees to organize the Conference, in close co-operation with the United Nations Development Programme and with the organs, specialized agencies and other organizations of the United Nations system, in co-ordination with the Preparatory Committee, bearing in mind the third point of the San Salvador communiqué on the Central American refugees;

10. *Requests* the Secretary-General, in co-operation with the High Commissioner, to report to the Economic and Social Council at its second regular session of 1989 and to the General Assembly at its forty-fourth session on the implementation of the present resolution.

General Assembly resolution 43/118

8 December 1988   Meeting 75   Adopted without vote

Approved by Third Committee (A/43/874) without vote, 23 November (meeting 51); 31-nation draft (A/C.3/43/L.60), orally revised; agenda item 102.
Sponsors: Argentina, Bolivia, Brazil, Chile, Colombia, Costa Rica, Denmark, Dominican Republic, Ecuador, El Salvador, Finland, Guatemala, Haiti, Honduras, Iceland, Italy, Japan, Malaysia, Mexico, Morocco, Nicaragua, Norway, Pakistan, Panama, Peru, Spain, Sweden, Thailand, United States, Uruguay, Venezuela.
Meeting numbers. GA 43rd session: 3rd Committee 44, 45, 47, 48, 50, 51; plenary 75.

South-West Asia, North Africa and the Middle East

During 1988, UNHCR took steps to prepare for the voluntary repatriation of Afghans, including signing agreements with Afghanistan and Pakistan and holding discussions with Iran and representatives of the Afghan refugees to define the conditions of voluntary repatriation and to outline the material assistance needed. UNHCR's role included protecting the refugees and spontaneous returnees, building the capacity to respond to large-scale repatriation movements and providing direct support to the returnees in Afghanistan. A total of $12 million was obligated for those activities during 1988.

In Pakistan, preparations for the repatriation of more than 3 million Afghan refugees were accelerated during the second half of the year, especially in the areas of health and training, even as assistance continued to be delivered to newly arriving refugees from the border areas of Afghanistan where military conflict had intensified.

In Iran, UNHCR contributed $10.6 million towards the care and maintenance of Afghan refugees, in addition to Iran's own considerable contribution. In addition, at the request of Iran, UNHCR provided $8.3 million in assistance to some 70,000 Kurdish refugees from Iraq, primarily for medical supplies, shelter and other basic necessities.

A large number of Somalis entered the Persian Gulf region during the year, and the UNHCR regional office at Beirut, Lebanon, continued to provide assistance to some 5,900 stateless refugees. Other groups receiving UNHCR assistance in the area during the year included 1,000 refugees of Eritrean origin living on the coast of the Red Sea and a group of 70,000-80,000 persons in Yemen from Democratic Yemen. In connection with the peace plan proposed in 1988 by the Secretary-General and OAU to end the dispute in Western Sahara (see PART FOUR, Chapter I), wherein UNHCR was called on to participate in the census of Western Saharan refugees, UNHCR was preparing a contingency plan towards their repatriation. Meanwhile, it continued to assist vulnerable Sahraoui groups in Algeria.

REFERENCES

[1]A/44/12. [2]YUN 1987, p. 885, GA res. 42/107, 7 Dec. 1987. [3]A/43/533. [4]YUN 1984, p. 943. [5]YUN 1978, p. 915, SC res. 435(1978), 29 Sep. 1978. [6]YUN 1987, p. 891, GA res. 42/132, 7 Dec. 1987. [7]A/43/536. [8]YUN 1987, p. 886, GA res. 42/106, 7 Dec. 1987. [9]A/43/717 & Corr.1 & Add.1. [10]YUN 1987, p. 888, GA res. 42/138, 7 Dec. 1987. [11]A/43/594. [12]YUN 1987, p. 889, GA res. 42/128, 7 Dec. 1987. [13]A/43/593 & Add.1. [14]YUN 1987, p. 890, GA res. 42/126, 7 Dec. 1987. [15]A/43/592. [16]YUN 1987, p. 890, GA res. 42/139, 7 Dec. 1987. [17]A/43/595. [18]YUN 1987, p. 893, GA res. 42/127, 7 Dec. 1987. [19]A/43/535. [20]YUN 1987, p. 894, GA res. 42/129, 7 Dec. 1987. [21]A/43/534. [22]A/43/510-S/20091. [23]A/43/12/Add.1. [24]YUN 1951, p. 520. [25]YUN 1967, p. 769. [26]A/C.3/43/6. [27]A/43/591. [28]A/43/729-S/20234.

Chapter XVI

Drugs of abuse

The abuse of drugs remained a serious threat to all countries and segments of society in 1988. Health hazards were heightened by a trend towards the simultaneous consumption of two or more drugs and by the emergence of more potent narcotic substances. In its annual report, the International Narcotics Control Board (INCB) stated that the illicit production and trafficking of drugs by internationally linked criminal organizations continued to undermine the integrity of national economies and imperil the security of some countries. During the year, heavy emphasis was placed on bringing to justice the master-minds of criminal syndicates involved in the illicit production, manufacture and distribution of drugs.

In an effort to address the upsurge in illicit trafficking and associated criminal activity, work continued throughout 1988 on preparing a draft convention against illicit traffic in narcotic drugs and psychotropic substances. The United Nations Conference for the Adoption of a Convention against Illicit Traffic in Narcotic Drugs and Psychotropic Substances was convened at Vienna from 25 November to 20 December and adopted the text of the Convention, which was opened for signature on 20 December.

The General Assembly strongly condemned the involvement of children in drug trafficking and urged the establishment of national and international programmes to protect children from the illicit consumption of drugs and from involvement in illicit production and trafficking (resolution 43/121).

The Economic and Social Council recommended follow-up activities to the 1987 International Conference on Drug Abuse and Illicit Trafficking (resolution 1988/9), including the establishment of an international drug assessment system and the convening of a second interregional meeting of Heads of National Drug Law Enforcement Agencies to promote implementation of the 1988 Convention against Illicit Trafficking.

The Commission on Narcotic Drugs, the principal policy-making body of the United Nations on drug control issues, considered matters relating to the reduction of illicit demand and drug law enforcement, and made recommendations to the Economic and Social Council for adoption. INCB continued its evaluation and overall supervision of the implementation of drug control treaties.

Drug abuse and international control

The Secretary-General, in his annual progress report[1] on international co-operation in drug abuse control, submitted in response to a 1979 General Assembly request,[2] outlined the activities of the various United Nations entities involved in drug abuse control, particularly the follow-up to the 1987 International Conference on Drug Abuse and Illicit Trafficking.[3]

During 1988, the Division of Narcotic Drugs focused its efforts on fostering and strengthening international co-operation to cope more effectively with drug abuse. It expanded its activities to meet increasing demands for services and advice from Member States, requests for material, and for supportive action and legal advice.

The Division established and strengthened national laboratory services in Member States, developing a network of laboratories at regional and international levels and facilitating scientific information exchanges. National laboratories in Chile, Ghana, Madagascar and Uruguay received laboratory equipment, chemicals and reagents. With the financial support of the United Nations Fund for Drug Abuse Control (UNFDAC), the Division launched a regional project for Africa to establish 19 laboratories over a three-year period. Five of the laboratories were targeted for assistance in 1988.

The Division produced and distributed drug identification kits, updated its reference standard collection and provided Governments with samples of the reference standards. It issued a working manual on the identification of the most commonly trafficked drugs, established regional training centres in forensic analysis and developed a network of collaborative laboratories to provide advanced training in methods of drug analysis for biological fluids. The Division also started work on the establishment of the International Drug Abuse Assessment System.

Information activities included quarterly summaries of drug seizures and trends in illicit trafficking and updating of the list of national bodies authorizing the import/export of narcotic drugs and psychotropic substances, as well as the list of authorized national manufacturers of such substances.

The United Nations Development Programme (UNDP) assisted in the execution of projects financed by UNFDAC and others and provided funding for programmes from its own resources. UNDP's support to the Fund continued under the agreement signed by both bodies in 1987.[4] Under its interregional programme, UNDP contributed $120,000 to the United Nations Social Defence Research Institute (UNSDRI) for a research project on drug abuse in the context of development: prevention, treatment and rehabilitation.

Four projects were carried out by UNDP in Asia and the Pacific, providing training in treatment and rehabilitation techniques, law enforcement and narcotics detection, and aviation security. At the national level, UNDP funded projects in Indonesia and Sri Lanka. In Thailand, UNDP, UNFDAC, the United Nations Environment Programme and the United Nations Children's Fund were financing an integrated rural development project to replace opium/poppy cultivation with food and cash crop production.

In Latin America and the Caribbean, UNDP provided administrative support through its field offices to UNFDAC-supported drug control programmes and served as executing agency for its projects in Barbados, Bolivia, Brazil, Colombia, Ecuador, Paraguay and Peru.

The World Health Organization (WHO) promoted a public health approach to reduce the harm caused by psychoactive substances, and its European Regional Office co-operated with the Commission of European Communities and the Council of Europe in a multi-country project to stimulate health promotion at the community level.

WHO also supported prevention initiatives in Jordan, Malaysia, the Marshall Islands and the Republic of Palau, by improving education on substance abuse for health professionals. It developed strategies to meet the needs of high-risk groups, collected data on drug-related mortality and morbidity and, in collaboration with other United Nations agencies, prepared guidelines on drug abuse reporting systems, with special emphasis on health aspects.

WHO produced training materials for community health workers in developing countries on drug abuse assessment and on the organization of primary health-care services for drug abusers. It acted as the executing agent for national programmes in Afghanistan, the Bahamas, Burma, China, Colombia, Jamaica, Mauritius and Sri Lanka, and its regional offices participated in evaluation, treatment and rehabilitation projects in Africa, South-East Asia and the Western Pacific.

The International Labour Organisation (ILO) focused on the rehabilitation and social reintegration of recovering addicts and the reduction of drug and alcohol problems in the workplace. It developed a drug and alcohol education campaign for incorporation into the workers education programme. The post of Inter-regional Adviser on Alcohol and Drug-related Matters was created on 1 January 1988 to support ILO assistance and technical advice at the regional level.

Assistance in vocational and social rehabilitation programmes, and projects to combat drug and alcohol abuse among workers, was provided to Bolivia, Colombia, Ecuador, India, Malaysia, Nigeria, Pakistan, Peru, the Philippines, Somalia, Sri Lanka and Thailand. ILO continued its project in Bolivia to eliminate illicit plantings of drugs, as well as its projects in Burma, Thailand, Zimbabwe and the countries of South-East Asia, on the selection of appropriate treatment and rehabilitation programmes and social reintegration of former addicts.

Activities of the United Nations Educational, Scientific and Cultural Organization (UNESCO) in 1988 included a role as executing agency for UNFDAC-financed projects in Africa and Asia; the preparation of audio-visual materials for community programmes in Benin; and the production of education materials on drug addiction for a project in Burma. Through its Caribbean Network of Education Innovation for Development (CARNEID), UNESCO collaborated closely with the Caribbean Community to formulate preventive education projects.

The International Civil Aviation Organization (ICAO) concentrated on legal, technical and other means of suppressing the illicit transportation of drugs by air. The ICAO Council requested the Air Navigation Commission to study targets identified in the Comprehensive Multidisciplinary Outline of Future Activities in Drug Abuse Control[5] related to the prevention of drug abuse in the workplace; the surveillance of air approaches to frontiers; and controls over aircraft in international airspace.

The Economic and Social Commission for Asia and the Pacific (ESCAP) reviewed the drug situation in the region with a view to creating a regional drug information network. A workshop was held at Bangkok, Thailand (15-19 February), as part of an ongoing project to standardize the format for data collection and analysis of drug abuse treatment and rehabilitation in the region.

Other drug control-related activities were carried out by the Crime Prevention and Criminal Justice Branch of the Centre for Social Development and Humanitarian Affairs, the United Nations Committee on Crime Prevention and Control, UNSDRI, the World Food Programme, the Food and Agriculture Organization of the United Nations and the International Maritime Organization.

GENERAL ASSEMBLY ACTION

On 8 December, by **decision 43/428**, the General Assembly, on the recommendation of the Third (Social, Humanitarian and Cultural) Committee, took note of the Secretary-General's report on international co-operation in drug abuse control.[1]

UN Fund for Drug Abuse Control

During 1988, the United Nations Fund for Drug Abuse Control continued to expand its programmes, intensify activities in key areas, and improve the quality of its services. The UNFDAC programme budget for 1988 was $60.4 million, a 52 per cent increase over 1987 ($39.8 million). Technical co-operation activities were extended to 40 countries through 88 projects for area development operations, preventive education and public information, treatment and rehabilitation of drug-dependent persons, and law enforcement. There were also 33 regional and global projects providing training, research, advisory services and information exchange.

Among new UNFDAC initiatives in 1988 were: the launching of a $20 million project to control drug abuse and illicit trafficking in India; the design of a new programme of co-operation with the Lao People's Democratic Republic; the initiation of direct collaboration with the co-ordinator for the United Nations Humanitarian and Economic Assistance Programmes in Afghanistan; the expansion of operations in Bolivia with a $4 million project for basic rural sanitation services and an agreement to match the Bolivian Government's efforts to eradicate illicit coca production; a $22.2 million integrated rural development and crop substitution project and a project to strengthen prevention and treatment services in Colombia; two integrated rural development projects in Peru at a total cost of $15 million; the implementation of a $12 million multi-sectoral project in Brazil; the signing of a memorandum of understanding with the Government of Mexico for a $15 million drug control programme; and the successful completion of a customs inspection facility in Yugoslavia. UNFDAC's programme activities in the Caribbean were strengthened by the establishment of an office to assist in the design of master plans and the completion of an $800,000 regional telecommunications system for the control of illicit drug traffic. An intensive effort to address the drug problem in Africa led to the formulation and implementation of projects in 17 countries with a multi-year global commitment of $7.5 million. This activity included a $2.6 million multi-sectoral project in Morocco and two projects in Nigeria at a total cost of about $2 million.

Review of UN drug control programmes

In March, the Secretary-General submitted a report[6] to the Committee for Programme and Co-ordination (CPC) in which it reviewed the implementation of CPC's decisions by substantive secretariat units of United Nations drug control programmes. The review was also intended to assist the Committee in its examination of future medium-term plans and programme budgets of drug control programmes.

The evaluators reported mixed success in implementing CPC's recommendations. They observed that while some efforts had been successful, others had been affected by a lack of resources and still others depended on the capacity of Member States. They recommended that the Secretariat should: systematically collect bilateral and multilateral conventions relating to the tracing, freezing and seizing of illegally acquired assets and the extradition of persons arrested for drug crimes; strengthen the technical capability of the Division of Narcotic Drugs in drug demand reduction and pursue preventive education efforts and information dissemination campaigns with the involvement of local communities, non-governmental organizations and relevant specialized agencies; and effectively implement existing arrangements for co-ordination and co-operation among United Nations drug control entities.

CPC consideration. In May,[7] CPC endorsed the recommendations contained in the Secretary-General's report and recommended that the question of a possible merger of the Division of Narcotic Drugs and the secretariat of INCB should be further explored.

ECONOMIC AND SOCIAL COUNCIL ACTION

On 25 May 1988, the Economic and Social Council, on the recommendation of its Second (Social) Committee, adopted **resolution 1988/13** without vote.

Strengthening of co-operation and co-ordination in international drug control

The Economic and Social Council,

Considering that the implementation of the Single Convention on Narcotic Drugs of 1961, as amended by the 1972 Protocol Amending the Single Convention on Narcotic Drugs of 1961, and the Convention on Psychotropic Substances of 1971, forms the basis for national and international drug control,

Aware that the adherence of as many States as possible to the existing international drug control treaties is essential to achieving regional and international co-operation and co-ordination in reducing illicit demand for drugs, in suppressing illicit trafficking, in improving training, administrative practices and data collection, and in undertaking joint activities,

1. *Urges* all States that have not already done so to accede to the existing international drug control treaties;

2. *Also urges* parties to those treaties to implement the provisions thereof;

3. *Invites* Governments to establish appropriate national mechanisms for the adequate co-ordination of activities and co-operation between agencies engaged in drug abuse prevention, treatment and rehabilitation, the control of the supply of illicit drugs and the suppression of illicit trafficking;

4. *Recommends* that Governments, where they have not already done so, seek to establish at the regional level an organizational structure to stimulate, where appropriate, common activities and training seminars and workshops

on drug control, to be held at regular intervals, for the following purposes:

(a) To undertake research and surveys to assess the nature and extent of drug abuse;

(b) To provide training in drug law enforcement and improve administrative practices;

(c) To introduce programmes to prevent drug abuse at the national and regional levels, having due regard to the prevailing socio-cultural and socio-economic conditions;

(d) To exchange experiences and consult on innovative policies, measures or experiments regarding the reduction of drug supply and demand;

(e) To make use of any expert knowledge and other resources in the region and solicit expertise from other regions, where appropriate;

5. *Recommends* that Governments and international organizations, as appropriate, consider the following activities in greater detail, with a view to implementing them:

(a) Studies of patterns of illicit consumption, with a view to bringing about greater awareness of the problem and sharing of information and providing policy guidance on effective countermeasures;

(b) The development of public education programmes, including the use of kits, publications and audio-visual equipment, to reduce the demand for illicit drugs in specific target groups and to make the general population aware of the hazards of drug abuse;

(c) Programmes in prevention, law enforcement and administrative practices required by the international drug control treaties, including the production and dissemination of manuals and other training materials, where appropriate, as well as programme evaluation;

(d) The detection and identification of narcotic drugs and psychotropic substances and their origins, as well as precursors and essential chemicals that could be diverted to illicit use, and the provision of equipment for these purposes;

(e) The constitution of *ad hoc* groups to co-ordinate, on a multilateral basis and among police forces, strategies to identify and immobilize drug trafficking organizations;

(f) The development of a methodology for the collection and analysis of data on illicit trafficking;

(g) The establishment of mechanisms for the speedy and secure exchange of information between drug law enforcement authorities locally, nationally and across common borders, and the provision of appropriate communications equipment where needed;

(h) The improvement of co-ordination among all agencies concerned with regard to the scope, content and scheduling of seminars and other training programmes, in order to enhance their effectiveness;

6. *Requests* the specialized agencies and other organizations of the United Nations system, in particular the Division of Narcotic Drugs of the United Nations Secretariat and the United Nations Fund for Drug Abuse Control, as well as the International Criminal Police Organization and the Customs Co-operation Council, to support, whenever possible, the efforts and initiatives undertaken by Governments as recommended in the present resolution;

7. *Requests* the Secretary-General to transmit the text of the present resolution to all Governments, specialized agencies and other intergovernmental organizations

concerned for consideration and implementation, as appropriate.

Economic and Social Council resolution 1988/13

25 May 1988   Meeting 13   Adopted without vote

Approved by Second Committee (E/1988/87) without vote, 5 May (meeting 3); draft by Commission on Narcotic Drugs (E/1988/13); agenda item 13.

Resources for UN drug control programmes

INCB, in its 1988 report,[8] stated that the financial crisis facing the United Nations had imposed constraints on its operating programmes. This had resulted in a freeze on recruitment and lower priority being accorded to activities related to voluntary control measures for psychotropic substances and the monitoring of precursors and essential chemicals. The Director-General of the United Nations Office at Vienna informed the tenth special session of the Commission on Narcotic Drugs (8-19 February) of her concern about the budgetary and staffing situations of the Division of Narcotic Drugs and the secretariat of INCB and their devastating effects on the capacity of both bodies to deal with the work-load imposed on them by the international community.

Action by the Commission on Narcotic Drugs. On 12 February,[9] the Commission concluded that any reduction below the approved total appropriation for the programme budget for the biennium 1986-1987 relating to INCB and the Division of Narcotic Drugs would be irreconcilable with the efforts of Governments and the United Nations to intensify the global struggle against drug abuse. It urged all States to make urgent representations to the Secretary-General in support of this conclusion. The Commission recommended that CPC should maintain and possibly strengthen the level of resources available to the drug control units.

International campaign

Report of the Secretary-General. In an October report,[10] submitted in response to a 1987 General Assembly request,[11] the Secretary-General informed the Assembly of the status of the international campaign against drug abuse and illicit trafficking. The report summarized action taken by the Commission on Narcotic Drugs, the Economic and Social Council and the Secretariat's Division of Narcotic Drugs with regard to drug control programmes and the resources available for them. He also reported that on 25 February 1988 he had received the Commission's delegation to discuss its conclusions on the financial situation of the United Nations drug control units.

Follow-up to the International Conference on Drug Abuse and Illicit Trafficking

In 1987,[12] the General Assembly welcomed the Declaration and the Comprehensive Multidisciplinary Outline for Future Activities in Drug Abuse Control (CMO), adopted by the 1987 International Conference on Drug Abuse and Illicit Trafficking (Vienna, 17-26 June 1987),[3] and requested the Commission on Narcotic Drugs to identify suitable measures for follow-up. In February, the Secretary-General submitted a note[13] to the Commission outlining inter-agency follow-up to the Conference, action taken by the General Assembly, and proposals for the Commission to consider in identifying suitable modalities for implementing the recommendations of the Conference. The Secretary-General also discussed the question of the adequacy of resources for United Nations drug control entities and noted the need to restore those resources to their former level and to allocate further resources to cover additional activities envisaged in CMO. He added that the level and scope of programmes and activities of the Secretariat would be determined by its mandates and by the financial resources available from the regular budget and extrabudgetary resources. He also noted the need to strengthen the Office of the Director-General of the United Nations Office at Vienna to assist in the general co-ordination and follow-up of CMO.

In later addenda,[14] the Secretary-General outlined action taken or planned by the Division of Narcotic Drugs, INCB, other agencies and programmes of the United Nations system and the regional commissions to implement the relevant recommendations of the Conference. The Commission, at its tenth special session (Vienna, 8-19 February),[15] recommended to the Economic and Social Council for adoption follow-up activities to be taken by Member States and agencies of the United Nations system.

ECONOMIC AND SOCIAL COUNCIL ACTION

On 25 May 1988, the Economic and Social Council, on the recommendation of its Second Committee, adopted **resolution 1988/9** without vote.

International Conference on Drug Abuse and Illicit Trafficking

The Economic and Social Council,

Welcoming the successful conclusion of the International Conference on Drug Abuse and Illicit Trafficking, in particular the adoption of the Declaration and the Comprehensive Multidisciplinary Outline of Future Activities in Drug Abuse Control,

Affirming its commitment to the Declaration of the Conference as an expression of the political will of nations to combat the drug menace,

Noting that in the Declaration of the Conference the Secretary-General was requested to make proposals, in the context of the United Nations programme and budget and within available resources, that reflect the priority attached to the field of drug abuse control,

Noting also that in the Declaration of the Conference, the Commission on Narcotic Drugs was requested to examine the most suitable modalities for following up

the activities referred to in the Declaration and the Comprehensive Multidisciplinary Outline, as appropriate, at the international level,

Urging Governments to take early action to conclude a new convention against illicit traffic in narcotic drugs and psychotropic substances, to which the General Assembly and the Conference have attached high priority,

Recognizing the important contributions of the United Nations drug control bodies and their distinct mandates and responsibilities, and welcoming the Secretary-General's efforts to increase co-ordination of activities related to drug control following the Conference,

Recalling that the General Assembly, in its resolution 42/112 of 7 December 1987, *inter alia*, requested the Commission on Narcotic Drugs, as the principal United Nations policy-making body on drug control, to identify suitable measures for follow-up to the Conference and, in that context, to give appropriate consideration to the report of the Secretary-General on the Conference,

1.   *Urges* Governments and organizations to adhere to the principles set forth in the Declaration of the International Conference on Drug Abuse and Illicit Trafficking and to utilize the recommendations of the Comprehensive Multidisciplinary Outline of Future Activities in Drug Abuse Control in guiding the development of national and regional strategies and particularly bilateral, regional and international co-operative arrangements;

2.   *Welcomes* the prompt action taken by the Secretary-General to identify suggestions for activities to build upon the achievements of the Conference;

3.   *Urges* those Member States that have not yet done so to accede to the Single Convention on Narcotic Drugs of 1961, as amended by the 1972 Protocol Amending the Single Convention on Narcotic Drugs of 1961, and the Convention on Psychotropic Substances of 1971;

4.   *Urges* Governments, as a priority goal in the follow-up of the Conference, to provide additional resources to the United Nations Fund for Drug Abuse Control in order to enable it to strengthen its co-operation with the developing countries in their efforts to implement drug control programmes;

5.   *Invites* intergovernmental and regional and international non-governmental organizations that are referred to under the particular targets of the Comprehensive Multidisciplinary Outline to provide to the Commission on Narcotic Drugs, at future sessions, information on activities undertaken in pursuit of those targets;

6.   *Requests* the Secretary-General to review the procedure for the submission of written reports on drug matters in the United Nations and to report thereon to the Commission;

7.   *Requests* the Secretary-General to review, within available resources, current information systems in the United Nations drug control units and to develop an information strategy and submit it, with its financial implications, to the Commission on Narcotic Drugs at its thirty-third session, with a view to the creation, within existing United Nations structures, of an information system integrating input from national, regional and international sources in a computerized data base, so as to facilitate the linkage, retrieval and dissemination of information on all aspects of narcotic drugs, psychotropic substances and the chemicals used in their illicit processing and manufacturing;

8.   *Invites* the Secretary-General to support, within available resources, the activities of relevant non-governmental organizations in the drive against drug abuse and to co-ordinate the activities of the appropriate United Nations agencies with them;

9.   *Urges* the Secretary-General to ensure continued inter-agency co-operation in implementing and reporting on activities related to the targets established in the Comprehensive Multidisciplinary Outline and to ensure that the *ad hoc* inter-agency meetings on co-ordination in matters of international drug abuse control consider how such activities can be included by each specialized agency in its regular programme and budget, and to continue to report on such inter-agency co-operation;

10.   *Invites* the regional meetings of heads of national drug law enforcement agencies to take the Comprehensive Multidisciplinary Outline into account in their discussions, with a view to enhancing co-operation to combat illicit drug trafficking;

11.   *Recommends* that the Secretary-General convene a second interregional meeting of heads of national drug law enforcement agencies at an appropriate time following the adoption of the convention against illicit traffic in narcotic drugs and psychotropic substances, with a view to promoting co-operation in the implementation of the convention;

12.   *Recommends* that, in developing activities to implement the guiding principles contained in the Declaration of the Conference and the targets of the Comprehensive Multidisciplinary Outline, the United Nations drug control bodies, specialized agencies and other intergovernmental organizations give particular emphasis in the coming year to the activities identified in the annex to the present resolution;

13.   *Decides* to keep under review the action taken with respect to the Declaration and the Comprehensive Multidisciplinary Outline adopted by the Conference.

ANNEX
Suggested activities for follow-up to the International Conference on Drug Abuse and Illicit Trafficking by organizations of the United Nations system and other international organizations

A.   Prevention and reduction of demand

1.   The Division of Narcotic Drugs of the United Nations Secretariat, in collaboration with other United Nations drug control bodies and the World Health Organization, should help Governments improve data collection, should establish valid, reliable and practical procedures that national authorities may adopt and should undertake other activities identified in targets 1 and 2 of the Comprehensive Multidisciplinary Outline of Future Activities in Drug Abuse Control.

2.   The United Nations Educational, Scientific and Cultural Organization, in collaboration with the World Health Organization and appropriate United Nations bodies, should solicit, compile and analyse information on educational and public information methods that have been proved effective in the prevention of drug abuse, and disseminate this material to States on request.

3.   The International Labour Organisation should supply resource kits for the promotion and implementation of programmes to reduce drug abuse in the workplace, and monitor their effectiveness.

4.   Non-governmental organizations with special expertise in the field of drugs should collaborate with Governments and appropriate United Nations bodies to ensure that effective education and prevention activities are identified and information on them is widely disseminated.

B.   Control of supply

5.   The International Narcotics Control Board, in collaboration with the World Health Organization and other competent entities, should assist countries, on request, in improving their capacity for monitoring the manufacture, importation, dispensing and distribution of substances under international control.

6.   The World Health Organization, in collaboration with the Division of Narcotic Drugs of the Secretariat and the International Narcotics Control Board, should assist national drug regulatory authorities in developing and strengthening their pharmaceutical administrations and control laboratories in order to enable them to control pharmaceutical preparations containing narcotic drugs and psychotropic substances.

7.   The World Health Organization, in collaboration with United Nations drug control bodies, non-governmental organizations and others involved in the rational use of pharmaceutical preparations containing narcotic drugs and psychotropic substances, should assist national educational authorities in developing training materials and conducting training courses to ensure that medical practitioners and other health personnel are well trained in the rational use and prescription of narcotic drugs and psychotropic substances.

8.   The Customs Co-operation Council should continue to develop, as a high priority, an internationally recognized customs nomenclature for selected precursors, specified chemicals and equipment.

9.   The Division of Narcotic Drugs of the Secretariat, in collaboration with development assistance bodies and other bodies with relevant experience and in consultation and agreement with the Governments concerned, should support crop surveys and monitoring efforts, using such technologies as high-resolution satellite imagery and aerial photography.

10.   The United Nations Fund for Drug Abuse Control should continue to encourage contributions and develop master plans for narcotics control, including the eradication of illicit crops and, where appropriate, the substitution of those crops through integrated rural development programmes.

11.   The Division of Narcotics Drugs of the Secretariat should convene an expert group to make recommendations on the eradication of illicit plants using methods that do not harm the environment or humans.

12.   International financing institutions should contribute more to integrated rural development in support of the eradication of illicit plantings and crop substitution programmes.

13.   The Food and Agriculture Organization of the United Nations, in collaboration with the United Nations Fund for Drug Abuse Control and other United Nations bodies, should improve methodological approaches to integrated rural development, eradication of illicit crops and crop substitution.

C.   Suppression of illicit trafficking

14.   The Division of Narcotic Drugs of the Secretariat, in co-operation with the International

Criminal Police Organization, the Customs Co-operation Council and with other United Nations drug control bodies, should continue to organize appropriate training courses for law enforcement personnel, making the most effective use of available information sources.

15. The Division of Narcotic Drugs of the Secretariat should continue to give high priority to its programme of scientific and technical assistance to Member States that have limited resources, and should collaborate with the World Health Organization in this regard. The programme should include the establishment and strengthening of national laboratory services, an expanded training programme involving qualified national laboratories, the development of recommended methods of testing, and the provision of pure reference standards and scientific and technical information.

16. The International Criminal Police Organization and the Customs Co-operation Council should co-ordinate the dissemination of profiles of drug trafficking organizations and information on their methods of operation.

17. The International Civil Aviation Organization, the International Maritime Organization, the World Tourism Organization, the International Air Transport Association and the International Chamber of Shipping should, if they have not already done so, consider and set standards, in co-operation with the Customs Co-operation Council, to improve the control of movements of passengers and goods, with a view to curbing illicit traffic in drugs.

18. The Universal Postal Union should study ways to prevent the use of the international mails for drug trafficking and make recommendations for action to combat this problem.

19. The United Nations Fund for Drug Abuse Control and regional and bilateral programmes should, on request, assist countries in equipping and strengthening their law enforcement authorities.

D. Treatment and rehabilitation

20. The World Health Organization, in collaboration with other organizations of the United Nations system, non-governmental and other relevant bodies, should, on request, provide Governments with the basic information they need to develop clear policies for treatment and rehabilitation programmes appropriate to their national needs.

21. The World Health Organization, the Division of Narcotic Drugs of the Secretariat and other competent international bodies, including non-governmental organizations, should solicit, compile, analyse and disseminate information on treatment modalities and techniques that have been proved effective and on appropriate evaluation methodologies that could be easily adapted for national use.

22. The World Health Organization, in collaboration with other competent international bodies, including non-governmental organizations, should solicit, compile, analyse and disseminate material that has been found effective in the training of personnel who treat and help rehabilitate former drug addicts.

23. The International Labour Organisation should prepare and publish guidelines for programmes to reintegrate former addicts in occupational activities or vocational training.

24. The World Health Organization should continue to explore with Governments and report on the development of:

(a) Preventive and health education programmes as a means of interrupting the transmission through intravenous drug abuse of the human immunodeficiency virus (HIV);

(b) Appropriate treatment and counselling for drug misusers who are HIV positive or who have developed acquired immunodeficiency syndrome (AIDS).

Economic and Social Council resolution 1988/9

25 May 1988   Meeting 13   Adopted without vote

Approved by Second Committee (E/1988/87) without vote, 5 May (meeting 3); draft by Commission on Narcotic Drugs (E/1988/13); agenda item 13.

Report of the Secretary-General. In an October report,[16] the Secretary-General, responding to a 1987 General Assembly request,[12] informed the Assembly of action taken by the Commission on Narcotic Drugs, the Economic and Social Council and the Secretary-General as follow-up to the Conference. He indicated that, as requested by the Assembly, the Declaration and CMO were issued in all official languages of the United Nations and that the first annual International Day against Drug Abuse and Illicit Trafficking was observed on 26 June 1988 in many parts of the world.

The Secretary-General reported that the *Ad Hoc* Inter-Agency Meeting on the Co-ordination of International Drug Abuse Control of the Administrative Committee on Co-ordination held two sessions in 1988 (Vienna, 13 February;[17] Geneva, 1 and 2 September[18]). In September, participating entities considered, among other items, the follow-up to the International Conference on Drug Abuse and Illicit Trafficking and CMO and ways to make their related activities more effective. Particular attention was given to the immediate steps recommended by the Economic and Social Council in May for follow-up to the Conference (see above). They also discussed the gap between the resources available to the United Nations system as a whole and the actions required of it by CMO. They agreed to attempt, on an experimental basis, to quantify the level of resources allocated by two of the main specialized agencies for drug abuse control programmes, as well as the expanded activities recommended by the Conference, to give Member States a clearer idea of the financial implications of effective United Nations follow-up to the Conference.

GENERAL ASSEMBLY ACTION

On 8 December, the General Assembly, on the recommendation of the Third Committee, adopted **resolution 43/122** without vote.

International campaign against drug abuse and illicit trafficking

The General Assembly,

Recalling its resolutions 40/122 of 13 December 1985, 41/125 of 4 December 1986, 42/112 and 42/113 of 7 December 1987 and the relevant resolutions of the Commission on Narcotic Drugs and the Economic and Social Council adopted to implement the international campaign against drug abuse and illicit trafficking,

Recalling with satisfaction the successful conclusion of the International Conference on Drug Abuse and Illicit Trafficking, in particular the adoption of the Declaration, as an expression of the political will of nations to combat the drug menace, and the Comprehensive Multidisciplinary Outline of Future Activities in Drug Abuse Control, a compendium of recommendations for implementation,

Conscious that the global problem of illicit trafficking in and illicit production and abuse of narcotic drugs and psychotropic substances continues to have a devastating effect on individuals and on States,

Emphasizing that the connections between drug trafficking and international criminal organizations and the violence and corruption associated with them are highly detrimental to the democratic institutions, national security and economic, social and cultural structures of States,

Bearing in mind the need to ensure the implementation of the courses of action recommended in the Comprehensive Multidisciplinary Outline, particularly in the areas of education and public information with regard to the abuse of narcotic drugs and psychotropic substances,

Noting that the collective responsibility of all States for the international campaign against drug abuse and illicit trafficking was highlighted in the Declaration,

Recognizing that measures to prevent and control supply and to combat illicit trafficking can be effective only if they take into consideration the close link between illicit traffic in narcotic drugs and psychotropic substances, including illicit production and abuse, and the social, economic and cultural conditions in the States affected, and are formulated and implemented in the context of the social and economic policies of States, taking due account of community traditions and the harmonious development and conservation of the environment,

Reiterating that the transit routes used by drug traffickers are constantly changing and that an increasing number of countries in all regions of the world, and even entire areas, are particularly vulnerable to the illicit transit traffic because of their geographical location and other considerations,

Emphasizing that, in order to stop the illicit transit traffic in narcotic drugs and psychotropic substances, regional and interregional co-operation and action and necessary support and assistance are required to strengthen the capability of States and regions, including those hitherto unaffected,

Noting that the new convention against illicit traffic in narcotic drugs and psychotropic substances, when adopted, should, together with the existing international instruments, greatly enhance the international campaign against drug abuse and illicit trafficking,

Taking note of Commission on Narcotic Drugs resolution 4(S-X) of 12 February 1988 concerning the financial and human resources available to the Division of Narcotic Drugs of the Secretariat and the secretariat of the International Narcotics Control Board,

Considering the importance of the United Nations Fund for Drug Abuse Control as a major source of multilateral funding and expertise for drug abuse control efforts of the developing countries and the Fund's success in fund-raising and its improved operations,

Recalling its decision to observe 26 June each year as the International Day Against Drug Abuse and Illicit Trafficking,

I

*International campaign against drug abuse
and illicit trafficking*

1.   *Takes note* of the report of the Secretary-General;

2.   *Reiterates* its condemnation of international drug trafficking as a criminal activity, and encourages all States to continue to demonstrate the political will to enhance international co-operation to stop illicit trafficking in narcotic drugs and psychotropic substances, including illicit production and consumption;

3.   *Urges* all States to take appropriate action in regard to drug abuse control, in accordance with international drug control instruments, recognizing the collective responsibility of States, to provide appropriate resources for the elimination of illicit production, trafficking and drug abuse, as set forth in the Declaration of the International Conference on Drug Abuse and Illicit Trafficking;

4.   *Acknowledges* that, despite serious economic constraints, particularly in developing countries, Governments continue to make determined efforts to cope with the increasing abuse of and illicit traffic in narcotic drugs and psychotropic substances, especially with the destructive activities of international criminal organizations;

5.   *Notes with satisfaction* the valuable work of the meetings of Heads of National Drug Law Enforcement Agencies, in particular the Second Meeting of Heads of National Drug Law Enforcement Agencies, African Region, held at Dakar from 18 to 22 April 1988, the Second Meeting of Heads of National Drug Law Enforcement Agencies, Latin American and Caribbean Region, held at Lima from 12 to 16 September 1988, and the Fourteenth Meeting of Heads of National Drug Law Enforcement Agencies, Asia and the Pacific Region, held at Bangkok from 3 to 7 October 1988;

6.   *Requests* that consideration be given to the convening of regional meetings of heads of national drug law enforcement agencies in regions where they have not yet been held;

7.   *Notes with satisfaction* that the Second Interregional Meeting of Heads of National Drug Law Enforcement Agencies is to be held in 1989 and encourages it to consider the reports and achievements of all the regional meetings;

8.   *Urges* the Interregional Meeting to discuss ways and means of enhancing law enforcement training, especially in those areas that would require new knowledge and skills for the implementation of the provisions of the new convention against illicit traffic in narcotic drugs and psychotropic substances;

9.   *Encourages* States to use the meetings of the working group of the Commission on Narcotic Drugs and other forums for the purpose of exchanging experiences in the fight against the illicit transit of drugs and psychotropic substances and to increase regional and interregional co-operation on this aspect of the drug problem;

10.   *Reiterates once again its request* to the Secretary-General to continue to make the necessary arrangements

for holding, within the framework of advisory services, interregional seminars on the experience gained within the United Nations system in integrated rural development programmes that include the substitution of illegal crops in affected areas, including the Andean region;

11. *Endorses* Commission on Narcotic Drugs resolution 4(S-X), the implementation of which is essential for the adequate functioning of the Division of Narcotic Drugs and the secretariat of the International Narcotics Control Board;

12. *Commends* the United Nations Fund for Drug Abuse Control for the productive work that it has done as one of the main bodies of the United Nations system providing technical co-operation and funding in the field of drug abuse control;

13. *Appeals* to Member States to continue to provide additional resources to the Fund to enable it to continue its activities, giving particular attention to requests for assistance from developing countries;

14. *Once again calls upon* the Governments of countries facing problems of drug abuse, particularly those most seriously affected, as part of their national strategies, to take the necessary measures to reduce significantly the illicit demand for narcotic drugs and psychotropic substances with the aim of creating societies that deeply respect health, fitness and well-being, and to provide appropriate information and advice on the harmful effects of drug abuse, through adequate community action, to all sectors of their communities;

15. *Requests* the Secretary-General to take steps to ensure that the Department of Public Information of the Secretariat includes in its publications information designed to prevent the abuse of narcotic drugs and psychotropic substances, especially by young people;

II

International Conference on Drug Abuse and Illicit Trafficking

1. *Takes note* of the report of the Secretary-General;

2. *Urges* Governments and organizations to adhere to the principles set forth in the Declaration of the International Conference on Drug Abuse and Illicit Trafficking and to utilize the recommendations of the Comprehensive Multidisciplinary Outline of Future Activities in Drug Abuse Control in developing national and regional strategies, particularly to promote bilateral, regional and international co-operative arrangements;

3. *Recommends* that, in developing activities to implement the guiding principles contained in the Declaration and the targets of the Comprehensive Multidisciplinary Outline, the United Nations drug control bodies, specialized agencies and other intergovernmental organizations should give particular emphasis to activities identified in the annex to Economic and Social Council resolution 1988/9 of 25 May 1988;

4. *Requests* the Secretary-General, within the available resources, to review current information systems in the United Nations drug control units and to develop an information strategy and submit it, with its financial implications, to the Commission on Narcotic Drugs at its thirty-third session;

5. *Requests* the Commission to consider the review by the Secretary-General and to advise on the creation, within existing United Nations structures, of an information system to integrate inputs from national, regional and international sources, so as to facilitate the linkage, retrieval and dissemination of information on all aspects of narcotic drugs, psychotropic substances and the chemicals used in their illicit processing and manufacturing;

6. *Invites* the Secretary-General to support, within the available resources, the activities of non-governmental organizations concerned and, in recognition of the latter's experience and expertise, to co-ordinate United Nations activities in this field with the organizations concerned;

7. *Requests* the Secretary-General to ensure continued inter-agency co-ordination in drug abuse control activities, in particular by rotating the venue of inter-agency meetings on co-ordination, which will enhance efforts by the Commission to implement follow-up activities to the Conference;

8. *Calls upon* the Commission to keep under review action taken with respect to the Declaration and the Comprehensive Multidisciplinary Outline;

9. *Requests* the Secretary-General to report to the General Assembly at its forty-fourth session on the implementation of the present resolution and decides to include in the provisional agenda of that session the item entitled "International campaign against traffic in drugs".

General Assembly resolution 43/122

8 December 1988   Meeting 75   Adopted without vote

Approved by Third Committee (A/43/875) without vote, 17 November (meeting 46); 49-nation draft (A/C.3/43/L.43), orally revised; agenda item 103.

Sponsors: Angola, Argentina, Austria, Bahamas, Barbados, Bolivia, Botswana, Brazil, Brunei Darussalam, Burkina Faso, Chile, Colombia, Costa Rica, Côte d'Ivoire, Cuba, Dominican Republic, Ecuador, Egypt, El Salvador, Fiji, France, Germany, Federal Republic of, Ghana, Greece, Guatemala, India, Indonesia, Italy, Jamaica, Malaysia, Malta, Mexico, Morocco, Nicaragua, Pakistan, Panama, Paraguay, Peru, Philippines, Samoa, Senegal, Singapore, Spain, Thailand, Trinidad and Tobago, Turkey, Uruguay, Venezuela, Yugoslavia.

Meeting numbers. GA 43rd session: 3rd Committee 30, 32-35, 42, 46; plenary 75.

Supply and demand

Narcotic raw materials for licit use

The Economic and Social Council, in resolutions adopted in 1986[19] and 1987,[20] requested INCB to continue to monitor the implementation of its resolutions aimed at re-establishing and maintaining a world-wide balance between demand for a supply of opiates for medical and scientific purposes and, in particular, at reducing excessive stocks of opiate raw materials for licit purposes, as provided for in the 1961 Single Convention on Narcotic Drugs.[21] However, the Board had to defer the implementation of the Council's resolutions so as to devote its reduced resources to other treaty-based functions which had been accorded higher priority.

INCB reported[8] that global consumption of opiates had stabilized since the mid-1970s at approximately 200 tonnes per year in morphine equivalent. Since 1980, production of opiate raw materials had been in approximate balance with the consumption of opiates. The consumption of pholcodine and ethylmorphine declined and the demand for codeine levelled off despite the abundance of raw materials and low prices. World consumption of dihydrocodeine continued to increase, and the demand for morphine doubled in recent years as a result of its increased use for the treatment of terminally ill patients.

ECONOMIC AND SOCIAL COUNCIL ACTION

On 25 May, on the recommendation of its Second Committee, the Economic and Social Council adopted **resolution 1988/10** without vote.

Demand and supply of opiates for medical and scientific purposes

The Economic and Social Council,

Recalling its resolutions 1979/8 of 9 May 1979, 1980/20 of 30 April 1980, 1981/8 of 6 May 1981, 1982/12 of 30 April 1982, 1983/3 of 24 May 1983, 1984/21 of 24 May 1984, 1985/16 of 28 May 1985, 1986/9 of 21 May 1986 and 1987/31 of 26 May 1987,

Re-emphasizing the central role in the control of the production of and trade in opiates played by the Single Convention on Narcotic Drugs of 1961, as amended by the 1972 Protocol Amending the Single Convention on Narcotic Drugs of 1961,

Reaffirming the fundamental need for international co-operation and solidarity in all activities relating to the control of narcotic drugs,

Bearing in mind that the maintenance of a world-wide balance between the licit supply of and the legitimate demand for opiates for medical and scientific purposes is an important aspect of an international strategy and policy for drug abuse control,

Concerned that large stocks of opiate raw materials held by traditional supplier countries continue to impose heavy financial and other burdens on them,

Having considered the section of the report of the International Narcotics Control Board for 1987 on the demand for and supply of opiates for medical and scientific purposes, including the observation that world demand and production have been in approximate balance and that, over the next several years, the demand for opiates will remain at the present level,

1. _Urges_ all Governments seriously to consider ways of resolving the problem of excess stocks in order to bring about an expeditious improvement in the current situation;

2. _Requests_ the International Narcotics Control Board to review the available information on the problem and to enter into a dialogue with interested Governments and other parties in order to develop a practical and effective solution, which may involve international development assistance organizations;

3. _Requests_ the Secretary-General to transmit the present resolution to all Governments and appropriate international agencies for consideration and implementation.

Economic and Social Council resolution 1988/10

25 May 1988   Meeting 13   Adopted without vote

Approved by Second Committee (E/1988/87) without vote, 5 May (meeting 3); draft by Commission on Narcotic Drugs (E/1988/13); agenda item 13.

Demand reduction

The Division of Narcotic Drugs, in its programme for the prevention and reduction of the illicit demand for drugs, provided assistance to national authorities, particularly through the programme for the utilization of community resources for the prevention and reduction of drug abuse which was supported by UNFDAC. Under the programme, seminars and workshops were held, including the Workshop on the Utilization of Community Resources for the Prevention and Reduction of Drug Abuse for Asia and the Pacific Region (Manila, Philippines, 7-11 December 1987). The Division also encouraged the development of national pilot programmes and projects.

Action by the Commission on Narcotic Drugs. On 16 February,[22] the Commission urged professional pharmacy bodies and associations to offer patients information on the appropriate and safe use of pharmaceuticals containing narcotic drugs and psychotropic substances, and to develop mechanisms for detecting and preventing the use of such drugs or substances for non-medical purposes. It requested schools of pharmacy and post-graduate education institutions to emphasize in their curricula the control and rational use of psychoactive substances and control of the distribution chain, and to expand, in collaboration with other entities and the pharmaceutical industry, research into trends of abuse of such substances.

On 18 February,[23] the Commission recommended that the Division of Narcotic Drugs extend the programme on the utilization of community resources to prevent and reduce drug abuse through regional workshops, and called for more financial support for that programme.

On 19 February,[24] the Commission recommended that the Secretary-General establish an international drug abuse assessment system for the collection, analysis, evaluation and assessment of drug abuse information so as to improve the quality of data submitted to the Commission; develop data and classification procedures; and provide training in the handling and reporting of drug abuse data.

ECONOMIC AND SOCIAL COUNCIL ACTION

On 25 May, on the recommendation of its Second Committee, the Economic and Social Council adopted **resolution 1988/16** without vote.

Improved measures for reduction of the illicit demand for narcotic drugs and psychotropic substances

The Economic and Social Council,

Recalling that the General Assembly, in its resolution 42/112 of 7 December 1987, welcomed the successful conclusion of the International Conference on Drug Abuse and Illicit Trafficking and, in particular, the adoption of the Declaration and the Comprehensive Multidisciplinary Outline of Future Activities in Drug Abuse Control,

Concerned about the growing abuse of drugs in most parts of the world,

Recognizing that measures for prevention, public awareness, treatment, rehabilitation and social reintegration are essential in curbing drug abuse,

Aware that existing strategies for the reduction of the illicit demand for narcotic drugs and psychotropic substances and conventional methods for the evaluation of preventive measures and methods of treatment have not always been effective owing to the complexity of the causes of the phenomenon,

1. *Urges* all Governments to foster, through national policies, the best possible conditions for the healthy development of, and a meaningful life for, all young people and to facilitate their integration into the community, so as to mitigate the social and economic circumstances that encourage abuse of narcotic drugs and psychotropic substances;

2. *Recommends* that scientific research into the factors that might promote or prevent drug dependence should be strengthened and that the methodologies and results of such research should be made available to all States;

3. *Appeals* to all Governments to develop and implement comprehensive national strategies for drug abuse prevention and public awareness that are designed to meet the particular situation and needs of the target groups and provide for long-term and continuous measures;

4. *Also appeals* to all Governments to create a national network of counselling and treatment services to advise high-risk groups and help misusers by providing appropriate treatment, rehabilitation and social reintegration programmes aimed at reducing the harm associated with drug abuse and leading to a drug-free life;

5. *Calls upon* all Governments to engage non-governmental organizations as partners in the development and implementation of prevention strategies and the establishment of counselling and treatment services, in view of the importance of community commitment to demand reduction programmes;

6. *Requests* Governments to take suitable measures, as part of their national strategies in their campaigns against drug abuse, to reduce excessive and inappropriate use of medicinal products containing narcotic drugs and psychotropic substances, including such measures as special education and training of medical, pharmaceutical and paramedical personnel on all aspects of the abuse problem and the rational use of such drugs;

7. *Calls upon* the Governments of countries facing problems of drug abuse to take, when appropriate, the necessary measures to reduce significantly the illicit demand for narcotic drugs and psychotropic substances;

8. *Requests* the Secretary-General to invite all Governments to implement the present resolution in accordance with the Declaration of the International Conference on Drug Abuse and Illicit Trafficking and the Comprehensive Multidisciplinary Outline of Future Activities in Drug Abuse Control.

Economic and Social Council resolution 1988/16

25 May 1988   Meeting 13   Adopted without vote

Approved by Second Committee (E/1988/87) without vote, 5 May (meeting 3); draft by Commission on Narcotic Drugs (E/1988/13); agenda item 13.

Illicit traffic

Preparation of convention against illicit traffic

On 5 February 1988, by **decision 1988/102**, the Economic and Social Council, pursuant to a 1987 General Assembly resolution,[25] requested the Commission on Narcotic Drugs to consider and,

if possible, approve at its tenth special session the draft convention against illicit traffic in narcotic drugs and psychotropic substances, and to prepare recommendations on the next measures necessary to conclude the preparation of the convention.

In February,[15] the Commission had before it the initial draft convention prepared by the Division of Narcotic Drugs, which included a draft preamble, implementation articles and final clauses. It also had before it comments on the draft received from Governments and an account of the Commission's deliberations at its 1987 session.[26] In addition, the Commission had the revised text of articles completed by the open-ended intergovernmental expert group on the preparation of a draft convention at its 1987[27] and 1988 sessions (Vienna, 25 January–5 February 1988),[28] a summary of comments from Governments on the expert group's revised text,[29] and a background note by the Secretary-General on progress in preparing the new convention.[30]

The Commission recommended that the Council convene a conference of plenipotentiaries to adopt the convention, preceded by a meeting of a review group to continue its preparation.

ECONOMIC AND SOCIAL COUNCIL ACTION

On 25 May 1988, the Economic and Social Council, on the recommendation of its Second Committee, adopted **resolution 1988/8** without vote.

Preparation of an international convention against illicit traffic in narcotic drugs and psychotropic substances

The Economic and Social Council,

Recalling General Assembly resolution 39/141 of 14 December 1984, in which the Commission on Narcotic Drugs was requested to initiate, as a matter of priority, the preparation of a draft convention against illicit traffic in narcotic drugs and psychotropic substances,

Recalling also General Assembly resolutions 33/168 of 20 December 1978, 35/195 of 15 December 1980, 36/132 of 14 December 1981, 37/198 of 18 December 1982, 38/93 and 38/122 of 16 December 1983, 39/143 of 14 December 1984, 40/120, 40/121 and 40/122 of 13 December 1985, 41/125, 41/126 and 41/127 of 4 December 1986 and other relevant resolutions,

Recalling further that the Commission, pursuant to resolution 1(S-IX) of 14 February 1986, considered an initial draft convention, which included fourteen articles, and the comments of Governments thereon, at its thirty-second session, held from 2 to 11 February 1987,

Considering that, as provided for in Economic and Social Council resolution 1987/27 of 26 May 1987, the open-ended Intergovernmental Expert Group met twice in 1987 to review the working document which consolidated the draft convention and, wherever possible, to reach agreement on the articles of the convention, and prepared revised working documents,

Considering also that the General Assembly, in its resolution 42/111 of 7 December 1987, requested the

Secretary-General to consider convening a further meeting of the Intergovernmental Expert Group for a period of two weeks immediately prior to the tenth special session of the Commission on Narcotic Drugs in order to continue revision of the working paper on the draft convention, and also requested the Commission to consider and, if possible, approve the draft convention at its tenth special session and to prepare recommendations on measures to be taken to conclude the preparation of the convention, including the possibility of convening a plenipotentiary conference in 1988 for its adoption,

Recalling the Declaration of the International Conference on Drug Abuse and Illicit Trafficking, in which the Conference called for the urgent but careful preparation and finalization of the draft convention to ensure its entry into force at the earliest possible date,

Having received the report of the Commission on Narcotic Drugs on its tenth special session,

Bearing in mind the Quito Declaration against Traffic in Narcotic Drugs of 11 August 1984, the New York Declaration against Drug Trafficking and the Illicit Use of Drugs of 1 October 1984 and the Lima Declaration of 29 July 1985, in which profound alarm was expressed at the seriousness of the problem,

1. *Expresses its appreciation* to the Secretary-General for the excellent preparation of the working documents on the draft convention, which have been circulated to States for consideration at the meetings of the Intergovernmental Expert Group, as requested by the Economic and Social Council in its resolution 1987/27;

2. *Expresses its thanks* to States that have submitted their comments on the working documents on the draft convention or proposals for textual changes thereto;

3. *Expresses its thanks* to the Intergovernmental Expert Group for the work accomplished during its meetings held from 29 June to 10 July 1987, from 5 to 16 October 1987 and from 25 January to 5 February 1988;

4. *Reminds* States of the importance and urgency of proceeding with the work on the preparation of the draft convention in the most expeditious manner, with a view to ensuring that the convention is effective, widely acceptable and enters into force at the earliest possible time;

5. *Takes note* of the report of the Commission on Narcotic Drugs on its tenth special session, annex II to which contains texts of draft articles for the proposed convention;

6. *Requests* the Secretary-General to transmit by 15 March 1988 for consideration the relevant parts of the report of the Commission, with any relevant annexes and such background documentation considered pertinent, to all States, the specialized agencies, the International Narcotics Control Board and the International Criminal Police Organization and other interested intergovernmental organizations;

7. *Decides* to convene, in accordance with Article 62, paragraph 4, of the Charter of the United Nations and within the provisions of General Assembly resolution 366(IV) of 3 December 1949, a conference of plenipotentiaries for the adoption of a convention against illicit traffic in narcotic drugs and psychotropic substances;

8. *Also decides* to convene, within available resources, a review group for the conference to meet for a period of up to two weeks, preferably at Vienna, not later than mid-June 1988, the proceedings of which shall be governed, *mutatis mutandis*, by the rules of procedure of the functional commissions of the Economic and Social Council;

9. *Instructs* the review group:

(a) To review the texts of draft articles 1 to 6 with a view to submitting them to the plenipotentiary conference; in addition, the group may review the remaining draft articles and related texts with a view to making those changes that may be necessary to achieve overall consistency in the text of the draft convention to be submitted to the plenipotentiary conference;

(b) To consider organizational matters relating to the conference and the draft provisional rules of procedure to be prepared by the Secretary-General;

10. *Requests* the Secretary-General:

(a) To arrange for the conference to be held in 1988, not sooner than four months after the meeting of the review group;

(b) To invite to participate in the conference and the meeting of the review group:

(i) All States;

(ii) Specialized agencies and intergovernmental organizations interested in the matter, with the same rights as they have at sessions of the Economic and Social Council;

(iii) The International Narcotics Control Board, with the same rights as it has at sessions of the Economic and Social Council;

(c) To transmit, immediately after the meeting of the review group, the text of the draft convention and related documents to all States and other interested parties;

(d) To prepare provisional rules of procedure for the conference;

(e) To provide summary records of the meetings of the conference and its committees.

Economic and Social Council resolution 1988/8

25 May 1988   Meeting 13   Adopted without vote

Approved by Second Committee (E/1988/87) without vote, 5 May (meeting 3); draft by Commission on Narcotic Drugs (E/1988/13); agenda item 13.

Conference for the adoption of the international convention against illicit traffic

On 25 May, by **decision 1988/120**, the Economic and Social Council decided to hold a conference of plenipotentiaries for the adoption of a convention against illicit traffic in narcotic drugs and psychotropic substances at Vienna from 25 November to 20 December 1988.

The review group established by the Council (Vienna, 27 June–8 July) reviewed articles 1 to 6 of the draft convention and considered organizational matters concerning the plenipotentiary conference.[31] It recommended to the conference the revised draft convention and further proposals relating to its text, the draft provisional rules of procedure of the conference, and a draft provisional agenda. It also recommended that a one-day consultation be held immediately preceding the conference to settle organizational and procedural questions.

On 26 July, by **decision 1988/159**, the Economic and Social Council authorized the holding of one-day pre-conference consultations immediately prior to the opening of the conference.

In an October report[32] submitted in response to a 1987 General Assembly request,[25] the Secretary-General informed the Assembly of progress in preparing the draft convention and preparations for the conference and the convention's adoption. He indicated that a one-day pre-conference consultation was to be held on 23 November 1988, and that he had designated the Director of the Secretariat's Division of Narcotic Drugs as executive secretary of the conference.

GENERAL ASSEMBLY ACTION

On 8 December, the General Assembly, on the recommendation of the Third Committee, adopted **resolution 43/120** without vote.

Preparation of a draft convention against illicit traffic in narcotic drugs and psychotropic substances

The General Assembly,

Recalling its resolutions 33/168 of 20 December 1978, 35/195 of 15 December 1980, 36/132 of 14 December 1981, 36/168 of 16 December 1981, 37/168 of 17 December 1982, 37/198 of 18 December 1982, 38/93 and 38/122 of 16 December 1983, 39/141 and 39/143 of 14 December 1984, 40/120, 40/121 and 40/122 of 13 December 1985, 41/125, 41/126 and 41/127 of 4 December 1986, 42/111, 42/112 and 42/113 of 7 December 1987 and other relevant provisions,

Emphasizing the importance of the contribution that will be made by the convention in supplementing the existing international instruments on the subject, namely, the Single Convention on Narcotic Drugs of 1961, as amended by the 1972 Protocol Amending the Single Convention on Narcotic Drugs of 1961, and the Convention on Psychotropic Substances of 1971,

Underlining the importance of the appeal made in paragraph 3 of the Declaration of the International Conference on Drug Abuse and Illicit Trafficking, in which the Conference called for the urgent and careful finalization of the preparation of the draft convention against illicit traffic in narcotic drugs and psychotropic substances, which today becomes more urgent owing to the continuous aggravation of the problem,

Noting with appreciation the progress made by the Commission on Narcotic Drugs at its tenth special session in the preparation of the draft convention,

Underlining the importance of the valuable contribution of the Secretary-General, the useful observations of the Member States and the work of the open-ended Intergovernmental Expert Group, which met twice during 1987 and once during 1988 and which prepared revised working papers, and the conclusions of the Review Group convened at Vienna from 27 June to 8 July 1988,

Taking into consideration that the Economic and Social Council in its resolution 1988/8 and in its decision 1988/120 of 25 May 1988 decided to convene at Vienna, from 25 November to 20 December 1988, the Conference of plenipotentiaries for the adoption of a convention against illicit traffic in narcotic drugs and psychotropic substances,

Having considered the report of the Secretary-General on the progress achieved in the preparation of the draft convention,

1. *Welcomes with appreciation* Economic and Social Council resolution 1988/8, in which it decided to convene the Review Group in mid-June 1988 at Vienna, with the mandate of continuing the preparation of the draft convention and preparing the organizational aspects of the Conference of plenipotentiaries for the adoption of a convention against illicit traffic in narcotic drugs and psychotropic substances;

2. *Takes note with satisfaction* of the report of the Secretary-General, and the report of the Commission on Narcotic Drugs on its tenth special session and the recommendations therein, approved by the Economic and Social Council in its resolution 1988/8 and decisions 1988/118 and 1988/120 of 25 May 1988 and 1988/159 of 26 July 1988, in which it decided, *inter alia*, to convene the Conference of plenipotentiaries to adopt the convention, and to extend to ten working days the thirty-third session of the Commission on Narcotic Drugs in order to allow it to consider suitable measures to be taken prior to the entry into force of the convention;

3. *Requests* the Commission on Narcotic Drugs, as the principal United Nations policy-making body on drug abuse control, to identify suitable measures to be taken prior to the entry into force of the convention;

4. *Urges* all States to adopt a constructive approach with a view to resolving any outstanding differences over the text of the convention;

5. *Requests* all States, while reaffirming their commitment to the Declaration of the International Conference on Drug Abuse and Illicit Trafficking as an expression of the political will of nations to combat the drug problem, to assign the highest priority to the Conference of plenipotentiaries and to participate actively in it, at the highest possible level, for the adoption of the convention;

6. *Expresses its appreciation* to the Secretary-General, the Commission on Narcotic Drugs and all related organs established by the Commission for their effectiveness in responding to its request to prepare the draft convention;

7. *Once again urges* all States that have not yet done so to ratify or to accede to the Single Convention on Narcotic Drugs of 1961, as amended by the 1972 Protocol Amending the Single Convention on Narcotic Drugs of 1961, and the Convention on Psychotropic Substances of 1971;

8. *Requests* the Secretary-General to report to the General Assembly at its forty-fourth session on the implementation of the present resolution, particularly on the conclusions of the Conference of plenipotentiaries for the adoption of a convention against illicit traffic in narcotic drugs and psychotropic substances.

General Assembly resolution 43/120

8 December 1988   Meeting 75   Adopted without vote

Approved by Third Committee (A/43/875) without vote, 17 November (meeting 46); 56-nation draft (A/C.3/43/L.39); agenda item 103.

Sponsors: Angola, Argentina, Australia, Bahamas, Bangladesh, Barbados, Belgium, Bolivia, Brazil, Canada, Chile, China, Colombia, Costa Rica, Côte d'Ivoire, Cuba, Dominican Republic, Ecuador, Egypt, El Salvador, Fiji, German Democratic Republic, Germany, Federal Republic of, Ghana, Greece, Guatemala, Guyana, Honduras, Hungary, India, Indonesia, Italy, Jamaica, Madagascar, Malaysia, Malta, Mexico, Morocco, Nicaragua, Pakistan, Panama, Paraguay, Peru, Philippines, Poland, Senegal, Spain, Trinidad and Tobago,

Turkey, United Kingdom, United States, Uruguay, Venezuela, Yugoslavia, Zaire, Zambia.

Meeting numbers. GA 43rd session: 3rd Committee 30, 32-35, 42, 46; plenary 75.

The United Nations Conference for the Adoption of a Convention against Illicit Traffic in Narcotic Drugs and Psychotropic Substances (Vienna, 25 November–20 December 1988)[33] was attended by representatives of 106 States. It was also attended by representatives of the Pan Africanist Congress of Anzania and the South West Africa People's Organization, as well as by a number of specialized agencies, intergovernmental organizations, United Nations organs and related bodies, and non-governmental organizations (NGOs). On 19 December,[34] the Conference adopted the text of the Convention, which was opened for signature on 20 December 1988.

The Convention, which was subject to ratification, acceptance, approval or act of formal confirmation and was open for accession, was to remain open for signature at Vienna until 28 February 1989 and, thereafter, in New York until 20 December 1989, the Secretary-General being the depositary. As at 31 December 1988, 44 States had signed the Convention.[35] The Convention required 20 ratifications prior to its entry into force.

The Conference also adopted its Final Act,[36] containing three resolutions recommending the widest possible use of the records and communication system of the International Criminal Police Organization to address the goals of the Convention; the provisional application of the Convention before its entry into force; and the provision of sufficient resources to the Division of Narcotic Drugs and the secretariat of INCB to enable them to discharge their tasks under international drug control treaties.

Drug law enforcement

INCB noted that the drafting of a new international treaty to combat illicit drug trafficking was at an advanced stage and that Governments were already enacting legislation to prevent money-laundering and to confiscate traffickers' assets. Regional and international co-operation among enforcement agencies had seriously disrupted traffickers' operations and offered the best prospects for confronting international criminal organizations. During the year, countries in Eastern and Western Europe and North America had concluded formal co-operative agreements and had achieved significant results, including the destruction of traffickers' networks.

The Commission on Narcotic Drugs considered recommendations from the three regional meetings of Heads of National Drug Law Enforcement Agencies (HONLEAs) held during 1987 in Africa, Asia, and Latin America and the Caribbean, and

the work of the Sub-Commission on Illicit Drug Traffic and Related Matters in the Near and Middle East. HONLEA, Africa,[37] had recommended, *inter alia*, the establishment of national mechanisms to monitor trends in drug abuse; the co-ordination of preventive measures and the collection of data for drug abuse assessment; the development of relevant training programmes; the creation of a regional drug control organization; and the expansion of international co-operation to provide information, equipment, financial resources and training.

ECONOMIC AND SOCIAL COUNCIL ACTION

On 25 May 1988, the Economic and Social Council, on the recommendation of its Second Committee, adopted **resolution 1988/15** without vote.

Meetings of Heads of National Drug Law Enforcement Agencies: Asia and the Pacific, Africa, and Latin America and the Caribbean

The Economic and Social Council,

Recalling its resolution 1845(LVI) of 15 May 1974, in which it requested the Secretary-General to convene regular meetings of the heads of national drug law enforcement agencies of the countries in the Asia and Pacific region, its resolution 1985/11 of 28 May 1985, in which it requested the Secretary-General to convene regular meetings of the heads of the national drug control and law enforcement agencies of States in the African region, and its resolution 1987/34 of 26 May 1987, in which it invited Governments of Latin American and Caribbean countries to participate in a regional meeting, with a view to establishing regular meetings of heads of national drug law enforcement agencies in that region,

Recalling also that the General Assembly, in its resolution 37/198 of 18 December 1982, requested the Secretary-General to explore the feasibility of establishing, on a continuing basis, co-ordination mechanisms for drug law enforcement in regions where they did not exist,

Noting that these regional meetings have been granted the status of subsidiary organs of the Commission on Narcotic Drugs, to which they report,

Bearing in mind that three regional meetings of heads of national drug law enforcement agencies were successfully convened in 1987,

Recognizing the valuable contribution that these meetings have made, and can continue to make, to international co-operation and co-ordination, on a regional and interregional basis, in the field of drug law enforcement and other areas of international drug control,

1. *Confirms,* in the light of the terminology used at the First Interregional Meeting of Heads of National Drug Law Enforcement Agencies, held at Vienna from 28 July to 1 August 1986, that each of the three regional meetings should in future be designated "Meeting of Heads of National Drug Law Enforcement Agencies", followed by an indication of the region;

2. *Requests* the Secretary-General to take the necessary measures to convene these three regional meetings at the capitals of States in the respective regions that may wish to act as host or at the headquarters of the

regional commission concerned, annually, beginning in 1988, except in years when an interregional meeting is held, to provide the financial resources required from available resources and, if necessary, to seek additional extrabudgetary resources;

3. *Also requests* the Secretary-General, at his discretion, to invite States outside the region that request observer status and that are actively involved in countering the illicit drug traffic in, through or from the region to send observers to the meetings, on the understanding that any expense would be borne by the States concerned;

4. *Requests* the Commission on Narcotic Drugs to include in the agenda of its regular and special sessions a separate item entitled "Development and promotion of more effective action against illicit drug trafficking through regional co-operation in drug law enforcement", under which it should consider reports or recommendations of the meetings of heads of national drug law enforcement agencies and the Sub-Commission on Illicit Drug Traffic and Related Matters in the Near and Middle East and take appropriate action.

Economic and Social Council resolution 1988/15

25 May 1988	Meeting 13	Adopted without vote

Approved by Second Committee (E/1988/87) without vote, 5 May (meeting 3); draft by Commission on Narcotic Drugs (E/1988/13); agenda item 13.

Also on 25 May, on the recommendation of its Second Committee, the Council adopted **resolution 1988/12** without vote.

Reduction of the illicit supply of drugs

The Economic and Social Council,

Recognizing that drug law enforcement training is critical to the fight against illicit drug trafficking and in the promotion of international co-operation and co-ordination,

Emphasizing the need for international and up-to-date drug law enforcement training,

Reaffirming Commission on Narcotic Drugs resolutions 5(XXXII) and 6(XXXII) of 10 February 1987,

1. *Reaffirms* the recommendations of the First Meeting of Heads of National Drug Law Enforcement Agencies, Africa;

2. *Requests* the Division of Narcotic Drugs of the United Nations Secretariat, in co-operation with the International Criminal Police Organization, the Customs Co-operation Council, other interested organizations and Member States, to establish, as a matter of high priority, a long-term international drug law enforcement training strategy, aimed, *inter alia*, at the improvement of appropriate training techniques, tools and materials;

3. *Also requests* the Division of Narcotic Drugs of the Secretariat to establish an annual plan and a regular schedule for drug law enforcement training programmes and activities, to co-ordinate them with interested intergovernmental organizations and national agencies in different regions and to encourage Governments, especially those of transit States and developing countries, to take adequate advantage of these programmes and activities;

4. *Urges* Member States to increase the funds available to the United Nations Fund for Drug Abuse Con-

trol to support drug law enforcement training programmes and activities.

Economic and Social Council resolution 1988/12

25 May 1988	Meeting 13	Adopted without vote

Approved by Second Committee (E/1988/87) without vote, 5 May (meeting 3); draft by Commission on Narcotic Drugs (E/1988/13); agenda item 13.

GENERAL ASSEMBLY ACTION

On 8 December, the General Assembly, on the recommendation of the Third Committee, adopted **resolution 43/121** without vote.

Use of children in the illicit traffic in narcotic drugs and rehabilitation of drug-addicted minors

The General Assembly,

Recalling its resolutions 41/127 of 4 December 1986 and 42/113 of 7 December 1987, as well as the relevant resolutions of the Commission on Narcotic Drugs and of the Economic and Social Council adopted to implement the international campaign against drug abuse and illicit trafficking,

Recalling the provisions of the Declaration of the International Conference on Drug Abuse and Illicit Trafficking and the guidelines contained in the Comprehensive Multidisciplinary Outline of Future Activities in Drug Abuse Control,

Alarmed by the fact that drug dealers' organizations are making use of children in their illicit production of and trafficking in drugs, and by the increase in the number of drug-addicted children,

Conscious of the physical and psychological damage inflicted on children by the illicit use of narcotic drugs and of its serious effects both on their potential for development and on their relationships with their families and society,

Having in mind the provisions of the Declaration of the Rights of the Child,[a]

Reaffirming the provisions of its resolution 42/101 of 7 December 1987 on the question of a convention on the rights of the child, which affirm that children's rights require special protection and call for continuous improvement of the situation of children all over the world, as well as their development and education,

1. *Strongly condemns* drug trafficking in all its forms, particularly those criminal activities which involve children in the use, production and illicit sale of narcotic drugs and psychotropic substances;

2. *Urges* all States to join together in order to establish national and international programmes to protect children from the illicit consumption of drugs and psychotropic substances and from involvement in illicit production and trafficking;

3. *Invites* the Governments of those Member States which are most affected by drug use among their child population to adopt urgent additional measures, as part of their national strategies, to prevent, reduce and eliminate drug use by children, with the aim of ensuring for children a social and family environment that will preserve their health, physical fitness and well-being;

4. *Calls upon* all States to promote the adoption, by their competent legislative organs, of measures provid-

---

[a]YUN 1959, p. 198, GA res. 1386(XIV), 19 Oct. 1959.

ing for suitably severe punishment of drug-trafficking crimes that involve children;

5.   *Urges* all Governments, competent international organizations and non-governmental organizations to give high priority, in their campaigns to prevent drug addiction among children and to rehabilitate children so addicted, to the dissemination of necessary information and the provision of appropriate advice for all sectors of their communities with regard to the serious effects of the illicit use of drugs among children, as well as to the promotion of appropriate community action;

6.   *Appeals* to the competent international agencies and the United Nations Fund for Drug Abuse Control to assign high priority to financial support for prevention campaigns and programmes to rehabilitate drug-addicted minors conducted by government bodies dealing with such matters, and also appeals to all competent international and national agencies to provide all possible support to the non-governmental organizations engaged in such action;

7.   *Requests* the Secretary-General to ensure that the Department of Public Information of the Secretariat includes in its publications, as a matter of priority, information designed to prevent the use of narcotic drugs and psychotropic substances among children.

General Assembly resolution 43/121

8 December 1988   Meeting 75   Adopted without vote

Approved by Third Committee (A/43/875) without vote, 17 November (meeting 46); 37-nation draft (A/C.3/43/L.42); agenda item 103.

Sponsors: Argentina, Austria, Bahamas, Barbados, Bolivia, Colombia, Costa Rica, Cuba, Dominican Republic, Ecuador, Germany, Federal Republic of, Ghana, Greece, Honduras, India, Indonesia, Malaysia, Mexico, Morocco, Nepal, Nicaragua, Nigeria, Norway, Pakistan, Panama, Paraguay, Peru, Philippines, Poland, Portugal, Romania, Samoa, Singapore, Turkey, Uruguay, Venezuela, Yugoslavia.

Meeting numbers. GA 43rd session: 3rd Committee 30, 32-35, 42, 46; plenary 75.

Regional issues

Africa

In its 1988 report,[8] INCB stated that drug abuse and illicit trafficking were expanding rapidly in the African region. Nationals of a large number of countries were actively participating in the traffic, which was spilling over into previously unaffected States.

Illicit cultivation of cannabis increased throughout the region. In addition to Morocco, cultivation was noted in Côte d'Ivoire, Ghana, Kenya, Madagascar, Mauritius and Nigeria, and in other parts of eastern and southern Africa. An alarming trend was the emergence in some areas of cannabis varieties with a higher content of tetrahydrocannabinol.

Heroin addiction was on the rise in many African countries, especially in Kenya, Mauritius and Nigeria. Much of the heroin, however, mainly from India and Pakistan, was trafficked onwards to markets in Europe and North America.

The appearance of cocaine in illicit African channels was another ominous development. The drug, which originated in South America, was trafficked through Côte d'Ivoire, Ghana, Morocco and Nigeria. Cocaine seizures were also reported in Cameroon, Kenya, Mali, Mauritania, Rwanda, Tunisia and some countries in the southern subregion. Nigeria also reported cases of cocaine abuse.

Psychotropic substances such as methaqualone, amphetamines, secobarbital, diazepam and flunitrazepam continued to be routed in millions of tablets to Africa's illicit markets. Although diversions of methaqualone from licit channels had almost ceased, illicit trafficking continued from clandestine laboratories in India and, recently, within Africa itself. Cases of psychotropic substance abuse were reported with increasing frequency. Enormous quantities of pemoline, a psychoactive substance not yet under international control, were being routed towards western Africa, and WHO had recommended its inclusion in Schedule IV of the 1971 Convention on Psychotropic Substances.[38]

The INCB report noted that a majority of African countries did not have effective drug control administrations. It recommended that, among other things, Governments enact adequate drug control legislation; restrict distribution channels for drugs and substances required for licit purposes; strengthen law enforcement services; and provide treatment and rehabilitation services for addicts.

The second meeting of HONLEA, Africa, was held at Dakar, Senegal (18-22 April). It recommended the establishment of regional structures for the co-ordination of drug control programmes; adherence to international drug control treaties; and the creation of national administrations to apply those treaties.

ECONOMIC AND SOCIAL COUNCIL ACTION

On 25 May, on the recommendation of its Second Committee, the Economic and Social Council adopted **resolution 1988/11** without vote.

Co-ordination of drug control activities in the African region

The Economic and Social Council,

Having examined the report of the International Narcotics Control Board for 1987, specifically paragraphs 125 to 139 concerning drug abuse and illicit trafficking in Africa,

Concerned that several States of the African region are not yet parties to the international conventions on narcotic drugs and psychotropic substances,

Also concerned at the increasing incidence of drug abuse and illicit trafficking in the African region,

Considering that there is a need to strengthen preventive arrangements and control machinery at the national and regional levels,

1.   *Calls upon* those States of the African region that have not yet done so to accede to the existing interna-

tional conventions on narcotic drugs and psychotropic substances;

2. *Requests* the Secretary-General to establish, within the limits of the resources available and within the structure of the Economic Commission for Africa, a focal point to be responsible for co-ordinating and promoting measures to combat drug misuse and abuse and illicit traffic in drugs throughout the entire African region;

3. *Urges* the States of the African region that have not yet done so to establish national agencies with responsibility for co-ordinating action to combat drug misuse and abuse and illicit traffic in drugs, in accordance with article 35 of the Single Convention on Narcotic Drugs of 1961, as amended by the 1972 Protocol Amending the Single Convention on Narcotic Drugs of 1961, and article 21 of the Convention on Psychotropic Substances of 1971;

4. *Also requests* the Secretary-General to report to the Commission on Narcotic Drugs at its thirty-third session on the measures taken to implement the present resolution.

Economic and Social Council resolution 1988/11

25 May 1988   Meeting 13   Adopted without vote

Approved by Second Committee (E/1988/87) without vote, 5 May (meeting 3); draft by Commission on Narcotic Drugs (E/1988/13); agenda item 13.

Asia

East and South-East Asia. Despite campaigns to eradicate opium poppy cultivation, opium production in the region remained high, facilitating the manufacture of heroin in clandestine laboratories operating near the borders of Burma, the Lao People's Democratic Republic and Thailand. In Thailand, opium production for the 1987/1988 crop year was estimated at 27 tonnes, and the number of heroin abusers nationally remained at between 200,000 and 300,000. Thailand continued to be a transit country for much of the opiates produced in the region. In Malaysia, opium and heroin continued to be trafficked across the northern borders and coastline. Opium and heroin from the region were also trans-shipped through Hong Kong for domestic consumption and for markets in Australia, Europe and North America. Attempts to traffic drugs through China were also reported.

Control programmes in the region resulted in the destruction of some 1,740 hectares of poppy in Thailand during the 1987/1988 crop year, and large seizures of heroin. In the Lao People's Democratic Republic, 50 illicit drug producers and traffickers were arrested and convicted in June. A Dangerous Drugs (Forfeiture of Property) Act, enacted in Malaysia, provided for the confiscation of assets derived from trafficking. The countries of the Association of South-East Asian Nations continued to strengthen drug control programmes with emphasis on the training of law enforcement and drug rehabilitation officials.

In Hong Kong, more than 400 kilograms of heroin were seized during the first half of the year, and seizures of cannabis from the Philippines as well as cannabis resin from Nepal also increased. In 1988, new regulations required that records be kept of receipts and disposals of all psychotropic substances and export declarations for substances controlled under Schedule III of the 1971 Convention on Psychotropic Substances.[38] The Dangerous Drugs Ordinance, amended in 1987, extended the presumption of trafficking in cases of possession to cocaine, amphetamines, methaqualone and quinalbarbitone.

South Asia. New regulations were enacted in India, providing for preventive detention for illicit drug activity and more stringent controls over the manufacture and movement of acetic anhydride used in the production of heroin. To combat escalating drug abuse, especially in heroin, the Government surveyed the extent of abuse, and established demand reduction programmes. In March, INCB held consultations with India on the expiration of the transitional reservations relating to the non-medical use of cannabis, and on the implementation of Economic and Social Council resolutions regarding the demand and supply of opiates for medical and scientific needs.

Bangladesh and Nepal reported an increase in drug abuse. In Nepal, the number of abusers was estimated at 20,000, most of whom were under 30 years of age. Bangladesh amended its legislation to provide severe penalties for drug offences.

Oceania

Drug abuse created a major problem in Australia, where heroin, cocaine and psychotropic substances, particularly amphetamines, remained available. Heroin was mainly trafficked from South-East Asia and the Near and Middle East, but was also locally manufactured from codeine tablets. During 1987 and the first half of 1988, approximately 7 tonnes of cannabis and 9.5 tonnes of cannabis resin were seized and four heroin and eight amphetamine laboratories were destroyed. A nation-wide cocaine data collection system to monitor the extent of abuse was being established as part of a national campaign against drug abuse, which also incorporated a strategy for the prevention and treatment of cocaine abuse.

The detection and eradication of cannabis cultivation continued in New Zealand, where cannabis abuse accounted for 90 per cent of all drug offences. The number of cocaine seizures remained significant, however, and a marked increase in the illicit traffic of lysergic acid diethylamide (LSD) was reported.

The fourteenth meeting of HONLEA, Asia and the Pacific, was held at Bangkok (3-7 October 1988).

Near and Middle East

Huge quantities of opium, heroin and cannabis resin seized within the Near and Middle East and abroad reflected the scale of the region's production. Trafficking in heroin to Europe continued, while large quantities of psychotropic substances, in particular fenetylline, were trafficked in the opposite direction. During the first half of 1988, Jordan reported seizures of more than 11,000 depressant tablets, and Kuwait more than 500,000 stimulant tablets. Also in the first six months of the year, almost half a tonne of opium was seized in Iran. Turkey remained a transit country for heroin into Europe and the Government was aware of the need to strengthen controls. Illicit cultivation of cannabis and opium poppy continued in Egypt, Lebanon and Pakistan, where opium production might have doubled during the 1987/1988 growing year.

INCB emphasized the need for financial and technical assistance from the international community to implement supply/demand reduction measures, to establish treatment and rehabilitation services in the region, and to develop co-operative drug control programmes with neighbouring countries.

The Sub-Commission on Illicit Traffic and Related Matters in the Near and Middle East held its twenty-third session in 1988 (Vienna, 3-4 February).[39] The Sub-Commission recommended that the incidence and patterns of drug abuse be studied and evaluated to provide policy guidance on effective countermeasures. It also recommended the establishment of information exchange mechanisms among local drug law enforcement authorities and a long-term international drug law enforcement training strategy to standardize training techniques, tools and materials. The Sub-Commission called on Member States to allocate more funds for United Nations drug control programmes, discussed the possible expansion of its membership and decided to refer the issue to the Commission on Narcotic Drugs. At its February session,[15] the Commission, noting the interest of Egypt, India and Jordan in full membership in the Sub-Commission, recommended to the Economic and Social Council that the membership of the Sub-Commission be enlarged.

ECONOMIC AND SOCIAL COUNCIL ACTION

On 25 May, the Economic and Social Council, on the recommendation of its Second Committee, adopted **resolution 1988/14** without vote.

Enlargement of the Sub-Commission on Illicit Drug Traffic and Related Matters in the Near and Middle East

The Economic and Social Council,

Recalling its resolution 1775 (LIV) of 18 May 1973, by which it authorized the establishment of the Sub-Commission on Illicit Drug Traffic and Related Matters in the Near and Middle East,

Taking note of the report of the Sub-Commission on its twenty-third session, particularly paragraph 8 thereof,

Noting the interest expressed at the tenth special session of the Commission on Narcotic Drugs by three States from the geographic area of the Sub-Commission in participating actively in the deliberations of the Sub-Commission,

Welcoming all forms of international co-operation at the regional level that tend to reinforce co-ordination of the fight against the illicit traffic in narcotic drugs and psychotropic substances,

1. *Decides* that the Sub-Commission on Illicit Drug Traffic and Related Matters in the Near and Middle East shall continue to meet annually at a capital in the region, whenever possible, and at the United Nations Office at Vienna prior to regular or special sessions of the Commission on Narcotic Drugs;

2. *Welcomes and authorizes* the enlargement of the Sub-Commission;

3. *Endorses* the membership of Egypt, India and Jordan in the Sub-Commission;

4. *Requests* the Secretary-General, at his discretion, to invite States outside the region that request observer status and that are actively involved in countering the illicit drug traffic in, through or from the region to send observers to the meetings of the Sub-Commission, on the understanding that the expenses would be borne by the States concerned.

Economic and Social Council resolution 1988/14

25 May 1988   Meeting 13   Adopted without vote

Approved by Second Committee (E/1988/87) without vote, 5 May (meeting 3); draft by Commission on Narcotic Drugs (E/1988/13); agenda item 13.

Europe

Eastern Europe. Although drug addiction did not constitute a major public health problem in Eastern Europe, some countries intensified activities to prevent the abuse of certain narcotic drugs and psychotropic substances diverted from local sources, and increased efforts to suppress transit traffic along the Balkan route and through the USSR. A seminar (Tashkent, USSR, June), attended by representatives of Bulgaria, Czechoslovakia, Hungary, Poland and the USSR, worked out a common approach to the assessment of drug addiction in those countries. Abuse of certain pharmaceuticals and toxic inhalants recently increased in Hungary, although the number of addicts remained small. In its efforts to curtail the abuse of alkaloid decoctions illicitly prepared from poppy straw, Poland reduced the area licensed for legitimate poppy cultivation. As a result of wide-ranging campaigns for the early identification of drug abusers, the number of registered addicts in the USSR increased to nearly 51,000. Cases of abuse of organic solvents, predominantly by teenagers, were also reported in the Soviet Union. Co-operation among Soviet, Western European and North American authorities resulted in the confiscation of several tonnes of cannabis and the arrest of some major traffickers.

Western Europe. Drug abuse and illicit trafficking remained widespread throughout the region, leading to a sharp increase in drug-related deaths, mainly from heroin and psychoactive substances. Cocaine seizures were on the rise, and a number of coca paste–refining laboratories were detected and destroyed in Spain. There were indications that the abuse of cannabis was stabilizing or in decline in most Western European countries but the quantity of heroin seized increased. Psychotropic substances were trafficked from the region to other parts of the world in large quantities, and some substances of licit origin, including diazepam, flunitrazepam and benzodiazepines, were increasingly abused in Western Europe itself. The abuse of stimulants and amphetamines in particular was a major concern in Scandinavian countries, where the average age of abusers declined. An INCB study revealed that large amounts of phenobarbital manufactured in Europe were exported to Afghanistan and Pakistan to be used as an adulterant for heroin.

There were a number of legislative initiatives on drug control. On 31 December 1987, France made it illegal to aid and abet the laundering of funds derived from drug trafficking. In March 1988, Spain extended the scope of its penal laws to investigate bank accounts and confiscate assets from trafficking. Similar provisions had been introduced earlier by Italy, Portugal and the United Kingdom, and most other Western European countries were preparing legislative amendments to the same effect.

North America

In 1988, new legislation was enacted in the United States to provide additional education, treatment and rehabilitation programmes as well as stringent new penalties for both drug traffickers and users. It established the cabinet-level post of Director of National Drug Control Policy and created a system of recording and tracing sales by United States manufacturers of specific chemicals and precursors used to process raw materials into drugs. A survey among high-school and college students showed a 20 per cent decline in cocaine abuse, although the quantity of cocaine seized was on the rise. Seizures of heroin remained at the same level as in 1987. Cannabis eradication activities continued throughout the country, together with the confiscation of drug traffickers' assets. During the year, the United States participated in a number of international enforcement operations which seriously disrupted organized drug trafficking and resulted in substantial seizures of assets.

Cannabis and its derivatives continued to be the most abused drugs in Canada, but cocaine abuse was increasing. Ample quantities of heroin were available on the illicit market, and the clandestine manufacture of some psychotropic substances continued. Canada expanded its drug control programmes and increased their emphasis on financial aspects of drug trafficking.

In Mexico, opium poppy cultivation was expanded, with smaller fields being planted in remote areas at high altitude to reduce the effectiveness of aerial eradication efforts. Despite severe economic problems, Mexico gave the highest priority to its drug law enforcement campaign and dedicated an increasing percentage of its budget to that goal. The Mexican armed forces became more involved in drug control efforts, with 25,000 soldiers engaged full time in manual eradication. During the first half of 1988, nearly 1,500 hectares of opium poppy and 1,000 hectares of cannabis were destroyed manually and by aerial spraying. The Mexican navy conducted interdiction operations in territorial waters and was responsible for crop eradication in some coastal areas. A number of major traffickers were arrested during the year, and there were significant seizures of assets.

Latin America and the Caribbean

Increasing drug abuse and the expansion of illicit production and trafficking, mainly of cocaine, affected more and more countries in Latin America and the Caribbean in 1988. Despite eradication efforts, illicit coca cultivation spread significantly in the Andean countries and elsewhere in the region. In response, national authorities intensified their anti-drug activities with: coca and cannabis eradication campaigns; co-ordinated drug seizure operations; treatment and rehabilitation programmes for drug abusers; and strengthened banking regulations for the seizure of traffickers' assets. Several countries placed precursors—essential chemicals and solvents used in the illicit manufacture of cocaine—under control. Bolivia and Peru, the world's two main coca-producing countries, made further inroads on the vast and uncontrolled cultivation of the coca bush with the aim of reducing production to levels required for legitimate medical and industrial purposes. Bolivia prohibited all coca bush cultivation in excess of 12,000 hectares, and encouraged crop substitution in areas of excessive production. In Peru, authorities eradicated nearly 700 hectares of illicit coca, destroyed 30 laboratories and seized more than 2 tonnes of coca paste during the first half of 1988. Other efforts included the development of drug interdiction programmes for the pan-American and central highways as well as for the Amazon River and its principal tributaries, and a drug prevention curriculum for public schools.

Enforcement operations and the aerial eradication of cannabis in Colombia resulted in increased seizures of clandestine laboratories and cocaine base. Aerial reconnaissance established that almost all coca cultivation had been destroyed in Ecuador. However, Ecuador remained a major transit country and drug abuse was rapidly increasing, particularly in the coastal areas. Large-scale cannabis cultivation and trafficking continued in Paraguay, which also served as a transit country for cocaine from Bolivia. A conference was held in July to heighten public awareness of drug issues.

In Central America and the Caribbean, 211 hectares of illicitly cultivated opium poppy were destroyed in Guatemala, and nearly 400 drug-related arrests were made in Belize during the first half of the year. Panama reported seizures of drugs in transit and of chemicals. The Caribbean, with free ports and insufficiently strict banking controls in some countries, provided ready facilities for international drug trafficking and money-laundering. Cocaine trafficking via the Bahamas to the United States was on the rise, but there was a marked decline in cannabis traffic. Local cocaine and cannabis abuse increased alarmingly, and the Board sent a mission to the Bahamas at the invitation of its Government late in the year. Jamaica continued intensive cannabis eradication operations and took action to combat the violation of its airspace by traffickers. Illegal airstrips were destroyed and, in July, the Government announced plans for legislation to permit the seizure of traffickers' assets.

The second meeting of HONLEA, Latin America and the Caribbean, was held at Lima, Peru (12-16 September 1988).

Conventions

INCB reported that, during 1988, Somalia, Uganda and the United Arab Emirates acceded to the 1961 Single Convention on Narcotic Drugs,[21] bringing the total number of States parties to the Convention in its original or amended forms to 125.[35] Since the Board's last report, the German Democratic Republic and Uganda became parties to the 1972 Protocol[40] amending the Convention, bringing the number of States parties to 81. The number of States parties to the 1971 Convention on Psychotropic Substances[38] rose to 92, with the adherence in 1988 of Canada, Czechoslovakia, Uganda and the United Arab Emirates.

INCB noted that certain control measures required for psychotropic substances under the 1971 Convention had not yet been adequately implemented due to human resource and financial difficulties in national drug control administrations. To improve the monitoring of international trade and reduce the diversion of psychotropic substances into illicit channels, INCB recommended the extension of the import/export authorization system.

The Commission on Narcotic Drugs, on 8 February, decided that acetyl-alpha-methylfentanyl,[41] alpha-methylfentanyl,[42] 3-methylfentanyl,[43] 1-phenethyl-4-phenyl-4-piperidinol acetate (ester) (also referred to as PEPAP)[44] and 1-methyl-4-phenyl-4-piperidinol propionate (ester) (also referred to as MPPP)[45] should be included in Schedules I and IV of the Single Convention on Narcotic Drugs. It also decided that methamphetamine racemate[46] should be included in Schedule II of the Convention on Psychotropic Substances, and that 5-allyl-5-(1-methylbutyl) barbituric acid (secobarbital)[47] should be transferred from Schedule III to Schedule II of that Convention.

On the same date, the Commission decided,[48] in accordance with article 3, paragraph 4, of the Convention on Psychotropic Substances, to terminate in part the exemptions granted by Finland to the preparations of Gastrodyn comp. and Trimigrin, so that the requirements of article 8, paragraph 1, and of article 11, paragraph 5, should also apply to those two preparations.

Organizational questions

Commission on Narcotic Drugs

The Commission on Narcotic Drugs held its tenth special session at Vienna from 8 to 19 February 1988.[15]

On 25 May, by **decision 1988/119**, the Economic and Social Council took note of the Commission's report on its tenth special session.

Also on 25 May, the Council, by **decision 1988/118**, extended the duration of the Commission's thirty-third (1989) session to 10 working days and included in its agenda an item on the development and promotion of more effective action against illicit drug trafficking through regional cooperation in drug law enforcement.

Functioning of the Commission
and its subsidiary bodies

In 1987,[49] the Economic and Social Council established a Special Commission on the In-depth Study of the United Nations Intergovernmental Structure and Functions in the Economic and Social Fields and requested all subsidiary bodies of the General Assembly and the Council to submit to the Special Commission their views and proposals on the recommendations of the 1986 Group of High-level Intergovernmental Experts to Review the Efficiency of the Administrative and Financial Functioning of the United Nations[50] regarding their functioning. On 19 February,[51] responding to that request, the Commission on Narcotic Drugs transmitted to the Special Commission its views and proposals on its functioning and that of its subsidiary machinery. It considered that there was no need to change the functioning or to amend the existing terms of reference or reporting channels of the Commission on Narcotic Drugs or its subsidiary organs, but decided to keep its functioning under continuous review for possible improvement.

International Narcotics Control Board

In 1988, INCB held its forty-third and forty-fourth sessions at Vienna, from 24 May to 3 June and from 10 to 21 October, respectively.

On 25 May, by **decision 1988/117**, the Economic and Social Council took note of the INCB report for 1987.[52]

REFERENCES

[1]A/43/770. [2]YUN 1979, p. 933, GA res. 34/177, 17 Dec. 1979. [3]YUN 1987, p. 900. [4]*Ibid.*, p. 904. [5]*Ibid.*, p. 901. [6]A/AC.51/1988/5. [7]A/43/16. [8]*Report of the International Narcotics Control Board for 1988* (E/INCB/1988/1), Sales No. E.88.XI.4. [9]E/1988/13 (res. 4(S-X)). [10]A/43/684. [11]YUN 1987, p. 912, GA res. 42/113, 7 Dec. 1987. [12]*Ibid.*, p. 902, GA res. 42/112, 7 Dec. 1987. [13]E/CN.7/1988/4. [14]E/CN.7/1988/4/Add.1-3. [15]E/1988/13. [16]A/43/679. [17]ACC/1988/PG/3. [18]ACC/1988/PG/10. [19]YUN 1986, p. 864, ESC res. 1986/9, 21 May 1986. [20]YUN 1987, p. 908, ESC res. 1987/31, 26 May 1987. [21]YUN 1961, p. 382. [22]E/1988/13 (res. 1(S-X)). [23]*Ibid.* (res. 2(S-X)). [24]*Ibid.* (res. 3(S-X)). [25]YUN 1987, p. 911, GA res. 42/111, 7 Dec. 1987. [26]*Ibid.*, p. 909. [27]*Ibid.*, p. 911. [28]E/CN.7/1988/2 (Part IV) & Corr.1,2 & Add.1. [29]E/CN.7/1988/2 (Part III) & Add.1,2. [30]E/CN.7/1988/2 (Part I) & Corr.1. [31]E/CONF.82/3. [32]A/43/678. [33]A/44/572. [34]E/CONF.82/15. [35]*Multilateral Treaties Deposited with the Secretary-General: Status as at 31 December 1988* (ST/LEG/SER.E/7), Sales No. E.89.V.3. [36]E/CONF.82/14. [37]E/CN.7/1988/3. [38]YUN 1971, p. 380. [39]E/CN.7/1988/13. [40]YUN 1972, p. 397. [41]E/1988/13 (dec. 1(S-X)). [42]*Ibid.* (dec. 2(S-X)). [43]*Ibid.* (dec. 3(S-X)). [44]*Ibid.* (dec. 4(S-X)). [45]*Ibid.* (dec. 5(S-X)). [46]*Ibid.* (dec. 7(S-X)). [47]*Ibid.* (dec. 6(S-X)). [48]*Ibid.* (dec. 8(S-X)). [49]YUN 1987, p. 948, ESC dec. 1987/112, 6 Feb. 1987. [50]YUN 1986, p. 1024, GA res. 41/213, 19 Dec. 1986. [51]E/1988/13 (dec. 9(S-X)). [52]YUN 1987, p. 903.

Chapter XVII

Statistics

During 1988, the Statistical Office of the United Nations continued to focus on further developing the System of National Accounts, revising and harmonizing international economic classifications, improving the demographic, social and environment statistics of developing countries and pursuing its technical co-operation activities, particularly training activities related to a future population and housing census.

In June, the Sub-Committee on Statistical Activities of the Administrative Committee on Co-ordination discussed policy issues and other matters relating to United Nations statistical activities. The Secretary-General issued a number of reports for consideration by the Statistical Commission in 1989. The Commission, which meets biennially, did not meet in 1988.

In July, the Economic and Social Council, in **decision 1988/181**, took note of a number of reports on international economic and social policy, including regional and sectoral developments, which were of relevance to the United Nations work in the field of statistics.

UN statistical bodies

ACC Sub-Committee

The Sub-Committee on Statistical Activities of the Administrative Committee on Co-ordination (ACC) (twenty-second session, Geneva, 6-10 June 1988)[1] considered co-ordination questions related to work being planned or carried out by the organizations of the United Nations system. They included the processing and dissemination of trade statistics, publication and dissemination policy, revision of the System of National Accounts (SNA), service statistics, indicative patterns of consumption, population and housing censuses, tourism and migration statistics, social statistics and indicators, environment statistics, status in employment classification, price statistics, harmonization of economic classifications, co-ordination of technical co-operation in statistics and co-ordination of *ad hoc* statistical inquiries to countries from non-statistical units of international organizations.

The Sub-Committee also considered the National Household Survey Capability Programme, the Living Standards Measurement Study and the Social Dimensions of Adjustment Study. It reviewed the base year for statistics, the Directory of United Nations Serial Publications and the functioning of the ACC machinery. In addition, it reviewed inter-agency inputs into preparations for the twenty-fifth (1989) session of the Statistical Commission.

The Sub-Committee agreed that, in the light of technological changes, high priority should be given to the intensification of co-operation with respect to data dissemination policies and practices. It considered as one of its objectives the achievement of a consistent dissemination policy among international organizations to ensure that their statistical data were available to as wide a range of users as possible.

Economic statistics

Energy, environment and industry statistics

An October report by the Secretary-General[2] outlined progress made by the Statistical Office in energy and industry statistics since the 1987 session of the Statistical Commission.

As a follow-up to its activities in new and renewable sources of energy, the Office prepared a project proposal to assist developing countries in expanding and improving their statistical data base for energy planning. Funds were being sought for the project, which was expected to be co-ordinated with regional projects of a similar nature. In the area of training, two workshops on energy statistics methodology were planned for China.

In the area of industrial statistics, a new computerized system was created to compile, process and disseminate the results of the 1983 world programme in industrial statistics. A review of the industrial statistics programme was being conducted to identify additional indicators suitable for the annual data collection. The data were being sought by supplementary questionnaires, and, as at March 1988, 83 additional tables had been supplied by developing countries.

In a report on environment statistics in 1988,[3] the Secretary-General described the Statistical Office's ongoing methodological work, which focused on the preparation of *A Framework for the Development of Environment Statistics*[4] and technical reports on statistics of the environmental aspects of human settlements and of the natural environment. *Concepts and Methods of Environment Statistics: Human Settlements Statistics—A Technical Report*[5] was published and a report on statistics of the natural environment was in the process of preparation.

The Office, following a recommendation by the SNA expert group meeting on production accounts and input-output tables (see below) that environmental accounts be developed as satellite accounts to SNA, elaborated a framework for environmental accounts. This was discussed at a joint United Nations Environment Programme/World Bank expert group meeting on environmental accounting and SNA (Paris, 21 and 22 November), which made recommendations on the structure, concepts and classifications of an environmental accounting framework.

The development of the proposed global programme of environment statistics continued. In this regard, the Office revised past and current activities of the regional commissions and other international organizations. The Office did not envisage any comprehensive data collection at the global level until a sufficient number of regional and national programmes of environment statistics had been established.

National accounts and balances

The Secretary-General submitted a progress report on the revision of the System of National Accounts, which continued to be co-ordinated, planned and organized by the Inter-Secretariat Working Group on National Accounts, composed of the Statistical Office of the United Nations and those of the Organisation for Economic Co-operation and Development, the European Communities, the International Monetary Fund (IMF), the World Bank and the United Nations regional commissions.

Global expert meetings were held on public sector accounts (Washington, D.C., 25-29 January), which made recommendations to harmonize SNA guidelines with IMF government finance statistics; on production accounts and input-output tables (Vienna, 21-30 March), which made recommendations to redefine concepts relating to statistical units, taxes and secondary products, to make them more operational; and on financial flows and balances (Washington, D.C., 6-14 September), which made recommendations on redefining the financial sector to reflect new developments in financial institutions, markets and instruments and give new guidelines on national and sectoral balance sheets.

Work on preparation of the first draft of the revised SNA commenced and the Inter-Secretariat Working Group (Washington, D.C., 16 and 17 September) discussed the first set of chapters and reviewed those SNA issues remaining to be resolved. The Group also prepared a work programme for further work on SNA.

During 1988, the Statistical Office continued work on links between SNA and the System of Balances of the National Economy (MPS) with special attention to the problems linking the concepts and classifications of the two systems.[7] Both national accounting systems underwent intensive development processes. A revised version of MPS was published and implementation of the changes started. However, progress on linking was limited in the revision of a publication on comparisons of SNA and MPS.

A note by the Secretary-General[8] outlined the direction of the work related to MPS carried out by the Standing Commission for Co-operation in the Field of Statistics of the Council for Mutual Economic Assistance (CMEA), in particular with respect to the development of a unified methodology for the computation of gross domestic product for CMEA member countries and the adaptation of the updated MPS for the improvement and elaboration of the methodology used in international comparisons of the major indicators of the development of the economies of CMEA countries.

Price statistics

The Statistical Office continued to co-ordinate the International Comparison Programme (ICP), involving comparisons in price statistics, used for assessing the relative economic development of countries. A report by the Secretary-General[9] indicated that progress achieved in phase V of ICP was slower than expected in 1988. In particular, difficulties were encountered with respect to core comparisons. Concerning the methodology of ICP, a compromise agreement was reached by international organizations on the question of fixity, and an expert group on ICP met (Luxembourg, 6-10 June) to review the entire methodology in the light of the experiences of regionalization and the method of aggregation to be used. Plans and prospects for phase VI of ICP were also elaborated.

Service statistics

Although the increasing importance of the service sector in the world economy, particularly in production and trade, had been widely recognized, statistics on services, in both developed and developing countries, needed significant improvement. That need for better statistics in the field of international trade in services became apparent in the framework of the Uruguay Round of multilateral trade negotiations (see PART THREE, Chapter IV). The Secretary-General, in an October report,[10] informed of the activities of the Statistical Office, which had allocated special priority to the development of statistics in services, both in collecting information on national practices and in elaborating classifications, the conceptual background and various organizational and methodological problems. In particular, the Office circulated a questionnaire to national statistical offices on the collection, availability and use of service statistics. The report also outlined a programme of work at the international level covering the next several years and proposed the creation of an intersecretariat working group on service statistics within the framework of the ACC Sub-Committee on Statistical Activities.

The third meeting of the Voorburg Group on service statistics (Wiesbaden, Federal Republic of Germany, 4-6 October 1988) discussed statistics of trade in services and the problems of quantity and price indices of services. The Group agreed to continue its activities in view of the many unresolved problems in services statistics and the limitations on the development of a methodology.

Preliminary summaries of the United Nations/IMF survey on trade in services statistics and on the United Nations survey on quantity and price indices of services were prepared and circulated to national statistical offices.

Trade statistics

Consequent to Standard International Trade Classification (SITC) Revision 3, work was completed on a classification by broad economic categories—defined in terms of SITC Revision 3—and volume I of the commodity indexes for SITC Revision 3 was planned to be completed by the end of 1988.

The Statistical Office continued work on volume II of *Methods Used in Compiling the United Nations Price Indexes for External Trade*, covering descriptions of the unit value and quantum indexes of exports of machinery and transport equipment, manufactured goods, fuel, and raw materials and imports of minerals, fuel and related materials and exports and imports of market economies.

A draft description of the methodology for the indexes for exports of manufactured goods was compiled, and work continued on describing the methodologies for other indexes and on improving the index of machinery and transport equipment.

International economic classifications

The Secretary-General submitted in October 1988 a progress report on the harmonization of international economic classifications.[11] The report indicated that the final draft of the third revision of the International Standard Industrial Classification (ISIC) of all economic activities,[12] used both nationally and internationally in classifying data according to economic activity in the fields of population, production, employment, national income and other economic statistics, was completed and circulated. The final draft (provisional) of the Central Product Classification (CPC),[13] providing a framework for international comparison of statistics dealing with goods, services and

assets, was also completed. Both documents were being considered by countries and international organizations to ensure harmonization between national and various international economic classifications. The report also summarized some conceptual issues relating to ISIC and CPC dealing with non-transportable goods and services.

The third United Nations Expert Group Meeting on Harmonization of Economic Classifications (New York, 25-29 April) agreed to recommend the two documents to the Statistical Commission for approval in 1989. The Group also pointed out the need to maintain co-ordination among the classifications, including the procedures to maintain and update ISIC and CPC as well as the Harmonized Commodity Description and Coding System of the Customs Co-Operation Council. The Group made proposals on how to develop the explanatory notes for the services part of CPC, which were taken up by the Statistical Office. It was expected that draft explanatory notes would be available to the Commission in 1989.

Social and demographic statistics

Social indicators

The Secretary-General submitted in December 1988 a report on current activities in international work on social statistics.[14] The report reviewed recent work on general sources and methods and on indicators in selected subject-matter fields, as reported by international agencies, and described methods and objectives of current international work on social and related statistical classifications. In particular, it described the key roles of the United Nations framework for the integration of social, demographic and related statistics and of the illustrative basic classifications for indicators in the United Nations *Handbook on Social Indicators*. It outlined the current work of the Statistical Office on the development of statistics and indicators on women and special population groups and on international compilation and dissemination of social statistics. In addition, the United Nations Department of Technical Co-operation for Development (DTCD) and the Statistical Office, in co-operation with other interested offices and organizations, implemented an active programme of technical co-operation and training in developing countries in social statistics and indicators, especially concerning the situation of women and disabled persons.

In another report,[15] the Secretary-General provided information on work undertaken by the Statistical Office and the International Research and Training Institute for the Advancement of Women towards the preparation of a technical report on the development of statistical concepts and methods and their relation to the SNA, to assist countries to compile statistics systematically so as to identify and measure women's contribution to the economy.

The International Labour Office also submitted a report[16] on the International Classification of Status in Employment (ICSE). It examined the departures in national practice from the existing international classification, discussed some problems of concept and application, and made proposals for future work on a possible revision of ICSE.

Population and housing census

In an October report,[2] the Secretary-General described the developments which had occurred and the preparations made by the Statistical Office, regional commissions and countries towards carrying out a population and housing census in the 1990s. In an annex to the report, a census calendar was presented indicating dates of national population and/or housing censuses taken or anticipated during the decade 1985-1994.

Supplementary principles and recommendations for population and housing censuses were being finalized for publication, and the International Labour Organisation adopted the revised International Standard Classification of Occupations.

The regional commissions for Asia and the Pacific, for Latin America and the Caribbean, for Africa and for Europe held meetings to review or evaluate national experiences in conducting the 1980 censuses in order to achieve further improvements in the quality and coverage of censuses, and to consider recommendations for the 1990 round of censuses.

Civil registration and vital statistics

A proposal for an International Programme for Accelerating the Improvement of Vital Statistics and Civil Registration Systems, developed by the Statistical Office, the World Health Organization and the International Institute for Vital Registration and Statistics, was prepared and forwarded to several international organizations for comment.

The programme would help to promote, support and encourage developing countries in accelerating the development and improvement of their civil registration and vital statistics systems during the 1990s, so that they would become a component of the socio-demographic data base needed for monitoring population trends and development.

Patterns of consumption

The Secretary-General and the United Nations Research Institute for Social Development re-ported on the development of indicators on patterns of consumption: qualitative aspects of development.[17] The report summarized the work undertaken on three national case-studies and the responses of Governments to the inquiry by the Secretariat on their experiences and views, including information provided on data sources, dissemination and timeliness of socio-economic indicators on patterns of consumption.

National Household Survey Capability Programme

In a November 1988 report,[18] the Secretary-General submitted proposals on the long-range future of the National Household Survey Capability Programme (NHSCP). The report described the progress made in programme implementation and arrangements for programme co-ordination and management. It reviewed NHSCP training activities and the execution of technical studies. The work programme for the biennium 1989-1990 was also outlined. A draft plan of operations, providing for the extension of NHSCP through 1991 and containing suggestions on possible avenues for development beyond 1991, was presented to the Programme Review Committee.

World Bank household survey initiatives

A World Bank report[19] reviewed its initiatives in the design and implementation of permanent integrated household surveys: the Living Standards Measurement Study (LSMS) programme, aimed at providing the means of assessing living standards in developing countries, and the Social Dimensions of Adjustment (SDA) programme, designed to assist in minimizing the impact of macro-economic adjustment measures on sub-Saharan Africa. The report provided the rationale and background for the two initiatives, reviewed and evaluated LSMS surveys and detailed the orientations of the SDA project and its organizational and operational status. The report also described steps taken by the Bank to coordinate its activities with those of other international agencies, including NHSCP.

Other statistical activities

Technical co-operation

The Secretary-General summarized the technical co-operation programmes in statistics of organizations of the United Nations system and several multilateral and bilateral organizations outside the system for the period 1985-1988.[20] DTCD and the regional commissions assisted developing countries to strengthen and extend national services and capabilities for collecting, processing, disseminating and using a broad range of development-related statistics. Projects covered such topics as general economic statistics and national accounts, social and demographic statistics, statistics on women and special population groups and integrated statistical services. The main activities of DTCD in 1988 included work related to the 1990 round of population and housing censuses, the promotion of NHSCP, assisting developing countries least advanced in statistics and promoting the use of microcomputers in statistical work.[21]

In 1988, the total United Nations technical cooperation programme in statistics provided technical support for the formulation and execution of country projects at an estimated cost of $24 million.

Special issues

In a report on the current state of statistics and statistical development in developing countries,[22] the Secretary-General presented an overview of long-term trends in statistical development and reviewed national experiences in carrying out selected major statistical activities through the relevant regional commissions and specialized agencies. The report concluded that the overall availability of data from developing countries had improved, but, although achievements had been considerable and had contributed to capability-building, they had not been the same for all developing countries. Moreover, the amount of external resources devoted to statistical development had generally formed a minor part of technical cooperation efforts of multilateral and bilateral agencies. Accordingly, the report proposed strategies for accelerating statistical development and for better mobilizing needed human and financial resources.

Programme questions

In an overall review of the statistical activities of the United Nations system, the World Tourism Organization and the Inter-American Statistical Institute for the period 1986 to mid-1988,[23] the Secretary-General described major achievements, activities cancelled and those significantly modified. The Secretary-General also submitted updated information on the work of the Statistical Office[24] and reports on recurrent statistical publications of the United Nations,[25] on the recruitment and selection of professional staff for work in national statistical offices and statistical services of the United Nations,[26] and on the proposed work programme of the Statistical Office for 1990-1991 and the preliminary proposals for the medium-term plan for 1992-1997.[27]

REFERENCES

[1]ACC/1988/PG/11. [2]E/CN.3/1989/15. [3]E/CN.3/1989/13. [4]*A Framework for the Development of Environment Statistics*, Sales No. E.84.XVII.12. [5]*Concepts and Methods of Environment Statistics: Human Settlements Statistics—A Technical Report* (ST/ESA/STAT/SER.F/51), Sales No. E.88.XVII.14. [6]E/CN.3/1989/4. [7]E/CN.3/1989/6. [8]E/CN.3/1989/5 & Corr.1. [9]E/CN.3/1989/10. [10]A/CN.3/1989/7. [11]E/CN.3/1989/8. [12]ST/ESA/STAT/SER.M/4/Rev.3 & Add.1,2. [13]ST/ESA/STAT/SER.M/77 & Add.1. [14]E/CN.3/1989/11. [15]E/CN.3/1989/12. [16]E/CN.3/1989/9. [17]E/CN.3/1989/14. [18]E/CN.3/1989/18. [19]E/CN.3/1989/19. [20]E/CN.3/1989/16. [21]DP/1989/46/Add.1. [22]E/CN.3/1989/17. [23]E/CN.3/1989/21. [24]E/CN.3/1989/22. [25]E/CN.3/1989/3. [26]E/CN.3/1989/2. [27]E/CN.3/1989/24.

OTHER PUBLICATIONS

Development of Statistical Concepts and Methods on Disability for Household Surveys, Sales No. E.88.XVII.4. *Handbook of National Accounting: Public Sector Accounts*, Sales No. E.88.XVII.5. *Improving Statistics and Indicators on Women Using Household Surveys*, Sales No. E.88.XVII.11. *United Nations Disability Statistics Data Base 1975-1986: Technical Manual*, Sales No. E.88.XVII.12. *Demographic Yearbook 1988*, Sales No. E/F.89.XIII.1. *Energy Statistics Yearbook, 1988* (ST/ESA/STAT/SER.J/32), Sales No. E/F.90.XVII.4. *International Trade Statistics Yearbook, 1988*, vols. I and II (ST/ESA/STAT/SER.6/37 & Add.1), Sales No. E/F.90.XVII.6. *Industrial Statistics Yearbook, 1988*, vol. I: *General Industrial Statistics* (ST/ESA/STAT/SER.P/28 (vol. I)), Sales No. E.90.XVII.12; vol. II: *Commodity Production Statistics* (ST/ESA/STAT/SER.P/28 (vol. II)), Sales No. E/F.90.XVII.13. *Energy Balances and Electricity Profiles, 1988* (ST/ESA/STAT/SER.W/5), Sales No. E/F.90.XVII.15. *National Accounts Statistics: Main Aggregates and Detailed Tables, 1988*, vols. I and II, Sales No. E.90.XVII.18. *Compendium of Social Statistics and Indicators, 1988*, Sales No. E/F.91.XVII.6. *Commodity Trade Statistics*, vol. XXXVIII (ST/ESA/STAT/SER.D/103).

Chapter XVIII

Institutional arrangements

In 1988, a Special Commission of the Economic and Social Council completed an in-depth study of the United Nations intergovernmental structure and functions in the economic and social fields. The Chairman of the Commission reported that it had diagnosed the problems but much ground remained to be covered on the means for effective and practical reform.

In December, the General Assembly adopted resolution 43/174 reviewing the efficiency of the administrative and financial functioning of the United Nations in the economic and social fields and requesting the Secretary-General to seek the views of all Member States.

The Economic and Social Council, meanwhile, reviewed its structure and functioning. In July, the Council adopted resolution 1988/77, which set forth measures aimed at revitalizing its policy formulation, monitoring, operational activities, co-ordination, working methods and organization of work. The Council also adopted guidelines for the selection of subjects for and the timing of international decades and the procedures for proclaiming them (1988/63).

The Administrative Committee on Co-ordination (ACC) and the Committee for Programme and Co-ordination (CPC) held Joint Meetings in July on the response of the United Nations system to development problems.

Restructuring questions

Report of the Secretary-General. In an April 1988 progress report,[1] the Secretary-General described action he had taken to implement recommendation 25 of the Group of High-level Intergovernmental Experts to Review the Efficiency of the Administrative and Financial Functioning of the United Nations. Recommendation 25, relating to economic and social matters, was one of 60 recommendations aimed at the reform and renewal of the United Nations, adopted by the General Assembly in 1986.[2] The Secretary-General stated that the Secretariat had reviewed its programmes but would await the outcome of the in-depth study being conducted by the Special Commission of the Economic and Social Council before making specific recommendations. The Special Commission was

established in 1987 to study the United Nations intergovernmental structure and functions in the economic and social fields. The Secretary-General said that the Secretariat's programme review had indicated that there was less overlapping of analytical work being done on the world economy than had been suggested, but that there was room for streamlining activities such as the short- to medium-term analysis of the economic situation and prospects. He said that more emphasis would be given to regular monitoring and the integrated study of major economic, social and environmental trends, as well as to substantive and operational activities within the Secretariat in some fields. Consultations were taking place among the entities concerned to streamline their activities and strengthen co-operation. In this context, the Department of International Economic and Social Affairs and the United Nations Conference on Trade and Development (UNCTAD) had identified possibilities for strengthening their co-operation in analytical work on the world economy and in the development of data bases for that purpose. They were also changing their internal structures to give greater focus and coherence to their responses to intergovernmental mandates. A study was also being carried out on the future role and activities of the regional commissions.

In a later report[3] to the Fifth (Administrative and Budgetary) Committee, the Secretary-General reported on the implementation of recommendation 29 of the Group of High-level Intergovernmental Experts. As requested by the Assembly in 1987,[4] he reviewed his decision to assign to the Office of the Under-Secretary-General for Political and General Assembly Affairs and Secretariat Services the functions of the Office of Secretariat Services for Economic and Social Matters relating to the technical secretariat servicing of intergovernmental and related meetings and special conferences. He concluded, after considering the recommendations of the Experts and those of the Assembly on restructuring the economic and social sectors of the United Nations system, that the goal of avoiding duplication and of ensuring effective servicing of intergovernmental meetings and conferences could best be achieved by consolidating the related technical servicing functions in one office, as he had done.

CPC action. CPC considered the report of the Secretary-General and recommended that he keep the matter under review, taking fully into account the outcome of the in-depth study of the United

Nations intergovernmental structure and functions in the economic and social fields.[5]

Special Commission's study. In accordance with a 1987 Economic and Social Council decision,[6] a Special Commission of the Council submitted in June 1988 a report[7] on the in-depth study of the United Nations intergovernmental structure and functions in the economic and social fields. The study had been called for in 1986 by the General Assembly,[2] which approved the recommendations of the Group of 18 to improve the Organization's administrative and financing functions. The in-depth study (recommendation 8)[8] was a priority recommendation.

The Special Commission, which met in New York between 2 March 1987 and 23 May 1988, was attended by the representatives and observers of 104 States, eight specialized agencies, the International Atomic Energy Agency, the European Community and two non-governmental organizations (NGOs)—the International Chamber of Commerce and the International Confederation of Free Trade Unions.

Its report covered the work of nine sessions which, among other things, considered the organization of the Commission's work and methodology for the study; reviewed informal working papers prepared by the Secretariat; established an informal working group of the whole for an exchange of views on the functioning of the General Assembly and the Economic and Social Council; was briefed on consultations held with executive heads of United Nations organizations; approved a programme of work for 1988; reviewed the functioning of individual bodies of the United Nations in the economic, social and related fields; and requested that the Chairman prepare a consolidated discussion paper on proposals related to the functioning of those bodies. The paper was issued on 21 April and was the subject of informal consultations. On 29 April, the Commission requested the Chairman to prepare a text on its draft conclusions and recommendations. The Chairman stated that the Commission had diagnosed the problems, but because there was insufficient common ground on various issues, he would have to exercise his judgement in putting together a balanced package for possible implementation.

At the ninth session (2-6, 11 and 23 May), the Commission had before it the Chairman's text. On 11 May, the Chairman informed members of the outcome of informal consultations on the draft conclusions and recommendations, during which sentiments had been expressed that the divergent views on major outstanding issues could not be reconciled. The Chairman said that while this was disappointing, he could not impose an agreement on Commission members.

On 24 May, the Economic and Social Council, by **decision 1988/112**, took note of an oral pro-gress report made on 13 May by the Chairman of the Special Commission on the in-depth study. On 29 July, by **decision 1988/182**, the Council took note of the report of the Special Commission on the in-depth study and transmitted it to the General Assembly for consideration at its 1988 session.

GENERAL ASSEMBLY ACTION

On 9 December 1988, the General Assembly adopted without vote **resolution 43/174**.

Review of the efficiency of the administrative and financial functioning of the United Nations in the economic and social fields

The General Assembly,

Recalling its resolutions 32/197 of 20 December 1977 on the restructuring of the economic and social sectors of the United Nations system, 41/213 of 19 December 1986 on the review of the efficiency of the administrative and financial functioning of the United Nations, 42/170 of 11 December 1987 on the implementation of General Assembly resolution 41/213 in the economic and social fields, and 42/211 of 21 December 1987 on the implementation of General Assembly resolution 41/213,

Recalling also Economic and Social Council resolution 1988/77 of 29 July 1988 on the revitalization of the Council,

Emphasizing that the financial stability of the Organization will facilitate the orderly, balanced and well co-ordinated implementation of resolution 41/213 in all its parts,

Emphasizing also that the work of the United Nations should be enhanced and streamlined in order to make the United Nations more effective and responsive to the needs of Member States, particularly developing countries,

Conscious of the fact that the reform of the economic and social sectors of the United Nations is a continuing process aimed at strengthening the effectiveness of the United Nations in dealing with those issues and requires further attention,

Taking note of the report of the Special Commission of the Economic and Social Council on the In-depth Study of the United Nations Intergovernmental Structure and Functions in the Economic and Social Fields and its Secretariat support structures, and recognizing that, although the Special Commission had conducted the in-depth study entrusted to it, the Special Commission was unable to reach agreed recommendations,

1. *Stresses* the common interest of all countries in the effective functioning of the United Nations in the economic and social fields so that it is more responsive not only to current issues, but also to emerging problems and issues, particularly those related to the development of developing countries;

2. *Requests* the Secretary-General to consult with all Member States and seek their views on ways and means of achieving a balanced and effective implementation of recommendations 2 and 8 of the Group of High-level Intergovernmental Experts to Review the Efficiency of the Administrative and Financial Functioning of the United Nations, taking into consideration all relevant reports, including the report of the Special Commission of the Economic and Social Council on the In-depth Study of the United Nations Intergovernmental Structure and Functions in the Economic and Social Fields, as well as the outcome of the discussions in 1989 on the revitalization

of the Economic and Social Council, and to submit to the General Assembly at its forty-fourth session a detailed report in order to enable Member States to consider and take appropriate action with a view to enhancing the effectiveness of the intergovernmental structure and its Secretariat support structures as well as programme delivery in the economic and social fields;

3. *Decides* to consider, at its forty-fourth session, the report of the Secretary-General called for in paragraph 2 above, and his final report on the implementation of resolution 41/213, under the item entitled "Review of the efficiency of the administrative and financial functioning of the United Nations".

General Assembly resolution 43/174

9 December 1988   Meeting 76   Adopted without vote

Draft by Malta (A/43/L.48); agenda item 49.
Meeting numbers. GA 43rd session: plenary 46, 76.

Revitalization of the Economic and Social Council

The Economic and Social Council examined the question of its structure and functioning during its second regular session of 1988 (Geneva, 6-29 July).

On 29 July, it adopted without vote **resolution 1988/77**.

Revitalization of the Economic and Social Council

The Economic and Social Council,

Recalling General Assembly resolutions 41/213 of 19 December 1986, 42/170 of 11 December 1987 and 42/211 of 21 December 1987, concerning the review of the efficiency of the administrative and financial functioning of the United Nations,

Recalling also General Assembly resolution 32/197 of 20 December 1977 on the restructuring of the economic and social sectors of the United Nations system,

Recalling further section IV of General Assembly resolution 33/202 of 29 January 1979, concerning the role of the Director-General for Development and International Economic Cooperation,

Recalling Economic and Social Council resolutions 1458(XLVII) of 8 August 1969 and 1982/50 of 28 July 1982,

Recognizing that the process of reforming the economic and social sectors of the United Nations aims at contributing to the full implementation of General Assembly resolution 41/213 and requires continued attention,

Aware that the work of the Economic and Social Council should be enhanced and streamlined in order to make the United Nations system more responsive to the challenges of development, in particular of developing countries, and to the needs of Member States in the coming years,

Fully aware of the urgent need to revitalize the Council in order to enable it, under the authority of the General Assembly, to exercise effectively its functions and powers as set out in the Charter of the United Nations and relevant resolutions of the General Assembly and the Council,

Having heard statements by the President of the Economic and Social Council and by Member States on the revitalization of the Council as the principal organ of the United Nations under the Charter in the economic and social fields,

1. *Affirms* that the Economic and Social Council should make an important contribution to the major issues and concerns facing the international community, in particular,

the economic and social development of developing countries;

2. *Decides* to adopt the following measures aimed at revitalizing the Council, improving its functioning and enabling it to exercise effectively its functions and powers as set out in Chapters IX and X of the Charter of the United Nations:

Policy formulation

(*a*) With a view to formulating and elaborating action-oriented recommendations:

(i)   The annual general discussion of "international economic and social policy, including regional and sectoral developments" should take place during the first five working days of the second regular session and should allow enough time for a dialogue and an exchange of views between members and executive heads of the organizations of the United Nations system;

(ii) The Council should undertake annually in-depth discussions of previously identified major policy themes, to be selected on the basis of a multi-year work programme derived, *inter alia*, from the priorities set out in the medium-term plan of the United Nations and the work programmes of other relevant United Nations bodies;

(iii) The Council shall, as and when necessary, address urgent and emerging issues relating to acute international economic and social problems, possibly as one of the themes identified in accordance with subparagraph (ii) above;

(iv) In the context of the above:

a. The executive heads of the specialized agencies or their senior representatives should participate actively in the deliberations of the Council;

b. The specialized agencies should be invited to resume submission of analytical summaries of their annual reports for the consideration of the Council;

Monitoring

(*b*) The Council shall monitor the implementation of the overall strategies, policies and priorities established by the General Assembly in the economic, social and related fields as set out in relevant resolutions of the Assembly and the Council; it shall also consider all appropriate modalities for carrying out the recommendations of the Assembly on matters falling within the Council's competence; in this regard:

(i)   The Secretary-General should circulate each year to Member States and all organizations of the United Nations system, as well as to the Council at its organizational session, a consolidated note on the decisions adopted by the General Assembly in the economic, social and related fields, highlighting matters that require action by them;

(ii) The Council shall obtain information from the specialized agencies on the steps taken to give effect to the recommendations of the General Assembly and the Council on economic, social and related matters that fall within their respective mandates and areas of competence; such information is to be included in the analytical summaries of their annual reports;

(*c*) With a view to submitting appropriate recommendations to the General Assembly on the overall and programme priorities of the United Nations in the economic, social and related fields, the Council shall examine in depth the relevant chapters of the proposed medium-term plan and sections of the proposed programme budget of the United Nations in the light of the recommendations of the Committee for Programme and Co-ordination;

Operational activities

(d) The Council shall recommend to the General Assembly overall priorities and policy guidelines for operational activities for development undertaken by the United Nations system; for that purpose:

(i) The Council, as part of its co-ordination functions, shall define, as and when necessary, overall priorities and specific activities for the organizations of the United Nations system, within their respective mandates, so that the operational activities for development of the United Nations system are carried out in a coherent and effective manner;

(ii) The Council shall deal, each year, with a limited number of policy co-ordination issues, including those identified in General Assembly resolution 42/196 of 11 December 1987; the executive heads of the organizations concerned should be invited to participate actively in such discussions;

(iii) Once every three years the Council shall conduct a comprehensive policy review of the operational activities for development of the United Nations system, which shall be one of its major policy themes and shall be undertaken in connection with the triennial policy review of operational activities carried out by the General Assembly;

(iv) The Council shall monitor the follow-up to its recommendations; organizations of the United Nations system should report to the Council on progress made in the implementation of those recommendations;

Co-ordination

(e) The Council shall carry out its functions of co-ordinating the activities of the United Nations system in the economic, social and related fields as an integral part of its work; to this effect:

(i) Co-ordination instruments, such as cross-organizational reports, the Joint Meetings of the Committee for Programme and Co-ordination and the Administrative Committee on Co-ordination, and reports of the Administrative Committee on Co-ordination and its subsidiary bodies, should be rationalized in order to enable the Council to carry out its co-ordination functions in an effective manner, based on the measures contained in the present resolution; the Committee for Programme and Co-ordination should assist the Council in this regard and submit specific proposals thereon to the Council at its second regular session of 1989;

(ii) The Administrative Committee on Co-ordination, through its Consultative Committee on Substantive Questions (Operational Activities), and the Joint Consultative Group on Policy should prepare suggestions to assist the Council in fulfilling its central co-ordinating role in the field of operational activities for development and should submit them to the Council at its second regular session of 1989;

(iii) The Council shall consider the activities and programmes of the organs, organizations and bodies of the United Nations system, in order to ensure, through consultation with and recommendations to the agencies, that the activities and programmes of the United Nations and its agencies are compatible and mutually complementary, and shall recommend to the General Assembly relative priorities for the activities of the United Nations system in the economic and social fields; for that purpose, cross-organizational programme analyses shall be discontinued in their present form and be replaced by brief analyses on major issues in the medium-term plan, as referred to in subparagraph (a) (ii) above, to be considered directly by the Council; immediately after the General Assembly adopts the next medium-term plan, the Secretary-General should submit to the Council draft proposals on a multi-year programme for such analyses;

(iv) In considering the question of regional co-operation, the Council shall concentrate on the policy review and co-ordination of activities, particularly with respect to issues of common interest to all regions and matters relating to interregional co-operation;

Working methods and organization of work

(f) In formulating its biennial programme of work, the Council shall, to the extent possible, consolidate similar or closely related issues under a single agenda item, in order to consider and take action on them in an integrated manner; the Council shall pay particular attention to bringing the economic and the social activities of the United Nations system closer together; to this effect:

(i) In proposing future calendars of conferences, the Secretary-General should ensure that meetings of the subsidiary bodies of the Council will end at least eight weeks before the session of the Council at which their reports are to be considered; the Committee on Conferences should be requested to act accordingly;

(ii) The Council shall further continue to consider the biennialization of the sessions of its subsidiary bodies and items on its own agenda and programme of work, taking into account the need for a balance between economic and social issues;

(iii) The Secretariat shall prepare for the Council, on the basis of reports submitted by the relevant organs, organizations and bodies of the United Nations system, issue-oriented consolidated reports on economic, social and related questions that the Council will consider under the consolidated agenda items;

(iv) All reports submitted to the Council should be prefaced by an analytical executive summary that highlights the main issues addressed and the recommendations made in the report;

(v) The six-week rule for the circulation of substantive reports of the Secretariat and the eight-week rule for the annotated agenda of the Council should be strictly observed;

(vi) The Council shall report to the General Assembly on the outcome of its work in a manner that will enable the Assembly, in its Main Committees, to consider the recommendations made by the Council in an integrated manner;

(vii) The Council shall review all relevant documentation prepared for the consideration of questions in the economic, social and related fields;

(g) The Secretary-General, in the context of the implementation of General Assembly resolution 41/213, should submit to the Council, at its second regular session of 1989, proposals on the structure and composition of a separate and identifiable secretariat support structure for the Council, which would undertake the substantive functions and technical servicing that will be required to implement subparagraphs *(b)* (i), *(b)* (ii), *(e)* (iii) and *(f)* (iii) above;

(h) To achieve better and more effective co-ordination of the economic, social and related activities of the United Nations system, including operational activities for development, the Office of the Director-General for Development and International Economic Co-operation should be strengthened; in this context, the relevant provisions of General Assembly resolutions 32/197 and 33/202, including those concerning improved policy planning, should be fully implemented;

(i) In the recruitment of staff for the United Nations Secretariat in the economic and social fields, due consideration should be given to the principle of equitable geographical representation;

(j) The Third (Programme and Co-ordination) Committee of the Council shall henceforth focus on:

(i) Operational activities for development of the United Nations system and system-wide co-ordination of those activities;

(ii) Programme questions;

(iii) Co-ordination of the activities of the United Nations and the United Nations system;

(k) The Council shall elect its President and Bureau early in the calendar year, prior to the organizational session of the Council;

(l) Prior to the organizational session, the President, with the co-operation of the other members of the Bureau, should arrange for consultations with members of the Council on the draft programme of work and provisional agenda prepared by the Secretary-General and on the allocation of agenda items and make proposals thereon for consideration by the Council; the duration of the organizational session of the Council could consequently be shortened;

3. *Requests* the Secretary-General to submit a report to the Economic and Social Council at its second regular session of 1989 on the feasibility and comparative costs of holding at the United Nations, with the present insessional arrangements, one consolidated or two regular sessions of the Council;

4. *Decides* to include an item entitled "Revitalization of the Economic and Social Council" in the provisional agenda for its second regular session of 1989 and to consider under that item a report of the Secretary-General on progress in the implementation of the present resolution;

5. *Requests* the Secretary-General to report to the Economic and Social Council at its second regular session of 1989 on the progress made in the implementation of the relevant paragraphs of the present resolution and on proposals for incorporating in the biennial programme of work of the Council measures to implement the present resolution;

6. *Also requests* the Secretary-General, in order to enable the Council to continue discussions on how its work can be enhanced so as to make it more responsive to the challenge of development in the coming years, to submit to the Council at its second regular session of 1989 a note on:

(a) The functioning of the Council and its subsidiary bodies in relation to the relevant chapters of the medium-term plan, using the following categories: (i) policy formulation, co-ordination and monitoring, (ii) operations and implementation, (iii) technical support;

(b) The mandates of the bodies established to assist the Council in carrying out its functions, listed according to the same three categories.

Economic and Social Council resolution 1988/77

29 July 1988   Meeting 41   Adopted without vote

Draft by Tunisia, for Group of 77 (E/1988/L.45/Rev.1), orally corrected; agenda item 3 *(b)*.

Meeting numbers. ESC 30, 37, 39, 41.

GENERAL ASSEMBLY ACTION

By **decision 43/432** of 20 December, the General Assembly endorsed the Council's resolution on its revitalization.

A note by the Secretary-General submitted to the General Assembly in October[9] reproduced the text of a draft resolution entitled "Implementation of section II of the annex to General Assembly resolution 32/197 on the restructuring of the economic and social sectors of the United Nations system". On 20 December, the Assembly, by **decision 43/433**, decided to consider the draft resolution at its forty-fifth (1990) session.

Other organizational matters

Co-operation with other organizations

Non-governmental organizations

The Committee on Non-Governmental Organizations met twice in 1988: in New York on 3 May[10] and at Geneva on 6 July.[11] At both meetings, it heard requests from NGOs with consultative status to address the Economic and Social Council or its committees in connection with items on the Council's agenda. In May, the Committee recommended that five NGOs be heard by the Council or its committees, and in July, that three NGOs be heard.

In 1988, the number of NGOs in consultative status with the Council remained at 827.[12] They were divided into three groups: category I—organizations representative of major population segments in a large number of countries, involved with the economic and social life of the areas they represented; category II—international organizations having special competence in a few of the Council's areas of activity; and organizations on the Roster—considered able to make occasional and useful contributions to the Council's work.

Intergovernmental organizations

During 1988, 31 intergovernmental organizations were designated by the Economic and Social Council under rule 79ᵃ of the rules of procedure for participation in the Council's deliberations on questions within the scope of their activities. Of these, 24 were participating on a continuing basis and seven on an *ad hoc* basis.[13]

Work programme for 1988-1989

At its 1988 organizational session, held in New York from 2 to 5 February and on 3 March, the Economic and Social Council considered its draft basic programme of work for 1988 and 1989 as submitted by the Secretary-General.[14] On the basis of the draft, the Council on 5 February adopted **decision 1988/101**.

By section I of the decision, the Council approved the list of items for consideration in 1988—15 items at the first regular session and 20 at the second regular session—and allocated the items to be considered at the first session to its sessional committees and plenary meetings. It requested its Bureau, in organizing the programme of work of the first regular session, to take into account also the programme of work of the Council's Special Commission on the In-depth Study of the United Nations Intergovernmental Structure and Functions in the Economic and Social Fields, and to submit proposals on the organization of work of its second regular session, including arrangements for consideration of the item on international co-operation and co-ordination within the United Nations system. The Council further decided to give priority consideration at its second regular session to the question of multilateral responses to structural imbalances in the world economy and their impact on developing countries, and to undertake an in-depth review of the report of the Commission on Human Settlements.

With regard to the reports of the Council of the United Nations University, the World Food Council and the Committee on the Development and Utilization of New and Renewable Sources of Energy, the Council decided to consider only specific recommendations requiring its action or relating to the co-ordination aspects of the work covered, and not to consider the part of the report of the UNDP Governing Council dealing with the United Nations Population Fund, except for recommendations requiring Council action.

Under the item on regional co-operation, the Council decided to consider the question of interregional co-operation in transport problems. It would also consider the report of the Trade and Development Board of the United Nations Conference on Trade and Development on the second part of its thirty-fourth session, but authorized the Secretary-General to transmit the Board's report on the first part of its thirty-fifth session directly to the General Assembly. The Council decided to review its recurrent and other documentation to determine whether any document had become redundant, lost its usefulness, or could be issued at less frequent intervals. The Council reiterated the request to its subsidiary bodies to review their recurrent publications and to discontinue those no longer serving a useful purpose.

Acting on a note by the Secretary-General,[15] the Council deferred consideration of the report of the Secretary-General and the Director-General of UNESCO on the World Decade for Cultural Development (1988-1997) until its 1989 second regular session and recommended that the Assembly do likewise. It transmitted to the Special Commission on the In-depth Study of the United Nations Intergovernmental Structure and Functions in the Economic and Social Fields a draft resolution entitled ''Implementation of section II of the annex to General Assembly resolution 32/197 on the restructuring of the economic and social sectors of the United Nations system''.

By section II of the decision, the Council took note of the list of questions for inclusion in its 1989 work programme.

The Council held its first regular session in New York from 3 to 27 May, its second regular session at Geneva from 6 to 29 July, and its resumed second regular session in New York on 17 October, convened pursuant to **decision 1988/183** of 29 July. The Council's Committee on Economic, Social and Cultural Rights met during the organizational session. The First (Economic) and Second (Social) Committees met during the first session and the First and the Third (Programme and Co-ordination) Committees met during the second session.

Agenda of 1988 sessions

On 2 February 1988, the Economic and Social Council adopted a five-item annotated agenda for its organizational session.[16] The agenda for the first regular session, as annotated,[17] was adopted on 3 May and listed the items approved by the Council in **decision 1988/101**, with the addition of a question on the fight against the locust and grasshopper infestation in Africa under agenda item 1 (Adoption of the agenda and other organizational matters).

By **decision 1988/151** of 27 May, the Council approved the draft provisional agenda and the draft programme of work for its second regular session,[18] as orally revised. It deferred until its second regular session consideration of the draft decision on international co-operation to integrate women in development,[19] allocating it under item

---

ᵃRule 79 of the Council's rules of procedure states: ''Representatives of intergovernmental organizations accorded permanent observer status by the General Assembly and of other intergovernmental organizations designated on an *ad hoc* or a continuing basis by the Council on the recommendation of the Bureau, may participate, without the right to vote, in the deliberations of the Council on questions within the scope of the activities of the organizations.''

1 of the provisional agenda, on adoption of the agenda and other organizational matters. By the same decision, draft resolutions on a system-wide medium-term plan for the advancement of women: equality, development and peace, and on system-wide co-ordination of activities to advance the status of women and to integrate women in development[20] were to be considered at the second session under item 17 of the provisional agenda, on international co-operation and co-ordination within the United Nations system.

By **decision 1988/152**, the Council on 6 July adopted the agenda of its second session and approved the organization of work for the session.[21] It decided to transmit the report of the United Nations High Commissioner for Refugees to the 1988 General Assembly session, and to consider in plenary meeting the question of the draft introduction to the next medium-term plan. In addition, the Council on 8 July decided to devote one plenary meeting to a discussion of the economic aspects of women in development within the context of its general discussion of international economic and social policy, including regional and sectoral developments.

For the agenda lists, see APPENDIX IV.

Calendar of meetings

By **decision 1988/103** of 5 February 1988, the Economic and Social Council, pursuant to a 1987 General Assembly resolution,[22] invited the Committee on Conferences to review the Council's draft biennial calendar of conferences and meetings, beginning with the calendar for 1990-1991, and to submit its recommendations to the Council (see PART SIX, Chapter III).

Limitation of documentation

On 8 April 1988,[23] the Secretariat reported on the status of preparation of documentation for the first regular session of the Economic and Social Council, and on 22 June[24] for the second regular session. The reports were submitted pursuant to 1979 Council resolutions[25] on the limitation of documentation and its circulation in all working languages six weeks in advance of the sessions of the Council and its subsidiary bodies.

The reports noted that, to allow adequate time for policy and other clearances and editing, documentation for the first session should have been submitted by 16 February and circulated by 22 March, and, for the second session, submitted by 20 April and circulated by 25 May. A table on the status of documentation, annexed to each report, showed the documents that failed to make the circulation dates. Explanations for the delays were to be provided by the offices concerned.

Financial implications of resolutions and decisions

In September 1988,[26] the Secretary-General submitted to the Fifth   Committee of the General Assembly revised estimates resulting from resolutions and decisions adopted by the Economic and Social Council in 1988. The estimates of requirements for items other than conference-servicing amounted to $3,518,100 for the 1988-1989 biennium, of which $562,000 was expected to be provided from extrabudgetary resources and $2,373,000 from resources appropriated by the Assembly in 1987. The remaining $583,100 had been revised downward and an amount of $550,800 was being requested on a non-recurrent basis under budget sections 1 (overall policy-making, direction and co-ordination), 6B (Centre for Social Development and Humanitarian Affairs), 9 (United Nations Centre on Transnational Corporations) and 19 (United Nations Centre for Human Settlements).

On 9 November,[27] the Fifth Committee approved by recorded vote additional appropriations of $53,000 under section 6B, $185,900 under section 9 (revised downward from $271,600), and $121,500 under section 19 (down from $127,500) of the 1988-1989 programme budget. The Fifth Committee also approved an appropriation of $10,900 under section 31 (staff assessment), to be offset by an increase in the same amount under income section 1.

Earlier, on 7 October,[28] the Secretary-General reported to the Council that conference-servicing requirements were estimated at $5,471,100 for 1988-1989. On 17 October, the Council revised the requirements upward to $5,507,300. Also, on 17 October, the Council, by **decision 1988/186**, took note of the Secretary-General's report,[28] as orally revised.

Report for 1988

The work of the Economic and Social Council at its organizational session and two regular sessions in 1988 was summarized in its annual report to the General Assembly.[13] Parts of the report were considered by the Assembly and others by its Second and Fifth Committees.

On 20, 21 and 22 December, respectively, the Assembly, by **decisions 43/430, 43/449 and 43/456**, took note of the Council's report. On 20 December, acting on the recommendation of the Second Committee, the Assembly also took note of a number of documents relating to the report (**decision 43/435**).

REFERENCES
[1]A/43/286 & Corr.1. [2]YUN 1986, p. 1024, GA res. 41/213, 19 Dec. 1986. [3]A/C.5/43/1/Add.3. [4]YUN 1987, p. 1098, GA res. 42/211, 21 Dec. 1987. [5]A/43/16. [6]YUN 1987, p. 948,

ESC dec. 1987/112, 6 Feb. 1987. [7]E/1988/75. [8]YUN 1986, p. 891. [9]A/C.2/43/L.4. [10]E/1988/83. [11]E/1988/101. [12]YUN 1987, p. 937. [13]A/43/3/Rev.1. [14]E/1988/1 & Add.1. [15]E/1988/44. [16]E/1988/2. [17]E/1988/30. [18]E/1988/L.20. [19]E/1988/L.29. [20]E/1988/15/Rev.1. [21]E/1988/100. [22]YUN 1987, p. 1171, GA res. 42/207 B, 11 Dec. 1987. [23]E/1988/L.16/Rev.1. [24]E/1988/L.27. [25]YUN 1979, pp. 1217 & 1218, ESC res. 1979/1 & 1979/69, 9 Feb. & 2 Aug. 1979. [26]A/C.5/43/5. [27]A/43/980. [28]E/1988/119.

Co-ordination in the UN system

ACC activities

In 1988, ACC considered issues related to the preparation and elaboration of an international development strategy for the fourth United Nations development decade, including suggestions concerning the objectives of such a strategy, its scope and targets, as well as related long-term plans established within the United Nations system. ACC requested its Task Force on Long-term Development Objectives to review the ongoing work in the system on trends and problems relating to the 1990s, to identify any additional studies that were needed, and to suggest ways in which those studies could be prepared through co-operative efforts. In addition, the Director-General for Development and International Economic Co-operation convened a meeting of senior officials of United Nations organizations on 7 October to carry out further work in the area. Reviewing the work of its Task Force and the discussions at the meeting of senior officials, ACC decided that the work on long-term issues should be reviewed in order to enhance its complementarity.

Other related questions considered by ACC included debt and development, structural adjustment, sustainable and environmentally sound development, and operational activities for development. ACC agreed that greater co-operation among the relevant agencies of the system was needed with regard to analytical work in the field of debt and development.

The results of a High-level Meeting on Employment and Structural Adjustment, convened by the International Labour Organisation (ILO) in November 1987 and attended by representatives of 20 Governments, 10 employer and 10 worker organizations, United Nations organizations, and the Organisation for Economic Co-operation and Development (OECD), were considered by ACC in April 1988. ACC welcomed the outcome of the Meeting, which concluded that successful adjustment policies required action at all levels of the economy and in international economic relations.

Ways to mitigate the negative social effects of adjustment policies were discussed by ACC's Consultative Committee on Substantive Questions (Operational Activities) (CCSQ(OPS)) in April. The achievement of a stronger social consensus was described as an important condition for effective adjustment programmes. ACC called for increased collaboration among United Nations organizations in achieving social and political consensus by promoting greater public awareness, developing social indicators and monitoring impacts on living standards. The question of structural adjustment was again discussed by ACC in October, on the basis of a paper prepared by the World Bank and supplemented by the International Monetary Fund (IMF).

ACC emphasized the need to correct financial imbalances among the industrialized countries, since they had a negative impact on the international economic environment through, among other things, the perpetuation of high interest rates, the paucity of finance for development and protectionist measures.

Problems of co-ordination, particularly at the country level, were taken up by ACC. Consideration was given to the role and function of resident co-ordinators; programming of the operational activities of the United Nations system; co-operation with the World Bank; integration of food aid and emergency assistance into other development aid; and the flexibility, simplification and harmonization of procedures.

In the area of programmes, an *ad hoc* inter-agency meeting on women was convened to review the decisions of the Commission on the Status of Women, immediately after its thirty-second session in March 1988. ACC also monitored support activities for the World Decade for Cultural Development (1988-1997), the International Literacy Year (1990), the Global Strategy for Shelter to the Year 2000, and the co-ordination of activities in the field of disarmament. In December, a sixth *ad hoc* inter-agency meeting on the United Nations Decade of Disabled Persons discussed a mid-Decade review of the implementation of the World Programme of Action concerning Disabled Persons. Other *ad hoc* inter-agency meetings during the year dealt with international drug abuse control activities; system-wide co-ordination of policies and programmes in the field of aging; co-operation in the area of demographic estimates and projections; and the prevention of crime and treatment of offenders.

ACC continued to keep under review family-related activities. The Consultative Committee on Substantive Questions (Programme Matters) (CCSQ(PROG)) reviewed the follow-up action to the 1987 Interregional Consultation on Developmental Social Welfare Policies and Programmes. The ACC Sub-Committee on Nutrition examined a wide range of questions, including priority issues of nutrition in times of disaster, the United Nations programme to combat vitamin-A deficiency, the behavioural consequences of iron deficiency, uses of anthropometric measures in nutrition, and primary health care and the identification of nutrition issues for the year 2000. The ACC Sub-Committee on Statistical Activities surveyed the work plans of the system's organizations, publication and dissemination policy, processing and dissemination of trade statistics, and ongoing statistical programmes. Other areas considered by ACC were the harmonization at the country level of activities in science and technology for development, rural development and water resources.

With respect to management and institutional policy issues, ACC reviewed the conditions of service of staff of the Professional and higher categories, conditions of service in the field, and the functioning of the International Civil Service Commission.

ACC also considered issues related to action in response to Assembly resolutions on the policies of *apartheid* of South Africa, co-ordination of outer space activities, co-operation within the United Nations system in the field of archives, public information activities and the co-ordination of information systems.

At the direction of ACC, its Organizational Committee continued to review the functioning of ACC machinery, its interaction with intergovernmental bodies and its contribution to the revitalization of the Economic and Social Council, based on the recommendations of the Council's Special Commission (see below).

ACC described the foregoing activities in its annual overview report for 1988.[1] It met during the year in a first regular session (Geneva, 20 and 21 April) and a second regular session (New York, 25 and 26 October), at which it adopted 31 decisions[2] relating to the topics mentioned above and to ACC machinery.

ACC's principal subsidiary bodies met as follows:

Organizational Committee (New York, 23 and 24 February, 10-12 October; Geneva, 11-13 and 22 April, 29 and 30 June); Consultative Committee on Administrative Questions (CCAQ) (Personnel and General Administrative Questions—PER) (sixty-eighth session, Rome, Italy, 29 February–18 March; sixty-ninth session, New York, 5-22 July); CCAQ (Financial and Budgetary Questions—FB) (sixty-eighth session, Rome, 7-11 March; sixty-ninth session, New York, 12-16 September); joint CCAQ(PER)/(FB) meeting (Rome, 9 March); CCSQ(OPS) (first regular session, Geneva, 6-8 April; second regular session, New York, 21-23 September); CCSQ (Programme Matters) (PROG) (New York, 3-5 October).

Bodies on specific subjects met as follows:

Ad hoc inter-agency meeting on co-ordination in matters of international drug abuse control, Vienna, 13 February, Geneva, 1-2 September; Sub-Committee on Nutrition, fourteenth session, Geneva, 22-26 February; Task Force on Science and Technology for De-

velopment, ninth session, New York, 7-10 March; informal inter-agency working group on youth at the technical level, Vienna, 8 and 9 March; *ad hoc* inter-agency meeting on system-wide co-ordination of policies and programmes in the field of aging, Vienna, 10 and 11 March; *ad hoc* inter-agency meeting on women and development, Vienna, 24 and 25, 28 and 29 March; Joint United Nations Information Committee, fifteenth session, Geneva, 29-31 March; Task Force on Rural Development, sixteenth meeting, New York, 11-13 May; eighth Inter-agency Consultation on the Follow-up to the Substantial New Programme of Action for the 1980s for the Least Developed Countries, Geneva, 16 and 17 May; *ad hoc* inter-agency working group on demographic estimates and projections, Geneva, 16-18 May; Sub-Committee on Statistical Activities, twenty-second session, Geneva, 6-10 June; inter-agency meeting on the follow-up to the Seventh United Nations Congress on the Prevention of Crime and the Treatment of Offenders, Vienna, 1 and 2 September; Task Force on Long-term Development Objectives, sixteenth session, New York, 13-16 September; World Bank meeting on the implementation of Bank-funded projects, Washington, D.C., 19 and 20 September; *ad hoc* inter-agency meeting on outer space activities, Geneva, 3-5 October; Intersecretariat Group for Water Resources, ninth session, Geneva, 17-21 October; sixth *ad hoc* inter-agency meeting on the United Nations Decade of Disabled Persons, Vienna, 5-7 December.

Report for 1987

The ACC annual overview report for 1987[3] was considered on 27 May 1988 by CPC,[4] which noted improvements in the report's presentation. The Committee agreed on the need for greater efforts in following up ACC's recommendations and recommended that ACC keep its subsidiary machinery under review. CPC further noted that future annual overview reports would focus on a new critical analysis of such issues as improvements in coordination and of the problems faced by the United Nations system in carrying out its functions.

By **decision 1988/167** of 27 July, the Economic and Social Council took note of the ACC report.

CPC activities

In 1988, CPC met in New York, for an organizational meeting on 28 March and for its twenty-eighth session, from 2 May to 3 June for the first part and from 6 to 19 September for the second part.[4] At its organizational meeting, the Committee decided to begin the session on 2 May instead of 25 April.

During the first part of the session, CPC considered a report by the Secretary-General on programme performance of the United Nations for the biennium 1986-1987[5] and examined revised estimates of the 1988-1989 programme budget, including the Secretary-General's plans for implementing recommendations of the Group of 18,[6] as requested by the General Assembly in a 1987 resolution.[7] It discussed in that connection the Secretary-General's note[8] on the use and operation of the contingency fund set up in 1986[9] to accommodate additional expenditures within the overall budget. In addition, it examined reports on the location of the functions related to liaison with NGOs and on measures relating to the priority assigned by the Secretary-General to the United Nations Programme of Action for African Economic Recovery and Development 1986-1990. The Committee also examined the proposed revisions to the medium-term plan for the period 1984-1989 (extended to 1991), setting out its conclusions and recommendations on the chapters covered.

CPC considered a number of other reports by the Secretary-General. They included: a second progress report on implementation of the 1986 General Assembly resolution approving the recommendations of the Group of 18 to improve the Organization's administrative and financial functioning;[9] in-depth evaluations of the programme on development issues and policies and the human settlements programme; a report on the application of evaluation findings in programme design, delivery and policy directives; and progress reports on CPC recommendations regarding the work of the Department of Public Information and the drug control programme. Consideration of a report on mailing lists and registers maintained by the United Nations was deferred until CPC's 1989 session.

CPC also took note of the report of the Joint United Nations Information Committee (JUNIC) on policies for distributing material through United Nations information centres and discussed, in addition to a follow-up report, three reports and a note by the Secretary-General dealing with cross-organizational programme analyses (see below). It gave its assessment of the 1987 ACC annual overview report and the 1988 work programme of the Joint Inspection Unit (JIU), also incorporating the nucleus of the JIU work programme for 1989-1990. A JIU report on monitoring, evaluation and management review components in reporting on the performance and results of United Nations programmes was referred to the Fifth Committee of the General Assembly.

During the second part of the session, CPC focused on the programme aspects as set forth in the outline of the proposed 1990-1991 programme budget, in line with reform measures called for in the 1986 General Assembly resolution.[9] It considered a note[10] by the Secretary-General on the draft introduction to the medium-term plan for the period starting in 1992, transmitted to CPC by Economic and Social Council **decision 1988/168** of 27 July. Also before the Committee was the calendar of consultations on the medium-term plan. CPC further examined revised estimates for the public information section of the 1988-1989

programme budget and an in-depth evaluation of the major programme on political and Security Council affairs.

ECONOMIC AND SOCIAL COUNCIL ACTION

On 27 July 1988, acting on the recommendation of its Third (Programme and Co-ordination) Committee, the Economic and Social Council adopted without vote **resolution 1988/62**.

Report of the Committee for Programme and Co-ordination

The Economic and Social Council,

Having considered the report of the Committee for Programme and Co-ordination on the work of its twenty-eighth session,

Recalling the provisions of Chapters IX and X of the Charter of the United Nations and, in particular, the role of the Economic and Social Council in co-ordination in the economic and social fields within the United Nations system,

Reaffirming the importance of the programming and co-ordinating functions carried out by the Committee for Programme and Co-ordination as the main subsidiary organ of the Economic and Social Council and the General Assembly for planning, programming and co-ordination,

Noting the importance of the additional responsibilities in the budgetary process assigned to the Committee for Programme and Co-ordination by the General Assembly in its resolution 41/213 of 19 December 1986,

Recognizing that the medium-term plan should continue to serve as the principal policy directive of the United Nations and, _inter alia_, as a tool for co-ordination in the economic and social fields,

Recognizing also that programme performance reports, programme evaluations and cross-organizational programme analyses are significant instruments for promoting efficiency and integrating the programming and co-ordination processes,

1. _Takes note with appreciation_ of the report of the Committee for Programme and Co-ordination on the work of its twenty-eighth session, and endorses the conclusions and recommendations contained therein;

2. _Authorizes_ the Committee, subject to established procedure, to resume its twenty-eighth session from 6 to 19 September 1988 in order to consider those pending items of the agenda indicated in the Committee's report;

3. _Requests_ the Secretary-General to ensure that the documentation necessary for the Committee to complete its work is provided in good time.

Economic and Social Council resolution 1988/62

27 July 1988   Meeting 39   Adopted without vote

Approved by Third Committee (E/1988/114) without vote, 19 July (meeting 10); draft by Trinidad and Tobago (E/1988/C.3/L.7), orally revised; agenda items 17 & 18.
Financial implications. A/43/16/Add.1.

By **decision 1988/184** of 17 October, the Council endorsed the conclusions and recommendations of CPC on the introduction to the medium-term plan for the period beginning in 1992 and the calendar of consultations on the medium-term plan, as contained in the CPC report on its resumed twenty-eighth session.[4]

Joint Meetings of CPC and ACC

The twenty-third series of Joint Meetings of CPC and ACC was held at Geneva on 4 and 5 July.[11] The topic for consideration was the response of the United Nations system to development problems, with special attention to the implementation of the United Nations Programme of Action for African Economic Recovery and Development 1986-1990. As a basis for discussion, the Committees had before them a background paper prepared by ACC. Matters considered at the Meetings included: development as an integrated process; the alleviation of poverty; the social impact of structural adjustment; the need to strengthen infrastructure in developing countries and ensure that they benefit from technological advances; the development of early warning and forecasting systems; co-ordination of activities, especially at the country level; economic recovery and the development of human resources; and the preparation of an international development strategy for the fourth United Nations development decade.

The framework of future Joint Meetings was also discussed. The Secretary-General, as ACC Chairman, suggested that the Meetings consider: adopting a multi-year programme of work so that the necessary preparations could be made by members of both Committees; rescheduling the Meetings for October in New York in conjunction with the second regular session of ACC; and ensuring effective follow-up to the conclusions and recommendations of the Meetings.

ECONOMIC AND SOCIAL COUNCIL ACTION

On 27 July, acting on the recommendation of its Third Committee, the Economic and Social Council adopted without vote **resolution 1988/64**.

Joint Meetings of the Committee for Programme and Co-ordination and the Administrative Committee on Co-ordination

The Economic and Social Council,

Recalling its resolutions 1982/50 of 28 July 1982, 1986/50 of 22 July 1986 and 1987/82 of 8 July 1987, as well as Chapters IX and X of the Charter of the United Nations,

Stressing the importance of periodic meetings between Member States and the executive heads of organizations of the United Nations system in promoting better understanding and co-ordination of the activities of the system in the economic and social fields and of the role of the Joint Meetings of the Committee for Programme and Co-ordination and the Administrative Committee on Co-ordination in that regard,

Reiterating the need for further improvement in the functioning of the Joint Meetings, relating in particular to the timing, participation, agenda and follow-up,

Having considered the report of the Chairmen of the Committee for Programme and Co-ordination and the Administrative Committee on Co-ordination on the twenty-third series of Joint Meetings of the two Committees, including the suggestions made concerning the functioning of the Joint Meetings, particularly those made by the Secretary-General of the United Nations,

1. *Takes note* of the report of the Chairmen of the Committee for Programme and Co-ordination and the Administrative Committee on Co-ordination on the twenty-third series of Joint Meetings of the two Committees, in particular the comments made on the timing, venue and conduct of the Joint Meetings;

2. *Decides* that, in future, the Joint Meetings should be held in New York in conjunction with the autumn session of the Administrative Committee on Co-ordination, in order to facilitate the participation of the members of the Committee for Programme and Co-ordination at a high level as well as the participation of the executive heads of the specialized agencies and United Nations programmes, and that the duration of the Meetings should be sufficient to allow for an adequate exchange of views among participants;

3. *Decides also* that the Joint Meetings should take the following measures relating to their work:

(a) Members of the two Committees should identify well in advance the specific issues for discussion under each topic and hold a concrete exchange of views, focusing on practical measures to solve the co-ordination problems identified;

(b) The background papers prepared by the Administrative Committee on Co-ordination should include appropriate action-oriented proposals, so as to assist the Joint Meetings in achieving concrete results;

(c) Steps should be taken to ensure effective follow-up at the intergovernmental and intersecretariat levels of the conclusions and recommendations of the Joint Meetings;

4. *Decides* that appropriate measures for effective intergovernmental and intersecretariat follow-up of the conclusions and recommendations of the Joint Meetings should be reported, through the Committee for Programme and Co-ordination, to the Economic and Social Council at its second regular session in the following year;

5. *Requests* the Secretary-General to submit a report to the Council at its organizational session for 1989 on the measures taken to implement the present resolution;

6. *Decides* to review the implementation of the present resolution at its second regular session of 1991 in the context of the study of the United Nations intergovernmental structure and functions in the economic and social fields.

Economic and Social Council resolution 1988/64

27 July 1988   Meeting 39   Adopted without vote

Approved by Third Committee (E/1988/114) without vote, 22 July (meeting 14); 9-nation draft (E/1988/C.3/L.12), orally revised; agenda item 17.
Sponsors: Australia, Canada, China, German Democratic Republic, Italy, Japan, Norway, Tunisia, United States.

Cross-organizational programme analyses

In March 1988,[12] the Secretary-General submitted a report to the Economic and Social Council on measures taken to implement the recommendations of CPC concerning the cross-organizational programme analysis (COPA) on economic and social research, pursuant to a Council resolution of 1986.[13] The measures were intended to improve the flow of information on research findings; to improve the effectiveness of research and its responsiveness to the needs of intergovernmental bodies; and to strengthen relationships between the organizations of the United Nations system, the United Nations University and United Nations institutes.

ACC's consultative subsidiary body, CCSQ(PROG), reviewed follow-up to the COPA of economic and social research and policy analysis, based on the recommendations of CPC regarding co-ordination of research activities and future research planning within the United Nations system. It surveyed progress made in the preparation of the COPA on the system's activities related to the advancement of women, and considered the proposed scope and approach of a COPA on industrial development for submission to CPC. It also examined the provisions of Economic and Social Council **resolution 1988/77** to replace COPAs in their current form by brief analyses on major priority themes identified in the medium-term plan.

CPC also considered three reports by the Secretary-General dealing with other COPAs. One concerned a proposed analysis of industrial development; another provided the scope and approach of the COPA on United Nations activities related to the advancement of women; and the third was an analysis of environmental activities. A note presented a follow-up to a COPA on economic and social research in the United Nations system; another, a synoptic table on the implementation of CPC's recommendations regarding the analysis of human settlements activities. The Committee stressed the need for clarity, consistency and an absence of ambiguity in the definition and presentation of data included in COPAs, and requested that future analyses be prepared in a way that would enable CPC to reach clear conclusions and make precise recommendations.

Medium-term plans

In 1988, in response to a 1987 resolution of the Economic and Social Council,[14] ACC prepared a report on the implementation of the system-wide medium-term plan for women and development for the period 1990-1995, to be submitted to the Council through the Commission on the Status of Women. It also approved the preparation schedule for the plan for 1996-2001, the formulation of which was to be considered in 1992. Relevant sections of the 1988 report of the Commission on the Status of Women were before CPC for consideration at its first regular session. It also had before it proposed revisions to the medium-term plan for

1984-1989 extended to 1991, and the draft introduction to the medium-term plan for the period beginning in 1992.

REFERENCES

[1]E/1989/18. [2]ACC/1988/DEC/1-18, ACC/1988/DEC/19-31. [3]E/1988/42. [4]A/43/16. [5]A/43/326. [6]YUN 1986, p. 880. [7]YUN 1987, p. 1098, GA res. 42/211, 21 Dec. 1987. [8]A/43/324. [9]YUN 1986, p. 1024, GA res. 41/213, 19 Dec. 1986. [10]A/43/329. [11]E/1988/79. [12]E/1988/47. [13]YUN 1986, p. 884, ESC res. 1986/51, 22 July 1986. [14]YUN 1987, p. 840, ESC res. 1987/86, 8 July 1987.

Other institutional arrangements

Work programmes of General Assembly's Second and Third Committees

Second Committee

In 1988, a draft biennial programme of work for 1989-1990 for the General Assembly's Second Committee was before that Committee for consideration and approval. It was submitted in a Secretariat note[1] in keeping with an Assembly practice established in 1984[2] to improve complementarity between the work of the Assembly and that of the Economic and Social Council.

By **decision 43/448** of 20 December 1988, the Assembly, on the recommendation of its President, deferred consideration of the Second Committee's biennial programme of work for 1989-1990 to its resumed forty-third session.

Third Committee

In November 1988, the Third Committee had before it a note from the Secretariat[3] transmitting a draft decision concerning its programme of work. Submitted in 1986 by Côte d'Ivoire, Morocco and Zaire, the draft had been deferred for consideration until 1987 and again until 1988.[4]

By **decision 43/426** of 8 December, the General Assembly, on the recommendation of the Third Committee,[5] deferred consideration of the draft until 1989.

As originally submitted, the draft would have had the Assembly decide to consider the following items every two years, beginning at its 1986 session: the question of aging; implementation of the World Programme of Action concerning Disabled Persons and the United Nations Decade of Disabled Persons; elimination of all forms of religious intolerance; human rights and scientific and technological developments; and alternative approaches and ways and means within the United Nations system for improving the effective enjoyment of human rights and fundamental freedoms (with the exception of the question related to the right of development).

International decades

In April 1988, the Secretary-General reported to the Economic and Social Council on the guidelines for international decades. Submitted in response to a 1987 General Assembly request,[6] the report[7] provided recommendations concerning the selection of subjects for, and the timing of, international decades, requirements and procedures for proclaiming them, and review and appraisal of implementation of the programme of action for the decade. Annexed to the report was a list of international decades proclaimed by the General Assembly since 1961.

ECONOMIC AND SOCIAL COUNCIL ACTION

On 27 July, on the recommendation of its Third Committee, the Economic and Social Council adopted without vote **resolution 1988/63**.

Guidelines for international decades

The Economic and Social Council,

Recalling its resolution 1980/67 of 25 July 1980, in which it adopted guidelines for international years and anniversaries,

Noting General Assembly resolution 42/171 of 11 December 1987, in which the Assembly requested the Council to submit recommendations on guidelines for the designation of future international decades,

Having considered the report of the Secretary-General on guidelines for international decades,

Recommends that the General Assembly adopt the guidelines for international decades contained in the annex to the present resolution on the understanding that these guidelines are not intended to apply to United Nations development decades.

ANNEX
Guidelines for international decades

A. *Selection of subjects for and timing of international decades*

1. The subject proposed for a decade should be consistent with the purposes and principles of the United Nations, as stated in the Charter. It should be of priority concern in the political, economic, social, cultural, humanitarian or human rights field, and should require long-term action at the international or regional level and at the national level. Action on the subject should contribute to the development of international co-operation or the strengthening of universal peace.

2. In areas where effective programmes already exist, international decades should be proclaimed only if they can be expected to produce results that would not otherwise be achieved.

3. As a rule, overlapping of decades should be avoided. A new international decade should be initiated only if it is clear that the United Nations system has the substantive, administrative and financial capacity to play an effective role in the implementation of a programme for the decade.

4. Before a new decade is proposed, consideration should be given to the possibility of an observance for a shorter period of time.

B. *Requirements for the proclamation of international decades*

5. Proposals for international decades should include a draft programme of action with well-defined objectives and activities to be carried out at the international, regional and national levels. The activities should be designed to lead to clearly identifiable results. The draft programme of action should indicate the proposed organizational arrangements and modalities for financing, from both budgetary and extrabudgetary sources, as well as procedures for monitoring implementation. Provision should also be made for public information activities.

6. The draft programme of action should indicate a lead agency or agencies for the decade and the mechanisms to be used for co-ordinating the activities of the organizations of the United Nations system, as well as those of the other intergovernmental and non-governmental organizations concerned.

7. At the national level, the programme of action should provide for the establishment of national committees or other mechanisms to mobilize public support and carry out activities connected with the decade.

C. *Procedures for the proclamation of international decades*

8. Proposals for international decades should be submitted to the Economic and Social Council so that it may review the purpose and timing, drawing on the views of the Committee for Programme and Co-ordination and other intergovernmental bodies concerned.

9. The General Assembly should proclaim an international decade after the proposal has been thoroughly reviewed by the intergovernmental bodies concerned and the views of all Member States and of the non-governmental organizations concerned have been taken into account. For this purpose there should be an interval of two years between the introduction of the proposal in the Economic and Social Council and the proclamation of the decade by the General Assembly.

10. There should be sufficient time between the proclamation of the decade by the General Assembly and the start of the decade to allow for preparatory work at the international, regional and national levels.

11. When a second decade on a particular subject is proposed, the following should be taken into consideration:

(a) There should be a two-year preparatory period between the end of the first decade and the start of the second for drafting the programme of action for the second decade;

(b) Steps should be taken to ensure that the expertise and experience acquired during the first decade are retained, in order to ensure the prompt implementation of activities once a second decade is launched;

(c) The mid-term and end-term reviews of the first decade should be used as a baseline for the programme of action for the second decade;

(d) A second decade should be proclaimed only if the objectives of the first decade have not been fully attained and if there are good prospects for attaining them, particularly in cases where projects or programmes of the first decade have reached an advanced stage of implementation.

D. *Review and appraisal of the implementation of the programme of action of the decade*

12.   The implementation of the programme of action of the decade should normally be reviewed by an appropriate intergovernmental body at the mid-point and end of the decade. When a world conference on the subject of an international decade is convened within the period of the decade, such a conference should serve, *inter alia*, as an instrument for the review and appraisal of the implementation of the programme of action of the decade.

Economic and Social Council resolution 1988/63

27 July 1988   Meeting 39   Adopted without vote

Approved by Third Committee (E/1988/114) without vote, 21 July (meeting 13); draft by Chairman (E/1988/C.3/L.11), orally revised; agenda item 17.

GENERAL ASSEMBLY ACTION

By **decision 43/434** of 20 December, the General Assembly, acting on the recommendation of the Second Committee, referred the issue to the Council for further consideration in 1989, with a view to enabling the Assembly at its forty-fourth (1989) session to consider and take the appropriate action on guidelines for international decades.

REFERENCES

[1]A/C.2/43/L.71. [2]YUN 1984, p. 986, GA res. 39/217, 18 Dec. 1984. [3]A/C.3/43/L.3. [4]YUN 1987, p. 953, GA dec. 42/423, 7 Dec. 1987. [5]A/43/868. [6]YUN 1987, p. 953, GA res. 42/171, 11 Dec. 1987. [7]E/1988/58 & Corr.1.

PART FOUR

Trusteeship and decolonization

Chapter I

Questions relating to decolonization

The subject of decolonization continued to be actively pursued by the United Nations throughout 1988, in particular by the General Assembly's Special Committee on the Situation with regard to the Implementation of the Declaration on the Granting of Independence to Colonial Countries and Peoples (Committee on colonial countries). The Committee examined the status of the implementation of the Declaration by international organizations as well as action by foreign economic and military interests to impede it.

The Committee examined other general decolonization questions and made recommendations on the situations in the Trust Territory of the Pacific Islands (see next chapter); Namibia (see PART FOUR, Chapter III); and other Non-Self-Governing Territories, such as East Timor, the Falkland Islands (Malvinas), New Caledonia and Western Sahara, as well as a number of small island Territories, mostly under the administration of the United Kingdom or the United States. The question of Puerto Rico was also considered.

The General Assembly requested the Committee to continue seeking means to implement the Declaration on independence for colonial countries (resolution 43/45) and reaffirmed that the United Nations system ought to contribute to its implementation (43/30).

The Assembly called for wider dissemination of information on decolonization (43/46) and requested administering Powers to continue transmitting information on their Territories to the Secretary-General as prescribed in the Charter of the United Nations (43/28). Those Powers were also urged to safeguard the right of colonial peoples to the natural resources of their Territories (43/29).

The Assembly condemned military activities and arrangements in colonial Territories as detrimental to the rights and interests of colonial peoples and called for an end to such activities (decision 43/410). States were again invited to make offers of study and training facilities to the inhabitants of those Territories (43/32).

The Economic and Social Council reaffirmed the need for United Nations assistance to the peoples of colonial Territories and their national liberation movements, deplored the collaboration of the International Monetary Fund with South Africa and called on the Fund to cease such operations (resolution 1988/53).

As recommended by the Movement of Non-Aligned Countries, the Assembly declared the period 1990-2000 as the International Decade for the Eradication of Colonialism (43/47). It requested the Secretary-General to submit an action plan aimed at ushering in the twenty-first century in a world free from colonialism.

1960 Declaration on colonial countries

During 1988, the United Nations continued to focus its efforts on decolonizing Territories in implementation of the 1960 Declaration on the Granting of Independence to Colonial Countries and Peoples.[1] As the main body dealing with the issue, the Committee on colonial countries considered various aspects of its implementation.

The Committee held two sessions in 1988, in New York—the first on 2 February, at which it considered organizational questions, and the second from 1 to 16 August.[2] Its Sub-Committee on Petitions, Information and Assistance held meetings between 8 March and 27 May, and the Sub-Committee on Small Territories met between 9 March and 2 June. On their recommendations, the Committee took action on the implementation of the Declaration by international organizations, on the dissemination of information on decolonization and on reports on the Territories supplied by the administering Powers and by visiting missions of the Committee.

Implementation of the Declaration

On 22 November 1988, the General Assembly adopted **resolution 43/45** by recorded vote.

Implementation of the Declaration on the Granting of Independence to Colonial Countries and Peoples

The General Assembly,

Having examined the report of the Special Committee on the Situation with regard to the Implementation of the Declaration on the Granting of Independence to Colonial Countries and Peoples,

Recalling its resolutions 1514(XV) of 14 December 1960, containing the Declaration on the Granting of Independence to Colonial Countries and Peoples, 2621(XXV) of 12 October 1970, containing the programme of action for the full implementation of the Declaration, and 35/118 of 11 December 1980, the annex to which contains the Plan of Action for the Full Implementation of the Declaration, as well as 40/56 of 2 December 1985 on the twenty-fifth anniversary of the Declaration,

Recalling all its previous resolutions concerning the implementation of the Declaration, in particular resolution 42/71 of 4 December 1987, as well as the relevant resolutions of the Security Council,

Recalling its resolution S-14/1 of 20 September 1986 on the question of Namibia and taking into account the Declaration adopted by the World Conference on Sanctions against Racist South Africa, and the Declaration of the International Conference for the Immediate Independence of Namibia and the Programme of Action on Namibia adopted by the Conference,

Condemning the continued colonialist and racist repression of Africans, particularly in Namibia, by the Government of South Africa through its persistent, illegal occupation of the international Territory, and its intransigent attitude towards all efforts being made to bring about an internationally acceptable solution to the situation obtaining in the Territory,

Deeply conscious of the urgent need to take all necessary measures to eliminate forthwith the last vestiges of colonialism, particularly in respect of Namibia where desperate attempts by South Africa to perpetuate its illegal occupation have brought untold suffering and bloodshed to the people,

Strongly condemning the policies of those States which, in defiance of the relevant resolutions of the United Nations, have continued to collaborate with the Government of South Africa in its domination of the people of Namibia,

Reiterating its conviction that the total eradication of racial discrimination, *apartheid* and violations of the basic human rights of the peoples of colonial Territories will be achieved most expeditiously by the faithful and complete implementation of the Declaration, particularly in Namibia, and by the speediest possible complete elimination of the presence of the illegal occupying régime therefrom,

Conscious that the success of national liberation struggles and the resultant international situation have provided the international community with a unique opportunity to make a decisive contribution towards the total elimination of colonialism in all its forms and manifestations in Africa,

Noting with satisfaction the work accomplished by the Special Committee with a view to securing the effective and complete implementation of the Declaration contained in General Assembly resolution 1514(XV) and other relevant resolutions of the United Nations,

Noting also with satisfaction the co-operation and active participation of the administering Powers concerned in the relevant work of the Special Committee, as well as their continued readiness to receive United Nations visiting missions in the Territories under their administration,

Stressing the importance of the participation of the administering Powers in the related work of the Special Committee and noting with concern the negative impact which the non-participation of certain administering Powers has had on the work of the Special Committee, depriving it of an important source of information on the Territories under their administration,

Keenly aware of the pressing need of the newly independent and emerging States for assistance from the United Nations and its system of organizations in the economic, social and other fields,

Mindful that the year 1990 will mark the thirtieth anniversary of the Declaration on the Granting of Independence to Colonial Countries and Peoples,

1. *Reaffirms* its resolution 1514(XV) and all other resolutions on decolonization and calls upon the administering Powers, in accordance with those resolutions, to take all necessary steps to enable the dependent peoples of the Territories concerned to exercise fully and without further delay their inalienable right to self-determination and independence;

2. *Affirms once again* that the continuation of colonialism in all its forms and manifestations—including racism, *apartheid*, those activities of foreign economic and other interests contrary to the Charter of the United Nations and the Declaration on the Granting of Independence to Colonial Countries and Peoples, as well as the violations of the right to self-determination and basic human rights of the peoples of colonial Territories and continuous policies and practices to suppress legitimate national liberation movements—is incompatible with the Charter, the Universal Declaration of Human Rights and the Declaration on the Granting of Independence to Colonial Countries and Peoples and poses a serious threat to international peace and security;

3. *Reaffirms its determination* to take all necessary steps with a view to the complete and speedy eradication of colonialism and to the faithful and strict observance by all States of the relevant provisions of the Charter, the Declaration on the Granting of Independence to Colonial Countries and Peoples and the guiding principles of the Universal Declaration of Human Rights;

4. *Affirms once again* its recognition of the legitimacy of the struggle of the peoples under colonial and alien domination to exercise their right to self-determination and independence by all the necessary means at their disposal;

5. *Approves* the report of the Special Committee on the Situation with regard to the Implementation of the Declaration on the Granting of Independence to Colonial Countries and Peoples covering the work during 1988, including the programme of work envisaged for 1989;

6. *Calls upon* all States, in particular the administering Powers, as well as the specialized agencies and other organizations of the United Nations system within their respective spheres of competence, to give effect to the recommendations contained in the report of the Special Committee for the speedy implementation of the Declaration contained in General Assembly resolution 1514(XV) and other relevant resolutions of the United Nations;

7. *Condemns* the continuing activities of foreign economic and other interests which are impeding the implementation of the Declaration with respect to the colonial Territories, particularly Namibia;

8. *Strongly condemns* all collaboration, particularly in the nuclear and military fields, with the Government of South Africa and calls upon the States concerned to cease forthwith all such collaboration;

9. *Requests* all States, directly and through their action in the specialized agencies and other organizations of the United Nations system, to withhold assistance of

any kind from the Government of South Africa until the inalienable right of the people of Namibia to self-determination and independence within a united Namibia, including Walvis Bay, has been restored, and to refrain from taking any action which might imply recognition of the legitimacy of the illegal occupation of Namibia by that régime;

10. *Calls upon* the colonial Powers to withdraw immediately and unconditionally their military bases and installations from colonial Territories, to refrain from establishing new ones and not to involve those Territories in any offensive acts or interference against other States;

11. *Urges* all States, directly and through their action in the specialized agencies and other organizations of the United Nations system, to provide all moral and material assistance to the oppressed people of Namibia and, in respect of the other Territories, requests the administering Powers, in consultation with the Governments of the Territories under their administration, to take steps to enlist and make effective use of all possible assistance, on both a bilateral and a multilateral basis, in the strengthening of the economies of those Territories;

12. *Requests* the Special Committee to continue to seek suitable means for the immediate and full implementation of General Assembly resolution 1514(XV) in all Territories that have not yet attained independence and, in particular:

(a) To formulate specific proposals for the elimination of the remaining manifestations of colonialism and to report thereon to the General Assembly at its forty-fourth session;

(b) To make concrete suggestions which could assist the Security Council in considering appropriate measures under the Charter with regard to developments in colonial Territories that are likely to threaten international peace and security;

(c) To continue to examine the compliance of Member States with resolution 1514(XV) and other relevant resolutions on decolonization, particularly those relating to Namibia;

(d) To continue to pay special attention to the small Territories, in particular through the dispatch of visiting missions to those Territories whenever the Special Committee deems it appropriate, and to recommend to the General Assembly the most suitable steps to be taken to enable the populations of those Territories to exercise their right to self-determination and independence;

(e) To take all necessary steps to enlist world-wide support among Governments, as well as national and international organizations having a special interest in decolonization, for the achievement of the objectives of the Declaration and the implementation of the relevant resolutions of the United Nations, particularly as concerns the oppressed people of Namibia;

(f) To prepare and submit to the General Assembly at its forty-fourth session, preparatory to the commemoration of the thirtieth anniversary of the Declaration in 1990 and in order to further enhance the process of decolonization, recommendations on appropriate programmes of activities to be undertaken by the United Nations, Member States and intergovernmental and non-governmental organizations in the course of the commemoration year;

13. *Calls upon* the administering Powers to continue to co-operate with the Special Committee in the discharge of its mandate and to permit the access of visiting missions to the Territories to secure first-hand information and ascertain the wishes and aspirations of their inhabitants and urges, in particular, those administering Powers which do not participate in the work of the Special Committee to do so at its 1989 session;

14. *Requests* the Secretary-General and the specialized agencies and other organizations of the United Nations system to provide or continue to provide to the newly independent and emerging States all possible assistance in the economic, social and other fields;

15. *Requests* the Secretary-General to provide the Special Committee with the facilities and services required for the implementation of the present resolution, as well as of the various resolutions and decisions on decolonization adopted by the General Assembly and the Special Committee.

General Assembly resolution 43/45

22 November 1988   Meeting 59   147-2-7 (recorded vote)

36-nation draft (A/43/L.23 and Add.1); agenda item 18.

Sponsors: Afghanistan, Algeria, Angola, Benin, Burkina Faso, Byelorussian SSR, Congo, Cuba, Cyprus, Czechoslovakia, Democratic Yemen, Ethiopia, German Democratic Republic, Ghana, Hungary, India, Iran, Lao People's Democratic Republic, Libyan Arab Jamahiriya, Madagascar, Mali, Mongolia, Nicaragua, Papua New Guinea, Sierra Leone, Sudan, Syrian Arab Republic, Tunisia, Ukrainian SSR, United Republic of Tanzania, Vanuatu, Venezuela, Viet Nam, Yugoslavia, Zambia, Zimbabwe.

Financial implications. 5th Committee, A/43/843; S-G, A/C.5/43/37.

Meeting numbers. GA 43rd session: 5th Committee 36; plenary 57-59.

Recorded vote in Assembly as follows:

In favour: Afghanistan, Albania, Algeria, Angola, Antigua and Barbuda, Argentina, Australia, Austria, Bahamas, Bahrain, Bangladesh, Barbados, Belize, Benin, Bhutan, Bolivia, Botswana, Brazil, Brunei Darussalam, Bulgaria, Burkina Faso, Burma, Burundi, Byelorussian SSR, Cameroon, Cape Verde, Central African Republic, Chad, Chile, China, Colombia, Comoros, Congo, Costa Rica, Côte d'Ivoire, Cuba, Cyprus, Czechoslovakia, Democratic Kampuchea, Democratic Yemen, Denmark, Djibouti, Dominica, Dominican Republic, Ecuador, Egypt, El Salvador, Equatorial Guinea, Ethiopia, Fiji, Finland, Gabon, Gambia, German Democratic Republic, Ghana, Greece, Grenada, Guatemala, Guinea, Guinea-Bissau, Guyana, Haiti, Honduras, Hungary, Iceland, India, Indonesia, Iran, Iraq, Ireland, Jamaica, Japan, Jordan, Kenya, Kuwait, Lao People's Democratic Republic, Lebanon, Lesotho, Liberia, Libyan Arab Jamahiriya, Madagascar, Malawi, Malaysia, Maldives, Mali, Malta, Mauritania, Mauritius, Mexico, Mongolia, Morocco, Mozambique, Nepal, New Zealand, Nicaragua, Niger, Nigeria, Norway, Oman, Pakistan, Panama, Papua New Guinea, Peru, Philippines, Poland, Portugal, Qatar, Romania, Rwanda, Saint Kitts and Nevis, Saint Lucia, Saint Vincent and the Grenadines, Samoa, Sao Tome and Principe, Saudi Arabia, Senegal, Seychelles, Sierra Leone, Singapore, Solomon Islands, Somalia, Spain, Sri Lanka, Sudan, Suriname, Swaziland, Sweden, Syrian Arab Republic, Thailand, Togo, Trinidad and Tobago, Tunisia, Turkey, Uganda, Ukrainian SSR, USSR, United Arab Emirates, United Republic of Tanzania, Uruguay, Vanuatu, Venezuela, Viet Nam, Yemen, Yugoslavia, Zaire, Zambia, Zimbabwe.

Against: United Kingdom, United States.

Abstaining: Belgium, Canada, Germany, Federal Republic of, Israel, Italy, Luxembourg, Netherlands.

The Assembly took related action in **resolution 43/105**, by which it reaffirmed that the universal realization of the right of all peoples to self-determination was a fundamental condition for the guarantee of human rights.

Implementation of the Declaration by UN organizations

In response to a 1987 request by the General Assembly,[3] the Secretary-General invited 25 specialized agencies and other international organizations to submit information on their activities aimed at implementing the 1960 Declaration. He submitted a report in May 1988, with three later addenda,[4] which summarized the responses received from 18 of the organizations.

The issue of implementation by the specialized agencies and international institutions associated with the United Nations was the subject of consultations between the President of the Economic and Social Council and the Chairman of the Committee on colonial countries. In a report describing the consultations,[5] held in response to a 1987 request by the Council,[6] the two officers noted that several international agencies and organizations had continued to extend assistance in varying degrees to the peoples of Non-Self-Governing Territories (NSGTs). However, they remarked that the assistance had been far from adequate in terms of the critical needs of the peoples concerned, particularly those in southern Africa. They considered it imperative that the organizations should intensify their assistance to those peoples.

The Committee on colonial countries considered the issue and adopted a resolution[7] which was the basis of a draft forwarded to the Assembly for consideration.

ECONOMIC AND SOCIAL COUNCIL ACTION

On 26 July, the Economic and Social Council adopted by roll-call vote **resolution 1988/53**, as recommended by its Third (Programme and Co-ordination) Committee.

Implementation of the Declaration on the Granting of Independence to Colonial Countries and Peoples by the specialized agencies and the international institutions associated with the United Nations

The Economic and Social Council,

Having examined the report of the Secretary-General and the report of the President of the Economic and Social Council concerning the question of the implementation of the Declaration on the Granting of Independence to Colonial Countries and Peoples by the specialized agencies and the international institutions associated with the United Nations,

Having heard the statements made by the Chairman of the Special Committee on the Situation with regard to the Implementation of the Declaration on the Granting of Independence to Colonial Countries and Peoples and by the Vice-Chairman of the Special Committee against *Apartheid,*

Recalling General Assembly resolution 1514(XV) of 14 December 1960, containing the Declaration on the Granting of Independence to Colonial Countries and Peoples, and all other resolutions adopted by United Nations bodies on this subject, in particular General Assembly resolution 42/75 of 4 December 1987 and Economic and Social Council resolution 1987/78 of 8 July 1987,

Recalling also General Assembly resolutions S-14/1 of 20 September 1986 and 42/14 of 6 November 1987 on the question of Namibia and 42/23 of 20 November 1987

on the policies of *apartheid* of the Government of South Africa,

Deeply concerned that the objectives of the Charter of the United Nations and the Declaration on the Granting of Independence to Colonial Countries and Peoples have not been fully achieved as regards the peoples under colonial and alien domination, particularly those struggling in Namibia and South Africa under the repressive rule of the racist régime of Pretoria,

Reaffirming the responsibility of the specialized agencies and other organizations within the United Nations system to take all effective measures, within their respective spheres of competence, to assist in the full and speedy implementation of the Declaration and other relevant resolutions of United Nations bodies,

Noting with deep concern that South Africa continues to present a serious threat to international peace and security owing to its practice of *apartheid,* its illegal occupation of Namibia and its acts of aggression and destabilization against the front-line and neighbouring States,

Strongly condemning the continuing breach by South Africa of the obligations assumed by it under the Charter of the United Nations and its persistent non-compliance with the relevant resolutions and decisions of the United Nations,

Reaffirming that the denial of full political and civil rights to the majority of the population of South Africa is the result of the continuation of a colonial situation in that country,

Deeply conscious of the continuing critical need of the people of Namibia and their national liberation movement, the South West Africa People's Organization, for concrete assistance from the specialized agencies and the international institutions associated with the United Nations in their struggle for liberation from the illegal occupation of their country by the racist minority régime of South Africa,

Appreciating that progress has been maintained in the extension of assistance to refugees from southern Africa through the continuing efforts of the United Nations High Commissioner for Refugees,

Deeply concerned that the action taken thus far by the organizations concerned in the provision of assistance to the people of Namibia is still far from adequate to meet their urgent and growing needs,

Gravely concerned at the continued financial and other links of the International Monetary Fund with the Government of South Africa, in disregard of relevant General Assembly resolutions,

Noting with satisfaction the continuing efforts of the United Nations Development Programme in the extension of assistance to Namibia and the national liberation movement concerned, and commending the initiative taken by that organization in establishing channels for closer, periodic contacts and consultations between the specialized agencies and United Nations institutions and the Organization of African Unity and the national liberation movement in the formulation of assistance programmes,

1. *Takes note* of the report of the President of the Economic and Social Council, and endorses the observations and suggestions contained therein;

2. *Reaffirms* that the recognition by the General Assembly, the Security Council and other United Nations organs of the legitimacy of the struggle of colonial peoples to exercise their right to self-determination and in-

dependence entails, as a corollary, the extension by the United Nations system of organizations of all the necessary moral and material assistance to the peoples of Namibia and South Africa and their national liberation movements;

3. *Expresses its appreciation* to those specialized agencies and other organizations within the United Nations system that have continued to co-operate in varying degrees with the United Nations and the Organization of African Unity in the implementation of the Declaration on the Granting of Independence to Colonial Countries and Peoples and other relevant resolutions of United Nations bodies, and urges all the specialized agencies and other organizations within the United Nations system, in particular the World Bank, the International Finance Corporation and the International Monetary Fund, to contribute to the full and speedy implementation of the relevant provisions of those resolutions;

4. *Requests* the specialized agencies and other organizations within the United Nations system, in the light of the intensification of the liberation struggle in Namibia, to do everything possible as a matter of urgency to render increased assistance to the people of Namibia, in consultation with the Organization of African Unity and the United Nations Council for Namibia, in particular in connection with the Nationhood Programme for Namibia;

5. *Requests* the specialized agencies and other organizations within the United Nations system, in view of the deteriorating situation in South Africa and the acts of aggression and destabilization by the *apartheid* régime against States in the region, to increase their assistance to the front-line and neighbouring States and to the liberation movements in South Africa;

6. *Also requests* the specialized agencies and other organizations within the United Nations system to continue to take, in accordance with the relevant resolutions of the General Assembly and the Security Council, all necessary measures to withhold any financial, economic, technical or other assistance from the Government of South Africa until that Government restores to the people of Namibia their inalienable right to self-determination and independence, and to refrain from taking any action that might imply recognition of, or support for, the illegal occupation of Namibia by that régime;

7. *Further requests* the specialized agencies and other organizations within the United Nations system, in accordance with the relevant resolutions of the General Assembly and the Security Council on the policies of *apartheid* of the Government of South Africa, to intensify their support for the oppressed people of South Africa and to take such measures as will totally isolate the *apartheid* régime and mobilize world public opinion against *apartheid;*

8. *Condemns* the persistent non-compliance of the Government of South Africa with United Nations resolutions and decisions, in particular Security Council resolution 435(1978) of 29 September 1978 containing the United Nations plan for the independence of Namibia, and declares illegal and null and void the installation on 17 June 1985 of a so-called interim government at Windhoek;

9. *Deeply deplores* the financial and other links of the International Monetary Fund with the Government of South Africa, in disregard of repeated General Assembly resolutions to the contrary, and urgently calls upon the Fund to put an end to such links;

10. *Recommends once again* that a separate item on assistance to national liberation movements recognized by the Organization of African Unity be included in the agenda of future high-level meetings of the General Secretariat of the Organization of African Unity and the secretariats of the United Nations and other organizations within the United Nations system, with a view to strengthening further the existing measures for co-ordination of action to ensure the best use of available resources for assistance to the peoples of the colonial Territories;

11. *Notes with satisfaction* the inclusion of Namibia, represented by the United Nations Council for Namibia, in the membership of various organizations within the United Nations system, and urges those that have not yet granted full membership to the United Nations Council for Namibia to do so without delay;

12. *Notes with satisfaction also* the arrangements made by several specialized agencies and United Nations institutions that enable representatives of the national liberation movements recognized by the Organization of African Unity to participate fully as observers in proceedings relating to matters concerning their countries, and calls upon those international institutions that have not yet done so to make such arrangements without delay, including arrangements to defray the cost of the participation of those representatives;

13. *Recommends* that all States intensify their efforts in the specialized agencies and other organizations within the United Nations system of which they are members to ensure the full and effective implementation of the Declaration on the Granting of Independence to Colonial Countries and Peoples and other relevant resolutions of United Nations bodies;

14. *Urges* the governing bodies of those specialized agencies and other organizations within the United Nations system that have not already done so to include in the agenda of their regular sessions a separate item on the progress made and action to be taken by their organization in the implementation of the Declaration on the Granting of Independence to Colonial Countries and Peoples and other relevant resolutions of United Nations bodies;

15. *Also urges* the executive heads of the specialized agencies and other organizations within the United Nations system to formulate, with the active co-operation of the Organization of African Unity, and to submit, as a matter of priority, to their governing and legislative organs concrete proposals for the full implementation of the relevant United Nations decisions;

16. *Draws the attention* of the Special Committee on the Situation with regard to the Implementation of the Declaration on the Granting of Independence to Colonial Countries and Peoples and the Special Committee against *Apartheid* to the present resolution and to the discussion on the subject at the second regular session of 1988 of the Economic and Social Council;

17. *Requests* the President of the Economic and Social Council to continue consultations on these matters with the Chairman of the Special Committee on the Situation with regard to the Implementation of the Declaration on the Granting of Independence to Colonial Countries and Peoples and the Chairman of the Spe-

cial Committee against *Apartheid* and to report thereon to the Council;

18. *Requests* the Secretary-General to follow the implementation of the present resolution, with particular attention to co-ordination and integration arrangements for maximizing the efficiency of the assistance activities undertaken by various organizations of the United Nations system aimed at enabling the Namibian people to achieve their independence speedily, and to report thereon to the Council at its second regular session of 1989;

19. *Decides* to keep these questions under continuous review.

Economic and Social Council resolution 1988/53

26 July 1988   Meeting 38   38-1-12 (roll-call vote)

Approved by Third Committee (E/1988/107) by vote (33-1-12), 15 July (meeting 8); 22-nation draft (E/1988/C.3/L.2); agenda item 19.

Sponsors: Afghanistan, Bulgaria, Cuba, Djibouti, Egypt, Ethiopia, German Democratic Republic, Ghana, Guinea, Iran, Iraq, Mozambique, Pakistan, Peru, Sierra Leone, Somalia, Sudan, Syrian Arab Republic, Trinidad and Tobago, Tunisia, United Republic of Tanzania, Yugoslavia.

Roll-call vote in Council as follows:

In favour: Bolivia, Bulgaria, Byelorussian SSR, China, Colombia, Cuba, Egypt, German Democratic Republic, Ghana, Guinea, India, Iran, Iraq, Jamaica, Lesotho, Liberia, Libyan Arab Jamahiriya, Mozambique, Norway, Oman, Pakistan, Panama, Peru, Philippines, Poland, Rwanda, Saudi Arabia, Sierra Leone, Somalia, Sri Lanka, Sudan, Syrian Arab Republic, Trinidad and Tobago, USSR, Uruguay, Vanuatu, Venezuela, Yugoslavia, Zaire.

Against: United States.

Abstaining: Australia, Belgium, Canada, Denmark, France, Germany, Federal Republic of, Greece, Ireland, Italy, Japan, Portugal, United Kingdom.

The Council held separate roll-call votes on three paragraphs. The seventh preambular paragraph was adopted by 37 votes to 2, with 11 abstentions, the thirteenth preambular paragraph by 36 to 1, with 13 abstentions, and paragraph 9 by 36 to 1, with 13 abstentions. The Third Committee had approved the paragraphs by votes of 34-2-9, 33-1-13 and 33-1-13, respectively.

GENERAL ASSEMBLY ACTION

On 22 November, acting on the recommendation of the Fourth Committee, the General Assembly adopted by recorded vote **resolution 43/30**.

Implementation of the Declaration on the Granting of Independence to Colonial Countries and Peoples by the specialized agencies and the international institutions associated with the United Nations

The General Assembly,

Having considered the item entitled ''Implementation of the Declaration on the Granting of Independence to Colonial Countries and Peoples by the specialized agencies and the international institutions associated with the United Nations'',

Having considered the reports submitted on the item by the Secretary-General, and the Chairman of the Special Committee on the Situation with regard to the Implementation of the Declaration on the Granting of Independence to Colonial Countries and Peoples,

Recalling the Declaration on the Granting of Independence to Colonial Countries and Peoples, contained in its resolution 1514(XV) of 14 December 1960, the Plan of Action for the Full Implementation of the Declaration, contained in the annex to its resolution 35/118 of 11 December 1980, and its resolution 40/56 of 2 December 1985 on the twenty-fifth anniversary of the Declaration, as well as all other relevant General Assembly resolutions, including in particular resolution 42/75 of 4 December 1987,

Recalling also its resolutions ES-8/2 of 14 September 1981, S-14/1 of 20 September 1986 and 42/14 A to E of 6 November 1987 on the question of Namibia,

Taking into account the relevant provisions of the Declaration of the International Conference for the Immediate Independence of Namibia and the Programme of Action on Namibia, the Declaration adopted by the World Conference on Sanctions against Racist South Africa, the Luanda Declaration and Programme of Action adopted by the United Nations Council for Namibia at its extraordinary plenary meetings held at Luanda from 18 to 22 May 1987, and the final communiqué adopted by the United Nations Council for Namibia at its ministerial meeting held in New York on 2 October 1987,

Bearing in mind the relevant provisions of the final documents of the Eighth Conference of Heads of State or Government of Non-Aligned Countries, held at Harare from 1 to 6 September 1986, and of the resolution on the question of Namibia adopted by the Council of Ministers of the Organization of African Unity at its forty-eighth ordinary session, held at Addis Ababa from 19 to 23 May 1988,

Aware that the struggle of the people of Namibia for self-determination and independence is in its crucial stage and has sharply intensified as a consequence of the stepped-up aggression of the illegal colonialist régime of Pretoria against the people of the Territory and the increased support rendered to that régime by its allies, coupled with efforts to deprive the Namibian people of their hard-won victories in the liberation struggle, and that it is therefore incumbent upon the entire international community decisively to intensify concerted action in support of the people of Namibia and their sole and authentic representative, the South West Africa People's Organization, for the attainment of their goal,

Concerned that the policy of ''constructive engagement'' with the *apartheid* régime of South Africa and the ''linkage'', as well as economic and military collaboration maintained by certain Western Powers, Israel and other countries with Pretoria, have only encouraged and strengthened the racist régime in its continued illegal occupation and massive militarization and exploitation of Namibia in violation of the relevant resolutions and decisions of the United Nations,

Gravely concerned at the continued imperialist and neo-colonialist support for South Africa's oppressive and aggressive policies in Namibia and with respect to independent States in southern Africa, in particular the front-line States, as exemplified by the discussions and resolutions of the Security Council,

Conscious of the worsening of the situation in southern Africa because of South Africa's racist policies of oppression, aggression and occupation, which constitute a clear threat to world peace and security, and condemning the continuing breach by South Africa of the obligations assumed by it under the Charter of the United Nations and its persistent non-compliance with the relevant resolutions and decisions of the United Nations,

Deeply conscious of the continuing critical need of the Namibian people and their national liberation movement, the South West Africa People's Organization, and of the peoples of other colonial Territories for concrete assistance from the specialized agencies and other organizations of the United Nations system in their struggle for liberation from colonial rule and in their efforts to achieve and consolidate their national independence,

Deeply concerned that, although there has been progress in the extension of assistance to refugees from Namibia, the actions taken hitherto by the organizations concerned in providing assistance to the people of the Territory through their national liberation movement, the South West Africa People's Organization, still remain inadequate to meet the urgent and growing needs of the Namibian people,

Reaffirming the responsibility of the specialized agencies and other organizations of the United Nations system to take all the necessary measures, within their respective spheres of competence, to ensure the full and speedy implementation of General Assembly resolution 1514(XV) and other relevant resolutions of the United Nations, particularly those relating to the provision of moral and material assistance, on a priority basis, to the peoples of the colonial Territories and their national liberation movements,

Expressing its firm belief that closer contacts and consultations between the specialized agencies and other organizations of the United Nations system, on the one hand, and the Organization of African Unity and the South West Africa People's Organization, on the other, will help these agencies and organizations to overcome procedural and other difficulties which have impeded or delayed the implementation of some assistance programmes,

Recalling its resolution 42/14 C of 6 November 1987 in which it requested all specialized agencies and other organizations of the United Nations system to grant full membership to Namibia, represented by the United Nations Council for Namibia, so that the Council may participate as the legal Administering Authority for Namibia in the work of those agencies and organizations,

Expressing its appreciation to the General Secretariat of the Organization of African Unity for the continued co-operation and assistance it has extended to the specialized agencies and other organizations of the United Nations system in connection with the implementation of the relevant resolutions of the United Nations,

Expressing its appreciation to the Governments of the front-line States for the steadfast support extended to the people of Namibia and their national liberation movement, the South West Africa People's Organization, in their just and legitimate struggle for the attainment of freedom and independence despite increased armed attacks by the forces of the racist régime of South Africa, and aware of the particular needs of those Governments for assistance in that connection,

Noting the support given by the specialized agencies and other organizations of the United Nations system to the implementation of the Nationhood Programme for Namibia, in accordance with General Assembly resolution 32/9 A of 4 November 1977,

Deploring the continued co-operation with and assistance rendered to South Africa by certain specialized agencies in the financial, economic, technical and other fields in contravention of the relevant resolutions of the United Nations, thus enhancing neo-colonialist practices in the system of international relations,

Bearing in mind the importance of the activities of non-governmental organizations aimed at putting an end to the assistance which is still being rendered to South Africa by some specialized agencies,

Mindful of the imperative need to keep under continuous review the activities of the specialized agencies and other organizations of the United Nations system in the implementation of the various United Nations decisions relating to decolonization,

1. *Approves* the chapter of the report of the Special Committee on the Situation with regard to the Implementation of the Declaration on the Granting of Independence to Colonial Countries and Peoples relating to the item;

2. *Reaffirms* that the specialized agencies and other organizations and institutions of the United Nations system should continue to be guided by the relevant resolutions of the United Nations in their efforts to contribute, within their spheres of competence, to the full and speedy implementation of the Declaration on the Granting of Independence to Colonial Countries and Peoples;

3. *Reaffirms also* that the recognition by the General Assembly, the Security Council and other United Nations organs of the legitimacy of the struggle of colonial peoples to exercise their right to self-determination and independence entails, as a corollary, the extension by the specialized agencies and other organizations of the United Nations system of all the necessary moral and material assistance to those peoples and their national liberation movements;

4. *Expresses its appreciation* to those specialized agencies and other organizations of the United Nations system that have continued to co-operate in varying degrees with the United Nations and the Organization of African Unity in the implementation of General Assembly resolution 1514(XV) and other relevant resolutions of the United Nations, and urges all the specialized agencies and other organizations of the United Nations system to accelerate the full and speedy implementation of the relevant provisions of those resolutions;

5. *Expresses its concern* that the assistance extended thus far by certain specialized agencies and other organizations of the United Nations system to the colonial peoples, particularly the people of Namibia and their national liberation movement, the South West Africa People's Organization, is far from adequate in relation to the actual needs of the peoples concerned;

6. *Reiterates its conviction* that the specialized agencies and other organizations and bodies of the United Nations system should refrain from taking any action that might imply recognition of, or support for, the legitimacy of the domination of the Territory of Namibia by the racist régime of South Africa;

7. *Requests* all specialized agencies and other organizations and bodies of the United Nations system, in accordance with the relevant resolutions of the General Assembly and of the Security Council, to take all necessary measures to withhold from the racist régime of South Africa any form of co-operation and assistance in the financial, economic, technical and other fields and to discontinue all support to that régime until the people of Namibia have exercised fully their inalienable right to self-determination, freedom and national independence in a united Namibia and until the inhuman system of *apartheid* has been totally eradicated;

8. *Regrets* that the World Bank and the International Monetary Fund continue to maintain links with the racist régime of Pretoria, expresses the view that all links should be discontinued and, pending that action, calls upon those organizations not to extend any support or loans to that régime;

9. *Urges once again* the executive heads of the World Bank and the International Monetary Fund to draw the particular attention of their governing bodies to the present resolution with a view, *inter alia*, to formulating specific programmes beneficial to the peoples of the colonial Territories, particularly Namibia;

10. *Requests* the specialized agencies and other organizations of the United Nations system to render or continue to render, as a matter of urgency, all possible moral and material assistance to the colonial peoples struggling for liberation from colonial rule, bearing in mind that such assistance should not only meet their immediate needs but also create conditions for development after they have exercised their right to self-determination and independence;

11. *Requests once again* the specialized agencies and other organizations of the United Nations system to continue to provide all moral and material assistance to the newly independent and emerging States so as to enable them to achieve genuine economic independence;

12. *Reiterates its recommendation* that the specialized agencies and other organizations of the United Nations system should initiate or broaden contacts and co-operation with the colonial peoples and their national liberation movements directly or, where appropriate, through the Organization of African Unity, and review and introduce greater flexibility in their procedures with respect to the formulation and preparation of assistance programmes and projects so as to be able to extend the necessary assistance without delay to help the colonial peoples and their national liberation movements in their struggle to exercise their inalienable right to self-determination and independence in accordance with General Assembly resolution 1514(XV);

13. *Recommends* that a separate item on assistance to national liberation movements recognized by the Organization of African Unity should be included in the agenda of future high-level meetings between the General Secretariat of the Organization of African Unity and the secretariats of the United Nations and other organizations of the United Nations system, with a view to strengthening further the existing measures of co-ordination of action to ensure the best use of available resources for assistance to the peoples of the colonial Territories;

14. *Urges* the specialized agencies and other organizations of the United Nations system that have not already done so to include in the agenda of the regular meetings of their governing bodies a separate item on the progress they have made in the implementation of resolution 1514(XV) and the other relevant resolutions of the United Nations;

15. *Urges* the specialized agencies and other organizations and institutions of the United Nations system to extend, as a matter of priority, substantial material assistance to the Governments of the front-line States in order to enable them to support more effectively the struggle of the people of Namibia for freedom and independence and to resist the violation of their territorial integrity by the armed forces of the racist régime of South Africa directly or, as in Angola and Mozambique, through puppet groups in the service of Pretoria;

16. *Welcomes* the establishment by the non-aligned countries of the Action for Resisting Invasion, Colonialism and *Apartheid* Fund and invites the specialized agencies and other organizations of the United Nations system to co-operate with the Fund in the common objective of providing emergency assistance to the front-line States and national liberation movements in southern Africa in their struggle against the *apartheid* régime;

17. *Notes with satisfaction* the arrangements made by several specialized agencies and other organizations of the United Nations system to enable representatives of the national liberation movements recognized by the Organization of African Unity to participate fully as observers in the proceedings relating to matters concerning their respective countries, and calls upon those agencies and organizations that have not yet done so to follow this example and to make the necessary arrangements without delay;

18. *Urges* the specialized agencies and other organizations and institutions of the United Nations system to assist in accelerating progress in all sectors of the national life of colonial Territories, particularly in the development of their economies;

19. *Draws the particular attention* of the specialized agencies and other organizations of the United Nations system to Security Council resolution 566(1985) of 19 June 1985, in which the Council condemned the racist régime of South Africa for its installation of a so-called interim government in Namibia and declared that action to be illegal and null and void;

20. *Recommends* that all Governments should intensify their efforts in the specialized agencies and other organizations of the United Nations system of which they are members to ensure the full and effective implementation of General Assembly resolution 1514(XV) and other relevant resolutions of the United Nations and, in that connection, should accord priority to the question of providing assistance on an emergency basis to the peoples of the colonial Territories and their national liberation movements;

21. *Draws the attention* of the specialized agencies and other organizations of the United Nations system to the Plan of Action for the Full Implementation of the Declaration on the Granting of Independence to Colonial Countries and Peoples, contained in the annex to General Assembly resolution 35/118, in particular to those provisions calling upon the agencies and organizations to render all possible moral and material assistance to the peoples of the colonial Territories and to their national liberation movements;

22. *Urges* the executive heads of the specialized agencies and other organizations of the United Nations system, having regard to the provisions of paragraph 13 above, to formulate, with the active co-operation of the Organization of African Unity where appropriate, and to submit, as a matter of priority, to their governing and legislative organs concrete proposals for the full implementation of the relevant United Nations decisions, in particular specific programmes of assistance to the peoples of the colonial Territories and their national liberation movements;

23. *Requests* the Secretary-General to continue to assist the specialized agencies and other organizations of the United Nations system in working out appropriate

measures for implementing the relevant resolutions of the United Nations and to prepare for submission to the relevant bodies, with the assistance of those agencies and organizations, a report on the action taken in implementation of the relevant resolutions, including the present resolution, since the circulation of his previous report;

24. *Requests* the Economic and Social Council to continue to consider, in consultation with the Special Committee on the Situation with regard to the Implementation of the Declaration on the Granting of Independence to Colonial Countries and Peoples, appropriate measures for co-ordination of the policies and activities of the specialized agencies and other organizations of the United Nations system in implementing the relevant resolutions of the General Assembly;

25. *Requests* the specialized agencies to report periodically to the Secretary-General on their implementation of the present resolution;

26. *Requests* the Special Committee to continue to examine the question and to report thereon to the General Assembly at its forty-fourth session.

General Assembly resolution 43/30

22 November 1988   Meeting 59   124-4-27 (recorded vote)

Approved by Fourth Committee (A/43/788) by recorded vote (118-3-26), 25 October (meeting 13); draft by Committee on colonial countries (A/43/23); agenda items 110 & 12.

Meeting numbers. GA 43rd session: 4th Committee 7-14; plenary 59.

Recorded vote in Assembly as follows:

In favour: Afghanistan, Albania, Algeria, Angola, Antigua and Barbuda, Argentina, Bahamas, Bahrain, Bangladesh, Barbados, Belize, Benin, Bhutan, Bolivia, Botswana, Brazil, Brunei Darussalam, Bulgaria, Burkina Faso, Burma, Burundi, Byelorussian SSR, Cape Verde, Chad, Chile, China, Colombia, Comoros, Congo, Cuba, Cyprus, Czechoslovakia, Democratic Kampuchea, Democratic Yemen, Djibouti, Dominican Republic, Ecuador, Egypt, Ethiopia, Fiji, Gambia, German Democratic Republic, Ghana, Greece, Grenada, Guatemala, Guinea, Guinea-Bissau, Guyana, Haiti, Hungary, India, Indonesia, Iran, Iraq, Jamaica, Jordan, Kenya, Kuwait, Lao People's Democratic Republic, Lebanon, Lesotho, Liberia, Libyan Arab Jamahiriya, Madagascar, Malawi, Malaysia, Maldives, Mali, Mauritania, Mauritius, Mexico, Mongolia, Morocco, Mozambique, Nepal, Nicaragua, Niger, Nigeria, Oman, Pakistan, Panama, Papua New Guinea, Peru, Philippines, Poland, Qatar, Romania, Rwanda, Saint Kitts and Nevis, Saint Lucia, Saint Vincent and the Grenadines, Samoa, Sao Tome and Principe, Saudi Arabia, Senegal, Seychelles, Sierra Leone, Singapore, Solomon Islands, Somalia, Sri Lanka, Sudan, Suriname, Swaziland, Syrian Arab Republic, Thailand, Togo, Trinidad and Tobago, Tunisia, Uganda, Ukrainian SSR, USSR, United Arab Emirates, United Republic of Tanzania, Uruguay, Vanuatu, Venezuela, Viet Nam, Yemen, Yugoslavia, Zaire, Zambia, Zimbabwe.

Against: Germany, Federal Republic of,* Israel, United Kingdom, United States.

Abstaining: Australia, Austria, Belgium, Canada, Central African Republic, Costa Rica, Côte d'Ivoire, Denmark, Dominica, El Salvador, Equatorial Guinea, Finland, France, Honduras, Iceland, Ireland, Italy, Japan, Luxembourg, Malta, Netherlands, New Zealand, Norway, Portugal, Spain, Sweden, Turkey.

*Later advised the Secretariat it had intended to abstain.

In the Fourth Committee, Israel requested a separate vote on the word ''Israel'' in the eighth preambular paragraph; the word was retained by a recorded vote of 72 to 38, with 29 abstentions.

In **resolution 43/46**, the Assembly requested the specialized agencies and other United Nations organizations to disseminate information on decolonization. In **resolution 43/45**, it called on the agencies to give effect to the recommendations of the Committee on colonial countries.

Foreign interests impeding implementation of the Declaration

In 1988, the Committee on colonial countries continued to consider the activities of foreign economic, financial and other interests operating in colonial Territories, particularly in southern Africa, which it said were obstructing the political independence of indigenous populations. It reaffirmed its concern about those activities and adopted a resolution[8] which became the basis of a draft it recommended to the General Assembly.

GENERAL ASSEMBLY ACTION

On 22 November, the General Assembly, acting on the recommendation of the Fourth Committee, adopted **resolution 43/29** by recorded vote.

Activities of foreign economic and other interests which are impeding the implementation of the Declaration on the Granting of Independence to Colonial Countries and Peoples in Namibia and in all other Territories under colonial domination and efforts to eliminate colonialism, *apartheid* and racial discrimination in southern Africa

The General Assembly,

Having considered the item entitled ''Activities of foreign economic and other interests which are impeding the implementation of the Declaration on the Granting of Independence to Colonial Countries and Peoples in Namibia and in all other Territories under colonial domination and efforts to eliminate colonialism, *apartheid* and racial discrimination in southern Africa'',

Having examined the chapter of the report of the Special Committee on the Situation with regard to the Implementation of the Declaration on the Granting of Independence to Colonial Countries and Peoples relating to the item,

Taking into consideration the relevant chapters of the report of the United Nations Council for Namibia,

Recalling its resolutions 1514(XV) of 14 December 1960, containing the Declaration on the Granting of Independence to Colonial Countries and Peoples, 2621(XXV) of 12 October 1970, containing the programme of action for the full implementation of the Declaration, 35/118 of 11 December 1980, the annex to which contains the Plan of Action for the Full Implementation of the Declaration, and 40/56 of 2 December 1985 on the twenty-fifth anniversary of the Declaration, as well as all other resolutions of the United Nations relating to the item,

Reaffirming the solemn obligation of the administering Powers under the Charter of the United Nations to promote the political, economic, social and educational advancement of the inhabitants of the Territories under their administration and to protect the human and natural resources of those Territories against abuses,

Reaffirming that any economic or other activity that impedes the implementation of the Declaration on the Granting of Independence to Colonial Countries and Peoples and obstructs efforts aimed at the elimination of colonialism, *apartheid* and racial discrimination in southern Africa and other colonial Territories is in direct violation of the rights of the inhabitants and of the principles of the Charter and all relevant resolutions of the United Nations,

Reaffirming that the natural resources of all Territories under colonial and racist domination are the heritage of the peoples of those Territories and that the depletive exploitation of those resources by foreign economic interests, in particular in Namibia, in association with the occupying régime of South Africa, constitute a direct violation of the rights of the peoples and of the principles of the Charter and all relevant resolutions of the United Nations,

Bearing in mind the relevant provisions of the final communiqué of the Meeting of Ministers for Foreign Affairs and Heads of Delegation of Non-Aligned Countries to the forty-second session of the General Assembly, held in New York from 5 to 7 October 1987, and the relevant resolutions adopted by the Assembly of Heads of State and Government of the Organization of African Unity at its twenty-fourth ordinary session, held at Addis Ababa from 25 to 28 May 1988,

Taking into account the relevant provisions of the documents adopted by the World Conference on Sanctions against Racist South Africa and the International Conference for the Immediate Independence of Namibia, and of the Luanda Declaration and Programme of Action adopted by the United Nations Council for Namibia at its extraordinary plenary meetings held at Luanda from 18 to 22 May 1987, and the final communiqué adopted by the United Nations Council for Namibia at its ministerial meeting held in New York on 2 October 1987,

Noting with profound concern that the colonial Powers and certain States, through their activities in the colonial Territories, have continued to disregard United Nations decisions on the subject and that they have failed to implement, in particular, the relevant provisions of General Assembly resolutions 2621(XXV) of 12 October 1970 and 42/74 of 4 December 1987, by which the Assembly called upon the colonial Powers and those Governments that had not yet done so to take legislative, administrative or other measures in respect of their nationals and the bodies corporate under their jurisdiction that own and operate enterprises in colonial Territories, particularly in Africa, that are detrimental to the interests of the inhabitants of those Territories, in order to put an end to such enterprises and to prevent new investments that run counter to the interests of the inhabitants of those Territories,

Condemning the intensified activities of those foreign economic, financial and other interests that continue to exploit the natural and human resources of the colonial Territories and to accumulate and repatriate huge profits to the detriment of the interests of the inhabitants, particularly in the case of Namibia, thereby impeding the realization by the peoples of the Territories of their legitimate aspirations for self-determination and independence,

Strongly condemning the support that the racist minority régime of South Africa continues to receive from those foreign economic, financial and other interests that are collaborating with the régime in the exploitation of the natural and human resources of the international Territory of Namibia, in the further entrenchment of its illegal racist domination over the Territory and in the strengthening of its system of *apartheid,*

Strongly condemning the investment of foreign capital in the production of uranium and the collaboration by certain Western and other countries with the racist minority régime of South Africa in the nuclear field which, by providing that régime with nuclear equipment and technology, enable it to develop nuclear and military capabilities and to become a nuclear Power, thereby promoting South Africa's continued illegal occupation of Namibia,

Reaffirming that the natural resources of Namibia, including its marine resources, are the inviolable and incontestable heritage of the Namibian people and that the exploitation and depletion of those resources, particularly the uranium deposits, as a result of their plunder by South Africa and certain Western and other foreign economic interests, in violation of the Charter, of the relevant resolutions of the General Assembly and the Security Council and of Decree No. 1 for the Protection of the Natural Resources of Namibia, enacted by the United Nations Council for Namibia on 27 September 1974, and in disregard of the advisory opinion of the International Court of Justice of 21 June 1971, are considered to be illegal, that they contribute to the maintenance of the illegal occupation régime and are a grave threat to the integrity and prosperity of an independent Namibia,

Recalling its endorsement of the decision by the United Nations Council for Namibia that, in the exercise of the Council's rights under the United Nations Convention on the Law of the Sea, the Council would proclaim an exclusive economic zone for Namibia, the outer limit of which would be 200 miles, and recalling also its statement that any action regarding the implementation of the Council's decision should be taken in consultation with the South West Africa People's Organization, the sole and authentic representative of the Namibian people,

Expressing its support for the initiation by the United Nations Council for Namibia of legal proceedings in the domestic courts of States against corporations or individuals involved in the exploitation, transport, processing or purchase of Namibia's natural resources, as part of the efforts of the Council to give effect to Decree No. 1 for the Protection of the Natural Resources of Namibia,

Concerned about any foreign economic, financial and other activities which continue to deprive the indigenous populations of colonial Territories, including certain Territories in the Caribbean and the Pacific Ocean regions, of their rights over the wealth of their countries, where the inhabitants of those Territories continue to suffer from a loss of land ownership as a result of the failure of the administering Powers concerned to restrict the sale of land to foreigners, despite the repeated appeals of the General Assembly,

Conscious of the continuing need to mobilize world public opinion against the involvement of foreign economic, financial and other interests in the exploitation of natural and human resources, which impedes the independence of colonial Territories and the elimination of racism, particularly in South Africa and Namibia, and emphasizing the importance of action by local authorities, trade unions, religious bodies, academic institutions, mass media, solidarity movements and other nongovernmental organizations, as well as individuals, in applying pressure on transnational corporations to refrain from any investment or activity in South Africa and Namibia, in encouraging a policy of systematic divestment of any financial or other interest in corporations doing business with South Africa and in counteracting all forms of collaboration with the occupation régime in Namibia,

1. *Reaffirms* the inalienable right of the peoples of dependent Territories to self-determination and independence and to the enjoyment of the natural resources of their Territories, as well as their right to dispose of those resources in their best interests;

2. *Reiterates* that any administering or occupying Power that deprives the colonial peoples of the exercise of their legitimate rights over their natural resources or subordinates the rights and interests of those peoples to foreign economic and financial interests violates the solemn obligations it has assumed under the Charter of the United Nations;

3. *Reaffirms* that, by their depletive exploitation of natural resources, the continued accumulation and repatriation of huge profits and the use of those profits for the enrichment of foreign settlers and the perpetuation of colonial domination and racial discrimination in the Territories, the activities of foreign economic, financial and other interests operating at present in the colonial Territories, particularly in Namibia, constitute a major obstacle to political independence and racial equality, as well as to the enjoyment of the natural resources of those Territories by the indigenous inhabitants;

4. *Condemns* the activities of foreign economic and other interests in the colonial Territories which impede the implementation of the Declaration on the Granting of Independence to Colonial Countries and Peoples and the efforts to eliminate colonialism, *apartheid* and racial discrimination;

5. *Condemns* the policies of Governments that continue to support or collaborate with those foreign economic and other interests engaged in exploiting the natural and human resources of the Territories, in particular, illegally exploiting Namibia's mineral and sea resources, violating the political, economic and social rights and interests of the indigenous peoples and thus obstructing the full and speedy implementation of the Declaration in respect of those Territories;

6. *Strongly condemns* the collaboration of the Governments of certain Western and other countries with the racist minority régime of South Africa in the nuclear field and calls upon those and all other Governments concerned to refrain from supplying that régime, directly or indirectly, with installations, equipment or material that might enable it to produce uranium, plutonium and other nuclear materials, reactors or military equipment;

7. *Strongly condemns* the collaboration with the racist minority régime of South Africa of certain Western and other countries as well as transnational corporations that continue to make new investments in South Africa and supply the régime with armaments, nuclear technology and all other materials that are likely to buttress it and thus aggravate the threat to world peace;

8. *Calls upon* all States, in particular certain Western and other States, to take urgent, effective measures to terminate all collaboration with the racist régime of South Africa in the political, economic, trade, military and nuclear fields and to refrain from entering into other relations with that régime in violation of the relevant resolutions of the United Nations and of the Organization of African Unity;

9. *Calls once again upon* all Governments that have not yet done so to take legislative, administrative or other measures in respect of their nationals and the bodies corporate under their jurisdiction that own and operate enterprises in colonial Territories, particularly in Africa, that are detrimental to the interests of the inhabitants of those Territories, in order to put an end to such enterprises and to prevent new investments that run counter to the interests of the inhabitants of those Territories;

10. *Calls upon* all States to terminate, or cause to have terminated, any investments in Namibia or loans to the racist minority régime of South Africa and to refrain from any agreements or measures to promote trade or other economic relations with that régime;

11. *Requests* all States that have not yet done so to take effective measures to end the supply of funds and other forms of assistance, including military supplies and equipment, to the racist minority régime of South Africa, which uses such assistance to repress the people of Namibia and their national liberation movement;

12. *Strongly condemns* South Africa for its continued exploitation and plundering of the natural resources of Namibia, leading to the rapid depletion of such resources, in complete disregard of the legitimate interests of the Namibian people, for the creation in the Territory of an economic structure dependent essentially upon its mineral resources and for its illegal extension of the territorial sea and its proclamation of an economic zone off the coast of Namibia;

13. *Reiterates* that all activities of foreign economic interests in Namibia are considered to be illegal under international law and declares that consequently South Africa and all the foreign economic interests operating in Namibia are liable to pay damages to the future legitimate Government of an independent Namibia, and recalls that the General Assembly called upon the United Nations Council for Namibia, in pursuance of the relevant provisions of Decree No. 1 for the Protection of the Natural Resources of Namibia, to continue to take the necessary steps to compile statistical information on the wealth illegally extracted from Namibia, with a view to assessing the extent of compensation eventually due to an independent Namibia;

14. *Calls upon* those oil-producing and oil-exporting countries that have not yet done so to take effective measures against the oil companies concerned so as to terminate the supply of crude oil and petroleum products to the racist régime of South Africa;

15. *Reiterates* that the exploitation and plundering of the marine and other natural resources of Namibia by South African and other foreign economic interests, including the activities of those transnational corporations that are engaged in the exploitation and export of the Territory's uranium ores and other resources, in violation of the relevant resolutions of the General Assembly and the Security Council and of Decree No. 1 for the Protection of the Natural Resources of Namibia, are considered to be illegal, that they contribute to the maintenance of the illegal occupation régime and are a grave threat to the integrity and prosperity of an independent Namibia;

16. *Condemns* the plunder of Namibian uranium and calls upon the Governments of all States, particularly those whose nationals and corporations are involved in the mining and processing of Namibian uranium, to take

all appropriate measures in compliance with the provisions of Decree No. 1 for the Protection of the Natural Resources of Namibia, including the practice of requiring negative certificates of origin, to prohibit and prevent State-owned and other corporations, together with their subsidiaries, from dealing in Namibian uranium and from engaging in uranium-prospecting activities in Namibia;

17. *Requests* the Governments of the Federal Republic of Germany, the Netherlands and the United Kingdom of Great Britain and Northern Ireland, which operate the Urenco uranium enrichment plant, to have Namibian uranium specifically excluded from the Treaty of Almelo, which regulates the activities of Urenco;

18. *Reiterates its request* to all States, pending the imposition of comprehensive mandatory sanctions against South Africa, to take legislative, administrative and other measures, individually or collectively, as appropriate, in order effectively to isolate South Africa politically, economically, militarily and culturally, in accordance with the relevant resolutions of the General Assembly, the most recent of which being resolutions 42/14 A to E of 6 November 1987, and encourages those Governments that have recently taken certain unilateral sanction measures against the South African régime to take further measures;

19. *Calls once again upon* all States to discontinue all economic, financial and trade co-operation with the racist minority régime of South Africa concerning Namibia and to refrain from entering into any relations with South Africa, purporting to act on behalf of or concerning Namibia, that may lend support to its continued illegal occupation of that Territory;

20. *Invites* all Governments and organizations of the United Nations system, having regard to the relevant provisions of the Declaration on the Establishment of a New International Economic Order, contained in General Assembly resolution 3201(S-VI) of 1 May 1974, and of the Charter of Economic Rights and Duties of States, contained in Assembly resolution 3281(XXIX) of 12 December 1974, to ensure, in particular, that the permanent sovereignty of the colonial Territories over their natural resources is fully respected and safeguarded;

21. *Urges* the administering Powers concerned to take effective measures to safeguard and guarantee the inalienable right of the peoples of the colonial Territories to their natural resources and to establish and maintain control over their future development and requests the administering Powers to take all necessary steps to protect the property rights of the peoples of those Territories;

22. *Calls upon* the administering Powers concerned to abolish all discriminatory and unjust wage systems and working conditions prevailing in the Territories under their administration and to apply in each Territory a uniform system of wages to all the inhabitants without any discrimination;

23. *Requests* the Secretary-General to undertake, through the Department of Public Information of the Secretariat, a sustained and broad campaign with a view to informing world public opinion of the facts concerning the pillaging of natural resources in colonial Territories and the exploitation of their indigenous populations by foreign economic interests and, in respect of Namibia, the support they render to the racist minority régime of South Africa;

24. *Appeals* to mass media, trade unions and non-governmental organizations, as well as individuals, to co-ordinate and intensify their efforts to mobilize international public opinion against the policy of the *apartheid* régime of South Africa and to work for the enforcement of economic and other sanctions against that régime and for encouraging a policy of systematic and genuine divestment from corporations doing business in South Africa;

25. *Decides* to continue to monitor closely the situation in the remaining colonial Territories so as to ensure that all economic activities in those Territories are aimed at strengthening and diversifying their economies in the interests of the indigenous peoples, at promoting the economic and financial viability of those Territories and at speeding their accession to independence and, in that connection, requests the administering Powers concerned to ensure that the peoples of the Territories under their administration are not exploited for political, military and other purposes detrimental to their interests;

26. *Requests* the Special Committee on the Situation with regard to the Implementation of the Declaration on the Granting of Independence to Colonial Countries and Peoples to continue to examine this question and to report thereon to the General Assembly at its forty-fourth session.

General Assembly resolution 43/29

22 November 1988   Meeting 59   133-9-14 (recorded vote)

Approved by Fourth Committee (A/43/761) by recorded vote (79-10-12), 10 October (meeting 6); draft by Committee on colonial countries (A/43/23); agenda item 109.

Meeting numbers. GA 43rd session: 4th Committee 2-6; plenary 59.

Recorded vote in Assembly as follows:

In favour: Afghanistan, Albania, Algeria, Angola, Antigua and Barbuda, Argentina, Australia, Bahamas, Bahrain, Bangladesh, Barbados, Belize, Benin, Bhutan, Bolivia, Botswana, Brazil, Brunei Darussalam, Bulgaria, Burkina Faso, Burma, Burundi, Byelorussian SSR, Cape Verde, Central African Republic, Chad, Chile, China, Colombia, Comoros, Congo, Costa Rica, Cuba, Cyprus, Czechoslovakia, Democratic Kampuchea, Democratic Yemen, Djibouti, Dominican Republic, Ecuador, Egypt, El Salvador, Equatorial Guinea, Ethiopia, Fiji, Gabon, Gambia, German Democratic Republic, Ghana, Grenada, Guatemala, Guinea, Guinea-Bissau, Guyana, Haiti, Honduras, Hungary, India, Indonesia, Iran, Iraq, Jamaica, Jordan, Kenya, Kuwait, Lao People's Democratic Republic, Lebanon, Lesotho, Liberia, Libyan Arab Jamahiriya, Madagascar, Malawi, Malaysia, Maldives, Mali, Malta, Mauritania, Mauritius, Mexico, Mongolia, Morocco, Mozambique, Nepal, New Zealand, Nicaragua, Niger, Nigeria, Oman, Pakistan, Panama, Papua New Guinea, Peru, Philippines, Poland, Qatar, Romania, Rwanda, Saint Kitts and Nevis, Saint Lucia, Saint Vincent and the Grenadines, Samoa, Sao Tome and Principe, Saudi Arabia, Senegal, Seychelles, Sierra Leone, Singapore, Solomon Islands, Somalia, Sri Lanka, Sudan, Suriname, Swaziland, Syrian Arab Republic, Thailand, Togo, Trinidad and Tobago, Tunisia, Turkey, Uganda, Ukrainian SSR, USSR, United Arab Emirates, United Republic of Tanzania, Uruguay, Vanuatu, Venezuela, Viet Nam, Yemen, Yugoslavia, Zaire, Zambia, Zimbabwe.

Against: Belgium, France, Germany, Federal Republic of, Italy, Luxembourg, Netherlands, Portugal, United Kingdom, United States.

Abstaining: Austria, Canada, Côte d'Ivoire, Denmark, Dominica, Finland, Greece, Iceland, Ireland, Israel, Japan, Norway, Spain, Sweden.

During its consideration of the topic, the Fourth Committee heard a statement by J. A. González-González, a journalist, after approving his request for a hearing.[9]

Military activities in colonial countries

Pursuant to a 1987 request by the General Assembly,[10] the Committee on colonial countries continued in 1988 to consider military activities and bases in colonial countries. On 8 August, it approved a decision on the subject,[11] which became the basis for a draft recommendation to the Assembly. On 11 August,[12] the Committee Chairman transmitted the decision to the Security Council, drawing attention to a paragraph in which the Committee urged the Council to make the arms embargo against South Africa more effective and comprehensive.

GENERAL ASSEMBLY ACTION

In November, the General Assembly adopted **decision 43/410** by recorded vote.

Military activities and arrangements by colonial Powers in Territories under their administration which might be impeding the implementation of the Declaration on the Granting of Independence to Colonial Countries and Peoples

At its 59th plenary meeting, on 22 November 1988, the General Assembly, on the recommendation of the Fourth Committee, adopted the following text:

"1. The General Assembly, having considered the chapter of the report of the Special Committee on the Situation with regard to the Implementation of the Declaration on the Granting of Independence to Colonial Countries and Peoples relating to an item on the agenda of the Special Committee entitled 'Military activities and arrangements by colonial Powers in Territories under their administration which might be impeding the implementation of the Declaration on the Granting of Independence to Colonial Countries and Peoples' and recalling its decision 42/417 of 4 December 1987 on the question, deplores the fact that the colonial Powers concerned have taken no steps to implement the request that the Assembly has repeatedly addressed to them, most recently in paragraph 10 of its resolution 42/71 of 4 December 1987, to withdraw immediately and unconditionally their military bases and installations from colonial Territories and to refrain from establishing new ones.

"2. In recalling its resolution 1514(XV) of 14 December 1960 and all other relevant resolutions and decisions of the United Nations relating to military bases and installations in colonial and Non-Self-Governing Territories, the General Assembly reaffirms its strong conviction that the presence of military bases and installations in the colonial and Non-Self-Governing Territories could constitute a major obstacle to the implementation of the Declaration on the Granting of Independence to Colonial Countries and Peoples and that it is the responsibility of the administering Powers to ensure that the existence of such bases and installations does not hinder the populations of the Territories from exercising their right to self-determination and independence in conformity with the purposes and principles of the Charter of the United Nations and the Declaration. Furthermore, aware of the presence of military bases and installations of the administering Powers concerned and other countries in those Territories, the Assembly urges the administering Powers concerned to continue to take all necessary measures not to involve those Territories in any offensive acts or interference against other States and to comply fully with the purposes and principles of the Charter, the Declaration and the resolutions and decisions of the United Nations relating to military activities and arrangements by colonial Powers in Territories under their administration.

"3. The General Assembly reiterates its condemnation of all military activities and arrangements by colonial Powers in Territories under their administration that are detrimental to the rights and interests of the colonial peoples concerned, especially their right to self-determination and independence. The Assembly once again calls upon the colonial Powers concerned to terminate immediately and unconditionally such activities and to eliminate such military bases in compliance with the relevant resolutions of the Assembly, in particular with paragraph 9 of the Plan of Action for the Full Implementation of the Declaration on the Granting of Independence to Colonial Countries and Peoples, contained in the annex to Assembly resolution 35/118 of 11 December 1980.

"4. The General Assembly reiterates that the colonial Territories and areas adjacent thereto should not be used for nuclear testing, dumping of nuclear wastes or deployment of nuclear and other weapons of mass destruction.

"5. The General Assembly notes with serious concern that, in southern Africa in general, and in and around Namibia in particular, a critical situation continues to prevail as a result of South Africa's continued illegal occupation of the Territory and its inhuman repression of the people of South Africa. The racist régime has resorted to desperate measures in order to suppress by force the legitimate aspirations of those peoples and, in its escalating war against them and their national liberation movements, struggling for freedom, justice and independence, the régime has repeatedly committed acts of armed aggression against the neighbouring independent African States, Angola, Botswana, Lesotho, Mozambique, Zambia and Zimbabwe, which have caused extensive loss of human lives and destruction of the economic infrastructure. The Assembly condemns the racist régime of South Africa for its utilization of the illegally occupied international Territory of Namibia as a springboard for perpetrating armed invasions, subversion, destabilization and aggression against neighbouring African States, in particular Angola; and declares that the policy of aggression and destabilization pursued by Pretoria not only undermines the peace and stability of the southern African region but also constitutes a threat to international peace and security, and demands the cessation forthwith of all such acts of aggression.

"6. The General Assembly strongly condemns South Africa for its military buildup in Namibia, its persistent acts of aggression and subversion against neighbouring African States, its introduction of compulsory military service for Namibians, its proclamation of a so-called security zone in Namibia, its forced recruitment and training of Namibians for tribal armies, its use of mercenaries to suppress the Namibian people and carry out its attacks against independent African States, in particular the front-line States, its illegal use of Namibian territory for acts of aggression against independent African States and its forcible displacement of Namibians from their homes. The Assembly calls upon all States to take effective measures to prevent the recruitment, training, financing and transit of mercenaries for service in Namibia. It condemns the continued military, nuclear and intelligence collaboration between South Africa and certain countries, which constitutes a violation of the arms embargo imposed against South Africa by the Security Council in its resolution 418(1977) of 4 November 1977, and which poses a threat to international peace and security. The Assembly urges that the Security Council consider, as a matter of urgency, the report of the Committee established under its resolution 421(1977) of 9 December 1977 and that it adopt further measures to widen the scope of resolution 418(1977) in order to make it more effective and comprehensive. The Assembly also calls for the scrupulous observance of Security Council resolution 558(1984) of 13 December 1984 enjoining all States to refrain from importing armaments from South Africa. The Assembly is particularly mindful in that regard of a series of resolutions adopted by the Security Council, the General Assembly, the Special Committee on the Situation with regard to the Implementation of the Declaration on the Granting of Independence to Colonial Countries and Peoples, the Special Committee against *Apartheid* and the United Nations Council for Namibia, as well as the Movement of Non-Aligned Countries, the Organization of African Unity, the Commonwealth and a number of intergovernmental and regional organizations.

"7. The General Assembly demands the urgent dismantling of all military bases in the international Territory of Namibia and calls for the immediate cessation of the war of oppression waged by the racist minority régime against the people of Namibia and their national liberation movement, the South West Africa People's Organization, their sole and authentic representative. Reaffirming the legitimacy of the struggle of the people of Namibia to achieve their freedom and independence, the Assembly appeals to all States to render sustained and increased moral and political support, as well as assistance in all fields, to the South West Africa People's Organization to enable it to intensify its struggle for the liberation of Namibia.

"8. The General Assembly considers that the acquisition of nuclear-weapon capability by the racist régime of South Africa, with its infamous record of violence and aggression, constitutes a further effort on its part to terrorize and intimidate independent States in the region into submission while also posing a threat to all mankind. The Assembly condemns the continuing support to the racist régime of South Africa in the military and nuclear fields. In this context, the Assembly expresses its concern at the grave consequences for international peace and security of the collaboration between the racist régime of South Africa and certain Western Powers, Israel and other countries in the military and nuclear fields. It calls upon the States concerned to end all such collaboration and, in particular, to halt the supply to South Africa of equipment, technology, nuclear materials and related training, which increases its nuclear capability.

"9. The General Assembly, noting that the militarization of Namibia and the regimentation of its people have led to forced conscription, to a greatly increasing flow of refugees and to a tragic disorganization of the family life of the Namibian people, strongly condemns the forcible and wholesale displacement of Namibians from their homes for military and political purposes and the introduction of compulsory military service for Namibians and declares that all measures by the illegal occupation régime to enforce military conscription in Namibia are null and void. In this connection, the Assembly urges all Governments, the specialized agencies and other intergovernmental organizations to provide increased material assistance to the thousands of refugees who have been forced by the *apartheid* régime's oppressive policies in Namibia and South Africa to flee into the neighbouring States.

"10. The General Assembly, in recalling its resolutions ES-8/2 of 14 September 1981 and S-14/1 of 20 September 1986, by which it strongly urged States to cease forthwith, individually and collectively, all collaboration with the racist régime of South Africa in order totally to isolate it politically, economically, militarily and culturally, strongly condemns the continuing collaboration of certain countries with the racist régime in the political, economic, military and nuclear fields. The Assembly expresses its conviction that continuing military collaboration strengthens the aggressive military machinery of the Pretoria régime and thus constitutes a hostile action against the people of Namibia and the front-line States. Furthermore, such collaboration is in contravention of the arms embargo imposed against South Africa under Security Council resolution 418(1977), undermines international solidarity against the *apartheid* régime and helps to perpetuate that régime's illegal occupation of Namibia. The Assembly thus calls for the termination forthwith of all such collaboration.

"11. The General Assembly deprecates the continued alienation of land in colonial Territories for military installations. The large-scale utilization of local economic and manpower resources for this purpose diverts resources that could be more beneficially utilized in promoting the economic development of the Territories concerned and is thus contrary to the interests of their populations.

"12. The General Assembly requests the Secretary-General to continue, through the Department of Public Information of the Secretariat, an intensified campaign of publicity with a view to informing world public opinion of the facts concerning the military activities and arrangements in colonial Territories which are impeding the implementation of the Declaration on the Granting of Independence to Colonial Countries and Peoples, contained in Assembly resolution 1514(XV).

"13. The General Assembly requests the Special Committee on the Situation with regard to the Implementation of the Declaration on the Granting of Independence to Colonial Countries and Peoples to continue to examine this question and to report thereon to the Assembly at its forty-fourth session."

General Assembly decision 43/410

128-12-15 (recorded vote)

Approved by Fourth Committee (A/43/761) by recorded vote (76-11-13), 10 October (meeting 6); draft by Committee on colonial countries (A/43/23); agenda item 109.

Meeting numbers. GA 43rd session: 4th Committee 2-6; plenary 59.

Recorded vote in Assembly as follows:

In favour: Afghanistan, Albania, Algeria, Angola, Antigua and Barbuda, Argentina, Bahamas, Bahrain, Bangladesh, Barbados, Belize, Benin, Bhutan, Bolivia, Botswana, Brazil, Brunei Darussalam, Bulgaria, Burkina Faso, Burma, Burundi, Byelorussian SSR, Cape Verde, Central African Republic, Chad, China, Colombia, Comoros, Congo, Costa Rica, Cuba, Cyprus, Czechoslovakia, Democratic Kampuchea, Democratic Yemen, Djibouti, Dominican Republic, Ecuador, Egypt, El Salvador, Equatorial Guinea, Ethiopia, Fiji, Gabon, Gambia, German Democratic Republic, Ghana, Grenada, Guatemala, Guinea, Guinea-Bissau, Guyana, Haiti, Honduras, Hungary, India, Indonesia, Iran, Iraq, Jamaica, Jordan, Kenya, Kuwait, Lao People's Democratic Republic, Lebanon, Lesotho, Liberia, Libyan Arab Jamahiriya, Madagascar, Malawi, Malaysia, Maldives, Mali, Mauritania, Mauritius, Mexico, Mongolia, Morocco, Mozambique, Nepal, Nicaragua, Niger, Nigeria, Oman, Pakistan, Panama, Papua New Guinea, Peru, Philippines, Poland, Qatar, Romania, Rwanda, Saint Kitts and Nevis, Saint Lucia, Saint Vincent and the Grenadines, Samoa, Sao Tome and Principe, Saudi Arabia, Senegal, Seychelles, Sierra Leone, Singapore, Solomon Islands, Somalia, Sri Lanka, Sudan, Suriname, Swaziland, Syrian Arab Republic, Thailand, Togo, Trinidad and Tobago, Tunisia, Uganda, Ukrainian SSR, USSR, United Arab Emirates, United Republic of Tanzania, Uruguay, Vanuatu, Venezuela, Viet Nam, Yemen, Yugoslavia, Zaire, Zambia, Zimbabwe.

Against: Belgium, Canada, France, Germany, Federal Republic of, Israel, Italy, Japan, Luxembourg, Netherlands, Portugal, United Kingdom, United States.

Abstaining: Australia, Austria, Côte d'Ivoire, Denmark, Dominica, Finland, Greece, Iceland, Ireland, Malta, New Zealand, Norway, Spain, Sweden, Turkey.

Information dissemination

The Committee on colonial countries considered the question of dissemination of information on decolonization in August 1988.[2] Among its speakers were representatives of liberation movements, namely, the South West Africa People's Organization, the National Congress of South Africa and the Pan Africanist Congress of Azania. It considered reports of the Sub-Committee on Petitions, Information and Assistance on its consultations with the United Nations Secretariat,[13] non-governmental organizations (NGOs),[14] and the Organization of African Unity (OAU) and national liberation movements.[15] It endorsed the conclusions and recommendations contained therein with the understanding that the reservations expressed by members would be reflected in the record of the meeting.

Among those recommendations, the Committee requested the relevant United Nations departments to intensify publicity efforts regarding decolonization, to disseminate more widely information on the remaining colonial Territories, to counteract the hostile campaign by South Africa and some Western countries depicting national liberation movements as terrorist organizations, and to strengthen co-operation with the Pool of Non-Aligned News Agencies. The Committee urged all States to increase their support to the peoples of Namibia and South Africa and their liberation movements.

GENERAL ASSEMBLY ACTION

On 22 November, the General Assembly adopted **resolution 43/46** by recorded vote.

Dissemination of information on decolonization
The General Assembly,

Having examined the chapter of the report of the Special Committee on the Situation with regard to the Implementation of the Declaration on the Granting of Independence to Colonial Countries and Peoples relating to the dissemination of information on decolonization and publicity for the work of the United Nations in the field of decolonization,

Recalling its resolution 1514(XV) of 14 December 1960, containing the Declaration on the Granting of Independence to Colonial Countries and Peoples, and all other resolutions and decisions of the United Nations concerning the dissemination of information on decolonization, in particular General Assembly resolution 42/72 of 4 December 1987,

Reiterating the importance of publicity as an instrument for furthering the aims and purposes of the Declaration and mindful of the continuing pressing need to take all possible steps to acquaint world public opinion with all aspects of the problems of decolonization with a view to assisting effectively the peoples of the colonial Territories in achieving self-determination, freedom and independence,

Noting with deep concern the increased measures of censorship imposed by the racist régime of South Africa upon the local and international media with respect to all aspects of the policies and practices of *apartheid* and developments in Namibia,

Aware of the increasingly important role being played in the widespread dissemination of relevant information by a number of non-governmental organizations having a special interest in decolonization, and noting with satisfaction the intensified efforts of the Special Committee in enlisting the support of those organizations in that regard,

1. *Approves* the chapter of the report of the Special Committee on the Situation with regard to the Implementation of the Declaration on the Granting of Independence to Colonial Countries and Peoples relating to the dissemination of information on decolonization and publicity for the work of the United Nations in the field of decolonization;

2. *Considers* it incumbent upon the United Nations to continue to play an active role in the process of self-determination and independence and to intensify its efforts for the widest possible dissemination of information on decolonization, with a view to the further mobilization of international public opinion in support of complete decolonization;

3. *Requests* the Secretary-General, having regard to the suggestions of the Special Committee, to continue to take concrete measures through all the media at his disposal, including publications, radio and television, to give widespread and continuous publicity to the work of the United Nations in the field of decolonization, and, *inter alia:*

(a) To continue, in consultation with the Special Committee, to collect, prepare and disseminate basic material, studies and articles relating to the problems of decolonization and, in particular, to continue to publish the periodical *Objective: Justice* and other publications, special articles and studies, including the *Decolonization* series, and to select from them appropriate material for wider dissemination by means of reprints in various languages;

(b) To seek the full co-operation of the administering Powers concerned in the discharge of the tasks referred to above;

(c) To intensify the activities of all United Nations information centres;

(d) To maintain a close working relationship with the Organization of African Unity by holding periodic consultations and by systematically exchanging relevant information with that organization;

(*e*) To enlist, with the close co-operation of United Nations information centres, the support of non-governmental organizations having a special interest in decolonization in the dissemination of the relevant information;

(*f*) To continue to provide full press release coverage for all meetings of the Special Committee and its subsidiary bodies;

(*g*) To ensure the availability of the necessary facilities and services to that end;

(*h*) To report to the Special Committee on the measures taken in implementation of the present resolution;

4. *Requests* all States, in particular the administering Powers, the specialized agencies and other organizations of the United Nations system and non-governmental organizations having a special interest in decolonization to undertake or intensify, in co-operation with the Secretary-General and within their respective spheres of competence, the large-scale dissemination of the information referred to in paragraph 2 above;

5. *Requests* the Special Committee to follow the implementation of the present resolution and to report thereon to the General Assembly at its forty-fourth session.

General Assembly resolution 43/46

22 November 1988   Meeting 59   149-2-5 (recorded vote)

37-nation draft (A/43/L.24 and Add.1); agenda item 18.

Sponsors: Afghanistan, Algeria, Angola, Benin, Burkina Faso, Byelorussian SSR, Congo, Cuba, Cyprus, Czechoslovakia, Democratic Yemen, Ethiopia, German Democratic Republic, Ghana, Hungary, India, Iran, Lao People's Democratic Republic, Libyan Arab Jamahiriya, Madagascar, Mali, Mongolia, Nicaragua, Papua New Guinea, Samoa, Sierra Leone, Sudan, Syrian Arab Republic, Tunisia, Ukrainian SSR, United Republic of Tanzania, Vanuatu, Venezuela, Viet Nam, Yugoslavia, Zambia, Zimbabwe.

Financial implications. 5th Committee, A/43/843; S-G, A/C.5/43/37.

Meeting numbers. GA 43rd session: 5th Committee 36; plenary 57-59.

Recorded vote in Assembly as follows:

In favour: Afghanistan, Albania, Algeria, Angola, Antigua and Barbuda, Argentina, Australia, Austria, Bahamas, Bahrain, Bangladesh, Barbados, Belize, Benin, Bhutan, Bolivia, Botswana, Brazil, Brunei Darussalam, Bulgaria, Burkina Faso, Burma, Burundi, Byelorussian SSR, Cameroon, Canada, Cape Verde, Central African Republic, Chad, Chile, China, Colombia, Comoros, Congo, Costa Rica, Côte d'Ivoire, Cuba, Cyprus, Czechoslovakia, Democratic Kampuchea, Democratic Yemen, Denmark, Djibouti, Dominica, Dominican Republic, Ecuador, Egypt, El Salvador, Equatorial Guinea, Ethiopia, Fiji, Finland, Gabon, Gambia, German Democratic Republic, Ghana, Greece, Grenada, Guatemala, Guinea, Guinea-Bissau, Guyana, Haiti, Honduras, Hungary, Iceland, India, Indonesia, Iran, Iraq, Ireland, Jamaica, Japan, Jordan, Kenya, Kuwait, Lao People's Democratic Republic, Lebanon, Lesotho, Liberia, Libyan Arab Jamahiriya, Luxembourg, Madagascar, Malawi, Malaysia, Maldives, Mali, Malta, Mauritania, Mauritius, Mexico, Mongolia, Morocco, Mozambique, Nepal, New Zealand, Nicaragua, Niger, Nigeria, Norway, Oman, Pakistan, Panama, Papua New Guinea, Peru, Philippines, Poland, Portugal, Qatar, Romania, Rwanda, Saint Kitts and Nevis, Saint Lucia, Saint Vincent and the Grenadines, Samoa, Sao Tome and Principe, Saudi Arabia, Senegal, Seychelles, Sierra Leone, Singapore, Solomon Islands, Somalia, Spain, Sri Lanka, Sudan, Suriname, Swaziland, Sweden, Syrian Arab Republic, Thailand, Togo, Trinidad and Tobago, Tunisia, Turkey, Uganda, Ukrainian SSR, USSR, United Arab Emirates, United Republic of Tanzania, Uruguay, Vanuatu, Venezuela, Viet Nam, Yemen, Yugoslavia, Zaire, Zambia, Zimbabwe.

Against: United Kingdom, United States.

Abstaining: Belgium, Germany, Federal Republic of, Israel, Italy, Netherlands.

In **resolution 43/29**, the Assembly requested the United Nations Secretariat to inform world public opinion about the pillaging of natural resources in colonial Territories and the exploitation of their indigenous populations by foreign economic interests. In **decision 43/410**, it requested the Secretariat to inform world public opinion about the military activities in colonial Territories which were impeding implementation of the 1960 Declaration.

Week of solidarity with the peoples of Namibia and other colonial Territories

In May 1988, a series of public information activities was undertaken by the United Nations Secretariat, assisted by United Nations information centres throughout the world, in observance of the Week of Solidarity with the Peoples of Namibia and All Other Colonial Territories, as well as Those in South Africa, Fighting for Freedom, Independence and Human Rights.[2] Events included photo exhibitions, film screenings and briefings for NGOs. In a statement issued on 20 May, the Chairman of the Committee on colonial countries reviewed developments regarding decolonization, particularly in southern Africa, and appealed to Member States and the United Nations system, as well as NGOs, to mobilize support for dependent peoples.

Role of NGOs

The Sub-Committee on Petitions, Information and Assistance held consultations with a number of NGOs, which provided information on their particular areas of concern. In its conclusions and recommendations,[14] adopted by the Committee on colonial countries on 1 August, the Sub-Committee stated that NGOs played an important role in decolonization, particularly by disseminating information and by assisting colonial peoples and their liberation movements. It encouraged NGOs to intensify their efforts in this regard.

The General Assembly, in **resolution 43/46**, requested the Secretary-General to publicize the work of the United Nations on decolonization and to enlist the support of NGOs in such dissemination.

International Decade for the Eradication of Colonialism

The Conference of Foreign Ministers of Non-Aligned Countries (Nicosia, Cyprus, 7-10 September) adopted a political statement containing a proposal that the General Assembly should declare the 1990-2000 period as the International Decade for the Eradication of Colonialism.[16] According to the statement, the Ministers agreed to suggest to the Assembly that it adopt an action plan aimed at inaugurating the twenty-first century with a world free from colonialism.

GENERAL ASSEMBLY ACTION

On 22 November, the General Assembly adopted **resolution 43/47** by recorded vote.

International Decade for the Eradication of Colonialism

The General Assembly,

Recalling that the year 1990 will mark the thirtieth anniversary of the Declaration on the Granting of Independence to Colonial Countries and Peoples,

Bearing in mind the related recommendation contained in the Final Document adopted by the Conference of Foreign Ministers of Non-Aligned Countries, held at Nicosia from 7 to 10 September 1988,

Bearing in mind also the important contribution of the United Nations in the field of decolonization, in particular through the Special Committee on the Situation with regard to the Implementation of the Declaration on the Granting of Independence to Colonial Countries and Peoples,

1. *Declares* the period 1990-2000 as the International Decade for the Eradication of Colonialism;

2. *Requests* the Secretary-General to submit to the General Assembly at its forty-fourth session a report that would enable the Assembly to consider and adopt an action plan aimed at ushering in the twenty-first century, a world free from colonialism.

General Assembly resolution 43/47

22 November 1987   Meeting 59   135-1-20 (recorded vote)

80-nation draft (A/43/L.28/Rev.1 & Add.1); agenda item 18.

Sponsors: Afghanistan, Algeria, Angola, Argentina, Bangladesh, Barbados, Benin, Botswana, Brunei Darussalam, Burkina Faso, Burundi, Cameroon, Cape Verde, Central African Republic, Chad, Colombia, Comoros, Congo, Côte d'Ivoire, Cuba, Cyprus, Democratic Yemen, Djibouti, Ecuador, Egypt, Ethiopia, Gabon, Ghana, Guinea, Guinea-Bissau, Guyana, India, Indonesia, Iran, Iraq, Jordan, Kenya, Kuwait, Lao People's Democratic Republic, Lesotho, Liberia, Libyan Arab Jamahiriya, Madagascar, Malawi, Malaysia, Maldives, Mali, Mauritania, Morocco, Mozambique, Nepal, Nicaragua, Niger, Nigeria, Pakistan, Panama, Peru, Qatar, Rwanda, Senegal, Seychelles, Sierra Leone, Somalia, Sri Lanka, Sudan, Swaziland, Syrian Arab Republic, Togo, Tunisia, Uganda, United Arab Emirates, United Republic of Tanzania, Vanuatu, Venezuela, Viet Nam, Yemen, Yugoslavia, Zaire, Zambia, Zimbabwe.

Meeting numbers. GA 43rd session: plenary 57-59.

Recorded vote in Assembly as follows:

In favour: Afghanistan, Albania, Algeria, Angola, Antigua and Barbuda, Argentina, Australia, Bahamas, Bahrain, Bangladesh, Barbados, Belize, Benin, Bhutan, Bolivia, Botswana, Brazil, Brunei Darussalam, Bulgaria, Burkina Faso, Burma, Burundi, Byelorussian SSR, Cameroon, Cape Verde, Central African Republic, Chad, Chile, China, Colombia, Comoros, Congo, Costa Rica, Côte d'Ivoire, Cuba, Cyprus, Czechoslovakia, Democratic Kampuchea, Democratic Yemen, Djibouti, Dominica, Dominican Republic, Ecuador, Egypt, El Salvador, Equatorial Guinea, Ethiopia, Fiji, Gabon, Gambia, German Democratic Republic, Ghana, Guatemala, Guinea, Guinea-Bissau, Guyana, Haiti, Honduras, Hungary, India, Indonesia, Iran, Iraq, Jamaica, Jordan, Kenya, Kuwait, Lao People's Democratic Republic, Lebanon, Lesotho, Liberia, Libyan Arab Jamahiriya, Madagascar, Malawi, Malaysia, Maldives, Mali, Malta, Mauritania, Mauritius, Mexico, Mongolia, Morocco, Mozambique, Nepal, New Zealand, Nicaragua, Niger, Nigeria, Oman, Pakistan, Panama, Papua New Guinea, Peru, Philippines, Poland, Qatar, Romania, Rwanda, Saint Kitts and Nevis, Saint Lucia, Saint Vincent and the Grenadines, Samoa, Sao Tome and Principe, Saudi Arabia, Senegal, Seychelles, Sierra Leone, Singapore, Solomon Islands, Somalia, Sri Lanka, Sudan, Suriname, Swaziland, Syrian Arab Republic, Thailand, Togo, Trinidad and Tobago, Tunisia, Turkey, Uganda, Ukrainian SSR, USSR, United Arab Emirates, United Republic of Tanzania, Uruguay, Vanuatu, Venezuela, Viet Nam, Yemen, Yugoslavia, Zaire, Zambia, Zimbabwe.

Against: United States.

Abstaining: Austria, Belgium, Canada, Denmark, Finland, France, Germany, Federal Republic of, Greece, Iceland, Ireland, Israel, Italy, Japan, Luxembourg, Netherlands, Norway, Portugal, Spain, Sweden, United Kingdom.

Puerto Rico

In August 1988, the Committee on colonial countries considered, as a separate item, its 1987 decision on Puerto Rico.[17] It heard statements by 30 representatives of organizations, mainly Puerto Rican. On 16 August, it adopted a resolution[18] by 9 votes to 2, with 11 abstentions, in which it reaffirmed the inalienable right of the people of Puerto Rico to self-determination and independence, in conformity with the 1960 Decla-

ration,[1] and expressed the hope that the people of Puerto Rico might exercise that right without hindrance. The text of the resolution was transmitted to the United States.

REFERENCES

[1]YUN 1960, p. 49, GA res. 1514(XV), 14 Dec. 1960. [2]A/43/23. [3]YUN 1987, p. 961, GA res. 42/75, 4 Dec. 1987. [4]A/43/355 & Add.1-3. [5]E/1988/81 & Add.1. [6]YUN 1987, p. 958, ESC res. 1987/78, 8 July 1987. [7]A/43/23 (A/AC.109/970). [8]*Ibid.* (A/AC.109/968). [9]A/C.4/43/6. [10]YUN 1987, p. 968, GA dec. 42/417, 4 Dec. 1987. [11]A/43/23, (A/AC.109/969). [12]S/20118. [13]A/AC.109/L.1650. [14]A/AC.109/L.1666. [15]A/AC.109/L.1667. [16]A/43/667-S/20212. [17]YUN 1987, p. 972. [18]A/43/23 (A/AC.109/973).

Other general questions concerning NSGTs

Scholarships

In accordance with a 1987 General Assembly request,[1] the Secretary-General reported on offers by Member States of study and training facilities for inhabitants of NSGTs.[2] The report, covering the period from 1 September 1987 to 31 August 1988, listed the following 37 Member States as having over the years offered scholarships: Austria, Brazil, Bulgaria, Cyprus, Czechoslovakia, Egypt, German Democratic Republic, Federal Republic of Germany, Ghana, Greece, Hungary, India, Iran, Ireland, Israel, Italy, Libyan Arab Jamahiriya, Malawi, Malta, Mexico, New Zealand, Pakistan, Philippines, Poland, Romania, Sri Lanka, Sudan, Syrian Arab Republic, Tunisia, Turkey, Uganda, USSR, United Arab Emirates, United Kingdom, United States, Uruguay, Yugoslavia. Information about these offers was included in the twenty-fifth edition of the handbook *Study Abroad*, published by the United Nations Educational, Scientific and Cultural Organization. The scholarships were for study and training of university standard as well as for post-primary, technical and vocational training of immediate practical value.

In the period under review, 160 students, most of them not inhabitants of NSGTs, requested information and application forms from the United Nations. Applications from NSGTs were transmitted to the offering States and, for information, to the respective administering Power. Applications from Namibian students were referred to the Office of the United Nations Commissioner for Namibia and to the United Nations Educational and Training Programme for Southern Africa, as well as to offering Governments.

A number of countries reported to the Secretary-General on current scholarships and study awards granted to inhabitants of NSGTs. Cyprus offered a two-year scholarship every other year, Czechoslovakia offered 20 in 1989/90, Egypt granted 50 in 1988/89 and the German Democratic Republic provided five each year. The Federal Republic of Germany reported that 75 Namibians were currently studying there and a further 185 had been granted on-the-spot scholarships enabling them to study outside the Federal Republic. Malta offered training to 15 Namibian students in trade schools, Pakistan had offered seven scholarships in 1987/88, out of which five had been utilized, the Sudan would grant one scholarship in 1988/89 and Turkey awarded two to Namibians. The USSR provided education for 177 students from NSGTs, as well as training for over 200 specialists, and the United Kingdom had awarded 442 scholarships to students from British dependent Territories from 1985 to 1987 and intended to offer 73 new ones to Namibians during 1988/89.

GENERAL ASSEMBLY ACTION

On 22 November, the General Assembly, on the recommendation of the Fourth Committee, adopted **resolution 43/32** without vote.

Offers by Member States of study and training facilities for inhabitants of Non-Self-Governing Territories

The General Assembly,

Recalling its resolution 42/77 of 4 December 1987,

Having examined the report of the Secretary-General on offers by Member States of study and training facilities for inhabitants of Non-Self-Governing Territories, prepared pursuant to General Assembly resolution 845(IX) of 22 November 1954,

Conscious of the importance of promoting the educational advancement of the inhabitants of Non-Self-Governing Territories,

Strongly convinced that the continuation and expansion of offers of scholarships is essential in order to meet the increasing need of students from Non-Self-Governing Territories for educational and training assistance, and considering that students in those Territories should be encouraged to avail themselves of such offers,

1. *Takes note* of the report of the Secretary-General;

2. *Expresses its appreciation* to those Member States that have made scholarships available to the inhabitants of Non-Self-Governing Territories;

3. *Invites* all States to make or continue to make generous offers of study and training facilities to the inhabitants of those Territories that have not yet attained self-government or independence and, wherever possible, to provide travel funds to prospective students;

4. *Urges* the administering Powers to take effective measures to ensure the widespread and continuous dissemination in the Territories under their administration of information relating to offers of study and training facilities made by States and to provide all the necessary facilities to enable students to avail themselves of such offers;

5. *Requests* the Secretary-General to report to the General Assembly at its forty-fourth session on the implementation of the present resolution;

6. *Draws the attention* of the Special Committee on the Situation with regard to the Implementation of the Declaration on the Granting of Independence to Colonial Countries and Peoples to the present resolution.

General Assembly resolution 43/32

22 November 1988   Meeting 59   Adopted without vote

Approved by Fourth Committee (A/43/790) without vote, 25 October (meeting 13); 42-nation draft (A/C.4/43/L.4); agenda item 112.

Sponsors: Algeria, Argentina, Australia, Bahamas, Brazil, Cameroon, Chile, China, Colombia, Congo, Costa Rica, Cuba, Cyprus, Egypt, Fiji, Ghana, Guinea, India, Indonesia, Jamaica, Japan, Liberia, Madagascar, Mali, New Zealand, Nicaragua, Pakistan, Papua New Guinea, Philippines, Saint Vincent and the Grenadines, Samoa, Sri Lanka, Sudan, Sweden, Thailand, Togo, Trinidad and Tobago, Tunisia, Turkey, United States, Venezuela, Yugoslavia.

Meeting numbers. GA 43rd session: 4th Committee 7-13; plenary 59.

Information to the United Nations

States responsible for the administration of Territories which had not attained full self-government continued to be required, under Article 73 *e* of the United Nations Charter, to transmit regularly to the Secretary-General information on the Territories' economic, social and educational conditions. In 1987, the General Assembly had requested the fullest possible information on political and constitutional developments.[3] In a September 1988 report,[4] the Secretary-General stated that he had received information from administering countries with respect to the following NSGTs:

New Zealand: Tokelau

United Kingdom: Anguilla, Bermuda, British Virgin Islands, Cayman Islands, Falkland Islands (Malvinas), Gibraltar, Montserrat, Pitcairn, St. Helena, Turks and Caicos Islands

United States: American Samoa, Guam, United States Virgin Islands

The Secretary-General noted that Spain had informed him in 1976[5] that it had terminated its presence in Western Sahara and considered itself exempt from any international responsibility in connection with that Territory's administration. On 15 March 1988,[6] Portugal informed the Secretary-General that it had nothing to add to the information it had provided in 1979[7] when it had stated that conditions in East Timor had prevented it from assuming its responsibilities for the Territory's administration.

The Committee on colonial countries considered the question of information from NSGTs and, on 3 August, adopted a resolution,[8] which became the basis for a draft recommended to the General Assembly.

GENERAL ASSEMBLY ACTION

On 22 November, the General Assembly, on the recommendation of the Fourth Committee, adopted by recorded vote **resolution 43/28**.

Information from Non-Self-Governing Territories transmitted under Article 73 *e* of the Charter of the United Nations

The General Assembly,

Having examined the chapter of the report of the Special Committee on the Situation with regard to the Implementation of the Declaration on the Granting of Independence to Colonial Countries and Peoples relating to the information from Non-Self-Governing Territories transmitted under Article 73 *e* of the Charter of the United Nations and the action taken by the Special Committee in respect of that information,

Having also examined the report of the Secretary-General on this item,

Recalling its resolution 1970(XVIII) of 16 December 1963, in which it requested the Special Committee to study the information transmitted to the Secretary-General in accordance with Article 73 *e* of the Charter and to take such information fully into account in examining the situation with regard to the implementation of the Declaration on the Granting of Independence to Colonial Countries and Peoples, contained in General Assembly resolution 1514(XV) of 14 December 1960,

Recalling also its resolution 42/73 of 4 December 1987, in which it requested the Special Committee to continue to discharge the functions entrusted to it under resolution 1970(XVIII),

Stressing the importance of timely transmission by the administering Powers of adequate information under Article 73 *e* of the Charter, in particular in relation to the preparation by the Secretariat of the working papers on the Territories concerned,

1. *Approves* the chapter of the report of the Special Committee on the Situation with regard to the Implementation of the Declaration on the Granting of Independence to Colonial Countries and Peoples relating to the information from Non-Self-Governing Territories transmitted under Article 73 *e* of the Charter of the United Nations;

2. *Reaffirms* that, in the absence of a decision by the General Assembly itself that a Non-Self-Governing Territory has attained a full measure of self-government in terms of Chapter XI of the Charter, the administering Power concerned should continue to transmit information under Article 73 *e* of the Charter with respect to that Territory;

3. *Requests* the administering Powers concerned to continue to transmit to the Secretary-General the information prescribed in Article 73 *e* of the Charter, as well as the fullest possible information on political and constitutional developments in the Territories concerned, within a maximum period of six months following the expiration of the administrative year in those Territories;

4. *Requests* the Secretary-General, in connection with the preparation by the Secretariat of the working papers for the Special Committee on the Territories concerned, to continue to ensure that adequate information is drawn from all available published sources;

5. *Requests* the Special Committee to continue to discharge the functions entrusted to it under General Assembly resolution 1970(XVIII), in accordance with established procedures, and to report thereon to the Assembly at its forty-fourth session.

General Assembly resolution 43/28

22 November 1988   Meeting 59   154-0-2 (recorded vote)

Approved by Fourth Committee (A/43/787) by recorded vote (140-0-2), 25 October (meeting 13); draft by Committee on colonial countries (A/43/23); agenda item 108.

Meeting numbers. GA 43rd session: 4th Committee 7-13; plenary 59.

Recorded vote in Assembly as follows:

In favour: Afghanistan, Albania, Algeria, Angola, Antigua and Barbuda, Argentina, Australia, Austria, Bahamas, Bahrain, Bangladesh, Barbados, Belgium, Belize, Benin, Bhutan, Bolivia, Botswana, Brazil, Brunei Darussalam, Bulgaria, Burkina Faso, Burma, Burundi, Byelorussian SSR, Canada, Cape Verde, Central African Republic, Chad, Chile, China, Colombia, Comoros, Congo, Costa Rica, Côte d'Ivoire, Cuba, Cyprus, Czechoslovakia, Democratic Kampuchea, Democratic Yemen, Denmark, Djibouti, Dominica, Dominican Republic, Ecuador, Egypt, El Salvador, Equatorial Guinea, Ethiopia, Fiji, Finland, Gabon, Gambia, German Democratic Republic, Germany, Federal Republic of, Ghana, Greece, Grenada, Guatemala, Guinea, Guinea-Bissau, Guyana, Haiti, Honduras, Hungary, Iceland, India, Indonesia, Iran, Iraq, Ireland, Israel, Italy, Jamaica, Japan, Jordan, Kenya, Kuwait, Lao People's Democratic Republic, Lebanon, Lesotho, Liberia, Libyan Arab Jamahiriya, Luxembourg, Madagascar, Malawi, Malaysia, Maldives, Mali, Malta, Mauritania, Mauritius, Mexico, Mongolia, Morocco, Mozambique, Nepal, Netherlands, New Zealand, Nicaragua, Niger, Nigeria, Norway, Oman, Pakistan, Panama, Papua New Guinea, Paraguay, Peru, Philippines, Poland, Portugal, Qatar, Romania, Rwanda, Saint Kitts and Nevis, Saint Lucia, Saint Vincent and the Grenadines, Samoa, Sao Tome and Principe, Saudi Arabia, Senegal, Seychelles, Sierra Leone, Singapore, Solomon Islands, Somalia, Spain, Sri Lanka, Sudan, Suriname, Swaziland, Sweden, Syrian Arab Republic, Thailand, Togo, Trinidad and Tobago, Tunisia, Turkey, Uganda, Ukrainian SSR, USSR, United Arab Emirates, United Republic of Tanzania, Uruguay, Vanuatu, Venezuela, Viet Nam, Yemen, Yugoslavia, Zaire, Zambia, Zimbabwe.

Against: None.

Abstaining: United Kingdom, United States.

Visiting missions

The Chairman of the Committee on colonial countries, as requested by the Committee in 1987, continued consultations with the administering Powers of NSGTs on the question of permitting access of visiting missions to the Territories. In a July 1988 report,[9] he stated that New Zealand and the United States had reiterated their readiness to continue to provide all relevant information, to participate in the work of the Committee and to receive visiting missions. While noting that in the past the United Kingdom had permitted visiting missions to Territories under its administration, the Chairman appealed to it to reconsider its decision not to take part in the work of the Committee.

On 3 August, the Committee adopted a resolution[10] in which it stressed the need to dispatch periodic visiting missions to colonial Territories and called on administering Powers concerned to continue to co-operate with the United Nations in that regard. It urged the United Kingdom to permit the access of visiting missions to Territories under its administration and to reconsider its decision not to participate in the Committee's work. The appeal was transmitted to the United Kingdom.

In **resolution 43/45**, the General Assembly called on administering Powers to co-operate with the Committee and to permit the access of visiting missions to the Territories to secure first-hand information and ascertain the wishes and aspirations of their inhabitants. It urged, in particular, those administering Powers which did not participate in the Committee's work to do so in 1989.

The Assembly also dealt with the topic in resolutions on individual Territories (see below).

Closure of the Trust Fund for Assistance to Colonial Countries and Peoples

The Governing Council of the United Nations Development Programme (UNDP), at its 1988 regular session, considered a report of the UNDP Administrator on trust funds established by him in 1987[11] and the report of the Advisory Committee on Administrative and Budgetary Questions thereon,[12] as well as a note by the Administrator containing his recommendation that the Trust Fund for Assistance to Colonial Countries and Peoples be closed.[13] The Administrator reported that the resources of the Fund had been almost fully utilized and that no further contributions to it were expected. On 1 July,[14] the Council agreed with his recommendation that the Fund be closed and that its unspent balance be transferred to UNDP general resources. It requested him to submit that proposal to the General Assembly.

The Assembly acted on the proposal on 20 December by adopting **decision 43/446**, thereby taking note of the Council's decision to close the Fund and to transfer the remaining balance of $900 to UNDP general resources.

REFERENCES
[1]YUN 1987, p. 973, GA res. 42/77, 4 Dec. 1987. [2]A/43/677. [3]YUN 1987, p. 974, GA res. 42/73, 4 Dec. 1987. [4]A/43/658. [5]YUN 1976, p. 738. [6]A/43/219. [7]YUN 1979, p. 1117. [8]A/43/23 (A/AC.109/966). [9]A/AC.109/L.1672. [10]A/43/23 (A/AC.109/965). [11]DP/1988/53. [12]DP/1988/58. [13]DP/1988/57. [14]E/1988/19 (dec. 88/47).

Colonial Territories

The peaceful settlement of the dispute over the Falkland Islands (Malvinas), the conflict in Western Sahara, the questions of New Caledonia and East Timor, and the situation in a number of other small colonial Territories continued to be considered in 1988 by the Committee on colonial countries. Other United Nations bodies considered the Trust Territory of the Pacific Islands (see next chapter) and Namibia (see PART FOUR, Chapter III).

Falkland Islands (Malvinas)

In a press communiqué of 11 February 1988, transmitted to the Secretary-General the next day,[1] Argentina noted the planned military exercise of British forces in the area of the Malvinas

Islands between 7 and 31 March and said that they showed the arbitrary attitude of the United Kingdom, which was particularly striking at a time when initiatives were being undertaken, through friendly countries, to achieve a relaxation of tension in the area. Responding on 25 February,[2] the United Kingdom said that it was a routine reinforcement exercise. The reinforcement capability had enabled the United Kingdom to reduce its garrison in the Falkland Islands, thereby lowering tension in the region, and it remained committed to restoring more normal relations with Argentina while standing by its commitments to the islanders. On 3 March,[3] Argentina said that the exercises, in addition to violating the sovereign right of Argentina over the islands, ran counter to relevant United Nations resolutions. Argentina would maintain vigilance during any military activities and, where necessary, put defence plans into operation.

SECURITY COUNCIL CONSIDERATION

By a letter of 11 March,[4] Argentina requested a meeting of the Security Council to consider the situation created in the South Atlantic by the decision of the United Kingdom to conduct military manoeuvres. The Council met twice on 17 March. *Meeting numbers.* SC 2800, 2801.

Addressing the Council, Argentina said that since the restoration of democracy in 1983, it had displayed its determination to seek a negotiated solution to its dispute with the United Kingdom over the Malvinas; however, the United Kingdom, by its show of force in the area, at a time when indirect contacts had been under way to improve the situation, was posing a threat to international peace. The United Kingdom had consistently refused to consider the matter of sovereignty.

In response, the United Kingdom said it was determined to prevent another catastrophe such as the 1982 invasion of the islands by over 10,000 Argentine troops. It chose to meet its obligation to safeguard the security of the people of the islands by maintaining the smallest possible garrison there while establishing the means to reinforce it rapidly. Since 1982 the United Kingdom had made clear that occasional reinforcement exercises would be necessary; the current one involved a small number of aircraft and fewer than 1,000 troops, which could hardly be considered a threat. Its forces in the Falkland Islands were there to defend the islands from attack, and over the past two years the reinforcement capability had allowed the United Kingdom to halve the number of troops it kept there.

Action by the Committee on colonial countries. The Falkland Islands (Malvinas) question was considered by the Committee on colonial countries at its August session,[5] during which it heard statements by Argentina, Cuba, two representatives of the Falkland Islands Legislative Council and one other petitioner. The United Kingdom, the administering Power, in conformity with its 1986 decision,[6] did not participate.

The Committee, in a resolution of 11 August,[7] reiterated that the way to end the special and particular colonial situation was through a negotiated settlement. It regretted that the implementation of the Assembly resolutions on the question had not started, urged the parties to resume negotiations and reiterated its support for the renewed good offices mission of the Secretary-General.

Report of the Secretary-General. The Secretary-General, responding to a 1987 Assembly resolution,[8] submitted in November 1988 a report[9] stating that, during 1988, he discussed the question of the Falkland Islands (Malvinas) on a number of occasions with the two parties and concluded that the positions of the two Governments remained substantially unchanged. Conditions had not therefore sufficiently evolved for him to carry out the Assembly's mandate. The United Kingdom remained committed to seeking more normal relations with Argentina while standing by its commitments to the Falkland Islanders; it had proposed setting aside the sovereignty issue because of the fundamentally opposed positions, while making progress on practical and beneficial matters, such as fisheries. Argentina expressed readiness to comply with the 1987 Assembly resolution and to initiate negotiations to resolve the differences between the two sides, including all questions concerning the future of the islands. While both parties had exercised restraint, the Secretary-General regretted that they had not entered into dialogue consistent with the 1987 resolution. He was all the more disappointed in view of the length of time that had elapsed since the 1982 conflict and the current trend towards seeking peaceful solutions to international disputes.

GENERAL ASSEMBLY ACTION

On 17 November, the General Assembly adopted **resolution 43/25** by recorded vote.

Question of the Falkland Islands (Malvinas)
The General Assembly,

Having considered the question of the Falkland Islands (Malvinas) and having received the report of the Secretary-General,

Aware of the interest of the international community in the peaceful and definitive settlement by the Governments of Argentina and the United Kingdom of Great Britain and Northern Ireland of all their differences, in accordance with the Charter of the United Nations,

Taking note of the interest repeatedly expressed by both parties in normalizing their relations,

Convinced that such purpose would be facilitated by a global negotiation between both Governments that will

allow them to rebuild mutual confidence on a solid basis and to resolve the pending problems, including all aspects on the future of the Falkland Islands (Malvinas),

1. *Reiterates its request* to the Governments of Argentina and the United Kingdom of Great Britain and Northern Ireland to initiate negotiations with a view to finding the means to resolve peacefully and definitively the problems pending between both countries, including all aspects on the future of the Falkland Islands (Malvinas), in accordance with the Charter of the United Nations;

2. *Requests* the Secretary-General to continue his renewed mission of good offices in order to assist the parties in complying with the request made in paragraph 1 above, and to take the necessary measures to that end;

3. *Also requests* the Secretary-General to submit to the General Assembly at its forty-fourth session a report on the progress made in the implementation of the present resolution;

4. *Decides* to include in the provisional agenda of its forty-fourth session the item entitled "Question of the Falkland Islands (Malvinas)".

General Assembly resolution 43/25

17 November 1988   Meeting 54   109-5-37 (recorded vote)

14-nation draft (A/43/L.27 & Add.1); agenda item 34.

Sponsors: Bolivia, Brazil, Colombia, Cuba, Dominican Republic, Ghana, Honduras, India, Mexico, Peru, Uruguay, Venezuela, Yugoslavia, Zimbabwe.

Recorded vote in Assembly as follows:

In favour: Afghanistan, Albania, Algeria, Angola, Argentina, Australia, Austria, Bahamas, Barbados, Benin, Bolivia, Botswana, Brazil, Bulgaria, Burkina Faso, Burma, Burundi, Byelorussian SSR, Cameroon, Canada, Cape Verde, Central African Republic, Chad, Chile, China, Colombia, Comoros, Congo, Costa Rica, Côte d'Ivoire, Cuba, Cyprus, Czechoslovakia, Democratic Kampuchea, Democratic Yemen, Djibouti, Dominican Republic, Ecuador, Egypt, El Salvador, Ethiopia, France, Gabon, German Democratic Republic, Ghana, Greece, Guatemala, Guinea, Guinea-Bissau, Guyana, Haiti, Honduras, Hungary, India, Indonesia, Iran, Iraq, Italy, Japan, Kuwait, Lao People's Democratic Republic, Lebanon, Liberia, Libyan Arab Jamahiriya, Madagascar, Malaysia, Mali, Mauritania, Mexico, Mongolia, Nepal, Netherlands, Nicaragua, Niger, Nigeria, Norway, Pakistan, Panama, Paraguay, Peru, Philippines, Poland, Romania, Rwanda, Sao Tome and Principe, Seychelles, Sierra Leone, Singapore, Somalia, Spain, Sudan, Suriname, Sweden, Syrian Arab Republic, Togo, Tunisia, Uganda, Ukrainian SSR, USSR, United Republic of Tanzania, United States, Uruguay, Venezuela, Viet Nam, Yemen, Yugoslavia, Zaire, Zambia, Zimbabwe.

Against: Belize, Gambia, Oman, Sri Lanka, United Kingdom.

Abstaining: Antigua and Barbuda, Bahrain, Belgium, Bhutan, Brunei Darussalam, Denmark, Dominica, Fiji, Finland, Germany, Federal Republic of, Grenada, Iceland, Ireland, Israel, Jamaica, Jordan, Kenya, Lesotho, Luxembourg, Malawi, Maldives, Malta, New Zealand, Papua New Guinea, Portugal, Saint Kitts and Nevis, Saint Lucia, Saint Vincent and the Grenadines, Saudi Arabia, Senegal, Solomon Islands, Swaziland, Thailand, Trinidad and Tobago, Turkey, United Arab Emirates, Vanuatu.

Also, on 17 November, the Assembly, by **decision 43/409**, took note of the report of the Fourth Committee on the question.[10] The Committee heard statements by four petitioners.

Western Sahara

The decolonization of Western Sahara and the right of its people to self-determination remained a concern of the United Nations in 1988.

Action by the Commission on Human Rights. The Commission on Human Rights, on 22 February,[11] reaffirmed that the question of Western Sahara was one of decolonization and again requested the parties to the conflict, Morocco and the Frente Popular para la Liberación de Saguia el-Hamra y de Río de Oro (POLISARIO Front), to negotiate a cease-fire and create the necessary conditions for a referendum for self-determination. The Commission welcomed the efforts of the Secretary-General and the Chairman of the Assembly of Heads of State and Government of OAU to promote a solution and decided to consider the situation in 1989 as a high-priority matter.

Consideration by the Committee on colonial countries. The Committee on colonial countries considered the question of Western Sahara at its August session,[5] during which it heard a statement by the POLISARIO Front, among others. The Committee had before it a working paper prepared by the Secretariat on political and military developments in the Territory.[12] In November 1987, the Secretary-General had dispatched a technical mission to Western Sahara, headed by the Under-Secretary-General for Special Political Questions, Regional Co-operation, Decolonization and Trusteeship. In May 1988, the Secretary-General expressed his satisfaction at the restoration of diplomatic relations between Algeria and Morocco and hoped that the move would help his mission of good offices, with a view to achieving a solution to the Western Sahara conflict. The paper mentioned two major attacks by the "Saharan People's Liberation Army" against Moroccan soldiers, one on 18 November 1987 and the other in January 1988, killing several hundred.

SECURITY COUNCIL ACTION

On 20 September, the Security Council considered the question of Western Sahara and heard a statement by the Secretary-General, who said that Morocco and the POLISARIO Front had accepted the peace proposals submitted by him and the OAU Chairman, aimed at promoting a just and definitive solution. The proposals offered a framework for bringing about a cease-fire and creating the conditions necessary for holding a credible referendum organized and supervised by the United Nations in co-operation with OAU (see below).

On the basis of the Secretary-General's report, the Council unanimously adopted **resolution 621(1988)**.

The Security Council,

Having heard a report by the Secretary-General of the United Nations on his mission of good offices, pursued jointly with the current Chairman of the Assembly of Heads of State and Government of the Organization of African Unity, in conformity with General Assembly resolution 40/50 of 2 December 1985, with a view to settling the question of Western Sahara,

Taking note of the agreement in principle given by the Kingdom of Morocco and the Frente Popular para la Liberación de Saguia el-Hamra y de Río de Oro on 30 August 1988 to the joint proposals of the Secretary-

General and the current Chairman of the Organization of African Unity,

Anxious to support these efforts with a view to the holding of a referendum for self-determination of the people of Western Sahara, organized and supervised by the United Nations in co-operation with the Organization of African Unity,

1. *Decides* to authorize the Secretary-General to appoint a special representative for Western Sahara;

2. *Requests* the Secretary-General to transmit to it as soon as possible a report on the holding of a referendum for self-determination of the people of Western Sahara and on ways and means to ensure the organization and supervision of such a referendum by the United Nations in co-operation with the Organization of African Unity.

Security Council resolution 621(1988)

20 September 1988   Meeting 2826   Adopted unanimously

Draft prepared in consultations among Council members (S/20193).

Report of the Secretary-General. The Secretary-General, pursuant to a 1987 General Assembly resolution,[13] reported in October 1988[14] on the results of meetings he and the OAU Chairman had held between April and September 1988 with Morocco and the POLISARIO Front. The Secretary-General and the OAU Chairman were satisfied with the progress achieved as the two parties had agreed to their proposals for restoring peace in the region. Under the proposals, during a transition period between the beginning of the cease-fire and the results of the referendum, the Secretary-General's Special Representative would be the sole authority, particularly with regard to all questions pertaining to the referendum. He would be assisted by a support group comprising a civilian unit, a military unit and a security unit. A contingent of United Nations observers would verify the cessation of hostilities, the implementation of the cease-fire, the exchange of prisoners, the determining of the positions of the parties at the time of the cease-fire and the consigning of their troops to sites to be determined by the Special Representative. The proposals provided for Morocco gradually to reduce its troops in Western Sahara, with the remainder stationed at sites designated by the Special Representative. Similarly, POLISARIO troops would be stationed at sites also determined by the Special Representative and under United Nations surveillance.

The Secretary-General said he was currently working with the OAU Chairman to finalize details of the peace plan, and it was necessary to preserve the momentum of the process. Consequently, he had requested the Security Council to authorize him to proceed to the appointment of a Special Representative. After finalization of the plan, he would seek the Council's approval of the required number of observers and civilian and military personnel.

The Secretary-General estimated the total cost of the initial phase of implementing the peace plan at $687,900.[15]

Pursuant to Security Council resolution 621(1988), in December 1988 the Secretary-General appointed Hector Gros Espiel of Uruguay as his Special Representative for Western Sahara.

GENERAL ASSEMBLY ACTION

In October, the General Assembly's Fourth Committee heard two petitioners at their request,[16] representatives of the POLISARIO Front and the American Association of Jurists.

On 22 November, on the recommendation of the Fourth Committee, the Assembly adopted **resolution 43/33** by recorded vote.

Question of Western Sahara

The General Assembly,

Having considered in depth the question of Western Sahara,

Recalling the inalienable right of all peoples to self-determination and independence, in accordance with the principles set forth in the Charter of the United Nations and in General Assembly resolution 1514(XV) of 14 December 1960, containing the Declaration on the Granting of Independence to Colonial Countries and Peoples,

Recalling its resolution 42/78 of 4 December 1987 on the question of Western Sahara,

Recalling resolution AHG/Res.104(XIX) on Western Sahara, adopted by the Assembly of Heads of State and Government of the Organization of African Unity at its nineteenth ordinary session, held at Addis Ababa from 6 to 12 June 1983,

Taking note with appreciation of the part concerning Western Sahara of the final documents adopted by the Conference of Ministers for Foreign Affairs of the Non-Aligned Countries, held at Nicosia from 7 to 10 September 1988,

Having examined the chapter of the report of the Special Committee on the Situation with regard to the Implementation of the Declaration on the Granting of Independence to Colonial Countries and Peoples relating to Western Sahara,

Having examined the report of the Secretary-General on the question of Western Sahara,

Noting with appreciation the continuation of the joint good offices process initiated in New York on 9 April 1986 by the current Chairman of the Assembly of Heads of State and Government of the Organization of African Unity and the Secretary-General of the United Nations with a view to implementing resolution AHG/Res.104(XIX) and General Assembly resolution 40/50 of 2 December 1985,

1. *Takes note with appreciation* of the report of the Secretary-General on the question of Western Sahara;

2. *Reaffirms* that the question of Western Sahara is a question of decolonization which remains to be completed on the basis of the exercise by the people of Western Sahara of their inalienable right to self-determination and independence;

3. *Reaffirms also* that the solution of the question of Western Sahara lies in the implementation of resolution

AHG/Res.104(XIX) of the Assembly of Heads of State and Government of the Organization of African Unity, in which ways and means were established for a just and definitive political solution to the Western Sahara conflict;

4. *Again requests,* to that end, the two parties to the conflict, the Kingdom of Morocco and the Frente Popular para la Liberación de Saguia el-Hamra y de Río de Oro, to undertake direct negotiations in the shortest possible time, with a view to bringing about a cease-fire to create the necessary conditions for a peaceful and fair referendum for self-determination of the people of Western Sahara, a referendum without any administrative or military constraints, under the auspices of the Organization of African Unity and the United Nations;

5. *Welcomes* the efforts of the current Chairman of the Assembly of Heads of State and Government of the Organization of African Unity and the Secretary-General of the United Nations to promote a just and definitive solution of the question of Western Sahara, in accordance with General Assembly resolution 40/50;

6. *Also welcomes* the agreement in principle given on 30 August 1988 by the Kingdom of Morocco and the Frente Popular para la Liberación de Saguia el-Hamra y de Río de Oro to the joint proposals of the current Chairman of the Assembly of Heads of State and Government of the Organization of African Unity and the Secretary-General of the United Nations with a view to the holding of a referendum for self-determination of the people of Western Sahara, organized and supervised by the United Nations in co-operation with the Organization of African Unity;

7. *Further welcomes* the unanimous adoption of Security Council resolution 621(1988) of 20 September 1988, by which the Council authorized the Secretary-General to appoint a special representative for Western Sahara;

8. *Invites* the current Chairman of the Assembly of Heads of State and Government of the Organization of African Unity and the Secretary-General of the United Nations to continue to exert every effort to persuade the two parties to the conflict, the Kingdom of Morocco and the Frente Popular para la Liberación de Saguia el-Hamra y de Río de Oro, to negotiate, in the shortest possible time and in accordance with resolution AHG/Res.104(XIX), General Assembly resolution 40/50 and the present resolution, the terms of a cease-fire and the modalities for organizing the said referendum;

9. *Expresses its support* for the efforts of the current Chairman of the Assembly of Heads of State and Government of the Organization of African Unity and the Secretary-General of the United Nations with a view to promoting a just and lasting solution of the question of Western Sahara, in accordance with General Assembly resolution 40/50;

10. *Appeals* to the Kingdom of Morocco and the Frente Popular para la Liberación de Saguia el-Hamra y de Río de Oro to display the political will necessary to implement resolution AHG/Res.104(XIX), General Assembly resolutions 40/50 of 2 December 1985, 41/16 of 31 October 1986 and 42/78 of 4 December 1987 and the present resolution;

11. *Reaffirms* the determination of the United Nations to co-operate fully with the Organization of African Unity with a view to implementing the relevant deci-

sions of that organization, in particular resolution AHG/Res.104(XIX);

12. *Requests* the Special Committee on the Situation with regard to the Implementation of the Declaration on the Granting of Independence to Colonial Countries and Peoples to continue to consider the situation in Western Sahara as a matter of priority and to report thereon to the General Assembly at its forty-fourth session;

13. *Invites* the Secretary-General of the Organization of African Unity to keep the Secretary-General of the United Nations informed of the progress achieved in the implementation of the decisions of the Organization of African Unity relating to Western Sahara;

14. *Invites* the Secretary-General to follow the situation in Western Sahara closely with a view to the implementation of the present resolution and to report thereon to the General Assembly at its forty-fourth session.

General Assembly resolution 43/33

22 November 1988   Meeting 59   86-0-53 (recorded vote)

Approved by Fourth Committee (A/43/797 & Corr.1) by recorded vote (87-0-53), 25 October (meeting 13); 46-nation draft (A/C.4/43/L.2); agenda item 18.

Sponsors: Afghanistan, Albania, Algeria, Antigua and Barbuda, Barbados, Belize, Benin, Botswana, Burkina Faso, Burundi, Congo, Cuba, Cyprus, Democratic Yemen, Ethiopia, Ghana, Guyana, India, Iran, Lao People's Democratic Republic, Lesotho, Libyan Arab Jamahiriya, Madagascar, Malawi, Mali, Mauritania, Mexico, Mozambique, Nicaragua, Nigeria, Panama, Papua New Guinea, Rwanda, Saint Kitts and Nevis, Seychelles, Sierra Leone, Suriname, Swaziland, Syrian Arab Republic, Uganda, United Republic of Tanzania, Vanuatu, Viet Nam, Yugoslavia, Zambia, Zimbabwe.

Meeting numbers. GA 43rd session: 4th Committee 7-13; plenary 59.

Recorded vote in Assembly as follows:

In favour: Afghanistan, Albania, Algeria, Antigua and Barbuda, Argentina, Australia, Austria, Bahamas, Barbados, Belize, Benin, Bhutan, Bolivia, Botswana, Brazil, Bulgaria, Burkina Faso, Burundi, Byelorussian SSR, Colombia, Congo, Cuba, Cyprus, Czechoslovakia, Democratic Yemen, Ecuador, El Salvador, Ethiopia, Fiji, Finland, Gambia, German Democratic Republic, Ghana, Greece, Guatemala, Guyana, Honduras, Hungary, Iceland, India, Iran, Ireland, Jamaica, Kenya, Lao People's Democratic Republic, Lesotho, Libyan Arab Jamahiriya, Madagascar, Malawi, Mali, Mauritania, Mauritius, Mexico, Mongolia, Mozambique, New Zealand, Nicaragua, Nigeria, Norway, Panama, Papua New Guinea, Peru, Philippines, Poland, Rwanda, Saint Kitts and Nevis, Seychelles, Spain, Suriname, Swaziland, Sweden, Syrian Arab Republic, Togo, Trinidad and Tobago, Tunisia, Uganda, Ukrainian SSR, USSR, United Republic of Tanzania, Uruguay, Vanuatu, Venezuela, Viet Nam, Yugoslavia, Zambia, Zimbabwe.

Against: None.

Abstaining: Bahrain, Bangladesh, Belgium, Brunei Darussalam, Burma, Canada, Central African Republic, Chile, Costa Rica, Côte d'Ivoire, Denmark, Djibouti, Dominica, Dominican Republic, Egypt, Equatorial Guinea, France, Gabon, Germany, Federal Republic of, Guinea, Haiti, Indonesia, Israel, Italy, Japan, Jordan, Luxembourg, Malaysia, Maldives, Malta, Netherlands, Oman, Pakistan, Paraguay, Portugal, Qatar, Saint Lucia, Saint Vincent and the Grenadines, Samoa, Saudi Arabia, Sierra Leone, Singapore, Solomon Islands, Somalia, Sri Lanka, Sudan, Thailand, Turkey, United Arab Emirates, United Kingdom, United States, Yemen, Zaire.

New Caledonia

In 1986,[17] the General Assembly had determined that New Caledonia, a group of islands in the south-west Pacific Ocean, was an NSGT within the meaning of the United Nations Charter and affirmed the right of the people to self-determination and independence in accordance with the 1960 Declaration on colonial countries;[18] however, France, the administering Power, did not consider New Caledonia an NSGT. It had organized a referendum on 13 September 1987 in which, it maintained, the people of the Territory had had the opportunity to express their views.[19]

France reported that the referendum had resulted in a vote in favour of remaining with France. According to a Secretariat working paper of August 1988,[20] a Statute of Autonomy for the Territory, approved by the Council of Ministers of France, was to come into force after the holding of elections on 24 April 1988. Despite some incidents of violence and a boycott by the Front de libération nationale kanak et socialiste (FLNKS), elections were held and won by the Rassemblement pour la Calédonie dans la République (RPCR). In May, France dispatched a mission to the Territory charged with the responsibility of presenting proposals for its future. Discussions were held with representatives of political parties and other officials and, as a result, the two sides accepted a set of proposals known as the Matignon Agreement.

The Agreement covered a wide range of arrangements for the governing of the Territory, including the following: after a one-year period of direct French administration, New Caledonia would be divided into three provinces, each with its own elected Assembly and Executive Council; matters of common concern would be dealt with by a territorial Congress consisting of the three provincial Assemblies and headed by the High Commissioner, who would be responsible for the overall administration of the Territory; France would be responsible for foreign trade, defence, maintenance of law and order, justice and secondary and higher education; the territorial Government would be responsible for co-ordination between France and local institutions, budget matters, infrastructure and primary education; and another referendum on self-determination would be held in 1998. Both FLNKS and RPCR endorsed the proposals conditionally. Discussions continued to be held between France and the parties concerned with a view to implementing the Agreement.

Action by the Committee on colonial countries. The Committee on colonial countries considered the question of New Caledonia at two meetings in August 1988.[5] It had before it the Secretariat working paper (see above) and background information relating to the Territory prepared by the Evangelical Church of New Caledonia.[21]

On 10 August,[22] the Committee noted with satisfaction the dialogue initiated under the auspices of the French authorities on the status of the Territory and urged all parties involved to continue their dialogue and refrain from acts of violence. The text of the resolution, which was transmitted to France, was the basis of a draft recommended to the General Assembly.

GENERAL ASSEMBLY ACTION

On 22 November, the General Assembly adopted without vote **resolution 43/34**, as recommended by the Fourth Committee.

Question of New Caledonia

The General Assembly,

Having considered the question of New Caledonia,

Having examined the chapter of the report of the Special Committee on the Situation with regard to the Implementation of the Declaration on the Granting of Independence to Colonial Countries and Peoples relating to New Caledonia,

Recalling its resolutions 1514(XV) of 14 December 1960 and 1541(XV) of 15 December 1960,

Noting with satisfaction the dialogue initiated under the auspices of the French authorities on the status of the Territory,

Noting also that the French authorities were taking positive measures to promote political, economic and social development in New Caledonia to provide a framework for the peaceful progress of the Territory to self-determination,

1. *Approves* the chapter of the report of the Special Committee on the Situation with regard to the Implementation of the Declaration on the Granting of Independence to Colonial Countries and Peoples relating to New Caledonia;

2. *Urges* all the parties involved, in the interest of all the people of New Caledonia, to continue their dialogue and to refrain from acts of violence;

3. *Invites* all the parties involved to continue promoting a framework for the peaceful progress of the Territory to self-determination;

4. *Requests* the Special Committee to continue the examination of this question at its next session and to report thereon to the General Assembly at its forty-fourth session.

General Assembly resolution 43/34

22 November 1988   Meeting 59   Adopted without vote

Approved by Fourth Committee (A/43/797 & Corr.1) without objection, 25 October (meeting 14); draft by Committee on colonial countries (A/43/23); agenda item 18.

Meeting numbers. GA 43rd session: 4th Committee 7-14; plenary 59.

East Timor

Although the General Assembly by **decision 43/402** of 23 September deferred consideration of the question of East Timor until 1989, it was taken up by the Committee on colonial countries in 1988. The Secretary-General continued his substantive high-level talks with Portugal—considered by the United Nations to be the legal administering Power—and Indonesia, which maintained that decolonization in East Timor was complete and that its people had chosen independence through integration with Indonesia.

Consideration by the Committee on colonial countries. The Committee on colonial countries considered the East Timor question at four meetings between 1 and 12 August.[5] It heard statements by Indonesia, Guinea-Bissau (on behalf also of Angola, Cape Verde, Mozambique, and Sao Tome and Principe) and Portugal (as the administering Power). Additionally, it heard statements by representatives of the Frente Revolucionária de Timor Leste Independente and NGOs. The Committee had before it a Secretariat working paper on political developments, the human rights situation and economic and social conditions.[23] The paper mentioned reports of an increase in the Indonesian military presence in the Territory during July 1987, bringing the total to some 13,000 to 15,000 troops.

In letters to the Committee Chairman of 11 April, 29 July and 5 August,[24] Indonesia reiterated its opposition to the appearance of petitioners to discuss East Timor, stating that the decolonization process there had been carried out in conformity with the provisions of the United Nations Charter and Assembly resolutions on decolonization, and that, since East Timor had been formally integrated into Indonesia in 1976, the Committee's consideration of the question would constitute interference in a sovereign State's internal affairs.

Other communications. On 15 March,[25] Portugal informed the Secretary-General that it had nothing to add to the information it had provided in 1979,[26] as required by Article 73 *e* of the Charter.

Indonesia and Portugal, in letters to the Assembly President, again expressed their differing opinions on East Timor. On 8 June,[27] in response to a statement that day to the fifteenth special session of the Assembly by the Portuguese President, Indonesia refuted the Portuguese call for negotiations to find a solution that was internationally acceptable. Portugal responded on 23 June,[28] reiterating the position taken by its President, stating its commitment to safeguard the right to self-determination and expressing support for the Secretary-General's efforts to hold consultations on the issue.

Report of the Secretary-General. In a September progress report,[29] the Secretary-General stated that during the preceding year he had held substantive talks on several occasions with officials of Indonesia and Portugal with a view to giving effect to a 1987 proposal for a visit by a Portuguese parliamentary delegation to East Timor in order to obtain first-hand information on the situation. The two parties agreed in principle to such a visit, subject to the elaboration of mutually acceptable terms of reference. They agreed further that the Permanent Representatives of the two countries should resume their contacts under the Secretary-General's auspices with a view to reaching agreement on the terms, modalities and timing of the proposed visit. The Secretary-General reported that humanitarian programmes were being carried out for the benefit of the East Timorese people. Under a programme for the repatriation of former Portuguese civil servants and their dependants, carried out through the International Committee of the Red Cross with funding from the Office of the United Nations High Commissioner for

Refugees, approximately 405 persons had been repatriated to Portugal. Repatriation of the remaining few cases was expected to be completed within a few months.

Further communication. In a letter of 25 October to the Secretary-General,[30] Portugal said that the planned visit on 1 and 2 November of the President of Indonesia to East Timor would have serious implications at a time when talks were under way on the terms of reference for a possible visit by Portuguese parliamentarians to East Timor.

Other Territories

American Samoa

The Committee on colonial countries considered the question of American Samoa on 1 August and had before it a working paper prepared by the Secretariat on developments in the Territory.[31]

On 22 November, on the recommendation of the Fourth Committee, the General Assembly adopted **resolution 43/43** without vote.

Question of American Samoa

The General Assembly,

Having considered the question of American Samoa,

Having examined the relevant chapters of the report of the Special Committee on the Situation with regard to the Implementation of the Declaration on the Granting of Independence to Colonial Countries and Peoples,

Recalling its resolution 1514(XV) of 14 December 1960, containing the Declaration on the Granting of Independence to Colonial Countries and Peoples, and all resolutions and decisions of the United Nations relating to American Samoa, in particular General Assembly resolution 42/88 of 4 December 1987,

Conscious of the need to promote progress towards the full implementation of the Declaration in respect of American Samoa,

Having heard the statement of the representative of the United States of America, as the administering Power,

Aware of the special circumstances of the geographical location and economic conditions of the Territory and bearing in mind the necessity of diversifying and strengthening further its economy as a matter of priority in order to promote economic stability,

Recalling the dispatch in 1981 of a United Nations visiting mission to the Territory,

Mindful that United Nations visiting missions provide an effective means of ascertaining the situation in the small Territories and emphasizing the desirability of sending, at an appropriate time, a further visiting mission to American Samoa,

1. *Approves* the chapter of the report of the Special Committee on the Situation with regard to the Implementation of the Declaration on the Granting of Independence to Colonial Countries and Peoples relating to American Samoa;

2. *Reaffirms* the inalienable right of the people of American Samoa to self-determination and independence in conformity with the Declaration on the Granting of Independence to Colonial Countries and Peoples;

3. *Reiterates the view* that such factors as territorial size, geographical location, size of population and limited natural resources should in no way delay the speedy exercise by the people of the Territory of their inalienable right to self-determination and independence in conformity with the Declaration, which fully applies to American Samoa;

4. *Calls upon* the Government of the United States of America, as the administering Power, to take all necessary steps, bearing in mind the rights, interests and wishes of the people of American Samoa as expressed freely in any act of self-determination, to expedite the process of decolonization of the Territory in accordance with the relevant provisions of the Charter of the United Nations and the Declaration and reaffirms the importance of fostering an awareness among the people of American Samoa of the possibilities open to them in the exercise of their right to self-determination and independence;

5. *Reaffirms* the responsibility of the administering Power, under the Charter, to promote the economic and social development of American Samoa and calls upon the administering Power to intensify its efforts to strengthen and diversify the economy of the Territory;

6. *Urges* the administering Power, in co-operation with the territorial Government, to take effective measures to safeguard and guarantee the inalienable right of the people of American Samoa to own and dispose of the natural resources of the Territory, including marine resources, and to establish and maintain control over the future development of those resources;

7. *Also urges* the administering Power to continue to foster close relations between the Territory and other island communities in the region and promote co-operation between the territorial Government and regional institutions, as well as the specialized agencies and other organizations of the United Nations system;

8. *Requests* the Special Committee to continue the examination of this question at its next session, including the possible dispatch of a further visiting mission to American Samoa at an appropriate time and in consultation with the administering Power, taking into account, in particular, the wishes of the people of the Territory, and to report thereon to the General Assembly at its forty-fourth session.

General Assembly resolution 43/43

22 November 1988   Meeting 59   Adopted without vote

Approved by Fourth Committee (A/43/797 & Corr.1) without objection, 25 October (meeting 14); draft by Committee on colonial countries (A/43/23); agenda item 18.

Meeting numbers. GA 43rd session: 4th Committee 7-14; plenary 59.

Anguilla

On 1 August 1988, the Committee on colonial countries considered the question of Anguilla, having before it working papers by the Secretariat on developments concerning the Territory[32] and foreign economic and other interests.[33]

On 22 November, on the recommendation of the Fourth Committee, the General Assembly adopted **resolution 43/36** without vote.

Question of Anguilla

The General Assembly,

Having considered the question of Anguilla,

Having examined the relevant chapters of the report of the Special Committee on the Situation with regard to the Implementation of the Declaration on the Granting of Independence to Colonial Countries and Peoples,

Recalling its resolution 1514(XV) of 14 December 1960, containing the Declaration on the Granting of Independence to Colonial Countries and Peoples, and all resolutions and decisions of the United Nations relating to Anguilla, including in particular General Assembly resolution 42/80 of 4 December 1987,

Conscious of the need to ensure the full and speedy implementation of the Declaration in respect of the Territory,

Having heard the statement of the representative of the United Kingdom of Great Britain and Northern Ireland, as the administering Power,

Noting the stated policy of the Government of the United Kingdom, the administering Power, that it remains ready to respond positively to the express wish of the people of the Territory on the question of independence,

Noting the impending consideration by the Territory's House of Assembly and by the Government of the United Kingdom of the recommendations of the Constitutional Review Committee and noting the priority accorded by the territorial Government to the revision of the laws of Anguilla,

Aware of the special circumstances of the geographical location and economic conditions of the Territory and bearing in mind the necessity of diversifying and strengthening further its economy as a matter of priority in order to promote economic stability,

Reaffirming the responsibility of the administering Power to promote the economic and social development of the Territory and noting the continued growth of the Territory's economy due largely to the expansion in the tourism and construction industries,

Expressing its concern at the continued illegal operation of foreign fishing vessels within the territorial waters of Anguilla and welcoming the measures taken by the territorial Government to protect and conserve marine resources,

Stressing the importance of an efficient and effective civil service and noting the measures being taken by the territorial Government aimed at alleviating the problem of unemployment and providing increased job opportunities,

Noting with concern the vulnerability of the Territory to drug trafficking and related activities,

Noting the contribution to the development of the Territory by specialized agencies and other organizations of the United Nations system, in particular the United Nations Development Programme,

Noting also that in 1987 Anguilla became a member of the Eastern Caribbean Central Bank and that it continued to participate and maintain an active interest in the related activities of other regional organizations,

Recalling the dispatch in 1984 of a United Nations visiting mission to the Territory,

Mindful that United Nations visiting missions provide an effective means of ascertaining the situation in the small Territories and considering that the possibility of sending a further visiting mission to Anguilla at an appropriate time should be kept under review,

1. *Approves* the chapter of the report of the Special Committee on the Situation with regard to the Implementation of the Declaration on the Granting of Independence to Colonial Countries and Peoples relating to Anguilla;

2. *Reaffirms* the inalienable right of the people of Anguilla to self-determination and independence in conformity with the Declaration on the Granting of Independence to Colonial Countries and Peoples;

3. *Reiterates the view* that such factors as territorial size, geographical location, size of population and limited natural resources should in no way delay the speedy exercise by the people of the Territory of their inalienable right to self-determination and independence in conformity with the Declaration, which fully applies to Anguilla;

4. *Reiterates* that it is the responsibility of the United Kingdom of Great Britain and Northern Ireland, as the administering Power, to create such conditions in Anguilla as will enable its people to exercise freely and without interference, from a well-informed standpoint as to the available options, their inalienable right to self-determination and independence in accordance with resolution 1514(XV), and all other relevant resolutions of the General Assembly;

5. *Reaffirms* that it is ultimately for the people of Anguilla themselves to determine freely their future political status in accordance with the relevant provisions of the Charter of the United Nations and the Declaration and, in that connection, reaffirms the importance of fostering an awareness among the people of the Territory of the possibilities open to them in the exercise of their right to self-determination and independence;

6. *Calls upon* the administering Power to continue, in co-operation with the territorial Government, to take measures with a view to strengthening and diversifying the Territory's economy;

7. *Urges* the administering Power, in co-operation with the territorial Government, to continue the assistance necessary to increase employment of the local population in the civil service and other sectors of the economy;

8. *Also urges* the administering Power, in co-operation with the territorial Government, to take effective measures to safeguard and guarantee the inalienable right of the people of Anguilla to own and dispose of the natural resources of the Territory, including marine resources, and to establish and maintain control over the future development of those resources;

9. *Calls upon* the administering Power to continue to take all necessary measures, in co-operation with the territorial Government, to counter problems related to drug trafficking;

10. *Reiterates its request* to the administering Power to continue to enlist the assistance of the specialized agencies and other organizations of the United Nations system, as well as other international and regional bodies, in the development and strengthening of the economy of Anguilla;

11. *Also reiterates its request* to the administering Power to continue to make every effort to facilitate and encourage the participation of the Territory in regional and international organizations;

12. *Requests* the Special Committee to continue the examination of this question at its next session, including the possible dispatch of a further visiting mission to Anguilla at an appropriate time and in consultation with the administering Power, and to report thereon to the General Assembly at its forty-fourth session.

General Assembly resolution 43/36
22 November 1988   Meeting 59   Adopted without vote

Approved by Fourth Committee (A/43/797 & Corr.1) without objection, 25
   October (meeting 14); draft by Committee on colonial countries (A/43/23);
   agenda item 18.
Meeting numbers. GA 43rd session: 4th Committee 7-14; plenary 59.

Bermuda

The Committee on colonial countries considered the question of Bermuda on 1 August, including working papers by the Secretariat on developments concerning the Territory[34] and on foreign economic and other interests[35] and military activities.[36]

On 22 November, on the recommendation of the Fourth Committee, the General Assembly adopted without vote **resolution 43/39.**

Question of Bermuda

The General Assembly,

Having considered the question of Bermuda,

Having examined the relevant chapters of the report of the Special Committee on the Situation with regard to the Implementation of the Declaration on the Granting of Independence to Colonial Countries and Peoples,

Recalling its resolution 1514(XV) of 14 December 1960, containing the Declaration on the Granting of Independence to Colonial Countries and Peoples, and all resolutions and decisions of the United Nations relating to Bermuda, in particular General Assembly resolution 42/86 of 4 December 1987,

Conscious of the need to ensure the full and speedy implementation of the Declaration in respect of the Territory,

Having heard the statement of the representative of the United Kingdom of Great Britain and Northern Ireland, as the administering Power,

Noting the stated policy of the Government of the United Kingdom, the administering Power, that it remains ready to respond positively to the express wish of the people of the Territory on the question of independence,

Noting the active discussions in the Territory, both within and outside the territorial Government, on the future status of Bermuda,

Aware of the special circumstances of the geographical location and economic conditions of the Territory and bearing in mind the necessity of diversifying and strengthening further its economy as a matter of priority in order to promote economic stability,

Noting with concern the vulnerability of the Territory to drug trafficking and related activities,

Noting with appreciation the assistance extended to the Territory by the United Nations Development Programme,

Mindful that United Nations visiting missions provide an effective means of ascertaining the situation in the small Territories and considering that the possibility of sending a visiting mission to Bermuda at an appropriate time should be kept under review,

1. *Approves* the chapter of the report of the Special Committee on the Situation with regard to the Implementation of the Declaration on the Granting of Independence to Colonial Countries and Peoples relating to Bermuda;

2. *Reaffirms* the inalienable right of the people of Bermuda to self-determination and independence in conformity with the Declaration on the Granting of Independence to Colonial Countries and Peoples;

3. *Reiterates the view* that such factors as territorial size, geographical location, size of population and limited natural resources should in no way delay the speedy exercise by the people of the Territory of their inalienable right to self-determination and independence in conformity with the Declaration, which fully applies to Bermuda;

4. *Reiterates* that it is the responsibility of the United Kingdom of Great Britain and Northern Ireland, as the administering Power, to create such conditions in the Territory as will enable the people of Bermuda to exercise freely and without interference their inalienable right to self-determination and independence in accordance with General Assembly resolution 1514(XV) and, in that connection, reaffirms the importance of fostering an awareness among the people of Bermuda of the possibilities open to them in the exercise of that right;

5. *Reaffirms* that it is ultimately for the people of Bermuda themselves to determine their own future political status in accordance with the relevant provisions of the Charter of the United Nations and the Declaration;

6. *Reaffirms its strong conviction* that the presence of military bases and installations in the Territory could constitute a major obstacle to the implementation of the Declaration and that it is the responsibility of the administering Power to ensure that the existence of such bases and installations does not hinder the population of the Territory from exercising its right to self-determination and independence in conformity with the purposes and principles of the Charter;

7. *Urges* the administering Power to continue to take all necessary measures not to involve Bermuda in any offensive acts or interference directed against other States and to comply fully with the purposes and principles of the Charter, the Declaration and the resolutions and decisions of the General Assembly relating to military activities and arrangements by colonial Powers in Territories under their administration;

8. *Also urges* the administering Power, in co-operation with the territorial Government, to take effective measures to safeguard and guarantee the inalienable right of the people of Bermuda to own and dispose of the natural resources of the Territory, including marine resources, and to establish and maintain control over the future development of those resources;

9. *Further urges* the administering Power, in co-operation with the territorial Government, to continue to provide assistance for increased employment of the local population in the civil service, particularly at senior levels;

10. *Calls upon* the administering Power to continue to take all necessary measures, in co-operation with the territorial Government, to counter problems related to drug trafficking;

11. *Invites* the specialized agencies and other organizations of the United Nations system to continue to provide assistance for the development needs of Bermuda;

12. *Emphasizes* the desirability of sending a visiting mission to the Territory and requests the administering Power to facilitate the dispatch of such a mission at the earliest possible opportunity;

13. *Requests* the Special Committee to continue the examination of this question at its next session, including the possible dispatch of a visiting mission to Bermuda at an appropriate time and in consultation with the administering Power, and to report thereon to the General Assembly at its forty-fourth session.

General Assembly resolution 43/39

22 November 1988   Meeting 59   Adopted without vote

Approved by Fourth Committee (A/43/797 & Corr.1) without objection, 25 October (meeting 14); draft by Committee on colonial countries (A/43/23); agenda item 18.
Meeting numbers. GA 43rd session: 4th Committee 7-14; plenary 59.

British Virgin Islands

The Committee on colonial countries considered the question of the British Virgin Islands on 1 August. It had before it a working paper by the Secretariat on developments concerning the Territory.[37]

On 22 November, on the recommendation of the Fourth Committee, the General Assembly adopted **resolution 43/41** without vote.

Question of the British Virgin Islands
The General Assembly,

Having considered the question of the British Virgin Islands,

Having examined the relevant chapters of the report of the Special Committee on the Situation with regard to the Implementation of the Declaration on the Granting of Independence to Colonial Countries and Peoples,

Recalling its resolution 1514(XV) of 14 December 1960, containing the Declaration on the Granting of Independence to Colonial Countries and Peoples, and all resolutions and decisions of the United Nations relating to the British Virgin Islands, including in particular General Assembly resolution 42/82 of 4 December 1987,

Conscious of the need to ensure the full and speedy implementation of the Declaration in respect of the Territory,

Having heard the statement of the representative of the United Kingdom of Great Britain and Northern Ireland, as the administering Power,

Noting the stated policy of the Government of the United Kingdom, the administering Power, that it remains ready to respond positively to the express wish of the people of the Territory on the question of independence,

Aware of the special circumstances of the geographical location and economic conditions of the Territory and bearing in mind the necessity of diversifying and strengthening further its economy as a matter of priority in order to promote economic stability,

Reaffirming that it is the responsibility of the administering Power to promote the economic and social development of the Territory and noting the decline in the Territory's economic activities, with the exception of tourism,

Noting with concern the continued illegal operations of foreign fishing vessels within the territorial waters and noting the measures being taken by the territorial Government in that regard,

Noting the critical need for the cadre training of nationals in all fields and noting with satisfaction the measures being taken by the territorial Government in that connection,

Noting with concern the vulnerability of the Territory to drug trafficking and related activities,

Welcoming the contribution to the development of the Territory by the specialized agencies and other organizations of the United Nations system, particularly the United Nations Development Programme, as well as by regional organizations,

Noting the continued participation of the Territory in regional and other international organizations,

Recalling the dispatch in 1976 of a United Nations visiting mission to the Territory,

Mindful that United Nations visiting missions provide an effective means of ascertaining the situation in the small Territories and considering that the possibility of sending a further visiting mission to the British Virgin Islands at an appropriate time should be kept under review,

1. *Approves* the chapter of the report of the Special Committee on the Situation with regard to the Implementation of the Declaration on the Granting of Independence to Colonial Countries and Peoples relating to the British Virgin Islands;

2. *Reaffirms* the inalienable right of the people of the British Virgin Islands to self-determination and independence in conformity with the Declaration on the Granting of Independence to Colonial Countries and Peoples;

3. *Reiterates the view* that such factors as territorial size, geographical location, size of population and limited natural resources should in no way delay the speedy exercise by the people of the Territory of their inalienable right to self-determination and independence in conformity with the Declaration, which fully applies to the British Virgin Islands;

4. *Reiterates* that it is the responsibility of the United Kingdom of Great Britain and Northern Ireland, as the administering Power, to create such conditions in the Territory as will enable the people of the British Virgin Islands to exercise freely and without interference their inalienable right to self-determination and independence in accordance with resolution 1514(XV) and all other relevant resolutions of the General Assembly;

5. *Reaffirms* that it is ultimately for the people of the British Virgin Islands themselves to determine freely their future political status in accordance with the relevant provisions of the Charter of the United Nations and the Declaration and, in that connection, reaffirms the importance of fostering an awareness among the people of the Territory of the possibilities open to them in the exercise of their right to self-determination;

6. *Calls upon* the administering Power to continue, in co-operation with the Government of the British Virgin Islands, to take measures with a view to strengthening and diversifying the Territory's economy;

7. *Urges* the administering Power, in co-operation with the territorial Government, to take effective measures to safeguard and guarantee the inalienable right of the people of the British Virgin Islands to own and dispose of the natural resources of the Territory, including marine resources, and to establish and maintain control over the future development of those resources;

8. *Calls upon* the administering Power, in co-operation with the territorial Government, to take further measures in the cadre training of nationals so as to facilitate their wider participation in the decision-making process in all sectors;

9. _Also calls upon_ the administering Power to continue to take all necessary measures, in co-operation with the territorial Government, to counter problems related to drug trafficking;

10. _Reiterates its call_ upon the administering Power to continue to facilitate the participation of the British Virgin Islands in various international and regional organizations and in other organizations of the United Nations system;

11. _Urges_ the specialized agencies and other organizations of the United Nations system, as well as the regional organizations concerned, to intensify measures to accelerate progress in the social and economic development of the Territory;

12. _Requests_ the Special Committee to continue the examination of this question at its next session, including the possible dispatch of a further visiting mission to the British Virgin Islands at an appropriate time and in consultation with the administering Power, and to report thereon to the General Assembly at its forty-fourth session.

General Assembly resolution 43/41

22 November 1988   Meeting 59   Adopted without vote

Approved by Fourth Committee (A/43/797 & Corr.1) without objection, 25 October (meeting 14); draft by Committee on colonial countries (A/43/23); agenda item 18.

Meeting numbers. GA 43rd session: 4th Committee 7-14; plenary 59.

Cayman Islands

The Committee on colonial countries, on 1 August, considered the question of the Cayman Islands. It had before it two working papers by the Secretariat—one on developments concerning the Territory[38] and another on foreign economic and other interests.[39]

On 22 November, on the recommendation of the Fourth Committee, the General Assembly adopted without vote **resolution 43/37**.

Question of the Cayman Islands

The General Assembly,

Having considered the question of the Cayman Islands,

Having examined the relevant chapters of the report of the Special Committee on the Situation with regard to the Implementation of the Declaration on the Granting of Independence to Colonial Countries and Peoples,

Recalling its resolution 1514(XV) of 14 December 1960, containing the Declaration on the Granting of Independence to Colonial Countries and Peoples, and all resolutions and decisions of the United Nations relating to the Cayman Islands, in particular General Assembly resolution 42/85 of 4 December 1987,

Conscious of the need to ensure the full and speedy implementation of the Declaration in respect of the Territory,

Having heard the statement of the representative of the United Kingdom of Great Britain and Northern Ireland, as the administering Power,

Noting the stated policy of the Government of the United Kingdom, the administering Power, that it remains ready to respond positively to the express wish of the people of the Territory on the question of independence,

Aware of the special circumstances of the geographical location and economic conditions of the Territory and

bearing in mind the necessity of diversifying and strengthening further its economy as a matter of priority in order to promote economic stability,

Noting the measures being taken by the territorial Government to promote agricultural production with a view to reducing the Territory's dependence on imported provisions,

Expressing its concern that property and land continue to be owned and developed largely by investors from abroad,

Noting that a large proportion of the labour force of the Territory consists of expatriates,

Noting with concern the vulnerability of the Territory to drug trafficking and related activities,

Noting with appreciation the continued contribution of the United Nations Development Programme, as well as regional institutions, to the development of the Territory,

Recalling the dispatch in 1977 of a United Nations visiting mission to the Territory,

Mindful that United Nations visiting missions provide an effective means of ascertaining the situation in the small Territories and considering that the possibility of sending a further visiting mission to the Cayman Islands at an appropriate time should be kept under review,

1. _Approves_ the chapter of the report of the Special Committee on the Situation with regard to the Implementation of the Declaration on the Granting of Independence to Colonial Countries and Peoples relating to the Cayman Islands;

2. _Reaffirms_ the inalienable right of the people of the Cayman Islands to self-determination and independence in conformity with the Declaration on the Granting of Independence to Colonial Countries and Peoples;

3. _Reiterates the view_ that such factors as territorial size, geographical location, size of population and limited natural resources should in no way delay the speedy exercise by the people of the Territory of their inalienable right to self-determination and independence in conformity with the Declaration, which fully applies to the Cayman Islands;

4. _Reiterates_ that it is the responsibility of the United Kingdom of Great Britain and Northern Ireland, as the administering Power, to create such conditions in the Territory as will enable the people of the Cayman Islands to exercise freely and without interference their inalienable right to self-determination and independence in accordance with resolution 1514(XV) and all other relevant resolutions of the General Assembly;

5. _Reaffirms_ that it is ultimately for the people of the Cayman Islands themselves to determine their future political status in accordance with the relevant provisions of the Charter of the United Nations and the Declaration and, in that connection, reaffirms the importance of fostering an awareness among the people of the Territory of the possibilities open to them in the exercise of their right to self-determination and independence;

6. _Calls upon_ the administering Power, in consultation with the territorial Government, to facilitate and promote increased participation by the local population in the decision-making process in the affairs of the Territory;

7. _Reaffirms_ the responsibility of the administering Power to promote the economic and social development of the Territory and recommends that priority should

continue to be given to the diversification of the Territory's economy;

8. *Urges* the administering Power, in co-operation with the territorial Government, to take effective measures to safeguard and guarantee the inalienable right of the people of the Cayman Islands to own and dispose of the natural resources of the Territory, including marine resources, and to establish and maintain control over the future development of those resources;

9. *Calls upon* the administering Power to continue to take all necessary measures, in co-operation with the territorial Government, to counter problems related to drug trafficking;

10. *Invites* the specialized agencies and other organizations of the United Nations system, as well as other international and regional institutions, to continue to take all necessary measures to accelerate progress in the social and economic life of the Territory;

11. *Requests* the Special Committee to continue the examination of this question at its next session, including the possible dispatch of a further visiting mission to the Cayman Islands at an appropriate time and in consultation with the administering Power, and to report thereon to the General Assembly at its forty-fourth session.

General Assembly resolution 43/37

22 November 1988   Meeting 59   Adopted without vote

Approved by Fourth Committee (A/43/797 & Corr.1) without objection, 25 October (meeting 14); draft by Committee on colonial countries (A/43/23); agenda item 18.
Meeting numbers. GA 43rd session: 4th Committee 7-14; plenary 59.

Gibraltar

On 12 August, the Committee on colonial countries considered the question of Gibraltar. It had before it a working paper by the Secretariat on developments concerning the Territory.[40] Taking into account the continuing discussions between the parties concerned, the Committee decided to continue its consideration of Gibraltar in 1989, subject to General Assembly directives.

GENERAL ASSEMBLY ACTION

In November, the General Assembly adopted **decision 43/411** without vote.

Question of Gibraltar

At its 59th plenary meeting, on 22 November 1988, the General Assembly, on the recommendation of the Fourth Committee, adopted the following text as representing the consensus of the members of the Assembly:

"The General Assembly, recalling its decision 42/418 of 4 December 1987 and recalling at the same time that the Brussels statement, agreed to on 27 November 1984 by the Governments of Spain and the United Kingdom of Great Britain and Northern Ireland, states, *inter alia*, the following:

'The establishment of a negotiating process aimed at overcoming all the differences between them over Gibraltar and at promoting co-operation on a mutually beneficial basis on economic, cultural, touristic, aviation, military and environmental matters. Both sides accept that the issues of sovereignty will be discussed in that process. The

British Government will fully maintain its commitment to honour the wishes of the people of Gibraltar as set out in the preamble of the 1969 Constitution',

"takes note of the fact that, as part of this process, the Ministers for Foreign Affairs met at Madrid on 5 and 6 December 1985, in London on 13 and 14 January 1987, at Madrid on 27 and 28 November 1987 and in London on 2 December 1987, on the last of which occasions they reached agreement on arrangements for co-operation over the use of Gibraltar airport, resumption of the ferry service between Gibraltar and Algeciras and improving the flow of surface traffic between Spain and Gibraltar; regrets that these measures have not yet been brought into effect; and urges both Governments to continue their negotiations with the object of reaching a definitive solution to the problem of Gibraltar in the light of relevant resolutions of the General Assembly and in the spirit of the Charter of the United Nations."

General Assembly decision 43/411

Adopted without vote

Approved by Fourth Committee (A/43/797 & Corr.1) without objection, 25 October (meeting 14); draft consensus (A/C.4/L.6); agenda item 18.
Meeting numbers. GA 43rd session: 4th Committee 7-14; plenary 59.

Guam

The Committee on colonial countries, on 1 August, considered the question of Guam. It had before it working papers prepared by the Secretariat on developments concerning the Territory[41] and on military activities.[42]

On 22 November, on the recommendation of the Fourth Committee, the General Assembly adopted **resolution 43/42** without vote.

Question of Guam

The General Assembly,

Having considered the question of Guam,

Having examined the relevant chapters of the report of the Special Committee on the Situation with regard to the Implementation of the Declaration on the Granting of Independence to Colonial Countries and Peoples,

Recalling its resolution 1514(XV) of 14 December 1960, containing the Declaration on the Granting of Independence to Colonial Countries and Peoples, and all resolutions and decisions of the United Nations relating to Guam, in particular General Assembly resolution 42/87 of 4 December 1987,

Conscious of the need to ensure the full and speedy implementation of the Declaration in respect of the Territory,

Having heard the statement of the representative of the United States of America, as the administering Power,

Noting the approval, in referendums held in Guam in 1987, of a draft Commonwealth Act, which, upon its enactment by the United States Congress, would confer upon Guam a full measure of internal self-government,

Aware of the special circumstances of the geographical location and economic conditions of the Territory and bearing in mind the necessity of diversifying and strengthening further its economy as a matter of priority in order to promote economic stability,

Taking note of the statement of the representative of the administering Power that the draft Commonwealth Act seeks to promote economic development by establishing a free trade zone between Guam and the United States,

Taking note also of the statement of the representative of the administering Power that the cultural identity of the Chamorro people, the indigenous inhabitants of Guam, would be recognized under the draft Commonwealth Act,

Recalling the dispatch in 1979 of a United Nations visiting mission to the Territory,

Mindful that United Nations visiting missions provide an effective means of ascertaining the situation in the small Territories and reiterating that the possibility of sending a further visiting mission to Guam at an appropriate time should be kept under review,

1. *Approves* the chapter of the report of the Special Committee on the Situation with regard to the Implementation of the Declaration on the Granting of Independence to Colonial Countries and Peoples relating to Guam;

2. *Reaffirms* the inalienable right of the people of Guam to self-determination and independence in conformity with the Declaration on the Granting of Independence to Colonial Countries and Peoples;

3. *Reaffirms its conviction* that such factors as territorial size, geographical location, size of population and limited natural resources should in no way delay the implementation of the Declaration, which fully applies to Guam;

4. *Reaffirms* the importance of fostering an awareness among the people of Guam of the possibilities open to them with regard to their right to self-determination and calls upon the United States of America, as the administering Power, in co-operation with the territorial Government, to expedite the process of decolonization strictly in accordance with the expressed wishes of the people of the Territory;

5. *Reaffirms its strong conviction* that the presence of military bases and installations in the Territory could constitute a major obstacle to the implementation of the Declaration and that it is the responsibility of the administering Power to ensure that the existence of such bases and installations does not hinder the population of the Territory from exercising its right to self-determination and independence in conformity with the purposes and principles of the Charter of the United Nations;

6. *Urges* the administering Power to continue to take all necessary measures not to involve the Territory in any offensive acts or interference against other States and to comply fully with the purposes and principles of the Charter, the Declaration and the resolutions and decisions of the General Assembly relating to military activities and arrangements by colonial Powers in Territories under their administration;

7. *Reaffirms* the responsibility of the administering Power, under the Charter, to promote the economic and social development of Guam and, in that connection, calls upon the administering Power to take further steps to strengthen and diversify the economy of the Territory, particularly in the fields of agriculture and fisheries;

8. *Reiterates* that one of the obstacles to economic growth in Guam is the holding of large tracts of land by the United States federal authorities, and calls upon the administering Power, in co-operation with the territorial Government, to expedite the transfer of land to the people of the Territory and to take the necessary steps to safeguard their property rights;

9. *Urges* the administering Power, in co-operation with the territorial Government, to take effective measures to safeguard and guarantee the inalienable right of the people of Guam to own and dispose of the natural resources of the Territory, including marine resources, and to establish and maintain control over the future development of those resources;

10. *Reaffirms* the importance of continued efforts by the territorial Government, with the support of the administering Power, towards promoting the Chamorro language and culture and urges the administering Power to give full recognition to the status and rights of the Chamorro people as provided for in the draft Commonwealth Act;

11. *Requests* the Special Committee to continue the examination of this question at its next session, including the possible dispatch of a further visiting mission to Guam at an appropriate time and in consultation with the administering Power, and to report thereon to the General Assembly at its forty-fourth session.

General Assembly resolution 43/42

22 November 1988   Meeting 59   Adopted without vote

Approved by Fourth Committee (A/43/797 & Corr.1) without objection, 25 October (meeting 14); draft by Committee on colonial countries (A/43/23); agenda item 18.
Meeting numbers. GA 43rd session: 4th Committee 7-14; plenary 59.

Montserrat

The Committee on colonial countries, on 1 August, considered the question of Montserrat, having before it working papers by the Secretariat on developments concerning the Territory[43] and on foreign economic and other interests.[44]

On 22 November, on the recommendation of the Fourth Committee, the General Assembly adopted **resolution 43/38** without vote.

Question of Montserrat

The General Assembly,

Having considered the question of Montserrat,

Having examined the relevant chapters of the report of the Special Committee on the Situation with regard to the Implementation of the Declaration on the Granting of Independence to Colonial Countries and Peoples,

Recalling its resolution 1514(XV) of 14 December 1960, containing the Declaration on the Granting of Independence to Colonial Countries and Peoples, and all resolutions and decisions of the United Nations relating to Montserrat, including in particular General Assembly resolution 42/81 of 4 December 1987,

Conscious of the need to ensure the full and speedy implementation of the Declaration in respect of the Territory,

Having heard the statement of the representative of the United Kingdom of Great Britain and Northern Ireland, as the administering Power,

Noting the stated policy of the Government of the United Kingdom, the administering Power, that it remains ready to respond positively to the express wish of the people of the Territory on the question of independence,

Taking note of the agreement in principle by the Heads of Authority of the Organization of Eastern Caribbean States at its eleventh meeting held at Tortola, British Virgin Islands on 26 and 27 May 1987, for the establishment, subject to approval through a referendum of the peoples of the countries concerned, of a political union among its members and noting the stated position of the Government of Montserrat in favour of independence and of participation in such a political union,

Aware of the special circumstances of the geographical location and economic conditions of the Territory and bearing in mind the necessity of diversifying and strengthening further its economy as a matter of priority in order to promote economic stability,

Noting the continued growth of the Territory's economy in 1986 and the commitment of the Government of Montserrat to the strengthening and diversification of the Territory's economy,

Noting the measures being taken by the territorial Government to improve the efficiency of the civil service, the priority it places on cadre training and the strengthening of the educational system and its efforts to promote the integration of women in all phases of national development, and drawing attention to the need to associate the Territory in the related work of the United Nations bodies concerned in that regard,

Welcoming the contribution to the development of the Territory by the specialized agencies and other organizations of the United Nations system operating in Montserrat, in particular the United Nations Development Programme and the United Nations Children's Fund,

Noting with concern the continued dissociation of the Territory from the activities of the United Nations Educational, Scientific and Cultural Organization since the withdrawal by the administering Power of the associate membership of Montserrat from that organization in 1983, and aware of the active interest of the Government of Montserrat in the readmission of the Territory as an associate member of the agency,

Recalling the dispatch in 1975 and 1982 of United Nations visiting missions to the Territory,

Mindful that United Nations visiting missions provide an effective means of ascertaining the situation in the small Territories and considering that the possibility of sending a further visiting mission to Montserrat at an appropriate time should be kept under review,

1. *Approves* the chapter of the report of the Special Committee on the Situation with regard to the Implementation of the Declaration on the Granting of Independence to Colonial Countries and Peoples relating to Montserrat;

2. *Reaffirms* the inalienable right of the people of Montserrat to self-determination and independence in conformity with the Declaration on the Granting of Independence to Colonial Countries and Peoples;

3. *Reiterates the view* that such factors as territorial size, geographical location, size of population and limited natural resources should in no way delay the speedy exercise by the people of the Territory of their inalienable right to self-determination and independence in conformity with the Declaration, which fully applies to Montserrat;

4. *Reiterates* that it is the responsibility of the United Kingdom of Great Britain and Northern Ireland, as the administering Power, to create such conditions in the Territory as will enable the people of Montserrat to exercise freely and without interference their inalienable right to self-determination and independence in accordance with resolution 1514(XV) and all other relevant resolutions of the General Assembly;

5. *Reaffirms* that it is ultimately for the people of Montserrat themselves to determine their future political status in accordance with the relevant provisions of the Charter of the United Nations and the Declaration, and reiterates its call upon the administering Power to launch programmes, in co-operation with the territorial Government, to foster an awareness among the people of Montserrat of the possibilities available to them in the exercise of their right to self-determination and independence;

6. *Reaffirms* the responsibility of the administering Power to promote the economic and social development of Montserrat and calls upon the administering Power to continue, in co-operation with the territorial Government, to strengthen the economy of the Territory and to increase its assistance to programmes of diversification;

7. *Urges* the administering Power, in co-operation with the territorial Government, to take effective measures to safeguard and guarantee the inalienable right of the people of Montserrat to own and dispose of the natural resources of the Territory, including marine resources, and to establish and maintain control over the future development of those resources;

8. *Reiterates its call* upon the administering Power, in co-operation with the territorial Government, to continue the assistance necessary for the employment of the local population in the civil service, particularly at senior levels;

9. *Urges* the administering Power, in co-operation with the territorial Government, to overcome shortages in human resources by providing appropriate incentives to assist nationals in finding better opportunities at home and to attract qualified nationals from abroad;

10. *Invites* the specialized agencies and other organizations of the United Nations system, as well as other international and regional organizations, to intensify their efforts to accelerate progress in the economic and social life of the Territory;

11. *Calls upon* the administering Power, in co-operation with the territorial Government, to take urgent steps to facilitate the readmission of Montserrat as an associate member of the United Nations Educational, Scientific and Cultural Organization;

12. *Requests* the Special Committee to continue the examination of this question at its next session, including the possible dispatch of a further visiting mission to Montserrat at an appropriate time and in consultation with the administering Power, and to report thereon to the General Assembly at its forty-fourth session.

General Assembly resolution 43/38

22 November 1988   Meeting 59   Adopted without vote

Approved by Fourth Committee (A/43/797 & Corr.1) without objection, 25 October (meeting 14); draft by Committee on colonial countries (A/43/23); agenda item 18.

Meeting numbers. GA 43rd session: 4th Committee 7-14; plenary 59.

Pitcairn

The Committee on colonial countries, during its discussion of the question of Pitcairn on 1 August, considered a working paper by the Secretariat on developments concerning the Territory.[45]

In November, the General Assembly adopted without vote **decision 43/412**.

Question of Pitcairn

At its 59th plenary meeting, on 22 November 1988, the General Assembly, on the recommendation of the Fourth Committee, adopted the following text as representing the consensus of the members of the Assembly:

"The General Assembly, having examined the chapter of the report of the Special Committee on the Situation with regard to the Implementation of the Declaration on the Granting of Independence to Colonial Countries and Peoples relating to Pitcairn, reaffirms the inalienable right of the people of Pitcairn to self-determination in conformity with the Declaration on the Granting of Independence to Colonial Countries and Peoples, which fully applies to the Territory. The Assembly further reaffirms the responsibility of the administering Power to promote the economic and social development of the Territory. The Assembly urges the administering Power to continue to respect the lifestyle that the people of the Territory have chosen and to preserve, promote and protect it. The Assembly requests the Special Committee to continue to examine the question at its next session and to report thereon to the Assembly at its forty-fourth session."

General Assembly decision 43/412

Adopted without vote

Approved by Fourth Committee (A/43/797 & Corr.1) without objection, 25 October (meeting 14); draft by Committee on colonial countries (A/43/23); agenda item 18.
Meeting numbers. GA 43rd session: 4th Committee 7-14; plenary 59.

St. Helena

The Committee on colonial countries, which considered a working paper by the Secretariat on developments concerning St. Helena,[46] discussed the question of the Territory on 1 August.

In November, the General Assembly adopted by recorded vote **decision 43/413**.

Question of St. Helena

At its 59th plenary meeting, on 22 November 1988, the General Assembly, on the recommendation of the Fourth Committee, having examined the relevant chapters of the report of the Special Committee on the Situation with regard to the Implementation of the Declaration on the Granting of Independence to Colonial Countries and Peoples, reaffirmed the inalienable right of the people of St. Helena to self-determination and independence in conformity with the Declaration on the Granting of Independence to Colonial Countries and Peoples, contained in Assembly resolution 1514(XV) of 14 December 1960. The Assembly urged the administering Power, in consultation with the Legislative Council and other representatives of the people of St. Helena, to continue to take all necessary steps to ensure the speedy implementation of the Declaration in respect of the Territory and, in that connection, reaffirmed the importance of promoting an awareness among the people of St. Helena of the possibilities open to them in the exercise of their right to self-determination. The Assembly expressed the view that the administering Power

should continue to implement infrastructure and community development projects aimed at improving the general welfare of the community and to encourage local initiative and enterprise. The Assembly, in view of the serious developments in South Africa, noted with concern the trade and transportation dependency of the Territory on South Africa. The Assembly reaffirmed that continued development assistance from the administering Power, together with any assistance that the international community might be able to provide, constituted an important means of developing the economic potential of the Territory and of enhancing the capacity of its people to realize fully the goals set forth in the relevant provisions of the Charter of the United Nations. The Assembly, in that connection, welcomed the assistance rendered by the United Nations Development Programme and invited other organizations of the United Nations system to assist in the development of the Territory. The Assembly noted with deep concern the continued presence of military facilities on the dependency of Ascension Island and, in that regard, recalled all the United Nations resolutions and decisions concerning military bases and installations in colonial and Non-Self-Governing Territories. The Assembly urged the administering Power to take all the necessary measures not to involve the Territory in any offensive acts or interference against neighbouring States by the racist régime of South Africa. The Assembly considered that the possibility of dispatching a United Nations visiting mission to St. Helena at an appropriate time should be kept under review, and requested the Special Committee to continue to examine the question of St. Helena at its next session and to report thereon to the Assembly at its forty-fourth session.

General Assembly decision 43/413

123-2-30 (recorded vote)

Approved by Fourth Committee (A/43/797 & Corr.1) by recorded vote (108-2-25), 25 October (meeting 14); draft by Committee on colonial countries (A/43/23); agenda item 18.
Meeting numbers. GA 43rd session: 4th Committee 7-14; plenary 59.

Recorded vote in Assembly as follows:

In favour: Afghanistan, Albania, Algeria, Angola, Antigua and Barbuda, Argentina, Bahamas, Bahrain, Bangladesh, Barbados, Belize, Benin, Bhutan, Bolivia, Botswana, Brazil, Brunei Darussalam, Bulgaria, Burkina Faso, Burma, Burundi, Byelorussian SSR, Cape Verde, Central African Republic, Chad, China, Colombia, Comoros, Congo, Costa Rica, Côte d'Ivoire, Cuba, Cyprus, Czechoslovakia, Democratic Kampuchea, Democratic Yemen, Djibouti, Dominica, Ecuador, Egypt, El Salvador, Ethiopia, Fiji, Gabon, Gambia, German Democratic Republic, Ghana, Grenada, Guatemala, Guinea, Guinea-Bissau, Guyana, Haiti, Hungary, India, Indonesia, Iran, Iraq, Jamaica, Jordan, Kenya, Kuwait, Lao People's Democratic Republic, Lesotho, Liberia, Libyan Arab Jamahiriya, Madagascar, Malawi, Malaysia, Maldives, Mali, Mauritania, Mauritius, Mexico, Mongolia, Morocco, Mozambique, Nepal, Nicaragua, Niger, Nigeria, Oman, Pakistan, Panama, Papua New Guinea, Peru, Philippines, Poland, Qatar, Romania, Rwanda, Saint Lucia, Samoa, Sao Tome and Principe, Saudi Arabia, Seychelles, Sierra Leone, Singapore, Solomon Islands, Somalia, Sri Lanka, Sudan, Suriname, Swaziland, Syrian Arab Republic, Thailand, Togo, Trinidad and Tobago, Tunisia, Uganda, Ukrainian SSR, USSR, United Arab Emirates, United Republic of Tanzania, Uruguay, Vanuatu, Venezuela, Viet Nam, Yemen, Yugoslavia, Zaire, Zambia, Zimbabwe.

Against: United Kingdom, United States.

Abstaining: Australia, Austria, Belgium, Canada, Denmark, Dominican Republic, Equatorial Guinea, Finland, France, Germany, Federal Republic of, Greece, Honduras, Iceland, Ireland, Israel, Italy, Japan, Lebanon, Luxembourg, Malta, Netherlands, New Zealand, Norway, Paraguay, Portugal, Saint Vincent and the Grenadines,[a] Senegal, Spain, Sweden, Turkey.

[a]Later advised the Secretariat it had intended to vote in favour.

In the Fourth Committee, a separate recorded vote was taken on the seventh sentence, referring to the continued presence of military facilities on Ascension Island. The sentence was retained by 82 votes to 28, with 19 abstentions.

Tokelau

The Committee on colonial countries on 1 August considered the question of Tokelau. It had before it a working paper prepared by the Secretariat on developments concerning the Territory.[47]

On 22 November, on the recommendation of the Fourth Committee, the General Assembly adopted without vote **resolution 43/35**.

Question of Tokelau

The General Assembly,

Having considered the question of Tokelau,

Having examined the relevant chapters of the report of the Special Committee on the Situation with regard to the Implementation of the Declaration on the Granting of Independence to Colonial Countries and Peoples,

Recalling its resolution 1514(XV) of 14 December 1960, containing the Declaration on the Granting of Independence to Colonial Countries and Peoples, and all resolutions and decisions of the United Nations relating to Tokelau, in particular General Assembly resolution 42/84 of 4 December 1987,

Having heard the statement of the representative of New Zealand, the administering Power,

Noting the continuing devolution of power to the local authority, the General *Fono* (Council), and mindful that the cultural heritage and traditions of the people of Tokelau should be taken fully into account in the evolution of Tokelau's political institutions,

Noting with satisfaction the continued progress in the preparation of a legal code to conform with the traditional laws and cultural values of Tokelau and noting the express wish that the General *Fono* share additional responsibility in the process of law-making,

Aware of the special circumstances of the geographical location and economic conditions of the Territory and bearing in mind the necessity of diversifying and strengthening further its economy as a matter of priority in order to promote economic stability,

Reaffirming the responsibility of the administering Power to promote the economic and social development of the Territory and noting the measures being taken by the Government of New Zealand in that regard,

Noting the decision of the General *Fono* to include Tokelau in a fisheries treaty between countries in the region and stressing the importance of safeguarding the right of the people of Tokelau to the full enjoyment of their marine resources,

Noting also the strong opposition expressed by the people of Tokelau to nuclear testing in the Pacific region and their concern that those tests constitute a grave threat to the natural resources of the Territory and its social and economic development,

Noting with appreciation the assistance extended to Tokelau by the administering Power, other States Members of the United Nations and organizations of the United Nations system, in particular by the United Nations Development Programme, for the rehabilitation and reconstruction of the islands following the natural disasters in 1987,

Recalling the dispatch in 1976, 1981 and 1986 of United Nations visiting missions to the Territory,

Mindful that United Nations visiting missions provide an effective means of ascertaining the situation in the small Territories and considering that the possibility of sending a further visiting mission to Tokelau at an appropriate time should be kept under review,

1. *Approves* the chapter of the report of the Special Committee on the Situation with regard to the Implementation of the Declaration on the Granting of Independence to Colonial Countries and Peoples relating to Tokelau;

2. *Reaffirms* the inalienable right of the people of Tokelau to self-determination and independence in accordance with the Declaration on the Granting of Independence to Colonial Countries and Peoples;

3. *Reiterates the view* that such factors as territorial size, geographical location, size of population and limited natural resources should in no way delay the implementation of the Declaration, which fully applies to Tokelau;

4. *Urges* the Government of New Zealand, the administering Power, to continue to respect fully the wishes of the people of Tokelau, in carrying out the Territory's political and economic development, in order to preserve their social, cultural and traditional heritage;

5. *Calls upon* the administering Power, in consultation with the General *Fono* (Council) of Tokelau, to continue to expand its development assistance to Tokelau;

6. *Urges* the administering Power, other Member States and organizations of the United Nations system to continue to extend to Tokelau the maximum assistance possible for the rehabilitation and reconstruction of the islands in order to overcome the losses incurred in natural disasters in 1987;

7. *Invites* the specialized agencies and other organizations of the United Nations system, as well as other international and regional institutions, to extend or continue to extend all possible assistance to Tokelau, in consultation with the administering Power and the people of Tokelau;

8. *Requests* the Special Committee to continue the examination of this question at its next session, including the possible dispatch of a further visiting mission to Tokelau at an appropriate time and in consultation with the administering Power, and to report thereon to the General Assembly at its forty-fourth session.

General Assembly resolution 43/35

22 November 1988   Meeting 59   Adopted without vote

Approved by Fourth Committee (A/43/797 & Corr.1) without objection, 25 October (meeting 14); draft by Committee on colonial countries (A/43/23); agenda item 18.

Meeting numbers. GA 43rd session: 4th Committee 7-14; plenary 59.

Turks and Caicos Islands

The Committee on colonial countries on 1 August considered the question of the Turks and Caicos Islands. It had before it working papers prepared by the Secretariat on developments concerning the Territory[48] and on foreign economic and other interests.[49]

On 22 November, on the recommendation of the Fourth Committee, the General Assembly adopted **resolution 43/40** without vote.

Question of the Turks and Caicos Islands

The General Assembly,

Having considered the question of the Turks and Caicos Islands,

Having examined the relevant chapters of the report of the Special Committee on the Situation with regard to the Implementation of the Declaration on the Granting of Independence to Colonial Countries and Peoples,

Recalling its resolution 1514(XV) of 14 December 1960, containing the Declaration on the Granting of Independence to Colonial Countries and Peoples, and all resolutions and decisions of the United Nations relating to the Turks and Caicos Islands, including in particular General Assembly resolution 42/83 of 4 December 1987,

Conscious of the need to ensure the full and speedy implementation of the Declaration in respect of the Territory,

Having heard the statement of the representative of the United Kingdom of Great Britain and Northern Ireland, as the administering Power,

Noting the stated policy of the Government of the United Kingdom, the administering Power, that it remains ready to respond positively to the express wish of the people of the Territory on the question of independence,

Noting the elections for the Legislative Council, held in March 1988 under the new territorial Constitution,

Aware of the special circumstances of the geographical location and economic conditions of the Turks and Caicos Islands and bearing in mind the necessity of diversifying and strengthening further its economy as a matter of priority in order to promote economic stability and develop a wider economic base for the Territory,

Noting with concern the vulnerability of the Territory to drug trafficking and related activities,

Noting the continuing contribution of the United Nations Development Programme to the development of the Territory,

Recalling the dispatch in 1980 of two United Nations visiting missions to the Territory,

Mindful that United Nations visiting missions provide an effective means of ascertaining the situation in the small Territories and considering that the possibility of sending a further visiting mission to the Turks and Caicos Islands at an appropriate time should be kept under review,

1. *Approves* the chapter of the report of the Special Committee on the Situation with regard to the Implementation of the Declaration on the Granting of Independence to Colonial Countries and Peoples relating to the Turks and Caicos Islands;

2. *Reaffirms* the inalienable right of the people of the Turks and Caicos Islands to self-determination and independence in conformity with the Declaration on the Granting of Independence to Colonial Countries and Peoples;

3. *Reiterates the view* that such factors as territorial size, geographical location, size of population and limited natural resources should in no way delay the speedy exercise by the people of the Territory of their inalienable right to self-determination and independence in conformity with the Declaration, which fully applies to the Turks and Caicos Islands;

4. *Reiterates* that it is the responsibility of the United Kingdom of Great Britain and Northern Ireland, as the administering Power, to create such conditions in the Territory as will enable the people of the Turks and Caicos Islands to exercise freely and without interference their inalienable right to self-determination and independence in accordance with resolution 1514(XV) and all other relevant resolutions of the General Assembly;

5. *Reaffirms* that it is the responsibility of the administering Power under the Charter of the United Nations to develop its dependent Territories economically and socially and urges the administering Power, in consultation with the Government of the Turks and Caicos Islands, to take the necessary measures to promote the economic and social development of the Territory and, in particular, to accelerate the diversification of the economy;

6. *Urges* the administering Power, in co-operation with the territorial Government, to take effective measures to safeguard and guarantee the inalienable right of the people of the Turks and Caicos Islands to own and dispose of the natural resources of the Territory, including marine resources, and to establish and maintain control over the future development of those resources;

7. *Also urges* the administering Power, in consultation with the territorial Government, to continue to provide the necessary asssistance for the localization of the civil service at all levels and for the training of local personnel;

8. *Calls upon* the administering Power to continue to take all necessary measures, in co-operation with the territorial Government, to counter problems related to drug trafficking;

9. *Invites* the specialized agencies and other organizations of the United Nations system, as well as the regional institutions concerned, to continue to pay special attention to the development needs of the Turks and Caicos Islands;

10. *Requests* the Special Committee to continue the examination of this question at its next session, including the possible dispatch of a further visiting mission to the Turks and Caicos Islands at an appropriate time and in consultation with the administering Power, and to report thereon to the General Assembly at its forty-fourth session.

General Assembly resolution 43/40

22 November 1988   Meeting 59   Adopted without vote

Approved by Fourth Committee (A/43/797 & Corr.1) without objection, 25 October (meeting 14); draft by Committee on colonial countries (A/43/23); agenda item 18.
Meeting numbers. GA 43rd session: 4th Committee 7-14; plenary 59.

United States Virgin Islands

At three meetings between 1 and 5 August, the Committee on colonial countries considered the question of the United States Virgin Islands, having before it working papers by the Secretariat on developments concerning the Territory[50] and on foreign economic and other interests[51] and military activities.[52]

On 22 November, on the recommendation of the Fourth Committee, the General Assembly adopted **resolution 43/44** without vote.

Question of the United States Virgin Islands

The General Assembly,

Having considered the question of the United States Virgin Islands,

Having examined the relevant chapters of the report of the Special Committee on the Situation with regard to the Implementation of the Declaration on the Granting of Independence to Colonial Countries and Peoples,

Recalling its resolution 1514(XV) of 14 December 1960, containing the Declaration on the Granting of Independence to Colonial Countries and Peoples, and all resolutions and decisions of the United Nations relating to the United States Virgin Islands, including in particular General Assembly resolution 42/89 of 4 December 1987,

Conscious of the need to ensure the full and speedy implementation of the Declaration in respect of the Territory,

Having heard the statement of the representative of the United States of America, as the administering Power,

Taking note of the statement of the representative of the administering Power that the people of the Territory of the United States Virgin Islands, through their democratically elected legislature and executive, exercise responsibility for local government and control of their future, including the possibility of modifying their present relationship with the United States and that the Government of the United States stands ready to respond to their wishes whenever they so decide in that regard,

Noting that the Government of the United States Virgin Islands is reviewing the possibility of further devolution of power thereto, taking due account of the related experience of other Non-Self-Governing Territories,

Welcoming the enactment of legislation, in March 1988, providing for a referendum, to be held in November 1989, on options available for the Territory's future status, namely, statehood, independence, free association, incorporated territory, *status quo*, commonwealth and compact of federal relations,

Aware of the special circumstances of the geographical location and economic conditions of the Territory and bearing in mind the necessity of diversifying and strengthening further its economy as a matter of priority in order to promote economic stability,

Noting the measures being taken by the territorial Government with a view to strengthening the Territory's financial viability and facilitating its economic development,

Noting also the stated position of the Government of the United States Virgin Islands on the disposition of Water Island, as well as the need for the Territory to exercise control over its own resources,

Noting further the concern expressed by a petitioner at the reclamation and development of submerged land at Long Bay in the Charlotte Amalie Harbour, which should be addressed by the administering Power,

Noting with concern the vulnerability of the Territory to drug trafficking and related activities,

Noting the active interest of the Government of the United States Virgin Islands in participating in the related work of the international and regional organizations concerned,

Recalling the dispatch in 1977 of a United Nations visiting mission to the Territory,

Mindful that United Nations visiting missions provide an effective means of assessing the situation in the small Territories and considering that the possibility of sending a further visiting mission to the United States Virgin Islands at an appropriate time should be kept under review,

1. *Approves* the chapter of the report of the Special Committee on the Situation with regard to the Implementation of the Declaration on the Granting of Independence to Colonial Countries and Peoples relating to the United States Virgin Islands;

2. *Reaffirms* the inalienable right of the people of the United States Virgin Islands to self-determination and independence in conformity with the Declaration on the Granting of Independence to Colonial Countries and Peoples;

3. *Reiterates the view* that such factors as territorial size, geographical location, size of population and limited natural resources should in no way delay the speedy exercise by the people of the Territory of their inalienable right to self-determination and independence in conformity with the Declaration, which fully applies to the United States Virgin Islands;

4. *Reiterates* that it is the responsibility of the United States of America, as the administering Power, to continue to create such conditions in the United States Virgin Islands as will enable the people of the Territory to exercise freely and without interference their inalienable right to self-determination and independence in conformity with resolution 1514(XV);

5. *Reaffirms* that it is ultimately for the people of the United States Virgin Islands themselves to determine their future political status in accordance with the relevant provisions of the Charter of the United Nations, the Declaration and the relevant resolutions of the General Assembly and, in that connection, calls upon the administering Power, in co-operation with the territorial Government, to facilitate programmes of political education in the Territory in order to foster an awareness among the people of the possibilities open to them in the exercise of their right to self-determination;

6. *Reaffirms* the responsibility of the administering Power under the Charter to continue to promote the economic and social development of the United States Virgin Islands, and urges the administering Power, in co-operation with the territorial Government, to continue to take measures with a view to strengthening and diversifying the Territory's economy;

7. *Urges* the administering Power, in co-operation with the territorial Government, to take effective measures to safeguard and guarantee the inalienable right of the people of the United States Virgin Islands to own and dispose of the natural resources of the Territory, including marine resources, and to establish and maintain control over the future development of those resources;

8. *Calls upon* the administering Power to continue to take all necessary measures, in co-operation with the territorial Government, to counter problems related to drug trafficking;

9. *Urges* the administering Power to facilitate the participation of the United States Virgin Islands in various international and regional organizations;

10. *Also urges* the administering Power to continue to take all necessary measures to comply fully with the purposes and principles of the Charter, the Declaration and the relevant resolutions and decisions of the General Assembly relating to military activities and arrangements by colonial Powers in Territories under their administration;

11. *Requests* the Special Committee to continue the examination of this question at its next session, including the possible dispatch of a further visiting mission to the United States Virgin Islands at an appropriate time and in consultation with the administering Power, and to report thereon to the General Assembly at its forty-fourth session.

General Assembly resolution 43/44

22 November 1988　　　Meeting 59　　　Adopted without vote

Approved by Fourth Committee (A/43/797 & Corr.1) without objection, 25 October (meeting 14); draft by Committee on colonial countries (A/43/23); agenda item 18.

Meeting numbers. GA 43rd session: 4th Committee 7-14; plenary 59.

REFERENCES

[1]A/43/138-S/19500. [2]A/43/169-S/19541. [3]A/43/203-S/19579. [4]S/19604. [5]A/43/23. [6]YUN 1986, p. 967. [7]A/43/23 (A/AC.109/972). [8]YUN 1987, p. 1027, GA res. 42/19, 17 Nov. 1987. [9]A/43/799. [10]A/43/801. [11]E/1988/12 (res. 1988/5). [12]A/AC.109/959. [13]YUN 1987, p. 1032, GA res. 42/78, 4 Dec. 1987. [14]A/43/680. [15]A/C.5/43/59. [16]A/C.4/43/3 & Add.1. [17]YUN 1986, p. 913, GA res. 41/41 A, 2 Dec. 1986. [18]YUN 1960, p. 49, GA res. 1514(XV), 14 Dec. 1960. [19]YUN 1987, p. 1030. [20]A/AC.109/964. [21]A/AC.109/939. [22]A/43/23 (A/AC.109/971). [23]A/AC.109/961. [24]A/AC.109/951 & Add.1,2. [25]A/43/219. [26]YUN 1979, p. 1117. [27]A/S-15/38. [28]A/S-15/49. [29]A/43/588. [30]A/AC.109/974. [31]A/AC.109/953. [32]A/AC.109/934. [33]A/AC.109/935. [34]A/AC.109/942. [35]A/AC.109/947. [36]A/AC.109/948. [37]A/AC.109/940. [38]A/AC.109/941. [39]A/AC.109/943. [40]A/AC.109/963. [41]A/AC.109/945 & Add.1,2. [42]A/AC.109/949. [43]A/AC.109/944 & Corr.1. [44]A/AC.109/946. [45]A/AC.109/936. [46]A/AC.109/938. [47]A/AC.109/937 & Corr.1. [48]A/AC.109/950. [49]A/AC.109/952 & Corr.1. [50]A/AC.109/955. [51]A/AC.109/956. [52]A/AC.109/954.

Chapter II

International Trusteeship System

In 1988, the Trusteeship Council, on behalf of the Security Council, continued to supervise the one Trust Territory remaining under the International Trusteeship System—the Trust Territory of the Pacific Islands, a strategic territory administered by the United States.

The Trusteeship Council held its fifty-fifth regular session in New York from 10 May to 19 July. It considered the Administering Authority's annual report, heard 15 petitioners and examined 41 written petitions and 10 communications regarding the Territory. Of its five members (China, France, USSR, United Kingdom, United States), China did not participate.

In May, the Council recommended that the United States, the Administering Authority, in consultation with the constitutional Government of Palau, complete the process of approval of the Compact of Free Association for Palau at the earliest possible date. The Council noted with satisfaction the assurances given by the Administering Authority that it would continue fulfilling its responsibilities under the Charter of the United Nations and the Trusteeship Agreement.

Trust Territory of the Pacific Islands

Constitutional developments

The Trust Territory of the Pacific Islands, designated as a strategic area and administered by the United States in accordance with the Trusteeship Agreement approved by the Security Council in 1947,[1] comprises three archipelagos of more than 2,100 islands and atolls (about 100 of which are inhabited) scattered over some 7.8 million square kilometres of the western Pacific Ocean, north of the Equator. The Territory, collectively known as Micronesia, had 168,431 inhabitants in 1986. The Territory had four constitutional Governments— the Federated States of Micronesia, the Marshall Islands, the Northern Mariana Islands and Palau—each, as a result of referendums, with its own popularly elected legislature and executive head.

The United States had signed in 1986[2] legislation enacting the Compact of Free Association with the Marshall Islands and with the Federated States of Micronesia, which had entered into force the same year. Also in 1986, the Commonwealth Covenant with the Northern Mariana Islands had entered into force, and plebiscites were held in Palau to vote on the Compact of Free Association, under the observation of the Trusteeship Council.

On 31 March 1988,[3] a legal challenge to the constitutional amendment approved by the people of Palau on 4 August 1987 by a 72 per cent majority was filed in Palau's Supreme Court, thereby reinstituting a lawsuit that had been withdrawn in September 1987. On 22 April, the Supreme Court of Palau ruled that, because there was no inconsistency between the Compact of Free Association and the Constitution of Palau, the Government of Palau could not amend the Constitution through use of its article relating to inconsistencies. However, as the law authorizing the 4 August 1987 referendum suffered from procedural deficiencies, its results, i.e., the approval on 21 August 1987 of the Compact by a 73 per cent majority, were therefore null and void.

With regard to this Supreme Court decision, the Administering Authority assured the Council that it was up to Palau's Government to resolve the internal questions concerning political status and that the United States was prepared to respect whatever decision was rendered by the people and their Government.

In accordance with a 1986 Trusteeship Council resolution,[4] the United States continued to pursue the constitutional steps necessary to bring into force the Compact with Palau. On 28 March 1988, the United States Senate unanimously adopted legislation authorizing the entry into force of the Compact as soon as Palau had completed constitutional procedures to approve it. Similar legislation was also before the United States House of Representatives.

The United States informed the Council that the Office of the High Commissioner of the Trust Territory of the Pacific Islands had been abolished as of 10 July 1987 and the remaining functions transferred to the Office of Territorial and International Affairs, Department of the Interior, except for some federal transitional and capital improvement programmes which were being carried out by the recently created Office of Transition at Saipan. The United States stated that, while it would welcome free association with Palau, such association could only come about after Palau had ratified the Compact in accordance with its own constitutional procedures.

On 27 May 1988, the Council recommended that the process of approval of the Compact be completed at the earliest possible date. In response, the Administering Authority stated that the United States Congress had considered legislation to implement the Compact. It added that the Palau Supreme Court's decision pronouncing the 1987 referendum null and void had clarified how the people of Palau could approve the Compact under their Constitution.

Conditions in the Territory

In a working paper submitted to the Trusteeship Council in May 1988,[5] the Secretariat described conditions in the Trust Territory, covering political, economic, social and educational developments. The information was updated by a similar report issued a year later.[6] In addition to describing constitutional developments and progress towards self-government (see above), the paper summarized the structure of the four constitutional Governments, each of which had a legislature, executive, state or municipal government and a civil service. Following the abolition of the Office of the High Commissioner in 1987, a residual Office of Transition with a staff of 10 to 15 was located in the Northern Mariana Islands to complete property transfers and programmes. Under the new status arrangements, the Marshall Islands and the Federated States of Micronesia were ''sovereign and self-governing'' and the Northern Mariana Islands was ''self-governing''.

Funding for government operations in the Trust Territory was derived mainly from an annual grant provided by the Department of the Interior. The second and third largest sources of income were federal grants and locally collected revenues from taxation. For fiscal year 1988, the grant from the Administering Authority totalled $33 million and annual expenditures in the Territory amounted to $41 million. Local revenues totalled $8.2 million. The tight financial situation that existed was expected to be worked out satisfactorily, pending the long-term solution of the political status situation.

As regards war claims, the United States had appropriated $12.5 million in fiscal year 1988 for the Title I claims (damages sustained by the indigenous inhabitants during the Second World War) still pending, which represented 50 per cent of the total due. Payments were scheduled to begin in July on the basis of judgements rendered by the Micronesian Claims Commission in 1976.

Considerable development was made in the private sector economy, particularly in the area of tourism and marine resources.

The Trusteeship Council held its fifty-fifth session in New York from 10 May to 19 July 1988. It had before it the annual report of the Administering Authority for the year ending 30 September 1987[7] and a working paper prepared by the Secretariat.[5] By a note of 2 May,[8] the Secretary-General transmitted the report to the Security Council.

On 19 July, the Trusteeship Council adopted its report to the Security Council covering the period 17 December 1987 to 19 July 1988.[3] In proposing that the process of approval of the Compact of Free Association for Palau be completed at the earliest possible date, the Council noted that the people of the Trust Territory, in exercise of their right to self-government, had elected to assume full responsibility for administration in the economic, social and educational fields. The Council considered that any difficulties over the interpretation of the new status agreements should be resolved bilaterally by the parties concerned in accordance with the procedures mutually agreed and laid down in the relevant new status agreements. It noted with satisfaction the assurances given by the Administering Authority that it would continue to fulfil its responsibilities under the Charter and the Trusteeship Agreement.

Consideration by the Committee on colonial countries. The General Assembly's Special Committee on the Situation with regard to the Implementation of the Declaration on the Granting of Independence to Colonial Countries and Peoples (Committee on colonial countries)[9] considered the question of the Trust Territory on 1 August 1988 and adopted the conclusions and recommendations made by its Sub-Committee on Small Territories.[10] In considering the question, the Committee had before it a Secretariat working paper on developments in the Territory.[11]

The Committee reaffirmed the right of the people of the Territory to self-determination and independence in conformity with the Charter and the 1960 Declaration on the Granting of Independence to Colonial Countries and Peoples.[12] It reiterated that such factors as territorial size, geographical location, size of population and limited natural resources should in no way delay the implementation of the Declaration. Noting the Administering Authority's intention to terminate the Trusteeship Agreement, the Committee urged that it be done in strict conformity with the Charter. Recognizing that it was ultimately for the Micronesians to decide their political destiny, the Committee called on the Administering Authority not to fragment the Territory or take any action against the wishes of its people; to ensure that the existence of military bases and installations did not hinder the Territory's people from exercising their right to self-determination; and not to involve the Territory in any offensive acts or interference against other States. The Committee urged the Authority to accelerate the resolution of the problem of unpaid war claims.

In transmitting the conclusions and recommendations to the President of the Security Council on 22 August,[13] the Committee's Acting Chairman observed that the Security Council was empowered, under Article 83 of the Charter, to exercise all United Nations functions relating to strategic areas. Also on 22 August,[14] the conclusions and recommendations were transmitted to the President of the Trusteeship Council.

GENERAL ASSEMBLY CONSIDERATION

On 25 October, the Chairman of the General Assembly's Fourth Committee, following consultations with the Chairman of the Committee on colonial countries and with concerned delegations, suggested that no action be taken on a draft resolution recommended by the latter Committee. That suggestion was adopted without objection.[15]

Hearings

On 11 and 12 May, the Trusteeship Council heard 15 petitioners on various issues concerning conditions in, and the future status of, the Trust Territory.[3] The Committee on colonial countries heard one petitioner on 1 August, while its Sub-Committee on Small Territories heard three petitioners on 13 May.[9]

On 12 October, the General Assembly's Fourth Committee heard two petitioners. The United States expressed reservations about granting the hearings since, according to Article 83 of the Charter, functions relating to strategic areas such as the Trust Territory should be exercised exclusively by the Security Council and the Trusteeship Council. Similarly, Finland, on behalf of the five Nordic countries, said that granting the hearings did not mean that the Nordic countries accepted the view that the Assembly was entitled to deal with the matter.

Petitions and communications

On 18 and 23 May, the Trusteeship Council considered 41 written petitions and 10 communications. It decided to take note of those communications and included them in an annex to its report to the Security Council.[3]

REFERENCES
[1]YUN 1946-47, p. 398. [2]YUN 1986, p. 917. [3]S/20168. [4]YUN 1986, p. 918, TC res. 2183(LIII), 28 May 1986. [5]T/L.1265. [6]T/L.1269. [7]T/1923. [8]S/19855. [9]A/43/23. [10]A/AC.109/L.1663. [11]A/AC.109/957. [12]YUN 1960, p. 49, GA res. 1514(XV), 14 Dec. 1960. [13]S/20146. [14]T/1927. [15]A/43/797 & Corr.1.

Other aspects of the International Trusteeship System

Fellowships and scholarships

Under a scholarship programme launched by the General Assembly in 1952,[1] 11 Member States had in past years made scholarships available for students from Trust Territories: Czechoslovakia, Hungary, Indonesia, Italy, Mexico, Pakistan, Philippines, Poland, Tunisia, USSR, Yugoslavia. In a report to the Trusteeship Council covering the period from 12 May 1987 to 17 May 1988,[2] the Secretary-General stated that he had requested up-to-date information concerning scholarships made available under the programme and had received information only from the USSR, which said that no inhabitant from the Trust Territory was studying in the USSR in 1987/88.

Information dissemination

A report of the Secretary-General covering the period from 1 May 1987 to 30 April 1988[3] described the distribution by the United Nations Department of Public Information (DPI) of United Nations documents, official records and information materials, including taped radio programmes, throughout the Trust Territory. Those activities, primarily carried out through the United Nations Information Centre (UNIC) at Tokyo, were aimed at keeping the people of the Territory aware of United Nations activities, particularly with respect to the Trusteeship System.

Information material provided by DPI consisted of press releases in English and French dealing with the Trusteeship Council, and photo coverage of the proceedings of the Council. DPI also prepared for the *UN Chronicle* reports on the Council's deliberations and on the visiting missions to observe the plebiscites on the Compact of Free Association for Palau.[4]

In January, the Director of the UNIC at Tokyo visited the Territory and reported that there was a significant demand for information on the United Nations, particularly in relation to disarmament, control of nuclear weapons, law of the sea, and economic and social development.

In the Trusteeship Council, the USSR suggested that a central file of material disseminated in the Territory be compiled in order to enable the Council to assess its contents and quality and, in that regard, copies of relevant United Nations basic instruments not mentioned in the list should be made available to the Territory. The USSR noted the absence in the Secretary-General's report of details on the nature of the co-operation between

DPI and the Administering Authority as regards dissemination of information, as well as the absence of an evaluation of the visit to the Territory by the Director of the UNIC at Tokyo.

The DPI representative responded that the creation within DPI of a new division for dissemination would permit more accurate and up-to-date monitoring of all material distributed on a subject-by-subject basis. Regarding the evaluation of the Director's visit, the Director had reported on the availability of relevant material in the Territory. The representative indicated that additional copies of information material would be supplied whenever necessary.

Co-operation with the
Committee on colonial countries

At its 1988 session, the Trusteeship Council again considered together the question of the attainment of self-government and independence by the Trust Territory and co-operation with the Committee on colonial countries.

During the discussion in the Council, the USSR noted that despite the repeated requests of the Committee, the Administering Authority had refused to participate in its work and to provide it with necessary information. Moreover, in its reports and statements to the Council, the Authority had provided no information within the context of the 1960 Declaration on the Granting of Independence to Colonial Countries and Peoples.[5] In the view of the USSR, the refusal of the Authority and the majority of members of the Council to co-operate with the General Assembly and the Committee were in contradiction with the 1960 Declaration and other United Nations decisions.

On 26 May,[6] the Trusteeship Council drew the Security Council's attention to the proceedings of the Trusteeship Council concerning the at-

tainment of self-government or independence by the Trust Territory and to the statement made by the USSR.

Co-operation with CERD and the
Decade against racial discrimination

In 1988, the Trusteeship Council again considered together the question of co-operation with the Committee on the Elimination of Racial Discrimination (CERD) and the Second Decade to Combat Racism and Racial Discrimination (1983-1993).

During the debate, the USSR stressed the importance of studying how the Programme of Action for the Second Decade was being implemented in the Territory, expressing the hope that the Administering Authority would submit relevant information for consideration at the current session and include such information in its future annual report, as well as in its report to CERD.

The United States said that, for all practical purposes, racism was non-existent in the Trust Territory and that allegations of human rights violations were untenable. The United Kingdom stated that from petitions and all documents received over the past years, as well as reports and statements of the Administering Authority, there was no evidence that racial discrimination or racism existed in the Territory.

On 26 May,[6] the Council took note of the statements made by its members.

REFERENCES

[1]YUN 1951, p. 788, GA res. 557(VI), 18 Jan. 1952. [2]T/1926. [3]T/1924 & Corr.1. [4]YUN 1987, p. 977. [5]YUN 1960, p. 49, GA res. 1514(XV), 14 Dec. 1960. [6]S/20168.

PUBLICATION

Index to Proceedings of the Trusteeship Council, Fifty-fifth Session—1988 (ST/LIB/SER.B/T.49), Sales No. E.89.I.6.

Chapter III

Namibia

Throughout 1988, the United Nations continued to work for the independence of Namibia, occupied by South Africa and the largest Territory remaining under colonial rule.

During the year, significant progress was made towards national independence and self-determination for Namibia, as Angola, Cuba and South Africa reached agreement in July on the principles for a peaceful settlement of conflicts in south-western Africa. The South West Africa People's Organization (SWAPO), for its part, agreed to comply with the cessation of all hostile acts.

This resulted in the Protocol of Brazzaville, in which Angola, Cuba and South Africa agreed to recommend to the Secretary-General that 1 April 1989 be established as the date for implementation of Security Council resolution 435(1978), the United Nations plan for a peaceful settlement, and to meet in December in New York for signature of the tripartite agreement and for signature by Angola and Cuba of a bilateral agreement.

The Security Council, noting Angola's and Cuba's decision to redeploy and withdraw Cuban troops from Angola, on 20 December established, under its authority, the United Nations Angola Verification Mission for a period of 31 months. The actual signing of the bilateral agreement to redeploy and withdraw troops from Angola took place on 22 December. Also on 22 December, Angola, Cuba and South Africa signed the tripartite agreement, in which they requested the Secretary-General to seek authority from the Security Council to commence implementation of resolution 435(1978) on 1 April 1989. This agreement provided for the departure of South African military forces from Namibia, as provided for in the 1978 resolution, and the co-operation of South Africa and Angola with the Secretary-General to ensure the independence of Namibia through free and fair elections. The agreement further stressed the territorial integrity and inviolability of Namibia's borders and the need for all parties to refrain from the threat or use of force.

At its 1988 session, the General Assembly continued to pursue the objective of independence for Namibia and adopted five resolutions on the question, similar to those of previous years. The Assembly condemned South Africa for its continued illegal occupation of Namibia, reiterated that Namibia was the direct responsibility of the United Nations until independence, and reaffirmed that SWAPO was the sole and authentic representative of the Namibian people and that Security Council resolution 435(1978) was the only internationally accepted basis for a peaceful settlement. South Africa was condemned for its imposition of a so-called interim government and for its utilization of Namibian territory as a springboard for armed invasions against neighbouring States, and the Security Council was urged to impose comprehensive and mandatory sanctions against South Africa (resolution 43/26 A).

The Assembly demanded that South Africa comply fully and unconditionally with resolutions of the Security Council relating to Namibia, and rejected attempts to establish a linkage between the independence of Namibia and any extraneous issues (43/26 B). The Assembly approved the work programme of the United Nations Council for Namibia (43/26 C) and requested the Council to increase the dissemination of information supporting the cause of Namibia (43/26 D). It appealed for increased contributions to the United Nations Fund for Namibia, urged United Nations organizations to expedite the execution of projects in favour of Namibians, and decided to allocate $1.5 million from the regular United Nations budget to the Fund (43/26 E).

Various United Nations programmes continued to provide assistance to Namibians outside their country, financed primarily by voluntary contributions and administered by the United Nations Fund for Namibia. In 1988, the Fund spent more than $12.8 million for assistance to Namibia, with 35 States contributing nearly $8 million.

Namibia question

Activities of the UN Council for Namibia. During 1988, the United Nations Council for Namibia continued to carry out its mandate as the legal Administering Authority for Namibia until independence, to work to bring an end to the occupation of Namibia by South Africa and to protect the rights and interests of Namibia and its people.[1] Its report to the Assembly on the situation in Namibia and on its activities covered the period from 1 September 1987 to 31 August 1988,[2] with later 1988 activities being detailed in its 1989 report.[3] The Council participated in Security Council meetings on Namibia and took part in the proceedings of other United Nations bodies, in particular the Special Committee on the Situation with regard to the Implementation of the Declaration on the Granting of Independence to Colonial Countries and Peoples (Committee on colonial countries) and the Special Committee against *Apartheid*, and similarly invited those bodies to its own meetings and events.

The activities of the Council extended to the promotion of Namibia's interests in specialized agencies and other United Nations bodies and conferences where it represented Namibia. The Council co-operated closely with the Organization of African Unity (OAU) and the Movement of Non-Aligned Countries by taking part in their meetings.

In the course of the year, the Council was also represented at various meetings and conferences sponsored by other international organizations and conferences, including the Association of West European Parliamentarians for Action against *Apartheid* Conference (Lusaka, Zambia, and Harare, Zimbabwe, 23-30 March), the Fifth National Conference of the National Alliance of Third World Journalists (Atlanta, United States, 21-24 April), the World Council of Churches Hearings on Namibia (Washington, D.C., 2-4 May), the Week of Solidarity with the People of Namibia and People under *Apartheid* (Bamako, Mali, 7-14 November), and the Seventh Congress of the Afro-Asian Peoples' Solidarity Organization (New Delhi, India, 24-28 November).

Two seminars were held by the Council in 1988. The Seminar on the International Responsibility for Namibia's Independence (Istanbul, Turkey, 21-25 March), in adopting the Istanbul Declaration and Call for Action,[4] recommended urgent measures to be taken by non-governmental organizations (NGOs), parliamentarians and legislators, the media and the Council in support of the immediate independence of Namibia. It requested the Secretary-General to pursue his diplomatic initiatives for the implementation of Security Council resolution 435(1978)[5] and called, in particular, for the severance of all links with South Africa, for increased pressure on Governments that co-operated with it, for the intensification of peoples' and workers' sanctions, and for further steps to enforce Decree No. 1 for the Protection of the Natural Resources of Namibia.[6] The Seminar on Efforts to Implement the United Nations Plan for the Independence of Namibia (Toronto, Canada, 7-11 September), in its final document,[7] urged the international community to provide increased political and moral support, as well as material assistance, in order to enable SWAPO to lead effec-

tively the struggle of the Namibian people for self-determination and national independence.

On 25 May, the Council attended activities commemorating the twenty-fifth anniversary of OAU. The Council commemorated Namibia Day on 26 August[8] and, in accordance with a 1976 Assembly resolution,[9] commemorated on 27 October the Week of Solidarity with the People of Namibia and their Liberation Movement, SWAPO. In observance of that Week, the Council held two meetings; messages of solidarity were received from a number of heads of State or Government, Governments and various organizations.[10]

In accordance with a 1987 Assembly resolution,[11] the Council continued to consult with SWAPO in the formulation and implementation of its programme of work, and to channel assistance to Namibians through the United Nations Fund for Namibia. In addition, the Council reported on political, economic, military and social contacts between Member States and South Africa[12] (see below) since the adoption of another 1987 Assembly resolution.[13]

Missions. Pursuant to a 1987 General Assembly resolution,[11] the Council sent missions of consultation in 1988 to Asia, Latin America, and Australia and New Zealand to co-ordinate efforts for the implementation of United Nations resolutions on Namibia and to exchange views on initiatives that could be taken towards implementation of those resolutions.

In India (30 and 31 May), the Council was briefed by senior officials on the state of the Action for Resisting Invasion, Colonialism and *Apartheid* (AFRICA) Fund, which was currently assisting 46 Namibian refugees. The President of the Council and the Permanent Representative of SWAPO to India addressed a press conference organized by the New Delhi United Nations Information Centre. The mission to Thailand (2-6 June) was informed that Thailand had severed all government contacts with South Africa and all economic contacts in the private sector. Thailand announced pledges to the United Nations Fund for Namibia. While in Malaysia (7-10 June), the President of the Council participated in a discussion at the Institute of Strategic and International Studies on issues that threatened international peace, including the situation in southern Africa. In Indonesia (10-15 June), the Government offered training to Namibian students in agriculture, fisheries, shipping, telecommunications and remote sensing. The mission to Singapore (16-18 June) held consultations with officials, who stated that Singapore would continue to co-ordinate action on the Namibian question with the other members of the Association of South-East Asian Nations.

The Council visited four countries in South America from 7 to 20 July.[14] In Chile (7 and 8

July), the Government announced an offer of scholarships for Namibians to study at the Chilean diplomatic academy, and to provide training in sea biology, oceanography, sea farming and other fields. In a joint communiqué,[14] the mission and Chile strongly urged South Africa to put an end to the illegal occupation of Namibia in order to pave the way for implementation of resolution 435(1978). In Peru (10-12 July), the Government pointed out to the mission that its recognition of SWAPO as the sole and authentic representative of the Namibian people had taken the form of establishing diplomatic relations with that organization. Further, Peru offered to provide fellowships to Namibians for study in its diplomatic academy. Venezuela, during the visit of the mission (13-15 July), rejected efforts to impose preconditions which were at variance with resolution 435(1978). Brazil, for its part, announced to the mission (17-20 July) its willingness to intensify co-operation with SWAPO through, *inter alia*, holding plenary meetings of the Council, and expressed its readiness to receive a SWAPO delegation to discuss modalities of co-operation.

The mission to New Zealand (29 and 30 August) agreed with the Government that the imposition of sanctions was the only means of compelling South Africa to negotiate. In a meeting with the SWAPO representative, New Zealand agreed to sponsor a tour of New Zealand by the SWAPO Ndilimani Cultural Troupe. The mission to Australia (1-3 September) agreed with Government officials that the issue of concern was whether the momentum towards a solution of the Namibian question could be sustained.

Report of the Secretary-General. The Secretary-General, in an October 1988 report,[15] forwarded to the General Assembly replies he had received from 14 Governments on action towards the implementation of two 1987 Assembly resolutions: one on the situation in Namibia resulting from the illegal occupation of the Territory by South Africa,[13] and the other relating to the implementation of resolution 435(1978).[16]

Action by the Committee on colonial countries. The Committee on colonial countries held five meetings in 1988 devoted to Namibia, with SWAPO and the Council for Namibia participating. By an 8 August consensus,[17] the Committee reiterated that South Africa, by not complying with United Nations resolutions, was responsible for creating a situation that threatened international peace and security. Its intransigence made it more imperative than ever for the United Nations to reassert its direct responsibility over Namibia until independence. The Committee condemned South Africa for its imposition of the so-called interim government in Namibia and declared the administration and its laws and

proclamations null and void. The Committee rejected attempts to link implementation of resolution 435(1978) and extraneous issues, particularly the presence of Cuban troops in Angola. It demanded that South Africa release all Namibian political prisoners and account for all "disappeared" Namibians.

The Committee condemned the activities of all foreign economic interests exploiting the natural resources of Namibia, especially its uranium and diamond deposits, and demanded that they comply with United Nations resolutions and withdraw from the Territory. South Africa was further condemned for its military buildup in Namibia and its utilization of the Territory as a springboard for armed aggression against neighbouring States, particularly Angola. The Committee recommended that the Security Council impose sanctions against South Africa.

The Committee noted the activities of NGOs to promote the severance of economic and other links with South Africa as well as other measures taken by Governments in compliance with United Nations resolutions, which helped to mobilize support for the Namibian cause.

On 9 August,[18] the text of the consensus was transmitted to the President of the Security Council.

Action by the Commission on Human Rights. The Commission on Human Rights, in a resolution of 23 February on the situation in southern Africa,[19] reaffirmed the right of the Namibian people to self-determination and independence, and rejected the so-called constitutional initiative, including the recently announced "statutory council", which fell short of accepting the "one man, one vote" principle. The Commission declared that South Africa's occupation of Namibia was aggression against the Namibian people and a threat to international peace and security.

In a resolution of 29 February on the situation of human rights in Namibia,[20] the Commission condemned South Africa for the militarization of Namibia, the use of mercenaries to suppress the Namibians, using Namibians for tribal armies, the forcible displacement of Namibians from their homes, torture of political prisoners, and the exploitation of Namibia's natural resources. It reiterated its demand that South Africa co-operate with the United Nations to implement resolution 435(1978), without raising extraneous issues, so that the people of Namibia could enjoy their human rights as well as exercise their right to self-determination. It deplored the establishment by South Africa of so-called Namibia information offices in Paris, Bonn, London and Washington, among other cities, aimed at legitimizing its puppet institutions in Namibia, in particular the so-called interim government. It condemned the collaboration of certain States and international institutions with South Africa as well as foreign economic interests operating in Namibia, and urged States to take action to ensure compliance with Decree No. 1. The Commission demanded that South Africa release all Namibian political prisoners and that captured freedom fighters be accorded prisoner-of-war status. In addition, it demanded that South Africa account for all disappeared Namibians.

ECONOMIC AND SOCIAL COUNCIL ACTION

In **resolution 1988/53**, the Economic and Social Council requested the specialized agencies and other organizations within the United Nations system to render increased support to the people of Namibia, to withhold any assistance from South Africa until it restored to the people of Namibia their right to self-determination and independence, and to refrain from any action which might imply recognition of the illegal occupation of Namibia. The Council condemned South Africa's persistent non-compliance with Security Council resolution 435(1978) and declared null and void its installation of a so-called interim government. In **resolution 1988/56**, on the activities of transnational corporations (TNCs) in South Africa and Namibia, the Council urged Governments of home countries of TNCs that had not done so to ensure that those corporations ceased to contribute to maintaining the *apartheid* policies of South Africa and its illegal occupation of Namibia.

Political aspects

The Council for Namibia, which continued in 1988 to monitor the political situation in and relating to Namibia, reported that progress was made towards a negotiated settlement for the Territory.[3] Its Standing Committee II submitted in July a report on the subject.[21]

Throughout the year, South Africa maintained its illegal occupation of Namibia in defiance of the United Nations, through its unilaterally installed interim administration. The Council reported that on 8 April, Pieter W. Botha, the President of South Africa, announced during a visit to Windhoek that he was strengthening the powers of the South African Administrator-General in Namibia. The latter was authorized to call ethnically based elections in the Territory and to block any attempt to diminish the powers of the "second-tier" ethnic authorities. He was also authorized to take steps against the local media which were allegedly promoting subversion and terrorism.

Despite South Africa's repressive measures, the Namibian people continued its struggle for self-determination. To this end, rallies and mass demonstrations were held in Namibia during 1988, many of which were broken up when the military and police attacked the participants. On 1 May, rallies were held in 10 towns under the auspices of the National Union of Namibian Workers (NUNW) to commemorate International Workers' Day. A crowd of 6,000 people gathered at Windhoek for the May Day celebration, at which NUNW launched its "Campaign for a Living Wage". On 4 May, some 5,000 schoolchildren marched at Katatura township in Windhoek to commemorate the massacre by South Africa at the Kassinga (Angola) refugee camp on 4 May 1978. The schoolchildren were attacked by police using tear-gas, rubber bullets and truncheons.

SWAPO continued to provide political leadership to the people of Namibia at home and abroad, working, with the support of the international community, to provide for the needs of Namibian refugees and create a basis for nation-building in preparation for an independent Namibia.

The year 1988 was marked, however, by important political and diplomatic progress towards Namibian independence, reflecting the new atmosphere of co-operation between the two super-Powers. Angola, Cuba and South Africa, with the United States as mediator and the USSR as an observer, began negotiations on a regional peace settlement including the implementation of the United Nations plan, Security Council resolution 435(1978).[5] The first round of these negotiations, which came to be referred to as the tripartite talks, took place in London on 3 and 4 May. The London meetings were followed by bilateral talks between Angola and South Africa at Brazzaville, Congo, on 12 and 13 May, at which preliminary ideas and opening positions on the timetable of Cuban withdrawal from Angola were exchanged. Angola proposed a four-year timetable while South Africa put forward the view that all Cuban forces should leave Angola within one year of the commencement of the implementation of resolution 435(1978).

On 18 and 19 May, senior officials of the USSR and the United States met at Lisbon, Portugal, to discuss ways that they might facilitate a general settlement of the problems in south-western Africa. The discussions were continued during a summit meeting in Moscow between the Presidents of the USSR and the United States from 29 May to 1 June. The negotiations gained momentum with the holding of three further rounds of talks in Cairo (24 and 25 June), New York (11-13 July) and Geneva (2-5 August).

Following the general advance on 27 June of Angolan and Cuban troops to southern Angola in the aftermath of the battles for control of Cuito Cuanavale, a serious armed clash took place at Calueque, near the Angola-Namibia border, where several South African soldiers were killed. Once again, South Africa threatened to withdraw from the tripartite talks.

From 11 to 13 July, however, the tripartite talks resumed at the level of expert in New York. Agreement was reached on a set of principles for the establishment of peace in south-western Africa. On 20 July, following approval by the Governments involved, the text of the 14 principles was released.[22] The three Governments agreed to: fix a date for commencement of the implementation of resolution 435(1978); abstain from action that could prevent a settlement; arrange withdrawal of Cuban troops from Angola with verification by the United Nations; respect the sovereignty of States and the inviolability of borders; abstain from the threat or use of force against States; accept responsibility not to allow their territory to be used for aggression; verify and monitor compliance with the obligations of a settlement; resolve differences through negotiations; recognize the role of the permanent members of the Security Council as guarantors for implementing their agreements; and recognize the mediating role of the United States. This agreement was followed by talks involving high-level military delegations from the three countries on 22 and 23 July at Sal Island, Cape Verde.

Further progress was made during a round of negotiations in Geneva from 2 to 5 August. In a joint statement issued on 8 August, known as the Geneva Protocol,[23] the parties agreed on a sequence of steps to achieve peace in south-western Africa. Angola, Cuba, South Africa and the United States also agreed to recommend to the Secretary-General 1 November 1988 as the date for commencement of the implementation of resolution 435(1978). Another significant feature of the statement was the declaration of a *de facto* cessation of hostilities in Namibia and Angola with immediate effect. The parties also pledged to reach agreement by 1 September 1988 on a timetable for the staged and total withdrawal of Cuban troops from Angola.

On 12 August,[24] the President of SWAPO informed the Secretary-General that his organization had agreed to comply with the cessation of all hostile acts in accordance with the Geneva agreement, and was ready to abide by that agreement until the formal cease-fire under resolution 435(1978) took effect.

The first meetings of a joint military commission, composed of military officers from Angola, Cuba and South Africa, to supervise the cease-fire took place on 15 August at Ruacana on the Angola-Namibia border. On 22 August, the commission signed a formal cease-fire agreement. A Joint Military Monitoring Commission was established to supervise and determine the rules under which the cease-fire would operate, as well as to decide on action to be taken in case of violations.

The tripartite talks, which resumed at Brazzaville from 24 to 26 August, covered the timetable for Cuban troop withdrawal, and were adjourned until September. On 31 August, pursuant to the understandings reached at Geneva in early August, South African troops completed their withdrawal from southern Angola.

From 21 to 23 September, the Secretary-General visited South Africa to discuss preparations for the implementation of resolution 435(1978) and related matters. He visited Angola on 23 and 24 September to discuss with the Angolan President the situation in south-western Africa, and, while in Luanda, also met with the President of SWAPO and informed him of the outcome of his visit to Pretoria.

A series of meetings at Brazzaville during November and December produced on 13 December an agreement on the final elements for a tripartite agreement[25] relating to the implementation of resolution 435(1978), beginning on 1 April 1989, and the outlines of a related bilateral treaty between Angola and Cuba[26] specifying a schedule for the phased total withdrawal of Cuban troops from Angola. The Protocol of Brazzaville[25] committed the parties to signing these treaties and established a joint commission in which the United States and the USSR were invited to participate as observers.

Eight months of continuous negotiation between Angola, Cuba and South Africa, with the United States as mediator, culminated in the signing on 22 December in New York of the tripartite[27] and bilateral agreements referred to above, as agreed in the Geneva and Brazzaville Protocols (see below).

GENERAL ASSEMBLY ACTION

The General Assembly's continuing concern over Namibia's independence struggle was expressed in five 1988 resolutions (43/26 A-E).

On 17 November, the Assembly adopted **resolution 43/26 A** by recorded vote.

Situation in Namibia resulting from the illegal occupation of the Territory by South Africa

The General Assembly,

Recalling its resolution 1514(XV) of 14 December 1960, containing the Declaration on the Granting of Independence to Colonial Countries and Peoples,

Recalling also its resolution 2145(XXI) of 27 October 1966, by which it terminated the Mandate of South Africa over Namibia and placed the Territory under the direct responsibility of the United Nations,

Recalling further its resolution 2248(S-V) of 19 May 1967, by which it established the United Nations Council for Namibia as the legal Administering Authority for Namibia until independence,

Having examined the report of the United Nations Council for Namibia,

Having examined also the relevant chapter of the report of the Special Committee on the Situation with regard to the Implementation of the Declaration on the Granting of Independence to Colonial Countries and Peoples,

Recalling other resolutions and decisions declaring the illegality of the continued occupation of Namibia by South Africa, in particular Security Council resolutions 284(1970) of 29 July 1970 and 301 (1971) of 20 October 1971, and the advisory opinion of the International Court of Justice of 21 June 1971,

Recalling also its resolutions 3111(XXVIII) of 12 December 1973 and 31/146 and 31/152 of 20 December 1976, in which, *inter alia*, it recognized the South West Africa People's Organization as the sole and authentic representative of the Namibian people and granted observer status to it,

Recalling further its resolutions ES-8/2 of 14 September 1981 and 36/121 B of 10 December 1981, by which it called upon States to cease forthwith, individually and collectively, all dealings with South Africa in order totally to isolate it politically, economically, militarily and culturally,

Recalling the debates held at its special session on the question of Namibia and its resolution S-14/1 of 20 September 1986, adopted at that session,

Taking note of debates held by the Security Council from 28 to 30 October 1987 on the question of Namibia, and of its resolution 601(1987) of 30 October 1987,

Welcoming the final documents and communiqués of the Assembly of Heads of State and Government of the Organization of African Unity at its twenty-fourth ordinary session, held at Addis Ababa from 25 to 28 May 1988, the Fifth Islamic Summit Conference, held at Kuwait from 26 to 29 January 1987, the Conference of Foreign Ministers of Non-Aligned Countries, held at Nicosia from 7 to 10 September 1988, the Council of Ministers of the Organization of African Unity at its forty-seventh and forty-eighth ordinary sessions, held at Addis Ababa from 22 to 27 February 1988 and from 19 to 23 May 1988, respectively, the Seminar on the International Responsibility for Namibia's Independence, held at Istanbul, Turkey, from 21 to 25 March 1988, and the Seminar on Efforts to Implement the United Nations Plan for the Independence of Namibia, held at Toronto, Canada, from 7 to 11 September 1988,

1. *Approves* the report of the United Nations Council for Namibia;

2. *Reaffirms* the inalienable right of the people of Namibia to self-determination, freedom and national independence in a united Namibia, in accordance with the Charter of the United Nations and as recognized by the General Assembly in its resolutions 1514(XV) and 2145(XXI) and in subsequent resolutions of the Assembly relating to Namibia;

3. *Strongly condemns* the South African régime for its continued illegal occupation of Namibia in defiance of the resolutions of the United Nations relating to Namibia;

4. *Declares* that South Africa's illegal occupation of Namibia constitutes an act of aggression against the Namibian people in terms of the Definition of Aggression contained in General Assembly resolution 3314(XXIX) of 14 December 1974, and supports the legitimate struggle of the Namibian people by all means at their disposal, under the leadership of the South West Africa People's Organization, to repel South Africa's aggression and to achieve self-determination, freedom and national independence in a united Namibia;

5. *Declares also* that the liberation struggle in Namibia is a conflict of an international character in terms of article 1, paragraph 4, of Additional Protocol I to the Geneva Conventions of 12 August 1949, and demands that South Africa accord prisoner-of-war status to all captured freedom fighters as called for by the Geneva Convention relative to the Treatment of Prisoners of War and the Additional Protocol thereto;

6. *Reiterates* that, in accordance with its resolution 2145(XXI), Namibia is the direct responsibility of the United Nations until genuine self-determination and national independence are achieved in the Territory and reaffirms the mandate of the United Nations Council for Namibia as the legal Administering Authority for Namibia until independence under its resolution 2248(S-V) and subsequent resolutions of the General Assembly;

7. *Reaffirms* its decision that the United Nations Council for Namibia, in pursuance of its mandate, should proceed to establish its administration in Namibia with a view to terminating racist South Africa's illegal occupation of the Territory;

8. *Also reaffirms* that the South West Africa People's Organization, the national liberation movement of Namibia, is the sole and authentic representative of the Namibian people and only with its direct and full participation can the genuine independence of Namibia be achieved;

9. *Solemnly reaffirms* that Namibia's independence must be with its territorial integrity intact, including Walvis Bay, the Penguin Islands and other offshore islands, and reiterates that, in accordance with the resolutions of the United Nations, any attempt by South Africa to annex them is, therefore, illegal, null and void;

10. *Calls upon* the Security Council to declare categorically that Walvis Bay is an integral part of Namibia and that the question should not be left as a matter for negotiation between an independent Namibia and South Africa;

11. *Reaffirms* its solidarity with, and support for, the South West Africa People's Organization, the sole and authentic representative of the Namibian people, and pays tribute to that organization for the sacrifices that it has made in the field of battle and also for the spirit of statesmanship, co-operation and far-sightedness that it has displayed in the political and diplomatic arena despite the most extreme provocations on the part of the racist Pretoria régime;

12. *Commends* the South West Africa People's Organization for its continued intensification of the struggle on all fronts, including the armed struggle, and for its commitment to embrace all Namibian patriots in an effort further to strengthen national unity so as to ensure the territorial integrity and sovereignty of a united Namibia, and welcomes the consolidation of unity in action by the patriotic forces in Namibia, as clearly demonstrated by the combined actions of workers, youth, students, parents, churches and various professional organizations during this critical phase of their struggle for national and social liberation;

13. *Reaffirms* that the United Nations plan for the independence of Namibia, embodied in Security Council resolutions 385(1976) of 30 January 1976 and 435(1978) of 29 September 1978, is the only internationally accepted basis for a peaceful settlement of the Namibian question and demands its immediate implementation without pre-condition or modification;

14. *Strongly condemns* South Africa for obstructing the implementation of the resolutions of the United Nations,

in particular Security Council resolutions 385(1976), 435(1978), 439(1978) of 13 November 1978, 532(1983) of 31 May 1983, 539(1983) of 28 October 1983, 566(1985) of 19 June 1985 and 601(1987), and for its manœuvres, in contravention of these resolutions, designed to consolidate its colonial and neo-colonial interests at the expense of the legitimate aspirations of the Namibian people for genuine self-determination, freedom and national independence in a united Namibia;

15. *Expresses its dismay* at the failure to date of the Security Council to discharge effectively its responsibilities for the maintenance of peace and security in southern Africa, owing to the vetoes of two of its Western permanent members;

16. *Urges* the Security Council to act decisively in fulfilment of the direct responsibility of the United Nations over Namibia and to take, without further delay, appropriate action to ensure that the United Nations plan, as embodied in Council resolution 435(1978), is not undermined or modified in any way and that it is fully respected and implemented;

17. *Reiterates its conviction* that racist South Africa's continued illegal occupation of Namibia, its defiance of the resolutions of the United Nations, its brutal repression of the Namibian people, its acts of destabilization and aggression against independent African States and its policies of *apartheid* constitute a threat to international peace and security;

18. *Denounces* all fraudulent constitutional and political schemes by which the illegal racist régime of South Africa attempts to perpetuate its colonial domination of Namibia, and, in particular, calls upon the international community to refrain from according any recognition or extending any co-operation to any régime imposed by the illegal South African administration upon the Namibian people in violation of Security Council resolutions 385(1976), 435(1978), 439(1978), 532(1983), 539(1983), 566(1985) and 601(1987) and of other relevant resolutions of the General Assembly and of the Council;

19. *Strongly condemns* the Pretoria régime for the imposition of the so-called interim government in Namibia on 17 June 1985, declares this measure null and void and affirms that it constitutes a direct affront and a clear defiance of the resolutions of the Security Council, particularly resolutions 435(1978) and 439(1978), and further affirms that this manœuvre by South Africa of creating puppet institutions subservient to the interests of the racist régime is intended to consolidate Pretoria's colonial stranglehold over Namibia and to prolong the oppression of the Namibian people;

20. *Reiterates* that there are only two parties to the conflict in Namibia, namely, the Namibian people represented by the South West Africa People's Organization, their sole and authentic representative, and the racist régime of South Africa, which illegally occupies Namibia;

21. *Strongly rejects and condemns* the persistent attempts made by the Pretoria régime and its ally to establish a "linkage" between the implementation of Security Council resolution 435(1978) and extraneous and irrelevant issues, particularly the presence of Cuban forces in Angola, which is a ploy intended to delay the independence of Namibia and to jeopardize the responsibility of the United Nations for this Territory and constitutes interference in the internal affairs of that independent and sovereign State;

22. *Expresses its appreciation* to the front-line States and the South West Africa People's Organization for their statesmanlike and constructive attitude in the efforts aimed at implementing Security Council resolution 435(1978);

23. *Rejects* all attempts to distort the question of Namibia by portraying it as part of a global East-West confrontation rather than one of decolonization that must be resolved in accordance with the provisions of the Charter and the Declaration on the Granting of Independence to Colonial Countries and Peoples;

24. *Firmly condemns and rejects* the policy of "constructive engagement", which encourages the racist régime of South Africa to continue its defiance of the decisions of the international community on Namibia, and its policy of *apartheid*, which is a crime against humanity;

25. *Strongly condemns* the continuing collaboration between South Africa and certain Western and other States in the political, economic, diplomatic, military, cultural and financial fields, and expresses its conviction that such collaboration helps to prolong South Africa's domination and control over the people and Territory of Namibia;

26. *Deplores*, in this context, the establishment and operation by racist South Africa of the so-called Namibia information offices in France, the Federal Republic of Germany, the United Kingdom of Great Britain and Northern Ireland and the United States of America, aimed at legitimizing its puppet institutions in Namibia, in particular the so-called interim government for which the racist régime has been condemned by the Security Council and the international community, and demands their immediate closure;

27. *Strongly condemns also* the sinister and slanderous campaign of disinformation by the racist régime of South Africa and its agents, including the so-called International Society for Human Rights, against the just struggle of the Namibian people for self-determination and national independence;

28. *Notes with appreciation* the measures taken by some States, international organizations, parliamentarians, institutions and non-governmental organizations to exert pressure on the racist régime of South Africa and calls upon them to redouble and intensify their efforts to force the racist régime to comply with the resolutions and decisions of the United Nations relating to Namibia and South Africa;

29. *Calls once again upon* all Governments, especially those that have close links with South Africa, to support, in co-operation with the United Nations Council for Namibia, the actions of the United Nations to defend the national rights of the Namibian people until independence and to isolate the racist régime of South Africa;

30. *Urges* Governments that have in the past used their veto or cast negative votes in the Security Council in regard to the question of the imposition of comprehensive and mandatory sanctions against South Africa to support and respond positively to the international call to isolate racist South Africa;

31. *Calls upon* the members of the European Economic Community to strengthen and extend, as a matter of urgency, the economic sanctions that they have imposed on the Pretoria régime, so as to include their application to illegally occupied Namibia;

32. *Calls upon* the Government of the Federal Republic of Germany, as a measure of its recognition of the direct responsibility of the United Nations over Namibia and the United Nations Council for Namibia as the sole legal Administering Authority for the Territory until independence, to discontinue all programmes of development aid and assistance to illegally occupied Namibia, and urges all States to consult the United Nations Council for Namibia regarding any such assistance, in order to ensure that it will not prolong the illegal occupation of Namibia by the Pretoria régime and the colonial institutions in the Territory;

33. *Strongly condemns* South Africa for its use of mercenaries to suppress the Namibian people and to carry out its military attacks against independent African States, and reiterates its call upon all States to take legislative and other appropriate measures to prohibit the recruitment, training, financing and transit of mercenaries for service in Namibia;

34. *Also strongly condemns* South Africa for its military buildup in Namibia, its imposition of military conscription of all Namibian males between seventeen and fifty-five years of age into the occupying colonial army, its forcible displacement of Namibians from their homes and its proclamation of a so-called security zone in Namibia, and declares that all such measures taken by racist South Africa are illegal, null and void;

35. *Demands once again* that South Africa immediately release all Namibian political prisoners, including all those imprisoned or detained under the so-called internal security laws, martial law or any other arbitrary measures, whether such Namibians have been charged or tried or are being held without charge in Namibia or South Africa;

36. *Demands* that South Africa account for all "disappeared" Namibians and declares that South Africa shall be liable to compensate the victims, their families and the future lawful Government of an independent Namibia for the losses sustained;

37. *Calls upon* Member States to render sustained and increased support, as well as material, financial, military and other assistance, to the South West Africa People's Organization so as to enable it to intensify its struggle for the liberation of Namibia;

38. *Calls upon* the specialized agencies and other organizations of the United Nations system to render sustained and increased material, financial and other assistance to the South West Africa People's Organization so as to enable it to intensify its struggle for the liberation of Namibia;

39. *Urges* all Governments and the specialized agencies and other intergovernmental organizations to provide increased material assistance to the thousands of Namibian refugees who have been forced by the oppressive policies of the *apartheid* régime to flee Namibia, especially into the neighbouring front-line States;

40. *Reaffirms its conviction* that the solidarity and support of the front-line States for the Namibian cause continue to be factors of paramount importance in the efforts to bring genuine independence to the Territory;

41. *Strongly condemns* the racist régime of South Africa for its utilization of the illegally occupied international Territory of Namibia as a springboard for perpetrating armed invasions, subversion, destabilization and aggression against neighbouring African States, in particular Angola;

42. *Denounces* the acts of aggression by the racist régime against Angola, Botswana, Mozambique, Zambia and Zimbabwe, declares that the Pretoria régime's policy of aggression and destabilization not only undermines the peace and stability of the southern African region but also constitutes a threat to international peace and security, and calls upon South Africa to cease all acts of aggression against the neighbouring African States;

43. *Strongly urges* the international community to increase, as a matter of urgency, humanitarian assistance and financial, material, military and political support to the front-line States so as to enable them to resolve their own economic difficulties, which are largely a consequence of the Pretoria régime's policies of aggression and subversion, and to defend themselves better against South Africa's persistent attempts to destabilize them;

44. *Requests* Member States urgently to extend all necessary assistance to Angola and other front-line States in order to enable them to strengthen their defence capacities against acts of aggression by South Africa;

45. *Expresses its grave concern* at the acquisition of nuclear-weapon capability by the racist régime of South Africa and declares that such acquisition constitutes a threat to peace and security in Africa while posing a danger to all mankind;

46. *Condemns*, and calls for an immediate end to, the continuing military collaboration on the part of certain Western countries with the racist régime of South Africa, and expresses its conviction that such collaboration, in addition to strengthening the aggressive military machinery of the Pretoria régime, thereby constituting a hostile action against the people of Namibia and the front-line States, is also in violation of the arms embargo imposed against South Africa under Security Council resolution 418(1977) of 4 November 1977;

47. *Declares* that such collaboration encourages the Pretoria régime in its defiance of the international community and obstructs efforts to eliminate *apartheid* and bring South Africa's illegal occupation of Namibia to an end, and calls for the immediate cessation of such collaboration;

48. *Calls upon* the Security Council to adopt the necessary measures to tighten the arms embargo imposed against South Africa under Council resolution 418(1977), to ensure its application to illegally occupied Namibia and to ensure strict compliance with the embargo by all States;

49. *Also calls upon* the Security Council to implement, as a matter of urgency, the recommendations contained in the report of the Security Council Committee established in pursuance of Council resolution 421(1977) of 9 December 1977;

50. *Condemns* all collaboration with the Pretoria régime in the nuclear field, and calls upon all States that do so to terminate such collaboration, including refraining from supplying the racist minority régime of South Africa, directly or indirectly, with installations, equipment or material that might enable it to produce uranium, plutonium or other nuclear materials or reactors;

51. *Endorses* the decision taken by the United Nations Council for Namibia that it will, in the exercise of its rights under the United Nations Convention on the Law of the Sea, proclaim an exclusive economic zone for Namibia, the outer limit of which shall be 200 miles, and states that any action for the implementation of that de-

cision should be taken in consultation with the South West Africa People's Organization, the representative of the Namibian people;

52. *Reaffirms* that the natural resources of Namibia, including its marine resources, are the inviolable heritage of the Namibian people, and expresses its deep concern at the depletion of these resources, particularly its uranium deposits, as a result of their plunder by South Africa and certain Western and other foreign economic interests, in violation of the pertinent resolutions of the General Assembly and of the Security Council, of Decree No. 1 for the Protection of the Natural Resources of Namibia, enacted by the United Nations Council for Namibia on 27 September 1974, and in disregard of the advisory opinion of the International Court of Justice of 21 June 1971;

53. *Declares* that all activities of foreign economic interests in Namibia are illegal under international law and that all the foreign economic interests operating in Namibia are liable to pay damages to the future legitimate Government of an independent Namibia;

54. *Calls upon* the United Nations Council for Namibia, in pursuance of the relevant provisions of Decree No. 1 for the Protection of the Natural Resources of Namibia, to continue to take the necessary steps to compile statistical information on the wealth illegally extracted from Namibia with a view to assessing the extent of compensation eventually due to an independent Namibia;

55. *Strongly condemns* the activities of all foreign economic interests operating in Namibia which are illegally exploiting the resources of the Territory, and demands that these interests comply with all the relevant resolutions and decisions of the United Nations by immediately withdrawing from the Territory and by putting an end to their co-operation with the illegal South African administration;

56. *Declares* that, by their incessant exploitation of the human and natural resources of the Territory and their continued accumulation and repatriation of huge profits, the foreign economic, financial and other interests operating in Namibia constitute a major obstacle to its independence;

57. *Once again requests* all Member States, particularly those States whose corporations are engaged in the exploitation of Namibian resources, to take all appropriate measures, including legislative and enforcement action, to ensure the full application of, and compliance by all corporations and individuals within their jurisdiction with, the provisions of Decree No. 1 for the Protection of the Natural Resources of Namibia;

58. *Calls upon* the Governments of all States, particularly those whose corporations are involved in the mining and processing of Namibian uranium, to take all appropriate measures in compliance with resolutions and decisions of the United Nations and Decree No. 1 for the Protection of the Natural Resources of Namibia, including the practice of requiring negative certificates of origin, to prohibit State-owned and other corporations, together with their subsidiaries, from dealing in Namibian uranium and from engaging in any uranium-prospecting activities in Namibia;

59. *Reiterates* its approval of the initiation by the United Nations Council for Namibia of legal proceedings in the domestic courts of States against corporations or individuals involved in the exploitation, transport, processing or purchase of Namibia's natural resources, as part of its efforts to give effect to Decree No. 1 for the Protection of the Natural Resources of Namibia;

60. *Requests* the Governments of the Federal Republic of Germany, the Netherlands and the United Kingdom of Great Britain and Northern Ireland, which operate the Urenco uranium-enrichment plant, to have Namibian uranium specifically excluded from the Treaty of Almelo, which regulates the activities of Urenco;

61. *Urges* the United Nations Council for Namibia, in its capacity as the legal Administering Authority for Namibia until independence, to consider the promulgation of additional legislation in order to protect and promote the interests of the people of Namibia and to implement effectively all its legislation;

62. *Calls upon* all specialized agencies, in particular the International Monetary Fund, to ensure the termination of all collaboration with, and assistance to, the racist régime of South Africa, since such assistance serves to augment the military capability of the Pretoria régime, thus enabling it not only to continue the brutal repression in Namibia and South Africa itself, but also to commit acts of aggression against independent neighbouring States;

63. *Requests* all States that have not already done so, pending the imposition of comprehensive and mandatory sanctions against South Africa, to take legislative, administrative and other measures individually and collectively, as appropriate, in order effectively to isolate South Africa politically, economically, militarily and culturally, in accordance with General Assembly resolutions ES-8/2 and 36/121 B, and its resolution 37/233 A of 20 December 1982;

64. *Requests* the United Nations Council for Namibia, in its implementation of paragraph 15 of General Assembly resolution ES-8/2 and of the relevant provisions of Assembly resolutions 36/121 B and 37/233 A, to continue to monitor the boycott of South Africa and to submit to the Assembly at its forty-fourth session a comprehensive report on all contacts between Member States and South Africa containing an analysis of the information received from Member States and other sources on the continuing political, economic, financial and other relations of States and their economic and other interest groups with South Africa and of measures taken by States to terminate all dealings with the racist régime of South Africa;

65. *Requests* all States to co-operate fully with the United Nations Council for Namibia in the fulfilment of its task concerning the implementation of General Assembly resolutions ES-8/2, 36/121 B and 37/233 A and to report to the Secretary-General by the forty-fourth session of the Assembly on the measures taken by them in the implementation of those resolutions;

66. *Strongly urges* the Security Council, in view of the persistent refusal by the racist régime of South Africa to comply with the resolutions and decisions of the United Nations on the question of Namibia, particularly Council resolutions 385(1976), 435(1978), 539(1983) and 566(1985), and, in the light of the serious threat to international peace and security posed by South Africa, to impose comprehensive and mandatory sanctions against that régime as provided for in Chapter VII of the Charter;

67. *Expresses its appreciation* to the Secretary-General for his personal commitment to Namibia's independence and for his efforts aimed at the implementation of resolutions and decisions of the United Nations on the question of Namibia, particularly Security Council resolution 435(1978), and urges him to continue those efforts;

68. *Requests* the Secretary-General to report to the General Assembly at its forty-fourth session on the implementation of the present resolution.

General Assembly resolution 43/26 A

17 November 1988   Meeting 54   130-0-23 (recorded vote)

Draft by Council for Namibia (A/43/24); agenda item 29.
Financial implications. 5th Committee, A/43/818; S-G, A/C.5/43/34 & Add.1.
Meeting numbers. GA 43rd session: 4th Committee 4-8; 5th Committee 33; plenary 47-52, 54.

Recorded vote in Assembly as follows:

In favour: Afghanistan, Albania, Algeria, Angola, Antigua and Barbuda, Argentina, Bahamas, Bahrain, Bangladesh, Barbados, Benin, Bhutan, Bolivia, Botswana, Brazil, Brunei Darussalam, Bulgaria, Burkina Faso, Burma, Burundi, Byelorussian SSR, Cameroon, Cape Verde, Central African Republic, Chad, Chile, China, Colombia, Comoros, Congo, Côte d'Ivoire, Cuba, Cyprus, Czechoslovakia, Democratic Kampuchea, Democratic Yemen, Djibouti, Dominica, Dominican Republic, Ecuador, Egypt, El Salvador, Ethiopia, Fiji, Gabon, Gambia, German Democratic Republic, Ghana, Grenada, Guatemala, Guinea, Guinea-Bissau, Guyana, Haiti, Honduras, Hungary, India, Indonesia, Iran, Iraq, Jamaica, Jordan, Kenya, Kuwait, Lao People's Democratic Republic, Lebanon, Lesotho, Liberia, Libyan Arab Jamahiriya, Madagascar, Malawi, Malaysia, Maldives, Mali, Malta, Mauritius, Mexico, Mongolia, Morocco, Mozambique, Nepal, Nicaragua, Niger, Nigeria, Oman, Pakistan, Panama, Papua New Guinea, Peru, Philippines, Poland, Qatar, Romania, Rwanda, Saint Kitts and Nevis, Saint Lucia, Saint Vincent and the Grenadines, Samoa, Sao Tome and Principe, Saudi Arabia, Senegal, Seychelles, Sierra Leone, Singapore, Solomon Islands, Somalia, Sri Lanka, Sudan, Suriname, Swaziland, Syrian Arab Republic, Thailand, Togo, Trinidad and Tobago, Tunisia, Turkey, Uganda, Ukrainian SSR, USSR, United Arab Emirates, United Republic of Tanzania, Uruguay, Vanuatu, Venezuela, Viet Nam, Yemen, Yugoslavia, Zaire, Zambia, Zimbabwe.

Against: None.

Abstaining: Australia, Austria, Belgium, Canada, Denmark, Finland, France, Germany, Federal Republic of, Greece, Iceland, Ireland, Israel, Italy, Japan, Luxembourg, Netherlands, New Zealand, Norway, Portugal, Spain, Sweden, United Kingdom, United States.

In related action, the General Assembly condemned the installation of an interim government and the linkage issue in **resolution 43/26 B**.

The Assembly, in **resolution 43/30**, reiterated its position that the specialized agencies and other United Nations organizations should refrain from taking any action that might imply recognition of, or support for, the legitimacy of South Africa's domination of Namibia. They were requested to withhold all forms of co-operation and assistance from South Africa until the Namibian people had exercised their right to self-determination, freedom and national independence.

By **decision 43/408** of 14 November, the Assembly took note of the report on Namibia of its Fourth Committee.[28] The Committee, noting that the Assembly had decided to consider the question of Namibia directly in plenary meeting, stated that on 12 and 18 October it had heard, at their request,[29] petitioners of the following organizations: International Confederation of Free Trade Unions, Lutheran World Federation, United States Out of Southern Africa Network, Namibia Support Committee, SWAPO Support Committee, *United States World Journal*.

Military aspects

The Council for Namibia also reviewed the military situation in and relating to Namibia in its 1988[2] and 1989 reports;[3] its Standing Committee II submitted a report on the matter in July 1988.[30] In a November report on contacts between Member States and South Africa,[12] the Council reported that contacts in the military and nuclear fields remained unchanged.

According to the Council, South Africa continued to face opposition inside Namibia and within its own borders, as well as large-scale isolation as a result of measures adopted by the international community. Pretoria responded by increasing its defence budget by 40 per cent, and escalating its military aggression and policy of destabilizing neighbouring States. In 1988, its policies directly affected all States in the region and caused the death of civilians and economic and social disruption on an unprecedented scale.

The extent of South Africa's military involvement in southern Africa was believed to have been one of the factors that pushed it towards a political settlement in Namibia. In particular, the escalating cost of its military occupation and intervention, which was reported to have risen to $1 billion annually by 1988, was a deciding factor. Moreover, police and defence allocations in the Namibian budget were increased to 17 per cent of total expenditures for fiscal year 1987/88. The illegal occupation of Namibia was estimated to absorb nearly 10 per cent of all spending by the South African Government. These economic factors and the fact that South Africa sustained heavy losses in men and equipment during its incursions into Angola, as well as defections, mutinies and widespread indiscipline among its troops, forced the régime to increase white recruitment to replace black conscripts, resulting in high casualties among white soldiers and making the war increasingly unpopular among white segments of the population. Nevertheless, South Africa continued to strengthen its military presence in Namibia, particularly along the northern border where 50,000 South African troops were concentrated.

Even after SWAPO announced a unilateral cease-fire on 1 September, the northern part of the country remained a security zone, with reports of violence against civilians increasing. Wider effects of the war included the dislocation of entire communities and disruption of the traditional economy.

The Council reported that Israel was collaborating with South Africa in several areas of weapons development, aircraft production, training and direct military involvement. During 1988, South African companies were reported to have been actively trying to recruit engineers and skilled personnel made redundant by Israeli defence manufacturers. According to SWAPO, Israeli military personnel were involved with South African Defence Forces (SADF) in Angola, some engaged in actual fighting in the provinces of Cunene and Cuando Cubango, while some Israeli technicians were involved in jamming radar, enabling the South Africa air force to bomb Lubango in southern Angola in February.

In January 1988, SADF launched a massive attack on Cuito Cuanavale, a strategic garrison town and rail centre in south-eastern Angola, approximately 300 kilometres north of the Namibian border in Cuando Cubango province.

On 22 August, Angola, Cuba and South Africa signed a formal cease-fire at Ruacana (see above). Consequently, South Africa, on 30 August, announced its military withdrawal from Angola. Following its defeat at Cuito Cuanavale, the União Nacional para a Independência Total de Angola, the opposition group fighting in southern Angola, moved its troops north and was reported to be based largely in Zaire.

Angola, Cuba and South Africa signed an agreement on 22 December which, as provided for in resolution 435(1978), stipulated that South Africa would withdraw all its forces from Namibia.

The Committee on colonial countries also considered the military situation in Namibia. On 8 August[17] it reiterated its conviction that the armed liberation struggle of the Namibian people, led by SWAPO, continued to be an important and decisive factor in their efforts to achieve independence in a united Namibia. It strongly condemned South Africa for its military buildup in Namibia and for its utilization of Namibia as a springboard for attacks against neighbouring States. The Committee called on all States to prevent the recruitment, training and transit of mercenaries for service in Namibia, and on all specialized agencies, in particular the International Monetary Fund, to terminate all collaboration with and assistance to South Africa which could augment its military capability.

By **decision 43/410**, the General Assembly took similar action.

In **resolution 43/26 A**, the Assembly commended SWAPO for its continued intensification of the struggle on all fronts, including the armed struggle, and condemned South Africa for its military buildup in Namibia and its imposition of military conscription of Namibian males. South Africa was further condemned for its utilization of Namibian territory as a springboard for perpetrating armed invasions against neighbouring States and for its use of mercenaries to suppress the Namibian people.

Implementation of resolution 435(1978)

Geneva and Brazzaville Protocols

After holding a series of negotiations in 1988, Angola, Cuba and South Africa reached agreement on the principles for a peaceful settlement of the conflict in south-western Africa. The three countries and the United States, having met from 2 to 5 August at Geneva, issued, on 8 August, a joint statement, known as the Geneva Protocol.[23] In the statement, they announced their agreement on a sequence of steps necessary to prepare the way for the independence of Namibia in accordance with Security Council resolution 435(1978) and to achieve peace in south-western Africa. In addition to the recommendation that resolution 435(1978) be implemented beginning 1 November 1988, the parties approved, *ad referendum* to their respective Governments, the text of a tripartite agreement that embodied the principles negotiated in New York and formally approved by the Governments on 20 July (see above). On their side, Angola and Cuba reiterated their decision to subscribe to a bilateral accord, which would include a timetable acceptable to all parties, for the staged and total withdrawal of Cuban troops from Angola. The parties further approved steps that would enhance mutual confidence, reduce the risk of military confrontation and create the conditions in the region necessary to conclude the negotiations. With the approval of these measures, a *de facto* cessation of hostilities came into effect.

On 17 August,[24] Tunisia and Zambia transmitted to the Secretary-General a letter by Sam Nujoma, President of SWAPO, in which SWAPO agreed to comply with the cessation of all hostile acts, which had been put into effect as of 10 August in Angola. He expressed SWAPO's willingness to continue to abide by the agreement until the formal cease-fire under resolution 435(1978) was signed between SWAPO and South Africa. In SWAPO's view, South Africa should be called on to refrain from repressing SWAPO members and supporters inside Namibia during that period. SWAPO, in accepting 1 November 1988 as the date for the commencement of implementation of resolution 435(1978), urged the Secretary-General to avail himself, as part of his good offices, of this opportunity to initiate consultations with the parties concerned.

On 13 December, Angola, Cuba and South Africa signed the Protocol of Brazzaville, the text of which was conveyed to the Secretary-General the following day by the United States.[25] By the Protocol, the three signatories agreed to recommend to the Secretary-General that 1 April 1989 be established as the date for implementation of resolution 435(1978). They agreed to meet on 22 December 1988 in New York for the signing of the tripartite agreement and for the signing by Angola and Cuba of their bilateral agreement. By that date, Angola and Cuba expected to have reached agreement with the

Secretary-General on verification arrangements to be approved by the Security Council. The parties further agreed to exchange prisoners of war and to establish a Joint Commission responsible for the resolution of any dispute regarding the interpretation or implementation of the tripartite agreement. The United States and the USSR were invited to participate as observers in the work of the Commission, and it was agreed that Namibia, once it became independent, would become a full member of the Commission. The Commission was to be constituted within 30 days of the signing of the tripartite agreement and was in no way to function as a substitute for the United Nations Transition Assistance Group in Namibia or for the United Nations entity performing verification in Angola.

In a declaration issued at Athens, Greece, on 16 December,[31] the 12 members of the European Community (EC) welcomed the signing of the Brazzaville Protocol, which, they said, brought the independence of Namibia on the basis of resolution 435(1978) closer than ever before. They reaffirmed their intention to promote economic and social development in Namibia by providing it with substantial economic assistance once it became independent, as well as their willingness to receive from an independent Namibia an application for accession to the Lomé Convention.

Tripartite agreement

A tripartite agreement signed by Angola, Cuba and South Africa on 22 December in New York was transmitted to the Secretary-General by the United States the same day.[27] The parties agreed to request immediately the Secretary-General to seek authority from the Security Council to commence implementation of resolution 435(1978) on 1 April 1989. All South African military forces were to depart Namibia in accordance with that resolution. South Africa and Angola were to co-operate with the Secretary-General to ensure the independence of Namibia through free and fair elections and to abstain from any action that could prevent the execution of the resolution. The parties also agreed to respect the territorial integrity and inviolability of the borders of Namibia and ensure that their territories were not used in connection with acts of war, aggression or violence against the territorial integrity or inviolability of Namibia's borders. Angola and Cuba were to implement the bilateral agreement providing for the redeployment towards the north and the eventual total withdrawal of Cuban troops from Angola, and the on-site verification of that withdrawal through arrangements made with the Security Council. Consistent with their obligations under the United Nations Charter, the parties were to refrain from the threat or use of force and to respect the principle of non-interference in the internal affairs of the States of south-western Africa.

SECURITY COUNCIL ACTION (September)

On 27 September,[32] Zambia requested that the Security Council be convened to consider the situation in Namibia. As a result of consultations among Council members on 29 September, the President made the following statement:[33]

"Ten years ago, on 29 September 1978, the Security Council adopted resolution 435(1978) in order to ensure an early independence of Namibia, through free elections under the supervision and control of the United Nations.

"The members of the Security Council express grave concern that such a long time after the adoption of resolution 435(1978) the Namibian people have not yet attained their self-determination and independence.

"Reaffirming the pertinent resolutions of the Security Council and the legal responsibility of the United Nations with regard to Namibia, the members of the Council once again call upon South Africa to comply at last with these resolutions and to cease its illegal occupation of Namibia. In this respect, they stress the Security Council's continuing commitment to discharge its particular responsibility for furthering the interests of the people of Namibia and their aspirations for peace, justice and independence through a full and definitive implementation of resolution 435(1978).

"They support the resolute action led by the Secretary-General with a view to the implementation of resolution 435(1978) and encourage him to continue his efforts to that end.

"The Council notes developments in recent weeks in efforts by a number of parties to find a peaceful solution to the conflict in south-western Africa that are reflected in the joint statement of 8 August 1988 by the Governments of Angola, Cuba, South Africa and the United States, which has been circulated as a Security Council document.

"The Council also notes the expressed readiness of the South West Africa People's Organization to sign and observe a cease-fire agreement with South Africa, as stated in document S/20129 of 17 August 1988, in order to pave the way for the implementation of resolution 435(1978). On this tenth anniversary of the adoption of resolution 435(1978), its early implementation is the common aspiration of the international community. The members of the Council urge the parties to display the necessary political will to translate the commitments they have made into reality in order to bring about a peaceful settlement of the Namibian question and peace and stability in the region.

"In particular, they strongly urge South Africa to comply forthwith with the Security Council's resolutions and decisions, particularly resolution 435(1978), and to co-operate with the Secretary-General in its immediate, full and definitive implementation. To this end, the Council urges States Members of the United Nations to render all necessary assistance to the Secretary-General and his staff in the administrative and other practical steps necessary for the emplacement of the United Nations Transition Assistance Group.''

Meeting number. SC 2827.

SECURITY COUNCIL ACTION (December)

Angola[34] and Cuba[35] informed the Secretary-General on 17 December that it was their intention to sign on 22 December a bilateral agreement providing for the redeployment to the north and withdrawal of the Cuban troops from Angola, in accordance with a timetable agreed upon by both countries, and for the verification of that withdrawal by the United Nations. The Secretary-General was requested to recommend to the Security Council that a United Nations military observer group be set up to carry out that mandate.

The Council, having noted the decision of Angola and Cuba to conclude the bilateral agreement, adopted on 20 December **resolution 626(1988)**, by which it decided, among other things, to establish under its authority a United Nations Angola Verification Mission for a period of 31 months. The arrangements for the establishment of the Mission were to enter into force as soon as the tripartite agreement between Angola, Cuba and South Africa, on the one hand, and the bilateral agreement between Angola and Cuba, on the other, were signed. (See PART TWO, Chapter I.)

GENERAL ASSEMBLY ACTION

On 17 November, the General Assembly adopted **resolution 43/26 B** by recorded vote.

Implementation of Security Council resolution 435(1978)

The General Assembly,

Noting that the Secretary-General has reported that all the necessary conditions for the implementation of Security Council resolution 435(1978) of 29 September 1978 have already been fulfilled,

Indignant that ten years after the adoption of Security Council resolution 435(1978) the Namibian people have not yet exercised their right to self-determination and attained independence,

Expressing grave concern at the lack of progress in implementing Security Council resolution 435(1978), as indicated in the further reports of the Secretary-General dated 29 December 1983, 6 June 1985, 6 September 1985, 26 November 1985, 31 March 1987 and 27 October 1987 concerning the implementation of Council resolution 435(1978) and resolution 439(1978) of 13 November 1978,

Recalling Security Council resolution 601(1987) of 30 October 1987 by which the Council, *inter alia*, decided to authorize the Secretary-General to proceed to arrange a cease-fire between South Africa and the South West Africa People's Organization in order to undertake the administrative and other practical steps necessary for the emplacement of the United Nations Transition Assistance Group,

1. *Reiterates* that Security Council resolutions 385(1976) of 30 January 1976 and 435(1978), embody-

ing the United Nations plan for the independence of Namibia, constitute the only internationally accepted basis for a peaceful settlement of the question of Namibia and demands their immediate and unconditional implementation;

2. *Strongly condemns* racist South Africa for obstructing the implementation of Security Council resolutions 385(1976), 435(1978), 439(1978), 532(1983) of 31 May 1983, 539(1983) of 28 October 1983, 566(1985) of 19 June 1985 and 601(1987);

3. *Demands* that South Africa urgently comply fully and unconditionally with the resolutions of the Security Council, in particular resolutions 385(1976) and 435(1978) and subsequent resolutions of the Council relating to Namibia;

4. *Emphasizes once again* that the only parties to the conflict in Namibia are, on the one hand, the Namibian people represented by the South West Africa People's Organization, their sole and authentic representative, and, on the other, the racist régime of South Africa which illegally occupies the Territory;

5. *Strongly condemns* the racist régime of South Africa for the installation of a so-called interim government in Namibia on 17 June 1985, in defiance of resolutions and decisions of the United Nations, and declares this measure null and void, and reiterates its call upon the international community to continue to refrain from according any recognition or extending any co-operation to any régime imposed by the illegal South African administration upon the Namibian people;

6. *Firmly rejects and condemns* the persistent attempts to establish a ''linkage'' or ''parallelism'' between the independence of Namibia and any extraneous and irrelevant issues, in particular the presence of Cuban forces in Angola, and emphasizes unequivocally that all such attempts are designed to delay further the independence of Namibia in accordance with Security Council resolution 435(1978), and that they constitute a gross and unwarranted interference in the internal affairs of Angola;

7. *Urgently calls upon* the international community to act resolutely against the intransigent stance of the Pretoria régime, and stresses the responsibility of the Security Council concerning the implementation of its resolutions on Namibia in view of the threat to regional and international peace and security created by the racist régime of South Africa;

8. *Notes with satisfaction* the statement by the Security Council on the occasion of the tenth anniversary of the adoption of resolution 435(1978) in which the members of the Council, *inter alia*, strongly urged South Africa to comply forthwith with the resolutions and decisions of the Security Council, particularly resolution 435(1978), and to co-operate with the Secretary-General in its immediate, full and definitive implementation;

9. *Expresses* its appreciation to the Secretary-General for his personal commitment to the independence of Namibia and for his efforts aimed at the implementation of resolutions and decisions of the United Nations on the question of Namibia, particularly Security Council resolution 435(1978), and urges him to continue those efforts;

10. *Requests* the Secretary-General to report to the General Assembly at its forty-fourth session on the implementation of the present resolution.

General Assembly resolution 43/26 B
17 November 1988   Meeting 54   140-0-13 (recorded vote)

Draft by Council for Namibia (A/43/24); agenda item 29.
Financial implications. 5th Committee, A/43/818; S-G, A/C.5/43/34 & Add.1.
Meeting numbers. GA 43rd session: 5th Committee 33; plenary 47-52, 54.

Recorded vote in Assembly as follows:

In favour: Afghanistan, Albania, Algeria, Angola, Antigua and Barbuda, Argentina, Australia, Austria, Bahamas, Bahrain, Bangladesh, Barbados, Benin, Bhutan, Bolivia, Botswana, Brazil, Brunei Darussalam, Bulgaria, Burkina Faso, Burma, Burundi, Byelorussian SSR, Cameroon, Cape Verde, Central African Republic, Chad, Chile, China, Colombia, Comoros, Congo, Côte d'Ivoire, Cuba, Cyprus, Czechoslovakia, Democratic Kampuchea, Democratic Yemen, Denmark, Djibouti, Dominican Republic, Ecuador, Egypt, El Salvador, Ethiopia, Fiji, Finland, Gabon, Gambia, German Democratic Republic, Ghana, Greece, Grenada, Guatemala, Guinea, Guinea-Bissau, Guyana, Haiti, Honduras, Hungary, Iceland, India, Indonesia, Iran, Iraq, Ireland, Jamaica, Jordan, Kenya, Kuwait, Lao People's Democratic Republic, Lebanon, Lesotho, Liberia, Libyan Arab Jamahiriya, Madagascar, Malawi, Malaysia, Maldives, Mali, Malta, Mauritius, Mexico, Mongolia, Morocco, Mozambique, Nepal, New Zealand, Nicaragua, Niger, Nigeria, Norway, Oman, Pakistan, Panama, Papua New Guinea, Peru, Philippines, Poland, Qatar, Romania, Rwanda, Saint Kitts and Nevis, Saint Lucia, Saint Vincent and the Grenadines, Samoa, Sao Tome and Principe, Saudi Arabia, Senegal, Seychelles, Sierra Leone, Singapore, Solomon Islands, Somalia, Spain, Sri Lanka, Sudan, Suriname, Swaziland, Sweden, Syrian Arab Republic, Thailand, Togo, Trinidad and Tobago, Tunisia, Turkey, Uganda, Ukrainian SSR, USSR, United Arab Emirates, United Republic of Tanzania, Uruguay, Vanuatu, Venezuela, Viet Nam, Yemen, Yugoslavia, Zaire, Zambia, Zimbabwe.

Against: None.

Abstaining: Belgium, Canada, Dominica, France, Germany, Federal Republic of, Israel, Italy, Japan, Luxembourg, Netherlands, Portugal, United Kingdom, United States.

Related action was taken by the Assembly in **resolution 43/106**, by which it reaffirmed the inalienable right of the Namibian people to self-determination and national independence and condemned those Governments that did not recognize those rights. In **resolution 43/29**, the Assembly called again on all States to discontinue all economic, financial and trade co-operation with South Africa concerning Namibia that might lend support to its continued illegal occupation.

Information dissemination

The Council for Namibia, in co-operation with the Department of Public Information (DPI) and in consultation with SWAPO, continued in 1988 to disseminate information to Governments, leading opinion makers, the media, political and academic institutions, NGOs, cultural organizations and others to mobilize world public opinion in support of Namibia's independence.[2] Much of its work in dissemination of information was carried out by its Standing Committee III.[36]

The Council produced and disseminated folders and acquired and disseminated materials on diverse matters concerning Namibia's struggle for independence and self-determination. Among those materials was an updated compendium of major resolutions of the General Assembly and of the Security Council, resolutions adopted by OAU, excerpts from declarations and communiqués adopted by the Movement of Non-Aligned Countries, and reports of the Secretary-General on the question of Namibia. The Council gave special consideration to publicizing its two 1988 seminars

(see above) and two journalists' encounters organized in advance of them.

Activities of the Council were publicized through press releases in English and French, and disseminated to the press, delegations and NGOs at United Nations Headquarters and to United Nations information centres (UNICs) throughout the world. Daily press coverage in English and French was provided for Security Council meetings and the General Assembly debate on Namibia, as well as for seminars and missions undertaken by the Council during the reporting period. Material on the question of Namibia was also provided regularly to the Pool of Non-Aligned News Agencies.

Information on the situation in Namibia and the work of the Council was disseminated through two periodical publications, the *UN Chronicle* and *Objective: Justice*, and was contained in *Basic Facts about the United Nations* and the *Yearbook of the United Nations*. Nearly 13,000 publications and 1,500 copies of wall sheets and posters were distributed by UNICs in 1987/88. The background booklet *A Trust Betrayed: Namibia* was revised for reprinting.

"Namibia's Independence, Ten Years after Security Council Resolution 435(1978)" was the title of a *Perspective* radio feature programme produced in May. United Nations Radio provided full coverage of the World Council of Churches hearings on Namibia held in May in Washington, D.C., and material from the hearings was used in news telephone feeds and news magazine programmes, including *South African Review* and the *Namibia Up-date* series. Coverage of the 6 May plenary meeting of the Council included a special programme entitled "The Council for Namibia to visit Windhoek?", which focused on discussions between the President of SWAPO and Council members. The special *Namibia Up-date* radio series was produced in the Spanish and Herero languages. A feature programme on the United Nations Institute for Namibia was produced in French, and two feature programmes on solidarity with Namibians were produced in Russian.

A total of 63 television news packages on Namibia were prepared for international syndicators. A *UN In Action* television programme entitled *Namibia Exiles*, produced in Arabic, Chinese, English, French, Japanese, Russian and Spanish, dealt with the occupation and exploitation of Namibia by South Africa and described the Council's role in providing education and training programmes for the country. The film *Free Namibia*, available in Arabic, English, French, Portuguese and Spanish, was screened 69 times, while the film *Namibia: A Trust Betrayed*, in the same five languages, was screened 72 times.

As part of its programme of co-operation with NGOs, and under the terms of a 1987 Assembly resolution,[37] the Council, in consultation with SWAPO, made financial contributions to a number of NGOs to enable them to promote the cause of freedom of the Namibian people by producing information materials on the situation there.

The Office of the United Nations Commissioner for Namibia continued to serve as an additional source of information on the situation in Namibia and the activities of the Council. In this regard, it prepared the *Namibia Bulletin*, a monthly review, and *Namibia in the News*, a weekly newsletter. The Commissioner's Office undertook the distribution of some 350,000 copies in English and 175,000 copies in other languages of various United Nations and other publications, including an information kit on Namibia.

The Committee on colonial countries, on 8 August,[17] reiterated its request to the Secretary-General to intensify his efforts to mobilize world public opinion against South Africa's policies concerning Namibia and, in particular, to increase world-wide information dissemination on the Namibian liberation struggle. The Committee emphasized the importance of action by local authorities, trade unions, religious bodies, academic institutions, the mass media, solidarity movements and others in mobilizing Governments and public opinion in support of that struggle, in exerting pressure on TNCs to refrain from any investment or activity in Namibia and in counteracting all forms of collaboration with South Africa.

GENERAL ASSEMBLY ACTION

On 17 November, the General Assembly adopted **resolution 43/26 D by recorded vote.**

Dissemination of information and mobilization of international public opinion in support of the immediate independence of Namibia

The General Assembly,

Gravely concerned at the total black-out of news on Namibia imposed by the illegal régime of South Africa, in particular regarding the increased repression of the Namibian people by that régime,

Gravely concerned at the campaign of slander and disinformation against the United Nations and the liberation struggle of the Namibian people for self-determination and national independence led by the South West Africa People's Organization, their sole and authentic representative,

Stressing the urgent need to mobilize international public opinion on a continuous basis with a view to assisting effectively the people of Namibia in the achievement of self-determination, freedom and independence in a united Namibia and, in particular, to intensify the worldwide and continuous dissemination of information on the struggle for liberation being waged by the people of Namibia under the leadership of the South West Africa People's Organization,

Reiterating the importance of intensifying publicity on all aspects of the question of Namibia as an instrument for furthering the mandate given by the General Assembly to the United Nations Council for Namibia,

Recognizing the important role that non-governmental organizations are playing in the dissemination of information on Namibia and in the mobilization of international public opinion in support of the immediate independence of Namibia,

1. *Requests* the United Nations Council for Namibia, in co-operation with the Department of Public Information of the Secretariat and in consultation with the South West Africa People's Organization, the sole and authentic representative of the Namibian people, in pursuance of its international campaign in support of the struggle of the Namibian people for national independence:

(a) To continue to consider effective ways and means of increasing the dissemination of information relating to Namibia in order to intensify the international campaign in favour of the cause of Namibia;

(b) To focus its activities towards greater mobilization of public opinion in Western countries, particularly the United States of America, the United Kingdom of Great Britain and Northern Ireland and the Federal Republic of Germany, as well as in Japan;

(c) To counteract the total news black-out on Namibia imposed by the illegal South African régime, which forbids foreign journalists from entering and reporting from the Territory;

(d) To intensify the international campaign for the imposition of comprehensive and mandatory sanctions against South Africa under Chapter VII of the Charter of the United Nations;

(e) To organize an international campaign to boycott products from Namibia and South Africa, in co-operation with non-governmental organizations;

(f) To expose and denounce collaboration with the racist régime of South Africa in all fields;

(g) To organize exhibitions on Namibia and the struggle of the Namibian people for independence;

(h) To prepare and disseminate publications on the political, economic, military and social consequences of the illegal occupation of Namibia by South Africa, on legal matters, on the question of the territorial integrity of Namibia and on contacts between Member States and South Africa;

(i) To prepare periodic reports on the brutalities committed by the racist régime of South Africa against the Namibian people and ensure their widest possible distribution;

(j) To produce and disseminate radio and television programmes designed to draw the attention of world public opinion to the current situation in and around Namibia;

(k) To produce and disseminate, in both the English language and the local languages of Namibia, radio programmes designed to counter the hostile propaganda and disinformation campaign of the racist régime of South Africa;

(l) To produce and disseminate posters;

(m) To ensure full coverage through advertisements in newspapers and magazines, press releases, press conferences and press briefings of all activities of the United Nations regarding Namibia in order to maintain a constant flow of information to the public on all aspects of the question of Namibia;

(n) To prepare and disseminate a thematic atlas on Namibia;

(o) To reproduce and disseminate the comprehensive economic map of Namibia;

(p) To produce and disseminate booklets on the activities of the Council;

(q) To update and disseminate widely a compendium of resolutions of the General Assembly and of the Security Council relating to Namibia and of relevant documents of the Movement of Non-Aligned Countries and the Organization of African Unity, as well as decisions, declarations and communiqués of the front-line States on the question of Namibia;

(r) To update, publicize and distribute the indexed reference book on transnational corporations that plunder the human and natural resources of Namibia, and on the profits they extract from the Territory;

(s) To produce and disseminate widely, on a monthly basis, a bulletin containing analytical and updated information intended to mobilize maximum support for the Namibian cause;

(t) To produce and disseminate, on a weekly basis, an information newsletter containing updated information on developments in and relating to Namibia, in support of the Namibian cause;

(u) To acquire books, pamphlets and other materials relating to Namibia for dissemination;

(v) To prepare, in consultation with the South West Africa People's Organization, a list of Namibian political prisoners;

(w) To assist the South West Africa People's Organization in the production and distribution of material on Namibia;

2. *Also requests* the United Nations Council for Namibia to continue to organize, in co-operation with the Department of Public Information, media encounters on developments relating to Namibia, particularly prior to activities of the Council during 1989;

3. *Further requests* the United Nations Council for Namibia to exert all efforts to counteract the campaign of slander and disinformation against the United Nations and the liberation struggle in Namibia carried out by South African agents from the so-called information offices established in several Western countries;

4. *Requests* the United Nations Council for Namibia to co-operate closely with relevant intergovernmental organizations, in order to increase the awareness of the international community of the direct responsibility of the United Nations over Namibia and the continued illegal occupation of that Territory by the racist régime of South Africa;

5. *Calls upon* the United Nations Council for Namibia to continue to co-operate with non-governmental organizations in its efforts to mobilize international public opinion in support of the liberation struggle of the Namibian people, under the leadership of the South West Africa People's Organization;

6. *Also requests* the United Nations Council for Namibia to prepare, update and disseminate lists of non-governmental organizations, in particular those in the major Western countries, in order to ensure better co-operation and co-ordination among non-governmental organizations working in support of the Namibian cause and against *apartheid;*

7. *Further requests* the United Nations Council for Namibia to organize workshops for non-governmental or-

ganizations, parliamentarians, trade unionists, academics and media representatives at which the participants will consider how they can contribute to the implementation of the decisions of the United Nations relating to the dissemination of information on Namibia;

8. *Decides* to allocate the sum of $500,000 to be used by the United Nations Council for Namibia for its programme of co-operation with non-governmental organizations, including support to conferences and workshops in solidarity with Namibia arranged by those organizations, dissemination of conclusions of such conferences and workshops and support to such other activities as will promote the cause of the liberation struggle of the Namibian people, subject to decisions to be taken by the Council in each individual case in consultation with the South West Africa People's Organization;

9. *Requests* the United Nations Council for Namibia to continue to contact and inform leading opinion makers, media leaders, academic institutions, trade unions, legislators and parliamentarians, cultural organizations, support groups and other concerned persons and non-governmental organizations about the objectives and functions of the United Nations Council for Namibia and the struggle of the Namibian people under the leadership of the South West Africa People's Organization;

10. *Also requests* the United Nations Council for Namibia to co-operate with the specialized agencies and other organizations of the United Nations system in the promotion of a campaign of information on the question of Namibia, in their respective fields;

11. *Appeals* to non-governmental organizations and associations, institutions, support groups and individuals sympathetic to the Namibian cause:

(a) To increase the awareness of their national communities and legislative bodies concerning South Africa's illegal occupation of Namibia, the liberation struggle being waged by the Namibian people under the leadership of the South West Africa People's Organization, the gross violation of basic human rights by the South African régime in Namibia and the plunder of the Territory's resources by foreign economic interests;

(b) To mobilize in their countries broad public support for the national liberation of Namibia by holding hearings, seminars and public presentations on various aspects of the Namibian question, as well as by producing and distributing pamphlets, films and other information material;

(c) To expose and campaign against the political, economic, financial, military and cultural collaboration of certain Western Governments with the South African régime, as well as official visits to and from South Africa;

(d) To intensify public pressure for the immediate withdrawal from Namibia of foreign economic interests that are exploiting the human and natural resources of the Territory;

(e) To continue and develop campaign and research work, in order to expose the involvement and operations of certain Western-based oil companies in the supply of petroleum products to Namibia and South Africa;

(f) To step up their efforts to persuade universities, local governments, trade unions and churches and other institutions to divest themselves of all investments in firms doing business in Namibia and South Africa;

(g) To intensify the campaign for the immediate and unconditional release of all Namibian political prisoners

and detainees and the granting of prisoner-of-war status to all Namibian freedom fighters, in accordance with the Geneva Convention relative to the Treatment of Prisoners of War and the Additional Protocol thereto;

12. *Requests* Member States to broadcast programmes on their national radio and television networks and to publish material in their official news media about the situation in and around Namibia and the obligation of Governments and peoples to assist in every possible way in the struggle of the Namibian people for independence;

13. *Requests* all Member States to observe Namibia Day in a befitting manner by giving the widest possible publicity to and ensuring the dissemination of information on the struggle of the people of Namibia, including the issuance of special postage stamps for the occasion;

14. *Requests* the Secretary-General to direct the Department of Public Information to assist the United Nations Council for Namibia in the implementation of its programme of dissemination of information and to ensure that all activities of the United Nations on dissemination of information on the question of Namibia follow the policy guidelines laid down by the United Nations Council for Namibia as the legal Administering Authority for the Territory;

15. *Requests* the Secretary-General to continue to assist, as a matter of priority, the United Nations Council for Namibia in the implementation of its programme of dissemination of information;

16. *Also requests* the Secretary-General to provide the United Nations Council for Namibia with the work programme of the Department of Public Information for 1989 covering the activities of dissemination of information on the question of Namibia, followed by periodic reports on the programme undertaken, including details of expenses incurred;

17. *Further requests* the Secretary-General to direct the Department of Public Information to disseminate, in 1989, the list of Namibian political prisoners prepared by the United Nations Council for Namibia in consultation with the South West Africa People's Organization, in order to intensify international pressure for their immediate and unconditional release.

General Assembly resolution 43/26 D

17 November 1988   Meeting 54   129-0-23 (recorded vote)

Draft by Council for Namibia (A/43/24); agenda item 29.
Financial implications. 5th Committee, A/43/818; S-G, A/C.5/43/34 & Add.1.
Meeting numbers. GA 43rd session: 5th Committee 33; plenary 47-52, 54.

Recorded vote in Assembly as follows:

In favour: Afghanistan, Albania, Algeria, Angola, Antigua and Barbuda, Argentina, Australia, Bahamas, Bahrain, Bangladesh, Barbados, Benin, Bhutan, Bolivia, Botswana, Brazil, Brunei Darussalam, Bulgaria, Burkina Faso, Burma, Burundi, Byelorussian SSR, Cameroon, Cape Verde, Central African Republic, Chad, Chile, China, Colombia, Comoros, Congo, Côte d'Ivoire, Cuba, Cyprus, Czechoslovakia, Democratic Kampuchea, Democratic Yemen, Djibouti, Dominica, Dominican Republic, Ecuador, Egypt, El Salvador, Ethiopia, Fiji, Gabon, Gambia, German Democratic Republic, Ghana, Guatemala, Guinea, Guinea-Bissau, Guyana, Haiti, Honduras, Hungary, India, Indonesia, Iran, Iraq, Jamaica, Jordan, Kenya, Kuwait, Lao People's Democratic Republic, Lebanon, Liberia, Libyan Arab Jamahiriya, Madagascar, Malawi, Malaysia, Maldives, Mali, Malta, Mauritius, Mexico, Mongolia, Morocco, Mozambique, Nepal, Nicaragua, Niger, Nigeria, Oman, Pakistan, Panama, Papua New Guinea, Peru, Philippines, Poland, Qatar, Romania, Rwanda, Saint Kitts and Nevis, Saint Lucia, Saint Vincent and the Grenadines, Samoa, Sao Tome and Principe, Saudi Arabia, Senegal, Seychelles, Sierra Leone, Singapore, Solomon Islands, Somalia, Sri Lanka, Sudan, Suriname, Swaziland, Syrian Arab Republic, Thailand, Togo, Trinidad and Tobago, Tunisia, Turkey, Uganda, Ukrainian SSR, USSR, United Arab Emirates, United Republic of Tanzania, Uruguay, Vanuatu, Venezuela, Viet Nam, Yemen, Yugoslavia, Zaire, Zambia, Zimbabwe.

Against: None.
Abstaining: Austria, Belgium, Canada, Denmark, Finland, France, Germany, Federal Republic of, Greece, Iceland, Ireland, Israel, Italy, Japan, Lesotho, Luxembourg, Netherlands, New Zealand, Norway, Portugal, Spain, Sweden, United Kingdom, United States.

In **resolution 43/60 A**, the General Assembly requested the Secretary-General to ensure that DPI further intensified its efforts to alert world public opinion to the illegal occupation of Namibia and to disseminate information relating to the struggle of Namibia's oppressed people for self-determination, national independence and freedom, as well as to the need for the full and speedy implementation of the United Nations independence plan.

In **resolution 43/106**, the Assembly condemned South Africa for the news black-out in Namibia, the repeated destruction of editorial offices of independent papers such as *The Namibian* and the arrest of their staff members.

Work programme of the Council for Namibia

On 17 November, the Assembly adopted **resolution 43/26 C** by recorded vote.

Programme of work of the United Nations Council for Namibia

The General Assembly,

Having examined the report of the United Nations Council for Namibia,

Convinced of the need for continued consultations with the South West Africa People's Organization in the formulation and implementation of the programme of work of the United Nations Council for Namibia, as well as in any matter of interest to the Namibian people,

1. *Approves* the report of the United Nations Council for Namibia, including the recommendations contained therein, and decides to make adequate financial provision for their implementation;

2. *Decides* that the United Nations Council for Namibia, in the discharge of its responsibilities as the legal Administering Authority for Namibia until independence, shall:

(a) Continue to mobilize international support in order to press for the speedy withdrawal of the illegal South African administration from Namibia in accordance with the resolutions of the United Nations relating to Namibia;

(b) Counter the policies of South Africa against the Namibian people and the United Nations, as well as against the United Nations Council for Namibia as the legal Administering Authority for Namibia;

(c) Denounce and seek the rejection by all States of all kinds of schemes through which South Africa attempts to perpetuate its illegal presence in Namibia;

(d) Ensure non-recognition of any administration or entity installed in Namibia not ensuing from free elections conducted under the supervision and control of the United Nations, in accordance with the relevant resolutions of the Security Council, in particular resolutions 385(1976) of 30 January 1976, 435(1978) of 29 September 1978, 439(1978) of 13 November 1978, 532(1983) of 31 May 1983, 539(1983) of 28 October 1983, 566(1985) of 19 June 1985, and 601(1987) of 30 October 1987;

(*e*) Make a concerted effort to counter the attempts to establish a "linkage" or "parallelism" between the independence of Namibia and extraneous issues, such as the withdrawal of Cuban forces from Angola;

3. *Decides* that the United Nations Council for Namibia shall hold extraordinary plenary meetings in Latin America or southern Africa and that such meetings shall be provided with verbatim records;

4. *Decides also* that the United Nations Council for Namibia shall send missions of consultation to Governments in order to co-ordinate efforts for the implementation of resolutions of the United Nations on the question of Namibia and to mobilize support for the Namibian cause;

5. *Decides further* that the United Nations Council for Namibia shall represent Namibia at United Nations conferences and meetings of intergovernmental and non-governmental organizations, bodies and conferences to ensure that the rights and interests of Namibia shall be adequately protected;

6. *Decides* that Namibia, represented by the United Nations Council for Namibia, shall participate as a full member in all conferences and meetings organized by the United Nations to which all States or, in the case of regional conferences and meetings, all African States are invited;

7. *Requests* all committees and other subsidiary bodies of the General Assembly and of the Economic and Social Council to continue to invite the United Nations Council for Namibia to participate whenever the rights and interests of Namibians are discussed, and to consult closely with the United Nations Council for Namibia before submitting any draft resolution that may involve such rights and interests;

8. *Reiterates its request* to all specialized agencies and other organizations of the United Nations system to grant full membership to Namibia, represented by the United Nations Council for Namibia, so that the Council may participate as the legal Administering Authority for Namibia in the work of those agencies and organizations;

9. *Reiterates its request* to all specialized agencies and other organizations of the United Nations system that have not yet done so to grant a waiver of the assessment of Namibia during the period in which it is represented by the United Nations Council for Namibia;

10. *Again requests* all intergovernmental organizations, bodies and conferences to ensure that the rights and interests of Namibia are protected and to invite Namibia, represented by the United Nations Council for Namibia, to participate as a full member, whenever such rights and interests are involved;

11. *Requests* the United Nations Council for Namibia, in its capacity as the legal Administering Authority for Namibia, to accede to any international conventions as it may deem appropriate in close consultation with the South West Africa People's Organization;

12. *Decides* that the United Nations Council for Namibia shall:

(*a*) Consult regularly with the leaders of the South West Africa People's Organization by inviting them to New York and by sending high-level missions to the provisional headquarters of that organization, which will visit Namibian refugee centres whenever necessary;

(*b*) Prepare and publish reports on the political, economic, military, legal and social situation in and relating to Namibia;

(*c*) Review the progress of the liberation struggle in Namibia in its political, military and social aspects and prepare comprehensive and analytical periodic reports related thereto;

(*d*) Review the compliance of Member States with the relevant resolutions and decisions of the United Nations relating to Namibia and, taking into account the advisory opinion of the International Court of Justice of 21 June 1971, prepare annual reports on the subject with a view to recommending appropriate policies to the General Assembly, in order to counter the support that some States give to the illegal South African administration in Namibia;

(*e*) Continue taking measures to ensure the full implementation of Decree No. 1 for the Protection of the Natural Resources of Namibia, including legal proceedings in the domestic courts of States, in accordance with paragraph 59 of resolution 43/26 A;

(*f*) Consider the illegal activities of foreign economic interests, particularly the transnational corporations operating in Namibia, including the exploitation of and trade in Namibian uranium, with a view to recommending appropriate policies to the General Assembly, in order to put an end to such activities;

(*g*) Take measures to ensure the closure of the so-called information offices created by the illegal South African occupation régime in certain Western countries for promoting its puppet institutions in Namibia, in violation of resolutions and decisions of the United Nations on the question of Namibia;

(*h*) Notify the Governments of States whose corporations, whether public or private, operate in Namibia of the illegality of such operations and urge them to take measures to end such operations;

(*i*) Consider sending missions of consultation to Governments of States whose corporations have investments in Namibia in order to persuade them to take all possible measures to terminate such investments;

(*j*) Contact institutions and municipalities to encourage them to divest themselves of their investments in Namibia and South Africa;

(*k*) Contact specialized agencies and other international institutions associated with the United Nations, in particular the International Monetary Fund, with a view to protecting Namibia's interests;

(*l*) Draw the attention of States, the specialized agencies and private corporations to Decree No. 1 for the Protection of the Natural Resources of Namibia, with a view to ensuring their compliance with the Decree;

(*m*) Organize international and regional activities, as required, in order to obtain relevant information on all aspects of the situation in and relating to Namibia, in particular the exploitation of the people and resources of Namibia by South African and other foreign economic interests, and to expose such activities, with a view to intensifying active support for the Namibian cause;

(*n*) Secure the territorial integrity of Namibia as a unitary State, including Walvis Bay, the Penguin Islands and other offshore islands of Namibia;

13. *Decides* to make adequate financial provision in the section of the programme budget of the United Nations relating to the United Nations Council for Namibia for the financing of the office of the South

West Africa People's Organization in New York, in order to ensure appropriate representation of the people of Namibia at the United Nations through the South West Africa People's Organization;

14. *Decides also* to continue to defray the expenses of representatives of the South West Africa People's Organization, whenever the United Nations Council for Namibia so decides;

15. *Requests* the United Nations Council for Namibia to continue to consult with the South West Africa People's Organization in the formulation and implementation of its programme of work, as well as on all matters of interest to the Namibian people;

16. *Also requests* the United Nations Council for Namibia to facilitate the participation of the liberation movements recognized by the Organization of African Unity in meetings of the Council away from United Nations Headquarters, whenever such participation is deemed necessary;

17. *Decides* that, in order to expedite the training of the personnel required for an independent Namibia, qualified Namibians should be given opportunities to develop further their skills in the work of the United Nations Secretariat and the specialized agencies and other organizations of the United Nations system, and authorizes the United Nations Council for Namibia, in consultation with the South West Africa People's Organization, to take, on an urgent basis, necessary action towards that end;

18. *Takes note* of the consolidation of the Office of the United Nations Commissioner for Namibia and the secretariat of the United Nations Council for Namibia and in this regard requests the Secretary-General, in consultation with the President of the United Nations Council for Namibia, to ensure that the Council is provided with adequate secretariat assistance to help it to continue to discharge fully and effectively all tasks and functions arising out of its mandate.

General Assembly resolution 43/26 C

17 November 1988   Meeting 54   147-0-6 (recorded vote)

Draft by Council for Namibia (A/43/24); agenda item 29.
Financial implications. 5th Committee, A/43/818; S-G, A/C.5/43/34 & Add.1.
Meeting numbers. GA 43rd session: 5th Committee 33; plenary 47-52, 54.

Recorded vote in Assembly as follows:

In favour: Afghanistan, Albania, Algeria, Angola, Antigua and Barbuda, Argentina, Australia, Austria, Bahamas, Bahrain, Bangladesh, Barbados, Belgium, Benin, Bhutan, Bolivia, Botswana, Brazil, Brunei Darussalam, Bulgaria, Burkina Faso, Burma, Burundi, Byelorussian SSR, Cameroon, Cape Verde, Central African Republic, Chad, Chile, China, Colombia, Comoros, Congo, Côte d'Ivoire, Cuba, Cyprus, Czechoslovakia, Democratic Kampuchea, Democratic Yemen, Denmark, Djibouti, Dominica, Dominican Republic, Ecuador, Egypt, El Salvador, Ethiopia, Fiji, Finland, Gabon, Gambia, German Democratic Republic, Ghana, Greece, Grenada, Guatemala, Guinea, Guinea-Bissau, Guyana, Haiti, Honduras, Hungary, Iceland, India, Indonesia, Iran, Iraq, Ireland, Israel, Italy, Jamaica, Japan, Jordan, Kenya, Kuwait, Lao People's Democratic Republic, Lebanon, Lesotho, Liberia, Libyan Arab Jamahiriya, Luxembourg, Madagascar, Malawi, Malaysia, Maldives, Mali, Malta, Mauritius, Mexico, Mongolia, Morocco, Mozambique, Nepal, New Zealand, Nicaragua, Niger, Nigeria, Norway, Oman, Pakistan, Panama, Papua New Guinea, Peru, Philippines, Poland, Portugal, Qatar, Romania, Rwanda, Saint Kitts and Nevis, Saint Lucia, Saint Vincent and the Grenadines, Samoa, Sao Tome and Principe, Saudi Arabia, Senegal, Seychelles, Sierra Leone, Singapore, Solomon Islands, Somalia, Spain, Sri Lanka, Sudan, Suriname, Swaziland, Sweden, Syrian Arab Republic, Thailand, Togo, Trinidad and Tobago, Tunisia, Turkey, Uganda, Ukrainian SSR, USSR, United Arab Emirates, United Republic of Tanzania, Uruguay, Vanuatu, Venezuela, Viet Nam, Yemen, Yugoslavia, Zaire, Zambia, Zimbabwe.

Against: None.

Abstaining: Canada, France, Germany, Federal Republic of, Netherlands, United Kingdom, United States.

In **resolution 43/213**, the General Assembly invited the Secretary-General, in connection with the 1986 recommendation of the Group of High-level Intergovernmental Experts to Review the Efficiency of the Administrative and Financial Functioning of the United Nations,[38] to proceed with the reclassification of the post of the Secretary of the Council from the D-1 to the D-2 level, as he had suggested in an October report on implementation of the recommendation.[39] The Group had recommended that the support activities of the Council and of the Office of the Commissioner for Namibia be consolidated.

UN Commissioner for Namibia

Activities of the Commissioner

The United Nations Commissioner for Namibia continued in 1988 to perform the administrative and executive tasks entrusted to him by the Council for Namibia. Acting through his offices at United Nations Headquarters (New York), Gaborone (Botswana), Luanda (Angola) and Lusaka (Zambia), he was involved in the protection of Namibian interests, including the travel documents programme and efforts to ensure implementation of Decree No. 1 for the Protection of the Natural Resources of Namibia.[6] In this regard, the Commissioner continued to distribute publicity material on the plunder of Namibian resources in violation of the Decree. The Office of the Commissioner issued and renewed travel documents in Africa, North America and Western Europe. It collected and analysed information relating to Namibia and closely followed internal political, economic and legal developments in South Africa affecting Namibia.

The Office administered assistance programmes under the United Nations Fund for Namibia, which comprised three major components: the Nationhood Programme, the United Nations Institute for Namibia, and educational, social and relief activities. Under the third component, the Office carried out 16 projects.

The Office continued to undertake a number of studies, which included a revised version of a study on TNCs operating in Namibia, a summarized version of a demographic study of the Namibian population, and studies dealing with the socio-economic and legal situation prevailing in Namibia as well as the incomes and profits made by foreign economic interests operating illegally in the country.

The Luanda office served as a focal point for the co-ordination of assistance to Namibians and in this regard worked with agencies of the United Nations system represented in Angola to ensure a well-integrated inter-agency approach. The office organized inter-agency meetings on programme activities, missions to Angola and Namibian matters. Luanda being the provisional headquarters for SWAPO, the office was also a focal point for the appraisal of project ideas, formulation and evaluation. The major activities of the office therefore involved the management of ongoing projects under the Nationhood Programme (see below) and the implementation in Angola of seven newly approved projects. The office coordinated activities of bilateral and multilateral missions whose purpose was to select Namibians for training in various institutions, and participated in the field-attachment programme by securing the placement with the Angolan national airline, TAAG, of Namibian aircraft maintenance technicians. In close co-operation with SWAPO, the office assisted the Vocational Training Centre at Cuacra, Angola, as well as the Namibian Secondary Technical School at Loudima, Congo, which had become fully operational. The office also continued to co-ordinate assistance to SWAPO settlements and provided support for seminars on the establishment of the Namibian press agency, NAMPA, and on diplomacy for SWAPO cadres.

The Gaborone office continued to monitor political developments in Namibia and the region and to co-operate closely with SWAPO. It maintained close contacts with the Government of Botswana, diplomatic missions accredited to Botswana and other institutions on matters considered vital for the promotion of Namibian interests. From September 1987 to August 1988, the office issued 39 United Nations Council for Namibia travel and identity documents to Namibians, and extended the validity of 35 others. It also assisted in obtaining visas for Namibians wishing to transit through neighbouring countries.

The Lusaka office monitored and reported on the situation in southern Africa and worked closely with SWAPO. The management, monitoring, reappraisal and reporting on projects under the Nationhood Programme and the General Account of the Fund for Namibia continued to be its main task. Visits by various heads of State and Government, Foreign Ministers, heads of United Nations agencies and religious figures led to enhanced support for the office and contributions to the Nationhood Programme, as evidenced by the offers of financial assistance by EC to the Institute for Namibia and the field-attachment programme for Namibians. Similar contacts with the Association of West European Parliamentarians for Action against *Apartheid* resulted in an offer of financial assistance for agricultural activities in SWAPO settlements. The office maintained close relations with regional organizations, such as the Southern African Development Co-ordination Conference, the Multinational Programming and Operational Centres of the Economic Commission for Africa,

the preferential trade area, and the Eastern and Southern Africa Management Institute, as well as NGOs and private voluntary organizations. From June 1987 to August 1988, the office issued 907 new travel and identity documents and effected 1,857 renewals and 192 cancellations. Being an important operational centre for the field-attachment and individual scholarship programmes, the office succeeded in securing the agreement of a number of African Governments and parastatals to accept over 70 Namibian trainee graduates.

Extension of the Commissioner's appointment

On the Secretary-General's proposal,[40] the General Assembly, by **decision 43/311** of 17 November 1988, extended the appointment of Bernt Carlsson as United Nations Commissioner for Namibia for a one-year term beginning on 1 January 1989. His initial appointment, for six months, had begun on 1 July 1987.

On 21 December 1988, Mr. Carlsson was killed in an aeroplane crash.

REFERENCES

[1]YUN 1967, p. 709, GA res. 2248(S-V), 19 May 1967. [2]A/43/24. [3]A/44/24. [4]A/AC.131/279. [5]YUN 1978, p. 915, SC res. 435(1978), 29 Sep. 1978. [6]YUN 1974, p. 152. [7]A/AC.131/294. [8]A/AC.131/309. [9]YUN 1976, p. 789, GA res. 31/150, 20 Dec. 1976. [10]A/AC.131/301 & Corr.1. [11]YUN 1987, p. 1008, GA res. 42/14 C, 6 Nov. 1987. [12]A/AC.131/297. [13]YUN 1987, p. 997, GA res. 42/14 A, 6 Nov. 1987. [14]A/AC.131/289. [15]A/43/724. [16]YUN 1987, p. 1004, GA res. 42/14 B, 6 Nov. 1987. [17]A/43/23 (A/AC.109/967 & Corr.1.). [18]S/20110. [19]E/1988/12 (res. 1988/8). [20]*Ibid.* (res. 1988/10). [21]A/AC.131/284. [22]S/20412. [23]A/43/521-S/20109. [24]S/20129. [25]A/43/964-S/20325. [26]S/20345. [27]A/43/989-S/20346. [28]A/43/780. [29]A/C.4/43/7 & Add.1-5. [30]A/AC.131/283. [31]A/43/986-S/20342. [32]S/20203. [33]S/20208. [34]S/20336. [35]S/20337. [36]A/AC.131/282. [37]YUN 1987, p. 1012, GA res. 42/14 D, 6 Nov. 1987. [38]YUN 1986, p. 943. [39]A/C.5/43/1/Rev.1/Add.1. [40]A/43/807.

Economic and social conditions

Foreign investment and natural resources

The United Nations Council for Namibia, in its 1988 report to the General Assembly,[1] and its Standing Committee II in a July report[2] characterized the basic structure of the Namibian economy as typically colonial, almost exclusively tailored to the needs and demands of foreign capital, and highly skewed towards the production of primary export commodities. The three principal extractive industries—mining, farming and fishing—accounted for more than 40 per cent of the gross domestic product (GDP), generated more than 90 per cent of exports and engaged over 80 per cent of all paid employment. In terms of economic ties, Namibia had been kept totally dependent on South Africa, which treated the Territory virtually as its fifth province, as a repository of physical wealth and as a captive annexed market for its own economy.

The economic history of Namibia showed a consistent pattern of collusion and mutual support between South Africa and TNCs operating in the Territory. The *apartheid* régime maintained conditions under which foreign interests could reap large profits from exploitation of Namibia's economic resources. TNCs, in turn, assisted South Africa in its illegal occupation by paying taxes, providing fuel and other supplies for the occupation forces and collaborating with South Africa in its violation of international law.

Namibia was endowed with abundant natural wealth, including uranium, gem diamonds, copper, lead, zinc, manganese and other metals, as well as agricultural and fishery products. These resources, however, were exclusively controlled and illegally exploited by South African and other foreign economic interests.

Namibia's mineral wealth included a wide range of base metals and other precious metals of strategic importance, which made up 20 per cent of the total output of the mining sector in value. Almost all of the zinc, tin, lead, vanadium and tungsten extracted from the Territory went to South Africa and its Western allies.

Over 70 per cent of Namibia's base metal production came from the Tsumeb Corporation, Ltd., which produced blister copper, refined lead, zinc, gold, silver and other minerals. Gold Fields of South Africa (GFSA) owned 47 per cent of Tsumeb, the Newmont Mining Corporation of the United States owned 31 per cent and British Petroleum Minerals International owned 14 per cent, with the rest being owned mainly by South African firms. In April 1988, Newmont Mining Corporation reportedly sold its entire share to GFSA.

All of the uranium produced in Namibia was exported. Given the illegal nature of the distribution and processing of that uranium, most transport companies and processing plants sought to conceal their involvement. One of the major processing companies in Europe was Urenco, Ltd., a joint venture of Uranisotopenenttrennungsgesellschaft (URANIT) of the Federal Republic of Germany, Ultra-Centrifugue Nederland (UCN) of the Netherlands and British Nuclear Fuels.

In an effort to implement Decree No. 1 for the Protection of the Natural Resources of Namibia,[3] the Council had instituted in 1987[4] legal proceedings in a district court of The Hague against Urenco Nederland V.O.F., UCN and the Government of the Netherlands, seeking to prevent Urenco from carrying out orders based on purchases of Namibian uranium. Following the defendants' submission of statements of defence on 3 May 1988, the court adjourned the case to allow the lawyers representing the Council to submit their reply.

The exploitation of Namibia's diamonds was monopolized by Consolidated Diamond Mines (CDM), one of the world's largest gem diamond producers and the oldest and largest of the mining companies operating in the Territory. CDM was a wholly owned subsidiary of De Beers Consolidated Mines, Ltd., of South Africa, which itself was 30 per cent owned by the Anglo-American Corporation of South Africa, Ltd.

International banks had a long history of involvement in Namibia without necessarily maintaining commercial operations there. Many towns in Namibia had been transformed into army camps, and financial services were part of the infrastructure that had been developed to sustain the military occupation.

Namibia's commercial and manufacturing sectors produced 10 to 15 per cent of its GDP and, like the service sector, were dominated by South African and other foreign economic interests which exploited Namibia's raw materials, transferred them elsewhere for processing and used the Territory as a captive market for manufactured goods. Some 80 per cent of those manufactured goods were produced in South Africa, with the balance originating in third countries and imported into Namibia by South African–owned trading companies. The unrestricted entry of South African goods into Namibia inhibited the growth of local industry and perpetuated its dependence on South Africa.

Livestock farming accounted for 80 to 90 per cent of the overall value of commercial agriculture, but had been severely affected by the drought conditions over the previous 10 years. Most of the cattle produced in Namibia were taken to South Africa on the hoof or after being slaughtered at local abattoirs. The remainder were shipped to Western European markets in the form of frozen cuts and canned beef. The sole meat-processing concern in the country was Swavleis, which operated plants at Okahandja and Windhoek.

South African companies had virtually monopolized the Namibian fishing industry over the previous 25 years, holding 11 of the 12 pelagic licences as well as the entire lobster concession, and receiving 80 per cent of the fishing quotas. Fishing in the offshore waters of Namibia was regulated by the International Commission for South-East Atlantic Fisheries (ICSEAF) and the International Commission for the Conservation of Atlantic Tunas (ICCAT). In view of the early accession of the Council for Namibia to the 1982 United Nations Convention on the Law of the Sea,[5] the

Council expected ICSEAF and ICCAT members to conduct their operations with due regard to that instrument and in the interests of the Namibian people.

As requested in 1987 by the Economic and Social Council,[6] the Secretary-General submitted to the Commission on Transnational Corporations, in February 1988,[7] a report summarizing the activities of TNCs in South Africa and Namibia (see PART TWO, Chapter I). Another report[8] dealt with the responsibilities of home countries with respect to TNCs operating in the region in violation of United Nations resolutions. A third report[9] listed TNCs with interests in companies in South Africa and Namibia which had disposed of or reduced their interests or were in the process of so doing.

The Committee on colonial countries, in a consensus of 8 August,[10] condemned the activities of all foreign economic interests operating in Namibia and demanded their immediate withdrawal, declaring that, by their exploitation of resources and accumulation of profits, they constituted a major obstacle to Namibia's independence. It demanded that those States whose TNCs continued to operate in Namibia comply with United Nations resolutions by ensuring the immediate withdrawal of all investments from Namibia and putting an end to co-operation of such corporations with the illegal South African administration. The Committee reaffirmed that the activities of foreign economic interests were considered to be illegal under international law and that they would be liable to pay damages to a future lawful Namibian Government. It further reaffirmed that Namibia's natural resources were the inviolable heritage of the Namibian people and expressed deep concern at their depletion in violation of United Nations resolutions and Decree No. 1. In addition, the Committee condemned the exploitation of Namibian uranium by State-owned or State-controlled corporations, and supported the initiation by the Council of legal proceedings.

The General Assembly, by **resolution 43/29**, reaffirmed that, by the exploitation of Namibia's natural resources and the repatriation of huge profits, foreign economic, financial and other interests constituted a major obstacle to political independence and racial equality in Namibia. The Assembly called on States to terminate investments in Namibia and loans to South Africa, reiterated that all foreign economic interests in Namibia were illegal, and declared that consequently South Africa and such interests would be liable to pay damages to the future legitimate Government of an independent Namibia. The Assembly condemned South Africa for its continued plundering of Namibia's natural resources, in complete disregard of the legitimate interests of the Namib-

ian people. It also condemned the plunder of Namibian uranium and called on all States, particularly those whose nationals and corporations were involved in mining and processing Namibian uranium, to comply with Decree No. 1.

In **resolution 43/26 A**, the Assembly demanded that all foreign economic interests in Namibia comply with relevant United Nations resolutions by immediatcly withdrawing from the Territory. It reaffirmed that the natural resources of Namibia were the inviolable heritage of its people, and expressed deep concern at their depletion, particularly the uranium deposits. All Member States were requested to comply with Decree No. 1.

The Assembly, in **resolution 43/26 C**, decided that the Council for Namibia should continue taking measures to ensure the implementation of Decree No. 1, including taking legal proceedings in domestic courts, and consider the illegal activities of foreign economic interests, particularly TNCs operating in Namibia.

Social conditions and exploitation of labour

The Council for Namibia[1] and its Standing Committee II[11] reviewed the social conditions in Namibia. They reported that during 1988, the conditions continued to deteriorate as a result of South Africa's occupation and its repressive policies and practices.

In 1964, South Africa had begun to impose its *apartheid* policy of fragmentation on Namibia, dividing it into several "homelands". That policy was expanded in 1980 when Namibians were divided into 11 mutually exclusive groups on the basis of racial, ethnic and tribal origins. The system of "Bantu education" was also designed to perpetuate white supremacy by training blacks for subservient jobs in the local economy. Basic education was compulsory for white but not for black children. The allocation for education of a white child was seven times greater than that for a black child. The disparity in the statistics of black and white students who completed high school was even more glaring, since almost all black Namibians were forced to forgo high school education in order to work and help support their families. A good number were expelled because of their opposition to South Africa's occupation and their support for SWAPO.

The health sector in Namibia was also linked to the *apartheid* system and was consequently characterized by gross inequalities. Health services for the black majority were rudimentary at best and in many areas virtually non-existent. South Africa's policies of racial fragmentation and mandatory inferior living conditions for the blacks were major underlying causes of the wide disparity in the health conditions between blacks and whites. With the exception of commercial farmers, whites lived in urban areas where housing was of high quality and they were assured clean water, sewage disposal facilities and all conveniences of modern living. Blacks, on the other hand, were forced to live in squalid, unhygienic conditions in the "homelands".

Malnutrition, abject poverty, overcrowded living conditions and an unsanitary environment contributed to the spread of diseases almost unknown among whites. The difference between the health facilities provided for whites and blacks was manifested in infant mortality and life expectancy rates: the infant mortality rate of blacks was more than eight times that of whites, and life expectancy for blacks ranged from 42 to 52 years, compared to 68 to 72 years for whites. Health services continued to deteriorate, clinics were closed and the number of medical personnel was reduced.

The general public continued to suffer from the repression and violation of human rights under the South African administration. The terrorization of the population through killings, systematic torture, abductions, detentions without trial and disappearances of civilians were carried out by paramilitary squads such as *Koevoet*, *Takkies* and *Etango*. Their atrocities were facilitated by the information black-out throughout Namibia.

An attempt was made to silence the newspaper *The Namibian*, which had been critical of South Africa's administration in Namibia. An arson attack on 10 October destroyed its offices in Windhoek.

At hearings convened in Washington, D.C., from 2 to 4 May, the President of the National Council of the Churches of Christ in the United States testified that Ignatius Nambodi, a Catholic mission worker detained by South African authorities on 2 February and found dead in his cell 20 days later, was never allowed a visit by a lawyer, a member of the clergy or even his family.

On 6 May, the President of SWAPO informed the Council that 16 schools had been destroyed recently in north-western and north-eastern Namibia. He said that occupation police and army were empowered to kill people and destroy property.

The Council reported several cases where the South African military and police committed atrocities against Namibians,[12] including the rape of women and children, as well as beatings.

The fact that many Namibians had been dispossessed of their land and the continuing state of war and repression had resulted in large numbers of Namibians fleeing their native land to seek refuge in neighbouring countries, particularly Angola and Zambia. The Office of the United Nations High Commissioner for Refugees (UNHCR) estimated that there were 70,000 to 80,000 Namibian refugees in Angola, Zambia and other neigh-

bouring countries. Refugee camps in Angola were a principal target of attack by South African occupation forces based in Namibia.

The *apartheid* system in Namibia continued to ensure a cheap labour force, with the greater part of the black labour force made up of migrants on short-term contracts. Many employers continued to hire workers without guarantees of renewals, and to house them in large all-male dormitories known as compounds or hostels. These were usually isolated from local communities and in many cases controlled by armed guards.

The conditions under which Namibian labourers worked were extremely exploitative. They had no statutory rights to a pension, set pay, holiday pay or maternity leave. A worker could be dismissed without prior notice and such occurrences were frequent. Furthermore, they were not legally entitled to compensation for dismissal or to unemployment benefits. Working conditions were often dangerous and unhealthy, exposing them to racism, abuse and beatings in their workplaces. On farms, there had been numerous cases in which workers had been brutally assaulted or killed by employers for minor misdemeanours.

Black trade unions faced harassment and repression, and worker's protests had been violently suppressed by the police and army. It was also illegal for registered trade unions to assist or be affiliated with any political party.

In 1988, labour activities of the National Union of Namibian Workers centred around the "Campaign for a Living Wage". The membership of the Union rose to an estimated 40,000 in 1988. An agreement concerning wages and working conditions was signed by the Mineworkers Union of Namibia (MUN) and Consolidated Diamond Mines on 14 December. Rössing Uranium signed a recognition agreement with MUN endorsing collective bargaining, freedom of association and dispute procedures. Lalandil, a large employer in the seasonal crayfish industry in Lüderitz, reached agreement with the Namibian Food and Allied Workers Union (NAFAU) on wages and conditions of employment for seasonal fisheries and factory workers. Another Lüderitz firm, SWAFIL, signed a recognition agreement with NAFAU but did not resolve issues on transport, job security and pension.

The Secretary-General submitted to the Commission on the Status of Women in 1988 a report on developments in the situation of women under *apartheid* in South Africa and Namibia[13] (see PART THREE, Chapter XIII).

ECONOMIC AND SOCIAL COUNCIL ACTION

On 26 May, the Economic and Social Council, on the recommendation of its Second (Social) Committee, adopted **resolution 1988/24** by recorded vote.

Women and children in Namibia

The Economic and Social Council,

Recalling its resolution 1986/23 of 23 May 1986,

Recalling also the Nairobi Forward-looking Strategies for the Advancement of Women, in particular paragraph 259, which calls for the speedy and effective implementation of Security Council resolution 435(1978) of 29 September 1978 concerning the independence of Namibia,

Gravely concerned about the delay in the implementation of Security Council resolution 435(1978) regarding the withdrawal of South Africa's illegal administration from Namibia and the holding of elections under the supervision of the United Nations,

Deeply concerned about the perpetual suffering of Namibian women under the illegal occupation of the racist South African régime, and further concerned about the use of Namibian territory as a springboard for attacking and destabilizing neighbouring States,

Having considered the report of the Secretary-General on new developments concerning the situation of women under *apartheid* in South Africa and Namibia and measures of assistance to women from South Africa and Namibia who have become refugees as a result of the practice of *apartheid,*

1. *Condemns,* in no uncertain terms, the racist régime of South Africa for its installation of a so-called interim Government at Windhoek;

2. *Denounces* the forcible conscription of Namibian men and women between the ages of 17 and 55 years into the racist army, as well as the detention of children, practices which consolidate and facilitate widespread repression throughout the country;

3. *Rejects* South Africa's insistence on linking the independence of Namibia to the withdrawal of Cuban troops from Angola;

4. *Demands* the release of all political prisoners, among whom are included women and children, and the lifting of the state of emergency imposed by South Africa for more than twelve years;

5. *Demands* that South Africa refrain from using Namibia as a base from which to infiltrate Angola and other independent neighbouring countries;

6. *Calls upon* all women of the world to support and assist all bodies struggling to put an end to colonialism in Namibia;

7. *Requests* the Secretary-General to submit to the Commission on the Status of Women at its thirty-third session a comprehensive report on monitoring the implementation of the Nairobi Forward-looking Strategies for the Advancement of Women with regard to women and children in Namibia.

Economic and Social Council resolution 1988/24

26 May 1988	Meeting 15	44-0-9 (recorded vote)

Approved by Second Committee (E/1988/90) by recorded vote (38-0-9), 13 May (meeting 9); draft by Commission on women (E/1988/15); agenda item 11.

Recorded vote in Council as follows:

In favour: Australia, Bolivia, Bulgaria, Byelorussian SSR, China, Colombia, Cuba, Denmark, Djibouti, Egypt, Gabon, German Democratic Republic, Ghana, Greece, Guinea, India, Iran, Iraq, Ireland, Jamaica, Lesotho, Liberia, Libyan Arab Jamahiriya, Mozambique, Norway, Oman, Pakistan, Panama, Peru, Philippines, Poland, Rwanda, Saudi Arabia, Sierra Leone, Somalia, Sri Lanka, Sudan, Syrian Arab Republic, Trinidad and Tobago, USSR, Uruguay, Venezuela, Yugoslavia, Zaire.

Against: None.

Abstaining: Belgium, Canada, France, Germany, Federal Republic of, Italy, Japan, Portugal, United Kingdom, United States.

GENERAL ASSEMBLY ACTION

The General Assembly, in **resolution 43/106**, condemned South Africa for its increased brutal repression of the Namibian people, as manifested by arrest and detention without trial of SWAPO leaders, trade unionists and church leaders, the cold-blooded murder and torture of children, women and the elderly, and the bombing and destruction of social and educational institutions. In **resolution 43/134**, the Assembly expressed outrage at and condemned the detention, torture and inhuman treatment of children in Namibia. **Resolution 43/116** included the Assembly's call on the international community to increase assistance to the countries of southern Africa to enable them to provide facilities and services to refugees, returnees and displaced persons.

REFERENCES

[1]A/43/24. [2]A/AC.131/286. [3]YUN 1974, p. 152. [4]YUN 1987, p. 1019. [5]YUN 1982, p. 181. [6]YUN 1987, p. 148, ESC res. 1987/56, 28 May 1987. [7]E/C.10/1988/7. [8]E/C.10/1988/8. [9]E/1988/23 & Corr.1-3. [10]A/43/23 (A/AC.109/967 & Corr.1). [11]A/AC.131/285. [12]A/44/24. [13]E/CN.6/1988/2.

International assistance

Throughout 1988, the Council for Namibia and other United Nations bodies continued to provide and co-ordinate assistance to the Namibian freedom struggle. Most of the funding, mainly voluntary contributions, was provided through the United Nations Fund for Namibia, while additional funding was provided through the United Nations regular budget, the United Nations Development Programme (UNDP) and specialized agencies. The Fund operated the Nationhood Programme for Namibia, financing training programmes and surveys of the economic and social sectors in preparation for independence, and the United Nations Institute for Namibia, involving research, training and planning activities. In addition, the Fund had a programme for educational, social and relief assistance dealing with the immediate needs of Namibians.

Appeals for increased assistance to deal with the growing needs of Namibia were made by several organs of the United Nations. On 8 August,[1] the Committee on colonial countries urged all Governments, specialized agencies and other intergovernmental organizations to increase material assistance to the Namibian refugees who had been forced to flee Namibia, especially into the neighbouring front-line States.

The Economic and Social Council, in **resolution 1988/53**, requested United Nations organizations, as a matter of urgency, to render increased assistance to the Namibian people, in consultation with OAU and the Council for Namibia, in particular in connection with the Nationhood Programme.

The General Assembly, in **decision 43/410**, appealed to all States to render sustained and increased moral and political support, as well as assistance in all fields, to SWAPO to enable it to intensify its struggle. In **resolution 43/30**, the Assembly expressed concern that the assistance extended thus far by certain United Nations organizations to the Namibian people and SWAPO was far from adequate in relation to actual needs. Those organizations were urged, as a matter of priority, to extend substantial material assistance to the front-line States to enable them to support more effectively the Namibian freedom struggle.

UN Fund for Namibia

Activities of the Fund

The United Nations Fund for Namibia, for which voluntary contributions were the major financial source, continued to serve in 1988 as the main instrument through which the Council for Namibia, acting as its trustee, channelled assistance to Namibians. The Fund had three main programmes with separate accounts: the Nationhood Programme for Namibia; the United Nations Institute for Namibia; and educational, social and relief assistance (General Account).

The United Nations Commissioner for Namibia submitted progress reports for the Nationhood Programme and activities under the General Account as at 30 June[2] and 31 December[3] 1988. While the Nationhood Programme and the Institute were set up with particular reference to the future attainment of independence, the establishment of State machinery and the assumption of administrative responsibilities, the General Account provided individual scholarships and catered to the immediate needs and the welfare of Namibians in their independence struggle. Fund expenditures for the three programmes totalled $12,832,050 in 1988 as follows: Nationhood Programme, $2,389,679; Institute, $6,355,902; and General Account, $4,086,469.

Nationhood Programme

The Nationhood Programme consisted of two major components: manpower training programmes, and surveys and analyses of Namibian economic and social sectors, including identification of development tasks and policy options. Through the Programme, hundreds of Namibians continued their training at various institutions,

mostly in African countries. Fields of training included mining and marine engineering, pilot training, aircraft maintenance, nurses' training, remedial training in English, mathematics and physics, public administration, journalism, agriculture, railway operations and fisheries.

A total of 16 new projects and 26 project revisions were approved in 1988 by the Council for Namibia, for which a total of $3,674,118 was approved from the Nationhood Programme Account. More than 350 Namibians completed their training in 1988 with an equal number of new students having enrolled.

At the end of June 1988, more than 60 Namibians were undergoing attachment training in Ethiopia, Kenya, Nigeria, the United Republic of Tanzania, Zambia and Zimbabwe. Areas of training included civil aviation, telecommunications, postal services, railway operations, tropical disease control, law, fisheries, agriculture and meat packing.

The United Nations Vocational Training Centre at Cuacra, Angola, operated at full capacity with an enrolment of about 200 trainees in auto mechanics, machine shop and fitting, electrical installations, plumbing, carpentry, and building and construction. A group of 81 trainees graduated in December.

UN Institute for Namibia

The United Nations Institute for Namibia, at Lusaka, continued to train middle-level skilled manpower for an independent Namibia and carried out applied research in a variety of sectors of the Namibian economy. The research programme was intended to make available basic documentation for policy formulation by the future Government of an independent Namibia. In 1988, 157 new students were admitted to programmes of the Institute, which included management and development studies, teacher-training upgrading, and a secretarial programme. This brought the total student body to 562. The ninth graduating group, comprising 113 students, received diplomas in management and development studies, bringing the number of graduates in this field to 757. The Institute's diplomas were underwritten by the University of Zambia. In addition, 29 students were awarded teaching diplomas in basic education and 26 students received certificates in the secretarial training programmes, bringing the Institute's total number of graduates since its inception to 1,020. The Namibian Extension Unit, an autonomous body established in 1981, continued to expand its distance education programme for Namibians who had been denied education in Namibia. It was currently serving several thousand Namibian adults and youths in Zambia and Angola.

General Account

Educational, social and relief assistance, particularly in the form of scholarships, was the main activity financed by the Fund's General Account. It also financed vocational and technical training; provided assistance in health and medical care, nutrition and social welfare; acquired books and periodicals for Namibian refugee camps and SWAPO offices; and facilitated the attendance of Namibian representatives at international seminars, meetings and conferences.

Between 1 July 1987 and 30 June 1988, the demand for scholarships continued to increase and 87 new awards were approved. As at 30 June 1988, 266 Namibians were being sponsored under the scholarship programme in 17 countries, with the majority in the United States. Most educational assistance was granted at the post-secondary level, but a few students were sponsored at primary and secondary levels. Fields of study included education, agriculture, business administration, economics, accounting, journalism, engineering, public administration, animal husbandry, motor mechanics and tailoring.

All new training activities were constituted as projects. Since the beginning of 1988, nine new projects and nine project revisions had been approved by the Committee on the United Nations Fund for Namibia. Those projects provided for the education and training of Namibians at various levels, among them diploma and degree programmes in Barbados, Guyana, the United Kingdom and Zimbabwe. A group of trainees continued their course in video and cinematography, and radio broadcasters continued in-service training at various African radio stations. The Fund also became increasingly involved in the financing of the operational costs of the Namibian Technical Secondary School of Loudima, Congo, which in mid-1988 had 247 students.

Financing of the Fund

The major source of financing of the United Nations Fund for Namibia remained voluntary contributions. In 1988, 35 countries paid nearly $8 million to the Fund: $2,060,966 to the Nationhood Programme, $4,513,041 to the Institute, and $1,339,579 to the General Account. In addition, the Fund was financed from the United Nations regular budget. For 1988, the General Assembly allocated $1.5 million, as determined in a 1987 resolution.[(4)] Funding was also provided by UNDP. On 1 July,[(5)] the UNDP Governing Council increased the indicative planning figure for Namibia for the 1987-1991 programming cycle to $10.6 million.

On 8 August,[(1)] the Committee on colonial countries urgently called on all States and the United Nations system to support the Fund for Namibia and all programmes of assistance organized by the Council to benefit the Namibian people and to prepare them for the responsibilities of independent nationhood.

GENERAL ASSEMBLY ACTION

On 17 November, the General Assembly adopted **resolution 43/26 E** by recorded vote.

United Nations Fund for Namibia

The General Assembly,

Having examined the parts of the report of the United Nations Council for Namibia relating to the United Nations Fund for Namibia,

Recalling its resolution 2679(XXV) of 9 December 1970, by which it established the United Nations Fund for Namibia,

Recalling its resolution 3112(XXVIII) of 12 December 1973, by which it appointed the United Nations Council for Namibia trustee of the United Nations Fund for Namibia,

Recalling also its resolution 31/153 of 20 December 1976, by which it decided to launch the Nationhood Programme for Namibia,

Recalling further its resolution 34/92 A of 12 December 1979, by which it approved the charter of the United Nations Institute for Namibia, and its resolution 37/233 E of 20 December 1982, by which it approved amendments to the charter,

1. *Takes note* of the relevant parts of the report of the United Nations Council for Namibia;

2. *Decides* that the United Nations Council for Namibia shall:

(a) Continue to formulate policies of assistance to Namibians and co-ordinate assistance for Namibia provided by the specialized agencies and other organizations and institutions of the United Nations system;

(b) Continue to act as trustee of the United Nations Fund for Namibia and, in this capacity, administer and manage the Fund;

(c) Continue to provide broad guidelines and formulate principles and policies for the United Nations Institute for Namibia;

(d) Continue to co-ordinate, plan and direct the Nationhood Programme for Namibia, in consultation with the South West Africa People's Organization, with the aim of consolidating all measures of assistance by the specialized agencies and other organizations and institutions of the United Nations system into a comprehensive assistance programme;

(e) Continue to consult with the South West Africa People's Organization in the formulation and implementation of assistance programmes for Namibians;

(f) Report to the General Assembly at its forty-fourth session on the programmes and activities undertaken through the United Nations Fund for Namibia;

3. *Decides* that the United Nations Fund for Namibia, which comprises the General Account, the United Nations Institute for Namibia Account and the Nationhood Programme Account, shall be the primary source of development assistance to Namibians;

4. *Expresses its appreciation* to all States, specialized agencies and other organizations of the United Nations system, governmental and non-governmental organizations and individuals that have made contributions to

the United Nations Fund for Namibia to support the activities under the General Account, the activities of the United Nations Institute for Namibia and the Nationhood Programme for Namibia, and calls upon them to increase their assistance to Namibians through those channels;

5. *Requests* the Secretary-General and the President of the United Nations Council for Namibia to intensify appeals to Governments, intergovernmental and non-governmental organizations and individuals for more generous voluntary contributions to the General Account, the Nationhood Programme Account and the United Nations Institute for Namibia Account of the United Nations Fund for Namibia in view of the increased activities undertaken through the Fund for Namibia, and, in this connection, emphasizes the need for contributions in order to increase the number of scholarships awarded to Namibians under the United Nations Fund for Namibia;

6. *Invites* Governments to appeal once more to their national organizations and institutions for voluntary contributions to the United Nations Fund for Namibia;

7. *Decides* to allocate as a temporary measure to the United Nations Fund for Namibia the sum of 1.5 million dollars from the regular budget of the United Nations for 1989;

8. *Requests* the United Nations Commissioner for Namibia, in order to mobilize additional resources, to continue to formulate, in consultation with the South West Africa People's Organization, projects of assistance to the Namibian people to be co-financed by Governments and non-governmental organizations;

9. *Requests* the specialized agencies and other organizations and institutions of the United Nations system, in the light of the urgent need to strengthen the programmes of assistance to the Namibian people, to make every effort to expedite the execution of projects under the Nationhood Programme for Namibia and other projects in favour of Namibians on the basis of procedures which will reflect the role of the United Nations Council for Namibia as the legal Administering Authority for Namibia;

10. *Expresses its appreciation* to those specialized agencies and other organizations and institutions of the United Nations system that have contributed to the Nationhood Programme for Namibia, and calls upon them to continue their participation in the Programme by:

(a) Implementing projects approved by the United Nations Council for Namibia;

(b) Planning and initiating new project proposals in co-operation with, and at the request of, the Council;

(c) Allocating funds from their own financial resources for the implementation of the projects approved by the Council;

11. *Commends* the progress made in the implementation of the pre-independence components of the Nationhood Programme for Namibia, and requests the United Nations Council for Namibia to continue to elaborate and consider policies and contingency plans regarding the transitional and post-independence phases of the Programme;

12. *Requests* the United Nations Council for Namibia to continue and to intensify its field attachment programme, enabling Namibians trained under various programmes to gain practical on-the-job experience in Governments and institutions in diverse countries, particularly in Africa;

13. *Appeals* to all Governments, specialized agencies and other organizations and institutions of the United Nations system, non-governmental organizations and individuals to make generous contributions to the United Nations Fund for Namibia in order to support the field attachment programme and to meet its financial requirements;

14. *Expresses its appreciation* to the United Nations Development Programme for its increased contribution to the financing and administration of the Nationhood Programme for Namibia and the financing of the United Nations Institute for Namibia, and calls upon it to continue to allocate, at the request of the United Nations Council for Namibia, funds from the indicative planning figure for Namibia for the projects under the Nationhood Programme and for the Institute, taking into consideration that Namibia remains a unique responsibility of the United Nations, and to exercise maximum flexibility and understanding in approving projects funded from the indicative planning figure;

15. *Expresses its appreciation* for the assistance provided by the United Nations Children's Fund, the Office of the United Nations High Commissioner for Refugees and the World Food Programme to Namibian refugees, and requests them to expand their assistance in order to provide for the basic needs of the refugees;

16. *Expresses its appreciation* to those specialized agencies and other organizations of the United Nations system which have waived agency support costs in respect of projects in favour of Namibians, financed from the United Nations Fund for Namibia and other sources, and urges those that have not yet done so to take appropriate steps in this regard;

17. *Decides* that Namibians shall continue to be eligible for assistance through the United Nations Educational and Training Programme for Southern Africa and the United Nations Trust Fund for South Africa;

18. *Commends* the United Nations Institute for Namibia for the effectiveness of its training programmes for Namibians and its research activities on Namibia, which contribute substantially to the struggle for freedom of the Namibian people and to the establishment of an independent State of Namibia;

19. *Urges* the specialized agencies and other organizations and institutions of the United Nations system to co-operate closely with the United Nations Institute for Namibia in strengthening its programme of activities;

20. *Requests* the United Nations Council for Namibia, in consultation with the South West Africa People's Organization, to finalize and publish, at an early date, a demographic study of the Namibian population;

21. *Requests* the Secretary-General to continue to provide the Office of the United Nations Commissioner for Namibia with the necessary resources for the performance of the responsibilities entrusted to it by the United Nations Council for Namibia as the co-ordinating authority for the implementation of the Nationhood Programme for Namibia, as well as other assistance programmes.

General Assembly resolution 43/26 E

17 November 1988   Meeting 54   148-0-5 (recorded vote)

Draft by Council for Namibia (A/43/24); agenda item 29.
Financial implications. 5th Committee, A/43/818; S-G, A/C.5/43/34 & Add.1.
Meeting numbers. GA 43rd session: 5th Committee 33; plenary 47-52, 54.

Recorded vote in Assembly as follows:

In favour: Afghanistan, Albania, Algeria, Angola, Antigua and Barbuda, Argentina, Australia, Austria, Bahamas, Bahrain, Bangladesh, Barbados, Belgium, Benin, Bhutan, Bolivia, Botswana, Brazil, Brunei Darussalam, Bulgaria, Burkina Faso, Burma, Burundi, Byelorussian SSR, Cameroon, Cape Verde, Central African Republic, Chad, Chile, China, Colombia, Comoros, Congo, Côte d'Ivoire, Cuba, Cyprus, Czechoslovakia, Democratic Kampuchea, Democratic Yemen, Denmark, Djibouti, Dominica, Dominican Republic, Ecuador, Egypt, El Salvador, Ethiopia, Fiji, Finland, Gabon, Gambia, German Democratic Republic, Ghana, Greece, Grenada, Guatemala, Guinea, Guinea-Bissau, Guyana, Haiti, Honduras, Hungary, Iceland, India, Indonesia, Iran, Iraq, Ireland, Israel, Italy, Jamaica, Japan, Jordan, Kenya, Kuwait, Lao People's Democratic Republic, Lebanon, Lesotho, Liberia, Libyan Arab Jamahiriya, Luxembourg, Madagascar, Malawi, Malaysia, Maldives, Mali, Malta, Mauritius, Mexico, Mongolia, Morocco, Mozambique, Nepal, Netherlands, New Zealand, Nicaragua, Niger, Nigeria, Norway, Oman, Pakistan, Panama, Papua New Guinea, Peru, Philippines, Poland, Portugal, Qatar, Romania, Rwanda, Saint Kitts and Nevis, Saint Lucia, Saint Vincent and the Grenadines, Samoa, Sao Tome and Principe, Saudi Arabia, Senegal, Seychelles, Sierra Leone, Singapore, Solomon Islands, Somalia, Spain, Sri Lanka, Sudan, Suriname, Swaziland, Sweden, Syrian Arab Republic, Thailand, Togo, Trinidad and Tobago, Tunisia, Turkey, Uganda, Ukrainian SSR, USSR, United Arab Emirates, United Republic of Tanzania, Uruguay, Vanuatu, Venezuela, Viet Nam, Yemen, Yugoslavia, Zaire, Zambia, Zimbabwe.

Against: None.

Abstaining: Canada, France, Germany, Federal Republic of, United Kingdom, United States.

Other UN assistance

UN Educational and Training Programme. In a report to the General Assembly,[6] the Secretary-General stated that the United Nations Educational and Training Programme for Southern Africa (see PART TWO, Chapter I), during the period 1 October 1987 to 31 August 1988, granted 201 new scholarships to Namibians and extended 278, in addition to those financed by the United Nations Fund for Namibia.

UNDP activities. According to a 1989 report[7] of the UNDP Administrator, UNDP provided assistance to SWAPO in 1988 through eight projects totalling $1,928,000. The projects included assistance to SWAPO settlements in Zambia and Angola, the securing of a food supply to the United Nations Vocational Training Centre for Namibia at Cuacra, the training of SWAPO teachers, external aid management and administration, promotion of women's participation in development, health service, and maintenance and mechanical repair services.

Agency assistance. United Nations specialized agencies and other organizations continued to provide assistance to colonial countries, including Namibia. The Secretary-General reported on such assistance in 1988,[8] with a follow-up report in 1989.[9]

Among those agencies reporting on their assistance to Namibians, the United Nations Educational, Scientific and Cultural Organization (UNESCO) stated that it undertook social sciences research, increased public awareness of the situation in Namibia and provided training in its fields of competence to Namibian cadres. UNESCO assistance was designed to combat South African propaganda, mobilize public opinion and provide a basis for planning a post-*apartheid* society. Two books were published in 1988 with UNESCO as-

sistance: *A History of Resistance in Namibia* and *De l'ethnicisme comme moyen d'enfermement des populations sudafricaines*, which had one chapter on Namibia.

The International Civil Aviation Organization (ICAO) continued to co-operate with the Council for Namibia, invited it to its relevant meetings and participated in the Nationhood Programme. ICAO advised the Commissioner for Namibia regarding placement of trained personnel in the civil aviation departments and airlines of other African countries to obtain practical experience.

UNHCR, within the terms of its humanitarian and non-political mandate, continued to deliver material assistance for the benefit of Namibian refugees. In Angola, where some 69,000 Namibians had sought refuge by mid-1988, the main emphasis of UNHCR assistance was placed on self-sufficiency and productivity. Areas of activity included agriculture, a textile workshop, mechanical and teacher training, as well as general education. Smaller numbers of Namibian refugees in Botswana, Mozambique, Zambia and Zimbabwe received similar support. Some 400 Namibian students were transferred in 1988 from Luanda to Lusaka. In Zambia, assistance was provided to Nyango Farm, for Namibian refugees under the care of SWAPO. UNHCR also maintained its annual contribution of $30,000 to the United Nations Institute for Namibia, which trained professional cadres in preparation for Namibian independence.

The International Labour Organisation (ILO), of which Namibia was a full member, maintained active collaboration with the United Nations Commissioner for Namibia, especially as regards programmes of technical assistance within the framework of the Nationhood Programme. ILO activities covered vocational training, rehabilitation, employment planning and creation, rural development, labour administration, workers' education, small enterprise development, migrant workers and fellowship schemes. In the field of vocational training, courses in several trades were held at the Pilot Vocational Training Centre for Namibians at Cuacra. The Centre's second batch of students, of whom 60 per cent were women, graduated in December. Under a project on vocational rehabilitation of war victims and other disabled persons, 45 disabled Namibians completed both basic education and skills training in a number of Zambian institutions.

The Food and Agriculture Organization of the United Nations carried out surveys and policy analyses on various aspects of Namibia's agriculture. Projects included preparation of agrarian reform and settlement programmes, formulation of plans for the protection of food supplies and nutrition, contingency plans for fisheries, formulation of programmes for agricultural education, and an assessment of land suitability for various types of agricultural activity.

The World Health Organization provided a substantial number of fellowships to Namibians for training as physicians, nurses, sanitary engineers and health administrators, among others. Funds were provided to enable Namibians to participate in international health-related courses. Transport and equipment were purchased for maternal and child care programmes and for epidemiological surveillance.

REFERENCES

[1]A/43/23 (A/AC.109/967 & Corr.1). [2]A/AC.131/303. [3]A/AC.131/316. [4]YUN 1987, p. 1023, GA res. 42/14 E, 6 November 1987. [5]E/1988/19 (dec. 88/31 A). [6]A/43/681 & Corr.1. [7]DP/1989/21. [8]A/43/355 & Add.1-3. [9]A/44/297 & Add.1,2.

PART FIVE

Legal questions

Chapter I

International Court of Justice

In 1988, the International Court of Justice continued to consider four contentious cases and a fifth case was referred to it. The Court delivered one Judgment, one advisory opinion and a number of Orders.

Judicial work of the Court

In the contentious case concerning border and transborder armed actions (Nicaragua v. Honduras), the Court in 1988 delivered a Judgment on its jurisdiction and the admissibility of the Application. In an advisory case concerning the applicability of the obligation to arbitrate under section 21 of the 1947 Agreement between the United Nations and the United States of America regarding the Headquarters of the United Nations,[1] the Court made an Order and delivered an advisory opinion.

One new case, concerning maritime delimitation between Greenland and Jan Mayen Island (Denmark v. Norway), was referred to the Court.

The 1988 activities of the Court were described in two reports to the General Assembly, one covering the period from 1 August 1987 to 31 July 1988[2] and the other from 1 August 1988 to 31 July 1989.[3] By **decision 43/405** of 17 October 1988, the Assembly took note of the 1987/88 report.

Military and paramilitary activities in and against Nicaragua

The question of responsibility for military and paramilitary activities in and against Nicaragua had been before the Court since 1984[4] when Nicaragua instituted proceedings against the United States. In 1986,[5] the Court delivered a Judgment by which it found that the United States was obliged to make reparation to Nicaragua for injury caused by breaches of obligations under international law. In 1987, Nicaragua requested the Court to pursue the case as no agreement had been reached between the parties as to the form and amount of reparation.

By a 1987 Order,[6] the Court fixed time-limits for filing a Memorial (written pleading) by Nicaragua and a Counter-Memorial by the United States. Earlier, the United States had informed the Court of its view that the Court was without jurisdiction to entertain the dispute.

While the Memorial of Nicaragua was duly filed within the time-limit on 29 March 1988, that of the United States was not received by the fixed date, 29 July 1988.

The Secretary-General, in a report to the General Assembly of October 1988,[7] stated that there had been no new developments in the situation since the Assembly's adoption in 1987[8] of a resolution calling for compliance with the Judgment.

GENERAL ASSEMBLY ACTION

On 25 October 1988, the General Assembly adopted **resolution 43/11** by recorded vote.

Judgment of the International Court of Justice of 27 June 1986 concerning military and paramilitary activities in and against Nicaragua: need for immediate compliance

The General Assembly,

Recalling Security Council resolutions 530(1983) of 19 May 1983 and 562(1985) of 10 May 1985, and its resolutions 41/31 of 3 November 1986 and 42/18 of 12 November 1987,

Aware that, under the Charter of the United Nations, the International Court of Justice is the principal judicial organ of the United Nations and that each Member undertakes to comply with the decision of the Court in any case to which it is a party,

Considering that Article 36, paragraph 6, of the Statute of the Court provides that "in the event of a dispute as to whether the Court has jurisdiction, the matter shall be settled by the decision of the Court",

Taking note of the Judgment of the International Court of Justice of 27 June 1986 in the case of "Military and Paramilitary Activities in and against Nicaragua",

Having considered the events that have taken place in and against Nicaragua since the Judgment was rendered, in particular the continued financing by the United States of America of military and other activities in and against Nicaragua,

Emphasizing the obligation of States, under customary international law, not to intervene in the internal affairs of other States,

1. *Urgently calls* for full and immediate compliance with the Judgment of the International Court of Justice of 27 June 1986 in the case of "Military and Paramilitary Activities in and against Nicaragua" in conformity with the relevant provisions of the Charter of the United Nations;

2. *Requests* the Secretary-General to keep the General Assembly informed on the implementation of the present resolution;

3. *Decides* to include in the provisional agenda of its forty-fourth session the item entitled "Judgment of the International Court of Justice of 27 June 1986 concern-

ing military and paramilitary activities in and against Nicaragua: need for immediate compliance''.

General Assembly resolution 43/11

25 October 1988   Meeting 36   89-2-48 (recorded vote)

Draft by Nicaragua (A/43/L.14); agenda item 33.

Recorded vote in Assembly as follows:

In favour: Afghanistan, Albania, Algeria, Argentina, Australia, Austria, Bahamas, Barbados, Belize, Benin, Bhutan, Bolivia, Botswana, Brazil, Bulgaria, Burkina Faso, Burma, Burundi, Byelorussian SSR, Cameroon, Canada, Cape Verde, China, Colombia, Congo, Cuba, Cyprus, Czechoslovakia, Democratic Yemen, Denmark, Ecuador, Ethiopia, Finland, German Democratic Republic, Ghana, Greece, Guinea-Bissau, Haiti, Hungary, Iceland, India, Indonesia, Iran, Iraq, Ireland, Kenya, Kuwait, Lao People's Democratic Republic, Lesotho, Libyan Arab Jamahiriya, Madagascar, Malawi, Maldives, Mali, Mexico, Mongolia, Mozambique, Nepal, New Zealand, Nicaragua, Nigeria, Norway, Pakistan, Panama, Papua New Guinea, Peru, Philippines, Poland, Romania, Sao Tome and Principe, Seychelles, Spain, Sudan, Swaziland, Sweden, Syrian Arab Republic, Trinidad and Tobago, Uganda, Ukrainian SSR, USSR, United Arab Emirates, United Republic of Tanzania, Uruguay, Vanuatu, Venezuela, Viet Nam, Yugoslavia, Zambia, Zimbabwe.

Against: Israel, United States.

Abstaining: Antigua and Barbuda, Bahrain, Belgium, Brunei Darussalam, Central African Republic, Chad, Costa Rica, Côte d'Ivoire, Dominica, Dominican Republic, Egypt, El Salvador, Equatorial Guinea, France, Germany, Federal Republic of, Grenada, Guatemala, Honduras, Italy, Jamaica, Japan, Jordan, Lebanon, Liberia, Luxembourg, Malaysia, Malta, Mauritius, Morocco, Netherlands, Niger, Oman, Portugal, Rwanda, Saint Kitts and Nevis, Saint Vincent and the Grenadines, Samoa, Saudi Arabia, Senegal, Sierra Leone, Somalia, Sri Lanka, Togo, Tunisia, Turkey, United Kingdom, Yemen, Zaire.

Border and transborder armed actions (Nicaragua v. Honduras)

In 1986[9] and 1987,[10] the Court had dealt with border and transborder armed actions between Nicaragua and Honduras, in proceedings instituted by Nicaragua. Nicaragua alleged that Honduras had given assistance to *contras* who were carrying out armed actions against Nicaragua.

On 21 March 1988, Nicaragua filed with the Court a request for the indication of interim measures of protection; however, it withdrew the request 10 days later. That day, 31 March, the President of the Court made an Order[11] recording the withdrawal.

With the agreement of both sides, 6 June 1988 was fixed for the opening of oral proceedings on the issues of jurisdiction and admissibility. At six public meetings thereafter, statements were made on behalf of both States.

On 20 December, the Court delivered a Judgment[12] on its jurisdiction and the admissibility of the Application, whose operative provisions read as follows:

> *The Court,*
>
> (1) Unanimously,
>
> *Finds* that it has jurisdiction under Article XXXI of the Pact of Bogotá to entertain the Application filed by the Government of the Republic of Nicaragua on 28 July 1986;
>
> (2) Unanimously,
>
> *Finds* that the Application of Nicaragua is admissible.

Judge Lachs appended a declaration to the Judgment and Judges Oda, Schwebel and Shahabuddeen appended separate opinions.

Request for advisory opinion

In a dispute between the United Nations and its host country, the United States attempted to apply its domestic Anti-Terrorism Act of 1987 in such a manner as to force closure of the Permanent Observer Mission of the Palestine Liberation Organization (PLO) to the United Nations. On 2 March 1988, the General Assembly adopted **resolution 42/229 B**, requesting the Court to give an advisory opinion in the matter. The advisory opinion was to clarify the question whether the United States, in the light of facts reflected in 1988 reports of the Secretary-General concerning the Committee on Relations with the Host Country,[13] as a party to the 1947 United Nations Headquarters Agreement,[1] was under an obligation to enter into arbitration in accordance with section 21 of that Agreement (see PART FIVE, Chapter V).

By an Order of 9 March 1988,[14] the Court fixed 25 March 1988 as the time-limit for the submission of written statements by the United Nations and the United States, as well as by any other State party to the Statute of the Court which wished to do so. By the same Order, the Court decided to hold hearings, opening on 11 April 1988, at which oral comments on written statements might be submitted by the United Nations, the United States or other States having presented written statements. Written statements were filed within the time-limit by the United Nations, the United States, the German Democratic Republic and the Syrian Arab Republic.

On 26 April, at a public sitting, the Court delivered its advisory opinion,[15] the operative part of which read as follows:

> *The Court,*
>
> Unanimously,
>
> *Is of the opinion* that the United States of America, as a party to the Agreement between the United Nations and the United States of America regarding the Headquarters of the United Nations of 26 June 1947, is under an obligation, in accordance with section 21 of that Agreement, to enter into arbitration for the settlement of the dispute between itself and the United Nations.

Judge Elias appended a declaration to the advisory opinion. Separate opinions were appended by Judges Oda, Schwebel and Shahabuddeen.

On 13 May, the General Assembly, by **resolution 42/232**, took note of and endorsed the Court's advisory opinion, urged the host country to abide by its obligations and requested the Secretary-General to continue his efforts to ensure the constitution of the arbitral tribune provided for under section 21 of the Agreement.

Meanwhile, the United States had initiated legal proceedings in a domestic court in order to obtain judicial authorization to close the PLO Observer Mission as required by the Anti-Terrorism Act. On 29 June, the United States District Court for the Southern District of New York rejected the authorization sought by the United States. In his report of 13 September 1988,[16] the Secretary-General welcomed the decision by the United States not to appeal the case, thus bringing to an end the dispute between the United Nations and its host country.

Frontier dispute between El Salvador and Honduras

El Salvador and Honduras submitted to the Court in 1986 a land, island and maritime frontier dispute; the following year the Court acceded to their request for a special Chamber to deal with the case.[10] The Court fixed 1 June 1988 as the time-limit for the filing of Memorials and both parties complied. The next step in the written proceedings was the filing of Counter-Memorials by 1 February 1989.

Case concerning Elettronica Sicula S.p.A. (United States v. Italy)

In 1987, the United States had instituted proceedings against Italy, arising from Italy's requisition of the plant and related assets of Elettronica Sicula S.p.A. (ELSI), an Italian company stated to be 100 per cent owned by two United States corporations.

By a 1987 Order,[10] the Chamber had fixed 18 March 1988 as the time-limit for the filing of a Reply by the United States to a 1987 Italian Counter-Memorial, and 18 July 1988 for the filing of a Rejoinder by Italy to a 1987 United States Memorial. Both the Reply and the Rejoinder were filed within the prescribed time-limits. Oral proceedings were scheduled to begin in early 1989.

Composition of the Chamber

By an Order of 20 December 1988,[17] the Court decided on the composition of the Chamber, originally constituted in 1987,[10] having

elected Judge Ruda to fill the vacancy left by the death of Judge Nagendra Singh (see APPENDIX III). By the Rules of Court, Judge Ruda became President of the Chamber.

Maritime delimitation in the area between Greenland and Jan Mayen (Denmark v. Norway)

On 16 August 1988, Denmark filed in the Registry of the Court an Application instituting proceedings against Norway, stating that, despite negotiations conducted since 1980, a dispute had continued with regard to the delimitation of Denmark's and Norway's fishing zones and continental shelf areas in the waters between the east coast of Greenland and the Norwegian island of Jan Mayen. Denmark therefore requested the Court to decide, in accordance with international law, where a line of delimitation should be drawn in that area.

By an Order of 14 October 1988,[18] the Court fixed 1 August 1989 as the time-limit for the Memorial of Denmark and 15 May 1990 for the Counter-Memorial of Norway.

REFERENCES

[1]YUN 1947-48, p. 199, GA res. 169(II), 31 Oct. 1947. [2]A/43/4. [3]A/44/4. [4]YUN 1984, p. 1084. [5]YUN 1986, p. 981. [6]YUN 1987, p. 1047. [7]A/43/728. [8]YUN 1987, p. 191, GA res. 42/18, 12 Nov. 1987. [9]YUN 1986, p. 983. [10]YUN 1987, p. 1048. [11]*Case concerning Border and Transborder Armed Actions (Nicaragua v. Honduras), Request for the Indication of Provisional Measures, Order of 31 March 1988*, I.C.J. Sales No. 542. [12]*Ibid., Judgment of 20 December 1988*, I.C.J. Sales No. 547. [13]A/42/915 & Add.1-3. [14]*Case concerning Applicability of the Obligation to Arbitrate under Section 21 of the United Nations Headquarters Agreement of 26 June 1947, Order of 9 March 1988*, I.C.J. Sales No. 541. [15]*Ibid., Advisory Opinion of 26 April 1988*, I.C.J. Sales No. 543; A/42/952. [16]A/42/915/Add.5. [17]*Case concerning Elettronica Sicula S.p.A. (ELSI) (United States of America v. Italy), Order of 20 December 1988*, I.C.J. Sales No. 548. [18]*Case concerning Maritime Delimitation in the Area between Greenland and Jan Mayen (Denmark v. Norway), Order of 14 October 1988*, I.C.J Sales No. 544.

OTHER PUBLICATIONS

International Court of Justice: Reports of Judgments, Advisory Opinions and Orders, Index 1988, I.C.J. Sales No. 551. *International Court of Justice Yearbook 1987-1988*, No. 42, I.C.J. Sales No. 546; *1988-1989*, No. 43, I.C.J. Sales No. 568.

Chapter II

Legal aspects of international political relations

As part of its continuing efforts to develop legal measures for promoting friendly relations among States, the General Assembly, in December 1988, approved the Declaration on the Prevention and Removal of Disputes and Situations Which May Threaten International Peace and Security and on the Role of the United Nations in this Field, as drafted by the Special Committee on the topic (resolution 43/51).

Also in December, the Assembly urged States to observe the 1982 Manila Declaration on the Peaceful Settlement of International Disputes and stressed the need to settle such disputes through progressive development and codification of international law and through enhancing the role of the United Nations in this field (resolution 43/163). The Assembly decided that its Sixth (Legal) Committee should complete, in 1990, the identification of the elements of good-neighbourliness between States and begin elaborating an international document on strengthening that concept (resolution 43/171 A and B). In addition, the Assembly invited the International Law Commission (ILC) to continue its elaboration of the draft Code of Crimes against the Peace and Security of Mankind (resolution 43/164) and the *Ad Hoc* Committee on the Drafting of an International Convention against the Recruitment, Use, Financing and Training of Mercenaries to submit such a draft convention in 1989 (resolution 43/168). ILC also continued drafting articles on the law of the non-navigational uses of international watercourses.

The Assembly considered that, because of its complexity, additional time should be given to Governments for thorough study of draft articles and for determining their respective positions on the procedure for future work on the international law on most-favoured-nation clauses (decision 43/429).

Maintenance of international peace and security

The Special Committee on the Charter of the United Nations and on the Strengthening of the Role of the Organization, which met in New York from 22 February to 11 March 1988,[1] accorded priority to the question of the maintenance of international peace and security in all its aspects in order to strengthen the role of the United Nations, in particular the Security Council, in accordance with a 1987 request of the General Assembly.[2] The Committee thus completed in 1988 the draft Declaration on the Prevention and Removal of Disputes and Situations Which May Threaten International Peace and Security and the Role of the United Nations in this Field and submitted the draft to the Assembly.

GENERAL ASSEMBLY ACTION

On 5 December 1988, the General Assembly, on the recommendation of the Sixth Committee, adopted **resolution 43/51** without vote.

Declaration on the Prevention and Removal of Disputes and Situations Which May Threaten International Peace and Security and on the Role of the United Nations in this Field

The General Assembly,

Recalling its resolutions 38/141 of 19 December 1983, 39/88 of 13 December 1984, 40/78 of 11 December 1985, 41/83 of 3 December 1986 and 42/157 of 7 December 1987,

Taking note of the report of the Special Committee on the Charter of the United Nations and on the Strengthening of the Role of the Organization, which met in New York from 22 February to 11 March 1988 and completed a draft Declaration on the Prevention and Removal of Disputes and Situations Which May Threaten International Peace and Security and on the Role of the United Nations in this Field,

Convinced that the adoption of the Declaration on the Prevention and Removal of Disputes and Situations Which May Threaten International Peace and Security and on the Role of the United Nations in this Field will contribute towards strengthening the role and enhancing the effectiveness of the United Nations in maintaining international peace and security,

Considering the need to ensure a wide dissemination of the text of the Declaration,

1. *Approves* the Declaration on the Prevention and Removal of Disputes and Situations Which May Threaten International Peace and Security and on the Role of the United Nations in this Field, the text of which is annexed to the present resolution;

2. *Expresses its appreciation* to the Special Committee on the Charter of the United Nations and on the Strengthening of the Role of the Organization for its important contribution to the elaboration of the text of the Declaration;

3. *Requests* the Secretary-General to inform the Governments of the States Members of the United Nations or members of specialized agencies, and the Security Council, of the adoption of the Declaration;

4. *Urges* that every effort be made to ensure that the Declaration becomes generally known and fully implemented.

ANNEX
Declaration on the Prevention and Removal of Disputes and Situations Which May Threaten International Peace and Security and on the Role of the United Nations in this Field

The General Assembly,

Recognizing the important role that the United Nations and its organs can play in the prevention and removal of international disputes and situations which may lead to international friction or give rise to an international dispute, the continuance of which may threaten the maintenance of international peace and security (hereafter: "disputes" or "situations"), within their respective functions and powers under the Charter of the United Nations,

Convinced that the strengthening of such a role of the United Nations will enhance its effectiveness in dealing with questions relating to the maintenance of international peace and security and in promoting the peaceful settlement of international disputes,

Recognizing the fundamental responsibility of States for the prevention and removal of disputes and situations,

Recalling that the peoples of the United Nations are determined to practise tolerance and live together in peace with one another as good neighbours,

Bearing in mind the right of all States to resort to peaceful means of their own choice for the prevention and removal of disputes or situations,

Reaffirming the Declaration on Principles of International Law concerning Friendly Relations and Co-operation among States in accordance with the Charter of the United Nations, the Manila Declaration on the Peaceful Settlement of International Disputes and the Declaration on the Enhancement of the Effectiveness of the Principle of Refraining from the Threat or Use of Force in International Relations,

Recalling that it is the duty of States to refrain in their international relations from military, political, economic or any other form of coercion against the political independence or territorial integrity of any State,

Calling upon States to co-operate fully with the relevant organs of the United Nations and to support actions taken by them in accordance with the Charter relating to the prevention or removal of disputes and situations,

Bearing in mind the obligation of States to conduct their relations with other States in accordance with international law, including the principles of the United Nations,

Reaffirming the principle of equal rights and self-determination of peoples,

Recalling that the Charter confers on the Security Council the primary responsibility for the maintenance of international peace and security, and that Member States have agreed to accept and carry out its decisions in accordance with the Charter,

Recalling also the important role conferred by the Charter on the General Assembly and the Secretary-General in the maintenance of international peace and security,

1. *Solemnly declares* that:

1. States should act so as to prevent in their international relations the emergence or aggravation of disputes or situations, in particular by fulfilling in good faith their obligations under international law;

2. In order to prevent disputes or situations, States should develop their relations on the basis of the sovereign equality of States and in such a manner as to enhance the effectiveness of the collective security system through the effective implementation of the provisions of the Charter of the United Nations;

3. States should consider the use of bilateral or multilateral consultations in order better to understand each other's views, positions and interests;

4. States party to regional arrangements or members of agencies referred to in Article 52 of the Charter should make every effort to prevent or remove local disputes or situations through such arrangements and agencies;

5. States concerned should consider approaching the relevant organs of the United Nations in order to obtain advice or recommendations on preventive means for dealing with a dispute or situation;

6. Any State party to a dispute or directly concerned with a situation, particularly if it intends to request a meeting of the Security Council, should approach the Council, directly or indirectly, at an early stage and, if appropriate, on a confidential basis;

7. The Security Council should consider holding from time to time meetings, including at a high level with the participation, in particular, of Ministers for Foreign Affairs, or consultations to review the international situation and search for effective ways of improving it;

8. In the course of the preparation for the prevention or removal of particular disputes or situations, the Security Council should consider making use of the various means at its disposal, including the appointment of the Secretary-General as rapporteur for a specified question;

9. When a particular dispute or situation is brought to the attention of the Security Council without a meeting being requested, the Council should consider holding consultations with a view to examining the facts of the dispute or situation and keeping it under review, with the assistance of the Secretary-General when needed; the States concerned should have the opportunity of making their views known;

10. In such consultations, consideration should be given to employing such informal methods as the Security Council deems appropriate, including confidential contacts by its President;

11. In such consultations, the Security Council should consider, *inter alia:*

(a) Reminding the States concerned to respect their obligations under the Charter;

(b) Making an appeal to the States concerned to refrain from any action which might give rise to a dispute or lead to the deterioration of the dispute or situation;

(c) Making an appeal to the States concerned to take action which might help to remove, or to prevent the continuation or deterioration of, the dispute or situation;

12. The Security Council should consider sending, at an early stage, fact-finding or good offices missions or establishing appropriate forms of United Nations presence, including observers and peace-keeping operations, as a means of preventing the further deterioration of the dispute or situation in the areas concerned;

13. The Security Council should consider encouraging and, where appropriate, endorsing efforts

at the regional level by the States concerned or by regional arrangements or agencies to prevent or remove a dispute or situation in the region concerned;

14. Taking into consideration any procedures that have already been adopted by the States directly concerned, the Security Council should consider recommending to them appropriate procedures or methods of settlement of disputes or adjustment of situations, and such terms of settlement as it deems appropriate;

15. The Security Council, if it is appropriate for promoting the prevention and removal of disputes or situations, should, at an early stage, consider making use of the provisions of the Charter concerning the possibility of requesting the International Court of Justice to give an advisory opinion on any legal question;

16. The General Assembly should consider making use of the provisions of the Charter in order to discuss disputes or situations, when appropriate, and, in accordance with Article 11 and subject to Article 12 of the Charter, making recommendations;

17. The General Assembly should consider, where appropriate, supporting efforts undertaken at the regional level by the States concerned or by regional arrangements or agencies, to prevent or remove a dispute or situation in the region concerned;

18. If a dispute or situation has been brought before it, the General Assembly should consider including in its recommendations making more use of fact-finding capabilities, in accordance with Article 11 and subject to Article 12 of the Charter;

19. The General Assembly, if it is appropriate for promoting the prevention and removal of disputes or situations, should consider making use of the provisions of the Charter concerning the possibility of requesting the International Court of Justice to give an advisory opinion on any legal question;

20. The Secretary-General, if approached by a State or States directly concerned with a dispute or situation, should respond swiftly by urging the States to seek a solution or adjustment by peaceful means of their own choice under the Charter and by offering his good offices or other means at his disposal, as he deems appropriate;

21. The Secretary-General should consider approaching the States directly concerned with a dispute or situation in an effort to prevent it from becoming a threat to the maintenance of international peace and security;

22. The Secretary-General should, where appropriate, consider making full use of fact-finding capabilities, including, with the consent of the host State, sending a representative or fact-finding missions to areas where a dispute or a situation exists; where necessary, the Secretary-General should also consider making the appropriate arrangements;

23. The Secretary-General should be encouraged to consider using, at as early a stage as he deems appropriate, the right that is accorded to him under Article 99 of the Charter;

24. The Secretary-General should, where appropriate, encourage efforts undertaken at the regional level to prevent or remove a dispute or situation in the region concerned;

25. Should States fail to prevent the emergence or aggravation of a dispute or situation, they shall continue to seek a settlement by peaceful means in accordance with the Charter;

2. *Declares* that nothing in the present Declaration shall be construed as prejudicing in any manner the provisions of the Charter, including those contained in Article 2, paragraph 7, thereof, or the rights and duties of States, or the scope of the functions and the powers of United Nations organs under the Charter, in particular those relating to the maintenance of international peace and security;

3. *Also declares* that nothing in the present Declaration could in any way prejudice the right to self-determination, freedom and independence of peoples forcibly deprived of that right and referred to in the Declaration on Principles of International Law concerning Friendly Relations and Co-operation among States in accordance with the Charter of the United Nations, particularly peoples under colonial or racist régimes or other forms of alien domination.

General Assembly resolution 43/51

5 December 1988   Meeting 68   Adopted without vote

Approved by Sixth Committee (A/43/886) without vote, 4 November (meeting 30); 6-nation draft (A/C.6/43/L.6); agenda item 135.
Sponsors: Colombia, Cyprus, Czechoslovakia, Finland, Ghana, Venezuela.
Meeting numbers. GA 43rd session: 6th Committee 14-20, 30; plenary 68.

Peaceful settlement of disputes between States

In 1988, the General Assembly again considered the peaceful settlement of disputes. In this regard, it had before it the Secretary-General's report on implementation of the 1982 Manila Declaration on the Peaceful Settlement of International Disputes.[3] In December, the Assembly urged States to observe the provisions of the Declaration.

Special Committee consideration. The Special Committee on the Charter of the United Nations and on the Strengthening of the Role of the Organization, at its February/March 1988 session,[1] continued work on the peaceful settlement of disputes and considered proposals on rationalizing the existing procedures of the United Nations.

The question of peaceful settlement of disputes was considered by an open-ended Working Group of the Committee, which examined a working paper originally submitted in 1983 by Nigeria, the Philippines and Romania and revised in 1987 by Romania.[4] The paper contained a proposal on the resort to a commission of good offices, mediation or conciliation within the United Nations for the peaceful settlement of international disputes, and the Committee issued an informal revised version of that proposal. The original proposal of creating a commission[5] was considered by the Committee in each of the intervening years. In 1988, following the consideration of the informal proposal, Romania submitted a further revised version.[6] The consensus of the Working Group was that progress on the topic had been achieved and that work on the proposal should continue at the Committee's next session with a view to reaching agreement on conclusions to be submitted to the General Assembly in 1989.

The Working Group also examined a progress report by the Secretary-General on the preparation of a handbook on the peaceful settlement of disputes between States,[7] which had been initiated at the Assembly's request in 1983.[8] A consultative group had reviewed the drafts prepared by the Secretariat on the portions dealing with inquiry, mediation and conciliation. The Secretary-General explained that the preparation of the handbook had so far been carried out exclusively by regular Secretariat staff. He recognized this was a long-term assignment requiring extensive research and that its implementation had been hampered by the current financial situation of the United Nations.

Report of the Secretary-General. The Secretary-General, as requested by the General Assembly in 1987,[9] submitted in September 1988 a report with later addenda[10] containing replies received from nine Member States and 10 international intergovernmental organizations on the implementation of the Manila Declaration on the Peaceful Settlement of International Disputes and on ways and means of increasing its effectiveness. The replies, which included proposals and considerations for a broader implementation of the Declaration, were from Argentina, Botswana, the Federal Republic of Germany (on behalf of the 12 States members of the European Community (EC)), Mexico, Nigeria, Peru, the Philippines, Romania and the USSR. Replies were also received from United Nations specialized agencies, EC and the Council of Europe.

GENERAL ASSEMBLY ACTION

On 9 December 1988, the General Assembly, on the recommendation of the Sixth Committee, adopted **resolution 43/163** by recorded vote.

Peaceful settlement of disputes between States

The General Assembly,

Having considered the item entitled "Peaceful settlement of disputes between States",

Recalling its resolution 37/10 of 15 November 1982, by which it approved the Manila Declaration on the Peaceful Settlement of International Disputes, annexed thereto,

Recalling also its resolutions 38/131 of 19 December 1983, 39/79 of 13 December 1984, 40/68 of 11 December 1985, 41/74 of 3 December 1986 and 42/150 of 7 December 1987,

Deeply concerned at the continuation of conflict situations and the emergence of new sources of disputes and tension in international life, and especially at the growing tendency to resort to force or the threat of the use of force and to intervention in internal affairs, and at the escalation of the arms race, which gravely endanger the independence and security of States as well as international peace and security,

Taking into account the need to exert the utmost effort in order to settle any situations and disputes between States on the basis of sovereign equality and exclusively by peaceful means, in conformity with the Charter of the United Nations, and to avoid any military actions and hostilities against other States, which can only make more difficult the solution of existing problems,

Considering that the question of the peaceful settlement of disputes should represent one of the central concerns for States and for the United Nations and that efforts for strengthening the process of peaceful settlement of disputes should be continued,

Emphasizing the responsibility of every State to promote a policy of respect for the national independence and sovereignty of other States, non-interference in internal affairs and good understanding and co-operation, which is a basic requirement for reducing tension and for establishing a climate of peace and mutual confidence in the world,

Taking note with interest of the report of the Secretary-General, submitted in accordance with resolution 42/150, which contains useful opinions, proposals and considerations for a broader implementation of the Manila Declaration,

1. *Again urges* all States to observe and promote in good faith the provisions of the Manila Declaration on the Peaceful Settlement of International Disputes in the settlement of their international disputes;

2. *Stresses* the need to continue efforts to strengthen the process of the peaceful settlement of disputes through progressive development and codification of international law and through enhancing the effectiveness of the United Nations in this field;

3. *Calls upon* Member States to make full use, in accordance with the Charter of the United Nations, of the framework provided by the United Nations for the peaceful settlement of disputes and international problems;

4. *Requests* the Secretary-General to submit to the General Assembly at its forty-fourth session a further report containing the replies of Member States, relevant United Nations bodies and specialized agencies, regional intergovernmental organizations and interested international legal bodies on the implementation of the Manila Declaration and on ways and means of increasing the effectiveness of this instrument;

5. *Decides* that the question of the peaceful settlement of disputes between States shall be considered at its forty-fourth session as a separate agenda item, in conjunction with the item of the provisional agenda entitled "Report of the Special Committee on the Charter of the United Nations and on the Strengthening of the Role of the Organization".

General Assembly resolution 43/163

9 December 1988   Meeting 76   132-0-22 (recorded vote)

Approved by Sixth Committee (A/43/882) by roll-call vote (90-0-20), 21 November (meeting 45); 53-nation draft (A/C.6/43/L.8); agenda item 129.

Sponsors: Angola, Bahrain, Bangladesh, Barbados, Benin, Bolivia, Botswana, Burkina Faso, Burundi, Cape Verde, Central African Republic, Colombia, Costa Rica, Cyprus, Democratic Yemen, Dominican Republic, Ecuador, Guatemala, Guinea, Guyana, Haiti, Honduras, India, Indonesia, Lesotho, Liberia, Madagascar, Malaysia, Mali, Mauritius, Morocco, Mozambique, Nepal, Nicaragua, Niger, Nigeria, Pakistan, Panama, Paraguay, Philippines, Romania, Sierra Leone, Singapore, Somalia, Sri Lanka, Sudan, Swaziland, Togo, Trinidad and Tobago, Uganda, Uruguay, Yugoslavia, Zaire.

Meeting numbers. GA 43rd session: 6th Committee 14-20, 42, 45; plenary 76.

Recorded vote in Assembly as follows:

In favour: Afghanistan, Albania, Algeria, Angola, Antigua and Barbuda, Argentina, Austria, Bahamas, Bahrain, Barbados, Belize, Benin, Bhutan, Bolivia, Botswana, Brazil, Brunei Darussalam, Bulgaria, Burkina Faso, Burma, Burundi, Byelorussian SSR, Cameroon, Cape Verde, Central African Republic, Chad, Chile, China, Colombia, Congo, Costa Rica, Côte d'Ivoire, Cuba, Cyprus, Czechoslovakia, Democratic Kampuchea, Democratic Yemen, Djibouti, Dominican Republic, Ecuador, Egypt, El Salvador, Equatorial Guinea, Ethiopia, Fiji, Gabon, Gambia, German Democratic Republic, Ghana, Greece, Grenada, Guatemala, Guinea, Guinea-Bissau, Guyana, Honduras, Hungary, India, Indonesia, Iran, Iraq, Ireland, Kenya, Kuwait, Lao People's Democratic Republic, Lebanon, Lesotho, Liberia, Libyan Arab Jamahiriya, Madagascar, Malawi, Malaysia, Maldives, Mali, Malta, Mauritania, Mauritius, Mexico, Mongolia, Morocco, Mozambique, Nepal, New Zealand, Nicaragua, Niger, Nigeria, Oman, Pakistan, Panama, Papua New Guinea, Paraguay, Peru, Philippines, Poland, Qatar, Romania, Rwanda, Saint Kitts and Nevis, Saint Lucia, Saint Vincent and the Grenadines, Samoa, Sao Tome and Principe, Saudi Arabia, Senegal, Seychelles, Sierra Leone, Singapore, Solomon Islands, Somalia, Sri Lanka, Sudan, Suriname, Swaziland, Syrian Arab Republic, Thailand, Togo, Trinidad and Tobago, Tunisia, Uganda, Ukrainian SSR, USSR, United Arab Emirates, United Republic of Tanzania, Uruguay, Vanuatu, Venezuela, Viet Nam, Yemen, Yugoslavia, Zaire, Zambia, Zimbabwe.

Against: None.

Abstaining: Australia, Belgium, Canada, Denmark, Dominica, Finland, France, Germany, Federal Republic of, Iceland, Israel, Italy, Japan, Jordan, Luxembourg, Netherlands, Norway, Portugal, Spain, Sweden, Turkey, United Kingdom, United States.

The Assembly retained paragraphs 4 and 5 by recorded votes of 118 to 9, with 22 abstentions, and of 121 to 19, with 10 abstentions, respectively. The Sixth Committee had approved those paragraphs by roll-call votes of 78 to 7, with 23 abstentions, and of 82 to 17, with 10 abstentions.

Good-neighbourliness between States

In December 1988, the General Assembly decided to complete, in 1990, the task of identifying and clarifying the elements of good-neighbourliness between States and to begin elaborating a suitable international document on the development and strengthening of that concept.

Sub-Committee consideration. On 26 September 1988, the Assembly's Sixth Committee re-established its Sub-Committee on Good-Neighbourliness, in response to a 1987 Assembly request[11] that it complete in 1988 the task of identifying and clarifying good-neighbourliness and begin the elaboration of a suitable international document on the development and strengthening of good-neighbourliness between States. The Sub-Committee held eight meetings in October and November,[12] at which it considered its 1987 report[13] to the Sixth Committee, containing a list under the heading "Legal and other elements relating to the development and strengthening of good-neighbourliness", and two conference room papers by the United Kingdom, containing a proposed amendment and a proposed addition to the list of elements. The list was divided into four major sections: legal and other elements; areas of co-operation; ways and means; and action of international organizations. It was understood that the list was not exhaustive and that the positioning of the points in the list was provisional. The

Sub-Committee did not conclude its consideration of proposals regarding the list of elements.

GENERAL ASSEMBLY ACTION

On 9 December 1988, the General Assembly, on the recommendation of the Sixth Committee, adopted two resolutions on the development and strengthening of good-neighbourliness between States. **Resolution 43/171 A** was adopted by recorded vote.

The General Assembly,

Bearing in mind the determination of the peoples of the United Nations, as expressed in the Charter of the United Nations, to practise tolerance and live together in peace with one another as good neighbours,

Recalling the Declaration on Principles of International Law concerning Friendly Relations and Co-operation among States in accordance with the Charter of the United Nations, approved by its resolution 2625(XXV) of 24 October 1970,

Considering that the great changes of a political, economic and social nature, as well as the scientific and technological advances that have taken place in the world and led to unprecedented interdependence of nations, have given new dimensions to good-neighbourliness in the conduct of States and increased the need to develop and strengthen it,

1. *Takes note* of the report of the Sub-Committee on Good-Neighbourliness, established by the Sixth Committee during the forty-third session of the General Assembly;

2. *Decides* to include in the provisional agenda of its forty-fifth session the item entitled "Development and strengthening of good-neighbourliness between States".

General Assembly resolution 43/171 A

9 December 1988   Meeting 76   67-9-65 (recorded vote)

Approved by Sixth Committee (A/43/887) by vote (28-20-64), 29 November (meeting 51); 10-nation draft (A/C.6/43/L.14/Rev.1); agenda item 136.
Sponsors: Austria, Canada, Denmark, Finland, Iceland, Ireland, Netherlands, Norway, Sweden, United Kingdom.
Meeting numbers. GA 43rd session: 6th Committee 43, 44, 48, 49, 51; plenary 76.

Recorded vote in Assembly as follows:

In favour: Antigua and Barbuda, Argentina, Australia, Austria, Bangladesh,[a] Belgium, Belize, Benin, Canada, Cape Verde,[b] Costa Rica, Denmark, Djibouti, Dominica, Dominican Republic, Ecuador,[a] El Salvador, Equatorial Guinea, Fiji, Finland, France, Gabon,[a] Germany, Federal Republic of, Greece, Grenada, Guinea, Guinea-Bissau,[b] Haiti, Iceland, Ireland, Israel, Italy, Japan, Jordan, Kenya, Lebanon, Luxembourg, Malawi, Malta, Mozambique,[b] Netherlands, New Zealand, Nigeria,[a] Norway, Oman,[a] Papua New Guinea, Portugal, Rwanda,[a] Saint Kitts and Nevis, Saint Lucia, Saint Vincent and the Grenadines, Samoa, Sao Tome and Principe,[b] Senegal,[a] Seychelles, Sierra Leone, Solomon Islands, Somalia,[a] Spain, Suriname,[a] Sweden, Syrian Arab Republic, Trinidad and Tobago, Turkey, United Kingdom, United States, Venezuela.

Against: Bulgaria,[a] Cameroon, Lao People's Democratic Republic, Madagascar, Mongolia, Philippines, Romania, Sudan, Viet Nam.

Abstaining: Afghanistan, Algeria, Angola, Bahamas, Bahrain, Barbados, Botswana, Brazil, Brunei Darussalam, Burkina Faso, Burma, Burundi, Byelorussian SSR, Central African Republic, Chad, Chile, China, Colombia, Congo, Côte d'Ivoire, Cuba, Cyprus, Czechoslovakia, Egypt, Ethiopia, German Democratic Republic, Ghana, Guatemala, Guyana, Honduras, Hungary, India, Indonesia, Iran, Iraq, Kuwait, Lesotho, Liberia, Libyan Arab Jamahiriya, Mali, Mexico, Nepal, Nicaragua, Niger, Pakistan, Panama, Paraguay, Peru, Poland, Saudi Arabia, Singapore, Sri Lanka, Swaziland, Thailand, Tunisia, Uganda, Ukrainian SSR, USSR, United Arab Emirates, Uruguay, Vanuatu, Yugoslavia, Zaire, Zambia, Zimbabwe.

[a]Later advised the Secretariat it had intended to abstain.
[b]Later advised the Secretariat it had intended not to participate in the vote.

Resolution 43/171 B was also adopted by recorded vote.

The General Assembly,

Bearing in mind the determination of the peoples of the United Nations, as expressed in the Charter of the United Nations, to practise tolerance and live together in peace with one another as good neighbours,

Recalling the Declaration on Principles of International Law concerning Friendly Relations and Co-operation among States in accordance with the Charter of the United Nations, approved by its resolution 2625(XXV) of 24 October 1970,

Recalling also its resolutions 1236(XII) of 14 December 1957, 1301(XIII) of 10 December 1958, 2129(XX) of 21 December 1965, 34/99 of 14 December 1979, 36/101 of 9 December 1981, 37/117 of 16 December 1982, 38/126 of 19 December 1983, 39/78 of 13 December 1984, 41/84 of 3 December 1986 and 42/158 of 7 December 1987, as well as its decision 40/419 of 11 December 1985,

Bearing in mind that, for various reasons, there are particularly favourable opportunities for co-operation and mutual advantage between neighbouring countries in many fields and various forms, and that the development of such co-operation may have a positive influence on international relations as a whole,

Considering that the great changes of a political, economic and social nature, as well as the scientific and technological advances that have taken place in the world and led to unprecedented interdependence of nations, have given new dimensions to good-neighbourliness in the conduct of States and increased the need to develop and strengthen it,

Taking into account the working papers concerning the development and strengthening of good-neighbourliness between States, as well as the written replies sent by States and international organizations on the content of good-neighbourliness and on ways and means to enhance it, the views expressed by States on this subject and the reports of the Sub-Committee on Good-Neighbourliness established by the Sixth Committee,

Recalling its opinion that it is necessary to continue to examine the question of good-neighbourliness in order to strengthen and develop its content, as well as ways and modalities to enhance its effectiveness, and that the results of this examination could be included, at an appropriate time, in a suitable international document,

1. *Reaffirms* that good-neighbourliness fully conforms with the purposes of the United Nations and shall be founded upon the strict observance of the principles of the United Nations as embodied in the Charter and in the Declaration on Principles of International Law concerning Friendly Relations and Co-operation among States in accordance with the Charter of the United Nations, and so presupposes the rejection of any acts seeking to establish zones of influence or domination;

2. *Calls once again upon* States, in the interest of the maintenance of international peace and security, to develop good-neighbourly relations, acting on the basis of these principles;

3. *Reaffirms* that the generalization of the long practice of good-neighbourliness and of principles and rules pertaining to it is likely to strengthen friendly relations and co-operation among States in accordance with the Charter;

4. *Takes note* of the report of the Sub-Committee on Good-Neighbourliness, which functioned within the Sixth Committee during the forty-third session of the General Assembly;

5. *Decides* to continue and to complete at its forty-fifth session, on the basis of the present resolution and the report of the Sub-Committee, the task of identifying and clarifying the elements of good-neighbourliness and to begin the elaboration of a suitable international document on the development and strengthening of good-neighbourliness between States within the framework of a sub-committee on good-neighbourliness;

6. *Decides* to include in the provisional agenda of its forty-fifth session the item entitled "Development and strengthening of good-neighbourliness between States".

General Assembly resolution 43/171 B

9 December 1988   Meeting 76   124-8-22 (recorded vote)

Approved by Sixth Committee (A/43/887) by vote (100-9-18), 29 November (meeting 51); 39-nation draft (A/C.6/43/L.20); agenda item 136.

Sponsors: Angola, Bangladesh, Benin, Bolivia, Bulgaria, Burundi, Cameroon, Cape Verde, Colombia, Cuba, Dominican Republic, German Democratic Republic, Guatemala, Guinea, Guyana, Honduras, Iraq, Kenya, Liberia, Madagascar, Malaysia, Mali, Mauritius, Mongolia, Mozambique, Nicaragua, Panama, Philippines, Poland, Romania, Rwanda, Sudan, Suriname, Swaziland, Uganda, USSR, Viet Nam, Yugoslavia, Zaire.

Meeting numbers. GA 43rd session: 6th Committee 43, 44, 48, 49, 51; plenary 76.

Recorded vote in Assembly as follows:

In favour: Afghanistan, Albania, Algeria, Angola, Antigua and Barbuda, Argentina, Bahamas, Bahrain, Bangladesh, Barbados, Belize, Benin, Bhutan, Bolivia, Botswana, Brunei Darussalam, Bulgaria, Burkina Faso, Burma, Burundi, Byelorussian SSR, Cameroon, Cape Verde, Central African Republic, Chad, Chile, China, Colombia, Congo, Costa Rica, Côte d'Ivoire, Cuba, Cyprus, Czechoslovakia, Democratic Kampuchea, Democratic Yemen, Djibouti, Dominican Republic, Ecuador, Egypt, El Salvador, Equatorial Guinea, Ethiopia, Fiji, Gabon, Gambia, German Democratic Republic, Ghana, Greece, Grenada, Guatemala, Guinea, Guinea-Bissau, Guyana, Haiti, Honduras, India, Indonesia, Iran, Iraq, Kenya, Kuwait, Lao People's Democratic Republic, Lebanon, Lesotho, Liberia, Libyan Arab Jamahiriya, Madagascar, Malawi, Malaysia, Maldives, Mali, Malta, Mauritania, Mauritius, Mexico, Mongolia, Morocco, Mozambique, Nepal, Nicaragua, Niger, Nigeria, Oman, Pakistan, Panama, Papua New Guinea, Paraguay, Peru, Philippines, Poland, Qatar, Romania, Rwanda, Saint Kitts and Nevis, Saint Lucia, Saudi Arabia, Senegal, Seychelles, Sierra Leone, Singapore, Somalia, Sri Lanka, Sudan, Suriname, Swaziland, Syrian Arab Republic, Thailand, Togo, Trinidad and Tobago, Tunisia, Turkey, Uganda, Ukrainian SSR, USSR, United Arab Emirates, Uruguay, Vanuatu, Viet Nam, Yemen, Yugoslavia, Zaire, Zambia, Zimbabwe.

Against: Belgium, France, Germany, Federal Republic of, Luxembourg, Netherlands, Portugal, United Kingdom, United States.

Abstaining: Australia, Austria, Brazil, Canada, Denmark, Dominica, Finland, Hungary, Iceland, Ireland, Israel, Italy, Japan, Jordan, New Zealand, Norway, Saint Vincent and the Grenadines, Samoa, Solomon Islands, Spain, Sweden, Venezuela.

The Assembly retained paragraph 5 and the last preambular paragraph of resolution 43/171 B by recorded votes of 111 to 21, with 19 abstentions, and of 114 to 21, with 17 abstentions, respectively. The Sixth Committee had approved those paragraphs by votes of 97 to 21, with 8 abstentions, and of 98 to 21, with 7 abstentions.

Draft code of crimes against peace and security

In 1988, at its fortieth session,[14] the International Law Commission continued elaborating the draft Code of Crimes against the Peace and Security of Mankind. In December, the General Assembly invited ILC to continue work on the topic, on which ILC had resumed work in 1982[15] and whose title in English had been amended by the Assembly in 1987,[16] replacing the word "offences" by "crimes" in order to achieve greater uniformity and equivalence between different language versions. The draft Code, originally prepared by ILC in 1954[17] in response to a 1947 Assembly request,[18] defined crimes under international law for which the responsible individual was to be punished.

ILC consideration. ILC considered in 1988 the sixth report by its Special Rapporteur on the topic, Doudou Thiam (Senegal).[19] The report comprised three parts, of which the first dealt with crimes against peace in the 1954 draft Code, in particular aggression, annexation, the sending of armed bands to the territory of another State, and intervention in the internal and external affairs of a State. The second part covered new characterizations of crimes against peace, in particular colonial domination and mercenarism, while the third part presented draft article 11 on "acts constituting crimes against peace". Following a discussion of the report, ILC decided to refer to the Drafting Committee the new version of draft article 11. After considering the report of the Drafting Committee, ILC provisionally adopted articles 4 (obligation to try or extradite), 7 (*non bis in idem*), 8 (non-retroactivity), 10 (responsibility of the superior), 11 (official position and criminal responsibility) and 12 (aggression).

The six articles provisionally adopted in 1988 were transmitted to the General Assembly by the Secretary-General in August.[20]

In **resolution 43/169** on the work of ILC, the Assembly recommended that, taking into account the comments of Governments, ILC should continue its work on the topic.

Report of the Secretary-General. The Secretary-General submitted to the General Assembly in August 1988 a report with a later addendum,[21] containing replies from 11 Governments in response to the Assembly's invitation for views on the 1987 conclusions of ILC.[16]

GENERAL ASSEMBLY ACTION

On 9 December, on the recommendation of the Sixth Committee, the General Assembly adopted **resolution 43/164** by recorded vote.

Draft Code of Crimes against the Peace and Security of Mankind

The General Assembly,

Mindful of Article 13, paragraph 1 *a*, of the Charter of the United Nations, which provides that the General Assembly shall initiate studies and make recommendations for the purpose of encouraging the progressive development of international law and its codification,

Recalling its resolution 177(II) of 21 November 1947, by which it directed the International Law Commission

to prepare a draft code of offences against the peace and security of mankind,

Having considered the draft Code of Offences against the Peace and Security of Mankind prepared by the Commission and submitted to the General Assembly in 1954,

Recalling its belief that the elaboration of a code of offences against the peace and security of mankind could contribute to strengthening international peace and security and thus to promoting and implementing the purposes and principles set forth in the Charter,

Recalling also its resolution 36/106 of 10 December 1981, in which it invited the Commission to resume its work with a view to elaborating the draft Code and to examine it with the required priority in order to review it, taking into account the results achieved by the process of the progressive development of international law,

Bearing in mind that the Commission should fulfil its task on the basis of early elaboration of draft articles thereof,

Having considered chapter IV of the report of the Commission on the work of its fortieth session,

Taking note of the report of the Secretary-General on the subject,

Taking into account the views expressed during the debate on this item at its forty-third session,

Recognizing the importance and urgency of the subject,

1. *Invites* the International Law Commission to continue its work on the elaboration of the draft Code of Crimes against the Peace and Security of Mankind including the elaboration of a list of crimes, taking into account the progress made at its fortieth session, as well as the views expressed during the forty-third session of the General Assembly;

2. *Notes* the approach currently envisaged by the Commission in dealing with the judicial authority to be assigned for the implementation of the provisions of the draft Code, and encourages the Commission to explore further all possible alternatives on the question;

3. *Requests* the Secretary-General to continue to seek the views of Member States regarding the conclusions contained in paragraph 69 *(c)* (i) of the Commission's report on the work of its thirty-fifth session;

4. *Also requests* the Secretary-General to include the views received from Member States in accordance with paragraph 3 above in a report to be submitted to the General Assembly at its forty-fourth session;

5. *Decides* to include in the provisional agenda of its forty-fourth session the item entitled "Draft Code of Crimes against the Peace and Security of Mankind", to be considered in conjunction with the examination of the report of the Commission.

General Assembly resolution 43/164

9 December 1988   Meeting 76   137-5-13 (recorded vote)

Approved by Sixth Committee (A/43/883) by vote (104-5-13), 25 November (meeting 48); 24-nation draft (A/C.6/43/L.21); agenda item 130.

Sponsors: Algeria, Angola, Bulgaria, Burundi, Cameroon, Chad, Cuba, Cyprus, Czechoslovakia, Egypt, Ethiopia, German Democratic Republic, Kenya, Mali, Mongolia, Philippines, Poland, Qatar, Romania, Rwanda, Senegal, Sudan, Tunisia, Viet Nam.

Meeting numbers. GA 43rd session: 6th Committee 25-40, 48; plenary 76.

Recorded vote in Assembly as follows:

In favour: Afghanistan, Albania, Algeria, Angola, Antigua and Barbuda, Argentina, Australia, Austria, Bahamas, Bahrain, Barbados, Belize, Benin, Bhutan, Bolivia, Botswana, Brazil, Brunei Darussalam, Bulgaria, Burkina Faso, Burma, Burundi, Byelorussian SSR, Cameroon, Canada,[a] Cape Verde, Central African Republic, Chad, Chile, China, Colombia, Congo, Costa Rica, Côte d'Ivoire, Cuba, Cyprus, Czechoslovakia, Democratic Kampuchea, Democratic Yemen, Djibouti, Dominica, Dominican Republic, Ecuador,

Draft convention against mercenaries

The General Assembly, in 1988, invited the *Ad Hoc* Committee on the Drafting of an International Convention against the Recruitment, Use, Financing and Training of Mercenaries to complete its work and to submit a draft convention, if possible in 1989. The question of the use of mercenaries as a means of impeding the exercise of the right of peoples to self-determination was also considered in a report by the Special Rapporteur of the Commission on Human Rights. The report examined the current state of international law in the field, noted the lack of rules of positive international law directly condemning mercenary practices and recommended the drafting of an international convention in this respect (see PART THREE, Chapter X).

Ad Hoc Committee consideration. The *Ad Hoc* Committee against mercenaries held its seventh session in New York from 25 January to 12 February 1988.⁽²²⁾ In addition to documents considered at previous sessions, the Committee had before it draft articles contained in its 1987 report⁽²³⁾ as a second revised consolidated negotiating basis of a convention against mercenaries. In 1988, the Committee established a working group and a drafting group, both of which met during the session. The Committee recognized the progress made in 1988 in preparing the third revised consolidated negotiating basis and recommended that the Assembly invite the Committee to continue work in 1989 with the goal of drafting, at the earliest possible date, an international convention.

The Committee's 1988 report⁽²²⁾ included the report of the working group, a statement by the drafting group's Chairman, a draft preamble proposed by the Committee's Chairman and the third revised consolidated negotiating basis of a convention against mercenaries. On 12 February, the report was approved by the Committee.

GENERAL ASSEMBLY ACTION

On 9 December 1988, the General Assembly, on the recommendation of the Sixth Committee, adopted **resolution 43/168** without vote.

Report of the *Ad Hoc* Committee on the Drafting of an International Convention against the Recruitment, Use, Financing and Training of Mercenaries

The General Assembly,

Recalling its resolutions, particularly resolutions 2395(XXIII) of 29 November 1968, 2465(XXIII) of 20 December 1968, 2548(XXIV) of 11 December 1969, 2708(XXV) of 14 December 1970 and 3103(XXVIII) of 12 December 1973, and its resolution 1514(XV) of 14 December 1960, as well as Security Council resolutions 405(1977) of 14 April 1977, 419(1977) of 24 November 1977, 496(1981) of 15 December 1981 and 507(1982) of 28 May 1982, in which the United Nations denounced the practice of using mercenaries, in particular against developing countries and national liberation movements,

Recalling in particular its resolution 42/155 of 7 December 1987, by which it decided to renew the mandate of the *Ad Hoc* Committee on the Drafting of an International Convention against the Recruitment, Use, Financing and Training of Mercenaries,

Bearing in mind the need for strict observance of the principles of sovereign equality, political independence, territorial integrity of States and self-determination of peoples, enshrined in the Charter of the United Nations and developed in the Declaration on Principles of International Law concerning Friendly Relations and Co-operation among States in accordance with the Charter of the United Nations,

Bearing in mind also that every State has the duty to refrain from organizing or encouraging the organization of irregular forces or armed bands, including mercenaries, for incursion into another State,

Recognizing that the recruitment, use, financing and training of mercenaries by States is contrary to fundamental principles of international law, such as the duty to refrain from the threat or use of force, non-intervention in the internal affairs, territorial integrity or political independence of other States, and seriously impedes the process of self-determination of people struggling against colonialism, racism and *apartheid* and all forms of foreign domination,

Bearing in mind the pernicious impact that the activities of mercenaries have on international peace and security,

Considering that the progressive development and codification of the rules of international law on the activities of mercenaries would contribute immensely to the implementation of the purposes and principles of the Charter,

Welcoming the wide and effective participation of members of the *Ad Hoc* Committee in the work of the Committee and the participation of a large number of observers in that work,

Taking into account the work done so far by the *Ad Hoc* Committee,

Reaffirming the need for the conclusion, at the earliest possible date, of an international convention against the recruitment, use, financing and training of mercenaries,

1. *Takes note* of the report of the *Ad Hoc* Committee on the Drafting of an International Convention against the Recruitment, Use, Financing and Training of Mercenaries;

2. *Decides* to renew the mandate of the *Ad Hoc* Committee with a view to completing as soon as possible a draft international convention against the recruitment, use, financing and training of mercenaries;

3. *Requests* the *Ad Hoc* Committee, in the fulfilment of its mandate, to use the draft articles contained in chapter III of its report, entitled "Third revised consolidated negotiating basis of a convention against the recruitment, use, financing and training of mercenaries" as a basis for future negotiation on the text of the proposed international convention;

4. *Invites* the *Ad Hoc* Committee to take into account the suggestions and proposals of Member States submitted to the Secretary-General on the subject and the views and comments expressed at the fortieth, forty-first, forty-second and forty-third sessions of the General Assembly during the debate in the Sixth Committee devoted to the consideration of the report of the *Ad Hoc* Committee;

5. *Decides* that the *Ad Hoc* Committee shall hold its eighth session from 30 January to 17 February 1989;

6. *Also decides* that the *Ad Hoc* Committee shall accept the participation of observers of Member States, including participation in the meetings of its drafting and working groups;

7. *Requests* the Secretary-General to provide, on a priority basis, the *Ad Hoc* Committee with any assistance and facilities it may require to hold its eighth session;

8. *Reaffirms* the importance that pre-session consultations among the members of the *Ad Hoc* Committee and other interested States may have in facilitating the smooth conduct of its work towards the fulfilment of its task, *inter alia*, as regards the composition of the Bureau and the organization of work;

9. *Invites* the *Ad Hoc* Committee to make every effort to submit its final report containing a draft international convention against the recruitment, use, financing and training of mercenaries to the General Assembly if possible at its forty-fourth session;

10. *Decides* to include in the provisional agenda of its forty-fourth session the item entitled "Report of the *Ad Hoc* Committee on the Drafting of an International Convention against the Recruitment, Use, Financing and Training of Mercenaries".

General Assembly resolution 43/168

9 December 1988   Meeting 76   Adopted without vote

Approved by Sixth Committee (A/43/884) by vote (122-0-3), 29 November (meeting 51); 40-nation draft (A/C.6/43/L.13); agenda item 133.

Sponsors: Algeria, Angola, Benin, Burundi, Cuba, Egypt, Ethiopia, German Democratic Republic, Ghana, Guinea, India, Kenya, Lao People's Democratic Republic, Liberia, Libyan Arab Jamahiriya, Madagascar, Mali, Mexico, Mongolia, Morocco, Mozambique, Nicaragua, Nigeria, Panama, Philippines, Romania, Rwanda, Senegal, Sudan, Suriname, Syrian Arab Republic, Togo, Tunisia, Uganda, Ukrainian SSR, Viet Nam, Yugoslavia, Zaire, Zambia, Zimbabwe.

Financial implications. 5th Committee, A/43/943; S-G, A/C.5/43/53, A/C.6/43/L.19.

Meeting numbers. GA 43rd session: 5th Committee 43; 6th Committee 22-24, 46, 47, 49, 51; plenary 76.

The Sixth Committee approved the draft resolution as a whole after retaining the fifth preambular paragraph by 100 votes to 9, with 15 abstentions.

On 8 December, the Assembly adopted **resolution 43/107** on the use of mercenaries as a means to violate human rights and impede the exercise of the right to self-determination.

Draft articles on non-navigational uses of international watercourses

In 1988, ILC continued work on the law of the non-navigational uses of international watercourses,[14] as recommended by the General Assembly in 1987.[24] It had before it the fourth report by its Special Rapporteur, Stephen C. McCaffrey (United States),[25] containing three chapters—status of work on the topic and plan for future work; exchange of data and information; and environmental protection, pollution and related matters. In chapter I, the Special Rapporteur provided a preliminary outline for the treatment of the topic as a whole: part I (introduction) consisted of articles 1 to 5; part II (general principles) contained articles 6 and 7; part III (new uses and changes in existing uses) contained articles 11 to 15; part IV consisted of a single article, dealing with the exchange of data and information; part V dealt with environmental protection, pollution and related matters; part VI with water-related hazards and dangers; and part VII with the relationship between non-navigational and navigational uses. Under the heading of other matters, the outline contained a list of subjects which would, in the view of the Rapporteur, be more appropriately dealt with in annexes to the draft.

On the recommendation of the Drafting Committee, ILC provisionally adopted 14 articles which it had discussed at previous sessions and which were transmitted in August 1988 to the General Assembly by the Secretary-General.[20]

Most-favoured-nation clauses

In response to a 1985 General Assembly request,[26] the Secretary-General submitted a report[27] containing comments received as at 15 August 1988—from one Member State (Kuwait) and one specialized agency (United Nations Industrial Development Organization)—on the draft articles on most-favoured-nation clauses adopted by ILC in 1978,[28] on the procedure for completing work on the topic and on the forum for future discussion.

GENERAL ASSEMBLY ACTION

On 9 December 1988, the General Assembly, by **decision 43/429**, took note of the complexity of codification or progressive development of the international law on most-favoured-nation clauses, and considered that additional time should be given to Governments for thorough study of draft articles and for determining their respective positions on the most appropriate procedure for future work, including the forum for further discussion. It decided to take up the question again in 1991.

REFERENCES

[1]A/43/33. [2]YUN 1987, p. 1072, GA res. 42/157, 7 Dec. 1987. [3]YUN 1982, p. 1372, GA res. 37/10, annex, 15 Nov. 1982. [4]YUN 1987, p. 1051. [5]YUN 1983, p. 1106. [6]A/AC.182/L.52/Rev.2. [7]A/AC.182/L.58. [8]YUN 1983, p. 1106, GA res. 38/131, 19 Dec. 1983. [9]YUN 1987, p. 1052, GA res. 42/150, 7 Dec. 1987. [10]A/43/530 & Add.1,2. [11]YUN 1987, p. 1053, GA res. 42/158, 7 Dec. 1987. [12]A/C.6/43/L.11. [13]YUN 1987, p. 1053. [14]A/43/10. [15]YUN 1982, p. 1375. [16]YUN 1987, p. 1058, GA res. 42/151, 7 Dec. 1987. [17]YUN 1954, p. 411. [18]YUN 1947-48, p. 215, GA res. 177(II), 21 Nov. 1947. [19]A/CN.4/411 & Corr.1,2. [20]A/43/539. [21]A/43/525 & Add.1. [22]A/43/43. [23]YUN 1987, p. 1060. [24]*Ibid.*, p. 1086, GA res. 42/156, 7 Dec. 1987. [25]A/CN.4/412 & Add.1,2 & Corr.1-3. [26]YUN 1985, p. 1194, GA res. 40/65, 11 Dec. 1985. [27]A/43/526. [28]YUN 1978, p. 945.

Chapter III

States and international law

The General Assembly, in December 1988, alarmed by repeated violent acts against diplomatic and consular representatives as well as against representatives to international intergovernmental organizations, urged States to ensure their safety and to prevent such acts (resolution 43/167).

The International Law Commission continued work on the status of the diplomatic courier and the diplomatic bag not accompanied by diplomatic courier, as well as on international liability for injurious consequences arising out of acts not prohibited by international law.

The Secretariat continued its depository functions for agreements deposited with the Secretary-General.

Diplomatic relations

Protection of diplomats

As at 31 December 1988, the number of parties to the various international instruments relating to the protection of diplomats and diplomatic and consular relations was as follows:[1] 152 States were parties to the 1961 Vienna Convention on Diplomatic Relations,[2] with Albania ratifying it in 1988; 42 States were parties to the Optional Protocol concerning the acquisition of nationality[3] and 52 were parties to the Optional Protocol concerning the compulsory settlement of disputes.[3]

The 1963 Vienna Convention on Consular Relations[4] had 120 parties, with Antigua and Barbuda succeeding and Guinea and Saudi Arabia acceding in 1988; 34 States were parties to the Optional Protocol concerning the acquisition of nationality[5] and 41 were parties to the Optional Protocol concerning the compulsory settlement of disputes.[5]

The 1973 Convention on the Prevention and Punishment of Crimes against Internationally Protected Persons, including Diplomatic Agents,[6] had 74 States parties, the Netherlands, Oman and the Syrian Arab Republic having acceded in 1988.

Report of the Secretary-General. Pursuant to a 1987 General Assembly resolution,[7] the Secretary-General requested States to submit information on serious violations of the protection, security and safety of diplomatic and consular missions and representatives and to inform him of their views with respect to any measures needed to enhance such protection and safety. In August, the Secretary-General submitted to the Assembly a report, with later addenda,[8] containing such information and views from 24 States, as well as a list of States parties, as at 9 August 1988, to the relevant conventions (see above).

Australia reported that one person had been convicted for offences related to the November 1986 bombing of the Turkish Consulate at Melbourne, and one violation had occurred at Canberra involving a South African diplomat. Belgium reported that the official investigation into the October 1987 attack perpetrated on a diplomat of the Syrian Arab Republic in Brussels had not been completed.

The Federal Republic of Germany charged Chile with failing to fulfil its international obligation to observe the immunity from jurisdiction of two German diplomats, a Minister Counsellor and a Consul, by initiating judicial proceedings against them. By ignoring diplomatic and consular immunity, the judicial authorities of Chile were, according to the Federal Republic of Germany, violating important provisions of the Vienna Conventions on diplomatic and consular relations. Chile replied that the rulings of its courts in this case did not in any way affect the immunity and jurisdiction referred to in the Vienna Conventions. Chile confirmed its adherence to the principles of international law, and therefore to the provisions of those Conventions. Furthermore, Chile said it would always guarantee the immunity of diplomatic and consular agents accredited in its territory. Chile also reported several violations which took place in 1987 against its diplomatic missions or representatives: an attack in September on its Embassy in Argentina by a group of approximately 400 persons, causing damage to its premises and injuring some policemen; in August, a group of 20 persons forced entry into its Consulate in Amsterdam, Netherlands; in November, a similar attempt was made against its Consulate in Tacna, Peru; in August, the armed robbery of the residence of its naval attaché in Brazil; and in November, the theft of two automobiles belonging to its diplomats in El Salvador and Paraguay.

Mexico reported that a United States national had regularly demonstrated offensive and provocative behaviour against the Mexican Consulate and consular officials in Los Angeles; it added that the United States, in some cases, had not done enough to curb those activities. It further mentioned that the diplomatic missions in Mexico of France, Greece and Denmark had been occupied briefly by non-violent protesters who dispersed quickly once their demands had been heard.

Norway provided information on the September 1987 violent occupation of the Iranian Embassy in Oslo by 11 Iranian citizens and the subsequent sentencing and expelling of the perpetrators from Norway. Cyprus reported that in May 1988 an automobile had been blown up near the Israeli Embassy in Nicosia, killing 4 persons, including the driver, and injuring 16 others. A suspect was arrested the same day. Israel reported three 1988 bomb explosions near its embassies: one in February in Manila, Philippines; another in March in Tokyo, Japan; and the third in May in Nicosia.

Greece reported the killing of a United States naval attaché in June 1988 in Athens. Lebanon listed two February 1988 incidents: the damaging of the residence of the Ambassador of Côte d'Ivoire by two hand-grenades, and the looting of the Chancellery of the Moroccan Mission.

In regard to the views on effective measures to enhance the protection, security and safety of diplomatic and consular representatives, the Republic of Korea suggested introducing into the existing system of domestic law provisions placing heavy punishment on offenders and increasing security around the premises of diplomatic and consular missions. The Byelorussian SSR felt that international legal guarantees for the entire area of inter-State relations should be improved through the addition of specific measures to strengthen existing international legal instruments, and that work should be continued on the codification and progressive development of diplomatic law. Australia, the Byelorussian SSR, Mexico, Poland, the Republic of Korea, the Ukrainian SSR and the USSR expressed support for the principles of effective measures to enhance the protection, security and safety of diplomatic and consular representatives and missions.

GENERAL ASSEMBLY ACTION

On 9 December, the General Assembly, on the recommendation of the Sixth (Legal) Committee, adopted **resolution 43/167** without vote.

Consideration of effective measures to enhance the protection, security and safety of diplomatic and consular missions and representatives

The General Assembly,

Having considered the report of the Secretary-General,

Conscious of the need to develop and strengthen friendly relations and co-operation among States,

Convinced that respect for the principles and rules of international law governing diplomatic and consular relations is a basic prerequisite for the normal conduct of relations among States and for the fulfilment of the purposes and principles of the Charter of the United Nations,

Alarmed by the repeated acts of violence against diplomatic and consular representatives, as well as against representatives to international intergovernmental organizations and officials of such organizations, which endanger or take innocent lives and seriously impede the normal work of such representatives and officials,

Concerned at the failure to respect the inviolability of diplomatic and consular missions and representatives,

Also concerned at the abuse of diplomatic or consular privileges and immunities, particularly if acts of violence are involved,

Emphasizing the duty of States to take all appropriate measures as required by international law, including measures of a preventive nature, and to bring offenders to justice,

Welcoming measures already taken by States to this end in conformity with their international obligations,

Convinced that the role of the United Nations, which includes the reporting procedures established under General Assembly resolution 35/168 of 15 December 1980 and further elaborated in later Assembly resolutions, is important in promoting efforts to enhance the protection, security and safety of diplomatic and consular missions and representatives,

Reaffirming its resolution 42/154 of 7 December 1987,

1. *Takes note* of the report of the Secretary-General;

2. *Strongly condemns* acts of violence against diplomatic and consular missions and representatives, as well as against missions and representatives to international intergovernmental organizations and officials of such organizations, and emphasizes that such acts can never be justified;

3. *Urges* States to observe, implement and enforce the principles and rules of international law governing diplomatic and consular relations and, in particular, to ensure, in conformity with their international obligations, the protection, security and safety of the missions, representatives and officials mentioned in paragraph 2 above officially present in territories under their jurisdiction, including practical measures to prohibit in their territories illegal activities of persons, groups and organizations that encourage, instigate, organize or engage in the perpetration of acts against the security and safety of such missions, representatives and officials;

4. *Also urges* States to take all necessary measures at the national and international levels to prevent any acts of violence against the missions, representatives and officials mentioned in paragraph 2 above, and to bring offenders to justice;

5. *Recommends* that States should co-operate closely through, *inter alia*, contacts between the diplomatic and consular missions and the receiving State, with regard to practical measures designed to enhance the protection, security and safety of diplomatic and consular missions and representatives and with regard to exchange of information on the circumstances of all serious violations thereof;

6. *Calls upon* States that have not yet done so to consider becoming parties to the instruments relevant to

the protection, security and safety of diplomatic and consular missions and representatives;

7. *Also calls upon* States, in cases where a dispute arises
in connection with a violation of their international obligations concerning the protection of the missions or
the security of the representatives and officials mentioned in paragraph 2 above, to make use of the means
for peaceful settlement of disputes, including the good
offices of the Secretary-General, and requests the
Secretary-General, when he deems it appropriate, to
offer his good offices to the States directly concerned;

8. *Requests* all States to report to the Secretary-
General in accordance with the provisions of resolution
42/154;

9. *Requests* the Secretary-General to issue a report
on the item, in accordance with paragraph 12 of resolution 42/154, on an annual basis, as well as to proceed
with his other tasks pursuant to the same resolution;

10. *Decides* to include in the provisional agenda of its
forty-fifth session the item entitled ''Consideration of
effective measures to enhance the protection, security
and safety of diplomatic and consular missions and
representatives: report of the Secretary-General''.

General Assembly resolution 43/167

9 December 1988   Meeting 76   Adopted without vote

Approved by Sixth Committee (A/43/821) without vote, 14 November (meet-
ing 41); 19-nation draft (A/C.6/43/L.7); agenda item 132.
Sponsors: Argentina, Australia, Austria, Bulgaria, Canada, Denmark, Finland,
Germany, Federal Republic of, Hungary, Iceland, Japan, Mongolia, Nether-
lands, Norway, Philippines, Sierra Leone, Sweden, Turkey, Uruguay.
Meeting numbers. GA 43rd session: 6th Committee 7-10, 41, 47; plenary 76.

Status of diplomatic bags and couriers

The International Law Commission (ILC), at its
1988 session,[9] considered the eighth report[10] of
the Special Rapporteur, Alexander Yankov (Bulgaria), on the status of the diplomatic courier and
the diplomatic bag not accompanied by diplomatic
courier. In response to a 1987 General Assembly
request,[11] 28 Member States and Switzerland[12]
submitted to ILC their views on the set of 33 draft
articles dealing with the issue, which had been
provisionally adopted by ILC in 1986.[13]

In his report, the Special Rapporteur analysed
the observations submitted by Governments and
summarized the main trends and proposals for
each of the draft articles. After considering the report, ILC referred the draft articles to its Drafting Committee for a second reading, together with
the proposals made by the Special Rapporteur and
those formulated in the plenary, on the understanding that he could make new proposals to the
Committee if he deemed it appropriate.

REFERENCES

[1]*Multilateral Treaties Deposited with the Secretary-General: Status as at
31 December 1988* (ST/LEG/SER.E/7), Sales No. E.89.V.3.
[2]YUN 1961, p. 512. [3]*Ibid.*, p. 516. [4]YUN 1963, p. 510.
[5]*Ibid.*, p. 512. [6]YUN 1973, p. 775, GA res. 3166(XXVIII),
annex, 14 Dec. 1973. [7]YUN 1987, p. 1068, GA res. 42/154,
7 Dec. 1987. [8]A/43/527 & Add.1-3. [9]A/43/10.
[10]A/CN.4/417 & Corr.1,2. [11]YUN 1987, p. 1086, GA
res. 42/156, 7 Dec. 1987. [12]A/CN.4/409 & Corr.1,2 & Add.1-
5. [13]YUN 1986, p. 996.

State immunities, liability and responsibility

In response to the Assembly's 1987 recommendation,[1] ILC, in 1988,[2] took up three aspects of
international law concerning States: jurisdictional
immunities of States and their property, international liability for injurious consequences arising
out of acts not prohibited by international law, and
State responsibility for internationally wrongful
acts.

In December, the Assembly recommended that,
taking into account government comments, ILC
should continue its work on those topics (**resolution 43/169**).

Draft articles on State immunities

At its 1988 session, ILC had before it the
preliminary report[3] of its Special Rapporteur,
Motoo Ogiso (Japan), on jurisdictional immunities of States and their property, which attempted
to analyse the comments of 23 Member States and
Switzerland[4] on a set of 28 draft articles which
the Commission had provisionally adopted in
1986.[5] Comments by five other Member States
were received later.[6]

Due to lack of time, ILC was unable to consider
the topic, but allowed the Special Rapporteur to
introduce his report to expedite its future work. The
Rapporteur made comments of a general nature
concerning the distinction between two kinds of acts
of States, namely *acta jure imperii* and *acta jure gestionis*,
noting that there were fundamental differences of
views in both ILC and in the Assembly's Sixth
Committee, as well as in Governments' comments
on the conclusion that the jurisdictional immunity
could be applied only to the *acta jure imperii* and not
to the *acta jure gestionis*. The theoretical differences
of view were between those countries that favoured
the so-called restrictive theory of State immunity
and those that supported the absolute theory.

Draft articles on State liability

In 1988, ILC[2] continued consideration of draft
articles on international liability for injurious consequences arising out of acts not prohibited by international law. It had before it the fourth report[7]
of the Special Rapporteur on the topic, Julio Barboza (Argentina), containing 10 draft articles. Chapter I (general provisions) contained articles 1 to 5
and chapter II (principles) contained articles 6 to
10. The draft articles dealt with: scope of the articles; use of terms; attribution; relationship between
the articles and other international agreements; absence of effect on other rules of international law;
freedom of action and the limits thereto; co-operation;
participation; prevention; and reparation.

After discussing the articles, ILC referred the articles to its Drafting Committee, together with the comments made by ILC members on specific aspects. It stated that it would welcome the views of Governments on the topic, particularly on the role which risk and harm should play.

Draft articles on State responsibility

In 1988, ILC[2] had before it the preliminary report[8] of its Special Rapporteur, Gaetano Arangio-Ruiz (Italy), on State responsibility, as well as observations on the topic received from one Government,[9] in response to a 1980 General Assembly request.[10]

ILC was unable to consider the topic in 1988 due to lack of time, but allowed the Special Rapporteur to introduce his report to expedite its future work. The report dealt with the remaining Part Two (content, forms and degrees of State responsibility) and Part Three (peaceful settlement of disputes arising from an alleged internationally wrongful act). It also re-examined articles 6 (cessation of an internationally wrongful act of a continuing character) and 7 (restitution in kind) of Part Two.

REFERENCES
[1]YUN 1987, p. 1086, GA res. 42/156, 7 Dec. 1987. [2]A/43/10. [3]A/CN.4/415 & Corr.1. [4]A/CN.4/410 & Add.1. [5]YUN 1986, p. 997. [6]A/CN.4/410/Add.2-5. [7]A/CN.4/413 & Corr.1. [8]A/CN.4/416 & Corr.1,2 & Add.1 & Add.1/Corr.1,2. [9]A/CN.4/414. [10]YUN 1980, p. 1129, GA res. 35/163, 15 Dec. 1980.

Treaties and agreements

In 1988, the Secretariat continued its depository functions for bilateral and multilateral agreements deposited with the Secretary-General.

Treaties involving international organizations

The 1986 Vienna Convention on the Law of Treaties between States and International Organizations or between International Organizations[1] was, in 1988, acceded to by Bulgaria and Hungary, and ratified by Mexico and Sweden.[2]

Registration and publication of treaties by the United Nations

During 1988, some 1,025 international agreements and 305 subsequent actions were received by the Secretariat for registration or filing and recording. In addition, there were 273 registrations of formalities concerning agreements for which the Secretary-General performs depositary functions.

The texts of international agreements registered or filed and recorded are published in the United Nations *Treaty Series* in the original languages, with translations into English and French where necessary. In 1988, the following volumes of the *Treaty Series* covering treaties registered or filed in 1978, 1979, 1980 and 1981 were issued:

1066, 1096, 1123, 1124, 1134, 1136, 1138, 1148, 1152, 1156, 1158, 1162, 1166, 1167, 1169, 1177, 1181, 1182, 1185, 1186, 1197, 1206, 1235.

Multilateral treaties

New multilateral treaties concluded under United Nations auspices

The following treaties, concluded under United Nations auspices, were deposited with the Secretary-General during 1988:[2]

Protocol to the 1979 Convention on Long-Range Transboundary Air Pollution concerning the Control of Emissions of Nitrogen Oxides or their Transboundary Fluxes, concluded at Sofia on 31 October 1988

Convention on International Bills of Exchange and International Promissory Notes, adopted by the General Assembly of the United Nations on 9 December 1988

United Nations Convention Against Illicit Traffic in Narcotic Drugs and Psychotropic Substances, concluded at Vienna on 20 December 1988

Regulation No. 74: Uniform provisions concerning the approval of mopeds with regard to the installation of lighting and light-signalling devices; Regulation No. 75: Uniform provisions concerning the approval of pneumatic tyres for motor cycles; Regulation No. 76: Uniform provisions concerning the approval of headlamps for mopeds emitting a driving beam and a passing beam; Regulation No. 77: Uniform provisions concerning the approval of parking lamps for power-driven vehicles; Regulation No. 78: Uniform provisions concerning the approval of vehicles of category L with regard to braking; Regulation No. 79: Uniform provisions concerning the approval of vehicles with regard to the steering equipment; Regulation No. 80: Uniform provisions concerning the approval of seats of large passenger vehicles and of these vehicles with regard to the strength of their seats and their anchorages; Regulation No. 81: Uniform provisions concerning the approval of rear-view mirrors, and of two-wheeled power-driven vehicles with or without side car with regard to the installation of rear-view mirrors on handlebars; Regulation No. 82: Uniform provisions concerning the approval of moped headlamps equipped with filament halogen lamps (HS2)—all annexed to the *Agreement concerning the Adoption of Uniform Conditions of Approval and Reciprocal Recognition of Approval for Motor Vehicle Equipment and Parts*, done at Geneva on 20 March 1958

Multilateral treaties deposited with the Secretary-General

The number of multilateral treaties for which the Secretary-General performed depositary functions stood at 351 at the end of 1988. During the year, 75 signatures were affixed to treaties for which the Secretary-General performed depositary functions and 374 instruments of ratification, accession, acceptance and approval or notification were transmitted to him. In addition, he received 167 communications from States expressing observations or declarations and reservations made at the time of signature, ratification or accession.

The following multilateral treaties in respect of which the Secretary-General acts as depositary came into force during 1988:[2]

International Convention against Apartheid in Sports, adopted by the General Assembly of the United Nations on 10 December 1985

Convention on the Limitation Period in the International Sale of Goods, concluded at New York on 14 June 1974, as amended by the Protocol of 11 April 1980

United Nations Convention on Contracts for the International Sale of Goods, concluded at Vienna on 11 April 1980

Regulation No. 72: Uniform provisions concerning the approval of motor-cycle headlamps emitting an asymmetrical passing beam and a driving beam and equipped with halogen lamps (HS1 lamps); Regulation No. 73: Uniform provisions concerning the approval of goods vehicles, trailers and semi-trailers with regard to their lateral protection; Regulation No. 74: Uniform provisions concerning the approval of mopeds with regard to the installation of lighting and light-signalling devices; Regulation No. 75: Uniform provisions concerning the approval of pneumatic tyres for motor cycles; Regulation No. 76: Uniform provisions concerning the approval of headlamps for mopeds emitting a driving beam and a passing beam; Regulation No. 77:
Uniform provisions concerning the approval of parking lamps for power-driven vehicles; Regulation No. 78: Uniform provisions concerning the approval of vehicles of category L with regard to braking; Regulation No. 79: Uniform provisions concerning the approval of vehicles with regard to the steering equipment—all annexed to the *Agreement concerning the Adoption of Uniform Conditions of Approval and Reciprocal Recognition of Approval for Motor Vehicle Equipment and Parts*, done at Geneva on 20 March 1958

Protocol to the 1979 Convention on Long-Range Transboundary Air Pollution on Long-Term Financing of the Co-operative Programme for Monitoring and Evaluation of the Long-Range Transmission of Air Pollutants in Europe (EMEP), concluded at Geneva on 28 September 1984

Vienna Convention for the Protection of the Ozone Layer, concluded at Vienna on 22 March 1985

REFERENCES

[1]YUN 1986, p. 1006. [2]*Multilateral Treaties Deposited with the Secretary-General: Status as at 31 December 1988* (ST/LEG/SER.E/7), Sales No. E.89.V.3.

PUBLICATION

Statement of Treaties and International Agreements. Registered or filed and recorded with the Secretariat during 1988, ST/LEG/SER.A/491-502 (monthly).

Chapter IV

Law of the sea

The landmark 1982 United Nations Convention on the Law of the Sea continued to fulfil its role of establishing a legal order for the seas and oceans. The number of ratifications increased to 37 in 1988 and some 106 States were claiming a territorial sea of 12 nautical miles.

The Secretary-General emphasized that without international law respected by all States, there could be no stable framework for multilateral co-operation in a highly complex world of sovereign nations and conflicting interests. It was natural therefore that States should continue to urge early ratification of, or accession to, the Convention, emphasizing its importance not only for ocean uses and resources, but also for the maintenance of peace and security and the strengthening of international co-operation in many areas.

In November, the General Assembly, by resolution 43/18, noted the progress being made by the Preparatory Commission for the International Sea-Bed Authority and for the International Tribunal for the Law of the Sea and expressed its satisfaction with the historic 1987 decisions of the Preparatory Commission to register the four pioneer investors sponsored respectively by India, France, Japan and the USSR, and to designate reserved areas for the Authority.

UN Convention on the Law of the Sea

Signatures and ratifications

During 1988, the number of ratifications of the United Nations Convention on the Law of the Sea increased to 37,[1] with the addition of Brazil and Cyprus. The Convention was to enter into force 12 months after receipt of the sixtieth instrument of ratification or accession.

The Convention, adopted by the Third United Nations Conference on the Law of the Sea in 1982,[2] closed for signature in 1984, having received a total of 159 signatures.[3]

Developments relating to the Convention

In response to a 1987 General Assembly resolution,[4] the Secretary-General reported in October 1988[5] on developments pertaining to the Convention and on the implementation of that resolution. The two-part report gave an overview of developments relating to the law of the sea and outlined the activities of the Office for Ocean Affairs and the Law of the Sea.

The report reflected the increasing concern of the international community with the protection of the global environment and expressed the growing need for enhanced international co-operation to protect the seas and oceans, particularly in relation to international security, economic development and environmental balance. The focus and scope of international co-operation involving ocean issues had also been influenced by the emergence of the new concept of environmentally sound and sustainable development, as well as by new concerns over global climate and ecological balance.

The report stated that the year had seen considerable legislative activity in various intergovernmental forums, particularly on unlawful acts at sea and on environmental protection questions, including those concerning responsibility and liability. In all such cases, the Convention had been instrumental in helping to promote the development of law and policy, and in helping to ensure compatibility in the various related fields of international law.

The Convention continued to receive broad national and international support. States continued to use the Convention not only as a model for enacting their maritime laws and regulations, but as an instrument for providing norms for assessing the validity of maritime claims by other States. In this sense, the Convention fulfilled its role of establishing a legal order for the seas and oceans. At the international level, the Fourth Special Antarctic Treaty Consultative Meeting on Antarctic Mineral Resources stated that the geographic extent of the continental shelf as referred to in the 1988 Convention on the Regulation of the Antarctic Mineral Resource Activities would be determined by reference to the relevant paragraphs of article 76 of the United Nations Convention on the Law of the Sea. The Convention had also influenced a number of forums in their work on the law of the non-navigational uses of international watercourses.

The general acceptance of a 12-mile territorial sea, as provided for in the Convention, was acknowledged to be a major contribution to international law, as the move towards establishing or recognizing the 12-mile limit became more widespread. Some 106 States had extended their territorial sea to 12 nautical miles, with Belgium,

Ireland and the United Kingdom[5] being the most recent to have done so.

According to the report, it was established law that, in the exclusive economic zone, a coastal State had sovereign rights for the purposes of exploring and exploiting, conserving and managing the natural resources, whether living or non-living, of the waters superjacent to the sea-bed and of the sea-bed and its subsoil. In addition, the coastal States had jurisdiction in the zone over artificial islands, installations and structures, marine scientific research and the protection and preservation of the marine environment. All other States enjoyed certain basic freedoms of the high seas, including freedom of navigation and overflight, the freedom to lay submarine cables and pipelines, and other internationally lawful uses of the sea related to those freedoms.

In 1988, 90 coastal States had enacted legislation claiming jurisdiction over marine research activities and 24 had promulgated detailed regulations and procedures for those activities within the terms of article 246 of the Convention.[6]

As States continued to implement the norms contained in the Convention, the need to delimit their maritime boundaries became increasingly important. The delimitation of maritime boundaries by the agreement of the coastal States concerned was one of the prescribed modes of settling such disputes and several agreements were concluded in 1988. Among them were agreements between Sweden and the USSR on principles for delimiting sea areas in the Baltic Sea (13 January); between Solomon Islands and Australia establishing certain sea and sea-bed boundaries (11 September); between France and the United Kingdom relating to delimiting the territorial sea in the Strait of Dover (2 November); and between the United Kingdom and Ireland concerning the delimitation of areas of the continental shelf between them (7 November).

However, the International Court of Justice remained seized of the 1986 dispute between El Salvador and Honduras concerning their land, island and maritime frontier.[7] Likewise, the dispute between Guinea-Bissau and Senegal as to their maritime frontier was still before an arbitral tribunal. Since August 1988, the Court had also been seized of the dispute concerning the delimitation of Denmark's and Norway's fishing zones and continental shelf areas between the east coast of Greenland and the Norwegian island of Jan Mayen.

Other developments relating to the law of the sea reviewed in the report included peaceful uses of the seas, maritime law, world shipping, protection and preservation of the marine environment, marine science and technology, and fisheries management and development.

With respect to peaceful uses of the seas, there was considerable support for the development of a multilateral agreement for the prevention of incidents at sea beyond the territorial sea. Such an agreement would be in addition to those bilateral agreements already existing, including the new 1988 agreement between the Federal Republic of Germany and the USSR concerning the prevention of incidents at sea beyond the territorial sea.

On 20 December 1988, the United Nations Convention against Illicit Traffic in Narcotic Drugs and Psychotropic Substances was adopted and article 17 dealt explicitly with illicit traffic by sea.

A draft Convention for the Suppression of Unlawful Acts against the Safety of Maritime Navigation, as well as a draft Protocol for the Suppression of Unlawful Acts against the Safety of Fixed Platforms Located on the Continental Shelf, were considered at a diplomatic conference convened by the International Maritime Organization (IMO) in Rome in March 1988. On 10 March, the Conference adopted both instruments, which filled an important gap in international law, inasmuch as they dealt with unlawful acts (terrorism) on the high seas that fell outside the crime of piracy, as defined in article 101 of the United Nations Convention on the Law of the Sea. By June 1988, 23 countries had signed the Convention and 21 had signed the Protocol.

One hundred countries had ratified the 1974 International Convention for the Safety of Life at Sea (SOLAS)[8] and the 1972 Convention on the International Regulations for Preventing Collisions at Sea.[9] The Collision Regulations currently applied to 94 per cent of the world's merchant tonnage and SOLAS to 95 per cent. SOLAS had recently been amended to deal directly with roll-on/roll-off ferries, in response to the disaster of the *Herald of Free Enterprise* in Belgium. One of the most important innovations in the Collision Regulations had been the recognition given to traffic separation schemes. Amendments due to enter into force on 19 November 1989 concerned changes in these schemes, procedures for crossing traffic lanes and the use of inshore traffic lanes. Other rules concerned the operation of vessels in narrow channels, the conduct of vessels manœuvre in restricted visibility and provisions concerning vessels constrained by their draught.

Several international 1988 conferences[10] adopted protocols, amending both SOLAS and the 1978 SOLAS Protocol and the 1966 Load Lines Convention[11] in order to introduce a Global Maritime Distress and Safety System (GMDSS), and a new harmonized system of survey and certifications for ships. These protocols were expected to enter into force on 1 February 1992. GMDSS had been developed over the course of many years and after a great deal of discussion involving IMO, the International Telecommunication Union (ITU) and the International Maritime Satellite Organization (INMARSAT). The basic concept of the system was that search and rescue authorities ashore, as well as shipping in the immediate vicinity of the ship in distress, would be rapidly alerted to a distress incident so that they could assist in a co-ordinated search and rescue operation with the minimum delay. The search itself would also be conducted according to procedures laid down by the 1979 International Convention on Maritime Search and Rescue,[12] as amplified in the IMO Manual on Search and Rescue. GMDSS, for its part, would provide the means of communication regardless of the area in which the ship was located. The system would also provide emergency and safety communications and maritime safety information, including navigational and meteorological warnings. Although satellites would play an important role through INMARSAT, they would not completely replace existing maritime radio communications.

As at 26 July 1988, 62 Governments had ratified or acceded to the London Dumping Convention (LDC). The current work of the contracting parties was focused on substantial strengthening of the global régime for dumping and incineration at sea, with implications also for the regional dumping protocols. The work done within the LDC framework had broad significance, considering that LDC parties constituted the only specialized global forum for environmental law, outside of IMO meetings on the 1978 Protocol (MARPOL 73/78)[13] to the 1973 International Convention for the Prevention of Pollution from Ships,[14] and that dumping issues were in large part a reflection of growing problems with waste management in general. An important feature also of the LDC forum was the role played by its scientific group in developing the scientific aspects of environmental regulatory systems.

Regarding incineration at sea, the 1988 consultative meeting of States parties to LDC agreed that States that had not used this method of disposal should consider alternative land-based options with a view to developing safer and more environmentally acceptable solutions. The meeting also called for an immediate halt to exports of liquid wastes by parties for burning in the waters of non-contracting States. The parties further agreed to take all possible steps to minimize or reduce substantially the marine incineration of noxious liquid wastes by 1 January 1991 and to re-evaluate the situation in 1992, with a view to ending the practice by 31 December 1994. It was further agreed that there were no fundamental inconsistencies between the United Nations Convention on the Law of the Sea and LDC that would suggest the need for amendment. LDC should therefore be interpreted in the light of developments of international law since its adoption in 1972, including those established in part XII of the Convention.

As for fisheries management and development, the 1987 Treaty between the the United States and members of the South Pacific Forum Fisheries Agency, covering fishing both inside and outside areas of coastal State jurisdiction, was currently in force by virtue of the United States ratification of 15 June 1988. Similar regional agreements were being sought with other distant water fleets operating in the region. The Committee for Eastern Central Atlantic Fisheries, at its 1988 session, adopted two important management recommendations which froze the harvesting of several stocks (cephalopods, mackerels and horse mackerels) in the northern area and regulated the mesh opening of beach seines in the Gulf of Guinea.

Preparatory Commission

In 1988, the Preparatory Commission for the International Sea-Bed Authority and for the International Tribunal for the Law of the Sea held its sixth session at Kingston, Jamaica, from 14 March to 8 April, and met in New York from 15 August to 2 September.[5] The major issues considered were the implementation of the obligations of pioneer investors and certifying States under resolution II[15] on the registration of pioneer investors in deep sea-bed mining, adopted in 1982 by the Third United Nations Conference on the Law of the Sea, and the preparation of the rules, regulations and procedures relating to the organs of the Authority.[16]

During the period under review, the Preparatory Commission focused its attention on the obligations, flowing from registration, of the pioneer investors and the certifying States. An informal consultation group was established to deal with the implementation of those obligations. It held five meetings and, at the Commission's summer meeting, the issues involved were also discussed in informal consultations between the Commission's Chairman and the various interest groups. The issues related to the training of personnel designated by the Commission (paragraph 12 (*a*) of resolution II); the implementation of paragraph 12 (*a*) of resolution II and paragraph 14 of another document[17] related to the exploration of minerals for the Enterprise; and the payment by pioneer investors of an annual fixed fee of $1 million (paragraph 7 (*b*) of resolution II).[18]

The Commission completed consideration of the draft rules of procedure of the Legal and Technical Commission and of the Economic Planning Commission and provisionally approved all, with the exception of those relating to elections, decision-making on questions of substance and observers, and matters which constituted some of the "hard-core issues" before the informal plenary. Draft rules of procedure of the Assembly and of the Council that did not fall under the category of "hard-core issues" were also examined and several were provisionally adopted. The Commission also reviewed draft rules of the Legal and Technical Commission that dealt with special procedures relating to the approval of plans of work. Due note was taken of the relevant provisions in the draft regulations on prospecting, exploration and exploitation of polymetallic nodules in the area,[19] but further consideration of this matter was postponed pending informal consultations to be undertaken by the Chairman.

A February paper[20] prepared by the Secretariat discussed the current status of deep sea-bed exploration and mining technology. Topics examined in the paper included exploration technology, mining technology, technology acquisition and future directions. A comparison of hydraulic mining subsystems and their complexity was contained in the annex.

The Special Representative of the Secretary-General for the Law of the Sea to the Commission submitted in March[21] a report on administrative action by the Secretary-General regarding the registration of pioneer investors under resolution II.

Special Commissions

The Preparatory Commission's four Special Commissions continued to work in accordance with their respective mandates.

Developing land-based producer States

The mandate of Special Commission 1 was to study the problems that would be encountered by the developing land-based producer States likely to be most seriously affected by sea-bed mineral production. In April,[22] the Special Commission's Chairman reported on its current work on the following issues: establishment of a compensation fund and/or system; the subsidization of sea-bed mining; the projection of demand, supply and prices for key metals; the categorizing of serious adverse effects of sea-bed production; isolation of the effects of sea-bed production; and the use of quantifiable yardsticks to identify the developing land-based producer States likely to be most seriously affected by sea-bed production. The Special Commission requested the Secretariat to prepare working papers on each of the topics and submit

recommendations to the Authority, through the Preparatory Commission.

In his September statement on the progress of the Commission's[23] work, the Special Commission Chairman noted, among other things, that discussion on these topics had identified gaps which needed to be covered in order to fulfil the overall work programme of the Commission. These pertained to: the recycling of copper, nickel, cobalt and manganese, with emphasis on the latter three metals; the substitution of these metals by other metals or materials and vice versa; the projection of future supply, demand and prices for these metals, along with a continuous updating of data on the mineral situation; bilateral trade in these metals, including barter trade; and commodity agreements with relevance for these metals. The statement also took note of the Third Regional Conference on the Development and Utilization of Mineral Resources in Africa (Kampala, Uganda, June), which addressed the growing difficulties faced by the African mining sector and solutions that might be found through strengthened regional co-operation.

The Enterprise

Special Commission 2, dealing with the establishment of the Enterprise—the Authority's operational arm—allocated much time to its *Ad Hoc* Working Group on Training, in accordance with the special priority established for the work of this Group, following the registration of the first group of pioneer investors. The Working Group, established in 1987, had succeeded in formulating a set of draft principles and policies that should govern a Preparatory Commission training programme.[24] Other meetings of the Commission were devoted to the item on structure and organization of the Enterprise, for which the Secretariat had prepared a working paper.[25] In April,[26] the Chairman reported on its progress of work, covering three subjects: assumptions; training; and structure and organization of the Enterprise. As for the latter, the Commission again affirmed that the Enterprise, at whatever phase of its development, must be a model organization as regards the competency of its staff, the efficiency of its management, and its ability to respond quickly and effectively to developments in the future sea-bed mining industry. It was again emphasized that its operations and final organizational configuration must await decisions that could only be made by the Enterprise itself.

A further Chairman's September progress report[27] dealt with exploration questions, assumptions about the behaviour of the metals market and training. The experts dwelt at some length on the special environmental problems they envisaged with sea-bed mining. It was pointed out that pollution problems with land-based mining tended to be localized, whereas sea-bed mining had the potential for wide-scale environmental disturbance. In addition, very little was known about the ecology of the deep sea and about the recovery rates of living organisms, which were assumed to be very slow. There was also the problem of pollution from sediment brought to the surface.

Sea-bed mining code

Special Commission 3, which was to prepare the rules, regulations and procedures for the exploration and exploitation of the deep sea-bed, continued its consideration of amendments[28] to a document[29] on financial terms of contract. The Commission held a first detailed reading[30] of the draft regulations on the transfer of technology prepared by the Secretariat,[31] together with amendments submitted by Belgium, the Federal Republic of Germany, Italy, Japan, the Netherlands and the United Kingdom.[32] Particular attention was given to the scope of the regulations, the use of terms, undertakings in contracts on the transfer of technology which the contractor was legally entitled to transfer, as well as those technologies that the contractor was not legally entitled to transfer, and the procedure for obtaining technology. In September,[33] the Commission's Chairman stated that the co-sponsors of the amendments agreed that the obligation of the contractor was a last-resort obligation; that the obligation ceased after the tenth year of commercial production by the Enterprise; and that if the obligation was invoked the resulting sale of technology by the contractor was to be at a fair and reasonable price.

A Seminar on the Current Status of Developments in Deep Sea-Bed Mining Technology (18-22 August) was also reviewed, with experts from various countries participating. The Seminar dealt with various aspects of deep-sea mining technology and was held, in part, to assist Special Commission 3 in its consideration of complex technology transfer issues, in particular the availability of deep sea-bed mining technology on the open market.

International Tribunal

Special Commission 4, which was mandated to prepare recommendations for the establishment of the International Tribunal for the Law of the Sea, completed in 1988[34] its article-by-article examination of the draft Headquarters Agreement between the International Tribunal and the host country, the Federal Republic of Germany,[35] a revised draft of which was prepared by the Secretariat in August.[36] Revised draft Rules of the Tribunal were submitted to the plenary by the Chairman of Commission 4 in February.[37] In addition, Commission 4 began examining the draft

Convention/Protocol on the Privileges and Immunities of the Tribunal.[38] It also substantially concluded consideration of procedures to be adopted for the prompt release of vessels and crews. In March,[39] the Chairman reported on the August 1987 visit by the Bureau of Special Commission 4 and Secretariat officials to the host country.

The Federal Republic of Germany communicated to the Special Representative of the Secretary-General for the Law of the Sea its intention to hold an international architectural competition for the design and construction of the building to house the Tribunal in Hamburg-Nienstedten. The Government proposed to invite about 20 national and international architects to submit designs. Estimates and assumptions as to the required space and facilities for the building had been made by government authorities in consultation with the United Nations. An international jury was to be established and to make its award in 1989.

The Chairman held informal consultations with interested delegations from all regional groups on matters relating to the seat of the Tribunal, in the event that the Federal Republic of Germany did not accede to the Convention before its entry into force.

Functions of the Secretary-General

Office for Ocean Affairs and the Law of the Sea

Following the consolidation in 1987 of marine affairs activities in the Office for Ocean Affairs and the Law of the Sea (OALOS),[40] the Office was responsible for implementing major programme 25 of the medium-term plan (1984-1989), comprising programme 1 (Law of the sea), and programme 2 (Economic and technical aspects of marine affairs). In addition, it had been entrusted with certain activities formerly carried out by the Department of Political and Security Council Affairs.[5]

The Office continued to provide integrated services to the Preparatory Commission, a substantial part of which involved the continuous preparation of studies and draft legal texts and the provision of information, data and analysis on matters dealt with by the different bodies of the Commission. Among important developments with regard to the Office's assistance programme was an increasing number of requests from Member States on planning and programming for maritime areas under national jurisdiction. They included requests from Mauritania, Senegal and the United Republic of Tanzania.

Given the comprehensive nature and complexity of the Convention, the Office endeavoured to strengthen its co-operation within the United

Nations system. To this end it convened, in July, the first *Ad Hoc* Inter-Agency Consultation on Ocean Affairs at which 14 organizations and bodies were represented. The consultation was convened on a recommendation of ICSPRO (the Intergovernmental Oceanographic Commission with UNESCO, IMO, FAO, WMO and OALOS). Because of its limited membership and mandate, ICSPRO felt that a wider forum was needed for consultations encompassing the broad spectrum of marine activities, including a review of global and regional developments. The discussions demonstrated that it was extremely important for the United Nations system to consult regularly on matters of common interest.

The Office was also represented at, and in most cases prepared papers for, numerous meetings of governmental and non-governmental organizations.

The third Hamilton Shirley Amerasinghe Memorial Fellowship on the Law of the Sea—established by the General Assembly in 1981[41] in honour of the first President of the Third United Nations Conference on the Law of the Sea and financed by voluntary contributions—was awarded to Maria Luisa Carvallo, of the Ministry of Foreign Affairs of Chile.[42] The fellowship, valued at about $20,000, provided six months of postgraduate university study or research and a three-month internship with OALOS.

A new mineral data base (MINDAT) was added to the computerized Law of the Sea Information System, and would also be used for the work of the Preparatory Commission. MINDAT, currently containing 25 categories of information on copper, nickel, manganese and cobalt, by country and with global totals, also detailed the production, consumption and import and export of the minerals in various forms for the period 1971-1986.

GENERAL ASSEMBLY ACTION

On 1 November, the General Assembly adopted **resolution 43/18** by recorded vote.

Law of the sea

The General Assembly,

Reaffirming its resolutions 37/66 of 3 December 1982, 38/59 A of 14 December 1983, 39/73 of 13 December 1984, 40/63 of 10 December 1985, 41/34 of 5 November 1986 and 42/20 of 18 November 1987, regarding the law of the sea,

Recognizing that, as stated in the third preambular paragraph of the United Nations Convention on the Law of the Sea, the problems of ocean space are closely interrelated and need to be considered as a whole,

Convinced that it is important to safeguard the unified character of the Convention and related resolutions adopted therewith and to refrain from applying their provisions selectively, in a manner inconsistent with their object and purpose,

Emphasizing the need for States to ensure consistent application of the Convention, as well as the need for harmonization of national legislation with the provisions of the Convention,

Considering that, in its resolution 2749(XXV) of 17 December 1970, it proclaimed that the sea-bed and ocean floor, and the subsoil thereof, beyond the limits of national jurisdiction (hereinafter referred to as "the Area"), as well as the resources of the Area, are the common heritage of mankind,

Recalling that the Convention provides the régime to be applied to the Area and its resources,

Emphasizing that no State should undermine the Convention and related resolutions of the Third United Nations Conference on the Law of the Sea,

Recognizing also the need for co-operation in the early and effective implementation by the Preparatory Commission for the International Sea-Bed Authority and for the International Tribunal for the Law of the Sea of resolution II of the Third United Nations Conference on the Law of the Sea,

Noting with satisfaction the progress made in the Preparatory Commission since its inception, including the registration in 1987 as pioneer investors of Institut français de recherche pour l'exploitation de la mer (IFREMER), the Government of India, Deep Ocean Resources Development Co., Ltd. (DORD) and Yuzhmorgeologiya, whose applications were submitted by the Governments of France, India, Japan and the Union of Soviet Socialist Republics respectively, bearing in mind that such registration entails both rights and obligations,

Noting also with satisfaction the designation by the Preparatory Commission of reserved areas for the Authority from the application areas submitted by the pioneer investors pursuant to resolution II,

Noting also that the Preparatory Commission has decided to hold its seventh regular session at Kingston from 27 February to 23 March 1989 and to hold a summer meeting in 1989,

Noting further the increasing needs of countries, especially developing countries, for information, advice and assistance in the implementation of the Convention and in their developmental process for the full realization of the benefits of the comprehensive legal régime established by the Convention,

Recognizing that the Convention encompasses all uses and resources of the sea and that all related activities within the United Nations system need to be implemented in a manner consistent with it,

Noting with appreciation the important initiative of the Secretary-General in convening an inter-agency meeting on international and regional developments in ocean affairs and the law of the sea,

Deeply concerned at the current state of the marine environment,

Taking note of activities carried out in 1988 under the major programme on marine affairs, set forth in chapter 25 of the medium-term plan for the period 1984-1989, in accordance with the report of the Secretary-General, as approved in General Assembly resolution 38/59 A, and the report of the Secretary-General,

Recalling its approval of the financing of the expenses of the Preparatory Commission from the regular budget of the United Nations,

Taking special note of the report of the Secretary-General prepared in pursuance of paragraph 14 of General Assembly resolution 42/20,

1. *Recalls* the historic significance of the United Nations Convention on the Law of the Sea as an important contribution to the maintenance of peace, justice and progress for all peoples of the world;

2. *Expresses its satisfaction* at the increasing and overwhelming support for the Convention, as evidenced, *inter alia*, by the one hundred and fifty-nine signatures and thirty-five of the sixty ratifications or accessions required for entry into force of the Convention;

3. *Calls upon* all States that have not done so to consider ratifying or acceding to the Convention at the earliest possible date to allow the effective entry into force of the new legal régime for the uses of the sea and its resources;

4. *Calls upon* all States to safeguard the unified character of the Convention and related resolutions adopted therewith;

5. *Also calls upon* States to observe the provisions of the Convention when enacting their national legislation;

6. *Further calls upon* States to desist from taking actions which undermine the Convention or defeat its object and purpose;

7. *Notes* the progress being made by the Preparatory Commission for the International Sea-Bed Authority and for the International Tribunal for the Law of the Sea in all areas of its work;

8. *Expresses its satisfaction* at the historic decisions of the Preparatory Commission of 17 August and 17 December 1987 to register the four pioneer investors sponsored respectively by India, France, Japan and the Union of Soviet Socialist Republics and to designate reserved areas for the Authority;

9. *Looks forward* to the early and satisfactory conclusion of the current consultations in the Preparatory Commission on the implementation of the obligations of the registered pioneer investors and the certifying States;

10. *Expresses its appreciation* to the Secretary-General for his efforts in support of the Convention and for the effective execution of the major programme on marine affairs set forth in chapter 25 of the medium-term plan for the period 1984-1989;

11. *Also expresses its appreciation* for the report of the Secretary-General prepared in pursuance of General Assembly resolution 42/20 and requests him to continue to carry out the activities outlined therein, as well as those aimed at the strengthening of the legal régime of the sea, special emphasis being placed on the work of the Preparatory Commission, including the implementation of resolution II of the Third United Nations Conference on the Law of the Sea;

12. *Calls upon* the Secretary-General to continue to assist States in the implementation of the Convention and in the development of a consistent and uniform approach to the legal régime thereunder, as well as in their national, subregional and regional efforts towards the full realization of the benefits therefrom, and invites the organs and organizations of the United Nations system to co-operate and lend assistance in these endeavours;

13. *Approves* the decision of the Preparatory Commission to hold its seventh regular session at Kingston from 27 February to 23 March 1989 and to hold a summer meeting in 1989;

14. *Requests* the Secretary-General to report to the General Assembly at its forty-fourth session on developments pertaining to the Convention and all related activities and on the implementation of the present resolution;

15. *Also requests* the Secretary-General to prepare for the General Assembly at its forty-fourth session a special report on recent developments related to the protection and preservation of the marine environment in the light of the relevant provisions of the United Nations Convention on the Law of the Sea;

16. *Decides* to include in the provisional agenda of its forty-fourth session the item entitled "Law of the sea".

General Assembly resolution 43/18

1 November 1988   Meeting 41   135-2-6 (recorded vote)

52-nation draft (A/43/L.18 & Add.1); agenda item 35.

Sponsors: Algeria, Australia, Austria, Bahamas, Brazil, Bulgaria, Byelorussian SSR, Cameroon, Canada, Cape Verde, Chile, China, Côte d'Ivoire, Denmark, Egypt, Ethiopia, Fiji, Finland, German Democratic Republic, Ghana, Iceland, India, Indonesia, Ireland, Jamaica, Kuwait, Madagascar, Malaysia, Malta, Mexico, New Zealand, Nigeria, Norway, Oman, Pakistan, Philippines, Portugal, Romania, Senegal, Sierra Leone, Singapore, Solomon Islands, Sri Lanka, Sudan, Sweden, Thailand, Trinidad and Tobago, Tunisia, Ukrainian SSR, United Republic of Tanzania, Uruguay, Vanuatu.

Recorded vote in Assembly as follows:

In favour: Algeria, Angola, Antigua and Barbuda, Argentina, Australia, Austria, Bahamas, Bahrain, Bangladesh, Barbados, Belgium, Belize, Benin, Bhutan, Bolivia, Botswana, Brazil, Brunei Darussalam, Bulgaria, Burkina Faso, Burma, Burundi, Byelorussian SSR, Cameroon, Cape Verde, Central African Republic, Chad, Chile, China, Colombia, Congo, Costa Rica, Côte d'Ivoire, Cuba, Cyprus, Czechoslovakia, Democratic Kampuchea, Democratic Yemen, Denmark, Djibouti, Dominican Republic, Egypt, El Salvador, Equatorial Guinea, Ethiopia, Fiji, Finland, France, Gabon, German Democratic Republic, Ghana, Greece, Grenada, Guinea, Guinea-Bissau, Guyana, Hungary, Iceland, India, Indonesia, Iran, Iraq, Ireland, Israel,[a] Italy, Jamaica, Japan, Jordan, Kenya, Kuwait, Lao People's Democratic Republic, Lebanon, Lesotho, Liberia, Libyan Arab Jamahiriya, Luxembourg, Madagascar, Malawi, Malaysia, Maldives, Mali, Malta, Mauritania, Mauritius, Mexico, Mongolia, Morocco, Mozambique, Nepal, Netherlands, New Zealand, Nicaragua, Niger, Nigeria, Norway, Oman, Pakistan, Panama, Papua New Guinea, Paraguay, Philippines, Poland, Portugal, Qatar, Romania, Saint Lucia, Samoa, Sao Tome and Principe, Saudi Arabia, Senegal, Seychelles, Sierra Leone, Singapore, Solomon Islands, Somalia, Spain, Sri Lanka, Sudan, Swaziland, Sweden, Thailand, Togo, Trinidad and Tobago, Tunisia, Ukrainian SSR, USSR, United Arab Emirates, United Republic of Tanzania, Uruguay, Vanuatu, Viet Nam, Yemen, Yugoslavia, Zaire, Zambia.

Against: Turkey, United States.

Abstaining: Ecuador, Germany, Federal Republic of, Guatemala, Peru, United Kingdom, Venezuela.

[a]Later advised the Secretariat it had intended to abstain.

REFERENCES

[1]*Multilateral Treaties Deposited with the Secretary-General: Status as at 31 December 1988* (ST/LEG/SER.E/7), Sales No. E.89.V.3. [2]YUN 1982, p. 178. [3]YUN 1984, p. 108. [4]YUN 1987, p. 112, GA res. 42/20, 18 Nov. 1987. [5]A/43/718. [6]YUN 1982, p. 195. [7]YUN 1986, p. 984. [8]YUN 1974, p. 1030. [9]YUN 1972, p. 812. [10]A/44/461. [11]YUN 1966, p. 1058. [12]YUN 1979, p. 1317. [13]YUN 1978, p. 1161. [14]YUN 1973, p. 964. [15]YUN 1982, p. 216. [16]LOS/PCN/L.62 & Corr.1, LOS/PCN/L.67/Rev.1. [17]LOS/PCN/L.41/Rev.1. [18]LOS/PCN/L.67/Rev.1. [19]LOS/PCN/SCN.3/WP.6/Rev.1. [20]LOS/PCN/L.56 & Corr.1,2. [21]LOS/PCN/L.57. [22]LOS/PCN/L.58. [23]LOS/PCN/L.63. [24]LOS/PCN/SCN.2/1988/CRP.3. [25]LOS/PCN/SCN.2/WP.15. [26]LOS/PCN/L.60. [27]LOS/PCN/L.65. [28]LOS/PCN/SCN.3/WP.11 & Corr.1, LOS/PCN/SCN.3/WP.12. [29]LOS/PCN/SCN.3/WP.6/Add.2. [30]LOS/PCN/L.59. [31]LOS/PCN.3/WP.6/Add.4. [32]LOS/PCN/SCN.3/WP.13/Rev.1. [33]LOS/PCN/L.64. [34]LOS/PCN/L.66. [35]LOS/PCN/SCN.4/L.11/Add.1. [36]LOS/PCN/SCN.4/WP.5/Rev.1 & Corr.1. [37]LOS/PCN/SCN.4/L.10/Add.1 & Corr.1. [38]LOS/PCN/SCN.4/WP.6. [39]LOS/PCN.4/L.12. [40]YUN 1987, p. 111. [41]YUN 1981, p. 1268. [42]A/44/650 & Corr.1.

OTHER PUBLICATION

The Law of the Sea: A Select Bibliography (LOS/LIB/3), Sales No. E.88.V.2.

Chapter V

Other legal questions

In 1988, the United Nations continued to address various aspects of international law and international economic law.

The Assembly requested the Special Committee on the Charter of the United Nations and on the Strengthening of the Role of the Organization to give priority to the question of maintaining international peace and security in all its aspects in order to strengthen the United Nations role and to continue its work on the peaceful settlement of disputes between States (resolution 43/170).

The Assembly resumed its forty-second (1987) session in 1988 to consider the situation arising from the announced closing by the United States of the Palestine Liberation Organization (PLO) Observer Mission to the United Nations under its 1987 Anti-Terrorism Act. In March, the Assembly considered that a dispute existed between the United Nations and the host country concerning the interpretation or application of the 1947 Headquarters Agreement between the United Nations and the United States. It reaffirmed that the PLO mission was covered by the provisions of that Agreement and called on the host country to abide by it (42/229 A). It also decided to request an advisory opinion from the International Court of Justice (ICJ) as to whether the United States was obliged to enter into arbitration under the Agreement (42/229 B).

In November, the United States refused an entry visa for PLO Chairman Yasser Arafat to enable him to participate in the forty-third (1988) session of the Assembly. In December, the Assembly deplored the failure of the host country to respond favourably to its request to reverse the decision (43/48) and decided to consider the question of Palestine at the United Nations Office at Geneva from 13 to 15 December (43/49).

The Assembly recommended that the International Law Commission—responsible for the progressive development and codification of international law—continue working on all topics in its current programme (43/169).

The Assembly also called on States concerned to accord to national liberation movements recognized by the Organization of African Unity and/or the League of Arab States the facilities, privileges and immunities necessary for their functioning and decided that PLO and the South West Africa People's Organization were entitled to have their communications relating to the General Assem-bly issued and circulated without intermediary, as official Assembly documents (43/160 B).

Legal aspects of international economic law and the new international economic order continued to be considered by the United Nations Commission on International Trade Law (UNCITRAL) and the Sixth (Legal) Committee of the General Assembly. In December, the Assembly adopted and opened for signature or accession the United Nations Convention on International Bills of Exchange and International Promissory Notes, thereby putting the seal on more than 16 years of work by UNCITRAL (43/165). The Assembly recommended that UNCITRAL continue working on the topics in its work programme (43/166) and that the Sixth Committee make a final decision at the forty-fourth (1989) session of the Assembly on the appropriate forum to complete the codification and progressive development of the legal principles and norms relating to the new international economic order (43/162).

International organizations and international law

Strengthening the role of the United Nations

The Secretary-General, in his annual report on the work of the Organization, noted that on matters of international peace and security, the principal organs of the United Nations increasingly functioned as envisaged in the Charter. The working relationship of the Security Council and the Secretary-General had rarely if ever been closer. He stated that a number of international problems —Afghanistan, Cambodia, Cyprus, Iran-Iraq, Namibia and Western Sahara—in their different contexts, had moved towards solutions in consonance with the principles of the Charter. He observed that during the first four decades of its existence, the United Nations had been unable to put in place the reliable system of collective security that its Charter envisaged because developments during the early years of the Organization went contrary to expectations. However, if the United Nations was often brought to an impasse in maintaining international peace and security by the inability of permanent members of the Security Council to develop a common approach, the Organization had not allowed this to block its endeavours. With ingenuity and realism, it had found other ways of at least defusing conflicts. If, in one aspect, the United Nations had fallen short of the Charter's objectives, it had kept pace with, and often served as a catalyst to, rapid and peaceful change in other respects. Even when politically disabled by differences among permanent Council members, it had displayed a capacity for innovation, and had played a role that on no reckoning could be considered peripheral.

The Secretary-General said that while the great Powers, like other nations, normally resolved or reduced their differences through negotiations outside the United Nations, they needed the Organization to come to grips with issues that concerned other nations and that, in one way or another, impinged on their own relationships as well. All this argued for greater, not less, support for the United Nations. He stressed the need to adjust political attitudes on all sides to the double requirement of making United Nations resolutions more purposeful and of respecting them as genuine expressions or reminders of widely shared concerns.

Noting that there had been a reassuring and unanimous interest in restoring the Security Council's peacemaking capacity, the Secretary-General emphasized that the Council's effectiveness required that all Member States give it their full support, not only by accepting an agreed determination, but also by providing full diplomatic backing for it.

The Secretary-General said that while United Nations peace-keeping had proved to be a necessity in many conflicts, success depended not only on the consent of the parties, but also on: consistent support for the Council; a clear and practical mandate; the readiness of Member States to volunteer troops; and adequate financial arrangements. A cohesive approach in the spirit of the Charter, regardless of differences of perception, interest or ideology, was indispensable for resolving conflicts. Peace-keeping, however, could only be a palliative if it did not serve as a prelude to, or accompany negotiations towards, a comprehensive settlement.

The Secretary-General said that the Charter obligation of settling international disputes by peaceful means in conformity with the principles of justice and international law would imply that these disputes be kept under constant review by the Security Council.

The principle that treaties must be complied with in good faith was basic to the Charter, he said. Respect for international agreements was not only a fundamental principle of international law, it was the foundation of the organized international community. If this principle were abandoned, the superstructure of contemporary international law and organization, including the functioning of the United Nations, the effectiveness of its decisions and resort to international arbitration or judicial settlement of disputes, would collapse. It was thus in the equal interest of all States to work towards a world where nations would operate within a complete, coherent and viable system of law. The Secretary-General appealed to Governments to refer justiciable cases to the International Court of Justice (ICJ).

The Secretary-General welcomed the resolution by the Economic and Social Council on its revitalization which, when implemented, could greatly enhance its ability to give policy guidelines as well as to monitor and co-ordinate the economic and social activities of the United Nations system.

He stressed that the financial health of the Organization needed to be immediately restored. The impact of the Organization's financial crisis was heightened by increasing responsibilities for peace-making and peace-keeping. He asked that the General Assembly urgently consider both the cash and reserves aspects of the crisis, including new ways of raising money.

Activities of the Special Committee. The Special Committee on the Charter of the United Nations and on the Strengthening of the Role of the Organization[1] convened in accordance with a resolution by the General Assembly of 1987[2] (New York, 22 February–11 March) to consider proposals on the maintenance of international peace and security, and the peaceful settlement of disputes between States. It also had before it a progress report on a draft handbook on peaceful dispute settlement (see PART FIVE, Chapter II).

The Special Committee's Working Group considered a draft document on the prevention and removal of threats to peace and of situations that might lead to international friction or give rise to a dispute. Its deliberations were based on paragraphs which were provisionally adopted at its 1987 session.[3] The Committee subsequently submitted the draft Declaration on the Prevention and Removal of Disputes Which May Threaten International Peace and Security and the Role of the United Nations in this Field to the Assembly, which considered and adopted it as **resolution 43/51** (see PART FIVE, Chapter II).

The Working Group also had before it a further revised 1987 working paper on the rationalization of existing United Nations procedures, first submitted in 1985[4] by France and the United Kingdom. In presenting the paper, one of the co-sponsors indicated that, if annexed to the rules of procedure of the General Assembly, it would contribute to the efficiency of the Assembly's work.

GENERAL ASSEMBLY ACTION

On 9 December, the General Assembly, on the recommendation of the Sixth (Legal) Committee, adopted **resolution 43/170** without vote.

Report of the Special Committee on the Charter of the United Nations and on the Strengthening of the Role of the Organization

The General Assembly,

Recalling its resolution 3499(XXX) of 15 December 1975, by which it established the Special Committee on the Charter of the United Nations and on the Strengthening of the Role of the Organization, and its relevant resolutions adopted at subsequent sessions,

Taking note of the reports of the Secretary-General on the work of the Organization submitted to the General Assembly at its thirty-seventh, thirty-ninth, fortieth, forty-first, forty-second and forty-third sessions, as well as of the views and comments expressed on them by Member States,

Having considered the report of the Special Committee on the Charter of the United Nations and on the Strengthening of the Role of the Organization on the work of its session held in 1988,

Expressing its deep appreciation to the Special Committee for the progress achieved during its 1988 session, which led to the completion of the draft Declaration on the Prevention and Removal of Disputes and Situations Which May Threaten International Peace and Security and on the Role of the United Nations in this Field, and for submitting it to the General Assembly at its forty-third session for adoption,

Mindful of the desirability of further work being done by the Special Committee in the field of the maintenance of international peace and security,

Noting with satisfaction that tangible progress has been achieved in the Special Committee on the proposal concerning the resort to a commission of good offices, mediation or conciliation within the United Nations,

Noting also with satisfaction the progress achieved in the elaboration of the draft handbook on the peaceful settlement of disputes between States,

1. *Takes note* of the report of the Special Committee on the Charter of the United Nations and on the Strengthening of the Role of the Organization;

2. *Decides* that the Special Committee shall hold its next session from 27 March to 14 April 1989;

3. *Requests* the Special Committee, at its session in 1989, taking into account the provisions of paragraph 5 below:

    (a) To accord priority to the question of the maintenance of international peace and security in all its aspects in order to strengthen the role of the United Nations, and, in this context, to consider:

    (i) Proposals concerning fact-finding activities by the United Nations;

    (ii) Other proposals relating to the maintenance of international peace and security that might be submitted to the Special Committee at its session in 1989;

    (b) To continue its work on the question of the peaceful settlement of disputes between States, and, in this context:

    (i) To complete its consideration of the proposal on the resort to a commission of good offices, mediation or conciliation within the United Nations and to submit conclusions thereon, in an appropriate form, to the General Assembly at its forty-fourth session;

    (ii) To examine the progress report of the Secretary-

General on the elaboration of the draft handbook on the peaceful settlement of disputes between States;

4. *Requests* the Special Committee to keep the question of the rationalization of the procedures of the United Nations under active review;

5. *Also requests* the Special Committee to be mindful of the importance of reaching general agreement whenever that has significance for the outcome of its work;

6. *Decides* that the Special Committee shall accept the participation of observers of Member States, including in the meetings of its working group;

7. *Requests* the Secretary-General to continue, on a priority basis, the preparation of the draft handbook on the peaceful settlement of disputes between States, on the basis of the outline elaborated by the Special Committee and in the light of the views expressed in the course of the discussions in the Sixth Committee and in the Special Committee, and to report to the Special Committee at its session in 1989 on the progress of work, before submitting to it the draft handbook in its final form, with a view to its approval at a later stage;

8. *Also requests* the Secretary-General to render all assistance to the Special Committee;

9. *Requests* the Special Committee to submit a report on its work to the General Assembly at its forty-fourth session;

10. *Decides* to include in the provisional agenda of its forty-fourth session the item entitled "Report of the Special Committee on the Charter of the United Nations and on the Strengthening of the Role of the Organization".

General Assembly resolution 43/170

9 December 1988   Meeting 76   Adopted without vote

Approved by Sixth Committee (A/43/886) without vote, 22 November (meeting 46); 24-nation draft (A/C.6/43/L.15); agenda item 135.

Sponsors: Argentina, Belgium, Colombia, Cyprus, Czechoslovakia, Ecuador, Egypt, Germany, Federal Republic of, Ghana, Indonesia, Italy, Japan, Kenya, Morocco, New Zealand, Oman, Philippines, Poland, Romania, Senegal, Spain, Venezuela, Yugoslavia, Zambia.

Financial implications. 5th Committee, A/43/944; S-G, A/C.5/43/52, A/C.6/43/L.18.

Meeting numbers. GA 43rd session: 5th Committee 43; 6th Committee 14-20, 46; plenary 76.

Publication of Repertories of Practice

Pursuant to a request by the General Assembly of 1981[5] that the Secretary-General give priority to updating the supplements to the *Repertory of Practice of United Nations Organs* and the *Repertoire of the Practice of the Security Council*, a March 1988 note by the Secretariat[6] to the Special Committee on the Charter of the United Nations and on the Strengthening of the Role of the Organization—updating a corresponding note of 1987[7]—gave the current status of work on the above publications.

According to the note, *Supplement No. 5* of the *Repertory* (covering 1970-1978) was completed, with three volumes having been published in English and the two remaining volumes being scheduled for publication in English in 1989. Regarding *Supplement No. 6* (covering 1979-1984), the preliminary draft of one volume was completed and the drafting of another volume was near completion. The *Supplement for 1975-1980* of the *Repertoire* was published in English in 1987 and its French version was scheduled for publication in 1989. The manuscripts for the *Supplement for 1981-1984* were close to completion. It was noted that publication of the *Repertoire*, as with the *Repertory*, depended on the continued availability of financial and human resources. Reductions in both had already affected the preparatory work.

Host country relations

Pursuant to a General Assembly request of 1987,[8] the Committee on Relations with the Host Country continued to devote attention to relations between the United Nations diplomatic community and the United States, its host country. At five meetings between 5 May and 23 November,[9] the Committee considered: the security of missions and the safety of their personnel; the question of privileges and immunities; and matters relating to transportation. In connection with the implementation of the 1947 Headquarters Agreement between the United Nations and the United States,[10] the Committee discussed: host country legislation concerning the use of the premises of foreign missions; travel regulations; entry visas; the acceleration of immigration and customs procedures; the possibility of establishing a commissary at United Nations Headquarters to assist diplomatic personnel and staff; and the advisory opinion of ICJ of 26 April 1988 (see below, under ''Relations between the host country and PLO''; for the ICJ advisory opinion, see PART FIVE, Chapter I).

On 5 May, Bulgaria and the Libyan Arab Jamahiriya drew the Committee's attention to travel restrictions imposed by the host country on members and dependants of their respective missions. By letters of 9 June,[11] 25 July[12] and 7 November,[13] Bulgaria, Czechoslovakia, the German Democratic Republic and Poland brought to the attention of the Secretary-General the fact that, in a note verbale of 18 May, the United States had advised those missions, in addition to the mission of Albania, that, with immediate effect, their personnel and dependants were required to submit, in writing, requests for travel beyond a 25-mile radius outside New York City. Although the Permanent Representatives and their families were exempt from such notification, they were required to use the Foreign Missions Service for booking public transportation and accommodation. In their joint letters, they called for the Secretary-General's active assistance and intervention with the relevant United States authorities to have those measures revoked. By notes verbales dated 22 August and 20 September, the United States advised Hungary and Romania that similar travel regulations would apply to the personnel of their missions, effective 29 August and 20 September, respectively.

The Libyan Arab Jamahiriya complained in May about delays in the issuance of visas for members of its delegation to attend official United Nations meetings. The United States replied that a long-standing government policy required 10 to 15 working days for the processing of single-entry visas. The Committee considered a letter of 22 September by Nicaragua[14] denouncing the refusal by the United States to grant entry visas to a significant number of members of its delegation to the forty-third (1988) session of the General Assembly, to be headed by President Ortega. It stated that, in the light of that action, President Ortega had been obliged to cancel his visit to the Assembly. In response, the United States denied attempting to influence the composition of the Nicaraguan delegation. The representative of the United States said that 67 individuals had requested visas and 30 visas had been authorized and delivered before President Ortega announced he would not participate in the session. There was no question that President Ortega had the right to speak before the Assembly.

Among its recommendations and conclusions, the Committee urged the host country to take all necessary measures to prevent criminal acts, including harassment and activities that violated the security of missions and the safety of their personnel or their property, and to apprehend, bring to justice and punish all those responsible for criminal acts against missions accredited to the United Nations. Regarding travel regulations, the Committee urged the United States to continue honouring its obligations to facilitate the functioning of the United Nations and its missions. It suggested that the Secretariat and others work together to solve outstanding difficulties concerning unpaid bills by certain missions, and appealed to the host country to review the measures relating to diplomatic vehicles with a view to responding to the needs of the diplomatic community.

GENERAL ASSEMBLY ACTION

On 9 December 1988, the General Assembly, on the recommendation of the Sixth Committee, adopted **resolution 43/172** without vote.

Report of the Committee on Relations with the Host Country

The General Assembly,

Having considered the report of the Committee on Relations with the Host Country,

Recalling Article 105 of the Charter of the United Nations, the Convention on the Privileges and Immunities of the United Nations and the Agreement between the United Nations and the United States of America regarding the Headquarters of the United Nations,

Recalling also that the problems related to the privileges and immunities of all missions accredited to the United Nations, the security of the missions and the safety of their personnel are of great importance and concern to Member States, as well as the primary responsibility of the host country,

Recognizing that effective measures should continue to be taken by the competent authorities of the host country, in particular to prevent any acts violating the security of missions and the safety of their personnel,

Conscious of the increased interest shown by Member States in participating in the work of the Committee,

1. *Endorses* the recommendations and conclusions of the Committee on Relations with the Host Country contained in paragraph 81 of its report;

2. *Reaffirms its condemnation* of any criminal acts violating the security of missions accredited to the United Nations and the safety of their personnel;

3. *Urges* the host country to take all necessary measures to continue to prevent criminal acts, including harassment and violations of the security of missions and the safety of their personnel or infringements of the inviolability of their property, in order to ensure the existence and functioning of all missions, including practicable measures to prohibit illegal activities of persons, groups and organizations that encourage, instigate, organize or engage in the perpetration of acts and activities against the security and safety of such missions and representatives;

4. *Reiterates its request* to the parties concerned to follow consultations with a view to reaching solutions to the issues raised by certain Member States concerning the size of their missions, in accordance with the Agreement between the United Nations and the United States of America regarding the Headquarters of the United Nations and in the spirit of co-operation;

5. *Urges* the host country, in the light of the consideration by the Committee of travel regulations issued by the host country, to continue to honour its obligations to facilitate the functioning of the United Nations and the missions accredited to it;

6. *Stresses* the importance of a positive perception of the work of the United Nations, expresses concern about a negative public image and, therefore, urges that efforts be continued to build up public awareness by explaining, through all available means, the importance of the role played by the United Nations and the missions accredited to it in the strengthening of international peace and security;

7. *Requests* the Secretary-General to remain actively engaged in all aspects of the relations of the United Nations with the host country and to continue to stress the importance of effective measures to avoid acts of terrorism, violence and harassment against the missions and their personnel, as well as the need for any pertinent legislation adopted by the host country to be in accord with the Agreement and its other relevant obligations;

8. *Requests* the Committee to continue its work, in conformity with General Assembly resolution 2819(XXVI) of 15 December 1971;

9. *Decides* to include in the provisional agenda of its forty-fourth session the item entitled ''Report of the Committee on Relations with the Host Country''.

General Assembly resolution 43/172

9 December 1988   Meeting 76   Adopted without vote

Approved by Sixth Committee (A/43/900/Add.1) without vote, 1 December (meeting 52); draft by Cyprus (A/C.6/43/L.23), orally revised; agenda item 137.

Meeting numbers. GA 43rd session: 6th Committee 51, 52; plenary 76.

Relations between the host country and PLO

Responding to requests by Bahrain for the Arab Group (19 February),[15] Zimbabwe for the Non-Aligned Countries (22 February),[16] Kuwait on behalf of the Organization of the Islamic Conference (22 February)[17] and the Chairman of the Committee on the Exercise of the Inalienable Rights of the Palestinian People (24 February),[18] the Assembly reconvened in 1988 its forty-second (1987) session (29 February to 13 May) to complete consideration of relations with the host country.

Apprised of action being considered in the United States that might impede maintenance of the PLO Observer Mission to the United Nations, the General Assembly had, by a resolution of 1987,[19] reiterated that the PLO Mission was covered by the 1947 Headquarters Agreement between the United Nations and the United States[10] and requested the host country to abide by its obligations under the Agreement. Pursuant to that resolution, which also requested the Secretary-General to take effective measures to ensure full respect for the Agreement, the Secretary-General reported on the matter on 10 February 1988.[20]

The report stated that, on 5 January, the United States confirmed that the Foreign Relations Authorization Act, Fiscal Years 1988 and 1989, Title X, the Anti-Terrorism Act of 1987, which *inter alia* prohibited PLO from maintaining offices within the United States, signed on 22 December 1987 by President Reagan, would take effect 90 days thereafter. On 14 January, the Secretary-General pointed out to the United States that, as the assurance he had sought since December 1987 regarding existing arrangements for the PLO Observer Mission had not been forthcoming, it had to be concluded that a dispute existed between the United Nations and the United States concerning interpretation and application of the Headquarters Agreement. Accordingly, he invoked the Agreement's dispute settlement procedure and proposed that the negotiations phase commence on 20 January, while a series of legal consultations between the United Nations and the United States which had begun on 7 January should continue.

In the course of those consultations, the United Nations Legal Counsel was informed that the United States was unwilling to enter formally into the dispute settlement procedure and had not yet concluded that a dispute existed between it and the United Nations. Its Executive Branch was examining the possibility of interpreting the law in conformity with its obligations under the Agreement, or alternatively providing assurances that would set aside the 90-day period for the legislation's entry into force. The position presented by the United Nations Legal Counsel was that the question was one of compliance with international law. The Headquarters Agreement, he said, was a binding international instrument which was being violated by the United States legislation in question. The Secretary-General stated on 2 February that the procedure laid out in section 21 of the Agreement was the only legal remedy available to the United Nations in the matter.

In a follow-up report of 25 February,[21] the Secretary-General informed the Assembly that, on 11 February, the Legal Counsel had communicated to the United States the United Nations choice of Eduardo Jiménez de Aréchaga, the former President of ICJ, as arbitrator. No communication was thus far received from the United States regarding its choice of an arbitrator.

GENERAL ASSEMBLY ACTION (March)

The General Assembly, on 2 March 1988, adopted **resolution 42/229 A** by recorded vote.

The General Assembly,

Having considered the reports of the Secretary-General of 10 and 25 February 1988,

Recalling its resolution 42/210 B of 17 December 1987,

Reaffirming the applicability to the Permanent Observer Mission of the Palestine Liberation Organization to the United Nations in New York of the provisions of the Agreement between the United Nations and the United States of America regarding the Headquarters of the United Nations, dated 26 June 1947,

Having been apprised of the provisions of the Foreign Relations Authorization Act, Fiscal Years 1988 and 1989, which was signed on 22 December 1987, Title X of which establishes certain prohibitions regarding the Palestine Liberation Organization, *inter alia,* a prohibition "to establish or maintain an office, headquarters, premises, or other facilities or establishments within the jurisdiction of the United States at the behest or direction of, or with funds provided by the Palestine Liberation Organization or any of its constituent groups, any successor to any of those, or any agents thereof",

Bearing in mind that that provision takes effect on 21 March 1988,

Taking note of the position of the Secretary-General in which he concluded that a dispute existed between the United Nations and the United States of America concerning the interpretation or application of the Agreement,

Noting that the Secretary-General invoked the dispute settlement procedure set out in section 21 of the Agreement and proposed that the negotiations phase of the procedure commence on 20 January 1988,

Noting also from the report of the Secretary-General of 10 February 1988 that the United States was not in a position and was not willing to enter formally into the dispute settlement procedure under section 21 of the Agreement, that the United States was still evaluating the situation, and that the Secretary-General had sought assurances that the present arrangements for the Permanent Observer Mission of the Palestine Liberation Organization would not be curtailed or otherwise affected,

Affirming that the United States of America, the host country, is under a legal obligation to enable the Permanent Observer Mission of the Palestine Liberation Organization to establish and maintain premises and adequate functional facilities and to enable the personnel of the Mission to enter and remain in the United States to carry out their official functions,

1. *Supports* the efforts of the Secretary-General and expresses its great appreciation for his reports;

2. *Reaffirms* that the Permanent Observer Mission of the Palestine Liberation Organization to the United Nations in New York is covered by the provisions of the Agreement between the United Nations and the United States of America regarding the Headquarters of the United Nations and that it should be enabled to establish and maintain premises and adequate functional facilities and that the personnel of the Mission should be enabled to enter and remain in the United States of America to carry out their official functions;

3. *Considers* that the application of Title X of the Foreign Relations Authorization Act, Fiscal Years 1988 and 1989, in a manner inconsistent with paragraph 2 above would be contrary to the international legal obligations of the host country under the Agreement;

4. *Considers* that a dispute exists between the United Nations and the United States of America, the host country, concerning the interpretation or application of the Agreement, and that the dispute settlement procedure set out in section 21 of the Agreement should be set in operation;

5. *Calls upon* the host country to abide by its treaty obligations under the Agreement and to provide assurance that no action will be taken that would infringe on the current arrangements for the official functions of the Permanent Observer Mission of the Palestine Liberation Organization to the United Nations in New York;

6. *Requests* the Secretary-General to continue in his efforts in pursuance of the provisions of the Agreement, in particular section 21 thereof, and to report without delay to the Assembly;

7. *Decides* to keep the matter under active review.

General Assembly resolution 42/229 A

2 March 1988   Meeting 104   143-1 (recorded vote)

57-nation draft (A/42/L.46 & Add.1); agenda item 136.

Sponsors: Afghanistan, Algeria, Bahrain, Bangladesh, Botswana, Brunei Darussalam, Bulgaria, Burkina Faso, Byelorussian SSR, Comoros, Cuba, Czechoslovakia, Democratic Yemen, Djibouti, German Democratic Republic, Ghana, Guyana, India, Indonesia, Iran, Iraq, Jordan, Kuwait, Lao People's Democratic Republic, Lebanon, Libyan Arab Jamahiriya, Madagascar, Malaysia, Mali, Malta, Mauritania, Mongolia, Morocco, Nicaragua, Oman, Pakistan, Philippines, Poland, Qatar, Saudi Arabia, Senegal, Sierra Leone, Somalia, Sudan, Syrian Arab Republic, Tunisia, Turkey, Uganda, Ukrainian SSR, USSR, United Arab Emirates, Vanuatu, Viet Nam, Yemen, Yugoslavia, Zambia, Zimbabwe.

Meeting numbers. GA resumed 42nd session: plenary 104.

Recorded vote in Assembly as follows:

In favour: Afghanistan, Albania, Algeria, Angola, Antigua and Barbuda, Argentina, Australia, Austria, Bahamas, Bahrain, Bangladesh, Barbados, Belgium, Belize, Bhutan, Bolivia, Botswana, Brazil, Brunei Darussalam, Bulgaria, Burkina Faso, Burma, Burundi, Byelorussian Soviet Socialist Republic, Cameroon, Canada, Cape Verde, Chile, China, Colombia, Comoros, Costa Rica, Côte d'Ivoire, Cuba, Cyprus, Czechoslovakia, Democratic Kampuchea, Democratic Yemen, Denmark, Djibouti, Ecuador, Egypt, Ethiopia, Fiji, Finland, France, Gabon, German Democratic Republic, Germany, Federal Republic of, Ghana, Greece, Guatemala, Guinea, Guinea-Bissau, Guyana, Haiti, Honduras, Hungary, Iceland, India, Indonesia, Iran, Iraq, Ireland, Italy, Jamaica, Japan, Jordan, Kenya, Kuwait, Lao People's Democratic Republic, Lebanon, Lesotho, Liberia, Libyan Arab Jamahiriya, Luxembourg, Madagascar, Malawi, Malaysia, Maldives, Mali, Malta, Mauritania, Mauritius, Mexico, Mongolia, Morocco, Mozambique, Nepal, Netherlands, New Zealand, Nicaragua, Niger, Nigeria, Norway, Oman, Pakistan, Panama, Papua New Guinea, Paraguay, Peru, Philippines, Poland, Portugal, Qatar, Rwanda, Saint Kitts and Nevis, Saint Lucia, Saint Vincent and the Grenadines, Samoa, Saudi Arabia, Senegal, Seychelles, Sierra Leone, Singapore, Solomon Islands, Somalia, Spain, Sri Lanka, Sudan, Suriname, Swaziland, Sweden, Syrian Arab Republic, Thailand, Togo, Trinidad and Tobago, Tunisia, Turkey, Uganda, Ukrainian SSR, USSR, United Arab Emirates, United Kingdom, United Republic of Tanzania, Uruguay, Venezuela, Viet Nam, Yemen, Yugoslavia, Zaire, Zambia, Zimbabwe.

Against: Israel.

On the same date, the Assembly adopted **resolution 42/229 B**, also by recorded vote.

The General Assembly,

Recalling its resolution 42/210 B of 17 December 1987 and bearing in mind its resolution 42/229 A above,

Having considered the reports of the Secretary-General of 10 and 25 February 1988,

Affirming the position of the Secretary-General that a dispute exists between the United Nations and the host country concerning the interpretation or application of the Agreement between the United Nations and the United States of America regarding the Headquarters of the United Nations, dated 26 June 1947, and noting his conclusions that attempts at amicable settlement were deadlocked and that he had invoked the arbitration procedure provided for in section 21 of the Agreement by nominating an arbitrator and requesting the host country to nominate its own arbitrator,

Bearing in mind the constraints of time that require the immediate implementation of the dispute settlement procedure in accordance with section 21 of the Agreement,

Noting from the report of the Secretary-General of 10 February 1988 that the United States of America was not in a position and was not willing to enter formally into the dispute settlement procedure under section 21 of the Agreement and that the United States was still evaluating the situation,

Taking into account the provisions of the Statute of the International Court of Justice, in particular Articles 41 and 68 thereof,

Decides, in accordance with Article 96 of the Charter of the United Nations, to request the International Court of Justice, in pursuance of Article 65 of the Statute of the Court, for an advisory opinion on the following question, taking into account the time constraint:

In the light of facts reflected in the reports of the Secretary-General, is the United States of America, as a party to the Agreement between the United Nations and the United States of America regarding the Headquarters of the United Nations, under an obligation to enter into arbitration in accordance with section 21 of the Agreement?

General Assembly resolution 42/229 B

2 March 1988   Meeting 104   143-0 (recorded vote)

57-nation draft (A/42/L.47 & Add.1); agenda item 136.

Sponsors: Afghanistan, Algeria, Bahrain, Bangladesh, Botswana, Brunei Darussalam, Bulgaria, Burkina Faso, Byelorussian SSR, Comoros, Cuba, Czechoslovakia, Democratic Yemen, Djibouti, German Democratic Republic, Ghana, Guyana, India, Indonesia, Iran, Iraq, Jordan, Kuwait, Lao People's Democratic Republic, Lebanon, Libyan Arab Jamahiriya, Madagascar, Malaysia, Mali, Malta, Mauritania, Mongolia, Morocco, Nicaragua, Oman, Pakistan, Philippines, Poland, Qatar, Saudi Arabia, Senegal, Sierra Leone, Somalia, Sudan, Syrian Arab Republic, Tunisia, Uganda, Ukrainian SSR, USSR, United Arab Emirates, Vanuatu, Viet Nam, Yemen, Yugoslavia, Zambia, Zimbabwe.

Meeting numbers. GA resumed 42nd session: plenary 104.

Recorded vote in Assembly as follows:

In favour: Afghanistan, Albania, Algeria, Angola, Antigua and Barbuda, Argentina, Australia, Austria, Bahamas, Bahrain, Bangladesh, Barbados, Belgium, Belize, Bhutan, Bolivia, Botswana, Brazil, Brunei Darussalam, Bulgaria, Burkina Faso, Burma, Burundi, Byelorussian SSR, Cameroon, Canada, Cape Verde, Chile, China, Colombia, Comoros, Costa Rica, Côte d'Ivoire, Cuba, Cyprus, Czechoslovakia, Democratic Kampuchea, Democratic Yemen, Denmark, Djibouti, Ecuador, Egypt, Ethiopia, Fiji, Finland, France, Gabon, German Democratic Republic, Germany, Federal Republic of, Ghana, Greece, Guatemala, Guinea, Guinea-Bissau, Guyana, Haiti, Honduras, Hungary, Iceland, India, Indonesia, Iran, Iraq, Ireland, Italy, Jamaica, Japan, Jordan, Kenya, Kuwait, Lao People's Democratic Republic, Lebanon, Lesotho, Liberia, Libyan Arab Jamahiriya, Luxembourg, Madagascar, Malawi, Malaysia, Maldives, Mali, Malta, Mauritania, Mauritius, Mexico, Mongolia, Morocco, Mozam-

bique, Nepal, Netherlands, New Zealand, Nicaragua, Niger, Nigeria, Norway, Oman, Pakistan, Panama, Papua New Guinea, Paraguay, Peru, Philippines, Poland, Portugal, Qatar, Rwanda, Saint Kitts and Nevis, Saint Lucia, Saint Vincent and the Grenadines, Samoa, Saudi Arabia, Senegal, Seychelles, Sierra Leone, Singapore, Solomon Islands, Somalia, Spain, Sri Lanka, Sudan, Suriname, Swaziland, Sweden, Syrian Arab Republic, Thailand, Togo, Trinidad and Tobago, Tunisia, Turkey, Uganda, Ukrainian SSR, USSR, United Arab Emirates, United Kingdom, United Republic of Tanzania, Uruguay, Venezuela, Viet Nam, Yemen, Yugoslavia, Zaire, Zambia, Zimbabwe.

Against: None.

Also on 2 March, the Assembly, by **decision 42/461**, decided to keep the matter under active review, to permit expeditious consideration should developments so require, upon receipt of the report of the Secretary-General requested in paragraph 6 of **resolution 42/229 A**.

The Secretary-General reported on 11 March[22] that the United States Attorney General had informed him in a letter of the same date that he was required by the Anti-Terrorism Act of 1987 to close the office of the Permanent Observer Mission of PLO to the United Nations irrespective of any obligations the United States might have under the Headquarters Agreement. Under the circumstances, the United States believed that submission of the matter to arbitration would not serve a useful purpose. The Secretary-General protested to the United States on 16 March[23] that the United States decision constituted a clear violation of the Headquarters Agreement, raising serious implications given the responsibilities of the United States as the host country. He could not accept that the United States might act irrespective of its obligations under the Agreement.

The Secretary-General further noted[22] that on 11 March the Permanent Observer of PLO was notified by the United States Attorney General that, as at 21 March, maintenance of the PLO Mission would be unlawful and, should PLO fail to comply with the requirements of the 1987 Anti-Terrorism Act, the Department of Justice would take action in Federal Court to ensure compliance. With regard to the request for an advisory opinion of ICJ contained in **resolution 42/229 B**, the Secretary-General informed the Assembly that on the same date he and the Legal Counsel transmitted to the Court certified texts of that resolution and the request for an advisory opinion. The Registrar of ICJ transmitted on 9 March to the Secretary-General a Court order, inviting him to supply relevant documents at the earliest possible date and fixing the time-limit for the submission of written statements by the United Nations, the United States and other parties to the ICJ Statute at 25 March.

On 18 March,[24] Tunisia requested the Secretary-General to have circulated, as an official document of the Assembly, the text of the Headquarters Agreement. On 22 March,[25] it transmitted the text of a letter to the Secretary-General by which the Permanent Observer of PLO had informed the United States on 14 March that PLO maintained its Mission in pursuance of resolutions by the Assembly of 1974,[26] 1987[27] and 1988 (**resolution 42/229 A**, see above), and was in no sense accredited to the United States but present in the United States solely as invitees of the United Nations within the meaning of the Headquarters Agreement. Also annexed to Tunisia's communication was a letter of 14 March by the United States Attorney General, notifying the Permanent Observer of PLO that the United States Congress had chosen, irrespective of international law, to ban the presence of all PLO offices in the country. In discharging his obligation to enforce the law, the only responsible course was to respect and follow that decision.

ICJ advisory opinion

On 29 April,[28] the Secretary-General forwarded to the Assembly the advisory opinion of 26 April of the International Court of Justice on the applicability of the obligation to arbitrate under section 21 of the United Nations Headquarters Agreement of 26 June 1947, as requested by the Assembly in its **resolution 42/229 B** (see above). The advisory opinion unanimously determined that the United States was under an obligation to enter into arbitration for settling the dispute between itself and the United Nations (see PART FIVE, Chapter I). In May, the Assembly endorsed the Court's advisory opinion.

GENERAL ASSEMBLY ACTION (March)

On 23 March 1988, the General Assembly adopted **resolution 42/230** by recorded vote.

Report of the Committee on Relations with the Host Country

The General Assembly,

Having considered the reports of the Secretary-General of 11 and 16 March 1988,

Guided by the purposes and principles of the Charter of the United Nations and, in particular, the provisions of Chapter XVI,

Recalling its resolutions 42/210 B of 17 December 1987 and 42/229 A and B of 2 March 1988,

Recalling that the United Nations was created with the aim, *inter alia*, as defined in the Charter, "to establish conditions under which justice and respect for the obligations arising from treaties and other sources of international law can be maintained",

Recalling that the Agreement between the United Nations and the United States of America regarding the Headquarters of the United Nations, dated 26 June 1947, was drawn up in accordance with the Charter, in particular Articles 28 and 105 thereof,

Concerned that the application to and enforcement against the Permanent Observer Mission of the Palestine Liberation Organization to the United Nations in New York of Title X of the Foreign Relations Authorization Act, Fiscal Years 1988 and 1989, would impede the realization of the aims of the United Nations,

Expressing its appreciation to the International Court of Justice for having unanimously adopted an order on 9 March 1988 accelerating its procedure on the request submitted by the General Assembly for its advisory opinion on "the applicability of the obligation to arbitrate under section 21 of the United Nations Headquarters Agreement of 26 June 1947",

Expressing grave concern about the attitude of the Government of the host country as expressed in the letter dated 11 March 1988 from the Acting Permanent Representative of the United States of America to the Secretary-General, which states, *inter alia*, that "the Attorney General of the United States has determined that he is required by the Anti-Terrorism Act of 1987 to close the office of the Palestine Liberation Organization Observer Mission to the United Nations in New York, irrespective of any obligations the United States may have under the Agreement between the United Nations and the United States regarding the Headquarters of the United Nations",

Expressing serious alarm at the warning contained in that letter that "if the PLO does not comply with the Act, the Attorney General will initiate legal action to close the PLO Observer Mission on or about March 21 1988",

1. *Strongly supports* the position taken by the Secretary-General and expresses its great appreciation for his reports;

2. *Reaffirms* that the Permanent Observer Mission of the Palestine Liberation Organization to the United Nations in New York is covered by the provisions of the Agreement between the United Nations and the United States of America regarding the Headquarters of the United Nations and that the Palestine Liberation Organization has the right to establish and maintain premises and adequate functional facilities and that the personnel of the Mission should be enabled to enter and remain in the United States to carry out their official functions;

3. *Affirms* the crucial importance of the Agreement and consequently the arrangements mentioned in paragraph 2 above concerning the functioning of the organs of the United Nations, including the General Assembly, at Headquarters in New York;

4. *Determines* that the application to and enforcement against the Permanent Observer Mission of the Palestine Liberation Organization to the United Nations in New York of Title X of the Foreign Relations Authorization Act, Fiscal Years 1988 and 1989, is inconsistent with paragraph 2 above and is contrary to the international legal obligations of the host country under the Agreement;

5. *Reaffirms* that a dispute exists between the United Nations and the United States of America, the host country, concerning the interpretation or application of the Agreement, and that the dispute settlement procedure provided for under section 21 of the Agreement, which constitutes the only legal remedy to solve the dispute, should be set in operation, and requests the host country to name its arbitrator to the arbitral tribunal;

6. *Requests* the Secretary-General to continue his efforts to ensure the proper constitution of the arbitral tribunal provided for under section 21 of the Agreement;

7. *Deplores* the failure of the host country to comply with its obligations under the Agreement;

8. *Urges* the host country to abide by its international legal obligations and to desist from taking any action inconsistent with paragraph 2 above;

9. *Notes* the fact that, within the text of its order, the International Court of Justice on 9 March 1988 took note of paragraph 5 of General Assembly resolution 42/229 A;

10.　*Requests* the Secretary-General to take adequate measures on a preliminary basis, if necessary, in order to ensure the discharge of the official functions of the Permanent Observer Mission of the Palestine Liberation Organization to the United Nations in New York;

11.　*Further requests* the Secretary-General to report to the General Assembly without delay on developments in this matter;

12.　*Decides* to keep the matter under active review.

General Assembly resolution 42/230

23 March 1988　　　　Meeting 109　　　148-2 (recorded vote)

63-nation draft (A/42/L.48 & Add.1); agenda item 136.
Sponsors: Afghanistan, Algeria, Bahrain, Bangladesh, Benin, Brunei Darussalam, Bulgaria, Burkina Faso, Byelorussian SSR, Colombia, Comoros, Congo, Cuba, Czechoslovakia, Democratic Yemen, Djibouti, Ethiopia, German Democratic Republic, Ghana, Guyana, India, Indonesia, Iran, Iraq, Jordan, Kuwait, Lao People's Democratic Republic, Lebanon, Libyan Arab Jamahiriya, Madagascar, Malaysia, Mali, Malta, Mauritania, Mexico, Mongolia, Morocco, Nepal, Nicaragua, Oman, Pakistan, Panama, Peru, Philippines, Poland, Qatar, Saudi Arabia, Senegal, Sierra Leone, Somalia, Sudan, Syrian Arab Republic, Tunisia, Uganda, Ukrainian SSR, USSR, United Arab Emirates, Vanuatu, Viet Nam, Yemen, Yugoslavia, Zambia, Zimbabwe.
Meeting numbers. GA 42nd session: plenary 104-109.

Recorded vote in Assembly as follows:

In favour: Afghanistan, Albania, Algeria, Angola, Antigua and Barbuda, Argentina, Australia, Austria, Bahamas, Bahrain, Bangladesh, Barbados, Belgium, Belize, Benin, Bhutan, Bolivia, Botswana, Brazil, Brunei Darussalam, Bulgaria, Burkina Faso, Burma, Burundi, Byelorussia, Cameroon, Canada, Cape Verde, Central African Republic, Chad, Chile, China, Colombia, Comoros, Congo, Costa Rica, Côte d'Ivoire, Cuba, Cyprus, Czechoslovakia, Democratic Kampuchea, Democratic Yemen, Denmark, Djibouti, Ecuador, Egypt, Ethiopia, Fiji, Finland, France, Gabon, German Democratic Republic, Federal Republic of Germany, Ghana, Greece, Grenada, Guatemala, Guinea, Guinea-Bissau, Guyana, Honduras, Hungary, Iceland, India, Indonesia, Iran, Iraq, Ireland, Italy, Jamaica, Japan, Jordan, Kenya, Kuwait, Lao People's Democratic Republic, Lebanon, Lesotho, Liberia, Libya, Luxembourg, Madagascar, Malawi, Malaysia, Maldives, Mali, Malta, Mauritania, Mauritius, Mexico, Mongolia, Morocco, Mozambique, Nepal, Netherlands, New Zealand, Nicaragua, Niger, Nigeria, Norway, Oman, Pakistan, Panama, Papua New Guinea, Paraguay, Peru, Philippines, Poland, Portugal, Qatar, Rwanda, Saint Lucia, Saint Vincent, Samoa, Saudi Arabia, Senegal, Seychelles, Sierra Leone, Singapore, Solomon Islands, Somalia, Spain, Sri Lanka, St. Kitts and Nevis, Sudan, Suriname, Swaziland, Sweden, Syria, Thailand, Togo, Trinidad and Tobago, Tunisia, Turkey, Uganda, Ukraine, USSR, United Arab Emirates, United Kingdom, United Republic of Tanzania, Uruguay, Vanuatu, Venezuela, Viet Nam, Yemen, Yugoslavia, Zaire, Zambia, Zimbabwe.

Against: Israel, United States.

On the same date, the Assembly decided that consultations would continue on reconvening the Assembly before 11 April to resume consideration of the relations with the host country (**decision 42/462**).

Responding to the request contained in **resolution 42/230**, the Secretary-General reported to the Assembly on 11 May[29] that he had, on 24 March, authorized the Legal Counsel to present written and oral statements on his behalf to ICJ on its advisory opinion of 26 April concerning the applicability of the obligation to arbitrate under the Headquarters Agreement. Subsequently, the Legal Counsel made an oral statement to the Court on 11 April and answered questions at a public sitting on 12 April.

GENERAL ASSEMBLY ACTION (May)

On 13 May 1988, the General Assembly adopted **resolution 42/232** by recorded vote.

Report of the Committee on Relations with the Host Country

The General Assembly,

Having requested, in its resolution 42/229 B of 2 March 1988, an advisory opinion from the International Court of Justice regarding the applicability of the obligation to arbitrate under section 21 of the Agreement between the United Nations and the United States of America regarding the Headquarters of the United Nations, dated 26 June 1947,

Having noted that, in its advisory opinion of 26 April 1988, the Court was unanimously of the opinion that "the United States of America, as a party to the Agreement between the United Nations and the United States of America regarding the Headquarters of the United Nations of 26 June 1947, is under an obligation, in accordance with section 21 of that Agreement, to enter into arbitration for the settlement of the dispute between itself and the United Nations'',

Having noted also that the Court pointed out that "the purpose of the arbitration procedure envisaged by that Agreement is precisely the settlement of such disputes as may arise between the Organization and the host country without any prior recourse to municipal courts, and it would be against both the letter and the spirit of the Agreement for the implementation of that procedure to be subjected to such prior recourse'',

Having noted also that the Court recalled "the fundamental principle of international law that international law prevails over domestic law'',

1.　*Expresses its appreciation* to the International Court of Justice for having "found that an early answer to the request'' submitted by the General Assembly on 2 March 1988 "for advisory opinion would be desirable'', and for having accelerated its procedure on the said request;

2.　*Takes note of and endorses* the advisory opinion of the International Court of Justice of 26 April 1988, concerning the applicability of the obligation to arbitrate under section 21 of the Agreement between the United Nations and the United States of America regarding the Headquarters of the United Nations, dated 26 June 1947;

3.　*Urges* the host country to abide by its international legal obligations and to act consistently with the advisory opinion of the International Court of Justice of 26 April 1988, and accordingly to name its arbitrator to the arbitral tribunal provided for under section 21 of the Agreement;

4.　*Requests* the Secretary-General to continue his efforts to ensure the constitution of the arbitral tribunal provided for under section 21 of the Agreement;

5.　*Further requests* the Secretary-General to report to the General Assembly without delay on developments in this matter;

6.　*Decides* to keep the matter under active review.

General Assembly resolution 42/232

13 May 1988　　　　Meeting 113　　　136-2 (recorded vote)

65-nation draft (A/42/L.50); agenda item 136.
Sponsors: Afghanistan, Algeria, Angola, Bahrain, Bangladesh, Barbados, Benin, Brunei Darussalam, Bulgaria, Burkina Faso, Byelorussian SSR, Colombia, Comoros, Cuba, Czechoslovakia, Democratic Yemen, Djibouti, Ethiopia, German Democratic Republic, Ghana, Guyana, India, Indonesia, Iran, Iraq, Jordan, Kuwait, Lao People's Democratic Republic, Lebanon, Libyan Arab Jamahiriya, Madagascar, Malaysia, Mali, Malta, Mauritania, Mexico, Mongolia, Morocco, Nepal, Nicaragua, Oman, Pakistan, Panama, Peru, Philippines, Poland, Qatar, Saudi Arabia, Senegal, Sierra Leone, Soma-

lia, Sudan, Syrian Arab Republic, Tunisia, Turkey, Uganda, Ukrainian SSR, USSR, United Arab Emirates, United Republic of Tanzania, Vanuatu, Viet Nam, Yemen, Yugoslavia, Zambia.

Meeting numbers. GA 42nd session: plenary 104-109, 113.

Recorded vote in Assembly as follows:

In favour: Afghanistan, Albania, Algeria, Angola, Antigua and Barbuda, Argentina, Australia, Austria, Bahamas, Bahrain, Bangladesh, Barbados, Belgium, Belize, Benin, Bhutan, Bolivia, Botswana, Brazil, Brunei Darussalam, Bulgaria, Burkina Faso, Burma, Burundi, Byelorussia, Canada, Cape Verde, Central African Republic, Chad, Chile, China, Colombia, Comoros, Congo, Costa Rica, Côte d'Ivoire, Cuba, Cyprus, Czechoslovakia, Democratic Kampuchea, Democratic Yemen, Denmark, Djibouti, Ecuador, Egypt, Ethiopia, Fiji, Finland, France, Gabon, German Democratic Republic, Federal Republic of Germany, Ghana, Greece, Grenada, Guinea, Guinea-Bissau, Guyana, Haiti, Honduras, Hungary, Iceland, Indonesia, Iran, Iraq, Ireland, Italy, Jamaica, Japan, Jordan, Kenya, Kuwait, Lao People's Democratic Republic, Lebanon, Lesotho, Liberia, Libya, Madagascar, Malaysia, Maldives, Mali, Malta, Mauritania, Mauritius, Mexico, Mongolia, Morocco, Mozambique, Nepal, Netherlands, New Zealand, Nicaragua, Nigeria, Norway, Oman, Pakistan, Panama, Papua New Guinea, Paraguay, Peru, Philippines, Poland, Portugal, Qatar, Rwanda, Samoa, Saudi Arabia, Senegal, Seychelles, Sierra Leone, Singapore, Somalia, Spain, Sri Lanka, Sudan, Sweden, Syria, Thailand, Togo, Trinidad and Tobago, Tunisia, Turkey, Uganda, Ukraine, USSR, United Arab Emirates, United Kingdom, United Republic of Tanzania, Uruguay, Venezuela, Viet Nam, Yemen, Yugoslavia, Zaire, Zambia, Zimbabwe.

Against: Israel, United States.

Legal proceedings

As requested by **resolution 42/232**, the Secretary-General communicated to the Assembly in September[(30)] that, at the time of the adoption of that resolution, the United States had already initiated legal proceedings in domestic court against PLO[(29)] to obtain judicial authorization to close its Observer Mission as required under the 1987 Anti-Terrorism Act. On 8 June, the United States District Court heard arguments of counsel in the case *United States of America v. The Palestine Liberation Organization, et al.* At that hearing the United Nations was formally admitted as *amicus curiae* in the case.

On 29 June, the District Court rejected the authorization sought by the United States. The Court noted that United States statutes and treaties were both supreme law of the land and that its Constitution set forth no order of precedence to differentiate between them. In the present case, the Court found that the Headquarters Agreement obligated the United States to allow PLO transit, entry and access to the United Nations, in addition to the use of offices. The 1987 Anti-Terrorism Act did not alter the United States obligations under the Agreement for it failed to disclose the clear legislative intent necessary for the Court to act in its contravention. The Court further rejected the argument that it should defer to the advisory opinion of ICJ regarding the United States obligation to arbitrate.

After the United States announced on 29 August that it had decided not to appeal the Court's decision, the Secretary-General concluded that the dispute between the United Nations and its host country concerning the PLO Observer Mission had thus come to an end.

Visa application of PLO Chairman Yasser Arafat

On 23 November, the attention of the Committee on Relations with the Host Country[(31)] was drawn by the PLO Permanent Observer to the fact that, on 8 December, the General Assembly would begin its debate on Palestine and PLO Chairman Yasser Arafat, intending to participate in that debate, would submit the appropriate forms for an entry visa into the United States. On 28 November, the Committee discussed the denial by the United States of the visa to Yasser Arafat, to permit the PLO Chairman to attend the forty-third (1988) session of the Assembly.

The United States explained in the Committee that there was evidence that PLO was engaged in terrorism against the United States after it had forsworn terrorism in 1985. Having evidence that Yasser Arafat knew of and condoned terrorism against the United States, the Government had denied him a visa. This was consistent with the Headquarters Agreement. The United Nations Legal Counsel noted[(32)] a difference of opinion between the United Nations and the United States on the legal character and validity in international law of the so-called security reservation contained in United States public law. Yasser Arafat's visa application was solely to allow him to visit the United Nations Headquarters district and fell within the scope of sections 11, 12 and 13 of the Headquarters Agreement, which provided that invitees of the United Nations should not be impeded in their access to the Headquarters district irrespective of the state of bilateral relations with the host country. The United States Department of State did not make the point that the presence of the PLO Chairman in the United States would *per se* in any way threaten the country's security. He expressed the opinion that the host country was under obligation to grant the visa request of the Chairman of PLO.

In summing up the debate, the Committee Chairman concluded that the majority of speakers had expressed the opinion that denial of the application violated the Headquarters Agreement and the host country should be asked to urgently review and reverse its decision to enable Yasser Arafat to participate in the Assembly debate as scheduled.

GENERAL ASSEMBLY ACTION (November)

On 30 November, the General Assembly, on the recommendation of the Sixth Committee, adopted **resolution 43/48** by roll-call vote.

Report of the Committee on Relations with the Host Country

The General Assembly,

Recalling Article 105 of the Charter of the United Nations and the Agreement between the United Nations and the United States of America regarding the Headquarters of the United Nations, dated 26 June 1947,

Recalling also its resolution 3237(XXIX) of 22 November 1974, in which, *inter alia,* it invited the Palestine Liberation Organization to participate in the sessions and the work of the General Assembly in the capacity of observer,

Affirming the right of Member States and observers freely to designate the members of their delegation to participate in the sessions and the work of the General Assembly,

Having been apprised that the Palestine Liberation Organization, in conformity with the usual practice, had requested through the Secretary-General an entry visa for Mr. Yasser Arafat, Chairman of the Executive Committee of the Palestine Liberation Organization, in order to participate in the forty-third session of the General Assembly,

Having been informed of the decision of the host country to deny the requested visa, in violation of its international legal obligations under the Agreement,

Endorsing the opinion of the Legal Counsel of the United Nations rendered on 28 November 1988,

1. _Affirms_ the right of the Palestine Liberation Organization freely to designate the members of its delegation to participate in the sessions and the work of the General Assembly;

2. _Deplores_ the failure by the host country to approve the granting of the requested entry visa;

3. _Considers_ that this decision by the Government of the United States of America, the host country, constitutes a violation of the international legal obligations of the host country under the Agreement between the United Nations and the United States of America regarding the Headquarters of the United Nations;

4. _Urges_ the host country to abide scrupulously by the provisions of the Agreement and to reconsider and reverse its decision;

5. _Requests_ the Secretary-General to submit a report on the developments in this matter no later than 1 December 1988.

General Assembly resolution 43/48

30 November 1988   Meeting 65   151-2-1 (roll-call vote)

Approved by Sixth Committee (A/43/900 & Corr.1) by vote (121-2-1), 29 November (meeting 51); draft by Brunei Darussalam, India, Indonesia, Jordan (for League of Arab States), Malaysia, Yugoslavia, Zambia, Zimbabwe (A/C.6/43/L.25), orally revised; agenda item 137.

Roll-call vote in Assembly as follows:

In favour: Afghanistan, Albania, Algeria, Angola, Antigua and Barbuda, Argentina, Australia, Austria, Bahamas, Bahrain, Bangladesh, Barbados, Belgium, Belize, Benin, Bhutan, Bolivia, Botswana, Brazil, Brunei Darussalam, Bulgaria, Burkina Faso, Burma, Burundi, Byelorussian SSR, Cameroon, Canada, Cape Verde, Central African Republic, Chad, Chile, China, Colombia, Comoros, Congo, Costa Rica, Côte d'Ivoire, Cuba, Cyprus, Czechoslovakia, Democratic Kampuchea, Democratic Yemen, Denmark, Djibouti, Dominican Republic, Ecuador, Egypt, El Salvador, Equatorial Guinea, Ethiopia, Fiji, Finland, France, Gabon, Gambia, German Democratic Republic, Germany, Federal Republic of, Ghana, Greece, Guatemala, Guinea, Guinea-Bissau, Guyana, Haiti, Honduras, Hungary, Iceland, India, Indonesia, Iran, Iraq, Ireland, Italy, Jamaica, Japan, Jordan, Kenya, Kuwait, Lao People's Democratic Republic, Lebanon, Lesotho, Liberia, Libyan Arab Jamahiriya, Luxembourg, Madagascar, Malawi, Malaysia, Maldives, Mali, Malta, Mauritania, Mauritius, Mexico, Mongolia, Morocco, Mozambique, Nepal, Netherlands, New Zealand, Nicaragua, Niger, Nigeria, Norway, Oman, Pakistan, Panama, Papua New Guinea, Peru, Philippines, Poland, Portugal, Qatar, Romania, Rwanda, Saint Lucia, Saint Vincent and the Grenadines, Samoa, Sao Tome and Principe, Saudi Arabia, Senegal, Seychelles, Sierra Leone, Singapore, Solomon Islands, Somalia, Spain, Sri Lanka, Sudan, Suriname, Swaziland, Sweden, Syrian Arab Republic, Thailand, Togo, Trinidad and Tobago, Tunisia, Turkey, Uganda, Ukrainian SSR, USSR, United Arab Emirates, United Republic of Tanzania, Uruguay, Vanuatu, Venezuela, Viet Nam, Yemen, Yugoslavia, Zaire, Zambia, Zimbabwe.

Against: Israel, United States.

Abstaining: United Kingdom.

Pursuant to the reporting request contained in **resolution 43/48**, the Secretary-General informed the Assembly on 1 December[33] that by a note verbale of the same date addressed to him, the United

States reiterated that it considered the reasons for denying the PLO Chairman compelling and fully consistent with the Headquarters Agreement and saw no basis for changing its decision.

GENERAL ASSEMBLY ACTION (December)

On 2 December, the General Assembly, in adopting **resolution 43/49** by recorded vote, decided to meet in plenary at the United Nations Office at Geneva to consider the question of Palestine, during which PLO Chairman Yasser Arafat addressed the Assembly.

Report of the Committee on Relations with the Host Country

The General Assembly,

Recalling its resolution 43/48 of 30 November 1988, in which, _inter alia_, it urged the host country to abide scrupulously by the provisions of the Agreement between the United Nations and the United States of America regarding the Headquarters of the United Nations, dated 26 June 1947, and to reconsider and reverse its decision to deny the visa requested for Mr. Yasser Arafat, Chairman of the Executive Committee of the Palestine Liberation Organization,

Having considered the report of the Secretary-General of 1 December 1988 in which it is stated that the host country informed him that ''we see no basis for changing our decision'',

Affirming the right of persons mentioned in section 11 of the Agreement to enter the United States of America without any impediment for the purpose of transit to or from the headquarters district,

1. _Deplores_ the failure of the host country to respond favourably to the request of the General Assembly contained in its resolution 43/48;

2. _Decides_, in the present compelling circumstances and without prejudice to normal practice, to consider the question of Palestine, item 37 of the agenda of the forty-third session of the General Assembly, in plenary, at the United Nations Office at Geneva during the period from 13 to 15 December 1988;

3. _Requests_ the Secretary-General to make the necessary arrangements for the implementation of the present resolution, and authorizes him to adjust the schedule of meetings at the United Nations Office at Geneva during those days as required.

General Assembly resolution 43/49

2 December 1988   Meeting 67   154-2-1 (recorded vote)

28-nation draft (A/43/L.43 & Add.1); agenda items 137 & 8.

Sponsors: Algeria, Bahrain, Bangladesh, Cuba, Democratic Yemen, Djibouti, India, Iraq, Jordan, Kuwait, Lebanon, Libyan Arab Jamahiriya, Malaysia, Mauritania, Morocco, Oman, Pakistan, Qatar, Saudi Arabia, Somalia, Sudan, Syrian Arab Republic, Tunisia, United Arab Emirates, Yemen, Yugoslavia, Zambia, Zimbabwe.

Financial implications. 5th Committee, A/43/910; S-G, A/C.5/43/57.

Meeting numbers. GA 43rd session: 5th Committee 40; plenary 67.

Recorded vote in Assembly as follows:

In favour: Afghanistan, Albania, Algeria, Angola, Antigua and Barbuda, Argentina, Australia, Austria, Bahamas, Bahrain, Bangladesh, Barbados, Belgium, Belize, Benin, Bhutan, Bolivia, Botswana, Brazil, Brunei Darussalam, Bulgaria, Burkina Faso, Burma, Burundi, Byelorussian SSR, Cameroon, Canada, Cape Verde, Central African Republic, Chad, Chile, China, Colombia, Comoros, Congo, Costa Rica, Côte d'Ivoire, Cuba, Cyprus, Czechoslovakia, Democratic Kampuchea, Democratic Yemen, Denmark, Djibouti, Dominican Republic, Ecuador, Egypt, El Salvador, Equatorial Guinea, Ethiopia, Fiji, Finland, France, Gabon, Gambia, German Democratic Republic, Ger-

many, Federal Republic of, Ghana, Greece, Grenada, Guatemala, Guinea, Guinea-Bissau, Guyana, Haiti, Honduras, Hungary, Iceland, India, Indonesia, Iran, Iraq, Ireland, Italy, Jamaica, Japan, Jordan, Kenya, Kuwait, Lao People's Democratic Republic, Lebanon, Lesotho, Liberia, Libyan Arab Jamahiriya, Luxembourg, Madagascar, Malawi, Malaysia, Maldives, Mali, Malta, Mauritania, Mauritius, Mexico, Mongolia, Morocco, Mozambique, Nepal, Netherlands, New Zealand, Nicaragua, Niger, Nigeria, Norway, Oman, Pakistan, Panama, Papua New Guinea, Paraguay, Peru, Philippines, Poland, Portugal, Qatar, Romania, Rwanda, Saint Kitts and Nevis, Saint Lucia, Saint Vincent and the Grenadines, Samoa, Sao Tome and Principe, Saudi Arabia, Senegal, Seychelles, Sierra Leone, Singapore, Solomon Islands, Somalia, Spain, Sri Lanka, Sudan, Suriname, Swaziland, Sweden, Syrian Arab Republic, Thailand, Togo, Trinidad and Tobago, Tunisia, Turkey, Uganda, Ukrainian SSR, USSR, United Arab Emirates, United Republic of Tanzania, Uruguay, Vanuatu, Venezuela, Viet Nam, Yemen, Yugoslavia, Zaire, Zambia, Zimbabwe.
Against: Israel, United States.
Abstaining: United Kingdom.

Observer status of national liberation movements

In accordance with a resolution by the General Assembly of 1986,[34] the Secretary-General issued, in October 1988, a report with later addenda[35] containing replies from Czechoslovakia, the Byelorussian SSR, the Ukrainian SSR, the USSR and Yugoslavia on the implementation of the resolution concerning the observer status of national liberation movements recognized by the Organization of African Unity and/or by the League of Arab States. By the 1986 resolution, the Assembly had urged all States to accede to the 1975 Vienna Convention on the Representation of States in Their Relations with International Organizations of a Universal Character,[36] and requested those States hosting international organizations or conferences to accord the facilities, privileges and immunities necessary for the performance of their functions to delegations of national liberation movements.

GENERAL ASSEMBLY ACTION

On 9 December 1988, the General Assembly, on the recommendation of the Sixth Committee, adopted two resolutions on the matter. **Resolution 43/160 A** was adopted by recorded vote.

The General Assembly,
Recalling its resolutions 35/167 of 15 December 1980, 37/104 of 16 December 1982, 39/76 of 13 December 1984 and 41/71 of 3 December 1986,
Taking note of the report of the Secretary-General,
Recalling also its resolution 3237(XXIX) of 22 November 1974, by which it granted observer status to the Palestine Liberation Organization,
Recalling further its resolution 31/152 of 20 December 1976, by which it granted observer status to the South West Africa People's Organization,
Desirous of enhancing the effective role played by these national liberation movements,
Bearing in mind the necessity of facilitating the work of these organizations,
1. *Decides* that the Palestine Liberation Organization and the South West Africa People's Organization are entitled to have their communications relating to the sessions and work of the General Assembly issued and circulated directly, and without intermediary, as official documents of the Assembly;

2. *Decides also* that the Palestine Liberation Organization and the South West Africa People's Organization are entitled to have their communications relating to the sessions and work of all international conferences convened under the auspices of the General Assembly of the United Nations issued and circulated directly, and without intermediary, as official documents of these conferences;
3. *Authorizes* the Secretariat to issue and circulate as official documents of the United Nations, under the appropriate symbol of other organs or conferences of the United Nations, communications submitted directly, without intermediary, by the Palestine Liberation Organization and the South West Africa People's Organization, on matters relative to the work of these organs and conferences;
4. *Requests* the Secretary-General to take the necessary steps for the implementation of the present resolution.

General Assembly resolution 43/160 A

9 December 1988   Meeting 76   117-2-31 (recorded vote)

Approved by Sixth Committee (A/43/880) by vote (81-2-25), 28 November (meeting 50); 25-nation draft (A/C.6/43/L.10/Rev.1), orally revised; agenda item 126.
Sponsors: Afghanistan, Algeria, Angola, Bahrain, Bangladesh, Cuba, Democratic Yemen, Djibouti, Iraq, Jordan, Kuwait, Lebanon, Libyan Arab Jamahiriya, Mauritania, Morocco, Oman, Qatar, Saudi Arabia, Somalia, Sudan, Syrian Arab Republic, Tunisia, United Arab Emirates, Yemen, Zambia.
Meeting numbers. GA 43rd session: 6th Committee 21, 22, 50; plenary 76.

Recorded vote in Assembly as follows:

In favour: Afghanistan, Albania, Algeria, Angola, Antigua and Barbuda, Argentina, Bahrain, Barbados, Belize, Benin, Bhutan, Bolivia, Botswana, Brazil, Brunei Darussalam, Bulgaria, Burkina Faso, Burma, Burundi, Byelorussian SSR, Cameroon, Cape Verde, Central African Republic, Chad, China, Colombia, Congo, Cuba, Cyprus, Czechoslovakia, Democratic Kampuchea, Democratic Yemen, Djibouti, Dominican Republic, Ecuador, Egypt, Equatorial Guinea, Ethiopia, Fiji, Gabon, Gambia, German Democratic Republic, Ghana, Grenada, Guatemala, Guinea, Guinea-Bissau, Guyana, Hungary, India, Indonesia, Iran, Iraq, Jordan, Kuwait, Lao People's Democratic Republic, Lebanon, Lesotho, Liberia, Libyan Arab Jamahiriya, Madagascar, Malawi, Malaysia, Maldives, Mali, Mauritius, Mexico, Mongolia, Morocco, Nepal, Nicaragua, Niger, Nigeria, Oman, Pakistan, Panama, Papua New Guinea, Peru, Philippines, Poland, Qatar, Romania, Rwanda, Saint Lucia, Saint Vincent and the Grenadines, Sao Tome and Principe, Saudi Arabia, Senegal, Seychelles, Sierra Leone, Singapore, Solomon Islands, Somalia, Sri Lanka, Sudan, Suriname, Swaziland, Syrian Arab Republic, Thailand, Togo, Trinidad and Tobago, Tunisia, Turkey, Uganda, Ukrainian SSR, USSR, United Arab Emirates, United Republic of Tanzania, Uruguay, Vanuatu, Venezuela, Viet Nam, Yemen, Yugoslavia, Zaire, Zambia.
Against: Israel, United States.
Abstaining: Australia, Austria, Bahamas, Belgium, Canada, Costa Rica, Cote d'Ivoire, Denmark, Dominica, El Salvador, Finland, France, Germany, Federal Republic of, Greece, Honduras, Iceland, Ireland, Italy, Japan, Kenya, Luxembourg, Malta, Netherlands, New Zealand, Norway, Paraguay, Portugal, Samoa, Spain, Sweden, United Kingdom.

Resolution 43/160 B was also adopted by recorded vote.

The General Assembly,
Recalling its resolutions 35/167 of 15 December 1980, 37/104 of 16 December 1982, 39/76 of 13 December 1984 and 41/71 of 3 December 1986,
Recalling also its resolutions 3237(XXIX) of 22 November 1974, 3280(XXIX) of 10 December 1974 and 31/152 of 20 December 1976,
Taking note of the report of the Secretary-General,
Bearing in mind the resolution of the United Nations Conference on the Representation of States in Their Relations with International Organizations relating to the observer status of national liberation movements recognized by the Organization of African Unity and/or by the League of Arab States,

Noting that the Vienna Convention on the Representation of States in Their Relations with International Organizations of a Universal Character, of 14 March 1975, regulates only the representation of States in their relations with international organizations,

Taking into account the current practice of inviting the above-mentioned national liberation movements to participate as observers in the sessions of the General Assembly, specialized agencies and other organizations of the United Nations system and in the work of the conferences held under the auspices of such international organizations,

Convinced that the participation of the national liberation movements referred to above in the work of international organizations helps to strengthen international peace and co-operation,

Desirous of ensuring the effective participation of the above-mentioned national liberation movements as observers in the work of international organizations and of regulating, to that end, their status and the facilities, privileges and immunities necessary for the performance of their functions,

Noting that many States have recognized those national liberation movements and have granted them facilities, privileges and immunities in their countries,

1.   *Urges* all States that have not done so, in particular those which act as host to international organizations or to conferences convened by, or held under the auspices of, international organizations of a universal character, to consider as soon as possible the question of ratifying, or acceding to, the Vienna Convention on the Representation of States in Their Relations with International Organizations of a Universal Character;

2.   *Calls once more upon* the States concerned to accord to the delegations of the national liberation movements recognized by the Organization of African Unity and/or by the League of Arab States and accorded observer status by international organizations, the facilities, privileges and immunities necessary for the performance of their functions, in accordance with the provisions of the Vienna Convention on the Representation of States in Their Relations with International Organizations of a Universal Character;

3.   *Requests* the Secretary-General to report to the General Assembly at its forty-fifth session on the implementation of the present resolution.

General Assembly resolution 43/160 B

9 December 1988   Meeting 76   124-9-18 (recorded vote)

Approved by Sixth Committee (A/43/880) by vote (87-9-14), 28 November (meeting 50); 26-nation draft (A/C.6/43/L.24 & Corr.1); agenda item 126.
Sponsors: Afghanistan, Algeria, Angola, Bahrain, Bangladesh, Cuba, Democratic Yemen, Djibouti, Iraq, Kuwait, Lebanon, Libyan Arab Jamahiriya, Madagascar, Mauritania, Nicaragua, Oman, Qatar, Saudi Arabia, Somalia, Sudan, Syrian Arab Republic, Tunisia, Uganda, United Arab Emirates, Yemen, Yugoslavia.
Meeting numbers. GA 43rd session: 6th Committee 21, 22, 50; plenary 76.

Recorded vote in Assembly as follows:

In favour: Afghanistan, Albania, Algeria, Angola, Antigua and Barbuda, Argentina, Bahamas, Bahrain, Barbados, Belize, Benin, Bhutan, Bolivia, Botswana, Brazil, Brunei Darussalam, Bulgaria, Burkina Faso, Burma, Burundi, Byelorussian SSR, Cameroon, Cape Verde, Central African Republic, Chad, Chile, China, Colombia, Congo, Costa Rica, Cuba, Cyprus, Czechoslovakia, Democratic Kampuchea, Democratic Yemen, Djibouti, Dominican Republic, Ecuador, Egypt, Equatorial Guinea, Ethiopia, Fiji, Gabon, Gambia, German Democratic Republic, Ghana, Greece, Grenada, Guatemala, Guinea, Guinea-Bissau, Guyana, Hungary, India, Indonesia, Iran, Iraq, Jordan, Kenya, Kuwait, Lao People's Democratic Republic, Lebanon, Lesotho, Liberia, Libyan Arab Jamahiriya, Madagascar, Malawi, Malaysia, Maldives, Mali, Malta, Mauritania, Mauritius, Mexico, Mongo-

lia, Morocco, Nepal, Nicaragua, Niger, Nigeria, Oman, Pakistan, Panama, Papua New Guinea, Peru, Philippines, Poland, Qatar, Romania, Rwanda, Saint Lucia, Saint Vincent and the Grenadines, Samoa, Sao Tome and Principe, Saudi Arabia, Senegal, Seychelles, Sierra Leone, Singapore, Solomon Islands, Somalia, Sri Lanka, Sudan, Suriname, Swaziland, Syrian Arab Republic, Thailand, Togo, Trinidad and Tobago, Tunisia, Turkey, Uganda, Ukrainian SSR, USSR, United Arab Emirates, United Republic of Tanzania, Uruguay, Vanuatu, Venezuela, Viet Nam, Yemen, Yugoslavia, Zaire, Zambia.
Against: Belgium, France, Germany, Federal Republic of, Israel, Italy, Luxembourg, Netherlands, United Kingdom, United States.
Abstaining: Australia, Austria, Canada, Côte d'Ivoire, Denmark, Dominica, El Salvador, Finland, Honduras, Iceland, Ireland, Japan, New Zealand, Norway, Paraguay, Portugal, Spain, Sweden.

Asian-African Legal Consultative Committee

Pursuant to a General Assembly request of 1986,[37] the Secretary-General submitted, in October 1988, a report[38] on co-operation between the United Nations and the Asian-African Legal Consultative Committee (AALCC), an organization which the Assembly had invited in 1980[39] to participate in its sessions and work in the capacity of a permanent observer.

The report reviewed the activities of the Committee in the context of a 1987 programme of co-operation in the following areas: co-operative framework; representation at meetings and conferences; strengthening the role of the United Nations through rationalization of functional modalities; measures designed to further the work of the Assembly's Sixth Committee; facilitation of the work of ILC and the United Nations Commission on International Trade Law (UNCITRAL); law of the sea; international economic co-operation for development; refugee questions; zones of peace and international co-operation; and illicit traffic in narcotic drugs. The Committee also dealt with criteria for the distinction between terrorism and people's struggle for liberation, and the deportation of Palestinians as a violation of international law, particularly the 1949 Geneva Conventions.

GENERAL ASSEMBLY ACTION

On 17 October 1988, the General Assembly adopted **resolution 43/1** without vote.

Co-operation between the United Nations and the Asian-African Legal Consultative Committee
The General Assembly,

Recalling its resolutions 36/38 of 18 November 1981, 37/8 of 29 October 1982, 38/37 of 5 December 1983, 39/47 of 10 December 1984, 40/60 of 9 December 1985 and 41/5 of 17 October 1986,

Having considered the report of the Secretary-General on co-operation between the United Nations and the Asian-African Legal Consultative Committee,

Having heard the statement made on 17 October 1988 by the Secretary-General of the Asian-African Legal Consultative Committee on the steps taken by the Committee to ensure continuing, close and effective co-operation between the two organizations,

1.   *Takes note with appreciation* of the report of the Secretary-General;

2. *Notes with appreciation* the continuing efforts of the Asian-African Legal Consultative Committee towards strengthening the role of the United Nations and its various organs, including the International Court of Justice, through programmes and initiatives undertaken by the Committee;

3. *Notes with satisfaction* the commendable progress achieved towards enhancing co-operation between the United Nations and the Asian-African Legal Consultative Committee in wider areas;

4. *Requests* the Secretary-General to submit to the General Assembly at its forty-fifth session a report on co-operation between the United Nations and the Asian-African Legal Consultative Committee;

5. *Decides* to include in the provisional agenda of its forty-fifth session the item entitled "Co-operation between the United Nations and the Asian-African Legal Consultative Committee".

General Assembly resolution 43/1

17 October 1988   Meeting 32   Adopted without vote

21-nation draft (A/43/L.4 & Add.1); agenda item 20.
Sponsors: Australia, Canada, China, Cyprus, Egypt, Ghana, India, Indonesia, Iran, Iraq, Jamaica, Japan, Jordan, Kenya, Mongolia, Nepal, New Zealand, Romania, Sudan, Thailand, United Republic of Tanzania.

REFERENCES

[1]A/43/33. [2]YUN 1987, p. 1072, GA res. 42/157, 7 Dec. 1987. [3]*Ibid.*, p. 1072. [4]YUN 1985, p. 1177. [5]YUN 1981, p. 1240, GA res. 36/123, 11 Dec. 1981. [6]A/AC.182/L.57. [7]YUN 1987, p. 1073. [8]*Ibid.*, p. 1074, GA res. 42/210 A, 17 Dec. 1987. [9]A/43/26. [10]YUN 1947-48, p. 199, GA res. 169(II), 31 Oct. 1947. [11]A/42/956. [12]A/42/958. [13]A/C.6/43/6. [14]A/C.6/43/3. [15]A/42/919. [16]A/42/921. [17]A/42/922. [18]A/42/924. [19]YUN 1987, p. 1075, GA res. 42/210 B, 17 Dec. 1987. [20]A/42/915. [21]A/42/915/Add.1. [22]A/42/915/Add.2. [23]A/42/915/Add.3. [24]A/42/932. [25]A/42/939. [26]YUN 1974, p. 227, GA res. 3237(XXIX), 22 Nov. 1974. [27]YUN 1987, p. 1075, GA res. 42/210 B, 17 Dec. 1987. [28]A/42/952. [29]A/42/915/Add.4. [30]A/42/915/Add.5. [31]A/43/26 & Corr.1 & Add.1 & Add.1/Corr.1. [32]A/C.6/43/7. [33]A/43/909. [34]YUN 1986, p. 1003, GA res. 41/71, 3 Dec. 1986. [35]A/43/528 & Add.1,2. [36]YUN 1975, p. 880. [37]YUN 1986, p. 1016, GA res. 41/5, 17 Oct. 1986. [38]A/43/640. [39]YUN 1980, p. 469, GA res. 35/2, 13 Oct. 1980.

International Law Commission

ILC, at its fortieth session (Geneva, 9 May-29 July 1988),[1] continued its work on the progressive development and codification of international law. In accordance with its 1987[2] General Assembly mandate, the Commission provisionally adopted in 1988 six articles of the draft Code of Crimes against the Peace and Security of Mankind, on which the Assembly subsequently invited ILC to continue to work (**resolution 43/164**). The Commission also considered non-navigational uses of international watercourses and provisionally adopted 14 draft articles on the subject. In August,[3] the Secretary-General transmitted to the Assembly the articles adopted by ILC in 1988 on both topics (see PART FIVE, Chapter II). ILC also examined the jurisdictional immunities of States and their property; in-

ternational liability for injurious consequences arising out of acts not prohibited by international law; and the status of the diplomatic courier and the diplomatic bag not accompanied by diplomatic courier. It was unable to consider State responsibility due to lack of time (see PART FIVE, Chapter III), and did not consider relations between States and international organizations, noting the intent of the Special Rapporteur to submit a report at the Commission's next session.

The Commission held 54 public meetings. Its Drafting Committee held 41 meetings; the Enlarged Bureau, 3; and the Planning Group of the Enlarged Bureau, 5. ILC continued in 1988 to co-operate with AALCC, the European Committee on Legal Co-operation, and the Inter-American Juridical Committee.

The Secretariat prepared for the Commission's attention in 1989 a topical summary of the Sixth Committee's discussion in 1988[4] of the 1988 ILC report.

ILC work programme and working methods

As requested by the Assembly in 1987,[2] the Commission discussed, in 1988, matters relating to its programme, procedures, working methods and documentation in the framework of the Bureau's Planning Group and the Enlarged Bureau itself.

In July, it observed—based on recommendations of the Enlarged Bureau resulting from discussions in the Planning Group—that the two topics on which it could achieve maximum progress in the next three years were the status of the diplomatic courier and the diplomatic bag not accompanied by diplomatic courier; and jurisdictional immunities of States and their property. The Commission decided to concentrate in 1989 and 1990 on these topics without excluding others. It was convinced that the streamlining of its agenda would be conducive to higher productivity. It also intended to establish a small Working Group to identify and propose possible topics for inclusion in a long-term programme of work.

ILC recalled that it consistently aimed to produce texts that were sufficiently precise to form the basis of a convention or other legal instrument while leaving the Assembly freedom to decide the form which the end product of the Commission's work would eventually take. ILC was aware that commentaries on draft articles were of crucial importance for the analysis and interpretation of their corresponding texts, and that they should reflect the collective understanding of members. To help achieve this, it encouraged Special Rapporteurs to hold consultations in the framework of the Drafting Committee before draft commentaries were submitted in plenary. It believed it would also be worthwhile to further examine the possibility of giving the Drafting Committee computerized assistance.

Other issues addressed included: the desire to maintain the normal arrangements for a 12-week session; the need for ILC to receive in a timely manner United Nations communications relevant to topics on its work programme; the ability of the Sixth Committee to submit to the Special Rapporteurs in a timely manner the necessary documentation; and the production of reports and the ILC *Yearbook* in all official United Nations languages.[(1)]

In considering ways to make it easier for delegations to the Sixth Committee to acquaint themselves with the content of its report, ILC decided that its general work description at the start of the report should be expanded to include an indication of concrete results and footnoted references to the meetings at which each topic was considered. Finally, the Commission considered the possibility of enabling Special Rapporteurs to attend the Sixth Committee debate on the report so they could have a comprehensive view of existing positions, take note of observations made and prepare their reports earlier.

In response to the same Assembly resolution,[(2)] the Sixth Committee decided in 1988[(5)] to establish an open-ended *Ad Hoc* Working Group to consider improvements in the way the ILC report was considered in the Sixth Committee. The *Ad Hoc* Working Group held six meetings between 3 and 14 November and its Chairman gave an oral report on its work on 11 November.

GENERAL ASSEMBLY ACTION

On 9 December 1988, the General Assembly, on the recommendation of the Sixth Committee, adopted **resolution 43/169** without vote.

Report of the International Law Commission on the work of its fortieth session

The General Assembly,

Having considered the report of the International Law Commission on the work of its fortieth session,

Emphasizing the need for the progressive development of international law and its codification in order to make it a more effective means of implementing the purposes and principles set forth in the Charter of the United Nations and in the Declaration on Principles of International Law concerning Friendly Relations and Cooperation among States in accordance with the Charter of the United Nations and to give increased importance to its role in relations among States,

Recognizing the importance of referring legal and drafting questions to the Sixth Committee, including topics that might be submitted to the International Law Commission, and of enabling the Sixth Committee and the Commission further to enhance their contributions to the progressive development of international law and its codification,

Recalling the need to keep under review those topics of international law which, given their new or renewed interest for the international community, may be suitable

for the progressive development and codification of international law and therefore may be included in the future programme of work of the International Law Commission,

Considering that experience has demonstrated the usefulness of structuring the debate on the report of the International Law Commission in the Sixth Committee in such a manner that conditions are provided for concentrated attention on each of the main topics dealt with in the report, and that this process is facilitated when the Commission indicates specific issues on which expressions of views by Governments are of particular interest for the continuation of its work,

1.   *Takes note* of the report of the International Law Commission on the work of its fortieth session;

2.   *Expresses its appreciation* to the International Law Commission for the work accomplished at that session;

3.   *Recommends* that, taking into account the comments of Governments, whether in writing or expressed orally in debates in the General Assembly, the International Law Commission should continue its work on the topics in its current programme, listed as items 2 to 8 in paragraph 7 of its report;

4.   *Expresses its satisfaction* with the efforts of the International Law Commission to improve its procedures and methods of work and to formulate proposals on its future programme of work;

5.   *Requests* the International Law Commission:

(a)   To keep under review the planning of its activities for the term of office of its members, bearing in mind the desirability of achieving as much progress as possible in the preparation of draft articles on specific topics;

(b)   To consider further its methods of work in all their aspects, bearing in mind that the staggering of the consideration of some topics might contribute, *inter alia*, to a more effective consideration of its report in the Sixth Committee;

(c)   To indicate in its annual report, for each topic, those specific issues on which expressions of views by Governments, either in the Sixth Committee or in written form, would be of particular interest for the continuation of its work;

6.   *Recommends* the continuation of efforts to improve the ways in which the report of the International Law Commission is considered in the Sixth Committee, with a view to providing effective guidance for the Commission in its work;

7.   *Expresses its satisfaction* at the useful informal discussions held in the framework of the *Ad Hoc* Working Group provided for under paragraph 6 of General Assembly resolution 42/156 of 7 December 1987, which dealt with questions of improving the ways in which the report of the International Law Commission is considered in the Sixth Committee, with a view to providing effective guidance for the Commission in its work, and takes note of the oral report of the Chairman of the *Ad Hoc* Working Group;

8.   *Decides* that the Sixth Committee, in structuring its debate on the report of the International Law Commission at the forty-fourth session of the General Assembly, should bear in mind the possibility of reserving time for informal exchanges of views on matters relating to the Commission;

9.   *Takes note* of the comments of the International Law Commission on the question of the duration of its session, as presented in paragraph 569 of its report, and expresses the view that the requirements of the work for

the progressive development of international law and its codification and the magnitude and complexity of the subjects on the agenda of the Commission make it desirable that the usual duration of its sessions be maintained;

10. *Reaffirms* its previous decisions concerning the increased role of the Codification Division of the Office of Legal Affairs of the Secretariat and those concerning the summary records and other documentation of the International Law Commission;

11. *Urges* Governments and, as appropriate, international organizations to respond in writing as fully and expeditiously as possible to the requests of the International Law Commission for comments, observations and replies to questionnaires and for materials on topics in its programme of work;

12. *Reaffirms its wish* that the International Law Commission continue to enhance its co-operation with intergovernmental legal bodies whose work is of interest for the progressive development of international law and its codification;

13. *Once again expresses the wish* that seminars will continue to be held in conjunction with the sessions of the International Law Commission and that an increasing number of participants from developing countries will be given the opportunity to attend those seminars, appeals to States that can do so to make the voluntary contributions that are urgently needed for the holding of the seminars, and expresses the hope that every effort will be made by the Secretary-General, within existing resources, to provide the seminars with adequate services, including interpretation, as required;

14. *Requests* the Secretary-General to forward to the International Law Commission, for its attention, the records of the debate on the report of the Commission at the forty-third session of the General Assembly and to prepare and distribute a topical summary of the debate.

General Assembly resolution 43/169

9 December 1988   Meeting 76   Adopted without vote

Approved by Sixth Committee (A/43/885) without vote, 21 November (meeting 45); 46-nation draft (A/C.6/43/L.12); agenda item 134.
Sponsors: Algeria, Argentina, Australia, Austria, Brazil, Bulgaria, Canada, Cape Verde, Chile, China, Cyprus, Denmark, Egypt, Ethiopia, Finland, France, German Democratic Republic, Germany, Federal Republic of, Greece, Guatemala, Guinea, Iceland, Ireland, Italy, Jamaica, Japan, Jordan, Kenya, Mali, Mexico, Morocco, New Zealand, Norway, Peru, Philippines, Poland, Romania, Senegal, Spain, Sweden, Tunisia, United Kingdom, United States, Venezuela, Viet Nam, Yugoslavia.
Meeting numbers. GA 43rd session: 6th Committee 25-40, 45; plenary 76.

UN Programme for the teaching and study of international law

The twenty-fourth session of the International Law Seminar—for post-graduate students and young professors or government officials dealing with international law—was held during the ILC session (Geneva, 6-24 June), with four United Nations Institute for Training and Research (UNITAR) fellows and 18 other participants, mostly from developing countries. The participants attended ILC meetings and lectures specifically organized for them. Argentina, Austria, Denmark, the Federal Republic of Germany, Finland and Sweden had made voluntary financial contributions, thus making it possible to award nine fellowships. Since the first seminar in 1964, fellowships had been awarded to 264 of the 536 participants, representing 122 nationalities.

Other activities

Additional training courses were offered as part of the United Nations Programme of Assistance in the Teaching, Study, Dissemination and Wider Appreciation of International Law.[6] Under the annual joint United Nations–UNITAR fellowship programme, 20 middle-grade governmental legal officers and young teachers of international law attended courses for six weeks at the Hague Academy of International Law (Netherlands), as well as seminars organized by UNITAR. Some fellows also participated in the International Law Seminar in Geneva (see above), while others received three months practical training at legal offices of the United Nations, its specialized agencies and other bodies. Topics of the special seminars were: the new international economic order; the United Nations Convention on the Law of the Sea; legal aspects of international trade; dispute settlement in international commercial transactions; legal aspects of development financing; international humanitarian law; international régime for refugee protection; human rights protection; the codification process of international law at the United Nations; negotiations and drafting of treaties and other international legal instruments; and the settlement of international conflicts.

In accordance with a General Assembly request of 1987,[7] UNITAR organized a two-week regional training and refresher course in international law for the Latin America and Caribbean region (Brasília, Brazil, 21 November–1 December) with 28 participants from 21 countries. Within the framework of its Major Programme XIII (Peace, international understanding, human rights and the law of nations), the United Nations Educational, Scientific and Cultural Organization (UNESCO) organized a regional post-graduate training course (Bujumbura, Burundi, 7-13 January). The seminar was attended by some 60 participants from Burundi, Cameroon, Gabon and Zaire, including six teachers, public officials, ministerial advisers, judges and legal advisers and about 30 final-year law students. The first 1988 issue of the UNESCO liaison bulletin *International Law* was published (Bangkok, June), with news and information from Asia and the Pacific region.

In 1988, the third award of the Hamilton Shirley Amerasinghe Memorial Fellowship on the Law of the Sea was bestowed on the legal adviser to the Ministry of Foreign Affairs of Chile (see PART FIVE, Chapter IV).

In response to a request by the Assembly of 1987,[7] the Secretary-General recommended that sessions of the Geneva International Law Seminar (see above) should be scheduled to make it financially possible for United Nations–UNITAR fellows to participate in the programmed sessions. He recommended that 1990-1991 activities should continue along the same lines as in the past, leaving room for new initiatives. If extra funds became available, the matters should be looked at afresh.

As to the UNITAR fellowship programme, he recommended that it be continued during the 1990-1991 biennium with a minimum of 15 fellowships each year to be awarded under the United Nations regular budget. Given the Organization's ongoing financial crisis, maximum use should be made of existing human and material resources of the United Nations so as to achieve the best results within a policy of maximum financial restraint, he said. To the extent possible, teaching experts for special seminars should be recruited from among staff, thereby reducing consultants' fees and travel expenses to a minimum.

REFERENCES

[1]A/43/10. [2]YUN 1987, p. 1086, GA res. 42/156, 7 Dec. 1987. [3]A/43/539. [4]A/CN.4/L.431. [5]A/43/885. [6]A/44/712. [7]YUN 1987, p. 1087, GA res. 42/148, 7 Dec. 1987.

International economic law

In 1988, legal aspects of international economic law and the new international economic order (NIEO) continued to be considered by the United Nations Commission on International Trade Law (UNCITRAL) and by the Sixth Committee of the General Assembly.

International trade law

Report of UNCITRAL

The twenty-first session of UNCITRAL (New York, 11-22 April 1988)[1] considered under international payments: electronic fund transfers; the draft Convention on International Bills of Exchange and International Promissory notes; and stand-by letters of credit and guarantees. The Commission also examined the liability of operators of transport terminals; international countertrade; and its future programme and co-ordination of work. It also considered the status of conventions and the promotion of texts of the Commission, and the promotion of the Legal Guide on Drawing Up International Contracts for the Construction of Industrial Works. Its Working Group on NIEO (Vienna, 17-28 October) discussed procurement (see below, under "Legal aspects of the new international economic order").

As in previous years, UNCITRAL's annual report was forwarded to the United Nations Conference on Trade and Development for comments.

Unification of trade law

International payments

In considering the preparation of Model Rules on electronic funds transfers, the Commission had before it in 1988 the report of its Working Group on International Payments on the work of its sixteenth (1987) session.[2] The Working Group considered a list of legal issues for possible inclusion in the Model Rules contained in a report by the UNCITRAL secretariat. The Commission agreed that the Model Rules should concentrate on problems arising in international fund transfers while considering both domestic and international aspects of such transactions.

The Commission took note of a resolution by the Assembly of 1987[3] concerning the draft Convention on International Bills of Exchange and International Promissory Notes. The Assembly had requested the Secretary-General to ask all States to submit their observations and proposals on the draft before 30 April 1988, with the intention of adopting the Convention at its forty-third (1988) session. A working group was established within the framework of the Sixth Committee on 23 September and, in the course of eight meetings between 26 and 30 September,[4] it considered the observations and proposals of States, as contained in a June report by the Secretary-General.[5] The working group recommended the adoption of the draft Convention, with modifications, in the form in which it had been adopted by UNCITRAL during its twentieth (1987) session.[6]

GENERAL ASSEMBLY ACTION

On 9 December, the General Assembly, on the recommendation of the Sixth Committee, adopted without vote and opened for signature or accession the United Nations Convention on International Bills of Exchange and International Promissory Notes as **resolution 43/165**, thereby putting the seal on more than 16 years of work by UNCITRAL.

United Nations Convention on International Bills of Exchange and International Promissory Notes

The General Assembly,

Recalling its resolution 2205(XXI) of 17 December 1966, by which it created the United Nations Commission on International Trade Law with a mandate to further the progressive harmonization and unification of the law of international trade and in that respect to bear in mind the interests of all peoples, in particular those of developing countries, in the extensive development of international trade,

Aware that the free circulation of bills of exchange and promissory notes facilitates international trade and finance,

Convinced that the adoption of a convention on international bills of exchange and international promissory notes will facilitate the use of such instruments,

Taking note with satisfaction of the decision of the United Nations Commission on International Trade Law at its twentieth session to transmit the text of the draft Convention on International Bills of Exchange and International Promissory Notes to the General Assembly for its consideration,

Recalling its resolution 42/153 of 7 December 1987, in which it requested the Secretary-General to draw the attention of all States to the draft Convention, to ask them to submit the observations and proposals they wished to make on the draft Convention and to circulate those observations and proposals to all Member States,

Recalling also that in the same resolution it decided to consider, at its forty-third session, the draft Convention, with a view to its adoption at that session, and to create to that end a working group, in the framework of the Sixth Committee, to consider the observations and proposals made by States,

Satisfied with the modifications in the draft Convention proposed by the open-ended Working Group on the draft Convention on International Bills of Exchange and International Promissory Notes, and expressing its appreciation for the efforts of the Working Group,

1. *Expresses its appreciation* to the United Nations Commission on International Trade Law for preparing the text of the draft Convention on International Bills of Exchange and International Promissory Notes;

2. *Adopts* and opens for signature or accession the United Nations Convention on International Bills of Exchange and International Promissory Notes contained in the annex to the present resolution;

3. *Calls upon* all Governments to consider becoming party to the Convention.

ANNEX
United Nations Convention on International Bills of Exchange and International Promissory Notes

Chapter I. Sphere of application
and form of the instrument

Article 1

1. This Convention applies to an international bill of exchange when it contains the heading ''International bill of exchange (UNCITRAL Convention)'' and also contains in its text the words ''International bill of exchange (UNCITRAL Convention)''.

2. This Convention applies to an international promissory note when it contains the heading ''International promissory note (UNCITRAL Convention)'' and also contains in its text the words ''International promissory note (UNCITRAL Convention)''.

3. This Convention does not apply to cheques.

Article 2

1. An international bill of exchange is a bill of exchange which specifies at least two of the following places and indicates that any two so specified are situated in different States:

(*a*) The place where the bill is drawn;

(*b*) The place indicated next to the signature of the drawer;

(*c*) The place indicated next to the name of the drawee;

(*d*) The place indicated next to the name of the payee;

(*e*) The place of payment,

provided that either the place where the bill is drawn or the place of payment is specified on the bill and that such place is situated in a Contracting State.

2. An international promissory note is a promissory note which specifies at least two of the following places and indicates that any two so specified are situated in different States:

(*a*) The place where the note is made;

(*b*) The place indicated next to the signature of the maker;

(*c*) The place indicated next to the name of the payee;

(*d*) The place of payment,

provided that the place of payment is specified on the note and that such place is situated in a Contracting State.

3. This Convention does not deal with the question of sanctions that may be imposed under national law in cases where an incorrect or false statement has been made on an instrument in respect of a place referred to in paragraph 1 or 2 of this article. However, any such sanctions shall not affect the validity of the instrument or the application of this Convention.

Article 3

1. A bill of exchange is a written instrument which:

(*a*) Contains an unconditional order whereby the drawer directs the drawee to pay a definite sum of money to the payee or to his order;

(*b*) Is payable on demand or at a definite time;

(*c*) Is dated;

(*d*) Is signed by the drawer.

2. A promissory note is a written instrument which:

(*a*) Contains an unconditional promise whereby the maker undertakes to pay a definite sum of money to the payee or to his order;

(*b*) Is payable on demand or at a definite time;

(*c*) Is dated;

(*d*) Is signed by the maker.

Chapter II. Interpretation

Section 1. General provisions

Article 4

In the interpretation of this Convention, regard is to be had to its international character and to the need to promote uniformity in its application and the observance of good faith in international transactions.

Article 5

In this Convention:

(*a*) ''Bill'' means an international bill of exchange governed by this Convention;

(*b*) ''Note'' means an international promissory note governed by this Convention;

(*c*) ''Instrument'' means a bill or a note;

(*d*) ''Drawee'' means a person on whom a bill is drawn and who has not accepted it;

(*e*) ''Payee'' means a person in whose favour the drawer directs payment to be made or to whom the maker promises to pay;

(*f*) ''Holder'' means a person in possession of an instrument in accordance with article 15;

(*g*) ''Protected holder'' means a holder who meets the requirements of article 29;

(*h*) ''Guarantor'' means any person who undertakes an obligation of guarantee under article 46, whether governed by paragraph 4 *(b)* ("guaranteed") or paragraph 4 *(c)* ("*aval*") of article 47;

(i) "Party" means a person who has signed an instrument as drawer, maker, acceptor, endorser or guarantor;

(j) "Maturity" means the time of payment referred to in paragraphs 4, 5, 6 and 7 of article 9;

(k) "Signature" means a handwritten signature, its facsimile or an equivalent authentication effected by any other means; "forged signature" includes a signature by the wrongful use of such means;

(l) "Money" or "currency" includes a monetary unit of account which is established by an intergovernmental institution or by agreement between two or more States, provided that this Convention shall apply without prejudice to the rules of the intergovernmental institution or to the stipulations of the agreement.

Article 6

For the purposes of this Convention, a person is considered to have knowledge of a fact if he has actual knowledge of that fact or could not have been unaware of its existence.

Section 2. Interpretation of formal requirements

Article 7

The sum payable by an instrument is deemed to be a definite sum although the instrument states that it is to be paid:

(a) With interest;

(b) By instalments at successive dates;

(c) By instalments at successive dates with a stipulation in the instrument that upon default in payment of any instalment the unpaid balance becomes due;

(d) According to a rate of exchange indicated in the instrument or to be determined as directed by the instrument; or

(e) In a currency other than the currency in which the sum is expressed in the instrument.

Article 8

1. If there is a discrepancy between the sum expressed in words and the sum expressed in figures, the sum payable by the instrument is the sum expressed in words.

2. If the sum is expressed more than once in words, and there is a discrepancy, the sum payable is the smaller sum. The same rule applies if the sum is expressed more than once in figures only, and there is a discrepancy.

3. If the sum is expressed in a currency having the same description as that of at least one other State than the State where payment is to be made, as indicated in the instrument, and the specified currency is not identified as the currency of any particular State, the currency is to be considered as the currency of the State where payment is to be made.

4. If an instrument states that the sum is to be paid with interest, without specifying the date from which interest is to run, interest runs from the date of the instrument.

5. A stipulation stating that the sum is to be paid with interest is deemed not to have been written on the instrument unless it indicates the rate at which interest is to be paid.

6. A rate at which interest is to be paid may be expressed either as a definite rate or as a variable rate. For a variable rate to qualify for this purpose, it must vary in relation to one or more reference rates of interest in accordance with provisions stipulated in the instrument and each such reference rate must be published or otherwise available to the public and not be subject, directly or indirectly, to unilateral determination by a person who is named in the instrument at the time the bill is drawn or the note is made, unless the person is named only in the reference rate provisions.

7. If the rate at which interest is to be paid is expressed as a variable rate, it may be stipulated expressly in the instrument that such rate shall not be less than or exceed a specified rate of interest, or that the variations are otherwise limited.

8. If a variable rate does not qualify under paragraph 6 of this article or for any reason it is not possible to determine the numerical value of the variable rate for any period, interest shall be payable for the relevant period at the rate calculated in accordance with paragraph 2 of article 70.

Article 9

1. An instrument is deemed to be payable on demand:

(a) If it states that it is payable at sight or on demand or on presentment or if it contains words of similar import; or

(b) If no time of payment is expressed.

2. An instrument payable at a definite time which is accepted or endorsed or guaranteed after maturity is an instrument payable on demand as regards the acceptor, the endorser or the guarantor.

3. An instrument is deemed to be payable at a definite time if it states that it is payable:

(a) On a stated date or at a fixed period after a stated date or at a fixed period after the date of the instrument;

(b) At a fixed period after sight;

(c) By instalments at successive dates; or

(d) By instalments at successive dates with the stipulation in the instrument that upon default in payment of any instalment the unpaid balance becomes due.

4. The time of payment of an instrument payable at a fixed period after date is determined by reference to the date of the instrument.

5. The time of payment of a bill payable at a fixed period after sight is determined by the date of acceptance or, if the bill is dishonoured by non-acceptance, by the date of protest or, if protest is dispensed with, by the date of dishonour.

6. The time of payment of an instrument payable on demand is the date on which the instrument is presented for payment.

7. The time of payment of a note payable at a fixed period after sight is determined by the date of the visa signed by the maker on the note or, if his visa is refused, by the date of presentment.

8. If an instrument is drawn, or made, payable one or more months after a stated date or after the date of the instrument or after sight, the instrument is payable on the corresponding date of the month when payment must be made. If there is no corresponding date, the instrument is payable on the last day of that month.

Article 10

1. A bill may be drawn:

(a) By two or more drawers;

(b) Payable to two or more payees.

2. A note may be made:

(a) By two or more makers;

(b) Payable to two or more payees.

3. If an instrument is payable to two or more payees in the alternative, it is payable to any one of them and any one of them in possession of the instrument may exercise the rights of a holder. In any other case the instrument is payable to all of them and the rights of a holder may be exercised only by all of them.

Article 11

A bill may be drawn by the drawer:

(a) On himself;

(b) Payable to his order.

Section 3. Completion of an incomplete instrument

Article 12

1. An incomplete instrument which satisfies the requirements set out in paragraph 1 of article 1 and bears the signature of the drawer or the acceptance of the drawee, or which satisfies the requirements set out in paragraph 2 of article 1 and paragraph 2 (d) of article 3, but which lacks other elements pertaining to one or more of the requirements set out in articles 2 and 3, may be completed, and the instrument so completed is effective as a bill or a note.

2. If such an instrument is completed without authority or otherwise than in accordance with the authority given:

(a) A party who signed the instrument before the completion may invoke such lack of authority as a defence against a holder who had knowledge of such lack of authority when he became a holder;

(b) A party who signed the instrument after the completion is liable according to the terms of the instrument so completed.

Chapter III. Transfer

Article 13

An instrument is transferred:

(a) By endorsement and delivery of the instrument by the endorser to the endorsee; or

(b) By mere delivery of the instrument if the last endorsement is in blank.

Article 14

1. An endorsement must be written on the instrument or on a slip affixed thereto (*"allonge"*). It must be signed.

2. An endorsement may be:

(a) In blank, that is, by a signature alone or by a signature accompanied by a statement to the effect that the instrument is payable to a person in possession of it;

(b) Special, that is, by a signature accompanied by an indication of the person to whom the instrument is payable.

3. A signature alone, other than that of the drawee, is an endorsement only if placed on the back of the instrument.

Article 15

1. A person is a holder if he is:

(a) The payee in possession of the instrument; or

(b) In possession of an instrument which has been endorsed to him, or on which the last endorsement is in blank, and on which there appears an uninterrupted series of endorsements, even if any endorsement was forged or was signed by an agent without authority.

2. If an endorsement in blank is followed by another endorsement, the person who signed this last endorsement is deemed to be an endorsee by the endorsement in blank.

3. A person is not prevented from being a holder by the fact that the instrument was obtained by him or any previous holder under circumstances, including incapacity or fraud, duress or mistake of any kind, that would give rise to a claim to, or a defence against liability on, the instrument.

Article 16

The holder of an instrument on which the last endorsement is in blank may:

(a) Further endorse it either by an endorsement in blank or by a special endorsement;

(b) Convert the blank endorsement into a special endorsement by indicating in the endorsement that the instrument is payable to himself or to some other specified person; or

(c) Transfer the instrument in accordance with sub-paragraph (b) of article 13.

Article 17

1. If the drawer or the maker has inserted in the instrument such words as "not negotiable", "not transferable", "not to order", "pay (X) only", or words of similar import, the instrument may not be transferred except for purposes of collection, and any endorsement, even if it does not contain words authorizing the endorsee to collect the instrument, is deemed to be an endorsement for collection.

2. If an endorsement contains the words "not negotiable", "not transferable", "not to order", "pay (X) only", or words of similar import, the instrument may not be transferred further except for purposes of collection, and any subsequent endorsement, even if it does not contain words authorizing the endorsee to collect the instrument, is deemed to be an endorsement for collection.

Article 18

1. An endorsement must be unconditional.

2. A conditional endorsement transfers the instrument whether or not the condition is fulfilled. The condition is ineffective as to those parties and transferees who are subsequent to the endorsee.

Article 19

An endorsement in respect of a part of the sum due under the instrument is ineffective as an endorsement.

Article 20

If there are two or more endorsements, it is presumed, unless the contrary is proved, that each endorsement was made in the order in which it appears on the instrument.

Article 21

1. If an endorsement contains the words "for collection", "for deposit", "value in collection", "by procuration", "pay any bank", or words of similar import authorizing the endorsee to collect the instrument, the endorsee is a holder who:

(a) May exercise all rights arising out of the instrument;

(b) May endorse the instrument only for purposes of collection;

(c) Is subject only to the claims and defences which may be set up against the endorser.

2. The endorser for collection is not liable on the instrument to any subsequent holder.

Article 22

1. If an endorsement contains the words "value in security", "value in pledge", or any other words indicating a pledge, the endorsee is a holder who:

(*a*) May exercise all rights arising out of the instrument;

(*b*) May endorse the instrument only for purposes of collection;

(*c*) Is subject only to the claims and defences specified in article 28 or article 30.

2. If such an endorsee endorses for collection, he is not liable on the instrument to any subsequent holder.

Article 23

The holder of an instrument may transfer it to a prior party or to the drawee in accordance with article 13; however, if the transferee has previously been a holder of the instrument, no endorsement is required, and any endorsement which would prevent him from qualifying as a holder may be struck out.

Article 24

An instrument may be transferred in accordance with article 13 after maturity, except by the drawee, the acceptor or the maker.

Article 25

1. If an endorsement is forged, the person whose endorsement is forged, or a party who signed the instrument before the forgery, has the right to recover compensation for any damage that he may have suffered because of the forgery against:

(*a*) The forger;

(*b*) The person to whom the instrument was directly transferred by the forger;

(*c*) A party or the drawee who paid the instrument to the forger directly or through one or more endorsees for collection.

2. However, an endorsee for collection is not liable under paragraph 1 of this article if he is without knowledge of the forgery:

(*a*) At the time he pays the principal or advises him of the receipt of payment; or

(*b*) At the time he receives payment, if this is later, unless his lack of knowledge is due to his failure to act in good faith or to exercise reasonable care.

3. Furthermore, a party or the drawee who pays an instrument is not liable under paragraph 1 of this article if, at the time he pays the instrument, he is without knowledge of the forgery, unless his lack of knowledge is due to his failure to act in good faith or to exercise reasonable care.

4. Except as against the forger, the damages recoverable under paragraph 1 of this article may not exceed the amount referred to in article 70 or article 71.

Article 26

1. If an endorsement is made by an agent without authority or power to bind his principal in the matter, the principal, or a party who signed the instrument before such endorsement, has the right to recover compensation for any damage that he may have suffered because of such endorsement against:

(*a*) The agent;

(*b*) The person to whom the instrument was directly transferred by the agent;

(*c*) A party or the drawee who paid the instrument to the agent directly or through one or more endorsees for collection.

2. However, an endorsee for collection is not liable under paragraph 1 of this article if he is without knowledge that the endorsement does not bind the principal:

(*a*) At the time he pays the principal or advises him of the receipt of payment; or

(*b*) At the time he receives payment, if this is later, unless his lack of knowledge is due to his failure to act in good faith or to exercise reasonable care.

3. Furthermore, a party or the drawee who pays an instrument is not liable under paragraph 1 of this article if, at the time he pays the instrument, he is without knowledge that the endorsement does not bind the principal, unless his lack of knowledge is due to his failure to act in good faith or to exercise reasonable care.

4. Except as against the agent, the damages recoverable under paragraph 1 of this article may not exceed the amount referred to in article 70 or article 71.

Chapter IV. Rights and liabilities

Section 1. The rights of a holder and of a protected holder

Article 27

1. The holder of an instrument has all the rights conferred on him by this Convention against the parties to the instrument.

2. The holder may transfer the instrument in accordance with article 13.

Article 28

1. A party may set up against a holder who is not a protected holder:

(*a*) Any defence that may be set up against a protected holder in accordance with paragraph 1 of article 30;

(*b*) Any defence based on the underlying transaction between himself and the drawer or between himself and his transferee, but only if the holder took the instrument with knowledge of such defence or if he obtained the instrument by fraud or theft or participated at any time in a fraud or theft concerning it;

(*c*) Any defence arising from the circumstances as a result of which he became a party, but only if the holder took the instrument with knowledge of such defence or if he obtained the instrument by fraud or theft or participated at any time in a fraud or theft concerning it;

(*d*) Any defence which may be raised against an action in contract between himself and the holder;

(*e*) Any other defence available under this Convention.

2. The rights to an instrument of a holder who is not a protected holder are subject to any valid claim to the instrument on the part of any person, but only if he took the instrument with knowledge of such claim or if he obtained the instrument by fraud or theft or participated at any time in a fraud or theft concerning it.

3. A holder who takes an instrument after the expiration of the time-limit for presentment for payment is subject to any claim to, or defence against liability on, the instrument to which his transferor is subject.

4. A party may not raise as a defence against a holder who is not a protected holder the fact that a third person has a claim to the instrument unless:

(*a*) The third person asserted a valid claim to the instrument; or

(*b*) The holder acquired the instrument by theft or forged the signature of the payee or an endorsee, or participated in the theft or the forgery.

Article 29

"Protected holder" means the holder of an instrument which was complete when he took it or which was incomplete within the meaning of paragraph 1 of article 12 and was completed in accordance with authority given, provided that when he became a holder:

(a) He was without knowledge of a defence against liability on the instrument referred to in paragraphs 1 (a), (b), (c) and (e) of article 28;

(b) He was without knowledge of a valid claim to the instrument of any person;

(c) He was without knowledge of the fact that it had been dishonoured by non-acceptance or by non-payment;

(d) The time-limit provided by article 55 for presentment of that instrument for payment had not expired;

(e) He did not obtain the instrument by fraud or theft or participate in a fraud or theft concerning it.

Article 30

1. A party may not set up against a protected holder any defence except:

(a) Defences under paragraph 1 of article 33, article 34, paragraph 1 of article 35, paragraph 3 of article 36, paragraph 1 of article 53, paragraph 1 of article 57, paragraph 1 of article 63 and article 84 of this Convention;

(b) Defences based on the underlying transaction between himself and such holder or arising from any fraudulent act on the part of such holder in obtaining the signature on the instrument of that party;

(c) Defences based on his incapacity to incur liability on the instrument or on the fact that he signed without knowledge that his signature made him a party to the instrument, provided that his lack of knowledge was not due to his negligence and provided that he was fraudulently induced so to sign.

2. The rights to an instrument of a protected holder are not subject to any claim to the instrument on the part of any person, except a valid claim arising from the underlying transaction between himself and the person by whom the claim is raised.

Article 31

1. The transfer of an instrument by a protected holder vests in any subsequent holder the rights to and on the instrument which the protected holder had.

2. Those rights are not vested in a subsequent holder if:

(a) He participated in a transaction which gives rise to a claim to, or a defence against liability on, the instrument;

(b) He has previously been a holder, but not a protected holder.

Article 32

Every holder is presumed to be a protected holder unless the contrary is proved.

Section 2. Liabilities of the parties

A. General provisions

Article 33

1. Subject to the provisions of articles 34 and 36, a person is not liable on an instrument unless he signs it.

2. A person who signs an instrument in a name which is not his own is liable as if he had signed it in his own name.

Article 34

A forged signature on an instrument does not impose any liability on the person whose signature was forged. However, if he consents to be bound by the forged signature or represents that it is his own, he is liable as if he had signed the instrument himself.

Article 35

1. If an instrument is materially altered:

(a) A party who signs it after the material alteration is liable according to the terms of the altered text;

(b) A party who signs it before the material alteration is liable according to the terms of the original text. However, if a party makes, authorizes or assents to a material alteration, he is liable according to the terms of the altered text.

2. A signature is presumed to have been placed on the instrument after the material alteration unless the contrary is proved.

3. Any alteration is material which modifies the written undertaking on the instrument of any party in any respect.

Article 36

1. An instrument may be signed by an agent.

2. The signature of an agent placed by him on an instrument with the authority of his principal and showing on the instrument that he is signing in a representative capacity for that named principal, or the signature of a principal placed on the instrument by an agent with his authority, imposes liability on the principal and not on the agent.

3. A signature placed on an instrument by a person as agent but who lacks authority to sign or exceeds his authority, or by an agent who has authority to sign but who does not show on the instrument that he is signing in a representative capacity for a named person, or who shows on the instrument that he is signing in a representative capacity but does not name the person whom he represents, imposes liability on the person signing and not on the person whom he purports to represent.

4. The question whether a signature was placed on the instrument in a representative capacity may be determined only by reference to what appears on the instrument.

5. A person who is liable pursuant to paragraph 3 of this article and who pays the instrument has the same rights as the person for whom he purported to act would have had if that person had paid the instrument.

Article 37

The order to pay contained in a bill does not of itself operate as an assignment to the payee of funds made available for payment by the drawer with the drawee.

B. The drawer

Article 38

1. The drawer engages that upon dishonour of the bill by non-acceptance or by non-payment, and upon any necessary protest, he will pay the bill to the holder, or to any endorser or any endorser's guarantor who takes up and pays the bill.

2. The drawer may exclude or limit his own liability for acceptance or for payment by an express stipulation in the bill. Such a stipulation is effective only with respect to the drawer. A stipulation excluding or limiting liability for payment is effective only if another party is or becomes liable on the bill.

C. The maker

Article 39

1. The maker engages that he will pay the note in accordance with its terms to the holder, or to any party who takes up and pays the note.

2. The maker may not exclude or limit his own liability by a stipulation in the note. Any such stipulation is ineffective.

D. The drawee and the acceptor

Article 40

1. The drawee is not liable on a bill until he accepts it.

2. The acceptor engages that he will pay the bill in accordance with the terms of his acceptance to the holder, or to any party who takes up and pays the bill.

Article 41

1. An acceptance must be written on the bill and may be effected:

(*a*) By the signature of the drawee accompanied by the word "accepted" or by words of similar import; or

(*b*) By the signature alone of the drawee.

2. An acceptance may be written on the front or on the back of the bill.

Article 42

1. An incomplete bill which satisfies the requirements set out in paragraph 1 of article 1 may be accepted by the drawee before it has been signed by the drawer, or while otherwise incomplete.

2. A bill may be accepted before, at or after maturity, or after it has been dishonoured by non-acceptance or by non-payment.

3. If a bill drawn payable at a fixed period after sight, or a bill which must be presented for acceptance before a specified date, is accepted, the acceptor must indicate the date of his acceptance; failing such indication by the acceptor, the drawer or the holder may insert the date of acceptance.

4. If a bill drawn payable at a fixed period after sight is dishonoured by non-acceptance and the drawee subsequently accepts it, the holder is entitled to have the acceptance dated as of the date on which the bill was dishonoured.

Article 43

1. An acceptance must be unqualified. An acceptance is qualified if it is conditional or varies the terms of the bill.

2. If the drawee stipulates in the bill that his acceptance is subject to qualification:

(*a*) He is nevertheless bound according to the terms of his qualified acceptance;

(*b*) The bill is dishonoured by non-acceptance.

3. An acceptance relating to only a part of the sum payable is a qualified acceptance. If the holder takes such an acceptance, the bill is dishonoured by non-acceptance only as to the remaining part.

4. An acceptance indicating that payment will be made at a particular address or by a particular agent is not a qualified acceptance, provided that:

(*a*) The place in which payment is to be made is not changed;

(*b*) The bill is not drawn payable by another agent.

E. The endorser

Article 44

1. The endorser engages that upon dishonour of the instrument by non-acceptance or by non-payment, and upon any necessary protest, he will pay the instrument to the holder, or to any subsequent endorser or any endorser's guarantor who takes up and pays the instrument.

2. An endorser may exclude or limit his own liability by an express stipulation in the instrument. Such a stipulation is effective only with respect to that endorser.

F. The transferor by endorsement or by mere delivery

Article 45

1. Unless otherwise agreed, a person who transfers an instrument, by endorsement and delivery or by mere delivery, represents to the holder to whom he transfers the instrument that:

(*a*) The instrument does not bear any forged or unauthorized signature;

(*b*) The instrument has not been materially altered;

(*c*) At the time of transfer, he has no knowledge of any fact which would impair the right of the transferee to payment of the instrument against the acceptor of a bill or, in the case of an unaccepted bill, the drawer, or against the maker of a note.

2. Liability of the transferor under paragraph 1 of this article is incurred only if the transferee took the instrument without knowledge of the matter giving rise to such liability.

3. If the transferor is liable under paragraph 1 of this article, the transferee may recover, even before maturity, the amount paid by him to the transferor, with interest calculated in accordance with article 70, against return of the instrument.

G. The guarantor

Article 46

1. Payment of an instrument, whether or not it has been accepted, may be guaranteed, as to the whole or part of its amount, for the account of a party or the drawee. A guarantee may be given by any person, who may or may not already be a party.

2. A guarantee must be written on the instrument or on a slip affixed thereto ("*allonge*").

3. A guarantee is expressed by the words "guaranteed", "*aval*", "good as *aval*" or words of similar import, accompanied by the signature of the guarantor. For the purposes of this Convention, the words "prior endorsements guaranteed" or words of similar import do not constitute a guarantee.

4. A guarantee may be effected by a signature alone on the front of the instrument. A signature alone on the front of the instrument, other than that of the maker, the drawer or the drawee, is a guarantee.

5. A guarantor may specify the person for whom he has become guarantor. In the absence of such specification, the person for whom he has become guarantor is the acceptor or the drawee in the case of a bill, and the maker in the case of a note.

6. A guarantor may not raise as a defence to his liability the fact that he signed the instrument before it was signed by the person for whom he is a guarantor, or while the instrument was incomplete.

Article 47

1. The liability of a guarantor on the instrument is of the same nature as that of the party for whom he has become guarantor.

2. If the person for whom he has become guarantor is the drawee, the guarantor engages:

(*a*) To pay the bill at maturity to the holder, or to any party who takes up and pays the bill;

(*b*) If the bill is payable at a definite time, upon dishonour by non-acceptance and upon any necessary protest, to pay it to the holder, or to any party who takes up and pays the bill.

3. In respect of defences that are personal to himself, a guarantor may set up:

(*a*) Against a holder who is not a protected holder only those defences which he may set up under paragraphs 1, 3 and 4 of article 28;

(*b*) Against a protected holder only those defences which he may set up under paragraph 1 of article 30.

4. In respect of defences that may be raised by the person for whom he has become a guarantor:

(*a*) A guarantor may set up against a holder who is not a protected holder only those defences which the person for whom he has become a guarantor may set up against such holder under paragraphs 1, 3 and 4 of article 28;

(*b*) A guarantor who expresses his guarantee by the words ''guaranteed'', ''payment guaranteed'' or ''collection guaranteed'', or words of similar import, may set up against a protected holder only those defences which the person for whom he has become a guarantor may set up against a protected holder under paragraph 1 of article 30;

(*c*) A guarantor who expresses his guarantee by the words ''*aval*'' or ''good as *aval*'' may set up against a protected holder only:

(i) The defence, under paragraph 1 (*b*) of article 30, that the protected holder obtained the signature on the instrument of the person for whom he has become a guarantor by a fraudulent act;

(ii) The defence, under article 53 or article 57, that the instrument was not presented for acceptance or for payment;

(iii) The defence, under article 63, that the instrument was not duly protested for non-acceptance or for non-payment;

(iv) The defence, under article 84, that a right of action may no longer be exercised against the person for whom he has become guarantor;

(*d*) A guarantor who is not a bank or other financial institution and who expresses his guarantee by a signature alone may set up against a protected holder only the defences referred to in subparagraph (*b*) of this paragraph;

(*e*) A guarantor which is a bank or other financial institution and which expresses its guarantee by a signature alone may set up against a protected holder only the defences referred to in subparagraph (*c*) of this paragraph.

Article 48

1. Payment of an instrument by the guarantor in accordance with article 72 discharges the party for whom he became guarantor of his liability on the instrument to the extent of the amount paid.

2. The guarantor who pays the instrument may recover from the party for whom he has become guarantor and from the parties who are liable on it to that party the amount paid and any interest.

Chapter V.   Presentment, dishonour by non-acceptance or non-payment, and recourse

Section 1.   Presentment for acceptance and dishonour by non-acceptance

Article 49

1. A bill may be presented for acceptance.

2. A bill must be presented for acceptance:

(*a*) If the drawer has stipulated in the bill that it must be presented for acceptance;

(*b*) If the bill is payable at a fixed period after sight; or

(*c*) If the bill is payable elsewhere than at the residence or place of business of the drawee, unless it is payable on demand.

Article 50

1. The drawer may stipulate in the bill that it must not be presented for acceptance before a specified date or before the occurrence of a specified event. Except where a bill must be presented for acceptance under paragraph 2 (*b*) or (*c*) of article 49, the drawer may stipulate that it must not be presented for acceptance.

2. If a bill is presented for acceptance notwithstanding a stipulation permitted under paragraph 1 of this article and acceptance is refused, the bill is not thereby dishonoured.

3. If the drawee accepts a bill notwithstanding a stipulation that it must not be presented for acceptance, the acceptance is effective.

Article 51

A bill is duly presented for acceptance if it is presented in accordance with the following rules:

(*a*) The holder must present the bill to the drawee on a business day at a reasonable hour;

(*b*) Presentment for acceptance may be made to a person or authority other than the drawee if that person or authority is entitled under the applicable law to accept the bill;

(*c*) If a bill is payable on a fixed date, presentment for acceptance must be made before or on that date;

(*d*) A bill payable on demand or at a fixed period after sight must be presented for acceptance within one year of its date;

(*e*) A bill in which the drawer has stated a date or time-limit for presentment for acceptance must be presented on the stated date or within the stated time-limit.

Article 52

1. A necessary or optional presentment for acceptance is dispensed with if:

(*a*) The drawee is dead, or no longer has the power freely to deal with his assets by reason of his insolvency, or is a fictitious person, or is a person not having capacity to incur liability on the instrument as an acceptor; or

(*b*) The drawee is a corporation, partnership, association or other legal entity which has ceased to exist.

2. A necessary presentment for acceptance is dispensed with if:

(*a*) A bill is payable on a fixed date, and presentment for acceptance cannot be effected before or on that date due to circumstances which are beyond the control of the holder and which he could neither avoid nor overcome; or

(*b*) A bill is payable at a fixed period after sight, and presentment for acceptance cannot be effected within one ear of its date due to circumstances which are beyond the control of the holder and which he could neither avoid nor overcome.

3. Subject to paragraphs 1 and 2 of this article, delay in a necessary presentment for acceptance is excused, but presentment for acceptance is not dispensed with, if the bill is drawn with a stipulation that it must be presented for acceptance within a stated time-limit, and the delay in presentment for acceptance is caused by circumstances which are beyond the control of the holder and which he could neither avoid nor overcome. When the cause of the delay ceases to operate, presentment must be made with reasonable diligence.

Article 53

1. If a bill which must be presented for acceptance is not so presented, the drawer, the endorsers and their guarantors are not liable on the bill.

2. Failure to present a bill for acceptance does not discharge the guarantor of the drawee of liability on the bill.

Article 54

1. A bill is considered to be dishonoured by non-acceptance:

(a) If the drawee, upon due presentment, expressly refuses to accept the bill or acceptance cannot be obtained with reasonable diligence or if the holder cannot obtain the acceptance to which he is entitled under this Convention;

(b) If presentment for acceptance is dispensed with pursuant to article 52, unless the bill is in fact accepted.

2. *(a)* If a bill is dishonoured by non-acceptance in accordance with paragraph 1 *(a)* of this article, the holder may exercise an immediate right of recourse against the drawer, the endorsers and their guarantors, subject to the provisions of article 59.

(b) If a bill is dishonoured by non-acceptance in accordance with paragraph 1 *(b)* of this article, the holder may exercise an immediate right of recourse against the drawer, the endorsers and their guarantors.

(c) If a bill is dishonoured by non-acceptance in accordance with paragraph 1 of this article, the holder may claim payment from the guarantor of the drawee upon any necessary protest.

3. If a bill payable on demand is presented for acceptance, but acceptance is refused, it is not considered to be dishonoured by non-acceptance.

Section 2. Presentment for payment and dishonour by non-payment

Article 55

An instrument is duly presented for payment if it is presented in accordance with the following rules:

(a) The holder must present the instrument to the drawee or to the acceptor or to the maker on a business day at a reasonable hour;

(b) A note signed by two or more makers may be presented to any one of them, unless the note clearly indicates otherwise;

(c) If the drawee or the acceptor or the maker is dead, presentment must be made to the persons who under the applicable law are his heirs or the persons entitled to administer his estate;

(d) Presentment for payment may be made to a person or authority other than the drawee, the acceptor or the maker if that person or authority is entitled under the applicable law to pay the instrument;

(e) An instrument which is not payable on demand must be presented for payment on the date of maturity or on one of the two business days which follow;

(f) An instrument which is payable on demand must be presented for payment within one year of its date;

(g) An instrument must be presented for payment:

(i) At the place of payment specified on the instrument;

(ii) If no place of payment is specified, at the address of the drawee or the acceptor or the maker indicated in the instrument; or

(iii) If no place of payment is specified and the address of the drawee or the acceptor or the maker is not indicated, at the principal place of business or habitual residence of the drawee or the acceptor or the maker;

(h) An instrument which is presented at a clearing-house is duly presented for payment if the law of the place where the clearing-house is located or the rules or customs of that clearing-house so provide.

Article 56

1. Delay in making presentment for payment is excused if the delay is caused by circumstances which are beyond the control of the holder and which he could neither avoid nor overcome. When the cause of the delay ceases to operate, presentment must be made with reasonable diligence.

2. Presentment for payment is dispensed with:

(a) If the drawer, an endorser or a guarantor has expressly waived presentment; such waiver:

(i) If made on the instrument by the drawer, binds any subsequent party and benefits any holder;

(ii) If made on the instrument by a party other than the drawer, binds only that party but benefits any holder;

(iii) If made outside the instrument, binds only the party making it and benefits only a holder in whose favour it was made;

(b) If an instrument is not payable on demand, and the cause of delay in making presentment referred to in paragraph 1 of this article continues to operate beyond thirty days after maturity;

(c) If an instrument is payable on demand, and the cause of delay in making presentment referred to in paragraph 1 of this article continues to operate beyond thirty days after the expiration of the time-limit for presentment for payment;

(d) If the drawee, the maker or the acceptor has no longer the power freely to deal with his assets by reason of his insolvency, or is a fictitious person or a person not having capacity to make payment, or if the drawee, the maker or the acceptor is a corporation, partnership, association or other legal entity which has ceased to exist;

(e) If there is no place at which the instrument must be presented in accordance with subparagraph *(g)* of article 55.

3. Presentment for payment is also dispensed with as regards a bill, if the bill has been protested for dishonour by non-acceptance.

Article 57

1. If an instrument is not duly presented for payment, the drawer, the endorsers and their guarantors are not liable on it.

2. Failure to present an instrument for payment does not discharge the acceptor, the maker and their guarantors or the guarantor of the drawee of liability on it.

Article 58

1. An instrument is considered to be dishonoured by non-payment:

(a) If payment is refused upon due presentment or if the holder cannot obtain the payment to which he is entitled under this Convention;

(b) If presentment for payment is dispensed with pursuant to paragraph 2 of article 56 and the instrument is unpaid at maturity.

2. If a bill is dishonoured by non-payment, the holder may, subject to the provisions of article 59, exercise a right of recourse against the drawer, the endorsers and their guarantors.

3. If a note is dishonoured by non-payment, the holder may, subject to the provisions of article 59, exercise a right of recourse against the endorsers and their guarantors.

Section 3. Recourse

Article 59

If an instrument is dishonoured by non-acceptance or by non-payment, the holder may exercise a right of recourse only after the instrument has been duly protested for dishonour in accordance with the provisions of articles 60 to 62.

A. Protest

Article 60

1. A protest is a statement of dishonour drawn up at the place where the instrument has been dishonoured and signed and dated by a person authorized in that respect by the law of that place. The statement must specify:

(a) The person at whose request the instrument is protested;

(b) The place of protest;

(c) The demand made and the answer given, if any, or the fact that the drawee or the acceptor or the maker could not be found.

2. A protest may be made:

(a) On the instrument or on a slip affixed thereto ("*allonge*"); or

(b) As a separate document, in which case it must clearly identify the instrument that has been dishonoured.

3. Unless the instrument stipulates that protest must be made, a protest may be replaced by a declaration written on the instrument and signed and dated by the drawee or the acceptor or the maker, or, in the case of an instrument domiciled with a named person for payment, by that named person; the declaration must be to the effect that acceptance or payment is refused.

4. A declaration made in accordance with paragraph 3 of this article is a protest for the purpose of this Convention.

Article 61

Protest for dishonour of an instrument by non-acceptance or by non-payment must be made on the day on which the instrument is dishonoured or on one of the four business days which follow.

Article 62

1. Delay in protesting an instrument for dishonour is excused if the delay is caused by circumstances which are beyond the control of the holder and which he could neither avoid nor overcome. When the cause of the delay ceases to operate, protest must be made with reasonable diligence.

2. Protest for dishonour by non-acceptance or by non-payment is dispensed with:

(a) If the drawer, an endorser or a guarantor has expressly waived protest; such waiver:

(i) If made on the instrument by the drawer, binds any subsequent party and benefits any holder;

(ii) If made on the instrument by a party other than the drawer, binds only that party but benefits any holder;

(iii) If made outside the instrument, binds only the party making it and benefits only a holder in whose favour it was made;

(b) If the cause of the delay in making protest referred to in paragraph 1 of this article continues to operate beyond thirty days after the date of dishonour;

(c) As regards the drawer of a bill, if the drawer and the drawee or the acceptor are the same person;

(d) If presentment for acceptance or for payment is dispensed with in accordance with article 52 or paragraph 2 of article 56.

Article 63

1. If an instrument which must be protested for non-acceptance or for non-payment is not duly protested, the drawer, the endorsers and their guarantors are not liable on it.

2. Failure to protest an instrument does not discharge the acceptor, the maker and their guarantors or the guarantor of the drawee of liability on it.

B. Notice of dishonour

Article 64

1. The holder, upon dishonour of an instrument by non-acceptance or by non-payment, must give notice of such dishonour:

(a) To the drawer and the last endorser;

(b) To all other endorsers and guarantors whose addresses the holder can ascertain on the basis of information contained in the instrument.

2. An endorser or a guarantor who receives notice must give notice of dishonour to the last party preceding him and liable on the instrument.

3. Notice of dishonour operates for the benefit of any party who has a right of recourse on the instrument against the party notified.

Article 65

1. Notice of dishonour may be given in any form whatever and in any terms which identify the instrument and state that it has been dishonoured. The return of the dishonoured instrument is sufficient notice, provided it is accompanied by a statement indicating that it has been dishonoured.

2. Notice of dishonour is duly given if it is communicated or sent to the party to be notified by means appropriate in the circumstances, whether or not it is received by that party.

3. The burden of proving that notice has been duly given rests upon the person who is required to give such notice.

Article 66

Notice of dishonour must be given within the two business days which follow:

(a) The day of protest or, if protest is dispensed with, the day of dishonour; or

(b) The day of receipt of notice of dishonour.

Article 67

1. Delay in giving notice of dishonour is excused if the delay is caused by circumstances which are beyond

the control of the person required to give notice, and which he could neither avoid nor overcome. When the cause of the delay ceases to operate, notice must be given with reasonable diligence.

2. Notice of dishonour is dispensed with:

(a) If, after the exercise of reasonable diligence, notice cannot be given;

(b) If the drawer, an endorser or a guarantor has expressly waived notice of dishonour; such waiver:

(i) If made on the instrument by the drawer, binds any subsequent party and benefits any holder;

(ii) If made on the instrument by a party other than the drawer, binds only that party but benefits any holder;

(iii) If made outside the instrument, binds only the party making it and benefits only a holder in whose favour it was made;

(c) As regards the drawer of the bill, if the drawer and the drawee or the acceptor are the same person.

Article 68

If a person who is required to give notice of dishonour fails to give it to a party who is entitled to receive it, he is liable for any damages which that party may suffer from such failure, provided that such damages do not exceed the amount referred to in article 70 or article 71.

Section 4. Amount payable

Article 69

1. The holder may exercise his rights on the instrument against any one party, or several or all parties, liable on it and is not obliged to observe the order in which the parties have become bound. Any party who takes up and pays the instrument may exercise his rights in the same manner against parties liable to him.

2. Proceedings against a party do not preclude proceedings against any other party, whether or not subsequent to the party originally proceeded against.

Article 70

1. The holder may recover from any party liable:

(a) At maturity: the amount of the instrument with interest, if interest has been stipulated for;

(b) After maturity:

(i) The amount of the instrument with interest, if interest has been stipulated for, to the date of maturity;

(ii) If interest has been stipulated to be paid after maturity, interest at the rate stipulated, or, in the absence of such stipulation, interest at the rate specified in paragraph 2 of this article, calculated from the date of presentment on the sum specified in subparagraph *(b)* (i) of this paragraph;

(iii) Any expenses of protest and of the notices given by him;

(c) Before maturity:

(i) The amount of the instrument with interest, if interest has been stipulated for, to the date of payment; or, if no interest has been stipulated for, subject to a discount from the date of payment to the date of maturity, calculated in accordance with paragraph 4 of this article;

(ii) Any expenses of protest and of the notices given by him.

2. The rate of interest shall be the rate that would be recoverable in legal proceedings taken in the jurisdiction where the instrument is payable.

3. Nothing in paragraph 2 of this article prevents a court from awarding damages or compensation for additional loss caused to the holder by reason of delay in payment.

4. The discount shall be at the official rate (discount rate) or other similar appropriate rate effective on the date when recourse is exercised at the place where the holder has his principal place of business, or, if he does not have a place of business, his habitual residence, or, if there is no such rate, then at such rate as is reasonable in the circumstances.

Article 71

A party who pays an instrument and is thereby discharged in whole or in part of his liability on the instrument may recover from the parties liable to him:

(a) The entire sum which he has paid;

(b) Interest on that sum at the rate specified in paragraph 2 of article 70, from the date on which he made payment;

(c) Any expenses of the notices given by him.

Chapter VI. Discharge

Section 1. Discharge by payment

Article 72

1. A party is discharged of liability on the instrument when he pays the holder, or a party subsequent to himself who has paid the instrument and is in possession of it, the amount due pursuant to article 70 or article 71:

(a) At or after maturity; or

(b) Before maturity, upon dishonour by non-acceptance.

2. Payment before maturity other than under paragraph 1 *(b)* of this article does not discharge the party making the payment of his liability on the instrument except in respect of the person to whom payment was made.

3. A party is not discharged of liability if he pays a holder who is not a protected holder, or a party who has taken up and paid the instrument, and knows at the time of payment that the holder or that party acquired the instrument by theft or forged the signature of the payee or an endorsee, or participated in the theft or the forgery.

4. *(a)* A person receiving payment of an instrument must, unless agreed otherwise, deliver:

(i) To the drawee making such payment, the instrument;

(ii) To any other person making such payment, the instrument, a receipted account, and any protest.

(b) In the case of an instrument payable by instalments at successive dates, the drawee or a party making a payment, other than payment of the last instalment, may require that mention of such payment be made on the instrument or on a slip affixed thereto (''*allonge*'') and that a receipt therefor be given to him.

(c) If an instrument payable by instalments at successive dates is dishonoured by non-acceptance or by non-payment as to any of its instalments and a party, upon dishonour, pays the instalment, the holder who receives such payment must give the party a certified copy of the instrument and any necessary authenticated protest in order to enable such party to exercise a right on the instrument.

(d) The person from whom payment is demanded may withhold payment if the person demanding payment does not deliver the instrument to him. Withholding payment in these circumstances does not constitute dishonour by non-payment under article 58.

(e) If payment is made but the person paying, other than the drawee, fails to obtain the instrument, such person is discharged but the discharge cannot be set up as a defence against a protected holder to whom the instrument has been subsequently transferred.

Article 73

1. The holder is not obliged to take partial payment.

2. If the holder who is offered partial payment does not take it, the instrument is dishonoured by non-payment.

3. If the holder takes partial payment from the drawee, the guarantor of the drawee, or the acceptor or the maker:

(a) The guarantor of the drawee, or the acceptor or the maker is discharged of his liability on the instrument to the extent of the amount paid;

(b) The instrument is to be considered as dishonoured by non-payment as to the amount unpaid.

4. If the holder takes partial payment from a party to the instrument other than the acceptor, the maker or the guarantor of the drawee:

(a) The party making payment is discharged of his liability on the instrument to the extent of the amount paid;

(b) The holder must give such party a certified copy of the instrument and any necessary authenticated protest in order to enable such party to exercise a right on the instrument.

5. The drawee or a party making partial payment may require that mention of such payment be made on the instrument and that a receipt therefor be given to him.

6. If the balance is paid, the person who receives it and who is in possession of the instrument must deliver to the payor the receipted instrument and any authenticated protest.

Article 74

1. The holder may refuse to take payment at a place other than the place where the instrument was presented for payment in accordance with article 55.

2. In such case if payment is not made at the place where the instrument was presented for payment in accordance with article 55, the instrument is considered to be dishonoured by non-payment.

Article 75

1. An instrument must be paid in the currency in which the sum payable is expressed.

2. If the sum payable is expressed in a monetary unit of account within the meaning of subparagraph *(l)* of article 5 and the monetary unit of account is transferable between the person making payment and the person receiving it, then, unless the instrument specifies a currency of payment, payment shall be made by transfer of monetary units of account. If the monetary unit of account is not transferable between those persons, payment shall be made in the currency specified in the instrument or, if no such currency is specified, in the currency of the place of payment.

3. The drawer or the maker may indicate in the instrument that it must be paid in a specified currency other than the currency in which the sum payable is expressed. In that case:

(a) The instrument must be paid in the currency so specified;

(b) The amount payable is to be calculated according to the rate of exchange indicated in the instrument. Failing such indication, the amount payable is to be calculated according to the rate of exchange for sight drafts (or, if there is no such rate, according to the appropriate established rate of exchange) on the date of maturity:

(i) Ruling at the place where the instrument must be presented for payment in accordance with subparagraph *(g)* of article 55, if the specified currency is that of that place (local currency); or

(ii) If the specified currency is not that of that place, according to the usages of the place where the instrument must be presented for payment in accordance with subparagraph *(g)* of article 55;

(c) If such an instrument is dishonoured by non-acceptance, the amount payable is to be calculated:

(i) If the rate of exchange is indicated in the instrument, according to that rate;

(ii) If no rate of exchange is indicated in the instrument, at the option of the holder, according to the rate of exchange ruling on the date of dishonour or on the date of actual payment;

(d) If such an instrument is dishonoured by non-payment, the amount payable is to be calculated:

(i) If the rate of exchange is indicated in the instrument, according to that rate;

(ii) If no rate of exchange is indicated in the instrument, at the option of the holder, according to the rate of exchange ruling on the date of maturity or on the date of actual payment.

4. Nothing in this article prevents a court from awarding damages for loss caused to the holder by reason of fluctuations in rates of exchange if such loss is caused by dishonour for non-acceptance or by non-payment.

5. The rate of exchange ruling at a certain date is the rate of exchange ruling, at the option of the holder, at the place where the instrument must be presented for payment in accordance with subparagraph *(g)* of article 55 or at the place of actual payment.

Article 76

1. Nothing in this Convention prevents a Contracting State from enforcing exchange control regulations applicable in its territory and its provisions relating to the protection of its currency, including regulations which it is bound to apply by virtue of international agreements to which it is a party.

2. *(a)* If, by virtue of the application of paragraph 1 of this article, an instrument drawn in a currency which is not that of the place of payment must be paid in local currency, the amount payable is to be calculated according to the rate of exchange for sight drafts (or, if there is no such rate, according to the appropriate established rate of exchange) on the date of presentment ruling at the place where the instrument must be presented for payment in accordance with subparagraph *(g)* of article 55.

(b) (i) If such an instrument is dishonoured by non-acceptance, the amount payable is to be calculated, at the option of the holder, at the rate of exchange ruling on the date of dishonour or on the date of actual payment.

(ii) If such an instrument is dishonoured by non-payment, the amount is to be calculated, at the option of the holder, according to the rate of exchange ruling on the date of presentment or on the date of actual payment.

(iii)   Paragraphs 4 and 5 of article 75 are applicable where appropriate.

Section 2.   Discharge of other parties

Article 77

1.   If a party is discharged in whole or in part of his liability on the instrument, any party who has a right on the instrument against him is discharged to the same extent.

2.   Payment by the drawee of the whole or a part of the amount of a bill to the holder, or to any party who takes up and pays the bill, discharges all parties of their liability to the same extent, except where the drawee pays a holder who is not a protected holder, or a party who has taken up and paid the bill, and knows at the time of payment that the holder or that party acquired the bill by theft or forged the signature of the payee or an endorsee, or participated in the theft or the forgery.

Chapter VII.   Lost instruments

Article 78

1.   If an instrument is lost, whether by destruction, theft or otherwise, the person who lost the instrument has, subject to the provisions of paragraph 2 of this article, the same right to payment which he would have had if he had been in possession of the instrument. The party from whom payment is claimed cannot set up as a defence against liability on the instrument the fact that the person claiming payment is not in possession of the instrument.

2.   (a)   The person claiming payment of a lost instrument must state in writing to the party from whom he claims payment:

(i)   The elements of the lost instrument pertaining to the requirements set forth in paragraph 1 or paragraph 2 of articles 1, 2 and 3; for this purpose the person claiming payment of the lost instrument may present to that party a copy of that instrument;

(ii)   The facts showing that, if he had been in possession of the instrument, he would have had a right to payment from the party from whom payment is claimed;

(iii) The facts which prevent production of the instrument.

(b)   The party from whom payment of a lost instrument is claimed may require the person claiming payment to give security in order to indemnify him for any loss which he may suffer by reason of the subsequent payment of the lost instrument.

(c)   The nature of the security and its terms are to be determined by agreement between the person claiming payment and the party from whom payment is claimed. Failing such an agreement, the court may determine whether security is called for and, if so, the nature of the security and its terms.

(d)   If the security cannot be given, the court may order the party from whom payment is claimed to deposit the sum of the lost instrument, and any interest and expenses which may be claimed under article 70 or article 71, with the court or any other competent authority or institution, and may determine the duration of such deposit. Such deposit is to be considered as payment to the person claiming payment.

Article 79

1.   A party who has paid a lost instrument and to whom the instrument is subsequently presented for payment by another person must give notice of such presentment to the person whom he paid.

2.   Such notice must be given on the day the instrument is presented or on one of the two business days which follow and must state the name of the person presenting the instrument and the date and place of presentment.

3.   Failure to give notice renders the party who has paid the lost instrument liable for any damages which the person whom he paid may suffer from such failure, provided that the damages do not exceed the amount referred to in article 70 or article 71.

4.   Delay in giving notice is excused when the delay is caused by circumstances which are beyond the control of the person who has paid the lost instrument and which he could neither avoid nor overcome. When the cause of the delay ceases to operate, notice must be given with reasonable diligence.

5.   Notice is dispensed with when the cause of delay in giving notice continues to operate beyond thirty days after the last day on which it should have been given.

Article 80

1.   A party who has paid a lost instrument in accordance with the provisions of article 78 and who is subsequently required to, and does, pay the instrument, or who, by reason of the loss of the instrument, then loses his right to recover from any party liable to him, has the right:

(a)   If security was given, to realize the security; or

(b)   If an amount was deposited with the court or other competent authority or institution, to reclaim the amount so deposited.

2.   The person who has given security in accordance with the provisions of paragraph 2 (b) of article 78 is entitled to obtain release of the security when the party for whose benefit the security was given is no longer at risk to suffer loss because of the fact that the instrument is lost.

Article 81

For the purpose of making protest for dishonour by non-payment, a person claiming payment of a lost instrument may use a written statement that satisfies the requirements of paragraph 2 (a) of article 78.

Article 82

A person receiving payment of a lost instrument in accordance with article 78 must deliver to the party paying the written statement required under paragraph 2 (a) of article 78, receipted by him, and any protest and a receipted account.

Article 83

1.   A party who pays a lost instrument in accordance with article 78 has the same rights which he would have had if he had been in possession of the instrument.

2.   Such party may exercise his rights only if he is in possession of the receipted written statement referred to in article 82.

Chapter VIII.   Limitation (prescription)

Article 84

1.   A right of action arising on an instrument may no longer be exercised after four years have elapsed:

(a)   Against the maker, or his guarantor, of a note payable on demand, from the date of the note;

(b) Against the acceptor or the maker or their guarantor of an instrument payable at a definite time, from the date of maturity;

(c) Against the guarantor of the drawee of a bill payable at a definite time, from the date of maturity or, if the bill is dishonoured by non-acceptance, from the date of protest for dishonour or, where protest is dispensed with, from the date of dishonour;

(d) Against the acceptor of a bill payable on demand or his guarantor, from the date on which it was accepted or, if no such date is shown, from the date of the bill;

(e) Against the guarantor of the drawee of a bill payable on demand, from the date on which he signed the bill or, if no such date is shown, from the date of the bill;

(f) Against the drawer or an endorser or their guarantor, from the date of protest for dishonour by non-acceptance or by non-payment or, where protest is dispensed with, from the date of dishonour.

2.   A party who pays the instrument in accordance with article 70 or article 71 may exercise his right of action against a party liable to him within one year from the date on which he paid the instrument.

Chapter IX.   Final provisions

Article 85
The Secretary-General of the United Nations is hereby designated as the Depositary for this Convention.

Article 86
1.   This Convention is open for signature by all States at the Headquarters of the United Nations, New York, until 30 June 1990.

2.   This Convention is subject to ratification, acceptance or approval by the signatory States.

3.   This Convention is open for accession by all States which are not signatory States as from the date it is open for signature.

4.   Instruments of ratification, acceptance, approval and accession are to be deposited with the Secretary-General of the United Nations.

Article 87
1.   If a Contracting State has two or more territorial units in which, according to its constitution, different systems of law are applicable in relation to the matters dealt with in this Convention, it may, at the time of signature, ratification, acceptance, approval or accession, declare that this Convention is to extend to all its territorial units or only to one or more of them, and may amend its declaration by submitting another declaration at any time.

2.   These declarations are to be notified to the Depositary and are to state expressly the territorial units to which the Convention extends.

3.   If a Contracting State makes no declaration under paragraph 1 of this article, the Convention is to extend to all territorial units of that State.

Article 88
1.   Any State may declare at the time of signature, ratification, acceptance, approval or accession that its courts will apply the Convention only if both the place indicated in the instrument where the bill is drawn, or the note is made, and the place of payment indicated in the instrument are situated in Contracting States.

2.   No other reservations are permitted.

Article 89
1.   This Convention enters into force on the first day of the month following the expiration of twelve months after the date of deposit of the tenth instrument of ratification, acceptance, approval or accession.

2.   When a State ratifies, accepts, approves or accedes to this Convention after the deposit of the tenth instrument of ratification, acceptance, approval or accession, this Convention enters into force in respect of that State on the first day of the month following the expiration of twelve months after the date of deposit of its instrument of ratification, acceptance, approval or accession.

Article 90
1.   A Contracting State may denounce this Convention by a formal notification in writing addressed to the Depositary.

2.   The denunciation takes effect on the first day of the month following the expiration of six months after the notification is received by the Depositary. Where a longer period for the denunciation to take effect is specified in the notification, the denunciation takes effect upon the expiration of such longer period after the notification is received by the Depositary. The Convention remains applicable to instruments drawn or made before the date at which the denunciation takes effect.

DONE at . . . , this . . . day of . . . , one thousand nine hundred and . . . in a single original, of which the Arabic, Chinese, English, French, Russian and Spanish texts are equally authentic.

IN WITNESS WHEREOF the undersigned plenipotentiaries, being duly authorized by their respective Governments, have signed this Convention.

General Assembly resolution 43/165

9 December 1988   Meeting 76   Adopted without vote

Approved by Sixth Committee (A/43/820) without vote, 7 October (meeting 10); draft by Mexico (A/C.6/43/L.3); agenda item 131.
Meeting numbers. GA 43rd session: 6th Committee 4-6, 10; plenary 76.

Stand-by letters of credit and guarantees

UNCITRAL had before it the March report of the Secretary-General on stand-by letters of credit and guarantees[7] and considered in particular its conclusions and suggestions as to the possible future work of the Commission in this field. The report described the functions and characteristics of the stand-by letter of credit and independent guarantees, provided an overview of the legal framework comprising statutory provisions of law, case law and uniform rules, and legal issues that may arise. The report concluded that there was considerable disparity and uncertainty in respect of the legal rules governing the two instruments.

The Commission agreed to envisage future work in two stages: the first relating to contractual rules of model terms and the second pertaining to statutory law. It welcomed the work of the International Chamber of Commerce (ICC) in preparing draft Uniform Rules on Guarantees. It concluded that the Commission, at its twenty-second (1989) session, would take a final decision on whether a uniform law should be prepared and, if so, what its scope and contents should be.

Liability of operators of transport terminals

The Commission, having before it the report of the Working Group on International Contract Practices on the work of its eleventh session,[8] noted that the Working Group had completed a draft text of uniform rules on the liability of operators of transport terminals and had recommended their adoption in the form of a convention. UNCITRAL decided to consider at its twenty-second (1989) session, with a view to its adoption, the draft Convention prepared by the Working Group. It requested the Secretary-General to transmit the draft to all States and interested international organizations for comments, and requested the Secretariat to prepare and distribute a compilation of those comments as early as possible. It was suggested that a diplomatic conference for the conclusion of a Convention on the Liability of Operators of Transport Terminals in International Trade might present a good opportunity to consider a possible revision of the limits of liability and provisions pertaining to the 1978 United Nations Convention on the Carriage of Goods by Sea (Hamburg Rules).

International countertrade

In 1988, UNCITRAL had before it a preliminary study of legal issues in international countertrade.[9] It contained a description of contractual approaches to countertrade and an enumeration of the important legal issues involved. The Commission decided that it would be desirable to prepare a legal guide for drafting countertrade contracts. The Secretariat was requested to prepare a draft outline of the guide for the Commission's next session so that it could decide what future action might be taken.

Co-ordination of work

In considering its co-ordination of work, the Commission had before it a report of the Secretary-General containing a register of international organizations active in the field of international trade law.[10] The report concentrated on those organizations that were forming agencies, but included some organizations of particular importance to the development of international trade law in other ways. UNCITRAL observed that co-ordination among international organizations depended in large measure on co-ordination at the national level among the various government ministries and branches active in different international organizations. Statements before the Commission were made by the International Institute for the Unification of Private Law (UNIDROIT); the Secretary-General of the Hague Conference on Private International Law; AALCC; the United Nations Conference on Trade and Development/General Agreement on Tariffs and Trade (UNCTAD/GATT) International Trade Centre (ITC); and the Latin American Federation of Banks (FELABAN).

Status and promotion of texts of the Commission

Having adopted in 1987[11] the UNCITRAL *Legal Guide on Drawing Up International Contracts for the Construction of Industrial Works*, the Commission had requested the Secretary-General to take effective measures for the Guide's widespread distribution and promotion. In a 1988 note[12] to the Commission, the Secretariat indicated that the English version of the *Legal Guide* was published in February 1988 and the five other official United Nations language versions would soon appear.

Training and assistance

In accordance with a 1987[13] Assembly resolution, the UNCITRAL secretariat organized a seminar on international trade law (Maseru, Lesotho, 25-30 July) for 34 participants from 14 countries of the southern African region. UNCITRAL also co-sponsored with the Cairo Regional Arbitration Centre a seminar on international commercial arbitration (Cairo, Egypt, 28-31 March). A two-week workshop on international trade law and practice for enterprise personnel was held (Quingdao, China, 11-22 July) in co-operation with the Economic and Social Commission for Asia and the Pacific (ESCAP). A note by the Secretariat[14] stated that in order for UNCITRAL to carry on a viable programme of training and assistance, adequate funds had to be available. UNCITRAL noted difficulties planning a seminar or symposium when funds were not available far enough in advance to make the necessary commitments and when the level of contribution was inadequate.

GENERAL ASSEMBLY ACTION

On 9 December, the General Assembly, on the recommendation of the Sixth Committee, adopted **resolution 43/166** without vote.

Report of the United Nations Commission on International Trade Law on the work of its twenty-first session

The General Assembly,

Recalling its resolution 2205(XXI) of 17 December 1966, by which it created the United Nations Commission on International Trade Law with a mandate to further the progressive harmonization and unification of the law of international trade and in that respect to bear in mind the interests of all peoples, in particular those of developing countries, in the extensive development of international trade,

Recalling also its resolutions 3201(S-VI) of 1 May 1974, 3281(XXIX) of 12 December 1974 and 3362(S-VII) of 16 September 1975,

Reaffirming its conviction that the progressive harmonization and unification of international trade law, in reducing or removing legal obstacles to the flow of international trade, especially those affecting the developing countries, would significantly contribute to universal economic co-operation among all States on a basis of equality, equity and common interest and to the elimination of discrimination in international trade and, thereby, to the well-being of all peoples,

Having regard for the need to take into account the different social and legal systems in harmonizing and unifying international trade law,

Stressing the value of participation by States at all levels of economic development, including developing countries, in the process of harmonizing and unifying international trade law,

Having considered the report of the United Nations Commission on International Trade Law on the work of its twenty-first session,

Recognizing the success of the seminar on international trade law held at Maseru from 25 to 30 July 1988 in co-operation with the Preferential Trade Area of Eastern and Southern African States,

Recognizing the need for the Commission to have adequate sources of funding for its programme of training and assistance in international trade law,

Noting that the Convention on the Limitation Period in the International Sale of Goods, of 14 June 1974, came into force on 1 August 1988,

Aware that the United Nations Convention on the Carriage of Goods by Sea, of 31 March 1978, was prepared at the request of developing countries and is likely to come into force in the near future,

Convinced that widespread adherence to the conventions emanating from the work of the Commission would benefit the peoples of all States,

1. *Takes note with appreciation* of the report of the United Nations Commission on International Trade Law on the work of its twenty-first session;

2. *Commends* the Commission for the progress made in its work and for having reached decisions by consensus;

3. *Calls upon* the Commission to continue to take account of the relevant provisions of the resolutions concerning the new international economic order, as adopted by the General Assembly at its sixth and seventh special sessions;

4. *Reaffirms* the mandate of the Commission, as the core legal body within the United Nations system in the field of international trade law, to co-ordinate legal activities in this field in order to avoid duplication of effort and to promote efficiency, consistency and coherence in the unification and harmonization of international trade law, and, in this connection, recommends that the Commission, through its secretariat, should continue to maintain close co-operation with the other international organs and organizations, including regional organizations, active in the field of international trade law;

5. *Reaffirms also* the importance, in particular for developing countries, of the work of the Commission concerned with training and assistance in the field of international trade law and the desirability for it to sponsor seminars and symposia, in particular those organized on a regional basis, to promote such training and assistance, and, in this connection:

(a) Expresses its appreciation to the Kingdom of Lesotho and the Preferential Trade Area of Eastern and Southern African States for their collaboration with the secretariat of the Commission in organizing the seminar on international trade law held at Maseru and to the Governments whose contributions enabled the seminar to take place;

(b) Welcomes the initiatives being undertaken by the Commission and its secretariat to collaborate with other organizations and institutions in the organization of regional seminars;

(c) Invites Governments, the relevant United Nations organs, organizations, institutions and individuals to make voluntary contributions to the United Nations Commission on International Trade Law symposia, where appropriate, to the financing of special projects, and otherwise to assist the secretariat of the Commission in financing and organizing seminars and symposia, in particular in developing countries, and for the award of fellowships to candidates from developing countries to enable them to participate in such seminars and symposia;

6. *Repeats its invitation* to those States which have not yet done so to consider ratifying or acceding to the following conventions:

(a) Convention on the Limitation Period in the International Sale of Goods, of 14 June 1974;

(b) Protocol amending the Convention on the Limitation Period in the International Sale of Goods, of 11 April 1980;

(c) United Nations Convention on the Carriage of Goods by Sea, of 31 March 1978;

(d) United Nations Convention on Contracts for the International Sale of Goods, of 11 April 1980;

7. *Welcomes* the decision of the Commission to collect and disseminate court decisions and arbitral awards relating to legal texts emanating from its work so as to further the uniformity of their application in practice;

8. *Renews its request* to the Secretary-General to make increased efforts to promote the adoption and use of the texts emanating from the work of the Commission;

9. *Recommends* that the Commission should continue its work on the topics included in its programme of work;

10. *Expresses its appreciation* for the important role played by the International Trade Law Branch of the Office of Legal Affairs of the Secretariat, as the substantive secretariat of the Commission, in assisting in the structuring and implementation of the work programme of the Commission, and invites the Secretary-General to consider taking whatever measures may be necessary, within existing resources, to provide the Commission with adequate substantive secretariat support.

General Assembly resolution 43/166

9 December 1988   Meeting 76   Adopted without vote

Approved by Sixth Committee (A/43/820) without vote, 24 October (meeting 21); 28-nation draft (A/C.6/43/L.4); agenda item 131.

Sponsors: Argentina, Australia, Austria, Brazil, Canada, Cyprus, Czechoslovakia, Denmark, Egypt, Finland, France, German Democratic Republic, Germany, Federal Republic of, Greece, Guyana, Hungary, Italy, Japan, Kenya, Lesotho, Libyan Arab Jamahiriya, Netherlands, Sierra Leone, Spain, Sweden, Turkey, United Kingdom, Yugoslavia.

Meeting numbers. GA 43rd session: 6th Committee 4-6, 10; plenary 76.

Legal aspects of the new international economic order

Report of the Secretary-General. Pursuant to a General Assembly resolution of 1987,[15] the Secretary-General submitted in August a report with a later addendum[16] containing views and comments by eight Governments in response to his March 1988 note concerning the most appropriate procedures to be adopted with regard to a 1984 study by UNITAR[17] relating to NIEO.

On 9 December 1988, on the recommendation of the Sixth Committee, the General Assembly adopted **resolution 43/162** by recorded vote.

Progressive development of the principles and norms of international law relating to the new international economic order

The General Assembly,

Bearing in mind that, in accordance with the Charter of the United Nations, the General Assembly is called upon to initiate studies and make recommendations for the purpose of encouraging the progressive development of international law and its codification,

Recalling its resolutions 3201(S-VI) and 3202(S-VI) of 1 May 1974, containing the Declaration and the Programme of Action on the Establishment of a New International Economic Order, 3281(XXIX) of 12 December 1974, containing the Charter of Economic Rights and Duties of States, 3362(S-VII) of 16 September 1975 on development and international economic co-operation and 35/56 of 5 December 1980, the annex to which contains the International Development Strategy for the Third United Nations Development Decade,

Recalling also its resolutions 34/150 of 17 December 1979 and 35/166 of 15 December 1980, entitled "Consolidation and progressive development of the principles and norms of international economic law relating in particular to the legal aspects of the new international economic order", and its resolutions 36/107 of 10 December 1981, 37/103 of 16 December 1982, 38/128 of 19 December 1983, 39/75 of 13 December 1984, 40/67 of 11 December 1985, 41/73 of 3 December 1986 and 42/149 of 7 December 1987, entitled "Progressive development of the principles and norms of international law relating to the new international economic order",

Bearing in mind the urgent need to adopt measures to reactivate the process of international economic co-operation and the negotiations undertaken for that purpose, particularly in view of the economic difficulties encountered by the developing countries,

Considering the close link between the establishment of a just and equitable international economic order and the existence of an appropriate legal framework,

Recognizing the need for the codification and progressive development of the principles and norms of international law relating to the new international economic order,

Recalling the analytical study submitted to the General Assembly at its thirty-ninth session by the United Nations Institute for Training and Research,

1. *Notes with appreciation* the views and comments submitted by Governments pursuant to resolutions 40/67, 41/73 and 42/149;

2. *Requests* the Secretary-General:

(a) To continue to seek proposals of Member States concerning the most appropriate procedures to be adopted with regard to the consideration of the analytical study, as well as the codification and progressive development of the principles and norms of international law relating to the new international economic order;

(b) To include the proposals received in accordance with subparagraph *(a)* above in a report to be submitted to the General Assembly at its forty-fourth session;

3. *Recommends* that the Sixth Committee should consider making a final decision at the forty-fourth session of the General Assembly on the question of the appropriate forum within its framework which would undertake the task of completing the elaboration of the process of codification and progressive development of the principles and norms of international law relating to the new international economic order, taking into account the proposals and suggestions which have been or will be submitted by Member States on the matter;

4. *Decides* to include in the provisional agenda of its forty-fourth session the item entitled "Progressive development of the principles and norms of international law relating to the new international economic order".

General Assembly resolution 43/162

9 December 1988   Meeting 76   129-0-24 (recorded vote)

Approved by Sixth Committee (A/43/881) by vote (81-0-23), 22 November (meeting 46); 22-nation draft (A/C.6/43/L.16); agenda item 128.
Sponsors: Barbados, Chile, Colombia, Cuba, Egypt, Jamaica, Mali, Mexico, Niger, Pakistan, Panama, Paraguay, Peru, Philippines, Romania, Samoa, Senegal, Tunisia, Uganda, Venezuela, Viet Nam, Zambia.
Meeting numbers. GA 43rd session: 6th Committee 41, 42, 46; plenary 76.

Recorded vote in Assembly as follows:

In favour: Afghanistan, Albania, Algeria, Angola, Antigua and Barbuda, Argentina, Bahamas, Bahrain, Barbados, Belize, Benin, Bhutan, Bolivia, Botswana, Brazil, Brunei Darussalam, Bulgaria, Burkina Faso, Burma, Burundi, Byelorussian SSR, Cameroon, Cape Verde, Central African Republic, Chad, Chile, China, Colombia, Congo, Costa Rica, Côte d'Ivoire, Cuba, Cyprus, Czechoslovakia, Democratic Kampuchea, Democratic Yemen, Djibouti, Dominica, Dominican Republic, Ecuador, Egypt, El Salvador, Equatorial Guinea, Ethiopia, Fiji, Gabon, Gambia, German Democratic Republic, Ghana, Grenada, Guatemala, Guinea, Guinea-Bissau, Guyana, Honduras, Hungary, India, Indonesia, Iran, Iraq, Jordan, Kenya, Kuwait, Lao People's Democratic Republic, Lebanon, Lesotho, Liberia, Libyan Arab Jamahiriya, Madagascar, Malawi, Malaysia, Maldives, Mali, Malta, Mauritania, Mauritius, Mexico, Mongolia, Morocco, Mozambique, Nepal, Nicaragua, Niger, Nigeria, Oman, Pakistan, Panama, Papua New Guinea, Paraguay, Peru, Philippines, Poland, Qatar, Romania, Rwanda, Saint Kitts and Nevis, Saint Lucia, Saint Vincent and the Grenadines, Samoa, Sao Tome and Principe, Saudi Arabia, Senegal, Seychelles, Sierra Leone, Singapore, Solomon Islands, Somalia, Sri Lanka, Sudan, Suriname, Swaziland, Syrian Arab Republic, Thailand, Togo, Trinidad and Tobago, Tunisia, Uganda, Ukrainian SSR, USSR, United Arab Emirates, United Republic of Tanzania, Uruguay, Vanuatu, Venezuela, Viet Nam, Yemen, Yugoslavia, Zaire, Zambia.

Against: None.

Abstaining: Australia, Austria, Belgium, Canada, Denmark, Finland, France, Germany, Federal Republic of, Greece, Iceland, Ireland, Israel, Italy, Japan, Luxembourg, Netherlands, New Zealand, Norway, Portugal, Spain, Sweden, Turkey, United Kingdom, United States.

REFERENCES

[1]A/43/17. [2]A/CN.9/297. [3]YUN 1987, p. 1081, GA res. 42/153, 7 Dec. 1987. [4]A/C.6/43/L.2. [5]A/43/405 & Add.1-3. [6]YUN 1987, p. 1081. [7]A/CN.9/301. [8]A/CN.9/298. [9]A/CN.9/302. [10]A/CN.9/303. [11]YUN 1987, p. 1082. [12]A/CN.9/310. [13]YUN 1987, p. 1079, GA res. 42/152, 7 Dec. 1987. [14]A/CN.9/311. [15]YUN 1987, p. 1083, GA res. 42/149, 7 Dec. 1987. [16]A/43/529 & Add.1. [17]YUN 1984, p. 1115.

PART SIX

Administrative and budgetary questions

Chapter I

United Nations financing and programming

Throughout 1988, the United Nations continued to grapple with a financial crisis that resulted from the withholding of assessed contributions by a number of Member States to both the Organization's regular budget and to that for peace-keeping operations. The crisis coincided with an expansion of the Organization's responsibilities for peace-keeping, thus placing new strains on its already precarious financial stability. An analysis of the financial situation presented in November by the Secretary-General projected a net short-term deficit of $319.4 million. One Member State owed a total of $337.3 million, including nearly $122.4 million in arrears from previous years. Of the $1,111 million in contributions to the United Nations regular budget payable by 1 January 1988, $716.5 million had been collected at the end of 1988, leaving some $395 million outstanding.

To avoid defaulting on its day-to-day financial commitments, the Organization exhausted both its Working Capital Fund and its Special Account during 1988, and resorted to temporary borrowing from peace-keeping funds.

Appropriations for the 1988-1989 biennium were raised by $19 million to $1,789 million by the General Assembly in December (resolution 43/218 A). Income estimates for 1988-1989 were revised upward by about $7.1 million to $344.4 million over 1987 estimates (43/218 B). To finance appropriations for 1989, Member States were assessed $747 million net of staff assessment (43/218 C).

The Assembly decided that the Secretary-General should prepare his proposed programme budget for 1990-1991 on the basis of a total preliminary estimate of $1,767,060,000 at 1988 rates. The contingency fund, used to accommodate additional expenditures, was consequently set at 0.75 per cent of the 1990-1991 budget estimates (43/214).

The Assembly approved the scale of assessments for 1989-1991 (43/223 A) and requested the Committee on Contributions to improve the methodology used in the scale's preparation and to seek more comprehensive data on the external debt of Member States (43/223 B). The Assembly also approved a method for collecting assessments from non-member States (43/223 C).

The accounts and financial statements for either the year or biennium ending 31 December 1987, for the United Nations and 80 voluntarily financed programmes, were accepted by the As-

sembly together with the opinions of the United Nations Board of Auditors (43/216).

Further action was taken during 1988 to improve United Nations programme planning, budgeting and evaluation. By resolution 43/219, the Assembly adopted revisions to the 1984-1989 medium-term plan, extended to 1991. It decided that the next plan would cover 1992-1997, and endorsed a number of recommendations by the Joint Inspection Unit (JIU) and the Committee for Programme and Co-ordination concerning the monitoring and evaluation of United Nations programmes. The Assembly also considered various aspects of the work of JIU (43/221).

United Nations financing

Financial situation

Reports of the Secretary-General. In November 1988, the Secretary-General submitted to the General Assembly an analysis of the financial situation of the United Nations.[1] He characterized the Organization's financial position as grave and said that the primary means of resolving the problem, and the one that would result in the lowest cost to Member States, remained that of prompt payment by every Member State, early in the year, of all assessed contributions. Unless that were done, the Organization would continue to face the very real risk of defaulting on its daily financial commitments.

According to the Secretary-General, the United Nations combined short-term deficit was estimated at $319.7 million by the end of 1988, compared with $356 million for 1987. The 1988 deficit included amounts to be repaid or credited to Member States from surplus accounts for contributions to the first United Nations Emergency Force (UNEF I) (1956) and the United Nations Operations in the Congo (ONUC). The deficit was composed of: amounts outstanding as a result of withholdings by some Member States of their shares of assessed contributions in respect of certain items in the regular budget; unpaid assessments for peace-keeping operations, which were transferred to a special account pursuant to Assembly resolutions of 1972[2] and 1981;[3] withholdings of assessments in respect of UNEF II (1973), the United Nations Disengagement Observer Force (UNDOF) and the United Nations Interim Force in Lebanon (UNIFIL) by certain Member States; net obligations incurred in excess of available funds in respect of UNEF I and ONUC; and the repayment due to Member States for credits in surplus accounts for UNEF I and ONUC. The short-term deficit, therefore, included any unpaid assessments pertaining to the regular budget and to peace-keeping operations which had not been characterized by Member States as withholdings.

The projected decrease of $36.3 million between 1987 and 1988 resulted from full and partial payments to be made by several Member States and partial payments of funds previously withheld from their assessed contributions to the regular budget, and the partial payment to peace-keeping operations by five Member States of money previously withheld. An increase in the level of the Special Account was also expected due to an additional contribution from one Member State and interest earned on the balance.

In addition to the short-term deficit, the financial difficulties of the Organization were compounded by delays in payment or non-payment by a number of States of assessed contributions to the regular budget and to peace-keeping operations. The level of outstanding contributions had increased dramatically over the previous four years.

According to the Secretary-General, unpaid debts to Member States that had participated in peace-keeping operations under agreements that included reimbursement for services rendered, mainly the provision of troops, would amount to $310.6 million as at 31 December 1988. Currently, the Organization's peace-keeping activities were able to continue only because the troop-contributing Member States continued to bear the full burden of the deficit.

The shortfall in payments to the regular budget created an immediate day-to-day cash shortage to cover the Organization's payroll and payments to vendors. Because the shortfall in regular budget payments was so large, other sources of funding were often required to meet daily cash needs. To meet its obligations, the Organization had used the $100 million Working Capital Fund plus funds in the Special Account (estimated at $109.8 million by year-end 1988) and, occasionally, had resorted to temporary borrowing from peace-keeping funds. Amounts realized from the suspension by the General Assembly in 1987 of three financial regulations related to surpluses in the regular budget had also been utilized, when available, to meet some of the cash requirements for the regular budget.

The Secretary-General had sent out letters of assessment to all Member States before the end

of December 1987. These were followed up with additional letters in early March 1988, meetings with all regional groups, and subsequent letters to Foreign Ministers in June. Positive responses were received from many Member States, and data showed that a number of them had made efforts to pay earlier in the year.

Member States withheld payments towards certain items in the regular budget in the amount of a projected $63.8 million, and held back a total of $237.3 million towards peace-keeping operations. One Member State made a $5 million voluntary contribution in 1988 to the United Nations Special Account, which was used to supplement the Working Capital Fund to meet the Organization's daily expenses.

In his December report on the financial crisis,[4] the Secretary-General said that the expanding responsibilities of the Organization for peacemaking and peace-keeping had placed new strains on the already precarious financial situation. More than ever, it was essential that the Organization's financial stability be assured. He requested the Assembly to give urgent attention to both the cash and the reserves aspects of the crisis and find ways to ensure that a workable long-term solution was achieved. Throughout 1988, the United Nations had confronted the possibility of imminent bankruptcy and had narrowly managed to avoid it.

As at 30 November 1988, $269.2 million, or 35.5 per cent of the year's total regular budget assessments of $758 million, remained unpaid. Together with arrears of $180.9 million for prior years, total assessed contributions outstanding amounted to $450.1 million, of which $337.3 million, including nearly $122.4 million in arrears from prior years, was owed by one Member State. Cash reserves to meet the shortfall in payment of contributions, defined as the Working Capital Fund and the Special Account, totalling $209.8 million, were replenished only once, in the first quarter of 1988, and had been drawn down since to meet current operating expenses.

By the end of November, only 79 Member States had paid their assessed contributions in full. Of the 80 countries in arrears, 40 owed more than their 1988 assessments, 11 owed an amount equal to them and 29 owed less than their 1988 assessments. During the first 11 months of 1988, 14 Member States made no payments at all.

The Secretary-General reported that, notwithstanding the projected 1989 regular budget cash flow, the Organization's financial situation would remain fragile so long as its reserves were not fully funded. He said that the financial situation could deteriorate rapidly if additional demands for existing or new peace-keeping operations were made on those depleted reserves or if there were acute currency fluctuations or inflation. Unless and until the basic legal obligation of full and timely payment of assessed contributions was honoured by all Member States without exception, the United Nations would continue to confront financial uncertainty.

In an oral report before the Fifth (Administrative and Budgetary) Committee on 12 December, the Chairman of the Advisory Committee on Administrative and Budgetary Questions (ACABQ) said that the forecasted amounts and timing of contributions for 1989 were based on the experience of 1988, but also assumed that the major contributor would pay an amount approximately equal to its total 1989 regular budget assessment. The 1989 disbursement forecast was also based on the experience of 1988 and the Organization would manage to avoid insolvency if those assumptions held true, but only by once again utilizing its reserves to meet cash requirements at many points during the year.

GENERAL ASSEMBLY ACTION

On 19 September, by **decision 42/464**, the General Assembly included in the draft agenda of its forty-third (1988) session the item on the current financial crisis of the United Nations.

On 21 December, on the recommendation of the Fifth Committee, the Assembly adopted without vote **resolution 43/215**.

Current financial crisis of the United Nations
The General Assembly,
Recalling the purposes and principles of the Charter of the United Nations and, in particular, Article 17,
Recalling also its resolutions 41/213 of 19 December 1986 and 42/211 and 42/212 of 21 December 1987,
Deeply concerned about the current financial crisis, caused by the non-fulfilment by some Member States of their obligations under the Charter, which threatens the financial solvency, stability and work of the Organization,
Noting the renewed efforts by some Member States to pay their assessed contributions in full or to reduce the level of their outstanding contributions,
Reaffirming the need for a durable, reliable and lasting financial foundation for the Organization, in accordance with the Charter,
Taking note of the report of the Secretary-General on the current financial crisis of the United Nations,
Taking note also of the views expressed by Member States in the Fifth Committee on the current financial crisis of the United Nations,
1. *Reaffirms* the obligation of all Member States, under the Charter of the United Nations, to finance the expenses of the Organization as apportioned by the General Assembly, and calls upon them to pay all their assessed contributions in full and in a timely manner;
2. *Urges* all Member States that have not done so to fulfil their financial obligations under the Charter;
3. *Requests* the Secretary-General to continue to monitor the financial situation of the United Nations and

to keep the President of the General Assembly and the chairmen of the regional groups informed so as to facilitate consideration by Member States if the situation so requires;
4. *Also requests* the Secretary-General to communicate to all Member States the latest information on the magnitude of the current financial crisis facing the Organization and to report thereon in a timely and comprehensive manner to the General Assembly at its forty-fourth session.

General Assembly resolution 43/215

21 December 1988   Meeting 84   Adopted without vote

Approved by Fifth Committee (A/43/952) without vote, 19 December (meeting 51); draft by Fiji (A/C.5/43/L.22) following informal consultations; agenda item 50.
Meeting numbers. GA 43rd session: 5th Committee 45-47, 49, 51; plenary 84.

On the same date, also on the Fifth Committee's recommendation and without vote, the Assembly adopted **resolution 43/220**.

Financial emergency of the United Nations
The General Assembly,
Recalling its resolutions 3049 A (XXVII) of 19 December 1972, 3538(XXX) of 17 December 1975, 32/104 of 14 December 1977, 35/113 of 10 December 1980, 36/116 B of 10 December 1981, 37/13 of 16 November 1982, 38/228 B of 20 December 1983, 39/239 B of 18 December 1984, 40/241 A and B of 18 December 1985, 41/204 A of 11 December 1986 and 42/216 A of 21 December 1987,
Mindful of the report of the Negotiating Committee on the Financial Emergency of the United Nations and of the views expressed by Member States thereon in the Fifth Committee at the thirty-second session of the General Assembly,
Having considered the report of the Secretary-General on the analysis of the financial situation of the United Nations, and the comments thereon made by the Chairman of the Advisory Committee on Administrative and Budgetary Questions in his introductory statement,
Noting with concern that the short-term deficit of the Organization, though marginally reduced during the year, is expected to reach approximately 320 million United States dollars as at 31 December 1988,
Noting also with concern that delays in and partial payment of assessed contributions continue to create serious cash-flow problems for the Organization,
Concerned also at the increasingly precarious financial situation of peace-keeping operations, and noting that peace-keeping activities remain in operation to a large extent because the current and former troop-contributing Member States, particularly the developing-country troop contributors, continue to bear most of the burden of the deficit,
Reiterating earlier appeals to Member States, without prejudice to their position of principle, to make voluntary contributions to the Special Account referred to in annex VI to the report of the Secretary-General on the analysis of the financial situation of the United Nations,
Noting recent developments concerning the financial situation of the Organization, in particular the progress being made towards liquidating the long-standing arrears in peace-keeping operations and the offers of volun-

tary contributions by some Member States in response to the Secretary-General's appeals,

Considering the possibility that for many Member States a calendar difference between the national fiscal year and that of the Organization may be among contributory factors in the delay in the payment of assessed contributions,

Taking into account the views expressed by Member States in the Fifth Committee during the forty-third session,

1. *Reaffirms* its commitment to seek a comprehensive and generally acceptable solution to the financial problems of the United Nations, based on the principle of the collective financial responsibility of Member States and in strict compliance with the Charter of the United Nations;

2. *Urges* all Member States to meet their financial obligations under the Charter;

3. *Renews its appeal* to all Member States to make their best efforts to overcome constraints to the prompt payment of all assessed contributions and advances to the Working Capital Fund;

4. *Expresses its appreciation* to all Member States that pay their assessed contributions in full within thirty days of the receipt of the Secretary-General's communication, in accordance with regulation 5.4 of the Financial Regulations of the United Nations;

5. *Requests* the Secretary-General, in addition to sending his official communications to the permanent representatives of Member States, to approach, as and when appropriate, the Governments of Member States for the purpose of encouraging expeditious payment in full of all assessed contributions, in compliance with regulation 5.4 of the Financial Regulations of the United Nations;

6. *Invites* Member States to provide information regarding their expected pattern of payments, in order to facilitate the financial planning by the Secretary-General;

7. *Requests* the Negotiating Committee on the Financial Emergency of the United Nations to keep the financial situation of the Organization under review and to report, as and when appropriate, to the General Assembly;

8. *Requests* the Secretary-General to submit to the General Assembly at its forty-fourth session a comprehensive report on the financial situation of the United Nations, including updated information on the practices of other organizations of the United Nations system for achieving prompt and full payment of assessed contributions.

General Assembly resolution 43/220

21 December 1988   Meeting 84   Adopted without vote

Approved by Fifth Committee (A/43/953) without vote, 19 December (meeting 51); draft by Fiji (A/C.5/43/L.21) following informal consultations; agenda item 116.

Meeting numbers. GA 43rd session: 5th Committee 45-47, 49, 51; plenary 84.

Review of the efficiency of the administrative and financial functioning of the United Nations

In April 1988,[5] the Secretary-General submitted his second progress report on implementation of a 1986 General Assembly resolution[6] adopted on the basis of a report of the Group of High-level Intergovernmental Experts to Review the Efficiency of the Administrative and Financial Functioning of the United Nations (Group of 18). The Secretary-General's report reflected action taken and progress made during the first 15 months of the three-year period envisaged by the Assembly for implementation of the recommendations of the Group in the following areas: political affairs, economic and social matters, co-ordination in the United Nations system, information, conference services, administration and finance, and personnel.

The Secretary-General stated that extensive restructuring was complete in the political and administrative areas and was well under way in the Department of Public Information (DPI). Final restructuring in the economic and social fields had to await the results of reviews undertaken by the intergovernmental bodies. Many recommendations aimed at streamlining the Secretariat and ensuring greater efficiency in its activities, whether in substantive or servicing functions, had already been fully implemented or were to be put into effect during the remainder of the reform period. The Secretary-General acknowledged the outstanding co-operation of the staff in that regard.

Delivering mandated programmes in the most efficient and cost-effective manner remained the most important task of the Secretariat, the Secretary-General said. By the same token, it was essential that Member States supported the endeavour to strengthen the Organization and the services it rendered to the international community.

ACABQ's comments on the Secretary-General's report were contained in an October report.[7]

In the context of its consideration of programme questions, the Committee for Programme and Co-ordination (CPC), at its 1988 session,[8] also discussed matters pertaining to the implementation of recommendations of the Group of 18.

GENERAL ASSEMBLY ACTION

On 21 December, on the recommendation of the Fifth Committee, the General Assembly adopted **resolution 43/213** without vote.

Implementation of General Assembly resolution 41/213: progress report and revised estimates for the biennium 1988-1989

The General Assembly,

Recalling its resolution 41/213 of 19 December 1986 on the review of the efficiency of the administrative and financial functioning of the United Nations and its resolution 42/211 of 21 December 1987 on the implementation of General Assembly resolution 41/213,

Reaffirming that measures to improve the efficiency of the administrative and financial functioning of the United Nations and to improve the planning, programming and budgeting process should aim at and contribute to strengthening the effectiveness of the Organization in dealing with political, economic and social issues in order better to achieve the purposes of and respect for the principles set out in the Charter of the United Nations,

Noting from the report of the Secretary-General on the work of the Organization that the emerging world situation is bound to impose additional responsibilities on the United Nations,

Reaffirming also that all Member States must honour, promptly and in full, their financial obligations as set out in the Charter,

Re-emphasizing that the financial stability of the Organization will facilitate the orderly, balanced and well co-ordinated implementation of resolution 41/213 in all its parts,

Having considered the relevant reports of the Secretary-General,

Having considered also the relevant parts of the report of the Committee for Programme and Co-ordination on the work of its twenty-eighth session and of the reports of the Advisory Committee on Administrative and Budgetary Questions,

Taking into account the views expressed by Member States during the consideration of this item at its forty-third session,

1. *Renews its appeal* to Member States to demonstrate their commitment to the United Nations by, *inter alia*, meeting their financial obligations on time and in full, in accordance with the Charter and the Financial Regulations of the United Nations;

2. *Stresses* that, in order to carry out successfully the process of reform and restructuring, it is essential that the present financial uncertainties be dispelled;

3. *Welcomes* the determination of the Secretary-General to continue his efforts to implement fully the recommendations of the Group of High-level Intergovernmental Experts to Review the Efficiency of the Administrative and Financial Functioning of the United Nations which fall within his purview, as adopted in resolution 41/213 and in accordance with paragraph 7 of resolution 42/211;

4. *Reiterates* its support for the Secretary-General in the fulfilment of his responsibilities as chief administrative officer of the Organization;

5. *Stresses* that the implementation of its resolution 41/213 must not have a negative impact on mandated programmes and activities;

6. *Emphasizes* in this respect that, in accordance with the existing regulations and rules, while output revisions in programme budgets may be proposed in order to comply more efficiently with the objectives of those programmes and activities, outputs specifically requested in mandates should be fully delivered;

7. *Requests* the Secretary-General to submit his proposed revisions referred to in paragraph 6 above to the General Assembly in the context of proposed programme budgets;

8. *Reiterates* that further implementation of its resolution 41/213 should be carried out in a balanced way and with flexibility so as to improve the structure and composition of the Secretariat;

9. *Endorses* the recommendations of the Committee for Programme and Co-ordination on the Secretary-General's report on the implementation of recommen-

dation 15 of the Group of High-level Intergovernmental Experts, as adjusted by a 10 per cent reduction in the staffing of conference services in New York and Geneva entailing an overall post reduction of 12.1 per cent by the end of the biennium 1988-1989; and further endorses the recommendation of the Advisory Committee on Administrative and Budgetary Questions that the adjustment under section 29 of the programme budget should entail the restoration of 100 posts on the understanding that this restoration would not require additional appropriations for the biennium 1988-1989;

10. *Requests* the Secretary-General to submit, in the context of his proposed programme budget for the biennium 1990-1991, concrete recommendations for absorbing the costs of the posts referred to above including, to the maximum extent possible, through the elimination of additional posts, under the criteria set out in paragraphs 5, 8, and 9 above and paragraphs 11 to 13 below;

11. *Endorses* the recommendations of the Committee for Programme and Co-ordination and the Advisory Committee on Administrative and Budgetary Questions pertaining to small offices, regional commissions and other units referred to therein, and also requests the Secretary-General to keep in mind the concerns expressed by Member States in the Fifth Committee on proposed reductions of staff in small units such as the United Nations Environment Programme and the United Nations Centre for Human Settlements (Habitat);

12. *Concurs* with the comments and observations of the Advisory Committee on Administrative and Budgetary Questions in paragraph 33 of its report regarding the organization, functions and staffing of the administrative and common services unit at Nairobi;

13. *Requests* the Secretary-General in further implementing recommendation 15 to continue to take into account the following guidelines:

(a) This recommendation should be implemented flexibly taking due account of work-load analyses, where applicable;

(b) Its implementation should have no negative impact on programmes;

(c) Its implementation should have no adverse effect on the structure and composition of the Secretariat bearing in mind the necessity of securing the highest standards of efficiency, competence and integrity of staff with due regard to equitable geographical distribution;

(d) It should be implemented in a balanced manner, taking into account recommendations 41, 46, 47 and 54;

14. *Invites* the Secretary-General to continue the implementation of recommendations 41, 46, 47 and 54 and to report thereon to the General Assembly at its forty-fourth session in the context of the report referred to in paragraph 18 below;

15. *Invites* the Secretary-General, as regards recommendation 19, to proceed with the reclassification of the post as indicated in paragraph 7 of his report;

16. *Endorses* the recommendations of the Committee for Programme and Co-ordination and the Advisory Committee on Administrative and Budgetary Questions as regards recommendation 25, relating to the location of the liaison functions with non-governmental organizations, and recommendation 29;

17. *Invites* the Secretary-General to implement recommendation 37 in accordance with the recommendations of the Committee for Programme and Co-

ordination as contained in paragraphs 82 to 88 of its report and the comments and observations of the Advisory Committee on Administrative and Budgetary Questions as contained in paragraphs 40 to 60 of its report;

18. *Requests* the Secretary-General and the Committee for Programme and Co-ordination to report to the General Assembly on the implementation of resolution 41/213 in accordance with recommendation 71, taking into account the views expressed in the Fifth Committee;

19. *Also requests* the Secretary-General to submit to the General Assembly at its forty-fifth session an analytical report assessing the effect of the implementation of resolution 41/213 on the Organization and its activities as a whole, and the way in which it has enhanced the efficiency of its administrative and financial functioning.

General Assembly resolution 43/213

21 December 1988   Meeting 84   Adopted without vote

Approved by Fifth Committee (A/43/951) without vote, 18 December (meeting 50); draft by Vice-Chairman (A/C.5/43/L.19); agenda item 49.
Meeting numbers. GA 43rd session: 5th Committee 7, 10-12, 14, 16, 18, 19, 21, 23, 24, 46-48, 50; plenary 84.

UN budget

Budget for 1988-1989

Appropriations

The General Assembly in December 1988 approved an increase of $19,160,000 in the United Nations programme budget for 1988-1989, raising appropriations for the biennium to $1,788,746,300 and authorizing a number of expenditures over the initial amount approved in 1987.[9] In approving the increase, the Assembly followed recommendations by the Fifth Committee on the revised estimates submitted by the Secretary-General in his first performance report on the 1988-1989 budget,[10] as well as on the programme budget implications adopted by the Assembly under items considered by other Main Committees or in respect of items dealt with in plenary meetings.

The largest overall increases were approved for the following activities: political and Security Council affairs: peace-keeping activities, $18.8 million; the Economic Commission for Africa, $7 million; overall policy making, direction and co-ordination, $5.3 million; the Economic and Social Commission for Western Asia, $4.2 million; the Economic and Social Commission for Asia and the Pacific, $2.4 million; the Department of Technical Co-operation for Development, $2 million; the Department of International Economic and Social Affairs, $2 million; political affairs, trusteeship and decolonization, $1.6 million; public information, $1.3 million; and the International Trade Centre, $1.2 million.

Notable decreases in appropriations were approved in the area of common support services, with deductions of $8.8 million from conference and library services and $6 million from administration and management. Appropriations for the Office of the United Nations High Commissioner for Refugees (UNHCR) and for staff assessment were adjusted downward by $3.5 million and $3.4 million, respectively.

ACABQ, in its report on the revised estimates,[11] recommended a series of compensatory measures, in view of which, it noted, there should be no need to request additional appropriations in the second programme budget performance report for 1988-1989.

ACABQ, in December 1988,[12] recommended approval of the revisions to the appropriations and estimates of income as contained in the Secretary-General's report.

In its comments on the 1988-1989 budget performance report,[13] ACABQ noted that more than half of the additional expenditure appropriation requested by the Secretary-General was earmarked for adjustments in average realized salary levels within grades, while the remainder was requested for changes in the percentage rate of common staff. The Advisory Committee questioned why, in view of the need to control recruitment to reach the target levels of the staffing table, the Secretary-General had not anticipated continuation of the salary-level trend in 1988 and therefore included the necessary resources when the 1988-1989 programme budget was recosted. It urged him to re-examine his methodology with a view to refining and improving his methods for forecasting and budgeting for such increases.

GENERAL ASSEMBLY ACTION

On 21 December, on the recommendation of the Fifth Committee, the General Assembly adopted **resolution 43/218 A** without vote.

Revised budget appropriations for the biennium 1988-1989

The General Assembly

Resolves that for the biennium 1988-1989 the amount of 1,769,586,300 United States dollars appropriated by its resolution 42/226 A of 21 December 1987 shall be adjusted by 19,160,000 dollars as follows:

Section	Amount appropriated by resolution 42/226 A	Increase or (decrease)	Revised appropriation
	(United States dollars)		
PART I. *Overall policy-making, direction and co-ordination*			
1. Overall policy-making, direction and co-ordination	44,932,900	5,280,800	50,213,700
Total, PART I	44,932,900	5,280,800	50,213,700

	Amount appropriated by resolution 42/226 A	Increase or (decrease)	Revised appropriation
	(United States dollars)		

Section

PART II. *Political and Security Council affairs; peace-keeping activities*

2A. Political and Security Council affairs; peace-keeping activities	80,462,100	18,796,900	99,259,000
2B. Disarmament affairs activities	9,430,600	817,000	10,247,600
Total, PART II	89,892,700	19,613,900	109,506,600

PART III. *Political affairs, trusteeship and decolonization*

3. Political affairs, trusteeship and decolonization	31,824,500	1,594,800	33,419,300
Total, PART III	31,824,500	1,594,800	33,419,300

PART IV. *Economic, social and humanitarian activities*

4. Policy-making organs (economic and social activities)	2,040,600	(58,200)	1,982,400
5A. Office of the Director-General for Development and International Economic Co-operation	3,840,100	232,700	4,072,800
5B. Regional Commissions Liaison Office	641,000	114,900	755,900
6A. Department of International Economic and Social Affairs	40,280,500	1,956,200	42,236,700
6B. Activities on global social development issues	12,007,100	(1,745,200)	10,261,900
7. Department of Technical Co-operation for Development	19,922,900	1,994,200	21,917,100
9. Transnational corporations	9,529,200	349,500	9,878,700
10. Economic Commission for Europe	35,797,400	(1,178,400)	34,619,000
11. Economic and Social Commission for Asia and the Pacific	33,483,000	2,365,000	35,848,000
12. Economic Commission for Latin America and the Caribbean	43,069,900	(258,900)	42,811,000
13. Economic Commission for Africa	44,234,600	6,972,600	51,207,200
14. Economic and Social Commission for Western Asia	32,599,900	4,166,300	36,766,200
15. United Nations Conference on Trade and Development	78,936,000	(1,977,800)	76,958,200
16. International Trade Centre	12,242,800	1,166,300	13,409,100
17. Centre for Science and Technology for Development	3,971,300	(147,300)	3,824,000
18. United Nations Environment Programme	10,651,100	(59,800)	10,591,300
19. United Nations Centre for Human Settlements (Habitat)	8,356,100	366,400	8,722,500
20. International drug control	8,750,200	(1,316,600)	7,433,600
21. Office of the United Nations High Commissioner for Refugees	39,444,400	(3,512,400)	35,932,000

	Amount appropriated by resolution 42/226 A	Increase or (decrease)	Revised appropriation
	(United States dollars)		
22. Office of the United Nations Disaster Relief Co-ordinator	7,289,400	(344,600)	6,944,800
23. Human Rights	17,008,800	(71,600)	16,937,200
24. Regular programme of technical co-operation	32,346,100	72,300	32,418,400
Total, PART IV	496,442,400	9,085,600	505,528,000

PART V. *International justice and law*

25. International Court of Justice	12,527,700	723,100	13,250,800
26. Legal activities	16,706,000	(72,000)	16,634,000
Total, PART V	29,233,700	651,100	29,884,800

PART VI. *Public information*

27. Public information	77,001,700	1,254,100	78,255,800
Total, PART VI	77,001,700	1,254,100	78,255,800

PART VII. *Common support services*

28. Administration and management	377,150,000	(5,999,200)	371,150,800
29. Conference and library services	333,779,200	(8,828,800)	324,950,400
Total, PART VII	710,929,200	(14,828,000)	696,101,200

PART VIII. *Special expenses*

30. United Nations bond issue	3,520,800	–	3,520,800
Total, PART VIII	3,520,800	–	3,520,800

PART IX. *Staff assessment*

31. Staff assessment	266,605,900	(3,385,800)	263,220,100
Total, PART IX	266,605,900	(3,385,800)	263,220,100

PART X. *Capital expenditures*

32. Construction, alteration, improvement and major maintenance of premises	19,202,500	(106,500)	19,096,000
Total, PART X	19,202,500	(106,500)	19,096,000
GRAND TOTAL	1,769,586,300	19,160,000	1,788,746,300

General Assembly resolution 43/218 A

21 December 1988   Meeting 84   Adopted without vote

Approved by Fifth Committee (A/43/980) without vote, 19 December (meeting 51); agenda item 114.

Meeting numbers. GA 43rd session: 5th Committee 7, 10-12, 14, 16, 18, 19, 21, 23, 24, 27, 29-31, 33, 36, 37, 39-48, 50, 51; plenary 84.

On the same date, the Assembly, by **resolution 43/217, section XIII**, concurred with the observations of ACABQ as contained in its reports.

Income

In December 1988, the General Assembly approved revised income estimates for 1988-1989 totalling $344.4 million, or about $7.1 million more than the amount approved in 1987.[14] Income from staff assessment decreased by about $3.4 million, while general income increased by $8.5 million and that from revenue-producing activities was raised by approximately $2.1 million. Reasons for the increases were mainly due to higher revenues gained from the rental of United Nations premises, and also as a result of favourable exchange-rate movements.

GENERAL ASSEMBLY ACTION

On 21 December, on the recommendation of the Fifth Committee, the General Assembly adopted **resolution 43/218 B** without vote.

Revised income estimates for the biennium 1988-1989

The General Assembly

Resolves that for the biennium 1988-1989 the estimates of income of 337,330,200 United States dollars approved by its resolution 42/226 B of 21 December 1987 shall be increased by 7,113,100 dollars as follows:

	Amount approved by resolution 42/226 B	Increase or (decrease)	Revised estimates
		(United States dollars)	
Income Section			
PART I. *Income from staff assessment*			
1. Income from staff assessment	271,019,900	(3,438,400)	267,581,500
Total, PART I	271,019,900	(3,438,400)	267,581,500
PART II. *Other income*			
2. General income	54,542,300	8,492,900	63,035,200
3. Revenue-producing activities	11,768,000	2,058,600	13,826,600
Total, PART II	66,310,300	10,551,500	76,861,800
GRAND TOTAL	337,330,200	7,113,100	344,443,300

General Assembly resolution 43/218 B

21 December 1988   Meeting 84   Adopted without vote

Approved by Fifth Committee (A/43/980) without vote, 19 December (meeting 51); agenda item 114.

Meeting numbers. GA 43rd session: 5th Committee 7, 10-12, 14, 16, 18, 19, 21, 23, 24, 27, 29-31, 33, 36, 37, 39-48, 50, 51; plenary 84.

Financing 1989 appropriations

By **resolution 43/218 C**, the General Assembly specified the amounts to be obtained from each major income section to finance appropriations for 1989. Member States were assessed $747,074,062 net of staff assessment.

GENERAL ASSEMBLY ACTION

On 21 December, on the recommendation of the Fifth Committee, the General Assembly adopted **resolution 43/218 C** without vote.

Financing of appropriations for the year 1989

The General Assembly

Resolves that for the year 1989:

1. Budget appropriations in a total amount of 900,853,150 United States dollars, consisting of 884,793,150 dollars, being half of the appropriations initially approved for the biennium 1988-1989 by General Assembly resolution 42/226 A of 21 December 1987,

plus 19,160,000 dollars, being the increase in appropriations approved during the forty-third session by resolution A above, less 3,100,000 dollars, being the reduction resulting from savings in the liquidation of obligations for the biennium 1984-1985 surrendered in accordance with Assembly resolution 40/239 A, paragraph 6, shall be financed in accordance with regulations 5.1 and 5.2 of the Financial Regulations of the United Nations as follows:

(a) 35,706,650 dollars consisting of:

(i) 25,155,150 dollars, being half of the estimated income approved for the biennium 1988-1989 by Assembly resolution 42/226 B of 21 December 1987 other than staff assessment income and excluding the estimated income in income section 2 (16 million dollars) in respect of the repayment of the loan to the United Nations Industrial Development Organization;

(ii) 10,551,500 dollars, being the increase in estimated income other than staff assessment income approved by resolution B above;

(b) 865,146,500 dollars, being the assessment on Member States in accordance with Assembly resolution 43/223 A of 21 December 1988 on the scale of assessments for the years 1989, 1990 and 1991;

2. There shall be set off against the assessment on Member States, in accordance with the provisions of General Assembly resolution 973(X) of 15 December 1955, their respective share in the Tax Equalization Fund in the total amount of 118,072,438 dollars, consisting of:

(a) 135,509,950 dollars, being half of the estimated staff assessment income approved by Assembly resolution 42/226 B;

(b) Less 3,438,400 dollars, being the estimated decrease in income from staff assessment approved by resolution B above;

(c) Less 13,999,112 dollars, being the decrease in income from staff assessment compared to the revised estimates for the biennium 1986-1987, approved by Assembly resolution 42/213 B of 21 December 1987.

General Assembly resolution 43/218 C

21 December 1988   Meeting 84   Adopted without vote

Approved by Fifth Committee (A/43/980) without vote, 19 December (meeting 51); agenda item 114.

Meeting numbers. GA 43rd session: 5th Committee 7, 10-12, 14, 16, 18, 19, 21, 23, 24, 27, 29-31, 33, 36, 37, 39-48, 50, 51; plenary 84.

Loan to UNIDO

The General Assembly decided, by **resolution 43/217, section V**, of 21 December 1988, to continue with the special arrangements made in 1987[15] regarding repayment of a loan by the United Nations Industrial Development Organization (UNIDO). It accepted UNIDO's proposal to commence repayment in 1990 at an annual minimum rate of $1 million. The loan, granted by the Assembly in 1985,[16] was originally to be for $24 million to finance the initial operations of the agency until it received sufficient contributions from its members. That amount was adjusted downward in 1986 to $16 million to reflect UNIDO's actual requirements.[17] The conditions of the loan called for repayment of $8 million in 1986 and the remaining $8 million by 1987.

However, due to financial difficulties, UNIDO had been unable to make any payments on the loan in 1986 or 1987. In October 1988,[18] the Secretary-General reported that he had been informed by UNIDO that outstanding assessed contributions to it as at 31 December 1987 amounted to $26 million and that estimates for collection of the 1988-1989 assessments did not indicate that the level of outstanding contributions would decrease. It would appear that UNIDO would be unable to make any repayments of the loan during 1988-1989. In June 1988, the Industrial Development Board adopted a proposal by the Director-General, giving him the authority to renegotiate the terms of the loan. Under the proposed terms, a payment of $1 million would be made annually, starting in 1990. Additional payments accelerating that schedule could be negotiated pending the condition of UNIDO's Working Capital Fund.

That proposal, the Secretary-General concluded, would unilaterally convert what was originally a two-year, short-term bridging facility to a long-term loan that could take up to 19 years to repay, which was not what Member States had intended when the appropriations for the original financing were approved. In his view, the maximum time such a loan should continue to be borne by Member States was five more years. Repayment should be at the rate of either $3.2 million annually, beginning in 1989, or $4 million a year, starting 1990. Also, in view of the changed nature of the loan, a reasonable interest rate should be charged. In the absence of an agreement on a firm modality for repayment in the current biennium and in view of the current financial situation of the United Nations, the Secretary-General proposed that the special arrangement made in 1987 regarding assessments on Member States[19] be continued for 1989. Under the 1987 resolution, a waiver had been set on financial regulation 5.2 *(b)* (stipulating an $8 million reduction in the assessments on Member States in 1988 and a further $8 million in 1989). The loan was to be considered separately in the annual financing resolutions for the budget. Further, 1988 assessments would not be reduced by any part of the loan and those for 1989 would be reduced only by the amount actually repaid.

ACABQ observed in November 1988[20] that the Secretary-General's proposals for repayment of the loan within five years and his suggestion for including interest payments did not take full account of UNIDO's current and projected financial difficulties. The Advisory Committee recommended that both organizations continue to negotiate modalities for repayment—in particular, procedures for accelerated payments—and

that the Assembly accept UNIDO's proposal to commence repaying the loan in 1990 at the minimum rate of $1 million per year.

Report of ACABQ

During 1988, ACABQ met in New York (12 April–27 May), The Hague, Netherlands (30 and 31 May), Geneva (1-10 June) and Rome, Italy (13-17 June). It considered reports of the Secretary-General on the programme budget for 1988-1989 and other budget-related matters. By **resolution 43/217, section III**, the General Assembly, on 21 December 1988, took note with appreciation of ACABQ's first report.[21]

Proposed programme budget for 1990-1991

As called for by the Assembly in 1986,[22] the Secretary-General submitted in August 1988 a report on the proposed programme budget outline for 1990-1991,[23] with preliminary estimates of resources to which a contingency fund for additional expenditures would be added.

Indicative estimates of recurrent resources for 1990-1991 at 1988 rates, excluding adjustments for currency fluctuations and inflation, were $1,705.5 million, or 9.6 per cent lower than the revalued resource base of $1,886.6 million for 1988-1989. Non-recurrent resources for 1990-1991 were estimated at $58.1 million, or 158 per cent higher than the similar provision in 1988-1989. The estimate represented a 9.6 per cent decline in the relative growth rate.

The Secretary-General proposed that the contingency fund be set at a level of 0.75 per cent of the 1990-1991 budget, excluding expenditures arising from the impact of extraordinary expenses as well as fluctuations in rates of exchange and inflation. He also suggested that the Assembly continue to keep the appropriateness and adequacy of that level under review.

ACABQ,[24] countering the Secretary-General's proposal, recommended that the 1990-1991 programme budget be estimated at $1,982,523,700. This estimate was based on a preliminary estimate of $1,763,700,000, recosted first at 1989 and then at 1990-1991 currency fluctuation and inflation rates. The Advisory Committee also took into account its own recommendation to increase the vacancy rate for Professional and higher-level posts to 5 per cent, and the net addition of 50 posts as called for in the ACABQ report on the revised estimates for 1988-1989 (see PART SIX, Chapter II).

ACABQ did not object to the level of the contingency fund being set at 0.75 per cent, or about $15 million, of the preliminary estimates for the 1990-1991 budget. It recommended that appropriations for the fund should not be made in advance, but that limited amounts should be appropriated as needed. The fund should remain at the level set in the budget outline, with the understanding that the approved amount need not be reached but could not be exceeded.

At its 1988 session,[8] CPC compiled four lists of priorities related to political, economic, social and legal matters for the proposed 1990-1991 programme budget, in accordance with a 1986 Assembly resolution.[6] CPC noted that future budget outlines would benefit from full implementation of the provisions concerning priorities for the medium-term plan starting in 1992. It requested that the Secretary-General report in 1989 on the approach for identifying priorities that reflected broad sectoral trends.

GENERAL ASSEMBLY ACTION

On 21 December 1988, on the recommendation of the Fifth Committee, the General Assembly adopted **resolution 43/214** without vote.

Proposed programme budget outline for the biennium 1990-1991 and use and operation of the contingency fund

The General Assembly,

Recalling its resolution 41/213 of 19 December 1986, by which, *inter alia*, it requested the Secretary-General to submit in off-budget years an outline of the programme budget for the following biennium and to include in the programme budget a contingency fund and recognized the necessity of finding a comprehensive solution to the problem of all additional expenditures, including those deriving from inflation and currency fluctuation,

Recalling also its resolution 42/211 of 21 December 1987 in which it decided to consider at its forty-third session the question of a comprehensive solution to the problem of all additional expenditures, including those deriving from inflation and currency fluctuation,

Having considered the report of the Secretary-General, the relevant parts of the report of the Committee for Programme and Co-ordination and the report of the Advisory Committee on Administrative and Budgetary Questions,

Taking into account the views expressed by Member States during the consideration of this item at its forty-second and forty-third sessions,

1. *Emphasizes* that sound programme budgeting, including a greater level of predictability of resources required, is not fully achievable until the current financial crisis is fully brought to an end by the full and prompt payment of assessments by Member States;

2. *Recognizes* that the outline of the proposed programme budget is part of the process of improving the efficiency and effectiveness of the Organization;

3. *Affirms* that the outline, being a part of the new budget process defined in its resolution 41/213, is in a developmental period, that its methodology requires further improvement and that the whole exercise should be applied with flexibility, in accordance with resolutions 41/213 and 42/211;

4. *Recognizes also* that the outline should provide a greater level of predictability of resources required for the following biennium, while ensuring that such resources are adequate for the fulfilment of the objectives, programmes and activities of the Organization, as mandated by the relevant legislative bodies of the United Nations, thereby facilitating the widest possible agreement on the programme budget;

5. *Decides* that the Secretary-General should prepare his proposed programme budget for the biennium 1990-1991 on the basis of the total preliminary estimate of 1,767,060,000 United States dollars at 1988 rates (equivalent to 1,982,523,700 dollars at 1990-1991 rates) as shown in paragraph 16 of the report of the Advisory Committee on Administrative and Budgetary Questions;

6. *Decides also* that the contingency fund of the programme budget for the biennium 1990-1991 shall be established at a level of 0.75 per cent of the preliminary estimate at 1990-1991 rates referred to above, i.e., 15 million dollars, shall be appropriated as needed and shall be used according to the purpose and procedures set out in the annexes to its resolutions 41/213 and 42/211 and relevant regulations and rules;

7. *Decides further* to keep under review, during the implementation of the programme budget for the biennium 1990-1991 and in the light of the evolving situation, the appropriateness and adequacy of the level of the contingency fund, as well as its mode of operation;

8. *Reaffirms* the need for a comprehensive and satisfactory solution to the problem of controlling the effects of inflation and currency fluctuation on the budget of the United Nations;

9. *Notes with appreciation* the work undertaken on this issue by the Advisory Committee on Administrative and Budgetary Questions and its observations on the establishment of a reserve that would cover additional requirements due to currency fluctuation, non-staff costs inflation and statutory cost increases for staff;

10. *Agrees* to the concept of a reserve as described in paragraph 9 above, requests the Secretary-General to formulate a set of procedures for the operation of the reserve to be submitted through the Advisory Committee on Administrative and Budgetary Questions to the General Assembly at its forty-fourth session, and agrees to address further at that time the question of setting up such a reserve for the biennium 1990-1991;

11. *Stresses* the importance of indicating in the outline of the proposed programme budget priorities reflecting general trends of a broad sectoral nature, endorses the recommendations of the Committee for Programme and Co-ordination in this regard, and requests the Secretary-General to submit a report on all aspects of priority-setting in future outlines to the General Assembly at its forty-fourth session through the Committee for Programme and Co-ordination;

12. *Requests* the Secretary-General to present his proposed programme budget for the biennium 1990-1991 in accordance with the present resolution and paragraph 10 of resolution 43/213 of 21 December 1988.

General Assembly resolution 43/214

21 December 1988   Meeting 84   Adopted without vote

Approved by Fifth Committee (A/43/951) without vote, 19 December (meeting 51); draft by India (A/C.5/43/L.20) following informal consultations, orally revised; agenda item 49.

Meeting numbers. GA 43rd session: 5th Committee 7, 10-12, 14, 16, 18, 19, 21, 23, 24, 46-48, 50, 51; plenary 84.

REFERENCES

[1]A/C.5/43/29 & Corr.1. [2]YUN 1972, p. 720, GA res. 3049 C (XXVII), 19 Dec. 1972. [3]YUN 1981, p. 1299, GA res. 36/116 A, 10 Dec. 1981. [4]A/43/932. [5]A/43/286 & Corr.1. [6]YUN 1986, p. 1024, GA res. 41/213, 19 Dec. 1986. [7]A/43/651. [8]A/43/16. [9]YUN 1987, p. 1101, GA res. 42/213 A, 21 Dec. 1987. [10]A/C.5/43/30 & Add.1. [11]A/43/651. [12]A/43/7/Add.11,12. [13]A/43/7/Add.11. [14]YUN 1987, p. 1103, GA res. 43/213 B, 21 Dec. 1987. [15]*Ibid.*, p. 1109. [16]YUN 1985, p. 1207, GA res. 40/253 A, 18 Dec. 1985. [17]YUN 1986, p. 1037, GA res. 41/209, 11 Dec. 1986. [18]A/C.5/43/17 & Corr.1. [19]YUN 1987, p. 1108, GA res. 43/226 C, 21 Dec. 1987. [20]A/43/7/Add.5. [21]A/43/7 & Add.1-13. [22]YUN 1986, p. 1025, GA res. 41/213, annex I, 19 Dec. 1986. [23]A/43/524. [24]A/43/929.

Contributions

The forty-eighth session of the Committee on Contributions was held in New York from 6 June to 1 July 1988.[1] Responding to a 1987 General Assembly resolution,[2] the Committee prepared a scale of assessments for 1989-1991, reviewed limits in the scheme to avoid excessive variations of individual assessment rates between successive scales and continued its work on improving the methodology for drafting future scales. In addition, the Committee proposed interim arrangements for the collection of assessed contributions from non-member States.

Scale of assessments

In its 1988 report,[1] the Committee on Contributions presented its recommendations for the scale of assessment for the apportionment of United Nations expenses for the years 1989, 1990 and 1991. The report showed the unadjusted and adjusted machine scales used by the Committee in establishing those recommendations and the results of the mitigation process. Reservations by two Committee members regarding the proposed scale were also included in the report.

Under the new scale, 79 Member States were assessed at 0.01 per cent, 9 at 0.02 and 6 at 0.03. A total of 94 Member States, i.e., 59 per cent of the membership, were thus assessed at or below 0.03 per cent. Assessment rates for the Group of 77 developing countries as a whole increased from 9.67 to 10.01 per cent.

GENERAL ASSEMBLY ACTION

On 21 December 1988, on the recommendation of the Fifth Committee, the General Assembly adopted **resolution 43/223 A** without vote.

The General Assembly,

Recognizing the obligation of Member States, under Article 17 of the Charter of the United Nations, to bear the expenses of the Organization as apportioned by the General Assembly,

Bearing in mind rule 160 of the rules of procedure of the General Assembly,

1. *Resolves* that the scale of assessments for the contributions of Member States to the regular budget of the United Nations for 1989 and 1990, and also 1991 unless a new scale is approved earlier by the General Assembly on the recommendation of the Committee on Contributions in response to resolution B below, shall be as follows:

Member State	Per cent	Member State	Per cent	Member State	Per cent
Afghanistan	0.01	Chile	0.08	Greece	0.40
Albania	0.01	China	0.79	Grenada	0.01
Algeria	0.15	Colombia	0.14	Guatemala	0.02
Angola	0.01	Comoros	0.01	Guinea	0.01
Antigua and Barbuda	0.01	Congo	0.01	Guinea-Bissau	0.01
Argentina	0.66	Costa Rica	0.02	Guyana	0.01
Australia	1.57	Côte d'Ivoire	0.02	Haiti	0.01
Austria	0.74	Cuba	0.09	Honduras	0.01
Bahamas	0.02	Cyprus	0.02	Hungary	0.21
Bahrain	0.02	Czechoslovakia	0.66	Iceland	0.03
Bangladesh	0.01	Democratic Kampuchea	0.01	India	0.37
Barbados	0.01	Democratic Yemen	0.01	Indonesia	0.15
Belgium	1.17	Denmark	0.69	Iran (Islamic Republic of)	0.69
Belize	0.01	Djibouti	0.01	Iraq	0.12
Benin	0.01	Dominica	0.01	Ireland	0.18
Bhutan	0.01	Dominican Republic	0.03	Israel	0.21
Bolivia	0.01	Ecuador	0.03	Italy	3.99
Botswana	0.01	Egypt	0.07	Jamaica	0.01
Brazil	1.45	El Salvador	0.01	Japan	11.38
Brunei Darussalam	0.04	Equatorial Guinea	0.01	Jordan	0.01
Bulgaria	0.15	Ethiopia	0.01	Kenya	0.01
Burkina Faso	0.01	Fiji	0.01	Kuwait	0.29
Burma	0.01	Finland	0.51	Lao People's Democratic	
Burundi	0.01	France	6.25	Republic	0.01
Byelorussian Soviet		Gabon	0.03	Lebanon	0.01
Socialist Republic	0.33	Gambia	0.01	Lesotho	0.01
Cameroon	0.01	German Democratic		Liberia	0.01
Canada	3.09	Republic	1.28	Libyan Arab Jamahiriya	0.28
Cape Verde	0.01	Germany, Federal		Luxembourg	0.06
Central African Republic	0.01	Republic of	8.08	Madagascar	0.01
Chad	0.01	Ghana	0.01	Malawi	0.01

Member State	Per cent	Member State	Per cent	Member State	Per cent
Malaysia	0.11	Qatar	0.05	Trinidad and Tobago	0.05
Maldives	0.01	Romania	0.19	Tunisia	0.03
Mali	0.01	Rwanda	0.01	Turkey	0.32
Malta	0.01	Saint Kitts and Nevis	0.01	Uganda	0.01
Mauritania	0.01	Saint Lucia	0.01	Ukrainian Soviet	
Mauritius	0.01	Saint Vincent and the		Socialist Republic	1.25
Mexico	0.94	Grenadines	0.01	Union of Soviet Socialist	
Mongolia	0.01	Samoa	0.01	Republics	9.99
Morocco	0.04	Sao Tome and Principe	0.01	United Arab Emirates	0.19
Mozambique	0.01	Saudi Arabia	1.02	United Kingdom of	
Nepal	0.01	Senegal	0.01	Great Britain and	
Netherlands	1.65	Seychelles	0.01	Northern Ireland	4.86
New Zealand	0.24	Sierra Leone	0.01	United Republic of	
Nicaragua	0.01	Singapore	0.11	Tanzania	0.01
Niger	0.01	Solomon Islands	0.01	United States of	
Nigeria	0.20	Somalia	0.01	America	25.00
Norway	0.55	South Africa	0.45	Uruguay	0.04
Oman	0.02	Spain	1.95	Vanuatu	0.01
Pakistan	0.06	Sri Lanka	0.01	Venezuela	0.57
Panama	0.02	Sudan	0.01	Viet Nam	0.01
Papua New Guinea	0.01	Suriname	0.01	Yemen	0.01
Paraguay	0.03	Swaziland	0.01	Yugoslavia	0.46
Peru	0.06	Sweden	1.21	Zaire	0.01
Philippines	0.09	Syrian Arab Republic	0.04	Zambia	0.01
Poland	0.56	Thailand	0.10	Zimbabwe	0.02
Portugal	0.18	Togo	0.01		100.00

2. *Requests* the Committee on Contributions, in accordance with its mandate and the rules of procedure of the General Assembly, to consider representations made by Member States during the forty-third session on their respective assessments and to advise the Assembly of its recommendations for possible adjustments to allow the Assembly to take a decision at its forty-fourth session;

3. *Resolves further* that:

(a) In accordance with rule 160 of the rules of procedure of the General Assembly, the scale of assessments given in paragraph 1 above shall be reviewed by the Committee on Contributions in 1991, or earlier as specified in paragraph 1 above, when a report shall be submitted to the Assembly for consideration at its forty-sixth session;

(b) Notwithstanding the terms of regulation 5.5 of the Financial Regulations of the United Nations, the Secretary-General shall be empowered to accept, at his discretion and after consultation with the Chairman of the Committee on Contributions, a portion of the contributions of Member States for the calendar years 1989, 1990 and 1991 in currencies other than United States dollars;

(c) In accordance with rule 160 of the rules of procedure of the General Assembly, States which are not members of the United Nations but which participate in certain of its activities shall be called upon to contribute towards the 1989, 1990 and 1991 expenses of such activities on the basis of the following rates, unless modified as specified in paragraph 1 above:

Non-member State	Per cent
Democratic People's	
Republic of Korea	0.05
Holy See	0.01
Liechtenstein	0.01
Monaco	0.01
Nauru	0.01
Republic of Korea	0.22
San Marino	0.01
Switzerland	1.08
Tonga	0.01
Tuvalu	0.01

General Assembly resolution 43/223 A

21 December 1988   Meeting 84   Adopted without vote

Approved by Fifth Committee (A/43/981) without vote, 19 December (meeting 51); draft by Canada (A/C.5/43/L.17, part A) following informal consultations; agenda item 120.

Meeting numbers. GA 43rd session: 5th Committee 9-12, 14-18, 21, 51; plenary 84.

Scale preparation

In its 1988 report,[1] the Committee on Contributions noted that the fundamental criteria of the current methodology for scale preparation was the capacity to pay. Continuing the practice of using a 10-year statistical base period, capacity was measured in terms of the average national income of Member States from 1977-1986. Average national incomes were modified by a low per capita income allowance based on the same parameters used for the current scale, i.e., an upper per capita income limit of $2,200 and a relief gradient of 85 per cent. Ceiling and floor rates were limited to 25 per cent and 0.01 per cent, respectively, and there was a provision that prevented an increased assessment on the least developed countries, as called for by the General Assembly in 1981.[3]

After considering data presented by the Secretariat on total and public external debt restricted to developing countries, the Committee determined the eligibility for debt relief for all developing and centrally-planned economy countries for which data on total debt, both public and private, were available. As a result, 118 countries were identified as eligible, compared with 37 in 1985. Deductions for those 118 countries were based on the repayment of principle only, as interest payments were already reflected in national income estimates. However, as reliable data on debt service were not available, the Committee decided to approximate debt by using a working hypothesis on the ratio of debt service due to total external debt accumulation, resulting in a rate of 12 per cent. The ratio was determined in consultation with the International Monetary Fund (IMF), which suggested that the methodology be refined in the future based on a study of the length of repayment periods.

The Statistical Office of the Secretariat also presented a document on price-adjusted rates of exchange (PARE) to give the Committee an alternative for the *ad hoc* method applied in 1985.[5] The document focused on the effects of price-exchange-rate distortions on per capita income expressed in United States dollars.

The Committee tested PARE adjustments for a selected group of 32 countries based on the ratio between the actual exchange rate and the PARE-adjusted rate. As that test showed that the adjustments would result in a considerable transfer of points between countries, the Committee reduced the effect of PARE uniformly for the selected countries by weighting it with the actual exchange rate. However, due to several anomalies that arose from the PARE methodology, the Committee then decided to adjust national income only for debt relief. Countries with significant exchange-rate distortions, identified by the PARE analysis, were borne in mind when drawing up the final scale of assessments.

Suggestions on how to adjust the national income concept for factors that were not taken into account in the current national income definition were also discussed by the Committee. Among other things, questions were raised about the treatment of large-scale transfers of capital which were included in the national income of the host country. A further question arose as to whether the national income concept used by the Committee was the most appropriate means of measuring capacity to pay. The Committee stated its intention to return to this matter in 1989.

GENERAL ASSEMBLY ACTION

On 21 December 1988, on the recommendation of the Fifth Committee, the General Assembly without vote adopted **resolution 43/223 B**.

The General Assembly,

Recalling all its previous resolutions on the scale of assessments, in particular resolutions 39/247 B of 12 April 1985 and 42/208 of 11 December 1987,

Having considered the report of the Committee on Contributions and noting with appreciation the efforts of the Committee,

Bearing in mind the evolution of the world economic situation and its impact on the capacity to pay of Member States,

Taking into account the views expressed in the Fifth Committee during the forty-third session, in particu-

lar on the need for a substantial improvement of the existing methodology and criteria for the determination of the scale of assessments, and the need for information on the steps taken in the preparation of the scale of assessments,

Also taking into account the views expressed in the Fifth Committee during the forty-third session on the ceiling and floor levels,

1 *Reconfirms* that the capacity to pay of Member States is the fundamental criterion for determining the scale of assessments;

2. *Requests* the Committee on Contributions, in order to ensure fairness and equity in the scale and to make the methodology transparent, easily understandable, stable over time and as simple as possible, to undertake a comprehensive review of all aspects of the existing methodology, and to this end:

(a) To continue to monitor the improvements in the area of the availability and comparability of national income data, and to continue its work on the price-adjusted rates of exchange methodology;

(b) To seek more comprehensive and systematic information on external debt with a view to ensuring that this factor is adequately taken into account in the calculations for determining the capacity to pay;

(c) To undertake a comprehensive review of the upper limit of the low per capita income allowance formula and the application of the formula;

(d) To review, in the light of the proposals made in the Fifth Committee:

(i) The statistical base period and its application;

(ii) The scheme to avoid excessive variations of individual rates between successive scales;

(iii) The possibility of excluding allocation of any additional points as a result of the application of the scheme of limits to those Member States with a very low per capita income;

and to include in its report the implications of the various options considered;

(e) To limit the use of *ad hoc* adjustments in the preparation of the scale to the minimum possible, keeping in mind that in case such *ad hoc* adjustments are necessary, they should be made on the basis of objective, rational and transparent considerations, applied uniformly, and to include in its reports on the preparation of future scales of assessments explicit information on the basis of which such *ad hoc* adjustments were made;

3. *Requests* the Committee on Contributions to examine, as a means of improving the current methodology, the possible use of other factors, including the situation of those countries:

(a) Whose economies depend on one or a few products or income sources;

(b) Which suffered a real loss of income as a result of deteriorating terms of trade;

(c) Which experience serious balance-of-payments (trade) problems or a negative net flow of resources;

(d) Which have limited capacity to acquire convertible currencies;

4. *Also requests* the Committee on Contributions to continue its study on the concept of national income, as indicated in paragraph 47 of its report;

5. *Further requests* the Committee on Contributions, in conducting the studies and reviews indicated in paragraphs 2 and 3 above, to examine also the interrelationship of each of the elements as part of the overall

methodology, bearing in mind the need to avoid duplication and negative impact of each individual element on the others in order to reflect capacity to pay;

6. *Requests* the Committee on Contributions to submit a report on the above-mentioned reviews and their implications for future scales of assessments, with illustrative examples, to the General Assembly at its forty-fourth session;

7. *Requests* the Secretary-General to provide the Committee on Contributions with the facilities it requires to carry out its work, including supplementary assistance if necessary.

General Assembly resolution 43/223 B

21 December 1988   Meeting 84   Adopted without vote

Approved by Fifth Committee (A/43/981) without vote, 19 December (meeting 51); draft by Canada (A/C.5/43/L.17, part B) following informal consultations; agenda item 120.
Meeting numbers. GA 43rd session: 5th Committee 9-12, 14-18, 21, 51; plenary 84.

Budget contributions in 1988

Of the $1,111.5 million in contributions to the United Nations regular budget payable as at 1 January 1988, $716.5 million had been collected by 31 December, leaving almost $395 million outstanding. Of the total amount payable, $758 million was assessed for 1988 alone, while the remaining $353 million was outstanding from previous years. Budget assessments were in accordance with scales for 1986-1988 approved by the General Assembly in 1985.[6]

At the resumption of the General Assembly's 1987 session, the Secretary-General informed the Assembly President on 29 February 1988[7] that 12 Member States—Benin, Central African Republic, Congo, Dominica, Dominican Republic, El Salvador, Equatorial Guinea, Gambia, Nicaragua, Romania, Sao Tome and Principe, South Africa—were more than two years in arrears in the payment of their budget contributions.

On 1 and 18 March, 16 August and 19 September,[8] the Secretary-General reported that Benin, the Central African Republic, the Congo, Dominica, the Dominican Republic, El Salvador, Equatorial Guinea, the Gambia, Nicaragua, Romania, and Sao Tome and Principe had made the necessary payments to reduce their arrears below the two-year limit to maintain voting privileges, as specified in Article 19 of the United Nations Charter. On 20 September 1988,[9] he stated that South Africa remained $33,940,541 in arrears.

Contributions from non-member States

In 1988,[1] the Committee on Contributions decided that the Secretariat should examine the question of contributions by non-member States and prepare a note for consideration at its 1989 session. In the mean time, it proposed that non-member States pay at the beginning of each calendar year an amount equivalent to their average annual contribution during the previous 10 years, with a later adjustment for their actual level of participation during that year.

On 21 December, the General Assembly, by **resolution 43/223 C**, took note of the Committee's proposal concerning the procedures for the collection of contributions from non-member States.

REFERENCES

[1]A/43/11 & Corr.1. [2]YUN 1987, p. 1112, GA res. 42/208, 11 Dec. 1987. [3]YUN 1981, p. 1292, GA res. 36/231 A, 18 Dec. 1981. [4]YUN 1985, p. 1214, GA res. 39/247 B, 12 Apr. 1985. [5]*Ibid.*, p. 1215. [6]*Ibid.*, p. 1216, GA res. 40/248, 15 Dec. 1985. [7]A/42/925. [8]A/42/925/Add.1-4. [9]A/43/618.

Accounts and auditing

The accounts and financial statements for the year or biennium ended 31 December 1987 for the United Nations and eight voluntarily financed programmes were accepted by the General Assembly together with the audit opinions of the United Nations Board of Auditors. The Assembly also endorsed the observations of the Board and of ACABQ.

The Secretary-General transmitted to the Board on 31 March 1988 his financial reports on the accounts for the United Nations, including the International Trade Centre (ITC) (jointly sponsored by the United Nations Conference on Trade and Development (UNCTAD) and the General Agreement on Tariffs and Trade (GATT)) and the United Nations University, for the 1986-1987 biennium.

The programmes for which financial reports and audited financial statements were submitted were: the United Nations Development Programme (UNDP),[2] the United Nations Children's Fund,[3] the United Nations Relief and Works Agency for Palestine Refugees in the Near East (UNRWA),[4] the United Nations Institute for Training and Research (UNITAR),[5] the voluntary funds administered by the United Nations High Commissioner for Refugees (UNHCR),[6] the Fund of the United Nations Environment Programme (UNEP),[7] the United Nations Population Fund (UNFPA)[8] and the United Nations Habitat and Human Settlements Foundation.[9]

Recommendations and observations were made by the Board on various aspects of those programmes. Among the topics considered were cash management, budgetary control, payroll and personnel systems, procurement practices, computer operations, project management, peace-keeping operations, trust funds, revenue-producing activities, accounting procedures and financial reporting systems.

The Board of Auditors gave qualified audit opinions on the financial statements of the United Nations, UNDP and UNFPA.

In the case of the United Nations, the Board noted that most of the unpaid assessed contributions from Member States, including $353.2 million owed to the United Nations alone as of December 1987, had been outstanding for several years. The Board's opinion on the financial statements, therefore, was subject to the ultimate realization of those assets.

Regarding UNDP's financial statement, the Board found that the delineation between programme, programme support and operating costs was not adequately reflected. It also recommended that, at least for UNDP core activities, administrative expenditures be recorded on a gross rather than a net basis, as was the current practice, without off-setting administrative costs, regardless of funding source.

Concerning UNFPA, the Board stated that, other than expenditures executed by UNFPA itself, there was inadequate documentation to support programme expenditures made by executing agencies.

The Board also issued qualified audit opinions on compliance with the financial regulations and legislative authority of the Organization by UNWRA and ITC. This was due to procedural errors in the implementation of previous audit recommendations and to certain practices which needed review.

A summary of the Board's principal findings and conclusions for remedial action were transmitted to the Assembly in July 1988.[10] Comments on the Board's reports for the financial period ending 31 December 1987 were made by ACABQ in October.[11]

In addition, ACABQ examined the Board's report on its expanded audit of the financial report and accounts of UNICEF for the year ended 31 December 1986,[12] which was submitted pursuant to a 1987 General Assembly request.[13] As a result of the expanded audit, the Board rendered a clean opinion of the UNICEF accounts for 1986.

GENERAL ASSEMBLY ACTION

On 21 December 1988, acting on the recommendation of the Fifth Committee, the General Assembly adopted **resolution 43/216** without vote.

Financial reports and audited financial statements, and reports of the Board of Auditors

The General Assembly,

Having considered the financial reports and audited financial statements for the period ended 31 December 1987 of the United Nations, including the International Trade Centre and the United Nations University, the United Nations Development Programme, the United Nations Children's Fund, the United Nations Relief and Works Agency for Palestine Refugees in the Near East, the United Nations Institute for Training and Research, the voluntary funds administered by the United Nations High Commissioner for Refugees, the Fund of the United Nations Environment Programme, the United Nations Population Fund, and the United Nations Habitat and Human Settlements Foundation, the reports and audit opinions of the Board of Auditors, the concise summary of the principal findings and conclusions of common interest contained in the reports of the Board of Auditors, and the report of the Advisory Committee on Administrative and Budgetary Questions,

Having also considered the report of the Board of Auditors on its expanded audit of the financial report and accounts of the United Nations Children's Fund for the year ended 31 December 1986,

Recognizing the progress made in the implementation of General Assembly resolution 42/206 of 11 December 1987,

Noting with concern that the Board of Auditors, for the reasons stated in its reports, issued qualified audit opinions on the financial statements of the United Nations, the United Nations Development Programme and the United Nations Population Fund, and also issued qualified audit opinions on compliance with the Financial Regulations and legislative authority in the transactions of the United Nations Relief and Works Agency for Palestine Refugees in the Near East and the International Trade Centre,

Noting also with concern the delay in the issuance of the reports of the Board of Auditors for consideration by the General Assembly at its forty-third session,

Taking into consideration the views expressed by delegations, by the Board of Auditors, by the Advisory Committee on Administrative and Budgetary Questions and by representatives of the United Nations organizations and programmes during the debate in the Fifth Committee on this item, and the widely expressed support for measures to improve the efficiency, management, financial accountability and budgetary control of the United Nations organizations and programmes concerned,

Recognizing that the qualifications on the certification of programme expenditures in the audit opinions on the United Nations Development Programme and the United Nations Population Fund accounts are technical in nature and require co-ordinated action by the administrations and governing bodies of the Programme and the Fund and the executing agencies concerned,

1. *Accepts* the financial reports and audited financial statements and the audit opinions and reports of the Board of Auditors regarding the aforementioned organizations;

2. *Requests* the governing bodies of the United Nations Development Programme, the United Nations Population Fund, the United Nations Relief and Works Agency for Palestine Refugees in the Near East and the International Trade Centre to require the executive heads concerned to take immediate steps within their competence to correct the situations or conditions that gave rise to the qualification of audit opinions of the Board of Auditors;

3.   *Urges* the panel of external auditors, administrations, governing bodies of the executing agencies and other parties concerned to solve the problem with regard to the certification of programme expenditures executed and reported by United Nations executing agencies in co-operation with the United Nations Development Programme as well as with the United Nations Population Fund;

4.   *Endorses* the concurring observations and recommendations of the Board of Auditors and the Advisory Committee on Administrative and Budgetary Questions as contained in their respective reports, duly taking into account the divergent views expressed in the Fifth Committee on the question of the Multinational Programming and Operational Centres and the Pan-African Documentation and Information System;

5.   *Requests* the competent governing bodies to ensure that the executive heads concerned take necessary steps on a priority basis to implement the recommendations of the Board of Auditors and the Advisory Committee on Administrative and Budgetary Questions as contained in their respective reports, and to report thereon to the General Assembly at its forty-fourth session;

6.   *Requests* the Secretary-General and the executive heads of United Nations organizations and programmes concerned to take without delay appropriate measures within their competence in the light of the comments, observations and recommendations of the Board of Auditors and the Advisory Committee on Administrative and Budgetary Questions, including those relating to financial reporting, budgetary controls, unliquidated obligations, cash management, trust funds, and hiring of consultants, experts and temporary assistance, and to report to the General Assembly at its forty-fourth session, through the governing bodies of these organizations and programmes;

7.   *Also requests* the Secretary-General and the executive heads of United Nations organizations and programmes concerned to report to the General Assembly at its forty-fourth session, through the Board of Auditors and the Advisory Committee on Administrative and Budgetary Questions, specific measures taken to implement previous recommendations of the Board, and requests the Board and the Advisory Committee to evaluate the efficacy of those measures;

8.   *Recommends* that all future reports of the Board of Auditors continue to include separate sections that summarize recommendations for corrective action to be taken by the organizations and programmes concerned, with an indication of relative urgency;

9.   *Also recommends* that the Board of Auditors continue to submit to the General Assembly a concise document summarizing its principal findings, conclusions and recommendations of common interest, classified by audit area and, where appropriate, identifying the audited organization;

10.   *Requests* the Board of Auditors and the Advisory Committee on Administrative and Budgetary Questions to continue to cover in their reviews of the organizations and programmes, including peace-keeping operations, the areas relating to the efficiency and effectiveness of the financial procedures and controls, the accounting system and related administrative and management areas, in accordance with regulation 12.5 of the Financial Regulations of the United Nations, and

to recommend measures, as appropriate, to strengthen financial and management controls;

11.   *Also requests* the Board of Auditors to study the desirability and feasibility of conducting its reviews as stipulated in regulation 12.5 of the Financial Regulations of the United Nations in a more comprehensive manner and to report thereon to the General Assembly at its forty-fourth session;

12.   *Stresses* the need to standardize the presentation and format of financial statements and accounting policies among United Nations organizations and programmes;

13.   *Requests* the Secretary-General and the executive heads of United Nations organizations and programmes and other relevant entities, in consultation with the Board of Auditors, to explore the possibility of standardizing the presentation and format of financial statements and accounting policies of all audited organizations and programmes, taking into account previous relevant studies, and to report with proposals thereon to the General Assembly at its forty-fourth session;

14.   *Invites* the administrations of the United Nations, the United Nations Development Programme and the United Nations Population Fund to review their accounting policy with respect to unliquidated obligations taking into account generally accepted accounting principles;

15.   *Requests* the Secretary-General to reflect the results of the reorganization of the United Nations Postal Administration, as well as the status of implementation of the recommendations of the Board of Auditors, in the proposed programme budget for the biennium 1990-1991;

16.   *Invites* Governments that are represented on the governing bodies of organizations and programmes for which audited financial statements have been considered by the General Assembly to ensure that full consideration is given to the reports of the Board of Auditors and the Advisory Committee on Administrative and Budgetary Questions and the comments made thereon in the Fifth Committee;

17.   *Encourages* governing bodies of organizations and programmes to invite a representative of the Board of Auditors to be present at their meetings when considering the reports of the Board;

18.   *Underlines* the importance of an effective internal audit function in the organizations and programmes reported on, and requests the Secretary-General and the executive heads of United Nations organizations and programmes concerned to ensure that their respective internal audit units carry out follow-up audit work to assess the corrective action taken by the administrations in response to the main recommendations of the Board of Auditors;

19.   *Requests* the Board of Auditors and the administrations concerned to co-operate and ensure that all reports under this item are issued in time in accordance with existing rules.

General Assembly resolution 43/216

21 December 1988   Meeting 84   Adopted without vote

Approved by Fifth Committee (A/43/803) without vote, 10 November (meeting 28); draft by Canada (A/C.5/43/L.4) following informal consultations; agenda item 113.

Meeting numbers. GA 43rd session: 5th Committee 7-10, 12-14, 27, 28; plenary 84.

REFERENCES

[1]A/43/5, vols. I-III. [2]A/43/5/Add.1. [3]A/43/5/Add.2. [4]A/43/5/Add.3. [5]A/43/5/Add.4. [6]A/43/5/Add.5. [7]A/43/5/Add.6. [8]A/43/5/Add.7. [9]A/43/5/Add.8. [10]A/43/445. [11]A/43/674 & Corr.1. [12]A/42/5/Add.2. [13]YUN 1987, p. 1115, GA res. 42/206, 11 Dec. 1987.

United Nations programmes

Efforts to improve programme planning and performance, together with programme evaluation, continued throughout 1988.

Programme planning and performance

Programme performance 1986-1987

Report of the Secretary-General. A report on the programme performance of the United Nations for 1986-1987 was submitted by the Secretary-General in April 1988.[1] The report stated that following CPC's 1986 consideration of the 1984-1985 programme performance,[2] action had been taken to facilitate regular performance reporting by departments and offices. CPC's observations were taken into account, particularly as they related to questions of reporting methodology.

Regarding methodology, the Secretary-General noted that there were basically three categories of activities that, by virtue of their distinct nature, required different reporting formats: substantive activities (including reports, publications and public information); servicing bodies; and other activities for which programmatic descriptions were not sufficiently detailed to permit reporting by either of the other two formats. Tables in the report gave summaries of programmed output by category of activity, comparisons of programmed outputs for 1986-1987 with those for 1984-1985, and outputs postponed from 1984-1985.

Concerning all the programmes covered, the overall implementation rate in 1986-1987 lagged behind that of the previous biennium by 6.6 per cent, the most likely cause being the appreciably higher vacancy rate in a number of departments due to the Organization's freeze on recruitment imposed in reaction to the current financial crisis. Vacancies in the Professional category during 1986-1987 averaged 13 per cent and reached 15 per cent by the end of 1987.

In a July addendum,[3] the Secretary-General gave a breakdown of the programme performance of all 29 sections of the 1986-1987 programme budget.

CPC consideration. CPC considered the Secretary-General's report at its 1988 session[4] and noted the adjustments in methodology and presentation. It expressed concern that the overall programme delivery rate had decreased by about 7 per cent compared with the previous biennium. Noting that all outputs, regardless of type, were treated similarly, CPC recommended that the methodology be refined to present a qualitative and quantitative classification. It expressed concern over the high rates of postponed and terminated outputs, recommending that future reports give the reasons and authority for these actions and also indicate the future status of those outputs postponed. CPC also recommended that the Secretary-General further review the definition for termination of outputs and that the General Assembly give due consideration to the addendum to the report, which, because of its late issuance, CPC was unable to take into account.

In **resolution 1988/62**, the Economic and Social Council endorsed CPC's conclusions and recommendations.

JIU consideration. In January 1988, the Joint Inspection Unit (JIU) reported on the performance and results of United Nations programmes, which included monitoring, evaluation and management review.[5]

JIU recommended, among other things, that the Secretary-General replace the current programme performance report with one that analysed progress and results against the established objectives for each United Nations subprogramme.

It also recommended (recommendation 2) that the Secretary-General assess the staffing of the Central Evaluation Unit to ensure it had the necessary resources; add at least one more Professional staff member to the Central Monitoring Unit in the Office of Programme Planning, Budget and Finance; and strengthen the evaluation capacity of the United Nations in general. It was further recommended that ACABQ, the Fifth Committee and the Committee on Conferences consider requesting an annual in-depth Secretariat report on management improvement actions (recommendation 3). JIU stated that high priority should be given by the Secretary-General to establishing a computerized management information system which integrated both performance and financial information (recommendation 4).

In May,[6] the Secretary-General said the JIU recommendation to replace the current programme performance report would be considered, but he pointed out that a summary in a revised format would be at variance with the rules governing programme planning, and would create a voluminous report of some 500 pages for the Assembly and CPC to examine since there were some 470 subprogrammes. The Secretary-General said that the matter of staffing had been taken into account in the recent restructuring of the office in question.

Regarding the annual review report on management improvement actions, the Secretary-General stated that once the question of an integrated management information system for the entire Secretariat had been dealt with by the General Assembly and was operational, such reporting would be one of its outputs. He added that, in developing that system, consideration would be given to computerization.

Medium-term plan revisions and extension

The medium-term plan for 1984-1989, covering the entire range of United Nations activities, was first adopted by the General Assembly in 1982[7] and revised in 1984[8] and 1986.[9] In 1987,[10] the Assembly had endorsed the recommendations of the Secretary-General and CPC[11] to extend the medium-term plan to cover 1990 and 1991.

In April 1988,[12] the Secretary-General submitted revisions to extend the medium-term plan to cover 1990-1991; to incorporate new developments or mandates; and to provide a framework for the proposed 1990-1991 programme budget. He proposed revisions to 27 of the 31 major budget programmes.

Three types of revisions were suggested: completely new subprogrammes, substantive revisions of existing programmes or subprogrammes, and small textual revisions. One hundred and fifty-two programmes were identified under the 31 major programmes, with the Secretary-General proposing the creation of one additional programme on research and the collection of information. Of the 485 subprogrammes (averaging eight per programme), he proposed that 105 be revised and 19 be deleted. He also proposed that 12 new subprogrammes be added to the current plan.

The 19 subprogrammes suggested for deletion, with their work reassigned to other programmes, were under the following programmes: Division of Narcotic Drugs; public information; human settlements; Economic Commission for Western Asia (ESCWA); international trade; development finance; Economic Commission for Latin America and the Caribbean (ECLAC); statistics; programme planning, budgeting and financial services; human resources management; communications; technical support services; and programme planning and co-ordination.

The 12 new subprogrammes would be created under research and the collection of information; Economic and Social Commission for Asia and the Pacific (ESCAP); Economic Commission for Africa (ECA); social development and humanitarian affairs; programme planning, budgeting and financial services; and technical support services.

On 16 November 1988,[13] the Chairman of the Fifth Committee forwarded to the Assembly the comments of the Chairmen of the Assembly's six other Main Committees on the proposed revisions. Each Chairman set out the views of his Committee on those chapters which concerned it and indicated comments by individual Member States or groups of States. Annexed were the views of six States expressed in the First Committee on the questions of disarmament and nuclear weapons as they related to the medium-term plan.

In its recommendations on the Secretary-General's proposed revisions to the medium-term plan,[4] CPC called for a new and more practical type of presentation of the plan and its revisions. It felt the report lacked clarity, due in part to a selective inclusion of legislative mandates and to technical deficiencies. The Committee gave detailed suggestions by chapter for textual changes to the proposed revised plan.

According to ACABQ,[14] it was difficult to assess the effects of all the latest proposed revisions. The Committee recalled that the current medium-term plan had been substantially revised since first being issued, a situation which impaired the plan's utility, gave rise to serious confusion and was to be avoided in future. Revisions and addenda should be issued when additions, subtractions, substitutions or modifications were required. ACABQ strongly believed that the mere reorganization, merger or deletion of organizational units that did not materially affect the programme of work or related priorities should not lead to the publication of revisions. The Secretariat should submit to CPC and ACABQ proposals on the best way of handling revisions to future medium-term plans.

Preparation of the 1992-1997 medium-term plan

In 1988, the Secretary-General continued to put forward his proposals for the medium-term plan beginning in 1992. Following up on his 1987 note,[15] he submitted in May 1988, at the Assembly's 1987 request,[16] a draft introduction to the plan.[17]

He suggested that the plan be simplified and that the current division into four "parts"— political, legal and humanitarian, public information, and economic and social—lacked practical significance and unnecessarily complicated the structure. Restructuring did not imply any overall reduction of the Organization's role, he said. On the contrary, it should help clarify the Organization's aims and enhance its performance.

The basic priorities of the Organization as laid down in the Charter had not changed, the Secretary-General said. The plan would comprise four major programmes: peace, security, disarmament (especially nuclear disarmament) and self-determination of peoples; international law, human rights and fundamental freedoms; economic and social advancement of all peoples; and information and common services. Among priorities for the 1990s were the reinforcement of the abilities of the Security Council, a comprehensive just and lasting settlement of the Arab-Israeli conflict, ending *apartheid* and restoring freedom and independence in southern Africa, resolving the critical economic situation in Africa, and reducing poverty worldwide.

A suggested calendar of consultations on the 1992-1997 medium-term plan was put forward by the Secretary-General in September 1988.[18] The consultations were to take place during 1989 with the intergovernmental bodies concerned. The Secretary-General recommended that the Assembly authorize him to issue instructions for the preparation of the plan, and to request the sectoral, functional and regional bodies to recommend priorities among subprogrammes in their field of competence. CPC recommended approval of the calendar.[4]

ACABQ stated, also in September,[14] that the Secretary-General should attempt to streamline the calendar of consultations further, particularly when preparing future medium-term plans. It felt that the Secretariat otherwise might become so involved in the cycle of preparations for the plan that it would lose sight of other imperatives, such as monitoring its implementation. ACABQ suggested the adoption of the calendar as submitted by the Secretary-General.

GENERAL ASSEMBLY ACTION

On 21 December, on the recommendation of the Fifth Committee, the General Assembly adopted without vote **resolution 43/219**.

Programme planning

The General Assembly,

Recalling its resolutions 31/93 of 14 December 1976, 32/197 of 20 December 1977, 37/234 of 21 December 1982, 38/227 A and B of 20 December 1983, 40/240 of 18 December 1985, 41/213 of 19 December 1986 and 42/215 of 21 December 1987 and Economic and Social Council resolutions 2008(LX) of 14 May 1976, 1988/62 and 1988/64 of 27 July 1988 and 1988/77 of 29 July 1988,

Having considered the report of the Committee for Programme and Co-ordination on the work of its twenty-eighth session and the relevant parts of the report of the Economic and Social Council for 1988,

Having considered also the proposed revisions to the medium-term plan for the period 1984-1989, the reports of the Secretary-General on the programme performance of the United Nations for the biennium 1986-1987 and on the application of evaluation findings in programme design, delivery and policy directives, and the notes by the Secretary-General on the preparation of the next medium-term plan and on the calendar of consultations on the medium-term plan for the period starting in 1992,

Having considered further the views expressed in the Main Committees of the General Assembly on the proposed revisions to the medium-term plan for the period 1984-1989 (extended to 1991) and on the draft introduction to the medium-term plan for the period beginning in 1992,

Taking note of the report of the Advisory Committee on Administrative and Budgetary Questions on the proposed revisions to the medium-term plan for the period 1984-1989, the calendar of consultations on the medium-term plan for the period starting in 1992 and the preparation of the next medium-term plan,

Taking note also of the report of the Joint Inspection Unit entitled ''Reporting on the performance and results of United Nations programmes: monitoring, evaluation and management review components'' and the comments of the Secretary-General thereon,

Reaffirming the importance of the programming and co-ordinating functions within the United Nations carried out by the Committee for Programme and Co-ordination as the main subsidiary organ of the General Assembly and the Economic and Social Council for planning, programming and co-ordination,

Reiterating the need to improve continuously the programme planning, budgeting, monitoring and evaluation process in the Organization and the need for the participation of Member States from an early stage and throughout the process,

Emphasizing that future programme performance and evaluation reports should assist Member States in measuring results against established objectives,

I

Regulations and rules governing programme planning, the programme aspects of the budget, the monitoring of implementation and the methods of evaluation

Stresses the need to implement fully all the provisions of the Regulations and Rules Governing Programme Planning, the Programme Aspects of the Budget, the Monitoring of Implementation and the Methods of Evaluation;

II

Programme planning

1. *Reiterates* the importance of the medium-term plan as the principal policy directive of the United Nations;

2. *Stresses* the role of the medium-term plan in contributing to the improvement of the efficiency and the effectiveness of the United Nations in the implementation of its mandated activities, and thus to the enhancement of the role of the United Nations as set out in the Charter of the United Nations;

3. *Adopts* the revisions to the medium-term plan for the period 1984-1989 (extended to 1991), as modified by the recommendations made by the Committee for Programme and Co-ordination at its twenty-eighth session and the Economic and Social Council at its second regular session of 1988, taking into account the views expressed in the Main Committees of the General Assembly, and taking note of the observations made by the Advisory Committee on Administrative and Budgetary Questions;

4. *Decides* that the next medium-term plan of the United Nations shall cover the period 1992-1997;

5. *Requests* the Secretary-General to ensure effective co-ordination with the specialized agencies, including

those having a different planning cycle, and to review, through the Administrative Committee on Co-ordination, the question of harmonization of planning and budgeting cycles in the United Nations system;

6. *Endorses* the recommendations of the Committee for Programme and Co-ordination on the calendar of consultations proposed by the Secretary-General for the preparation of the medium-term plan for the period 1992-1997 in the light of the recommendations of the Advisory Committee on Administrative and Budgetary Questions to the extent that they are feasible;

7. *Requests* the Secretary-General, in revising his draft introduction and preparing the proposed medium-term plan for the period 1992-1997, including its structure, to take into account the views expressed by Member States on the preparation of the next medium-term plan and to act in full accordance with the pertinent Regulations and Rules Governing Programme Planning, the Programme Aspects of the Budget, the Monitoring of Implementation and the Methods of Evaluation concerning the content, formulation and presentation of the medium-term plan;

8. *Invites* all intergovernmental bodies, when considering in 1989 the pertinent portions of the proposed medium-term plan for the period 1992-1997, to give due attention to the most appropriate structure for the major programme or major programmes, programmes and sub-programmes submitted for their consideration, as compared with the current structure and in the light of an analysis of the objectives, trends and general orientations derived from the mandates of the intergovernmental bodies, to be provided by the Secretary-General;

9. *Requests* the Secretary-General to provide intergovernmental bodies with relevant evaluation studies as approved by the General Assembly, where available, to facilitate their consideration of pertinent portions of the proposed medium-term plan for the period 1992-1997;

10. *Also requests* the Secretary-General to submit to the General Assembly, through the Committee for Programme and Co-ordination and the Advisory Committee on Administrative and Budgetary Questions, a consolidated summary of the comments and recommendations made by Member States and the intergovernmental bodies referred to above, in particular concerning the structure of the plan, together with his proposed medium-term plan for the period 1992-1997;

11. *Endorses* the recommendations of the Committee for Programme and Co-ordination and the Advisory Committee on Administrative and Budgetary Questions regarding the need for a new and more practical type of presentation of the medium-term plan and of its revisions, preferably in loose leaf format, in order to improve the utility of the plan document and to facilitate its review and use by the intergovernmental bodies concerned and by the Secretariat;

III
Monitoring, evaluation and reports of the Joint Inspection Unit

1. *Stresses again* the need for improving the monitoring and evaluation functions in the United Nations in accordance with the Regulations and Rules Governing Programme Planning, the Programme Aspects of the Budget, the Monitoring of Implementation and the Methods of Evaluation, so as to provide adequate feed-back for the formulation of the medium-term plan and of programme budgets and for the effective implementation of programmes, as well as to provide Member States with a basis for more informed decision-making;

2. *Requests* the Secretary-General to submit a report on the methodological and practical aspects concerning implementation of recommendation 1 of the Joint Inspection Unit as contained in its report entitled "Reporting on the performance and results of United Nations programmes: monitoring, evaluation and management review components", with some specific examples using the sample form contained in annex II to the report;

3. *Endorses* recommendation 2 of the Joint Inspection Unit in the light of the comments of the Secretary-General thereon;

4. *Requests* the Secretary-General to submit concrete proposals on the means of implementing recommendation 3 of the Joint Inspection Unit in the current circumstances;

5. *Takes note* of recommendation 4 of the Joint Inspection Unit and endorses the views of the Secretary-General thereon;

6. *Endorses* the conclusions and recommendations of the Committee for Programme and Co-ordination contained in paragraphs 86 and 87 of its report and requests the Secretary-General to present a timetable for the implementation of the recommendations on self-evaluation contained in his report on the application of evaluation findings in programme design, delivery and policy directives as well as for completing initial evaluation training and providing central evaluation services;

7. *Requests* the Secretary-General to submit to the General Assembly at its forty-fourth session, through the Committee for Programme and Co-ordination, a consolidated progress report on the various requests contained in section III of the present resolution;

8. *Reiterates its request* to the Secretary-General that the programme performance and in-depth evaluation reports, together with the conclusions and recommendations of the Committee for Programme and Co-ordination thereon, as endorsed by the General Assembly, be submitted to the relevant intergovernmental and expert bodies to ensure follow-up action;

IV
Joint meetings of the Committee for Programme and Co-ordination and the Administrative Committee on Co-ordination

Takes note of Economic and Social Council resolution 1988/64;

V
Other conclusions and recommendations

Endorses those other conclusions and recommendations formulated by the Committee for Programme and Co-ordination at its twenty-eighth session which have not otherwise been approved by the General Assembly at its forty-third session.

General Assembly resolution 43/219

21 December 1988   Meeting 84   Adopted without vote

Approved by Fifth Committee (A/43/979) without vote, 18 December (meeting 50); draft by Cuba (A/C.5/43/L.18) following informal consultations; agenda item 115.
Meeting numbers. GA 43rd session: 5th Committee 19, 25, 26, 29, 31, 34, 50; plenary 84.

Programme evaluation

In his ongoing efforts to improve the evaluation of United Nations programmes, the Secretary-General in March 1988[19] submitted to the General Assembly through CPC a report on the application of evaluation findings in programme design, delivery and policy directives. The report, the first of its kind on a biennial basis, was conducted in accordance with the Regulations and Rules Governing Programme Planning, the Programme Aspects of the Budget, the Monitoring of Implementation and the Methods of Evaluation, which called for self-evaluation and in-depth studies. In 1987, the Assembly had endorsed CPC's recommendation that evaluation methodology continue to be refined.[16]

The Secretary-General noted that in-depth studies were conducted at the major programme level by an external unit, and that in-depth evaluations by the Central Evaluation Unit, at the request of CPC, covered programmes at Headquarters, the regional commissions and sectoral bodies.

He noted also that the self-evaluation system established in 1986[20] required all programme managers to ensure its systematic integration in each stage of programme planning. The system also highlighted the importance of managerial accountability. The Secretary-General concluded that the machinery for evaluation was in place and its integration into the whole programme planning, budgeting and monitoring cycle was proceeding gradually. Its slow but steady introduction would require further attention to enable it to function effectively, and constant efforts would be needed to ensure that it was viewed as a tool for assisting programme managers and not for detecting failures or reducing funding. The Secretary-General suggested that CPC might wish to recommend that he strengthen the programme planning, budgeting, monitoring and evaluation components for integrated management and policy-making.

CPC considered the Secretary-General's report in May 1988.[4] It recommended further strengthening of evaluation and agreed to endorse the Secretary-General's recommendations. It also agreed that evaluation should be fully integrated into the programme planning, budgeting and monitoring process.

The General Assembly, in adopting **resolution 43/219**, endorsed CPC's recommendations and requested the Secretary-General to present a timetable for implementing his recommendations on self-evaluation as well as for completing initial evaluation training and providing central evaluation services.

Joint Inspection Unit

Throughout 1988, the Joint Inspection Unit continued to issue reports addressing various aspects of the inspection, review or evaluation of selected programmes of the United Nations system. In its January report on the performance and results of United Nations programmes: monitoring evaluation and management review components,[21] JIU stated that the method currently used to review programmes was still incomplete, as there was no systematic reporting on performance and results. The biennial programme performance reports conducted by the Secretariat were neither timely nor analytical and were scarcely used.

In late 1986, the report said, the Secretariat had introduced a new system of built-in self-evaluation. Unfortunately, CPC had received only a brief biennial report summarizing general conclusions about evaluation and programme design. JIU felt it was critical that the new framework be used to produce reports that would firmly integrate evaluation into programme decision-making; provide timely information on programme progress; establish accountability for performance; and help Member States ensure the most cost-effective use of scarce programme funds.

The report suggested that the Secretary-General replace the current output-counting programme performance report with one that analysed progress made and results achieved against the established objectives for each United Nations subprogramme. Even though the Secretariat-wide evaluation system called for by the Assembly in 1981[22] would most likely never be established, certain actions should be taken to strengthen the existing system. Those measures included adequate staffing of central units and strengthened evaluation and performance reporting in major units.

Noting that although administration, management and conference services support functions consumed almost half the United Nations regular budget, JIU pointed out that they provided almost no reporting to intergovernmental bodies on actual gains achieved in efficiency, service quality or productivity. JIU suggested that the relevant intergovernmental bodies consider requesting an in-depth review report annually in a selected administrative support or conference services area.

In September 1988,[23] JIU submitted to the General Assembly its report on the representation of organizations of the United Nations system at conferences and meetings. It highlighted what it felt were inefficiencies in the conference invitation procedure and the need to streamline the process, particularly in view of the Organization's financial crisis. It suggested also that significant savings in travel expenses could be made by increasing the use of field and liaison offices as meeting places.

In 1987,[24] the Assembly had invited JIU to introduce several suggestions for self-improvement

that it had made in its report on its July 1986–
June 1987 activities.[25] The implementation of
those improvements was followed up in JIU's report on its work from 1 July 1987 to 30 June
1988.[26] JIU stated that its 1988 work programme
had been reviewed by CPC in 1988 and, in June,
it had a fruitful discussion with ACABQ on a number
of studies in the work programme. The achievement of a more collective approach to JIU business
had been discussed thoroughly and its current report had been significantly broadened in response
to the Assembly's 1987 request[24] that the Unit include a section on JIU's findings regarding implementation of its recommendations.

In response to another Assembly request, the
report included the guidelines JIU followed for
selecting, conducting and reporting on its inspections. Under those guidelines, it prepared reports,
notes and confidential letters on the work of its
participating organizations only, i.e., those that
had accepted its statute. JIU's work programme,
formally approved by the JIU Inspectors each
January, included at least one item of interest to
each participating organization. A reasonable
number of studies were to be addressed to the
major intergovernmental bodies with inter-agency
responsibilities, such as the Economic and Social
Council, CPC and the Governing Council of
UNDP, as well as to the Fifth Committee.

The guidelines also called for some items to be
chosen from each of the following subject areas:
substantive programmes, technical co-operation,
personnel questions, administration, conference
services, and programme planning and budgeting. Studies should have a direct bearing on the
efficiency of services, substantively as well as ad-
ministratively, and should aim to improve
management methods, attain common or comparable standards and achieve greater co-
ordination among organizations.

The 1988 JIU work programme was submitted
by the Secretary-General to the Assembly in
February,[27] together with the nucleus of the
Unit's work programme for 1989-1990.

The Secretary-General reported on the implementation of the 1987 recommendations of JIU
in September 1988.[28] In June,[29] he commented
on JIU's 1987 report on autonomous research institutes of the United Nations.[30]

Regarding membership of JIU, the Administrative Committee on Co-ordination (ACC), in April
1988,[31] requested its Organizational Committee
to examine the consultation procedure with regard
to reviewing candidates for appointment. The
Committee was to use the proposals made by the
United Nations Educational, Scientific and Cultural Organization (UNESCO) as the basis of its review, and submit recommendations for enhancing the participation of ACC in those procedures

to the Committee in 1988. In October,[32] ACC
requested the Secretary-General, as ACC Chairman, to bring its concerns regarding the current
procedures of the appointment of JIU members to
the attention of the President of the General Assembly and invite him to consult with the regional
groups on those concerns.

GENERAL ASSEMBLY ACTION

On 21 December, on the recommendation of
the Fifth Committee, the General Assembly
adopted **resolution 43/221** without vote.

Joint Inspection Unit

The General Assembly,

Recalling its resolutions 40/259 of 18 December 1985,
41/213 of 19 December 1986 and, in particular, 42/218
of 21 December 1987,

Having considered the report of the Joint Inspection Unit
on its activities during the period 1 July 1987 to 30 June
1988, together with the report of the Secretary-General
on the implementation of the recommendations of the
Unit,

1. *Takes note* of the report of the Joint Inspection
Unit;

2. *Welcomes* the measures introduced thus far in improving the quality, effectiveness and presentation of
the reports of the Joint Inspection Unit pursuant to
General Assembly resolution 42/218;

3. *Encourages* the Joint Inspection Unit to continue
its efforts towards this end, particularly with regard to
a section in its annual report on its findings concerning
the implementation of its recommendations;

4. *Also encourages* the Joint Inspection Unit when
drawing up future reports to limit where possible the
narrative part and to expand the evaluative part therein,
while offering recommendations for improvement that
are both practical and feasible;

5. *Takes note* of the work programme of the Joint
Inspection Unit for 1988 and the nucleus of its proposed
work programme for 1989-1990;

6. *Requests* the Joint Inspection Unit to consider a
more selective approach in drawing up its work programme with a view to limiting the quantity and improving the quality of its reports;

7. *Invites* the Joint Inspection Unit, taking into account its other responsibilities, to include in its proposed
work programme the provision of advice to participating organizations on their methods of internal evaluation and the undertaking of more *ad hoc* evaluations of
programmes and activities, with due regard to programmatic aspects identified by the Committee for Programme and Co-ordination and taking fully into account the mandates of the organizations concerned;

8. *Also invites* the Joint Inspection Unit, in this respect, to give greater attention to management, budgetary and administrative issues, including those identified by the Advisory Committee on Administrative and
Budgetary Questions in its reports on the administrative and budgetary co-ordination of the United Nations
with the specialized agencies and the International
Atomic Energy Agency and by the Board of Auditors
in its audit opinions and reports, as well as those areas
of the United Nations system undergoing reform;

9. *Requests* the Secretary-General and the Joint Inspection Unit, in bringing to the attention of the appropriate bodies of the United Nations system all reports of the Unit on matters within their respective spheres of competence, to arrange for the earliest possible introduction of reports of the Unit;

10. *Requests* the Joint Inspection Unit to recommend new procedures designed to encourage more detailed consideration of its reports by the appropriate bodies of the United Nations system;

11. *Expresses its appreciation* to the Secretary-General for the improved content and format of his report on the implementation of the recommendations of the Joint Inspection Unit;

12. *Invites* the Secretary-General, in his capacity as Chairman of the Administrative Committee on Co-ordination and in consultation with the Joint Inspection Unit, to ensure the maintenance of an efficient and effective research capability within the secretariat of the Unit;

13. *Underlines* the importance of applying the highest standards in selecting candidates for appointment as inspectors, as stipulated in chapter 2 of the statute of the Joint Inspection Unit, and of giving special emphasis to experience in national or international administrative and financial matters, including management questions and, where possible, knowledge of the United Nations or other international organizations;

14. *Also underlines*, in this respect, the importance of the consultation process for reviewing the qualifications of the proposed candidates in accordance with article 3, paragraph 2, of the statute of the Joint Inspection Unit;

15. *Requests* the Secretary-General to bring the present resolution to the attention of the executive heads of the participating organizations of the Joint Inspection Unit;

16. *Requests* the Joint Inspection Unit to take into account the guidelines outlined above in finalizing its work programme for 1989-1990 and to report to the General Assembly at its forty-fourth session on the progress made in the implementation of the present resolution.

General Assembly resolution 43/221

21 December 1988   Meeting 84   Adopted without vote

Approved by Fifth Committee (A/43/738) without vote, 20 October (meeting 12); draft by Vice-Chairman (A/C.5/43/L.3) following informal consultations; agenda item 118.
Meeting numbers. GA 43rd session: 5th Committee 4-7, 12; plenary 84.

REFERENCES
(1)A/43/326 & Corr.1. (2)YUN 1986, p. 1045. (3)A/43/326/Add.1 & Corr.1,2. (4)A/43/16. (5)A/43/124. (6)A/43/124/Add.1. (7)YUN 1982, p. 1430, GA res. 37/234, 21 Dec. 1982. (8)YUN 1984, p. 1138, GA res. 39/238, 18 Dec. 1984. (9)YUN 1986, p. 1041, GA res. 41/203, 11 Dec. 1986. (10)YUN 1987, p. 1118, GA res. 42/215, 21 Dec. 1987. (11)*Ibid.*, p. 1122. (12)A/43/6 & Corr.1. (13)A/C.5/43/36. (14)A/43/626 & Corr.1. (15)YUN 1987, p. 1123. (16)*Ibid.*, p. 1118, GA res. 42/215, 21 Dec. 1987. (17)A/43/329. (18)A/43/329/Add.1. (19)A/43/179. (20)YUN 1986, p. 1043. (21)A/43/124. (22)YUN 1981, p. 1312, GA res. 36/228 B, 18 Dec. 1981. (23)A/43/586. (24)YUN 1987, p. 1126, GA res. 42/218, 21 Dec. 1987. (25)*Ibid.*, p. 1124. (26)A/43/34. (27)A/43/161. (28)A/43/556. (29)A/43/397. (30)A/42/540. (31)ACC/1988/DEC/1-18 (dec. 1988/9). (32)ACC/1988/DEC/19-31 (dec. 1988/26).

Administrative and budgetary co-ordination in the UN system

The administrative and budgetary co-ordination of the United Nations with the specialized agencies and the International Atomic Energy Agency (IAEA) was the subject of a report submitted to the General Assembly on 31 October 1988 by ACABQ.[1] In accordance with its terms of reference, ACABQ met with executive heads of 13 organizations whose agreements with the United Nations provided for transmittal of their budgets for review by the General Assembly.

Those organizations were ILO, FAO, UNESCO, ICAO, UPU, WHO, ITU, WMO, IMO, WIPO, IFAD, UNIDO and IAEA.

The impact of currency fluctuations and inflation was the special topic taken up by the Advisory Committee during its deliberations with the organizations in question. Also contained in the report were data on the following: total amounts of the approved budgets, including supplementary estimates, 1980-1989; total net contributions of Member States actually payable under approved regular budgets, including supplementary estimates, 1980-1989; established posts, 1987-1989; regular budget contributions to technical co-operation activities, 1987-1989; extrabudgetary funds administered by the United Nations system of organizations, both contributions and expenditures, 1986-1987; working capital funds for 1989; scales of assessment applicable in 1989; and collection of contributions, 1987-1988.

The regular budgets of the Organization, the specialized agencies (excluding IFAD) and IAEA for 1989 amounted to $2,121,970,975, of which $2,008,756,760 was to be covered by assessed contributions, the report said. Also, depending on decisions made by the Assembly and the Security Council, further assessed contributions for the United Nations were likely to arise in 1989 for peace-keeping operations. For the 12-month period through October 1988, the total amount assessed for peace-keeping operations was $205.4 million.

As at 30 September 1988, the total of all outstanding budget contributions was $1,156,713,200, or 58.01 per cent of total net contributions of Member States actually payable in respect of that year, as compared with $1,078,557,800, or 65.3 per cent as at the same date in 1987.

According to the report, cash payments received by the United Nations system of organizations from voluntary contributions, which are labelled extra-budgetary funds, totalled $2,974,955,500 for 1987, and $2,562,238,100 in 1986. Of that, Member States contributed $2,796,237,700 in 1987 and $2,408,531,200 in 1986. Some $84,414,200 came from non-member States in 1987, while $71,888,000 was forthcoming from them in 1986. Expenditure of extrabudgetary funds administered by the United Nations system of organizations totalled $3,647,415,500 in 1987, compared with $3,527,801,000 in 1986.

The total number of established posts authorized or requested under the regular budgets of the specialized agencies (excluding IFAD) and IAEA for 1989 was 13,605, which was 36 more than the 1988 total of 13,569. The number of established posts authorized or requested under the regular budget of the United Nations for 1989 was 11,169, unchanged from 1988. Therefore, a grand total of 24,774 established posts for 1989 had been authorized or requested under the regular budgets of the United Nations, the specialized agencies (excluding IFAD) and IAEA.

In extensive comments on the budgets of each of the specialized agencies and of IAEA, the Ad-

visory Committee discussed, among other things: appropriations for 1986-1987; actual expenditure; actual income collected and cash deficit; appropriations for 1988-1989; the working capital funds; measures taken by each to deal with the savings or loss due to currency fluctuations; and posts under the regular budget.

GENERAL ASSEMBLY ACTION

By **decision 43/451** of 21 December 1988, the General Assembly took note with appreciation of ACABQ's report and requested the Secretary-General to refer it to the executive heads of the organizations of the United Nations system, through ACC. Also, it decided to transmit the report to the Board of Auditors, CPC, the International Civil Service Commission and JIU.

REFERENCE

(1)A/43/760.

Chapter II

United Nations officials

In 1988, the Secretary-General presented a detailed plan to reduce the number of posts in the United Nations. The reductions would affect the work of the Organization and the volume of its programmed activities would have to be reduced.

The Organization continued to operate under a recruitment freeze, introduced in 1986 as part of the response to the United Nations financial crisis. However, in February, the Secretary-General introduced limited recruitment where qualified internal candidates could not be found and in departments and offices with high vacancy rates.

The Secretary-General also reported a disturbing overall increase in the number of officials of the United Nations system who had been arrested and detained, or who had disappeared.

The presence and position of women in the Secretariat improved during 1988, despite the limited recruitment policy. The Secretary-General appointed a senior-level woman as a focal point for the action programme to improve the status of women in the Secretariat, and the Economic and Social Council requested each organization in the United Nations system to designate a similar high-level co-ordinator.

The International Civil Service Commission made several recommendations affecting United Nations personnel and submitted a preliminary report on conditions of service of staff in the Professional and higher categories. The General Assembly set out guidelines to be used by the Commission to complete the report (resolution 43/226).

The Secretary-General reported that marked progress in streamlining the Headquarters Joint Appeals Board had resulted in the virtual elimination of the case backlog. The Assembly requested that a fully revised internal justice system be established by the end of 1989 (43/224 B).

Personnel management

In early 1988, the Secretary-General, in view of the General Assembly's 1987 decision[1] that he review the freeze on recruitment of external candidates introduced in 1986,[2] and the recommendation of the Group of High-level Intergovernmental Experts to Review the Efficiency of the Administrative and Financial Functioning of the United Nations (Group of 18)[3] concerning the reduction of posts in the Secretariat, decided to introduce limited recruitment for vacant posts for which qualified internal candidates could not be identified through the vacancy management system. He also decided that flexibility in recruitment would continue for departments and offices with high vacancy rates, in particular the secretariats of regional commissions (see below).

Efforts were made to increase the mobility of Professional staff through the vacancy management and staff redeployment programme and this resulted in a significant number of staff movements between duty stations. The Secretary-General approved measures to facilitate this mobility, including enhanced entitlements for staff assigned or transferred to duty stations with high vacancy rates.

He also discussed the realignment of the periodic competitive examinations and reported that, during the period from 30 July 1987 to 1 June 1988, one internal competitive examination resulted in the selection of 21 candidates for promotion to the Professional level. An external exam was held in 1987 in four Member States—Greece, Japan, Mexico and the USSR—and 25 candidates were selected. Offers of appointment had been made to 23 (11 women and 12 men) so far.

Many components of the career development system, including counselling and succession planning, were deferred due to the Organization's financial crisis. However, special efforts were made to design some components of the career development plan for staff in the General Service and related categories. An emphasis on training was also incorporated in the staff reorganization to build a more efficient and effective Secretariat.

The Secretary-General submitted for consideration by the Assembly's Fifth (Administrative and Budgetary) Committee the views of the staff unions and associations of the United Nations Secretariat[4] on a number of personnel matters, including the functioning of the International Civil Service Commission (ICSC), the re-establishment of a climate of confidence through direct negotiations, and a comprehensive review of the conditions of service of the Professional and higher categories.

Staff composition

In October 1988, the Secretary-General presented to the General Assembly his annual report on the composition of the United Nations Secretariat —by nationality, sex and type of appointment —for the period covering 1 July 1987 to 30 June 1988.[5] The total number of staff of the United Nations Secretariat as at 30 June was 13,534, of whom 10,203 were paid from the regular budget and 3,331 from extrabudgetary sources.

Staff in the Professional category and above numbered 3,750; staff in the General Service and related categories were 8,777, and project personnel numbered 1,007.

During the reporting period, 66 appointments were made to Professional posts subject to geographical distribution.

On 30 June 1988, there were 10 unrepresented Member States, a number unchanged since 1 July 1987. There were 27 underrepresented Member States compared with 25 the previous year. Changes in representation stemmed not only from staff appointments and separations from service, but also from changes in the status of some staff members; reduced recruitment activities; and the introduction of new desirable ranges which incorporated the population factor in the ranges of individual Member States.

During the reporting period, 19 women were appointed to posts subject to geographical distribution, representing 28.8 per cent of the appointments made. This compared with a 28.6 per cent share of the appointments during the previous period.

GENERAL ASSEMBLY ACTION

On 21 December, on the recommendation of the Fifth Committee, the General Assembly adopted without vote **resolution 43/224 A.**

Composition of the Secretariat

The General Assembly,

Recalling Articles 100 and 101 of the Charter of the United Nations,

Reaffirming its resolutions 33/143 of 20 December 1978, 35/210 of 17 December 1980, 41/213 of 19 December 1986 and 42/220 A of 21 December 1987,

Emphasizing the independent international status of the staff of the Secretariat of the United Nations,

Taking note of the report of the Secretary-General on the composition of the Secretariat,

Noting that nationals of some Member States who served primarily on fixed-term contracts now accept long-term and permanent contracts for service with the Secretariat,

Concerned about a further deterioration in equitable geographical distribution of posts in the Secretariat, particularly at the higher echelons,

Bearing in mind the views on personnel questions expressed by Member States in the Fifth Committee during the forty-third session,

1. *Reiterates* its full support for the Secretary-General as chief administrative officer of the Organization and his prerogatives and responsibilities under the Charter of the United Nations;

2. *Requests* the Secretary-General to strengthen the role and emphasize the authority of the Office of Human Resources Management of the Secretariat in accordance with recommendation 41 of the Group of High-level Intergovernmental Experts to Review the Efficiency of the Administrative and Financial Functioning of the United Nations;

3. *Also requests* the Secretary-General, in order to preserve the principles of equitable geographical distribution and of rotation in the upper echelons of the Secretariat, to ensure that equal opportunity is given to candidates of all Member States when making appointments to all posts in the upper echelons, and not to extend, as a rule, the services of under-secretaries-general or assistant secretaries-general for a period exceeding ten years;

4. *Urges* the Secretary-General, whenever making appointments to posts subject to geographical distribution, to make every effort to recruit nationals of unrepresented and underrepresented Member States and candidates successful in the national competitive examinations, taking into consideration also paragraph 4 of resolution 41/206 A of 11 December 1986, in order to ensure that all such countries come closer to the midpoint of their desirable ranges;

5. *Reaffirms* the principle of equal opportunity, in accordance with the Charter, and the principle that no post should be considered the exclusive preserve of any Member State or group of States, and requests the Secretary-General to apply these principles faithfully, with due regard to the principle of equitable geographical distribution, which applies to all Member States;

6. *Urges* the Secretary-General to take additional measures to ensure that the nationals of developing countries are duly represented at the senior levels in accordance with the relevant resolutions of the General Assembly;

7. *Also urges* the Secretary-General, in addition to the action taken under paragraph 6 above to ensure that the nationals of other countries are also duly represented at the senior levels, in accordance with the relevant resolutions of the General Assembly;

8. *Requests* the Secretary-General to monitor closely the effects of the reduction of posts on geographical distribution, particularly at the higher levels, and to take appropriate measures to redress any imbalances;

9. *Also requests* the Secretary-General to give special attention to the filling of posts in organizational units with high vacancy rates, particularly the regional commissions;

10. *Further requests* the Secretary-General to continue his efforts aimed at the improvement of the composition of the Secretariat by ensuring a wide geographical distribution of staff at the Professional and higher levels in all main departments and offices;

11. *Urges* the Secretary-General to intensify his efforts towards the development of a comprehensive career development plan, based, *inter alia*, on competitive selection, for all staff, including General Service staff, in accordance with section III of the annex to General Assembly resolution 35/210, Assembly resolution 37/126 of 17 December 1982 and section I, paragraph 4, of resolution 42/220 A and the relevant Staff Regulations and Rules;

12. *Also urges* the Secretary-General to intensify his efforts towards increasing the mobility of staff and strengthening the training and retraining capabilities of the Secretariat;

13.   *Requests* the Secretary-General to complete the full realignment of internal and external examinations and to study their effect on geographical distribution and to submit proposals to the General Assembly as appropriate;

14.   *Also requests* the Secretary-General to report on the progress achieved on personnel matters to the General Assembly at its forty-fifth session.

General Assembly resolution 43/224 A

21 December 1988   Meeting 84   Adopted without vote

Approved by Fifth Committee (A/43/954) without vote, 15 December (meeting 48); draft by Sweden (A/C.5/43/L.12) following informal consultations; agenda item 121 *(a)*.

Meeting numbers. GA 43rd session: 5th Committee 14, 16, 18, 20, 22-26, 28, 30, 35, 48; plenary 84.

Post reductions

In April 1988,[6] the Secretary-General announced his plans to reduce the number of posts in the United Nations, as requested by the General Assembly in 1987[7] on the recommendation of the Group of 18.[3]

The Secretary-General proposed a target of 1,465 regularly funded posts for abolition by year-end 1989: 486 in the Professional category and above, and 979 at the General Service and other levels. This represented 13.02 per cent of 11,255 posts approved under the regular budget for 1988-1989. Besides a 25 per cent reduction of posts at the level of Under-Secretary-General and Assistant Secretary-General, proportionately greater cuts were proposed for the levels P-5 (Professional-5) to D-2 (Director-2). The only increase would be at the P-3 and P-2/P-1 levels. General Service and other level posts would decrease from 62.2 per cent to 61.6 per cent of the total number of posts.

The reductions ranged from 14.8 per cent (669 posts) in common services to 4.6 per cent (13 posts) in overall policy-making, direction and co-ordination.

For the Department of Conference Services at the two main conference centres—New York and Geneva—the Secretary-General proposed a target of 14.1 per cent, which would require a substantial reduction in the number of conferences and meetings planned for 1990-1991. Alternatively, he suggested that an overall 10 per cent post reduction could be achieved in the staffing of Conference Services in New York and Geneva without an excessive reduction in the conference-servicing capacity of the Organization.

The proposed post reductions were to be implemented through a combination of attrition, redeployment and controlled recruitment.

The Secretary-General said that programmes for 1990-1991 would have to be prepared in relation to a smaller Secretariat; however, there was not an automatic link, in all cases, between a smaller Secretariat and a reduced role for the Organization. Efficiency could be further improved through technological innovations and upgrades in management procedures, as well as through the consolidation of programmes and units.

In its report on the 1988-1989 programme budget,[8] the Advisory Committee on Administrative and Budgetary Questions (ACABQ) considered that to achieve the most realistic staff reductions in the Department of Conference Services, the target set by the Secretary-General should be adjusted downward, with "restoration" of 100 of the total 357 posts originally proposed for elimination. The restoration would bring the target for reductions under that budget section from 14.1 per cent to about 10.1 per cent. Full biennial costs of the 100 posts would amount to $12,893,900 net of staff assessment. ACABQ further recommended that the restoration be partially offset by a reduction of 50 posts in other areas, thereby bringing the total reduction for the Secretariat to 12.57 per cent instead of 13.02 per cent. The financing of the remaining 50 restored posts would not require additional appropriations.

The General Assembly, by **resolution 43/213** of 21 December, endorsed the recommendations of ACABQ.

High vacancy rates

In response to a 1987 General Assembly request,[9] the Secretary-General also reported on measures taken to improve the situation in the regional commissions and in those units of the Secretariat with the highest vacancy rates. In 1987, ACABQ had concluded that the average vacancy rates to be achieved over 1988-1989 to facilitate post reductions were likely to be significantly higher than those represented by the adjustment proposal of the Secretary-General. The Advisory Committee[2] recommended a greater turnover deduction of 2.5 per cent for all categories of staff. The vacancy rate for the Secretariat as at 29 February 1988 was 16 per cent.

The most seriously affected units were: the World Food Council with 31.3 per cent; the units located at Nairobi (the United Nations Environment Programme and the United Nations Centre for Human Settlements (Habitat)) with 28.3 per cent; the Economic Commission for Latin America and the Caribbean with 28.1 per cent; the Economic and Social Commission for Western Asia with 26.8 per cent; and the Economic Commission for Africa with 22.1 per cent.

The Secretary-General noted that posts vacated at the regional commissions remained unencumbered for longer periods than in the rest of the Secretariat due to their specialized or technical nature, and the mobility of staff among stations had been difficult to achieve. Twenty-five vacancies had been filled under the vacancy management and staff redeployment programme. Exceptions to the suspension of external recruitment to those units with high vacancy rates had been granted on a limited basis, accounting for 23 of the 84 authorized exceptions to the freeze. According to the Secretary-General's report, there were currently 127 vacancies in Secretariat units with high vacancy rates. The Secretary-General stated that he had authorized the regional commissions to recruit staff for short-term assignments of up to 11 months.

ACABQ[8] requested that updated information be provided to the Assembly at its current session, including specific data on recruitment at the P-1/P-2 levels.

Temporary recurrent posts

The Secretary-General proposed[10] that the 253 temporary recurrent posts financed under the regular budget be converted to established posts. The change, he said, would not affect the level of appropriation for the 1988-1989 biennium nor the targeted reductions of posts. The Secretary-General explained that most original mandates that had called for temporary posts had become permanent mandates and part of the regular work programme. In addition, the incumbents of temporary posts had not necessarily been assigned exclusively to the duties initially identified when their posts were created and the rationale for retaining the distinction between established and temporary posts had become rather tenuous.

ACABQ noted that 24 of the temporary recurrent posts had been proposed for abolition, thereby reducing the number of temporary recurrent posts being prepared for conversion to 229. It stated that it could not recommend a "blanket" conversion. Instead, it recommended that the proposal be resubmitted in the context of the programme budget for 1990-1991 so that each conversion proposal could be reviewed to determine if the functions were permanent enough to warrant establishing a permanent post.

Status of women in the Secretariat

The Secretary-General, responding to a 1985 resolution[11] by which the General Assembly had approved an action programme to address obstacles to the improvement of women's status in the United Nations Secretariat, submitted to the Fifth Committee in October 1988 a progress report.[12] The Group of 18[3] had recommended in 1986 that additional measures be taken to increase the proportion of women in the Professional categories, particularly at the higher levels.

According to the report, some progress had been achieved. As at 30 June 1988, the percentage of women occupying posts subject to geographical distribution in the United Nations Secretariat rose to 26.3 per cent, compared with 25.7 per cent in the previous period. An upward trend in the representation of women at the D-1 level and above also continued, but the distribution of women across various United Nations organizational units remained uneven, particularly in the regional commissions and in the United Nations Conference on Trade and Development (UNCTAD).

The institutional arrangements for continuation of the action programme were reviewed, as called for by the Assembly in 1987.[13] The Co-ordinator for the Improvement of the Status of Women in the Secretariat of the United Nations identified obstacles to the advancement of women and proposed policy changes. The review also monitored operational activities and the integration of new approaches and measures.

On 27 May, the Economic and Social Council, by **decision 1988/124**, requested the Secretary-General to extend the mandate of the Office of the Co-ordinator until the end of the 1988-1989 biennium, to review the situation at the end of that period, and to continue taking the necessary measures to ensure implementation of the action programme. In response to that request, the Secretary-General established a focal point within the immediate office of the Assistant Secretary-General for Human Resources Management to ensure co-ordination of the programme's implementation and to provide secretariat services to the Steering Committee for the Improvement of the Status of Women in the United Nations.

A further review of the action programme by the Steering Committee noted some improvement in the status of women and priorities for further action, including: the recruitment, assignment and promotion of women at senior levels; establishment of a career development system; and strengthening of training programmes and human resource planning systems.

The Secretary-General reported that several elements of the 1988-1989 work programme, based on the Steering Committee's recommendations, were being implemented, but there had been problems in establishing a career development system for the General Service staff in New York and at duty stations away from Headquarters.

In 1988,[14] ICSC continued to review progress with special measures for the recruitment of women.

United Nations organizations reported little progress in carrying out the 1985 ICSC recommendations.[15] While most made commitments to the principle of improving women's status, that was not always translated into action. The highest success rates had occurred in organizations that had set specific targets and established monitoring programmes.

The Commission requested its Chairman to invite governing bodies—particularly those that had shown little progress—to take up the matter at their next meetings and report to the Commission in 1989. ICSC also recommended that the organizations: stress the importance of commitment at the highest level to employ and promote more women, especially at the decision-making and policy level, and establish specific goals if they had not already done so; broaden and strengthen contacts with national recruitment services; amend personal history forms so that they could be shared with other agencies; and amend staff rules to allow the recruitment of spouses for established posts.

ECONOMIC AND SOCIAL COUNCIL ACTION

On 26 May, on the recommendation of its Second (Social) Committee, the Economic and Social Council adopted **resolution 1988/17** without vote.

Improvement of the status of women in the secretariats of the United Nations system

The Economic and Social Council,

Recalling that the Charter of the United Nations provides that no restrictions shall be placed on the eligibility of women and men to participate in any capacity and under conditions of equality in the work of the principal and subsidiary organs of the United Nations,

Noting the importance attached to the appointment of women at senior decision-making and managerial levels in paragraphs 306, 315, 356 and 358 of the Nairobi Forward-looking Strategies for the Advancement of Women,

Mindful of recommendation 46 of the Group of High-level Intergovernmental Experts to Review the Efficiency of the Administrative and Financial Functioning of the United Nations,

Referring to the report of the Secretary-General on the improvement of the status of women in the United Nations Secretariat,

Sharing the concern of the Secretary-General expressed in that report that the interests of women in the Secretariat should not suffer disproportionately from the impact of the restructuring and retrenchment measures being applied in the Secretariat,

1. *Requests* each organization of the United Nations system to designate, within existing resource allocations for personnel services, a high-level co-ordinator for the improvement of the status of women within that organization;

2. *Recommends* that each organization adopt specific action programmes and work plans outlining the measures to be taken to improve the status of women in its secretariat;

3. *Also recommends* that the Secretary-General take the necessary measures to ensure that current financial restraints and retrenchment measures do not have disproportionately negative consequences for women;

4. *Further recommends* that all organizations of the United Nations system take measures to ensure a greater proportion of women in the Professional category and above, especially at higher levels, in accordance with paragraph 358 of the Nairobi Forward-looking Strategies for the Advancement of Women, General Assembly resolution 40/258 B of 18 December 1985 and paragraph 8 of Assembly resolution 41/111 of 4 December 1986;

5. *Requests* the Secretary-General, in his capacity as Chairman of the Administrative Committee on Coordination, to report biennially in even-numbered years, within existing resources, to the Commission on the

Status of Women on progress made by the organizations of the United Nations system in improving the level of recruitment, conditions of service, career development and promotion opportunities of women;

6. *Also requests* the Secretary-General to continue to report to the General Assembly on the situation of women in the United Nations Secretariat and to transmit to the Commission on the Status of Women on a regular basis:

(*a*) The report of the Secretary-General on the improvement of the status of women in the United Nations Secretariat;

(*b*) Relevant sections of the annual report of the Secretary-General on the composition of the United Nations Secretariat;

(*c*) Relevant sections of background reports to the International Civil Service Commission;

(*d*) Relevant resolutions, decisions, reports and employment guidelines of the organizations of the United Nations common system, including information on the distribution of female staff members by nationality and by level.

Economic and Social Council resolution 1988/17

26 May 1988   Meeting 15   Adopted without vote

Approved by Second Committee (E/1988/90) without vote, 13 May (meeting 9); draft by Commission on women (E/1988/15); agenda item 11.

GENERAL ASSEMBLY ACTION

On 8 December, on the recommendation of the Third (Social, Humanitarian and Cultural) Committee, the General Assembly adopted without vote **resolution 43/103**.

Improvement of the status of women in the Secretariat

The General Assembly,

Taking into consideration the decision of the Secretary-General, in order to implement the action programme for the improvement of the status of women in the Secretariat by 1990 and the commitments to further action referred to in General Assembly resolution 42/62 of 30 November 1987, to deploy on a full-time basis a senior-level position with appropriate support, within existing resources, to the Office of the Assistant Secretary-General for Human Resources Management,

1. *Invites* the Secretary-General, as a matter of high priority, to implement fully the above-mentioned decision;

2. *Urges* the Secretary-General to consider, in accordance with the priorities contained in the fourth report of the Steering Committee for the Improvement of the Status of Women in the Secretariat, the appointment of a senior-level woman to the position designated as a focal point to ensure the implementation of the action programme for the improvement of the status of women in the Secretariat;

3. *Requests* the Secretary-General to report to the General Assembly at its forty-fourth session on the progress achieved in the implementation of the action programme for the improvement of the status of women in the Secretariat and that such information be submitted to the Commission on the Status of Women at its thirty-third session for comment.

General Assembly resolution 43/103

8 December 1988   Meeting 75   Adopted without vote

Approved by Third Committee (A/43/813) without vote, 11 November (meeting 40); 20-nation draft (A/C.3/43/L.28); agenda item 95.

Sponsors: Australia, Costa Rica, Cuba, Cyprus, Ghana, Greece, Guatemala, India, Indonesia, Iraq, Italy, Mexico, Morocco, New Zealand, Nicaragua, Philippines, Samoa, United States, Venezuela, Yugoslavia.

Meeting numbers. GA 43rd session: 3rd Committee 15, 23-30, 36, 40; plenary 75.

On 21 December, on the recommendation of the Fifth Committee, the General Assembly adopted without vote **resolution 43/224 C.**

Improvement of the status of women in the Secretariat

The General Assembly,

Recalling Articles 8, 100 and 101 of the Charter of the United Nations,

Recalling also all relevant resolutions on the improvement of the status of women in the Secretariat,

Recalling the relevant paragraphs of the Nairobi Forward-looking Strategies for the Advancement of Women, in particular paragraphs 315, 356 and 358,

Reaffirming the goal of increasing the number of women in posts subject to geographical distribution to 30 per cent of the total by 1990,

Noting with satisfaction that the question of the improvement of the status of women in the secretariats of the United Nations system continues to be a standing item on the agenda of the Administrative Committee on Co-ordination,

1. *Takes note* of the report of the Secretary-General and of his decision to deploy, on a full-time basis, a senior-level position, within existing resources, as focal point within the Office of Human Resources Management of the Secretariat, to monitor and facilitate the improvement of the status of women in the Secretariat;

2. *Requests* the Secretary-General to continue his efforts and to consider the introduction of additional measures, if necessary, in order to increase the number of women in posts subject to geographical distribution with a view to achieving, to the extent possible, an overall participation rate of 30 per cent of the total by 1990, without prejudice to the principle of equitable geographical distribution of posts, as was requested in paragraph 3 of resolution 40/258 B of 18 December 1985;

3. *Urges* the Secretary-General to increase his efforts to ensure an equitable representation of women from developing countries in posts subject to geographical distribution;

4. *Requests* the Secretary-General to intensify his efforts to increase the percentage of women in posts at the senior and policy-formulating levels, in particular the number of women from developing countries in these posts;

5. *Reiterates its request* to all Member States to continue to support the efforts of the United Nations and the specialized agencies to increase the proportion of women in the Professional category and above by, *inter alia,* nominating more women candidates and encouraging women to apply for vacant posts and to participate in national competitive examinations;

6. *Requests* the Secretary-General to submit a complete report to the General Assembly at its forty-fourth session on the continued implementation of the action programme for the improvement of the status of women in the Secretariat, in particular on the respective roles of the focal point and the Steering Committee for the Improvement of the Status of Women in the Secretariat, and on progress achieved in the implementation of the recommendations of the Steering Committee as contained in its fourth report, and to ensure that that information is presented to the Commission on the Status of Women at its thirty-third session.

General Assembly resolution 43/224 C

21 December 1988   Meeting 84   Adopted without vote

Approved by Fifth Committee (A/43/954) without vote, 15 December (meeting 48); draft by Sweden (A/C.5/43/L.12) following informal consultations; agenda item 121.

Meeting numbers. GA 43rd session: 5th Committee 14, 16, 18, 20, 22-26, 28, 30, 35, 48; plenary 84.

Staff language training

In 1988, the General Assembly again took up the question of working languages of the Secretariat and language training. In a 1984 report,[16] the Secretary-General had noted that the financial and other incentives offered to encourage the broader use of official languages had not fully met their objectives.

GENERAL ASSEMBLY ACTION

On 21 December 1988, on the recommendation of the Fifth Committee, the General Assembly adopted **resolution 43/224 D** without vote.

Working languages of the Secretariat and language training

The General Assembly,

Aware of the importance of the linguistic capability of the Secretariat for the efficient and effective functioning of the Organization,

Recalling its resolutions 2(I) of 1 February 1946, 2241 B (XXI) of 20 December 1966, 2359 B (XXII) of 19 December 1967 and 2480 B (XXIII) of 21 December 1968 on the use of working languages in the Secretariat,

Recalling also section III of its resolution 38/232 of 20 December 1983, and the report of the Secretary-General on the status of the linguistic skills of the United Nations staff, submitted pursuant to that resolution,

Desirous that the rules governing the use of the working languages of the Secretariat be fully applied in practice,

1. *Encourages* the Secretary-General, in the context of his efforts to ensure a better use of the working languages of the Secretariat, to take the measures available so as to enable staff to use the appropriate working languages in their written and oral communications, bearing in mind the particular situation at the regional commissions where other working languages are also used;

2. *Requests* the Secretary-General to encourage staff members, particularly those occupying posts subject to geographical distribution, to make full use of existing language training facilities, with a view to broadening their knowledge of all the languages of the Organization, and to continue to implement the provisions of section XVII of General Assembly resolution 36/235 of 18 December 1981;

3. *Invites* Member States to continue to make voluntary contributions, in line with existing procedures, to the existing language training facilities of the United Nations;

4. *Invites* the Secretary-General to submit to the General Assembly at its forty-fifth session a report on the implementation of the present resolution.

General Assembly resolution 43/224 D

21 December 1988   Meeting 84   Adopted without vote

Approved by Fifth Committee (A/43/954) without vote, 15 December (meeting 48); draft by Sweden (A/C.5/43/L.12, part D) following informal consultations; agenda item 121.
Meeting numbers. GA 43rd session: 5th Committee 14, 16, 18, 20, 22-26, 28, 30, 35, 48; plenary 84.

Staff rules

In September 1988,[17] the Secretary-General submitted his annual report to the General Assembly containing the texts of provisional amendments made to the staff rules of the United Nations since his previous report in 1987.[18] The changes—applicable to all staff except technical co-operation project personnel, staff members specifically engaged for conferences and other short-term service, and special interns—concerned education grants; assignment allowances; standards of accommodation for travel; terminal expenses; and scales for salary, pensionable remuneration and computation of separation payments.

The General Assembly, by **decision 43/454** of 21 December 1988, took note of the Secretary-General's report.

International Civil Service Commission

The International Civil Service Commission (ICSC) held its twenty-seventh session at Rome, Italy (7 January–24 March), and its twenty-eighth session in New York (11-29 July). The Commission examined issues derived from General Assembly decisions as well as from its own statute. A summary of its deliberations, recommendations and decisions was provided in its fourteenth annual report to the Assembly.[14] Total financial implications of ICSC's 1988 decisions and recommendations for the United Nations common system were approximately $14.1 million. Of that, $7.4 million related to programmes financed through regular budgets, while the remaining $6.7 million related to programmes paid for by voluntary contributions.

Functioning of ICSC

In response to a 1987 General Assembly request,[19] ICSC considered its functioning and relations between it and staff representatives.[14] It examined various points raised in the Fifth Committee and decided to shorten its annual report and improve the format, and to consider at a future session other issues raised by that Committee. The Commission also reviewed its working methods, noting that a number of problems interfered with its effective functioning, including insufficient information about complex issues prior to sessions and crowded agendas which limited discussion on important matters. It also noted criticism by staff organizations that the current arrangements did not allow for their views to be adequately taken into account. ICSC agreed to arrange its work programme so as to take up during the first week priority items on which decisions and recommendations to the General Assembly were required. It also agreed on a number of organizational procedures to streamline its work.

The Commission was informed by the Federation of International Civil Servants' Associations (FICSA) and by the Co-ordinating Committee for Independent Staff Unions and Associations of their decision to suspend participation in all activities of the Commission. ICSC deemed it important that staff representatives participate in its work and expressed regret over their absence.

GENERAL ASSEMBLY ACTION

On 21 December 1988, on the recommendation of the Fifth Committee, the General Assembly adopted **resolution 43/226** without vote.

United Nations common system: report of the International Civil Service Commission

The General Assembly,

Having considered the fourteenth annual report of the International Civil Service Commission and other related reports,

I

Comprehensive review of the conditions of service of the staff in the Professional and higher categories

Recalling that, in section III of its resolution 42/221 of 21 December 1987, it requested the International Civil Service Commission to undertake a comprehensive review of the conditions of service of the staff in the Professional and higher categories in order to provide a sound and stable methodological basis for their remuneration,

Reaffirming the guidelines provided in section III, paragraph 1, of resolution 42/221,

Recalling also that, in section III, paragraph 2, of resolution 42/221, the Commission was requested to submit to the General Assembly at its forty-third session a preliminary report on the comprehensive review containing an analysis of the subject, together with an outline of one or more possible alternatives,

Noting that the preliminary report on the comprehensive review contained in chapter III, section C, of the report of the Commission, does not contain the analysis requested,

Bearing in mind that the Commission should allocate the highest priority to the comprehensive review in its programme of work for 1989,

Recognizing that the scope of the review should not necessarily be limited to the four areas identified by the Commission in its preliminary report,

Mindful of the interrelationship between these four areas and of the need for conditions of service whose component parts are appropriately balanced,

Emphasizing, in the light of the long-term consequences of this review, the desirability in the review process for close co-operation between the Commission, the organizations of the United Nations common system and the staff representatives,

1. *Requests* the International Civil Service Commission, as a priority, to pursue the comprehensive review and, if necessary, to adjust its programme of work and schedule of meetings for 1989, in order to provide conditions for substantive discussion and finalization of the comprehensive review at its second session of 1989;

2. *Invites* the Commission to make arrangements to allow for the fullest participation of organizations and staff representatives in all aspects and at all stages of the comprehensive review;

3. *Also requests* the Commission to submit a comprehensive report to the General Assembly at its forty-fourth session together with a preliminary assessment of the impact of the relevant recommendations therein on pensionable remuneration;

4. *Further requests* the Commission in its review to be guided by the following:

(*a*) The Commission should examine all elements of the present conditions of service, and after identifying problems related to staff recruitment, retention and mobility should propose solutions to these problems;

(*b*) The proposed solutions should be accompanied by an indication of their financial implications, together with an estimate of the overall costs;

(*c*) The overall costs should, as far as possible, be comparable to the costs of the current remuneration system;

(1) *Comparator*

(*a*) The Noblemaire principle should continue to serve as the basis of comparison between United Nations emoluments and those of the highest-paying civil service—currently the United States federal civil service—which, by its size and structure, lends itself to such comparison;

(*b*) The Commission should review how best the application of the Noblemaire principle can ensure the competitiveness of United Nations remuneration without resorting to comparison with the private sector;

(*c*) In this connection the Commission should undertake a comparative study of the concept of the margin including the way in which it is intended to compensate for expatriation;

(2) *Remuneration system*

(*a*) A single world-wide salary scale should be a fundamental goal of the remuneration system. Within this framework, a review should be made of how best special recruitment needs can be accommodated. The Commission should look into the present multiplicity of salary scales with a view to their correlation and possible amalgamation;

(*b*) In the context of equalizing purchasing power, the Commission should consider among other alternatives:

(i) The division of the pay package into its major component parts, one of which would be housing, reflecting the spending patterns of staff;

(ii) Major simplification of the post adjustment system, including eliminating negative post adjustment, separating out the housing component, streamlining the cost-of-living survey and computation process;

(*c*) The Commission should also review the rationale and magnitude of all elements of remuneration;

(3) *Motivation and productivity*

Consideration should be given to enhancing productivity through the introduction of incentives for merit and rewards on promotion payable on a one-time basis, coupled with less financial reward for longevity, which should be linked to a more rigorous performance appraisal system. Consideration should also be given to the introduction of administrative arrangements and of other non-monetary awards for meritorious service. The Commission should review and report on the current practice of automatic advancement to the next step without rigorous performance appraisal as well as on existing and new possible non-monetary awards for meritorious performance;

(4) *Mobility and hardship*

The Commission should analyse how best adequate incentives can be provided for mobility and for service in hardship duty stations. It should take into account the particular needs of those organizations whose programmes require that staff be reassigned to and from headquarters and field locations. In reviewing the scope and purpose of all the current allowances payable in cases of mobility and hardship, the entitlements provided by the comparator for non-diplomatic expatriates may serve as a general point of reference. In this respect, the Commission should, bearing in mind the different types of contractual arrangements existing in the system, review whether incentives should be provided by way of lump sums on transfers in lieu of or as well as ongoing payments in the form of allowances to compensate for hardships;

5. *Requests* the Commission to analyse the feasibility of utilizing existing data sources; in this regard, consideration should be given to both public and private sources which publish up-to-date and accurate data on relevant subjects;

II

Functioning of the International Civil
Service Commission

Recalling paragraph 1 of its resolution 3042(XXVII) of 19 December 1972, whereby it decided to establish in principle an international civil service commission consisting of independent experts having the requisite qualifications and experience who would be appointed in their individual capacities by the General Assembly,

Recalling also the subsequent establishment of the International Civil Service Commission by General Assembly resolution 3357(XXIX) of 18 December 1974,

Reaffirming the importance of the role of the Commission as an independent technical body answerable to the General Assembly,

Recalling further its request made in section VIII of resolution 42/221 that the Commission should undertake a study of its functioning with a view to enhancing its work,

Expressing concern over the position taken by the staff representatives to suspend their participation in the work of the Commission,

Noting that the Commission has not found it possible to undertake a more in-depth review of its functioning,

Noting also the need to undertake, as soon as possible, a full review of the functioning of the Commission, including the definition of the role of the Commission in relation to the determination of the conditions of service of the staff, and the Commission's relation to the General Assembly,

1. *Requests* the International Civil Service Commission to expand the review of its functioning in consultation with the organizations of the United Nations common system and staff representatives and to present proposals thereon to the General Assembly at its forty-fifth session;

2. *Invites* the Commission to review its rules of procedure at the earliest opportunity to allow for the fullest possible consultations with organizations and staff representatives and, to the greatest extent possible, their presence in its deliberations;

3. *Requests* the Secretary-General, in the context of article 4 of the statute of the Commission, to propose to the General Assembly an appropriate deadline for the submission of candidatures for appointment to the Commission so as to allow for full and timely consultations with the three parties concerned;

4. *Also requests* the Secretary-General, in his report to the General Assembly, to reflect the views resulting from the consultations referred to in paragraph 3 above;

5. *Urges* the two staff representative bodies to resume participation in the work of the Commission at the earliest possible opportunity;

III
Decisions and recommendations contained in the report of the International Civil Service Commission

A. *Functioning of the post adjustment within the margin range*

Recalling that in its resolution 40/244 of 18 December 1985 it approved the range of 110 to 120, with a desirable mid-point of 115, for the net remuneration margin, on the understanding that the margin would be maintained at a level around the desirable mid-point of 115 over a period of time,

Recalling also that in section I, paragraph 1, of its resolution 42/221 it decided to maintain the methodology described in annex I to the report of the International Civil Service Commission to the General Assembly at its fortieth session for the calculation of the margin between the net remuneration of staff in the Professional and higher categories of the United Nations and that of the comparator civil service, which should continue to be applied for the time being,

Confirming that the decisions of the Commission contained in paragraph 17 of its report are in conformity with the decision of the General Assembly contained in section I, paragraph 1, of resolution 42/221,

Noting that the determination of parameters for the operation of the post adjustment system within the margin range should be considered as a principle under article 10 *(a)* of the statute of the Commission,

Noting also that, under the four-month rule currently in operation, when a post adjustment index increases by 5 per cent above the level corresponding to the class of post adjustment currently being paid, a new class of post adjustment at Headquarters becomes effective only after a waiting period of four months, during which the

post adjustment index must not have fallen below the level corresponding to the new class,

1. *Takes note* of the guidelines to be followed for the maintenance of the net remuneration margin around the desirable mid-point of 115 over a period of time, contained in paragraph 23 of the report of the International Civil Service Commission, and decides that the resulting margin referred to in paragraphs 23 *(b)* and *(c)* relates to the average of the successive margins reported to the General Assembly beginning with the margin period 1 October 1985 to 30 September 1986 and continuing until the submission of the report on the margin methodology requested in resolution 42/221 for presentation to the Assembly at its forty-fifth session;

2. *Decides*, as an interim measure and until the forty-fifth session of the General Assembly, that the application of the above guidelines should not result in the granting of successive classes of post adjustment in New York at less than four-month intervals;

B. *Allowances*

Having reviewed chapters V and XIII of the report of the International Civil Service Commission,

1. *Requests* the International Civil Service Commission to include, as an integral part of the comprehensive review, a study of:

(a) The purpose and conditions of an education grant;

(b) The purpose and methodology for dependency allowances for staff in the Professional and higher categories;

2. *Approves*, as an interim measure and until a revised system based on the above study is adopted:

(a) The recommendations of the Commission concerning the education grant as contained in paragraph 75 of its report;

(b) The recommendations of the Commission concerning the children's allowance for the Professional and higher categories as contained in paragraph 79 *(a)* of its report;

3. *Approves* consequently the relevant amendments to staff regulations 3.2 and 3.4 *(a)* (i);

C. *Others*

Recalling its resolutions 40/244 of 18 December 1985 and 41/207 of 11 December 1986, and concerned about the uneven progress achieved by the organizations of the United Nations common system regarding implementation of the recommendations of the International Civil Service Commission approved by the General Assembly in 1985,

Recalling also section II of its resolution 37/126 of 17 December 1982 and section VII of its resolution 42/221,

1. *Endorses* the recommendations of the International Civil Service Commission contained in paragraph 91 of its report concerning special measures to be undertaken by the organizations for the recruitment of women, and requests the Commission to report to the General Assembly at its forty-fifth session on the progress made in this regard, with supporting data for each organization of the United Nations common system;

2. *Requests* the Commission to continue its review of the practices of supplementary payments and deductions, to pursue its collection of information on these practices and to include such information in its report to the General Assembly at its forty-fourth session.

General Assembly resolution 43/226
21 December 1988   Meeting 84   Adopted without vote

Approved by Fifth Committee (A/43/977) without vote, 18 December (meeting 50); draft by Vice-Chairman (A/C.5/43/L.14) following informal consultations; agenda item 122.
Meeting numbers. GA 43rd session: 5th Committee 13, 16, 20, 22, 24, 25, 32, 50; plenary 84.

Privileges and immunities

In response to a 1987 General Assembly request,[20] the Secretary-General submitted to the Fifth Committee, on behalf of and with the approval of the Administrative Committee on Co-ordination (ACC), a November 1988 report[21] on respect for the privileges and immunities of officials of the United Nations system. He noted that during the period from 1 July 1987 to 30 June 1988, a total of 168 cases of arrest and detention or disappearance of officials were reported. There was a significant increase in cases affecting officials of the United Nations Relief and Works Agency for Palestine Refugees in the Near East (UNRWA), which reported 151 cases. He stated that United Nations officials continued to experience difficulty in receiving timely information on pending cases.

The Secretary-General also reported on restrictions on official and private travel by host countries, which affected staff members of UNRWA travelling to the West Bank and the Gaza Strip. Restrictions were also imposed by the United States on staff members from Albania, Bulgaria, Czechoslovakia, the German Democratic Republic, Hungary, Poland and Romania. He also reported on unauthorized taxation of officials by some Member States and the introduction of regulations and directives which affected his authority to establish the terms and conditions of local recruitment by United Nations organizations. The Secretary-General stated that he would continue to explore through his security co-ordinator further measures to strengthen the response of the system to violations of the privileges and immunities of staff members.

GENERAL ASSEMBLY ACTION

On 21 December, on the recommendation of the Fifth Committee, the General Assembly adopted **resolution 43/225** without vote.

Respect for the privileges and immunities of officials of the United Nations and the specialized agencies and related organizations

The General Assembly,

Recalling that, under Article 100 of the Charter of the United Nations, each Member of the United Nations undertakes to respect the exclusively international character of the responsibilities of the Secretary-General and the staff and not to seek to influence them in the discharge of their responsibilities,

Recalling that, under Article 105 of the Charter, all officials of the Organization shall enjoy in the territory of each of its Member States such privileges and immunities as are necessary for the independent exercise of their functions in connection with the Organization,

Recalling the Convention on the Privileges and Immunities of the United Nations, the Convention on the Privileges and Immunities of the Specialized Agencies, the Agreement on the Privileges and Immunities of the International Atomic Energy Agency and the United Nations Development Programme Standard Basic Assistance Agreements,

Recalling also its resolution 76(I) of 7 December 1946, in which it approved the granting of the privileges and immunities referred to in articles V and VII of the Convention on the Privileges and Immunities of the United Nations to all members of the staff of the United Nations,

Recalling its resolution 43/173 of 9 December 1988 containing, *inter alia*, a body of principles for the protection of all persons under any form of detention or imprisonment, including the principle that all persons under arrest or detention be provided whenever necessary with medical care and treatment,

Reiterating the obligation of all officials of the Organization in the conduct of their duties to observe fully the laws and regulations of Member States,

Mindful of the responsibilities of the Secretary-General to safeguard the functional immunity of all United Nations officials,

Mindful also of the importance in this respect of the provision by Member States of adequate and timely information concerning the arrest and detention of staff members and, more particularly, their granting of access to them,

Bearing in mind the wider considerations of the Secretary-General to guarantee minimum standards of justice and due process to United Nations officials,

Reaffirming its previous resolutions, in particular resolution 42/219 of 21 December 1987,

1. *Takes note with concern* of the report of the Secretary-General, submitted on behalf of the Administrative Committee on Co-ordination, and of the developments indicated therein, in particular the significant number of new cases of arrest and detention and those regarding previously reported cases under this category;

2. *Also takes note with concern* of the restrictions on duty travel of officials as indicated in the report of the Secretary-General;

3. *Further takes note with concern* of the information contained in the report of the Secretary-General related to taxation and the status, privileges and immunities of officials;

4. *Deplores* the increase in the number of cases where the functioning, safety and well-being of officials have been adversely affected;

5. *Also deplores* the increasing number of cases in which the lives and well-being of officials have been placed in jeopardy during the exercise of their official functions;

6. *Calls upon* all Member States scrupulously to respect the privileges and immunities of all officials of the United Nations and the specialized agencies and related organizations and to refrain from any acts that would impede such officials in the performance of their functions, thereby seriously affecting the proper functioning of the Organization;

7. *Calls upon* those Member States holding under arrest or detention officials of the United Nations and the specialized agencies and related organizations to enable the Secretary-General or the executive head of the organization concerned to exercise fully the right of functional protection inherent in the relevant multilateral conventions and bilateral agreements, particularly with respect to immediate access to detained staff members;

8. *Calls upon* all Member States otherwise impeding officials of the United Nations and the specialized agencies and related organizations in the proper discharge of their duties to review the cases and to co-ordinate efforts with the Secretary-General or the executive head of the organization concerned to resolve each case with all due speed;

9. *Calls upon* the staff of the United Nations and the specialized agencies and related organizations to comply with the obligations resulting from the Staff Regulations and Rules of the United Nations, in particular regulation 1.8, and from the equivalent provisions governing the staff of the other agencies;

10. *Calls upon* the Secretary-General to use all such means as are available to him to bring about an expeditious solution of the cases still pending, which were referred to in the report;

11. *Also calls upon* the Secretary-General, as chief administrative officer of the United Nations, to continue personally to act as the focal point in promoting and ensuring the observance of the privileges and immunities of officials of the United Nations and the specialized agencies and related organizations by using all such means as are available to him;

12. *Urges* the Secretary-General to give priority, through the United Nations Security Co-ordinator and his other special representatives, to the reporting and prompt follow-up of cases of arrest, detention and other possible matters relating to the security and proper functioning of officials of the United Nations and the specialized agencies and related organizations;

13. *Requests* the Secretary-General, as Chairman of the Administrative Committee on Co-ordination, to review and appraise the measures already taken to enhance the proper functioning, safety and protection of international civil servants and to modify them where necessary.

General Assembly resolution 43/225

21 December 1988   Meeting 84   Adopted without vote

Approved by Fifth Committee (A/43/954) without vote, 18 December (meeting 50); draft by Chairman (A/C.5/43/L.13) following informal consultations; agenda item 121 *(b)*.
Meeting numbers. GA 43rd session: 5th Committee 14, 16, 18, 20, 22-26, 28, 30, 35, 50; plenary 84.

REFERENCES
[1]YUN 1987, p. 1132, GA res. 42/220 A, 21 Dec. 1987. [2]YUN 1986, p. 1018. [3]YUN 1986, p. 1050. [4]A/C.5/43/21 & Add.1. [5]A/43/659. [6]A/C.5/43/1. [7]YUN 1987, p. 1098, GA res. 42/211, 21 Dec. 1986. [8]A/43/651. [9]YUN 1987, p. 1139, GA res. 40/258, 18 Dec. 1985. [10]A/C.5/43/1/Rev.1. [11]YUN 1985, p. 1139, GA res. 40/258, 18 Dec. 1985. [12]A/C.5/43/14. [13]YUN 1987, p. 1136, GA res. 42/220 C, 21 Dec. 1987. [14]A/43/30 & Corr.1. [15]YUN 1987, p. 1134. [16]YUN 1984, p. 1157. [17]A/C.5/43/6. [18]YUN 1987, p. 1143. [19]*Ibid.*, p. 1144, GA res. 42/221, 21 Dec. 1987. [20]*Ibid.*, p. 1149, GA res. 42/219, 21 Dec. 1987. [21]A/C.5/43/18.

Staff costs

Salaries and allowances

In response to a 1987 General Assembly request that ICSC conduct a comprehensive review of the conditions of service of staff in the Professional and higher categories, in order to provide a sound and stable methodology for determining remuneration[1] and to propose one or more possible alternatives, ICSC in 1988 submitted a preliminary report,[2] in which it noted that the current remuneration system had operated reasonably well for many years, but had been impaired by such factors as extreme currency fluctuations, volatile inflation rates, budgetary and other domestic considerations of the comparator country on the overall level of remuneration in the common system and increasing problems affecting working conditions at many duty stations. As a result, it had become difficult to respond in a predictable and timely manner to the needs of organizations in the common system.

The Commission identified four priority areas for review: the basis for determining the level of remuneration—the definition of the comparator; the remuneration system, including post adjustment; motivation and productivity; and mobility and hardship incentives. In reviewing each of the areas, the Commission outlined a number of options for further study and expressed the hope that the Assembly would provide directives and guidelines for it to follow during the substantive work involved in a comprehensive review.

Post adjustment

Under its standing mandate, ICSC reviewed the relationship between the levels of net remuneration of the United Nations and the United States federal civil service during 1988.[2] Specifically, it conducted a detailed review of the lifting of the post adjustment freeze in New York and, in that connection, considered the impact of the revised methodology introduced by the Commission in 1987[3] for calculating the out-of-area price progression factor in post adjustment.

The Commission stated that it had not been foreseen that the revised methodology would also impact on the cost-of-living differential between New York and Washington, D.C., and thus affect the margin calculation. The change had also directly affected the date of implementation of class 8 of post adjustment in New York. Under the new methodology, it would have become due on 1 February 1988, as compared to 1 June 1988 under the previous methodology.

Bearing in mind that in 1987[1] the Assembly had requested that ICSC maintain the methodology for calculation of the net remuneration margin it described in its 1985 annual report,[4] the Commission decided that the previous methodology for calculation of the out-of-area price progression factor should continue to apply for New York and Washington, D.C.

ICSC also decided that the post adjustment index (PAI) for both New York and Washington, D.C., should be updated from October 1982, the date of the last comprehensive survey, using the consumer price index (CPI) of the United States Bureau of Labor Statistics to adjust the in-area expenditures and the old out-of-area price progression factored in the calculation methodology in effect until 31 August 1987 to adjust out-of-area expenditures.

Those PAIs should be used to determine the post adjustment classifications for New York and Washington, D.C., and thus used in the calculation of the net remuneration margin. Also, the revised out-of-area price progression factor introduced by the Commission as from 1 September 1987 should continue to be used for calculating PAIs for all other duty stations until 31 August 1988.

The Commission decided that post adjustment increases in New York should take effect either on or after the date of the increase in the United States federal civil service salaries, or on the date when the revised post adjustment class became due in New York. In either case, the resulting margin should remain between 114 and 116. However, if it did not lie inside those parameters, an alternative implementation date for a post adjustment increase in New York would be selected to ensure that the resulting margin remained around 115.

Education grant and children's allowance

Increases in the education grant for staff members were recommended by ICSC in 1988,[2] based on a proposal submitted by the Consultative Committee on Administrative Questions (CCAQ) of ACC and the views of the International Fund for Agricultural Development (IFAD). CCAQ's proposal had been made in the light of increased expenditures for education reported in 1987 and of further increases in the fees charged by schools attended by children of international staff of the common system stationed at Headquarters.

The Commission recommended that $9,000 per annum be the maximum amount admissible as educational expenses, up from $6,000 previously. Thus, the maximum grant would rise from $4,500 to $6,750. Within the maximum grant, the ceiling for boarding costs should be increased from $1,500 to $2,000. The maximum additional reimbursement of boarding costs over and above the full grant for staff members at designated duty stations should be maintained at $1,500 per year.

Also, for disabled children, the grant should be set at 100 per cent of admissible expenses, up to a maximum of $9,000. The total costs of those decisions were estimated by ICSC at $4.6 million, using exchange rates in effect on 1 April 1988.

For countries where it had decided that the remuneration correction factor was applicable, ICSC made similar adjustments, with the increased amounts to be payable in local currency.

The Commission also examined the current status of children's, spouses' and secondary dependants' allowances. It recommended, for the Professional and higher categories, effective 1 January 1989, that the children's allowance be increased to $1,050 and the secondary dependants' allowance to $450. For countries where the remuneration correction factor was applicable, the Commission recommended an increase of 50 per cent to the amount payable in local currency as of 1 April 1988. The Commission also decided that these allowances should be considered in the context of the comprehensive review of the conditions of staff in the Professional and higher categories. For the General Service and related categories, it recommended no change in the current level of the allowance.

The total cost of these decisions was estimated at $8.17 million for the children's allowance and $120,000 for the secondary dependants' allowance.

Separation payments

The scale for separation payments—including commutation of accrued annual leave, repatriation grant, death grant and termination indemnity—for the Professional and higher categories had been established by the Assembly in 1981.[5] However, ACABQ noted in a December 1988 report[6] that a proposal for establishing such a scale for the Director-General for Development and International Economic Co-operation and for the Administrator of the United Nations Development Programme (UNDP) had never been submitted to the Assembly. The Advisory Committee therefore recommended that the payments be established with effect from 1 April 1988 at a gross amount of $150,000, with a corresponding net dependant rate of $87,800 and net without dependant rate of $76,530. Those payments were approved by the Assembly on 21 December 1988 by **decision 43/450**.

Supplementary payments and deductions by Governments

At its March 1988 session,[2] ICSC continued to study the issue of supplementary payments to and deductions from the remuneration of common system staff by certain Member States. In 1987,[1] the General Assembly had requested those States and common system organizations to provide ICSC with information on the subject. As at 1 July 1988,

73 Member States and Switzerland had responded to that request.

The Commission expressed regret over the insufficient response, drew the Assembly's attention to the fact that supplementary payments were on the rise and decided to include the issue in its comprehensive review of conditions of service of the Professional and higher categories (see above).

On 21 December, the General Assembly, by **resolution 43/226**, requested ICSC to continue its review of supplementary payments and deductions and to report further on the subject in 1989.

Emoluments of ICJ members

In a November 1988 report[7] on emoluments of the members of the International Court of Justice (ICJ), ACABQ noted that, in April, ICSC had introduced the concept of a local currency floor (and ceiling) at a certain number of duty stations, including The Hague, Netherlands, to protect the cost-of-living supplement from currency exchange variations. This meant that the salaries of all ICJ members, including the Registrar, were protected in local currency terms in the event of a weakening of the US dollar below a certain exchange rate.

Although no direct link existed between the emoluments of the Judges and those of senior Secretariat officials, the Advisory Committee believed that extending the application of such a guideline to the emoluments of the Judges warranted consideration. The financial implications of introducing the floor/ceiling concept, with the floor calculation based on the 1986 emoluments and an exchange rate 4 per cent below the average 1986 exchange rate, would depend on the most current exchange rate. The ceiling rate would be calculated using the 1986 emoluments as a base and an exchange rate of 2.8 guilders per dollar.

ACABQ had been informed that the current exchange rate was 2 guilders per dollar, i.e., below the floor rates. Therefore, should the rate remain at that level, the additional 1989 payments for all Judges would total $73,800, and the emolument for each Judge would total $100,720.

On 21 December, by **resolution 43/217, section VI**, the General Assembly approved ACABQ's recommendations.

Pensions

During 1988, the number of participants in the United Nations Joint Staff Pension Fund increased from 53,968 to 54,006. As at 31 December, there were 28,362 periodic benefits in award: 9,528 retirement benefits, 4,753 early retirement benefits, 5,067 deferred retirement benefits, 3,489 widows' and widowers' benefits, 4,910 children's benefits, 570 disability benefits and 45 secondary dependants' benefits. In the course of the year, 3,662 lump-sum withdrawal and other settlements were paid. The principal of the Fund increased from $6,113,333,746 to $6,810,774,123. Investment income totalled $697,367,860, comprising $395,536,601 in interest and dividends and $301,831,259 in net profit on sales of investments. After deduction of investment management costs of $6,600,111, net investment income was $690,767,749.

Over the previous 38 years, the total book value of the portfolio had risen from $13 million to $6,199 million, a compound increase of 17.6 per cent a year. During the 1987 calendar year, investment income from interest and dividends amounted to $354.5 million, an increase of 7.7 per cent over 1986. The total of new funds which became available for investment amounted to $360 million (contributions plus investment income, minus benefit payments and less investment expenses). Realized capital gains amounted to $698 million, an increase of 19.4 per cent.

As the 21-member United Nations Joint Staff Pension Board held no session during 1988, its Standing Committee met at Geneva (20-24 June). The major items it dealt with were: continued study of measures to restore over the long term the actuarial balance of the Fund; methodology and assumptions to be used in the actuarial balance of the Fund as at 31 December 1988; impact of currency fluctuations on pensionable remuneration and consequent pensions of staff in the General Service and other locally recruited categories; and membership of the World Tourism Organization in the Fund. The focus on those particular items had been requested by the Assembly in 1987.[8]

The Standing Committee also considered the management of the Fund's investments, the financial statements and schedules for the year ended 31 December 1987, the administrative expenses of the Fund and amendments to the Fund's rules of procedure governing attendance and participation at sessions of the Board.

ACABQ submitted its comments[9] on the 1988 report of the Board and the report of the Secretary-General on the Fund's investments (see below). It noted that responsibility for studies of pensionable remuneration, as called for by the Standing Committee in 1988, lay primarily with ICSC; however, such studies should be done in full collaboration with the Board.

Pension Fund investments

The annual report for the year ended 31 March 1988 on the investments of the United Nations Joint Staff Pension Fund was submitted to the Assembly by the Secretary-General in September.[10]

The market value of the Fund's assets increased to $7,229 million from $7,016 million a year earlier, an increase of $213 million or 3 per cent, and $919 million above the book value.

Total investment return for the year ending 31 March 1988 was 3.1 per cent which, after adjusting for inflation, represented a "real" rate of return of −0.8 per cent.

The Fund remained one of the most diversified pension funds in the world. Investments were held in 27 currencies and 44 countries; 51 per cent of the assets were invested in currencies other than the United States dollar, the Fund's unit of account. The decline in the relative value of the dollar during the year influenced the market value of investments outside the United States when expressed in dollars, and also enhanced the positive rates of return in local currencies after translation into dollars.

Equities constituted 43 per cent of the assets as at 31 March, down 51 per cent from the previous year. Bonds accounted for 34 per cent compared with 27 per cent the previous year, while real estate-related securities amounted to 11 per cent.

The Secretary-General stated that the investment return to the Fund, which was considerably lower than in recent years, needed to be viewed against the background of the economic and financial conditions existing during the period under review. With the sharp decline of stock market prices in October 1987 plus the volatility of global financial markets thereafter, the return could be considered satisfactory, comparing well with similar pension funds.

Actuarial balance

In 1988,[7] the Fund's Standing Committee continued studying measures to restore the Fund's actuarial balance in response to the 1987 request of the General Assembly.[8] The Standing Committee took into account the view of the Committee of Actuaries, which noted that there had been actuarial savings resulting from measures already adopted by the Assembly, including two increases in contribution rates. However, increased actuarial costs had arisen from changes in certain demographic assumptions and from accumulated interest on the past imbalance. Among the factors that had contributed to increased costs over the years were: economic developments, including inflation and currency fluctuations and the combined effect of maintaining the mandatory age of separation at 60, and increased life expectancy which had lengthened the period of payments. There had also been a significant rise in the number of early retirements in recent years.

To curb the deterioration of the Fund's actuarial balance, the Committee of Actuaries again recommended—as it had since 1983—raising the rate of contributions to meet the increased costs of the system. The Standing Committee agreed with the Committee of Actuaries that there should be a study on the possible extension of participation in the Fund to employees excluded by the terms of their appointment. Differing views had emerged on the merits of pursuing modifications of the mandatory age of separation, of the normal retirement age and of the early retirement provisions, and it was recommended that more extensive studies be performed on those items in 1989.

Regarding restoration of the Fund's actuarial balance, ACABQ, in October 1988,[9] expressed the hope that the Board would not limit itself only to the Standing Committee's recommendations.

Administrative expenses

A total of $22,877,400 net had been approved by the Assembly in 1987[8] for the administrative expenses of the Pension Fund during the 1988-1989 biennium. ACABQ noted in an October 1988 report[9] that no supplementary expenses had been requested for the current year. However, adjustments in the post levels in the Board's staffing table were required in respect of three posts in the Fund's secretariat. Those adjustments would cost $22,800 to implement, but the Secretary-General had stated that they could be met from within resources already approved for the current biennium. Based on that arrangement, ACABQ approved the changes.

GENERAL ASSEMBLY ACTION

On 21 December, on the recommendation of the Fifth Committee, the General Assembly adopted **resolution 43/227** without vote.

United Nations pension system
The General Assembly,

Recalling its resolution 42/222 of 21 December 1987,

Having considered the report of the United Nations Joint Staff Pension Board for 1988 to the General Assembly and to the member organizations of the United Nations Joint Staff Pension Fund, the report of the Secretary-General on the investments of the United Nations Joint Staff Pension Fund, and the related report of the Advisory Committee on Administrative and Budgetary Questions,

I

Measures to restore the actuarial balance of the
United Nations Joint Staff Pension Fund

1. *Takes note* of section III.A of the report of the United Nations Joint Staff Pension Board, which contains the interim report of the Board on its study of all possible measures to restore the actuarial balance of the Fund over the long term;

2. *Requests* the Board to continue its work in implementing section I, paragraph 2, of resolution 42/222;

II

Administrative expenses

Approves the revised staffing table for the secretariat of the United Nations Joint Staff Pension Fund for the biennium 1988-1989, as contained in annex IV to the report of the United Nations Joint Staff Pension Board, on the understanding that the additional costs will be met within the expenses approved for the biennium 1988-1989;

III

Takes note of the remaining sections of the report of the United Nations Joint Staff Pension Board;

IV

Investments of the United Nations
Joint Staff Pension Fund

Takes note with appreciation of the report of the Secretary-General on the investments of the United Nations Joint Staff Pension Fund.

General Assembly resolution 43/227

21 December 1988   Meeting 84   Adopted without vote

Approved by Fifth Committee (A/43/846 & Add.1) without vote, 16 December (meeting 49); draft by Vice-Chairman following informal consultations (A/C.5/43/L.5), orally amended by USSR; agenda item 123.
Meeting numbers. GA 43rd session: 5th Committee 13, 20, 22, 24, 36, 49; plenary 84.

REFERENCES

[1]YUN 1987, p. 1144, GA res. 42/221, 21 Dec. 1987. [2]A/43/30 & Corr.1. [3]YUN 1987, p. 1153. [4]YUN 1985, p. 1245. [5]YUN 1981, p. 1342, GA dec. 36/459, 18 Dec. 1981. [6]A/43/7/Add.13. [7]A/43/7/Add.6. [8]YUN 1987, p. 1158, GA res. 42/222, 21 Dec. 1987. [9]A/43/712. [10]A/C.5/43/3.

Administration of justice

As requested by the General Assembly in 1987,[1] the Secretary-General in October 1988[2] submitted a report on improving the administration of justice in the Secretariat. The report outlined the principles underlying the programme and progress made in reforming procedures to resolve staff disputes and appeals made within the United Nations system. In 1986,[3] the Group of 18 had also recommended that procedures to administrate justice be simplified to render the system more efficient and less costly.

The Secretary-General said that in order to have a fair and successful redress system, it was desirable, as far as possible, to separate the offices taking decisions which led to appeals from those with responsibility for evaluating such appeals, and to strengthen the authority of the system through effective staff participation. In 1988, steps were taken to strengthen staff participation, especially through the Joint Appeals Board (JAB) and the Joint Disciplinary Committee, and to give those bodies greater authority. On 1 February, the Under-Secretary-General for Administration and Management was placed in direct charge of the system, since that office was normally distanced from the day-to-day administrative decisions from which most appeals originated.

The first step taken to reform the system was to eliminate the backlog of cases before JAB, which had in recent years seriously undermined the system's effectiveness. The initial focus was on the Board in New York where, with the aid of recurrent "task force" resources, the number of cases, including "old" ones, was reduced to their lowest level since 1972. All cases lodged prior to 1988 either had been dealt with or were being examined and, by the end of the year, the Board estimated it would have only current cases on its books. The Board had also set a target of six months for processing cases.

The success in New York was attributed to the nomination of a new 52-member JAB representing the Secretariat on a geographical, gender and grading basis; the appointment of a temporary full-time presiding officer; and the provision of additional alternate secretaries. "Interim guidelines" for JAB procedures were issued to new Board members and the strict enforcement of time-limits for dealing with cases had a critical impact on the Board's productivity.

Revisions were also made to JAB membership at Geneva and Nairobi, with the aim of disposing of case backlogs at those duty stations by the end of 1988.

Decisions of the Board currently went directly to the Under-Secretary-General for Administration and Management for consideration and advice to the Secretary-General, who had a target of seven working days for notification of his decision. New administrative instructions on the role of counsel in the Organization were issued and membership of the Panel of Counsel increased significantly.

The next stage of the reform process would entail the establishment, by 1989, of a fully revised system to deal with staff grievances and disciplinary cases with enhanced objectivity, fairness and speed.

Commenting on the report, ACABQ[4] expressed satisfaction over the reduction in cases pending, but cautioned that speed in resolving them should not compromise the quality of consideration afforded each case. Also, the Secretary-General should define what would constitute a "frivolous" application to the Board so as to avoid a subjective rejection. ACABQ noted that problems remained in the appellate process in Nairobi, and called on the Secretary-General to ensure that the backlog was dealt with promptly. The Secretary-General was also requested to submit at the earliest stage any proposal to revise the Staff Regulations and/or Rules, and to make proposals for the adequate staffing of JAB in the 1990-1991 budget.

GENERAL ASSEMBLY ACTION

On 21 December, on the recommendation of the Fifth Committee, the General Assembly adopted **resolution 43/224 B** without vote.

Administration of justice in the Secretariat

The General Assembly,

Noting the importance of a just and efficient internal justice system in the Secretariat,

Having considered the report of the Secretary-General on the administration of justice in the Secretariat and the related report of the Advisory Committee on Administrative and Budgetary Questions,

Welcoming the improvement in the internal justice system and the considerable progress achieved during the current year, including the disposal of the backlog of cases of the Headquarters Joint Appeals Board and the streamlining of the appeals procedures,

1. *Endorses* the report of the Secretary-General and the related report of the Advisory Committee on Administrative and Budgetary Questions;

2. *Requests* the Secretary-General to establish by the end of 1989 a fully revised internal justice system as proposed in his report pursuant to recommendation 60 of the Group of High-level Intergovernmental Experts to Review the Efficiency of the Administrative and Financial Functioning of the United Nations and to report thereon to the General Assembly at its forty-fourth session;

3. *Calls upon* the Secretary-General to finish putting into place improved disciplinary rules and procedures at the earliest stage, as well as revised appellate procedures, in accordance with paragraphs 18 and 19 of his report, and to report thereon to the General Assembly at its forty-fourth session.

General Assembly resolution 43/224 B

21 December 1988   Meeting 84   Adopted without vote

Approved by Fifth Committee (A/43/954) without vote, 15 December (meeting 48); draft by Sweden (A/C.5/43/L.12) following informal consultations; agenda item 121.

Meeting numbers. GA 43rd session: 5th Committee 14, 16, 18, 20, 22-26, 28, 30, 35, 48; plenary 84.

Feasibility of establishing a single administrative tribunal

In October 1988, the Secretary-General, in response to a 1987 General Assembly request,[5] submitted a report[6] on consultations held during 1988 on the feasibility of establishing a single administrative tribunal for the International Labour Organisation (ILO) and the United Nations. He had been requested in 1978[7] to study this question, when the Assembly became concerned that the jurisprudence of the ILO Administrative Tribunal and that of the United Nations were diverging. The Secretary-General convened 14 consultative meetings between 8 March and 7 July 1988, at which proposed amendments to the statutes of the two tribunals were examined. He outlined the substantive conclusions relating to proposed changes in the statutes, as set out in two annexes to his report. Also annexed was a proposed draft resolution on harmonization and further development of the statutes, rules and practices of the two tribunals.

On 21 December, the Assembly, by **decision 43/452,** invited Member States to comment on the Secretary-General's proposals by 31 May 1989 and

requested the Secretary-General to report those comments in 1989.

Administrative Tribunal Judgement on remuneration correction factor

In 1986,[8] ICSC had decided to introduce, on an interim basis with effect from 1 September 1986, a remuneration correction factor (RCF) to the post adjustment. Its objective was to minimize upwards or downwards variations of take-home pay in local currency resulting from exchange rate fluctuations. However, due to the Organization's serious financial crisis, the Secretary-General had decided to defer implementing the RCF at Geneva and Vienna, while indicating that he would lift the deferment as soon as practicable. Subsequently, he decided to implement the RCF at those duty stations from 1 January 1987.

Four staff members appealed the validity of the deferment and, in May 1988, the Administrative Tribunal delivered its Judgement (No. 421), by which it ordered that the four claimants and similarly situated staff in the Professional and higher categories be paid for the period 1 September to 31 December 1986.

The Secretary-General therefore reported[9] that the financial implications of the Judgement amounted to a total of $597,200, including $439,400 under the regular budget and $157,800 from other sources. He therefore proposed to charge $439,400 in additional expenditures against the overall balance of appropriations for the 1986-1987 biennium. ACABQ concurred with those recommendations.[4]

GENERAL ASSEMBLY ACTION

On 21 December, on the recommendation of the Fifth Committee, the General Assembly adopted without vote **resolution 43/217, section IV.**

> **Judgement No. 421 of the United Nations Administrative Tribunal related to the application of the remuneration correction factor to post adjustment at Geneva and Vienna as at 1 September 1986**
>
> [*The General Assembly . . .*]
>
> *Approves* the proposal of the Secretary-General to charge the additional expenditures resulting from Judgement No. 421 of the United Nations Administrative Tribunal against the overall balance of appropriations for the biennium 1986-1987 to be retained as a result of the suspension of regulations 4.3, 4.4 and 5.2 *(d)* of the Financial Regulations of the United Nations;
>
> . . .

General Assembly resolution 43/217, section IV

21 December 1988   Meeting 84   Adopted without vote

Approved by Fifth Committee (A/43/980) without vote, 15 November (meeting 31); oral proposal by Chairman; agenda item 114.

REFERENCES

[1]YUN 1987, p. 1163, GA res. 42/220 B, 21 Dec. 1987.
[2]A/C.5/43/25. [3]YUN 1986, p. 1075. [4]A/43/7/Add.4.
[5]YUN 1987, p. 1164, GA res. 42/217, 21 Dec. 1987.
[6]A/43/704. [7]YUN 1978, p. 995, GA res. 33/119, 19
Dec. 1978. [8]YUN 1986, p. 1067. [9]A/C.5/43/9.

Travel

Official travel

In 1988, the Secretary-General continued to keep under review the travel and related entitlements of representatives of Member States attending United Nations meetings, as requested by the General Assembly in 1987.[1] Over the years, the Assembly had taken several actions to modify those travel entitlements and in 1986 endorsed the recommendation[2] of the Group of 18 to limit travel reimbursement costs to representatives of the least developed countries (LDCs) attending the Assembly.[3]

In an August 1988 report,[4] the Secretary-General informed the Assembly that travel expenses were currently being paid for no more than five representatives from each LDC attending regular Assembly sessions. Travel and subsistence expenses were paid for members of bodies and subsidiary bodies of the United Nations who served in an individual personal capacity and not as representatives of Governments. Travel but not subsistence expenses were paid for one representative of each Member State participating in a functional commission of the Economic and Social Council, or in a sub-commission or sub-committee of a functional commission. In the case of governmental experts appointed directly by their Governments, travel and subsistance were paid only on the express authorization of the General Assembly.

ACABQ[5] suggested, as a further refinement of the current provisions, the discontinuation of the daily $8 allowance granted to eligible members while travelling by a direct route, by ship, aeroplane or train, as of 1 January 1988.

On 21 December, by **resolution 43/217, section IX**, the General Assembly endorsed ACABQ's recommendation and deferred action on the other issues in the Secretary-General's report.

Standard of accommodation
for air travel

The Secretary-General submitted in November 1988[6] a report on expenditures by the United Nations for first-class travel, as called for by the General Assembly in 1987.[7] The expenditures related to travel of one member of each delegation attending sessions of the Assembly (LDCs

only); other travel by non-Secretariat officials; and travel of Secretariat officials other than the Secretary-General.

Total additional costs incurred by the Organization as a result of exceptions to the standard rules of travel, as authorized by the Secretary-General from 1 July 1987 to 30 June 1988, were $68,911, compared with the corresponding additional cost of $35,650 in the previous reporting period.[8]

Observing that the provisions of the Assembly's 1987 resolution[7] had been applied only during the second six-month period of the 12-month reporting period (July 1987–June 1988), ACABQ[5] cautioned against attempting to draw any conclusions from the preliminary data provided by the Secretary-General, as the full effects of the Assembly's 1987 provisions were not currently known.

On 21 December, by **resolution 43/217, section X**, the General Assembly took note of the report of the Secretary-General.

Contractual agreements

In September 1988, the Secretary-General reported on the organization of official travel,[9] as requested by the General Assembly in 1987.[10] Noting that information on the subject had already been provided in his report on implementing recommendations of the Joint Inspection Unit (JIU),[11] the Secretary-General said that the only significant development relating to travel since issuance of that report related to travel agency arrangements in the United Nations Office at Geneva.

He stated that the lowest bidder for the travel agency contract to be awarded by that office had not pursued contract negotiations with the Organization. At the same time, it was learned that Midland Bank PLC, parent company of Thomas Cook S.A., had disposed of its interests in South Africa and submitted documented proof to the United Nations. As the bank would be removed from the list of transnational corporations with interests in South Africa, and Thomas Cook S.A. had been the second lowest bidder for the travel agency contract, it was expected that a three-year contract would soon be awarded to it. In 1987, JIU had recommended terminating the contract with Thomas Cook S.A.[12]

On 21 December 1988, by **resolution 43/217, section XI**, the General Assembly took note of the Secretary-General's report.

REFERENCES

[1]YUN 1987, p. 1166, GA res. 42/225, sect. VI, 21 Dec. 1987.
[2]YUN 1986, p. 1024, GA res. 41/213, 19 Dec. 1986. [3]Ibid.,
p. 1080. [4]A/C.5/43/4 & Corr.1. [5]A/43/7/Add.8.
[6]A/C.5/43/31. [7]YUN 1987, p. 1165, GA res. 42/214, 21
Dec. 1987. [8]Ibid., p. 1165. [9]A/C.5/43/54. [10]YUN 1987,
p. 1165, GA dec. 42/453, 21 Dec. 1987. [11]A/43/556. [12]YUN
1987, p. 1164.

Other UN officials

Experts and consultants

Pursuant to a 1987 General Assembly decision,[1] the Secretary-General submitted a report in October 1988 on the use of consultants and participants in *ad hoc* expert groups during 1986-1987.[2] The report also gave data on former staff over 55 years of age who were re-engaged in 1987 and were receiving a United Nations pension. In 1986, the Group of 18 had recommended a 30 per cent reduction in consultancies and that the hiring of former staff be abolished.[3]

Expenditures for the 1986-1987 biennium for consultants totalled $8,300,600—$5,137,800 under the regular budget and $3,162,800 under extrabudgetary resources—representing a 46.7 per cent reduction in regular budget expenditure from 1984-1985, and an increase in extrabudgetary spending of 45.1 per cent. Overall, there was a reduction of 36.9 per cent, or $4,868,400, in overall spending for consultants.

Expenditures for *ad hoc* expert groups during 1986-1987 were $1,256,700 from the regular budget and $959,000 in extrabudgetary funds. There was an overall decrease of $1,523,800, or 40.7 per cent, compared with the previous biennium.

There were 415 former staff over 55 years old re-engaged during 1987 at all duty stations throughout the Secretariat. In 89 cases, an annual payment of over $12,000 was made, which was the limit determined as an interim measure by the Assembly in 1982.[4]

In its comments on the report,[5] ACABQ noted that while reductions had been made in the use of regular budget funds, they had been partially offset by increased expenditure under extrabudgetary resources. It had also learned that requests for payments to consultants and *ad hoc* experts had to be accompanied by a certification of satisfactory completion of service, which was done by or on behalf of the head of the department to which the service was provided. According to the Secretary-General, payment had been withheld in nine cases during the biennium. Regarding the practice of re-engaging former staff, ACABQ said that its 1987 comments remained valid.[6]

On 21 December 1988, by **resolution 43/217, section I**, the General Assembly took note of the Secretary-General's report and the related report of ACABQ.

REFERENCES

[1]YUN 1987, p. 1167, GA res. 42/452, 21 Dec. 1987. [2]A/C.5/43/13. [3]YUN 1986, p. 1080. [4]YUN 1982, p. 1489, GA res. 37/237, sect. VIII, 21 Dec. 1982. [5]A/43/7/Add.2. [6]YUN 1987, p. 1167.

Chapter III

Other administrative and management questions

In 1988, the Committee on Conferences continued to examine ways in which conference resources within the United Nations system could be used more effectively. In December, the General Assembly decided to retain the Committee as a permanent subsidiary organ (resolution 43/222 B). The Assembly requested the Secretary-General to continue his efforts to ensure respect for equal treatment of the official languages of the United Nations (43/222 E) and appealed to Member States to keep the length of communications to a minimum (43/222 C). The Assembly approved the implementation of phase I of an integrated management information system and the 1989 budget estimate of the International Computing Centre at Geneva (43/217, sections XII and II).

Conferences and meetings

In 1988, the Committee on Conferences approved the draft calendar of conferences and meetings of United Nations organs for 1989.[1] Other matters dealt with by the Committee were its own status, the control and limitation of documentation, the possibility of central planning and coordination of all organizational aspects of conference servicing, a review of proposals relating to the schedule of conferences made at sessions of the General Assembly and an evaluation of the 1987 International Conference on Drug Abuse and Illicit Trafficking.

At its organizational session on 10 February, the Committee agreed to meet as required to take up matters related to the calendar of conferences. Its substantive session was held in New York from 17 to 26 August. In its report, the Committee submitted three draft resolutions, which served as the bases for Assembly **resolutions 43/222 A-C**.

Report of the Secretary-General. In April,[2] the Secretary-General issued his second progress report on the implementation of a 1986 Assembly resolution[3] calling for greater efficiency in the Organization's administrative and financial functioning. Referring to the call for a strengthened Committee on Conferences with broadened responsibilities (recommendation 1),[4] the Secretary-General noted that the Committee had achieved consensus on many important points. Some success had been

achieved in staggering conferences and meetings throughout the year in order to make better use of facilities and resources (recommendation 1 (e)). With regard to the call for a reduction in the number and duration of meetings and conferences (recommendation 2),[5] it was noted that the calendar of conferences for the biennium 1988-1989 did not reflect a diminished level of meeting activity. The report stated that, as mandated by the Assembly in 1987,[6] conference services must be provided with adequate personnel, with due respect for the equal treatment of all official languages of the United Nations.

Mandate of the Committee on Conferences

The Committee on Conferences resumed consideration of the question of changing its status to that of a permanent intergovernmental body, as requested by the Assembly in 1986.[7]

The Committee recommended that it become a permanent subsidiary body of the Assembly, whose members would be appointed for a term of office of three years, with one third retiring each year; that members should be eligible for reappointment; and that the Assembly, on the basis of existing practice, would decide on how to stagger the membership. The Committee agreed that the mode of selecting its members should remain unchanged.

GENERAL ASSEMBLY ACTION

On 21 December, the Assembly, acting on the recommendation of the Fifth (Administrative and Budgetary) Committee, adopted **resolution 43/222 B** by recorded vote.

Status of the Committee on Conferences

The General Assembly

1. *Decides* to retain the Committee on Conferences as a permanent subsidiary organ;

2. *Decides* that the Committee on Conferences shall be composed of twenty-one members to be appointed by the President of the General Assembly, after consultations with the chairmen of the regional groups, for a period of three years, on the basis of the following geographical distribution:

   (a) Six members from African States;

   (b) Five members from Asian States;

   (c) Four members from Latin American and Caribbean States;

   (d) Two members from Eastern European States;

(e) Four members from Western European and other States;

3. *Decides* that one third of the Committee's membership shall retire annually and that retiring members may be reappointed;

4. *Decides* that the Committee on Conferences shall have the following terms of reference:

(a) To advise the General Assembly on all matters pertaining to the organization of conferences in the United Nations;

(b) To plan and co-ordinate conferences and meetings in close consultation with the Secretariat and all relevant bodies in the preparation of the draft calendar, in particular by staggering conferences and meetings throughout the year, and to avoid to the maximum extent possible the overlapping of meetings related to the same sector of activity in the same conference location;

(c) In this connection, to examine the proposals of the Secretary-General on the draft calendar prepared on the basis of his budgetary proposals and to recommend to the General Assembly a draft calendar of conferences and meetings designed to meet the needs of the United Nations and to ensure the optimum utilization of conference-servicing resources. With respect to the proposed departures from the approved calendar of conferences and meetings that have administrative and financial implications, to act on behalf of the Assembly, in conformity with the budgetary process in force and with full respect for the mandates of other bodies;

(d) To determine the ways and means that might ensure the optimum utilization of conference facilities and services, including documentation, and to present appropriate recommendations to the General Assembly;

(e) To advise the General Assembly on the current and future requirements of the Organization for conference services, facilities and documentation;

(f) To make recommendations as appropriate to the General Assembly on means to ensure an improved co-ordination of conferences within the United Nations system, including conference services and facilities, and to conduct the appropriate consultations in that regard;

(g) To monitor the implementation of all General Assembly resolutions on the organization and servicing of, and documentation for, conferences and meetings;

(h) To monitor the policy of the Organization on publications, with the assistance of the Publications Board of the Secretariat and taking into account the positions adopted by the Committee on Information and other relevant bodies;

(i) To report annually thereon to the General Assembly.

General Assembly resolution 43/222 B

21 December 1988   Meeting 84   129-4-14 (recorded vote)

Approved by Fifth Committee (A/43/963) by recorded vote (91-3-13), 13 December (meeting 46); draft by Committee on Conferences (A/43/32 & Corr.1,2), amended by Argentina (A/C.5/43/L.10); agenda item 119.
Financial implications. 5th Committee, A/43/959; S-G, A/C.5/43/11.
Meeting numbers. GA 43rd session: 5th Committee 3-6, 36, 45, 46; plenary 84.

Recorded vote in Assembly as follows:

In favour: Afghanistan, Algeria, Angola, Antigua and Barbuda, Argentina, Bahamas, Bahrain, Bangladesh, Barbados, Belize, Benin, Bhutan, Bolivia, Botswana, Brazil, Brunei Darussalam, Burkina Faso, Burma, Burundi, Byelorussian SSR, Cameroon, Canada, Central African Republic, Chad, Chile, China, Colombia, Comoros, Congo, Costa Rica, Côte d'Ivoire, Cuba, Cyprus, Czechoslovakia, Democratic Yemen, Djibouti, Dominican Republic, Ecuador, Egypt, Ethiopia, Fiji, Finland, Gabon, Gambia, German Democratic Republic, Ghana, Guatemala, Guinea, Guinea-Bissau, Guyana, Haiti, Honduras, Hungary, Iceland, India, Indonesia, Iran, Iraq, Jamaica, Japan, Jordan, Kenya, Kuwait, Lao People's Democratic Republic, Lebanon, Lesotho, Liberia, Libyan Arab Jamahiriya, Madagascar, Malawi, Malaysia, Maldives, Mali, Mauritania, Mauritius, Mexico, Mongolia, Morocco, Mozambique, Nepal, New Zealand, Nicaragua, Niger, Nigeria, Norway, Oman, Pakistan, Panama, Papua New Guinea, Paraguay, Peru, Philippines, Poland, Qatar, Romania, Rwanda, Saint Lucia, Saint Vincent and the Grenadines, Samoa, Sao Tome and Principe, Saudi Arabia, Senegal, Sierra Leone, Singapore, Solomon Islands, Somalia, Sri Lanka, Sudan, Swaziland, Sweden, Syrian Arab Republic, Thailand, Togo, Trinidad and Tobago, Tunisia, Uganda, Ukrainian SSR, USSR, United Arab Emirates, United Republic of Tanzania, Uruguay, Vanuatu, Venezuela, Viet Nam, Yemen, Yugoslavia, Zaire, Zambia, Zimbabwe.
Against: Germany, Federal Republic of, Israel, United Kingdom, United States.
Abstaining: Australia, Austria, Belgium, Bulgaria, Denmark, France, Greece, Ireland, Italy, Luxembourg, Netherlands, Portugal, Spain, Turkey.

Uganda proposed that the Fifth Committee inform the Assembly that action on the draft resolution was taken on the understanding that nothing in paragraph 4 *(c)* should be construed as giving the Committee on Conferences any role in the budgetary process or authority to override decisions on programmes and on meetings and conferences duly decided upon by United Nations legislative organs. The proposal was adopted by a recorded vote of 78 to 14, with 15 abstentions.

Calendar of meetings

In response to a 1986 request of the Assembly,[8] the Committee on Conferences in 1988[1] discussed the pattern of future meetings of the Advisory Board on Disarmament Studies. The Board had repeatedly sought authorization from the Assembly to meet at United Nations Headquarters during Assembly sessions, as mandated by a 1985 resolution.[9]

The Secretariat explained that efforts made by the Board to adjust its meeting pattern had been hampered by the fact that a number of the Board members were also representatives to the Conference on Disarmament at Geneva, which was not scheduled to end until mid-September 1988. Consequently, Board meetings could not be held before that time. The Committee recommended that the Assembly authorize the Board to meet during the forty-third session of the Assembly, but it also urged the Board to make greater efforts to avoid meeting during Assembly sessions in the future.

Calendar for 1988-1989

In February 1988, the Secretariat circulated a note[10] containing the calendar of conferences and meetings of the United Nations and of the principal organs of the specialized agencies and the International Atomic Energy Agency for 1988 and 1989. In 1988, the Committee on Conferences approved a draft revised calendar for 1989 and submitted it to the Assembly for approval.[1] A draft calendar of conferences and meetings for 1988 and 1989 had been adopted by the Assembly in 1987.[11]

Calendar for 1990-1991

By **decision 1988/103** of 5 February, pursuant to a 1987 request by the Assembly,[11] the Economic and Social Council invited the Committee on Conferences to review the Council's draft biennial calendar beginning with the calendar for 1990-1991 and to submit its recommendations.

In August, the Committee on Conferences was informed that a detailed draft biennial calendar of conferences for 1990-1991 could not be submitted to it until the Economic and Social Council had finalized its calendar of meetings in July 1989.[1] The Committee, invited to decide whether it required an earlier draft with fewer details of the proposed dates and venues of meetings, indicated that it would prefer to have the most detailed and up-to-date draft possible, even if it meant receiving the draft later than in previous years.

GENERAL ASSEMBLY ACTION

On 21 December, the Assembly, on the recommendation of the Fifth Committee, adopted **resolution 43/222 D** without vote.

Programme of work of the Committee on Conferences
The General Assembly

Requests the Secretary-General to submit information to the Committee on Conferences at its organizational session in 1989 to assist the Committee in establishing its work programme on a biennial basis in line with the programme budget and the medium-term plan of the United Nations, taking into account the views expressed by delegations during the forty-third session of the General Assembly.

General Assembly resolution 43/222 D

21 December 1988   Meeting 84   Adopted without vote

Approved by Fifth Committee (A/43/963) without vote, 13 December (meeting 46); draft by Vice-Chairman following informal consultations (A/C.5/43/L.9); agenda item 119.
Meeting numbers. GA 43rd session: 5th Committee 3-6, 45, 46; plenary 84.

Conference and meeting services

The Committee on Conferences considered a report issued in March by the Secretary-General[12] on the utilization of conference-servicing resources by certain United Nations bodies meeting in New York, Geneva and Vienna in 1987. The report indicated that the bodies listed had collectively improved their utilization of conference resources compared to previous years. The utilization factor was 74 per cent for bodies meeting in New York, 84 per cent for those meeting at Geneva and 85 per cent for Vienna.

The Committee requested the Chairman to ask the chairmen of bodies that had not adequately utilized the resources provided to them

to bring the matter to the attention of their members so that they could consider a review of their meeting patterns. The Committee recommended that the Assembly urge United Nations organs that had failed to make adequate use of the conference-servicing resources provided to them to consider reducing the number of meetings they requested in their future programmes of work. It further requested the Chairman and the Secretary-General to assist those organs to make better use of their services.

The Assembly had also requested[11] the Secretary-General to examine the possibility of having all organizational aspects of conference servicing in the United Nations centrally planned and co-ordinated, with a view to optimizing efficiency and cost-effectiveness. The Secretary-General was to take into account the recommendations of the Economic and Social Council's Special Commission on the in-depth study of the United Nations intergovernmental structure and functions in the economic and social fields and submit his findings to the Assembly through the Committee on Conferences. The Special Commission issued its report in June,[13] but the Secretariat informed the Committee in August that, pending a decision by the Assembly or the Council on the outcome of the Commission's deliberations, it was unable to comply with the Assembly's request.

GENERAL ASSEMBLY ACTION

On 21 December, the Assembly, on the recommendation of the Fifth Committee, adopted **resolution 43/222 A** without vote.

Report of the Committee on Conferences
The General Assembly,

Having considered the report of the Committee on Conferences,

1. *Takes note with appreciation* of the report of the Committee on Conferences;

2. *Approves* the draft revised calendar of conferences and meetings of the United Nations for 1989 as submitted by the Committee on Conferences;

3. *Authorizes* the Committee on Conferences to make adjustments in the calendar of conferences and meetings for 1989 that may become necessary as a result of action and decisions taken by the General Assembly at its forty-third session;

4. *Notes with appreciation* that there has been a considerable improvement in the utilization of conference resources by a number of United Nations organs;

5. *Urges* those United Nations organs which have failed to make adequate use of the conference-servicing resources provided to them to consider reducing the number of meetings they request in their future programmes of work;

6. *Requests* the Chairman of the Committee on Conferences and the Secretary-General to maintain their contacts with United Nations organs that have failed to make adequate use of the conference-

servicing resources provided to them in order to assist those organs in making better use of their services;

7. *Requests* the Committee on Conferences to remain seized of the matter on the basis of further reports from the Secretary-General.

General Assembly resolution 43/222 A

21 December 1988   Meeting 84   Adopted without vote

Approved by Fifth Committee (A/43/963) without vote, 13 December (meeting 46); draft by Committee on Conferences (A/43/32 & Corr.1,2); agenda item 119.
Meeting numbers. GA 43rd session: 5th Committee 3-6, 45, 46; plenary 84.

Language and interpretation services

The Secretary-General in September 1988[14] issued a report on the implementation of a 1987 Assembly resolution[6] requesting the Secretary-General to provide adequate conference-servicing personnel to ensure equal treatment of all the official languages of the United Nations (Arabic, Chinese, English, French, Russian, Spanish). The Secretary-General noted that severe cuts had already been made in the translation and interpretation services and that, in order to ensure the provision of interpretation and other services despite those cuts, sufficient temporary assistance funds would have to be made available so that free-lancers could be recruited as necessary.

GENERAL ASSEMBLY ACTION

On 21 December, the Assembly, on the recommendation of the Fifth Committee, adopted **resolution 43/222 E** without vote.

Implementation of General Assembly resolution 42/207 C

The General Assembly,

Reaffirming its resolution 42/207 C of 11 December 1987,

Taking note of the report of the Secretary-General on the implementation of resolution 42/207 C,

1. *Requests* the Secretary-General to continue his valuable efforts to implement resolution 42/207 C;

2. *Also requests* the Secretary-General to report on this matter to the General Assembly at its forty-fourth session.

General Assembly resolution 43/222 E

21 December 1988   Meeting 84   Adopted without vote

Approved by Fifth Committee (A/43/963) without vote, 13 December (meeting 46); draft by Vice-Chairman following informal consultations (A/C.5/43/L.9); agenda item 119.
Meeting numbers. GA 43rd session: 5th Committee 3-6, 45, 46; plenary 84.

Conference reports

In accordance with 1982 Assembly guidelines for preparing United Nations special conferences,[15] a Conference Management Committee was established to guide and co-ordinate Secretariat activities for the 1987 International Conference on Drug Abuse and Illicit Trafficking.[16] At its August session, the Committee on Conferences endorsed the Conference Management Committee's recommendation[17] that a standard format be established for final reports of major conferences and that guidelines be provided for preparing and editing reports.

Representation at conferences

In September, the Secretary-General transmitted to the Assembly a report of the Joint Inspection Unit (JIU) on the representation of United Nations organizations at conferences and meetings.[18] The report was a result of a JIU study to examine the effectiveness of the participation by Secretariat staff members in meetings and to recommend ways of increasing efficiency and reducing the costs involved.

JIU recommended the restructuring of the Representation Unit of the Executive Office of the Secretary-General, which was responsible for the direction and control of official travel, in order to increase its ability to implement the current co-ordinating and approval procedures. It also recommended that the practice of non-participatory attendance be considerably reduced, that attendance of United Nations departments at conferences and meetings be limited to one person, and that wherever liaison or field offices existed in the venue of a meeting, travel from Headquarters not be allowed unless the meeting were highly specialized. JIU further recommended that the length of attendance at meetings held away from Headquarters be kept to a minimum, that rules and practices in the financial area be made uniform and that United Nations departments and offices constantly review and evaluate overall representational activity in a comprehensive and critical manner. It was recommended that the Secretary-General further request departments and offices to observe strictly procedures regarding representation at conferences and meetings, with particular emphasis on the time-limits for the issuance of invitations and the submission of authorization requests.

REFERENCES

[1]A/43/32 & Corr.1,2. [2]A/43/286. [3]YUN 1986, p. 1024, GA res. 41/213, 19 Dec. 1986. [4]*Ibid.*, p. 1083. [5]*Ibid.*, p. 1084. [6]YUN 1987, p. 1173, GA res. 42/207 C, 11 Dec. 1987. [7]YUN 1986, p. 1083, GA res. 41/177 B, 5 Dec. 1986. [8]*Ibid.*, p. 1085, GA res. 41/177 A, 5 Dec. 1986. [9]YUN 1985, p. 1256, GA res. 40/243, 18 Dec. 1985. [10]A/AC.172/125. [11]YUN 1987, p. 1171, GA res. 42/207 B, 11 Dec. 1987. [12]A/AC.172/88/Add.6. [13]E/1988/75. [14]A/43/628. [15]YUN 1982, p. 1498, GA res. 37/14 B, annex, 16 Nov. 1982. [16]YUN 1987, p. 900. [17]A/AC.172/126. [18]A/43/586.

Documents and publications

Documents limitation

In May, the Secretary-General published an updated version of a note[1] setting forth the policies laid down by the General Assembly regarding the control and limitation of documentation, as requested by the Assembly in 1969.[2] The note, which took into account policy decisions adopted by the Assembly up to the end of 1987, was distributed to all Member States.

Those policies applied for the most part to the documentation of the Assembly and its subsidiary bodies, although other United Nations organs, in particular the Economic and Social Council and bodies such as the Trade and Development Board of the United Nations Conference on Trade and Development, had been invited to apply the same policies.

The document included specific recommendations for the control of meeting records, statements, reports and studies, annexes and supplements to official records, documentation for treaty bodies and special conferences, and statements of programme budget implications. Annexes to the note contained a list of meeting record entitlements and revised guidelines for the format and contents of the reports of subsidiary organs of the Assembly, as well as guidelines for the control and limitation of documentation for special conferences of the United Nations.

Pursuant to a 1986 request of the Assembly[3] that the Committee on Conferences examine the number of communications from Member States circulated as United Nations documents, the Committee requested the Secretariat to report on the matter. In May 1988, the Secretariat issued a report,[4] listing all such documents circulated between February 1987 and March 1988 and noting the country of origin and the number of pages of each document.

The Committee resumed consideration of the question in August.[5] The Secretariat, in introducing the report, stated that the vast majority of communications issued as United Nations documents were less than three pages long, and that of the 1,126 documents listed, only 15 exceeded 24 pages.

The Committee recommended that the Assembly renew its appeal to Member States to exercise restraint in requesting the circulation of communications as United Nations documents, and that they endeavour to keep the length of communications to a minimum. The Committee agreed to keep the matter under review and to discuss it again in 1990 on the basis of an updated report from the Secretariat.

Also in May, the Secretary-General issued a report[6] on the compliance of subsidiary organs of the Assembly with the 32-page limit for reports set in 1982.[7] The report noted that the total volume of supplements to the *Official Records of the General Assembly* issued by subsidiary organs in 1987 amounted to 2,936 pages, some 600 more than in 1986. This was a reversal from the period 1978 to 1986, when the number of pages had fallen from 4,209 to 2,323.

On the basis of that report, the Committee on Conferences took up the matter in August.[5] It was aware that some bodies, owing to the nature of their work, faced difficulties in complying with the 32-page limit. It recognized that it was too early to tell whether the 1987 increase represented a reversal of the earlier trend towards a reduction in the volume of supplements. The Committee therefore decided to request its Chairman to maintain his contacts with the chairmen of those bodies whose reports had exceeded 32 pages, stressing the need for brevity.

GENERAL ASSEMBLY ACTION

On 21 December, the Assembly, on the recommendation of the Fifth Committee, adopted **resolution 43/222 C** without vote.

Control and limitation of documentation

The General Assembly,

Recalling its resolutions 2292(XXII) of 8 December 1967, 2538(XXIV) of 11 December 1969, 3415(XXX) of 8 December 1975, 34/50 of 23 November 1979, 35/10 B of 3 November 1980, 36/117 of 10 December 1981, 37/14 C of 16 November 1982, 40/243, section III, of 18 December 1985, 41/177 D of 5 December 1986 and 42/207 of 11 December 1987,

1. *Renews its appeal* to Member States to exercise restraint in their requests for the circulation of communications as United Nations documents;

2. *Appeals* to Member States making such requests to endeavour to keep the length of the communications to a minimum;

3. *Requests* the Committee on Conferences to keep this matter under review and to report thereon to the General Assembly at its forty-fifth session;

4. *Requests* the Secretary-General to establish a standard format for final reports of special conferences of the United Nations and to provide guidelines for the preparation and editing of those reports;

5. *Again requests* that subsidiary organs should strive to keep their reports to the General Assembly within the desirable limit of thirty-two pages;

6. *Invites* the Committee on Conferences to remain seized of this matter on the basis of further reports from the Secretary-General.

General Assembly resolution 43/222 C

21 December 1988   Meeting 84   Adopted without vote

Approved by Fifth Committee (A/43/963) without vote, 13 December (meeting 46); draft by Committee on Conferences (A/43/32 & Corr.1,2); agenda item 119.

Meeting numbers. GA 43rd session: 5th Committee 3-6, 45, 46; plenary 84.

REFERENCES

(1)A/INF/43/1. (2)YUN 1969, p. 830, GA res. 2538(XXIV), 11 Dec. 1969. (3)YUN 1986, p. 1090, GA res. 41/177 D, 5 Dec. 1986. (4)A/AC.172/127. (5)A/43/32 & Corr.1,2. (6)A/AC.172/128. (7)YUN 1982, p. 1500, GA res. 37/14 C, 16 Nov. 1982.

UN premises

Conference facilities at Addis Ababa and Bangkok

A report of the Secretary-General on the construction of conference facilities at Addis Ababa, Ethiopia, and Bangkok, Thailand, was submitted to the Fifth Committee in October 1988.(1) It outlined the status and development of the two projects and contained updated timetables for their construction, approved by the General Assembly in 1984.(2) The report noted that no new appropriation would be required for the projects during the biennium 1988-1989.

Activities related to the expansion of conference facilities of the Economic Commission for Africa at Addis Ababa through September 1988 included the negotiation of contracts with the quantity surveyor and the architect/engineer, and the preparation of up-to-date project cost estimates by the quantity surveyor. The cost of construction, excluding contingency and administrative costs, was estimated at $71,534,700. As the provision for contingency and administrative costs was usually 5 to 10 per cent, it was unclear whether the original estimated total project cost of $73,501,000 as approved by the Assembly could be maintained.

Regarding the conference facilities of the Economic and Social Commission for Asia and the Pacific at Bangkok, the activities undertaken during the first nine months of 1988 included remobilization of the quantity surveyor and architectural/engineering consultants engaged for the project, a ground-breaking ceremony presided over by the Prime Minister of Thailand, and the preparation of up-to-date project cost estimates. The estimated construction cost was $40,327,800, so it was estimated that the total project cost of $44,177,700 already approved by the Assembly would be sufficient to cover the contingency and administrative costs.

On 21 December, the Assembly, by **resolution 43/217, section VIII**, took note of the Secretary-General's report.

REFERENCES

(1)A/C.5/43/16. (2)YUN 1984, pp. 620 & 628, GA res. 39/236, sects. III & XI, 18 Dec. 1984.

Information systems and computers

Technological innovations

In November, in accordance with a recommendation of the Advisory Committee on Administrative and Budgetary Questions (ACABQ), the Secretary-General issued a report(1) containing revised estimates for the establishment of an integrated management information system (IMIS). It described the existing situation, explained the objectives, stages, scope and benefits of IMIS and outlined the proposed method of financing the project.

The report stated that there was widespread dissatisfaction with the current data-processing systems supporting the administrative functions of the Organization, particularly in the financial and personnel areas. Where they existed at all, they rarely shared common data and were old and unresponsive. IMIS would be a highly integrated computer system covering all functional areas in administration and management, entailing a substantial cost for the Organization. Its major benefit would be an improvement in the overall quality of management of the United Nations. It would eventually result in substantial productivity gains, after the system had undergone a shakedown period.

In its December report on the establishment of IMIS,(2) ACABQ recommended that the Assembly approve the implementation of phase I of the project within a three-and-one-half-year period at a total cost not exceeding $28 million at 1988 rates. That represented a reduction of $3,593,500 from the Secretary-General's projected cost of $31,593,500. ACABQ recommended that the Secretary-General's request for additional appropriations for the project in the amount of $6,204,200 for the biennium 1988-1989 be reduced to $3,425,700.

ACABQ was not fully convinced by some of the explanations submitted by the Secretariat concerning the projected cost of phase I of the IMIS project. It stated that certain costs should be lower after competitive bidding and that the Secretary-General's rationale in concluding that 2,000 terminals would be required for the IMIS system was not readily apparent.

In its appraisal of the Secretary-General's proposal, ACABQ cautioned that, while it accepted the need for improved information systems in the Secretariat, the mere advent of new technology would not achieve the intended objectives if there was no accompanying clear management direction that would make optimum use of such technological innovations. Cost estimates for phases II and

III of the IMIS project were $9,301,000, bringing the cost of the entire project to $40,894,500.

The Fifth Committee recommended that the Assembly approve the implementation of phase I of the project at the revised level of $28 million.[3] The Committee took its decision on the understanding that the Secretary-General, in implementing the project, would endeavour to contain costs, take measures to bring about effective co-ordination among the centres concerned and ensure that the experience of other United Nations organizations was taken into account.

GENERAL ASSEMBLY ACTION

On 21 December, the Assembly, on the recommendation of the Fifth Committee, adopted **resolution 43/217, section XII**, without vote.

Establishment of an integrated management information system

[*The General Assembly . . .*]

1. *Approves* the implementation, within a three-and-one-half-year period, of phase I of the integrated management information system project at a total cost not to exceed 28 million dollars at 1988 rates;

2. *Authorizes* the Secretary-General to administer flexibly and to allocate among the cost centres identified in his report the total cost established for the project;

3. *Approves* the Secretary-General's understanding concerning the use and application of voluntary funds as contained in paragraph 53 of his report;

. . .

General Assembly resolution 43/217, section XII

21 December 1988   Meeting 84   Adopted without vote

Approved by Fifth Committee (A/43/980) by recorded vote (83-4-21), 12 December (meeting 45); oral proposal by Chairman; agenda item 114.
Meeting numbers. GA 43rd session: 5th Committee 42, 44, 45; plenary 84.

Co-ordination of information systems

In April,[4] the Administrative Committee on Co-ordination (ACC) approved the revised work programme and budget of the Advisory Committee for the Co-ordination of Information Systems (ACCIS) for the biennium 1988-1989.[5] The budget remained within the limit directed by ACC and the Economic and Social Council, and was structured on a base of $1,939,500.

The work programme of ACCIS for the biennium had three subprogrammes: information resources of the United Nations system, tools for improving the information infrastructure within the United Nations system and basic co-ordination services.

The main objective of the first subprogramme was to develop and make available a number of data bases and printed products that provided information on existing information resources and activities of United Nations organizations. The Secretariat proceeded with plans to make a system-wide *Register of Development Activities* operational, as requested by the Assembly in 1982.[6] The *Directory of United Nations Data Bases and Information Systems* continued to be the basic information resource for other ACCIS activities. ACCIS guides to United Nations information sources on the environment, trade and health were to be produced during 1988-1989. In addition, ACCIS decided to prepare a data base of non-governmental data collections held by the United Nations.

The second subprogramme was concerned with tools for making more efficient use of existing resources. The use of computer networking along with or as a substitute for telegraph, telex, post or even travel was likely to be the area of greatest impact in improving information infrastructure at the United Nations. It was decided not to pursue a study of the feasibility of developing a common communication network facility, as proposed in the 1986-1987 work programme. Instead, that programme element would be reoriented towards enhancing the use of readily available communication links and solving hardware and software problems.

Under the third subprogramme, advisory services on information systems would continue to be provided by ACCIS. The *ACCIS Newsletter*, which had 2,000 subscribers, was to continue to report on the progress of the ACCIS work programme, new developments in information technology and other relevant information.

Archives

In October,[7] the Organizational Committee of ACC considered a report by the Section of Archivists of International Organizations of the International Council of Archives, which called for promoting the preservation of the archives of the United Nations and the specialized agencies.

Also in October,[8] ACC recommended that all organizations of the United Nations system establish, with appropriate formal authorization, an archives and records management service in order to ensure the preservation of their archives. It also decided to draw to the attention of the organizations of the system three further studies prepared by the United Nations Educational, Scientific and Cultural Organization and the work and recommendations of the Technical Panel on Records Management of ACCIS.

International Computing Centre

In September, the Secretary-General submitted to the Fifth Committee the 1989 budget estimates of the International Computing Centre at Geneva.[9] The estimates amounted to $11,775,000, as compared to $9,025,600 for 1988. The five organizations/programmes that were projected to use the Centre most in 1989 were, in order of money to be spent: the United Nations High Commissioner for Refugees, the United Nations, the World Health Organization, the World Food Programme and the World Intellectual Property Organization. Together, those organizations accounted for over three quarters of the funding for the Centre's operations.

On 21 December, the Assembly, by resolution **43/217, section II**, approved the 1989 budget estimates of ICC.

REFERENCES

(1)A/C.5/43/24. (2)A/43/7/Add.10. (3)A/43/980. (4)ACC/1988/DEC/1-18 (dec. 1988/11). (5)ACC/1988/10. (6)YUN 1982, p. 624, GA res. 37/226, 20 Dec. 1982. (7)ACC/1988/2/Add.3. (8)ACC/1988/DEC/19-31 (dec. 1988/29). (9)A/C.5/43/8 & Corr.1.

UN Postal Administration

In 1988, gross revenue of the United Nations Postal Administration (UNPA) from the sale of philatelic items at United Nations Headquarters and at overseas offices totalled more than $12.6 million. Revenue from the sale of stamps for philatelic purposes was retained by the United Nations. Under the terms of an agreement between the United Nations and the United States, revenue from the sale of United States dollar–denominated stamps used for postage from Headquarters was reimbursed to the United States Postal Service. Similarly, postal agreements between the United Nations and the Governments of Switzerland and Austria required that revenue derived from the sale of Swiss franc– and Austrian schilling–denominated stamps for postage use be reimbursed to the Swiss and Austrian postal authorities, respectively.

Six commemorative stamp issues, two definitive stamps and two souvenir cards were released by UNPA during the year.

The first commemorative issue, released on 29 January in denominations of 22 and 33 United States cents, 0.35 and 1.40 Swiss francs (SwF) and 4 and 6 Austrian schillings (S), was on the theme "IFAD—For a World Without Hunger". Two definitive stamps with denominations of 3 cents and SwF 0.50 were issued on the same day.

On 18 March, commemorative stamps were released in a mini-sheet format of 12 stamps to commemorate "Survival of the Forests". The stamps, which were in a vertical *se-tenant* pair format, carried denominations of 25 and 44 cents, SwF 0.50 and 1.10 and S 4 and 5.

The third commemorative issue, carrying the slogan "International Volunteer Day", was released on 6 May. The stamps were in denominations of 25 and 50 cents, SwF 0.80 and 0.90 and S 6 and 7.50. A souvenir card accompanied the issue.

"Health in Sports" was the theme of the fourth commemorative issue for the year. Issued on 17 June, the six stamps carried denominations of 25 and 38 cents, SwF 0.50 and 1.40 and S 6 and 8. A souvenir card accompanied the issue.

The ninth set of 16 stamps in the "Flag Series" was released on 15 September. Each stamp carried a denomination of 25 cents.

On 9 December, a set of three stamps and three souvenir sheets were released to commemorate the fortieth anniversary of the Universal Declaration of Human Rights.[1] The stamps carried denominations of 25 cents, SwF 0.90 and S 5. The souvenir sheets, in denominations of $1, SwF 2 and S 11, carried the complete text of the preamble to the Declaration in English, French and German, respectively.

A total of 67,747,324 stamps were printed in 1988, and 2,993,035 envelopes received cancellation on the first day of issue.

REFERENCE

(1)YUN 1948-49, p. 535, GA res. 217 A (III), 10 Dec. 1948.

PART SEVEN

Intergovernmental organizations
related to the United Nations

Chapter I

International Atomic Energy Agency (IAEA)

In 1988, the activities of the International Atomic Energy Agency (IAEA) in nuclear safety and radiation protection increased due to growing interest by its member States. The thirty-second session of the IAEA General Conference (Vienna, 19-23 September) called for measures to strengthen international co-operation in nuclear safety and radiological protection and for sharing safety-related information.

The Conference condemned all nuclear waste dumping practices that would infringe on the sovereignty of States and/or would endanger the environment or public health of other countries, and called on all member States to ensure that no such practices occurred. It requested the IAEA Director General to establish a technical working group of experts to elaborate an internationally agreed code of practice for international transactions involving nuclear wastes based on, among other things, a review of current national and international laws and regulations on waste disposal.

On 21 September 1988, the Joint Protocol relating to the Application of the 1963 Vienna Convention on Civil Liability for Nuclear Damage[a] and the 1960 Paris Convention on Third Party Liability in the Field of Nuclear Energy was adopted and opened for signature.

IAEA's efforts to strengthen the infrastructure for nuclear power projects in its developing member States continued through interregional and national training courses, seminars, workshops, technical co-operation projects, advisory missions, guidebooks, manuals and technical committee meetings.

During the year, IAEA continued to foster research and development in the peaceful uses of nuclear energy and the exchange of scientific and technical information, to establish and administer safeguards, to provide technical assistance to its member States and to establish health and safety standards.

The IAEA Board of Governors met six times in 1988, once in each of February, May, June and December and twice in September.

IAEA membership remained at 113 throughout 1988 (see Annex I).

Nuclear safety and radiation protection

In 1988, IAEA strengthened its safety evaluation and information exchange services for nuclear power plants and research reactors.

Six operational safety review team (OSART) missions carried out in-depth reviews of management programmes, plant operation, maintenance, personnel training, technical support, plant chemistry, radiological protection and emergency capability at nuclear plants in six countries (France, Hungary, Italy, Japan, Sweden, USSR). OSART guidelines were published and a report was prepared on OSART findings based on the results of missions between June 1987 and June 1988. Under the operational safety indicators programme, a set of plant-specific indicators, which helped identify key areas for in-depth investigation, were used in conjunction with OSART missions. The number of reports to IAEA's incident reporting system on unusual operating, surveillance and maintenance events at nuclear plants increased from 421 to 613.

Experts of the integrated safety assessment of research reactors programme visited reactor facilities in five countries (Colombia, Iraq, Norway, Republic of Korea, Venezuela). IAEA initiated in 1988 a three-year publication programme, which would include a safety standard report, several safety guides and safety practices. The 326 research reactors operating in 55 countries in 1988 had a cumulative operating experience of 9,814 reactor years.

The International Nuclear Safety Advisory Group completed its work on basic safety principles for nuclear power plants. In the area of probabilistic safety assessment, a personal computer software package developed for fault-tree and event-tree analysis was distributed to more than 50 users in member States. The package was being adapted for use as a tool for the safety management of nuclear power plants, in co-operation with member States.

Progress was made on implementing an interagency (IAEA/United Nations Industrial Development Organization (UNIDO)/United Nations Environment Programme/World Health Organization (WHO)) project for assessing and managing the health and environmental risks of energy and other complex industrial systems. Case-studies were initiated in eight member States.

In the area of radiation protection, through an IAEA/Nuclear Energy Agency of the Organisation for Economic Co-operation and Development meeting (Vienna), an international consensus was

[a]YUN 1963, p. 595.

achieved on the exemption of radiation sources and practices from regulatory control. Following the 1986 accident at the Chernobyl nuclear power plant in the Ukrainian SSR, member States supplied IAEA with measurements of radioactivity in environmental materials; the task of entering the information into the Agency's data base was completed in 1988.

As a result of requests, radiation protection advisory teams reviewed infrastructures in 12 countries (Bangladesh, Costa Rica, Côte d'Ivoire, Ethiopia, Greece, Guatemala, Indonesia, Jamaica, Madagascar, Nigeria, Senegal, Viet Nam) and recommended long-term strategies for co-operation and assistance. Three other countries (Libyan Arab Jamahiriya, Qatar, Zambia) received missions to advise on measures for ensuring the existence and implementation of effective radiation protection legislation. Two missions to Jordan assessed the radiation protection services at medical installations. Support for the establishment of national radiation protection services was provided by 37 technical co-operation projects.

Nuclear power

The total installed nuclear power-generating capacity in the world increased by about 4.3 per cent during 1988, reaching 311 gigawatts (electrical) by the end of the year. At that time, there were 429 nuclear power plants in operation, accounting for some 17 per cent of the world's electricity generation and representing an accumulated operating experience of about 5,000 reactor years.

Fourteen nuclear power plants came on line during the year, in France, the Federal Republic of Germany, Japan, the Republic of Korea, Spain, the USSR, the United Kingdom and the United States, and construction started on six plants, in China, France, Japan, the USSR and the United Kingdom. Two reactors with a total capacity of 335 megawatts (electrical) were permanently shut down in the USSR and the United Kingdom.

IAEA provided technical support for energy, electricity and nuclear power planning studies in Egypt, Indonesia, Malaysia, Thailand, Tunisia, Turkey, Viet Nam and Yugoslavia. Co-operation between IAEA and the World Bank in planning energy and electric power systems in developing countries continued, with joint World Bank/ United Nations Development Programme (UNDP) activities undertaken in Egypt, Morocco, Turkey and Yugoslavia. IAEA provided technical support for feasibility studies and infrastructure development planning projects in China, Malaysia, Morocco and Tunisia. Various training courses were held in China, the Federal Republic of Germany, Indonesia, Malaysia, Morocco, Poland, the Republic of Korea, Romania and the United States.

At the end of 1988, the IAEA power reactor information system (PRIS) contained data for about 3,800 years of power reactor operation and on some 27,700 outages. During the year, data sets were supplied on request to contributing member States and detailed background information was provided for OSART missions. Using PRIS data, IAEA published editions of *Nuclear Power Reactors in the World* and *Operating Experience with Power Reactors in Member States (1987)*.

Nuclear fuel cycle

Sixty-five IAEA members were involved in fuel cycle technology activities. New projects included an international study on water reactor extended burn-up, a project on post-accident management of severely damaged nuclear fuel and radioactive waste arising; and a study on safety aspects of production, handling, transport and storage of uranium hexafluoride. An analysis was completed on the status and trends in the world nuclear fuel cycle and on the methodology of work performed by IAEA, emphasizing expected changes and corresponding probable directions for international co-operation. Technical assistance was provided to 33 members.

With reactor-related uranium requirements of some 38,600 tons in 1988, uranium production remained below requirements. Large inventories, estimated at three to four years of forward requirements, filled the gap and were expected to do so for a number of years. Thirty-three technical co-operation projects on uranium exploration and resource development in 31 countries were supported. The first *World Atlas of Uranium Occurrences and Deposits*, containing over 6,000 records of uranium occurrences in 96 countries, was published.

Fourteen technical co-operation projects were supported in nine countries in research reactor modernization, nuclear fuel fabrication, nuclear fuel and materials study, nuclear fuel cycle technology, nuclear fuel developments and simulation of radiation damage. Projects jointly supported with the IAEA Division of Nuclear Power included reactor physics, nuclear power stations and research reactors.

Radioactive waste management

IAEA increased its involvement in the waste management problems of developing countries. The national radioactive waste management policies, plans and activities of 12 developing countries were reviewed under the waste management advisory programme. IAEA provided support for 26 technical co-operation projects in 19 member States in waste management, the majority of which related to handling, treatment, conditioning and storage, reflecting the main current concerns of developing countries.

The Technical Review Committee on Underground Disposal, which had guided the programme on underground waste disposal for the preceding 10 years, was disbanded to make way for the International Radioactive Waste Management Advisory Committee, which was to have wider terms of reference and provide advice to IAEA on the whole of its radioactive waste management programme.

IAEA co-operated with the Commission of the European Communities in organizing an international symposium on the management of low- and intermediate-level radioactive wastes (Stockholm, Sweden, May), which was attended by more than 300 experts from 32 countries and 6 international organizations.

Other activities focused on handling, treatment, conditioning and storage of radioactive wastes, decontamination and decommissioning of nuclear facilities, and environmental aspects of radioactive waste management.

Food and agriculture

In the area of food and agriculture, IAEA, through the joint Food and Agriculture Organization of the United Nations (FAO)/IAEA Division, continued to assist developing member States to improve their agriculture and food production through the application of isotopes, ionizing radiation and related techniques, especially biotechnology.

Assistance was provided by IAEA in soil fertility, irrigation and crop production through 49 research contracts and agreements and 69 technical co-operation projects. In the field of plant breeding and genetics, assistance to 35 member States was provided through 36 national and 2 regional projects. Training in technologies needed for the application of nuclear techniques in plant improvement was arranged for 62 scientists from 36 member States through fellowships or courses. In agrochemicals and residues, assistance to member States continued through 62 research contracts and agreements and 13 technical co-operation projects. In food preservation, member States received assistance through 52 research contracts and agreements and 23 technical co-operation projects.

Research and training continued at IAEA's Agricultural Laboratory at Siebersdorf, Austria, in animal reproduction, disease diagnostics and nutrition. The Laboratory also supported insect and pest control, particularly Mediterranean fruit fly (medfly) reduction and tsetse fly eradication.

An International Conference on the Acceptance, Control of and Trade in Irradiated Foods (Geneva, December), jointly sponsored with FAO, WHO and the International Trade Centre, aimed at achieving a consensus on the acceptance and control of irradiated foods among member States. The Conference was attended by more than 250 experts designated by some 60 member States and 14 intergovernmental and non-governmental organizations. An international document on food irradiation, adopted by consensus, indicated that some 60 Governments had recognized food irradiation as a method of processing food to reduce food losses and illness caused by certain food-borne pathogens and to facilitate wider trade of food items.

Life sciences

In the life sciences, assistance continued to be provided to member States on the application of nuclear techniques in medicine, applied radiation biology and radiotherapy, radiation dosimetry, and nutritional and health-related environmental studies. Many of these activities were carried out in co-operation with WHO.

Training courses in nuclear medicine included an interregional training course (Moscow); a regional training course on medical scintigraphy (Havana, Cuba); a regional seminar on nuclear techniques in parasitic and communicable diseases for Asia and the Pacific (Bombay, India); and a seminar on training in nuclear medicine in developing countries (Vienna). Technical advice and assistance in nuclear medicine were provided through 67 research contracts and agreements and for 116 technical co-operation projects.

In applied radiation biology and radiotherapy, 14 participants from 11 developing member States were trained during a course for the Asia and Pacific region on radiation sterilization of tissue grafts for safe clinical use (Taiyuan, China). Sixteen participants attended an interregional seminar on new approaches in practices for radiation sterilization of medical supplies (Canada). Technical advice was provided for 65 research contracts and agreements and 15 technical co-operation projects.

A video film on IAEA dosimetry activity was completed in Chinese, English and Spanish. The performance test of the transportable reference-class ionization chamber dosimeter system for use in radiation therapy was completed and another system for the comparison of radiation protection level secondary standard dosimeters was developed. Assistance to member States in radiation dosimetry continued through 28 research contracts and agreements and 41 technical co-operation projects.

Research co-ordination meetings reviewed progress on nuclear techniques for toxic elements in foodstuffs and nuclear and nuclear-related techniques in the study of environmental pollution associated with solid wastes. An advisory group meeting was held on nuclear techniques in background air pollution monitoring. Assistance continued in nutritional and health-related environmental studies through 72 research contracts and agreements in 42 member States.

Physical and earth sciences

IAEA continued to promote the exchange of information in the physical and earth sciences and to assist countries with the application of nuclear techniques in experimental physics, analytical and radiation chemistry, non-destructive testing, radiation processing, industrial process control, geology, mining and hydrology.

In 1988, there were 325 research reactors operating in 54 member States, including 71 in 34 developing countries. The International Thermonuclear Experimental Reactor (ITER) was inaugurated during the year and its secretariat established at Vienna.

IAEA supported 193 technical co-operation projects for 48 countries to promote the transfer of nuclear technologies employed in industry.

In isotope hydrology, IAEA supported 57 technical co-operation projects in 50 member States, providing assistance in nuclear techniques in water resources assessment, geothermal resource exploration, strengthening analytical capabilities and the establishment of isotope laboratories, and the application of nuclear techniques to specific hydrological projects such as those related to sediment transport, leakage from dams and reservoirs, lake dynamics and water pollution.

Technical assistance

During 1988, 1,009 projects were operational and 88 training courses were held, involving 2,023 expert assignments and training for 1,947 IAEA fellows, visiting scientists and other participants.

Of the assistance delivered, the largest portion (20 per cent) related to the application of isotopes and radiation in agriculture. Other important fields were nuclear safety and radiation protection (19 per cent), applications of isotopes and radiation in industry and hydrology (16 per cent), nuclear engineering and technology (15 per cent), nuclear physics (8 per cent) and nuclear medicine (8 per cent).

Total new resources available for technical co-operation increased by 10 per cent over 1987 to $45.6 million. The IAEA Technical Assistance and Co-operation Fund accounted for 75.7 per cent of the total available resources, extrabudgetary funds for 12.5 per cent, UNDP for 6.7 per cent and assistance in kind for 5.1 per cent. Disbursements were highest in equipment procurement, accounting for just under 50 per cent of total delivery; the remaining provisions were nearly evenly split between training and expert services.

Scientific research and support

The IAEA Laboratories at Seibersdorf provided the experimental back-up services to programmes in food and agriculture, and physical, chemical and life sciences. They offered in-service training for individual fellows, organized training courses and supplied officers for technical co-operation projects.

Training, research and service activities were performed in areas such as soil fertility, irrigation, crop mutation, insect and pest control, pesticide analysis and formulation, animal nutrition, health and reproduction, and analytical chemistry, radiation dosimetry, electronics, instrumentation and isotope hydrology. In addition, the Laboratories provided analytical services for safeguards. The Safeguards Analytical Laboratory received 1,180 samples of nuclear material, reducing the total time needed to conclude verifications by destructive analysis by 17 per cent.

The International Laboratory of Marine Radioactivity (Monaco) conducted two world-wide intercalibration exercises for concentrations of man-made and natural radio-nuclides in natural samples. More than 40 laboratories participated in the analysis of a fish-flesh reference standard and a marine sediment sample. Comprehensive technical support was given for regional and global marine pollution assessments in co-operation with other United Nations agencies.

The International Centre for Theoretical Physics (Trieste, Italy) carried out research and training-for-research in fundamental physics, condensed matter, atomic and molecular physics, mathematics, physics and energy, physics and the environment, physics of the living state, applied physics and high technology, and physics and development. Some 4,100 scientists took part in the activities of the Centre and in the programme for training at laboratories in Italy.

Agency safeguards and responsibilities

As in previous years, the secretariat, in carrying out the IAEA safeguards obligations, did not detect any event which would indicate the diversion of a significant amount of safeguarded nuclear material—or the misuse of facilities, equipment or non-nuclear material subject to safeguards under certain agreements—for the manufacture of any nuclear weapon or explosive device, or for any other military purpose, or for purposes unknown. It was considered reasonable to conclude that the nuclear material under IAEA safeguards remained in peaceful nuclear activities or was otherwise adequately accounted for. During the year, 2,128 inspections were performed.

As at 31 December 1988, there were 168 safeguards agreements in force with 99 States, a safeguards agreement with Nigeria pursuant to the 1968 Treaty on the Non-Proliferation of Nuclear Weapons[b] (NPT) having entered into force in February and unilateral submission agreements with Albania and India having entered into force in March and September, respectively. Also agreements were concluded with Panama pursuant to NPT and the Treaty for the Prohibition of Nuclear Weapons in Latin America (Tlatelolco Treaty), and with Saint Lucia pursuant to NPT. Bahrain and Saudi Arabia acceded to NPT, bringing the total number of States parties to it at the end of 1988 to 139.

IAEA and China concluded an agreement relating to the latter's voluntary offer to place some of its peaceful nuclear installations under Agency safeguards.

Safeguards were applied in 41 States under agreements pursuant to NPT or to NPT and the Tlatelolco Treaty, and in one State pursuant to the Tlatelolco Treaty. NPT safeguards agreements had been concluded with 10 of the 11 States signatories of the South Pacific Nuclear Free Zone Treaty;[c] safeguards were applied in one of them pursuant to an NPT agreement. At the end of 1988, there were 511 nuclear facilities under safeguards or containing safeguarded nuclear material, 8 of which were in nuclear-weapon States. There were also 407 locations outside facilities containing small amounts of safeguarded material and two safeguarded non-nuclear installations.

Nuclear information

Costa Rica, Jordan, Morocco and UNIDO joined the International Nuclear Information System, bringing its membership to 78 IAEA member States and 15 international organizations. By the end of the year, the bibliographic data base of nuclear literature contained 1,266,075 records.

The data base of the Agricultural Information System, covering 130 national and 17 international organizations, totalled 1.5 million references in November.

Secretariat

At the end of 1988, the number of staff members of the secretariat was 2,079—797 in the Professional and higher categories (drawn from 77 countries), 1,150 in the General Service category and 132 in the Maintenance and Operatives Service category. (For senior secretariat officers, see Annex II.)

Budget

The regular budget for 1988 was $156,182,000, of which $146,838,000 was financed from contributions by member States on the basis of the 1988 scale of assessment, $5,366,000 from income from work for others and $3,978,000 from other miscellaneous income.

NOTE: For further information, see *The Annual Report for 1988*, prepared by IAEA.

[b]YUN 1968, p. 17, GA res. 2373(XXII), annex, 12 June 1968.
[c]YUN 1985, p. 58.

Annex I.   MEMBERSHIP OF THE INTERNATIONAL ATOMIC ENERGY AGENCY
(As at 31 December 1988)

Afghanistan, Albania, Algeria, Argentina, Australia, Austria, Bangladesh, Belgium, Bolivia, Brazil, Bulgaria, Burma, Byelorussian SSR, Cameroon, Canada, Chile, China, Colombia, Costa Rica, Côte d'Ivoire, Cuba, Cyprus, Czechoslovakia, Democratic Kampuchea, Democratic People's Republic of Korea, Denmark, Dominican Republic, Ecuador, Egypt, El Salvador, Ethiopia, Finland, France, Gabon, German Democratic Republic, Germany, Federal Republic of, Ghana, Greece, Guatemala, Haiti, Holy See, Hungary, Iceland, India, Indonesia, Iran, Iraq, Ireland, Israel, Italy, Jamaica, Japan, Jordan, Kenya, Kuwait, Lebanon, Liberia, Libyan Arab Jamahiriya, Liechtenstein, Luxembourg, Madagascar, Malaysia, Mali, Mauritius, Mexico, Monaco, Mongolia, Morocco, Namibia, Netherlands, New Zealand, Nicaragua, Niger, Nigeria, Norway, Pakistan, Panama, Paraguay, Peru, Philippines, Poland, Portugal, Qatar, Republic of Korea, Romania, Saudi Arabia, Senegal, Sierra Leone, Singapore, South Africa, Spain, Sri Lanka, Sudan, Sweden, Switzerland, Syrian Arab Republic, Thailand, Tunisia, Turkey, Uganda, Ukrainian SSR, USSR, United Arab Emirates, United Kingdom, United Republic of Tanzania, United States, Uruguay, Venezuela, Viet Nam, Yugoslavia, Zaire, Zambia, Zimbabwe.

Annex II.   OFFICERS AND OFFICES OF THE INTERNATIONAL ATOMIC ENERGY AGENCY

BOARD OF GOVERNORS
(For the period October 1988—September 1989)

OFFICERS
Chairman: Michael Shenstone (Canada).
Vice-Chairmen: Hocine Mesloub (Algeria), Georg Sitzlack (German Democratic Republic).

MEMBERS
Algeria, Argentina, Australia, Brazil, Canada, China, Colombia, Côte d'Ivoire, Cuba, Denmark, Egypt, France, German Democratic Republic, Germany, Federal Republic of, Ghana, Hungary, India, Indonesia, Japan, Korea, Kuwait, Libyan Arab Jamahiriya, Malaysia, Mexico, Netherlands, Pakistan, Peru, Senegal, Spain, Switzerland, Turkey, USSR, United Kingdom, United States, Yugoslavia.

MAIN COMMITTEES OF THE BOARD OF GOVERNORS

ADMINISTRATIVE AND BUDGETARY COMMITTEE
Participation in the Administrative and Budgetary Committee is open to all members of the Board of Governors.

TECHNICAL ASSISTANCE COMMITTEE
Participation in the Technical Assistance Committee is open to all members of the Board of Governors.

COMMITTEE ON ASSURANCES OF SUPPLY
Participation in the Committee on Assurances of Supply is open to all IAEA member States.

SENIOR SECRETARIAT OFFICERS

Director General: Hans Blix.
Special Assistants to the Director General: Nina Alonso, Robert Skjoeldebrand, Tadeusz Wojcik.
Secretary of the Policy-making Organs: Muttusamy Sanmuganathan.
Deputy Director General for Safeguards: Jon Jennekens.

Deputy Director General for Nuclear Energy and Safety: Leonard Konstantinov.
Deputy Director General for Administration: William J. Dircks.
Deputy Director General for Technical Co-operation: Noramly bin Muslim.
Deputy Director General for Research and Isotopes: Maurizio Zifferero.

HEADQUARTERS AND OTHER OFFICES

HEADQUARTERS
International Atomic Energy Agency
Wagramerstrasse 5
(P.O. Box 100, Vienna International Centre)
A-1400 Vienna, Austria
  Cable address: INATOM VIENNA
  Telephone: (43) (1) 23600
  Telex: 1-12645 ATOM A
  Facsimile: (43) (1) 234564

LIAISON OFFICE
International Atomic Energy Agency
Liaison Office at the United Nations
1 United Nations Plaza, Room 1155
New York, N.Y. 10017, United States
  Telephone: (1) (212) 963-6010, 6011, 6012
  Telex: 42 05 44 UNH
  Facsimile: (1) (212) 751-4117

IAEA also maintained offices at Geneva, Tokyo and Toronto, Canada. IAEA-supported laboratories and research centres were located at Monaco; Seibersdorf, Austria; and Trieste, Italy.

Chapter II

International Labour Organisation (ILO)

The International Labour Organisation (ILO) continued in 1988 to promote policies to create employment and satisfy basic human needs; develop human resources; improve working conditions; and promote social security. It sought to strengthen industrial relations and tripartite (government/ employer/worker) co-operation and to advance human rights and international labour standards. The main instruments of action continued to be standard-setting, technical co-operation activities, research and publishing. ILO membership remained at 150 (see Annex I).

Meetings

The seventy-fifth session of the International Labour Conference (Geneva, 1-22 June) was attended by some 1,900 delegates and advisers from 141 countries. The Conference adopted new conventions and recommendations on safety and health in the construction industry, employment promotion and protection against unemployment, and discussed a revision of the Indigenous and Tribal Populations Convention, scheduled for its 1989 session.

A tripartite committee examined the application of ILO conventions and recommendations by member States and reviewed the application of ILO standards concerning equality of opportunity and treatment in employment and occupation. The Conference also reviewed promotion of rural employment, highlighting the key role of rural economies in both developed and developing countries in the search for a solution to unemployment.

Forty-one countries were represented at ILO's Seventh African Regional Conference (Harare, Zimbabwe, 29 November-7 December), which adopted two main sets of conclusions regarding rural and urban training and the role of co-operatives. Resolutions were adopted on promotion of the co-operative movement in Africa; southern Africa and *apartheid*; economic development and social progress in Africa; promotion of women workers' activities within the ILO Plan of Action on Equality and Opportunity and Treatment of Men and Women in Employment; protection of the working and general environment in Africa; and respect for human rights and fundamental freedoms.

The Coal Mines Committee, at its twelfth session (Geneva, 13-21 April), adopted conclusions on manpower planning, training and retraining in the light of technological change and occupational health services and social facilities in the industry. Resolutions were adopted on social security, wages and legislation in the mining industry, as well as on the role of coal in an energy policy.

The Committee on Conditions of Work in the Fishing Industry (Geneva, 4-13 May) adopted conclusions on systems of remuneration and earnings, occupational adaptation to technical changes and the social and economic needs of small-scale fishermen and rural fishing communities, as well as resolutions on protecting the livelihood of fishermen, working and living conditions in the fishing industry and hours of work and staffing.

Conclusions of the tenth session of the Chemical Industries Committee (Geneva, 5-13 October) concerned shiftwork and the impact of new technology on safety and health protection. The Committee also adopted resolutions on control and avoidance of toxic waste, chemical hazards and industrial accidents in the chemical industry.

The Joint Committee on the Public Service (Geneva, 23 November-1 December) adopted two sets of conclusions—on joint consultation, negotiating and collective bargaining rights with regard to determining pay and conditions of employment in public service, and on social security, including social protection of employees in respect of invalidity, retirement and survivors' benefits. It also adopted a resolution on trade union rights.

The Metal Trades Committee, at its twelfth session (Geneva, 7-15 December), adopted conclusions on productivity and on the special problems of young workers in the metal trades. Resolutions adopted concerned the industrial environment, safety and health, further education and training of metal workers (emphasizing equality between men and women), labour policies for conversion and diversification, multinational enterprises and ratification and application of ILO basic human rights standards.

Working environment

The ILO International Programme for the Improvement of Working Conditions and Environment provided technical co-operation to member States for the promotion of occupational safety and health (India, Morocco, Pakistan, Poland, Thailand and Zimbabwe), mine safety (China, India, Indonesia, Turkey and Viet Nam), major hazard control (India, Indonesia and Thailand) and training in occupational safety and health (Malaysia). Short-term consultancies were carried out in Argentina, Costa Rica, India, Pakistan, Republic of Korea, Senegal, Singapore and Tunisia, and fellowships and study tours were granted to government officials from China and the Comoros and to members of the Employers' Federation of Pakistan.

Regional activities in Asia included projects on construction safety and information services and a workshop on occupational safety and health administration. Sectoral activities were emphasized, as evidenced by regional seminars on safety and health in agriculture (Damascus, Syrian Arab Republic, April) and chemical safety (Amman, Jordan, September) and a symposium on chemical accidents and occupational health (Mombasa, Kenya, December). The Seventh International Conference on Pneumoconiosis was also held (Pittsburgh, United States, August).

Technical co-operation activities in the areas of working conditions and welfare facilities included a seminar on work-related facilities for trade unionists from French-speaking countries in Africa, organized in co-operation with the All-Union Central Council of Trade Unions of the USSR (Tashkent, USSR, September), and an Asian subregional tripartite seminar on the protection of homeworkers (Manila, Philippines, December). National training courses for small entrepreneurs on the improvement of working conditions and productivity were organized in India, Mexico, Peru and Thailand. Technical advisory services were provided to India on the design of child labour action programmes and to the National Workers' Confederation in Zaire on welfare facilities and services for women workers. A pilot project on welfare facilities for women workers, financed by the Netherlands, was implemented in Indonesia.

Services provided by the International Occupational Safety and Health Information Centre (CIS) were expanded, and included the provision of records on compact disc, the first of its kind to be used in the United Nations system. The ILO/CIS bulletin *Safety and Health at Work* emphasized legislative and training materials, chemical safety and practical information for developing countries.

World Employment Programme

The World Employment Programme (WEP) assisted ILO member States in implementing policies to promote full, productive and freely chosen employment and to reduce poverty. Through its action-oriented research, technical advisory services, national projects and regional teams in Africa, Asia and Latin America, WEP focused on longer-term rural development problems and the rapidly growing urban informal sector. In response to the economic crisis and the growth in unemployment during the 1980s, WEP was devoting a major part of its work to achieving greater equity in structural adjustment programmes. Among the areas covered were employment and poverty monitoring, direct employment creation and income generation for vulnerable groups; linkages between macro- and micro-economic interventions; technological change; and labour market problems.

Field activities

In 1988, total ILO operational expenditures stood at $125.1 million (an increase of 11.4 per cent over 1987). Assistance was provided for activities promoting employment, developing human resources and social institutions and improving living and working conditions. The United Nations Development Programme remained the largest source of funding for ILO programmes, providing nearly $60 million. The ILO regular budget provided $11.6 million, while expenditures funded from trust funds, including the United Nations Fund for Population Activities, accounted for $53.5 million.

The employment and development programme spent some $44.4 million on projects in support of infrastructure/rural works and employment planning/population. ILO training programmes expended $40.4 million to promote vocational training and management development programmes. The third largest ILO technical co-operation programme ($17.2 million) concerned sectoral activities, within which operational activities in support of co-operatives alone provided over two thirds of the total for sectoral activities.

Educational activities

The ILO training programme assisted its member States in formulating training strategies and programmes to prepare people for productive employment and to help workers to update and improve their skills. Special emphasis was given to improving the cost-effectiveness of national training systems and improving training and employment opportunities for youth, women, older workers and disabled persons. The largest component of the programme continued to be technical co-operation activities in member States. Some 40 per cent of the projects for vocational training, management development and vocational rehabilitation were executed in least developed countries. Other important components of the programme included analytical and research activities, technical advisory services on policy and operational issues, information dissemination and collaboration with the ILO regional vocational training centres and other international agencies and institutions.

The International Institute for Labour Studies at Geneva, the ILO centre for education and research, held its twenty-third international internship course on active labour policy development (Geneva, 6 May–3 June). The Institute, together with the ILO Bureau for Employers' Activities, organized an international course on the active role of managers in industrial relations (Geneva, 6 April–4 May). Under its new industrial organization programme, the Institute identified major patterns of industrial reorganization and analysed their implications for labour and ILO. Activities included setting up networks of practitioners and researchers. Under the labour markets programme, activities included promotion of research networks, synthesis of existing research through reviews and seminars, pilot methodological and conceptual studies aimed at improving analytical techniques and educational activities to upgrade national capacity for labour market analysis.

Four issues of the Institute's journal *Labour and Society* (in English and French) were published in 1988; two were special issues dealing with the future of trade unionism in industrialized market economies and labour markets.

During 1988, the International Centre for Advanced Technical and Vocational Training at Turin, Italy, organized 79 courses and seminars attended by 1,448 participants and administered 676 fellowships. The Centre conducted advanced programmes on the management of training institutions and focused on improving management for co-operatives, small enterprises, human resources and technical co-operation.

Training in the social aspects of labour, covering a comparative analysis of labour relations and the training of trainers of trade union instructors were undertaken for Africa, the Arab States and Latin America. A new course on the management of social and economic services of trade unions was conducted.

Increased efforts were made to promote the participation of women in the development process; three courses were held specifically for women in the field of co-operatives, training technology and small enterprise development in addition to an evaluation seminar for trade union women instructors from Central America.

Secretariat

As at 31 December 1988, the total number of full-time staff under permanent, fixed-term and short-term appointments at ILO headquarters and elsewhere was 3,047. Of these, 1,399 were in the Professional and higher categories, and 1,648 were in the General Service or Maintenance categories. Of the Professional staff, 668 were assigned to technical co-operation projects.

Budget

The International Labour Conference in June 1987 adopted a budget of $324.9 million for the 1988-1989 biennium.

NOTE: For further information on ILO see *Report of the Director-General: Activities of the ILO, 1988.*

Annex I.   MEMBERSHIP OF THE INTERNATIONAL LABOUR ORGANISATION
   (As at 31 December 1988)

Afghanistan, Algeria, Angola, Antigua and Barbuda, Argentina, Australia, Austria, Bahamas, Bahrain, Bangladesh, Barbados, Belgium, Belize, Benin, Bolivia, Botswana, Brazil, Bulgaria, Burkina Faso, Burma, Burundi, Byelorussian SSR, Cameroon, Canada, Cape Verde, Central African Republic, Chad, Chile, China, Colombia, Comoros, Congo, Costa Rica, Côte d'Ivoire, Cuba, Cyprus, Czechoslovakia, Democratic Kampuchea, Democratic Yemen, Denmark, Djibouti, Dominica, Dominican Republic, Ecuador, Egypt, El Salvador, Equatorial Guinea, Ethiopia, Fiji, Finland, France, Gabon, German Democratic Republic, Germany, Federal Republic of, Ghana, Greece, Grenada, Guatemala, Guinea, Guinea-Bissau, Guyana, Haiti, Honduras, Hungary, Iceland, India, Indonesia, Iran, Iraq, Ireland, Israel, Italy, Jamaica, Japan, Jordan, Kenya, Kuwait, Lao People's Democratic Republic, Lebanon, Lesotho, Liberia, Libyan Arab Jamahiriya, Luxembourg, Madagascar, Malawi, Malaysia, Mali, Malta, Mauritania, Mauritius, Mexico, Mongolia, Morocco, Mozambique, Namibia, Nepal, Netherlands, New Zealand, Nicaragua, Niger, Nigeria, Norway, Pakistan, Panama, Papua New Guinea, Paraguay, Peru, Philippines, Poland, Portugal, Qatar, Romania, Rwanda, Saint Lucia, San Marino, Sao Tome and Principe, Saudi Arabia, Senegal, Seychelles, Sierra Leone, Singapore, Solomon Islands, Somalia, Spain, Sri Lanka, Sudan, Suriname, Swaziland, Sweden, Switzerland, Syrian Arab Republic, Thailand, Togo, Trinidad and Tobago, Tunisia, Turkey, Uganda, Ukrainian SSR, USSR, United Arab Emirates, United Kingdom, United Republic of Tanzania, United States, Uruguay, Venezuela, Yemen, Yugoslavia, Zaire, Zambia, Zimbabwe.

Annex II.   OFFICERS AND OFFICES OF THE INTERNATIONAL LABOUR ORGANISATION

(As at 31 December 1988)

MEMBERSHIP OF THE GOVERNING BODY OF THE INTERNATIONAL LABOUR OFFICE

Chairman: N. G. Mensah (Benin), Government Group.
Vice-Chairmen: Jean-Jacques Oechslin (France), Employers' Group; Gerd Muhr (Federal Republic of Germany), Workers' Group.

REGULAR MEMBERS

Government members
Antigua and Barbuda, Argentina, Australia, Benin, Botswana, Brazil,* Burundi, Canada, China,* Colombia, Cuba, Czechoslovakia, France,* Germany, Federal Republic of,* Greece, India,* Italy,* Japan,* Kuwait, Liberia, Libyan Arab Jamahiriya, Malaysia, Sri Lanka, United Republic of Tanzania, USSR,* United Kingdom,* United States,* Yugoslavia.

Employers' members
M. Eurnekian (Argentina), Henri Georget (Niger), Johan von Holten (Sweden), A. Katz (United States), Wolf-Dieter Lindner (Federal Republic of Germany), A. M. Mackie (United Kingdom), Marwan Nasr (Lebanon), Jean-Jacques Oechslin (France), Tom D. Owuor (Kenya), Aurelio Periquet (Philippines), Najib Said (Tunisia), J. Santos Neves (Brazil), Naval H. Tata (India), H. Tsujino (Japan).

Workers' members
H. Adiko (Côte d'Ivoire), Ali Ibrahim (Somalia), J. E. Baker (United States), S. Crean (Australia), J. J. Delpino (Venezuela), M. Diop (Senegal), Y. Maruyama

(Japan), R. Mercier (Canada), J. Morton (United Kingdom), Gerd Muhr (Federal Republic of Germany), A. G. Mukherjee (India), Alfonso Sánchez Madariaga (Mexico), John Svenningsen (Denmark), G. I. Yanaev (USSR).

DEPUTY MEMBERS

Government deputy members
Bangladesh, Byelorussian SSR, Cameroon, Ecuador, German Democratic Republic, Guinea, Iran, Lesotho, Morocco, Nicaragua, Somalia, Sweden, Switzerland, Thailand, Turkey, Uganda, Uruguay, Venezuela.

Employers' deputy members
A. Al-Jassem (Kuwait), F. Diaz Garaycoa (Ecuador), A. Gazarin (Egypt), C. Hak (Netherlands), N. Kouadio (Côte d'Ivoire), J. M. Lacasa Aso (Spain), F. Moukoko Kingue (Cameroon), G. C. Okogwu (Nigeria), J. de Regil Gómez (Mexico), J. W. Rowe (New Zealand), Lucia Sasso-Mazzufferi (Italy), F. C. Sumbwe (Zambia), J. William (Barbados).

Workers' deputy members
K. Ahmed (Pakistan), M. Allini (Gabon), R. A. Baldassini (Argentina), Marc Blondel (France), A. Chiroma (Nigeria), V. David (Malaysia), H. M. Eid (Egypt), Fang Jiade (China), Heribert Maier (Austria), D. T. Mendoza (Philippines), Jozsef Timmer (Hungary), Raffaelo Vanni (Italy), Frank Walcott (Barbados), N. L. Zimba (Zambia).

*Member holding a non-elective seat as a State of chief industrial importance.

SENIOR OFFICIALS OF THE INTERNATIONAL LABOUR OFFICE

Director-General: Francis Blanchard
Deputy Directors-General: Bertil Bolin, David Taylor.
Assistant Directors-General: V. G. Chkounaev, F. Ji.

Director of the International Centre for Advanced Technical and Vocational Training: Jean-François Trémeaud.
Director of the International Institute for Labour Studies: P. Gopinath.

HEADQUARTERS, LIAISON AND OTHER OFFICES

HEADQUARTERS

International Labour Office
4 Route des Morillons
CH-1211 Geneva 22, Switzerland
Cable address: INTERLAB GENEVE
Telephone: (22) 799-6111
Telex: 415647 ILO CH
Facsimile: (22) 798-8686

LIAISON OFFICE

International Labour Organisation Liaison Office with the United Nations
820 Second Avenue, 18th floor
New York, N.Y. 10017, United States

ILO also maintained regional offices at Addis Ababa, Ethiopia; Bangkok, Thailand; Geneva; and Lima, Peru; as well as other liaison offices with the European Communities at Brussels, Belgium, and the Economic Commission for Latin America and the Caribbean at Santiago, Chile.

Chapter III

Food and Agriculture Organization of the United Nations (FAO)

The 49-member Council of the Food and Agriculture Organization of the United Nations (FAO) the organization's governing body between biennial meetings of the FAO Conference, held its ninety-fourth session in 1988 (Rome, Italy, 15-26 November). The Council drew attention to the critical economic situation of developing countries and urged that they be assisted through significant concessions on debt. It supported the Director-General's proposal that FAO assist in formulating new guidelines for food and agriculture. The Council urged a timely conclusion of the Uruguay Round of multilateral trade negotiations, recognizing the objectives and principles of the 1986 Ministerial Declaration on the Uruguay Round.[a]

The Council also called for increased international support to countries that had suffered natural disasters and appealed for the replenishment of the International Emergency Food Reserve— the one multilateral food scheme for use in time of disasters—which had been exhausted.

The importance of sustainability in agriculture and rural development was stressed repeatedly during the Council session. It recommended that economic remedies be found that would allow developing countries to implement appropriate environmental protection programmes. The Council considered of equal urgency the introduction of measures to protect biodiversity, halt land degradation and involve people at the grass-roots level in conservation and development.

The Council gave unanimous support to the Plan of Action for the Integration of Women in Development, submitted by the Director-General. It urged immediate attention to identify the type of activities and timetable required to implement the Plan, and requested the training of FAO staff to heighten awareness of issues related to women. The Council also expressed support for activities geared towards increasing the access of rural women to training, credit, market and extension services.

The nineteenth FAO Conference for the Near East (Muscat, Oman, March) called on member Governments to incorporate rural energy planning as an integral part of their rural and agricultural plans. It requested FAO assistance in carrying out a detailed assessment of energy resources in the light of shrinking fuelwood supplies. Issues related to immigration and immigrant labour were also discussed, and participants were encouraged to formulate national immigration policies with a

regional perspective. The Conference also called for an increase in the region's aquaculture production, which accounted for only 1 per cent of world output.

FAO's fifteenth Conference for Africa (Port Louis, Mauritius, April), representing 48 African countries, called for an increase in human, material and financial resources for anti-locust operations and recommended early warning, prevention and monitoring activities. The Conference highlighted the need for increased investment in fisheries and requested FAO assistance to African coastal States in monitoring, control and surveillance of their exclusive economic zones. The need for credit in farm mechanization and the further development of indigenous food crops were also discussed.

Despite an impressive increase in the region's food production, malnutrition continued to plague certain parts of Asia and the Pacific, which was underscored during the region's nineteenth Conference (Bangkok, Thailand, July). The Conference urged FAO to continue helping the poor and called on Governments in the region to curb deforestation and soil erosion. Participants also voiced concern about a fall in cereals production and a 20-million-ton drop in cereal stocks during 1987/88.

The sixteenth FAO Conference for Europe (Krakow, Poland, August) recommended that Governments reorient policies to reflect environmental concerns. The European countries called for further strengthening of FAO activities in the region and recommended that it maintain its role as a catalyst for agricultural co-operation.

Ministers of Agriculture gathered for the twentieth FAO Conference for Latin America and the Caribbean (Recife, Brazil, October). The 33-member Conference unanimously adopted the Recife Declaration, calling for action to eliminate trade protectionism and to suppress the use of food as an instrument of political pressure.

During 1988, FAO general membership and that of its Council remained unchanged at 158 and 49 countries respectively (see Annexes I and II).

Funding

The regular programme budget, which provided for services and technical assistance, was

[a]YUN 1986, p. 1211.

financed by FAO member countries (see below, under "Budget").

Advice and assistance in the field were provided through the field programme, funded largely from extrabudgetary sources such as the United Nations Development Programme (45 per cent) and the various trust funds made available by donor Governments and international financing institutions (47 per cent). FAO administered a technical co-operation programme financed from its regular budget to provide short-term projects; in 1988, the programme amounted to $26.9 million, or 8 per cent of total field expenditure.

FAO's 1988-1989 work programme was affected by a sharp decline in the value of the United States dollar, on which the organization's budget was based, and a delay in payment of assessed contributions by member countries. At the beginning of the year FAO faced a deficit of $47 million, forcing cuts in services and the adoption of austerity measures totalling some $20 million.

Activities in 1988

Food emergencies and rehabilitation

In the worst plague recorded since the 1950s, desert locusts swept across northern Africa in 1988 and penetrated as far as Iran, southern Europe and the Caribbean. The most serious outbreaks occurred in north-west Africa, the Sahel, Saudi Arabia and the Sudan. FAO responded with a call for intensified ground and aerial spraying. Meetings of donors helped generate some $200 million in funding for anti-locust operations. Massive spraying operations to bring the plague under control treated a total of 14.5 million hectares of land, including almost 5 million hectares in Morocco alone.

While civil strife caused famine in southern Sudan and serious food shortages in Mozambique, many African countries needed emergency assistance to manage crop surpluses. Abundant and well-distributed rains produced above-average harvests throughout the region. In the drought-prone Sahel, cereal output reached a record 9 million metric tons, 20 per cent higher than the previous record harvest of 1986.

FAO sent teams of experts to Ethiopia, the Sudan and nine Sahelian countries to estimate crop production. It also drew donor attention to opportunities to redistribute surpluses through local purchases and swaps and to fund inter-country transactions. Food shortages, however, continued in many areas. In November, Angola, Ethiopia, Malawi, Mozambique and the Sudan needed exceptional food aid totalling 3 million tons.

FAO and the World Health Organization trained veterinary staff from six West African countries to meet the threat of Rift Valley fever, a serious disease of people and cattle previously found in eastern and southern Africa. West African outbreaks were first reported in Mauritania in 1987. FAO also helped set up national diagnostic and surveillance systems to prepare the subregion for recurrences of the disease.

Four million Indonesian farmers financed a series of FAO projects for urgent agricultural rehabilitation in Africa. Through donations from Indonesia's National Key Farmers organization more than $6 million was raised for 41 projects.

Field programmes

The majority of FAO's field projects continued to be directed at increasing crop production. Other activities focused on rural development, natural resources, forestry, livestock, agricultural policy analysis, fisheries, research and technology development, and nutrition.

FAO carried out 2,493 field projects at an annual cost of $341.5 million. During the year, FAO's Investment Centre, which assisted developing countries to attract investment for agricultural development, prepared 44 projects, which received international financing worth $1,668.8 million, of which $1,025.2 million was in external loans.

The regional distribution of field projects in 1988 was Africa, 1,073; Asia and the Pacific, 602; the Near East, 305; Latin America and the Caribbean, 300; Europe, 68; and 145 in interregional or global initiatives.

Environment

An FAO draft strategy for the rehabilitation and conservation of African lands, aimed at halting widespread land degradation, proposed ways to implement conservation-based resource development. It was decided to broaden the strategy into an international scheme to include concrete proposals for action.

In the light of the accelerating erosion of plant genetic resources and the extinction of some species, FAO supported pilot projects aimed at conserving endangered species in their original habitats. One such project, under way in Cameroon, Malaysia and Peru, sought to map the distribution of several species, determine their presence in protected areas and in managed forest reserves, and formulate practical measures for their conservation.

As part of its efforts to preserve endangered livestock breeds, FAO supported the establishment of regional animal gene banks to conserve the semen and embryos of cattle, sheep, pigs and goats. Following a survey of the facilities in developing countries, FAO launched a series of projects to train gene-bank staff and provide equipment and expert advice.

A 1988 FAO report on improved tree fallows reviewed environment-friendly farming systems in the sub-tropics. Case-studies were conducted in Africa, Colombia, Mexico and the Peruvian Andes on systems that rotated crops with trees.

Crops

Weak cereals output in the main producing countries renewed concern over world food security. Global cereal stocks fell in 1988 to 399.5 million tons, from well over 400 million tons the previous year. World stocks, however, represented 24 per cent of consumption by year's end, well above the 18 per cent considered adequate by FAO for world food security.

FAO launched a project to assist the Democratic People's Republic of Korea to boost its rice production, under which 12 Korean rice scientists undertook overseas study tours on a wide variety of topics. During 1988, FAO implemented 30 field projects to improve rice cultivation in developing countries. In Sierra Leone, for example, a project that introduced semi-dwarf varieties facilitated the cultivation, for the first time, of two rice crops a year.

FAO expanded seed-production projects in Nepal to increase vegetable output in 15 areas. The project included formulation of proposals to improve the marketing network and to develop an information system for farmers based on baseline surveys of production costs and the market capacity for fresh vegetables.

A project in El Salvador distributed 2,500 low-cost galvanized iron granaries to farmers. Each granary held 1 ton of maize and kidney beans, while offering protection from pests and fungal diseases.

A project in Latin America and the Caribbean distributed lines and cultivars of the legume pigeon pea for trials in 14 countries. The trials were part of a series of FAO-supported activities to foster basic food production in the region; similar trials were conducted using tomato, garlic, yams and cassava.

A meeting convened by several United Nations bodies, including FAO and the International Atomic Energy Agency, adopted an international document on food irradiation. The participants agreed that irradiation could reduce post-harvest food losses and pathogen contamination and help international trade when used as a quarantine treatment. (See also PART SEVEN, Chapter I.)

Fisheries

To help boost aquaculture production in Latin America and the Caribbean, an FAO project funded by Italy helped to strengthen aquaculture management capacities by training planners, technicians and administrators. The project, named AQUILA, conducted a three-month course on planning and management in Mexico, attended by 22 people from 13 countries. AQUILA sponsored studies on aquaculture in 19 countries and courses in Bolivia and Peru on molluscs, in Venezuela on the exploitation of coastal lagoons, and in Panama on the prevention of crustacean diseases.

FAO's European Inland Fisheries Advisory Commission published codes of practice and procedures for introducing or transferring marine and freshwater organisms. Its inland fisheries committees in Africa, Latin America and the Caribbean, and Asia and the Pacific considered adopting the recommendations as they applied to each region.

FAO developed microcomputer software to help developing countries assess the state of their fish stocks. It distributed the first copies of LFSA and ANACO, programs that analysed catch data by length and age group, respectively. Other software packages compiled and analysed biological and socio-economic data to improve fisheries management.

Forestry

FAO completed an in-depth study of development potential in Latin America and the Caribbean and a plan for management of the region's tropical forests. The study found that despite the region's ample natural resources, development was hampered by external debt, low commodity prices, trade barriers and urban bias in economic and social policies. A plan of action based on the report was adopted by the twentieth FAO Conference for Latin America and the Caribbean (see above).

FAO's proposals for forestry development were based on the 1986 Tropical Forestry Action Plan.[b]

Land use

Work began on a major programme for land-use planning in the Brazilian Amazon. Following a request from Brazil, FAO began assessing the agricultural potential of agro-ecological zones in the 5 million square kilometre area of the Amazon basin. An FAO mission outlined a long-term perspective on economically and ecologically sustainable land use. It also examined the adequacy of existing land resources and proposed a methodology for land-use planning.

Trade reform

FAO's Committee on World Food Security, composed of 85 countries, met in April to assess the global food situation and to recommend measures to improve the poor's access to food supplies. It noted

[b]YUN 1986, p. 1118.

that per capita staple food consumption had declined in 32 of 64 low-income, food-deficit countries, and that their food-aid needs had increased substantially during 1987/88. The Committee urged action to balance the long-term interests of cereal-producing and -consuming countries and to improve access to export markets to boost the foreign exchange earnings of developing countries.

Rural youth

World Food Day, celebrated on 16 October 1988, focused on the contributions, needs and aspirations of the developing world's rural youth. The Day, established by the FAO Conference and observed since 1981, aimed at bringing key issues in food and agriculture to the attention of Governments, institutions and the general public.

Rural youth were celebrated at a special ceremony at FAO headquarters and through activities sponsored by Governments, non-governmental organizations and educational institutions throughout the world. In Mexico, a national meeting of rural youth was jointly organized by the Ministry of Agriculture and the National Peasants' Association. Youth clubs in Swaziland displayed agricultural products and handicrafts, Thailand inaugurated a tree-planting campaign and the Philippines approved a five-year programme to benefit youth.

Information

FAO developed a communications strategy and supplied media materials to 34 African countries as part of a region-wide effort to eradicate the cattle disease rinderpest. Regional workshops and training for African radio producers took place and communications activities were designed in five countries. FAO produced a communication kit, which included television spots, radio programmes, posters, flip-charts, postage stamps and photographs.

FAO's statistical information system, AGROSTAT, became available to a limited number of external users in seven government and international agencies through a network dubbed AGROTEL. The computer contained the world's most comprehensive bank of agricultural information and statistics.

FAO's Global Information and Early Warning System on Food and Agriculture (GIEWS) was strengthened with the installation at FAO headquarters of one of the world's most advanced environmental monitoring systems. The system, ARTEMIS (Africa Real-Time Environmental Monitoring using Imaging Satellites), processed data from orbiting and stationary satellites to provide continuous monitoring of rainfall and vegetation conditions across Africa, the Near East and South-West Asia. The addition of ARTEMIS along with agrometeorological data from FAO's Agriculture Department had improved the capacity of GIEWS to monitor crop conditions and evaluate food supplies. GIEWS supervised 21 projects to set up subregional or national early warning systems.

A computer-based Geographic Information System (GIS) played an increasingly important role in land and water development. The system allowed the combination of geographical information (for example, on soils, climate, geology and population) and "attribute data", such as statistics. The results, in graphic, map and table form, helped planners to assess resources and trends. FAO included vegetation maps of Africa, as well as South and South-East Asia, into the system's data base and began digitizing a new 1:1 million scale soil base map for East Africa's Intergovernmental Authority on Drought and Development. GIS also helped to plan irrigation systems in Cyprus and five Latin American countries and to analyse land-use potential in the Philippines.

FAO's Food and Nutrition Division completed a manual for planners and nutritionists on calculating human energy requirements. Publication of the manual and an accompanying microcomputer program was planned for 1989. Each of FAO's technical divisions produced dozens of position papers, training manuals and studies. The Information Division produced a wide variety of media materials, among them film strips, booklets and video and computer programs.

Secretariat

At the end of 1988, the number of staff employed at FAO headquarters was 3,411, of whom 1,255 were in the Professional and higher categories. Field project personnel and those in regional and country offices numbered 2,892: 1,256 in the Professional and higher categories and 1,636 in the General Service category. In addition, 379 associate experts worked for FAO, of whom 67 were at headquarters and 312 in the field or regional and country offices. (For officers of FAO, see Annex III.)

Budget

The regular programme budget was financed by FAO's 158 member countries according to a scale of contributions set by the FAO Conference. For 1988-1989, funding for the FAO programme of work and budget was set at $492 million.

NOTE: For details of FAO activities, see *FAO in 1988*, issued by FAO.

Annex I.   MEMBERSHIP OF THE FOOD AND AGRICULTURE ORGANIZATION
           (As at 31 December 1988)

Afghanistan, Albania, Algeria, Angola, Antigua and Barbuda, Argentina, Australia, Austria, Bahamas, Bahrain, Bangladesh, Barbados, Belgium, Belize, Benin, Bhutan, Bolivia, Botswana, Brazil, Bulgaria, Burkina Faso, Burma, Burundi, Cameroon, Canada, Cape Verde, Central African Republic, Chad, Chile, China, Colombia, Comoros, Congo, Cook Islands, Costa Rica, Côte d'Ivoire, Cuba, Cyprus, Czechoslovakia, Democratic Kampuchea, Democratic People's Republic of Korea, Democratic Yemen, Denmark, Djibouti, Dominica, Dominican Republic, Ecuador, Egypt, El Salvador, Equatorial Guinea, Ethiopia, Fiji, Finland, France, Gabon, Gambia, Germany, Federal Republic of, Ghana, Greece, Grenada, Guatemala, Guinea, Guinea-Bissau, Guyana, Haiti, Honduras, Hungary, Iceland, India, Indonesia, Iran, Iraq, Ireland, Israel, Italy, Jamaica, Japan, Jordan, Kenya, Kuwait, Lao People's Democratic Republic, Lebanon, Lesotho, Liberia, Libyan Arab Jamahiriya, Luxembourg, Madagascar, Malawi, Malaysia, Maldives, Mali, Malta, Mauritania, Mauritius, Mexico, Mongolia, Morocco, Mozambique, Namibia, Nepal, Netherlands, New Zealand, Nicaragua, Niger, Nigeria, Norway, Oman, Pakistan, Panama, Papua New Guinea, Paraguay, Peru, Philippines, Poland, Portugal, Qatar, Republic of Korea, Romania, Rwanda, Saint Kitts and Nevis, Saint Lucia, Saint Vincent and the Grenadines, Samoa, Sao Tome and Principe, Saudi Arabia, Senegal, Seychelles, Sierra Leone, Solomon Islands, Somalia, Spain, Sri Lanka, Sudan, Suriname, Swaziland, Sweden, Switzerland, Syrian Arab Republic, Thailand, Togo, Tonga, Trinidad and Tobago, Tunisia, Turkey, Uganda, United Arab Emirates, United Kingdom, United Republic of Tanzania, United States, Uruguay, Vanuatu, Venezuela, Viet Nam, Yemen, Yugoslavia, Zaire, Zambia, Zimbabwe.

Annex II.   MEMBERS OF THE COUNCIL OF THE FOOD AND AGRICULTURE ORGANIZATION
            (As at 31 December 1988)

Algeria, Argentina, Australia, Bangladesh, Brazil, Cameroon, Canada, China, Colombia, Cuba, Egypt, Finland, France, Gabon, Gambia, Germany, Federal Republic of, Guinea, Hungary, India, Indonesia, Iran, Iraq, Italy, Japan, Kenya, Lebanon, Lesotho, Libyan Arab Jamahiriya, Madagascar, Malaysia, Mexico, Nicaragua, Niger, Nigeria, Pakistan, Peru, Philippines, Saudi Arabia, Spain, Switzerland, Thailand, Trinidad and Tobago, Turkey, United Kingdom, United States, Venezuela, Yugoslavia, Zaire, Zambia.

Annex III.   OFFICERS AND OFFICES OF THE FOOD AND AGRICULTURE ORGANIZATION

OFFICERS

OFFICE OF THE DIRECTOR-GENERAL
Director-General: Edouard Saouma.
Deputy Director-General: Vacant.

DEPARTMENTS
Assistant Director-General, Administration and Finance Department: Dean K. Crowther.
Assistant Director-General, Agriculture Department: C. H. Bonte-Friedheim.
Assistant Director-General, Development Department: R. Rinville.
Assistant Director-General, Economic and Social Department: R. Moreno, a.i.
Assistant Director-General, Fisheries Department: A. Lindquist, a.i.
Assistant Director-General, Forestry Department: C. H. Murray.

Assistant Director-General, Department of General Affairs and Information: M. Alessi.

REGIONAL REPRESENTATIVES OF THE DIRECTOR-GENERAL
Officer-in-charge, Regional Office for Africa: N. Doumandji.
Assistant Director-General and Regional Representative for Asia and the Pacific: L. I. J. Silva.
Assistant Director-General and Regional Representative for Latin America and the Caribbean: M. E. Jalil.
Assistant Director-General and Regional Representative for the Near East: A. S. Jum'a.
Regional Representative for Europe: A. Bozzini.

HEADQUARTERS AND OTHER OFFICES

HEADQUARTERS
Food and Agriculture Organization
Via delle Terme di Caracalla
00100 Rome, Italy
  Cable address: FOODAGRI ROME
  Telephone: (39) (6) 57971
  Telex: 610181 FAO 1
  Facsimile: (39) (6) 5797-3152

LIAISON OFFICES
Food and Agriculture Organization Liaison Office with the United Nations
United Nations Headquarters, Room DC1-1125
New York, N.Y. 10017, United States
  Cable address: FOODAGRI NEW YORK
  Telephone: (1) (212) 963-6036
  Facsimile: (1) (212) 888-6188

Food and Agriculture Organization Liaison Office for North America
1001 22nd Street, N.W., Suite 300
Washington, D.C. 20437, United States
  Cable address: FOODAGRI WASHINGTON
  Telephone: (1) (202) 653-2400
  Telex: 64255
  Facsimile: (1) (202) 653-5760

FAO also maintained regional offices at Accra, Ghana; Bangkok, Thailand; and Santiago, Chile.

Chapter IV

United Nations Educational, Scientific and Cultural Organization (UNESCO)

The United Nations Educational, Scientific and Cultural Organization (UNESCO) in 1988 continued to promote co-operation among nations through education, natural and social sciences, culture and communication.

During the year, UNESCO membership remained unchanged at 158, plus three associate members (see Annex I).

Education

In 1988, UNESCO's major educational programmes focused on education for all, the formulation and application of education policies, and education, training and society.

Under education for all, the fight against illiteracy and the renewal and expansion of primary education received high priority. In accordance with a 1987 General Assembly resolution[a] proclaiming 1990 as International Literacy Year (ILY), UNESCO acted as lead organization for the Year, establishing a special ILY secretariat and an intersectoral task force. Each principal UNESCO regional office—Amman, Jordan; Bangkok, Thailand; Dakar, Senegal; Santiago, Chile—had created a task force for ILY and for activities related to the implementation of a 10-year plan of action to be launched in 1990 for the eradication of illiteracy by the year 2000. In response to an appeal of the UNESCO Director-General, more than 40 States established national committees or other structures to plan and carry out programmes for the Year.

UNESCO co-operated with other United Nations agencies in the area of education. It participated in the preparation of the World Conference on Education for All (Jomtien, Thailand, 1990), organized jointly with the World Bank, the United Nations Development Programme (UNDP) and the United Nations Children's Fund (UNICEF), and made efforts to improve concerted planning and co-ordination with those and other agencies implementing projects in member States.

In 1988, the regional programme of publications in African languages was launched. The programme aimed at translating creative works from the original language into other languages of the same subregion.

Action to promote the democratization of education focused on a study in Asia and the Pacific, which analysed the obstacles to completing primary education.

Adult education focused on training adult educators and the use of new information technologies in literacy training and adult education. A regional expert meeting on the role of adult education in agriculture for imparting new scientific knowledge to farmers was organized (Morocco, December). Two pilot experimental projects were established, one in the German Democratic Republic and the other in Nepal, to promote occupationally oriented non-formal adult education programmes. The quarterly publication, *Adult Education—Information Notes*, was issued in six languages. UNESCO also promoted measures to intensify existing education and training activities for disabled persons, refugees, national liberation movements and migrant workers and their families.

Activities to promote equality of educational opportunity for girls and women focused on identifying obstacles to educational equality between men and women, promoting general access to education for girls and women, and enhancing their equal access to scientific studies and to all levels of technical and vocational training.

Development of education in rural areas included studies, workshops, seminars and pilot projects. Under the programme on the formulation and application of education policies, the fourth Conference of Ministers of Education of Member States of the Europe Region (Paris, 21-27 September) addressed the prospects and tasks of educational development in Europe, specifically in relation to the humanistic, cultural and international dimension of education and the impact of new information and communication technologies in education.

The programme on education, training and society aimed at improving the teaching of science and technology, enhancing interaction between secondary systems and productive work, promoting physical education and sport, and integrating training and research activities.

Natural sciences

UNESCO promoted international co-operation in science and technology for development. It

---

[a]YUN 1987, p. 654, GA res. 42/104, 7 Dec. 1987.

organized training and research courses and workshops and seminars for specialists, many from developing countries, on various mathematical topics, physics, chemistry, biology, biotechnology and informatics. In the engineering sciences, UNESCO developed training materials and held training seminars and post-graduate training courses. Steps were taken to create the first UNESCO masters degree course in energy engineering. Studies in engineering education included "Structures of technological education and contributing social factors" and "Women in engineering education".

Short-term training courses were organized with research institutions to strengthen theoretical and practical teaching of informatics in higher education and raise the skills of about 200 specialists from developing countries through grants, fellowships and study tours.

The International Geological Correlation Programme (IGCP), with 87 established national committees, continued to stimulate international collaboration in the earth sciences. It had undertaken 120 scientific research projects, 52 of them ongoing. Twelve new projects were started, among them coastal evolution in the Quaternary, the most recent geological period. During the year, IGCP initiated regional projects such as geology for development in Africa and Quaternary geology and human survival in South-East Asia. Activities concerning natural hazards included development of scientific and technical knowledge to assess better and predict such events. UNESCO participated in the preparatory work for the International Decade for Natural Disaster Reduction (1990-1999).

Under the Man and the Biosphere programme (MAB), pilot projects focused on arid zone ecology in Kenya, Lesotho and Tunisia, pastoral management training in the Sahel and a new mountain development project in the Sierra del Rosario (Cuba). Efforts continued to expand the international network of biosphere reserves set up to promote integrated conservation, experimentation, research on and comparison of the structure, functioning and dynamics of ecosystems, and training; in 1988, there were 273 sites for biosphere reserves in 70 countries. During the year, the MAB book series was launched.

The International Hydrological Programme continued its third phase (1984-1989). Postgraduate courses in hydrology and water resources were sponsored, mainly for participants from developing countries, and several seminars, training courses and workshops took place. UNESCO cooperated with the United Nations, the Food and Agriculture Organization of the United Nations and Italy to organize a course on the application of remote sensing to water resources development. Several symposia and workshops were held dealing with urban hydrological problems and the question of sensitizing politicians, decision makers and planners. Regional activities included the preparation of the hydrogeological and water-balance maps of South and Central America, Mexico and the Caribbean.

The Intergovernmental Oceanographic Commission (IOC) continued efforts to encourage international co-operation in oceanic research; develop, recommend and co-ordinate international programmes for scientific investigation; and strengthen education, training and assistance in marine science and technology. To help understand and forecast climatic changes, including those of a potentially catastrophic nature, IOC co-operated with the International Council of Scientific Unions and the World Meteorological Organization in implementing the world climate research programme, stepping up its ship-of-opportunity programme and the deployment of drifting buoys for oceanographic and meteorological purposes. About 20 new stations were added to the IOC global sea-level observing system. An international conference (Paris, November) laid the grounds for the new world ocean circulation experiment. The Commission continued its study of environmental factors affecting fish-stock abundance, red tides and associated mass mortality of marine organisms, as well as sedimentary environments, sea-level changes, tectonics and resources.

UNESCO supported research programmes, the development of marine scientific manpower and local research infrastructures, particularly in the developing countries. The major coastal marine project, research and training leading to the integrated management of coastal marine systems, was further developed; in Africa, a new research network of scientists was set up. Training in the marine sciences included fellowships, travel grants, workshops and short training courses. A workshop on training and education in marine science for the year 2000 (Paris, 6-10 June) offered an international forum for those responsible for marine science teaching.

One of the ongoing projects under UNESCO's programme on human settlements concerned the rehabilitation of the Barrio Rio Salado in La Romana, Dominican Republic. Operational from the summer of 1988, the project associated local populations in decision-making concerning their communities. Among the expected results were the establishment of a school and a clinic, bringing the inhabitants primary education and medical care.

In the area of environmental education and information, UNESCO organized and supported meetings for educational decision makers, planners, administrators, curriculum developers and teacher educators on issues such as: teacher education in environmental education; developing national strategies and action plans in environmental education; integrating environmental education into university general education; the use of findings of environmental research in environmental education; networking of environmental education institutions; environment ethics; and the interrelationships between education, the environment and development. Training courses were held, studies and pilot projects were conducted and educational materials were produced.

Social sciences

An international meeting of experts on trends in an evaluation of peace and conflict research in the social and human sciences (Lima, Peru, 21-25 November) concluded that peace research should further examine the causes and consequences of North-South disparities and the issues relating to the emergence of regional conflicts and new trouble spots.

UNESCO co-operated with the Austrian National Commission to hold a conference (Burg Schlaiwing, Austria) on establishing a European university centre for peace studies. It also co-operated with the University of Burundi in organizing a regional post-graduate training seminar in international law (Bujumbura). The seminar was attended by some 60 teachers, civil servants, ministerial and legal advisers and doctoral students.

UNESCO trained teachers and members of all those professions necessitating a particular sensitivity to human rights and prepared relevant teaching materials. An international training seminar on the handling of documentation in the field of human rights (Tokyo, 21-24 November) was held, as was a meeting of experts on action in the field of education and information concerning children in situations of armed conflict (San José, Costa Rica, 3-7 May). The biannual bulletin, *Human Rights Teaching*, was published in English and French. The 1988 UNESCO Prize for Peace Education was awarded to Brother Roger, who founded the ecumenical community of Taizé, France, where thousands of young people are sensitized to human rights, peace and the sharing of cultures.

The UNESCO associated schools project promoted education on international co-operation at the national, regional and international levels. In 1988, the project included some 2,246 institutions in 97 countries.

Studies and research were conducted on prejudice, intolerance and racism. Emphasis was placed on strengthening action against prejudice, intolerance, racism and discrimination through teacher training, guidelines for teachers and supporting studies on discriminatory stereotypes in school textbooks and children's books. A meeting of experts was held (Manila, Philippines, 21-25 November) to assess the effects of cultural exchange and exchange of teachers on prejudice and attitude towards race, religion and ethnicity. Activities concerning the strug-

gle against *apartheid* included a study on the impact of the state of emergency in South Africa on newsgathering and dissemination and the awarding of post-graduate scholarships for study on women's education in a post-*apartheid* South Africa.

UNESCO also addressed the concerns and aspirations of young people. It organized a consultation of youth non-governmental organizations (NGOs) (Paris, October) on the participation of young people in the World Decade for Cultural Development (see below).

The status of women programme included a regional seminar (Rabat, Morocco) for women journalists specializing in international relations and case-studies on a wide variety of subjects relating to women. A book entitled *Pacific Women: Role and Status of Women in Pacific Societies* was published. Under a programme of co-operation between UNESCO and UNICEF, a study on women's education in Africa was issued.

Culture

On 21 January, the United Nations Secretary-General and the UNESCO Director-General launched the World Decade for Cultural Development (1988-1997). The United Nations had entrusted UNESCO to be the lead agency to implement the Plan of Action for the Decade, to follow it up and co-ordinate activities. A meeting of experts concerning the strategy for the implementation of the Decade (Paris, 23 and 24 March) was held. In the context of the Decade, some 25 youth NGOs participated in a meeting organized by UNESCO to prepare projects to encourage active participation by young people in cultural life. A newsletter for the Decade, *Culture* +, was published.

The implementation of international campaigns for safeguarding cultural heritage continued in the context of the Decade. Two new campaigns were launched to safeguard the principal monuments and sites of Ethiopia and the Jesuit Missions of the Guaranis in Argentina, Brazil and Paraguay. Activities were carried out in regard to the other 21 campaigns.

The World Heritage Committee, established under the 1972 Convention concerning the Protection of the World Cultural and Natural Heritage, held its twelfth session (Paris, 14-17 June). It inscribed 27 additional sites on the World Heritage List, bringing to 315 the number of cultural and natural properties protected by the Convention, to which 108 States were parties in 1988.

UNESCO contributed to preserving cultural identities and making known the world's diverse culture through the publication of the second volume of the *General History of Africa* in Italian, the third volume in English and the fourth volume in Portuguese. Translations of literary works written in less widely spoken languages were published in the

"UNESCO Collection of Representative Works", which in 1988 comprised more than 900 titles. During the year, two new series were launched, the *UNESCO Library of World Poetry* and *Art Albums*. The *Index Translationum*, a bibliography on the translations of works published each year in UNESCO member States, had 36 volumes. A programme was launched to improve the mutual knowledge of peoples through the collection and dissemination of oral traditions, dances, music and rites around the central theme "The stages of life". The journal *Museum* was published in Arabic, English, French, Russian and Spanish.

UNESCO launched a five-year project to study the significance of the three Silk Roads—those of the steppes and the oases and the sea routes—linking Chang'an, the capital of China under the Tlang dynasty, with Rome and later Venice. The Roads made possible the exchange of many commodities, cultural values and philosophical and religious ideas.

Activities to promote the arts continued, with the organization of an international symposium on the dynamic role of Latin American and Caribbean literatures in world literature (Brasília, Brazil, 18-21 April), a symposium on dance in Africa (Yamoussoukro, Côte d'Ivoire, 9-15 October) and a symposium on the status of the artist (Madrid, Spain, 7-10 November).

Communications

UNESCO focused on the socio-cultural impact of new communication technologies, the free flow and wider and better balanced dissemination of information and the development of communications.

Collaborative studies were produced by a network of institutions on socio-cultural, economic and legal aspects of new communication technologies.

Concerning the free flow of information, UNESCO published *The Watchdog Role of the Press*, a collection of case-studies drawn from all parts of the world. UNESCO assisted professional media organizations to enable journalists and producers to discuss common concerns and encouraged the creation of data banks and programme exchange mechanisms.

As to women in the media, UNESCO organized a seminar (Beijing, China, May) which brought together 20 senior media women from Asia to consider the role and problems of women in that profession.

The 35-member Intergovernmental Council of the International Programme for the Development of Communication (IPDC) (ninth session, Paris, 2-8 February) met to evaluate a range of projects from governmental and non-governmental sources. Since its creation in 1980, IPDC had funded 370 projects in 85 countries and had secured funds of nearly $16 million for its Special Account, and just over $16 million had gone to projects under the funds-in-trust programme. The total budget allocated for 1988 was $2.5 million, with $1.95 million allocated

to projects. In 1988, there were 50 communication projects (13 in Africa, 6 in Arab States, 14 in Asia and the Pacific, 17 in Latin America and the Caribbean).

General Information Programme

Activities under the General Information Programme were aimed at helping UNESCO member States build scientific information systems, documentation centres, libraries and archives, and promote the flow of specialized information. The Programme assisted member States, particularly developing countries, in the use of the most modern information-handling techniques. China, India and Morocco were helped to set up on-line information services providing access to international data bases in science and technology through special long-distance telecommunication facilities. Similarly, many developing countries received advice and assistance to build their own data bases.

The Programme was involved in the revival of the Alexandria Library of the Ptolemies (Egypt) and responded to the need for aid to the collections of the Library of the Academy of Sciences (Leningrad, USSR) damaged by fire in February.

Action for development

Activities under the programme on principles, methods and strategies of action for development focused on the study and planning of development, identifying priority projects for development and implementing action for development.

UNESCO supported two seminars (Conakry, Guinea; Quito, Ecuador), which provided 42 development leaders and workers with training in ways to boost public participation in the execution of development projects.

The mobilization of youth for development was highlighted through a number of meetings. Some 27 representatives of governmental and non-governmental organizations (Taoumasina, Madagascar, August) met to promote the exchange of information on youth activities. UNESCO lent technical support for training 35 youth officials in the design and execution of educational and social schemes (Madagascar, April). An information day for young people on the problems of drug abuse was organized (Reims, France) in co-operation with a youth NGO and was attended by over 300 participants.

In 1988, UNESCO published *Goals of Development*.

Technical assistance

Participation Programme

Allocations approved by the Director-General for 1988-1989 under the UNESCO Participation Programme, through which member States and organizations participate in technical assistance activities, amounted to $10,037,400.

Extrabudgetary programmes

Amounts obligated in 1988 in respect of projects for which UNESCO served as executing agency, financed by UNDP, the United Nations Population Fund and other extrabudgetary sources totalled $63.4 million.

Secretariat

As at 31 December 1988, the number of full-time staff employed by UNESCO on permanent, fixed-term and short-term appointments was 2,936, of whom 1,131 were in the Professional or higher categories drawn from 128 nationalities and 1,805 were in the General Service category.

Budget

The 1987 session of the UNESCO General Conference approved a budget of $350,386,000 for 1988-1989. The level of the Working Capital Fund was fixed at $15,000,000 and the total assessment of member States (after deducting miscellaneous income) at $335,875,360.

NOTE: For details of UNESCO activities in 1988, see *Report of the Director-General, 1988-1989.*

Annex I. MEMBERSHIP OF THE UNITED NATIONS EDUCATIONAL, SCIENTIFIC AND CULTURAL ORGANIZATION
(As at 31 December 1988)

Afghanistan, Albania, Algeria, Angola, Antigua and Barbuda, Argentina, Australia, Austria, Bahamas, Bahrain, Bangladesh, Barbados, Belgium, Belize, Benin, Bhutan, Bolivia, Botswana, Brazil, Bulgaria, Burkina Faso, Burma, Burundi, Byelorussian SSR, Cameroon, Canada, Cape Verde, Central African Republic, Chad, Chile, China, Colombia, Comoros, Congo, Costa Rica, Côte d'Ivoire, Cuba, Cyprus, Czechoslovakia, Democratic Kampuchea, Democratic People's Republic of Korea, Democratic Yemen, Denmark, Dominica, Dominican Republic, Ecuador, Egypt, El Salvador, Equatorial Guinea, Ethiopia, Fiji, Finland, France, Gabon, Gambia, German Democratic Republic, Germany, Federal Republic of, Ghana, Greece, Grenada, Guatemala, Guinea, Guinea-Bissau, Guyana, Haiti, Honduras, Hungary, Iceland, India, Indonesia, Iran, Iraq, Ireland, Israel, Italy, Jamaica, Japan, Jordan, Kenya, Kuwait, Lao People's Democratic Republic, Lebanon, Lesotho, Liberia, Libyan Arab Jamahiriya, Luxembourg, Madagascar, Malawi, Malaysia, Maldives, Mali, Malta, Mauritania, Mauritius, Mexico, Monaco, Mongolia, Morocco, Mozambique, Namibia, Nepal, Netherlands, New Zealand, Nicaragua, Niger, Nigeria, Norway, Oman, Pakistan, Panama, Papua New Guinea, Paraguay, Peru, Philippines, Poland, Portugal, Qatar, Republic of Korea, Romania, Rwanda, Saint Kitts and Nevis, Saint Lucia, Saint Vincent and the Grenadines, Samoa, San Marino, Sao Tome and Principe, Saudi Arabia, Senegal, Seychelles, Sierra Leone, Somalia, Spain, Sri Lanka, Sudan, Suriname, Swaziland, Sweden, Switzerland, Syrian Arab Republic, Thailand, Togo, Tonga, Trinidad and Tobago, Tunisia, Turkey, Uganda, Ukrainian SSR, USSR, United Arab Emirates, United Republic of Tanzania, Uruguay, Venezuela, Viet Nam, Yemen, Yugoslavia, Zaire, Zambia, Zimbabwe.

Associate members:
Aruba, British Virgin Islands, Netherlands Antilles.

Annex II. OFFICERS AND OFFICES OF THE UNITED NATIONS EDUCATIONAL, SCIENTIFIC AND CULTURAL ORGANIZATION
(As at 31 December 1988)

MEMBERS OF THE EXECUTIVE BOARD

Chairman: José Israel Vargas (Brazil).
Vice-Chairmen: Mohamed Brahimi El-Mili (Algeria), Aurelio Caicedo Ayerbe (Colombia), Youri E. Karlov (USSR), Swaran Singh (India), Alemayehu Teferra (Ethiopia), Brigitta Ulvhammar (Sweden).

Members: Paul Yao Akoto (Côte d'Ivoire), Yahya Aliyu (Nigeria), Fahd J. H. Al Thani (Qatar), Anwar Ibrahim (Malaysia), Léon Louis Boissier-Palun (Benin), Hilaire Bouhoyi (Congo), Marie-Claude Cabana (France), Brown B. Chimphamba (Malawi), Georges-Henri Dumont (Belgium), Federico Edjo Ovono (Equatorial Guinea), Mohamed Fathallah El-Khatib (Egypt), Walter Gelhoff (Federal Republic of Germany), Alfredo Guevara (Cuba), Reuben H. Harris (Antigua and Barbuda), Luis Bernardo Honwana (Mozambique), Siegfried Kaempf (German Democratic Republic), Mumtaz Ali Kazi (Pakistan), Elsa D. R. Kelly (Argentina), Mizuo Kuroda (Japan), Allan S. Li Fo Sjoe (Suriname), Abdelsalam A. Majali (Jordan), N'Tji Idriss Mariko (Mali), Margaretha Mickwitz (Finland), Milan Milanov (Bulgaria), Abdullahi Mohamed Mireh (Somalia), Eugenio L. Moore (Trinidad and Tobago), Franz Muheim (Switzerland), Adamou Ndam Njoya (Cameroon), Bethwell Allan Ogot (Kenya), Mohamed M. Ould Weddady (Mauritania), Maria Luisa Paronetto Valier (Italy), Luis Manual Peñalver (Venezuela), Luis Ramallo (Spain), Komlavi Fofoli Seddoh (Togo), Stella Soulioti (Cyprus), Iba Der Thiam (Senegal), Doddy Achdiat Tisna Amidjaja (Indonesia), Alberto Wagner de Reyna (Peru), Asavia Wandira (Uganda), Edward Gough Whitlam (Australia), Nissanka P. Wijeyeratne (Sri Lanka), Suk-heun Yun (Republic of Korea), Zhao Fusan (China), Kazimierz Zygulski (Poland).

PRINCIPAL OFFICERS OF THE SECRETARIAT

Director-General: Federico Mayor.
Deputy Directors-General: Eduardo Portella, Chaman-Lal Sharma.

Assistant Directors-General: Sorin Dumitresco, Thomas Keller, Youri N. Kochubey, Julio Labastida, Henri Lopes, Sylvain Lourié, Colin N. Power, Zhaochun Xu.

HEADQUARTERS AND OTHER OFFICE

HEADQUARTERS
UNESCO House
7 place de Fontenoy
75700 Paris, France
  Cable address: UNESCO PARIS
  Telephone: (33) (1) 45-68-10-00
  Telex: 204461
  Facsimile: (33) (1) 45-67-16-90

NEW YORK OFFICE
United Nations Educational, Scientific and Cultural Organization
2 United Nations Plaza, Room 900
New York, N.Y. 10017, United States
  Cable address: UNESCORG NEWYORK
  Telephone: (1) (212) 963-5995

Chapter V

World Health Organization (WHO)

The World Health Assembly, the governing body of the World Health Organization (WHO), at its forty-first annual session (Geneva, 2-13 May 1988), approved a revised budget of $609 million for the 1988-1989 biennium. The Assembly endorsed the Director-General's proposals concerning the main approaches of WHO's work with its member States, namely, strengthening the basic infrastructure of health systems based on primary health care; improving management, information support and research capabilities; ensuring the development and transfer of appropriate technology to countries; developing and reorienting human resources in line with new strategies; and mobilizing and making the best use of all possible financial and material resources for sustainable development. The Assembly endorsed the London Declaration on AIDS (acquired immunodeficiency syndrome) Prevention, adopted by the World Summit of Ministers of Health on Programmes for AIDS Prevention (London, 26-28 January 1988) (see below and PART THREE, Chapter XI), and adopted a resolution on avoidance of discrimination in relation to people infected with the human immunodeficiency virus (HIV) and people with AIDS.

The Assembly called for the eradication of poliomyelitis by the year 2000 and stressed the importance of greater involvement of all people, as well as mobilizing all potential resources, if the goal of health for all by the year 2000 was to be achieved.

The Assembly appointed a new WHO Director-General, Dr. Hiroshi Nakajima (Japan), who assumed office in July.

WHO celebrated its fortieth anniversary, as well as the tenth anniversary of the adoption of the Declaration of Alma-Ata (USSR, 1978)[a] and of the global eradication of smallpox.

In 1988, the membership of WHO remained at 166, with one associate member (see Annex I).

Strategy for health for all

The 1988 World Health Assembly adopted a five-point "declaration of personal commitment" to health for all.

In November, a new Office of International Co-operation was created with the aim of achieving better integration and co-ordination of WHO's programmes in countries and at all levels of WHO.

In the African region, several countries requested reviews of their national health plans to strengthen the positions of the national authorities vis-à-vis donors interested in supporting health measures. In the Americas, technical support was given to Guatemala for health systems management, outreach activities and health care financing. In South-East Asia and the western Pacific, major studies of country health resources were undertaken. In the eastern Mediterranean region, several country missions were planned.

Health system infrastructure

Health system development and research

The Health Systems Research Advisory Group (Gaborone, Botswana, June) reviewed research activities and discussed the establishment of focal points in ministries of health, research consultancies and training, and institution-strengthening. Members of the Group and WHO consultants co-operated in situation analyses and in formulating national plans for action, with support given to Botswana, Kenya, Malaysia, Mauritius and Senegal.

Workshops for health systems research training were organized in Argentina, Brazil, Colombia and Mexico. A meeting on health systems research in local health systems (Washington, D.C., September) developed a plan of action, including research information networks. In Europe, a health systems research workshop was organized for French-speaking participants (France, June). In order to strengthen health systems research in Africa, consultative meetings for policy makers and research workers were organized in Mauritius, Swaziland, the United Republic of Tanzania, Zambia and Zimbabwe. With support from the Danish International Development Agency, a long-term interregional health systems research training programme was developed and an interregional workshop was held (Kuala Lumpur, Malaysia, August), bringing together senior managers responsible for health research from 17 countries.

Primary health care systems

Twenty-two senior international health experts gathered (Riga, USSR, March) to review developments since the International Conference on Pri-

[a]YUN 1978, p. 1107.

mary Health Care (Alma-Ata, 1978) and to assess the prospects of achieving the goal of health for all by the year 2000. The experts found that the least developed countries had made very limited progress and had been more seriously affected by the economic crisis of the 1980s than other countries; health problems were increasingly acute in very poor urban areas; and major weaknesses in the organization and management of health services persisted—particularly at the district level—resulting in waste or misuse of meagre resources.

The second African regional meeting on health development (Brazzaville, Congo, February) served as an important step towards clarifying the regional strategy for accelerating the achievement of health for all, setting priorities and defining roles. In South-East Asia, a regional conference on health and development was preceded and followed by country consultations.

Health manpower

A joint meeting with the King's Fund Centre for Health Services Development (London, December) discussed the preparation of nurse practitioners as a cost-effective way to improve the quantity and quality of health services for communities. A European Conference on Nursing (Vienna, June) addressed the need to make the 3.5 million nurses in Europe aware of the concept of health for all and the primary health care approach. It recommended action to reorient nursing training and service to the changing health needs of the region.

A World Conference on Medical Education (Edinburgh, United Kingdom, August), jointly organized by WHO and the World Federation for Medical Education, was attended by 150 experts and culminated in the Edinburgh Declaration calling for changes in medical education to make it more socially relevant.

A WHO consultation (Geneva, March) agreed to resume the collection of data on numbers and categories of health personnel. Priority was to be given to co-operation with countries to develop such statistics, aimed at improving the relevance of health personnel policy and management decisions.

Public information and education for health

In addition to the observance of World Health Day on 7 April 1988, which was celebrated under the theme "Health for all—all for health", the World Health Assembly decided to extend the impact of health information by marking annually a world-wide No-Tobacco Day on 31 May and a World AIDS Day on 1 December. A new WHO Division of Health Education and Health Promotion was established to reflect a stronger commitment to the development policy in the area. Among

other activities, the Division collaborated with the health promotion unit of the Global Programme on AIDS, supporting national information and education activities. A second international conference on health promotion took place (Adelaide, Australia, April), focusing on the theme "healthy public policy".

The role of young people in health promotion continued to be emphasized. Intercountry workshops on involvement of young people in promotional aspects of health development were organized (Mali, October), where recommendations were elaborated for the attention of ministries and non-governmental organizations (NGOs), especially youth organizations.

In all WHO regions, school health education was emphasized and training programmes in health education were strengthened.

Environmental health

Five external experts (Geneva, April) concerned with development and environment reviewed the major environmental health challenges and provided WHO with guidance for reappraising its activities and adjusting them to changing needs. Representatives of the United Nations Development Programme (UNDP), the United Nations Children's Fund, the World Bank and WHO met with Congolese authorities (March) to set priorities for action in water supply and sanitation, define needs for joint activities, review the strategy in that area and provide advice to the Government. A meeting on the International Drinking Water Supply and Sanitation Decade (1981-1990), organized by Portugal with the support of WHO, UNDP and the Agency for Technical Co-operation (Federal Republic of Germany), was held (Lisbon, Portugal, April) for Portuguese-speaking African countries, to discuss their progress and needs.

Since the mid-1970s, WHO, in collaboration with the United Nations Environment Programme (UNEP), had been operating global networks for monitoring air and water quality and food contamination and collecting information on environmental conditions and human exposure levels in different parts of the world. In 1988, that information, supplemented with other data, was compiled and analysed and an assessment made of global and regional levels and trends. The results showed that, while general pollution was decreasing or unchanged in most industrialized countries, it was increasing in most of the developing world.

In April, UNEP, the International Labour Organisation and WHO renewed for six years their Memorandum of Understanding relating to co-operation in the International Programme on Chemical Safety. A meeting of directors of 32 institutions participating in the Programme (North

Carolina, United States, September) reviewed the contributions of the participating institutions to the achievements of the Programme over the previous five years and defined the activities that would be carried out during the next few years.

A WHO consultation (Geneva, April) on health surveillance and management procedures for food-handling personnel concluded that contamination of food by human "carriers" might have been greatly exaggerated and recommended that current procedures be discontinued and replaced by such measures as education and training of food personnel in personal hygiene, safe food-handling practices and food-borne disease surveillance. As regards pesticide residues in food, WHO, in collaboration with UNEP and the Food and Agriculture Organization of the United Nations (FAO), issued guidelines for predicting dietary intake.

Also in collaboration with FAO, WHO published *Food Irradiation: A Technique for Preserving and Improving the Safety of Food.* With FAO, the International Atomic Energy Agency, the United Nations Conference on Trade and Development and the General Agreement on Tariffs and Trade, WHO convened an international conference on the acceptance of trade in and control of irradiated food (Geneva, December). The conference reached an agreement in principle on the acceptance of irradiated food in trade under strict control provisions by competent national authorities.

Health promotion and care

Malnutrition in South-East Asia was tackled by a combination of strategies, including development of national nutritional policies, nutrition improvement through primary health care, improved capability for nutrition surveillance, national control programmes, information exchange and nutrition research. Vitamin-A and iodine deficiency were vigorously tackled in all WHO member countries of the region.

The partnership between WHO and the International Dental Federation became effective and their collaborative activities intensified. Many countries were involved in the international collaborative oral health development programme; joint working groups continued to deal with a variety of technical areas, such as alternative systems of delivery of periodontal care, economic factors in oral health, oral health in adolescents and oral manifestations of HIV infection.

The WHO regional office for the eastern Mediterranean held a consultation on accident prevention at which representatives of health departments and other departments established the basis for promoting consistent policies and programmes.

The WHO regional office for the western Pacific collaborated with member States to improve emergency services. In China, where road traffic injuries were a heavy burden on medical care services,

a detailed study of such accidents and of emergency services was undertaken and a national workshop was convened in Shenyang. The first WHO Collaborating Centre for Prevention and Control of Road Traffic Accidents in the region was designated at the Road Accident Research Unit of the University of Adelaide.

Health of specific population groups

WHO increased its technical and managerial support to national maternal and child health, including family planning (MCH/FP), programmes in more than 90 developing countries, in close collaboration with the United Nations Population Fund (UNFPA). At the global level, support focused on the development of technology; training and research related to maternal health; newborn and child health; family planning; adolescent health; and management, evaluation and information for such programmes. In view of the need to improve the quality of MCH/FP care, specific activities were undertaken to devise locally appropriate methods for its rapid evaluation.

A WHO consultation on maternal infections and infections of the newborn (Geneva, November/December) reviewed data on perinatal infections, including tetanus, hepatitis B, group B beta-streptococcal infections, syphilis, gonorrhoea and chlamydial infections, and developed approaches for identifying, preventing and managing them in primary health care at the first referral level. The World Health Assembly approved the co-sponsorship of the Special Programme of Research, Development and Research Training in Human Reproduction by UNDP, UNFPA and the World Bank.

An international conference on ethics and human values in family planing was held in collaboration with the Council for International Organizations of Medical Sciences (Bangkok, Thailand, June); over 100 participants from different professions discussed the rights and responsibilities of individuals, social entities and Governments in decisions affecting human reproduction.

A scientific committee of the International Commission on Occupational Health held an international workshop (Stockholm, Sweden, October) on occupational exposure of agricultural workers to organic dusts.

As to the health of the elderly, a meeting (Brazzaville, Congo, January) for co-ordinated action by WHO and NGOs concluded that policies relating to social security generally covered only a small proportion of population in Africa and excluded most of the elderly; the meeting called for promotion of care and related studies.

Protection and promotion of mental health

A series of instruments for assessing mental disorders was produced and tested in centres world-wide. The first was intended for use in epidemiological surveys of the general population, the second for the assessment of mental states by clinicians and research workers and the third for cross-culturally comparable assessment of personality disorders. The instruments were being tested in 54 centres in 33 countries, using 16 different languages. In addition, WHO continued its work on the enhancement of training of health professionals in mental health. A curriculum guide for nursing schools was developed and tested. A set of teaching materials for medical undergraduates concerning psychiatric problems found in general medical care was also developed. WHO prepared an annotated listing of mental health manuals to assist those developing training materials, especially for general health workers. Three posters—on epilepsy, alcohol policies and sensory deficit—were widely distributed.

Support for the needs of the chronically mentally ill continued. Two meetings convened by WHO were attended by participants from 24 countries in five WHO regions. While the first meeting was concerned with a broad range of issues, the second focused on mechanisms to ensure greater involvement of users in the planning and management of services.

A working group of experts from all WHO regions produced a consensus statement on health policies to combat drug and alcohol abuse (Canberra, Australia, March). With the financial support of the United Nations Fund for Drug Abuse Control (UNFDAC), training material was prepared to assist community health workers dealing with drug and alcohol abuse.

Diagnostic, therapeutic and rehabilitative technology

In pursuance of the Global Blood Safety Initiative, launched in 1988 by WHO in co-operation with other intergovernmental organizations and NGOs, WHO compiled a data base on blood transfusion services, prepared proposals for the development of integrated transfusion services and organized workshops on safe blood and blood products in the African, South-East Asian, eastern Mediterranean and western Pacific regions.

An international consultation on the conservation of medicinal plants (Chiang-Mai, Thailand, March), convened in association with the International Union for the Conservation of Nature and Natural Resources and the World Wildlife Fund, adopted the Chiang-Mai Declaration calling for the establishment of programmes to conserve medicinal plants, which provided traditional and modern drugs.

Concerning essential drugs and vaccines, WHO provided technical co-operation to some 40 countries with operational national programmes. A small number of the more populous countries (Indonesia, Nigeria, Pakistan, the Philippines, Viet Nam and several Andean States) took decisive steps to reformulate their national drug policies, including strategies for increased self-reliance in domestic production. *Guidelines for Developing National Drug Policies* and *Ethical Criteria for Medicinal Drug Promotion* were published during the year, as were *The Use of Essential Drugs* and *The International Pharmacopoeia* (vol. 3 of the third edition).

As to rehabilitation, WHO began implementing a new programme for services related to the delivery of orthopaedic appliances in developing countries. The basic idea was the creation of an "orthopaedic workshop without machines".

A new programme on deafness set up collaborating centres to mobilize the resources needed to develop its activities, among which were studies of community ear health, courses for district doctors in essential ear care, and the development of a low-cost hearing aid for children with moderate to severe impairment.

Disease prevention and control

AIDS

The World Summit of Ministers of Health on Programmes for AIDS Prevention (London, 26-28 January), organized jointly by WHO and the United Kingdom and attended by 114 ministers of health and delegates from 148 countries, adopted the London Declaration on AIDS Prevention, which emphasized the importance of information and education in national AIDS programmes and the need for urgent action to implement WHO's global AIDS strategy. The annual International Conference on AIDS, the major forum of information exchange, was held (Stockholm, June).

The Second African Regional Conference on AIDS was held (Kinshasa, Zaire, October), and provincial AIDS committees were being developed to help decentralize prevention and control. WHO and the United Nations Educational, Scientific and Cultural Organization (UNESCO) worked on including HIV and AIDS prevention in school curricula in East, West and Central Africa. Three centres for AIDS information collection and exchange were established in Cameroon, Nigeria and the United Republic of Tanzania. The Second Pan American Teleconference on AIDS (Rio de Janeiro, Brazil, December) was broadcast to over 41,000 health care workers throughout the Americas.

Cancer

In 1988, the mortality rate of cancer in the developing world reached 8 per cent, the same as that of the industrialized world.

National programmes to combat tobacco consumption were put into effect in several member States, since the effectiveness of anti-smoking campaigns was evidenced by experience in Finland and the United Kingdom, where lung cancer mortality rates among males had fallen by 17 per cent over the preceding 10 years.

WHO collaborated in a field intervention trial with hepatitis B vaccine for the prevention of hepatitis B and liver cancer in China, where both diseases were prevalent. More than 23,000 newborns in the Qidong area were vaccinated as part of the joint study of WHO with the Chinese Academy of Medical Sciences and the British Imperial Cancer Research Fund.

Guidelines were established for early detection of cervical cancer and WHO emphasized the importance of appropriate coverage of high-risk groups.

WHO collaborating centres were designated for palliative cancer care (Oxford, United Kingdom), for comprehensive cancer control (Reykjavik, Iceland), for cancer control and lymphoma research (Kuwait) and for quality of life in cancer care (Winnipeg, Canada).

Cardiovascular diseases

The WHO cardiovascular diseases programme emphasized prevention. A report of the Expert Committee on Prevention in Childhood and Youth of Adult Cardiovascular Diseases, presented at Geneva in October, called for each member State to make cardiovascular disease prevention part of their national health programmes and to include it in school education. A meeting on development of methodology for prevention and control of hypertension in developing countries (Geneva, June) drew attention to the high prevalence of hypertension and stroke in those countries and emphasized that action was urgently needed to prevent an epidemic of coronary heart disease by the end of the century. A campaign was launched at the time of the meeting to draw attention to that growing problem, under the theme ''Heart attacks are developing in developing countries—prevent them now''.

Several countries adopted national plans to prevent coronary heart disease which was increasing in the developing world, while mortality from it was declining in the industrialized world. The WHO collaborating centre in Prague, Czechoslovakia, began publishing a newsletter to exchange information on progress and disseminate recommendations on prevention.

In October, the fifth meeting of principal investigators of the WHO/MONICA (multinational monitoring of trends and determinants in cardiovascular diseases) project was held (Augsburg, Federal Republic of Germany, October) to review progress and plan future activities.

Diarrhoeal diseases

In 1988, it was considered that 99 per cent of the developing world population lived in countries having a well-planned diarrhoeal diseases control programme carried out as a major component of primary health care. The number of packets of oral rehydration salts produced world-wide stayed relatively stable at 350 million litre equivalents, some 75 per cent of which were produced by developing countries.

A set of teaching materials on diarrhoeal diseases control to be used at training units was completed and distributed, and a package of materials designed to strengthen the teaching of diarrhoeal diseases control in medical and paramedical schools was successfully field-tested. The Third International Conference on Oral Rehydration Therapy (Washington, D.C., December), stressing the theme of sustainability of national programmes, was attended by over 300 participants from 51 developing countries. Two scientific meetings were held to review knowledge and propose priorities for research, one on improved infant-feeding practices to prevent diarrhoea and the other on the development of vaccines for cholera and enterotoxigenic *Escherichia coli* diarrhoea. Progress was made in developing a rotavirus vaccine containing rhesus-human reassortant viruses for each of the four main human serotypes.

Immunization

Immunization services were reaching some 60 per cent of children in the developing world with a third dose of poliovirus and/or combined diphtheria, pertussis and tetanus vaccines. Immunization in developing countries each year prevented paralysis from poliomyelitis in almost 250,000 children, and nearly 2 million deaths from measles, neonatal tetanus and pertussis.

In May, the World Health Assembly called for the eradication of poliomyelitis by the year 2000. The Plan of Action for the Global Eradication of Poliomyelitis by the Year 2000 emphasized poliovirus vaccine and all other antigens in national immunization programmes to cover at least 80 per cent of infants by their first birthday and through the age group of 1-4 years, the necessary services being provided in each district; improving disease surveillance; strengthening laboratory capabilities; creating and maintaining public awareness; providing information and education, especially for parents; improving poliomyelitis rehabilitation services; and promoting research for better eradication strategies, including the development of improved poliovirus vaccines or vaccine combinations.

The WHO Regional Committee for Africa called for the elimination of neonatal tetanus from the region by 1995. The goal of eliminating poliomyelitis from the Americas was expected to be completed by the end of 1990. In the western Pacific, overall progress was achieved and China achieved a target of 85 per cent immunization coverage at the provincial level.

Leprosy

Leprosy control strategy continued to be based on secondary prevention through treatment of patients with multidrug therapy. The WHO-recommended regimens were reported to be feasible in a variety of countries and in different control programmes. According to government data, 32.7 per cent of the total number of registered cases were undergoing multidrug therapy. The result was that, for the first time, the number of registered leprosy cases decreased by over 7 per cent. The Thirteenth International Leprosy Congress (the Hague, Netherlands, September), co-sponsored by WHO, stressed the need for continued co-ordination and initiated plans for accelerated coverage by multidrug therapy. A revised edition of *A Guide to Leprosy Control* was published.

In South-East Asia, WHO extended technical support and guidance to nine member countries, having an estimated 5.3 million cases, or more than 45 per cent of the world total.

In September, the WHO Regional Committee for Africa requested its member States to review their leprosy control programmes and to replace sulfone monotherapy with WHO-recommended multidrug regimens.

At a consultation on leprosy control within urban primary health care (Alexandria, Egypt, November), leprosy control experts discussed methods and strategies which were expected to facilitate the organization of leprosy control in urban areas.

Malaria

According to the latest data, there were about 100 million clinical malaria cases in the world each year, and the prevalence of infection was estimated to be some 260 million parasite carriers, of whom 85 per cent were accounted for by Africa alone.

WHO provided technical co-operation to Governments, especially in those countries reporting major epidemics during the year, to control and possibly prevent future outbreaks.

WHO continued to expand its support to training programmes aimed at establishing and strengthening national "core" expertise for malaria control. A new international malaria course was organized in the United Republic of Tanzania and the USSR to meet the needs of English-speaking African countries. Inter-country and national workshops were also organized in all regions where malaria posed a major threat. In the Americas, more than 3,000 persons received training in malariology and malaria control. In the western Pacific, a new Malaria Training Research Centre was opened in Solomon Islands with funding from Japan. An informal consultation on malaria parasite resistance (Manila, Philippines), held for countries of the western Pacific and South-East Asia, reviewed different systems for monitoring and managing the problem and explored ways of integrating them into health services.

Epidemiological research related to malaria control was initiated in selected African countries in collaboration with the WHO collaborating centre on the epidemiology and control of malaria at the University of Rome, Italy.

Tuberculosis

In developing countries, about half the adult population was infected with *Mycobacterium tuberculosis*. In order to evaluate current and alternative measures and strategies for tuberculosis control, a comprehensive intervention study was started in Thailand. It included the assessment of a variety of case-holding and case-finding activities applicable within primary health care activities, of short-course therapeutic and prophylactic regimens, and of new diagnostic techniques.

In the chemotherapy research programme co-ordinated by WHO, some 30 new compounds were tested *in vitro* for their activity against *Mycobacterium tuberculosis* and strains of the *Mycobacterium avium intercellulare* complex.

The transfer of clinical research technology to developing countries was started by strengthening bacteriological laboratories in China and Thailand.

Secretariat

As at 31 December 1988, the total number of full-time staff employed by WHO stood at 4,441 on permanent and fixed-term contracts. Of these, 1,446 staff members, drawn from 128 nationalities, were in the Professional and higher categories and 2,995 were in the General Service category. Of the total number of staff, 76 were in posts financed by UNDP, UNEP, UNFDAC and UNFPA. (For senior officers of the secretariat, see Annex II.)

Budget

The fortieth (1987) World Health Assembly had approved an effective working budget of $634 million for the biennium 1988-1989, divided into allocations for the WHO work programme as follows: health system infrastructure, 32 per cent; health promotion and care, 18 per cent; disease prevention and control, 14 per cent; programme support, 24 per cent; and direction, co-ordination and management, 12 per cent. In May, in anticipation of potential financial difficulties, the Director-General recommended a reduction in the effective working budget for 1988-1989 of $25 million. The World Health Assembly approved that request, reducing the working budget to $609 million. In addition, the Director-General stated his intention to maintain provisional programme budget implementation reductions of $25 million, but without a corresponding reduction in the level of the effective working budget.

NOTE: For further information on WHO, see *The Work of WHO, 1988-1989, Biennial Report of the Director-General*.

Annex I. MEMBERSHIP OF THE WORLD HEALTH ORGANIZATION
(As at 31 December 1988)

Afghanistan, Albania, Algeria, Angola, Antigua and Barbuda, Argentina, Australia, Austria, Bahamas, Bahrain, Bangladesh, Barbados, Belgium, Benin, Bhutan, Bolivia, Botswana, Brazil, Brunei Darussalam, Bulgaria, Burkina Faso, Burma, Burundi, Byelorussian SSR, Cameroon, Canada, Cape Verde, Central African Republic, Chad, Chile, China, Colombia, Comoros, Congo, Cook Islands, Costa Rica, Côte d'Ivoire, Cuba, Cyprus, Czechoslovakia, Democratic Kampuchea, Democratic People's Republic of Korea, Democratic Yemen, Denmark, Djibouti, Dominica, Dominican Republic, Ecuador, Egypt, El Salvador, Equatorial Guinea, Ethiopia, Fiji, Finland, France, Gabon, Gambia, German Democratic Republic, Germany, Federal Republic of, Ghana, Greece, Grenada, Guatemala, Guinea, Guinea-Bissau, Guyana, Haiti, Honduras, Hungary, Iceland, India, Indonesia, Iran, Iraq, Ireland, Israel, Italy, Jamaica, Japan, Jordan, Kenya, Kiribati, Kuwait, Lao People's Democratic Republic, Lebanon, Lesotho, Liberia, Libyan Arab Jamahiriya, Luxembourg, Madagascar, Malawi, Malaysia, Maldives, Mali, Malta, Mauritania, Mauritius, Mexico, Monaco, Mongolia, Morocco, Mozambique, Nepal, Netherlands, New Zealand, Nicaragua, Niger, Nigeria, Norway, Oman, Pakistan, Panama, Papua New Guinea, Paraguay, Peru, Philippines, Poland, Portugal, Qatar, Republic of Korea, Romania, Rwanda, Saint Kitts and Nevis, Saint Lucia, Saint Vincent and the Grenadines, Samoa, San Marino, Sao Tome and Principe, Saudi Arabia, Senegal, Seychelles, Sierra Leone, Singapore, Solomon Islands, Somalia, South Africa, Spain, Sri Lanka, Sudan, Suriname, Swaziland, Sweden, Switzerland, Syrian Arab Republic, Thailand, Togo, Tonga, Trinidad and Tobago, Tunisia, Turkey, Uganda, Ukrainian SSR, USSR, United Arab Emirates, United Kingdom, United Republic of Tanzania, United States, Uruguay, Vanuatu, Venezuela, Viet Nam, Yemen, Yugoslavia, Zaire, Zambia, Zimbabwe.

Associate Member: Namibia.

Annex II. OFFICERS AND OFFICES OF THE WORLD HEALTH ORGANIZATION
(As at 31 December 1988)

OFFICERS OF THE FORTY-FIRST WORLD HEALTH ASSEMBLY

President: D. Ngandu-Kabeya (Zaire).
Vice-Presidents: M. A. Matin (Bangladesh), Dr. C. Hernandez Gil (Spain), Dr. P. Papageorgiou (Cyprus), Dr. T. Maoate (Cook Islands), Dr. E. Mohs (Costa Rica).
Chairman, Committee A: A. R. Y. Abdul Razak (Kuwait).
Chairman, Committee B: Dr. T. Mork (Norway).

*MEMBERS OF THE EXECUTIVE BOARD**

Chairman: Dr. A. Grech (Malta).
Vice-Chairmen: W. J. Rudowski (Poland), J. Abi-Saleh (Lebanon), Dr. M. Quijano Narezo (Mexico).
Rapporteurs: Dr. H. K. M. A. Hye (Bangladesh), S. Rakotomanga (Madagascar).

Members were designated by: Australia, Brazil, Canada, China, Cuba, Cyprus, Democratic Yemen, France, Germany, Federal Republic of, Guyana, Indonesia, Italy, Japan, Jordan, Lesotho, Liberia, Malawi, Mali, Mauritania, Mauritius, Saudi Arabia, Sri Lanka, Sweden, USSR, United States.

*The Board consists of 31 persons designated by member States elected by the World Health Assembly.

SENIOR OFFICERS OF THE SECRETARIAT

Director-General: Dr. Hiroshi Nakajima.
Deputy Director-General: Dr. Mohammed L. Abdelmoumène.
Assistant Directors-General: Dr. T. Bektimirov, Warren W. Furth, Dr. Hu Ching-Li, Dr. Jean-Paul Jardel.
Director, Regional Office for Africa: Dr. Gottlieb L. Monekosso.

Director, Regional Office for the Americas (Pan American Sanitary Bureau): Dr. Carlyle Guerra de Macedo.
Director, Regional Office for South-East Asia: Dr. U Ko Ko.
Director, Regional Office for Europe: Dr. Jo Eirik Asvall.
Director, Regional Office for the Eastern Mediterranean: Dr. Hussein A. Gezairy.
Director, Regional Office for the Western Pacific: Dr. Sang Tae Han.

HEADQUARTERS AND OTHER OFFICES

HEADQUARTERS
World Health Organization
20 Avenue Appia
1211 Geneva 27, Switzerland
Cable address: UNISANTE GENEVA
Telephone: (41) (22) 791-21-11
Telex: 415416
Facsimile: (41) (22) 791-07-46

WHO OFFICE AT THE UNITED NATIONS
World Health Organization
2 United Nations Plaza, Rooms 956-976
New York, N.Y. 10017, United States
Cable address: UNSANTE NEWYORK
Telephone: (1) (212) 963-6004
Telex: 234292
Facsimile: (1) (212) 223-2920

WHO also maintained regional offices at Alexandria, Egypt; Brazzaville, Congo; Copenhagen, Denmark; Manila, Philippines; New Delhi, India; and Washington, D.C.

Chapter VI

International Bank for Reconstruction and Development (World Bank)

During the fiscal year 1 July 1987 to 30 June 1988, the International Bank for Reconstruction and Development (World Bank) and its affiliate, the International Development Association (IDA), continued to help developing countries to raise their standard of living by channelling financial resources to them from developed countries.

The World Bank furthered the pledges made by its President to reinvigorate its role in assisting the heavily indebted, middle-income countries to grow out of debt and recession; in containing and managing the economic crisis in sub-Saharan Africa and in instituting sustained adjustment programmes to foster the entrepreneurial and productive potential of Africa's economies and peoples; and in supporting governmental strategies to eliminate by the year 2000 the worst aspects of absolute poverty in the populous, poor countries of Asia. The Bank did so by setting record levels of lending totalling $14,762 million ($574 million more than in 1987), both for project investments and for adjustment. Of the total, 43 per cent was committed to the highly indebted, middle-income countries. IDA credits rose by almost $1 billion, to $4,458.7 million, about half of which went to countries of sub-Saharan Africa. Together, the Bank and IDA approved loans and credits amounting to $19,220.7 million, while a second affiliate, the International Finance Corporation, approved gross investments totalling $1,270 million.

The Bank strengthened its catalytic role in addressing the concerns of the heavily indebted countries, significantly increased its lending to adjusting African countries and secured pledges of increased co-financing funds to them, and focused, in highly operational terms, on the formulation of an expanded programme of action to help alleviate poverty in the low-income countries of Asia and elsewhere.

The Bank began to develop country strategies and new instruments, including separate operations, in direct support of private-sector development. It launched a series of private-sector assessments to pinpoint the obstacles to its growth and the barriers that limited its contribution to overall economic development.

The Bank also expanded the scope of its work concerning the environment, focusing on the environmental impact of development projects and

identifying projects aimed at environmental problems.

As at 31 December 1988, membership of the World Bank remained unchanged at 151 (see Annex I).

Lending operations

In the fiscal year ending 30 June 1988, the World Bank made 118 loans amounting to $14,762 million to 37 countries, bringing the cumulative total of loan commitments since the Bank's inception in 1946 to $155,048.8 million.

Agriculture and rural development

The Bank made 27 loans for agriculture and rural development to 18 countries, amounting to $2,932.1 million. Of the $975.5 million provided to Brazil, $300 million was to implement a strategy to replace most subsidized farm credit with commercial lending at market rates. India received $350 million, of which $200 million was to expand the number of village dairy co-operatives, as well as dairy processing and marketing infrastructure. Mexico was granted a loan of $300 million to support reforms in the areas of consumer food subsidies and their targeting, improvement of producer-pricing policies, privatization of parastatals, and agricultural and agro-industry trade liberalization. Indonesia received $234 million to support government policies in irrigation, calling for increased efforts at efficient operation and maintenance, the introduction of direct cost-recovery mechanisms and rationalization of existing and programmed investments.

Development finance companies

Six countries received $1,490 million to assist development finance companies. Two loans were made to Mexico amounting to $800 million, of which $500 million was to support the Government's strategy of trade liberalization. Turkey received $400 million to support its continuing financial-sector reform during 1988-1989, focusing on improved financial policies, strengthening the commercial banking system and further development of money and capital markets. A loan of $120 million went to Yugoslavia for an export industries project designed to expedite growth of efficient exporting.

Education

The Bank made 10 loans totalling $654.9 million for education projects in nine countries. Of two loans made to Indonesia totalling $253.3 million, $140.3 million was to support selected activities in the Government's higher education programme. Turkey received $115.8 million to strengthen its capacity to plan and co-ordinate technician and technical/vocational teacher-training programmes; the Turkish Ministry of Culture and Tourism was also to be assisted in developing and implementing a national plan for tourism occupations. Mexico received a loan of $80 million to strengthen employment services, assist enterprises to provide in-service training and upgrade training institutions.

Energy

Fifteen energy projects—in oil, gas, coal and power—were assisted in 13 countries at a cost of $2,233.1 million. Of three loans totalling $905 million to India, $350 million went to improve the operational performance of the state electricity board in Uttar Pradesh. The remaining $555 million was to develop an offshore gas field at South Bassein and to support state and national efforts to alleviate power shortages in the southern region. A $300 million loan was extended to Colombia to continue its reform programme in the power sector, designed to improve the efficiency of power generation, transmission and distribution. A loan of $165 million was extended to China to alleviate a power shortage in eastern China, and to make more effective use of coal reserves through the development of large coal-fired thermal power-generating units.

Industry

Nine countries received 12 loans totalling $2,062.7 million for the industrial sector. Mexico received $665 million, of which $400 million financed imports of input materials and steel products to carry out needed restructuring actions. Argentina was granted $400 million to support reforms to the banking sector. India was extended a loan of $360 million to provide technical and financial support to two development finance institutions to help them meet their requirements for long-term resources, strengthen their capacity to appraise projects in a less-regulated environment and cope with portfolio-management problems stemming from the adjustment process.

Non-project

Six non-project loans totalling $1,020 million were extended to six countries. Indonesia received a $300 million adjustment loan to support trade policy reforms, Chile was granted $250 million to support the Government's medium-term adjustment programme and the Philippines received $200 million to support an ongoing reform programme for government corporations.

Population, health and nutrition

One loan of $109 million was made to Brazil to help arrest an increasing prevalence of three major endemic diseases and to develop a programme for the acquired immunodeficiency syndrome (AIDS), including AIDS testing in blood banks and AIDS education.

Small-scale enterprises

The Bank made three loans totalling $493 million to assist small-scale enterprises in three countries. Turkey received $300 million to finance private export-oriented investments and to provide credit to participating commercial banks. Funds amounting to $165 million given to Indonesia were to finance projects that would export at least 40 per cent of production resulting from the investments. Tunisia was granted $28 million to finance eligible small- and medium-sized investment projects through a credit line to three commercial banks and two development banks.

Technical assistance

One loan of $15.2 million was made to the Congo to acquire the technical and administrative capacity to implement public enterprise reforms and to improve public enterprise management.

Most of the Bank's direct funding of technical assistance was for components in support of investment projects. During 1988, technical assistance components of loans and credits for other purposes totalled $1,095.1 million in 175 operations, compared with $1,022.3 million in 186 operations during 1987.

The Bank continued to serve as executing agency for projects financed by the United Nations Development Programme (UNDP). At the end of 1988, the number of projects in progress stood at 154, for a total allocation of $234.8 million, compared with 149, for an allocation of $223.9 million, on 31 December 1987.

Telecommunications

The Bank made one loan to Jordan of $36 million to assist the Government to improve the policy and institutional framework for the efficient long-term development of telecommunications.

Transportation

Twenty-three loans totalling $2,117.2 million were made to 16 countries to develop transportation systems. Of five loans totalling $459 million received by China, $200 million supported the Government's objective of increasing railway capacity and improving its operations and efficiency. Nigeria received $250 million to support the Federal Highway Department to define and execute an appropriate and sustainable programme of rehabilitation, upgrading and maintenance. India was lent $390 million to renew and upgrade railway tracks on heavy-density freight routes.

Urban development

In fiscal 1988, 10 loans totalling $1,108.5 million were made to 10 countries for urban development projects. India received $250 million for its only private housing-finance company to support some 30 per cent of the company's programme over three and a half years. Brazil received $175 million for urgent reconstruction and rehabilitation necessitated by floods and landslides in Rio de Janeiro. A loan of $160 million to the Philippines provided support for immediate imports of construction material to initiate subdivision development.

Water supply and sewerage

The Bank made five loans totalling $490.3 million to five countries for water supply and sewerage projects. Turkey received $218 million to acquire sewerage and sewage-treatment facilities to continue a pollution-abatement programme started under a loan made in 1982 for $88.1 million. A $150 million loan was granted to Colombia to implement its water-supply and sewerage-sector reform programme, which included the provision of water-supply services to some 1.9 million people and sewerage services to about 1.3 million people.

Economic Development Institute

New approaches in the training and institution-building activities of the Economic Development Institute (EDI) were introduced. For the first time, EDI organized senior policy seminars on the financial sector and on the social impact of adjustment. With support from Japan, it organized a seminar (Washington, D.C.) for senior officials of developing countries' core ministries and of bilateral aid agencies to explore collaborative approaches in the design and implementation of structural adjustment programmes. EDI launched a new series of annual seminars, including public-sector management seminars for the South Pacific and courses on project analysis and implementation for South-East Asia. It embarked on a major three-year programme, with substantial core funding from UNDP, to strengthen higher-level management-training institutes in sub-Saharan Africa. Re-

sponding to the Bank's increased emphasis on women in development, EDI launched a programme of activities to enhance trainers' and policy makers' understanding and awareness of the issue and of the differential effect of alternative policy options on men and women.

Of the 88 courses and seminars held, 20 were senior policy seminars for development policy makers and advisers. EDI organized 41 economic and sector-management seminars for senior officials in economic and sectoral ministries.

Collaboration with other external sources of support for high-level training in developing countries further expanded, and the total volume of co-financing reached about $5 million for the year. The largest increase came from bilateral sources, notably Australia, France, Italy and Japan.

Co-financing

In fiscal 1988, the volume of co-financing continued to increase, reaching $6.6 billion, nearly $1.4 billion over 1987. As in previous years, almost half of all Bank-assisted projects attracted some form of co-financing. The Bank contributed $3,516.3 million for 96 projects, a decline of almost $1,500 million. The largest source of co-financing continued to be official bilateral aid agencies and multilateral development institutions, which together accounted for $3,233 million during the year, some $500 million more than in fiscal 1987.

The third and final year of implementation of the Special Facility for sub-Saharan Africa yielded 87 million special drawing rights (SDR) in special facility credits and SDR 182 million in special joint financing. Under a newly established special programme of assistance (SPA) for the debt-distressed, low-income countries of sub-Saharan Africa, about $6.4 billion had been pledged, of which more than half was to be made available by the donor community through co-financing Bank projects during 1988-1990. Approximately $200 million was committed for such co-financing under SPA.

Financing activities

Total borrowings by the Bank in fiscal 1988 amounted to the equivalent of $10,832 million, consisting of $10,537 million of new medium- and long-term borrowings plus $295 million of incremental short-term central bank facility borrowings. The total was made up of $3,545 million in United States dollars, $2,364 million in Japanese yen, $1,167 million in deutsche mark, $1,117 million in Swiss francs, $590 million in pounds sterling, $215 million in Netherlands guilders and $1,833 million in Australian dollars, Austrian schillings, Belgian francs, Canadian dollars, Danish kroner, European currency units, Finnish markkaa, French francs, Italian lire, Kuwaiti dinars, Luxembourg francs and Spanish pesetas. This excluded $4,400 million of refinancings of prepaid borrowings.

Twenty-four currency-swap transactions were completed, aggregating $1,795 million. Of the swaps completed, 52 per cent were into Swiss francs, 20 per cent into deutsche mark, 14 per cent into Japanese yen and 14 per cent into Netherlands guilders.

Capitalization

On 27 April 1988, the Bank's Board of Governors authorized a general capital increase of $74.8 billion, bringing the Bank's total authorized capital to $171.4 billion. As at 30 June 1988, 142 World Bank members, representing 79.1 per cent of shareholder power, had voted to approve the increase.

The Bank's capital stock was expressed in SDR as it was valued in terms of United States dollars immediately before the introduction of the basket method (the value based on a basket of 16 major currencies) of valuing the SDR on 1 July 1974 (SDR 1 = $US 1.20635).

The subscribed capital of the Bank on 30 June 1988 was $91,436 million, an increase of $6,205 million from fiscal 1987.

Income and expenditures

The Bank's gross revenues, generated primarily from loans and investments, increased by $860 million, or 11 per cent, to a total of $8,549 million in fiscal 1988. Net income was $1,004 million, despite a $421.5 million provision for potential losses on loans to eight Bank members that were in arrears on debt service.

Expenses totalled $7,492 million, an increase of 15 per cent over the previous fiscal year. Administrative costs were $476 million, an increase of $41 million over fiscal 1987.

Secretariat

As at 30 June 1988, the staff of the World Bank numbered 5,654, of whom 3,596 were in the Professional or higher categories, drawn from 116 nationalities. (For principal officers, see Annex II.)

NOTE: For details of the Bank's activities, see *The World Bank Annual Report 1988.*

Annex I.   MEMBERS OF THE WORLD BANK
(As at 30 June 1988)

Afghanistan, Algeria, Antigua and Barbuda, Argentina, Australia, Austria, Bahamas, Bahrain, Bangladesh, Barbados, Belgium, Belize, Benin, Bhutan, Bolivia, Botswana, Brazil, Burkina Faso, Burma, Burundi, Cameroon, Canada, Cape Verde, Central African Republic, Chad, Chile, China, Colombia, Comoros, Congo, Costa Rica, Côte d'Ivoire, Cyprus, Democratic Kampuchea, Democratic Yemen, Denmark, Djibouti, Dominica, Dominican Republic, Ecuador, Egypt, El Salvador, Equatorial Guinea, Ethiopia, Fiji, Finland, France, Gabon, Gambia, Germany, Federal Republic of, Ghana, Greece, Grenada, Guatemala, Guinea, Guinea-Bissau, Guyana, Haiti, Honduras, Hungary, Iceland, India, Indonesia, Iran, Iraq, Ireland, Israel, Italy, Jamaica, Japan, Jordan, Kenya, Kiribati, Kuwait, Lao People's Democratic Republic, Lebanon, Lesotho, Liberia, Libyan Arab Jamahiriya, Luxembourg, Madagascar, Malawi, Malaysia, Maldives, Mali, Malta, Mauritania, Mauritius, Mexico, Morocco, Mozambique, Nepal, Netherlands, New Zealand, Nicaragua, Niger, Nigeria, Norway, Oman, Pakistan, Panama, Papua New Guinea, Paraguay, Peru, Philippines, Poland, Portugal, Qatar, Republic of Korea, Romania, Rwanda, Saint Kitts and Nevis, Saint Lucia, Saint Vincent and the Grenadines, Samoa, Sao Tome and Principe, Saudi Arabia, Senegal, Seychelles, Sierra Leone, Singapore, Solomon Islands, Somalia, South Africa, Spain, Sri Lanka, Sudan, Suriname, Swaziland, Sweden, Syrian Arab Republic, Thailand, Togo, Tonga, Trinidad and Tobago, Tunisia, Turkey, Uganda, United Arab Emirates, United Kingdom, United Republic of Tanzania, United States, Uruguay, Vanuatu, Venezuela, Viet Nam, Yemen, Yugoslavia, Zaire, Zambia, Zimbabwe.

Annex II.   EXECUTIVE DIRECTORS AND ALTERNATES, OFFICERS AND OFFICES OF THE WORLD BANK
(As at 30 June 1988)

EXECUTIVE DIRECTORS AND ALTERNATES

Appointed Director	Appointed Alternate	Casting the vote of
Robert B. Keating	(vacant)	United States
Mitsukazu Ishikawa	Yukio Yoshimura	Japan
Gerhard Boehmer	Michael von Harpe	Federal Republic of Germany
Hélène Ploix	Olivier Debains	France
Frank Cassell	J. A. L. Faint	United Kingdom
Elected Director	*Elected Alternate*	*Casting the votes of*
Frank Potter (Canada)	Horace Barber (Jamaica)	Antigua and Barbuda, Bahamas, Barbados, Belize, Canada, Dominica, Grenada, Guyana, Ireland, Jamaica, Saint Kitts and Nevis, Saint Lucia, Saint Vincent and the Grenadines

Elected Director	Elected Alternate	Casting the votes of
Mercedes Rubio (Spain)	Francisco Vannini (Nicaragua)	Costa Rica, El Salvador, Guatemala, Honduras, Mexico, Nicaragua, Panama, Spain, Suriname, Venezuela
Jacques de Groote (Belgium)	Heiner Luschin (Austria)	Austria, Belgium, Hungary, Luxembourg, Turkey
Mourad Benachenhou (Algeria)	Salem Mohamed Omeish (Libyan Arab Jamahiriya)	Afghanistan, Algeria, Democratic Yemen, Ghana, Iran, Libyan Arab Jamahiriya, Morocco, Tunisia
C. R. Krishnaswamy Rao Sahib (India)	M. Mustafizur Rahman (Bangladesh)	Bangladesh, Bhutan, India, Sri Lanka
Fawzi Hamad Al-Sultan (Kuwait)	Mohamed W. Hosny (Egypt)	Bahrain, Egypt, Iraq, Jordan, Kuwait, Lebanon, Maldives, Oman, Pakistan, Qatar, Syrian Arab Republic, United Arab Emirates, Yemen
Paul Arlman (Netherlands)	Cvitan Dujmovic (Yugoslavia)	Cyprus, Israel, Netherlands, Romania, Yugoslavia
C. Ulrik Haxthausen (Denmark)	Veikko Kantola (Finland)	Denmark, Finland, Iceland, Norway, Sweden
Mitiku Jembere (Ethiopia)	J. S. A. Funna (Sierra Leone)	Botswana, Burundi, Ethiopia, Gambia, Guinea, Kenya, Lesotho, Liberia, Malawi, Mozambique, Nigeria, Seychelles, Sierra Leone, Sudan, Swaziland, Trinidad and Tobago, Uganda, United Republic of Tanzania, Zambia, Zimbabwe
Mario Draghi (Italy)	Rodrigo M. Guimarães (Portugal)	Greece, Italy, Malta, Portugal
Xu Naijiong (China)	Zhang Junyi (China)	China
Jobarah E. Suraisry (Saudi Arabia)	Abdulaziz Al-Sehail (Saudi Arabia)	Saudi Arabia
Murray A. Sherwin (New Zealand)	Robert G. Carling (Australia)	Australia, Kiribati, New Zealand, Papua New Guinea, Republic of Korea, Samoa, Solomon Islands, Vanuatu
Pedro Sampaio Malan (Brazil)	Carlos Sanclemente (Colombia)	Brazil, Colombia, Dominican Republic, Ecuador, Haiti, Philippines
Mohd. Ramli Wajib (Malaysia)	Kikham Vongsay (Lao People's Democratic Republic)	Burma, Fiji, Indonesia, Lao People's Democratic Republic, Malaysia, Nepal, Singapore, Thailand, Tonga, Viet Nam
Félix Alberto Camarasa (Argentina)	Claudio A. Pardo (Chile)	Argentina, Bolivia, Chile, Paraguay, Peru, Uruguay
André Milongo (Congo)	Jean-Pierre Le Bouder (Central African Republic)	Benin, Burkina Faso, Cameroon, Cape Verde, Central African Republic, Chad, Comoros, Congo, Côte d'Ivoire, Djibouti, Equatorial Guinea, Gabon, Guinea-Bissau, Madagascar, Mali, Mauritania, Mauritius, Niger, Rwanda, Sao Tome and Principe, Senegal, Somalia, Togo, Zaire

NOTE: Democratic Kampuchea, Poland and South Africa did not participate in the 1986 regular election of Executive Directors.

PRINCIPAL OFFICERS*

President: Barber B. Conable.
Senior Vice President, Policy, Planning and Research: W. David Hopper.
Senior Vice President, Operations: Moeen A. Qureshi.
Senior Vice President, Finance: Ernest Stern.
Senior Vice President, External Affairs and Administration: Willi A. Wapenhans.
Vice President and Controller: Sune B. Carlsson.
Vice President and Treasurer: Donald Roth.
Vice President, Financial Policy and Risk Management: D. Joseph Wood.
Vice President, Latin America and the Caribbean Regional Office: S. Shahid Husain.
Vice President, Co-financing: Kinihiko Inakage.

Vice President, Africa Regional Office: Edward V. K. Jaycox.
Vice President, Asia Regional Office: Attila Karaosmanoglu.
Vice President, Europe, Middle East and North Africa Regional Office: Wilfried P. Thalwitz.
Vice President, Financial Intermediation Services: Vacant.
Vice President, Development Economics and Chief Economist: Stanley Fischer.
Vice President, Sector Policy and Research: Visvanathan Rajagopalan.
Director-General, Operations Evaluation: Yves Rovani.
Vice President and General Counsel: Ibrahim F. I. Shihata.
Vice President and Secretary: Timothy T. Thahane.
Vice President, Personnel: William J. Cosgrove.

*The World Bank and IDA had the same officers and staff.

HEADQUARTERS AND OTHER OFFICES

HEADQUARTERS
The World Bank
1818 H Street, N.W.
Washington, D.C. 20433, United States
 Cable address: INTBAFRAD WASHINGTONDC
 Telephone: (1) (202) 477-1234
 Telex: RCA 248423 WORLDBK
 Facsimile: (1) (202) 477-6391

NEW YORK OFFICE
The World Bank Mission to the United Nations
809 United Nations Plaza, Suite 900
New York, N.Y. 10017, United States
 Cable address: INTBAFRAD NEWYORK
 Telephone: (1) (212) 963-6008
 Facsimile: (1) (212) 697-7020

The Bank also maintained major regional offices at Abidjan, Côte d'Ivoire; Bangkok, Thailand; Geneva; Nairobi, Kenya; Paris; and Tokyo.

Chapter VII

International Finance Corporation (IFC)

The International Finance Corporation (IFC), established in 1956, furthers economic growth in developing member countries by promoting private sector investment. It is a member of the World Bank Group, which also includes the International Bank for Reconstruction and Development (World Bank), the International Development Association and the Multilateral Investment Guarantee Agency. However, IFC operates independently, with its own Articles of Agreement, shareholders, management, staff and financial structure. Its share capital is provided by its member countries, which collectively also determine its policies and activities. In addition, it raises most of the funds for its lending activities through bond issues in the international financial markets and from returns on profitable investments.

IFC shares full project risks with its partners, enabling it to play an important role in mobilizing additional project funding from other investors and lenders, either through co-financing or loan syndications, underwritings and guarantees. In addition to project finance and resource mobilization, it provides advisory services and technical assistance to private businesses and Governments in order to create an environment hospitable to private investment.

During the fiscal year ending 30 June 1988, the IFC Board of Directors approved 95 investments totalling $1.3 billion, an increase of 38 per cent over 1987. In connection with those approvals, it was expected that $1.04 billion would be invested for IFC's own account and that $231.3 million would be arranged and underwritten for other investors. Of that total, $1.05 billion was for loans and $221.8 million for equity investments. IFC estimated that the total capital cost of projects it would help to finance was more than $5 billion, meaning that, for every $1 invested by IFC, others would invest more than $4.

Disbursements during fiscal 1988 were $2,288 million in loans and equity and quasi-equity investments. The disbursed loan portfolio grew by 21 per cent to $1,900 million as at 30 June 1988. IFC's net income for the year reached $100.6 million, representing a return on its net worth of 8.6 per cent.

During fiscal 1988, Poland joined IFC, bringing its membership to 133 countries (see Annex I).

Regional projects

IFC approved 95 investments; 93 were located in 40 countries, one was regional and one was worldwide in scope.

Africa

IFC continued to support reform efforts in Africa and to develop new initiatives to stimulate economic growth. It approved investments totalling $134.95 million for 23 business ventures in Africa, including capital markets projects. At the end of fiscal 1988, it had committed investments of $604.4 million in 127 ventures in 34 countries in the region.

The Africa Project Development Facility (APDF), established by IFC, the United Nations Development Programme and the African Development Bank, provided technical assistance to entrepreneurs. By the end of fiscal 1988, APDF had secured financing for 25 projects.

IFC's capital markets projects included the establishment of Côte d'Ivoire's first venture capital company and an additional loan to udc Limited, Zimbabwe's largest hire-purchase and factoring company. As a co-investor, IFC was to help establish udc-Botswana Finance Company, which would specialize in lease financing.

In the mining sector, IFC approved four investments in Western and Central Africa. The largest was a $32 million loan to Compagnie Minière de l'Ogooué in Gabon for an $80.4 million project to improve its infrastructure and to acquire transport equipment for its manganese ore.

For food and agribusiness, Cameroon received $2.3 million to rehabilitate and privatize a banana plantation. Zambia received $8 million for a commercial farming project using modern centre-pivot irrigation techniques.

During the year, IFC worked on the financial restructuring of companies in Nigeria, Senegal and Zambia.

The Foreign Investment Advisory Service (FIAS) strengthened its programme of assistance to developing countries. It advised and assisted Ghana, Guinea, Kenya, Madagascar, Senegal and Togo on strategies to promote foreign investment, stimulate domestic investment and develop export industries. FIAS began preparing regional reports on issues such as developing techniques to promote foreign investment in priority sectors, overcoming the problem of small markets that limited foreign investment and reconciling the desires of countries for local ownership and management to attract foreign investment.

Asia

IFC approved investments totalling $305.94 million for 29 projects in Asia. At the end of the fiscal year, it had committed investments of $647.9 million in 102 business ventures in 12 countries in the region.

IFC approved an equity investment of $15.55 million in a producer of semi-conductors in the Republic of Korea to support the company's medium-term expansion and diversification plans. It also approved an investment of $24 million in the Philippine Long Distance Telephone Company to assist in the installation of a modern digital switching system and expansion into the international financial markets. In India, IFC focused on equity and approved three investments in start-up projects involving the transfer of technology.

In the petrochemical sector, IFC approved a loan of $15 million to the Thai National Petrochemical Company to help finance the construction of an import/export jetty and storage facility.

During the year, FIAS provided additional assistance to Bangladesh, China, Indonesia, Malaysia, Papua New Guinea, the Philippines and Thailand, following the completion of initial projects. At the regional level, FIAS co-operated with the Committee on Industry, Minerals and Energy of the Association of South-East Asian Nations (ASEAN) to harmonize investment incentives among ASEAN member States. In collaboration with the Asian Development Bank, it organized a major conference at Manila, Philippines, on trends and prospects for foreign direct investment in the region.

Europe and the Middle East

IFC approved investments totalling $205.67 million for 16 business ventures in Europe and the Middle East, including capital markets. At the end of the fiscal year, it had committed investments of $682 million in 68 ventures in 11 countries.

IFC identified areas where it believed it could effectively support the economy of Poland. It supported a $66.6 million joint venture in Turkey to manufacture nylon and approved four investments in tourism projects there, totalling $27.49 million, to develop coastal hotels. In Egypt, it participated in the financial restructuring of the Luxor Hotel.

IFC approved the financing of its fourth major joint venture in Hungary, in the amount of $30.87 million. The foreign investor, Montedison of Italy, was to assist in establishing a $78.7 million project to produce 65,000 tons of polystyrene per year.

Latin America and the Caribbean

IFC approved investments of $618.51 million for 26 projects in Latin America and the Caribbean.

At the end of the fiscal year, it had investments of $1.4 billion in 150 ventures in 21 countries.

In Mexico, IFC launched a major initiative to support the private sector through corporate restructuring. It provided a loan of $46 million to one of Mexico's leading cement producers to enable it to repurchase more than $200 million of debt and reduce its total debt to about $70 million. IFC purchased a food and food processing company's entire debt of $69 million in exchange for an IFC loan of $20 million and equity in the company.

IFC syndicated a loan package of $74.76 million to assist a private sector venture in Venezuela to lease a closed-down direct-reduction plant from the Government, re-equip the plant and operate it to convert local iron ore to hot briquettes for export.

In Colombia, it assisted a synthetic-fibre producer to expand its existing facilities with a loan of $40 million, of which $30 million was for its own account, and restructured, with an investment of $1.65 million, the external debts of a coal-mining venture that had experienced difficulties.

IFC approved six investments in Brazil with an aggregate of $193.6 million for its own account. These included an $80 million credit line to three private commercial or investment banks for onlending to companies in need of foreign exchange for the purchase of equipment to expand or modernize their operations. IFC also provided a $40 million loan and $5 million in equity to Brazil's only producer of float glass to help finance construction of a second plant. It approved three investments in the chemical petrochemical sector, making two loans to producers of polypropylene and PVC (polyvinyl chloride) and exercising its equity subscription rights in a producer of fine chemicals. It also approved both loan and equity investments in the expansion of a major producer of textiles.

Financial operations

IFC's net income in fiscal 1988 reached a record high of $100.6 million, nearly double the income of 1987. Its total operating income was $345.6 million, compared with $285.4 million in fiscal 1987.

Capital and retained earnings

During fiscal 1988, member countries paid in capital of $128 million. As at 30 June 1988, total paid-in capital reached $850.2 million and retained earnings came to $438.2 million, bringing IFC's net worth to $1.3 billion.

Secretariat

IFC had 523 staff members drawn from 67 countries, including 50 developing countries (for principal officers, see Annex III).

NOTE: For details of IFC activities, see *International Finance Corporation Annual Report 1988*.

Annex I. MEMBERS OF THE INTERNATIONAL FINANCE CORPORATION
(As at 30 June 1988)

Afghanistan, Antigua and Barbuda, Argentina, Australia, Austria, Bahamas, Bangladesh, Barbados, Belgium, Belize, Benin, Bolivia, Botswana, Brazil, Burkina Faso, Burma, Burundi, Cameroon, Canada, Chile, China, Colombia, Congo, Costa Rica, Côte d'Ivoire, Cyprus, Denmark, Djibouti, Dominica, Dominican Republic, Ecuador, Egypt, El Salvador, Ethiopia, Fiji, Finland, France, Gabon, Gambia, Germany, Federal Republic of, Ghana, Greece, Grenada, Guatemala, Guinea, Guinea-Bissau, Guyana, Haiti, Honduras, Hungary, Iceland, India, Indonesia, Iran, Iraq, Ireland, Israel, Italy, Jamaica, Japan, Jordan, Kenya, Kiribati, Kuwait, Lebanon, Lesotho, Liberia, Libyan Arab Jamahiriya, Luxembourg, Madagascar, Malawi, Malaysia, Maldives, Mali, Mauritania, Mauritius, Mexico, Morocco, Mozambique, Nepal, Netherlands, New Zealand, Nicaragua, Niger, Nigeria, Norway, Oman, Pakistan, Panama, Papua New Guinea, Paraguay, Peru, Philippines, Poland, Portugal, Republic of Korea, Rwanda, Saint Lucia, Samoa, Saudi Arabia, Senegal, Seychelles, Sierra Leone, Singapore, Solomon Islands, Somalia, South Africa, Spain, Sri Lanka, Sudan, Swaziland, Sweden, Syrian Arab Republic, Thailand, Togo, Tonga, Trinidad and Tobago, Tunisia, Turkey, Uganda, United Arab Emirates, United Kingdom, United Republic of Tanzania, United States, Uruguay, Vanuatu, Venezuela, Viet Nam, Yemen, Yugoslavia, Zaire, Zambia, Zimbabwe.

Annex II. EXECUTIVE DIRECTORS AND ALTERNATES OF THE INTERNATIONAL FINANCE CORPORATION
(As at 30 June 1988)

Appointed Director	*Appointed Alternate*	*Casting the vote of*
Robert B. Keating	(vacant)	United States
Gerhard Boehmer	Michael von Harpe	Federal Republic of Germany
Frank Cassell	J. A. L. Faint	United Kingdom
Hélène Ploix	Olivier Debains	France
Mitsukazu Ishikawa	Yukio Yoshimura	Japan

Elected Director	*Elected Alternate*	*Casting the votes of*
Frank Potter (Canada)	Horace Barber (Jamaica)	Antigua and Barbuda, Bahamas, Barbados, Belize, Canada, Dominica, Grenada, Guyana, Ireland, Jamaica, Saint Lucia
C. R. Krishnaswamy Rao Sahib (India)	M. Mustafizur Rahman (Bangladesh)	Bangladesh, India, Sri Lanka
Jacques de Groote (Belgium)	Heiner Luschin (Austria)	Austria, Belgium, Hungary, Luxembourg, Turkey
Mario Draghi (Italy)	Rodrigo M. Guimarães (Portugal)	Greece, Italy, Portugal
C. Ulrik Haxthausen (Denmark)	Veikko Kantola (Finland)	Denmark, Finland, Iceland, Norway, Sweden
Mercedes Rubio (Spain)	Francisco Vannini (Nicaragua)	Costa Rica, El Salvador, Guatemala, Honduras, Mexico, Nicaragua, Panama, Spain, Venezuela
Paul Arlman (Netherlands)	Cvitan Dujmovic (Yugoslavia)	Cyprus, Israel, Netherlands, Yugoslavia
Murray A. Sherwin (New Zealand)	Robert G. Carling (Australia)	Australia, Kiribati, New Zealand, Papua New Guinea, Republic of Korea, Samoa, Solomon Islands, Vanuatu
Pedro Sampaio Malan (Brazil)	Carlos Sanclemente (Colombia)	Brazil, Colombia, Dominican Republic, Ecuador, Haiti, Philippines
Félix Alberto Camarasa (Argentina)	Claudio A. Pardo (Chile)	Argentina, Bolivia, Chile, Paraguay, Peru, Uruguay
Mohd. Ramli Wajib (Malaysia)	Kikham Vongsay (Lao People's Democratic Republic)	Burma, Fiji, Indonesia, Malaysia, Nepal, Singapore, Thailand, Tonga, Viet Nam
Mitiku Jembere (Ethiopia)	J. S. A. Funna (Sierra Leone)	Botswana, Burundi, Ethiopia, Gambia, Guinea, Kenya, Lesotho, Liberia, Malawi, Mozambique, Nigeria, Seychelles, Sierra Leone, Sudan, Swaziland, Trinidad and Tobago, Uganda, United Republic of Tanzania, Zambia, Zimbabwe
Fawzi Hamad Al-Sultan (Kuwait)	Mohamed W. Hosny (Egypt)	Egypt, Iraq, Jordan, Kuwait, Lebanon, Maldives, Oman, Pakistan, Syrian Arab Republic, United Arab Emirates, Yemen
Jobarah E. Suraisry (Saudi Arabia)	Abdulaziz Al-Sehail (Saudi Arabia)	Saudi Arabia
André Milongo (Congo)	Jean-Pierre Le Bouder (Central African Republic)	Benin, Burkina Faso, Cameroon, Congo, Côte d'Ivoire, Djibouti, Gabon, Guinea-Bissau, Madagascar, Mali, Mauritania, Mauritius, Niger, Rwanda, Senegal, Somalia, Togo, Zaire
Mourad Benachenhou (Algeria)	Salem Mohamed Omeish (Libyan Arab Jamahiriya)	Afghanistan, Ghana, Iran, Libyan Arab Jamahiriya, Morocco, Tunisia
Xu Naijiong (China)	Zhang Junyi (China)	China

NOTE: South Africa and Poland did not participate in the 1986 election of Executive Directors.

Annex III.   OFFICERS AND OFFICES
             OF THE INTERNATIONAL FINANCE CORPORATION
             (As at 1 July 1988)

PRINCIPAL OFFICERS

President: Barber B. Conable.*
Executive Vice-President: William S. Ryrie.
Vice-President, Investment Operations: Judhvir Parmar.
Vice-President, Portfolio Operations: Wilfried E. Kaffenberger.
Vice President, Finance and Planning: Richard H. Frank.
Vice-President and General Counsel: José E. Camacho.
Vice-President, Engineering: Makarand V. Dehejia.
Secretary: Timothy T. Thahane.*
Director, Department of Investments, Africa I: André G. Hovaguimian.
Director, Department of Investments, Africa II: M. Azam K. Alizai.
Director, Department of Investments, Asia I: Torstein Stephansen.
Director, Department of Investments, Asia II: Jamal-ud-din Kassum.
Director, Department of Investments, Europe and the Middle East: Douglas Gustafson.
Director, Department of Investments, Latin America and Caribbean I: Helmut Paul.
Director, Department of Investments, Latin America and Caribbean II: Everett J. Santos.
Director, Capital Markets Department: Vacant.
Director, Business Development and Syndications: Irving Kuczynski.

Director and Chief Economic Adviser, Economics Department: Guy Pierre Pfeffermann.
Deputy Director, Engineering Department: David B. Minch.
Deputy General Counsel, Legal Department: Walter F. Norris.
Principal Financial Adviser, Finance and Planning Department: Vasant H. Karmarkar.
Special Representative in Tokyo: Sugio Hatanaka.
Special Representative in Europe, London: Giovanni Vacchelli.
Special Representative in Europe, Paris: Gunter H. Kreuter.
Regional Mission in Eastern and Southern Africa: Ernest M. Kepper.
Regional Mission in India: Mohan Wikramanayake.
Regional Mission in Indonesia: Mumtaz Kahn.
Regional Mission in the Middle East: John H. Stewart.
Regional Mission in Nigeria: Bahadurali Jetha.
Regional Mission in North Africa: Sami Haddad.
Regional Mission in the Philippines: Richard L. Ranken.
Regional Mission in Thailand: Carlos M. Tan.
Regional Mission in Turkey: Reynaldo Ortiz.
Regional Mission in Western Africa: Vacant.

*Held the same position in the World Bank.

HEADQUARTERS AND OTHER OFFICES

HEADQUARTERS
International Finance Corporation
1818 H Street, N.W.
Washington, D.C. 20433, United States
  Cable address: CORINTFIN WASHINGTONDC
  Telephone: (1) (202) 477-1234
  Telex: ITT 440098, RCA 248423, WUI 64145
  Facsimile: (1) (202) 477-6391

  IFC also had major offices in London, Paris and Tokyo.

NEW YORK OFFICE
International Finance Corporation
809 United Nations Plaza, Suite 900
New York, N.Y. 10017, United States
  Cable address: CORINTFIN NEWYORK
  Telephone: (1) (212) 963-6008
  Facsimile: (1) (212) 697-7020

Chapter VIII

International Development Association (IDA)

The International Development Association (IDA) was established in 1960 as an affiliate of the International Bank for Reconstruction and Development (World Bank) to provide assistance for the same purposes as the Bank, but primarily to low-income countries. Though legally and financially distinct from the Bank, IDA shares the same staff.

The funds used by IDA, called credits to distinguish them from World Bank loans, come mostly from subscriptions in convertible currencies from members, general replenishments from its more industrialized and developed members, and transfers from the Bank's net earnings.

During fiscal year 1988 (1 July 1987–30 June 1988), IDA concentrated on the very poor countries, those with an annual per capita gross national product of less than $835 (in 1986 United States dollars). IDA's 99 approved credits were distributed among 36 countries in fiscal 1988. Credits were made only to Governments and were interest-free, with a service charge to cover administrative costs of 0.75 per cent on disbursed and 0.5 per cent on undisbursed balances. After an initial grace period of 10 years, the credits were repayable in 35 to 40 years.

The bulk of IDA funds for lending is provided by its Part I (industrial) member countries and several Part II (developing) countries under a series of replenishment agreements. The eighth replenishment of resources, which provided IDA with funds for commitment in fiscal years 1988-1990,[a] became effective on 4 March 1988, when IDA received notifications of participation from donors whose aggregate contributions amounted to 80 per cent of the replenishment.

Membership of IDA rose to 137 in 1988 with the admission of Poland (see Annex I).

Lending operations (credits)

At the end of fiscal 1988, IDA cumulative commitments totalled $47,766.4 million. Commitments during the fiscal year amounted to $4,458.7 million, of which $2,203.6 million went to 25 countries in Africa and $1,918 million to eight countries in Asia. India was the largest borrower, with four credits amounting to $717.2 million, followed by China with nine credits ($639.9 million) and Ghana with six ($261.1 million).

Agriculture and rural development

As in previous years, in fiscal 1988 the number of credits for agriculture and rural development accounted for the largest portion of IDA lending; 34 credits totalling $1,561.8 million were committed in 26 countries.

Of five credits totalling $489.9 million to China, $170 million was for a rural credit project to stimulate the growth and diversification of agriculture and increase the operational efficiency of the Agricultural Bank. India received two credits amounting to $360 million, of which $200 million supported the costs and reconstruction/rehabilitation requirements resulting from drought. Pakistan received $79.5 million to increase farm income and agricultural production by improving the reliability and equitability of irrigation-water supplies and reducing crop losses from rain flooding.

The Sudan was granted two credits totalling $104.7 million, of which $85 million was to provide financial and technical support to the Government's economic recovery programme and address efforts in irrigation. A credit of $81.5 million to Bangladesh was expected to increase food production by protecting agricultural land against floods, preventing salt-water intrusion, improving drainage and providing water for irrigation.

Development finance companies

IDA extended five credits amounting to $222.5 million to assist development finance companies. A $100 million credit was extended to Ghana to support a programme to develop a well-functioning and broadly based financial sector through the implementation of in-depth policy and institutional reforms. A credit of $70 million was granted to Bolivia to support reforms aimed at increasing confidence in the banking system and resource mobilization, strengthening the financial condition of banks and reducing the high cost of credit. Senegal received $33 million to support an industrial restructuring programme, by making credit available for fixed investments and working capital in existing and new enterprises.

Education

Nine education credits totalling $209.1 million were granted in fiscal 1988. Ethiopia received $70

[a]YUN 1986, p. 1152.

million to improve the quality and volume of manpower training, continue educational quality and equity and strengthen institutional development in the education sector. A credit of $50 million went to China to address urgent needs for an expanded and improved national lower secondary teacher-training system to meet the mandate for a nine-year universal basic education programme by the year 2000. Burundi received $31.5 million to increase access to basic education and improve the quality of primary and general secondary education.

Energy

In fiscal 1988, five countries received credits amounting to $161.9 million for energy-related projects. A $63 million credit was granted to Burma to help alleviate the growing shortage of petroleum by supporting further development of the Payagon gas field. Sri Lanka received $40.5 million to finance a five-year time-slice of the Ceylon Electricity Board's expenditures to rehabilitate, develop and expand distribution systems. The Niger was extended a $31.5 million credit to assist in promoting fuelwood conservation, substitution of sources for household energy and more effective management of natural forest cover.

Industry

Four countries received credits totalling $161.9 million for industrial projects. A credit of $102 million went to Kenya to provide support to the first phase (1988-1990) of the Government's medium-term adjustment programme for the industrial sector. Ghana received $40 million for a mining-sector rehabilitation project.

Non-project

IDA granted 11 non-project credits amounting to $667 million in fiscal 1988. Madagascar received $125 million to support the country's adjustment programme, designed to promote an early transition to per capita growth with increased social equity. A credit of $90 million was granted to Burundi to assist in its structural adjustment programme, aimed at accelerating economic growth and increasing per capita income and consumption levels. Mozambique received $70 million to support its economic rehabilitation programme.

Population, health and nutrition

Seven credits for population, health and nutrition totalling $195.9 million were granted during fiscal 1988. India received $57 million to support its family welfare strategy to improve coverage and accessibility of services among urban slum populations. A credit of $42.5 million was extended to Uganda to re-establish the provision of health serv-

ices by rehabilitating a number of strategically located hospitals and health centres. Ethiopia was granted a credit of $33 million to increase the quality, coverage and cost-effectiveness of maternal and child health services.

Small-scale enterprises

Sri Lanka received $20 million to provide credit through the banking system to small- and medium-scale private manufacturers and to contribute to policy reform and institutional strengthening in the areas of tariff administration, export promotion and financial sector operations.

Technical assistance

IDA granted eight technical assistance credits amounting to $80.5 million in fiscal 1988. Senegal received $17 million to carry out administrative reforms to strengthen its economic and financial management capacity. A credit of $12.8 million was granted to Chad to enhance its capacity to define and implement its development programme, carry out effective economic and financial management, monitor economic performance and improve revenue collection. Ghana received $10.5 million to formulate and implement sector-wide State-owned enterprise reforms and to initiate managerial and operational improvements in key public enterprises.

Transportation

Fifteen credits to 12 countries totalling $525.3 million were granted for the transportation sector. Of three credits totalling $100 million made to China, $50 million assisted in expanding the road capacity between Chengdu, the capital of Sichuan province, and Chongqing, the major industrial centre and river port of the province, as well as improving two rural roads. Bangladesh received $87.3 million, of which $62.3 million was to develop rural infrastructure in eight northwestern districts. A $60 million credit was extended to Ghana to rehabilitate roads and railways, including infrastructure rehabilitation, support for sector institutions and reforms, and pilot programmes in support of small-scale private road transport and low-cost rural transport.

Urban development

Eight urban projects were assisted in fiscal 1988 at a cost of $607.8 million. India received $300.2 million to assist the 10 largest cities in Tamil Nadu State, by strengthening institutions involved with the programming and delivery of urban services and the implementation of urban investments. Pakistan received $90 million to improve the living standards, environmental quality and productivity of people living in Lahore. A credit of $78 million was granted to Sri Lanka to reconstruct or rehabilitate affected infrastructure, revive economic activities and restore essential services.

Water supply and sewerage

Zaire received $45 million to develop new water-supply systems in 18 semi-rural centres, reinforce the water-supply system in Likasi, and provide technical assistance and consulting services to the State-owned water utility.

Secretariat

The principal officers, staff, headquarters and other offices of IDA are the same as those of the World Bank (see PART SEVEN, Chapter VI).

NOTE: For details of IDA activities during fiscal 1988, see *The World Bank Annual Report 1988*.

Annex I. MEMBERS OF THE INTERNATIONAL DEVELOPMENT ASSOCIATION
(As at 30 June 1988)

Part I (industrial) members

Australia, Austria, Belgium, Canada, Denmark, Finland, France, Germany, Federal Republic of, Iceland, Ireland, Italy, Japan, Kuwait, Luxembourg, Netherlands, New Zealand, Norway, South Africa, Sweden, United Arab Emirates, United Kingdom, United States.

Part II (developing) members

Afghanistan, Algeria, Argentina, Bangladesh, Belize, Benin, Bhutan, Bolivia, Botswana, Brazil, Burkina Faso, Burma, Burundi, Cameroon, Cape Verde, Central African Republic, Chad, Chile, China, Colombia, Comoros, Congo, Costa Rica, Côte d'Ivoire, Cyprus, Democratic Kampuchea, Djibouti, Dominica, Dominican Republic, Ecuador, Egypt, El Salvador, Equatorial Guinea, Ethiopia, Fiji, Gabon, Gambia, Ghana, Greece, Grenada, Guatemala, Guinea, Guinea-Bissau, Guyana, Haiti, Honduras, Hungary, India, Indonesia, Iran, Iraq, Israel, Jordan, Kenya, Kiribati, Lao People's Democratic Republic, Lebanon, Lesotho, Liberia, Libyan Arab Jamahiriya, Madagascar, Malawi, Malaysia, Maldives, Mali, Mauritania, Mauritius, Mexico, Morocco, Mozambique, Nepal, Nicaragua, Niger, Nigeria, Oman, Pakistan, Panama, Papua New Guinea, Paraguay, Peru, Philippines, Poland, Republic of Korea, Rwanda, Saint Kitts and Nevis, Saint Lucia, Saint Vincent and the Grenadines, Samoa, Sao Tome and Principe, Saudi Arabia, Senegal, Sierra Leone, Solomon Islands, Somalia, Spain, Sri Lanka, Sudan, Suriname, Swaziland, Syrian Arab Republic, Thailand, Togo, Tonga, Trinidad and Tobago, Tunisia, Turkey, Uganda, United Republic of Tanzania, Vanuatu, Viet Nam, Yemen, Yugoslavia, Zaire, Zambia, Zimbabwe.

Annex II. EXECUTIVE DIRECTORS AND ALTERNATES AND OFFICES OF THE INTERNATIONAL DEVELOPMENT ASSOCIATION
(As at 30 June 1988)

EXECUTIVE DIRECTORS AND ALTERNATES

Appointed Director	*Appointed Alternate*	*Casting the vote of*
Robert B. Keating	(vacant)	United States
Mitsukazu Ishikawa	Yukio Yoshimura	Japan
Gerhard Boehmer	Michael von Harpe	Federal Republic of Germany
Hélène Ploix	Olivier Debains	France
Frank Cassell	J. A. L. Faint	United Kingdom

Elected Director	*Elected Alternate*	*Casting the votes of*
Frank Potter (Canada)	Horace Barber (Jamaica)	Belize, Canada, Dominica, Grenada, Guyana, Ireland, Saint Kitts and Nevis, Saint Lucia, Saint Vincent and the Grenadines
Mercedes Rubio (Spain)	Francisco Vannini (Nicaragua)	Costa Rica, El Salvador, Guatemala, Honduras, Mexico, Nicaragua, Panama, Spain
Jacques de Groote (Belgium)	Heiner Luschin (Austria)	Austria, Belgium, Hungary, Luxembourg, Turkey
Mourad Benachenhou (Algeria)	Salem Mohamed Omeish (Libyan Arab Jamahiriya)	Afghanistan, Algeria, Democratic Yemen, Ghana, Iran, Libyan Arab Jamahiriya, Morocco, Tunisia
C. R. Krishnaswamy Rao Sahib (India)	M. Mustafizur Rahman (Bangladesh)	Bangladesh, Bhutan, India, Sri Lanka
Fawzi Hamad Al-Sultan (Kuwait)	Mohamed W. Hosny (Egypt)	Egypt, Iraq, Jordan, Kuwait, Lebanon, Maldives, Oman, Pakistan, Syrian Arab Republic, United Arab Emirates, Yemen
Paul Arlman (Netherlands)	Cvitan Dujmovic (Yugoslavia)	Cyprus, Israel, Netherlands, Yugoslavia
C. Ulrik Haxthausen (Denmark)	Veikko Kantola (Finland)	Denmark, Finland, Iceland, Norway, Sweden
Mitiku Jembere (Ethiopia)	J. S. A. Funna (Sierra Leone)	Botswana, Burundi, Ethiopia, Gambia, Guinea, Kenya, Lesotho, Liberia, Malawi, Mozambique, Nigeria, Sierra Leone, Sudan, Swaziland, Trinidad and Tobago, Uganda, United Republic of Tanzania, Zambia, Zimbabwe
Mario Draghi (Italy)	Rodrigo M. Guimarães (Portugal)	Greece, Italy
Xu Naijiong (China)	Zhang Junyi (China)	China

Elected Director	*Elected Alternate*	*Casting the votes of*
Jobarah E. Suraisry (Saudi Arabia)	Abdulaziz Al-Sehail (Saudi Arabia)	Saudi Arabia
Murray A. Sherwin (New Zealand)	Robert G. Carling (Australia)	Australia, Kiribati, New Zealand, Papua New Guinea, Republic of Korea, Samoa, Solomon Islands, Vanuatu
Pedro Sampaio Malan (Brazil)	Carlos Sanclemente (Colombia)	Brazil, Colombia, Dominican Republic, Ecuador, Haiti, Philippines
Mohd. Ramli Wajib (Malaysia)	Kikham Vongsay (Lao People's Democratic Republic)	Burma, Fiji, Indonesia, Lao People's Democratic Republic, Malaysia, Nepal, Thailand, Tonga, Viet Nam
Félix Alberto Camarasa (Argentina)	Claudio A. Pardo (Chile)	Argentina, Bolivia, Chile, Paraguay, Peru
André Milongo (Congo)	Jean-Pierre Le Bouder (Central African Republic)	Benin, Burkina Faso, Cameroon, Cape Verde, Central African Republic, Chad, Comoros, Congo, Côte d'Ivoire, Djibouti, Equatorial Guinea, Gabon, Guinea-Bissau, Madagascar, Mali, Mauritania, Mauritius, Niger, Rwanda, Sao Tome and Principe, Senegal, Somalia, Togo, Zaire

NOTE: Democratic Kampuchea, Poland and South Africa did not participate in the 1986 regular election of Executive Directors.

HEADQUARTERS AND OTHER OFFICES

HEADQUARTERS
International Development Association
1818 H Street, N.W.
Washington, D.C. 20433, United States
  Cable address: INDEVAS WASHINGTONDC
  Telephone: (1) (202) 477-1234
  Telex: RCA 248423 INDEVAS
  Facsimile: (1) (202) 477-6391

NEW YORK OFFICE
International Development Association
809 United Nations Plaza, Suite 900
New York, N.Y. 10017, United States
  Cable address: INDEVAS NEWYORK
  Telephone: (1) (212) 963-6008
  Facsimile: (1) (212) 697-7020

IDA also had major regional offices at Abidjan, Côte d'Ivoire; Bangkok, Thailand; Geneva; Nairobi, Kenya; Paris; and Tokyo.

Chapter IX

International Monetary Fund (IMF)

The International Monetary Fund (IMF), a forum in which its member States discuss global monetary issues and related economic matters, aims to assist them to develop sound policies and so engender a stable international economic and financial environment. The Fund provides members with advice on economic and financial policies, lends money to members that are undertaking economic reforms to overcome balance-of-payments difficulties and makes available to them information and technical assistance.

Each member contributes to IMF's pool of financial resources an amount of money, called a quota subscription, roughly proportional to its standing in the world economy. As at December 1988, aggregate quotas, measured in special drawing rights (SDRs)—the Fund's unit of account—amounted to SDR 90 billion ($130 billion). The amount a member has contributed determines its voting power and how much it can borrow from the Fund.

The IMF Board of Governors—the minister of finance or the head of the central bank of each member country—is the highest decision-making body in the Fund. The 22 Executive Directors, representing all IMF members, see to it that the decisions of the Board are carried out by the IMF staff.

During fiscal year 1988 (1 May 1987 to 30 April 1988), IMF continued to fulfil its surveillance mandate of the international monetary system, particularly the exchange rate policies of its members, by examining each member's policies and performance and through regular discussions of the world economic outlook.

IMF holds regular consultations with each member country, which allows it to appraise the country's overall economic situation and policies, discuss policy options and make recommendations. Consultations continued in response to modifications to the guidelines on the frequency of consultations introduced in 1987.[a] The number of consultations concluded in 1988 fell to 110 (74 per cent of membership) from 115 (75 per cent) in 1987.

At the end of 1988, the membership of IMF remained unchanged at 151 (see Annex I).

IMF facilities and policies

IMF provided member States with financial resources in support of programmes of economic adjustment. The facilities and policies through which it provided such support differed, depending on the nature of the macro-economic and structural problems to be addressed and the terms and degree of conditionality attached to them.

Stand-by arrangements, typically covering periods of one or two years, focus on specific macro-economic policies, such as exchange rate and interest policies, aimed at overcoming balance-of-payments difficulties. Extended arrangements, which support medium-term programmes generally running for three years, are available to overcome more intractable balance-of-payment difficulties, attributable to structural as well as macro-economic problems.

In September, the Interim Committee of the Board of Governors on the International Monetary System, a 22-member advisory body representing the same constituencies as in the Fund's Executive Board (see Annex II), recommended the continuation of the enlarged access policy, financed by borrowed resources, and the maintenance of the limits on the use of Fund resources in effect. Under the enlarged access policy, the limit on annual access under a stand-by or an extended arrangement continued to be 90 per cent or 110 per cent of quota; the cumulative access limit remained at 400 or 440 per cent of quota, depending on the size and nature of the member's balance-of-payments need and the strength of its adjustment efforts.

The structural adjustment facility (SAF), launched in 1986,[b] continued to provide loans on concessional terms to low-income countries facing protracted balance-of-payments problems.

In April 1988, the enhanced structural adjustment facility (ESAF), established in 1987[c] to provide additional assistance to low-income countries undertaking structural adjustments, became operational. Access under ESAF was expected to average 150 per cent of quota over a three-year programme period, with provision for up to 350 per cent in exceptional circumstances.

The compensatory financing facility, designed to help stabilize the earnings of countries exporting primary commodities, was superseded in Au-

[a]YUN 1987, p. 1251.
[b]YUN 1986, p. 1159.
[c]YUN 1987, p. 1252.

gust by the compensatory and contingency financing facility, which added a mechanism for contingency financing of member States that had entered into adjustment programmes supported by the Fund. Under the compensatory features of the facility, the Fund compensated members for levels of export earnings or cereal import costs that deviated from medium-term trends. Under the contingency features, the Fund provided additional financing to countries whose programmes might be threatened by external disruptions that might cause economic variables to deviate from those originally forecasted under the adjustment programme.

Under the buffer stock financing facility, IMF provided resources to help finance members' contributions to approved buffer stocks of commodities.

Financial assistance

During 1988, there were sharp increases in the use of Fund resources by members under the compensatory financing facility. Drawings by seven members totalled SDR 1.5 billion (compared to purchases by eight members of SDR 593 million in fiscal year 1987). Amounts agreed under stand-by and extended arrangements and SAF totalled SDR 4.54 billion.

The number of IMF financial arrangements in effect increased to 45 at the end of fiscal 1988, compared to 34 at the end of 1987. As at 30 April 1988, there were 18 stand-by arrangements (Argentina, Central African Republic, Costa Rica, Côte d'Ivoire, Ecuador, Egypt, Gabon, Guinea, Jamaica, Kenya, Malawi, Mauritania, Philippines, Senegal, Somalia, Togo, Tunisia, Zaire); 2 extended arrangements (Chile, Ghana); and 25 SAF arrangements (Bangladesh, Bolivia, Burundi, Central African Republic, Chad, Dominica, Gambia, Ghana, Guinea, Guinea-Bissau, Haiti, Kenya, Madagascar, Mauritania, Mozambique, Nepal, Niger, Senegal, Sierra Leone, Somalia, Sri Lanka, Togo, Uganda, United Republic of Tanzania, Zaire).

At the end of fiscal year 1988, credit outstanding in the General Resources Account was SDR 27.83 billion, a decline of SDR 3.8 billion compared to 1987.

Purchases, or drawings, on IMF's resources included SDR 1.7 billion under stand-by arrangements, SDR 260 million under extended arrangements and SDR 1.54 billion under the compensatory financing facility. Two countries had purchases outstanding totalling SDR 3 million in the buffer stock financing facility. As at 30 April 1988, loan disbursements under SAF totalled SDR 1.36 billion, with undisbursed commitments totalling SDR 0.77 billion.

Liquidity

As at 30 April 1988, the Fund's usable ordinary resources totalled SDR 41 billion, compared with SDR 39.3 billion at the end of the preceding fiscal year.

The Fund borrowed from official lenders to supplement its resources and to finance members' purchases under the enlarged access policy. The total amount of borrowed resources available at the end of fiscal 1988 declined to SDR 5.3 billion from SDR 7.1 billion at the end of fiscal 1987.

The Fund borrowed SDR 1.3 billion and repaid SDR 4.9 billion, resulting in a net decrease in total outstanding borrowing of SDR 3.6 billion, from SDR 12.7 billion at the end of fiscal 1987 to SDR 9.1 billion at the end of fiscal 1988.

SDR activity

Total transfers of SDRs increased in 1988 to SDR 19.9 billion from SDR 15.6 in 1987. While transactions with designation continued to decline, voluntary transfers among participants and prescribed holders increased sharply by 87 per cent, resulting in a 50 per cent rise in total transfers among them to SDR 9.5 billion. The volume of SDR transfers involving prescribed holders nearly tripled, to SDR 1.9 billion from SDR 0.68 billion during fiscal 1987.

The amount of SDRs transferred between participants and IMF increased by 12 per cent over the previous fiscal year. Transfers from participants to the General Resources Account increased by 8 per cent to SDR 4.61 billion. Transfers from that Account to participants in purchases, remuneration payments, sales to members needing SDRs for payments of charges, and interest payments on and repayments of Fund borrowings increased by 15 per cent to SDR 5.8 billion.

Policy on arrears

The continued delay by some members in discharging financial obligations to the Fund was of increasing concern during the fiscal year. Total overdue obligations rose from SDR 1.19 billion at the end of fiscal 1987 to SDR 1.94 billion at the end of fiscal 1988. The number of members in arrears by six months or more rose by one, to nine. During 1988, three members were declared ineligible to use the general resources of the Fund in view of their overdue obligations to the General Department. Earlier declarations of ineligibility with respect to five members remained in effect.

Concerned by the continued increase of overdue obligations, the Interim Committee in April 1988 requested the Executive Board to prepare a report on measures to reduce, and eventually eliminate, arrears to the Fund.

Technical assistance and training

Technical assistance continued to be an important part of IMF services to its members, focusing on general economic policy, balance-of-payments adjustment programmes, legal matters, debt management, problems arising from inflation, exchange and trade systems, public finance issues, financial sector issues, accounting, statistics and data processing.

Training of officials from member countries was provided by the IMF Institute through courses and seminars in economic analysis and policy. During fiscal 1988, the Institute conducted 14 courses and one seminar at IMF headquarters (Washington, D.C.) on financial analysis and policy, financial programming and policy, public finance, techniques of economic analysis, balance-of-payments methodology, money and banking statistics, government finance statistics and the role of IMF in the international monetary system. The Institute's training abroad included three seminars—on financial analysis and policy (Lao People's Democratic Republic), financial programming and policy (Sierra Leone) and financial analysis (Algeria). It also provided lecturing assistance to international, regional and national organizations.

IMF–World Bank collaboration

Collaboration between IMF and the World Bank intensified during fiscal 1988. Co-operation consisted of joint participation in missions, attendance at each other's Executive Board meetings, the regular exchange of documents and information, and attendance at and participation in conferences and seminars.

The two institutions also co-operated in support of low-income countries in terms of SAF and ESAF.

The Fund and Bank staff collaborated closely in efforts to encourage the flow of resources from donor Governments to member States.

Secretariat

As at 31 December 1988, the total full-time staff of IMF—including permanent, fixed-term and temporary employees—was 1,713, drawn from over 100 nationalities. (For senior officers, see Annex III.)

NOTE: For details of IMF activities in 1988, see *International Monetary Fund, Annual Report of the Executive Board for the Financial Year Ended April 30, 1988* and *International Monetary Fund, Annual Report of the Executive Board for the Financial Year Ended April 30, 1989*, published by the Fund.

Annex I. MEMBERSHIP OF THE INTERNATIONAL MONETARY FUND
(As at 31 December 1988)

Afghanistan, Algeria, Antigua and Barbuda, Argentina, Australia, Austria, Bahamas, Bahrain, Bangladesh, Barbados, Belgium, Belize, Benin, Bhutan, Bolivia, Botswana, Brazil, Burkina Faso, Burma, Burundi, Cameroon, Canada, Cape Verde, Central African Republic, Chad, Chile, China, Colombia, Comoros, Congo, Costa Rica, Côte d'Ivoire, Cyprus, Democratic Kampuchea, Democratic Yemen, Denmark, Djibouti, Dominica, Dominican Republic, Ecuador, Egypt, El Salvador, Equatorial Guinea, Ethiopia, Fiji, Finland, France, Gabon, Gambia, Germany, Federal Republic of, Ghana, Greece, Grenada, Guatemala, Guinea, Guinea-Bissau, Guyana, Haiti, Honduras, Hungary, Iceland, India, Indonesia, Iran, Iraq, Ireland, Israel, Italy, Jamaica, Japan, Jordan, Kenya, Kiribati, Kuwait, Lao People's Democratic Republic, Lebanon, Lesotho, Liberia, Libyan Arab Jamahiriya, Luxembourg, Madagascar, Malawi, Malaysia, Maldives, Mali, Malta, Mauritania, Mauritius, Mexico, Morocco, Mozambique, Nepal, Netherlands, New Zealand, Nicaragua, Niger, Nigeria, Norway, Oman, Pakistan, Panama, Papua New Guinea, Paraguay, Peru, Philippines, Poland, Portugal, Qatar, Republic of Korea, Romania, Rwanda, Saint Kitts and Nevis, Saint Lucia, Saint Vincent and the Grenadines, Sao Tome and Principe, Samoa, Saudi Arabia, Senegal, Seychelles, Sierra Leone, Singapore, Solomon Islands, Somalia, South Africa, Spain, Sri Lanka, Sudan, Suriname, Swaziland, Sweden, Syrian Arab Republic, Thailand, Togo, Tonga, Trinidad and Tobago, Tunisia, Turkey, Uganda, United Arab Emirates, United Kingdom, United Republic of Tanzania, United States, Uruguay, Vanuatu, Venezuela, Viet Nam, Yemen, Yugoslavia, Zaire, Zambia, Zimbabwe.

Annex II. EXECUTIVE DIRECTORS AND ALTERNATES
OF THE INTERNATIONAL MONETARY FUND
(As at 31 December 1988)

Appointed Director	*Appointed Alternate*	*Casting the vote of*
Charles H. Dallara	Charles S. Warner	United States
Frank Cassell	Charles Enoch	United Kingdom
Guenter Grosche	Bernd Goos	Federal Republic of Germany

Appointed Director	Appointed Alternate	Casting the vote of
Hélène Ploix	Dominique Marcel	France
Koji Yamazaki	Shinichi Yoshikuni	Japan
Yusuf A. Nimatallah	Ibrahim Al-Assaf	Saudi Arabia

Elected Director	Elected Alternate	Casting the votes of
Renato Filosa (Italy)	Nikos Kyriazidis (Greece)	Greece, Italy, Malta, Poland, Portugal
Leonor Filardo (Venezuela)	Miguel A. Fernández Ordóñez (Spain)	Costa Rica, El Salvador, Guatemala, Honduras, Mexico, Nicaragua, Spain, Venezuela
G. A. Posthumus (Netherlands)	G. P. J. Hogeweg (Netherlands)	Cyprus, Israel, Netherlands, Romania, Yugoslavia
Jacques de Groote (Belgium)	Johann Prader (Austria)	Austria, Belgium, Hungary, Luxembourg, Turkey
Mohamed Finaish (Libyan Arab Jamahiriya)	Abdul Moneim Othman (Iraq)	Bahrain, Democratic Yemen, Egypt, Iraq, Jordan, Kuwait, Lebanon, Libyan Arab Jamahiriya, Maldives, Oman, Pakistan, Qatar, Somalia, Syrian Arab Republic, United Arab Emirates, Yemen
Marcel Massé (Canada)	Dara McCormack (Ireland)	Antigua and Barbuda, Bahamas, Barbados, Belize, Canada, Dominica, Grenada, Ireland, Jamaica, Saint Kitts and Nevis, Saint Lucia, Saint Vincent and the Grenadines
C. R. Rye (Australia)	Chang-Yuel Lim (Republic of Korea)	Australia, Kiribati, New Zealand, Papua New Guinea, Philippines, Republic of Korea, Samoa, Seychelles, Solomon Islands, Vanuatu
Jorgen Ovi (Denmark)	Markus Fogelholm (Finland)	Denmark, Finland, Iceland, Norway, Sweden
Bimal Jalan (India)	L. Eustace N. Fernando (Sri Lanka)	Bangladesh, Bhutan, India, Sri Lanka
Alexandre Kafka (Brazil)	Jerry Hospedales (Trinidad and Tobago)	Brazil, Colombia, Dominican Republic, Ecuador, Guyana, Haiti, Panama, Suriname, Trinidad and Tobago
J. E. Ismael (Indonesia)	Ekamol Kiriwat (Thailand)	Burma, Fiji, Indonesia, Lao People's Democratic Republic, Malaysia, Nepal, Singapore, Thailand, Tonga, Viet Nam
El Tayeb El Kogali (Sudan)	L. B. Monyake (Lesotho)	Botswana, Burundi, Ethiopia, Gambia, Kenya, Lesotho, Liberia, Malawi, Mozambique, Nigeria, Sierra Leone, Sudan, Swaziland, Uganda, United Republic of Tanzania, Zambia, Zimbabwe
Dai Qianding (China)	Zhang Zhixiang (China)	China
Ernesto V. Feldman (Argentina)	Ricardo J. Lombardo (Uruguay)	Argentina, Bolivia, Chile, Paraguay, Peru, Uruguay
Mohammad Reza Ghasimi (Iran)	Omar Kabbaj (Morocco)	Afghanistan, Algeria, Ghana, Iran, Morocco, Tunisia
Mawakani Samba (Zaire)	Corentino V. Santos (Cape Verde)	Benin, Burkina Faso, Cameroon, Cape Verde, Central African Republic, Chad, Comoros, Congo, Côte d'Ivoire, Djibouti, Equatorial Guinea, Gabon, Guinea, Guinea-Bissau, Madagascar, Mali, Mauritania, Mauritius, Niger, Rwanda, Sao Tome and Principe, Senegal, Togo, Zaire

NOTE: Democratic Kampuchea and South Africa did not participate in the 1988 regular election of Executive Directors.

Annex III. OFFICERS AND OFFICES OF THE INTERNATIONAL MONETARY FUND
(As at 31 December 1988)

SENIOR OFFICERS

Managing Director: Michel Camdessus.
Deputy Managing Director: Richard D. Erb.
Economic Counsellor: Jacob A. Frenkel.
Counsellors: Mamoude Touré, Leo Van Houtven, L. A. Whittome.
Director, Administration Department: Graeme F. Rea.
Director, African Department: Mamoude Touré.
Director, Asian Department: P. R. Narvekar.
Director, Central Banking Department: J. B. Zulu.
Director, European Department: Massimo Russo.
Director, Exchange and Trade Relations Department: L. A. Whittome.
Director, External Relations Department: Azizali F. Mohammed.
Director, Fiscal Affairs Department: Vito Tanzi.
Director, IMF Institute: Gérard M. Teyssier.

General Counsel, Legal Department: François P. Gianviti.
Director, Middle Eastern Department: A. Shakour Shaalan.
Director, Research Department: Jacob A. Frenkel.
Secretary, Secretary's Department: Leo Van Houtven.
Treasurer, Treasurer's Department: F. Gerhard Laske.
Director, Western Hemisphere Department: Sterie T. Beza.
Director, Bureau of Computing Services: Warren N. Minami.
Director, Bureau of Language Services: Alan Wright.
Director, Bureau of Statistics: John B. McLenaghan.
Director, Office in Europe (Paris): Andrew J. Beith.
Director, Office in Geneva: Jack P. Barnouin (Acting).

HEADQUARTERS AND OTHER OFFICES

HEADQUARTERS
International Monetary Fund
700 19th Street N.W.
Washington, D.C. 20431, United States
Cable address: INTERFUND WASHINGTONDC
Telephone: (1) (202) 623-7000
Telex: (RCA) 248331 IMF UR, (MCI) 64111 IMF UW,
    (TRT) 197677 FUND UT
Facsimile: (1) (202) 623-4661

OFFICE IN NEW YORK
International Monetary Fund
1 United Nations Plaza, Room 1140
New York, N.Y. 10017, United States
Cable address: INTERFUND NEW YORK
Telephone: (1) (212) 963-6009
Facsimile: (1) (212) 319-9040

IMF also maintained offices at Geneva and in Paris.

Chapter X

International Civil Aviation Organization (ICAO)

The International Civil Aviation Organization (ICAO) facilitates the safety and efficiency of civil air transport. As an intergovernmental regulatory organization, its objectives are set down in annexes to the Convention on International Civil Aviation (Chicago, United States, 1944), which prescribe standards, recommended practices and procedures for facilitating civil aviation operations.

In 1988, ICAO estimated total traffic of the world's scheduled airlines to be some 212 billion tonne-kilometres, an increase of 7.6 per cent over 1987. The airlines carried in excess of 1 billion passengers, 4.6 per cent more than in 1987. The number of seats offered increased at a lower rate than passengers carried, raising the estimated passenger load factor to 68 per cent, 1 per cent higher than in 1987. Air freight increased by some 11 per cent to more than 53 billion tonne-kilometres. Airmail traffic increased by 2.4 per cent.

During the year, the ICAO Council held three regular sessions and one extraordinary session. On 25 March, it condemned the destruction by an act of sabotage of a Korean Air Lines civil aircraft during a scheduled international flight in November 1987, resulting in the loss of all 115 persons on board. The Council's extraordinary session (13 and 14 July) was convened at the request of Iran, following the shooting down on 3 July of an Iran Air Airbus, which resulted in the loss of 290 lives.

In 1988, membership of ICAO rose to 160 with the admission of the Federated States of Micronesia, the Marshall Islands and San Marino (see Annex I).

Activities in 1988

Air navigation

ICAO's efforts in air navigation continued to be directed towards updating and implementing ICAO specifications, guidance material and regional plans. ICAO specifications consisted of International Standards and Recommended Practices contained in 18 technical annexes to the Chicago Convention, and of Procedures for Air Navigation Services in three documents. Guidance material was contained in some 100 technical manuals, circulars and other documents, the purpose of which was to assist States in establishing and maintaining an up-to-date and effective aeronautical infrastructure. ICAO regional plans set

forth air navigation facilities and services required in the nine ICAO regions.

Six air navigation meetings covering a wide range of subjects recommended changes to ICAO specifications. ICAO regional offices assisted States in implementing the regional plans. Their efforts were supplemented by the work of experts sent to advise States on the installation of new facilities and services and the operation of existing ones.

During the year, special attention was given to accident investigation and prevention, aerodromes, aeronautical information services, audio-visual training aids, aviation medicine, flight safety and human factors, illicit transport of drugs, meteorology, operation of aircraft, personnel licensing and training, rules of the air and air traffic services, search and rescue, future air navigation systems, telecommunications and transport of dangerous goods. Safeguarding of international civil aviation against acts of unlawful interference was accorded particular emphasis.

Air transport

ICAO continued its programmes of economic studies, collecting and publishing air transport statistics and promoting greater facilitation in international air transport.

The tenth session of the Facilitation Division (Montreal, Canada, 7-23 September) made a comprehensive review of new subjects, such as facilities for elderly and disabled passengers, the prevention of narcotics trafficking, procedures for inadequately documented passengers and courier and express shipments. The eleventh meeting of the Panel on Fares and Rates (Montreal, 5-15 April) reviewed current developments in the fares and rates field. Workshops were held on airport and route facility management (Montevideo, Uruguay, 24-28 October), on international fares and rates (Budapest, Hungary, 11-15 April; Nairobi, Kenya, 4-8 July) and on statistics (Mexico City, 30 May–3 June; Nuku'alofa, Tonga, 24-28 October).

ICAO publications included a digest of bilateral air transport agreements, guidance material on the regulation of computer reservation systems, the 1988 edition of the manual of airport and air navigation facility tariffs, the regular series of digests of civil aviation statistics, the yearbook on world civil aviation statistics, a study of regional differences in fares, rates and costs for international air transport in 1986 and a survey of international air transport fares and rates in 1987.

Following a 1982 conference to amend the 1956 Danish and Icelandic joint financing agreements for air navigation services in Greenland and the Faeroe Islands and in Iceland, the two agreements, as amended, were provisionally applied from 1 January 1983. By the end of 1988, the protocols of amendment had been accepted by 17 of the 22 Governments that were parties to the agreements.

Legal matters

An International Conference on Air Law (Montreal, 9-24 February) adopted the Protocol for the Suppression of Unlawful Acts of Violence at Airports Serving International Civil Aviation, Supplementary to the Convention for the Suppression of Unlawful Acts against the Safety of Civil Aviation, done at Montreal on 23 September 1971. The Protocol was opened for signature at Montreal on 24 February 1988 and by year's end had been signed by 61 States. The Protocol added to the 1971 Convention's definition of ''offence'' unlawful and intentional acts of violence against persons at an airport serving international civil aviation which caused or were likely to cause serious injury or death; similarly, destruction or serious damage to the facilities of such an airport, to an aircraft not in service located thereon or disruption of the services of the airport would constitute offences punishable by severe penalties; the qualifying element of such offences was the fact that such an act endangered or was likely to endanger safety at that airport.

The Final Act of the Conference, signed on behalf of 77 States, included the text of a resolution which addressed preventive measures and urged States to take all possible measures for the suppression of acts of violence at airports serving international civil aviation, including such preventive measures as were required or recommended under annex 17 to the Chicago Convention.

On 29 June, the general work programme of the Legal Committee was approved by the ICAO Council and contained the following items in priority order: the 1982 United Nations Convention on the Law of the Sea[a] and its implications, if any, for the application of the Chicago Convention, its annexes and other international air law instruments; liability of air traffic control agencies; institutional and legal aspects of future air navigation systems; legal aspects of global air-ground communications; and preparation of a draft instrument on the interception of civil aircraft.

The following conventions and protocols on international air law concluded under ICAO auspices were ratified or adhered to by the member States listed below during 1988:

Convention for the Unification of Certain Rules relating to International Carriage by Air, signed at Warsaw on 12 October 1929
    Equatorial Guinea, Peru
Convention on the International Recognition of Rights in Aircraft (Geneva, 1948)
    Bangladesh, Guatemala
Protocol to Amend the Convention for the Unification of Certain Rules relating to International Carriage by Air signed at Warsaw on 12 October 1929 (The Hague, 1955)
    Peru
Convention, Supplementary to the Warsaw Convention, for the Unification of Certain Rules relating to International Carriage by Air Performed by a Person Other than the Contracting Carrier (Guadalajara, 1961)
    Peru
Convention on Offences and Certain Other Acts Committed on Board Aircraft (Tokyo, 1963)
    Byelorussian SSR, Cameroon, Ukrainian SSR, USSR
Convention for the Suppression of Unlawful Seizure of Aircraft (The Hague, 1970)
    Bhutan, Cameroon, Maldives
Protocol to Amend the Convention for the Unification of Certain Rules Relating to International Carriage by Air signed at Warsaw on 12 October 1929 as amended by the Protocol done at The Hague on 28 September 1955 (Guatemala City, 1971)
    Niger
Convention for the Suppression of Unlawful Acts against the Safety of Civil Aviation (Montreal, 1971)
    Bhutan, Maldives
Additional Protocol No. 1 to Amend the Convention for the Unification of Certain Rules relating to International Carriage by Air signed at Warsaw on 12 October 1929 (Montreal, 1975) (not in force)
    Greece
Additional Protocol No. 2 to Amend the Convention for the Unification of Certain Rules relating to International Carriage by Air signed at Warsaw on 12 October 1929 as amended by the Protocol done at The Hague on 28 September 1955 (Montreal, 1975) (not in force)
    Greece
Additional Protocol No. 3 to Amend the Convention for the Unification of Certain Rules relating to International Carriage by Air signed at Warsaw on 12 October 1929 as amended by the Protocols done at The Hague on 28 September 1955 and at Guatemala City on 8 March 1971 (Montreal, 1975) (not in force)
    Denmark, Finland, Greece, Israel, Norway, Sweden
Montreal Protocol No. 4 to Amend the Convention for the Unification of Certain Rules relating to International Carriage by Air signed at Warsaw on 12 October 1929 as amended by the Protocol done at The Hague on 28 September 1955 (Montreal, 1975) (not in force)
    Denmark, Finland, Greece, Israel, Norway, Sweden
Protocol to Amend the Convention on Damage Caused by Foreign Aircraft to Third Parties on the Surface signed at Rome on 7 October 1952 (Montreal, 1978) (not in force)
    Niger

Technical assistance

ICAO provided technical co-operation to 114 States; in 52 of them there were resident missions

[a]YUN 1982, p. 181.

consisting of one or more experts. Co-operation was also provided in the form of equipment, fellowships and scholarships and through short missions by experts.

ICAO employed 489 experts (some in two or more programmes) from 51 countries during all or part of 1988, 383 on assignment under the United Nations Development Programme (UNDP) and 115 on trust fund projects (including 7 under the associate experts programme). There were also 30 United Nations Volunteers. The number of experts in the field at the end of 1988 was 200.

A total of 1,507 fellowships were awarded (1,162 in 1987), of which 1,419 were implemented.

Equipment purchases and sub-contracts continued to represent a substantial proportion of the technical co-operation programme. In addition to UNDP and trust fund projects, 52 Governments or organizations had registered with ICAO under its Civil Aviation Purchasing Service. The total for equipment and sub-contracts committed amounted to some $23.4 million.

The following were recipients of UNDP country projects executed by ICAO:

Africa: Benin, Botswana, Burkina Faso, Burundi, Cameroon, Central African Republic, Chad, Congo, Equatorial Guinea, Gabon, Gambia, Ghana, Guinea, Guinea-Bissau, Kenya, Lesotho, Malawi, Mali, Mauritania, Mauritius, Mozambique, Niger, Nigeria, Rwanda, Sao Tome and Principe, Senegal, Seychelles, Sierra Leone, Swaziland, Togo, Uganda, United Republic of Tanzania, Zaire, Zambia, Zimbabwe.

Americas: Antigua and Barbuda, Argentina, Bahamas, Brazil, Cayman Islands, Chile, Dominican Republic, Ecuador, El Salvador, Honduras, Panama, Peru, Turks and Caicos Islands, Uruguay.

Asia/Pacific: Afghanistan, Bangladesh, Bhutan, Burma, China, Democratic People's Republic of Korea, India, Indonesia, Kiribati, Lao People's Democratic Republic, Malaysia, Maldives, Nepal, Niue, Pakistan, Philippines, Republic of Korea, Singapore, Sri Lanka, Thailand, Tonga, Viet Nam.

Europe, Mediterranean and the Middle East: Democratic Yemen, Djibouti, Egypt, Jordan, Kuwait, Lebanon, Oman, Poland, Portugal, Qatar, Romania, Saudi Arabia, Somalia, Sudan, Turkey, United Arab Emirates, Yemen.

Trust fund projects executed by ICAO were conducted in Argentina, Bolivia, Brunei Darussalam, Cape Verde, Colombia, Côte d'Ivoire, Iraq, Jordan, the Libyan Arab Jamahiriya, Maldives, Nigeria, Peru, Saudi Arabia, Senegal, Sierra Leone, Yemen and Zambia, and an inter-country project with the Central American Corporation for Air Navigation Services.

Secretariat

As at 31 December 1988, the total number of staff members employed in the ICAO secretariat stood at 813: 296 in the Professional and higher categories, drawn from 74 nationalities, and 517 in the General Service and related categories. Of those, 208 persons were employed in regional offices. In addition, there were 131 in the Professional category serving as technical experts on UNDP field projects. (For principal officers of the secretariat, see Annex II).

Budget

Appropriations for the 1988 financial year, including amounts carried over from previous years, totalled $32.5 million.

NOTE: For details of ICAO activities, see *Annual Report of the Council—1988*, published by ICAO.

Annex I.   MEMBERSHIP OF THE INTERNATIONAL CIVIL AVIATION ORGANIZATION
            (As at 31 December 1988)

Afghanistan, Algeria, Angola, Antigua and Barbuda, Argentina, Australia, Austria, Bahamas, Bahrain, Bangladesh, Barbados, Belgium, Benin, Bolivia, Botswana, Brazil, Brunei Darussalam, Bulgaria, Burkina Faso, Burma, Burundi, Cameroon, Canada, Cape Verde, Central African Republic, Chad, Chile, China, Colombia, Comoros, Congo, Cook Islands, Costa Rica, Côte d'Ivoire, Cuba, Cyprus, Czechoslovakia, Democratic Kampuchea, Democratic People's Republic of Korea, Democratic Yemen, Denmark, Djibouti, Dominican Republic, Ecuador, Egypt, El Salvador, Equatorial Guinea, Ethiopia, Fiji, Finland, France, Gabon, Gambia, Germany, Federal Republic of, Ghana, Greece, Grenada, Guatemala, Guinea, Guinea-Bissau, Guyana, Haiti, Honduras, Hungary, Iceland, India, Indonesia, Iran, Iraq, Ireland, Israel, Italy, Jamaica, Japan, Jordan, Kenya, Kiribati, Kuwait, Lao People's Democratic Republic, Lebanon, Lesotho, Liberia, Libyan Arab Jamahiriya, Luxembourg, Madagascar, Malawi, Malaysia, Maldives, Mali, Malta, Marshall Islands, Mauritania, Mauritius, Mexico, Micronesia (Federated States of), Monaco, Morocco, Mozambique, Nauru, Nepal, Netherlands, New Zealand, Nicaragua, Niger, Nigeria, Norway, Oman, Pakistan, Panama, Papua New Guinea, Paraguay, Peru, Philippines, Poland, Portugal, Qatar, Republic of Korea, Romania, Rwanda, Saint Lucia, Saint Vincent and the Grenadines, San Marino, Sao Tome and Principe, Saudi Arabia, Senegal, Seychelles, Sierra Leone, Singapore, Solomon Islands, Somalia, South Africa, Spain, Sri Lanka, Sudan, Suriname, Swaziland, Sweden, Switzerland, Syrian Arab Republic, Thailand, Togo, Tonga, Trinidad and Tobago, Tunisia, Turkey, Uganda, USSR, United Arab Emirates, United Kingdom, United Republic of Tanzania, United States, Uruguay, Vanuatu, Venezuela, Viet Nam, Yemen, Yugoslavia, Zaire, Zambia, Zimbabwe.

Annex II. OFFICERS AND OFFICES OF THE INTERNATIONAL CIVIL AVIATION ORGANIZATION
(As at 31 December 1988)

ICAO COUNCIL

OFFICERS
President: Assad Kotaite (Lebanon).
First Vice-President: J. Pérez y Bouras (Mexico).
Second Vice-President: Group Capt. J. O. Koranteng (Rtd.) (Ghana).
Third Vice-President: A. Boediman (Indonesia).
Secretary: Dr. Shivinder Singh Sidhu (India).

MEMBERS
Argentina, Australia, Brazil, Canada, China, Cuba, Czechoslovakia, Egypt, France, Germany, Federal Republic of, Ghana, India, Indonesia, Iraq, Italy, Japan, Kenya, Mexico, Nigeria, Pakistan, Panama, Peru, Saudi Arabia, Senegal, Spain, Sweden, Switzerland, Tunisia, USSR, United Kingdom, United Republic of Tanzania, United States, Venezuela.

PRINCIPAL OFFICERS OF THE SECRETARIAT

Secretary-General: Dr. Shivinder Singh Sidhu.
Director, Technical Assistance Bureau: M. J. Challons.
Director, Legal Bureau: M. Milde.

Director, Bureau of Administration and Services: M. Pereyra.
Director, Air Transport Bureau: V. D. Zubkov.
Director, Air Navigation Bureau: W. Fromme.

HEADQUARTERS AND OTHER OFFICES

HEADQUARTERS
International Civil Aviation Organization
1000 Sherbrooke Street West
Montreal, Quebec, Canada H3A 2R2
  Cable address: ICAO MONTREAL
  Telephone: (1) (514) 285-8219
  Telex: 05-24513
  Facsimile: (1) (514) 288-4772

ICAO also maintained regional offices at Bangkok, Thailand; Cairo, Egypt; Dakar, Senegal; Lima, Peru; Mexico City; Nairobi, Kenya; and Neuilly-sur-Seine, France.

Chapter XI

Universal Postal Union (UPU)

The Universal Postal Union (UPU), established in 1874 for the reciprocal exchange of postal services between nations, is one of the oldest international intergovernmental organizations. It promotes the organization and improvement of postal services and international collaboration. At the request of its members it participates in various forms of postal technical assistance.

In 1988, UPU membership increased to 169 with the admission of Saint Kitts and Nevis (see Annex I).

Activities of UPU organs

Universal Postal Congress

The Universal Postal Congress, composed of all member States, is the supreme legislative authority of UPU and normally meets every five years. The most recent Congress (the nineteenth) took place at Hamburg, Federal Republic of Germany, in 1984 and the twentieth was scheduled to meet in Washington, D.C., in 1989.

The work of the Congress consists mainly of examining and revising the Acts of the Union based on proposals submitted by member States, the Executive Council or the Consultative Council for Postal Studies (CCPS), and of making administrative arrangements for UPU activities. The Acts in force since 1 January 1986 were those of the 1984 Congress.

Executive Council

At its 1988 session (Berne, 19 April–4 May), the Executive Council—which carries out the work of UPU between sessions of the Congress by maintaining close contact with postal administrations, exercising control over the International Bureau (see below), promoting technical assistance and working with the United Nations and other organizations—considered administrative matters and examined studies concerning international mail referred to it by the 1984 Congress.

The Council considered proposals to be submitted to the 1989 Congress in the areas of rate-fixing, terminal dues and rates. It also examined changes which UPU would have to make to adapt its operations to current commercial and technical demands.

Consultative Council for Postal Studies

In 1988, CCPS continued its studies of various technical, economic and operational problems affecting postal administrations of UPU member States, including matters of particular interest to new and developing countries.

At its final session of the five-year period 1984-1989 (Berne, 17-28 October 1988), CCPS considered the results of studies and proposals stemming from them for submission to the 1989 Congress. It also considered two comprehensive reports for submission to that Congress—the CCPS report covering the period from 1984 to 1989 and the joint Executive Council, CCPS and International Bureau report on implementation of the Declaration of Hamburg. It concentrated on the 1989-1994 CCPS work programme as well as proposals for improving the organization and operation of CCPS after the 1989 Congress.

International Bureau

Under the general supervision of the Government of the Swiss Confederation, the International Bureau—the UPU secretariat—continued to serve the postal administrations of member States as an organ for liaison, information and consultation. The Bureau co-ordinated, published and disseminated international postal service information. At the request of postal administrations, it also conducted inquiries and acted as a clearing-house for settling certain accounts between them.

As at 31 December 1988, the number of permanent and temporary staff members employed by the UPU secretariat was 143, of whom 60 were in the Professional and higher categories (drawn from 47 countries) and 83 in the General Service category. Also, as French remained the sole official UPU language, 14 officials were employed in the Arabic, English, Portuguese, Russian and Spanish translation services. (For officers of the Bureau, see Annex II.)

Technical co-operation

In 1988, technical co-operation provided by UPU was financed for the most part by the United Nations Development Programme (UNDP); UNDP/UPU project expenditures amounted to some $2.2 million. Assistance was also provided through the UPU Special Fund (voluntary contributions in cash and kind from member States) and the regular budget. Total expenditures from these two sources amounted to approximately $1.5 million. In addition, postal administrations provided assistance on a bilateral and multi-lateral basis.

The Special Fund and the regular budget funded missions by consultants, scholarships for training, instruction materials and equipment. During 1988, 49 consultants carried out technical missions in 44 postal administrations and 247 fellowships were granted for training courses and technical meetings. Fellowships and training courses were also offered by several countries.

Budget

Under UPU's self-financing system, contributions are payable in advance by member States based on the following year's budget. At its 1988 session, the Executive Council approved the 1989 budget at a total of 27,319,500 Swiss francs.

NOTE: For details of UPU activities, see *Report on the Work of the Union, 1988*, published by UPU.

Annex I. MEMBERSHIP OF THE UNIVERSAL POSTAL UNION
(As at 31 December 1988)

Afghanistan, Albania, Algeria, Angola, Argentina, Australia, Austria, Bahamas, Bahrain, Bangladesh, Barbados, Belgium, Belize, Benin, Bhutan, Bolivia, Botswana, Brazil, Brunei Darussalam, Bulgaria, Burkina Faso, Burma, Burundi, Byelorussian SSR, Cameroon, Canada, Cape Verde, Central African Republic, Chad, Chile, China, Colombia, Comoros, Congo, Costa Rica, Côte d'Ivoire, Cuba, Cyprus, Czechoslovakia, Democratic Kampuchea, Democratic People's Republic of Korea, Democratic Yemen, Denmark, Djibouti, Dominica, Dominican Republic, Ecuador, Egypt, El Salvador, Equatorial Guinea, Ethiopia, Fiji, Finland, France, Gabon, Gambia, German Democratic Republic, Germany, Federal Republic of, Ghana, Greece, Grenada, Guatemala, Guinea, Guinea-Bissau, Guyana, Haiti, Honduras, Hungary, Iceland, India, Indonesia, Iran, Iraq, Ireland, Israel, Italy, Jamaica, Japan, Jordan, Kenya, Kiribati, Kuwait, Lao People's Democratic Republic, Lebanon, Lesotho, Liberia, Libyan Arab Jamahiriya, Liechtenstein, Luxembourg, Madagascar, Malawi, Malaysia, Maldives, Mali, Malta, Mauritania, Mauritius, Mexico, Monaco, Mongolia, Morocco, Mozambique, Nauru, Nepal, Netherlands, Netherlands Antilles, New Zealand, Nicaragua, Niger, Nigeria, Norway, Oman, Pakistan, Panama, Papua New Guinea, Paraguay, Peru, Philippines, Poland, Portugal, Qatar, Republic of Korea, Romania, Rwanda, Saint Kitts and Nevis, Saint Lucia, Saint Vincent and the Grenadines, San Marino, Sao Tome and Principe, Saudi Arabia, Senegal, Seychelles, Sierra Leone, Singapore, Solomon Islands, Somalia, Spain, Sri Lanka, Sudan, Suriname, Swaziland, Sweden, Switzerland, Syrian Arab Republic, Thailand, Togo, Tonga, Trinidad and Tobago, Tunisia, Turkey, Tuvalu, Uganda, Ukrainian SSR, USSR, United Arab Emirates, United Kingdom, United Kingdom Overseas Territories, United Republic of Tanzania, United States, Uruguay, Vanuatu, Vatican City State, Venezuela, Viet Nam, Yemen, Yugoslavia, Zaire, Zambia, Zimbabwe.

Annex II. ORGANS, OFFICERS AND OFFICE OF THE UNIVERSAL POSTAL UNION
(As at 31 December 1988)

EXECUTIVE COUNCIL
(Elected to hold office until the twentieth (1989) Universal Postal Congress)

Chairman: Federal Republic of Germany.
Vice-Chairmen: Benin, Jordan, Mexico, USSR.
Secretary-General: Adwaldo Cardoso Botto de Barros, Director-General of the International Bureau.

Members: Algeria, Australia, Belgium, Benin, Brazil, Cameroon, Chile, Colombia, Côte d'Ivoire, Egypt, Ethiopia, France, Gabon, Germany, Federal Republic of, Honduras, Hungary, India, Iraq, Ireland, Japan, Jordan, Lebanon, Madagascar, Mexico, New Zealand, Nigeria, Norway, Pakistan, Peru, Poland, Portugal, Romania, Saudi Arabia, Senegal, Switzerland, Thailand, USSR, United States, Uruguay, Zambia.

CONSULTATIVE COUNCIL FOR POSTAL STUDIES
(Elected to hold office until the twentieth (1989) Universal Postal Congress)

Chairman: Tunisia.
Vice-Chairman: Canada.
Secretary-General: Adwaldo Cardoso Botto de Barros, Director-General of the International Bureau.

Members: Algeria, Argentina, Australia, Austria, Bangladesh, Belgium, Brazil, Canada, China, Cuba, Egypt, Finland, France, Germany, Federal Republic of, India, Indonesia, Italy, Japan, Kenya, Morocco, Netherlands, New Zealand, Pakistan, Spain, Sri Lanka, Sudan, Switzerland, Thailand, Tunisia, USSR, United Kingdom, United Republic of Tanzania, United States, Yugoslavia, Zimbabwe.

INTERNATIONAL BUREAU

SENIOR OFFICERS
Director-General: Adwaldo Cardoso Botto de Barros.
Deputy Director-General: Félix Cicéron.
Assistant Directors-General: Jaime Ascandoni, Abdel Kader Baghdadi, El Mostafa Gharbi.

HEADQUARTERS
Universal Postal Union
Weltpoststrasse 4
Berne, Switzerland
  Postal address: Union postale universelle
    Case postale
    3000 Berne 15, Switzerland
  Cable address: UPU BERNE
  Telephone: (41) (31) 43 22 11
  Telex: 912761 UPU CH
  Facsimile: (41) (31) 43 22 10

Chapter XII

International Telecommunication Union (ITU)

In 1988, the Administrative Council of the International Telecommunication Union (ITU) held its forty-third session (Geneva, 20 June–1 July), during which it reviewed administrative and financial matters, considered reports on ITU activities and examined and discussed a new basic instrument for the Union (draft constitution and draft convention). It also examined the report of a group of experts on the long-term future of the International Frequency Registration Board (IFRB).

The Council took note of the results of consultations conducted within the entire ITU membership concerning: the agenda for the second session of the Regional Administrative Conference for the planning of VHF/UHF (very high frequency/ultra-high frequency) television broadcasting in the African broadcasting area and neighbouring countries (AFBC-2) (Geneva, November 1989); and the agenda of a two-day Regional Administrative Conference during the third week of AFBC-2 for the purpose of abrogating the parts relating to the VHF/UHF television broadcasting plan of 1963,[a] which could still be in force at that time.

During 1988, membership of ITU rose to 166 with the admission of Bhutan, Samoa and Vanuatu (see Annex I).

Administrative radio conferences

The second session of the World Administrative Radio Conference (WARC) on the use of the geostationary-satellite orbit and the planning of space services utilizing it (Geneva, 29 August–6 October) established an allotment plan for certain bands of the fixed-satellite service; drew up associate procedures to enable the implementation of the plan; adopted procedures to improve the coordination process in certain bands between countries that would be affected by the installation of new satellites; and simplified, for the unplanned bands, the procedures that had been followed to access the geostationary-satellite orbit.

The World Administrative Telegraph and Telephone Conference (Melbourne, Australia, 28 November–9 December) focused on how international economic progress and the interests of telecommunication service providers could best be fostered to their satisfaction and that of an ever-increasing group of users. The Conference endorsed the role of special arrangements that would

include the agreed financial, technical and operational conditions to be observed by the parties to such arrangements. It considered the recognition given to the importance of interconnection/interconnectivity and the reciprocal exchange of information through the ITU General Secretariat. Measures were adopted to ensure the continued availability of traditional international services to those areas and countries that might not be in a position to adopt new and advanced services in the near future.

At its second session (Rio de Janeiro, Brazil, 23 May–8 June), the Regional Administrative Radio Conference to establish a plan for the broadcasting service in the frequency band 1,605-1,705 kHz (kilohertz) in Region 2 (the Americas) adopted a frequency allotment plan making available 10 channels. Region 2 was divided into allotment areas to each of which a minimum number of channels would be attributed. Each country would be entitled to use one or more of the channels. The Conference also adopted a schedule for introducing the newly planned broadcasting service and the provisions that could be included in the Radio Regulations by a future WARC to govern the use of the frequency band 1,605-1,705 kHz.

International consultative committees

The second series of interim study group meetings (Geneva, 11 April–10 May) for the 1986-1990 International Radio Consultative Committee (CCIR) study period considered spectrum utilization and monitoring; propagation in non-ionized media; propagation in ionized media; standard frequencies and time-signals; and mobile, radio-determination and amateur radio. A new recommendation and report were developed on future public land mobile telecommunication systems. At the first meeting of the interim working party on mobile satellite studies, progress was made towards recommendations on satellite news gathering and on digital television transmission in networks. New editions of CCIR handbooks on computer utilization in frequency management and on satellite communication were published, as were new software and a handbook on VHF/UHF antenna design for broadcasting. Under technical cooperation, CCIR provided assistance regarding

[a]YUN 1963, p. 659.

radio problems put forward by administrations of developing countries. It also participated in the selection panel for experts, participated in seminars and training courses and reviewed several project documents and reports involving radiocommunication issues.

Since 1988 was the last year of the 1985-1988 International Telegraph and Telephone Consultative Committee (CCITT) study period, CCITT activities centred mainly around the final meetings, during which reports and recommendations were prepared for the ninth CCITT Plenary Assembly (Melbourne, 14-25 November). The Plenary Assembly, following consideration by 15 study groups, approved 368 new draft recommendations and 388 amended recommendations and made changes in the structure of CCITT study groups. It set up an *ad hoc* group to develop scientific proposals designed to ensure that CCITT continued to maintain its leading world position in telecommunications standardization. In view of the rapid changes in telecommunication technology and services, the Plenary Assembly adopted an accelerated procedure for approving new and revised recommendations in the interval between plenary assemblies. In the area of technical assistance, CCITT continued to participate in selecting experts for technical co-operation development projects. At the end of 1988, 226 private companies and 37 international organizations were registered as participants in the work of CCITT in addition to ITU member administrations.

International Frequency Registration Board

The major activities of IFRB during 1988 included follow-up action on decisions of: WARC-79 relating to the review of assignments in the Master International Frequency Register; the 1981 Regional Administrative MF (medium frequency) Broadcasting Conference (Region 2); the 1984 Regional Administrative Radio Conference for FM (frequency modulation) sound broadcasting in the frequency band 87.5-108 MHz (megahertz) (Region 1—Africa and Europe—and certain countries in Region 3—Asia and Australasia); the 1985 Regional Administrative Conference for the planning of the MF maritime mobile and aeronautical radionavigation services (Region 1); the 1986 Regional Administrative Radio Conference to establish a plan for the broadcasting service in the band 1,605-1,705 kHz in Region 2; and the 1987 session of WARC on high frequency broadcasting.

Other activities related to the implementation of further modules for the IFRB frequency management system and continuing development of the system with a view to improving and rationalizing services to administrations; continuation of intersessional work and participation in the work of the second (1988) session of WARC on the use of the geostationary-satellite orbit and the planning of space services utilizing it; participation in the second (1988) session of the Regional Administrative Radio Conference to establish a plan for the broadcasting service in the band 1,605-1,705 kHz; continuation of intersessional work of the 1986 Regional Administrative Radio Conference for the planning of VHF/UHF television broadcasting in the African broadcasting area and neighbouring countries; application of the decisions of the 1987 WARC for the mobile services; and participation in the interim meetings of study groups and working parties of CCIR.

Technical co-operation

In 1988, under various ITU technical co-operation programmes in developing countries, 591 expert missions were carried out, 876 fellows were undergoing training abroad and equipment valued at $12.2 million was delivered, mainly to telecommunication training centres. Nineteen projects were being implemented, either partially or entirely under contract. Total assistance amounted to $31.4 million for 188 projects.

The following countries and territories were aided:

Africa: Algeria, Botswana, Burkina Faso, Burundi, Cameroon, Cape Verde, Central African Republic, Chad, Côte d'Ivoire, Djibouti, Gambia, Guinea, Liberia, Mali, Malawi, Morocco, Mauritania, Mozambique, Rwanda, Senegal, Somalia, Swaziland, Togo, Zaire, Zambia, Zimbabwe.

Americas: Brazil, Belize, Chile, Colombia, Ecuador, El Salvador, Haiti, Honduras, Mexico, Netherlands Antilles, Nicaragua, Panama, Peru, Saint Lucia, Suriname, Trinidad and Tobago, Venezuela.

Asia and the Pacific: Afghanistan, Bangladesh, Bhutan, Burma, India, Indonesia, Iran, Lao People's Democratic Republic, Malaysia, Nepal, Republic of Korea, Samoa, Sri Lanka, Tokelau.

Europe and the Middle East: Albania, Bulgaria, Democratic Yemen, Hungary, Jordan, Kuwait, Lebanon, Malta, Poland, Portugal, Qatar, Romania, Saudi Arabia, Syrian Arab Republic, Turkey, Yemen.

The three main objectives of ITU technical co-operation activities continued to be: promoting the development of regional telecommunications networks in Africa, the Americas, Asia, the Pacific, the Middle East and the Mediterranean basin; strengthening the telecommunication technical and administrative services in developing countries; and developing human resources required for telecommunications.

ITU continued to promote the development of telecommunication networks and their integration into the world-wide telecommunication system, in accordance with the objectives established by its World Plan Committee and regional plan committees.

The Pan-African Telecommunications Network (PANAFTEL), with its basic structure designed to interconnect the countries in Africa without transit beyond the continent, required attention; apart from the subregion of Central Africa, for which much remained to be done, the main PANAFTEL network structures had been installed. In addition to the land and submarine cable network, 41 of the 45 countries south of the Sahara had satellite earth stations. Financing was needed for the four missing earth stations. The United Nations Development Programme (UNDP) approved an extension for the fourth programming cycle (1987-1991) of the two PANAFTEL projects: operation and extension of the network, and network maintenance and rehabilitation. Regarding maintenance and rehabilitation, 15 national plans to improve maintenance (NPIMs), two rehabilitation projects and three overall maintenance improvement schemes were completed by the end of 1988; six NPIMs were under preparation, three at the final stage.

The feasibility study for the regional African satellite communication system, with an estimated budget of $7.5 million and co-financed by contributions from UNDP, the Organization of African Unity, ITU, the United Nations Educational, Scientific and Cultural Organization, Italy, the Federal Republic of Germany and a technical assistance grant from the African Development Bank, commenced in 1988. The study was to include terrestrial and satellite aspects and use, to a certain degree, inputs from country-study reports. Consultancy services were to be used to undertake part of the regional activity, particularly its space component.

In the area of strengthening national telecommunications technical and administrative services, Guinea received assistance to set up automatic telephone calls with a large number of countries; Cameroon, to analyse bids for the modernization and extension of switching exchanges; Togo, to draft technical specifications for the purchase and installation of digital switching equipment; and Burkina Faso, to prepare technical specifications for a new international transit centre and an earth station. To meet the needs of expanding, operating and maintaining their telecommunication networks, most administrations in Africa made efforts to develop their own national training facilities, often with the assistance of UNDP-financed projects. ITU continued its participation in projects to develop and/or strengthen training centres and activities in Algeria, Angola, Burkina Faso, Burundi, the Central African Republic, Chad, Djibouti, Malawi, Somalia, Togo, Zaire and Zimbabwe.

At the subregional level, a UNDP/ITU project supported the establishment of the African Advanced Level Telecommunications Institute (AFRALTI), which started its training activities in May. AFRALTI acted as a focal point to promote and organize various forms of co-operation with and between telecommunication training centres at the higher training levels. Subregional projects, especially in the context of the PANAFTEL implementation and maintenance projects, continued to contribute to the overall learning process.

In the Americas, ITU continued to promote development of a telecommunication network by assisting national and regional organizations responsible for such activity. A project document to improve the telecommunication network of the Caribbean subregion was prepared and discussed with the Caribbean Community and national authorities. Two projects for the Central American region, one for the Central American Bank/Regional Technical Committee for Telecommunications in Central America and another for a regional centre for the development of telecommunications software, were also discussed. In addition, a project document to improve the radio and television broadcasting network for 18 countries of the Latin American and Caribbean Broadcasting Union was prepared and discussed with Governments and Union authorities. Most of the projects in the region were devoted to the development and strengthening of administrative and planning services. Many administrations made efforts to introduce the computer-aided telecommunication network planning software. Several projects valued at $1.5 million were introducing modern methods and technologies in producing training aids by the use of computers.

Technical co-operation activities in Asia and the Pacific focused on the adoption of improved maintenance practices and computer-aided management techniques. The activities were undertaken mostly through six regional projects: networking of test and development centres (Seoul, Republic of Korea); telecommunications computer software training (Beijing); regional telecommunications planning (Bangkok, Thailand); telecommunications development and planning in the South Pacific; development of maritime radiocommunications (Asia); and cellular radio telephone systems application (countries of the Association of South-East Asian Nations).

Support to strengthen national telecommunication services in Asia and the Pacific was provided through a number of UNDP-financed projects, covering such areas as networking of test and development centres, network planning, maintenance and operations, rural and coastal communications, computer-aided billing, introduction of new services and management of telecommunication services.

As to the development of human resources, at the intercountry level a number of meetings and workshops were organized through training-oriented projects within the framework of UNDP. At the country level, ITU continued to be involved in UNDP-funded training projects in Bangladesh, Burma, India, Indonesia and Sri Lanka.

The second Steering Committee meeting of the European telecommunications development project (Geneva, January) identified six areas of collaboration, each to be the responsibility of a lead country assisted by other members. The work plan for each area was approved and the following meetings took place: feasibility study on computer-aided network planning (Bulgaria, two meetings); preparation of draft agreements on the use or joint development of special devices developed and used individually by each member country (Portugal); strategy for the transition from analogue to digital techniques (Yugoslavia); and the use or joint design of software programmes in six identified fields (Greece, two meetings). For the remaining two areas of collaboration—economic and financial aspects of telecommunications and joint working activities for research and development—Malta and Hungary, respectively, were designated as lead countries.

In addition, the following national projects were geared towards the strengthening of technical and managerial capabilities: in Albania, the planning and installation of two pilot microwave projects with Italy and Greece, as well as the creation of a measurement centre for telecommunication research; in Bulgaria, expansion of the activities of the research centre in new services; in Democratic Yemen, building up of a modern telecommunication infrastructure and the creation of a nucleus of a training centre and transition to digital technique in the Aden network; in Kuwait, planning of telecommunication facilities for the Ministry of the Interior and planning of transmission systems, new services and computerization of data base; in Malta, preparation of a master plan; in Qatar, promotion of radio and television services and their efficient operation; in Romania, microwave design techniques for parts of a satellite earth station for meteorology reception; in Saudi Arabia, planning of telecommunication facilities for radio broadcasting and national satellite communication for the Ministry of Information, as well as assistance in frequency management (terminated in early 1988); in Turkey, management and organization with emphasis on introducing computers in the training process; and in Yemen, assistance in implementing the second five-year development plan for telecommunications and frequency planning for MF, FM and television coverage.

A new regional project on co-ordination of telecommunication development in the least developed countries in the Arab region and Ethiopia, in which Democratic Yemen, Djibouti, Ethiopia, Somalia, the Sudan and Yemen participated,

with Egypt and Saudi Arabia as sponsors, terminated one year of its activities at the end of 1988, having achieved all objectives for that year. During the first project meeting (Djibouti, March), the detailed work plan of the project was reviewed and approved; joint transit tariff rates for all project members were agreed in June (Sanaa, Yemen). A maintenance co-ordination meeting was held (Aden, Democratic Yemen, July) to improve maintenance activities of the subregional microwave network and to agree on end-to-end measurements of each link, as was a training course on maintenance of the regional microwave links (Sanaa, August-October).

National projects in the Middle East involving training included assistance to the Jordanian Telecommunication Corporation in establishing a Telecommunication College; to Lebanon to organize fellowship programmes outside the country in various telecommunication fields; to the Qatar Telecommunication Training Centre in implementing an expansion programme, initiating the training of instructors, upgrading training standards and institutionalizing a management system and procedures; to Saudi Arabia in running telecommunication training institutes in Riyadh and Jeddah; to the Syrian Training Centre for Telecommunications; and to the Yemen Telecommunication Corporation in establishing and organizing a modern telecommunication training institute.

Training activities

By the end of 1988, 492 training courses were available through the ITU sharing system and 591 were being developed.

The third regional meeting for the co-ordination of training activities of French-speaking African countries was held with ITU assistance (Dakar, Senegal, 24-28 October) and a regional seminar on computer-based training took place (Brasilia, Brazil, 31 October-5 November). In addition, the Training Committee of the African Regional Telecommunications Conference of Eastern and Southern Africa met (Kampala, Uganda, 12-14 September). ITU's training division held workshops in which 578 individuals participated. Missions to assist in formulating training projects were carried out in Bhutan, Ghana, Guatemala, the Libyan Arab Jamahiriya, Nigeria and Uruguay. Numerous other missions were undertaken to provide advice on training.

The computerized data base of training opportunities was updated, reaching a total of 503 courses open to foreign trainees.

Centre for Telecommunications Development

The activities of the Centre for Telecommunications Development (CTD), which became operational in April 1987, were financed entirely by voluntary contributions in cash and kind from the public and private sectors.

In response to 56 requests for assistance received from developing countries, 29 missions were organized to study the telecommunication sector and to identify requirements. Small-scale projects were completed in Malta, Rwanda, Uruguay and Zanzibar. Other projects were prepared for implementation in Malta and Mozambique.

Progress continued on the CTD InfoBase, which, in addition to information on the telecommunication sector, including planned, ongoing and completed projects, would also contain socio-economic and development indicators. Over 50 per cent of the required data had been entered.

Secretariat

As at 31 December 1988, 759 officials (excluding staff on short-term contracts and project staff) were employed by ITU either at its headquarters or in the field. Of those, 9 were elected officials, 586 had permanent contracts and 164 had fixed-term contracts; 74 nationalities were represented in those posts subject to geographical distribution. (For principal officers, see Annex II.)

Budget

The 1987 ITU Administrative Council had adopted a budget of 127,430,621.28 Swiss francs (based on an exchange rate of $US 1.00 = SwF 1.29) for 1988. Regular budget expenditure for the year amounted to SwF 107,853,171.52. In addition, SwF 11,953,420.88 was programmed for technical co-operation and SwF 6,173,925.88 for the publication budget. Another SwF 1,450,163 was allocated for regional administrative conferences.

NOTE: For further information regarding ITU activities, see the *Report on the Activities of the International Telecommunication Union in 1988.*

Annex I. MEMBERSHIP OF THE INTERNATIONAL TELECOMMUNICATION UNION
(As at 31 December 1988)

Afghanistan, Albania, Algeria, Angola, Antigua and Barbuda, Argentina, Australia, Austria, Bahamas, Bahrain, Bangladesh, Barbados, Belgium, Belize, Benin, Bhutan, Bolivia, Botswana, Brazil, Brunei Darussalam, Bulgaria, Burkina Faso, Burma, Burundi, Byelorussian SSR, Cameroon, Canada, Cape Verde, Central African Republic, Chad, Chile, China, Colombia, Comoros, Congo, Costa Rica, Côte d'Ivoire, Cuba, Cyprus, Czechoslovakia, Democratic Kampuchea, Democratic People's Republic of Korea, Democratic Yemen, Denmark, Djibouti, Dominican Republic, Ecuador, Egypt, El Salvador, Equatorial Guinea, Ethiopia, Fiji, Finland, France, Gabon, Gambia, German Democratic Republic, Germany, Federal Republic of, Ghana, Greece, Grenada, Guatemala, Guinea, Guinea-Bissau, Guyana, Haiti, Honduras, Hungary, Iceland, India, Indonesia, Iran, Iraq, Ireland, Israel, Italy, Jamaica, Japan, Jordan, Kenya, Kiribati, Kuwait, Lao People's Democratic Republic, Lebanon, Lesotho, Liberia, Libyan Arab Jamahiriya, Liechtenstein, Luxembourg, Madagascar, Malawi, Malaysia, Maldives, Mali, Malta, Mauritania, Mauritius, Mexico, Monaco, Mongolia, Morocco, Mozambique, Namibia, Nauru, Nepal, Netherlands, New Zealand, Nicaragua, Niger, Nigeria, Norway, Oman, Pakistan, Panama, Papua New Guinea, Paraguay, Peru, Philippines, Poland, Portugal, Qatar, Republic of Korea, Romania, Rwanda, Saint Vincent and the Grenadines, Samoa, San Marino, Sao Tome and Principe, Saudi Arabia, Senegal, Sierra Leone, Singapore, Solomon Islands, Somalia, South Africa, Spain, Sri Lanka, Sudan, Suriname, Swaziland, Sweden, Switzerland, Syrian Arab Republic, Thailand, Togo, Tonga, Trinidad and Tobago, Tunisia, Turkey, Uganda, Ukrainian SSR, USSR, United Arab Emirates, United Kingdom, United Republic of Tanzania, United States, Uruguay, Vanuatu, Vatican City State, Venezuela, Viet Nam, Yemen, Yugoslavia, Zaire, Zambia, Zimbabwe.

Annex II. OFFICERS AND OFFICE OF THE INTERNATIONAL TELECOMMUNICATION UNION

ADMINISTRATIVE COUNCIL, INTERNATIONAL FREQUENCY REGISTRATION BOARD AND PRINCIPAL OFFICERS

PRINCIPAL OFFICERS OF THE UNION
Secretary-General: Richard E. Butler.
Deputy Secretary-General: Jean Jipguep.

ITU ADMINISTRATIVE COUNCIL
Algeria, Argentina, Australia, Benin, Brazil, Cameroon, Canada, China, Colombia, Egypt, Ethiopia, France, German Democratic Republic, Germany, Federal Republic of, India, Indonesia, Italy, Japan, Kenya, Kuwait, Lebanon, Mexico, Morocco, Nigeria, Pakistan, Peru, Philippines, Romania, Saudi Arabia, Senegal, Spain, Sweden, Switzerland, Thailand, USSR, United Kingdom, United Republic of Tanzania, United States, Venezuela, Yugoslavia, Zambia.

INTERNATIONAL FREQUENCY REGISTRATION BOARD
Chairman: Yoshitaka Kurihara (Japan).
Vice-Chairman: Abderrazak Berrada (Morocco).
Members: Gary C. Brooks (Canada), William H. Bellchambers (United Kingdom), Vladimir V. Kozlov (USSR).

OFFICERS OF THE INTERNATIONAL CONSULTATIVE COMMITTEES
Director, International Radio Consultative Committee: Richard C. Kirby (United States).
Director, International Telegraph and Telephone Consultative Committee: Theodor Irmer (Federal Republic of Germany).

HEADQUARTERS

General Secretariat of the International Telecommunication Union
Place des Nations
1211 Geneva 20, Switzerland
Cable address: BURINTERNA GENEVA
Telephone: (41) (22) 730-5111
Telex: 421000 UIT CH
Facsimile: (41) (22) 733-7256

Chapter XIII

World Meteorological Organization (WMO)

In 1988, the World Meteorological Organization (WMO) carried out its activities in accordance with the programme and budget adopted in 1987 for the period 1988-1991 by its highest body, the World Meteorological Congress, which meets at least once every four years. The 36-member Executive Council meets annually to supervise the implementation of programmes and regulations.

As at 31 December 1988, the membership of WMO remained at 160—155 States and 5 Territories (see Annex I).

World Weather Watch

In 1988, the World Weather Watch (WWW), the basic programme of WMO, continued to provide support to other WMO programmes in the areas of applications and research. Its essential elements were the Global Observing System (GOS), whereby observational data were obtained; the Global-Data Processing System (GDPS), which provided for the processing, storage and retrieval of observational data and made available processed information; and the Global Telecommunications System (GTS), consisting of 280 point-to-point circuits providing telecommunication facilities for the rapid collection, exchange and distribution of observational data and processed information.

The activities of GOS continued under its two sub-systems, one surface-based and the other space-based. The surface-based sub-system was composed of the regional basic synoptic networks, other observational networks on land and at sea (at the national level), meteorological observations from aircraft, climatological stations, agricultural meteorological stations and special stations, such as those monitoring ozone and radiation. The space-based sub-system included near-polar-orbiting and geostationary meteorological satellites. In order to meet national needs, the surface-based sub-system included supplementary observing stations. In 1988, there were some 5,500 observing stations of that kind, of which more than 570 also made pilot-balloon observations; also in operation were 331 automatic weather stations. In the space-based sub-system, both polar-orbiting and geostationary meteorological satellites took direct observations. GOS continued to provide members with quantitative information derived from instrument measurements, such as atmospheric pressure, humidity, air temperature and wind velocity, and qualitative information aimed at describing phenomena by providing information on the state of the sky, forms of clouds and types of precipitation. The satellite systems operated by WMO members continued to provide valuable information for use by meteorological and hydrological services. Progress was made in developing new technology for improving the global coverage of observational data, such as the aircraft-to-satellite data relay system and the Automated Shipboard Aerological Programme for upper-air observations from merchant ships and drifting-buoy systems.

Tropical Cyclone Programme

The Tropical Cyclone Programme (TCP) continued to establish national and regionally co-ordinated systems to prevent loss of life and mitigate damage caused by tropical cyclones. During the year, TCP focused on upgrading observational and telecommunication networks, applying advances in satellite technology and improving forecasting and warning systems.

Several members of the Economic and Social Commission for Asia and the Pacific (ESCAP)/WMO Typhoon Committee took steps to improve the networks of weather radars and upper-air stations as well as telecommunications for national data collection and for exchange of data and processed products. Activities under the hydrological component continued to concentrate on monitoring designated flood-forecasting systems, flood loss prevention and management and flood risk analysis and mapping.

In March, the WMO/ESCAP Panel on Tropical Cyclones reviewed the progress made under its programme, including the installation of cyclone-detection radars and an automatic warning by satellite system. It endorsed several recommendations made by a consultancy mission on storm-surges to assess national and regional capabilities, requirements and activities related to storm surge prediction and by the second (1987) Regional Workshop on Cyclone Storm Surge. Based on the information and advice of a consultancy mission to its members in early 1988, the Panel decided to implement the first phase of its regional computer network project, with installation during 1988-1989 of turnkey microcomputer-based systems in three of its member countries.

Instruments and Methods of Observation Programme

In 1988, the Instruments and Methods of Observation Programme (IMOP) organized and conducted regional and global intercomparisons of instruments such as hygrometers, solid precipitation measurement instruments and digital barometers. Efforts were made to implement the programme on a global level by the Commission for Instruments and Methods of Observation (CIMO) and on a regional level through WMO regional associations. Other activities included updating regulatory and guidance materials and developing algorithms for automated surface and upper-air measurements.

At the WMO Technical Conference on Meteorological Instruments and Methods of Observation (TECO-88) (Leipzig, German Democratic Republic, 16-20 May), 50 papers were presented on sensor developments, improvements in automation, remote sensing, instrument intercomparison, data quality, training, maintenance and network aspects.

The first session of the CIMO Advisory Working Group (Potsdam, German Democratic Republic, 24-27 May) reviewed IMOP and evaluated the results of TECO-88.

World Climate Programme

The Tenth World Meteorological Congress (1987) had decided that the World Climate Programme (WCP), instituted in 1979 to aid nations in applying climate information to human activities and to warn of changes in climate that might significantly affect economic and social activities, should continue to receive high priority. The four components of WCP were the World Climate Data Programme (WCDP), the World Climate Applications Programme (WCAP), the World Climate Impact Studies Programme (WCIP), and the World Climate Research Programme (WCRP).

During the year, activities of the Programme focused on establishing a WMO/United Nations Environment Programme (UNEP) Intergovernmental Panel on Climate Change (IPCC), which would aim at developing a realistic and effective strategy for addressing climate change. The first session of IPCC (Geneva, 9-11 November) adopted an 18-month schedule for its consideration of the climate change issue, including broad aspects of science, impacts and policy.

A major project under WCDP was the implementation of the data rescue project (DARE), which was procuring micrographic systems for members in Africa. The International DARE Coordination Centre was established at Brussels, with the support of Belgium. The Commission on Climatology Working Group on Climate Data Management began preparing manuals on how to perform a particular sequence of climate data

management tasks. The publication *Statistics on Regional Networks of Climatological Stations* was issued and the *CSM Monthly Bulletin* continued to be published.

Within WCAP, activities related to food, water and energy continued to receive priority. Attention was also given to areas such as urban and building climatology, transportation and human health. WMO continued to provide support to the Solar Power Committee of the World Energy Conference (WEC) in preparing a report to the next WEC Congress, to be held at Toronto, Canada, in September 1989. WMO also co-operated with the Economic Commission for Europe Committee on Gas in preparing for a study on the importance and significance of meteorology, including climatological information and weather forecasts in gas operations. WMO participated in a Conference on Healthy Buildings (Stockholm, Sweden, 5-8 September), which discussed meteorological and climatological aspects of buildings and constructions. At planning meetings for the International Decade for Natural Disaster Reduction (1990s), WMO contributed to discussions on how to mitigate loss of life and property caused by natural disasters.

Within WCIP, greenhouse gases continued to receive major attention. Preparations continued for the Second World Climate Conference (1990), focusing on the global issues associated with possible climate changes and the benefits of climate applications. A major activity of the Programme was the joint WMO/UNEP invitation to Governments to serve on IPCC and the establishment of a joint secretariat for the Panel at WMO headquarters. A WMO/UNEP International Council of Scientific Unions Advisory Group on Greenhouse Gases (June) developed the basis for a new UNEP project in co-operation with the Beijer Institute involving the establishment of three working groups to consider various aspects of policy response to climate change.

An *ad hoc* working group on world climate impact studies (Bangkok, Thailand, 11-15 January) met to carry out a comparative study between the global climate anomalies connected with the 1986/87 El Niño event and those of the one occurring during 1982/83.

WCRP focused on determining the extent of climate predictability and man's influence on climate. In 1988, the Executive Council endorsed the recommendations of the joint scientific committee to prepare a global energy and water cycle experiment, which would result in the establishment of a firmer physical basis for medium- and long-term weather forecasting. During the year, the main WCRP projects involved global climate analysis, studies of atmospheric general circulation models, research on individual climate processes, study of the tropical ocean and global atmosphere, a world ocean circulation experiment and studies of climate forcings and of changes in the ecosystems.

Research and development

The WMO Research and Development Programme covered weather prediction research, tropical meteorology research, environmental pollution monitoring and research and cloud physics and weather modification research. The responsibility for promoting and co-ordinating such activities lay with the Commission for Atmospheric Sciences (CAS).

Priority continued to be assigned to weather prediction research on all time-scales, with particular attention being given to the development of various numerical weather prediction models in the tropics. The monitoring of atmospheric composition parameters continued to be strengthened through the Background Air Pollution Monitoring Network (BAPMoN) and Global Ozone Observing Stations, and further action was taken to advance knowledge of cloud physics and prospects to modify it. The WMO Technical Conference on Regional Weather Prediction with Emphasis on the Use of Global Products, held at the European Centre for Medium-range Weather Forecasts (Reading, United Kingdom, 18-22 April), discussed global and regional forecasting, including the use of direct model output and statistical enhancement methods.

The third session of the CAS working group on tropical meteorology, held at WMO headquarters (28-31 March), reviewed the implementation of the Tropical Meteorological Research Programme and its six major components: tropical cyclone monsoons, semi-arid-zone meteorology, tropical droughts, tropical rain-producing systems (other than cyclones), tropical limited-area modelling and the interaction between tropical and mid-latitude systems. The group updated and revised the overall programme. The second WMO Regional Workshop on Asian Winter Monsoon (Kuala Lumpur, Malaysia, 27 June–1 July), co-sponsored by the Malaysian Ministry of Science, Technology and Environment and the Association of Scientific Co-operation in Asia, stressed the continued importance of further research in monsoon meteorology and the availability and dissemination of data for monsoon-affected countries.

The 1988 WMO Research Award for Young Scientists was conferred upon Silas C. Michaelides (Cyprus) for his work on limited-area energetics of Genoa cyclogenesis.

The Executive Council Panel of Experts/CAS working group on environmental pollution and atmospheric chemistry (Hilo, Hawaii, 27-31 March) focused on possible changes in atmospheric ozone and other constituents of the atmosphere and on measurements, modelling and further studies of the long-range transport of pollutants. A re-evaluation of BAPMoN was being carried out by leading authorities in atmospheric chemistry to ensure its ability to provide information on possible changes in the composition of the atmosphere in the coming decades.

The main objectives of the WMO Cloud Physics and Weather Modification Research Programme were to promote sound scientific foundations for weather modification and to provide the rationale for all aspects of weather modification. The second International Cloud Modelling Workshop (Toulouse, France, 8-12 August) attracted 81 participants from 18 countries.

Applications of meteorology

The WMO Applications of Meteorology Programme comprised agricultural, marine and aeronautical meteorology.

Agricultural meteorology

The Agricultural Meteorology Programme assisted WMO members in organizing and strengthening their agrometeorological services, enabling them to make optimum use of meteorological and hydrological information and knowledge in agricultural production and protection. The Commission for Agricultural Meteorology (CAgM) provided advice on different aspects of the programme and close collaboration was maintained with the Food and Agriculture Organization of the United Nations (FAO).

During 1988, the major activity was the response of WMO to the invasion of many parts of western and northern Africa by huge swarms of desert locusts, which threatened the food resources of the region. In co-operation with FAO and other international organizations and with support from bilateral donors, WMO took various urgent actions to combat the locust plague. Activities included a joint expert mission to the areas concerned to define the meteorological data requirements for locust control and to assist in further developing the subregional meteorological activities in the fight against the locusts. A joint FAO/WMO workshop on the provision of agrometeorological information for locust control was held at Tunis, Tunisia, from 26 to 29 July.

A meeting of the Regional Association II (Asia) working group on agricultural meteorology (New Delhi, India, 11-15 January) considered draft reports on agroclimatology of the banana and ground-nut crops, agroclimatological zoning, and drought and desertification. A meeting of the Regional Association VI (Europe) working group on agricultural meteorology (Geneva, 10-14 October) finalized reports on operational agrometeorological services for the potato crop, weather and climate and the quality of production, agrometeorological data banks and the development of agrometeorological services in areas under stressful conditions. A workshop on agrometeorological information for planning and operation in agriculture with special reference to plant protection (Calcutta, India, 22-26 August) discussed the influence of meteorological factors on plant epidemic development, modelling of crop growth and development, crop monitoring and forecasting, modelling of pest outbreaks, modelling of weed development, meteorological factors influencing pesticide behaviour, economic benefits of forecasting models and remote-sensing applications in plant-protection activities.

WMO participated in a joint meeting of the Co-ordination and Advisory Committee and the Executive Committee of the regional training centre for agrometeorology and operational hydrology and their applications (programme for the Sahelian countries) (AGRHYMET) (8-17 January). The meeting proposed the use of operational forecasts by the National Services of the Gambia and Mali. WMO contributed to those efforts, on an experimental basis to adapt such forecasts to agriculture, in the context of the AGRHYMET programme.

At a meeting of the CAgM working group on monitoring, assessment and combat of drought and desertification (Florence, Italy, 5-9 April), the final report of the working group was adopted, which included methods and practical techniques for operational use in the fight against drought and desertification. Roving seminars on potential primary production of natural pastures and the resulting carrying capacity were organized (Zambia 20 June-1 July; Ethiopia, 12-13 December).

Marine meteorology

The Marine Meteorology Programme promoted marine meteorological services for the high seas and coastal areas and the application of marine climatological information to planning marine activities.

The International Maritime Satellite Organization (INMARSAT) system for the collection of ships' weather reports by satellite continued to expand, with some 7,200 ships, including 1,161 voluntary observing ships, equipped with INMARSAT ship earth stations by mid-year.

A course on ocean waves and tides, co-sponsored by WMO at the International Centre for Theoretical Physics (Trieste, Italy, September/October), discussed wave and tide theory, air-sea interactions, wave measurements, wave modelling and wave and tidal data analysis.

The Integrated Global Ocean Services System (IGOSS) was planned, developed and co-ordinated jointly by WMO and the Intergovernmental Oceanographic Commission (IOC) of the United Nations Educational, Scientific and Cultural Organization for the global collection and exchange of oceanic data and the timely preparation and dissemination of oceanic products and services for both operational and research activities. Its three main elements were the IGOSS Observing System, the IGOSS Data Processing and Services System, and the IGOSS Telecommunication Arrangements. The fifth session of the IOC/WMO Working Committee for IGOSS (Paris, 14-23 November) considered and adopted the new IGOSS plan and implementation programme for 1989-1995.

During the year, expert consultancy missions to advise on further development of national meteorological services took place in Chile, Iran and Morocco.

Aeronautical meteorology

The Aeronautical Meteorology Programme—aimed at assisting members to plan, establish and operate the aeronautical meteorological services required to ensure the safety, efficiency and economy of air navigation—was carried out in close collaboration with the International Civil Aviation Organization (ICAO) and other international organizations.

In 1988, activities included the development of regulatory material for updating volume II of the WMO *Technical Regulations—Meteorological Service for International Air Navigation*; preparation of other guidance material; further co-ordination of action, at the regional and national levels, for the implementation of standardized global and regional practices; and co-operation with other international organizations, particularly ICAO, in the application of meteorology to aviation.

The second session of the Commission for Aeronautical Meteorology (CAeM) working group on meteorological observations and information distribution arrangements for local aeronautical users (Geneva, 25-27 May) focused on reviewing the draft version of the *Guide on Meteorological Observation and Information Distribution Systems at Airports*. The fifth session of the CAeM working group on the provision of meteorological information required before and during flight (10-14 October) discussed the current state of implementation of the World Area Forecast System (WAFS), the depiction of wind speeds in kilometres per hour on WAFS upper-air charts, proposed changes to aeronautical meteorological codes, change groups in aerodome forecasts, the concept of area meteorological watch, aeronautical requirements for observational data and products and a proposed guide to aeronautical meteorological office practices. The CAeM working group on advanced techniques applied to aeronautical meteorology issued its first newsletter in June 1988, reporting on research and development activities relevant to aeronautical meteorology.

Hydrology and water resources

The Hydrology and Water Resources Programme promoted world-wide co-operation in evaluating water resources and assisted in their development through the co-ordination of hydrological services, including data collection and processing, forecasting and warnings, and supply of meteorological and hydrological data for design purposes. Its three components were the Operational Hydrology Programme (OHP) applications and services to water resources and co-operation with water-related programmes of other international organizations.

The Operational Hydrology Programme (OHP) was executed mainly by the Commission for Hydrology, which reviewed its work from 1984 to 1988 (Geneva, 24 October–4 November). Working groups were established for data acquisition and processing systems; hydrological forecasting and applications for water management; and operational hydrology, climate and the environment.

A major activity within OHP was the Hydrological Operational Multipurpose Subprogramme (HOMS), which aimed to provide an efficient means of transferring operational hydrological technology and an international framework for the integration of techniques for collecting and processing hydrological data.

Two United Nations Development Programme (UNDP)–funded projects in support of the final UNDP-funded HOMS/Asia workshop of the integrated systems in hydrology were held at the Asian Institute of Technology (Bangkok, Thailand, December), while the HOMS/Europe project continued its series of training seminars to support the transfer of components among the participating countries.

In 1988, the number of HOMS National Reference Centres and focal points increased to 105. The *HOMS Reference Manual* contained 391 components, 16 sequences and 4 users' requirements. The programme on applications and services to water resources provided technical support for the water-related activities of TCP and WCP.

The Fourth Planning Meeting on the water component of WCP, organized jointly by UNESCO and WMO (Paris, 12-16 September), reviewed the progress of existing programmes and suggested future activities for the Programme.

Education and training

Educational and training activities in meteorology and operational hydrology included promoting high standards in the technical and scientific training of all WMO personnel; awarding fellowships; organizing training courses, seminars and workshops; and preparing training publications.

The thirteenth session of the Executive Council Panel of Experts on Education and Training, scheduled for 1988, was postponed for financial reasons; it was expected to be held in 1989.

The regional meteorological training centres continued to provide education and training to personnel from developing countries. Activities included having visiting scientists assist some centres with specific aspects of training programmes and providing textbooks and other publications. Some of the training centres organized or hosted special training events.

A course on the management of meteorological training centres (Turin, Italy, 4-22 July) provided participants with updated information on management techniques, such as planning, organizing, staffing and controlling institutional performances, management of training courses and operations, curriculum design and development and modern trends in training methods.

Under fellowship funds from various sources administered by WMO, 308 fellows were trained. Financial assistance was also provided to 55 participants in various WMO-supported training events under the fellowship programme.

Technical co-operation

Under the WMO Technical Co-operation Programme, assistance was provided to 133 member countries through UNDP, the WMO Voluntary Co-operation Programme (VCP), trust funds and the WMO regular budget.

UNDP assistance was provided to 124 countries at an estimated value of $125 million. In addition to ongoing projects, 20 new country projects were approved during the year. UNDP sectoral adviser missions in meteorology and operational hydrology were undertaken to 38 countries at the request of UNDP resident representatives and government authorities to assist in planning and formulating new projects.

The project for assistance to drought-stricken countries in eastern and southern Africa and the project for strengthening the agrometeorological and hydrological services of the Sahelian countries continued. Other large-scale projects focused on the evaluation of water resources, flood forecasting, meteorological services for agriculture, meteorological training, research and improvement of facilities for the detection and warning of tropical cyclones.

VCP was maintained by voluntary contributions of members, in the form of equipment and services or cash. In 1988, 98 countries received an estimated $6.9 million in aid under VCP. A total of

57 VCP projects, mostly in support of WWW activities, were completed during the year.

Under the regular WMO budget, 90 countries were assisted and 30 fellowships were awarded in 1988. Financial support was also given for participation in group training, technical conferences and study tours.

Under a trust fund project with Italy, assistance to the AGRHYMET project continued with several activities, including assistance to a pilot project in agrometeorology in the Niger and a workshop in telecommunication and hydrological equipment maintenance for specialists from the Sahelian countries. Other trust fund arrangements, with Belgium, Finland, Honduras, Italy, Netherlands, Switzerland and the United States continued to be implemented. Under the Technical Co-operation Programme, 567 fellows received training—247 under UNDP programmes, 206 under VCP, 64 under the regular budget and 50 under trust funds.

Secretariat

On 31 December 1988, WMO employed 275 full-time staff members. Of those, 123 were in the Professional and higher categories, 143 were in the General Service and related categories and 9 were supernumerary staff, made up of both categories.

Budget

Nineteen eighty-eight was the beginning of the tenth financial period (1988-1991). The Tenth WMO Congress (1987) had approved significant changes in the financial regulations of the Organization, including budgeting in Swiss francs (SwF) and changing from annual to biennial budgets. It had established a maximum expenditure of SwF 170 million for the four-year financial period. The WMO Executive Council, in June 1987, had approved a budget of SwF 82,128,300 for the 1988-1989 biennium.

In June, the Executive Council approved supplementary estimates of SwF 506,100 to cover the anticipated deficit in support costs for technical co-operation activities.

NOTE: For more details on WMO, see *Annual Report of the World Meteorological Organization, 1988.*

Annex I.   MEMBERSHIP OF THE WORLD METEOROLOGICAL ORGANIZATION
(Membership as at 31 December 1988)

Afghanistan, Albania, Algeria, Angola, Argentina, Australia, Austria, Bahamas, Bahrain, Bangladesh, Barbados, Belgium, Belize, Benin, Bolivia, Botswana, Brazil, Brunei Darussalam, Bulgaria, Burkina Faso, Burma, Burundi, Byelorussian SSR, Cameroon, Canada, Cape Verde, Central African Republic, Chad, Chile, China, Colombia, Comoros, Congo, Costa Rica, Côte d'Ivoire, Cuba, Cyprus, Czechoslovakia, Democratic Kampuchea, Democratic People's Republic of Korea, Democratic Yemen, Denmark, Djibouti, Dominica, Dominican Republic, Ecuador, Egypt, El Salvador, Ethiopia, Fiji, Finland, France, Gabon, Gambia, German Democratic Republic, Germany, Federal Republic of, Ghana, Greece, Guatemala, Guinea, Guinea-Bissau, Guyana, Haiti, Honduras, Hungary, Iceland, India, Indonesia, Iran, Iraq, Ireland, Israel, Italy, Jamaica, Japan, Jordan, Kenya, Kuwait, Lao People's Democratic Republic, Lebanon, Lesotho, Liberia, Libyan Arab Jamahiriya, Luxembourg, Madagascar, Malawi, Malaysia, Maldives, Mali, Malta, Mauritania, Mauritius, Mexico, Mongolia, Morocco, Mozambique, Nepal, Netherlands, New Zealand, Nicaragua, Niger, Nigeria, Norway, Oman, Pakistan, Panama, Papua New Guinea, Paraguay, Peru, Philippines, Poland, Portugal, Qatar, Republic of Korea, Romania, Rwanda, Saint Lucia, Sao Tome and Principe, Saudi Arabia, Senegal, Seychelles, Sierra Leone, Singapore, Solomon Islands, Somalia, South Africa,* Spain, Sri Lanka, Sudan, Suriname, Swaziland, Sweden, Switzerland, Syrian Arab Republic, Thailand, Togo, Trinidad and Tobago, Tunisia, Turkey, Uganda, Ukrainian SSR, USSR, United Arab Emirates, United Kingdom, United Republic of Tanzania, United States, Uruguay, Vanuatu, Venezuela, Viet Nam, Yemen, Yugoslavia, Zaire, Zambia, Zimbabwe.

*Suspended by the Seventh (1975) Congress from exercising the rights and privileges of a member.

Territories:
British Caribbean Territories, French Polynesia, Hong Kong, Netherlands Antilles, New Caledonia.

Annex II.   OFFICERS AND OFFICE OF THE WORLD METEOROLOGICAL ORGANIZATION

MEMBERS OF THE WMO EXECUTIVE COUNCIL

President: Zou Jingmeng (China).
First Vice-President: J. W. Zillman (Australia).
Second Vice-President: S. Alaimo (Argentina).
Third Vice-President: J. T. Houghton (United Kingdom).
Members: A. I. Abandah (Jordan), L. K. Ahialegbedzi (Togo), M. Bautista Pérez (Spain), M. Boulama (Niger), C. Candanedo (Panama), A. M. El-Masry (Egypt), H. L. Ferguson (Canada), E. W. Friday (United States), C. A. Grezzi (Uruguay), J. A. Izrael (USSR), Y. Kikuchi (Japan), R. L. Kintanar (Philippines), A. Lebeau (France), K. Mostefa Kara (Algeria), S. Palmieri (Italy), F. M. Q. Malik (Pakistan), E. F. de Queiroz (Brazil), H. Reiser (Federal Republic of Germany), V. Richter (Czechoslovakia), R. P. Sarker (India), S. E. Tandoh (Ghana), P. Toubbe (Cameroon), E. Zarate Hernandez (Costa Rica), M. C. Zinyowera (Zimbabwe).

NOTE: The Executive Council is composed of four elected officers; the six Presidents of the regional associations (see below), who are *ex officio* members; and 26 elected members. Members serve in their personal capacities, not as representatives of Governments.

SENIOR OFFICERS OF THE SECRETARIAT

Secretary-General: G. O. P. Obasi.
Deputy Secretary-General: J. P. Bruce (acting).
Assistant Secretary-General: R. Czelnai.
Director, World Weather Watch Department: T. D. Potter.
Director, Research and Development Programme Department: J. P. N. Labrousse.
Director, Hydrology and Water Resources Department: J. C. Rodda.
Director, Technical Co-operation Department: E. Basso (acting).
Director, Education and Training Department: G. V. Necco.
Director, Administration Department: J. K. Murithi.

Director, Languages, Publications and Conferences Department: A. W. Kabakibo.
Director, World Climate Programme Department: V. G. Boldirev.
Director, Basic Systems: S. Mildner.
Director, World Climate Research Programme: P. Morel.
Regional Director for Africa: S. Chacowry.
Regional Director for the Americas: G. Lizano Vindas.
Regional Director for Asia and the South-West Pacific: T. Y. Ho.
Special Assistant to the Secretary-General: R. A. de Guzman.
Executive Assistant to the Secretary-General: J. B. L. Breslin.

PRESIDENTS OF REGIONAL ASSOCIATIONS AND TECHNICAL COMMISSIONS

REGIONAL ASSOCIATIONS
I. Africa: W. Degefu (Ethiopia).
II. Asia: I. Hussain Al-Majed (Qatar).
III. South America: Vacant.
IV. North and Central America: C. E. Berridge (British Caribbean Territories).
V. South-West Pacific: H. P. A. Jaafar (acting) (Brunei Darussalam).
VI. Europe: E. J. Jatila (acting) (Finland).

TECHNICAL COMMISSIONS
Aeronautical Meteorology: J. Kastelein (Netherlands).
Agricultural Meteorology: A. Kassar (Tunisia).
Atmospheric Sciences: F. Mesinger (Yugoslavia).
Basic Systems: A. A. Vasiliev (USSR).
Climatology: J. J. Rasmussen (United States).
Hydrology: O. Starosolszky (Hungary).
Instruments and Methods of Observation: S. Huovila (Finland).
Marine Meteorology: F. Gérard (France).

HEADQUARTERS

World Meteorological Organization
41, Avenue Giuseppe Motta
(Case postale No. 2300)
CH-1211, Geneva 2, Switzerland
Cable address: METEOMOND GENEVA
Telephone: (41) (22) 730-81-11
Telex: 414199 OMM CH
Facsimile: (41) (22) 734-23-26

Chapter XIV

International Maritime Organization (IMO)

In 1988, several legal instruments were adopted under the auspices of the International Maritime Organization (IMO)—the Convention for the Suppression of Unlawful Acts against the Safety of Maritime Navigation and a Protocol for the Suppression of Unlawful Acts against the Safety of Fixed Platforms Located on the Continental Shelf. Protocols also were adopted to the International Convention for the Safety of Life at Sea, 1974 (SOLAS Convention) and the 1978 SOLAS Protocol and the International Convention on Load Lines, 1966.

IMO membership rose to 132 during 1988 following the admission of the Solomon Islands on 27 June; the organization also had one associate member (see Annex I).

Activities in 1988

The IMO Council, the organization's governing body between sessions of its biennial Assembly, chose James Cowley (United Kingdom) as the winner of the International Maritime Prize for 1987. The Prize is awarded annually to the individual or organization judged to have made the most significant contribution to IMO's work and objectives.

The theme for World Maritime Day, which was celebrated at IMO headquarters on 22 September, was "Shipboard management for maritime safety and pollution prevention".

Training facilities

The World Maritime University at Malmö, Sweden, had a total enrolment of 102 students, the maximum number that the University could accommodate. Eight new countries were represented in the class—Burma, the Democratic People's Republic of Korea, Kiribati, Malta, Namibia, the Niger, Oman and Sao Tome and Principe. Some 97 countries had sent students to the University since its opening in 1983. The University was established under IMO auspices to provide advanced training for senior personnel, mainly from developing countries, involved in maritime administration, technical management of shipping companies and maritime education.

During the year, two more institutions were established as the result of co-operation between IMO and its member States. The first, the IMO International Maritime Academy (Trieste, Italy), was to provide short-term training courses in various aspects of shipping and act as the apex for the implementation of IMO's model courses programme

(see below). The IMO International Maritime Law Institute (Valetta, Malta), established to provide post-graduate training in maritime law to suitably qualified law graduates, particularly those from developing countries, was inaugurated on 6 October.

The first titles in a series of model courses, designed to assist maritime institutes—especially in developing countries—to organize and introduce new training courses and improve existing material, were published by IMO. The model courses were intended to assist the implementation of IMO conventions, codes and other standards and to help ensure that a common agreed minimum standard was achieved by all maritime States.

Prevention of pollution

Annex V of the International Convention for the Prevention of Pollution from Ships, 1973, as modified by the 1978 Protocol (MARPOL 73/78), entered into force on 31 December 1988. It contained measures to prevent pollution at sea by dumping garbage, including the ban on the dumping of all plastics, such as synthetic ropes, synthetic fishing nets and plastic garbage bags. Other forms of garbage could be dumped under strictly controlled conditions. IMO's Marine Environment Protection Committee (London, 5-9 September) agreed that the North Sea should be made a Special Area under annex V. Certain seas were designated as Special Areas under the annex because of their unique environmental problems. In those areas the dumping of plastics and garbage was completely banned and the disposal of food wastes was strictly controlled.

Meeting at IMO headquarters (3-7 October), contracting parties to the Convention on the Prevention of Marine Pollution by Dumping of Wastes and Other Matter (London Dumping Convention) agreed to end incineration at sea by the end of 1994. They further agreed not to export wastes intended for incineration at sea to any State which was not a party to the Convention, nor to allow their disposal in other ways which were harmful to the environment. Measures were also adopted to prevent the unrestricted use of tributyltin compounds, which were often used as anti-fouling paint on ships.

Ship security and safety of life at sea

A conference convened by IMO (Rome, Italy, 1-10 March 1988) adopted two international treaties designed to combat unlawful acts against shipping and other maritime activities: the Convention for the Suppression of Unlawful Acts against the Safety of Maritime Navigation and a Protocol for the Suppression of Unlawful Acts against the Safety of Fixed Platforms Located on the Continental Shelf. The Convention dealt with offences against the safety of ships and persons on board and the supplementary Protocol with offences against fixed platforms.

The 1974 SOLAS Convention was amended by the Maritime Safety Committee (London, 11-22 April). The amendments were designed to improve the safety of roll-on/roll-off passenger ships and were expected to enter into force on 22 October 1989 under the Convention's "tacit acceptance" procedures. On 28 October, further amendments, also concerning the safety of roll-on/roll-off ships, were adopted at a special session of the Committee. They were expected to enter into force on 29 April 1990.

IMO model courses, available from the IMO Publications Section, dealt with oil tanker familiarization, radar observation and plotting, the operational use of automatic radar-plotting aids, radar simulator, basic stability, personnel survival, maritime search and rescue, mission co-ordinator, maritime search and rescue administrator, maritime search and rescue co-ordinator, port state control, basic fire fighting, planned fleet maintenance and hull protection, and marine accident and incident investigation.

Secretariat

As at 31 December 1988, the IMO secretariat employed 256 full-time staff members (excluding those on technical assistance projects). Of these, 99 were in the Professional and higher categories and 157 were in the General Service and related categories. There were 12 Professional and 23 General Service staff employed on technical assistance projects. (For principal officers of the secretariat, see Annex II.)

Budget

In 1987, the IMO Assembly had resolved that the budget appropriations and assessments be denominated in pounds sterling. The Assembly adopted a budget of 21,627,200 pounds for the 1988-1989 biennium, with an appropriation of 10,574,100 pounds for 1988 and 11,053,100 pounds for 1989. The 1989 budget was recalculated in November 1988 to 10,564,700 pounds, giving a revised total appropriation for the biennium of 21,138,800 pounds. The assessments of member States for 1988 totalled 9,353,300 pounds.

NOTE: For details of IMO activities in 1988, see the magazine of IMO, *IMO News*, Nos. 1-4.

Annex I. **MEMBERSHIP OF THE INTERNATIONAL MARITIME ORGANIZATION**
          (As at 31 December 1988)

Algeria, Angola, Antigua and Barbuda, Argentina, Australia, Austria, Bahamas, Bahrain, Bangladesh, Barbados, Belgium, Benin, Bolivia, Brazil, Brunei Darussalam, Bulgaria, Burma, Cameroon, Canada, Cape Verde, Chile, China, Colombia, Congo, Costa Rica, Côte d'Ivoire, Cuba, Cyprus, Czechoslovakia, Democratic Kampuchea, Democratic People's Republic of Korea, Democratic Yemen, Denmark, Djibouti, Dominica, Dominican Republic, Ecuador, Egypt, El Salvador, Equatorial Guinea, Ethiopia, Fiji, Finland, France, Gabon, Gambia, German Democratic Republic, Germany, Federal Republic of, Ghana, Greece, Guatemala, Guinea, Guinea-Bissau, Guyana, Haiti, Honduras, Hungary, Iceland, India, Indonesia, Iran, Iraq, Ireland, Israel, Italy, Jamaica, Japan, Jordan, Kenya, Kuwait, Lebanon, Liberia, Libyan Arab Jamahiriya, Madagascar, Malaysia, Maldives, Malta, Mauritania, Mauritius, Mexico, Morocco, Mozambique, Nepal, Netherlands, New Zealand, Nicaragua, Nigeria, Norway, Oman, Pakistan, Panama, Papua New Guinea, Peru, Philippines, Poland, Portugal, Qatar, Republic of Korea, Romania, Saint Lucia, Saint Vincent and the Grenadines, Saudi Arabia, Senegal, Seychelles, Sierra Leone, Singapore, Solomon Islands, Somalia, Spain, Sri Lanka, Sudan, Suriname, Sweden, Switzerland, Syrian Arab Republic, Thailand, Togo, Trinidad and Tobago, Tunisia, Turkey, USSR, United Arab Emirates, United Kingdom, United Republic of Tanzania, United States, Uruguay, Vanuatu, Venezuela, Viet Nam, Yemen, Yugoslavia, Zaire.

Associate member: Hong Kong.

Annex II. **OFFICERS AND OFFICE OF THE INTERNATIONAL MARITIME ORGANIZATION**
           (As at 31 December 1988)

IMO COUNCIL AND MARITIME SAFETY COMMITTEE

IMO COUNCIL
Chairman: W. A. O'Neil (Canada).
Members: Algeria, Argentina, Australia, Brazil, Canada, China, Cyprus, Egypt, France, Germany, Federal Republic of, Greece, India, Indonesia, Italy, Japan, Kuwait, Lebanon, Liberia, Morocco, Nigeria, Norway, Pakistan, Panama, Peru, Poland, Saudi Arabia, Spain, Sweden, Trinidad and Tobago, USSR, United Kingdom, United States.

MARITIME SAFETY COMMITTEE
Chairman: E. Jansen (Norway).

Membership in the Maritime Safety Committee is open to all IMO member States.

OFFICERS AND OFFICE

PRINCIPAL OFFICERS OF IMO SECRETARIAT
Secretary-General: Chandrika Prasad Srivastava.
Assistant Secretary-General: T. A. Mensah.
Secretary, Maritime Safety Committee: Y. Sasamura.

HEADQUARTERS
International Maritime Organization
4 Albert Embankment
London SE1 7SR, England
  Cable address: INTERMAR LONDON, SE1
  Telephone: (44) (71) 735-7611
  Telex: 23588
  Facsimile: (44) (71) 587-3210

Chapter XV

World Intellectual Property Organization (WIPO)

During 1988, the membership of the World Intellectual Property Organization (WIPO) increased to 121 with the accessions to the 1967 Convention establishing WIPO of Ecuador, Guinea-Bissau, Swaziland and Trinidad and Tobago (see Annex I). The number of States party to the Paris Convention for the Protection of Industrial Property rose to 98 with the accession of Guinea-Bissau. The number of States party to the Berne Convention for the Protection of Literary and Artistic Works rose to 79 with the accession of Colombia, Peru and Trinidad and Tobago. The Republic of Korea became party to the Budapest Treaty on the International Recognition of the Deposit of Micro-organisms for the Purposes of Patent Procedure, bringing the number of contracting States to 22. Burkina Faso became party to the Rome Convention for the Protection of Performers, Producers of Phonograms and Broadcasting Organizations, bringing the number of contracting States to 32. Burkina Faso and Trinidad and Tobago became party to the Geneva Convention for the Protection of Producers of Phonograms against Unauthorized Duplication of Their Phonograms, bringing the total number to 42. At the end of the year, the total membership of WIPO, including that of the various Unions administered by it, was 132.

Seventeen treaties in the two main fields of intellectual property were administered by WIPO in 1988. They are listed below in order of adoption:

Industrial property: Paris Convention for the Protection of Industrial Property; Madrid Agreement for the Repression of False or Deceptive Indications of Source on Goods; Madrid Agreement concerning the International Registration of Marks; The Hague Agreement concerning the International Deposit of Industrial Designs; Nice Agreement concerning the International Classification of Goods and Services for the Purpose of the Registration of Marks; Lisbon Agreement for the Protection of Appellations of Origin and Their International Registration; Locarno Agreement establishing an International Classification for Industrial Designs; Patent Co-operation Treaty (PCT); Strasbourg Agreement concerning the International Patent Classification (IPC); Trademark Registration Treaty; Vienna Agreement establishing an International Classification of the Figurative Elements of Marks; Budapest Treaty on the International Recognition of the Deposit of Micro-organisms for the Purpose of Patent Procedure; Nairobi Treaty on the Protection of the Olympic Symbol.

Copyright and neighbouring rights: Berne Convention for the Protection of Literary and Artistic Works; Rome Convention for the Protection of Performers, Producers

of Phonograms and Broadcasting Organizations; Geneva Convention for the Protection of Producers of Phonograms against Unauthorized Duplication of Their Phonograms; Brussels Convention relating to the Distribution of Programme-Carrying Signals Transmitted by Satellite.

The governing bodies of WIPO and the Unions administered by it held their nineteenth series of meetings (Geneva, 26 September–3 October 1988).

Activities in 1988

Development co-operation

WIPO co-operated with developing countries and with intergovernmental organizations in their development projects relating to intellectual property, by providing assistance in the preparation of legislation, or establishment or modernization of national or regional institutions, including patent documentation and information services.

Three WIPO permanent programmes, supervised by intergovernmental permanent committees, provided the framework for development co-operation relating to industrial property, patent information and copyright and neighbouring rights.

Regarding industrial property, WIPO organized national, regional, subregional and interregional meetings, in co-operation with Governments and/or organizations, at its headquarters in Geneva and at Luanda (Angola), Canberra (Australia), Rio de Janeiro (Brazil), Varna (Bulgaria), Ouagadougou (Burkina Faso), Beijing (China), Abidjan (Côte d'Ivoire), Cairo (Egypt), San Salvador (El Salvador), Bordeaux, Paris and Strasbourg (France), Munich (Federal Republic of Germany), Accra (Ghana), Hong Kong, New Delhi (India), Tōkyō (Japan), Amman (Jordan), Vientiane (Lao People's Democratic Republic), Monrovia (Liberia), Tripoli (Libyan Arab Jamahiriya), Rabat (Morocco), The Hague (Netherlands), Seoul (Republic of Korea), Singapore, Stockholm (Sweden), Lomé (Togo), Washington, D.C. (United States), Caracas (Venezuela), Ho Chi Minh City (Viet Nam), Belgrade and Dubrovnik (Yugoslavia) and Harare (Zimbabwe).

Medals and prizes for inventors and promoters of innovation were awarded by WIPO at national and international exhibitions or contests for inventors and special ceremonies held in Belgium, Benin, Bulgaria, Burkina Faso, Canada, China, Colombia, Côte d'Ivoire, Czechoslovakia, the Democratic People's Republic of Korea, Ethiopia, Iraq, Japan, Mongolia, Switzerland, the Syrian Arab Republic, the USSR, Yugoslavia and Zimbabwe.

Continuing a programme started in 1975, 447 state-of-the-art search reports on technology disclosed in patent documents and related literature were provided to developing countries free of charge under agreements concluded between WIPO and contributing industrial property offices in developed countries. The reports were prepared by the patent offices of Australia, Austria, Finland, the German Democratic Republic, the Federal Republic of Germany, Japan, Sweden, Switzerland, the USSR, the United Kingdom and the International Bureau—the WIPO secretariat.

Regarding copyright and related fields, WIPO organized national, regional, subregional and interregional meetings at WIPO headquarters and at Buenos Aires (Argentina), Bogotá (Colombia), Blantyre (Malawi), Kuala Lumpur (Malaysia), Lagos (Nigeria), Lima (Peru) and Zurich (Switzerland).

Under training, 291 fellowships were granted to nationals of 92 countries and seven organizations in industrial property and 50 fellowships to nationals of 36 developing countries and one organization in copyright. In the industrial property sector, 32 countries, four intergovernmental organizations and two other institutions provided individual and group training; 16 countries and one institution provided such training in copyright.

Industrial property

A world-wide forum on the impact of emerging technologies on the law of intellectual property (Geneva, September) examined the interrelationship of advanced or new technologies and the law of intellectual property, and dealt with biotechnology, computer technology, and new techniques of reproduction and communication.

The International Bureau of WIPO prepared two documents, one on model provisions for national laws and another on provisions in the Paris, Berne and Neighbouring Rights Conventions for a meeting of the Committee of Experts on Measures against Counterfeiting and Piracy (Geneva, April). Wide support was expressed for WIPO's initiative to combat counterfeiting and piracy and to establish model provisions, which could serve as a basis for preparing national laws in that area.

The Committee of Experts on Biotechnological Inventions and Industrial Property (Geneva, October) based its discussions on material prepared by the International Bureau. It was recommended that a meeting of WIPO and the International Union for the Protection of New Varieties of Plants be convened to discuss the interface between patent protection and plant variety rights.

A symposium organized jointly by WIPO and the French National Institute of Industrial Property (Bordeaux, November) dealt with the protection of appellations of origin and indications of source and their relevance to internal and external trade. The symposium considered, in particular, questions relating to natural products such as wine, cheese, coffee, tea and tobacco.

Other expert committees dealt with the harmonization of certain provisions in laws for the protection of inventions and intellectual property in respect of integrated circuits. In addition, work continued on updating IPC and other classifications concerning industrial designs or registration of trade and service marks.

During 1988, 11,996 international applications under PCT were received by the International Bureau from 28 receiving offices. The *PCT Gazette* was published fortnightly and special issues were published in January and July to consolidate general information. The total number of registrations of marks under the Madrid Agreement was 13,016. To that figure should be added 4,538 renewals. The total number of registrations and renewals effected was therefore 17,554.

Copyright and neighbouring rights

Activities in copyright and neighbouring rights included the convening, jointly with the United Nations Educational, Scientific and Cultural Organization, of committees of governmental experts on photographic works (Paris, April) and on the evaluation and synthesis of principles on various categories of works (Geneva, June/July). In addition, committees of experts met on the establishment of an international register of audio-visual works (Geneva, March) and to prepare for a diplomatic conference for the conclusion of a treaty on the international registration of audio-visual works (Geneva, November/December).

Secretariat

As at 31 December 1988, WIPO employed 319 full-time staff members. Of these, 107 were in the Professional and higher categories (drawn from 40 member States) and 212 were in the General Service category.

Budget

The principal sources of the WIPO budget—107,082,000 Swiss francs for the 1988-1989 biennium—are ordinary and special contributions from member States and income derived from international registration services (primarily under PCT and the Madrid Agreement). Ordinary contributions are paid on the basis of a class-and-unit system by members of the Paris, Berne, IPC, Nice, Locarno and Vienna Unions and by WIPO member States not belonging to any of the Unions.

NOTE: For details of WIPO activities, see *Governing Bodies of WIPO and the Unions Administered by WIPO: Report of the Director General.*

Annex I. MEMBERSHIP OF THE WORLD INTELLECTUAL PROPERTY ORGANIZATION
(As at 31 December 1988)

Algeria, Angola, Argentina, Australia, Austria, Bahamas, Bangladesh, Barbados, Belgium, Benin, Brazil, Bulgaria, Burkina Faso, Burundi, Byelorussian SSR, Cameroon, Canada, Central African Republic, Chad, Chile, China, Colombia, Congo, Costa Rica, Côte d'Ivoire, Cuba, Cyprus, Czechoslovakia, Democratic People's Republic of Korea, Denmark, Ecuador, Egypt, El Salvador, Fiji, Finland, France, Gabon, Gambia, German Democratic Republic, Germany, Federal Republic of, Ghana, Greece, Guatemala, Guinea, Guinea-Bissau, Haiti, Holy See, Honduras, Hungary, Iceland, India, Indonesia, Iraq, Ireland, Israel, Italy, Jamaica, Japan, Jordan, Kenya, Lebanon, Lesotho, Libyan Arab Jamahiriya, Liechtenstein, Luxembourg, Malawi, Mali, Malta, Mauritania, Mauritius, Mexico, Monaco, Mongolia, Morocco, Netherlands, New Zealand, Nicaragua, Niger, Norway, Pakistan, Panama, Paraguay, Peru, Philippines, Poland, Portugal, Qatar, Republic of Korea, Romania, Rwanda, Saudi Arabia, Senegal, Sierra Leone, Somalia, South Africa, Spain, Sri Lanka, Sudan, Suriname, Swaziland, Sweden, Switzerland, Togo, Trinidad and Tobago, Tunisia, Turkey, Uganda, Ukrainian SSR, USSR, United Arab Emirates, United Kingdom, United Republic of Tanzania, United States, Uruguay, Venezuela, Viet Nam, Yemen, Yugoslavia, Zaire, Zambia, Zimbabwe.

Annex II. OFFICERS AND OFFICES OF THE WORLD INTELLECTUAL PROPERTY ORGANIZATION
(As at 31 December 1988)

GENERAL ASSEMBLY

OFFICERS
Chairman: Juan de Villafranca (Mexico).
Vice-Chairmen: J. H. André Gariépy (Canada), Joachim Hemmerling (German Democratic Republic).

MEMBERS
Algeria, Argentina, Australia, Austria, Bahamas, Barbados, Belgium, Benin, Brazil, Bulgaria, Burkina Faso, Burundi, Cameroon, Canada, Central African Republic, Chad, Chile, China, Colombia, Congo, Costa Rica, Côte d'Ivoire, Cuba, Cyprus, Czechoslovakia, Democratic People's Republic of Korea, Denmark, Egypt, Fiji, Finland, France, Gabon, German Democratic Republic, Germany, Federal Republic of, Ghana, Greece, Guinea, Guinea-Bissau, Haiti, Holy See, Hungary, Iceland, India, Indonesia, Iraq, Ireland, Israel, Italy, Japan, Jordan, Kenya, Lebanon, Libyan Arab Jamahiriya, Liechtenstein, Luxembourg, Malawi, Malaysia, Mali, Malta, Mauritania, Mauritius, Mexico, Monaco, Mongolia, Morocco, Netherlands, New Zealand, Niger, Norway, Pakistan, Peru, Philippines, Poland, Portugal, Republic of Korea, Rwanda, Senegal, South Africa, Spain, Sri Lanka, Sudan, Suriname, Sweden, Switzerland, Togo, Trinidad and Tobago, Tunisia, Turkey, Uganda, USSR, United Kingdom, United Republic of Tanzania, United States, Uruguay, Venezuela, Viet Nam, Yugoslavia, Zaire, Zambia, Zimbabwe.

CO-ORDINATION COMMITTEE

OFFICERS
Chairman: Gao Lulin (China).
Vice-Chairmen: Joachim Hemmerling (German Democratic Republic), Fumitake Yoshida (Japan).

MEMBERS
Algeria, Argentina, Australia, Austria, Bangladesh, Brazil, Bulgaria, Cameroon, Canada, Chile, China, Colombia, Côte d'Ivoire, Cuba, Czechoslovakia, Egypt, France, German Democratic Republic, Germany, Federal Republic of, Hungary, India, Indonesia, Italy, Jamaica, Japan, Kenya, Mexico, Morocco, Netherlands, Nicaragua, Pakistan, Poland, Republic of Korea, Saudi Arabia, Senegal, Spain, Sweden, Switzerland, Syrian Arab Republic, Turkey, USSR, United Kingdom, United Republic of Tanzania, United States, Uruguay, Venezuela.

SENIOR OFFICERS OF THE INTERNATIONAL BUREAU

Director General: Arpad Bogsch.
Deputy Directors General: Shahid Alikhan, Lev Efremovich Kostikov, Alfons Schäfers.
Legal Counsel: Gust Ledakis.
Director, Office of the Director General: François Curchod.
Director, Copyright and Public Information Department: Henry Olsson.
Directors, Development Co-operation and External Relations Bureau: Rubén Beltrán (Latin America and the Caribbean), Kamil Idris (Arab countries), Ibrahima Thiam (Africa).

Director, Developing Countries (Copyright) Division: Carlos Fernández Ballesteros.
Director, Industrial Property Division: Ludwig Baeumer.
Director, Patent Co-operation Treaty Division: Daniel Bouchez.
Director, Patent Information and Classifications Division: Paul Claus.
Director, Copyright Law Division: Mihály Ficsor.
Controller and Director, Budget and Finance Division: Thomas A. J. Keefer.
Director, General Administration Division: Richard Yung.

HEADQUARTERS AND OTHER OFFICE

HEADQUARTERS
World Intellectual Property Organization
34, Chemin des Colombettes
1211 Geneva 20, Switzerland
  Cable address: WIPO Geneva *or* OMPI Genève
  Telephone: (41) (22) 730-9111
  Telex: 412912 OMPI CH
  Facsimile: (41) (22) 733-5428

WIPO OFFICE AT THE UNITED NATIONS
2 United Nations Plaza, Room 560
New York, N.Y. 10017, United States
  Telephone: (1) (212) 963-6813
  Telex: 420544 UNH UI
  Facsimile: (1) (212) 963-4801

Chapter XVI

International Fund for Agricultural Development (IFAD)

In 1988, the International Fund for Agricultural Development (IFAD) continued to provide concessional assistance to finance agricultural projects in low-income, food-deficit countries. The Fund, aimed at increasing food production, reducing malnutrition and alleviating rural poverty, concentrated on the poorest farmers, providing them with the necessary production means and institutional support. Particular attention was given to restoring agricultural development capacity to sub-Saharan countries. IFAD also focused on women in development, cooperation with non-governmental organizations (NGOs) and the environment.

Two newly funded programmes were introduced during the year—the Extended Co-operation Programme (ECP) with NGOs, which for the first time afforded a direct functional link between IFAD and NGOs, with government consent, and the Special Programme for Women in Development, designed to enhance the Fund's technical capacity to address the problems of poor rural women.

The IFAD Executive Board held three regular sessions in 1988 (April, September and November), approving 24 loans for 23 projects, including five loans under the Special Programme for Sub-Saharan African Countries Affected by Drought and Desertification (SPA) and 31 technical assistance grants.

The Board authorized the IFAD President to negotiate and sign a co-operation agreement with the Office of the United Nations High Commissioner for Refugees. The agreement was finalized during the year, as was a co-operation agreement with the United Nations Industrial Development Organization, for which the Board had given its authorization in 1987.

The Board approved the submission of two reports to the United Nations Economic and Social Council, on operational activities for development and on IFAD's contribution to the United Nations Programme of Action for African Economic Recovery and Development 1986-1990.[a]

Membership of IFAD rose to 143 in 1988, with the admission of Trinidad and Tobago on 24 March. Of the current members, 20 were in Category I (developed countries), 12 in Category II (oil-exporting developing countries) and 111 in Category III (other developing countries) (see Annex I).

Resources

Initial resources and contributions to the first replenishment provided IFAD with about $2.1 billion to cover operations for two 3-year periods from 1978 to 1983. Because of delay in concluding negotiations on the second replenishment of resources, the first had to be stretched over four years (1981-1984) instead of three years. The second replenishment, to which IFAD members had pledged $488 million, came into effect on 27 November 1986.

Contributions and firm pledges to SPA, which became effective in May 1986, exceeded the three-year target of $300 million as at 31 January 1988. However, subsequent appreciation of the United States dollar reduced the value to $253 million.

Activities in 1988

The new loans approved for 23 projects, denominated in special drawing rights (SDRs), totalled SDR 176.5 million ($229.8 million), including five loans amounting to SDR 40.5 million ($52.4 million) under SPA. The 31 technical assistance grants came to SDR 9.8 million ($12.8 million), including 11 grants of SDR 2.5 million ($3.2 million) from SPA resources and one of SDR 29,230 ($38,000) under ECP. The total financial assistance provided in 1988 amounted to SDR 186.3 million ($242.5 million), as compared to SDR 175.2 million ($226.6 million) in 1987.

Of the 23 projects approved, 22 were IFAD-initiated, of which 14, or 63.6 per cent, attracted co-financing from other donors amounting to $46.7 million.

During the year, 10 projects were approved for the Africa region, for a lending total of SDR 81.5 million ($105.6 million) under SPA and the Regular Programme combined. The projects dealt with agricultural and rural development, rehabilitation of drought-affected areas (including assistance to nomadic pastoralists), livestock development and artisanal fisheries.

The seven projects approved for Asia, involving SDR 41.2 million ($53.8 million), emphasized credit for smallholder farmers and the landless (especially women) and livestock and small-scale fisheries development.

The three projects for Latin America and the Caribbean, obtaining loans of SDR 19.5 million ($25.9 million), aimed to meet the credit needs of small farmers in poor regions.

In the Near East and North Africa, three projects were approved under SPA and the Regular Pro-

[a]YUN 1986, p. 446, GA res. S-13/2, annex, 1 June 1986.

gramme, involving loans of SDR 35.1 million ($46 million). They dealt with dry-land farming and irrigation improvement, co-operative credit, and protection and development of a degraded watershed crossing the border between Algeria and Tunisia.

Under the Regular Programme, a total of $9.5 million was approved in grants for all technical assistance activities: $7.3 million for agricultural research, $1.4 million for project preparation and $0.8 million for training. Under SPA, technical assistance grants totalling $3.2 million were approved: $0.4 million for project preparation, $1.6 million for technical experts and training in IFAD-financed projects and $1.2 million from the Special Operations Facility designed to speed and facilitate project start-up. In addition, for the first time, a technical assistance grant of $38,000 was approved under ECP. Total grants amounted to $12.8 million.

IFAD continued its special programming missions, which focused on creating a policy dialogue with Governments on the general framework for smallholder development, developing country strategies as a guide to the Fund's investment allocation and identifying specific projects and programmes. Three missions were carried out in Brazil, Ethiopia and Rwanda. In addition, a rural development review mission went to Oman to take a first look at entrenched rural poverty problems and to evolve a possible role for IFAD.

Secretariat

At the end of 1988, the IFAD secretariat totalled 189 staff members, of whom 76 were in the Professional category and above—drawn from 37 nationalities—and 113 in the General Service category. (For senior secretariat officers, see Annex II.)

Income and expenditure

Total revenue under the Regular Programme in 1988 was $91.8 million, consisting of $65.6 million in investment income, including gains of $1.9 million resulting from active portfolio management, and $26.2 million from interest and service charges on loans. Total operational and administrative expenses for the year amounted to $27.9 million (including an exchange rate gain on operations of $0.87 million), compared with a budget, before contingency, of $35 million. The excess of revenue over expenses for the year was $63.9 million.

Total revenue under SPA was $8.8 million, consisting of $8.7 million in investment income and $0.1 million from interest and service charges on loans. Total expenses for the year amounted to $2.2 million, compared with a budget, before contingency, of $3.7 million.

NOTE: For details of IFAD activities in 1988, see *IFAD Annual Report 1988.*

Annex I.   MEMBERSHIP OF THE INTERNATIONAL FUND FOR AGRICULTURAL DEVELOPMENT
           (As at 31 December 1988)

Category I: Australia, Austria, Belgium, Canada, Denmark, Finland, France, Germany, Federal Republic of, Ireland, Italy, Japan, Luxembourg, Netherlands, New Zealand, Norway, Spain, Sweden, Switzerland, United Kingdom, United States.
Category II: Algeria, Gabon, Indonesia, Iran, Iraq, Kuwait, Libyan Arab Jamahiriya, Nigeria, Qatar, Saudi Arabia, United Arab Emirates, Venezuela.
Category III: Afghanistan, Angola, Antigua and Barbuda, Argentina, Bangladesh, Barbados, Belize, Benin, Bhutan, Bolivia, Botswana, Brazil, Burkina Faso, Burundi, Cameroon, Cape Verde, Central African Republic, Chad, Chile, China, Colombia, Comoros, Congo, Costa Rica, Côte d'Ivoire, Cuba, Cyprus, Democratic People's Republic of Korea, Democratic Yemen, Djibouti, Dominica, Dominican Republic, Ecuador, Egypt, El Salvador, Equatorial Guinea, Ethiopia, Fiji, Gambia, Ghana, Greece, Grenada, Guatemala, Guinea, Guinea-Bissau, Guyana, Haiti, Honduras, India, Israel, Jamaica, Jordan, Kenya, Lao People's Democratic Republic, Lebanon, Lesotho, Liberia, Madagascar, Malawi, Maldives, Mali, Malta, Mauritania, Mauritius, Mexico, Morocco, Mozambique, Nepal, Nicaragua, Niger, Oman, Pakistan, Panama, Papua New Guinea, Paraguay, Peru, Philippines, Portugal, Republic of Korea, Romania, Rwanda, Saint Kitts and Nevis, Saint Lucia, Saint Vincent and the Grenadines, Samoa, Sao Tome and Principe, Senegal, Seychelles, Sierra Leone, Solomon Islands, Somalia, Sri Lanka, Sudan, Suriname, Swaziland, Syrian Arab Republic, Thailand, Togo, Tonga, Trinidad and Tobago, Tunisia, Turkey, Uganda, United Republic of Tanzania, Uruguay, Viet Nam, Yemen, Yugoslavia, Zaire, Zambia, Zimbabwe.

Annex II.   OFFICERS AND OFFICES OF THE
            INTERNATIONAL FUND FOR AGRICULTURAL DEVELOPMENT
            (As at 31 December 1988)

EXECUTIVE BOARD

Chairman: Idriss Jazairy.

MEMBERS
Category I: Finland, France, Japan, Switzerland, United Kingdom, United States. *Alternates:* Austria, Canada, Germany, Federal Republic of, Netherlands, Norway.

Category II: Iraq, Kuwait, Libyan Arab Jamahiriya, Nigeria, Saudi Arabia, Venezuela. *Alternates:* Algeria, Gabon, Indonesia, Iran, Qatar, United Arab Emirates.

Category III: Brazil, Congo, Cuba, Cyprus, Madagascar, Republic of Korea. *Alternates:* Bangladesh, Colombia, Liberia, Mexico, Nepal, Zambia.

SENIOR OFFICERS OF THE SECRETARIAT

President: Idriss Jazairy.
Vice President: Donald S. Brown.
Assistant President, Economic and Planning Department: Vacant.
Assistant President, Project Management Department: Moise Mensah.
Assistant President, General Affairs Department: Enrique ter Horst.

Controller, Financial Services Division: Desmond Saldanha.
Treasurer, Financial Services Division: My Huynh Cong.
Director, Legal Services Division: Mohammed Nawaz.
Internal Auditor: Tor Myrvang.

HEADQUARTERS AND OTHER OFFICE

HEADQUARTERS
International Fund for Agricultural Development
107 Via del Serafico
00142 Rome, Italy
  Cable address: IFAD ROME
  Telephone: (39) (6) 54591
  Telex: 620330
  Facsimile: 5043463

LIAISON OFFICE
International Fund for Agricultural Development
1889 F Street, N.W.
Washington, D.C. 20006, United States
  Telephone: (1) (202) 289-3812
  Facsimile: (1) (202) 289-4267

Chapter XVII

United Nations Industrial Development Organization (UNIDO)

In 1988, the United Nations Industrial Development Organization (UNIDO) continued its activities in industrial operations, strategies and promotion. Special programmes included the Industrial Development Decade for Africa (IDDA) (1980s), assistance to the least developed countries (LDCs), industrial co-operation among developing countries, the integration of women in industrial development and co-operation with industrial enterprises and non-governmental organizations.

The Industrial Development Board, at its fourth regular session (Vienna, Austria, 10-18 October), considered, among other things, IDDA, UNIDO's contribution to the United Nations Programme of Action for African Economic Recovery and Development 1986-1990,[a] restructuring of world industrial production and redeployment, industrialization of LDCs, technical assistance to the Namibian and Palestinian peoples and to South African national liberation movements and UNIDO's contributions to environment and industrial development.

At its second special session (Vienna, 21 June), the Board elected a new Vice-President and appointed a deputy Director-General of Administration (see Annex II).

At the end of December, 151 States were members of UNIDO, including Australia, which withdrew from the Organization effective 31 December 1988. New members in 1988 were Albania and the Maldives (see Annex I).

Industrial strategies and operations

A total of 1,784 projects, valued at $119.8 million, were implemented or being implemented in 1988. Activities were funded from the United Nations Development Programme (UNDP) (64.3 per cent), the regular UNIDO budget (2.1 per cent), UNDP-administered trust funds (0.8 per cent) and other funds (32.8 per cent).

Africa, including the African Arab States, accounted for 32.1 per cent of technical assistance delivered by UNIDO during the year; the Americas, 9 per cent; non-African Arab States, 15 per cent; Asia and the Pacific, 36.7 per cent; Europe, 3.6 per cent; and global and interregional projects, 14.3 per cent.

Chemical industries accounted for $31.4 million of technical co-operation expenditures; institutional infrastructure, $15.8 million; engineering in-

dustries, $13.7 million; agro-industries, $11.6 million; metallurgical industries, $8 million; training, $6.7 million; industrial management and rehabilitation, $6 million; industrial planning, $5.8 million; feasibility studies, $4.9 million; and other activities, $15.9 million.

By project component, personnel accounted for $49.2 million (41.1 per cent); equipment, $35.8 million (29.9 per cent); fellowships and training, $17.9 million (15 per cent); sub-contracts, $13.4 million (11.2 per cent); and miscellaneous, $3.4 million (2.8 per cent).

Implementation of industrial operations

Agro-industries. Technical co-operation expenditures for agro-industries amounted to $11.6 million, with some 62 per cent financed by UNDP. Africa accounted for 23.2 per cent of the total; the Americas, 7 per cent; the non-African Arab States, 7.7 per cent; Asia and the Pacific, 57.9 per cent; Europe, 1.5 per cent; and interregional/global, 9.7 per cent. A total of 136 projects were completed or being implemented.

Activities focused on textile and garment production; improvement of existing industrial structures; replacement of imported raw materials with local products; food development, processing and packaging; and improvements in leather production and marketing.

Chemical industries. Technical co-operation expenditures for chemical industries amounted to $31.4 million, with about 67 per cent financed by UNDP. Africa accounted for 37.8 per cent; the Americas, 4.3 per cent; the non-African Arab States, 27.7 per cent; Asia and the Pacific, 48.1 per cent; Europe, 3.7 per cent; and interregional/global, 5 per cent. A total of 349 projects were completed or being implemented.

Activities focused on cement, lime and related industries; production of building materials using locally available materials; ceramics and glass; petrochemicals and petroleum refining; fertilizer; pharmaceuticals; biotechnology; pulp and paper; energy, fuel technology and pollution control; and the environment.

Engineering industries. In the engineering industries, technical co-operation expenditures amounted to $13.7 million, with about 92 per cent financed by UNDP. Africa accounted for 29.1 per

---

[a]YUN 1986, p. 446, GA res. S-13/2, 1 June 1986.

cent; the Americas, 10.2 per cent; the non-African Arab States, 3.1 per cent; Asia and the Pacific, 51.9 per cent; Europe, 6.4 per cent; and interregional/global, 0.4 per cent. A total of 198 projects were completed or being implemented, covering agricultural machinery and equipment; metalworking and machine tools; industrial design and production automation; and land- and water-transport equipment.

Feasibility studies. Technical co-operation expenditures for feasibility studies amounted to $4.9 million, with some 68 per cent financed by UNDP. Africa accounted for 54.5 per cent; the Americas, 1.4 per cent; the non-African Arab States, 24.5 per cent; Asia and the Pacific, 21.3 per cent; and interregional/global, 8.2 per cent. During the year, 106 projects were completed or being implemented.

Some 80 opportunity, pre-feasibility and feasibility studies were implemented, leading to new investment projects and the rehabilitation or expansion of existing enterprises. The UNIDO methodology for industrial investment project preparation, evaluation and financing and the application of a computer model for feasibility analysis and reporting were the subjects of 30 seminars at which more than 800 professionals from development banks, consulting firms and ministries were trained.

Industrial management and rehabilitation. Technical co-operation expenditures on industrial management and rehabilitation amounted to $6 million, with some 88 per cent financed by UNDP. Africa accounted for 36.5 per cent; the Americas, 15.1 per cent; the non-African Arab States, 19.1 per cent; Asia and the Pacific, 36.0 per cent; Europe, 4.3 per cent; and interregional/global, 0.7 per cent. A total of 115 projects were completed or being completed.

Efforts to modernize management structures and to apply computers to management continued. In addition, energy conservation and management activities were undertaken, and rehabilitation and restructuring in the wood sector were emphasized.

Industrial planning. Technical co-operation expenditures for industrial planning amounted to $5.8 million, with about 72 per cent financed by UNDP. Africa accounted for 54.9 per cent; the Americas, 21.1 per cent; the non-African Arab States, 4.1 per cent; Asia and the Pacific, 15 per cent; Europe, 2.2 per cent; and interregional/global, 2.8 per cent. A total of 89 projects were completed or being implemented.

Several major projects aimed at industrial restructuring, while others dealt with improving the decision support structure, upgrading industrial statistical systems and introducing management information systems. In addition, several industrial master plans, sectoral surveys and sectoral plans were carried out.

Institutional infrastructure. In the area of institutional infrastructure, technical co-operation expenditures totalled $15.8 million, with some 84 per cent financed by UNDP. Africa accounted for 37.7 per cent; the Americas, 15.2 per cent; the non-African Arab States, 22.9 per cent; Asia and the Pacific, 21.8 per cent; Europe, 3.1 per cent; and interregional/global, 4.9 per cent. During the year, 191 projects were completed or being implemented.

Technical co-operation in this field was characterized by demand for a comprehensive package of technical services. The promotion and development of small- and medium-scale industries continued to be the predominant programme element. Special activities and projects in support of such industries were strengthened, including enterprise-to-enterprise co-operation, national and international sub-contracting assistance to chambers of commerce and adaptation of products for export.

Metallurgical industries. Technical co-operation expenditures for metallurgical industries amounted to $8 million, with some 90 per cent financed by UNDP. Africa accounted for 20.4 per cent; the Americas, 9.7 per cent; the non-African Arab States, 6.8 per cent; Asia and the Pacific, 63.2 per cent; Europe, 3.6 per cent; and interregional/global, 2.3 per cent. A total of 135 projects were completed or being implemented.

Emphasis was placed on developing the bauxite-processing sector for aluminium and alumina production; developing the foundry industry; various aspects of copper production; strengthening and developing centres for metallurgical technology; and developing environmentally sound projects.

Training. Expenditures for fellowships and training components in all technical co-operation projects implemented by UNIDO amounted to $17.9 million, with some 17.8 per cent financed by UNDP. Of that total, $12.2 million was spent on fellowships and study tours and $5.7 million on group training and meetings. Africa accounted for 28.3 per cent; the Americas, 9.8 per cent; the non-African Arab States, 4.3 per cent; Asia and the Pacific, 5.2 per cent; Europe, 2.7 per cent; and interregional/global, 53.9 per cent. A total of 176 projects were implemented or being implemented.

Industrial promotion

Industrial promotion continued to focus on reinforcing links between activities related to industrial investment, consultations and development, and the transfer of technology.

System of Consultations. The UNIDO System of Consultations, a mechanism for achieving the goals of restructuring world industry and increasing the share of developing countries in world production, as set out in the Lima Declaration and Plan of Action on Industrial Development and

Co-operation,[b] held two consultations: the First Interregional Consultation on the Food-Processing Industry with Emphasis on Sugar-cane Processing (Havana, Cuba, 26-30 September) and the Regional Consultation on the Phosphatic Fertilizers and Pesticides Industries in Africa (Yamoussoukro, Côte d'Ivoire, 12-16 December). Preparatory meetings were held for consultations in 1989 on fruit and vegetable processing, small- and medium-scale enterprises and the electronics industry.

Development and transfer of technology. Preparation began, in co-operation with the Eastern and Southern African Management Institute, to establish an informatics development centre for that subregion. In June, under a project funded by Italy, preparations began to establish an international centre for science and high technology at Trieste, Italy.

Two national workshops were prepared in the area of technology policies (Tunisia and the United Republic of Tanzania), and UNIDO contributed to a national workshop on science and technology organized by Ethiopia.

A workshop on protein engineering and a forum of scientists from 21 member countries of the International Centre for Genetic Engineering and Biotechnology (ICGEB) were held (Trieste, March). In May, the New Delhi component of ICGEB began functioning. ICGEB provided advisory services and assistance in biotechnology to Argentina, Egypt, Kuwait and Viet Nam. A programme for a meeting on biotechnology in the Arab region was developed in co-operation with the Economic and Social Commission for Western Asia.

Steps were taken to establish a network of materials-related centres for developing countries, emphasizing new materials and materials testing and control. In response to a request by Brazil, discussions were intitiated on establishing an international material assessment and applications centre.

Activities related to new and renewable sources of energy concentrated on expanding the system of networks for research and development training and for information exchange among institutions in developing countries. Technical manuals for the design, standardization and fabrication of equipment for small hydropower stations were completed in co-operation with the Latin American Energy Organization. A new technology for small-scale alcohol production from sugar was introduced in Kenya with assistance from Brazil, and a demonstration project for the gasification of agricultural waste was started in Zimbabwe.

In the area of technology acquisition and negotiation, technical advisory services were expanded, and a number of workshops and seminars were held. Country profiles on regulations and practices regarding technology acquisition in developing countries were finalized. Within the Technological Information Exchange System, the Computerized Registry Information System, designed to handle technology-transfer information intended as a tool for effective policy-making, strategic planning, evaluation and monitoring of contract implementation, was installed in Indonesia, Malaysia, Philippines, Thailand and Tunisia. In addition, a promotional programme for strengthening basic technological infrastructure was initiated, with special attention directed to Africa and Central America.

At the end of 1988, the Industrial and Technological Information Bank (INTIB) networking system had more than 50 participating national and four regional focal points. Guidelines were being prepared to clarify their role, *modus operandi* and internal organization. Screenmail, an electronic mail system, was being used to facilitate communication between INTIB and its focal points. A workshop on information networking and co-operation was held in Moscow. Training in the use of INTIB and other UNIDO information systems and data bases was organized, and projects to strengthen national information organizations and their link with INTIB were being implemented in Algeria, Cameroon, Mongolia, Nigeria, Poland, Senegal and Viet Nam.

The Industrial Inquiry Service supplied assessed information in response to more than 1,500 inquiries. Directories on research and technological institutions dealing with sugar and sugar by-products and with fruits and vegetables were published. At year's end, the Technology Supply Data Base had more than 2,000 entries.

Investment promotion. UNIDO continued to assist developing countries in identifying sound investment projects with local sponsors and in finding foreign partners to provide a share of the financial and other resources required in their implementation. A total of 476 new investment projects were identified and formulated; 121 industrial investment projects were successfully promoted, representing a total investment of $413.8 million.

UNIDO launched a project development facility at the UNIDO Investment Promotion Service (Cologne, Federal Republic of Germany), financed by the Federal Republic of Germany, to facilitate the development of small- and medium-scale industries in developing countries.

In Africa, UNIDO prepared, together with the Centre for Industrial Development of the European Economic Community, and participated in the Eighth Industrial Forum for West Africa (Dakar, Senegal), which was attended by some 650 project sponsors and potential foreign partners. Assistance was provided to the Chamber of Commerce and Industry of Zambia to strengthen the role of private industry. Preparations began for two invest-

[b]YUN 1975, p. 473.

ment project promotion forums—one for the Gambia, Ghana, Liberia, Nigeria and Sierra Leone, and the other for the member States of the Preferential Trade Area for Eastern and Southern Africa.

In the Arab region, an industrial investment programme was approved for implementation for the electronics industry, covering Algeria, Egypt, Iraq, Jordan, Kuwait, Morocco, Saudi Arabia, Syrian Arab Republic, Tunisia and United Arab Emirates. Assistance was provided to the Sudan in promoting a large cotton-spinning project for which the pre-investment study was prepared by the Arab Industrial Development Organization.

In Asia and the Pacific, follow-up activities focused on China, Indonesia, the Philippines and Thailand. The Investors' Forum for Indonesia resulted in some 20 projects that were under negotiation. At an investment projects promotion forum for the Philippines held at Manila, 140 projects were identified and promoted by UNIDO and were discussed among Philippine project sponsors and potential foreign partners. The forum led to the signing of 72 letters of intent for investment projects with a total investment value of some $220 million.

In the Latin American and Caribbean region, industrial investment activities were based on a strategy aimed at addressing the range of issues relevant to foreign investment. Attention was given in particular to evaluating investment projects in the context of their particular subsectors; investment legislation and incentives; the competence of local sponsors; improving the quality of project formulation and screening; effective marketing and promotion strategies; and establishing a computerized investment project management system. At the regional level, a programme was designed for the Andean group under which the support of a leading development finance institution and UNDP was enlisted.

Assistance to LDCs

As food production and food security continued to be the dominant problems in the LDCs, the bulk of UNDP-financed technical assistance was channelled to agriculture. Projects approved under all sources of funds totalled $20.5 million, of which $16.8 million accounted for new projects. The total resources allocated to the industrial sector in LDCs almost doubled in 1988.

The main thrust of UNIDO's assistance continued to be the development and promotion of small- and medium-scale industries using locally available raw materials, industrial planning and programming and the preparation of pre-feasibility and feasibility studies for investment projects. Projects dealing with food processing, food preservation, and research and development on food production technology received high priority.

Industrial co-operation among developing countries

More than 40 co-operation agreements were reached in such areas as food processing, industrial training, feasibility studies, small-scale production enterprises, leather processing, aquaculture, quality control and technical infrastructural development at the Solidarity Ministerial Meeting for Co-operation in the Industrial Development of Cape Verde (Praia, Cape Verde, 6-10 June). Other activities included the promotion of various bilateral industrial co-operation projects, including co-operation between China and Egypt in phosphate mining and processing as well as in rare-earth extraction; co-operation between Burundi and Romania in the construction of two small industrial units in Burundi; a programme of co-operation between Cuba and China in micro- and mini-hydroelectric plants and the production of newsprint from bagasse; establishment of carpentry and exercise book workshops in the United Republic of Tanzania in co-operation with Turkey; a programme of co-operation between Senegal and Brazil in the field of fruit conservation and processing; co-operation between Ethiopia and India in the small-scale industry sector; and co-operation between Rwanda and Yugoslavia in the establishment of an industrial estate in Rwanda.

At a working group meeting on co-operative arrangements among selected developing countries (Buenos Aires, Argentina, 31 May–4 June), nearly 50 participants from 19 countries identified 43 technical and other co-operation projects. The meeting was organized in co-operation with the Argentine Association of Machine Tools, Accessories and Ancillaries and the Argentine National Institute of Industrial Technology.

Two technical workshops were held in Yugoslavia: one at Ljubljana, where experts from eight developing countries met with Yugoslav experts and agreed on measures to ensure a permanent flow of information among them in the area of small- and medium-scale industries, and the other at Novi Sad, where the focus was on agricultural machinery and agro-industries and where participants from 21 countries identified 35 industrial projects for follow-up action and implementation. At an expert group meeting on the processing of raw materials (Vienna, 22-26 August), 16 experts from developing countries and representatives of international organizations prepared conclusions and recommendations on food processing, non-metallic minerals and textile fibres in preparation for the Action Committee on Raw Materials, scheduled to meet in Nigeria in April 1989.

Other promotional activities included negotiations with the Korean Institute for Economics and Technology to prepare the way for an industrial forum on enterprise-to-enterprise co-operation in

Asia; preparations for a meeting on establishing multinational production enterprises among developing countries; initial work on a programme of inventories to help match the industrial requirements of developing countries by drawing on the industrial and service capacities of other developing countries; and preparatory work on a data base to be operated within INTIB and made available to regional information centres.

Industrial Development Decade for Africa (1980s)

Under the IDDA programme, technical co-operation activities concentrated on establishing pilot and demonstration plants, the accelerated development of human resources and institutional infrastructure for industrial development. Technical co-operation programmes amounting to about $22 million, covering such areas as leather products, food and agro-industries, telecommunications, industrial rehabilitation and training, were formulated and promoted among potential donors.

Intra-African industrial co-operation continued to be prominent in IDDA activities. Meetings on the promotion of intra-African industrial co-operation for the Northern and Eastern/Southern African subregions were organized by UNIDO in co-operation with the Economic Commission for Africa (ECA) and relevant intergovernmental organizations. Both meetings adopted a revised subregional programme consisting of investment and support projects, along with a strategy to accelerate its implementation.

UNIDO hosted the eighth meeting of the Joint Committee on IDDA of the secretariats of ECA and the Organization of African Unity (OAU) in February. It also contributed, at the request of OAU, to the Fifth All-Africa Trade Fair (Kinshasa, Zaire, July) in the form of a seminar on IDDA focusing on the link between agriculture and industry, demonstrations of African-developed food-processing technologies and general information about UNIDO.

Integration of women in industrial development

The number of technical co-operation projects targeting women increased in 1988, with 21 projects valued at over $3.1 million being implemented and 13 projects valued at $8.5 million in the pipeline.

Attention was given to the problems involved in the development and dissemination of appropriate food-processing technologies for rural women, and research was carried out on how UNIDO should deal with those problems in co-operation with the International Fund for Agricultural Development and the United Nations Development Fund for Women (UNIFEM).

Following recognition of the need for a more methodological approach to statistics and data collection on women's participation in specific industrial subsectors, UNIDO entered into consultations with the United Nations Statistical Office, the United Nations Centre for Social Development and Humanitarian Affairs at Vienna, UNDP, the International Research and Training Institute for the Advancement of Women, the International Labour Organisation, the United Nations Educational, Scientific and Cultural Organization and UNIFEM, as well as with relevant intergovernmental, national, non-governmental and research organizations producing statistics on women. An exchange of statistical and other information on women in industrial activities was agreed upon.

Secretariat

As at 31 December 1988, the UNIDO secretariat totalled 1,257 staff members: 423 in the Professional and higher categories and 834 in the General Service and related categories. (See Annex II for UNIDO officers.)

SIDFAs

Senior Industrial Development Field Advisers (SIDFAs) continued to assist in programming and implementing technical co-operation projects.

In 1988, among the main activities of the Field Representative Advisory Committee were laying the groundwork for a set of guidelines for establishing work targets and introducing periodic work programmes for SIDFAs and Junior Professional Officers (JPOs).

UNIDO was represented by 36 SIDFAs, working with UNDP resident representatives; 24 were financed by UNDP: 9 from the regular budget and 3 from voluntary contributions.

The JPOs provided valuable support to the technical co-operation and other programmes of UNIDO. A total of 74 JPOs, including 8 nationals of developing countries, were employed by the end of 1988. The programme was supported by Austria, Belgium, Denmark, Finland, France, Federal Republic of Germany, Italy, Japan, Netherlands, Norway, Sweden and Switzerland.

Budget

For 1988, total expenditures were $191.5 million, comprising $119.8 million for technical co-operation programmes and $71.7 million for headquarters expenditures. The latter was financed largely from the regular budget ($56.9 million) and supplemented by $14.8 million derived from a 13 per cent reimbursement for technical assistance delivery.

For the 1988-1989 biennium, the UNIDO General Conference approved net appropriations of $154.3 million.

NOTE: For more details on UNIDO activities in 1988, see *Annual Report of UNIDO 1988*.

Annex I.   MEMBERSHIP OF THE UNITED NATIONS
INDUSTRIAL DEVELOPMENT ORGANIZATION
(As at 31 December 1988)

Afghanistan, Albania, Algeria, Angola, Argentina, Australia, Austria, Bahamas, Bahrain, Bangladesh, Barbados, Belgium, Belize, Benin, Bhutan, Bolivia, Botswana, Brazil, Bulgaria, Burkina Faso, Burundi, Byelorussian SSR, Cameroon, Canada, Cape Verde, Central African Republic, Chile, China, Colombia, Comoros, Congo, Costa Rica, Côte d'Ivoire, Cuba, Cyprus, Czechoslovakia, Democratic People's Republic of Korea, Democratic Yemen, Denmark, Dominica, Dominican Republic, Ecuador, Egypt, Equatorial Guinea, Ethiopia, Fiji, Finland, France, Gabon, Gambia, German Democratic Republic, Germany, Federal Republic of, Ghana, Greece, Grenada, Guatemala, Guinea, Guinea-Bissau, Guyana, Haiti, Honduras, Hungary, India, Indonesia, Iran, Iraq, Ireland, Israel, Italy, Jamaica, Japan, Jordan, Kenya, Kuwait, Lao People's Democratic Republic, Lebanon, Lesotho, Libyan Arab Jamahiriya, Luxembourg, Madagascar, Malawi, Malaysia, Maldives, Mali, Malta, Mauritania, Mauritius, Mexico, Mongolia, Morocco, Mozambique, Namibia,* Nepal, Netherlands, New Zealand, Nicaragua, Niger, Nigeria, Norway, Oman, Pakistan, Panama, Papua New Guinea, Paraguay, Peru, Philippines, Poland, Portugal, Qatar, Republic of Korea, Romania, Rwanda, Saint Kitts and Nevis, Saint Lucia, Saint Vincent and the Grenadines, Sao Tome and Principe, Saudi Arabia, Senegal, Seychelles, Sierra Leone, Somalia, Spain, Sri Lanka, Sudan, Suriname, Swaziland, Sweden, Switzerland, Syrian Arab Republic, Thailand, Togo, Tonga, Trinidad and Tobago, Tunisia, Turkey, Uganda, Ukrainian SSR, USSR, United Arab Emirates, United Kingdom, United Republic of Tanzania, United States, Uruguay, Vanuatu, Venezuela, Viet Nam, Yemen, Yugoslavia, Zaire, Zambia, Zimbabwe.

*Represented by the United Nations Council for Namibia; assessment waived in accordance with General Assembly resolution 36/121 D of 10 December 1981.

Annex II.   OFFICERS AND OFFICES OF THE UNITED NATIONS
INDUSTRIAL DEVELOPMENT ORGANIZATION
(As at 31 December 1988)

INDUSTRIAL DEVELOPMENT BOARD

OFFICERS
President: R. E Guyer (Argentina).
Vice-Presidents: E. A. Al-Nowaiser (Saudi Arabia), B. wa Mwenda (Zaire), E. Ybañez (Spain).
Rapporteur: Y. V. Kostenko, Ukrainian SSR.

MEMBERS
Algeria, Argentina, Australia, Austria, Bangladesh, Belgium, Botswana, Brazil, Bulgaria, Cameroon, Chile, China, Côte d'Ivoire, Cuba, Denmark, Ecuador, Egypt, France, German Democratic Republic, Germany, Federal Republic of, Ghana, Greece, Guinea, India, Indonesia, Iraq, Italy, Jamaica, Japan, Kenya, Malaysia, Mexico, Nigeria, Panama, Philippines, Republic of Korea, Saudi Arabia, Spain, Sweden, Switzerland, Thailand, Tunisia, Turkey, Ukrainian SSR, USSR, United Kingdom, United Republic of Tanzania, United States, Venezuela, Yugoslavia, Zaire, Zambia.

PROGRAMME AND BUDGET COMMITTEE

OFFICERS
Chairman: T. A. Mgbokwere (Nigeria).
Vice-Chairmen: G. E. Clark (United Kingdom), E. Ivan (Hungary), C. Valdivia Sesma (Cuba).
Rapporteur: A. S. Punia (India).

MEMBERS
Algeria, Angola, Argentina, Austria, Bangladesh, Brazil, China, Côte d'Ivoire, Cuba, Czechoslovakia, Finland, France, Germany, Federal Republic of, Hungary, India, Iran, Iraq, Italy, Japan, Morocco, Netherlands, Nigeria, Peru, USSR, United Kingdom, United States, Zimbabwe.

SENIOR SECRETARIAT OFFICERS

Director-General: Domingo L. Siazon, Jr.

Deputy Directors-General: Louis Alexandrenne, Alberto Araoz, Louis Faoro, Anatoli Vassiliev, Horst Paul Friedrich Wiesebach.

HEADQUARTERS AND OTHER OFFICES

HEADQUARTERS
United Nations Industrial Development Organization
Vienna International Centre
P.O. Box 300
A-1400 Vienna, Austria
  Cable address: UNIDO Vienna
  Telephone: (43) (1) 211310
  Telex: 135612
  Facsimile: (43) (1) 232156

  UNIDO also maintained a liaison office at Geneva.

LIAISON OFFICE
UNIDO Liaison Office
1 United Nations Plaza, Room 1110
New York, N.Y. 10017, United States
  Telephone: (1) (212) 963-6882

Chapter XVIII

Interim Commission for the International Trade Organization (ICITO) and the General Agreement on Tariffs and Trade (GATT)

The United Nations Conference on Trade and Employment (Havana, Cuba, November 1947–March 1948) drew up a charter for an International Trade Organization (ITO) and established an Interim Commission for the International Trade Organization (ICITO). Since the charter itself was never accepted, ITO was not established. However, while drawing up the charter, the members of the Conference's Preparatory Committee negotiated on tariffs among themselves, and also drew up the General Agreement on Tariffs and Trade (GATT)—a multilateral treaty embodying reciprocal rights and obligations, which is the only multilateral instrument that lays down agreed rules for international trade. It entered into force on 1 January 1948 with 23 contracting parties. Since then, ICITO has provided the GATT secretariat.

As at 31 December 1988, the number of contracting parties to GATT had risen to 96 with the addition of Lesotho (8 January) (see Annex I). One other country, Tunisia, had acceded provisionally. The contracting parties conducted about 90 per cent of all international trade; 28 other countries, to whose territories GATT had been applied before their independence, maintained a *de facto* application of GATT pending final decisions as to their future commercial policy.

Multilateral trade negotiations

Uruguay Round

Trade Negotiations Committee

In February 1988, the Trade Negotiations Committee, the body responsible for overseeing the Uruguay Round (GATT's eighth "round" of multilateral trade negotiations, launched in 1986[a]), decided to hold a mid-term review of the Round at a ministerial level meeting (Montreal, Canada, 5-9 December). More than 90 Ministers attended the meeting along with 1,000 delegates.

Among the decisions reached at the mid-term review were an agreed package of trade concessions on tropical products; an agreement on institutional changes negotiated in the groups on dispute settlement procedure and the functioning of the GATT system; and agreement on a far-reaching text on trade in services. An impasse on agricul-

ture could not be broken and therefore the Ministers decided that the nine subjects on which agreement had been secured should be put on hold and that the Committee should reconvene at senior-officials level in April 1989.

The Surveillance Body reported to the Committee and monitored two commitments contained in the 1986 Ministerial Declaration on the Uruguay Round:[b] a standstill (a freeze on any further restrictive trade inconsistent with GATT) and a rollback (the phasing out of measures inconsistent with GATT, or bringing them into conformity with GATT). By the end of 1988, the Surveillance Body had reported 24 notifications of alleged breaches of standstill from 11 participants against eight participants. Eighteen of the notifications came from developed countries and six from developing countries and covered quantitative restrictions, tariffs, import controls and prohibitions, export restrictions, internal taxes, production and export subsidies, and government procurement.

Group of Negotiations on Goods

The Group of Negotiations on Goods oversaw the work of the 14 negotiating groups which were established in 1987 to conduct the work outlined in part I of the 1986 Ministerial Declaration. The activities of the negotiating groups at the half-way mark of the Uruguay Round are listed below.

Tariffs. As in the past, the group was faced with the problem of finding a common method for cutting tariffs. In 1988, there was widespread support for a Tokyo Round (1973-1979—the seventh "round" of multilateral trade negotiations) formula for its ease of use and potential for achieving the widest and deepest cuts. At the mid-term review, the Ministers decided that: substantive tariff negotiations should begin not later than 1 July 1989, with the overall target amount of, at the minimum, the tariff reduction achieved by the formula participants in the Tokyo Round; the scope of tariff bindings should be substantially widened to provide greater security and predictability in international trade, with credit given for bindings

---

[a]YUN 1986, p. 1210.

[b]*Ibid.*, p. 1211.

and appropriate recognition accorded to liberalization measures adopted since 1 June 1986; and participation of developing countries would follow the general principles governing the negotiations, including those giving them special treatment.

Non-tariff measures. To move the negotiations forward, participants were invited to submit, by mid-year, proposals on what non-tariff measures should be included in the negotiations, classifying the measures under three negotiating approaches: through drafting of multilateral rules; use of a systematic formula method; and the traditional request-and-offer procedure.

In June, 15 industrial and developing countries put forth a proposal addressing the main issues facing the group. The sponsors, stressing the need for a clear negotiating framework in time for the mid-term review, favoured the general use of a systematic approach. The proposal suggested using a formula to reduce the effects of measures with a volume or price-restricting character. Still, some countries continued to prefer the request-and-offer procedure as the main negotiating tool. In December, the Ministers agreed that, to pave the way for substantive negotiations, the group must establish the necessary framework, including procedures, by June 1989. They listed a set of principles and guidelines to underpin that framework.

Natural resource–based products. It was generally recognized that the main trade barriers on resource products were also being negotiated in other groups. The group might have to wait for decisions on negotiating techniques and modalities by other groups, in particular those on tariffs and non-tariff measures, before it could formulate its own. That was also agreed by Ministers at the mid-term review.

Textiles and clothing. The group's main task was to negotiate the return of the textile and clothing sector to GATT rather than the members of the Multifibre Arrangement—the Arrangement regarding International Trade in Textiles—which had been regulating such trade since 1974.[c] During 1988, the group examined a number of proposals aimed at achieving that objective. At the mid-term review, Ministers were unable to agree on a text setting out points for action.

Agriculture. In 1988, participants examined 1987 proposals for the reform of agricultural trade and new submissions. Concerns were raised relating to other non-economic issues besides food security, including protection of the environment, maintenance of rural populations and rural development. The group made progress on the technical aspects of its work, establishing a technical group to facilitate further work on an aggregate measurement of government support for agriculture and related matters and a working group on sanitary and phytosanitary regulations and barriers.

Tropical products. The first concrete result of the Uruguay Round was a trade liberalization package for early implementation negotiated at the mid-term review. The "Montreal" package covered seven product groups: tropical beverages; spices, flowers and plants; certain oilseeds, vegetable oils and oilcakes; tobacco, rice and tropical roots; tropical fruits and nuts; tropical wood and rubber; and jute and hard fibres. The trade covered by the concessions amounted to some $20 billion.

Review of GATT articles. Suggestions were tabled on several articles of the General Agreement. In Montreal, the Ministers agreed that the group should define issues for negotiation with precision and clarity and that specific proposals should be brought forward as soon as possible, preferably not later than 31 December 1989.

Multinational trade negotiation agreements and arrangements. Discussion touched on six Tokyo Round codes dealing with anti-dumping, customs valuation, subsidies and countervailing measures, government procurement, technical barriers to trade, and import licensing procedures. The Ministers at the mid-term review agreed that the group should pursue its negotiations and encouraged participants to submit specific texts at an early date.

Safeguards. The group continued to discuss the following elements which could form the basis of a safeguards agreement: transparency, temporary nature of safeguard actions, degressivity and structural adjustment, compensation and retaliation, product and geographic coverage, "grey-area" measures, multilateral surveillance and dispute settlement, special and differential treatment for developing countries, and legal framework. The major difference to overcome had been the long-standing argument about "selectivity"—between those who favoured the idea of taking action against single suppliers (essentially large importing countries that had found export restraints so attractive) and those who sought an agreement on non-discriminatory application of safeguard measures (principally small and developing countries that felt most at risk from such measures). In 1988, the negotiating group received a variety of proposals; some continued to emphasize the importance of non-discrimination with respect to safeguard action taken at the border, some stressed the need to deal specifically with industries in "structural" difficulty, and some envisaged less stringent rules with respect to selectivity. An agreed text eluded Ministers in Montreal.

Subsidies and countervailing measures. Much of the work of the group in 1988 was devoted to developing a common negotiating basis which could help

[c]YUN 1974, p. 1043.

strike a balance between those countries that were mostly concerned with the use of subsidies and those that were concerned with the use of countervailing measures, or the countermeasures Governments were entitled to take against subsidized exports.

Trade-related aspects of intellectual property rights. The group continued to express different views on the extent to which new rules, within GATT, covering intellectual property protection should be negotiated. It considered the extent to which new rules could promote the protection of intellectual property and the relationship between its negotiations and activities in other organizations, such as the World Intellectual Property Organization. Specific proposals were tabled in the group. In Montreal, participants encountered serious difficulties in bridging their differences.

Trade-related investment measures. Discussions in the negotiating group focused on the contention made by several industrialized countries that the trade effects of many investment measures conflicted in some way with GATT articles. They envisaged confirming the applicability of certain articles and establishing GATT rules that could more clearly and effectively deal with the adverse trade effects of government investment requirements, such as local content, export performance, trade balancing, product mandating and domestic sales. In some countries those measures were not designed to distort trade, but were aimed at legitimate objectives including industrialization and development. They considered the adverse trade effects minimal, and suggested that the group examine problems on a case-by-case basis. The group examined submissions by some participants which sought to facilitate the examination of the effects of trade-related investment measures by classifying them into those which were clearly inconsistent with GATT and those which were not but which were relevant to its provisions. In Montreal, the Ministers asked that the group continue identifying trade-restrictive and distorting effects.

Dispute settlement. The dispute settlement system of GATT serves to resolve disputes once they occur and as a pressure on Governments to live up to their obligations as GATT members. Twenty-five formal proposals on behalf of 38 participants were approved by the Ministers in Montreal. Among the main features of the proposals were: specific time-limits on procedures for consultations; arbitration as an alternative to panel proceedings; dispute panels to be established at the first GATT Council meeting following the one at which the initial request for a panel was made; strict time-limits for determining terms of reference and composition of panels and a time-schedule for their work; avoidance of delays to the adoption of panel reports by the Council; and legal advice for developing contracting parties involved in a dispute.

Functioning of the GATT system. As called for in its negotiating plan, the group in 1988 established common working texts which became the basis of subsequent negotiations. In Montreal, the Ministers approved a new system of national trade policy surveillance in GATT. Under the new system, the GATT Council would conduct regular reviews of the totality of such policies for each GATT member, permitting a collective evaluation of their effects and impact on the multilateral trade system. The Ministers also agreed to be more active in the activities of the institution by holding meetings of the Contracting Parties at ministerial level once every two years.

Group of Negotiations on Services

During 1988, the Group of Negotiations on Services continued to discuss fundamental concepts which might underpin an agreement on services. It examined questions such as whether an agreement should be restricted to cross-border trade where the services crossed the border (for example, telephone services), or whether services provided through a physical commercial presence in a second country (for example, branch banking) should be covered. The promotion of development was central to the discussion. The Group discussed the principles which might form the basis of an agreement. In particular, it considered non-discrimination in the treatment of foreign services providers, national treatment under which foreign-owned services suppliers should be treated on the same basis as domestic suppliers and the concept of transparency, which opened up for public scrutiny the nature of regulations and laws affecting the services sector. At the mid-term review of the Uruguay Round, the Ministers established guidelines for the Group's future work.

Implementation of the Tokyo Round agreements

The agreements of the Tokyo Round provided an improved framework for the conduct of world trade and were adopted as an integral part of GATT. The Tokyo Round established a number of agreements or codes covering non-tariff measures and certain sectoral matters as well as securing major tariff cuts. Each of the agreements had an overseeing committee or council. Those bodies dealt with tariffs, anti-dumping practices, subsidies and countervailing measures, government procurement, technical barriers to trade, customs valuation, import licensing, bovine meat, dairy products and civil aircraft.

Other GATT activities

Contracting Parties regular session

The Contracting Parties held their forty-fourth regular session on 7 and 8 November 1988, focusing on the Uruguay Round and the importance of its success.

Council of Representatives

The Council of Representatives, GATT's highest body between sessions of the Contracting Parties, held two special meetings in 1988 to review developments in the trading system, as described in two reports, which gave an extensive compilation and analysis of measures taken by Governments. In June, the Council considered the first report, covering developments between October 1987 and March 1988, which noted that trade policy formulation had continued to be dominated by concerns over trade imbalances, exchange rate uncertainties, unemployment problems and slow growth in many industrialized countries, resistance to adjustment and the continuing debt-servicing difficulties of many developing countries. The Council also discussed measures, both liberalizing and restrictive, taken by GATT members, including trade-liberalization programmes of developing countries and their efforts towards structural adjustment.

For the Council's second special meeting, the report on developments between April and August 1988 noted that attention in the trade policy field focused on the passage of the Omnibus Trade and Competitiveness Act in the United States, which had aroused concern in many countries, and the veto by the President of the United States of the Textile and Apparel Act; the move towards the unification of the European market; and the progress of the Uruguay Round negotiations. Other developments included the application by the United States of measures aimed at strengthening protection of intellectual property rights and new European Community (EC) anti-dumping measures.

At the mid-term review of the Uruguay Round, tentative agreement was reached on a new comprehensive review mechanism which would replace the Council's reviews.

Trade and development

The Committee on Trade and Development continued to review, discuss and negotiate trade issues of interest to developing countries. It reviewed implementation of part IV of the General Agreement, dealing with special treatment for developing countries, and of the ''enabling clause'', an agreement resulting from the Tokyo Round providing for differential and more favourable treatment of developing countries in various areas of trade policy. The Committee kept track of GATT technical co-operation activities with developing countries, particularly in the context of the multilateral negotiations. It invited Governments and international organizations providing similar forms of assistance to report on their activities as well as on facilities that might be available.

The Sub-Committee on Trade of Least-Developed Countries, reactivated by the Committee in 1987, met in February and October 1988 to review developments in the Uruguay Round. At the October meeting, a number of issues were raised in connection with the mid-term review, including the need for predictability in the concession to be offered to the least developed countries as well as a guarantee of their long-term maintenance; to remedy any possible loss of preferential margins given to least developed countries; and a time-bound action in the implementation of measures.

Conciliation and settlement of disputes

The Ministers at the mid-term review of the Uruguay Round reached provisional agreement on a detailed plan to streamline the process of conciliation and settlement of disputes and the Council established 13 dispute-settlement panels, almost double the 1987 total—itself a record. All but one related to agricultural products. Three major disputes were settled through the adoption of panel reports: an EC complaint on the treatment of imported alcoholic drinks by Canadian provincial boards; a United States complaint on Canadian restrictions on exports of fresh salmon and herring; and an EC panel case against the Japan–United States semi-conductor agreement. Activation of the procedures in the Council helped bring about the resolution of four other disputes through amicable bilateral agreements. In May the Council agreed that, unless a party to a dispute opposed it, panel reports would be derestricted when adopted.

In November, the Contracting Parties extended by another year the permanent roster of non-governmental panelists established by them in 1984. The roster, composed of 35 prospective panelists agreed by the Council in 1985, and extended in 1986 and 1987, could be drawn upon by the Director-General should the disputing parties fail to agree to a panel's membership through the traditional consultative procedure.

Technical assistance

In 1988, the GATT secretariat's Technical Co-operation Division organized or participated in regional or subregional trade policy seminars held in Côte d'Ivoire, Indonesia, Kenya, Thailand and Zambia.

Training programme

From 1955 to the end of 1988, a total of 1,098 officials from 114 countries and 10 regional organizations had attended GATT trade policy courses. Twenty-four fellowships are granted for each course, following a decision by the 1982 ministerial meeting. Two such courses, one conducted in English and the other in Spanish were given in 1988.

International Trade Centre

The International Trade Centre, established by GATT in 1964 and jointly operated with the United Nations Conference on Trade and Development since 1968, continued providing trade information and trade promotion advisory services to developing countries. The Centre's technical co-operation activities amounted to $26.3 million in 1988. Some 127 national, 44 regional and 96 interregional projects were under implementation throughout the year, covering one or more of the Centre's eight programme areas: institutional infrastructure for national trade promotion, specialized national trade promotion services, export market development, commodity promotion, training, import operations and techniques, trade promotion for least developed countries and activities with national chambers of commerce.

Secretariat

As at 31 December 1988, the GATT secretariat employed 402 staff members—175 in the Professional and higher categories and 227 in the General Service category. (For senior officers of the secretariat, see Annex II.)

Financial arrangements

Member countries of GATT contribute to the budget in accordance with a scale assessed on the basis of each country's share in the total trade of the contracting parties and associated Governments. The budget for 1988 was 61,439,000 Swiss francs.

NOTE: For further information on GATT, see *GATT Activities 1988: An Annual Review of the Work of the GATT.*

Annex I.   CONTRACTING PARTIES TO THE GENERAL AGREEMENT ON TARIFFS AND TRADE
   (As at 31 December 1988)

Antigua and Barbuda, Argentina, Australia, Austria, Bangladesh, Barbados, Belgium, Belize, Benin, Botswana, Brazil, Burkina Faso, Burma, Burundi, Cameroon, Canada, Central African Republic, Chad, Chile, Colombia, Congo, Côte d'Ivoire, Cuba, Cyprus, Czechoslovakia, Denmark, Dominican Republic, Egypt, Finland, France, Gabon, Gambia, Germany, Federal Republic of, Ghana, Greece, Guyana, Haiti, Hong Kong, Hungary, Iceland, India, Indonesia, Ireland, Israel, Italy, Jamaica, Japan, Kenya, Kuwait, Lesotho, Luxembourg, Madagascar, Malawi, Malaysia, Maldives, Malta, Mauritania, Mauritius, Mexico, Morocco, Netherlands, New Zealand, Nicaragua, Niger, Nigeria, Norway, Pakistan, Peru, Philippines, Poland, Portugal, Republic of Korea, Romania, Rwanda, Senegal, Sierra Leone, Singapore, South Africa, Spain, Sri Lanka, Suriname, Sweden, Switzerland, Thailand, Togo, Trinidad and Tobago, Turkey, Uganda, United Kingdom, United Republic of Tanzania, United States, Uruguay, Yugoslavia, Zaire, Zambia, Zimbabwe.

Annex II.   OFFICERS AND OFFICE OF THE GENERAL AGREEMENT ON TARIFFS AND TRADE
   (As at 31 December 1988)

OFFICERS

OFFICERS OF THE CONTRACTING PARTIES*
Chairman of the Contracting Parties: Amir Habib Jamal (United Republic of
   Tanzania).
Vice-Chairman of the Contracting Parties: Janusz Kaczurba (Poland), Marko
   Kosin (Yugoslavia), Olli A. Mennander (Finland).
Chairman of the Council of Representatives: John M. Weekes (Canada).
Chairman of the Committee on Trade and Development: Rubens Ricupero
   (Brazil).

SENIOR OFFICERS OF THE SECRETARIAT
Director-General: Arthur Dunkel.
Deputy Directors-General: Charles R. Carlisle, Madan G. Mathur.

SENIOR OFFICERS OF THE
INTERNATIONAL TRADE CENTRE UNCTAD/GATT
Executive Director: Göran M. Engblom.
Deputy Executive Director: Said T. Harb.

   *Elected at the December 1988 session of Contracting Parties to hold office until the end of the next session.

HEADQUARTERS

GATT Secretariat
Centre William Rappard
154, rue de Lausanne
1211 Geneva 21, Switzerland
   Cable address: GATT GENEVA
   Telephone: (41) (22) 739-51-11
   Telex: 412 324 GATT CH
   Facsimile: (41) (22) 731-42-06

Appendices

Appendix I

Roster of the United Nations

(As at 31 December 1988)

MEMBER	DATE OF ADMISSION	MEMBER	DATE OF ADMISSION	MEMBER	DATE OF ADMISSION
Afghanistan	19 Nov. 1946	German Democratic		Papua New Guinea	10 Oct. 1975
Albania	14 Dec. 1955	Republic	18 Sep. 1973	Paraguay	24 Oct. 1945
Algeria	8 Oct. 1962	Germany, Federal		Peru	31 Oct. 1945
Angola	1 Dec. 1976	Republic of	18 Sep. 1973	Philippines	24 Oct. 1945
Antigua and Barbuda	11 Nov. 1981	Ghana	8 Mar. 1957	Poland	24 Oct. 1945
Argentina	24 Oct. 1945	Greece	25 Oct. 1945	Portugal	14 Dec. 1955
Australia	1 Nov. 1945	Grenada	17 Sep. 1974	Qatar	21 Sep. 1971
Austria	14 Dec. 1955	Guatemala	21 Nov. 1945	Romania	14 Dec. 1955
Bahamas	18 Sep. 1973	Guinea	12 Dec. 1958	Rwanda	18 Sep. 1962
Bahrain	21 Sep. 1971	Guinea-Bissau	17 Sep. 1974	Saint Kitts and Nevis	23 Sep. 1983
Bangladesh	17 Sep. 1974	Guyana	20 Sep. 1966	Saint Lucia	18 Sep. 1979
Barbados	9 Dec. 1966	Haiti	24 Oct. 1945	Saint Vincent and	
Belgium	27 Dec. 1945	Honduras	17 Dec. 1945	the Grenadines	16 Sep. 1980
Belize	25 Sep. 1981	Hungary	14 Dec. 1955	Samoa	15 Dec. 1976
Benin	20 Sep. 1960	Iceland	19 Nov. 1946	Sao Tome and Principe	16 Sep. 1975
Bhutan	21 Sep. 1971	India	30 Oct. 1945	Saudi Arabia	24 Oct. 1945
Bolivia	14 Nov. 1945	Indonesia[2]	28 Sep. 1950	Senegal	28 Sep. 1960
Botswana	17 Oct. 1966	Iran (Islamic		Seychelles	21 Sep. 1976
Brazil	24 Oct. 1945	Republic of)	24 Oct. 1945	Sierra Leone	27 Sep. 1961
Brunei Darussalam	21 Sep. 1984	Iraq	21 Dec. 1945	Singapore[3]	21 Sep. 1965
Bulgaria	14 Dec. 1955	Ireland	14 Dec. 1955	Solomon Islands	19 Sep. 1978
Burkina Faso	20 Sep. 1960	Israel	11 May 1949	Somalia	20 Sep. 1960
Burma	19 Apr. 1948	Italy	14 Dec. 1955	South Africa	7 Nov. 1945
Burundi	18 Sep. 1962	Jamaica	18 Sep. 1962	Spain	14 Dec. 1955
Byelorussian Soviet		Japan	18 Dec. 1956	Sri Lanka	14 Dec. 1955
Socialist Republic	24 Oct. 1945	Jordan	14 Dec. 1955	Sudan	12 Nov. 1956
Cameroon	20 Sep. 1960	Kenya	16 Dec. 1963	Suriname	4 Dec. 1975
Canada	9 Nov. 1945	Kuwait	14 May 1963	Swaziland	24 Sep. 1968
Cape Verde	16 Sep. 1975	Lao People's		Sweden	19 Nov. 1946
Central African		Democratic Republic	14 Dec. 1955	Syrian Arab Republic[1]	24 Oct. 1945
Republic	20 Sep. 1960	Lebanon	24 Oct. 1945	Thailand	16 Dec. 1946
Chad	20 Sep. 1960	Lesotho	17 Oct. 1966	Togo	20 Sep. 1960
Chile	24 Oct. 1945	Liberia	2 Nov. 1945	Trinidad and Tobago	18 Sep. 1962
China	24 Oct. 1945	Libyan Arab		Tunisia	12 Nov. 1956
Colombia	5 Nov. 1945	Jamahiriya	14 Dec. 1955	Turkey	24 Oct. 1945
Comoros	12 Nov. 1975	Luxembourg	24 Oct. 1945	Uganda	25 Oct. 1962
Congo	20 Sep. 1960	Madagascar	20 Sep. 1960	Ukrainian Soviet	
Costa Rica	2 Nov. 1945	Malawi	1 Dec. 1964	Socialist Republic	24 Oct. 1945
Côte d'Ivoire	20 Sep. 1960	Malaysia[3]	17 Sep. 1957	Union of Soviet	
Cuba	24 Oct. 1945	Maldives	21 Sep. 1965	Socialist Republics	24 Oct. 1945
Cyprus	20 Sep. 1960	Mali	28 Sep. 1960	United Arab Emirates	9 Dec. 1971
Czechoslovakia	24 Oct. 1945	Malta	1 Dec. 1964	United Kingdom of	
Democratic Kampuchea	14 Dec. 1955	Mauritania	27 Oct. 1961	Great Britain and	
Democratic Yemen	14 Dec. 1967	Mauritius	24 Apr. 1968	Northern Ireland	24 Oct. 1945
Denmark	24 Oct. 1945	Mexico	7 Nov. 1945	United Republic	
Djibouti	20 Sep. 1977	Mongolia	27 Oct. 1961	of Tanzania[4]	14 Dec. 1961
Dominica	18 Dec. 1978	Morocco	12 Nov. 1956	United States	
Dominican Republic	24 Oct. 1945	Mozambique	16 Sep. 1975	of America	24 Oct. 1945
Ecuador	21 Dec. 1945	Nepal	14 Dec. 1955	Uruguay	18 Dec. 1945
Egypt[1]	24 Oct. 1945	Netherlands	10 Dec. 1945	Vanuatu	15 Sep. 1981
El Salvador	24 Oct. 1945	New Zealand	24 Oct. 1945	Venezuela	15 Nov. 1945
Equatorial Guinea	12 Nov. 1968	Nicaragua	24 Oct. 1945	Viet Nam	20 Sep. 1977
Ethiopia	13 Nov. 1945	Niger	20 Sep. 1960	Yemen	30 Sep. 1947
Fiji	13 Oct. 1970	Nigeria	7 Oct. 1960	Yugoslavia	24 Oct. 1945
Finland	14 Dec. 1955	Norway	27 Nov. 1945	Zaire	20 Sep. 1960
France	24 Oct. 1945	Oman	7 Oct. 1971	Zambia	1 Dec. 1964
Gabon	20 Sep. 1960	Pakistan	30 Sep. 1947	Zimbabwe	25 Aug. 1980
Gambia	21 Sep. 1965	Panama	13 Nov. 1945		

(footnotes on next page)

(footnotes for preceding page)

[1]Egypt and Syria, both of which became Members of the United Nations on 24 October 1945, joined together—following a plebiscite held in those countries on 21 February 1958—to form the United Arab Republic. On 13 October 1961, Syria, having resumed its status as an independent State, also resumed its separate membership in the United Nations; it changed its name to the Syrian Arab Republic on 14 September 1971. The United Arab Republic continued as a Member of the United Nations and reverted to the name of Egypt on 2 September 1971.

[2]On 20 January 1965, Indonesia informed the Secretary-General that it had decided to withdraw from the United Nations. By a telegram of 19 September 1966, it notified the Secretary-General of its decision to resume participation in the activities of the United Nations. On 28 September 1966, the General Assembly took note of that decision and the President invited the representatives of Indonesia to take their seats in the Assembly.

[3]On 16 September 1963, Sabah (North Borneo), Sarawak and Singapore joined with the Federation of Malaya (which became a United Nations Member on 17 September 1957) to form Malaysia. On 9 August 1965, Singapore became an independent State and on 21 September 1965 it became a Member of the United Nations.

[4]Tanganyika was admitted to the United Nations on 14 December 1961, and Zanzibar, on 16 December 1963. Following ratification, on 26 April 1964, of the Articles of Union between Tanganyika and Zanzibar, the two States became represented as a single Member: the United Republic of Tanganyika and Zanzibar; it changed its name to the United Republic of Tanzania on 1 November 1964.

Appendix II

Charter of the United Nations and Statute of the International Court of Justice

Charter of the United Nations

NOTE: The Charter of the United Nations was signed on 26 June 1945, in San Francisco, at the conclusion of the United Nations Conference on International Organization, and came into force on 24 October 1945. The Statute of the International Court of Justice is an integral part of the Charter.

Amendments to Articles 23, 27 and 61 of the Charter were adopted by the General Assembly on 17 December 1963 and came into force on 31 August 1965. A further amendment to Article 61 was adopted by the General Assembly on 20 December 1971, and came into force on 24 September 1973. An amendment to Article 109, adopted by the General Assembly on 20 December 1965, came into force on 12 June 1968.

The amendment to Article 23 enlarges the membership of the Security Council from 11 to 15. The amended Article 27 provides that decisions of the Security Council on procedural matters shall be made by an affirmative vote of nine members (formerly seven) and on all other matters by an affirmative vote of nine members (formerly seven), including the concurring votes of the five permanent members of the Security Council.

The amendment to Article 61, which entered into force on 31 August 1965, enlarged the membership of the Economic and Social Council from 18 to 27. The subsequent amendment to that Article, which entered into force on 24 September 1973, further increased the membership of the Council from 27 to 54.

The amendment to Article 109, which relates to the first paragraph of that Article, provides that a General Conference of Member States for the purpose of reviewing the Charter may be held at a date and place to be fixed by a two-thirds vote of the members of the General Assembly and by a vote of any nine members (formerly seven) of the Security Council. Paragraph 3 of Article 109, which deals with the consideration of a possible review conference during the tenth regular session of the General Assembly, has been retained in its original form in its reference to a ''vote of any seven members of the Security Council'', the paragraph having been acted upon in 1955 by the General Assembly, at its tenth regular session, and by the Security Council.

WE THE PEOPLES
OF THE UNITED NATIONS
DETERMINED
to save succeeding generations from the scourge of war, which twice in our lifetime has brought untold sorrow to mankind, and
to reaffirm faith in fundamental human rights, in the dignity and worth of the human person, in the equal rights of men and women and of nations large and small, and
to establish conditions under which justice and respect for the obligations arising from treaties and other sources of international law can be maintained, and
to promote social progress and better standards of life in larger freedom,

AND FOR THESE ENDS
to practice tolerance and live together in peace with one another as good neighbours, and
to unite our strength to maintain international peace and security, and
to ensure, by the acceptance of principles and the institution of methods, that armed force shall not be used, save in the common interest, and
to employ international machinery for the promotion of the economic and social advancement of all peoples,

HAVE RESOLVED TO
COMBINE OUR EFFORTS TO
ACCOMPLISH THESE AIMS
Accordingly, our respective Governments, through representatives assembled in the city of San Francisco, who have exhibited their full powers found to be in good and due form, have agreed to the present Charter of the United Nations and do hereby establish an international organization to be known as the United Nations.

Chapter I
PURPOSES AND PRINCIPLES

Article 1

The Purposes of the United Nations are:

1. To maintain international peace and security, and to that end: to take effective collective measures for the prevention and removal of threats to the peace, and for the suppression of acts of aggression or other breaches of the peace, and to bring about by peaceful means, and in conformity with the principles of justice and international law, adjustment or settlement of international disputes or situations which might lead to a breach of the peace;

2. To develop friendly relations among nations based on respect for the principle of equal rights and self-determination of peoples, and to take other appropriate measures to strengthen universal peace;

3. To achieve international co-operation in solving international problems of an economic, social, cultural, or humanitarian character, and in promoting and encouraging respect for human rights and for fundamental freedoms for all without distinction as to race, sex, language, or religion; and

4. To be a centre for harmonizing the actions of nations in the attainment of these common ends.

Article 2

The Organization and its Members, in pursuit of the Purposes stated in Article 1, shall act in accordance with the following Principles.

1. The Organization is based on the principle of the sovereign equality of all its Members.

2. All Members, in order to ensure to all of them the rights and benefits resulting from membership, shall fulfil in good faith the obligations assumed by them in accordance with the present Charter.

3. All Members shall settle their international disputes by peaceful means in such a manner that international peace and security, and justice, are not endangered.

4. All Members shall refrain in their international relations from the threat or use of force against the territorial integrity or political independence of any state, or in any other manner inconsistent with the Purposes of the United Nations.

5. All Members shall give the United Nations every assistance in any action it takes in accordance with the present Charter, and shall refrain from giving assistance to any state against which the United Nations is taking preventive or enforcement action.

6. The Organization shall ensure that states which are not Members of the United Nations act in accordance with these Principles so far as may be necessary for the maintenance of international peace and security.

7. Nothing contained in the present Charter shall authorize the United Nations to intervene in matters which are essentially within the domestic jurisdiction of any state or shall require the Members to submit such matters to settlement under the present Charter; but this principle shall not prejudice the application of enforcement measures under Chapter VII.

Chapter II
MEMBERSHIP

Article 3

The original Members of the United Nations shall be the states which, having participated in the United Nations Conference on International Organization at San Francisco, or having previously signed the Declaration by United Nations of 1 January 1942, sign the present Charter and ratify it in accordance with Article 110.

Article 4

1. Membership in the United Nations is open to all other peace-loving states which accept the obligations contained in the present Charter and, in the judgment of the Organization, are able and willing to carry out these obligations.

2. The admission of any such state to membership in the United Nations will be effected by a decision of the General Assembly upon the recommendation of the Security Council.

Article 5

A Member of the United Nations against which preventive or enforcement action has been taken by the Security Council may be suspended from the exercise of the rights and privileges of membership by the General Assembly upon the recommendation of the Security Council. The exercise of these rights and privileges may be restored by the Security Council.

Article 6

A Member of the United Nations which has persistently violated the Principles contained in the present Charter may be expelled from the Organization by the General Assembly upon the recommendation of the Security Council.

Chapter III
ORGANS

Article 7

1. There are established as the principal organs of the United Nations: a General Assembly, a Security Council, an Economic and Social Council, a Trusteeship Council, an International Court of Justice, and a Secretariat.

2. Such subsidiary organs as may be found necessary may be established in accordance with the present Charter.

Article 8

The United Nations shall place no restrictions on the eligibility of men and women to participate in any capacity and under conditions of equality in its principal and subsidiary organs.

Chapter IV
THE GENERAL ASSEMBLY

Composition

Article 9

1. The General Assembly shall consist of all the Members of the United Nations.

2. Each Member shall have not more than five representatives in the General Assembly.

Functions and powers

Article 10

The General Assembly may discuss any questions or any matters within the scope of the present Charter or relating to the powers and functions of any organs provided for in the present Charter, and, except as provided in Article 12, may make recommendations to the Members of the United Nations or to the Security Council or to both on any such questions or matters.

Article 11

1. The General Assembly may consider the general principles of co-operation in the maintenance of international peace and security, including the principles governing disarmament and the regulation of armaments, and may make recommendations with regard to such principles to the Members or to the Security Council or to both.

2. The General Assembly may discuss any questions relating to the maintenance of international peace and security brought before it by any Member of the United Nations, or by the Security Council, or by a state which is not a Member of the United Nations in accordance with Article 35, paragraph 2, and, except as provided in Article 12, may make recommendations with regard to any such questions to the state or states concerned or to the Security Council or to both. Any such question on which action is necessary shall be referred to the Security Council by the General Assembly either before or after discussion.

3. The General Assembly may call the attention of the Security Council to situations which are likely to endanger international peace and security.

4. The powers of the General Assembly set forth in this Article shall not limit the general scope of Article 10.

Article 12

1. While the Security Council is exercising in respect of any dispute or situation the functions assigned to it in the present Charter, the General Assembly shall not make any recommendation with regard to that dispute or situation unless the Security Council so requests.

2. The Secretary-General, with the consent of the Security Council, shall notify the General Assembly at each session of any matters relative to the maintenance of international peace and security which are being dealt with by the Security Council and shall similarly notify the General Assembly, or the Members of the United Nations if the General Assembly is not in session, immediately the Security Council ceases to deal with such matters.

Article 13

1. The General Assembly shall initiate studies and make recommendations for the purpose of:
   a. promoting international co-operation in the political field and encouraging the progressive development of international law and its codification;
   b. promoting international co-operation in the economic, social, cultural, educational, and health fields, and assisting in the realization of human rights and fundamental freedoms for all without distinction as to race, sex, language, or religion.

2. The further responsibilities, functions and powers of the General Assembly with respect to matters mentioned in paragraph 1(b) above are set forth in Chapters IX and X.

Article 14

Subject to the provisions of Article 12, the General Assembly may recommend measures for the peaceful adjustment of any situation, regardless of origin, which it deems likely to impair the general welfare or friendly relations among nations, including situations resulting from a violation of the provisions of the present Charter setting forth the Purposes and Principles of the United Nations.

Article 15

1. The General Assembly shall receive and consider annual and special reports from the Security Council; these reports shall include an account of the measures that the Security Council has decided upon or taken to maintain international peace and security.
2. The General Assembly shall receive and consider reports from the other organs of the United Nations.

Article 16

The General Assembly shall perform such functions with respect to the international trusteeship system as are assigned to it under Chapters XII and XIII, including the approval of the trusteeship agreements for areas not designated as strategic.

Article 17

1. The General Assembly shall consider and approve the budget of the Organization.
2. The expenses of the Organization shall be borne by the Members as apportioned by the General Assembly.
3. The General Assembly shall consider and approve any financial and budgetary arrangements with specialized agencies referred to in Article 57 and shall examine the administrative budgets of such specialized agencies with a view to making recommendations to the agencies concerned.

Voting

Article 18

1. Each member of the General Assembly shall have one vote.
2. Decisions of the General Assembly on important questions shall be made by a two-thirds majority of the members present and voting. These questions shall include: recommendations with respect to the maintenance of international peace and security, the election of the non-permanent members of the Security Council, the election of the members of the Economic and Social Council, the election of members of the Trusteeship Council in accordance with paragraph 1(c) of Article 86, the admission of new Members to the United Nations, the suspension of the rights and privileges of membership, the expulsion of Members, questions relating to the operation of the trusteeship system, and budgetary questions.
3. Decisions on other questions, including the determination of additional categories of questions to be decided by a two-thirds majority, shall be made by a majority of the members present and voting.

Article 19

A Member of the United Nations which is in arrears in the payment of its financial contributions to the Organization shall have no vote in the General Assembly if the amount of its arrears equals or exceeds the amount of the contributions due from it for the preceding two full years. The General Assembly may, nevertheless, permit such a Member to vote if it is satisfied that the failure to pay is due to conditions beyond the control of the Member.

Procedure

Article 20

The General Assembly shall meet in regular annual sessions and in such special sessions as occasion may require. Special sessions shall be convoked by the Secretary-General at the request of the Security Council or of a majority of the Members of the United Nations.

Article 21

The General Assembly shall adopt its own rules of procedure. It shall elect its President for each session.

Article 22

The General Assembly may establish such subsidiary organs as it deems necessary for the performance of its functions.

Chapter V
THE SECURITY COUNCIL

Composition

Article 23[1]

1. The Security Council shall consist of fifteen Members of the United Nations. The Republic of China, France, the Union of Soviet Socialist Republics, the United Kingdom of Great Britain and Northern Ireland, and the United States of America shall be permanent members of the Security Council. The General Assembly shall elect ten other Members of the United Nations to be non-permanent members of the Security Council, due regard being specially paid, in the first instance to the contribution of Members of the United Nations to the maintenance of international peace and security and to the other purposes of the Organization, and also to equitable geographical distribution.
2. The non-permanent members of the Security Council shall be elected for a term of two years. In the first election of the non-permanent members after the increase of the membership of the Security Council from eleven to fifteen, two of the four additional members shall be chosen for a term of one year. A retiring member shall not be eligible for immediate re-election.
3. Each member of the Security Council shall have one representative.

Functions and powers

Article 24

1. In order to ensure prompt and effective action by the United Nations, its Members confer on the Security Council primary responsibility for the maintenance of international peace and security, and agree that in carrying out its duties under this responsibility the Security Council acts on their behalf.
2. In discharging these duties the Security Council shall act in accordance with the Purposes and Principles of the United Nations. The specific powers granted to the Security Council for the discharge of these duties are laid down in Chapters VI, VII, VIII, and XII.
3. The Security Council shall submit annual and, when necessary, special reports to the General Assembly for its consideration.

Article 25

The Members of the United Nations agree to accept and carry out the decisions of the Security Council in accordance with the present Charter.

Article 26

In order to promote the establishment and maintenance of international peace and security with the least diversion for armaments of the world's human and economic resources, the Security Council shall be responsible for formulating, with the

---

[1]Amended text of Article 23, which came into force on 31 August 1965. (The text of Article 23 before it was amended read as follows:

1. The Security Council shall consist of eleven Members of the United Nations. The Republic of China, France, the Union of Soviet Socialist Republics, the United Kingdom of Great Britain and Northern Ireland, and the United States of America shall be permanent members of the Security Council. The General Assembly shall elect six other Members of the United Nations to be non-permanent members of the Security Council, due regard being specially paid, in the first instance to the contribution of Members of the United Nations to the maintenance of international peace and security and to the other purposes of the Organization, and also to equitable geographical distribution.

2. The non-permanent members of the Security Council shall be elected for a term of two years. In the first election of non-permanent members, however, three shall be chosen for a term of one year. A retiring member shall not be eligible for immediate re-election.

3. Each member of the Security Council shall have one representative.)

assistance of the Military Staff Committee referred to in Article 47, plans to be submitted to the Members of the United Nations for the establishment of a system for the regulation of armaments.

Voting

Article 27 [2]

1. Each member of the Security Council shall have one vote.
2. Decisions of the Security Council on procedural matters shall be made by an affirmative vote of nine members.
3. Decisions of the Security Council on all other matters shall be made by an affirmative vote of nine members including the concurring votes of the permanent members; provided that, in decisions under Chapter VI, and under paragraph 3 of Article 52, a party to a dispute shall abstain from voting.

Procedure

Article 28

1. The Security Council shall be so organized as to be able to function continuously. Each member of the Security Council shall for this purpose be represented at all times at the seat of the Organization.
2. The Security Council shall hold periodic meetings at which each of its members may, if it so desires, be represented by a member of the government or by some other specially designated representative.
3. The Security Council may hold meetings at such places other than the seat of the Organization as in its judgment will best facilitate its work.

Article 29

The Security Council may establish such subsidiary organs as it deems necessary for the performance of its functions.

Article 30

The Security Council shall adopt its own rules of procedure, including the method of selecting its President.

Article 31

Any Member of the United Nations which is not a member of the Security Council may participate, without vote, in the discussion of any question brought before the Security Council whenever the latter considers that the interests of that Member are specially affected.

Article 32

Any Member of the United Nations which is not a member of the Security Council or any state which is not a Member of the United Nations, if it is a party to a dispute under consideration by the Security Council, shall be invited to participate, without vote, in the discussion relating to the dispute. The Security Council shall lay down such conditions as it deems just for the participation of a state which is not a Member of the United Nations.

Chapter VI
PACIFIC SETTLEMENT OF DISPUTES

Article 33

1. The parties to any dispute, the continuance of which is likely to endanger the maintenance of international peace and security, shall, first of all, seek a solution by negotiation, enquiry, mediation, conciliation, arbitration, judicial settlement, resort to regional agencies or arrangements, or other peaceful means of their own choice.
2. The Security Council shall, when it deems necessary, call upon the parties to settle their dispute by such means.

Article 34

The Security Council may investigate any dispute or any situation which might lead to international friction or give rise to a dispute, in order to determine whether the continuance of the dispute or situation is likely to endanger the maintenance of international peace and security.

Article 35

1. Any Member of the United Nations may bring any dispute, or any situation of the nature referred to in Article 34, to the attention of the Security Council or of the General Assembly.
2. A state which is not a Member of the United Nations may bring to the attention of the Security Council or of the General Assembly any dispute to which it is a party if it accepts in advance, for the purposes of the dispute, the obligations of pacific settlement provided in the present Charter.
3. The proceedings of the General Assembly in respect of matters brought to its attention under this Article will be subject to the provisions of Articles 11 and 12.

Article 36

1. The Security Council may, at any stage of a dispute of the nature referred to in Article 33 or of a situation of like nature, recommend appropriate procedures or methods of adjustment.
2. The Security Council should take into consideration any procedures for the settlement of the dispute which have already been adopted by the parties.
3. In making recommendations under this Article the Security Council should also take into consideration that legal disputes should as a general rule be referred by the parties to the International Court of Justice in accordance with the provisions of the Statute of the Court.

Article 37

1. Should the parties to a dispute of the nature referred to in Article 33 fail to settle it by the means indicated in that Article, they shall refer it to the Security Council.
2. If the Security Council deems that the continuance of the dispute is in fact likely to endanger the maintenance of international peace and security, it shall decide whether to take action under Article 36 or to recommend such terms of settlement as it may consider appropriate.

Article 38

Without prejudice to the provisions of Articles 33 to 37, the Security Council may, if all the parties to any dispute so request, make recommendations to the parties with a view to a pacific settlement of the dispute.

Chapter VII
ACTION WITH RESPECT TO THREATS TO THE PEACE, BREACHES OF THE PEACE, AND ACTS OF AGGRESSION

Article 39

The Security Council shall determine the existence of any threat to the peace, breach of the peace, or act of aggression and shall make recommendations, or decide what measures shall be taken in accordance with Articles 41 and 42, to maintain or restore international peace and security.

Article 40

In order to prevent an aggravation of the situation, the Security Council may, before making the recommendations or deciding upon the measures provided for in Article 39, call upon the parties concerned to comply with such provisional measures as it deems necessary or desirable. Such provisional measures shall be without prejudice to the rights, claims, or position of the parties concerned. The Security Council shall duly take account of failure to comply with such provisional measures.

---

[2]Amended text of Article 27, which came into force on 31 August 1965. (The text of Article 27 before it was amended read as follows:

1. Each member of the Security Council shall have one vote.
2. Decisions of the Security Council on procedural matters shall be made by an affirmative vote of seven members.
3. Decisions of the Security Council on all other matters shall be made by an affirmative vote of seven members including the concurring votes of the permanent members; provided that, in decisions under Chapter VI, and under paragraph 3 of Article 52, a party to a dispute shall abstain from voting.)

Article 41

The Security Council may decide what measures not involving the use of armed force are to be employed to give effect to its decisions, and it may call upon the Members of the United Nations to apply such measures. These may include complete or partial interruption of economic relations and of rail, sea, air, postal, telegraphic, radio, and other means of communication, and the severance of diplomatic relations.

Article 42

Should the Security Council consider that measures provided for in Article 41 would be inadequate or have proved to be inadequate, it may take such action by air, sea, or land forces as may be necessary to maintain or restore international peace and security. Such action may include demonstrations, blockade, and other operations by air, sea, or land forces of Members of the United Nations.

Article 43

1. All Members of the United Nations, in order to contribute to the maintenance of international peace and security, undertake to make available to the Security Council, on its call and in accordance with a special agreement or agreements, armed forces, assistance, and facilities, including rights of passage, necessary for the purpose of maintaining international peace and security.
2. Such agreement or agreements shall govern the numbers and types of forces, their degree of readiness and general location, and the nature of the facilities and assistance to be provided.
3. The agreement or agreements shall be negotiated as soon as possible on the initiative of the Security Council. They shall be concluded between the Security Council and Members or between the Security Council and groups of Members and shall be subject to ratification by the signatory states in accordance with their respective constitutional processes.

Article 44

When the Security Council has decided to use force it shall, before calling upon a Member not represented on it to provide armed forces in fulfilment of the obligations assumed under Article 43, invite that Member, if the Member so desires, to participate in the decisions of the Security Council concerning the employment of contingents of that Member's armed forces.

Article 45

In order to enable the United Nations to take urgent military measures, Members shall hold immediately available national airforce contingents for combined international enforcement action. The strength and degree of readiness of these contingents and plans for their combined action shall be determined, within the limits laid down in the special agreement or agreements referred to in Article 43, by the Security Council with the assistance of the Military Staff Committee.

Article 46

Plans for the application of armed force shall be made by the Security Council with the assistance of the Military Staff Committee.

Article 47

1. There shall be established a Military Staff Committee to advise and assist the Security Council on all questions relating to the Security Council's military requirements for the maintenance of international peace and security, the employment and command of forces placed at its disposal, the regulation of armaments, and possible disarmament.
2. The Military Staff Committee shall consist of the Chiefs of Staff of the permanent members of the Security Council or their representatives. Any Member of the United Nations not permanently represented on the Committee shall be invited by the Committee to be associated with it when the efficient discharge of the Committee's responsibilities requires the participation of that Member in its work.
3. The Military Staff Committee shall be responsible under the Security Council for the strategic direction of any armed forces placed at the disposal of the Security Council. Questions relating to the command of such forces shall be worked out subsequently.
4. The Military Staff Committee, with the authorization of the Security Council and after consultation with appropriate regional agencies, may establish regional sub-committees.

Article 48

1. The action required to carry out the decisions of the Security Council for the maintenance of international peace and security shall be taken by all the Members of the United Nations or by some of them, as the Security Council may determine.
2. Such decisions shall be carried out by the Members of the United Nations directly and through their action in the appropriate international agencies of which they are members.

Article 49

The Members of the United Nations shall join in affording mutual assistance in carrying out the measures decided upon by the Security Council.

Article 50

If preventive or enforcement measures against any state are taken by the Security Council, any other state, whether a Member of the United Nations or not, which finds itself confronted with special economic problems arising from the carrying out of those measures shall have the right to consult the Security Council with regard to a solution of those problems.

Article 51

Nothing in the present Charter shall impair the inherent right of individual or collective self-defence if an armed attack occurs against a Member of the United Nations, until the Security Council has taken measures necessary to maintain international peace and security. Measures taken by Members in the exercise of this right of self-defence shall be immediately reported to the Security Council and shall not in any way affect the authority and responsibility of the Security Council under the present Charter to take at any time such action as it deems necessary in order to maintain or restore international peace and security.

Chapter VIII
REGIONAL ARRANGEMENTS

Article 52

1. Nothing in the present Charter precludes the existence of regional arrangements or agencies for dealing with such matters relating to the maintenance of international peace and security as are appropriate for regional action, provided that such arrangements or agencies and their activities are consistent with the Purposes and Principles of the United Nations.
2. The Members of the United Nations entering into such arrangements or constituting such agencies shall make every effort to achieve pacific settlement of local disputes through such regional arrangements or by such regional agencies before referring them to the Security Council.
3. The Security Council shall encourage the development of pacific settlement of local disputes through such regional arrangements or by such regional agencies either on the initiative of the states concerned or by reference from the Security Council.
4. This Article in no way impairs the application of Articles 34 and 35.

Article 53

1. The Security Council shall, where appropriate, utilize such regional arrangements or agencies for enforcement action under its authority. But no enforcement action shall be taken under regional arrangements or by regional agencies without the authorization of the Security Council, with the exception of measures against any enemy state, as defined in paragraph 2 of this Article, provided for pursuant to Article 107 or in regional arrangements directed against renewal of aggressive policy on the part of any such state, until such time as the Organization may, on request of the Governments concerned, be charged with the responsibility for preventing further aggression by such a state.

2. The term enemy state as used in paragraph 1 of this Article applies to any state which during the Second World War has been an enemy of any signatory of the present Charter.

Article 54

The Security Council shall at all times be kept fully informed of activities undertaken or in contemplation under regional arrangements or by regional agencies for the maintenance of international peace and security.

Chapter IX
INTERNATIONAL ECONOMIC AND SOCIAL CO-OPERATION

Article 55

With a view to the creation of conditions of stability and well-being which are necessary for peaceful and friendly relations among nations based on respect for the principle of equal rights and self-determination of peoples, the United Nations shall promote:

a. higher standards of living, full employment, and conditions of economic and social progress and development;
b. solutions of international economic, social, health, and related problems; and international cultural and educational co-operation; and
c. universal respect for, and observance of, human rights and fundamental freedoms for all without distinction as to race, sex, language, or religion.

Article 56

All Members pledge themselves to take joint and separate action in co-operation with the Organization for the achievement of the purposes set forth in Article 55.

Article 57

1. The various specialized agencies, established by intergovernmental agreement and having wide international responsibilities, as defined in their basic instruments, in economic, social, cultural, educational, health, and related fields, shall be brought into relationship with the United Nations in accordance with the provisions of Article 63.

2. Such agencies thus brought into relationship with the United Nations are hereinafter referred to as specialized agencies.

Article 58

The Organization shall make recommendations for the co-ordination of the policies and activities of the specialized agencies.

Article 59

The Organization shall, where appropriate, initiate negotiations among the states concerned for the creation of any new specialized agencies required for the accomplishment of the purposes set forth in Article 55.

Article 60

Responsibility for the discharge of the functions of the Organization set forth in this Chapter shall be vested in the General Assembly and, under the authority of the General Assembly, in the Economic and Social Council, which shall have for this purpose the powers set forth in Chapter X.

Chapter X
THE ECONOMIC AND SOCIAL COUNCIL

Composition

Article 61[3]

1. The Economic and Social Council shall consist of fifty-four Members of the United Nations elected by the General Assembly.

2. Subject to the provisions of paragraph 3, eighteen members of the Economic and Social Council shall be elected each year for a term of three years. A retiring member shall be eligible for immediate re-election.

3. At the first election after the increase in the membership of the Economic and Social Council from twenty-seven to fifty-

four members, in addition to the members elected in place of the nine members whose term of office expires at the end of that year, twenty-seven additional members shall be elected. Of these twenty-seven additional members, the term of office of nine members so elected shall expire at the end of one year, and of nine other members at the end of two years, in accordance with arrangements made by the General Assembly.

4. Each member of the Economic and Social Council shall have one representative.

Functions and powers

Article 62

1. The Economic and Social Council may make or initiate studies and reports with respect to international economic, social, cultural, educational, health, and related matters and may make recommendations with respect to any such matters to the General Assembly, to the Members of the United Nations, and to the specialized agencies concerned.

2. It may make recommendations for the purpose of promoting respect for, and observance of, human rights and fundamental freedoms for all.

3. It may prepare draft conventions for submission to the General Assembly, with respect to matters falling within its competence.

4. It may call, in accordance with the rules prescribed by the United Nations, international conferences on matters falling within its competence.

Article 63

1. The Economic and Social Council may enter into agreements with any of the agencies referred to in Article 57, defining the terms on which the agency concerned shall be brought into relationship with the United Nations. Such agreements shall be subject to approval by the General Assembly.

2. It may co-ordinate the activities of the specialized agencies through consultation with and recommendations to such agencies and through recommendations to the General Assembly and to the Members of the United Nations.

Article 64

1. The Economic and Social Council may take appropriate steps to obtain regular reports from the specialized agencies. It may make arrangements with the Members of the United Nations and with the specialized agencies to obtain reports on the steps taken to give effect to its own recommendations and to recommendations on matters falling within its competence made by the General Assembly.

2. It may communicate its observations on these reports to the General Assembly.

Article 65

The Economic and Social Council may furnish information to the Security Council and shall assist the Security Council upon its request.

Article 66

1. The Economic and Social Council shall perform such functions as fall within its competence in connexion with the carrying out of the recommendations of the General Assembly.

---

[3]Amended text of Article 61, which came into force on 24 September 1973. (The text of Article 61 as previously amended on 31 August 1965 read as follows:

1. The Economic and Social Council shall consist of twenty-seven Members of the United Nations elected by the General Assembly.

2. Subject to the provisions of paragraph 3, nine members of the Economic and Social Council shall be elected each year for a term of three years. A retiring member shall be eligible for immediate re-election.

3. At the first election after the increase in the membership of the Economic and Social Council from eighteen to twenty-seven members, in addition to the members elected in place of the six members whose term of office expires at the end of that year, nine additional members shall be elected. Of these nine additional members, the term of office of three members so elected shall expire at the end of one year, and of three other members at the end of two years, in accordance with arrangements made by the General Assembly.

4. Each member of the Economic and Social Council shall have one representative.)

2. It may, with the approval of the General Assembly, perform services at the request of Members of the United Nations and at the request of specialized agencies.

3. It shall perform such other functions as are specified elsewhere in the present Charter or as may be assigned to it by the General Assembly.

Voting

Article 67

1. Each member of the Economic and Social Council shall have one vote.

2. Decisions of the Economic and Social Council shall be made by a majority of the members present and voting.

Procedure

Article 68

The Economic and Social Council shall set up commissions in economic and social fields and for the promotion of human rights, and such other commissions as may be required for the performance of its functions.

Article 69

The Economic and Social Council shall invite any Member of the United Nations to participate, without vote, in its deliberations on any matter of particular concern to that Member.

Article 70

The Economic and Social Council may make arrangements for representatives of the specialized agencies to participate, without vote, in its deliberations and in those of the commissions established by it, and for its representatives to participate in the deliberations of the specialized agencies.

Article 71

The Economic and Social Council may make suitable arrangements for consultation with non-governmental organizations which are concerned with matters within its competence. Such arrangements may be made with international organizations and, where appropriate, with national organizations after consultation with the Member of the United Nations concerned.

Article 72

1. The Economic and Social Council shall adopt its own rules of procedure, including the method of selecting its President.

2. The Economic and Social Council shall meet as required in accordance with its rules, which shall include provision for the convening of meetings on the request of a majority of its members.

Chapter XI
DECLARATION REGARDING
NON-SELF-GOVERNING TERRITORIES

Article 73

Members of the United Nations which have or assume responsibilities for the administration of territories whose peoples have not yet attained a full measure of self-government recognize the principle that the interests of the inhabitants of these territories are paramount, and accept as a sacred trust the obligation to promote to the utmost, within the system of international peace and security established by the present Charter, the well-being of the inhabitants of these territories, and, to this end:

a. to ensure, with due respect for the culture of the peoples concerned, their political, economic, social, and educational advancement, their just treatment, and their protection against abuses;

b. to develop self-government, to take due account of the political aspirations of the peoples, and to assist them in the progressive development of their free political institutions, according to the particular circumstances of each territory and its peoples and their varying stages of advancement;

c. to further international peace and security;

d. to promote constructive measures of development, to encourage research, and to co-operate with one another and,

when and where appropriate, with specialized international bodies with a view to the practical achievement of the social, economic, and scientific purposes set forth in this Article; and

e. to transmit regularly to the Secretary-General for information purposes, subject to such limitation as security and constitutional considerations may require, statistical and other information of a technical nature relating to economic, social, and educational conditions in the territories for which they are respectively responsible other than those territories to which Chapters XII and XIII apply.

Article 74

Members of the United Nations also agree that their policy in respect of the territories to which this Chapter applies, no less than in respect of their metropolitan areas, must be based on the general principle of good-neighbourliness, due account being taken of the interests and well-being of the rest of the world, in social, economic, and commercial matters.

Chapter XII
INTERNATIONAL TRUSTEESHIP SYSTEM

Article 75

The United Nations shall establish under its authority an international trusteeship system for the administration and supervision of such territories as may be placed thereunder by subsequent individual agreements. These territories are hereinafter referred to as trust territories.

Article 76

The basic objectives of the trusteeship system, in accordance with the Purposes of the United Nations laid down in Article 1 of the present Charter, shall be:

a. to further international peace and security;

b. to promote the political, economic, social, and educational advancement of the inhabitants of the trust territories, and their progressive development towards self-government or independence as may be appropriate to the particular circumstances of each territory and its peoples and the freely expressed wishes of the peoples concerned, and as may be provided by the terms of each trusteeship agreement;

c. to encourage respect for human rights and for fundamental freedoms for all without distinction as to race, sex, language, or religion, and to encourage recognition of the interdependence of the peoples of the world; and

d. to ensure equal treatment in social, economic, and commercial matters for all Members of the United Nations and their nationals, and also equal treatment for the latter in the administration of justice, without prejudice to the attainment of the foregoing objectives and subject to the provisions of Article 80.

Article 77

1. The trusteeship system shall apply to such territories in the following categories as may be placed thereunder by means of trusteeship agreements:

a. territories now held under mandate;

b. territories which may be detached from enemy states as a result of the Second World War; and

c. territories voluntarily placed under the system by states responsible for their administration.

2. It will be a matter for subsequent agreement as to which territories in the foregoing categories will be brought under the trusteeship system and upon what terms.

Article 78

The trusteeship system shall not apply to territories which have become Members of the United Nations, relationship among which shall be based on respect for the principle of sovereign equality.

Article 79

The terms of trusteeship for each territory to be placed under the trusteeship system, including any alteration or amendment, shall be agreed upon by the states directly concerned, including the mandatory power in the case of territories held under mandate by a Member of the United Nations, and shall be approved as provided for in Articles 83 and 85.

Article 80

1. Except as may be agreed upon in individual trusteeship agreements, made under Articles 77, 79, and 81, placing each territory under the trusteeship system, and until such agreements have been concluded, nothing in this Chapter shall be construed in or of itself to alter in any manner the rights whatsoever of any states or any peoples or the terms of existing international instruments to which Members of the United Nations may respectively be parties.

2. Paragraph 1 of this Article shall not be interpreted as giving grounds for delay or postponement of the negotiation and conclusion of agreements for placing mandated and other territories under the trusteeship system as provided for in Article 77.

Article 81

The trusteeship agreement shall in each case include the terms under which the trust territory will be administered and designate the authority which will exercise the administration of the trust territory. Such authority, hereinafter called the administering authority, may be one or more states or the Organization itself.

Article 82

There may be designated, in any trusteeship agreement, a strategic area or areas which may include part or all of the trust territory to which the agreement applies, without prejudice to any special agreement or agreements made under Article 43.

Article 83

1. All functions of the United Nations relating to strategic areas, including the approval of the terms of the trusteeship agreements and of their alteration or amendments, shall be exercised by the Security Council.

2. The basic objectives set forth in Article 76 shall be applicable to the people of each strategic area.

3. The Security Council shall, subject to the provisions of the trusteeship agreements and without prejudice to security considerations, avail itself of the assistance of the Trusteeship Council to perform those functions of the United Nations under the trusteeship system relating to political, economic, social, and educational matters in the strategic areas.

Article 84

It shall be the duty of the administering authority to ensure that the trust territory shall play its part in the maintenance of international peace and security. To this end the administering authority may make use of volunteer forces, facilities, and assistance from the trust territory in carrying out the obligations towards the Security Council undertaken in this regard by the administering authority, as well as for local defence and the maintenance of law and order within the trust territory.

Article 85

1. The functions of the United Nations with regard to trusteeship agreements for all areas not designated as strategic, including the approval of the terms of the trusteeship agreements and of their alteration or amendment, shall be exercised by the General Assembly.

2. The Trusteeship Council, operating under the authority of the General Assembly, shall assist the General Assembly in carrying out these functions.

Chapter XIII
THE TRUSTEESHIP COUNCIL

Composition

Article 86

1. The Trusteeship Council shall consist of the following Members of the United Nations:

a. those Members administering trust territories;
b. such of those Members mentioned by name in Article 23 as are not administering trust territories; and
c. as many other Members elected for three-year terms by the General Assembly as may be necessary to ensure that the total number of members of the Trusteeship Council is equally divided between those Members of the United Nations which administer trust territories and those which do not.

2. Each member of the Trusteeship Council shall designate one specially qualified person to represent it therein.

Functions and powers

Article 87

The General Assembly and, under its authority, the Trusteeship Council, in carrying out their functions, may:

a. consider reports submitted by the administering authority;
b. accept petitions and examine them in consultation with the administering authority;
c. provide for periodic visits to the respective trust territories at times agreed upon with the administering authority; and
d. take these and other actions in conformity with the terms of the trusteeship agreements.

Article 88

The Trusteeship Council shall formulate a questionnaire on the political, economic, social, and educational advancement of the inhabitants of each trust territory, and the administering authority for each trust territory within the competence of the General Assembly shall make an annual report to the General Assembly upon the basis of such questionnaire.

Voting

Article 89

1. Each member of the Trusteeship Council shall have one vote.

2. Decisions of the Trusteeship Council shall be made by a majority of the members present and voting.

Procedure

Article 90

1. The Trusteeship Council shall adopt its own rules of procedure, including the method of selecting its President.

2. The Trusteeship Council shall meet as required in accordance with its rules, which shall include provision for the convening of meetings on the request of a majority of its members.

Article 91

The Trusteeship Council shall, when appropriate, avail itself of the assistance of the Economic and Social Council and of the specialized agencies in regard to matters with which they are respectively concerned.

Chapter XIV
THE INTERNATIONAL COURT OF JUSTICE

Article 92

The International Court of Justice shall be the principal judicial organ of the United Nations. It shall function in accordance with the annexed Statute, which is based upon the Statute of the Permanent Court of International Justice and forms an integral part of the present Charter.

Article 93

1. All Members of the United Nations are *ipso facto* parties to the Statute of the International Court of Justice.

2. A state which is not a Member of the United Nations may become a party to the Statute of the International Court of Justice on conditions to be determined in each case by the General Assembly upon the recommendation of the Security Council.

Article 94

1. Each Member of the United Nations undertakes to comply with the decision of the International Court of Justice in any case to which it is a party.

2. If any party to a case fails to perform the obligations incumbent upon it under a judgment rendered by the Court, the other party may have recourse to the Security Council, which may, if it deems necessary, make recommendations or decide upon measures to be taken to give effect to the judgment.

Article 95

Nothing in the present Charter shall prevent Members of the United Nations from entrusting the solution of their differences to other tribunals by virtue of agreements already in existence or which may be concluded in the future.

Article 96

1. The General Assembly or the Security Council may request the International Court of Justice to give an advisory opinion on any legal question.

2. Other organs of the United Nations and specialized agencies, which may at any time be so authorized by the General Assembly, may also request advisory opinions of the Court on legal questions arising within the scope of their activities.

Chapter XV
THE SECRETARIAT

Article 97

The Secretariat shall comprise a Secretary-General and such staff as the Organization may require. The Secretary-General shall be appointed by the General Assembly upon the recommendation of the Security Council. He shall be the chief administrative officer of the Organization.

Article 98

The Secretary-General shall act in that capacity in all meetings of the General Assembly, of the Security Council, of the Economic and Social Council, and of the Trusteeship Council, and shall perform such other functions as are entrusted to him by these organs. The Secretary-General shall make an annual report to the General Assembly on the work of the Organization.

Article 99

The Secretary-General may bring to the attention of the Security Council any matter which in his opinion may threaten the maintenance of international peace and security.

Article 100

1. In the performance of their duties the Secretary-General and the staff shall not seek or receive instructions from any government or from any other authority external to the Organization. They shall refrain from any action which might reflect on their position as international officials responsible only to the Organization.

2. Each Member of the United Nations undertakes to respect the exclusively international character of the responsibilities of the Secretary-General and the staff and not to seek to influence them in the discharge of their responsibilities.

Article 101

1. The staff shall be appointed by the Secretary-General under regulations established by the General Assembly.

2. Appropriate staffs shall be permanently assigned to the Economic and Social Council, the Trusteeship Council, and, as required, to other organs of the United Nations. These staffs shall form a part of the Secretariat.

3. The paramount consideration in the employment of the staff and in the determination of the conditions of service shall be the necessity of securing the highest standards of efficiency, competence, and integrity. Due regard shall be paid to the importance of recruiting the staff on as wide a geographical basis as possible.

Chapter XVI
MISCELLANEOUS PROVISIONS

Article 102

1. Every treaty and every international agreement entered into by any Member of the United Nations after the present Charter comes into force shall as soon as possible be registered with the Secretariat and published by it.

2. No party to any such treaty or international agreement which has not been registered in accordance with the provisions of paragraph 1 of this Article may invoke that treaty or agreement before any organ of the United Nations.

Article 103

In the event of a conflict between the obligations of the Members of the United Nations under the present Charter and their obligations under any other international agreement, their obligations under the present Charter shall prevail.

Article 104

The Organization shall enjoy in the territory of each of its Members such legal capacity as may be necessary for the exercise of its functions and the fulfilment of its purposes.

Article 105

1. The Organization shall enjoy in the territory of each of its Members such privileges and immunities as are necessary for the fulfilment of its purposes.

2. Representatives of the Members of the United Nations and officials of the Organization shall similarly enjoy such privileges and immunities as are necessary for the independent exercise of their functions in connexion with the Organization.

3. The General Assembly may make recommendations with a view to determining the details of the application of paragraphs 1 and 2 of this Article or may propose conventions to the Members of the United Nations for this purpose.

Chapter XVII
TRANSITIONAL SECURITY ARRANGEMENTS

Article 106

Pending the coming into force of such special agreements referred to in Article 43 as in the opinion of the Security Council enable it to begin the exercise of its responsibilities under Article 42, the parties to the Four-Nation Declaration, signed at Moscow, 30 October 1943, and France, shall, in accordance with the provisions of paragraph 5 of that Declaration, consult with one another and as occasion requires with other Members of the United Nations with a view to such joint action on behalf of the Organization as may be necessary for the purpose of maintaining international peace and security.

Article 107

Nothing in the present Charter shall invalidate or preclude action, in relation to any state which during the Second World War has been an enemy of any signatory to the present Charter, taken or authorized as a result of that war by the Governments having responsibility for such action.

Chapter XVIII
AMENDMENTS

Article 108

Amendments to the present Charter shall come into force for all Members of the United Nations when they have been adopted by a vote of two thirds of the members of the General Assembly and ratified in accordance with their respective constitutional processes by two thirds of the Members of the United Nations, including all the permanent members of the Security Council.

Article 109 [4]

1.   A General Conference of the Members of the United Nations for the purpose of reviewing the present Charter may be held at a date and place to be fixed by a two-thirds vote of the members of the General Assembly and by a vote of any nine members of the Security Council. Each Member of the United Nations shall have one vote in the conference.

2.   Any alteration of the present Charter recommended by a two-thirds vote of the conference shall take effect when ratified in accordance with their respective constitutional processes by two thirds of the Members of the United Nations including all the permanent members of the Security Council.

3.   If such a conference has not been held before the tenth annual session of the General Assembly following the coming into force of the present Charter, the proposal to call such a conference shall be placed on the agenda of that session of the General Assembly, and the conference shall be held if so decided by a majority vote of the members of the General Assembly and by a vote of any seven members of the Security Council.

Chapter XIX
RATIFICATION AND SIGNATURE

Article 110

1.   The present Charter shall be ratified by the signatory states in accordance with their respective constitutional processes.

2.   The ratifications shall be deposited with the Government of the United States of America, which shall notify all the signatory states of each deposit as well as the Secretary-General of the Organization when he has been appointed.

3.   The present Charter shall come into force upon the deposit of ratifications by the Republic of China, France, the Union of Soviet Socialist Republics, the United Kingdom of Great Britain and Northern Ireland, and the United States of America, and by a majority of the other signatory states. A protocol of the ratifications deposited shall thereupon be drawn up by the Government of the United States

of America which shall communicate copies thereof to all the signatory states.

4.   The states signatory to the present Charter which ratify it after it has come into force will become original Members of the United Nations on the date of the deposit of their respective ratifications.

Article 111

The present Charter, of which the Chinese, French, Russian, English, and Spanish texts are equally authentic, shall remain deposited in the archives of the Government of the United States of America. Duly certified copies thereof shall be transmitted by that Government to the Governments of the other signatory states.

IN FAITH WHEREOF the representatives of the Governments of the United Nations have signed the present Charter.

DONE at the city of San Francisco the twenty-sixth day of June, one thousand nine hundred and forty-five.

---

[4]Amended text of Article 109, which came into force on 12 June 1968. (The text of Article 109 before it was amended read as follows:

1.   A General Conference of the Members of the United Nations for the purpose of reviewing the present Charter may be held at a date and place to be fixed by a two-thirds vote of the members of the General Assembly and by a vote of any seven members of the Security Council. Each Member of the United Nations shall have one vote in the conference.

2.   Any alteration of the present Charter recommended by a two-thirds vote of the conference shall take effect when ratified in accordance with their respective constitutional processes by two thirds of the Members of the United Nations including all the permanent members of the Security Council.

3.   If such a conference has not been held before the tenth annual session of the General Assembly following the coming into force of the present Charter, the proposal to call such a conference shall be placed on the agenda of that session of the General Assembly, and the conference shall be held if so decided by a majority vote of the members of the General Assembly and by a vote of any seven members of the Security Council.)

Statute of the International Court of Justice

Article 1

THE INTERNATIONAL COURT OF JUSTICE established by the Charter of the United Nations as the principal judicial organ of the United Nations shall be constituted and shall function in accordance with the provisions of the present Statute.

Chapter I
ORGANIZATION OF THE COURT

Article 2

The Court shall be composed of a body of independent judges, elected regardless of their nationality from among persons of high moral character, who possess the qualifications required in their respective countries for appointment to the highest judicial offices, or are jurisconsults of recognized competence in international law.

Article 3

1.   The Court shall consist of fifteen members, no two of whom may be nationals of the same state.

2.   A person who for the purposes of membership in the Court could be regarded as a national of more than one state shall be deemed to be a national of the one in which he ordinarily exercises civil and political rights.

Article 4

1.   The members of the Court shall be elected by the General Assembly and by the Security Council from a list of persons nominated by the national groups in the Permanent Court of Arbitration, in accordance with the following provisions.

2.   In the case of Members of the United Nations not represented in the Permanent Court of Arbitration, candidates shall be nominated by national groups appointed for this purpose by their governments under the same conditions as those prescribed for mem-

bers of the Permanent Court of Arbitration by Article 44 of the Convention of The Hague of 1907 for the pacific settlement of international disputes.

3.   The conditions under which a state which is a party to the present Statute but is not a Member of the United Nations may participate in electing the members of the Court shall, in the absence of a special agreement, be laid down by the General Assembly upon recommendation of the Security Council.

Article 5

1.   At least three months before the date of the election, the Secretary-General of the United Nations shall address a written request to the members of the Permanent Court of Arbitration belonging to the states which are parties to the present Statute, and to the members of the national groups appointed under Article 4, paragraph 2, inviting them to undertake, within a given time, by national groups, the nomination of persons in a position to accept the duties of a member of the Court.

2.   No group may nominate more than four persons, not more than two of whom shall be of their own nationality. In no case may the number of candidates nominated by a group be more than double the number of seats to be filled.

Article 6

Before making these nominations, each national group is recommended to consult its highest court of justice, its legal faculties and schools of law, and its national academies and national sections of international academies devoted to the study of law.

Article 7

1.   The Secretary-General shall prepare a list in alphabetical order of all the persons thus nominated. Save as provided in Article 12, paragraph 2, these shall be the only persons eligible.

2. The Secretary-General shall submit this list to the General Assembly and to the Security Council.

Article 8
The General Assembly and the Security Council shall proceed independently of one another to elect the members of the Court.

Article 9
At every election, the electors shall bear in mind not only that the persons to be elected should individually possess the qualifications required, but also that in the body as a whole the representation of the main forms of civilization and of the principal legal systems of the world should be assured.

Article 10
1. Those candidates who obtain an absolute majority of votes in the General Assembly and in the Security Council shall be considered as elected.

2. Any vote of the Security Council, whether for the election of judges or for the appointment of members of the conference envisaged in Article 12, shall be taken without any distinction between permanent and non-permanent members of the Security Council.

3. In the event of more than one national of the same state obtaining an absolute majority of the votes both of the General Assembly and of the Security Council, the eldest of these only shall be considered as elected.

Article 11
If, after the first meeting held for the purpose of the election, one or more seats remain to be filled, a second and, if necessary, a third meeting shall take place.

Article 12
1. If, after the third meeting, one or more seats still remain unfilled, a joint conference consisting of six members, three appointed by the General Assembly and three by the Security Council, may be formed at any time at the request of either the General Assembly or the Security Council, for the purpose of choosing by the vote of an absolute majority one name for each seat still vacant, to submit to the General Assembly and the Security Council for their respective acceptance.

2. If the joint conference is unanimously agreed upon any person who fulfils the required conditions, he may be included in its list, even though he was not included in the list of nominations referred to in Article 7.

3. If the joint conference is satisfied that it will not be successful in procuring an election, those members of the Court who have already been elected shall, within a period to be fixed by the Security Council, proceed to fill the vacant seats by selection from among those candidates who have obtained votes either in the General Assembly or in the Security Council.

4. In the event of an equality of votes among the judges, the eldest judge shall have a casting vote.

Article 13
1. The members of the Court shall be elected for nine years and may be re-elected; provided, however, that of the judges elected at the first election, the terms of five judges shall expire at the end of three years and the terms of five more judges shall expire at the end of six years.

2. The judges whose terms are to expire at the end of the above-mentioned initial periods of three and six years shall be chosen by lot to be drawn by the Secretary-General immediately after the first election has been completed.

3. The members of the Court shall continue to discharge their duties until their places have been filled. Though replaced, they shall finish any cases which they may have begun.

4. In the case of the resignation of a member of the Court, the resignation shall be addressed to the President of the Court for transmission to the Secretary-General. This last notification makes the place vacant.

Article 14
Vacancies shall be filled by the same method as that laid down for the first election, subject to the following provision: the Secretary-

General shall, within one month of the occurrence of the vacancy, proceed to issue the invitations provided for in Article 5, and the date of the election shall be fixed by the Security Council.

Article 15
A member of the Court elected to replace a member whose term of office has not expired shall hold office for the remainder of his predecessor's term.

Article 16
1. No member of the Court may exercise any political or administrative function, or engage in any other occupation of a professional nature.

2. Any doubt on this point shall be settled by the decision of the Court.

Article 17
1. No member of the Court may act as agent, counsel, or advocate in any case.

2. No member may participate in the decision of any case in which he has previously taken part as agent, counsel, or advocate for one of the parties, or as a member of a national or international court, or of a commission of enquiry, or in any other capacity.

3. Any doubt on this point shall be settled by the decision of the Court.

Article 18
1. No member of the Court can be dismissed unless, in the unanimous opinion of the other members, he has ceased to fulfil the required conditions.

2. Formal notification thereof shall be made to the Secretary-General by the Registrar.

3. This notification makes the place vacant.

Article 19
The members of the Court, when engaged on the business of the Court, shall enjoy diplomatic privileges and immunities.

Article 20
Every member of the Court shall, before taking up his duties, make a solemn declaration in open court that he will exercise his powers impartially and conscientiously.

Article 21
1. The Court shall elect its President and Vice-President for three years; they may be re-elected.

2. The Court shall appoint its Registrar and may provide for the appointment of such other officers as may be necessary.

Article 22
1. The seat of the Court shall be established at The Hague. This, however, shall not prevent the Court from sitting and exercising its functions elsewhere whenever the Court considers it desirable.

2. The President and the Registrar shall reside at the seat of the Court.

Article 23
1. The Court shall remain permanently in session, except during the judicial vacations, the dates and duration of which shall be fixed by the Court.

2. Members of the Court are entitled to periodic leave, the dates and duration of which shall be fixed by the Court, having in mind the distance between The Hague and the home of each judge.

3. Members of the Court shall be bound, unless they are on leave or prevented from attending by illness or other serious reasons duly explained to the President, to hold themselves permanently at the disposal of the Court.

Article 24
1. If, for some special reason, a member of the Court considers that he should not take part in the decision of a particular case, he shall so inform the President.

2. If the President considers that for some special reason one of the members of the Court should not sit in a particular case, he shall give him notice accordingly.

3. If in any such case the member of the Court and the President disagree, the matter shall be settled by the decision of the Court.

Article 25

1. The full Court shall sit except when it is expressly provided otherwise in the present Statute.

2. Subject to the condition that the number of judges available to constitute the Court is not thereby reduced below eleven, the Rules of the Court may provide for allowing one or more judges, according to circumstances and in rotation, to be dispensed from sitting.

3. A quorum of nine judges shall suffice to constitute the Court.

Article 26

1. The Court may from time to time form one or more chambers, composed of three or more judges as the Court may determine, for dealing with particular categories of cases; for example, labour cases and cases relating to transit and communications.

2. The Court may at any time form a chamber for dealing with a particular case. The number of judges to constitute such a chamber shall be determined by the Court with the approval of the parties.

3. Cases shall be heard and determined by the chambers provided for in this Article if the parties so request.

Article 27

A judgment given by any of the chambers provided for in Articles 26 and 29 shall be considered as rendered by the Court.

Article 28

The chambers provided for in Articles 26 and 29 may, with the consent of the parties, sit and exercise their functions elsewhere than at The Hague.

Article 29

With a view to the speedy dispatch of business, the Court shall form annually a chamber composed of five judges which, at the request of the parties, may hear and determine cases by summary procedure. In addition, two judges shall be selected for the purpose of replacing judges who find it impossible to sit.

Article 30

1. The Court shall frame rules for carrying out its functions. In particular, it shall lay down rules of procedure.

2. The Rules of the Court may provide for assessors to sit with the Court or with any of its chambers, without the right to vote.

Article 31

1. Judges of the nationality of each of the parties shall retain their right to sit in the case before the Court.

2. If the Court includes upon the Bench a judge of the nationality of one of the parties, any other party may choose a person to sit as judge. Such person shall be chosen preferably from among those persons who have been nominated as candidates as provided in Articles 4 and 5.

3. If the Court includes upon the Bench no judge of the nationality of the parties, each of these parties may proceed to choose a judge as provided in paragraph 2 of this Article.

4. The provisions of this Article shall apply to the case of Articles 26 and 29. In such cases, the President shall request one or, if necessary, two of the members of the Court forming the chamber to give place to the members of the Court of the nationality of the parties concerned, and, failing such, or if they are unable to be present, to the judges specially chosen by the parties.

5. Should there be several parties in the same interest, they shall, for the purpose of the preceding provisions, be reckoned as one party only. Any doubt upon this point shall be settled by the decision of the Court.

6. Judges chosen as laid down in paragraphs 2, 3 and 4 of this Article shall fulfil the conditions required by Articles 2, 17 (paragraph 2), 20, and 24 of the present Statute. They shall take part in the decision on terms of complete equality with their colleagues.

Article 32

1. Each member of the Court shall receive an annual salary.

2. The President shall receive a special annual allowance.

3. The Vice-President shall receive a special allowance for every day on which he acts as President.

4. The judges chosen under Article 31, other than members of the Court, shall receive compensation for each day on which they exercise their functions.

5. These salaries, allowances, and compensation shall be fixed by the General Assembly. They may not be decreased during the term of office.

6. The salary of the Registrar shall be fixed by the General Assembly on the proposal of the Court.

7. Regulations made by the General Assembly shall fix the conditions under which retirement pensions may be given to members of the Court and to the Registrar, and the conditions under which members of the Court and the Registrar shall have their travelling expenses refunded.

8. The above salaries, allowances, and compensation shall be free of all taxation.

Article 33

The expenses of the Court shall be borne by the United Nations in such a manner as shall be decided by the General Assembly.

Chapter II
COMPETENCE OF THE COURT

Article 34

1. Only states may be parties in cases before the Court.

2. The Court, subject to and in conformity with its Rules, may request of public international organizations information relevant to cases before it, and shall receive such information presented by such organizations on their own initiative.

3. Whenever the construction of the constituent instrument of a public international organization or of an international convention adopted thereunder is in question in a case before the Court, the Registrar shall so notify the public international organization concerned and shall communicate to it copies of all the written proceedings.

Article 35

1. The Court shall be open to the states parties to the present Statute.

2. The conditions under which the Court shall be open to other states shall, subject to the special provisions contained in treaties in force, be laid down by the Security Council, but in no case shall such conditions place the parties in a position of inequality before the Court.

3. When a state which is not a Member of the United Nations is a party to a case, the Court shall fix the amount which that party is to contribute towards the expenses of the Court. This provision shall not apply if such state is bearing a share of the expenses of the Court.

Article 36

1. The jurisdiction of the Court comprises all cases which the parties refer to it and all matters specially provided for in the Charter of the United Nations or in treaties and conventions in force.

2. The states parties to the present Statute may at any time declare that they recognize as compulsory *ipso facto* and without special agreement, in relation to any other state accepting the same obligation, the jurisdiction of the Court in all legal disputes concerning:

a. the interpretation of a treaty;

b. any question of international law;

c. the existence of any fact which, if established, would constitute a breach of an international obligation;

d. the nature or extent of the reparation to be made for the breach of an international obligation.

3. The declarations referred to above may be made unconditionally or on condition of reciprocity on the part of several or certain states, or for a certain time.

4. Such declarations shall be deposited with the Secretary-General of the United Nations, who shall transmit copies thereof to the parties to the Statute and to the Registrar of the Court.

5. Declarations made under Article 36 of the Statute of the Permanent Court of International Justice and which are still in force shall be deemed, as between the parties to the present Statute, to be acceptances of the compulsory jurisdiction of the International Court of Justice for the period which they still have to run and in accordance with their terms.

6. In the event of a dispute as to whether the Court has jurisdiction, the matter shall be settled by the decision of the Court.

Article 37

Whenever a treaty or convention in force provides for reference of a matter to a tribunal to have been instituted by the League of Nations, or to the Permanent Court of International Justice, the matter shall, as between the parties to the present Statute, be referred to the International Court of Justice.

Article 38

1. The Court, whose function is to decide in accordance with international law such disputes as are submitted to it, shall apply:

   a. international conventions, whether general or particular, establishing rules expressly recognized by the contesting states;

   b. international custom, as evidence of a general practice accepted as law;

   c. the general principles of law recognized by civilized nations;

   d. subject to the provisions of Article 59, judicial decisions and the teachings of the most highly qualified publicists of the various nations, as subsidiary means for the determination of rules of law.

2. This provision shall not prejudice the power of the Court to decide a case *ex aequo et bono*, if the parties agree thereto.

Chapter III
PROCEDURE

Article 39

1. The official languages of the Court shall be French and English. If the parties agree that the case shall be conducted in French, the judgment shall be delivered in French. If the parties agree that the case shall be conducted in English, the judgment shall be delivered in English.

2. In the absence of an agreement as to which language shall be employed, each party may, in the pleadings, use the language which it prefers; the decision of the Court shall be given in French and English. In this case the Court shall at the same time determine which of the two texts shall be considered as authoritative.

3. The Court shall, at the request of any party, authorize a language other than French or English to be used by that party.

Article 40

1. Cases are brought before the Court, as the case may be, either by the notification of the special agreement or by a written application addressed to the Registrar. In either case the subject of the dispute and the parties shall be indicated.

2. The Registrar shall forthwith communicate the application to all concerned.

3. He shall also notify the Members of the United Nations through the Secretary-General, and also any other states entitled to appear before the Court.

Article 41

1. The Court shall have the power to indicate, if it considers that circumstances so require, any provisional measures which ought to be taken to preserve the respective rights of either party.

2. Pending the final decision, notice of the measures suggested shall forthwith be given to the parties and to the Security Council.

Article 42

1. The parties shall be represented by agents.

2. They may have the assistance of counsel or advocates before the Court.

3. The agents, counsel, and advocates of parties before the Court shall enjoy the privileges and immunities necessary to the independent exercise of their duties.

Article 43

1. The procedure shall consist of two parts: written and oral.

2. The written proceedings shall consist of the communication to the Court and to the parties of memorials, counter-memorials and, if necessary, replies; also all papers and documents in support.

3. These communications shall be made through the Registrar, in the order and within the time fixed by the Court.

4. A certified copy of every document produced by one party shall be communicated to the other party.

5. The oral proceedings shall consist of the hearing by the Court of witnesses, experts, agents, counsel, and advocates.

Article 44

1. For the service of all notices upon persons other than the agents, counsel, and advocates, the Court shall apply direct to the government of the state upon whose territory the notice has to be served.

2. The same provision shall apply whenever steps are to be taken to procure evidence on the spot.

Article 45

The hearing shall be under the control of the President or, if he is unable to preside, of the Vice-President; if neither is able to preside, the senior judge present shall preside.

Article 46

The hearing in Court shall be public, unless the Court shall decide otherwise, or unless the parties demand that the public be not admitted.

Article 47

1. Minutes shall be made at each hearing and signed by the Registrar and the President.

2. These minutes alone shall be authentic.

Article 48

The Court shall make orders for the conduct of the case, shall decide the form and time in which each party must conclude its arguments, and make all arrangements connected with the taking of evidence.

Article 49

The Court may, even before the hearing begins, call upon the agents to produce any document or to supply any explanations. Formal note shall be taken of any refusal.

Article 50

The Court may, at any time, entrust any individual, body, bureau, commission, or other organization that it may select, with the task of carrying out an enquiry or giving an expert opinion.

Article 51

During the hearing any relevant questions are to be put to the witnesses and experts under the conditions laid down by the Court in the rules of procedure referred to in Article 30.

Article 52

After the Court has received the proofs and evidence within the time specified for the purpose, it may refuse to accept any further oral or written evidence that one party may desire to present unless the other side consents.

Article 53

1. Whenever one of the parties does not appear before the Court, or fails to defend its case, the other party may call upon the Court to decide in favour of its claim.

2. The Court must, before doing so, satisfy itself, not only that it has jurisdiction in accordance with Articles 36 and 37, but also that the claim is well founded in fact and law.

Article 54

1. When, subject to the control of the Court, the agents, counsel, and advocates have completed their presentation of the case, the President shall declare the hearing closed.

2. The Court shall withdraw to consider the judgment.

3. The deliberations of the Court shall take place in private and remain secret.

Article 55

1. All questions shall be decided by a majority of the judges present.

2. In the event of an equality of votes, the President or the judge who acts in his place shall have a casting vote.

Article 56

1. The judgment shall state the reasons on which it is based.

2. It shall contain the names of the judges who have taken part in the decision.

Article 57

If the judgment does not represent in whole or in part the unanimous opinion of the judges, any judge shall be entitled to deliver a separate opinion.

Article 58

The judgment shall be signed by the President and by the Registrar. It shall be read in open court, due notice having been given to the agents.

Article 59

The decision of the Court has no binding force except between the parties and in respect of that particular case.

Article 60

The judgment is final and without appeal. In the event of dispute as to the meaning or scope of the judgment, the Court shall construe it upon the request of any party.

Article 61

1. An application for revision of a judgment may be made only when it is based upon the discovery of some fact of such a nature as to be a decisive factor, which fact was, when the judgment was given, unknown to the Court and also to the party claiming revision, always provided that such ignorance was not due to negligence.

2. The proceedings for revision shall be opened by a judgment of the Court expressly recording the existence of the new fact, recognizing that it has such a character as to lay the case open to revision, and declaring the application admissible on this ground.

3. The Court may require previous compliance with the terms of the judgment before it admits proceedings in revision.

4. The application for revision must be made at latest within six months of the discovery of the new fact.

5. No application for revision may be made after the lapse of ten years from the date of the judgment.

Article 62

1. Should a state consider that it has an interest of a legal nature which may be affected by the decision in the case, it may submit a request to the Court to be permitted to intervene.

2. It shall be for the Court to decide upon this request.

Article 63

1. Whenever the construction of a convention to which states other than those concerned in the case are parties is in question, the Registrar shall notify all such states forthwith.

2. Every state so notified has the right to intervene in the proceedings; but if it uses this right, the construction given by the judgment will be equally binding upon it.

Article 64

Unless otherwise decided by the Court, each party shall bear its own costs.

Chapter IV
ADVISORY OPINIONS

Article 65

1. The Court may give an advisory opinion on any legal question at the request of whatever body may be authorized by or in accordance with the Charter of the United Nations to make such a request.

2. Questions upon which the advisory opinion of the Court is asked shall be laid before the Court by means of a written request containing an exact statement of the question upon which an opinion is required, and accompanied by all documents likely to throw light upon the question.

Article 66

1. The Registrar shall forthwith give notice of the request for an advisory opinion to all states entitled to appear before the Court.

2. The Registrar shall also, by means of a special and direct communication, notify any state entitled to appear before the Court or international organization considered by the Court, or, should it not be sitting, by the President, as likely to be able to furnish information on the question, that the Court will be prepared to receive, within a time limit to be fixed by the President, written statements, or to hear, at a public sitting to be held for the purpose, oral statements relating to the question.

3. Should any such state entitled to appear before the Court have failed to receive the special communication referred to in paragraph 2 of this Article, such state may express a desire to submit a written statement or to be heard; and the Court will decide.

4. States and organizations having presented written or oral statements or both shall be permitted to comment on the statements made by other states or organizations in the form, to the extent, and within the time limits which the Court, or, should it not be sitting, the President, shall decide in each particular case. Accordingly, the Registrar shall in due time communicate any such written statements to states and organizations having submitted similar statements.

Article 67

The Court shall deliver its advisory opinions in open court, notice having been given to the Secretary-General and to the representatives of Members of the United Nations, of other states and of international organizations immediately concerned.

Article 68

In the exercise of its advisory functions the Court shall further be guided by the provisions of the present Statute which apply in contentious cases to the extent to which it recognizes them to be applicable.

Chapter V
AMENDMENT

Article 69

Amendments to the present Statute shall be effected by the same procedure as is provided by the Charter of the United Nations for amendments to that Charter, subject however to any provisions which the General Assembly upon recommendation of the Security Council may adopt concerning the participation of states which are parties to the present Statute but are not Members of the United Nations.

Article 70

The Court shall have power to propose such amendments to the present Statute as it may deem necessary, through written communications to the Secretary-General, for consideration in conformity with the provisions of Article 69.

Appendix III

Structure of the United Nations

General Assembly

The General Assembly is composed of all the Members of the United Nations.

SESSIONS
Resumed forty-second session: 29 February–2 March, 18-23 March, 11-13 May, 16 and 17 August and 19 September 1988.
Fifteenth special session: 31 May–25 June 1988.
Forty-third session:[1] 20 September–22 December 1988 (suspended).

OFFICERS
Resumed forty-second session and fifteenth special session
President: Peter Florin (German Democratic Republic).[a]
Vice-Presidents:[b] Botswana, Cameroon, China, Comoros, France, Jordan, Mauritania, Mongolia, Netherlands, Nicaragua, Paraguay, Portugal, Saint Vincent and the Grenadines, Singapore, Sri Lanka, Syrian Arab Republic, Togo, Tunisia, USSR, United Kingdom, United States.

[a]On 31 May 1988 (decision S-15/12), the Assembly decided that the President at the forty-second session would serve in the same capacity at the fifteenth special session.
[b]On 31 May 1988 (decision S-15/14), the Assembly decided that the Vice-Presidents at the forty-second session would serve in the same capacity at the fifteenth special session.

Forty-third session
President: Dante Caputo (Argentina).[a]
Vice-Presidents:[b] Bahrain, China, Côte d'Ivoire, Cyprus, Denmark, Ecuador, El Salvador, France, Guinea-Bissau, Libyan Arab Jamahiriya, Malta, Nepal, Sao Tome and Principe, Swaziland, Thailand, USSR, United Kingdom, United Republic of Tanzania, United States, Vanuatu, Yugoslavia.

[a]Elected on 20 September 1988 (decision 43/302).
[b]Elected on 20 September 1988 (decision 43/304).

The Assembly has four types of committees: (1) Main Committees; (2) procedural committees; (3) standing committees; (4) subsidiary and *ad hoc* bodies. In addition, it convenes conferences to deal with specific subjects.

Main Committees

Seven Main Committees have been established as follows:

Political and Security Committee (disarmament and related international security questions) (First Committee)
Special Political Committee
Economic and Financial Committee (Second Committee)
Social, Humanitarian and Cultural Committee (Third Committee)
Trusteeship Committee (including Non-Self-Governing Territories) (Fourth Committee)
Administrative and Budgetary Committee (Fifth Committee)
Legal Committee (Sixth Committee)

The General Assembly may constitute other committees, on which all Members of the United Nations have the right to be represented.

OFFICERS OF THE MAIN COMMITTEES

Resumed forty-second session

Fifth Committee[a]
Chairman: Henrik Amneus (Sweden).
Vice-Chairmen: Deryck Murray (Trinidad and Tobago), Raj Singh (Fiji).
Rapporteur: Felix Aboly-Bi-Kouassi (Côte d'Ivoire).

[a]The only Main Committee to meet at the resumed session.

Fifteenth special session[a]

Committee of the Whole of the Fifteenth Special Session
Chairman: Mansur Ahmad (Pakistan).[b]
Vice-Chairmen: Argentina, Australia, Bahamas, Czechoslovakia, Hungary, Japan, Mongolia, Morocco, Netherlands, New Zealand, Norway, Romania, Sri Lanka, Sudan, Togo, Uruguay, Yugoslavia, Zaire.
Rapporteur: Pedro Núñez-Mosquera (Cuba).

[a]On 31 May 1988 (decision S-15/13), the Assembly decided that the Chairmen of the Main Committees at the forty-second session (YUN 1987, p. 1335) would serve in the same capacity at the fifteenth special session, on the understanding that the Chairmen of the Third and Sixth Committees would be replaced by another member of the same delegation.
[b]Elected by the Assembly on 31 May 1988 (decision S-15/15); other officers elected by the Committee on 3 June.

Forty-third session[a]

[a]Chairmen elected by the Main Committees; announced by the Assembly President on 20 September 1988 (decision 43/303).

First Committee
Chairman: Douglas Roche (Canada).
Vice-Chairmen: Victor G. Batiouk (Ukrainian SSR), Luvsandorjiin Bayart (Mongolia).
Rapporteur: Virgilio A. Reyes (Philippines).

Special Political Committee
Chairman: Eugeniusz Noworyta (Poland).
Vice-Chairmen: Orobola Fasehun (Nigeria), Horacio Nogues Zubizarreta (Paraguay).
Rapporteur: Jean Michel Veranneman de Watervliet (Belgium).

Second Committee
Chairman: Hugo Navajas-Mogro (Bolivia).
Vice-Chairmen: José Fernandez (Philippines), Eloho E. Otobo (Nigeria).
Rapporteur: Martin Walter (Czechoslovakia).

Third Committee
Chairman: Mohammad A. Abulhasan (Kuwait).
Vice-Chairmen: Mohamed Noman Galal (Egypt), Carlos Jativa (Ecuador).
Rapporteur: Carlos Casajuana (Spain).

Fourth Committee
Chairman: Jonathan C. Peters (Saint Vincent and the Grenadines).
Vice-Chairmen: Sverre J. Bergh Johansen (Norway), Denis Dangue-Rewaka (Gabon).
Rapporteur: Emmanuel Douma (Congo).

[1]The forty-third session of the General Assembly resumed in 1989 from 14 February to 7 March, from 18 to 20 April, on 11 July and on 18 September.

Fifth Committee
Chairman: Michael George Okeyo (Kenya).
Vice-Chairmen: Mojtaba Arastou (Iran), Tjaco T. van den Hout (Netherlands).
Rapporteur: Flor A. de Rodríguez (Venezuela).

Sixth Committee
Chairman: Achol Deng (Sudan).
Vice-Chairmen: Hameed Mohamed Ali (Democratic Yemen), Ioan Voicu (Romania).
Rapporteur: Carlos Velasco Mendiola (Peru).

Procedural committees

General Committee
The General Committee consists of the President of the General Assembly, as Chairman, the 21 Vice-Presidents and the Chairmen of the seven Main Committees.

Credentials Committee
The Credentials Committee consists of nine members appointed by the General Assembly on the proposal of the President.

Fifteenth special session[a]
Argentina *(Chairman)*, Barbados, Cape Verde, China, Germany, Federal Republic of, Kenya, Singapore, USSR, United States.

[a]On 31 May 1988 (decision S-15/11), the Assembly decided that the Credentials Committee at the fifteenth special session would have the same composition as at the forty-second session.

Forty-third session
Bolivia, China, Luxembourg *(Chairman)*, Thailand, Togo, Trinidad and Tobago, USSR, United States, Zimbabwe.[a]

[a]Appointed on 20 September 1988 (decision 43/301).

Standing committees

The two standing committees consist of experts appointed in their individual capacity for three-year terms.

Advisory Committee on Administrative and Budgetary Questions
Members:
To serve until 31 December 1988: Ahmad Fathi Al-Masri (Syrian Arab Republic); Ion Gorita (Romania); Ferguson O. Iheme (Nigeria); C. S. M. Mselle, *Chairman* (United Republic of Tanzania); Christopher R. Thomas (Trinidad and Tobago).
To serve until 31 December 1989: Michel Brochard (France); Luiz Sergio Gama Figueira (Brazil);[a] Tadanori Inomata (Japan); Ma Longde (China); Irmeli Mustonen (Finland); Banbit A. Roy (India).
To serve until 31 December 1990: Bagbeni Adeito Nzengeya (Zaire); Even Fontaine-Ortiz (Cuba); Richard Nygard (United States); Tjaco T. van den Hout (Netherlands); Viktor A. Vislykh (USSR).

[a]Until 30 June 1988; Maria Elisa de Bittencourt Berenguer (Brazil) was appointed by the General Assembly on 13 May (decision 42/312 B) for a term beginning on 1 July to fill the resultant vacancy.

On 9 December 1988 (decision 43/318), the General Assembly appointed the following five members for a three-year term beginning on 1 January 1989 to fill the vacancies occurring on 31 December 1988: Ahmad Fathi Al-Masri (Syrian Arab Republic), Ferguson O. Iheme (Nigeria), C. S. M. Mselle (United Republic of Tanzania), Jozsef Tardos (Hungary), Christopher R. Thomas (Trinidad and Tobago).

Committee on Contributions
Members:
To serve until 31 December 1988: Andrzej Abraszewski, *Vice Chairman* (Poland); Kenshiroh Akimoto (Japan); John Fox (United States); Elias M. C. Kazembe (Zambia); Adnan A. Yonis (Iraq); Assen Iliev Zlatanov (Bulgaria).
To serve until 31 December 1989: Bagbeni Adeito Nzengeya (Zaire); Carlos Antonio Bivero García (Venezuela); Peter Gregg (Australia); Atilio Norberto Molteni (Argentina); Dimitri Rallis (Greece); Omar Sirry (Egypt).
To serve until 31 December 1990: Amjad Ali, *Chairman* (Pakistan); Ernesto Battisti (Italy); Alain Catta (France); Yuri Chulkov (USSR); Mauro Sergio da Fonseca Costa Couto (Brazil);[a] Wang Liansheng (China).

[a]Resigned in December 1988; Carlos Moreira Garcia (Brazil) was appointed by the General Assembly on 21 December (decision 43/319 B) for a two-year term beginning on 1 January 1989 to fill the resultant vacancy.

On 9 December 1988 (decision 43/319 A), the General Assembly appointed the following six members for a three-year term beginning on 1 January 1989 to fill the vacancies occurring on 31 December 1988: Kenshiroh Akimoto (Japan), John Fox (United States), Ion Gorita (Romania), Elias M. C. Kazembe (Zambia), Vanu Gopala Menon (Singapore), Assen Iliev Zlatanov (Bulgaria).

Subsidiary and *ad hoc* bodies

The following subsidiary and *ad hoc* bodies were in existence or functioning in 1988, or were established during the General Assembly's forty-third session, held from 20 September to 22 December 1988. (For other related bodies, see p. 1030.)

Ad Hoc Committee of the General Assembly for the Announcement of Voluntary Contributions to the 1989 Programme of the United Nations High Commissioner for Refugees
As soon as practicable after the opening of each regular session of the General Assembly, an *ad hoc* committee of the whole of the Assembly meets, under the chairmanship of the President of the session, to enable Governments to announce pledges of voluntary contributions to the programme of UNHCR for the following year. Also invited to announce their pledges are States which are members of specialized agencies but not Members of the United Nations. In 1988, the *Ad Hoc* Committee met on 21 November.

Ad Hoc Committee of the General Assembly for the Announcement of Voluntary Contributions to the United Nations Relief and Works Agency for Palestine Refugees in the Near East
As soon as practicable after the opening of each regular session of the General Assembly, an *ad hoc* committee of the whole of the Assembly meets, under the chairmanship of the President of the session, to enable Governments to announce pledges of voluntary contributions to the programme of UNRWA for the following year. Also invited to announce their pledges are States which are members of specialized agencies but not Members of the United Nations. In 1988, the *Ad Hoc* Committee met on 21 November.

Ad Hoc Committee of the International Conference on Kampuchea
The *Ad Hoc* Committee of the International Conference on Kampuchea held five meetings between 12 January and 25 August 1988, at United Nations Headquarters.

Members: Belgium *(Vice-Chairman)*, Japan, Malaysia *(Rapporteur)*, Nepal, Nigeria, Peru, Senegal, Sri Lanka, Sudan, Thailand.

Chairman: Massamba Sarré (Senegal).

Ad Hoc Committee of the Whole for the Preparation of the International Development Strategy for the Fourth United Nations Development Decade
On 20 December 1988, the General Assembly established an *Ad Hoc* Committee of the Whole to prepare an international development strategy for the fourth United Nations development decade (1991-2000). The Committee did not meet in 1988.

Ad Hoc Committee of the Whole
of the General Assembly on the Review and Appraisal
of the United Nations Programme of Action
for African Economic Recovery and Development 1986-1990

The *Ad Hoc* Committee of the Whole on the Review and Appraisal of the United Nations Programme of Action for African Economic Recovery and Development 1986-1990[2] met at United Nations Headquarters from 12 to 23 September 1988.

Chairman: Tom Eric Vraalsen (Norway).
Vice-Chairmen: Lloyd M. H. Barnett (Jamaica), Gert Kueck (German Democratic Republic), Kishore Mahbubani (Singapore).
Rapporteur: G. B. Mbulo (Zambia).

Ad Hoc Committee on the Drafting of an International
Convention against the Recruitment, Use, Financing
and Training of Mercenaries

The 35-member *Ad Hoc* Committee on the Drafting of an International Convention against the Recruitment, Use, Financing and Training of Mercenaries held its seventh session at United Nations Headquarters from 25 January to 12 February 1988.

Members: Algeria, Angola, Bangladesh, Barbados, Benin, Bulgaria, Canada, Cuba, Democratic Yemen, Ethiopia, France, German Democratic Republic, Germany, Federal Republic of, Haiti, India, Italy, Jamaica, Japan, Mongolia, Nigeria,[a] Portugal, Seychelles, Spain, Suriname, Togo, Turkey, Ukrainian SSR, USSR, United Kingdom, United States, Uruguay, Viet Nam, Yugoslavia, Zaire, Zambia.

[a]Until 31 December 1988, when it withdrew in accordance with a schedule of rotation agreed on by the Group of African States. On 9 December (decision 43/317), the General Assembly confirmed the appointment by its President of Senegal, effective 1 January 1989, to fill the resultant vacancy.

Chairman: Werner H. W. Vreedzaam (Suriname).
Vice-Chairmen: Abdullahi N. Bage (Nigeria), Vladimir Y. Eltchenko (Ukrainian SSR), Tullio Treves (Italy).
Rapporteur: Hameed Mohamed Ali (Democratic Yemen).

Ad Hoc Committee on the Indian Ocean

In 1988, the 49-member *Ad Hoc* Committee on the Indian Ocean, continuing the preparatory work for the Conference on the Indian Ocean (scheduled for 1990 at Colombo, Sri Lanka), held two sessions, at United Nations Headquarters: from 11 to 15 April and from 11 to 22 July.

Members: Australia, Bangladesh, Bulgaria, Canada, China, Democratic Yemen, Djibouti, Egypt, Ethiopia, France, German Democratic Republic, Germany, Federal Republic of, Greece, India, Indonesia, Iran, Iraq, Italy, Japan, Kenya, Liberia, Madagascar, Malaysia, Maldives, Mauritius, Mozambique, Netherlands, Norway, Oman, Pakistan, Panama, Poland, Romania, Seychelles, Singapore, Somalia, Sri Lanka, Sudan, Thailand, Uganda, USSR, United Arab Emirates, United Kingdom, United Republic of Tanzania, United States, Yemen, Yugoslavia, Zambia, Zimbabwe.

Sweden, a major maritime user of the Indian Ocean, continued to participate in the meetings as an observer.

Chairman: Daya Perera (Sri Lanka).
Vice-Chairmen: Jill Courtney (Australia), Manuel dos Santos (Mozambique), Wilhelm Grundmann (German Democratic Republic), Isslamet Poernomo (Indonesia).
Rapporteur: Jean de Dieu Rakotozafy (Madagascar).

Ad Hoc Committee on the World Disarmament Conference

The 40-member *Ad Hoc* Committee on the World Disarmament Conference met at United Nations Headquarters on 14 January and 27 April 1988.

Members: Algeria, Argentina, Austria, Belgium, Brazil, Bulgaria, Burundi, Canada, Chile, Colombia, Czechoslovakia, Egypt, Ethiopia, Hungary, India, Indonesia, Iran, Italy, Japan, Lebanon, Liberia, Mexico, Mongolia, Morocco, Netherlands, Nigeria, Pakistan, Peru, Philippines, Poland, Romania, Spain, Sri Lanka, Sweden, Tunisia, Turkey, Venezuela, Yugoslavia, Zaire, Zambia.

The USSR participated in the work of the *Ad Hoc* Committee, while China, France, the United Kingdom and the United States maintained contact with it through its Chairman, pursuant to a 1973 General Assembly resolution.[3]

Chairman: Daya Perera (Sri Lanka).
Vice-Chairmen:[a] Kazimierz Tomaszewski (Poland).
Rapporteur: Francisco Viqueira (Spain).

[a]Two posts remained vacant.

WORKING GROUP
Members: Burundi, Egypt, Hungary, India, Iran, Italy, Mexico, Peru, Poland, Spain *(Chairman)*, Sri Lanka.

Advisory Committee on the United Nations Educational
and Training Programme for Southern Africa

Members: Byelorussian SSR, Canada, Denmark, India, Japan, Liberia, Nigeria, Norway, United Republic of Tanzania, United States, Venezuela, Zaire, Zambia.

Chairman: Tom Eric Vraalsen (Norway).
Vice-Chairman: Isaiah Zimba Chabala (Zambia).

Advisory Committee on the United Nations Programme
of Assistance in the Teaching, Study, Dissemination
and Wider Appreciation of International Law

The Advisory Committee on the United Nations Programme of Assistance in the Teaching, Study, Dissemination and Wider Appreciation of International Law held its twenty-third session at United Nations Headquarters on 14 December 1988.

Members (until 31 December 1991): Bangladesh, Cyprus, France, Ghana, Libyan Arab Jamahiriya, Mexico, Netherlands, Romania, Turkey, USSR, United Kingdom, Venezuela, Zaire.

Chairman: Clifford Nii Amon Kotey (Ghana).

Board of Auditors

The Board of Auditors consists of three members appointed by the General Assembly for three-year terms.

Members:
To serve until 30 June 1989: Senior President of the Audit Office of France.
To serve until 30 June 1990: Chairman of the Commission of Audit of the Philippines.
To serve until 30 June 1991: Auditor-General of Ghana.

On 9 December 1988 (decision 43/320), the General Assembly appointed the President of the Federal Court of Audit of the Federal Republic of Germany for a three-year term beginning on 1 July 1989.

Collective Measures Committee

Established in 1950 under the General Assembly's "Uniting for Peace" resolution,[4] the Collective Measures Committee reported three times to the Assembly. In noting the third report, to its ninth (1954) session, the Assembly directed the Committee to remain in a position to pursue such further studies as it may deem desirable to strengthen the capability of the United Nations to maintain peace and to report to the Security Council and to the Assembly as appropriate.[5]

---

[2]YUN 1986, p. 446, GA res. S-13/2, annex, 1 June 1986.
[3]YUN 1973, p. 18, GA res. 3183(XXVIII), 18 Dec. 1973.
[4]YUN 1950, p. 194, GA res. 377(V), part A, para. 11, 3 Nov. 1950.
[5]YUN 1954, p. 23, GA res. 809(IX), 4 Nov. 1954.

Members: Australia, Belgium, Brazil, Burma, Canada, Egypt, France, Mexico, Philippines, Turkey, United Kingdom, United States, Venezuela, Yugoslavia.

Committee for the United Nations Population Award

The Committee for the United Nations Population Award is composed of: *(a)* 10 representatives of United Nations Member States elected by the Economic and Social Council for a three-year period, with due regard for equitable geographical representation and the need to include Member States that had made contributions for the Award; *(b)* the Secretary-General and the UNFPA Executive Director, to serve *ex officio;* and *(c)* five individuals eminent for their significant contributions to population-related activities, selected by the Committee, to serve as honorary members in an advisory capacity for a renewable three-year term.

In 1988, the Committee held meetings at United Nations Headquarters on 25 January and 8 February.

Members (until 31 December 1988): Burundi, Colombia, Ecuador, Japan, Mexico, Pakistan, Spain, Sudan, Tunisia, Yugoslavia.
Ex-officio members: The Secretary-General and the UNFPA Executive Director.
Honorary members (until 31 December 1988): Takeo Fukuda, Edem Kodjo, Carmen Miro, Robert E. Turner III, Simone Veil.

Chairman: Ahmed Ghezal (Tunisia).

On 26 May and 28 July 1988 (decisions 1988/150 and 1988/176), the Economic and Social Council elected the following 10 States for a three-year term beginning on 1 January 1989 to fill the vacancies occurring on 31 December 1988: Byelorussian SSR, Ecuador, India, Japan, Mauritius, Mexico, Pakistan, Rwanda, Togo, Turkey.

Committee of Trustees of the United Nations Trust Fund for South Africa

Members: Chile, Morocco, Nigeria, Pakistan, Sweden.

Chairman: Jan K. Eliasson (Sweden).
Vice-Chairman: Joseph N. Garba (Nigeria).

Committee on Applications for Review of Administrative Tribunal Judgements

The Committee on Applications for Review of Administrative Tribunal Judgements held its thirty-first session at United Nations Headquarters on 9 February 1988.

Members (until 19 September 1988) (based on the composition of the General Committee at the General Assembly's forty-second session): Botswana, Cameroon, China, Comoros, Cyprus, France, German Democratic Republic, Jordan, Libyan Arab Jamahiriya, Mauritania, Mongolia, Netherlands, Nicaragua, Panama, Paraguay, Portugal, Qatar, Saint Vincent and the Grenadines, Singapore, Sri Lanka, Syrian Arab Republic, Sweden, Togo, Tunisia, Ukrainian SSR, USSR, United Kingdom, United States, Zaire.

Chairman: Rajab A. Azzarouk (Libyan Arab Jamahiriya).
Rapporteur: David M. Edwards (United Kingdom).

Members (from 20 September 1988) (based on the composition of the General Committee at the General Assembly's forty-third session): Argentina, Bahrain, Bolivia, Canada, China, Côte d'Ivoire, Cyprus, Denmark, Ecuador, El Salvador, France, Guinea-Bissau, Kenya, Kuwait, Libyan Arab Jamahiriya, Malta, Nepal, Poland, Saint Vincent and the Grenadines, Sao Tome and Principe, Sudan, Swaziland, Thailand, USSR, United Kingdom, United Republic of Tanzania, United States, Vanuatu, Yugoslavia.

Committee on Arrangements for a Conference for the Purpose of Reviewing the Charter

All Members of the United Nations are members of the Committee on Arrangements for a Conference for the Purpose of Reviewing the Charter.

The Committee, established in 1955, last met in 1967, following which the General Assembly decided to keep it in being.[6]

Committee on Conferences

The Committee on Conferences consisted of 22 Member States appointed by the President of the General Assembly on the basis of equitable geographical balance, to serve for a three-year term.

Members (until 31 December 1988): Algeria, Argentina, Austria, Bahamas, Byelorussian SSR, Chile, Cyprus, Egypt, France, German Democratic Republic, Germany, Federal Republic of, Indonesia, Japan, Kenya, Mexico, New Zealand, Senegal, Sri Lanka, Tunisia, USSR, United Kingdom, United States.

Chairman: Bernards A. N. Mudho (Kenya).
Vice-Chairmen: J. D. Ariyaratne (Sri Lanka), Jaime Bazan (Chile), Falk Meltke (German Democratic Republic).
Rapporteur: Franziska Friessnigg (Austria).

On 21 December 1988 (resolution 43/222 B), the General Assembly decided to retain the Committee as a permanent subsidiary organ, composed of 21 members appointed by the Assembly President, after consultation with the chairmen of the regional groups, on the basis of the following geographical distribution: six members from African States; five members from Asian States; four members each from Latin American and Caribbean States and from Western European and other States; and two members from Eastern European States. Members were to serve for a renewable three-year term, one third of the membership retiring annually. As a transitional arrangement, one third of the membership was to be appointed for one year, one third for two years and one third for three years.

The new members had not been appointed by the end of 1988.

Committee on Information

The 70-member Committee on Information held its tenth session at United Nations Headquarters from 27 June to 13 July and on 8 and 9 September 1988.

Members: Algeria, Argentina, Bangladesh, Belgium, Benin, Brazil, Bulgaria, Burundi, Chile, China, Colombia, Congo, Costa Rica, Côte d'Ivoire, Cuba, Cyprus, Denmark, Ecuador, Egypt, El Salvador, Ethiopia, Finland, France, German Democratic Republic, Germany, Federal Republic of, Ghana, Greece, Guatemala, Guinea, Guyana, India, Indonesia, Italy, Japan, Jordan, Kenya, Lebanon, Malta, Mexico, Mongolia, Morocco, Netherlands, Niger, Nigeria, Pakistan, Peru, Philippines, Poland, Portugal, Romania, Singapore, Somalia, Spain, Sri Lanka, Sudan, Syrian Arab Republic, Togo, Trinidad and Tobago, Tunisia, Turkey, Ukrainian SSR, USSR, United Kingdom, United Republic of Tanzania, United States, Venezuela, Viet Nam, Yemen, Yugoslavia, Zaire.

Chairman: Pablo Barrios (Spain).
Vice-Chairmen: Waguih Said Moustapha Hanafi (Egypt), Ricardo Lagorio (Argentina), Mansoor Suhail (Pakistan).
Rapporteur: Gerhard Haensel (German Democratic Republic).

On 6 December 1988, the General Assembly increased the Committee's membership from 70 to 73 (decision 43/418) and appointed Hungary, Ireland and Zimbabwe as members (decision 43/316).

Committee on Relations with the Host Country

Members: Bulgaria, Canada, China, Costa Rica, Côte d'Ivoire, France, Honduras, Iraq, Mali, Senegal, Spain, USSR, United Kingdom, United States (host country).

Chairman: Constantine Moushoutas (Cyprus).
Vice-Chairmen: Bulgaria, Canada, Côte d'Ivoire.
Rapporteur: Emilia Castro de Barish (Costa Rica).

Committee on the Development and Utilization of New and Renewable Sources of Energy

The Committee on the Development and Utilization of New and Renewable Sources of Energy, open to the participation of all States

---

[6]YUN 1967, p. 291, GA res. 2285(XXII), 5 Dec. 1967.

as full members, held its fourth session at United Nations Headquarters from 28 March to 8 April 1988.

Chairman: Boris N. Goudima (Ukrainian SSR).
Vice-Chairmen: Sjoerd Leenstra (Netherlands), Mohamed Mahmoud Ould El Gaouthe (Mauritania), Eduardo Praselj (Venezuela).
Rapporteur: G. B. A. Fernando (Sri Lanka).

Committee on the Exercise of the Inalienable Rights of the Palestinian People

Members: Afghanistan, Cuba, Cyprus, German Democratic Republic, Guinea, Guyana, Hungary, India, Indonesia, Lao People's Democratic Republic, Madagascar, Malaysia, Mali, Malta, Nigeria, Pakistan, Romania, Senegal, Sierra Leone, Tunisia, Turkey, Ukrainian SSR, Yugoslavia.

Chairman: Massamba Sarré (Senegal) (until 22 August 1988), Absa Claude Diallo (Senegal) (from 23 August).
Vice-Chairmen: Shah Mohammad Dost (Afghanistan), Oscar Oramas-Oliva (Cuba).
Rapporteur: Alexander Borg Olivier (Malta).

WORKING GROUP
Members: Afghanistan, Cuba, German Democratic Republic, Guinea, Guyana, India *(Vice-Chairman)*, Malta *(Chairman)*, Pakistan, Senegal, Tunisia, Turkey, Ukrainian SSR; Palestine Liberation Organization.

Committee on the Peaceful Uses of Outer Space

The 53-member Committee on the Peaceful Uses of Outer Space held its thirty-first session at United Nations Headquarters from 13 to 23 June 1988.

Members: Albania, Argentina, Australia, Austria, Belgium, Benin, Brazil, Bulgaria, Burkina Faso, Cameroon, Canada, Chad, Chile, China, Colombia, Czechoslovakia, Ecuador, Egypt, France, German Democratic Republic, Germany, Federal Republic of, Greece, Hungary, India, Indonesia, Iran, Iraq, Italy, Japan, Kenya, Lebanon, Mexico, Mongolia, Morocco, Netherlands, Niger, Nigeria, Pakistan, Philippines, Poland, Romania, Sierra Leone, Spain, Sudan, Sweden, Syrian Arab Republic, USSR, United Kingdom, United States, Uruguay, Venezuela, Viet Nam, Yugoslavia.

Chairman: Peter Jankowitsch (Austria).
Vice-Chairman: Petre Tanasie (Romania).
Rapporteur: Flavio Miragaia Perri (Brazil).

LEGAL SUB-COMMITTEE
The Legal Sub-Committee, a committee of the whole, held its twenty-seventh session at Geneva from 14 to 31 March 1988.

Chairman: Ludek Handl (Czechoslovakia).

SCIENTIFIC AND TECHNICAL SUB-COMMITTEE
The Scientific and Technical Sub-Committee, a committee of the whole, held its twenty-fifth session at United Nations Headquarters from 16 to 26 February 1988.

Chairman: John H. Carver (Australia).

Disarmament Commission

In 1988, the Disarmament Commission, composed of all the Members of the United Nations, held a series of meetings between 2 and 20 May and an organizational meeting on 1 December, all at United Nations Headquarters.

Chairman: Davidson L. Hepburn (Bahamas).
Vice-Chairmen: Australia, Austria, Cameroon, Czechoslovakia, Jordan, Togo, Uruguay.
Rapporteur: Istvan Sipos (Hungary).

High-level Committee on the Review of Technical Co-operation among Developing Countries

The High-level Committee on the Review of Technical Co-operation among Developing Countries, composed of all States participating in UNDP, did not meet in 1988.

Intergovernmental Committee on Science and Technology for Development

The Intergovernmental Committee on Science and Technology for Development, which reports to the General Assembly through the Economic and Social Council and is open to the participation of all States as full members, did not meet in 1988.

ADVISORY COMMITTEE ON SCIENCE
AND TECHNOLOGY FOR DEVELOPMENT
The 28-member Advisory Committee on Science and Technology for Development held its eighth session at Goa, India, from 26 to 30 September 1988.

Members:
To serve until 31 December 1989: Carlos Rafael Abeledo, *Vice-Chairman* (Argentina); Elisabeth Birman (Hungary); Harvey Brooks, *Vice-Chairman* (United States); Essam El-Din Galal (Egypt); Karl E. Ganzhorn (Federal Republic of Germany); Yoichi Kaya (Japan); Mumtaz Ali Kazi (Pakistan); Lydia P. Makhubu, *Vice-Chairman* (Swaziland); Lourival Carmo Monaco (Brazil); Salim Msangi (United Republic of Tanzania); James Mullin, *Rapporteur* (Canada); Yash Pal, *Vice-Chairman* (India); Nana Claris Efuah Pratt (Sierra Leone); Francisco R. Sagasti, *Chairman* (Peru).
To serve until 31 December 1990: Saleh Abdulrahman Al-Athel (Saudi Arabia); Ali Boussaha (Algeria); Robert Gyabaa Jones Butler (Ghana); Hyung Sup Choi (Republic of Korea); Elisabeth Helander (Finland); David Kear (New Zealand); Stefan Kwiatkowski, *Vice-Chairman* (Poland); Henry Isaac Cloore Lowe (Jamaica); Tansia Moldende Monkoy (Zaire); Daniel Resendiz Núñez (Mexico); Charles Herbert Geoffrey Oldham (United Kingdom); Omar bin Abdul Rahman (Malaysia); Alexander P. Vladislavlev (USSR); Wu Yikang (China).

Intergovernmental Group to Monitor the Supply and Shipping of Oil and Petroleum Products to South Africa

The Intergovernmental Group to Monitor the Supply and Shipping of Oil and Petroleum Products to South Africa is composed of 11 Member States appointed by the Assembly President, in consultation with the regional groups and the Chairman of the Special Committee against *Apartheid*, on the basis of equitable geographical distribution and ensuring representation of oil-exporting and -shipping States.

Members: Algeria, Cuba, German Democratic Republic, Indonesia, Kuwait, New Zealand, Nicaragua, Nigeria, Norway, Ukrainian SSR, United Republic of Tanzania.

Chairman: Tom Eric Vraalsen (Norway).
Vice-Chairman: Nabeela Al-Mulla (Kuwait).
Rapporteur: Wilbert K. Chagula (United Republic of Tanzania).

Interim Committee of the General Assembly

The Interim Committee of the General Assembly, on which each Member of the United Nations has the right to appoint one representative, was originally established by the Assembly in 1947 to function between the Assembly's regular sessions. It was re-established in 1948 for a further year and in 1949[7] for an indefinite period. The Committee has not met since 1961.[8]

International Civil Service Commission

The International Civil Service Commission consists of 15 members who serve in their personal capacity as individuals of recognized competence in public administration or related fields, par-

---

[7]YUN 1948-49, p. 411, GA res. 295(IV), 21 Nov. 1949.
[8]YUN 1961, p. 705.

ticularly in personnel management. They are appointed by the General Assembly, with due regard for equitable geographical distribution, for four-year terms.

The Commission held two sessions in 1988: its twenty-seventh at Rome, Italy, from 7 to 24 March, and its twenty-eighth at United Nations Headquarters from 11 to 29 July.

Members:
To serve until 31 December 1988: Ivan P. Aboimov (USSR); Amjad Ali (Pakistan); Francesca Yetunde Emanuel (Nigeria); Omar Sirry (Egypt); M. A. Vellodi (India).
To serve until 31 December 1989: Michel Jean Bardoux (France); Claudia Cooley (United States); Antônio Fonseca Pimentel (Brazil); Alexis Stephanou (Greece); Ku Tashiro (Japan).
To serve until 31 December 1990: Richard M. Akwei, *Chairman* (Ghana); Turkia Daddah (Mauritania); Karel Houska (Czechoslovakia); André Xavier Pirson (Belgium); Carlos S. Vegega, *Vice-Chairman* (Argentina).

On 9 December 1988 (decision 43/323), the General Assembly appointed the following members for a four-year term beginning on 1 January 1989 to fill the vacancies occurring on 31 December 1988: Amjad Ali (Pakistan), Francesca Yetunde Emanuel (Nigeria), Omar Sirry (Egypt), Vladislav Petrovich Terekhov (USSR), M. A. Vellodi (India).

ADVISORY COMMITTEE ON POST ADJUSTMENT QUESTIONS
The Advisory Committee on Post Adjustment Questions consists of six members, of whom five are chosen from the geographical regions of Africa, Asia, Latin America, Eastern Europe, and Western Europe and other States; and one, from ICSC, who serves *ex officio* as Chairman. Members are appointed by the ICSC Chairman to serve for four-year terms.

The Advisory Committee held its thirteenth session at Montreal, Canada, from 10 to 17 May 1988.

Members:
To serve until 31 December 1988: Saw Swee Hock (Singapore).
To serve until 31 December 1989: Jeremiah P. Banda (Zambia).
To serve until 31 December 1990: Hugues Picard (France).
To serve until 31 December 1991: Yuri Ivanov (USSR), Isaac Kerstenetzky (Brazil).
Ex-officio member: Carlos S. Vegega, *Chairman* (Argentina).

International Law Commission
The International Law Commission consists of 34 persons of recognized competence in international law, elected by the General Assembly to serve in their individual capacity for a five-year term. Vacancies occurring within the five-year period are filled by the Commission.

The Commission held its fortieth session at Geneva from 9 May to 29 July 1988.

Members (until 31 December 1991): Bola Adesumbo Ajibola (Nigeria); Hussain M. Al-Baharna (Bahrain); Awn S. Al-Khasawneh (Jordan); Riyadh Al-Qaysi (Iraq); Gaetano Arangio-Ruiz (Italy); Julio Barboza (Argentina); Yuri G. Barsegov (USSR); J. Alan Beesley (Canada); Mohamed Bennouna (Morocco); Boutros Boutros-Ghali (Egypt); Carlos Calero Rodrigues (Brazil); Leonardo Díaz-González, *Chairman* (Venezuela); Gudmundur Eiriksson (Iceland); Laurel B. Francis (Jamaica); Bernhard Graefrath, *First Vice-Chairman* (German Democratic Republic); Francis Mahon Hayes (Ireland); Jorge Enrique Illueca (Panama); Andreas J. Jacovides (Cyprus); Abdul G. Koroma (Sierra Leone); Ahmed Mahiou, *Second Vice-Chairman* (Algeria); Stephen C. McCaffrey (United States); Frank X. J. C. Njenga (Kenya); Motoo Ogiso (Japan); Stanislaw M. Pawlak (Poland); Pemmaraju Sreenivasa Rao (India); Edilbert Razafindralambo (Madagascar); Paul Reuter (France); Emmanuel J. Roucounas (Greece); César Sepúlveda Gutiérrez (Mexico); Shi Jiuyong, *Rapporteur* (China); Luis Solari Tudela (Peru); Doudou Thiam (Senegal); Christian Tomuschat (Federal Republic of Germany); Alexander Yankov (Bulgaria).

Investments Committee
The Investments Committee consists of nine members appointed by the Secretary-General, after consultation with the United Nations Joint Staff Pension Board and ACABQ, subject to confirmation by the General Assembly. Members serve for three-year terms.

Members:
To serve until 31 December 1988: Aloysio de Andrade Faria (Brazil); Braj Kumar Nehru, *Chairman* (India); Stanislaw Raczkowski (Poland).
To serve until 31 December 1989:[a] Yves Oltramare (Switzerland); Emmanuel Noi Omaboe (Ghana).
To serve until 31 December 1990: Jean Guyot, *Vice-Chairman* (France); George Johnston (United States); Michiya Matsukawa (Japan).

[a]One seat remained vacant in 1988.

In addition, during 1988, Ahmed Abdullatif (Saudi Arabia) and Juergen Reimnitz (Federal Republic of Germany) served in an *ad hoc* consultative capacity.

On 9 December 1988 (decision 43/321), the General Assembly confirmed the appointment by the Secretary-General of Aloysio de Andrade Faria (Brazil), Braj Kumar Nehru (India) and Stanislaw Raczkowski (Poland) as members for a three-year term, and of Juergen Reimnitz (Federal Republic of Germany) for a one-year term, all beginning on 1 January 1989.

Joint Advisory Group on the International Trade Centre UNCTAD/GATT
The Joint Advisory Group was established in accordance with an agreement between UNCTAD and GATT with effect from 1 January 1968, the date on which their joint sponsorship of the International Trade Centre commenced.

Participation in the Group is open to all States members of UNCTAD and to all contracting parties to GATT.

The Group held its twenty-first session at Geneva from 11 to 15 April 1988.

Chairman: de Montigny Marchand (Canada).
Vice-Chairmen: G. Nanovfszky (Hungary), B. M. Neele (Brazil).
Rapporteur: Li Enheng (China).

Joint Inspection Unit
The Joint Inspection Unit consists of not more than 11 Inspectors appointed by the General Assembly from candidates nominated by Member States following appropriate consultations, including consultations with the President of the Economic and Social Council and with the Chairman of ACC. The Inspectors, chosen for their special experience in national or international administrative and financial matters, with due regard for equitable geographical distribution and reasonable rotation, serve in their personal capacity for five-year terms.

Members:
To serve until 31 December 1989: Kahono Martohadinegoro, *Chairman* (Indonesia).
To serve until 31 December 1990: Enrique Ferrer Vieyra (Argentina); Alain Gourdon (France); Richard Vognild Hennes, *Vice-Chairman* (United States); Ivan Kojic (Yugoslavia); Kabongo Tunsala (Zaire).
To serve until 31 December 1992: Mohamed Salah Eldin Ibrahim (Egypt); Nasser Kaddour (Syrian Arab Republic);[a] Boris P. Prokofiev (USSR); Siegfried Schumm (Federal Republic of Germany); Norman Williams (Panama).

[a]Until 31 January 1988; replaced on 27 May 1988 by Adib Daoudy (Syrian Arab Republic), who had been appointed in 1987 (see YUN 1987, p. 1340).

On 22 December 1988 (decision 43/326), the General Assembly appointed Raúl Quijano (Argentina) for a term beginning on 1 April 1989 and expiring on 31 December 1993 (to replace Enrique Ferrer Vieyra (Argentina) who was to resign effective 1 April) and Kahono Martohadinegoro (Indonesia) for a five-year term beginning on 1 January 1990.

Negotiating Committee on the Financial Emergency of the United Nations

Established in 1975 by the General Assembly[9] to consist of 54 Member States appointed by its President on the basis of equitable geographical balance, the Negotiating Committee on the Financial Emergency of the United Nations has a membership of 48. It has not met since 1976.[10]

Members: Argentina, Austria, Bangladesh, Bolivia, Burkina Faso, Canada, Chad, Colombia, Cuba, Ecuador, Egypt, Finland, France, Gabon, German Democratic Republic, Germany, Federal Republic of, Ghana, Greece, Grenada, India, Indonesia, Iran, Ireland, Italy, Jamaica, Japan, Jordan, Kenya, Kuwait, Libyan Arab Jamahiriya, Malawi, Mexico, Morocco, Nigeria, Pakistan, Philippines, Poland, Spain, Sudan, Swaziland, Sweden, Trinidad and Tobago, Tunisia, Turkey, USSR, United Kingdom, United States, Venezuela.

Office of the United Nations High Commissioner for Refugees (UNHCR)

The United Nations High Commissioner for Refugees reports annually to the General Assembly through the Economic and Social Council.

EXECUTIVE COMMITTEE OF THE HIGH COMMISSIONER'S PROGRAMME

The Executive Committee held its thirty-ninth session at Geneva from 3 to 10 October 1988.

Members: Algeria, Argentina, Australia, Austria, Belgium, Brazil, Canada, China, Colombia, Denmark, Finland, France, Germany, Federal Republic of, Greece, Holy See, Iran, Israel, Italy, Japan, Lebanon, Lesotho, Madagascar, Morocco, Namibia (represented by the United Nations Council for Namibia), Netherlands, Nicaragua, Nigeria, Norway, Pakistan,[a] Somalia,[a] Sudan, Sweden, Switzerland, Thailand, Tunisia, Turkey, Uganda, United Kingdom, United Republic of Tanzania, United States, Venezuela, Yugoslavia, Zaire.

[a]Elected by the Economic and Social Council on 26 May 1988 (decision 1988/150), thereby increasing the membership to 43.

Chairman: Amir Habib Jamal (United Republic of Tanzania).
Vice-Chairman: Fredo Dannenbring (Federal Republic of Germany).
Rapporteur: Marilia Sardenberg Zelner Gonçalves (Brazil).

United Nations High Commissioner for Refugees: Jean-Pierre Hocké.[a]
Deputy High Commissioner: Arthur Eugene Dewey.

[a]Re-elected by the General Assembly on 29 November 1988 (decision 43/312) for a three-year term beginning on 1 January 1989.

SUB-COMMITTEE OF THE WHOLE
ON INTERNATIONAL PROTECTION

The Sub-Committee of the Whole on International Protection held its thirteenth meeting at Geneva from 27 to 30 September 1988.

Chairman: R. H. Robertson (Australia).

SUB-COMMITTEE ON
ADMINISTRATIVE AND FINANCIAL MATTERS

The Sub-Committee on Administrative and Financial Matters, which is composed of all members of the Executive Committee, held its eighth meeting at Geneva concurrently with the thirteenth meeting of the Sub-Committee of the Whole on International Protection.

Chairman: Amir Habib Jamal (United Republic of Tanzania).

Panel for Inquiry and Conciliation

The Panel for Inquiry and Conciliation was created by the General Assembly in 1949[11] to consist of qualified persons, designated by United Nations Member States, each to serve for a term of five years. Information concerning the Panel's composition had from time to time been communicated to the Assembly and the Security Council; the last consolidated list was issued by the Secretary-General in a note of 20 January 1961.

Panel of External Auditors

The Panel of External Auditors consists of the members of the United Nations Board of Auditors and the appointed external auditors of the specialized agencies and IAEA.

Panel of Military Experts

The General Assembly's "Uniting for Peace" resolution[12] called for the appointment of military experts to be available, on request, to United Nations Member States wishing to obtain technical advice on the organization, training and equipment of elements within their national armed forces which could be made available, in accordance with national constitutional processes, for service as a unit or units of the United Nations upon the recommendation of the Security Council or the Assembly.

Preparatory Committee for the Third Special Session of the General Assembly Devoted to Disarmament

The open-ended Preparatory Committee for the Third Special Session of the General Assembly Devoted to Disarmament held its third (final) session at United Nations Headquarters from 25 January to 5 February 1988.

Chairman: Mansur Ahmad (Pakistan).
Vice-Chairmen: Argentina, Australia, Bahamas, Czechoslovakia, Hungary, Japan, Mongolia, Morocco, Netherlands, New Zealand, Norway, Romania, Sri Lanka, Sudan, Togo, Uruguay, Yugoslavia, Zaire.
Rapporteur: Pedro Núñez-Mosquera (Cuba).

Special Committee against *Apartheid*

Members: Algeria, German Democratic Republic, Ghana, Guinea, Haiti, Hungary, India, Indonesia, Malaysia, Nepal, Nigeria, Peru, Philippines, Somalia, Sudan, Syrian Arab Republic, Trinidad and Tobago, Ukrainian SSR.

Chairman: Joseph N. Garba (Nigeria).
Vice-Chairmen: Yves L. Auguste (Haiti), Guennadi I. Oudovenko (Ukrainian SSR), Jai Pratap Rana (Nepal).
Rapporteur: Arif Shahid Khan (India).

In pursuance of its 1979 request that the Committee's membership be expanded,[13] the General Assembly, on 5 December 1988 (decision 43/315), confirmed the appointment by its President of Zimbabwe, with effect from 1 January 1989.

SUB-COMMITTEE ON PETITIONS AND INFORMATION
Members: Algeria *(Chairman)*, German Democratic Republic, Nepal, Somalia, Trinidad and Tobago.

SUB-COMMITTEE ON THE IMPLEMENTATION
OF UNITED NATIONS RESOLUTIONS
AND COLLABORATION WITH SOUTH AFRICA
Members: Ghana *(Chairman)*, Hungary, India, Indonesia, Peru, Sudan.

Special Committee on Peace-keeping Operations

In 1988, the 33-member Special Committee on Peace-keeping Operations met at United Nations Headquarters on 10 February and 25 August.

---

[9]YUN 1975, p. 957, GA res. 3538(XXX), 17 Dec. 1975.
[10]YUN 1976, pp. 889 and 1064.
[11]YUN 1948-49, p. 416, GA res. 268 D (III), 28 Apr. 1949.
[12]YUN 1950, p. 194, GA res. 377(V), part A, para. 10, 3 Nov. 1950.
[13]YUN 1979, p. 201, GA res. 34/93 R, 17 Dec. 1979.

Members: Afghanistan, Algeria, Argentina *(Vice-Chairman)*, Australia, Austria, Canada *(Vice-Chairman)*, Denmark, Egypt *(Rapporteur)*, El Salvador, Ethiopia, France, German Democratic Republic *(Vice-Chairman)*, Guatemala, Hungary, India, Iraq, Italy, Japan *(Vice-Chairman)*, Mauritania, Mexico, Netherlands, Nigeria *(Chairman)*, Pakistan, Poland, Romania, Sierra Leone, Spain, Thailand, USSR, United Kingdom, United States, Venezuela, Yugoslavia.

On 6 December 1988, the General Assembly increased the Special Committee's membership to 34 and approved China's request to become a member.

WORKING GROUP
Members: France, India, Mexico, Pakistan, USSR, United Kingdom, United States, and the officers of the Special Committee.

Special Committee on the Charter of the United Nations and on the Strengthening of the Role of the Organization

The 47-member Special Committee on the Charter of the United Nations and on the Strengthening of the Role of the Organization met at United Nations Headquarters from 22 February to 11 March 1988.

Members: Algeria, Argentina, Barbados, Belgium, Brazil, China, Colombia, Congo, Cyprus, Czechoslovakia, Ecuador, Egypt, El Salvador, Finland, France, German Democratic Republic, Germany, Federal Republic of, Ghana, Greece, Guyana, India, Indonesia, Iran, Iraq, Italy, Japan, Kenya, Liberia, Mexico, Nepal, New Zealand, Nigeria, Pakistan, Philippines, Poland, Romania, Rwanda, Sierra Leone, Spain, Tunisia, Turkey, USSR, United Kingdom, United States, Venezuela, Yugoslavia, Zambia.

Chairman: Bengt H. G. A. Broms (Finland).
Vice-Chairmen: Vaclav Mikulka (Czechoslovakia), Augustus Oboadum Tanoh (Ghana), Omar Zurita (Venezuela).
Rapporteur: James C. Droushiotis (Cyprus).

Special Committee on the Situation with regard to the Implementation of the Declaration on the Granting of Independence to Colonial Countries and Peoples

Members: Afghanistan, Bulgaria, Chile, China, Congo, Côte d'Ivoire, Cuba, Czechoslovakia, Ethiopia, Fiji, India, Indonesia, Iran, Iraq, Mali, Norway, Sierra Leone, Syrian Arab Republic, Trinidad and Tobago, Tunisia, USSR, United Republic of Tanzania, Venezuela, Yugoslavia.

Chairman: Tesfaye Tadesse (Ethiopia).
Vice-Chairmen: Sverre Bergh Johansen (Norway), Tatiana Brosnakova (Czechoslovakia), Oscar Oramas-Oliva (Cuba).
Rapporteur: Ahmad Farouk Arnouss (Syrian Arab Republic).

SUB-COMMITTEE ON PETITIONS,
INFORMATION AND ASSISTANCE
Members: Afghanistan, Bulgaria, Congo, Cuba, Czechoslovakia *(Chairman)*, Indonesia, Iran, Iraq, Mali, Sierra Leone, Syrian Arab Republic, Tunisia, United Republic of Tanzania.

SUB-COMMITTEE ON SMALL TERRITORIES
Members: Afghanistan, Bulgaria, Chile, Côte d'Ivoire, Cuba, Czechoslovakia, Ethiopia, Fiji, India, Indonesia, Iran, Iraq, Mali, Norway *(Rapporteur)*, Trinidad and Tobago, Tunisia *(Chairman)*, United Republic of Tanzania, Venezuela, Yugoslavia.

WORKING GROUP
In 1988, the Working Group of the Special Committee, which functions as a steering committee, consisted of: Congo, Fiji, Iran; the five officers of the Special Committee; and the Chairman and the Rapporteur of the Sub-Committee on Small Territories.

Special Committee to Investigate Israeli Practices Affecting the Human Rights of the Population of the Occupied Territories

Members: Senegal, Sri Lanka *(Chairman)*, Yugoslavia.

Special Committee to Select the Winners of the United Nations Human Rights Prize

The Special Committee to Select the Winners of the United Nations Human Rights Prize was established pursuant to a 1966 General Assembly resolution[14] recommending that a prize or prizes in the field of human rights be awarded not more often than at five-year intervals. Prizes were awarded for the fourth time on 10 December 1988.

Members: The President of the General Assembly, the President of the Economic and Social Council, the Chairman of the Commission on Human Rights, the Chairman of the Commission on the Status of Women and the Chairman of the Sub-Commission on Prevention of Discrimination and Protection of Minorities.

United Nations Administrative Tribunal

Members:
To serve until 31 December 1988: Ahmed Osman (Egypt); Roger Pinto, *First Vice-President* (France); Samarendranath Sen, *President* (India).
To serve until 31 December 1989: Jerome Ackerman (United States); Arnold Wilfred Geoffrey Kean, *Second Vice-President* (United Kingdom).
To serve until 31 December 1990: Francisco Forteza (Uruguay); Ioan Voicu (Romania).

On 9 December 1988 (decision 43/322), the General Assembly appointed Ahmed Osman (Egypt), Roger Pinto (France) and Samarendranath Sen (India) for a three-year term beginning on 1 January 1989 to fill the vacancies occurring on 31 December 1988.

United Nations Capital Development Fund

The United Nations Capital Development Fund was set up as an organ of the General Assembly to function as an autonomous organization within the United Nations framework, with the control of its policies and operations to be exercised by a 24-member Executive Board elected by the Assembly from Members of the United Nations or members of the specialized agencies or of IAEA. The chief executive officer of the Fund, the Managing Director, exercises his functions under the general direction of the Executive Board, which reports to the Assembly through the Economic and Social Council.

EXECUTIVE BOARD
The UNDP Governing Council acts as the Executive Board of the Fund—and the UNDP Administrator as its Managing Director—in conformity with measures the General Assembly adopted provisionally in 1967[15] and reconfirmed yearly thereafter. In 1981, the Assembly decided that UNDP should continue to provide the Fund with, among other things, all headquarters administrative support services;[16] the Fund thus continued to operate under the same arrangements, which remained unchanged in 1988.

Managing Director: William H. Draper III (UNDP Administrator).

United Nations Commission on International Trade Law (UNCITRAL)

The United Nations Commission on International Trade Law consists of 36 members elected by the General Assembly, in accordance with a formula providing equitable geographical representation and adequate representation of the principal economic and legal systems of the world. Members serve for six-year terms.

The Commission held its twenty-first session at United Nations Headquarters from 11 to 20 April 1988.

Members:
To serve until the day preceding the Commission's regular annual session in 1989: Algeria, Australia, Austria, Brazil, Central Afri-

[14]YUN 1966, p. 458, GA res. 2217 A (XXI), annex, 19 Dec. 1966.
[15]YUN 1967, p. 372, GA res. 2321(XXII), 15 Dec. 1967.
[16]YUN 1981, p. 469, GA res. 36/196, 17 Dec. 1981.

can Republic, China, Egypt, France, German Democratic Republic, Japan, Mexico, Nigeria, Singapore, Sweden, USSR, United Kingdom, United Republic of Tanzania.

To serve until the day preceding the Commission's regular annual session in 1992: Argentina, Chile, Cuba, Cyprus, Czechoslovakia, Hungary, India, Iran, Iraq, Italy, Kenya, Lesotho, Libyan Arab Jamahiriya, Netherlands, Sierra Leone, Spain, United States, Uruguay, Yugoslavia.

Chairman: Henry M. Joko-Smart (Sierra Leone).
Vice-Chairmen: Michael Joachim Bonell (Italy), Rafael Eyzaguirre (Chile), Kuchibhotla Venkataramiah (India).
Rapporteur: Ivan Szasz (Hungary).

On 19 October 1988 (decision 43/307), the General Assembly elected the following for a six-year term beginning on the first day of the regular annual session in 1989 (16 May) to fill the vacancies occurring the day before: Bulgaria, Cameroon, Canada, China, Costa Rica, Denmark, Egypt, France, Germany, Federal Republic of, Japan, Mexico, Morocco, Nigeria, Singapore, Togo, USSR, United Kingdom.

WORKING GROUP ON
INTERNATIONAL CONTRACT PRACTICES
In 1988, the Working Group on International Contract Practices, composed of all States members of UNCITRAL, held two sessions: its eleventh at United Nations Headquarters from 18 to 29 January, and its twelfth at Vienna from 21 to 30 November.

Chairman: Michael Joachim Bonell (Italy) (eleventh session), A. S. Hartkamp (Netherlands) (twelfth session).
Rapporteur: Kuchibhotha Venkatramiah (India) (eleventh session), Liu Dagui (China) (twelfth session).

WORKING GROUP ON INTERNATIONAL PAYMENTS
In 1988, the Working Group on International Payments, composed of all States members of UNCITRAL, held two sessions: its seventeenth at United Nations Headquarters from 5 to 15 July, and its eighteenth at Vienna from 5 to 16 December.

Chairman: José María Abascal Zamora (Mexico).
Rapporteur: Rose Burns (Australia) (seventeenth session), Veronique Ingram (Australia) (eighteenth session).

WORKING GROUP ON THE
NEW INTERNATIONAL ECONOMIC ORDER
The Working Group on the New International Economic Order, composed of all States members of UNCITRAL, held its tenth session at Vienna from 17 to 25 October 1988.

Chairman: Robert Hunja (Kenya).
Rapporteur: Adriana Aguilera de Rodriguez (Mexico).

United Nations Conciliation Commission for Palestine
Members: France, Turkey, United States.

United Nations Conference on Trade and Development (UNCTAD)
Members of UNCTAD are Members of the United Nations or members of the specialized agencies or of IAEA.

TRADE AND DEVELOPMENT BOARD
The Trade and Development Board is a permanent organ of UNCTAD. It reports to UNCTAD as well as annually to the General Assembly through the Economic and Social Council. Its membership is drawn from the following list of UNCTAD members.

Part A. Afghanistan, Algeria, Angola, Bahrain, Bangladesh, Benin, Bhutan, Botswana, Brunei Darussalam, Burkina Faso, Burma, Burundi, Cameroon, Cape Verde, Central African Republic, Chad, China, Comoros, Congo, Côte d'Ivoire, Democratic Kampuchea, Democratic People's Republic of Korea, Democratic Yemen, Djibouti, Egypt, Equatorial Guinea, Ethiopia, Fiji, Gabon, Gambia, Ghana, Guinea, Guinea-Bissau, India, Indonesia, Iran,

Iraq, Israel, Jordan, Kenya, Kuwait, Lao People's Democratic Republic, Lebanon, Lesotho, Liberia, Libyan Arab Jamahiriya, Madagascar, Malawi, Malaysia, Maldives, Mali, Mauritania, Mauritius, Mongolia, Morocco, Mozambique, Namibia, Nepal, Niger, Nigeria, Oman, Pakistan, Papua New Guinea, Philippines, Qatar, Republic of Korea, Rwanda, Samoa, Sao Tome and Principe, Saudi Arabia, Senegal, Seychelles, Sierra Leone, Singapore, Solomon Islands, Somalia, South Africa, Sri Lanka, Sudan, Swaziland, Syrian Arab Republic, Thailand, Togo, Tonga, Tunisia, Uganda, United Arab Emirates, United Republic of Tanzania, Vanuatu, Viet Nam, Yemen, Yugoslavia, Zaire, Zambia, Zimbabwe.

Part B. Australia, Austria, Belgium, Canada, Cyprus, Denmark, Finland, France, Germany, Federal Republic of, Greece, Holy See, Iceland, Ireland, Italy, Japan, Liechtenstein, Luxembourg, Malta, Monaco, Netherlands, New Zealand, Norway, Portugal, San Marino, Spain, Sweden, Switzerland, Turkey, United Kingdom, United States.

Part C. Antigua and Barbuda, Argentina, Bahamas, Barbados, Belize, Bolivia, Brazil, Chile, Colombia, Costa Rica, Cuba, Dominica, Dominican Republic, Ecuador, El Salvador, Grenada, Guatemala, Guyana, Haiti, Honduras, Jamaica, Mexico, Nicaragua, Panama, Paraguay, Peru, Saint Kitts and Nevis, Saint Lucia, Saint Vincent and the Grenadines, Suriname, Trinidad and Tobago, Uruguay, Venezuela.

Part D. Albania, Bulgaria, Byelorussian SSR, Czechoslovakia, German Democratic Republic, Hungary, Poland, Romania, Ukrainian SSR, USSR.

BOARD MEMBERS AND SESSIONS
The membership of the Board is open to all UNCTAD members. Those wishing to become members of the Board communicate their intention to the Secretary-General of UNCTAD for transmittal to the Board President, who announces the membership on the basis of such notifications.

The Board held the following sessions in 1988, at Geneva: the second part of its thirty-fourth session from 25 April to 6 May and on 10 May, and the first part of its thirty-fifth session from 19 to 30 September and on 5 October.

Members: Afghanistan, Algeria, Angola, Argentina, Australia, Austria, Bahrain, Bangladesh, Barbados, Belgium, Benin, Bhutan, Bolivia, Brazil, Bulgaria, Burkina Faso, Burma, Burundi, Byelorussian SSR, Cameroon, Canada, Central African Republic, Chad, Chile, China, Colombia, Congo, Costa Rica, Côte d'Ivoire, Cuba, Cyprus, Czechoslovakia, Democratic People's Republic of Korea, Democratic Yemen, Denmark, Dominican Republic, Ecuador, Egypt, El Salvador, Ethiopia, Finland, France, Gabon, German Democratic Republic, Germany, Federal Republic of, Ghana, Greece, Grenada, Guatemala, Guinea, Guyana, Haiti, Honduras, Hungary, India, Indonesia, Iran, Iraq, Ireland, Israel, Italy, Jamaica, Japan, Jordan, Kenya, Kuwait, Lebanon, Liberia, Libyan Arab Jamahiriya, Liechtenstein, Luxembourg, Madagascar, Malaysia, Mali, Malta, Mauritania, Mauritius, Mexico, Mongolia, Morocco, Namibia, Nepal, Netherlands, New Zealand, Nicaragua, Nigeria, Norway, Oman, Pakistan, Panama, Papua New Guinea, Paraguay, Peru, Philippines, Poland, Portugal, Qatar, Republic of Korea, Romania, Saudi Arabia, Senegal, Sierra Leone, Singapore, Somalia, Spain, Sri Lanka, Sudan, Suriname, Sweden, Switzerland, Syrian Arab Republic, Thailand, Togo, Trinidad and Tobago, Tunisia, Turkey, Uganda, Ukrainian SSR, USSR, United Arab Emirates, United Kingdom, United Republic of Tanzania, United States, Uruguay, Venezuela, Viet Nam, Yemen, Yugoslavia, Zaire, Zambia, Zimbabwe.

OFFICERS (BUREAU) OF THE BOARD
Thirty-fourth session
President: Georg Massion (Federal Republic of Germany) (until 29 April), Fredo Dannenbring (Federal Republic of Germany) (from 29 April).
Vice-Presidents: Gustavo Albin Santos (Mexico), José María Araneo (Uruguay), Tobgye S. Dorji (Bhutan), Oto Hlavacek (Czechoslovakia), Mogens Isaksen (Denmark), Farouk Kasrawi (Jordan), Joseph C. Petrone (United States), Samuel Ernest

Quarm (Ghana), Christoph Querner (Austria), Vladimir Tchekline (USSR).
Rapporteur: Mohammed Said Benryane (Morocco).

Thirty-fifth session
President: Tobgye S. Dorji (Bhutan).
Vice-Presidents: Emeka Ayo Azikiwe (Nigeria), Raul España Smith (Bolivia), Farouk Kasrawi (Jordan), Euripide P. Kerkinos (Greece), de Montigny Marchand (Canada), José Enrique Mejia Ucles (Honduras), Youssef Mokaddem (Tunisia), Joseph C. Petrone (United States), Gerald Philipp (German Democratic Republic), T. V. Teodorovich (USSR).
Rapporteur: Kees Klompenhouwer (Netherlands).

SUBSIDIARY ORGANS OF THE
TRADE AND DEVELOPMENT BOARD
The main committees of the Board are open to the participation of all interested UNCTAD members, on the understanding that those wishing to attend a particular session of one or more of the main committees communicate their intention to the Secretary-General of UNCTAD during the preceding regular session of the Board. On the basis of such notifications, the Board determines the membership of the main committees.

COMMITTEE ON COMMODITIES
The Committee on Commodities held its thirteenth session at Geneva from 5 to 13 December 1988.

Members: Algeria, Argentina, Australia, Austria, Bahrain, Bangladesh, Belgium, Bolivia, Brazil, Bulgaria, Burkina Faso, Burma, Burundi, Cameroon, Canada, Central African Republic, Chad, Chile, China, Colombia, Costa Rica, Côte d'Ivoire, Cuba, Cyprus, Czechoslovakia, Democratic People's Republic of Korea, Democratic Yemen, Denmark, Dominican Republic, Ecuador, Egypt, El Salvador, Ethiopia, Finland, France, Gabon, German Democratic Republic, Germany, Federal Republic of, Ghana, Greece, Guatemala, Guinea, Haiti, Honduras, Hungary, India, Indonesia, Iran, Iraq, Ireland, Israel, Italy, Jamaica, Japan, Jordan, Kenya, Kuwait, Liberia, Libyan Arab Jamahiriya, Madagascar, Malaysia, Malta, Mauritius, Mexico, Morocco, Netherlands, New Zealand, Nicaragua, Nigeria, Norway, Pakistan, Panama, Paraguay, Peru, Philippines, Poland, Portugal, Qatar, Republic of Korea, Romania, Rwanda, Saudi Arabia, Senegal, Somalia, Spain, Sri Lanka, Sudan, Sweden, Switzerland, Syrian Arab Republic, Thailand, Togo, Trinidad and Tobago, Tunisia, Turkey, Uganda, USSR, United Arab Emirates, United Kingdom, United Republic of Tanzania, United States, Uruguay, Venezuela, Viet Nam, Yemen, Yugoslavia, Zaire, Zimbabwe.

Chairman: Stéphane Gompertz (France).
Vice-Chairmen: Maciej Lebkowsky (Poland), Galo Leoro Franco (Ecuador), Kunihiko Makita (Japan), Hani Riad (Egypt), Wittayut Wongwarnij (Thailand).
Rapporteur: Emile M'Lingui Keffa (Côte d'Ivoire).

COMMITTEE ON TUNGSTEN
The Committee on Tungsten held its twentieth session at Geneva from 7 to 11 November 1988.

Members: Argentina, Australia, Austria, Belgium, Bolivia, Brazil, Canada, China, Cyprus, France, Gabon, Germany, Federal Republic of, Italy, Japan, Mexico, Netherlands, Peru, Poland, Portugal, Republic of Korea, Romania, Rwanda, Spain, Sweden, Thailand, Turkey, USSR, United Kingdom, United States.

Chairman: C. Cajka (Canada).
Vice-Chairman/Rapporteur: K. Natsume (Japan).

COMMITTEE ON ECONOMIC CO-OPERATION
AMONG DEVELOPING COUNTRIES
The Committee on Economic Co-operation among Developing Countries did not meet in 1988.

Members: Algeria, Argentina, Australia, Austria, Bahrain, Bangladesh, Belgium, Benin, Bolivia, Brazil, Bulgaria, Burma, Cameroon, Canada,

Central African Republic, Chile, China, Colombia, Costa Rica, Côte d'Ivoire, Cuba, Cyprus, Czechoslovakia, Democratic People's Republic of Korea, Democratic Yemen, Denmark, Dominican Republic, Ecuador, Egypt, El Salvador, Ethiopia, Finland, France, Gabon, German Democratic Republic, Germany, Federal Republic of, Ghana, Greece, Guatemala, Guyana, Haiti, Honduras, Hungary, India, Indonesia, Iran, Iraq, Ireland, Israel, Italy, Jamaica, Japan, Jordan, Kenya, Kuwait, Lebanon, Liberia, Libyan Arab Jamahiriya, Madagascar, Malaysia, Malta, Mauritius, Mexico, Morocco, Netherlands, New Zealand, Nicaragua, Nigeria, Norway, Oman, Pakistan, Panama, Paraguay, Peru, Philippines, Poland, Portugal, Qatar, Republic of Korea, Romania, Saudi Arabia, Senegal, Singapore, Somalia, Spain, Sri Lanka, Sudan, Suriname, Sweden, Switzerland, Syrian Arab Republic, Thailand, Togo, Trinidad and Tobago, Tunisia, Turkey, Uganda, USSR, United Arab Emirates, United Kingdom, United Republic of Tanzania, United States, Uruguay, Venezuela, Viet Nam, Yemen, Yugoslavia, Zaire, Zambia, Zimbabwe.

COMMITTEE ON INVISIBLES AND FINANCING RELATED TO TRADE
The Committee on Invisibles and Financing related to Trade did not meet in 1988.

Members: Algeria, Argentina, Australia, Austria, Bahrain, Bangladesh, Belgium, Bolivia, Brazil, Bulgaria, Burkina Faso, Burundi, Cameroon, Canada, Central African Republic, Chad, Chile, China, Colombia, Costa Rica, Côte d'Ivoire, Cuba, Czechoslovakia, Democratic People's Republic of Korea, Democratic Yemen, Denmark, Dominican Republic, Ecuador, Egypt, El Salvador, Ethiopia, Finland, France, German Democratic Republic, Germany, Federal Republic of, Ghana, Greece, Guatemala, Guinea, Honduras, Hungary, India, Indonesia, Iran, Iraq, Ireland, Israel, Italy, Jamaica, Japan, Jordan, Kenya, Kuwait, Lebanon, Liberia, Libyan Arab Jamahiriya, Madagascar, Malaysia, Mali, Malta, Mexico, Morocco, Netherlands, New Zealand, Nicaragua, Nigeria, Norway, Pakistan, Panama, Paraguay, Peru, Philippines, Poland, Portugal, Qatar, Republic of Korea, Romania, Saudi Arabia, Senegal, Somalia, Spain, Sri Lanka, Sudan, Sweden, Switzerland, Syrian Arab Republic, Thailand, Trinidad and Tobago, Tunisia, Turkey, Uganda, USSR, United Kingdom, United Republic of Tanzania, United States, Uruguay, Venezuela, Viet Nam, Yemen, Yugoslavia, Zaire, Zimbabwe.

COMMITTEE ON MANUFACTURES
The Committee on Manufactures did not meet in 1988.

Members: Algeria, Argentina, Australia, Austria, Bahrain, Bangladesh, Belgium, Bolivia, Brazil, Bulgaria, Burkina Faso, Cameroon, Canada, Central African Republic, Chile, China, Colombia, Costa Rica, Côte d'Ivoire, Cuba, Czechoslovakia, Democratic People's Republic of Korea, Democratic Yemen, Denmark, Dominican Republic, Ecuador, Egypt, El Salvador, Ethiopia, Finland, France, German Democratic Republic, Germany, Federal Republic of, Ghana, Greece, Guatemala, Haiti, Honduras, Hungary, India, Indonesia, Iran, Iraq, Ireland, Israel, Italy, Jamaica, Japan, Jordan, Kenya, Kuwait, Liberia, Libyan Arab Jamahiriya, Madagascar, Malaysia, Mali, Malta, Mauritius, Mexico, Morocco, Netherlands, New Zealand, Nicaragua, Nigeria, Norway, Pakistan, Panama, Paraguay, Peru, Philippines, Poland, Portugal, Qatar, Republic of Korea, Romania, Saudi Arabia, Senegal, Singapore, Somalia, Spain, Sri Lanka, Sudan, Sweden, Switzerland, Syrian Arab Republic, Thailand, Trinidad and Tobago, Tunisia, Turkey, USSR, United Kingdom, United Republic of Tanzania, United States, Uruguay, Venezuela, Viet Nam, Yemen, Yugoslavia, Zaire, Zambia, Zimbabwe.

COMMITTEE ON SHIPPING
The Committee on Shipping held its thirteenth session at Geneva from 14 to 22 March 1988.

Members: Algeria, Argentina, Australia, Bahrain, Bangladesh, Belgium, Benin, Bolivia, Brazil, Bulgaria, Burkina Faso, Cameroon, Canada, Central African Republic, Chile, China, Colombia,

Congo,[a] Costa Rica, Côte d'Ivoire, Cuba, Cyprus, Czechoslovakia, Democratic People's Republic of Korea, Democratic Yemen, Denmark, Dominican Republic, Ecuador, Egypt, El Salvador, Ethiopia, Finland, France, Gabon, German Democratic Republic, Germany, Federal Republic of, Ghana, Greece, Guatemala, Guinea, Honduras, Hungary, India, Indonesia, Iran, Iraq, Israel, Italy, Jamaica, Japan, Jordan, Kenya, Kuwait, Lebanon, Liberia, Libyan Arab Jamahiriya, Madagascar, Malaysia, Malta, Mauritius, Mexico, Morocco, Netherlands, New Zealand, Nicaragua, Nigeria, Norway, Oman, Pakistan, Panama, Paraguay, Peru, Philippines, Poland, Portugal, Qatar, Republic of Korea, Romania, Saudi Arabia, Senegal, Somalia, Spain, Sri Lanka, Sudan, Sweden, Switzerland, Syrian Arab Republic, Thailand, Trinidad and Tobago, Tunisia, Turkey, Uganda, USSR, United Arab Emirates, United Kingdom, United Republic of Tanzania, United States, Uruguay, Venezuela, Viet Nam, Yemen, Yugoslavia, Zaire.

[a]Elected by the Trade and Development Board on 25 April 1988, raising the Committee's membership to 103.

Chairman: Hugo Sommerkamp-Bernales (Peru).
Vice-Chairmen: Gosta Lind af Hageby (Sweden), Tadeusz Lodykowski (Poland), Douglas Pelkola (Canada), Roger Tchibota-Souamy (Gabon), Zhu Jianxin (China).
Rapporteur: I. Gusti Ngurah Swetja (Indonesia).

WORKING GROUP ON INTERNATIONAL SHIPPING LEGISLATION
The Working Group on International Shipping Legislation, whose membership is identical to that of the Committee on Shipping, did not meet in 1988.

COMMITTEE ON TRANSFER OF TECHNOLOGY
The Committee on Transfer of Technology did not meet in 1988.

Members: Algeria, Argentina, Australia, Austria, Bahrain, Bangladesh, Belgium, Bolivia, Brazil, Bulgaria, Burkina Faso, Cameroon, Canada, Chile, China, Colombia, Costa Rica, Côte d'Ivoire, Cuba, Czechoslovakia, Democratic People's Republic of Korea, Democratic Yemen, Denmark, Dominican Republic, Ecuador, Egypt, El Salvador, Ethiopia, Finland, France, German Democratic Republic, Germany, Federal Republic of, Ghana, Greece, Guatemala, Haiti, Honduras, Hungary, India, Indonesia, Iran, Iraq, Ireland, Israel, Italy, Jamaica, Japan, Jordan, Kenya, Kuwait, Liberia, Libyan Arab Jamahiriya, Madagascar, Malaysia, Malta, Mauritius, Mexico, Morocco, Netherlands, New Zealand, Nicaragua, Nigeria, Norway, Pakistan, Panama, Paraguay, Peru, Philippines, Poland, Portugal, Qatar, Republic of Korea, Romania, Saudi Arabia, Senegal, Sierra Leone, Somalia, Spain, Sri Lanka, Sudan, Sweden, Switzerland, Syrian Arab Republic, Thailand, Trinidad and Tobago, Tunisia, Turkey, USSR, United Arab Emirates, United Kingdom, United Republic of Tanzania, United States, Uruguay, Venezuela, Viet Nam, Yemen, Yugoslavia, Zaire, Zimbabwe.

SPECIAL COMMITTEE ON PREFERENCES
The Special Committee on Preferences, which is open to the participation of all UNCTAD members, held its fifteenth session at Geneva from 24 May to 1 June 1988.

Chairman: M. Lebkowski (Poland).
Vice-Chairmen: M. M. Abdel-Fattah (Egypt), P. García Donoso (Ecuador), E. A. Hoerig (Federal Republic of Germany), D. Shaw (Canada), G. Zrnic (Yugoslavia).
Rapporteur: A. Abba (Algeria).

United Nations Council for Namibia
Members: Algeria, Angola, Australia, Bangladesh, Belgium, Botswana, Bulgaria, Burundi, Cameroon, Chile, China, Colombia, Cyprus, Egypt, Finland, Guyana, Haiti, India, Indonesia, Liberia, Mexico, Nigeria, Pakistan, Poland, Romania, Senegal, Turkey, USSR, Venezuela, Yugoslavia, Zambia.
President: Peter D. Zuze (Zambia).

Vice-Presidents: Hocine Djoudi (Algeria), Chinmaya R. Gharekhan (India), Samuel R. Insanally (Guyana), Dragoslav Pejic (Yugoslavia), Ilter Turkmen (Turkey).

United Nations Commissioner for Namibia: Bernt Carlsson.[a]

[a]Reappointed by the General Assembly on 17 November 1988 (decision 43/311) for a one-year term beginning on 1 January 1989; however, he died on 21 December 1988.

COMMITTEE ON THE UNITED NATIONS FUND FOR NAMIBIA
Members: Australia, Finland, India, Nigeria, Romania, Senegal, Turkey, Venezuela *(Vice-Chairman/Rapporteur)*, Yugoslavia, Zambia; the President of the Council *(ex-officio Chairman)*.

STANDING COMMITTEE I
Members: Algeria, Cameroon *(Chairman)*, China, Colombia, Finland, Haiti, India,[a] Indonesia, Nigeria, Poland, Senegal, Turkey *(Vice-Chairman)*, USSR, Venezuela, Zambia.

[a]New member in 1988.

STANDING COMMITTEE II
Members: Algeria, Angola, Australia, Bangladesh, Botswana, Bulgaria, Chile, Colombia, Cyprus, Egypt, Finland, Guyana, India, Liberia, Mexico, Nigeria,[a] Pakistan *(Chairman)*, Romania, Zambia.

[a]New member in 1988.

STANDING COMMITTEE III
Members: Algeria, Angola, Australia, Belgium, Bulgaria *(Chairman)*, Burundi, Colombia, Cyprus, Egypt, India, Mexico *(Vice-Chairman)*, Nigeria, Pakistan, Romania, Venezuela, Yugoslavia, Zambia.

STEERING COMMITTEE
In 1988, the Steering Committee consisted of the Council's President and five Vice-Presidents, the Chairmen of its three Standing Committees and the Vice-Chairman/Rapporteur of the Committee on the United Nations Fund for Namibia.

United Nations Development Fund for Women (UNIFEM)
The United Nations Development Fund for Women is a separate entity in autonomous association with UNDP. The Director of the Fund, appointed by the UNDP Administrator, conducts all matters related to its mandate and the Administrator is accountable for its management and operations.

CONSULTATIVE COMMITTEE
The Consultative Committee on UNIFEM to advise the UNDP Administrator on all policy matters affecting the Fund's activities is composed of five Member States designated by the General Assembly President with due regard for the financing of the Fund from voluntary contributions and to equitable geographical distribution. Each State member of the Committee serves for a three-year term and designates a person with expertise in development co-operation activities, including those benefiting women.
The Committee held two sessions in 1988, at United Nations Headquarters: its twenty-third from 5 to 11 April, and its twenty-fourth from 6 to 12 September.

Members (to serve until 31 December 1988): Colombia, German Democratic Republic, India, Kenya, Norway.

Director of UNIFEM: Margaret Snyder.

On 9 December 1988 (decision 43/325), the General Assembly took note of the appointment by its President of the German Democratic Republic, India, Mexico, the Netherlands and Senegal for a three-year term beginning on 1 January 1989.

United Nations Environment Programme (UNEP)
GOVERNING COUNCIL
The Governing Council of UNEP consists of 58 members elected by the General Assembly.

Seats on the Governing Council are allocated as follows: 16 to African States, 13 to Asian States, 6 to Eastern European States, 10 to Latin American States, and 13 to Western European and other States.

The Governing Council, which reports to the Assembly through the Economic and Social Council, held its first special session at Nairobi, Kenya, from 14 to 18 March 1988.

Members:
To serve until 31 December 1988: Argentina, Australia, Barbados, Botswana, Bulgaria, Canada, Chile, China, Colombia, Congo, Czechoslovakia, Denmark, France, Ghana, India, Indonesia, Jamaica, Jordan, Kenya, Libyan Arab Jamahiriya, Malta, Mexico, Netherlands, Niger, Nigeria, Oman, Panama, Papua New Guinea, Poland, Sri Lanka, Swaziland, Syrian Arab Republic, Thailand, Tunisia, Turkey, Uganda, United Kingdom, Yugoslavia, Zambia.
To serve until 31 December 1989: Brazil, Burundi, Dominican Republic, Gabon, Germany, Federal Republic of, Greece, Iran, Iraq, Japan, Mauritania, Republic of Korea, Senegal, Sweden, Switzerland, Ukrainian SSR, USSR, United States, Venezuela, Zaire.

President: Jorge Enrique Illueca (Panama).
Vice-Presidents: Z. R. Ansari (India), C. J. Butale (Botswana), D. Protsenko (Ukrainian SSR).
Rapporteur: P. Sutter (Switzerland).

Executive Director of UNEP: Mostafa Kamal Tolba.[a]
Deputy Executive Director: William H. Mansfield III.

[a]Re-elected by the General Assembly on 2 December 1988 (decision 43/314) for a four-year term beginning on 1 January 1989.

On 24 October 1988 (decision 43/406), the General Assembly decided to elect at the current session 10 members for a one-year term and 29 members for a three-year term beginning on 1 January 1989, as part of the transitional arrangement for changing the term of office of members from three to four years, to elect 29 members in 1989 for a four-year term beginning on 1 January 1990 and to elect every other year half the total of 58 members. As a result, the Assembly, on 24 October (decision 43/308), elected, for terms beginning on 1 January 1989, the following for one year: Argentina, Australia, Barbados, China, France, Indonesia, Lesotho, Mauritius, Yugoslavia, Zimbabwe; and the following for three years: Bangladesh, Botswana, Bulgaria, Canada, Chile, Colombia, Costa Rica, Côte d'Ivoire, Czechoslovakia, Finland, Guyana, India, Jordan, Kenya, Libyan Arab Jamahiriya, Malta, Mexico, Netherlands, Oman, Pakistan, Poland, Rwanda, Saudi Arabia, Sri Lanka, Sudan, Togo, Turkey, Uganda, United Kingdom.

COMMITTEE OF PERMANENT REPRESENTATIVES
The open-ended Committee of Permanent Representatives consists of permanent representatives to UNEP and/or Government-designated officials, to consider administrative and budgetary and programme matters, and to review progress in implementing the programme and Council decisions. It meets with the Executive Director at least five times a year.

United Nations Institute for Disarmament Research (UNIDIR)

BOARD OF TRUSTEES
The Secretary-General's Advisory Board on Disarmament Studies, composed in 1988 of 24 eminent persons selected on the basis of their personal expertise and taking into account the principle of equitable geographical representation, functions as the Board of Trustees of UNIDIR; the Director of UNIDIR reports to the General Assembly and is an *ex-officio* member of the Advisory Board when it acts as the Board of Trustees.

Members: Oluyemi Adeniji (Nigeria); Hadj Benabdelkader Azzout (Algeria); Rolf Björnerstedt (Sweden); James E. Dougherty (United States); Omran El-Shafei (Egypt); Constantin Ene (Romania); Alfonso García Robles, *Chairman* (Mexico); Ignac Golob (Yugoslavia); A. C. Shahul Hameed (Sri Lanka); Ryukichi Imai (Japan); Boris P. Krasulin (USSR);[a] Bjorn Inge Kristvik (Norway); Carlos Lechuga

Hevia (Cuba); Liang Yufan (China); Sir Ronald Mason (United Kingdom); William Eteki Mboumoua (Cameroon); Manfred Mueller (German Democratic Republic); Carlos Ortiz de Rozas (Argentina); Edgard Pisani (France);[a] Maharajakrishna Rasgotra (India); Friedrich Ruth (Federal Republic of Germany); Amada Segarra (Ecuador); Agha Shahi (Pakistan); Tadeusz Strulak (Poland).

[a]Appointed in April and September 1988, respectively.

Director of UNIDIR: Jayantha Dhanapala.

United Nations Institute for Training and Research (UNITAR)
The Executive Director of UNITAR, in consultation with the Board of Trustees of the Institute, reports through the Secretary-General to the General Assembly and, as appropriate, to the Economic and Social Council and other United Nations bodies.

BOARD OF TRUSTEES
The Board of Trustees of UNITAR is composed of: *(a)* not less than 11 and not more than 30 members, which may include one or more officials of the United Nations Secretariat, appointed on a broad geographical basis by the Secretary-General, in consultation with the Presidents of the General Assembly and the Economic and Social Council; and *(b)* four *ex-officio* members.
The Board held its twenty-sixth session at United Nations Headquarters from 11 to 15 April 1988.

Members:
To serve until 31 December 1988: Andrés Aguilar (Venezuela); Rafeeuddin Ahmed (Secretariat); J. Isawa Elaigwu (Nigeria); Alexander F. Fesenko (USSR); Jacques Leprette (France); Missoum Sbih, *Vice-Chairman* (Algeria); S. Shah Nawaz, *Chairman* (Pakistan).
To serve until 31 December 1989: D. H. N. Alleyne (Trinidad and Tobago); Jaime de Piniés (Secretariat); Lucio García del Solar (Argentina); Kiyoaki Kikuchi (Japan); Franz E. Muheim (Switzerland); Ali A. Treiki (Libyan Arab Jamahiriya).
To serve until 31 December 1990: Lawrence S. Eagleburger (United States); Amara Essy (Côte d'Ivoire); Keijo Korhonen (Finland); Natarajan Krishnan (India); Umberto La Rocca (Italy).
Ex-officio members: The Secretary-General, the President of the General Assembly, the President of the Economic and Social Council and the Executive Director of UNITAR.

Executive Director of UNITAR: Michel Doo Kingué.

United Nations Joint Staff Pension Board
The United Nations Joint Staff Pension Board did not meet in 1988.

Members: United Nations, ILO, WHO, FAO, UNESCO, ICAO, IAEA, WMO, IMO, ITU, ICITO/GATT, WIPO, IFAD, UNIDO.

STANDING COMMITTEE OF THE PENSION BOARD
The Standing Committee met at Geneva from 20 to 24 June 1988.

Members (elected at the Board's 1987 session):

United Nations (Group I)
Representing the General Assembly: Member: Sol Kuttner. Alternates: Mario Majoli, Ulrich Kalbitzer, Yukio Takasu.
Representing the Secretary-General: Member: Kofi A. Annan. Alternates: J. Richard Foran, Matias de la Mota, Maryan Baquerot, Anthony J. Miller, Dulcie Bull.
Representing the Participants: Member: Susanna H. Johnston. Alternates: Gualtiero Fulcheri, Bruce C. Hillis, Lennox Bourne, Nancy L. Sadka.
Specialized agencies (Group II)
Representing the Governing Body: Member: William M. Yoffee (ILO). Alternate: E. Zador (UNIDO), *Chairman.*
Representing the Executive Head: Member: Warren W. Furth (WHO), *Second Vice-Chairman.* Alternate: John E. Morgan (WHO).
Representing the Participants: Member: W. E. Price (IAEA), *First Vice-Chairman.* Alternates: D. Bertaud (IMO), P. A. Traub (ITU), R. M. Perry (WMO).

Specialized agencies (Group III)
    Representing the Governing Body: Member: A. D. Weygandt (FAO).
    Representing the Executive Head: Member: A. Raffray (UNESCO).
    Representing the Participants: Member: G. Thorn (ICITO). Alternate: Gilles Frammery (WIPO).

COMMITTEE OF ACTUARIES

The Committee of Actuaries consists of five members, each representing one of the five geographical regions of the United Nations.

Members: Ajibola O. Ogunshola (Nigeria), *Region I* (African States); Kunio Takeuchi (Japan), *Region II* (Asian States); Evgeny M. Chetyrkin (USSR), *Region III* (Eastern European States); Gonzalo Arroba (Ecuador), *Region IV* (Latin American States); Robert J. Myers (United States), *Region V* (Western European and other States).

United Nations Population Fund (UNFPA)

The United Nations Population Fund, a subsidiary organ of the General Assembly, plays a leading role in the United Nations system in promoting population programmes and assists developing countries at their request in dealing with their population problems. It operates under the overall policy guidance of the Economic and Social Council and under the financial and administrative policy guidance of the Governing Council of UNDP.

Executive Director: Dr. Nafis I. Sadik.
Deputy Executive Director: Tatsuro Kunugi.

United Nations Relief and Works Agency for Palestine Refugees in the Near East (UNRWA)

ADVISORY COMMISSION OF UNRWA

In 1988, the Advisory Commission of UNRWA held an extraordinary meeting on 2 March and its regular meeting on 25 August, both at Vienna.

Members: Belgium, Egypt, France, Japan, Jordan, Lebanon, Syrian Arab Republic, Turkey *(Chairman)* (until 24 August), United Kingdom *(Chairman)* (from 25 August), United States.

WORKING GROUP ON THE FINANCING OF UNRWA

Members: France, Ghana, Japan, Lebanon, Norway *(Rapporteur)*, Trinidad and Tobago, Turkey *(Chairman)*, United Kingdom, United States.

Commissioner-General of UNRWA: Giorgio Giacomelli.
Deputy Commissioner-General: Robert S. Dillon (until July), William L. Eagleton (from October).

United Nations Scientific Advisory Committee

Established by the General Assembly in 1954 as a seven-member advisory committee on the International Conference on the Peaceful Uses of Atomic Energy (1955), the United Nations Scientific Advisory Committee was so renamed and its mandate revised by the Assembly in 1958,[17] retaining its original composition. The Committee has not met since 1956.[18]

Members: Brazil, Canada, France, India, USSR, United Kingdom, United States.

United Nations Scientific Committee on the Effects of Atomic Radiation

The 21-member United Nations Scientific Committee on the Effects of Atomic Radiation held its thirty-seventh session at Vienna from 6 to 17 June 1988.

Members: Argentina, Australia, Belgium, Brazil, Canada, China, Czechoslovakia, Egypt, France, Germany, Federal Republic of, India, Indonesia, Japan, Mexico, Peru, Poland, Sudan, Sweden, USSR, United Kingdom, United States.

Chairman: B. Lindell (Sweden).
Vice-Chairman: K. H. Lokan (Australia).
Rapporteur: J. Maisin (Belgium).

United Nations Special Fund

(to provide emergency relief and development assistance)

BOARD OF GOVERNORS

The activities of the United Nations Special Fund were suspended, *ad interim*, in 1978 by the General Assembly, which assumed the functions of the Board of Governors of the Fund. In 1981,[19] the Assembly decided to continue performing those functions, within the context of its consideration of the item on development and international economic co-operation, pending consideration of the question in 1983. However, no further action had been taken by the end of 1988.

United Nations Staff Pension Committee

The United Nations Staff Pension Committee consisted of three members elected by the General Assembly, three appointed by the Secretary-General and three elected by the participants in the United Nations Joint Staff Pension Fund. The term of office of the elected members is three years, or until the election of their successors.

Members:
Elected by Assembly (to serve until 31 December 1988): *Members:* Sol Kuttner *(Chairman)*, Mario Majoli, Michael George Okeyo. *Alternates:* Ulrich Kalbitzer, Miguel A. Ortega, Yukio Takasu.
Appointed by Secretary-General (to serve until further notice): *Members:* Kofi Annan, J. Richard Foran, Matias de la Mota. *Alternates:* Maryan Baquerot, Anthony J. Miller, Dulcie Bull.
Elected by Participants (to serve until 31 December 1989): *Members:* Susanna H. Johnston, Gualtiero Fulcheri, Bruce C. Hillis *(Vice-Chairman)*. *Alternates:* Lennox Bourne, Nancy L. Sadka, George Irving.

In accordance with its 1987 decision that the composition of the Committee change with effect from 1 January 1989,[20] the General Assembly, on 9 December 1988 (decision 43/324), elected the following for a three-year term beginning on 1 January 1989: *Members:* Yogesh Kumar Gupta (India), Sol Kuttner (United States), Michael George Okeyo (Kenya), Victor A. Vislykh (USSR); *Alternates:* Tadanori Inomata (Japan), Ulrich Kalbitzer (Federal Republic of Germany), Mohand Ladjouzi (Algeria), Teodoro Maus (Mexico).

United Nations University

COUNCIL OF THE UNITED NATIONS UNIVERSITY

The Council of the United Nations University, the governing board of the University, reports annually to the General Assembly, to the Economic and Social Council and to the UNESCO Executive Board through the Secretary-General and the UNESCO Director-General. It consists of: *(a)* 24 members appointed jointly by the Secretary-General and the Director-General of UNESCO, in consultation with the agencies and programmes concerned including UNITAR, who serve in their personal capacity for six-year terms; *(b)* the Secretary-General, the Director-General of UNESCO and the Executive Director of UNITAR, who are *ex-officio* members; and *(c)* the Rector of the University, who is normally appointed for a five-year term.

In 1988, the Council held two sessions: its thirty-first at Brasilia, Brazil, from 26 to 30 July, and its thirty-second in Tokyo from 6 to 10 December.

Members:
To serve until 2 May 1989: Bakr Abdullah Bakr (Saudi Arabia); Bashir Bakri, *Vice-Chairman* (Sudan); Marie-Thérèse Basse (Senegal); André Blanc-Lapierre (France); Mercedes B. Concep-

---

[17]YUN 1958, p. 31, GA res. 1344(XIII), 13 Dec. 1958.
[18]YUN 1956, p. 108.
[19]YUN 1981, p. 418, GA dec. 36/424, 4 Dec. 1981.
[20]YUN 1987, p. 1158, GA res. 42/222, 21 Dec. 1987.

ción (Philippines); Helge Gyllenberg, *Vice-Chairman* (Finland); Walter Joseph Kamba (Zimbabwe); Gerald Cecil Lalor (Jamaica); Maria de Lourdes Pintasilgo (Portugal); Yevgeniy M. Primakov (USSR); Alberto Wagner de Reyna (Peru); Zhao Dihua (China).
To serve until 2 May 1992: Mary F. Berry (United States); Alfonso Borrero (Colombia); Umberto Colombo, *Vice-Chairman* (Italy); Kuniyoshi Date (Japan); Keith B. Griffin (United Kingdom); Joseph Ki-Zerbo (Burkina Faso); Candido Mendes de Almeida (Brazil); M. G. K. Menon, *Vice-Chairman* (India); Martha V. Mvungi, *Vice-Chairman* (United Republic of Tanzania); Mihaly Simai, *Vice-Chairman* (Hungary); Rehman Sobhan (Bangladesh); Justin Thorens, *Chairman* (Switzerland).
Ex-officio members: The Secretary-General, the Director-General of UNESCO and the Executive Director of UNITAR.

Rector of the United Nations University: Heitor Gurgulino de Souza.

The Council maintained four standing committees during 1988: Committee on Finance and Budget; Committee on Institutional and Programmatic Development; Committee on Statutes, Rules and Guidelines; Committee on the Report of the Council.

United Nations Voluntary Fund for Indigenous Populations
The United Nations Voluntary Fund for Indigenous Populations provides financial assistance to representatives of indigenous communities and organizations to enable their participation in meetings of the Working Group on Indigenous Populations, a subsidiary of the Sub-Commission on Prevention of Discrimination and Protection of Minorities.

BOARD OF TRUSTEES
The Board of Trustees to advise the Secretary-General in his administration of the Fund consists of five members with relevant experience in issues affecting indigenous populations, appointed in their personal capacity by the Secretary-General for a three-year term. At least one member is a representative of a widely recognized organization of indigenous people.
The Board held its first session at Geneva from 25 to 30 April 1988.

Members: Leif Dunfjeld (Norway); Alioune Sène (Senegal); Hiwi Tauroa (New Zealand); Danilo Turk (Yugoslavia); Augusto Willemsen-Díaz, *Chairman* (Guatemala).

United Nations Voluntary Fund for Victims of Torture

BOARD OF TRUSTEES
The Board of Trustees to advise the Secretary-General in his administration of the United Nations Voluntary Fund for Victims of Torture consists of five members with wide experience in the field of human rights, appointed in their personal capacity by the Secretary-

General with due regard for equitable geographical distribution and in consultation with their Governments.
The Board held its seventh session at Geneva from 22 to 26 February 1988.

Members (to serve until 31 December 1988): Hans Danelius, *Chairman* (Sweden); Elizabeth Odio Benito (Costa Rica); Waleed M. Sadi (Jordan); Ivan Tosevski (Yugoslavia); Amos Wako (Kenya).

World Food Council
The World Food Council, at the ministerial or plenipotentiary level, functions as an organ of the United Nations and reports to the General Assembly through the Economic and Social Council. It consists of 36 members, nominated by the Economic and Social Council and elected by the Assembly according to the following pattern: nine members from African States, eight from Asian States, seven from Latin American States, four from socialist States of Eastern Europe and eight from Western European and other States. Members serve for three-year terms.
The Council held its fourteenth session at Nicosia, Cyprus, from 23 to 26 May 1988.

Members:
To serve until 31 December 1988: Antigua and Barbuda, Australia, Bangladesh, Cyprus, Dominican Republic, German Democratic Republic, Germany, Federal Republic of, Guinea, Honduras, Mali, Somalia, USSR.
To serve until 31 December 1989: Argentina, Burundi, Colombia, France, Hungary, India, Italy, Japan, Pakistan, Rwanda, Sweden, Tunisia.
To serve until 31 December 1990: Bulgaria, Canada, China, Côte d'Ivoire, Indonesia, Madagascar, Mexico, Thailand, Turkey, United States, Uruguay, Zambia.

President: Eduardo Pesqueira (Mexico).
Vice-Presidents: Abdirizak Mohamoud Abubakar (Somalia), Ibrahim Baluch (Pakistan), Mats Hellstrom (Sweden), Yovtcho Roussev (Bulgaria).

Executive Director: Gerald Ion Trant.

On 26 May 1988 (decision 1988/150), the Economic and Social Council nominated the following 14 States, 12 of which were to be elected by the General Assembly, for a three-year term beginning on 1 January 1989 to fill the vacancies occurring on 31 December 1988: Australia, Bangladesh, Cape Verde, Cyprus, Ecuador, German Democratic Republic, Germany, Federal Republic of, Guatemala, Iran, Niger, Paraguay, Syrian Arab Republic, USSR, Zimbabwe. All but Bangladesh and Iran were elected by the Assembly on 19 October 1988 (decision 43/305).

Security Council

The Security Council consists of 15 Member States of the United Nations, in accordance with the provisions of Article 23 of the United Nations Charter as amended in 1965.

MEMBERS
Permanent members: China, France, USSR, United Kingdom, United States.
Non-permanent members: Algeria, Argentina, Brazil, Germany, Federal Republic of, Italy, Japan, Nepal, Senegal, Yugoslavia, Zambia.

On 26 October 1988 (decision 43/309), the General Assembly elected Canada, Colombia, Ethiopia, Finland and Malaysia for a two-year term beginning on 1 January 1989, to replace Argentina, Federal Republic of Germany, Italy, Japan and Zambia, whose terms of office were to expire on 31 December 1988.

PRESIDENTS
The presidency of the Council rotates monthly, according to the English alphabetical listing of its member States. The following served as Presidents during 1988:

Month	*Member*	*Representative*
January	United Kingdom	Sir Crispin Tickell
February	United States	Vernon A. Walters
		Herbert S. Okun
March	Yugoslavia	Dragoslav Pejic
April	Zambia	Peter Dingi Zuze
May	Algeria	Hocine Djoudi
June	Argentina	Marcelo E. R. Delpech
July	Brazil	Paulo Nogueira-Batista
August	China	Li Luye
September	France	Pierre-Louis Blanc
October	Federal Republic of Germany	Alexander Count York von Wartenburg
November	Italy	Giovanni Migliuolo
		Mario Scialoja
December	Japan	Hideo Kagami

Military Staff Committee

The Military Staff Committee consists of the chiefs of staff of the permanent members of the Security Council or their representatives. It met fortnightly throughout 1988; the first meeting was held on 4 January and the last on 30 December.

Standing committees

Each of the three standing committees of the Security Council is composed of representatives of all Council members:

Committee of Experts (to examine the provisional rules of procedure of the Council and any other matters entrusted to it by the Council)
Committee on the Admission of New Members
Committee on Council Meetings Away from Headquarters

Ad hoc bodies

Ad Hoc Committee established under resolution 507(1982)
Members: France *(Chairman)*, Guyana,[a] Jordan,[a] Uganda.[a]

[a]Not Council members in 1988.

Ad Hoc Sub-Committee on Namibia
The *Ad Hoc* Sub-Committee on Namibia consists of all the members of the Security Council. It did not meet in 1988.

Committee of Experts established by the Security Council at its 1506th meeting
(on the question of micro-States)
The Committee of Experts consists of all the members of the Security Council. It did not meet in 1988.

Security Council Commission established under resolution 446(1979)
(to examine the situation relating to settlements in the Arab territories occupied since 1967, including Jerusalem)
Members: Bolivia,[a] Portugal,[a] Zambia.

[a]Not Council members in 1988.

Security Council Committee established by resolution 421(1977) concerning the question of South Africa
The Committee consists of all the members of the Security Council.

Chairman: Jai Patap Rana (Nepal).

PEACE-KEEPING OPERATIONS AND SPECIAL MISSIONS

United Nations Truce Supervision Organization (UNTSO)
Chief of Staff: Lieutenant-General Martin Vadset.

United Nations Military Observer Group in India and Pakistan (UNMOGIP)
Chief Military Observer: Brigadier-General James Parker.

United Nations Peace-keeping Force in Cyprus (UNFICYP)
Special Representative of the Secretary-General in Cyprus: James

Holger (until February 1988), Oscar Hector Camilión (from 29 February).
Force Commander: Major-General Günther G. Greindl.

United Nations Disengagement Observer Force (UNDOF)
Force Commander: Major-General Gustaf Welin (until 9 September 1988), Major-General Adolf Radauer (from 10 September).

United Nations Interim Force in Lebanon (UNIFIL)
Force Commander: Major-General Gustav Hägglund (until 30 June 1988), Major-General Lars-Eric Wahlgren (from 1 July).

United Nations Good Offices Mission in Afghanistan and Pakistan (UNGOMAP)
On 31 October 1988, the Security Council confirmed its April provisional agreement to establish a United Nations Good Offices Mission in Afghanistan and Pakistan to assist in the smooth and faithful implementation of the provisions of the Agreements on the Settlement of the Situation relating to Afghanistan and to consider alleged violations.

Representative of the Secretary-General: Diego Cordovez (from 14 April 1988).
Deputy to the Representative: Major-General Raúli Kalervo Helminen (from 14 April 1988).

United Nations Iran-Iraq Military Observer Group (UNIIMOG)
On 9 August 1988, the Security Council established under its authority a United Nations Iran-Iraq Military Observer Group to verify, confirm and supervise the cease-fire between Iran and Iraq and the withdrawal of all forces to the internationally recognized boundaries. UNIIMOG was established for six months.

Chief Military Observer: Major-General Slavko Jovic (from 11 August 1988).

United Nations Angola Verification Mission (UNAVEM)
On 20 December 1988, the Security Council established under its authority a United Nations Angola Verification Mission to verify the redeployment northwards and the phased and total withdrawal of Cuban troops from the territory of Angola in accordance with the timetable agreed between Angola and Cuba. UNAVEM was established for 31 months.

Chief Military Observer: Brigadier-General Péricles Ferreira Gomes (from 23 December 1988).

United Nations Transition Assistance Group (UNTAG)
Authorized by the Security Council in 1978,[21] the United Nations Transition Assistance Group had not been emplaced in Namibia by the end of 1988.

Special Representative of the Secretary-General: Martti Ahtisaari.
Commander-designate: Lieutenant-General Dewan Prem Chand.

---

[21]YUN 1978, p. 915, SC res. 435(1978), 29 Sep. 1978.

Economic and Social Council

The Economic and Social Council consists of 54 Member States of the United Nations, elected by the General Assembly, each for a three-year term, in accordance with the provisions of Article 61 of the United Nations Charter as amended in 1965 and 1973.

MEMBERS
To serve until 31 December 1988: Australia, Belgium, Byelorussian SSR, Djibouti, Egypt, Gabon, German Democratic Republic, Iraq, Italy, Jamaica, Mozambique, Pakistan, Panama, Peru, Philippines, Sierra Leone, Syrian Arab Republic, United States.

To serve until 31 December 1989: Belize, Bolivia, Bulgaria, Canada, China, Denmark, Iran, Norway, Oman, Poland, Rwanda, Somalia, Sri Lanka, Sudan, USSR, United Kingdom, Uruguay, Zaire.
To serve until 31 December 1990: Colombia, Cuba, France, Germany, Federal Republic of, Ghana, Greece, Guinea, India, Ireland, Japan, Lesotho, Liberia, Libyan Arab Jamahiriya, Portugal, Saudi Arabia, Trinidad and Tobago, Venezuela, Yugoslavia.

On 26 and 28 October 1988 (decision 43/310), the General Assembly elected the following 18 States for a three-year term beginning on 1 January 1989 to fill the vacancies occurring on 31 December 1988: Bahamas, Brazil, Cameroon, Czechoslovakia, Indonesia, Iraq, Italy, Jordan, Kenya, Netherlands, New Zealand, Nicaragua, Niger, Thailand, Tunisia, Ukrainian SSR, United States, Zambia.

SESSIONS

Organizational session for 1988: United Nations Headquarters, 2-5 February and 3 March.
First regular session of 1988: United Nations Headquarters, 3-27 May.
Second regular session of 1988: Geneva, 6-29 July.
Resumed second regular session of 1988: United Nations Headquarters, 17 October.

OFFICERS

President: Andrés Aguilar (Venezuela).
Vice-Presidents: Salim Bin Mohammed Al-Khussaiby (Oman); Finn Jonck (Denmark); Abdillahi Said Osman (Somalia) (until 5 July); Mampiti F. Nchapi (Lesotho) (from 6 July); Oleg N. Pashkevich (Byelorussian SSR).

Subsidiary and other related organs

SUBSIDIARY ORGANS

In addition to three regular sessional committees, the Economic and Social Council may, at each session, set up other committees or working groups, of the whole or of limited membership, and refer to them any items on the agenda for study and report.

Other subsidiary organs reporting to the Council consist of functional commissions, regional commissions, standing committees, expert bodies and *ad hoc* bodies.

The inter-agency Administrative Committee on Co-ordination also reports to the Council.

Sessional bodies

SESSIONAL COMMITTEES

Each of the sessional committees of the Economic and Social Council consists of the 54 members of the Council.

First (Economic) Committee. Chairman: Finn Jonck (Denmark).
Vice-Chairmen: Herbert Brauneis (German Democratic Republic), Gabriel N. Fernandez (Liberia).
Second (Social) Committee. Chairman: Salim Bin Mohammed Al-Khussaiby (Oman). *Vice-Chairmen:* Guy Trouveroy (Belgium), Marek Zawacki (Poland).
Third (Programme and Co-ordination) Committee. Chairman: Mampiti F. Nchapi (Lesotho).

Functional commissions

Commission for Social Development

The Commission for Social Development consists of 32 members, elected for four-year terms by the Economic and Social Council according to a specific pattern of equitable geographical distribution.

The Commission did not meet in 1988.

Members:
To serve until 31 December 1988: Chile, Denmark, Indonesia, Italy, Mali, Netherlands, Panama, Poland, Thailand, Zimbabwe.
To serve until 31 December 1990: Argentina, Austria, Bangladesh, Cyprus, Dominican Republic, German Democratic Republic, Ghana, Liberia, Libyan Arab Jamahiriya, Norway, Togo.
To serve until 31 December 1991: France, Germany, Federal Republic of, Guatemala, Haiti, Iraq, Pakistan, Romania, Sudan, Uganda, USSR, United States.

On 26 May 1988 (decision 1988/150), the Economic and Social Council elected the following for a four-year term beginning on 1 January 1989 to fill 9 of the 10 vacancies occurring on 31 December 1988: Cameroon, Chile, China, Ecuador, Finland, Malta,

Philippines, Poland, Spain. No further elections were held in 1988 to fill the remaining seat, allocated to a member from African States.

Commission on Human Rights

The Commission on Human Rights consists of 43 members, elected for three-year terms by the Economic and Social Council according to a specific pattern of equitable geographical distribution.

The Commission held its forty-fourth session at Geneva from 1 February to 11 March 1988.

Members:
To serve until 31 December 1988: Algeria, Bangladesh, Belgium, Byelorussian SSR, Colombia, Costa Rica, Cyprus, Ethiopia, India, Ireland, Mozambique, Nicaragua, Norway, USSR.
To serve until 31 December 1989: Brazil, France, German Democratic Republic, Iraq, Italy, Mexico, Pakistan, Philippines, Rwanda, Senegal, Somalia, Togo, United States, Yugoslavia.
To serve until 31 December 1990: Argentina, Botswana, Bulgaria, China, Gambia, Germany, Federal Republic of, Japan, Nigeria, Peru, Portugal, Sao Tome and Principe, Spain, Sri Lanka, United Kingdom, Venezuela.

Chairman: Alioune Sène (Senegal).
Vice-Chairmen: César Delgado Barreto (Peru), José D. Ingles (Philippines), Francesco Mezzalama (Italy).
Rapporteur: Gerhard Richter (German Democratic Republic).

On 26 May 1988 (decision 1988/150), the Economic and Social Council elected the following 14 members for a three-year term beginning on 1 January 1989 to fill the vacancies occurring on 31 December 1988: Bangladesh, Belgium, Canada, Colombia, Cuba, Cyprus, Ethiopia, India, Morocco, Panama, Swaziland, Sweden, Ukrainian SSR, USSR.

AD HOC WORKING GROUP OF EXPERTS
(established by Commission on Human
Rights resolution 2(XXIII) of 6 March 1967)
Members: Mikuin Leliel Balanda, *Chairman* (Zaire); Humberto Díaz-Casanueva, *Vice-Chairman* (Chile); Felix Ermacora (Austria); Branimir M. Jankovic (Yugoslavia); Elly Elikunda E. M'Tango (United Republic of Tanzania); Mulka Govinda Reddy (India).

GROUP OF THREE ESTABLISHED UNDER THE
INTERNATIONAL CONVENTION ON THE SUPPRESSION
AND PUNISHMENT OF THE CRIME OF *APARTHEID*
The Group of Three held its eleventh session at Geneva from 25 to 28 January 1988.

Members: Ethiopia, Nicaragua, Sri Lanka.

Chairman/Rapporteur: Gustavo Adolfo Vargas (Nicaragua).

SUB-COMMISSION ON PREVENTION OF
DISCRIMINATION AND PROTECTION OF MINORITIES
The Sub-Commission consists of 26 members elected by the Commission on Human Rights from candidates nominated by Member States of the United Nations, in accordance with a scheme to ensure equitable geographical distribution. Members serve in their individual capacity as experts, rather than as governmental representatives, each for a four-year term.

The Sub-Commission held its fortieth session at Geneva from 8 August to 2 September 1988.

Members:[a]
To serve until February 1990: Yawo Agboyibor (Togo); Awn Shawkat Al-Khasawneh (Jordan); Judith Sefi Attah (Nigeria); Murlidhar Chandrakant Bhandare, *Chairman* (India); Stanislav V. Chernichenko (USSR); Erica-Irene A. Daes (Greece); Leandro Despouy (Argentina); Louis Joinet (France); Fatma Zohra Ksentini, *Vice-Chairman* (Algeria); Claire Palley, *Vice-Chairman* (United Kingdom); Alejandro Sobarzo Loaiza (Mexico); Tian Jin (China); Luis Alberto Varela Quirós (Costa Rica).

To serve until February 1992: Miguel Alfonso Martínez (Cuba); Mary Concepción Bautista (Philippines); Ion Diaconu (Romania); Asbjorn Eide (Norway); Ribot Hatano (Japan); Aidid Abdillahi Ilkahanaf (Somalia); Ahmed Mohamed Khalifa (Egypt); Rafael Rivas Posada, *Vice Chairman* (Colombia); William W. Treat (United States); Danilo Turk, *Rapporteur* (Yugoslavia); Theodoor Cornelis van Boven (Netherlands); Halima Embarek Warzazi (Morocco); Fisseha Yimer (Ethiopia).

[a]Elected on 29 February 1988, in accordance with Economic and Social Council resolution 1986/35 (YUN 1986, p. 731) and decision 1987/102 (YUN 1987, p. 782).

Working Group
(established by resolution 2(XXIV) of 16 August 1971 of the Sub-Commission on Prevention of Discrimination and Protection of Minorities pursuant to Economic and Social Council resolution 1503(XLVIII))

The Working Group on Communications concerning human rights held its sixteenth session at Geneva from 25 July to 5 August 1988.

Members: Ribot Hatano (Japan); Teimuraz O. Ramishvili (USSR); Alejandro Sobarzo Loaiza (Mexico); Theodoor Cornelis van Boven (Netherlands); Fisseha Yimer, *Chairman/Rapporteur* (Ethiopia).

Working Group
(established on 21 August 1974 by resolution 11(XXVII) of the Sub-Commission on Prevention of Discrimination and Protection of Minorities)

The Working Group on Contemporary Forms of Slavery[a] held its thirteenth session at Geneva from 1 to 5 and on 12 August 1988.

[a]Formerly the Working Group on Slavery; name change endorsed by the Commission on 8 March 1988.

Members: Mary Concepción Bautista (Philippines); Ion Diaconu (Romania); Asbjorn Eide, *Chairman/Rapporteur* (Norway); Fatma Zohra Ksentini (Algeria); Luis Alberto Varela Quirós (Costa Rica).

Working Group on Detention
The Working Group on Detention met at Geneva between 10 and 26 August 1988.

Members: Miguel Alfonso Martínez, *Rapporteur* (Cuba); John Carey, *Chairman* (United States); Ribot Hatano (Japan); Aidid Abdillahi Ilkahanaf (Somalia); Danilo Turk (Yugoslavia).

Working Group on Indigenous Populations
The Working Group on Indigenous Populations held its sixth session at Geneva from 1 to 5 August 1988.

Members: Miguel Alfonso Martínez (Cuba); Erica-Irene A. Daes, *Chairman/Rapporteur* (Greece); Christy Mbonu (Nigeria); Tian Jin (China); Danilo Turk (Yugoslavia).

WORKING GROUP OF GOVERNMENTAL
EXPERTS ON THE RIGHT TO DEVELOPMENT

The Working Group of Governmental Experts on the Right to Development held its eleventh session at Geneva from 11 to 22 January 1988.

Members: Juan Alvarez Vita (Peru); Irina Bokova (Bulgaria); Kantilal Lallubhai Dalal, *Vice-Chairman/Rapporteur* (India); Riyadh Aziz Hadi (Iraq); Julio Heredia-Pérez, *Vice-Chairman* (Cuba); Fatma Zohra Ksentini (Algeria); Jean-Pierre Le Court (France); Mirta Saavedra Polo (Panama); Fahd Salim (Syrian Arab Republic); Alioune Sène, *Chairman* (Senegal); Kongit Singegiorgis (Ethiopia); Rais Touzmohammad (USSR); Danilo Turk, *Vice-Chairman* (Yugoslavia); Johannes Zandvliet (Netherlands).

WORKING GROUP ON ENFORCED
OR INVOLUNTARY DISAPPEARANCES

During 1988, the mandate of the Working Group on Enforced or Involuntary Disappearances was extended for two years by a Commission on Human Rights resolution of 8 March, as approved by the Economic and Social Council on 13 May (decision 1988/107).

The Working Group held three sessions in 1988: its twenty-fourth at United Nations Headquarters from 23 to 27 May, and its twenty-fifth and twenty-sixth at Geneva from 12 to 16 September and from 30 November to 9 December, respectively.

Members: Jonas Kwami Dotse Foli (Ghana); Agha Hilaly (Pakistan); Ivan Tosevski, *Chairman/Rapporteur* (Yugoslavia); Toine van Dongen (Netherlands); Luís Alberto Varela Quirós (Costa Rica) (twenty-fourth session), Diego García-Sayán (Peru) (twenty-fifth and twenty-sixth sessions).

WORKING GROUPS
(to study situations revealing a consistent pattern of gross violations of human rights)

Working Group established by Commission on Human Rights decision 1987/103 of 2 March 1987:
Members: Marc Bossuyt, *Chairman/Rapporteur* (Belgium); Todor Dichev (Bulgaria); Shaheen Amin Gilani (Pakistan); José Carlos Mariategui (Peru); Théoneste Mujyanama (Rwanda).

Working Group established by Commission on Human Rights decision 1988/103 of 2 March 1988:
Members: Antonio Costa Lobo (Portugal), Todor Dichev (Bulgaria), Roshdi Khaled Rashid (Iraq), Aregba Polo (Togo), Armando Villanueva del Campo (Peru).

WORKING GROUPS (OPEN-ENDED)

Working Group established by Commission on Human Rights decision 1985/112 of 14 March 1985
(to draft a declaration on the right and responsibility of individuals, groups and organs of society to promote and protect universally recognized human rights and fundamental freedoms):
Chairman/Rapporteur: Robert H. Robertson (Australia).

Working Group established by Commission on Human Rights resolution 1987/47 of 14 March 1987
(to draft a declaration on the rights of persons belonging to national, ethnic, religious and linguistic minorities):
Chairman/Rapporteur: Zagorka Ilic (Yugoslavia).

Working Group established by Commission on Human Rights resolution 1987/48 of 14 March 1987
(to draft a convention on the rights of the child):
Chairman/Rapporteur: Adam Lopatka (Poland).

Commission on Narcotic Drugs
The Commission on Narcotic Drugs consists of 40 members, elected for four-year terms by the Economic and Social Council from among the Members of the United Nations and members of the specialized agencies and the parties to the Single Convention on Narcotic Drugs, 1961, with due regard for the adequate representation of *(a)* countries which are important producers of opium or coca leaves, *(b)* countries which are important in the manufacture of narcotic drugs, and *(c)* countries in which drug addiction or the illicit traffic in narcotic drugs constitutes an important problem, as well as taking into account the principle of equitable geographical distribution.

The Commission held its tenth special session at Vienna from 8 to 19 February 1988.

Members:
To serve until 31 December 1989: Argentina, Australia, Belgium, Bulgaria, China, Ecuador, Hungary, Indonesia, Japan, Malaysia, Mali, Mexico, Nigeria, Senegal, Spain, Turkey, USSR, United Kingdom, Venezuela, Zambia.

To serve until 31 December 1991: Bolivia, Brazil, Canada, Côte d'Ivoire, Denmark, Egypt, France, Germany, Federal Republic of, India, Italy, Lebanon, Madagascar, Netherlands, Pakistan, Peru, Poland, Switzerland, Thailand, United States, Yugoslavia.

Chairman: Philip O. Emafo (Nigeria).
First Vice-Chairman: Dilshad Najmuddin (Pakistan).
Second Vice-Chairman: E. A. Babayan (USSR).
Rapporteur: R. J. Samsom (Netherlands).

SUB-COMMISSION ON ILLICIT DRUG TRAFFIC AND
RELATED MATTERS IN THE NEAR AND MIDDLE EAST
The Sub-Commission held its twenty-third session at Vienna on 3 and 4 February 1988.

Members: Afghanistan, Iran, Pakistan, Sweden, Turkey.

Chairman: Erdem Erner (Turkey).
Vice-Chairman: Dilshad Najmuddin (Pakistan).

On 25 May 1988, the Economic and Social Council endorsed the membership of Egypt, India and Jordan in the Sub-Commission.

MEETINGS OF HEADS OF NATIONAL
DRUG LAW ENFORCEMENT AGENCIES (HONLEA)

Interregional HONLEA

Interregional HONLEA examines in depth the most important aspects of the drug trafficking problem. All Member States are encouraged to participate, and competent bodies within the United Nations system as well as the International Criminal Police Organization (Interpol) and the Customs Co-operation Council are invited to offer their technical expertise.
Interregional HONLEA did not meet in 1988.

HONLEA, Africa

A meeting to co-ordinate regional activities against illicit drug traffic, convened annually (except when Interregional HONLEA meets), is open to any State in the region, as well as to observers from Interpol, the Customs Co-operation Council, other competent international and intergovernmental organizations, and INCB. Any interested Government which is actively involved in countering illicit drug traffic in the region may be invited by the Secretary-General to send an observer at its own expense.
HONLEA, Africa, held its second meeting at Dakar, Senegal, from 18 to 22 April 1988.

Chairman: El Hadj Malick Ba (Senegal).
First Vice-Chairman: Ahmed Fathy Nada (Egypt).
Second Vice-Chairman: Samson H. Makaurire (Zimbabwe).
Third Vice-Chairman: Tro Emile Gondo (Côte d'Ivoire).
Rapporteur: Winter A. Kabwiku (Zambia).

HONLEA, Asia and the Pacific

A meeting to co-ordinate regional activities against illicit drug traffic, convened annually (except when Interregional HONLEA meets) in one of the region's capitals, is open to any country or territory in the region approved by the Commission, as well as to observers from the Association of South-East Asian Nations, the Colombo Plan Bureau, the Customs Co-operation Council, Interpol and INCB. Any interested Government outside the region may be invited by the Secretary-General to send an observer at its own expense.
HONLEA, Asia and the Pacific, held its fourteenth meeting at Bangkok, Thailand, from 3 to 7 October 1988.

Chairman: Chavalit Yodmani (Thailand).
First Vice-Chairman: Zhou Nian Shan (China).
Second Vice-Chairman: Adrien Whiddett (Australia).
Third Vice-Chairman: B. V. Kumar (India).
Rapporteur: John A. Jamieson (New Zealand).

HONLEA, Latin America and the Caribbean

A meeting to co-ordinate regional activities against illicit drug traffic, convened annually (except when Interregional HONLEA meets) in one of the region's capitals, is open to any country or territory in the region approved by the Commission, as well as to observers from the Customs Co-operation Council, Interpol and INCB. Any interested Government outside the region may be invited by the Secretary-General to send an observer at its own expense.
HONLEA, Latin America and the Caribbean, held its second meeting at Lima, Peru, from 12 to 16 September 1988.

Chairman: Fernando Reyes Roca (Peru).
First Vice-Chairman: Jorge Alderete Rosales (Bolivia).
Second Vice-Chairman: Edward Hughes (Saint Kitts and Nevis).
Third Vice-Chairman: Oscar Rodolfo López (Argentina).
Fourth Vice-Chairman: José Ortega Padilla (Mexico).
Rapporteur: Eliseo Barrios Soto (Guatemala).

Commission on the Status of Women

The Commission on the Status of Women consists of 32 members, elected for four-year terms by the Economic and Social Council according to a specific pattern of equitable geographical distribution.
The Commission held its thirty-second session at Vienna from 14 to 23 March 1988.

Members:
To serve until 31 December 1988: Brazil, Byelorussian SSR, Canada, France, Greece, India, Japan, Mauritius, Sudan, Tunisia, Venezuela.
To serve until 31 December 1990: Australia, Bangladesh, Côte d'Ivoire, Czechoslovakia, Gabon, Italy, Mexico, Philippines, USSR, United States, Zaire.
To serve until 31 December 1991: Burkina Faso, China, Costa Rica, Cuba, German Democratic Republic, Guatemala, Lesotho, Pakistan, Sweden, Turkey.

Chairman: Lindsay Niemann (Canada).
Vice-Chairmen: Thereza Maria Machado Quintella (Brazil), Dagmar Molkova (Czechoslovakia), Wang Shuxian (China).
Rapporteur: Liliane Dubois (Mauritius).

On 26 May 1988 (decision 1988/150), the Economic and Social Council elected the following 11 members for a four-year term beginning on 1 January 1989 to fill the vacancies occurring on 31 December 1988: Austria, Brazil, Canada, Colombia, France, Japan, Morocco, Poland, Sudan, Thailand, United Republic of Tanzania.

Population Commission

The Population Commission, which consists of 27 members elected for four-year terms by the Economic and Social Council according to a specific pattern of equitable geographical distribution, did not meet in 1988.

Members:
To serve until 31 December 1988: Brazil, Cameroon, Colombia, Germany, Federal Republic of, Mauritius, Netherlands, Thailand, Turkey, Ukrainian SSR.
To serve until 31 December 1989: Burundi, China, Cuba, Iran, Malawi, Mexico, USSR, United Kingdom, United States.
To serve until 31 December 1991: Bolivia, France, Iraq, Japan, Nigeria, Poland, Rwanda, Sweden, Togo.

On 26 May 1988 (decision 1988/150), the Economic and Social Council elected the following for a four-year term beginning on 1 January 1989 to fill eight of the nine vacancies occurring on 31 December 1988: Bangladesh, Belgium, Brazil, Colombia, Egypt, Germany, Federal Republic of, Turkey, Ukrainian SSR. No further elections were held in 1988 to fill the remaining seat, allocated to a member from African States.

Statistical Commission

The Statistical Commission, which consists of 24 members elected for four-year terms by the Economic and Social Council according to a specific pattern of equitable geographical distribution, did not meet in 1988.

Members:
To serve until 31 December 1988: Brazil, Finland, India, Japan, Mexico, New Zealand, Ukrainian SSR, United Kingdom.
To serve until 31 December 1989: Argentina, Egypt, France, Germany, Federal Republic of, Spain, Togo, USSR, Zambia.
To serve until 31 December 1991: Bulgaria, China, Czechoslovakia, Ghana, Morocco, Pakistan, Panama, United States.

On 26 May 1988 (decision 1988/150), the Economic and Social Council elected the following eight members for a four-year term beginning on 1 January 1989 to fill the vacancies occurring on 31 December 1988: Brazil, Canada, Hungary, Iran, Japan, Mexico, Norway, United Kingdom.

WORKING GROUP ON INTERNATIONAL
STATISTICAL PROGRAMMES AND CO-ORDINATION
The Working Group consists of the Bureau of the Statistical Commission; the representatives to the Commission of the two major contributors to the United Nations budget, unless they are already represented in the Bureau; and one representative to the Commission from a developing country from among members of each of the following: ECA, ECLAC, ESCAP and ESCWA, unless they are also already represented in the Bureau. Members serve two-year terms.
The Working Group did not meet in 1988.

Regional commissions

Economic and Social Commission for Asia and the Pacific (ESCAP)
The Economic and Social Commission for Asia and the Pacific held its forty-fourth session at Jakarta, Indonesia, from 11 to 20 April 1988.

Members: Afghanistan, Australia, Bangladesh, Bhutan, Brunei Darussalam, Burma, China, Democratic Kampuchea, Fiji, France, India, Indonesia, Iran, Japan, Lao People's Democratic Republic, Malaysia, Maldives, Mongolia, Nauru, Nepal, Netherlands, New Zealand, Pakistan, Papua New Guinea, Philippines, Republic of Korea, Samoa, Singapore, Solomon Islands, Sri Lanka, Thailand, Tonga, Tuvalu, USSR, United Kingdom, United States, Vanuatu, Viet Nam.
Associate members: American Samoa,[a] Commonwealth of the Northern Mariana Islands, Cook Islands, Federated States of Micronesia, Guam, Hong Kong, Kiribati, Niue, Republic of the Marshall Islands, Republic of Palau.

[a]Became an associate member on 20 April 1988.

Switzerland, not a Member of the United Nations, participates in a consultative capacity in the work of the Commission.

Chairman: Ali Alatas (Indonesia).
Vice-Chairmen: John Amaratunge (Sri Lanka), Kwang Soo Choi (Republic of Korea), James Cecil Cocker (Tonga), Akoka Doi (Papua New Guinea), Kasitah Gaddam (Malaysia), Villiame S. J. Gonelevu (Fiji), Takujiro Hamada (Japan), Jose D. Ingles (Philippines), Prapas Limpabandhu (Thailand), Liu Shu-qing (China), Mahdi Mir Mo'ezzi (Iran), Mohammad A. Munim (Bangladesh), Mohan Man Sainju (Nepal), Tay Eng Soon (Singapore), Soubanh Srithilath (Lao People's Democratic Republic), Narayan Datt Tiwari (India), Paul J. Tovua (Solomon Islands), Tran Quang Co (Viet Nam).
Rapporteur: Saraswati Shrestha (Nepal).

Following are the main subsidiary and related bodies of the Commission:
Advisory body: Advisory Committee of Permanent Representatives and Other Representatives Designated by Members of the Commission.
Legislative bodies: Committee on Agricultural Development; Committee on Development Planning; Committee on Industry, Technology, Human Settlements and the Environment; Committee on Natural Resources; Committee on Population; Committee on Shipping, and Transport and Communications; Committee on Social Development; Committee on Statistics; Committee on Trade.
Subsidiary bodies: Governing Board, Asian and Pacific Centre for Transfer of Technology; Governing Board, Regional Co-ordination Centre for Research and Development of Coarse Grains, Pulses, Roots and Tuber Crops in the Humid Tropics of Asia and the Pacific.
Related intergovernmental bodies: Asian and Pacific Development Centre; Committee for Co-ordination of Joint Prospecting for Mineral Resources in Asian Offshore Areas; Committee for Co-ordination of Joint Prospecting for Mineral Resources in South Pacific Offshore Areas; Interim Committee for Co-ordination of Investigations of the Lower Mekong Basin; Typhoon Committee.
Regional institution: Statistical Institute for Asia and the Pacific.
Intergovernmental meeting convened by ESCAP: Special Body on Land-locked Countries.

Economic and Social Commission for Western Asia (ESCWA)
The Economic and Social Commission for Western Asia held its third special session at Baghdad, Iraq, on 8 June 1988.

Members: Bahrain, Democratic Yemen, Egypt, Iraq, Jordan, Kuwait, Lebanon, Oman, Qatar, Saudi Arabia, Syrian Arab Republic, United Arab Emirates, Yemen; Palestine Liberation Organization.

Chairman: Hisham Hassan Tawfiq (Iraq).
Vice-Chairmen: Abd al-Hamid Mubarak Khalifah al-Kubaysi (Qatar), Ibrahim Jasim al-Bahw (Kuwait).
Rapporteur: Mukhtar Hashim Uthman (Egypt).

The Commission's one main subsidiary organ, the Technical Committee, composed of all ESCWA members, reviews the Commission's programme of work.

Economic Commission for Africa (ECA)
The Economic Commission for Africa meets in annual session at the ministerial level known as the Conference of Ministers.
The Commission held its twenty-third session (fourteenth meeting of the Conference of Ministers) at Niamey, Niger, from 14 to 17 April 1988.

Members: Algeria, Angola, Benin, Botswana, Burkina Faso, Burundi, Cameroon, Cape Verde, Central African Republic, Chad, Comoros, Congo, Côte d'Ivoire, Djibouti, Egypt, Equatorial Guinea, Ethiopia, Gabon, Gambia, Ghana, Guinea, Guinea-Bissau, Kenya, Lesotho, Liberia, Libyan Arab Jamahiriya, Madagascar, Malawi, Mali, Mauritania, Mauritius, Morocco, Mozambique, Niger, Nigeria, Rwanda, Sao Tome and Principe, Senegal, Seychelles, Sierra Leone, Somalia, South Africa,[a] Sudan, Swaziland, Togo, Tunisia, Uganda, United Republic of Tanzania, Zaire, Zambia, Zimbabwe.

[a]On 30 July 1963, the Economic and Social Council decided that South Africa should not take part in the work of ECA until conditions for constructive co-operation had been restored by a change in South Africa's racial policy (YUN 1963, p. 274, ESC res. 974 D IV (XXXVI)).

Switzerland, not a Member of the United Nations, participates in a consultative capacity in the work of the Commission.

Chairman: Almoustapha Soumaila (Niger).
First Vice-Chairman: Béchir Gueblaoui (Tunisia).
Second Vice-Chairman: Gérard Niyibigira (Burundi).
Rapporteur: Amina Salum Ali (United Republic of Tanzania).

The Commission has established the following principal legislative organs:
Conference of Ministers; Technical Preparatory Committee of the Whole; sectoral ministerial conferences, each assisted by an appropriate committee of technical officials; Council of Ministers of each Multinational Programming and Operational Centre, assisted by its committee of officials.
The Commission has also established the following subsidiary bodies:

Joint Conference of African Planners, Statisticians and Demographers; Intergovernmental Committee of Experts for Science and Technology Development; Intergovernmental Regional Committee on Human Settlements and Environment; Africa Regional Co-ordinating Committee for the Integration of Women in Development; Technical Committee of the Pan-African Documentation and Information System.

Economic Commission for Europe (ECE)

The Economic Commission for Europe held its forty-third session at Geneva from 12 to 21 April 1988.

Members: Albania, Austria, Belgium, Bulgaria, Byelorussian SSR, Canada, Cyprus, Czechoslovakia, Denmark, Finland, France, German Democratic Republic, Germany, Federal Republic of, Greece, Hungary, Iceland, Ireland, Italy, Luxembourg, Malta, Netherlands, Norway, Poland, Portugal, Romania, Spain, Sweden, Switzerland, Turkey, Ukrainian SSR, USSR, United Kingdom, United States, Yugoslavia.

The Holy See, Liechtenstein and San Marino, which are not Members of the United Nations, participate in a consultative capacity in the work of the Commission.

Chairman: Peter Dietze (German Democratic Republic).
Vice-Chairman: Ercument Yavuzalp (Turkey).
Rapporteurs: Hans-Christian Kint (Belgium), Alexandre Sytchev (Byelorussian SSR).

Following are the principal subsidiary bodies of the Commission:
Chemical Industry Committee; Coal Committee; Committee on Agricultural Problems; Committee on Electric Power; Committee on Gas; Committee on Housing, Building and Planning; Committee on the Development of Trade; Conference of European Statisticians; Inland Transport Committee; Meeting of Government Officials Responsible for Standardization Policies; Senior Advisers to ECE Governments on Energy; Senior Advisers to ECE Governments on Environmental and Water Problems; Senior Advisers to ECE Governments on Science and Technology; Senior Economic Advisers to ECE Governments; Steel Committee; Timber Committee; Working Party on Engineering Industries and Automation.

Ad hoc meetings of experts are convened for sectors of activity not dealt with by these principal bodies.

Economic Commission for Latin America and the Caribbean (ECLAC)

The Economic Commission for Latin America and the Caribbean held its twenty-second session at Rio de Janeiro, Brazil, from 20 to 27 April 1988.

Members: Antigua and Barbuda, Argentina, Bahamas, Barbados, Belize, Bolivia, Brazil *(Chairman),* Canada, Chile *(Fourth Vice-Chairman),* Colombia, Costa Rica *(Rapporteur),* Cuba *(Third Vice-Chairman),* Dominica, Dominican Republic, Ecuador, El Salvador, France, Grenada, Guatemala, Guyana, Haiti, Honduras, Jamaica, Mexico, Netherlands, Nicaragua, Panama, Paraguay, Peru, Portugal, Saint Kitts and Nevis, Saint Lucia, Saint Vincent and the Grenadines, Spain *(Second Vice-Chairman),* Suriname, Trinidad and Tobago *(First Vice-Chairman),* United Kingdom, United States, Uruguay, Venezuela.
Associate members: Aruba,[a] British Virgin Islands, Montserrat, Netherlands Antilles, United States Virgin Islands.

[a]Became an associate member on 22 April 1988.

Switzerland, not a Member of the United Nations, participates in a consultative capacity in the work of the Commission.

The Commission has established the following principal subsidiary bodies:
Caribbean Development and Co-operation Committee; Central American Economic Co-operation Committee and its Inter-agency Committee; Committee of High-level Government Experts; Committee of the Whole; Regional Council for Planning,[a] Latin American and Caribbean Institute for Economic and Social Planning.

The Latin American Demographic Centre forms part of the ECLAC system as an autonomous institution.

[a]Formerly the Technical Committee; name change ratified by ECLAC on 27 April 1988.

Standing committees

Commission on Human Settlements

The Commission on Human Settlements consists of 58 members elected by the Economic and Social Council for four-year terms according to a specific pattern of equitable geographical distribution; it reports to the General Assembly through the Council.

The Commission held its eleventh session at New Delhi, India, from 6 to 12 April 1988.

Members:
To serve until 31 December 1988: Bolivia, Canada, Congo, Dominican Republic, France, Hungary, Indonesia, Iraq, Italy, Malawi, Malaysia, Morocco, Nepal,[a] Netherlands, Nigeria, Panama, Poland, Swaziland, Sweden.
To serve until 31 December 1990: Argentina, Brazil, Bulgaria, Cameroon, Colombia, Ecuador, Finland, Gabon, Iran, Japan, Madagascar, Pakistan, Philippines, Sierra Leone, Togo, Turkey, Uganda, USSR, United Kingdom, United States.
To serve until 31 December 1991: Bangladesh, Botswana, Burundi, Byelorussian SSR, Cyprus, Denmark,[b] Egypt, German Democratic Republic, Germany, Federal Republic of, Greece, India, Jamaica, Jordan, Kenya, Mexico, Norway, Peru, Sri Lanka, United Republic of Tanzania.

[a]Elected on 26 May 1988 (decision 1988/150).
[b]Elected on 28 July 1988 (decision 1988/176).

Chairman: Mohsina Kidwai (India).
Vice-Chairmen: Tiexeira Soares (Brazil), Derek Stroud (United Kingdom), Michael R. Tshipinare (Botswana).
Rapporteur: A. Lupina (Poland).

On 26 May 1988 (decision 1988/150), the Economic and Social Council elected the following 19 members for a four-year term beginning on 1 January 1989 to fill the vacancies occurring on 31 December 1988: Bolivia, Canada, China, France, Guatemala, Hungary, Indonesia, Iraq, Italy, Lesotho, Malawi, Netherlands, Paraguay, Somalia, Swaziland, Sweden, Syrian Arab Republic, Tunisia, Yugoslavia.

Commission on Transnational Corporations

The Commission on Transnational Corporations consists of 48 members, elected from all States for three-year terms by the Economic and Social Council according to a specific pattern of geographical distribution.

The Commission held its fourteenth session at United Nations Headquarters from 6 to 15 April 1988.

Members:
To serve until 31 December 1988: Antigua and Barbuda, Bangladesh, Benin, Brazil, Cuba, Cyprus, Indonesia, Kenya, Mexico, Netherlands, Nigeria, Norway, Swaziland, USSR, United Kingdom, United States.
To serve until 31 December 1989: China, Colombia, Czechoslovakia, Egypt, Fiji, France, German Democratic Republic, Germany, Federal Republic of, Iran, Japan, Peru, Sierra Leone, Suriname, Switzerland, Tunisia, Zaire.
To serve until 31 December 1990: Burundi, Byelorussian SSR, Cameroon, Canada, Ghana, India, Iraq, Italy, Jamaica, Philippines, Poland, Republic of Korea, Trinidad and Tobago, Turkey, Uganda, Venezuela.
Expert advisers (served through the fourteenth session): Mark Anderson (United States),[a] Thomas J. Bata (Canada), Ernst-Otto Czempiel (Federal Republic of Germany),[a] Kamal Hossain (Bangladesh),[a] Celso Lafer (Brazil), Luis Enrique Marius Martinez (Uruguay/Italy), Ali Mazrui (Kenya),[a] Brian Price (United King-

dom), John Bower Rhodes (United States), William Robbins (United Kingdom),[a] Hassan A. Sunmonu (Nigeria),[a] Kari Tapiola (Finland),[a] Teng Weizao (China), L. M. Thapar (India),[a] Raul Trajtenberg (Uruguay/Argentina),[a] Vasiliy P. Trepelkov (USSR).

[a]Selected by the Commission on 12 April 1988 to serve for a further two years, up to and including the sixteenth (1990) session. Selected on the same date for the same term were: Peter Frerk (Federal Republic of Germany), Roland Guyvarc'h (France), Laurence McQuade (United States), Alexis Sierralta (Venezuela), Wang Linsheng (China), Nikolai G. Zaitsev (USSR). José Maria Basagoiti (Mexico) was selected at a later date.

Chairman: James Victor Gbeho (Ghana).
Vice-Chairmen: H. H. de Brabander-Ypes (Netherlands), Horst Heininger (German Democratic Republic), Raj Singh (Fiji).
Rapporteur: Fernando P. de Mello Barreto Filho (Brazil).

On 26 May 1988 (decision 1988/150), the Economic and Social Council elected the following for a three-year term beginning on 1 January 1989 to fill 13 of the 16 vacancies occurring on 31 December 1988: Brazil, Costa Rica, Cuba, Cyprus, Gabon, Indonesia, Mexico, Netherlands, Norway, Swaziland, USSR, United Kingdom, United States. No further elections were held in 1988 to fill the remaining seats, allocated to two members from African States and one member from Asian States.

Committee for Programme and Co-ordination
The Committee for Programme and Co-ordination is the main subsidiary organ of the Economic and Social Council and of the General Assembly for planning, programming and co-ordination and reports directly to both. It consists of 34 members nominated by the Council and elected by the Assembly for three-year terms according to a specific pattern of equitable geographical distribution.
During 1988, the Committee held, at United Nations Headquarters, an organizational meeting on 28 March, and its twenty-eighth session from 2 May to 3 June and from 6 to 19 September.

Members:
To serve until 31 December 1988: Argentina, Benin, France, Peru, USSR, United States, Zambia.
To serve until 31 December 1989: Brazil, Burkina Faso, Cameroon, China, Indonesia, Japan, Tunisia.
To serve until 31 December 1990: Austria, Bahrain, Bangladesh, Canada, Colombia, Côte d'Ivoire, Cuba, Germany, Federal Republic of, India, Kenya, Mexico, Pakistan, Poland, Romania, Rwanda, Sweden, Trinidad and Tobago, United Kingdom, Uganda, Yugoslavia.

Chairman: Deryck Lance Murray (Trinidad and Tobago).
Vice-Chairmen: Miodrag Cabric (Yugoslavia) (until June), Goran Fejic (Yugoslavia) (September); Isaiah Zimba Chabala (Zambia), Wilfried Koschorreck (Federal Republic of Germany).
Rapporteur: Fauzia Mufti Abbas (Pakistan).

On 26 May 1988 (decision 1988/150), the Economic and Social Council nominated the following nine Member States, seven of which were to be elected by the General Assembly, for a three-year term beginning on 1 January 1989 to fill the vacancies occurring on 31 December 1988: Bahamas, Benin, Chile, France, Peru, USSR, United States, Venezuela, Zambia. All but Chile and Peru were elected by the Assembly on 19 October (decision 43/306).

Committee on Natural Resources
The Committee on Natural Resources consists of 54 members, elected by the Economic and Social Council for four-year terms in accordance with the geographical distribution of seats in the Council.
The Committee did not meet in 1988.

Members:
To serve until 31 December 1988:[a] Argentina, Bangladesh, Botswana, Brazil, Burundi, Canada, Chile, China, Colombia, Ecuador, Egypt, Ghana, Greece, India, Japan, Kenya, Libyan Arab

Jamahiriya, Malaysia, Morocco, Netherlands, Panama, Sudan, Ukrainian SSR, USSR, Uruguay, Venezuela.
To serve until 31 December 1990:[b] Bolivia, Byelorussian SSR, Côte d'Ivoire, Cuba, Finland, France, German Democratic Republic, Germany, Federal Republic of, Hungary, Iran, Nigeria, Pakistan, Philippines, Poland, Swaziland, Sweden, Thailand, Togo, Turkey, Uganda, United States, Zaire.

[a]One seat allocated to a member from Western European and other States remained unfilled in 1988.
[b]Five seats allocated to two members from Asian States and three members from Western European and other States remained unfilled in 1988.

On 26 May 1988 (decision 1988/150), the Economic and Social Council elected the following for a four-year term beginning on 1 January 1989 to fill 15 of the 27 vacancies occurring on 31 December 1988: Botswana, Chile, China, Ecuador, El Salvador, Guatemala, Guinea-Bissau, Haiti, Honduras, Japan, Paraguay, Sudan, Ukrainian SSR, USSR, Uruguay. No further elections were held in 1988 to fill the remaining seats, allocated to five members from African States, three members from Asian States and four members from Western European and other States.

Committee on Negotiations with Intergovernmental Agencies
The Committee on Negotiations with Intergovernmental Agencies, established by the Economic and Social Council on 16 February 1946, was reconstituted by the Council on 4 February 1983 for the purpose of negotiating a relationship agreement between the United Nations and UNIDO.
The Committee adjourned *sine die* on 20 November 1985 upon completion of its report on the negotiations.

Committee on Non-Governmental Organizations
The Committee on Non-Governmental Organizations consists of 19 members elected by the Economic and Social Council for a four-year term according to a specific pattern of equitable geographical representation.
In 1988, the Committee met at United Nations Headquarters on 3 May and 7 July.

Members (until 31 December 1990): Bulgaria, Burundi, Colombia, Costa Rica, Cuba, Cyprus, France, Greece, Kenya, Malawi, Nicaragua, Oman, Pakistan, Rwanda, Sao Tome and Principe, Sri Lanka, Sweden, USSR, United States.

Chairman: Célestin Kabanda (Rwanda).
Vice-Chairman: Emil Y. Golemanov (Bulgaria).
Rapporteur: Erato Kozakou-Marcoullis (Cyprus).

Expert bodies

Ad Hoc Group of Experts on International Co-operation in Tax Matters
The membership of the *Ad Hoc* Group of Experts on International Co-operation in Tax Matters—to consist of 25 members drawn from 15 developing and 10 developed countries, appointed by the Secretary-General to serve in their individual capacity—remained at 24 in 1988, with one member from a developing country still to be appointed.
The *Ad Hoc* Group, which normally meets biennially, did not meet in 1988.

Members: Julius Olasoji Akinmola (Nigeria), Mohamed Chkounda (Morocco), Maurice Hugh Collins (United Kingdom), Eivany Antonio Da Silva (Brazil), V. U. Eradi (India), Mordecai S. Feinberg (United States), José Ramón Fernández-Pérez (Spain), Antonio H. Figueroa (Argentina), Mayer Gabay (Israel), Hugo Hanisch-Ovalle (Chile), I. A. Imtiazi (Pakistan), Abdel Fatah Ismail (Egypt), Marwan Koudsi (Syrian Arab Republic), Dominique Lemaire (France), Daniel Lüthi (Switzerland), Reksoprajitno Mansury (Indonesia), Thomas Menck (Federal Republic of Germany), Canute R. Miller (Jamaica), Alfred Philipp (Austria), Aaron Schwartzman (Mexico), Rainer Söderholm (Finland), André

Titty (Cameroon), Koenraad Van der Heeden (Netherlands), Isao Watanabe (Japan).

Committee for Development Planning

The Committee for Development Planning is composed of 24 experts representing different planning systems. They are appointed by the Economic and Social Council, on nomination by the Secretary-General, to serve in their personal capacity for a term of three years.

The Committee held its twenty-fourth session at United Nations Headquarters from 12 to 15 April 1988.

Members (until 31 December 1989): Abdlatif Y. Al-Hamad, *Chairman* (Kuwait); Nicolás Ardito-Barletta (Panama); Gerasimos D. Arsenis (Greece); Edmar Bacha (Brazil); Bernard T. G. Chidzero (Zimbabwe); Hernando de Soto (Peru); Prithvi Nath Dhar (India); Adama Diallo (Senegal); Just Faaland, *Rapporteur* (Norway); Keith Broadwell Griffin (United Kingdom); Patrick Guillaumont (France); Mahbub ul Haq (Pakistan); Gerald K. Helleiner (Canada); Huan Xiang (China); Helen Hughes (Australia); Shinichi Ichimura (Japan); Solita Collas Monsod (Philippines);[a] Henry Nau (United States); G. O. Nwankwo (Nigeria); Jozef Pajestka (Poland); Mihaly Simai, *Vice-Chairman* (Hungary); Udo Ernst Simonis (Federal Republic of Germany);[a] Igor Sysoyev (USSR); Ferdinand Van Dam (Netherlands).

[a]Appointed 5 February 1988 (decision 1988/106).

Committee of Experts on the Transport of Dangerous Goods

The Committee of Experts on the Transport of Dangerous Goods is composed of experts from countries interested in the international transport of dangerous goods. The experts are made available by their Governments at the request of the Secretary-General. The membership, to be increased to 15 in accordance with a 1975 resolution of the Economic and Social Council,[22] was 13 in 1988.

The Committee held its fifteenth session at Geneva from 5 to 14 December 1988.

Members: Canada, China,[a] France, Germany, Federal Republic of, Italy, Japan, Netherlands, Norway, Poland, Sweden, USSR, United Kingdom, United States.

[a]Membership endorsed by the Economic and Social Council on 26 May 1988 (decision 1988/149).

Chairman: Alan Roberts (United States).
Vice-Chairman: L. Grainger (United Kingdom).

The Committee may alter, as required, the composition of its subsidiary bodies. In addition, any Committee member may participate in the work of and vote in those bodies provided such member notify the United Nations Secretariat of the intention to do so.

GROUP OF EXPERTS ON EXPLOSIVES

The Group of Experts on Explosives held its twenty-eighth session at Geneva from 1 to 5 August 1988.

Chairman: M. Mariat (France).
Vice-Chairman: L. Grainger (United Kingdom).

GROUP OF RAPPORTEURS OF THE COMMITTEE OF
EXPERTS ON THE TRANSPORT OF DANGEROUS GOODS

In 1988, the Group of Rapporteurs of the Committee of Experts on the Transport of Dangerous Goods held two sessions, at Geneva: its thirty-seventh from 7 to 11 March and its thirty-eighth from 8 to 12 August.

Chairman: L. Grainger (United Kingdom).
Vice-Chairman: J. Monteith (Canada).

Committee on Crime Prevention and Control

The Committee on Crime Prevention and Control consists of 27 members elected for four-year terms by the Economic and Social Council, according to a specific pattern of equitable geo-

graphical representation, from among experts nominated by Member States.

The Committee held its tenth session at Vienna from 22 to 31 August 1988.

Members:

To serve until 31 December 1988: Mohamed Boulasri (Morocco); David Faulkner (United Kingdom); Ronald L. Gainer (United States); Jozsef Godony (Hungary); Aura Guerra de Villaláz (Panama); A. R. Khandker (Bangladesh); Abdul Meguid Ibrahim Kharbit (Kuwait); Farouk A. Mourad (Saudi Arabia); Bertin Pandi (Central African Republic); Aregba Polo (Togo); Miguel A. Sánchez Méndez (Colombia); Abdel Aziz Abdalla Shiddo (Sudan); Bo Svensson, *Vice-Chairman* (Sweden).

To serve until 31 December 1990: Cheng Weiqiu (China); Roger S. Clark (New Zealand); Dusan Cotic, *Vice-Chairman* (Yugoslavia); Hedi Fessi (Tunisia); Eugène Jules Henri Frencken (Belgium); Vasily P. Ignatov (USSR);[a] Albert Llewelyn Olawole Metzger, *Rapporteur* (Sierra Leone); Benjamín Miguel-Harb (Bolivia);[b] Jorge Arturo Montero Castro, *Vice-Chairman* (Costa Rica); Abdul Karim Nasution (Indonesia); Victor Ramanitra (Madagascar); Simone Andrée Rozes (France); Minoru Shikita, *Chairman* (Japan); Adolfo Luis Tamini (Argentina).

[a]Elected on 5 February 1988 (decision 1988/106) to fill the vacancy created by the resignation of Aleksei Y. Kudryavtsev (USSR).
[b]Elected on 26 May 1988 (decision 1988/150).

On 26 May 1988 (decision 1988/150), the Economic and Social Council elected the following 13 members for a four-year term beginning on 1 January 1989 to fill the vacancies occurring on 31 December 1988: Ramón de la Cruz Ochoa (Cuba), Trevor Percival Frank De Silva (Sri Lanka), David Faulkner (United Kingdom), Ronald L. Gainer (United States), Nour El-Deen Khair (Jordan), Jacek Kubiak (Poland), Hama Mâmoudou (Niger), Farouk A. Mourad (Saudi Arabia), Salah Nour (Algeria), Bertin Pandi (Central African Republic), Gioacchino Polimeni (Italy), Miguel A. Sánchez Méndez (Colombia), Abdel Aziz Abdalla Shiddo (Sudan).

Committee on Economic, Social and Cultural Rights

The Committee on Economic, Social and Cultural Rights consists of 18 experts serving in their personal capacity, elected by the Economic and Social Council from among persons nominated by States parties to the International Covenant on Economic, Social and Cultural Rights. The experts have recognized competence in the field of human rights, with due consideration given to equitable geographical distribution and to the representation of different forms of social and legal systems. Members serve for four-year terms.

The Committee held its second session at Geneva from 8 to 25 February 1988.

Members:

To serve until 31 December 1988: Juan Alvarez Vita, *Vice-Chairman* (Peru); Mohamed Lamine Fofana (Guinea); María de los Angeles Jiménez Butragueño (Spain); Samba Cor Konate (Senegal); Vassil Mrachkov (Bulgaria); Wladyslaw Neneman, *Vice-Chairman* (Poland); Kenneth Osborne Rattray (Jamaica); Mikis Demetriou Sparsis (Cyprus); Philippe Texier (France).

To serve until 31 December 1990: Philip Alston, *Rapporteur* (Australia); Ibrahim Ali Badawi El-Sheikh, *Chairman* (Egypt); Adib Daoudy, *Vice-Chairman* (Syrian Arab Republic);[a] Jaime Alberto Marchan Romero (Ecuador); Alexandre Muterahejuru (Rwanda); Bruno Simma (Federal Republic of Germany); Eduard P. Sviridov (USSR);[b] Chikako Taya (Japan); Javier Wimer Zambrano (Mexico).

[a]Resigned on 11 May 1988; Sami Glaiel (Syrian Arab Republic) was elected on 28 July (decision 1988/176) to fill the resultant vacancy.
[b]Resigned on 19 February 1988; Valeri I. Kouznetsov (USSR) was elected on 26 May (decision 1988/150) to fill the resultant vacancy.

On 26 May 1988 (decision 1988/150), the Economic and Social Council re-elected, for a four-year term beginning on 1 Janu-

---

[22]YUN 1975, p. 734, ESC res. 1973(LIX), 30 July 1975.

ary 1989, the nine members whose terms were to expire on 31 December 1988.

Intergovernmental Working Group of Experts on International Standards of Accounting and Reporting

The Intergovernmental Working Group of Experts on International Standards of Accounting and Reporting, which reports to the Commission on Transnational Corporations, consists of 34 members, elected for three-year terms by the Economic and Social Council according to a specific pattern of equitable geographical distribution. Each State elected appoints an expert with appropriate experience in accounting and reporting.

The Group held its sixth session at United Nations Headquarters from 7 to 17 March 1988.

Members:

To serve until 31 December 1988:[a] Cyprus, Germany, Federal Republic of, India, Italy, Japan, Malawi, Netherlands, Nigeria, Panama, Tunisia, Uganda, United Kingdom, Uruguay.

To serve until 31 December 1990:[b] Brazil, Canada, China, France, Kenya, Norway, Spain, Swaziland, Switzerland,[c] USSR,[d] Zaire.

[a]Four seats allocated to one member each from Asian and Latin American and Caribbean States and two members from Eastern European States remained unfilled in 1988.
[b]Six seats allocated to two members each from African, Asian and Latin American and Caribbean States remained unfilled in 1988.
[c]Elected on 28 July 1988 (decision 1988/176).
[d]Elected on 3 March 1988 (decision 1988/106).

Chairman: Pieter A. Wessel (Netherlands).
Vice-Chairmen: V. P. Bogomolov (USSR), Eliseu Martins (Brazil), Theophilos Theophilou (Cyprus).
Rapporteur: G. B. Chiwaula (Malawi).

On 26 May 1988 (decision 1988/150), the Economic and Social Council elected the following for a three-year term beginning on 1 January 1989 to fill 11 of the 17 vacancies occurring on 31 December 1988: Cyprus, Czechoslovakia, Germany, Federal Republic of, India, Italy, Japan, Malawi, Netherlands, Nigeria, Uganda, United Kingdom. No further elections were held in 1988 to fill the seats allocated to one member each from African, Asian and Eastern European States, and three members from Latin American and Caribbean States.

United Nations Group of Experts on Geographical Names

The United Nations Group of Experts on Geographical Names represents various geographical/linguistic divisions, of which there were 17 in 1988, as follows: Africa Central; Africa East; Africa West; Arabic; Asia East (other than China); Asia South-East and Pacific South-West; Asia South-West (other than Arabic); China; Dutch- and German-speaking; East Central and South-East Europe; India; Latin America; Norden; Romano-Hellenic; Union of Soviet Socialist Republics; United Kingdom; United States of America/Canada.

The Group of Experts did not meet in 1988.

Ad hoc bodies

Special Commission of the Economic and Social Council on the In-depth Study of the United Nations Intergovernmental Structure and Functions in the Economic and Social Fields

The Special Commission of the Economic and Social Council on the In-depth Study of the United Nations Intergovernmental Structure and Functions in the Economic and Social Fields, open to the full participation of all Member States, held five sessions in 1988, at United Nations Headquarters: its fifth from 18 to 29 January, its sixth from 8 to 19 February, its seventh from 7 to 18 March, its eighth from 18 to 29 April, and its ninth (final) session from 2 to 6 and on 11 and 23 May.

Chairman: Abdel Halim Badawi (Egypt).
Vice-Chairmen: Chinmaya R. Gharekhan (India), Adriaan Jacobovits de Szeged (Netherlands), Lev I. Maksimov (Byelorussian SSR), Mario Moya-Palencia (Mexico).

Administrative Committee on Co-ordination

The Administrative Committee on Co-ordination held two sessions in 1988: the first at Geneva on 20 and 21 April, and the second at United Nations Headquarters on 25 and 26 October.

The membership of ACC, under the chairmanship of the Secretary-General of the United Nations, includes the executive heads of ILO, FAO, UNESCO, ICAO, WHO, the World Bank, IMF, UPU, ITU, WMO, IMO, WIPO, IFAD, UNIDO, IAEA and the secretariat of the Contracting Parties to GATT.

Also taking part in the work of ACC are the United Nations Director-General for Development and International Economic Co-operation; the Under-Secretaries-General for International Economic and Social Affairs, for Administration and Management, and for Technical Co-operation for Development; and the executive heads of UNCTAD, UNDP, UNEP, UNFPA, UNHCR, UNICEF, UNITAR, UNRWA and WFP.

ACC has established subsidiary bodies on organizational, administrative and substantive questions.

Other related bodies

International Research and Training Institute for the Advancement of Women (INSTRAW)

The International Research and Training Institute for the Advancement of Women, a body of the United Nations financed through voluntary contributions, functions under the authority of a Board of Trustees.

BOARD OF TRUSTEES

The Board of Trustees is composed of 11 members serving in their individual capacity, appointed by the Economic and Social Council on the nomination of States; and *ex-officio* members. Members serve for three-year terms, with a maximum of two terms.

The Board, which reports periodically to the Council and where appropriate to the General Assembly, held its eighth session at Santo Domingo, Dominican Republic, from 8 to 12 February 1988.

Members (until 30 June 1988):
To serve until 30 June 1988: Fabiola Cuvi Ortiz (Ecuador); Elena Atanassova Lagadinova (Bulgaria); Lin Shangzhen, *Rapporteur* (China); Victoria N. Okobi, *Vice President* (Nigeria); Kristin Tornes (Norway).
To serve until 30 June 1989: Inés Alberdi (Spain); Siga Seye (Senegal); Berta Torrijos de Arosemena (Panama).
To serve until 30 June 1990: Daniela Colombo, *President* (Italy); Tawhida O. Hadra (Sudan); Achie Sudiarti Luhulima (Indonesia).

On 26 May 1988 (decision 1988/150), the Economic and Social Council appointed the following five members for a three-year term beginning on 1 July 1988 to fill the vacancies occurring on 30 June: Fabiola Cuvi Ortiz (Ecuador), Awa Diallo (Mali), Elena Atanassova Lagadinova (Bulgaria), Gule Afruz Mahbub (Bangladesh), Kristin Tornes (Norway).

Members (from 1 July 1988):
To serve until 30 June 1989: Inés Alberdi (Spain), Siga Seye (Senegal), Berta Torrijos de Arosemena (Panama).
To serve until 30 June 1990: Daniela Colombo (Italy), Tawhida O. Hadra (Sudan), Achie Sudiarti Luhulima (Indonesia).
To serve until 30 June 1991: Fabiola Cuvi Ortiz (Ecuador), Awa Diallo (Mali), Elena Atanassova Lagadinova (Bulgaria), Gule Afruz Mahbub (Bangladesh), Kristin Tornes (Norway).

Ex-officio members: The Director of the Institute, and a representative of the Secretary-General, each of the regional commissions and the Institute's host country (Dominican Republic).
Director of the Institute: Dunja Pastizzi-Ferencic.

United Nations Children's Fund (UNICEF)

EXECUTIVE BOARD

The UNICEF Executive Board, which reports to the Economic and Social Council and, as appropriate, to the General Assembly, consists of 41 members elected by the Council from Member States of the United Nations or members of the specialized agencies or of IAEA, for three-year terms.

In 1988, the Board held an organizational session on 23 February, its regular session from 18 to 29 April and (with its composition as of 1 August) an organizational session on 6 June, all at United Nations Headquarters.

Members (until 31 July 1988):
To serve until 31 July 1988: Argentina, Bangladesh, Brazil, Bulgaria, Chile, Congo, Djibouti, Ethiopia, France, Gabon, Italy, Japan, Mali, Mexico, Netherlands, Oman, Pakistan, Tunisia, USSR, United Kingdom, United States.
To serve until 31 July 1989: Canada, China, Colombia, Germany, Federal Republic of, Guyana, Lesotho, Norway, Poland, Thailand, Turkey.
To serve until 31 July 1990: Australia, Belgium, Benin, India, Indonesia, Liberia, Philippines, Switzerland, Uruguay, Yugoslavia.

Chairman: A. P. Maruping (Lesotho).
First Vice-Chairman: Makoto Taniguchi (Japan).
Second Vice-Chairman: Stanislaw Trepczynski (Poland).
Third Vice-Chairman: Sidibé Aissata Cisse (Mali).
Fourth Vice-Chairman: Rawle Lucas (Guyana).

On 26 May 1988 (decision 1988/150), the Economic and Social Council elected the following 21 members for a three-year term beginning on 1 August 1988 to fill the vacancies occurring on 31 July: Bangladesh, Bolivia, Byelorussian SSR, Cameroon, Egypt, France, Italy, Japan, Mexico, Nicaragua, Nigeria, Oman, Pakistan, Republic of Korea, Sao Tome and Principe, Sudan, Sweden, Uganda, USSR, United Kingdom, United States.

Members (from 1 August 1988):
To serve until 31 July 1989: Canada, China, Colombia, Germany, Federal Republic of, Guyana, Lesotho, Norway, Poland, Thailand, Turkey.
To serve until 31 July 1990: Australia, Belgium, Benin, India, Indonesia, Liberia, Philippines, Switzerland, Uruguay, Yugoslavia.
To serve until 31 July 1991: Bangladesh, Bolivia, Byelorussian SSR, Cameroon, Egypt, France, Italy, Japan, Mexico, Nicaragua, Nigeria, Oman, Pakistan, Republic of Korea, Sao Tome and Principe, Sudan, Sweden, Uganda, USSR, United Kingdom, United States.

Chairman: Torild Skard (Norway).
First Vice-Chairman: Suyono Yahya (Indonesia).
Second Vice-Chairman: Stanislaw Trepczynski (Poland).
Third Vice-Chairman: Michael O. Ononaiye (Nigeria).
Fourth Vice-Chairman: Chandrashekhar Dasgupta (India).

Executive Director of UNICEF: James P. Grant.

COMMITTEE ON ADMINISTRATION AND FINANCE
The Committee on Administration and Finance is a committee of the whole of the UNICEF Executive Board.

Chairman: Suyono Yahya (Indonesia) (until 31 July), Nicole Senécal (Canada) (from 1 August).
Vice-Chairman: Nicole Senécal (Canada) (until 31 July), Rawle Lucas (Guyana) (from 1 August).

PROGRAMME COMMITTEE
The Programme Committee is a committee of the whole of the UNICEF Executive Board.

Chairman: Torild Skard (Norway) (until 31 July), Margarita Dieguez-Armas (Mexico) (from 1 August).
Vice-Chairman: Margarita Dieguez-Armas (Mexico) (until 31 July), Hoda Badran (Egypt) (from 1 August).

UNICEF/WHO Joint Committee on Health Policy
The UNICEF/WHO Joint Committee on Health Policy consists of: six members of the UNICEF Executive Board, among whom are the chairmen of the Executive Board and the Programme Committee who serve *ex officio;* and six members of the WHO Executive Board.

The Joint Committee, which meets biennially, did not meet in 1988.

United Nations Development Programme (UNDP)

GOVERNING COUNCIL
The Governing Council of UNDP, which reports to the Economic and Social Council and through it to the General Assembly, consists of 48 members, elected by the Council from Member States of the United Nations or members of the specialized agencies or of IAEA. Twenty-seven seats are allocated to developing countries as follows: 11 to African countries, 9 to Asian countries and Yugoslavia, and 7 to Latin American countries. Twenty-one seats are allocated to economically more advanced countries as follows: 17 to Western European and other countries, and 4 to Eastern European countries. The term of office is three years, one third of the members being elected each year.

In 1988, the Governing Council held an organizational meeting at United Nations Headquarters on 16 and 19 February, a special session at United Nations Headquarters from 17 to 19 February and its thirty-fifth session at Geneva from 6 June to 1 July.

Members:
To serve until the day preceding the February 1989 organizational session: Belgium, Brazil, Bulgaria, Burundi, Cameroon, Canada, Cape Verde, Denmark, France, Indonesia, Kuwait, Malawi, Mauritius, New Zealand, Republic of Korea, Spain.
To serve until the day preceding the February 1990 organizational session: Argentina, Burkina Faso, Colombia, Ecuador, Fiji, Finland, German Democratic Republic, Germany, Federal Republic of, India, Liberia, Netherlands, Poland, Sudan, Switzerland, Thailand, Turkey.
To serve until the day preceding the February 1991 organizational session: Austria, China, Cuba, Ghana, Guatemala, Italy, Japan, Libyan Arab Jamahiriya, Norway, Peru, Syrian Arab Republic, USSR, United Kingdom, United States, Yugoslavia, Zimbabwe.

President: Timon Sam Mangwazu (Malawi).
Vice-Presidents: Soemadi Brotodiningrat (Indonesia), Sjoerd Leenstra (Netherlands), Juan Salazar-Sancisi (Ecuador), Janusz Zielinski (Poland).

On 26 and 27 May (decision 1988/150) and on 28 July 1988 (decision 1988/176), the Economic and Social Council elected the following 16 members for a three-year term beginning on the first day of the February 1989 organizational session to fill the vacancies occurring the preceding day: Australia, Belgium, Brazil, Canada, Cyprus, France, Guinea-Bissau, Kenya, Mozambique, Pakistan, Philippines, Romania, Sao Tome and Principe, Spain, Sweden, Zaire.

Administrator of UNDP: William H. Draper III.
Associate Administrator: G. Arthur Brown.

BUDGETARY AND FINANCE COMMITTEE
The Budgetary and Finance Committee, a committee of the whole, held a series of meetings at Geneva between 6 June and 1 July 1988.

Chairman: Sjoerd Leenstra (Netherlands).
Rapporteur: Kwame Tengkorang (Ghana).

COMMITTEE OF THE WHOLE
The Governing Council resolved itself into a Committee of the Whole and held meetings on 17 and 18 February and between 7 June and 1 July 1988 to consider matters related to programme management. The President of the Council presided.

United Nations Research Institute for Social Development (UNRISD)

BOARD OF DIRECTORS
The Board of Directors of UNRISD reports to the Economic and Social Council through the Commission for Social Development.
The Board consists of:

The Chairman, appointed by the Secretary-General: Paul-Marc Henry (France) (until 1 October 1988), Keith Griffin (United Kingdom) (from 2 October);

Seven members, nominated by the Commission for Social Development and confirmed by the Economic and Social Council (to serve until 30 June 1989): Ismail Sabri Abdalla (Egypt), Sartaj Aziz (Pakistan), Vida Cok (Yugoslavia), Louis Emerij (Netherlands), Ulf Hannerz (Sweden), Sally Weaver (Canada);[a] (to serve until 30 June 1991): Lucio Kowarick (Brazil).

Seven other members, as follows: a representative of the Secretary-General, the Director of the Latin American Institute for Economic and Social Planning, the Director of the African Institute for Economic Development and Planning, the Executive Secretary of ESCWA, the Director of UNRISD *(ex officio)*, and the representatives of two of the following specialized agencies appointed as members and observers in annual rotation: UNESCO and WHO (members); ILO and FAO (observers).

[a]Resigned in July 1988.

Director of the Institute: Dharam Ghai.

World Food Programme

COMMITTEE ON FOOD AID POLICIES AND PROGRAMMES

The Committee on Food Aid Policies and Programmes, the governing body of WFP, reports annually to the Economic and Social Council, the FAO Council and the World Food Council. It consists of 30 members, of which 15 are elected by the Economic and Social Council and 15 by the FAO Council, from Member States of the United Nations or from members of FAO. Members serve for three-year terms.

The Committee held two sessions during 1988, at Rome, Italy: its twenty-fifth from 30 May to 9 June and its twenty-sixth on 12 December.

Members:

To serve until 31 December 1988:
  Elected by Economic and Social Council: Argentina, Cape Verde, Colombia, Finland, United Kingdom.
  Elected by FAO Council: Ethiopia, France, Germany, Federal Republic of, Sao Tome and Principe, Venezuela.
To serve until 31 December 1989:
  Elected by Economic and Social Council: Hungary, India, Italy, Sweden, Tunisia.
  Elected by FAO Council: Australia, Bangladesh *(Chairman)*, Canada, Saudi Arabia, United States *(First Vice-Chairman)*.
To serve until 31 December 1990:
  Elected by Economic and Social Council: Belgium, Japan, Kenya *(Second Vice-Chairman)*, Norway, Pakistan.
  Elected by FAO Council: Brazil, Cameroon, China, Madagascar, Netherlands.

On 26 May 1988 (decision 1988/150), the Economic and Social Council elected Colombia, Cuba, Denmark, the Niger and the United Kingdom, and, on 24 November, the FAO Council elected the Congo, France, the Federal Republic of Germany, Mexico and Zambia, all for a three-year term beginning on 1 January 1989 to fill the vacancies occurring on 31 December 1988.

Executive Director of WFP: James Charles Ingram.
Deputy Executive Director: Salahuddin Ahmed.

Conference

**United Nations Conference for the Adoption of a
Convention against Illicit Traffic in
Narcotic Drugs and Psychotropic Substances**

The United Nations Conference for the Adoption of a Convention against Illicit Traffic in Narcotic Drugs and Psychotropic Substances was held at Vienna from 25 November to 20 December 1988. Participating were the following 106 States:

Afghanistan, Albania, Algeria, Argentina, Australia, Austria, Bahamas, Bahrain, Bangladesh, Barbados, Belgium, Bolivia, Botswana, Brazil, Bulgaria, Burma, Byelorussian SSR, Cameroon, Canada, Cape Verde, Chile, China, Colombia, Costa Rica, Côte d'Ivoire, Cuba, Cyprus, Czechoslovakia, Denmark, Dominican Republic, Ecuador, Egypt, Ethiopia, Finland, France, German Democratic Republic, Germany, Federal Republic of, Ghana, Greece, Guatemala, Guinea, Holy See, Honduras, Hungary, India, Indonesia, Iran, Iraq, Ireland, Israel, Italy, Jamaica, Japan, Jordan, Kenya, Kuwait, Libyan Arab Jamahiriya, Luxembourg, Madagascar, Malaysia, Malta, Mauritania, Mauritius, Mexico, Monaco, Morocco, Nepal, Netherlands, New Zealand, Nicaragua, Nigeria, Norway, Oman, Pakistan, Panama, Papua New Guinea, Paraguay, Peru, Philippines, Poland, Portugal, Qatar, Republic of Korea, Saudi Arabia, Senegal, Spain, Sri Lanka, Sudan, Suriname, Sweden, Switzerland, Thailand, Tunisia, Turkey, Ukrainian SSR, USSR, United Arab Emirates, United Kingdom, United Republic of Tanzania, United States, Uruguay, Venezuela, Viet Nam, Yemen, Yugoslavia, Zaire.

President: Guillermo Bedregal-Gutiérrez (Bolivia).
Vice-Presidents: Algeria, Argentina, Bahamas, China, Côte d'Ivoire, France, Iran, Japan, Kenya, Malaysia, Mexico, Morocco, Nigeria, Pakistan, Philippines, Senegal, Sudan, Sweden, Turkey, USSR, United Kingdom, United States, Venezuela, Yugoslavia.
Rapporteur-General: Mervat Tallawy (Egypt).

Chairmen of committees:
  General Committee: The President of the Conference.
  Committee I: Gioacchino Polimeni (Italy).
  Committee II: Istvan Bayer (Hungary).
  Drafting Committee: M. V. N. Rao (India).
  Credentials Committee: Edouard Molitor (Luxembourg).

Trusteeship Council

Article 86 of the United Nations Charter lays down that the Trusteeship Council shall consist of the following:

Members of the United Nations administering Trust Territories;
Permanent members of the Security Council which do not administer Trust Territories;
As many other members elected for a three-year term by the General Assembly as will ensure that the membership of the Council is equally divided between United Nations Members which administer Trust Territories and those which do not.[a]

[a]During 1988, only one Member of the United Nations was an administering member of the Trusteeship Council, while four permanent members of the Security Council continued as non-administering members.

MEMBERS
Member administering a Trust Territory: United States.
Non-administering members: China, France, USSR, United Kingdom.

SESSION
Fifty-fifth session: United Nations Headquarters, 10 to 27 May and 19 July 1988.

OFFICERS
President: Jean-Michel Gaussot (France).
Vice-President: John A. Birch (United Kingdom).

International Court of Justice

Judges of the Court

The International Court of Justice consists of 15 Judges elected for nine-year terms by the General Assembly and the Security Council.

The following were the Judges of the Court serving in 1988, listed in the order of precedence:

Judge	Country of nationality	End of term[a]
José Maria Ruda, *President*[b]	Argentina	1991
Kéba Mbaye, *Vice-President*[b]	Senegal	1991
Manfred Lachs	Poland	1994
Nagendra Singh[c]	India	1991
Taslim Olawale Elias	Nigeria	1994
Shigeru Oda	Japan	1994
Roberto Ago	Italy	1997
Stephen M. Schwebel	United States	1997
Sir Robert Y. Jennings	United Kingdom	1991
Mohammed Bedjaoui	Algeria	1997
Ni Zhengyu	China	1994
Jens Evensen	Norway	1994
Nikolai K. Tarassov	USSR	1997
Gilbert Guillaume	France	1991
Mohamed Shahabuddeen	Guyana	1997

[a]Term expires on 5 February of the year indicated.
[b]Elected by the Court on 24 February 1988 for a three-year term.
[c]Died on 11 December 1988.

Registrar: Eduardo Valencia-Ospina.
Deputy Registrar: Bernard Noble.

Chamber formed in the case concerning
Elettronica Sicula S.p.A. (ELSI)
(United States of America v. Italy)

Members: Nagendra Singh *(President)* (until 11 December 1988), Shigeru Oda, Roberto Ago, Stephen M. Schwebel, Sir Robert Y. Jennings.

Chamber formed in the case concerning the *Land, Island and Maritime Frontier Dispute (El Salvador/Honduras)*

Members: José Sette Câmara *(President)*, Shigeru Oda, Sir Robert Y. Jennings.
Ad hoc members: Nicolas Valticos, Michel Virally.

Chamber of Summary Procedure
(as constituted by the Court on 24 February 1988)

Members: José Maria Ruda *(ex officio)*, Kéba Mbaye *(ex officio)*, Sir Robert Y. Jennings, Ni Zhengyu, Jens Evensen.
Substitute members: Gilbert Guillaume, Mohamed Shahabuddeen.

Parties to the Court's Statute

All Members of the United Nations are *ipso facto* parties to the Statute of the International Court of Justice. Also parties to it are the following non-members: Liechtenstein, Nauru,[a] San Marino, Switzerland.

[a]Became a party to the Statute on 29 January 1988.

States accepting the compulsory jurisdiction of the Court

Declarations made by the following States, a number with reservations, accepting the Court's compulsory jurisdiction (or made under the Statute of the Permanent Court of International Justice and deemed to be an acceptance of the jurisdiction of the International Court) were in force at the end of 1988:

Australia, Austria, Barbados, Belgium, Botswana, Canada, Colombia, Costa Rica, Cyprus,[a] Democratic Kampuchea, Denmark, Dominican Republic, Egypt, El Salvador, Finland, Gambia, Haiti, Honduras, India, Japan, Kenya, Liberia, Liechtenstein, Luxembourg, Malawi, Malta, Mauritius, Mexico, Nauru,[a] Netherlands, New Zealand, Nicaragua, Nigeria, Norway, Pakistan, Panama, Philippines, Portugal, Senegal, Somalia, Sudan, Suriname, Swaziland, Sweden, Switzerland, Togo, Uganda, United Kingdom, Uruguay.

[a]Filed its declaration of acceptance on 29 April and 29 January 1988, respectively.

United Nations organs and specialized and related agencies authorized to request advisory opinions from the Court

Authorized by the United Nations Charter to request opinions on any legal question: General Assembly, Security Council.
Authorized by the General Assembly in accordance with the Charter to request opinions on legal questions arising within the scope of their activities: Economic and Social Council, Trusteeship Council, Interim Committee of the General Assembly, Committee on Applications for Review of Administrative Tribunal Judgements, ILO, FAO, UNESCO, ICAO, WHO, World Bank, IFC, IDA, IMF, ITU, WMO, IMO, WIPO, IFAD, UNIDO, IAEA.

Committees of the Court

BUDGETARY AND ADMINISTRATIVE COMMITTEE
Members: José Maria Ruda *(ex officio)*, Kéba Mbaye *(ex officio)*, Taslim Olawale Elias, Stephen M. Schwebel, Mohammed Bedjaoui, Nikolai K. Tarassov, Gilbert Guillaume.

COMMITTEE ON RELATIONS
Members: Nagendra Singh (until 11 December 1988), Ni Zhengyu, Jens Evensen.

LIBRARY COMMITTEE
Members: Shigeru Oda, Sir Robert Y. Jennings, Ni Zhengyu.

RULES COMMITTEE
Members: Manfred Lachs, Kéba Mbaye, Shigeru Oda, Roberto Ago, Sir Robert Y. Jennings, Ni Zhengyu, Nikolai K. Tarassov, Mohamed Shahabuddeen.

Other United Nations–related bodies

The following bodies are not subsidiary to any principal organ of the United Nations but were established by an international treaty instrument or arrangement sponsored by the United Nations and are thus related to the Organization and its work. These bodies, often referred to as "treaty organs", are serviced by the United Nations Secretariat and may be financed in part or wholly from the Organization's regular budget, as authorized by the General Assembly, to which most of them report annually.

Committee against Torture

The Committee against Torture was established under the Convention against Torture and Other Cruel, Inhuman or Degrading Treat-ment or Punishment.[23] It consists of 10 experts elected for four-year terms by the States parties to the Convention to serve in their personal capacity, with due regard for equitable geographical distribution and for the usefulness of the participation of some persons having legal experience.

The Committee, which reports annually to the General Assembly, held its first session at Geneva from 18 to 22 April 1988.

Members:
To serve until 31 December 1989: Alexis Dipanda Mouelle, *Vice-Chairman* (Cameroon); Yuri A. Khitrin (USSR); Dimitar Nikolov

[23]YUN 1984, p. 815, GA res. 39/46, annex, article 17, 10 Dec. 1984.

Mikhailov, *Rapporteur* (Bulgaria); Bent Sorensen (Denmark); Joseph Voyame, *Chairman* (Switzerland).

To serve until 31 December 1991: Alfredo R. A. Bengzon (Philippines); Peter Thomas Burns (Canada); Christine Chanet (France); Socorro Díaz Palacios (Mexico); Ricardo Gil Lavedra, *Vice-Chairman* (Argentina).

Committee on the Elimination of Discrimination against Women

The Committee on the Elimination of Discrimination against Women was established under the Convention on the Elimination of All Forms of Discrimination against Women.[24] It consists of 23 experts elected for four-year terms by the States parties to the Convention to serve in their personal capacity, with due regard for equitable geographical distribution and for representation of the different forms of civilization and principal legal systems.

The Committee, which reports annually to the General Assembly through the Economic and Social Council, held its seventh session at United Nations Headquarters from 16 February to 4 March 1988.

Members:

To serve until 15 April 1988: Désirée P. Bernard, *Chairman* (Guyana); Marie Caron (Canada); Elizabeth Evatt (Australia); Aida González Martínez (Mexico); Chryssanthi Laiou-Antoniou (Greece); Alma Montenegro de Fletcher (Panama); Edith Oeser (German Democratic Republic); Maria Margarida Salema (Portugal); Kongit Singegiorgis (Ethiopia); Esther Véliz Díaz de Villalvilla (Cuba); Margareta Wadstein, *Rapporteur* (Sweden).

To serve until 15 April 1990: Ryoko Akamatsu, *Vice-Chairman* (Japan); Ivanka Corti (Italy); Hadja Assa Diallo Soumare, *Vice-Chairman* (Mali); Ruth Escobar (Brazil); Norma M. Forde (Barbados); Guan Minqian (China); Zagorka Ilic (Yugoslavia); Elvira Novikova, *Vice-Chairman* (USSR); Lily Pilataxi de Arenas (Ecuador); Pudjiwati Sayogyo (Indonesia);[a] Mervat Tallawy (Egypt); Rose N. Ukeje (Nigeria).

[a] Appointment approved by the Committee on 16 February 1988.

In March 1988, the States parties elected the following for a four-year term beginning on 16 April 1988 to fill the vacancies occurring on 15 April: Ana Maria Alfonsín de Fasan (Argentina), Désirée P. Bernard (Guyana), Carlota Bustelo García del Real (Spain), Elizabeth Evatt (Australia), Grethe Fenger-Möller (Denmark), Aida González Martínez (Mexico), Chryssanthi Laiou-Antoniou (Greece), Edith Oeser (German Democratic Republic), Hanna Beate Schöpp-Schilling (Federal Republic of Germany), Kongit Singegiorgis (Ethiopia), Kissem Walla-Tchangai (Togo).

Committee on the Elimination of Racial Discrimination

The Committee on the Elimination of Racial Discrimination was established under the International Convention on the Elimination of All Forms of Racial Discrimination.[25] It consists of 18 experts elected for four-year terms by the States parties to the Convention to serve in their personal capacity, with due regard for equitable geographical distribution and for representation of the different forms of civilization and principal legal systems.

The Committee, which reports annually to the General Assembly through the Secretary-General, held its thirty-sixth session at Geneva from 1 to 12 August 1988.

Members:

To serve until 19 January 1990: Mahmoud Aboul-Nasr (Egypt); Hamzat Ahmadu (Nigeria); Michael Parker Banton (United Kingdom); Mohamed Omer Beshir (Sudan); André Braunschweig (France); George O. Lamptey, *Chairman* (Ghana); Karl Josef Partsch, *Vice-Chairman* (Federal Republic of Germany); Agha Shahi (Pakistan); Michael E. Sherifis (Cyprus).

To serve until 19 January 1992:[a] Eduardo Ferrero Costa (Peru); Isi Foighel (Denmark); Ivan Garvalov, *Vice-Chairman* (Bulgaria); Yuri A. Reshetov (USSR); Jorge Rhenan Segura (Costa Rica); Shanti Sadiq Ali, *Rapporteur* (India); Song Shuhua (China); Kasimir Vidas (Yugoslavia); Mario Jorge Yutzis, *Vice-Chairman* (Argentina).

[a] Elected on 15 January 1988.

Conference on Disarmament

The Conference on Disarmament, the multilateral negotiating forum on disarmament, reports annually to the General Assembly and is serviced by the United Nations Secretariat. It was composed of 40 members in 1988.

During 1988, the Conference met at Geneva from 2 February to 29 April and from 7 July to 20 September.

Members: Algeria, Argentina, Australia, Belgium, Brazil, Bulgaria, Burma, Canada, China, Cuba, Czechoslovakia, Egypt, Ethiopia, France, German Democratic Republic, Germany, Federal Republic of, Hungary, India, Indonesia, Iran, Italy, Japan, Kenya, Mexico, Mongolia, Morocco, Netherlands, Nigeria, Pakistan, Peru, Poland, Romania, Sri Lanka, Sweden, USSR, United Kingdom, United States, Venezuela, Yugoslavia, Zaire.

The presidency, which rotates in English alphabetical order among the members, was held by the following in 1988: February, German Democratic Republic; March, Federal Republic of Germany; April and the recess between the first and second parts of the 1988 session, Hungary; July, India; August, Indonesia; September and the recess until the 1989 session, Iran.

Human Rights Committee

The Human Rights Committee was established under the International Covenant on Civil and Political Rights.[26] It consists of 18 experts elected by the States parties to the Covenant to serve in their personal capacity for four-year terms.

In 1988, the Committee, which reports annually to the General Assembly through the Economic and Social Council, held three sessions: its thirty-second at United Nations Headquarters from 21 March to 8 April, its thirty-third at Geneva from 11 to 29 July and its thirty-fourth at Geneva from 24 October to 11 November.

Members:

To serve until 31 December 1988: Andrés Aguilar (Venezuela); Rosalyn Higgins (United Kingdom); Rajsoomer Lallah (Mauritius); Andreas V. Mavrommatis (Cyprus); Anatoly P. Movchan (USSR); Fausto Pocar, *Vice-Chairman* (Italy); Alejandro Serrano Caldera (Nicaragua); S. Amos Wako (Kenya); Adam Zielinski (Poland).

To serve until 31 December 1990: Nisuke Ando (Japan); Christine Chanet (France); Joseph A. L. Cooray, *Vice-Chairman* (Sri Lanka); Vojin Dimitrijevic, *Rapporteur* (Yugoslavia); Omran El-Shafei (Egypt); Joseph A. Mommersteeg (Netherlands); Birame Ndiaye, *Vice-Chairman* (Senegal); Julio Prado Vallejo, *Chairman* (Ecuador); Bertil Wennergren (Sweden).

On 16 September 1988, the States parties elected the following for a four-year term beginning on 1 January 1989 to fill the vacancies occurring on 31 December 1988: Francisco José Aguilar Urbina (Costa Rica), Janos Fodor (Hungary), Rosalyn Higgins (United Kingdom), Rajsoomer Lallah (Mauritius), Andreas V. Mavrommatis (Cyprus), Rein A. Myullerson (USSR), Fausto Pocar (Italy), Alejandro Serrano Caldera (Nicaragua), S. Amos Wako (Kenya).

International Narcotics Control Board (INCB)

The International Narcotics Control Board, established under the Single Convention on Narcotic Drugs, 1961, as amended by the 1972 Protocol, consists of 13 members, elected by the Economic and Social Council for five-year terms, three from candidates nominated by WHO and 10 from candidates nominated by Members of the United Nations and parties to the Single Convention.

The Board held two sessions in 1988, at Vienna: its forty-third from 24 May to 3 June and its forty-fourth from 5 to 21 October.

Members:

To serve until 1 March 1990: Dr. Cai Zhi-ji (China); Dr. John C. Ebie (Nigeria);[a] Dr. Diego Garcés-Giraldo (Colombia); Ben J. A.

---

[24] YUN 1979, p. 898, GA res. 34/180, annex, article 17, 18 Dec. 1979.
[25] YUN 1965, p. 443, GA res. 2106 A (XX), annex, article 8, 21 Dec. 1965.
[26] YUN 1966, p. 427, GA res. 2200 A (XXI), annex, part IV, 16 Dec. 1966.

Huyghe-Braeckmans (Belgium); Mohsen Kchouk, *First Vice-President* (Tunisia); Sahibzada Raoof Ali Khan, *President* (Pakistan).

To serve until 1 March 1992: Sirad Atmodjo (Indonesia);[a] Dr. Nikolai K. Barkov (USSR); Dr. Abdullahi S. Elmi (Somalia); Betty C. Gough (United States); Dr. S. Oguz Kayaalp, *Second Vice-President* (Turkey);[a] Paul Reuter (France); Dr. Tulio Velasquez-Quevedo, *Rapporteur* (Peru).

[a]Elected from candidates nominated by WHO.

Preparatory Commission for the International Sea-Bed Authority and for the International Tribunal for the Law of the Sea

The Preparatory Commission for the International Sea-Bed Authority and for the International Tribunal for the Law of the Sea was established by the Third United Nations Conference on the Law of the Sea. It consists of States, Namibia (represented by the United Nations Council for Namibia), self-governing associated States, territories enjoying full internal self-government and international organizations which have signed or acceded to the United Nations Convention on the Law of the Sea. As at 31 December 1988, the Commission had 159 members.

In 1988, the Commission held the first part of its sixth session at Kingston, Jamaica, from 14 March to 8 April and the second part at United Nations Headquarters from 15 August to 2 September.

Members: Afghanistan, Algeria, Angola, Antigua and Barbuda, Argentina, Australia, Austria, Bahamas, Bahrain, Bangladesh, Barbados, Belgium, Belize, Benin, Bhutan, Bolivia, Botswana, Brazil, Brunei Darussalam, Bulgaria, Burkina Faso, Burma, Burundi, Byelorussian SSR, Cameroon, Canada, Cape Verde, Central African Republic, Chad, Chile, China, Colombia, Comoros, Congo, Cook Islands, Costa Rica, Côte d'Ivoire, Cuba, Cyprus, Czechoslovakia, Democratic Kampuchea, Democratic People's Republic of Korea, Democratic Yemen, Denmark, Djibouti, Dominica, Dominican Republic, Egypt, El Salvador, Equatorial Guinea, Ethiopia, European Economic Community, Fiji, Finland, France, Gabon, Gambia, German Democratic Republic, Ghana, Greece, Grenada, Guatemala, Guinea, Guinea-Bissau, Guyana, Haiti, Honduras, Hungary, Iceland, India, Indonesia, Iran, Iraq, Ireland, Italy, Jamaica, Japan, Kenya, Kuwait, Lao People's Democratic Republic, Lebanon, Lesotho, Liberia, Libyan Arab Jamahiriya, Liechtenstein, Luxembourg, Madagascar, Malawi, Malaysia, Maldives, Mali, Malta, Mauritania, Mauritius, Mexico, Monaco, Mongolia, Morocco, Mozambique, Namibia (United Nations Council for), Nauru, Nepal, Netherlands, New Zealand, Nicaragua, Niger, Nigeria, Niue, Norway, Oman, Pakistan, Panama, Papua New Guinea, Paraguay, Philippines, Poland, Portugal, Qatar, Republic of Korea, Romania, Rwanda, Saint Kitts and Nevis, Saint Lucia, Saint Vincent and the Grenadines, Samoa, Sao Tome and Principe, Saudi Arabia, Senegal, Seychelles, Sierra Leone, Singapore, Solomon Islands, Somalia, South Africa, Spain, Sri Lanka, Sudan, Suriname, Swaziland, Sweden, Switzerland, Thailand, Togo, Trinidad and Tobago, Tunisia, Tuvalu, Uganda, Ukrainian SSR, USSR, United Arab Emirates, United Republic of Tanzania, Uruguay, Vanuatu, Viet Nam, Yemen, Yugoslavia, Zaire, Zambia, Zimbabwe.

Chairman: José Luis Jesus (Cape Verde).
Vice-Chairmen: Algeria, Australia, Brazil, Cameroon, Chile, China, France, India, Iraq, Japan, Liberia, Nigeria, Sri Lanka, USSR.
Rapporteur-General: Kenneth O. Rattray (Jamaica).

CREDENTIALS COMMITTEE
Members: Austria, China, Colombia, Costa Rica, Côte d'Ivoire, Hungary, Ireland, Japan, Somalia.
Chairman: Karl Wolf (Austria).

GENERAL COMMITTEE
The General Committee consists of the Commission's Chairman, the 14 Vice-Chairmen, the Rapporteur-General and the 20 officers of the four Special Commissions.

SPECIAL COMMISSIONS
The four Special Commissions are each composed of all the members of the Commission:

Special Commission 1 (on the problem of land-based producers)
Chairman: Hasjim Djalal (Indonesia).
Vice-Chairmen: Austria, Cuba, Romania, Zambia.

Special Commission 2 (on the Enterprise)
Chairman: Lennox Ballah (Trinidad and Tobago).
Vice-Chairmen: Canada, Mongolia, Senegal, Yugoslavia.

Special Commission 3 (on the mining code)
Chairman: Jaap A. Walkate (Netherlands).
Vice-Chairmen: Gabon, Mexico, Pakistan, Poland.

Special Commission 4 (on the International Tribunal for the Law of the Sea)
Chairman: Günter Goerner (German Democratic Republic).
Vice-Chairmen: Colombia, Greece, Philippines, Sudan.

Principal members of the United Nations Secretariat

(as at 31 December 1988)

Secretariat

The Secretary-General: Javier Pérez de Cuéllar

Executive Office of the Secretary-General
Under-Secretary-General, Chef de Cabinet: Virendra Dayal
  Assistant Secretary-General, Executive Assistant to the Secretary-General: Alvaro de Soto
  Assistant Secretary-General, Chief of Protocol: Aly I. Teymour

Office of the Director-General for Development and International Economic Co-operation
Director-General: Jean Louis Ripert

Office of the Under-Secretaries-General for Special Political Affairs
Under-Secretaries-General: Diego Cordovez, Marrack I. Goulding

Office of the Under-Secretary-General for Political and General Assembly Affairs and Secretariat Services
Under-Secretary-General: Joseph Verner Reed

Office for Research and the Collection of Information
Assistant Secretary-General: James O. C. Jonah

Office of Legal Affairs
Under-Secretary-General, the Legal Counsel: Carl-August Fleischhauer

Office for Ocean Affairs and the Law of the Sea
Under-Secretary-General, Special Representative of the Secretary-General: Satya N. Nandan

Department of Political and Security Council Affairs
Under-Secretary-General: Vasiliy S. Safronchuk
  Assistant Secretary-General, Centre against Apartheid: Sotirios Mousouris

Department for Special Political Questions, Regional Co-operation, Decolonization and Trusteeship
Under-Secretary-General: Abdulrahim Abby Farah

OFFICE OF THE UNITED NATIONS COMMISSIONER FOR NAMIBIA
Assistant Secretary-General, Commissioner for Namibia: Bernt Carlsson

Department for Disarmament Affairs
Under-Secretary-General: Yasushi Akashi

Department of International Economic and Social Affairs
Under-Secretary-General: Rafeeuddin Ahmed
Assistant Secretary-General for Development Research and Policy Analysis: P. Göran Ohlin

Department of Technical Co-operation for Development
Under-Secretary-General: Xie Qimei

Centre for Science and Technology for Development
Assistant Secretary-General, Executive Director: Sergio C. Trindade

United Nations Centre on Transnational Corporations
Assistant Secretary-General, Executive Director: Peter Hansen

United Nations Conference on Trade and Development
Under-Secretary-General, Secretary-General of the Conference: Kenneth K. S. Dadzie (appointment extended by GA **decision 43/313** of 29 Nov. 1988 for three years from 1 Jan. 1989)
Assistant Secretary-General, Deputy Secretary-General of the Conference: Yves Berthelot

Office of the United Nations Disaster Relief Co-ordinator
Under-Secretary-General, Disaster Relief Co-ordinator: M'Hamed Essaafi

Office of the United Nations High Commissioner for Refugees
Under-Secretary-General, High Commissioner: Jean-Pierre Hocké
Assistant Secretary-General, Deputy High Commissioner: Arthur Eugene Dewey

United Nations Environment Programme
Under-Secretary-General, Executive Director: Mostafa Kamal Tolba
Assistant Secretary-General, Deputy Executive Director: William H. Mansfield III
Assistant Secretary-General, Assistant Executive Director, Office of the Environment Programme: Genady N. Golubev

United Nations Centre for Human Settlements
Under-Secretary-General, Executive Director: Arcot Ramachandran
Assistant Secretary-General, Deputy Administrator, United Nations Habitat and Human Settlements Foundation: Sumihiro Kuyama

Economic Commission for Europe
Under-Secretary-General, Executive Secretary: Gerald Hinteregger

Economic and Social Commission for Asia and the Pacific
Under-Secretary-General, Executive Secretary: Shah A. M. S. Kibria

Economic Commission for Latin America and the Caribbean
Under-Secretary-General, Executive Secretary: Gert Rosenthal

Economic Commission for Africa
Under-Secretary-General, Executive Secretary: Adebayo Adedeji

Economic and Social Commission for Western Asia
Under-Secretary-General, Executive Secretary: Mohamed Said Nabulsi

United Nations Relief and Works Agency for Palestine Refugees in the Near East
Under-Secretary-General, Commissioner-General: Giorgio Giacomelli
Assistant Secretary-General, Deputy Commissioner-General: William L. Eagleton

World Food Council
Assistant Secretary-General, Executive Director: Gerald Ion Trant

Department of Public Information
Under-Secretary-General: Thérèse P. Sévigny

Department of Conference Services
Under-Secretary-General for Conference Services and Special Assignments: Eugeniusz Wyzner

Department of Administration and Management
Under-Secretary-General: Martti Ahtisaari

OFFICE OF PROGRAMME PLANNING, BUDGET AND FINANCE
Assistant Secretary-General, Controller: Luis Maria Gómez

OFFICE OF HUMAN RESOURCES MANAGEMENT
Assistant Secretary-General: Kofi A. Annan

OFFICE OF GENERAL SERVICES
Assistant Secretary-General: J. Richard Foran

United Nations Office at Geneva
Under-Secretary-General, Director-General of the United Nations Office at Geneva and head of the Centre for Human Rights: Jan Martenson
Assistant Secretary-General, Personal Representative of the Secretary-General, Secretary-General of the Conference on Disarmament: Miljan Komatina

United Nations Office at Vienna
Under-Secretary-General, Director-General of the United Nations Office at Vienna and head of the Centre for Social Development and Humanitarian Affairs: Margaret Joan Anstee

Secretariats of subsidiary organs, special representatives and other related bodies

International Court of Justice Registry
Assistant Secretary-General, Registrar: Eduardo Valencia-Ospina

International Trade Centre UNCTAD/GATT
Assistant Secretary-General, Executive Director: Goran M. Engblom

Office of the Co-ordinator for United Nations Humanitarian and Economic Assistance Programmes relating to Afghanistan
Under-Secretary-General, Co-ordinator: Sadruddin Aga Khan

Office of the Special Representative of the Secretary-General for Co-ordination of Kampuchean Humanitarian Assistance Programmes
Assistant Secretary-General, Special Representative of the Secretary-General: Shah A. M. S. Kibria

Office of the Special Representative of the Secretary-General for Emergency Operations in Ethiopia
Assistant Secretary-General, Special Representative of the Secretary-General: Michael Priestley

Office of the Special Representative of the Secretary-General for Humanitarian Affairs in South-East Asia
Under-Secretary-General, Special Representative of the Secretary-General: Rafeeuddin Ahmed

Office of the Special Representative of the Secretary-General for Namibia
Under-Secretary-General, Special Representative of the Secretary-General: Martti Ahtisaari

Office of the Special Representative of the Secretary-General for the Promotion of the United Nations Decade of Disabled Persons
Assistant Secretary-General, Special Representative of the Secretary-General: Hans Hoegh

**Office of the Special Representative of the
Secretary-General for Western Sahara**
Assistant Secretary-General, Special Representative of the Secretary-General: Héctor Gros Espiel

United Nations Angola Verification Mission
Chief Military Observer: Brigadier-General Péricles Ferreira Gomes

**United Nations Assistance for the Reconstruction
and Development of Lebanon**
Special Representative for the Reconstruction and Development of Lebanon: Ragnar Gudmundsson

United Nations Children's Fund
Under-Secretary-General, Executive Director: James P. Grant
  Assistant Secretary-General, Deputy Executive Director, Operations: Karin Lokhaug
  Assistant Secretary-General, Deputy Executive Director, Programmes: Richard Jolly
  Assistant Secretary-General, Deputy Executive Director for External Relations: Marco Vianello-Chiodo

United Nations Development Programme
Administrator: William H. Draper III
  Associate Administrator: G. Arthur Brown
  Deputy Assistant Administrators and Directors, Bureau for Finance and Administration: M. Douglas Stafford, Eugene Youkel
  Assistant Administrator and Director, Bureau for Programme Policy and Evaluation: Ryokichi Hirono
  Executive Director, United Nations Population Fund: Dr. Nafis I. Sadik
  Deputy Executive Director, United Nations Population Fund: Tatsuro Kunugi
  Assistant Executive Director, United Nations Population Fund: Joseph Van Arendonk
  Assistant Administrator and Regional Director, Regional Bureau for Africa: Pierre-Claver Damiba
  Assistant Administrator and Regional Director, Regional Bureau for Arab States and European Programmes: Mohamed Abdalla Nour
  Assistant Administrator and Regional Director, Regional Bureau for Asia and the Pacific: Andrew J. Joseph
  Assistant Administrator and Regional Director, Regional Bureau for Latin America and the Caribbean: Augusto Ramirez-Ocampo

United Nations Disengagement Observer Force
Assistant Secretary-General, Force Commander: Major-General Adolf Radauer

United Nations Fund for Drug Abuse Control
Assistant Secretary-General, Executive Director: Giuseppe di Gennaro

**United Nations Good Offices Mission
in Afghanistan and Pakistan**
Under-Secretary-General, Representative of the Secretary-General: Diego Cordovez
  Assistant Secretary-General, Deputy to the Representative: Major-General Rauli Kalervo Helminen

United Nations Institute for Training and Research
Under-Secretary-General, Executive Director: Michel Doo Kingué

United Nations Interim Force in Lebanon
Assistant Secretary-General, Force Commander: Major-General Lars-Eric Wahlgren

United Nations Iran-Iraq Military Observer Group
Assistant Secretary-General, Chief Military Observer: Major-General Slavko Jovic

United Nations Military Observer Group in India and Pakistan
Chief Military Observer: Brigadier-General James Parker

United Nations Peace-keeping Force in Cyprus
Under-Secretary-General, Special Representative of the Secretary-General: Oscar Hector Camilión
  Assistant Secretary-General, Force Commander: Major-General Günther G. Greindl

United Nations Truce Supervision Organization
Assistant Secretary-General, Chief of Staff: Lieutenant-General Martin Vadset

United Nations University
Under-Secretary-General, Rector: Heitor Grugulino de Souza
  Assistant Secretary-General, Director, World Institute for Development Economics Research: Lalith R. U. Jayawardena

---

On 31 December 1988, the total number of staff of the United Nations holding permanent, probationary and fixed-term appointments with service or expected service of a year or more was 13,242. Of these, 4,677 were in the Professional and higher categories and 8,565 were in the General Service, Manual Worker and Field Service categories. Of the same total, 11,840 were regular staff serving at Headquarters or other established offices and 1,402 were assigned as project personnel to technical co-operation projects. In addition, UNRWA had some 17,097 local area staff, including temporary assistance. Figures do not include UNDP and UNICEF.

Appendix IV

Agenda of United Nations principal organs in 1988

This appendix lists the items on the agenda of the General Assembly, the Security Council, the Economic and Social Council and the Trusteeship Council during 1988. For the Assembly and the Economic and Social Council, the column headed "Allocation" indicates the assignment of each item to plenary meetings or committees.

Agenda item titles have been shortened by omitting mention of reports following the subject of the item. Thus, "Question of Cyprus: report of the Secretary-General" has been shortened to "Question of Cyprus". Where the subject-matter of the item is not apparent from its title, the subject is identified in square brackets; this is not part of the title.

General Assembly

Agenda items considered at the resumed forty-second session
(29 February–2 March, 18-23 March, 11-13 May,
16 and 17 August and 19 September 1988)

Item No.	Title	Allocation
2.	Minute of silent prayer or meditation.	Plenary
8.	Adoption of the agenda and organization of work.	Plenary
17.	Appointments to fill vacancies in subsidiary organs and other appointments: *(a)* Appointment of members of the Advisory Committee on Administrative and Budgetary Questions.	5th
28.	Armed Israeli aggression against the Iraqi nuclear installations and its grave consequences for the established international system concerning the peaceful uses of nuclear energy, the non-proliferation of nuclear weapons and international peace and security.	Plenary
34.	The situation in Central America: threats to international peace and security and peace initiatives.	Plenary
43.	Current financial crisis of the United Nations.	1
46.	Question of Cyprus.	Plenary
47.	Consequences of the prolongation of the armed conflict between Iran and Iraq.	Plenary
86.	Special programmes of economic assistance.	2
121.	Scale of assessments for the apportionment of the expenses of the United Nations.	1
136.	Report of the Committee on Relations with the Host Country.	3
145.	Financing of the United Nations Iran-Iraq Military Observer Group.[4]	5th

Agenda of the fifteenth special session
(31 May–25 June 1988)

Item No.	Title	Allocation
1.	Opening of the session by the Chairman of the delegation of the German Democratic Republic.	Plenary
2.	Minute of silent prayer or meditation.	Plenary
3.	Credentials of representatives to the fifteenth special session of the General Assembly: *(a)* Appointment of the members of the Credentials Committee; *(b)* Report of the Credentials Committee.	Plenary Plenary
4.	Election of the President of the General Assembly.	Plenary
5.	Organization of the session.	Plenary
6.	Report of the Preparatory Committee for the Third Special Session of the General Assembly Devoted to Disarmament.	Plenary
7.	Adoption of the agenda.	Plenary
8.	General debate.	Plenary

[1]Allocated to the Fifth Committee at the first part of the session in 1987 but considered only in plenary meeting at the resumed session.
[2]Allocated to the Second Committee at the first part of the session in 1987 but considered only in plenary meeting at the resumed session.
[3]Allocated to the Sixth Committee at the first part of the session in 1987 but considered only in plenary meeting at the resumed session.
[4]Item added at the resumed session.

Item No.	Title	Allocation
9.	Review and appraisal of the present international situation, especially in the light of the vital objective of terminating the arms race and the pressing need to achieve substantial progress in the field of disarmament.	Plenary
10.	Assessment of the implementation of the decisions and recommendations adopted by the General Assembly at its tenth and twelfth special sessions:	
	(a) Report of the Conference on Disarmament;	5
	(b) Report of the Disarmament Commission;	5
	(c) Resolutions of the General Assembly in the field of arms limitation and disarmament;	5
	(d) Status of negotiations on arms limitations and disarmament in bilateral and various multilateral forums.	5
11.	Consideration and adoption of the Comprehensive Programme of Disarmament.	5
12.	Assessment of developments and trends, including qualitative and quantitative aspects, relevant to the disarmament process, with a view to the elaboration of appropriate concrete and practical measures and, if necessary, additional principles, taking duly into account the principles and priorities established in the Final Document of the Tenth Special Session of the General Assembly, the first special session devoted to disarmament.	5
13.	Consideration of the role of the United Nations in the field of disarmament and of the effectiveness of the disarmament machinery.	5
14.	United Nations information and educational activities in the field of disarmament, including measures to mobilize world public opinion in favour of disarmament:	
	(a) World Disarmament Campaign;	5
	(b) Other public information activities.	5
15.	Relationship between disarmament and development, in the light of the action programme adopted at the International Conference.	5
16.	Adoption, in an appropriate format, of the document(s) of the fifteenth special session of the General Assembly.	Plenary

Agenda of the forty-third session
(first part, 20 September–22 December 1988)

Item No.	Title	Allocation
1.	Opening of the session by the Chairman of the delegation of the German Democratic Republic.	Plenary
2.	Minute of silent prayer or meditation.	Plenary
3.	Credentials of representatives to the forty-third session of the General Assembly:	
	(a) Appointment of the members of the Credentials Committee;	Plenary
	(b) Report of the Credentials Committee.	Plenary
4.	Election of the President of the General Assembly.	Plenary
5.	Election of the officers of the Main Committees.	Plenary
6.	Election of the Vice-Presidents of the General Assembly.	Plenary
7.	Notification by the Secretary-General under Article 12, paragraph 2, of the Charter of the United Nations.	Plenary
8.	Adoption of the agenda and organization of work.	Plenary
9.	General debate.	Plenary
10.	Report of the Secretary-General on the work of the Organization.	Plenary
11.	Report of the Security Council.	Plenary
12.	Report of the Economic and Social Council.	Plenary, 2nd, 3rd, 4th, 5th
13.	Report of the International Court of Justice.	Plenary
14.	Report of the International Atomic Energy Agency.	Plenary
15.	Elections to fill vacancies in principal organs:	
	(a) Election of five non-permanent members of the Security Council;	Plenary
	(b) Election of eighteen members of the Economic and Social Council;	Plenary
	(c) Election of a member of the International Court of Justice.	Plenary
16.	Elections to fill vacancies in subsidiary organs and other elections:	
	(a) Election of members of the Governing Council of the United Nations Environment Programme;	Plenary
	(b) Election of twelve members of the World Food Council;	Plenary
	(c) Election of seven members of the Committee for Programme and Co-ordination;	Plenary

---

[5]Allocated to the Committee of the Whole of the Fifteenth Special Session.

Item No.	Title	Allocation

(d) Election of seventeen members of the United Nations Commission on International Trade Law; — Plenary

(e) Election of the United Nations High Commissioner for Refugees; — Plenary

(f) Election of the Executive Director of the United Nations Environment Programme. — Plenary

17. Appointments to fill vacancies in subsidiary organs and other appointments:

   (a) Appointment of members of the Advisory Committee on Administrative and Budgetary Questions; — 5th

   (b) Appointment of members of the Committee on Contributions; — 5th

   (c) Appointment of a member of the Board of Auditors; — 5th

   (d) Confirmation of the appointment of members of the Investments Committee; — 5th

   (e) Appointment of members of the United Nations Administrative Tribunal; — 5th

   (f) Appointment of members of the International Civil Service Commission; — 5th

   (g) Appointment of members and alternate members of the United Nations Staff Pension Committee; — 5th

   (h) Appointment of a member of the Joint Inspection Unit; — Plenary

   (i) Appointment of the members of the Consultative Committee on the United Nations Development Fund for Women; — Plenary

   (j) Appointment of the United Nations Commissioner for Namibia; — Plenary

   (k) Confirmation of the appointment of the Secretary-General of the United Nations Conference on Trade and Development. — Plenary

18. Implementation of the Declaration on the Granting of Independence to Colonial Countries and Peoples. — Plenary, 4th

19. Admission of new Members to the United Nations. — Plenary

20. Co-operation between the United Nations and the Asian-African Legal Consultative Committee. — Plenary

21. Right of peoples to peace. — Plenary

22. The situation in Central America: threats to international peace and security and peace initiatives. — Plenary

23. The situation in Kampuchea. — Plenary

24. Co-operation between the United Nations and the Organization of the Islamic Conference. — Plenary

25. Co-operation between the United Nations and the League of Arab States. — Plenary

26. Co-operation between the United Nations and the Organization of African Unity. — Plenary

27. Co-operation between the United Nations and the Organization of American States. — Plenary

28. Co-operation between the United Nations and the Latin American Economic System. — Plenary

29. Question of Namibia. — Plenary, 4th[6]

30. The situation in Afghanistan and its implications for international peace and security. — Plenary

31. Zone of peace and co-operation of the South Atlantic. — Plenary

32. Question of the Comorian island of Mayotte. — Plenary

33. Judgment of the International Court of Justice of 27 June 1986 concerning military and paramilitary activities in and around Nicaragua: need for immediate compliance. — Plenary

34. Question of the Falkland Islands (Malvinas). — Plenary, 4th[7]

35. Law of the sea. — Plenary

36. Policies of *apartheid* of the Government of South Africa. — Plenary, SPC[7]

37. Question of Palestine. — Plenary

38. Fortieth anniversary of the Universal Declaration of Human Rights. — Plenary

39. Critical economic situation in Africa: United Nations Programme of Action for African Economic Recovery and Development 1986-1990. — Plenary

40. The situation in the Middle East. — Plenary

41. Implementation of the resolutions of the United Nations. — Plenary

42. Question of peace, stability and co-operation in South-East Asia. — Plenary

43. Declaration of the Assembly of Heads of State and Government of the Organization of African Unity on the aerial and naval military attack against the Socialist People's Libyan Arab Jamahiriya by the present United States Administration in April 1986. — Plenary

44. Launching of global negotiations on international economic co-operation for development. — Plenary

45. Question of equitable representation on and increase in the membership of the Security Council. — Plenary

46. Armed Israeli aggression against the Iraqi nuclear installations and its grave consequences for the established international system concerning the peaceful uses of nuclear energy, the non-proliferation of nuclear weapons and international peace and security. — Plenary

---

[6]Hearings of organizations.

[7]Hearings of organizations and individuals having an interest in the question.

Item No.	*Title*	*Allocation*
47.	Question of Cyprus.	8
48.	Consequences of the prolongation of the armed conflict between Iran and Iraq.	Plenary
49.	Review of the efficiency of the administrative and financial functioning of the United Nations.	Plenary, 5th
50.	Current financial crisis of the United Nations.	5th
51.	Implementation of General Assembly resolution 42/25 concerning the signature and ratification of Additional Protocol I of the Treaty for the Prohibition of Nuclear Weapons in Latin America (Treaty of Tlatelolco).	1st
52.	Cessation of all nuclear-test explosions.	1st
53.	Urgent need for a comprehensive nuclear-test-ban treaty.	1st
54.	Establishment of a nuclear-weapon-free zone in the region of the Middle East.	1st
55.	Establishment of a nuclear-weapon-free zone in South Asia.	1st
56.	Convention on Prohibitions or Restrictions on the Use of Certain Conventional Weapons Which May Be Deemed to Be Excessively Injurious or to Have Indiscriminate Effects.	1st
57.	Conclusion of effective international arrangements on the strengthening of the security of non-nuclear-weapon States against the use or threat of use of nuclear weapons.	1st
58.	Conclusion of effective international arrangements to assure non-nuclear-weapon States against the use or threat of use of nuclear weapons.	1st
59.	Prevention of an arms race in outer space.	1st
60.	Implementation of the Declaration on the Denuclearization of Africa.	1st
61.	Prohibition of the development and manufacture of new types of weapons of mass destruction and new systems of such weapons.	1st
62.	Reduction of military budgets.	1st
63.	Chemical and bacteriological (biological) weapons.	1st
64.	General and complete disarmament:	
	(a) Contribution of the specialized agencies and other organizations and programmes of the United Nations system to the cause of arms limitation and disarmament;	1st
	(b) Prohibition of the development, production, stockpiling and use of radiological weapons;	1st
	(c) Notification of nuclear tests;	1st
	(d) Conventional disarmament;	1st
	(e) Nuclear disarmament;	1st
	(f) Objective information on military matters;	1st
	(g) Implementation of General Assembly resolutions in the field of disarmament;	1st
	(h) Naval armaments and disarmament;	1st
	(i) Prohibition of the production of fissionable material for weapons purposes;	1st
	(j) Review of the role of the United Nations in the field of disarmament;	1st
	(k) Dumping of nuclear and industrial wastes in Africa.	1st
65.	Review and implementation of the Concluding Document of the Twelfth Special Session of the General Assembly:	
	(a) Review and implementation of the Concluding Document of the Twelfth Special Session of the General Assembly;	1st
	(b) Freeze on nuclear weapons;	1st
	(c) Convention on the Prohibition of the Use of Nuclear Weapons;	1st
	(d) United Nations Regional Centre for Peace and Disarmament in Asia;	1st
	(e) World Disarmament Campaign;	1st
	(f) Implementation of General Assembly resolution 42/39 H on a nuclear-arms freeze;	1st
	(g) United Nations disarmament fellowship, training and advisory services programme;	1st
	(h) United Nations Regional Centre for Peace and Disarmament in Africa;	1st
	(i) United Nations Regional Centre for Peace, Disarmament and Development in Latin America.	1st
66.	Review of the implementation of the recommendations and decisions adopted by the General Assembly at its fifteenth special session.	1st
67.	Review of the implementation of the recommendations and decisions adopted by the General Assembly at its tenth special session:	
	(a) Report of the Disarmament Commission;	1st
	(b) Report of the Conference on Disarmament;	1st
	(c) Status of multilateral disarmament agreements;	1st
	(d) Advisory Board on Disarmament Studies;	1st
	(e) United Nations Institute for Disarmament Research;	1st
	(f) Review and appraisal of the implementation of the Declaration of the 1980s as the Second Disarmament Decade;	1st
	(g) Climatic effects of nuclear war, including nuclear winter;	1st

---

[8]On 23 September 1988, the General Assembly adopted the General Committee's recommendation that the allocation of item 47 be deferred until an appropriate time in the future.

Item No.	Title	Allocation

(h) Economic and social consequences of the armaments race and its extremely harmful effects on world peace and security; — 1st

(i) Review of the implementation of the recommendations and decisions of the tenth special session; — 1st

(j) Non-use of nuclear weapons and prevention of nuclear war; — 1st

(k) Cessation of the nuclear-arms race and nuclear disarmament; — 1st

(l) Prevention of nuclear war; — 1st

(m) Disarmament Week; — 1st

(n) Implementation of the recommendations and decisions of the tenth special session. — 1st

68. Implementation of the Declaration of the Indian Ocean as a Zone of Peace. — 1st

69. Israeli nuclear armament. — 1st

70. Question of Antarctica. — 1st

71. Strengthening of security and co-operation in the Mediterranean region. — 1st

72. Review of the implementation of the Declaration on the Strengthening of International Security:

    (a) Need for result-oriented political dialogue to improve the international situation; — 1st

    (b) Review of the implementation of the Declaration on the Strengthening of International Security. — 1st

73. Comprehensive system of international peace and security. — 1st

74. Effects of atomic radiation. — SPC

75. International co-operation in the peaceful uses of outer space. — SPC

76. United Nations Relief and Works Agency for Palestine Refugees in the Near East. — SPC

77. Report of the Special Committee to Investigate Israeli Practices Affecting the Human Rights of the Population of the Occupied Territories. — SPC

78. Comprehensive review of the whole question of peace-keeping operations in all their aspects. — SPC

79. Questions relating to information. — SPC

80. Question of the Malagasy islands of Glorieuses, Juan de Nova, Europa and Bassas da India. — SPC

81. Question of the composition of the relevant organs of the United Nations. — SPC

82. Development and international economic co-operation:

    (a) International development strategy for the fourth United Nations development decade; — 2nd

    (b) Trade and development; — 2nd

    (c) Food problems; — 2nd

    (d) New and renewable sources of energy; — 2nd

    (e) Development of the energy resources of developing countries; — 2nd

    (f) Long-term trends in social and economic development; — 2nd

    (g) Long-term strategy for sustainable and environmentally sound development. — 2nd

83. External debt crisis and development. — 2nd

84. Operational activities for development:

    (a) Operational activities of the United Nations system; — 2nd

    (b) United Nations Development Programme; — 2nd

    (c) United Nations Population Fund; — 2nd

    (d) United Nations Children's Fund; — 2nd

    (e) World Food Programme. — 2nd

85. Training and research:

    (a) United Nations Institute for Training and Research; — 2nd

    (b) United Nations University. — 2nd

86. Special economic and disaster relief assistance:

    (a) Office of the United Nations Disaster Relief Co-ordinator; — 2nd

    (b) Special programmes of economic assistance. — 2nd

87. Implementation of the Programme of Action for the Second Decade to Combat Racism and Racial Discrimination. — 3rd

88. Adverse consequences for the enjoyment of human rights of political, military, economic and other forms of assistance given to the racist and colonialist régime of South Africa. — 3rd

89. Question of aging. — 3rd

90. Policies and programmes involving youth. — 3rd

91. Elimination of all forms of racial discrimination. — 3rd

92. Implementation of the World Programme of Action concerning Disabled Persons and the United Nations Decade of Disabled Persons. — 3rd

93. Crime prevention and criminal justice. — 3rd

94. Elimination of all forms of discrimination against women. — 3rd

95. Forward-looking strategies for the advancement of women to the year 2000:

    (a) Implementation of the Declaration on the Participation of Women in Promoting International Peace and Co-operation; — 3rd

    (b) Implementation of the Nairobi Forward-looking Strategies for the Advancement of Women; — 3rd

    (c) United Nations Development Fund for Women. — 3rd

Item No.	Title	Allocation

96. Importance of the universal realization of the right of peoples to self-determination and of the speedy granting of independence to colonial countries and peoples for the effective guarantee and observance of human rights. — 3rd

97. Elimination of all forms of religious intolerance. — 3rd

98. Human rights and scientific and technological developments. — 3rd

99. Question of a convention on the rights of the child. — 3rd

100. International Covenants on Human Rights. — 3rd

101. Reporting obligations of States parties to United Nations instruments on human rights. — 3rd

102. Office of the United Nations High Commissioner for Refugees:
   (a) International Conference on the Plight of Refugees, Returnees and Displaced Persons in Southern Africa; — 3rd
   (b) Second International Conference on Assistance to Refugees in Africa; — 3rd
   (c) Assistance to refugees, returnees and displaced persons of Central America. — 3rd

103. International campaign against traffic in drugs:
   (a) Draft convention against illicit traffic in narcotic drugs and psychotropic substances; — 3rd
   (b) International Conference on Drug Abuse and Illicit Trafficking; — 3rd
   (c) International campaign against drug abuse and illicit trafficking. — 3rd

104. Alternative approaches and ways and means within the United Nations system for improving the effective enjoyment of human rights and fundamental freedoms:
   (a) Respect for the right of everyone to own property alone as well as in association with others and its contribution to the economic and social development of Member States; — 3rd
   (b) Impact of property on the enjoyment of human rights and fundamental freedoms; — 3rd
   (c) Right to development; — 3rd
   (d) Development of public information activities in the field of human rights. — 3rd

105. New international humanitarian order. — 3rd

106. Torture and other cruel, inhuman or degrading treatment or punishment. — 3rd

107. Families in the development process. — 3rd

108. Information from Non-Self-Governing Territories transmitted under Article 73 *e* of the Charter of the United Nations. — 4th

109. Activities of foreign economic and other interests which are impeding the implementation of the Declaration on the Granting of Independence to Colonial Countries and Peoples in Namibia and in all other Territories under colonial domination and efforts to eliminate colonialism, *apartheid* and racial discrimination in southern Africa. — 4th

110. Implementation of the Declaration on the Granting of Independence to Colonial Countries and Peoples by the specialized agencies and the international institutions associated with the United Nations. — 4th

111. United Nations Educational and Training Programme for Southern Africa. — 4th

112. Offers by Member States of study and training facilities for inhabitants of Non-Self-Governing Territories. — 4th

113. Financial reports and audited financial statements, and reports of the Board of Auditors:
   (a) United Nations; — 5th
   (b) United Nations Development Programme; — 5th
   (c) United Nations Children's Fund; — 5th
   (d) United Nations Relief and Works Agency for Palestine Refugees in the Near East; — 5th
   (e) United Nations Institute for Training and Research; — 5th
   (f) Voluntary funds administered by the United Nations High Commissioner for Refugees; — 5th
   (g) Fund of the United Nations Environment Programme; — 5th
   (h) United Nations Population Fund; — 5th
   (i) United Nations Habitat and Human Settlements Foundation. — 5th

114. Programme budget for the biennium 1988-1989. — 5th

115. Programme planning. — 5th

116. Financial emergency of the United Nations. — 5th

117. Administrative and budgetary co-ordination of the United Nations with the specialized agencies and the International Atomic Energy Agency:
   (a) Report of the Advisory Committee on Administrative and Budgetary Questions on administrative and budgetary co-ordination; — 5th
   (b) Harmonization of the statutes, rules and practices of the administrative tribunals of the International Labour Organisation and of the United Nations. — 5th

118. Joint Inspection Unit. — 5th

119. Pattern of conferences. — 5th

120. Scale of assessments for the apportionment of the expenses of the United Nations. — 5th

121. Personnel questions:
   (a) Composition of the Secretariat; — 5th
   (b) Respect for the privileges and immunities of officials of the United Nations and the specialized agencies and related organizations; — 5th
   (c) Other personnel questions. — 5th

Item No.	*Title*	*Allocation*
122.	United Nations common system.	5th
123.	United Nations pension system.	5th
124.	Financing of the United Nations peace-keeping forces in the Middle East:	
	(a) United Nations Disengagement Observer Force;	5th
	(b) United Nations Interim Force in Lebanon.	5th
125.	Consideration of the draft articles on most-favoured-nation clauses.	6th
126.	Observer status of national liberation movements recognized by the Organization of African Unity and/or by the League of Arab States.	6th
127.	Status of the Protocols Additional to the Geneva Conventions of 1949 and relating to the protection of victims of armed conflicts.	6th
128.	Progressive development of the principles and norms of international law relating to the new international economic order.	6th
129.	Peaceful settlement of disputes between States.	6th
130.	Draft Code of Crimes against the Peace and Security of Mankind.	6th
131.	Report of the United Nations Commission on International Trade Law on the work of its twenty-first session.	6th
132.	Consideration of effective measures to enhance the protection, security and safety of diplomatic and consular missions and representatives.	6th
133.	Report of the *Ad Hoc* Committee on the Drafting of an International Convention against the Recruitment, Use, Financing and Training of Mercenaries.	6th
134.	Report of the International Law Commission on the work of its fortieth session.	6th
135.	Report of the Special Committee on the Charter of the United Nations and on the Strengthening of the Role of the Organization.	6th
136.	Development and strengthening of good-neighbourliness between States.	6th
137.	Report of the Committee on Relations with the Host Country.	6th
138.	Draft Body of Principles for the Protection of All Persons under Any Form of Detention or Imprisonment.	6th
139.	Verification in all its aspects.	1st
140.	Science and peace.	SPC
141.	Implementation of the conclusions of the Third Review Conference of the Parties to the Treaty on the Non-Proliferation of Nuclear Weapons and establishment of a preparatory committee for the Fourth Review Conference.	1st
142.	Observer status for the Agency for the Prohibition of Nuclear Weapons in Latin America and the Caribbean in the General Assembly.	Plenary
143.	Responsibility of States for the protection of the environment and prevention of environmental pollution as a result of the accumulation of toxic and radioactive wastes, and strengthening of international co-operation for the purpose of resolving the problem.	2nd
144.	Responsibility of States to ban in their territory, and to refrain from instigating or supporting in the territory of other States, chauvinistic, racist and other manifestations that may cause discord between peoples and involvement of Governments and the mass media in combating such manifestations and in educating peoples and youth in the spirit of peaceful co-operation and international entente; and evaluation of the implementation of the Declaration on the Promotion among Youth of the Ideals of Peace, Mutual Respect and Understanding between Peoples.	3rd
145.	Liability for the illegal transfer and/or use of prohibited weapons and weapons or substances which cause unnecessary human suffering.	1st
146.	Promotion of peace, reconciliation and dialogue in the Korean peninsula.	Plenary
147.	Financing of the United Nations Iran-Iraq Military Observer Group.	5th
148.	Conservation of climate as part of the common heritage of mankind.	Plenary, 2nd
149.	Emergency assistance to Jamaica.	Plenary
150.	Emergency assistance to the Sudan.	Plenary
151.	Short-term, medium-term and long-term solutions to the problems of natural disasters in Bangladesh.	Plenary
152.	Emergency assistance to Nicaragua, Costa Rica, Panama and other countries affected by hurricane Joan.	Plenary

Security Council
Agenda items considered during 1988

Item No.[9]	*Title*
1.	The situation in the occupied Arab territories.
2.	The situation in the Middle East.

---

[9]Numbers indicate the order in which items were taken up in 1988.

*Item
No.*   *Title*

3. Letter dated 10 February 1988 from the Permanent Observer of the Republic of Korea to the United Nations addressed to the President of the Security Council; letter dated 10 February 1988 from the Permanent Representative of Japan to the United Nations addressed to the President of the Security Council (1987 Korean Air Lines incident).

4. The question of South Africa.

5. The situation between Iran and Iraq.

6. Letter dated 11 March 1988 from the Permanent Representative of Argentina to the United Nations addressed to the President of the Security Council (situation in the South Atlantic).

7. Letter dated 17 March 1988 from the Chargé d'affaires a.i. of the Permanent Mission of Nicaragua to the United Nations addressed to the President of the Security Council (complaint against the United States).

8. Letter dated 19 April 1988 from the Permanent Representative of Tunisia to the United Nations addressed to the President of the Security Council (complaint against Israel).

9. The situation in Cyprus.

10. Letter dated 5 July 1988 from the Acting Permanent Representative of the Islamic Republic of Iran to the United Nations addressed to the President of the Security Council (complaint against the United States).

11. The situation concerning Western Sahara.

12. The situation in Namibia.

13. The situation relating to Afghanistan.

14. Letter dated 17 December 1988 from the Permanent Representative of Angola to the United Nations addressed to the Secretary-General; letter dated 17 December 1988 from the Permanent Representative of Cuba to the United Nations addressed to the Secretary-General (establishment of a United Nations Angola Verification Mission).

Economic and Social Council
Agenda of the organizational session for 1988
(2-5 February and 3 March 1988)

*Item
No.*   *Title*   *Allocation*

1. Election of the Bureau.   Plenary

2. Adoption of the agenda and other organizational matters.   Plenary

3. Basic programme of work of the Council for 1988 and 1989.   Plenary

4. Elections to subsidiary bodies of the Council and confirmation of representatives on the functional commissions.   Plenary

5. Provisional agenda for the first regular session of 1988 and related organizational matters.   Plenary

Agenda of the first regular session of 1988
(3-27 May 1988)

*Item
No.*   *Title*   *Allocation*

1. Adoption of the agenda and other organizational matters.   Plenary

2. Implementation of the Programme of Action for the Second Decade to Combat Racism and Racial Discrimination.   Plenary

3. International Covenants on Human Rights: *(a)* International Covenant on Civil and Political Rights; *(b)* International Covenant on Economic, Social and Cultural Rights.   Plenary

4. Convention on the Elimination of All Forms of Discrimination against Women.   Plenary

5. Consideration of the necessary arrangements for the meeting of the *Ad Hoc* Committee of the Whole of the General Assembly on the Review and Appraisal of the United Nations Programme of Action for African Economic Recovery and Development 1986-1990.   Plenary

6. United Nations University.   1st

7. International co-operation in tax matters.   1st

8. Public administration and finance.   1st

9. Cartography.   1st

10. Human rights.   2nd

Item No.	Title	Allocation
11.	Advancement of women.	2nd
12.	Social development.	2nd
13.	Narcotic drugs.	2nd
14.	Elections and nominations.	Plenary
15.	Consideration of the provisional agenda for the second regular session of 1988.	Plenary

Agenda of the second regular session of 1988
(6-29 July; resumed 17 October 1988)

Item No.	Title	Allocation
1.	Adoption of the agenda and other organizational matters.	Plenary[10]
2.	General discussion of international economic and social policy, including regional and sectoral developments.	Plenary
3.	In-depth study of the United Nations intergovernmental structure and functions in the economic and social fields: *(a)* report of the Special Commission of the Economic and Social Council on the In-depth Study of the United Nations Intergovernmental Structure and Functions in the Economic and Social Fields; *(b)* the Economic and Social Council.	Plenary
4.	Consideration of the necessary arrangements for the meeting of the *Ad Hoc* Committee of the Whole of the General Assembly on the Review and Appraisal of the United Nations Programme of Action for African Economic Recovery and Development 1986-1990.	Plenary
5.	International development strategy for the fourth United Nations development decade.	Plenary
6.	Permanent sovereignty over national resources in the occupied Palestinian and other Arab territories.	Plenary
7.	Regional co-operation.	1st
8.	Transnational corporations.	1st
9.	Food and agriculture.	1st
10.	Trade and development.	1st
11.	International co-operation on the environment.	1st
12.	International co-operation in the field of human settlements.	1st
13.	Development and utilization of new and renewable sources of energy.	1st
14.	Report of the United Nations High Commissioner for Refugees.	Plenary
15.	Special economic, humanitarian and disaster relief assistance.	3rd
16.	Operational activities for development.	3rd
17.	International co-operation and co-ordination within the United Nations system.	3rd
18.	Programme questions.	3rd[11]
19.	Implementation of the Declaration on the Granting of Independence to Colonial Countries and Peoples by the specialized agencies and the international institutions associated with the United Nations.	3rd
20.	Elections.	Plenary

Trusteeship Council
Agenda of the fifty-fifth session
(10 May–19 July 1988)

Item No.	Title
1.	Adoption of the agenda.
2.	Report of the Secretary-General on credentials.
3.	Election of the President and the Vice-President.
4.	Examination of the annual report of the Administering Authority for the year ended 30 September 1987: Trust Territory of the Pacific Islands.
5.	Examination of petitions listed in the annex to the agenda.
6.	Offers by Member States of study and training facilities for inhabitants of Trust Territories.

---

[10]Considered also at the resumed session.
[11]Considered only in plenary meeting at the resumed session.

Appendix V

United Nations Information Centres and Services

(As at July 1991)

ACCRA. United Nations Information Centre
Gamel Abdul Nassar/Liberia Roads
(Roman Ridge Ambassadorial Estate, Extension Area, Plot N78)
Accra, Ghana
Serving: Ghana, Sierra Leone

ADDIS ABABA. United Nations Information Service, Economic Commission for Africa
Africa Hall
(P.O. Box 3001)
Addis Ababa, Ethiopia
Serving: Ethiopia

ALGIERS. United Nations Information Centre
19 Avenue Chahid El Ouali Mustapha Sayed
(Boîte Postale 823, Alger-Gare, Algeria)
Algiers, Algeria
Serving: Algeria

ANKARA. United Nations Information Centre
197 Ataturk Bulvari
(P.K. 407)
Ankara, Turkey
Serving: Turkey

ANTANANARIVO. United Nations Information Centre
22 Rue Rainitovo, Antasahavola
(Boîte Postale 1348)
Antananarivo, Madagascar
Serving: Madagascar

ASUNCION. United Nations Information Centre
Casilla de Correo 1107
Asunción, Paraguay
Serving: Paraguay

ATHENS. United Nations Information Centre
36 Amalia Avenue
GR-10558 Athens, Greece
Serving: Cyprus, Greece, Israel

BAGHDAD. United Nations Information Service, Economic and Social Commission for Western Asia
Amiriya, Airport Street
(P.O. Box 27)
Baghdad, Iraq
Serving: Iraq

BANGKOK. United Nations Information Service, Economic and Social Commission for Asia and the Pacific
United Nations Building
Rajdamnern Avenue
Bangkok 10200, Thailand

Serving: Cambodia, Hong Kong, Lao People's Democratic Republic, Malaysia, Singapore, Thailand, Viet Nam

BEIRUT. United Nations Information Centre
Apt. No. 1, Fakhoury Building
Montée Bain Militaire, Ardati Street
(P.O. Box 4656)
Beirut, Lebanon
Serving: Jordan, Kuwait, Lebanon, Syrian Arab Republic

BELGRADE. United Nations Information Centre
Svetozara Markovica 58
(P.O. Box 157)
Belgrade, Yugloslavia YU-11001
Serving: Albania, Yugoslavia

BOGOTA. United Nations Information Centre
Calle 100 No. 8A-55, Of. 815
(Apartado Aéreo 058964)
Bogotá 2, Colombia
Serving: Colombia, Ecuador, Venezuela

BRAZZAVILLE. United Nations Information Centre
Avenue Foch, Case Ortf 15
(P.O. Box 13210)
Brazzaville, Congo
Serving: Congo

BRUSSELS. United Nations Information Centre and Liaison Office
Avenue de Broqueville 40
1200 Brussels, Belgium
Serving: Belgium, Luxembourg, Netherlands; liaison with EEC

BUCHAREST. United Nations Information Centre
16 Aurel Vlaic
(P.O. Box 1-701)
Bucharest, Romania
Serving: Romania

BUENOS AIRES. United Nations Information Centre
Junín 1940 (1er piso)
1113 Buenos Aires, Argentina
Serving: Argentina, Uruguay

BUJUMBURA. United Nations Information Centre
117 Avenue de la Poste
(Boîte Postale 2160)
Bujumbura, Burundi
Serving: Burundi

CAIRO. United Nations Information Centre
1 Osiris Street
Tagher Building (Garden City)
(Boîte Postale 262)
Cairo, Egypt
Serving: Egypt, Saudi Arabia, Yemen

COLOMBO. United Nations Information Centre
202-204 Bauddhaloka Mawatha
(P.O. Box 1505, Colombo)
Colombo 7, Sri Lanka
Serving: Sri Lanka

COPENHAGEN. United Nations Information Centre
37 H. C. Andersens Boulevard
DK-1553 Copenhagen V, Denmark
Serving: Denmark, Finland, Iceland, Norway, Sweden

DAKAR. United Nations Information Centre
72 Boulevard de la République
(Boîte Postale 154)
Dakar, Senegal
Serving: Cape Verde, Côte d'Ivoire, Gambia, Guinea, Guinea-Bissau, Mauritania, Senegal

DAR ES SALAAM. United Nations Information Centre
Samora Machel Avenue
Matasalamat Building (1st floor)
(P.O. Box 9224)
Dar es Salaam, United Republic of Tanzania
Serving: United Republic of Tanzania

DHAKA. United Nations Information Centre
House 25, Road 11
Dhanmandi
(G.P.O. Box 3658, Dhaka 1000)
Dhaka 1209, Bangladesh
Serving: Bangladesh

GENEVA. United Nations Information Service, United Nations Office at Geneva
Palais des Nations
1211 Geneva 10, Switzerland
Serving: Bulgaria, Poland, Switzerland

HARARE. United Nations Information Centre
Dolphin House (ground floor)
123 Moffat Street/Union Avenue
(P.O. Box 4408)
Harare, Zimbabwe
Serving: Zimbabwe

ISLAMABAD. United Nations Information
Centre
House No. 26
88th Street, Ramna 6/3
(P.O. Box 1107)
Islamabad, Pakistan
Serving: Pakistan

JAKARTA. United Nations Information
Centre
Gedung Dewan Pers (5th floor)
32-34 Jalan Kebon Sirih
Jakarta, Indonesia
Serving: Indonesia

KABUL. United Nations Information Centre
Shah Mahmoud Ghazi Watt
(P.O. Box 5)
Kabul, Afghanistan
Serving: Afghanistan

KATHMANDU. United Nations Information
Centre
Pulchowk, Patan
(P.O. Box 107, Pulchowk)
Kathmandu, Nepal
Serving: Nepal

KHARTOUM. United Nations Information
Centre
United Nations Compound
University Avenue
(P.O. Box 1992)
Khartoum, Sudan
Serving: Somalia, Sudan

KINSHASA. United Nations Information
Centre
Bâtiment Deuxième République
Boulevard du 30 Juin
(Boîte Postale 7248)
Kinshasa, Zaire
Serving: Zaire

LAGOS. United Nations Information Centre
17 Kingsway Road, Ikoyi
(P.O. Box 1068)
Lagos, Nigeria
Serving: Nigeria

LA PAZ. United Nations Information Centre
Edificio Naciones Unidas
Plaza Isabel La Católica
Planta Baja
(Apartado Postal 9072)
La Paz, Bolivia
Serving: Bolivia

LIMA. United Nations Information Centre
Mariscal Blas Cerdeña 450
San Isidro
(P.O. Box 14-0199, Lima)
Lima 27, Peru
Serving: Peru

LISBON. United Nations Information Centre
Rua Latino Coelho, 1
Ed. Aviz, Bloco. A-1, 10º
1000 Lisbon, Portugal
Serving: Portugal

LOME. United Nations Information Centre
107 Boulevard du 13 Janvier
(Boîte Postale 911)
Lomé, Togo
Serving: Benin, Togo

LONDON. United Nations Information Centre
20 Buckingham Gate
London SW1E 6LB, England
Serving: Ireland, United Kingdom

LUSAKA. United Nations Information Centre
P.O. Box 32905
Lusaka 10101, Zambia
Serving: Botswana, Malawi, Swaziland,
Zambia

MADRID. United Nations Information Centre
Avenida General Perón, 32-1
(P.O. Box 3400, 28080 Madrid)
28020 Madrid, Spain
Serving: Spain

MANAGUA. United Nations Information
Centre
De Plaza España
2 Cuadras Abajo, Bolonia
(P.O. Box 3260)
Managua, Nicaragua
Serving: Nicaragua

MANAMA. United Nations Information
Centre
House No. 131, Road 2803
Segaya 328
(P.O. Box 26004)
Manama, Bahrain
Serving: Bahrain, Qatar, United Arab
Emirates

MANILA. United Nations Information Centre
NEDA Building
106 Amorsolo Street
Legaspi Village, Makati
(P.O. Box 7285 (DAPO), 1300 Domestic
Road, Pasay City)
Metro Manila, Philippines
Serving: Papua New Guinea, Philippines,
Solomon Islands

MASERU. United Nations Information Centre
Corner Kingsway and Hilton Hill Road
opposite Sanlam Centre
(P.O. Box 301)
Maseru 100, Lesotho
Serving: Lesotho

MEXICO CITY. United Nations Information
Centre
Presidente Masaryk 29 (7º piso)
11570 México, D.F., Mexico
Serving: Cuba, Dominican Republic,
Mexico

MONROVIA. United Nations Information
Centre
LBDI Building
Tubman Boulevard
(P.O. Box 274)
Monrovia, Liberia
Serving: Liberia

MOSCOW. United Nations Information
Centre
4/16 Ulitsa Lunacharskogo
Moscow 121002, USSR
Serving: Byelorussian SSR, Ukrainian
SSR, USSR

NAIROBI. United Nations Information Centre
United Nations Office
Gigiri
(P.O. Box 34135)
Nairobi, Kenya
Serving: Kenya, Seychelles, Uganda

NEW DELHI. United Nations Information
Centre
55 Lodi Estate
New Delhi 110003, India
Serving: Bhutan, India

OUAGADOUGOU. United Nations Informa-
tion Centre
218 Rue de la Gare
Secteur No. 3
(Boîte Postale 135)
Ouagadougou 01, Burkina Faso
Serving: Burkina Faso, Chad, Mali, Niger

PANAMA CITY. United Nations Information
Centre
Urbanización Obarrio
Calle 54 y Avenida Tercera Sur, Casa No. 17
(P.O. Box 6-9083 El Dorado)
Panama City, Panama
Serving: Panama

PARIS. United Nations Information Centre
1 rue Miollis
75732, Paris Cedex 15, France
Serving: France

PORT OF SPAIN. United Nations Informa-
tion Centre
2nd floor, Bretton Hall
16 Victoria Avenue
(P.O. Box 130)
Port of Spain, Trinidad
Serving: Antigua and Barbuda, Ba-
hamas, Barbados, Belize, Dominica,
Grenada, Guyana, Jamaica, Netherlands
Antilles, Saint Kitts and Nevis, Saint Lucia,
Saint Vincent and the Grenadines, Suri-
name, Trinidad and Tobago

PRAGUE. United Nations Information Centre
Panska 5
11000 Prague 1, Czechoslovakia
Serving: Czechoslovakia

RABAT. United Nations Information Centre
Angle Charia Ibnouzaid et Zankat Round-
anat, No. 6
(Boîte Postale 601)
Rabat, Morocco
Serving: Morocco

RIO DE JANEIRO. United Nations Informa-
tion Centre
Palácio Itamaraty
Ave. Marechal Floriano 196
20080 Rio de Janeiro, RJ Brazil
Serving: Brazil

ROME. United Nations Information Centre
Palazzetto Venezia
Piazza San Marco 50
Rome, Italy
Serving: Holy See, Italy, Malta

SAN SALVADOR. United Nations Information Centre
Edificio Escalón (2º piso)
Paseo General Escalón y 87 Avenida Norte
Colonia Escalón
(Apartado Postal 2157)
San Salvador, El Salvador
Serving: El Salvador

SANTIAGO. United Nations Information Service, Economic Commission for Latin America and the Caribbean
Edificio Naciones Unidas
Avenida Dag Hammarskjöld
(Avenida Dag Hammarskjöld s/n, Casilla 179-D)
Santiago, Chile
Serving: Chile

SYDNEY. United Nations Information Centre
Suite 1, 125 York Street
(P.O. Box 4045, Sydney N.S.W. 2001)
Sydney N.S.W. 2000, Australia

Serving: Australia, Fiji, Kiribati, Nauru, New Zealand, Samoa, Tonga, Tuvalu, Vanuatu

TEHRAN. United Nations Information Centre
Avenue Boharest Maydan, Argantine No. 74
(P.O. Box 15875-4557, Tehran)
Tehran, 620 891, Iran
Serving: Iran

TOKYO. United Nations Information Centre
Shin Aoyama Building Nishikan (22nd floor)
1-1 Minami Aoyama 1-chome, Minato-ku
Tokyo 107, Japan
Serving: Japan, Trust Territory of the Pacific Islands

TRIPOLI. United Nations Information Centre
Muzzafar Al Aftas Street
Hay El-Andalous (2)
(P.O. Box 286)
Tripoli, Libyan Arab Jamahiriya
Serving: Libyan Arab Jamahiriya

TUNIS. United Nations Information Centre
61 Boulevard Bab-Benat
(Boîte Postale 863)
Tunis, Tunisia
Serving: Tunisia

VIENNA. United Nations Information Service, United Nations Office at Vienna
Vienna International Centre
Wagramer Strasse 5
(P.O. Box 500, A-1400 Vienna)
A-1220 Vienna, Austria
Serving: Austria, Germany, Hungary

WASHINGTON, D.C. United Nations Information Centre
1889 F Street, N.W.
Washington, D.C. 20006, United States
Serving: United States

YANGON. United Nations Information Centre
6 Natmauk Road
(P.O. Box 230)
Yangon, Myanmar
Serving: Myanmar

YAOUNDE. United Nations Information Centre
Immeuble Kamden
Rue Joseph Clère
(Boîte Postale 836)
Yaoundé, Cameroon
Serving: Cameroon, Central African Republic, Gabon

Indexes

Using the subject index

The index contains four types of entries:

Subject terms, including geographical names, are in bold face and, in most cases, are based on the subject descriptors used in the United Nations Bibliographical Information System (UNBIS), published in the *UNBIS Thesaurus* (United Nations Publication: Sales No. E.85.I.20). In order to minimize subentries, the index lists broad and narrow terms in their separate alphabetical positions; for example, "human rights", "racial discrimination" and "right to development". Subjects pertaining to the United Nations or the system as a whole, such as "contributions (UN)", "finances (UN)" and "staff (UN/UN system)", are indexed separately, with cross-references under "United Nations".

NAMES of organizations and subsidiary bodies, conferences, United Nations Secretariat departments and offices, programmes, and special decades and observances, are given in full in capitals and small capitals and are alphabetized in either of two ways: (1) Names of bodies, units and programmes that are part of the United Nations, names of subsidiary bodies of specialized agencies and of their affiliated institutions, and titles of special decades and observances, are indexed under their key word: APARTHEID, SPEC. CT. AGAINST; DEVELOPMENT DECADE, 3RD UN; LAW OF THE SEA, 3RD UN CF. ON THE; MARITIME DAY, WORLD; TECHNICAL CO-OPERATION FOR DEVELOPMENT, DEPARTMENT OF. (2) Names of specialized agencies and of non–United Nations organizations are alphabetized under the first word of their title: INTER-AMERICAN CS. ON HUMAN RIGHTS; WORLD METEOROLOGICAL ORGANIZATION.

Names of publications are italicized, with only those receiving relatively extensive treatment in *Yearbook* articles, such as *Trade and Development Report, 1988* and the *World Economic Survey 1988*, being listed.

Cross-references are not given to entries in close proximity; for example, there is a cross-reference to "economic development" under "development" but not to "development assistance".

———

Bodies/subjects/topics are listed only when substantive information is given.

Abbreviations

In addition to the abbreviations contained in the list on p. xv, the subject index uses the following:

ASG	Assistant Secretary-General
CD	Conference on Disarmament
cf(s).	conference(s)
cl(s).	council(s)
cs(s).	commission(s)
ct(s).	committee(s)
DC	Disarmament Commission
DG	Director-General
LOS	Law of the Sea
mtg(s).	meeting(s)
sess.	session
SCPDPM	Sub-Commission on Prevention of Discrimination and Protection of Minorities of the Commission on Human Rights
spec.	special
UNCLS	United Nations Conference on the Law of the Sea
UNJSPB	United Nations Joint Staff Pension Board
USG	Under-Secretary-General

Subject index

ing/fellowships, 952; world traffic, 950 (ICAO); *see also* air law; air navigation; air transport

CIVIL AVIATION, CONVENTION FOR THE SUPPRESSION OF UNLAWFUL ACTS AGAINST THE SAFETY OF *(1971)*: ratifications, 951

CIVIL AVIATION, INTERNATIONAL CONVENTION ON *(1944* Chicago Convention), 950; annexes, 950, 951; & LOS convention, 951

CIVIL AVIATION, PROTOCOL FOR THE SUPPRESSION OF UNLAWFUL ACTS OF VIOLENCE AT AIRPORTS SERVING INTERNATIONAL (Supplement to *1971* Montreal Convention): opened for signature, 951

CIVIL AVIATION PURCHASING SERVICE, 952

Civil Service Cs., International, *see* International Civil Service Cs.

Civilian Persons in Time of War, Convention on Protection of (4th Geneva Convention), *see under* Geneva Conventions

climate: & agriculture, 463 (UNEP); applications, 962; change in, 962; data management, 962; El Niño, effects of, *Ad Hoc* Working Group, 463, 962; global change in, **105**, 364; & greenhouse gases, 462-63, 962; as heritage of mankind, 463, **463-64**; impact studies, 463, 962; publications, 616; research, 921, 962-63; *see also* air pollution; atmosphere; meteorology

CLIMATE AND DEVELOPMENT, IST WORLD CONGRESS ON, 448 (UNEP/WMO)

CLIMATE CF., 2ND WORLD *(1990)*, 463, 962 (GA/WMO)

CLIMATE CHANGE, UNEP/WMO INTERGOVERNMENTAL PANEL ON (IPCC), 462-63, **464** (GA); Ist sess., 463, 962

CLIMATE DATA MANAGEMENT, CS. ON CLIMATOLOGY WORKING GROUP ON, 962

CLIMATE PROGRAMME, WORLD *(1979)*, 103 (COPUOS), **463-64** (GA), 962-63 (WMO); joint secretariat/working groups established, 962

Climate Applications Programme, World, 962

Climate Data Programme, World, 962; Referral Service/data rescue, 962

Climate Impact Studies Programme, World, 962

Climate Research Programme, World, 962-63

coal: trade/co-operation, 291, **292** (Coal Ct./ESC)

COAL CT. (ECE): 84th sess., 291

COAL MINES CT. (ILO): 12th sess., 911

COARSE GRAINS, PULSES, ROOTS AND TUBER CROPS IN HUMID TROPICS OF ASIA AND THE PACIFIC, REGIONAL CO-ORDINATION CENTRE FOR RESEARCH AND DEVELOPMENT (ESCAP); Governing Board, 1023

coastal waters, *see under* marine ecosystems

cocaine abuse/coca cultivation, 679 (UNFDAC); *see also regional entries*

COCOA AGREEMENT, *1986* INTERNATIONAL: ratifications/accessions, 411

COCOA CL., INTERNATIONAL, 411

COLLECTIVE MEASURES CT. (GA), 1007; members, 1008

Colombia: drug control/traffic, 679, 689 (UNFDAC), 696; energy, 933; IFC investment, 942; & involuntary disappearances, 522 (Working Group); Population Award, 476; water supply loan, 934 (World Bank)

COLOMBO PLAN BUREAU: co-operation with HONLEA, 1022

colonial countries, 719-56

decade on, proposed, 734, **734-35** (Foreign Ministers Cf./GA)

independence for, Declaration on, 719-30

information dissemination, 733, **733-34**, 734 (colonial countries Ct./GA)

military activities in, 730-31, **731-33** (colonial countries Ct./GA)

trust funds for, 738 (UNDP Cl./GA)

Week of Solidarity with peoples of, 734

see also International Trusteeship System; national liberation movements; Non-Self-Governing Territories; self-determination of peoples; *and names of territories and the following entries*

COLONIAL COUNTRIES AND PEOPLES, DECLARATION ON THE GRANTING OF INDEPENDENCE TO *(1960)*, 719-30; implementation (general aspects), **101-103** (colonial countries Ct./GA), 719; by UN organizations, 721-27 (colonial countries Ct., 722; ESC, **722-24**, 724; GA, **724-27**); foreign interests impeding, 727, **727-30**, 730 (colonial countries Ct./GA); 30th anniversary, *1990*, preparations, **721**

COLONIAL COUNTRIES AND PEOPLES, SPEC. CT. ON THE SITUATION WITH REGARD TO THE IMPLEMENTATION OF THE DECLARATION ON THE GRANTING OF INDEPENDENCE TO, 719, **720**; membership, 1012; officers, 1012; Sub-Ct. on Petitions, Information and Assistance, 719, 733, 734, 1012; Sub-Ct. on Small Territories, 719, 1012; visiting missions, 721 (GA); work programme, *1989*, 720 (GA); Working Group, 1012

COLONIAL COUNTRIES AND PEOPLES, TRUST FUND FOR ASSISTANCE TO (UNDP): closing of/balance transfer, 351, 738 (UNDP Cl./GA)

COLONIALISM, INTERNATIONAL DECADE FOR THE ERADICATION OF, *1990-2000* (proposed), 332, **734-35** (GA)

Committee . . . *for specific ct., see key word(s) of title*

commodities, 410 (Ct. on/GA), 411 (UNCTAD); agreements/arrangements, 285-86 (ESCAP), 410 (Working Party), 411-12; classification system (statistics), 700 (SG/Expert Group); compensatory/contingency facility, **371**, 945-46 (GA/IMF); consultations, 411; export diversification, **370**, 410 (GA/Commodities Ct.); *see also* metals; minerals; synthetics and substitutes; *and names of individual products*

COMMODITIES, CT. ON (TDB), 410; members/cts. of, 1014; Working Party on Processing, Marketing and Distribution, including Transportation, 410

COMMODITIES, COMMON FUND FOR: *1980* Agreement Establishing, **405** (GA); signatures/ratifications, 410-11; Second Account, in UNPAAERD review, **370** (GA)

COMMODITY DESCRIPTION AND CODING SYSTEM, HARMONIZED (Customs Co-operation Cl.), 412, 413, 700 (UN Expert Group)

COMMUNICATION, INTERNATIONAL PROGRAMME FOR THE DEVELOPMENT OF

(IPDC): implementation, 109, **109-10** (UNESCO DG/SG); Intergovernmental Cl., 9th sess., 109, **110** (GA), 923 (UNESCO); project allocations, 109 (Spec. Account)

communications, 273 (ECA), 923 (UNESCO/IPDC); & new technologies, 109; *see also* information dissemination; mass communication; new world information and communication order; public information; radio broadcasting; telecommunications

communications satellites, 103 (COPUOS), 109; low-cost receivers, 100 (UNISPACE-2); UN seminar on development of, 101; *see also* satellites; telecommunications; *and regional entries*

COMMUNICATIONS, WORKING GROUP ON (SCPDPM): members/Chairman, 1021

Comorian island of Mayotte, 162, **162-63** (SG/GA), **503** (GA)

Comoros, Islamic Federal Republic of, 162

computer technology, 446 (UNFSTD); & telecommunications, 959 (ITU); *see also* information systems; microcomputer technology; UN: information systems/computers

COMPUTING CENTRE, INTERNATIONAL (Geneva): budget, 901-902 (GA/SG)

CONFERENCE SERVICES, DEPARTMENT OF: USG, 1033

CONFERENCES, CT. ON, 895; status, 895, **895-96**, 896 (Ct./GA); members/officers, 1008; report, **897** (GA); work programme, **897** (GA)

conferences/meetings (UN), 14 (SG), 895-98

calendar of, 896-97 (Ct. on Cfs.); *1988-1989*, 896; *1990-1991*, 897, **897** (Ct. on Cfs./ESC/GA)

language/interpretation services, 898, **898** (SG/GA)

major cfs., final reports of, 898 (Cf. Management Ct./Ct. on Cfs.)

representation at, 898 (JIU)

servicing resources, 897, **897-98** (Ct. on Cfs./GA)

spec., guidelines for: Cf. Management Ct., establishment, 898

see also documents (UN); *and geographic and subject entries*

Congo: mineral exploration, 436 (France/UNRFNRE), 437 (UNRFNRE); technical assistance, 933 (World Bank)

conservation: biological diversity, proposed convention, 465-66 (expert mtg./ad hoc working group); endangered species, international trade, 466 (UNEP), status of, 458; marine mammals, 470 (UNEP); *see also* biosphere; ecosystems; plant genetic resources; regional seas programmes; wild animals

CONSERVATION MONITORING CENTRE, WORLD, 458

CONSERVATION OF MIGRATORY SPECIES OF WILD ANIMALS, CONVENTION ON THE: mtgs., Scientific Cl./Parties to, 466

CONSERVATION STRATEGY, WORLD: expansion/update, 465

construction industry: building materials, 482 (UNCHS); & low-income shelter/infrastructure, 482-83 (UNCHS)

consular missions: security/safety of, 806-807, **807-808** (SG/GA); *see also under* diplomatic relations

EUROPEAN ACT, SINGLE: in force *(1987)*, 288
EUROPEAN COMMUNITIES, CS. OF THE: radio-active waste management, symposium, 907
EUROPEAN COMMUNITY (EC): & common market *(1992)*, 288, 294; & Cyprus, 123; & Namibia, **767**, 772, 780
EUROPEAN CONVENTION FOR THE PREVENTION OF TORTURE AND INHUMAN OR DEGRADING TREATMENT OR PUNISHMENT *(1987)*, 515
EUROPEAN CT. ON LEGAL CO-OPERATION: co-operation with ILC, 831
EUROPEAN ECONOMIC COMMUNITY: & GSP, 407; Industrial Development Centre, 979
EUROPEAN FREE TRADE ASSOCIATION (EFTA), 290, 294
EUROPEAN INLAND FISHERIES ADVISORY CS., 917
EUROPEAN SPACE AGENCY (ESA), 101
EUROPEAN STATISTICIANS, CF. OF (36th sess.), 294
exchange rates, *see under* international monetary and financial affairs/system
exclusive economic zone: & LOS, 812 (SG); *see also* continental shelf; fisheries
experts, *see* UN: experts/consultants; *and* subject entries
Explosives, Group of Experts on, *see* Transport of Dangerous Goods, Ct. of Experts on the
exports, *see* commodities; GATT; international trade; trade
extra-legal executions, 519, **519-20**, 520-**21** (Spec. Rapporteur/Human Rights Cs./SCPDPM/ ESC/GA); prevention, 610, 613 (SG/Crime Prevention Ct.)

Faeroe Islands: Danish-Icelandic air navigation agreement, 951
Falkland Islands (Malvinas), 738-39 (communications/SC, 738; colonial countries Ct., 738-39; GA, **739**, 739; SG, 739); information to UN, 736
family, international year of the (proposed), 607, **607-608** (GA)
family planning: 302 (ECLAC), 473, 474 (UNFPA), 927 (WHO); & AIDS, 473 (WHO/UNFPA); & ethics/human values, Cf. on, 927; & fertility reduction, 356, 357 (DTCD)
FAMILY PLANNING, REGIONAL TRAINING CENTRE FOR (Mauritius), 473
FAMINE AND MALNUTRITION, UNDP TRUST FUND FOR COUNTRIES AFFLICTED BY: allocations, 420 (UNDP Administrator/Cl.); *see also* hunger and malnutrition
fascism, *see* nazism/fascism
Federated States of Micronesia, *see* Micronesia, Federated States of
fellowships, 357 (DTCD), 971 (WIPO), 977 (UNIDO), 985-86 (GATT); cartography, 444; civil aviation, 952 (ICAO); disarmament, 44, **44-45** (SG/GA); 97 (UNIDIR); international law, 833-34 (UN/UNITAR/ GA); LOS, 816, 833; meteorology, 965, 966 (WMO); Palestinians, 214 (UNDP); 261 (UNESCO); postal services, 955 (UPU); space applications, 101-102 (UN Programme); *see also regional and subject entries*

fertility, *see* family planning; human reproduction
FERTILIZER DEVELOPMENT CENTRE, INTERNATIONAL: & UNDP co-operation, 340
FERTILIZERS AND PESTICIDES INDUSTRIES IN AFRICA, REGIONAL CONSULTATION ON PHOSPHATIC, 978
fibres, *see* jute; textiles
Fiji: UNIFIL troop contribution, 220
FINANCIAL EMERGENCY OF THE UN, NEGOTIATING CT. ON THE: members, 1011
financial policy, *see* development finance; insurance; international monetary and financial affairs/system; public finance
financial situation (UN), 13-14 (SG), 853-56 (ACABQ, 855; GA, **855**, **855-56**; SG, 853-55); Group of 18 recommendations, implementation, 856-58 (SG/CPC/ ACABQ, 856; GA, **856-58**); *see also* budget (UN); contributions (UN)
Finland: troop contingents: UNDOF, 226, UNFICYP, 123, UNIFIL, 220, UNIIMOG, 195
fisheries, 917 (FAO); management/development, 813; & LOS Convention, 781-82; stocks & environmental factors, 921 (UNESCO/IOC); *see also* aquaculture; Namibia
FISHING INDUSTRY, CT. ON CONDITIONS OF WORK IN THE (ILO), 911
fissionable materials, prohibition of production, *see under* nuclear weapons
floods: impact on LDCs, 386 (UNCTAD); relief programmes, 386-90; *see also country names*
FLORA, FAUNA AND THEIR HABITATS, DECLARATION ON THE PROTECTION OF: adoption, 293 (ECE)
food, 593-99; composition, directory update/publication, 600; contamination levels, 459, 926 (WHO/UNEP); handling procedures, consultation, 927; pesticides guidelines, dietary intake, 927 (WHO/UNEP/ FAO); & trade protectionism, **596** (GA), 915, 917-18; use of as political pressure, **595**, 915 (GA/Recife Declaration); world situation, 593-94 (SG/ESC); *see also* agricultural development; commodities; grains; nutrition; *and names of food products*
food, right to, 530, **530-31** (Human Rights Cs./ESC)
food aid, 596 (GA), 597-99 (CFA, 597-98; WFP, 598); contributions/pledges, 598; development assistance, 598; emergency operations, 598; information systems, 598
FOOD AID CONVENTION *(1986)*: pledges, 598; parties to, 599
FOOD AID POLICIES AND PROGRAMMES, CT. ON (CFA), 597-98; annual report, 597; projects, 598; *see also* Food Programme, World (WFP)
food and agriculture, 270-71 (ECA), 304 (ECLAC), 313 (ESCWA), 340 (UNDP), 593-97, 915-18 (FAO); emergencies, 915, 916 (FAO); & environmental issues, 916-17 (FAO); FAO field projects, 916; guidelines for, proposed new, 915 (FAO DG); IDA replenishment, **597** (GA); & IFAD replenishment, **596** (ESC); information systems, 918; South-South co-operation, 594, **596** (UNDP/WFC/GA); technical co-operation, strengthening, 359, 594, **594-95** (WFC/

GA); *see also* hunger and malnutrition; *and regional entries*
FOOD AND AGRICULTURE, GLOBAL INFORMATION AND EARLY WARNING SYSTEM IN (FAO): monitoring system, installation of, 918
FOOD AND AGRICULTURE ORGANIZATION OF THE UN (FAO), 915-19
FOOD COUNCIL, WORLD (WFC), 594, **594** (ESC/GA); Exec. Director/Deputy, 1018, 1033; members/officers, 1018; 14th ministerial sess., 594, **596** (GA)
FOOD DATA SYSTEMS PROJECT, INTERNATIONAL, 600
FOOD DAY, WORLD, 1008
food industry: food-processing, 1st inter-regional consultation, 978 (UNIDO); technology transfer, **596** (GA)
food problems, 593-97 (FAO, 593-94; GA, **595-97**; SG/ESC/WFC, 594); information/early warning system, 918 (FAO); irradiation, cf./document on, 907, 917, 927 (IAEA/FAO/WHO/ITC)
FOOD PROGRAMME, WORLD (WFP): activities, 598; contributions/pledges, 598-99; Exec. Director/Deputy, 1029; Food Aid Ct. (governing body), 597, 1029 (members/officers); *1989-1990* pledging targets, **596** (GA)
FOOD RESERVE, INTERNATIONAL EMERGENCY (IEFR): contributions, 597, 599; replenishment, appeal for, 915
FOOD SECURITY, CT. ON WORLD (FAO): members/mtg., 917; trade reform, 917-18
FOODS, INTERNATIONAL CF. ON THE ACCEPTANCE, CONTROL OF AND TRADE IN IRRADIATED, 907, 917, 927 (FAO/ITC/WHO)
foreign trade, *see* international trade; trade
FOREST ECONOMICS AND STATISTICS, JOINT FAO/ECE WORKING PARTY ON, 293
forestry development, 917 (FAO); *see also* tropical forests
forests, 269 (ECA), 293 (ECE); commemorative stamps, 902; ecosystems, 458, 465; *see also* tropical forests
France: contingents, to UNIFIL, 220; pioneer investor, 811; *see also* Comorian island of Mayotte; Malagasy islands; New Caledonia; Suriname; *and under* territorial sea
francophone countries, *see under* Africa
freedom of movement, *see under* human rights
freedom of speech, *see under* human rights
FREQUENCY REGISTER BOARD, INTERNATIONAL, 956; *see also* radio broadcasting: frequency allocation
freshwater ecosystems, 468 (UNEP); Damman Aquifer action plan, 468; ground water, nitrates in/salinization of, 468 (UNEP/WHO); & World Climate Programme mtg., 468 (UNESCO/UNEP); *see also* inland waters; lakes; rivers/river basins; water resources
front-line States, 158-59, **768** *(Apartheid* Ct./colonial countries Ct./GA); emergency assistance to, **149**, 159, 784 (colonial countries Ct./GA); refugee assistance, 788 (UNHCR); spec. assistance to, 380, **380-81**, 781 (SG/GA); *see also* Lesotho; Malawi; Namibia; South Africa: & neighbouring States; Swaziland; *and names of States*
fuels, *see* coal; energy; gas; oil
fuelwood: crisis in, 440 (SG)

MARITIME SATELLITE ORGANIZATION, INTERNATIONAL, 813, 964
MARITIME SEARCH AND RESCUE, *1979* INTERNATIONAL CONVENTION ON, 813
MARITIME UNIVERSITY, WORLD (IMO), 968
marks: registration of, *see* trade marks
MARKS, MADRID AGREEMENT CONCERNING THE INTERNATIONAL REGISTRATION OF, 970; total registations under, 971
MARPOL, *see* Ships, International Convention for the Prevention of Pollution from
Marshall Islands: admission to ICAO, 950; Compact of Free Association, 757, 758; *see also* Trust Territory of the Pacific Islands (Micronesia)
mass communication, 108-10 (Information Ct.); *see also* new world information and communication order; public information; *and entries under* communication
mass exoduses, *see under* human rights violations
maternal and child health, 646 (UNICEF), 927 (WHO/UNFPA); & AIDS/HIV, 473, 474 (UNFPA/WHO); *see also* children; family planning
Mauritius: family planning training centre, 473 (UNFPA); science/technology, 272 (ECA)
Mayotte, *see* Comorian island of Mayotte
MEDICAL EDUCATION, WORLD CF. ON: Declaration, 926
medicinal plants: consultation on conservation of, 928
medicine/medical issues: education, 926 (WHO)
Mediterranean region: civil aviation, technical assistance, 952 (ICAO); economic co-operation in, 289 (ECE); monk seal protection, Action Plan, 470 (UNEP); regional seas programme (UNEP), 468-69; security/co-operation, 27-28, **28-29** (SG/GA); transport centres, 290 (ECE/ESC), 422; *see also country names*
meetings (UN), *see* conferences/mtgs. (UN)
MEKONG BASIN, INTERIM CT. FOR COORDINATION OF INVESTIGATIONS OF THE LOWER (ESCAP), 1023
Mekong River Basin: development, 438 (UNEP); food production, 468 (UNEP)
Members (UN), *see under* United Nations
mental health: promotion/protection of, 927-28 (WHO)
mercenaries: draft convention against use of, 803-804 (*Ad Hoc* Ct., 803; GA, **803-804**, 804); & self-determination, 505-508 (ESC, **506**; GA, **506-508**, 508; Human Rights Cs., 505-506); Spec. Rapporteur, 506, 803, 804 (*Ad Hoc* Ct./GA)
MERCENARIES, *AD HOC* CT. ON THE DRAFTING OF AN INTERNATIONAL CONVENTION AGAINST THE RECRUITMENT, USE, FINANCING AND TRAINING OF, 506, **507** (Spec. Rapporteur/GA), 803, **803** (GA); members/officers, 1007; 7th sess., 1007; working/drafting groups, establishment, 803
METAL TRADES CT. (ILO): 12th sess., 911
metallurgical industries: technical co-operation, 977 (UNIDO/UNDP)
metals, 781; *see also names of metals*
METEOROLOGICAL INSTRUMENTS AND METHODS OF OBSERVATION, PROGRAMME/ TECHNICAL CF. ON, 962
meteorology: Applications Programme, 618-19 (WMO); education/training, 965

(WMO); & environment, 963 (WMO); observation programme, 962 (Cs./Advisory Group); research/development, 963 (WMO); satellite use in, 961; technical co-operation, 619-20 (WMO); tropical, 963; *see also* agrometeorology; air pollution; atmosphere; climate; hydrology; oceans; weather; WMO
METEOROLOGY, CS. FOR AERONAUTICAL (WMO): President, 967; 2nd sess./Working Group, Advanced Techniques, 964
METEOROLOGY, CS. FOR AGRICULTURAL, 963- 64; President, 621
METEOROLOGY, CS. FOR MARINE: President, 967
METEOROLOGY PROGRAMME, AERONAUTICAL, 964-65 (WMO/ICAO)
METEOROLOGY RESEARCH PROGRAMME, TROPICAL (WMO), 963
Mexico, 629 (UNIFEM/UNDP/ILO); agriculture, 932 (World Bank); development finance, 932; drug control/opium cultivation, 679 (UNFDAC), 695; education, 933; fisheries planning, FAO course, 917; geothermal project, 436 (UNRFNRE); IFC investment, 938; industry, 933 (World Bank); refugees in, 674 (UNHCR)
MICROBIAL STRAIN DATA NETWORK WORKING GROUP, 465
MICROBIOLOGICAL RESOURCES CENTRES, 466 (UNEP)
microcomputer technology: use in statistics, 702 (DTCD)
Micronesia, *see* Trust Territory of the Pacific Islands (Micronesia)
Micronesia, Federated States of: admission to ICAO, 950; Compact of Free Association, 757, 758; *see also* Trust Territory of the Pacific Islands (Micronesia)
Micro-States: Ct. of Experts on (SC), members, 1019
microwave technology: & remote-sensing, workshop, 101 (UN/ESA)
Middle East: civil aviation, technical assistance, 952 (ICAO); drug law enforcement, 693-94; human rights violations, 575-77; investments in, 938 (IFC); refugees in, 656-57 (UNHCR); telecommunications, 957, 959 (ITU); UNICEF programmes, 645; *see also* Arab States; Economic and Social Cs. for Western Asia; nuclear-weapon-free zones; *and country names*
Middle East situation, 4 (SG), 201-66
    general aspects, 201-204 (GA, **202-204**; SG, 202); Arab peace plans, 202, **203** (SG/GA); implementation of *1987* GA resolutions, 202 (SG); UN peace-keeping operations/truce supervision, 207 (SG overview)
    proposed peace cf., 204-207 (GA, **206-207**; Palestinian rights Ct., 206; SG, 204-206)
    see also Disengagement Observer Force, UN; Golan Heights; Jerusalem; Lebanon, UN Interim Force in; Palestine question; territories occupied by Israel; UN Truce Supervision Organization; *and country names*
migrant workers: & children of, **487** (GA); discrimination against, **486**, **488** (ESC/ GA); draft convention on rights of, 496, **496-97** (Human Rights Cs./Working Group/GA)

MIGRANT WORKERS AND THEIR FAMILIES, WORKING GROUP ON THE DRAFTING OF AN INTERNATIONAL CONVENTION ON THE PROTECTION OF THE RIGHTS OF ALL, 496
military expenditures, *see under* disarmament
Military Experts, Panel of, *see* Peace, Uniting for
MILITARY STAFF CT. (SC), 1019
mineral resources, 271 (ECA), 299 (ECLAC), 356, 437 (DTCD); exploitation, 781 (Namibia Cl.); *see also* metals; mining; natural resources; sea-bed; *and names of minerals*
Mineral Resources Development Centre, Central African, *see under* Central Africa
Mineral Resources Development Centre, Eastern and Southern African, *see under* Eastern and southern Africa
mining, 269 (ECA); *see also* metals *and under* sea-bed
minorities, 497 (Human Rights Cs./ SCPDPM); rights of, working group on, 1021
MISSILE SYSTEMS, *1972* TREATY ON THE LIMITATION OF ANTI-BALLISTIC (ABM Treaty), **88** (GA)
MISSILES, US/USSR AGREEMENT ON NOTIFICATIONS OF LAUNCHES OF INTERCONTINENTAL BALLISTIC MISSILES AND SUBMARINE-LAUNCHED BALLISTIC, 33, 52
MISSILES, *1987* TREATY BETWEEN THE UNITED STATES AND THE UNION OF SOCIALIST REPUBLICS ON THE ELIMINATION OF THEIR INTERMEDIATE-RANGE AND SHORTER-RANGE (INF Treaty), 6, 10 (SG), 56; ratification, 56, **58** (CD/GA)
missing persons, *see* human rights: disappearance of persons; *and under* Cyprus
monetary policy, *see* international monetary and financial affairs/system
Mongolia: energy project, 441 (DTCD); zoonosis, control/prevention, 460
Monitoring and Assessment Research Centre, *see under* environmental monitoring
Monrovia Strategy for the Economic Development of Africa, Lagos Plan of Action for Implementation of the, *see* Africa, Lagos Plan of Action for the Implementation of the Monrovia Strategy for the Economic Development of Africa
monsoons: research/development, 963 (WMO)
Montreal Protocol on Substances that Deplete the Ozone Layer *(1987)*, *see under* ozone layer
Montserrat, 750, **750-51** (colonial countries Ct./GA); information to UN, 736
MOON AND OTHER CELESTIAL BODIES, AGREEMENT GOVERNING ACTIVITIES OF STATES ON THE *(1979)*: parties/signatories, 98 (SG), 99; *see also* outer space: treaties/ conventions on
Morocco: water quality project, 342 (UNDP); *see also* Western Sahara
most-favoured-nation clauses, *see under* international trade law
motor vehicles, multilateral treaties on, in force/deposited, 809, 810
MOTORWAY PROJECT, CT. OF THE TRANS-EUROPEAN NORTH-SOUTH, 294 (ECE/ UNDP)
mountain ecosystems: seminar on ecology/natural resources management, 465

nuclear disarmament, 6-7, 10 (SG), 34 (GA spec. sess.), 52-75
  bilateral negotiations, 56-59; & arms freeze, 63-64 (GA); Moscow summit, joint statement, 33; *1987* INF Treaty, ratification, 56, 58 (CD/GA); strategic arms reductions, 56, 58 (CD/GA); *see also entries under missiles*
  multilateral negotiations, consensus, 56, 56-57 (CD/GA)
  see also non-nuclear-weapon States; non-proliferation; peace and security, international; zones of peace; *and the following entries*
nuclear energy, 442-44 (GA, 443-44; IAEA DG, 442-43), 906; convention/protocol, status, 444, 905; *see also* Thermonuclear Experimental Reactor, International
NUCLEAR ENERGY, *1960* PARIS CONVENTION ON THIRD PARTY LIABILITY IN THE FIELD OF: Joint Protocol relating to, adoption, 443 (GA), 905
NUCLEAR ENERGY AGENCY (OECD), 905
Nuclear-Free Zone Treaty, South Pacific, *see* South Pacific Nuclear-Free Zone Treaty (1985 Treaty of Rarotonga)
NUCLEAR INFORMATION SYSTEM, INTERNATIONAL, 909
NUCLEAR MATERIAL, CONVENTION ON PHYSICAL PROTECTION OF, 444 (GA)
nuclear medicine, 907 (IAEA); *see also under* diseases
nuclear non-proliferation, *see under* non-proliferation; nuclear-weapon-free zones; zones of peace
nuclear power
  accidents: Chernobyl, 906 (IAEA); conventions on (Early Notification/Emergency Assistance), 444 (SG/GA); in space, 102-103 (COPUOS)
  fuel cycle, 906 (IAEA); publication, 906
  generating capacity, world, 442, 906 (IAEA); publications, 906
  information, 909; Power Reactor Information System, 906
  plants: attacks on, prohibition, 79, 80 (CD/*Ad Hoc* Ct./SG/GA); total in operation, 906
  research reactors, 908
  safeguards agreements, 443, 908-909 (IAEA); *see also country names*
  safety, 443, 444 (IAEA/GA), 905-906 (IAEA); Analytical Laboratory (IAEA), 908; incident reporting system, 905; of research reactors, 905; (operational safety review team) missions, 905 (IAEA)
  sources of: draft legal principles, 104 (COPUOS/Working Group)
  see also under radiation; radioactive waste management
NUCLEAR POWER, DIVISION OF (IAEA), 906
NUCLEAR RISK REDUCTION CENTRES, AGREEMENT BETWEEN THE UNITED STATES OF AMERICA AND THE UNION OF SOVIET SOCIALIST REPUBLICS ON THE ESTABLISHMENT OF/PROTOCOLS I, II *(1987)*, 33, 52
NUCLEAR SAFETY ADVISORY GROUP, INTERNATIONAL (IAEA), 905

nuclear war
  climatic/physical effects of: study on, 55, 55-56 (SG/expert group), 97, 98 (Advisory Board/GA)
  prevention, 52-53 (CD/DC, 52; GA, 53-54); *ad hoc* ct. on, proposed, 52, 53 (CD/GA); USSR-US agreements on, 52, 52-53 (CD/DC/GA)
nuclear-weapon-free zones, 34, 35 (GA spec. sess./Preparatory Ct.), 49, 66-74
  Africa, denuclearization: *1964* OAU Declaration, implementation, 66-67 67-68 (GA); *see also* South Africa: nuclear capability
  Balkans/Central & North Europe, 34, 66
  Latin America, 34 (GA spec. sess.), 69, 69-70 (GA)
  Middle East (proposed), 34, 70, 70-71 (SG/GA); *see also* Israel
  South Asia, 72, 72-73 (GA/SG)
  South Pacific, 34 (GA spec. sess.), 66
  see also arms race: outer space; sea-bed; zones of peace
NUCLEAR-WEAPON-FREE ZONES, INTERNATIONAL MTG. FOR, 66
nuclear-weapon tests: cessation, 60-62 (*Ad Hoc* Experts Group, 60-61; DC/CD/SG; 60; GA, 61); *ad hoc* ct. on, proposed, 60, 61 (CD/GA); explosions, annual register, 60 (SG); proposed comprehensive treaty on, 60, 62-63 (CD/GA); radiation from, 462 (UNSCEAR); 6-nation initiative, Stockholm Declaration, 60, 61, 62 (GA); *see also* seismic monitoring
NUCLEAR WEAPON TESTS IN THE ATMOSPHERE, IN OUTER SPACE AND UNDER WATER, TREATY BANNING *(1963)*: scope of, proposed amendment to, 60, 62 (communication/GA); parties to, 98
nuclear weapons
  fissionable material for, prohibition of production, 59, 59-60 (CD/GA)
  freeze (proposed), 60, 63, 63-64 (GA)
  intermediate-range nuclear forces, *1987* INF Treaty, 56; *see also* Missiles, *1987* Treaty between the US and the USSR
  1980 comprehensive study on, proposed update, 97-98 (Advisory Board/GA)
  non-proliferation of, 10 (SG), 66-75; *see also country names; regional entries*
  non-use of, proposed legal instrument on, 52, 52-53 (CD/GA)
  prohibition on use of, draft convention, 54-55 (GA)
  see also non-nuclear-weapon States; South Africa: nuclear capability; *and under* Missiles, *1987* Treaty between the US and the USSR
NUCLEAR WEAPONS, *1968* TREATY ON THE NON-PROLIFERATION OF (NPT), 10 (SG); & IAEA safeguards, 67, 909; *1990* Review Cf., preparations, 10 (SG), 74, 74-75 (GA); parties to, 98
NUCLEAR WEAPONS IN LATIN AMERICA, *1967* TREATY FOR THE PROHIBITION OF (Treaty of Tlatelolco), 129-30; parties to, 98; Protocol I, implementation, 69, 69-70 (GA); Protocol II, 69; safeguards agreements, 909

NUCLEAR WEAPONS IN LATIN AMERICA AND THE CARIBBEAN, AGENCY FOR THE PROHIBITION OF: observer status for, 129-30, 130 (GA)
nutrition: 599-600 (UNU/ACC); publication, 600; research/training, 600 (UNU); surveillance systems, 600; vitamin/mineral deficiencies, 600, 644, 646 (UNICEF); *see also* breast-feeding; food
NUTRITION, ACC SUB-CT./ADVISORY GROUP ON, 600, 711
NUTRITION SUPPORT PROGRAMME, WHO/ UNICEF JOINT, 643
NUTRITION SURVEILLANCE PROGRAMME, INTER-AGENCY FOOD AND (FAO/WHO/ UNICEF), 600

OCCUPATIONAL SAFETY AND HEALTH INFORMATION CENTRE, INTERNATIONAL, 912; *see also* working conditions
OCCUPATIONS, INTERNATIONAL STANDARD CLASSIFICATION OF (ILO), 701
ocean affairs, 921 (IOC); circulation experiment, world cf. on, 921 (IOC); co-operation in UN system, 815-16 (*Ad Hoc* Inter-agency Mtg.); drifting buoys/sea-level observation stations, 921; economics/technology, 815 (OALOS); environmental protection, 811, 817 (GA); & meteorology services, 964 (WMO/IOC); *see also* atmosphere; marine affairs; sea; sea-bed
OCEAN AFFAIRS, *AD HOC* INTER-AGENCY CONSULTATION ON, 816, 816 (GA)
OCEAN AFFAIRS AND THE LAW OF THE SEA, OFFICE FOR (OALOS): SG functions, 811, 815-16
OCEAN SERVICES SYSTEM, INTEGRATED GLOBAL: main components, 964; IOC/WMO Working Ct. for, 5th sess., 964
Oceania: drug abuse/traffic, 693; refugee assistance, 673 (UNHCR)
OCEANOGRAPHIC CS., INTERGOVERNMENTAL (IOC), 921 (UNESCO); & WMO, 921, 964
oil: investment in, 438-39 (SG); price decline/stabilization, effects of, 438-39 (SG); & Western Asia, 310, 312 (ESCWA); world demand, 439
OLYMPIC CT., INTERNATIONAL: declaration on *apartheid*, 142
Oman: poverty in, IFAD mission, 974; & TNCs in, 433 (ESCWA/TNCs Centre)
operational safety review team, *see under* nuclear power: safety
opium poppy cultivation, 678 (UNDP); *see also under country and regional entries*
ORAL REHYDRATION THERAPY, 3RD INTERNATIONAL CF. ON, 929 (WHO); *see also* diarrhoeal diseases
Organisation for Economic Co-operation and Development, *see* Economic Co-operation and Development, Organisation for (OECD)
ORGANIZATION OF AFRICAN UNITY (OAU)
  co-operation with UN, 164-65, 165-67, 167 (SG/GA/OAU-UN mtg.)
  statements/communications: & Africa economic situation, 166; colonization, information dissemination, 167 (GA); & Comoros, 162; & denuclearization, 167 (GA)

& housing census, 701 (SG); technical co-operation, 702 (SG)
policy formulation/evaluation, 473
programme monitoring/evaluation, 474 (UNDP Cl.)
publications, 476
spec. programmes, 473
& women in development, 475 (UNDP/UNFPA); training in, 473-74 (UNFPA)
world: total/growth, 472
see also demographic activities; family planning; fertility; *and regional and subject entries*
POPULATION, INTERNATIONAL CF. ON *(1984)*: follow-up, 472 (SG/UNFPA)
POPULATION AWARD, UN (6th): Ct. for, 1008 (Chairman/members); recipients 476; Trust Fund, status, 476
POPULATION CS. (ESC): members, 1022
POPULATION FUND, UN (UNFPA), 472-76; accounts *(1987)*, 476 (Board of Auditors/GA); budget *(1988-1989)*, revised, 475-76 (UNFPA/GA); contributions, 476; country/intercountry programmes, 474 (UNDP); Exec. Director/Deputy/Assistant, 1017, 1034; income/ expenditures, 473, 475; staffing, 476 (Exec. Director/UNDP Cl.); work programmes *(1990-1992)*, 475 (UNDP Cl./Exec. Director)
POPULATION INFORMATION NETWORK (POPIN), 505 (ECA), 535, 536 (ECLAC)
POPULATION STUDIES, REGIONAL INSTITUTE FOR, 505
ports, 420; training projects, 423 (UNCTAD/UNDP)
Portugal: ITU project, 959; observer, Expert Ct. on Dangerous Goods, 423; *see also* East Timor
Post Adjustment Questions, Advisory Ct. on, *see under* International Civil Service Cs.
POSTAL ADMINISTRATION, UN (UNPA): commemorative stamps, 902; revenue agreements, 902
postal services, international, 954-55 (UPU/UNDP); *1984* Hamburg Declaration, implementation, 954 (UPU)
Power Reactor Information System, *see* nuclear power: information systems
PREFERENCES, SPEC. CT. ON (TDB), 406-407; member/officers, 1015; Working Group on Rules of Origin, 407
premises (UN): cf. facilities (Addis Ababa/Bangkok), 900 (SG/GA); *see also* UN: offices
price statistics: International Comparison Project (ICP), Phase V, 699 (SG); Phase VI, 699 (SG); methodology of, expert group mtg., 699
primary health care: Alma Ata Cf. *(1978)*, review mtg., 925-26 (WHO); regional developments, 926 (WHO); *see also* children; maternal health care
prisoners, *see* detainees; extra-legal executions; torture and other cruel treatment; *and under* South Africa *and* territories occupied by Israel
prisoners of war, treatment of, *see under* Geneva Conventions
privileges and immunities (UN), 886, **886-87** (ACC/SG/GA)
PRIVILEGES AND IMMUNITIES OF THE UNITED NATIONS, *1946* CONVENTION ON THE: &

Romania, 582 (SCPDPM); & UNRWA staff, 257
Programme and Co-ordination, Ct. for, *see* Co-ordination, Ct. for Programme and
PROGRAMME PLANNING, BUDGET AND FINANCE, OFFICE OF: ASG, 1033
programmes (UN), 869-75
administrative/budgetary co-ordination, 875-76 (ACABQ/GA)
evaluation, **872**, 873 (GA/SG/CPC); & JIU, 873
performance, 869-70 (SG/CPC/JIU); medium-term plans: *1984-1989*, revisions/extensions, 869-70, **871** (SG/CPC/ACABQ/GA); *1992-1997*, 870-71, **871-72** (SG/CPC/ACABQ/GA)
see also co-ordination in UN system; Joint Inspection Unit (JIU)
prostitution, *see* children; slavery
protectionism, *see under* international trade
psychotropic substances, 692, 696 (INCB); illicit demand for, **687** (ESC); *see also* narcotic drugs; *and regional entries*
PSYCHOTROPIC SUBSTANCES, *1971* CONVENTION ON: accessions, **681**, **689** (ESC/GA); schedules/exemptions, 696 (Narcotic Drugs Cs.); States parties, 696
Psychotropic Substances, UN Cf. for the Adoption of a Convention against Illicit Traffic in Narcotic Drugs and, *see* Narcotic Drugs and Psychotropic Substances, UN Cf. for the Adoption of a Convention against Illicit Traffic in
public accounting, *see* accounts (UN) *and entries following* audit/auditing
public administration and finance, 277, **277-78** (ECA/ESC); DTCD projects, 327, 356
PUBLIC ADMINISTRATION AND FINANCE, UN PROGRAMME IN: 7th *(1984)* Mtg. of Experts, 277; 9th *(1989)* Mtg. of Experts, 277, 327
public information (UN system), 110-17; co-ordination in UN system, 112, **112-16**, 116 (JUNIC/GA); *see also* mass communication; new world information and communication order; radio/visual services; *entries under* information; *and organizational and subject entries*
PUBLIC INFORMATION, DEPARTMENT OF (DPI) (Secretariat), 108, 111, **112-15** (Information Ct./SG/GA); publications, 111, **115** (SG/GA); restructuring, 111, **115** (SG/CPC/GA); staff, geographical distribution, 111, **115** (SG/GA); training programmes, 111, **114** (SG/GA); USG, 1033; *see also Development Forum*; Information Centres (UN); Radio and Visual Services Division; *UN Chronicle*; *Yearbook of the United Nations*
Puerto Rico, 735 (colonial countries Ct.)

Qatar: electricity demand, 308; radio/television services/telecommunications training centre, 959 (ITU)

racial discrimination/racism, 484-91; global consultation, 485, **488** (CERD/GA); legislation, training in preparing, 485, **487-88** (SG/GA); private groups, role of, 485, **487** (SG/GA); recourse procedures for victims,

handbook, 485, **488** (Human Rights Cs./GA); *see also apartheid*; discrimination; human rights; migrant workers; nazism/fascism; religious intolerance
RACIAL DISCRIMINATION, CT. ON THE ELIMINATION OF (CERD), 489, **489-90** (SG/GA); financial situation, 489, **490** (SG/GA); members/officers, 1031; regional working groups, appointment of members, 489; 36th sess., 485, 489, 1031; TC, co-operation with, 489, 760
RACIAL DISCRIMINATION, INTERNATIONAL CONVENTION ON THE ELIMINATION OF ALL FORMS OF *(1965)*: accessions/ratifications, 488, **488-89** (SG/GA); implementation, 489, **489-90** (CERD/GA); States parties, 12th (emergency) mtg., 489, **490** (GA); violations under, communications, 489 (CERD)
RACIAL DISCRIMINATION, INTERNATIONAL DAY FOR THE ELIMINATION OF: observance, 155, 157 (DPI/*Apartheid* Ct.)
RACIAL DISCRIMINATION, 2ND DECADE TO COMBAT RACISM AND *(1983-1993)*: Action Programme, implementation, 484-88 (ESC, **485-86**; GA, **487-88**; Human Rights Cs./SCPDPM/CERD, 485; SG, 484-85); Rapporteur study, achievements/obstacles, 485, **486-87** (Human Rights Cs./SCPDPM/ESC)
RADIATION, UN SCIENTIFIC CT. ON THE EFFECTS OF ATOMIC (UNSCEAR): members/officers, 1017; sess./report, 116, **116** (GA); & UNEP, **117**, 462 (GA)
radiation effects, 116-17 (GA, **116-17**; UNSCEAR, 116); advisory team missions, 906 (IAEA); protection, 443 (IAEA), 905-906 (IAEA/OECD); technical co-operation projects, 906; *see also under* nuclear power: accidents
RADIO AND VISUAL SERVICES DIVISION (DPI), 111-12, **115** (Information Ct./GA)
radio broadcasting: administrative cfs., 956 (ITU); consultative cts., 956-57 (ITU); frequency allocation, 957 (ITU); *see also* mass communication; public information; telecommunications
RADIO CF., REGIONAL ADMINISTRATIVE: 2nd sess., 956
RADIO CFS., WORLD ADMINISTRATIVE, 956 (ITU); on geostationary orbit (2nd sess.), 957
RADIO CONSULTATIVE CT., INTERNATIONAL: handbooks, 956; study group mtgs., 956
RADIOACTIVE WASTE MANAGEMENT ADVISORY CT., INTERNATIONAL (IAEA), 907
radioactive wastes: low/intermediate-level, symposium, 907 (IAEA/EC); management of, 81, 906-907 (IAEA); nuclear/industrial dumping, 81, **82-83** (OAU/IAEA/UNEP/GA), 81-82, **82** (CD/GA), 443 (IAEA Board); & nuclear facilities, decommissioning, 907; underground disposal, Review Ct. disbanded, 907; *see also* marine environment; oceans; sea
radioactivity: marine, 908 (IAEA)
RADIOACTIVITY, INTERNATIONAL LABORATORY OF MARINE (Monaco), 908
Radiological Emergency, Convention on Assistance in the Case of a Nuclear Accident or, *see* Nuclear Accident or Radiological Emergency, Convention on Assistance in the Case of a

Index of resolutions and decisions

Numbers in italics indicate that the text is summarized rather than reprinted in full. (For dates of sessions, refer to Appendix III.)

How to obtain volumes of the *Yearbook*

The 1985 to 1988, 1991 and 1992 volumes of the *Yearbook of the United Nations* are sold and distributed in the United States, Canada and Mexico by Kluwer Academic Publishers, 101 Philip Drive, Norwell, Massachusetts 02061; in all other countries by Kluwer Academic Publishers Group, P.O. Box 322, 3300 AH Dordrecht, Netherlands.

Yearbook of the United Nations, 1992, Vol. 46, Sales No. E.93.I.1 $150.

Yearbook of the United Nations, 1991, Vol. 45, Sales No. E.92.I.1 $115.

Yearbook of the United Nations, 1987, Vol. 41, Sales No. E.91.I.1 $105.

Yearbook of the United Nations, 1986, Vol. 40, Sales No. E.90.I.1 $95.

Yearbook of the United Nations, 1985, Vol. 39, Sales No. E.88.I.1 $95.

Other recent volumes of the *Yearbook* may be obtained in many bookstores throughout the world and also from United Nations Publications. *Yearbook* Volumes 1-41 (1946-1987) are available in microfiche. Individual volumes are also available, and prices can be obtained by contacting the following: United Nations Publications, Sales Section, Room DC2-853, United Nations, New York, N.Y. 10017, or United Nations Publications, Palais des Nations, Office C-115, 1211 Geneva 10, Switzerland.

NOTES

NOTES

NOTES

NOTES

NOTES